S0-ARM-198

MIGRATION FROM THE RUSSIAN EMPIRE

Lists of Passengers Arriving at the Port of New York

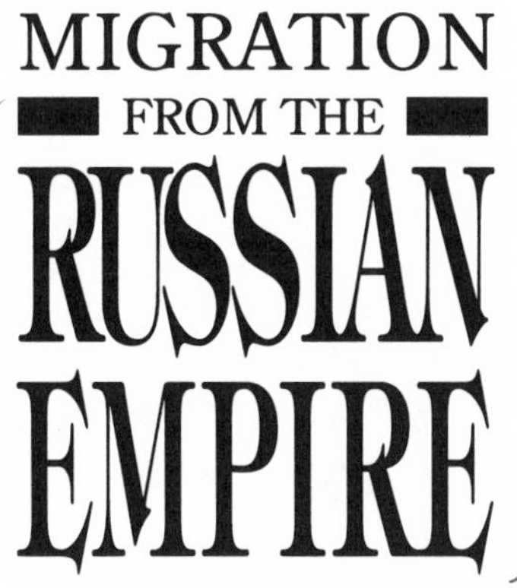

MIGRATION FROM THE RUSSIAN EMPIRE

Lists of Passengers Arriving at
the Port of New York

Volume 2

October 1882 – April 1886

Edited by
Ira A. Glazier
Director, Temple-Balch Center for Immigration Research

Library of Congress Catalogue Card Number 95-75722
International Standard Book Number, Volume 2: 0-8063-1475-3
Made in the United States of America

INTRODUCTION

This work contains data on passengers of Russian nationality who emigrated to the United States from Russian territories between 1875 and 1910. The information was extracted from the original ship manifests held at the Temple-Balch Center for Immigration Research in Philadelphia. From the year 1820, these manifests, or passenger lists, were filed by all vessels entering U.S. ports from abroad.

In this work, passenger lists are arranged in chronological order by date of arrival. The records of passengers of Russian nationality—Poles, Finns, and Russians—are given here in their entirety, while records of non-Russian nationals are excluded.

Information in the passenger lists regarding nationality changed several times during the nineteenth century. Until 1882 passenger lists gave the name of the country to which the passengers *belonged*. This was interpreted to mean either country of citizenship, country of last residence, or country of birth. Beginning in 1882, however, immigrants were required to name their *native country*, citizenship, or country of birth. From 1898 to 1934 passenger lists recorded aliens according to race, religion, or people, in addition to country of origin.

Passenger lists make possible a detailed reconstruction of population movements from the major sender countries by including information on the age, sex, occupation, nationality, residence, and intended destination of each passenger. This information enables the researcher to distinguish between U.S. citizens returning to their country of origin, persons traveling to destinations outside the United States, and immigrants. Manifests record deaths during the voyage, but information on mortality is not presented here. The lists also give the name of the ship, the port of embarkation, and the date of arrival in the U.S. port.

Historical Background and Causes of Russian Migration in the Nineteenth Century

The United States was the primary destination for Russian overseas migration between 1871 and 1910. Over 2.3 million migrants from Russia arrived between 1871 and 1910: approximately 600,000 between 1871 and 1898 and 1.7 million between 1899 and 1910 (Table 1). Almost all came from the western part of Russia. Several nationalities and ethnic groups, Slav and non-Slav, were represented—Poles, Byelorussians, Great Russians, Ukrainians, Jews, Finns, Lithuanians, Latvians, Estonians, and Germans[1]. Ethnic Russians migrated in far greater numbers than indigenous Russians. Of the 1.7 million emigrants who arrived in the U.S. between 1899 and 1910, 43 percent were Jews, 27 percent Poles, 9 percent Lithuanians, 8 percent Finns, 5 percent Germans, and 4 percent Russians (Tables 2 and 3).

Many factors contributed to migration from the Russian Empire at the end of the nineteenth century. The most important was the transition from a pre-industrial to a modern industrial State. This led to disruption of traditional agriculture and the demise of the small-scale, family economy. The transition started with the abolition of serfdom in the 1860s, the beginning of railroad construction, and government-financed industrial development. It led to mass overseas migration, first of Jews, Poles, Finns, and Germans, and later also of Russians.

The transition overlapped with a land tenure system that led to land scarcity and unemployment because of the persistence of the large *latifundia,* a worldwide agrarian depression, widening income differentials that led to pauperization of the rural population, and legal discrimination against ethnic and religious minorities.

In the last quarter of the nineteenth century, the Russian Empire underwent a demographic transition that had dramatic effects on the region. The population of the Polish lands doubled in the nineteenth century. New industries in Warsaw and Łódź, which were centers of Russian industrial development in the late nineteenth century, could not absorb this surplus population. Three million Poles migrated to other countries from Prussian, Austrian, and Russian Poland by World War I. The heaviest migration was from agricultural provinces in the north—Suwałki, Płock, and Łomża. Over 600,000 Poles migrated from Congress Poland (Russian Poland) to the U.S. between 1871 and 1914, 80 percent of them after 1900.

The population of Finland grew to 2.6 million between 1850 and 1900 as the rural population doubled in size. Finns migrated in the eighteenth century to Stockholm, other parts of Scandinavia, and St. Petersburg. In the 1870s, after a succession of poor harvests and a shift from arable farming to dairy farming, they began migrating to the U.S. Finnish migration grew rapidly between 1880 and 1893. The migration spread from north to south, rising to over a quarter of a million people between 1894 and 1914.

In Russian Baltic territories, Lithuanians migrated from Kovno, Suwałki and Vilna; Latvians from Courland, Livonia, and Vitebsk; and Estonians from the Russian provinces of Estonia. Estonians moved to underpopulated areas in Russia; Lithuanians to Latvia, St. Petersburg, Moscow, and Odessa, and also to England and Scotland.

In the northwestern region of Russia (Byelorussia), Russians migrated to the west from Vilna, Grodno, Minsk, and Mohilev—territories formerly under Polish-Lithuanian rule. In the South (Ukraine), migration was from Volhynia, Podolia, and Kiev, at first as seasonal migrants to European countries, and later to England, Argentina, Brazil, and North America. Over 90 percent of those who migrated overseas went to the United States as laborers, agricultural workers, and domestic servants.

In the late nineteenth century, overseas migration of Russians was relatively limited; it became a mass migration only between 1907 and 1914. Most Russian migration prior to 1907 was internal to industrial cities and settlements in the east, to farms in southern Russia, and to western Siberia.

Between 1875 and 1880 some 25,000 Russian Germans migrated to the U.S. These were Volga Germans, whose ancestors—from Hesse, Baden, Wuerttemburg, Alsace, and the Palatinate—had been invited in the second half of the eighteenth century by Catherine the Great to establish agricultural colonies in Russia. Many settled in the lower Volga and Black Sea regions. They were attracted by the promise of exemption from military service and religious toleration, which they had enjoyed for 150 years. When their status was changed in the 1870s they migrated to the U.S.[2] Many were Mennonites who went first to Mexico and afterwards to the U.S. The migration of Volga Germans to the U.S. slowed in the 1880s but revived in the 1890s during a period of poor harvests and hard times in Russia. Additional incentives to migrate came from the Russification policy of the government and pressure to convert to the Russian Orthodox Church. Over a quarter of a million Volga Germans migrated by the early twentieth century to Kansas, Minnesota, the Dakota Territories, and Nebraska.

The largest number of migrants from the Russian Empire were Poles and Russian Jews. The Jewish population in the Empire increased from 1.5 million to over 5.2 million by the end of the nineteenth century. About 1.5 million Jews emigrated to the United States between 1880 and 1914, while half a million went to South America, Canada, South Africa, Western Europe, and Palestine.

Jewish emigration originated in the 25 provinces of the Pale of Settlement. There were 4.9 million Jews living in the Pale, which extended from the Baltic to the Black Sea and consisted of Lithuania, Byelorussia, the southwestern provinces (Ukraine), and parts of Poland. The Pale had four main regions: ten Polish provinces (Suwałki, Siedlce, Łublin, Łomzȧ, Płock, Warsaw, Łódź, Kalisz, Radom, and Kielce), with 27 percent of the Jewish population; six provinces in northwest Russia (Kovno, Vilna, Grodno, Minsk, Mohilev, and Vitebsk), with 29 percent; five provinces in southwest Russia (Volhynia, Podolia, Kiev, Poltava, and Chernigov), with 29 percent; and four provinces in southern Russia (Bessarabia, Kherson, Tauria, and Ekaterinoslav), with 14 percent of the Jewish population.

The Polish provinces Suwałki, Łomzȧ, and Płock, together with the provinces of the northwest region, had the highest population density and were therefore the poorest in the Pale.

In addition to the general factors mentioned previously that contributed to migration from the Russian Empire, there were specific factors that affected the migration of Russian Jews. Emigration was heavily influenced by the role of the State in Russia. Jews had migrated to Poland in the Middle Ages and had been Russian subjects since the late eighteenth century. After 1835, however, they were allowed to settle only in the Pale. The prohibition against Jews buying land in Russia began with the Polish insurrection in 1864 and the May Laws of 1882. Jews were excluded from rural localities and also prohibited from settling in some cities in the Pale. These restrictions were sufficient to keep the majority of Russian Jews in non-agricultural activities.

Under Alexander II concessions were made to Jewish merchants, who could live outside the Pale, and Jews were given limited opportunities for social mobility. Under Alexander III and Nicholas II, however, there was a reactionary transformation of government policies concerning Jews.

Mass migration of Russian Jews began under Alexander III in 1881. There were two major waves: the first was between 1882 and 1892, the second between 1898 and 1906. Fluctuations in annual migration to the U.S. after 1880 reflected changing political and economic conditions in Russia. The May Laws of May 3, 1882 were promulgated as a result of a series of anti-Jewish pogroms and massacres in the Ukraine and Bessarabia in 1881. They prohibited further settlement of Jews in rural districts and prohibited Jews from buying or renting lands outside the cities and incorporated towns (*miestechkos*). A mass exodus followed the May Laws of 1882.

Another exodus occurred in 1887 when the government revived anti-Jewish policies with educational restrictions and expulsions. New migration peaks occurred in 1891 and 1892, following restrictions on residence and the wholesale expulsions of some 20,000 Jews from Moscow. Thousands of families of Jewish artisans and merchants were forced to leave Moscow and other interior cities to seek new homes in the cities of the Pale. In 1892 emigration was given official legal toleration by the State, but emigrants were forced to renounce their right to return.

A second, larger wave of migration began in 1898 and continued to 1906. It coincided with the start of a new period of economic depression, revolutionary terrorism, and anti-Jewish propaganda. Pogroms broke out throughout the Pale—starting with the massacres in Nikolaev (1902), Kischinev (1903), and Gomel (1904)—and spread in 1905 and 1906 into the Polish provinces of Bialystok and Siedlce. Almost half a million Russian Jews fled to the U.S. during the period of the Russo-Japanese War, the abortive revolution of 1905, and the anti-Jewish massacres in the Pale. By the outbreak of war in 1914, another 300,000 had followed.

Emigration was not legally regulated in Russia until 1892. Emigrants were thus at the mercy of shipping agents and speculators. After the May pogroms of 1881, many Jews who left Odessa for the U.S. traveled by way of Hamburg. There was direct rail communication to Bremen and Hamburg from the German border. Starting in 1888 there was also service from Libau, a Baltic port. However, direct embarkation from Russia was not feasible for most emigrants because of the high cost of passports. After 1898, Russian emigrants crossed the Russian German border at Eydtkuhnen, Prostken, and Tilsit, then traveled by rail to Hamburg and Bremen to board ships for America. About 70 percent of the migration from the Russian Empire between 1890 and 1910 went by way of Hamburg and Bremen[3].

Origins, Destinations, and Personal Characteristics of Migrants from the Russian Empire

Overseas migration of Poles from Russia began in the 1870s, accelerated during the 1890s, and continued until World War I. Migration from Congress (Russian) Poland reached its high point between 1895 and 1913 with over 450,000 emigrants to the U.S. The U.S. was the most important overseas destination, although Poles also migrated to Canada, Argentina, and Brazil.

The population of Russian Poland grew from 5 to 10 million between 1815 and 1910. Population increased more rapidly than urbanization, and agricultural production lagged because of excessive fragmentation of farms. Villages became overpopulated because peasants were unable to migrate to cities. In the early years of Polish migration, the main objective of the migrants was to save money to buy land. In later years migrants left in search of work, and the migrant population was more evenly distributed between peasants and workers. By the early twentieth century Polish peasants were buying land with immigrant remittances from the U.S.[4]

In addition to overseas migration, however, there was a massive seasonal movement of agricultural laborers from Congress Poland to the large Junker estates in eastern Germany and into the mines and metallurgical industries of Silesia. This internal east-west flow grew out of the increasing demand for labor created by Germany's industrial revolution.

Polish migrants to the U.S. came from low-wage agrarian districts on the Prussian border. Over two-thirds of the villagers were landless farmhands or owners of "dwarf" farms. About 12 to 15 percent were urban workers. Female migrants were largely servants. Poles migrated for the most part as singles. The proportion of females and children to adult males was low. Suwalki provided the heaviest overseas emigration between 1890 and 1904. Poles showed a high rate of return; about 30 percent of the migrants returned to Poland.

Russian overseas migration was similar in structure to Polish migration but was more of a temporary labor migration. It started later and reached a critical mass only between 1907 and 1914. Russians lived in close proximity to Lithuanians, Poles, and Jews. Overseas migrants originated in Byelorussia and the Ukraine. Vilna and Volhynia were major centers of Russian migration. Some 18,000 Russians emigrated from Vilna to the U.S. between 1908 and 1910. Immigrant remittances from Russians and

Lithuanians in the U.S. were one of the most important sources of income in the region. Overseas migration from the province of Minsk led to a shortage of agricultural labor and rising agricultural wages in 1910[5].

Russian migration intensified in 1907 with government repression of strikes of farmers and farm workers in western and southern Russia. The Stolypin agrarian reforms freed peasants from legal and economic obligations to the *mir* and started a wave of migration both internal to eastern Russia and overseas to the U.S.

Russian migrants were predominantly farm laborers, landless peasants, and small farmers who left parents and families at home. Forty percent were illiterate and one-third returned to Russia.

There were marked differences in migration patterns among Russian Jews in the Pale based on population densities, age, sex, and occupational background. Russian census data for 1897 suggest that the early wave of immigration to the U.S. was probably from Lithuania and Byelorussia. There was more poverty and overcrowding in the northwestern region where Jews constituted almost three-fifths of the urban population, hence a greater propensity to migrate. The northwest also had a larger share of Jews in handicrafts and manufacturing than in trade or commerce and a lower ratio of males in the prime migrating age group than in the south and southwest[6]. In the less-crowded southern and southwestern regions there were fewer restrictions on Jews and more employment opportunities as a result of industrial growth.

As with most other groups, the propensity to migrate among Russian Jews was higher among males than females, among people in prime working ages than the very young or very old, and among the lower income groups more vulnerable to dislocation in the transition to industrialization and modernization. Those who were oppressed by legal restrictions and persecution were also more likely to emigrate.[7]

Jews migrating from the interior regions of Russia into the Pale were economically stronger than those who had originally settled there. Older settlers were forced out and thus the first to migrate to the U.S. Economic conditions in the south were better. Jews began to migrate from the south and southwest only after the pogroms of the pre-World War I decade, which were concentrated there.

The exile of Jews from rural areas to the cities and towns of the Pale, and the limitations on their mobility, had long-term economic effects. Jews were excluded from employment in government and higher education.

Government-sponsored discriminatory policies deprived them of economic opportunities to enter new regions, markets, and areas of employment, which forced massive emigration abroad.

Russian Jewish immigrants were more urban, more married, and had a higher ratio of females to males than most other immigrant groups. A quarter were children under fourteen years of age. The high proportion of women and children indicates a movement of families.

Chain migration played an important role in Jewish immigration. Personal ties to family and friends in the community of origin were very important. Russian Jews left extended families at home and migrated to families of orientation (father, mother, sister, brother) and procreation (wife, husband, son, daughter)—that is to nuclear family networks already in the U.S.[8]

Russian Jewish immigration had a high proportion of skilled workers. Small craftsmen and skilled workers made up over two-thirds of the occupations of migrants, but they accounted for less than two-fifths of the census population. Small shopkeepers and peddlers accounted for 5 percent of migrant occupations, but were nearly one-third of the census population[9]. The large number of skilled laborers and artisans among immigrants reflected the overcrowded conditions of these trades, particularly in the northwest region of the Pale.

Because of discriminatory policies of the State, Jews did not benefit from the industrialization of Russia at the end of the nineteenth century. To relieve poverty and unemployment, Jewish workers had to move from petty trades and commerce into higher productivity sectors in industry and handicrafts.

The majority of Jewish immigrants were skilled workers. Almost half were garment workers—tailors, dressmakers, seamstresses, etc. Carpenters, cabinet makers, woodworkers, shoemakers, clerks, painters, glaziers, butchers, bakers, watch makers, metal workers, and machinists made up about 30 percent of the skilled workers. Farmers and unskilled laborers, on the other hand, accounted for only 25 percent of the labor force.

Large-scale migration of artisans to western Europe and to the U.S. made room for Jews to move from rural to urban areas and from commerce into industry and handicrafts. Interregional migration to southern Russia and the Polish districts from the densely populated northwest made possible the shift from unskilled to skilled occupations. Thus, while Jews were moving interregionally from north to south and from rural areas to towns in Russia, they were also moving overseas to commercial and manufacturing centers in the northeastern United States. The majority went to New York, Philadelphia, and Massachusetts. But others settled in New Jersey, Connecticut, Illinois, Ohio, and Maryland. The high concentration of Russian Jews in skilled crafts and trades explains to a large degree the occupational and urban distribution of Jewish immigrants in the U.S[10].

Conclusion

Historians and genealogists in the field of immigration research have relied on aggregate level data to examine the development, extent, and character of population movements. With information available in these volumes, researchers will be able to go beyond gross statistical profiles to study these movements at the level of microhistory—to follow individuals and families from their place of origin to their destination and to focus on personal circumstances. This will enable scholars to assess the push-and-pull factors that contributed to the migration phenomenon and to give a more human dimension to the mass movement.

The editor would like to take this opportunity to express his deep appreciation to Mr. Robert I. Silverman. Without his encouragement, understanding, and patience, and without the generous support that he and his associates provided, this work on Russian migration, preliminary as it is, could not have been undertaken. These volumes are therefore dedicated to him.

IRA A. GLAZIER

Director, Temple-Balch Institute
Center for Immigration Research

FOOTNOTES

1. V.V. Oblensky (Osinskyii), *Mezhdunarodnye i Mezhdukontinental 'nye migratsii dovoennoj Rossi i CCCR* (Moscow, 1928), 22–23.

2. N.L. Tudorianu, *Ocherki Rossiskoi Trudovoi Emigratsii Perioda Imperializma* (Kishinev, 1986), 124–25.

3. Ibid., 124–25, 138.

4. K. Groniowski, "Emigration from Poland to America," *Emigration from Northern Central and Southern Europe* (Cracow, 1981), 151–64.

5. R. Melville, "Permanent Emigration and Temporary Transnational Migration: Jewish, Polish and Russian Emigration From Tsarist Russia, 1861–1914," *Overseas Migration From East-Central and Southeastern Europe 1880–1940,* edited by J. Puskas (Budapest, 1990), 139–42.

6. S. Kuznets, "Immigration of Russian Jews to the United States: Background and Structure," *Perspectives in American History,* 9 (1975), 62–79.

7. Ibid., 93–112.

8. I.A. Glazier and R.J. Kleiner, "Analisi comparate degli emigranti dell 'Europa meridionale e orientale attraverso le liste passeggeri delle navi statunitensi," *Altreitalie,* 7 (1992), 115–25.

9. Oblensky, op. cit., 25.

10. A. Kahan, *Essays in Jewish Social and Economic History,* edited by R. Weiss (Chicago, 1986), 101–17.

Table 1

Emigration from the Russian Empire to the U.S. 1871–1910

Gross Immigration

Year	Russian Empire (1)	Poland (2)	Russian Hebrews (3)	Russian Hebrews to N.Y. (4)	Russian Hebrews as % of Russian Empire (5)=(3)/(1)
1871	673	535	121	—	18.0
1872	1018	1647	266	—	26.1
1873	1634	3338	497	—	30.4
1874	4073	1795	587	—	14.4
1875	7997	984	898	1796	11.2
1876	4775	925	570	1140	11.9
1877	6599	533	713	1426	10.8
1878	3048	547	360	719	11.8
1879	4453	489	494	988	11.1
1880	5014	2177	4165	4332	83.1
1881	5041	5614	5218	7949	—
1882	16918	4672	13249	9955	78.3
1883	9909	2011	7542	5269	76.1
1884	12689	4536	10248	11753	80.8
1885	17158	3085	12939	12095	75.4
1886	17800	3939	13646	12874	76.7
1887	30766	6128	23381	21404	76.0

Year	Russian Empire (1)	Poland (2)	Russian Hebrews (3)	Russian Hebrews to N.Y. (4)	Russian Hebrews as % of Russian Empire (5)=(3)/(1)
1888	33487	5826	25195	18784	75.2
1889	33916	4922	25265	17209	74.5
1890	35598	11073	28252	19557	79.4
1891	47426	24797	40662	39587	85.7
1892	82511	40536	69959	55996	84.8
1893	43310	16374	35246	20741	81.4
1894	39278	1941	28079	16731	71.5
1895	35907	709	25348	14152	70.6
1896	51445	691	36219	17617	70.4
1897	25816	4165	19325	11106	74.9
1898	29828	4726	22302	11581	74.8
1899	60982	*	24275	*	39.8
1900	90787	*	37011	*	40.8
1901	85257	*	37660	*	44.2
1902	107347	*	37846	*	35.2
1903	136093	*	47609	*	35.0
1904	145141	*	77544	*	53.4
1905	184897	*	92388	*	50.0
1906	215665	*	125234	*	58.1
1907	258943	*	114932	*	44.4
1908	156711	*	71922	*	45.9

1909	120460	*	39150	*	32.5
1910	186792	*	59824	*	32.0
Total	2357162	158715	1216141	334761	

* n.d.

Columns 1 and 2 are from the *Reports of the Immigration Commission*, vol. III (*Statistical Review of Immigration, 1819–1910*), 61st Cong., 3rd sess., S. Doc. 756 (Washington, D.C., 1911), Table 9, Pt. 2, Arno Press 1970. These data are compiled from official returns of the Bureau of Statistics, U.S. Treasury Department.

Column 2: Poland, a country without a State, was partitioned by the Austro-Hungarian, German, and Russian Empires for the third time in 1795. Between 1820 and 1898 Poland was recognized as an independent country only by American statisticians. From 1899 to 1919 Polish statistics are combined with the migration statistics of the countries to which she belonged.

Column 3: Annual series have been calculated from Columns 1 and 2 following S. Kuznets, "Immigration of Russian Jews to the United States: Background and Structure," *Perspectives in American History*, 9 (1975): 40–41. Immigration of Jews from the Russian Empire has been estimated at 70 percent of total immigration and from Poland at 43 percent of total immigration. The proportion of immigrants from Poland is based on the ratios of foreign born from Russian Poland in the U.S. Census of 1890. (*Statistical Review of Immigration*, Table 9, p.416). No allowance has been made for immigration from Canada. For 1899–1910, official data on race is from the *Statistical Review of Immigration.*

There are no official statistics on Jewish immigration between 1875 and 1898. S. Joseph has constructed a series from partial returns collected by the Hebrew immigrant aid societies of New York, Philadelphia, and Baltimore between 1886 and 1898 and has extrapolated his estimates back to 1881–1885. The statistical series on Russian Jewish arrivals in the *Evreiskaia Entsiklopedia,* vol. 3, "Amerika" (St. Petersburg, 1907) assumes mistakenly that migration from Russia consisted only of Russian Jews.

Column 4 is derived from ships' passenger lists: 1875–1879 arrivals include all U.S. ports; 1880–1898 is only for New York arrivals. Between 1875 and 1879 Russian Jewish arrivals are estimated at 20 percent of the combined totals of Columns 1 and 2. From 1881 to 1886 Russian Empire arrivals are deflated by a factor of 0.70 and Polish arrivals by 0.43. The anomaly of larger numbers to New York in 1880, 1881, and 1884 (Column 4) than to all U.S. ports (Column 3) results from New York being on a calendar year (January–December) rather than a fiscal year basis (July–June). From 1887 to 1898 data are from S. Joseph, *Jewish Immigration to United States*, Table V^1, 161. Official data on race after 1899 is reported in *Statistical Review of Immigration.*

Table 2

Immigration to the U.S. from the Russian Empire and Finland (by race or people and country of last permanent residence)

1899–1910

Year	Finnish	German	Jewish	Lithuanian	Polish	Russian
1899	6048	5383	24275	6838	15517	1657
1900	12515	5349	37011	10297	22500	1165
1901	9966	5643	37660	8805	21475	655
1902	13854	8452	37846	9975	33859	1536
1903	18776	10485	47689	14420	39548	3565
1904	10077	7128	77544	12707	32577	3907
1905	16671	6722	92388	17649	47224	3278
1906	13461	10279	125234	13697	46204	5282
1907	14311	13480	114932	24811	73122	16085
1908	6303	10009	71978	13270	37947	16324
1909	11202	7781	39150	14595	37770	9099
1910	14999	10016	59824	21676	63635	14768
Total	148183	100727	765531	168740	471378	77321

Source: *Reports of the Immigration Commission*, vol. III (*Statistical Review of Immigration 1819–1910*), 61st Cong., 3rd sess., S. Doc. 756 (Washington, D.C., 1911), Table 14, p. 62.

Table 3

Immigration to the U.S. from the Russian Empire (by race, people, and country of last permanent residence) 1899–1910 (percent)

Year	Finnish (1)	German (2)	Jewish (3)	Lithuanian (4)	Polish (5)	Russian (6)
1899	9.9	8.8	39.8	11.2	25.4	2.7
1900	13.8	5.9	40.8	11.3	24.8	1.3
1901	11.7	1.6	44.2	10.0	25.2	0.8
1902	12.9	8.0	35.3	9.3	31.5	1.4
1903	13.8	7.7	35.0	10.6	29.1	2.6
1904	7.0	5.0	53.9	8.8	22.6	2.7
1905	9.0	3.6	50.0	9.5	25.5	1.8
1906	6.2	4.8	58.1	6.4	21.4	2.4
1907	5.5	5.2	44.4	9.6	28.2	6.2
1908	4.0	6.4	45.9	8.5	24.2	10.4
1909	9.3	6.5	32.5	12.1	31.4	7.6
1910	8.0	5.4	32.1	11.6	34.1	2.9

Source: Calculated from *Reports of the Immigration Commission,* vol. III (*Statistical Review of Immigration 1819–1910*), 61st Cong., 3rd sess., S. Doc. 756 (Washington, D.C., 1911), Table 14, p.62.

BIBLIOGRAPHY

Dinnerstein, L. "East European Jewish Migration to the United States 1880–1914." *Les Migrations Internationale De La Fin Du XVIII Siecle a Nos Jours* (1980).

Evreisksaia Entsiklopedia. 16 vols. St. Petersburg, 1915.

Ferenczi, I., and W. Willcox. *International Migrations*. 2 vols. New York, 1931.

Glazier, I.A., and R.J. Kleiner. "Analisi comparate degli emigranti dell'Europa meridionale e orientale attraverso le liste passeggeri delle navi statunitensi." *Altreitalie*, 7 (1992).

Groniowski, K. "Emigration from Poland to America." *Emigration from Northern, Central and Southern Europe*. Cracow, 1981.

Joseph, S. *Immigration to the United States 1881–1910*. New York, 1914.

Just, M. *Ost und sudosteuropaische Amerika-wanderung 1881–1914*. Stuttgart, 1988.

Kahan, A. *Essays in Jewish Social and Economic History*. Edited by R. Weiss. Chicago, 1986.

Kuznets, S. "Immigration of Russian Jews to the United States: Background and Structure." *Perspectives in American History*, 9 (1975).

Melville, R. "Permanent Emigration and Temporary Transnational Migration: Jewish, Polish and Russian Emigration From Tsarist Russia, 1861–1914." *Overseas Migration From East-Central and Southeastern Europe 1880–1940*. Edited by J. Puskas. Budapest, 1990.

Oblensky (Osinskyii), V.V. *Mezhdunarodnye i Mezhdukontinental 'nye migratsii dovoennoj Rossi i CCCR*. Moscow, 1928.

________. "Emigration from and Immigration into Russia." *International Migrations*. Vol. 2. Edited by W. Willcox. New York, 1931.

Recueil De Materiaux Sur La Situation Economique Des Israelistes De Russie. 2 vols. Paris, 1906.

Reports of the Immigration Commission, vol. III. *(Statistical Review of Immigration, 1819-1910; Distribution of Immigrants 1850–1900)*. 61st Cong., 3rd sess., S. Doc., 756. Washington, D.C.: Government Printing Office, 1911.

Ritterband, P., B. Kosmin, and J. Scheckner. "Counting Jewish Populations: Methods and Problems." *American Jewish Year Book* 88 (1988).

Rubinow, I.M. "Economic Conditions of the Jews in Russia." *Bulletin of the Bureau of Labor* 72. Washington, D.C.: Department of Commerce and Labor, 1907.

Sarna, J. "The Myth of No Return: Jewish Return Migration to Eastern Europe 1881–1914." *Labor Migration in the Atlantic Economies*. Edited by D. Hoerder. Westport, Conn., 1985.

Stampfer, S. "The Geographic Background of East European Jewish Migration." *Migration Across Time and Nations*. Edited by I.A. Glazier and L. De Rosa. New York, 1986, 220–30.

Tudorianu, N.L. *Ocherki Rossiskoi Trudovoi Emigratsii Perioda Imperializma*. Kishinev, 1986.

Virtanen, Keijo. *Settlement or Return: Finnish Emigrants (1860–1930) in the International Overseas Return Migration Movement*. Turku, Finland: Migration Institute, 1979.

Wischnitzer, M. *To Dwell in Safety: The Story of Jewish Migration since 1800*. Philadelphia, 1948.

KEY *

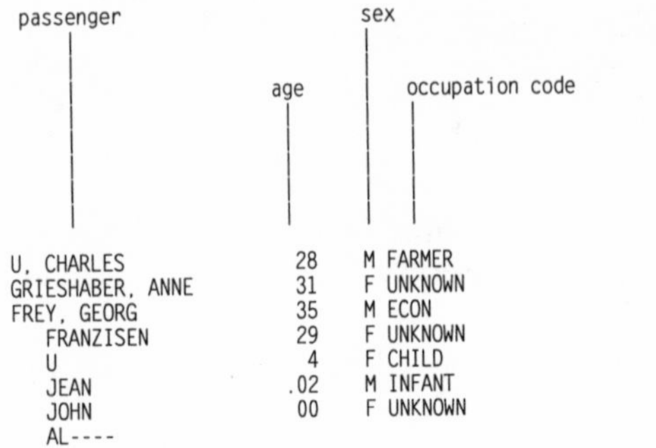

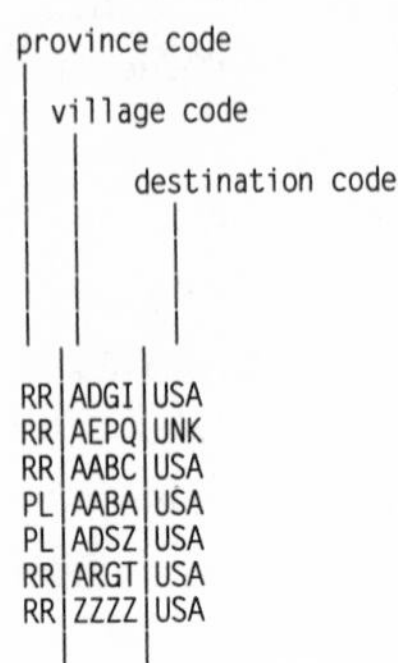

.02 - two month old infant
00 unknown age

UNK - unknown destination
ZZZZ - unknown village
UN - unknown province

--- letters illegible
U unknown last name
U unknown first name

* Information in the above fields is as it appears in the document. For this reason, information on the provinces and villages can often be the same. Information on occupation may also include data on personal status.

LIST OF PROVINCE (OR COUNTRY) CODES

RR RUSSIA
FN FINLAND
PL POLAND

LIST OF OCCUPATIONS WITH CODES

ACCT	ACCOUNTANT
ACHTT	ARCHITECT
ACROBAT	ACROBAT
ADJ	ADJUSTER
ADLR	ANTIQUE DEALER
ADV	ADVOCATE
AGNT	AGENT
AGNTTH	THEATRICAL AGENT
AGRC	AGRICULTURIST
AGRT	AGRICULTURALIST
AHR	AUTHOR
AMR	ARMOURER
ANT	AERONAUT
APDST	APPRENTICE
APTC	APOTHECARY
AR	ACTOR
ART	ARTIST
ASST	ASSISTANT
ATH	ATHLETE
ATR	ACTUARY
ATSN	ARTISAN
ATTNY	ATTORNEY
AUC	AUCTIONEER
AXMKR	AX MAKER
AY	ARMY
B	BROTHER
BALR	BAILER
BAR	BARRISTER
BARRELMKR	BARRELMAKER
BAT	BATTER
BBR	BARBER
BCHR	BUTCHER
BCK	BACKER
BCKM	BRICK MAKER
BCKMKR	BUCKLE MAKER
BDM	BIRD MAN
BDMKR	BEAD MAKER
BDS	BIRD SELLER
BGR	BAGGER
BILLPOSTER	BILL POSTER
BKBNDR	BOOKBINDER
BKLYR	BRICKLAYER
BKMR	BOOKMAKER
BKPR	BOOKKEEPER
BKR	BAKER
BKRB	BREAD BAKER
BKRC	CAKE BAKER
BKSL	BOOKSELLER
BL	BLEACHER
BLDMKR	BLADE MAKER
BLDR	BUILDER
BLKMKR	BLOCK MAKER
BLKSMH	BLACKSMITH
BLMN	BELLMAN
BLR	BOILER MAKER
BMKR	BROOM MAKER
BND	BINDER
BNKR	BANKER
BOAT	BOATMAN
BOMKR	BONNET MAKER
BOO	BOOKER
BOTT	BOTANIST
BRCMKR	BRACE MAKER
BRDE	BRIDE
BRDKP	BOARDINGHOUSE KEEPER
BRF	BRASS FOUNDER
BRFHR	BRASS FINISHER
BRG	BURGESS
BRK	BARKEEPER
BRKR	BROKER
BRKSTR	BRICK SETTER
BRM	BRUSH MAKER
BRN	BARON
BRR	BREWER
BRRGM	BARGEMAN
BRWKR	BRASS WORKER
BRZ	BRAZIER
BSCKMR	BISCUIT MAKER
BSKM	BASKETMAKER
BSP	BISHOP
BTC	BOOT CLOSER
BTDR	BARTENDER
BTH	BATHER
BTL	BUTLER
BTLMKR	BOTTLE MAKER
BTM	BIT MAKER
BTMK	BOATMAKER
BTMKR	BOOTMAKER
BTNM	BUTTON MAKER
BXMR	BOX MAKER
BY	BOY
BYR	BUYER
C	COUSIN
CADR	CARDER
CAGT	COMMERCIAL AGENT
CAND	CANDIDATE
CAR	CARRIER
CASEMAKER	CASE MAKER
CBDR	CABDRIVER
CBLDR	CARRIAGE BUILDER/MAKER
CBLR	COBBLER
CBMKR	CLOG AND BUTTON MAKER
CBTMKR	CABINET MAKER
CCHBLDR	COACH BUILDER
CCHMKR	COACH MAKER
CCHMN	COACHMAN
CCHPNTR	COACHPAINTER
CCMCHT	COMMERCIAL MERCHANT
CDN	COMEDIAN
CDR	CAR DRIVER
CDTR	CORD CUTTER
CDW	CORD WINDER
CDWN	CORDWAINER
CFEKPP	COFFEEHOUSE KEEPER
CGRMKR	CIGAR MAKER
CH	CHILD
CHAIR	CHAIR MAKER
CHBRMD	CHAMBER MAID
CHD	CHEESE DEALER
CHIMKR	CHINAMAKER
CHMAK	CHEESE MAKER
CHMGR	CHEESE MANAGER
CHMKR	CLOTH MAKER
CHMMTR	CHEMICAL MANUFACTURER
CHND	CHANDLER
CHND	CHILD MAID
CHR	CHASER
CHSWP	CHIMNEY SWEEPER
CHTMR	COACH TRIMMER
CHWKR	CLOTH WORKER
CK	COOK
CKCTR	CORK CUTTER
CKM	COOK MAID
CKR	CHECKER
CL	CLERK
CLDRS	CLOTH DRESSER
CLGYMN	CLERGYMAN
CLK	CLICKER
CLKMKR	CLOCK MAKER
CLLMN	CELLAR MAN
CLLR	COLLECTOR
CLMKR	COLOR MAKER
CLMNFTR	CLOTH MANUFACTURER
CLNT	COLONISATOR
CLR	COLLIER
CLRMKR	COLLAR MAKER
CLSH	CLOTH SHEARER
CMDR	COMMODORE
CMMSR	COMMISSIONER
CMN	COALMAN
CMP	COMPOSER
CMPR	COMPOSITOR
CMST	CHEMIST
CNDL	CANDLE MAKER

LIST OF OCCUPATIONS WITH CODES

CNF	CONFECTIONER
COL	COLONEL
COMP	COMPANION
CON	CONDUCTOR
COUM	COUCHMAN
COUMKR	COUCH MAKER
CPMKR	CAP MAKER
CPR	COOPER
CPRMNR	COPPER MINER
CPRSMH	COPPERSMITH
CPSPNGMKR	CAPSPRING MAKER
CPT	CAPTAIN
CPTLT	CAPITALIST
CPTR	CARPENTER
CPYR	COPIER
CRDMKR	CARD MAKER
CRMN	CAR MAN
CRPM	CARPET MAKER
CRR	COURIER
CRT	CARTER
CRTMK	CART MAKER
CRTMN	CARTMAN
CRTR	CROFTER
CSHR	CASHIER
CSL	CONSUL
CSLR	COUNSELOR
CSTR	CASTER
CTHR	CLOTHIER
CTL	CUTLER
CTLDLR	CATTLE DEALER
CTLDR	CATTLE DRIVER
CTLMN	CATTLE ATTENDANT
CTM	CATTLE MAN
CTNPTR	COTTON PRINTER
CTNSP	COTTON SPINNER
CTR	CUTTER
CTRMN	MOUNTAIN CUTTER
CTRV	COMMERCIAL TRAVELLER
CTTR	CONTRACTOR
CTW	CARTWRIGHT
CTYM	COUNTRY MAN
CULT	CULTIVATOR
CUR	CURRIER
CURE	CURER
CVER	CIVIL ENGINEER
CVR	CARVER
CVR-GLDR	CARVER AND GILDER
D	DAUGHTER
DARY	DAIRYMAN
DCT	DECORATOR
DETECTIVE	DETECTIVE
DFTMN	DRAFTSMAN
DGR	DIGGER
DIACTR	DIAMOND SETTER
DIP	DIPLOMAT
DIR	DIVER
DISP	DISPATCHER
DLR	DEALER
DMS	DOMESTIC
DNC	DANCING MASTER/TEACHER
DPR	DRAPER
DPRASST	DRAPER ASSISTANT
DR	DOCTOR
DRG	DRUGGIST
DRS	DRESSER
DRSMKR	DRESSMAKER
DRV	DROVER
DRVR	DRIVER
DSGR	DESIGNER
DSTLR	LIQUOR MAKER
DT	DENTIST
DTR	DIRECTOR
DYR	DYER
ECON	ECONOMIST
ED	EDITOR
EGR	ENGRAVER
ELN	ELECTRICIAN
EMBD	EMBROIDERER
EMBS	EMBOSSER
EMPL	EMPLOYEE
ENGD	ENGINE DRIVER
ENGR	ENGINEER
ENMKR	ENGINE MAKER
EQ	EQUESTRIAN
F	STEPDAUGHTER
FA	FATHER
FAB	FABRICANT
FCTR	FILE CUTTER
FDR	FOUNDER
FDRS	FUR DRESSER
FEFNDR	IRON FOUNDER
FELMO	FELLMONGER
FFMR	FRUIT GROWER
FGR	FIGURIST
FHAD	FARM HAND
FID	FIDDLER
FIL	FILER
FINA	FINANCE AGENT
FLABR	FARM LABORER
FLMLR	FLOUR MILLER
FLSH	FLESHER
FLSMH	FILE SMITH
FLST	FLORIST
FLUMR	FLUTE MAKER
FLWMKR	FLOWER MAKER
FLWSLR	FLOWER SELLER
FLXNR	FLAXENER
FMR	FARMER
FMR-MECH	FARMER AND MECHANIC
FMSTWD	FARM STEWARD
FNR	FANNER
FORMN	FOREMAN
FRD	FRUIT DEALER,SELLER
FRDYR	FUR DYER
FRG	FORGEMAN
FRMKR	FRAME MAKER
FRMN	FIREMAN
FRNGMR	FRINGE MAKER
FRR	FARRIER
FRWKR	FRAME WORKER
FSHMN	FISHERMAN
FSR	FORESTER
FSVNT	FARM SERVANT
FTMN	FOOTMAN
FTR	FITTER
FUL	FULLER
FUNSHR	FURNISHER
FUR	FURRIER
FURNM	FURNITURE MAKER
FWKR	FACTORY WORKER
FY	FOYER
FYMN	FOUNDRYMAN
G	STEPSON
GALVANIZER	GALVANIZER
GAMB	GAMBLER
GCR	GROCER
GCRCL	GROCERY CLERK
GDBT	GOLDBEATER
GDMRMK	GAS METER MAKER
GDNR	GARDENER,GROWER
GDR	GRINDER
GDSM	GOLDSMITH
GDWK	GOLDWORKER
GEN	GENERAL
GENT	GENTLEMAN
GEOL	GEOLOGIST
GEOM	GEOMETER
GKPR	GAMESKEEPER
GL	GIRL
GLABR	GOLD LABORER
GLDR	GILDER
GLMK	GLOVE MAKER
GLSBR	GLASS BLOWER
GLSCTR	GLASS CUTTER

LIST OF OCCUPATIONS WITH CODES

GLSGDR	GLASS GRINDER
GLSL	GLASS SELLER
GLSMKR	GLASS MAKER
GLSR	GLASSER
GLVR	GLOVER
GM	GROOM
GNGMKR	GINGER MAKER
GNMKR	GUN MAKER
GNR	GRAINER
GRL	GIRDLER
GRN-GCR	GREEN GROCER
GRVMKR	GROVE MAKER
GSF	GASFITTER
GSMH	GUNSMITH
GTFTR	GRATE FITTER
GUL	GUILDER
GUNNR	US NAVY GUNNER
GVNS	GOVERNESS
GVR	GRAVER
GVTS	GOVERNMENT SERVICES
GYP	GYPSER
GZR	GLAZIER
H	HUSBAND
HAMF	HAT MANUFACTURER
HARB	HARBOR MASTER
HBRDSR	HABERDASHER
HD	HERD
HDWMR	HARDWARE MERCHANT
HJNR	HOUSE JOINER
HKR	HACKER
HMRMN	HAMMER MAN
HNTR	HUNTER
HP	HELPER
HPNTR	HOUSE PAINTER
HRCTR	HAIRCUTTER
HRDRS	HAIRDRESSER
HRNSNR	HORN SHINER
HRSB	HARNESS MAKER
HRSDLR	HORSE DEALER
HRSM	HARNESS MAKER
HRSMN	HORSEMAN
HS	HOSIER
HSKPR	HOUSEKEEPER
HSMD	HOUSE MAID
HSPTR	HOUSE CARPENTER
HSTLR	HOSTLER
HSWF	HOUSEWIFE
HTDRS	HATDRESSER
HTL	UNKNOWN
HTLKPR	HOTEL KEEPER
HTLMGR	HOTEL MANAGER
HTR	HATTER
HTTR	HAT TRIMMER
HUSB	HUSBAND
HWK	HAWKER
IMKR	INSTRUMENT MAKER
IMPLIT	IMPRINTER, LITHOGRAPHER
IND	INDEPENDENT
INDT	INDUSTRIALIST
INF	INFANT
INKP	INNKEEPER
INMKR	IRON MAKER
INMNGR	IRON MONGER
INS	INSURANCE BROKER
INSTR	INSTITUTOR
INSTRU	INSTRUCTOR
INT-B	FAMILY-GOING TO BROTHER
INT-FA	INTENDING TO GO TO FAMILY
INT-H	FAMILY-GOING TO HUSBAND
INT-S	FAMILY-GOING TO SON
INTP	INTERPRETER
INWKR	IRON WORKER
IPTR	IMPORTER
IRGR	IRON GROVER
IRN	IRONER
IRNMLDR	IRON MOULDER
IRNT	IRON TURNER
IRSMH	IRON SMITH
ISP	INSPECTOR
JAP	JAPANNER
JCK	JOCKEY
JDG	JUDGE
JLR	JAILER
JNLST	JOURNALIST
JNR	JOINER
JRNM	JOURNEYMAN
JRNW	JOURNEYWOMAN
JRT	JURIST
JUR	JURIST
JWLR	JEWELLER
KEMK	KEY MAKER
KMNFTR	KNIFE MANUFACTURER
KNGR	KNIFE GRINDER
KNR	KEENER
KNSMH	KNIFESMITH
KNTR	KNITTER
KPR	KEEPER
KTM	KETTLE MAKER
L	IN LAW
LABR	LABORER
LAD	LAUNDRY WORKER
LANDMAN	LANDMAN
LCMKR	LACE MAKER
LDGHKPR	LODGINGHOUSE KEEPER
LDMA	LADY'S MAID
LDY	LADY
LEDLR	LEATHER DEALER
LITGR	LITHOGRAPHER
LKMKR	LOCKMAKER
LKSH	LOCKSMITH
LLD	LANDLORD
LMNFTR	LEATHER MANUFACTURER
LMP	LUMPER
LNG	LINGUIST
LNWVR	LINEN WEAVER
LPLTR	LAMP LIGHTER
LPMKR	LAMP MAKER
LPR	LAPPER
LRCTR	LEATHER CUTTER
LRDR	LARD RENDERER
LRDRS	LEATHER DRESSER
LSORT	LETTER SORTER
LSPNR	LACE SPINNER
LT	LIEUTENANT
LTRCRR	LETTER CARRIER
LTRMN	LITERARY MAN
LWYR	LAWYER
M	MOTHER
MA	MATRON
MACH	MACHINIST
MACHMKR	MACHINE MAKER
MAGISTRAT	MAGISTRATE
MARMSN	MARBLE MASON
MARN	MARINE
MARWKR	MARBLE WORKER
MAT	MATTRESS MAKER
MCHT	MERCHANT
MCHT-CL	MERCHANT AND CLERK
MCTR	MARBLE CUTTER
MD	PHYSICIAN
MDW	MIDWIFE
MECH	MECHANIC
MED	MEDICAL WORKER
MGR	MANAGER
MILT	MILITARY
MKDLR	MILK DEALER
MKMD	MILKMAID
MKMN	MILKMAN
MKR	MAKER
MLBLDR	MILL BUILDER
MLCCHR	MOLE CATCHER
MLDR	MOLDER
MLHND	MILL HAND
MLNR	MILLINER

LIST OF OCCUPATIONS WITH CODES

MLR	MILLER BAKER
MLW	MILL WORKER
MLWR	MILLWRIGHT
MMRNR	MASTER MARINER
MNFTR	MANUFACTURER
MNLG	MINERALOGIST
MNR	MINER
MNSTR	MINISTER
MNTL	MANTLE MAKER
MNTR	MOUNTER
MOD	MODELER
MODIST	MODIST
MODMKR	MODEL MAKER
MON	MONK
MPOL	MARBLE POLISHER
MRMKR	MIRROR MAKER
MRNR	MARINER
MSMK	MASON MAKER
MSN	MASON
MSNY	MISSIONARY
MST	MASTER
MSTMKR	MILLSTONE MAKER
MSVNT	MANSERVANT
MTE	MATE
MTH	MATCHMAKER
MTLDLR	METAL DEALER
MTMKR	MANTEAU MAKER
MTMLDR	METAL MOLDER
MTWKR	METAL WORKER
MUSMR	MASTER OF MUSIC
MUSN	MUSICIAN
MUSTCHR	MUSIC TEACHER
MYR	MAYOR
N	NIECE/NEPHEW
NDMKR	NEEDLEMAKER
NER	UNKNOWN
NLR	NAILER
NLRM	NAIL MAKER
NLSMH	NAILSMITH
NN	NONE
NOTPUB	NOTARY PUBLIC
NRS	NURSE
NRSYMN	NURSERYMAN
NTRL	NATURALIST
NVGT	NAVIGATOR
NVOF	NAVAL OFFICER
NVYLT	NAVY LIEUTENANT
NWP	NEWSPAPER
OFF	OFFICER
OGNBDR	ORGAN BUILDER
OGNMK	ORGAN MAKER
OGNST	ORGANIST
OLM	OILMAN
OLMKR	OIL MAKER
OLREF	OIL REFINER
OP	OPERATIVE
OPSGR	OPERA SINGER
OPTC	OPTICIAN
OST	OSTLER
OVRSR	OVERSEER
PASM	PASTRY MAKER
PBL	PUBLICAN
PDLR	PEDDLER
PFNL	PROFESSIONAL
PH	PHOTOGRAPHER
PHD	DOCTOR OF PHILOSOPHY
PHLG	PHILOLOGIST
PHRS	PHARMACIST
PHS	PHILOSOPHER
PIMK	PIPE MAKER
PINST	PIANIST
PK	PACKER
PKBCHR	PORK CUTTER
PLGM	PLOUGHMAN
PLH	PLOW HOLDER
PLMN	POLICEMAN
PLN	PLANER
PLNTR	PLANTER
PLR	PLAITER
PLSTR	PLASTERER
PLT	POLITICIAN
PLTR	POULTERER
PLTWKR	PLATE WORKER
PLTYR	PLATE LAYER
PMBR	PLUMBER
PMKR	PIANO MAKER
PMM	PORTMANTEAU MAKER
PMNFTR	PIANO MANUFACTURER
PNM	PIN MAKER
PNR	POINTER
PNTR	PAINTER
PORKMAN	PORK MAN
POST	POST OFFICER
POT	PILOT
PPHGR	PAPER HANGER
PPMFR	PAPER MANUFACTURER
PPMKR	PAPER MAKER
PPNTMKR	PRINT MAKER
PPNTR	PORTRAIT PAINTER
PPR	PIPER
PPTR	PROPRIETOR
PRCH	PREACHER
PREST	PRIEST
PRF	PERFUMER
PRNTR	PRINTER
PROF	PROFESSOR
PROF-MUS	PROFESSOR OF MUSIC
PRS	PRESSMAN
PRSR	PRESSER
PRTR	PORTER
PRWKR	PRINT WORKER
PSN	PARSON
PSNT	PEASANT
PSP	LAPIDARY
PST	PASTER
PSTR	PASTOR
PT	POTTER
PTMKR	PATTERN MAKER
PTNR	PIANO TUNER
PTR	PUTTER
PTYM	POTTERY MAKER
PUB	PUBLISHER
PUD	PUDDLER
PUMK	PUMP MAKER
PURMKR	PURSE MAKER
PVMT	PROVISION MERCHANT
PVR	PAVER
PVTM	PRIVATE MAN
PVTR	PRIVATIER
PVTW	PRIVATE WOMAN
QA	QUAY WORKER
QRYMN	QUARRYMAN
R	RELATIVE
RAB	RABBI
RBM	RIBBON MAKER
RCR	RANCHER
RDMKR	ROAD MAKER
RE	RELIGIOUS
RE-MERCY	SISTER OF MERCY
REF	REFINER
REST	RESTAURANTEUR
RFMK	ROOF MAKER
RGM	RAGMAN
RKCTR	ROCK CUTTER
RKMKR	RAKE MAKER
RMKR	RULE MAKER
RNGR	RANGER
RPR	ROPE MAKER
RPTR	REPORTER
RR	RENTER
RRCL	RAILWAY CLERK
RROFF	RAILWAY OFFICER
RRWKR	RAILWAY WORKER
RST	RESTORER

LIST OF OCCUPATIONS WITH CODES

RTR	RENTIER
RVR	RIVETER
RZMKR	RAZOR MAKER
S	SON
S-FRM	SON OF FARMER
SALT	SALTER
SCH	SCHOLAR
SCHM	SCHOOL MASTER
SCHMS	SCHOOL MISTRESS
SCMKR	SCREW MAKER
SCP	SCULPTOR
SCR	SCOURER
SCRBLR	SCRIBBLER
SDLMKR	SADDLE MAKER
SDLR	SADDLER
SDM	SEEDMAN
SDWM	SODA WATER MAKER
SDYR	SILK DYER
SEALMAKER	SEAL MAKER
SEC	SECRETARY
SEMN	SEAMAN
SGL	SINGLE
SGN	SURGEON
SGNMKR	SIGN MAKER
SHAGNT	SHIP AGENT
SHCHND	SHIP CHANDLER
SHDL	SHEEP JOBBER
SHFM	SHEPHERD
SHGLR	SHINGLER
SHIBRO	SHIP BROKER
SHMK	SHOEMAKER
SHMST	SHIP MASTER
SHPAST	SHOP ASSISTANT
SHPC	SHIP'S CARPENTER
SHPKR	SHOPKEEPER
SHPMKR	SHIP MAKER
SHPNTR	SHIP PAINTER
SHPO	SHIP OWNER
SHPR	SHIPPER
SHPWRT	SHIPWRIGHT
SHR	SHEARER
SHV	SHAVER
SHW	SHOWMAN
SI	SISTER
SING	SINGER
SKDR	SKIN DRESSER
SKR	SKINNER
SLD	SOLDIER
SLKDRS	SILK DRESSER
SLKP	SALOON KEEPER
SLL	SELLER
SLMK	SAIL MAKER
SLMKR	SAIL MAKER
SLPL	SILVER PLATER
SLR	SAILOR
SLSMH	SILVERSMITH
SLSMN	SALESMAN
SLT	SLATER
SMH	SMITH
SML	SMELTER
SMSTS	SEAMSTRESS
SP	SPINSTER
SPB	SOAP BOILER
SPDLR	SOAP DEALER
SPM	SOAP MAKER
SPMNFTR	SOAP MANUFACTURER
SPNMSTR	SPINNING MASTER
SPNR	SPINNER
SPNTR	SIGN PAINTER
SPRTMN	SPORTSMAN
SRTMKR	SHIRT MAKER
SSPNR	SILK SPINNER
STAMKR	STAMP MAKER
STB	STONE BREAKER
STBLR	STABLER
STCL	STORE CLERK
STCLR	STREET CLEANER
STCTR	STONE CUTTER
STDNT	STUDENT
STDR	STAGE DRIVER
STGKPR	STAGE KEEPER
STK	STOKER
STKPR	STOREKEEPER
STKW	STOCKING WEAVER
STLMN	STABLEMAN
STLR	STONE LAYER
STMAKR	STICK MAKER
STMKR	STEEL MAKER
STMN	STATESMAN
STMSN	STONE MASON
STNER	STATIONER
STNG	STENOGRAPHER
STNR	STONER
STPLH	STONE POLISHER
STRK	STRIKER
STRW	SILK THROWSTER
STRY	STATUARY MAKER
STVMKR	STOVE MANUFACTURER
STWD	STEWARD
STWPR	STRAW PRESSER
STWS	STEWARDESS
SUGB	SUGAR BAKER
SUGBBLR	SUGAR BOILER
SUGF	SUGAR REFINER
SUGM	SUGAR MAKER
SVNT	SERVANT
SVYR	SURVEYOR
SWMKR	SAW MAKER
SWP	SWEEPER
SWR	SAWYER
SWVR	SILK WEAVER
TBCL	TOBACCO LABORER
TBCMNFTR	TOBACCO MANUFACTURER
TBCNST	TOBACCONIST
TBKR	TABLE MAKER
TCH	TECHNICIAN
TCHR	TEACHER
TCHRL	TEACHER OF LANGUAGES
TDR	TRADER
TECH	TECHNICIAN
TELG	TELEGRAPHER
TER	TEAMSTER
TERM	TERRACE MAKER
THEO	THEOLOGIAN
THPROF	THEOLOGY PROFESSOR
THR	THATCHER
TIL	TILLER
TILM	TILE MAKER
TIR	TINNER
TKMKR	TRUNK MAKER
TKR	TINKER
TLKPR	TOLL KEEPER
TLR	TAILOR
TLRW	WAISTCOAT MAKER
TMKR	THREAD MAKER
TNM	TINMAN
TNMICH	TIN MAN, IRON WORKER, COPPER SMITH
TNMK	TIN MAKER
TNR	TANNER
TNSTH	TINSMITH
TPCTR	TYPE CUTTER
TPGPH	TYPOGRAPHER
TPMK	TAPE MAKER
TPS	TYPESETTER
TR	TILER
TRDM	MAN OF TRADE
TRDSMN	TRADESMAN
TRMM	TRIMMING MAKER
TRMR	TRIMMER
TRNR	TRAINER
TRSR	TREASURER
TRVLR	TRAVELLER
TSLMK	TASSEL MAKER
TT	TOURIST

LIST OF OCCUPATIONS WITH CODES

TU	TURNER
TUT	TUTOR
TVN	TAVERNER
TYMN	TOYMAN
U	UNCLE
UMKR	UMBRELLA MAKER
UNDTKR	UNDERTAKER
UPHST	UPHOLSTERER
VAL	VALET
VAR	VARNISHER
VET	VETERINARIAN
VIOL	VIOLINIST
VLNTR	VOLUNTEER
VLR	UNKNOWN
VLT	VELVET WORKER
VNDRS	VINE-DRESSER
VNT	VINTNER
VSGN	VETERINARIAN SURGEON
W	WIFE
W-FMR	WIFE OF FARMER
W-SHMK	WIFE OF SHOEMAKER
WCHMKR	WATCHMAKER
WDCDR	WOOD CORDER
WDCTR	WOOD CUTTER
WDCV	WOOD CARVER
WDMCHT	WOOD MERCHANT
WDMN	WOOD MAN
WDRNGR	WOOD RANGER
WDTU	WOOD TURNER
WET	WATERMAN
WGGM	WAGON MAKER
WGHR	WEIGHER
WGNR	WAGONER
WGR	WINE GROWER
WGT	WRIGHT
WHLR	WHEELER
WHR	WHEELWRIGHT
WI	WIDOW/WIDOWER
WI-FMR	WIDOW/WIDOWER-FARMER
WIDR	WIRE DRAWER
WIWKR	WIRE WORKER
WLCR	WALL CLEANER
WLD	WELDER
WLDPR	WOOL DRAPER
WLS	WOOL SPINNER
WLSR	WOOL SORTER
WLST	WOOL STAPLER
WLWRK	WOOL WORKER
WMCHT	WINE MERCHANT
WMN	WATCHMAN
WO	WOMAN
WPRTR	WINE PORTER
WRHSMN	WAREHOUSE MAN
WRMKR	WIRE MAKER
WRT	WRITER
WSHR	WASHER
WSMH	WHITESMITH
WTR	WAITER
WTRPR	WATERPROOF MAKER
WTRS	WAITRESS
WVR	WEAVER
WWSH	WHITE WASHER
WXM	WAX MAKER
Y	GRANDPARENT

LIST OF VILLAGE CODES

Code	Village
****	BORN-AT-SEA
AADE	ALTONA
AADQ	AMSTERDAM
AAEC	ANTWERP
AAER	ARNSTEIN
AAHU	BASEL
AAJV	BERGA
AAJX	BERGEN
AAKH	BERLIN
AAMJ	BILLIGHEIM
AAQH	BOSTON
AARR	BREMEN
AAXF	CASSEL
AAXL	CHICAGO
AAYK	COPENHAGEN
AAYZ	CULM
AAZF	DAHLEN
AAZQ	DANZIG
ABBX	DOBRA
ABHT	ELBERFELD
ABIJ	ALSACE
ABPN	FREUDENTHAL
ABPS	FRIEDENSDORF
ABQB	FRIEDRICHSTADT
ABUT	GNESEN
ABVE	GOERLITZ
ACBD	HAMBERG
ACBF	HAMBURG
ACBR	HANNOVER
ACDS	HAVRE
ACDU	HECHINGEN
ACNZ	JOHANNISTHAL
ACON	KALISCH
ACOV	KANDEL
ACSD	KOENIGSBERG
ACSX	KONITZ
ACTC	KRAKAU
ACTQ	KROTOSCHIN
ACWP	LAUFFEN
ACXZ	LEMBERG
ACZG	LICHTENTHAL
ADAT	LISSA
ADAX	LIVERPOOL
ADBQ	LONDON
ADCR	LUEBECK
ADDQ	MAGDEBURG
ADED	MANCHESTER
ADGO	MEMEL
ADIJ	MINDEN
ADIM	MIROSLAW
ADJJ	MOLLEN
ADNB	NEUDORF
ADNI	NEUENKIRCHEN
ADOI	NEUSTADT
ADQU	NORDEL
ADWH	OSTELSHEIM
ADXW	PARIS
ADYN	PETERSBERG
ADZU	POLZIN
AEAB	POSEN
AEAP	PRUSSIA
AEFL	RIGA
AEGC	RODEN
AEGT	ROHRBACH
AEHV	ROTHENBERG
AEIY	RUSSDORF
AEMA	SCHLAWE
AEQH	SEDLETZ
AEQQ	SEIDEL
AERS	SILESIA
AESF	SMOLENSK
AESM	SOLINGEN
AETS	SPEYER
AETV	SPIEKA
AETZ	SPRINGFELD
AEUW	STADELHOFEN
AEWM	STETTIN
AEWS	STOCKHOLM
AEXK	STRASSBURG
AFAJ	TORGAU
AFDK	VEGESACK
AFQV	WORMS
AFTM	AUSTRIA
AFTP	BELFAST
AFTS	BOHEMIA
AFVG	ODESSA
AFVH	OXFORD
AFWJ	WARSAW
AFZD	POLAND
AGAL	WUERTEMBERG
AGDD	WIELITZ
AGDU	CZERSK
AGFI	LIBAU
AGHK	NUSSDORF
AGQK	POPOWO
AGQX	RUNOWO
AGRA	SCHADOW
AGRH	SITTARD
AGRT	WILNA
AGUZ	GOTHENBURG
AGVP	LANDER
AHCJ	BURGEN
AHDV	TEREK
AHLP	ROGOWO
AHNX	BARDISCHEW
AHNY	BARDISCHEW
AHOA	BELAK
AHOC	COSSE-LE-VIVIEN
AHOJ	KICHINEV
AHOK	KIEV
AHOO	MOSCOW
AHPZ	SMOLK
AHQC	ST PETERSBURG
AHQD	ST PETERSBURG
AHQE	SZERENCA
AHQF	URSK
AHQH	ST PETERSBURG
AHQO	DOBEROW
AHQP	ELISAVETGRAD
AHQQ	GOTTIN
AHQR	KIRSANOV
AHQU	GRODNO
AHRF	NERCHINSK
AHRK	POLTAWA
AHRM	SIBERIA
AHRS	TEREK
AHRW	ZUDOWKA
AHRY	ASKUTO
AHRZ	AUGUSTOWO
AHSA	BECKLOROWA
AHSB	BERDIANSK
AHSC	BOLESLAWA
AHSD	DEKOV
AHSE	DERSCHUMISCHOK
AHSF	DOMBRA
AHSG	DRUSCHKOPOL
AHSH	DUBNO
AHSI	DULUTH
AHSJ	FARIOW
AHSK	GALJEWO
AHSL	GEORGENBURG
AHSM	GIKULA
AHSN	GLOGOW
AHSO	GORDISCHZE
AHSP	GRAJEWO
AHSQ	GRINSCHOK
AHSR	HABODKE
AHSS	HAGDEN
AHST	IANOWA
AHSU	JABLONOWA
AHSV	JULIANOWO
AHSW	KALWARY
AHSX	KAMENETZ
AHSY	KAROCZIN
AHSZ	KEDAN
AHTA	KELM
AHTB	KOBRIN
AHTC	KOJDONOWO
AHTD	KOLO
AHTE	KORONOW
AHTF	KOWNO
AHTG	KRASNOPOL
AHTH	KURTSCHOW
AHTI	LANGENOW
AHTJ	LESCHOW
AHTK	LIPNO
AHTL	LIPSK
AHTM	LITTOWA
AHTN	LODZ
AHTO	LOMZA
AHTP	LOSDEY
AHTQ	LUDWINOWO
AHTR	MARIANPOL
AHTS	MERETZ
AHTT	MEROKNOW
AHTU	MINSK
AHTV	MISCHINETZ
AHTW	MLAWA
AHTX	MOHILEW
AHTY	OPALEWO
AHTZ	OZEROV
AHUA	PAJURA
AHUB	PAPESCHKY
AHUC	PASKOVE-GUSKI
AHUD	PIEWICK
AHUE	PINSK
AHUF	PLOCK
AHUG	PLONSK
AHUH	PLOTZ
AHUI	PLOTZK
AHUJ	POLOTZK
AHUK	RADISCHKOWITZ
AHUL	REPIN
AHUM	RETOWA
AHUN	ROSKOW
AHUO	ROWNO
AHUP	SACKY
AHUQ	SALUNDSK
AHUR	SARATOV
AHUS	SERY
AHUT	SIERPE
AHUU	SIMNO
AHUV	SLABODKA
AHUW	SMITZKOWO
AHUX	SNOWSK
AHUY	SOKOLOW
AHUZ	STANIN
AHVA	TAUROGGEN
AHVB	TERECZEWO
AHVC	WARANKOW
AHVD	WARTA
AHVE	WEMPIELSK
AHVF	WERNEWITZ
AHVG	WIDERNIK
AHVH	WIERZOW
AHVI	WIESNEWSK
AHVJ	WILCOWICK
AHVK	WILKEWISK
AHVL	WILKOMIR
AHVM	WISCHNOVE
AHVN	WISS
AHVO	WIZAN
AHVP	WODZLAWEK
AHVQ	WOLOSIN
AHVR	ZANOWO
AHVS	ZEMPLIN
AHVT	ZIPLISCHOK
AHVU	BIALYSTOCK
AHVV	BIELSK
AHVW	BOLTA
AHVX	BREST LITOVSK

LIST OF VILLAGE CODES

AHVY	CHERNIGOV
AHVZ	CHMELNIK
AHWA	DIMABURG
AHWB	DOLZY
AHWC	DOMBROWNO
AHWD	DRAZGOWO
AHWE	DUNABURG
AHWF	ELIZABETHGRAD
AHWG	GRISCHKEBUDE
AHWH	GUDELI
AHWI	GUMBIN
AHWJ	ILGE
AHWK	JESNE
AHWL	KALICH
AHWM	KALWARY
AHWN	KAMENETZ
AHWO	KELLEM
AHWP	KIBARTI
AHWQ	KISHINEV
AHWR	KOLA
AHWS	KOLACZY
AHWT	KORZUN
AHWU	KOWEL
AHWV	KOWIN
AHWW	KOZLOW
AHWX	KRAKINOF
AHWY	KREMENCZUG
AHWZ	KROTINGEN
AHXA	KRUIM
AHXB	LAHTI
AHXC	LANDEROW
AHXD	LASZICE
AHXE	LERCY
AHXF	LESCHANOWA
AHXG	LESNOV
AHXH	LIBAU
AHXI	LIDE
AHXJ	LINKOW
AHXK	MAHOWA
AHXL	MARIANPOL
AHXM	MESBICH
AHXN	MULOW
AHXO	NAROWOSK
AHXP	NAWARODOWZ
AHXQ	NEWOGRODNE
AHXR	NICZIN
AHXS	OSCMANIE
AHXT	OSINOWKA
AHXU	PANIEWA
AHXV	PILLWESCHKOW
AHXW	PILWISCHKY
AHXX	PODOLSK
AHXY	PORSCHA
AHXZ	PRASNITZ
AHYA	PRETZKOW
AHYB	PRZEMYSL
AHYC	REPIN
AHYD	RITTOWO
AHYE	ROMANOWO
AHYF	ROSSIN
AHYG	ROTNITZA
AHYH	SANDOWDZ
AHYI	SCHARKOW
AHYJ	SCHUEBIN
AHYK	SELTZ
AHYL	SHERWINSK
AHYM	SLUZEWO
AHYN	SMOALK
AHYO	SPOLSKI
AHYP	STRALZEWO
AHYQ	STUSTZIN
AHYR	SUCHOWOLA
AHYS	SYDA
AHYT	TELEPOWA
AHYU	WALKOMIR
AHYV	WALKOWICH
AHYW	WALOCZIN
AHYX	WASSERY
AHYY	WEICHE
AHYZ	WISAN
AHZA	WISHEGRAD
AHZB	WLADOWA
AHZC	ZICHAWOWA
AHZD	DOBREZYN
AHZE	FRISCHEK
AHZF	GRUTA
AHZG	LAPINECZ
AHZH	OSTROLENKA
AHZI	PLUMGIAN
AHZJ	PONIEWESH
AHZK	OLSIN
AHZL	RATZKE
AHZM	RIPPIN
AHZN	ROSZAN
AHZO	RUTZEWITZ
AHZP	SCHAULEN
AHZQ	SKUDVILL
AHZR	STAWISCHE
AHZS	SUWALKEN
AHZT	WAMPIELSKI
AHZU	WLADISLAWO
ZZZZ	UNKNOWN

LIST OF DESTINATION CODES

Code	Destination
ABG	ALTENBURG
ACC	APPLE CREEK
ADD	ADDISON
ADR	ADRIAN
AGT	AGRENTINA
AIO	ALBION
AL	ALABAMA
ALB	ALBANY
ALX	ALEXANDRIA
ANT	ATLANTIC
AOA	AURORA
AR	ARKANSAS
ASH	ASHLAND
AST	ASTORIA
ATL	ATLANTA
ATO	ALTON
AUB	AUBURN
AUS	AUSTRIA
BAD	BADEN
BAL	BALTIMORE
BAV	BAVARIA
BCK	BECKUM
BEL	BELLEVILLE
BET	BETHLEHEM
BEV	BELLEVUE
BGL	BURLINGTON
BGM	BELGIUM
BIL	BILBAO
BIS	BLUE ISLAND
BKL	BUNKER HILL
BLO	BLOOMINGTON
BLV	BELLVILLE
BMG	BIRMINGHAM
BNG	BRANDENBURG
BO	BOSTON
BOL	BOLLINGTON
BOO	BLOOMFIELD
BRA	BRAZIL
BRE	BREMEN
BRI	BRISTOL
BRL	BERLIN
BRO	BROOKLYN
BTL	BUTLER
BUF	BUFFALO
CA	CENTRAL AMERICA
CAL	CALIFORNIA
CAN	CANADA
CAT	CANTON
CBA	CUBA
CDE	CAMDEN
CER	CANTERBURY
CGD	CAPE GIRARDEAU
CH	CHICAGO
CHE	CHESTER
CHR	CHARLESTON
CIA	CHRISTIAN
CIN	CINCINNATI
CLE	CLEVELAND
CO	COLORADO
COC	COLCHESTER
COL	COLUMBIA
COS	COSTA RICA
COU	COLUMBUS
COV	COVINGTON
CPO	CITYPOINT
CRC	COSTA RICA
CRE	CIRCLEVILLE
CRS	CHARLESTOWN
CT	CONNECTICUT
CUM	CUMBERLAND
CVL	CHARLESVILLE
DAV	DAVENPORT
DBQ	DUBUQUE
DE	DELAWARE
DEE	DUNDEE
DET	DETROIT
DKK	DUNKIRK
DMK	DENMARK
DOR	DORCHESTER
DUB	DUBLIN
DYT	DAYTON
EB	ELZABETH
EBT	ELIZABETHTOWN
EI	EAST INDIES
EMA	ELMIRA
EN	ENGLAND
ERE	ERIE
EVA	EVANSVILLE
FDE	FREDONIA
FKL	FRANKLIN GROVE
FL	FLORIDA
FR	FRANCE
FRK	FRANKLIN
FRO	FERNANDO
FRP	FREEPORT
FTL	FORT LANDING
FTM	FORT MADISON
FTP	FORT PLAIN
FUL	FULTON
FWY	FORT WAYNE
GA	GEORGIA
GAL	GALVESTON
GBY	GREEN BAY
GES	GREEN ISLAND
GFD	GREENFIELD
GHV	GRAND HAVEN
GLA	GALENA
GLO	GLOUCESTER
GR	GERMANY
GRE	GREENWICH
GTR	GERMANTOWN
GUT	GUTTENBERG
GVE	GREENVILLE
HAK	HACKENSACK
HAL	HALIFAX
HAM	HAMBURG
HAN	HENDERSON
HAR	HARRISBURG
HAS	HASTINGS
HAT	HAMILTON
HBI	HANNIBAL
HBK	HOBOKEN
HDT	HERMANNSTADT
HFT	HATFIELD
HLU	HONOLULU
HMN	HARMON
HMR	HOMER
HMY	HARMONY
HOL	HOLLAND
HON	HUNGARY
HOU	HOUSTON
HRL	HARLEM
HRW	HAVERSTRAW
HTD	HARTFORD
HTI	HAITI
HTO	HAMPTON
HTT	HUNTINGTON
HUD	HUDSON
HUR	HURON
HVA	HAVANA
HVR	HANNOVER
IA	IOWA
ICE	ICELAND
IL	ILLINOIS
IN	INDIANA
INA	INDIA
IND	INDIANAPOLIS
IRE	IRELAND
IVH	IVANHOE
JAI	JAMAICA
JAS	JASONVILLE
JDA	JORDAN
JEF	JEFFERSON
JER	JERSEY
JKS	JACKSON
JOH	JOHNSTON
JRV	JERSEYVILLE
JSB	JAMESBURG
KAL	KALAMAZOO
KIN	KINGSTON
KS	KANSAS
KY	KENTUCKY
LA	LOUISIANA
LAN	LANCASTER
LEB	LEBANON
LEX	LEXINGTON
LGH	LONGHILL
LIB	LIBERTY
LIP	LIVERPOOL
LIS	LONG ISLAND
LOB	LOUISBURG
LON	LONDON
LOU	LOUISVILLE
LPE	LA PORTE
LPR	LA PRAIRIE
LRT	LITTLE ROCK
LUX	LUXEMBURG
LWG	LAWRENCEBURG
LYE	LAFAYETTE
MA	MASSACHUSETTS
MAH	MARSHFIELD
MAR	MARION
MAS	MANSFIELD
MAT	MATAMOROS
MCL	MOUNT CARMEL
MD	MARYLAND
ME	MAINE
MEC	MECKLENBURG
MET	METROPOLIS
MI	MICHIGAN
MID	MIDDLETOWN
MIL	MILWAUKEE
MLL	MARSHALLTOWN
MN	MINNESOTA
MO	MISSOURI
MOB	MOBILE
MOL	MOLINE
MPS	MEMPHIS
MRE	MONROE
MRL	MONTREAL
MRQ	MARQUETTE
MRR	MORRIS
MS	MISSISSIPPI
MSN	MADISON
MT	MONTANA
MTA	MANITOBA
MTO	MILTON
MTR	MONTROSE
MTS	MARTINSBURG
MTV	MOUNT VERNON
MVL	MELVILLE
MX	MEXICO
NAS	NASHVILLE
NBG	NEWBURG
NBH	NEWBURGH
NBR	NEW BERLIN
NC	NORTH CAROLINA
NCY	NEW CITY
NDF	NEW BREDFORD
NE	NEBRASKA
NEZ	NATCHEZ
NFA	NIAGARA FALLS
NFF	NEW BUFFALO
NFK	NORFOLK
NFL	NEW BRAUNFELS
NGD	NEW GRANADA
NH	NEW HAMPSHIRE
NHB	NEW HAMBURG
NJ	NEW JERSEY
NLB	NEW ALBANY
NLO	NEW LONDON

LIST OF DESTINATION CODES

NME NEW BREMEN
NO NEW ORLEANS
NOL NEW HOLSTEIN
NPO NAPOLEON
NPT NEWPORT
NRD NEW MADRID
NRW NORWICH
NSS NASSAU BAHAMAS
NSS NASSAU
NST NEW AMSTERDAM
NUE NEUSTADT
NUL NEW ULM
NUV NEUVILLE
NV NEVADA
NVE NEW HAVEN
NW NEWARK
NWK NEW BRUNSWICK
NWY NORWEY
NY NEW YORK
NZL NEW ZEALAND
OH OHIO
OLY OLNY
OR OREGON
ORG ORANGE
OSW OSWEGO
OTT OTTAWA
OWS OWENS
OXF OXFORD
PA PENNSYLVANIA
PAL PALMYRA
PAN PANAMA
PAT PATERSON
PE PERU
PEO PEORIA
PET PETERSBURG
PHI PHILADELPHIA
PIT PITTSBURGH
PJV PORT JERVIS
PKE POUGHKEEPSIE
PLR PALMER
PLY PLYMOUTH
PMT PYRMONT
POR PORTUGAL
POT POTTSVILLE
PRI PRINCETON
PRU PRUSSIA
PSN PATTERSON
PTL PORTLAND
PTS PORTSMOUTH
PTT PITTSFIELD
PTW PORT WASHINGTON
PUR PORT HURON
PVD PROVIDENCE
PVX PHOENIXVILLE
QBC QUEBEC
QUI QUINCY
RBI RUBICON
RCI ROCK ISLAND
RDE RIO DE JANEIRO
RDG READING
RDT RONDOUT
RIC RICHMOND
RIS RHODE ISLAND
RKV ROCKVILLE
RME ROME
ROC ROCHESTER
ROS ROSEVILLE
RSS RUSSIA
SAA SAARLOUIS
SAL SALISBURY
SAN SANDUSKY
SAR SARATOGA
SAV SAVANNAH
SBG SHEBOYGAN
SC SOUTH CAROLINA
SCT SCOTLAND
SDH SANDWICH ISLAND
SFC SAN FRANCISCO
SGN SOUTHINGTON
SHH SOUTHAMPTON
SIS STATEN ISLAND
SLG STERLING
SP ST.PAUL
SPI SPAIN
SPR SPRINGFIELD
SRE SACRAMENTO
SRY ST.MARY
SSB STRASBOURG
STC ST.CHARLES
STF STRATFORD
STL ST.LOUIS
STZ SCHWEIDNITZ
SVT ST.VINCENT
SW SWITZERLAND
SWD SWEDEN
SY SYRACUSE
TFF TIFFIN
THT TERRE HAUTE
TKY TURKEY
TN TENNESSEE
TOL TOLEDO
TOR TORONTO
TRE TRENTON
TRI TRINIDAD
TRY TROY
TWD TONAWANDA
TX TEXAS
UNK UNKNOWN
UON UNION
UPC UPPER CANADA
USA UNITED STATES
UT UTICA
VA VIRGINIA
VAC VERACRUZ
VCK VICKSBURG
VLP VALPORAISO
VMT VERMONT
VZU VENEZUELA
WAE WATERTOWN
WAS WASHINGTON
WAT WATERLOO
WBK WESTBROOK
WDC WASHINGTON D.C.
WDV WOODVILLE
WEB WEBSTER
WEI WELLINGTON
WFD WATERFORD
WGT WILLINGTON
WHE WHEELING
WI WISCONSIN
WIL WILLIAMSBURG
WIT WILMINGTON
WOO WOODSTOCK
WPA WESTPHALIA
WPT WEST POINT
WRR WATERBURY
WRT WUERTTEMBERG
WTM WESTMINSTER
WTP WESTPORT
*** DIED ON BOARD

MIGRATION FROM THE RUSSIAN EMPIRE

Lists of Passengers Arriving at the Port of New York

PASSENGER	AGE	SEX	OCCUPATION	PRIV	VILS	DES

SHIP: HABSBURG

FROM: BREMEN
TO: NEW YORK
ARRIVED: 02 OCTOBER 1882

PASSENGER	AGE	SEX	OCCUPATION	PV VIL	DES
RAUCH, JOHANN	21	M	TU	RRZZZZ	USA

SHIP: ANCHORIA

FROM: GLASGOW
TO: NEW YORK
ARRIVED: 04 OCTOBER 1882

PASSENGER	AGE	SEX	OCCUPATION	PV VIL	DES
JONASON, JOHN	44	M	LABR	RRZZZZ	USA
ZERVI, JOH.HERM.	25	M	LABR	RRZZZZ	USA
CHRISTIAN	19	M	LABR	RRZZZZ	USA
ULLIANOFF, ANDR.	52	M	FARMER	RRZZZZ	USA
E.MRS	26	F	NN	RRZZZZ	USA

SHIP: GELLERT

FROM: HAMBURG AND HAVRE
TO: NEW YORK
ARRIVED: 04 OCTOBER 1882

PASSENGER	AGE	SEX	OCCUPATION	PV VIL	DES
BRINSKENHOFF, ARON	20	M	PNTR	RRZZZZ	USA
NAUMANN, JOHANNE	20	F	SGL	RRZZZZ	USA
ZILINCK, PAUL	17	M	LABR	RRZZZZ	USA
KALLMEYER, CAESAR	25	M	MCHT	RRZZZZ	USA
GRUENWOLD, MAX	42	M	TLR	RRZZZZ	USA
SKYNBYS, JOSEF	20	M	LABR	RRZZZZ	USA
EIGE, SARA	42	F	W	RRZZZZ	USA
CHANE	10	F	CH	RRZZZZ	USA
JOSEF	5	M	CHILD	RRZZZZ	USA
JANKEL	3	M	CHILD	RRZZZZ	USA
SCHLOME	1	F	CHILD	RRZZZZ	USA
PONORKOWSKY, IGNATZ	19	M	LABR	RRZZZZ	USA
KLIP--, JOHANN	23	M	LABR	RRZZZZ	USA
HERNER, GAETAN	29	M	MCHT	RRZZZZ	USA

SHIP: PEREIRE

FROM: HAVRE
TO: NEW YORK
ARRIVED: 04 OCTOBER 1882

PASSENGER	AGE	SEX	OCCUPATION	PV VIL	DES
MALCKONSKI, U	36	M	MSNY	PLZZZZ	OH

SHIP: NECKAR

FROM: BREMEN
TO: NEW YORK
ARRIVED: 07 OCTOBER 1882

PASSENGER	AGE	SEX	OCCUPATION	PV VIL	DES
DEMBICKI, MAX	30	M	MCHT	RRZZZZ	RSS
JESSY	24	F	NN	RRZZZZ	RSS
KOKES, SWATOPLUK	33	M	HTR	RRZZZZ	USA
KAMENZ, LOUISE	48	F	NN	RRZZZZ	USA
FERDINAND	10	M	NN	RRZZZZ	USA
ANNA	7	F	CHILD	RRZZZZ	USA

SHIP: SILESIA

FROM: HAMBURG
TO: NEW YORK
ARRIVED: 07 OCTOBER 1882

PASSENGER	AGE	SEX	OCCUPATION	PV VIL	DES
DIMAN, LEA	21	F	W	RRZZZZ	USA
CHAIE	.11	M	INFANT	RRZZZZ	USA
SAPIRSTEIN, BARUCH	21	M	NN	RRZZZZ	USA
SUESSKEND, MARCUS	19	M	GDSM	RRZZZZ	USA
SEGARVIK, MARCUS	33	M	LABR	RRZZZZ	USA
BARUCHOWITZ, TRADEL	19	F	SGL	RRZZZZ	USA
KAJRAITYS, JAN	15	M	LABR	RRZZZZ	USA
JULIUS	9	M	CHILD	RRZZZZ	USA
BALEWICZ, MARIEN	18	M	LABR	RRZZZZ	USA
KOPUSCHINSKI, MARIANNE	39	F	W	RRZZZZ	USA
ANTON	9	M	CHILD	RRZZZZ	USA
JAN	8	M	CHILD	RRZZZZ	USA
ANTONIE	6	F	CHILD	RRZZZZ	USA
FRANZ	3	M	CHILD	RRZZZZ	USA
MARIANNE	.06	F	INFANT	RRZZZZ	USA
LIEF, TOBIAS	40	M	LABR	RRZZZZ	USA
KUSSON, TOBIAS	25	M	LABR	RRZZZZ	USA
LAPEHN, GEORG	17	M	LABR	RRZZZZ	USA
STERBINSKI, ELISABETH	30	F	W	RRZZZZ	USA
ADOLF	6	M	CHILD	RRZZZZ	USA
ELISABETH	.11	F	INFANT	RRZZZZ	USA
KLAWANSKI, MIREL	24	F	W	RRZZZZ	USA
FRUME	.11	F	INFANT	RRZZZZ	USA
WEHMANN, ISRAEL	21	M	LABR	RRZZZZ	USA
SENGER, SCHEWI	22	F	SGL	RRZZZZ	USA
GROCHOWALSKI, AGNISKA	27	F	W	RRZZZZ	USA
ANTONIE	7	F	CHILD	RRZZZZ	USA
ANTON	3	M	CHILD	RRZZZZ	USA
JOSEF	.11	M	INFANT	RRZZZZ	USA
VOSS, HUGO	26	M	MCHT	RRZZZZ	USA

SHIP: CITY OF CHESTER

FROM: LIVERPOOL
TO: NEW YORK
ARRIVED: 09 OCTOBER 1882

PASSENGER	AGE	SEX	OCCUPATION	PV VIL	DES
MIERSWAISKI, SIG.	40	M	GENT	PLZZZZ	USA
ALEXANDER	29	M	SVNT	PLZZZZ	USA
BERGLIE, MADL.	30	F	SP	RRZZZZ	USA

SHIP: INDIA

FROM: HAMBURG
TO: NEW YORK
ARRIVED: 09 OCTOBER 1882

PASSENGER	AGE	SEX	OCCUPATION	PRV VIL DES
STROSKA, R.	33	F	WO	RRZZZZUSA
OLINE	8	F	CHILD	RRZZZZUSA
LEIKE	7	F	CHILD	RRZZZZUSA
FEIGE	3	F	CHILD	RRZZZZUSA
MOISCHE	2	F	CHILD	RRZZZZUSA
DREYE, E.	24	F	SGL	RRZZZZUSA
BELLSKY, M.	19	F	UNKNOWN	RRZZZZUSA
RUSCH, CHANE	30	F	WO	RRZZZZUSA
ANNA	3	F	CHILD	RRZZZZUSA
LEM, H.	20	M	TRDSMN	RRZZZZUSA

SHIP: LABRADOR

FROM: HAVRE
TO: NEW YORK
ARRIVED: 12 OCTOBER 1882

PASSENGER	AGE	SEX	OCCUPATION	PRV VIL DES
SHAL, HARRIS	30	F	UNKNOWN	RRZZZZNY
ABRAHAM	10	M	UNKNOWN	RRZZZZNY
JACOB	9	M	CHILD	RRZZZZNY
JOSEPH	6	M	CHILD	RRZZZZNY
ANNA	3	F	CHILD	RRZZZZNY
DAVID	00	M	INF	RRZZZZNY

SHIP: STATE OF NEBRASKA

FROM: GLASGOW
TO: NEW YORK
ARRIVED: 12 OCTOBER 1882

PASSENGER	AGE	SEX	OCCUPATION	PRV VIL DES
SILBERG, M.	30	F	W	PLZZZZUSA
LIBE	6	M	CHILD	PLZZZZUSA
BEILE	4	M	CHILD	PLZZZZUSA
CHAINI	3	F	CHILD	PLZZZZUSA
PUNSE, MALI	10	F	UNKNOWN	PLZZZZUSA
ROTTI	7	F	CHILD	PLZZZZUSA
BRAUN, J.	11	M	UNKNOWN	PLZZZZUSA

SHIP: SUEVIA

FROM: HAMBURG
TO: NEW YORK
ARRIVED: 12 OCTOBER 1882

PASSENGER	AGE	SEX	OCCUPATION	PRV VIL DES
CIDZIK, ADAM	30	M	LABR	RRZZZZUSA
SINGER, BENE	39	M	JNR	RRZZZZUSA
RAFAEL	20	M	UNKNOWN	RRZZZZUSA
SCHMIDT, EMILIE	17	F	SGL	RRZZZZUSA
HARTMANN, BERNHD.	26	M	LABR	RRZZZZUSA
ROSALIE	26	F	W	RRZZZZUSA
ADOLF	.03	M	INFANT	RRZZZZUSA
LESSLAN, MARIE	8	F	CHILD	RRZZZZUSA
MARIENHOT, IDA	49	F	W	RRZZZZUSA
JOSEF	8	M	CHILD	RRZZZZUSA
REBECCA	6	F	CHILD	RRZZZZUSA
MASCHE	.11	F	INFANT	RRZZZZUSA
KROMANN, NATHAN	26	M	MCHT	RRZZZZUSA
RABYJENAS, KAZIS	26	M	UNKNOWN	RRZZZZUSA
MIKOLAITES, JONAS	24	M	UNKNOWN	RRZZZZUSA
GELGOTYR, VERONIKA	26	F	SGL	RRZZZZUSA
STERN, LEOPOLD	24	M	MCHT	RRZZZZUSA

SHIP: NEDERLAND

FROM: ANTWERP
TO: NEW YORK
ARRIVED: 14 OCTOBER 1882

PASSENGER	AGE	SEX	OCCUPATION	PRV VIL DES
CABE, IWAWOON	30	M	UNKNOWN	RRZZZZUSA

SHIP: HELVETIA

FROM: LIVERPOOL AND QUEENSTOWN
TO: NEW YORK
ARRIVED: 16 OCTOBER 1882

PASSENGER	AGE	SEX	OCCUPATION	PRV VIL DES
PYKE, ABRAM	51	M	LABR	RRZZZZUSA
LOKANDER, MICHAEL	49	M	LABR	RRZZZZUSA
KUMARA, SERAFIA	18	F	SP	RRZZZZUSA
FORSTI, JOHAN	46	M	LABR	RRZZZZUSA
MATTS	44	M	LABR	RRZZZZUSA
LENDGUIST, JACOB	18	M	LABR	RRZZZZUSA

SHIP: CATALONIA

FROM: LIVERPOOL AND QUEENSTOWN
TO: NEW YORK
ARRIVED: 19 OCTOBER 1882

PASSENGER	AGE	SEX	OCCUPATION	PRV VIL DES
LIVAK, ANDRAS	28	M	LABR	PLZZZZUSA
GERA, MICHAL	25	M	LABR	PLZZZZUSA
ILKO, JANOS	33	M	LABR	PLZZZZUSA
DWARAWO, MICHL.	11	M	CH	PLZZZZUSA
HAWLIK, ANDREAS	10	M	CH	PLZZZZUSA
JURCYS, MICHAL	11	M	CH	PLZZZZUSA
WATNIK, MARIA	10	F	CH	PLZZZZUSA
TIENA, MICHAL	22	M	LABR	PLZZZZUSA
LISAK, MICHAL	28	M	LABR	PLZZZZUSA
WASEL, JANOS	30	M	LABR	PLZZZZUSA
LITRO, STEFAN	11	M	CH	PLZZZZUSA
KRANITH, ANDRAS	11	M	CH	PLZZZZUSA
GERA, JANOS	23	M	LABR	PLZZZZUSA
BODNER, JURA	10	M	CH	PLZZZZUSA
JURCAK, ANDRAS	9	M	CHILD	PLZZZZUSA
STANISLAUS, SALVAN	32	M	LABR	PLZZZZUSA
BUDEY, JATRAN	38	M	LABR	PLZZZZUSA
FEDOR, JOSEF	21	M	LABR	PLZZZZUSA
JATRAN	24	M	LABR	PLZZZZUSA
FOOT, JANOS	23	M	LABR	PLZZZZUSA
PAUL, SANDRO	11	M	CH	PLZZZZUSA
JORG, STANISLAUS	28	M	CH	PLZZZZUSA
OSTWACH, JOSEF	29	M	CH	PLZZZZUSA
KOSAK, ANDRAS	10	M	CH	PLZZZZUSA

PASSENGER	AGE	SEX	OCCUPATION	PRV VIL DES
MARKOS, ANDRAS	11	M	CH	PLZZZZUSA
ROMAN, JANOS	50	M	LABR	PLZZZZUSA
PETER, JANOS	27	M	LABR	PLZZZZUSA
FENNE, PAUL	11	M	CH	PLZZZZUSA
PETERTA, JORG.	33	M	LABR	PLZZZZUSA
SEDLAK, MILVAL	40	M	LABR	PLZZZZUSA
ANDRAISEY, JANOS	11	M	CH	PLZZZZUSA
IVERBAK, SETRAN	38	M	LABR	PLZZZZUSA
OBERSKI, MICHAL	45	M	LABR	PLZZZZUSA
JOSEF	35	M	LABR	PLZZZZUSA
TIANKOWSKY, JANKO	11	M	CH	PLZZZZUSA
MITREK, JANOS	38	M	LABR	PLZZZZUSA
BARACH, MICKO	10	M	LABR	PLZZZZUSA
PIROSCHKO, GUILA	32	M	LABR	PLZZZZUSA
HARULLA, MICHAL	24	M	LABR	PLZZZZUSA
WORDA, GEORG	24	M	LABR	PLZZZZUSA
DINOS, JANKO	11	M	CH	PLZZZZUSA
KRAVETZ, TURKI	10	M	CH	PLZZZZUSA
ANDRASCHEK, TURKI	33	M	LABR	PLZZZZUSA
SZALAI, GEORG	29	M	LABR	PLZZZZUSA
PRAWLENSKY, JOSEF	30	M	LABR	PLZZZZUSA
MONLA, PAUL	11	M	CH	PLZZZZUSA
PESTA, NIKLO	26	M	LABR	PLZZZZUSA
ISAYONDER, JANOS	24	M	LABR	PLZZZZUSA

SHIP: WIELAND

FROM: HAMBURG AND HAVRE
TO: NEW YORK
ARRIVED: 19 OCTOBER 1882

PASSENGER	AGE	SEX	OCCUPATION	PRV VIL DES
SAGEWICZ, JACOB	21	M	LABR	RRZZZZUSA
KOSKY, MARY	23	F	W	RRZZZZUSA
CHRISTIAN	.11	M	INFANT	RRZZZZUSA
ELISE	.01	M	INFANT	RRZZZZUSA
SKIELSKI, ANTON	18	M	MCHT	RRZZZZUSA
STELLM--, MARIE	30	F	SGL	RRZZZZUSA

SHIP: BOHEMIA

FROM: HAMBURG
TO: NEW YORK
ARRIVED: 23 OCTOBER 1882

PASSENGER	AGE	SEX	OCCUPATION	PRV VIL DES
WILKOWSKY, WOLF	17	M	DLR	RRZZZZUSA
JOSEPH	17	M	DLR	RRZZZZUSA
WASILEWSKY, ANTONIN	21	M	LABR	RRZZZZUSA
RACUS, VICENTZ	20	M	LABR	RRZZZZUSA
JUKA, JANUS	49	M	LABR	RRZZZZUSA
WEITSCHULIS, ANTON	21	M	LABR	RRZZZZUSA
DOBINUS, STANISL.	29	M	LABR	RRZZZZUSA
DITZBAUM, JOH.	23	M	LABR	RRZZZZUSA
BAHR, LUDW.	24	M	LABR	RRZZZZUSA
MANKE, HERRM.	23	M	LABR	RRZZZZUSA
HOBUS, PAULINE	22	F	SGL	RRZZZZUSA
WETZEL, ALBERTINE	22	F	SGL	RRZZZZUSA
CAROLINE	16	F	SGL	RRZZZZUSA
LAWERENTZ, WILH.	37	M	FARMER	RRZZZZUSA
FRIDR.	36	F	W	RRZZZZUSA
FRANZ	9	M	CHILD	RRZZZZUSA
EMILIE	8	F	CHILD	RRZZZZUSA
GUSTAV	7	M	CHILD	RRZZZZUSA
OTTO	5	M	CHILD	RRZZZZUSA
ANNA	.11	F	INFANT	RRZZZZUSA
SPIERING, CARL	23	M	FARMER	RRZZZZUSA
FRDKE.	26	F	W	RRZZZZUSA
METSCHULEIS, JOH.	23	M	LABR	RRZZZZUSA
ENSCOLT, GUSTAV	18	M	LABR	RRZZZZUSA
BANIENE, AGATHA	30	F	W	RRZZZZUSA
JOH.	7	M	CHILD	RRZZZZUSA
JOSEF	4	M	CHILD	RRZZZZUSA
PICES	.11	M	INFANT	RRZZZZUSA
LUKASZEWIEZ, AGATHA	20	F	SGL	RRZZZZUSA
MINEUWIEZA, STASIS	30	M	SGL	RRZZZZUSA
WICZLICKE, MARIEN	20	M	LABR	RRZZZZUSA
LAUKATPT, STASIS	26	M	LABR	RRZZZZUSA
MARIA	18	F	W	RRZZZZUSA

SHIP: EGYPT

FROM: LIVERPOOL
TO: NEW YORK
ARRIVED: 23 OCTOBER 1882

PASSENGER	AGE	SEX	OCCUPATION	PRV VIL DES
CRAMER, S.	30	M	LABR	RRZZZZUSA
FRIDMAN, J.	11	M	CH	RRZZZZUSA
MARELYAK, MARTIN	34	M	LABR	RRZZZZUSA

SHIP: POLYNESIA

FROM: HAMBURG
TO: NEW YORK
ARRIVED: 23 OCTOBER 1882

PASSENGER	AGE	SEX	OCCUPATION	PRV VIL DES
WOLFSON, E.B.	18	F	SGL	RRZZZZUSA
KRIKYANSKE, JOHS.	16	M	TRDSMN	RRZZZZUSA
SIMCHE, KOSSB.	50	M	LABR	RRZZZZUSA
WOLF	6	M	CHILD	RRZZZZUSA
RABINOWITZ, H.	38	M	TLR	RRZZZZUSA
BEILE	28	F	W	RRZZZZUSA
ABRAHAM	.09	M	INFANT	RRZZZZUSA
ROSENTHAL, G.	19	F	WO	RRZZZZUSA

SHIP: WERRA

FROM: BREMEN
TO: NEW YORK
ARRIVED: 23 OCTOBER 1882

PASSENGER	AGE	SEX	OCCUPATION	PRV VIL DES
SCHWANDT, FRIEDR.	29	M	LLD	RRZZZZNY
AUGUSTE	20	F	UNKNOWN	RRZZZZNY
MINNA	22	F	UNKNOWN	RRZZZZNY
HUGO	.11	M	INFANT	RRZZZZNY
ELISABETH	.11	F	INFANT	RRZZZZNY

PASSENGER	AGE	SEX	OCCUPATION	PRVL	VILL	DES

SHIP: WESTPHALIA

FROM: HAMBURG AND HAVRE
TO: NEW YORK
ARRIVED: 24 OCTOBER 1882

DULCKI, JOSEF	20	M	LABR	RR	ZZZZ	USA
KOBELLKO, MATHS.	20	M	LABR	RR	ZZZZ	USA
PIETERKOWSKE, HERM.	19	M	TLR	RR	ZZZZ	USA

SHIP: CANADA

FROM: HAVRE
TO: NEW YORK
ARRIVED: 25 OCTOBER 1882

KLIMECKI, U-MR	46	M	UNKNOWN	PL	ZZZZ	USA

SHIP: CIRCASSIA

FROM: GLASGOW
TO: NEW YORK
ARRIVED: 25 OCTOBER 1882

HAMMS, A.	32	M	FARMER	RR	ZZZZ	USA
WILHELMINA, A.	30	M	UNKNOWN	RR	ZZZZ	USA
OGST, J.	21	M	UNKNOWN	RR	ZZZZ	USA

SHIP: MAIN

FROM: BREMEN
TO: NEW YORK
ARRIVED: 28 OCTOBER 1882

LYNOUIS, EVA	25	F	UNKNOWN	RR	ZZZZ	USA
ANNA	5	F	CHILD	RR	ZZZZ	USA
MINNA	.06	F	INFANT	RR	ZZZZ	USA

SHIP: CITY OF BERLIN

FROM: LIVERPOOL AND QUEENSTOWN
TO: NEW YORK
ARRIVED: 30 OCTOBER 1882

TWOMOLA, JOHAN	23	M	LABR	RR	ZZZZ	USA
FINNETTI, W.	29	M	UNKNOWN	RR	ZZZZ	USA
TANNOLA, FANELLE	26	M	UNKNOWN	RR	ZZZZ	USA
MELLELA, PATEDA	19	M	UNKNOWN	RR	ZZZZ	USA

SHIP: GRECIAN MONARCH

FROM: LONDON
TO: NEW YORK
ARRIVED: 02 NOVEMBER 1882

ILMUESKY, L.	22	M	LABR	PL	ZZZZ	USA
GERSLER, J.	22	M	LABR	PL	ZZZZ	USA
FREEDMAN, SARAH	35	F	NN	PL	ZZZZ	USA
ROSE	11	F	CH	PL	ZZZZ	USA
LEAH	10	F	CH	PL	ZZZZ	USA
ANNE	9	F	CHILD	PL	ZZZZ	USA
RACHEL	6	F	CHILD	PL	ZZZZ	USA
MARY	4	F	CHILD	PL	ZZZZ	USA
ABRAHAM	2	M	CHILD	PL	ZZZZ	USA
COHEN, LEAH	31	F	NN	PL	ZZZZ	USA
U	6	F	CHILD	PL	ZZZZ	USA
MURSET, U	58	F	NN	PL	ZZZZ	USA
NEUMAN, M.	30	M	LABR	PL	ZZZZ	USA
KATE	25	F	W	PL	ZZZZ	USA
PARCHUT, M.	26	M	LABR	PL	ZZZZ	USA
ZONIN, A.	23	M	LABR	PL	ZZZZ	USA
ASHFELD, JUS.	28	M	LABR	PL	ZZZZ	USA
ANNE	21	F	W	PL	ZZZZ	USA
SZTRASSEN, JOH.	35	M	LABR	PL	ZZZZ	USA
MARTHER, A.	34	M	LABR	PL	ZZZZ	USA
MARIA	25	F	W	PL	ZZZZ	USA
MARIA	7	F	CHILD	PL	ZZZZ	USA
MARTJAN	3	F	CHILD	PL	ZZZZ	USA
JULIE	.09	F	INFANT	PL	ZZZZ	USA
KAFIRE	.09	F	INFANT	PL	ZZZZ	USA

SHIP: FRANCE

FROM: HAVRE
TO: NEW YORK
ARRIVED: 03 NOVEMBER 1882

EROSTORFF, U-MISS	27	F	LDY	RR	ZZZZ	NY

SHIP: JASON

FROM: AMSTERDAM
TO: NEW YORK
ARRIVED: 03 NOVEMBER 1882

SOLODKE, JAN	20	M	LABR	RR	AEFL	USA

SHIP: VANDALIA

FROM: HAMBURG
TO: NEW YORK
ARRIVED: 03 NOVEMBER 1882

ARCHIHOWSKA, EMILIE	20	F	SGL	RR	ZZZZ	USA
NADELFIN, MALKE	23	F	W	RR	ZZZZ	USA
ITZIG	.11	M	INFANT	RR	ZZZZ	USA
JOH.	.01	M	INFANT	RR	ZZZZ	USA
DEUTSCH, MALI	30	F	W	RR	ZZZZ	USA

PASSENGER	AGE	SEX	OCCUPATION	PRV VIL DES
MINDUS	6	M	CHILD	RRZZZZUSA
LEIB	.11	M	INFANT	RRZZZZUSA
LEFKOWITZ, MARIE	16	F	SGL	RRZZZZUSA
BERKOWITZ, CHAIM	30	M	DLR	RRZZZZUSA
NADELFIN, ABR.	21	M	MCHT	RRZZZZUSA
ESTE	18	F	W	RRZZZZUSA
JASINSKA, MARG.	30	F	W	RRZZZZUSA
JOSEPHA	5	F	CHILD	RRZZZZUSA
THEKLA	2	F	CHILD	RRZZZZUSA
KRUCZNOWSKI, MATTHS.	22	M	LABR	RRZZZZUSA
JERVOSKY, ANNA	28	F	SGL	RRZZZZUSA
DEUTSCH, FANNY	9	F	CHILD	RRZZZZUSA
FUTTERMANN, GEORG	19	M	LABR	RRZZZZUSA
SCHRAMM, CAROLE.	37	F	W	RRZZZZUSA
WANDA	9	F	CHILD	RRZZZZUSA
OSCAR	3	M	CHILD	RRZZZZUSA
LIECK, EMILIE	24	F	SGL	RRZZZZUSA
MOWSCHER, LEIB	24	M	DLR	RRZZZZUSA
FRIKHOLZ, ROSA	17	F	SGL	RRZZZZUSA
DAWID, LEWI	16	M	FARMER	RRZZZZUSA
KAPDOWITZ, BARNET	56	M	DLR	RRZZZZUSA
SELMIS, MIHAEL	22	M	LABR	RRZZZZUSA
BERNATOVIC, JOSEF	20	M	LABR	RRZZZZUSA
JACUSCZLS, FRANZ	19	M	LABR	RRZZZZUSA

SHIP: COLON

FROM: PANAMA
TO: NEW YORK
ARRIVED: 04 NOVEMBER 1882

PASSENGER	AGE	SEX	OCCUPATION	PRV VIL DES
GAINSBURG, SAML.	32	M	MCHT	RRZZZZRSS
WM.	35	M	MCHT	RRZZZZRSS

SHIP: ENGLAND

FROM: LIVERPOOL AND QUEENSTOWN
TO: NEW YORK
ARRIVED: 04 NOVEMBER 1882

PASSENGER	AGE	SEX	OCCUPATION	PRV VIL DES
LACKMAN, P.	30	M	LABR	FNZZZZUSA
ANVALA, ANDERS	20	M	LABR	FNZZZZUSA
ENGHAN, E.	19	M	LABR	FNZZZZUSA
LEWANON, A.	27	M	LABR	FNZZZZUSA
ROSARIN, NILS	25	M	LABR	FNZZZZUSA
LENANIN, MATTS.	25	M	LABR	FNZZZZUSA

SHIP: HEKLA

FROM: COPENHAGEN
TO: NEW YORK
ARRIVED: 07 NOVEMBER 1882

PASSENGER	AGE	SEX	OCCUPATION	PRV VIL DES
LIND, SARAH-F.	16	F	NN	RRZZZZUSA

SHIP: FRISIA

FROM: HAMBURG AND HAVRE
TO: NEW YORK
ARRIVED: 08 NOVEMBER 1882

PASSENGER	AGE	SEX	OCCUPATION	PRV VIL DES
BEHRENDT, ISIDOR	17	M	MCHT	RRZZZZUSA
ZILMSKY, ANTON	39	M	FARMER	RRZZZZUSA
MARIE	34	F	W	RRZZZZUSA
MARIE	9	F	CHILD	RRZZZZUSA
ANNA	7	F	CHILD	RRZZZZUSA
ANTON	4	M	CHILD	RRZZZZUSA
VINCENT	.11	M	INFANT	RRZZZZUSA
ABRAMS, MOSES	54	M	MCHT	RRZZZZUSA
REBECCA	28	F	W	RRZZZZUSA
ANNA	7	F	CHILD	RRZZZZUSA
ARON	5	M	CHILD	RRZZZZUSA
GRUSCHEWSKI, ISAAC	38	M	DLR	RRZZZZUSA
WEINGAERTNER, AUGUST	24	M	SLR	RRZZZZUSA

SHIP: AUSTRALIA

FROM: HAMBURG
TO: NEW YORK
ARRIVED: 09 NOVEMBER 1882

PASSENGER	AGE	SEX	OCCUPATION	PRV VIL DES
BERUSTEIN, RIWKE	26	F	WO	RRZZZZUSA
SCH.	5	M	CHILD	RRZZZZUSA
GOLDE	.11	F	INFANT	RRZZZZUSA
DEBORAH	.01	F	INFANT	RRZZZZUSA
UNANSKY, ITTA	29	F	WO	RRZZZZUSA
ESTER	7	F	CHILD	RRZZZZUSA
SOHANDAL	.11	F	INFANT	RRZZZZUSA
BENJ.	.01	M	INFANT	RRZZZZUSA
BRENER, NALLKI	29	F	WO	RRZZZZUSA
REGINA	7	F	CHILD	RRZZZZUSA
BERTHA	6	F	CHILD	RRZZZZUSA
CHAINE	4	F	CHILD	RRZZZZUSA
ADAM	.11	F	INFANT	RRZZZZUSA
ABRAHAM	.01	M	INFANT	RRZZZZUSA
SKOLADA, IANKO	40	M	UNKNOWN	RRZZZZUSA
CHARKOVOSKY, WASLOW	18	M	UNKNOWN	RRZZZZUSA
SCHAFRAW, DAVID	33	M	MCHT	RRZZZZUSA
KIFER, CARL	25	M	SGL	RRZZZZUSA
PESSKY, MINNA	38	F	SGL	RRZZZZUSA
REWINSKY, ARON	19	M	UNKNOWN	RRZZZZUSA
JOOH.	18	F	UNKNOWN	RRZZZZUSA
PERSLEY, FRIMANT	15	F	SGL	RRZZZZUSA
JAKOB	8	M	CHILD	RRZZZZUSA
KIAV	7	F	CHILD	RRZZZZUSA
RACHEL	5	F	CHILD	RRZZZZUSA
JOSHUA	.06	M	INFANT	RRZZZZUSA
LEWIN, JOSEF	26	M	UNKNOWN	RRZZZZUSA
KRONEGELD, SCHEWE	33	F	WO	RRZZZZUSA
ANNA	4	F	CHILD	RRZZZZUSA
HELENE	.06	F	INFANT	RRZZZZUSA
CHARWITZ, LESSEL	50	M	LABR	RRZZZZUSA
HECKSTEIN, A.	17	M	MCHT	RRZZZZUSA
FRENNDLECH, M.	19	M	TRDM	RRZZZZUSA
ZALLTUER, F.	8	M	CHILD	RRZZZZUSA
KANTROWY, DORA	23	F	WO	RRZZZZUSA
ISAAK	.06	M	INFANT	RRZZZZUSA
FRIEDMAN, LAISER	8	M	CHILD	RRZZZZUSA
KATERSKA, ROSA	41	F	WO	RRZZZZUSA
LUTZEN	.06	M	INFANT	RRZZZZUSA

PASSENGER	AGE	SEX	OCCUPATION	PV RIVL	DES

SHIP: STRASSBURG

FROM: BREMEN
TO: NEW YORK
ARRIVED: 09 NOVEMBER 1882

PASSENGER	AGE	SEX	OCCUPATION	PV RIVL	DES
CENPREJANOWSKY, WLADISL	22	M	BLKSMH	RRZZZ	ZUSA

SHIP: ALLEMANIA

FROM: HAMBURG
TO: NEW YORK
ARRIVED: 10 NOVEMBER 1882

PASSENGER	AGE	SEX	OCCUPATION	PV RIVL	DES
TUWIN, ISRAEL	18	M	DLR	RRZZZ	ZUSA
ROBINSON, MOSES	21	M	UNKNOWN	RRZZZ	ZUSA
DOROSZYNSKA, MARIANNE	22	F	W	RRZZZ	ZUSA
JOSEF	.11	M	INFANT	RRZZZ	ZUSA
LIPSCHITZ, JOSSEL	20	M	LABR	RRZZZ	ZUSA
DISYEWO, HINDE	19	F	SGL	RRZZZ	ZUSA
GOLDSTEIN, NACHMANN	20	M	LABR	RRZZZ	ZUSA
KATWET, MARIE	18	F	SGL	RRZZZ	ZUSA

SHIP: SCYTHIA

FROM: LIVERPOOL
TO: NEW YORK
ARRIVED: 10 NOVEMBER 1882

PASSENGER	AGE	SEX	OCCUPATION	PV RIVL	DES
FRESSACH, E.	18	M	LABR	RRZZZ	ZUSA
IDELSKY, A.	45	M	LABR	PLZZZ	ZUSA

SHIP: ERIN

FROM: LIVERPOOL AND QUEENSTOWN
TO: NEW YORK
ARRIVED: 11 NOVEMBER 1882

PASSENGER	AGE	SEX	OCCUPATION	PV RIVL	DES
BEY, JOHAN	34	M	LABR	FNZZZ	ZUSA
KUSTAFSCKI, J.	18	M	LABR	FNZZZ	ZUSA
HENRICKSON, JACOB	26	M	LABR	FNZZZ	ZUSA
FITHPULA, MATTA	22	M	LABR	FNZZZ	ZUSA
FIKKELA, JOHAN	36	M	LABR	FNZZZ	ZUSA
MENLI, MATTS	21	M	LABR	FNZZZ	ZUSA
RAMELZ, CARL	27	M	LABR	FNZZZ	ZUSA
KASALIN, HEINRICH	29	M	LABR	FNZZZ	ZUSA
LAGER, ANDERS	26	M	LABR	FNZZZ	ZUSA
KANI, JOHAN	19	M	LABR	FNZZZ	ZUSA
STEMI, JOHAN	24	M	LABR	FNZZZ	ZUSA
KOSKOLA, JOHAN	44	M	LABR	FNZZZ	ZUSA
KUMTI, JACOB	44	M	LABR	FNZZZ	ZUSA
YUALA, SIMON	36	M	LABR	FNZZZ	ZUSA
STANZBERG, GUSTAV	36	M	LABR	FNZZZ	ZUSA
PAROLI, STOKI	24	M	CPTR	FNZZZ	ZUSA
SCHOPE, GUSTAV	28	M	LABR	FNZZZ	ZUSA
KOPIAKA, JACOB	44	M	LABR	FNZZZ	ZUSA
NISSILA, MATHIAS	24	M	LABR	FNZZZ	ZUSA
JUNTI, ADOLPH	19	M	LABR	FNZZZ	ZUSA
KARKAUS, MATTS	38	M	LABR	FNZZZ	ZUSA
WALNI, SOFIA	22	F	SP	FNZZZ	ZUSA
HARKARS, JOHAN	38	M	LABR	FNZZZ	ZUSA

SHIP: STATE OF INDIANA

FROM: GLASGOW AND LARNE
TO: NEW YORK
ARRIVED: 11 NOVEMBER 1882

PASSENGER	AGE	SEX	OCCUPATION	PV RIVL	DES
BERGER, ABRAHAM	17	M	LABR	RRZZZ	ZUSA
ROSENBLUM, JUDE	15	M	NN	RRZZZ	ZUSA
SCHANDLER, SCHAMAIE	23	M	LABR	RRZZZ	ZUSA
CHLAMIE	23	M	LABR	RRZZZ	ZUSA
DRATZ, EPHRAIM	20	M	LABR	RRZZZ	ZUSA
ROSENTHAL, MARCUS	55	M	LABR	RRZZZ	ZUSA
FEIGE	14	F	W	RRZZZ	ZUSA
MARIA	13	F	NN	RRZZZ	ZUSA
LOSSELOWITZ, ITZIG	11	M	NN	RRZZZ	ZUSA
FRIED, EPHRAIM	36	M	LABR	RRZZZ	ZUSA
RUBEN	11	M	NN	RRZZZ	ZUSA
PERLMANN, MOSES	24	M	LABR	RRZZZ	ZUSA
CHEIKLOWITZ, RADESH	20	M	LABR	RRZZZ	ZUSA
ZNIKER, ISAAK	20	M	LABR	RRZZZ	ZUSA
LEPSCHUTZ, JACOB	20	M	LABR	RRZZZ	ZUSA

SHIP: CIMBRIA

FROM: HAMBURG AND HAVRE
TO: NEW YORK
ARRIVED: 13 NOVEMBER 1882

PASSENGER	AGE	SEX	OCCUPATION	PV RIVL	DES
JAMBERKY, J.	32	M	UNKNOWN	RRZZZ	ZUSA
SWOLUCK, LEIB	18	M	LABR	RRZZZ	ZUSA
YAEG, SCHAJE	19	M	SGL	RRZZZ	ZUSA
HETMANN, MINNA	27	F	W	RRZZZ	ZUSA
DORA	.11	F	INFANT	RRZZZ	ZUSA
HERM.	.01	M	INFANT	RRZZZ	ZUSA
JABALOWSKY, APPE.	39	M	W	RRZZZ	ZUSA
WEITZLOWSKY, ZESLAW	16	M	LABR	RRZZZ	ZUSA
FEDEROW, NICEF.	36	M	UNKNOWN	RRZZZ	ZUSA
SCHIKAROWITZ, JOS.	19	M	UNKNOWN	RRZZZ	ZUSA
SCHUMSKA, STAN.	26	M	W	RRZZZ	ZUSA
JOH.	.03	M	INFANT	RRZZZ	ZUSA
LAUBACH, FRZ.	32	M	FARMER	RRZZZ	ZUSA
CATH.	27	F	W	RRZZZ	ZUSA
CARL	7	M	CHILD	RRZZZ	ZUSA
HCH.	3	M	CHILD	RRZZZ	ZUSA
JAC.	.11	M	INFANT	RRZZZ	ZUSA
ROSENBLUM, HIRSCH	19	M	DLR	RRZZZ	ZUSA
WILRHINSKI, RUBIN	21	M	UNKNOWN	RRZZZ	ZUSA

SHIP: POLLUX

FROM: AMSTERDAM
TO: NEW YORK
ARRIVED: 13 NOVEMBER 1882

PASSENGER	AGE	SEX	OCCUPATION	PV RIVL	DES
JUNGST, WILHELM	29	M	LABR	RRZZZ	ZUSA
MATSON, O.L.	38	M	LABR	RRZZZ	ZUSA

PASSENGER	AGE	SEX	OCCUPATION	PRV IL	DES

SHIP: RHEIN

FROM: BREMEN
TO: NEW YORK
ARRIVED: 13 NOVEMBER 1882

STELANIK, STANISLAWA	16	F	NN	RRZZZZ	USA

SHIP: ANCHORIA

FROM: GLASGOW
TO: NEW YORK
ARRIVED: 14 NOVEMBER 1882

BALTAZAROWICZ, ALEX	32	M	LABR	RRZZZZ	USA

SHIP: LESSING

FROM: HAMBURG
TO: NEW YORK
ARRIVED: 16 NOVEMBER 1882

ZEMANSKY, RACHEL	20	F	SGL	RRZZZZ	USA
MAX	18	M	CK	RRZZZZ	USA
NATHAN	13	M	UNKNOWN	RRZZZZ	USA
KELMANN, RUHLIE	25	F	W	RRZZZZ	USA
MAZUR, STOZ	9	M	CHILD	RRZZZZ	USA

SHIP: BOTHNIA

FROM: LIVERPOOL
TO: NEW YORK
ARRIVED: 17 NOVEMBER 1882

ULGENS, JOSEPH	18	M	LABR	RRZZZZ	USA
AORSYV, OTTO	36	M	LABR	RRZZZZ	USA
KALLMAN, JOHANN	28	M	LABR	RRZZZZ	USA
BACKMAN, ALF.	23	M	LABR	RRZZZZ	USA

SHIP: SPAIN

FROM: LIVERPOOL AND QUEENSTOWN
TO: NEW YORK
ARRIVED: 17 NOVEMBER 1882

ROSENBLOOM, S.MR	23	M	GENT	RRZZZZ	USA
WALANDIMIRSKY, U-MR	22	M	GENT	RRZZZZ	USA
STUTZEN, W.MR	22	M	GENT	RRZZZZ	USA
GAVRILENKO, U-MR	22	M	GENT	RRZZZZ	USA
RAKESDOWSKY, A.MR	23	M	GENT	RRZZZZ	USA
KLEINBERGER, JOSEPH	26	M	GENT	RRZZZZ	USA
ROTH, MOZE	25	F	SVNT	RRZZZZ	USA
LEPKOWITZ, LEO	17	M	LABR	RRZZZZ	USA
URAR, SAMUEL	17	M	LABR	RRZZZZ	USA

PASSENGER	AGE	SEX	OCCUPATION	PRV IL	DES
SALMONVIRTZ, LEO	36	M	LABR	RRZZZZ	USA
MOKONOWITZ, MENDEL	24	M	LABR	RRZZZZ	USA
SALMONOWITZ, BERNHARD	36	M	LABR	RRZZZZ	USA

SHIP: RHYNLAND

FROM: ANTWERP
TO: NEW YORK
ARRIVED: 18 NOVEMBER 1882

SCHWARZ, CHRISTA.	25	F	NN	RRZZZZ	USA
MARGD.	.06	F	INFANT	RRZZZZ	USA

SHIP: STATE OF NEVADA

FROM: GLASGOW AND LARNE
TO: NEW YORK
ARRIVED: 18 NOVEMBER 1882

SUSNITIKY, LIESEN	19	F	SVNT	PLZZZZ	USA
SIMON, OSCHER	10	M	NN	PLZZZZ	USA
LURIE, MOSES	20	M	LABR	PLZZZZ	USA
BLAIN, ISRAEL	25	M	LABR	PLZZZZ	USA
MANTARILISK, HIRSCH	19	F	SVNT	PLZZZZ	USA
MEYER	11	M	NN	PLZZZZ	USA
LASCHOVENTY, FELIX	32	M	LABR	PLZZZZ	USA
DORMON, ADOLPH	22	M	LABR	PLZZZZ	USA
OSITEL	11	M	NN	PLZZZZ	USA
MENDELOWITZ, ABRAHAM	31	M	FARMER	PLZZZZ	USA
LABRACHAMOWICK, SARAH	15	F	NN	PLZZZZ	USA
BRAUN, JOSTE.	18	F	SVNT	PLZZZZ	USA

SHIP: HELVETIA

FROM: LIVERPOOL
TO: NEW YORK
ARRIVED: 23 NOVEMBER 1882

SONERAY, RUEBEN	20	M	LABR	RRZZZZ	USA
KARLIN, WILHELM	20	M	LABR	RRZZZZ	USA
WRITANNA, MATTS.	30	M	LABR	RRZZZZ	USA
RITOMAKI, JOHAN	27	M	LABR	RRZZZZ	USA
SEMAIN, HENRIK-B.	29	M	LABR	RRZZZZ	USA
ANDERSON, JOHN	28	M	LABR	RRZZZZ	USA
JOHANSON, DAVID	27	M	LABR	RRZZZZ	USA
SUNDIN, A.W.	18	M	LABR	RRZZZZ	USA
THULIN, GUSTAVE	38	M	LABR	RRZZZZ	USA
SODERHAHN, GUSTAVE-A.	20	M	LABR	RRZZZZ	USA

PASSENGER	AGE	SEX	OCCUPATION	PRV VIL DES

SHIP: POLARIA

FROM: HAMBURG
TO: NEW YORK
ARRIVED: 23 NOVEMBER 1882

PASSENGER	AGE	SEX	OCCUPATION	PRV VIL DES
GOLDENSOHN, HASKEL	20	M	TRDSMN	RRZZZZUSA
RABINOWIZ, DAVID	55	M	TRDSMN	RRZZZZUSA
ISSER	29	M	S	RRZZZZUSA
SCHEMATZKY, ABRAH.	20	M	TRDSMN	RRZZZZUSA
ERNESTINE	22	F	W	RRZZZZUSA
GUTMANN, MOSES	23	M	TRDSMN	RRZZZZUSA
CHAIS	20	F	W	RRZZZZUSA
ORKUSCH, JACOB	20	M	TRDSMN	RRZZZZUSA
KURANER, SOPHIE	18	F	SGL	RRZZZZUSA
FEINSBERG, DAVID	17	M	TRDSMN	RRZZZZUSA

SHIP: SILESIA

FROM: HAMBURG
TO: NEW YORK
ARRIVED: 23 NOVEMBER 1882

PASSENGER	AGE	SEX	OCCUPATION	PRV VIL DES
HOFFMANN, MEYER	18	M	PNR	RRZZZZUSA
SMITH, CHAIE	18	F	SGL	RRZZZZUSA
RUBENSTEIN, GOLDE	20	F	SGL	RRZZZZUSA
LEWIN, HOSCHER	20	M	TLR	RRZZZZUSA
ASCHER, JUDEL	60	M	UNKNOWN	RRZZZZUSA
AHASCHE	60	F	W	RRZZZZUSA
LEVY, FECHWED	30	M	LABR	RRZZZZUSA
LEIB	4	M	CHILD	RRZZZZUSA
ZOS--OW, HANNE	25	F	W	RRZZZZUSA
BEILE	4	F	CHILD	RRZZZZUSA
PESCHE	.11	F	INFANT	RRZZZZUSA
STAROPOLSKY, DINA	9	F	CHILD	RRZZZZUSA
FRIEDMANN, MALE	18	F	SGL	RRZZZZUSA
FINKELSTEIN, MOSES	50	M	DLR	RRZZZZUSA
HANNE	45	F	W	RRZZZZUSA
CHEIE	17	F	CH	RRZZZZUSA
LOEB	9	M	CHILD	RRZZZZUSA
HIRSCH	8	M	CHILD	RRZZZZUSA
PASIDOLSKI, CHIFRE	60	F	W	RRZZZZUSA
ESTHER	18	F	D	RRZZZZUSA
EPHRAIM	9	M	CHILD	RRZZZZUSA
EIDELSOHN, JOEL	20	M	DLR	RRZZZZUSA
STRALKOOWSKY, BERKO	22	M	UNKNOWN	RRZZZZUSA
MIASZKOWSKY, ZSIEL	18	F	SGL	RRZZZZUSA
NUSSBAUM, DINE	18	F	UNKNOWN	RRZZZZUSA
BAKOWSKI, RIEWE	19	F	SGL	RRZZZZUSA
SCHILIBOLSKI, JOSUAH	21	M	LABR	RRZZZZUSA
BASCHE	20	F	W	RRZZZZUSA
SALEWETZKY, HANNE	45	F	UNKNOWN	RRZZZZUSA
KANTOR, ESTHER	25	F	UNKNOWN	RRZZZZUSA
LIEBE	.11	F	INFANT	RRZZZZUSA
RASA	.01	F	INFANT	RRZZZZUSA
MARHORAS, LEA	35	F	W	RRZZZZUSA
SALOMON	4	M	CHILD	RRZZZZUSA
JENTA	.11	F	INFANT	RRZZZZUSA
DAVID	.01	M	INFANT	RRZZZZUSA
KRISCHMANSKI, MARASCHE	19	F	W	RRZZZZUSA
MOSES	.06	M	INFANT	RRZZZZUSA
CHEVEL, PERLE	41	F	W	RRZZZZUSA
HANNE	16	F	CH	RRZZZZUSA
RACHEL	9	F	CHILD	RRZZZZUSA
ABRAHAM	8	M	CHILD	RRZZZZUSA
RUBIN, ETTA	38	F	W	RRZZZZUSA
RUBEN	14	M	CH	RRZZZZUSA
BERTHA	3	F	CHILD	RRZZZZUSA
PITAFFSKY, HARRIS	19	M	LABR	RRZZZZUSA
JASKULSKI, ALEX.	24	M	UNKNOWN	RRZZZZUSA
VICTORIA	22	F	W	RRZZZZUSA
SALOME	.11	F	INFANT	RRZZZZUSA
ODCUZ, MOSES	19	M	LABR	RRZZZZUSA
SUDWAISKY, SCHOENE	18	F	SGL	RRZZZZUSA
NATOWSKI, ISAAK	18	M	LABR	RRZZZZUSA
GOLDMANN, LEISER	17	M	UNKNOWN	RRZZZZUSA
HOFFMANN, JULIUS	46	M	FARMER	RRZZZZUSA
JOSEPHA	45	F	W	RRZZZZUSA
EMILIE	9	F	CHILD	RRZZZZUSA
LORENY, AGNES	19	F	SGL	RRZZZZUSA
FRIEDI, FERD.	22	M	FARMER	RRZZZZUSA
LOUISE	18	F	SGL	RRZZZZUSA
SCHTACHLSCHEIDER, HERM.	22	M	FARMER	RRZZZZUSA
KOSCH, MICHAEL	21	M	UNKNOWN	RRZZZZUSA
STOEKE, FRIEDR.	19	M	UNKNOWN	RRZZZZUSA
EUPHROSZINE	21	F	SGL	RRZZZZUSA
BRUNKOL, JACOB	21	M	FARMER	RRZZZZUSA
EISWALD, MICHAEL	21	M	UNKNOWN	RRZZZZUSA

SHIP: STELLA

FROM: AMSTERDAM
TO: NEW YORK
ARRIVED: 23 NOVEMBER 1882

PASSENGER	AGE	SEX	OCCUPATION	PRV VIL DES
MACRUM, JON	25	M	LABR	PLZZZZUSA
DOMBROWSKY, JON	20	M	LABR	PLZZZZUSA
GERMIES, MACICY	20	M	LABR	PLZZZZUSA
KRVEZE, JALTZIE	22	F	NN	PLZZZZUSA
MENHAUS, WILHELM	30	M	LABR	PLZZZZUSA
CENZER, MARIE	30	F	UNKNOWN	PLAHXAUSA
WACRON	8	M	CHILD	PLAHXAUSA
CORNELIA	8	F	CHILD	PLAHXAUSA
LULINSKY, EDWARD	16	M	UNKNOWN	PLAHXTUSA

SHIP: CATALONIA

FROM: LIVERPOOL AND QUEENSTOWN
TO: NEW YORK
ARRIVED: 25 NOVEMBER 1882

PASSENGER	AGE	SEX	OCCUPATION	PRV VIL DES
GOLDBERG, B.MR	41	M	MCHT	PLZZZZUSA

SHIP: ST. OF PENNSYLVANIA

FROM: GLASGOW AND LARNE
TO: NEW YORK
ARRIVED: 25 NOVEMBER 1882

PASSENGER	AGE	SEX	OCCUPATION	PRV VIL DES
URCHISKI, CHAINE	21	M	PDLR	RRZZZZUSA
BIRABOSH, JACOB	22	M	LABR	RRZZZZUSA
PAUKANI, W.	26	M	LABR	RRZZZZUSA
G.	52	F	W	RRZZZZUSA
WASKUTI, FRITZ	26	M	LABR	RRZZZZUSA
OLSAYSKI, ALON	18	M	PDLR	RRZZZZUSA
KARONORONSKI, SELISENAU	18	M	LABR	RRZZZZUSA
BAUCISH, W.	21	M	BCHR	RRZZZZUSA
BUCKWITZ, ISIDOR	48	M	FARMER	RRZZZZUSA
LENA	33	F	W	RRZZZZUSA

PASSENGER	AGE	SEX	OCCUPATION	PRV VIL DES
JONI	7	M	CHILD	RRZZZZUSA
P.	5	M	CHILD	RRZZZZUSA
M.	1	F	CHILD	RRZZZZUSA
SCHWARTZ, MARIA	11	F	NN	RRZZZZUSA
ABRARIEWICZ, ROSI	9	M	CHILD	RRZZZZUSA
HEDRICK, JOS.	25	M	LABR	RRZZZZUSA
KARAELL, --IRH	33	M	LABR	RRZZZZUSA
WEBER, JOS.	39	M	LABR	RRZZZZUSA
OHLANDER, PET.	23	F	W	RRZZZZUSA
OSKAR	.09	M	INFANT	RRZZZZUSA
HEDSIG, JAS.	30	M	LABR	RRZZZZUSA
FRANKI, J.	35	M	LABR	RRZZZZUSA
STICKER, C.	41	F	W	RRZZZZUSA
LEVI, M.	37	M	LABR	RRZZZZUSA
TAIN, M.	37	M	LABR	RRZZZZUSA
SABAGDER, JAS.	40	M	LABR	RRZZZZUSA
MAGNRIZAETT, DIEDR.	24	M	LABR	RRZZZZUSA
HAGNER, M.	28	M	LABR	RRZZZZUSA
ISRAELSEN, ISRAEL	63	M	FARMER	RRZZZZUSA
JUGI	59	F	W	RRZZZZUSA
ALMA	28	F	W	RRZZZZUSA
OSCAR	11	M	NN	RRZZZZUSA
DESA, M.	28	M	LABR	RRZZZZUSA
SPAN, JAS.	38	M	LABR	RRZZZZUSA
KULTERSTRAND, P.	24	M	LABR	RRZZZZUSA
PLESCHMIDT, P.	28	M	LABR	RRZZZZUSA
STOCKER, JOS.	42	M	FARMER	RRZZZZUSA
A.MARIA	42	F	W	RRZZZZUSA
SOPHA	17	F	W	RRZZZZUSA
CHRISTIAN	15	M	NN	RRZZZZUSA
CARL	11	M	NN	RRZZZZUSA
PAULSIN, GUSTAV	22	M	LABR	RRZZZZUSA
KULLERSTRADT, J.	18	M	LABR	RRZZZZUSA
ABRAHAMHAUSEN, HANS	19	M	LABR	RRZZZZUSA
ISRAELSEN, CARL	26	M	LABR	RRZZZZUSA
ALFRED	16	M	LABR	RRZZZZUSA
SPRAGEN, A.O.	30	F	W	RRZZZZUSA
MATILDA	9	F	CHILD	RRZZZZUSA
F.	8	F	CHILD	RRZZZZUSA
IDA	6	F	CHILD	RRZZZZUSA

SHIP: NEDERLAND

FROM: ANTWERP
TO: NEW YORK
ARRIVED: 27 NOVEMBER 1882

PASSENGER	AGE	SEX	OCCUPATION	PRV VIL DES
NURWICZ, RATAVZE	18	M	FARMER	PLZZZZUSA
JANKO, POSKUMAK	17	M	FARMER	PLZZZZUSA
GULAS, ANNA	22	F	FARMER	PLZZZZUSA
HALKA	.06	F	INFANT	PLZZZZUSA
LASTOFSKA, MARG.	22	F	FARMER	PLZZZZUSA
U	.10	M	INFANT	PLZZZZUSA

SHIP: SUEVIA

FROM: HAMBURG
TO: NEW YORK
ARRIVED: 27 NOVEMBER 1882

PASSENGER	AGE	SEX	OCCUPATION	PRV VIL DES
MORRIS, JOHN	22	M	LABR	RRZZZZUSA
BERMANN, HASSE	36	F	W	RRZZZZUSA
PESCHE	9	F	CHILD	RRZZZZUSA
GITTEL	5	M	CHILD	RRZZZZUSA
CHANNE	3	F	CHILD	RRZZZZUSA

PASSENGER	AGE	SEX	OCCUPATION	PRV VIL DES
WASSILEWSKI, VINCENT	26	M	LABR	RRZZZZUSA
STANISL.	19	M	LABR	RRZZZZUSA
AUG.	21	M	LABR	RRZZZZUSA
MORRIS, ABRAH.	16	M	LABR	RRZZZZUSA
WIZSCHINSKI, JACOB	18	M	LABR	RRZZZZUSA
SCHALMANN, JAN	24	M	PNTR	RRZZZZUSA
UBENSKY, MOSCHY	21	M	LABR	RRZZZZUSA
ROSENBERG, BENJ.	25	M	DLR	RRZZZZUSA
WIESNER, JOHANNA	14	F	SGL	RRZZZZUSA
REICHERT, MORED	17	M	DLR	RRZZZZUSA
BERKOWITZ, HERRND.	33	M	LABR	RRZZZZUSA
ROSA	22	F	W	RRZZZZUSA
KOWATKOWSKY, ROSALIE	30	F	SGL	RRZZZZUSA
FROSNISKI, CHASKEL	21	M	DLR	RRZZZZUSA
BASCHE	22	F	W	RRZZZZUSA
RAIZE	.06	F	INFANT	RRZZZZUSA
GRUNBERG, FEIGEL	17	F	SGL	RRZZZZUSA
ROSA	9	F	CHILD	RRZZZZUSA
MUDENSTEIN, ISRAEL	21	M	DLR	RRZZZZUSA
RACHEL	21	F	W	RRZZZZUSA
SARA	.06	F	INFANT	RRZZZZUSA
HURWITZ, CHAIM	18	M	DLR	RRZZZZUSA
BERKOWITZ, BERPI	.08	F	INFANT	RRZZZZUSA

SHIP: EGYPT

FROM: LIVERPOOL
TO: NEW YORK
ARRIVED: 28 NOVEMBER 1882

PASSENGER	AGE	SEX	OCCUPATION	PRV VIL DES
KOBA, F.	36	M	LABR	RRZZZZUSA
KUGER, AUG.	41	M	LABR	RRZZZZUSA
ALBERT	10	M	CH	RRZZZZUSA
E.	8	M	CHILD	RRZZZZUSA
A.	4	M	CHILD	RRZZZZUSA
A.	3	M	CHILD	RRZZZZUSA
FRANZ	00	M	INF	RRZZZZUSA
FRANECH, DAVID	35	M	LABR	RRZZZZUSA
ROSSIT, SOLOMIN	22	M	LABR	RRZZZZUSA
IREES, BARNETT	45	M	LABR	RRZZZZUSA
FRONUAN, JULIA	35	F	SP	RRZZZZUSA

SHIP: GALLIA

FROM: LIVERPOOL AND QUEENSTOWN
TO: NEW YORK
ARRIVED: 29 NOVEMBER 1882

PASSENGER	AGE	SEX	OCCUPATION	PRV VIL DES
DAMBY, DAVID	22	M	JNR	RRZZZZUSA
ROSE	23	F	W	RRZZZZUSA

SHIP: KATIE

FROM: STETTIN
TO: NEW YORK
ARRIVED: 29 NOVEMBER 1882

PASSENGER	AGE	SEX	OCCUPATION	PRV VIL DES
WARHOWSKY, MICHAEL	20	M	LABR	RRZZZZUSA
HEPPOLA, HENRICK	30	M	FARMER	RRZZZZUSA

PASSENGER	AGE	SEX	OCCUPATION	PRVIL	DES

SHIP: GELLERT

FROM: HAMBURG, HAVRE AND PLYMOUTH
TO: NEW YORK
ARRIVED: 02 DECEMBER 1882

PASSENGER	AGE	SEX	OCCUPATION	PRVIL	DES
KLACZOWSKY, ISRAEL	23	M	LABR	RRZZZZ	USA
WITKIN, OSIP	27	M	DLR	RRZZZZ	USA
MATIN, FEIGE	20	F	W	RRZZZZ	USA
BRENIE	.06	M	INFANT	RRZZZZ	USA
SHAKIN, BENZEL	23	M	DLR	RRZZZZ	USA
TOLLUS, VALERIA	26	F	W	RRZZZZ	USA
WLADISLAV	6	M	CHILD	RRZZZZ	USA
MARIANNE	5	F	CHILD	RRZZZZ	USA
LEWY, BER.	21	M	LABR	RRZZZZ	USA
ENGELBRECHT, ANNA	14	F	NN	RRZZZZ	USA
CAROLINE	9	F	CHILD	RRZZZZ	USA
JOHANNE	8	F	CHILD	RRZZZZ	USA
MARIA	7	F	CHILD	RRZZZZ	USA
SCHLESINGER, GRUME	22	F	SGL	RRZZZZ	USA
SCHUMSTEY, BERKO	20	M	LABR	RRZZZZ	USA
KIDAERSKY, SIMON	20	M	LABR	RRZZZZ	USA
FEIGE	18	F	SGL	RRZZZZ	USA
WACHENBERG, SALOMON	18	M	MCHT	RRZZZZ	USA
BEREBEIZEK, LEIB	17	M	TLR	RRZZZZ	USA
SILBERMANN, ROSA	9	F	CHILD	RRZZZZ	USA
WARNGORIS, GEORG	27	M	LABR	RRZZZZ	USA
SCHREYDECK, LUDWIG	22	M	JNR	RRZZZZ	USA
WARNGORIS, EVA	26	F	W	RRZZZZ	USA
LEWIN, CHATZKEL	12	M	BY	RRZZZZ	USA
GRUEBERG, SIGM.	30	M	DR	RRZZZZ	USA

SHIP: ELBE

FROM: BREMEN AND SOUTHAMPTON
TO: NEW YORK
ARRIVED: 04 DECEMBER 1882

PASSENGER	AGE	SEX	OCCUPATION	PRVIL	DES
GROENBERG, OSSIAN	20	M	SEMN	RRZZZZ	USA

SHIP: NECKAR

FROM: BREMEN
TO: NEW YORK
ARRIVED: 05 DECEMBER 1882

PASSENGER	AGE	SEX	OCCUPATION	PRVIL	DES
HAEFENFELS, EMILIE	20	F	W	RRZZZZ	USA
EMIL	3	M	CHILD	RRZZZZ	USA

SHIP: ZEELAND

FROM: ANTWERP
TO: NEW YORK
ARRIVED: 05 DECEMBER 1882

PASSENGER	AGE	SEX	OCCUPATION	PRVIL	DES
KOBER, CONRAD	22	M	LABR	PLZZZZ	CAN
COUPONMANN, S.	44	M	MCHT	RRZZZZ	NY

SHIP: DEVONIA

FROM: GLASGOW AND MOVILLE
TO: NEW YORK
ARRIVED: 06 DECEMBER 1882

PASSENGER	AGE	SEX	OCCUPATION	PRVIL	DES
LASTIKA, JUKE	21	M	LABR	FNZZZZ	USA
METALU, MALBS.	25	M	LABR	FNZZZZ	USA
RUSENKO, RETY	35	M	LABR	PLZZZZ	USA

SHIP: STATE OF ALABAMA

FROM: GLASGOW
TO: NEW YORK
ARRIVED: 06 DECEMBER 1882

PASSENGER	AGE	SEX	OCCUPATION	PRVIL	DES
CZICHOWSKIE, SAM	19	M	LABR	PLZZZZ	USA
KOBELSKI, JUDEL	21	M	UNKNOWN	PLZZZZ	USA
FEDERMAN, A.	22	M	UNKNOWN	PLZZZZ	USA
WEILKEWITZ, M.	22	M	UNKNOWN	PLZZZZ	USA
SCHARTZENSTACH, J.	18	M	UNKNOWN	PLZZZZ	USA
CICHMANN, MEYER	17	M	UNKNOWN	PLZZZZ	USA

SHIP: ABYSSINIA

FROM: LIVERPOOL AND QUEENSTOWN
TO: NEW YORK
ARRIVED: 07 DECEMBER 1882

PASSENGER	AGE	SEX	OCCUPATION	PRVIL	DES
PERSSON, ANDEN	18	M	LABR	FNZZZZ	USA
URIDALA, JACOB	28	M	LABR	FNZZZZ	USA
FORRALA, JOS.	24	M	LABR	FNZZZZ	USA
OLKONEN, AUG.	26	M	LABR	FNZZZZ	USA
JERRELA, ELAIAS	27	M	LABR	FNZZZZ	USA
MONNEIKOELA, ELIAS	47	M	LABR	FNZZZZ	USA
RITTO, ABRAM	32	M	LABR	FNZZZZ	USA
ESKOLA, JOHAN	25	M	LABR	FNZZZZ	USA
LINNINGA, FRANS-O.	29	M	LABR	FNZZZZ	USA

SHIP: WIELAND

FROM: HAMBURG AND HAVRE
TO: NEW YORK
ARRIVED: 07 DECEMBER 1882

PASSENGER	AGE	SEX	OCCUPATION	PRVIL	DES
FEINSTEIN, HIRSCH	18	M	DLR	RRZZZZ	USA
KUSCHEWSKY, PENTE	30	F	W	RRZZZZ	USA
MENDEL	.11	M	INFANT	RRZZZZ	USA
BERL	.11	M	INFANT	RRZZZZ	USA
PORESNEFSKI, JUDEL	21	M	DLR	RRZZZZ	USA
FAIN, SALMAN	14	M	BY	RRZZZZ	USA
RUDOWSKY, ABRAHAM	65	M	DLR	RRZZZZ	USA
SARA	33	F	W	RRZZZZ	USA
MOSES	9	M	CHILD	RRZZZZ	USA
BEILE	6	M	CHILD	RRZZZZ	USA
GOLDE	.11	F	INFANT	RRZZZZ	USA
WEISS, MARRUS	19	M	HTR	RRZZZZ	USA
JERAKOWITZ, AIHEINE	25	F	SGL	RRZZZZ	USA
DEGUTZKI, MOSES	17	M	DLR	RRZZZZ	USA

PASSENGER	AGE	SEX	OCCUPATION	PV RIV L	DES
GITTEL	9	F	CHILD	RRZZZZ	USA
LEIBE	8	M	CHILD	RRZZZZ	USA
LIEBAMANN	6	M	CHILD	RRZZZZ	USA
ELIAS	5	M	CHILD	RRZZZZ	USA
AREUD, WOLF	16	M	LABR	RRZZZZ	USA
BARANROK, DAVID	27	M	MCHT	RRZZZZ	USA
WILEZEK, SCHILLEM	18	M	LABR	RRZZZZ	USA
LENDON, MOSES	9	M	CHILD	RRZZZZ	USA
JACOBSON, ANDR.	20	M	LABR	RRZZZZ	USA
MASIEKO, ANDR.	41	M	LABR	RRZZZZ	USA
PASIL, JOSEF	19	M	LABR	RRZZZZ	USA
GORESGENI, JOH.	32	M	FARMER	RRZZZZ	USA
MAZUR, MORDCHE	19	M	LABR	RRZZZZ	USA
ZUIKER, PHIL.	23	M	MCHT	RRZZZZ	USA
GALISCHEFSKI, THOMAS	30	M	LABR	RRZZZZ	USA
JOSEF	20	M	LABR	RRZZZZ	USA
DOEL, HEINRICH	34	M	LABR	RRZZZZ	USA
BOZEWSKA, CATH.	36	F	W	RRZZZZ	USA
ANTONIE	9	F	CHILD	RRZZZZ	USA
HANSLAUS	7	F	CHILD	RRZZZZ	USA
JOH.	6	F	CHILD	RRZZZZ	USA
ANDREUS	5	F	CHILD	RRZZZZ	USA
FELIX	.11	F	INFANT	RRZZZZ	USA

SHIP: STATE OF FLORIDA

FROM: GLASGOW AND LARNE
TO: NEW YORK
ARRIVED: 08 DECEMBER 1882

PASSENGER	AGE	SEX	OCCUPATION	PV RIV L	DES
MAURY, JOS.	35	M	MCHT	RRZZZZ	USA
SYTNER, JUDAS	28	M	TLR	RRZZZZ	USA
SARAH	1	F	CHILD	RRZZZZ	USA
NOCHE	1	F	CHILD	RRZZZZ	USA
FATTEL	7	M	CHILD	RRZZZZ	USA
SKALKA, DAD.	22	M	TLR	RRZZZZ	USA

SHIP: CASTOR

FROM: AMSTERDAM
TO: NEW YORK
ARRIVED: 09 DECEMBER 1882

PASSENGER	AGE	SEX	OCCUPATION	PV RIV L	DES
BACKER, FREDK.	18	M	LABR	RRZZZZ	USA
ANTON, MACHIS	56	M	LABR	RRZZZZ	USA
THERESA	56	F	NN	RRZZZZ	USA
GEORG	21	M	LABR	RRZZZZ	USA
KULLMAN, DANIEL	23	M	NN	RRZZZZ	USA
PHILLIPINE	18	F	NN	RRZZZZ	USA
MATHIS, ANNA	29	F	NN	RRZZZZ	USA
MICHAEL	4	F	CHILD	RRZZZZ	USA
HAIZMANN, ANTON	23	F	NN	RRZZZZ	USA
ULSCHNIDER, ANTON	31	M	LABR	RRZZZZ	USA
KONALSKY, STENI	26	M	LABR	RRZZZZ	USA
SCHULZE, EDWD.	26	M	LABR	RRZZZZ	USA
SCHILOWSKY, ANTON	33	M	NN	RRZZZZ	USA
AUGUSTA	28	F	NN	RRZZZZ	USA
LEWENDOWSKI, MARG.	20	F	NN	RRZZZZ	USA
PRALL, JOSEPHE	25	F	NN	RRZZZZ	USA
ANTAZA, FRANCIS	22	F	NN	PLZZZZ	USA
BULGEES, ADAM	57	M	NN	PLZZZZ	USA
GERTRUD	26	F	NN	PLZZZZ	USA
ALBERS, WED.	26	F	NN	PLZZZZ	USA
HAINDL, WENZEL	20	M	NN	PLZZZZ	USA
HACKE, PAUL	40	M	NN	PLZZZZ	USA

PASSENGER	AGE	SEX	OCCUPATION	PV RIV L	DES
ENGBERT, GEO.	24	M	NN	PLZZZZ	USA
KUNZ, FRANZ	25	M	NN	PLZZZZ	USA
REMHARD, ANNA	27	F	NN	PLZZZZ	USA
MULLER, HERMANN	8	M	CHILD	PLZZZZ	USA
KEPPELEIN, WNS.	30	M	LABR	PLZZZZ	USA
SCHENK, CHRIS	30	M	LABR	PLZZZZ	USA
PELERSON, GUSTAV	41	M	LABR	RRZZZZ	USA
ANNA	8	F	CHILD	RRZZZZ	USA
ELVIRA	7	F	CHILD	RRZZZZ	USA
WM.	5	M	CHILD	RRZZZZ	USA
MARIE	.06	F	INFANT	RRZZZZ	USA

SHIP: CITY OF RICHMOND

FROM: LIVERPOOL
TO: NEW YORK
ARRIVED: 09 DECEMBER 1882

PASSENGER	AGE	SEX	OCCUPATION	PV RIV L	DES
JAPHA, ALBERT	32	M	LABR	RRZZZZ	USA
GABORN	24	F	W	RRZZZZ	USA

SHIP: CANADA

FROM: LONDON
TO: NEW YORK
ARRIVED: 11 DECEMBER 1882

PASSENGER	AGE	SEX	OCCUPATION	PV RIV L	DES
SCHWARZ, RUB.	38	F	TLR	PLZZZZ	USA
KITTY	18	F	SVNT	PLZZZZ	USA
SARA	16	F	SVNT	PLZZZZ	USA
ABRM.	11	M	CH	PLZZZZ	USA
SAOL.	4	M	CHILD	PLZZZZ	USA
RACHEL	.07	F	INFANT	PLZZZZ	USA
ALEXANDER, MORIS	24	M	LABR	PLZZZZ	USA
LOIDKE, THEOD.	30	M	LABR	RRZZZZ	USA
MAFOSSE, MAT.	23	M	LABR	RRZZZZ	USA
HISTLA, MAX	38	M	LABR	RRZZZZ	USA
SALO, JOH.	23	M	JNR	RRZZZZ	USA
KAKARI, MAT.	22	M	JNR	RRZZZZ	USA
ERIK	37	M	JNR	RRZZZZ	USA
SAVLY, JOSEF	24	M	LABR	RRZZZZ	USA
FODLASKY, CHORA	28	M	LABR	RRZZZZ	USA
HONFAS, MAT.	22	M	LABR	RRZZZZ	USA
DAVIDSON, MAT.	31	M	LABR	RRZZZZ	USA
SISSALA, AND.	31	M	TLR	RRZZZZ	USA
ROINSKI, GUS.	25	M	TLR	RRZZZZ	USA
MALYNEK, JACOB	31	M	TLR	RRZZZZ	USA
HERBERT, PETER	24	M	TLR	RRZZZZ	USA

SHIP: LAKE CHAMPLAIN

FROM: LIVERPOOL
TO: NEW YORK
ARRIVED: 11 DECEMBER 1882

PASSENGER	AGE	SEX	OCCUPATION	PV RIV L	DES
JAMENHOFF, LUDWIG	21	M	LABR	RRZZZZ	CAN
KIEHNMOISKI, AMAYLA	25	F	W	PLZZZZ	USA
EMELIA	3	F	CHILD	PLZZZZ	USA
AMAYLA	.07	F	INFANT	PLZZZZ	USA

PASSENGER	AGE	SEX	OCCUPATION	PRIV	DES

SHIP: INDIA

FROM: HAMBURG
TO: NEW YORK
ARRIVED: 12 DECEMBER 1882

PASSENGER	AGE	SEX	OCCUPATION	PRIV	DES
HERMANN, CARL	26	M	HTR	RR	ZZZZUSA
ADAM	24	M	HTR	RR	ZZZZUSA
PATTELENOWSKY, JOSEF	18	M	LABR	RR	ZZZZUSA
BENDMANSKY, JOSEF	22	M	LABR	RR	ZZZZUSA

SHIP: ERIN

FROM: LIVERPOOL AND QUEENSTOWN
TO: NEW YORK
ARRIVED: 13 DECEMBER 1882

PASSENGER	AGE	SEX	OCCUPATION	PRIV	DES
DABULEVITSCH, JOHN	18	M	UNKNOWN	RR	ZZZZUSA
BOYANONFSKA, AGATHA	20	F	SVNT	RR	ZZZZUSA
WOITTEOWEICZ, ANTON	24	M	LABR	RR	ZZZZUSA

SHIP: RUGIA

FROM: HAMBURG
TO: NEW YORK
ARRIVED: 13 DECEMBER 1882

PASSENGER	AGE	SEX	OCCUPATION	PRIV	DES
WARGA, ANTON	19	M	LABR	RR	ZZZZUSA
SCHUMES, ISAAC	35	M	UNKNOWN	RR	ZZZZUSA
SARA	25	F	W	RR	ZZZZUSA
EPHRAIM, PAULIN	25	F	W	RR	ZZZZUSA
FANNY	2	F	CHILD	RR	ZZZZUSA
LOUIS	.06	M	INFANT	RR	ZZZZUSA
PITLANSKY, SCHOLEM	37	M	LABR	RR	ZZZZUSA
EVA, IAFFE	40	F	W	RR	ZZZZUSA
CHANNE	18	F	CH	RR	ZZZZUSA
MINNA	18	F	UNKNOWN	RR	ZZZZUSA
REBECCA	16	F	UNKNOWN	RR	ZZZZUSA
RAHEL	15	F	UNKNOWN	RR	ZZZZUSA
JEDIJE	9	F	CHILD	RR	ZZZZUSA
FAUST, WLADISL.	30	M	UNKNOWN	RR	ZZZZUSA
LAZANNA	28	F	W	RR	ZZZZUSA
TASCHMANN, GUTMAN	20	M	SHMK	RR	ZZZZUSA
GOLDSTEIN, ARIEL	20	M	TLR	RR	ZZZZUSA
KAHN, NANNE	20	M	DLR	RR	ZZZZUSA
BORNSTEIN, DAVID	20	M	UNKNOWN	RR	ZZZZUSA
PIBELSKI, CHAIM	20	M	UNKNOWN	RR	ZZZZUSA
SIMANSKI, ABRAH.	20	M	UNKNOWN	RR	ZZZZUSA
LAPINSKY, LEA	30	F	W	RR	ZZZZUSA
ALTER	.04	M	INFANT	RR	ZZZZUSA
SAMUEL	.01	M	INFANT	RR	ZZZZUSA
JUDES, JANKEL	47	M	JNR	RR	ZZZZUSA
KRAEMER, LAIB	45	M	DLR	RR	ZZZZUSA
MALZ, JOSET	20	M	DLR	RR	ZZZZUSA
URBANOWICZ, JAN.	19	M	UNKNOWN	RR	ZZZZUSA
WACINKOWIC, KASIMIR	15	M	UNKNOWN	RR	ZZZZUSA
SINKEWICZ, CARL	22	M	LABR	RR	ZZZZUSA
PREUS, MOSES	16	M	DLR	RR	ZZZZUSA
BERNSTEIN, JUDEL	21	M	DLR	RR	ZZZZUSA
ZIOASOHN, ELIAS	20	M	LABR	RR	ZZZZUSA
BERNSTEIN, SOLAMAN	9	M	CHILD	RR	ZZZZUSA

SHIP: BOHEMIA

FROM: HAMBURG
TO: NEW YORK
ARRIVED: 15 DECEMBER 1882

PASSENGER	AGE	SEX	OCCUPATION	PRIV	DES
HARRIS, ANNA	28	F	W	RR	ZZZZUSA
LEA	3	F	CHILD	RR	ZZZZUSA
JANKEL	.10	M	INFANT	RR	ZZZZUSA
LAZOWKIEWIEZ, PETRONELL	18	F	SGL	RR	ZZZZUSA
BAWELKEYS, ANDREW	22	M	LABR	RR	ZZZZUSA
MIKODIMOWITZ, STANISL.	30	M	LABR	RR	ZZZZUSA
FRANZISKA	28	F	W	RR	ZZZZUSA
MARIANNE	4	F	CHILD	RR	ZZZZUSA
USALIS, MATEUS	31	M	LABR	RR	ZZZZUSA
MASCKANIS, ANTON	24	M	LABR	RR	ZZZZUSA
JANKOWSKY, JAN	30	M	LABR	RR	ZZZZUSA
JUDINSKY, ALEX	48	M	LABR	RR	ZZZZUSA
ASSONOWIEZ, JOSSEL	14	M	BY	RR	ZZZZUSA
BOROWSKY, JOS.	46	M	LABR	RR	ZZZZUSA
SCHEINE	9	F	CHILD	RR	ZZZZUSA
SAMUEL	7	M	CHILD	RR	ZZZZUSA
SCUTE	5	F	CHILD	RR	ZZZZUSA
KRAPIWSKY, ANNA	21	F	SGL	RR	ZZZZUSA
BROWSKY, SCHEINE	46	F	W	RR	ZZZZUSA
BLUME	.11	M	INFANT	RR	ZZZZUSA
PATOWSKI, JOHANN	20	F	SGL	RR	ZZZZUSA
STUREN, SCHAINE	35	M	JNR	RR	ZZZZUSA
LITERNICAS, JANOS	32	M	LABR	RR	ZZZZUSA
STANKOWITSCH, JOSEPH	24	M	LABR	RR	ZZZZUSA
SOMINSKI, FRANS	21	M	LABR	RR	ZZZZUSA
ZIONSKY, JOSEF	21	M	LABR	RR	ZZZZUSA
ANSZO, JONAS	20	M	LABR	RR	ZZZZUSA
ZUCKUS, JONAS	21	M	LABR	RR	ZZZZUSA
REISS, CARL	26	M	LABR	RR	ZZZZUSA
MARIANE	18	F	W	RR	ZZZZUSA
RUBIN, CHAIM	20	M	LABR	RR	ZZZZUSA
GOLDBERG, MEIER	16	M	LABR	RR	ZZZZUSA

SHIP: FRISIA

FROM: HAMBURG AND HAVRE
TO: NEW YORK
ARRIVED: 15 DECEMBER 1882

PASSENGER	AGE	SEX	OCCUPATION	PRIV	DES
KIAFKOTSKI, JOSEF	26	M	LABR	RR	ZZZZUSA
KLEINMANN, MINDEL	25	F	SGL	RR	ZZZZUSA
DAVID	18	M	LABR	RR	ZZZZUSA
KASTER, ISRAEL	21	M	LABR	RR	ZZZZUSA
BLADT, ROMAN	24	M	MCHT	RR	ZZZZUSA
OSTROWSKI, PETER	31	M	LABR	RR	ZZZZUSA
JADWIGA	25	F	W	RR	ZZZZUSA
STANISLAUS	3	M	CHILD	RR	ZZZZUSA
ANTONIE	.11	F	INFANT	RR	ZZZZUSA
BUCHMANN, DAVID	22	M	MCHT	RR	ZZZZUSA
GROSSMANN, AMSCHEL	9	M	CHILD	RR	ZZZZUSA
GORDON, DAVIS	38	M	JWLR	RR	ZZZZUSA

SHIP: STATE OF NEBRASKA

FROM: GLASGOW AND LARNE
TO: NEW YORK
ARRIVED: 15 DECEMBER 1882

PASSENGER	AGE	SEX	OCCUPATION	PRV VIL DES
RUBEL, M.	22	M	PDLR	RRZZZZUSA
GARBUSKY, N.G.	20	M	PDLR	RRZZZZUSA
FELDSTEIN, E.	19	F	SP	RRZZZZUSA
FARBER, U-MRS	24	F	W	RRZZZZUSA
PESSE.	.06	F	INFANT	RRZZZZUSA
KANTROWIDZ, S.	42	M	SGN	RRZZZZUSA
U-MRS	38	F	W	RRZZZZUSA
SAMUEL	19	M	LABR	RRZZZZUSA
WOLF	16	M	LABR	RRZZZZUSA
ISRIAL	10	M	NN	RRZZZZUSA
CHAIE	9	F	CHILD	RRZZZZUSA
BELLE	8	M	CHILD	RRZZZZUSA
FREDDIE	7	M	CHILD	RRZZZZUSA
SHAKEWSKI, D.	50	M	PDLR	RRZZZZUSA
DAVID, M.	46	M	BBR	RRZZZZUSA
U-MRS	36	F	W	RRZZZZUSA
BASCHE	18	F	SP	RRZZZZUSA
A.	16	M	LABR	RRZZZZUSA
JABLOWSKY, J.	24	M	SHMK	RRZZZZUSA

SHIP: RHEIN

FROM: BREMEN AND SOUTHAMPTON
TO: NEW YORK
ARRIVED: 19 DECEMBER 1882

PASSENGER	AGE	SEX	OCCUPATION	PRV VIL DES
LADA, CIPRIAN	31	M	DLR	RRZZZZUSA
MARKS, AUGUST	21	M	LABR	RRZZZZUSA
KARPINSKY, JOH.	21	M	LABR	RRZZZZUSA
GEISSLER, BRUNO	52	M	LABR	RRZZZZUSA
HELENE	45	F	W	RRZZZZUSA
OLAD	19	F	NN	RRZZZZUSA
ALEXANDER	16	M	NN	RRZZZZUSA

SHIP: ANCHORIA

FROM: GLASGOW
TO: NEW YORK
ARRIVED: 21 DECEMBER 1882

PASSENGER	AGE	SEX	OCCUPATION	PRV VIL DES
POWLACK, JOSEF	44	M	BTMKR	RRZZZZUSA
DWORYCEKI, LUDWIG	25	M	BKR	RRZZZZUSA

SHIP: STATE OF GEORGIA

FROM: GLASGOW AND LARNE
TO: NEW YORK
ARRIVED: 21 DECEMBER 1882

PASSENGER	AGE	SEX	OCCUPATION	PRV VIL DES
TUBLONSKY, JOSIEL	21	M	FARMER	PLZZZZUSA
DEMBINTGKI, MARE	11	F	NN	PLZZZZUSA
HEISER, FRIEDRICK	27	M	LABR	PLZZZZUSA
WINKLER, CHRISTIAN	33	M	LABR	PLZZZZUSA
GOLUBSKY, ANTON	25	M	LABR	PLZZZZUSA
WOILUGOSSKER, MARIANNE	30	F	NN	PLZZZZUSA
MURASSKY, MARTIN	25	M	FARMER	PLZZZZUSA
CZELINSKY, ADAM	22	M	FARMER	PLZZZZUSA

SHIP: VANDALIA

FROM: HAMBURG
TO: NEW YORK
ARRIVED: 21 DECEMBER 1882

PASSENGER	AGE	SEX	OCCUPATION	PRV VIL DES
SALOMON, DAVID	17	M	MCHT	RRZZZZUSA
JENISZEWSKI, MARG.	40	F	W	RRZZZZUSA
JOSEF	15	M	CH	RRZZZZUSA
JULIANE	9	F	CHILD	RRZZZZUSA
ANTONIE	5	F	CHILD	RRZZZZUSA
STANISL.	3	M	CHILD	RRZZZZUSA
MICHAEL	.11	M	INFANT	RRZZZZUSA
GRUNWALD, JACOB	20	M	LABR	RRZZZZUSA
WARSCHAWSKY, GUSCHE	28	F	W	RRZZZZUSA
CHASE	9	F	CHILD	RRZZZZUSA
ABRA.	.11	M	INFANT	RRZZZZUSA
JAWSCHINSKI, BASHI	63	F	W	RRZZZZUSA
SCHMIEGE, MEILICH	17	M	BCHR	RRZZZZUSA
SCHAPIRA, MEYER	37	M	DLR	RRZZZZUSA
CHANNE	32	F	W	RRZZZZUSA
MENDEL	8	M	CHILD	RRZZZZUSA
KIELE	6	F	CHILD	RRZZZZUSA
SARA	4	F	CHILD	RRZZZZUSA
MOSES	.11	M	INFANT	RRZZZZUSA
OREL	.01	M	INFANT	RRZZZZUSA
HARMS, MARG.	34	F	W	RRZZZZUSA
OLBETER, LEOP.	23	M	LABR	RRZZZZUSA
BANDER, GEORG	20	M	LABR	RRZZZZUSA
BULLER, HEINR.	24	M	LABR	RRZZZZUSA
CHAIKE, PETER	25	M	FARMER	RRZZZZUSA
HAMMERBACH, ADOLPH	9	M	CHILD	RRZZZZUSA
FEEBER, SARA	22	F	W	RRZZZZUSA
FANNY	16	F	SGL	RRZZZZUSA
BERTHA	9	F	CHILD	RRZZZZUSA
LEVIN	8	M	CHILD	RRZZZZUSA
JOHANNE	7	F	CHILD	RRZZZZUSA
JACOB	6	M	CHILD	RRZZZZUSA

SHIP: CIMBRIA

FROM: HAMBURG AND HAVRE
TO: NEW YORK
ARRIVED: 22 DECEMBER 1882

PASSENGER	AGE	SEX	OCCUPATION	PRV VIL DES
KALIAMSKY, ANTON	20	M	LABR	RRZZZZUSA

SHIP: GRECIAN MONARCH

FROM: LONDON
TO: NEW YORK
ARRIVED: 22 DECEMBER 1882

PASSENGER	AGE	SEX	OCCUPATION	PRV VIL DES
AUSELL, SAMUEL	28	M	LABR	PLZZZZUSA
BRUN, HEYMAN	28	M	LABR	PLZZZZUSA

PASSENGER	AGE	SEX	OCCUPATION	PRV VIL DES
SHEIN, WEGMAN	24	M	LABR	PLZZZZUSA
BRODD, RACHEL	46	F	UNKNOWN	PLZZZZUSA
MIRIAM	9	F	CHILD	PLZZZZUSA
FOCUS, BETSY	20	F	UNKNOWN	PLZZZZUSA
GOLDBERG, BETSY	23	F	UNKNOWN	PLZZZZUSA
ELISABETH	1	F	CHILD	PLZZZZUSA

SHIP: LAKE HURON

FROM: LIVERPOOL AND QUEENSTOWN
TO: NEW YORK
ARRIVED: 22 DECEMBER 1882

PASSENGER	AGE	SEX	OCCUPATION	PRV VIL DES
WILENZIG, K.	30	M	LABR	RRZZZZUSA

SHIP: SWITZERLAND

FROM: ANTWERP
TO: NEW YORK
ARRIVED: 22 DECEMBER 1882

PASSENGER	AGE	SEX	OCCUPATION	PRV VIL DES
SCHINDER, PAULINE	26	F	DMS	RRZZZZUSA
MARIA	23	F	UNKNOWN	RRZZZZUSA
MUELLEROCHOW, MARIA	36	F	UNKNOWN	RRZZZZUSA

SHIP: ENGLAND

FROM: LIVERPOOL AND QUEENSTOWN
TO: NEW YORK
ARRIVED: 24 DECEMBER 1882

PASSENGER	AGE	SEX	OCCUPATION	PRV VIL DES
STARBROWITZ, JAN.	25	M	LABR	PLZZZZUSA
STEFAN, JONAS	33	M	LABR	PLZZZZUSA

SHIP: NEVADA

FROM: LIVERPOOL
TO: NEW YORK
ARRIVED: 26 DECEMBER 1882

PASSENGER	AGE	SEX	OCCUPATION	PRV VIL DES
KOSKLER, M.	21	M	LABR	FNZZZZUSA

SHIP: SILESIA

FROM: HAMBURG AND HAVRE
TO: NEW YORK
ARRIVED: 29 DECEMBER 1882

PASSENGER	AGE	SEX	OCCUPATION	PRV VIL DES
FISCHKIN, ISRAEL	20	M	TLR	RRZZZZUSA
REINES, SALOMON	9	M	CHILD	RRZZZZUSA
SILBERMANN, SARA	27	F	W	RRZZZZUSA
FENNY	9	F	CHILD	RRZZZZUSA
RASCHE	8	F	CHILD	RRZZZZUSA
HANNA	4	F	CHILD	RRZZZZUSA
SELIG	.11	M	INFANT	RRZZZZUSA
REISCHEL	.01	F	INFANT	RRZZZZUSA
NAWROTSKY, STAN.	39	M	UNKNOWN	RRZZZZUSA
MARIE	5	F	CHILD	RRZZZZUSA
MEIER, MINNA	21	F	SGL	RRZZZZUSA
BUKOWSKY, GEORG	28	M	UNKNOWN	RRZZZZUSA
LESTER, SARA-G.	17	F	SGL	RRZZZZUSA
HERZ, SAMUEL	21	M	DLR	RRZZZZUSA
DANNIECEWITZ, MARTIN	30	M	LABR	RRZZZZUSA
WILSZINSKI, LOUIS	34	M	GLSR	RRZZZZUSA
WASILEWSKY, VINCENTI	27	M	LABR	RRZZZZUSA
PRIZEWITSCH, JAN	20	M	UNKNOWN	RRZZZZUSA
GONSCHUR, SALOMON	20	M	DLR	RRZZZZUSA
HOPP, AMALIE	19	F	SGL	RRZZZZUSA
BLUMENTHAL, HEINRICH	28	M	LABR	RRZZZZUSA
SCHILL, RUDOLPH	29	M	SEMN	RRZZZZUSA
KUBILUS, JOSEF	21	M	UNKNOWN	RRZZZZUSA
JOSEPHER, ISRAEL	19	M	MCHT	RRZZZZUSA

SHIP: WAESLAND

FROM: ANTWERP
TO: NEW YORK
ARRIVED: 29 DECEMBER 1882

PASSENGER	AGE	SEX	OCCUPATION	PRV VIL DES
BOJEWSK, JOSEPH	30	M	LABR	PLZZZZNY
CATH.	26	F	LABR	PLZZZZNY
FRANCISCA	.10	F	INFANT	PLZZZZNY
ZWOLINSKA, MARDANNA	61	F	LABR	PLZZZZNY
SPYSHAWA, MICHEL	18	M	LABR	PLZZZZNY
JOCKEWITZ, U.	18	M	LABR	PLZZZZNY
MAURAK, ANTON	23	M	LABR	PLZZZZNY
CULBUTZ, JAN	23	M	LABR	PLZZZZNY
ZWOLINSKI, PAUL	19	M	LABR	PLZZZZNY
DEDL, CYONIN	23	M	TLR	RRZZZZUNK
SAWINSKY, JOH.	33	M	BCHR	PLZZZZNY
JOSEPH	00	M	BCHR	PLZZZZNY
MARIE	4	F	CHILD	PLZZZZNY
ALOISIA	3	F	CHILD	PLZZZZNY
LANKODIA	.11	F	INFANT	PLZZZZNY
SAWANSKY, MICH.	2	M	CHILD	PLZZZZNY
SZULACZEWIZ, MAGD.	24	F	UNKNOWN	PLZZZZUNK
MARIANNA	2	F	CHILD	PLZZZZUNK
JOSEF	.11	M	INFANT	PLZZZZUNK

SHIP: POLYNESIA

FROM: HAMBURG
TO: NEW YORK
ARRIVED: 30 DECEMBER 1882

PASSENGER	AGE	SEX	OCCUPATION	PRV VIL DES
KORTENBACH, ANTONIE	37	F	WO	RRZZZZUSA
ANNA	8	F	CHILD	RRZZZZUSA
HELENE	7	F	CHILD	RRZZZZUSA
MILTELMAN, IGN.	45	M	LABR	RRZZZZUSA
BRETZLEZKER, HACK.	29	M	TRDSMN	RRZZZZUSA
PANKEIUS, WANNZIS	21	M	TRDSMN	RRZZZZUSA
MOFSON, ISAAC	8	M	CHILD	RRZZZZUSA
RUFAHL, ERNESTINE	68	F	WO	RRZZZZUSA
AUGUSTA	28	F	WO	RRZZZZUSA
HEINRICH	7	M	CHILD	RRZZZZUSA

PASSENGER	AGE	SEX	OCCUPATION	PRV	VIL	DES
SPIEGELMANN, B.	20	F	SGL	RR	ZZZZ	USA
KLANOWSKY, ALEX	26	M	UNKNOWN	RR	ZZZZ	USA
RIECHER, FRITZ	22	M	SMH	RR	ZZZZ	USA

SHIP: BRITANNIC

FROM: LIVERPOOL AND QUEENSTOWN
TO: NEW YORK
ARRIVED: 01 JANUARY 1883

PASSENGER	AGE	SEX	OCCUPATION	PRV	VIL	DES
DE-STRUVE, MONS	32	M	DIP	RR	ZZZZ	USA
NISHIGORN, L.	20	M	SVNT	RR	ZZZZ	USA

SHIP: ODER

FROM: BREMEN AND SOUTHAMPTON
TO: NEW YORK
ARRIVED: 01 JANUARY 1883

PASSENGER	AGE	SEX	OCCUPATION	PRV	VIL	DES
LASKI, VINCENZ	26	M	MCHT	RR	ZZZZ	USA

SHIP: GELLERT

FROM: HAMBURG AND HAVRE
TO: NEW YORK
ARRIVED: 05 JANUARY 1883

PASSENGER	AGE	SEX	OCCUPATION	PRV	VIL	DES
SATZYNSKI, JAN	18	M	LABR	RR	ZZZZ	USA
SCHAPIRA, JERUCHEM	9	M	CHILD	RR	ZZZZ	USA
STAROST, ZIWIC	19	M	SGL	RR	ZZZZ	USA
GIEBER, ALTE	9	M	CHILD	RR	ZZZZ	USA
BLOCH, FEIWEL	20	M	DLR	RR	ZZZZ	USA
GARANCHI, MORDCHE	19	M	LABR	RR	ZZZZ	USA
LOKSCH, JOS.	20	M	LABR	RR	ZZZZ	USA
SONNESCHEIN, JOS.	29	M	LABR	RR	ZZZZ	USA
SCHLITZER, JOEL	36	M	DLR	RR	ZZZZ	USA
ESTHER	15	F	D	RR	ZZZZ	USA
SCHAPIRA, WOLF	46	M	DLR	RR	ZZZZ	USA
NITTEN	9	M	CHILD	RR	ZZZZ	USA
GIBIANSKI, RACHEL	9	F	CHILD	RR	ZZZZ	USA
SIEROTA, DINA	20	F	SGL	RR	ZZZZ	USA
SCHWARZ, ELIA	19	M	TLR	RR	ZZZZ	USA

SHIP: ST. OF PENNSYLVANIA

FROM: GLASGOW AND LARNE
TO: NEW YORK
ARRIVED: 05 JANUARY 1883

PASSENGER	AGE	SEX	OCCUPATION	PRV	VIL	DES
LEO, ADOLF	32	M	PNTR	RR	ZZZZ	USA
ANNA	24	F	W	RR	ZZZZ	USA

SHIP: DONAU

FROM: BREMEN
TO: NEW YORK
ARRIVED: 08 JANUARY 1883

PASSENGER	AGE	SEX	OCCUPATION	PRV	VIL	DES
KARPUS, KAZ.	24	M	LABR	RR	ZZZZ	USA

SHIP: CITY OF RICHMOND

FROM: LIVERPOOL AND QUEENSTOWN
TO: NEW YORK
ARRIVED: 09 JANUARY 1883

PASSENGER	AGE	SEX	OCCUPATION	PRV	VIL	DES
MURAWSKA, KATARINA	39	F	W	PL	ZZZZ	USA
JOE.	11	M	CH	PL	ZZZZ	USA
JOHN	4	M	CHILD	PL	ZZZZ	USA
MARCUNINCK, WOG.	50	F	UNKNOWN	PL	ZZZZ	USA
CECELIE	14	F	UNKNOWN	PL	ZZZZ	USA
JOHN	3	M	CHILD	PL	ZZZZ	USA
MARIANNE	1	M	CHILD	PL	ZZZZ	USA

SHIP: CIRCASSIA

FROM: GLASGOW
TO: NEW YORK
ARRIVED: 11 JANUARY 1883

PASSENGER	AGE	SEX	OCCUPATION	PRV	VIL	DES
STAGNAS, ANDERS	29	M	FARMER	RR	ZZZZ	USA
BACKLUM, ABRAHAM	37	M	UNKNOWN	RR	ZZZZ	USA
NYBACK, MORTON	27	M	UNKNOWN	RR	ZZZZ	USA
STAGNES, K.M.	36	M	UNKNOWN	RR	ZZZZ	USA
FAND, E.J.	37	M	UNKNOWN	RR	ZZZZ	USA

SHIP: AUSTRALIA

FROM: HAMBURG
TO: NEW YORK
ARRIVED: 15 JANUARY 1883

PASSENGER	AGE	SEX	OCCUPATION	PRV	VIL	DES
OYENBACH, N.	20	M	TRDSMN	RR	ZZZZ	USA
LANG, SIMON	24	M	LABR	RR	ZZZZ	USA
JULIE	27	F	W	RR	ZZZZ	USA
GINSELA	5	F	CHILD	RR	ZZZZ	USA
ERNESTINE	2	F	CHILD	RR	ZZZZ	USA
ASCHER, LEWIS	50	M	PH	RR	ZZZZ	USA
PODHASKI, PETER	22	M	CL	RR	ZZZZ	USA
GRENWITZ, FRIEDR.	24	M	LABR	RR	ZZZZ	USA
HELENE	29	F	W	RR	ZZZZ	USA
HEINUCL	6	M	CHILD	RR	ZZZZ	USA
ANNA	.10	F	INFANT	RR	ZZZZ	USA
MIKOLSCH, PASIA	10	F	SGL	RR	ZZZZ	USA
MILHA	7	F	CHILD	RR	ZZZZ	USA

PASSENGER	AGE	SEX	OCCUPATION	PV VIL DES

SHIP: RHYNLAND

FROM: ANTWERP
TO: NEW YORK
ARRIVED: 15 JANUARY 1883

PASSENGER	AGE	SEX	OCCUPATION	PV VIL DES
LUDERITZ, DORA	22	F	BKR	RRZZZZUSA
OTTE, CHRISTINA	27	F	UNKNOWN	RRZZZZUSA

SHIP: SPAIN

FROM: LIVERPOOL AND QUEENSTOWN
TO: NEW YORK
ARRIVED: 15 JANUARY 1883

PASSENGER	AGE	SEX	OCCUPATION	PV VIL DES
WIESYANSKI, JACOB	21	M	UNKNOWN	RRZZZZUSA
ROSENSTEIN, NELLY	32	F	W	RRZZZZUSA
LOUIS	6	M	CHILD	RRZZZZUSA
GOLDBERG, ABRAHAM	24	M	UNKNOWN	RRZZZZUSA
SARAH	18	F	W	RRZZZZUSA
ISAAC	.04	M	INFANT	RRZZZZUSA
LOWENBERG, HYMAN	56	M	LABR	RRZZZZUSA
HANNAH	50	F	W	RRZZZZUSA
TORNA	15	F	SP	RRZZZZUSA
GOLDSTEIN, ARON	22	M	LABR	RRZZZZUSA

SHIP: WIELAND

FROM: HAMBURG
TO: NEW YORK
ARRIVED: 15 JANUARY 1883

PASSENGER	AGE	SEX	OCCUPATION	PV VIL DES
SEMPLINER, CHEIN	9	M	CHILD	RRZZZZUSA
AIDERSKI, JOSEF	20	M	DLR	RRZZZZUSA
LINDGUIST, JULIUS	24	M	MCHT	FNZZZZUSA
KATZ, SCHMUL	22	M	TLR	RRZZZZUSA
ACHEGAL, MOSES	19	M	MCHT	RRZZZZUSA
BOCHER, BENZE	17	M	TLR	RRZZZZUSA
LEBOWITZ, MOSES	18	M	MCHT	RRZZZZUSA
LANGE, CESAR	21	M	MCHT	RRZZZZUSA
WOSKUBOMIK, SIMON	15	M	MCHT	RRZZZZUSA
BADANE	42	F	SGL	RRZZZZUSA
CEYANDER, CARL	24	M	STDNT	FNZZZZUSA
ZOSTKOW, RIWKE	21	F	W	RRZZZZUSA
AILPE	9	F	CHILD	RRZZZZUSA
MOSES	.11	M	INFANT	RRZZZZUSA
NEHERUJE	22	M	LABR	RRZZZZUSA
TUWIM, MOSES	17	M	DLR	RRZZZZUSA
KAHN, GALI	28	F	W	RRZZZZUSA
PROLEZKA, JOSEF	29	M	LABR	RRZZZZUSA

SHIP: RUGIA

FROM: HAMBURG AND HAVRE
TO: NEW YORK
ARRIVED: 18 JANUARY 1883

PASSENGER	AGE	SEX	OCCUPATION	PV VIL DES
MICHALOWITZ, BARUCH	52	M	MCHT	RRZZZZUSA
SARAH	22	F	SGL	RRZZZZUSA
EHRLICH, WILH.	14	M	LABR	RRZZZZUSA
PLOFS, KARL	34	M	LABR	RRZZZZUSA
MARTHA	2	F	CHILD	RRZZZZUSA
ARONOWSKI, DOBRE	38	F	W	RRZZZZUSA
MEILACH	14	F	CH	RRZZZZUSA
SAMUEL	9	M	CHILD	RRZZZZUSA

SHIP: STATE OF ALABAMA

FROM: GLASGOW
TO: NEW YORK
ARRIVED: 18 JANUARY 1883

PASSENGER	AGE	SEX	OCCUPATION	PV VIL DES
FRIEDELSEED, M.	18	M	LABR	RRZZZZUSA
LANECK, W.	27	M	UNKNOWN	RRZZZZUSA
LEISS, M.	18	M	UNKNOWN	RRZZZZUSA
ROSENBERG, M.	29	M	UNKNOWN	RRZZZZUSA
ZGAW, GEZEL	25	M	UNKNOWN	RRZZZZUSA
PRESS, HERMANN	42	M	UNKNOWN	RRZZZZUSA

SHIP: STATE OF FLORIDA

FROM: GLASGOW AND LARNE
TO: NEW YORK
ARRIVED: 19 JANUARY 1883

PASSENGER	AGE	SEX	OCCUPATION	PV VIL DES
MOROKAS, N.	25	M	LABR	RRZZZZUSA
ORMSCHKA, J.	28	M	LABR	RRZZZZUSA
G.	25	M	LABR	RRZZZZUSA
SAGULUZ, G.	25	M	LABR	RRZZZZUSA
BAJZA, S.	00	M	LABR	RRZZZZUSA
KIRUAK, A.	26	M	LABR	RRZZZZUSA
DAISKA, A.	27	M	LABR	RRZZZZUSA

SHIP: LAKE MANITOBA

FROM: LIVERPOOL
TO: NEW YORK
ARRIVED: 22 JANUARY 1883

PASSENGER	AGE	SEX	OCCUPATION	PV VIL DES
PERLSTEIN, SIMSON	36	M	PDLR	RRZZZZNY

SHIP: WISCONSIN

FROM: LIVERPOOL AND QUEENSTOWN
TO: NEW YORK
ARRIVED: 22 JANUARY 1883

PASSENGER	AGE	SEX	OCCUPATION	PV VIL DES
LUKASG, ANDREAS	20	M	LABR	FNZZZZUSA

PASSENGER	AGE	SEX	OCCUPATION	PRV	VIL	DES
SHIP: FRISIA						
FROM: HAMBURG						
TO: NEW YORK						
ARRIVED: 27 JANUARY 1883						
PATEMKIEVING, ANTON	14	M	LABR	RR	ZZZZ	USA
PALIWODA, SCHEBSEL	24	M	MCHT	RR	ZZZZ	USA
NAUMANN, ISAAS	18	M	CL	RR	ZZZZ	USA
FEBBERG, MOSES	20	M	DLR	RR	ZZZZ	USA
GELBERTH, CHASHEL	30	M	DLR	RR	ZZZZ	USA
GLAGOEV, SHLONE	24	M	TLR	RR	ZZZZ	USA
ELKONIN, ELLE	30	M	PNTR	RR	ZZZZ	USA
KOZLOVSKY, ANDR.	24	M	LABR	RR	ZZZZ	USA
HIRSCHKO, MERE	22	F	W	RR	ZZZZ	USA
ILON	.09	M	INFANT	RR	ZZZZ	USA
SCHAIVITZKY, ISAAC	23	M	MCHT	RR	ZZZZ	USA
RAPHAEL, ISAAC	50	M	MCHT	RR	ZZZZ	USA
SCHNEIDER, SALOMON	46	M	DLR	RR	ZZZZ	USA
MOSES	16	M	TLR	RR	ZZZZ	USA
LEWIN, GUSTE	18	F	SGL	RR	ZZZZ	USA
RESZENSKY, ROSA	15	F	SGL	RR	ZZZZ	USA
BLUM, MORITZ	29	M	LABR	RR	ZZZZ	USA
PRENSKY, NOSHEMJE	39	M	LABR	RR	ZZZZ	USA
SHIP: BELGENLAND						
FROM: ANTWERP						
TO: NEW YORK						
ARRIVED: 29 JANUARY 1883						
AVSEPH, VIDAVER	27	M	UNKNOWN	RR	ZZZZ	NY
SHIP: HOLLAND						
FROM: LONDON						
TO: NEW YORK						
ARRIVED: 30 JANUARY 1883						
MEINER, ELKA	28	F	W	RR	ZZZZ	USA
LEAH	8	F	CHILD	RR	ZZZZ	USA
REGINE	7	F	CHILD	RR	ZZZZ	USA
JACOB	5	M	CHILD	RR	ZZZZ	USA
TIEWEL	3	M	CHILD	RR	ZZZZ	USA
EPHRAIM	00	M	INF	RR	ZZZZ	USA
COHEN, LOZUS	23	M	LABR	PL	ZZZZ	USA
SHIP: WESTPHALIA						
FROM: HAMBURG AND HAVRE						
TO: NEW YORK						
ARRIVED: 08 FEBRUARY 1883						
DANILEWITZ, MARCIN	22	M	LABR	RR	ZZZZ	NY
PREGER, ESTHER	42	F	W	RR	ZZZZ	PHI
SLATE	14	F	CH	RR	ZZZZ	PHI
PEREL	9	M	CHILD	RR	ZZZZ	PHI
SIMON, GEWIN	15	M	DLR	RR	ZZZZ	PHI
EHATZKEI, SHMUL	30	M	DLR	RR	ZZZZ	NY
KOMELEWSKY, ADAM	26	M	DLR	RR	ZZZZ	NY
SUCKEWITZ, THOMAS	25	M	DLR	RR	ZZZZ	NY
SIGINSKY, ANDREAS	24	M	DLR	RR	ZZZZ	NY
TREGIS, ANTON	26	M	DLR	RR	ZZZZ	NY
NOVEMBER, FISCHEL	22	M	BKBNDR	RR	ZZZZ	NY
IGLOWSKY, CHAIM	27	M	DLR	RR	ZZZZ	IA
SHIP: GRECIAN MONARCH						
FROM: LONDON						
TO: NEW YORK						
ARRIVED: 12 FEBRUARY 1883						
KATZ, MOSES	26	M	LABR	PL	ZZZZ	NY
LENA	21	F	W	PL	ZZZZ	NY
WEIN, JOSEPH	28	M	LABR	PL	ZZZZ	NY
MALKE	27	F	W	PL	ZZZZ	NY
MIRESEN, SHERE	44	M	LABR	PL	ZZZZ	NY
MORRIS	16	M	LABR	PL	ZZZZ	NY
DAVIS, ISAAK	38	M	LABR	PL	ZZZZ	NY
FELSBER, FRIEDMAN	22	M	LABR	PL	ZZZZ	NY
MILNER, CHAYA	00	F	UNKNOWN	PL	ZZZZ	NY
RUBEN	6	M	CHILD	PL	ZZZZ	NY
ABRAHAM	2	M	CHILD	PL	ZZZZ	NY
MOSES	.02	M	INFANT	PL	ZZZZ	NY
HYMAU, ASCHOR	19	M	LABR	PL	ZZZZ	NY
SCHAPE, ABRAHAM	21	M	LABR	PL	ZZZZ	NY
SCHONFEL, MAX	22	M	LABR	PL	ZZZZ	NY
WENE, ISAAK	17	M	LABR	PL	ZZZZ	NY
LICHTENSTEIN, ABR.	26	M	LABR	PL	ZZZZ	NY
SILLERSTEIN, JACOB	20	M	LABR	PL	ZZZZ	NY
SHIP: LABRADOR						
FROM: HAVRE						
TO: NEW YORK						
ARRIVED: 12 FEBRUARY 1883						
LAMANOFF, MICHAEL	26	M	OFF	RR	ZZZZ	PHI
GOLDBERG, ISRAEL	21	M	TLR	RR	ZZZZ	NY
KAMA	18	F	UNKNOWN	RR	ZZZZ	NY
SHIP: LAKE HURON						
FROM: LIVERPOOL						
TO: NEW YORK						
ARRIVED: 12 FEBRUARY 1883						
BLOOM, LEVI	28	M	UNKNOWN	PL	ZZZZ	USA

PASSENGER	AGE	SEX	OCCUPATION	PRIV	DES

SHIP: WAESLAND

FROM: ANTWERP
TO: NEW YORK
ARRIVED: 12 FEBRUARY 1883

PASSENGER	AGE	SEX	OCCUPATION	PRIV	DES
KOSWOSKI, JOH.	29	M	UNKNOWN	RRZZZZ	NY
MISLONSKI, FRG.	38	M	UNKNOWN	RRZZZZ	NY
CHALI, A.	27	M	BBR	RRZZZZ	NY

SHIP: STATE OF INDIANA

FROM: GLASGOW AND LARNE
TO: NEW YORK
ARRIVED: 13 FEBRUARY 1883

PASSENGER	AGE	SEX	OCCUPATION	PRIV	DES
CHAIMSOHN, JOSEL	23	M	LABR	RRZZZZ	USA
KLIEN, IGNATZ	33	M	LABR	RRZZZZ	USA
SOBUCH, HINDE	34	F	W	RRZZZZ	USA
SO--KU--D	12	M	NN	RRZZZZ	USA
CHATZKE	10	F	NN	RRZZZZ	USA
ESTHER	8	F	CHILD	RRZZZZ	USA
SCHLAPOBERSKY, REBEKKA	17	M	LABR	RRZZZZ	USA
BALZICK, HERMAN	22	M	SLR	RRZZZZ	USA
FANNY	22	F	W	RRZZZZ	USA
LEVEZ, ABRAHAM	21	M	LABR	RRZZZZ	USA
SCHULAM, SALMON	10	M	NN	RRZZZZ	USA
HELTER, RINKE	37	F	W	RRZZZZ	USA
GITTEL	9	F	CHILD	RRZZZZ	USA

SHIP: POLARIA

FROM: HAMBURG
TO: NEW YORK
ARRIVED: 15 FEBRUARY 1883

PASSENGER	AGE	SEX	OCCUPATION	PRIV	DES
BRAUN, JOHS.	40	F	WO	RRZZZZ	USA
JOHAN.	15	F	UNKNOWN	RRZZZZ	USA

SHIP: SILESIA

FROM: HAMBURG AND HAVRE
TO: NEW YORK
ARRIVED: 19 FEBRUARY 1883

PASSENGER	AGE	SEX	OCCUPATION	PRIV	DES
LUBEWIK, FRANT	25	M	UNKNOWN	RRZZZZ	USA
RODINSKY, VICENTY	26	M	UNKNOWN	RRZZZZ	USA
DREBIN, ROSA	35	F	W	RRZZZZ	USA
LIESE	9	F	CHILD	RRZZZZ	USA
IDA	8	F	CHILD	RRZZZZ	USA
LEIB	7	M	CHILD	RRZZZZ	USA
HANNE	3	F	CHILD	RRZZZZ	USA
GRUENWALD, ADOLF	23	M	LABR	RRZZZZ	USA
LEVY, HIRSCH	20	M	FARMER	RRZZZZ	USA
LASKIN, ISRAEL	30	M	LABR	RRZZZZ	USA
REVINEKY, STANISL.	19	M	LABR	RRZZZZ	USA
WOLINEE, JAN	22	M	UNKNOWN	RRZZZZ	USA
IVAJAN, JAN	22	M	UNKNOWN	RRZZZZ	USA
JESKAU, ADOLF	34	M	UNKNOWN	RRZZZZ	USA
RAVINEKY, LEOPOLD	18	M	UNKNOWN	RRZZZZ	USA
KOLICKEVIC, ANTON	26	M	UNKNOWN	RRZZZZ	USA
SCHMIDTKE, JARSIS	25	M	UNKNOWN	RRZZZZ	USA
RUDANSKY, MOSES	34	M	LABR	RRZZZZ	USA
BRUNSCH, ANNA	30	F	W	RRZZZZ	USA
EMILIE	9	F	CHILD	RRZZZZ	USA
KOCH, NATALIE	20	F	W	RRZZZZ	USA
ROBERT	.11	M	INFANT	RRZZZZ	USA
CARL	.01	M	INFANT	RRZZZZ	USA
COHN, FEIGE	35	F	W	RRZZZZ	USA
MEIER	9	M	CHILD	RRZZZZ	USA
ELIAS	6	M	CHILD	RRZZZZ	USA
CHASHKES, ETTEL	20	F	SGL	RRZZZZ	USA
LUETKE, HEINR.	38	M	UNKNOWN	RRZZZZ	USA
LEWIN, HERMANN	22	M	CGRMKR	RRZZZZ	USA
REBECCA	17	F	W	RRZZZZ	USA
DAVID, SCHMUEL	19	M	WCHMKR	RRZZZZ	USA
GRUENBLATT, ABRAHAM	18	M	DLR	RRZZZZ	USA
BIGALSKI, WILHELM	17	M	TLR	RRZZZZ	USA

SHIP: ABYSSINIA

FROM: LIVERPOOL
TO: NEW YORK
ARRIVED: 20 FEBRUARY 1883

PASSENGER	AGE	SEX	OCCUPATION	PRIV	DES
ODBACKER, DAVID	26	M	UNKNOWN	FNZZZZ	USA
BJORKAREN, MATTS	28	M	UNKNOWN	FNZZZZ	USA
KANGAS, PIETARI-M.	23	M	LABR	FNZZZZ	USA
MYLLOGOGNAS, JOSA	36	M	UNKNOWN	FNZZZZ	USA
SONGVIST, JOHAN	27	M	UNKNOWN	FNZZZZ	USA
SALLA, MARTULUS	25	M	UNKNOWN	FNZZZZ	USA
HAAZAJARVI, ELIAS	22	M	UNKNOWN	FNZZZZ	USA
RUORA, HENRIK	20	M	UNKNOWN	FNZZZZ	USA
HINKKALOA, ELIAS	30	M	UNKNOWN	FNZZZZ	USA
ANNALA, JAAKOP	25	M	UNKNOWN	FNZZZZ	USA
JARVENPAA, KUSTAA	34	M	UNKNOWN	FNZZZZ	USA
MUSTAPAA, MATTI	25	M	UNKNOWN	FNZZZZ	USA
MARTILLA, ISSAK	25	M	UNKNOWN	FNZZZZ	USA
KUSTAA	35	M	UNKNOWN	FNZZZZ	USA
SURILA, ELIAS	31	M	UNKNOWN	FNZZZZ	USA

SHIP: DONAU

FROM: BREMEN AND SOUTHAMPTON
TO: NEW YORK
ARRIVED: 21 FEBRUARY 1883

PASSENGER	AGE	SEX	OCCUPATION	PRIV	DES
BOSMAKOWSKI, FRANZ	25	M	MCHT	RRZZZZ	USA

SHIP: ST. OF PENNSYLVANIA

FROM: GLASGOW AND LARNE
TO: NEW YORK
ARRIVED: 21 FEBRUARY 1883

PASSENGER	AGE	SEX	OCCUPATION	PRIV	DES
FEVASKOWITZ, FRESIS	26	M	FARMER	RRZZZZ	USA
ZNINDZINSKY, JOHANN	36	M	TLR	RRZZZZ	USA
AGNES	24	F	W	RRZZZZ	USA
WAN--KY, MENDEL	22	M	LABR	RRZZZZ	USA

PASSENGER	AGE	SEX	OCCUPATION	PRVL	VIL	DES
JAEWITZ, NISER	35	M	GCR	RR	ZZZZ	USA
SCHEMEDOWITZ, HESEL	22	M	GCR	RR	ZZZZ	USA
LOCZINSKY, ABRAM	33	M	TLR	RR	ZZZZ	USA
GANRONSKY, LEIB	24	M	PDLR	RR	ZZZZ	USA
BREMER, LOUIS	40	M	PDLR	RR	ZZZZ	USA
LEIB	7	M	CHILD	RR	ZZZZ	USA
STZIKOSOHN, HIRSCH	10	M	NN	RR	ZZZZ	USA

SHIP: NEDERLAND

FROM: ANTWERP
TO: NEW YORK
ARRIVED: 22 FEBRUARY 1883

PASSENGER	AGE	SEX	OCCUPATION	PRVL	VIL	DES
POKOISKI, ANSON	5	M	CHILD	PL	ZZZZ	PHI

SHIP: BOHEMIA

FROM: HAMBURG
TO: NEW YORK
ARRIVED: 23 FEBRUARY 1883

PASSENGER	AGE	SEX	OCCUPATION	PRVL	VIL	DES
DAVILEFSKI, CHAIE	48	F	W	RR	ZZZZ	USA
SCHIFRE	7	F	CHILD	RR	ZZZZ	USA
POGORSKI, MICHALINE	27	F	W	RR	ZZZZ	USA
IWAN	.08	M	INFANT	RR	ZZZZ	USA
DWORSKI, NECHAME	22	F	SGL	RR	ZZZZ	USA
MICKNOWSKY, LAIBA	24	F	SGL	RR	ZZZZ	USA
SCHARGAN, BAER	23	M	DLR	RR	ZZZZ	USA
ALAWSKY, BEILE	22	F	SGL	RR	ZZZZ	USA
MUELLER, JOHANNES	17	M	LABR	RR	ZZZZ	USA

SHIP: ENGLAND

FROM: LIVERPOOL AND QUEENSTOWN
TO: NEW YORK
ARRIVED: 23 FEBRUARY 1883

PASSENGER	AGE	SEX	OCCUPATION	PRVL	VIL	DES
FRANKEL, LOUIS	40	M	LABR	RR	ZZZZ	USA

SHIP: ALASKA

FROM: LIVERPOOL AND QUEENSTOWN
TO: NEW YORK
ARRIVED: 26 FEBRUARY 1883

PASSENGER	AGE	SEX	OCCUPATION	PRVL	VIL	DES
GRANBACKA, MATTS-J.	32	M	LABR	FN	ZZZZ	USA
TWEL, ANDERS-H.	38	M	LABR	FN	ZZZZ	USA
PUATS, MATTS-M.	23	M	LABR	FN	ZZZZ	USA
KAPELA, MATTS-J.	46	M	LABR	FN	ZZZZ	USA
STENBACKA, MAN-M.	28	M	LABR	FN	ZZZZ	USA
SIEMALA, ERITE-S.	26	M	LABR	FN	ZZZZ	USA
JOHANSON, NICLAS	19	M	LABR	FN	ZZZZ	USA
SOMARS, ABEL-M.	31	M	LABR	FN	ZZZZ	USA
PAA, ISATE-K.	26	M	LABR	FN	ZZZZ	USA
KANTALA, JOHAN	32	M	LABR	FN	ZZZZ	USA
ERIKSON, ERITE	29	M	LABR	FN	ZZZZ	USA
SAWES, JOHAN	33	M	LABR	FN	ZZZZ	USA
HUTAMARNE, JOHAN	27	M	LABR	FN	ZZZZ	USA
KANGES, JOHAN-J.	28	M	LABR	FN	ZZZZ	USA
RURTAMATEE, MATTS	33	M	LABR	FN	ZZZZ	USA
SAHOOLA, WILHELM	30	M	LABR	FN	ZZZZ	USA
MATEE, ERIK-E.	24	M	LABR	FN	ZZZZ	USA
MAKEE, JOHAN-M.	27	M	LABR	FN	ZZZZ	USA
JERVI, EDUARD	28	M	LABR	FN	ZZZZ	USA
JOHANSEN, GUSTAF	17	M	LABR	FN	ZZZZ	USA
JACOB	27	M	LABR	FN	ZZZZ	USA
SALS, ERIK	35	M	LABR	FN	ZZZZ	USA
KREAPAA, MATTS-M.	25	M	LABR	FN	ZZZZ	USA
GUSTAFSSON, JOHAN	26	M	LABR	FN	ZZZZ	USA

SHIP: CANADA

FROM: HAVRE
TO: NEW YORK
ARRIVED: 01 MARCH 1883

PASSENGER	AGE	SEX	OCCUPATION	PRVL	VIL	DES
CRUSEN, U-MR	55	M	UNKNOWN	RR	ZZZZ	USA

SHIP: FURNESSIA

FROM: GLASGOW
TO: NEW YORK
ARRIVED: 01 MARCH 1883

PASSENGER	AGE	SEX	OCCUPATION	PRVL	VIL	DES
BENSKI, SIMON	18	M	CGRMKR	RR	ZZZZ	USA
KRUSHEWICZ, IAN	51	M	FARMER	RR	ZZZZ	USA
PRUSKI, BART	38	M	FARMER	RR	ZZZZ	USA
MATTRUCK, AND.	34	M	FARMER	RR	ZZZZ	USA
DAHLCARL, GUSTAF	30	M	FARMER	RR	ZZZZ	USA
BRANSKI, GUDAL	37	M	LABR	RR	ZZZZ	USA

SHIP: VANDALIA

FROM: HAMBURG
TO: NEW YORK
ARRIVED: 02 MARCH 1883

PASSENGER	AGE	SEX	OCCUPATION	PRVL	VIL	DES
JOHN, BEHR	25	M	LABR	RR	ZZZZ	USA
ROMANOWSKI, IAN	24	M	LABR	RR	ZZZZ	USA
FRIEDLINDER, ISAAC	24	M	DLR	RR	ZZZZ	USA
HARRIS, LOUIS	16	M	LABR	RR	ZZZZ	USA
KAFKE, JULKE	18	M	LABR	RR	ZZZZ	USA
BREZINSKI, ABRAHAM	23	M	SHMK	RR	ZZZZ	USA
YAROCZEK, LEIB	24	M	CL	RR	ZZZZ	USA
KOSWEN, MOSES	31	M	DLR	RR	ZZZZ	USA
ANNA	30	F	DLR	RR	ZZZZ	USA
REPPIN, FRIED	21	M	MCHT	RR	ZZZZ	USA
FEDER, CHAJE	21	F	SGL	RR	ZZZZ	USA
HIMMELHOCHE, SAMUELE	28	F	W	RR	ZZZZ	USA
SALMON	.09	M	INFANT	RR	ZZZZ	USA
IUDELSANG, IOHANNE	22	F	W	RR	ZZZZ	USA
RAPHAELA	.08	F	INFANT	RR	ZZZZ	USA
SEGAL, MENDEL	55	M	DLR	RR	ZZZZ	USA
KROCHMALNIK, LEIB	23	M	MCHT	RR	ZZZZ	USA

PASSENGER	AGE	SEX	OCCUPATION	PRIVL	DES
RACHEL	22	F	W	RRZZZZ	USA
WALOCHEWSKY, IOSEF	16	M	LABR	RRZZZZ	USA
ZEBROWSKY, DANIEL	26	M	LABR	RRZZZZ	USA
HRISZKO, IOHANN	30	M	LABR	RRZZZZ	USA

SHIP: PENNLAND

FROM: ANTWERP
TO: NEW YORK
ARRIVED: 03 MARCH 1883

PASSENGER	AGE	SEX	OCCUPATION	PRIVL	DES
CAPLAN, JUDEL	33	M	CPTR	RRZZZZ	USA
RUTECKA, THEOPHILA	25	F	NN	RRZZZZ	USA
U	.11	F	INFANT	RRZZZZ	USA
WARNAGIRIS, U	33	M	CLGYMN	RRZZZZ	USA

SHIP: WIELAND

FROM: HAMBURG AND HAVRE
TO: NEW YORK
ARRIVED: 05 MARCH 1883

PASSENGER	AGE	SEX	OCCUPATION	PRIVL	DES
MICHELSEN, SAMUEL	40	M	MCHT	RRZZZZ	USA
ARON	12	M	S	RRZZZZ	USA
ATNICK, MENDEL	21	M	MCHT	RRZZZZ	USA
KATZ, ABEL	19	F	SGL	RRZZZZ	USA
SCHIMANSKY, DWORE	18	F	SGL	RRZZZZ	USA
SLATE	9	F	CHILD	RRZZZZ	USA
LEWITZ, ABRAH.	49	M	LABR	RRZZZZ	USA
NOSSEN	18	M	LABR	RRZZZZ	USA
BOGNIOWO, CHANNE	24	F	W	RRZZZZ	USA
BLUME	.11	F	INFANT	RRZZZZ	USA
FEIGE	.01	F	INFANT	RRZZZZ	USA
CZIWETZ, KAUFMANN	29	M	LABR	RRZZZZ	USA
JORIN, DAVID	26	M	LABR	RRZZZZ	USA
BERMAN, ISAAC	38	M	LABR	RRZZZZ	USA
REIHE, MORDCHE	19	M	LABR	RRZZZZ	USA
ROTHHOWSKY, WULF	23	M	LABR	RRZZZZ	USA
KOJEK, STANISLAUS	48	M	LABR	RRZZZZ	USA
HEINRICH, JAN	25	M	LABR	RRZZZZ	USA
LANSCHALL, HIRSCH	19	M	LABR	RRZZZZ	USA
SPIRO, MENDEL	53	M	MCHT	RRZZZZ	USA
KOLTANSKI, JACOB	21	M	MCHT	RRZZZZ	USA
AWIN, MARCUS	25	M	MCHT	RRZZZZ	USA
GROLLMANN, CHAIE	29	F	WO	RRZZZZ	USA
ALTER	5	M	CHILD	RRZZZZ	USA
JOSSEL	.11	M	INFANT	RRZZZZ	USA
JANKELOWITZ, ABRAHAM	19	M	LABR	RRZZZZ	USA
REBEKKA	19	F	W	RRZZZZ	USA
SAMSCHER	5	M	CHILD	RRZZZZ	USA
PESCHE	.11	M	INFANT	RRZZZZ	USA
LOWENTHAL, NECHE	40	F	WO	RRZZZZ	USA
SCHIE	8	M	CHILD	RRZZZZ	USA
RIEWE	6	F	CHILD	RRZZZZ	USA
GREIEFSKI, FRANZ	31	M	LABR	RRZZZZ	USA
BLASKEWSCH, JOH.	28	M	LABR	RRZZZZ	USA
KALINOWSKI, MICHAEL	29	M	LABR	RRZZZZ	USA
DUSCHINSKI, JOSEF	30	M	LABR	RRZZZZ	USA
KOSEWSKI, LUDWIG	25	M	LABR	RRZZZZ	USA
DRANOWSKI, LUDWIG-FRANZ	18	M	LABR	RRZZZZ	USA
SWANKOWSKY, JOHANN	23	M	LABR	RRZZZZ	USA
MALZAKEN, JOHANN	20	M	LABR	RRZZZZ	USA
GISCHITSKI, JULIAN	39	M	LABR	RRZZZZ	USA
SWADOWSKI, FRANZ	23	M	LABR	RRZZZZ	USA

SHIP: POLYNESIA

FROM: HAMBURG
TO: NEW YORK
ARRIVED: 06 MARCH 1883

PASSENGER	AGE	SEX	OCCUPATION	PRIVL	DES
BARER, ISAAC	22	M	TRDSMN	RRZZZZ	USA
BANDEL	18	F	SVNT	RRZZZZ	USA
JONESSHOWITZ, NACH.	42	M	TRDSMN	RRZZZZ	USA
KELTSOHN, GEORGE	58	M	TCHR	RRZZZZ	USA
ROSENBAUM, SCHEYER	20	M	MCHT	RRZZZZ	USA
ESTI, LESSER	28	M	LABR	RRZZZZ	USA

SHIP: GREECE

FROM: LONDON
TO: NEW YORK
ARRIVED: 09 MARCH 1883

PASSENGER	AGE	SEX	OCCUPATION	PRIVL	DES
SOLBE, SOLOMON	19	M	UNKNOWN	RRZZZZ	USA
ROSENTHAL, JACOB	25	M	UNKNOWN	RRZZZZ	USA

SHIP: CALIFORNIA

FROM: HAMBURG
TO: NEW YORK
ARRIVED: 10 MARCH 1883

PASSENGER	AGE	SEX	OCCUPATION	PRIVL	DES
MILBOR, SENDER	17	M	TLR	PLZZZZ	USA
HELLER, CHAIE	25	F	WO	PLZZZZ	USA
MORITZ	.09	M	INFANT	PLZZZZ	USA
BREMER, JS.	24	M	TRDSMN	PLZZZZ	USA
LEISER	22	M	UNKNQWN	PLZZZZ	USA
FRANZBLUM, S.	28	M	UNKNOWN	PLZZZZ	USA
MARCUS, F.	23	M	UNKNOWN	PLZZZZ	USA
MARTINSEN, CATHA.	33	F	WO	PLZZZZ	USA
ANA	.09	F	INFANT	PLZZZZ	USA
JUNGBLUT, LINA	33	F	WO	PLZZZZ	USA
GISCHE	.10	F	INFANT	PLZZZZ	USA
BENJAMIN, ROB.	26	F	WO	PLZZZZ	USA
SABINE	5	F	CHILD	PLZZZZ	USA
BENJAMINE	.03	F	INFANT	PLZZZZ	USA
OLOZEWSKI, JOS.	26	M	SMH	PLZZZZ	USA
BOHLING, FR.	23	M	LABR	PLZZZZ	USA
SIEG, FRIEDR.	29	M	UNKNOWN	PLZZZZ	USA
JULIUS	28	M	UNKNOWN	PLZZZZ	USA
PASSELT, GEORG	32	M	UNKNOWN	PLZZZZ	USA
BABLEE, DARIS	26	F	SGL	PLZZZZ	USA
HELCK, WILHELM.	22	M	LABR	PLZZZZ	USA
PETERS, H.	22	M	UNKNOWN	PLZZZZ	USA
DIRGES, LOUIS	22	M	UNKNOWN	PLZZZZ	USA

SHIP: SUEVIA

FROM: HAMBURG
TO: NEW YORK
ARRIVED: 10 MARCH 1883

PASSENGER	AGE	SEX	OCCUPATION	PRV VIL DES
BEILIM, CHAIE	20	F	SGL	RRZZZZUSA
CHAIM	18	M	LABR	RRZZZZUSA
SCHEIP--, LEIB	20	M	LABR	RRZZZZUSA
MAZUTZ--, RIWKE	9	F	CHILD	RRZZZZUSA
ZERINSKY, CHANNE	23	F	W	RRZZZZUSA
HERRM.	.11	M	INFANT	RRZZZZUSA
LEVIN	.01	M	INFANT	RRZZZZUSA
DIDELEITES, VICENTI	18	M	LABR	RRZZZZUSA
MARKOVIE, VICENTI	23	M	LABR	RRZZZZUSA
WABELEITES, JOS.	18	M	LABR	RRZZZZUSA
SMIKENSKY, JOS.	24	M	LABR	RRZZZZUSA
TEOFILA	26	F	W	RRZZZZUSA
DULINSKA, ELSBETA	30	F	SGL	RRZZZZUSA
SZEZESNY, MICHAEL	22	M	LABR	RRZZZZUSA
JODNOWSKI, THOMS.	28	M	LABR	RRZZZZUSA
LIPINSKY, ANTON	36	M	LABR	RRZZZZUSA
ROGINSKY, PAVEL	23	M	LABR	RRZZZZUSA
HRIBOWSKY, KAZIMIR	23	M	LABR	RRZZZZUSA
LIDRICH, CARL	23	M	LABR	RRZZZZUSA
KARL	45	M	LABR	RRZZZZUSA
LEOPOLDINE	46	F	W	RRZZZZUSA
AMALIE	22	F	CH	RRZZZZUSA
GUSTAV	4	M	CHILD	RRZZZZUSA
KARL	.11	M	INFANT	RRZZZZUSA
MAZUSKY, ESTHER	35	F	SGL	RRZZZZUSA
CZERTOH, DAVID	20	M	TLR	RRZZZZUSA
PINKOWSKY, SIMON	20	M	LABR	RRZZZZUSA
WOLF	16	M	LABR	RRZZZZUSA
KALISKY, JOHE.	21	F	W	RRZZZZUSA
TAUBE	.11	F	INFANT	RRZZZZUSA
SCHWEITZER, BERNHD.	21	M	BKBNDR	RRZZZZUSA
REGINE	21	F	W	RRZZZZUSA
SCHOENFELD, LEA	21	F	SGL	RRZZZZUSA
SCHEPILEWSKI, LEON	40	M	LABR	RRZZZZUSA
VINCENT	14	M	CH	RRZZZZUSA
ANTON	9	M	CHILD	RRZZZZUSA
DOMINO	8	M	CHILD	RRZZZZUSA
JOSEF	3	M	CHILD	RRZZZZUSA
SAMUELSON, MENDEL	30	M	LABR	RRZZZZUSA
WYATER, JACOB	23	M	LABR	RRZZZZUSA
KLEBANSKY, SELDE	19	F	W	RRZZZZUSA
PEREL	9	M	CHILD	RRZZZZUSA
PESACH	.06	M	INFANT	RRZZZZUSA
KAPANSKY, JUDEL	18	M	LABR	RRZZZZUSA
WEIBELOWSKY, MARIE	46	F	W	RRZZZZUSA
FEIGE	15	F	CH	RRZZZZUSA
SARAH	9	F	CHILD	RRZZZZUSA
ASTROM, SAMUEL	34	M	LABR	RRZZZZUSA
FRANK, HEINRICH	18	M	LABR	RRZZZZUSA
DAVID, NATHAN	36	M	LABR	RRZZZZUSA
ROSENKOWITZ, BEHR.	34	M	LABR	RRZZZZUSA
PINKUS, CHAIM	18	M	LABR	RRZZZZUSA
BLUM, ABRAHAM	18	M	MCHT	RRZZZZUSA
WOICHEIOWSKY, PETER	22	M	LABR	RRZZZZUSA
FELIX	28	M	LABR	RRZZZZUSA
DRAGASHIS, ANTONA	30	M	LABR	RRZZZZUSA
MASCHEIHAS, SEBASTIAN	17	M	LABR	RRZZZZUSA
WOICZEK	16	M	LABR	RRZZZZUSA

SHIP: GERMANIC

FROM: LIVERPOOL
TO: NEW YORK
ARRIVED: 12 MARCH 1883

PASSENGER	AGE	SEX	OCCUPATION	PRV VIL DES
DE-KOBATH, N.	40	M	GENT	RRZZZZFR

SHIP: HAMMONIA

FROM: HAMBURG AND HAVRE
TO: NEW YORK
ARRIVED: 12 MARCH 1883

PASSENGER	AGE	SEX	OCCUPATION	PRV VIL DES
WALIZEREVICZ, JOH.	26	M	FARMER	RRZZZZUSA
KERPO--, ---H	24	M	UNKNOWN	RRZZZZUSA
ZYLINSKI, JOSEPH	20	M	LABR	RRZZZZUSA
SZYTOWSKA, JOSEPH	20	M	LABR	RRZZZZUSA
PEPELONUS, FRANZ	55	M	LABR	RRZZZZUSA
GENESCWITZ, JOH.	20	M	W	RRZZZZUSA
SZEIWINSKI, GEORG	19	M	LABR	RRZZZZUSA
DUDUSKIWICZ, VINCENZ	23	M	UNKNOWN	RRZZZZUSA
WCIZIKOWSKY, WAORINEE	20	M	UNKNOWN	RRZZZZUSA
ZSCHARIASCH, MAIE	25	F	W	RRZZZZUSA
SARA	6	F	CHILD	RRZZZZUSA
TAUBE	.11	F	INFANT	RRZZZZUSA
NETSCHE	.01	F	INFANT	RRZZZZUSA

SHIP: AUSTRALIA

FROM: HAMBURG
TO: NEW YORK
ARRIVED: 13 MARCH 1883

PASSENGER	AGE	SEX	OCCUPATION	PRV VIL DES
KOWALSKI, IGNATZ	33	M	LABR	RRZZZZUSA
SCHWAN, ADAM	22	M	LABR	PLZZZZUSA
TEMKOWSKI, A.	22	M	LABR	PLZZZZUSA
SESCHNEWSKI, FELIX	21	M	LABR	PLZZZZUSA
BRANITZKI, W.	22	M	LABR	PLZZZZUSA
SCHULKEWSKI, ANTEH	22	M	LABR	PLZZZZUSA
JUSKEWICZ, IOH.	20	M	LABR	PLZZZZUSA
VRINKE, CH.	26	F	WO	RRZZZZUSA
MARIANNE	.10	F	INFANT	RRZZZZUSA
GAWERSKI, EMIL	24	M	LKSH	PLZZZZUSA
AVROWSKI, GAB.	22	M	UNKNOWN	PLZZZZNO

SHIP: BOLIVIA

FROM: GLASGOW
TO: NEW YORK
ARRIVED: 15 MARCH 1883

PASSENGER	AGE	SEX	OCCUPATION	PRV VIL DES
EPHRAMOVSKY, LEVY	25	M	FARMER	RRZZZZUSA
SCHAFLE, JOHN	34	M	MCHT	RRZZZZUSA
KRUGER, ADOLF	28	M	FARMER	RRZZZZUSA
KOOZOROVSKI, H.	33	M	FARMER	PLZZZZUSA
MARIE	24	F	NN	PLZZZZUSA
LUDWIG	4	F	CHILD	PLZZZZUSA
MANARINA	3	F	CHILD	PLZZZZUSA

PASSENGER	AGE	SEX	OCCUPATION	PRV	VIL	DES
WALEGAT, MICHAL	34	M	SHMK	PL	ZZZZ	USA
CARL	27	F	NN	PL	ZZZZ	USA
MARIE	8	F	CHILD	PL	ZZZZ	USA
STANISLAUS	4	M	CHILD	PL	ZZZZ	USA
JOHANNA	3	F	CHILD	PL	ZZZZ	USA
KUST, MANA--	54	F	FARMER	PL	ZZZZ	USA
FRANZ	10	M	NN	PL	ZZZZ	USA

SHIP: CATALONIA

FROM: LIVERPOOL AND QUEENSTOWN
TO: NEW YORK
ARRIVED: 15 MARCH 1883

PASSENGER	AGE	SEX	OCCUPATION	PRV	VIL	DES
MYSEL, MARKS	27	M	WCHMKR	PL	ZZZZ	PHI
FANNY-B.	24	F	W	PL	ZZZZ	PHI

SHIP: ELBE

FROM: BREMEN AND SOUTHAMPTON
TO: NEW YORK
ARRIVED: 17 MARCH 1883

PASSENGER	AGE	SEX	OCCUPATION	PRV	VIL	DES
MANOWSKI, MICHEL	24	M	FARMER	RR	ZZZZ	USA
ROSCHACK, ALBERT	28	M	FARMER	RR	ZZZZ	USA
PLASCHENSKY, JOSEF	32	M	FARMER	RR	ZZZZ	USA
KUSCHERA, ANDR.	25	M	FARMER	RR	ZZZZ	USA
BUDIG, WILH.	32	M	FARMER	RR	ZZZZ	USA
REIMSCHREIBER, ALB.	24	M	LABR	RR	ZZZZ	USA

SHIP: GELLERT

FROM: HAMBURG
TO: NEW YORK
ARRIVED: 21 MARCH 1883

PASSENGER	AGE	SEX	OCCUPATION	PRV	VIL	DES
BOGERTHAL, LEIB	16	M	UNKNOWN	RR	ZZZZ	USA
RAKI, HIRSCH	32	M	DLR	RR	ZZZZ	USA
POTCHFERDOWSKY, FRANZ	24	M	LABR	RR	ZZZZ	USA
SOWCUZ, MERI	28	F	SGL	RR	ZZZZ	USA
HARMIKOWSKI, PAULINE	24	F	UNKNOWN	RR	ZZZZ	USA
ROSENBAUM, MEIER	23	M	DLR	RR	ZZZZ	USA
BERKOWSKY, PERL	22	F	SGL	RR	ZZZZ	USA
KLOZOWSKI, LEON	27	M	LABR	RR	ZZZZ	USA
FETIKOWSKI, NICOLAI	27	M	UNKNOWN	RR	ZZZZ	USA
GELBERG, LEISER	40	M	UNKNOWN	RR	ZZZZ	USA
SAMSEBER, ABRAH.	36	M	UNKNOWN	RR	ZZZZ	USA
BOCK, ELLE	19	F	SGL	RR	ZZZZ	USA
KUBINSKY, ANTON	21	M	LABR	RR	ZZZZ	USA
KARPAN, SIMON	19	M	FUR	RR	ZZZZ	USA

SHIP: WAESLAND

FROM: ANTWERP
TO: NEW YORK
ARRIVED: 23 MARCH 1883

PASSENGER	AGE	SEX	OCCUPATION	PRV	VIL	DES
ROBRECKY, SUSANNA	60	F	UNKNOWN	PL	ZZZZ	USA
ZNAINA, VALENTY	23	M	UNKNOWN	PL	ZZZZ	USA
SAWALZKI, MICH.	31	M	LABR	RR	ZZZZ	USA
RETZA, MARTKA	6	F	CHILD	RR	ZZZZ	USA
BACKOS, JOH.	47	M	UNKNOWN	RR	ZZZZ	USA

SHIP: INDIPENDENTE

FROM: PALERMO
TO: NEW YORK
ARRIVED: 24 MARCH 1883

PASSENGER	AGE	SEX	OCCUPATION	PRV	VIL	DES
RIPLAT, D.MICHEL-MR	38	M	MCHT	RR	ZZZZ	USA
JOSEPH	26	M	UNKNOWN	RR	ZZZZ	USA
JOHN	20	M	UNKNOWN	RR	ZZZZ	USA
GALM, J.FORD	42	M	UNKNOWN	RR	ZZZZ	USA

SHIP: NEVADA

FROM: GLASGOW AND LARNE
TO: NEW YORK
ARRIVED: 26 MARCH 1883

PASSENGER	AGE	SEX	OCCUPATION	PRV	VIL	DES
HOLOPSKY, JOSEPH	40	M	LABR	PL	ZZZZ	USA
JENNE	24	F	SVNT	PL	ZZZZ	USA
CHASSE	1	M	CHILD	PL	ZZZZ	USA
KRAUSSE, WILHELM	31	M	LABR	PL	ZZZZ	USA
JAKULOWSKY, VALENTINE	43	M	LABR	PL	ZZZZ	USA
LING, JULIUS	18	M	LABR	PL	ZZZZ	USA
SATOLZIG, ANDERS	24	M	LABR	PL	ZZZZ	USA
ZIELK, ANDERS	30	M	LABR	PL	ZZZZ	USA
ROK, JANOS	11	M	LABR	PL	ZZZZ	USA
MAKOK, FRANOK	35	M	LABR	PL	ZZZZ	USA
ANDRAS, MAX	25	M	LABR	PL	ZZZZ	USA
JOSEPHER, CHANNE	45	M	LABR	PL	ZZZZ	USA
MILARSKY, ANDRAS	30	M	LABR	PL	ZZZZ	USA
SEGEL, SCHINGE	44	M	LABR	PL	ZZZZ	USA
DATKONIEZ, IGNACY	23	M	LABR	PL	ZZZZ	USA
KASCHEL, MOSES	35	M	LABR	PL	ZZZZ	USA
KLAM, JOSEF	19	M	LABR	PL	ZZZZ	USA
CROSS, HERMAN	18	M	LABR	PL	ZZZZ	USA
SHON, JONAS	23	M	LABR	PL	ZZZZ	USA
SASHITZKY, JOUL	30	F	W	PL	ZZZZ	USA
BRODTSKY, SOLOMON	00	M	LABR	PL	ZZZZ	USA
MILATZKY, MOSES	00	M	LABR	PL	ZZZZ	USA
IMITZKY, ABRAHAM	00	M	LABR	PL	ZZZZ	USA

SHIP: SERVIA

FROM: LIVERPOOL
TO: NEW YORK
ARRIVED: 26 MARCH 1883

PASSENGER	AGE	SEX	OCCUPATION	PRV	VIL	DES
HOODKA, JAN	42	M	LABR	RR	ZZZZ	USA
FRANZ	18	M	LABR	RR	ZZZZ	USA
STREWE, OTTO	63	M	MCHT	RR	ZZZZ	USA
HERMAN	28	M	SGN	RR	ZZZZ	USA

SHIP: ROTTERDAM

FROM: ROTTERDAM
TO: NEW YORK
ARRIVED: 27 MARCH 1883

PASSENGER	AGE	SEX	OCCUPATION	PRV	VIL	DES
ZERNEN, WILHELM	30	M	FARMER	PL	ZZZZ	USA
WUNICH, GATH.	48	M	FARMER	PL	ZZZZ	USA
JOSEF	9	M	CHILD	PL	ZZZZ	USA

SHIP: WESTPHALIA

FROM: HAMBURG AND HAVRE
TO: NEW YORK
ARRIVED: 27 MARCH 1883

PASSENGER	AGE	SEX	OCCUPATION	PRV	VIL	DES
GOSKA, PETER	30	M	LABR	RR	ZZZZ	NE
VERONIKA	24	F	NN	RR	ZZZZ	NE
FRANZ	4	M	CHILD	RR	ZZZZ	NE
MARIE	.11	F	INFANT	RR	ZZZZ	NE
WISNEWSKY, JAN	27	M	LABR	RR	ZZZZ	NE
GERSACKI, J.	30	M	LABR	RR	ZZZZ	NY
LEWANDOWSKY, ANTON	43	M	LABR	RR	ZZZZ	NY
JANNSZEWSKY, ANTON	37	M	LABR	RR	ZZZZ	NY
DERECZKIE, FRANZISKA	19	F	SGL	RR	ZZZZ	NY
RUBMANN, DANIEL	21	M	SHMK	RR	ZZZZ	NY
FISICK, MORITZ	24	M	LABR	RR	ZZZZ	NY
BURSTEIN, EISICK	28	M	PNTR	RR	ZZZZ	NY
RIWKE	23	F	W	RR	ZZZZ	NY
KRINITZKI, MATSCHI	21	M	LABR	RR	ZZZZ	NY
PLAKEWITZ, VALENTIN	35	M	LABR	RR	ZZZZ	NY
PLOCHARSKY, STANISLAUS	40	M	LABR	RR	ZZZZ	NY
WOLPE, MAX	22	M	DLR	RR	ZZZZ	NY
STANAZTIS, ANDREAS	40	M	LABR	RR	ZZZZ	NY
KUTOVSKY, ANDREAS	23	M	LABR	RR	ZZZZ	NY
ODOMAITIS, OSIF	38	M	LABR	RR	ZZZZ	NY
PURCE, KASIMIR	19	M	LABR	RR	ZZZZ	NY
BOCKUS, KASIMIR	26	M	LABR	RR	ZZZZ	NY
BUCET, PETRA	23	F	W	RR	ZZZZ	NY
MARIANE	.06	F	INFANT	RR	ZZZZ	NY
STOPECK, JANKEL	17	M	TLR	RR	ZZZZ	NY
GITTELSOHN, SARAH	24	F	WO	RR	ZZZZ	NY
JUDELSOHN, CHAIE	40	F	WO	RR	ZZZZ	NY
SARA	19	F	CH	RR	ZZZZ	NY
ABRAHAM	9	M	CHILD	RR	ZZZZ	NY
SHANE	7	F	CHILD	RR	ZZZZ	NY
RAPHAELSOHN, HIRSCH	50	M	MCHT	RR	ZZZZ	NY
RAPHAEL	16	M	S	RR	ZZZZ	NY
GINSBERG, ABRAHAM	16	M	MCHT	RR	ZZZZ	NY
MISKUTSCHEN, CHANNE	60	F	WO	RR	ZZZZ	NY
JUDELSOHN, MOSES	4	M	CHILD	RR	ZZZZ	NY
JANKEL	3	M	CHILD	RR	ZZZZ	NY
WALLERSTEIN, LINE	20	F	SGL	RR	ZZZZ	NY

SHIP: AMERIQUE

FROM: HAVRE
TO: NEW YORK
ARRIVED: 28 MARCH 1883

PASSENGER	AGE	SEX	OCCUPATION	PRV	VIL	DES
DE-KONTSKI, A.MR	60	M	CMPR	RR	ZZZZ	NY
FREIND, MICHEL	31	M	BLKMKR	PL	ZZZZ	NY
DEBARA	32	M	UNKNOWN	PL	ZZZZ	NY
ISRAEL	4	M	CHILD	PL	ZZZZ	NY
ABRAHAM	00	M	INF	PL	ZZZZ	NY
MINNA	7	F	CHILD	PL	ZZZZ	NY

SHIP: AMERIQUE

FROM: HAVRE
TO: NEW YORK
ARRIVED: 28 MARCH 1883

PASSENGER	AGE	SEX	OCCUPATION	PRV	VIL	DES
KAMINSKI, JOSEPH	25	M	MCHT	RR	ZZZZ	USA
GROSMINSKI, SAMUEL	46	M	MCHT	RR	ZZZZ	USA
KESNER, MOSES	60	M	MCHT	RR	ZZZZ	USA

SHIP: CIRCASSIA

FROM: GLASGOW
TO: NEW YORK
ARRIVED: 28 MARCH 1883

PASSENGER	AGE	SEX	OCCUPATION	PRV	VIL	DES
KARNOWSKI, FRANZ	37	M	FARMER	RR	ZZZZ	USA

SHIP: WYOMING

FROM: LIVERPOOL AND QUEENSTOWN
TO: NEW YORK
ARRIVED: 28 MARCH 1883

PASSENGER	AGE	SEX	OCCUPATION	PRV	VIL	DES
JOHANSSON, ERIK	30	M	FARMER	FN	ZZZZ	USA
ANNA	32	F	W	FN	ZZZZ	USA
JOHAN	9	M	CHILD	FN	ZZZZ	USA
SVEN	3	F	CHILD	FN	ZZZZ	USA
SVENSON, ERIK	46	M	LABR	FN	ZZZZ	USA
FORSELL, JOHANN	38	M	LABR	FN	ZZZZ	USA
NYMAN, ERIK	30	M	LABR	FN	ZZZZ	USA
NYSTROM, ANDERS	21	M	LABR	FN	ZZZZ	USA
NYLAND, ALEXANDER	27	M	LABR	FN	ZZZZ	USA
STROM, ANDERS	23	M	LABR	FN	ZZZZ	USA
SPARF, JOHAN	40	M	LABR	FN	ZZZZ	USA
SUNDGVEST, ALEXANDER	25	M	LABR	FN	ZZZZ	USA
JACOBSON, ALEXANDER	19	M	LABR	FN	ZZZZ	USA
NYLAND, JOHAN	21	M	LABR	FN	ZZZZ	USA
FINNEL, ALFRED-A.	30	M	LABR	FN	ZZZZ	USA

SHIP: GRECIAN MONARCH

FROM: LONDON
TO: NEW YORK
ARRIVED: 29 MARCH 1883

PASSENGER	AGE	SEX	OCCUPATION	PRV VIL DES
COHEN, DAVIS	20	M	UNKNOWN	PLZZZZUSA
WEINER, ISAAC	42	M	UNKNOWN	PLZZZZUSA
PEISAJ	11	M	UNKNOWN	PLZZZZUSA
U	00	M	UNKNOWN	PLZZZZUSA
MINNA	25	F	UNKNOWN	PLZZZZUSA
W.	3	M	CHILD	PLZZZZUSA
HELENA	.07	F	INFANT	PLZZZZUSA
BLUME, ISAAC	22	M	UNKNOWN	PLZZZZUSA
LIPMANN, W.	24	M	UNKNOWN	PLZZZZUSA
DAVIS, R.	11	M	UNKNOWN	PLZZZZUSA
ROSENBLATT, BEN	42	M	UNKNOWN	PLZZZZUSA
LAZARUS, DAVIS	28	M	UNKNOWN	PLZZZZUSA
JANE	25	F	UNKNOWN	PLZZZZUSA
HENRY	4	M	CHILD	PLZZZZUSA
ISRAEL	2	M	CHILD	PLZZZZUSA
BARNETT	.04	M	INFANT	PLZZZZUSA
ADDIS, A.	34	M	UNKNOWN	PLZZZZUSA
SALOMON	27	M	UNKNOWN	PLZZZZUSA
ISAACS, SARAH	26	F	UNKNOWN	PLZZZZUSA
KATY	20	F	UNKNOWN	PLZZZZUSA
JEOZE	5	F	CHILD	PLZZZZUSA
CHAYNNIE	3	F	CHILD	PLZZZZUSA

SHIP: ST. OF PENNSYLVANIA

FROM: GLASGOW AND LARNE
TO: NEW YORK
ARRIVED: 29 MARCH 1883

PASSENGER	AGE	SEX	OCCUPATION	PRV VIL DES
GRAJEWSKE, JUDEL	21	M	UNKNOWN	RRZZZZUSA
SCHWARZ, H.	23	M	UNKNOWN	RRZZZZUSA
GRUEN, JOSEF	18	M	UNKNOWN	RRZZZZUSA
COLOVUSKER, ISTVAN	33	M	UNKNOWN	RRZZZZUSA

SHIP: HABSBURG

FROM: BREMEN AND SOUTHAMPTON
TO: NEW YORK
ARRIVED: 02 APRIL 1883

PASSENGER	AGE	SEX	OCCUPATION	PRV VIL DES
VOLAK, ADALBERT	30	M	LABR	PLZZZZUSA
MARIANNE	20	F	W	PLZZZZUSA
MICHAEL	3	M	CHILD	PLZZZZUSA
JOSEF	.06	M	INFANT	PLZZZZUSA
JEZSIWA, JOSEF	00	M	LABR	PLZZZZUSA
WIATER, WASZINA	00	F	W	PLZZZZUSA
GEKOF, MARTIN	00	M	FARMER	PLZZZZUSA
MARIANNE	30	F	W	PLZZZZUSA
FRANZISKA	4	F	CHILD	PLZZZZUSA
AGATHA	.10	F	INFANT	PLZZZZUSA
SKROWON, STANISLAUS	36	M	LABR	PLZZZZUSA
OLECHOSKY, JOSEF	34	M	LABR	PLZZZZUSA

SHIP: SARDINIAN

FROM: LIVERPOOL AND QUEENSTOWN
TO: NEW YORK
ARRIVED: 02 APRIL 1883

PASSENGER	AGE	SEX	OCCUPATION	PRV VIL DES
JACGUET, MARIEL	28	M	LABR	RRZZZZUSA
RAUL, JOSEPH	43	M	FARMER	RRZZZZUSA

SHIP: SILESIA

FROM: HAMBURG AND HAVRE
TO: NEW YORK
ARRIVED: 02 APRIL 1883

PASSENGER	AGE	SEX	OCCUPATION	PRV VIL DES
LEWIN, CHANNE	27	F	W	RRZZZZUSA
SALOMON	9	M	CHILD	RRZZZZUSA
JENTE	.11	F	INFANT	RRZZZZUSA
KATZ, MELACH	18	M	LABR	RRZZZZUSA
ITTE	16	F	SI	RRZZZZUSA
LEIB	9	M	CHILD	RRZZZZUSA
FRANK, JENTE	25	F	W	RRZZZZUSA
LINA	.11	F	INFANT	RRZZZZUSA
FIN, ABEL	26	M	DLR	RRZZZZUSA
JARWAKOWSKI, HERSCH	59	M	DLR	RRZZZZUSA
KOPEL, CARL	16	M	DLR	RRZZZZUSA
GOLDENSOHN, BASCHE	47	F	W	RRZZZZUSA
CHEIE	9	F	CHILD	RRZZZZUSA
CHEIM	4	M	CHILD	RRZZZZUSA
MALINOWSKY, FRANZ	22	M	LABR	RRZZZZUSA
LISEKY, KAROL	25	M	LABR	RRZZZZUSA
MELONA, ANTON	28	M	LABR	RRZZZZUSA
LISEKY, AUGUST	22	M	LABR	RRZZZZUSA
SOIDOS, VICENTI	30	M	LABR	RRZZZZUSA
KOWALEWSKI, PAUL	35	M	LABR	RRZZZZUSA
PRUSINCKY, JAN	25	M	LABR	RRZZZZUSA
BOYSEN, SOEREN	59	M	FARMER	RRZZZZUSA
ANNA	58	F	W	RRZZZZUSA
MARIE	24	F	CH	RRZZZZUSA
ANNA	22	F	CH	RRZZZZUSA
HANS	7	M	CHILD	RRZZZZUSA
JOHNSEN, FRITZ	20	M	FARMER	RRZZZZUSA
FESO, DEMETER	26	M	LABR	PLZZZZUSA
BARILKA, MICHALY	27	M	LABR	PLZZZZUSA
POLIVKA, MICHALY	27	M	LABR	PLZZZZUSA
HUDAK, PETER	29	M	LABR	PLZZZZUSA
HONZA, MICHALY	33	M	LABR	PLZZZZUSA
KAPSCAK, JOHANN	33	M	LABR	PLZZZZUSA
MENOM, JOHAN-JONAS	23	M	LABR	PLZZZZUSA
GURICHA, MICHALY	26	M	LABR	PLZZZZUSA
DEREMBY, MICHALY	29	M	LABR	PLZZZZUSA
HAVRYLA, JANOS	16	M	LABR	PLZZZZUSA
ROSNITZKY, RESI	18	F	SGL	RRZZZZUSA
NARWA, SCHMUL-F.	20	M	LABR	RRZZZZUSA
FREMKI, RACHEL	9	F	CHILD	RRZZZZUSA

SHIP: FRISIA

FROM: HAMBURG AND HAVRE
TO: NEW YORK
ARRIVED: 04 APRIL 1883

PASSENGER	AGE	SEX	OCCUPATION	PRV VIL DES
EDELMANN, MEYER	18	M	LABR	RRZZZZUSA
WOLSCHINSKI, ANTON	20	M	LABR	RRZZZZUSA

PASSENGER	AGE	SEX	OCCUPATION	PRIVL	DES
GRUDKANTZKI, ANDR.	20	M	LABR	RRZZZZ	USA
NIKLAUS, JULIANE	50	F	W	RRZZZZ	USA
HELENE	28	F	W	RRZZZZ	USA
ANNA	5	F	CHILD	RRZZZZ	USA
JULIE	.11	F	INFANT	RRZZZZ	USA
BERNSTEIN, MARG.BEILE	17	F	SGL	RRZZZZ	USA
ARON	9	M	CHILD	RRZZZZ	USA
WILINSKI, STANISL.	28	M	LABR	RRZZZZ	USA
DEMANTEWITZ, ABRAHAM	30	M	LABR	RRZZZZ	USA
TIREL, ESTHER	17	F	SGL	RRZZZZ	USA
TAUBE	9	F	CHILD	RRZZZZ	USA
GUTMANN, JUHIEL	19	M	LABR	RRZZZZ	USA
FEUX, JETTE	25	F	SGL	RRZZZZ	USA
FRIEDMANN, ISAAC	28	M	MCHT	RRZZZZ	USA

SHIP: NEPIGON

FROM: LIVERPOOL AND QUEENSTOWN
TO: NEW YORK
ARRIVED: 04 APRIL 1883

PASSENGER	AGE	SEX	OCCUPATION	PRIVL	DES
OBEVSTEIN, MEYER	20	M	UNKNOWN	PLZZZZ	NY

SHIP: SCYTHIA

FROM: LIVERPOOL AND QUEENSTOWN
TO: NEW YORK
ARRIVED: 04 APRIL 1883

PASSENGER	AGE	SEX	OCCUPATION	PRIVL	DES
BELHMAN, GUSTAF	23	M	LABR	RRZZZZ	USA

SHIP: RHYNLAND

FROM: ANTWERP
TO: NEW YORK
ARRIVED: 07 APRIL 1883

PASSENGER	AGE	SEX	OCCUPATION	PRIVL	DES
CZEKALLA, HERM.	19	M	LABR	PLZZZZ	CH
BITSCHKOWAS, IGNATZ	23	M	LABR	PLZZZZ	NY
IWAN	31	M	LABR	PLZZZZ	NY
CHUDZINSKI, FRANZ	20	M	LABR	PLZZZZ	NY
MAHROWSKI, KAZIMIR	17	M	LABR	PLZZZZ	MIL
CZIACZIALOWSKI, THOM.	25	M	NN	PLZZZZ	MIL
KOWITZKI, FRIEDR.	48	M	FARMER	PLZZZZ	MIL
WILHELMINA	53	F	NN	PLZZZZ	MIL
AUGUSTA	18	F	NN	PLZZZZ	MIL
ARMA	00	F	INF	PLZZZZ	MIL

SHIP: STATE OF FLORIDA

FROM: GLASGOW AND LARNE
TO: NEW YORK
ARRIVED: 07 APRIL 1883

PASSENGER	AGE	SEX	OCCUPATION	PRIVL	DES
NICHTER, ANNETTE	34	F	W	RRZZZZ	USA
RESCHILLA	11	F	UNKNOWN	RRZZZZ	USA
RUTNER, EIDEL	35	F	UNKNOWN	RRZZZZ	USA
REISEL	11	F	UNKNOWN	RRZZZZ	USA
SELDE	9	F	CHILD	RRZZZZ	USA
ESTHER	6	F	CHILD	RRZZZZ	USA
MACHLSCH	5	M	CHILD	RRZZZZ	USA
JOSEPH	00	M	UNKNOWN	RRZZZZ	USA
SARAH	00	F	UNKNOWN	RRZZZZ	USA
MALZSCHEIK, MATZALDR	49	M	LABR	RRZZZZ	USA
RATER, JOSEPH	48	M	UNKNOWN	RRZZZZ	USA
STANISLAW, MATZALDOR	30	M	UNKNOWN	RRZZZZ	USA
GORDON, SAMUEL	34	M	UNKNOWN	RRZZZZ	USA

SHIP: FRANCE

FROM: HAVRE
TO: NEW YORK
ARRIVED: 12 APRIL 1883

PASSENGER	AGE	SEX	OCCUPATION	PRIVL	DES
POSNECK, JOSEPH	22	M	LABR	RRZZZZ	NY
GROS, ARON	24	M	UNKNOWN	RRZZZZ	NY

SHIP: WIELAND

FROM: HAMBURG AND HAVRE
TO: NEW YORK
ARRIVED: 13 APRIL 1883

PASSENGER	AGE	SEX	OCCUPATION	PRIVL	DES
YAEKEL, DOROTHEA	40	F	W	RRZZZZ	USA
ODELINE	17	F	CH	RRZZZZ	USA
JOH.	15	M	CH	RRZZZZ	USA
KARL	9	M	CHILD	RRZZZZ	USA
OTTILIE	6	F	CHILD	RRZZZZ	USA
ALBERT	4	M	CHILD	RRZZZZ	USA
OLGA	2	F	CHILD	RRZZZZ	USA
SIMON	.11	M	INFANT	RRZZZZ	USA
SILBERMANN, CHAIE	24	F	W	RRZZZZ	USA
ABRAH.	.11	M	INFANT	RRZZZZ	USA
BURMESTER, DOROTHEA	65	F	W	RRZZZZ	USA
KURSCHAU, BEILE	17	F	SGL	RRZZZZ	USA
CALENBRUM, HEINR.	48	M	LABR	RRZZZZ	USA
VICTORIA	35	F	W	RRZZZZ	USA
BIRK, THEOD.	22	M	STDNT	RRZZZZ	USA

SHIP: LYDIAN MONARCH

FROM: LONDON
TO: NEW YORK
ARRIVED: 14 APRIL 1883

PASSENGER	AGE	SEX	OCCUPATION	PRIVL	DES
ROTHSTEIR, MOSES	30	M	LABR	RRZZZZ	NY
LESTINSKY, MARK	20	M	LABR	PLZZZZ	BO

PASSENGER	AGE	SEX	OCCUPATION	PRV VIL DES
PETTERSEN, OWEN-G.	46	M	CPTR	RRZZZZPIT
JOHANNA	38	F	NN	RRZZZZPIT
SAMUEL	18	M	NN	RRZZZZPIT
AXEL	11	M	NN	RRZZZZPIT
HILDA	10	F	NN	RRZZZZPIT
SELINA	7	F	CHILD	RRZZZZPIT
POREN-C.	5	M	CHILD	RRZZZZPIT
ASKAR	2	M	CHILD	RRZZZZPIT
EMIL	.06	F	INFANT	RRZZZZPIT

SHIP: BOHEMIA

FROM: HAMBURG
TO: NEW YORK
ARRIVED: 16 APRIL 1883

PASSENGER	AGE	SEX	OCCUPATION	PRV VIL DES
PRESS, MENUCHE	24	F	W	RRZZZZUSA
BEHR	.11	M	INFANT	RRZZZZUSA
SCHATT, RIWE	18	F	SGL	RRZZZZUSA
GORDON, JACOB	9	M	CHILD	RRZZZZUSA
FINKELSTEIN, BEHR	14	M	LABR	RRZZZZUSA
REINES, LIPSE	16	F	SGL	RRZZZZUSA
ROSENBERG, JUDES	9	M	CHILD	RRZZZZUSA
POMIANSKY, GITTEL	31	F	W	RRZZZZUSA
ALTE	8	F	CHILD	RRZZZZUSA
SELDE	5	F	CHILD	RRZZZZUSA
CHANNE	3	F	CHILD	RRZZZZUSA
RABINOWITZ, LEA	53	F	W	RRZZZZUSA
HANNE	19	F	D	RRZZZZUSA
MILLER, NACHAME	23	F	W	RRZZZZUSA
HAIE	.11	M	INFANT	RRZZZZUSA
ABR.	.01	M	INFANT	RRZZZZUSA
MARCUSSON, MEIE	36	F	W	RRZZZZUSA
EMILIE	9	F	CHILD	RRZZZZUSA
SCHMUL	3	M	CHILD	RRZZZZUSA
GOLDBERG, HIELEL	16	M	LABR	RRZZZZUSA
RASNITZKY, LEISER	58	M	LABR	RRZZZZUSA
EDE	45	F	W	RRZZZZUSA
KARABELNIK, MARCUS	45	M	UNKNOWN	RRZZZZUSA
CIRLE	44	F	W	RRZZZZUSA
OTE	9	F	CHILD	RRZZZZUSA
ABR.	8	M	CHILD	RRZZZZUSA
CHASKEL	.11	M	INFANT	RRZZZZUSA
PFEFFER, VINCENT	23	M	MCHT	RRZZZZUSA
CHARON, REISE	33	F	W	RRZZZZUSA
LARE	8	F	CHILD	RRZZZZUSA
BEILE	7	F	CHILD	RRZZZZUSA
SCHMUL	.11	M	INFANT	RRZZZZUSA
MENKEWITZ, KASIMIR	28	M	LABR	RRZZZZUSA
HEIER, ROBERT	33	M	JWLR	RRZZZZUSA
MITKA, JAN	23	M	LABR	RRZZZZUSA
KAMINSKI, JAN	22	M	UNKNOWN	RRZZZZUSA
BZEZINSKI, ANTON	21	M	UNKNOWN	RRZZZZUSA
KALBIN, LEANHD.	33	M	LABR	RRZZZZUSA
MARGE.	32	F	W	RRZZZZUSA
CATHE.	.11	F	INFANT	RRZZZZUSA
SLODOWSKI, FR.	20	M	FARMER	RRZZZZUSA
GROZDE, JOH.	24	M	UNKNOWN	RRZZZZUSA

SHIP: SPAIN

FROM: LIVERPOOL AND QUEENSTOWN
TO: NEW YORK
ARRIVED: 16 APRIL 1883

PASSENGER	AGE	SEX	OCCUPATION	PRV VIL DES
WEINSTEIN, CHANE	45	F	W	PLZZZZUSA
SCHOLEN	11	M	CH	PLZZZZUSA
SIMON	9	M	CHILD	PLZZZZUSA
FINKELSTEIN, SARAH	27	F	W	PLZZZZUSA
BEILE	.11	M	INFANT	PLZZZZUSA
RIVALSKI, SAMUEL	30	M	LABR	PLZZZZUSA

SHIP: RHAETIA

FROM: HAMBURG AND HAVRE
TO: NEW YORK
ARRIVED: 19 APRIL 1883

PASSENGER	AGE	SEX	OCCUPATION	PRV VIL DES
SIDERSKI, DAVID	31	M	LABR	RRZZZZUSA
BERNSTEIN, TOBIAS	41	M	LABR	RRZZZZUSA
ROSAITSKY, MEIER	24	M	LABR	RRZZZZUSA
STEINISLAWSKI, WICTORIA	30	F	W	RRZZZZUSA
THOMAS	.06	M	INFANT	RRZZZZUSA
RANKOSKA, ANTOINE	50	F	SGL	RRZZZZUSA
KASIMIR	16	M	CH	RRZZZZUSA
WLADISLAW	9	M	CHILD	RRZZZZUSA

SHIP: STATE OF NEBRASKA

FROM: GLASGOW AND LARNE
TO: NEW YORK
ARRIVED: 19 APRIL 1883

PASSENGER	AGE	SEX	OCCUPATION	PRV VIL DES
CHUAN, U-MR	23	M	TLR	RRZZZZUSA
RAHOW, L.	23	M	PDLR	RRZZZZUSA

SHIP: LAKE MANITOBA

FROM: LIVERPOOL AND QUEENSTOWN
TO: NEW YORK
ARRIVED: 20 APRIL 1883

PASSENGER	AGE	SEX	OCCUPATION	PRV VIL DES
HARASMAS, PAVEL	33	M	LABR	PLZZZZNY
TERESA	22	F	W	PLZZZZNY
MICHAL	1	M	CHILD	PLZZZZNY
ZELAK, ANDRACH	21	M	LABR	PLZZZZNY

PASSENGER	AGE	SEX	OCCUPATION	PRVL	VILE	DES

SHIP: FULDA

FROM: BREMEN
TO: NEW YORK
ARRIVED: 21 APRIL 1883

PASSENGER	AGE	SEX	OCCUPATION	PRV	VIL	DES
SZALWIENSKI, WOICEK	39	M	LABR	RR	ZZZZ	USA
MATECKI, MATHEUS	29	M	LABR	RR	ZZZZ	USA
GUSOWSKI, JOSEF	21	M	LABR	RR	ZZZZ	USA
MURAWSKI, JOSEF	24	M	LABR	RR	ZZZZ	USA
KURZINSKI, JAN	18	M	LABR	RR	ZZZZ	USA
FRANZ	20	M	LABR	RR	ZZZZ	USA
OLESZEWSKI, THEOPHIL	20	M	LABR	RR	ZZZZ	USA
FUTZZYNSKI, ANTON	24	M	LABR	RR	ZZZZ	USA
GUSTAVSON, AARON	38	M	LABR	RR	ZZZZ	USA
SLAWINSKA, KATARZYN	28	M	LABR	RR	ZZZZ	USA
LEWANDOWSKI, JOSEF	30	M	LABR	RR	ZZZZ	USA

SHIP: ODER

FROM: BREMEN AND SOUTHAMPTON
TO: NEW YORK
ARRIVED: 21 APRIL 1883

PASSENGER	AGE	SEX	OCCUPATION	PRV	VIL	DES
WORTEMANN, LEBREIHT	28	M	LABR	RR	ZZZZ	USA

SHIP: FLAMBOROUGH

FROM: UNKNOWN
TO: NEW YORK
ARRIVED: 23 APRIL 1883

PASSENGER	AGE	SEX	OCCUPATION	PRV	VIL	DES
TEZELL, F.S.	24	M	LABR	RR	ZZZZ	USA

SHIP: ITALY

FROM: LIVERPOOL AND QUEENSTOWN
TO: NEW YORK
ARRIVED: 23 APRIL 1883

PASSENGER	AGE	SEX	OCCUPATION	PRV	VIL	DES
SCHELMASKY, JOSEF	28	M	LABR	PL	ZZZZ	USA
MICHAELINA	22	M	LABR	PL	ZZZZ	USA
WILKOWSKY, VINZENT	43	M	LABR	PL	ZZZZ	USA
NOWRASKY, THOS.	26	M	LABR	PL	ZZZZ	USA
JADWIGA	30	F	W	PL	ZZZZ	USA
ANDREW	00	M	INF	PL	ZZZZ	USA
ANDERS	00	M	INF	PL	ZZZZ	USA
KOSELAIK, VERONI	20	F	W	PL	ZZZZ	USA
STANELS	7	M	CHILD	PL	ZZZZ	USA
DRAWEISK, MARIA	30	F	SP	PL	ZZZZ	USA
FABIAN, MARIA	32	F	W	PL	ZZZZ	USA
JOSKA	00	F	INF	PL	ZZZZ	USA
MARSARA, MICHAEL	24	M	LABR	PL	ZZZZ	USA
ZABUBREK, U-MRS	48	F	W	PL	ZZZZ	USA
VALENTIN	50	M	LABR	PL	ZZZZ	USA
MECKIWKIA	20	F	SP	PL	ZZZZ	USA
MICHL.	9	M	CHILD	PL	ZZZZ	USA
FRANZ	11	M	CH	PL	ZZZZ	USA
JOSEF	23	M	LABR	PL	ZZZZ	USA
KASENSKY, JAN	32	M	LABR	PL	ZZZZ	USA
LACHONZKI, VIRS.	23	M	LABR	PL	ZZZZ	USA
SOBERZASKI, JOHAN	26	M	LABR	PL	ZZZZ	USA
ELIZABETH	21	F	W	PL	ZZZZ	USA
FRANZ	00	M	INF	PL	ZZZZ	USA
BRIAVISKY, MARTIN	32	M	LABR	PL	ZZZZ	USA
ATZANAWIKI, MARIANA	36	F	W	PL	ZZZZ	USA
WINZENT	10	M	CH	PL	ZZZZ	USA
VICTORIA	8	F	CHILD	PL	ZZZZ	USA
POLLACK, ANDERS	26	M	LABR	PL	ZZZZ	USA
MIKOLENZEK, VALENTIN	29	M	LABR	PL	ZZZZ	USA
PERIKOFF, J.	24	M	GENT	RR	ZZZZ	USA

SHIP: SUEVIA

FROM: HAMBURG
TO: NEW YORK
ARRIVED: 23 APRIL 1883

PASSENGER	AGE	SEX	OCCUPATION	PRV	VIL	DES
SCHIDERSKY, CHAIE	25	F	W	RR	ZZZZ	USA
CHANNE	.11	F	INFANT	RR	ZZZZ	USA
JOSSEL	.01	M	INFANT	RR	ZZZZ	USA
BASCHE	20	F	SGL	RR	ZZZZ	USA
BUDOWSKY, JOSEF	43	M	LABR	RR	ZZZZ	USA
RINETZKY, JAN	33	M	LABR	RR	ZZZZ	USA
SCHILINSKY, MATHIAS	36	M	LABR	RR	ZZZZ	USA
KAZEWSKI, JOSEF	42	M	LABR	RR	ZZZZ	USA
MIRNATZKI, FR.	21	M	LABR	RR	ZZZZ	USA
BETLEJEWSKI, JOH.	28	M	LABR	RR	ZZZZ	USA

SHIP: HAMMONIA

FROM: HAMBURG AND HAVRE
TO: NEW YORK
ARRIVED: 25 APRIL 1883

PASSENGER	AGE	SEX	OCCUPATION	PRV	VIL	DES
KLUSAYTES, HELENE	22	F	SGL	RR	ZZZZ	USA
BARTZ, ADOLF	21	M	LABR	RR	ZZZZ	USA
ZAHN, PAULINE	32	F	W	RR	ZZZZ	USA
BRUNO	8	M	CHILD	RR	ZZZZ	USA
HELENE	7	F	CHILD	RR	ZZZZ	USA
HENRIETTE	4	F	CHILD	RR	ZZZZ	USA
PETCZULIS, VINCENT	28	M	LABR	RR	ZZZZ	USA
PETCULIS, ANNA	28	F	SGL	RR	ZZZZ	USA
IWAROWICZ, OTTI	28	M	LABR	RR	ZZZZ	USA

SHIP: POLARIA

FROM: HAMBURG
TO: NEW YORK
ARRIVED: 25 APRIL 1883

PASSENGER	AGE	SEX	OCCUPATION	PRV	VIL	DES
ABRAMOWITS, SCHEKE	38	F	WO	RR	ZZZZ	NY
RAHEL	18	F	D	RR	ZZZZ	NY
TAUBE	14	F	D	RR	ZZZZ	NY
ELTERMANN, MARIE	40	F	WO	RR	ZZZZ	NY
KUCHEN	8	F	CHILD	RR	ZZZZ	NY
BARUCH	7	M	CHILD	RR	ZZZZ	NY
CHARKE	5	F	CHILD	RR	ZZZZ	NY
BOKARAZA, HEINR.JOS.	30	M	LABR	RR	ZZZZ	NY

PASSENGER	AGE	SEX	OCCUPATION	PRV	VIL	DES
EVA	24	F	W	RR	ZZZZ	NY
SZCKANKOWSKI, LAX	30	M	LABR	PL	ZZZZ	NY

SHIP: ABYSSINIA

FROM: LIVERPOOL
TO: NEW YORK
ARRIVED: 26 APRIL 1883

PASSENGER	AGE	SEX	OCCUPATION	PRV	VIL	DES
PALKO, ANNA	28	F	W	PL	ZZZZ	USA
SMARKO, JOS.	14	M	MNR	PL	ZZZZ	USA
POLKO, ANNA	7	F	CHILD	PL	ZZZZ	USA
JURO	.09	M	INFANT	PL	ZZZZ	USA
BACKMAN, GUSTAF	28	M	CL	RR	ZZZZ	USA
KALKOLA, PAULAS	23	M	LABR	RR	ZZZZ	USA
HONTCO, PAUL	23	M	LABR	RR	ZZZZ	USA

SHIP: PAVONIA

FROM: LIVERPOOL AND QUEENSTOWN
TO: NEW YORK
ARRIVED: 26 APRIL 1883

PASSENGER	AGE	SEX	OCCUPATION	PRV	VIL	DES
OSTREM, NICOLAI	20	M	LABR	PL	ZZZZ	USA
LAZASIZIK, JOHAN	39	M	FARMER	PL	ZZZZ	USA
BELACY, GEO.	31	M	FARMER	PL	ZZZZ	USA
MURI, ANDREAS	40	M	FARMER	PL	ZZZZ	USA
BANDJAK, MICHAL	47	M	FARMER	PL	ZZZZ	USA
KARIZ, MICHAL	47	M	FARMER	PL	ZZZZ	USA
CIRAY, LAJOZ	10	M	CH	PL	ZZZZ	USA
KIFER, JOHAN	11	M	CH	PL	ZZZZ	USA
BAUER, CARL	47	M	LABR	PL	ZZZZ	USA
SOHAK, JANKI	48	M	LABR	PL	ZZZZ	USA
DIPSZE, JANOS	36	M	LABR	PL	ZZZZ	USA
WASIL	41	M	LABR	PL	ZZZZ	USA
BAUER, CARL	9	M	CHILD	PL	ZZZZ	USA
TUBACY, JOSEF	34	M	LABR	PL	ZZZZ	USA
HORNIK, JANOS	11	M	CH	PL	ZZZZ	USA
BRIDASY, AND.	40	M	LABR	PL	ZZZZ	USA
JOCHUDI, ALVIS	25	M	LABR	PL	ZZZZ	USA
KOKOLI, JOHAN	26	M	LABR	PL	ZZZZ	USA
BIRYZ, JOHAN	45	M	LABR	PL	ZZZZ	USA
ELIZBETH	39	F	W	PL	ZZZZ	USA
JOSEF	10	M	CH	PL	ZZZZ	USA
JOHAN	7	M	CHILD	PL	ZZZZ	USA
MARIE	5	F	CHILD	PL	ZZZZ	USA
AUGUST	.11	M	INFANT	PL	ZZZZ	USA
JAWLOWSKI, IGNEZ	54	M	LABR	PL	ZZZZ	USA
EMMA	43	F	W	PL	ZZZZ	USA
MARIE	14	F	SVNT	PL	ZZZZ	USA
PLENSKY, ALBINE	23	F	SVNT	PL	ZZZZ	USA

SHIP: DENMARK

FROM: LONDON
TO: NEW YORK
ARRIVED: 28 APRIL 1883

PASSENGER	AGE	SEX	OCCUPATION	PRV	VIL	DES
STOLKEL, J.	39	M	CL	PL	ZZZZ	USA
LTEPOEWUSKI, F.	42	M	UNKNOWN	PL	ZZZZ	USA

SHIP: DEVONIA

FROM: GLASGOW AND MOVILLE
TO: NEW YORK
ARRIVED: 01 MAY 1883

PASSENGER	AGE	SEX	OCCUPATION	PRV	VIL	DES
KALINSUSKY, PEITZ	24	M	LABR	PL	ZZZZ	USA
JACHARSTKE, S.	36	M	LABR	PL	ZZZZ	USA
OWYARJIK, VULKULNE	26	M	LABR	PL	ZZZZ	USA
ANKIEWIEZ, SADDLUS	31	M	BCHR	PL	ZZZZ	USA
KRITSCHEK, W.	26	M	LABR	PL	ZZZZ	USA
PARADOWSKE, ANDRYZ	26	M	LABR	PL	ZZZZ	USA
BETKEWSKY, FRANZ	28	M	LABR	PL	ZZZZ	USA
ROWOHZKY, FRANZ	18	M	LABR	PL	ZZZZ	USA
MUSSELL, ADALBERT	41	M	LABR	PL	ZZZZ	USA
STACHOWITZ, IGNATZ	23	M	LABR	PL	ZZZZ	USA
RYZEWSKY, ADALBERT	26	M	LABR	PL	ZZZZ	USA
KONOZINSKY, MICHL.	27	M	LABR	PL	ZZZZ	USA
PETRONSKY, FRANK	33	M	LABR	PL	ZZZZ	USA
MARIE	28	F	NN	PL	ZZZZ	USA
STEFEMSKY, K.	40	M	LABR	PL	ZZZZ	USA
JENDREZAY, ANDERS	38	M	LABR	PL	ZZZZ	USA
SYLOYUTE, SYLO	28	M	TLR	PL	ZZZZ	USA
MATULEWITZ, ANTON	21	M	LABR	PL	ZZZZ	USA
MELOWAKY, MARTIN	29	M	LABR	PL	ZZZZ	USA
WAYRZYWIK, JACOB	32	M	DRV	PL	ZZZZ	USA
MICHALINA	26	F	NN	PL	ZZZZ	USA
ANDRIS	4	M	CHILD	PL	ZZZZ	USA
HONSTANS	2	M	CHILD	PL	ZZZZ	USA
THANZ	.03	M	INFANT	PL	ZZZZ	USA
ALSCHWARZ, ADOLF	24	M	MCHT	PL	ZZZZ	USA
ALSCHNAEZ, MARIE	18	F	NN	PL	ZZZZ	USA
RETHOUKA, CATH.	24	F	NN	PL	ZZZZ	USA
THEODA	7	M	CHILD	PL	ZZZZ	USA
JON	6	M	CHILD	PL	ZZZZ	USA
WLADYSLAW	4	M	CHILD	PL	ZZZZ	USA
STANISLAW	.06	M	INFANT	PL	ZZZZ	USA
ORLIK, ANDERS	32	M	LABR	PL	ZZZZ	USA
MYHALINA	26	F	NN	PL	ZZZZ	USA
PEETA	.01	M	INFANT	PL	ZZZZ	USA
MASCHKURVIZ, MICH.	23	M	LABR	PL	ZZZZ	USA
DUNNANT, FRANZ	60	M	LABR	PL	ZZZZ	USA
ALVISIA	24	M	LABR	PL	ZZZZ	USA
PEKOWSKY, HEINRICH	16	M	LABR	PL	ZZZZ	USA
PELLIEZCK, PETRONELLA	58	M	LABR	PL	ZZZZ	USA
OZESKO, ILGO	21	M	LABR	PL	ZZZZ	USA
ZILZEVNSKY, V.	21	M	LABR	PL	ZZZZ	USA
KUDIZRVA, ANDRES	30	M	LABR	PL	ZZZZ	USA
SYOVSKY, VOGT.	23	M	LABR	PL	ZZZZ	USA
JANERS, FRANZ	42	M	LABR	PL	ZZZZ	USA
ELIZA	19	F	NN	PL	ZZZZ	USA
KEEHAR, MORITZ	40	M	MCHT	RR	ZZZZ	USA
KALWSKY, JOHANN	39	M	LABR	PL	ZZZZ	USA
STROME, STANISLOUS	.06	M	INFANT	PL	ZZZZ	USA

SHIP: GELLERT

FROM: HAMBURG AND HAVRE
TO: NEW YORK
ARRIVED: 01 MAY 1883

PASSENGER	AGE	SEX	OCCUPATION	PRV	VIL	DES
SCHALOWSKY, TETRUS	22	M	LABR	RR	ZZZZ	USA
BERNADEZ, JOSEF	21	M	LABR	RR	ZZZZ	USA
YONKOWSKA, VINCENTA	46	F	W	RR	ZZZZ	USA
STEFAN	9	M	CHILD	RR	ZZZZ	USA
BUCHHOLZ, WILH.	58	M	LABR	RR	ZZZZ	USA
WILHE.	50	F	W	RR	ZZZZ	USA
WILH.	24	M	CH	RR	ZZZZ	USA
IDA	8	F	CHILD	RR	ZZZZ	USA

PASSENGER	AGE	SEX	OCCUPATION	PRIV	DES
SOZAWINSKI, VALENTIN	24	M	LABR	RRZZZZ	USA
ROGALSKY, JAN	24	M	LABR	RRZZZZ	USA
SCHOENFELDT, MORITZ	35	M	MCHT	RRZZZZ	USA
EMILIE	19	F	W	RRZZZZ	USA
VICTORINE	2	F	CHILD	RRZZZZ	USA
HERRM.	1	M	CHILD	RRZZZZ	USA

SHIP: OHIO

FROM: BREMEN
TO: NEW YORK
ARRIVED: 01 MAY 1883

PASSENGER	AGE	SEX	OCCUPATION	PRIV	DES
WAZSILEWSKI, FRANZ	27	M	LABR	RRZZZZ	USA
MALOSKOFSKA, JOSEFA	6	F	CHILD	RRZZZZ	USA
WUSACHKOFSKI, IGNATZ	23	M	LABR	RRZZZZ	USA
JELENSKI, MARTIN	31	M	LABR	RRZZZZ	USA
TILENDA, IOSEF	27	M	LABR	RRZZZZ	USA
SWOLAWSKI, STEFAN	22	M	LABR	RRZZZZ	USA
MASSAKOWSKA, SOPHIA	61	F	NN	RRZZZZ	USA
VALINE	.11	F	INFANT	RRZZZZ	USA
LASAR	.11	M	INFANT	RRZZZZ	USA
HALLASKOWSKI, MARIANNE	26	F	UNKNOWN	RRZZZZ	USA
FRANZISKE	.10	F	INFANT	RRZZZZ	USA

SHIP: SERVIA

FROM: LIVERPOOL
TO: NEW YORK
ARRIVED: 01 MAY 1883

PASSENGER	AGE	SEX	OCCUPATION	PRIV	DES
BRENIER, ELLE	24	M	MCHT	RRZZZZ	USA

SHIP: WAESLAND

FROM: ANTWERP
TO: NEW YORK
ARRIVED: 04 MAY 1883

PASSENGER	AGE	SEX	OCCUPATION	PRIV	DES
VONCONBE, J.MR	30	M	AGNT	RRZZZZ	USA
BIERDA, JOH.	24	M	LABR	PLZZZZ	USA
ANNA	40	F	NN	PLZZZZ	USA
BROSZKI, SOFIA	23	F	NN	PLZZZZ	BUF
PALAZOWSKA, WEOBSKO	25	M	LABR	PLZZZZ	BUF
THEOPHIL	4	M	CHILD	PLZZZZ	BUF
STANISLAS	2	M	CHILD	PLZZZZ	BUF
MEDESLAV	.03	M	INFANT	PLZZZZ	BUF
DYCHOWSKI, JOH.	23	M	LABR	PLZZZZ	IL
ZWALENSKY, MARIA	31	F	NN	PLZZZZ	UNK
STEPHAN	4	M	CHILD	PLZZZZ	UNK
LOREAZ	1	F	CHILD	PLZZZZ	UNK
STANISLAS	.03	M	INFANT	PLZZZZ	UNK
MATUSLEWITZ, W.	47	M	LABR	PLZZZZ	UNK
O.	20	F	NN	PLZZZZ	UNK
NICOLAS	15	M	NN	PLZZZZ	UNK
SDIENOWITSCH, LEIB	18	M	NN	RRZZZZ	NY
TUNNICH, ALB.	18	M	NN	RRZZZZ	IL
THRENREICH, FRZ.	14	M	NN	RRZZZZ	PHI
ZIOLBOWSKI, F.	18	M	NN	PLZZZZ	NY
BIANIONE, EVA	22	F	NN	PLZZZZ	NY

PASSENGER	AGE	SEX	OCCUPATION	PRIV	DES
MARY	.11	F	INFANT	PLZZZZ	NY
RUTAFOZUK, VALENTZ	19	M	NN	PLZZZZ	NY

SHIP: HERMANN

FROM: BREMEN
TO: NEW YORK
ARRIVED: 07 MAY 1883

PASSENGER	AGE	SEX	OCCUPATION	PRIV	DES
NUMSKE, JULIUS	33	M	LABR	RRZZZZ	USA
STOPKO, TON	25	M	LABR	RRZZZZ	USA
DORA, U	00	M	LABR	RRZZZZ	USA
KEMENZ, FERV.	46	M	FARMER	RRZZZZ	USA
KONYOAZKI, ADAM	36	M	FARMER	RRZZZZ	USA
NEUMANN, CARL	12	M	NN	RRZZZZ	USA
BRECHELLIES, HENRIETH	41	M	LABR	RRZZZZ	USA

SHIP: NUERNBERG

FROM: BREMEN AND SOUTHAMPTON
TO: NEW YORK
ARRIVED: 07 MAY 1883

PASSENGER	AGE	SEX	OCCUPATION	PRIV	DES
KRZYKWO, MICH.	30	M	LABR	RRZZZZ	IL
KIZICH, GUISEPPE	33	M	FARMER	RRZZZZ	IL

SHIP: RUGIA

FROM: HAMBURG
TO: NEW YORK
ARRIVED: 07 MAY 1883

PASSENGER	AGE	SEX	OCCUPATION	PRIV	DES
DANKSCHES, THOMAS	46	M	LABR	RRZZZZ	USA
SLIKNA, MACAJUS	24	M	LABR	RRZZZZ	USA
RACZINS, JOSEF	27	M	LABR	RRZZZZ	USA
PAZELA, CARL	23	M	FARMER	RRZZZZ	USA
SIKORA, PETER	34	M	SMH	RRZZZZ	USA
WORRICCOSKY, VAEL	25	M	LABR	RRZZZZ	USA
REFEROVSKY, SIG.	22	M	LABR	RRZZZZ	USA
ZEIHEWITZ, SIMON	20	M	LABR	RRZZZZ	USA
KODUKEWIDZ, MICHAL	22	M	LABR	RRZZZZ	USA
RUDZEICZ, APOLINIA	24	F	SGL	RRZZZZ	USA
MALESKI, THOMAS	22	M	LABR	RRZZZZ	USA
BUNDINOWITZ, JOS.	26	M	LABR	RRZZZZ	USA
FOGELSKY, JOS.	28	M	LABR	RRZZZZ	USA
NIEBERT, JOH.	34	M	LABR	RRZZZZ	USA
JOH.	16	M	LABR	RRZZZZ	USA
STAPRISL-BORGEWICZ, KAS	16	M	LABR	RRZZZZ	USA
WANZENSKI, KAS.	46	M	LABR	RRZZZZ	USA
SALENSKI, JOS.	22	M	LABR	RRZZZZ	USA
BENDER, JUL.	23	M	LABR	RRZZZZ	USA
PALVIS, SIMON	24	M	LABR	RRZZZZ	USA
HUBINSKI, JOHN	26	M	LABR	RRZZZZ	USA
STIRNITZKO, ALBT.	22	M	LABR	RRZZZZ	USA
SCHICHAZEWSKY, ALBT.	34	M	LABR	RRZZZZ	USA
HALMOWSKY, JOH.	24	M	LABR	RRZZZZ	USA
FEINOJOLD, HOSKO	31	M	DLR	RRZZZZ	USA
FRICE	20	F	W	RRZZZZ	USA

PASSENGER	AGE	SEX	OCCUPATION	PV RI VL / DES

SHIP: WESTPHALIA

FROM: HAMBURG AND HAVRE
TO: NEW YORK
ARRIVED: 08 MAY 1883

PASSENGER	AGE	SEX	OCCUPATION	PV RI VL / DES
WINIK, ISRAEL	39	M	TLR	RRZZZZNY
FUERGES, JULIUS	20	M	LABR	RRZZZZNY
WOITECHOWSKI, ANTON	30	M	LABR	RRZZZZNY
CATHARINA	30	F	W	RRZZZZNY
ANTONIE	.11	F	INFANT	RRZZZZNY
MARKOWICH, JOHANN	30	M	LABR	RRZZZZNY
DERBISEWSKI, FRANZ	38	M	LABR	RRZZZZNY
KUZEWSKI, FRANZ	33	M	LABR	RRZZZZNY

SHIP: CITY OF CHESTER

FROM: LIVERPOOL AND QUEENSTOWN
TO: NEW YORK
ARRIVED: 12 MAY 1883

PASSENGER	AGE	SEX	OCCUPATION	PV RI VL / DES
CARLSON, GUSTAF	25	M	LABR	FNZZZZUSA
THOMASEN, JOHAN	39	M	LABR	FNZZZZUSA
MUKELSEN, JOH.	40	M	LABR	FNZZZZUSA
MATTSEN, GUSTAF	44	M	LABR	FNZZZZUSA
MATTSON, RESSIANE	32	M	LABR	FNZZZZUSA
ABESEN, GUSTAF	22	M	LABR	FNZZZZUSA
JOHANSEN, MATS.	21	M	LABR	FNZZZZUSA
PALM, ANDERS	28	M	LABR	FNZZZZUSA
ANDERSEN, HERMAN	22	M	LABR	FNZZZZUSA
HEROLLD, JOHN	21	M	LABR	FNZZZZUSA
MATTSEN, GUSTAF	28	M	LABR	FNZZZZUSA
HERMAN	27	M	LABR	FNZZZZUSA
CHRISTIENSEN, GUST.	36	M	LABR	FNZZZZUSA
JOHANSEN, JACOB	27	M	LABR	FNZZZZUSA
JACOBSEN, ALEX	41	M	LABR	FNZZZZUSA
MIKELSEN, ELIAS	30	M	LABR	FNZZZZUSA
JOHANSEN, ANDERS	40	M	LABR	FNZZZZUSA
GUSTAFSEN, JOHN	30	M	LABR	FNZZZZUSA
ISAACSON, JOHN	38	M	LABR	FNZZZZUSA
ANDERSEN, ERIC	27	M	LABR	FNZZZZUSA
JOHANSEN, GABRIEL	20	M	LABR	FNZZZZUSA
GUSTAFSEN, GUSTAF	38	M	LABR	FNZZZZUSA
GORANSEN, GUSTAF	48	M	LABR	FNZZZZUSA
NILSEN, LARS	47	M	LABR	FNZZZZUSA
LARSEN, JOHN-A.	25	M	LABR	FNZZZZUSA
ANIETT	24	F	SP	FNZZZZUSA

SHIP: AUSTRALIA

FROM: HAMBURG
TO: NEW YORK
ARRIVED: 14 MAY 1883

PASSENGER	AGE	SEX	OCCUPATION	PV RI VL / DES
ZEUKORKEI, AUG.	24	M	LABR	RRZZZZUSA
CASPERSKI, N.	25	M	LABR	RRZZZZUSA
JANKE, GUSTAV	27	M	LABR	RRZZZZUSA
CHARMINSKI, FRANK	40	M	TRDSMN	RRZZZZUSA
KARNIACK, JANOS	45	M	TRDSMN	RRZZZZUSA
DEVKOSKI, P.	38	M	TRDSMN	RRZZZZUSA
WINGNEROWITZ, JOSEF	43	M	LABR	RRZZZZUSA
OSTROSKY, IGN.	8	M	CHILD	RRZZZZUSA
INGROWITZ, FELIX	21	M	LABR	RRZZZZUSA
JUSCHKEWIEZ, BIGITISCH	35	M	LABR	RRZZZZUSA

PASSENGER	AGE	SEX	OCCUPATION	PV RI VL / DES

PASSENGER	AGE	SEX	OCCUPATION	PV RI VL / DES
ABRAMOWITZ, VINC.	7	M	CHILD	RRZZZZUSA
ANDRANOWICZ, A.	22	M	LABR	RRZZZZUSA
RAWITZKI, ANTON	24	M	LABR	RRZZZZUSA
ANRASCHEWIZ, FRANZ	27	M	LABR	RRZZZZUSA
KOWOLSKY, C.	8	M	CHILD	RRZZZZUSA
ABRAMOWIZ, STANISL.	25	M	LABR	RRZZZZUSA
HAUSE, NICOL.	34	M	LABR	RRZZZZUSA
JACOBOVSKI, AMBROS.	30	M	LABR	RRZZZZUSA
VICTORIA	20	F	W	RRZZZZUSA
ORSCHELSKA	.11	F	INFANT	RRZZZZUSA
ANDSCHA	.01	F	INFANT	RRZZZZUSA
WERSCHBITZKI, STANISL.	35	M	LABR	RRZZZZUSA
SCHIERKEWICZ, JOS.	28	M	LABR	RRZZZZUSA
WACHILOVSKIWIEZ, CHAS.	23	M	LABR	RRZZZZUSA
KOSA, M.	60	M	LABR	RRZZZZUSA
JOHANN	24	M	LABR	RRZZZZUSA
JOSEF	8	M	CHILD	RRZZZZUSA
KOWALKI, MIHAL	42	M	FARMER	PLZZZZUSA
SELMER, EMIL	33	M	MCHT	PLZZZZUSA
MARIE	26	F	W	PLZZZZUSA
DUDECK, REGINE	50	F	WO	PLZZZZUSA
WLADISLAWA	8	M	CHILD	PLZZZZUSA
JULIANE	7	F	CHILD	PLZZZZUSA
BROZINSKI, JANOS	25	M	LABR	PLZZZZUSA
LUDWIKA	25	F	W	PLZZZZUSA
PETRONELLA	.09	F	INFANT	PLZZZZUSA
TENNSACZ, TEOFIL	47	M	LABR	RRZZZZUSA
JOSEF	8	M	CHILD	RRZZZZUSA
KALMORSKI, JAC.	28	M	LABR	RRZZZZUSA
KURTINEITS, KARL	33	M	LABR	RRZZZZUSA
WAWIKATSCH, VINC.	23	M	LABR	RRZZZZUSA
MILEWITSCH, VINC.	25	M	LABR	RRZZZZUSA
MIKOLEWITZ, HIPPOLYT	27	M	LABR	RRZZZZUSA

SHIP: HELVETIA

FROM: LIVERPOOL AND QUEENSTOWN
TO: NEW YORK
ARRIVED: 14 MAY 1883

PASSENGER	AGE	SEX	OCCUPATION	PV RI VL / DES
KRELLIKTER, MATTHEW	20	M	LABR	RRZZZZUSA
KALLYONHLI, ISAK	31	M	LABR	RRZZZZUSA
KEMPENEN, MATTS.	25	M	LABR	RRZZZZUSA
LEIKO, JOHAN	30	M	LABR	RRZZZZUSA
HANISKASKI, ISAK	33	M	LABR	RRZZZZUSA
MLILUWAKA, JOHAN	36	M	LABR	RRZZZZUSA
D--HARE, JACOB	28	M	LABR	RRZZZZUSA
WALLI, --IAS	32	M	LABR	RRZZZZUSA
LOULLI, GUS.	46	M	LABR	RRZZZZUSA
HALLAMAKI, GUS.	36	M	LABR	RRZZZZUSA
SCHIWERSTEFF, ETIENE	34	M	LABR	RRZZZZUSA

SHIP: SILESIA

FROM: HAMBURG AND HAVRE
TO: NEW YORK
ARRIVED: 14 MAY 1883

PASSENGER	AGE	SEX	OCCUPATION	PV RI VL / DES
DANGELOWICZ, JULIANE	18	F	SGL	RRZZZZUSA
MANTHEY, CHRIST.	23	M	LABR	RRZZZZUSA
DANIELOWITZ, JAN	24	M	LABR	RRZZZZUSA
DICEPIC, WLADISLAW	18	M	LABR	RRZZZZUSA
VICTOROVIC, ANNA	21	F	SGL	RRZZZZUSA
SAKEVIC, ADAM	34	M	LABR	RRZZZZUSA
ANTROVICZ, JERZI	21	M	LABR	RRZZZZUSA

PASSENGER	AGE	SEX	OCCUPATION	PRV VIL DES
STADULSKA, ANTONIE	23	F	W	RRZZZZUSA
PETRUS	8	M	CHILD	RRZZZZUSA
JAN	3	M	CHILD	RRZZZZUSA
JAN	.11	M	INFANT	RRZZZZUSA
GANS, JAN	19	M	LABR	RRZZZZUSA
BORT, MARTEL	18	M	LABR	RRZZZZUSA
SLOCK, MICHEL	23	M	LABR	RRZZZZUSA
SKUNDA, JAN	25	M	LABR	RRZZZZUSA
GALIZKY, OSOF	20	M	LABR	RRZZZZUSA
IVANOWICKY, CASIM.	21	M	LABR	RRZZZZUSA
PODZON, STANISLAUS	27	M	LABR	PLZZZZUSA
CATHA.	24	F	W	PLZZZZUSA
SUMIK, GRAZUL	20	M	LABR	PLZZZZUSA
SMITH, MICHAEL	20	M	LABR	RRZZZZUSA
KOWALEWSKI, STEFAN	23	M	LABR	RRZZZZUSA
MATKOWSKY, SZYMON	33	M	LABR	RRZZZZUSA
PODGEISKY, PAWEL	28	M	LABR	RRZZZZUSA

SHIP: ETHIOPIA

FROM: GLASGOW AND MOVILLE
TO: NEW YORK
ARRIVED: 16 MAY 1883

PASSENGER	AGE	SEX	OCCUPATION	PRV VIL DES
SMITH, SAMUEL	33	M	PDLR	PLZZZZUSA
PYHALATI, ANDERS-E.	24	M	LABR	FNZZZZUSA
HENDRICKSEN, CARL	35	M	LABR	FNZZZZUSA
JAKKALA, ANDERS-A.	50	M	JNR	FNZZZZUSA
BENGO, JACOB	25	M	LABR	FNZZZZUSA
HIRKKALA, JOHAN	27	M	LABR	FNZZZZUSA
MARIA	18	F	HP	FNZZZZUSA
KATTILLA, LINA-K.	23	F	HP	FNZZZZUSA

SHIP: EGYPTIAN MONARCH

FROM: LONDON
TO: NEW YORK
ARRIVED: 19 MAY 1883

PASSENGER	AGE	SEX	OCCUPATION	PRV VIL DES
OLINSKI, DAVID	4	M	CHILD	PLZZZZNY

SHIP: NECKAR

FROM: BREMEN
TO: NEW YORK
ARRIVED: 19 MAY 1883

PASSENGER	AGE	SEX	OCCUPATION	PRV VIL DES
RUDZEKOWA, LUDW.	22	F	NN	RRZZZZUSA
GABRIS, JUSTINE	22	F	NN	RRZZZZUSA
GRUDZINSKI, JOS.	36	M	LABR	RRZZZZUSA

SHIP: RHYNLAND

FROM: ANTWERP
TO: NEW YORK
ARRIVED: 19 MAY 1883

PASSENGER	AGE	SEX	OCCUPATION	PRV VIL DES
VONRAMATOWSKY, FRZ.	18	M	PNTR	PLZZZZNY
BUBOWSKA, CATH.	20	F	SVNT	PLZZZZPHI
PAWELSKI, EMILIE	20	F	SVNT	PLZZZZUNK
INLOWSKY, CLARA	29	F	SVNT	PLZZZZNY
CARL	8	M	CHILD	PLZZZZNY
PAUL	.06	M	INFANT	PLZZZZNY
ANNA	4	F	CHILD	PLZZZZNY
MATHILDE	2	F	CHILD	PLZZZZNY
ANNA	60	F	UNKNOWN	PLZZZZNY
GOMBREWISKI, LEONT.	22	F	BCHR	PLZZZZNY
MOTINSKA, MAG.	27	M	CK	PLZZZZNY
JULIA	3	F	CHILD	PLZZZZNY
WLADISLAW	4	M	CHILD	PLZZZZNY
JOHANN	.09	M	INFANT	PLZZZZNY
FIRKA, JADINIKA	28	F	CK	PLZZZZNY
JOSEPH	4	M	CHILD	PLZZZZNY
JOSEPHA	.05	F	INFANT	PLZZZZNY
KODENSKA, JOHANNA	20	F	CK	PLZZZZNY
ANTON	3	M	CHILD	PLZZZZNY
SCHEWAKOWSKI, JOS.	17	M	FARMER	PLZZZZNY

SHIP: GERMANIC

FROM: LIVERPOOL AND QUEENSTOWN
TO: NEW YORK
ARRIVED: 21 MAY 1883

PASSENGER	AGE	SEX	OCCUPATION	PRV VIL DES
LONAKE, J.J.	24	M	LABR	PLZZZZUSA
KOSKI, J.J.	26	M	LABR	PLZZZZUSA
AMALA, J.J.	34	M	LABR	PLZZZZUSA
KOSALA, J.P.	21	M	LABR	PLZZZZUSA
KORION, ANDRUS	40	M	LABR	PLZZZZUSA
WORGELIC, P.P.	32	M	LABR	PLZZZZUSA
PAKO, P.S.	34	M	LABR	PLZZZZUSA
SORKHAMPKI, J.H.	26	M	LABR	PLZZZZUSA

SHIP: BOTHNIA

FROM: LIVERPOOL AND QUEENSTOWN
TO: NEW YORK
ARRIVED: 23 MAY 1883

PASSENGER	AGE	SEX	OCCUPATION	PRV VIL DES
WAZBONSKI, FRANS	30	M	LABR	PLZZZZUSA
WITBONSKI, J.MR	50	M	MCHT	PLZZZZUSA

SHIP: CALIFORNIA

FROM: HAMBURG
TO: NEW YORK,
ARRIVED: 23 MAY 1883

PASSENGER	AGE	SEX	OCCUPATION	PRV VIL DES
PETERSEN, MATHILDE	18	F	SGL	RRZZZZUSA
SIMOW, SIEGFRIED	16	M	LABR	RRZZZZUSA

PASSENGER	AGE	SEX	OCCUPATION	PRV VIL DES
BARTH, FRIEDA	8	F	CHILD	PLZZZZUSA
JAGILSKI, MARIE	45	F	SGL	RRZZZZUSA
GRUENBAUM, HERMANN	24	M	LABR	PLZZZZUSA
SALI	23	F	W	PLZZZZUSA
MORITZ	.07	M	INFANT	PLZZZZUSA
CYYMANN, CHRIST	46	M	LABR	RRZZZZUSA
CAROLINE	44	F	WO	RRZZZZUSA
SAMLEWITZ, ABRAM	8	M	CHILD	RRZZZZUSA
ISAAK	7	M	CHILD	RRZZZZUSA
JIKANOWITZ, ANTON	48	M	TRDSMN	RRZZZZUSA
SILBER, CHASIN	00	M	TDR	PLZZZZUSA
SABULEWSKI, ROSELIE	24	F	W	RRZZZZUSA
MARIE	9	F	CHILD	RRZZZZUSA
WEINFELD, HANNI	21	F	WO	RRZZZZUSA
ETTEL	6	F	CHILD	RRZZZZUSA
MAISCHEWITZ, CASIMIR	29	M	SMH	RRZZZZUSA
DRESCHER, JULIUS	21	M	UNKNOWN	RRZZZZUSA
WOEZELWISCH, MICHEL	39	M	UNKNOWN	RRZZZZUSA

SHIP: FRANCE

FROM: HAVRE
TO: NEW YORK
ARRIVED: 23 MAY 1883

PASSENGER	AGE	SEX	OCCUPATION	PRV VIL DES
JABRONOWSKI, ABBE	54	M	CUR	PLZZZZNY
PAESMARENS, BENJAMIN	40	M	TLR	RRZZZZNY
CHARIPA, SIMON	22	M	UNKNOWN	RRZZZZNY
MARIE	20	F	UNKNOWN	RRZZZZNY
ROSEMBERG, MOREL	22	M	FARMER	RRZZZZNY
STRATOWSKI, HENRI	21	M	UNKNOWN	RRZZZZNY
PRINZ, SALOMON	16	M	UNKNOWN	RRZZZZNY
ARON	12	M	UNKNOWN	RRZZZZNY

SHIP: HOHENZOLLERN

FROM: BREMEN
TO: NEW YORK
ARRIVED: 23 MAY 1883

PASSENGER	AGE	SEX	OCCUPATION	PRV VIL DES
KAMNISKI, CARL	20	M	FARMER	RRZZZZUSA
PLUSZINSKY, AUGUST	40	M	LABR	RRZZZZUSA
VALENTIN	43	M	LABR	RRZZZZUSA
WILIZEWSKI, MICHAEL	32	M	LABR	RRZZZZUSA
FEIGE, GUSTAV	26	M	LABR	RRZZZZUSA

SHIP: PENNLAND

FROM: ANTWERP
TO: NEW YORK
ARRIVED: 23 MAY 1883

PASSENGER	AGE	SEX	OCCUPATION	PRV VIL DES
KARPUS, WINCAS	21	M	LABR	RRZZZZUNK
LEIZOL, C.	19	M	BCHR	RRZZZZUNK

SHIP: WIELAND

FROM: HAMBURG
TO: NEW YORK
ARRIVED: 23 MAY 1883

PASSENGER	AGE	SEX	OCCUPATION	PRV VIL DES
ISRAEL, ELIAS	26	M	BKR	RRZZZZUSA
BATAVID, MARCUS	30	M	MCHT	RRZZZZUSA
AMALIE	26	F	W	RRZZZZUSA
BERNHD.	9	M	CHILD	RRZZZZUSA
AGATIN, LYDIA	16	F	SGL	RRZZZZUSA
ARCADIUS	14	M	LABR	RRZZZZUSA
SZAJINOWIEZ, ISRAEL	18	M	CL	RRZZZZUSA

SHIP: ASSYRIAN MONARCH

FROM: LONDON
TO: NEW YORK
ARRIVED: 24 MAY 1883

PASSENGER	AGE	SEX	OCCUPATION	PRV VIL DES
BORTFOSHUNSKY, SIMON	18	M	LABR	PLZZZZUSA

SHIP: STATE OF GEORGIA

FROM: GLASGOW AND LARNE
TO: NEW YORK
ARRIVED: 24 MAY 1883

PASSENGER	AGE	SEX	OCCUPATION	PRV VIL DES
WILENSKY, LOUISA	23	M	WCHMKR	RRZZZZUSA
KOSBILIK, JOHAN	32	M	LABR	RRZZZZUSA
KANNENGUEISER, SALKE	40	M	LABR	RRZZZZUSA
MENDEL	16	M	LABR	RRZZZZUSA
IDES	41	F	W	RRZZZZUSA
NUSON	12	M	CH	RRZZZZUSA
BARASCH	8	M	CHILD	RRZZZZUSA
ROSE	8	F	CHILD	RRZZZZUSA
ELLI	1	F	CHILD	RRZZZZUSA
GLUCKLISCH, MOSES	24	M	LABR	RRZZZZUSA
FUCK, MEYER	26	M	LABR	RRZZZZUSA
GUMBAUM, JOS.	30	M	LABR	RRZZZZUSA
BERGER, JAN	25	M	LABR	RRZZZZUSA
PEPPI	20	F	W	RRZZZZUSA
AROSTER, LEO	10	M	CH	RRZZZZUSA
POLACYCK, MORITZ	30	M	PDLR	RRZZZZUSA
KOLNID, JANOS	30	M	PDLR	RRZZZZUSA
GEIGER, MARIE	20	F	DMS	RRZZZZUSA
DEMKO, ELIZ.	28	F	DMS	RRZZZZUSA
SCOTS, ANNA	30	F	W	RRZZZZUSA
ANNA	7	F	CHILD	RRZZZZUSA
AGNES	2	F	CHILD	RRZZZZUSA
JUDICSAK, SOPHIE	30	F	W	RRZZZZUSA
CLARA	6	F	CHILD	RRZZZZUSA
SCHIFF--, JOSEPH	39	M	LABR	RRZZZZUSA
KAUFMANN, PRICHES	43	M	LABR	RRZZZZUSA
ELKE	45	F	W	RRZZZZUSA
PEISCH	11	F	CH	RRZZZZUSA
CHAIM	8	M	CHILD	RRZZZZUSA
GOTTHEL, WILHELM	23	M	PDLR	RRZZZZUSA
DER--, JOHANN	25	M	PDLR	RRZZZZUSA

SHIP: ODER

FROM: BREMEN AND SOUTHAMPTON
TO: NEW YORK
ARRIVED: 25 MAY 1883

PASSENGER	AGE	SEX	OCCUPATION	PRV VIL DES
KOSENSKI, STANISLAS	30	M	FARMER	RRZZZZUSA
STANKIEWITZ, FRANZ	26	M	LABR	RRZZZZUSA
MICHALSKI, JOSEPH	23	M	MLR	RRZZZZUSA
STANKIEWICZ, FRZ.	26	M	MCHT	RRZZZZUSA

SHIP: LYDIAN MONARCH

FROM: LONDON
TO: NEW YORK
ARRIVED: 29 MAY 1883

PASSENGER	AGE	SEX	OCCUPATION	PRV VIL DES
SILVERMAN, FANNY	30	F	UNKNOWN	RRZZZZNY
REBECCA	5	F	CHILD	RRZZZZNY
ANNIE	2	F	CHILD	RRZZZZNY
LEAH	1	M	CHILD	RRZZZZNY
JASCPLE, JORSCPTO	29	M	CGRMKR	RRZZZZNY
JULIA	20	F	UNKNOWN	RRZZZZNY
SYMONS, SARAH	34	F	UNKNOWN	RRZZZZNY
SAMUEL	8	M	CHILD	RRZZZZNY
ABRAHAM	4	M	CHILD	RRZZZZNY
RACHEL	4	F	CHILD	RRZZZZNY
SOPHIA	4	F	CHILD	RRZZZZNY
MORRIS	1	M	CHILD	RRZZZZNY
HYMANN, HARRIS	28	M	HTR	PLZZZZNY
SARAH	29	F	UNKNOWN	PLZZZZNY
SAMUEL	3	M	CHILD	PLZZZZNY
ISAAC	1	M	CHILD	PLZZZZNY
COHEN, RACHEL	33	F	UNKNOWN	PLZZZZNY
ESTHER	8	F	CHILD	PLZZZZNY
MENDE	4	M	CHILD	PLZZZZNY
SARAH	5	F	CHILD	PLZZZZNY

SHIP: PAVONIA

FROM: LIVERPOOL AND QUEENSTOWN
TO: NEW YORK
ARRIVED: 30 MAY 1883

PASSENGER	AGE	SEX	OCCUPATION	PRV VIL DES
BALA, GEORGE	33	M	LABR	PLZZZZUSA
ANNA	26	F	MA	PLZZZZUSA
JANKS	.04	M	INFANT	PLZZZZUSA
JOHAN	10	M	UNKNOWN	PLZZZZUSA
DUNKE, STEFAN	34	M	LABR	PLZZZZUSA
BALI, JANAS	26	M	UNKNOWN	PLZZZZUSA
LETZON, JANAS	35	M	UNKNOWN	PLZZZZUSA
DAVIDSON, JOSEF	11	M	CH	PLZZZZUSA
NALEPA, JANOS	39	M	LABR	PLZZZZUSA
ORLA, NUHAL	36	M	UNKNOWN	PLZZZZUSA
FARKOS, JOSEF	38	M	UNKNOWN	PLZZZZUSA
PARSCHUK, PAUL	11	M	CH	PLZZZZUSA
HURBASC, WENDELIN	42	M	LABR	PLZZZZUSA
ANNA	35	F	MA	PLZZZZUSA
ANNA	5	F	CHILD	PLZZZZUSA
LATZEH	.11	F	INFANT	PLZZZZUSA
JULIE	.11	F	INFANT	PLZZZZUSA

SHIP: STATE OF NEBRASKA

FROM: GLASGOW
TO: NEW YORK
ARRIVED: 31 MAY 1883

PASSENGER	AGE	SEX	OCCUPATION	PRV VIL DES
KATZ, M.	26	M	LABR	PLZZZZUSA
SIMON	18	M	UNKNOWN	PLZZZZUSA
MANN, A.	24	M	PDLR	PLZZZZUSA
SENDIK, I.	24	M	UNKNOWN	PLZZZZUSA
KERN, S.	34	M	UNKNOWN	PLZZZZUSA
COHN, S.	24	M	UNKNOWN	PLZZZZUSA
KREILONSTEIN, B.	22	M	UNKNOWN	PLZZZZUSA
SEFKA, W.	29	M	UNKNOWN	PLZZZZUSA
DUVORSKA, E.	24	M	UNKNOWN	PLZZZZUSA
SAMUEL, F.	17	M	CH	PLZZZZUSA
DAVID, S.	15	M	PDLR	PLZZZZUSA
SCHRAZOWSKY, E.	44	M	PDLR	PLZZZZUSA
LEWIN, S.	16	M	UNKNOWN	PLZZZZUSA
FILEKAMSKI, C.	34	M	UNKNOWN	PLZZZZUSA
BENJAMIN	10	M	CH	PLZZZZUSA
BLOCK, I.	18	M	PDLR	PLZZZZUSA
MEDWICK, H.	20	M	PDLR	PLZZZZUSA
RAGONE, I.	20	M	UNKNOWN	PLZZZZUSA
ALLISCHEWITZ, L.	25	M	UNKNOWN	PLZZZZUSA
STOLEJASKA, I.	18	M	UNKNOWN	PLZZZZUSA
BRIKER, M.	25	M	UNKNOWN	PLZZZZUSA
BRUDERMANN, T.	20	M	UNKNOWN	PLZZZZUSA
REUBEN, I.	21	M	UNKNOWN	PLZZZZUSA
ASCHROD, I.	18	M	UNKNOWN	PLZZZZUSA
GRIBRANSKY, M.	45	M	PDLR	PLZZZZUSA
SVIE, M.	25	M	PDLR	PLZZZZUSA
LAMPSRIL, I.	25	M	UNKNOWN	PLZZZZUSA
DRESER, C.	60	M	PDLR	PLZZZZUSA
RABENSTEIN, E.	24	M	PDLR	PLZZZZUSA
TROMMER, I.	35	M	UNKNOWN	PLZZZZUSA
SCHER, S.	18	M	UNKNOWN	PLZZZZUSA
ROSE, S.	19	M	UNKNOWN	PLZZZZUSA
ORZEWSKY, A.	25	M	UNKNOWN	PLZZZZUSA
KWZUWANSKI, N.	36	M	LABR	PLZZZZUSA

SHIP: SUEVIA

FROM: HAMBURG
TO: NEW YORK
ARRIVED: 31 MAY 1883

PASSENGER	AGE	SEX	OCCUPATION	PRV VIL DES
SCHNEPISKY, BERIL	20	F	UNKNOWN	RRZZZZUSA
MER---, STANISLAW	00	M	LABR	RRZZZZUSA
KORU--, MARIE	19	F	SGL	RRZZZZUSA
KONUESARSKI, RACHEL	17	F	SGL	RRZZZZUSA
AUGUSTOWSKY, RACHEL	47	F	W	RRZZZZUSA
ZAELEL	.11	F	INFANT	RRZZZZUSA
LEIB	.01	M	INFANT	RRZZZZUSA
GARFUNFEL, REBECCA	18	F	SGL	RRZZZZUSA
WEIN, HENE	32	F	W	RRZZZZUSA
JANKEL	8	M	CHILD	RRZZZZUSA
SARA	6	F	CHILD	RRZZZZUSA
RACHEL	5	F	CHILD	RRZZZZUSA
JETTE	3	F	CHILD	RRZZZZUSA
GUMBINER, LIUBA	20	F	SGL	RRZZZZUSA
JACOB	8	M	CHILD	RRZZZZUSA
MISKIN, OSKAR	7	M	CHILD	RRZZZZUSA
KOWINSKI, MOSES	38	M	FARMER	RRZZZZUSA
JEGLINIKOWSKI, JUDEL	17	M	UNKNOWN	RRZZZZUSA
SCHNEPISKY, ROSA	21	F	SGL	RRZZZZUSA
SLIZEVSKY, VAOVINZE	40	M	LABR	RRZZZZUSA
BOKSA, ANTON	28	M	UNKNOWN	RRZZZZUSA
LISKEVIE, MARTIN	19	M	UNKNOWN	RRZZZZUSA

PASSENGER	AGE	SEX	OCCUPATION	PV D / RI E / VL S
POTOCKY, ANDR.	20	M	UNKNOWN	RRZZZZUSA
DAVID, FRANZ	30	M	UNKNOWN	RRZZZZUSA
ZONAS, TOMAS	25	M	UNKNOWN	RRZZZZUSA
MAZURKEVIL, BARTH.	25	M	UNKNOWN	RRZZZZUSA
ANNA	25	F	W	RRZZZZUSA
JENCEVIE, VINCENT	24	M	LABR	RRZZZZUSA
DERESKEVIE, ANDRE	25	M	UNKNOWN	RRZZZZUSA
KRAKENIE, SIMON	23	M	UNKNOWN	RRZZZZUSA
RUSKEVIE, CASIMIR	28	M	LABR	RRZZZZUSA
ANDREI	24	M	UNKNOWN	RRZZZZUSA
PETER	18	M	UNKNOWN	RRZZZZUSA
WINCE, KOLAR	38	M	UNKNOWN	RRZZZZUSA
ANDREKUS, MATH.	32	M	LABR	RRZZZZUSA
MUELER, VICTORIA	39	F	W	RRZZZZUSA
LOEFFLER, KARL	35	M	LABR	RRZZZZUSA
SCHULTZ, ADOLPH	50	M	LABR	RRZZZZUSA
HENNRICH, JACOB	18	M	UNKNOWN	RRZZZZUSA
MUELLER, LUDWIG	38	M	SDLR	RRZZZZUSA
FLOCKEN, ALBERT	36	M	FARMER	RRZZZZUSA
MENDE, HEINR.	22	M	LABR	RRZZZZUSA
HAMSNER, HUGO	16	M	UNKNOWN	RRZZZZUSA
FISCHER, SAMUEL	8	M	CHILD	RRZZZZUSA
KARPOW, JOH.	40	M	LABR	RRZZZZUSA

SHIP: CITY OF ROME

FROM: LIVERPOOL
TO: NEW YORK
ARRIVED: 01 JUNE 1883

PASSENGER	AGE	SEX	OCCUPATION	PV D / RI E / VL S
ZECH, JOSEFA	40	F	MA	PLZZZZUSA
JOSEFA	12	F	NN	PLZZZZUSA
URANIA	4	M	CHILD	PLZZZZUSA
PETER	.04	M	INFANT	PLZZZZUSA
KLACK, WILHELM	41	M	LABR	PLZZZZUSA
FLORENTINE	28	F	W	PLZZZZUSA
PAULINE	6	F	CHILD	PLZZZZUSA
MICHAEL	3	M	CHILD	PLZZZZUSA
LEON	.06	M	INFANT	PLZZZZUSA
XESYOPOLSKI, ADELBERT	50	M	LABR	PLZZZZUSA
MARY-ANN	50	F	MA	PLZZZZUSA
ANNA	19	M	LABR	PLZZZZUSA

SHIP: DE RUYTER

FROM: ANTWERP
TO: NEW YORK
ARRIVED: 01 JUNE 1883

PASSENGER	AGE	SEX	OCCUPATION	PV D / RI E / VL S
SCHUCHIN, JOH.	62	M	FARMER	RRZZZZUSA
WISLER, WINZES	33	M	UNKNOWN	RRZZZZUSA
SCHULZ, WILHELM	37	M	PNR	RRZZZZUSA
LEIBER, GATZ.	56	M	TLR	RRZZZZUSA
LEWIN, LEIBE	45	M	LABR	RRZZZZUSA
DARSCHKE, ANSCHEL	22	M	UNKNOWN	RRZZZZUSA

SHIP: GEISER

FROM: COPENHAGEN
TO: NEW YORK
ARRIVED: 02 JUNE 1883

PASSENGER	AGE	SEX	OCCUPATION	PV D / RI E / VL S
KAUEFFMANN, KURT	22	M	FARMER	RRZZZZUSA

SHIP: CITY OF PARIS

FROM: LIVERPOOL AND QUEENSTOWN
TO: NEW YORK
ARRIVED: 04 JUNE 1883

PASSENGER	AGE	SEX	OCCUPATION	PV D / RI E / VL S
JOHNSON, OTTO-S.	25	M	LABR	FNZZZZUSA

SHIP: BOHEMIA

FROM: HAMBURG AND HAVRE
TO: NEW YORK
ARRIVED: 05 JUNE 1883

PASSENGER	AGE	SEX	OCCUPATION	PV D / RI E / VL S
ZADURSKY, WLADIMIR	22	M	UNKNOWN	RRZZZZUSA
GRODSKOWSKY, GITTEL	30	F	SGL	RRZZZZUSA
STEINBERG, ROESSEL	22	F	W	RRZZZZUSA
JACOB	.06	M	INFANT	RRZZZZUSA
LINKEWICZ, THERESE	18	F	SGL	RRZZZZUSA
ROSENBAUM, JACOB	37	M	LABR	RRZZZZUSA
LEISSER	9	M	CHILD	RRZZZZUSA
CHEIM	8	M	CHILD	RRZZZZUSA
LEA	6	F	CHILD	RRZZZZUSA
CHASCHE	4	F	CHILD	RRZZZZUSA
EVERSKA, SELIG	37	M	DLR	RRZZZZUSA
KANEL, WALF	35	M	UNKNOWN	RRZZZZUSA
WEISS, ROSA	50	F	W	RRZZZZUSA
BERTHA	18	F	D	RRZZZZUSA
PISKIN, JANTEL	40	M	UNKNOWN	RRZZZZUSA
GALD, LINE	20	F	SGL	RRZZZZUSA
GALDBERGER, HANNE	18	F	UNKNOWN	RRZZZZUSA
GABARSKY, SALTIEL	19	M	TLR	RRZZZZUSA
TRAINE	21	F	W	RRZZZZUSA
ALTMANN, ETTEL	28	F	W	RRZZZZUSA
RUBEN	7	M	CHILD	RRZZZZUSA
RICOKE	.11	M	INFANT	RRZZZZUSA
HINDE	.01	F	INFANT	RRZZZZUSA
GEISLER, ABRAHAM	15	M	LABR	RRZZZZUSA
GOLDSCHMIDT, ADA	22	F	SGL	RRZZZZUSA
ITZIG, DAVID	25	M	TLR	RRZZZZUSA
YODES, WOLF	32	M	UNKNOWN	RRZZZZUSA
LEWITA, CHAIME	28	F	SGL	RRZZZZUSA
SARA	20	F	UNKNOWN	RRZZZZUSA
PALEWSKY, ALTER	26	F	UNKNOWN	RRZZZZUSA
WJORST, HILLEL	33	M	LABR	RRZZZZUSA
MOSES	36	M	UNKNOWN	RRZZZZUSA
PISIK, MEYER	43	M	UNKNOWN	RRZZZZUSA
ON, NACHEM	17	M	UNKNOWN	RRZZZZUSA
LANFER, BERNHARR	28	M	UNKNOWN	RRZZZZUSA
FEIN, RUBIN	19	M	CGRMKR	RRZZZZUSA
FISCHER, LEIB	40	M	DLR	RRZZZZUSA
JASINOWSKA, ZOLLEL	9	M	CHILD	RRZZZZUSA
ZAKASAI, LEISSER	37	M	TLR	RRZZZZUSA
CHAIM	9	M	CHILD	RRZZZZUSA
ELSAN, ISE	65	F	W	RRZZZZUSA
KLOPER, ELIAS	18	M	DLR	RRZZZZUSA

PASSENGER	AGE	SEX	OCCUPATION	PRV	VIL	DES
GOLDSCHMIDT, ZLATE	30	F	W	RR	ZZZZ	USA
ETKOWSKY, MENASCHE	53	M	TLR	RR	ZZZZ	USA
CHANNE	17	F	W	RR	ZZZZ	USA
LUDWIN, JANKEL	19	M	DLR	RR	ZZZZ	USA
SAKOWSKI, MOSES	18	M	UNKNOWN	RR	ZZZZ	USA
ZIBULARSCH, HERSCHEL	21	M	TLR	RR	ZZZZ	USA
SLOMINSKY, JACOB	14	M	UNKNOWN	RR	ZZZZ	USA
WELLER, ISAAC	17	M	JNR	RR	ZZZZ	USA
HIRSHBERG, SALOMON	9	M	CHILD	RR	ZZZZ	USA
FEIERMANN, JOSSEL	17	M	DLR	RR	ZZZZ	USA
BERLINSKY, MORDCHE	17	M	TLR	RR	ZZZZ	USA
MARKEWITZ, SIMON	25	M	UNKNOWN	RR	ZZZZ	USA
SCHAPIRA, SCHEPSEL	34	M	SMH	RR	ZZZZ	USA
ZEPKA, MARIANE	36	F	W	RR	ZZZZ	USA
ANNA	.11	F	INFANT	RR	ZZZZ	USA
KITTEL, WILH.	33	M	WVR	RR	ZZZZ	USA
GRONAU, FRANZ	25	M	SHMK	RR	ZZZZ	USA
PAULINE	24	F	W	RR	ZZZZ	USA
OWOTZKY, FRANZ	24	M	LABR	RR	ZZZZ	USA
SABOZINSKY, MATHS.	23	M	UNKNOWN	RR	ZZZZ	USA
CERZESKY, WOICZIK	18	M	UNKNOWN	RR	ZZZZ	USA
STADTSINGER, MENDEL	17	M	CGRMKR	RR	ZZZZ	USA
POCH, LORANZ	34	F	LABR	RR	ZZZZ	USA
SAUK, KAZIMIR	25	M	LABR	RR	ZZZZ	USA
DACH, IVAN	27	M	UNKNOWN	RR	ZZZZ	USA
BALTROSCHAJT, WILEM	30	M	UNKNOWN	RR	ZZZZ	USA
LIPSCHONSKY, ABRAHAM	20	M	LABR	RR	ZZZZ	USA
HENNY	26	F	W	RR	ZZZZ	USA
ALY	.06	M	INFANT	RR	ZZZZ	USA
BAUMGART, JOHAIM	26	M	LABR	RR	ZZZZ	USA
EMILIE	21	F	W	RR	ZZZZ	USA
FRIED, ISRAEL	24	M	TNR	RR	ZZZZ	USA
REIBSTEIN, LUSCHE	50	M	TLR	RR	ZZZZ	USA
GETZ, GELE	17	F	SGL	RR	ZZZZ	USA
KAPLAN, MART	50	M	LABR	RR	ZZZZ	USA
JECKEL	9	M	CHILD	RR	ZZZZ	USA
LICHTENSTEIN, ISAAC	26	M	DLR	RR	ZZZZ	USA
MATZEJWSKI, CASIMIR	44	M	LABR	RR	ZZZZ	USA
ZEGLETZKY, JOSEF	30	M	UNKNOWN	RR	ZZZZ	USA
SIKORSKY, PETER	23	M	LABR	RR	ZZZZ	USA
SLAVICKY, JOSEF	20	M	UNKNOWN	RR	ZZZZ	USA
MAGDA.	22	F	W	RR	ZZZZ	USA
BOGDANOWIC, JAN	27	M	LABR	RR	ZZZZ	USA
IWANOWSKY, HIERONYMUS	36	M	LKSH	RR	ZZZZ	USA
JANOW, ANDR.	20	M	LABR	RR	ZZZZ	USA
SOBEL, VICTOR	43	M	TLR	RR	ZZZZ	USA
RABSTEIN, VICTOR	45	M	UNKNOWN	RR	ZZZZ	USA
HERZIG, CHEIM	24	M	TLR	RR	ZZZZ	USA
SIEF, LEA	50	F	W	RR	ZZZZ	USA
REBECCA	18	F	SGL	RR	ZZZZ	USA
MUENZ, IDA	23	F	SGL	RR	ZZZZ	USA
LEVIN, MARKE	18	F	SGL	RR	ZZZZ	USA
BRANNER, LOEB	16	M	MCHT	RR	ZZZZ	USA
JOSKOWITZ, MEYER	25	M	LABR	RR	ZZZZ	USA
BALTOVSAJTIS, ANDRY	25	M	LABR	RR	ZZZZ	USA
SACKAVTY, JORGIS	26	M	UNKNOWN	RR	ZZZZ	USA
JAKUCVIE, JOSEF	24	M	UNKNOWN	RR	ZZZZ	USA
ROMONOWSKY, JOSEF	26	M	UNKNOWN	RR	ZZZZ	USA
EDELSTEIN, MARIE	9	F	CHILD	RR	ZZZZ	USA

SHIP: HAMMONIA

FROM: HAMBURG
TO: NEW YORK
ARRIVED: 05 JUNE 1883

PASSENGER	AGE	SEX	OCCUPATION	PRV	VIL	DES
BOHM, SALOMON	21	M	SHMK	RR	ZZZZ	USA
WROCZYNSKI, SIMON	30	M	LABR	RR	ZZZZ	USA
JOS.	24	M	LABR	RR	ZZZZ	USA
ROSALIE	24	F	W	RR	ZZZZ	USA
ANTON	.11	M	INFANT	RR	ZZZZ	USA
KOPNER, FRANZISKA	29	F	W	RR	ZZZZ	USA
CARL	7	M	CHILD	RR	ZZZZ	USA
MROCZYNSKY, AGNES.	30	F	W	RR	ZZZZ	USA
JOSEF	.10	M	INFANT	RR	ZZZZ	USA
ANTONIE	10	F	INF	RR	ZZZZ	USA
JILLES, EREN	38	M	BCHR	RR	ZZZZ	USA
LEIB	16	M	S	RR	ZZZZ	USA

SHIP: MAIN

FROM: BREMEN
TO: NEW YORK
ARRIVED: 05 JUNE 1883

PASSENGER	AGE	SEX	OCCUPATION	PRV	VIL	DES
LBIKOSKI, WLADISLAW	17	M	LABR	RR	ZZZZ	USA
URBANOWICZ, PETER	19	M	FARMER	RR	ZZZZ	USA

SHIP: SERVIA

FROM: LIVERPOOL
TO: NEW YORK
ARRIVED: 05 JUNE 1883

PASSENGER	AGE	SEX	OCCUPATION	PRV	VIL	DES
BORODIN, ANT.	36	M	ENGR	RR	ZZZZ	USA
DOLEOSANKE, ALEX	34	M	GENT	RR	ZZZZ	USA
PHILIPOFF, JOHN	14	M	STDNT	RR	ZZZZ	USA

SHIP: CITY OF PARA

FROM: PANAMA
TO: NEW YORK
ARRIVED: 06 JUNE 1883

PASSENGER	AGE	SEX	OCCUPATION	PRV	VIL	DES
FALANNSKIA, D.	42	M	UNKNOWN	PL	ZZZZ	USA
U-MRS	36	F	UNKNOWN	PL	ZZZZ	USA
U-MISS	7	F	CHILD	PL	ZZZZ	USA
U	5	M	CHILD	PL	ZZZZ	USA

SHIP: FRANCE

FROM: LONDON
TO: NEW YORK
ARRIVED: 06 JUNE 1883

PASSENGER	AGE	SEX	OCCUPATION	PRV	VIL	DES
FRUST, FRANTISCH	36	M	LABR	PL	ZZZZ	UNK
ANNA	29	F	W	PL	ZZZZ	UNK
ANNA	14	F	CH	PL	ZZZZ	UNK
EMILY	1	F	CHILD	PL	ZZZZ	UNK
RASPER, JOSEF	34	M	LABR	PL	ZZZZ	UNK
ANTONISS	47	M	LABR	PL	ZZZZ	UNK
DRAZIL, VINCENT	18	M	LABR	PL	ZZZZ	UNK
FRANTISK	9	M	CHILD	PL	ZZZZ	UNK
TERINZIE	25	F	SP	PL	ZZZZ	UNK

PASSENGER	AGE	SEX	OCCUPATION	PRIV	VIL	DES
SHIP: INDIA						
FROM: HAMBURG						
TO: NEW YORK						
ARRIVED: 06 JUNE 1883						
BENJAMINSOHN, WILF	23	M	MCHT	RR	ZZZZ	NY
JUHNOWICZ, GERSCH	23	M	TLR	RR	ZZZZ	NY
SIHIMM, CHAIM	19	M	CL	RR	ZZZZ	NY
STRENGER, MORITZ	25	M	GZR	RR	ZZZZ	NY
BURHOWITZ, HILLER	19	M	CPTR	RR	ZZZZ	NY
BLOCH, B.	24	M	CL	RR	ZZZZ	NY
CALL, MENDEL	63	M	TLR	RR	ZZZZ	NY
HUSCHOWITZ, MEYER	25	M	MLR	RR	ZZZZ	UNK
TROMME	18	F	W	RR	ZZZZ	UNK
BERGENBAUM, JAC.	29	M	BKBNDR	RR	ZZZZ	NY
LINK, JOSEF	28	M	GDSM	RR	ZZZZ	NY
LEIBOWITZ, ESLY	26	F	WO	RR	ZZZZ	NY
IGNATZ	00	M	S	RR	ZZZZ	NY
JUDA	.09	F	INFANT	RR	ZZZZ	NY
SOMMEROWITZ, JOS.	32	M	TRDSMN	RR	ZZZZ	NY
WEISS, HANNY	18	F	WO	RR	ZZZZ	NY
ABRAHAM	8	M	CHILD	RR	ZZZZ	NY
JUDA	3	F	CHILD	RR	ZZZZ	NY
ARONOWITZ, H.	16	F	SGL	RR	ZZZZ	NY
JURKOWITZ, M.	30	M	TRDSMN	RR	ZZZZ	NY
BESI	18	F	W	RR	ZZZZ	NY
DAWIDOWITZ, PEPY	18	F	SGL	RR	ZZZZ	NY
JANOSDI, HANDSCHE	34	M	TRDSMN	RR	ZZZZ	NY
LANDESMANN, ADOLF	17	M	TRDSMN	RR	ZZZZ	NY
FRIEDMANN, BEHR	54	M	TRDSMN	RR	ZZZZ	NY
FLACHSMANN, WOLF	17	M	TRDSMN	RR	ZZZZ	NY
SOLNITZKY, LEHAYE	19	M	TRDSMN	RR	ZZZZ	NY
LEWIN, SIMON	37	M	TRDSMN	RR	ZZZZ	NY
RUBENSTEIN, LECH.	25	F	WO	RR	ZZZZ	NY
TEGIMOSCHITZ, ENOCH	18	M	TRDSMN	RR	ZZZZ	NY
DOLMSHY, GEDALJE	49	M	TRDSMN	RR	ZZZZ	NY
KELEIN, MORITZ	41	M	TRDSMN	RR	ZZZZ	NY
REGU	38	F	W	RR	ZZZZ	NY
ROSEE	8	F	CHILD	RR	ZZZZ	NY
ADOLF	5	M	CHILD	RR	ZZZZ	NY
DAVID	6	M	CHILD	RR	ZZZZ	NY
JUDITH	4	F	CHILD	RR	ZZZZ	NY
ARON	.02	M	INFANT	RR	ZZZZ	NY
MEALY	.11	F	INFANT	RR	ZZZZ	NY
WERNER, LEIB	34	M	MCHT	RR	ZZZZ	NY
CHASON, JACOB	40	M	TNR	RR	ZZZZ	NY
IZIK	31	M	TNR	RR	ZZZZ	NY
OBRAMOWITZ, ISEK	26	M	SMH	RR	ZZZZ	NY
ALTTUEL, SIM.	18	M	SMH	RR	ZZZZ	NY
KLEIN, SCHLOME	28	M	SMH	RR	ZZZZ	NY
WEINER, S.	23	M	LABR	RR	ZZZZ	NY
CH--, MOSES	22	M	LABR	RR	ZZZZ	NY
SCHOFF, PAUL	26	M	LABR	RR	ZZZZ	NY
ELISABETH	21	F	W	RR	ZZZZ	NY
PAUL	.10	M	INFANT	RR	ZZZZ	NY
BROSOWSKI, M.	18	F	SGL	RR	ZZZZ	NY
FEIWEL	8	F	CHILD	RR	ZZZZ	NY
BRINOWITZ, ANTON	36	M	LABR	RR	ZZZZ	NY
HEN, ABR.	16	M	TNR	PL	ZZZZ	NY
FRIEDMANN, MOSES	34	M	TRDSMN	RR	ZZZZ	NY
KAREBELNIK, H.	21	M	TRDSMN	RR	ZZZZ	NY
FALIK, M.	16	M	TRDSMN	RR	ZZZZ	BAL
LURIS, BENJ.	84	M	TRDSMN	RR	ZZZZ	BAL
GRODNEIK, JUDEL	21	M	TRDSMN	RR	ZZZZ	NY
LUBASKI, CHANE	50	F	WO	RR	ZZZZ	NY
ESTER	17	F	WO	RR	ZZZZ	NY
ROSAZ, JAROS	24	M	LABR	RR	ZZZZ	NY
BENDRIK, VINCENT	21	M	LABR	RR	ZZZZ	NY
SEZNIZKI, JOS.	22	M	LABR	RR	ZZZZ	CH
ZIRC, LEA	20	F	WO	RR	ZZZZ	CH
FRIEDMANN, ISRAEL	22	M	TLR	RR	ZZZZ	NY
RANEL	20	F	W	RR	ZZZZ	NY
KLEIN, ALTER	32	M	LABR	PL	ZZZZ	NY
MICHAL, JANOS	21	M	CPTR	RR	ZZZZ	NY
DAVIDSOHN, LEIB	40	M	TRDSMN	RR	ZZZZ	NY
MERBER, CHAIM	15	M	CL	RR	ZZZZ	NY
BLOCH, ISRAEL	18	M	CL	RR	ZZZZ	NY
MOSCHKOWITZ, ROSI	8	F	CHILD	RR	ZZZZ	NY
STRUMPF, MOSES	18	M	LABR	RR	ZZZZ	NY
RAMH, SIFRA	20	F	WO	PL	ZZZZ	NY
RINOTA	.09	F	INFANT	PL	ZZZZ	NY
SEMMLER, ALEX	26	M	LABR	RR	ZZZZ	NY
GASS, HEINR.	24	M	LABR	RR	ZZZZ	NY
SWINTOI, JENDIES	26	M	LABR	PL	ZZZZ	CH
BARBARA	44	F	W	PL	ZZZZ	CH
EVA	8	F	CHILD	PL	ZZZZ	CH
AGNES	4	F	CHILD	PL	ZZZZ	CH
KOSTELESKI, JOHS.	37	M	LABR	PL	ZZZZ	NY
MUSKA, ANDR.	25	M	LABR	PL	ZZZZ	NY
TORBA, BLANISS	25	M	LABR	PL	ZZZZ	NY
KOHANN, STANISL.	24	M	LABR	PL	ZZZZ	NY
MAKOS, SLEMIS	34	M	LABR	PL	ZZZZ	NY
MOSKAL, ANTON	24	M	LABR	PL	ZZZZ	NY
ZUCKOWSKI, ANTON	27	M	LABR	RR	ZZZZ	NY
FELICIA	19	F	W	RR	ZZZZ	NY
MANDEL, LIEBE	8	F	CHILD	RR	ZZZZ	NY
MORRIS, U-MISS	50	F	WO	RR	ZZZZ	CAN
SCHAMPA, ARON	17	M	LABR	RR	ZZZZ	NY
LYIPMANN, JOS.	23	M	TLR	RR	ZZZZ	NY
ACHSELROTH, DAVID	21	M	TLR	RR	ZZZZ	NY
SLAKEWITZ, JACOB	23	M	TLR	RR	ZZZZ	NY
WOLOWITZ, MORTJE	22	M	TLR	RR	ZZZZ	NY
RAFALOWITZ, MOSES	21	M	TLR	RR	ZZZZ	NY
GORDON, SCHLEIME	36	F	WO	RR	ZZZZ	NY
JAFSKON, SCHINCE	28	M	SMH	RR	ZZZZ	NY
KOSCHINSKI, MORITZ	28	M	SMH	RR	ZZZZ	NY
HOBRANO, JURA	40	M	LABR	PL	ZZZZ	NY
BIALITZ, WILLIAM	18	M	LABR	PL	ZZZZ	NY
SHIP: WYOMING						
FROM: LIVERPOOL AND QUEENSTOWN						
TO: NEW YORK						
ARRIVED: 06 JUNE 1883						
DANIELSON, ANDERS	30	M	CBTMKR	FN	ZZZZ	USA
KRESTINE	49	F	W	FN	ZZZZ	USA
KERSTIN	18	F	SP	FN	ZZZZ	USA
PERDSON, HALMERS-M.	33	M	FARMER	FN	ZZZZ	USA
BRITTA	36	F	W	FN	ZZZZ	USA
PER	29	M	FARMER	FN	ZZZZ	USA
ANNA	10	F	CH	FN	ZZZZ	USA
ANDERS	8	M	CHILD	FN	ZZZZ	USA
CARL	3	M	CHILD	FN	ZZZZ	USA
AXEL	1	M	CHILD	FN	ZZZZ	USA
CUBLA, AUG.	26	M	LABR	FN	ZZZZ	USA
MOCK, JULIUN	21	M	UNKNOWN	FN	ZZZZ	USA
BRAZEL, JOHAN	27	M	UNKNOWN	FN	ZZZZ	USA
FRICK, BABETTI	30	F	SP	FN	ZZZZ	USA
HEDIGER, JOHAN	44	M	LABR	FN	ZZZZ	USA
FLEIG, MARIE	25	F	SP	FN	ZZZZ	USA
FORDEIA, MICHAEL	24	M	LABR	FN	ZZZZ	USA
PFIRMANN, FRANZ	25	M	LABR	FN	ZZZZ	USA

SHIP: STATE OF NEVADA

FROM: GLASGOW AND LARNE
TO: NEW YORK
ARRIVED: 08 JUNE 1883

PASSENGER	AGE	SEX	OCCUPATION	PRV VIL DES
TAUB, CHAIM	19	M	UNKNOWN	RRZZZZUSA
BASCHISTI, SAMUIL	39	M	MCHT	RRZZZZUSA
RUTIN, ARON	30	M	UNKNOWN	RRZZZZUSA
ISAACSOHN, JANKIL	36	M	UNKNOWN	RRZZZZUSA
ALPERNIN, ABRAHAM	33	M	UNKNOWN	RRZZZZUSA
SCHWAIG	20	F	W	RRZZZZUSA
ISRAEL	37	M	MCHT	RRZZZZUSA
SCHLASENE, SCHLOM	34	M	UNKNOWN	RRZZZZUSA
SCHPULAS, JUDEL	31	M	UNKNOWN	RRZZZZUSA
LAPUK, AREN	21	M	UNKNOWN	RRZZZZUSA
MORDICA	16	M	UNKNOWN	RRZZZZUSA
LAKS, LEIB	19	M	UNKNOWN	RRZZZZUSA
ABRAMOVITZ, BEHR.	32	M	MCHT	RRZZZZUSA
ELPERIN, SAMUEL	31	M	UNKNOWN	RRZZZZUSA
ALTERMANN, JOHAN	14	M	UNKNOWN	RRZZZZUSA
HAWAHB, ISAAC	16	M	UNKNOWN	RRZZZZUSA
MARJHEN, FRANZ	22	M	MCHT	PLZZZZUSA
KRUPMAN, DAVID	25	M	UNKNOWN	PLZZZZUSA
SITEWEITZKY, SCHWUACH	39	M	UNKNOWN	PLZZZZUSA
SAMUEL	12	M	UNKNOWN	PLZZZZUSA
KAHN, ELISKEN	32	F	W	PLZZZZUSA
PARMIN, WOLF	31	M	LABR	PLZZZZUSA
ABRAHAM	22	M	UNKNOWN	PLZZZZUSA
SCHOW, JOSSEL	19	M	UNKNOWN	PLZZZZUSA
FRUD, JESEV	22	F	SVNT	PLZZZZUSA
SILBERTSTEIN, JEWEL	17	F	UNKNOWN	PLZZZZUSA
ARMANSIZ, MATHIAS	37	M	LABR	PLZZZZUSA
STEINDMAN, GERSON	20	M	UNKNOWN	PLZZZZUSA
FRIDRICH, SPRING	22	M	UNKNOWN	PLZZZZUSA
ZUWENTSKY, ESTER	28	F	W	PLZZZZUSA
ISAAC	17	M	UNKNOWN	PLZZZZUSA
MIRKE	11	F	UNKNOWN	PLZZZZUSA
MOSES	7	M	CHILD	PLZZZZUSA
CHANE	6	F	CHILD	PLZZZZUSA
ELKE	.06	F	INFANT	PLZZZZUSA
SIMDERSEN, SARAH	26	F	W	PLZZZZUSA
MEYER	2	M	CHILD	PLZZZZUSA
FRANKEL, CHAIM	22	M	LABR	PLZZZZUSA
JUDEL	26	F	W	PLZZZZUSA
ISAAC	3	M	CHILD	PLZZZZUSA
WALKA	1	M	CHILD	PLZZZZUSA
HARSIS, SAMUEL	31	M	TRVLR	PLZZZZUSA
GALBMSKY, BEHR.	20	M	LABR	PLZZZZUSA
LOOHN, EDWARD	30	M	UNKNOWN	PLZZZZUSA
M.	34	F	W	PLZZZZUSA

SHIP: ST GERMAIN

FROM: HAVRE
TO: NEW YORK
ARRIVED: 09 JUNE 1883

PASSENGER	AGE	SEX	OCCUPATION	PRV VIL DES
RAPPE, JOSEPHE	22	M	CLKMKR	RRZZZZUSA
BOGOLAWSKY, EPHRAME	24	M	MUSN	RRZZZZUSA
DABROWSKY, ELIAS	33	M	UNKNOWN	RRZZZZUSA
GUMBUS, JOSEPH	33	M	UNKNOWN	RRZZZZUSA
HOFFMANN, JOSEPH	32	M	ENGR	RRZZZZUSA
OSTROWSKY, JEAN	31	M	TPGPH	RRZZZZUSA

SHIP: ALASKA

FROM: LIVERPOOL AND QUEENSTOWN
TO: NEW YORK
ARRIVED: 11 JUNE 1883

PASSENGER	AGE	SEX	OCCUPATION	PRV VIL DES
BANGAURATI, ISAK	31	M	CPTR	FNZZZZUSA
LILJEROOS, ISAK	31	M	UNKNOWN	FNZZZZUSA
INBERG, EMIL	24	M	CPTR	FNZZZZUSA
KAUKAS, JOHAN-J.	20	M	LABR	FNZZZZUSA
VASARMAKI, OSEAR	17	M	LABR	FNZZZZUSA
TREUHARA, EDWARD	25	M	FARMER	FNZZZZUSA
JACOBSON, SOLOMON	28	M	BKLYR	FNZZZZUSA
JACKSON, VICTOR	19	M	BKLYR	FNZZZZUSA
LIUD, JOHAN-V.	19	M	BKLYR	FNZZZZUSA
REUHOLM, HENRIK	30	M	LABR	FNZZZZUSA
LUNDGREN, FRANS	41	M	LABR	FNZZZZUSA
LEHTONEN, JOHAN	24	M	FARMER	FNZZZZUSA
LILIUS, JOHAN	31	M	FARMER	FNZZZZUSA
SJOGVIST, NESTOR	36	M	FARMER	FNZZZZUSA
ANNA	35	F	W	FNZZZZUSA
ANDERSON, ANDERS-J.	24	M	LABR	FNZZZZUSA
BJOIKMANN, CARL-P.	26	M	FARMER	FNZZZZUSA
ANNA	23	F	W	FNZZZZUSA
GERDA	2	F	CHILD	FNZZZZUSA
LILJEGRON, JOHAN	28	M	LABR	FNZZZZUSA
KLINT, CARL	31	M	STMSN	FNZZZZUSA
VICKMANN, JOHANN	26	M	STMSN	FNZZZZUSA
JOHANSSON, ERIK	25	M	JNR	FNZZZZUSA
FORSTENSSON, AXEL	24	M	JNR	FNZZZZUSA

SHIP: BRITANNIC

FROM: LIVERPOOL
TO: NEW YORK
ARRIVED: 11 JUNE 1883

PASSENGER	AGE	SEX	OCCUPATION	PRV VIL DES
VONDESROPP, ALFRED	25	M	ENGR	RRZZZZUSA

SHIP: RHAETIA

FROM: HAMBURG AND HAVRE
TO: NEW YORK
ARRIVED: 11 JUNE 1883

PASSENGER	AGE	SEX	OCCUPATION	PRV VIL DES
BREISGIELSKI, GERSON	19	M	WMN	RRZZZZUSA
KREINSEHN, JACOB	25	M	LABR	RRZZZZUSA
KRUPINSKY, FEIGEL	24	F	W	RRZZZZUSA
SARA	.11	F	INFANT	RRZZZZUSA
PALTOEL	.01	F	INFANT	RRZZZZUSA
SILANSKY, JULS.	17	M	LABR	RRZZZZUSA
EPSTEIN, SANDEL	19	M	LABR	RRZZZZUSA
FELDSTEIN, JACOB	30	M	LABR	RRZZZZUSA
JRAELEWSKY, ABRAHAM	20	M	LABR	RRZZZZUSA
ROSENKOWSKY, SIMON	45	M	LABR	RRZZZZUSA
--HA--, ABEL	27	M	LABR	RRZZZZUSA
SILBERMAHN, GABRIEL	17	M	LABR	RRZZZZUSA
SKLAROWSKY, MOSES	19	M	LABR	RRZZZZUSA
ROSENKOWSKY, CHATZKEL	16	M	LABR	RRZZZZUSA
WESTERMANN, MARCUS	21	M	LABR	RRZZZZUSA
MEYER, BENZIEN	19	M	LABR	RRZZZZUSA
ZUCKER, MOSES	27	M	LABR	RRZZZZUSA
PEPERD, JANKEL	18	M	LABR	RRZZZZUSA
FELDSTEIN, OSCHER	17	M	LABR	RRZZZZUSA

PASSENGER	AGE	SEX	OCCUPATION	PRV VIL DES
RUBINSKY, ABRAHAM	40	M	LABR	RRZZZZUSA
SKLAUSKY, IZOK	18	M	LABR	RRZZZZUSA
BLOCH, JUDEL	9	M	CHILD	PLZZZZUSA
BRZCJAN, ANNA	54	F	W	PLZZZZUSA
MAGD.	18	F	CH	PLZZZZUSA
JAN	16	M	CH	PLZZZZUSA
JOSEF	8	M	CHILD	PLZZZZUSA
GOSEIEMSKI, WOLEK	20	M	LABR	PLZZZZUSA
MOSBACH, FEIGE	55	F	W	PLZZZZUSA
REICHEL	20	F	D	PLZZZZUSA
SCHULMANN, MIRJEM	25	M	DLR	PLZZZZUSA
BRUSAKOWSKI, JOSEPH	30	M	LABR	PLZZZZUSA
SZISCUSKI, FRANZ	25	M	LABR	PLZZZZUSA
RYSZINSKI, JOSEPH	30	M	LABR	PLZZZZUSA
DAVIDOWICZ, HERRM.	16	M	CL	PLZZZZUSA
SILBERMANN, MOSES	20	M	FARMER	PLZZZZUSA
DWORSKY, MOSES	20	M	FARMER	PLZZZZUSA
WOLUTKCWI, JAN	42	M	LABR	PLZZZZUSA
PICULIS, JOSEF	19	M	LABR	PLZZZZUSA
ROZONY, VICENTI	27	M	LABR	PLZZZZUSA
FABER, ADOLF	18	M	LABR	PLZZZZUSA
PICULIS, ANTON	17	M	LABR	PLZZZZUSA
SIMULEWIC, ANDR.	20	M	LABR	PLZZZZUSA
MOKUCEVIC, VICENTI	26	M	LABR	PLZZZZUSA
SKYNKYS, ADAM	19	M	LABR	PLZZZZUSA
BRANAITIS, STANISLAUS	20	M	LABR	PLZZZZUSA
WOITMAS, IVAN	24	M	LABR	PLZZZZUSA
REFSKI, DAVID	18	M	LABR	PLZZZZUSA
BUGDEROWICZ, ANTONIE	37	F	W	PLZZZZUSA
BLUM, ARON	19	M	TLR	PLZZZZUSA
KAPLAN, ESTER	33	F	W	PLZZZZUSA
LEA	9	F	CHILD	PLZZZZUSA
FANNY	7	F	CHILD	PLZZZZUSA
BHRISTE.	5	F	CHILD	PLZZZZUSA
SCHONE	3	F	CHILD	PLZZZZUSA
PESSE	.11	F	INFANT	PLZZZZUSA
SILBERSTEIN, GERSON	30	M	LABR	PLZZZZUSA
DORFMANN, FEIGE	23	F	W	PLZZZZUSA
ABRAM	.11	M	INFANT	PLZZZZUSA
RUCIN, FEIGE	23	F	W	PLZZZZUSA
MUNKE	.11	M	INFANT	PLZZZZUSA
GRUMVALD, CARELINE	21	F	SGL	PLZZZZUSA
LEMBCKE, AUGUST.	17	M	LABR	PLZZZZUSA
SILLER, GABRIEL	45	M	LABR	PLZZZZUSA
GENITZKI, OSCAR.	31	M	DLR	PLZZZZUSA
RIEDE, DOBE	19	F	SGL	PLZZZZUSA
LANGE, WILH	35	M	FARMER	PLZZZZUSA
LOUISE	40	F	W	PLZZZZUSA
JULIUS	9	M	CHILD	PLZZZZUSA
WILHELM	8	M	CHILD	PLZZZZUSA
BERTHA	7	F	CHILD	PLZZZZUSA
CARL	5	M	CHILD	PLZZZZUSA
ANNA	3	F	CHILD	PLZZZZUSA

SHIP: SWITZERLAND

FROM: ANTWERP
TO: NEW YORK
ARRIVED: 11 JUNE 1883

PASSENGER	AGE	SEX	OCCUPATION	PRV VIL DES
ROSENFELD, MOSES	25	M	TLR	PLZZZZNY
TIKALSKA, MAGDALENA	11	F	MCHT	RRZZZZCH

SHIP: CIRCASSIA

FROM: GLASGOW AND MOVILLE
TO: NEW YORK
ARRIVED: 12 JUNE 1883

PASSENGER	AGE	SEX	OCCUPATION	PRV VIL DES
LOPHIN, ANNA	28	F	DMS	FNZZZZUSA
BUCHUMAN, MAG.	30	M	LABR	FNZZZZUSA
EMUBER, LEANDER	21	M	LABR	FNZZZZUSA
LEMGNIST, F.E.	38	M	LABR	FNZZZZUSA
ARBIRS, C.A.	20	M	LABR	FNZZZZUSA
JACOBSON, LEA	24	M	LABR	FNZZZZUSA
MATSON, F.W.	33	M	LABR	FNZZZZUSA
GUSTAFSON, E.G.F.	21	M	LABR	FNZZZZUSA
L.A.	26	M	LABR	FNZZZZUSA
DEFORTU, MAGNUS	25	M	LABR	FNZZZZUSA

SHIP: GELLERT

FROM: HAMBURG AND HAVRE
TO: NEW YORK
ARRIVED: 12 JUNE 1883

PASSENGER	AGE	SEX	OCCUPATION	PRV VIL DES
MORAWSHY, JOSEF	25	M	LABR	RRZZZZUSA
WOLINITZ, VISENTI	30	M	LABR	RRZZZZUSA
DOZNIAK, PISTER	26	M	LABR	RRZZZZUSA
LIPSKY, MORDCHE	20	M	SHMK	RRZZZZUSA
NISCHELKOWSKY, EISIK	25	M	TLR	RRZZZZUSA
GROZELEWSKY, EHAM	39	M	SHMK	RRZZZZUSA
ISE	9	M	CHILD	RRZZZZUSA
BIATATOTZKI, BLUME	28	F	W	RRZZZZUSA
HENACH	15	M	CH	RRZZZZUSA
RACHEL	7	F	CHILD	RRZZZZUSA
CHAMME	9	F	CHILD	RRZZZZUSA
DOMBROWSKY, LEA	24	F	SGL	RRZZZZUSA
EGELSHI, ISAAK	50	M	DLR	RRZZZZUSA
KLAASEN, ABRAHAM	30	M	FARMER	RRZZZZUSA
SUSANNE	28	F	W	RRZZZZUSA
HELENE	5	F	CHILD	RRZZZZUSA
ABRAHAM	3	M	CHILD	RRZZZZUSA
LESER	.11	M	INFANT	RRZZZZUSA
DELESHI, HEINR.	44	M	FARMER	RRZZZZUSA
CATH.	52	F	W	RRZZZZUSA
MARIE	20	F	D	RRZZZZUSA
ELIS.	56	F	W	RRZZZZUSA
PENNER, ISAAK	41	M	FARMER	RRZZZZUSA
CATH.	36	F	W	RRZZZZUSA
ISAAK	16	M	CH	RRZZZZUSA
FRANZ	8	M	CHILD	RRZZZZUSA
JACOB	2	M	CHILD	RRZZZZUSA
BARB.	.03	F	INFANT	RRZZZZUSA
HUNJOS, ED.	32	M	MCHT	RRZZZZUSA
HEDEMANN, ED.	27	M	OFF	RRZZZZUSA
SCHAJEWITZ, LAIB	20	M	DLR	RRZZZZUSA
RABINOWITZ, ELIAS	19	M	DLR	RRZZZZUSA
ELPERN, NOFSEN	20	M	DLR	RRZZZZUSA
PESCHE	20	F	W	RRZZZZUSA
SCHIMELOWITZ, HILLEL	19	M	DLR	RRZZZZUSA
KALATZNIK, SIMON	8	M	CHILD	RRZZZZUSA
WILENSKY, ISAAC	50	M	LABR	RRZZZZUSA
GISSEL	23	F	W	RRZZZZUSA
BUHAVSHY, HESCHEL	18	M	SGL	RRZZZZUSA
ZWIC, MORDCHE	17	M	LABR	RRZZZZUSA
TRYWUSCH, ROSALIE	24	F	SGL	RRZZZZUSA
SARA	20	F	SGL	RRZZZZUSA
ADOMISIN, ANNA	22	F	SGL	RRZZZZUSA
ESTERSOHN, DWORE	34	F	W	RRZZZZUSA
RAHEL	8	F	CHILD	RRZZZZUSA
ISAAC	5	M	CHILD	RRZZZZUSA

PASSENGER	AGE	SEX	OCCUPATION	PRV VIL DES
ABRAHAM	.11	M	INFANT	RRZZZZUSA
CHASEN, SCHONE	22	F	SGL	RRZZZZUSA
JADSEN, ELHE	19	F	SGL	RRZZZZUSA
SCHARF, MATHE	19	F	SGL	RRZZZZUSA
WOLOWICH, ITZIG	19	M	LABR	RRZZZZUSA
RACHEL	22	F	W	RRZZZZUSA
DWORE	.06	F	INFANT	RRZZZZUSA
MAHICWICZ, VICENTY	24	M	FARMER	RRZZZZUSA
MAMROSCH, PORFERG	36	M	LABR	PLZZZZUSA
MARTICIN, JAN	20	M	LABR	PLZZZZUSA
KOPEC, SAC	28	M	LABR	PLZZZZUSA
WATO, MIHAL	27	M	LABR	PLZZZZUSA
SESTAC, MIHAL	30	M	LABR	PLZZZZUSA
MEZA, JURA	29	M	LABR	PLZZZZUSA
IUAN, PAL	25	M	LABR	PLZZZZUSA
IRCHA, JANOS	20	M	LABR	PLZZZZUSA
LABOWSKI, JOH.	40	M	LABR	PLZZZZUSA
ANNA	30	F	W	PLZZZZUSA
STRONHA, ONUFRY	44	M	LABR	PLZZZZUSA
JURCAH, ANNA	24	F	W	PLZZZZUSA
FALHSTEIN, HANNY	29	F	W	PLZZZZUSA
FROMEL	10	M	CH	PLZZZZUSA
LAIB	5	M	CHILD	PLZZZZUSA
STEC, FLORIAN	30	M	LABR	PLZZZZUSA
MAGD.	25	F	W	PLZZZZUSA
MARIANNE	24	F	W	PLZZZZUSA
VICTORIA	10	F	D	PLZZZZUSA
SZHALUBA, SZEPAN	30	M	LABR	PLZZZZUSA
VICTORIA	20	F	W	PLZZZZUSA
SZEPAN	12	M	CH	PLZZZZUSA
JOSEFA	6	F	CHILD	PLZZZZUSA
PETER	5	M	CHILD	PLZZZZUSA
MARIANNE	2	F	CHILD	PLZZZZUSA
HANNA	.01	F	INFANT	PLZZZZUSA
ZIMAITIS, ADAM	40	M	LABR	RRZZZZUSA
PROBULIS, DOMINIH	34	M	LABR	RRZZZZUSA
GROZEWIC, IGNATZ	15	M	LABR	RRZZZZUSA
KAZLOWSKY, MICAS	19	M	LABR	RRZZZZUSA

SHIP: NIAGARA

FROM: HAVANA
TO: NEW YORK
ARRIVED: 12 JUNE 1883

PASSENGER	AGE	SEX	OCCUPATION	PRV VIL DES
STEINMESTER, I.MRS	38	F	LDY	RRZZZZUSA
U, U	4	M	CHILD	RRZZZZUSA

SHIP: PERSIAN MONARCH

FROM: LONDON
TO: NEW YORK
ARRIVED: 12 JUNE 1883

PASSENGER	AGE	SEX	OCCUPATION	PRV VIL DES
AARONS, SARAH	23	F	DRSMKR	PLZZZZUSA
RACHAEL	8	F	CHILD	PLZZZZUSA
ELISABETH	2	F	CHILD	PLZZZZUSA
PODLASKY, SARAH	33	F	UNKNOWN	PLZZZZUSA
LINA	5	F	CHILD	PLZZZZUSA
MARTHA	3	F	CHILD	PLZZZZUSA
ALBERT	1	M	CHILD	PLZZZZUSA
KIANA, THINA	44	F	UNKNOWN	PLZZZZUSA

SHIP: POLARIA

FROM: HAMBURG
TO: NEW YORK
ARRIVED: 13 JUNE 1883

PASSENGER	AGE	SEX	OCCUPATION	PRV VIL DES
SASS, WILHELM	40	M	LABR	RRZZZZUNK
AMALIA	30	F	W	RRZZZZUNK
MARIE	8	F	CHILD	RRZZZZUNK
ERNST	7	M	CHILD	RRZZZZUNK
WILHELM	4	M	CHILD	RRZZZZUNK
ALBERT	.06	M	INFANT	RRZZZZUNK
GIERLICH, FRANZ	50	M	LABR	RRZZZZUNK
CAROLINE	59	F	W	RRZZZZUNK
MARIE	21	F	D	RRZZZZUNK
FRANZ	19	M	S	RRZZZZUNK
CAROLINE	17	F	D	RRZZZZUNK
KORKOW, HERMANN	20	M	LABR	RRZZZZUNK
SCHLOMOWITZ, FEIGE	35	F	WO	RRZZZZNY
BLOCK, ALBERT	25	M	LABR	RRZZZZUNK
ERNESTINE	23	F	W	RRZZZZUNK
NETTLE, JOHANN	85	M	LABR	RRZZZZUNK
BECKER, AUGUST	36	M	LABR	RRZZZZPIT
HENRIETTE	31	F	W	RRZZZZPIT
CARL	8	M	CHILD	RRZZZZPIT
ANNA	7	F	CHILD	RRZZZZPIT
AUGUST	5	M	CHILD	RRZZZZPIT
MARIA	3	F	CHILD	RRZZZZPIT
OLGA	.05	F	INFANT	RRZZZZPIT
WILHELM	.02	M	INFANT	RRZZZZPIT
HEINKE, ALBERT	36	M	LABR	RRZZZZUNK
AUGUSTE	26	F	W	RRZZZZUNK
LOUISE	.02	F	INFANT	RRZZZZUNK
RUDOLF	.11	M	INFANT	RRZZZZUNK
AUGUSTE	20	F	D	RRZZZZUNK
CAROLINE	53	F	UNKNOWN	RRZZZZUNK
SCHULTZ, LUDWIG	48	M	FARMER	RRZZZZPIT
FRIEDERIKE	48	F	W	RRZZZZPIT
LUDWIG	00	M	S	RRZZZZPIT
SCHRODER, CARL	30	M	LABR	RRZZZZUNK
AUGUSTE	31	F	W	RRZZZZUNK
ELSA	.02	F	INFANT	RRZZZZUNK
KOCH, CARL	24	M	LABR	RRZZZZUNK
FRIDA	25	F	W	RRZZZZUNK
FISCHER, HEINR.	64	M	LABR	RRZZZZUNK
FRIEDERIKE	60	F	W	RRZZZZUNK
HERRMAN	18	M	S	RRZZZZUNK
FRIEDERIKE	21	F	D	RRZZZZUNK
HEITSCHMIDT, CARL	60	M	LABR	RRZZZZPIT
SOFIE	60	F	W	RRZZZZPIT
AXEL, WILHELM	30	M	LABR	RRZZZZUNK
CAROLINE	28	F	W	RRZZZZUNK
CAROLINA	7	F	CHILD	RRZZZZUNK
CARL	5	M	CHILD	RRZZZZUNK
LOUISE	3	F	CHILD	RRZZZZUNK
PAULINE	.06	F	INFANT	RRZZZZUNK
MAI--, MENDEL	26	M	TLR	RRZZZZNY
LUBELSKI, MORDCHE	50	F	WO	RRZZZZNY
ESTER	55	F	D	RRZZZZNY
CHAIE	7	F	CHILD	RRZZZZNY
NECHE, SCHLOVE	23	M	TRDSMN	RRZZZZNY
WESCHENGROD, ITZIK	44	M	TLR	RRZZZZNY
DOBRAJANSKO, BENI	26	M	TLR	RRZZZZNY
MOLLER, ISAAC	38	M	TLR	RRZZZZNY
WILCZIEN, EISIK	18	M	TLR	RRZZZZNY
DOHREN, HEINR.	17	M	UNKNOWN	RRZZZZCH
FALCK, ROSA	27	F	SGL	RRZZZZNY
WEIN, JETTE	30	F	WO	RRZZZZNY
WIGDOROWITZ, LEIB	20	F	LABR	RRZZZZNY
SCHNEIDER, DAVID	7	M	CHILD	RRZZZZNY
ALEXANDROWITZ, MANA	18	F	W	RRZZZZNY
GITELEWITSCH, JONAS	22	M	LABR	RRZZZZNY
BREITES, JONAS	24	M	LABR	RRZZZZNY
GRANOWSKY, GRADUS	22	M	LABR	RRZZZZNY

PASSENGER	AGE	SEX	OCCUPATION	PRIV	VIL	DES
BLUMENTHAL, ELKA	15	F	SGL	PL	ZZZZ	NY
GUTAMNN, PEPI	15	F	SGL	PL	ZZZZ	NY
FISCHER, LIPOT	22	M	TRDSMN	RR	ZZZZ	NY
FREITMANN, ISAAK	15	F	SGL	RR	ZZZZ	NY
CHEINE	8	F	CHILD	RR	ZZZZ	NY
IDA	6	F	CHILD	RR	ZZZZ	NY
SCHACHNER, ITZIG	26	M	MCHT	RR	ZZZZ	NY
SCHWALK, OSCHER	19	M	MCHT	RR	ZZZZ	NY
RUDNITZKI, BERSCHE	28	M	MCHT	RR	ZZZZ	NY
GIRSON, JOSEF-L.	25	M	MCHT	RR	ZZZZ	NY
LEVIN, JANKEL	42	M	MCHT	RR	ZZZZ	NY
KOWALSKI, LEIBE	20	F	SGL	RR	ZZZZ	NY
WIEN, LEISER	18	M	TRDSMN	RR	ZZZZ	NY
HERSCH	26	M	TRDSMN	RR	ZZZZ	NY
BEELE	24	F	W	RR	ZZZZ	NY
GUGURZIK, JONAS	50	M	TRDSMN	RR	ZZZZ	NY
TAUBE	50	F	W	RR	ZZZZ	NY
IETTE	8	F	CHILD	RR	ZZZZ	NY
ISAAC	7	M	CHILD	RR	ZZZZ	NY
SACHNAWSKI, LENI	24	F	SGL	RR	ZZZZ	NY
BERNSTEIN, MOSES	17	M	TRDSMN	RR	ZZZZ	NY
BIALEBLOTZKI, ABR.	33	M	TRDSMN	RR	ZZZZ	NY
RODZANSKI, CIREL	21	F	SGL	RR	ZZZZ	NY
CIKLAUSKI, MERTE	22	F	SGL	RR	ZZZZ	NY
GOLDSCHMIDT, PESCHE	35	F	WO	PL	ZZZZ	NY
NESCHE	.09	F	INFANT	PL	ZZZZ	NY
JOCHEWO	.09	M	INFANT	PL	ZZZZ	NY
NIERVETZKY, SARA	20	F	WO	PL	ZZZZ	NY
LEA	.10	F	INFANT	PL	ZZZZ	NY
ISAAC	.10	M	INFANT	PL	ZZZZ	NY
KOSSEL, JACOB	17	M	TRDSMN	RR	ZZZZ	NY
GLASLEUS, ANDR.	17	M	LABR	RR	ZZZZ	NY
DRIESCHMANN, FRIEDR.	54	M	LABR	RR	ZZZZ	NY
WILHELM	16	M	S	RR	ZZZZ	NY
GEORG	15	M	S	RR	ZZZZ	NY
MARIE	20	F	D	RR	ZZZZ	NY
WERNER, CHRIST	55	M	LABR	RR	ZZZZ	NY
LOUISE	44	F	W	RR	ZZZZ	NY
HERRMANN	4	M	CHILD	RR	ZZZZ	NY
WILHELM	.09	M	INFANT	RR	ZZZZ	NY
MARCUS, BEHR	18	M	TRDSMN	RR	ZZZZ	NY
GINTSCHAUSKY, LEISER	18	M	TRDSMN	RR	ZZZZ	NY
PLETZKY, THOMAS	26	M	TRDSMN	RR	ZZZZ	NY
SCHARBEWSKA, ISA	24	F	SGL	RR	ZZZZ	NY
RUBENSTEIN, SCHEPSEL	31	M	TRDSMN	RR	ZZZZ	NY
JASLOWSKY, MEIER	55	M	TRDSMN	RR	ZZZZ	NY
WITKOVSKY, M.	33	M	TRDSMN	RR	ZZZZ	NY
STERNSCHUSS, N.	19	M	TRDSMN	RR	ZZZZ	NY
HARWITZ, CHAIM	17	M	TRDSMN	RR	ZZZZ	NY
MATILSKY, PESCHE	19	F	SGL	RR	ZZZZ	NY
WATELSKI, CHANE	20	F	TRDSMN	RR	ZZZZ	NY
IGNER, HERMANN	51	M	TRDSMN	RR	ZZZZ	NY
FELD, LEISER	35	M	TRDSMN	RR	ZZZZ	NY
EPHRAIM	7	M	CHILD	RR	ZZZZ	NY
ROTH, WILH.	24	M	FARMER	RR	ZZZZ	NY
MIHR, AUG.	23	M	FARMER	RR	ZZZZ	NY
KOSCHENKO, CHAIE	17	F	SGL	RR	ZZZZ	NY
EPPSTEIN, JOS.	24	M	TRDSMN	RR	ZZZZ	NY
IGARSKI, B.	30	M	TRDSMN	RR	ZZZZ	NY
JANOTZKI, JS.	18	M	TRDSMN	RR	ZZZZ	NY
BRASELSKI, JOS.	20	M	TRDSMN	RR	ZZZZ	NY
SCHMIATZKI, J.	28	M	TRDSMN	RR	ZZZZ	NY
GRIESKA, SALI	24	F	WO	RR	ZZZZ	NY
MARA	.06	F	INFANT	RR	ZZZZ	NY
KAUFMANN, MOSES	25	M	TRDSMN	RR	ZZZZ	NY
ROSCHANSKI, CHAWE	50	F	WO	RR	ZZZZ	NY
RADOWSKI, ZALE	38	F	WO	RR	ZZZZ	NY
MINE	18	F	D	RR	ZZZZ	NY
BROSCHE	7	F	CHILD	RR	ZZZZ	NY
RUBEN	5	M	CHILD	RR	ZZZZ	NY
ISRAEL	4	M	CHILD	RR	ZZZZ	NY
GORDON, DEBORA	38	F	WO	RR	ZZZZ	NY
BEILE	6	F	CHILD	RR	ZZZZ	NY
EISECK	.09	M	INFANT	RR	ZZZZ	NY
LIEBERT, ISAC	21	M	TRDSMN	RR	ZZZZ	NY
GRA---, CHAIE	00	F	CH	RR	ZZZZ	NY

SHIP: AMERIQUE

FROM: HAVRE
TO: NEW YORK
ARRIVED: 14 JUNE 1883

PASSENGER	AGE	SEX	OCCUPATION	PRIV	VIL	DES
SILBERMANN, ISRAEL	13	M	UNKNOWN	RR	ZZZZ	USA
HILF, JEHIEL	19	M	UNKNOWN	RR	ZZZZ	USA
SEGALSWITSK, HEINRICH	13	M	UNKNOWN	RR	ZZZZ	USA
GRUNSTEIN, JOSEPH	13	M	UNKNOWN	RR	ZZZZ	USA
UNIGLICHT, ISRAEL	58	M	UNKNOWN	RR	ZZZZ	USA
BENI	12	M	UNKNOWN	RR	ZZZZ	USA
GRUNSTEIN, BARACK	19	M	UNKNOWN	RR	ZZZZ	USA

SHIP: DENMARK

FROM: LONDON
TO: NEW YORK
ARRIVED: 14 JUNE 1883

PASSENGER	AGE	SEX	OCCUPATION	PRIV	VIL	DES
MICH, LOAREL	30	M	LABR	PL	ZZZZ	USA

SHIP: WAESLAND

FROM: ANTWERP
TO: NEW YORK
ARRIVED: 14 JUNE 1883

PASSENGER	AGE	SEX	OCCUPATION	PRIV	VIL	DES
U, ISAAC	36	M	LABR	RR	ZZZZ	PA
LEIN, JOHN	21	M	LABR	PL	ZZZZ	CH

SHIP: STATE OF INDIANA

FROM: GLASGOW AND LARNE
TO: NEW YORK
ARRIVED: 15 JUNE 1883

PASSENGER	AGE	SEX	OCCUPATION	PRIV	VIL	DES
SOMALEWOWSKY, FRANZ	28	M	LABR	RR	ZZZZ	USA
DOGEREWIZ, SIMON	18	M	LABR	RR	ZZZZ	USA
BOGAWIC, JOSEF	21	M	LABR	RR	ZZZZ	USA
BURNALES, HATZI	25	M	LABR	RR	ZZZZ	USA
SECYOFSKY, JOSEPH	20	M	LABR	RR	ZZZZ	USA
MASCHLOWSKY, CHAIE	21	M	LABR	RR	ZZZZ	USA

PASSENGER	AGE	SEX	OCCUPATION	PRIVL	DES

SHIP: HABSBURG

FROM: BREMEN
TO: NEW YORK
ARRIVED: 16 JUNE 1883

PASSENGER	AGE	SEX	OCCUPATION	PRIVL	DES
HABERT, EMILIE	18	F	SVNT	RRZZZZ	USA
HOFFMANN, CAROLINE	60	F	HSKPR	RRZZZZ	USA
BRAUSTROM, ANDERS	20	M	BBR	RRZZZZ	MI
SIWANDER, ROBERT	48	M	LABR	RRZZZZ	WI
SODERSTROM, PETER	38	M	LABR	RRZZZZ	NY
JOSEFINA	32	F	W	RRZZZZ	NY
CARL	7	M	CHILD	RRZZZZ	NY
ERIC	5	M	CHILD	RRZZZZ	NY
OSCAR	2	M	CHILD	RRZZZZ	NY
NORDGRIST, MICHEL	38	M	FARMER	RRZZZZ	NY
ANDERSON, MARTEN	28	M	LABR	RRZZZZ	NY
KANNARS, ALFRED	41	M	LABR	RRZZZZ	NY
WITKOWSKI, PAWEL	22	M	FARMER	RRZZZZ	NY
LEVANDOWSKI, JAN	55	M	FARMER	RRZZZZ	NY
BERZSELAWCZIK, VALENTIN	35	M	FARMER	RRZZZZ	NY
FRANKEL, DANIEL	16	M	FARMER	RRZZZZ	NY
MORIZ	15	M	FARMER	RRZZZZ	NY

SHIP: CITY OF CHESTER

FROM: LIVERPOOL AND QUEENSTOWN
TO: NEW YORK
ARRIVED: 18 JUNE 1883

PASSENGER	AGE	SEX	OCCUPATION	PRIVL	DES
OSTMAN, HENRIK	20	M	LABR	FNZZZZ	USA
BALKEMAN, ZABNEL-A.	19	M	LABR	FNZZZZ	USA
ANDERSON, URLEHLIN	25	M	LABR	FNZZZZ	USA
MATTSON, MATH.	26	M	LABR	FNZZZZ	USA
BACK, CARL-U.	21	M	LABR	FNZZZZ	USA
AUG.J.	21	M	LABR	FNZZZZ	USA

SHIP: GALLIA

FROM: LIVERPOOL AND QUEENSTOWN
TO: NEW YORK
ARRIVED: 18 JUNE 1883

PASSENGER	AGE	SEX	OCCUPATION	PRIVL	DES
SROAN, MATEIS	28	M	LABR	RRZZZZ	USA
NEMWIERM, JACOB	31	M	LABR	RRZZZZ	USA
JANSO, MATLIER	20	M	LABR	RRZZZZ	USA
CRIKSEN, JOHAN	33	M	LABR	RRZZZZ	USA
CATTSON, ERIK-M.	18	M	LABR	RRZZZZ	USA
CARLSON, AUG.R.	25	M	LABR	RRZZZZ	USA
LASFILD, HANS-S.	20	M	LABR	RRZZZZ	USA
YAMPSA, MIKKEL-M.	22	M	LABR	RRZZZZ	USA
CHALSON, AUGT.	20	M	LABR	RRZZZZ	USA

SHIP: WESTPHALIA

FROM: HAMBURG AND HAVRE
TO: NEW YORK
ARRIVED: 19 JUNE 1883

PASSENGER	AGE	SEX	OCCUPATION	PRIVL	DES
WILKOWSKY, CIPE	50	F	W	RRZZZZ	NY
MEIER	16	M	CH	RRZZZZ	NY
DAVID	9	M	CHILD	RRZZZZ	NY
JOSEF, MARIA	18	F	SGL	RRZZZZ	NY
JACOBS, FANNY	30	F	W	RRZZZZ	NY
ANNA	9	F	CHILD	RRZZZZ	NY
JETTE	4	F	CHILD	RRZZZZ	NY
ABRAHAM	.11	M	INFANT	RRZZZZ	NY
EDELSTEIN, GUSTAV	15	M	LABR	RRZZZZ	NY
BARNAR, JOH.	24	M	LABR	FNZZZZ	NY
ANDERSON, JOHANNA	22	F	SGL	FNZZZZ	NY
RIGEL, RUBIN	18	M	LABR	RRZZZZ	NY
BANK, SALOMON	18	M	TNMK	RRZZZZ	NY
SARATA, ANDREN	33	M	LABR	RRZZZZ	NY
LEANORE	28	F	W	RRZZZZ	NY
VICENTE	29	M	LABR	RRZZZZ	NY
HELENE	9	F	CHILD	RRZZZZ	NY
STUZECK	5	M	CHILD	RRZZZZ	NY
ROSA	.11	F	INFANT	RRZZZZ	NY
WAZETER, ANTON	57	M	LABR	RRZZZZ	NY
VOTH, JOHANN	38	M	LABR	RRZZZZ	NE
CAROLINE	32	F	W	RRZZZZ	NE
JOHANN	25	M	LABR	RRZZZZ	NE
ANDREAS	8	M	CHILD	RRZZZZ	NE
HELENE	7	F	CHILD	RRZZZZ	NE
CAROLINE	.03	F	INFANT	RRZZZZ	NE
KLEIN, EPHRAIM	52	M	LABR	RRZZZZ	MI
WILHE.	46	F	W	RRZZZZ	MI
JOHANN	23	M	CH	RRZZZZ	MI
JUSTE	21	F	CH	RRZZZZ	MI
EPHRAIM	17	M	CH	RRZZZZ	MI
JACOB	15	M	CH	RRZZZZ	MI
WILHE.	7	F	CHILD	RRZZZZ	MI
PETER	62	M	LABR	RRZZZZ	MI
VOTH, CARL	46	M	LABR	RRZZZZ	NE
FLORENTINE	41	F	W	RRZZZZ	NE
HEINRICH	17	M	CH	RRZZZZ	NE
WILHE.	16	F	CH	RRZZZZ	NE
CARL	9	M	CHILD	RRZZZZ	NE
WILH.	8	M	CHILD	RRZZZZ	NE
JOHN	7	M	CHILD	RRZZZZ	NE
EDUARD	6	M	CHILD	RRZZZZ	NE
ANDREAS	5	M	CHILD	RRZZZZ	NE
FRIEDR.	.11	M	INFANT	RRZZZZ	NE
FRICHTING, THEODOR	42	M	LABR	RRZZZZ	UNK
ELISABETH	32	F	W	RRZZZZ	UNK
FRIEDR.	17	M	CH	RRZZZZ	UNK
ANDREAS	8	M	CHILD	RRZZZZ	UNK
ELISABETH	7	F	CHILD	RRZZZZ	UNK
HELENE	6	F	CHILD	RRZZZZ	UNK
EDUARD	5	M	CHILD	RRZZZZ	UNK
CATHRINA	4	F	CHILD	RRZZZZ	UNK
THEODORE	.11	F	INFANT	RRZZZZ	UNK
JOHN	.01	M	INFANT	RRZZZZ	UNK
KOZLOVSKY, MARTIN	44	M	LABR	RRZZZZ	UNK
HELENE	44	F	W	RRZZZZ	UNK
JOHANN	8	M	CHILD	RRZZZZ	UNK
MARTIN	7	M	CHILD	RRZZZZ	UNK
PETER	4	M	CHILD	RRZZZZ	UNK
MARIA	.02	F	INFANT	RRZZZZ	UNK
DZERKOWSKY, JOHANN	22	M	LABR	RRZZZZ	NY
HENTSCHKA, MARIA	75	F	W	RRZZZZ	NY
FRIEDSTEIN, SAUL	17	M	LABR	RRZZZZ	NY
MILLER, DWORE	26	F	W	RRZZZZ	NY
BERTJE	5	F	CHILD	RRZZZZ	NY
ABE	.11	M	INFANT	RRZZZZ	NY

SHIP: GRECIAN MONARCH

FROM: LONDON
TO: NEW YORK
ARRIVED: 20 JUNE 1883

PASSENGER	AGE	SEX	OCCUPATION	PRV VIL DES
ROSENBERG, MORRIS	58	M	LABR	PLZZZZUSA
LEAL	52	F	W	PLZZZZUSA
ABRAHAM	16	M	NN	PLZZZZUSA
SARAH	13	F	NN	PLZZZZUSA
RACHEL	11	F	NN	PLZZZZUSA
GRECIN, SIMON	30	M	LABR	PLZZZZUSA
ESTER	30	F	W	PLZZZZUSA
RACHEL	10	F	NN	PLZZZZUSA
ABRAHAM	8	M	CHILD	PLZZZZUSA
MORRIS	.05	M	INFANT	PLZZZZUSA
REPTOWSKY, SAMSON	41	M	LABR	PLZZZZUSA
KASUR, HRG.	45	M	LABR	PLZZZZUSA
HUSTIFELD, AARON	20	M	LABR	PLZZZZUSA
COHEN, MORRIS	22	M	LABR	PLZZZZUSA
BETSY	47	F	W	PLZZZZUSA
RAPHAEL	18	M	NN	PLZZZZUSA
SARAH	17	F	NN	PLZZZZUSA
LEAH	16	F	NN	PLZZZZUSA
JACOB	00	M	NN	PLZZZZUSA
LEWIS, RACHEL	42	F	NN	PLZZZZUSA
SIMON	18	M	NN	PLZZZZUSA
REBECCA	15	F	NN	PLZZZZUSA
FRANK	10	M	NN	PLZZZZUSA
JACOB	5	M	CHILD	PLZZZZUSA
MANKS, RACHEL	30	F	NN	PLZZZZUSA
DEBORAH	6	F	CHILD	PLZZZZUSA
JOSEF	4	M	CHILD	PLZZZZUSA
RACHEL	.03	F	INFANT	PLZZZZUSA
JEROSKY, JANE	50	F	NN	PLZZZZUSA
COHEN, SARAH	21	F	NN	PLZZZZUSA

SHIP: ETHIOPIA

FROM: LIVERPOOL
TO: NEW YORK
ARRIVED: 21 JUNE 1883

PASSENGER	AGE	SEX	OCCUPATION	PRV VIL DES
BIGGAI, ELIES	24	M	LABR	RRZZZZUSA
DALLACK, ANDER.	25	M	LABR	RRZZZZUSA
GPERMORK, JAKOB	40	M	LABR	RRZZZZUSA
SAKAJAWE, ERIK	22	M	LABR	RRZZZZUSA
MATTS.	26	M	LABR	RRZZZZUSA
A.	30	M	LABR	RRZZZZUSA
NORRINER, JONAS.	60	M	LABR	RRZZZZUSA
ASPHOLM, JOHAN-A.	33	M	LABR	RRZZZZUSA
KROPIDLOWSKI, C.AUD.	25	M	LABR	PLZZZZUSA
KRONSON, MARKS	19	M	TRVLR	PLZZZZUSA
KENETZ, EVA	38	F	UNKNOWN	PLZZZZUSA
JUNITZO	9	M	CHILD	PLZZZZUSA
JURKO	9	M	CHILD	PLZZZZUSA
KIZEMMSKI, JOSEF	24	M	LABR	PLZZZZUSA
MARGANA	22	F	UNKNOWN	PLZZZZUSA
CHANE	31	F	UNKNOWN	PLZZZZUSA
SARA	9	F	CHILD	PLZZZZUSA
MOSES	7	M	CHILD	PLZZZZUSA
REGINA	6	F	CHILD	PLZZZZUSA
MAX	4	M	CHILD	PLZZZZUSA
ELLIA	2	F	CHILD	PLZZZZUSA
ISSAC	1	M	CHILD	PLZZZZUSA
LEVY, JACOB	20	M	TLR	PLZZZZUSA
ROGULZLIE, ANTON	20	M	LABR	PLZZZZUSA

SHIP: ST. OF PENNSYLVANIA

FROM: GLASGOW AND LARNE
TO: NEW YORK
ARRIVED: 21 JUNE 1883

PASSENGER	AGE	SEX	OCCUPATION	PRV VIL DES
ADELSOHN, GERSON	14	M	LABR	RRZZZZUSA
KATZ, JOHANNA	18	F	TLR	RRZZZZUSA
GROFS, IGNATZ	22	M	TLR	RRZZZZUSA
MACUJUNSKY, ISAAC	17	M	LABR	RRZZZZUSA
SUFAMANN, W.	17	M	LABR	RRZZZZUSA
LEWITAN, SANDER	20	M	LABR	RRZZZZUSA
LEWIN, MOSES	19	M	AGNT	RRZZZZUSA
FREUDE	24	F	W	RRZZZZUSA
KADESCHOLM, SCHEMI	28	F	W	RRZZZZUSA
JACKE	1	M	CHILD	RRZZZZUSA
LI--	1	M	CHILD	RRZZZZUSA
DANTOWISZ, LEIB	55	M	PNTR	RRZZZZUSA
GUTMANN, PESACH	32	M	LABR	RRZZZZUSA
PLETOWNICK, JOSEPH	22	M	LABR	RRZZZZUSA
NEUMANN, JOSEPH	16	M	LABR	RRZZZZUSA
RESMANN, FOSSEL	29	M	LABR	RRZZZZUSA
SACK, LEIB	22	M	LABR	RRZZZZUSA
BERTA	00	F	W	RRZZZZUSA
WEINSTEIN, GABRIEL	19	M	LABR	RRZZZZUSA
WEINGARTEN, HEIMANN	25	M	TLR	RRZZZZUSA
SCHER, RUKUS	20	M	TBCNST	RRZZZZUSA
SOHMUKLES, ASNEL	31	M	TLR	RRZZZZUSA
FRIEDMAN, WOLFF	18	M	WCHMKR	RRZZZZUSA

SHIP: THINGVALLA

FROM: COPENHAGEN
TO: NEW YORK
ARRIVED: 21 JUNE 1883

PASSENGER	AGE	SEX	OCCUPATION	PRV VIL DES
PETTERSSON, JOSEF-W.	20	M	LABR	FNZZZZUSA
JOHANNA	17	F	SGL	FNZZZZUSA
HEIKKILA, FRANS-W.H.	20	M	LABR	FNZZZZUSA
HENDRIKSEN-HANNUS, O.W.	19	M	LABR	FNZZZZUSA
HENDRIKSEN-SADERGRENARR	19	M	LABR	FNZZZZUSA

SHIP: POLYNESIA

FROM: HAMBURG
TO: NEW YORK
ARRIVED: 22 JUNE 1883

PASSENGER	AGE	SEX	OCCUPATION	PRV VIL DES
LFRAUK, JUDI	28	M	TRDSMN	RRZZZZUSA
RUBEN, PESSI	20	F	WO	RRZZZZUSA
JOCHWALD	8	M	CHILD	RRZZZZUSA
HEM	7	F	CHILD	RRZZZZUSA
RADOWSKY, BERH	28	M	TRDSMN	RRZZZZUSA
GIETEL	18	F	W	RRZZZZUSA
OCHALCK, ANTONIE	20	F	SGL	RRZZZZUSA
RINGEL, R.	18	M	TRDSMN	RRZZZZUSA
SCHELLER, ROSALIE	18	F	SGL	RRZZZZUSA
NEWMANN, SALI	18	M	TRDSMN	RRZZZZUSA
WERSLOWITZ, ERNEST.	17	F	SGL	RRZZZZUSA
MORITZ	7	M	CHILD	RRZZZZUSA
KLEIN, LUDWIG	8	M	CHILD	RRZZZZUSA
ROSENBERG, H.	51	M	TRDSMN	RRZZZZUSA
LENE	44	F	W	RRZZZZUSA
MINNA	12	F	D	RRZZZZUSA

PASSENGER	AGE	SEX	OCCUPATION	PRIV	VIL	DES
RESI	8	F	CHILD	RR	ZZZZ	USA
MILDER, RESI	50	F	WO	RR	ZZZZ	USA
TONI	16	F	D	RR	ZZZZ	USA
KUBOWITZ, ABRAH.	18	M	TRDSMN	RR	ZZZZ	USA
TISPAK, GYURA	50	M	TRDSMN	RR	ZZZZ	USA
SUSANNE	50	F	W	RR	ZZZZ	USA
MACKS	28	F	W	RR	ZZZZ	USA
HELENE	8	F	CHILD	RR	ZZZZ	USA
JANOS	7	M	CHILD	RR	ZZZZ	USA
JACKO	5	M	CHILD	RR	ZZZZ	USA
NEBEL, MEYER	33	M	TRDSMN	RR	ZZZZ	USA
WLISSMANN, WOLFF	26	M	TRDSMN	RR	ZZZZ	USA
SELKO	22	F	W	RR	ZZZZ	USA
ARMIN	.06	M	INFANT	RR	ZZZZ	USA
REICHEL	.02	M	INFANT	RR	ZZZZ	USA
MALZ, BONUH	29	M	TRDSMN	RR	ZZZZ	USA
LEFKOWITZ, SAM.	18	M	TRDSMN	RR	ZZZZ	USA
BERNSTEIN, CHJENE	38	F	WO	RR	ZZZZ	USA
CHJENE	20	F	D	RR	ZZZZ	USA
ISAAC	16	M	S	RR	ZZZZ	USA
MALHE	8	F	CHILD	RR	ZZZZ	USA
SARAH	7	F	CHILD	RR	ZZZZ	USA
ARON	4	M	CHILD	RR	ZZZZ	USA
CHAWE	.05	F	INFANT	RR	ZZZZ	USA
LONDON, GISA	20	F	SGL	RR	ZZZZ	USA
DEUTSCH, ISSER	8	F	CHILD	RR	ZZZZ	USA
ROTHSTEIN, IAUHE	18	F	SGL	RR	ZZZZ	USA
FEINMANN, MOS.	22	M	MCHT	RR	ZZZZ	USA
SCHWARZ, CH.	17	M	MCHT	RR	ZZZZ	USA
KALISCH, KLEIM	40	M	MCHT	RR	ZZZZ	USA
JEFSMITH, JOS.	24	M	LABR	RR	ZZZZ	USA
WOELKEWICZ, KAYETON	55	M	LABR	RR	ZZZZ	USA
FERTL, FREMENT	25	F	WO	PL	ZZZZ	USA
SAMUEL	.07	M	INFANT	PL	ZZZZ	USA
BEEK, SARAH	23	F	WO	PL	ZZZZ	USA
ISAAK	.02	M	INFANT	PL	ZZZZ	USA
HEILPERN, NEOCH	22	M	TRDSMN	RR	ZZZZ	USA
JANOWSKI, CHAIM	8	M	CHILD	RR	ZZZZ	USA
PERLSTEIN, ABRAH.	18	M	LABR	RR	ZZZZ	USA
MULLER, JOH.	36	M	LABR	RR	ZZZZ	USA
EVA	27	F	W	RR	ZZZZ	USA
ADAM	.05	M	INFANT	RR	ZZZZ	USA
RADZEWITZ, KASLAS	30	M	LABR	RR	ZZZZ	USA
STRUMPT, SALOM	27	M	LABR	RR	ZZZZ	USA
EITHER	16	F	W	RR	ZZZZ	USA
SCHMALZBA--, JACOB	30	M	TRDSMN	RR	ZZZZ	USA
STRAMMER, BERL	22	M	TRDSMN	RR	ZZZZ	USA
WEINEROWITZ, FEIGE	20	F	WO	RR	ZZZZ	USA
MALHE	7	F	CHILD	RR	ZZZZ	USA
BENJAMIN	.04	M	INFANT	RR	ZZZZ	USA
SALOMO	.10	M	INFANT	RR	ZZZZ	USA
KACHANOWITZ, D.	16	M	TRDSMN	RR	ZZZZ	USA
WINECK, BLUME	40	F	WO	RR	ZZZZ	USA
CHANE	7	F	CHILD	RR	ZZZZ	USA
RUWEN	6	F	CHILD	RR	ZZZZ	USA
ELIAS	5	M	CHILD	RR	ZZZZ	USA
ESTER	.04	F	INFANT	RR	ZZZZ	USA
GERDENSTEIN, FRUME	19	M	TRDSMN	RR	ZZZZ	USA
SPARBER, JOSEF	45	M	TRDSMN	PL	ZZZZ	USA
ROCHEL	39	F	W	PL	ZZZZ	USA
GITEL	8	F	CHILD	PL	ZZZZ	USA
LEISER	7	M	CHILD	PL	ZZZZ	USA
SALOMON	4	M	CHILD	PL	ZZZZ	USA
ABRAHAM	2	M	CHILD	PL	ZZZZ	USA
JACOB	.11	M	INFANT	PL	ZZZZ	USA
BLATT, MARAUS	35	M	TRDSMN	PL	ZZZZ	USA
SCHEINDEL	26	F	W	PL	ZZZZ	USA
GERBEL, GITEL	14	F	SGL	PL	ZZZZ	USA
FISCHER, JUDA	17	F	SGL	PL	ZZZZ	USA
MARCUS, LAZARUS	24	M	CGRMKR	PL	ZZZZ	USA
PICOTROWSKA, ALWINE	38	F	SGL	PL	ZZZZ	USA
SEILER, LOUISE	22	F	SGL	PL	ZZZZ	USA
SINGER, ESTER	40	F	WO	PL	ZZZZ	USA
MANDEL	18	F	D	PL	ZZZZ	USA
LAIE	.04	F	INFANT	PL	ZZZZ	USA
GROFS, PEPI	30	F	SGL	PL	ZZZZ	USA
JUSCHOCHELLER, S.M.	19	M	TRDSMN	RR	ZZZZ	USA
SZTARAS, JOS.	28	M	TRDSMN	RR	ZZZZ	USA
BIALOCKEWSKI, ETTEL	21	F	WO	RR	ZZZZ	USA
WOLF	.04	M	INFANT	RR	ZZZZ	USA
BEBOZERKOVSKI, RACHEL	25	F	WO	RR	ZZZZ	USA
ZATKE	7	F	CHILD	RR	ZZZZ	USA
BEREL	3	F	CHILD	RR	ZZZZ	USA
CHANE	.06	F	INFANT	RR	ZZZZ	USA
CHAM	.11	F	INFANT	RR	ZZZZ	USA
GRIENBLATT, MALKE	19	F	SGL	PL	ZZZZ	USA
EISIG	00	F	SGL	PL	ZZZZ	USA
BEILE	25	F	SGL	PL	ZZZZ	USA
VALLECK, MARCUS	19	M	TRDSMN	PL	ZZZZ	USA
RIEDLER, SALOM.	18	M	TRDSMN	PL	ZZZZ	USA
SCHUKLOWSKY, ABRAHAM	40	M	TRDSMN	RR	ZZZZ	USA
ALEXANDER, MORDSCHE	18	F	WO	RR	ZZZZ	USA
MATULEWITZ, JAN	30	M	TRDSMN	RR	ZZZZ	USA
LOWENTHAL, CHAIE	23	F	WO	RR	ZZZZ	USA
SALAMON	.06	M	INFANT	RR	ZZZZ	USA
HERR, CHAIE	7	F	CHILD	RR	ZZZZ	USA
FRASECK, JACOB	18	M	TRDSMN	RR	ZZZZ	USA
FRIEDMAN, LIEBE	30	F	WO	RR	ZZZZ	USA
HINDE	7	F	CHILD	RR	ZZZZ	USA
EINHOVN, HERSCH	30	M	TRDSMN	RR	ZZZZ	USA
ROMANON, VINCENT	20	M	TRDSMN	RR	ZZZZ	USA
BRODER, MOSES	23	M	TRDSMN	RR	ZZZZ	USA
ZELZ, FRAM	20	M	TRDSMN	RR	ZZZZ	USA
NORMEL, MOSES	23	M	TRDSMN	RR	ZZZZ	USA
GUSSMANN, MARIE	28	F	WO	RR	ZZZZ	USA
SALI	3	F	CHILD	RR	ZZZZ	USA
FERRI	.02	M	INFANT	RR	ZZZZ	USA
ARMIN	.02	M	INFANT	RR	ZZZZ	USA
RUBIN, ABRAHAM	15	M	TRDSMN	RR	ZZZZ	USA
WIGRAMSKA, ELIOKMA	23	M	TRDSMN	RR	ZZZZ	USA
PREICS, SAMUEL	31	M	TRDSMN	RR	ZZZZ	USA
WANGREITIST, MATH.	18	M	LABR	RR	ZZZZ	USA
GOTTWARD, LOUIS	36	M	TRDSMN	RR	ZZZZ	USA
KALK, FRIED.	21	M	LABR	RR	ZZZZ	USA
WARMBIER, CARL	21	M	LABR	RR	ZZZZ	USA
KRAULITKA, OSCAR	45	M	TRDSMN	RR	ZZZZ	USA
HUSCHEL	7	M	CHILD	RR	ZZZZ	USA
PLECHETZKO, ROSCHEL	15	F	SGL	RR	ZZZZ	USA
LEISER	7	M	CHILD	RR	ZZZZ	USA
GLUCK, BETTY	55	M	LABR	RR	ZZZZ	USA
SAMUEL	18	M	S	RR	ZZZZ	USA
ISIDOR	8	M	CHILD	RR	ZZZZ	USA
BOLTRONE, GRABLIK	23	M	TRDSMN	RR	ZZZZ	USA
MARCWICZ, MATHEUS	20	M	TRDSMN	RR	ZZZZ	USA
SARATHA, FRANZ	30	M	TRDSMN	RR	ZZZZ	USA
FRANZISKA	20	F	W	RR	ZZZZ	USA
ALEXANDRA	.06	M	INFANT	RR	ZZZZ	USA
TIKELSKA, ROSALIE	17	F	SGL	RR	ZZZZ	USA
MARKUS, ODEUS	22	M	TRDSMN	RR	ZZZZ	USA
LEISE	50	F	W	RR	ZZZZ	USA
KAPLAND, DANIEL	45	M	LABR	RR	ZZZZ	USA
ODEUS, PIUKUS	40	M	LABR	RR	ZZZZ	USA
BETNAR, SUSANNA	28	F	WO	RR	ZZZZ	USA
FRANZISKA	4	F	CHILD	RR	ZZZZ	USA
U	00	M	S	RR	ZZZZ	USA
MARTHA	.01	F	INFANT	RR	ZZZZ	USA
STERN, MAX	24	M	MCHT	RR	ZZZZ	USA

PASSENGER	AGE	SEX	OCCUPATION	PRIV	VIL	DES

SHIP: CITY OF RICHMOND

FROM: LIVERPOOL AND QUEENSTOWN
TO: NEW YORK
ARRIVED: 23 JUNE 1883

PASSENGER	AGE	SEX	OCCUPATION	PRIV	VIL	DES
HAGSTROM, SOPHIA	20	F	SP	FN	ZZZZ	MI
MOTTENEN, MARKUS	33	M	LABR	FN	ZZZZ	MI
ABRAHAMSON, JACOB	34	M	LABR	FN	ZZZZ	MI
WECKAPAKKA, JOH.	28	M	LABR	FN	ZZZZ	MI
MANNER, AMANDA	17	F	SP	FN	ZZZZ	MN
WESS, LEANDER	18	M	LABR	FN	ZZZZ	MN
BRASK, AND.	20	M	LABR	FN	ZZZZ	MN
PASARINA, JOSEF.	26	F	W	FN	ZZZZ	MN
JOHA.	4	F	CHILD	FN	ZZZZ	MN
MANUELLA, GRETA	27	F	SP	FN	ZZZZ	MN
PAKAKALAR, IINA	21	F	SP	FN	ZZZZ	MN

SHIP: EGYPTIAN MONARCH

FROM: LONDON
TO: NEW YORK
ARRIVED: 23 JUNE 1883

PASSENGER	AGE	SEX	OCCUPATION	PRIV	VIL	DES
ABRAHAMSKI, JACOB	19	M	CNF	PL	ZZZZ	NY
ABRAHAMS, SOLOMON	19	M	TLR	PL	ZZZZ	NY
BARNELT, SARAH	26	F	TLR	PL	ZZZZ	NY
AARON	4	M	CHILD	PL	ZZZZ	NY
EVA	.07	F	INFANT	PL	ZZZZ	NY
GILLIER, REBECCA	18	F	UNKNOWN	RR	ZZZZ	NY
WALKENBREIT, MORIS	31	M	CGRMKR	RR	ZZZZ	NY
LENA	26	F	UNKNOWN	RR	ZZZZ	NY
LOUIS	2	M	CHILD	RR	ZZZZ	NY
GEETA	.04	F	INFANT	RR	ZZZZ	NY
BERNSTEIN, MOSES	27	M	MCHT	RR	ZZZZ	NY
WILLFER, ISAK	18	M	FARMER	RR	ZZZZ	MN
LAA, ANDRES-WILHELM	17	M	UNKNOWN	RR	ZZZZ	WI
VEIKOR, JOH.ERIK	38	M	UNKNOWN	RR	ZZZZ	WI
WATTLE, JOH.	33	M	UNKNOWN	RR	ZZZZ	WI
ROMBERG, HENN.ISAC	25	M	UNKNOWN	RR	ZZZZ	MI
ANLETLA, KATTE	23	F	UNKNOWN	RR	ZZZZ	WI
JOHANNA	18	F	SVNT	RR	ZZZZ	WI
GRINSPUN, ABRAHAM	40	M	MLR	RR	ZZZZ	CH
SCHNEIDER, MORDESHAI	23	M	BRR	RR	ZZZZ	LAN
LIVINGSTORN, NICOLAUS	20	M	CL	RR	ZZZZ	NY
SAFMONS, WOOLF	33	M	TLR	RR	ZZZZ	UNK
MARY	31	F	UNKNOWN	RR	ZZZZ	UNK
HYAMS, ELIZA	60	F	UNKNOWN	RR	ZZZZ	UNK
SYMONS, SOLOMON	7	M	CHILD	RR	ZZZZ	UNK
JACOB	5	M	CHILD	RR	ZZZZ	UNK
ROSY	2	F	CHILD	RR	ZZZZ	UNK
SIMON, JULES	38	M	TLR	RR	ZZZZ	NY
DORA	36	F	UNKNOWN	RR	ZZZZ	NY
NATHAN	14	M	UNKNOWN	RR	ZZZZ	NY
ABRAHAM	9	M	CHILD	RR	ZZZZ	NY
ROSA	7	F	CHILD	RR	ZZZZ	NY
WYMAN	4	M	CHILD	RR	ZZZZ	NY
MORIS	2	M	CHILD	RR	ZZZZ	NY
FANNY	.10	F	INFANT	RR	ZZZZ	NY
LEWIS, HYMAN	23	M	UNKNOWN	RR	ZZZZ	NY
HENRIETTA	27	F	UNKNOWN	RR	ZZZZ	NY
HUDALH, B.JOHANN	22	F	SVNT	RR	ZZZZ	NY
HEINBERG, MARIE	22	F	UNKNOWN	RR	ZZZZ	NY

SHIP: NEDERLAND

FROM: ANTWERP
TO: NEW YORK
ARRIVED: 23 JUNE 1883

PASSENGER	AGE	SEX	OCCUPATION	PRIV	VIL	DES
LECHEMOWITSCH, MONYK	30	M	FARMER	PL	ZZZZ	NY
SCHWALENSKI, FRANZ	30	M	BBR	PL	ZZZZ	NY
BALAINGER, KATTIE	20	F	NN	PL	ZZZZ	NY
VERUSIBLA, SAVEL	33	M	UNKNOWN	PL	ZZZZ	UNK
GABRILEWIZ, ALEX	17	M	UNKNOWN	PL	ZZZZ	UNK

SHIP: RUGIA

FROM: HAMBURG
TO: NEW YORK
ARRIVED: 23 JUNE 1883

PASSENGER	AGE	SEX	OCCUPATION	PRIV	VIL	DES
MALINA, ADOLF	17	M	APTC	RR	ZZZZ	USA
LEWRESOW, ELKE	20	F	SGL	RR	ZZZZ	USA
DWORE	16	F	SGL	RR	ZZZZ	USA
LEIB	9	M	CHILD	RR	ZZZZ	USA
BERG, HIRSCH	17	M	DLR	RR	ZZZZ	USA
KIETUTZ, PERL	45	F	W	RR	ZZZZ	USA
EISICH	9	M	CHILD	RR	ZZZZ	USA
KWASCHNIK, JOH.	46	M	FARMER	RR	ZZZZ	USA
ANNA	42	F	W	RR	ZZZZ	USA
DANIEL	20	M	S	RR	ZZZZ	USA
CAROLINE	22	F	SGL	RR	ZZZZ	USA
JOHANN	18	M	S	RR	ZZZZ	USA
MAGDAL	9	F	CHILD	RR	ZZZZ	USA
SOPHIE	6	F	CHILD	RR	ZZZZ	USA
CHRISTINE	.11	F	INFANT	RR	ZZZZ	USA
JOH	.01	M	INFANT	RR	ZZZZ	USA
DANIEL	44	M	FARMER	RR	ZZZZ	USA
CHRISTINE	36	F	W	RR	ZZZZ	USA
JOH.	20	M	S	RR	ZZZZ	USA
GOTTLIEB	18	M	S	RR	ZZZZ	USA
WILHELM	16	M	S	RR	ZZZZ	USA
LOUISE	14	F	D	RR	ZZZZ	USA
CHRISTINE	6	F	CHILD	RR	ZZZZ	USA
FROKE.	4	F	CHILD	RR	ZZZZ	USA
PAULINE	2	F	CHILD	RR	ZZZZ	USA
LOUISE	7	F	CHILD	RR	ZZZZ	USA
SCHEZERLACK, CHANNE	50	F	W	RR	ZZZZ	USA
CHAM	17	M	S	RR	ZZZZ	USA
CHAIE	9	F	CHILD	RR	ZZZZ	USA
SCHNITTER, SLATE	38	F	W	RR	ZZZZ	USA
RACHEL	5	F	CHILD	RR	ZZZZ	USA
ARON	.11	M	INFANT	RR	ZZZZ	USA
ARNOFSKY, GOLDE	50	F	W	RR	ZZZZ	USA
AESER	9	M	CHILD	RR	ZZZZ	USA
RACHEL	8	F	CHILD	RR	ZZZZ	USA
JUDITH	7	F	CHILD	RR	ZZZZ	USA
NECHE	.11	F	INFANT	RR	ZZZZ	USA
JUDKE	.01	F	INFANT	RR	ZZZZ	USA
SCHITZEL, JENNY	20	F	W	RR	ZZZZ	USA
ARON	.11	M	INFANT	RR	ZZZZ	USA
ARONS, FEIGE	23	F	W	RR	ZZZZ	USA
NECHAME	.11	F	INFANT	RR	ZZZZ	USA
BERLINER, GOLDE	20	F	SGL	RR	ZZZZ	USA
MERSON, ISRAEL	30	M	LABR	RR	ZZZZ	USA
KRAFT, KEILE	28	F	SGL	RR	ZZZZ	USA
FREKER, ISAAC	20	M	LABR	RR	ZZZZ	USA
SCHULEN, MARIANE	18	F	SGL	RR	ZZZZ	USA
MULLER, SAM.	30	M	LABR	RR	ZZZZ	USA
WEISS, NAFTALI	18	M	LABR	RR	ZZZZ	USA
KOWALSKI, JAN	22	M	JNR	RR	ZZZZ	USA
LANDOW, DORA	17	F	SGL	RR	ZZZZ	USA

PASSENGER	AGE	SEX	OCCUPATION	PV RIVL	DES
LICHTENBERG, MARCUS	15	M	LABR	RRZZZZ	USA
MIRCZINSKI, VICTOR	19	M	LABR	RRZZZZ	USA
SUPROWSKI, LUD.	14	M	BY	RRZZZZ	USA
GORNIK, CHANNE	25	F	SGL	RRZZZZ	USA
ANITE, ZALKO	21	F	W	RRZZZZ	USA
JACOB	.11	M	INFANT	RRZZZZ	USA
LAZAR, SALI	40	F	W	RRZZZZ	USA
ISIDOR	9	M	CHILD	RRZZZZ	USA
LENE	8	F	CHILD	RRZZZZ	USA
MORITZ	6	M	CHILD	RRZZZZ	USA
HERRM.	3	M	CHILD	RRZZZZ	USA
RUFF, RAHEL	18	F	SGL	RRZZZZ	USA
WALLERSTEIN, BEILE	32	F	W	RRZZZZ	USA
DOBRE	9	F	CHILD	RRZZZZ	USA
ADOLF	.11	M	INFANT	RRZZZZ	USA
MURD.	.01	M	INFANT	RRZZZZ	USA
SCHILEKTOR, RASCHE	19	F	SGL	RRZZZZ	USA
ARON	9	M	CHILD	RRZZZZ	USA
WOLNIAEWE, VICTORIA	25	F	SGL	RRZZZZ	USA
WOLLMIENICZ, FRANZISKA	21	F	W	RRZZZZ	USA
JOSEF	.11	M	INFANT	RRZZZZ	USA
BERKSOHN, SAMUEL	28	M	MCHT	RRZZZZ	USA
KACSIC, ANTON	48	M	LABR	RRZZZZ	USA
HRONGIS, GEORG	44	M	LABR	RRZZZZ	USA
GRUNSPAN, JOEL	21	M	PRNTR	RRZZZZ	USA

SHIP: WERRA

FROM: BREMEN
TO: NEW YORK
ARRIVED: 23 JUNE 1883

PASSENGER	AGE	SEX	OCCUPATION	PV RIVL	DES
OTTO, ELISE	39	F	UNKNOWN	RRZZZZ	NY
KRUSZYNSKA, TEOFILA	23	F	UNKNOWN	RRZZZZ	NY
JOSEFA	.08	F	INFANT	RRZZZZ	NY
SANDSTEIN, Y.E.K	35	M	LABR	FNZZZZ	NY
SUNDENA, CLARIEN	18	F	LKSH	RRZZZZ	NY
GULMETS, ADRIAN	19	M	LABR	FNZZZZ	NY
SWEDEN, CHARLES	24	M	LABR	FNZZZZ	NY
NORDGRAM, BRUNO	19	M	LABR	FNZZZZ	NY
BERNAS, ELISA	23	F	UNKNOWN	FNZZZZ	NY
KEISA	19	F	UNKNOWN	FNZZZZ	NY
STOITAS, PETER	21	M	LABR	FNZZZZ	NY
BERNAS, JOHANN	42	M	LABR	FNZZZZ	NY
LISE-ANNE	21	F	UNKNOWN	FNZZZZ	NY
CLARA	19	F	UNKNOWN	FNZZZZ	NY
CARL	36	M	UNKNOWN	FNZZZZ	NY

SHIP: ARIZONA

FROM: LIVERPOOL AND QUEENSTOWN
TO: NEW YORK
ARRIVED: 25 JUNE 1883

PASSENGER	AGE	SEX	OCCUPATION	PV RIVL	DES
JAPIS, ANDERS	36	M	FLABR	RRZZZZ	USA
RANTOLS, JACOB	23	M	FLABR	RRZZZZ	USA
KONFI, MICHAEL	25	M	FLABR	RRZZZZ	USA
MAITLY, JOHN	23	M	FLABR	RRZZZZ	USA
EKMAN, JACOB	35	M	FLABR	RRZZZZ	USA
KAKOLA, JOHAN	30	M	FLABR	RRZZZZ	USA
SELLAMPA, JOHAN	46	M	FARMER	RRZZZZ	USA
NASKALA, MATTS	28	M	PRNTR	RRZZZZ	USA
VATILO, ANDERS	28	M	JNR	RRZZZZ	USA
PALLAKA, SUSANNAH	20	F	SP	RRZZZZ	USA
JACKO, HERMAN	25	M	MNR	RRZZZZ	USA
KAAPE, JOHAN	33	M	MNR	RRZZZZ	USA
NAPOLO, ELIAS	29	M	CL	RRZZZZ	USA
HENRIH	35	M	CPTR	RRZZZZ	USA

SHIP: SPAIN

FROM: LIVERPOOL AND QUEENSTOWN
TO: NEW YORK
ARRIVED: 25 JUNE 1883

PASSENGER	AGE	SEX	OCCUPATION	PV RIVL	DES
KUTSKI, MAGELAL.	40	M	LABR	FNZZZZ	USA
MORIS, TOMAS	23	M	LABR	FNZZZZ	USA
SELEYSLA, REUSH	26	M	LABR	FNZZZZ	USA
OPOLISKY, FELIX	22	M	LABR	PLZZZZ	USA
DAMEJONGH, FRANK	23	M	LABR	PLZZZZ	USA
HOASSA, HERMAN	35	M	LABR	FNZZZZ	USA
SUSANNAH	36	F	W	FNZZZZ	USA
ELMA	8	F	CHILD	FNZZZZ	USA
JAKULA, ANNA	25	F	SP	FNZZZZ	USA
PESPA, LENA	27	F	W	FNZZZZ	USA
MILMA	.06	F	INFANT	FNZZZZ	USA
BULHELMA, HENRICK	18	M	LABR	FNZZZZ	USA
SEEKAMYS, FRID	24	M	LABR	FNZZZZ	USA
LUKARELLA, DAVID	19	M	LABR	FNZZZZ	USA
KARRO, KARL	35	M	LABR	FNZZZZ	USA
PEEPKUS, CHAIM	30	M	LABR	FNZZZZ	USA
DEDORA	20	F	W	FNZZZZ	USA
SHEE	7	F	CHILD	FNZZZZ	USA
ERKEH, JAKOB	21	M	LABR	FNZZZZ	USA
RUSSKO, MARIE	23	F	SP	FNZZZZ	USA
OLLIKALA, HANSON	41	M	LABR	FNZZZZ	USA
IRHULA, MATHAS	35	M	LABR	FNZZZZ	USA
LARTINSEN, JAKOB	25	M	LABR	FNZZZZ	USA
SAKARI, EVA	28	F	SP	FNZZZZ	USA
HONKAMIEN, JAKOB	27	M	LABR	FNZZZZ	USA
LEKMANN, HADDA	31	M	LABR	FNZZZZ	USA
JUMSI, HERKA	28	M	LABR	FNZZZZ	USA
EBBA	31	M	LABR	FNZZZZ	USA
ZIGLHA, KAROLINA	19	M	LABR	FNZZZZ	USA
MAKELA, JAKOB	34	M	LABR	FNZZZZ	USA
LEBAM, ALEX	25	M	LABR	FNZZZZ	USA
MARIE	19	F	W	FNZZZZ	USA
HUYSKA, ISRAEL	25	M	LABR	FNZZZZ	USA
KARTMAN, KALLI	25	M	LABR	FNZZZZ	USA
SOKO, ANNA	22	F	SP	FNZZZZ	USA
JOREN, JOHAN	30	M	LABR	FNZZZZ	USA
LAYMANN, ARVIA	18	F	SP	FNZZZZ	USA
JORNGVEST, FRANZ	17	M	LABR	FNZZZZ	USA
KAKKONEN, OSCAR	23	M	LABR	FNZZZZ	USA
AILI, ISAK	26	M	LABR	FNZZZZ	USA
KUWALSKY, ESTHER	25	F	W	FNZZZZ	USA
ISAAC	8	M	CHILD	FNZZZZ	USA
CHAIM	.01	M	INFANT	FNZZZZ	USA
OREZIK	.05	M	INFANT	FNZZZZ	USA
WIBBA, JOHAN	22	M	LABR	FNZZZZ	USA
HAIGATATAND, JOHAN	22	M	LABR	FNZZZZ	USA
WASMEN, RIKA	53	M	LABR	FNZZZZ	USA
MARKOLA, MATHAS	26	M	LABR	FNZZZZ	USA
LELBERI, JOHAN	28	M	LABR	FNZZZZ	USA
SUSANNAH	27	F	W	FNZZZZ	USA
HUIKALAMEN, LISA	18	F	SP	FNZZZZ	USA
HAINENKI, JAKOB	41	M	LABR	FNZZZZ	USA
SOKO, SELMA	19	M	LABR	FNZZZZ	USA
BOTTA, ERIKI	19	M	LABR	FNZZZZ	USA
KORTENAA, HERM.	21	M	LABR	FNZZZZ	USA
BYNTARI, MATTE	22	F	W	FNZZZZ	USA
ERKELA, HERMAN	32	M	LABR	FNZZZZ	USA
LENYOKI, ABRAMIS	19	M	LABR	FNZZZZ	USA
HARMA, I.	19	M	LABR	FNZZZZ	USA
NISKANEN, RIKKA	31	M	LABR	FNZZZZ	USA

PASSENGER	AGE	SEX	OCCUPATION	PRV VIL DES
JUSTINA	37	F	W	FNZZZZUSA
LAMELHA, HERMANN	44	M	LABR	FNZZZZUSA
LARTENEN, HERMAN	28	M	LABR	FNZZZZUSA
ULLKONIEMS, Y.J.	21	M	LABR	FNZZZZUSA
HUTAKELO, R.	25	M	LABR	FNZZZZUSA
PROPPA, AN.	30	M	LABR	FNZZZZUSA
HARTMAN, M.	21	M	LABR	FNZZZZUSA
JOLKANDES, M.	25	M	LABR	FNZZZZUSA
HILDA, DOTT	.06	M	INFANT	FNZZZZUSA
ALAKOTILA, E.	34	F	W	FNZZZZUSA
JUHAN, SONEO	11	M	CH	FNZZZZUSA
DOTTREN, ELLIN	10	F	CH	FNZZZZUSA
ANNA	4	F	CHILD	FNZZZZUSA
IHE, ANNA	3	F	CHILD	FNZZZZUSA
JONI	.05	M	INFANT	FNZZZZUSA
MANSEPP, ISAK	15	M	LABR	FNZZZZUSA
PAZAKANQUS, H.	27	M	LABR	FNZZZZUSA
GALMA, A.	3	M	CHILD	FNZZZZUSA
HUMALALUMY, M.	32	M	LABR	FNZZZZUSA
BERTKELA, M.	20	M	LABR	FNZZZZUSA
SERKOLA, H.	28	F	W	FNZZZZUSA
MARE	.05	F	INFANT	FNZZZZUSA
PUSANEAN, P.K.	40	M	LABR	FNZZZZUSA
DORA	17	F	SP	FNZZZZUSA
JULIAN	11	M	CH	FNZZZZUSA
AHLOREN, HERMAN	30	M	LABR	FNZZZZUSA
JYRHA, SAMUEL	25	M	LABR	FNZZZZUSA
DOGERSOHN, B.L.	21	M	LABR	FNZZZZUSA
MANTIMEMA, C.	20	M	LABR	FNZZZZUSA
HOLKKA, J.	33	M	LABR	FNZZZZUSA
AUTTO, P.C.	23	M	LABR	FNZZZZUSA
KORTEMISD, J.	28	M	LABR	FNZZZZUSA
KANTO, SOPHIA	20	F	SP	FNZZZZUSA
KOKALSKY, MENDEL	40	M	LABR	FNZZZZUSA

SHIP: FRISIA

FROM: HAMBURG AND HAVRE
TO: NEW YORK
ARRIVED: 26 JUNE 1883

PASSENGER	AGE	SEX	OCCUPATION	PRV VIL DES
NARKUS, MARIANNE	20	F	SGL	RRZZZZUSA
KOPRONSKI, JOH.	24	M	LABR	RRZZZZUSA
ARNOTOWA, CRISE	45	F	W	RRZZZZUSA
ROSA	6	F	CHILD	RRZZZZUSA
LACKZEKAI, FREIDE	20	F	SGL	RRZZZZUSA
JACOB	9	M	CHILD	RRZZZZUSA
BLUM, ESTER	48	F	W	RRZZZZUSA
MALC	5	F	CHILD	RRZZZZUSA
MERES	.11	F	INFANT	RRZZZZUSA
POP, ETTEL	21	F	SGL	RRZZZZUSA
SCHAPIRA, JACOB	40	M	DLR	RRZZZZUSA
RUDNER, ISAAC	23	M	JNR	RRZZZZUSA
KOHN, MOSES	19	M	TLR	RRZZZZUSA
BERZINSKI, SARA	36	F	SGL	RRZZZZUSA
MIKULIS, VICENTI	25	M	LABR	RRZZZZUSA
KATYLAS, VINCENTI	20	M	LABR	RRZZZZUSA
RUGELS, ANTON	18	M	LABR	RRZZZZUSA
CEPOLONIS, JULS.	14	M	LABR	RRZZZZUSA
SCROTEVIC, MAGDAL.	20	F	SGL	RRZZZZUSA
DRONSELANTY, MARIE	20	F	SGL	RRZZZZUSA
BURIEKA, PAULINE	20	F	SGL	RRZZZZUSA
KOPKO, CASIMIR	20	M	LABR	RRZZZZUSA
LOPUCELIZ, JAN	30	M	LABR	RRZZZZUSA
MIX, JOH.	28	M	FARMER	RRZZZZUSA
WEISS, JOH.	20	M	FARMER	RRZZZZUSA
LEIP, SELIG	21	M	MCHT	RRZZZZUSA
MATTSON, JOH.	34	M	LABR	FNZZZZUSA
KREZELL, PAVEL	32	M	LABR	PLZZZZUSA
ANNA	26	F	W	PLZZZZUSA
JAN	5	M	CHILD	PLZZZZUSA
BROZINA, JAN	40	M	LABR	PLZZZZUSA
KREZEK, TOMAS	39	M	LABR	PLZZZZUSA
PAUL	33	M	LABR	PLZZZZUSA
AGATHE	33	F	W	PLZZZZUSA
FRANZ, WOJTECH	24	M	LABR	PLZZZZUSA
PRIBILEVSKY, VINCENT	23	M	LABR	PLZZZZUSA
MUSEL, WOJTECH	28	M	LABR	PLZZZZUSA
BAJKO, WASIL	38	M	LABR	PLZZZZUSA
PAJA, VINCENTI	44	M	LABR	PLZZZZUSA
MARIANNE	40	F	W	PLZZZZUSA
PAVEL	26	F	SI	PLZZZZUSA
ODA	15	F	CH	PLZZZZUSA
ANNA	11	F	CH	PLZZZZUSA
VICTORIA	8	F	CHILD	PLZZZZUSA
CATHARINA	5	F	CHILD	PLZZZZUSA
YAVON, MICHAL	44	M	LABR	PLZZZZUSA
STACHUVOSKI, FRANZ	23	M	LABR	PLZZZZUSA
ROSZINYAK, YANOS	44	M	LABR	PLZZZZUSA
MROEZKA, JOHANN	35	M	LABR	PLZZZZUSA
KITILENSKY, JOSEF	25	M	LABR	PLZZZZUSA
WEYDER, JOSEF	25	M	LABR	PLZZZZUSA
PAL, YANOS	25	M	LABR	PLZZZZUSA
BRACKA, JOSEF	26	M	LABR	PLZZZZUSA
MROCKA, GRZEGORG	38	M	LABR	PLZZZZUSA
MARIANNE	35	F	W	PLZZZZUSA
TOMAS	8	M	CHILD	PLZZZZUSA
CAROLINE	6	F	CHILD	PLZZZZUSA
MARTIN	3	M	CHILD	PLZZZZUSA
AGATA	1	F	CHILD	PLZZZZUSA
GILAB, MICHAL	50	M	LABR	PLZZZZUSA
KATHARINE	45	F	W	PLZZZZUSA
ANNA	23	F	CH	PLZZZZUSA
PAVEL	14	M	CH	PLZZZZUSA
MARIANNE	11	F	CH	PLZZZZUSA
YASEK	9	M	CHILD	PLZZZZUSA
AGA	7	F	CHILD	PLZZZZUSA
TEKLA	4	F	CHILD	PLZZZZUSA
WOJTECH	.03	M	INFANT	PLZZZZUSA
RUSZINSKI, JOSEPH	17	M	LABR	PLZZZZUSA
MATHIAS	60	M	LABR	PLZZZZUSA
MARIANNE	58	F	W	PLZZZZUSA
CATHARINE	19	F	CH	PLZZZZUSA
ELAMA	18	F	CH	PLZZZZUSA
MAGDALEM	15	F	CH	PLZZZZUSA
SILICKIEZO, PETER	26	M	LABR	RRZZZZUSA

SHIP: BOTHNIA

FROM: LIVERPOOL AND QUEENSTOWN
TO: NEW YORK
ARRIVED: 27 JUNE 1883

PASSENGER	AGE	SEX	OCCUPATION	PRV VIL DES
JACOBSON, JACOB	24	M	LABR	RRZZZZUSA
MARKUSSON, HERMAN	24	M	LABR	RRZZZZUSA
HAAJSALA, MALIS	20	M	LABR	FNZZZZUSA
ISAACSON, OSKAR	20	M	LABR	FNZZZZUSA
NOTTBECH, C.MISS	29	F	SP	RRZZZZUSA

PASSENGER	AGE	SEX	OCCUPATION	PRIVL	DES

SHIP: BARK LEA

FROM: CAPE TOWN
TO: NEW YORK
ARRIVED: 28 JUNE 1883

PASSENGER	AGE	SEX	OCCUPATION	PRIVL	DES
FRANKLYN, U	35	M	LABR	PLZZZZ	USA

SHIP: CANADA

FROM: HAVRE
TO: NEW YORK
ARRIVED: 28 JUNE 1883

PASSENGER	AGE	SEX	OCCUPATION	PRIVL	DES
STEIN, HERMANN	29	M	SHMK	RRZZZZ	NY
HASENFRATZ, R.	23	M	SHMK	RRZZZZ	NY
MEYER, C.	27	M	SHMK	RRZZZZ	UNK
KARCH, J.MISS	20	F	UNKNOWN	RRZZZZ	UNK
HOFFMANN, T.MR	9	M	CHILD	RRZZZZ	NY
GRUMBERG, KISSIG	13	M	UNKNOWN	RRZZZZ	NY
TELBERG, M.	21	M	LKSH	RRZZZZ	NY

SHIP: HEIMDAL

FROM: UNKNOWN
TO: NEW YORK
ARRIVED: 29 JUNE 1883

PASSENGER	AGE	SEX	OCCUPATION	PRIVL	DES
VANDAWGUD, MICHAL	31	M	MCHT	RRZZZZ	USA

SHIP: STATE OF FLORIDA

FROM: GLASGOW AND LARNE
TO: NEW YORK
ARRIVED: 29 JUNE 1883

PASSENGER	AGE	SEX	OCCUPATION	PRIVL	DES
ALEXEIDES, J.	21	M	LABR	RRZZZZ	USA
SEVANIK, J.	30	M	LABR	RRZZZZ	USA
RADOICKOWSER, S.	20	M	LABR	RRZZZZ	USA
LESEHMSKE, C.	30	M	LABR	RRZZZZ	USA
BORHNITZKY, M.	28	M	LABR	RRZZZZ	USA
SCHMIJGELL, J.	24	M	LABR	RRZZZZ	USA
USNIGER, J.	25	M	LABR	RRZZZZ	USA
MICHALSKY, M.	33	M	LABR	RRZZZZ	USA
DANSKE, A.	23	M	LABR	RRZZZZ	USA
A.	18	F	UNKNOWN	RRZZZZ	USA
LASCHEITS, F.	19	F	UNKNOWN	RRZZZZ	USA
KARAMER, B.	53	M	LABR	RRZZZZ	USA
B.	32	F	UNKNOWN	RRZZZZ	USA
D.	8	M	CHILD	RRZZZZ	USA
S.	7	F	CHILD	RRZZZZ	USA
JOS.	5	M	CHILD	RRZZZZ	USA
ABRAHAMSEN, M.	19	M	LABR	RRZZZZ	USA
MIKLAND, L.KLEIN	21	F	UNKNOWN	RRZZZZ	USA
ROSE, S.F.	26	F	UNKNOWN	RRZZZZ	USA
GOLEBOCK, H.	29	F	UNKNOWN	RRZZZZ	USA
KARANOWSKY, W.	17	F	UNKNOWN	RRZZZZ	USA
LENTZ, G.	22	M	LABR	RRZZZZ	USA
JOS.	10	M	UNKNOWN	RRZZZZ	USA
KATZ, A.	41	M	LABR	RRZZZZ	USA
J.	34	F	UNKNOWN	RRZZZZ	USA
B.	17	F	UNKNOWN	RRZZZZ	USA
S.	10	F	UNKNOWN	RRZZZZ	USA
S.	6	F	CHILD	RRZZZZ	USA
M.	3	M	CHILD	RRZZZZ	USA
J.	.08	F	INFANT	RRZZZZ	USA
GRENES, M.	45	M	LABR	RRZZZZ	USA
A.	45	F	UNKNOWN	RRZZZZ	USA
I.	17	F	UNKNOWN	RRZZZZ	USA
E.	10	F	UNKNOWN	RRZZZZ	USA
J.	4	F	CHILD	RRZZZZ	USA
PISMEK, F.	42	M	LABR	RRZZZZ	USA
R.	38	F	UNKNOWN	RRZZZZ	USA
S.	16	F	UNKNOWN	RRZZZZ	USA
P.	12	F	UNKNOWN	RRZZZZ	USA
H.	10	F	UNKNOWN	RRZZZZ	USA
DWD.	8	M	CHILD	RRZZZZ	USA
S.	.06	M	INFANT	RRZZZZ	USA
BRATZKY, H.	22	F	UNKNOWN	RRZZZZ	USA
BERK, H.	18	F	UNKNOWN	RRZZZZ	USA
SUSSMANWITZ, P.	28	F	UNKNOWN	RRZZZZ	USA
MULLER, DVD.	22	M	LABR	RRZZZZ	USA
J.	20	F	UNKNOWN	RRZZZZ	USA
L.	20	F	UNKNOWN	RRZZZZ	USA
GARBER, B.	10	M	UNKNOWN	RRZZZZ	USA
EWGEL, P.	18	F	UNKNOWN	RRZZZZ	USA
RATH, M.	18	F	UNKNOWN	RRZZZZ	USA
FAKSCHEIT, M.	20	F	UNKNOWN	RRZZZZ	USA
PRINZ, E.	18	F	UNKNOWN	RRZZZZ	USA
KATZ, F.	24	M	LABR	RRZZZZ	USA
W.	22	F	UNKNOWN	RRZZZZ	USA
AB.	.10	M	INFANT	RRZZZZ	USA
SCHMONROLZKY, M.	26	M	LABR	RRZZZZ	USA
F.	23	F	UNKNOWN	RRZZZZ	USA
SWIKHUSKI, J.	43	F	UNKNOWN	RRZZZZ	USA

SHIP: RHYNLAND

FROM: ANTWERP
TO: NEW YORK
ARRIVED: 30 JUNE 1883

PASSENGER	AGE	SEX	OCCUPATION	PRIVL	DES
LAWATSCHEK, ELISE	29	F	UNKNOWN	PLZZZZ	NY
STANKOZKA, MALZUZATA	60	F	LABR	PLZZZZ	NY
PELEOFIA	33	F	UNKNOWN	PLZZZZ	NY
KLEMENTO	29	F	UNKNOWN	PLZZZZ	NY
DEKER, JOHANNA	17	F	UNKNOWN	PLZZZZ	NY
MARKOWSKA, FRANCISCA	20	F	UNKNOWN	PLZZZZ	PLY
U	15	F	UNKNOWN	PLZZZZ	CH

SHIP: ANCHORIA

FROM: GLASGOW
TO: NEW YORK
ARRIVED: 01 JULY 1883

PASSENGER	AGE	SEX	OCCUPATION	PRIVL	DES
HRERLINSKI, FAT.	23	F	SVNT	RRZZZZ	USA

SHIP: BERLIN

FROM: LIVERPOOL
TO: NEW YORK
ARRIVED: 02 JULY 1883

PASSENGER	AGE	SEX	OCCUPATION	PRV VIL DES
GUSTAFSEN, JULIUS	30	M	LABR	RRZZZZMN
MOJAVA, JOHN-P.	23	M	LABR	RRZZZZMI
DYNE, MATIS	26	M	LABR	RRZZZZMI
FORNUVAARA, DANL	32	M	LABR	RRZZZZMI
RONAKOSKI, THOS.	31	M	LABR	RRZZZZMI
JOHANSON, JACOB	25	M	LABR	RRZZZZMI
MICKELSON, JOHAN	27	M	LABR	RRZZZZMI
JOHANSEN, WILHELM	21	M	LABR	RRZZZZMI
MATTSON, JACOB	25	M	LABR	RRZZZZMI
MULKUMENI, ANDRES	38	M	LABR	RRZZZZMI
MALKOSAN, THOS.	30	M	LABR	RRZZZZMI
JOHANSON, JACOB	25	M	LABR	RRZZZZMI
KWIMAKI, JOHN	28	M	LABR	RRZZZZMI
ISACSON, ISAAC	24	M	LABR	RRZZZZMI
NETMAN, WILLIAM	28	M	LABR	RRZZZZMI
GUSTAFSON, GUSTAF	30	M	LABR	RRZZZZMI
LOPPI, MATHIAS	24	M	LABR	RRZZZZMI
MERNETI, EMMANUEL	23	M	LABR	RRZZZZMI
JACOBSON, ANDREAS	48	M	LABR	RRZZZZMI
WATTERLA, KULLA-M.	25	F	SP	RRZZZZNY

SHIP: THE QUEEN

FROM: LIVERPOOL
TO: NEW YORK
ARRIVED: 02 JULY 1883

PASSENGER	AGE	SEX	OCCUPATION	PRV VIL DES
PERHAN, ALEXANDER	32	M	LABR	RRZZZZUSA
JOUTTI, JULIA	27	F	SP	FNZZZZUSA
LISSA, HUSTMA	27	F	SP	FNZZZZUSA
HURTILA, SUSANNA	23	F	SP	FNZZZZUSA
ALBERY, HELENA	45	F	W	FNZZZZUSA
DROTTIEN	11	F	CH	FNZZZZUSA
POLAKKA, MIKKI	34	M	LABR	FNZZZZUSA
LAKONSIR, GRITTA	18	F	SP	FNZZZZUSA
ASHAMALA, ANNA	24	F	SP	FNZZZZUSA
KOTHKILA, ANNA	16	F	SP	FNZZZZUSA
RUDINEN, ANNA	25	F	SP	FNZZZZUSA
HILLUNEN, JOHAN	30	M	LABR	FNZZZZUSA
ABEL	24	M	LABR	FNZZZZUSA
JOHAN	30	M	LABR	FNZZZZUSA
MURSON, MATTHIAS	29	M	LABR	FNZZZZUSA
WAISANEN, JAKOB	26	M	LABR	FNZZZZUSA
MORLANSEN, KASA	23	F	W	FNZZZZUSA
IDA	5	F	CHILD	FNZZZZUSA
IERKINSKA, KASA	30	F	W	FNZZZZUSA
ANNA	7	F	CHILD	FNZZZZUSA
ADAM	8	M	CHILD	FNZZZZUSA
KORPINER, JAKOB	23	M	LABR	FNZZZZUSA
ANNA	25	F	SP	FNZZZZUSA
KASSON	7	M	CHILD	FNZZZZUSA
ANNA	2	F	CHILD	FNZZZZUSA
HITTENGEN, JOHAN	17	M	LABR	FNZZZZUSA
SIMLINA, WILLIAM	21	M	LABR	FNZZZZUSA
KERANON, WALBORN	18	F	SP	FNZZZZUSA
MAGARAMEN, JOHAN	45	M	LABR	FNZZZZUSA
SAPPANSEN, WALBORG	30	F	SP	FNZZZZUSA
LESHILA, MARIA	25	F	SP	FNZZZZUSA
KUPPA, ISAAK	36	M	LABR	FNZZZZUSA
KOUPUTA, GANURE	44	M	LABR	FNZZZZUSA
OLSON, STEFFU	34	M	LABR	FNZZZZUSA
SAMUELSEN, OSKAR	19	M	LABR	FNZZZZUSA
JYNFAMMAKA, HENDRIK	38	M	LABR	FNZZZZUSA
HISULA, JUHA	43	M	LABR	FNZZZZUSA
PALMERM, CARL	21	M	LABR	FNZZZZUSA
SVENSON, JOHAN	33	M	LABR	FNZZZZUSA
ANNA	32	F	W	FNZZZZUSA
EMMA	4	F	CHILD	FNZZZZUSA
JOHANSON, LOUGEREKRAN	26	F	SP	FNZZZZUSA
CARL	26	M	LABR	FNZZZZUSA
CARLSEN, IDA	18	F	SP	FNZZZZUSA
NILSDOTTER, ANNA	59	F	W	FNZZZZUSA
JANSEN, ANDERS	26	M	LABR	FNZZZZUSA
CHRISTOFFISON, CAROLINE	24	F	W	FNZZZZUSA
U	00	F	INF	FNZZZZUSA
SERTENSEN, LARS	21	M	LABR	FNZZZZUSA
NILSON, MARTINUS	20	M	LABR	FNZZZZUSA
JOHANSEN, AUGUST	22	M	LABR	FNZZZZUSA
ERIKSON, JOHAN	4	M	CHILD	FNZZZZUSA
STRANGE, MATTIE	35	F	W	FNZZZZUSA
MARI	38	F	W	FNZZZZUSA
ERIK	31	M	LABR	FNZZZZUSA
ANNIE	31	F	W	FNZZZZUSA
SIKLA, ANA	36	M	LABR	FNZZZZUSA
LIDSTRAGE, MATTI	19	M	LABR	FNZZZZUSA
BRINK, MIKKI	21	M	LABR	FNZZZZUSA
MANI, HERMAN	20	M	LABR	FNZZZZUSA
MAKI, HERMAN	25	M	LABR	FNZZZZUSA
RAULAMAKI, MARTI	16	M	LABR	FNZZZZUSA
SUSANNA	25	F	W	FNZZZZUSA
LAKSI, JACOB	23	M	LABR	FNZZZZUSA
MAMMI, HENDRIK	35	M	LABR	FNZZZZUSA
HASKALD, MATH.	28	M	LABR	FNZZZZUSA
MUILN, JOHAN	28	M	LABR	FNZZZZUSA
KARAA, JAKOB	23	M	LABR	FNZZZZUSA
MAKINEN, HERMAN	27	M	LABR	FNZZZZUSA
SATTELA, JOHAN	23	M	LABR	FNZZZZUSA
RANANGARVI, GUSBY	24	M	LABR	FNZZZZUSA
LUOMANBERN, GUSTAF	44	M	LABR	FNZZZZUSA
JOHAN	18	M	LABR	FNZZZZUSA
ANTI	20	M	LABR	FNZZZZUSA
BERTITI, JOHAN	35	M	LABR	FNZZZZUSA
JUNTI, JOHAN	29	M	LABR	FNZZZZUSA
JOHANSEN, ERIK	30	M	LABR	FNZZZZUSA
KERMUNEND, ISAK	29	M	LABR	FNZZZZUSA
JOHANSEN, JAKOB	21	M	LABR	FNZZZZUSA
METTARAVINGI, JIHAN	24	M	LABR	FNZZZZUSA
FORNBERY, JOHAN	21	M	LABR	FNZZZZUSA
KERMUMI, JOHAN	22	M	LABR	FNZZZZUSA
HEIKKALA, MATTI	38	M	LABR	FNZZZZUSA
ISACKTON, JACOB	30	M	LABR	FNZZZZUSA
KOWS, MARIE	23	F	SP	FNZZZZUSA
EDIN, ERIK	23	M	LABR	FNZZZZUSA
SVENSON, SELMA	22	M	LABR	FNZZZZUSA
ELIASEN, JOHAN	29	M	LABR	FNZZZZUSA
WALKAA, JOHAN	30	M	LABR	FNZZZZUSA
GUNAGVIRT, ANDERS	41	M	LABR	FNZZZZUSA
MAKI, JOHAN	30	M	LABR	FNZZZZUSA
MARIE	34	F	W	FNZZZZUSA
JOHAN	8	M	CHILD	FNZZZZUSA
BILLAYAMAKI, KISA	16	M	LABR	FNZZZZUSA
MANSTROM, KALLI	26	M	LABR	FNZZZZUSA
MILSSALD, JOHAN	32	M	LABR	FNZZZZUSA
MAKI, JOHAN	19	M	LABR	FNZZZZUSA
KERALLA, JOHAN	53	M	LABR	FNZZZZUSA
MAYA	52	F	W	FNZZZZUSA
MAYA	11	F	CH	FNZZZZUSA
KERRALD, FRANZ	25	M	LABR	FNZZZZUSA
NINA	23	F	W	FNZZZZUSA
LIVAROS, JOHAN	45	M	LABR	FNZZZZUSA
SUCKENTHALEN, JOSEF	22	M	LABR	FNZZZZUSA
MOLDZ, ROB	37	M	GZR	FNZZZZUSA
ARDV, WILH.	16	M	LABR	FNZZZZUSA
FAVER, LVAVIZ	29	M	LABR	FNZZZZUSA
BLUHM, FRED	22	M	LABR	FNZZZZUSA
SUTTNER, FOTTLIEB	54	M	LABR	FNZZZZUSA
OTTO	23	M	LABR	FNZZZZUSA
MASSEN, JEUS	25	M	LABR	FNZZZZUSA

PASSENGER	AGE	SEX	OCCUPATION	PRV VIL DES
DENK, JOSEPH	24	M	LABR	FNZZZZUSA
WESNER, JULIUS	27	M	LABR	FNZZZZUSA
WOLFF, EDWARD	25	M	LABR	FNZZZZUSA
FRED.	31	M	LABR	FNZZZZUSA

SHIP: FRANCE

FROM: HAVRE
TO: NEW YORK
ARRIVED: 05 JULY 1883

PASSENGER	AGE	SEX	OCCUPATION	PRV VIL DES
JACASSY, J.F.	39	M	TDR	RRZZZZNY
ABOLNIKOFF, MOSES	21	M	SHMK	RRZZZZNY
ROSENSTEIN, LOUIS	28	M	UNKNOWN	RRZZZZNY
BAGDANOFF, HIRSCH	21	M	PNR	RRZZZZNY
LEIBMANN, JULES	28	M	UNKNOWN	RRZZZZNY
MARIE	25	F	UNKNOWN	RRZZZZNY
PASSERO, BATTISTE	25	M	CL	RRZZZZNY

SHIP: LESSING

FROM: HAMBURG AND HAVRE
TO: NEW YORK
ARRIVED: 05 JULY 1883

PASSENGER	AGE	SEX	OCCUPATION	PRV VIL DES
TRAUBE, MORITZ	16	M	DLR	RRZZZZUSA
GOLDSTEIN, ARON	43	M	MCHT	RRZZZZUSA
BORDOWITZ, SIMON	32	M	MCHT	RRZZZZUSA
MAJEWSKI, MARIAM	24	M	LABR	RRZZZZUSA
KOMINSKI, STANISL.	19	M	LABR	RRZZZZUSA
DOMAROTZKI, VINCENT	36	M	LABR	RRZZZZUSA
VICTORIA	35	F	W	RRZZZZUSA
LUDOVIKA	5	F	CHILD	RRZZZZUSA
VINCENT	.03	M	INFANT	RRZZZZUSA
WOLASEWITZ, GEORG	26	M	LABR	RRZZZZUSA
GUTOW, WASIL	40	M	LABR	RRZZZZUSA
URBANOWITZ, CASIMIR	22	M	LABR	RRZZZZUSA
DICK, JOHANN	35	M	FARMER	RRZZZZUSA
CATH.	28	F	W	RRZZZZUSA
CATH.	8	F	CHILD	RRZZZZUSA
JOH.	7	M	CHILD	RRZZZZUSA
SARA	4	F	CHILD	RRZZZZUSA
GERHARD	.03	M	INFANT	RRZZZZUSA
NICKEL, HEDWIG	28	F	W	RRZZZZUSA
CATH.	26	F	W	RRZZZZUSA
SARA	.06	F	INFANT	RRZZZZUSA
MARTENTZ, CORNELIUS	28	M	LABR	RRZZZZUSA
ABRAH.	26	M	LABR	RRZZZZUSA
HENRICH	23	M	LABR	RRZZZZUSA
ABR.	22	M	LABR	RRZZZZUSA
KISSEN, PETER	29	M	LABR	RRZZZZUSA
CATH.	31	F	W	RRZZZZUSA
CATH.	8	F	CHILD	RRZZZZUSA
ANNA	7	F	CHILD	RRZZZZUSA
JOHS.	6	M	CHILD	RRZZZZUSA
PIETRICH	5	M	CHILD	RRZZZZUSA
PETRUS	2	M	CHILD	RRZZZZUSA
HEINR.	.06	M	INFANT	RRZZZZUSA
ROSENTHAL, ISAAC	26	M	LABR	RRZZZZUSA
DROZEDOWITZ, MARTA	36	F	W	RRZZZZUSA
MALKE	16	F	D	RRZZZZUSA
EDLIA	60	F	WO	RRZZZZUSA
JACOB	8	M	CHILD	RRZZZZUSA
CHAIE	7	M	CHILD	RRZZZZUSA
RACHEL	6	F	CHILD	RRZZZZUSA
ELLA	4	F	CHILD	RRZZZZUSA
EHMER, EUGEN	24	M	MCHT	RRZZZZUSA
CEDERBANN, HERRM.	24	M	MCHT	RRZZZZUSA
TAUCHER, EMILIE	19	F	SGL	RRZZZZUSA
PETSCHKIESS, JOH.	31	M	LABR	RRZZZZUSA
LIPSCHAK, MORCHEL	37	M	BCHR	RRZZZZUSA
KRAKOWER, SCHIFFRA	37	F	W	RRZZZZUSA
PREISE, CHASKEL	55	M	DLR	RRZZZZUSA
BREZING, BERTHA	21	F	SGL	RRZZZZUSA
MOLOWITCH, ALEXANDER	6	M	CHILD	RRZZZZUSA
AMALIE	4	F	CHILD	RRZZZZUSA
KUKOWER, ESTHER	16	F	SGL	RRZZZZUSA
MICHELSON, RIWKE	8	F	CHILD	RRZZZZUSA
GOLDBLATT, CHEIE	30	F	W	RRZZZZUSA
ALTER	.11	M	INFANT	RRZZZZUSA
LICHTHARZ, HERSCH	20	M	TLR	RRZZZZUSA
OHRENBACH, ARON	40	M	LABR	RRZZZZUSA
KULICK, ESTER	25	F	SGL	RRZZZZUSA
LULZER, MARIE	24	F	SGL	RRZZZZUSA
LIPSCHUTZ, ABRAHAM	27	M	LABR	RRZZZZUSA
ENDEL, CHAIE	25	F	W	RRZZZZUSA
LEA	.11	M	INFANT	RRZZZZUSA
BEILE	.11	M	INFANT	RRZZZZUSA
ALEXANDROWITZ, DAVID	17	M	BCHR	RRZZZZUSA
ZIPKE	17	F	SGL	RRZZZZUSA
SCHULDNER, HIRSCH	27	M	SMH	RRZZZZUSA
KANN, JACOB	19	M	MCHT	RRZZZZUSA
LEIDECK, ISAAK	18	M	BCHR	RRZZZZUSA
WLADISLAWA, ELEONORE	36	F	SGL	RRZZZZUSA
SEMBRUNOWSKA, CAECILIE	27	F	SGL	RRZZZZUSA
FOBLANSKA, JAN	38	M	LABR	RRZZZZUSA
NICHTMANN, HEIMANN	21	M	JNR	RRZZZZUSA

SHIP: AUSTRALIA

FROM: HAMBURG
TO: NEW YORK
ARRIVED: 06 JULY 1883

PASSENGER	AGE	SEX	OCCUPATION	PRV VIL DES
GARFINKEL, DINE	25	F	SGL	RRZZZZUSA
SAKEWITZ, MARIE	27	F	WO	RRZZZZUSA
EVA	5	F	CHILD	RRZZZZUSA
JOSEF	3	M	CHILD	RRZZZZUSA
ALEXANDER	.06	M	INFANT	RRZZZZUSA
NICOLAUS, SIMON.	29	F	WO	RRZZZZUSA
VIERIKEWITZ, LEIBISCH	28	M	TRDSMN	RRZZZZUSA
RUBIN, SALOMON	20	M	CGRMKR	RRZZZZUSA
SCHLANGER, HERM.	40	M	TLR	RRZZZZUSA
KLEIMVACHER, AUG.	28	M	FARMER	RRZZZZUSA
VILOMANCHUS, JONAS	29	M	FARMER	RRZZZZUSA
CATHARINA	27	F	W	RRZZZZUSA
HUBNER, ISAAK	22	M	TLR	RRZZZZUSA
AUGUST	25	M	FARMER	RRZZZZUSA
LEWIN, MARIA	22	F	SGL	RRZZZZUSA
BOKAWITZKI, IDA	14	F	CH	RRZZZZUSA
CHAIM	8	M	CHILD	RRZZZZUSA
BIRKENBAUM, DERSON	28	M	TRDSMN	PLZZZZUSA
KAUFTEIL, ELIAS	25	M	TRDSMN	PLZZZZUSA
CORNEGEN, AUGUST	28	M	LABR	PLZZZZUSA
BEWZ, AUGUST	32	M	LABR	PLZZZZUSA

SHIP: PENNLAND

FROM: ANTWERP
TO: NEW YORK
ARRIVED: 06 JULY 1883

PASSENGER	AGE	SEX	OCCUPATION	PRV VIL DES
ALTER, L.	21	M	PNTR	RRZZZZPHI
GOLDSTEIN, ESTHER	18	F	UNKNOWN	RRZZZZPHI
ABEL	20	M	LABR	RRZZZZDAV

SHIP: MAIN

FROM: BREMEN
TO: NEW YORK
ARRIVED: 07 JULY 1883

PASSENGER	AGE	SEX	OCCUPATION	PRV VIL DES
SCHAFF, DAVID	18	M	MCHT	RRZZZZUSA
FIRENPIANSKI, BENJ.	28	M	DLR	RRZZZZUSA
NEWMANN, MOSES	21	M	DLR	RRZZZZUSA
KAN, LOESER	44	M	DLR	RRZZZZUSA
HOSCOSKO	19	M	DLR	RRZZZZUSA
HYMAN, ISIDOR	21	M	JNR	RRZZZZUSA
ISRA	.06	F	INFANT	RRZZZZUSA

SHIP: WYOMING

FROM: LIVERPOOL AND QUEENSTOWN
TO: NEW YORK
ARRIVED: 10 JULY 1883

PASSENGER	AGE	SEX	OCCUPATION	PRV VIL DES
THRONDSEN, ANNE	59	F	W	FNZZZZUSA
THOWALD	18	F	SP	FNZZZZUSA
LORENTZEN, JORGEN	20	M	LABR	FNZZZZUSA
PEDERSEN, MAUS	47	M	LABR	FNZZZZUSA
RENDAHL, JOHANUS	32	M	LABR	FNZZZZUSA

SHIP: LYDIAN MONARCH

FROM: LONDON
TO: NEW YORK
ARRIVED: 11 JULY 1883

PASSENGER	AGE	SEX	OCCUPATION	PRV VIL DES
ZETRICKER, ANNA	9	F	CHILD	PLZZZZNY
LENA	4	F	CHILD	PLZZZZNY
ISAAC, SARAH	40	F	W	PLZZZZNY
RAPHAEL	16	F	CH	PLZZZZNY
THOEBE	14	F	CH	PLZZZZNY
IENDLEWITZ, LEAH	25	F	W	PLZZZZNY
BETSY	3	F	CHILD	PLZZZZNY
CHIEB	1	M	CHILD	PLZZZZNY
CHAIN	.06	F	INFANT	PLZZZZNY
IACOBS, RACHEL	33	F	W	PLZZZZNY
MORRIS	11	M	CH	PLZZZZNY
ASHER	10	M	CH	PLZZZZNY
LEAPIER, WOOLF	19	M	UNKNOWN	PLZZZZNY
GABER, BARNETT	38	M	LABR	PLZZZZNY
BETSY	34	F	W	PLZZZZNY
MENDEL	11	M	CH	PLZZZZNY
ABRAHAMS	5	M	CHILD	PLZZZZNY
MARKS	3	M	CHILD	PLZZZZNY
JACOB	.06	M	INFANT	PLZZZZNY
GENTLEMAN, LEO	20	M	BTMKR	PLZZZZNY
BROWN, W.F.	44	M	CPTR	PLZZZZTOR
U-MRS	40	F	W	PLZZZZTOR
ANNIE	14	F	CH	PLZZZZTOR
GEORGE	15	M	CH	PLZZZZTOR
JANE	6	F	CHILD	PLZZZZTOR
GORDON	4	M	CHILD	PLZZZZTOR
ACKERMAN, LEO	45	M	LABR	PLZZZZPHI
ZAMBERG, SIMON	30	M	TLR	PLZZZZNY
SARAH	26	F	W	PLZZZZNY
WOLF	4	M	CHILD	PLZZZZNY
ELIZA	5	F	CHILD	PLZZZZNY
ALEXANDER	2	M	CHILD	PLZZZZNY
SENLOWITZ, PEREZ	20	M	TLR	RRZZZZNY
ZELIMEBER, RACHEL	40	F	LDY	RRZZZZNY
LUKA	15	F	LDY	RRZZZZNY
JACOBS, FANNY	40	F	LDY	PLZZZZNY
ANE	21	F	LDY	PLZZZZNY
MALTA, WALBE	24	M	LABR	PLZZZZMI
MARKS, LOUIS	40	M	TLR	RRZZZZNY
SARAH	39	F	W	RRZZZZNY
ESTER	15	F	CH	RRZZZZNY
JESSIE	8	F	CHILD	RRZZZZNY
ABRAHAMS, JOSEPH	29	M	LABR	RRZZZZNY
RACHEL	28	F	W	RRZZZZNY
ABRAHAM	9	M	CHILD	RRZZZZNY
ESTER	7	F	CHILD	RRZZZZNY
LEAH	.04	M	INFANT	RRZZZZNY
MITYMAN, KILLIE	36	F	W	RRZZZZNY
AMELIA	14	F	CH	RRZZZZNY
MATHON	9	F	CHILD	RRZZZZNY
JANE	7	F	CHILD	RRZZZZNY
BETSY	5	F	CHILD	RRZZZZNY
ABRAHAM	2	M	CHILD	RRZZZZNY
MORRIS	.06	M	INFANT	RRZZZZNY
JACOBS, MORRIS	50	M	TLR	RRZZZZNY
JANE	48	F	W	RRZZZZNY
LEWIS	11	M	CH	RRZZZZNY
BARREL	11	M	CH	RRZZZZNY
SAMUEL	5	M	CHILD	RRZZZZNY
FRIEND, MOS.	40	M	TLR	RRZZZZNY
FANNY	33	F	W	RRZZZZNY
LOUIS	9	M	CHILD	RRZZZZNY
EMANUEL	7	M	CHILD	RRZZZZNY
CILIA	4	M	CHILD	RRZZZZNY
FILCIA	2	M	CHILD	RRZZZZNY
FLORENCE	.06	F	INFANT	RRZZZZNY
COHEN, ISAAK	48	M	TLR	RRZZZZNY

SHIP: STATE OF NEBRASKA

FROM: GLASGOW AND LARNE
TO: NEW YORK
ARRIVED: 11 JULY 1883

PASSENGER	AGE	SEX	OCCUPATION	PRV VIL DES
GWAS, S.	42	M	LABR	PLZZZZUSA
SKURA, S.	37	M	LABR	PLZZZZUSA
RUBENSKI, L.	20	M	LABR	PLZZZZUSA
CHAIE	20	F	SP	PLZZZZUSA
ARLAMOWTZ, U	30	M	LABR	PLZZZZUSA
LEWITZ, U	16	M	LABR	PLZZZZUSA
LIPSCHITZ, M.	28	M	LABR	PLZZZZUSA
CHMILEWSKY, U-MRS.	23	F	W	PLZZZZUSA
SELDE	1	F	CHILD	PLZZZZUSA
LICHTENBERG, U-MRS.	50	F	W	PLZZZZUSA
CHAIE	12	F	CH	PLZZZZUSA
JOUEL	9	M	CHILD	PLZZZZUSA
ABRAM	7	M	CHILD	PLZZZZUSA

PASSENGER	AGE	SEX	OCCUPATION	PRV VIL DES
CHAIM	2	M	CHILD	PLZZZZUSA
SAJONTSCHICK, A.	36	M	PDLR	PLZZZZUSA
SIMONSON, F.	36	M	CPTR	PLZZZZUSA
SALZMANN, U-MRS.	35	F	W	PLZZZZUSA
XENNE	10	F	CH	PLZZZZUSA
CHAIE	5	F	CHILD	PLZZZZUSA
MARIA	3	F	CHILD	PLZZZZUSA
ROCHEL	.06	F	INFANT	PLZZZZUSA
KLAPECK, M.	38	M	PDLR	PLZZZZUSA
ODLER, C.	18	M	LABR	PLZZZZUSA
GDALKOWSKY, M.	36	M	PDLR	PLZZZZUSA
LUMBINSKY, I.	19	M	LABR	PLZZZZUSA
KLEINFUSS, A.	40	M	PDLR	PLZZZZUSA
BARNOWITZ, B.	38	M	PDLR	PLZZZZUSA
LIPOWITZ, F	30	M	BCHR	PLZZZZUSA
ROTHENBERG, B.	40	M	PDLR	PLZZZZUSA
RAGOWSKY, C.	21	M	PDLR	PLZZZZUSA
BEREND, S.	17	M	PDLR	PLZZZZUSA
SELZER, M.	18	M	PDLR	PLZZZZUSA
WISSIGRETSKY, J.	32	M	TLR	PLZZZZUSA
GROSSMANN, M.	10	M	CH	PLZZZZUSA
LIEMANN, S.	25	M	TLR	PLZZZZUSA
KAPLAN, D.	19	M	SHMK	PLZZZZUSA
RIZEL, I.	50	M	PDLR	PLZZZZUSA
SARENBERG, A.	45	M	PDLR	RRZZZZUSA
ABRAMOWITZ, H.	17	M	PDLR	RRZZZZUSA
LEIBSOHN, I.	23	M	PDLR	RRZZZZUSA
STUHR, H.	36	M	PDLR	RRZZZZUSA
HOFSTELER, M.	16	M	PDLR	RRZZZZUSA
SCHIDOWSKY, W.	19	M	PDLR	RRZZZZUSA
COHEN, CHANE	28	F	W	RRZZZZUSA
MILNER, L.	20	M	JNR	RRZZZZUSA
BODIL, M.	30	M	PDLR	RRZZZZUSA
MAMCHAWSKY, CHAIM	29	M	PDLR	RRZZZZUSA
LINITZKI, J.	29	M	BY	RRZZZZUSA
GOLD, S.	46	M	PDLR	RRZZZZUSA
MERSON, J.	24	M	PDLR	RRZZZZUSA
A.	25	M	PDLR	RRZZZZUSA
SUSFMANN, I.	22	M	TNR	RRZZZZUSA
JOSSELSOHN, J.	41	M	LABR	RRZZZZUSA
MAGID, M.	27	M	SHMK	RRZZZZUSA
LUBINSKY, B.	24	M	PDLR	RRZZZZUSA
SCHMILK, I.	17	M	PDLR	RRZZZZUSA
FRICHS, S.	34	M	PDLR	RRZZZZUSA
BINDER, H.	17	M	SHMK	RRZZZZUSA
SCHWERIMG, M.	17	M	PDLR	RRZZZZUSA
MORWISCH, H.	22	M	PDLR	RRZZZZUSA
BERZOWSKIE, U-MRS.	34	F	W	RRZZZZUSA
SARAH	11	F	CH	RRZZZZUSA
MOSES	10	M	CH	RRZZZZUSA
FEIGEL	9	F	CHILD	RRZZZZUSA
ABRAM	8	M	CHILD	RRZZZZUSA
SALMON	6	M	CHILD	RRZZZZUSA
WOLFF	2	M	CHILD	RRZZZZUSA
KESKITALO, F.	19	M	FARMER	FNZZZZUSA
HALNNEN, I.	43	M	FARMER	FNZZZZUSA
A.	36	M	FARMER	FNZZZZUSA
RAUTIS, S.	25	M	FARMER	FNZZZZUSA
VAIHOJA, I.	20	M	FARMER	FNZZZZUSA
PIRTTIKOSKY, J.	18	M	FARMER	FNZZZZUSA
JAAKOLA, J.	19	M	FARMER	FNZZZZUSA
MATTILA, I.	34	M	FARMER	FNZZZZUSA
MARIA	27	F	SP	FNZZZZUSA
HEIKKOLA, A.	25	M	FARMER	FNZZZZUSA
JOENTAKANEN, M.	36	M	FARMER	FNZZZZUSA
AKERSFON, S.	27	M	LABR	FNZZZZUSA
AHLFONS, F.A.	33	M	CPTR	FNZZZZUSA
KAROLINE	00	F	W	FNZZZZUSA
HAAG, ELLEN	18	F	SP	FNZZZZUSA

SHIP: LABRADOR

FROM: HAVRE
TO: NEW YORK
ARRIVED: 12 JULY 1883

PASSENGER	AGE	SEX	OCCUPATION	PRV VIL DES
MEDVEDNIKOW, ANDRE	26	M	MCHT	RRZZZZNY
WOLF, MALNI	23	M	TLR	RRZZZZNY
SARAH	21	F	UNKNOWN	RRZZZZNY
JACOB	.02	M	INFANT	RRZZZZNY
JANKELEWICZ, JUDE	22	M	TLR	RRZZZZNY
LUNSKY, SAMUEL	24	M	CPTR	RRZZZZNY
LEA	22	F	UNKNOWN	RRZZZZNY
GUSS, BERLE	45	M	TLR	RRZZZZNY
GOLDE	40	F	UNKNOWN	RRZZZZNY
DAVID	20	M	UNKNOWN	RRZZZZNY

SHIP: CALIFORNIA

FROM: HAMBURG
TO: NEW YORK
ARRIVED: 13 JULY 1883

PASSENGER	AGE	SEX	OCCUPATION	PRV VIL DES
WIESE, SELIG	36	M	TLR	RRZZZZUSA
WASILEWSKY, STASIS	21	M	TRDSMN	RRZZZZUSA
STRUPINSKY, JES.	30	M	TRDSMN	PLZZZZUSA
ANNA	19	F	W	PLZZZZUSA
PAZISKI, ISAAK	27	M	TRDSMN	PLZZZZUSA
PEIFER, JOS.	24	M	TRDSMN	RRZZZZUSA
PLEIN, HERSCH	22	M	TRDSMN	RRZZZZUSA
FEINBERG, WICH	32	F	WO	RRZZZZUSA
EISICH	8	F	CHILD	RRZZZZUSA
SARAH	6	F	CHILD	RRZZZZUSA
ROSATZKY, CHAIE	44	F	WO	RRZZZZUSA
RINE	7	F	CHILD	RRZZZZUSA
JERUHM	6	M	CHILD	RRZZZZUSA
HERZ, CHINYE	28	F	WO	PLZZZZUSA
GOLDE	5	M	CHILD	PLZZZZUSA
DONINGER, LIEBE	25	F	WO	PLZZZZUSA
GOLDE	.06	M	INFANT	PLZZZZUSA
ELEBOGEN, GITEL	16	F	SGL	PLZZZZUSA
PRINOWITZ, RACHEL	18	F	SGL	RRZZZZUSA
USPITZ, MERIAM	7	F	CHILD	RRZZZZUSA
SAMUEL	6	M	CHILD	RRZZZZUSA
FINKOBERK, MARKI	21	M	LABR	PLZZZZUSA
HERZ, FREDIE	6	F	CHILD	PLZZZZUSA
ISRAEL	5	M	CHILD	PLZZZZUSA
MELNIKOW, PESCHKE	20	F	WO	RRZZZZUSA
KAPLAN, MICHEL	19	M	TRDSMN	RRZZZZUSA
GOLDSTEIN, GOLDE	25	F	SGL	RRZZZZUSA
SCHMALHEIZER, MAX	7	M	CHILD	RRZZZZUSA
MARIE	5	F	CHILD	RRZZZZUSA
WEINSTEIN, SCHEFTEL	22	M	TRDSMN	RRZZZZUSA
SILBER, MORDSCHE	19	M	TRDSMN	RRZZZZUSA
PERLSTEIN, MOSES	36	M	TRDSMN	RRZZZZUSA
RACHOWITZ, JUDEL	45	F	WO	RRZZZZUSA
HERTZ	18	M	S	RRZZZZUSA
BRAUN, DOBE	19	F	SGL	RRZZZZUSA
GORDON, LINCHE	33	F	WO	RRZZZZUSA
ELIESER	6	M	CHILD	RRZZZZUSA
MOSCOWITZ, MARITZ	22	M	TRDSMN	RRZZZZUSA
NUFSBAUM, ZILLI	17	F	SGL	RRZZZZUSA
MIHAL, MORRIS	23	M	TRDSMN	RRZZZZUSA
SWAN, MORRIS	23	M	TRDSMN	RRZZZZUSA
SIF, THEODOR	20	M	TRDSMN	RRZZZZUSA
ROSENBLUTT, NACHM.	20	M	TRDSMN	RRZZZZUSA
UHRBACH, SIEGM.	25	M	TRDSMN	RRZZZZUSA
EVRES, EISIK	42	M	TRDSMN	RRZZZZUSA
BRUCKNER, ZIMCHE	29	M	TRDSMN	RRZZZZUSA

PASSENGER	AGE	SEX	OCCUPATION	PRV VIL DES
BENOUSOHN, JACOB	35	M	TRDSMN	RRZZZZUSA
ROSENZWEIG, DANIEL	19	M	TRDSMN	RRZZZZUSA
MUGLEISEN, NACHIM	20	M	LABR	RRZZZZUSA
GRIM, JACOB	43	M	LABR	RRZZZZUSA
SCHEFFLER, RIFKE	18	M	LABR	RRZZZZUSA
LEITNER, FRIMET	28	M	LABR	RRZZZZUSA
FISCHBEIN, SALY	20	M	LABR	RRZZZZUSA
HIRSCH, ANNA	7	F	CHILD	RRZZZZUSA
STREIMM, SCHAREM	7	M	CHILD	RRZZZZUSA
BOLLMAN, ERNST	26	M	MCHT	RRZZZZUSA
SLOWICKI, IGN.	18	M	LABR	RRZZZZUSA
ZIMMERMAN, LEIB	43	M	TLR	RRZZZZUSA
RIEBECK, BERREL	46	M	LABR	RRZZZZUSA
BRANDJE, MOSES	7	M	CHILD	RRZZZZUSA
BAROWSKI, TAUBE	43	F	WO	RRZZZZUSA
ABRAHAM	7	M	CHILD	RRZZZZUSA
PESCHE	6	F	CHILD	RRZZZZUSA
SCHORE	.04	F	INFANT	RRZZZZUSA
SONKAP, JOHANNA	60	F	WO	RRZZZZUSA
JOSEF	17	M	S	RRZZZZUSA
SKARDA, JOHANN	39	M	LABR	RRZZZZUSA
WOLPE, MEIER	22	M	LABR	RRZZZZUSA
KOWINSKI, HIRSCH	17	M	TRDSMN	RRZZZZUSA
BERMANN, MEIER	18	M	TRDSMN	RRZZZZUSA
KANN, SCHOLEM	17	M	TRDSMN	RRZZZZUSA
SCHALET, BERKO	16	M	TRDSMN	RRZZZZUSA
GOLDSTEIN, ABRAM	7	M	CHILD	RRZZZZUSA
ARGANOWITS, HANNE	18	F	SGL	RRZZZZUSA
SCHLEPOWITS, SALOM.	18	M	TRDSMN	RRZZZZUSA
JOSEF	20	M	TRDSMN	RRZZZZUSA
SCHLEIER, PESCHE	35	F	WO	RRZZZZUSA
BETTI	.09	F	INFANT	RRZZZZUSA
JACOBSOHN, HERZ	66	M	TRDSMN	RRZZZZUSA
MICHLE	69	F	W	RRZZZZUSA
ANDORSKI, LEA	18	F	SGL	RRZZZZUSA

SHIP: SUEVIA

FROM: HAMBURG
TO: NEW YORK
ARRIVED: 13 JULY 1883

PASSENGER	AGE	SEX	OCCUPATION	PRV VIL DES
WODNICK, MINDS.	18	F	SGL	RRZZZZUSA
THERESE	9	F	CHILD	RRZZZZUSA
MILLER, BERUCH	50	M	MLR	RRZZZZUSA
NATHAN, ABE	16	M	WCHMKR	RRZZZZUSA
RADONSKY, ANTON	21	M	LABR	RRZZZZUSA
STORPIRISTER, JOSEF	25	M	LABR	RRZZZZUSA
BARZDAITIZ, AUZE	22	M	LABR	RRZZZZUSA
JAROSIK, ADOLF	24	M	LABR	RRZZZZUSA
TOBOLAUZKI, CHASCHE	15	F	SGL	RRZZZZUSA
ROSEK, ASRIEL	19	M	TLR	RRZZZZUSA
MEYERS, ASRIEL	50	F	W	RRZZZZUSA
MOSES	9	M	CHILD	RRZZZZUSA
ABROMAITIS, ISAAC	46	M	DLR	RRZZZZUSA
DOLNITZKI, KUSSIEL	30	M	DLR	RRZZZZUSA
MINTZ, JUDEL	60	M	DLR	RRZZZZUSA
BRENNER, SLAWE	15	M	LABR	RRZZZZUSA
URBANOWITZ, VINCENT	23	M	LABR	RRZZZZUSA
AMBROSEWICZKOWA, MAGD.	30	F	SGL	RRZZZZUSA
HEINRICK, ANT.	40	M	LABR	RRZZZZUSA
DIEZBAL, JAN	27	M	LABR	RRZZZZUSA
AUZE, MALIS	22	M	LABR	RRZZZZUSA
KASACO, ANTON	24	M	LABR	RRZZZZUSA
ZAGARNISKY, MACH.	21	M	LABR	RRZZZZUSA
MIROCS, ABRAH.	16	M	LABR	RRZZZZUSA
BALLEZIEZ, ANDRAS	20	M	LABR	RRZZZZUSA
SAWITZKY, PIMIS	18	M	LABR	RRZZZZUSA
CZARUE	9	M	CHILD	RRZZZZUSA
FRUGEL, GETTEL	15	F	SGL	RRZZZZUSA

PASSENGER	AGE	SEX	OCCUPATION	PRV VIL DES
BUTKOWSKY, MARTIN	24	M	LABR	RRZZZZUSA
DIENN, GUSTAV	27	M	LABR	RRZZZZUSA
NEWMARK, LEIB	21	M	BRR	RRZZZZUSA
HASKEL, MORITZ	18	M	MCHT	RRZZZZUSA
EPSTEIN, ESTER	19	F	SGL	RRZZZZUSA
ZICHANOWSKI, JOSEF	28	M	LABR	RRZZZZUSA
FRYD, HIRSCH	13	M	BY	RRZZZZUSA
BIRUBAUM, ISRAEL	22	M	LABR	RRZZZZUSA
SCHIFF, LEISER	14	M	LABR	RRZZZZUSA
SCHIE	9	M	CHILD	RRZZZZUSA
JEVJENSKI, GROMAN	34	M	DLR	RRZZZZUSA
DULSKI, MENDEL	9	M	CHILD	RRZZZZUSA
PHILIPOWITZ, SIGMUND	27	M	LABR	RRZZZZUSA
STANISLAWA	22	F	W	RRZZZZUSA
STOWALSKY, JUDAS	17	M	MCHT	RRZZZZUSA
KOLWENSKY, MOSES	23	M	LABR	RRZZZZUSA
GINDSBURG, MENDEL	19	M	LABR	RRZZZZUSA
HOLZMAN, MOSES	23	M	LABR	RRZZZZUSA
KETZER, MOSES	23	M	LABR	RRZZZZUSA
HOLLAND, SALUSCH	25	M	MUSN	RRZZZZUSA
RUBINOWITZ, ZLATE	40	F	W	RRZZZZUSA
LEIE	8	F	CHILD	RRZZZZUSA
SARA	6	F	CHILD	RRZZZZUSA
CHAIM	.11	M	INFANT	RRZZZZUSA
RINGELHAUFT, SARA	20	F	SGL	RRZZZZUSA
HIRSCH	9	M	CHILD	RRZZZZUSA
BRALOSENSKI, ISAAC	21	M	UNKNOWN	RRZZZZUSA
PALKI, MARIE	23	F	SGL	FNZZZZUSA
BAREUDT, ANNA	39	F	W	RRZZZZUSA
LEVIN, LOUIS	17	M	DLR	RRZZZZUSA
SCHLOM, ROSA	27	F	SGL	RRZZZZUSA
EFRATH, GITTEL	23	F	SGL	RRZZZZUSA
KABACKOS, ETTI	12	F	CH	RRZZZZUSA
POSKER, ALEXANDER	35	M	LABR	RRZZZZUSA
LITTI	40	F	W	RRZZZZUSA
SARA	8	F	CHILD	RRZZZZUSA
ROSA	7	F	CHILD	RRZZZZUSA
CHANNE	4	F	CHILD	RRZZZZUSA
FEIGE	3	F	CHILD	RRZZZZUSA
LINUKY, IRAN	32	M	LABR	RRZZZZUSA
PUSTILA, JACOB	28	M	LABR	RRZZZZUSA
NEVECKY, ANTON	35	M	LABR	RRZZZZUSA
MANHEIM, DAVID	30	M	LABR	RRZZZZUSA
MISCHKEWE--, HIRSCH	23	M	LABR	RRZZZZUSA
BUBELS, MORDCHE	29	M	LABR	RRZZZZUSA
SZIPOWSKI, LEA	45	F	WO	RRZZZZUSA
SCHOLEM	19	M	CH	RRZZZZUSA
SAMUEL	9	M	CHILD	RRZZZZUSA
KAPLAN, ITTE	35	F	WO	RRZZZZUSA
CHEIE	9	F	CHILD	RRZZZZUSA
HANNE	7	F	CHILD	RRZZZZUSA
NOCHIM	5	M	CHILD	RRZZZZUSA
JACOB	.11	M	INFANT	RRZZZZUSA
REGER, ISAAC	26	M	TLR	RRZZZZUSA
KOWADLA, RUBEN	21	M	TLR	RRZZZZUSA
LANKIDES, CASIMIR	20	M	TLR	RRZZZZUSA
BUTELONIS, ADAM	20	M	TLR	RRZZZZUSA
MENEZINSKI, MOSES	28	M	MCHT	RRZZZZUSA
FRIEDMAN, SALOMON	9	M	CHILD	RRZZZZUSA
LEWIN, ANNA	18	F	SGL	RRZZZZUSA
ABRAMOWITZ, MEITE	19	M	SGL	RRZZZZUSA
MENKULSKI, ISRAEL	21	M	SHMK	RRZZZZUSA
POTASCHINSKI, ISAAC	21	M	SMH	RRZZZZUSA
RUDNITZKI, MOSES	21	M	BCHR	RRZZZZUSA
SCHILANSKI, JOSSEL	21	M	BRM	RRZZZZUSA
LIEBERMANN, ISAAC	17	M	BRM	RRZZZZUSA
FITEFSKI, SARA	29	F	WO	RRZZZZUSA
MORDCHE	.11	F	INFANT	RRZZZZUSA
KACZAKOWITZ, WSTER	29	F	WO	RRZZZZUSA
HENE	8	F	CHILD	RRZZZZUSA
TUBO--, BLUME	21	F	WO	RRZZZZUSA
MALKE	.11	F	INFANT	RRZZZZUSA
SARA	8	F	CHILD	RRZZZZUSA
CHANNE	4	F	CHILD	RRZZZZUSA
ZIPA	7	F	CHILD	RRZZZZUSA

PASSENGER	AGE	SEX	OCCUPATION	PRV VIL DES
JOSEF	.11	M	INFANT	RRZZZZUSA
BEILES, ABRAHAM	26	M	LABR	RRZZZZUSA
JERMANOWSKA, SARA	21	F	SGL	RRZZZZUSA
REBECCA	22	F	SGL	RRZZZZUSA
ALTSCHUL--, HIRSCH	28	M	TCHR	RRZZZZUSA
SIMON, DORA	24	F	WO	RRZZZZUSA
BERTHA	.11	F	INFANT	RRZZZZUSA
IDE	.01	F	INFANT	RRZZZZUSA
MENIKER, DAVID	19	M	LABR	RRZZZZUSA

SHIP: SILESIA

FROM: HAMBURG
TO: NEW YORK
ARRIVED: 16 JULY 1883

PASSENGER	AGE	SEX	OCCUPATION	PRV VIL DES
HEYMANN, ARON	18	M	TLR	RRZZZZUSA
FISCHELOWITZ, WOLF	20	M	MCHT	RRZZZZUSA
META	18	F	W	RRZZZZUSA
BLEIWEISS, MOSES	24	M	TLR	RRZZZZUSA
DAVID	16	M	LABR	RRZZZZUSA
GROSSMANN, MOSES	20	M	LABR	RRZZZZUSA
SEGALLA, BERTHA	16	F	SGL	RRZZZZUSA
DOBROWSKY, KAREL	28	M	LABR	RRZZZZUSA
NEUMANN, ADOLF	19	M	LABR	RRZZZZUSA
FILDEJOSEF, ABRAH.	26	M	LABR	RRZZZZUSA
BLOCKY, ISAAC	18	M	LABR	RRZZZZUSA
GUTMANN, SAM.W.	18	M	LABR	RRZZZZUSA
KONOPACK, ANIELA	27	F	W	RRZZZZUSA
LUCIAN	.11	M	INFANT	RRZZZZUSA
BRONISLAWA	.01	F	INFANT	RRZZZZUSA
HOLPERIEN, EIGE	40	F	W	RRZZZZUSA
SCHLOME	9	M	CHILD	RRZZZZUSA
CHANNE	8	F	CHILD	RRZZZZUSA
NOTE	7	F	CHILD	RRZZZZUSA
SENDER	3	M	CHILD	RRZZZZUSA
DWORE	.11	M	INFANT	RRZZZZUSA
BOROWSKY, ISAAC	37	M	LABR	RRZZZZUSA
KURNICKY, FELIX	31	M	LABR	RRZZZZUSA
PETRINE, MORITZ	20	M	LKSH	RRZZZZUSA
BORG, MORDCHE	20	M	DLR	RRZZZZUSA
JUDURSKI, CHAIM	17	M	DLR	RRZZZZUSA
BOGIN, BARUCH	16	M	DLR	RRZZZZUSA
MAROWSKY, MORDCHE	16	M	TLR	RRZZZZUSA
VOGEL, HAUNE	15	F	W	RRZZZZUSA
TAUBE	9	F	CHILD	RRZZZZUSA
DINA	8	F	CHILD	RRZZZZUSA
HENACH	6	M	CHILD	RRZZZZUSA
RUWEN	5	M	CHILD	RRZZZZUSA
BEILE	.11	F	INFANT	RRZZZZUSA
MOLOWITZKY, OWSCHE	23	F	TLR	RRZZZZUSA
WILENEZIK, LEA	22	F	SGL	RRZZZZUSA
MALKE	21	F	SGL	RRZZZZUSA
GLAUBIGER, JACOB	30	M	MCHT	RRZZZZUSA
KUBA, KOL	26	M	FARMER	RRZZZZUSA
PATWIEKY, ABRAHAM	30	M	MCHT	RRZZZZUSA
SILEWICZ, CASIMIR	24	M	LABR	RRZZZZUSA
KABATZNIK, CAECILIE	22	F	W	RRZZZZUSA
SAMUEL	.11	M	INFANT	RRZZZZUSA
GOLDSTEIN, CHANNE	21	F	SGL	RRZZZZUSA
KRONENBERG, ISAAC	62	M	DYR	RRZZZZUSA
FARBER, FEWEL	22	M	DYR	RRZZZZUSA
JACOBOWICZ, ROSA	20	F	SGL	RRZZZZUSA
BANDER, RIWEL	30	M	BCHR	RRZZZZUSA
JERUSALEMSKY, WOLF	21	M	LABR	RRZZZZUSA
SARETZKY, SELIG	25	M	MCHT	RRZZZZUSA
HOLIBACH, TOBIAS	35	M	LABR	RRZZZZUSA
KOLNETZKI, FELIX	25	M	LABR	RRZZZZUSA
NYSTROM, CARL	18	M	MCHT	FNZZZZUSA

SHIP: ENGLAND

FROM: LIVERPOOL AND QUEENSTOWN
TO: NEW YORK
ARRIVED: 17 JULY 1883

PASSENGER	AGE	SEX	OCCUPATION	PRV VIL DES
HURT, JUO.	20	M	LABR	RRZZZZUSA
WENEREKKA, JUO.	22	M	LABR	RRZZZZUSA
HURTZ, SAKER	20	M	LABR	RRZZZZUSA
LAITZ, HENNITZ	36	M	LABR	RRZZZZUSA
RAISAINER, SOLOMON	18	M	LABR	RRZZZZUSA
VEROHARDE, JOLOMAN	36	M	LABR	RRZZZZUSA
JAINFERRI, MATTAS	27	M	LABR	RRZZZZUSA
BYCKNER, JOSEPH	23	M	LABR	RRZZZZUSA
SAPPANER, JAKOB	30	M	LABR	RRZZZZUSA
GRETZ	28	F	W	RRZZZZUSA
KAPANA	4	F	CHILD	RRZZZZUSA
JOKAB	2	M	CHILD	RRZZZZUSA
ANNA	00	U	INF	RRZZZZUSA
FANHENEN, JOS.	25	M	LABR	RRZZZZUSA
ROPPO, SIMARD	28	M	LABR	RRZZZZUSA
SAPPANE, JOSEPH	32	M	LABR	RRZZZZUSA
U, LISH	30	M	LABR	RRZZZZUSA
JOHNSA, KRESTINA	8	F	CHILD	RRZZZZUSA
U, CIRL	6	F	CHILD	RRZZZZUSA
ELIS	4	F	CHILD	RRZZZZUSA
PENTSON, SOPHA	20	F	SP	RRZZZZUSA
JOHNSON, KILINA	15	F	CH	RRZZZZUSA
HOLENSBERG, F.W.	15	M	LABR	RRZZZZUSA
JOHNSON, JIN.	43	M	LABR	RRZZZZUSA
HUNTER, CARYL	25	M	LABR	RRZZZZUSA
JOHNSON, J.H.	30	M	LABR	RRZZZZUSA
U, MESIDORA	25	F	W	RRZZZZUSA
RAISANEN, ANTI	50	M	LABR	RRZZZZUSA
ANNA	25	F	SP	RRZZZZUSA
BUSKA, HILKE	37	M	LABR	RRZZZZUSA
BENRA, JUO.	3	M	CHILD	RRZZZZUSA
KESALA, JAKOB	27	M	LABR	RRZZZZUSA
ANTTINOGA, JAKOB	28	M	LABR	RRZZZZUSA
MULATKEN, ANDERS	21	M	LABR	RRZZZZUSA
KARLSON, W.	2	M	CHILD	RRZZZZUSA
KURLSON, G.	35	M	LABR	RRZZZZUSA
NORDBURG, MARIA	32	M	LABR	RRZZZZUSA
CARLSON, JOSEF	27	M	LABR	RRZZZZUSA
WANBERG, GABRIEL	27	M	LABR	RRZZZZUSA
HANSON, ERIN	28	M	LABR	RRZZZZUSA
HACKUNSEN, PEN	25	M	LABR	RRZZZZUSA

SHIP: HAMMONIA

FROM: HAMBURG AND HAVRE
TO: NEW YORK
ARRIVED: 18 JULY 1883

PASSENGER	AGE	SEX	OCCUPATION	PRV VIL DES
BEIDEN, GOLDE	35	F	W	RRZZZZUSA
HASE	14	F	CH	RRZZZZUSA
ELKA	8	F	CHILD	RRZZZZUSA
DENSON, BERSCHA	24	F	W	RRZZZZUSA
GOLDMAN, CHASE	18	F	SGL	RRZZZZUSA
KORHONEN, THOMAS	24	M	LABR	FNZZZZUSA
CAHN, ALBE-JESCHIEL	32	F	W	RRZZZZUSA
TABUSCH	.11	M	INFANT	RRZZZZUSA
MENDEL, BINA	32	F	W	RRZZZZUSA
JOSEF	9	M	CHILD	RRZZZZUSA
SARA	8	F	CHILD	RRZZZZUSA
MALKES, LEIB	33	M	LABR	RRZZZZUSA
KOHN, TAUBE	25	F	SGL	RRZZZZUSA
TEKOZINSKI, SAML.	23	M	LABR	RRZZZZUSA
SCHWARZMANN, JACOB	18	M	LABR	RRZZZZUSA

PASSENGER	AGE	SEX	OCCUPATION	PRV	VIL	DES
RUBENSTEIN, AIZIK	17	M	LABR	RRZZZZUSA		
REISE	21	F	SGL	RRZZZZUSA		
GABA, LIEBE	27	F	W	RRZZZZUSA		
HIRSCH	3	M	CHILD	RRZZZZUSA		
WEINER, ZEMACH	23	M	LABR	RRZZZZUSA		
VOGELSON, ABRAHAM	20	M	LABR	RRZZZZUSA		
RODSCHUTZKY, MOSES	28	M	LABR	RRZZZZUSA		
MISKE	20	F	W	RRZZZZUSA		
WEIBERG, SEILIG	20	M	LABR	RRZZZZUSA		
EISENSCHMIDT, CHAIE	34	F	W	RRZZZZUSA		
REBECCA	7	F	CHILD	RRZZZZUSA		
TAUBE	5	F	CHILD	RRZZZZUSA		
ARON	.11	M	INFANT	RRZZZZUSA		
NOCHIM	.01	M	INFANT	RRZZZZUSA		
EFRAIKE, BENJAMIN	30	M	MCHT	RRZZZZUSA		
LEIB	24	M	MCHT	RRZZZZUSA		
LEIB	22	M	MCHT	RRZZZZUSA		
SCHON, BEILE	15	F	SGL	RRZZZZUSA		
ELIASCHOWITZ, ISAAC	25	M	LABR	RRZZZZUSA		
LEA	22	F	W	RRZZZZUSA		
CHAIE	.11	F	INFANT	RRZZZZUSA		
HERM.	.01	M	INFANT	RRZZZZUSA		
ONEL, JUDEL	18	M	LABR	RRZZZZUSA		
DINER, LEVIN	60	M	LABR	RRZZZZUSA		
LIMRU	23	M	LABR	RRZZZZUSA		
SCHENKER, CHAIM	34	M	GZR	RRZZZZUSA		
FARBER, JOEL	35	M	TCHR	RRZZZZUSA		
FINKELSTEIN, SAMUEL	16	M	LABR	RRZZZZUSA		

SHIP: ST GERMAIN

FROM: HAVRE
TO: NEW YORK
ARRIVED: 18 JULY 1883

PASSENGER	AGE	SEX	OCCUPATION	PRV	VIL	DES
STEINBERG, JACOB	49	M	NN	PLZZZZNY		

SHIP: STATE OF NEVADA

FROM: GLASGOW AND LARNE
TO: NEW YORK
ARRIVED: 18 JULY 1883

PASSENGER	AGE	SEX	OCCUPATION	PRV	VIL	DES
LEWINSKY, SIMON	23	M	MCHT	PLZZZZUSA		
TORWIG, FRED	26	M	MCHT	PLZZZZUSA		
SWITINSKY, SCHONE	25	F	W	PLZZZZUSA		
SARAH	3	F	CHILD	PLZZZZUSA		
SELIG	00	M	NN	PLZZZZUSA		
SILKERMANN, MAX	00	M	LABR	PLZZZZUSA		
ALBINSKY, CHACE	21	F	NN	PLZZZZUSA		
ITTE	1	F	CHILD	PLZZZZUSA		
CHANE	.06	M	INFANT	PLZZZZUSA		
SLOWTONSKY, JOSEL	44	M	MCHT	PLZZZZUSA		
BONOWSKY, MOSES	19	M	MCHT	PLZZZZUSA		
CHAIE	22	F	W	PLZZZZUSA		
BARCHE	.02	M	INFANT	PLZZZZUSA		
MOLTIN, ISAAC	68	M	PDLR	PLZZZZUSA		
RIVEKKA	20	F	SVNT	PLZZZZUSA		
SCHELINSKY, KERZUCH	20	M	PDLR	PLZZZZUSA		
GUSCHPAN, JOSEPH	20	M	PDLR	PLZZZZUSA		
MEYERSITZ, SALMEN	37	M	PDLR	PLZZZZUSA		
KADMEZAS, SAMUEL	32	M	PDLR	PLZZZZUSA		
GURALSKY, CHTZKEL	35	M	PDLR	PLZZZZUSA		
SARAH	27	F	W	PLZZZZUSA		
ABRAHAM	.02	M	INFANT	PLZZZZUSA		
SMOLNITZKY, HR-ER.	20	M	PDLR	PLZZZZUSA		
MARKINSKY, ABRAHAM	20	M	PDLR	PLZZZZUSA		
SARAH	20	F	W	PLZZZZUSA		
LESER	19	M	PDLR	PLZZZZUSA		
JANKEL	.03	M	INFANT	PLZZZZUSA		
KALM, MARCUS	50	M	PDLR	PLZZZZUSA		
VANDOWSKY, SIMON	00	M	PDLR	PLZZZZUSA		
HUSCHEL	10	M	NN	PLZZZZUSA		
NILTOLERA, SUSANNE	18	F	SVNT	FNZZZZUSA		
JAMISKO, EVA	25	F	SVNT	FNZZZZUSA		

SHIP: BOHEMIA

FROM: HAMBURG AND HAVRE
TO: NEW YORK
ARRIVED: 23 JULY 1883

PASSENGER	AGE	SEX	OCCUPATION	PRV	VIL	DES
TRUPANSKY, WOLF	24	M	UNKNOWN	RRZZZZUSA		
SAPPENSTEIN, JACOB	9	M	CHILD	RRZZZZUSA		
GWEINSKI, SARA	20	F	SGL	RRZZZZUSA		
SANMEL	13	M	B	RRZZZZUSA		
BEN	33	M	SDLR	RRZZZZUSA		
EICHWEDEL, FERD	33	M	SDLR	RRZZZZUSA		
STREICH, ALTE	40	F	W	RRZZZZUSA		
LEILE	20	F	CH	RRZZZZUSA		
CHAIE	7	F	CHILD	RRZZZZUSA		
ALBERT	6	F	CHILD	RRZZZZUSA		
CHRISTINE	3	F	CHILD	RRZZZZUSA		
PETERSEN, PETER	18	M	FARMER	RRZZZZUSA		
YENS	15	M	FARMER	RRZZZZUSA		
NIELSEN, H.P.	37	M	FARMER	RRZZZZUSA		
PETERSEN, MARIANE	42	F	W	RRZZZZUSA		
CAROLINE	9	F	CHILD	RRZZZZUSA		
RASMINE	8	F	CHILD	RRZZZZUSA		
ELLEN	5	F	CHILD	RRZZZZUSA		
OTTO	.10	M	INFANT	RRZZZZUSA		
DAHLGAARD, C.J.	32	M	FARMER	RRZZZZUSA		
CHRISTINE	24	F	W	RRZZZZUSA		
MAREN	4	M	CHILD	RRZZZZUSA		
YENS	3	M	CHILD	RRZZZZUSA		
OTTO	.10	M	INFANT	RRZZZZUSA		
REISSE, DOROTHEA	27	F	SGL	RRZZZZUSA		
SCHERER, JULS.	17	M	DLR	RRZZZZUSA		
JULS.	17	M	DLR	RRZZZZUSA		
HAASE, REGINE	31	F	W	RRZZZZUSA		
VALENTIN	2	F	CHILD	RRZZZZUSA		
LIERMANN, FRIEDER	54	M	FARMER	RRZZZZUSA		
FRIEDERICE	52	F	W	RRZZZZUSA		
AUGUSTE	15	F	D	RRZZZZUSA		
BADUNZEL, GUSTAV	34	M	FARMER	RRZZZZUSA		
WILHMINE	35	F	W	RRZZZZUSA		
FRANK	8	F	CHILD	RRZZZZUSA		
EMILIE	5	F	CHILD	RRZZZZUSA		
ANNA	4	F	CHILD	RRZZZZUSA		
AUGUSTE	.09	F	INFANT	RRZZZZUSA		
UHRENSOHN, MOSES	42	M	BKR	RRZZZZUSA		
EKE	42	F	W	RRZZZZUSA		
CHANNE	17	F	CH	RRZZZZUSA		
SIMON	9	F	CHILD	RRZZZZUSA		
SCHEIN	8	F	CHILD	RRZZZZUSA		
ISAAC	4	F	CHILD	RRZZZZUSA		
JOSCHWED	.11	F	INFANT	RRZZZZUSA		
DASCHE	.01	F	INFANT	RRZZZZUSA		
HOLLANDER, SENDER	20	M	LABR	RRZZZZUSA		
FEIGE	20	F	W	RRZZZZUSA		
JUSELSTEIN, HEINRICH	20	M	MCHT	RRZZZZUSA		
KRUGER, AUGUST	39	M	LABR	RRZZZZUSA		
JULIANNE	33	F	W	RRZZZZUSA		
U, WILH	9	F	CHILD	RRZZZZUSA		
EMILIE	7	F	CHILD	RRZZZZUSA		

PASSENGER	AGE	SEX	OCCUPATION	PRV VIL DES
EMIL	4	M	CHILD	RRZZZZUSA
EMMA	2	F	CHILD	RRZZZZUSA
PAUL	.09	U	INFANT	RRZZZZUSA
NETZLER, FRIEDER	16	M	FSHMN	RRZZZZUSA
BOECK, CAROLINE	67	F	W	RRZZZZUSA
MULLER, WILH	20	M	LABR	RRZZZZUSA
ROMUS, FERD	26	M	FARMER	RRZZZZUSA
JASDSEWSKA, JOSEFINE	50	F	SGL	RRZZZZUSA
LINKE, MARIA	21	F	SGL	RRZZZZUSA
KRIGER, CHATHO	23	F	SGL	RRZZZZUSA
AZARKA, PENZEL	9	F	CHILD	RRZZZZUSA
PERLMANN, CHAIN	20	M	LABR	RRZZZZUSA
ZEUDKERMANN, JETTE	24	F	W	RRZZZZUSA
LEIB	.11	F	INFANT	RRZZZZUSA
SZULCZERKA, ANTONIA	18	F	SGL	RRZZZZUSA
OPALKOWSKI, MAX	29	M	SHMK	RRZZZZUSA
RUBURK, WOLF	24	M	LABR	RRZZZZUSA
ETTEL	24	F	W	RRZZZZUSA
SARA	7	F	CHILD	RRZZZZUSA
BENJA	.03	F	INFANT	RRZZZZUSA
BASEL	43	M	LABR	RRZZZZUSA
JACOB	15	M	CH	RRZZZZUSA
BENJAMIN	9	M	CHILD	RRZZZZUSA
KRISCHISKY, REISEL	9	M	CHILD	RRZZZZUSA
WEISS, FRIEDERICH	40	M	FARMER	RRZZZZUSA
ELONORE	40	F	W	RRZZZZUSA
JOHANNE	19	F	CH	RRZZZZUSA
GOTTFRIED	17	M	CH	RRZZZZUSA
SAMUEL	11	M	CH	RRZZZZUSA
LIDA	8	F	CHILD	RRZZZZUSA
SANDLIERT	2	F	CHILD	RRZZZZUSA
DUX, JOHANN	22	M	FARMER	RRZZZZUSA
RATBMANN, NAFTALI	55	M	FARMER	RRZZZZUSA
JETTE	17	F	SGL	RRZZZZUSA
SENDOROWITZ, MARCUS	24	M	LABR	RRZZZZUSA
KOSWEN, SCHMERL	18	M	LABR	RRZZZZUSA

SHIP: GENERAL WERDER

FROM: BREMEN
TO: NEW YORK
ARRIVED: 23 JULY 1883

PASSENGER	AGE	SEX	OCCUPATION	PRV VIL DES
VYMANN, ANNA	14	F	NN	RRZZZZUSA
JAKIMACI, GRETA	37	F	W	RRZZZZUSA
HEKKALA, WYS.	19	F	DMS	RRZZZZUSA
IDA	16	F	DMS	RRZZZZUSA
SAPHIE	12	F	CH	RRZZZZUSA
WILJAM	8	M	CHILD	RRZZZZUSA
TARRIMAA, ERIK	27	M	LABR	RRZZZZUSA
HONNUJUNTI, GUSTAVA	29	F	W	RRZZZZUSA
MARIANNE	4	F	CHILD	RRZZZZUSA
WILJAM	2	M	CHILD	RRZZZZUSA
CZASKA, ANDREAS	46	M	LABR	RRZZZZUSA
CIROSKA, PETER	47	M	LABR	RRZZZZUSA
ALBANUS, STANISLAW	23	M	LABR	RRZZZZUSA

SHIP: GELLERT

FROM: HAMBURG AND HAVRE
TO: NEW YORK
ARRIVED: 24 JULY 1883

PASSENGER	AGE	SEX	OCCUPATION	PRV VIL DES
PLIHINS, MASIS	26	M	DLR	RRZZZZUSA
LELJANSKY, RUBIN	32	M	DLR	RRZZZZUSA
YESENACH, PESCHAH	30	M	DLR	RRZZZZUSA
SOLEWSKI, FRANZ	28	M	DLR	RRZZZZUSA
BOROWSKI, MORITZ	24	M	DLR	RRZZZZUSA
SINBERG, NASHAN	30	M	DLR	RRZZZZUSA
MOROWITZ, MOSES	17	M	UNKNOWN	RRZZZZUSA
MIX, JOH.	28	M	LABR	RRZZZZUSA
ANSONIE	16	F	SGL	RRZZZZUSA
KOMENDAWSKY, PETER	26	M	LABR	RRZZZZUSA
ROLIHOWSKY, CASPAR	26	M	LABR	RRZZZZUSA
ERDMAN, MOSES	9	M	CHILD	RRZZZZUSA
LEVINSTAN, SARA	20	F	W	RRZZZZUSA
ABR.	.11	M	INFANT	RRZZZZUSA
SCHILEM, SCHLOM	45	M	LABR	RRZZZZUSA
ESSE	8	F	CHILD	RRZZZZUSA
LEWINSTEIN, ISAAC	22	M	LABR	RRZZZZUSA
JACOB	.11	M	INFANT	RRZZZZUSA
MELL, HIRSCH	21	M	LABR	RRZZZZUSA
MIRCE	.11	M	INFANT	RRZZZZUSA
SUSSMANN, JACOB	20	M	LABR	RRZZZZUSA
SCHILLEM, SUSSE	9	M	CHILD	RRZZZZUSA
CLIASOHN, SARA	25	F	W	RRZZZZUSA
ITE	4	F	CHILD	RRZZZZUSA
MOSES	.11	M	INFANT	RRZZZZUSA
HERZLICH, JACOB	15	M	LABR	RRZZZZUSA
KAUFMANN, LOUIS	18	M	LABR	RRZZZZUSA
PEISACH	56	M	LABR	RRZZZZUSA
WEINER, MOSES	26	M	LABR	RRZZZZUSA
KAMINOWSKY, ROSEL	40	F	WO	RRZZZZUSA
CHAIE	14	F	CH	RRZZZZUSA
ITZIK	9	M	CHILD	RRZZZZUSA
GISSEL	8	M	CHILD	RRZZZZUSA
MARIASCHE	7	F	CHILD	RRZZZZUSA
HIRSCH	5	M	CHILD	RRZZZZUSA
GRASGRIM, SIMON	60	M	LABR	RRZZZZUSA
FANNY	56	F	W	RRZZZZUSA
LEIZERWITZ, JACOB	24	M	LABR	RRZZZZUSA
ERSCHTER, MORDCHE	9	M	CHILD	RRZZZZUSA
GARSNER, JOE	24	M	GDSM	RRZZZZUSA
ELFENBEIN, SAIE	20	F	SGL	RRZZZZUSA
KALM, GABRIEL	24	M	SLR	RRZZZZUSA
STEIN, MOSES	23	M	SLR	RRZZZZUSA
SANDLER, LEIB	32	M	SLR	RRZZZZUSA
EPSTEIN, ARON	22	M	SLR	RRZZZZUSA
OPPENBAUER, LIEBE	50	F	W	RRZZZZUSA
RACSHE	30	F	W	RRZZZZUSA
CHAME	13	F	CH	RRZZZZUSA
SARAH	6	F	CHILD	RRZZZZUSA
LUBLUDERSKY, SARAH	52	F	W	RRZZZZUSA
LUPEL, LEIB	50	M	UNKNOWN	RRZZZZUSA
KOLINSKY, SARAH	25	M	LABR	RRZZZZUSA
TAPNACH, MOSES	17	M	LABR	RRZZZZUSA
HOREWITZ, LIEBE	20	F	SGL	RRZZZZUSA
ABRAMOWSKY, SELIG	15	M	LABR	RRZZZZUSA
TAPNACH, FRD.	18	M	LABR	RRZZZZUSA
SLASOWITZ, SCHAIE	21	M	LABR	RRZZZZUSA
ELFENBEIN, CHASE	2	F	CHILD	RRZZZZUSA

SHIP: PERSIAN MONARCH

FROM: LONDON
TO: NEW YORK
ARRIVED: 25 JULY 1883

PASSENGER	AGE	SEX	OCCUPATION	PRV VIL DES
KATZ, HANNAH	00	F	W	PLZZZZNY
C.	22	F	DMS	PLZZZZNY
G.	17	M	LABR	PLZZZZNY
CELIA	11	F	CH	PLZZZZNY
F.	9	M	CHILD	PLZZZZNY
BERT	23	M	LABR	PLZZZZNY
SARAH	20	F	DMS	PLZZZZNY

PASSENGER	AGE	SEX	OCCUPATION	PRIV	VIL	DES
KELF, A.	21	M	LABR	PL	ZZZZ	NY
SHEINBERG, J.	22	M	LABR	PL	ZZZZ	NY
BRUKLYN, B.	22	M	LABR	RR	ZZZZ	NY
STERNWISKY, A.	40	M	LABR	PL	ZZZZ	NY
BLAN, B.	26	M	LABR	PL	ZZZZ	NY
TROMPETER, H.	31	M	LABR	PL	ZZZZ	NY
PENKARS, P.	32	M	LABR	RR	ZZZZ	NY
HUPFER, H.	46	M	LABR	PL	ZZZZ	NY
WEIRISKSKY, W.	28	M	LABR	PL	ZZZZ	NY
SCHEIRER, S.	32	M	LABR	PL	ZZZZ	NY
KRENDT, J.B.	28	F	DMS	PL	ZZZZ	NY
P.	32	M	LABR	PL	ZZZZ	NY
SOAMUTESFA, A.	21	M	LABR	RR	ZZZZ	UNK
HAGLAND, A.	40	M	LABR	RR	ZZZZ	NY
AUGUSTRUCKY, M.	11	M	CH	PL	ZZZZ	NY
YATZ, L.	36	F	DMS	FN	ZZZZ	NY
M.	4	M	CHILD	FN	ZZZZ	NY
JOHANNA	2	F	CHILD	FN	ZZZZ	NY
ISAK	1	M	CHILD	FN	ZZZZ	NY
JACOBS, RACHAEL	46	F	DMS	PL	ZZZZ	NY
MARY	00	F	CH	PL	ZZZZ	NY
HYMAN	00	M	LABR	PL	ZZZZ	NY
RACHAEL	11	F	CH	PL	ZZZZ	NY
MORRIS	9	M	CHILD	PL	ZZZZ	NY
LCAH	7	F	CHILD	PL	ZZZZ	NY
GOLDEN	4	M	CHILD	PL	ZZZZ	NY
LAKI, LAUNCDOT	28	M	LABR	PL	ZZZZ	NY
MARY	26	F	W	PL	ZZZZ	NY
L.J.	.01	M	INFANT	PL	ZZZZ	NY
HANSTENTEIN, D.	24	M	LABR	PL	ZZZZ	NY
BRONSKI, S.	24	M	LABR	PL	ZZZZ	NY
SMALISKI, NATHAN	25	M	LABR	PL	ZZZZ	NY
SARAH	23	F	W	PL	ZZZZ	NY
SIMON, A.	32	M	LABR	PL	ZZZZ	NY
SARAH	20	F	W	PL	ZZZZ	NY
HARRIS	1	M	CHILD	PL	ZZZZ	NY
HYMAN	1	M	CHILD	PL	ZZZZ	NY
MANGEL, MAX	30	M	LABR	PL	ZZZZ	NY
HIRSCH, ABRAHAM	30	M	LABR	PL	ZZZZ	NY
WOLFMANN, J.	30	M	LABR	PL	ZZZZ	NY
HEWCHAUSER, H.	30	M	LABR	PL	ZZZZ	NY
MAHLER, JACOB	26	M	LABR	PL	ZZZZ	NY

SHIP: STATE OF INDIANA

FROM: GLASGOW AND LARNE
TO: NEW YORK
ARRIVED: 26 JULY 1883

PASSENGER	AGE	SEX	OCCUPATION	PRIV	VIL	DES
PERNIS, SCHIR.	22	M	PDLR	RR	ZZZZ	USA
MICHELMANN, ABRAHAM	21	M	UNKNOWN	RR	ZZZZ	USA
SCHIDHWSKI, SAHNON	17	M	UNKNOWN	RR	ZZZZ	USA
PRENSKI, SARA	50	F	W	RR	ZZZZ	USA
MERDCHE-A.	11	M	UNKNOWN	RR	ZZZZ	USA
STOWZLN, NICOFRUME	24	F	DMS	RR	ZZZZ	USA
KRAKM---TY, DANE	22	F	W	RR	ZZZZ	USA
MIRE	.05	F	INFANT	RR	ZZZZ	USA
STESCHOWSKY, MAZKA	24	M	LABR	RR	ZZZZ	USA
RUZONSKY, SIMON	54	M	PDLR	RR	ZZZZ	USA
ARONSOHN, HINDE	40	F	W	RR	ZZZZ	USA
BERL	11	F	UNKNOWN	RR	ZZZZ	USA
SAUL	7	M	CHILD	RR	ZZZZ	USA
BAVER, NICOLAUS	24	M	LABR	RR	ZZZZ	USA
WIGNA, GUISEPPE	25	M	UNKNOWN	RR	ZZZZ	USA
SAROLNUZKI, ABRAHAM	30	M	UNKNOWN	RR	ZZZZ	USA
IGNAZWIC, H.	29	F	DMS	RR	ZZZZ	USA
RZESCHEWSKI, ISAAC	49	M	LABR	RR	ZZZZ	USA
CHANE	10	M	UNKNOWN	RR	ZZZZ	USA
GOSPODAUK, STANISTAN	39	M	LABR	RR	ZZZZ	USA
JANUSKO, JOHN	35	M	LABR	RR	ZZZZ	USA

PASSENGER	AGE	SEX	OCCUPATION	PRIV	VIL	DES
MANINKA, KRESTA-L.	30	F	W	RR	ZZZZ	USA
ANNA	3	F	CHILD	RR	ZZZZ	USA
RUTA	.03	F	INFANT	RR	ZZZZ	USA
HANNULA, CARL	18	M	LABR	RR	ZZZZ	USA
RAISANEN, CARL	21	M	UNKNOWN	RR	ZZZZ	USA
BRETA	10	F	UNKNOWN	RR	ZZZZ	USA
KAISA	9	F	CHILD	RR	ZZZZ	USA
KAYNAMEN, LUBA	28	F	DMS	RR	ZZZZ	USA
LORNBERG, HENRY	57	M	FARMER	RR	ZZZZ	USA
WALBERG	57	F	W	RR	ZZZZ	USA
JACOB	18	M	LABR	RR	ZZZZ	USA
HARTEMANN, HEINRICH	19	M	UNKNOWN	RR	ZZZZ	USA
PASCHEK, PETTER	19	M	CL	RR	ZZZZ	USA
WOLTKE, CARL	30	M	PDLR	RR	ZZZZ	USA
SCHAIKA, FRANZ	26	M	UNKNOWN	RR	ZZZZ	USA
HENDSCHELL, JOHANN	29	M	WCHMKR	RR	ZZZZ	USA
BERDLMGMEIRL, ANTON	59	M	LABR	RR	ZZZZ	USA
GRUSKE, KARL	50	M	UNKNOWN	RR	ZZZZ	USA
BOBKO, MOSES	10	M	UNKNOWN	RR	ZZZZ	USA

SHIP: WAESLAND

FROM: ANTWERP
TO: NEW YORK
ARRIVED: 26 JULY 1883

PASSENGER	AGE	SEX	OCCUPATION	PRIV	VIL	DES
STERN, FREDERIKA-MRS	62	F	NN	RR	ZZZZ	NY
PAULA-MISS	25	F	NN	RR	ZZZZ	NY
OLGA-MISS	22	F	NN	RR	ZZZZ	NY
AGNES-MISS	21	F	NN	RR	ZZZZ	NY
DETLAFF, HELENA	48	F	SVNT	PL	ZZZZ	CH
HELENA	16	F	SVNT	PL	ZZZZ	CH
KARPINSKI, ABR.	00	M	LABR	PL	ZZZZ	NY

SHIP: RHAETIA

FROM: HAMBURG AND HAVRE
TO: NEW YORK
ARRIVED: 28 JULY 1883

PASSENGER	AGE	SEX	OCCUPATION	PRIV	VIL	DES
MICHELSKY, CHAIE	24	F	W	RR	ZZZZ	USA
HIRSCH	.11	M	INFANT	RR	ZZZZ	USA
LEVINSON, CHAIE	30	F	W	RR	ZZZZ	USA
MOSES	.11	M	INFANT	RR	ZZZZ	USA
DAWIDOWITZ, BERNT.	24	M	DLR	RR	ZZZZ	USA
BETTI	24	F	SGL	RR	ZZZZ	USA
GUTTMANN, MEYER	20	M	CL	RR	ZZZZ	USA
SCHEINKER, MERE	20	F	SGL	RR	ZZZZ	USA
SCHEINE	18	F	CH	RR	ZZZZ	USA
HERSCHFELD, JOSEPH	25	M	DLR	RR	ZZZZ	USA
SCHWALL, DEBORAH	16	F	W	RR	ZZZZ	USA
WERRIEX, LEISER	14	M	LABR	RR	ZZZZ	USA
STEIN, JACAB	9	M	CHILD	RR	ZZZZ	USA
LIPSKY, SEHEINE	24	F	W	RR	ZZZZ	USA
ESTHER	6	F	CHILD	RR	ZZZZ	USA
ETTEL	4	F	CHILD	RR	ZZZZ	USA
BERNSTEIN, JOEHEL	31	M	DLR	RR	ZZZZ	USA
LEWINTHAL, LEIB	23	M	LABR	RR	ZZZZ	USA
HANNE	24	F	W	RR	ZZZZ	USA
LIEBE	3	F	CHILD	RR	ZZZZ	USA
WARANKA, JOH.	21	M	LABR	RR	ZZZZ	USA
NAGRUNOWSKY, WILH	9	M	CHILD	RR	ZZZZ	USA
ZUCKERMANN, ROSA	25	F	SGL	RR	ZZZZ	USA
FREINKEL, MEIER	17	M	DLR	RR	ZZZZ	USA
ALTERMANN, MALKE	9	F	CHILD	RR	ZZZZ	USA

PASSENGER	AGE	SEX	OCCUPATION	PRV VIL DES
SARA	9	F	CHILD	RRZZZZUSA
GERSCHOWITZ, CHAIM	16	M	DLR	RRZZZZUSA
GOLDVSCHER, SUSSE	30	M	LABR	RRZZZZUSA
GENI	22	F	W	RRZZZZUSA
DWOSE	4	F	CHILD	RRZZZZUSA
ISRAEL	.11	M	INFANT	RRZZZZUSA
SELIG	20	M	LABR	RRZZZZUSA
LINEZKA, ARON	35	M	LABR	RRZZZZUSA
GITTEL	30	F	W	RRZZZZUSA
SELVE	9	F	CHILD	RRZZZZUSA
DWORE	6	F	CHILD	RRZZZZUSA
SPRINZE	4	F	CHILD	RRZZZZUSA
ROSA	.11	F	INFANT	RRZZZZUSA
SHIMANOW, BERE	33	M	LABR	RRZZZZUSA
REISEL	25	F	W	RRZZZZUSA
ARON	9	M	CHILD	RRZZZZUSA
REBECCA	7	F	CHILD	RRZZZZUSA
MALI	5	F	CHILD	RRZZZZUSA
CHANNE	3	F	CHILD	RRZZZZUSA
WITEL	.11	F	INFANT	RRZZZZUSA
TUDOROWITZ, ESTHER	48	F	W	RRZZZZUSA
KLEISSMANN, IGNATZ	43	M	DLR	RRZZZZUSA
HANNE	42	F	W	RRZZZZUSA
ROSA	7	F	CHILD	RRZZZZUSA
MORITZ	8	M	CHILD	RRZZZZUSA
SALLY	.09	F	INFANT	RRZZZZUSA
SIROVNAK, ANNA	18	F	SGL	RRZZZZUSA
NEUMAM, MARCUS	25	M	LABR	RRZZZZUSA
BERKOWITZ, JOSEPH	14	M	FARMER	RRZZZZUSA
KATI, PERL	9	F	CHILD	RRZZZZUSA
ROSA	9	F	CHILD	RRZZZZUSA
BUXHAUM, LEOPOLD	17	M	CL	RRZZZZUSA
SIMON, LASAR	9	M	CHILD	RRZZZZUSA
KATZ, JANOS	35	M	LABR	RRZZZZUSA
STEIN, ABRAHAM	55	M	FARMER	RRZZZZUSA
ROSENHAUM, EMANUEL	23	M	LABR	RRZZZZUSA
DANGEL, MORVCHEL	39	M	LABR	RRZZZZUSA
LIBERK, NOSCHEN	21	M	LABR	RRZZZZUSA
GELZOWSKI, CHEIE	18	F	SGL	RRZZZZUSA
LURIE, JENNY	29	F	W	RRZZZZUSA
HERZ	8	F	CHILD	RRZZZZUSA
MEILE	5	F	CHILD	RRZZZZUSA
MEIER	.11	F	INFANT	RRZZZZUSA
ISRAEL	18	M	LABR	RRZZZZUSA
BLOCK, ELKE	15	F	SGL	RRZZZZUSA
MERESLAWSKY, DEVORE	21	F	SGL	RRZZZZUSA
SHLAROWSKY, RAPHAEL	18	M	LABR	RRZZZZUSA
GOLDBE--, SCHEPSEL	42	M	BKR	RRZZZZUSA
ZIBUTSKI, SEELIG	18	M	JNR	RRZZZZUSA
MAKIR, SOLEIN	18	M	DLR	RRZZZZUSA
KARTONY--M, ANNIE	23	F	SGL	RRZZZZUSA
EHRLICH, FOIGE	28	F	W	RRZZZZUSA
MORDECHE	6	F	CHILD	RRZZZZUSA
CHANNE	4	F	CHILD	RRZZZZUSA
JACHE	.11	F	INFANT	RRZZZZUSA
PETREKAT, CAROLINE	28	F	SGL	RRZZZZUSA
ROSENBLETH, HEREM.	30	M	DLR	RRZZZZUSA
SCHAPIRA, ISAAK	44	M	DLR	RRZZZZUSA

SHIP: SPAIN

FROM: LIVERPOOL AND QUEENSTOWN
TO: NEW YORK
ARRIVED: 28 JULY 1883

PASSENGER	AGE	SEX	OCCUPATION	PRV VIL DES
DRUCOMANITZ, SPERIDONN	40	M	UNKNOWN	FNZZZZUSA
KOHKONEN, PETTER	30	M	UNKNOWN	FNZZZZUSA
SARA	30	F	UNKNOWN	FNZZZZUSA
ANNA	4	F	CHILD	FNZZZZUSA
JOHANN	2	M	CHILD	FNZZZZUSA
TOBIAS	.06	M	INFANT	FNZZZZUSA
KORMELAMEN, KAZA	24	F	SP	FNZZZZUSA
PANSEN, ANNA	29	F	UNKNOWN	FNZZZZUSA
RAKANEN, MARI	19	F	UNKNOWN	FNZZZZUSA
FOLIVK, REMERT	17	M	LABR	FNZZZZUSA
LANGJOR, OLE-D.	28	M	UNKNOWN	FNZZZZUSA
OMERZ, MICHEAB	41	M	UNKNOWN	FNZZZZUSA
LAPPOLLETE, MEOLC	20	M	UNKNOWN	FNZZZZUSA
BJORKGREST, JOHN	21	M	UNKNOWN	FNZZZZUSA
MAALA, TOMAS	25	M	UNKNOWN	FNZZZZUSA
NUMNER, JOS.	24	M	UNKNOWN	FNZZZZUSA
BASTRON, HENA	24	M	UNKNOWN	FNZZZZUSA
MAATES, MANNA	25	M	UNKNOWN	FNZZZZUSA
KALTULA, JOHAN	24	M	UNKNOWN	FNZZZZUSA
SOLOMEN, GUSTAF	18	M	UNKNOWN	FNZZZZUSA
WAHTALD, FELIX	16	M	UNKNOWN	FNZZZZUSA
MARTOVARRE, ANTTB.	27	M	UNKNOWN	FNZZZZUSA
KATASA, PETER	24	M	UNKNOWN	FNZZZZUSA
KONTWARRE, GUSTAF	22	M	UNKNOWN	FNZZZZUSA
POLO, AMANDEN	11	M	CH	FNZZZZUSA
HOLVARSEN, ABEL	20	M	LABR	FNZZZZUSA
HANS	17	M	UNKNOWN	FNZZZZUSA
KAENPPAEMN, ANNA	30	F	W	FNZZZZUSA
ANNA	11	F	CH	FNZZZZUSA
JAKOB	4	M	CHILD	FNZZZZUSA
MATHIAS	2	M	CHILD	FNZZZZUSA
LENA	.06	F	INFANT	FNZZZZUSA
BJCKONEN, A.	15	M	LABR	FNZZZZUSA
PYYKKONEN, ISAK	20	M	UNKNOWN	FNZZZZUSA
BJERKLUNGL, AXEL	19	M	UNKNOWN	FNZZZZUSA
KRALL, VIKTOR	19	M	UNKNOWN	FNZZZZUSA
HELLBUNEN, HENRIK	25	M	UNKNOWN	FNZZZZUSA
HERANON, ADAM	25	M	UNKNOWN	FNZZZZUSA
MORLANEN, BERTHOLD	35	M	UNKNOWN	FNZZZZUSA
KAUJOR, LANDEN	27	M	UNKNOWN	FNZZZZUSA
KOLEMAMAR, JAKOB	30	M	UNKNOWN	FNZZZZUSA
LUPPOREN, ERIK	35	M	UNKNOWN	FNZZZZUSA
HANTOLA, DAVID	33	M	UNKNOWN	FNZZZZUSA
MATTS.	11	M	CH	FNZZZZUSA
MAYANER, JOHAN	21	M	LABR	FNZZZZUSA
WAGRUNEN, ELIAS	23	M	UNKNOWN	FNZZZZUSA
MUSTAPPA, JOHAN	21	M	UNKNOWN	FNZZZZUSA
PAESANEN, KAISA	35	F	W	FNZZZZUSA
ZANTUMY, MARIA	22	F	UNKNOWN	FNZZZZUSA
KUNANEN, BEEDA	22	F	SP	FNZZZZUSA

SHIP: FURNESSIA

FROM: LIVERPOOL AND QUEENSTOWN
TO: NEW YORK
ARRIVED: 30 JULY 1883

PASSENGER	AGE	SEX	OCCUPATION	PRV VIL DES
RONGREW, JOHAN	18	M	LABR	RRZZZZUSA
HEIKE, JACOB	20	M	UNKNOWN	RRZZZZUSA
SMED, CARL	20	M	UNKNOWN	RRZZZZUSA

SHIP: WESTPHALIA

FROM: HAMBURG AND HAVRE
TO: NEW YORK
ARRIVED: 31 JULY 1883

PASSENGER	AGE	SEX	OCCUPATION	PRV VIL DES
KISSIN, ELIAS	30	M	DLR	RRZZZZNY
ROSENTHAL, SIMON	22	M	DLR	RRZZZZNY
GOLDANSKY, GIEZI	30	F	W	RRZZZZNY

PASSENGER	AGE	SEX	OCCUPATION	PRV VIL DES
CHAIM	7	M	CHILD	RRZZZZNY
MOSES	5	M	CHILD	RRZZZZNY
MIREL	.11	F	INFANT	RRZZZZNY
MARIA	.01	F	INFANT	RRZZZZNY
JSCHKOWISH, JACOB	17	M	TLR	RRZZZZNY
SIROTKIN, ABRAHAM	26	M	UNKNOWN	RRZZZZNY
SUBOTNIK, BAER	45	M	UNKNOWN	RRZZZZNY
GRUENBERG, JACOB	21	M	LABR	RRZZZZNY
GRAJEWSKY, JAN	48	M	UNKNOWN	RRZZZZNY
LEWIN, HERMANN	12	M	BY	RRZZZZNY
MEMLOWSKY, GALIE	30	F	W	RRZZZZNY
SANDEL	6	M	CHILD	RRZZZZNY
SELIG	4	M	CHILD	RRZZZZNY
CHAIE	.11	F	INFANT	RRZZZZNY
EIDESBERG, DAVID	49	M	BCHR	RRZZZZNY
BACK, SARA	21	F	SGL	RRZZZZNY
GARFUNKEL, CHAIE	58	F	W	RRZZZZNY
ABRAHAMS, ABRAHAM	44	M	MCHT	RRZZZZNY
SPOHN, ALBERT	25	M	UNKNOWN	RRZZZZNY
CIRWIN, SARA	33	F	WO	RRZZZZNY
SHEIE	9	F	CHILD	RRZZZZNY
JOSSIE	8	F	CHILD	RRZZZZNY
KUSIEL	6	F	CHILD	RRZZZZNY
ABRAHAM	.11	M	INFANT	RRZZZZNY
ROSENTHAL, ABEL	48	M	MCHT	RRZZZZNY
BLOCH, ABRAHAM	29	M	UNKNOWN	RRZZZZNY
BERGMANN, OLGA	31	F	SGL	RRZZZZPHI
HANNE	24	F	UNKNOWN	FNZZZZPHI

SHIP: AMERIQUE

FROM: HAVRE
TO: NEW YORK
ARRIVED: 02 AUGUST 1883

PASSENGER	AGE	SEX	OCCUPATION	PRV VIL DES
WOGSTCHAL, WOLF	29	M	MCHT	RRZZZZUSA
CHASSIS, ISAAC	23	M	BCHR	RRZZZZUSA
BERTHE	18	F	UNKNOWN	RRZZZZUSA
FINKELSTEIN, PAUL	20	M	TLR	RRZZZZUSA
SUSSMANN, VICTOR	21	M	CL	RRZZZZUSA
FRIEDMANN, ABRAHAM	50	M	MCHT	RRZZZZUSA

SHIP: POLARIA

FROM: HAMBURG
TO: NEW YORK
ARRIVED: 02 AUGUST 1883

PASSENGER	AGE	SEX	OCCUPATION	PRV VIL DES
RIBUKI, ABR.	16	M	TRDSMN	RRZZZZNY
ROSENTHAL, P.LEAH	34	F	WO	RRZZZZNY
FREIDE	8	F	CHILD	RRZZZZNY
MINNA	6	F	CHILD	RRZZZZNY
RIWE	5	F	CHILD	RRZZZZNY
CHAIM	2	M	CHILD	RRZZZZNY
PESCHE	.03	F	INFANT	RRZZZZNY
JOSCHHSON, PAULINE	36	F	WO	RRZZZZNY
JOSEF	17	M	S	RRZZZZNY
TINE	7	F	CHILD	RRZZZZNY
SJELK	6	F	CHILD	RRZZZZNY
BOTHOWSKY, S.	18	M	WCHMKR	RRZZZZNY
REICHER, HERM.	16	M	UNKNOWN	PLZZZZCLE
MARIA	18	F	SI	PLZZZZCLE
GENDZNER, HENNE	18	F	UNKNOWN	PLZZZZNY
GUDAT, JOSEPH	18	M	LABR	RRZZZZNY
PODURGIRL, M.JOSEFA	28	F	WO	RRZZZZNY
ANTERNI	.02	M	INFANT	RRZZZZNY
BOLESLAWA	.11	M	INFANT	RRZZZZNY
SZCESSAN	6	F	CHILD	RRZZZZNY
STANISLAUS	5	M	CHILD	RRZZZZNY
KLEMENTINE	.02	F	INFANT	RRZZZZNY
DANILAWITZ, ELKE	19	F	SGL	RRZZZZNY
SCHNEPS, JACOB	28	M	LABR	PLZZZZNY
OBRIMESKEW, FR.	32	F	WO	RRZZZZNY
PESE	.04	F	INFANT	RRZZZZNY
GLASMER, SCHEINDEL	18	F	SGL	PLZZZZNY
SABINSKY, WOLF	7	M	CHILD	RRZZZZNY
RASMUSSEN, NILS	27	M	FARMER	RRZZZZUNK
MARIANNE	26	F	W	RRZZZZUNK
KIRSTINE	3	F	CHILD	RRZZZZUNK
PETER	.04	M	INFANT	RRZZZZUNK
THORBEN	.11	M	INFANT	RRZZZZUNK
HAUSEN, ROSMUS	33	M	FARMER	RRZZZZNY
BOBBES, LEIB	40	M	TLR	RRZZZZCH
NIZINISKI, FRANZ	50	M	LABR	PLZZZZNY
GUZIG, FRANZ	35	M	UNKNOWN	PLZZZZNY
POLUKAINK, JAN	40	M	UNKNOWN	PLZZZZNY
HOVANETZ, ANDR.	17	M	UNKNOWN	PLZZZZNY
BACH, ALBERT	26	M	UNKNOWN	PLZZZZNY
GOMPIER, MICH.	28	M	UNKNOWN	PLZZZZNY
BAUMGARTEN, HEINR.	24	M	UNKNOWN	RRZZZZNY
BIGORITZ, WITTSCHACK	54	M	TRDSMN	RRZZZZNY
MARIANNE	42	F	W	RRZZZZNY
ROSALIE	18	F	D	RRZZZZNY
VICTORIE	13	F	UNKNOWN	RRZZZZNY
JOHANN	6	M	CHILD	RRZZZZNY
FRANZISECK	5	M	CHILD	RRZZZZNY
BRAGOWITZ, KATY	.04	F	INFANT	RRZZZZNY
SERWINSKI, STANISL.	25	M	TRDSMN	RRZZZZNY
MATLOWSKI, AGN.	18	F	SGL	RRZZZZNY
KURZWEIL, SALOMEI	34	M	TRDSMN	RRZZZZNY
KEGEL, FISCHEL	23	M	UNKNOWN	RRZZZZNY
KALBERG, JULIE	17	F	WO	RRZZZZNY
LEIB	7	M	CHILD	RRZZZZNY
SKRENTA, STANISL.	28	M	TRDSMN	RRZZZZNY
RITSCHAK, STANISL.	24	M	UNKNOWN	RRZZZZNY
FRANZISKA	17	F	W	RRZZZZNY
WITISDRAKET	37	F	SI	RRZZZZNY
GLOWA, STEFAN	28	M	TRDSMN	RRZZZZNY
FRANK, SCHONE	20	F	W	RRZZZZNY
CHANE	.04	F	INFANT	RRZZZZNY
LEIB, ARON	24	M	TRDSMN	RRZZZZNY
WEINSTEIN, MOSES	44	F	UNKNOWN	RRZZZZNY
RESCHE	16	F	D	RRZZZZNY
CHIWONZIK, CHASKEL	40	F	WO	RRZZZZCIN
LEISE	19	M	S	RRZZZZCIN
JACOBOWITZ, VICTOR	44	M	TRDSMN	RRZZZZNY
ALTER	6	M	CHILD	RRZZZZNY
EWENZAPIER, SEIWEL	19	F	SGL	RRZZZZNY
SLOTINSKY, ABR.	25	M	TRDSMN	RRZZZZNY

SHIP: ST. OF PENNSYLVANIA

FROM: GLASGOW AND LARNE
TO: NEW YORK
ARRIVED: 03 AUGUST 1883

PASSENGER	AGE	SEX	OCCUPATION	PRV VIL DES
HOSHBRADSKI, M.	19	M	LABR	RRZZZZUSA
HUSCHKEWITZ, HIZIG	32	M	MCHT	RRZZZZUSA
TUBES, LEIB	19	M	TLR	RRZZZZUSA
TONF, HIZIG	35	M	TLR	RRZZZZUSA
SPEIGEL, ESTY	11	M	UNKNOWN	RRZZZZUSA
SCHAPIN, ABRAHAM	27	M	LABR	RRZZZZUSA
GOLGUT, BENJAMIN	19	M	LABR	RRZZZZUSA
CALMANN, PROIDEL	19	M	JWLR	RRZZZZUSA
PYFKONNEN, LARS	20	M	LABR	RRZZZZUSA

PASSENGER	AGE	SEX	OCCUPATION	PRV VIL DES
DAWIDSON, E.G.	36	M	LABR	RRZZZZUSA
SGURSTRA, FRANZ	23	M	LABR	RRZZZZUSA

SHIP: CITY OF BERLIN

FROM: LIVERPOOL
TO: NEW YORK
ARRIVED: 06 AUGUST 1883

PASSENGER	AGE	SEX	OCCUPATION	PRV VIL DES
DAVIDSON, PETTER	33	M	LABR	RRZZZZMI
ANDERSON, ANDERS	24	M	LABR	RRZZZZMI
JOHANSON, ANDERS	24	M	LABR	RRZZZZMI
ERIKSON, JOHAN	34	M	LABR	RRZZZZMI
SOTALI, FELIX	18	M	LABR	RRZZZZMI
ERICKSON, ALVAN	30	M	LABR	RRZZZZMI
NEMICKSON, JOHAN	32	M	LABR	RRZZZZMN
PER.	29	M	LABR	RRZZZZMN
KAWKARGAWIE, IDA	00	F	INF	PLZZZZWI
GRETA	25	F	W	PLZZZZWI

SHIP: FRISIA

FROM: HAMBURG AND HAVRE
TO: NEW YORK
ARRIVED: 07 AUGUST 1883

PASSENGER	AGE	SEX	OCCUPATION	PRV VIL DES
SAPIRO, MARIASSE	50	F	W	RRZZZZUSA
WUNEROWSKY, WULF	60	M	TNR	RRZZZZUSA
PERZON, MICHAEL	56	M	DLR	RRZZZZUSA
LEA	54	F	W	RRZZZZUSA
REISEL	9	F	CHILD	RRZZZZUSA
RAPERPORT, PAULINE	16	F	SGL	RRZZZZUSA
ACHTABOWSKI, ANTON	18	M	LABR	RRZZZZUSA
PICKKOLA, JOHANNE	28	F	W	FNZZZZUSA
JOSEFINE	25	F	SI	FNZZZZUSA
JENNY	2	F	CHILD	FNZZZZUSA
MARGA.	.11	F	INFANT	FNZZZZUSA
FREID, CHANNE	22	F	W	RRZZZZUSA
SCHEINE	18	F	SGL	RRZZZZUSA
GOLDSTEIN, SAMUEL	23	M	DLR	RRZZZZUSA
DWORKOWITSCH, MOSES	45	M	DLR	RRZZZZUSA
BUDA, CHAWE	20	F	W	RRZZZZUSA
SCHIMSCHEN	.11	F	INFANT	RRZZZZUSA
MICHELSON, ISAAC	21	M	LABR	RRZZZZUSA
GOLDSTEIN, GONEL	30	M	DLR	RRZZZZUSA
BASS, CHASCHE	40	F	W	RRZZZZUSA
LIEBE	17	F	CH	RRZZZZUSA
SCHEPSEL	9	M	CHILD	RRZZZZUSA
LEA	8	F	CHILD	RRZZZZUSA
SCHMUL	.11	M	INFANT	RRZZZZUSA
DWERKOWITZ, MENACHE	45	F	W	RRZZZZUSA
ABRAM	15	M	CH	RRZZZZUSA
ELIAS	9	M	CHILD	RRZZZZUSA
STIREL	7	M	CHILD	RRZZZZUSA
IERHIEL	5	M	CHILD	RRZZZZUSA
JUK.	.11	M	INFANT	RRZZZZUSA
FUHRMANN, ED.	20	M	STDNT	RRZZZZUSA
ZIBART, JOH.	35	M	FARMER	RRZZZZUSA
WILHE.	38	F	W	RRZZZZUSA
JOH.	8	M	CHILD	RRZZZZUSA
JOSEF	6	M	CHILD	RRZZZZUSA
ADAM	4	M	CHILD	RRZZZZUSA
REBECCA	2	F	CHILD	RRZZZZUSA
EVA	2	F	CHILD	RRZZZZUSA
MIX, WILHE.	50	F	W	RRZZZZUSA
CARL	11	M	CH	RRZZZZUSA
MARIE	13	F	CH	RRZZZZUSA
FRIEDRICH, CAROLINE	65	F	W	RRZZZZUSA
ZWEIFUSS, SCHEINDEL	51	F	W	RRZZZZUSA
SCHWEITZER, CHEIE	36	F	W	RRZZZZUSA
MARIE	9	F	CHILD	RRZZZZUSA
SCHWARZBERG, LEIB	52	M	TLR	RRZZZZUSA
ROSCHE	52	F	W	RRZZZZUSA
GROSSMANN, ELKE	40	F	W	RRZZZZUSA
LEA	14	F	CH	RRZZZZUSA
CHANNE	9	F	CHILD	RRZZZZUSA
ETTEL	7	F	CHILD	RRZZZZUSA
JOSSEL	5	M	CHILD	RRZZZZUSA
BERNSTEIN, BEINES.	20	M	LABR	RRZZZZUSA
SARAH	19	F	W	RRZZZZUSA
BLUMENTHAL, SALOMON	19	M	LABR	RRZZZZUSA
FRISCHMANN, JOSSEL	19	M	LABR	RRZZZZUSA
GROSSMANN, LIEBE	26	F	W	RRZZZZUSA
SALOMON	.11	M	INFANT	RRZZZZUSA
GOLDMANN, ARON	19	M	DLR	RRZZZZUSA
TAUBE	18	F	W	RRZZZZUSA
SMILINGOWSKY, NISSEN	20	M	LABR	RRZZZZUSA
LEA	20	F	W	RRZZZZUSA
RUBINSTEIN, SARAH	21	F	W	RRZZZZUSA
, DAVID	.11	M	INFANT	RRZZZZUSA
LAWNER, SARAH	19	F	SGL	RRZZZZUSA
DAGUTSKI, ABRAM	17	M	LABR	RRZZZZUSA
MOSES	19	M	LABR	RRZZZZUSA
FRIEDMANN, RUBIN	9	M	CHILD	RRZZZZUSA
KRIWITZKI, JOSEPH	29	M	LABR	RRZZZZUSA
DEMKO, DAVID-E.	20	M	LABR	RRZZZZUSA
DUBERSTEIN, EISIK	23	M	LABR	RRZZZZUSA
ROBIN, RAHL.B.	20	F	SGL	RRZZZZUSA
SCHMIDT, GEORG	64	M	LABR	RRZZZZUSA
STOMINSKI, STANISL.	28	M	LABR	RRZZZZUSA
STACHOWSKI, ANDR.	25	M	LABR	RRZZZZUSA
KRUSCHLOWSKI, IGNATZ	22	M	LABR	RRZZZZUSA
GLADSTEIN, MOSES	31	M	BCHR	RRZZZZUSA
MASCHE	9	F	CHILD	RRZZZZUSA
FINKELSTEIN, CHAIE	24	F	W	RRZZZZUSA
MINDEL	.10	M	INFANT	RRZZZZUSA
LAZOWSKI, BASCHE	20	F	SGL	RRZZZZUSA
TOPOROWSKI, CIREL	24	F	W	RRZZZZUSA
MOSES	.11	M	INFANT	RRZZZZUSA
MORDCHE	.01	F	INFANT	RRZZZZUSA
PERLOWITZ, DWORE	29	F	W	RRZZZZUSA
CHAIE	.11	F	INFANT	RRZZZZUSA
RASCHBAN, JOCHRE	42	F	W	RRZZZZUSA
SARA	9	F	CHILD	RRZZZZUSA
ROSA	6	F	CHILD	RRZZZZUSA
NACHE	5	F	CHILD	RRZZZZUSA
ISRAEL	.11	M	INFANT	RRZZZZUSA
SCHACHNEROWICZ, PESSE	19	F	SGL	RRZZZZUSA

SHIP: ABYSSINIA

FROM: LIVERPOOL AND QUEENSTOWN
TO: NEW YORK
ARRIVED: 08 AUGUST 1883

PASSENGER	AGE	SEX	OCCUPATION	PRV VIL DES
NYLUND, KARL-J.	26	M	LABR	FNZZZZUSA
ISAKSSON, BRITTA-L.	37	F	W	FNZZZZUSA
ISAAK	15	M	LABR	FNZZZZUSA
ERIK	11	M	CH	FNZZZZUSA
RAGSA	9	F	CHILD	FNZZZZUSA
SODERLUND, BRITTA	33	F	W	FNZZZZUSA
HEDIN, RABERT-F.	19	M	LABR	FNZZZZUSA
KAMPIA, MIKKA-M.	17	M	MNR	FNZZZZUSA
NYSTTI, MIKKI-M.	25	M	LABR	FNZZZZUSA
FORSBURG, FRANS	29	M	LABR	FNZZZZUSA

PASSENGER	AGE	SEX	OCCUPATION	PRV VIL DES
HIKKILA, ABEL	25	M	LABR	FNZZZZUSA
GUNTAR, ISAK	27	M	LABR	FNZZZZUSA
HEIKKILA, ISAK	19	M	LABR	FNZZZZUSA
LOHTEENKORVA, FRANS	20	M	LABR	FNZZZZUSA
MIKKOLA, JACOB	26	M	LABR	FNZZZZUSA
KYAMPAA, JOHAN	29	M	LABR	FNZZZZUSA
KORPI, JOHAN	29	M	LABR	FNZZZZUSA
MATTILA, HENRIK	29	M	JNR	FNZZZZUSA
SIROS, SAML.	20	M	LABR	FNZZZZUSA
JOHAN	20	M	CL	FNZZZZUSA
KORHIAMKI, FRANS	19	M	JNR	FNZZZZUSA

SHIP: CANADA

FROM: HAVRE
TO: NEW YORK
ARRIVED: 08 AUGUST 1883

PASSENGER	AGE	SEX	OCCUPATION	PRV VIL DES
DE-STRUVE, U-MR.	00	M	CSL	RRZZZZWAS
U-MRS.	32	F	UNKNOWN	RRZZZZWAS
U	7	F	CHILD	RRZZZZWAS
U	6	F	CHILD	RRZZZZWAS
U	4	F	CHILD	RRZZZZWAS
U	3	F	CHILD	RRZZZZWAS
U	1	M	CHILD	RRZZZZWAS
U, U	33	M	MSVNT	RRZZZZWAS
U	28	M	MSVNT	RRZZZZWAS
MORANSKI, LUDOMIR	24	M	NN	RRZZZZNY
PAWLAWSKI, JACQUS	22	M	CL	RRZZZZNY
SPALAWSKI, DAVID	22	M	CL	RRZZZZNY
BERCOVITCH, ABRAHAM	19	M	ENGR	RRZZZZNY

SHIP: GRECIAN MONARCH

FROM: LONDON
TO: NEW YORK
ARRIVED: 08 AUGUST 1883

PASSENGER	AGE	SEX	OCCUPATION	PRV VIL DES
ROSENTHAL, S.	27	M	TLR	RRZZZZUSA
LEVINSOHN, U.	16	M	LABR	RRZZZZUSA
HARRIS, J.	20	M	CGRMKR	RRZZZZUSA
KRETZKANS, M.	18	M	LABR	RRZZZZUSA
ADELSHON, B.	30	M	UNKNOWN	PLZZZZUSA
BETSY	31	F	W	PLZZZZUSA
ISAAC	9	M	CHILD	PLZZZZUSA
MORRIS	7	M	CHILD	PLZZZZUSA
CATHERINE	3	F	CHILD	PLZZZZUSA
SAMUEL	.01	M	INFANT	PLZZZZUSA
MALAWSKI, ISIG	74	M	LABR	PLZZZZUSA
SELLIWEITE, FEMILL	24	M	UNKNOWN	PLZZZZUSA
WISCELKA	24	F	W	PLZZZZUSA
NULHADO, AG.	31	M	CGRMKR	PLZZZZUSA
WELTZER, ISAAC	34	M	TLR	PLZZZZUSA
POLITA, OSYP	20	M	LABR	PLZZZZUSA
LUGOSIEWICZ, J.	20	M	UNKNOWN	PLZZZZUSA
SALOMON, D.	24	M	UNKNOWN	PLZZZZUSA
RACHEL	25	F	W	PLZZZZUSA
ADA	3	F	CHILD	PLZZZZUSA
SIMON	.10	M	INFANT	PLZZZZUSA

SHIP: STATE OF FLORIDA

FROM: GLASGOW AND LARNE
TO: NEW YORK
ARRIVED: 08 AUGUST 1883

PASSENGER	AGE	SEX	OCCUPATION	PRV VIL DES
WANGAGES, SARO.	32	M	LABR	RRZZZZUSA
KLINCK, JOHAN	42	M	LABR	RRZZZZUSA
WOITILA, ANDREAS	45	M	LABR	RRZZZZUSA
LUBINSKY, MICHAEL	18	M	LABR	RRZZZZUSA
GRUNSTEIN, LEIB	32	M	LABR	RRZZZZUSA
MASODER, PIEVEN	19	M	NN	RRZZZZUSA
CHESSEZ, MASCHE	20	M	LABR	RRZZZZUSA
ISRAELOWIEZ, CHEINE	20	F	W	RRZZZZUSA
CHEFEZ, JUDAS	20	M	LABR	RRZZZZUSA
MARGNOSKY, STANISLAV	19	M	LABR	RRZZZZUSA
ANTONINA	19	F	W	RRZZZZUSA
MARIANNA	60	F	NN	RRZZZZUSA
HRICHS, MENDEL	31	M	LABR	RRZZZZUSA
RUBENSTEIN, JACOB	29	M	LABR	RRZZZZUSA
JUDEL	21	M	LABR	RRZZZZUSA
SPEINGARN, ISAAC	60	M	LABR	RRZZZZUSA
JEPPE	65	F	W	RRZZZZUSA
SCHARERER, JOSEPH	42	M	FARMER	RRZZZZUSA
CHARLOTTE	20	F	SP	RRZZZZUSA
BERDSCHE	14	M	FARMER	RRZZZZUSA
MARIE	11	F	CH	RRZZZZUSA
SCHANDER	9	M	CHILD	RRZZZZUSA
KATHE.	7	F	CHILD	RRZZZZUSA
LEA	1	M	CHILD	RRZZZZUSA
JULIA	4	F	CHILD	RRZZZZUSA
ROSINA	2	F	CHILD	RRZZZZUSA
THERESA	.06	F	INFANT	RRZZZZUSA
LEPOHITZ, LOZER	23	M	LABR	RRZZZZUSA
MARGULIS, SALMEN	47	M	LABR	RRZZZZUSA
MEYER, JOHANN	27	M	LABR	RRZZZZUSA
CHWELOWSKY, JANKEL	44	M	LABR	RRZZZZUSA
TADUSCHITZ, ROSMER	48	M	LABR	RRZZZZUSA
ROTENSKI, MAX	17	M	LABR	RRZZZZUSA
MORASKY, CHAIE	45	M	PDLR	RRZZZZUSA
ALTI	18	F	SP	RRZZZZUSA
FEIGE	8	F	CHILD	RRZZZZUSA
DRUGENITZ, OLEIS	27	M	LABR	RRZZZZUSA
RESLER, SAMUEL	41	M	LABR	RRZZZZUSA
ETTE	44	M	LABR	RRZZZZUSA
ETTE	42	F	W	RRZZZZUSA
BEILE	6	M	CHILD	RRZZZZUSA
GETTEL	.03	F	INFANT	RRZZZZUSA
KMUTTER, MORDCHE	33	M	LABR	RRZZZZUSA
SANDELIA, MARIA	23	F	NN	RRZZZZUSA
KISKA, LEANDER-M.	18	M	LABR	RRZZZZUSA
AMONDSON, JONAS	44	M	PDLR	PLZZZZUSA
WALLEMANN, OLLE	18	M	LABR	RRZZZZUSA
JAMESJARN, JOHN	22	M	LABR	RRZZZZUSA
LAMPSA, DANL.	20	M	LABR	RRZZZZUSA
KOCHANOWSKI, JOSEPH	29	M	LABR	RRZZZZUSA
PAVLUS, WLADISLAUS	22	M	LABR	PLZZZZUSA
LARSCHKEWITZ, ALFONS	25	M	LABR	RRZZZZUSA
BRANDE, MORITZ	18	M	PDLR	RRZZZZUSA
RADKOWSKI, ALEX.	25	M	PDLR	RRZZZZUSA
ANTONIE	22	F	W	RRZZZZUSA
KOMTSCHEN, FRANZISKA	12	F	NN	RRZZZZUSA
WEINGECHER, MENDEL	30	M	LABR	RRZZZZUSA
OSHOKLOWITZ, SCHOLASTIK	27	F	W	RRZZZZUSA
OSHOKLOWITZ, URSULA	8	F	CHILD	RRZZZZUSA
SIEVEN	4	F	CHILD	RRZZZZUSA
MARIAN	.06	F	INFANT	RRZZZZUSA
MARY-ANN	1	F	CHILD	RRZZZZUSA
MISKOWITZ, MORITZ	34	M	LABR	RRZZZZUSA
GRUMBERG, ABRAHAM	20	M	LABR	RRZZZZUSA
MATHAN, ABRAHAM	17	M	LABR	RRZZZZUSA
USTYCH, JOSEF-F.	37	M	LABR	RRZZZZUSA
MILLIAN, ABRAHAM	54	M	LABR	RRZZZZUSA
THIEDLAND, BEILE	30	F	W	RRZZZZUSA

PASSENGER	AGE	SEX	OCCUPATION	PRIVL	DES
JANTRAMAN, MICHEL	18	M	LABR	RRZZZZ	USA

SHIP: RHYNLAND

FROM: ANTWERP
TO: NEW YORK
ARRIVED: 10 AUGUST 1883

PASSENGER	AGE	SEX	OCCUPATION	PRIVL	DES
KOSCHONK, JULIUS	20	M	FARMER	PLZZZZ	USA
BURIAN, LOUISA	20	F	UNKNOWN	PLZZZZ	USA
KLOZOWSKI, MATH.	59	M	FARMER	PLZZZZ	USA
BARB.	57	F	UNKNOWN	PLZZZZ	USA
GUAN, AD.	21	M	SMH	PLZZZZ	USA
AUGUSTA	23	F	UNKNOWN	PLZZZZ	USA
LENGER, THEOPHILE	22	M	UNKNOWN	PLZZZZ	USA
REPTISKI, FRANZ	25	M	FARMER	PLZZZZ	USA
NEWACK, VINCENT	22	M	UNKNOWN	PLZZZZ	USA
RASKOWSKY, ROSALIE	18	F	UNKNOWN	PLZZZZ	USA
JOS.	15	M	UNKNOWN	PLZZZZ	USA
WISCOLOWA, FRANCISCA	30	F	UNKNOWN	PLZZZZ	USA
WEIGA, MARG.	30	F	UNKNOWN	PLZZZZ	USA
FRANCOIN	10	M	UNKNOWN	PLZZZZ	USA
MARG.	5	F	CHILD	PLZZZZ	USA
JOHANNA	.05	F	INFANT	PLZZZZ	USA

SHIP: RUGIA

FROM: HAMBURG
TO: NEW YORK
ARRIVED: 11 AUGUST 1883

PASSENGER	AGE	SEX	OCCUPATION	PRIVL	DES
KORETZKY, CARL	29	M	FARMER	RRZZZZ	USA
TOHBER, CHRISTIAN	23	M	LABR	RRZZZZ	USA
OTTILIE	21	F	W	RRZZZZ	USA
AMANDA	.03	F	INFANT	RRZZZZ	USA
LASKOWITZ, RUBIN	30	M	LABR	RRZZZZ	USA
BENZEL, SAMUEL	23	M	LABR	RRZZZZ	USA
MOSES, FANKEL	9	M	CHILD	RRZZZZ	USA
WEINGROWITZ, SARA	24	F	W	RRZZZZ	USA
SCHAWE	.11	F	INFANT	RRZZZZ	USA
ROSENTHAL, GITTEL	25	F	W	RRZZZZ	USA
LEIB	.11	M	INFANT	RRZZZZ	USA
BERL	.01	M	INFANT	RRZZZZ	USA
RELSKY, JALLEL	17	M	LABR	RRZZZZ	USA
JSAAKSON, SALMEN	22	M	DLR	RRZZZZ	USA
DOW, MIREL	30	F	W	RRZZZZ	USA
MARCUS	9	M	CHILD	RRZZZZ	USA
SIMCHE	8	F	CHILD	RRZZZZ	USA
JAKOB	7	M	CHILD	RRZZZZ	USA
SIDERSKY, ISAAK	23	M	LABR	RRZZZZ	USA
KIEWE	9	M	CHILD	RRZZZZ	USA
ROSENTHAL, HIRSCH	44	M	LABR	RRZZZZ	USA
CHAROSZITZ, GEDALIA	9	F	CHILD	RRZZZZ	USA
PAUSA, MATWE	27	M	LABR	RRZZZZ	USA
SMOLITZCHANSKY, RUBEN	20	M	UNKNOWN	RRZZZZ	USA
BERKSOHN, MEIER	19	M	UNKNOWN	RRZZZZ	USA
JABLONOWSKY, MERE	26	F	W	RRZZZZ	USA
RACHEL	5	F	CHILD	RRZZZZ	USA
ARON	.11	M	INFANT	RRZZZZ	USA
ALKAN	.01	M	INFANT	RRZZZZ	USA
CIGANOWITZ, ABRAM	25	M	TLR	RRZZZZ	USA
SAKS, BENZEL	24	M	TNMK	RRZZZZ	USA
IATKOWSKY, JOSSEL	15	M	SHMK	RRZZZZ	USA
WYRBINCKY, IGNATZ	25	M	LABR	RRZZZZ	USA
BARGSTEIN, BASCHE	25	F	SGL	RRZZZZ	USA
BEDASCH, MICHEL	68	M	LABR	RRZZZZ	USA
DWORA	58	F	W	RRZZZZ	USA
ALPERN, ROSALIE	19	F	SGL	RRZZZZ	USA
BLUMBERG, JANKEL	15	M	DLR	RRZZZZ	USA
REINKOWSKY, ETTEL	24	F	W	RRZZZZ	USA
ABRAHAM	.11	M	INFANT	RRZZZZ	USA
STRATT, BEYLE	17	F	SGL	RRZZZZ	USA
SCHOENMANN, RIWKE	38	F	W	RRZZZZ	USA
HIRSCH	18	M	CH	RRZZZZ	USA
MERE	9	F	CHILD	RRZZZZ	USA
ISRAEL	7	M	CHILD	RRZZZZ	USA
WOLFF	5	M	CHILD	RRZZZZ	USA
RAHEL	.11	F	INFANT	RRZZZZ	USA
GUTFARB, SCHOLEM	19	M	DLR	RRZZZZ	USA
SCHOENE	18	F	W	RRZZZZ	USA
KOMESARSKY, RIWKE	16	F	SGL	RRZZZZ	USA
COHN, JOSEF	38	M	DLR	RRZZZZ	USA
LIBOWSKY, CHAIE	9	F	CHILD	RRZZZZ	USA
SCHNEIDERSTEIN, MSES	40	M	TLR	RRZZZZ	USA
FINKELSTEIN, LEISER	26	M	UNKNOWN	RRZZZZ	USA
BLUMBERG, RAPHAEL	59	M	DLR	RRZZZZ	USA
GOLDE	50	F	W	RRZZZZ	USA
LAKER, ELIAS	19	M	TLR	RRZZZZ	USA
FAIN, DOBE	28	F	W	RRZZZZ	USA
SLATE	8	F	CHILD	RRZZZZ	USA
NECHAME	5	F	CHILD	RRZZZZ	USA
NOTE	.11	F	INFANT	RRZZZZ	USA
BEILE	.01	F	INFANT	RRZZZZ	USA
NAVIASKY, NESCHE	17	F	SGL	RRZZZZ	USA
BEILSON, MICHEL	16	M	SHMK	RRZZZZ	USA
LEA	18	F	SGL	RRZZZZ	USA
KUPER, DINE	23	F	W	RRZZZZ	USA
NECHAME	.11	F	INFANT	RRZZZZ	USA
RIWE	.01	F	INFANT	RRZZZZ	USA
AHRONSOHN, LEOP.	19	M	STDNT	RRZZZZ	USA
ZABER, CASIMIR	20	M	LABR	RRZZZZ	USA
MITRIKAS, JOAN	19	M	LABR	RRZZZZ	USA
SCHNEIDER, FEIBEL	22	M	LABR	RRZZZZ	USA
PEHL	20	F	W	RRZZZZ	USA
LESER	6	M	CHILD	RRZZZZ	USA
SILBERSTEIN, CHAIE	25	F	W	RRZZZZ	USA
BENJAMIN	.11	M	INFANT	RRZZZZ	USA
WEISS, CHANNE	19	F	SGL	RRZZZZ	USA
DAVIDSOHN, THEODOR	21	M	UNKNOWN	RRZZZZ	USA
JOSEFSOHN, MOSES	21	M	UNKNOWN	RRZZZZ	USA

SHIP: LESSING

FROM: HAMBURG AND HAVRE
TO: NEW YORK
ARRIVED: 14 AUGUST 1883

PASSENGER	AGE	SEX	OCCUPATION	PRIVL	DES
DERENCZ, ANTON	33	M	LABR	RRZZZZ	USA
NOWIECKY, VINCENT	24	M	LABR	RRZZZZ	USA
BORKHOFF, ELISE	27	F	W	RRZZZZ	USA
WERA	8	F	CHILD	RRZZZZ	USA
ALEXDER	5	M	CHILD	RRZZZZ	USA
MARKIEWICZ, ANNA	19	F	SGL	RRZZZZ	USA
CAMINSKY, SIMON	21	M	MCHT	RRZZZZ	USA
BLUM, SCHMERL	16	M	LABR	RRZZZZ	USA
JAFFE, SELDA	20	F	SGL	RRZZZZ	USA
PRITZKON, LORENZ	28	M	WDMN	RRZZZZ	USA
CHRISTINE	20	F	W	RRZZZZ	USA
JOH.	.08	M	INFANT	RRZZZZ	USA
PERLSTEIN, ISACK	19	M	LABR	RRZZZZ	USA
KAPLAN, BLUME	20	M	SGL	RRZZZZ	USA
WOLLENBERG, AMALIE	20	F	SGL	RRZZZZ	USA
THERESE	16	F	SGL	RRZZZZ	USA
RACZKOWSKI, SCHEPSEL	20	M	TLR	RRZZZZ	USA
PESTKI, SALOMON	20	M	DLR	RRZZZZ	USA

PASSENGER	AGE	SEX	OCCUPATION	PV VIL DES
SOPRAN, HODES	25	F	W	RRZZZZUSA
ELIAS	.11	M	INFANT	RRZZZZUSA
LOEWENBERG, MAX	21	M	TLR	RRZZZZUSA
DRIBEN, JOSEF	17	M	LABR	RRZZZZUSA
FREIDMANN, ELISE	31	F	WO	RRZZZZUSA
SCHLOME	5	M	CHILD	RRZZZZUSA
CHAINE	4	F	CHILD	RRZZZZUSA
SCHEIMAN, HIRSCH	24	M	MCHT	RRZZZZUSA
TEPLITZ, ARON	24	M	LABR	RRZZZZUSA
GESELES, GITTEL	28	F	WO	RRZZZZUSA
HANNE	4	F	CHILD	RRZZZZUSA
BEN.	2	M	CHILD	RRZZZZUSA
ERLIN	.01	M	INFANT	RRZZZZUSA
HILLE, MENDEL	60	M	MCHT	RRZZZZUSA
HERRM.	40	M	MCHT	RRZZZZUSA
LIEBER, DAVID	19	M	MCHT	RRZZZZUSA
SOMMBOWSKI, ABRAHAM	23	M	MCHT	RRZZZZUSA
MOLACH, SALOMON	21	M	MCHT	RRZZZZUSA
SLATE	19	F	WO	RRZZZZUSA
FRANKEL, CHIESCHE	20	F	SGL	RRZZZZUSA
PRENSKE, MEIER	19	M	MCHT	RRZZZZUSA
MOLLIN, LEIB	25	M	MCHT	RRZZZZUSA
KIWE	22	F	WO	RRZZZZUSA
RAHEL	.06	F	INFANT	RRZZZZUSA
GORDON, SCHLOME	9	M	CHILD	RRZZZZUSA
SPIEGELSKY, MORDCKE	45	M	MCHT	RRZZZZUSA
FAKTEROWSKY, DAVID	9	M	CHILD	RRZZZZUSA
JANOWSKY, CHAIM	22	M	MCHT	RRZZZZUSA
GITTEL	21	F	W	RRZZZZUSA
JASSADZ, JACOB	23	M	LABR	RRZZZZUSA
FRANK, NACHUM	9	M	CHILD	RRZZZZUSA
WIENER, MAX	20	M	LABR	RRZZZZUSA
KRAHM, MARCUS	29	M	LABR	RRZZZZUSA
ZALKIND, PESCHE	21	F	WO	RRZZZZUSA
FISCHEL	.11	F	INFANT	RRZZZZUSA
GRINGARD, MARCUS	19	M	BCHR	RRZZZZUSA
DWORE	18	F	W	RRZZZZUSA
FREIDMANN, SIMON	18	M	MCHT	RRZZZZUSA

SHIP: FRANCE

FROM: HAVRE
TO: NEW YORK
ARRIVED: 15 AUGUST 1883

PASSENGER	AGE	SEX	OCCUPATION	PV VIL DES
LEFLER, HERMANN	22	M	ENGR	RRZZZZNY
RUCHERT, LOUIS	41	M	UNKNOWN	RRZZZZIN

SHIP: INDIA

FROM: HAMBURG
TO: NEW YORK
ARRIVED: 16 AUGUST 1883

PASSENGER	AGE	SEX	OCCUPATION	PV VIL DES
GOLDBERG, JOH.	24	F	WO	RRZZZZNY
JENNY	5	F	CHILD	RRZZZZNY
GREWE, MINNA	25	F	SGL	RRZZZZNY
KREMONT, JACOB	48	M	MCHT	RRZZZZNY
HELLMANN, ISAAC	23	M	TLR	RRZZZZNY
IDA	22	F	W	RRZZZZNY
HOLLMANN, H.	30	M	LABR	RRZZZZNY
JACOSCHINSKI, M.	17	M	LABR	RRZZZZNY
SAEGER, JACOB	26	M	MCHT	RRZZZZNY
NEUHOF, SEM.	24	M	TLR	RRZZZZNY
SCHLOEGMANN, M.	18	M	TRDSMN	RRZZZZNY
KOTZ, ABRAH.	23	M	TRDSMN	RRZZZZNY
GRUENSTEIN, CHAIM	18	M	TLR	RRZZZZNY
CHAWE	19	F	SGL	RRZZZZNY
ROSE	20	F	SGL	RRZZZZNY
STRIKOWSKI, CH.	30	M	TRDSMN	RRZZZZNY
GOLDFELDER, BERNHD.	26	M	TLR	RRZZZZNY
HANNY	23	F	W	RRZZZZNY
MALWINE	.11	F	INFANT	RRZZZZNY
MORITZ	.01	M	INFANT	RRZZZZNY
KERBEL, ARON	26	M	SHMK	RRZZZZNY
JAZOMBEAK, P.	26	M	LABR	RRZZZZNY
SALENDER, M.	26	M	LABR	RRZZZZNY
KIDIN, GINISTRO	30	M	LABR	RRZZZZNY
SCHOLVETZ, JOEL	29	M	LABR	RRZZZZNY
KELEIN, MEYER	28	M	TRDSMN	RRZZZZNY
FALCK, MEYER	28	M	TRDSMN	RRZZZZNY
KRESCH, JOEL	52	M	TRDSMN	RRZZZZNY
CHOYKE, BERNHARD	30	M	MCHT	RRZZZZNY
ROCHMANN, HANNA	30	F	WO	RRZZZZNY
SARA	7	F	CHILD	RRZZZZNY
CHAIE	5	F	CHILD	RRZZZZNY
WARENKIEWICZ, MARIE	18	F	SGL	RRZZZZNY
BECKER, BEILE	25	F	WO	RRZZZZNY
MORTJE	2	F	CHILD	RRZZZZNY
ISRAEL	.09	M	INFANT	RRZZZZNY
GUESCHE	40	F	WO	RRZZZZNY
FREIDE	7	F	CHILD	RRZZZZNY
MOSES	6	M	CHILD	RRZZZZNY
THOEN, EDUARD	32	M	SDLR	RRZZZZNY
GEIDO, ADOLF	24	M	SDLR	RRZZZZNY
WOLFF, FEIGE	24	F	WO	RRZZZZNY
MARIE	3	F	CHILD	RRZZZZNY
SCHOEL	.09	F	INFANT	RRZZZZNY
WEIZNER, REGIE	50	F	WO	RRZZZZNY
EMANUEL	13	M	S	RRZZZZNY
MARCUS	7	M	CHILD	RRZZZZNY
EHRENREICH, MARCUS	21	M	TRDSMN	RRZZZZNY
HUROCZACK, PHILIPP	30	M	LABR	RRZZZZNY
KORANZKI, ALBIN	30	M	LABR	RRZZZZNY
JANKO, SIESZAK	20	M	LABR	RRZZZZNY
SCHNEIZER, HERMANN	48	M	TRDSMN	PLZZZZNY
SCHMERR, JACOB	35	M	TRDSMN	PLZZZZNY
KAINO, ABRAM	20	M	TRDSMN	RRZZZZNY
ROSENTHAL, JUDE	7	M	CHILD	RRZZZZNY
HIRSCH, JACOB	28	M	TRDSMN	RRZZZZNY
GITTEL	25	F	W	RRZZZZNY
FICHTENBAUM, JOSEF	40	M	TRDSMN	RRZZZZNY
GAERTNER, JOCHE	36	F	WO	RRZZZZNY
JACOB	.09	M	INFANT	RRZZZZNY
LEIB	.09	M	INFANT	RRZZZZNY
FIEBER, SOFIE	28	F	WO	RRZZZZNY
ANNA	6	F	CHILD	RRZZZZNY
LEIMANN, SIMON	26	M	TRDSMN	RRZZZZNY
PLAPLA, MINNA	11	F	CH	RRZZZZNY
MORSCHE	7	M	CHILD	RRZZZZNY
GEIGER, ROSALIE	48	F	WO	RRZZZZNY
LOTTE	16	F	D	RRZZZZNY
MORITZ	18	M	S	RRZZZZNY
FANNI	12	F	D	RRZZZZNY
IGNATZ	7	M	CHILD	RRZZZZNY
MALI	6	F	CHILD	RRZZZZNY
SAMUEL	5	M	CHILD	RRZZZZNY
MINNA	4	F	CHILD	RRZZZZNY
LUTERKORT, ESTER	46	F	WO	RRZZZZNY
CLARA	6	F	CHILD	RRZZZZNY
LINA	5	F	CHILD	RRZZZZNY
ZARILIE	4	F	CHILD	RRZZZZNY
PINCUS, SARA	19	F	SGL	RRZZZZNY
LIBOWITZ, BEILE	19	F	SGL	RRZZZZNY
SINBERG, LEIB	26	M	TRDSMN	RRZZZZNY
SZAREWITZ, LUDWIG	49	M	LABR	RRZZZZNY
CHAZKEL, RACH.	24	F	WO	RRZZZZNY
MEYER	.06	M	INFANT	RRZZZZNY

PASSENGER	AGE	SEX	OCCUPATION	PRIVL	DES
SHIP: PENNLAND					
FROM: ANTWERP					
TO: NEW YORK					
ARRIVED: 16 AUGUST 1883					
ROBINSON, HARRIS	25	M	HAMF	RR	ZZZZNY
JENNY	25	F	UNKNOWN	RR	ZZZZNY
SHIP: STATE OF NEBRASKA					
FROM: GLASGOW AND LARNE					
TO: NEW YORK					
ARRIVED: 22 AUGUST 1883					
SHAPERIRA, M.	24	M	PDLR	PL	ZZZZUSA
ROSENBERG, I.	29	M	UNKNOWN	PL	ZZZZUSA
KOHN, L.	24	M	UNKNOWN	PL	ZZZZUSA
HURWITZ, D.	19	M	UNKNOWN	PL	ZZZZUSA
FENER, D.	21	M	UNKNOWN	PL	ZZZZUSA
CHAJMOWITZ, M.	45	M	TLR	RR	ZZZZUSA
BERGAMOWITZ, S.	33	M	PDLR	RR	ZZZZUSA
FLEISCHER, G.	26	M	TLR	RR	ZZZZUSA
ULITZKY, G.	23	M	CGRMKR	RR	ZZZZUSA
KRAUWITZKY, J.	17	M	PDLR	RR	ZZZZUSA
ERBSTEIN, G.	19	M	TLR	RR	ZZZZUSA
SHIP: POLYNESIA					
FROM: HAMBURG					
TO: NEW YORK					
ARRIVED: 25 AUGUST 1883					
ROSENBERG, ADOLF	19	M	TRDSMN	RR	ZZZZNY
LIPKOVITZ, JAK.	20	M	UNKNOWN	RR	ZZZZNY
DAVIDERITS, D.	25	M	UNKNOWN	RR	ZZZZNY
PAPEVITS, ELIAS	28	M	UNKNOWN	RR	ZZZZNY
DURCHSCHLAG, M.	19	M	UNKNOWN	RR	ZZZZNY
WEIFS, HANE	12	F	UNKNOWN	RR	ZZZZNY
REINSBERG, HANS	39	M	MCHT	RR	ZZZZNY
MARY	27	F	W	RR	ZZZZNY
HANNY	7	F	CHILD	RR	ZZZZNY
ABROMOWITZ, CH.	22	M	TRDSMN	RR	ZZZZNY
HIRSCHBERG, ABR.	22	M	UNKNOWN	RR	ZZZZNY
GOLDBERG, ISRAEL	28	M	UNKNOWN	RR	ZZZZBAL
NODELSTECHER, SAMUEL	26	M	TNMK	RR	ZZZZBAL
DAVID	18	M	UNKNOWN	RR	ZZZZBAL
KUKLEWITZ, STANISLAUS	19	M	LABR	RR	ZZZZNY
GLOWARTZ, RASCHE	40	F	WO	RR	ZZZZNY
SARA	7	F	CHILD	RR	ZZZZNY
NASEN	5	M	CHILD	RR	ZZZZNY
SAMUEL	4	M	CHILD	RR	ZZZZNY
KAPLAN, ADOLF	23	M	TRDSMN	RR	ZZZZNY
LAPIDISER, ANNA	19	F	SGL	RR	ZZZZNY
MOWSOHN, CHAIKEL	18	M	MCHT	RR	ZZZZNY
BIGELEISEN, LAZAR	22	M	MCHT	PL	ZZZZNY
TRAUGOTT, JOACHIM	26	M	MCHT	PL	ZZZZNY
DEBORA	22	F	SGL	PL	ZZZZNY
LEISER	19	M	TRDSMN	PL	ZZZZNY
KLEINER, LOEB.	29	M	MCHT	PL	ZZZZNY
EICHENSTEIN, MORITZ	33	M	TRDSMN	PL	ZZZZNY
LICHTENSTEIN, SAL.	36	M	UNKNOWN	RR	ZZZZNY
SIW, MEIER	17	M	CGRMKR	RR	ZZZZNY
ANNA	17	F	SI	RR	ZZZZNY
HANNEL, ABR.H.	35	M	TRDSMN	PL	ZZZZNY
WIEDHOFF, ABRAH.	20	M	UNKNOWN	PL	ZZZZNY
SALZMANN, DAV.	7	M	CHILD	PL	ZZZZNY
CHINDEL, CH.	34	M	TRDSMN	PL	ZZZZNY
HEFSE, FRIEDR.	33	M	LABR	RR	ZZZZNY
JUNDINE	29	F	W	RR	ZZZZNY
ERNST	.11	M	INFANT	RR	ZZZZNY
ELNA	.01	F	INFANT	RR	ZZZZNY
SHIP: SILESIA					
FROM: HAMBURG AND HAVRE					
TO: NEW YORK					
ARRIVED: 27 AUGUST 1883					
WOKSEN, ARNOLD	30	M	MCHT	RR	ZZZZUSA
SENDER, AUGUSTE	20	F	SGL	RR	ZZZZUSA
SLAMINSKY, ANNA	21	F	SGL	RR	ZZZZUSA
REBECCA	18	F	SGL	RR	ZZZZUSA
ERBSTEIN, DAVID	30	M	MCHT	RR	ZZZZUSA
TRILLING, ABRAHAM	50	M	LABR	RR	ZZZZUSA
MARIE	50	F	W	RR	ZZZZUSA
CHANNE	20	F	CH	RR	ZZZZUSA
JANKEL	18	M	CH	RR	ZZZZUSA
LEIBISCH, HIRSCH	32	M	DLR	RR	ZZZZUSA
GOLDMANN, JOSEF	20	M	CL	RR	ZZZZUSA
DOMBROWSKI, ANTONIA	28	F	SGL	RR	ZZZZUSA
BENEDICTO	9	M	CHILD	RR	ZZZZUSA
GROSSMANN, ISRAEL	20	M	SMH	RR	ZZZZUSA
FROMBERG, SCHAIC	9	M	CHILD	RR	ZZZZUSA
JACOBSOHN, SIMON	27	M	LABR	RR	ZZZZUSA
HERTZBERG, HENRY	29	M	LABR	RR	ZZZZUSA
REICH, CAROLINE	26	F	W	RR	ZZZZUSA
NAFTALIE	7	F	CHILD	RR	ZZZZUSA
EMILIE	4	F	CHILD	RR	ZZZZUSA
HELENE	.11	F	INFANT	RR	ZZZZUSA
STIMMEL, CZIWE	56	F	W	RR	ZZZZUSA
ROSCHE	9	F	CHILD	RR	ZZZZUSA
MORITZ	8	M	CHILD	RR	ZZZZUSA
WALLOSCHINSKI, SAM.	18	M	DLR	RR	ZZZZUSA
BESMANOWITZ, BASCHE	20	F	W	RR	ZZZZUSA
SALMEN	9	M	CHILD	RR	ZZZZUSA
BENJAMIN	8	M	CHILD	RR	ZZZZUSA
LESCHKE	7	F	CHILD	RR	ZZZZUSA
RIWE	.11	M	INFANT	RR	ZZZZUSA
FRANKELSTEIN, MENDEL	35	M	LABR	RR	ZZZZUSA
SCHILNITZKI, SCHLOME	20	M	LABR	RR	ZZZZUSA
WERNER, YRDKE	45	F	W	RR	ZZZZUSA
AGNES	8	F	CHILD	RR	ZZZZUSA
KORNISCHKA, ERNESTINE	45	F	W	RR	ZZZZUSA
ALBERT	8	M	CHILD	RR	ZZZZUSA
OTTO	6	M	CHILD	RR	ZZZZUSA
MARTHA	18	F	SGL	RR	ZZZZUSA
MUNCKHAGEN, ALBERT	30	M	SDLR	RR	ZZZZUSA
ROSENBERG, ISRAEL	20	M	LABR	RR	ZZZZUSA
ROCHEC	20	F	W	RR	ZZZZUSA
SCHNEIDER, DAVID	21	M	TLR	RR	ZZZZUSA
SCHKOSS, JOCHIM	38	M	MCHT	RR	ZZZZUSA
POMOZNIK, MOSES	42	M	DLR	RR	ZZZZUSA
LISTER, ZALKE	25	F	SGL	RR	ZZZZUSA
KLARA	20	F	SGL	RR	ZZZZUSA
EBERT, MARIE	31	F	SGL	RR	ZZZZUSA

PASSENGER	AGE	SEX	OCCUPATION	PRV VIL DES

SHIP: AUSTRALIA

FROM: HAMBURG
TO: NEW YORK
ARRIVED: 31 AUGUST 1883

PASSENGER	AGE	SEX	OCCUPATION	PRV VIL DES
KALBACH, BEIL	36	M	TRDSMN	PLZZZZNY
JENNE	40	F	W	PLZZZZNY
MOSES	6	M	CHILD	PLZZZZNY
GROSS, GETHE	17	F	SGL	PLZZZZNY
KALBACH, JOSEF	18	M	TLR	PLZZZZNY
JACOB	17	M	TRDSMN	PLZZZZNY
EIGNER, JETTE	35	F	WO	PLZZZZNY
NACHUM	7	M	CHILD	PLZZZZNY
HANDEL	6	M	CHILD	PLZZZZNY
FANNE	3	F	CHILD	PLZZZZNY
GRUENBAUM, HANNI	23	F	WO	PLZZZZNY
MARIA	4	F	CHILD	PLZZZZNY
JACOB	.08	M	INFANT	PLZZZZNY
MEYER, BENJ.	19	M	SHMK	RRZZZZNY
NOTES, MARCUS	20	M	TRDSMN	RRZZZZNY
RACHEL	18	F	W	RRZZZZNY
CHWAXZEWSKA, RACH.	30	F	WO	RRZZZZNY
JACOB	6	M	CHILD	RRZZZZNY
FREIDE	4	F	CHILD	RRZZZZNY
GLUTHE	.10	F	INFANT	RRZZZZNY
DIETRICH, BARL.	33	M	TLR	PLZZZZ***
ASCH, NUSIM	16	M	TRDSMN	RRZZZZNY

SHIP: FURNESSIA

FROM: LIVERPOOL AND QUEENSTOWN
TO: NEW YORK
ARRIVED: 03 SEPTEMBER 1883

PASSENGER	AGE	SEX	OCCUPATION	PRV VIL DES
POTTALA, LOUISA	19	F	SVNT	RRZZZZUSA
PERCTULA, JOHANA	28	F	W	RRZZZZUSA
IDA	.09	F	INFANT	RRZZZZUSA

SHIP: GELLERT

FROM: HAMBURG AND HAVRE
TO: NEW YORK
ARRIVED: 05 SEPTEMBER 1883

PASSENGER	AGE	SEX	OCCUPATION	PRV VIL DES
JA--OWSKY, BARUCH	24	M	UNKNOWN	RRZZZZUSA
EID---KY, ALEK.	22	M	UNKNOWN	RRZZZZUSA
U, REINHD.	15	M	UNKNOWN	RRZZZZUSA
DEUTSCH, LEIBE	22	F	TNMK	RRZZZZUSA
GUIP, MORDCHE	55	M	SHMK	RRZZZZUSA
BARNET, KALMAN	32	M	TLR	RRZZZZUSA
SCHEER, EISICK	33	M	UNKNOWN	RRZZZZUSA
DWORKOWSKY, RAPHAEL	27	M	UNKNOWN	RRZZZZUSA
LEIZEROWITZ, LUDWIG	23	M	UNKNOWN	RRZZZZUSA
CEGIELSKY, JAN	40	M	LABR	RRZZZZUSA
SCHULZ, JOHAN	49	M	LABR	RRZZZZUSA
GULIANNE	42	F	W	RRZZZZUSA
HENR.	12	M	CH	RRZZZZUSA
EUPHROSINE	6	F	CHILD	RRZZZZUSA
AMALIE	3	F	CHILD	RRZZZZUSA
SCHMIDT, BERTHA	22	F	SGL	RRZZZZUSA
SANDER, GUSTINE	19	F	UNKNOWN	RRZZZZUSA
BONKOWSKY, EDWARD	20	M	LABR	RRZZZZUSA
LUNGE, ADOLF	25	M	UNKNOWN	RRZZZZUSA
LANDAU, FRIEDR.	20	M	UNKNOWN	RRZZZZUSA
SONNENBERG, FRIEDR.	24	M	UNKNOWN	RRZZZZUSA
HOFFMANN, FRIEDR.	17	M	UNKNOWN	RRZZZZUSA
LANGE, EDWARD	21	M	UNKNOWN	RRZZZZUSA
SZELSKI, GEORG.	38	M	UNKNOWN	RRZZZZUSA
SZELSKA, PAULINE	28	F	SGL	RRZZZZUSA
ADAMS, PAUL.	22	F	W	RRZZZZUSA
AUGST.	2	F	CHILD	RRZZZZUSA
BAUM, JULS.	21	M	LABR	RRZZZZUSA
SEGAL, ELIAS	16	M	BBR	RRZZZZUSA
KREIS, MICHAEL	24	M	LABR	RRZZZZUSA
GENSINSKI, STANISL.	22	M	UNKNOWN	RRZZZZUSA
LITKE, ANTON	22	M	UNKNOWN	RRZZZZUSA
PUZ, MANEIY	23	M	UNKNOWN	RRZZZZUSA
ABRAMOVITZ, ROSA	28	F	W	RRZZZZUSA
BASSERLE	3	F	CHILD	RRZZZZUSA
SIMON	.11	M	INFANT	RRZZZZUSA
EYTRON, LOUIS	20	M	LABR	RRZZZZUSA
GUTMANN, MINNA	23	F	W	RRZZZZUSA
WOLF	.11	M	INFANT	RRZZZZUSA
LEWITH, LEA	22	F	W	RRZZZZUSA
CHASCHE	.11	F	INFANT	RRZZZZUSA
ELI	.01	M	INFANT	RRZZZZUSA
BOELSER, CHINE	18	F	SGL	RRZZZZUSA
LACHMANN, CHAIM	17	M	CL	RRZZZZUSA
DIEMER, FEIGE	37	F	W	RRZZZZUSA
BASCHE	16	F	CH	RRZZZZUSA
JUDA	7	M	CHILD	RRZZZZUSA
CHEIE	6	F	CHILD	RRZZZZUSA
ELIAS	.11	M	INFANT	RRZZZZUSA
LEIBE	.01	M	INFANT	RRZZZZUSA
ECKSTEIN, HEINR.	26	M	LABR	RRZZZZUSA
ROSENBERG, FANNY	23	F	SGL	RRZZZZUSA
BORNSTEIN, JOSEF	24	M	UNKNOWN	RRZZZZUSA
BERKOWITZ, MENASCHE	20	M	SGL	RRZZZZUSA
TREIGANG, GUSTAV	24	M	SHMK	RRZZZZUSA
LEWINSTEIN, MALKE	53	F	W	RRZZZZUSA
KATE	17	F	D	RRZZZZUSA
AJIN, BERNHD.	20	M	LABR	RRZZZZUSA
LIPPSCHEITZ, CHANNE	18	F	SGL	RRZZZZUSA
REITTENBERG, SARAH	50	F	UNKNOWN	RRZZZZUSA
SADIC	21	F	CH	RRZZZZUSA
SAMUEL	9	M	CHILD	RRZZZZUSA
RACHEL	8	F	CHILD	RRZZZZUSA
KLUGEMANN, ELKE	17	F	SGL	RRZZZZUSA
BRACK, BASCHE	18	F	SGL	RRZZZZUSA
BURNSTEIN, CHAIE	42	F	W	RRZZZZUSA
JACOB	9	M	CHILD	RRZZZZUSA
ABRAH.	8	M	CHILD	RRZZZZUSA
SELIG	.11	M	INFANT	RRZZZZUSA
EPSTEIN, JANKEL	18	M	DLR	RRZZZZUSA
FELDMANN, SAM.	20	M	LABR	RRZZZZUSA
KAPLAN, JACOB	17	M	TLR	RRZZZZUSA
ISAACSOHN, ISAAC	20	M	UNKNOWN	RRZZZZUSA
BOTWENIK, MORDUCH	20	M	SHMK	RRZZZZUSA
SAGOR, NOAK.	19	M	UNKNOWN	RRZZZZUSA
BERELOWITZ, DOBRE	26	F	W	RRZZZZUSA
FREIDE.	.11	F	INFANT	RRZZZZUSA
DAVID	.01	M	INFANT	RRZZZZUSA
EPPSTEIN, JOSEF	9	M	CHILD	RRZZZZUSA
ROSENZWEIG, SALOMON	21	M	LABR	RRZZZZUSA
CIRL	18	F	W	RRZZZZUSA
ROSENBLUM, GOSIK	15	M	LABR	RRZZZZUSA
BESTERMANN, ISAAC	17	M	WVR	RRZZZZUSA
FRANK, CHAIE	40	F	W	RRZZZZUSA
PERKE	7	F	CHILD	RRZZZZUSA
MOSES	5	M	CHILD	RRZZZZUSA
FREIDE	.11	F	INFANT	RRZZZZUSA
JUDES	.01	M	INFANT	RRZZZZUSA
DEMBOWITZ, MEYER	25	M	DLR	RRZZZZUSA
MILANER, ARTHUR	21	M	CPR	RRZZZZUSA
KLUGERMANN, JECHIEL	50	M	LABR	RRZZZZUSA
RACHEL	50	F	W	RRZZZZUSA
DAVID	9	M	CHILD	RRZZZZUSA
CHANNE	8	F	CHILD	RRZZZZUSA

PASSENGER	AGE	SEX	OCCUPATION	PRV VIL DES
KABATZNIK, FEIWEL	16	M	LABR	RRZZZZUSA
BREGMANN, ELIAS	9	M	CHILD	RRZZZZUSA
KAHAN, JUDEL	21	F	CGRMKR	RRZZZZUSA
ARMAN, MERE	14	F	SGL	RRZZZZUSA
FARBER, LEA	18	F	UNKNOWN	RRZZZZUSA
WARSCHAUER, TAUBE	50	F	W	RRZZZZUSA
CHANNE	16	F	D	RRZZZZUSA
GOLDGARN, BERNHD.	21	M	LABR	RRZZZZUSA
MISTOWSKY, ISAAC	59	M	UNKNOWN	RRZZZZUSA
FEIGE	55	F	W	RRZZZZUSA
SCHULTZ, JOH.	49	M	FARMER	RRZZZZUSA
MUELLER, ARMAND	30	M	CKR	RRZZZZUSA
CATHA.	25	F	W	RRZZZZUSA
ARMAND	6	M	CHILD	RRZZZZUSA
WOLSCHIN, KATI	17	F	SGL	RRZZZZUSA

SHIP: STATE OF INDIANA

FROM: GLASGOW AND LARNE
TO: NEW YORK
ARRIVED: 06 SEPTEMBER 1883

PASSENGER	AGE	SEX	OCCUPATION	PRV VIL DES
SCHURPUNSCH, LUDWIGA	44	F	W	RRZZZZUSA
ANTON	9	M	CHILD	RRZZZZUSA
JOSEPH	5	M	CHILD	RRZZZZUSA
SAMITOWSKI, SIMON	45	M	LABR	RRZZZZUSA
MARIA	47	F	W	RRZZZZUSA
FLORA	18	F	DMS	RRZZZZUSA
LUDWIG	4	M	CHILD	RRZZZZUSA
MADGA.	6	F	CHILD	RRZZZZUSA
PASSANDOWSKY, ELHKUM	28	M	LABR	RRZZZZUSA
LUSNOFOSKY, JACOB	32	M	LABR	RRZZZZUSA
MAGDALINE	28	F	W	RRZZZZUSA
MARIA	1	F	CHILD	RRZZZZUSA

SHIP: CALIFORNIA

FROM: HAMBURG
TO: NEW YORK
ARRIVED: 07 SEPTEMBER 1883

PASSENGER	AGE	SEX	OCCUPATION	PRV VIL DES
SALZMANN, TESCHAL	30	F	WO	RRZZZZNY
SAMUEL-BASSE	7	M	CHILD	RRZZZZNY
BASSE	6	M	CHILD	RRZZZZNY
LIEBE	4	M	CHILD	RRZZZZNY
SCHAWE	3	F	CHILD	RRZZZZNY
LINE	.06	F	INFANT	RRZZZZNY
BRITZ, ISAAC	22	M	TRDSMN	RRZZZZNY
NATHANSON, NATHAN	58	M	TRDSMN	RRZZZZNY
MARIE	54	F	W	RRZZZZNY
RACHEL	20	M	S	RRZZZZNY
EMMA	17	F	D	RRZZZZNY
SARA	14	F	D	RRZZZZNY
LURIAL, SANDER	19	M	TRDSMN	RRZZZZNY
GRUENBAUM, MORITZ	58	M	TRDSMN	RRZZZZNY
BORSCHINSKI, SEBE	24	F	SGL	RRZZZZNY
SEGAL, MINE	20	F	SGL	RRZZZZNY
BECKER, ZALLEL	23	M	TRDSMN	PLZZZZNY
KRULEWITZ, MASCHE	16	F	SGL	PLZZZZNY
FISS, ALBERT	26	M	TLR	RRZZZZNY
MELTZER, SCHLEIME	46	M	TLR	RRZZZZNY
SCHNEIDER, ITZIG	22	M	TLR	RRZZZZNY
IDA	20	F	SGL	RRZZZZNY
BEHMER, MARG.	35	F	WO	RRZZZZNY
ABRAHAM	6	M	CHILD	RRZZZZNY

PASSENGER	AGE	SEX	OCCUPATION	PRV VIL DES
BEIRACH, M.	40	F	WO	RRZZZZNY
ANNA	7	F	CHILD	RRZZZZNY
TRIME	6	F	CHILD	RRZZZZNY
WEINGARTEN, JAC.	50	M	TLR	PLZZZZNY
SCHINDLER, JOSEF	42	M	MCHT	PLZZZZNY
SPIEGEL, BRONCE	17	F	SGL	PLZZZZNY
NACHHAUSER, SAM.	20	M	MCHT	PLZZZZNY
FELDMANN, PISACH	18	M	MCHT	PLZZZZNY
KLAPSAU, ISAAC	17	M	TLR	PLZZZZNY
WERNER, ALBERT	22	M	MCHT	PLZZZZNY
KLEIMANN, MEND.	18	M	TRDSMN	RRZZZZNY
REDER, LEISER	23	M	TRDSMN	PLZZZZNY
EIGE	26	F	WO	PLZZZZNY
PINCHOS	.05	M	INFANT	PLZZZZNY
LEICHTER, PERL	23	F	SGL	PLZZZZNY
KUPFERMANN, M.	15	F	SGL	PLZZZZNY
BRENNER, REWKE	18	F	SGL	PLZZZZNY
BRONHEIM, ISAAC	17	M	TRDSMN	PLZZZZNY
EIL, ABRAH.	7	M	CHILD	PLZZZZNY
ERTSCHEK, ISRAEL	25	M	GZR	PLZZZZNY
TAUBE	22	F	W	PLZZZZNY
CHAIM	.11	M	INFANT	PLZZZZNY
CHAI	.01	F	INFANT	PLZZZZNY
ROTH, ROSA	21	F	SGL	PLZZZZNY
IGNATZ, JOHANN	21	M	LABR	PLZZZZNY
BERLINER, SAM.	17	M	LABR	PLZZZZNY
SALY	20	M	LABR	PLZZZZNY
BASSOR, FERENZ	21	M	LABR	PLZZZZNY
SIRBUS, CLARA	17	F	SGL	PLZZZZNY
WENDIK, MARIA	20	F	WO	PLZZZZNY
JOHANN	.10	M	INFANT	PLZZZZNY
JOSEF	23	M	LABR	PLZZZZNY
BARUCH, LEIB	34	M	TLR	RRZZZZNY
SUWALKI, ESTER-RACHEL	24	F	WO	RRZZZZNY
OKERINSEWSKI, FEIWE	00	M	TRDSMN	PLZZZZNY
BER-GULBINSKI, NOTE	26	M	TRDSMN	PLZZZZNY
SCHINDLER, ISSER	24	M	TRDSMN	PLZZZZNY
TIGER, BEREL	55	M	TRDSMN	PLZZZZNY
PARZELAN, MEYER	40	M	TRDSMN	PLZZZZNY
KOCH, JOS.	17	M	TRDSMN	PLZZZZNY
BRUCK, ISIDOR	26	M	WCHMKR	PLZZZZNY
KAPLAN, ELIAS	19	M	LABR	RRZZZZNY
RECHO, MORITZ	19	M	LABR	RRZZZZNY
SCHER, KASIMIR	38	M	TLR	RRZZZZNY
SCHAPEWITZ, MOSES	7	M	CHILD	RRZZZZNY
SCHARTSCHUK, NECHEMIE	25	M	TRDSMN	RRZZZZNY
JAN, BOLESLAV	23	M	TRDSMN	RRZZZZNY
BRAUN, RACHMIEL	18	M	TRDSMN	RRZZZZNY
BEHR	16	M	TRDSMN	RRZZZZNY
PERTINSKY, ISRAEL	19	M	TRDSMN	RRZZZZNY
SCHONI	18	F	W	RRZZZZNY
ALTKRUG, SCHOENE	20	F	WO	RRZZZZNY
GECTEL	.06	F	INFANT	RRZZZZNY
DEMBICER, TRADEL	17	M	TRDSMN	RRZZZZNY
NEUSTAEDTER, MELAH	16	M	TRDSMN	RRZZZZNY
MANDEL, TRADEL	17	M	TRDSMN	RRZZZZNY
FARGOLSCHIN, MARCUS	19	M	TRDSMN	RRZZZZNY
GRABOWSKI, LEHA	30	F	WO	RRZZZZNY
SOSCHE	.10	F	INFANT	RRZZZZNY
FRANKE, ABRAHAM	18	M	TRDSMN	RRZZZZNY
LIPMANN, JULIUS	42	M	TRDSMN	RRZZZZNY
GREFSMANN, ABRAHAM	28	M	TRDSMN	RRZZZZNY
LENA	24	F	W	RRZZZZNY
HINDE	.09	F	INFANT	RRZZZZNY
RADISCHKAUSKI, JOSEF	24	M	LABR	RRZZZZNY

SHIP: BOHEMIA

FROM: HAMBURG
TO: NEW YORK
ARRIVED: 10 SEPTEMBER 1883

PASSENGER	AGE	SEX	OCCUPATION	PRV VIL DES
SACHARFF, MOSES	16	M	LABR	RRZZZZUSA
KLEMPNER, REISE	19	F	SGL	RRZZZZUSA
FEIGENSOHN, DOBE	16	F	SGL	RRZZZZUSA
RONBEN, DINA	54	F	W	RRZZZZUSA
HENKE, EMILIE	20	F	W	RRZZZZUSA
FINGELBURG, MOSES	17	M	LABR	RRZZZZUSA
BROZOWSKI, HIRSCH	18	M	DLR	RRZZZZUSA
SUDARSKI, LEA	35	F	SGL	RRZZZZUSA
SCHLACKETZKI, RACHEL	31	F	W	RRZZZZUSA
ALTE	7	F	CHILD	RRZZZZUSA
POLTI	5	F	CHILD	RRZZZZUSA
KEILE	.11	F	INFANT	RRZZZZUSA
PERESTKOWSKI, EYSTER	25	M	DLR	RRZZZZUSA
ROMEHEWITZ, CONSTANTIEN	22	M	DLR	RRZZZZUSA
SOGURSKI, LOUIS	22.	M	LABR	RRZZZZUSA
BUBINSTEIN, SLAMA	9	F	CHILD	RRZZZZUSA
BERS, MARITZ	30	M	LABR	RRZZZZUSA
POCKERNIK, ANNA	33	F	W	RRZZZZUSA
GEORG	9	M	CHILD	RRZZZZUSA
DWOROWSKI, MORDECHE	20	M	DLR	RRZZZZUSA
SCHULBERG, MORDESCHE	20	M	DLR	RRZZZZUSA
ANGOSTOWSKY, ABRAHAM	58	M	LABR	RRZZZZUSA
CHANNE	55	F	W	RRZZZZUSA
SIMON, LIEBE	14	F	SGL	RRZZZZUSA
GOLDSTEIN, JOSEL	53	M	DLR	RRZZZZUSA
MALKE	20	M	CH	RRZZZZUSA
BASCHE	18	M	CH	RRZZZZUSA
ISAC	9	M	CHILD	RRZZZZUSA
FILIKOWSKI, MARIE	23	F	W	RRZZZZUSA
SCHAFRANSKI, SELIG	60	M	DLR	RRZZZZUSA
EIGE	60	F	W	RRZZZZUSA
SMOLINSKY, SARA	26	F	W	RRZZZZUSA
JACOB	5	M	CHILD	RRZZZZUSA
FEIGE	.11	M	INFANT	RRZZZZUSA
SEPKE	20	F	SGL	RRZZZZUSA
REINZOHN, RASCHE	54	F	W	RRZZZZUSA
SIMON	9	M	CHILD	RRZZZZUSA
DAVIEL	5	M	CHILD	RRZZZZUSA
FRIED, SIEFS	54	F	W	RRZZZZUSA
MAFSCHOWICZ, SAMUEL	25	F	SGL	RRZZZZUSA
SCHAPIRO, HEINRICH	24	M	BKBNDR	RRZZZZUSA
SUCHOZELSCHI, ALD	26	F	SGL	RRZZZZUSA
RUBINSTEIN, DINE	22	F	SGL	RRZZZZUSA
ZUPITZKI, LEIZER	26	M	DLR	RRZZZZUSA
LEISER, JOHANNE	22	M	DLR	RRZZZZUSA
ZIEGEL, HIRSH	16	M	DLR	RRZZZZUSA
BABELNIK, LEIB	17	M	DLR	RRZZZZUSA
SAKOLSKI, ARON	30	M	DLR	RRZZZZUSA
SALOMON	9	M	CHILD	RRZZZZUSA
KAPLAN, SCHIELEN	39	M	DLR	RRZZZZUSA
DLUGOWSKI, AUGUST	55	M	DLR	RRZZZZUSA
YNWINSKI, CHAIN	17	F	SGL	RRZZZZUSA
RECHAME	9	F	CHILD	RRZZZZUSA
BADY, DORA	17	F	SGL	RRZZZZUSA
SCHULTZ, ERNESTI	46	F	SGL	RRZZZZUSA
KLIPPEL, ELISE	24	F	SGL	RRZZZZUSA
SCHULTZ, PAULINE	.11	F	INFANT	RRZZZZUSA
RABKOWSKA, EVA	67	F	W	RRZZZZUSA
SPIELMANN, JACOB	24	M	LABR	RRZZZZUSA
GOLDMANN, ISIDOR	19	M	LABR	RRZZZZUSA
LIPINSKI, ANTON	26	M	LABR	RRZZZZUSA
WALTER, FRIDR.	30	M	LKSH	RRZZZZUSA
SCHULTZ, OTTO	29	M	BCHR	RRZZZZUSA
PIETRKOWSKY, ARON	16	F	SGL	RRZZZZUSA
GRUNEWITZ, SARA	30	M	LABR	RRZZZZUSA
DWOE	9	F	CHILD	RRZZZZUSA
KUEIN, DOVA	45	M	LABR	RRZZZZUSA
FILIKOWSKI, CHAIN	.09	M	INFANT	RRZZZZUSA

SHIP: ENGLAND

FROM: LIVERPOOL AND QUEENSTOWN
TO: NEW YORK
ARRIVED: 11 SEPTEMBER 1883

PASSENGER	AGE	SEX	OCCUPATION	PRV VIL DES
FORSTI, NARMID-GRETA	53	F	SP	RRZZZZUSA
SERAFIA	11	F	CH	RRZZZZUSA
HAISEN, MARIE	39	F	W	RRZZZZUSA
JOHAN	11	M	CH	RRZZZZUSA
MARTHA	9	F	CHILD	RRZZZZUSA
MATHILDE	6	F	CHILD	RRZZZZUSA
JENSINE	00	F	INF	RRZZZZUSA
BRITTAKA, JOHAN	27	M	LABR	RRZZZZUSA
MARIA	26	F	W	RRZZZZUSA
THOMAS, AUGUSTA	30	F	W	RRZZZZUSA
GUSTAF	7	M	CHILD	RRZZZZUSA
HELENE	5	F	CHILD	RRZZZZUSA
CLARA	4	F	CHILD	RRZZZZUSA
ANNA	00	F	INF	RRZZZZUSA

SHIP: WESTPHALIA

FROM: HAMBURG AND HAVRE
TO: NEW YORK
ARRIVED: 11 SEPTEMBER 1883

PASSENGER	AGE	SEX	OCCUPATION	PRV VIL DES
YODZIS, DOMINICK	20	M	LABR	RRZZZZNY
STANKIEWICZ, JACOB	18	M	LABR	RRZZZZNY
KOZLOWSKA, AGATHE	20	F	SGL	RRZZZZNY
COHN, ISAAC	18	M	LABR	RRZZZZNY
BROCKMANN, ABRAHAM	46	M	DLR	RRZZZZNY
MELON, FRANZ	24	M	LABR	RRZZZZNY
CAROLINE	23	F	W	RRZZZZNY
ANTON	23	M	LABR	RRZZZZNY
FUHRMANN, PERL	14	F	SGL	RRZZZZNY
LACHZINSK, RACHEL	25	F	W	RRZZZZNY
RUBEN	.11	M	INFANT	RRZZZZNY
FEIWEL	.01	M	INFANT	RRZZZZNY
FRIEDMANN, HANNE	36	F	W	RRZZZZNY
NOSSEN	9	M	CHILD	RRZZZZNY
ETTEL	5	F	CHILD	RRZZZZNY
ABRAH.	4	M	CHILD	RRZZZZNY
MOSES	.11	M	INFANT	RRZZZZNY
GROV, SALOMON	30	M	DLR	RRZZZZNY
GILZINSKY, HENDE	43	F	W	RRZZZZNY
BASCHENIA	9	F	CHILD	RRZZZZNY
CHANNE	7	F	CHILD	RRZZZZNY
ABRAH	.02	M	INFANT	RRZZZZNY
LEWIT, PESCHE	39	F	W	RRZZZZNY
MASCHE	8	F	CHILD	RRZZZZNY
JOSSEL	4	M	CHILD	RRZZZZNY
SAMUEL	.11	M	INFANT	RRZZZZNY
GERSON	.01	M	INFANT	RRZZZZNY
SCHLACHTER, HIRSCH	17	M	MCHT	RRZZZZNY
LIPCKE, HIRSCH	17	M	TLR	RRZZZZNY
RAPKIN, HIRSCH	20	M	TNR	RRZZZZNY
ROSENSKY, FEIWEL	26	M	MSN	RRZZZZNY
KREISSMANN, ABRAH.	42	M	DLR	PLZZZZNY
ADAM	16	M	S	PLZZZZNY
BOBLAWSKY, SAL.	27	M	TLR	RRZZZZNY
BERACHOWITSCH, SORACH	31	F	MCHT	RRZZZZNY
FEIGENBAUM, SARAH	24	F	MCHT	RRZZZZNY
WOLF	4	M	CHILD	RRZZZZNY
SCHLOMARES, JACOB	20	M	TLR	RRZZZZNY
BITNER, JACOB	20	M	LABR	RRZZZZNY
PAMINNUSKY, LEIB	60	M	SHMK	RRZZZZNY
FRIEDE	50	F	W	RRZZZZNY
ABRAHAM	20	M	CH	RRZZZZNY

PASSENGER	AGE	SEX	OCCUPATION	PRIV	VIL	DES
RIWE	19	F	CH	RR	ZZZZ	NY
FABIAN, BER.	40	M	LABR	RR	ZZZZ	NY
GORDANSKY, ALTER	22	M	LABR	RR	ZZZZ	NY
ROSENBERG, NOHE	22	M	LABR	RR	ZZZZ	NY
KATZ, MOSCHE	49	M	LABR	RR	ZZZZ	NY
SPIELER, CHOZEK	20	M	LABR	RR	ZZZZ	NY
FRIEDMANN, SHOLEM	20	M	LABR	RR	ZZZZ	NY
BUDWISKY, ABRAH.	30	M	LABR	RR	ZZZZ	NY
SIEMENSKY, LIEBE	18	F	SGL	RR	ZZZZ	NY
KANTALOWSKY, ETTEL	18	F	SGL	RR	ZZZZ	NY
GRINBERG, MENDEL	28	M	MCHT	RR	ZZZZ	NY
FRIEDMANN, LEISER	14	M	BY	RR	ZZZZ	NY

SHIP: AMERIQUE

FROM: HAVRE AND PLYMOUTH
TO: NEW YORK
ARRIVED: 13 SEPTEMBER 1883

PASSENGER	AGE	SEX	OCCUPATION	PRIV	VIL	DES
KAHN, ISAAC	19	M	HTR	PL	ZZZZ	USA
FINKELSTEIN, JACOB	16	M	MCHT	PL	ZZZZ	USA
ZAHK, LEIB	23	M	CPTR	RR	ZZZZ	USA
GISEL	19	F	UNKNOWN	RR	ZZZZ	USA
GOLDSTEIN, DLOSES	23	M	BCHR	RR	ZZZZ	USA
MALKE	22	F	UNKNOWN	RR	ZZZZ	USA
FELDMANN, JACOB	19	M	SHMK	RR	ZZZZ	USA
BEISEL	00	F	UNKNOWN	RR	ZZZZ	USA
ZAREBSCHEWRSKY, RUBENS	28	M	LKSH	RR	ZZZZ	USA
BLUME	24	F	UNKNOWN	RR	ZZZZ	USA
GERMAIN, ABRAHAM	30	M	FARMER	RR	ZZZZ	USA
HENRIETTE	28	F	UNKNOWN	RR	ZZZZ	USA
SONI	7	F	CHILD	RR	ZZZZ	USA
GRIENSTEIN, SALOMON	21	M	UNKNOWN	RR	ZZZZ	USA
SCHECKTMANN, ABRAHAM	23	M	BCHR	RR	ZZZZ	USA
CHAYES	19	F	UNKNOWN	RR	ZZZZ	USA
RECLE	00	F	INF	RR	ZZZZ	USA

SHIP: BOLIVIA

FROM: GLASGOW AND MOVILLE
TO: NEW YORK
ARRIVED: 13 SEPTEMBER 1883

PASSENGER	AGE	SEX	OCCUPATION	PRIV	VIL	DES
GOLA, JANOS	24	M	LABR	RR	ZZZZ	USA
FODA, GEO.	12	M	NN	RR	ZZZZ	USA
PRABUTER, HARRIS	45	M	SHMK	RR	ZZZZ	USA
COHEN, SALOMON	46	M	SHMK	RR	ZZZZ	USA
KRIEWINSKI, FRANZ	19	M	TLR	RR	ZZZZ	USA

SHIP: CANADA

FROM: HAVRE
TO: NEW YORK
ARRIVED: 13 SEPTEMBER 1883

PASSENGER	AGE	SEX	OCCUPATION	PRIV	VIL	DES
MENINCREZ, JACOB-MR.	32	M	LKSH	RR	ZZZZ	NY
JULE-MRS.	28	M	NN	RR	ZZZZ	NY
MOSES	4	M	CHILD	RR	ZZZZ	NY
SARA	1	F	CHILD	RR	ZZZZ	NY
MI-------R, ISAAK-MR.	23	M	NN	RR	ZZZZ	NY
HENRI-MRS.	20	M	NN	RR	ZZZZ	NY
MARE	1	M	CHILD	RR	ZZZZ	NY
GOLDENBERG, MINETCHA-MR	26	M	CPTR	RR	ZZZZ	NY
GOLDENBERG, SARA-MRS.	23	F	NN	RR	ZZZZ	NY
HECHT, MOSES-MR.	21	M	CBTMKR	RR	ZZZZ	NY
FRACHTENBERG, JACOB	24	M	NN	RR	ZZZZ	NY
REBECCA-MRS.	22	F	NN	RR	ZZZZ	NY
PEREL	.04	M	INFANT	RR	ZZZZ	NY
KAPLAN, ISAAK-MR.	22	M	NN	RR	ZZZZ	NY
CHANE-MRS.	18	F	NN	RR	ZZZZ	NY
STEIN, ABRAHAM-MR.	24	M	NN	RR	ZZZZ	NY
MALI-MRS.	20	F	NN	RR	ZZZZ	NY
SARA	.01	F	INFANT	RR	ZZZZ	NY
BRENNER, HENRI-MR.	48	M	SHMK	RR	ZZZZ	NY
LOUISE-MRS.	19	F	NN	RR	ZZZZ	NY
MOSES-MR.	14	M	NN	RR	ZZZZ	NY
AUGUSTIN	.06	M	INFANT	RR	ZZZZ	NY
OREZKI, ZUDECK-MR.	23	M	TLR	RR	ZZZZ	NY
LEONIS-MRS.	20	F	NN	RR	ZZZZ	NY
ANNA	2	F	CHILD	RR	ZZZZ	NY
ACHST, BENJAMIN-MR.	30	M	SMH	RR	ZZZZ	NY
SITTEL-MR.	29	M	SMH	RR	ZZZZ	NY
ROSTOWSKY, SAMUEL-MR.	23	M	SMH	RR	ZZZZ	NY
MASCHIN, JACOB-MR.	24	M	CPTR	RR	ZZZZ	NY

SHIP: ST. OF PENNSYLVANIA

FROM: GLASGOW AND LARNE
TO: NEW YORK
ARRIVED: 14 SEPTEMBER 1883

PASSENGER	AGE	SEX	OCCUPATION	PRIV	VIL	DES
ELSSAS, FEIGE	26	F	SVNT	RR	ZZZZ	NY
BERKOWITZ, PAUL	20	M	LABR	RR	ZZZZ	NY
ADETRAD, OSCKAR	21	M	LABR	RR	ZZZZ	NY
CHEITZ, JACOB	24	M	LABR	RR	ZZZZ	NY
ISCHERSCHER, SIMON	32	M	UNKNOWN	RR	ZZZZ	NY
ISACSOHN, MEIR	24	M	LABR	RR	ZZZZ	NY
LEWIN, MOSES	24	M	LABR	RR	ZZZZ	NY
GRIENHAUS, FEIGE	18	F	SVNT	RR	ZZZZ	NY
LEWIN, SAMUEL	19	M	MLR	RR	ZZZZ	NY
SEPAN, JOSEKK	36	M	SHMK	RR	ZZZZ	NY
RATZKONSKY, SALOMON	17	M	SHMK	RR	ZZZZ	NY
LEIRIE, RIWE	40	F	W	RR	ZZZZ	BO
CHAIE	18	F	NN	RR	ZZZZ	BO
JARCKEL	9	M	CHILD	RR	ZZZZ	BO
ABRAHAM	4	M	CHILD	RR	ZZZZ	BO
RANKEWIZ, PINCUS	17	M	LABR	RR	ZZZZ	BO
GRANN, CHONE	22	M	TLR	RR	ZZZZ	NY
RUDERMANN, U	26	M	TLR	RR	ZZZZ	NY
HODER, ARON	20	M	LABR	RR	ZZZZ	NY
MYLINSKY, M.	37	M	BKBNDR	RR	ZZZZ	NY
WISHLFSON, M.	18	M	LABR	RR	ZZZZ	NY
SCHOHOR, G.	22	M	LABR	RR	ZZZZ	NY
MOLOTOFSKI, MARCUS	21	M	LABR	RR	ZZZZ	NY
LESKIENICK, TERTZY	20	M	LABR	RR	ZZZZ	NY
KREKSKENSKY, S.	30	M	TLR	RR	ZZZZ	NY
YANIKS, AD--	25	M	LABR	RR	ZZZZ	NY
ABBERMAN, MOSES	16	M	LABR	RR	ZZZZ	NY

PASSENGER	AGE	SEX	OCCUPATION	PRIV	VIL	DES

SHIP: NEDERLAND

FROM: ANTWERP
TO: NEW YORK
ARRIVED: 17 SEPTEMBER 1883

PASSENGER	AGE	SEX	OCCUPATION	PV	VIL	DES
MARYNINSKY, ANT.	26	M	UNKNOWN	RR	ZZZZ	USA
HARTWICH, ANT.	24	M	UNKNOWN	RR	ZZZZ	USA

SHIP: RHAETIA

FROM: HAMBURG AND HAVRE
TO: NEW YORK
ARRIVED: 18 SEPTEMBER 1883

PASSENGER	AGE	SEX	OCCUPATION	PV	VIL	DES
KAPLAN, CHANNE	50	F	W	RR	ZZZZ	USA
NOCHUM	9	M	CHILD	RR	ZZZZ	USA
WEISSWASSER, DEBORAH	18	F	SGL	RR	ZZZZ	USA
WIELEN, MARCUS	20	M	MCHT	RR	ZZZZ	USA
MAEDUFF, WILLIAM	20	M	ENGR	RR	ZZZZ	USA
STEIN, MORDSCHE	25	M	LKSH	RR	ZZZZ	USA
MERIN, JOSEPH	22	M	CGRMKR	RR	ZZZZ	USA
GIMNUSKI, SCHARIE	20	M	UNKNOWN	RR	ZZZZ	USA
BRAWMANN, ISAAC	26	M	DLR	RR	ZZZZ	USA
BLOCH, MICHAL	18	M	TLR	RR	ZZZZ	USA
SCHNEIDER, SCHMEREL	19	M	SHMK	RR	ZZZZ	USA
ROSSEINER, ABRAHAM	45	M	SING	RR	ZZZZ	USA
SALMEN	21	M	CH	RR	ZZZZ	USA
JOSEPH	9	M	CHILD	RR	ZZZZ	USA
SAMUEL	8	M	CHILD	RR	ZZZZ	USA
CHAIM	9	M	CHILD	RR	ZZZZ	USA
SEIDENWERK, ABRAHAM	21	M	LABR	RR	ZZZZ	USA
MOSES, HIRSCH	45	M	DLR	RR	ZZZZ	USA
COHEN, PINGUIS	50	M	TCHR	RR	ZZZZ	USA
MERE	50	F	W	RR	ZZZZ	USA
GROSSMANN, WOLF.	20	M	DLR	RR	ZZZZ	USA
RASCHE	20	F	W	RR	ZZZZ	USA
JACOBS, LOUIS	18	M	LABR	RR	ZZZZ	USA
LIBANOWITSCH, IDEL	28	F	W	RR	ZZZZ	USA
MENDEL	1	M	CHILD	RR	ZZZZ	USA
BERMANN, SLOMAN	20	M	JNR	RR	ZZZZ	USA
GOLDBERGER, JENS	28	M	DLR	RR	ZZZZ	USA
SARABOWSKI, BEILE	20	F	SGL	RR	ZZZZ	USA
KAENTROWITZ, KALMAN	15	M	TLR	RR	ZZZZ	USA
GRODZIN, ABRAHAM	23	M	DLR	RR	ZZZZ	USA
BEHR, CHAIM	43	M	TLR	RR	ZZZZ	USA
SCHNEID, ELIAS	43	M	UNKNOWN	RR	ZZZZ	USA
BUERGANF, CHANNE	21	F	SGL	RR	ZZZZ	USA
RIWKE	18	F	UNKNOWN	RR	ZZZZ	USA
BUTINSKY, ISAAC	15	M	DLR	RR	ZZZZ	USA
KUCZINSKI, LESSER	29	M	DLR	RR	ZZZZ	USA
JETTE	28	F	W	RR	ZZZZ	USA
WILLI	.11	M	INFANT	RR	ZZZZ	USA
CHAITER, MOSES	20	M	DLR	RR	ZZZZ	USA
SCHAIE	18	F	W	RR	ZZZZ	USA
BREINE	28	F	UNKNOWN	RR	ZZZZ	USA
SAMUEL	.11	M	INFANT	RR	ZZZZ	USA
SCHAPIRA, LEIB	55	F	DLR	RR	ZZZZ	USA
ABELMANN, JACOB	20	M	UNKNOWN	RR	ZZZZ	USA
RACHEL	20	F	W	RR	ZZZZ	USA
CHAIC	.11	F	INFANT	RR	ZZZZ	USA
BARTNITZKI, RACHEL	40	F	W	RR	ZZZZ	USA
MEIER	14	M	CH	RR	ZZZZ	USA
CHAIE	9	F	CHILD	RR	ZZZZ	USA
KOELEW	8	M	CHILD	RR	ZZZZ	USA
RAESCHE	7	F	CHILD	RR	ZZZZ	USA
JUDES	6	M	CHILD	RR	ZZZZ	USA
GIBIANSKI, HIRSCH	20	M	DLR	RR	ZZZZ	USA
GORDON, JANKEL-HERZ	18	M	TLR	RR	ZZZZ	USA
KOEHN, ALTER	9	M	CHILD	RR	ZZZZ	USA
SAX, ABRAHAM	18	M	LABR	RR	ZZZZ	USA
DEECTOR, ROLE	18	F	SGL	RR	ZZZZ	USA
KOEHN, OLGA	9	F	CHILD	RR	ZZZZ	USA
GLUECKMANN, RACHEL	28	F	W	RR	ZZZZ	USA
SCHMUEL	.11	M	INFANT	RR	ZZZZ	USA
ROSA	1	F	CHILD	RR	ZZZZ	USA
NOTES, SALOMON	20	M	TLR	RR	ZZZZ	USA
SPIELER, KAEPPEL	27	M	UNKNOWN	RR	ZZZZ	USA
GOLDBERG, ABRAHAM	40	M	UNKNOWN	RR	ZZZZ	USA
SELIGMAN, MOSES	17	M	UNKNOWN	RR	ZZZZ	USA
FEINBLUM, SCHMUEL	16	M	TU	RR	ZZZZ	USA
KAETENOWSKY, JANNE	18	F	SGL	RR	ZZZZ	USA
CHEIE	14	F	UNKNOWN	RR	ZZZZ	USA
BER	4	M	CHILD	RR	ZZZZ	USA
HIRSCH, OFEA	20	F	CGRMKR	RR	ZZZZ	USA
MIHAL, JANOS	18	M	LABR	PL	ZZZZ	USA
RIZ, BASALEGA	40	M	UNKNOWN	PL	ZZZZ	USA
SMOS, SEMON	30	M	UNKNOWN	PL	ZZZZ	USA
SOROGA, PETRO	27	M	UNKNOWN	PL	ZZZZ	USA
SUPSKY, VICTOR	23	M	UNKNOWN	PL	ZZZZ	USA

SHIP: FRANCE

FROM: HAVRE
TO: NEW YORK
ARRIVED: 19 SEPTEMBER 1883

PASSENGER	AGE	SEX	OCCUPATION	PV	VIL	DES
GALLOL, L.	29	M	UNKNOWN	RR	ZZZZ	NY
SCHNEIDER, DAVID	53	M	UNKNOWN	RR	ZZZZ	NY
MENI-MISS	22	F	UNKNOWN	RR	ZZZZ	NY
BERL	18	M	UNKNOWN	RR	ZZZZ	NY
ABRAHAM	21	M	UNKNOWN	RR	ZZZZ	NY
FRISCHKE	14	M	UNKNOWN	RR	ZZZZ	NY
ZIPCEVA	11	F	UNKNOWN	RR	ZZZZ	NY
ISAAC	7	M	CHILD	RR	ZZZZ	NY
MAGALEWSKI, DAVID	24	M	SCP	RR	ZZZZ	NY
SUFTER, LEIB	34	M	JWLR	RR	ZZZZ	NY
GENTE	25	M	UNKNOWN	RR	ZZZZ	NY
MOSES	4	M	CHILD	RR	ZZZZ	NY
MANILOFF, BENJAMIN	26	M	UNKNOWN	RR	ZZZZ	NY
MARIE	24	F	UNKNOWN	RR	ZZZZ	NY
SARAH	1	F	CHILD	RR	ZZZZ	NY
BERBECK, DAVID	23	M	SHMK	RR	ZZZZ	NY
SPINNZA	20	F	UNKNOWN	RR	ZZZZ	NY
MARIE	1	F	CHILD	RR	ZZZZ	NY
BERGER, BERL	24	M	CPTR	RR	ZZZZ	NY
LIEBE	19	M	UNKNOWN	RR	ZZZZ	NY
GRIBINIASSET, WOLFF	21	M	TLR	PL	ZZZZ	NY
MARIUS, CHARLES	13	M	UNKNOWN	RR	ZZZZ	CAN
SCHTEIN, MASKEL	14	M	UNKNOWN	RR	ZZZZ	CHR
MERMANN, DARON	14	M	UNKNOWN	RR	ZZZZ	NY
BILOCHKORFF, JOSEPH	17	M	UNKNOWN	RR	ZZZZ	UNK
ABRAHAM	12	M	UNKNOWN	RR	ZZZZ	UNK
ZONKEL	9	M	CHILD	RR	ZZZZ	UNK
KANELSKY, MOSES	35	M	UNKNOWN	RR	ZZZZ	NY
DIVINA	29	F	UNKNOWN	RR	ZZZZ	NY

PASSENGER	AGE	SEX	OCCUPATION	PRV	VIL	DES
SHIP: GRECIAN MONARCH						
FROM: LONDON						
TO: NEW YORK						
ARRIVED: 19 SEPTEMBER 1883						
SKLAR, MICHLA	28	F	W	PL	ZZZZ	USA
BEARL	6	M	CHILD	PL	ZZZZ	USA
MOSES	4	M	CHILD	PL	ZZZZ	USA
SARAH	1	F	CHILD	PL	ZZZZ	USA
ABRAHAMS, ISIDOR	36	M	TLR	PL	ZZZZ	USA
SOPHIA	28	F	W	PL	ZZZZ	USA
MILLY	4	F	CHILD	PL	ZZZZ	USA
SHATTIN, MEYER	22	M	TLR	PL	ZZZZ	USA
LIPMAN, LOUIS	31	M	HTR	PL	ZZZZ	USA
FACHS, JOHANNA	34	F	W	PL	ZZZZ	USA
HENRIETTA	9	F	CHILD	PL	ZZZZ	USA
LOUIS	7	M	CHILD	PL	ZZZZ	USA
GARCINOWITCH, ALBERT	22	M	LABR	PL	ZZZZ	USA
ZANTTS, ARON	35	M	LABR	PL	ZZZZ	USA
ROSENFELT, HYMEN	28	M	LABR	PL	ZZZZ	USA
SCHWARZBERG, LEISER	20	M	LABR	PL	ZZZZ	USA
GOLDSTEINDER, MORRIS	48	M	LABR	PL	ZZZZ	USA
BLUMENTHAL, MORRIS	26	M	FUR	PL	ZZZZ	USA
DOLINSKY, MEYER	18	M	TLR	PL	ZZZZ	USA
FLACHS, ITZIG	20	M	BCHR	PL	ZZZZ	USA
SPAMER, ISRAEL	18	M	BCHR	PL	ZZZZ	USA
GRINWOLD, MINDE	47	F	W	PL	ZZZZ	USA
SIMON	8	M	CHILD	PL	ZZZZ	USA
FROMME	5	F	CHILD	PL	ZZZZ	USA
SALOMON, SELIG	23	M	TLR	PL	ZZZZ	USA
SARAH	19	F	W	PL	ZZZZ	USA
SHEER, DAVIS	26	M	LABR	PL	ZZZZ	USA
GRINBERG, SALOMON	28	M	LABR	PL	ZZZZ	USA
SZEWERYK, PALKS	25	M	LABR	PL	ZZZZ	USA
GONDA, STEPHEN	21	M	LABR	PL	ZZZZ	USA
DIKE, MICHAL	27	M	LABR	PL	ZZZZ	USA
BONAFF, PARIS	21	M	TLR	PL	ZZZZ	USA
ADOLF	18	M	TLR	PL	ZZZZ	USA
KORTSCH, JONAS	31	M	BKR	PL	ZZZZ	USA
ROSENWEIG, SALOMON	29	M	CGRMKR	PL	ZZZZ	USA
SIGMUND	21	M	CGRMKR	PL	ZZZZ	USA
HOLLANDER, ISAAC	32	M	CGRMKR	PL	ZZZZ	USA
BOCK, DAVID	18	M	LABR	PL	ZZZZ	USA
PELSA, BLUMA	25	F	W	PL	ZZZZ	USA
JACOB	5	M	CHILD	PL	ZZZZ	USA
SALOMON	3	M	CHILD	PL	ZZZZ	USA
LEONARD	.09	M	INFANT	PL	ZZZZ	USA
ROSENBLATT, HIRSCH	35	M	DLR	PL	ZZZZ	USA
RACHEL	34	F	W	PL	ZZZZ	USA
FEITEL	17	F	NN	PL	ZZZZ	USA
SIMON	12	M	NN	PL	ZZZZ	USA
HIRSCH	5	M	CHILD	PL	ZZZZ	USA
ROSA	4	F	CHILD	PL	ZZZZ	USA
SALOMON	1	M	CHILD	PL	ZZZZ	USA
LEA	1	F	CHILD	PL	ZZZZ	USA
JANICK, JOSEF	19	M	LABR	PL	ZZZZ	USA
POLAK, MORRIS	27	M	CGRMKR	PL	ZZZZ	USA
ESTHER	25	F	W	PL	ZZZZ	USA
PHOEBE	7	F	CHILD	PL	ZZZZ	USA
SARAH	4	F	CHILD	PL	ZZZZ	USA
MALINOWSKY, VICTOR	26	M	LABR	PL	ZZZZ	USA
ROSENBLATT, RACHEL	30	F	W	PL	ZZZZ	USA
SALOMON	14	M	NN	PL	ZZZZ	USA
ISABELLA	8	F	CHILD	PL	ZZZZ	USA
ROSE	7	F	CHILD	PL	ZZZZ	USA
LEA	6	F	CHILD	PL	ZZZZ	USA
ABR.	4	M	CHILD	PL	ZZZZ	USA
JOSEPH	3	M	CHILD	PL	ZZZZ	USA
REBECCA	1	F	CHILD	PL	ZZZZ	USA
WISEBARD, ISAAC	34	M	PNTR	PL	ZZZZ	USA
HENRIKOWSKY, ANDR.	23	M	LABR	PL	ZZZZ	USA
KUASCHIE, MAURICE	30	M	LABR	PL	ZZZZ	USA
BOROTLAN, THOMAS	26	M	TLR	PL	ZZZZ	USA
BLANSTEIN, ISAAC	32	M	LABR	PL	ZZZZ	USA
SPIELMAN, FANNY	38	F	W	PL	ZZZZ	USA
AARON	15	M	CH	PL	ZZZZ	USA
MORRIS	11	M	CH	PL	ZZZZ	USA
KOPZACKER, SAML.	32	M	LABR	PL	ZZZZ	USA
HANNAH	24	F	W	PL	ZZZZ	USA
ESTHER	1	F	CHILD	PL	ZZZZ	USA
SILBERBERG, ISAAC	19	M	TLR	PL	ZZZZ	USA
DAVIS, RACHEL	46	F	W	PL	ZZZZ	USA
CHRIS.	18	M	LABR	PL	ZZZZ	USA
LEWIS	15	M	LABR	PL	ZZZZ	USA
DAVIS	10	M	CH	PL	ZZZZ	USA
RUEBEN	8	M	CHILD	PL	ZZZZ	USA
BILSOUL, FANNY	33	F	W	PL	ZZZZ	USA
LEWIS	8	M	CHILD	PL	ZZZZ	USA
ANNIE	7	F	CHILD	PL	ZZZZ	USA
MICHAEL	5	M	CHILD	PL	ZZZZ	USA
ROSE	4	F	CHILD	PL	ZZZZ	USA
JOSEPH	2	M	CHILD	PL	ZZZZ	USA
SAMUEL	.10	M	INFANT	PL	ZZZZ	USA
FRIEDMANN, ABM.	21	M	LABR	PL	ZZZZ	USA
CHAYA	26	F	W	PL	ZZZZ	USA
REBECCA	1	F	CHILD	PL	ZZZZ	USA
GEDLIVER, JACOB	24	M	LABR	PL	ZZZZ	USA
KATE	22	F	W	PL	ZZZZ	USA
FANNY	.10	F	INFANT	PL	ZZZZ	USA
MENTLICK, RAPHAEL	29	M	LABR	PL	ZZZZ	USA
EVA	27	F	W	PL	ZZZZ	USA
REVALSKY, HANNAH	30	F	W	PL	ZZZZ	USA
JUDUH	9	M	CHILD	PL	ZZZZ	USA
LAZARUS	8	M	CHILD	PL	ZZZZ	USA
SARAH	5	F	CHILD	PL	ZZZZ	USA
FANNY	3	F	CHILD	PL	ZZZZ	USA
KALISKY, JOSEPH	23	M	LABR	PL	ZZZZ	USA
DORA	22	F	W	PL	ZZZZ	USA
LEVY, AARON	26	M	LABR	PL	ZZZZ	USA
RAHEL	25	F	W	PL	ZZZZ	USA
HANNAH	6	F	CHILD	PL	ZZZZ	USA
ZALIE	4	F	CHILD	PL	ZZZZ	USA
SARAH	2	F	CHILD	PL	ZZZZ	USA
SHIP: STATE OF FLORIDA						
FROM: GLASGOW AND LARNE						
TO: NEW YORK						
ARRIVED: 20 SEPTEMBER 1883						
DREWITZ, LEIB	21	M	LABR	RR	ZZZZ	USA
MENKUFSKY, BENJAMIN	40	M	LABR	RR	ZZZZ	USA
GUTMANN, LEIB	21	M	LABR	RR	ZZZZ	USA
LANDBERG, JULIUS	18	M	LABR	RR	ZZZZ	USA
RUBENSTEIN, CHANE	16	F	NN	RR	ZZZZ	USA
RAUFER, ZEIGI-G.	36	F	W	RR	ZZZZ	USA
JENTE	11	F	CH	RR	ZZZZ	USA
MERC.	10	F	CH	RR	ZZZZ	USA
DAVID	8	M	CHILD	RR	ZZZZ	USA
RUSCHE	6	M	CHILD	RR	ZZZZ	USA
S--	1	M	CHILD	RR	ZZZZ	USA
DAVIDESITZ, ELNI	12	F	NN	RR	ZZZZ	USA
LEWIN, SINCHE	26	M	PDLR	RR	ZZZZ	USA
LAZEWNITZ, MOSCHE	33	M	PDLR	RR	ZZZZ	USA
KLUGMANN, ELIAS	21	M	LABR	RR	ZZZZ	USA
FISCHE, LESIER	38	M	LABR	RR	ZZZZ	USA
KRONER, JODUS	34	M	LABR	RR	ZZZZ	USA
FRIEDHOPPER, RESE	35	F	W	RR	ZZZZ	USA
BEREL	.10	M	INFANT	RR	ZZZZ	USA
LICHTENBERG, CHANNE	26	F	W	RR	ZZZZ	USA
DIENE	.08	M	INFANT	RR	ZZZZ	USA
BISRITZKI, MOSES	43	M	LABR	RR	ZZZZ	USA
ROCHEL	41	F	W	RR	ZZZZ	USA

PASSENGER	AGE	SEX	OCCUPATION	PRV	VIL	DES
SARAH	10	F	CH	RR	ZZZZ	USA
SAMUEL	3	M	CHILD	RR	ZZZZ	USA
BEILA	1	F	CHILD	RR	ZZZZ	USA
LICHTBLAU, JULIUS	34	M	LABR	RR	ZZZZ	USA
MERKEL, ISRAEL	27	M	LABR	RR	ZZZZ	USA
CHANNA	24	F	W	RR	ZZZZ	USA
DORE	.11	M	INFANT	RR	ZZZZ	USA
SAML.	.11	F	INFANT	RR	ZZZZ	USA

SHIP: RHYNLAND

FROM: ANTWERP
TO: NEW YORK
ARRIVED: 21 SEPTEMBER 1883

PASSENGER	AGE	SEX	OCCUPATION	PRV	VIL	DES
DOMBZALSKI, ALBERTINE	41	F	UNKNOWN	PL	ZZZZ	USA
FRANCISCA	20	F	UNKNOWN	PL	ZZZZ	USA
IGNATZ	10	M	UNKNOWN	PL	ZZZZ	USA
LEOCASHIE	17	F	UNKNOWN	PL	ZZZZ	USA
ROSALIA	3	F	CHILD	PL	ZZZZ	USA
CHUST, JOH.	17	M	FARMER	PL	ZZZZ	USA
PANKOZLIS, THS.	20	M	UNKNOWN	PL	ZZZZ	USA

SHIP: ELBE

FROM: BREMEN AND SOUTHAMPTON
TO: NEW YORK
ARRIVED: 22 SEPTEMBER 1883

PASSENGER	AGE	SEX	OCCUPATION	PRV	VIL	DES
STERN, JEAN	38	M	UNKNOWN	RR	ZZZZ	USA
EMMA	25	F	W	RR	ZZZZ	USA
BERNHARD	2	M	CHILD	RR	ZZZZ	USA
ROSA	.09	F	INFANT	RR	ZZZZ	USA
WOICHOSKI, HENDRIK	21	M	LABR	RR	ZZZZ	USA
KOSKISLA, ANNA-K.	45	F	W	FN	ZZZZ	USA
ANTON	20	M	FARMER	FN	ZZZZ	USA

SHIP: RICHMOND HILL

FROM: LONDON
TO: NEW YORK
ARRIVED: 25 SEPTEMBER 1883

PASSENGER	AGE	SEX	OCCUPATION	PRV	VIL	DES
MAGATH, M.	24	M	STDNT	RR	ZZZZ	USA

SHIP: RUGIA

FROM: HAMBURG
TO: NEW YORK
ARRIVED: 25 SEPTEMBER 1883

PASSENGER	AGE	SEX	OCCUPATION	PRV	VIL	DES
KUSACABAGE, MARIANE	24	F	SGL	RR	ZZZZ	USA
COHEN, JANE	25	F	W	RR	ZZZZ	USA
CHEIM	6	F	CHILD	RR	ZZZZ	USA
BASCHE	5	F	CHILD	RR	ZZZZ	USA
BEISACH	.08	M	INFANT	RR	ZZZZ	USA
ITZIG, JUDEL	18	M	PT	RR	ZZZZ	USA
FEINBERG, BONE	34	F	UNKNOWN	RR	ZZZZ	USA
FEIGE	9	F	CHILD	RR	ZZZZ	USA
TEWE	8	F	CHILD	RR	ZZZZ	USA
SCHOLEM	7	M	CHILD	RR	ZZZZ	USA
ISSRIEL	.11	M	INFANT	RR	ZZZZ	USA
FILIKOWSKIE, CHAIE	54	F	W	RR	ZZZZ	USA
ETTE	20	F	D	RR	ZZZZ	USA
KAPLAN, HERRM.	26	M	CGRMKR	RR	ZZZZ	USA
SEHER, RACHEL	18	M	SGL	RR	ZZZZ	USA
EINHORN, ISSER	17	F	DLR	RR	ZZZZ	USA
SPEKTORSKY, LEA	50	F	W	RR	ZZZZ	USA
MORITZ	18	M	CH	RR	ZZZZ	USA
ABRAHAM	8	M	CHILD	RR	ZZZZ	USA
ESTER	6	F	CHILD	RR	ZZZZ	USA
MAYERSOHN, SIMON	9	M	CHILD	RR	ZZZZ	USA
U, U	35	F	UNKNOWN	RR	ZZZZ	USA
U	9	M	CHILD	RR	ZZZZ	USA
RACHEL	8	M	CHILD	RR	ZZZZ	USA
CANNE	7	F	CHILD	RR	ZZZZ	USA
PESACH	6	M	CHILD	RR	ZZZZ	USA
SALMEN	.11	M	INFANT	RR	ZZZZ	USA
SZABOWITZ, BELA	20	F	SGL	RR	ZZZZ	USA
PREISS, ANNA	18	F	UNKNOWN	RR	ZZZZ	USA
WISBANER, EMILIE	53	F	W	RR	ZZZZ	USA
OBERLAENDER, AUGUST	55	M	WVR	RR	ZZZZ	USA
OSCAR	26	M	FARMER	RR	ZZZZ	USA
POSNANSKY, GOLDA	64	F	SGL	RR	ZZZZ	USA
SCHOENBERG, LEA	18	F	UNKNOWN	RR	ZZZZ	USA
RACHMANN, MINE	25	F	W	RR	ZZZZ	USA
CHANNE	.11	F	INFANT	RR	ZZZZ	USA
JANUS, ISAAC	38	M	LABR	RR	ZZZZ	USA
SCHMULK, CHAIE	35	F	SGL	RR	ZZZZ	USA
PETRO---Y, PETER	22	M	LABR	RR	ZZZZ	USA
RACUMA, TOMAS	21	M	UNKNOWN	RR	ZZZZ	USA
GRIGONIS, JOSEF	20	M	UNKNOWN	RR	ZZZZ	USA
GRINOVIC, TOMAS	22	M	UNKNOWN	RR	ZZZZ	USA
CERUSS, DONIZI	48	M	UNKNOWN	RR	ZZZZ	USA
HOPPE, STEPHAN	25	M	UNKNOWN	RR	ZZZZ	USA
SIMICHOVA, ANNA	20	F	UNKNOWN	RR	ZZZZ	USA
SEIMES, ADAM	40	M	UNKNOWN	RR	ZZZZ	USA
DIEMISKI, RACHEL	58	F	UNKNOWN	RR	ZZZZ	USA
RACHE	6	F	CHILD	RR	ZZZZ	USA
ARON, JOSEPH	9	M	CHILD	RR	ZZZZ	USA
KRACZUSKY, TITUS	40	M	MCHT	RR	ZZZZ	USA
WOSSKEBOWNIK, SURA	40	F	UNKNOWN	RR	ZZZZ	USA
RACHEL	9	F	CHILD	RR	ZZZZ	USA
ARON	7	M	CHILD	RR	ZZZZ	USA
CHAIM	4	M	CHILD	RR	ZZZZ	USA
SELIG	.11	M	INFANT	RR	ZZZZ	USA
KOLWENSKY, SARAH	20	F	SGL	RR	ZZZZ	USA
STEINBERG, SARAH	24	F	SGL	RR	ZZZZ	USA
HANK, JOH.	26	M	LABR	RR	ZZZZ	USA
LEWIN, FREUNET	23	M	LABR	RR	ZZZZ	USA
HELENE	22	F	W	RR	ZZZZ	USA
LESLAN, BASCHE	16	F	SGL	RR	ZZZZ	USA
CHERITOWITS, CHANNE	24	F	W	RR	ZZZZ	USA
CHAIM	.11	M	INFANT	RR	ZZZZ	USA
GLDBERGER, BEILE	36	F	W	RR	ZZZZ	USA
JUDAS	9	M	CHILD	RR	ZZZZ	USA
CHANNE	8	F	CHILD	RR	ZZZZ	USA
SARAH	6	F	CHILD	RR	ZZZZ	USA
ZIZCHOK	.04	M	INFANT	RR	ZZZZ	USA
MEYER	.11	M	INFANT	RR	ZZZZ	USA
KOSWEN, SCHMEREL	18	M	DLR	RR	ZZZZ	USA
GOTOWSKY, MARTIN	21	M	TLR	RR	ZZZZ	USA
FEIGE	21	F	W	RR	ZZZZ	USA
LESCHZINSKI, HERSCHELL	21	M	TLR	RR	ZZZZ	USA
KARIGANZKY, C.	18	M	LABR	RR	ZZZZ	USA
BEIK, METASCH	30	M	UNKNOWN	RR	ZZZZ	USA
MAGDALENE	30	F	W	RR	ZZZZ	USA
ANTON	3	M	CHILD	RR	ZZZZ	USA
CASAK	.01	M	INFANT	RR	ZZZZ	USA
WINKELSTEIN, NETTE	17	F	SGL	RR	ZZZZ	USA

PASSENGER	AGE	SEX	OCCUPATION	PRV	VIL	DES
SAMEL, ABR.	17	M	MCHT	RR	ZZZ	USA
SOBOLOWSKI, SINE	17	F	W	RR	ZZZ	USA
BEILE	.11	M	INFANT	RR	ZZZ	USA
POPLOWSKI, DAVID	27	M	MCHT	RR	ZZZ	USA
ESTHER	26	F	W	RR	ZZZ	USA
LWINKE	.11	F	INFANT	RR	ZZZ	USA
HUEBSCHMANN, JUNKEL	9	M	CHILD	RR	ZZZ	USA
MAUSCHEL	8	M	CHILD	RR	ZZZ	USA
MILCHDINES, HERSCH	20	M	TLR	RR	ZZZ	USA
HOHMANN, JETTE	17	F	SGL	RR	ZZZ	USA
LOKOLSKI, CHANNE	26	F	W	RR	ZZZ	USA
BARUCH	.11	M	INFANT	RR	ZZZ	USA
BALL, PAULINE	16	F	SGL	RR	ZZZ	USA
JUDISCH, ANNA	30	F	W	RR	ZZZ	USA
SARA	.08	F	INFANT	RR	ZZZ	USA
STEIN, MOSES	30	M	MCHT	RR	ZZZ	USA
MATNICK, HANNE	23	F	W	RR	ZZZ	USA
MEIER	.11	M	INFANT	RR	ZZZ	USA
JUSCHCZAK, ERZA	33	F	SGL	RR	ZZZ	USA
ANERAN, ESTHER	55	F	W	RR	ZZZ	USA
WEWZLOWSKI, NOAK	21	M	LABR	RR	ZZZ	USA
ROTHSTEIN, GUTE	48	F	W	RR	ZZZ	USA
ALEXANDER, ANNE	26	F	W	RR	ZZZ	USA
ROSA	6	F	CHILD	RR	ZZZ	USA
SCHOENEWALD, ABRAHAM	20	M	LABR	RR	ZZZ	USA
ESTHER	20	F	W	RR	ZZZ	USA
WEINBERGER, ISRAEL	42	M	LABR	RR	ZZZ	USA
BETTI	25	F	W	RR	ZZZ	USA
BENZY	6	M	CHILD	RR	ZZZ	USA
FURMANN	.11	M	INFANT	RR	ZZZ	USA
GOLDBLATT, MALI	16	F	SGL	RR	ZZZ	USA
MASCHKOWITZ, LILE	16	F	UNKNOWN	RR	ZZZ	USA
GRUENBERGER, BERHARD	19	M	LABR	RR	ZZZ	USA
LEFKOWITZ, EMANUEL	40	M	LABR	RR	ZZZ	USA
GOTE	30	F	W	RR	ZZZ	USA
SEISEL	8	F	CHILD	RR	ZZZ	USA
ESTI	6	F	CHILD	RR	ZZZ	USA
MARIE	.11	F	INFANT	RR	ZZZ	USA
SIMON, REBECCA	38	F	W	RR	ZZZ	USA
HINDE	16	F	D	RR	ZZZ	USA
HANNE	9	F	CHILD	RR	ZZZ	USA
DAVID	.11	M	INFANT	RR	ZZZ	USA
SOLMK, ABEL	28	M	LABR	RR	ZZZ	USA
BJORKMANN, TH.	30	M	MCHT	FN	ZZZ	USA

SHIP: LABRADOR

FROM: HAVRE
TO: NEW YORK
ARRIVED: 26 SEPTEMBER 1883

PASSENGER	AGE	SEX	OCCUPATION	PRV	VIL	DES
RABINOWITSCH, SOPHIE	20	F	TCHR	RR	ZZZ	ZNY
HORIVITZ, JOSEPH	27	M	ENGR	RR	ZZZ	ZNY
SCHENFF, J.EU.	29	M	TLR	PL	ZZZ	ZMO
ZWOLINSKI, JOSEPH	27	M	TLR	PL	ZZZ	ZNY

SHIP: POLARIA

FROM: HAMBURG
TO: NEW YORK
ARRIVED: 26 SEPTEMBER 1883

PASSENGER	AGE	SEX	OCCUPATION	PRV	VIL	DES
PATASCHINSKI, LAISER	17	M	TRDSMN	RR	ZZZ	ZNY
MASLOWSKI, JOSZI	30	M	TRDSMN	RR	ZZZ	ZNY
MICHALMA	30	F	W	RR	ZZZ	ZNY
STANISLAW	.11	M	INFANT	RR	ZZZ	ZNY
LEWANDOWSKI, VALENTIN	28	M	TRDSMN	RR	ZZZ	ZNY
CAROLINE	20	F	W	RR	ZZZ	ZNY
ANNA	.07	F	INFANT	RR	ZZZ	ZNY
FISCH, KOPEL	41	M	TLR	PL	ZZZ	ZNY
REC, CHATZKEL	45	M	TRDSMN	PL	ZZZ	ZNY
EIDEL	7	F	CHILD	PL	ZZZ	ZNY
RAPPEPORT, FEISEL	42	M	FARMER	PL	ZZZ	ZNY
SARAH	7	F	CHILD	PL	ZZZ	ZNY
HALPERM, MICHAL	33	M	FARMER	RR	ZZZ	ZNY
BARBALITZ, JURA	32	M	FARMER	RR	ZZZ	ZNY
ILLA, MARZINKO	26	F	WO	RR	ZZZ	ZNY
SELLA	.11	F	INFANT	RR	ZZZ	ZNY
BALKO, MARISSA	21	F	WO	RR	ZZZ	ZNY
FREMANN, MOSES	36	M	FARMER	PL	ZZZ	ZNY
ARON, WULF	17	M	TLR	RR	ZZZ	ZNY
MILO, JENECH	55	M	FARMER	RR	ZZZ	ZNY
BARDT, CHANNE	35	F	WO	RR	ZZZ	ZCH
NESSEN	7	M	CHILD	RR	ZZZ	ZCH
MOCISCHE	6	M	CHILD	RR	ZZZ	ZCH
MARIANNA	.11	F	INFANT	RR	ZZZ	ZCH
PESSIL	.01	F	INFANT	RR	ZZZ	ZCH
REIMER, BENJAMIN	31	M	LABR	RR	ZZZ	ZCH
GEISEKS, JAN	30	M	LABR	RR	ZZZ	ZCH
NEDZALCK, LEON	40	M	LABR	RR	ZZZ	ZCH
SZEPKOSKA, JOSEPH	37	M	LABR	RR	ZZZ	ZCH
ULCASCH, CARL	7	M	CHILD	RR	ZZZ	ZCH
MULLER, GEORG	28	M	FARMER	RR	ZZZ	ZCH
LENA	25	F	W	RR	ZZZ	ZCH
MAX	.11	M	INFANT	RR	ZZZ	ZCH
KOPPEL, MARYAM	30	F	WO	PL	ZZZ	ZNY
CHAIS	.09	F	INFANT	PL	ZZZ	ZNY
NOTH, RESI	30	F	SGL	PL	ZZZ	ZNY
SCHAPPENS, LADOMIR	13	M	CH	RR	ZZZ	ZNY
ANTON	7	M	CHILD	RR	ZZZ	ZNY
SCHELEIM, ISRAEL	26	M	TRDSMN	RR	ZZZ	ZNY
LEWIKOWSKI, SAMUEL	18	M	UNKNOWN	RR	ZZZ	ZNY
MULLER, MEIER	19	M	LABR	RR	ZZZ	ZIL
SITOWISZ, HINZ	20	M	TRDSMN	RR	ZZZ	ZCH
BIETZ, BERTHA	19	F	SGL	RR	ZZZ	ZMIL
BLOCH, SIM.	18	M	CL	RR	ZZZ	ZNY
WARGO, JANOS	25	M	LABR	RR	ZZZ	ZNY
PETROTZI, MICHEL	20	M	LABR	RR	ZZZ	ZNY
LEVINSKY, SCHLAUME	20	M	TRDSMN	RR	ZZZ	ZNY
RIFKE	19	F	W	RR	ZZZ	ZNY
RESIM, ABRAH.	17	M	TRDSMN	RR	ZZZ	ZNY
LICBERT, LORNE	50	F	WO	RR	ZZZ	ZNY
ROCHEL	20	F	D	RR	ZZZ	ZNY
FRANKENSTEIN, BEILE	36	F	WO	RR	ZZZ	ZNY
WOCUH	7	F	CHILD	RR	ZZZ	ZNY
BLUME	5	M	CHILD	RR	ZZZ	ZNY
ABRAHAM	11	M	S	RR	ZZZ	ZNY
ROSE	.01	F	INFANT	RR	ZZZ	ZNY
FIRSCHFELD, FELIX	28	M	TLR	PL	ZZZ	ZNY

SHIP: PENNLAND

FROM: ANTWERP
TO: NEW YORK
ARRIVED: 27 SEPTEMBER 1883

PASSENGER	AGE	SEX	OCCUPATION	PRV	VIL	DES
SILVIRSTEIN, SALOMON	23	M	TLR	RR	ZZZ	ZNY
COHEN, CH.	23	M	SHMK	RR	ZZZ	ZNY
KATAFIAN, MICH.	30	M	LABR	RR	ZZZ	ZNY

PASSENGER	AGE	SEX	OCCUPATION	PRIV	VIL	DES

SHIP: RHEIN

FROM: BREMEN AND SOUTHAMPTON
TO: NEW YORK
ARRIVED: 29 SEPTEMBER 1883

GRABATTEN, ANNA	26	F	NN	RR	ZZZ	USA
CARL	.11	M	INFANT	RR	ZZZ	USA
MANDELKORN, LOUIS	22	M	MCHT	RR	ZZZ	USA

SHIP: FULDA

FROM: BREMEN
TO: NEW YORK
ARRIVED: 30 SEPTEMBER 1883

GORDINK, GREGOR	30	M	FARMER	RR	ZZZ	USA
EULALIA	29	F	NN	RR	ZZZ	USA
WASILI	8	F	CHILD	RR	ZZZ	USA
GREGOR	2	M	CHILD	RR	ZZZ	USA

SHIP: CELTIC

FROM: LIVERPOOL AND QUEENSTOWN
TO: NEW YORK
ARRIVED: 01 OCTOBER 1883

VALLENWOLSKE, THOMAS	26	M	LABR	PL	ZZZ	USA
KREMTEISER, ANTON	25	M	LABR	PL	ZZZ	USA
SZERDNISKE, ANTON	20	M	LABR	PL	ZZZ	USA
GOTTLIEB, GLAUSS	22	M	LABR	PL	ZZZ	USA

SHIP: HELVETIA

FROM: LIVERPOOL AND QUEENSTOWN
TO: NEW YORK
ARRIVED: 01 OCTOBER 1883

SIMON, MAIER	28	M	LABR	PL	ZZZ	USA
SOMPPI, ESAYAS	27	M	LABR	RR	ZZZ	USA
LIPPOLA, ISAK	30	M	LABR	RR	ZZZ	USA
SOMPPI, JACOB	27	M	LABR	RR	ZZZ	USA
ROBELL, ERNEST	23	M	LABR	RR	ZZZ	USA
SILBERMAN, L.	20	M	LABR	RR	ZZZ	USA

SHIP: LYDIAN MONARCH

FROM: LONDON
TO: NEW YORK
ARRIVED: 01 OCTOBER 1883

BIKUCM, HARRIS	21	M	NN	PL	ZZZ	USA
SZYMAWOWICH, JESUA	42	M	UNKNOWN	PL	ZZZ	USA
GRANIASKY, ABRAHAM	36	M	LABR	PL	ZZZ	USA
LEIORER	12	M	LABR	PL	ZZZ	USA
SALOMON	9	M	CHILD	PL	ZZZ	USA
GROSSMAN, SALOMON	28	M	LABR	PL	ZZZ	USA
FERBER, LEWIS	23	M	LABR	RR	ZZZ	USA
PERLMANN, MEYER	19	M	LABR	PL	ZZZ	USA
OKEIL, SCHMERL	22	M	LABR	PL	ZZZ	USA
CHAIM	12	M	NN	PL	ZZZ	USA
PHILIP	11	M	NN	PL	ZZZ	USA
ABRHAM, FRANCIS	18	M	NN	PL	ZZZ	USA
ROSENBLATT, DANIEL	38	M	LABR	PL	ZZZ	USA
ISRAEL	12	M	NN	PL	ZZZ	USA
SYLVESTON, MICHAEL	33	M	SHMK	PL	ZZZ	USA
DAVIS, SARAH	28	F	SGL	PL	ZZZ	USA
FANNY	17	F	SGL	PL	ZZZ	USA

SHIP: NORMANDIE

FROM: HAVRE
TO: NEW YORK
ARRIVED: 01 OCTOBER 1883

RYKOSKY, J.MR.	54	M	NN	RR	ZZZ	NY

SHIP: ETHIOPIA

FROM: GLASGOW AND MOVILLE
TO: NEW YORK
ARRIVED: 03 OCTOBER 1883

SAREMENN, PETER	29	M	LABR	FN	ZZZ	USA

SHIP: STATE OF NEBRASKA

FROM: GLASGOW AND MOVILLE
TO: NEW YORK
ARRIVED: 03 OCTOBER 1883

LEBOWITZ, SARAH	20	F	SP	RR	ZZZ	USA
MIKHSCHANSKY, U-MRS	26	F	W	RR	ZZZ	USA
CHAIE	7	M	CHILD	RR	ZZZ	USA
PERL--, U	00	M	CH	RR	ZZZ	USA
LIPSCHITS, M.	20	M	PDLR	RR	ZZZ	USA
STEIN, U-MRS	38	F	W	RR	ZZZ	USA
BEILE	17	F	CH	RR	ZZZ	USA
LEAH	5	F	CHILD	RR	ZZZ	USA
FREIDEL	3	F	CHILD	RR	ZZZ	USA
GRUNSTEIN, J.	20	M	PDLR	RR	ZZZ	USA
APIRGAN, S.	25	M	PDLR	RR	ZZZ	USA
FRANK, M.	19	M	PDLR	RR	ZZZ	USA
BRANDY, H.	35	M	PDLR	RR	ZZZ	USA
KUTZKEL, N.	19	M	PDLR	RR	ZZZ	USA
RABINOWITZ, U-MRS	28	F	W	RR	ZZZ	USA
SARAH	12	F	CH	RR	ZZZ	USA
MAX	9	M	CHILD	RR	ZZZ	USA
ROSENBAUM, H.	23	M	PDLR	RR	ZZZ	USA
JANKEL	20	M	PDLR	RR	ZZZ	USA
LACHMANN, U-MRS	25	F	W	RR	ZZZ	USA
JISKE	.06	M	INFANT	RR	ZZZ	USA
SCHMIEGER, N.	26	M	DLR	PL	ZZZ	USA
SHILOSHATZKY, M.	38	M	DLR	PL	ZZZ	USA

PASSENGER	AGE	SEX	OCCUPATION	PRIV	VIL	DES
COHN, C.	32	M	DLR	PL	ZZZZ	USA
SLOMINSKY, M.	25	M	DLR	PL	ZZZZ	USA
MOSESSOHN, C.	26	M	LABR	PL	ZZZZ	USA
CHASAN, S.	29	M	LABR	PL	ZZZZ	USA
STOLINSKY, J.	26	M	PDLR	PL	ZZZZ	USA
RUSSLAENDER, H.	21	M	PDLR	PL	ZZZZ	USA
CHACHRON, U-MRS	41	F	W	PL	ZZZZ	USA
MICHAL	8	M	CHILD	PL	ZZZZ	USA
CHAIM	5	M	CHILD	PL	ZZZZ	USA
ISSER	4	M	CHILD	PL	ZZZZ	USA
ESTHER	2	F	CHILD	PL	ZZZZ	USA
FRIEDRICH, M.	16	M	CL	PL	ZZZZ	USA
DIGOLZ, M.	21	M	PDLR	PL	ZZZZ	USA
KOSUL, C.	21	M	PDLR	PL	ZZZZ	USA
SKUSABALSKY, U-MRS	20	F	W	PL	ZZZZ	USA
CHANE	.06	F	INFANT	PL	ZZZZ	USA
RABLANSKY, U-MRS	35	F	W	PL	ZZZZ	USA
LEIB	11	M	CH	PL	ZZZZ	USA
RIVE	8	F	CHILD	PL	ZZZZ	USA
MOSES	5	M	CHILD	PL	ZZZZ	USA
CHANNE	2	F	CHILD	PL	ZZZZ	USA
FROUME	1	F	CHILD	PL	ZZZZ	USA
SCHLAFRON, CHASKEL	.02	M	INFANT	PL	ZZZZ	USA
BLOCH, U-MRS	29	F	W	PL	ZZZZ	USA
LEAH	1	F	CHILD	PL	ZZZZ	USA
ROGATZ, ISSER	12	M	CH	PL	ZZZZ	USA

SHIP: SUEVIA

FROM: HAMBURG
TO: NEW YORK
ARRIVED: 05 OCTOBER 1883

PASSENGER	AGE	SEX	OCCUPATION	PRIV	VIL	DES
HIRSCHKAWITZ, ISAAK	24	M	SHMK	RR	ZZZZ	USA
SKIBESKY, SCHMUL	20	M	LABR	RR	ZZZZ	USA
STEINHARDT, RACHEL	26	F	W	RR	ZZZZ	USA
DWORA	.11	F	INFANT	RR	ZZZZ	USA
BOMSEN, JANKEL	50	M	FELMO	RR	ZZZZ	USA
RACHEL	50	F	W	RR	ZZZZ	USA
KOHN, SCHEINE	24	F	W	RR	ZZZZ	USA
PESCHE	00	F	INF	RR	ZZZZ	USA
MUSSIN, GERSON	30	M	DLR	RR	ZZZZ	USA
GITTEL	30	F	W	RR	ZZZZ	USA
SARA	16	F	CH	RR	ZZZZ	USA
ZIWIE	9	F	CHILD	RR	ZZZZ	USA
LEA	8	F	CHILD	RR	ZZZZ	USA
HENE	5	F	CHILD	RR	ZZZZ	USA
NIEMZOW, JOSEF	18	M	SDLR	RR	ZZZZ	USA
HEBBE, AMALIE	24	F	W	RR	ZZZZ	USA
EMMA	3	F	CHILD	RR	ZZZZ	USA
ASEP------, FRANZISKA	19	F	SGL	RR	ZZZZ	USA
HODWIG	17	F	SGL	RR	ZZZZ	USA
KLAURCKI, ANTONINE	38	F	W	RR	ZZZZ	USA
MARIANNE	7	F	CHILD	RR	ZZZZ	USA
VINCENT	5	M	CHILD	RR	ZZZZ	USA
BRONISLAWA	3	F	CHILD	RR	ZZZZ	USA
HELENE	.11	F	INFANT	RR	ZZZZ	USA
MALITZKY, JOH.	60	M	LABR	RR	ZZZZ	USA
MARIANNE	56	F	W	RR	ZZZZ	USA
SABINE	15	F	D	RR	ZZZZ	USA
GRZEBOWSKY, VINCENT	41	M	LABR	RR	ZZZZ	USA
SPIRO, JOHE.	18	F	SGL	RR	ZZZZ	USA
KURKOWSKIE, WATZLAV	35	M	LABR	RR	ZZZZ	USA
LIEBERMANN, HEINR.	17	M	DLR	RR	ZZZZ	USA
ARTMANN, ROSALIE	45	F	W	RR	ZZZZ	USA
EDUARD	9	M	CHILD	RR	ZZZZ	USA
MATHILDE	6	F	CHILD	RR	ZZZZ	USA
HERZ, ERNESTINE	42	F	W	RR	ZZZZ	USA
ANNE	8	F	CHILD	RR	ZZZZ	USA
SARA	6	F	CHILD	RR	ZZZZ	USA
SUSANNE	4	F	CHILD	RR	ZZZZ	USA
WAGALIN, EVA	35	F	W	RR	ZZZZ	USA
LEOPOLD	8	M	CHILD	RR	ZZZZ	USA
ALBERTINE	3	F	CHILD	RR	ZZZZ	USA
PELAGIA	00	F	INF	RR	ZZZZ	USA
BUMSKA, MARIE	29	F	W	RR	ZZZZ	USA
DIAMANT, SCHEINE	.11	F	INFANT	RR	ZZZZ	USA
SKALMER, ESTHER	52	F	W	RR	ZZZZ	USA
RACHEL	9	F	CHILD	RR	ZZZZ	USA
SARA	7	F	CHILD	RR	ZZZZ	USA
KOHN, JUDEL-S.	15	M	DLR	RR	ZZZZ	USA
BLUHMEN, AUGUST-V.	29	M	RR	RR	ZZZZ	USA
CLARA	23	F	W	RR	ZZZZ	USA
LILIENTHAL, FANNY	18	F	SGL	RR	ZZZZ	USA

SHIP: CITY OF RICHMOND

FROM: LIVERPOOL
TO: NEW YORK
ARRIVED: 06 OCTOBER 1883

PASSENGER	AGE	SEX	OCCUPATION	PRIV	VIL	DES
LUKOWA, JULIANA	24	F	SP	PL	ZZZZ	USA
SKRADI, JOSEF	25	M	LABR	PL	ZZZZ	USA
VAWREMEC, MALISK	70	F	SP	PL	ZZZZ	USA
CINA, JOSEF	50	F	W	PL	ZZZZ	USA
VICTORIA	12	F	CH	PL	ZZZZ	USA
TEKLA	11	F	UNKNOWN	PL	ZZZZ	USA
JAN	10	M	UNKNOWN	PL	ZZZZ	USA
PETER	9	M	CHILD	PL	ZZZZ	USA
MARIANNA	7	F	CHILD	PL	ZZZZ	USA
JAROCHOGKA, AGNES	25	F	SP	PL	ZZZZ	USA
GALASKA, SIMON	27	M	LABR	PL	ZZZZ	USA
CIBULA, JOSEF	24	M	UNKNOWN	PL	ZZZZ	USA
SIMON, ANDNICA	24	F	SP	PL	ZZZZ	USA
ALLRECHT, C.	12	M	CH	PL	ZZZZ	USA
REPKA, JOSEF	24	M	LABR	PL	ZZZZ	USA
SURO, LAW.	12	M	CH	PL	ZZZZ	USA
BREYER, VORTLECK	35	M	LABR	PL	ZZZZ	USA
VASIL, ULIAS	29	M	UNKNOWN	PL	ZZZZ	USA
MIKLOS, RTULIP	40	M	UNKNOWN	PL	ZZZZ	USA
MIKALEC	29	M	UNKNOWN	PL	ZZZZ	USA
KUCA, BLUJI	29	M	UNKNOWN	PL	ZZZZ	USA
PEAK, MARCI	25	M	UNKNOWN	PL	ZZZZ	USA
GERZEL, RUZAK	25	M	UNKNOWN	PL	ZZZZ	USA
HYDAK, JOSEF	40	M	UNKNOWN	PL	ZZZZ	USA
HARAKEL, MARTIN	12	M	CH	PL	ZZZZ	USA
ADAMZAK, M.	12	M	UNKNOWN	PL	ZZZZ	USA
WIATER, WOREZECK	24	M	LABR	PL	ZZZZ	USA
HOLMSTRORN, A.E.	23	M	UNKNOWN	PL	ZZZZ	USA
LUDEN, P.C.	32	M	UNKNOWN	PL	ZZZZ	USA
SWANSON, FRITIOF	71	M	UNKNOWN	PL	ZZZZ	USA

SHIP: FURNESSIA

FROM: LIVERPOOL AND QUEENSTOWN
TO: NEW YORK
ARRIVED: 08 OCTOBER 1883

PASSENGER	AGE	SEX	OCCUPATION	PRIV	VIL	DES
AGANENE, PAULIN-N.	25	M	LABR	RR	ZZZZ	USA

SHIP: SALIER

FROM: BREMEN
TO: NEW YORK
ARRIVED: 08 OCTOBER 1883

PASSENGER	AGE	SEX	OCCUPATION	PRV VIL DES
ZENTFEST, JOHANNES	42	M	DLR	RRZZZZUSA
MARIE	38	F	W	RRZZZZUSA
HEINR.	5	M	CHILD	RRZZZZUSA
MARIE	9	F	CHILD	RRZZZZUSA
JOHANN	7	M	CHILD	RRZZZZUSA
MIRJAN	3	M	CHILD	RRZZZZUSA
SZYNOKOWSKI, FRZ.	25	M	FARMER	RRZZZZUSA
JULIANE	25	F	W	RRZZZZUSA
MARIANNE	2	F	CHILD	RRZZZZUSA
NASTIZY	.06	F	INFANT	RRZZZZUSA
BARTKOWSKI, JAN	25	M	SHMK	RRZZZZUSA
ANNA	24	F	W	RRZZZZUSA
STANISLAUS	10	M	CH	RRZZZZUSA

SHIP: SILESIA

FROM: HAMBURG AND HAVRE
TO: NEW YORK
ARRIVED: 08 OCTOBER 1883

PASSENGER	AGE	SEX	OCCUPATION	PRV VIL DES
GRUENBLATT, SARA	38	F	W	RRZZZZUSA
SCHEINE	18	F	CH	RRZZZZUSA
ISRAEL	14	M	CH	RRZZZZUSA
CHEINE	9	F	CHILD	RRZZZZUSA
HIRSCH	8	M	CHILD	RRZZZZUSA
ARIL	6	M	CHILD	RRZZZZUSA
SERESEWSKI, ORES	35	M	PNTR	RRZZZZUSA
SEGALL, MORITZ	9	M	CHILD	RRZZZZUSA
WASILKOWE, BESCHE	24	F	W	RRZZZZUSA
MOSES	.11	M	INFANT	RRZZZZUSA
WOLF	.01	M	INFANT	RRZZZZUSA
GORVEL	24	M	MCHT	RRZZZZUSA
LIPPMANN, GOLDE	30	F	W	RRZZZZUSA
JUDEL	9	F	CHILD	RRZZZZUSA
CHAIE	8	F	CHILD	RRZZZZUSA
EPHRAIM	7	M	CHILD	RRZZZZUSA
FRUMMEL	4	F	CHILD	RRZZZZUSA
CHANNE	.11	F	INFANT	RRZZZZUSA
RASTOLSKY, LEA	20	F	W	RRZZZZUSA
BLOCH, RASCHEL	9	F	CHILD	RRZZZZUSA
KUKIS, HELENE	27	F	W	RRZZZZUSA
MIHAL	2	M	CHILD	RRZZZZUSA
BERNSTEIN, MALKE	28	F	W	RRZZZZUSA
LESER	8	M	CHILD	RRZZZZUSA
HIRSCH	7	M	CHILD	RRZZZZUSA
BREINE	.11	F	INFANT	RRZZZZUSA
KOPAZNIK, SARA	21	F	W	RRZZZZUSA
DINE	.11	F	INFANT	RRZZZZUSA
KAPLAN, SCHIFRA	30	F	W	RRZZZZUSA
SARA	8	F	CHILD	RRZZZZUSA
SCHOLEM	6	M	CHILD	RRZZZZUSA
EIDE	4	F	CHILD	RRZZZZUSA
PESCHE	2	F	CHILD	RRZZZZUSA
HASS, ANTON	19	M	LABR	RRZZZZUSA
ULIEWIECZ, HEINR.	26	M	LABR	RRZZZZUSA
ABRAMOWITZ, LEISER	22	M	DLR	RRZZZZUSA
FRUMME	20	F	W	RRZZZZUSA
BREUER, MOSES	30	M	DLR	RRZZZZUSA
SCHIFMANN, CHASCHE	20	F	SGL	RRZZZZUSA
KOLOMANSKY, SELIG	19	M	DLR	RRZZZZUSA
ITSCHKOWSKY, PIETSCH	17	M	DLR	RRZZZZUSA
RUTKOWSKY, BALTRIUS	21	M	DLR	RRZZZZUSA
BERMANN, ETTEL	22	M	DLR	RRZZZZUSA
GRUENBERG, ITE	38	F	W	RRZZZZUSA
SALOMON	9	M	CHILD	RRZZZZUSA
LEA	8	F	CHILD	RRZZZZUSA
HERSCHEL	6	M	CHILD	RRZZZZUSA
RIEWKE	.11	M	INFANT	RRZZZZUSA
CHEMIL	.01	M	INFANT	RRZZZZUSA
SLOTOLOW, RIEWKE	38	F	W	RRZZZZUSA
ESTER	16	F	CH	RRZZZZUSA
MORDCHE	17	M	CH	RRZZZZUSA
ISAAC	9	M	CHILD	RRZZZZUSA
MATES	7	M	CHILD	RRZZZZUSA
SALOMON	5	M	CHILD	RRZZZZUSA
MEIER	.11	M	INFANT	RRZZZZUSA
LEA	.01	F	INFANT	RRZZZZUSA
MILLMANN, REBECCA	20	F	SGL	RRZZZZUSA
MOSEROWITZ, CHANNE	18	F	SGL	RRZZZZUSA
RABINOWITZ, JANKEL	9	M	CHILD	RRZZZZUSA
KLEINFUSS, CHASCHE	19	F	SGL	RRZZZZUSA
JAFFE, WOLF	26	M	DLR	RRZZZZUSA
GRAUSASS, MICHAL	23	M	LABR	RRZZZZUSA
LASTOWSKI, JOSEF	21	M	LABR	RRZZZZUSA
BARTKEWITZ, BARTOL.	21	M	LABR	RRZZZZUSA
KAPLAN, MEIER	20	M	DLR	RRZZZZUSA
CHANNE	20	F	W	RRZZZZUSA
BERELOWITZ, ROSA	22	F	SGL	RRZZZZUSA
BAK, BASCHE	50	F	W	RRZZZZUSA
LINDE, ELIAS	21	M	DLR	RRZZZZUSA
ARMINAS, MATTH.	20	M	LABR	RRZZZZUSA
SIMANN, PESCHE	16	F	SGL	RRZZZZUSA
SAMUEL	9	M	CHILD	RRZZZZUSA
BASCHE	9	F	CHILD	RRZZZZUSA
BINE	6	F	CHILD	RRZZZZUSA
SCHAPIRA, SARA	17	F	SGL	RRZZZZUSA
SZARKOPSKI, ANDR.	24	M	LABR	RRZZZZUSA
STANKIEWICZ, JOSEF	22	M	LABR	RRZZZZUSA
STOZKOS, JOSEF	23	M	LABR	RRZZZZUSA
MILLER, ANNA	20	F	W	RRZZZZUSA
ABRAH.	.11	M	INFANT	RRZZZZUSA
BERNSTEIN, CHAIE	24	F	W	RRZZZZUSA
SCHOLEM	.11	M	INFANT	RRZZZZUSA
SAWOL, JOSEF	20	M	LABR	RRZZZZUSA
BREZOWSKY, ANDR.	22	M	LABR	RRZZZZUSA
BALEZENSKI, BAJTRUK	37	M	LABR	RRZZZZUSA
PESTKE, JOSEF	22	M	LABR	RRZZZZUSA
JOSEF	23	M	LABR	RRZZZZUSA
BESSERGLUECK, CHANNE	18	F	SGL	RRZZZZUSA
STANKEWICZ, MATTHIAS	21	M	LABR	RRZZZZUSA
SORPOLES, PETER	20	M	LABR	RRZZZZUSA
MARY	18	F	SGL	RRZZZZUSA
LUKASKI, MIHAL	20	M	LABR	RRZZZZUSA
PFEIFER, ANNA	24	F	W	RRZZZZUSA
AUGUST	.11	M	INFANT	RRZZZZUSA
AMBURSKY, SCHMUL	17	M	LABR	RRZZZZUSA
BOWER, EIDEL	18	F	SGL	RRZZZZUSA

SHIP: SPAIN

FROM: LIVERPOOL
TO: NEW YORK
ARRIVED: 08 OCTOBER 1883

PASSENGER	AGE	SEX	OCCUPATION	PRV VIL DES
JURVI, JARROLE	30	M	UNKNOWN	FNZZZZUSA
LAIY, ANDERS	14	M	UNKNOWN	FNZZZZUSA
JUNLINNEN, ISRAIL	30	M	UNKNOWN	FNZZZZUSA
HAYCHUN, TH.	31	M	UNKNOWN	FNZZZZUSA
FANTAIN, JACOB	21	M	UNKNOWN	FNZZZZUSA
NUINI, SAMUEL	33	M	UNKNOWN	FNZZZZUSA
HAKALA, MARIA	23	F	SP	FNZZZZUSA
KAUPPI, ANNA-L.	24	F	UNKNOWN	FNZZZZUSA
JARVI, GABRIEL	33	M	LABR	FNZZZZUSA

PASSENGER	AGE	SEX	OCCUPATION	PRV VIL DES
LANG, IVAN	23	M	UNKNOWN	FNZZZZUSA
BORG, MIKKEL	32	M	UNKNOWN	FNZZZZUSA
WUSCHELDIE, C.A.	25	M	UNKNOWN	FNZZZZUSA
VICKLAUDER, EMMA	20	F	SP	FNZZZZUSA
JOHAN	25	M	LABR	FNZZZZUSA
KRYANPAW, WILIMINA	39	F	W	FNZZZZUSA
JACOB	14	M	LABR	FNZZZZUSA
JUSHNA	11	F	CH	FNZZZZUSA
VIKTER	7	M	CHILD	FNZZZZUSA
GUSTAF	5	M	CHILD	FNZZZZUSA
SUSANNA	.03	F	INFANT	FNZZZZUSA
HOPPE, HEINR.	36	M	LABR	FNZZZZUSA

SHIP: ANCHORIA

FROM: GLASGOW
TO: NEW YORK
ARRIVED: 09 OCTOBER 1883

PASSENGER	AGE	SEX	OCCUPATION	PRV VIL DES
NOSAK, MICHAL	40	M	LABR	RRZZZZUSA
RAPPOPORT, MAX	18	M	LABR	RRZZZZUSA
PROHASKA, SOPHIA	19	F	SVNT	RRZZZZUSA

SHIP: HAMMONIA

FROM: HAMBURG
TO: NEW YORK
ARRIVED: 09 OCTOBER 1883

PASSENGER	AGE	SEX	OCCUPATION	PRV VIL DES
RODA, RACHA	25	F	W	RRZZZZUSA
BERTHA	.11	F	INFANT	RRZZZZUSA
KUCHER, RIWKE	23	F	W	RRZZZZUSA
BENG	.11	M	INFANT	RRZZZZUSA
U, VICTORIA	53	M	UNKNOWN	RRZZZZUSA
JOSEF	55	F	UNKNOWN	RRZZZZUSA
SOHE.	24	M	UNKNOWN	RRZZZZUSA
ADOLF	26	F	UNKNOWN	RRZZZZUSA
GRAMI-, ESTHER	00	F	UNKNOWN	RRZZZZUSA
KELKIN, LIESE	22	F	W	RRZZZZUSA
CHAIE	.11	F	INFANT	RRZZZZUSA
PALY, MATEL	35	M	W	RRZZZZUSA
CHANNE	8	F	CHILD	RRZZZZUSA
CHANNE	7	F	CHILD	RRZZZZUSA
PERLE	3	F	CHILD	RRZZZZUSA
CHAIM	.11	M	INFANT	RRZZZZUSA
ITE	.01	M	INFANT	RRZZZZUSA
KREINE	30	F	W	RRZZZZUSA
ISRAEL	8	M	CHILD	RRZZZZUSA
SIMON	7	M	CHILD	RRZZZZUSA
CHANNE	6	F	CHILD	RRZZZZUSA
NISSEN	5	M	CHILD	RRZZZZUSA
CHAJE	.11	F	INFANT	RRZZZZUSA
RIWKE	18	F	W	RRZZZZUSA
RACHEL	.11	F	INFANT	RRZZZZUSA
REINISCH, ETTI	35	F	W	RRZZZZUSA
LEA	7	F	CHILD	RRZZZZUSA
LEISSER	5	M	CHILD	RRZZZZUSA
JUDEL	.11	M	INFANT	RRZZZZUSA
RASSL, GEORG	51	M	LABR	RRZZZZUSA
ELISABETH	42	F	W	RRZZZZUSA
ANNA	18	F	CH	RRZZZZUSA
THERESE	15	F	CH	RRZZZZUSA
JOSEF	8	M	CHILD	RRZZZZUSA
LEOPOLD	3	M	CHILD	RRZZZZUSA

SHIP: ASSYRIAN MONARCH

FROM: LONDON
TO: NEW YORK
ARRIVED: 10 OCTOBER 1883

PASSENGER	AGE	SEX	OCCUPATION	PRV VIL DES
HARRI, EVA	33	F	UNKNOWN	RRZZZZUSA
IDA	11	F	CH	RRZZZZUSA
HERMANN	9	M	CHILD	RRZZZZUSA
ISAAK	4	M	CHILD	RRZZZZUSA
ANNA	2	F	CHILD	RRZZZZUSA
AXEL	1	M	CHILD	RRZZZZUSA
PONOCRANTZ, JACOB	00	M	LABR	PLZZZZUSA
FLACHS, C.	36	M	LABR	RRZZZZUSA
ZILANSKA, MOSES	12	M	UNKNOWN	RRZZZZUSA
NENITZ, MEIER	45	M	UNKNOWN	RRZZZZUSA
JOSEF	12	M	UNKNOWN	RRZZZZUSA
JALZAL, JURA	39	M	LABR	PLZZZZUSA
HOLD.	35	F	W	PLZZZZUSA
ANNA	8	F	CHILD	PLZZZZUSA
G.	3	F	CHILD	PLZZZZUSA
JANOS, ALNTA	21	M	LABR	PLZZZZUSA
CZEK, ADAM	25	M	UNKNOWN	PLZZZZUSA
HAKOOIS, JANOS	30	M	UNKNOWN	PLZZZZUSA
MEROWICZ, E.	44	F	UNKNOWN	PLZZZZUSA
BLOCK, KIWE	24	M	LABR	RRZZZZUSA
BARJEY, EDW.	12	M	LABR	RRZZZZUSA
KUVZWEIL, ISAAC	50	M	UNKNOWN	RRZZZZUSA
LAX, HERM.	18	M	UNKNOWN	PLZZZZUSA
FIEDMANN, MARCUS	23	M	UNKNOWN	RRZZZZUSA
BROWITZ, ANNA	26	F	UNKNOWN	PLZZZZUSA
KRINS, G.	23	M	UNKNOWN	PLZZZZUSA
PETN, G.	25	M	UNKNOWN	PLZZZZUSA
DIRGOD, JANOS	19	M	UNKNOWN	PLZZZZUSA
PURNA, GEO.	22	M	UNKNOWN	PLZZZZUSA
LUSKA, F.	28	F	UNKNOWN	PLZZZZUSA
JANOS	6	M	CHILD	PLZZZZUSA
GEO.	1	M	CHILD	PLZZZZUSA
HASCHULD, JANOS	23	M	LABR	RRZZZZUSA
GALESCHOWITZY, P.	43	M	UNKNOWN	RRZZZZUSA
EVA	42	F	W	RRZZZZUSA
KAROL	7	M	CHILD	RRZZZZUSA
SOFIA	5	F	CHILD	RRZZZZUSA
MARIE	1	F	CHILD	RRZZZZUSA
KURSAVER, M.F.	23	M	UNKNOWN	RRZZZZUSA
BRUDKEINOS, V.	13	M	UNKNOWN	RRZZZZUSA
ANNUDORWITZ, I.	25	M	LABR	RRZZZZUSA
WAICOLATRIES, D.	36	M	UNKNOWN	RRZZZZUSA
STANATES, M.	26	M	UNKNOWN	RRZZZZUSA

SHIP: STATE OF NEVADA

FROM: GLASGOW AND LARNE
TO: NEW YORK
ARRIVED: 11 OCTOBER 1883

PASSENGER	AGE	SEX	OCCUPATION	PRV VIL DES
ISKUR, ANDREAS	19	M	FARMER	FNZZZZUSA
KOK, GUSTAF	18	M	FARMER	FNZZZZUSA
BUKER, AUGUST	25	M	FARMER	FNZZZZUSA
LUVINSKY, HURDE	27	F	HSWF	RRZZZZUSA
REBEKKA	2	F	CHILD	RRZZZZUSA
SARAH	.06	F	INFANT	RRZZZZUSA
ROST, JOSEPH	24	M	PDLR	PLZZZZUSA
MARESCHEWITZ, ESTER	26	F	W	PLZZZZUSA
SCHONE	1	F	CHILD	PLZZZZUSA
SMILK, FUGE	22	M	PDLR	PLZZZZUSA
ICOCAK, MICHAL	22	M	PDLR	PLZZZZUSA
JIDKE, AYE	00	M	PDLR	PLZZZZUSA
NISSEL	00	M	NN	PLZZZZUSA

PASSENGER	AGE	SEX	OCCUPATION	PRIVL	DES
GRUESNER, ANNA	00	F	PDLR	PLZZZZ	USA
SKIRSABOLSKY, ABRAHAM	20	M	PDLR	PLZZZZ	USA
LEWY, SCHAUL	60	M	PDLR	PLZZZZ	USA
LATINUZ, ICZEK	32	M	PDLR	PLZZZZ	USA
SMORKOWITZ, ELIAK	17	M	PDLR	PLZZZZ	USA
HASEL, MENDEL	19	M	PDLR	PLZZZZ	USA
SKADKOWSKY, APOLONIA	17	M	PDLR	PLZZZZ	USA
BUZEZOWSKY, JOSEPF	22	M	PDLR	PLZZZZ	USA
SUMIE, JOSEPH	22	M	PDLR	PLZZZZ	USA
DURBAN, AUGUST	28	M	PDLR	PLZZZZ	USA

SHIP: INDIA

FROM: HAMBURG
TO: NEW YORK
ARRIVED: 12 OCTOBER 1883

PASSENGER	AGE	SEX	OCCUPATION	PRIVL	DES
MROCZ, MARIE	34	F	WO	PLZZZZ	NY
AGATHE	25	F	SI	PLZZZZ	NY
ZABANOWSKY, JOSEFA	18	F	SGL	RRZZZZ	NY
TOMPOWSKI, ETTE	42	F	WO	RRZZZZ	NY
ROSA	7	F	CHILD	RRZZZZ	NY
LINA	5	F	CHILD	RRZZZZ	NY
ROBSTEIN, SALC	16	M	TLR	RRZZZZ	NY
GOTTLIEB, ANNIE	20	F	SGL	RRZZZZ	NY
TZIANOWSKI, BENJAMIN	20	M	TRDSMN	RRZZZZ	NY
SZESTAKOWSKI, FRANCISKA	30	F	WO	RRZZZZ	NY
ANNA	5	F	CHILD	RRZZZZ	NY
KIRSCHENBAUM, B.	36	M	TLR	PLZZZZ	NY
STASKEL, VINCENT	29	M	LABR	RRZZZZ	NY
LABINOFSKY, THEO.	22	M	LABR	RRZZZZ	NY
JAN	17	M	LABR	RRZZZZ	NY

SHIP: SWITZERLAND

FROM: ANTWERP
TO: NEW YORK
ARRIVED: 12 OCTOBER 1883

PASSENGER	AGE	SEX	OCCUPATION	PRIVL	DES
HERMANN, IGN.	29	M	SVNT	RRZZZZ	OH

SHIP: CITY OF NEVADA

FROM: HAVANA AND MEXICAN PORTS
TO: NEW YORK
ARRIVED: 13 OCTOBER 1883

PASSENGER	AGE	SEX	OCCUPATION	PRIVL	DES
ARTSUWICH, B.	38	M	MECH	RRZZZZ	RSS

SHIP: DONAU

FROM: BREMEN
TO: NEW YORK
ARRIVED: 13 OCTOBER 1883

PASSENGER	AGE	SEX	OCCUPATION	PRIVL	DES
PENNER, CORNEL	46	M	FARMER	RRZZZZ	USA
ANNA	22	F	CH	RRZZZZ	USA
HELENE	21	F	UNKNOWN	RRZZZZ	USA
CATH.	16	F	UNKNOWN	RRZZZZ	USA
ICH.	17	M	UNKNOWN	RRZZZZ	USA
CORNEL	11	M	UNKNOWN	RRZZZZ	USA
HIBERT, --LAAS	47	M	FARMER	RRZZZZ	USA
CATH.	40	F	W	RRZZZZ	USA
HEINR.	11	M	CH	RRZZZZ	USA
CATH.	10	F	UNKNOWN	RRZZZZ	USA
PETER	9	M	CHILD	RRZZZZ	USA
NICOLAI	7	M	CHILD	RRZZZZ	USA
DIEDR.	4	M	CHILD	RRZZZZ	USA
GAEHR, WILH.	21	M	UNKNOWN	RRZZZZ	USA
CROM, GEORG	21	M	UNKNOWN	RRZZZZ	USA
BOHNER, HUGO	22	M	UNKNOWN	RRZZZZ	USA

SHIP: AMERIQUE

FROM: HAVRE
TO: NEW YORK
ARRIVED: 15 OCTOBER 1883

PASSENGER	AGE	SEX	OCCUPATION	PRIVL	DES
PAHER, SALOMON	21	M	HTR	PLZZZZ	USA
ROSENBLUM, JACOB	29	M	TLR	RRZZZZ	USA
REBECCA	18	F	UNKNOWN	RRZZZZ	USA
U	00	F	INF	RRZZZZ	USA
UBERTALLI, SECONDO	21	M	HRDRS	RRZZZZ	USA
KANALSK, ABRAHAM	23	M	TLR	RRZZZZ	USA
PARVER, MOSES	23	M	UNKNOWN	RRZZZZ	USA
SCHEVA	20	F	UNKNOWN	RRZZZZ	USA
U	00	F	INF	RRZZZZ	USA
MARKIEWIG, MARCUS	26	M	MD	RRZZZZ	USA

SHIP: CITY OF BERLIN

FROM: LIVERPOOL AND QUEENSTOWN
TO: NEW YORK
ARRIVED: 15 OCTOBER 1883

PASSENGER	AGE	SEX	OCCUPATION	PRIVL	DES
JOHANSON, NILS	39	M	LABR	FNZZZZ	USA

SHIP: BOLIVIA

FROM: GLASGOW AND MOVILLE
TO: NEW YORK
ARRIVED: 16 OCTOBER 1883

PASSENGER	AGE	SEX	OCCUPATION	PRIVL	DES
DONEHOWSKI, STAN.	33	M	LABR	PLZZZZ	USA
SINKASZ, JURIUS	30	M	SHMK	PLZZZZ	USA
STRASDASZ, SIMON	40	M	LABR	PLZZZZ	USA
KARSITIS, CHRISTOPH.	24	M	LABR	PLZZZZ	USA

SHIP: LESSING

FROM: HAMBURG AND HAVRE
TO: NEW YORK
ARRIVED: 16 OCTOBER 1883

PASSENGER	AGE	SEX	OCCUPATION	PRV VIL DES
WENZUS, PETER	18	M	LABR	RRZZZZUSA
KABUS, TIOTER	17	M	LABR	RRZZZZUSA
JURKEWITZ, DOROTHEA	22	F	W	RRZZZZUSA
MARIE	.11	F	INFANT	RRZZZZUSA
VERBIL, MARTIN	20	M	LABR	RRZZZZUSA
KARNER, ALOIS	28	M	LABR	RRZZZZUSA
LOTYWNYK, JOSEF	50	M	LABR	RRZZZZUSA
CATH.	50	F	W	RRZZZZUSA
WIENS, DANIEL	38	M	FARMER	RRZZZZUSA
MARG.	29	F	W	RRZZZZUSA
MARIE	8	F	CHILD	RRZZZZUSA
CATH.	7	F	CHILD	RRZZZZUSA
ANNA	6	F	CHILD	RRZZZZUSA
HELENE	4	F	CHILD	RRZZZZUSA
FRANZ	.11	M	INFANT	RRZZZZUSA
MACZULSKY, JACOB	20	M	LABR	RRZZZZUSA
WOCHNICK, JOH.	27	M	LABR	RRZZZZUSA
FUHRMANN, WM.	23	M	STWD	RRZZZZUSA
GEISZTEROFSKY, ARON	13	M	BY	RRZZZZUSA
LEIB	8	M	CHILD	RRZZZZUSA
HUSA, HILDA	25	F	SGL	FNZZZZUSA
BROKASS, JOH.	21	M	SHMK	RRZZZZUSA
HOSETUS, STANISL.	22	M	LABR	RRZZZZUSA
KREWINSKY, ELISABETH	34	F	W	RRZZZZUSA
KOHN, BERL.	20	M	CGRMKR	RRZZZZUSA
ZAKIM, PAIL	19	F	SGL	RRZZZZUSA
MADDAUS, AUGUSTE	33	F	W	RRZZZZUSA
ELSA	6	F	CHILD	RRZZZZUSA
OSKAR	5	M	CHILD	RRZZZZUSA
INGO	4	M	CHILD	RRZZZZUSA
SENDA	3	F	CHILD	RRZZZZUSA
FRIEDA	2	F	CHILD	RRZZZZUSA
HARALD	.06	M	INFANT	RRZZZZUSA

SHIP: PAVONIA

FROM: LIVERPOOL AND QUEENSTOWN
TO: NEW YORK
ARRIVED: 17 OCTOBER 1883

PASSENGER	AGE	SEX	OCCUPATION	PRV VIL DES
BUDETCHEVESKI, ITZGA	40	M	LABR	RRZZZZUSA

SHIP: CANADA

FROM: HAVRE
TO: NEW YORK
ARRIVED: 18 OCTOBER 1883

PASSENGER	AGE	SEX	OCCUPATION	PRV VIL DES
STAMM, ABEL	38	M	TLR	RRZZZZNY
ZABAROUSKI, SARA	55	F	UNKNOWN	RRZZZZNY
LEON	13	M	UNKNOWN	RRZZZZNY
PRASENTHAL, ZARUCH	17	M	HTR	RRZZZZNY
CAUFS, MARYM	21	F	UNKNOWN	RRZZZZNY
BEILE	5	F	CHILD	RRZZZZNY
ROTHENSTEIN, ISAAK	9	M	CHILD	RRZZZZNY
ABRAM	7	M	CHILD	RRZZZZNY
WOLZOK, MOSES	48	M	TLR	RRZZZZNY
GILT	32	F	UNKNOWN	RRZZZZNY
SAMUEL	5	M	CHILD	RRZZZZNY
ROSA	3	F	CHILD	RRZZZZNY
SARA	.03	F	INFANT	RRZZZZNY

SHIP: PERSIAN MONARCH

FROM: LONDON
TO: NEW YORK
ARRIVED: 18 OCTOBER 1883

PASSENGER	AGE	SEX	OCCUPATION	PRV VIL DES
BLUMENTHAL, ALBERT	30	M	UNKNOWN	PLZZZZUSA
JACUBOWITZ, BERNARD	37	M	LABR	PLZZZZUSA
KORSCHAK, LEWIT	20	M	UNKNOWN	PLZZZZUSA
RECZONIK, KEEZE	25	M	UNKNOWN	PLZZZZUSA
SAM.	17	M	UNKNOWN	PLZZZZUSA
COHN, LINA	20	M	UNKNOWN	PLZZZZUSA
JOSEL	19	M	UNKNOWN	PLZZZZUSA
LAIF, BARAN	22	M	UNKNOWN	PLZZZZUSA
WIENER, ISRAEL	32	M	UNKNOWN	PLZZZZUSA

SHIP: STATE OF INDIANA

FROM: GLASGOW AND LARNE
TO: NEW YORK
ARRIVED: 18 OCTOBER 1883

PASSENGER	AGE	SEX	OCCUPATION	PRV VIL DES
KAPLANSKY, HERMAN	28	M	LABR	RRZZZZUSA
NORIN, OLGA-F.	34	F	DMS	RRZZZZUSA
STROM, MARIA	36	F	W	RRZZZZUSA
HUGO	9	M	CHILD	RRZZZZUSA
ADOLF	8	M	CHILD	RRZZZZUSA
HJALMAR	4	F	CHILD	RRZZZZUSA
ONELLA, ISAAK	45	M	LABR	RRZZZZUSA
KULI, MARIA-L.	35	F	W	RRZZZZUSA
ALEXANDRA	11	F	NN	RRZZZZUSA
MARIA-S.	4	F	CHILD	RRZZZZUSA
ISTOK, ANDREAS	24	M	LABR	RRZZZZUSA

SHIP: WAESLAND

FROM: ANTWERP
TO: NEW YORK
ARRIVED: 18 OCTOBER 1883

PASSENGER	AGE	SEX	OCCUPATION	PRV VIL DES
WILGAERT, JAC.	27	M	FARMER	RRZZZZUSA

SHIP: CITY OF ROME

FROM: LIVERPOOL AND QUEENSTOWN
TO: NEW YORK
ARRIVED: 19 OCTOBER 1883

PASSENGER	AGE	SEX	OCCUPATION	PRV VIL DES
MATULEWITCH, L.	20	M	NN	RRZZZZNY

SHIP: ELBE

FROM: BREMEN AND SOUTHAMPTON
TO: NEW YORK
ARRIVED: 20 OCTOBER 1883

PASSENGER	AGE	SEX	OCCUPATION	PRV VIL DES
SEEGER, EMILIE	28	F	NN	RRZZZZUSA

SHIP: NECKAR

FROM: BREMEN
TO: NEW YORK
ARRIVED: 20 OCTOBER 1883

PASSENGER	AGE	SEX	OCCUPATION	PRV VIL DES
TESLOSKI, MARIANA	35	F	NN	RRZZZZUSA
BRONISLAW	11	F	NN	RRZZZZUSA
VICENTI	10	M	NN	RRZZZZUSA
STEFENA	9	F	CHILD	RRZZZZUSA
STEFAN	1	M	CHILD	RRZZZZUSA
WALCHOMIZ, VALMIZ	22	M	LABR	RRZZZZUSA
KOWALSKY, VOYSEK	36	M	LABR	RRZZZZUSA
WESCHNEWSKY, JOSEF	21	M	LABR	RRZZZZUSA
SKUNERSKY, CATH.	21	F	NN	RRZZZZUSA
KUESNOSIERS, ANTON	25	M	BCHR	RRZZZZUSA
MARIANNE	21	F	W	RRZZZZUSA
ZABLOWITZ, APPOLONIA	38	F	NN	RRZZZZUSA
CAMELA	11	F	NN	RRZZZZUSA
JULIANE	7	F	CHILD	RRZZZZUSA
SIGMUND	2	M	CHILD	RRZZZZUSA
WADATZSKI, SONIA	20	F	NN	RRZZZZUSA
DZCKOSKI, JAN	40	M	LABR	RRZZZZUSA

SHIP: CITY OF MONTREAL

FROM: LIVERPOOL AND QUEENSTOWN
TO: NEW YORK
ARRIVED: 22 OCTOBER 1883

PASSENGER	AGE	SEX	OCCUPATION	PRV VIL DES
ROLOWOSKY, MELLIAN	30	F	W	PLZZZZCH
JULIAN	11	M	CH	PLZZZZCH
LOKESEWICK, J.	30	M	LABR	PLZZZZCH
SCALESKY, JUN.	33	M	LABR	PLZZZZCH
DONKAL, JEN	22	M	LABR	PLZZZZCH
IURSCHI, HENR.	11	M	CH	PLZZZZCH
KRYNAK, LEO	32	M	LABR	PLZZZZCH
KUNKAL, JOH.	27	M	LABR	PLZZZZCH
JOSFIK, FRANZ	24	M	LABR	PLZZZZCH
BOROWITZ, WOLTER	29	M	LABR	PLZZZZCH
JURKOWSKY, JAN	12	M	CH	PLZZZZCH
THOMAN, W.	25	M	LABR	PLZZZZCH
SHAUM, MAX	23	M	LABR	PLZZZZCH
HERENZ, WOITECH	27	M	LABR	PLZZZZCH
WONK, ANDRAY	31	M	LABR	PLZZZZCH
DONVART, CEFTER	31	M	LABR	PLZZZZCH
RASAENCZKY, WASSIL	11	M	CH	PLZZZZCH
STECKLA, ULVAN	29	M	LABR	PLZZZZCH
VASRIN, DUNAN	11	M	CH	PLZZZZCH
KOROLICK, PETER	10	M	CH	PLZZZZCH
STECKLA, VANO	30	M	LABR	PLZZZZCH
CHADYNCK, OSEF	11	M	CH	PLZZZZCH
WIDE, MARCUS	35	M	CL	RRZZZZBAL

SHIP: DEVONIA

FROM: GLASGOW
TO: NEW YORK
ARRIVED: 23 OCTOBER 1883

PASSENGER	AGE	SEX	OCCUPATION	PRV VIL DES
BRYLA, LEON	22	M	UNKNOWN	PLZZZZUSA
JANASCHIK, ANDRAS	31	M	LABR	PLZZZZUSA
PRYBISCIEN, TEDRZEL	40	M	LABR	PLZZZZUSA
KATEIRYNA	32	F	UNKNOWN	PLZZZZUSA
JAN	7	M	CHILD	PLZZZZUSA
MARYANKA	10	F	UNKNOWN	PLZZZZUSA
JOSEF	1	M	CHILD	PLZZZZUSA
STANISLAW	.01	M	INFANT	PLZZZZUSA
PYANEVZKI, WAACIEY	33	M	LABR	PLZZZZUSA
ANNA	31	F	UNKNOWN	PLZZZZUSA
FRANCISSICK	9	M	CHILD	PLZZZZUSA
WOJCIECH	6	M	CHILD	PLZZZZUSA
JOSEF	3	M	CHILD	PLZZZZUSA
JAN	1	M	CHILD	PLZZZZUSA
POWEL	.02	M	INFANT	PLZZZZUSA
RYBERZYK, GOFIL	38	M	UNKNOWN	PLZZZZUSA
ANNA	36	F	UNKNOWN	PLZZZZUSA
MARYANNA	.08	F	INFANT	PLZZZZUSA
MAGDALENA	28	F	UNKNOWN	PLZZZZUSA
KOVAI, PAULI	40	M	MNR	PLZZZZUSA
SUSANNA	39	F	UNKNOWN	PLZZZZUSA
HALEK, MARTIN	35	M	LABR	PLZZZZUSA
FREDERICKA	24	F	UNKNOWN	PLZZZZUSA
ANNA	12	F	UNKNOWN	PLZZZZUSA
LONGAVER, ANTON	58	M	MNR	PLZZZZUSA
MARIE	20	F	UNKNOWN	PLZZZZUSA
BOLAK, JANOS	23	M	LABR	PLZZZZUSA
BUSCHANZGI, JOSEF	50	M	MNR	PLZZZZUSA
MARIA	40	F	UNKNOWN	PLZZZZUSA
PYANOWSKI, JONAS	27	M	LABR	PLZZZZUSA
MARYANNA	25	F	UNKNOWN	PLZZZZUSA
FRANCISCHA	12	F	UNKNOWN	PLZZZZUSA

SHIP: HEIMDAL

FROM: UNKNOWN
TO: NEW YORK
ARRIVED: 23 OCTOBER 1883

PASSENGER	AGE	SEX	OCCUPATION	PRV VIL DES
SAUDERS, ERIK	23	M	LABR	FNZZZZUSA
CARLSON, ERIK	23	M	LABR	FNZZZZUSA

SHIP: WESTPHALIA

FROM: HAMBURG
TO: NEW YORK
ARRIVED: 23 OCTOBER 1883

PASSENGER	AGE	SEX	OCCUPATION	PRV VIL DES
KAMINSKY, ISAAC	13	M	SCH	RRZZZZNY
MAREZINSKY, FRANZ	40	M	LABR	RRZZZZNY
MACKLEINSKY, FRANZ	40	M	LABR	RRZZZZNY
ELISABETH	40	F	W	RRZZZZNY
DWASDINTIS, MACCI	38	M	LABR	RRZZZZNY
SHAPIRO, MARION	25	F	W	RRZZZZNY
NOTE	.11	F	INFANT	RRZZZZNY
CHNELEWSKY, HIRSCH	19	M	DLR	RRZZZZNY
FRIEDMANN, SAMUEL	26	M	LABR	RRZZZZNY
RESI	19	F	W	RRZZZZNY

PASSENGER	A G E	S E X	OCCUPATION	P V D R I E V L S
KUERSUER, JACOB	20	F	DLR	RRZZZZNY
ANDZIEWICZ, JERSEY	28	F	LABR	RRZZZZNY
RABINOWICZ, JANKEL	17	F	LABR	RRZZZZNY
MERE	19	F	SGL	RRZZZZNY
POLANSKY, GUTURANN	25	F	SGL	RRZZZZNY
MARY	25	F	W	RRZZZZNY
GALISROSKY, MOSES	8	M	CHILD	RRZZZZNY

SHIP: POLYNESIA

FROM: HAMBURG
TO: NEW YORK
ARRIVED: 25 OCTOBER 1883

PASSENGER	A G E	S E X	OCCUPATION	P V D R I E V L S
HOMEIK, JOHN	18	M	LABR	RRZZZZNY
LARFELZUS, EVA	32	F	WO	RRZZZZNY
ADAM	7	M	CHILD	RRZZZZNY
EVA	3	F	CHILD	RRZZZZNY
ANNA	00	F	INF	RRZZZZNY
SCHAMANEK, GEORG	22	M	LABR	RRZZZZNY
ALNES--, LUDIE	30	F	WO	RRZZZZNY
JOHA.	7	M	CHILD	RRZZZZNY
MOSKY, ANDR.	32	M	LABR	RRZZZZUNK
CHRISTIANE	34	F	W	RRZZZZUNK
CHRISTIANE	7	F	CHILD	RRZZZZUNK
CHRISTINE	5	F	CHILD	RRZZZZUNK
EMANUEL	.11	M	INFANT	RRZZZZUNK
JOHANNE	.01	F	INFANT	RRZZZZUNK
BAYER, MICHAEL	28	M	LABR	RRZZZZUNK
SOFIA	25	F	W	RRZZZZUNK
MICHAEL	5	F	CHILD	RRZZZZUNK
CHRISTINE	3	F	CHILD	RRZZZZUNK
WILHELM	.10	M	INFANT	RRZZZZUNK
WINKOSKY, CASIMIR	25	M	LABR	RRZZZZNY
GORASCHOFSKY, VALERIAN	60	M	LABR	PLZZZZMO
MALWINA	26	F	W	PLZZZZMO
LEONDINA	24	F	SGL	PLZZZZMO
GABORSKY, JAN	34	M	LABR	RRZZZZNY
ANDRASCH, LESCHMAK	27	M	LABR	RRZZZZNY
SCHUKALA, WOJECH	27	M	LABR	RRZZZZNY
WONGWESSIN, BRON.	30	F	WO	RRZZZZNY
MEIER	.11	M	INFANT	RRZZZZNY
TOBIAS	.01	M	INFANT	RRZZZZNY
WITTKOWSKI, JOS.	18	M	LABR	RRZZZZNY
JULESWI, FRANZ	21	M	LABR	RRZZZZNY
CAIBUS, EVA	20	F	SGL	RRZZZZNY
HENDZUBA, ANDR.	36	M	TLR	RRZZZZNY
SZERBA, STEFEN	38	M	LABR	RRZZZZNY
RISCHOLTER, JUS.	26	M	LABR	RRZZZZNY
WOSZECK, M.	25	M	LABR	RRZZZZNY
STAWITZKI, JOH.	28	M	LABR	RRZZZZNY
BUDNIK, JOS.	22	M	BCHR	RRZZZZNY
GRUETER, JOH.	17	M	LABR	RRZZZZNY
BOGDANOWITZ, MATH.	28	M	LABR	RRZZZZNY
GUENTHER, JOS.	25	M	LABR	RRZZZZNY
MARIA	26	F	W	RRZZZZNY
BALDWAETZ, MART.	17	M	LABR	RRZZZZNY
SKAHNEN, MARIA	19	F	SGL	RRZZZZNY
WUBICK, STEF.	19	M	LABR	PLZZZZNY
POVELANSKI, EDM.	40	M	LABR	RRZZZZNY
LEONORA	35	F	W	RRZZZZNY
PETER	3	M	CHILD	RRZZZZNY
JANOSCHEWSKI, JOS.	17	M	LABR	RRZZZZNY
NOWAK, STANISLAUS	23	M	FARMER	PLZZZZPHI
REGWICZ, LADISL.	25	M	FARMER	PLZZZZPHI
HEIMROTH, JOS.	29	M	LABR	PLZZZZNY
GOLDBERG, JOSEF	38	M	TRDSMN	RRZZZZNY
ISAACSOHN, JS.	50	M	TLR	RRZZZZNY
REDERBENTEK, SIEGM.	20	M	LABR	PLZZZZNY
LACHMANN, PETRO	15	M	BY	RRZZZZNY

SHIP: BOHEMIA

FROM: HAMBURG
TO: NEW YORK
ARRIVED: 29 OCTOBER 1883

PASSENGER	A G E	S E X	OCCUPATION	P V D R I E V L S
STACKMANN, FRIEDR.	43	M	LABR	RRZZZZUSA
HENZ, HEINRICH	37	M	FARMER	RRZZZZUSA
MARIE	29	F	W	RRZZZZUSA
JOH.	9	F	CHILD	RRZZZZUSA
CAROLINE	5	F	CHILD	RRZZZZUSA
MARIE	3	F	CHILD	RRZZZZUSA
HANNEMANN, JOH.	35	M	FARMER	RRZZZZUSA
LENE	28	F	W	RRZZZZUSA
FRIEDRICH	5	M	CHILD	RRZZZZUSA
HELENE	3	F	CHILD	RRZZZZUSA
AUGUSTE	1	F	CHILD	RRZZZZUSA
JOH.	.11	M	INFANT	RRZZZZUSA
FILCKER, LUDWIG	50	M	FARMER	RRZZZZUSA
EMA	47	F	W	RRZZZZUSA
MARGA.	20	F	CH	RRZZZZUSA
FRANKA.	17	F	CH	RRZZZZUSA
GOTTLIEB	8	M	CHILD	RRZZZZUSA
MARIE	7	F	CHILD	RRZZZZUSA
PETER	6	M	CHILD	RRZZZZUSA
REITER, FRIEDRICH	37	M	FARMER	RRZZZZUSA
COVENTINE	27	F	W	RRZZZZUSA
FRIEDRICH	8	M	CHILD	RRZZZZUSA
WILHELM	5	M	CHILD	RRZZZZUSA
HANNEMANN, PETER	38	M	FARMER	RRZZZZUSA
EMMA	34	F	W	RRZZZZUSA
PETER	9	M	CHILD	RRZZZZUSA
WILHELM	5	M	CHILD	RRZZZZUSA
MARIE	.11	F	INFANT	RRZZZZUSA
RIEDKE, LOUISE	16	F	SGL	RRZZZZUSA
HARNIES, MARIANNE	54	F	W	RRZZZZUSA
CATHAR.	9	F	CHILD	RRZZZZUSA
AGATHE	8	F	CHILD	RRZZZZUSA
JURAK	7	M	CHILD	RRZZZZUSA
JEPKE	6	M	CHILD	RRZZZZUSA
ANNA	2	F	CHILD	RRZZZZUSA
KARPEL, SCHLOME	24	M	LABR	RRZZZZUSA
RUSCHTIK, PAULINE	37	F	SGL	RRZZZZUSA
BLEIENRADT, FRIED.	68	M	FARMER	RRZZZZUSA
DOROTHEA	61	F	W	RRZZZZUSA
CHRISTINE	19	F	CH	RRZZZZUSA
LUDWIG	29	F	CH	RRZZZZUSA
LOUISE	26	F	CH	RRZZZZUSA
JACOB	4	M	CHILD	RRZZZZUSA
CHRISTINE	2	F	CHILD	RRZZZZUSA
JULIENNE	32	F	W	RRZZZZUSA
LUECK, CONRAD	33	M	FARMER	RRZZZZUSA
JOH.	4	M	CHILD	RRZZZZUSA
JULIANNE	5	F	CHILD	RRZZZZUSA
CHRISTINE	2	F	CHILD	RRZZZZUSA
SAMUEL	.04	M	INFANT	RRZZZZUSA
FRIEDR.	28	M	FARMER	RRZZZZUSA
LOUISE	25	F	W	RRZZZZUSA
JOH.	2	M	CHILD	RRZZZZUSA
PETER	.09	M	INFANT	RRZZZZUSA
JAENICKE, AUG.	19	M	FARMER	RRZZZZUSA
EILRICH, PETER	23	M	LABR	RRZZZZUSA
NORD, KATHA.	21	F	SGL	RRZZZZUSA
ZIMMERMANN, JOH.	23	M	LABR	RRZZZZUSA
NIELSEN, NIELS	29	M	MCHT	RRZZZZUSA
HADRASSOW, ADOLP.	22	M	LABR	RRZZZZUSA
JECHJE	25	F	W	RRZZZZUSA
MARGADISCH	9	F	CHILD	RRZZZZUSA
KNITTEL, WILH.	46	M	LABR	RRZZZZUSA
DOROTHEA	37	F	W	RRZZZZUSA
GOTTFRIED	14	M	CH	RRZZZZUSA
MARIE	13	F	CH	RRZZZZUSA
CATHA.	9	F	CHILD	RRZZZZUSA
EDUARD	4	F	CHILD	RRZZZZUSA

PASSENGER	AGE	SEX	OCCUPATION	PRIV	VIL	DES
WILHELM	.11	F	INFANT	RR	ZZZZ	USA
WASSERMANN, ESTER	30	F	W	RR	ZZZZ	USA
MARRIS	9	F	CHILD	RR	ZZZZ	USA
WESCHE	8	F	CHILD	RR	ZZZZ	USA
RISEWITZ, ISAAK	55	M	LABR	RR	ZZZZ	USA
BASCHE	50	F	W	RR	ZZZZ	USA
JOEL	9	M	CHILD	RR	ZZZZ	USA
SARABSKY, DAVID	19	M	LABR	RR	ZZZZ	USA
CUDEPSKI, ANTON	20	M	LABR	RR	ZZZZ	USA
STAMIROWSKI, HILAR	20	M	LABR	RR	ZZZZ	USA
MENCZYNSKY, MAGDALENA	24	F	SGL	RR	ZZZZ	USA
STOCKLISCHKI, LIEBE	23	F	W	RR	ZZZZ	USA
HENACH	.11	M	INFANT	RR	ZZZZ	USA
FRIEDLAENDER, MOSES	17	M	LABR	RR	ZZZZ	USA
KAPLAN, RIWE	48	F	W	RR	ZZZZ	USA
JACOB	8	F	CHILD	RR	ZZZZ	USA
REISEL	7	F	CHILD	RR	ZZZZ	USA
ENI	6	F	CHILD	RR	ZZZZ	USA
AMBRULEWITZ, FABIAN	30	M	LABR	RR	ZZZZ	USA
MAIEWSKY, JULIAN	21	M	LABR	RR	ZZZZ	USA
BOPSWITZ, HEINRICH	22	M	LABR	RR	ZZZZ	USA
KRICHGUNIS, PETER	21	M	LABR	RR	ZZZZ	USA
LUCKMALIS, MICHAL	21	M	LABR	RR	ZZZZ	USA
WISNEWSKY, ANTON	4	M	CHILD	RR	ZZZZ	USA
DAMANSKY, FRIEDR.	2	M	CHILD	RR	ZZZZ	USA
ALEXANDRA	60	F	W	RR	ZZZZ	USA
PODHAI--, VINCENTI	35	M	LABR	RR	ZZZZ	USA
PUROWSKY, PAUL	24	M	LABR	RR	ZZZZ	USA
KUSINSKY, FRANZ	29	M	LABR	RR	ZZZZ	USA
SUSENSKY, SPRIRIT	23	M	LABR	RR	ZZZZ	USA
LICKO, JAN	21	M	LABR	RR	ZZZZ	USA
KOTIL, VAEL	19	M	LABR	RR	ZZZZ	USA
BUDREWIC, PITRO	22	M	LABR	RR	ZZZZ	USA
DAHLKO, MATH.	24	M	LABR	RR	ZZZZ	USA
KLUENOWICK, ANTON	27	M	LABR	RR	ZZZZ	USA
PALISIN, JAN	23	M	LABR	RR	ZZZZ	USA
KOCHMANN, ANDREAS	16	M	LABR	RR	ZZZZ	USA
RUBINSTEIN, SAMUEL	28	M	LABR	RR	ZZZZ	USA
MEYER, JOSEF	49	M	JNR	RR	ZZZZ	USA
EPSTEIN, MAX	29	M	DLR	RR	ZZZZ	USA
BERTHA	23	F	W	RR	ZZZZ	USA
ISIDOR	.06	F	INFANT	RR	ZZZZ	USA
RUBINSTEIN, AMALIE	24	F	W	RR	ZZZZ	USA
MEIER, FRANZ	29	M	TNR	RR	ZZZZ	USA
RUBINSTEIN, DORA	.11	F	INFANT	RR	ZZZZ	USA
BUTTKOWSKA, MAGTA.	.11	F	INFANT	RR	ZZZZ	USA
DRESSURAN, STRATT.	20	M	LABR	RR	ZZZZ	USA
STERNMOTZ, ANDREAS	27	M	LABR	RR	ZZZZ	USA
GORZPA, JAN	30	M	LABR	RR	ZZZZ	USA

SHIP: CITY OF CHESTER

FROM: LIVERPOOL AND QUEENSTOWN
TO: NEW YORK
ARRIVED: 29 OCTOBER 1883

PASSENGER	AGE	SEX	OCCUPATION	PRIV	VIL	DES
MOISIS, SAM-N.	30	M	LABR	RR	ZZZZ	WI

SHIP: NEDERLAND

FROM: ANTWERP
TO: NEW YORK
ARRIVED: 29 OCTOBER 1883

PASSENGER	AGE	SEX	OCCUPATION	PRIV	VIL	DES
BAROWSKA, MARIANNA	28	F	UNKNOWN	RR	ZZZZ	USA
JOHANN	10	F	UNKNOWN	RR	ZZZZ	USA
PETER	5	M	CHILD	RR	ZZZZ	USA

SHIP: ODER

FROM: UNKNOWN
TO: NEW YORK
ARRIVED: 29 OCTOBER 1883

PASSENGER	AGE	SEX	OCCUPATION	PRIV	VIL	DES
HALZANA, GEORGE	30	M	WVR	RR	ZZZZ	USA
NICKEL, JACOB	30	M	LABR	RR	ZZZZ	USA
ANNA	30	F	NN	RR	ZZZZ	USA
JOHANN	.03	M	INFANT	RR	ZZZZ	USA

SHIP: THE QUEEN

FROM: LIVERPOOL
TO: NEW YORK
ARRIVED: 29 OCTOBER 1883

PASSENGER	AGE	SEX	OCCUPATION	PRIV	VIL	DES
BOSRU, H.	34	M	LABR	FN	ZZZZ	USA
PAUK, FR.	27	M	FARMER	FN	ZZZZ	USA
BRAUNI, MATTI	35	M	LABR	FN	ZZZZ	USA
CLUANE, CARL	28	M	LABR	FN	ZZZZ	USA
LUASTAKI, GUSTAF	26	M	LABR	FN	ZZZZ	USA
LERASTARI, JACOB	26	M	LABR	FN	ZZZZ	USA
NEVAMFEERA, GUSTAF	29	M	LABR	FN	ZZZZ	USA
HOTMESMAKI, ANTI	42	M	LABR	FN	ZZZZ	USA
RORPIFAN, JAKOB	29	M	LABR	FN	ZZZZ	USA
BONIKARI, JOHAN	22	M	LABR	FN	ZZZZ	USA
LAPINKAYAS, JAKOB	21	M	LABR	FN	ZZZZ	USA
AREHEROWSKI, ERIK	56	M	LABR	PL	ZZZZ	USA
SARA	55	F	W	PL	ZZZZ	USA
MERE	25	F	SP	PL	ZZZZ	USA
PREKE	7	F	CHILD	PL	ZZZZ	USA
RACHEL	00	F	INF	PL	ZZZZ	USA
SZERSKI, RACHEL	19	F	W	PL	ZZZZ	USA
CHAIE	00	F	INF	PL	ZZZZ	USA

SHIP: AUSTRALIA

FROM: HAMBURG
TO: NEW YORK
ARRIVED: 30 OCTOBER 1883

PASSENGER	AGE	SEX	OCCUPATION	PRIV	VIL	DES
MUDRA, MICHAL	22	M	FARMER	PL	ZZZZ	NY
GUMBA, LEISA	28	M	UNKNOWN	PL	ZZZZ	NY
NEMERZ, ANNA	18	F	SGL	PL	ZZZZ	NY
BELANI, MICHAL	7	M	CHILD	PL	ZZZZ	NY
MELKO, JURE	22	M	LABR	PL	ZZZZ	NY
KOHAN, BARBARA	17	F	SGL	PL	ZZZZ	NY
BILLIG, MMIRJANNE	18	F	UNKNOWN	PL	ZZZZ	NY

PASSENGER	AGE	SEX	OCCUPATION	PRIVL	DES
JULIANE, TRAJAN	32	F	WO	PLZZZZ	NY
NAWLINE	6	F	CHILD	PLZZZZ	NY
MAYA	.10	F	INFANT	PLZZZZ	NY
SARASPOLANI, CLARA	40	F	WO	PLZZZZ	NY
KARLO	7	M	CHILD	PLZZZZ	NY
LASSAS	5	M	CHILD	PLZZZZ	NY
ALBERT	3	M	CHILD	PLZZZZ	NY
LANDES, JOSEPH	34	M	WCHMKR	PLZZZZ	NY
STANIEWICZ, MARTHA	24	F	SGL	RRZZZZ	NY

SHIP: MAASDAM

FROM: ROTTERDAM
TO: NEW YORK
ARRIVED: 30 OCTOBER 1883

PASSENGER	AGE	SEX	OCCUPATION	PRIVL	DES
BAYANOFF, R.	34	M	EGR	RRZZZZ	USA

SHIP: GELLERT

FROM: HAMBURG AND HAVRE
TO: NEW YORK
ARRIVED: 01 NOVEMBER 1883

PASSENGER	AGE	SEX	OCCUPATION	PRIVL	DES
POLTER, ADELE.	28	F	W	RRZZZZ	USA
ADEL.	2	F	CHILD	RRZZZZ	USA
GUSTAV	.06	M	INFANT	RRZZZZ	USA
HOFFMANN, LIESE	25	F	SGL	RRZZZZ	USA
SKALSJKA, VICTORIA	27	F	W	RRZZZZ	USA
ANTONIE	.11	F	INFANT	RRZZZZ	USA
ASOWITZKA, ABR.	20	M	DLR	RRZZZZ	USA
KOWALEWSKI, PETER	27	M	LABR	RRZZZZ	USA
KORDSKI, MICHAEL	27	M	UNKNOWN	RRZZZZ	USA
BOROWSKY, MICHAEL	22	M	LABR	RRZZZZ	USA
PAWLOKAREICZ, VINCENT	27	M	UNKNOWN	RRZZZZ	USA
KREPITZKI, JULIAN	28	M	UNKNOWN	RRZZZZ	USA
STACKIEWICZ, JOSEF	24	M	UNKNOWN	RRZZZZ	USA
DORA, DAL	26	M	UNKNOWN	RRZZZZ	USA
STESSNA, VERONICA	19	F	SGL	RRZZZZ	USA
PERET, FRIEDR.	46	M	FARMER	RRZZZZ	USA
MARIE	30	F	W	RRZZZZ	USA
MARGA.	18	F	UNKNOWN	RRZZZZ	USA
SOFIE	15	F	UNKNOWN	RRZZZZ	USA
FRIEDR.	7	M	CHILD	RRZZZZ	USA
JOH.	2	M	CHILD	RRZZZZ	USA
GEORG.	.11	M	INFANT	RRZZZZ	USA
LEGAL, ISAAC	21	M	TLR	RRZZZZ	USA
NEUMARK, HIRSCH	45	M	MCHT	RRZZZZ	USA
CHEIE	40	F	W	RRZZZZ	USA
REBECA	9	F	CHILD	RRZZZZ	USA
SUSANNE	4	F	CHILD	RRZZZZ	USA
SCHUBOWSKY, IGNATZ	20	M	LABR	RRZZZZ	USA
POZAW---, JESCHI	20	M	UNKNOWN	RRZZZZ	USA
MAMKAS, VIECENTI	24	M	UNKNOWN	RRZZZZ	USA
LANKE, FRIEDR.	35	M	LABR	RRZZZZ	USA
SCHMIDT, RICHARD	30	M	BKR	RRZZZZ	USA
AUGST.	63	M	UNKNOWN	RRZZZZ	USA
NEUMANN, JOH.	36	M	UNKNOWN	RRZZZZ	USA
KALIZEWSKI, MATHIAS	37	M	UNKNOWN	RRZZZZ	USA
MATULENIC, MAGDL.	23	F	W	RRZZZZ	USA
VERONIKA	.11	F	INFANT	RRZZZZ	USA
RUTIGENY, MAGDL.	27	F	SGL	RRZZZZ	USA
KERT, ESTHER	30	F	W	RRZZZZ	USA
MOSES	6	M	CHILD	RRZZZZ	USA
SARA	5	F	CHILD	RRZZZZ	USA

PASSENGER	AGE	SEX	OCCUPATION	PRIVL	DES
LEINE	3	F	CHILD	RRZZZZ	USA
CHROMAKA, STEFAN	26	M	LABR	RRZZZZ	USA
SKAMANSKY, TIMKO	44	M	UNKNOWN	RRZZZZ	USA

SHIP: GRECIAN MONARCH

FROM: LONDON
TO: NEW YORK
ARRIVED: 01 NOVEMBER 1883

PASSENGER	AGE	SEX	OCCUPATION	PRIVL	DES
KASPAR, JACOB	36	M	TLR	PLZZZZ	USA
GOLDSTEIN, LEISER	27	M	LABR	PLZZZZ	USA
FANY	25	F	W	PLZZZZ	USA
ANNIE	2	F	CHILD	PLZZZZ	USA
KATZ, ROSALIE	42	F	W	PLZZZZ	USA
EMMA	18	F	CH	PLZZZZ	USA
FAMI	16	M	CH	PLZZZZ	USA
EMIL	12	M	CH	PLZZZZ	USA
AUG.	7	M	CHILD	PLZZZZ	USA
ROSA	4	F	CHILD	PLZZZZ	USA
LISMAN, ALBERT	27	M	CGRMKR	PLZZZZ	USA
FANNY	26	F	W	PLZZZZ	USA
JULIA	1	F	CHILD	PLZZZZ	USA

SHIP: STATE OF FLORIDA

FROM: GLASGOW AND LARNE
TO: NEW YORK
ARRIVED: 02 NOVEMBER 1883

PASSENGER	AGE	SEX	OCCUPATION	PRIVL	DES
BILEVLORD, PUER	22	M	LABR	PLZZZZ	USA
EVA	24	F	W	PLZZZZ	USA
WIGENTI	1	F	CHILD	PLZZZZ	USA
SCHNAPINAN, SARAH	42	F	DRSMKR	RRZZZZ	USA
JUDAS	22	M	LABR	RRZZZZ	USA
JETTEL	20	F	W	RRZZZZ	USA
GOLDSTEIN, KARPEL	20	M	PDLR	RRZZZZ	USA
BELSON, RAHEL	45	F	W	RRZZZZ	USA
HECNBERG, SCHONE	23	F	NN	RRZZZZ	USA
JUDEL	.04	M	INFANT	RRZZZZ	USA
CHANNE	.04	F	INFANT	RRZZZZ	USA

SHIP: MAIN

FROM: BREMEN
TO: NEW YORK
ARRIVED: 03 NOVEMBER 1883

PASSENGER	AGE	SEX	OCCUPATION	PRIVL	DES
VIECZKOWSKI, JAN	33	M	LABR	RRZZZZ	USA
AUSIAUNS, TR.	26	M	LABR	RRZZZZ	USA
MAGDA.	26	F	W	RRZZZZ	USA
JOSEPF	.11	M	INFANT	RRZZZZ	USA

SHIP: P CALAND

FROM: ROTTERDAM
TO: NEW YORK
ARRIVED: 03 NOVEMBER 1883

PASSENGER	AGE	SEX	OCCUPATION	PRV VIL DES
REPACK, JOSEPH	41	M	LABR	PLZZZZUSA
JOHANN	42	M	LABR	PLZZZZUSA
HUTISA, ADAM	23	M	LABR	PLZZZZUSA
PALULIAK, JOHANN	18	M	LABR	PLZZZZUSA
REPACK, STEPHEN	27	M	LABR	PLZZZZUSA
GACIK, JOSEF	23	M	LABR	PLZZZZUSA
FROLLA, PETER	10	M	LABR	PLZZZZUSA
GOWAMBIEWISCZ, TEPIE	23	M	TLR	PLZZZZUSA

SHIP: RHYNLAND

FROM: ANTWERP
TO: NEW YORK
ARRIVED: 03 NOVEMBER 1883

PASSENGER	AGE	SEX	OCCUPATION	PRV VIL DES
GRABOWSKI, JOS.	21	M	FARMER	PLZZZZUSA
RUSZATA, JOS.	20	M	UNKNOWN	PLZZZZUSA
SUKAJEWITZ, JOH.	30	M	UNKNOWN	PLZZZZUSA
MAGD.	35	F	UNKNOWN	PLZZZZUSA
THOMAS	9	M	CHILD	PLZZZZUSA
MAGD.	6	F	CHILD	PLZZZZUSA
JOH.	6	M	CHILD	PLZZZZUSA
MATULEWICZ, URSULA	46	F	UNKNOWN	PLZZZZUSA
VINCENT	17	M	FARMER	PLZZZZUSA
MATSCHEK, SEBAST.	24	M	FARMER	PLZZZZUSA
BUSCHTA, JOS.	39	M	UNKNOWN	PLZZZZUSA
MUSKARI, MARIE	34	F	UNKNOWN	PLZZZZUSA
MALEKUSCH, ANTON	33	M	FARMER	PLZZZZUSA
JOHANNA	30	F	UNKNOWN	PLZZZZUSA
KUZEMA, MICHELMA	21	F	UNKNOWN	PLZZZZUSA
PILACHONSKA, MICHLINA	20	F	UNKNOWN	PLZZZZUSA
----SY	.06	M	INFANT	PLZZZZUSA

SHIP: CITY OF CHICAGO

FROM: LIVERPOOL AND QUEENSTOWN
TO: NEW YORK
ARRIVED: 05 NOVEMBER 1883

PASSENGER	AGE	SEX	OCCUPATION	PRV VIL DES
HEDSTROM, GUSTAF	19	M	LABR	RRZZZZNY

SHIP: FRISIA

FROM: HAMBURG AND HAVRE
TO: NEW YORK
ARRIVED: 05 NOVEMBER 1883

PASSENGER	AGE	SEX	OCCUPATION	PRV VIL DES
AKERMANN, ADIM	21	F	SGL	FNZZZZUSA
GESTRIN, GEORG	24	M	FARMER	FNZZZZUSA
THORS, WENDLA	24	F	SGL	FNZZZZUSA
BICKEL, FRIEDR.	45	M	FARMER	RRZZZZUSA
CATHE.	40	F	W	RRZZZZUSA
ALEXANDER	23	M	CH	RRZZZZUSA
JACOB	21	M	CH	RRZZZZUSA
FRIEDR.	19	M	CH	RRZZZZUSA
MARTIN	15	M	CH	RRZZZZUSA
JOH.	5	M	CHILD	RRZZZZUSA
CATHE.	22	F	CH	RRZZZZUSA
EMILIE	9	F	CHILD	RRZZZZUSA
SOPHIE	7	F	CHILD	RRZZZZUSA
OCHSNER, JACOB	46	M	FARMER	RRZZZZUSA
CATHE	34	F	W	RRZZZZUSA
MARGA.	17	F	CH	RRZZZZUSA
JOH.	15	M	CH	RRZZZZUSA
JACOB	9	M	CHILD	RRZZZZUSA
SCHRIST.	7	M	CHILD	RRZZZZUSA
ROSINE	5	F	CHILD	RRZZZZUSA
ADAM	4	M	CHILD	RRZZZZUSA
PHILIPP	2	M	CHILD	RRZZZZUSA
HEINR.	.11	M	INFANT	RRZZZZUSA
KUSZLER, GEORG	43	M	FARMER	RRZZZZUSA
ELIZABETH	42	F	W	RRZZZZUSA
ELIZABETH	20	F	CH	RRZZZZUSA
CARL	18	M	CH	RRZZZZUSA
GEORG	15	M	CH	RRZZZZUSA
JOH.	9	M	CHILD	RRZZZZUSA
HEINR.	6	M	CHILD	RRZZZZUSA
FRIEDR.	3	M	CHILD	RRZZZZUSA
SOPHIE	2	F	CHILD	RRZZZZUSA
PAULINE	.11	F	INFANT	RRZZZZUSA
MANCH, JOH.	20	M	FARMER	RRZZZZUSA
GOTTL.	18	M	FARMER	RRZZZZUSA
ELISABETH	54	F	M	RRZZZZUSA

SHIP: RHAETIA

FROM: HAMBURG
TO: NEW YORK
ARRIVED: 05 NOVEMBER 1883

PASSENGER	AGE	SEX	OCCUPATION	PRV VIL DES
SOPRANK, SARA	28	F	W	RRZZZZUSA
ANNA	7	F	CHILD	RRZZZZUSA
SCHMERE	6	F	CHILD	RRZZZZUSA
SCHMIEL	3	M	CHILD	RRZZZZUSA
HASSE	.03	F	INFANT	RRZZZZUSA
MAKOWSKI, SCHANL	17	M	TLR	RRZZZZUSA
KUPEZINSKY, MARCUS	18	M	LABR	RRZZZZUSA
RANDIS, MATH.	22	M	LABR	RRZZZZUSA
OMBROWSKI, JOH.	23	M	UNKNOWN	RRZZZZUSA
SACHSAROWSKI, ANTON	19	M	UNKNOWN	RRZZZZUSA
AMBROJOS, EVA	32	F	W	RRZZZZUSA
JOSEF	4	M	CHILD	RRZZZZUSA
HELENE	15	F	W	RRZZZZUSA
JAVEK	.03	M	INFANT	RRZZZZUSA
KRABVIE, IVAN	30	M	LABR	RRZZZZUSA
ZAVORSKY, IVAN	24	M	UNKNOWN	RRZZZZUSA
MAZURKEVIC, MIHAL	24	M	UNKNOWN	RRZZZZUSA
STEDROWSKY, PAUL	30	M	UNKNOWN	RRZZZZUSA
TOMPOWSKY, IWAN	21	M	UNKNOWN	RRZZZZUSA
OTILUS, JOSEF	18	M	UNKNOWN	RRZZZZUSA
OSPUNTO, VINC.	21	M	UNKNOWN	RRZZZZUSA
SCHELEIKO, IWAN	30	M	UNKNOWN	RRZZZZUSA
TOMALAITIS, MARTIN	21	M	UNKNOWN	RRZZZZUSA
KAJETAN, ALEX	33	M	UNKNOWN	RRZZZZUSA
OHRLIB, MIX.	25	M	LABR	RRZZZZUSA
KOBILUS, IWAN	18	M	UNKNOWN	RRZZZZUSA
KLEIN, SIGMUND	32	M	MCHT	RRZZZZUSA
PROCZYNSKI, STANISL.	25	M	SMH	RRZZZZUSA
SCHONKOVSKY, VICENTI	36	M	LABR	RRZZZZUSA
PISNOJ, SCHOLEM	26	M	CGRMKR	RRZZZZUSA
MARG.	27	F	W	RRZZZZUSA
SOSCHE	.11	F	INFANT	RRZZZZUSA
CHATZKEL	.01	F	INFANT	RRZZZZUSA

PASSENGER	AGE	SEX	OCCUPATION	PRV	VIL	DES
GRAUS, AUG.	36	M	LABR	RR	ZZZZ	USA
CZIKOWSKY, VICTOR	30	M	UNKNOWN	RR	ZZZZ	USA
SIWOLIVKA, LUDOVIKA	24	F	W	RR	ZZZZ	USA
ANSKAITIS, JOSEF	22	M	UNKNOWN	RR	ZZZZ	USA

SHIP: FRANCE

FROM: LONDON
TO: NEW YORK
ARRIVED: 07 NOVEMBER 1883

PASSENGER	AGE	SEX	OCCUPATION	PRV	VIL	DES
SISSON, ABRAHAM	20	M	TLR	RR	ZZZZ	NY
LEGERSON, BARNETT	35	M	CL	RR	ZZZZ	NY

SHIP: GALLIA

FROM: LIVERPOOL
TO: NEW YORK
ARRIVED: 07 NOVEMBER 1883

PASSENGER	AGE	SEX	OCCUPATION	PRV	VIL	DES
NUROK, BERNARD	37	M	CL	RR	ZZZZ	USA

SHIP: PENNLAND

FROM: ANTWERP
TO: NEW YORK
ARRIVED: 09 NOVEMBER 1883

PASSENGER	AGE	SEX	OCCUPATION	PRV	VIL	DES
WODTKE, AUG.	27	M	SMH	PL	ZZZZ	CH
SALENSKY, CHARLOTTE	33	F	UNKNOWN	PL	ZZZZ	UNK
AUGUSTE	.11	F	INFANT	PL	ZZZZ	UNK
REBZITZKY, CAROL.	21	F	UNKNOWN	PL	ZZZZ	NY
KRIESE, ALBERT	18	M	LABR	PL	ZZZZ	UNK
GUTSCHE, FRITZ	20	M	UNKNOWN	PL	ZZZZ	UNK
MASKOWIAK, ANDR.	14	M	UNKNOWN	PL	ZZZZ	PLY
IGNACE	10	M	UNKNOWN	PL	ZZZZ	PLY

SHIP: STATE OF GEORGIA

FROM: GLASGOW AND LARNE
TO: NEW YORK
ARRIVED: 09 NOVEMBER 1883

PASSENGER	AGE	SEX	OCCUPATION	PRV	VIL	DES
OFSCHOWITZ, CHAIM	30	M	PDLR	RR	ZZZZ	USA
MOSES	23	M	PDLR	RR	ZZZZ	USA
FEIGEL, REUWEN	00	M	TLR	RR	ZZZZ	USA
MARGOLIS, LUBE	00	F	SP	RR	ZZZZ	USA
ADELSOHN, SIMON	00	M	PDLR	RR	ZZZZ	USA
PETERSEN, HEINRICH	00	M	REST	RR	ZZZZ	USA
ANNA	00	F	W	RR	ZZZZ	USA
WILHELM	.09	M	INFANT	RR	ZZZZ	USA
KARTAZAPINA, SOBIA	00	F	SP	PL	ZZZZ	USA
KORIPAUTA, ANNA	00	F	SP	PL	ZZZZ	USA

SHIP: FRANCE

FROM: HAVRE
TO: NEW YORK
ARRIVED: 11 NOVEMBER 1883

PASSENGER	AGE	SEX	OCCUPATION	PRV	VIL	DES
JADOWSKY, LEISER	25	M	SHMK	PL	ZZZZ	NY
NISIN	23	M	UNKNOWN	PL	ZZZZ	NY
FREDI	25	M	UNKNOWN	PL	ZZZZ	NY
ISAAC	15	M	UNKNOWN	PL	ZZZZ	NY
DEBORA	1	F	CHILD	PL	ZZZZ	NY

SHIP: GENERAL WERDER

FROM: BREMEN
TO: NEW YORK
ARRIVED: 12 NOVEMBER 1883

PASSENGER	AGE	SEX	OCCUPATION	PRV	VIL	DES
SUMERAKA, JULIANE	28	F	W	RR	ZZZZ	USA
AMELA	4	F	CHILD	RR	ZZZZ	USA
JOSEFINE	3	F	CHILD	RR	ZZZZ	USA
WLADISLAUS	1	M	CHILD	RR	ZZZZ	USA

SHIP: GERMANIC

FROM: LIVERPOOL
TO: NEW YORK
ARRIVED: 12 NOVEMBER 1883

PASSENGER	AGE	SEX	OCCUPATION	PRV	VIL	DES
BOBISCO, WALDEMAR	23	M	GENT	RR	ZZZZ	USA

SHIP: SPAIN

FROM: LIVERPOOL AND QUEENSTOWN
TO: NEW YORK
ARRIVED: 12 NOVEMBER 1883

PASSENGER	AGE	SEX	OCCUPATION	PRV	VIL	DES
SIGG, JOHANNA-A.	17	F	SP	FN	ZZZZ	USA
HATAJA, HERMAN	19	M	LABR	FN	ZZZZ	USA
KAND, ABRAM	32	M	LABR	FN	ZZZZ	USA
PULKMEN, EMANUEL	26	M	LABR	FN	ZZZZ	USA

SHIP: RUGIA

FROM: HAMBURG
TO: NEW YORK
ARRIVED: 17 NOVEMBER 1883

PASSENGER	AGE	SEX	OCCUPATION	PRV	VIL	DES
AMBROSZIEWICZ, FR.	24	M	LABR	RR	ZZZZ	USA
SAWITZ, SALOMON	20	M	LABR	RR	ZZZZ	USA
BATCHEN, SCHAIE	19	M	LABR	RR	ZZZZ	USA
WISCHNEWSKY, VICENTI	25	M	LABR	RR	ZZZZ	USA
ROSALIE	21	F	W	RR	ZZZZ	USA
ROSENTHAL, MAX	20	M	LABR	RR	ZZZZ	USA

PASSENGER	AGE	SEX	OCCUPATION	PRV	VIL	DES
FARMULOWSKY, TEKLA	18	F	SGL	RR	ZZZZ	USA
U, U	00	F	SGL	RR	ZZZZ	USA
FUBER, FRANZ	19	M	GDNR	RR	ZZZZ	USA
PAUNECK, ANTON	17	M	GDNR	RR	ZZZZ	USA
BEJANKY, LABE	20	M	LABR	RR	ZZZZ	USA
SAWILSKER, ISAAC	25	M	TLR	RR	ZZZZ	USA
MARYSCH, BREINE	23	F	W	RR	ZZZZ	USA
CHANNE	.11	M	INFANT	RR	ZZZZ	USA
LABOSZYNSKA, MOSES-IWAN	20	M	TLR	RR	ZZZZ	USA
LIPSCHUETZ, ELIAS	35	M	TLR	RR	ZZZZ	USA
SIMON, SOLOMON	22	M	MCHT	RR	ZZZZ	USA
HARBERG, MARCUS	50	M	LABR	RR	ZZZZ	USA
LICHTER, MICHAEL	43	M	LABR	RR	ZZZZ	USA
JUB.	7	M	CHILD	RR	ZZZZ	USA
JETTE	6	F	CHILD	RR	ZZZZ	USA
PRIETKOWSKI, ABRAHAM	20	M	LABR	RR	ZZZZ	USA
KOWALEWSKA, VICTORIEN	22	F	W	RR	ZZZZ	USA
TADDAUS	.11	M	INFANT	RR	ZZZZ	USA
KI--STEIN, LEIB	48	M	LABR	RR	ZZZZ	USA
LEA, LEIB	44	F	W	RR	ZZZZ	USA
KIRSTEIN, HIRSCH	18	M	LABR	RR	ZZZZ	USA
ZALKE	7	F	CHILD	RR	ZZZZ	USA
BURZE	7	F	CHILD	RR	ZZZZ	USA
WILKOWISKY, RAHLA	20	F	SGL	RR	ZZZZ	USA
WEYERT, ALEXANDER	23	M	MCHT	RR	ZZZZ	USA
WILZONN, VICTOR	20	M	MCHT	RR	ZZZZ	USA

SHIP: STATE OF NEBRASKA

FROM: GLASGOW
TO: NEW YORK
ARRIVED: 17 NOVEMBER 1883

PASSENGER	AGE	SEX	OCCUPATION	PRV	VIL	DES
ABRAMOWITCH, S.	30	M	DLR	PL	ZZZZ	USA
JOSEPHSON, J.H.	45	M	FARMER	FN	ZZZZ	USA
CARLSON, C.Z.	21	M	UNKNOWN	FN	ZZZZ	USA

SHIP: WESTERNLAND

FROM: ANTWERP
TO: NEW YORK
ARRIVED: 17 NOVEMBER 1883

PASSENGER	AGE	SEX	OCCUPATION	PRV	VIL	DES
GINTOWITZ, PELAGIE	26	M	LABR	PL	ZZZZ	UNK

SHIP: CALIFORNIA

FROM: HAMBURG
TO: NEW YORK
ARRIVED: 19 NOVEMBER 1883

PASSENGER	AGE	SEX	OCCUPATION	PRV	VIL	DES
THOMAN, JSTW.	26	M	TRDSMN	PL	ZZZZ	NY
SCHRETNOWSKI, JAN	24	M	UNKNOWN	PL	ZZZZ	NY
SIMON, ESCHA	50	M	SGL	PL	ZZZZ	NY
TOWASCHKO, H.	21	M	UNKNOWN	PL	ZZZZ	NY
SCKIN, JANOS	30	M	TRDSMN	PL	ZZZZ	NY
VINCCUS, MARIA	36	F	WO	PL	ZZZZ	NY
STEFAN	4	M	CHILD	PL	ZZZZ	NY
SIBELOWSKI, CASIMIR	22	M	TRDSMN	RR	ZZZZ	NY
BUTHCWICZ, FRANZ.	24	M	UNKNOWN	RR	ZZZZ	NY
RENTSCHIN, ANTON	23	M	UNKNOWN	RR	ZZZZ	NY
SCHMUL, GOLDST	18	M	SHMK	RR	ZZZZ	NY
SCHNEIDER, CHANE	35	F	WO	RR	ZZZZ	NY
SOPHIE	7	F	CHILD	RR	ZZZZ	NY
MINNE	6	F	CHILD	RR	ZZZZ	NY
ISAAC	5	M	CHILD	RR	ZZZZ	NY
MOSES	4	M	CHILD	RR	ZZZZ	NY
MARCUS	.11	M	INFANT	RR	ZZZZ	NY
CHAIM	.11	M	INFANT	RR	ZZZZ	NY
MENDEL	.01	M	INFANT	RR	ZZZZ	NY
SAMULEWECZ, BARTHOMY	40	M	LABR	RR	ZZZZ	UNK
STEFFENS, CHRIST	35	M	LABR	RR	ZZZZ	UNK
HEREN, KAUSCHEL	35	F	WO	RR	ZZZZ	NY
GOLDE	.06	F	INFANT	RR	ZZZZ	NY
BERENBERG, DAVID	23	M	TNMK	RR	ZZZZ	NY
KANTROWITSCH, ALEXAND.	22	M	UNKNOWN	RR	ZZZZ	NY
SZCZYRANKA, JAN	25	M	FARMER	PL	ZZZZ	NY
JULIA	30	F	W	PL	ZZZZ	NY
STERN, HEINR.	17	M	LABR	PL	ZZZZ	NY
STASCHAWA, HANNA	19	F	SGL	PL	ZZZZ	NY
SRIEVMANN, HANNA	21	F	WO	PL	ZZZZ	NY
FEIGEL	.03	F	INFANT	PL	ZZZZ	NY
WOELCK, CHAINE	19	M	TRDSMN	PL	ZZZZ	NY
KESSLER, LAZAR	25	M	LABR	PL	ZZZZ	NY
BERNHARD	7	M	CHILD	PL	ZZZZ	NY
DESEWSKY, PETER	25	M	TRDSMN	PL	ZZZZ	NY
MEIROMITZ, ALEZ.	21	M	UNKNOWN	PL	ZZZZ	NY
EHREN, SARAH	7	F	CHILD	RR	ZZZZ	NY
GIETEL	6	F	CHILD	RR	ZZZZ	NY
CHAIM	5	M	CHILD	RR	ZZZZ	NY

SHIP: AMERIQUE

FROM: HAVRE
TO: NEW YORK
ARRIVED: 20 NOVEMBER 1883

PASSENGER	AGE	SEX	OCCUPATION	PRV	VIL	DES
FRENKEL, MARIUS	25	M	CL	RR	ZZZZ	USA
DAVID, LONDON	20	M	UNKNOWN	RR	ZZZZ	USA
SCHWARZMANN, PENCHA	36	M	TLR	RR	ZZZZ	USA
SARAH	30	F	UNKNOWN	RR	ZZZZ	USA
LUCIE	10	F	UNKNOWN	RR	ZZZZ	USA
NEHANNA	4	F	CHILD	RR	ZZZZ	USA
HELLEN	00	F	INF	RR	ZZZZ	USA
GORDON, ABRAHAM	41	M	JNR	RR	ZZZZ	USA
SCHEIW	40	F	UNKNOWN	RR	ZZZZ	USA
AARON	4	M	CHILD	RR	ZZZZ	USA
DIVA	00	F	INF	RR	ZZZZ	USA
KREIN	00	F	INF	RR	ZZZZ	USA
WOLFF, HECHT	28	M	CULT	RR	ZZZZ	USA
LEA	24	F	UNKNOWN	RR	ZZZZ	USA
CHAZKIEL	00	F	INF	RR	ZZZZ	USA
ADESSKI, KOPPEL	30	M	TNR	RR	ZZZZ	USA
FEIGE	24	F	UNKNOWN	RR	ZZZZ	USA
CHARKA	00	F	INF	RR	ZZZZ	USA

SHIP: SILESIA

FROM: HAMBURG
TO: NEW YORK
ARRIVED: 20 NOVEMBER 1883

PASSENGER	AGE	SEX	OCCUPATION	PRV	VIL	DES
MUSKE, GUSTAV	18	M	LABR	RR	ZZZZ	USA
JAHN, CARL	27	M	FARMER	RR	ZZZZ	USA
NEUMANN, FLERKA	23	F	SGL	RR	ZZZZ	USA

PASSENGER	A G E	S E X	OCCUPATION	P R V	V I L	D E S
DAVID	18	M	TLR	RR	ZZZZ	USA
FISCHER, LOUIS	21	M	SMH	RR	ZZZZ	USA
SCHONZEIT, ABRAM	30	M	LABR	RR	ZZZZ	USA
SCHULNOWITZ, CHAIM	46	M	TLR	RR	ZZZZ	USA
MILKE	33	F	W	RR	ZZZZ	USA
HIRSCH	7	M	CHILD	RR	ZZZZ	USA
RACHEL	8	F	CHILD	RR	ZZZZ	USA
HIRSCHBERGER, WILH.	34	M	SDLR	RR	ZZZZ	USA
MICHELSON, JACOB	21	M	LABR	RR	ZZZZ	USA
BECKER, LEIB	21	M	LABR	RR	ZZZZ	USA
LEVY, BENNY	25	M	BCHR	RR	ZZZZ	USA
SLOMJAK, CHAIM	21	M	TLR	RR	ZZZZ	USA
GERTNER, ISAAC	20	M	SHMK	RR	ZZZZ	USA
SCHUL, CHAIE	24	F	SGL	RR	ZZZZ	USA
BINDER, MOSES	22	F	TLR	RR	ZZZZ	USA
RANLINAITIS, MICHAEL	17	F	LABR	RR	ZZZZ	USA
WALDMANN, MEIER	20	F	JWLR	RR	ZZZZ	USA
KAPLAN, BUNE	25	F	W	RR	ZZZZ	USA
SCHEINE	.11	F	INFANT	RR	ZZZZ	USA
KLINKOWSTEIN, MOSES	36	M	FELMO	RR	ZZZZ	USA
ELIAS	9	M	CHILD	RR	ZZZZ	USA
SCHUNROWSKI, SCHEWACH	18	M	FELMO	RR	ZZZZ	USA
LEWIT, KEILE	22	F	W	RR	ZZZZ	USA
REBECCA	.11	F	INFANT	RR	ZZZZ	USA
ELINEWSKI, MARCUS	9	M	CHILD	RR	ZZZZ	USA
WLADISLANOWSKY, ESRI	35	F	W	RR	ZZZZ	USA
SCHUMBERG, GEDALJE	20	M	LABR	RR	ZZZZ	USA
REIZE	20	F	W	RR	ZZZZ	USA
SCHUPNITZKY, JACOB	20	M	LABR	RR	ZZZZ	USA
TIKOTZKI, JANKEL	20	M	TLR	RR	ZZZZ	USA
GRINSTEIN, MOSES	18	M	TLR	RR	ZZZZ	USA
PIWEROWSKY, PALTIEL	19	M	LABR	RR	ZZZZ	USA
JALKUS, SCHLOME	35	M	LABR	RR	ZZZZ	USA
OPPEN, JOSEF	21	M	LABR	RR	ZZZZ	USA
TAWER, LEIB	20	M	LABR	RR	ZZZZ	USA
MARMELSTEIN, LEIB	9	M	CHILD	RR	ZZZZ	USA
KRUTSINSKY, SIMON	48	M	LABR	RR	ZZZZ	USA
WILINSKY, ABRAHAM	41	M	LABR	RR	ZZZZ	USA
GABRILOWITZ, ANTON	23	M	LABR	RR	ZZZZ	USA
LUKOSCHEWITZ, CARL	21	M	LABR	RR	ZZZZ	USA
SCHULMANN, RUBEN	22	M	LABR	RR	ZZZZ	USA
TEITELOWITZ, SCHLOME	32	M	LABR	RR	ZZZZ	USA
FALK, SAMUEL	21	M	LABR	RR	ZZZZ	USA
MELMANN, ABEL	21	M	LABR	RR	ZZZZ	USA
LICHTENSTEIN, SCHOLEM	21	M	LABR	RR	ZZZZ	USA
GOLDBERG, MOSES	20	M	LABR	RR	ZZZZ	USA
KATZ, LINE	18	F	SGL	RR	ZZZZ	USA
SCHULOM, ABRAHAM	32	M	LABR	RR	ZZZZ	USA
ARSCHINOWITZ, MOSES	15	M	LABR	RR	ZZZZ	USA
JABLONSKY, ROSA	50	F	W	RR	ZZZZ	USA
LEWINSKY, MOSES	25	M	LABR	RR	ZZZZ	USA
JACOB	20	M	LABR	RR	ZZZZ	USA
MISCHKINSKY, ISAAC	20	M	LABR	RR	ZZZZ	USA
MARCUS, GEDALIE	22	F	SGL	RR	ZZZZ	USA
KODISKY, ISAAC	18	M	LABR	RR	ZZZZ	USA
GESIS, MOSES	20	M	LABR	RR	ZZZZ	USA
JACHENOWSKY, NOCHEM	20	M	LABR	RR	ZZZZ	USA
EINSON, ABRAM	21	M	LABR	RR	ZZZZ	USA
RUBIN, BEHR	19	M	LABR	RR	ZZZZ	USA
TAMOWSKY, EMMY	18	F	SGL	RR	ZZZZ	USA
KURLANSKY, LEIB	18	M	LABR	RR	ZZZZ	USA
WILLENSKY, HILLEL	20	M	LABR	RR	ZZZZ	USA
FEIGE	17	F	SGL	RR	ZZZZ	USA
WARTOWSKY, MOSES	21	M	LABR	RR	ZZZZ	USA
SCHLASKY, DAVID	50	M	LABR	RR	ZZZZ	USA
GEBESCH, FERENZ	40	M	LABR	RR	ZZZZ	USA
MILEWSKY, ANTON	22	M	LABR	RR	ZZZZ	USA
ANNA	23	F	W	RR	ZZZZ	USA
RUSKOWSKY, PETRO	22	M	LABR	RR	ZZZZ	USA
CASICK, ALEXANDER	29	M	LABR	RR	ZZZZ	USA
MATULEVIC, VICENTY	19	M	LABR	RR	ZZZZ	USA
MEROVUS, JOSEF	21	M	LABR	RR	ZZZZ	USA
CHAMSKI, FRANZ	23	M	LABR	RR	ZZZZ	USA
CARMIEWSKI, LUDWIG	21	M	LABR	RR	ZZZZ	USA
YALLOWITCH, JOEL	63	M	LABR	RR	ZZZZ	USA
TAUBE	63	F	W	RR	ZZZZ	USA
FOULB, RACHMIEL	29	M	LABR	RR	ZZZZ	USA
COHN, DANIEL	20	M	LABR	RR	ZZZZ	USA
NEUMANN, LIBBIE	21	F	SGL	RR	ZZZZ	USA
LINKOWITZ, DAVID	23	F	JNR	RR	ZZZZ	USA
ZODIKOW, JACOB	21	F	SHMK	RR	ZZZZ	USA
KAPATE, ARON	20	F	MCHT	RR	ZZZZ	USA
JAKOBSCHEK, HIRSCH	28	F	SMH	RR	ZZZZ	USA
LEWIN, NOTE	26	F	SMH	RR	ZZZZ	USA
LOWIN, JOSEF	21	F	SHMK	RR	ZZZZ	USA
SCHAFIR, AUSTER	22	F	JNR	RR	ZZZZ	USA
KANTEROWITZ, DAVID	18	F	TLR	RR	ZZZZ	USA
MALKE	19	F	SGL	RR	ZZZZ	USA
AXELROD, GERSON	28	M	TLR	RR	ZZZZ	USA
MELAMED, JACOB	22	M	SHMK	RR	ZZZZ	USA
SCHMITMAN, NECHE	20	F	SGL	RR	ZZZZ	USA
ISAACSOHN, LABIN	22	M	DLR	RR	ZZZZ	USA
KAHN, HIRSCH	36	M	JNR	RR	ZZZZ	USA
ABRACH, NISSEN	27	M	DLR	RR	ZZZZ	USA
LEWIN, SAMUEL	20	M	MCHT	RR	ZZZZ	USA
LOSCHOS, CHAIE	20	M	MCHT	RR	ZZZZ	USA
MUSWENDT, BENSEL	24	M	MCHT	RR	ZZZZ	USA
ROSAITZKI, ARON	18	M	MCHT	RR	ZZZZ	USA
KRITZKOW, MICHEL	18	M	MCHT	RR	ZZZZ	USA
SENBERG, ABRAHAM	18	M	MCHT	RR	ZZZZ	USA
RABBINOWITZ, LUCIE	25	F	SGL	RR	ZZZZ	USA
RADER, GEORG	33	M	LABR	RR	ZZZZ	USA
SPIRO, JANI	19	F	SGL	RR	ZZZZ	USA
JAMBLOWSKI, KEILE	30	F	W	RR	ZZZZ	USA
MESSIAS	9	M	CHILD	RR	ZZZZ	USA
ELIAS	8	M	CHILD	RR	ZZZZ	USA
MERE	.11	F	INFANT	RR	ZZZZ	USA
DEMBROWITZ, MARIANNE	20	F	W	RR	ZZZZ	USA
SARA	.11	F	INFANT	RR	ZZZZ	USA
GRUNBERG, LEIB	20	M	DLR	RR	ZZZZ	USA
FRANKEL, ISAAC	20	M	DLR	RR	ZZZZ	USA
LIBOWSKY, CHAINE	19	M	DLR	RR	ZZZZ	USA
FINKELSTEIN, MOSES	65	M	DLR	RR	ZZZZ	USA
BRICKER, NASANNE	.45	F	W	RR	ZZZZ	USA
SAMUEL	9	M	CHILD	RR	ZZZZ	USA
JOSEFER, ABC.	50	M	LABR	RR	ZZZZ	USA
NEUHAUSER, BETTY	18	F	SGL	RR	ZZZZ	USA
KRZINSANSKY, JOSSEL	21	M	LABR	RR	ZZZZ	USA
RIMKOWSKY, SAMUEL	20	M	LABR	RR	ZZZZ	USA
WAVILIWITZ, ANTON	25	M	LABR	RR	ZZZZ	USA
MUNZINSKY, FRANZ	26	M	LABR	RR	ZZZZ	USA
SCHIERGINSKI, FRANZ	25	M	LABR	RR	ZZZZ	USA
GURZINSKY, STANISL.	20	M	LABR	RR	ZZZZ	USA
RADZINSKI, JOHANN	30	M	LABR	RR	ZZZZ	USA
SMALLINSKY, LAZAR	22	M	JNR	RR	ZZZZ	USA
MERLIS, MOSES	23	M	LABR	RR	ZZZZ	USA
ROSENFELD, JACOB	30	M	DLR	RR	ZZZZ	USA
GRIGELLIS, GEORG	21	M	LABR	RR	ZZZZ	USA
GUTOWSKI, AUGUSTIN	22	M	LABR	RR	ZZZZ	USA
LEHNREITIS, WILH.	19	M	FARMER	RR	ZZZZ	USA
RAND, ANTON	25	M	LABR	RR	ZZZZ	USA
JOSEF	25	M	LABR	RR	ZZZZ	USA
WITKIN, HIRSCH	21	M	DLR	RR	ZZZZ	USA
SELDE	20	F	W	RR	ZZZZ	USA
DEMLER, WOLF	17	M	LABR	RR	ZZZZ	USA
GERSON, COHEN	17	M	LABR	RR	ZZZZ	USA
BOROSKY, SAMUEL	18	M	LABR	RR	ZZZZ	USA
CHUDYK, CATHARINE	40	F	W	PL	ZZZZ	USA

SHIP: GREECE

FROM: LONDON
TO: NEW YORK
ARRIVED: 21 NOVEMBER 1883

PASSENGER	AGE	SEX	OCCUPATION	PRV VIL DES
FREEDMAN, ADELINE	25	F	SP	RRZZZZNY
JACOB, JOSEPH	20	M	LABR	RRZZZZNY
ROSENBERG, BENJ.	32	M	LABR	RRZZZZNY
BERKOWITZ, M.	38	M	LABR	RRZZZZNY

SHIP: HABSBURG

FROM: BREMEN
TO: NEW YORK
ARRIVED: 22 NOVEMBER 1883

PASSENGER	AGE	SEX	OCCUPATION	PRV VIL DES
SCHMIDT, JUSCHKO	31	M	FARMER	RRZZZZUSA

SHIP: HAMMONIA

FROM: HAMBURG
TO: NEW YORK
ARRIVED: 22 NOVEMBER 1883

PASSENGER	AGE	SEX	OCCUPATION	PRV VIL DES
PODHAISKY, CARL	28	M	MCHT	RRZZZZUSA
GOLDING, SAMUEL	40	M	DLR	RRZZZZUSA
DLUGATZ, BENJAMIN	37	M	DLR	RRZZZZUSA
SARA	35	F	W	RRZZZZUSA
SCHOCHE	15	F	CH	RRZZZZUSA
RAHEL	12	F	CH	RRZZZZUSA
ZIPPE	5	F	CHILD	RRZZZZUSA
KLEINBERG, SOCHAR	20	M	SMH	RRZZZZUSA
BRAUN, SCHLOME	18	M	LABR	RRZZZZUSA
FUCKS, CHAIZI--A	30	F	W	RRZZZZUSA
ISRAEL	4	M	CHILD	RRZZZZUSA
STONKIEWICZ, PAUL	25	M	LABR	RRZZZZUSA
MERKOWITZ, ABRAHAM	18	M	DLR	RRZZZZUSA
EINSOHN, LEA	8	F	CHILD	RRZZZZUSA
BRENNER, RUEBIN	20	M	DLR	RRZZZZUSA
BAIER, JOSEF	19	M	DLR	RRZZZZUSA
MIGANZ, ISRAEL	19	M	DLR	RRZZZZUSA
FREID, SIMON	19	M	SHMK	RRZZZZUSA
SPAETER, SAMUEL	28	M	MCHT	RRZZZZUSA
KEMPE, KREINDEL	60	F	W	RRZZZZUSA
FUCHS, ABRAH.	27	M	TLR	RRZZZZUSA
PACKELTSCHICK, HINDE	19	F	SGL	RRZZZZUSA
WARSCHAMSKI, DAVID	8	M	CHILD	RRZZZZUSA
CHAIE	7	F	CHILD	RRZZZZUSA
SICHER, WOLF	23	M	LABR	RRZZZZUSA
ROSENKRANZ, ISAAC	47	M	DLR	RRZZZZUSA
LAEB	21	M	DLR	RRZZZZUSA
PREUER, ELIAS	47	M	DLR	RRZZZZUSA
KOERNER, MOSES	23	M	TLR	RRZZZZUSA
REISE	20	F	W	RRZZZZUSA
TOMPACKI, JANOS	20	M	LABR	RRZZZZUSA
GOLDSTEIN, ISRAEL	8	M	CHILD	RRZZZZUSA
LIESETZKA, FRANZISKA	26	F	W	RRZZZZUSA
WLADISLAUS	.03	M	INFANT	RRZZZZUSA
APPELBAUM, ITZIG	21	M	BCHR	RRZZZZUSA
FRANKEL, JOSEF	17	M	LABR	RRZZZZUSA
WERTELSKY, MEIER	16	M	LABR	RRZZZZUSA
GALLINES, WINZES	20	M	LABR	RRZZZZUSA
BARTSCHEWSKY, VINCENTI	23	M	LABR	RRZZZZUSA
PUNDZIS, TURAS	30	M	LABR	RRZZZZUSA
KUKUCANI, ANTON	23	M	LABR	RRZZZZUSA
RADEWIC, JAN	24	M	LABR	RRZZZZUSA
HELENE	19	F	W	RRZZZZUSA
KACHNOUSKY, FRANZ	23	M	LABR	RRZZZZUSA
SADLOUSKY, STANISL.	32	M	LABR	RRZZZZUSA
KISINSKY, WLADIMIR	21	M	LABR	RRZZZZUSA
SMILLINSKY, CHAIE	18	F	SGL	RRZZZZUSA
ROSENBERG, JANKEL	22	M	DLR	RRZZZZUSA
RADLOWSKY, GOSSEL	45	M	TLR	RRZZZZUSA
KOHN, ABRAHAM	25	M	TLR	RRZZZZUSA
RUDANSKI, ZALKE	21	M	DLR	RRZZZZUSA
BASCHE	21	F	W	RRZZZZUSA
DRENSTHIEWSKI, ABRAHAM	23	M	JNR	RRZZZZUSA
LIEBER, MALKE	20	F	SGL	RRZZZZUSA
ANNA	13	F	SGL	RRZZZZUSA
BERKOWITZ, ULRICH	26	M	LABR	RRZZZZUSA
WISANSKY, LEIB	37	M	LABR	RRZZZZUSA
RUBENSTEIN, MENDL	20	M	LABR	RRZZZZUSA
CHAIE	20	F	W	RRZZZZUSA
RACHEL	.03	F	INFANT	RRZZZZUSA
LEWINSKY, MEIER	50	M	LABR	RRZZZZUSA
BITTERMANN, JACOB	18	M	CGRMKR	RRZZZZUSA
WERBELOWSKY, LEWIN	50	M	LABR	RRZZZZUSA
LEA	45	F	W	RRZZZZUSA
CHASKEL	17	M	NN	RRZZZZUSA
WOICZEKUS, WICENTI	26	M	LABR	RRZZZZUSA
JAFFE, CHEIM	30	M	MCHT	RRZZZZUSA

SHIP: PAVONIA

FROM: LIVERPOOL AND QUEENSTOWN
TO: NEW YORK
ARRIVED: 22 NOVEMBER 1883

PASSENGER	AGE	SEX	OCCUPATION	PRV VIL DES
STEIN, FANNY	33	F	SP	PLZZZZUSA

SHIP: BOLIVIA

FROM: GLASGOW AND MOVILLE
TO: NEW YORK
ARRIVED: 23 NOVEMBER 1883

PASSENGER	AGE	SEX	OCCUPATION	PRV VIL DES
MATUSAS, F.	35	M	LABR	PLZZZZUSA
PSYLYTOWICZ, JOSEF	24	M	SHMK	PLZZZZUSA
CATARINA	18	F	NN	PLZZZZUSA
WYDZGOWSKY, JOH.	44	M	LABR	PLZZZZUSA
ZACKMAN, ABRAHAM	19	M	TRVLR	RRZZZZUSA
HARRIS	22	M	TRVLR	RRZZZZUSA
LEVY, SARA	24	F	NN	RRZZZZUSA
LOUIS	3	M	CHILD	RRZZZZUSA
JUNN.	.09	M	INFANT	RRZZZZUSA

PASSENGER	AGE	SEX	OCCUPATION	PRIV	VIL	DES

SHIP: CANADA

FROM: HAVRE
TO: NEW YORK
ARRIVED: 24 NOVEMBER 1883

PASSENGER	AGE	SEX	OCCUPATION	PRIV VIL DES
RAPOPOX, WOLFANG	24	M	PRNTR	RRZZZZNY
LESER, SOHUS	22	M	TLR	RRZZZZNY
BARASCH, ARON	26	M	TLR	RRZZZZNY
CHESNE	22	F	NN	RRZZZZNY
GLUCKMANN, ABRAHAM	26	M	TLR	RRZZZZNY

SHIP: ASSYRIAN MONARCH

FROM: LONDON
TO: NEW YORK
ARRIVED: 26 NOVEMBER 1883

PASSENGER	AGE	SEX	OCCUPATION	PRIV VIL DES
MICHAELSON, LEAH	30	F	NN	PLZZZZUSA
RACHEL	2	F	CHILD	PLZZZZUSA
DEBORAH	.07	F	INFANT	PLZZZZUSA
LEVY, LEAH	22	F	NN	PLZZZZUSA
PELTA	4	F	CHILD	PLZZZZUSA
SARAH	2	F	CHILD	PLZZZZUSA
DEBORAH	.09	F	INFANT	PLZZZZUSA
HANNAH	60	F	NN	PLZZZZUSA
BLZANSKY, LEIB	54	M	LABR	RRZZZZUSA
BASIL	46	F	W	RRZZZZUSA
MINKA	12	M	CH	RRZZZZUSA
JUDA	10	F	CH	RRZZZZUSA
PALE, RISZ	30	M	LABR	PLZZZZUSA
ISAAC, KAUPLAN	16	M	LABR	RRZZZZUSA
MARGUIS, PRIEKER	19	M	LABR	RRZZZZUSA
LIPSCHICK, F.	32	M	LABR	PLZZZZUSA
REICHENSTOLL, F.	32	M	LABR	PLZZZZUSA
BALUK, A.	32	M	LABR	PLZZZZUSA
SILVERSTEIN, J.	27	M	LABR	PLZZZZUSA

SHIP: DONAU

FROM: BREMEN
TO: NEW YORK
ARRIVED: 26 NOVEMBER 1883

PASSENGER	AGE	SEX	OCCUPATION	PRIV VIL DES
RADAWTZKY, IGNATZ	25	M	LABR	RRZZZZUSA
GACKO, KASIMIR	20	M	UNKNOWN	RRZZZZUSA
LUKASZEWIEC, ANTHON	22	M	UNKNOWN	RRZZZZUSA
JAWOWICZ, JAN	26	M	UNKNOWN	RRZZZZUSA

SHIP: FULDA

FROM: BREMEN
TO: NEW YORK
ARRIVED: 26 NOVEMBER 1883

PASSENGER	AGE	SEX	OCCUPATION	PRIV VIL DES
KADES, ISAK	24	M	FARMER	RRZZZZUSA
PURITZ, AUGUST	44	M	FARMER	RRZZZZUSA
CAROLINE	10	F	UNKNOWN	RRZZZZUSA
AMALIE	9	F	CHILD	RRZZZZUSA

PASSENGER	AGE	SEX	OCCUPATION	PRIV VIL DES
JULIE	7	F	CHILD	RRZZZZUSA
STURM, HEDWIG	18	F	UNKNOWN	PLZZZZUSA
WENZEL, LIEBER	22	M	LABR	PLZZZZUSA
FUCHS, HERM.	28	M	UNKNOWN	PLZZZZUSA

SHIP: SWITZERLAND

FROM: ANTWERP
TO: NEW YORK
ARRIVED: 26 NOVEMBER 1883

PASSENGER	AGE	SEX	OCCUPATION	PRIV VIL DES
INTAL, JOS.	24	M	FARMER	RRZZZZNY

SHIP: CITY OF MONTREAL

FROM: LIVERPOOL
TO: NEW YORK
ARRIVED: 27 NOVEMBER 1883

PASSENGER	AGE	SEX	OCCUPATION	PRIV VIL DES
ALPHERN, JOS.	9	M	CHILD	RRZZZZMI
SARAH	38	F	W	RRZZZZMI
MARIA	6	F	CHILD	RRZZZZMI
HANNAH	4	F	CHILD	RRZZZZMI
MOROWSKY, ANTON	25	M	LABR	RRZZZZNY
WASILIF, LEON	11	M	CH	RRZZZZNY
HANILOWICK, VINCENT	40	M	FARMER	RRZZZZNY
ANNA	38	F	W	RRZZZZNY
BERTHA	1	F	CHILD	RRZZZZNY
VICTORIA	1	F	CHILD	RRZZZZNY
GOTTGEVA, MARIANN	25	F	SVNT	PLZZZZNY
GRABOWOSKY, BARBARA	20	F	UNKNOWN	PLZZZZNY
GRUNGULIB, SIMON	24	M	LABR	PLZZZZNY
MARIANA	20	F	W	PLZZZZNY
DINDULLA, VINCENT	12	M	CH	PLZZZZNY

SHIP: ENGLAND

FROM: LIVERPOOL AND QUEENSTOWN
TO: NEW YORK
ARRIVED: 27 NOVEMBER 1883

PASSENGER	AGE	SEX	OCCUPATION	PRIV VIL DES
GODRICK, JOS.	45	M	UNKNOWN	PLZZZZUSA
CATHERINE	34	F	W	PLZZZZUSA

SHIP: LESSING

FROM: HAMBURG AND HAVRE
TO: NEW YORK
ARRIVED: 28 NOVEMBER 1883

PASSENGER	AGE	SEX	OCCUPATION	PRIV VIL DES
BESKER, LEIBUSCH	17	M	CGRMKR	RRZZZZUSA
SILBERBERG, MIRJAM	27	F	W	RRZZZZUSA
MOSES	.11	M	INFANT	RRZZZZUSA
STERNSCHIYS, LEISER	21	M	DLR	RRZZZZUSA
HEILPERN, ELIAS	24	M	SMH	RRZZZZUSA

PASSENGER	AGE	SEX	OCCUPATION	PRV	VIL	DES
RIGER, ELIAS	24	M	MLR	RR	ZZZZ	USA
SCHMIDTMANN, ALTER	20	M	SMH	RR	ZZZZ	USA
LIPSCHUETZ, ABRAHAM	22	M	TLR	RR	ZZZZ	USA
POSKEWITZ, FEIWUESCH	16	M	LABR	RR	ZZZZ	USA
BRONEWITZ, FEIWUESCH	24	M	SHMK	RR	ZZZZ	USA
ROSOWSKY, MARCUS	24	M	JNR	RR	ZZZZ	USA
SCHAPPIRE, NISSEN	23	M	DLR	RR	ZZZZ	USA
AXELROD, CHAIM	23	M	LABR	RR	ZZZZ	USA
LAPIDES, ABRAHAM	19	M	JNR	RR	ZZZZ	USA
KRUEL, LEIBUSCH	53	M	LABR	RR	ZZZZ	USA
WOLF, PINCUS	18	M	LABR	RR	ZZZZ	USA
ALEF, CHANNE	28	F	W	RR	ZZZZ	USA
ISAAC	6	M	CHILD	RR	ZZZZ	USA
ARON	5	M	CHILD	RR	ZZZZ	USA
JACOB	.11	M	INFANT	RR	ZZZZ	USA
ESSEL, IOSSEL	24	M	DLR	RR	ZZZZ	USA
ALESLIN, ABRAHAM	15	M	UNKNOWN	RR	ZZZZ	USA
GOLDSCHMIDT, MEIER	16	M	DLR	RR	ZZZZ	USA
WENDER, SAMUEL	4	M	CHILD	RR	ZZZZ	USA
KROCHMAL, FREIDE	35	F	SGL	RR	ZZZZ	USA
MEISLIN, CHEIM	17	M	DLR	RR	ZZZZ	USA
LERNER, KUVE	18	F	UNKNOWN	RR	ZZZZ	USA
MOGULEWITZ, MOSES	31	M	TLR	RR	ZZZZ	USA
MUCHLITZKY, ANTON	00	M	UNKNOWN	RR	ZZZZ	USA
KOBATZINK, DAVID	00	M	UNKNOWN	RR	ZZZZ	USA
JALKOWSKY, JACOB	21	M	UNKNOWN	RR	ZZZZ	USA
ABRAHAMSOHN, JOSEF	21	M	TLR	RR	ZZZZ	USA
GOBARSKY, MICHLE	18	F	SGL	RR	ZZZZ	USA
ROMMER, BEILE	22	F	UNKNOWN	RR	ZZZZ	USA
KARPAL, CHAIE	32	F	W	RR	ZZZZ	USA
JANKEL	8	F	CHILD	RR	ZZZZ	USA
SALMEN	6	F	CHILD	RR	ZZZZ	USA
CHANA	.11	M	INFANT	RR	ZZZZ	USA
SUESSMONOWITZ, BERL	28	M	TLR	RR	ZZZZ	USA
MOLOWITZ, CHEMJA	19	M	UNKNOWN	RR	ZZZZ	USA
PERLMANN, ESTHER	30	F	W	RR	ZZZZ	USA
ETTA	7	F	CHILD	RR	ZZZZ	USA
SARAH	5	F	CHILD	RR	ZZZZ	USA
ISRAELOWITZ, SCHEINE	24	F	SGL	RR	ZZZZ	USA
COHN, CHAIE	25	F	SGL	RR	ZZZZ	USA
HERSCHINSKY, JACOB	19	M	LABR	RR	ZZZZ	USA
COHN, ISRAEL	20	M	UNKNOWN	RR	ZZZZ	USA
SOFER, ISAAC	30	M	UNKNOWN	RR	ZZZZ	USA
SARA	28	F	W	RR	ZZZZ	USA
BUTTJER, POPPE	53	M	UNKNOWN	RR	ZZZZ	USA
SARA	48	F	W	RR	ZZZZ	USA
SCHULBERG, BLUME	18	F	SGL	RR	ZZZZ	USA
EPHRAIM	20	M	DLR	RR	ZZZZ	USA
VORSTADT, SCHMEREL	30	M	DLR	RR	ZZZZ	USA
STROKOWSKY, MICH.	32	M	LABR	RR	ZZZZ	USA
MINNA	21	F	W	RR	ZZZZ	USA
FRIEDR.	7	M	CHILD	RR	ZZZZ	USA
STROKOVSKY, JOSEPH	5	M	CHILD	RR	ZZZZ	USA
JOHN	3	M	CHILD	RR	ZZZZ	USA
PAULINE	.11	F	INFANT	RR	ZZZZ	USA
GOTTLIEB	70	M	LABR	RR	ZZZZ	USA
AEPFELBAUM, MALIE	50	F	W	RR	ZZZZ	USA
ALTE	20	F	D	RR	ZZZZ	USA
WITTENBERG, JACOB	22	M	MCHT	RR	ZZZZ	USA
ABRATIS, JAN	19	M	LABR	RR	ZZZZ	USA
ANTON	9	M	CHILD	RR	ZZZZ	USA
MARIANNE	8	F	CHILD	RR	ZZZZ	USA
HELMANSKY, MOSES	40	M	TLR	RR	ZZZZ	USA
ARENSOHN, JACOB	38	M	UNKNOWN	RR	ZZZZ	USA
MERE	18	F	D	RR	ZZZZ	USA
CHOZI	9	F	CHILD	RR	ZZZZ	USA
HURWITZ, MORDCHE	18	M	LABR	RR	ZZZZ	USA
BINSKY, JANKEL	22	M	JNR	RR	ZZZZ	USA
HEILE	22	F	W	RR	ZZZZ	USA
JAKOWITZ, CHANNE	20	F	SGL	RR	ZZZZ	USA
SIBURSKY, FEIWEL	18	M	LABR	RR	ZZZZ	USA
JINKELBRANDT, NOCHEM	34	M	LABR	RR	ZZZZ	USA
WALTER, SOPHIE	23	F	SGL	RR	ZZZZ	USA
SCHIMILOWITZ, MARE	20	F	SGL	RR	ZZZZ	USA
LEVY, JUDEL	15	M	LABR	RR	ZZZZ	USA
SCHEINBERG, LISSEL	42	F	W	RR	ZZZZ	USA
ESTHER	9	F	CHILD	RR	ZZZZ	USA
DAVID	4	M	CHILD	RR	ZZZZ	USA
KAPLAN, JANKEL	22	M	TLR	RR	ZZZZ	USA
PLACHS, SARAH	24	F	SGL	RR	ZZZZ	USA
KOPOLA, HENRIK	25	M	LABR	RR	ZZZZ	USA
HELMANSKY, CHATZEL	26	M	LABR	RR	ZZZZ	USA
LEWINSOHN, CHAIM	9	M	CHILD	RR	ZZZZ	USA
KRZYNKOWSKI, EDWARD	21	M	PNR	RR	ZZZZ	USA
WOJNOWSKI, AND.	21	M	LABR	RR	ZZZZ	USA
KOWALSKI, HIRSCH	18	M	LABR	RR	ZZZZ	USA
WOELFELSOHN, JACOB	20	M	UNKNOWN	RR	ZZZZ	USA
HIRSCHOWITZ, JANKEL	26	M	TLR	RR	ZZZZ	USA
SEGALOWITZ, CHEIM	17	M	LABR	RR	ZZZZ	USA
ROSENBERG, MOSES	9	M	CHILD	RR	ZZZZ	USA
HLPERN, JOSEPH	20	M	LABR	RR	ZZZZ	USA
LAPIDUS, SCHOEL	18	M	UNKNOWN	RR	ZZZZ	USA
HOLPERN, ZALELL	19	M	UNKNOWN	RR	ZZZZ	USA
KOWALSKY, MOSES	17	M	UNKNOWN	RR	ZZZZ	USA
ROSENBERG, DINE	15	F	SGL	RR	ZZZZ	USA
SCHAPIRO, CHAIM	9	M	CHILD	RR	ZZZZ	USA
LEIB	9	M	CHILD	RR	ZZZZ	USA
SCHEINBERG, BROCHE	25	F	UNKNOWN	RR	ZZZZ	USA
BINE	.11	F	INFANT	RR	ZZZZ	USA
WEISSBORD, ISAAC	23	M	SHMK	RR	ZZZZ	USA
SAWADDA, JOSSIL	18	M	UNKNOWN	RR	ZZZZ	USA
UGGERT, SELMA	20	F	SGL	RR	ZZZZ	USA
ZUNSKI, MICHAEL	21	M	LABR	RR	ZZZZ	USA
AMDURSKY, JACOB	16	M	UNKNOWN	RR	ZZZZ	USA
BAYLIE	18	F	SGL	RR	ZZZZ	USA
CLONEITZ, ABRAHAM	21	M	MSN	RR	ZZZZ	USA
MAWROZKA, WANDA	30	F	W	RR	ZZZZ	USA
IRMA	9	F	CHILD	RR	ZZZZ	USA
KINISCHINSKY, BEHR	40	M	DLR	RR	ZZZZ	USA
DWORE	9	F	CHILD	RR	ZZZZ	USA
KIMKEWITSCH, ABRAM	20	M	TLR	RR	ZZZZ	USA
LUPOLD, GITTEL	24	F	SGL	RR	ZZZZ	USA
MAKOWSKY, CSOIE	25	F	W	RR	ZZZZ	USA
IRA	.11	F	INFANT	RR	ZZZZ	USA
JABLON, JACOB	20	M	LABR	RR	ZZZZ	USA
WOLKOWSKY, ISRAEL	17	M	LABR	RR	ZZZZ	USA
OSCHER	14	M	UNKNOWN	RR	ZZZZ	USA
BEHR	9	M	CHILD	RR	ZZZZ	USA
MISCHKOWSKY, CHAIM	21	M	LABR	RR	ZZZZ	USA
EISENBERG, LEIB	21	M	UNKNOWN	RR	ZZZZ	USA
DAVIDSON, CHONE	21	M	UNKNOWN	RR	ZZZZ	USA
LANGMANN, LEIB	25	M	UNKNOWN	RR	ZZZZ	USA
BARAINSKY, BARTHOLOMY	16	M	LABR	RR	ZZZZ	USA
PERLSTEIN, SAMUEL	16	M	UNKNOWN	RR	ZZZZ	USA
HANNE	4	F	CHILD	RR	ZZZZ	USA
ROSENSOHN, HYMAN	19	M	LABR	RR	ZZZZ	USA
FEIM, SARA	15	F	SGL	RR	ZZZZ	USA

SHIP: POLARIA

FROM: HAMBURG
TO: NEW YORK
ARRIVED: 28 NOVEMBER 1883

PASSENGER	AGE	SEX	OCCUPATION	PRV	VIL	DES
BOWITSCHECK, MEICH	37	M	LABR	PL	ZZZZ	NY
KARAT, MIHAL	45	M	LABR	PL	ZZZZ	NY
SWAN, PURTZO	19	M	LABR	PL	ZZZZ	NY
COHN, EDUASA	26	M	TRDSMN	PL	ZZZZ	NY
LOUIS	26	M	TRDSMN	PL	ZZZZ	NY
LANBERFELD, SIMON	22	M	LABR	PL	ZZZZ	NY
STANISLAUS, MISUNAS	32	M	LABR	PL	ZZZZ	NY
SCHOZINSKI, JONAS	25	M	LABR	PL	ZZZZ	NY
SCHWARTIS, JOSEF	23	M	LABR	PL	ZZZZ	NY
BEIEVONOS, DOMINIK	16	M	LABR	PL	ZZZZ	NY
SCHWAGITZ, STABAU	25	M	LABR	PL	ZZZZ	NY

PASSENGER	AGE	SEX	OCCUPATION	PRV VIL DES
SALOMOK, WASIL	00	M	LABR	PLZZZZNY
BOGUS, FRANZISCHOK	00	M	LABR	PLZZZZNY
ANNA	00	F	W	PLZZZZNY
KORDOA, THOMAS	28	M	LABR	PLZZZZNY
MICHAL, BERTA	24	M	LABR	PLZZZZNY
PAWEL	24	M	LABR	PLZZZZNY
DUDAS	20	M	LABR	PLZZZZNY
PUHAS	57	M	LABR	PLZZZZNY
DUDAS, JOSEPH	29	M	LABR	PLZZZZNY
MORJAK, THOMAS	33	M	LABR	PLZZZZNY
DUDAS, LESVAW	25	M	LABR	PLZZZZNY
MICHAL, KIS	58	M	LABR	PLZZZZNY
BROSCHNISKA, AGNIS	20	M	LABR	PLZZZZNY
URBAN, JANOS	30	M	LABR	PLZZZZNY
KANO, GEORG	18	M	LABR	PLZZZZNY
MAZLAGA, MIHAL	28	M	LABR	PLZZZZNY
WORLOVSKI, IGNATZ	27	M	LABR	PLZZZZNY
ANNA	18	F	W	PLZZZZNY
SCHOST, JAN	29	M	LABR	PLZZZZNY
KLIM, WASSER	26	M	LABR	PLZZZZNY
REIZKO, MICHAL	24	M	LABR	PLZZZZNY
HONZA, WASSIG	7	M	CHILD	PLZZZZNY
HUPZE, JANOS	16	M	UNKNOWN	PLZZZZNY
CHIRNEZER, WASSER	7	M	CHILD	PLZZZZNY
KARRAS, ISTWAN	33	M	UNKNOWN	PLZZZZNY
MICHOWICZ, IWAN	7	M	CHILD	PLZZZZNY
TABATZKO, JANOS	32	M	LABR	PLZZZZNY
HOLMMIZ, IVAN	6	M	CHILD	PLZZZZNY
RETZ, RAD	27	M	LABR	PLZZZZNY
MASOR	27	M	LABR	PLZZZZNY
MASKORI, GASPER	25	M	LABR	PLZZZZNY
HALUPA, MIKOLAI	26	M	LABR	PLZZZZNY
GARBITZKI, ANDRE	25	M	LABR	PLZZZZNY
HALUPA, PHILIPP	7	M	CHILD	PLZZZZNY
RECMITZER, FETZOR	00	M	LABR	PLZZZZNY
SCISCHOSCHSKI, JANTONI	42	M	LABR	PLZZZZNY
KORBELOK, DAVID	6	M	CHILD	PLZZZZNY
KORAR, FEMIA	26	M	LABR	PLZZZZNY
DETOSKA, MAMROSCH	20	M	LABR	PLZZZZNY
KORBELOK, OZEF	40	M	LABR	PLZZZZNY
HAULUPA, PAWEL	27	M	LABR	PLZZZZNY
MELITSCHAK, INIHAL	30	M	LABR	PLZZZZNY
RETZ, PINSEH	24	M	LABR	PLZZZZNY
BOWICK, DOMHA	16	M	LABR	PLZZZZNY
WENSCHENAK, VICENTI	30	M	LABR	PLZZZZNY
WIELOSCH, VICTORIA	23	M	LABR	PLZZZZNY
JANHOWICZ, JANOS	21	M	LABR	PLZZZZNY
RUDICK, VALENTIN	24	M	LABR	PLZZZZNY
HAUSCHICK, MIHAL	22	M	LABR	PLZZZZNY
PALLSCHIK, JOSEF	24	M	LABR	PLZZZZNY
BIRESCH, JANKO	43	M	LABR	PLZZZZNY
PIONTROWSKI, FRANZ	14	M	CL	RRZZZZNY
FUHRMANN, MOSES	18	M	LABR	RRZZZZNY
BANER, FRIEDR.W.	40	M	LABR	RRZZZZNY
SCHEWE, ISAAK	28	M	TRDSMN	RRZZZZNY
PEILER, MOSES	28	M	JNR	RRZZZZNY
KARMANN, ERRY	40	M	PNTR	RRZZZZNY
SCHNEIDERMANN, A.	19	M	TLR	RRZZZZNY
DULLINSKY, A.	32	M	TLR	RRZZZZNY
SCHLESNIGER, GEDALIE	18	M	TLR	RRZZZZNY
RESSIN, LEWIN	23	M	TLR	RRZZZZNY
HOFFMAN, MOSES	32	M	TLR	RRZZZZNY
SKUT, BEREL	18	M	TLR	RRZZZZNY
GUTTSTEIN, FEIWEL	18	M	TLR	RRZZZZNY
ROSTHOWSKY, SELIK	42	M	TLR	RRZZZZNY
ROWIN	7	M	CHILD	RRZZZZNY
GELLKER, SCHEBSCHE	23	M	TLR	RRZZZZNY
LIEBERMANN, GEROSCH	17	M	TLR	RRZZZZNY
PESIMKES, BENJ.	33	M	TLR	RRZZZZNY
TANSCHEIN, BENJ.	39	M	TLR	RRZZZZNY
JOETZOW, CHAIM-H.	26	M	TLR	RRZZZZNY
WOTNEWSKY, ITZIZ	18	M	TLR	RRZZZZNY
LIEBERMANN, ARID	19	M	TLR	RRZZZZNY
WERNER, CARL	38	M	FARMER	RRZZZZNY
FRANZBLAN, G.A.	27	M	TRDSMN	RRZZZZNY
ORTSMANN, U	35	M	TRDSMN	RRZZZZNY
KURZER, ESTER	24	F	WO	RRZZZZNY
PALCK, GIETEL	25	F	WO	RRZZZZNY
SAMUEL	.10	M	INFANT	RRZZZZNY
GREMFELS, ROSA	30	F	WO	RRZZZZNY
ABICTAM	16	M	S	RRZZZZNY
MARLE	7	F	CHILD	RRZZZZNY
ESTE	5	F	CHILD	RRZZZZNY
MARGES	.10	M	INFANT	RRZZZZNY
HURWITZ, LEIB	35	M	MCHT	RRZZZZNY
JAPP, SCHORE	30	F	WO	RRZZZZNY
ITZIG	.10	M	INFANT	RRZZZZNY
CHATZPEL, LEIB	18	M	TRDSMN	RRZZZZNY
BASANOWSKY, STANISL.	20	M	TRDSMN	RRZZZZNY
KROHOWSKY, JULIUS	26	M	TRDSMN	RRZZZZNY
WAIDA, FR.	30	M	TRDSMN	RRZZZZNY
MOSME	30	F	W	RRZZZZNY
PROTER	7	M	CHILD	RRZZZZNY
JAN	.11	M	INFANT	RRZZZZNY
MARIAMM	.01	F	INFANT	RRZZZZNY
MARGNAZ, JULIUS	26	M	TRDSMN	RRZZZZNY
BAZSZICRA, PAWEL	32	M	TRDSMN	RRZZZZNY
LOCWENSTEIN, WALF	27	M	TRDSMN	RRZZZZNY
WICHMANN, WILH.	35	M	FARMER	RRZZZZNY
LEONNE	32	F	W	RRZZZZNY
ERNST	.10	M	INFANT	RRZZZZNY
MARIA	22	F	SI	RRZZZZNY
FILHENSTEM, L.B.	18	M	TRDSMN	RRZZZZNY
SCHINIDLER, RASSEL	55	F	WO	RRZZZZNY
LEPALSCHNISKY, LEISER	21	M	TRDSMN	RRZZZZNY
HITTE, RASSEL	27	F	WO	RRZZZZNY
GOLDE	.06	F	INFANT	RRZZZZNY
ROSAKOWSKY, LEIB	20	M	LABR	RRZZZZNY
MALTROWSKY, JACOB	18	M	LABR	RRZZZZNY
DUBLOWSKY, CHAIM	24	M	LABR	RRZZZZNY
GOLDBROD, LEIB	20	M	TNR	RRZZZZBAL
REICH, ROSALIE	26	F	WO	RRZZZZNY
RELLI	4	F	CHILD	RRZZZZNY
LEOPOLD	.11	M	INFANT	RRZZZZNY
GESELLA	.01	F	INFANT	RRZZZZNY

SHIP: GERMAIN

FROM: HAVRE
TO: NEW YORK
ARRIVED: 30 NOVEMBER 1883

PASSENGER	AGE	SEX	OCCUPATION	PRV VIL DES
WEBER, CARLO	19	F	UNKNOWN	PLZZZZMX
LADESLAS	30	M	ENGR	PLZZZZMX
HULERMANN, JACOB	21	M	HTR	PLZZZZNY
BERTHA	26	F	UNKNOWN	PLZZZZNY
MOISE	3	M	CHILD	PLZZZZNY
AGASTINI	2	M	CHILD	PLZZZZNY
LEONTINE	1	F	CHILD	PLZZZZNY
JUDE, SIMON	20	M	TLR	PLZZZZNY
ANNA	21	F	UNKNOWN	PLZZZZNY
RATTSTEIN, MORITZ	26	M	TLR	RRZZZZNY
RISKI	22	F	UNKNOWN	RRZZZZNY
ABRAHAM	1	M	CHILD	RRZZZZNY
KAUFFMAN, CHANE	26	M	UNKNOWN	RRZZZZNY
FCEICHT, LIB.	26	M	CPTR	RRZZZZNY
CHARE	22	F	UNKNOWN	RRZZZZNY
LUSCH	1	M	CHILD	RRZZZZNY
PANLOWSKI, PURAL	24	M	TLR	RRZZZZNY
LITHER	22	F	UNKNOWN	RRZZZZNY
BERL	3	M	CHILD	RRZZZZNY
LAUR	.06	F	INFANT	RRZZZZNY
GLAUR, WOLF	36	M	UNKNOWN	RRZZZZNY
SARAH	20	F	UNKNOWN	RRZZZZNY
HIRSH	.03	M	INFANT	RRZZZZNY

PASSENGER	AGE	SEX	OCCUPATION	PRV	VIL	DES
MANRELIE, LIBEL	24	M	TLR	RR	ZZZZ	NY
RASCHE, C.	20	F	UNKNOWN	RR	ZZZZ	NY
GNEWITZ, NICOL	42	M	UNKNOWN	RR	ZZZZ	NY
CHANNE	42	F	UNKNOWN	RR	ZZZZ	NY
BEZEL	9	M	CHILD	RR	ZZZZ	NY
ELKIN, LIB.	23	M	TNMK	RR	ZZZZ	NY
RACHEL	18	F	UNKNOWN	RR	ZZZZ	NY
ZURAFSKY, RUBIN	23	M	MCHT	RR	ZZZZ	NY
GISEL	20	F	UNKNOWN	RR	ZZZZ	NY
ORENS, JEREMIE	24	M	MCHT	RR	ZZZZ	NY

SHIP: DEVONIA

FROM: GLASGOW
TO: NEW YORK
ARRIVED: 01 DECEMBER 1883

PASSENGER	AGE	SEX	OCCUPATION	PRV	VIL	DES
LUDWIN, PETER	40	M	LABR	PL	ZZZZ	USA
GUDESKY, ANTON	31	M	UNKNOWN	PL	ZZZZ	USA
DERR, JULIAN	23	M	UNKNOWN	PL	ZZZZ	USA
OKRAMORAG, ANT.	40	M	UNKNOWN	PL	ZZZZ	USA
MYALES, JAN	23	M	UNKNOWN	PL	ZZZZ	USA
KGOB, JAN	4	M	CHILD	PL	ZZZZ	USA
RAKLIN, KASIMIR	20	M	LABR	PL	ZZZZ	USA
CASNES, VINCENZ	50	M	FARMER	PL	ZZZZ	USA
BARBARA	50	F	UNKNOWN	PL	ZZZZ	USA
THOMAS	25	M	FARMER	PL	ZZZZ	USA
MARIANNA	19	F	UNKNOWN	PL	ZZZZ	USA
ANTON	12	M	UNKNOWN	PL	ZZZZ	USA

SHIP: CHATEAN LAFFITE

FROM: BORDEAUX
TO: NEW YORK
ARRIVED: 03 DECEMBER 1883

PASSENGER	AGE	SEX	OCCUPATION	PRV	VIL	DES
WALLNAN, M.	27	M	TT	RR	ZZZZ	NY
WALLNANN, MMDE.	20	F	UNKNOWN	RR	ZZZZ	NY

SHIP: CITY OF CHESTER

FROM: LIVERPOOL AND QUEENSTOWN
TO: NEW YORK
ARRIVED: 03 DECEMBER 1883

PASSENGER	AGE	SEX	OCCUPATION	PRV	VIL	DES
ABRAHAMSON, OSKAR-M.	34	M	UNKNOWN	RR	ZZZZ	MI
AXELSON, AXEL-A.	17	M	UNKNOWN	RR	ZZZZ	MI
JOHANSON, VICTOR-A.	24	M	UNKNOWN	FN	ZZZZ	MI

SHIP: NECKAR

FROM: BREMEN
TO: NEW YORK
ARRIVED: 03 DECEMBER 1883

PASSENGER	AGE	SEX	OCCUPATION	PRV	VIL	DES
ROGOSCHINSKI, JOS.	21	M	UNKNOWN	RR	ZZZZ	USA

SHIP: STATE OF INDIANA

FROM: GLASGOW
TO: NEW YORK
ARRIVED: 03 DECEMBER 1883

PASSENGER	AGE	SEX	OCCUPATION	PRV	VIL	DES
SCHILINSKY, HIRSCH	20	M	LABR	RR	ZZZZ	USA
SCHOMLENSKI, CHANKEL	17	M	UNKNOWN	RR	ZZZZ	USA
POTANSKI, BARZIG	20	M	UNKNOWN	RR	ZZZZ	USA
STRAUS, MOSES	17	M	UNKNOWN	RR	ZZZZ	USA
BRIKER, JOSEPH	40	M	FARMER	RR	ZZZZ	USA
LAWENSKI, HIRSCH	29	M	LABR	RR	ZZZZ	USA
GETTEL	28	F	W	RR	ZZZZ	USA
ABRAHAM	7	M	CHILD	RR	ZZZZ	USA
BEILE	.07	F	INFANT	RR	ZZZZ	USA
CHAIE	.07	F	INFANT	RR	ZZZZ	USA
LAPIDUS, HIRSCH	15	M	LABR	RR	ZZZZ	USA
WEINER, LESER	35	M	UNKNOWN	RR	ZZZZ	USA
LAPKIN, CHAIM	12	M	UNKNOWN	RR	ZZZZ	USA
BERNSTEIN, MOSES	18	M	LABR	RR	ZZZZ	USA
ESTEL	20	F	W	RR	ZZZZ	USA
HERR, MARCUS	30	M	UNKNOWN	RR	ZZZZ	USA
WEMSTOK, LESER	17	M	UNKNOWN	RR	ZZZZ	USA
GUMPELOWITZ, SAMUEL	20	M	LABR	RR	ZZZZ	USA
SCHMITTMANNE, LEHWE	26	M	PDLR	RR	ZZZZ	USA
SCHESTAK, BEWZIEN	24	M	UNKNOWN	RR	ZZZZ	USA
HEKER, WACHMAN	25	M	LABR	RR	ZZZZ	USA
BATME, ELIGI	27	M	UNKNOWN	RR	ZZZZ	USA
KATZ, LEIBE	29	M	UNKNOWN	RR	ZZZZ	USA
JENGIEL, MARCUS	33	M	UNKNOWN	RR	ZZZZ	USA
NUCKEL, MOSES	17	M	UNKNOWN	RR	ZZZZ	USA
SCHMOLSKY, JEWEL	20	M	LABR	RR	ZZZZ	USA
KAZONITZ, HUSCH	23	M	UNKNOWN	RR	ZZZZ	USA
JURIN, CHAIM	23	M	UNKNOWN	RR	ZZZZ	USA
ROFIS, CHAIM	35	M	UNKNOWN	RR	ZZZZ	USA
SCHEMAN, JOSEPH	00	M	UNKNOWN	RR	ZZZZ	USA
SCHNIDEL, SALEMON	29	M	LABR	RR	ZZZZ	USA
SCHWARZ, DAVID	21	M	UNKNOWN	RR	ZZZZ	USA
SILBERMANN, WOLF	50	M	UNKNOWN	RR	ZZZZ	USA
WACHUMWOITZ, HARZ	14	M	PDLR	RR	ZZZZ	USA
DEUTSCH, NACHMAN	18	M	UNKNOWN	RR	ZZZZ	USA
FINK, MARDEL	25	M	LABR	RR	ZZZZ	USA
HINDE	28	F	W	RR	ZZZZ	USA
SUSSKIND	.06	F	INFANT	RR	ZZZZ	USA
BOTSCHAN, NATHAN	45	M	FARMER	RR	ZZZZ	USA
OBEINSHON, MIRELSCHE	41	M	LABR	RR	ZZZZ	USA
BENJAMIN	11	M	UNKNOWN	RR	ZZZZ	USA
KLAWANSKY, ELIAS	45	M	FARMER	RR	ZZZZ	USA
GLASER, ABRAHAM	37	M	UNKNOWN	RR	ZZZZ	USA
SACHS, ISSER	38	M	UNKNOWN	RR	ZZZZ	USA
LESKER, STEFAN	35	M	UNKNOWN	RR	ZZZZ	USA
LATNIS, IGNATZ	28	M	UNKNOWN	RR	ZZZZ	USA
CYALTINSKIS, JOHANN	30	M	UNKNOWN	RR	ZZZZ	USA
LATINS, JOHANN	23	M	UNKNOWN	RR	ZZZZ	USA

PASSENGER	AGE	SEX	OCCUPATION	PRV	VIL	DES

SHIP: ODER

FROM: BREMEN AND SOUTHAMPTON
TO: NEW YORK
ARRIVED: 04 DECEMBER 1883

PASSENGER	AGE	SEX	OCCUPATION	PRV	VIL	DES
ANTOWOSKI, JACOB	28	M	LABR	RR	ZZZZ	USA

SHIP: PERSIAN MONARCH

FROM: LONDON
TO: NEW YORK
ARRIVED: 04 DECEMBER 1883

PASSENGER	AGE	SEX	OCCUPATION	PRV	VIL	DES
GELLSTRUNK, ISADOR	20	M	LABR	PL	ZZZZ	NY
REISMAN, BERNHARD	29	M	UNKNOWN	PL	ZZZZ	NY
FRIEDMAN, LUDWIG	45	M	UNKNOWN	PL	ZZZZ	NY
JOHANNA	44	F	W	PL	ZZZZ	NY
JANE	15	F	UNKNOWN	PL	ZZZZ	NY
ALEXANDER	9	M	CHILD	PL	ZZZZ	NY
MOSCO, RACHAEL	26	F	W	PL	ZZZZ	NY
HENRY	2	M	CHILD	PL	ZZZZ	NY
ANNA	.09	F	INFANT	PL	ZZZZ	NY
SLADUWITZ, JACOB	33	M	UNKNOWN	PL	ZZZZ	NY
ROMANEWITZ, ANTON	33	M	UNKNOWN	PL	ZZZZ	NY
MALINOSKY, T.	33	M	UNKNOWN	PL	ZZZZ	NY
LIWONAYKIS, V.	26	M	UNKNOWN	PL	ZZZZ	NY
GIEDSUM, MATHEIS	21	M	UNKNOWN	PL	ZZZZ	NY
JAKUTZ, VINCENTO	26	M	UNKNOWN	PL	ZZZZ	NY
MARIE	30	F	UNKNOWN	PL	ZZZZ	NY
ANNA	.10	F	INFANT	PL	ZZZZ	NY
WALLUKANES, M.	23	M	LABR	PL	ZZZZ	NY
BUTKOWSKY, A.	27	M	UNKNOWN	PL	ZZZZ	NY
MILEWSKY, A.	36	M	UNKNOWN	PL	ZZZZ	NY
FRIED, J.	29	M	UNKNOWN	PL	ZZZZ	NY
JOZTWAN, W.	39	M	UNKNOWN	PL	ZZZZ	NY
DAHI, D.	40	M	UNKNOWN	RR	ZZZZ	NY
GOLD, M.	26	M	UNKNOWN	PL	ZZZZ	NY
KULWINSKY, M.	19	M	UNKNOWN	PL	ZZZZ	NY
GLUCHOWITZ, J.	33	M	UNKNOWN	PL	ZZZZ	NY
DEBOWITZ, S.	26	M	UNKNOWN	PL	ZZZZ	NY
SCHARIE, N.	33	M	UNKNOWN	PL	ZZZZ	NY
C.	12	M	UNKNOWN	PL	ZZZZ	NY
MINTZER, MEYER	37	M	LABR	PL	ZZZZ	NY
AARON	12	M	CH	PL	ZZZZ	NY
KAPLAN, ELIA	44	M	LABR	PL	ZZZZ	NY
KISCHNER, MYER	24	M	UNKNOWN	PL	ZZZZ	NY
LINKA, FRANTISH	32	M	UNKNOWN	PL	ZZZZ	NY
LITRAGTYS, M.	25	M	UNKNOWN	RR	ZZZZ	NY
POJAWIS, J.	43	M	UNKNOWN	PL	ZZZZ	NY
PELAREWSKY, J.	25	M	UNKNOWN	PL	ZZZZ	NY
DZERMEYKA, S.	21	M	UNKNOWN	PL	ZZZZ	NY
BIELSKY, K.	27	M	UNKNOWN	PL	ZZZZ	NY
PASKEWITZ, A.	24	M	UNKNOWN	PL	ZZZZ	NY
PAJEWIS, J.	38	M	UNKNOWN	PL	ZZZZ	NY
RZEPSKY, W.	40	M	UNKNOWN	RR	ZZZZ	NY
WAWSZKOWIG, P.	26	M	UNKNOWN	PL	ZZZZ	NY
SCHLEBITSCH, H.	50	M	UNKNOWN	PL	ZZZZ	NY
STANISKY, F.	19	M	UNKNOWN	PL	ZZZZ	NY
XAWEC, E.	21	M	UNKNOWN	PL	ZZZZ	NY
BROWA, P.	12	M	CH	PL	ZZZZ	NY
MASETSKY, J.	32	M	LABR	PL	ZZZZ	NY
BEROWICH, D.	20	M	UNKNOWN	PL	ZZZZ	NY
TSEBATSCH, B.	12	M	CH	PL	ZZZZ	NY
SCHISHOWITZ, S.	11	M	UNKNOWN	PL	ZZZZ	NY
POWIAK, T.	36	M	LABR	PL	ZZZZ	NY
A.	5	M	CHILD	PL	ZZZZ	NY
PEPPER, ISAAC	50	M	LABR	PL	ZZZZ	NY
EVA	66	F	W	PL	ZZZZ	NY

SHIP: WAESLAND

FROM: ANTWERP
TO: NEW YORK
ARRIVED: 04 DECEMBER 1883

PASSENGER	AGE	SEX	OCCUPATION	PRV	VIL	DES
SPEWACK, FRANY	24	M	FARMER	RR	ZZZZ	DET
TESSACK, GEORGE	17	M	FARMER	RR	ZZZZ	DET

SHIP: CIRCASSIA

FROM: GLASGOW
TO: NEW YORK
ARRIVED: 05 DECEMBER 1883

PASSENGER	AGE	SEX	OCCUPATION	PRV	VIL	DES
LANDON, FEIGE	32	F	W	RR	ZZZZ	USA
SARAH	11	F	UNKNOWN	RR	ZZZZ	USA
DIBORE	10	F	UNKNOWN	RR	ZZZZ	USA
RIETTE	8	F	CHILD	RR	ZZZZ	USA
NATHAN	6	M	CHILD	RR	ZZZZ	USA
ETTIE	4	F	CHILD	RR	ZZZZ	USA
JETTE	.10	F	INFANT	RR	ZZZZ	USA

SHIP: MORAVIA

FROM: HAMBURG AND HAVRE
TO: NEW YORK
ARRIVED: 05 DECEMBER 1883

PASSENGER	AGE	SEX	OCCUPATION	PRV	VIL	DES
SCHIMKOWITZ, EISICK	45	M	UNKNOWN	RR	ZZZZ	USA
BLECHARSCH, ELION	21	M	UNKNOWN	RR	ZZZZ	USA
NACHUM	18	M	UNKNOWN	RR	ZZZZ	USA
LUBER, SCHLOME	18	M	TLR	RR	ZZZZ	USA
LIPKOWITZ, JOSEF	35	M	HAMF	RR	ZZZZ	USA
BORAX, SAMUEL	24	M	JNR	RR	ZZZZ	USA
SIMONSKY, ITZEK	19	M	SHMK	RR	ZZZZ	USA
SCHIMSCHOWITZ, KODISCH	19	M	TNMK	RR	ZZZZ	USA
BECHER, CHAIM	24	M	UNKNOWN	RR	ZZZZ	USA
RUDMANN, ARON	22	M	UNKNOWN	RR	ZZZZ	USA
MEYER	43	M	UNKNOWN	RR	ZZZZ	USA
STAKER, ALEXANDRE	20	M	UNKNOWN	RR	ZZZZ	USA
WOJECHOSKA, ANNA	19	F	SGL	RR	ZZZZ	USA
LEIBOWITZ, RAPHAEL	23	M	TLR	RR	ZZZZ	USA
LERAK, ABRAH.	18	M	UNKNOWN	RR	ZZZZ	USA
TANEL, SCHOLEM	50	M	CGRMKR	RR	ZZZZ	USA
MERE	16	F	D	RR	ZZZZ	USA
MARGOWSKI, EPHRAIM	18	M	PTR	RR	ZZZZ	USA
ZERSTNER, NACHIM	19	M	MSN	RR	ZZZZ	USA
SOFAR, JOSEF	50	M	LABR	RR	ZZZZ	USA
MARIASCHE	45	F	W	RR	ZZZZ	USA
LIEB--N, MORDSCHE	39	M	BCHR	RR	ZZZZ	USA
KRUMINS, KARNI	23	M	LABR	RR	ZZZZ	USA
SCHUSTER, CHAIM	37	M	UNKNOWN	RR	ZZZZ	USA
EPSTEIN, JOEL	23	M	UNKNOWN	RR	ZZZZ	USA
BRAUDY, ISRAEL	18	M	UNKNOWN	RR	ZZZZ	USA
LEWITANSKI, HERZ.	17	M	DLR	RR	ZZZZ	USA
JACOB	18	M	UNKNOWN	RR	ZZZZ	USA
KIWIANSKI, HIRSCH	21	M	UNKNOWN	RR	ZZZZ	USA
LIWINOSKI, PESACH	21	M	UNKNOWN	RR	ZZZZ	USA
METS, LUDWIG	18	M	UNKNOWN	RR	ZZZZ	USA
STEINERT, MATES	26	M	UNKNOWN	RR	ZZZZ	USA
LEWINSKI, SAMUEL	28	M	UNKNOWN	RR	ZZZZ	USA
ZIRALSKI, DAVID	22	M	UNKNOWN	RR	ZZZZ	USA
SCHELBOLSKI, SALOMON	18	M	UNKNOWN	RR	ZZZZ	USA

PASSENGER	AGE	SEX	OCCUPATION	PRV	VIL	DES
SCHMIGELSKI, SCHOLEM	28	M	LABR	RR	ZZZZ	USA
HUDOSCH, JANKEL	15	M	UNKNOWN	RR	ZZZZ	USA
SABOL, ANNETTE	22	F	SGL	RR	ZZZZ	USA
MEYER, FRANK	41	M	LABR	RR	ZZZZ	USA
MERKEL, FEIWEL	35	M	UNKNOWN	RR	ZZZZ	USA
FINKEL, SIMSON	32	M	UNKNOWN	RR	ZZZZ	USA
HORWETZ, JANKEL	32	M	LABR	RR	ZZZZ	USA
BELKOWITSCH, FEIGEL	36	M	UNKNOWN	RR	ZZZZ	USA
RINOMOWITSCH, JOSCHEL	49	M	UNKNOWN	RR	ZZZZ	USA
SOCHOWSKI, JAN	33	M	DLR	RR	ZZZZ	USA
SCHOENKRET, HENOCH	70	M	UNKNOWN	RR	ZZZZ	USA
RIEVE	65	F	W	RR	ZZZZ	USA
RISOWSKI, ITOCHY	20	M	LABR	RR	ZZZZ	USA
BUDREWITZ, AUGUST	36	M	UNKNOWN	RR	ZZZZ	USA
JESCHOWOFSKI, JAN	26	M	LABR	RR	ZZZZ	USA
SCHER, RIEFKE	28	F	W	RR	ZZZZ	USA
CHANNE	4	F	CHILD	RR	ZZZZ	USA
SARA	.11	F	INFANT	RR	ZZZZ	USA
LEWUSSON, WITTE	37	F	W	RR	ZZZZ	USA
OREL	23	M	DLR	RR	ZZZZ	USA
SAMUEL	6	M	CHILD	RR	ZZZZ	USA
JOCHWED	4	M	CHILD	RR	ZZZZ	USA
SPRINZE	2	M	CHILD	RR	ZZZZ	USA
FEIN, ISAAI	23	M	DLR	RR	ZZZZ	USA
GUZ----, SIMON	19	M	LABR	RR	ZZZZ	USA
EVA	24	F	SGL	RR	ZZZZ	USA
MASSIKAT, OSCAR	24	M	LABR	RR	ZZZZ	USA
STANKOWAIT, FRANZ	26	M	UNKNOWN	RR	ZZZZ	USA
BOLDIJA, ALEXANDER	34	M	LABR	RR	ZZZZ	USA
GUSZEWSKI, WLADISLAW	20	M	UNKNOWN	RR	ZZZZ	USA
SANKIEWICZ, STANISLAUS	25	M	UNKNOWN	RR	ZZZZ	USA
MARIANE	30	F	W	RR	ZZZZ	USA
JONAS, JACOB	20	M	CGRMKR	RR	ZZZZ	USA
GOLDFARB, TAUBE	25	F	W	RR	ZZZZ	USA
SCHEINE	.11	F	INFANT	RR	ZZZZ	USA
SIMANSKI, LEA	18	F	SGL	RR	ZZZZ	USA
SALODOCHIN, VIGDAR	35	M	UNKNOWN	RR	ZZZZ	USA
SCHIMANZEK, MOSES	18	M	SHMK	RR	ZZZZ	USA
FRANK, BERL	14	M	UNKNOWN	RR	ZZZZ	USA
BREKSTEIN, ISRAEL	18	M	UNKNOWN	RR	ZZZZ	USA
DISNICKY, GABRIEL	25	F	UNKNOWN	RR	ZZZZ	USA
UELWER, SCHLOME	30	M	TLR	RR	ZZZZ	USA
PRANKOWSKI, TEWIE	34	F	SGL	RR	ZZZZ	USA
RILINSKY, CHANNE	20	F	UNKNOWN	RR	ZZZZ	USA
SKRZYNSKI, SCHMUL	20	M	LABR	RR	ZZZZ	USA
KOLIFAR, FRUNNE	18	F	SGL	RR	ZZZZ	USA
MALOCZNIK, BENZEL	20	M	LABR	RR	ZZZZ	USA
BEINIMOWITZ, SCHMUEL	56	M	UNKNOWN	RR	ZZZZ	USA
SCHIE, HOFMAN	20	M	UNKNOWN	RR	ZZZZ	USA
KOUKIL, FRANZISKA	22	F	SGL	RR	ZZZZ	USA
KRUSZEWSKA, MARIE	27	F	W	RR	ZZZZ	USA
JAN	7	M	CHILD	RR	ZZZZ	USA
FRANZ	5	M	CHILD	RR	ZZZZ	USA
JOSEF	.09	M	INFANT	RR	ZZZZ	USA
LINITZKY, CHAIE	31	F	W	RR	ZZZZ	USA
DOBE	.11	F	INFANT	RR	ZZZZ	USA
RACHEL	.01	F	INFANT	RR	ZZZZ	USA
SOFAR, ELKE	9	F	CHILD	RR	ZZZZ	USA
KAUFFMANN, LEO	24	F	W	RR	ZZZZ	USA
HERSCHEL	6	M	CHILD	RR	ZZZZ	USA
JOCHWED	.11	M	INFANT	RR	ZZZZ	USA
RIWKE	.11	M	INFANT	RR	ZZZZ	USA
LIPA, SALOMON	44	M	TLR	RR	ZZZZ	USA
BUXBAUM, MARIUS	47	M	DLR	RR	ZZZZ	USA
EIDEL	44	F	W	RR	ZZZZ	USA
REFKA	9	F	CHILD	RR	ZZZZ	USA
MINKA	8	F	CHILD	RR	ZZZZ	USA
CHOLE	7	F	CHILD	RR	ZZZZ	USA
LECHNER, LEIB	40	M	DLR	RR	ZZZZ	USA
SEELING, CAROLINE	19	F	SGL	RR	ZZZZ	USA

SHIP: WESTPHALIA

FROM: HAMBURG AND HAVRE
TO: NEW YORK
ARRIVED: 05 DECEMBER 1883

PASSENGER	AGE	SEX	OCCUPATION	PRV	VIL	DES
LIKER, BARNCH	17	M	UNKNOWN	RR	ZZZZ	NY
FUHRMANN, MEIER	37	M	DLR	RR	ZZZZ	NY
BRUSK, ANG.	22	M	LABR	RR	ZZZZ	NY
SACOWISZ, DOMINIC	29	M	LABR	RR	ZZZZ	NY
KRUPPINSKY, PETER	17	M	LABR	RR	ZZZZ	NY
BILDA, CASIMIR	35	M	LABR	RR	ZZZZ	NY
KONNINECZ, VINCENT	24	M	LABR	RR	ZZZZ	NY
SAKRZEWSKI, VINCENT	26	M	LABR	RR	ZZZZ	NY
BILDA, JOSEF	18	M	LABR	RR	ZZZZ	NY
KOSSAKOFSKI, JOSEF	18	M	LABR	RR	ZZZZ	NY
OSERMANN, WULF	31	M	LABR	RR	ZZZZ	NY
ARKIN, ROSA	19	F	SGL	RR	ZZZZ	NY
MENDEL, PAULINE	20	F	SGL	RR	ZZZZ	NY
SIRER, MOSES	16	M	LABR	RR	ZZZZ	NY
ILIANSKY, ABRAHAM	34	M	DLR	RR	ZZZZ	NY
FUNDLIER, MOSES	17	M	CL	RR	ZZZZ	NY
WIRNSKY, VINCENTE	18	M	LABR	RR	ZZZZ	NY
EISENBERG, SCHEINE	16	F	SGL	RR	ZZZZ	NY
NACHUMSON, MOSES	18	M	DLR	RR	ZZZZ	NY
LADICKON, RASCHE	18	F	SGL	RR	ZZZZ	NY
LEVINSON, CHENNIE	20	M	DLR	RR	ZZZZ	NY
SCHLOSSBERG, MOSES	18	M	DLR	RR	ZZZZ	NY
NARKUNSKY, JANKEL	20	M	DLR	RR	ZZZZ	NY
YNST, PAUL	28	M	ENGR	RR	ZZZZ	NY
SOHEMISS, ANDR.	24	M	LABR	RR	ZZZZ	NY
GOMANTZKY, JOSES	21	M	LABR	RR	ZZZZ	NY
MISKOVIE, ANTONIN	24	M	LABR	RR	ZZZZ	NY
GEWIAK, VINCENT	20	M	LABR	RR	ZZZZ	NY
KEVLECK, PETER	18	M	LABR	RR	ZZZZ	NY
GOVESDAZ, JAN	24	M	LABR	RR	ZZZZ	NY
SEIDENBERG, CARL	20	M	LABR	RR	ZZZZ	NY
COHN, ARNOLD	9	M	CHILD	RR	ZZZZ	NY
KAPLAN, ARON	20	M	LABR	RR	ZZZZ	NY
KAHN, JOHANN	21	M	DLR	RR	ZZZZ	NY
HIRSCHSOHN, HILLEL	20	M	DLR	RR	ZZZZ	NY
GLUCKMANN, ZIPPE	24	F	W	RR	ZZZZ	NY
ELIAS	.11	M	INFANT	RR	ZZZZ	NY
MAKAREWICZ, WLADISL.	20	M	LABR	RR	ZZZZ	NY
BOCHHENK, JOH.	20	M	LABR	RR	ZZZZ	NY
GOVDZIENSKY, LEIB	40	M	LABR	RR	ZZZZ	NY
ITTE	9	F	CHILD	RR	ZZZZ	NY
FREUND, SCHMUHL	21	M	DLR	RR	ZZZZ	NY
ABRAHMOWITZ, SALMON	30	M	DLR	RR	ZZZZ	NY
KAMINSKY, PIOL	28	M	LABR	RR	ZZZZ	NY
MANDL, JETTE	20	F	SGL	RR	ZZZZ	NY
ETTELSEN, MALKE	38	F	W	RR	ZZZZ	NY
RASHE	9	F	CHILD	RR	ZZZZ	NY
ZIWIE	8	F	CHILD	RR	ZZZZ	NY
PESHE	7	F	CHILD	RR	ZZZZ	NY
DINE	5	F	CHILD	RR	ZZZZ	NY
DEBORA	3	F	CHILD	RR	ZZZZ	NY
HERSCH	.11	M	INFANT	RR	ZZZZ	NY
VESISEVACKY, BEILE	26	F	W	RR	ZZZZ	NY
SIMON	4	M	CHILD	RR	ZZZZ	NY
SZEDLINSKY, JOSEL	55	M	LABR	RR	ZZZZ	NY
WYSOCKI, GABRIEL	20	M	FARMER	RR	ZZZZ	NY
SAFFE, SALOMON	55	M	LABR	RR	ZZZZ	NY
MATLE	50	F	W	RR	ZZZZ	NY
MOSES	9	M	CHILD	RR	ZZZZ	NY
HIRSCH	8	M	CHILD	RR	ZZZZ	NY
CITRINBLATT, FEIGE	40	F	W	RR	ZZZZ	NY
ETTEL	9	F	CHILD	RR	ZZZZ	NY
SLATE	8	F	CHILD	RR	ZZZZ	NY
DAVID	.11	M	INFANT	RR	ZZZZ	NY
SARA	.01	F	INFANT	RR	ZZZZ	NY
LIWAJ, SALOMON	23	M	LABR	RR	ZZZZ	NY
LICHT, FEIWE	23	M	LABR	RR	ZZZZ	NY
SEIGER, MEIER	16	M	LABR	RR	ZZZZ	NY

PASSENGER	AGE	SEX	OCCUPATION	PRV	VIL	DES
KAUFMANN, CHAJE	19	M	LABR	RR	ZZZZ	NY
SCHMULG, MEIER	20	M	LABR	RR	ZZZZ	NY
SABAWICK, LANRENZ	26	M	LABR	RR	ZZZZ	NY
WOBITZKI, JOSEF	40	M	LABR	RR	ZZZZ	NY
ECKSTEIN, AARON	29	M	LABR	RR	ZZZZ	NY
WITOWSKY, H.	40	M	HAMF	RR	ZZZZ	NY
SELZER, FANNY	9	F	CHILD	RR	ZZZZ	NY

SHIP: FRANCE

FROM: HAVRE
TO: NEW YORK
ARRIVED: 07 DECEMBER 1883

PASSENGER	AGE	SEX	OCCUPATION	PRV	VIL	DES
CADISCH, JACOB	22	M	UNKNOWN	PL	ZZZZ	UNK
KUSTIN, MOSES	28	M	UNKNOWN	PL	ZZZZ	NY
SARAH	25	F	UNKNOWN	PL	ZZZZ	NY
LUBARSKY, MOSES	23	M	TLR	PL	ZZZZ	NY
REBECCA	21	F	UNKNOWN	PL	ZZZZ	NY
LINETZKI, JACOB	35	M	SHMK	PL	ZZZZ	NY
ROSA	28	F	UNKNOWN	PL	ZZZZ	NY
FUGES	3	M	CHILD	PL	ZZZZ	NY
GEDMANN, MOSES	29	M	LABR	PL	ZZZZ	NY
CHAGE	27	M	UNKNOWN	PL	ZZZZ	NY
LEB.	1	M	CHILD	PL	ZZZZ	NY
ROSEFELD, ZADOKS	34	M	LABR	PL	ZZZZ	NY
AMALIE	29	F	UNKNOWN	PL	ZZZZ	NY
BELLA	5	F	CHILD	PL	ZZZZ	NY
WECHSLER, CHANNA	41	M	UNKNOWN	PL	ZZZZ	CH
GOLDE	38	F	UNKNOWN	PL	ZZZZ	CH
CHASCHE	1	M	CHILD	PL	ZZZZ	CH

SHIP: CITY OF CHICAGO

FROM: LIVERPOOL AND QUEENSTOWN
TO: NEW YORK
ARRIVED: 08 DECEMBER 1883

PASSENGER	AGE	SEX	OCCUPATION	PRV	VIL	DES
RUNDSHAN, HENRIK-S.	37	M	UNKNOWN	RR	ZZZZ	NY

SHIP: MAIN

FROM: BREMEN
TO: NEW YORK
ARRIVED: 08 DECEMBER 1883

PASSENGER	AGE	SEX	OCCUPATION	PRV	VIL	DES
MAJEWSKI, LEOPOLD	26	M	FARMER	RR	ZZZZ	USA
PLUCINSKA, CATHR.	30	F	W	RR	ZZZZ	USA
VERONIKA	7	F	CHILD	RR	ZZZZ	USA
LUCIE	3	F	CHILD	RR	ZZZZ	USA
VICTORIA	.11	F	INFANT	RR	ZZZZ	USA

SHIP: SCHIEDAM

FROM: ROTTERDAM
TO: NEW YORK
ARRIVED: 10 DECEMBER 1883

PASSENGER	AGE	SEX	OCCUPATION	PRV	VIL	DES
ANDROLEWITZ, JACOB	44	M	FARMER	PL	ZZZZ	USA
MAGDALENA	25	F	UNKNOWN	PL	ZZZZ	USA
MARIA	6	F	CHILD	PL	ZZZZ	USA
ZERRIDUWSKY, MARTYN	20	M	LABR	PL	ZZZZ	USA
KLITSCHIN, SALOMON	21	M	MCHT	PL	ZZZZ	USA
LEWIN, MOSES	33	M	MCHT	PL	ZZZZ	USA
KOSNIKOWSKY, ISRAEL	17	M	MCHT	PL	ZZZZ	USA
KEBERT, ANTON	24	M	TLR	PL	ZZZZ	USA
JOHANN	20	M	TLR	PL	ZZZZ	USA
SAGERUT, BERNH.	25	M	NN	PL	ZZZZ	USA

SHIP: THE QUEEN

FROM: LIVERPOOL
TO: NEW YORK
ARRIVED: 10 DECEMBER 1883

PASSENGER	AGE	SEX	OCCUPATION	PRV	VIL	DES
SABALASKI, ABIN	20	M	CGRMKR	RR	ZZZZ	USA

SHIP: GELLERT

FROM: HAMBURG AND HAVRE
TO: NEW YORK
ARRIVED: 11 DECEMBER 1883

PASSENGER	AGE	SEX	OCCUPATION	PRV	VIL	DES
WOLAJTYS, ANDRYZ	24	M	LABR	RR	ZZZZ	USA
MARGOLINS, CACILIE	36	F	W	RR	ZZZZ	USA
WARSCHOWICK, ISAAC	18	M	CL	RR	ZZZZ	USA
ROMANOWSKY, FRANZKA.	23	F	W	RR	ZZZZ	USA
EVA	.11	F	INFANT	RR	ZZZZ	USA
CBLOJINA, KALMAN	33	M	TLR	RR	ZZZZ	USA
BRAND, SALMAN	44	M	UNKNOWN	RR	ZZZZ	USA
GLEICHER, MOZES	42	M	UNKNOWN	RR	ZZZZ	USA
GOLDINGER, ABRAH.	19	M	GDSM	RR	ZZZZ	USA
MOSES	9	M	CHILD	RR	ZZZZ	USA
MENDELSOHN, MEIER	20	M	DLR	RR	ZZZZ	USA
GOLDSTEIN, ALTER	20	M	TNMK	RR	ZZZZ	USA
FINKELSTEIN, LEISER	32	M	TNMK	RR	ZZZZ	USA
HOELFMANN, ARON	19	M	DLR	RR	ZZZZ	USA
HEVEZKA, WICENTI	21	M	UNKNOWN	RR	ZZZZ	USA
BINEWITZ, MAREIN	29	M	UNKNOWN	RR	ZZZZ	USA
BOLUNAS, SYLVESTER	23	M	LABR	RR	ZZZZ	USA
KAZEMIKS, FRANZ	23	M	UNKNOWN	RR	ZZZZ	USA
KARASKA, IVAN	24	M	UNKNOWN	RR	ZZZZ	USA
BUSCHKEWITZ, KARL	49	M	UNKNOWN	RR	ZZZZ	USA
THERESE	38	F	W	RR	ZZZZ	USA
KESPEROWITZ, WILH.	24	M	LABR	RR	ZZZZ	USA
MIGATZ, HEINR.	22	M	CGRMKR	RR	ZZZZ	USA
SPEISCHAENDER, KALMAN	21	M	SHMK	RR	ZZZZ	USA
MARKUSEWITZ, JUDEL	17	M	MCHT	RR	ZZZZ	USA
YARGAITIS, KASIMIR	24	M	LABR	RR	ZZZZ	USA
GRAUSLIS, PETER	21	M	FARMER	RR	ZZZZ	USA
PAROSELSKI, MOSES	9	M	CHILD	RR	ZZZZ	USA
PAPLER, WOLF	40	M	TLR	RR	ZZZZ	USA
PIMSTEIN, ELTER	35	M	BKBNDR	RR	ZZZZ	USA
GAETNER, ADOLF	30	M	TNR	RR	ZZZZ	USA
RECHTER, JOSEF	30	M	TLR	RR	ZZZZ	USA
CHAIE	28	F	W	RR	ZZZZ	USA

PASSENGER	AGE	SEX	OCCUPATION	PRV	VIL	DES
MISKY, ANTON	31	M	UNKNOWN	RR	ZZZZ	USA
DOMENIKA	24	F	W	RR	ZZZZ	USA
KEJZ, JAN	17	M	LABR	RR	ZZZZ	USA
LIRUZ, AGATHE	25	F	SGL	RR	ZZZZ	USA
MARGAITIS, JACOB	32	M	LABR	RR	ZZZZ	USA
KIN, LUDWIG	40	M	UNKNOWN	RR	ZZZZ	USA
JUNG, KARL	24	M	UNKNOWN	RR	ZZZZ	USA
GEUSINSKY, ANTON	30	M	UNKNOWN	RR	ZZZZ	USA
GEJUSISCH, MICHAEL	26	M	UNKNOWN	RR	ZZZZ	USA
BONATH, GEORG	42	M	UNKNOWN	RR	ZZZZ	USA
MARIE	9	F	CHILD	RR	ZZZZ	USA
BUSCHKEWITZ, IGNATZ	.02	M	INFANT	RR	ZZZZ	USA
HOWITZ, CHEIE	23	F	SGL	RR	ZZZZ	USA
EISENBERG, HEYMANN	18	M	DLR	RR	ZZZZ	USA
MENDELSOHN, CHAIM	19	M	BCHR	RR	ZZZZ	USA
EISENBERG, ROSA	19	F	SGL	RR	ZZZZ	USA
ABERMANN, NOSSEN	19	M	DLR	RR	ZZZZ	USA
SILBERMANN, NATHAN	20	M	UNKNOWN	RR	ZZZZ	USA
WEINBERG, HANNE	62	F	FARMER	RR	ZZZZ	USA
ROSENDORF, MENDEL	20	M	UNKNOWN	RR	ZZZZ	USA
IDELS, MAUCHEL	20	M	UNKNOWN	RR	ZZZZ	USA
ADAMOWICH, MAGDA.	20	F	SGL	RR	ZZZZ	USA
BROTZKI, CHAIE	40	F	W	RR	ZZZZ	USA
CHAIE	35	F	UNKNOWN	RR	ZZZZ	USA
SARA	9	F	CHILD	RR	ZZZZ	USA
SMOLINSKI, BENJAMIN	21	M	BRR	RR	ZZZZ	USA
ARKEIN, CHANE	28	F	W	RR	ZZZZ	USA
CHANNE	.11	F	INFANT	RR	ZZZZ	USA
MOSES	.01	M	INFANT	RR	ZZZZ	USA
BLUM, CHANEL	20	M	LABR	RR	ZZZZ	USA
KLAWANSKY, CHAIM	47	M	UNKNOWN	RR	ZZZZ	USA
FULWMANN, KALMAN	18	M	UNKNOWN	RR	ZZZZ	USA
RAHEL	20	F	SGL	RR	ZZZZ	USA
HUTZLEY, HERRM.	20	M	LABR	RR	ZZZZ	USA
JAWITZ, NOCHUM	9	M	CHILD	RR	ZZZZ	USA
KUBILLUS, JOSEF	30	M	LABR	RR	ZZZZ	USA
DEVILLUS, LOUIS	29	M	UNKNOWN	RR	ZZZZ	USA
NOWICKI, KANSTANTIN	28	M	UNKNOWN	RR	ZZZZ	USA
MINZOT, MAZE	25	M	FARMER	RR	ZZZZ	USA
EPPSTEIN, PESCHE	29	F	W	RR	ZZZZ	USA
SARAH	9	F	CHILD	RR	ZZZZ	USA
DAVID	8	M	CHILD	RR	ZZZZ	USA
WOLF	7	M	CHILD	RR	ZZZZ	USA
ETTE	5	F	CHILD	RR	ZZZZ	USA
BARUCH	.11	M	INFANT	RR	ZZZZ	USA
ELKES, FEIWUSCH	18	M	UNKNOWN	RR	ZZZZ	USA
MARIANE	23	F	UNKNOWN	RR	ZZZZ	USA
RIBATZKI, ISAAC	18	M	FELMO	RR	ZZZZ	USA
RACHEL	20	F	W	RR	ZZZZ	USA
CZENSTOCHOWSKY, MARCUS	20	M	SHMK	RR	ZZZZ	USA
EPPSTEIN, WOLF	12	M	BY	RR	ZZZZ	USA

SHIP: ERIN

FROM: LONDON
TO: NEW YORK
ARRIVED: 12 DECEMBER 1883

PASSENGER	AGE	SEX	OCCUPATION	PRV	VIL	DES
DAVIS, SOL.	24	M	CGRMKR	PL	ZZZZ	USA

SHIP: INDIA

FROM: HAMBURG
TO: NEW YORK
ARRIVED: 12 DECEMBER 1883

PASSENGER	AGE	SEX	OCCUPATION	PRV	VIL	DES
GISA, JAN	36	M	LABR	PL	ZZZZ	NY
KAUFMANN, JACOB	21	M	MCHT	RR	ZZZZ	NY
FOLCH, LOUIS	38	M	TRDSMN	RR	ZZZZ	NY
NACHME	15	F	D	RR	ZZZZ	NY
LERANEWICZ, MANIKA	21	F	SGL	RR	ZZZZ	UNK
BIRON, NAFTOLM	40	M	TRDSMN	RR	ZZZZ	NY
PESSEL	16	M	S	RR	ZZZZ	NY
KIENWICZ, JAN	40	M	TRDSMN	RR	ZZZZ	NY
NENCENTEA	24	F	W	RR	ZZZZ	NY
MARIANNE	.07	F	INFANT	RR	ZZZZ	NY
FESCHER, SOARAL-M.	21	M	MCHT	RR	ZZZZ	NY

SHIP: LABRADOR

FROM: HAVRE
TO: NEW YORK
ARRIVED: 12 DECEMBER 1883

PASSENGER	AGE	SEX	OCCUPATION	PRV	VIL	DES
FRIEDMANN, CH.SEIB	18	M	TLR	RR	ZZZZ	NY

SHIP: BELGENLAND

FROM: ANTWERP
TO: NEW YORK
ARRIVED: 13 DECEMBER 1883

PASSENGER	AGE	SEX	OCCUPATION	PRV	VIL	DES
KEISEC, PAUL	20	M	SVNT	PL	ZZZZ	MN
WASTIZLIEK, VAL.	38	M	SMH	PL	ZZZZ	MN
SEHEROWSKY, JOHN	20	M	GDNR	PL	ZZZZ	MN

SHIP: LAKE HURON

FROM: LIVERPOOL
TO: NEW YORK
ARRIVED: 13 DECEMBER 1883

PASSENGER	AGE	SEX	OCCUPATION	PRV	VIL	DES
FREEDMAN, H.	25	F	W	RR	ZZZZ	CAN
LILY	11	F	CH	RR	ZZZZ	CAN
JAS.	8	M	CHILD	RR	ZZZZ	CAN
JUO.	2	M	CHILD	RR	ZZZZ	CAN
ROBUKE, JOKAL	17	M	UNKNOWN	RR	ZZZZ	CAN
COHEN, HORRIER	21	M	UNKNOWN	RR	ZZZZ	CAN

PASSENGER	AGE	SEX	OCCUPATION	PRVL	VIL	DES

SHIP: STATE OF GEORGIA

FROM: GLASGOW AND LARNE
TO: NEW YORK
ARRIVED: 13 DECEMBER 1883

PASSENGER	AGE	SEX	OCCUPATION	PV DES
SERVIANSKY, DAVID	24	M	PDLR	RRZZZZUSA
KATZ, SAUL	24	M	UNKNOWN	RRZZZZUSA
SCHMIGER, SIMON	39	M	UNKNOWN	RRZZZZUSA
DWORE	21	F	W	RRZZZZUSA
FEIWEL	12	M	CH	RRZZZZUSA
ABE	7	M	CHILD	RRZZZZUSA
SARAH	6	F	CHILD	RRZZZZUSA
JUDE	2	M	CHILD	RRZZZZUSA
ITTE	1	F	CHILD	RRZZZZUSA
HERSHKPWITZ, ABRAH.	19	M	PDLR	RRZZZZUSA
WILANTSHECK, GITEL	24	F	SP	RRZZZZUSA
SEGAL, JOSSEL	00	M	PDLR	RRZZZZUSA
KLEINFUSS, SIME	17	F	CH	RRZZZZUSA
POELOSISKY, SAMUEL	18	M	PDLR	RRZZZZUSA
SARAH	15	F	SP	RRZZZZUSA
WIEDERMANN, NATGI	18	M	CL	RRZZZZUSA
BERNH.	00	M	BY	RRZZZZUSA
WOLPER, M.	00	M	PDLR	RRZZZZUSA
MARKUS, B.	00	M	MLR	RRZZZZUSA
GULBINUS, IVAN	00	M	LABR	RRZZZZUSA
TAMISKY, IVAN	00	M	UNKNOWN	RRZZZZUSA
SAMENTOSKY, NACHME	21	M	TLR	RRZZZZUSA
KREMER, M.	21	M	UNKNOWN	RRZZZZUSA
KUPER, DANL.	32	M	UNKNOWN	RRZZZZUSA

SHIP: ETHIOPIA

FROM: GLASGOW AND MOVILLE
TO: NEW YORK
ARRIVED: 14 DECEMBER 1883

PASSENGER	AGE	SEX	OCCUPATION	PV DES
FELORICK, JOHAN	40	M	LABR	RRZZZZUSA
ANNA	38	F	UNKNOWN	RRZZZZUSA
JOHAN	10	M	UNKNOWN	RRZZZZUSA
ANNA	2	F	CHILD	RRZZZZUSA
FRANZ	.09	M	INFANT	RRZZZZUSA
FREUND, ALEXANDER	27	M	UNKNOWN	RRZZZZUSA

SHIP: GRECIAN MONARCH

FROM: LONDON
TO: NEW YORK
ARRIVED: 14 DECEMBER 1883

PASSENGER	AGE	SEX	OCCUPATION	PV DES
DE-ROTCHKOFF, NADIA	22	F	BRN	RRZZZZUSA
STAGNOT, MATHEW	53	M	LABR	PLZZZZUSA
CIZAGA, FINKS	32	M	SHMK	PLZZZZUSA
CHINSHOWSKY, WOISEK	28	M	LABR	PLZZZZUSA
ANTONIE	21	M	UNKNOWN	PLZZZZUSA
MATTHEUS	21	M	UNKNOWN	PLZZZZUSA
WIBIANIOK, CAROLINE	22	F	UNKNOWN	PLZZZZUSA
FRICHOLZ, MEYER	22	M	SHMK	PLZZZZUSA
JALOSKY, STANISLAUS	21	M	LABR	PLZZZZUSA
BUDZYKUS, PISTV	47	M	UNKNOWN	PLZZZZUSA
LUDWIKE	39	F	W	PLZZZZUSA
WLEDISLEV	12	M	CH	PLZZZZUSA
SALOMAN	10	M	UNKNOWN	PLZZZZUSA
MECHELINA	6	M	CHILD	PLZZZZUSA
JOSEF	4	M	CHILD	PLZZZZUSA
DESEMER	3	M	CHILD	PLZZZZUSA
LUDWIKE	.06	F	INFANT	PLZZZZUSA
ROTTEWITZ, PINS	26	M	LABR	PLZZZZUSA
BLOMAN, SIMON	28	M	TLR	PLZZZZUSA
FOLCER, ABR.	24	M	UNKNOWN	PLZZZZUSA
ELLIS, ABR.	23	M	UNKNOWN	PLZZZZUSA
LITKE, MYER	21	M	LABR	PLZZZZUSA
ENUER	23	M	UNKNOWN	PLZZZZUSA
GOLDE, DEBORAH	30	F	W	PLZZZZUSA
LEIB	2	M	CHILD	PLZZZZUSA
RUCHEL	.09	F	INFANT	PLZZZZUSA
LOZORAS, JACOB	41	M	LABR	PLZZZZUSA
NATHAN, CHAS	26	M	CL	PLZZZZUSA
GEO.	24	M	UNKNOWN	PLZZZZUSA
FREINUSCH, ISAAC	44	M	LABR	PLZZZZUSA
LIEBE	42	F	W	PLZZZZUSA
JENNY	20	F	UNKNOWN	PLZZZZUSA
ELISE	19	F	UNKNOWN	PLZZZZUSA
DAVID	9	M	CHILD	PLZZZZUSA
RACHEL	6	F	CHILD	PLZZZZUSA
JULIE	4	F	CHILD	PLZZZZUSA
EVE	.07	F	INFANT	PLZZZZUSA
PRECHNER, ISAC	31	M	SING	PLZZZZUSA
BEATE	30	F	W	PLZZZZUSA
DAVID	12	M	CH	PLZZZZUSA
JACOB	10	M	UNKNOWN	PLZZZZUSA
WITTKE, SCHIEDEL	40	F	W	PLZZZZUSA
MOTZE	10	M	CH	PLZZZZUSA
SARAH	4	F	CHILD	PLZZZZUSA
MARTHA	2	F	CHILD	PLZZZZUSA
GREEAB----, HENA	17	F	UNKNOWN	PLZZZZUSA
WOLF	3	F	CHILD	PLZZZZUSA
YENA	1	F	CHILD	PLZZZZUSA
SEIGR, NATHAN	20	M	BKR	PLZZZZUSA
GOLDBERG, LAZARUS	32	M	SHMK	PLZZZZUSA
ANNIE	29	F	W	PLZZZZUSA
LEAH	2	F	CHILD	PLZZZZUSA
MORRIS	.11	M	INFANT	PLZZZZUSA
GORABIN, MOSES	36	M	LABR	PLZZZZUSA
CATHERINE	34	F	W	PLZZZZUSA
RACHEL	11	F	UNKNOWN	PLZZZZUSA
SALOMON	10	M	UNKNOWN	PLZZZZUSA
BETSY	8	M	CHILD	PLZZZZUSA
ADELAIDE	7	F	CHILD	PLZZZZUSA
WOLF	5	M	CHILD	PLZZZZUSA
ASHEN	3	M	CHILD	PLZZZZUSA
MEYER	.09	M	INFANT	PLZZZZUSA
OLLENBERG, MIRIAM	33	F	W	PLZZZZUSA
MILLY	9	F	CHILD	PLZZZZUSA
ABRAHAM	7	M	CHILD	PLZZZZUSA
SARAH	4	F	CHILD	PLZZZZUSA
LEAH	3	F	CHILD	PLZZZZUSA
REBBECCA	1	F	CHILD	PLZZZZUSA
HORWITZ, MOSES	23	M	LABR	PLZZZZUSA
WOLFGANG, ABR.	19	M	CPMKR	PLZZZZUSA
EHRITCHMANN, WOOLF	23	M	CPTR	RRZZZZUSA
ERIEN, ABR.	19	M	CVR	RRZZZZUSA

SHIP: RHEIN

FROM: BREMEN
TO: NEW YORK
ARRIVED: 15 DECEMBER 1883

PASSENGER	AGE	SEX	OCCUPATION	PV DES
LENDZCK, EUGEN	26	M	LABR	RRZZZZUSA
NERMANN, RENNHOLD	36	M	LABR	RRZZZZUSA
HWIATKOWSKI, CARL	21	M	LABR	RRZZZZUSA

PASSENGER	AGE	SEX	OCCUPATION	PRV VIL DES

SHIP: ELBE

FROM: BREMEN AND SOUTHAMPTON
TO: NEW YORK
ARRIVED: 17 DECEMBER 1883

PASSENGER	AGE	SEX	OCCUPATION	PRV VIL DES
WITKOSKA, STANISLAWA	23	F	W	RRZZZZUSA
BRONISLAWA	.11	F	INFANT	RRZZZZUSA

SHIP: ARIZONA

FROM: LIVERPOOL
TO: NEW YORK
ARRIVED: 18 DECEMBER 1883

PASSENGER	AGE	SEX	OCCUPATION	PRV VIL DES
OLTOLS, JACOB	74	M	MNR	FNZZZZUSA
KARRI, JOHAN-M.	26	M	UNKNOWN	FNZZZZUSA
MUSTILA, HENRIK	23	M	UNKNOWN	FNZZZZUSA

SHIP: BOHEMIA

FROM: HAMBURG AND HAVRE
TO: NEW YORK
ARRIVED: 18 DECEMBER 1883

PASSENGER	AGE	SEX	OCCUPATION	PRV VIL DES
TUROWICZ, KASIMIR	21	M	LABR	RRZZZZUSA
MALINOWSKI, JOSEF	21	M	LABR	RRZZZZUSA
GLEICHMANN, HIRSCH	32	M	DLR	RRZZZZUSA
PETROSCHEWITZ, THOMAS	21	M	LABR	RRZZZZUSA
DURKOWSKI, JOH.	21	M	LABR	RRZZZZUSA
GIBIROWSKI, ISRAEL	20	M	LABR	RRZZZZUSA
SZATEL-IK, MASRIE	41	M	SHMK	RRZZZZUSA
DUBRES, SAMUEL	41	M	GZR	RRZZZZUSA
STOLL, MOSCHE	20	M	TLR	RRZZZZUSA
WORNER, JOSEL	22	M	TLR	RRZZZZUSA
DRIBIN, DWOSCHE	30	F	W	RRZZZZUSA
SCHEINE	4	F	CHILD	RRZZZZUSA
JOSSEL	.11	F	INFANT	RRZZZZUSA
SKUWCENICZ, ISTWAN	23	M	LABR	RRZZZZUSA
COHN, JUDITH	28	F	W	RRZZZZUSA
MINKE	.11	M	INFANT	RRZZZZUSA
HIRSCH	.01	M	INFANT	RRZZZZUSA
ZADNORANSKI, JUDEL	29	M	DLR	RRZZZZUSA
KOHN, TEWJE	28	M	DLR	RRZZZZUSA
LIEBE	25	F	W	RRZZZZUSA
CHESCHE	7	M	CHILD	RRZZZZUSA
GUTE	5	F	CHILD	RRZZZZUSA
CHAIM	4	M	CHILD	RRZZZZUSA
NACHMANN	.11	M	INFANT	RRZZZZUSA
MANTEL	.01	F	INFANT	RRZZZZUSA
RUSCHANSKY, CHONE	36	M	DLR	RRZZZZUSA
AROWSKY, ABRAHAM	28	M	DLR	RRZZZZUSA
KRIWERUTZKY, YANKEL	25	M	TLR	RRZZZZUSA
FRANKOWSKY, MOSES	25	M	TLR	RRZZZZUSA
MALKE	24	F	W	RRZZZZUSA
MEIER	.11	F	INFANT	RRZZZZUSA
ROSA	.01	F	INFANT	RRZZZZUSA
FRANKEL, NOAK	46	M	DLR	RRZZZZUSA
EPHRAIN	43	M	DLR	RRZZZZUSA
NACHMANOWITZ, ABE	25	M	DLR	RRZZZZUSA
EISEN, BENSIN	32	M	DLR	RRZZZZUSA
KATZENBERGER, LASTAR	19	M	DLR	RRZZZZUSA
GRODSKY, MEYER	19	M	DLR	RRZZZZUSA
WISEMUSKY, RAMIEL	20	M	DLR	RRZZZZUSA
GRUNSTEIN, JUDES	32	F	W	RRZZZZUSA
RACHEL	9	F	CHILD	RRZZZZUSA
MOSES	8	F	CHILD	RRZZZZUSA
LEIB	7	F	CHILD	RRZZZZUSA
MEYER	4	F	CHILD	RRZZZZUSA
CHAIC	.11	F	INFANT	RRZZZZUSA
DWORKOWITZ, CHAIM	19	M	CGRMKR	RRZZZZUSA
GRUBNER, ISAAC	20	M	DLR	RRZZZZUSA
YEVJENSKI, MEYER	18	M	TNMK	RRZZZZUSA
DWORE	18	F	W	RRZZZZUSA
SCHINDOWITZ, ISAAC	19	M	DLR	RRZZZZUSA
DINER, MENDEL	9	M	CHILD	RRZZZZUSA
KOPER, SARA	23	F	W	RRZZZZUSA
HINDE	.11	F	INFANT	RRZZZZUSA
SCHOSCHES, MENDEL	19	M	BKBNDR	RRZZZZUSA
LORBER, ESTER	50	F	W	RRZZZZUSA
HENE	9	F	CHILD	RRZZZZUSA
ROSENBLUM, BASCHE	24	F	W	RRZZZZUSA
JACHIME	3	F	CHILD	RRZZZZUSA
JACOB	.09	M	INFANT	RRZZZZUSA
SKIRSOBOLSKI, MORSCHE	19	M	LABR	RRZZZZUSA
STREEMBIGLOWSKY, ZALLEL	21	M	LABR	RRZZZZUSA
BLANSTEIN, JANKEL	20	M	LABR	RRZZZZUSA
ETTKIN, ARON	18	M	LABR	RRZZZZUSA
SAWATZKY, ABRAM	25	M	LABR	RRZZZZUSA
ELKES, ARON	19	M	LABR	RRZZZZUSA
GASMISE, HERRSEL	20	M	DLR	RRZZZZUSA
KORSNEK, PETER	25	M	LABR	RRZZZZUSA
HELENE	25	F	W	RRZZZZUSA
WEBER, ANDR.	53	M	LABR	RRZZZZUSA
CATHA.	4	F	CHILD	RRZZZZUSA
GRUN, LEOPOLD	40	M	LABR	RRZZZZUSA
EHRLICH, SAMUEL	20	M	LABR	RRZZZZUSA
WEINBERG, NISSEN	17	M	DLR	RRZZZZUSA
LEWIN, NOCHUM	21	M	CNF	RRZZZZUSA
DILACHERS, IWAN	30	M	LABR	RRZZZZUSA
BENDER, HAMILS	19	M	LABR	RRZZZZUSA
LIPSTACK, GEORG	21	M	LABR	RRZZZZUSA
JASELWIZ, FRIEDERICH	41	M	LABR	RRZZZZUSA
DOWITZ, JOSEF	40	M	LABR	RRZZZZUSA
MICHAEL	40	M	LABR	RRZZZZUSA
KOHN, TABIUS	21	M	LABR	RRZZZZUSA

SHIP: BOTHNIA

FROM: LIVERPOOL
TO: NEW YORK
ARRIVED: 20 DECEMBER 1883

PASSENGER	AGE	SEX	OCCUPATION	PRV VIL DES
PLIT, EMANUEL	30	M	UNKNOWN	RRZZZZUSA
ABRAHAM	18	M	UNKNOWN	RRZZZZUSA
HOFF, AWNER	36	M	UNKNOWN	RRZZZZUSA
HATZ, GERSON	44	M	UNKNOWN	RRZZZZUSA
EIDUSCH, MEYER	11	M	CH	RRZZZZUSA
KOT, HERSCHEL	10	M	UNKNOWN	RRZZZZUSA

SHIP: RHAETIA

FROM: HAMBURG AND HAVRE
TO: NEW YORK
ARRIVED: 21 DECEMBER 1883

PASSENGER	AGE	SEX	OCCUPATION	PRV VIL DES
SALANUS, CARL	25	M	LABR	RRZZZZUSA
OSECHOW, ITZIG	40	M	UNKNOWN	RRZZZZUSA
LEIB	9	M	CHILD	RRZZZZUSA

PASSENGER	A G E	S E X	OCCUPATION	P V R I V L	D E S
SCHLOSBERG, MATES	40	M	DLR	RRZZZZ	USA
WOLF	20	M	UNKNOWN	RRZZZZ	USA
ROSENBUM, ALTER	28	M	UNKNOWN	RRZZZZ	USA
BLUCH, SALOMON	20	M	UNKNOWN	RRZZZZ	USA
ISRAELSKI, ORUSCH	16	M	UNKNOWN	RRZZZZ	USA
KATZ, CHAIE	20	F	W	RRZZZZ	USA
OLIZKI, BENDET	20	M	DLR	RRZZZZ	USA
LISSMANN, JACOB	20	M	DLR	RRZZZZ	USA
ROTHSCHILD, SAMUEL	24	M	UNKNOWN	RRZZZZ	USA
BERMAN, MOSES	45	M	DLR	RRZZZZ	USA
BARGEMUTH, CHAIM	20	M	UNKNOWN	RRZZZZ	USA
BADOWSKY, LITTMANN	19	M	UNKNOWN	RRZZZZ	USA
FISTEL, MORDSCHE	38	M	LABR	RRZZZZ	USA
RAHEL	16	F	CH	RRZZZZ	USA
ABEL	9	M	CHILD	RRZZZZ	USA
STUTZKEWITZ, ANTON	24	M	LABR	RRZZZZ	USA
ROMANOW, SCHEWAL	29	M	UNKNOWN	RRZZZZ	USA
GLATTSTEIN, MOSES	28	M	UNKNOWN	RRZZZZ	USA
BONN, ZERNE	30	F	W	RRZZZZ	USA
ABRAHAM	4	M	CHILD	RRZZZZ	USA
SARAH	.11	F	INFANT	RRZZZZ	USA
BUERKER, JACOB	18	M	CL	RRZZZZ	USA
NYGAARD, JOHANNA	35	F	SGL	RRZZZZ	USA
WIHMANN, MARIE	30	F	W	RRZZZZ	USA
HILDA	7	F	CHILD	RRZZZZ	USA
ANDERS	5	M	CHILD	RRZZZZ	USA
STANSKI, CONSTANTIN	22	M	LABR	RRZZZZ	USA
SCHILLING, JOHANNE	30	F	SGL	RRZZZZ	USA
STANSKI, CONSTANTIN	22	M	SHMK	RRZZZZ	USA
EICHLER, THEODOR	28	M	SMH	RRZZZZ	USA
SILBERMANN, ISRAEL	40	M	MCHT	RRZZZZ	USA
KLEWIS, CHAIM	20	M	UNKNOWN	RRZZZZ	USA
TRETKOWSKI, DAVID	20	M	UNKNOWN	RRZZZZ	USA
MIRCHEL, MATH.	40	M	UNKNOWN	RRZZZZ	USA
DOROTHEA	40	F	W	RRZZZZ	USA
JOH.	9	M	CHILD	RRZZZZ	USA
AUGUST	8	M	CHILD	RRZZZZ	USA
MATH.	6	M	CHILD	RRZZZZ	USA
MARIE	4	F	CHILD	RRZZZZ	USA
CAROLINE	.11	F	INFANT	RRZZZZ	USA
KAMINSKI, EIDEL	60	F	W	RRZZZZ	USA
TAFET, JOSEF	21	M	UNKNOWN	RRZZZZ	USA
KARPOWITZ, MORDSCHE	26	M	SMH	RRZZZZ	USA
DEIMENT, SCHOEL	21	M	TLR	RRZZZZ	USA
FRIEDMANN, NACHUM	23	M	MCHT	RRZZZZ	USA
EKSTEROWITZ, CHANNE	25	F	W	RRZZZZ	USA
HERM.	8	M	CHILD	RRZZZZ	USA
CHAIE	6	F	CHILD	RRZZZZ	USA
IDA	.11	F	INFANT	RRZZZZ	USA
LEWIN, MORDSCHE	20	M	LABR	RRZZZZ	USA
LIMAITES, ANTON	26	M	UNKNOWN	RRZZZZ	USA
BLUM, SCHOPSI	18	M	UNKNOWN	RRZZZZ	USA
LEWIN, HIRSCH	20	M	UNKNOWN	RRZZZZ	USA

SHIP: FLORIDA

FROM: GLASGOW
TO: NEW YORK
ARRIVED: 22 DECEMBER 1883

PASSENGER	A G E	S E X	OCCUPATION	P V R I V L	D E S
BANDLURG, LARENZ	00	M	LABR	PLZZZZ	USA
GALIMOUDSKY, ANDRE.	00	M	LABR	PLZZZZ	USA
ONYIANI, THS.	00	M	LABR	PLZZZZ	USA
GRAJEWSKY, FRANZ	00	M	LABR	PLZZZZ	USA
MARIANA	00	F	W	PLZZZZ	USA
JOSEF	.06	M	INFANT	PLZZZZ	USA
PRYLEIDSKY, JOSEF	33	M	LABR	PLZZZZ	USA
SCHEDCTZREICH, JETTE	00	F	HP	PLZZZZ	USA
STOLPE, MARTIN	46	M	LABR	PLZZZZ	USA
ZOFSZIG, JOHAN	33	M	LABR	PLZZZZ	USA
HELLIG, PAUL	30	M	LABR	PLZZZZ	USA
WYSAZLOW, FRANZ	27	M	LABR	PLZZZZ	USA
MAGDALENA	25	F	W	PLZZZZ	USA
ALBERT	.11	M	INFANT	PLZZZZ	USA

SHIP: POLYNESIA

FROM: HAMBURG
TO: NEW YORK
ARRIVED: 22 DECEMBER 1883

PASSENGER	A G E	S E X	OCCUPATION	P V R I V L	D E S
KAMOSCHEIK, VINCENT	39	M	UNKNOWN	PLZZZZ	NY
MISKSCHES, NICOLAI	22	M	UNKNOWN	PLZZZZ	NY
WASSILOVSKI, ADAM	29	M	UNKNOWN	PLZZZZ	NY
BORLOSSKI, THOMAS	28	M	UNKNOWN	PLZZZZ	NY
BARTOMI, DONL	23	M	UNKNOWN	PLZZZZ	NY
STRUMUEHL, ALEXANDER	21	M	UNKNOWN	PLZZZZ	NY
WILLISCH, JOSEPH	25	M	UNKNOWN	PLZZZZ	NY
SCHWEDSCHUBER, CARL	29	M	UNKNOWN	PLZZZZ	NY
ISANSKI, STANISLAUS	27	M	LABR	PLZZZZ	NY
DORAN, MICHAL	34	M	UNKNOWN	PLZZZZ	NY
SEBOSHAI, PAPIN	41	M	UNKNOWN	PLZZZZ	NY
SCHUMORSKY, TH.	34	M	UNKNOWN	PLZZZZ	NY
KRULL, WOICZICH	25	M	UNKNOWN	PLZZZZ	NY
NITSCH, JOSEPH	25	M	TRDSMN	PLZZZZ	NY
REICGEL, ANTON	29	M	UNKNOWN	PLZZZZ	NY
RECICHER, WOJCIK	27	M	LABR	PLZZZZ	NY
HOYSZ, JANOS	29	M	UNKNOWN	PLZZZZ	NY
HANSCHIN, ANDRAUH	25	M	UNKNOWN	PLZZZZ	NY
MACICH, KATSCHA	38	M	UNKNOWN	PLZZZZ	NY
KUDLOFSKY, WAHIL	24	M	UNKNOWN	PLZZZZ	NY
JADLOVTISCH, THEOD.	24	M	UNKNOWN	PLZZZZ	NY
VAPIL, MARTIN	25	M	UNKNOWN	PLZZZZ	NY
IGNATZ, JORES	20	M	UNKNOWN	PLZZZZ	NY
PETROVITS, MALHEAS	26	M	UNKNOWN	PLZZZZ	NY
SORGCS, JAKOBAFTES	22	M	UNKNOWN	PLZZZZ	NY
LIPTOK, JANOS	26	M	UNKNOWN	PLZZZZ	NY
STOFANIK, ANDS.	14	M	UNKNOWN	PLZZZZ	NY
MINARCIK, DOROTHEA	17	F	SGL	PLZZZZ	NY
KALMANN, SALEI	36	M	TRDSMN	PLZZZZ	NY
CHEMERA, WOYCUEH	51	M	UNKNOWN	PLZZZZ	NY
MOREIN, ROMAN	27	M	UNKNOWN	PLZZZZ	NY
TEHLA, CHIMIRA	19	F	SGL	PLZZZZ	NY
MENUK, JOSEF	50	M	LABR	PLZZZZ	NY
MOWKOWITZ, JAN	27	M	UNKNOWN	PLZZZZ	NY
MNUK, JEDJU	7	M	CHILD	PLZZZZ	NY
SCHARKEIMSKIU, SAISEL	22	M	LABR	RRZZZZ	NY
BONURSKY, HANAH	27	M	UNKNOWN	RRZZZZ	NY
SCHLOSBERG, JUDEL	18	M	UNKNOWN	RRZZZZ	NY
WILENZIK, ELIAS	26	M	UNKNOWN	RRZZZZ	NY
HOLDA, BARBARA	50	F	WO	PLZZZZ	NY
CASPAR	27	M	S	PLZZZZ	NY
JACOB	22	M	UNKNOWN	PLZZZZ	NY
THEKLA	7	F	CHILD	PLZZZZ	NY
JOSEF	6	M	CHILD	PLZZZZ	NY
SERANT, LUDOWIKA	22	F	SGL	PLZZZZ	NY
KAVZIS, ADAM	33	M	LABR	PLZZZZ	NY
MILUS, ANTON	22	M	UNKNOWN	PLZZZZ	NY
KRIWORSKI, JOSEF	25	M	UNKNOWN	PLZZZZ	NY
RACHEL	20	F	W	PLZZZZ	NY
PRYBOROWSKY, KATHARINA	18	F	SGL	RRZZZZ	NY
CHIMOCHOWSKI, JAN	20	M	LABR	RRZZZZ	NY
ARENBERG, SIMCHE	20	M	UNKNOWN	RRZZZZ	NY
KIEWWICZ, JAN	40	M	LABR	RRZZZZ	NY
VINCENTIA	24	F	W	RRZZZZ	NY
MARIANNA	.06	F	INFANT	RRZZZZ	NY
MARKSON, LABEL	7	M	CHILD	RRZZZZ	NY
VOIGTS, HEINR	31	M	CPTR	RRZZZZ	UNK
STEFANUK, JACOB	50	M	UNKNOWN	PLZZZZ	UNK
DZOK, JOSEF	40	M	UNKNOWN	PLZZZZ	UNK

PASSENGER	AGE	SEX	OCCUPATION	PRV	VIL	DES
POPITESZ, THOS.	32	M	UNKNOWN	PL	ZZZZ	UNK
MATHIAS, PETER	44	M	UNKNOWN	RR	ZZZZ	UNK
RACKI, JOSEF	22	M	UNKNOWN	RR	ZZZZ	UNK
METTLOWSKY, JOH.	19	M	UNKNOWN	RR	ZZZZ	UNK
PILLGINES, VINC.	40	M	UNKNOWN	RR	ZZZZ	UNK
BELSKI, ADAM	22	M	UNKNOWN	RR	ZZZZ	UNK
KEDISCH, IGNATZ	22	M	UNKNOWN	RR	ZZZZ	UNK
BELEWSKI, AN.	29	M	UNKNOWN	RR	ZZZZ	UNK
RALTENEWICZ, CAS.	34	M	TRDSMN	RR	ZZZZ	UNK
FRANZISKA	22	F	W	RR	ZZZZ	UNK
GESDI	.11	M	INFANT	RR	ZZZZ	UNK
HANNI	.01	F	INFANT	RR	ZZZZ	UNK
PITTEMIEWICZ, JAN	25	M	FARMER	RR	ZZZZ	UNK
SILBERMANN, AD.	28	M	LABR	PL	ZZZZ	UNK
FANNY	22	F	W	PL	ZZZZ	UNK
PEPI	.07	F	INFANT	PL	ZZZZ	UNK
BECKTLAFF, PHILIPP	24	M	TLR	PL	ZZZZ	UNK
RYMON, JULIAN	27	M	LABR	PL	ZZZZ	UNK
CZYRINCA, JAWODA	22	M	UNKNOWN	PL	ZZZZ	UNK
RECWANDOWSKY, STEFAN	29	M	UNKNOWN	PL	ZZZZ	UNK
KASAWAZKY, ADAM	24	M	UNKNOWN	PL	ZZZZ	UNK
RECICHST--, BERNHARD	17	M	BTL	RR	ZZZZ	UNK

SHIP: CITY OF BERLIN

FROM: LIVERPOOL AND QUEENSTOWN
TO: NEW YORK
ARRIVED: 24 DECEMBER 1883

PASSENGER	AGE	SEX	OCCUPATION	PRV	VIL	DES
EAGOIST, SMIL.	31	M	LABR	FN	ZZZZ	USA
JOSEFINA	27	F	W	FN	ZZZZ	USA
RANTAKAEGAS, ANTI	29	M	LABR	FN	ZZZZ	USA
WENAMAKI, JOHAN	27	M	LABR	FN	ZZZZ	USA
MAUNENIN, JOHAN	29	M	LABR	FN	ZZZZ	USA
HYYTENEIS, ERICK	32	M	LABR	FN	ZZZZ	USA
MUAMAKI, JOHAN	35	M	LABR	FN	ZZZZ	USA
HIBBERG, CHRISTINA	58	F	W	FN	ZZZZ	USA
MAI, AMBINSE	24	M	LABR	FN	ZZZZ	USA
GRIZELOWSKY, JOHN	22	M	LABR	FN	ZZZZ	USA

SHIP: GENERAL WERDER

FROM: BREMEN
TO: NEW YORK
ARRIVED: 24 DECEMBER 1883

PASSENGER	AGE	SEX	OCCUPATION	PRV	VIL	DES
KOWALSKI, FRANZESCA	30	F	W	RR	ZZZZ	USA
MARIA	4	F	CHILD	RR	ZZZZ	USA
DEMBROWSKA, ROSALIE	50	F	W	RR	ZZZZ	USA
PETROCK	26	M	FARMER	RR	ZZZZ	USA
AUGNIS	20	F	W	RR	ZZZZ	USA

SHIP: OLINDE RODRIGUES

FROM: HAVRE
TO: NEW YORK
ARRIVED: 24 DECEMBER 1883

PASSENGER	AGE	SEX	OCCUPATION	PRV	VIL	DES
SCHROIDER, MARIUS-MR.	21	M	TLR	RR	ZZZZ	NY
WEIMNANN, DAVID-MR.	00	M	PNTR	RR	ZZZZ	NY
FREDRIKE-MRS.	18	F	NN	RR	ZZZZ	NY
MANNI	2	F	CHILD	RR	ZZZZ	NY
BRONSCHLIN, LOB.MR.	22	M	BKBNDR	RR	ZZZZ	NY
GNENEL, JACOB-MR.	23	M	PNTR	RR	ZZZZ	NY
BROCHE-MRS.	18	F	NN	RR	ZZZZ	NY
MICHCLAS, JACOB-MR.	23	M	TLR	RR	ZZZZ	NY
ROSA-MRS.	21	F	NN	RR	ZZZZ	NY
MOISE	.10	M	INFANT	RR	ZZZZ	NY
ISAKO, CHAIN-MR.	23	M	TLR	RR	ZZZZ	NY
HOCHMANN, MISSIN-MR.	26	M	SHMK	RR	ZZZZ	NY
WINDISKY, JACOB-MR.	22	M	BLKSMH	RR	ZZZZ	NY
LIA-MRS.	20	F	NN	RR	ZZZZ	NY
REBEKA	9	F	CHILD	RR	ZZZZ	NY
ABRAHAM	1	M	CHILD	RR	ZZZZ	NY
KUPFERMANN, BAER-MR.	23	M	BLKSMH	RR	ZZZZ	NY
CARNE-MRS.	17	F	NN	RR	ZZZZ	NY
HENNE	.05	F	INFANT	RR	ZZZZ	NY
FIEDLER, HERZ-MR.	25	M	LABR	RR	ZZZZ	NY
CHAJE-MRS.	18	F	NN	RR	ZZZZ	NY
GITTEL	.04	F	INFANT	RR	ZZZZ	NY

SHIP: HELVETIA

FROM: LIVERPOOL AND QUEENSTOWN
TO: NEW YORK
ARRIVED: 26 DECEMBER 1883

PASSENGER	AGE	SEX	OCCUPATION	PRV	VIL	DES
GOLDMAN, HARRIS	26	M	LABR	PL	ZZZZ	USA
GULALUS, ADAM	24	M	LABR	PL	ZZZZ	USA
FENNFELD, EMIL	39	M	LABR	PL	ZZZZ	USA
HURTA, JOHAN	35	M	LABR	RR	ZZZZ	USA
ANNA	28	F	W	RR	ZZZZ	USA
MARIA	10	F	CH	RR	ZZZZ	USA
JOSEF.	7	F	CHILD	RR	ZZZZ	USA
ANN	4	F	CHILD	RR	ZZZZ	USA
JOHAN	.10	M	INFANT	RR	ZZZZ	USA
ROSINE	.10	F	INFANT	RR	ZZZZ	USA

SHIP: LAURENT

FROM: HAVRE
TO: NEW YORK
ARRIVED: 27 DECEMBER 1883

PASSENGER	AGE	SEX	OCCUPATION	PRV	VIL	DES
MUCKENSCHNABEN, JOSEPH	41	M	TLR	RR	ZZZZ	NY

SHIP: PAVONIA

FROM: LIVERPOOL
TO: NEW YORK
ARRIVED: 27 DECEMBER 1883

PASSENGER	AGE	SEX	OCCUPATION	PRV	VIL	DES
MISTITZKY, LEISER	40	M	WCHMKR	PL	ZZZZ	NY
COULSON, JOHN	47	M	MGR	RR	ZZZZ	NY

PASSENGER	AGE	SEX	OCCUPATION	PRV	VIL	DES

SHIP: WIELAND

FROM: HAMBURG
TO: NEW YORK
ARRIVED: 27 DECEMBER 1883

PASSENGER	AGE	SEX	OCCUPATION	PRV	VIL	DES
KRUK, JANKEL	35	M	LABR	RR	ZZZZ	USA
SCHLOMOWITZ, PELIG	9	M	CHILD	RR	ZZZZ	USA
LENITAN, MOSES	40	M	DLR	RR	ZZZZ	USA
ARONOWITZ, BASCHE	58	F	W	RR	ZZZZ	USA
KANOWSKY, CHANNE	18	F	SGL	RR	ZZZZ	USA
PASCINSKI, SCHACHNE	19	M	TLR	RR	ZZZZ	USA
GLEICHENHAUS, BERE	35	M	TLR	RR	ZZZZ	USA
BOGIN, GERSON	22	M	SHMK	RR	ZZZZ	USA
MENSOHN, MORDCHE	26	F	TLR	RR	ZZZZ	USA
RUBINSTEIN, JACOB	17	M	DLR	RR	ZZZZ	USA
SOLAR, ANTON	26	M	FARMER	RR	ZZZZ	USA
DOMANSKI, OLEAN	25	M	LABR	RR	ZZZZ	USA
JANKOWSKI, JOSEF	20	M	LABR	RR	ZZZZ	USA
BOSCHKI, JOH.	25	M	LABR	RR	ZZZZ	USA
MARKEL, JULS.	33	M	LABR	RR	ZZZZ	USA
AZAREWICZ, ALEXANDER	24	M	LABR	RR	ZZZZ	USA
JACOBSOHN, MOSES	19	M	MCHT	RR	ZZZZ	USA
MANFRIED, KIWE	33	M	DLR	RR	ZZZZ	USA
LEWIN, DAVID	22	M	TLR	RR	ZZZZ	USA
SCHER, MARCUS	38	M	MSN	RR	ZZZZ	USA
ARKIN, DAVID	34	M	DLR	RR	ZZZZ	USA
SCHAPIRSTEIA, KALMANN	36	M	DLR	RR	ZZZZ	USA
WOEFELD, CHAIE	22	M	CL	RR	ZZZZ	USA
LIPSCHITZ, MEYER	28	M	CL	RR	ZZZZ	USA
FEITES, GERSON	20	M	CL	RR	ZZZZ	USA
POLTIN, ABR.	18	M	CL	RR	ZZZZ	USA
FINN, ELIAS	17	M	LABR	RR	ZZZZ	USA
CZACHORSKI, STANISLAUS	35	M	SHMK	RR	ZZZZ	USA
MARIANNE	40	F	W	RR	ZZZZ	USA
MARIANNE	7	F	CHILD	RR	ZZZZ	USA
APOLIANNA	5	F	CHILD	RR	ZZZZ	USA
STANISLAWA	.11	F	INFANT	RR	ZZZZ	USA
EDMUND	.01	M	INFANT	RR	ZZZZ	USA
OKONEWITZ, JOEL	20	M	TLR	RR	ZZZZ	USA
ETTEL	20	F	W	RR	ZZZZ	USA
LOWIN, ABRAHAM	41	M	MCHT	RR	ZZZZ	USA
RIPS, ELIAS	25	M	MCHT	RR	ZZZZ	USA
SCISSERMAN, JACOB	25	M	JNR	RR	ZZZZ	USA
SARA	25	F	W	RR	ZZZZ	USA
BEILE	.11	F	INFANT	RR	ZZZZ	USA
NOSSEN	.01	M	INFANT	RR	ZZZZ	USA
DRUBERK, HERSCH	23	M	JNR	RR	ZZZZ	USA
SARA	23	F	W	RR	ZZZZ	USA
SCHUCHWALSKY, DAVID	22	M	PNTR	RR	ZZZZ	USA
KOPKA, ANTONIN	32	F	SGL	RR	ZZZZ	USA
ABRAHAM, ROSA	24	F	WO	RR	ZZZZ	USA
SELDE	.11	F	INFANT	RR	ZZZZ	USA
GUMSTEIN, JACOB	36	M	LKSH	RR	ZZZZ	USA
TOMBANK, SCHENIE	46	F	WO	RR	ZZZZ	USA
ALTER	9	M	CHILD	RR	ZZZZ	USA
SARA	8	F	CHILD	RR	ZZZZ	USA
TRUME	7	F	CHILD	RR	ZZZZ	USA
GRUNBERG, TENNI	33	F	WO	RR	ZZZZ	USA
RACHEL	8	F	CHILD	RR	ZZZZ	USA
CHAIE	.11	F	INFANT	RR	ZZZZ	USA
KAHN, FEIGE	38	F	WO	RR	ZZZZ	USA
MICHLE	8	M	CHILD	RR	ZZZZ	USA
KIWE	5	F	CHILD	RR	ZZZZ	USA
SAMUEL	5	M	CHILD	RR	ZZZZ	USA
DARKOWITZ, ABRAHAM	23	M	MCHT	RR	ZZZZ	USA
SCHEINKE, MOSES	21	M	JNR	RR	ZZZZ	USA
ABTER, HENORH	32	M	TLR	RR	ZZZZ	USA
ROTHENBERG, SCHEPSEL	33	M	LABR	RR	ZZZZ	USA
ROTHENSTEIN, MOSES	9	M	CHILD	RR	ZZZZ	USA
GOLDSTEIN, DAVID	35	M	LABR	RR	ZZZZ	USA
KRASKO, MOSSEL	55	M	LABR	RR	ZZZZ	USA
GOLDBERG, LEIB	9	M	CHILD	RR	ZZZZ	USA
BIALISTOTZKY, ABE	30	M	LABR	RR	ZZZZ	USA
PAWICGON, MORDCHE	45	M	LABR	RR	ZZZZ	USA
AUGUSTACH, JOSEF	40	M	LABR	RR	ZZZZ	USA
WAITUKAITIS, THOMAS	42	M	LABR	RR	ZZZZ	USA
OSTROWSKY, VICTORIA	20	F	WO	RR	ZZZZ	USA
ANNE	.11	F	INFANT	RR	ZZZZ	USA
MARIE	.11	F	INFANT	RR	ZZZZ	USA
SCHOLASCHEWICTZ, KASIMI	25	M	LABR	RR	ZZZZ	USA
LANE, RICHARD-VERKAMPF	21	M	MUSN	RR	ZZZZ	USA

SHIP: BELGRAVIA

FROM: GLASGOW AND MOVILLE
TO: NEW YORK
ARRIVED: 28 DECEMBER 1883

PASSENGER	AGE	SEX	OCCUPATION	PRV	VIL	DES
PERNSTEIN, L.	30	M	TLR	RR	ZZZZ	USA
SARAH	36	F	UNKNOWN	RR	ZZZZ	USA
ARON	5	M	CHILD	RR	ZZZZ	USA
RACHAEL	4	F	CHILD	RR	ZZZZ	USA
LOUIS	3	M	CHILD	RR	ZZZZ	USA
ISAAC	2	M	CHILD	RR	ZZZZ	USA
ERTEL	1	F	CHILD	RR	ZZZZ	USA

SHIP: STATE OF NEBRASKA

FROM: GLASGOW
TO: NEW YORK
ARRIVED: 31 DECEMBER 1883

PASSENGER	AGE	SEX	OCCUPATION	PRV	VIL	DES
COHN, I.	42	M	PDLR	RR	ZZZZ	USA
SHIFFMANN, M.	35	M	PDLR	RR	ZZZZ	USA
DAVID	12	M	CH	RR	ZZZZ	USA
BRODER, I.	23	M	PDLR	RR	ZZZZ	USA
SHENIE	19	F	W	RR	ZZZZ	USA
OFFEN, A.B.	00	M	PDLR	RR	ZZZZ	USA
ARKOWITZ, C.	00	M	UNKNOWN	RR	ZZZZ	USA
JOSCMIS, K.	00	M	UNKNOWN	RR	ZZZZ	USA
SACHAREWITCH, P.	00	M	UNKNOWN	RR	ZZZZ	USA
BRINES, K.	00	M	UNKNOWN	RR	ZZZZ	USA
MICHANES, I.	22	M	UNKNOWN	RR	ZZZZ	USA
BEHRMANN, M.	14	M	UNKNOWN	RR	ZZZZ	USA
SIEGEL, S.	19	M	UNKNOWN	RR	ZZZZ	USA

SHIP: AUSTRALIA

FROM: HAMBURG
TO: NEW YORK
ARRIVED: 02 JANUARY 1884

PASSENGER	AGE	SEX	OCCUPATION	PRV	VIL	DES
UKACZCK, CZUPICK	26	M	LABR	PL	ZZZZ	NY
LEHUKO, THYMKO	26	M	LABR	PL	ZZZZ	NY
HOWALETZ, MAXIN	26	M	LABR	PL	ZZZZ	NY
BANASZ, JOHANN	25	M	LABR	PL	ZZZZ	NY
FEDARSEK, CIPRUN	40	M	LABR	PL	ZZZZ	NY
PORG--, WANO	30	M	LABR	PL	ZZZZ	NY
PECKA, NIEZIFER	27	M	LABR	PL	ZZZZ	NY
SAFIA	20	F	W	PL	ZZZZ	NY
TOMACZ, A.	22	M	LABR	PL	ZZZZ	NY
WOYTOWITZ, M.	23	M	LABR	PL	ZZZZ	NY
MASELEWITZ, SERW.	40	M	LABR	PL	ZZZZ	NY

PASSENGER	AGE	SEX	OCCUPATION	PRIVL	DES
MAREK, BARES	35	M	LABR	PLZZZZ	NY
ANNA	26	F	W	PLZZZZ	NY
ADELMANN, SCHMUEL	28	M	TRDSMN	RRZZZZ	NY
SAGAL, LIBBIE	23	F	WO	RRZZZZ	NY
BEILE	.09	F	INFANT	RRZZZZ	NY
ADELMANN, LIEBE	24	F	WO	RRZZZZ	NY
EDDEL	.09	M	INFANT	RRZZZZ	NY
ABRAHAM	.09	M	INFANT	RRZZZZ	NY
FISCHER, ANNETTE	20	F	WO	RRZZZZ	NY
JACOB	7	M	CHILD	RRZZZZ	NY
TOCHALSKI, JAN	28	M	LABR	RRZZZZ	NY
JOSEFA	23	F	W	RRZZZZ	NY
BLADT, NOSSEN	20	M	TLR	RRZZZZ	NY
LEVY, OSIAS	14	M	TLR	RRZZZZ	NY
SCHIRANN, SIMON	22	M	TRDSMN	RRZZZZ	NY
BIELICH, KARL	44	M	TRDSMN	RRZZZZ	NY
FISCHER, HERSCH	40	M	TRDSMN	RRZZZZ	NY
BLEI, PAUL	26	M	BBR	RRZZZZ	MIL
MUKARM, A.	40	M	MCHT	RRZZZZ	NY
SCHIEFRAM, MATH.	25	M	TRDSMN	RRZZZZ	NY
BRAME	50	F	WO	RRZZZZ	NY
RACHEL	7	F	CHILD	RRZZZZ	NY
DVORA	6	F	CHILD	RRZZZZ	NY
BASE	3	F	CHILD	RRZZZZ	NY
BRAUN, RUDOLF	24	M	JNR	RRZZZZ	NY
KABLOWITZ, PERL	19	M	TRDSMN	RRZZZZ	NY
SMULOWSKI, SAUPEL	20	M	TRDSMN	RRZZZZ	NY
U, U	17	M	TRDSMN	RRZZZZ	NY
DAVID	7	M	CHILD	RRZZZZ	NY
KAHN, KUSSEL	26	M	TRDSMN	RRZZZZ	NY
KUZAK, JACOB	30	M	LABR	RRZZZZ	NY
DEMETRY, WOROBEL	32	M	LABR	RRZZZZ	NY
CZUPOK, MARIA	31	F	SGL	RRZZZZ	NY

SHIP: GALLIA

FROM: LIVERPOOL AND QUEENSTOWN
TO: NEW YORK
ARRIVED: 02 JANUARY 1884

PASSENGER	AGE	SEX	OCCUPATION	PRIVL	DES
GREGER, ALEXANDR	24	M	CGRMKR	RRZZZZ	USA
HINDRIK, ALFRED	25	M	UNKNOWN	RRZZZZ	USA

SHIP: LYDIAN MONARCH

FROM: LONDON
TO: NEW YORK
ARRIVED: 02 JANUARY 1884

PASSENGER	AGE	SEX	OCCUPATION	PRIVL	DES
GOLDESMANN, NACHSEN	48	M	PH	RRZZZZ	NY
JOZDMAN, ALEX	22	M	ENGR	RRZZZZ	NY
KALINKER, B.	21	M	TLR	PLZZZZ	NY
SOKSFERVSKI, MOSES	25	M	SHMK	PLZZZZ	NY
KOLCSKI, OSIAS	17	M	TLR	PLZZZZ	NY
GRABONSKA, I.	30	M	TLR	PLZZZZ	NY
MARCUS, JOSEF	58	M	SHMK	PLZZZZ	NY
MAKOWA, MOSES	30	M	TLR	PLZZZZ	NY
MYER, MOSES	40	M	LABR	PLZZZZ	NY
CHAIN, ABRAHAM	23	M	TLR	PLZZZZ	NY
SACKS, ISAAC	22	M	TLR	PLZZZZ	NY
ROSENBERG, LEIB	18	M	LABR	PLZZZZ	NY
PEISACH, CAIN	18	M	LABR	PLZZZZ	NY
BERNSTEIN, BOVEL	40	M	TLR	PLZZZZ	NY
SZYMOINEZ, MIRGIS	40	M	LABR	PLZZZZ	PA
ANNA	35	F	W	PLZZZZ	PA
SUBOSKA, JOSEF	43	M	LABR	PLZZZZ	PA
CATARINA	37	F	W	PLZZZZ	PA
CONSTANCE	2	F	CHILD	PLZZZZ	PA
SAPIRO, MERSCH	35	M	LABR	PLZZZZ	NY
KOWALSKI, SOL.	22	M	BLKSMH	PLZZZZ	NY
SOKITES, GURH.	20	M	LABR	PLZZZZ	NY
MALIKA, STANISL.	26	M	LABR	PLZZZZ	NY
SORISKA, KOSEF	21	M	LABR	PLZZZZ	NY

SHIP: WYOMING

FROM: LIVERPOOL AND QUEENSTOWN
TO: NEW YORK
ARRIVED: 02 JANUARY 1884

PASSENGER	AGE	SEX	OCCUPATION	PRIVL	DES
RISSONEN, J.W.	30	M	LABR	RRZZZZ	USA
JALSOO, HORMAN	24	M	LABR	RRZZZZ	USA
NIEMISTO, JACOB	30	M	LABR	RRZZZZ	USA
HUKKA, JOHAN-I.	24	M	LABR	RRZZZZ	USA

SHIP: AMERIQUE

FROM: HAVRE
TO: NEW YORK
ARRIVED: 03 JANUARY 1884

PASSENGER	AGE	SEX	OCCUPATION	PRIVL	DES
CRIANOWSKI, ALFRED	19	M	UNKNOWN	RRZZZZ	USA
WOGHALTER, LEON	19	M	UNKNOWN	RRZZZZ	USA
KOTSOWSKI, ISAAC	19	M	UNKNOWN	RRZZZZ	USA
LERNER, ISRAEL	17	M	CULT	RRZZZZ	USA
MAJER	13	M	UNKNOWN	RRZZZZ	USA

SHIP: RUGIA

FROM: HAMBURG
TO: NEW YORK
ARRIVED: 03 JANUARY 1884

PASSENGER	AGE	SEX	OCCUPATION	PRIVL	DES
FAIRMANN, HOACH	50	M	MCHT	RRZZZZ	USA
RACHEL	48	F	W	RRZZZZ	USA
JENTE	17	F	CH	RRZZZZ	USA
SOSCHE	9	F	CHILD	RRZZZZ	USA
CZERNE	.11	F	INFANT	RRZZZZ	USA
ABERELZKY, ABRAM	9	M	CHILD	RRZZZZ	USA
STOLLER, FEIGE	28	F	W	RRZZZZ	USA
CHANNE	.11	F	INFANT	RRZZZZ	USA
COHN, NECHENNIAS	46	M	DLR	RRZZZZ	USA
GOLDSCHMIDT, JOSEF	20	M	UNKNOWN	RRZZZZ	USA
FREIDE	19	F	W	RRZZZZ	USA
RASCHKES, REBECCA	25	F	UNKNOWN	RRZZZZ	USA
JUDEL	.11	F	INFANT	RRZZZZ	USA
ANENBERG, CHAIM	.09	M	INFANT	RRZZZZ	USA
FUNK, JANKEL	20	M	BCHR	RRZZZZ	USA
SCHALMANN, SABMEN	47	M	DLR	RRZZZZ	USA
HETBIN, SCHENNEL	22	M	UNKNOWN	RRZZZZ	USA
FRANK, DANIEL	49	M	UNKNOWN	RRZZZZ	USA
CHAIM	9	M	CHILD	RRZZZZ	USA
SUSSMANN, MOSES	27	M	TLR	RRZZZZ	USA
HOLAT, ABRAHAM	25	M	UNKNOWN	RRZZZZ	USA
PERLSTEIN, HILLEL	24	M	UNKNOWN	RRZZZZ	USA

PASSENGER	AGE	SEX	OCCUPATION	PRIV	VIL	DES
PITTERSOFF, ISAAC	26	M	UNKNOWN	RR	ZZZZ	USA
HOLPERN, WOLF	22	M	UNKNOWN	RR	ZZZZ	USA
SLOTKEN, MOSES	20	M	UNKNOWN	RR	ZZZZ	USA
BOTEWENICK, CHAIM	24	M	UNKNOWN	RR	ZZZZ	USA
SCHACHNOWITZ, JOSSEL	21	M	UNKNOWN	RR	ZZZZ	USA
SOCHARESKI, SARA	23	F	SGL	RR	ZZZZ	USA
SEGALOWITZ, SCHANEL	19	M	JNR	RR	ZZZZ	USA
ALICHEL, MEYER	48	M	BRM	RR	ZZZZ	USA
REDER, MENDEL	24	M	TLR	RR	ZZZZ	USA
KOHN, JACOB	22	M	DLR	RR	ZZZZ	USA
KOLINA, MEYER	25	M	TLR	RR	ZZZZ	USA
DANOWSKI, JACOB	21	M	DLR	RR	ZZZZ	USA
SCHMITT, NISSON	22	M	JNR	RR	ZZZZ	USA
MOSES	18	M	SHMK	RR	ZZZZ	USA
GALAIDE, JOSEPH	23	M	LABR	RR	ZZZZ	USA
BEHR, ISAAC	25	M	LABR	RR	ZZZZ	USA
MARENS, CHAIE	30	F	W	RR	ZZZZ	USA
CHANNE	9	F	CHILD	RR	ZZZZ	USA
BASCHE	.11	F	INFANT	RR	ZZZZ	USA
KATKISCHKE, CHANE	25	M	LABR	RR	ZZZZ	USA
BASCHE	25	F	W	RR	ZZZZ	USA
FREIDE	.11	F	INFANT	RR	ZZZZ	USA
NARAGELSKY, KUSIEL	30	M	LABR	RR	ZZZZ	USA
WIEGRANSKY, GUTEL	40	F	W	RR	ZZZZ	USA
ROSA	9	F	CHILD	RR	ZZZZ	USA
JODEL	8	F	CHILD	RR	ZZZZ	USA
FEEGE	4	F	CHILD	RR	ZZZZ	USA
KREINSOHN, SARA	44	F	W	RR	ZZZZ	USA
SAMUEL	18	M	CH	RR	ZZZZ	USA
HINDE	19	M	UNKNOWN	RR	ZZZZ	USA
GOLDE	00	F	UNKNOWN	RR	ZZZZ	USA
LEIB	00	M	UNKNOWN	RR	ZZZZ	USA
ISRAEL	00	M	UNKNOWN	RR	ZZZZ	USA
KOLESAR, JANOS	38	M	LABR	RR	ZZZZ	USA
JANOS	38	M	LABR	RR	ZZZZ	USA
MARIE	9	F	CHILD	RR	ZZZZ	USA
ANNA	6	F	CHILD	RR	ZZZZ	USA
HORWITZ, ELIAS	52	M	SHMK	RR	ZZZZ	USA
ABRAHMOWITZ, MEIER	30	M	SMH	RR	ZZZZ	USA
LUDERF, JOSEF	24	M	UNKNOWN	RR	ZZZZ	USA
CHRULSKY, VINCENT	21	M	UNKNOWN	RR	ZZZZ	USA
SONDER, JOSEF	21	M	LABR	RR	ZZZZ	USA
SILBERKNEST, ABRAH.	20	M	LABR	RR	ZZZZ	USA
KOPELOWITZ, CHANNE	19	F	SGL	RR	ZZZZ	USA
HALPEROWITZ, BENJAMIN	20	M	TLR	RR	ZZZZ	USA
MELTZER, CHAIM	18	M	UNKNOWN	RR	ZZZZ	USA
MUNICHES, DAVID	17	M	UNKNOWN	RR	ZZZZ	USA
FEINBERG, ISRAEL	19	M	LABR	RR	ZZZZ	USA
MAKAREINA, ANTON	21	M	LABR	RR	ZZZZ	USA
SCHEN, FRIEDR	23	M	LABR	RR	ZZZZ	USA
MARIE	22	F	W	RR	ZZZZ	USA
JESSIOWEK, ABRAM	51	M	DLR	RR	ZZZZ	USA
MARIE	50	F	W	RR	ZZZZ	USA
JOSEF	9	M	CHILD	RR	ZZZZ	USA
PELSEN, MORITZ	9	M	CHILD	RR	ZZZZ	USA
IST, MINNA	23	F	UNKNOWN	RR	ZZZZ	USA
FRIEDLOENDER, JACOB	17	M	MSN	RR	ZZZZ	USA
BRAME, ESTHER	25	F	W	RR	ZZZZ	USA
ROSENDAHL, JACOB	24	M	LABR	RR	ZZZZ	USA
BRENKE	20	F	W	RR	ZZZZ	USA
MENDEL	9	M	CHILD	RR	ZZZZ	USA
STEINERT, MATES	21	M	DLR	RR	ZZZZ	USA
ELISABETH	20	F	W	RR	ZZZZ	USA
FEINSTEIN, CHAIM	21	M	UNKNOWN	RR	ZZZZ	USA
ROSENKRAUZ, CHAIM	45	M	LABR	RR	ZZZZ	USA
FREIDE	8	F	CHILD	RR	ZZZZ	USA
SLATE	6	F	CHILD	RR	ZZZZ	USA
PERLMANN, NISSEN	21	M	MCHT	RR	ZZZZ	USA
GLASON, PAUL	32	M	UNKNOWN	RR	ZZZZ	USA

SHIP: CITY OF CHESTER

FROM: LIVERPOOL AND QUEENSTOWN
TO: NEW YORK
ARRIVED: 04 JANUARY 1884

PASSENGER	AGE	SEX	OCCUPATION	PRIV	VIL	DES
COCHIST, ANDREW	24	M	LABR	PL	ZZZZ	NY
MEEHAW, JOHN	18	M	LABR	PL	ZZZZ	NY
SVUNER, ISAK-J.	38	M	LABR	FN	ZZZZ	NY
LASSUS, ERIK-J.	25	M	LABR	FN	ZZZZ	NY

SHIP: P CALAND

FROM: ROTTERDAM
TO: NEW YORK
ARRIVED: 04 JANUARY 1884

PASSENGER	AGE	SEX	OCCUPATION	PRIV	VIL	DES
BEZEZINSKY, FRANZ	22	M	LABR	PL	ZZZZ	USA

SHIP: SWITZERLAND

FROM: ANTWERP
TO: NEW YORK
ARRIVED: 07 JANUARY 1884

PASSENGER	AGE	SEX	OCCUPATION	PRIV	VIL	DES
ABRAMSKI, JOS.	24	M	FARMER	RR	ZZZZ	NY
BENJAMIN, CHARLES	23	M	SHMK	RR	ZZZZ	NY
BROWN, TRILLIAN	28	M	TLR	RR	ZZZZ	NY
PATELSKI, JOACH.	26	M	FARMER	RR	ZZZZ	PHI

SHIP: CALIFORNIA

FROM: HAMBURG
TO: NEW YORK
ARRIVED: 08 JANUARY 1884

PASSENGER	AGE	SEX	OCCUPATION	PRIV	VIL	DES
LEMKOLZKY, RUSEL	33	M	TRDSMN	RR	ZZZZ	NY
LUBOW, HERMANN	30	M	TRDSMN	RR	ZZZZ	NY
REBECCA	6	F	CHILD	RR	ZZZZ	NY
BRITANIESCHSY, TAUBER	25	F	WO	RR	ZZZZ	NY
WOLF, CHAIM	27	M	TRDSMN	PL	ZZZZ	NY
PETER	24	F	W	PL	ZZZZ	NY
LIPSCHUTZ, SIMON	28	M	LABR	PL	ZZZZ	NY
SBEGENOW, JOSEF	17	M	LABR	PL	ZZZZ	NY
TANNENBAUM, HERM.	23	M	BTL	PL	ZZZZ	NY
LEONORE	23	F	W	PL	ZZZZ	NY
SCHABSES, AK.	18	M	TRDSMN	RR	ZZZZ	NY
GARUZICK, ASSAU	42	M	TRDSMN	RR	ZZZZ	NY
HOROWITZ, CHAIM	55	F	WO	RR	ZZZZ	NY
SLATE	20	F	D	RR	ZZZZ	NY
ABRAHAMOWITZ, DEBRA	35	F	WO	RR	ZZZZ	NY
CHAIE	7	F	CHILD	RR	ZZZZ	NY
GROSS, LENDIK	22	M	TRDSMN	RR	ZZZZ	NY
MASZOF, ABRAHAM	31	M	TRDSMN	RR	ZZZZ	NY
TONDER, JOACH.	28	M	TRDSMN	RR	ZZZZ	NY
BRUSCHKEWSKY, WLADIS.	23	M	TRDSMN	RR	ZZZZ	NY
SCHRA-E, SCH.	22	M	TRDSMN	RR	ZZZZ	NY
MEULKE	00	F	W	RR	ZZZZ	NY
WARMUND, JUDI	00	M	SHMK	RR	ZZZZ	NY

PASSENGER	AGE	SEX	OCCUPATION	PRIV	VIL	DES
DINER, AISSEN	24	M	MCHT	RR	ZZZZ	NY
LIKIEWITZ, MOSES	36	M	FARMER	RR	ZZZZ	NY
HONYS, VASLOW	00	M	FARMER	RR	ZZZZ	NY
MARIE	28	F	W	RR	ZZZZ	NY
MARIA	4	F	CHILD	RR	ZZZZ	NY
CATHARINA	.11	F	INFANT	RR	ZZZZ	NY
FRIEDERIKE	.01	F	INFANT	RR	ZZZZ	NY
ABERSOTT, AD.	42	M	LABR	RR	ZZZZ	NY
MARCUS, CHAIM	32	M	CGRMKR	RR	ZZZZ	NY
BLOCH, MARCUS	23	M	CGRMKR	RR	ZZZZ	NY
SAMUEL, GERSEN	19	M	CGRMKR	RR	ZZZZ	NY
URWITZ, SIMON	21	M	MCHT	RR	ZZZZ	NY
RULIES, HERMAN	28	M	MCHT	RR	ZZZZ	NY
NATHAN, ITZIG	21	M	MCHT	RR	ZZZZ	NY
U, U	26	M	LABR	PL	ZZZZ	NY
U	00	M	LABR	PL	ZZZZ	NY
BUCKY, WANO	22	M	LABR	PL	ZZZZ	NY
BURE, TOMDES	26	M	LABR	PL	ZZZZ	NY
BRUSKOWIZ, JAN	27	M	LABR	PL	ZZZZ	NY
BASISTOV, FRANZ	48	M	LABR	PL	ZZZZ	NY
KONSTANCIA	38	F	W	PL	ZZZZ	NY
JAN	18	M	S	PL	ZZZZ	NY
WOIZECH	7	M	CHILD	PL	ZZZZ	NY
JULIANA	5	F	CHILD	PL	ZZZZ	NY
KARTAZINA	3	F	CHILD	PL	ZZZZ	NY
MICHALINA	.11	F	INFANT	PL	ZZZZ	NY
OBZUDI, MARIANNE	53	F	WO	PL	ZZZZ	NY

SHIP: NECKAR

FROM: BREMEN
TO: NEW YORK
ARRIVED: 09 JANUARY 1884

PASSENGER	AGE	SEX	OCCUPATION	PRIV	VIL	DES
KATZEW, JOSEF	40	M	LABR	RR	ZZZZ	USA

SHIP: CANADA

FROM: HAVRE
TO: NEW YORK
ARRIVED: 10 JANUARY 1884

PASSENGER	AGE	SEX	OCCUPATION	PRIV	VIL	DES
STIEGLER, ABRAHAM-MR	42	M	TLR	RR	ZZZZ	NY
FRIEDE-MRS	38	F	NN	RR	ZZZZ	NY

SHIP: RHYNLAND

FROM: ANTWERP
TO: NEW YORK
ARRIVED: 11 JANUARY 1884

PASSENGER	AGE	SEX	OCCUPATION	PRIV	VIL	DES
SAMB, LOUIS	28	M	TLR	RR	ZZZZ	NY
COHEN, JOSEPH	24	M	ENGR	RR	ZZZZ	NY

SHIP: ASSYRIAN MONARCH

FROM: LONDON
TO: NEW YORK
ARRIVED: 12 JANUARY 1884

PASSENGER	AGE	SEX	OCCUPATION	PRIV	VIL	DES
JACOBOWITZ, CHAGA	25	F	NN	RR	ZZZZ	USA
JACOB	6	M	CHILD	RR	ZZZZ	USA
LEIBISH	4	F	CHILD	RR	ZZZZ	USA
JOSEPH	.09	M	INFANT	RR	ZZZZ	USA
PARNASS, BARNETT	28	M	LABR	RR	ZZZZ	USA
RACHEL	25	F	W	RR	ZZZZ	USA
ZIPPE	2	F	CHILD	RR	ZZZZ	USA
LANDOCORT, RAPHAEL	20	M	LABR	RR	ZZZZ	USA
COHEN, SOLOMON	26	M	LABR	PL	ZZZZ	USA
ELKA	24	F	W	PL	ZZZZ	USA
VELANSKY, LEO	00	M	LABR	RR	ZZZZ	USA
PRISCILLA	00	F	W	RR	ZZZZ	USA
MORRIS	.09	M	INFANT	RR	ZZZZ	USA
SIMONS, GOVA	31	F	NN	RR	ZZZZ	USA
MATILDA	11	F	CH	RR	ZZZZ	USA
MARY	10	F	CH	RR	ZZZZ	USA
SKOLINK, RACHAEL	22	F	NN	RR	ZZZZ	USA
JACOB	.10	M	INFANT	RR	ZZZZ	USA
ABERNAN, MOORIS	24	M	LABR	RR	ZZZZ	USA
REBECCA	22	F	W	RR	ZZZZ	USA
ELLEN	.10	F	INFANT	RR	ZZZZ	USA
FRANKELSTEIN, JACOB	21	M	LABR	RR	ZZZZ	USA
JACOBS, RACHAEL	29	F	NN	RR	ZZZZ	USA
SPOPSE	4	M	CHILD	RR	ZZZZ	USA
NATHAN	2	M	CHILD	RR	ZZZZ	USA
MALKE	.09	M	INFANT	RR	ZZZZ	USA
MALTHO, MARY	16	F	NN	RR	ZZZZ	USA
BERMANN, KITTY	37	F	NN	RR	ZZZZ	USA
FANNY	11	F	CH	RR	ZZZZ	USA
MARY	10	F	CH	RR	ZZZZ	USA
SARAH	9	F	CHILD	RR	ZZZZ	USA
JESSI	6	F	CHILD	RR	ZZZZ	USA
MARK	3	M	CHILD	RR	ZZZZ	USA
LEITWITZ, ISAAC	00	M	LABR	RR	ZZZZ	USA
LAPITOS, CARL	00	M	LABR	RR	ZZZZ	USA
GOLDSTEIN, FANNY	00	F	NN	RR	ZZZZ	USA
ANNI	3	F	CHILD	RR	ZZZZ	USA
MARY	.09	F	INFANT	RR	ZZZZ	USA
SKOWICK, LEIB	22	M	LABR	RR	ZZZZ	USA
FOX, JOS.	00	M	LABR	RR	ZZZZ	USA
BRIDICKI, JOS.	00	M	LABR	RR	ZZZZ	USA
MELLINCOFF, DAN.	00	M	LABR	RR	ZZZZ	USA
TOPOLSKY, ABR.	22	M	LABR	RR	ZZZZ	USA
ISTONN, DELINI	24	M	LABR	RR	ZZZZ	USA
SOKOLOWSKY, ABR.	48	M	LABR	RR	ZZZZ	USA
ROSYANSKY, HY.	24	M	LABR	RR	ZZZZ	USA
MARIE, OTTO	9	M	CHILD	RR	ZZZZ	USA
JOSEFER, BERNARD	20	M	LABR	RR	ZZZZ	USA
ROSENBERG, JOSEF-M.	48	M	LABR	RR	ZZZZ	USA
KURSEN, LEOH.	25	M	LABR	RR	ZZZZ	USA
GOLOMKOWITZ, FRANK	22	M	LABR	RR	ZZZZ	USA
SCHOTTEN, BRUNO	46	M	LABR	RR	ZZZZ	USA
MARIE	29	F	W	RR	ZZZZ	USA
STOLARSKI, IZIK	30	M	LABR	RR	ZZZZ	USA
KULEK, HY.F.	45	M	LABR	RR	ZZZZ	USA
LEWI, MARK	20	M	LABR	RR	ZZZZ	USA
LAZARUS, LOUIS	28	M	LABR	RR	ZZZZ	USA
COHEN, JACOB	32	M	LABR	RR	ZZZZ	USA
JACOB, SOLOMON	31	M	LABR	RR	ZZZZ	USA
SEGAL, MOSES	25	M	LABR	RR	ZZZZ	USA
LEBUWITZ, SOLOMON	23	M	LABR	RR	ZZZZ	USA
MEREMONT, HYMAN	25	M	LABR	RR	ZZZZ	USA
ADELE	26	F	W	RR	ZZZZ	USA
BERMANN, JACOB	26	M	LABR	RR	ZZZZ	USA
LORNIVER, MORRIS	24	M	LABR	RR	ZZZZ	USA
GOLDE	22	F	W	RR	ZZZZ	USA
SPILLFUNK, BLUMER	16	M	LABR	RR	ZZZZ	USA
GOLDBERG, MORRIS	23	M	LABR	RR	ZZZZ	USA

PASSENGER	AGE	SEX	OCCUPATION	PRIV	DES
MOSES, HYAM	25	M	LABR	RRZZZZ	USA
KLASEN, EDW.	30	M	LABR	RRZZZZ	USA
HORVITZ, MORRIS	28	M	LABR	RRZZZZ	USA
ST.	21	F	W	RRZZZZ	USA
MARKS	2	M	CHILD	RRZZZZ	USA
MOSES, ISAAK	00	M	LABR	RRZZZZ	USA

SHIP: STATE OF INDIANA

FROM: GLASGOW
TO: NEW YORK
ARRIVED: 12 JANUARY 1884

PASSENGER	AGE	SEX	OCCUPATION	PRIV	DES
JALSCHOWSKY, JOSEPH	18	M	LABR	RRZZZZ	USA
BUDNIKI, STANISLAUS	23	M	LABR	RRZZZZ	USA
GANORSKI, ANDRE	27	M	LABR	RRZZZZ	USA
ZIETLIN, C.A.H.	25	M	LABR	RRZZZZ	USA

SHIP: CITY OF CHICAGO

FROM: LIVERPOOL AND QUEENSTOWN
TO: NEW YORK
ARRIVED: 14 JANUARY 1884

PASSENGER	AGE	SEX	OCCUPATION	PRIV	DES
YELLER, CASL	36	M	LABR	RRZZZZ	NY
KRANKAWITZ, ANT.	30	M	LABR	RRZZZZ	NY
INPEHKEWIZ, FRANZ	12	M	LABR	RRZZZZ	NY

SHIP: CITY OF PARA

FROM: PANAMA
TO: NEW YORK
ARRIVED: 14 JANUARY 1884

PASSENGER	AGE	SEX	OCCUPATION	PRIV	DES
DOFACHEWSKY, U-MR	29	M	MCHT	RRZZZZ	RSS

SHIP: FRISIA

FROM: HAMBURG
TO: NEW YORK
ARRIVED: 14 JANUARY 1884

PASSENGER	AGE	SEX	OCCUPATION	PRIV	DES
KABATZNK, JANKEL	35	M	DLR	RRZZZZ	USA
GROBGELD, JACOB	30	M	UNKNOWN	RRZZZZ	USA
SAMORODECKY, DAVID	20	M	UNKNOWN	RRZZZZ	USA
BEILAND, MEYER	43	M	UNKNOWN	RRZZZZ	USA
CHAIE	42	F	W	RRZZZZ	USA
SCHAIE	9	M	CHILD	RRZZZZ	USA
ISAAC	8	M	CHILD	RRZZZZ	USA
SEGALL, CHATZKEL	33	M	DLR	RRZZZZ	USA
TROP, WOLF	24	M	FARMER	RRZZZZ	USA
PAWLOWSKI, VINCENTI	26	M	LABR	RRZZZZ	USA
KOSIZA	24	F	W	RRZZZZ	USA
MICHAEL	00	M	INF	RRZZZZ	USA
GLASER, FEIWEL	31	M	DLR	RRZZZZ	USA
EHSCHAN, ABRAHAM	29	M	TLR	RRZZZZ	USA
POLACK, LEIB	17	M	CGRMKR	RRZZZZ	USA
LUESSMANN, LIPMANN	21	M	DLR	RRZZZZ	USA
SCHEINBERG, ISAAC	44	M	LABR	RRZZZZ	USA
PESCHE	15	F	D	RRZZZZ	USA
BRENNER, WOLF	21	M	BKBNDR	RRZZZZ	USA
COHN, ABRAHAM	25	M	LABR	RRZZZZ	USA
SARA	24	F	W	RRZZZZ	USA
BROWARSKY, ANOCH	16	M	SHMK	RRZZZZ	USA
REICHFELDT, JONAS	29	M	DLR	RRZZZZ	USA
RUBINSTEIN, SCHEITEL	38	F	W	RRZZZZ	USA
RIWE	18	M	CH	RRZZZZ	USA
DOBAE	15	M	CH	RRZZZZ	USA
LIEBE	.11	F	INFANT	RRZZZZ	USA
ABRAHAM, PESSE	56	F	W	RRZZZZ	USA
FREIDEL	18	F	D	RRZZZZ	USA
CHEIE	16	F	UNKNOWN	RRZZZZ	USA
SCHAPIRA, DANIEL	26	M	DLR	RRZZZZ	USA
TODE, JACOB	19	M	UNKNOWN	RRZZZZ	USA
BLUMBERG, ERVSCHE	17	M	WCHMKR	RRZZZZ	USA
EPPSTEIN, SCHEINE	35	F	W	RRZZZZ	USA
NOACH	9	M	CHILD	RRZZZZ	USA
CHATZKEL	6	M	CHILD	RRZZZZ	USA
GLASMANN, SCHUEL	20	M	TLR	RRZZZZ	USA
PSENJAMINOWITZ, SALMEN	18	M	UNKNOWN	RRZZZZ	USA
CUKOR, DINA	29	F	W	RRZZZZ	USA
SELIG	8	M	CHILD	RRZZZZ	USA
PESSE	5	F	CHILD	RRZZZZ	USA
ABRAM	3	M	CHILD	RRZZZZ	USA
KOWNER, JACOB	38	M	DLR	RRZZZZ	USA
BEREBEICIK, LEIB	21	M	UNKNOWN	RRZZZZ	USA
JEDWABNITSKI, DAVID	19	M	UNKNOWN	RRZZZZ	USA
WILDSTEIN, FEIWUSCH	21	M	UNKNOWN	RRZZZZ	USA
MORACH, JUDEL	28	M	TLR	RRZZZZ	USA
KOWNER, JACOB	45	M	LABR	RRZZZZ	USA
RIWE	16	F	CH	RRZZZZ	USA
SCHEINE	8	F	CHILD	RRZZZZ	USA
RUBINOWITZ, LEA	36	F	W	RRZZZZ	USA
GITTEL	9	F	CHILD	RRZZZZ	USA
CHAIE	7	F	CHILD	RRZZZZ	USA
JAHUELIC, FRIEDR.	27	M	SMH	RRZZZZ	USA
BOROWSKI, LEOPOLD	28	M	LABR	RRZZZZ	USA
CARMOISIN, DAVID	21	M	UNKNOWN	RRZZZZ	USA
JAKOWSKY, SAM	33	M	FARMER	RRZZZZ	USA
SCHROD, ABRAM	33	M	FARMER	RRZZZZ	USA
GOLDBERG, DAVID	26	M	TLR	RRZZZZ	USA
KANER, HERSCH	23	M	UNKNOWN	RRZZZZ	USA
BRUNSTEIN, BARUCH	26	M	UNKNOWN	RRZZZZ	USA
GODZIK, JACOB	19	M	UNKNOWN	RRZZZZ	USA
SINGER, SARAH	25	F	UNKNOWN	RRZZZZ	USA
ARON, ABRAM	20	M	DLR	RRZZZZ	USA
MIMZER, MORDCHE	35	M	DLR	RRZZZZ	USA
GOLDBERG, JOSNA	30	F	WVR	RRZZZZ	USA
KOWNER, ITE	00	M	INF	RRZZZZ	USA
HEIDELMANN, ISRAEL	26	M	GZR	RRZZZZ	USA
KOHN, MARCUS	41	M	CPTR	RRZZZZ	USA
KRAEMER, JUDEL	33	M	DLR	RRZZZZ	USA
FEITELSOHN, CAERILIE	24	F	SGL	RRZZZZ	USA
MAJEWSKI, ROSALIE	25	F	SGL	RRZZZZ	USA
FRIEDMANN, SZEFTEL.	21	M	DLR	RRZZZZ	USA
SCHENKER, ISAAC	38	M	DLR	RRZZZZ	USA

SHIP: KATIE

FROM: STETTIN
TO: NEW YORK
ARRIVED: 16 JANUARY 1884

PASSENGER	AGE	SEX	OCCUPATION	PRIV	DES
MAYCHNACK, AGNES	21	F	UNKNOWN	RRZZZZ	USA
KAEZKONSKA, PIETRONELLA	30	F	UNKNOWN	RRZZZZ	USA

PASSENGER	AGE	SEX	OCCUPATION	PRV VIL DES
STACHONIAK, MARTIN	47	M	LABR	RRZZZZUSA
MARIANE	43	F	W	RRZZZZUSA
SZKUDLANEK, MICHAEL	30	M	LABR	RRZZZZUSA
METRUZENSKA, FRANZISKA	40	F	WO	RRZZZZUSA
LEONTINE	18	F	D	RRZZZZUSA
ANTONIE	7	F	CHILD	RRZZZZUSA
JOHAN	4	M	CHILD	RRZZZZUSA
GARSKI, JOHAN	37	M	LABR	RRZZZZUSA
JULIANA	46	F	W	RRZZZZUSA
SCHUTIST, ANNA	22	F	D	RRZZZZUSA
HINZ, VERONICA	21	F	D	RRZZZZUSA
WALOSCHEK, PAULINE	17	F	D	RRZZZZUSA
DOMKE, MARIE	00	F	CH	RRZZZZUSA
ANNA	10	F	CH	RRZZZZUSA
FRANZ	6	M	CHILD	RRZZZZUSA
GARSKI, ROSALIE	10	F	CH	RRZZZZUSA
VALENTINE	6	F	CHILD	RRZZZZUSA
SCHUTIST, MARIE	2	F	CHILD	RRZZZZUSA
MARTHA	.09	F	INFANT	RRZZZZUSA
HINZ, MARTIN	24	M	LABR	RRZZZZUSA

SHIP: CIRCASSIA

FROM: GLASGOW AND MOVILLE
TO: NEW YORK
ARRIVED: 17 JANUARY 1884

PASSENGER	AGE	SEX	OCCUPATION	PRV VIL DES
GERZIRIDA, HERM.M.	40	M	LABR	FNZZZZUSA

SHIP: CEPHALONIA

FROM: LIVERPOOL AND QUEENSTOWN
TO: NEW YORK
ARRIVED: 18 JANUARY 1884

PASSENGER	AGE	SEX	OCCUPATION	PRV VIL DES
ARONROHN, LOUS	20	M	CL	PLZZZZNY

SHIP: LESSING

FROM: HAMBURG
TO: NEW YORK
ARRIVED: 21 JANUARY 1884

PASSENGER	AGE	SEX	OCCUPATION	PRV VIL DES
MININKAS, ANNA	24	F	SGL	RRZZZZUSA
SCHULEWITZ, MENDEL	30	M	DLR	RRZZZZUSA
ROSENBLUM, SAMUEL	21	M	BKBNDR	RRZZZZUSA
RACHEL	20	F	W	RRZZZZUSA
KUSSEHEWITZ, MICHAEL	18	M	LABR	RRZZZZUSA
SIMONOWITZ, SIMON	23	M	JWLR	RRZZZZUSA
RUBINTSCHIK, CHAIM	23	M	LABR	RRZZZZUSA
BRESLAN, ELIAS	24	M	TLR	RRZZZZUSA
BALDANSKY, JUDEL	25	M	LABR	RRZZZZUSA
JOCHLER, FANY	23	F	SGL	RRZZZZUSA
SCHNEPESCHKI, MOSES	23	M	SHMK	RRZZZZUSA
KRYENSKY, ABRAM	30	M	TLR	RRZZZZUSA
SACHAREWITZ, ISRAEL	26	M	UNKNOWN	RRZZZZUSA
GRUENSPAN, EPHRAIM	25	M	UNKNOWN	RRZZZZUSA
JACUBOWITZ, JACOB	26	M	LABR	RRZZZZUSA
JUSCHKEWITZ, DOMINIK	23	M	UNKNOWN	RRZZZZUSA
SIMANSKY, BENEDIK	27	M	UNKNOWN	RRZZZZUSA
MAXIMOWITZ, SIMON	45	M	UNKNOWN	RRZZZZUSA
ZAIHARD, ISAAC	41	M	UNKNOWN	RRZZZZUSA
PRECHVOSKY, KAZIMIR	19	M	UNKNOWN	RRZZZZUSA
AUGUSTANOWITZ, FRANK	18	M	UNKNOWN	RRZZZZUSA
KRACKOOSKY, FRANT	20	M	UNKNOWN	RRZZZZUSA
ZESKEWITZ, BALESLAD	20	M	UNKNOWN	RRZZZZUSA
WOLSCONSKY, HAN	20	M	UNKNOWN	RRZZZZUSA
KNUDT, EMILIE	21	F	SGL	RRZZZZUSA
ACHIFT, ARON	36	M	TLR	RRZZZZUSA
MATZKEWITZ, CHAIKEL	25	M	TNMK	RRZZZZUSA
AYPOWITZ, SALMEN	37	M	LABR	RRZZZZUSA
MORDCHE	42	M	DLR	RRZZZZUSA
BOTWINIK, JACOB	36	M	GZR	RRZZZZUSA
MITLITZKI, LEWIN	32	M	MCHT	RRZZZZUSA
WEINSTEIN, TAUCHUM	37	M	UNKNOWN	RRZZZZUSA
CHASNOWITZ, HENOCH	32	M	UNKNOWN	RRZZZZUSA
WACLANIS, VICENTY	25	M	LABR	RRZZZZUSA
MILONCITZ, IGNATZ	18	M	UNKNOWN	RRZZZZUSA
BLASANTZKY, JOSES	33	M	UNKNOWN	RRZZZZUSA
JENNSCHANETZ, ANTONIS	40	M	UNKNOWN	RRZZZZUSA
MOSES, SAMUEL	27	M	MCHT	RRZZZZUSA
GRODOWSKI, CHAINE	9	M	CHILD	RRZZZZUSA
RINGINSKI, ABRAHAM	22	M	DLR	RRZZZZUSA
GORITZKI, FEIVEL	24	M	UNKNOWN	RRZZZZUSA
BIAL, ABEL	24	M	UNKNOWN	RRZZZZUSA
BAURZE, LIDOR	43	M	LABR	RRZZZZUSA
GERBER, LOSER	17	M	UNKNOWN	RRZZZZUSA
AILVIENSKI, MOSES	50	M	UNKNOWN	RRZZZZUSA
SCHNEIDER, CHAINE	.09	F	INFANT	RRZZZZUSA
SOREMBOWITSCH, ABRAHAM	22	M	BKBNDR	RRZZZZUSA
RABELSKI, FRUME	34	F	W	RRZZZZUSA
MAR---S, ELIAS	40	M	LABR	RRZZZZUSA
JOHE.	6	F	CHILD	RRZZZZUSA
BERTHA	.05	F	INFANT	RRZZZZUSA
HERSCHBECHER, SAUL	22	M	DLR	RRZZZZUSA
SCHWARZ, RISCHEL	19	F	SGL	RRZZZZUSA
WIESE, BERTHA	30	F	W	RRZZZZUSA
DAKOTZINSKY, ABRAHAM	19	M	DLR	RRZZZZUSA
SOFRANSKY, GITTEL	19	F	SGL	RRZZZZUSA
GARBOROWITZ, JACOB	15	M	LABR	RRZZZZUSA
LNDER, GABRIEL	42	M	LABR	RRZZZZUSA
ROSENTHAL, SELIG	41	M	UNKNOWN	RRZZZZUSA
GRINBERG, MORDCHE	24	M	UNKNOWN	RRZZZZUSA
MIKOLSKY, DAVID	15	M	UNKNOWN	RRZZZZUSA
UBOWITZ, BEHR	9	M	CHILD	RRZZZZUSA
MORAWER, FALK	60	M	LABR	RRZZZZUSA
JUDEL	22	M	UNKNOWN	RRZZZZUSA
SARA	14	F	SGL	RRZZZZUSA
CIRELSTEIN, MOSES	23	M	LABR	RRZZZZUSA
DAKOTZINSKY, SARA	.11	F	INFANT	RRZZZZUSA
TANNENBAUM, RIWE	24	F	W	RRZZZZUSA
LEISER	4	M	CHILD	RRZZZZUSA
PESCHE	.11	F	INFANT	RRZZZZUSA
SIDORAWITZ, MATES	40	M	UNKNOWN	RRZZZZUSA
BEILES, ISAAI	46	M	UNKNOWN	RRZZZZUSA
KRACANSKY, STEFAN	24	M	UNKNOWN	RRZZZZUSA
BELMAN, JACOB	23	M	UNKNOWN	RRZZZZUSA
WINKLER, BARUCH	24	M	UNKNOWN	RRZZZZUSA
ABRAHAM	29	M	UNKNOWN	RRZZZZUSA
ELENBURG, ARON	22	M	UNKNOWN	RRZZZZUSA
SCHULM, CHAIM	24	M	UNKNOWN	RRZZZZUSA
BACKE, JOSEF	33	M	UNKNOWN	RRZZZZUSA
GELARSEWSKI, MICHAEL	22	M	LABR	RRZZZZUSA
KOR, ELIAS	20	M	SHMK	RRZZZZUSA
KRAFT, AUGUST	23	M	LABR	RRZZZZUSA
KATZ, MOSES	24	M	UNKNOWN	RRZZZZUSA
SALOMON, ADOLF	23	M	LABR	RRZZZZUSA
DANSTEIN, MARCUS	24	M	UNKNOWN	RRZZZZUSA
JASKOWER, CHS.H.	33	M	UNKNOWN	RRZZZZUSA

SHIP: PERSIAN MONARCH

FROM: LONDON
TO: NEW YORK
ARRIVED: 21 JANUARY 1884

PASSENGER	AGE	SEX	OCCUPATION	PRV VIL DES
PECZKA, JAN	28	M	LABR	PLZZZZNY
JOSEFINE	24	F	W	PLZZZZNY
KONRAD	.08	M	INFANT	PLZZZZNY
BEROMKA	.08	M	INFANT	PLZZZZNY
MOSKOWITZ, C.S.	23	M	LABR	PLZZZZNY
DYZORONSKI, A.	21	M	LABR	PLZZZZNY
SUCHORATSKI, C.	21	M	LABR	PLZZZZNY
KAPLAN, LEIB	20	M	LABR	PLZZZZNY
KRANZ, L.H.	21	M	LABR	PLZZZZNY
ETTINGER, HIRSCH	34	M	LABR	PLZZZZNY
BERAMANN, S.	12	M	LABR	PLZZZZNY
TIOLER, I.	34	M	LABR	PLZZZZNY
BALMEAT, MEYER	29	M	LABR	PLZZZZNY
ZACHAWITZ, L.	12	M	LABR	PLZZZZNY
GANZ, C.	20	M	LABR	PLZZZZNY
KANNER, I.	25	M	LABR	PLZZZZNY
ETELSOHN, L.	11	M	CH	PLZZZZNY
DEBRIN, M.	10	M	CH	PLZZZZNY
RADYVSKY, M.	21	M	LABR	PLZZZZNY
BEITZ, L.	17	M	LABR	PLZZZZNY
SCHEIN, I.	48	M	LABR	PLZZZZNY
M.	12	M	LABR	PLZZZZNY
MULLNER, D.	18	F	DMS	PLZZZZNY
BRAMAN, I.	12	F	DMS	PLZZZZNY
RACZKOWSKY, A.	43	F	DMS	PLZZZZNY
GOLDBERG, H.	12	F	DMS	PLZZZZNY
FAUBKES, S.	13	F	DMS	PLZZZZNY
RUBINSKI, Z.	26	F	DMS	PLZZZZNY
WIPPEZ, S.	44	F	W	PLZZZZNY
S.	12	F	CH	PLZZZZNY
MICENSKY, M.	48	M	LABR	PLZZZZNY
C.	11	M	CH	PLZZZZNY
I.	10	M	CH	PLZZZZNY
RUBEN, SARAH	18	F	DMS	PLZZZZNY
SCHLATAIN, A.	30	M	LABR	PLZZZZNY

SHIP: SALIER

FROM: BREMEN
TO: NEW YORK
ARRIVED: 22 JANUARY 1884

PASSENGER	AGE	SEX	OCCUPATION	PRV VIL DES
KANKOWSKI, ALEXANDRA	26	F	NN	RRZZZZUSA
KRIEGER, LUDEWISKA	34	F	NN	RRZZZZUSA

SHIP: BOTHNIA

FROM: LIVERPOOL
TO: NEW YORK
ARRIVED: 23 JANUARY 1884

PASSENGER	AGE	SEX	OCCUPATION	PRV VIL DES
GOLDBERG, ELLIS-MR.	35	M	MCHT	RRZZZZUSA

SHIP: WESTPHALIA

FROM: HAMBURG AND HAVRE
TO: NEW YORK
ARRIVED: 23 JANUARY 1884

PASSENGER	AGE	SEX	OCCUPATION	PRV VIL DES
LEWI, AARON	19	M	MCHT	RRZZZZNY
SILBERMANN, HENE	50	F	W	RRZZZZNY
CHANNE	9	F	CHILD	RRZZZZNY
BRICK, MARIA	38	F	W	RRZZZZCH
ABRAHAM	9	M	CHILD	RRZZZZCH
ISIDOR	8	M	CHILD	RRZZZZCH
ALEXANDER	7	M	CHILD	RRZZZZCH
BARUCH	.11	M	INFANT	RRZZZZCH
ZUROWSKY, JANKEL	28	M	TLR	RRZZZZNY
SKUPSA, JOHANN	23	M	FARMER	RRZZZZNY
BOROVSKY, HERM.	19	M	CGRMKR	RRZZZZNY
SPRINGER, LEISER	17	M	CL	RRZZZZNY
FRIEDLAND, JANKEL	45	M	TLR	RRZZZZIL
WEBER, JACOB	28	M	DLR	RRZZZZNY
ZACHAROWITZ, MOSES	35	M	DLR	RRZZZZNY
JACZOWSKY, CHANNE	28	M	TLR	RRZZZZNY
GROSSMANN, CHAIN	35	M	SHMK	RRZZZZNY
KRUSCHINSKY, LEAR	56	M	LABR	RRZZZZNY
AUGUSTE	18	F	SGL	RRZZZZNY

SHIP: BELGENLAND

FROM: ANTWERP
TO: NEW YORK
ARRIVED: 24 JANUARY 1884

PASSENGER	AGE	SEX	OCCUPATION	PRV VIL DES
HEWONSKY, JOSEF	16	M	LABR	PLZZZZUNK
SPEGAA, FRANZ.	24	F	SVNT	PLZZZZUNK
THERA	00	F	INF	PLZZZZUNK
OWJDA, FRANZ	24	M	NN	PLZZZZCH
MALLCH, LES.	25	M	MLR	PLZZZZCH
LECOIS, ABR.	28	M	SHMK	PLZZZZMI
ESTER	24	F	NN	PLZZZZMI
DOREY	2	M	CHILD	PLZZZZMI
MILLY	00	F	INF	PLZZZZMI
KONINGSTOY, ISAAC	30	M	BRR	PLZZZZNY
KAPLAN, M.	22	M	TLR	RRZZZZUNK
WOLF, ABRAH.	21	M	TLR	RRZZZZUNK

SHIP: ACAPULCO

FROM: UNKNOWN
TO: NEW YORK
ARRIVED: 26 JANUARY 1884

PASSENGER	AGE	SEX	OCCUPATION	PRV VIL DES
ROSENCLAUS, MOSES	22	M	PDLR	RRZZZZUNK
FIELDBRAUT, JOS.	19	M	PDLR	RRZZZZUNK

PASSENGER	AGE	SEX	OCCUPATION	PVRIVL	DES
SHIP: GELLERT					
FROM: HAMBURG					
TO: NEW YORK					
ARRIVED: 29 JANUARY 1884					
MISKEWITZ, F.	64	F	W	RRZZZZ	USA
ROSALIE	23	F	D	RRZZZZ	USA
ARON	70	M	DLR	RRZZZZ	USA
SALZ, MOSES	20	M	DLR	RRZZZZ	USA
BOROWSKI, SAMUEL	30	M	PNTR	RRZZZZ	USA
HEILPERN, JACOB	23	M	JNR	RRZZZZ	USA
BRUDNER, ABRAH.	24	M	LKSH	RRZZZZ	USA
SCHWEIDEL, GERSON	21	M	JNR	RRZZZZ	USA
DINSTEIN, ABRAH.	30	M	LABR	RRZZZZ	USA
WERSCHEWSKY, LEOPOLD	18	M	UPHST	RRZZZZ	USA
MOKZABOWSKI, TEOFIL	26	M	LABR	RRZZZZ	USA
DOMBRAWSKY, FRANZ	23	M	LABR	RRZZZZ	USA
GLODOWSKY, W.	36	M	LABR	RRZZZZ	USA
TANTER, JACOB	30	M	LABR	RRZZZZ	USA
FREISCHEL, JOSEF	23	M	LABR	RRZZZZ	USA
KANTORSKY, JOH.	21	M	LABR	RRZZZZ	USA
TAMO, SALOMON	30	M	LABR	RRZZZZ	USA
ROBMANN, ELIAS	19	M	LABR	RRZZZZ	USA
MASUR, LIEBMANN	38	M	LABR	RRZZZZ	USA
FINTZELSTEIN, U	9	F	CHILD	RRZZZZ	USA
FEIERMANN, TABY	23	M	LABR	RRZZZZ	USA
KRINSKY, ABRAH.	41	M	LABR	RRZZZZ	USA
LIPTZIK, ISAAC	23	M	LABR	RRZZZZ	USA
LABOTZKY, FELIX	25	M	BCHR	RRZZZZ	USA
LEWIN, CHIEL	29	M	LABR	RRZZZZ	USA
ISAAC	16	M	LABR	RRZZZZ	USA
GABRIEL	9	M	CHILD	RRZZZZ	USA
LEVY, SAMUEL	25	M	LABR	RRZZZZ	USA
HIRSCH	23	M	LABR	RRZZZZ	USA
SCHAPIRO, MICHEL	48	M	LABR	RRZZZZ	USA
ERBSTEIN, SCHLOME	16	M	CGRMKR	RRZZZZ	USA
RUBRECHT, JOSEF	27	M	CGRMKR	RRZZZZ	USA
BARON, EISICH	24	M	CGRMKR	RRZZZZ	USA
LIME	20	F	W	RRZZZZ	USA
COSSLOWSKY, JUDEL	18	M	TLR	RRZZZZ	USA
HURWITZ, SIMON	33	M	TLR	RRZZZZ	USA
LEWIN, ITZIG	23	M	LKSH	RRZZZZ	USA
ROBMANN, MEIER	54	M	TLR	RRZZZZ	USA
ZENKO, CASIMIR	26	M	LABR	RRZZZZ	USA
BORNOWSKY, JAN	18	M	LABR	RRZZZZ	USA
BUCEWICZ, BENEDICT	22	M	LABR	RRZZZZ	USA
MATULEWICZ, JACOB	15	M	LABR	RRZZZZ	USA
SADES, JACOB	18	M	LABR	RRZZZZ	USA
BORNOWSKY, JOSEF	25	M	LABR	RRZZZZ	USA
KONEIS, ANTON	18	M	LABR	RRZZZZ	USA
VINCENT	23	M	LABR	RRZZZZ	USA
BACKO, STANISLAUS	27	M	LABR	RRZZZZ	USA
KILINSKY, STANISLAUS	27	M	LABR	RRZZZZ	USA
RUTZIEWSKY, PETER	31	M	LABR	RRZZZZ	USA
LENIJONIS, CASIMIR	41	M	LABR	RRZZZZ	USA
BRAUNSTEIN, ZELDE	45	F	W	RRZZZZ	USA
CACHOWSKY, FRANZ	19	F	SGL	RRZZZZ	USA
NOLASKOWSKY, JOSEFA	22	F	SGL	RRZZZZ	USA
JOHANNA	.11	F	INFANT	RRZZZZ	USA
KAPLAN, BERND.	22	M	LABR	RRZZZZ	USA
SVOGOWITZ, ARONHOLD	19	M	LABR	RRZZZZ	USA
SRAGOLSKI, SARA	20	F	SGL	RRZZZZ	USA
LEA	18	F	SGL	RRZZZZ	USA
MARKUS, BASCHE	28	F	SGL	RRZZZZ	USA
HOTNITZKI, HIRSCH	46	M	LABR	RRZZZZ	USA
RUBINOWITZ, LENDER	40	M	LABR	RRZZZZ	USA
LEIB	9	M	CHILD	RRZZZZ	USA
KILIKUS, MATH.	43	M	LABR	RRZZZZ	USA
GRUNBERG, GITTEL	20	F	W	RRZZZZ	USA
ANNE	16	F	SI	RRZZZZ	USA
RACHEL	.11	F	INFANT	RRZZZZ	USA
ZABORSKY, ARON	40	M	SHMK	RRZZZZ	USA
ZLOCZISTY, LEIB	26	M	TLR	RRZZZZ	USA
MOSES	33	M	TLR	RRZZZZ	USA
KATZ, BERL	25	M	LABR	RRZZZZ	USA
HEER, JOSEF	17	M	LABR	RRZZZZ	USA
MEIERMANN, LEWI.	21	M	DLR	RRZZZZ	USA
MILWIZKI, SCHEFSEL	26	M	DLR	RRZZZZ	USA
ANDREAS, VINCENTY	18	M	LABR	RRZZZZ	USA
KOCH, CARL	45	M	LABR	RRZZZZ	USA
NIADZINSKI, JAN	15	M	LABR	RRZZZZ	USA
BUCEWITZ, VINCENTY	16	M	LABR	RRZZZZ	USA
MEKLER, ABRAHAM	28	M	LABR	RRZZZZ	USA
SCHETLIS, KEIWE	41	M	LABR	RRZZZZ	USA
DEUTSCH, MINNA	18	F	SGL	RRZZZZ	USA
TEMPE, SARAH	26	F	W	RRZZZZ	USA
SHIP: POLARIA					
FROM: HAMBURG					
TO: NEW YORK					
ARRIVED: 29 JANUARY 1884					
RUBIN, WOLF	26	M	GZR	PLZZZZ	NY
SZESMAR, JURA	34	M	LABR	PLZZZZ	NY
MARIA	32	F	W	PLZZZZ	NY
MARIA	7	F	CHILD	PLZZZZ	NY
FEDOR	4	M	CHILD	PLZZZZ	NY
JULIA	.11	F	INFANT	PLZZZZ	NY
HAMINSKA	.01	F	INFANT	PLZZZZ	NY
FEDOR	6	M	CHILD	PLZZZZ	NY
RETZEK	45	M	LABR	PLZZZZ	NY
FENCIK	49	M	LABR	PLZZZZ	NY
URBAN, DEMICZEK	38	M	LABR	PLZZZZ	NY
ANDREKOWITZ, AND.	25	M	LABR	PLZZZZ	NY
BARBARA	22	F	W	PLZZZZ	NY
TUJDA, ANDRAS	32	M	LABR	PLZZZZ	NY
RISZKA, PETER	26	M	LABR	PLZZZZ	NY
HOLLENDER, LEIZER	43	M	LABR	PLZZZZ	NY
OSTRONSKI, F.	22	M	TNR	RRZZZZ	NY
MADLER, C.	15	M	BKR	RRZZZZ	NY
PATTELKOW, FRANZ	32	M	LABR	RRZZZZ	NY
BRIDA, STANISL.	24	M	LABR	PLZZZZ	NY
ZLOTCK, JAS.	24	M	LABR	PLZZZZ	NY
RADWANKA, JANOS	50	M	LABR	PLZZZZ	NY
LABIVANITZ, JOS.	24	M	LABR	PLZZZZ	NY
OLENIK, MARCIN	40	M	LABR	PLZZZZ	NY
PARNES, BARUCH	33	M	TRDSMN	RRZZZZ	NY
JANKEL	7	M	CHILD	RRZZZZ	NY
JAMISZEWSKI, SCHMUEL	23	M	TRDSMN	RRZZZZ	NY
LIEBERMANN, CH.D.	23	M	TRDSMN	RRZZZZ	NY
JAMISZEWSKI, LEIB	19	M	TRDSMN	RRZZZZ	NY
PUTTER, BENJ.	20	M	TRDSMN	RRZZZZ	NY
CHANE	20	F	W	RRZZZZ	NY
KURMES, MOSES-L.	39	M	TRDSMN	RRZZZZ	NY
KARCONECK, WOLF	31	M	TRDSMN	RRZZZZ	NY
DROZDKI, MORDCHE	26	M	TRDSMN	RRZZZZ	NY
LEMDAN, BERN.	32	M	TRDSMN	RRZZZZ	NY
SHIP: GENERAL WERDER					
FROM: BREMEN					
TO: NEW YORK					
ARRIVED: 31 JANUARY 1884					
WDENSEHUG, JOSEF	33	M	LABR	RRZZZZ	USA
THERESSA	20	F	W	RRZZZZ	USA
FRANZ	3	M	CHILD	RRZZZZ	USA

PASSENGER	AGE	SEX	OCCUPATION	PRV VIL DES
STEFAN	1	M	CHILD	RRZZZZUSA
WLADISLAW	.06	M	INFANT	RRZZZZUSA
JULIANNE	40	F	W	RRZZZZUSA

SHIP: PAVONIA

FROM: LIVERPOOL AND QUEENSTOWN
TO: NEW YORK
ARRIVED: 01 FEBRUARY 1884

PASSENGER	AGE	SEX	OCCUPATION	PRV VIL DES
CARLSON, CARL-JOHN.	25	M	SLR	FNZZZZNY
SCHNEIDER, EDW.	25	M	GENT	RRZZZZVA

SHIP: GALICIAN MONARCH

FROM: LONDON
TO: NEW YORK
ARRIVED: 02 FEBRUARY 1884

PASSENGER	AGE	SEX	OCCUPATION	PRV VIL DES
PURO, ABRAHAM	47	M	LABR	PLZZZZUSA
MARCUK, ABRAHAM	50	M	LABR	PLZZZZUSA
MAYER, SIMON	25	M	LABR	PLZZZZUSA
ROSENTHAL, MORITZ	30	M	LABR	PLZZZZUSA
SINGER, HENRY	29	M	LABR	PLZZZZUSA
JISCHOWSKI, JOSEF	36	M	LABR	PLZZZZUSA
MARIA	23	F	W	PLZZZZUSA
GUDELSKY, WOLFF	17	M	LABR	PLZZZZUSA
POPLER, M.	20	M	TLR	PLZZZZUSA
WIBLER, DAVIS	22	M	TLR	PLZZZZUSA
LEFKOWITZ, N.	22	M	TLR	PLZZZZUSA
TALKOWSKI, LEIB	25	M	LABR	RRZZZZUSA
POPOLSKI, OLE	21	M	LABR	RRZZZZUSA
MER, M.	31	M	LABR	RRZZZZUSA
OSTUKALSKI, JOSEL	47	M	LABR	RRZZZZUSA
JIKARSKI, JOSEF	24	M	LABR	RRZZZZUSA
RUPLAN, LEIB	30	M	LABR	RRZZZZUSA
FLEISCH, M.	38	M	LABR	RRZZZZUSA
OLENSKY, B.	48	M	LABR	RRZZZZUSA
GRINSBERG, J.	33	M	LABR	RRZZZZUSA
BABANSKI, J.	40	M	LABR	RRZZZZUSA
WESIERSKI, G.	21	M	LABR	RRZZZZUSA
LUBAWIN, L.	12	M	LABR	RRZZZZUSA
KANARSKY, SLOMON	22	M	TLR	RRZZZZUSA
GUSFMAN, JOSEPF	22	M	TLR	RRZZZZUSA
SALOMONS, RACHEL	26	F	WI	RRZZZZUSA
JACOB	.10	M	INFANT	RRZZZZUSA

SHIP: GALLIA

FROM: LIVERPOOL AND QUEENSTOWN
TO: NEW YORK
ARRIVED: 04 FEBRUARY 1884

PASSENGER	AGE	SEX	OCCUPATION	PRV VIL DES
MUVESKA-WICOLA, HERMAN-	27	M	LABR	RRZZZZUSA

SHIP: INDIA

FROM: HAMBURG
TO: NEW YORK
ARRIVED: 05 FEBRUARY 1884

PASSENGER	AGE	SEX	OCCUPATION	PRV VIL DES
SCHARKOWSKY, JOS.	21	M	LABR	RRZZZZNY
ENDELMANN, CHANE-M.	24	F	WO	RRZZZZNY
JACOBSOHN, JACOB	18	M	LABR	RRZZZZNY
ENDELMANN, LEIB	26	M	TRDSMN	RRZZZZNY
ELZIK	30	M	TRDSMN	RRZZZZNY
CILRYN, MALKE	16	F	SGL	RRZZZZNY
WEINSTEIN, ISAAK	16	M	BKBNDR	RRZZZZNY
GUNTHER, THOS.	50	M	FARMER	PLZZZZNY
GERTRUDE	50	F	W	PLZZZZNY
MAGDALENA	19	F	D	PLZZZZNY
DORAFSKY, JAN.	00	M	LABR	RRZZZZNY
LANDAN, BERNHD.	32	M	MCHT	PLZZZZNY
DASEFSKY, DOM.	19	M	LABR	PLZZZZNY
NARZESCHEFKY, STEFAN	22	M	LABR	PLZZZZNY
GEFFEN, ABR.	28	M	TRDSMN	RRZZZZNY
ANNA	22	F	W	RRZZZZNY
BRANTHOLD, TOBIAS	28	M	TRDSMN	RRZZZZNY
NEUMANN, ISRAEL	27	M	TRDSMN	RRZZZZNY
STORCH, FISCHEL	25	M	TRDSMN	PLZZZZNY
GROSHAUS, LESSER	26	M	TRDSMN	PLZZZZNY
CHAIME, ADOLF	28	M	TRDSMN	PLZZZZNY
ADELA	22	F	W	PLZZZZNY
GETEL	.05	F	INFANT	PLZZZZNY
KNECHT, LEOP.	24	M	LABR	PLZZZZNY
ROTTSTEIN, CH.-ABR.	19	M	LABR	RRZZZZNY
KILLOV, LUCH	36	M	LABR	RRZZZZNY
CATHARINA	21	F	W	RRZZZZNY
BACHUSG, FELIC	22	M	LABR	PLZZZZNY
PIOTCKOWSKI, MICHAL	49	M	LABR	RRZZZZNY
LADISLAUS	7	M	CHILD	RRZZZZNY
ANCZUKIEWICS, ALEXAND.	24	M	TRDSMN	RRZZZZNY
JIRSZAL, HENRIETTE	20	F	SGL	RRZZZZNY
POSWICTOWSKI, JENS	36	M	LABR	RRZZZZNY
MOROS	00	M	S	RRZZZZNY
JASKE, JOSEF	00	M	TRDSMN	RRZZZZNY
DAVIEDEZUK, VINCENT	00	M	LABR	RRZZZZNY
ANTONIE	30	F	W	RRZZZZNY
VINCENT	.09	M	INFANT	RRZZZZNY
PALUSCHAK, ANDR.	00	M	LABR	RRZZZZNY
ROLRINSKI, M.	30	M	LABR	RRZZZZNY
CEPA, JAN.	28	M	LABR	RRZZZZNY
GITTEL, R.	28	M	LABR	RRZZZZNY
JUCZKOWICZ, FRANZ	42	M	LABR	PLZZZZNY
ARMATA, JAN.	27	M	LABR	PLZZZZNY
JOWASZY, BERTA	29	M	LABR	PLZZZZNY
FELSOR, JOSEF	26	M	LABR	PLZZZZNY
WAJLOCHA, JOSEF	17	M	LABR	PLZZZZNY
CENTMAISKY, ANTON	22	M	LABR	PLZZZZNY
EGRESS, ANDR.	40	M	LABR	PLZZZZNY
STEFFAN, JASZ.	26	M	LABR	PLZZZZNY
BERTEK, STEFAN	24	M	LABR	PLZZZZNY
KLEYE, JOSEF	25	M	LABR	PLZZZZNY
KAPUSENISKY, JOS.	26	M	LABR	PLZZZZNY
KLENCA, ANDREAS	00	M	LABR	PLZZZZNY
K----, P-L	00	M	LABR	PLZZZZNY
KOWACZ, MICHAL	00	M	LABR	PLZZZZNY
ROMAN, MICHAL	40	M	LABR	PLZZZZNY
JURSKY, THOMAS	41	M	LABR	PLZZZZNY
POLITOSITZ, FRANZISEK	27	M	LABR	PLZZZZNY
KLEMENS, GURSKI	50	M	LABR	PLZZZZNY
MARKOWITZ, DANEL	43	M	LABR	PLZZZZNY
PYJOT, POLAK	36	M	LABR	PLZZZZNY
KADZIK, FRANZ.	15	M	LABR	PLZZZZNY
FRANZISEK, DYCNAL	17	M	LABR	PLZZZZNY
DREMLA, WOYSEK	30	M	LABR	PLZZZZNY
KARDZIK, ANTON	17	M	LABR	PLZZZZNY

PASSENGER	AGE	SEX	OCCUPATION	PRIV	VIL	DES

SHIP: ZEELAND

FROM: ANTWERP
TO: NEW YORK
ARRIVED: 06 FEBRUARY 1884

PASSENGER	AGE	SEX	OCCUPATION	PRIV VIL DES
WISNIEVZKI, MART.	40	M	FARMER	PLZZZZNY
JOSEFA	40	F	UNKNOWN	PLZZZZNY
ANTON	5	M	CHILD	PLZZZZNY
ANTONIA	3	F	CHILD	PLZZZZNY

SHIP: RHAETIA

FROM: HAMBURG AND HAVRE
TO: NEW YORK
ARRIVED: 08 FEBRUARY 1884

PASSENGER	AGE	SEX	OCCUPATION	PRIV VIL DES
BISTRUM, CONSTANTIN-BAR	42	M	PVTR	RRZZZZUSA
TENNENBAUM, SARAH	44	F	W	RRZZZZUSA
JUDES	9	F	CHILD	RRZZZZUSA
GESOWSKY, RUBEN	38	M	DLR	RRZZZZUSA
RAGOWIN, JUDEL	36	M	DLR	RRZZZZUSA
HERSCHSOHN, HENDEL	49	M	HTR	RRZZZZUSA
RAGOWIN, CHAIM	39	M	DLR	RRZZZZUSA
PERSKI, NOTE	18	M	BCHR	RRZZZZUSA
RAGOWIN, ARON	34	M	BCHR	RRZZZZUSA
PERSKI, MOSES	34	M	BCHR	RRZZZZUSA
GOTTFRIED, ISRAEL	25	M	DLR	RRZZZZUSA
GOLDSTEIN, JOSSEL	20	M	DLR	RRZZZZUSA
HAUSCHILD, JOH.	16	M	DLR	RRZZZZUSA
CYNAMEN, MOSES	22	M	LABR	RRZZZZUSA
PIASECKI, JAN	28	M	LABR	RRZZZZUSA
LAWISTOWSKI, JAN	34	M	LABR	RRZZZZUSA
DROSDOWSKI, JOSEF	9	M	CHILD	RRZZZZUSA
GRABOWSKY, FRANZ	25	M	LABR	RRZZZZUSA
BRON, CHAIM	25	M	DLR	RRZZZZUSA
BUNKOWSKA, JAGNA	35	F	W	RRZZZZUSA
JAN	4	M	CHILD	RRZZZZUSA
BRUDNIKI, JAN	23	M	LABR	RRZZZZUSA
MATZEITIS, FRANZ	24	M	LABR	RRZZZZUSA
LOWE---, MOSES	35	M	LABR	RRZZZZUSA
HURWITZ, BERL	29	M	TLR	RRZZZZUSA
BRIL, ISRAEL	22	M	TLR	RRZZZZUSA
KOLBURS, EDWARD	19	M	LABR	RRZZZZUSA
TANNELEMUS, TOMAS	24	M	MSN	RRZZZZUSA
LIBSCHITZ, BERL	48	M	DLR	RRZZZZUSA

SHIP: WESTERNLAND

FROM: ANTWERP
TO: NEW YORK
ARRIVED: 08 FEBRUARY 1884

PASSENGER	AGE	SEX	OCCUPATION	PRIV VIL DES
HYMANSON, BERN.	37	M	MCHT	RRZZZZNY
KOFFLER, ALB.	16	M	STDNT	RRZZZZNY
SISKOWSKY, BARB.	24	F	UNKNOWN	PLZZZZCLE
JOS.	10	F	UNKNOWN	PLZZZZCLE
KARL	00	M	INF	PLZZZZCLE
CEZAR, BOCHAS	48	M	LABR	PLZZZZNY
WALSKI, CAS.	39	M	FARMER	PLZZZZNY
CHAM.	29	M	FARMER	PLZZZZNY
VALENT.	45	F	UNKNOWN	PLZZZZNY
MAENSCHALK, JOH.	29	F	UNKNOWN	PLZZZZNY
JURANOWSKI, VAL.	23	F	UNKNOWN	PLZZZZNY

SHIP: CITY OF CHESTER

FROM: LIVERPOOL AND QUEENSTOWN
TO: NEW YORK
ARRIVED: 11 FEBRUARY 1884

PASSENGER	AGE	SEX	OCCUPATION	PRIV VIL DES
LILLKOCKS, MATH.H.	38	M	LABR	RRZZZZNY
LORMNI, MATHS.A.	31	M	UNKNOWN	RRZZZZNY
HABACKSI, MATHS.M.	27	M	UNKNOWN	RRZZZZNY
MANDELA, ALEX.	22	M	UNKNOWN	RRZZZZNY
RAJAH, JOH.ESIKSON	40	M	UNKNOWN	RRZZZZNY

SHIP: MORAVIA

FROM: HAMBURG
TO: NEW YORK
ARRIVED: 11 FEBRUARY 1884

PASSENGER	AGE	SEX	OCCUPATION	PRIV VIL DES
BUTRIMOWI--, JOHN	16	M	LABR	RRZZZZUSA
BUBIUS, ANZE	40	M	LABR	RRZZZZUSA
DINOWSKY, PIOTR	21	M	LABR	RRZZZZUSA
BUKAS, PIOTR	24	M	LABR	RRZZZZUSA
BOSALSK, JAN.	24	M	LABR	RRZZZZUSA
LEMAJTYS, MATOL.	27	M	LABR	RRZZZZUSA
MAGD.	23	F	SGL	RRZZZZUSA
MAGD.	.11	F	INFANT	RRZZZZUSA
JAN	.11	M	INFANT	RRZZZZUSA
DROGELIS, MATEUS	26	M	LABR	RRZZZZUSA
ZVINKEL, JOSEF	28	M	LABR	RRZZZZUSA
OSUP, JOSEF	27	M	LABR	RRZZZZUSA
JOHNA, MARIE	17	F	SGL	RRZZZZUSA
WITZKY, BEHR	28	F	SGL	RRZZZZUSA
EPSTEIN, DAVID	36	F	SGL	RRZZZZUSA
MICHALSKI, JAN	42	F	SGL	RRZZZZUSA
LISZUNSKI, JAN	25	F	SGL	RRZZZZUSA
GRUDOWSKI, ANTON	20	F	SGL	RRZZZZUSA
CHASANOWSKU, CHASKEL	50	F	DLR	RRZZZZUSA
MULLER, ISRAEL	37	F	DLR	RRZZZZUSA
NEUERMANN, SCHAOHNE	26	F	DLR	RRZZZZUSA
FRANK, ISRAEL	32	F	DLR	RRZZZZUSA
MULLER, MEER	45	F	DLR	RRZZZZUSA
PRITZ, BEIMUS	40	F	DLR	RRZZZZUSA
SIMKOWITZ, MENDEL	24	F	DLR	RRZZZZUSA
HELMER, WILH.	43	F	TLR	RRZZZZUSA
JABLONSKA, NECHEMIL	45	F	TCHR	RRZZZZUSA
LUCKERMANN, ARIL	28	F	DLR	RRZZZZUSA
DAVIDOWSKY, DAVID	35	F	LABR	RRZZZZUSA
GOLDBERG, RAPHAEL	28	F	LABR	RRZZZZUSA
BEHRMANN, CHATZEL	40	F	LABR	RRZZZZUSA
SAMUEL	25	F	LABR	RRZZZZUSA
RIEWKEN, CHASKEL	20	F	LABR	RRZZZZUSA
PALEI, CHAJE	35	F	SGL	RRZZZZUSA
REIMER, BERNH.	51	M	FARMER	RRZZZZUSA
SOVICKY, ADAM	20	M	LABR	RRZZZZUSA
IRASDORF, FRIEDR.	31	M	LABR	RRZZZZUSA
BORK, PETER	30	M	LABR	RRZZZZUSA
BATZENIS, JOSEF	23	M	LABR	RRZZZZUSA
MOTLEITIS, JOSEF	23	M	LABR	RRZZZZUSA
SOHATZ, SEIGE	26	F	W	RRZZZZUSA
CHAIE	6	F	CHILD	RRZZZZUSA
SELE	5	F	CHILD	RRZZZZUSA
LIPSCHITZ, ARON	20	M	LABR	RRZZZZUSA
WILKOWSKY, RUWEN	30	M	LABR	RRZZZZUSA
SEIDENBERG, SCHLOME	21	M	LABR	RRZZZZUSA
SIUHS, ROCHE	19	F	W	RRZZZZUSA
ETTENSOHN, CHAIM	20	M	LABR	RRZZZZUSA
MERGEL, HIRSCH	38	M	TLR	RRZZZZUSA
NICOLADES, MATHIAS	23	M	LABR	RRZZZZUSA

SHIP: STATE OF NEBRASKA

FROM: GLASGOW AND LARNE
TO: NEW YORK
ARRIVED: 12 FEBRUARY 1884

PASSENGER	AGE	SEX	OCCUPATION	PRV VIL DES
SACK, IGNATZ	24	M	MLR	RRZZZZUSA
GAIMT, MATH.	20	M	LABR	RRZZZZUSA
KRUEGER, LUDW.	24	M	LABR	RRZZZZUSA
BUECHNER, JOHN	23	M	UNKNOWN	RRZZZZUSA

SHIP: HABSBURG

FROM: BREMEN
TO: NEW YORK
ARRIVED: 13 FEBRUARY 1884

PASSENGER	AGE	SEX	OCCUPATION	PRV VIL DES
BURSTEIN, NIGAM	32	M	UNKNOWN	RRZZZZUSA
MICHAEL	6	M	CHILD	RRZZZZUSA

SHIP: NECKAR

FROM: BREMEN
TO: NEW YORK
ARRIVED: 13 FEBRUARY 1884

PASSENGER	AGE	SEX	OCCUPATION	PRV VIL DES
WEDLER, THOMAS	26	M	UNKNOWN	RRZZZZNY
HUDEREWITZ, SZYMAN	21	M	UNKNOWN	RRZZZZNY
BENTLER, JARUKE	35	M	FARMER	RRZZZZNY

SHIP: RUGIA

FROM: HAMBURG
TO: NEW YORK
ARRIVED: 13 FEBRUARY 1884

PASSENGER	AGE	SEX	OCCUPATION	PRV VIL DES
ROSEN, HECHE	18	F	SGL	RRZZZZUSA
KAMCHE, ISRAEL	44	M	BCHR	RRZZZZUSA
MOSES	19	M	BCHR	RRZZZZUSA
FRIEDMAND, ITSCHOK	25	M	TLR	RRZZZZUSA
LASSEK, HERSCH	20	M	TLR	RRZZZZUSA
MALETZKOWITZ, SIMON	23	M	SHMK	RRZZZZUSA
SCHULZER, JANKEL	19	M	TLR	RRZZZZUSA
ORZINSKY, STEPAN	24	M	FARMER	RRZZZZUSA
SWIDRINSKY, JONAS	33	M	FARMER	RRZZZZUSA
RUPINSKY, STANISLAUS	20	M	FARMER	RRZZZZUSA
SIMONAITIC, ADAM	27	M	FARMER	RRZZZZUSA
WEIKSCHNORAS, PETRAS	33	M	LABR	RRZZZZUSA
DUDZIS, JOSIAS	25	M	LABR	RRZZZZUSA
JURKONIS, WIZENTAS	18	M	LABR	RRZZZZUSA
HOFFAMANN, JACOB	17	M	CL	RRZZZZUSA
SUCHOTGEWSKY, NOCHUM	39	M	DLR	RRZZZZUSA
ALTER	16	M	S	RRZZZZUSA
SCHMIEGELSKY, FEIWEL	36	M	LABR	RRZZZZUSA
APPELBAUM, CHAIM	18	M	LABR	RRZZZZUSA
CHWAIT, JUDEL	50	M	TLR	RRZZZZUSA
STRICHOVOSKY, FRANZ	20	M	LABR	RRZZZZUSA
WERNOWSKY, STANISL.	20	M	LABR	RRZZZZUSA
LOBISINSKI, WOTEK	20	M	LABR	RRZZZZUSA
SURIN, PETER	17	M	LABR	RRZZZZUSA
MARNWASKI, LUDWIG	17	M	LABR	RRZZZZUSA
MISCKIEWICZ, MICHAEL	21	M	LABR	RRZZZZUSA
MILAVSKI, JOSEF	21	M	LABR	RRZZZZUSA
JORES, SIMON	21	M	LABR	RRZZZZUSA
POCZKIS, VINCENT	27	M	LABR	RRZZZZUSA
SIBVAISCH, KASIMIR	21	M	LABR	RRZZZZUSA
BROSCETIS, SIMON	27	M	LABR	RRZZZZUSA
GOLDSCHMIDT, SARA	18	F	SGL	RRZZZZUSA
SCHULOM, HINDA	17	F	W	RRZZZZUSA
MINNA	.06	F	INFANT	RRZZZZUSA
GOLDMANN, LOUIS	30	M	DLR	RRZZZZUSA
SCHEME	20	F	W	RRZZZZUSA
KULEBAKIN, ALEXANDER	18	M	DLR	RRZZZZUSA
GILIS, ANTONAS	22	M	LABR	RRZZZZUSA
BUCZAWICZAS, JOSIAS	23	M	LABR	RRZZZZUSA
ZELONIS, MADSCHUS	26	M	LABR	RRZZZZUSA
SKRANDZISKI, SCHINEN	21	M	DLR	RRZZZZUSA
KAHN, ELIAS	48	M	DLR	RRZZZZUSA
WEIGERT, PAUL	23	M	LABR	RRZZZZUSA
SINGER, PEREL	28	F	W	RRZZZZUSA
FUTERANSKY, JONA	19	M	DLR	RRZZZZUSA
GOLDE	16	F	W	RRZZZZUSA
PIOTROWSKI, IGNATZ	25	M	LABR	RRZZZZUSA
KRAUSE, WOITICH	24	M	LABR	RRZZZZUSA
KOCSMARSKI, VINCENTI	23	M	LABR	RRZZZZUSA
OKASCHEWSKI, WLADISLAW	23	M	LABR	RRZZZZUSA
ZABOTZKI, SARA	25	F	SGL	RRZZZZUSA
KRAMM, SUSSMANN	16	M	CL	RRZZZZUSA
POIS, JERUCHUM	24	M	DLR	RRZZZZUSA
KOBEROWSKA, JERUCHUM	26	M	DLR	RRZZZZUSA
BRANDE, JACOB	19	M	DLR	RRZZZZUSA
BERNER, ARON	21	M	DLR	RRZZZZUSA
DAWIDOWITZ, BOLTRUS	26	M	LABR	RRZZZZUSA
SEDEROWITZ, FELIX	25	M	LABR	RRZZZZUSA
WOITKEWITZ, FELIX	21	M	LABR	RRZZZZUSA
GUTSTEIN, SCHEPSEL	16	M	DLR	RRZZZZUSA
SMISKUS, JOSEF	25	M	LABR	RRZZZZUSA
POVELAJUS, JOSEF	33	M	LABR	RRZZZZUSA
KURKLINSKY, ISIDOR	22	M	LABR	RRZZZZUSA
SENNLIS, CONSTANTIN	18	M	LABR	RRZZZZUSA
LOSTANSKY, ANTON	20	M	LABR	RRZZZZUSA
GUKOVIC, JOHN	21	M	LABR	RRZZZZUSA
MORCKUCKY, OSIP	23	M	LABR	RRZZZZUSA
EIJROST, JOSEF	25	M	LABR	RRZZZZUSA
GAJDJURGIS, KASIMIR	22	M	LABR	RRZZZZUSA
WITARD, FRANZ	23	M	LABR	RRZZZZUSA
MAREOWICZ, RUD.	35	M	MCHT	RRZZZZUSA
SREIER, DAVID	24	M	TLR	RRZZZZUSA
OSTROVSKY, FRANK	43	M	LABR	RRZZZZUSA
STACHONITZ, PAVEL	25	M	LABR	RRZZZZUSA
JANOWSKY, JOSEF	30	M	LABR	RRZZZZUSA
ANNA	24	F	W	RRZZZZUSA
GOTTLIEB	.05	M	INFANT	RRZZZZUSA
BRIL, ISRAEL	22	M	TLR	RRZZZZUSA
ROTHSTEIN, BEIMISCH	23	M	TLR	RRZZZZUSA
TEITZ, JACOB	36	M	TLR	RRZZZZUSA
FRISCHKINDT, HIRSCH	48	M	TLR	RRZZZZUSA
KAPELOWITZ, ZADEK	28	M	TLR	RRZZZZUSA
SEGALOWITZ, MOSES	33	M	TLR	RRZZZZUSA
STEIN, SARA	40	F	W	RRZZZZUSA
CHAZKELS, MOSES	50	M	LABR	RRZZZZUSA
NIESCHEWSKI, HERM.	23	M	TLR	RRZZZZUSA
SAMAITIS, VINCENT	23	M	LABR	RRZZZZUSA
POSERA, MICHEL	30	M	LABR	RRZZZZUSA
WISGUT, MATES	22	M	LABR	RRZZZZUSA
MULLER, STEFAN	25	M	LABR	RRZZZZUSA
MALOWSKY, ROCHEL	23	F	W	RRZZZZUSA
SORE	.06	F	INFANT	RRZZZZUSA
ABKEWITZ, ABRAM	28	M	LABR	RRZZZZUSA
TRIKANSKY, WOLF	21	M	LABR	RRZZZZUSA
REIN, ZLATE	60	F	W	RRZZZZUSA
FRIEDMANN, FEIGELCHE	17	F	SGL	RRZZZZUSA
PALYCESKA, ANNA	24	F	W	RRZZZZUSA
KARL	.11	M	INFANT	RRZZZZUSA

PASSENGER	AGE	SEX	OCCUPATION	PRV	VIL	DES

SHIP: LYDIAN MONARCH

FROM: LONDON
TO: NEW YORK
ARRIVED: 14 FEBRUARY 1884

PASSENGER	AGE	SEX	OCCUPATION	PRV	VIL	DES
BLACHER, C.	37	M	TNMK	RR	ZZZZ	CIN
SEGAL, P.	26	M	TLR	RR	ZZZZ	CIN
REGAL, S.	18	M	UNKNOWN	RR	ZZZZ	CIN
MATILISKA, A.	19	F	W	RR	ZZZZ	CIN
HORWITZ, HN.	25	M	TRVLR	RR	ZZZZ	CH
MARK, K.	22	M	TLR	RR	ZZZZ	NY
MORRIS, AL.	36	M	GM	RR	ZZZZ	NY
MARKS, H.	30	M	TLR	RR	ZZZZ	NY
ABRAHAMS, N.	19	M	TLR	RR	ZZZZ	BO
YNDELCHON, M.	22	M	UNKNOWN	RR	ZZZZ	NY
GROVOWSKY, ISAAC	21	M	CL	RR	ZZZZ	NY
AZARKIN, KITTY	18	F	DRS	RR	ZZZZ	NY
LWENE, EM.	24	M	GZR	RR	ZZZZ	NY
BROWN, JACOB	21	M	TLR	RR	ZZZZ	NY
LINDENHAND, R.	23	M	TLR	RR	ZZZZ	PA
REBECCA	22	F	W	RR	ZZZZ	PA
KALICKY, H.	37	M	TCHR	RR	ZZZZ	WAS

SHIP: ODER

FROM: BREMEN
TO: NEW YORK
ARRIVED: 14 FEBRUARY 1884

PASSENGER	AGE	SEX	OCCUPATION	PRV	VIL	DES
FRIEDMAN, WILLIAM	20	M	DLR	RR	ZZZZ	USA
HEYDE, HERMAN	26	M	JNR	RR	ZZZZ	USA
EILITZ, AUGUST	25	M	TLR	RR	ZZZZ	USA
THOMAS, CARL	28	M	BCHR	RR	ZZZZ	USA
MUSZYNSKI, JOSEF	34	M	BKLYR	RR	ZZZZ	USA
VORBRECHT, FERDINAND	23	M	LABR	RR	ZZZZ	USA
ADAMCZAK, JOHAN	23	M	LABR	RR	ZZZZ	USA
SEIDL, ANTON	17	M	STDNT	RR	ZZZZ	USA

SHIP: POLYNESIA

FROM: HAMBURG
TO: NEW YORK
ARRIVED: 15 FEBRUARY 1884

PASSENGER	AGE	SEX	OCCUPATION	PRV	VIL	DES
OLVAR, JOSEF	27	M	UNKNOWN	RR	ZZZZ	UNK
HENMOSCH, JOSF	36	M	UNKNOWN	RR	ZZZZ	UNK
BECK, JANOS	25	M	UNKNOWN	RR	ZZZZ	UNK
HORIVAK, JANOS	24	M	UNKNOWN	RR	ZZZZ	UNK
KOWALEWSKI, MARZIN	40	M	LABR	RR	ZZZZ	UNK
MARIANNE	34	F	W	RR	ZZZZ	UNK
JOSEFA	5	F	CHILD	RR	ZZZZ	UNK
THEODORA	1	F	CHILD	RR	ZZZZ	UNK
URENBACH, ARON	24	M	TRDSMN	RR	ZZZZ	UNK
GRANZ, EPHRAIM	44	M	UNKNOWN	PL	ZZZZ	UNK
WYZYHOWSKI, ADALBERT	26	M	UNKNOWN	PL	ZZZZ	UNK
SACHAFCHEFSKI, HEIMAN	38	M	TLR	PL	ZZZZ	UNK
DAMULEWICZ, FRANZISCHEK	29	M	LABR	RR	ZZZZ	UNK

SHIP: DEVONIA

FROM: GLASGOW AND MOVILLE
TO: NEW YORK
ARRIVED: 18 FEBRUARY 1884

PASSENGER	AGE	SEX	OCCUPATION	PRV	VIL	DES
ANDREAS, JACOB	38	M	LABR	PL	ZZZZ	USA
STASICK, ISIDORE	30	M	LABR	PL	ZZZZ	USA
MICLE, VALENTINE	29	M	LABR	PL	ZZZZ	USA

SHIP: SWITZERLAND

FROM: ANTWERP
TO: NEW YORK
ARRIVED: 19 FEBRUARY 1884

PASSENGER	AGE	SEX	OCCUPATION	PRV	VIL	DES
DOBREZELEWSKI, ROB.	33	M	UNKNOWN	RR	ZZZZ	NY
EUGENIE	25	F	UNKNOWN	RR	ZZZZ	NY
ANIELE	9	F	CHILD	RR	ZZZZ	NY
FLORENTINOVON, BABECKA	42	F	UNKNOWN	RR	ZZZZ	NY
LOBETZKI, AUG.	40	M	LABR	RR	ZZZZ	UNK
JOSEPHA	33	F	UNKNOWN	RR	ZZZZ	NY
STROBLALIS, F.	35	M	LABR	RR	ZZZZ	UNK

SHIP: WIELAND

FROM: HAMBURG
TO: NEW YORK
ARRIVED: 19 FEBRUARY 1884

PASSENGER	AGE	SEX	OCCUPATION	PRV	VIL	DES
MUSINSKY, PESSE	25	F	W	RR	ZZZZ	USA
BASCHE	.11	F	INFANT	RR	ZZZZ	USA
KURNICKI, JOH.	21	M	LABR	RR	ZZZZ	USA
TULECKA, SMIKAS	24	M	LABR	RR	ZZZZ	USA
SAKOLOVSKI, ANTON	40	M	LABR	RR	ZZZZ	USA
ALABUND, ANTONIN	22	M	LABR	RR	ZZZZ	USA
STRUSAIS, PAVEL	34	M	LABR	RR	ZZZZ	USA
LIPINSKY, JAN	40	M	LABR	RR	ZZZZ	USA
MORRIS, GEDALJE	20	M	TLR	RR	ZZZZ	USA
ROSENOWITZ, ARON	47	M	TLR	RR	ZZZZ	USA
PARTNOI, JUDA	20	M	SHMK	RR	ZZZZ	USA
PUCHALSKY, ARON	27	M	TLR	RR	ZZZZ	USA
CENTNERSCHIRER, WOLF	25	M	TLR	RR	ZZZZ	USA
AKSANIT, NOCHEM	20	M	BCHR	RR	ZZZZ	USA
FRIEDMANN, SCHEMI	15	F	SGL	RR	ZZZZ	USA
SAKANOWITZ, ABRAHAM	40	M	TLR	RR	ZZZZ	USA
AHELSON, MOSE	24	M	TLR	RR	ZZZZ	USA
PILOWSKY, JANKEL	26	M	TLR	RR	ZZZZ	USA
BUBNUS, FRANZISKA	34	F	SGL	RR	ZZZZ	USA
SAMSOWITZ, ANTONI	38	F	W	RR	ZZZZ	USA
BALEWITZ, IVAN	50	M	LABR	RR	ZZZZ	USA
REKOS, MATHEI	19	M	LABR	RR	ZZZZ	USA
GAIDIS, CARL	30	M	LABR	RR	ZZZZ	USA
GABER, ADAM	26	M	LABR	RR	ZZZZ	USA
DABKUM, JOH.	21	M	LABR	RR	ZZZZ	USA
GAWINOWITSCH, SIMON	21	M	LABR	RR	ZZZZ	USA
GOLDFARB, MARCUS	25	M	FELMO	RR	ZZZZ	USA
ROSGAR, FEIBEL	36	M	TLR	RR	ZZZZ	USA
KOTSCHOK, ABRAM	19	M	TLR	RR	ZZZZ	USA
KIKOFKA, PESACH	24	M	TLR	RR	ZZZZ	USA
ABEL	23	M	TLR	RR	ZZZZ	USA
RAPHAELSOHN, ENSIG	47	M	DLR	RR	ZZZZ	USA
MENDEL	9	M	CHILD	RR	ZZZZ	USA
ARON	7	M	CHILD	RR	ZZZZ	USA

PASSENGER	AGE	SEX	OCCUPATION	PRV VIL DES
ROBALSKI, ISAAK	39	M	DLR	RRZZZZUSA
FRIEDMANN, ISRAEL	33	M	DLR	RRZZZZUSA
DOMBROWSKI, JOSAS	14	M	LABR	RRZZZZUSA
BUSZAMIS, MICHAEL	31	M	LABR	RRZZZZUSA
DABRUCKUS, AUGUST	28	M	LABR	RRZZZZUSA
BIELSKI, TOMA	29	M	LABR	RRZZZZUSA
MARTHA	30	F	W	RRZZZZUSA
MASSALIS, JOSIAS	25	M	LABR	RRZZZZUSA
SOWOKINAS, PETRUS	24	M	LABR	RRZZZZUSA
WOIWODE, MATHIAS	23	M	LABR	RRZZZZUSA
SIDANOWITZ, ADAM	18	M	LABR	RRZZZZUSA
DANILEWITZ, KASIMIR	17	M	LABR	RRZZZZUSA
LEWINSOHN, HESCHEL	34	M	LABR	RRZZZZUSA
RANCHMANN, HIRSCH	25	M	TLR	RRZZZZUSA
MOSS, SCHOLEM	20	M	TLR	RRZZZZUSA
KAPLAN, JOSSEL	16	M	DLR	RRZZZZUSA
JONE	25	M	DLR	RRZZZZUSA
LEWIN, ISRAEL	30	M	DLR	RRZZZZUSA
BADIN, ISAAK	40	M	DLR	RRZZZZUSA
SARA	17	F	CH	RRZZZZUSA
BEILE	9	F	CHILD	RRZZZZUSA
SCHINDER, ISRAEL	20	M	DLR	RRZZZZUSA
FRIED, NATHAN	19	M	DLR	RRZZZZUSA
GOLDSTEIN, ANNIE	22	F	W	RRZZZZUSA
MEYER	.10	M	INFANT	RRZZZZUSA
GRUNBERG, ISAAC	30	M	SHMK	RRZZZZUSA
REDZWITCH, JOSEPH	30	M	LABR	RRZZZZUSA
EVA	30	F	W	RRZZZZUSA
EVA	3	F	CHILD	RRZZZZUSA
ANDR.	.11	M	INFANT	RRZZZZUSA
BRESCHZINA, SAMUEL	18	M	DLR	RRZZZZUSA
KLIBARSKI, LEIB	44	M	SHMK	RRZZZZUSA
NEM, JANKEL	40	M	DLR	RRZZZZUSA
GOLDSTEIN, JANKEL	36	M	DLR	RRZZZZUSA
MASCHOTTAS, JOSEPH	22	M	STDNT	RRZZZZUSA
PANIMUNSKI, ARON	19	M	DLR	RRZZZZUSA
ROTHSCHILD, ABRAH.	21	M	DLR	RRZZZZUSA
SALOMON	9	M	CHILD	RRZZZZUSA
WEISGARBER, WOLF	27	M	SHMK	RRZZZZUSA
LIES, SCHLOME	50	M	LABR	RRZZZZUSA
SUEZYNSKI, ANTON	26	M	LABR	RRZZZZUSA
KLONOWSKI, FRANZ	26	M	LABR	RRZZZZUSA
SCHMIDT, AUGUST	23	M	LABR	RRZZZZUSA
JANISZEWSKI, JOSEF	30	M	LABR	RRZZZZUSA
CZEZYNSKI, JAN	21	M	LABR	RRZZZZUSA
KOCZYCZEWSKI, JAN	20	M	LABR	RRZZZZUSA
URMANOWITZ, SIMON	25	M	LABR	RRZZZZUSA
EPSTEIN, HIRSCH	25	M	DLR	RRZZZZUSA
DANIEL, WOLF	28	M	LABR	RRZZZZUSA
MULLER, JOHN	25	M	LABR	RRZZZZUSA
MARIANNA	23	F	W	RRZZZZUSA
JULIE	9	F	CHILD	RRZZZZUSA
JOHN	.11	M	INFANT	RRZZZZUSA
BAUMANN, CARL	25	M	LABR	RRZZZZUSA
JIVICKY, CATHA.	23	F	SGL	RRZZZZUSA
DANKSIS, IVAN	23	M	LABR	RRZZZZUSA
LAPUS, ANTON	39	M	LABR	RRZZZZUSA
MATINAJTYT, VALENT.	26	M	LABR	RRZZZZUSA
BLANK, WILH	21	M	LABR	RRZZZZUSA
SILBER, SCHMUEL	31	M	LABR	RRZZZZUSA
SEIER, FEIBEL	20	M	TLR	RRZZZZUSA
BJERILA, ALEXANDER	26	M	LABR	RRZZZZUSA
KULESCH, MOSES	24	M	LABR	RRZZZZUSA
LIGEWITSCH, NICODEM	23	M	FARMER	RRZZZZUSA
LOTONA, STANISLAUS	27	M	FARMER	RRZZZZUSA
HOCHSTEIN, GERSON	30	M	LABR	RRZZZZUSA
SAREFSKY, JOSEF	23	M	LABR	RRZZZZUSA
FLATAN, JACOB	22	M	WVR	RRZZZZUSA
NOWIK, NISSEN	24	M	DLR	RRZZZZUSA
SCHNEIDER, SIMON	34	M	SHMK	RRZZZZUSA
ROGOWIN, ARON	28	M	DLR	RRZZZZUSA
SOMMERFELD, TINA	18	F	SGL	RRZZZZUSA
MARKUS, CHAMI	31	M	DLR	RRZZZZUSA

SHIP: FRISIA

FROM: HAMBURG
TO: NEW YORK
ARRIVED: 20 FEBRUARY 1884

PASSENGER	AGE	SEX	OCCUPATION	PRV VIL DES
ZLOTOWSKI, STEFAN	17	M	LABR	RRZZZZUSA
JANISZEWSKA, LUDWIKA	39	F	W	RRZZZZUSA
WILIANE	5	F	CHILD	RRZZZZUSA
JOSEF	3	M	CHILD	RRZZZZUSA
ANNA	00	F	INF	RRZZZZUSA
SILBERSTEIN, L.W.	22	M	DLR	RRZZZZUSA
HERTZMANN, MEYER	23	M	DLR	RRZZZZUSA
SEIFFERT, GERSON	60	M	LABR	RRZZZZUSA
SCHILTTREFF, CONRAD	24	M	LABR	RRZZZZUSA
CATHA.	24	F	W	RRZZZZUSA
CONRAD	3	M	CHILD	RRZZZZUSA
JACOB	.03	M	INFANT	RRZZZZUSA
AMELITZKY, ANT.	30	M	FARMER	RRZZZZUSA
CZETCK, RIWKE	20	F	SGL	RRZZZZUSA
SZCHEJEVSKI, FRANZ.	24	M	LABR	RRZZZZUSA
GLUDKOFSKI, ANTON	42	M	UNKNOWN	RRZZZZUSA
KOLOZIVSKI, VALENTIN	21	M	UNKNOWN	RRZZZZUSA
JANKOFSKI, JAN	27	M	UNKNOWN	RRZZZZUSA
ISVAHC, HEINR.	38	M	UNKNOWN	RRZZZZUSA
ESKILA, ERIK	28	M	UNKNOWN	RRZZZZUSA
REMAR, JONAS	24	M	UNKNOWN	RRZZZZUSA
LEWINSOHN, NECHEMIL	28	M	DLR	RRZZZZUSA
JANISZEWSKA, JAN	00	M	INF	RRZZZZUSA
ISRELOWITZ, HERRSN.	25	M	DLR	RRZZZZUSA
NARBY, FEIWEL	33	M	LABR	RRZZZZUSA
BENDER, ABARAHAM	32	M	UNKNOWN	RRZZZZUSA
RAIGROTZKY, MOSES	40	M	UNKNOWN	RRZZZZUSA
GATTLER, HILLEL	32	M	UNKNOWN	RRZZZZUSA
CHARNASCH, ELIAS	40	M	DLR	RRZZZZUSA
SCHEI--, SAMUEL	40	M	MCHT	RRZZZZUSA
GOLDBERG, LIEBE	24	F	W	RRZZZZUSA
SARA	.11	F	INFANT	RRZZZZUSA
HINRICHSKI, MINNA	20	F	SGL	RRZZZZUSA
SCHEIN, ITZIG	50	M	UNKNOWN	RRZZZZUSA
SELDE	45	F	W	RRZZZZUSA
ABRAHAM	8	M	CHILD	RRZZZZUSA
ELIE	7	M	CHILD	RRZZZZUSA
BERMAN, LEISER	40	M	LABR	RRZZZZUSA
MERE	40	F	W	RRZZZZUSA
LEA	17	F	CH	RRZZZZUSA
ABRAHAM	8	M	CHILD	RRZZZZUSA
HILLEL	7	M	CHILD	RRZZZZUSA
SANDER	5	M	CHILD	RRZZZZUSA
JANKOWSKY, LEISER	20	M	LABR	RRZZZZUSA
KOPINSKY, STIRL	54	M	UNKNOWN	RRZZZZUSA
GURSKY, LEIB	40	M	UNKNOWN	RRZZZZUSA
LASDIN, BETTY	19	M	UNKNOWN	RRZZZZUSA
SCHEIN, ELIE	25	M	UNKNOWN	RRZZZZUSA
KOLCTZKI, RIEWE	14	F	SGL	RRZZZZUSA
WERBELOWSKI, ISAAC	17	M	TLR	RRZZZZUSA
RATKOWSKY, ISAAC	40	M	SHMK	RRZZZZUSA
KRZZWIANSKY, ISRAEL	22	M	UNKNOWN	RRZZZZUSA
SLOTNITZKI, LEIB	19	M	UNKNOWN	RRZZZZUSA
WERBOLCWSKI, MOSES	28	M	MCHT	RRZZZZUSA
SEIMANN, SIMSCHE	22	M	SMH	RRZZZZUSA
WOZNIACK, LUDWIGA	20	F	SGL	RRZZZZUSA

PASSENGER	AGE	SEX	OCCUPATION	PRV	VIL	DES

SHIP: CEPHALONIA

FROM: LIVERPOOL AND QUEENSTOWN
TO: NEW YORK
ARRIVED: 23 FEBRUARY 1884

PASSENGER	AGE	SEX	OCCUPATION	PRV VIL DES
HANSEN, HANS	46	M	FARMER	RRZZZZUSA
CATHARINA	44	F	W	RRZZZZUSA
BLICKHAN, ANNIE	29	F	W	RRZZZZUSA

SHIP: ETHIOPIA

FROM: GLASGOW AND MOVILLE
TO: NEW YORK
ARRIVED: 24 FEBRUARY 1884

PASSENGER	AGE	SEX	OCCUPATION	PRV VIL DES
LIFFEL, ARON	22	M	PDLR	RRZZZZUSA
MARGOLLIN, KALMAN	20	M	PDLR	RRZZZZUSA
LUBEL, KAPPEL	26	M	PDLR	RRZZZZUSA
BOTWINICK, SCHLOME-CHAI	22	M	PDLR	RRZZZZUSA
ROMANON, NISSEN	45	M	PDLR	RRZZZZUSA
LABUL, HIRSCH	30	M	PDLR	RRZZZZUSA
HODER, SCHMUEL	59	M	PDLR	RRZZZZUSA
ISRAEL, BENZE	32	M	PDLR	RRZZZZUSA
SCHNEIDER, PAUL	40	M	LABR	RRZZZZUSA
BONASSKI, JOSEL	26	M	TLR	RRZZZZUSA
RUBENSTEIN, JOSSEL	33	M	PNTR	RRZZZZUSA
DAWIDOP, LEIB	24	M	MLR	RRZZZZUSA
GRUNSCH, RUSCH	40	F	UNKNOWN	RRZZZZUSA
EPHRAIM	6	M	CHILD	RRZZZZUSA
ROSA	2	F	CHILD	RRZZZZUSA
KOHN, ISAK	22	M	PDLR	RRZZZZUSA
MISKO, PR.	32	M	LABR	RRZZZZUSA
DEMANS, A.S.	37	M	PDLR	RRZZZZUSA
SAKOLSKI, TEOFIL	31	M	MCHT	RRZZZZUSA
KOHN, MARIN.	27	F	HP	RRZZZZUSA

SHIP: EGYPTIAN MONARCH

FROM: LONDON
TO: NEW YORK
ARRIVED: 25 FEBRUARY 1884

PASSENGER	AGE	SEX	OCCUPATION	PRV VIL DES
LAATING, SAMUEL	20	M	CBTMKR	RRZZZZNY
COHN, SOLOMON	21	M	SHMK	RRZZZZNY
KOMBERY, LEWISS	45	M	BBR	RRZZZZNY
LEVERTON, PHILIP	19	M	TLR	RRZZZZPHI

SHIP: SALIER

FROM: BREMEN
TO: NEW YORK
ARRIVED: 25 FEBRUARY 1884

PASSENGER	AGE	SEX	OCCUPATION	PRV VIL DES
ZELINSKI, ANTONIE	32	F	W	RRZZZZUSA
GAHUKE, JOSEF	38	M	NN	RRZZZZUSA
CHRISTINE	27	F	W	RRZZZZUSA
ROBERT	3	M	CHILD	RRZZZZUSA
HULDA	.09	F	INFANT	RRZZZZUSA
REISS, BERTHA	17	F	NN	RRZZZZUSA

SHIP: HELVETIA

FROM: LIVERPOOL
TO: NEW YORK
ARRIVED: 27 FEBRUARY 1884

PASSENGER	AGE	SEX	OCCUPATION	PRV VIL DES
GURRACK, ALBERT	26	M	LABR	PLZZZZUSA
STANISLAW, KARAL	20	M	UNKNOWN	PLZZZZUSA
STREGWELL, JAN	21	M	UNKNOWN	RRZZZZUSA
PANNER, MATTHIA	30	M	UNKNOWN	RRZZZZUSA
HOLENBIRK, EMMANUEL	21	M	UNKNOWN	RRZZZZUSA

SHIP: ASSYRIAN MONARCH

FROM: LONDON
TO: NEW YORK
ARRIVED: 28 FEBRUARY 1884

PASSENGER	AGE	SEX	OCCUPATION	PRV VIL DES
BRAMSKY, A.	30	M	LABR	PLZZZZNY
F.	25	F	W	PLZZZZNY
R.	16	F	DMS	PLZZZZNY
B.	15	M	CH	PLZZZZNY
S.	13	F	UNKNOWN	PLZZZZNY
M.	12	F	UNKNOWN	PLZZZZNY
I.	10	M	UNKNOWN	PLZZZZNY
WEINER, ANNE	29	F	DMS	PLZZZZNY
COHEN, P.	35	M	LABR	PLZZZZNY
MARKOWITZ, I	20	M	UNKNOWN	PLZZZZNY
WARSHAWSKY, F.	30	M	UNKNOWN	PLZZZZNY
ROROLSKY, M.	35	M	UNKNOWN	PLZZZZNY
S.	40	F	W	PLZZZZNY
L.	30	M	LABR	PLZZZZNY
FINKLNSTEIN, S.	25	M	UNKNOWN	PLZZZZNY
MYERS, E.	20	M	UNKNOWN	PLZZZZNY
R.	19	F	W	PLZZZZNY
R.	20	M	LABR	PLZZZZNY
MYNS, S.	20	M	LABR	PLZZZZNY
CHATNSKY, L.	30	M	UNKNOWN	PLZZZZNY
STUDINGER, M.	45	M	UNKNOWN	PLZZZZNY
JAKELL, H.	40	M	UNKNOWN	PLZZZZNY
HAYDEN, A.	30	M	UNKNOWN	PLZZZZNY
TRASLER, I.T.	32	M	UNKNOWN	PLZZZZNY
KAZMEICHAL, JENDZAY	40	M	UNKNOWN	PLZZZZNY

SHIP: CITY OF MERIDA

FROM: VERA CRUZ
TO: NEW YORK
ARRIVED: 28 FEBRUARY 1884

PASSENGER	AGE	SEX	OCCUPATION	PRV VIL DES
RUDIGER, EARNESTO	27	M	UNKNOWN	PLZZZZNY

SHIP: FRANCE

FROM: HAVRE
TO: NEW YORK
ARRIVED: 28 FEBRUARY 1884

PASSENGER	AGE	SEX	OCCUPATION	PRV VIL DES
GLASTSTEIN, CHAISNE	24	M	ENGR	RRZZZZNY
BLOCH, BERNARD	21	M	TLR	RRZZZZNY

SHIP: HOHENSTAUFEN

FROM: BREMEN
TO: NEW YORK
ARRIVED: 28 FEBRUARY 1884

PASSENGER	AGE	SEX	OCCUPATION	PRV VIL DES
FURMENSKI, JAN	45	M	GDNR	RRZZZZUSA
JOS.	21	M	TNM	RRZZZZUSA
GRUDZENSKY, M.	22	M	LABR	RRZZZZUSA
WIKOWICZ, FRANZ	26	M	LABR	RRZZZZUSA
JAN	40	M	LABR	RRZZZZUSA
DOMBROWSKI, AUG.	50	M	LABR	RRZZZZUSA
GRATKOWSKI, JAN	44	M	LABR	RRZZZZUSA
GRAFMEYER, WILL.	7	M	CHILD	RRZZZZUSA
GYPIEWSKI, ADAM	44	M	LABR	RRZZZZUSA
STENDNER, LEOP.	23	M	LABR	RRZZZZUSA
GRUNFELD, ARON	39	M	LLD	RRZZZZUSA

SHIP: BOHEMIA

FROM: HAMBURG
TO: NEW YORK
ARRIVED: 29 FEBRUARY 1884

PASSENGER	AGE	SEX	OCCUPATION	PRV VIL DES
SCHAJES, JANKEL	21	M	LABR	RRZZZZUSA
MOSLEWECKJUTE, ALZBEBA	18	F	SGL	RRZZZZUSA
BAKUNAS, IGNACHOS	18	M	LABR	RRZZZZUSA
GOGOLIN, JUSTINE	22	F	SGL	RRZZZZUSA
SCHALLAU, EMILIE	17	F	SGL	RRZZZZUSA
OLUNG, FRIEDR.	26	M	LABR	FNZZZZUSA
MAGED, CAECILIE	16	F	SGL	RRZZZZUSA
NOTKEWITZ, JOSEF	23	M	LABR	RRZZZZUSA
SALETZKI, LEON	23	M	LABR	RRZZZZUSA
GOPPINGER, HERM.	21	M	LABR	RRZZZZUSA
KUHN, PAUL	35	M	LABR	RRZZZZUSA
JARUS, PAVEL	26	M	LABR	RRZZZZUSA
SKINSINIEWSKI, ADAM	29	M	LABR	RRZZZZUSA
KEMSURI, JOHANN	21	M	LABR	RRZZZZUSA
DESCHZEINSKI, ANDR.	34	M	LABR	RRZZZZUSA
TURCZINOWITZ, JOSEPH	20	M	LABR	RRZZZZUSA
RASWELOWITZ, MARTIN	28	M	LABR	RRZZZZUSA
SCHOWARZA, ADAM	20	M	LABR	RRZZZZUSA
PAULIKUNUS, ADAM	22	M	LABR	RRZZZZUSA
ANDROCESKAS, WINGAS	25	M	LABR	RRZZZZUSA
BULAWICZAS, ANDR.	19	M	LABR	RRZZZZUSA
STANZKIM, VINCENTAS	22	M	LABR	RRZZZZUSA
BOLANIS, SIMON	22	M	LABR	RRZZZZUSA
ULAN, MATHEAS	22	M	LABR	RRZZZZUSA
TURUTA, KASIMIR	50	M	LABR	RRZZZZUSA
TAUKIELEWITZ, MARCIN	25	M	LABR	RRZZZZUSA
MILKA	18	F	SGL	RRZZZZUSA
DYLINSKI, STANISLAW	24	M	LABR	RRZZZZUSA
PLYTNIK, ANTON	20	M	LABR	RRZZZZUSA
BALUKANIS, BOLTROMCY	20	M	LABR	RRZZZZUSA
BORONOWSKI, TOMAS	40	M	LABR	RRZZZZUSA
MOSALEWSKI, ADOLF	21	M	LABR	RRZZZZUSA
GUDELEWICZ, IGNAZ	25	M	LABR	RRZZZZUSA
GOLDSTEIN, MASCHEL	40	F	W	RRZZZZUSA
SPRUIDE	.11	F	INFANT	RRZZZZUSA
DAVID	.01	M	INFANT	RRZZZZUSA
PICUNAS, ALEXANDER	30	M	LABR	RRZZZZUSA
ANTYNOWITZ, PATHROS	40	M	LABR	RRZZZZUSA
TAMULENIS, PIOTR	25	M	LABR	RRZZZZUSA
KWEDEROWITZ, JOH.	25	M	LABR	RRZZZZUSA
WOITANIS, JOH.	25	M	LABR	RRZZZZUSA
MISKEL, THOMAS	31	M	LABR	RRZZZZUSA
BEIKILEWSKI, FRANZ	23	M	LABR	RRZZZZUSA
SKUPSKA, CAROLINE	25	F	SGL	RRZZZZUSA
MUHLSTEIN, RACHEL	20	F	SGL	RRZZZZUSA
SKOKOCZES, MAT-US	30	M	LABR	RRZZZZUSA
ROCKES, MICHAEL	24	M	LABR	RRZZZZUSA
GROSSBERG, MOSES	36	M	CGRMKR	RRZZZZUSA
LAV, DAVID	18	M	CGRMKR	RRZZZZUSA
GONENZKI, LEIB	17	M	CGRMKR	RRZZZZUSA
KAPLAN, BERE	42	M	CGRMKR	RRZZZZUSA
MEYERSOHN, HINDE	17	F	SGL	RRZZZZUSA
KUPERMANN, ISAAC	49	M	CGRMKR	RRZZZZUSA
MACHLES, MEYER	47	M	TLR	RRZZZZUSA
JUDEL	9	M	CHILD	RRZZZZUSA
HIRSCHKOWITZ, NOCHIM	26	M	TLR	RRZZZZUSA
MOWIANS, MATIS	29	M	LABR	RRZZZZUSA
MIKNEWITZ, FRANZ	40	M	LABR	RRZZZZUSA
KAKNEWITZ, MATUS	25	M	LABR	RRZZZZUSA
ROSENTHAL, KABNEN	15	M	CL	RRZZZZUSA
PEPLERSKI, SALEN	32	M	LABR	RRZZZZUSA
ASME	20	F	W	RRZZZZUSA
GRODEZKE, VICENTY	19	M	LABR	RRZZZZUSA
KOLWAIT, CHRISTIAN	22	M	LABR	RRZZZZUSA
DIAMANT, ABRAHAM	31	M	LABR	RRZZZZUSA
NOWAKOWSKI, JOMBE	26	M	SMH	RRZZZZUSA
MURAWSKY, FRANZ	37	M	LABR	RRZZZZUSA
SPINJELEWSKY, JAN	37	M	LABR	RRZZZZUSA
MARG.	36	F	W	RRZZZZUSA
KATZ, SCHIFFRE	18	F	SGL	RRZZZZUSA
CHITOCHEK, JANTREL	35	M	LABR	RRZZZZUSA
FURSTENBERG, EPHRAIM	34	M	LABR	RRZZZZUSA
LICHTENSTEIN, SIMON	25	M	LABR	RRZZZZUSA
RACHEL	26	F	SGL	RRZZZZUSA
RUTSECIN, DELLIC	57	M	TLR	RRZZZZUSA
KLASTEN, SARA	40	F	W	RRZZZZUSA
ROSA	19	F	CH	RRZZZZUSA
DAVID	17	M	CH	RRZZZZUSA
IVAN	9	M	CHILD	RRZZZZUSA
ANNA	4	F	CHILD	RRZZZZUSA
GOLDSTEIN, JEZNO	28	M	LABR	RRZZZZUSA
LEWY, SARAH	21	F	W	RRZZZZUSA
LEISER	.11	M	INFANT	RRZZZZUSA
PINSTEIN, ABRAHAM	32	M	LABR	RRZZZZUSA
WELWE, MICHAEL	26	M	LABR	RRZZZZUSA
LEWITS, JANKE	17	M	LABR	RRZZZZUSA
MERWITZ, MEYER	32	M	LABR	RRZZZZUSA
LUDIK, JURGIS	19	M	LABR	RRZZZZUSA
BASCH, MOSES	18	M	LABR	RRZZZZUSA
SAMETISIK, MATUS	27	M	LABR	RRZZZZUSA
MEROVITZ, JUDEL	22	M	LABR	RRZZZZUSA
JOWTZ, RICH.	28	M	LABR	RRZZZZUSA
MORIN, PETER	30	M	LABR	RRZZZZUSA
LOSOWSKY, FERSL	25	M	LABR	RRZZZZUSA
BELEWSKY, MICHAEL	54	M	LABR	RRZZZZUSA
ALMA	48	F	W	RRZZZZUSA
KREICHLER, MARTIN	25	F	PNTR	RRZZZZUSA
SILBERSTEIN, BERCK	33	F	TLR	RRZZZZUSA
BLASBERG, JONE	30	F	DLR	RRZZZZUSA
SOPOTKINSKI, JACOB	24	F	TLR	RRZZZZUSA
WITTENSTEIN, TAUCHEN	22	F	DLR	RRZZZZUSA
SELZER, ABRAHAM	22	F	DLR	RRZZZZUSA
PORAS, ISAAC	40	F	TLR	RRZZZZUSA
WLADIMIROW, RADIAN	49	F	LABR	RRZZZZUSA
IWAN	8	F	CHILD	RRZZZZUSA
LAZAROW, RIWE	15	F	SGL	RRZZZZUSA

PASSENGER	AGE	SEX	OCCUPATION	PRV VIL DES.
ABRAHA---, CHAIM	17	M	LABR	RRZZZZUSA
DWARGIRDOWA, ROSALIE	35	F	SGL	RRZZZZUSA
TSCHERNAVSKI, MARIANNE	30	F	W	RRZZZZUSA
ANTONIE	.04	F	INFANT	RRZZZZUSA
STIEDLIS, SALOMON	31	M	FELMO	RRZZZZUSA
NEYODA, PETER	33	M	LABR	RRZZZZUSA
KUNERT, JOSEF	25	M	LABR	RRZZZZUSA
ANKAJBYS, KASMIERS	28	M	LABR	RRZZZZUSA
KOJNATZKI, PIOTR	18	M	LABR	RRZZZZUSA
SORNSAITIS, PIOTR	30	M	LABR	RRZZZZUSA
LETMONK, JOSEF	22	M	LABR	RRZZZZUSA
RAIMIS, JOSEF	21	M	LABR	RRZZZZUSA
BATRUTZAITIS, JONAS	21	M	LABR	RRZZZZUSA
CZYBROWSKY, OSIP	23	M	LABR	RRZZZZUSA
SURMSAITIS, BALTHASAR	20	M	LABR	RRZZZZUSA
OWSCHAIR, ABEL	19	M	LABR	RRZZZZUSA
GUDEL, ISRAEL	20	M	LABR	RRZZZZUSA
SCHERESCHEWSKI, ISRAEL	40	M	LABR	RRZZZZUSA
URBUTIS, WINZIS	19	M	LABR	RRZZZZUSA
MEER, WULF	28	M	LABR	RRZZZZUSA
ROGALSKI, JOSEF	46	M	LABR	RRZZZZUSA
MARGOLIS, JUDEL	27	M	LABR	RRZZZZUSA
PLOTNOWSKI, PAUL	22	M	LABR	RRZZZZUSA
STERNETZ, MOSES	22	M	JNR	RRZZZZUSA
UTSEPIN, MEICE	43	M	LABR	RRZZZZUSA
MUSINSKI, GNESCHE	19	F	SGL	RRZZZZUSA
JUCINGILA, JONAS	24	M	LABR	RRZZZZUSA
LAZAROW, SARA	35	F	W	RRZZZZUSA
ETTEL	.11	F	INFANT	RRZZZZUSA
LEVINSOHN, MARIASCHE	17	F	SGL	RRZZZZUSA
LEIB	20	M	DLR	RRZZZZUSA
GOLDSTEIN, MASCHE	40	F	W	RRZZZZUSA
MATEL	.11	F	INFANT	RRZZZZUSA

SHIP: WESTERNLAND

FROM: ANTWERP
TO: NEW YORK
ARRIVED: 02 MARCH 1884

PASSENGER	AGE	SEX	OCCUPATION	PRV VIL DES.
PATTERSEI, JOS.	24	M	LABR	PLZZZZNY
WIDEZ, MART.	32	M	UNKNOWN	PLZZZZNY
GLOBOKA, JOH.	27	M	UNKNOWN	PLZZZZNY
SKAITES, ANT.	23	M	UNKNOWN	PLZZZZNY
JANNESKI, URUC.	25	M	UNKNOWN	PLZZZZNY
JOHON, J.	23	M	LABR	PLZZZZNY

SHIP: CALIFORNIA

FROM: HAMBURG
TO: NEW YORK
ARRIVED: 03 MARCH 1884

PASSENGER	AGE	SEX	OCCUPATION	PRV VIL DES.
ADAMASCHIEWA, BARB.	58	F	UNKNOWN	RRZZZZNY
PUTZADA, CASIEMIR	30	M	UNKNOWN	RRZZZZNY
ANNA	32	F	W	RRZZZZNY
ELISABETH	4	F	CHILD	RRZZZZNY
JAN	5	M	CHILD	RRZZZZNY
DOMEITER, VINCENT	31	M	TRDSMN	RRZZZZNY
MARIANNE	21	F	W	RRZZZZNY
JAN	.06	M	INFANT	RRZZZZNY
RUCZKEWICZ, JAN	53	M	TRDSMN	RRZZZZNY
PAFLOFSKI, WIDAL	26	M	UNKNOWN	RRZZZZNY
ROSEWICZ, ANTONIA	28	M	WO	RRZZZZNY
BOTZKEWICZ, IGNATZ	19	M	LABR	RRZZZZNY
PECHLITZ, STEFAN	24	M	UNKNOWN	RRZZZZNY
BALEWICZ, MECHAL	26	M	UNKNOWN	RRZZZZNY
KISSELES, PINS.	24	M	UNKNOWN	RRZZZZNY
ROHMER, HERSCH	31	M	UNKNOWN	PLZZZZNY
ULLMANN, ADOLF	18	F	SGL	PLZZZZNY
SALGA	15	F	SGL	PLZZZZNY
PAULOK, MITRO	42	M	UNKNOWN	PLZZZZNY
DUTKO, ELEAS	30	M	TRDSMN	PLZZZZNY
KA----S	30	M	UNKNOWN	PLZZZZNY
KOMORA, PETRO	28	M	UNKNOWN	PLZZZZNY
JENSCHI, SMARSCHIN	24	M	UNKNOWN	PLZZZZNY
JARKOFSKI, LEKO	24	M	UNKNOWN	PLZZZZNY
SCHERNAK, JACHO	37	M	UNKNOWN	PLZZZZNY
IADOSCH, PETER	25	M	LABR	PLZZZZNY
BREMUS, PETER	25	M	UNKNOWN	PLZZZZNY
WETZKO, MUSCHOLA	25	M	UNKNOWN	PLZZZZNY
FETSCHINA, JOS.	35	M	UNKNOWN	PLZZZZNY
JURKOFSKO, JAZKO	33	M	UNKNOWN	PLZZZZNY
WATIL, LEIDOSCH	23	M	UNKNOWN	PLZZZZNY
JENDSELLI, DUBKO	28	M	UNKNOWN	PLZZZZNY
KOPELCTZ, PAWEL	33	M	UNKNOWN	PLZZZZNY
HOREK, RITZ	33	M	UNKNOWN	PLZZZZNY
SUSCHKO, IWAN	27	M	UNKNOWN	PLZZZZNY
KOCHOLEK, JAZKO	36	M	UNKNOWN	PLZZZZNY
KADELLAK, HUMIFER	33	M	UNKNOWN	PLZZZZNY
RENKO, JUSKO	26	M	UNKNOWN	PLZZZZNY
WARIKOFSKI, WOJCEK	23	M	UNKNOWN	RRZZZZNY
RAKOTZ, ANTON	20	M	UNKNOWN	RRZZZZNY
PASSOWRE, JAN	37	M	LABR	PLZZZZNY
MUSCHUVECZ, JERCCHE	31	M	UNKNOWN	PLZZZZNY
VASCHEFSKI, WLADESLOF	19	M	UNKNOWN	PLZZZZNY
DIVUANESS, JORSCHE	54	M	UNKNOWN	PLZZZZNY
OLCAN	7	M	CHILD	PLZZZZNY
LEMIN, MATH.	38	F	WO	RRZZZZNY
GOLDA	7	F	CHILD	RRZZZZNY
SPINSK	6	F	CHILD	RRZZZZNY
LUBE	5	F	CHILD	RRZZZZNY
BERSCHE	3	F	CHILD	RRZZZZNY
SCHMKE	.10	F	INFANT	RRZZZZNY
KRASNE, SAMUEL	23	M	MSN	RRZZZZNY
ROEDER, JULIUS	30	M	LABR	RRZZZZNY
SCHABLANAS, JACOB	29	M	UNKNOWN	RRZZZZNY
WRABLEWSKY, TH.	27	M	UNKNOWN	RRZZZZNY
NARWATANISCH, TH.	31	M	UNKNOWN	RRZZZZNY
MAGNIZKI, FRANZ	24	M	UNKNOWN	RRZZZZNY
BALTSCHURK, AUB.	33	M	UNKNOWN	RRZZZZNY
STRAWNISKI, AUG.	40	M	UNKNOWN	RRZZZZNY
GELBFARB, DAVID	54	M	TRDSMN	RRZZZZNY
MASCHER, HONORATES	74	F	WO	RRZZZZNY
STANISLAUS	6	M	CHILD	RRZZZZNY
KRAKOWSKI, MAX	20	M	TRDSMN	RRZZZZNY
KOASOSKY, MOSES	18	M	TRDSMN	RRZZZZNY
LOFSER, ABRAH.	18	M	UNKNOWN	RRZZZZNY
DEMONT, SALOMON	33	M	UNKNOWN	RRZZZZNY
SOSLOVSKY, SCHEPL	30	M	UNKNOWN	RRZZZZNY
GODNICH, VINCENT	31	M	LABR	PLZZZZNY
BOCZEN, STEPHAN	27	M	LABR	PLZZZZNY
MASCHLER, BARE	55	M	TRDSMN	RRZZZZNY
ERNESTINE	23	F	D	RRZZZZNY
SCHIMECDA, W.	37	M	LABR	RRZZZZNY
LEWANDOWSKI, JOH.	29	M	FARMER	RRZZZZNY
MARKOWICZ, STIHW	29	M	UNKNOWN	PLZZZZNY
FEDORSCH, JANKO	30	M	UNKNOWN	PLZZZZNY
WEINBERGER, DAVID	32	M	UNKNOWN	PLZZZZNY
HERMANN	26	M	UNKNOWN	PLZZZZNY
SEISSER, MAX	30	M	TRDSMN	PLZZZZNY
BERTHA	23	F	W	PLZZZZNY
MIKLAS	.06	M	INFANT	PLZZZZNY
WENZEL, THERESE	27	F	WO	PLZZZZNY
WENISTEIN, ISAAC	26	M	WCHMKR	RRZZZZPA
REGALLOS, PETER	25	M	UNKNOWN	RRZZZZNY
PETROSCHKI, JACOB	26	M	TLR	RRZZZZNY

PASSENGER	AGE	SEX	OCCUPATION	PRV	VIL	DES

SHIP: RHEIN

FROM: BREMEN AND SOUTHAMPTON
TO: NEW YORK
ARRIVED: 03 MARCH 1884

PASSENGER	AGE	SEX	OCCUPATION	PRV	VIL	DES
SZYMANSKI, MARTIN	18	M	LABR	RR	ZZZZ	USA
KUCHNICKI, MARTIN	20	M	LABR	RR	ZZZZ	USA

SHIP: LESSING

FROM: HAMBURG AND HAVRE
TO: NEW YORK
ARRIVED: 04 MARCH 1884

PASSENGER	AGE	SEX	OCCUPATION	PRV	VIL	DES
WEIGANOT, JOHANN	54	M	FARMER	RR	ZZZZ	USA
CATHER	52	F	W	RR	ZZZZ	USA
MARGA	21	F	SGL	RR	ZZZZ	USA
CATHA	18	F	SGL	RR	ZZZZ	USA
JOH.	14	M	S	RR	ZZZZ	USA
FRIEDR.	9	M	CHILD	RR	ZZZZ	USA
HEINR.	7	M	CHILD	RR	ZZZZ	USA
KIVBES, ADAM	26	M	LABR	RR	ZZZZ	USA
BARRNCH, ESTHER	18	F	SGL	RR	ZZZZ	USA
RIDZEWSKI, FRANZISKA	20	F	SGL	RR	ZZZZ	USA
FRANZISKA	19	F	SGL	RR	ZZZZ	USA
LEIBINNES, IGNATZ	26	M	LABR	RR	ZZZZ	USA
AKAMOWITZ, ANTONOS	21	M	LABR	RR	ZZZZ	USA
JENZKINAS, MARTON	26	M	LABR	RR	ZZZZ	USA
LEIDKOWSKI, ALEXANDER	30	M	LABR	RR	ZZZZ	USA
MATUCKONIS, WINZAS	30	M	LABR	RR	ZZZZ	USA
BERKSOHN, WOLFF	23	M	LABR	RR	ZZZZ	USA
BOTH, ADOLF	24	M	DLR	RR	ZZZZ	USA
RESE	18	F	W	RR	ZZZZ	USA
PALM, CHAIN	17	M	DLR	RR	ZZZZ	USA
KAPLAN, KOSEHIEL	29	M	DLR	RR	ZZZZ	USA
NEUMANN, SUNDEL	30	M	TLR	RR	ZZZZ	USA
FREYKIND, MOSES	51	M	TLR	RR	ZZZZ	USA
KAPLAN, ELIAS	40	M	TLR	RR	ZZZZ	USA
JOTSIH, ERNST	25	M	LABR	RR	ZZZZ	USA
JETSIH, MAZINSKY	26	M	LABR	RR	ZZZZ	USA
SIHEIJOWITZ, FUHRMANN	26	M	TLR	RR	ZZZZ	USA
GROSSMAN, HIRSH	23	M	HAMF	RR	ZZZZ	USA
KALIKOWSKI, ABRAHAM	31	M	DLR	RR	ZZZZ	USA
JASALOWITZ, ARON	29	M	SHMK	RR	ZZZZ	USA
NORFTOMBROWSKI, ARON	40	M	SHMK	RR	ZZZZ	USA
ALEXANDEROWITZ, GERSON	32	M	SHMK	RR	ZZZZ	USA
MIKABOLSKY, MEIER	36	M	SHMK	RR	ZZZZ	USA
JERUCHIM	23	M	SHMK	RR	ZZZZ	USA
SCHAPIRO, MOSES	41	M	SHMK	RR	ZZZZ	USA
BEIKER, SUFSMANN	23	M	SHMK	RR	ZZZZ	USA
SFARKOWSKY, JUDEL	32	M	SHMK	RR	ZZZZ	USA
TANSEK, RUBEN	27	M	TLR	RR	ZZZZ	USA
PAWY, LEIB	20	M	TLR	RR	ZZZZ	USA
NISSEN	48	M	JNR	RR	ZZZZ	USA
GRUNBERG, SALOMON	40	M	DLR	RR	ZZZZ	USA
KELLER, RUMIN	27	M	DLR	RR	ZZZZ	USA
GOLDSTEIN, MOSES	38	M	LABR	RR	ZZZZ	USA
REMBA, MOSES	45	M	SHMK	RR	ZZZZ	USA
VALAITIS, ANTON	18	M	LABR	RR	ZZZZ	USA
ZURGANICK, MICH	27	M	LABR	RR	ZZZZ	USA
JANKO	18	M	LABR	RR	ZZZZ	USA
NOSICK, ABEL	34	M	FARMER	RR	ZZZZ	USA
SIHMERKES, LEISER	36	M	LABR	RR	ZZZZ	USA
ALTSEHUL, ELISA	21	M	CGRMKR	RR	ZZZZ	USA
SIMERNITZKI, JACOB	24	M	LABR	RR	ZZZZ	USA
HOLLUS, MOSES	36	M	LABR	RR	ZZZZ	USA
MARKOWITZ, MOSES	35	M	LABR	RR	ZZZZ	USA
NEWELEWSKI, KOPPEL	36	M	LABR	RR	ZZZZ	USA
MARGOLIN, BER	41	M	LABR	RR	ZZZZ	USA
BUDERMANN, CHAIN	30	M	LABR	RR	ZZZZ	USA
KOHN, MEIER	32	M	LABR	RR	ZZZZ	USA
GRUNHAUS, ABRAH.	33	M	TLR	RR	ZZZZ	USA
FISCHKE, ARON	22	M	TLR	RR	ZZZZ	USA
HONTOROWICZ, ASEHER	26	M	TLR	RR	ZZZZ	USA
BUNEMOWITZ, CHAIM	28	M	MCHT	RR	ZZZZ	USA
SCHMITKO, MARIUS	24	M	MCHT	RR	ZZZZ	USA
FRUMKIN, SCHLEIM	21	M	TLR	RR	ZZZZ	USA
SCHMUL	9	M	CHILD	RR	ZZZZ	USA
LIPSCHUTZ, ITZIG	19	M	TLR	RR	ZZZZ	USA
BAYER, ELIAS	16	M	CGRMKR	RR	ZZZZ	USA
HIRSOHN, CHAIN	45	M	DLR	RR	ZZZZ	USA
CHAIKEL, LEIB	56	M	DLR	RR	ZZZZ	USA
SCHULMANN, BAER	32	M	DLR	RR	ZZZZ	USA
BOBRONEITZ, JOSEF	27	M	LABR	RR	ZZZZ	USA
PILWELIS, MATHUS	24	M	LABR	RR	ZZZZ	USA
BINIMOWITZ, SAMUEL	36	M	TLR	RR	ZZZZ	USA
WOILANIS, FLORIN	20	M	LABR	RR	ZZZZ	USA
BLEISZIS, PECLIX	27	M	CL	RR	ZZZZ	USA
PROJIN, LEISER	16	M	CL	RR	ZZZZ	USA
SINOWESKI, AUGUST	34	M	LABR	RR	ZZZZ	USA
HERRMANEITIS, ANTOMUS	29	M	LABR	RR	ZZZZ	USA
KSIAZKI, JOSEF	24	M	LABR	RR	ZZZZ	USA
HANOWITZ, JOH.	31	M	LABR	RR	ZZZZ	USA
MASSONIS, THOMAS	23	M	LABR	RR	ZZZZ	USA
STUSIHKS, JOSEF	25	M	LABR	RR	ZZZZ	USA
PULNWIS, IGNAI	32	M	LABR	RR	ZZZZ	USA
PLUNGIS, JAN	28	M	MSN	RR	ZZZZ	USA
SCHMOLLIES, JUDAN	25	M	LABR	RR	ZZZZ	USA
BUSIHKOW, MORDCHAI	18	M	LABR	RR	ZZZZ	USA
BABULONIS, IVAN	44	M	LABR	RR	ZZZZ	USA
GAPLINSKA, MARIANE	20	F	SGL	RR	ZZZZ	USA
WYSOCKI, DAVID	48	M	HAMF	RR	ZZZZ	USA
SPEKTOR, DAVID	25	M	TLR	RR	ZZZZ	USA
GERBER, ISRAEL	25	M	TLR	RR	ZZZZ	USA
MEDOWINK, BERL	42	M	SHMK	RR	ZZZZ	USA
LEWICKY, MOSES	18	M	JNR	RR	ZZZZ	USA
LUBLIN, ISRAEL	25	M	FARMER	RR	ZZZZ	USA
KUSINTZKI, NIFSEN	31	M	TLR	RR	ZZZZ	USA
FLECZINSKY, JACOB	19	M	BKR	RR	ZZZZ	USA
LESINSKA, PAULINE	38	F	SGL	RR	ZZZZ	USA
LARSARSK, PAV.	23	M	LABR	RR	ZZZZ	USA
RUPINSKI, STANISL.	24	M	LABR	RR	ZZZZ	USA
KIRNOSILZKI, WLADISL.	37	M	LABR	RR	ZZZZ	USA
HARRESCH, MICHAEL	26	M	LABR	RR	ZZZZ	USA
CHANTOR, ANTON	19	M	LABR	RR	ZZZZ	USA
SOBOLARSIH, JANCEK	16	M	LABR	RR	ZZZZ	USA
SLOVIKOWSKI, ANTON	21	M	LABR	RR	ZZZZ	USA
STABATSKA, SARA	22	F	SGL	RR	ZZZZ	USA
ZEFF, FANY	26	F	W	RR	ZZZZ	USA
NACHUM	.11	M	INFANT	RR	ZZZZ	USA
PACEJKO, JOHANN	45	M	LABR	RR	ZZZZ	USA
GOLDBERG, ISAAC	24	M	DLR	RR	ZZZZ	USA
LEWIN, ISAAC	19	M	DLR	RR	ZZZZ	USA
HACKOWE, MORDCHE	44	M	DLR	RR	ZZZZ	USA
GULUMBECTZ, SAMUEL	36	M	DLR	RR	ZZZZ	USA
KISALOWITZ, ADOLF	24	M	LABR	RR	ZZZZ	USA
KWEDEROWITZ, ANDRZL.	23	M	LABR	RR	ZZZZ	USA
JAKUSCHEWITZ, MATIS	42	M	LABR	RR	ZZZZ	USA
PIETKOWITZ, PETER	24	M	LABR	RR	ZZZZ	USA
BROMBERG, ISAAK	23	M	DLR	RR	ZZZZ	USA
KAPLAN, GERSON	35	M	DLR	RR	ZZZZ	USA
SLESAK, VALT.	45	M	CPTR	RR	ZZZZ	USA
IWANSKY, CARL	33	M	SHMK	RR	ZZZZ	USA
MARTIN	39	M	SHMK	RR	ZZZZ	USA
DOKILLA, VINE	22	M	FARMER	RR	ZZZZ	USA
JIGINAT, JOS.	21	M	FARMER	RR	ZZZZ	USA
WATIKUNIS, ANDR.	22	M	FARMER	RR	ZZZZ	USA
SELAT, GASPAR	23	M	FARMER	RR	ZZZZ	USA
ANDR.	21	M	FARMER	RR	ZZZZ	USA
STRASIVNIS, JOH.	14	M	FARMER	RR	ZZZZ	USA
SCHUNSKAS, KAS.	30	M	FARMER	RR	ZZZZ	USA
WASILEWICZ, JURAS	35	M	FARMER	RR	ZZZZ	USA
LEVINGSTON, L.	24	M	UNKNOWN	RR	ZZZZ	USA

PASSENGER	AGE	SEX	OCCUPATION	PRIV	VIL	DES
SHIP: STATE OF INDIANA						
FROM: GLASGOW						
TO: NEW YORK						
ARRIVED: 04 MARCH 1884						
MANCRER, B.I.	42	M	PDLR	RR	ZZZZ	USA
BENZEL	10	M	CH	RR	ZZZZ	USA
POLAND, C.	20	M	PDLR	RR	ZZZZ	USA
STEIN, I.	20	M	UNKNOWN	RR	ZZZZ	USA
OSOGOWITZ, T.	34	M	UNKNOWN	RR	ZZZZ	USA
ADAM	12	M	UNKNOWN	RR	ZZZZ	USA
KALOWANSKY, M.	21	M	UNKNOWN	RR	ZZZZ	USA
MANRER, M.	22	M	UNKNOWN	RR	ZZZZ	USA
WEISSBOT, T.	27	M	UNKNOWN	RR	ZZZZ	USA
U-MRS	35	F	W	RR	ZZZZ	USA
HIRSH	10	M	UNKNOWN	RR	ZZZZ	USA
ZADEL	8	M	CHILD	RR	ZZZZ	USA
WOLOSWITZ, S.	40	M	PDLR	RR	ZZZZ	USA
STANKEWITZ, M.	22	F	SP	RR	ZZZZ	USA
HILLER, A.	20	M	PDLR	RR	ZZZZ	USA
FERTIG, R.	12	M	UNKNOWN	RR	ZZZZ	USA
TAUB, L.	27	M	SHMK	RR	ZZZZ	USA
RADLASKA, I.	20	M	TLR	RR	ZZZZ	USA
GALLINA, D.	35	M	UNKNOWN	RR	ZZZZ	USA
FUCHS, F.	22	M	PDLR	RR	ZZZZ	USA
SAWATSGY, A.	23	M	UNKNOWN	RR	ZZZZ	USA
LOWITT, M.	26	M	UNKNOWN	RR	ZZZZ	USA
POZA, M.	26	M	UNKNOWN	RR	ZZZZ	USA
RUMANN, GITEL	20	F	SP	RR	ZZZZ	USA
U-MRS	28	F	W	RR	ZZZZ	USA
GOLDE	3	F	CHILD	RR	ZZZZ	USA
MOSES	2	M	CHILD	RR	ZZZZ	USA
ROTHKE, A.	22	M	TLR	RR	ZZZZ	USA
SHIP: CATALONIA						
FROM: LIVERPOOL						
TO: NEW YORK						
ARRIVED: 06 MARCH 1884						
MAKELA, MATH.	31	M	LABR	FN	ZZZZ	NY
STORBACKY, MATHIAS	35	M	UNKNOWN	FN	ZZZZ	NY
GREDBACKER, JOHANNES	54	M	UNKNOWN	FN	ZZZZ	NY
WERSILA, I.	20	M	UNKNOWN	FN	ZZZZ	NY
MILTZAR, VOSUS	36	M	LABR	PL	ZZZZ	NY
PADELANCZKI, KOSIS	24	M	UNKNOWN	PL	ZZZZ	NY
SHIP: WESTPHALIA						
FROM: HAMBURG						
TO: NEW YORK						
ARRIVED: 06 MARCH 1884						
LIEGELINSKY, JACOB	24	M	DLR	RR	ZZZZ	NY
SCHAFIR, JOSEF	20	M	UNKNOWN	RR	ZZZZ	NY
HEPNER, SAMUEL	29	M	SVNT	RR	ZZZZ	NY
RIWKE	20	F	W	RR	ZZZZ	NY
ILGUNDS, JOSEF	21	M	UNKNOWN	RR	ZZZZ	NY
BORCHARDT, FRIEDR.	33	M	LABR	RR	ZZZZ	NY
NUKLIS, JOSEF	18	M	UNKNOWN	RR	ZZZZ	NY
GEORG	27	M	UNKNOWN	RR	ZZZZ	NY
BERNOTTI, VINCENTE	18	M	UNKNOWN	RR	ZZZZ	NY
BARTEL, JOH.	24	M	UNKNOWN	RR	ZZZZ	NY
BIELNNOS, CRESUS	36	M	UNKNOWN	RR	ZZZZ	NY
JOSKEWITZ, JIWGI	24	M	LABR	RR	ZZZZ	NY
GUTMANN, HIRSCH	18	M	WCHMKR	RR	ZZZZ	NY
KRONSIECK, LEVY	16	M	LABR	RR	ZZZZ	NY
COHN, MAX	27	M	TLR	RR	ZZZZ	NY
UNTERMANN, PAULINE	9	F	CHILD	RR	ZZZZ	NY
SPANZENKOPF, CHAIM	28	M	TLR	RR	ZZZZ	NY
KAPUSTA, TAMCHEN	25	M	LABR	RR	ZZZZ	NY
VITRIOL, SCHLOMI	39	M	PNR	RR	ZZZZ	NY
SARASOHN, ABRAM	17	M	PRNTR	RR	ZZZZ	NY
KARAFZEWITZ, ABRAM	27	M	TLR	RR	ZZZZ	NY
HIRSCH	28	M	UNKNOWN	RR	ZZZZ	NY
RIBATZKY, HINDE	30	F	W	RR	ZZZZ	NY
BEILE	18	F	SGL	RR	ZZZZ	NY
SCHOLEM	.11	M	INFANT	RR	ZZZZ	NY
KAMINOWITZ, LEON	18	M	TLR	RR	ZZZZ	NY
BIALISTOCK, JEZKO	30	M	UNKNOWN	RR	ZZZZ	NY
WOLF	37	M	UNKNOWN	RR	ZZZZ	NY
TSCHINSKY, SCHMUL	30	M	SHMK	RR	ZZZZ	NY
KOPITA, WOLF	33	M	UNKNOWN	RR	ZZZZ	NY
FRIEDELMANN, ISRAEL	18	M	TLR	RR	ZZZZ	NY
TIKUSZINSKY, HIRSCH	18	M	CTHR	RR	ZZZZ	NY
MANDIELZKY, RAFAEL	23	M	MSN	RR	ZZZZ	NY
RUZA, HIRSCH	31	M	UNKNOWN	RR	ZZZZ	NY
BERIL, SANDEL	31	M	UNKNOWN	RR	ZZZZ	NY
GIWNER, MOSES	36	M	TLR	RR	ZZZZ	NY
MICHELSOHN, SMUHL	18	M	SHMK	RR	ZZZZ	NY
KRAKOVSKI, STANISLAS	37	M	LABR	RR	ZZZZ	NY
WILEZENSKI, JULS.	24	M	FARMER	RR	ZZZZ	NY
LABARNI, CHEROMIN	33	M	UNKNOWN	RR	ZZZZ	NY
ROSALIE	35	F	W	RR	ZZZZ	NY
STANISLAV	7	M	CHILD	RR	ZZZZ	NY
CONSTANTIA	6	F	CHILD	RR	ZZZZ	NY
MURAWSKI, ANTON	27	M	UNKNOWN	RR	ZZZZ	NY
PODGURSKI, STANISL.	20	M	UNKNOWN	RR	ZZZZ	NY
MIEZERDITZ, ANTON	40	M	UNKNOWN	RR	ZZZZ	NY
ABRAMSKI, CONSTANTIN	17	M	UNKNOWN	RR	ZZZZ	NY
BALEZGUTH, METCDEI	20	M	UNKNOWN	RR	ZZZZ	NY
MALINOWSKY, MICHAEL	24	M	LABR	RR	ZZZZ	NY
GRUTKOWSKI, WOITECH	26	M	UNKNOWN	RR	ZZZZ	NY
KLEBS, AUGUST	23	M	UNKNOWN	RR	ZZZZ	NY
KRAMPITZ, CARL	18	M	UNKNOWN	RR	ZZZZ	NY
PICNICK, RACHEL	50	F	W	RR	ZZZZ	NY
FALK	19	M	S	RR	ZZZZ	NY
CAPLAN, MANUEL	25	M	LABR	RR	ZZZZ	NY
MARIE	26	F	W	RR	ZZZZ	NY
KOPITZKI, FRANZ	25	M	JNR	RR	ZZZZ	NY
BIERWITZKY, JOH.	32	M	UNKNOWN	RR	ZZZZ	NY
MUELLER, ZEWULIN	47	M	TLR	RR	ZZZZ	NY
LEWIE, SARAH	50	F	W	RR	ZZZZ	NY
DAVID	11	M	CH	RR	ZZZZ	NY
WOLF	11	M	CH	RR	ZZZZ	NY
GUTOWSKI, JOSEF	26	M	LABR	RR	ZZZZ	NY
ROGITZKI, VAL.	24	M	UNKNOWN	RR	ZZZZ	NY
SCHMANSKI, JUL.	19	M	UNKNOWN	RR	ZZZZ	NY
PORITZKI, ABRAHAM	50	M	UNKNOWN	RR	ZZZZ	NY
DAVIDOW, MOSES	8	M	CHILD	RR	ZZZZ	NY
SARATOW, ODER	22	M	LABR	RR	ZZZZ	NY
MARIE	18	F	W	RR	ZZZZ	NY
KUSAS, JOH.	20	M	LABR	RR	ZZZZ	NY
SUBATZ, FLORIAN	18	M	UNKNOWN	RR	ZZZZ	NY
LEWULIS, JOHANN	20	M	UNKNOWN	RR	ZZZZ	NY
MICHAEL	36	M	UNKNOWN	RR	ZZZZ	NY
WOLAMS, MATEI	26	M	UNKNOWN	RR	ZZZZ	NY
IGNATZ	23	M	UNKNOWN	RR	ZZZZ	NY
MICHALSKI, ABRAHAM	19	M	UNKNOWN	RR	ZZZZ	NY
PORITZKI, MOSES	17	M	UNKNOWN	RR	ZZZZ	NY
BRGEZAK, BERL	33	M	TLR	RR	ZZZZ	NY
LEWINSOHN, SCHEPSEL	19	M	TLR	RR	ZZZZ	NY
SKRODER, LEIB	22	M	UNKNOWN	RR	ZZZZ	NY
SCHNEIDER, MORDSCHE	21	M	CGRMKR	RR	ZZZZ	NY
KUHLINSKY, R----N	17	M	TLR	RR	ZZZZ	NY
PETRETGAR--, MARKUS	21	M	UNKNOWN	RR	ZZZZ	NY
ANSCHULEWITZ, CHOIN	24	M	SMH	RR	ZZZZ	NY
CAPLAN, SUMEN	25	M	TLR	RR	ZZZZ	NY

PASSENGER	AGE	SEX	OCCUPATION	PRV	VIL	DES
DEHN, PINCUS	24	M	TLR	RR	ZZZZ	NY

SHIP: LABRADOR

FROM: HAVRE
TO: NEW YORK
ARRIVED: 07 MARCH 1884

PASSENGER	AGE	SEX	OCCUPATION	PRV	VIL	DES
SZYMANSKI, EDWARD	25	M	ENGR	PL	ZZZZ	NY
GUNTHER, JULIEN	28	M	LKSH	PL	ZZZZ	NY

SHIP: PAVONIA

FROM: LIVERPOOL AND QUEENSTOWN
TO: NEW YORK
ARRIVED: 07 MARCH 1884

PASSENGER	AGE	SEX	OCCUPATION	PRV	VIL	DES
ZARONA, JANOS	38	M	FARMER	PL	ZZZZ	PIT
ZURESCHKO, MICHL.	28	M	FARMER	PL	ZZZZ	PIT
SCHOLTI, JANOS	39	M	FARMER	PL	ZZZZ	PIT
PIGA, STEFAN	11	M	CH	PL	ZZZZ	PIT
SIHIK, GEORGE	40	M	FARMER	PL	ZZZZ	PIT
POLOK, JONAS	34	M	FARMER	PL	ZZZZ	PIT
DANKS, ANDREAS	10	M	CH	PL	ZZZZ	PIT

SHIP: STATE OF GEORGIA

FROM: GLASGOW AND LARNE
TO: NEW YORK
ARRIVED: 08 MARCH 1884

PASSENGER	AGE	SEX	OCCUPATION	PRV	VIL	DES
ZINOWITZ, DAVID	00	M	TLR	PL	ZZZZ	USA
ISAAC	18	M	TLR	PL	ZZZZ	USA
TAUBER, BEHR	37	M	TLR	PL	ZZZZ	USA
RAHLA	30	F	W	PL	ZZZZ	USA
MALIE	19	F	SP	PL	ZZZZ	USA
LEOPOLD	10	M	CH	PL	ZZZZ	USA
JACOB	8	M	CHILD	PL	ZZZZ	USA
ANNA	6	F	CHILD	PL	ZZZZ	USA
ISIDOR	3	M	CHILD	PL	ZZZZ	USA
BEHRHOF, MOSES	33	M	PDLR	PL	ZZZZ	USA

SHIP: BELGENLAND

FROM: ANTWERP
TO: NEW YORK
ARRIVED: 10 MARCH 1884

PASSENGER	AGE	SEX	OCCUPATION	PRV	VIL	DES
GOYDGOWSKI, J.	19	M	LABR	PL	ZZZZ	NY
GANWEILER, SCH.	19	F	SVNT	PL	ZZZZ	NY
SCHNEIDER, I.	42	M	LABR	PL	ZZZZ	NY
KUPSKI, JOH.	30	M	LABR	PL	ZZZZ	CH

SHIP: BRITANNIC

FROM: LIVERPOOL AND QUEENSTOWN
TO: NEW YORK
ARRIVED: 10 MARCH 1884

PASSENGER	AGE	SEX	OCCUPATION	PRV	VIL	DES
WINZINSKY, B.	45	M	FARMER	PL	ZZZZ	USA
JOHANNA	47	F	W	PL	ZZZZ	USA
IDA	11	F	CH	PL	ZZZZ	USA
SIMON	10	M	CH	PL	ZZZZ	USA
REBECCA	6	F	CHILD	PL	ZZZZ	USA
VERGT, JULIUS	34	M	LABR	PL	ZZZZ	USA
PIONCKENNISKY, MCL.	29	M	LABR	PL	ZZZZ	USA
PORASCHINSKY, H.	27	M	LABR	PL	ZZZZ	USA
GOSTOWSKI, MCL.	28	M	LABR	PL	ZZZZ	USA
STACHKOWITZ, MARTIN	29	M	LABR	PL	ZZZZ	USA
MARIA	26	F	W	PL	ZZZZ	USA
MARTHA	.10	F	INFANT	PL	ZZZZ	USA
PRITRONSKI, MCL.	34	M	FARMER	PL	ZZZZ	USA
JOSEFA	33	F	W	PL	ZZZZ	USA
PAUL	8	M	CHILD	PL	ZZZZ	USA
CARL	6	M	CHILD	PL	ZZZZ	USA
JOHANNA	4	F	CHILD	PL	ZZZZ	USA
LESCHNISKY, JOSEPF	31	M	LABR	PL	ZZZZ	USA
GUSCHNISKY, MRD.	29	M	LABR	PL	ZZZZ	USA
GABRISCHAK, MCT.	27	M	LABR	PL	ZZZZ	USA
SUSCHITZKY, S.	29	M	LABR	PL	ZZZZ	USA

SHIP: PERSIAN MONARCH

FROM: LONDON
TO: NEW YORK
ARRIVED: 10 MARCH 1884

PASSENGER	AGE	SEX	OCCUPATION	PRV	VIL	DES
GRADETSKY, S.	22	M	LABR	PL	ZZZZ	NY
POLIANSKY, S.	19	M	LABR	PL	ZZZZ	NY

SHIP: WESER

FROM: BREMEN
TO: NEW YORK
ARRIVED: 10 MARCH 1884

PASSENGER	AGE	SEX	OCCUPATION	PRV	VIL	DES
BRENUER, SEBORA	22	F	UNKNOWN	RR	ZZZZ	PHI
ZABIKOSKA, JOSEFA	40	F	UNKNOWN	RR	ZZZZ	NY
LAURA	10	F	UNKNOWN	RR	ZZZZ	NY
JOSEPH	6	M	CHILD	RR	ZZZZ	NY
KRASZAVSKI, JOSEF	28	M	MLR	RR	ZZZZ	MN
MARIANNA	21	F	UNKNOWN	RR	ZZZZ	MN

SHIP: CITY OF MONTREAL

FROM: LIVERPOOL
TO: NEW YORK
ARRIVED: 11 MARCH 1884

PASSENGER	AGE	SEX	OCCUPATION	PRV	VIL	DES
SIBLESKEY, STANIS.	34	M	LABR	RR	ZZZZ	CH
ELLINBERGER, JOS.	28	M	UNKNOWN	PL	ZZZZ	CH
MEDOWSKY, SOLOMON	30	M	UNKNOWN	PL	ZZZZ	CH

SHIP: THE QUEEN

FROM: LIVERPOOL AND QUEENSTOWN
TO: NEW YORK
ARRIVED: 11 MARCH 1884

PASSENGER	AGE	SEX	OCCUPATION	PRV VIL DES
LEZEKKY, MALEM	32	M	TLR	PLZZZZUSA
REUTZ, MARTIN	41	M	TLR	PLZZZZUSA
RUBSTEIN, LUDVIE	41	M	TLR	PLZZZZUSA
KUBEKAR, PETER	30	M	TLR	PLZZZZUSA
BAFKULOIS, EMIL	27	M	TLR	PLZZZZUSA
LUBITH, WILH.	25	M	TLR	PLZZZZUSA
IEAU, GRUNAIS	31	M	TLR	PLZZZZUSA
RODERM, AUGUSTE	40	M	TLR	PLZZZZUSA
MERWITZ, MALVE	11	M	CH	PLZZZZUSA
EMIL	5	M	CHILD	PLZZZZUSA
SEPANIK, JAKOB	24	M	LABR	PLZZZZUSA
JABESE, MICH.	27	M	LABR	PLZZZZUSA
MINS, JANKEL	40	M	LABR	PLZZZZUSA
CREFAK, MARTIN	40	M	LABR	PLZZZZUSA
MURKAS, MARTIN	11	M	CH	PLZZZZUSA
CHLAP, JAKOB	27	M	LABR	PLZZZZUSA
SPONIAK, ROMZAN	25	M	LABR	PLZZZZUSA
REUP, AUS.	31	M	LABR	PLZZZZUSA
BARONK, SARAM	27	M	LABR	PLZZZZUSA
GIMISKI, LEO	11	M	CH	PLZZZZUSA
KORCUSKI, MARY	30	F	W	PLZZZZUSA
BAUFANI	8	M	CHILD	PLZZZZUSA
REBECCA	6	F	CHILD	PLZZZZUSA
ALRIBITA	.08	F	INFANT	PLZZZZUSA
MERWITZ, BATROME	37	M	LABR	PLZZZZUSA
CATH.	47	F	W	PLZZZZUSA
ALRITHA	7	F	CHILD	PLZZZZUSA
ARUSLA	.05	F	INFANT	PLZZZZUSA

SHIP: GALLIA

FROM: LIVERPOOL AND QUEENSTOWN
TO: NEW YORK
ARRIVED: 12 MARCH 1884

PASSENGER	AGE	SEX	OCCUPATION	PRV VIL DES
MISKA, LILY	38	F	W	RRZZZZUSA
JACOBSON-KNUOLA, JACOB	35	M	LABR	RRZZZZUSA
GUSTAFSON-RANTAVURA, HE	34	M	LABR	RRZZZZUSA
SIMONSON-LARNS, GUSTAV	30	M	LABR	RRZZZZUSA
GUSTAFSON-PAYHNSON, JOH	25	M	LABR	RRZZZZUSA

SHIP: GELLERT

FROM: HAMBURG
TO: NEW YORK
ARRIVED: 12 MARCH 1884

PASSENGER	AGE	SEX	OCCUPATION	PRV VIL DES
FEINBERG, DAVID	27	M	MCHT	RRZZZZUSA
SACHERCZUG, SARA	25	F	SGL	RRZZZZUSA
WOITANIS, WIZENTI	46	M	FARMER	RRZZZZUSA
SUCHINSKI, LUDWIG	40	M	UNKNOWN	RRZZZZUSA
BRZEZINSKI, KARL	22	M	UNKNOWN	RRZZZZUSA
WIZENTI	43	M	UNKNOWN	RRZZZZUSA
JURSZUKANIS, ANTON	36	M	UNKNOWN	RRZZZZUSA
ZYLANIS, KARL	42	M	UNKNOWN	RRZZZZUSA
BIALOBLOCKI, ANTON	35	M	UNKNOWN	RRZZZZUSA
SCHETZ, CHIENNE	30	F	SGL	RRZZZZUSA
GURIN, ELIAS	20	M	DLR	RRZZZZUSA
GEDRIS, PIETER	27	M	FARMER	RRZZZZUSA
LISOWSKI, DOMINIK	56	M	UNKNOWN	RRZZZZUSA
TUROWSKI, JAKOB	22	M	UNKNOWN	RRZZZZUSA
ADAM---TZ, MICHAL	25	M	UNKNOWN	RRZZZZUSA
U, U	29	M	UNKNOWN	RRZZZZUSA
KOLETZKY, SELIG	20	M	LABR	RRZZZZUSA
TRUMKIN, ELLIA	24	F	SGL	RRZZZZUSA
PARTNOI, SAUBEL	9	F	CHILD	RRZZZZUSA
GRUENBLATT, JOEL	38	M	GZR	RRZZZZUSA
LANDMANN, WOLF	20	M	SHMK	RRZZZZUSA
WEITZEN, ABEL	40	M	GZR	RRZZZZUSA
WALK, SUSSMANN	34	M	DLR	RRZZZZUSA
HERZOWITZ, JANKEL	17	M	UNKNOWN	RRZZZZUSA
GRAIEWER, LAIB	24	M	JNR	RRZZZZUSA
MANKOWITZ, ABRAH.	45	M	DLR	RRZZZZUSA
ISAAC	9	M	CHILD	RRZZZZUSA
BROCKEWIECZ, GEORG	21	M	FARMER	RRZZZZUSA
SIMONIS, JURAS	21	M	UNKNOWN	RRZZZZUSA
KOSAK, MATH.	30	M	UNKNOWN	RRZZZZUSA
KASOKEWITZ, TOMAS	45	M	UNKNOWN	RRZZZZUSA
SILBERMANN, JETTE	20	F	SGL	RRZZZZUSA
SCHAPIRO, ARON	45	M	DLR	RRZZZZUSA
SPRINGE	30	F	W	RRZZZZUSA
SUNDEL	.11	F	INFANT	RRZZZZUSA
WOIENLEWITZ, JOSEF	19	M	LABR	RRZZZZUSA
CHRISTINE	19	F	UNKNOWN	RRZZZZUSA
BENSCHICK, AUGUST	30	M	UNKNOWN	RRZZZZUSA
JESCHKEWICZ, JOSEF	28	M	UNKNOWN	RRZZZZUSA
FRANSISKA	23	F	W	RRZZZZUSA
MAGD.	.11	F	INFANT	RRZZZZUSA
VINCENZ	25	M	LABR	RRZZZZUSA
FRANZ.	25	F	W	RRZZZZUSA
MARIE	.09	F	INFANT	RRZZZZUSA
DORFMANN, SAMUEL	21	M	LABR	RRZZZZUSA
BEHM, MARCA	18	F	SGL	RRZZZZUSA
IRGELUNAS, STAN.	22	M	LABR	RRZZZZUSA
ARONOWITZ, ALTE	25	F	W	RRZZZZUSA
REBECCA	.11	F	INFANT	RRZZZZUSA
FRACK, MARCUS	38	M	TLR	RRZZZZUSA
CHOLEWA, LEA	26	F	SGL	RRZZZZUSA
MUELLER, MENDEL	19	M	LABR	RRZZZZUSA
BUCZOROWSKY, JAN	38	M	UNKNOWN	RRZZZZUSA
FLOCKER, LEIB	20	M	TLR	RRZZZZUSA
LIEBERS, ABRAM	25	M	LABR	RRZZZZUSA
SEMANOWITZ, ANTONIA	16	F	SGL	RRZZZZUSA
SALOMON	9	M	CHILD	RRZZZZUSA
SCHWARZ, MOSES	35	M	UNKNOWN	RRZZZZUSA
MEYROWITZ, HIRSCH	40	M	UNKNOWN	RRZZZZUSA
PUBROWITZ, SCHLOME	32	M	UNKNOWN	RRZZZZUSA
BERMANN, LEIB	35	M	UNKNOWN	RRZZZZUSA
ROCHL	30	F	W	RRZZZZUSA
CHOME	5	F	CHILD	RRZZZZUSA
BENZEL	.11	M	INFANT	RRZZZZUSA
SCHIMMELWITZ, MOSCHE	45	M	LABR	RRZZZZUSA
JAWBSOHN, LEISER	40	M	LABR	RRZZZZUSA
SEGALOWITZ, MEIER	30	M	BRR	RRZZZZUSA
MELZER, MORDCHE	45	M	LABR	RRZZZZUSA
DAVIDOWITZ, MOSES	22	M	DLR	RRZZZZUSA
LEWI, LEISER	17	M	CL	RRZZZZUSA
LEWIN, HERRM.	19	M	DLR	RRZZZZUSA
MOSLAWSKY, MOSES	18	M	UNKNOWN	RRZZZZUSA
EISCKOWITZ, SCHMUEL	32	M	UNKNOWN	RRZZZZUSA
GOLDBERG, MENDEL	19	M	TLR	RRZZZZUSA
POLATZKI, SCHOLEM	39	M	UNKNOWN	RRZZZZUSA
MORDCHE	9	M	CHILD	RRZZZZUSA
WISCHE, HENE	26	F	W	RRZZZZUSA
MORDCHE	7	M	CHILD	RRZZZZUSA
GOLDFUCHS, SUSSMANN	20	M	TLR	RRZZZZUSA
KELUCINSKY, ANTON	22	M	UNKNOWN	RRZZZZUSA
KAMINSKY, WITOLD	27	M	UNKNOWN	RRZZZZUSA
NARUSCHKEWITZ, SIMON	21	M	UNKNOWN	RRZZZZUSA
DOBKEWITZ, PAUSEL	40	M	UNKNOWN	RRZZZZUSA
MACKSCHIMOWITZ, ANDREI	36	M	UNKNOWN	RRZZZZUSA
JAUCZUK, FRANK	40	M	UNKNOWN	RRZZZZUSA
JAMILEWITZ, ANTON	23	M	UNKNOWN	RRZZZZUSA

PASSENGER	AGE	SEX	OCCUPATION	PRIVL	VIL	DES
GILIES, JOH.	24	M	UNKNOWN	RR	ZZZZ	USA
KLUEZINIK, POWEL	20	M	UNKNOWN	RR	ZZZZ	USA
JWAEZKA, MAREZI	24	M	UNKNOWN	RR	ZZZZ	USA
LABINSKY, PIETER	27	M	UNKNOWN	RR	ZZZZ	USA
GELLER, CZERNE	25	F	W	RR	ZZZZ	USA
ITE	.11	F	INFANT	RR	ZZZZ	USA
FELMANN, ARIE	38	M	BCHR	RR	ZZZZ	USA
DARIEN, DAVID	22	M	DLR	RR	ZZZZ	USA
SELWER, JOSEF	22	M	UNKNOWN	RR	ZZZZ	USA
NESCHE	22	F	SGL	RR	ZZZZ	USA
HEYMANN, MORDCHE	30	M	DLR	RR	ZZZZ	USA
WINZINOWITZ, ANTON	24	M	LABR	RR	ZZZZ	USA
ABRAMOWITZ, WLADISLAV	20	M	UNKNOWN	RR	ZZZZ	USA
KOWALEWSKY, BERNH	18	M	UNKNOWN	RR	ZZZZ	USA
RUSSINSKI, JOHANN	32	M	UNKNOWN	RR	ZZZZ	USA
KRZEWICZKI, BRONISLAV	19	M	LABR	RR	ZZZZ	USA
DULSKY, MARIE	34	F	W	RR	ZZZZ	USA
MINNA	5	F	CHILD	RR	ZZZZ	USA
JUDEL	3	F	CHILD	RR	ZZZZ	USA
SARA	.11	F	INFANT	RR	ZZZZ	USA
MARKOWSKY, JACOB	43	M	LABR	RR	ZZZZ	USA
WEGNER, JACOB	30	M	UNKNOWN	RR	ZZZZ	USA
JOH.	40	M	UNKNOWN	RR	ZZZZ	USA
LOBISCH, ANTON	38	M	UNKNOWN	RR	ZZZZ	USA
MACKEWICZ, FELIX	36	M	UNKNOWN	RR	ZZZZ	USA
PRZYBOROWSKI, JOSEF	22	M	UNKNOWN	RR	ZZZZ	USA
JIWOLINSKY, FRANZ	33	M	UNKNOWN	RR	ZZZZ	USA
BETLEWSKY, ANTON	19	M	UNKNOWN	RR	ZZZZ	USA
SAWORSKY, FRANZ	33	M	UNKNOWN	RR	ZZZZ	USA
KOWALSKY, FRANZ	48	M	UNKNOWN	RR	ZZZZ	USA
TZCHEKAITES, ANTON	23	M	UNKNOWN	RR	ZZZZ	USA
JOSES	29	M	UNKNOWN	RR	ZZZZ	USA
POSSLOWSKI, KAISES	19	M	UNKNOWN	RR	ZZZZ	USA
ROBETZKI, JAURS	21	M	UNKNOWN	RR	ZZZZ	USA
LOREDOWSKY, MIKAL	23	M	UNKNOWN	RR	ZZZZ	USA
KOWALSKI, JOSEF	21	M	UNKNOWN	RR	ZZZZ	USA
LALEWSKY, JAN	32	M	UNKNOWN	RR	ZZZZ	USA
PACZKOWSKY, FRANK	26	M	UNKNOWN	RR	ZZZZ	USA
OLSKOWSKI, FRANZ	23	M	UNKNOWN	RR	ZZZZ	USA
BORDZIKOWSKY, JOSEF	26	M	UNKNOWN	RR	ZZZZ	USA
JANIKE, MICHAEL	26	M	UNKNOWN	RR	ZZZZ	USA
NASS, PAUL	33	M	UNKNOWN	RR	ZZZZ	USA
THONES, JOH.	29	M	UNKNOWN	RR	ZZZZ	USA
BULKEWSKI, JOSEF	19	M	UNKNOWN	RR	ZZZZ	USA
SCHUELT, HEINR.	22	M	SHMK	RR	ZZZZ	USA
KLOSAWSKY, IGNAZ	25	M	LABR	RR	ZZZZ	USA
LEIDE, JAN	27	M	UNKNOWN	RR	ZZZZ	USA
KOSBUSKI, HENOFRE	38	M	UNKNOWN	RR	ZZZZ	USA
MILARSKI, FRANZ	35	M	UNKNOWN	RR	ZZZZ	USA
JOSCHINETZKI, FRANZ	49	M	UNKNOWN	RR	ZZZZ	USA
FUERSTENAN, WILH.	24	M	UNKNOWN	RR	ZZZZ	USA
SCHMIDT, ANTONE	23	F	SGL	RR	ZZZZ	USA
SONSKOWITZ, RAICHEL	19	F	SGL	RR	ZZZZ	USA
GERSON	25	M	LABR	RR	ZZZZ	USA
JUDEL	.09	F	INFANT	RR	ZZZZ	USA
FAHRENFELDT, AUG.	19	F	SGL	RR	ZZZZ	USA
EIDELBERG, ABRAH.	30	M	SHMK	RR	ZZZZ	USA
LASCHUCK, RACHEL	22	F	SGL	RR	ZZZZ	USA
ELTERMANN, ABRAH.	20	M	SHMK	RR	ZZZZ	USA
KATHEWITZ, SORACH	19	M	UNKNOWN	RR	ZZZZ	USA
KRIWIKE, NOACH	33	M	UNKNOWN	RR	ZZZZ	USA
BLUMENTHAL, LEA	31	F	W	RR	ZZZZ	USA
MOSES	13	M	CH	RR	ZZZZ	USA
ISAAC	9	M	CHILD	RR	ZZZZ	USA
MARIANNE	8	F	CHILD	RR	ZZZZ	USA
REBECCA	7	F	CHILD	RR	ZZZZ	USA
BEILE	5	F	CHILD	RR	ZZZZ	USA
ESTHER	.11	F	INFANT	RR	ZZZZ	USA
SALOM.	.01	M	INFANT	RR	ZZZZ	USA
KATZ, ISER	30	M	LABR	RR	ZZZZ	USA
KRUEGEL, WILH.	30	M	UNKNOWN	RR	ZZZZ	USA
AUGE.	22	F	W	RR	ZZZZ	USA
MINNA	.03	F	INFANT	RR	ZZZZ	USA
JOH.	42	M	LABR	RR	ZZZZ	USA
WILH.	38	F	W	RR	ZZZZ	USA

PASSENGER	AGE	SEX	OCCUPATION	PRIVL	VIL	DES
GALOW, WILH.	34	M	LABR	RR	ZZZZ	USA
CHRISTINE	30	F	W	RR	ZZZZ	USA
HERRW.	8	M	CHILD	RR	ZZZZ	USA
AUGUSTE	7	F	CHILD	RR	ZZZZ	USA
ANNA	6	F	CHILD	RR	ZZZZ	USA
BERTHA	4	F	CHILD	RR	ZZZZ	USA
MORITZ	.11	M	INFANT	RR	ZZZZ	USA
LAPIDUS, CHAINE	20	M	UNKNOWN	RR	ZZZZ	USA
FUNK, ISRAEL	19	M	UNKNOWN	RR	ZZZZ	USA

SHIP: FURNESSIA

FROM: GLASGOW AND MOVILLE
TO: NEW YORK
ARRIVED: 13 MARCH 1884

PASSENGER	AGE	SEX	OCCUPATION	PRIVL	VIL	DES
BALIZA, JOHAN	22	M	LABR	RR	ZZZZ	USA
THOMAS, MATHIAS	23	M	LABR	RR	ZZZZ	USA
GEORG, BELA	31	M	LABR	RR	ZZZZ	USA
ROSENBERG, JAN	19	M	PDLR	RR	ZZZZ	USA
ASCHOWAT, VALENTINE	41	M	ENGR	RR	ZZZZ	USA

SHIP: NURNBERG

FROM: BREMEN
TO: NEW YORK
ARRIVED: 13 MARCH 1884

PASSENGER	AGE	SEX	OCCUPATION	PRIVL	VIL	DES
SOSNOWSKI, VICENTE	38	M	LABR	RR	ZZZZ	USA
KOWALKOWSKI, BATLONI	30	M	LABR	RR	ZZZZ	USA
HONKE, THEODOR	21	M	LABR	RR	ZZZZ	USA
KATARZYNA	24	F	UNKNOWN	RR	ZZZZ	USA
HEINBERG, FRIEDR.	31	M	LABR	RR	ZZZZ	USA
WILHELMINE	37	F	UNKNOWN	RR	ZZZZ	USA
HERMAN	10	M	UNKNOWN	RR	ZZZZ	USA
BEHDE, AUGUST	24	M	LABR	RR	ZZZZ	USA
WIERSCHEWITZ, ALBERT	32	M	LABR	RR	ZZZZ	USA
DABEROCK, CARL	25	M	LABR	RR	ZZZZ	USA
THALL, LINA	20	F	UNKNOWN	RR	ZZZZ	USA
BREMER, SAMUEL	30	M	FARMER	RR	ZZZZ	USA

SHIP: DONAU

FROM: BREMEN
TO: NEW YORK
ARRIVED: 15 MARCH 1884

PASSENGER	AGE	SEX	OCCUPATION	PRIVL	VIL	DES
ROSENTHAL, GERH.	17	M	DLR	RR	ZZZZ	USA
CZOSKOW, MEIER	43	M	JNR	RR	ZZZZ	USA
KANRENOWSKY, MAREUS	25	M	DLR	RR	ZZZZ	USA
GRABOWSKY, LUKASZ	26	M	LABR	RR	ZZZZ	USA
GIZURSKI, PAWEL	23	M	LABR	RR	ZZZZ	USA
KUNISZEWSKY, JOS.	30	M	LABR	RR	ZZZZ	USA
BAGOJEWSKI, JOS.	23	M	LABR	RR	ZZZZ	USA
KOLINSKI, ADAM	23	M	LABR	RR	ZZZZ	USA
GOSOROWSKA, MARIANNA	28	F	NN	RR	ZZZZ	USA
ANNA	3	F	CHILD	RR	ZZZZ	USA

PASSENGER	AGE	SEX	OCCUPATION	PRV VIL DES

SHIP: GRECIAN MONARCH

FROM: LONDON
TO: NEW YORK
ARRIVED: 17 MARCH 1884

PASSENGER	AGE	SEX	OCCUPATION	PRV VIL DES
HELFER, H.	45	M	LABR	PLZZZZUSA
LIBERMANN, SIGMON	25	M	UNKNOWN	PLZZZZUSA
FANNY	26	F	W	PLZZZZUSA
HEYMAN, E.	26	M	LABR	PLZZZZUSA
HYMAN, REBECCA	25	F	W	PLZZZZUSA
LEWIS	7	M	CHILD	PLZZZZUSA
EVE	1	F	CHILD	PLZZZZUSA
LEWY, RACHEL	24	F	W	PLZZZZUSA
WOLF	1	M	CHILD	PLZZZZUSA
RIBECK, A.I.	17	M	LABR	PLZZZZUSA
POWEKANTZ, SIMA	27	F	W	PLZZZZUSA
ANNIL	6	F	CHILD	PLZZZZUSA
FANNY	4	F	CHILD	PLZZZZUSA
RACKBERG, WOLF	27	M	LABR	PLZZZZUSA
MARY	24	F	W	PLZZZZUSA
BETSY	3	F	CHILD	PLZZZZUSA
PINCUS	.11	M	INFANT	PLZZZZUSA
FRIEDMANN, MORITZ	30	M	LABR	PLZZZZUSA
ZUALE	26	F	W	PLZZZZUSA
JENH	4	F	CHILD	PLZZZZUSA
KATE	2	F	CHILD	PLZZZZUSA
SAMUEL	.02	M	INFANT	PLZZZZUSA

SHIP: REPUBLIC

FROM: LIVERPOOL AND QUEENSTOWN
TO: NEW YORK
ARRIVED: 17 MARCH 1884

PASSENGER	AGE	SEX	OCCUPATION	PRV VIL DES
KATZ, JOSEF	25	M	LABR	PLZZZZUSA
HAS, AUGUST	18	M	LABR	PLZZZZUSA
JEKEL, LEOPOLD	47	M	LABR	PLZZZZUSA
KLUIEWOSKI, JOS.	20	M	LABR	PLZZZZUSA
DORNOWECY, JOURS	25	M	LABR	PLZZZZUSA
DOWASKI, THOS.	25	M	LABR	PLZZZZUSA
SUSZYSA, PETRO	32	M	LABR	PLZZZZUSA
BALOKA, WASIL	16	M	LABR	PLZZZZUSA
SELESTURTZ, JOHARNES	24	M	LABR	PLZZZZUSA
SOSGOWCKI, MARTIN	25	M	LABR	PLZZZZUSA
THOS.	23	M	LABR	PLZZZZUSA
HAUGWELL, GUSTAFF.	26	M	LABR	PLZZZZUSA
GAY, MARTIN	26	M	LABR	PLZZZZUSA
GOLDA, JACOB	22	M	LABR	PLZZZZUSA
ADRIAN, MARTIN	27	M	LABR	PLZZZZUSA
WAITER, JOHAIE	27	M	FARMER	PLZZZZUSA
CATH.	24	F	W	PLZZZZUSA
JEASTAWORTZ, WOIZ.	28	M	LABR	PLZZZZUSA
AGNESS	23	F	W	PLZZZZUSA
KAGWISKI, MICHEL	29	M	LABR	PLZZZZUSA
JOHANNA	24	F	W	PLZZZZUSA
GABALACZ, ANDREAS	29	M	LABR	PLZZZZUSA
POCK, VALENTINE	28	M	LABR	PLZZZZUSA
STINGELLA, ANDREAS	29	M	LABR	PLZZZZUSA
ODERGECK, MARTIN	31	M	LABR	PLZZZZUSA
FUSKER, SP.	22	M	LABR	PLZZZZUSA
GIABAWSKY, JOSEL	36	M	LABR	PLZZZZUSA
BURGER, LASSI	19	M	LABR	PLZZZZUSA
WASSCHAFSKY, ARON	20	M	LABR	PLZZZZUSA
OSTANSKY, MEYER	22	M	LABR	PLZZZZUSA
BERGIN, MOSES	21	M	LABR	PLZZZZUSA
MIGAKOSCHISKY, LEISER	40	M	LABR	PLZZZZUSA
WEMOBLE, ABRAHAM	16	M	LABR	PLZZZZUSA
HANMER, WALDEMAR	35	M	LABR	PLZZZZUSA

PASSENGER	AGE	SEX	OCCUPATION	PRV VIL DES
SILERSEN, CHRISTIAN	29	M	LABR	PLZZZZUSA

SHIP: WAESLAND

FROM: ANTWERP
TO: NEW YORK
ARRIVED: 17 MARCH 1884

PASSENGER	AGE	SEX	OCCUPATION	PRV VIL DES
SEWUBER, F.	48	M	FARMER	RRZZZZNY
HUBIAK, FRZ.	25	M	MACH	RRZZZZNY
SCHURNOKOWSKI, STAN.	21	M	UNKNOWN	RRZZZZNY

SHIP: WERRA

FROM: BREMEN
TO: NEW YORK
ARRIVED: 17 MARCH 1884

PASSENGER	AGE	SEX	OCCUPATION	PRV VIL DES
GORECKI, JOS.	24	M	LABR	RRZZZZUSA
STACHARSKY, JOS.	23	M	LABR	RRZZZZUSA
FRAMKOWSKY, ISIDOR	34	M	LABR	RRZZZZUSA
ZABLOCKI, ANDRYS	30	M	LABR	RRZZZZUSA
MOHLENSKY, ANT.	24	M	LABR	RRZZZZUSA
SITTO, JAN	27	M	LABR	RRZZZZUSA
LEDKOWITCH, JAN	36	M	LABR	RRZZZZUSA
MALKOWSKY, ADAM	27	M	LABR	RRZZZZUSA
SADNISKI, WOJCACH	27	M	LABR	RRZZZZUSA
PRZESICKI, JOS.	20	M	LABR	RRZZZZUSA

SHIP: AUSTRALIA

FROM: HAMBURG
TO: NEW YORK
ARRIVED: 20 MARCH 1884

PASSENGER	AGE	SEX	OCCUPATION	PRV VIL DES
UHRICH, MOS.L.	28	M	TRDSMN	PLZZZZNY
SOPHIE	20	F	SI	PLZZZZNY
KRAEMER, ISRAEL	26	M	CPMKR	PLZZZZNY
BADER, MOS.	22	M	JNR	PLZZZZNY
ITKOWITSCH, ABR.	51	M	TRDSMN	RRZZZZNY
FUSCH, SOPHIE	18	F	SGL	PLZZZZNY
PUTLE--, MARIA	18	F	WO	PLZZZZNY
ANNA	7	F	CHILD	PLZZZZNY
JOSEF	00	M	S	PLZZZZNY
KOSLOWSKY, JAN	28	M	TLR	PLZZZZNY
STANISLAWA	21	F	W	PLZZZZNY
BERGER, DAVID	28	M	TRDSMN	PLZZZZNY
LEOPOLD	7	M	CHILD	PLZZZZNY
LIBSCHUETZ, LIB.	34	M	TRDSMN	RRZZZZNY
SIMON, ANNA	28	F	WO	RRZZZZNY
GITTEL	.06	F	INFANT	RRZZZZNY
ROSENBLUETH, KALM	22	M	TRDSMN	PLZZZZNY
KRIZISTOFZIK, JOS.	18	M	TRDSMN	RRZZZZNY
ZLOTIK, PHILIPP	25	M	TRDSMN	PLZZZZNY
POREBA, WOYCICH	40	M	LABR	PLZZZZNY
WOLAN, WOYCICH	45	M	UNKNOWN	PLZZZZNY
MAHARAN, HAJETAN	40	M	UNKNOWN	PLZZZZNY
NOWICKI, JOSEF	42	M	UNKNOWN	PLZZZZNY
BOCHORZ, STANISL.	27	M	UNKNOWN	PLZZZZNY
POREBA, KATH.	22	F	WO	PLZZZZNY

PASSENGER	AGE	SEX	OCCUPATION	PRV VIL DES
BRONISLAWA	.02	F	INFANT	PLZZZZNY
LUKASCHEWITZ, VICENTY	27	M	LABR	RRZZZZNY
SCHOMOKEITIS, MART.	27	M	UNKNOWN	RRZZZZNY
JANUSCHEFSKY, ANT.	26	M	LABR	RRZZZZNY
BROSSO, WLADISLAW	34	M	UNKNOWN	RRZZZZNY
NAMEWITZ, MATH.	18	M	LABR	RRZZZZNY
FERENZ, VICENTY	27	M	UNKNOWN	RRZZZZNY
STROTZKI, IASZKO	18	M	UNKNOWN	RRZZZZNY
SZABASTEWICZ, VINCENTY	25	M	LABR	RRZZZZNY
WISNEFSKY, MARCUS	32	M	TRDSMN	RRZZZZNY
BECKER, MEYER	34	M	UNKNOWN	RRZZZZNY
ALT, HIRSCH	20	M	UNKNOWN	RRZZZZNY
WORZEK, ABRAHAM	21	M	UNKNOWN	RRZZZZNY
ROSE	22	F	W	RRZZZZNY
WOLPERT, IANKEL	25	M	TRDSMN	RRZZZZNY
IENDREZIK, TH.	30	M	LABR	PLZZZZNY
GLIESGO, AGNES	30	F	WO	PLZZZZNY
HIRSCH, FRIEDR.	21	M	LABR	RRZZZZNY
AUGUSTE	21	M	UNKNOWN	RRZZZZNY
WILHELM	42	M	UNKNOWN	RRZZZZNY
JARALDIUS, PETER	39	M	UNKNOWN	RRZZZZNY
ANTON	21	M	UNKNOWN	RRZZZZNY
ZIBULSKI, JOSEF	20	M	UNKNOWN	RRZZZZNY
IURASCHEWITZ, PETER	20	M	UNKNOWN	RRZZZZNY
MAXIAMS, VINCENT	22	M	UNKNOWN	RRZZZZNY
GIWANOWSKI, CARL	23	M	UNKNOWN	RRZZZZNY
RULKOWSKI, JOSEF	19	M	UNKNOWN	RRZZZZNY
KUSES, JOSEF	20	M	UNKNOWN	RRZZZZNY

SHIP: BOTHNIA

FROM: LIVERPOOL
TO: NEW YORK
ARRIVED: 21 MARCH 1884

PASSENGER	AGE	SEX	OCCUPATION	PRV VIL DES
STEINBERG, SAML.	35	M	LABR	PLZZZZUSA
JUSI, CARL	33	M	LABR	RRZZZZUSA
GIOSEFFE	60	M	LABR	RRZZZZUSA
MARASI, INTIMATE	26	M	LABR	RRZZZZUSA
BARTUNEK, JOHAN	20	M	LABR	RRZZZZUSA
TESKE, FRANZ	19	M	LABR	RRZZZZUSA
LUTCHWSKY, ABRAHAM	33	M	LABR	RRZZZZUSA
BRAJACIK, STIFAN	37	M	LABR	RRZZZZUSA
FLURKE, JAN	22	M	LABR	RRZZZZUSA
WARGA, MICHL.	11	M	CH	RRZZZZUSA
RAHALSKI, JOSEF	9	M	CHILD	RRZZZZUSA
PASKY, WALENTIN	32	M	LABR	RRZZZZUSA
FLORIN	25	F	W	RRZZZZUSA
ELGASTH	.08	F	INFANT	RRZZZZUSA
STEFAN	.08	M	INFANT	RRZZZZUSA
FRUDMANN, JAN-R.	48	M	LABR	RRZZZZUSA
LOFUTAK, GEORG	40	M	LABR	RRZZZZUSA
KACWKA, ANDRAS	26	M	LABR	RRZZZZUSA
ANTAL, MATIA	11	M	CH	RRZZZZUSA
WANKAT, ANDRAS	10	M	CH	RRZZZZUSA
KARTIA, KORWA	32	M	FARMER	RRZZZZUSA
ZESMARIK, GEORG	28	M	FARMER	RRZZZZUSA
PAWTIK, MENDEL	42	M	FARMER	RRZZZZUSA
CHRISTOF, MARKA	11	M	CH	RRZZZZUSA
KOKATKA, PIROS	10	M	CH	RRZZZZUSA
WISKA, VINCENT	36	M	FARMER	RRZZZZUSA
MARIANNA	28	F	W	RRZZZZUSA
MAGDALINA	25	F	SP	RRZZZZUSA
JOSEF	.10	M	INFANT	RRZZZZUSA
STANISLAUS	.10	M	INFANT	RRZZZZUSA
TOCHAN, JANOS	36	M	FARMER	RRZZZZUSA
OSTIM, MICHL.	28	M	FARMER	RRZZZZUSA
LAKO, STEFEN	11	M	CH	RRZZZZUSA
TADT, MARCA	10	M	CH	RRZZZZUSA
RATNUSH, JOSEF	32	M	FARMER	RRZZZZUSA
MIKA, MICHAL	49	M	FARMER	RRZZZZUSA
TOKACY, JOSEF	44	M	FARMER	RRZZZZUSA
WUSI, PAUL	40	M	FARMER	RRZZZZUSA
MARKA, JURIK	26	M	FARMER	RRZZZZUSA
PETER, MICHAIL	30	M	FARMER	RRZZZZUSA
KNY, MICHAIL	39	M	FARMER	RRZZZZUSA
POZARER, MICHAIL	11	M	CH	RRZZZZUSA
MAZALA, MICHAIL	10	M	CH	RRZZZZUSA
PRENNCESER, THRURAS	24	M	FARMER	RRZZZZUSA
ANNA	22	F	SP	RRZZZZUSA
JOHAN	17	M	FARMER	RRZZZZUSA
GROMSKA, ANNA	20	F	SP	RRZZZZUSA
DIAMONT, LEON	30	M	LABR	PLZZZZUSA
JURKOWSKI, LEON	40	M	FARMER	PLZZZZUSA
CHRENETEWSKY, FRANZ	25	M	FARMER	PLZZZZUSA
CHOTLEYKY, STANISLAUS	21	M	FARMER	PLZZZZUSA
DABVZYNSKY, JOSEF	58	M	FARMER	PLZZZZUSA
POWATSKY, JOSEF	40	M	FARMER	PLZZZZUSA
PIATKOWSKY, FRANZ	33	M	FARMER	PLZZZZUSA
SCHITAPESWKY, WRYCISCH	25	M	FARMER	PLZZZZUSA
ROSINSKY, ANTON	11	M	CH	PLZZZZUSA
PRUSTUVICZ, NOYCESCH	24	M	FARMER	PLZZZZUSA
LOBOTSHEVICKY, JACOB	33	M	FARMER	PLZZZZUSA
MANELSKY, MICHAL	23	M	FARMER	PLZZZZUSA
WATKAWSKY, STANISLAUS	22	M	FARMER	PLZZZZUSA
OCRAWSKI, TAWEL	23	M	FARMER	PLZZZZUSA
SCHAMISKI, FRIEDMAN	30	M	FARMER	PLZZZZUSA
MOLLER, ANTON	11	M	CH	PLZZZZUSA
RUGISKY, SIMON	41	M	FARMER	PLZZZZUSA
AMELIA	27	F	SP	PLZZZZUSA
KLUZUS, ISLAS	20	M	LABR	PLZZZZUSA
SZWICIS, ANDER.	11	M	CH	PLZZZZUSA
RASZHARSKI, RAZMIR	10	M	CH	PLZZZZUSA
REDER, FREDWICK	52	M	LABR	PLZZZZUSA
DELGAR, AUGUST	38	M	LABR	PLZZZZUSA
FUCH, SAMUEL	28	M	LABR	PLZZZZUSA
BRUTKOWITZ, MARCIN	32	M	SDLR	PLZZZZUSA
MARIANA	24	F	W	PLZZZZUSA
KASIMIRA	.09	F	INFANT	PLZZZZUSA
SEACH, ALEXANDER	48	M	FARMER	RRZZZZUSA
MISAK, STEFAN	26	M	FARMER	RRZZZZUSA
HARCKO, WASIL	24	M	FARMER	RRZZZZUSA
ZBUR, WASIL	26	M	FARMER	RRZZZZUSA
WEDRER, JACOB	35	M	FARMER	RRZZZZUSA
STANSPER, HENRICH	26	M	FARMER	RRZZZZUSA
HORK, WASIL	11	M	CH	RRZZZZUSA
FELICKY, LUDWIG	10	M	CH	RRZZZZUSA
WAURIN, HANZEL	25	M	FARMER	RRZZZZUSA
WERNER, MOSES	27	M	FARMER	RRZZZZUSA
MAROWSKY, FRANZ	40	M	FARMER	RRZZZZUSA
RIBITZKY, FRANZ	40	M	FARMER	RRZZZZUSA
LALUSYKUMOCZ, JOSEF	30	M	FARMER	RRZZZZUSA
BUDINSKY, FERDINAND	9	M	CHILD	RRZZZZUSA
SILBER, SCHIMAR	11	M	CH	RRZZZZUSA
RAFINSKY, FRANZ	11	M	CH	RRZZZZUSA
PAWITSKY, JOSEF	10	M	CH	RRZZZZUSA
MARKULIS, JON	30	M	FARMER	RRZZZZUSA
MULLER, AUGUST	25	M	FARMER	RRZZZZUSA
KRAJNIK, FRANZ	34	M	FARMER	RRZZZZUSA
MULLER, FEITZ	26	M	FARMER	RRZZZZUSA
PASCHWESKY, JON	38	M	FARMER	RRZZZZUSA
DERANGAWSKY, SIMON	25	M	FARMER	RRZZZZUSA
KRAGSWISKY, JAN	31	M	FARMER	RRZZZZUSA
GALD, STOM	58	M	LABR	PLZZZZUSA
SADAWISKY, ANDER.	37	M	FARMER	RRZZZZUSA
BRERKWISKY, MICHL.	45	M	FARMER	RRZZZZUSA
TERENSKY, JAN	23	M	FARMER	RRZZZZUSA
LOHOLWISKY, MATIAS	34	M	FARMER	RRZZZZUSA
SCHONFULD, WILMUS	32	M	FARMER	RRZZZZUSA
AMLOKA, KUDI	8	F	CHILD	RRZZZZUSA
ROSENBERG, MOSES-L.	24	M	LABR	RRZZZZUSA
BERNHAN, SFOR	24	M	LABR	RRZZZZUSA
ARM, LINDER	28	M	LABR	RRZZZZUSA
JOSEF, GISCH	38	M	LABR	RRZZZZUSA

PASSENGER	AGE	SEX	OCCUPATION	PRV VIL DES

SHIP: CANADA

FROM: HAVRE
TO: NEW YORK
ARRIVED: 21 MARCH 1884

PASSENGER	AGE	SEX	OCCUPATION	PRV VIL DES
KAUFMANN, ANNA	24	F	UNKNOWN	RRZZZZNY

SHIP: RHAETIA

FROM: HAMBURG
TO: NEW YORK
ARRIVED: 21 MARCH 1884

PASSENGER	AGE	SEX	OCCUPATION	PRV VIL DES
FEITELBAUM, NACHUM	24	M	LABR	RRZZZZUSA
JASKULKA, MOSES	30	M	LABR	RRZZZZUSA
BALLRUSZEWICZ, AGATHE	21	F	SGL	RRZZZZUSA
SCHWANTNER, CHRIST.	26	M	FARMER	RRZZZZUSA
EMILIE	22	F	W	RRZZZZUSA
EMILIE	.04	F	INFANT	RRZZZZUSA
ROMIS, ETTEL	28	F	W	RRZZZZUSA
ALTE	4	F	CHILD	RRZZZZUSA
JUDE	.11	F	INFANT	RRZZZZUSA
TAUB, SALI	24	F	SGL	RRZZZZUSA
JAROWSKY, GABRIEL	21	M	BKR	RRZZZZUSA
SENDROWSKI, TEOFIE	31	M	LABR	RRZZZZUSA
MARCHLEWSKI, JOSEF	19	M	LABR	RRZZZZUSA
ROSNOCH, GUST.	22	M	LABR	RRZZZZUSA
WISNOWSKI, ANTON	38	M	LABR	RRZZZZUSA
SADENITZ, SARA	23	F	W	RRZZZZUSA
HIRSCH	8	M	CHILD	RRZZZZUSA
ESTHER	.06	F	INFANT	RRZZZZUSA
SCHOLIT, MANESCH	31	M	LABR	RRZZZZUSA
SARA	19	F	W	RRZZZZUSA
SACKIN, ISAAC	32	M	TLR	RRZZZZUSA
BOSCHWEDNITZKY, ISAAC	26	M	TLR	RRZZZZUSA
SAKOLSKY, ISAAC	24	M	LABR	RRZZZZUSA
KUSSELEWITZ, GETZEL	34	F	SGL	RRZZZZUSA
EYSENBERG, JENNY	20	F	SGL	RRZZZZUSA
KOHN, ISAAC	25	M	LABR	RRZZZZUSA
LEA	24	F	W	RRZZZZUSA
ABRAHAM, BEHR	21	M	LABR	RRZZZZUSA
KONOPNITZKY, BEREK	44	M	TLR	RRZZZZUSA
RIW--, SCHOLEM	35	M	SHMK	RRZZZZUSA
WEISSFELDE, CHAWE	13	F	SGL	RRZZZZUSA
BOREBEITSOLIK, HIRSCH	20	M	LABR	RRZZZZUSA
GRABENTSCHIK, BASCHE	19	F	SGL	RRZZZZUSA
MARCUS	22	M	LABR	RRZZZZUSA
RYLAKOWSKI, ANDR.	24	M	LABR	RRZZZZUSA
MARIANNE	18	F	W	RRZZZZUSA
BARTKOWSKI, FRANZ	20	M	LABR	RRZZZZUSA
KWIATKOWSKI, THOMAS	38	M	LABR	RRZZZZUSA
KALINOWSKI, JOH.	28	M	LABR	RRZZZZUSA
KANTORSKI, JOH.	26	M	LABR	RRZZZZUSA
SIMBORSKY, MARTIN	24	M	LABR	RRZZZZUSA
SLOVES, RACHEL	26	F	W	RRZZZZUSA
CHANE	6	F	CHILD	RRZZZZUSA
DOMBROWSKY, JAN	25	M	LABR	RRZZZZUSA
MARIANNE	28	F	W	RRZZZZUSA
STANISL.	9	M	CHILD	RRZZZZUSA
NEUSCHINSKY, ISAAC	18	M	LABR	RRZZZZUSA
BARZEWSKI, MART.	40	M	LABR	RRZZZZUSA
ULTISKI, THOMAS	42	M	LABR	RRZZZZUSA
FINKELBERG, FEWEL	50	M	SMH	RRZZZZUSA
DAVID	15	M	BBR	RRZZZZUSA
FEGOMASCH, JANKEL	53	M	FELMO	RRZZZZUSA
KAMBERG, ISRAEL	18	M	DLR	RRZZZZUSA
GORDON, SCHEIME	9	F	CHILD	RRZZZZUSA
RUESNA, HUGO	40	M	ENGR	RRZZZZUSA
AMALIE	35	F	W	RRZZZZUSA
JESONES, BALTRUS	27	M	LABR	RRZZZZUSA
KARDISCHOWSKY, JURI	28	M	LABR	RRZZZZUSA
PETROS	29	M	LABR	RRZZZZUSA
DIEKOW, DANIEL	29	M	LABR	RRZZZZUSA
ALOSLOWSKY, JACOB	42	M	LABR	RRZZZZUSA
SOPRANOWITZ, ANTON	37	M	LABR	RRZZZZUSA
LINDNIK, ALAZEI	33	M	LABR	RRZZZZUSA
GREGAROWITZ, MIHAL	19	M	SHMK	RRZZZZUSA
RINKO, CHAROL	19	F	W	RRZZZZUSA
FREUCK, JACOB	18	F	DLR	RRZZZZUSA
HIRSCHOWITZ, SHAIE	18	F	DLR	RRZZZZUSA
FEIN, ISAAC	23	F	DLR	RRZZZZUSA
MARIE	19	F	W	RRZZZZUSA
GROMANN, JUDEL	20	M	TLR	RRZZZZUSA
RUMS, PINKUS	23	M	TLR	RRZZZZUSA
JEUTE	22	F	W	RRZZZZUSA
ABEL	.11	M	INFANT	RRZZZZUSA
CHEME	.01	F	INFANT	RRZZZZUSA
KURAN, HIRSCH	23	M	DLR	RRZZZZUSA
SARA	21	F	W	RRZZZZUSA
ESTHER	.11	F	INFANT	RRZZZZUSA
MOSINTER, ISAAC	19	M	CL	RRZZZZUSA
MAYN.	20	M	CL	RRZZZZUSA
RABINOWITZ, MOSES	21	M	DLR	RRZZZZUSA
BACK, SCHMEREL	18	M	SMH	RRZZZZUSA
JAROWSKY, MEYER	20	M	DLR	RRZZZZUSA
LEWITH, ARON	20	M	DLR	RRZZZZUSA
URBANOWITZ, JOSEF	30	M	LABR	RRZZZZUSA
BRUSES, JAN	24	M	LABR	RRZZZZUSA
RUBINSKY, HENNE	25	F	W	RRZZZZUSA
CHAIE	.11	F	INFANT	RRZZZZUSA
GEUCK, MOSES	42	M	DLR	RRZZZZUSA
ANNA	30	F	W	RRZZZZUSA
ELIAS	28	M	DLR	RRZZZZUSA
RACHEL	20	F	W	RRZZZZUSA
LITWINSKES, ANTONAS	19	M	LABR	RRZZZZUSA
KATSCHERGAS, JONAS	24	M	LABR	RRZZZZUSA
JONAS	19	M	LABR	RRZZZZUSA
ABREITERS, JONAS	26	M	LABR	RRZZZZUSA
ABALSKI, JOH.	26	M	LABR	RRZZZZUSA
VERONICA	25	F	W	RRZZZZUSA
ZIMERMANN, HEINR.	25	M	LABR	RRZZZZUSA
NOWINSKY, PETER	27	M	LABR	RRZZZZUSA
BOJANOWSKY, WLADISLAW	23	M	LABR	RRZZZZUSA
DIONKIEWITZ, BARTHOL.	29	M	LABR	RRZZZZUSA
SCHAROFINAKI, FRANZ	25	M	LABR	RRZZZZUSA
MAJEWSKI, WILH.	30	F	W	RRZZZZUSA
AUG.	17	F	SGL	RRZZZZUSA
JOH.	8	M	CHILD	RRZZZZUSA
DEJANOWSKI, JOH.	21	M	LABR	RRZZZZUSA
ANTON.	24	F	W	RRZZZZUSA
NEUMAN, JUDEL	21	F	DLR	RRZZZZUSA
VOLANDT, CHRIST.	43	F	FARMER	RRZZZZUSA
U	33	F	W	RRZZZZUSA
BARB.	13	F	CH	RRZZZZUSA
CONRAD	8	M	CHILD	RRZZZZUSA
MARIE	7	F	CHILD	RRZZZZUSA
ANNA	3	F	CHILD	RRZZZZUSA
BARB.	.06	F	INFANT	RRZZZZUSA
FROHLICH, BARB.	19	F	SGL	RRZZZZUSA
RETTIG, BRUNO	23	M	TLR	RRZZZZUSA
LIST, GEORG	16	M	BCHR	RRZZZZUSA
EHRLICH, IDA	15	F	SGL	RRZZZZUSA
HANSEN, FRANZ	18	M	CK	RRZZZZUSA
DECKER--, U	18	M	SHMK	RRZZZZUSA
OHUHAUS, ADOLF	17	M	BKBNDR	RRZZZZUSA
SCHEIDERBERGER, JOH.	19	M	FARMER	RRZZZZUSA
AUSELMENT, JOSEF	16	M	FARMER	RRZZZZUSA
BURGER, KARL	29	M	FARMER	RRZZZZUSA
PELIKAN, RUDOLF	18	M	CPR	RRZZZZUSA
KOCH, DONALUS	30	M	MSN	RRZZZZUSA
VERONICA	31	F	W	RRZZZZUSA
ALBERT	.06	M	INFANT	RRZZZZUSA
RIEDE, ENGELBERT	27	M	FARMER	RRZZZZUSA

PASSENGER	AGE	SEX	OCCUPATION	PRV	VIL	DES
DANNECKER, ISIDOR	24	M	CPR	RR	ZZZZ	USA
MOSES, ROSA	19	F	SGL	RR	ZZZZ	USA
HETMANNSPERGER, JOH.	29	F	LABR	RR	ZZZZ	USA
KNOPFLER, THERESE	14	F	SGL	RR	ZZZZ	USA
VICTORIA	8	F	CHILD	RR	ZZZZ	USA
ALOIS	7	M	CHILD	RR	ZZZZ	USA
KNOBLAUCH, CARL	24	M	BKR	RR	ZZZZ	USA
MARSCHALITZKY, AUG.	29	F	SGL	RR	ZZZZ	USA
FRANCK, ANTON	42	M	MSN	RR	ZZZZ	USA
ANNA	25	F	SGL	RR	ZZZZ	USA
THERESE	16	F	CH	RR	ZZZZ	USA
JOSEF	8	M	CHILD	RR	ZZZZ	USA
LUDWIG	7	M	CHILD	RR	ZZZZ	USA
PAULINE	6	F	CHILD	RR	ZZZZ	USA
ANNA	5	F	CHILD	RR	ZZZZ	USA
KLAVESKI, JOH.	29	M	LABR	RR	ZZZZ	USA
MARIANNE	38	F	W	RR	ZZZZ	USA
JOH.	5	M	CHILD	RR	ZZZZ	USA
NENOLESKE, ANNE	17	F	SGL	RR	ZZZZ	USA
BRODZYNSKI, THEOFILO	27	M	LABR	RR	ZZZZ	USA
GOLLMISK, AUG.	25	M	LABR	RR	ZZZZ	USA

SHIP: BOLIVIA

FROM: GLASGOW
TO: NEW YORK
ARRIVED: 22 MARCH 1884

PASSENGER	AGE	SEX	OCCUPATION	PRV	VIL	DES
ANDREAS, SIMON	28	M	LABR	PL	ZZZZ	USA
ADAMSKI, WOYCIEK	29	M	UNKNOWN	PL	ZZZZ	USA
BISCHITZKI, VALI	25	M	UNKNOWN	PL	ZZZZ	USA
KOSACK, MARTIN	20	M	UNKNOWN	PL	ZZZZ	USA
CHANDOWSKI, SCHM.	22	M	UNKNOWN	PL	ZZZZ	USA
GENCKA, VAL.	24	M	CPTR	PL	ZZZZ	USA
CAJENSKY, CASPER	73	M	UNKNOWN	PL	ZZZZ	USA
GUSZSKI, ANTON	54	M	LABR	PL	ZZZZ	USA
TARSKY, JOS.	25	M	UNKNOWN	PL	ZZZZ	USA
HERSCHLOWITZ, ISRAEL	40	M	UNKNOWN	PL	ZZZZ	USA
JANUKI, VAL.	28	M	UNKNOWN	PL	ZZZZ	USA
GARSCHYAK, LORENZ	29	M	UNKNOWN	PL	ZZZZ	USA
HANTORSKI, JONAS	26	M	UNKNOWN	PL	ZZZZ	USA
KULINOWSKI, M.	20	M	UNKNOWN	PL	ZZZZ	USA
KROELIK, JOSEF	24	M	UNKNOWN	PL	ZZZZ	USA
MELAS, FRANCOIS	39	M	UNKNOWN	PL	ZZZZ	USA
MUSAJI, WOREN	28	M	MNR	PL	ZZZZ	USA
NORAKONCKI, JAN.	21	M	UNKNOWN	PL	ZZZZ	USA
PIETSCHALOS, ANTON	25	M	CPTR	PL	ZZZZ	USA
ANTON	20	M	UNKNOWN	PL	ZZZZ	USA
PRZYBYSZ, JOS.	30	M	MNR	PL	ZZZZ	USA
PIETSCHAK, WAYCICK	45	M	UNKNOWN	PL	ZZZZ	USA
KOSCHEK, STEFAN	26	M	UNKNOWN	PL	ZZZZ	USA
SCHOTZ, T.	29	M	UNKNOWN	PL	ZZZZ	USA
SULIK, DZURA	35	M	UNKNOWN	PL	ZZZZ	USA
SIMOWWSKY, FRANZ	46	M	UNKNOWN	PL	ZZZZ	USA
STRASCHEFSKY, JAN	26	M	LABR	PL	ZZZZ	USA
STEPARJAK, IGNATZ	26	M	UNKNOWN	PL	ZZZZ	USA
SOLENSKI, NICOL.	30	M	UNKNOWN	PL	ZZZZ	USA
SCHALITKY, FRANZ	22	M	UNKNOWN	PL	ZZZZ	USA
STELLSCHIKS, JOSEF	32	M	UNKNOWN	PL	ZZZZ	USA
SCHIAKOWSKI, JAN.	32	M	UNKNOWN	PL	ZZZZ	USA
JOCKSCHINSKY, IGNATZ	24	M	UNKNOWN	PL	ZZZZ	USA
JELESTOWITZ, ALIERTA	23	M	BCHR	PL	ZZZZ	USA
USCHAK, MARTIN	40	M	CNF	PL	ZZZZ	USA
VALETKA, STEFAN	24	M	LABR	PL	ZZZZ	USA
WESSOHOWSKI, MICH.	31	M	UNKNOWN	PL	ZZZZ	USA
SELENSKY, VINCENT	22	M	LABR	PL	ZZZZ	USA
DITHMIN, MARTIN	25	M	UNKNOWN	PL	ZZZZ	USA
HAVERA	18	M	UNKNOWN	PL	ZZZZ	USA
EVRLOWSKI, JAKUSZ	32	M	UNKNOWN	PL	ZZZZ	USA
PAULINE	33	F	UNKNOWN	PL	ZZZZ	USA

PASSENGER	AGE	SEX	OCCUPATION	PRV	VIL	DES
JGNASERAK, M.	29	M	UNKNOWN	PL	ZZZZ	USA
JOSEPHA	30	F	UNKNOWN	PL	ZZZZ	USA
STANISLAUS	1	M	CHILD	PL	ZZZZ	USA
KEDROWSKY, AUG.	25	M	UNKNOWN	PL	ZZZZ	USA
MARIAN	20	F	UNKNOWN	PL	ZZZZ	USA
LEOBADIA	2	F	CHILD	PL	ZZZZ	USA
FRANZ	.06	M	INFANT	PL	ZZZZ	USA
KACZMARCK, JOSEFA	22	F	UNKNOWN	PL	ZZZZ	USA

SHIP: FULDA

FROM: BREMEN
TO: NEW YORK
ARRIVED: 24 MARCH 1884

PASSENGER	AGE	SEX	OCCUPATION	PRV	VIL	DES
JOACHIM, GOTTL.	28	M	LLD	RR	ZZZZ	USA
DOROTHEA	26	F	UNKNOWN	RR	ZZZZ	USA
JACOB	.10	M	INFANT	RR	ZZZZ	USA
LINDEMANN, JOH.	33	M	LLD	RR	ZZZZ	USA
ROSINE	32	F	UNKNOWN	RR	ZZZZ	USA
JOHANN	4	M	CHILD	RR	ZZZZ	USA
GOTTLIEB	2	M	CHILD	RR	ZZZZ	USA
MAGDALINE	.11	F	INFANT	RR	ZZZZ	USA
LUETZ, LOUISE	21	F	UNKNOWN	RR	ZZZZ	USA
JOHANNS	2	M	CHILD	RR	ZZZZ	USA
GOTTLIEB	.10	M	INFANT	RR	ZZZZ	USA
WEICHSEL, PHIL.	25	M	LLD	RR	ZZZZ	USA
MARIE	23	F	UNKNOWN	RR	ZZZZ	USA
MARIA	.05	F	INFANT	RR	ZZZZ	USA
PFEIFFLE, JACOB	26	M	LLD	RR	ZZZZ	USA
CHRISTINE	26	F	UNKNOWN	RR	ZZZZ	USA
CATHARINE	.11	F	INFANT	RR	ZZZZ	USA
HUMANN, JACOB	26	M	LLD	RR	ZZZZ	USA
CHRISTIANA	25	F	UNKNOWN	RR	ZZZZ	USA
CONRAD	2	M	CHILD	RR	ZZZZ	USA
MARIA	.11	F	INFANT	RR	ZZZZ	USA
DOROTHEA	68	F	UNKNOWN	RR	ZZZZ	USA
RABINOWITZ, BERNH.	27	M	UNKNOWN	RR	ZZZZ	USA
HERMANN	16	M	UNKNOWN	RR	ZZZZ	USA

SHIP: STATE OF NEBRASKA

FROM: GLASGOW AND LARNE
TO: NEW YORK
ARRIVED: 24 MARCH 1884

PASSENGER	AGE	SEX	OCCUPATION	PRV	VIL	DES
WINKELSTEIN, NATE	00	M	LABR	RR	ZZZZ	USA
STANKOWITZ, PIATZ	00	M	UNKNOWN	RR	ZZZZ	USA
SELIWEK, DAVID	00	M	UNKNOWN	RR	ZZZZ	USA
STOCIKEWITZ, JAN	00	M	UNKNOWN	RR	ZZZZ	USA
WASCHILEWS-, WLADISLAW	41	M	UNKNOWN	RR	ZZZZ	USA
MARCHE-, STANISLAUS	22	M	UNKNOWN	RR	ZZZZ	USA
LUPTEBER, MARCUS	00	M	UNKNOWN	RR	ZZZZ	USA
CHANNIE	20	F	UNKNOWN	RR	ZZZZ	USA
SCHWARZ, MARCUS	40	M	LABR	PL	ZZZZ	USA
SIEGLIN, MASES	30	M	UNKNOWN	RR	ZZZZ	USA
GARAZAN---, ABRAHAM	00	M	UNKNOWN	RR	ZZZZ	USA
GOLDSTEIN, ISAAC	36	M	UNKNOWN	RR	ZZZZ	USA
PITZER, MALKE	24	F	W	RR	ZZZZ	USA
LEIL	00	F	INF	RR	ZZZZ	USA
WASCHILM--, STANNISL.	40	M	LABR	RR	ZZZZ	USA
TRAHEL, MALKE	54	F	W	RR	ZZZZ	USA
CAHN, RIWE	26	F	UNKNOWN	RR	ZZZZ	USA
REMME	00	F	INF	RR	ZZZZ	USA
MOSES	00	M	UNKNOWN	RR	ZZZZ	USA

PASSENGER	AGE	SEX	OCCUPATION	PRV	VIL	DES
MERSK--, ABRAH.	32	M	LABR	RR	ZZZZ	USA
WOLF.	10	M	CH	RR	ZZZZ	USA
NEUMAN, JANKEL	22	M	LABR	RR	ZZZZ	USA
HEFFNER, EDWARD	26	M	LABR	RR	ZZZZ	USA
GRAAZ, HERMANN	26	M	UNKNOWN	RR	ZZZZ	USA
WIRASK, MEYER	37	M	UNKNOWN	RR	ZZZZ	USA
ROGER, CHONEG	32	M	WVR	RR	ZZZZ	USA
TURECK, WALF	16	M	LABR	RR	ZZZZ	USA
MATISCHIK, WAITCHIK	48	M	LABR	RR	ZZZZ	USA
ASCHWEK, MICHAEL	35	M	UNKNOWN	RR	ZZZZ	USA
NISCHNEWSKY, PIAT	28	M	UNKNOWN	RR	ZZZZ	USA
SCHINKMAN, LEIB	47	M	LABR	RR	ZZZZ	USA
FUCHAS, MICH.	36	M	UNKNOWN	RR	ZZZZ	USA
SLURK, JANOS	27	M	LABR	RR	ZZZZ	USA
GRANO, HEF	26	M	UNKNOWN	RR	ZZZZ	USA
MARTOR, JANOS	50	M	UNKNOWN	RR	ZZZZ	USA
RESTOCK, KANITSCH	24	M	UNKNOWN	RR	ZZZZ	USA
SIMKA, KARLITZ	25	M	UNKNOWN	RR	ZZZZ	USA
SANDER, MARCUS	45	M	UNKNOWN	RR	ZZZZ	USA
PARKUCK, ASIES	00	M	CGRMKR	RR	ZZZZ	USA
SIME	00	F	UNKNOWN	RR	ZZZZ	USA
DMMER, BERL	00	M	LABR	RR	ZZZZ	USA
BRENDEL, JOSEPH.	00	M	GLSMKR	RR	ZZZZ	USA
SACHS, BERL	00	M	LABR	RR	ZZZZ	USA
KAPUL, KOPEL	00	M	UNKNOWN	RR	ZZZZ	USA
DROWITZ, NUGER	00	M	UNKNOWN	RR	ZZZZ	USA
RATHSTEIN, HERMANN	00	M	JWLR	RR	ZZZZ	USA
GELDMAN, MARCUS	00	M	LABR	RR	ZZZZ	USA
SCHAD, SCHAIE	00	F	SVNT	RR	ZZZZ	USA
KLATZKI, TAUCHMAN	00	M	LABR	RR	ZZZZ	USA
LEWIN, HIRSCH	00	M	UNKNOWN	RR	ZZZZ	USA
KLAAR, HIRSCH	00	M	JWLR	RR	ZZZZ	USA
SARAH	00	F	W	RR	ZZZZ	USA
ABRAHAM	00	M	CH	RR	ZZZZ	USA
RASCHE--	00	F	UNKNOWN	RR	ZZZZ	USA
SELIN, JACOB	26	M	LABR	RR	ZZZZ	USA
RAKUZ, VINCENZ	25	M	UNKNOWN	RR	ZZZZ	USA
ROGMILOWITZ, IGNATZ	17	M	UNKNOWN	RR	ZZZZ	USA
MIKELANIS, JULIUS	23	M	UNKNOWN	RR	ZZZZ	USA
NEURATANIS, JOSEPH	27	M	UNKNOWN	RR	ZZZZ	USA
LAZEWSKI, ADAM	33	M	UNKNOWN	RR	ZZZZ	USA
STAHINGES, PIOTR.	22	M	UNKNOWN	RR	ZZZZ	USA
NOWALSKI, FRANZISCHEK	24	M	UNKNOWN	RR	ZZZZ	USA
PAFSSIL, JOSAS	35	M	UNKNOWN	RR	ZZZZ	USA
SAROKI, WALDISCHOW	00	M	LABR	RR	ZZZZ	USA
MELKEWITZ, LEHON	26	M	UNKNOWN	RR	ZZZZ	USA
SOLENKA, LEIB	28	M	UNKNOWN	PL	ZZZZ	USA
NILSON, BARUCH	22	M	UNKNOWN	PL	ZZZZ	USA
LEWIS, JEIEWUS	42	M	UNKNOWN	RR	ZZZZ	USA
ABRAHAM	21	M	UNKNOWN	RR	ZZZZ	USA
JALHUSKY, NACHMAN	25	M	LABR	RR	ZZZZ	USA
BARSKOWIAK, ANTON	24	M	UNKNOWN	RR	ZZZZ	USA
ARON, HERZ	32	M	LABR	PL	ZZZZ	USA
RALOWSKI, SAEMER	25	M	UNKNOWN	PL	ZZZZ	USA
BRASAITIS, VINCENZ	00	M	UNKNOWN	PL	ZZZZ	USA
ANISCHA	00	F	W	PL	ZZZZ	USA
MASKA	00	F	INF	PL	ZZZZ	USA
BUDROWITZ, VINCENZ	00	M	LABR	PL	ZZZZ	USA
DAVIDOWITZ, VINCENZ	00	M	UNKNOWN	PL	ZZZZ	USA
MARIA	00	F	W	PL	ZZZZ	USA
ANNA	00	F	INF	PL	ZZZZ	USA
MATHEUS	00	M	UNKNOWN	PL	ZZZZ	USA
RADZULOWITZ, VINCENZ	26	M	LABR	PL	ZZZZ	USA
ELISE	33	F	W	PL	ZZZZ	USA
JAFTURK, EMILIE	00	F	UNKNOWN	PL	ZZZZ	USA
BENIGA	00	F	CH	PL	ZZZZ	USA
EMILIE	10	F	UNKNOWN	PL	ZZZZ	USA
PUCHOLSKI, CHUNE	00	M	UNKNOWN	PL	ZZZZ	USA
MILIET, ISRAEL	00	M	MCHT	PL	ZZZZ	USA
SIMELMANN, BERNHARD	23	M	LABR	RR	ZZZZ	USA

SHIP: CITY OF CHICAGO

FROM: LIVERPOOL
TO: NEW YORK
ARRIVED: 26 MARCH 1884

PASSENGER	AGE	SEX	OCCUPATION	PRV	VIL	DES
HABER, IGNATZ	42	M	UNKNOWN	PL	ZZZZ	NY
NARGE, JULIUS	36	M	UNKNOWN	PL	ZZZZ	NY
SCHLONPEUWD, MASEEY	20	M	UNKNOWN	PL	ZZZZ	NY
DANSKCHAIR, WLADISLAUS	23	M	BLKSMH	PL	ZZZZ	NY
RUSCHWSKI, ANDRE	23	M	WCHMKR	PL	ZZZZ	NY
BONDESWREZ, JOSEF	27	M	LABR	PL	ZZZZ	NY
MASULSERCKY, JOSEF	27	M	UNKNOWN	PL	ZZZZ	NY
CATH.	23	F	W	PL	ZZZZ	NY
URHANEEK, THR.	24	M	LABR	PL	ZZZZ	NY
WALITZKA, KARL	32	M	UNKNOWN	PL	ZZZZ	NY
MATUSCHAK, MARTIN	28	M	UNKNOWN	PL	ZZZZ	NY
KLEHAMMER, JOH.	16	M	UNKNOWN	PL	ZZZZ	NY
NAWATSCHAK, MICHAIL	26	M	UNKNOWN	PL	ZZZZ	NY
ZEHNEN, FENFIL	28	M	UNKNOWN	PL	ZZZZ	NY

SHIP: DEVONIA

FROM: GLASGOW AND MOVILLE
TO: NEW YORK
ARRIVED: 27 MARCH 1884

PASSENGER	AGE	SEX	OCCUPATION	PRV	VIL	DES
WISCHNEFSKY, VAL.	00	M	LABR	RR	ZZZZ	USA
ZINGBORSKY, A.	21	M	LABR	RR	ZZZZ	USA
SCHMIRSOWITZ, JOH.	19	M	LABR	RR	ZZZZ	USA
SOD, JANOS	17	M	LABR	RR	ZZZZ	USA
ANNIA	21	M	LABR	RR	ZZZZ	USA
SHALOWITZ, AUG.	30	M	LABR	RR	ZZZZ	USA
ANT.	28	M	LABR	RR	ZZZZ	USA
LEMENDOWSKY, A.	26	M	LABR	RR	ZZZZ	USA
YNDUSCHISKY, W.	41	M	LABR	RR	ZZZZ	USA
KUTOWITZ, JOH.	46	M	LABR	RR	ZZZZ	USA
WALIKOWSKY, M.	46	M	LABR	RR	ZZZZ	USA
BUTTNER, M.	28	M	LABR	RR	ZZZZ	USA
KUSEKIWITSCH, K.	44	M	LABR	RR	ZZZZ	USA
JURA	34	M	LABR	RR	ZZZZ	USA
ZUKOWSKI, M.	30	M	LABR	RR	ZZZZ	USA
ROSINSKI, M.	35	M	LABR	RR	ZZZZ	USA
MURKOSKI, M.	30	M	LABR	RR	ZZZZ	USA
GURNI, J.	45	M	LABR	RR	ZZZZ	USA
PAULINZKI, N.	24	M	LABR	RR	ZZZZ	USA
YARONI, PAUL	21	M	LABR	RR	ZZZZ	USA
MADORA, JOS.	23	M	LABR	RR	ZZZZ	USA
LYOHTZKY, IGNATZ	25	M	LABR	RR	ZZZZ	USA
SRIBOWITZ, NATHAN	34	M	LABR	RR	ZZZZ	USA
BINON, ANNI	32	M	LABR	RR	ZZZZ	USA
MANROSCHAK, AUG.	36	M	LABR	RR	ZZZZ	USA
STRAGOWSKI, PIETR.	00	M	LABR	RR	ZZZZ	USA
MAGIL, JOS.	26	M	LABR	RR	ZZZZ	USA
YAWOROWSKI, I.	00	M	LABR	RR	ZZZZ	USA
HIEKA, M.	00	M	LABR	RR	ZZZZ	USA
WITTKOWSKI, S.	27	M	LABR	RR	ZZZZ	USA
HALINOWSKY, A.	31	M	LABR	RR	ZZZZ	USA
CZUTKOWSKY, VIC.	31	M	LABR	RR	ZZZZ	USA
KOMOROSKY, JOS.	56	M	LABR	RR	ZZZZ	USA
WISNEWSKY, JAN	21	M	LABR	RR	ZZZZ	USA

SHIP: ENGLAND

FROM: LIVERPOOL AND QUEENSTOWN
TO: NEW YORK
ARRIVED: 27 MARCH 1884

PASSENGER	AGE	SEX	OCCUPATION	PRV VIL DES
SURN, MATTIE	22	F	SP	FNZZZZUSA
LISA	22	F	SP	FNZZZZUSA
KURVINIS, TUOMAS	25	M	LABR	FNZZZZUSA
SOFIA	24	F	W	FNZZZZUSA
TUOMAS	3	M	CHILD	FNZZZZUSA
KYNTAJA, JOH.	21	M	LABR	FNZZZZUSA
KINKIHOSKI, ISAEK	26	M	LABR	FNZZZZUSA
MAMRANJARVI, GUST.	25	M	LABR	FNZZZZUSA
SANONEN, MATTIE	26	M	LABR	FNZZZZUSA
PECKIGO, JOH.	23	M	LABR	FNZZZZUSA
KRAVE, HERMAN	22	M	LABR	FNZZZZUSA
HAGG, MATTIE-JAS.	38	M	LABR	FNZZZZUSA
HIRVI, WILHELM	18	M	LABR	FNZZZZUSA
MAMRUNAKI, JOSEPH	23	M	LABR	FNZZZZUSA
BERAA, JOHN	27	M	LABR	FNZZZZUSA
HARVI, JACOB	39	M	LABR	FNZZZZUSA
ROPI, JOH.	38	M	LABR	FNZZZZUSA
KARKIE, JOHAN	21	M	LABR	FNZZZZUSA

SHIP: MORAVIA

FROM: HAMBURG
TO: NEW YORK
ARRIVED: 27 MARCH 1884

PASSENGER	AGE	SEX	OCCUPATION	PRV VIL DES
BERGMANN, JACOB	45	M	DLR	RRZZZZUSA
AARON, CHONNE	60	M	UNKNOWN	RRZZZZUSA
SARA	52	F	W	RRZZZZUSA
FEIWEL	20	F	CH	RRZZZZUSA
JANKEL	8	M	CHILD	RRZZZZUSA
MIRKE	7	F	CHILD	RRZZZZUSA
MORDCHE	6	F	CHILD	RRZZZZUSA
ITZIG	5	M	CHILD	RRZZZZUSA
FEIDELSOHN, SCHENTE	25	F	W	RRZZZZUSA
CHANNE	.06	F	INFANT	RRZZZZUSA
BERINSTEIN, BERTHA	50	F	W	RRZZZZUSA
BERRIS, RACHEL	18	F	UNKNOWN	RRZZZZUSA
JANKEL	.11	M	INFANT	RRZZZZUSA
MICHALOWSKY, HENRICH	25	M	LABR	RRZZZZUSA
AMILIWICZ, ANDR.	20	M	UNKNOWN	RRZZZZUSA
AUGUSTOWSKY, ARON	43	M	UNKNOWN	RRZZZZUSA
RIWE	18	F	D	RRZZZZUSA
GRUSKY, KOLMAN	19	M	LABR	RRZZZZUSA
NIMELSTEIN, CHAIE	40	F	W	RRZZZZUSA
RAHEL	17	F	D	RRZZZZUSA
FRANK, CHANNE	50	F	W	RRZZZZUSA
SUEPELOWITZ, JOSSEL	34	M	DLR	RRZZZZUSA
SAFIRMANN, ABRAM	48	M	UNKNOWN	RRZZZZUSA
GRUENSPAN, NOSSEM	22	M	UNKNOWN	RRZZZZUSA
SINGER, MAMES	17	M	TLR	RRZZZZUSA
LAPIDUS, LEIB	44	M	LABR	RRZZZZUSA
WINARKOWSKY, RUBEN	56	M	UNKNOWN	RRZZZZUSA
DWORE	50	F	W	RRZZZZUSA
RACHEL	19	F	CH	RRZZZZUSA
SAMUEL	17	M	CH	RRZZZZUSA
CHONE	30	M	LABR	RRZZZZUSA
ITTE	30	F	W	RRZZZZUSA
MARCUS	.11	M	INFANT	RRZZZZUSA
STOLAR, CHANNE	26	F	W	RRZZZZUSA
MALKE	.11	F	INFANT	RRZZZZUSA
ROSENBERG, FREIDE	16	F	SGL	RRZZZZUSA
FLIEGEL, HIRSCH	24	M	DLR	RRZZZZUSA
GITTEL	23	F	W	RRZZZZUSA
GOLDE	.11	F	INFANT	RRZZZZUSA
PERL	.01	F	INFANT	RRZZZZUSA
BERNSTEIN, DWORE	20	F	SGL	RRZZZZUSA
BASCHE	9	F	CHILD	RRZZZZUSA
GOLDSTEIN, LEA	40	F	W	RRZZZZUSA
BLUME	9	F	CHILD	RRZZZZUSA
SARA	8	F	CHILD	RRZZZZUSA
COHN, ROSA	30	F	SGL	RRZZZZUSA
LEA	21	F	UNKNOWN	RRZZZZUSA
KAUFMANN, SCHEINE	25	F	W	RRZZZZUSA
DAVID	9	M	CHILD	RRZZZZUSA
SCHOLEM	8	M	CHILD	RRZZZZUSA
SCHLOME	8	M	CHILD	RRZZZZUSA
JACOB	6	M	CHILD	RRZZZZUSA
AUSENBERG, FRAVEL	40	F	W	RRZZZZUSA
MOSES, WOLF	36	M	DLR	RRZZZZUSA
LOMZKIEWITZ, HERSCH	20	M	UNKNOWN	RRZZZZUSA
GRIMZOWSKY, NOCHEM	25	M	UNKNOWN	RRZZZZUSA
HIRSCH	7	M	CHILD	RRZZZZUSA
KROSNOPOLSKY, GEDALIE	26	M	DLR	RRZZZZUSA
MEIRICH, SCHLOME	23	M	UNKNOWN	RRZZZZUSA
STAROLES, JANKEL	35	M	UNKNOWN	RRZZZZUSA
COHN, JOSEF	27	M	UNKNOWN	RRZZZZUSA
WEISS, FRANZ	18	M	LABR	RRZZZZUSA
DUSCHKAS, DAVID	33	M	DLR	RRZZZZUSA
LEWINSKY, MOSES	19	M	UNKNOWN	RRZZZZUSA
CHANNE	22	F	W	RRZZZZUSA
SWYTAI, AGNES	25	F	SGL	RRZZZZUSA
WALAIKO, MICHAEL	21	M	LABR	RRZZZZUSA
GOLDREICH, MALKE	19	F	SGL	RRZZZZUSA
STERNHEIM, JACOB	8	M	CHILD	RRZZZZUSA
ANMUTH, CHAIM	30	M	DLR	RRZZZZUSA
KIMCKE, SAUL	28	M	UNKNOWN	RRZZZZUSA
JATZER, ISRAEL	25	M	UNKNOWN	RRZZZZUSA
MINZEWITSCHAS, PETRUS	33	M	UNKNOWN	RRZZZZUSA
BALTREINANS, SCHABSE	28	M	UNKNOWN	RRZZZZUSA
DUGSCHIS, WINZOS	23	M	FARMER	RRZZZZUSA
BIELSKAS, JURGAS	40	M	UNKNOWN	RRZZZZUSA
GRIGEITAS, JURIOS	29	M	UNKNOWN	RRZZZZUSA
ROM, ELIAS	42	M	LABR	RRZZZZUSA
CIKANOWITZ, JURA	17	F	SGL	RRZZZZUSA
POCIENTA, MIHAL	18	M	LABR	RRZZZZUSA
KANOFSKI, ANDRZI	30	M	UNKNOWN	RRZZZZUSA
BARKSCHADT, JOH.FR.	22	M	UNKNOWN	RRZZZZUSA
FRANKFURT, MAX	16	M	LABR	RRZZZZUSA
MINZ, MASCHE	18	F	SGL	RRZZZZUSA
JUDAMY, SCHOLEM	20	M	LABR	RRZZZZUSA
GERSCHENOWITZ, BARUCH	30	M	DLR	RRZZZZUSA
SCHANSIS, JONAS	18	M	FARMER	RRZZZZUSA
MATSCHULAT, MATH.	19	M	UNKNOWN	RRZZZZUSA
BANZIKAUKAS, ADAM	26	M	UNKNOWN	RRZZZZUSA
SKUMINAS, MATHEAS	21	M	UNKNOWN	RRZZZZUSA
LEWINSOHN, LEIB	21	M	DLR	RRZZZZUSA
GUTTMANN, MOSES	21	M	UNKNOWN	RRZZZZUSA
ALIBER, HIRSCH	30	M	UNKNOWN	RRZZZZUSA
GITTELMANN, LEIB	22	M	UNKNOWN	RRZZZZUSA
ZUWINSKY, SARA	39	F	W	RRZZZZUSA
LIEBE	8	F	CHILD	RRZZZZUSA
ESTHER	7	F	CHILD	RRZZZZUSA
BASCHE	5	M	CHILD	RRZZZZUSA
ABEL	.11	M	INFANT	RRZZZZUSA
FEIGE	.01	F	INFANT	RRZZZZUSA
OPALKA, WILH.	27	M	LABR	RRZZZZUSA
GOTTL.	26	F	W	RRZZZZUSA
EMMA	.11	F	INFANT	RRZZZZUSA
KOSZAK, STANISL.	31	F	W	RRZZZZUSA
DYCHTOWIEZ, SOFIE	8	F	CHILD	RRZZZZUSA
KOSZAK, PAUL	4	M	CHILD	RRZZZZUSA
PROENOFSKI, IGNATZ	47	M	LABR	RRZZZZUSA
BOROFSKI, JULIAN	19	M	UNKNOWN	RRZZZZUSA
BOENOFSKI, JAN	31	M	UNKNOWN	RRZZZZUSA
ZENYTSKI, KASIMIR	36	M	UNKNOWN	RRZZZZUSA
SZULEWJESKI, MARIAM	44	M	UNKNOWN	RRZZZZUSA
POROEWEFSKI, MARIANE	17	F	SGL	RRZZZZUSA
GORALSKI, STANISL.	24	M	LABR	RRZZZZUSA

PASSENGER	AGE	SEX	OCCUPATION	PRVL	VIE	DES
FLOVKEWITSCH, ANTON	28	M	UNKNOWN	RR	ZZZZ	USA
MATINSCHEK, JOSEF	18	M	UNKNOWN	RR	ZZZZ	USA
PORTSCHISCHOWSKI, JOH.	27	M	UNKNOWN	RR	ZZZZ	USA
ALEXANDROWITZ, AUGUST	28	M	LABR	RR	ZZZZ	USA
VICTORIA	26	F	W	RR	ZZZZ	USA
MARTIN	.11	M	INFANT	RR	ZZZZ	USA
CHIMKEWITZ, JOSEF	21	M	LABR	RR	ZZZZ	USA
SCHWERKOWSKI, JOSEF	29	M	UNKNOWN	RR	ZZZZ	USA
PETRONELLI, ALWINE	23	F	W	RR	ZZZZ	USA
ANNA	.11	F	INFANT	RR	ZZZZ	USA
BIALISTOCKY, ITZIG	30	M	TLR	RR	ZZZZ	USA
MIKURAM, JANOS	32	M	UNKNOWN	RR	ZZZZ	USA
SIMENOWITZ, JONAS	28	M	LABR	RR	ZZZZ	USA
KREILIK, JOSIAS	22	M	UNKNOWN	RR	ZZZZ	USA
SEUSILOWOSKI, PETRUS	29	M	UNKNOWN	RR	ZZZZ	USA
ADAMEITIS, ANTON	38	M	UNKNOWN	RR	ZZZZ	USA
SUIVELIS, TOMAS	54	M	UNKNOWN	RR	ZZZZ	USA
KUPSCHUNUS, TOMAS	20	M	UNKNOWN	RR	ZZZZ	USA
ROSATIS, AUGUST	16	M	UNKNOWN	RR	ZZZZ	USA
WILKOS, JONAS	21	M	UNKNOWN	RR	ZZZZ	USA
KAHN, ISRAEL	21	M	UNKNOWN	RR	ZZZZ	USA
LESEWITZ, METZILAW	19	M	UNKNOWN	RR	ZZZZ	USA
MILEWSKI, KASIMIR	26	M	UNKNOWN	RR	ZZZZ	USA
KOSLOWSKI, TOMAS	32	M	UNKNOWN	RR	ZZZZ	USA
JOKOPINSCHIK, MICHEL	30	M	UNKNOWN	RR	ZZZZ	USA
JANIKOWSKI, FRANZ	30	M	UNKNOWN	RR	ZZZZ	USA
MARZINKOWITZ, ROSALIE	19	F	SGL	RR	ZZZZ	USA
AUGULOWITZ, WLADISLAUS	25	M	LABR	RR	ZZZZ	USA
NORAWESCH, ANTONAS	24	M	UNKNOWN	RR	ZZZZ	USA
BLAZIS, ANNA	28	F	W	RR	ZZZZ	USA
KOWAITIS, AUGUSTE	28	F	UNKNOWN	RR	ZZZZ	USA
KOWALESVSKI, DOMINIK	22	M	LABR	RR	ZZZZ	USA
NAWOZOTZKI, JOSEF	26	M	UNKNOWN	RR	ZZZZ	USA
DOMANOWSKI, FRANZ	27	M	UNKNOWN	RR	ZZZZ	USA
BUTZKO, FRANZ	27	M	UNKNOWN	RR	ZZZZ	USA
JAKUBOWSKI, ANDR.	22	M	UNKNOWN	RR	ZZZZ	USA
EITLIN, CHAIM	40	M	UNKNOWN	RR	ZZZZ	USA
RIVKE	37	F	W	RR	ZZZZ	USA
NECHAME	15	M	CH	RR	ZZZZ	USA
WIELEI	8	F	CHILD	RR	ZZZZ	USA
ABRAM	7	M	CHILD	RR	ZZZZ	USA
PESSE	.11	M	INFANT	RR	ZZZZ	USA
ZEMBA, EDWARD	20	M	LABR	RR	ZZZZ	USA
SCHENAL, MATHIAS	45	M	UNKNOWN	PL	ZZZZ	USA
CATH.	35	F	UNKNOWN	PL	ZZZZ	USA
WOJTUSCH	1	M	CHILD	PL	ZZZZ	USA
HOI, GREGOR	26	M	LABR	PL	ZZZZ	USA
BIESTAK, FRANZ	28	M	UNKNOWN	PL	ZZZZ	USA
IWAINSKI, JAN	37	M	UNKNOWN	PL	ZZZZ	USA
SOGALOWITZ, BERTHA	20	F	SGL	RR	ZZZZ	USA
KOBATZNIC, ISAAC	17	M	LABR	RR	ZZZZ	USA
AJEWSKY, ANTON	26	M	UNKNOWN	RR	ZZZZ	USA
SABORNI, JEUDRZE	37	M	LABR	RR	ZZZZ	USA
RUCHELLA, JAN	26	M	UNKNOWN	RR	ZZZZ	USA
CEBBUCKI, MARIAM	30	M	UNKNOWN	RR	ZZZZ	USA
OLESA, STANISL.	24	M	UNKNOWN	RR	ZZZZ	USA
FISCHER, GUSTAV	26	M	UNKNOWN	RR	ZZZZ	USA
PANTKOWSKI, MARTIN	29	M	UNKNOWN	RR	ZZZZ	USA
ANNA	25	F	SGL	RR	ZZZZ	USA
ZEPECKI, MARTIN	39	M	LABR	RR	ZZZZ	USA
JOSEPHINE	38	F	W	RR	ZZZZ	USA
MICHAEL	8	M	CHILD	RR	ZZZZ	USA
ROSALSKA, LEOKADIA	25	F	UNKNOWN	RR	ZZZZ	USA
LEON	.11	M	INFANT	RR	ZZZZ	USA
BUTCHINICK, ANTON	25	M	LABR	RR	ZZZZ	USA
GIMSCHALL, ANTON	26	M	UNKNOWN	RR	ZZZZ	USA
PAWLOWSKI, JOSEF	34	M	UNKNOWN	RR	ZZZZ	USA
BUTKIEWIEZ, ANTON	18	M	UNKNOWN	RR	ZZZZ	USA
SACKSCHERFSKI, JULIAN	28	M	UNKNOWN	RR	ZZZZ	USA
STANKEWITSCH, ALEX.	25	M	UNKNOWN	RR	ZZZZ	USA
MOSCHEIKA, PETER	42	M	LABR	RR	ZZZZ	USA
STANKEWITZ, RAULAI	40	M	UNKNOWN	RR	ZZZZ	USA
RUBINSKY, GEWE	24	M	UNKNOWN	RR	ZZZZ	USA
WISLINSKI, SAN	30	M	UNKNOWN	RR	ZZZZ	USA
DYLEWSKI, ALEX.	22	M	UNKNOWN	RR	ZZZZ	USA
ZEREVYNSKI, JAN	48	M	UNKNOWN	RR	ZZZZ	USA
MORZENSKI, IGNATZ	40	M	UNKNOWN	RR	ZZZZ	USA
NIKE, FRIEDR.	39	M	UNKNOWN	RR	ZZZZ	USA
GRUWALD, JULS.	22	M	UNKNOWN	RR	ZZZZ	USA
MALINROSK, FRANZ	19	M	UNKNOWN	RR	ZZZZ	USA
JOSKEWITZ, MATUS	22	M	JNR	RR	ZZZZ	USA
GERBER, ISRAEL	33	M	DLR	RR	ZZZZ	USA
WENGROWITZ, HERZ	25	M	LABR	RR	ZZZZ	USA
WISCHNI, RUBEN	35	M	DLR	RR	ZZZZ	USA
ZWICKLER, MOSES	20	M	TLR	RR	ZZZZ	USA
CHAIE	19	F	W	RR	ZZZZ	USA
PENTZATE, WOLF	20	M	DLR	RR	ZZZZ	USA
WALLERSTEIN, CHAIM	45	M	UNKNOWN	RR	ZZZZ	USA
JABLONKE, BUMIN	38	M	UNKNOWN	RR	ZZZZ	USA
BEHR	17	M	UNKNOWN	RR	ZZZZ	USA
RUBEN, MARCUS	31	M	UNKNOWN	RR	ZZZZ	USA
LEWIN, ESTHER	22	F	SGL	RR	ZZZZ	USA
RACHEL	18	F	UNKNOWN	RR	ZZZZ	USA
GORDON, MOSES	24	M	DLR	RR	ZZZZ	USA
SCHMUEL	19	M	UNKNOWN	RR	ZZZZ	USA
GRUENFELD, MAX	30	M	UNKNOWN	RR	ZZZZ	USA
ROSENBERG, ABR.	18	M	UNKNOWN	RR	ZZZZ	USA
LEWIN, MICHEL	24	M	TLR	RR	ZZZZ	USA
KROKOPOLSKI, SCHEWOK	22	M	LABR	RR	ZZZZ	USA
JZARSKI, ALTER	16	M	UNKNOWN	RR	ZZZZ	USA
BERMANN, BAAR	21	M	TNMK	RR	ZZZZ	USA
LOEWIN, HINDE	19	F	W	RR	ZZZZ	USA
ABRAH.	20	M	TLR	RR	ZZZZ	USA
RAULUS, BALEKA	28	M	LABR	RR	ZZZZ	USA
EICHENBERG, SALOMON	19	M	UNKNOWN	RR	ZZZZ	USA
HENI	20	M	FARMER	RR	ZZZZ	USA
PETROWSKY, JOH.	22	M	LABR	RR	ZZZZ	USA
BUNOWITZ, FELIX	40	M	UNKNOWN	RR	ZZZZ	USA
MICKLONIS, TOMAS	40	M	UNKNOWN	RR	ZZZZ	USA
BILEWSKY, ANTON	26	M	UNKNOWN	RR	ZZZZ	USA
RODISCHEWSKY, CARL	20	M	UNKNOWN	RR	ZZZZ	USA
JEWEROWSKY, AUGUST	30	M	UNKNOWN	RR	ZZZZ	USA
NOMIALIS, ANDR.	21	M	UNKNOWN	RR	ZZZZ	USA
BIELUNIS, PAUL	43	M	UNKNOWN	RR	ZZZZ	USA
SCHASKOWSKI, MIHAL	19	M	UNKNOWN	RR	ZZZZ	USA
MIMANSKI, PESCHE	35	F	W	RR	ZZZZ	USA
RACHEL	8	F	CHILD	RR	ZZZZ	USA
KOPPEL	7	F	CHILD	RR	ZZZZ	USA
CZEGOJEWSKI, MATH.	42	M	LABR	RR	ZZZZ	USA
SCHECHMOWSKY, LIESE	21	F	SGL	RR	ZZZZ	USA
PINEWSKI, ABRAM	24	M	DLR	RR	ZZZZ	USA
GALANT, ISRAEL	16	M	DLR	RR	ZZZZ	USA
BERNSTEIN, DORA	22	F	W	RR	ZZZZ	USA
LEA	.11	F	INFANT	RR	ZZZZ	USA
GELERNTER, WOLF	53	M	DLR	RR	ZZZZ	USA
DEMIKUS, JOSEF	28	M	UNKNOWN	RR	ZZZZ	USA
FOBORO--, ELISAB.	21	F	W	RR	ZZZZ	USA
CAMILA	.11	F	INFANT	RR	ZZZZ	USA
JAUKOWSKA, MARIANE	26	F	W	RR	ZZZZ	USA
JAN	.11	M	INFANT	RR	ZZZZ	USA
STEFFEN	.01	M	INFANT	RR	ZZZZ	USA
RUTKO---, U	28	M	UNKNOWN	RR	ZZZZ	USA
MIGUCKE, JOHANN	30	M	UNKNOWN	RR	ZZZZ	USA
ABRAMOWITZ, TOMAS	27	M	LABR	RR	ZZZZ	USA
STANKEWITZ, U	23	M	LABR	RR	ZZZZ	USA
KWALSKOWSKY, ADAM	28	M	LABR	RR	ZZZZ	USA
JOGIS, PAULUS	30	M	UNKNOWN	RR	ZZZZ	USA
BOGDANOWITZ, ADAM	39	M	UNKNOWN	RR	ZZZZ	USA
DOMBROWSKI, MIKOS	34	M	LABR	RR	ZZZZ	USA
JESNAS, JURI	21	M	UNKNOWN	RR	ZZZZ	USA
KILIVSKI, AMBRODJE	28	M	UNKNOWN	RR	ZZZZ	USA
JENKOWITZ, ANTON	19	M	UNKNOWN	RR	ZZZZ	USA
NURUSCHEWITZ, MARIE	30	F	W	RR	ZZZZ	USA
VAELAV	.11	F	INFANT	RR	ZZZZ	USA
GELWELOWSKI, SCHOLEM	50	M	UNKNOWN	RR	ZZZZ	USA
PESCHE	45	F	W	RR	ZZZZ	USA
EILER	29	M	LABR	RR	ZZZZ	USA
SCHIMNE	23	F	W	RR	ZZZZ	USA
ABEL	.11	M	INFANT	RR	ZZZZ	USA
BENJ.	16	M	CH	RR	ZZZZ	USA

PASSENGER	AGE	SEX	OCCUPATION	PRV VIL DES
EISIG	15	M	CH	RRZZZZUSA
CHAIE	6	F	CHILD	RRZZZZUSA
CHAIM	2	F	CHILD	RRZZZZUSA
RAHEL	.02	F	INFANT	RRZZZZUSA
JOSEF	19	M	LABR	RRZZZZUSA
FINKELSTEIN, JANKEL	22	M	UNKNOWN	RRZZZZUSA
SCHNEIDER, MOSES	50	M	UNKNOWN	RRZZZZUSA
SEZMANOWITZ, IGNATYS	21	M	LABR	RRZZZZUSA
SMOLSKY, FELIX	28	M	UNKNOWN	RRZZZZUSA
PILWISKY, JACOB	50	M	LABR	RRZZZZUSA
GARFINKEL, BENJAMIN	15	M	LABR	RRZZZZUSA
ERENSTEIN, JANKEL	34	M	UNKNOWN	RRZZZZUSA
SCHLOIS, DAVID	44	M	UNKNOWN	RRZZZZUSA
JANESCHKEWITZ, JACOBI	45	M	UNKNOWN	RRZZZZUSA
SCHINKEWITZ, KASIMIR	43	M	UNKNOWN	RRZZZZUSA
GOLDBERG, MORDCHE	27	M	UNKNOWN	RRZZZZUSA
JAFEZ, SCHEM	36	M	UNKNOWN	RRZZZZUSA
MAREIN	15	M	UNKNOWN	RRZZZZUSA
MERE	20	F	SGL	RRZZZZUSA
RACHEL	8	F	CHILD	RRZZZZUSA
ARONOWITZ, ABRAH.	19	M	LABR	RRZZZZUSA
ABRAMSON, ABRAH.	25	M	UNKNOWN	RRZZZZUSA
LIPKOWITZ, CHAIM	8	M	CHILD	RRZZZZUSA
LEWIN, MEIER	19	M	LABR	RRZZZZUSA
SEIDEL, TAUBE	20	F	SGL	RRZZZZUSA
RELTKOWSKY, FRANK	26	M	LABR	RRZZZZUSA
BOROVSKY, FRANZ	20	M	UNKNOWN	RRZZZZUSA
NOVAI, JAN	26	M	UNKNOWN	RRZZZZUSA
MARKEWITZ, MOSES	30	M	LABR	RRZZZZUSA
WASNIERSKI, GOTTL.	29	M	LABR	RRZZZZUSA
GORALSKI, THOMAS	25	M	UNKNOWN	RRZZZZUSA
MICHALAK, MICHAEL	24	M	UNKNOWN	RRZZZZUSA
SEGLEREWITSCH, THOMAS	18	M	UNKNOWN	RRZZZZUSA
JODECANSKY, CHANNE	30	F	W	RRZZZZUSA
CHAIE	8	F	CHILD	RRZZZZUSA
CHAIE	6	F	CHILD	RRZZZZUSA
MEYER	.11	M	INFANT	RRZZZZUSA
KRAKIN, DWORA	27	F	W	RRZZZZUSA
FEIWEL	8	F	CHILD	RRZZZZUSA
JOCHMED	7	M	CHILD	RRZZZZUSA
LEA	.11	F	INFANT	RRZZZZUSA
BLAZIS, MATHILDE	4	F	CHILD	RRZZZZUSA
JOSEF	.11	M	INFANT	RRZZZZUSA
KOWAITIS, ANTON	.11	M	INFANT	RRZZZZUSA

SHIP: ODER

FROM: BREMEN
TO: NEW YORK
ARRIVED: 28 MARCH 1884

PASSENGER	AGE	SEX	OCCUPATION	PRV VIL DES
BEHRENT, FRIEDRICH	24	M	LABR	RRZZZZUSA

SHIP: LYDIAN MONARCH

FROM: LONDON
TO: NEW YORK
ARRIVED: 29 MARCH 1884

PASSENGER	AGE	SEX	OCCUPATION	PRV VIL DES
COHEN, LEIB	24	F	UNKNOWN	RRZZZZNY
BALTAXEN, JOS.	20	M	LABR	RRZZZZNY
STOCK, PHILIP	26	M	TLR	RRZZZZNY
SOPHIA	26	F	W	RRZZZZNY
ASHER, PASECH	00	M	LABR	RRZZZZNY
KRIETZMAN, M.	28	M	TLR	PLZZZZNY
KACHAIL	24	F	W	PLZZZZNY
EMMANUEL	5	M	CHILD	PLZZZZNY
JOHN	3	M	CHILD	PLZZZZNY
REBECCA	1	F	CHILD	PLZZZZNY
GOLDBERG, A.	46	M	CCHMN	PLZZZZNY
GOLDSTEIN, H.	27	M	CCHMN	PLZZZZPHI
HISBERG, C.A.	55	F	W	PLZZZZCH
RACHAEL	17	F	CH	PLZZZZCH
ALTEN	12	M	CH	PLZZZZCH
SIRCA	10	F	CH	PLZZZZCH
PESTY	8	M	CHILD	PLZZZZCH

SHIP: CITY OF RICHMOND

FROM: LIVERPOOL
TO: NEW YORK
ARRIVED: 31 MARCH 1884

PASSENGER	AGE	SEX	OCCUPATION	PRV VIL DES
GOLDSTEIN, ABRAHAM	50	M	LABR	PLZZZZUSA
JEANETTE	4	F	CHILD	PLZZZZUSA
HEFMANN, HIRSCH	29	M	LABR	PLZZZZUSA
SLEWIN, IOSSEL	24	M	UNKNOWN	PLZZZZUSA
NANSEKANT, MICHUL	31	M	LABR	PLZZZZUSA
CHRISTINE	30	F	W	PLZZZZUSA
LINA	16	F	SP	PLZZZZUSA
AUGUSTA	3	F	CHILD	PLZZZZUSA
MARIE	00	F	INF	PLZZZZUSA
ABRAMOWIZ, SAM.	38	M	LABR	PLZZZZUSA
LEIB	11	M	CH	PLZZZZUSA
GOLKOWSKY, IOSSE	32	M	LABR	PLZZZZUSA
JANKO, FRIDA	35	F	W	PLZZZZUSA
GOLDBERG, BEAR	33	M	LABR	PLZZZZUSA
GONSKY, BARTOL	64	M	UNKNOWN	PLZZZZUSA
TORTLER, JOHAN	24	M	UNKNOWN	PLZZZZUSA

SHIP: EIDER

FROM: BREMERHAVEN AND SOUTHAMPTON
TO: NEW YORK
ARRIVED: 31 MARCH 1884

PASSENGER	AGE	SEX	OCCUPATION	PRV VIL DES
DESSAN, MORITZ	32	M	MCHT	RRZZZZRSS
U, U	00	U	UNKNOWN	RRZZZZUSA
GOHR, EMMA	27	F	W	RRZZZZUSA
OSCAR	3	M	CHILD	RRZZZZUSA
OTTO	.11	M	INFANT	RRZZZZUSA
JAGIELSKA, MARIANNA	11	F	CH	RRZZZZUSA
BALWA.	.11	F	INFANT	RRZZZZUSA
JABLONSKI, JAN	43	M	FARMER	RRZZZZUSA
BIENIEWICZ, JOSEF	25	M	FARMER	RRZZZZUSA
ANTONI	24	M	LABR	RRZZZZUSA
WANGA, STANISLAUS	24	M	LABR	PLZZZZUSA
GOLOMBIEWSKY, THOMAS	31	M	LABR	RRZZZZUSA
BARBA.	21	F	W	RRZZZZUSA
KANSCHETZKA, MARIA	21	F	NN	RRZZZZUSA
KAPLAN, ABRAHAM	23	M	LABR	RRZZZZUSA
PAWLOWEC, MATH.	00	M	LABR	PLZZZZUSA
EMICH, RUD.	00	U	UNKNOWN	PLZZZZUSA
REICHER, EMMA	00	U	UNKNOWN	PLZZZZUSA
FORST, W---L	00	U	UNKNOWN	PLZZZZUSA
U, U	00	U	UNKNOWN	PLZZZZUSA
GRABOWSKI, ANTONI	44	M	FARMER	RRZZZZUSA
BOBOWICZ, BENEDICT	21	M	FARMER	RRZZZZUSA
KOCHNOWSKI, JOSEF	24	M	LABR	RRZZZZUSA
SPERKA, JOSEPH	00	M	FARMER	RRZZZZUSA

PASSENGER	AGE	SEX	OCCUPATION	PRIV	VIL	DES
CONSTA.	00	F	W	RR	ZZZZ	USA
VICENTI	8	M	CHILD	RR	ZZZZ	USA
STEPHAN	3	M	CHILD	RR	ZZZZ	USA
---A	00	F	CH	RR	ZZZZ	USA
ANJECZOK, VALENT.	00	M	JNR	RR	ZZZZ	USA
MARGA	00	F	W	RR	ZZZZ	USA
JAN	00	M	CH	RR	ZZZZ	USA
MARIA	00	F	CH	RR	ZZZZ	USA

SHIP: POLARIA

FROM: HAMBURG
TO: NEW YORK
ARRIVED: 31 MARCH 1884

PASSENGER	AGE	SEX	OCCUPATION	PRIV	VIL	DES
BARON, PETER	39	M	LABR	PL	ZZZZ	NY
LECHFOR, JOHN	24	M	LABR	PL	ZZZZ	NY
STEFANIK, WOYCECH	32	M	LABR	PL	ZZZZ	NY
NEUMANN, FRIEDR.	26	M	LABR	PL	ZZZZ	NY
WALITZKI, JAN	50	M	LABR	PL	ZZZZ	NY
OSIN, KASIMIR	19	M	LABR	PL	ZZZZ	NY
FRASKOFSKI, ANDR.	27	M	LABR	PL	ZZZZ	NY
DEMBOFSKI, BAWEL	21	M	LABR	PL	ZZZZ	NY
PARLIH, MICHAL	40	M	LABR	PL	ZZZZ	NY
GOLDMANN, HIRSCH	35	M	TRDSMN	PL	ZZZZ	NY
ESTER	17	F	F	PL	ZZZZ	NY
FRUHMANN, WOLFF	41	M	TRDSMN	PL	ZZZZ	NY
ESTER	36	F	W	PL	ZZZZ	NY
SISSEI	7	F	CHILD	PL	ZZZZ	NY
FRADEL	6	M	CHILD	PL	ZZZZ	NY
ABRAHAM	3	M	CHILD	PL	ZZZZ	NY
DANIEL	.11	M	INFANT	PL	ZZZZ	NY
EPHRAIM	.01	M	INFANT	PL	ZZZZ	NY
FISCHGRUND, ISRAEL	48	M	TRDSMN	PL	ZZZZ	NY
HANNIE	37	F	W	PL	ZZZZ	NY
LILLI	7	F	CHILD	PL	ZZZZ	NY
SIMCKA	6	F	CHILD	PL	ZZZZ	NY
BEZI	5	F	CHILD	PL	ZZZZ	NY
ADOLPH	4	M	CHILD	PL	ZZZZ	NY
LALI	3	M	CHILD	PL	ZZZZ	NY
REGI	3	F	CHILD	PL	ZZZZ	NY
MEMNA	2	F	CHILD	PL	ZZZZ	NY
SZANI	.11	F	INFANT	PL	ZZZZ	NY
PAUL	.01	M	INFANT	PL	ZZZZ	NY
MICHLHAUSEN, ADOLPH	24	M	BCHR	PL	ZZZZ	NY
KOHA, JACOB	28	M	TRDSMN	PL	ZZZZ	NY
MENDEL, LAZAR	24	M	TRDSMN	PL	ZZZZ	NY
SETZ, CHAIM	23	M	TLR	RR	ZZZZ	NY
KLEINMANN, SCHONE	21	F	SGL	RR	ZZZZ	NY
ROGASCH, CARL	32	M	CPTR	RR	ZZZZ	NY
SOWINSKI, JOHANN	30	M	SHMK	RR	ZZZZ	NY
SKARBACK, WOYCICH	22	M	FARMER	PL	ZZZZ	NY
MAROZIN, SACK	24	M	FARMER	PL	ZZZZ	NY
MALOHINSKY, MIKOS	00	M	SHMK	PL	ZZZZ	NY
ANTONIA	22	F	W	PL	ZZZZ	NY
WAWRINEC, GOJDE	34	M	LABR	PL	ZZZZ	NY
VALENTZ, BOLK	30	M	LABR	PL	ZZZZ	NY
KORECI, JAN	24	M	LABR	PL	ZZZZ	NY
RECENECKY, JOSEF	19	M	LABR	PL	ZZZZ	NY
ROCHINTYNEK, JAY	26	M	LABR	PL	ZZZZ	NY
WARKOLAK, WASKO	27	M	LABR	PL	ZZZZ	NY
LAKASEK, DANKO	34	M	LABR	PL	ZZZZ	NY
LUKAC, JOSEF	18	M	LABR	PL	ZZZZ	NY
KLEPAC, MIKOS	21	M	LABR	PL	ZZZZ	NY
DUDAK, JUZEK	30	M	LABR	PL	ZZZZ	NY
SAT, ADAM	25	M	LABR	PL	ZZZZ	NY
NIZOLEK, JAN.	47	M	LABR	PL	ZZZZ	NY
JOSEF	24	M	LABR	PL	ZZZZ	NY
BARACZAK, JANOS	43	M	LABR	PL	ZZZZ	NY
FINCKELBERG, R.	18	F	SGL	RR	ZZZZ	NY
SCHWEINGRUBER, FR.	38	M	LABR	RR	ZZZZ	NY
MAKOVOTZ, WOLF	22	M	LABR	RR	ZZZZ	NY
ZEMAYTYS, JOSEF	24	M	LABR	RR	ZZZZ	NY
KALMAN, MARKNITZ	33	M	LABR	RR	ZZZZ	NY
BERGMANN, MOSES	22	M	LABR	RR	ZZZZ	NY
WINZEWITS, ANTON	20	M	LABR	RR	ZZZZ	NY
SOOROSKY, FELIX	28	M	LABR	RR	ZZZZ	NY
MARKEVITZ, JAN	24	M	LABR	RR	ZZZZ	NY
ZABYLOVITOC, JOSEF	17	M	LABR	RR	ZZZZ	NY
ROMANOWSKY, JULIAN	22	M	LABR	RR	ZZZZ	NY
POALSKY, M.	21	M	LABR	RR	ZZZZ	NY
VINGALLA, H.	36	M	FARMER	RR	ZZZZ	NY
GILLINENSKY, JULIUS	30	M	LABR	RR	ZZZZ	NY
CHORVORSCHEFSKY, A.	35	M	LABR	RR	ZZZZ	NY
PODGALSKY, FRANZ	46	M	LABR	RR	ZZZZ	NY
DOFSKOWSKY, LEON	25	M	LABR	RR	ZZZZ	NY
MILANOWSKY, JAN	34	M	LABR	RR	ZZZZ	NY
SOSNOWSKY, LUDWIG	22	M	LABR	RR	ZZZZ	NY
SLAWINSKY, SIMOS	24	M	LABR	RR	ZZZZ	NY
WROBLEWSKY, JOSEF	24	M	LABR	RR	ZZZZ	NY
KIESCHLING, PETER	46	M	LABR	RR	ZZZZ	NY
MARCYN	7	M	CHILD	RR	ZZZZ	NY
SOBOLEWSKY, THEOF.	29	M	LABR	RR	ZZZZ	NY
KRUSINSKI, AD.	42	M	LABR	RR	ZZZZ	NY
WIETHAT, JOS.	30	M	LABR	RR	ZZZZ	NY
WASELEWSKY, JULIAN	24	M	LABR	RR	ZZZZ	NY
GRUSCHOWSKY, TH.	30	M	LABR	RR	ZZZZ	NY
SOBOLEWSKY, VICENTY	24	M	LABR	RR	ZZZZ	NY
HOFF, LEIB	22	M	LABR	RR	ZZZZ	NY
LESCHEN, SAMUEL	22	M	LABR	RR	ZZZZ	NY
WASSELEFSKI, JOSEF	28	M	FARMER	RR	ZZZZ	NY
WOJTKOWIAK, ANDR.	27	M	FARMER	RR	ZZZZ	NY
CAPNIK, NEHEMIAN	21	M	LABR	RR	ZZZZ	NY
BROAK, DANA	19	F	SGL	PL	ZZZZ	NY
SCHOLTECK, ANDR.	42	M	LABR	PL	ZZZZ	NY
MARKEWITZ, STANISL.	28	M	LABR	PL	ZZZZ	NY
SALATOWSKY, FRANTA	24	M	LABR	PL	ZZZZ	NY
SCHUBRAK, FRANZ	48	M	LABR	PL	ZZZZ	NY
JENDRIKOWSKY, MICH.	40	M	LABR	PL	ZZZZ	NY
JOSEF	32	M	LABR	PL	ZZZZ	NY
MILEWSKY, JOHANN	23	M	LABR	PL	ZZZZ	NY
BRASINSKY, MATSCHE	17	M	LABR	PL	ZZZZ	NY
LUKOWSKY, ANDR.	21	M	LABR	PL	ZZZZ	NY
WOLUF, JOHANN	24	M	LABR	PL	ZZZZ	NY
ANDRE	21	M	LABR	PL	ZZZZ	NY
STANISLAW	23	M	LABR	PL	ZZZZ	NY
KRISCHITZKA, FRANZISCH	26	M	LABR	PL	ZZZZ	NY
OFSCHANITZ, MICH.	19	M	LABR	PL	ZZZZ	NY
RADIM, JOSEF	36	M	LABR	PL	ZZZZ	NY
WEI---L-, JACOB	33	M	LABR	PL	ZZZZ	NY
ABRAHAM	24	M	LABR	PL	ZZZZ	NY
KALLENDO, VINCENDES	22	M	LABR	PL	ZZZZ	NY
ACUKARTYS, ADAM	18	M	TRDSMN	PL	ZZZZ	NY
JELAT, KAREL	36	M	TRDSMN	PL	ZZZZ	NY
SOELGIN, JOHANN	21	M	TRDSMN	PL	ZZZZ	NY
TROSCHOWSKY, PETER	20	M	TRDSMN	PL	ZZZZ	NY
SUCHONET, JOSEF	23	M	TRDSMN	PL	ZZZZ	NY
KRISDITZKA, WLADISLAW	19	M	TRDSMN	PL	ZZZZ	NY
VINGELART, GIORGI	30	M	LABR	PL	ZZZZ	NY
POSERBSKY, P.	30	M	LABR	PL	ZZZZ	NY
MARIA	20	F	LABR	PL	ZZZZ	NY
VINCENTY	.04	M	INFANT	PL	ZZZZ	NY
SYLOWSKY, ANDR.	20	M	LABR	PL	ZZZZ	NY
VALARY, HELENE	20	F	LABR	PL	ZZZZ	NY
HRIMMALOWSKY, ANTON	40	M	LABR	PL	ZZZZ	NY
PARSCHKOFSKY, FRIEDR.	44	M	LABR	PL	ZZZZ	NY
CATHARINA	48	F	W	PL	ZZZZ	NY
KISCHKOFF, FRIEDR.	19	M	LABR	PL	ZZZZ	NY

SHIP: SWITZERLAND

FROM: ANTWERP
TO: NEW YORK
ARRIVED: 31 MARCH 1884

PASSENGER	AGE	SEX	OCCUPATION	PRV VIL DES
CULKOWSKI, IGN.	15	M	UNKNOWN	RRZZZZUSA
STANISLAOCK, ANT.	40	M	UNKNOWN	RRZZZZUSA

SHIP: WIELAND

FROM: HAMBURG
TO: NEW YORK
ARRIVED: 31 MARCH 1884

PASSENGER	AGE	SEX	OCCUPATION	PRV VIL DES
KOBIEKE, JACOB	30	M	DLR	RRZZZZUSA
CHANNE	23	F	W	RRZZZZUSA
RIEFKE	.06	F	INFANT	RRZZZZUSA
CZOKAITIS, MARIANNE	45	F	W	RRZZZZUSA
EVA	25	F	W	RRZZZZUSA
AUGUST	8	M	CHILD	RRZZZZUSA
JOSEF	7	M	CHILD	RRZZZZUSA
ALEX	2	M	CHILD	RRZZZZUSA
MILAWSKY, LEIB	18	M	LABR	RRZZZZUSA
GRUN, MARIANNE	23	F	W	RRZZZZUSA
FERD	.11	M	INFANT	RRZZZZUSA
RADMAND, JOHANNE	28	F	W	RRZZZZUSA
OLGA	3	F	CHILD	RRZZZZUSA
JOH.	.11	F	INFANT	RRZZZZUSA
SUPRANEZ, WOLF	17	M	LABR	RRZZZZUSA
ROBKOWSKY, ANTON	20	M	LABR	RRZZZZUSA
EVA	20	F	SGL	RRZZZZUSA
ELISABETH	18	F	SGL	RRZZZZUSA
KOMAROWSKY, ANTON	18	M	LABR	RRZZZZUSA
PRIECZKAILIS, WILH.	43	M	LABR	RRZZZZUSA
AMALIE	42	F	W	RRZZZZUSA
EDNARD	8	M	CHILD	RRZZZZUSA
GUSTAV	7	M	CHILD	RRZZZZUSA
PAULINE	6	F	CHILD	RRZZZZUSA
LEOPOLD	5	M	CHILD	RRZZZZUSA
EMIL	4	M	CHILD	RRZZZZUSA
LAPKEWICZ, MARIEL	30	M	LABR	RRZZZZUSA
SYPOK, LUKAS	27	M	LABR	RRZZZZUSA
FEIN, KLODE	45	F	W	RRZZZZUSA
MOSES	8	M	CHILD	RRZZZZUSA
REBECCA	21	F	W	RRZZZZUSA
SZUKLOWSKY, JUDEL	22	M	LABR	RRZZZZUSA
MACZI, JON	38	M	LABR	RRZZZZUSA
JANCK, MAX	22	M	LABR	RRZZZZUSA
COHN, ROSA	50	F	W	RRZZZZUSA
JOSSEL	8	M	CHILD	RRZZZZUSA
BERGMANN, LIEBE	26	F	W	RRZZZZUSA
SALOMON	.11	M	INFANT	RRZZZZUSA
RUDINSKY, JOSSEL	18	M	LABR	RRZZZZUSA
LAPIDUS, LEIB	40	M	LABR	RRZZZZUSA
HIRSCHFILD, SUNDEL	27	M	DLR	RRZZZZUSA
BREITMANN, NECHEMIE	30	M	LABR	RRZZZZUSA
GLIKSTEIN, LEIB	24	M	LABR	RRZZZZUSA
BOCZWINSKY, BARUCH	27	M	LABR	RRZZZZUSA
LEVY, HERZ	25	M	LABR	RRZZZZUSA
ANNE	20	F	W	RRZZZZUSA
MEYER	8	M	CHILD	RRZZZZUSA
SIMON	5	M	CHILD	RRZZZZUSA
NOWITZKY, JOSEPH	30	M	LABR	RRZZZZUSA
TILENDA, STANISLAV	26	M	LABR	RRZZZZUSA
SZUPIEN, JACOB	22	M	LABR	RRZZZZUSA
WOICECHOWAKY, KASIMIR	18	M	LABR	RRZZZZUSA
KOSCHEL, WILH.	24	M	LABR	RRZZZZUSA
AMALIE	22	F	W	RRZZZZUSA
STASCHULEWITZ, FRANZ	30	M	JNR	RRZZZZUSA
TABRISKE, RIWKE	26	F	W	RRZZZZUSA
ISRAEL	.11	M	INFANT	RRZZZZUSA
LEA	.01	F	INFANT	RRZZZZUSA
MIEZEWITZ, PETER	17	M	FARMER	RRZZZZUSA
WILKATIS, JOH.	32	M	FARMER	RRZZZZUSA
BAKUN, JACOB	26	M	FARMER	RRZZZZUSA
BLECHEWITZ, MOTUS	18	M	FARMER	RRZZZZUSA
IERUSCHEWITZ, KASIMIR	23	M	FARMER	RRZZZZUSA
BLECHEWITZ, JANOS	30	M	FARMER	RRZZZZUSA
DZERWA, VINCENT	18	M	FARMER	RRZZZZUSA
GRUBLIK, ADAM	28	M	FARMER	RRZZZZUSA
CZERNEWSKI, MATHEUS	25	M	FARMER	RRZZZZUSA
SUSCHUISKI, MATHS	24	M	FARMER	RRZZZZUSA
AUGUST	24	M	FARMER	RRZZZZUSA
NOWITZKAS, MATHS	35	M	FARMER	RRZZZZUSA
SIWLISS, THOMAS	54	M	FARMER	RRZZZZUSA
SELEDOMUS, VINCENT	36	M	FARMER	RRZZZZUSA
GIBAS, JOSEPH	24	M	FARMER	RRZZZZUSA
WADNITZKI, JERUCHEM	28	M	SHMK	RRZZZZUSA
SALOMON, SCHAHUE	39	M	DLR	RRZZZZUSA
FINKELSTEIN, LEIB	45	M	DLR	RRZZZZUSA
MARKOWITZ, ABE	31	M	MSN	RRZZZZUSA
TODRALSKY, MOSES	45	M	SHMK	RRZZZZUSA
HIMMELSTEIN, KALMAN	28	M	JNR	RRZZZZUSA
GRUNBERG, LEA	16	F	SGL	RRZZZZUSA
ETTE	18	F	SGL	RRZZZZUSA
RADINSKI, ISRAEL	22	M	DLR	RRZZZZUSA
RACHEL	19	F	W	RRZZZZUSA
KASCHDAN, JUDEL	30	F	SGL	RRZZZZUSA
PINASISKI, CHAIE	59	F	SGL	RRZZZZUSA
ZELESNIK, SARA	18	F	SGL	RRZZZZUSA
SIVKUS, PINCHAS	19	M	LABR	RRZZZZUSA
BRASOTIS, IWAN	29	M	LABR	RRZZZZUSA
MARIANNE	22	F	W	RRZZZZUSA
HORN, HENACH	28	M	DLR	RRZZZZUSA
WEITZONES, MATH.	40	M	FARMER	RRZZZZUSA
HERRMANN, KARL	40	M	FARMER	RRZZZZUSA
ARENTSCHEWITZ, ADOMAS	23	M	FARMER	RRZZZZUSA
KATH.	24	F	W	RRZZZZUSA
BUBNIS, ADAM	20	M	FARMER	RRZZZZUSA
WILZINSKY, JOH.	30	M	FARMER	RRZZZZUSA
MELLER, MOSES	25	M	LABR	RRZZZZUSA
GOSELA, FRANZ	33	M	LABR	RRZZZZUSA
SUEZIFASKI, FRANZ	40	M	LABR	RRZZZZUSA
PREIFER, JAN	38	M	LABR	RRZZZZUSA
SZEITKONSKI, ANTON	32	M	LABR	RRZZZZUSA
LUSZYNSKI, JOSEPH	24	M	LABR	RRZZZZUSA
SLAWITZKI, FRANZ	22	M	LABR	RRZZZZUSA
WYSNEWSKY, ANTON	21	M	LABR	RRZZZZUSA
RUTKOCZKI, IGNATZ	38	M	LABR	RRZZZZUSA
ROGANSKI, ALEXANDER	24	M	LABR	RRZZZZUSA
GRABKOWSKI, FRANZ	32	M	LABR	RRZZZZUSA
BUCHHOLZ, ANDR.	35	M	LABR	RRZZZZUSA
PELKOWSKI, ANTON	50	M	LABR	RRZZZZUSA
CZIEKANOWSKI, THOMAS	25	M	LABR	RRZZZZUSA
LEMKE, FERD.	24	M	LABR	RRZZZZUSA
RANKOWSKI, JOH.	26	M	LABR	RRZZZZUSA
WILDZINSKI, JOSEF	26	M	LABR	RRZZZZUSA
WODINCKI, SARA	35	F	W	RRZZZZUSA
NOCHE	8	M	CHILD	RRZZZZUSA
LEISER	7	M	CHILD	RRZZZZUSA
LEA	5	F	CHILD	RRZZZZUSA
ARON	3	M	CHILD	RRZZZZUSA
GRUNSPAN, ARON	21	M	SHMK	RRZZZZUSA
ZERINSKY, JACOB	26	M	WMN	RRZZZZUSA
SARA	24	F	W	RRZZZZUSA
ROBERT	.11	M	INFANT	RRZZZZUSA
SZKWACLA, SERWIN	35	M	FARMER	RRZZZZUSA
FMRIUSZKIONITZ, JAN	18	M	FARMER	RRZZZZUSA
SCHWACH, KINOEL	37	M	TLR	RRZZZZUSA
WEINBERGER, MORITZ	20	M	LABR	RRZZZZUSA
LOZUPKI, AUGUST	37	M	LABR	RRZZZZUSA
WERTSCHAT, JOHANN	37	M	LABR	RRZZZZUSA
DYRICH, CARL	25	M	LABR	RRZZZZUSA

PASSENGER	AGE	SEX	OCCUPATION	PRV VIL DES
BRAUD, CARL	26	M	LABR	RRZZZZUSA
SUSANNE	22	F	W	RRZZZZUSA
LEMKY, FRIEDR.	26	M	LABR	RRZZZZUSA
NAJASCHKA, JOH.	27	M	LABR	RRZZZZUSA
MARIANNE	27	F	W	RRZZZZUSA
EMILIE	7	F	CHILD	RRZZZZUSA
CARL	.11	M	INFANT	RRZZZZUSA
SCHWARZ, FRIEDR.	25	M	LABR	RRZZZZUSA
SCHULTZ, CARL	25	M	LABR	RRZZZZUSA
BECK, JULS.	23	M	LABR	RRZZZZUSA
POKRANT, ADOLPH	25	M	LABR	RRZZZZUSA
MUSAL, JAN	21	M	LABR	RRZZZZUSA
BARTEL, EVA	25	F	SGL	RRZZZZUSA
LEPKA, MICHAEL	28	M	LABR	RRZZZZUSA
SEITSTEIN, MARIUS	26	M	LABR	RRZZZZUSA
BERTHA	24	F	W	RRZZZZUSA
ANNA	.06	F	INFANT	RRZZZZUSA
LIPMANN, KOPPEL	56	M	LABR	RRZZZZUSA
LIPSCHITZ, BENZIER	30	M	LABR	RRZZZZUSA
NABOSNY, ISSER	25	M	LABR	RRZZZZUSA
BLUMENTHAL, TAUBE	25	F	W	RRZZZZUSA
CHEIM	.11	M	INFANT	RRZZZZUSA
WISOTZKI, WOJECK	25	M	LABR	RRZZZZUSA
GIDAM, SARA	16	F	SGL	RRZZZZUSA
MARCINKOWITZ, JOSEF	18	M	LABR	RRZZZZUSA
LEVI, CHAIE	21	F	W	RRZZZZUSA
MOSES	.11	M	INFANT	RRZZZZUSA
MILEWSKI, VINCENT	20	M	LABR	RRZZZZUSA
MAHNITZ, FELIX	27	M	LABR	RRZZZZUSA
RASNISKA, KATH.	23	F	SGL	RRZZZZUSA
GENEZUS, ANTON	25	M	LABR	RRZZZZUSA
UORAWASCH, ANTONAS	24	M	LABR	RRZZZZUSA
AUGULEWITZ, WLADISLAW	25	M	LABR	RRZZZZUSA
LIPSCHITZ, DWOSCHE	17	F	SGL	RRZZZZUSA
MICHEL	7	M	CHILD	RRZZZZUSA
WOLF	5	M	CHILD	RRZZZZUSA
KUROWSKY, JOSEF	25	M	LABR	RRZZZZUSA
GOLEMBIEWSKI, JAN	38	M	LABR	RRZZZZUSA
KULAKOWSKI, JOSEF	21	M	LABR	RRZZZZUSA
KAZILEWSKI, JAN	30	M	LABR	RRZZZZUSA
VALENTUKAMISS, PETER	25	M	LABR	RRZZZZUSA
AKRAMOWITZ, CARL	24	M	LABR	RRZZZZUSA
BITSCHOWSKI, WAWRZIN	27	M	LABR	RRZZZZUSA
DAUGERT, CHRIST	19	M	LABR	RRZZZZUSA
MAGNISS, JOSEF	20	M	LABR	RRZZZZUSA
WISNEWSKI, FRANZ	22	M	LABR	RRZZZZUSA
MICHALSKY, JOSEPH	23	M	LABR	RRZZZZUSA
LEWANDOWSKI, STANISL.	24	M	LABR	RRZZZZUSA
SEUDSKY	18	M	LABR	RRZZZZUSA
RUCZYNSKI, WOJCICH	26	M	JNR	RRZZZZUSA
GRITELEWITSCH, VINCENT	29	M	LABR	RRZZZZUSA
DAPKIEWICZ, LUDWIG	37	M	LABR	RRZZZZUSA
MATZESKAS, JOSEF	40	M	LABR	RRZZZZUSA
JOSEF	17	M	LABR	RRZZZZUSA
JAKUBOWITZ, ANTON	17	M	LABR	RRZZZZUSA
TONIKOWITZ, ANTON	20	M	LABR	RRZZZZUSA
KURSEN, JOSEF	48	M	LABR	RRZZZZUSA
WENSCHIWARTZ, VINCENT	19	M	LABR	RRZZZZUSA
TARLETZKI, JOSEF	23	M	LABR	RRZZZZUSA
MICHALEWITZ, FROME	28	F	W	RRZZZZUSA
CHANNE	5	F	CHILD	RRZZZZUSA
RACHEL	3	M	CHILD	RRZZZZUSA
LIEBMANN, SCHAPSE	19	F	SGL	RRZZZZUSA
PILTZ, SARA	23	F	W	RRZZZZUSA
CHAIE	.11	M	INFANT	RRZZZZUSA
BANK, BENJAMIN	19	M	LABR	RRZZZZUSA
HIRSCHOWITZ, MARIUS	28	M	LABR	RRZZZZUSA
KLEIN, GOLDE	20	F	SGL	RRZZZZUSA
JUDASKY, EFRAIM	61	M	LABR	RRZZZZUSA
PERECZANSKY, JANKEL	11	M	BY	RRZZZZUSA
RAMATH, CARL	40	M	BCHR	RRZZZZUSA

SHIP: SCHIEDAM

FROM: ROTTERDAM
TO: NEW YORK
ARRIVED: 01 APRIL 1884

PASSENGER	AGE	SEX	OCCUPATION	PRV VIL DES
ZALANOZEVOICZ, SAMINA	18	M	LABR	PLZZZZUSA
GOLMOLKE, JAN	30	M	LABR	PLZZZZUSA
HEMPITZ, SIMON	25	M	UNKNOWN	PLZZZZUSA

SHIP: SERVIA

FROM: LIVERPOOL
TO: NEW YORK
ARRIVED: 01 APRIL 1884

PASSENGER	AGE	SEX	OCCUPATION	PRV VIL DES
LEWI, ABRAM	22	M	TDR	RRZZZZUSA
LEWIS, SOLOMON	24	M	UNKNOWN	RRZZZZUSA
GORLI, JACOB	38	M	LABR	PLZZZZUSA
JASEPH, AND.	33	M	UNKNOWN	PLZZZZUSA
NUMERS, MIDA	24	F	SVNT	PLZZZZUSA
SKARMACHER, PAIEN	24	M	LABR	PLZZZZUSA
AND.	23	M	UNKNOWN	PLZZZZUSA
THOMAS, JANOS	32	M	UNKNOWN	PLZZZZUSA
BUSH, JOS.R.	47	M	MCHT	RRZZZZUSA

SHIP: FRANCE

FROM: HAVRE
TO: NEW YORK
ARRIVED: 02 APRIL 1884

PASSENGER	AGE	SEX	OCCUPATION	PRV VIL DES
OSIO, JOSEPH	20	M	UNKNOWN	RRZZZZNY

SHIP: RUGIA

FROM: HAMBURG
TO: NEW YORK
ARRIVED: 02 APRIL 1884

PASSENGER	AGE	SEX	OCCUPATION	PRV VIL DES
AUGSTRA, JAN	18	M	LABR	RRZZZZUSA
BOLEWSKY, BOLESLAW	19	M	LABR	RRZZZZUSA
POSILOWSKY, MATTHEI	26	M	UNKNOWN	RRZZZZUSA
MAUTHEY, GOTTLIEB	23	M	UNKNOWN	RRZZZZUSA
AUGUSTE	25	F	W	RRZZZZUSA
WERNICH, AUGUST	31	M	LABR	RRZZZZUSA
LEWKOWITZ, KIEWE	30	M	LABR	RRZZZZUSA
ROMANOWITZ, CHAIM	42	M	UNKNOWN	RRZZZZUSA
RETZKOWSKY, IGNATZ	34	M	LABR	RRZZZZUSA
MARSOLEWSKI, VINECENT	33	M	UNKNOWN	RRZZZZUSA
BOZELSKI, SANISL.	43	M	UNKNOWN	RRZZZZUSA
POLAKOWSKI, STANISL.	44	M	LABR	RRZZZZUSA
KREINSKI, ANTON	33	M	UNKNOWN	RRZZZZUSA
LIPERESCH, MATHIS	43	M	UNKNOWN	RRZZZZUSA
OMILIAN, JACOB	30	M	UNKNOWN	RRZZZZUSA
FRANZISKA	45	F	W	RRZZZZUSA
ANTONIA	.11	F	INFANT	RRZZZZUSA
FRANZISKA	.01	F	INFANT	RRZZZZUSA
GESTEROWSKI, ANTON	29	M	LABR	RRZZZZUSA

PASSENGER	AGE	SEX	OCCUPATION	PV RI VL	DES
ANNA	23	F	W	RRZZZZ	USA
MICHAEL	.11	M	INFANT	RRZZZZ	USA
POBUZESKY, JOH.	30	M	LABR	RRZZZZ	USA
MARIANNE	32	F	W	RRZZZZ	USA
JACOB	2	M	CHILD	RRZZZZ	USA
BROMISL	.03	M	INFANT	RRZZZZ	USA
KROSCINSKI, JULIAN	23	M	LABR	RRZZZZ	USA
MARIANNE	24	F	W	RRZZZZ	USA
LUBERETZKI, JACOB	32	M	UNKNOWN	RRZZZZ	USA
CATHA.	22	F	W	RRZZZZ	USA
JOSEF	.11	M	INFANT	RRZZZZ	USA
ANDR.	.01	M	INFANT	RRZZZZ	USA
KRONE, CASIMIR	43	M	LABR	RRZZZZ	USA
SCHWARZ, JANKEL	20	M	TLR	RRZZZZ	USA
ZWIEKA	22	F	W	RRZZZZ	USA
BRETTSTEIN, CHASKEL	42	M	DLR	RRZZZZ	USA
CHANNE	18	F	CH	RRZZZZ	USA
REISEL	15	F	UNKNOWN	RRZZZZ	USA
SCHUFRO, SARA	48	F	W	RRZZZZ	USA
MERE	8	F	CHILD	RRZZZZ	USA
WARONKER, JANKEL	39	M	LABR	RRZZZZ	USA
BOTWINIK, URI	39	M	GZR	RRZZZZ	USA
BERMANN, GITTEL	60	F	W	RRZZZZ	USA
CHANNE	18	F	D	RRZZZZ	USA
KALWIN, SARA	34	F	W	RRZZZZ	USA
DAVID	8	M	CHILD	RRZZZZ	USA
TAUBE	7	M	CHILD	RRZZZZ	USA
CHANNE	6	F	CHILD	RRZZZZ	USA
SCHEINE	.11	F	INFANT	RRZZZZ	USA
KRAJEWSKY, STAN.	50	M	UNKNOWN	RRZZZZ	USA
MICH.	8	M	CHILD	RRZZZZ	USA
DOBROWSKY, ANTON	27	M	LABR	RRZZZZ	USA
CHMIELEWSKY, STAN.	21	M	UNKNOWN	RRZZZZ	USA
RUTSCHINSKY, LEONH	25	M	LABR	RRZZZZ	USA
PUCHALSKY, IGNATZ	22	M	UNKNOWN	RRZZZZ	USA
BLUSEVIE, VALERIE	27	F	SGL	RRZZZZ	USA
TELKOWSKY, JOSEL	23	M	LABR	RRZZZZ	USA
BARON, JAN	24	M	LABR	RRZZZZ	USA
PACKOSCHOWSKY, MEER	45	F	W	RRZZZZ	USA
ONSCHO	16	M	LABR	RRZZZZ	USA
STASOLISCH, MATH.	32	M	FARMER	RRZZZZ	USA
WOHLGEMUTH, JULS.	32	M	SMH	RRZZZZ	USA
PURWINER, CHASCHE	20	F	SGL	RRZZZZ	USA
LEWIN, SALOMON	19	M	DLR	RRZZZZ	USA
FRIEDMANN, CHASCHE	20	F	SGL	RRZZZZ	USA
TOSCHMOWSKY, ISAAC	49	M	DLR	RRZZZZ	USA
BORASCHKOW, MOSES	50	M	WCHMKR	RRZZZZ	USA
GOLDENBERG, JACOB	30	M	LABR	RRZZZZ	USA
MENDEL	25	M	UNKNOWN	RRZZZZ	USA
ROSENBERG, CHAIM	26	M	UNKNOWN	RRZZZZ	USA
RAJEWSKY, CHEINE	40	F	W	RRZZZZ	USA
ROSENNBAUM, SCHEINE	30	F	UNKNOWN	RRZZZZ	USA
CHEIN	.11	M	INFANT	RRZZZZ	USA
RAJEWSKY, JACOB	20	M	LABR	RRZZZZ	USA
IMREWITZSCH, ANDRE	26	M	LABR	RRZZZZ	USA
LELOW, FRANZ	30	M	UNKNOWN	RRZZZZ	USA
SABITZKI, JOSEPH	35	M	UNKNOWN	RRZZZZ	USA
BINELEWITZ, STAN.	18	M	UNKNOWN	RRZZZZ	USA
HRIVITZKI, WOICICH	29	M	UNKNOWN	RRZZZZ	USA
ANNA	29	F	W	RRZZZZ	USA
HELENE	.11	F	INFANT	RRZZZZ	USA
STANISLAW	.01	M	INFANT	RRZZZZ	USA
RIMEWICZ, CASIMIR	24	M	LABR	RRZZZZ	USA
BALOTSCHANIS, MARTIN	23	M	UNKNOWN	RRZZZZ	USA
EISENSTARK, SARA	20	F	W	RRZZZZ	USA
ANNA	.11	F	INFANT	RRZZZZ	USA
IDA	2	F	CHILD	RRZZZZ	USA
GERSON	.11	M	INFANT	RRZZZZ	USA
ALBRECHTSENSKI, ED.	12	M	LABR	RRZZZZ	USA
SZIROEZYNSKY, AMALIE	40	F	W	RRZZZZ	USA
BORTELSTEIN, SARA	22	F	SGL	RRZZZZ	USA
BARASCHKOFF, SUSIE	42	F	W	RRZZZZ	USA
GINESIE	19	F	D	RRZZZZ	USA
KOCWILSKY, JANKEL	18	M	LABR	RRZZZZ	USA
HERZ, MATHES	48	M	UNKNOWN	RRZZZZ	USA

PASSENGER	AGE	SEX	OCCUPATION	PV RI VL	DES
SZESNY, MICHEL	30	M	UNKNOWN	RRZZZZ	USA
RUDAK, STAN.	22	M	LABR	RRZZZZ	USA
GROEHLER, FRIEDR.	51	M	UNKNOWN	RRZZZZ	USA
NEUMANN, JOH.	25	M	UNKNOWN	RRZZZZ	USA
BUEZINSKI, JOS.	26	M	UNKNOWN	RRZZZZ	USA
JASABABIES, VINCENTI	29	M	UNKNOWN	RRZZZZ	USA
GOLDBERG, FRUME	44	F	W	RRZZZZ	USA
JACOB	8	M	CHILD	RRZZZZ	USA
ABRAH	7	M	CHILD	RRZZZZ	USA
BEILE	5	F	CHILD	RRZZZZ	USA
SAWATZKI, PETER	23	F	LABR	RRZZZZ	USA
MILEWSKI, ANDR.	23	M	UNKNOWN	RRZZZZ	USA
MARCUZEWSKY, JOACH	19	M	UNKNOWN	RRZZZZ	USA
SCHUSTER, ADAM	25	M	UNKNOWN	RRZZZZ	USA
DZEM---, EDWARD	23	M	UNKNOWN	RRZZZZ	USA
LAPINSKI, LEMAN	24	M	UNKNOWN	RRZZZZ	USA
BARTOSCHWITZ, LUDWIG	23	M	UNKNOWN	RRZZZZ	USA
GRUSKI, LEIB	40	M	LABR	RRZZZZ	USA
LESELER, MOSES	26	M	UNKNOWN	RRZZZZ	USA
GOLDMANN, BENJAMIN	26	M	UNKNOWN	RRZZZZ	USA
RUBEN	21	M	UNKNOWN	RRZZZZ	USA
LEWIN, PESCHEL	22	M	UNKNOWN	RRZZZZ	USA
SCHULMANN, MOSES	23	M	CL	RRZZZZ	USA
HENKEL, CARL	28	M	CON	RRZZZZ	USA
JOSCHINSKI, PETER	25	M	OGNST	RRZZZZ	USA
SCHAPLICK, NICODEMUS	18	M	LABR	RRZZZZ	USA
WOLONGEWITZ, JOHN	22	M	UNKNOWN	RRZZZZ	USA
BOGUS, JOHN	20	M	UNKNOWN	RRZZZZ	USA
SCHIBEILE, JAN	18	M	UNKNOWN	RRZZZZ	USA
CHAROL, MICH.	26	M	UNKNOWN	RRZZZZ	USA
PINKALO, PAUL	42	M	UNKNOWN	RRZZZZ	USA
WISTINECKY, SARA	30	F	W	RRZZZZ	USA
RUOKE	8	F	CHILD	RRZZZZ	USA
CHAWE	7	F	CHILD	RRZZZZ	USA
FEIGE	3	F	CHILD	RRZZZZ	USA
SCHAPIR-, FEIGE	18	F	SGL	RRZZZZ	USA
KLEIN, CHAIM	18	M	UNKNOWN	RRZZZZ	USA
RADEZIKOWSKA, ANNA	22	F	SGL	RRZZZZ	USA
LABUTIS, ANDR.	24	M	LABR	RRZZZZ	USA
CARL	42	M	LABR	RRZZZZ	USA
WIZENTI	30	M	UNKNOWN	RRZZZZ	USA
JOSBALES, KATHA.	23	F	SGL	RRZZZZ	USA
WINECENT	.11	M	INFANT	RRZZZZ	USA
RIAZE--KI, WINCENT	27	M	LABR	RRZZZZ	USA
RADISCH--KI, JOSEPH	00	M	UNKNOWN	RRZZZZ	USA
BAUD-CH, MACEJ	19	M	UNKNOWN	RRZZZZ	USA
WEIZANES, FRANZ	21	M	UNKNOWN	RRZZZZ	USA
KAROSCHANSKI, JOSIAS	30	M	UNKNOWN	RRZZZZ	USA
SCHEGINSKI, MAX	28	M	UNKNOWN	RRZZZZ	USA
ASZILENE, ROSA	30	F	W	RRZZZZ	USA
JONAS	.11	M	INFANT	RRZZZZ	USA
BUEZINSKI, MARIE	20	F	SGL	RRZZZZ	USA
KATZMANN, FRANZ	21	M	UNKNOWN	RRZZZZ	USA
SCHANDOWSKI, STANISL.	50	M	UNKNOWN	RRZZZZ	USA
LORESON, KOHOS	32	M	UNKNOWN	RRZZZZ	USA
BROSMANN, SCHLOM.	25	M	LABR	RRZZZZ	USA
GARFUNKEL, CHEIN	28	M	UNKNOWN	RRZZZZ	USA
SKOWRONSKI, RUD.	35	M	MLR	RRZZZZ	USA
GOMISCHEWKI, ADAM	23	M	FARMER	RRZZZZ	USA
KURALO, LIM	32	M	UNKNOWN	RRZZZZ	USA

SHIP: FRANCE

FROM: LONDON
TO: NEW YORK
ARRIVED: 03 APRIL 1884

PASSENGER	AGE	SEX	OCCUPATION	PV RI VL	DES
TZEZESENKE, M.	23	M	LABR	RRZZZZ	NY

SHIP: SALIER

FROM: BREMEN
TO: NEW YORK
ARRIVED: 04 APRIL 1884

PASSENGER	AGE	SEX	OCCUPATION	PRV VIL DES
TIESENHAUSEN, PAUL	38	M	TT	RRZZZZUSA
SKARZENSKI, JAC.	34	M	LABR	RRZZZZUSA
PURITZ, FLORENTINE	35	F	W	RRZZZZUSA

SHIP: ELBE

FROM: BREMEN
TO: NEW YORK
ARRIVED: 05 APRIL 1884

PASSENGER	AGE	SEX	OCCUPATION	PRV VIL DES
REMPEL, ABRAH.F.	37	M	LABR	RRZZZZUSA
ANNA	21	F	W	RRZZZZUSA
ABRAH.	2	M	CHILD	RRZZZZUSA
DIETRICH	.06	M	INFANT	RRZZZZUSA
JAWELSKE, JACOB	11	M	NN	RRZZZZUSA
BOGACHI, JAN.	24	M	LABR	RRZZZZUSA

SHIP: EGYPTIAN MONARCH

FROM: LONDON
TO: NEW YORK
ARRIVED: 07 APRIL 1884

PASSENGER	AGE	SEX	OCCUPATION	PRV VIL DES
ISAAKS, MORIS	40	M	TRVLR	PLZZZZNY
ROSENSTEIN, ALEXANDER	24	M	CGRMKR	PLZZZZBAL
ROSENBERG, JOHN	23	M	LABR	PLZZZZNY
EDWARD	25	M	LABR	PLZZZZNY
LOSEN, PIETER	22	M	PDLR	PLZZZZMAS
BONUALO, ANGELO	26	M	PDLR	PLZZZZMAS

SHIP: HAMMONIA

FROM: HAMBURG AND HAVRE
TO: NEW YORK
ARRIVED: 07 APRIL 1884

PASSENGER	AGE	SEX	OCCUPATION	PRV VIL DES
DANGELWETZ, WLADISL.	45	M	LABR	RRZZZZUSA
ALJANE	30	F	W	RRZZZZUSA
KLARITAITIS, MAGD.	20	F	SGL	RRZZZZUSA
ZERNIK, JERKE	32	F	W	RRZZZZUSA
AUSTRE, JOSEPH	38	M	LABR	RRZZZZUSA
ZINK, AUGUST	27	M	LABR	RRZZZZUSA
GLEIZER, JULES	34	M	LABR	RRZZZZUSA
BREINOWITZ, SAMUEL	45	M	DLR	RRZZZZUSA
BIRGER, LEIBE	36	M	PNTR	RRZZZZUSA
BOIKOWITZ, ABRAH.	34	M	SHMK	RRZZZZUSA
STEIN, LINE	18	F	SGL	RRZZZZUSA
BASS, NECHMIE	27	M	LABR	RRZZZZUSA
CHEIE	30	F	W	RRZZZZUSA
SEINEKE	6	F	CHILD	RRZZZZUSA
MICHEL	5	M	CHILD	RRZZZZUSA
SEHEBSEL	.11	M	INFANT	RRZZZZUSA
GLATTSTEIN, SCHEINE	32	F	W	RRZZZZUSA
ESTHER	8	F	CHILD	RRZZZZUSA
RACHEL	7	F	CHILD	RRZZZZUSA
CHAIE	5	F	CHILD	RRZZZZUSA
FEIWEL	.11	M	INFANT	RRZZZZUSA
LEA	.01	F	INFANT	RRZZZZUSA
PALMAN, CHAIE	18	F	SGL	RRZZZZUSA
KLEIN, FR.	19	M	LABR	RRZZZZUSA
RODES, MOSES	60	M	LABR	RRZZZZUSA
CHANNE	55	F	W	RRZZZZUSA
SCHEINE	8	F	CHILD	RRZZZZUSA
REIN, ELKE	15	F	SGL	RRZZZZUSA
PRAZNISKY, SELIG	26	M	LABR	RRZZZZUSA
ELKE	22	F	W	RRZZZZUSA
GINSBERG, CZARRE	56	F	W	RRZZZZUSA
LAKI, BOZUMIL	22	F	MCHT	RRZZZZUSA
WILDONSKI, SIMON	40	F	LABR	RRZZZZUSA
SOHEIN, ELIAS	24	F	LABR	RRZZZZUSA
ALTER	8	F	CHILD	RRZZZZUSA
CHLIEWE, FELNEL	22	F	LABR	RRZZZZUSA
MISCHKOWSKY, JACOB	40	F	LABR	RRZZZZUSA
NOWODWORSKY, CHANNE	48	F	W	RRZZZZUSA
ROCHEL	8	F	CHILD	RRZZZZUSA
CHANNE	7	F	CHILD	RRZZZZUSA
ALASES	6	M	CHILD	RRZZZZUSA
STERNGFELD, CHEIM.	30	M	CGRMKR	RRZZZZUSA
AVERHORN, LEIBE	55	M	LABR	RRZZZZUSA
GOLDSTEIN, BEHR.	35	M	LABR	RRZZZZUSA
BEHRMANN, MOSES	42	M	LABR	RRZZZZUSA
CHEIPEZ, CHAIM	45	M	DLR	RRZZZZUSA
MARIASCHE	40	F	W	RRZZZZUSA
HANNE	.11	F	INFANT	RRZZZZUSA
RUBIN	.01	M	INFANT	RRZZZZUSA
WIETOROWITZ, ALEX	20	M	LABR	RRZZZZUSA
WOJDOWER, AGATHE	44	F	SGL	RRZZZZUSA
KEMERAITES, LUDWIG	48	M	LABR	RRZZZZUSA
WASZILEWSKA, MAGD.	22	F	SGL	RRZZZZUSA
ADAM	25	M	LABR	RRZZZZUSA
MATH.	28	M	LABR	RRZZZZUSA
SCHOTNER, VINCENTI	27	M	LABR	RRZZZZUSA
PUSCHKEWITZ, MATES	28	M	LABR	RRZZZZUSA
KLEINATSCHUNA, VICTOR	26	M	LABR	RRZZZZUSA
BIJANOWSKY, MICH.	22	M	LABR	RRZZZZUSA
BAREISKA, MARIANNE	23	F	SGL	RRZZZZUSA
JENSE	22	F	SGL	RRZZZZUSA
BRONSAN, MARTIN	25	M	LABR	RRZZZZUSA
CASIMIR	8	M	CHILD	RRZZZZUSA
MARTIN	7	M	CHILD	RRZZZZUSA
WEIDZULIS, VINCENT	25	M	LABR	RRZZZZUSA
BOSLEWITZ, VIN.	28	M	LABR	RRZZZZUSA
ANNA	22	F	W	RRZZZZUSA
BOLIMEITIS, VICENT	30	M	LABR	RRZZZZUSA
NORACH, FRANZ	24	M	LABR	RRZZZZUSA
SKARAPA, WLADISL.	28	M	LABR	RRZZZZUSA
BOBIN, MICHAEL	21	M	LABR	RRZZZZUSA
LIPSKI, MICHEL	42	M	LABR	RRZZZZUSA
MARIANNE	19	F	SGL	RRZZZZUSA
IASKALSKI, JAN	21	M	LABR	RRZZZZUSA
LIPKOWSKI, ALBERT	33	M	LABR	RRZZZZUSA
ZEVENKOFSKI, JAN	62	M	LABR	RRZZZZUSA
MARIANNE	30	F	W	RRZZZZUSA
JOSEFFA	5	F	CHILD	RRZZZZUSA
WARDOWSKI, S.	52	M	LABR	RRZZZZUSA
WAISECK, HEINR.	21	M	LABR	RRZZZZUSA
ZOLMER, FRANZ	22	M	LABR	RRZZZZUSA
JABLONSKI, JAN	35	M	LABR	RRZZZZUSA
GRONOWSKI, ANDR.	32	M	LABR	RRZZZZUSA
BUKOWSKI, JAN	44	M	LABR	RRZZZZUSA
LYBOWSKI, JOSEF	27	M	LABR	RRZZZZUSA
ZECHSEWSKI, JOSEF	27	M	LABR	RRZZZZUSA
DYKOWSKI, FRANZ	28	M	LABR	RRZZZZUSA
SWIRESYNK, PETER	26	M	LABR	RRZZZZUSA
DANGELOWITZ, R.	.11	M	INFANT	RRZZZZUSA
KLIMATSCHUNA, L.	.11	M	INFANT	RRZZZZUSA

PASSENGER	AGE	SEX	OCCUPATION	PRV VIL DES

SHIP: SPAIN

FROM: LIVERPOOL
TO: NEW YORK
ARRIVED: 07 APRIL 1884

PASSENGER	AGE	SEX	OCCUPATION	PRV VIL DES
INIGLEY, JAS.	21	M	LABR	PLZZZZUSA
BRUVIRSKY, ETTY	21	F	W	PLZZZZUSA
EV, LEV	17	M	LABR	PLZZZZUSA
ABE	00	F	INF	PLZZZZUSA
LEVI, HANS	19	M	LABR	PLZZZZUSA
RALNOFSKI, JOSEF	38	M	LABR	PLZZZZUSA

SHIP: FRISIA

FROM: HAMBURG
TO: NEW YORK
ARRIVED: 08 APRIL 1884

PASSENGER	AGE	SEX	OCCUPATION	PRV VIL DES
ANDRZIEJEWSKA, SALOMEA	28	F	W	RRZZZZUSA
MIHAL	3	M	CHILD	RRZZZZUSA
ADOLF	.11	M	INFANT	RRZZZZUSA
MARIENKOFF, HANNE	19	F	SGL	RRZZZZUSA
DANIEL	15	M	LABR	RRZZZZUSA
ROSAMOWICZ, VINCENTY	33	M	LABR	RRZZZZUSA
MAGDALINE	19	F	W	RRZZZZUSA
SZIMANOWICZ, ANDR.	18	M	LABR	RRZZZZUSA
ZOKSZEWSKI, ADAM	25	M	UNKNOWN	RRZZZZUSA
NIZEZEWSKI, FRANZ	25	M	UNKNOWN	RRZZZZUSA
JOSEF	20	M	UNKNOWN	RRZZZZUSA
PABELOWITZSCH, JAN	18	M	UNKNOWN	RRZZZZUSA
SCHINKEWITZSCH, ANNE	18	F	SGL	RRZZZZUSA
BENIMOWITZ, MEIER	38	M	UNKNOWN	RRZZZZUSA
DENTSCH, DAVID	24	M	UNKNOWN	RRZZZZUSA
JASCHINSKI, THEODOR	23	M	UNKNOWN	RRZZZZUSA
WICZNIEWSKI, JOSEF	28	M	LABR	RRZZZZUSA
BUNKOWSKI, ANTON	25	M	UNKNOWN	RRZZZZUSA
PAVLOWSKI, FRANZ	38	M	UNKNOWN	RRZZZZUSA
BIERNACHI, FRANZ	24	M	UNKNOWN	RRZZZZUSA
ZOLLMANN, JOSEPH	20	M	LABR	RRZZZZUSA
OBAROFSKI, VALENTIN	41	M	LABR	RRZZZZUSA
KOHELSKI, ANTON	23	M	UNKNOWN	RRZZZZUSA
HEISE, MICHAEL	42	M	UNKNOWN	RRZZZZUSA
STRASINSKI, JOSEF	23	M	LABR	RRZZZZUSA
CHODORBSKI, ANNA	29	F	SGL	RRZZZZUSA
DRENDEL, CARL	38	M	MSN	RRZZZZUSA
KRUEGER, AUGUSTE	28	F	SGL	RRZZZZUSA
SOMARZEWSKI, FELIX	26	M	UNKNOWN	RRZZZZUSA
APOLLONIA	25	F	W	RRZZZZUSA
SPONKOWSKI, MICH.	27	M	LABR	RRZZZZUSA
NARZYNSKA, ANTONIA	25	F	W	RRZZZZUSA
JOSEF	4	M	CHILD	RRZZZZUSA
RENSKI, JOSEF	26	M	LABR	RRZZZZUSA
FILITZKI, MARTIN	35	M	UNKNOWN	RRZZZZUSA
STEFANSKI, JOHANN	23	M	UNKNOWN	RRZZZZUSA

SHIP: INDIA

FROM: HAMBURG
TO: NEW YORK
ARRIVED: 08 APRIL 1884

PASSENGER	AGE	SEX	OCCUPATION	PRV VIL DES
RATKEWICZ, JOSEF	20	M	UNKNOWN	PLZZZZNY
SWINSEZKI, MATHES	20	M	UNKNOWN	PLZZZZNY
NESINSKI, STANISL.	20	M	UNKNOWN	PLZZZZNY
SIGELSKI, MISENTI	21	M	UNKNOWN	PLZZZZNY
WASTRINSKI, JOS.	60	M	UNKNOWN	PLZZZZNY
BANGRASZ, ADAM	36	M	UNKNOWN	PLZZZZNY
JANOS	7	M	CHILD	PLZZZZNY
MALBACH, JAN	25	M	UNKNOWN	PLZZZZNY
HONOPKA, FELIX	26	M	UNKNOWN	PLZZZZNY
ZURAWSKI, JOS.	42	M	UNKNOWN	PLZZZZNY
KIERZKI, SAREL	22	M	UNKNOWN	PLZZZZNY
MISETOWITZ, DOMINIK	17	M	UNKNOWN	PLZZZZNY
JESCHIKEWIZ, JOS.	18	M	UNKNOWN	PLZZZZNY
ROSINERSKY, FRANZ	24	M	UNKNOWN	PLZZZZNY
PASTINSKI, IGNAZ	38	M	UNKNOWN	PLZZZZNY
FECKLA	29	F	W	PLZZZZNY
ANCLO	6	F	CHILD	PLZZZZNY
JOSEF	5	M	CHILD	PLZZZZNY
STANISLAUS	.11	M	INFANT	PLZZZZNY
WLADILAW	1	M	CHILD	PLZZZZNY
TOGIN, GUSTAV	18	M	LABR	RRZZZZNY
LEIDO, ADRANH	22	M	UNKNOWN	RRZZZZNY
ROWINSKY, VALENT.	30	M	LABR	RRZZZZNY
EMILIE	30	F	W	RRZZZZNY
HELEN	7	F	CHILD	RRZZZZNY
BRONISLAW	5	M	CHILD	RRZZZZNY
HEDWIG	.09	F	INFANT	RRZZZZNY
SCHISSKA, MARIE	32	F	SGL	RRZZZZNY

SHIP: NORMANDIE

FROM: HAVRE
TO: NEW YORK
ARRIVED: 08 APRIL 1884

PASSENGER	AGE	SEX	OCCUPATION	PRV VIL DES
MARCUS, JOSEPH	23	M	HTR	RRZZZZNY
U, HEDWIG	42	F	NN	RRZZZZCAL

SHIP: CYTHIA

FROM: LIVERPOOL AND QUEENSTOWN
TO: NEW YORK
ARRIVED: 09 APRIL 1884

PASSENGER	AGE	SEX	OCCUPATION	PRV VIL DES
POTER, MALKE	37	F	W	RRZZZZUSA
RAWITSCH, K.	00	M	CMST	RRZZZZUSA
MIREL	15	F	W	RRZZZZUSA
BRETSCHIN, PETER	28	M	LABR	RRZZZZUSA
BELBZ, IVAN	42	M	LABR	RRZZZZUSA
IVANISCH, JOSO	30	M	LABR	RRZZZZUSA
KALULEK, JOSEF	42	M	LABR	RRZZZZUSA
KUSMA, JOSEF	40	M	LABR	RRZZZZUSA
MAKALKY, IGNAZ	24	M	LABR	RRZZZZUSA
PATRYK, IVAN	24	M	LABR	RRZZZZUSA
GREGOR	32	M	LABR	RRZZZZUSA
PUSZKAR, MICHAL	30	M	LABR	RRZZZZUSA
STARUCH, MICHAL	34	M	LABR	RRZZZZUSA
UVIN, GEORGE	23	M	LABR	RRZZZZUSA
VINC, KRORAIT	20	M	LABR	RRZZZZUSA
WORTH, JOACHIM	21	M	LABR	RRZZZZUSA
ZIWALISCH, BASSIL	24	M	LABR	RRZZZZUSA
BUKOWCYK, LUDVIG	34	M	LABR	PLZZZZUSA
BEYER, FRIED	29	M	LABR	PLZZZZUSA
BEMDENHEIMER, G.	36	M	LABR	PLZZZZUSA
CHAVINSKY, VICTOR	21	M	LABR	PLZZZZUSA
CHINSCHIK, STANISLAUS	33	M	LABR	PLZZZZUSA
CHONNAK, MICHAL	31	M	LABR	PLZZZZUSA

PASSENGER	AGE	SEX	OCCUPATION	PRVL	VIL	DES
CHUSSEK, JAN	28	M	LABR	PL	ZZZZ	USA
CHERITZ, WASYL	38	M	LABR	PL	ZZZZ	USA
LOJINSKY, ANTON	37	M	LABR	PL	ZZZZ	USA
DEPOWSKY, VINCENTY	56	M	LABR	PL	ZZZZ	USA
VICTOR	50	M	LABR	PL	ZZZZ	USA
AUGUS.	22	M	LABR	PL	ZZZZ	USA
DAINELOVSKY, EDUARD	48	M	LABR	PL	ZZZZ	USA
DZWONCZYK, ANDRAS	26	M	LABR	PL	ZZZZ	USA
FRANSECKI, ALIX	25	M	LABR	PL	ZZZZ	USA
MICAL	21	M	LABR	PL	ZZZZ	USA
GEGORSKY, HRANZ	22	M	LABR	PL	ZZZZ	USA
GORTZYNSKI, JAN	28	M	LABR	PL	ZZZZ	USA
HULIK, TEODOR	26	M	LABR	PL	ZZZZ	USA
JANUSKEWSKI, JOSEF	26	M	LABR	PL	ZZZZ	USA
BOTINZKI, FRANZ	18	M	LABR	PL	ZZZZ	USA
SHEKERSKY, ANTON	24	M	LABR	PL	ZZZZ	USA
SCHROEDER, WILHELM	27	M	LABR	PL	ZZZZ	USA
KRUGER, ROS.	21	M	LABR	PL	ZZZZ	USA
PAWITZ, METCHAIRE	49	M	LABR	PL	ZZZZ	USA
KOBILA, MICHAL	28	M	LABR	PL	ZZZZ	USA
KROJA, WASYL	26	M	LABR	PL	ZZZZ	USA
KRORTINATZ, KLIMAN	31	M	LABR	PL	ZZZZ	USA
KAMIDTKA, PETER	26	M	LABR	PL	ZZZZ	USA
KIWITKOWSKY, MARCIN	36	M	LABR	PL	ZZZZ	USA
KERSKY, JOSEF	21	M	LABR	PL	ZZZZ	USA
KARIS, STANISLAUS	18	M	LABR	PL	ZZZZ	USA
LEIMER, VICTOR	25	M	LABR	PL	ZZZZ	USA
LAVETZKY, AND.	21	M	LABR	PL	ZZZZ	USA
LIS, ADAM	28	M	LABR	PL	ZZZZ	USA
MATEREWICZ, P.	30	M	LABR	PL	ZZZZ	USA
KOTOSKY, J.	23	M	LABR	PL	ZZZZ	USA
LUGRER, E.	11	M	LABR	PL	ZZZZ	USA
BASARKO, JAN	10	M	LABR	PL	ZZZZ	USA
MANCAK, GEORGE	27	M	LABR	PL	ZZZZ	USA
MAIER, JAN	29	M	LABR	PL	ZZZZ	USA
MAREOWITZ, JAN	28	M	LABR	PL	ZZZZ	USA
ROSMAN, ANDREAS	32	M	LABR	PL	ZZZZ	USA
GROCAN, ANDREAS	26	M	LABR	PL	ZZZZ	USA
BOJNAK, ANDREAS	20	M	LABR	PL	ZZZZ	USA
ZILMSKY, JAN	30	M	LABR	PL	ZZZZ	USA
M.	24	M	LABR	PL	ZZZZ	USA
MIKLOSEVITZ, LUDVIG	40	M	LABR	PL	ZZZZ	USA
MURA, JOHAN	28	M	LABR	PL	ZZZZ	USA
JOHANNES	23	M	LABR	PL	ZZZZ	USA
SCHLAWA, JACOB	17	M	LABR	PL	ZZZZ	USA
NEMETZ, PETER	26	M	LABR	PL	ZZZZ	USA
PAWET, NICOL	44	M	LABR	PL	ZZZZ	USA
PAL, METERKO	24	M	LABR	PL	ZZZZ	USA
RITETZKY, MATUS	38	M	LABR	PL	ZZZZ	USA
IGNACIOUS	18	M	LABR	PL	ZZZZ	USA
RUSKEWITZ, LORENZ	26	M	LABR	PL	ZZZZ	USA
REITER, WASIL	42	M	LABR	PL	ZZZZ	USA
STOROSCHKO, MAX	27	M	LABR	PL	ZZZZ	USA
SKAVBO, JOSEF	53	M	LABR	PL	ZZZZ	USA
SIKORA, PAUL	32	M	LABR	PL	ZZZZ	USA
SCHOJAK, AGT.	25	M	LABR	PL	ZZZZ	USA
SCHLUCHARJIKZ, JOSEF	31	M	LABR	PL	ZZZZ	USA
SABALANTZKAS, WINCENTAS	25	M	LABR	PL	ZZZZ	USA
SAVADANZKAS, THOMAS	22	M	LABR	PL	ZZZZ	USA
SCHEWENTZ, JAN	26	M	LABR	PL	ZZZZ	USA
ANDREAS	33	M	LABR	PL	ZZZZ	USA
SIMON, LILAS	29	M	SHMK	PL	ZZZZ	USA
SILBUSKY, SYLVESTER	50	M	SHMK	PL	ZZZZ	USA
TULOK, MATHIAS	55	M	LABR	PL	ZZZZ	USA
TEREVLE, SERVI	21	M	LABR	PL	ZZZZ	USA
WAWRINCE, C.	33	M	LABR	PL	ZZZZ	USA
ZASANRITZ, JOSEF	24	M	LABR	PL	ZZZZ	USA
ZELUS, NICODEME	18	M	LABR	PL	ZZZZ	USA
ZITTZE, AMBROSIUS	27	M	JNR	PL	ZZZZ	USA
MICHEL	25	M	JNR	PL	ZZZZ	USA
ZABINSKY, JAN	25	M	JNR	PL	ZZZZ	USA
BEIECK, MICHAL	35	M	LABR	PL	ZZZZ	USA
SOPHIE	27	F	W	PL	ZZZZ	USA
JUDRA	.04	F	INFANT	PL	ZZZZ	USA
CSARNICH, JACOB	40	M	LABR	PL	ZZZZ	USA
REGINA	40	F	W	PL	ZZZZ	USA
MARIE	18	F	SP	PL	ZZZZ	USA
FEDERWITZ, MARCIUS	24	M	FARMER	PL	ZZZZ	USA
CATHARINA	24	F	W	PL	ZZZZ	USA
KLEMERA, JOSEF	31	M	LABR	PL	ZZZZ	USA
AGATHA	27	F	W	PL	ZZZZ	USA
JAN	1	M	CHILD	PL	ZZZZ	USA
STANISLAUS	37	M	SHMK	PL	ZZZZ	USA
MARIAN	30	F	W	PL	ZZZZ	USA
JOSEFA	4	F	CHILD	PL	ZZZZ	USA
JOHANNA	2	F	CHILD	PL	ZZZZ	USA
JAN	1	M	CHILD	PL	ZZZZ	USA
KRICHIGLOWSKI, BORT.	36	M	LABR	PL	ZZZZ	USA
ANTON	10	M	CH	PL	ZZZZ	USA
APOLINA	9	F	CHILD	PL	ZZZZ	USA
KATLAVSKY, MORIA	26	F	W	PL	ZZZZ	USA
MARCANA	5	M	CHILD	PL	ZZZZ	USA
JOSEF	3	M	CHILD	PL	ZZZZ	USA
PETER	.11	M	INFANT	PL	ZZZZ	USA
MERZINSKI, MATIAS	25	M	LABR	PL	ZZZZ	USA
AGATA	25	F	W	PL	ZZZZ	USA
RAISMEMD	1	F	CHILD	PL	ZZZZ	USA
MACALDO, JACOB	55	M	FARMER	PL	ZZZZ	USA
LUDWITA	35	F	W	PL	ZZZZ	USA
FRANZ	11	M	CH	PL	ZZZZ	USA
MORIAN	10	M	CH	PL	ZZZZ	USA
MICHAL	8	M	CHILD	PL	ZZZZ	USA
ANNA	1	F	CHILD	PL	ZZZZ	USA
OPALKA, MATH	49	M	LABR	PL	ZZZZ	USA
KATHARINA	50	F	W	PL	ZZZZ	USA
HERMAN	19	M	LABR	PL	ZZZZ	USA
JOHANN	16	M	LABR	PL	ZZZZ	USA
PATTA, MATTHIAS	33	M	LABR	PL	ZZZZ	USA
FRANCISCA	30	F	W	PL	ZZZZ	USA
FRANZ	8	M	CHILD	PL	ZZZZ	USA
JOHANN	4	M	CHILD	PL	ZZZZ	USA
ANTON	.08	M	INFANT	PL	ZZZZ	USA
SOCHO, FRANZ	26	M	LABR	PL	ZZZZ	USA
FRANCISCA	18	F	W	PL	ZZZZ	USA
APOLINA	.10	F	INFANT	PL	ZZZZ	USA
ZEWESKY, ADAM	27	M	LABR	PL	ZZZZ	USA
SARGER, MATHIAS	41	M	LABR	PL	ZZZZ	USA
WINCENSKY, W.	37	M	LABR	PL	ZZZZ	USA
AGATA	33	F	W	PL	ZZZZ	USA
ANTON	.09	M	INFANT	PL	ZZZZ	USA
FRANZ	.09	M	INFANT	PL	ZZZZ	USA

SHIP: ANCHORIA

FROM: GLASGOW
TO: NEW YORK
ARRIVED: 10 APRIL 1884

PASSENGER	AGE	SEX	OCCUPATION	PRVL	VIL	DES
DRAYNN, JOSEF	22	M	UNKNOWN	RR	ZZZZ	USA

SHIP: ERIN

FROM: LONDON
TO: NEW YORK
ARRIVED: 11 APRIL 1884

PASSENGER	AGE	SEX	OCCUPATION	PRVL	VIL	DES
DZENSOKEC, MOSES	40	M	LABR	PL	ZZZZ	NY
STEBEL, BERNHARD	28	M	WCHMKR	PL	ZZZZ	NY

PASSENGER	AGE	SEX	OCCUPATION	PRV	VIL	DES

SHIP: ST. OF PENNSYLVANIA

FROM: GLASGOW AND LARNE
TO: NEW YORK
ARRIVED: 11 APRIL 1884

PASSENGER	AGE	SEX	OCCUPATION	PRV VIL DES
ULMSKY, VALENTINE	25	M	LABR	RRZZZZUSA

SHIP: LESSING

FROM: HAMBURG AND HAVRE
TO: NEW YORK
ARRIVED: 12 APRIL 1884

PASSENGER	AGE	SEX	OCCUPATION	PRV VIL DES
MIKLOSZEWICZ, IWAN	34	M	UNKNOWN	RRZZZZUSA
KOSSINSKY, ALESSA	36	F	UNKNOWN	RRZZZZUSA
GRAJEFSKI, ARON.	52	M	DLR	RRZZZZUSA
BASCHE	52	F	W	RRZZZZUSA
JUTE	8	F	CHILD	RRZZZZUSA
SCHLAUME	7	M	CHILD	RRZZZZUSA
SA----, HIRSCH	29	M	UNKNOWN	RRZZZZUSA
MARIANNE	27	F	UNKNOWN	RRZZZZUSA
SCHMER, ARON	20	M	LABR	RRZZZZUSA
FRENDE	20	F	W	RRZZZZUSA
KERAZSEWESZ, STANISL.	25	M	LABR	RRZZZZUSA
TWERBERET, PAUL	24	M	UNKNOWN	RRZZZZUSA
POGSZEBA, ALB.	35	M	LABR	RRZZZZUSA
ANNA	23	F	W	RRZZZZUSA
PALMER, ALBERT	37	M	LABR	RRZZZZUSA
KARWIESKI, MICHAEL	45	M	LABR	RRZZZZUSA
CATH.	40	F	W	RRZZZZUSA
VICTORIA	15	F	CH	RRZZZZUSA
STANISL.	4	M	CHILD	RRZZZZUSA
OSTROWSKI, THEODOR	21	M	LABR	RRZZZZUSA
IWAN	18	M	UNKNOWN	RRZZZZUSA
WOJEISH	30	M	UNKNOWN	RRZZZZUSA
MATH.	41	M	UNKNOWN	RRZZZZUSA
TRIANOWSKI, JOSEPH	23	M	UNKNOWN	RRZZZZUSA
NIEMCEZOWSKI, JULIAN	20	M	UNKNOWN	RRZZZZUSA
NORKINWIESZ, ANTON	19	M	LABR	RRZZZZUSA
BOOMAN, FRIEDR.	17	M	CPR	RRZZZZUSA
LIPPE, MORITH	29	M	UNKNOWN	RRZZZZUSA
PAULINE	28	F	W	RRZZZZUSA
FRIEDOR	.11	M	INFANT	RRZZZZUSA
ALBERT	.01	M	INFANT	RRZZZZUSA
TOLDTZYK, ANDRE	20	M	LABR	RRZZZZUSA
JOHM, ROBERT	22	M	UNKNOWN	RRZZZZUSA
ZAREMBA, WADIM	21	M	UNKNOWN	RRZZZZUSA
NIMZ, EMILIE	35	F	W	RRZZZZUSA
BERTHA	8	F	CHILD	RRZZZZUSA
AUGUST	5	M	CHILD	RRZZZZUSA
MIKAS, DIELES	47	M	UNKNOWN	RRZZZZUSA
SIKOWITZ, ANTON	27	M	UNKNOWN	RRZZZZUSA
JOSES, DIELES	22	M	UNKNOWN	RRZZZZUSA
BUTHKEWITZ, JAN	42	M	UNKNOWN	RRZZZZUSA
SCHURSKI, STANISL.	24	M	UNKNOWN	RRZZZZUSA
PADEJENI, AUGUST	21	M	UNKNOWN	RRZZZZUSA
PRETKEWITZ, JACOB	40	M	UNKNOWN	RRZZZZUSA
JASKEWITZ, M-----I	20	M	UNKNOWN	RRZZZZUSA
GERTHSHANIV, PAUL	23	M	UNKNOWN	RRZZZZUSA
PALSCHI, FRANZ	25	M	UNKNOWN	RRZZZZUSA
WOSARIS, MUTSCHI	20	M	UNKNOWN	RRZZZZUSA
JUSCHK-LIS, KAISIS	22	M	UNKNOWN	RRZZZZUSA
POLOSCHIA, ANTONUS	24	M	UNKNOWN	RRZZZZUSA
POLOSCH-, CARL	28	M	UNKNOWN	RRZZZZUSA
ALERZANOS, MIRKOS	24	M	UNKNOWN	RRZZZZUSA
FRANZKOWSKI, IGNATZ	26	M	UNKNOWN	RRZZZZUSA

SHIP: NOORDLAND

FROM: ANTWERP
TO: NEW YORK
ARRIVED: 12 APRIL 1884

PASSENGER	AGE	SEX	OCCUPATION	PRV VIL DES
CHESKER, CONST.	25	M	FARMER	PLZZZZNY
JUL.	22	F	UNKNOWN	PLZZZZNY
KURKOWSKA, ANT.	19	M	UNKNOWN	PLZZZZNY
HESNIG, VERON.	9	M	CHILD	PLZZZZNY
KOLCZINSKI, VUF.	32	M	LABR	PLZZZZUNK
JOHN.	10	M	UNKNOWN	PLZZZZUNK
CARAS, CASIMIR	65	M	LABR	PLZZZZUNK
MAR.	60	F	UNKNOWN	PLZZZZUNK
KRINRATAYHS, J.	28	M	LABR	PLZZZZUNK
JANKONSKI, J.	28	M	UNKNOWN	PLZZZZUNK
BURRAVIRRE, JOH.	28	M	UNKNOWN	PLZZZZUNK
PRAWSIK, CAS.	22	M	LABR	PLZZZZUNK
SCHMAKEL, ALB.	29	M	UNKNOWN	PLZZZZUNK
HERM.	00	M	INF	PLZZZZUNK
KRZYZAGOSTI, TH.	21	M	UNKNOWN	PLZZZZUNK
JASZICK, ANNA	26	F	UNKNOWN	PLZZZZUNK
LACKRZENSKI, JAC.	28	M	UNKNOWN	PLZZZZUNK
BYEBKA, T.	27	M	UNKNOWN	PLZZZZUNK
SZARWAK, J.	22	M	UNKNOWN	PLZZZZUNK
BICZYNSKO, ANNA	33	F	UNKNOWN	PLZZZZUNK
PERSZ, MEAR	28	F	UNKNOWN	PLZZZZUNK
ANDECZICK, ANNA	00	F	INF	PLZZZZUNK

SHIP: VALENCIA

FROM: UNKNOWN
TO: NEW YORK
ARRIVED: 12 APRIL 1884

PASSENGER	AGE	SEX	OCCUPATION	PRV VIL DES
GROUSHEN, FELIX	30	M	BRKR	RRZZZZVZU

SHIP: ASSYRIAN MONARCH

FROM: LONDON
TO: NEW YORK
ARRIVED: 14 APRIL 1884

PASSENGER	AGE	SEX	OCCUPATION	PRV VIL DES
PHALAUD, E.A.	20	F	DMS	PLZZZZNY
LOHANSEN, C.	21	M	LABR	PLZZZZNY
BYRON, A.B.	25	M	UNKNOWN	PLZZZZNY
SCHLOUPT, VICTOR	30	M	UNKNOWN	PLZZZZNY
THEISER, PRENI	20	M	UNKNOWN	PLZZZZNY
ABRAHAMS, ADOLPHUS	20	M	UNKNOWN	PLZZZZNY
KOCH, C.	30	M	UNKNOWN	PLZZZZNY
DREHER, J.N.	21	M	DMS	PLZZZZNY
FELTZER, HENRY	20	M	LABR	PLZZZZNY
WEBER, PAUL	30	M	UNKNOWN	PLZZZZNY
AUSTENSEN, J.	21	M	UNKNOWN	PLZZZZNY

PASSENGER	AGE	SEX	OCCUPATION	PRIV	VIL	DES

SHIP: CITY OF MONTREAL

FROM: LIVERPOOL
TO: NEW YORK
ARRIVED: 14 APRIL 1884

PASSENGER	AGE	SEX	OCCUPATION	PRIV	VIL	DES
MOSER, JAS.	29	M	UNKNOWN	RR	ZZZZ	PHI
ASTWITZ, ONIFS-L.	45	M	UNKNOWN	RR	ZZZZ	NY
DAKABANSKY, ANDREAS	29	M	UNKNOWN	RR	ZZZZ	NY
KRABUR, CARL	19	M	UNKNOWN	RR	ZZZZ	NY
REBI, IWAN	33	M	UNKNOWN	RR	ZZZZ	NY
LANE, MARTIN	23	M	UNKNOWN	RR	ZZZZ	NY
BUCHALTER, JOHAN	23	M	UNKNOWN	RR	ZZZZ	NY
KUBELDIS, ODOLFO	22	M	UNKNOWN	RR	ZZZZ	PA
BROMISTAN	22	F	W	RR	ZZZZ	PA
PETROS	1	M	CHILD	RR	ZZZZ	PA
THEMAN, ESTHER	27	F	SVNT	RR	ZZZZ	NY
WAXNOSTNY, EVAN	46	M	LABR	RR	ZZZZ	NY
SELIGMAN, JOSEL	48	M	UNKNOWN	RR	ZZZZ	NY
ANAGE	45	F	W	RR	ZZZZ	NY
LACHOWOSKY, DAVID	24	M	LABR	RR	ZZZZ	NY
MIKE	19	F	W	RR	ZZZZ	NY
ANNA	1	F	CHILD	RR	ZZZZ	NY
KOW, ABRAHAM	40	M	LABR	RR	ZZZZ	NY
LOMAS, ANTON	25	M	UNKNOWN	RR	ZZZZ	NY
HEYDINGER, ADOLF	44	M	UNKNOWN	RR	ZZZZ	NY
ADMISKY, MARTIN	35	M	UNKNOWN	RR	ZZZZ	NY
TRUSMAN, AUGUST	21	M	UNKNOWN	RR	ZZZZ	NY
WASIT, BALENTIN	25	M	UNKNOWN	PL	ZZZZ	UNK
JANOWSKY, ANDREAS	47	M	UNKNOWN	PL	ZZZZ	UNK
JERANINSKY, STANISLAUS	36	M	UNKNOWN	PL	ZZZZ	SFC
JOSEFA	36	F	W	PL	ZZZZ	SFC
FRANZ	10	M	CH	PL	ZZZZ	SFC
CATH.	7	F	CHILD	PL	ZZZZ	SFC
IGNATZ	1	M	CHILD	PL	ZZZZ	SFC
SVIDALLA, SIMON	41	M	LABR	PL	ZZZZ	PA
ANTONIA	41	F	W	PL	ZZZZ	PA
MARIANA	11	F	CH	PL	ZZZZ	PA
JOHANNA	7	F	CHILD	PL	ZZZZ	PA
CATH.	1	F	CHILD	PL	ZZZZ	PA
ROSENBLUM, MICHL	46	M	LABR	PL	ZZZZ	NY
SLATE	60	F	W	PL	ZZZZ	NY
SARAH	40	F	UNKNOWN	PL	ZZZZ	NY
HINDE	11	F	CH	PL	ZZZZ	NY
LEISER	10	M	UNKNOWN	PL	ZZZZ	NY
ABRAM	8	M	CHILD	PL	ZZZZ	NY
CHAYE	6	F	CHILD	PL	ZZZZ	NY
REINKE, JOSES	22	M	LABR	PL	ZZZZ	NY
GESIMER, PETROS	22	M	UNKNOWN	PL	ZZZZ	NY
BEMATZKER, JONAS	31	M	UNKNOWN	PL	ZZZZ	NY
HAKENITZ, JONA	21	M	UNKNOWN	PL	ZZZZ	NY
BARONOWSKY, BASTROM	20	M	UNKNOWN	PL	ZZZZ	NY
ALEWITZ, MACEY-WAY	22	M	UNKNOWN	PL	ZZZZ	NY
KAZALAMESS, FERZ.	18	M	UNKNOWN	PL	ZZZZ	NY
WAICZMESS, JAN	25	M	UNKNOWN	PL	ZZZZ	NY
MATIV, JANS	23	M	UNKNOWN	PL	ZZZZ	NY
POHNOWSKY, JACOB	44	M	UNKNOWN	PL	ZZZZ	NY
SDOLIG, MACIEG	30	M	UNKNOWN	PL	ZZZZ	PA
MENEIS, JOSEF	18	M	UNKNOWN	PL	ZZZZ	PA
MACHINIS, JERRY	30	M	UNKNOWN	PL	ZZZZ	PA
KAWELOSKY, WIGAS	42	M	UNKNOWN	PL	ZZZZ	CIN
JULIENSKY, VINANT	36	M	UNKNOWN	PL	ZZZZ	CIN
JUSCHINKI, KASMER	50	M	UNKNOWN	PL	ZZZZ	CIN
ASSAN, CARL	22	M	UNKNOWN	PL	ZZZZ	CIN
RUSSINSKY, ANTON	20	M	UNKNOWN	PL	ZZZZ	CIN
MINNEWITZ, SIMON	41	M	LABR	PL	ZZZZ	PA
ADAM	16	M	UNKNOWN	PL	ZZZZ	PA
PAJOWIZ, MICHAS	25	M	UNKNOWN	PL	ZZZZ	NY
DANGLOW, VENCENT	23	M	UNKNOWN	PL	ZZZZ	NY
WATMAS, JEWZE	40	M	UNKNOWN	PL	ZZZZ	NY
BANROCK, JOSEF	36	M	UNKNOWN	PL	ZZZZ	NY
SARBI, JURAS	24	M	UNKNOWN	PL	ZZZZ	NY
FUSCHKY, PETRIUS	28	M	UNKNOWN	PL	ZZZZ	NY
ZIDERMANAS, ANTON	48	M	UNKNOWN	PL	ZZZZ	NY
MIKELANIS, PETRUS	26	M	UNKNOWN	PL	ZZZZ	NY
KULAK, ALEX	38	M	UNKNOWN	PL	ZZZZ	NY
MALLIS, ANTON	21	M	UNKNOWN	PL	ZZZZ	PA
BALA, JANATZ	20	M	UNKNOWN	PL	ZZZZ	NY
MICHLITZ, MICHAL	42	M	UNKNOWN	PL	ZZZZ	PA
VERONICA	36	F	W	PL	ZZZZ	PA
JOSEF	11	M	CH	PL	ZZZZ	PA
JOHANNA	10	F	UNKNOWN	PL	ZZZZ	PA
ANNA	9	F	CHILD	PL	ZZZZ	PA
MARIANNA	3	F	CHILD	PL	ZZZZ	PA
JOHANA	1	F	CHILD	PL	ZZZZ	PA
SCHULTZ, WILHELM	26	M	LABR	PL	ZZZZ	CH
LINIGLO, ALBERT	30	M	UNKNOWN	PL	ZZZZ	NY
UIZATE, ALBERT	35	M	UNKNOWN	PL	ZZZZ	NY
MARIA	35	F	W	PL	ZZZZ	NY
EDAMIC, ALX.	27	M	LABR	PL	ZZZZ	NY
PRYZBYLER, A.	30	M	UNKNOWN	PL	ZZZZ	NY

SHIP: CIRCASSIA

FROM: GLASGOW
TO: NEW YORK
ARRIVED: 16 APRIL 1884

PASSENGER	AGE	SEX	OCCUPATION	PRIV	VIL	DES
WUSZBUSKI, ST.	30	M	LABR	RR	ZZZZ	USA
JEKALIS, JAKOB	40	M	UNKNOWN	RR	ZZZZ	USA
KASCHANOWSKY, JAN	26	M	UNKNOWN	RR	ZZZZ	USA
BRIEWITZ, JULIUS	21	M	UNKNOWN	RR	ZZZZ	USA
PICH, JOHAN	28	M	UNKNOWN	RR	ZZZZ	USA
JACHEWITZ, CARL	26	M	UNKNOWN	RR	ZZZZ	USA
DOBUSCHNSKY, IWAN	26	M	UNKNOWN	RR	ZZZZ	USA
JULIAN	24	M	UNKNOWN	RR	ZZZZ	USA
LUDVIG	22	M	UNKNOWN	RR	ZZZZ	USA
IWANOWSKY, ALEX	24	M	UNKNOWN	RR	ZZZZ	USA
GOWACKI, FELIX	30	M	UNKNOWN	RR	ZZZZ	USA
LIS, JAKOB	29	M	UNKNOWN	RR	ZZZZ	USA
NONEURZ, ALEX	28	M	CL	RR	ZZZZ	USA
THALPUTH, MENDAL	16	M	CH	RR	ZZZZ	USA
MICHELSON, A.	29	M	UNKNOWN	RR	ZZZZ	USA
SWIK, FRANZ	25	M	LABR	RR	ZZZZ	USA
NIDZINSKY, OSEF	26	M	UNKNOWN	RR	ZZZZ	USA
KOSLIKOWSKY, THOS.	32	M	UNKNOWN	RR	ZZZZ	USA
WITCH, JOHAR	26	M	UNKNOWN	RR	ZZZZ	USA
BIEROMSKY, TOPHIL	28	M	UNKNOWN	RR	ZZZZ	USA
HIKULENWITCH, JOSEF	33	M	FARMER	RR	ZZZZ	USA
JOSEFA	28	F	W	RR	ZZZZ	USA
MANEL	26	M	UNKNOWN	RR	ZZZZ	USA
BOL.	.08	M	INFANT	RR	ZZZZ	USA
KOSLOWISKY, THOM.	44	M	FARMER	RR	ZZZZ	USA
ROSALIE	38	F	W	RR	ZZZZ	USA
CYPNIAN	11	M	UNKNOWN	RR	ZZZZ	USA
ANNA	8	F	CHILD	RR	ZZZZ	USA
FRANZWA	.11	M	INFANT	RR	ZZZZ	USA

SHIP: LABRADOR

FROM: HAVRE
TO: NEW YORK
ARRIVED: 17 APRIL 1884

PASSENGER	AGE	SEX	OCCUPATION	PRIV	VIL	DES
STOIRENKA, ANSELME	29	M	HTR	RR	ZZZZ	NY

PASSENGER	AGE	SEX	OCCUPATION	PRV	VIL	DES
SHIP: BOHEMIA						
FROM: HAMBURG						
TO: NEW YORK						
ARRIVED: 18 APRIL 1884						
ROREN, MORES	30	M	LABR	RR	ZZZZ	USA
PETROWSKI, PIADR.	20	M	UNKNOWN	RR	ZZZZ	USA
MALKOWSKI, ALEX.	20	M	UNKNOWN	RR	ZZZZ	USA
RUTCLANIS, JOSEF	20	M	UNKNOWN	RR	ZZZZ	USA
ZERGEWICZ, KUEZMAR	28	M	UNKNOWN	RR	ZZZZ	USA
ZIBULSKI, PANFIER	27	M	UNKNOWN	RR	ZZZZ	USA
MAXINOF, ARON	30	M	UNKNOWN	RR	ZZZZ	USA
SCHNWILL, ZICHAN	22	M	UNKNOWN	RR	ZZZZ	USA
PAAKOJINSKI, STANISL.	24	M	UNKNOWN	RR	ZZZZ	USA
BAHDANOWICZ, JULIAN	20	M	LABR	RR	ZZZZ	USA
PRUSKI, FRANZ	22	M	LABR	RR	ZZZZ	USA
ANDR.	18	M	UNKNOWN	RR	ZZZZ	USA
MIKULSKA, LUDWIG	42	M	LABR	RR	ZZZZ	USA
VERONIKA	16	F	CH	RR	ZZZZ	USA
MARIANNA	6	F	CHILD	RR	ZZZZ	USA
BRONISLAWA	3	F	CHILD	RR	ZZZZ	USA
ALEXANDER	00	M	INF	RR	ZZZZ	USA
WANZDAN, FERDINAND	36	M	LABR	RR	ZZZZ	USA
WILHELMINE	32	F	W	RR	ZZZZ	USA
EMIL	9	M	CHILD	RR	ZZZZ	USA
REINHOLD	7	M	CHILD	RR	ZZZZ	USA
AUGUST	5	M	CHILD	RR	ZZZZ	USA
MINNA	3	F	CHILD	RR	ZZZZ	USA
BERTHOLD	00	M	INF	RR	ZZZZ	USA
STOEBNER, ALBERT	34	M	SMH	RR	ZZZZ	USA
TANBENREIM, WILHELM	53	M	FARMER	RR	ZZZZ	USA
ZARADA, BLAJE	00	U	UNKNOWN	RR	ZZZZ	USA
KOFNATZKA, CANST.	00	U	UNKNOWN	RR	ZZZZ	USA
KOWALCZYK, JAC.	00	U	UNKNOWN	RR	ZZZZ	USA
GRAMS, GUSTAV	00	U	UNKNOWN	RR	ZZZZ	USA
SHIP: FULDA						
FROM: BREMEN						
TO: NEW YORK						
ARRIVED: 19 APRIL 1884						
JANSSEN, HCH.	22	M	UNKNOWN	RR	ZZZZ	USA
HELENE	20	F	UNKNOWN	RR	ZZZZ	USA
HCH.	.11	M	INFANT	RR	ZZZZ	USA
SHIP: GALLIA						
FROM: LIVERPOOL						
TO: NEW YORK						
ARRIVED: 19 APRIL 1884						
HELNER, GUSTAV	23	M	UNKNOWN	RR	ZZZZ	USA
SHIP: HOHENSTAUFEN						
FROM: BREMEN						
TO: NEW YORK						
ARRIVED: 19 APRIL 1884						
JABS, FERD.	26	M	UNKNOWN	RR	ZZZZ	USA
FINGER, PAULINE	20	F	UNKNOWN	RR	ZZZZ	USA
BANKOWSKI, FERD.	26	M	LABR	RR	ZZZZ	USA
SHIP: AURANIA						
FROM: LIVERPOOL AND QUEENSTOWN						
TO: NEW YORK						
ARRIVED: 21 APRIL 1884						
WINARS, ROSS-R.MR	33	M	GENT	RR	ZZZZ	USA
R.R.MRS	24	F	W	RR	ZZZZ	USA
SHIP: CALAND						
FROM: ROTTERDAM						
TO: NEW YORK						
ARRIVED: 21 APRIL 1884						
PORASKI, WLADISLAW	21	M	SHMK	PL	ZZZZ	USA
ALOIS	25	F	NN	PL	ZZZZ	USA
WLADA	22	F	DMS	PL	ZZZZ	USA
LUQUNSKY, JOSEPH	24	M	FARMER	PL	ZZZZ	USA
POZORSKI, PAULINA	21	F	SVNT	PL	ZZZZ	USA
BLANSCHKE, LOUISE	26	F	NN	PL	ZZZZ	USA
EMIL	4	M	CHILD	PL	ZZZZ	USA
FRANZ	4	M	CHILD	PL	ZZZZ	USA
SHIP: CITY OF CHESTER						
FROM: LIVERPOOL AND QUEENSTOWN						
TO: NEW YORK						
ARRIVED: 21 APRIL 1884						
VOSS, HEINRICH	25	M	LABR	PL	ZZZZ	NY
ZANKOWICZ, PIOTER	30	M	FARMER	PL	ZZZZ	NY
LERKOT, FEDOR	50	M	FARMER	PL	ZZZZ	NY
FERDRIS	11	M	CH	PL	ZZZZ	NY
LEWITEN, HIRSCH	19	M	LABR	RR	ZZZZ	NY
SIKORAWSKA, MARIE	48	F	W	PL	ZZZZ	NY
FRANTISEK	11	F	CH	PL	ZZZZ	NY
WOYTEK	8	F	CHILD	PL	ZZZZ	NY
GABRIEL, JAN	27	M	JWLR	PL	ZZZZ	NY
JOSEPF	20	M	JWLR	PL	ZZZZ	NY

PASSENGER	AGE	SEX	OCCUPATION	PRV	VIL	DES
SHIP: GELLERT						
FROM: HAMBURG AND HAVRE						
TO: NEW YORK						
ARRIVED: 21 APRIL 1884						
SZEZEPKOWSKI, LUDWIG	24	M	LABR	RR	ZZZZ	USA
MENZEL, FRANZ	18	M	WVR	RR	ZZZZ	USA
FRIEDLAND, ABRAH.	40	M	LABR	RR	ZZZZ	USA
LUKAITIS, BALTRUS	24	M	LABR	RR	ZZZZ	USA
LOBIKES, BARTH.	25	M	LABR	RR	ZZZZ	USA
SHIP: NEVADA						
FROM: LIVERPOOL						
TO: NEW YORK						
ARRIVED: 21 APRIL 1884						
RABUSOWEZ, ANSANUS	34	M	LABR	PL	ZZZZ	USA
FAMISTZA, RAWTAS	34	M	LABR	PL	ZZZZ	USA
WASILANSBUS, JONAS	25	M	LABR	PL	ZZZZ	USA
ROGELIS, MATHIMSHAS	30	F	W	PL	ZZZZ	USA
RINGONLIZAS, ANOSONING	27	M	LABR	PL	ZZZZ	USA
SAWIZZE, POINNES	27	M	LABR	PL	ZZZZ	USA
CHIHATSHI, M.CHATZ	25	M	LABR	PL	ZZZZ	USA
JOSWICEK, ANRIEAS	43	M	LABR	PL	ZZZZ	USA
ANSONI	36	F	W	PL	ZZZZ	USA
AUREAS	15	M	LABR	PL	ZZZZ	USA
ZATVICH	.09	M	INFANT	PL	ZZZZ	USA
MANGOIRSGI, JOSEF	28	M	LABR	PL	ZZZZ	USA
LICROTA, ANTON	49	M	LABR	PL	ZZZZ	USA
BUNAS, JAN	23	M	LABR	PL	ZZZZ	USA
MIVATAYOTZ, VINCENTY	30	M	LABR	PL	ZZZZ	USA
MAYDA	23	F	W	PL	ZZZZ	USA
MARIANE	.06	F	INFANT	PL	ZZZZ	USA
FEGAL, JOSEF	35	M	LABR	PL	ZZZZ	USA
AUGUSTINE, JANOS	46	F	W	PL	ZZZZ	USA
SERDA, WASIL	24	M	LABR	PL	ZZZZ	USA
STAIRISTZ, ANDREAS	38	M	LABR	PL	ZZZZ	USA
SUREZ, JANOS	25	F	W	PL	ZZZZ	USA
SERBERA, WSM.	43	M	LABR	PL	ZZZZ	USA
SRUBUS, FASLO	35	M	LABR	PL	ZZZZ	USA
HANNA	30	F	W	PL	ZZZZ	USA
WASEL	10	M	CH	PL	ZZZZ	USA
MARIA	9	F	CHILD	PL	ZZZZ	USA
TELKA	7	M	CHILD	PL	ZZZZ	USA
LASSO	.10	F	INFANT	PL	ZZZZ	USA
CLOOMMAH, U	24	M	LABR	PL	ZZZZ	USA
SEREBA, WASTI	28	M	LABR	PL	ZZZZ	USA
ALKIVATIN, JERIN	45	F	W	PL	ZZZZ	USA
VERONA	4	F	CHILD	PL	ZZZZ	USA
ROMAN, ERZE	18	M	LABR	PL	ZZZZ	USA
MILBRECK, FUZANCE	20	M	LABR	PL	ZZZZ	USA
FUNOKI, VALENTINI	34	F	W	PL	ZZZZ	USA
FRADORSKY, MARTIN	31	M	LABR	PL	ZZZZ	USA
ANTONI	23	F	W	PL	ZZZZ	USA
ANNIE	5	F	CHILD	PL	ZZZZ	USA

PASSENGER	AGE	SEX	OCCUPATION	PRV	VIL	DES
SHIP: POLYNESIA						
FROM: HAMBURG						
TO: NEW YORK						
ARRIVED: 21 APRIL 1884						
SUNDA, JOHANN	30	M	LABR	PL	ZZZZ	NY
POLTONYKA, JOHANN	30	M	LABR	PL	ZZZZ	IL
BARTUSKA, MATTHIAS	32	M	LABR	PL	ZZZZ	IL
ELISAB.	22	F	WO	PL	ZZZZ	IL
JOHANN	4	M	CHILD	PL	ZZZZ	IL
JOSEFA	.06	F	INFANT	PL	ZZZZ	IL
SHIP: FURNESSIA						
FROM: GLASGOW AND MOVILLE						
TO: NEW YORK						
ARRIVED: 22 APRIL 1884						
SCHOTT, JAN	36	M	LABR	PL	ZZZZ	USA
THERESE	30	F	W	PL	ZZZZ	USA
IWAN	2	M	CHILD	PL	ZZZZ	USA
N.ANIS.	.10	M	INFANT	PL	ZZZZ	USA
HONARHOWSKI, PHILIPP	47	M	LABR	PL	ZZZZ	USA
MARIANNE	44	F	W	PL	ZZZZ	USA
LUDWICKE	17	M	LABR	PL	ZZZZ	USA
AGNES	10	F	CH	PL	ZZZZ	USA
FRANCESKA	5	F	CHILD	PL	ZZZZ	USA
JACOB	2	M	CHILD	PL	ZZZZ	USA
FR.ZERBST	17	M	LABR	PL	ZZZZ	USA
REDWICK, ANDREAS	22	M	LABR	PL	ZZZZ	USA
RUSKOVSKI, STANISL.	29	M	LABR	PL	ZZZZ	USA
MICHL.	29	F	W	PL	ZZZZ	USA
MARIANNA	4	F	CHILD	PL	ZZZZ	USA
THEHEA	1	F	CHILD	PL	ZZZZ	USA
THOS.	.10	M	INFANT	PL	ZZZZ	USA
CATH.	3	F	CHILD	PL	ZZZZ	USA
WICHLAM, JOHANN	45	F	W	PL	ZZZZ	USA
PETER	23	M	LABR	PL	ZZZZ	USA
MARIA.	11	F	CH	PL	ZZZZ	USA
JOHANA	11	F	CH	PL	ZZZZ	USA
IGNATZ	8	M	CHILD	PL	ZZZZ	USA
MICHALSKI, JOS.	31	M	LABR	PL	ZZZZ	USA
EB.	28	F	W	PL	ZZZZ	USA
LEON	6	M	CHILD	PL	ZZZZ	USA
STANISL.	2	M	CHILD	PL	ZZZZ	USA
PETEGIA	.09	M	INFANT	PL	ZZZZ	USA
JULIANSWELLY, PROB.	28	M	LABR	PL	ZZZZ	USA
LEWANDOESKI, VALENTIN	32	M	LABR	PL	ZZZZ	USA
FRAN.	23	F	W	PL	ZZZZ	USA
HABAR.	4	M	CHILD	PL	ZZZZ	USA
IGNACY	2	M	CHILD	PL	ZZZZ	USA
MARIANA	.02	F	INFANT	PL	ZZZZ	USA
STACHOWICK, JAN	31	M	LABR	PL	ZZZZ	USA
MARIANA	36	F	W	PL	ZZZZ	USA
THOMAZ	6	M	CHILD	PL	ZZZZ	USA
VALENTIN	.10	M	INFANT	PL	ZZZZ	USA
SZIGO, JEDREZY	26	M	LABR	PL	ZZZZ	USA
HAROLINE	24	F	W	PL	ZZZZ	USA
ANNA	.08	F	INFANT	PL	ZZZZ	USA
RAKOS, THOS.	34	M	LABR	PL	ZZZZ	USA
JADENIGA	34	F	W	PL	ZZZZ	USA
CATH.	.11	F	INFANT	PL	ZZZZ	USA
BARRZUK, THEKLA	30	F	W	PL	ZZZZ	USA
MICHL.	.07	M	INFANT	PL	ZZZZ	USA
SNIKE, ANDRAZ	35	M	LABR	PL	ZZZZ	USA
SLEZ.	29	F	W	PL	ZZZZ	USA
FREDYK, FRANC	26	M	LABR	PL	ZZZZ	USA
URSULA	22	F	W	PL	ZZZZ	USA

PASSENGER	AGE	SEX	OCCUPATION	PRV VIL DES
ZELOHG, JOSEF	28	M	LABR	PLZZZZUSA
HATHRINA	25	F	W	PLZZZZUSA
GITZIN, ULRIKE	25	M	LABR	PLZZZZUSA
EUPH.	.10	F	INFANT	PLZZZZUSA
SYDAK, ANTON	47	M	LABR	PLZZZZUSA
JOHANNA	26	F	W	PLZZZZUSA
GRWAT, JAN	24	M	LABR	PLZZZZUSA
JAGN.	19	F	W	PLZZZZUSA
BEBLAK, DOM.	33	M	LABR	PLZZZZUSA
HARETEZKE, MARTIN	44	M	LABR	PLZZZZUSA
TORBA, PAWET	28	M	LABR	PLZZZZUSA
WIATROWSKI, LEON	60	M	LABR	PLZZZZUSA
GACZDA, PAVET	35	M	LABR	PLZZZZUSA
MUNICK, JAN	35	M	LABR	PLZZZZUSA
WOJTARCEZEK, MARTIN	28	M	LABR	PLZZZZUSA
WEGRYCIZN, MARTIN	40	M	LABR	PLZZZZUSA
CHERBACK, SIDOR	31	M	LABR	PLZZZZUSA
RISKO, JANKO	30	M	LABR	PLZZZZUSA
WEGRGYN, MARTIN	30	M	LABR	PLZZZZUSA
LEVER	46	M	LABR	PLZZZZUSA
BARYEK, JAN	26	M	LABR	PLZZZZUSA
ADRYAN, MARTIN	38	M	LABR	PLZZZZUSA
HUBISCHAK, ANDRE	40	M	LABR	PLZZZZUSA
LUKOWIAK, JOS.	27	M	LABR	PLZZZZUSA
LEPICH, PETER	33	M	LABR	RRZZZZUSA
FRANCISKOVIEK, A.	36	M	LABR	RRZZZZUSA
PINTER, MICHL.	23	M	LABR	RRZZZZUSA
GECAN, LORENZO	34	M	SEMN	RRZZZZUSA
PAPESICH, MARCUS	28	M	SEMN	RRZZZZUSA
SALGINZA, MIKULA	26	M	SEMN	RRZZZZUSA
BRIEDERMAN, JOSEF	24	M	LABR	PLZZZZUSA
FENSCHEL, SALO	19	M	LABR	PLZZZZUSA
SADWOKI, MATHEUS	47	M	LABR	PLZZZZUSA
HAWECKI, ANDREAS	43	M	LABR	PLZZZZUSA
BRAL, FRANZ	47	M	LABR	PLZZZZUSA
BENCZKI, MICHL.	28	M	LABR	PLZZZZUSA
MASCHLINSKI, FRANZ	23	M	LABR	PLZZZZUSA
DVOREK, WOLERTZ	38	M	LABR	PLZZZZUSA
ZULCYAK, FRANZ	22	M	LABR	PLZZZZUSA
MEREK, JOSEF	22	M	LABR	PLZZZZUSA
RANVORITZ, JOSEF	27	M	LABR	PLZZZZUSA
ANDRECYAK, JOS.	33	M	LABR	PLZZZZUSA
BENKUS, MICHL.	40	M	LABR	PLZZZZUSA
HABOCINSKY, FR.	30	M	LABR	PLZZZZUSA
SCHOLLIO, JOHANN	39	M	LABR	PLZZZZUSA
FRANKOWITZ, WOYT.	39	M	LABR	PLZZZZUSA
BENDEK, S.	30	M	LABR	PLZZZZUSA
HRAK, JAN	26	M	LABR	PLZZZZUSA
WALKOWSKY, WALENZ	24	M	LABR	PLZZZZUSA
CYGRANOWISKY, THOM.	45	M	LABR	PLZZZZUSA
RENAS, FELIX	42	M	LABR	PLZZZZUSA
GIRMAKA, C.W.	42	M	LABR	PLZZZZUSA
PETSASCHEL, JOSEF	32	M	LABR	PLZZZZUSA
JERDONEK, JOHAN	39	M	LABR	PLZZZZUSA
SIEGIN, JOSEF	50	M	LABR	PLZZZZUSA
HALICRACKA, SIM	30	M	LABR	PLZZZZUSA
MISKOWSKY, JONAS	33	M	LABR	PLZZZZUSA
ANDRASY, JANOS	25	M	LABR	PLZZZZUSA
CHERPAK, GEORG	20	M	LABR	PLZZZZUSA
NOLTSCHS, MICHL.	26	M	LABR	PLZZZZUSA
GINEZKA, IGNATZ	45	M	LABR	PLZZZZUSA
NEDINOKI, WINCINTA	35	M	LABR	PLZZZZUSA
ZIUNSCHWISKI, AUG.	40	M	LABR	PLZZZZUSA
BRADKOVSKI, MICH.	35	M	LABR	PLZZZZUSA
DOMOWELISCK, MATH.	29	M	LABR	PLZZZZUSA
GIELA, FRN.	38	M	LABR	PLZZZZUSA
MACEZKOWAIK, JACOB	23	M	LABR	PLZZZZUSA
HOLLORCKI, M.	28	M	LABR	PLZZZZUSA
WALGERCK, FRANZ	28	M	LABR	PLZZZZUNK
ROGANSKI, LORENZ	34	M	LABR	PLZZZZUNK
SLAWINSKI, DEMETRI	42	M	LABR	PLZZZZUNK
SCHLOPROCK, W.	23	M	LABR	PLZZZZUNK
SLOFSKY, JAS	28	M	LABR	PLZZZZUNK
GRAEFSKY, FRANZ	25	M	LABR	PLZZZZUNK
ROSINSKI, COUST.	24	M	LABR	PLZZZZUNK
UGNAZYCK, ANDREAS	38	M	LABR	PLZZZZUNK
SOMERFELD, MART	42	M	LABR	PLZZZZUNK
BAYONEZ, MARI	23	F	SVNT	PLZZZZUSA
ROSSI, FRANCISKA	20	F	SVNT	PLZZZZUSA
REDNARZIK, MARIE	18	F	SVNT	PLZZZZUSA
TIPER, JADWIGA	17	F	SVNT	PLZZZZUSA
PRYEWORAUGK, VICTORIA	20	F	SVNT	PLZZZZUSA
MORCYAK, HENRIETTE	26	F	SVNT	PLZZZZUSA
HORVAL, JOHAN	23	M	LABR	RRZZZZUSA
SLEKLA, THEO	11	M	CH	RRZZZZUSA
HERVAL, IROMLES	18	M	LABR	RRZZZZUSA
NAZARYCIK, MARKUS	34	M	LABR	RRZZZZUSA
SULITZ, HONSLAULIN	25	M	LABR	RRZZZZUSA
CHONZENKA, MAKE	24	M	LABR	RRZZZZUSA
RIKKO, LURA	36	M	LABR	RRZZZZUSA
GEMERTHCH, LAUR.	24	M	LABR	RRZZZZUSA
BOVALIK, JANOS	35	M	LABR	RRZZZZUSA
POONTEK, MARTIN	25	M	LABR	RRZZZZUSA

SHIP: ST LAURENT

FROM: HAVRE
TO: NEW YORK
ARRIVED: 22 APRIL 1884

PASSENGER	AGE	SEX	OCCUPATION	PRV VIL DES
BARAKOVITCH, MIRON-MR	24	M	FARMER	RRZZZZNY
EPSTEIN, ISARE-MR	19	M	FARMER	RRZZZZNY

SHIP: WESTPHALIA

FROM: HAMBURG
TO: NEW YORK
ARRIVED: 22 APRIL 1884

PASSENGER	AGE	SEX	OCCUPATION	PRV VIL DES
LEWIN, JACOB	24	M	DLR	RRZZZZNY
SWIRLIN, MARTIN	27	M	LABR	RRZZZZNY
FEINBERG, SALOMON	22	M	LABR	RRZZZZPHI

SHIP: CALIFORNIA

FROM: HAMBURG
TO: NEW YORK
ARRIVED: 24 APRIL 1884

PASSENGER	AGE	SEX	OCCUPATION	PRV VIL DES
BERNSTEIN, BERNHARD	34	M	TRDSMN	RRZZZZNY
ZATO, JOSEF	24	M	LABR	PLZZZZNY
FRANZ	61	M	LABR	PLZZZZNY
POBSYNSKI, UGUST	40	M	UNKNOWN	PLZZZZNY
DERENC, ANTON	29	M	UNKNOWN	PLZZZZNY
RAFSKY, MARTIN	52	M	UNKNOWN	PLZZZZNY
JANEK, SIMON	24	M	UNKNOWN	PLZZZZNY
GALUSKA, MATHIAS	26	M	UNKNOWN	PLZZZZNY
NIEMITZ, MATHEI	37	M	UNKNOWN	PLZZZZNY
SCHITKOWSKY, MATHEI	33	M	UNKNOWN	PLZZZZNY
LATKOWSKY, JOSEF	34	M	UNKNOWN	RRZZZZNY

SHIP: EIDER

FROM: BREMEN AND SOUTHAMPTON
TO: NEW YORK
ARRIVED: 25 APRIL 1884

PASSENGER	AGE	SEX	OCCUPATION	PRI VIL DES
PHILIPPENS, ABR.E.	54	M	AY	RRZZZZUSA
ROMIS, PHILIPP	40	M	FARMER	RRZZZZUSA
DESSAN, LEOPOLD	27	M	MCHT	RRZZZZUSA
CIRRI, MURDZA	25	F	UNKNOWN	PLZZZZUSA
PRESSLER, EMILIE	24	F	UNKNOWN	PLZZZZUSA
SMARINAK, FRANZ	23	M	LABR	PLZZZZUSA
DEJEWSKI, MARTIN	35	M	UNKNOWN	RRZZZZUSA
GEHRING, ROSINE	17	F	UNKNOWN	RRZZZZUSA
ROESSLER, GEORG	30	M	LABR	RRZZZZUSA
CAROL.	36	F	W	RRZZZZUSA
FRIEDR.	8	M	CHILD	RRZZZZUSA
ANNA	17	F	UNKNOWN	RRZZZZUSA
WITTMEYER, JOHANN	20	M	LABR	RRZZZZUSA
MAGD.	17	F	UNKNOWN	RRZZZZUSA
MARIA	20	F	UNKNOWN	RRZZZZUSA
GAEHRING, JACOB	33	M	LABR	RRZZZZUSA
CATH.	28	F	W	RRZZZZUSA
ANDREAS	8	M	CHILD	RRZZZZUSA
CAROL.	6	F	CHILD	RRZZZZUSA
CHRISTE	4	F	CHILD	RRZZZZUSA
ROSINA	2	F	CHILD	RRZZZZUSA
LOUISE	.09	F	INFANT	RRZZZZUSA
BECKER, ROBERT	15	M	UNKNOWN	RRZZZZUSA
HEER, ANDREAS	24	M	LABR	RRZZZZUSA
CAROL.	22	F	W	RRZZZZUSA
ELISAB.	.06	F	INFANT	RRZZZZUSA
PHILIPP	21	M	LABR	RRZZZZUSA
HEINR.	13	M	UNKNOWN	RRZZZZUSA
LOCHNER, NICOL.	31	M	LABR	RRZZZZUSA
BARBA.	28	F	W	RRZZZZUSA
ELISAB.	10	F	CH	RRZZZZUSA
JOHANN	8	M	CHILD	RRZZZZUSA
CATH.	4	F	CHILD	RRZZZZUSA
JOHANN	1	M	CHILD	RRZZZZUSA
ZUMBAUM, JOHANN	39	M	LABR	RRZZZZUSA
ROSINA	28	F	W	RRZZZZUSA
ROSINA	16	F	UNKNOWN	RRZZZZUSA
JACOB	11	M	CH	RRZZZZUSA
JOHANN	10	M	UNKNOWN	RRZZZZUSA
HEINR.	8	M	CHILD	RRZZZZUSA
MAGD.	.04	F	INFANT	RRZZZZUSA
DAIS, JACOB	30	M	LABR	RRZZZZUSA
BARBA.	26	F	W	RRZZZZUSA
MAGD.	3	F	CHILD	RRZZZZUSA
JACOB	9	M	CHILD	RRZZZZUSA
BURR, CHRIST.	28	M	LABR	RRZZZZUSA
ELISAB	24	F	W	RRZZZZUSA
ELISAB.	.03	F	INFANT	RRZZZZUSA
GEORG, FRIEDR.	42	M	LABR	RRZZZZUSA
ROSINA	36	F	W	RRZZZZUSA
JOHANN	8	M	CHILD	RRZZZZUSA
JACOB	4	M	CHILD	RRZZZZUSA
CHRISTIAN	.09	M	INFANT	RRZZZZUSA
FRIEDRICH	3	M	CHILD	RRZZZZUSA
VOLLMER, CONR.	30	M	LABR	RRZZZZUSA
EVA	28	F	W	RRZZZZUSA
CATH.	3	F	CHILD	RRZZZZUSA
HEINR.	.09	M	INFANT	RRZZZZUSA
SIELER, JOHANN	21	M	LABR	RRZZZZUSA
WALL, GEORG	35	M	UNKNOWN	RRZZZZUSA
CATH.	35	F	W	RRZZZZUSA
JACOB	12	M	CH	RRZZZZUSA
CATH.	10	F	UNKNOWN	RRZZZZUSA
CHRIST.	8	M	CHILD	RRZZZZUSA
MARIA	6	F	CHILD	RRZZZZUSA
GOTTFRIED	2	M	CHILD	RRZZZZUSA
ELISABETH	.09	F	INFANT	RRZZZZUSA
OTTNER, WILH.	28	M	LABR	RRZZZZUSA
MAGD.	24	F	W	RRZZZZUSA
WILH.	.09	M	INFANT	RRZZZZUSA
BURR, JACOB	35	M	LABR	RRZZZZUSA
SOPHIE	29	F	W	RRZZZZUSA
MAGD.	4	F	CHILD	RRZZZZUSA
ELISAB.	.09	F	INFANT	RRZZZZUSA
WINTER, JUTINA	19	F	W	RRZZZZUSA
BECKER, MINNA	11	F	CH	RRZZZZUSA
PRESSLER, FRIEDR.	34	M	LABR	RRZZZZUSA
MARG.	34	F	W	RRZZZZUSA
CHRISTE.	11	F	CH	RRZZZZUSA
CATH.	10	F	UNKNOWN	RRZZZZUSA
PHILIPP	7	M	CHILD	RRZZZZUSA
CAROL.	4	F	CHILD	RRZZZZUSA
BARBARA	3	F	CHILD	RRZZZZUSA
MAGD.	1	F	CHILD	RRZZZZUSA

SHIP: WAESLAND

FROM: ANTWERP
TO: NEW YORK
ARRIVED: 25 APRIL 1884

PASSENGER	AGE	SEX	OCCUPATION	PRI VIL DES
SCHURALT, JOS.	40	M	FARMER	PLZZZZNY
LELOISK, AUD.	37	M	FARMER	PLZZZZUNK
ANNA	38	F	UNKNOWN	PLZZZZUNK
MA.	17	F	UNKNOWN	PLZZZZUNK
PAUL	12	F	UNKNOWN	PLZZZZUNK
AUG.	9	M	CHILD	PLZZZZUNK
FR.	7	M	CHILD	PLZZZZUNK
LADES	5	M	CHILD	PLZZZZUNK
WASILEWSKI, A.	30	M	FARMER	PLZZZZUNK
MAR.	27	F	UNKNOWN	PLZZZZUNK
MAR.	2	F	CHILD	PLZZZZUNK
FRANCE	.06	M	INFANT	PLZZZZUNK
IGUMANSKI, F.	22	M	DR	PLZZZZNY
DESHUCY, M.	26	M	JNR	PLZZZZNY
GULURCH, AND.	19	M	JNR	PLZZZZCH
ROSPECL, AUG.	11	M	JNR	PLZZZZCH
CYRKEN, M.	27	M	FARMER	PLZZZZNY
LIERKOISKI, Y.	22	M	FARMER	PLZZZZNY
URBAN, PAUL.	17	M	FARMER	PLZZZZCH
BOSKISKI, M.	78	M	FARMER	PLZZZZCH
BRYEYENSKI, P.	18	M	FARMER	PLZZZZDET
CAYAKONSKI, Y.	33	M	FARMER	PLZZZZNY
JAS.	63	M	FARMER	PLZZZZNY
M.	4	M	CHILD	PLZZZZNY
FRANCK	3	M	CHILD	PLZZZZNY
JAC.	.06	M	INFANT	PLZZZZNY
SYMSKY, AND.	16	M	FARMER	PLZZZZCH
BALBIN, MUR.	19	F	UNKNOWN	PLZZZZUNK
DRANYGOLONKID, M.	20	M	FARMER	PLZZZZUNK
MEYER, LOUIS	25	M	TLR	PLZZZZNY
CANTISCH, JACOB	25	M	SMH	PLZZZZUNK

SHIP: BELGENLAND

FROM: ANTWERP
TO: NEW YORK
ARRIVED: 27 APRIL 1884

PASSENGER	AGE	SEX	OCCUPATION	PRI VIL DES
KEYRAITIS, EN.	22	M	LABR	PLZZZZUNK
SWOMMKOFF, E.	31	M	LWYR	RRZZZZNY
GOLEMBOURSKI, V.	34	M	MCHT	PLZZZZNY
M.	25	F	LABR	PLZZZZNY

PASSENGER	AGE	SEX	OCCUPATION	PRV	VIL	DES
ANNA	7	F	CHILD	PL	ZZZZ	NY
LOUISA	4	F	CHILD	PL	ZZZZ	NY
OMTO	00	F	INF	PL	ZZZZ	NY
KRUTZENA, JAC.	44	M	LABR	PL	ZZZZ	NY
PET.	44	M	LABR	PL	ZZZZ	NY
JOH.	6	M	CHILD	PL	ZZZZ	NY
JODW.	3	M	CHILD	PL	ZZZZ	NY
MARIAN	00	M	INF	PL	ZZZZ	NY
KLIMOWSKI, JOS.	50	M	LABR	PL	ZZZZ	NY
RAPLACHYK, STAN	21	M	FARMER	PL	ZZZZ	NY
IRZA	21	F	UNKNOWN	PL	ZZZZ	NY
IRZA	45	F	UNKNOWN	PL	ZZZZ	NY
PAPLAUZYCK, MAH.	54	M	FARMER	PL	ZZZZ	NY
ROINE, ERN.	31	M	LABR	PL	ZZZZ	NY
SZANBLEWSKI, W.	24	M	LABR	PL	ZZZZ	NY
AN.	25	M	LABR	PL	ZZZZ	NY
JOH.	3	M	CHILD	PL	ZZZZ	NY
BRAMIL	00	M	INF	PL	ZZZZ	***
MOCHAN, STAN.	38	M	LABR	PL	ZZZZ	DET
DERANGOWSKI, L.	55	M	LABR	PL	ZZZZ	IL
MAR.	50	F	UNKNOWN	PL	ZZZZ	IL
MARE	26	F	UNKNOWN	PL	ZZZZ	IL
TH.	24	M	UNKNOWN	PL	ZZZZ	IL
LEMCHEN, HUB.	24	M	CPTR	RR	ZZZZ	NY
JOH.	21	M	CPTR	RR	ZZZZ	NY

SHIP: AUSTRAL

FROM: LIVERPOOL
TO: NEW YORK
ARRIVED: 28 APRIL 1884

PASSENGER	AGE	SEX	OCCUPATION	PRV	VIL	DES
MERANGE, JANKEL	25	M	MCHT	RR	ZZZZ	NY
FRIEDMAN, CHAIM	25	M	UNKNOWN	RR	ZZZZ	NY

SHIP: CANADA

FROM: HAVRE
TO: NEW YORK
ARRIVED: 30 APRIL 1884

PASSENGER	AGE	SEX	OCCUPATION	PRV	VIL	DES
SIERAWSKI, T.	17	M	CL	RR	ZZZZ	NY
LEVINE, ISAAC	27	M	JWLR	RR	ZZZZ	NY
DELINSKI, HAYMANN	24	M	HTR	RR	ZZZZ	NY

SHIP: GRECIAN MONARCH

FROM: LONDON
TO: NEW YORK
ARRIVED: 30 APRIL 1884

PASSENGER	AGE	SEX	OCCUPATION	PRV	VIL	DES
GLUCKSBERG, MORIS	25	M	TLR	PL	ZZZZ	USA
WLADISLAWSKY, MARCUS	25	M	LABR	PL	ZZZZ	USA
REITZUK, JACOB	25	M	TLR	PL	ZZZZ	USA

SHIP: RHAETIA

FROM: HAMBURG
TO: NEW YORK
ARRIVED: 30 APRIL 1884

PASSENGER	AGE	SEX	OCCUPATION	PRV	VIL	DES
BUDZICK, GEORG.	21	M	FARMER	RR	ZZZZ	USA

SHIP: HOLLAND

FROM: LONDON
TO: NEW YORK
ARRIVED: 01 MAY 1884

PASSENGER	AGE	SEX	OCCUPATION	PRV	VIL	DES
WALTER, V.	22	M	CGRMKR	PL	ZZZZ	CAN
BARKUS, I.	23	M	CGRMKR	PL	ZZZZ	NY
MUCKLEVITCH, JUO.	28	M	CGRMKR	PL	ZZZZ	NY

SHIP: CITY OF RICHMOND

FROM: LIVERPOOL AND QUEENSTOWN
TO: NEW YORK
ARRIVED: 02 MAY 1884

PASSENGER	AGE	SEX	OCCUPATION	PRV	VIL	DES
JATZKO, JOSEF	20	M	UNKNOWN	PL	ZZZZ	USA
ROBARSKI, ANNA	16	F	SP	PL	ZZZZ	USA
FERENZ, ANNA	30	F	UNKNOWN	PL	ZZZZ	USA
PERTSCHAK, ADAM	33	M	LABR	PL	ZZZZ	USA
SCHOMSKY, MIKLOS	46	M	UNKNOWN	PL	ZZZZ	USA
WALKO, GEORGE	45	M	UNKNOWN	PL	ZZZZ	USA
WISTRO, PAB.	24	M	UNKNOWN	PL	ZZZZ	USA
UDAK, ANDREAS	33	M	UNKNOWN	PL	ZZZZ	USA
STAKEI, JAKA	26	M	UNKNOWN	PL	ZZZZ	USA
JONESA, JOSEPH	41	M	UNKNOWN	PL	ZZZZ	USA
DELINSKO, JOSEPH	40	M	UNKNOWN	PL	ZZZZ	USA
ROGITA, JANOS	33	M	UNKNOWN	PL	ZZZZ	USA
ROWALSKI, JOHAN	26	M	UNKNOWN	PL	ZZZZ	USA
LUDWIG	23	M	UNKNOWN	PL	ZZZZ	USA
ROSTEK, RUDOLPH	24	M	UNKNOWN	PL	ZZZZ	USA
CZERNITZKI, M.	28	M	UNKNOWN	PL	ZZZZ	USA
EVERTOPSKI, CASIMER	25	F	W	PL	ZZZZ	USA
HEDWIG	30	M	LABR	PL	ZZZZ	USA
C.	00	F	INF	PL	ZZZZ	USA
KOLODZINSKI, ANTON	00	M	LABR	PL	ZZZZ	USA
PAULINE	00	F	W	PL	ZZZZ	USA
MORAM.	7	M	CHILD	PL	ZZZZ	USA
CONSTANTINE	8	F	CHILD	PL	ZZZZ	USA
JOHAN	00	M	INF	PL	ZZZZ	USA
GLUSNER, ANDRIAS	37	M	LABR	PL	ZZZZ	USA
MATIAS	14	M	UNKNOWN	PL	ZZZZ	USA
MATSCHINDEKA, JANOS	30	M	UNKNOWN	PL	ZZZZ	USA

PASSENGER	AGE	SEX	OCCUPATION	PRV	IVL	DES

SHIP: NECKAR

FROM: BREMEN
TO: NEW YORK
ARRIVED: 02 MAY 1884

PASSENGER	AGE	SEX	OCCUPATION	PV RI VL	DES
SLAVINSKA, HELENE	8	F	CHILD	RRZZZZ	USA
JOSEPHA	6	F	CHILD	RRZZZZ	USA
JOHANN	4	M	CHILD	RRZZZZ	USA
VINCENT	.11	M	INFANT	RRZZZZ	USA
STANISL.	38	M	LABR	RRZZZZ	USA
MARIE	32	F	UNKNOWN	RRZZZZ	USA
WLADISLLAUS	15	M	LABR	RRZZZZ	USA
LUTZ, ROBERT	26	M	TLR	RRZZZZ	NY
CHORNOWSKY, JOH.	35	M	UNKNOWN	RRZZZZ	NY

SHIP: WIELAND

FROM: HAMBURG
TO: NEW YORK
ARRIVED: 02 MAY 1884

PASSENGER	AGE	SEX	OCCUPATION	PV RI VL	DES
TROJAN, STANISLAV	22	M	LABR	RRZZZZ	USA
FRITSCHE, RUD.	37	M	PNR	RRZZZZ	USA
SIKOLSKY, STAN.	21	M	UNKNOWN	RRZZZZ	USA
WELUNSKY, KARL	20	M	UNKNOWN	RRZZZZ	USA
KOCHENSKY, JAN	32	M	LABR	RRZZZZ	USA
SARNORSKY, MATEJ	42	M	UNKNOWN	RRZZZZ	USA
MATEJEOSKY, FRANZ	29	M	UNKNOWN	RRZZZZ	USA
WARLIK, JAN	26	M	UNKNOWN	RRZZZZ	USA
PAVLOWSKY, BARTH.	31	M	UNKNOWN	RRZZZZ	USA
KASLEWITZ, MARIAN	26	M	UNKNOWN	RRZZZZ	USA
CELMAR, JAN	20	M	UNKNOWN	RRZZZZ	USA
BREZINSKY, ROSALIE	60	F	W	RRZZZZ	USA
ONDREJ	58	M	LABR	RRZZZZ	USA
ANTON	8	M	CHILD	RRZZZZ	USA
WLADISL.	4	M	CHILD	RRZZZZ	USA
JOSEF	.11	M	INFANT	RRZZZZ	USA
POCHUTZKY, ARON	54	M	LABR	RRZZZZ	USA
ALTE	50	F	W	RRZZZZ	USA
HABERSACK, ADAM	43	M	UNKNOWN	RRZZZZ	USA
KELLER, MARTIN	37	M	UNKNOWN	RRZZZZ	USA
DETMER, JACOB	42	M	UNKNOWN	RRZZZZ	USA
ZUKOWSKY, JAN	58	M	UNKNOWN	RRZZZZ	USA
SOVKOWSKY, ANTON	41	M	UNKNOWN	RRZZZZ	USA
STANKE, JAN	43	M	UNKNOWN	RRZZZZ	USA
KOLODEFSKY, JACOB	23	M	UNKNOWN	RRZZZZ	USA
ZOLESKY, FRANK	27	M	UNKNOWN	RRZZZZ	USA
WYRDRASCHOWSKA, HELENE	23	F	W	RRZZZZ	USA
JOSEF	30	M	LABR	RRZZZZ	USA
VINCENTI	.11	M	INFANT	RRZZZZ	USA
SCHULZ, JOH.	25	M	LABR	RRZZZZ	USA
VOLGERMANN, RICH.	21	M	CPTR	RRZZZZ	USA
SCHRODT, RUD.	25	M	UNKNOWN	RRZZZZ	USA

SHIP: CRESCENT CITY

FROM: PANAMA
TO: NEW YORK
ARRIVED: 03 MAY 1884

PASSENGER	AGE	SEX	OCCUPATION	PV RI VL	DES
WASCHARER, G.	35	M	ENGR	RRZZZZ	FR

SHIP: SERVIA

FROM: LIVERPOOL
TO: NEW YORK
ARRIVED: 05 MAY 1884

PASSENGER	AGE	SEX	OCCUPATION	PV RI VL	DES
MASE, P.MR	31	M	GENT	RRZZZZ	USA
MART.L.	5	M	CHILD	RRZZZZ	USA
A.MISS	3	F	CHILD	RRZZZZ	USA
A.MISS	18	F	NRS	RRZZZZ	USA

SHIP: ELBE

FROM: BREMEN
TO: NEW YORK
ARRIVED: 06 MAY 1884

PASSENGER	AGE	SEX	OCCUPATION	PV RI VL	DES
PETRIKAT, MICHAEL	52	M	LABR	RRZZZZ	USA
STEINERT, GEORG	19	M	WHLR	RRZZZZ	USA
KOGEBR, AUGUSTE	22	F	UNKNOWN	RRZZZZ	USA
WINSZ, CARL	16	M	LABR	RRZZZZ	USA
PIETROWSKI, MARIAN	37	M	UNKNOWN	RRZZZZ	USA
DIKAN, MICHAEL	25	M	UNKNOWN	RRZZZZ	USA
PIETROWSKI, IGNAZI	26	M	UNKNOWN	RRZZZZ	USA
RUSS, ADAM	45	M	UNKNOWN	RRZZZZ	USA

SHIP: MORAVIA

FROM: HAMBURG
TO: NEW YORK
ARRIVED: 06 MAY 1884

PASSENGER	AGE	SEX	OCCUPATION	PV RI VL	DES
HARKOWITZ, MARIUS	20	M	LABR	RRZZZZ	USA
SLOPEBERSKY, ISRAEL	40	M	LABR	RRZZZZ	USA
BERTALLIS, MICH.	25	M	FARMER	RRZZZZ	USA
STACHOWIAK, MICH.	28	M	LABR	RRZZZZ	USA
JAN	26	M	LABR	RRZZZZ	USA
USARICH, CASIMIR	50	M	LABR	RRZZZZ	USA
ALEXAND.	44	M	LABR	RRZZZZ	USA
ADAM	23	M	LABR	RRZZZZ	USA
MELANIE	15	M	CH	RRZZZZ	USA
JAN	7	M	CHILD	RRZZZZ	USA
CASIMIR	5	M	CHILD	RRZZZZ	USA
BERSCHER, RAFAEL	40	M	LABR	RRZZZZ	USA
KOLINSKY, ARON	25	M	LABR	RRZZZZ	USA
GRANDUTER, MOSES	20	M	LABR	RRZZZZ	USA
PADRUZIK, LEIB	19	M	LABR	RRZZZZ	USA
PILOWITZ, MICHAL	45	M	LABR	RRZZZZ	USA
ISRAELOWITZ, ELIE	22	M	LABR	RRZZZZ	USA
OLENDERSK, MORDSCHE	20	M	LABR	RRZZZZ	USA
STONRONSKI, ANTON	19	M	LABR	RRZZZZ	USA
REMINSKI, BOLESLAV	26	M	LABR	RRZZZZ	USA
LUDOWIKA	26	M	LABR	RRZZZZ	USA
MIESKOFSKY, ADAM	40	M	LABR	RRZZZZ	USA
PRUSIKOVSKA, MARIANE	26	F	SGL	RRZZZZ	USA
FRANZ	37	M	LABR	RRZZZZ	USA
LIEBSCHINSKY, ABRAM	21	M	BKR	RRZZZZ	USA
MISCHKOWSKI, ARON	22	M	LABR	RRZZZZ	USA
LARZKY, JIRCHY	20	M	LABR	RRZZZZ	USA
BARTRUSZAYTYS, ANNA	30	F	W	RRZZZZ	USA
STANISL.	20	M	LABR	RRZZZZ	USA
STANISL.	8	M	CHILD	RRZZZZ	USA
VINCENT	6	M	CHILD	RRZZZZ	USA
ANNA	.11	F	INFANT	RRZZZZ	USA

PASSENGER	AGE	SEX	OCCUPATION	PRV VIL DES
ROTTSTEIN, RUBIN	6	M	CHILD	RRZZZZUSA
MALARANZY, MEYER	55	M	LABR	RRZZZZUSA
SONNEBERG, JOSEF	40	M	LABR	RRZZZZUSA
KOTESZUK, JOSEF	24	M	LABR	RRZZZZUSA
PLAWNER, ISAAI	24	M	LABR	RRZZZZUSA
MARIUS, DAVID	35	M	LABR	RRZZZZUSA
WILNER, GOLDE	20	F	SGL	RRZZZZUSA
KAHNOWITZ, SAMUEL	24	M	DLR	RRZZZZUSA
PAKELEZIK, LEIZER	44	M	LABR	RRZZZZUSA
SLATE	44	F	W	RRZZZZUSA
MOSES	9	M	CHILD	RRZZZZUSA
HIRSCH	8	M	CHILD	RRZZZZUSA
SCHEINE	7	F	CHILD	RRZZZZUSA
LEO	6	M	CHILD	RRZZZZUSA
CHANNE	.11	F	INFANT	RRZZZZUSA
RIVE	.01	F	INFANT	RRZZZZUSA
RACHEL	20	F	W	RRZZZZUSA
CHAIE	.11	F	INFANT	RRZZZZUSA
SMOLINSKI, HERM.	23	M	LABR	RRZZZZUSA
BJOSAVSKY, JULIAN	26	M	FARMER	RRZZZZUSA
DER, JOSEF	24	M	LABR	RRZZZZUSA
TSCHERNOVSKI, ROSALIE	19	F	SGL	RRZZZZUSA
BILAWSKY, JULIAN	30	M	LABR	RRZZZZUSA
ULEWIE, KLEMENS	24	M	LABR	RRZZZZUSA
SOIDEVSKI, MICH.	20	M	LABR	RRZZZZUSA
MOSEWSKY, JACOB	24	M	LABR	RRZZZZUSA
KUZEVSKY, ANTON	23	M	LABR	RRZZZZUSA
KRAL, LUDWIG	20	M	LABR	RRZZZZUSA
GAVRICH, PAUL	30	M	LABR	RRZZZZUSA
ANTONIE	27	F	W	RRZZZZUSA
PITZ, LUDW.	22	M	LABR	RRZZZZUSA
AMBROSIUS	17	M	LABR	RRZZZZUSA
DIDVALES, VINCENTY	26	M	LABR	RRZZZZUSA
GROL, GOTTFRIED	23	M	LABR	RRZZZZUSA
VICTOR, ANDR.	24	M	LABR	RRZZZZUSA
BOJONECK, ANTON	20	M	LABR	RRZZZZUSA
DELEWITZ, JAN	40	M	LABR	RRZZZZUSA
ANTON	37	M	LABR	RRZZZZUSA
URMANOWICZ, MATEUS	24	M	LABR	RRZZZZUSA
ADAM	18	M	LABR	RRZZZZUSA
BUZAS, ROOLAX	21	M	LABR	RRZZZZUSA
STODALIS, PIOTR.	28	M	FARMER	RRZZZZUSA
TOPIEL, L.	25	M	LABR	RRZZZZUSA
MISZKIEL, ANDR.	28	M	LABR	RRZZZZUSA
RADEITKY, JOSEF	39	M	LABR	RRZZZZUSA
JABLOWSKY, ANTON	22	M	LABR	RRZZZZUSA
NADOLIN, FRANZ	20	M	LABR	RRZZZZUSA
RUMINSKI, LEON	19	M	LABR	RRZZZZUSA
JANKIWSKY, JAN	30	M	LABR	RRZZZZUSA
BIZYNKOWSKI, IGNATZ	22	M	LABR	RRZZZZUSA
FLUSS, MARIANE	45	F	W	RRZZZZUSA
RUDOLF	9	M	CHILD	RRZZZZUSA
WILSERKOWSKI, FRANK	50	M	LABR	RRZZZZUSA
MARIANE	30	F	W	RRZZZZUSA
MICHAL	9	M	CHILD	RRZZZZUSA
STANISL.	3	M	CHILD	RRZZZZUSA
FRIEDRICH, MARTIN	36	M	LABR	RRZZZZUSA
TROTZKI, KAZIMIR	38	M	LABR	RRZZZZUSA
DZEMITKI, ADAM	33	M	LABR	RRZZZZUSA
SCHLASKI, PETER	19	M	LABR	RRZZZZUSA
ANLODONSKI, MACY	19	M	LABR	RRZZZZUSA
URBANOWITZ, KAZIMIR	32	M	LABR	RRZZZZUSA
KOCHEZINSKI, STANISL.	23	M	LABR	RRZZZZUSA
MIKNA, IGNOTAS	40	M	LABR	RRZZZZUSA
ANDRUSCHISS, ANNA	22	F	SGL	RRZZZZUSA
WALOITIS, MATHS.	27	M	LABR	RRZZZZUSA
DRUBOWSKI, ----Y	26	M	LABR	RRZZZZUSA
ROTTSTEIN, BER.	41	M	LABR	RRZZZZUSA
CAECILIC	9	F	CHILD	RRZZZZUSA
LINE	8	F	CHILD	RRZZZZUSA
ANNA	7	F	CHILD	RRZZZZUSA
SALOMON	9	M	CHILD	RRZZZZUSA
ABRAH.	8	M	CHILD	RRZZZZUSA
ALBRAM, MOSES	24	M	LABR	RRZZZZUSA
SABATZKY, MOSES	24	M	LABR	RRZZZZUSA

PASSENGER	AGE	SEX	OCCUPATION	PRV VIL DES
MALINOWSKI, JOH.	28	M	LABR	RRZZZZUSA
SCHNADOWSKI, MEYER	23	M	TLR	RRZZZZUSA
WERNER, DORA	32	F	W	RRZZZZUSA
INKNIEWITZ, WINZAS	27	M	LABR	RRZZZZUSA
BRUMBIVSKA, ANNA	20	F	SGL	RRZZZZUSA
MORDCHELOWITZ, HERRM.	25	M	DLR	RRZZZZUSA
KRAJUIK, THOM.	19	M	LABR	RRZZZZUSA
ZALNOWSKI, MIHAL	32	M	LABR	RRZZZZUSA
KREMEWIEZ, STANISL.	20	M	LABR	RRZZZZUSA
DAMBROWSKI, JOSEF	23	M	LABR	RRZZZZUSA
MISEWIEZ, FRANZA.	21	F	SGL	RRZZZZUSA
PAULINE	23	F	SGL	RRZZZZUSA
WAJSERZUG, MEYER	19	M	LABR	RRZZZZUSA
PINSSACK, ADOLF.	18	M	MCHT	RRZZZZUSA
BARONOW---, JOSEF	35	M	UNKNOWN	RRZZZZUSA
SCHIPULEN---, ANTON	24	M	UNKNOWN	RRZZZZUSA
ROWINS--, ADOLF.	23	M	UNKNOWN	RRZZZZUSA
MICHRIAV---, FRANZ	37	M	UNKNOWN	RRZZZZUSA
SCHNEIDEROWSKY, ZALLEL	29	M	TLR	RRZZZZUSA
LEWIN, RACHEL	22	F	SGL	RRZZZZUSA
BRZOZA, RACHEL	24	F	SGL	RRZZZZUSA
ZIBUSKI, STANISL.	29	M	SHMK	RRZZZZUSA

SHIP: DEVONIA

FROM: GLASGOW AND MOVILLE
TO: NEW YORK
ARRIVED: 07 MAY 1884

PASSENGER	AGE	SEX	OCCUPATION	PRV VIL DES
KLONOSKI, A.	30	M	LABR	RRZZZZUSA
VERONICA	26	F	UNKNOWN	RRZZZZUSA
ANDREAN	8	M	CHILD	RRZZZZUSA
HANNA	4	F	CHILD	RRZZZZUSA
FELIX	.06	M	INFANT	RRZZZZUSA
PRONDRINSKI, J.	31	M	LABR	RRZZZZUSA
CATH.	30	F	UNKNOWN	RRZZZZUSA
SCHULZ, CARL	85	M	UNKNOWN	RRZZZZUSA
TELIAN	2	M	CHILD	RRZZZZUSA
BRONESLOW	.06	M	INFANT	RRZZZZUSA
LABOROVSKI, M.	39	M	LABR	RRZZZZUSA
MARIANNE	36	F	UNKNOWN	RRZZZZUSA
EVA	5	F	CHILD	RRZZZZUSA
ANNA	3	F	CHILD	RRZZZZUSA
MILOK, W.	30	M	LABR	RRZZZZUSA
KOIECGINSKI, JOS.	30	M	UNKNOWN	RRZZZZUSA
CEMENSKI, P.	50	M	UNKNOWN	RRZZZZUSA
MAGDALENA	40	F	UNKNOWN	RRZZZZUSA
IDA	24	F	UNKNOWN	RRZZZZUSA
JONEK	10	M	UNKNOWN	RRZZZZUSA
JARET	9	F	CHILD	RRZZZZUSA
MEKLAS	7	M	CHILD	RRZZZZUSA
MARKIEWIG, THEO.	30	M	SMH	RRZZZZUSA
KASPRYAK, C.	29	M	LABR	RRZZZZUSA
MODZIEVSKI, AUG.	34	M	UNKNOWN	RRZZZZUSA
VICTORIA	32	F	UNKNOWN	RRZZZZUSA
JOHN	4	M	CHILD	RRZZZZUSA
PAUL	2	M	CHILD	RRZZZZUSA
VER.	.04	M	INFANT	RRZZZZUSA
KAS.	28	M	LABR	RRZZZZUSA
THS.	16	M	UNKNOWN	RRZZZZUSA
VICTOR	24	M	UNKNOWN	RRZZZZUSA
HASA	.11	F	INFANT	RRZZZZUSA
PRADZINOSKI, T.	35	M	LABR	RRZZZZUSA
ANNA	25	F	UNKNOWN	RRZZZZUSA
CAROLINE	16	F	UNKNOWN	RRZZZZUSA
ELZB.	18	F	UNKNOWN	RRZZZZUSA
PAWLEI, JOH.	14	M	UNKNOWN	RRZZZZUSA
SIKORSKI, P.	31	M	LABR	RRZZZZUSA
KALINICH, FRIED	60	M	UNKNOWN	RRZZZZUSA
HUGO	17	M	UNKNOWN	RRZZZZUSA

PASSENGER	AGE	SEX	OCCUPATION	PRIVIL	DES
CHEVIKOWSKI, CHRI.	27	M	UNKNOWN	RRZZZZ	USA
PEVLR.	26	F	UNKNOWN	RRZZZZ	USA
FRANGINK	31	M	LABR	RRZZZZ	USA
MARIANNA	25	F	UNKNOWN	RRZZZZ	USA
ANTONE	1	M	CHILD	RRZZZZ	USA
POLLOK, LYON-J.	38	M	LABR	RRZZZZ	USA
SLOWINSKI, M.	40	M	JNR	RRZZZZ	USA
FRANZ.	14	F	UNKNOWN	RRZZZZ	USA
MILOK, ANDERS	25	M	LABR	RRZZZZ	USA
LUSKASZEVIEZ, TH.	28	M	UNKNOWN	RRZZZZ	USA
FRANCISKA	26	F	UNKNOWN	RRZZZZ	USA
EVA	8	F	CHILD	RRZZZZ	USA
ELISABETH	4	F	CHILD	RRZZZZ	USA
JOHN	2	M	CHILD	RRZZZZ	USA
MARIKA	1	F	CHILD	RRZZZZ	USA
TREBIATOSKY, JOS.	53	M	LABR	RRZZZZ	USA
EVA	46	F	UNKNOWN	RRZZZZ	USA
VERE	18	M	UNKNOWN	RRZZZZ	USA
PAUL	16	M	UNKNOWN	RRZZZZ	USA
ANTONE	14	M	UNKNOWN	RRZZZZ	USA
VOC.	11	F	UNKNOWN	RRZZZZ	USA
LEE	2	M	CHILD	RRZZZZ	USA
ANNA	.09	F	INFANT	RRZZZZ	USA
SZYJKOWSKI, M.	28	M	LABR	RRZZZZ	USA
TANDECKE, FRANCE	28	M	UNKNOWN	RRZZZZ	USA
SWIKOWSKI, FR.	26	M	UNKNOWN	RRZZZZ	USA
STUCK, L.	22	M	UNKNOWN	RRZZZZ	USA
LAKOWSKI, JOAN	42	M	LABR	RRZZZZ	USA
STUCK, SIMON	22	M	UNKNOWN	RRZZZZ	USA
NOOCK, ANTON	24	M	UNKNOWN	RRZZZZ	USA
LUENSKI, MAREM	45	M	UNKNOWN	RRZZZZ	USA
ARVIGHT, ANTONIA	43	M	UNKNOWN	RRZZZZ	USA

SHIP: AMERIQUE

FROM: HAVRE
TO: NEW YORK
ARRIVED: 08 MAY 1884

PASSENGER	AGE	SEX	OCCUPATION	PRIVIL	DES
KAHN, BERNARD	21	M	CPMKR	RRZZZZ	USA
CHAVILSKI, ABRAHAM	36	M	SHMK	RRZZZZ	USA
HERZ, BACERIEE	29	F	WO	RRZZZZ	USA
EMMA	5	F	CHILD	RRZZZZ	USA
SARAH	00	F	INF	RRZZZZ	USA
ZUBERT, CHARLOTTE	20	F	SVNT	RRZZZZ	USA
GENISSE, SALOMON	26	M	TRVLR	RRZZZZ	USA
SKOULTCHIK, ISRAEL	23	M	TLR	RRZZZZ	USA

SHIP: AMERICA

FROM: BREMEN
TO: NEW YORK
ARRIVED: 09 MAY 1884

PASSENGER	AGE	SEX	OCCUPATION	PRIVIL	DES
KLENIA, JAN	18	M	FARMER	RRZZZZ	NY
KOPZYNSKI, FRANZISKA	28	F	UNKNOWN	RRZZZZ	NY
KOSZEIWSKI, JOS.	21	M	LABR	RRZZZZ	NY
FRANZIC.	22	F	W	RRZZZZ	NY
KASIMIRKOWSKI, STAN.	22	M	FARMER	RRZZZZ	NY
GURNE, JAN	40	M	UNKNOWN	RRZZZZ	NY
INKLONSKI, MEIK	25	M	UNKNOWN	RRZZZZ	NY
GUZINSKI, JAN.	29	M	UNKNOWN	RRZZZZ	NY
INKLINSKI, JAC.	30	M	UNKNOWN	RRZZZZ	NY
GUNS, CARL	30	M	UNKNOWN	RRZZZZ	NY
FRANCISKA	38	F	W	RRZZZZ	NY
LAZOWSWISKZ, JOSEF	28	M	LABR	RRZZZZ	NY
WISCHNOWSKZ, ANTON	37	M	UNKNOWN	RRZZZZ	NY
JANKOWSKZ, WLADISLAV	23	M	UNKNOWN	RRZZZZ	NY
THEOPOLIE	30	F	UNKNOWN	RRZZZZ	NY
MIKOJEWSKZ, VOJTECT	42	M	UNKNOWN	RRZZZZ	NY
WRUBLESKZ, IGNAS	41	M	UNKNOWN	RRZZZZ	NY
SCHAWENSKZ, IGNAS	12	M	UNKNOWN	RRZZZZ	NY
LAWANDROWSKI, STANISL.	42	M	LABR	RRZZZZ	NY
TURSKZ, STEFAN	34	M	UNKNOWN	RRZZZZ	NY
KNOLL, GUSTAV	24	M	UNKNOWN	RRZZZZ	NY
KAMAROWSKI, JOSEF	41	M	UNKNOWN	RRZZZZ	NY
WICERKOWSKI, PETER	38	M	UNKNOWN	RRZZZZ	NY

SHIP: ODER

FROM: BREMEN
TO: NEW YORK
ARRIVED: 09 MAY 1884

PASSENGER	AGE	SEX	OCCUPATION	PRIVIL	DES
MONDROCK, ANDREAS	25	M	UNKNOWN	RRZZZZ	USA
SYPOCZENSKI, FRANZ	23	M	UNKNOWN	RRZZZZ	USA
ALBRECHT, JOHAN	27	M	BCHR	RRZZZZ	USA

SHIP: PENNLAND

FROM: ANTWERP
TO: NEW YORK
ARRIVED: 09 MAY 1884

PASSENGER	AGE	SEX	OCCUPATION	PRIVIL	DES
KARASKA, JOS.	21	M	LABR	RRZZZZ	PLY
BLANNDZUN, G.	19	M	UNKNOWN	RRZZZZ	NY
STANROCZYN, STAN.	24	M	UNKNOWN	RRZZZZ	PLY
TAD	21	M	UNKNOWN	RRZZZZ	PLY
WITECKI, F.	27	M	BCHR	RRZZZZ	NY
RUAKIWICZ, VINZ.	22	M	UNKNOWN	RRZZZZ	NY
KABARINSKI, FRANZ	28	M	UNKNOWN	RRZZZZ	NY

SHIP: AUSTRALIA

FROM: HAMBURG
TO: NEW YORK
ARRIVED: 12 MAY 1884

PASSENGER	AGE	SEX	OCCUPATION	PRIVIL	DES
SWICS, CASIMIR	33	M	LABR	PLZZZZ	NY
MATAR, MICHEL	39	M	LABR	PLZZZZ	NY
KAMINSKY, ANTON	38	M	LABR	RRZZZZ	NY
MARIANNE	30	F	W	RRZZZZ	NY
MARIANNE	74	F	UNKNOWN	RRZZZZ	NY
WLADISLAW	6	M	CHILD	RRZZZZ	NY
SEMESKA, IGNATZ	31	M	LABR	RRZZZZ	NY
STURTINEITES, MICHEL	31	M	LABR	RRZZZZ	NY
SCHUKEITIN, VINCENT	22	M	LABR	RRZZZZ	NY

PASSENGER	AGE	SEX	OCCUPATION	PRIV	VIL	DES

SHIP: CITY OF BERLIN

FROM: LIVERPOOL AND QUEENSTOWN
TO: NEW YORK
ARRIVED: 12 MAY 1884

PASSENGER	AGE	SEX	OCCUPATION	PV	D
MORAWSKY, THOS.	43	M	UNKNOWN	PLZZZZ	USA
FRANS	40	F	W	PLZZZZ	USA
ANTONIA	7	F	CHILD	PLZZZZ	USA
STANISLAUS	4	M	CHILD	PLZZZZ	USA
VINCENTE	2	M	CHILD	PLZZZZ	USA
ANNA	1	F	CHILD	PLZZZZ	USA
KARNS, KARL	37	M	LABR	PLZZZZ	USA
CHRISTINE	30	F	W	PLZZZZ	USA
FREDRICH	10	M	CH	PLZZZZ	USA
KLEINICK, JAN	30	M	LABR	PLZZZZ	USA
JOS.	10	M	CH	PLZZZZ	USA
STANISLAW	11	M	UNKNOWN	PLZZZZ	USA
UROZOWSKY, MICH.	27	M	LABR	PLZZZZ	USA
KRAKOWSKY, ANTON	28	M	UNKNOWN	PLZZZZ	USA
POLAWSKY, KASIMIR	23	M	LABR	PLZZZZ	USA
SAVOLOWSKY, STANIS.	28	M	UNKNOWN	PLZZZZ	USA
FRANIZ, MAI.	11	F	CH	PLZZZZ	USA
LISKANIS, ANNA	26	F	SVNT	PLZZZZ	USA
GOTTLICH, FRANKEL	34	M	LABR	PLZZZZ	USA
HENRIETTA	28	F	W	PLZZZZ	USA
ANNA	7	F	CHILD	PLZZZZ	USA
KAROL	6	M	CHILD	PLZZZZ	USA
KRYZAEWSKY, IGNATZ	58	M	LABR	PLZZZZ	USA
BARBARA	57	F	W	PLZZZZ	USA
ANTON	27	M	CH	PLZZZZ	USA
BARBARA	12	F	CH	PLZZZZ	USA
ANNA	9	F	CHILD	PLZZZZ	USA
ZORNTZKY, JAN	20	M	LABR	PLZZZZ	USA
JAN	40	M	UNKNOWN	PLZZZZ	USA
JOHANA	36	F	W	PLZZZZ	USA
ANTON	10	M	CH	PLZZZZ	USA
FRANZ	8	M	CHILD	PLZZZZ	USA
TAFINSKY, FRANZ	44	M	LABR	PLZZZZ	USA
ANNA	36	F	W	PLZZZZ	USA
ANTON	8	M	CHILD	PLZZZZ	USA
JANKO, JOHANA	37	M	LABR	PLZZZZ	USA
SEKAC, MIKEL	29	M	UNKNOWN	PLZZZZ	USA
STAVECKY, JOS	40	M	UNKNOWN	PLZZZZ	USA
NOZAK, JOH.	46	M	UNKNOWN	PLZZZZ	USA
MALINSOWKY, EMIL	24	M	UNKNOWN	PLZZZZ	USA
SOPHIE	11	F	CH	PLZZZZ	USA
KRISKOWSKY, JAN	37	M	LABR	PLZZZZ	USA
ZELENSKY, STAN.	28	M	UNKNOWN	PLZZZZ	USA
BUSUCK, JAN	24	M	UNKNOWN	PLZZZZ	USA
KUSUCK, P.	35	M	UNKNOWN	PLZZZZ	USA
KESEDAY, GEO	32	M	UNKNOWN	PLZZZZ	USA
ANDERS, JAMBRICK	11	M	CH	PLZZZZ	USA
ANDRES, PEREMLA	45	M	FARMER	PLZZZZ	USA
PAK.MARIA	30	F	W	PLZZZZ	USA
JOSEF	1	M	CHILD	PLZZZZ	USA
JENNALAWITZ, PIAH	27	M	LABR	PLZZZZ	USA
HOPER	27	F	W	PLZZZZ	USA
TOMAS, KNIZ.	38	M	LABR	PLZZZZ	USA
GRADDA, MARIA	11	F	CH	PLZZZZ	USA
ROT, ANNA	11	M	UNKNOWN	PLZZZZ	USA
BLECHART, MARIA	10	M	UNKNOWN	PLZZZZ	USA
ZINDUCH, KRECH	30	M	LABR	PLZZZZ	USA
TONEAK, PIETER	11	M	CH	PLZZZZ	USA
KRONAK, MIHAL	50	M	LABR	PLZZZZ	USA
SWONTEN, J.P.	35	M	LABR	PLZZZZ	USA
WALA, ANDREAS	11	M	CH	PLZZZZ	USA
KOLK, SUSANA	20	F	W	PLZZZZ	USA
NOOWCKY, J.P.	22	M	LABR	PLZZZZ	USA
MYRNARKEY, KASPER	11	M	CH	PLZZZZ	USA
WONDOCKA, KRORITA	10	M	UNKNOWN	PLZZZZ	USA

SHIP: CITY OF ROME

FROM: LIVERPOOL
TO: NEW YORK
ARRIVED: 12 MAY 1884

PASSENGER	AGE	SEX	OCCUPATION	PV	D
KARSCHEFSKY, ST.	28	M	UNKNOWN	PLZZZZ	MI
PAWLACZAK, JOSEF	30	M	UNKNOWN	PLZZZZ	PA
ZALINSKE, ADAM	32	M	UNKNOWN	PLZZZZ	NY

SHIP: LYDIAN MONARCH

FROM: LONDON
TO: NEW YORK
ARRIVED: 12 MAY 1884

PASSENGER	AGE	SEX	OCCUPATION	PV	D
SILBERMANN, M.	31	M	PFNL	RRZZZZ	NY
LSTH.	26	F	UNKNOWN	RRZZZZ	NY
LIBERMANN, ISAAC	36	M	TLR	PLZZZZ	NY
HANNAH	34	F	W	PLZZZZ	NY
MEYER	17	M	UNKNOWN	PLZZZZ	NY
HARRI	11	M	UNKNOWN	PLZZZZ	NY
ISRAEL	9	M	CHILD	PLZZZZ	NY
SARAH	7	F	CHILD	PLZZZZ	NY
REBECCA	4	F	CHILD	PLZZZZ	NY
ABRAHAM	1	M	CHILD	PLZZZZ	NY
STEEF, AB.	24	M	TCHR	RRZZZZ	NY
LEWINSHON, SAL.	18	M	UNKNOWN	RRZZZZ	BAL
MILLAR, AB.	25	M	SHMK	RRZZZZ	UNK
GOEABERG, RACHAEL	22	F	W	RRZZZZ	UNK
COHEN, SAM	24	M	CGRMKR	RRZZZZ	UNK
L.	22	F	W	RRZZZZ	UNK
FANJOED, JACOB	38	M	CPR	PLZZZZ	PHI
GOEABERG, M.	27	M	TLR	RRZZZZ	BO
RAPHAUL, SARAH	20	F	TLR	PLZZZZ	NY
LARSCHAMMER, B.	31	M	UNKNOWN	PLZZZZ	NY
LLIZ.	32	F	W	PLZZZZ	NY
KABELKA, N.	20	M	UNKNOWN	PLZZZZ	PA
LARPROIT, B.	42	M	UNKNOWN	PLZZZZ	OH
MACIAS, J.	24	M	UNKNOWN	PLZZZZ	NY
LEBOWITZ, D.	50	M	TLR	PLZZZZ	NY
LUCHESWITZ, JONAS	35	M	UNKNOWN	RRZZZZ	NY
SANCZEVOSKY, J.	45	M	LABR	PLZZZZ	PA
BUTZKANZLES, J.	30	M	UNKNOWN	PLZZZZ	NY
ANNA	23	F	W	PLZZZZ	NY
SESCHSINK, JOSEF	23	M	LABR	PLZZZZ	NY
GRABOVSKY, I.	22	M	UNKNOWN	PLZZZZ	NY
LIBEROVSKY, M.	18	M	UNKNOWN	PLZZZZ	NY
MATANROSKY, S.	24	M	UNKNOWN	PLZZZZ	NY
A.	18	F	W	PLZZZZ	NY
SUCHOCK, PETER	28	M	LABR	PLZZZZ	NY
TANRIS, J.	27	M	UNKNOWN	PLZZZZ	NY
M.	23	F	W	PLZZZZ	NY
SIGSMUND, I.	35	M	LABR	PLZZZZ	NY
K.	23	F	W	PLZZZZ	NY
AUGUST, M.	46	M	LABR	PLZZZZ	NY
ZECHANOIC, J.	28	M	UNKNOWN	PLZZZZ	NY
RAGLIS, I.	24	M	UNKNOWN	PLZZZZ	NY
KANSEVOIE, A.	24	M	UNKNOWN	PLZZZZ	NY
ROSA	36	F	W	PLZZZZ	NY
NANGULIS, V.	24	M	LABR	PLZZZZ	NY
DALOVSKY, M.	36	M	UNKNOWN	PLZZZZ	NY
FUNK, A.	36	M	UNKNOWN	PLZZZZ	NY
A.	28	F	W	PLZZZZ	NY
ANNA	4	F	CHILD	PLZZZZ	NY
CAIN	5	M	CHILD	PLZZZZ	NY
ADA	.03	F	INFANT	PLZZZZ	NY
DEWISKEWICK, M.	46	M	LABR	PLZZZZ	NY
ANNA	44	F	W	PLZZZZ	NY

PASSENGER	AGE	SEX	OCCUPATION	PRV	DES
T.	22	F	UNKNOWN	PLZZZZ	NY
JOSEF	19	M	UNKNOWN	PLZZZZ	NY
R.	16	F	UNKNOWN	PLZZZZ	NY
DOEN	10	M	UNKNOWN	PLZZZZ	NY
ANNA	11	F	UNKNOWN	PLZZZZ	NY
M.	2	F	CHILD	PLZZZZ	NY
LAU.	.04	F	INFANT	PLZZZZ	NY
WEMGATH, AL.	23	M	WTRPR	RRZZZZ	NY
CHANVAITZ, MOSES	28	M	PROF	RRZZZZ	NY
SARAH	22	F	UNKNOWN	RRZZZZ	NY
JOSEPH	.11	M	INFANT	RRZZZZ	NY
BARVELKIN, SA.	30	M	PROF	RRZZZZ	NY
SARAH	26	F	UNKNOWN	RRZZZZ	NY
LATCINER, JOS.	25	M	UNKNOWN	RRZZZZ	NY
NORCHETAL, JOS.	21	M	UNKNOWN	RRZZZZ	NY
IHRENBERG, S.	28	M	UNKNOWN	RRZZZZ	NY
KARPO, M.	25	M	UNKNOWN	RRZZZZ	NY

SHIP: NEWPORT

FROM: HAVANA
TO: NEW YORK
ARRIVED: 12 MAY 1884

PASSENGER	AGE	SEX	OCCUPATION	PRV	DES
KRAWJEWSKI, F.MR	35	M	MCHT	PLZZZZ	USA

SHIP: WERRA

FROM: BREMEN
TO: NEW YORK
ARRIVED: 12 MAY 1884

PASSENGER	AGE	SEX	OCCUPATION	PRV	DES
HERBALD, MARTIN	40	M	FARMER	RRZZZZ	USA
ROSINE	36	F	UNKNOWN	RRZZZZ	USA
ANNA	22	F	UNKNOWN	RRZZZZ	USA
CHRISTINE	15	F	UNKNOWN	RRZZZZ	USA
FRIEDR.	14	M	UNKNOWN	RRZZZZ	USA
HEINR.	7	M	CHILD	RRZZZZ	USA
ROSINE	.07	F	INFANT	RRZZZZ	USA
SONNENFELD, JOHANN	22	M	FARMER	RRZZZZ	USA
RENNING, CARL	34	M	FARMER	RRZZZZ	USA
MARCYTHE	35	F	UNKNOWN	RRZZZZ	USA
SOFIE	6	F	CHILD	RRZZZZ	USA
HEINS, HEINR.	30	M	FARMER	RRZZZZ	USA
CHRISTINA	26	F	UNKNOWN	RRZZZZ	USA
CHRISTINA	6	F	CHILD	RRZZZZ	USA
DENTSCHER, JOH.	23	M	FARMER	RRZZZZ	USA
CAROLINE	21	F	UNKNOWN	RRZZZZ	USA
FRIEDR.	.05	M	INFANT	RRZZZZ	USA
SONNENFELD, JOHACMA	24	F	UNKNOWN	RRZZZZ	USA
ROST, EMILIE	20	F	UNKNOWN	RRZZZZ	USA
ELYER, MAGDALENA	54	F	UNKNOWN	RRZZZZ	USA
MARGTHE.	24	F	UNKNOWN	RRZZZZ	USA
ELISABTH.	18	F	UNKNOWN	RRZZZZ	USA
KARL	13	M	UNKNOWN	RRZZZZ	USA
MULLER, JACOB	50	M	FARMER	RRZZZZ	USA
CHRISTINE	48	F	UNKNOWN	RRZZZZ	USA
JACOB	20	M	FARMER	RRZZZZ	USA
JOHANN	18	M	FARMER	RRZZZZ	USA
FRIEDR.	7	M	CHILD	RRZZZZ	USA
EVA	17	F	UNKNOWN	RRZZZZ	USA
MARGTHE.	2	F	CHILD	RRZZZZ	USA
MANCH, WM.	33	M	FARMER	RRZZZZ	USA
SOFIE	27	F	UNKNOWN	RRZZZZ	USA
SOFIE	2	F	CHILD	RRZZZZ	USA

PASSENGER	AGE	SEX	OCCUPATION	PRV	DES
EVA	.11	F	INFANT	RRZZZZ	USA

SHIP: SPAIN

FROM: LIVERPOOL AND QUEENSTOWN
TO: NEW YORK
ARRIVED: 13 MAY 1884

PASSENGER	AGE	SEX	OCCUPATION	PRV	DES
ARENTAWSKY, JOLIOS	28	M	LABR	RRZZZZ	USA
LUGASRENWICZ, S.	40	M	LABR	RRZZZZ	USA
JENSON, JOHANES	30	M	LABR	PLZZZZ	USA
OBSDOTR, KARI	30	F	W	PLZZZZ	USA
JOHANSEN, JAS.	00	M	INF	PLZZZZ	USA
STOLEN, LARS	32	M	LABR	PLZZZZ	USA
LARSOTC, UNNIE	33	F	W	PLZZZZ	USA
JOHANNES	21	M	LABR	PLZZZZ	USA
RAZNILD	28	M	LABR	PLZZZZ	USA
KNUD	20	M	LABR	PLZZZZ	USA

SHIP: NORMANDIE

FROM: HAVRE
TO: NEW YORK
ARRIVED: 14 MAY 1884

PASSENGER	AGE	SEX	OCCUPATION	PRV	DES
GAIEWSKY, ANTON	33	M	SVNT	PLZZZZ	MX
HOLBACKZEWSKI, NICOLAS	47	M	CL	PLZZZZ	UNK
WIATOWSKI, STANISLAS.	21	M	TLR	PLZZZZ	NY

SHIP: SCYTHIA

FROM: LIVERPOOL AND QUEENSTOWN
TO: NEW YORK
ARRIVED: 14 MAY 1884

PASSENGER	AGE	SEX	OCCUPATION	PRV	DES
BAZAN, JAMES	25	M	LABR	PLZZZZ	USA
MIZAK, MIDA	28	M	LABR	PLZZZZ	USA
KYMAK, MICAL	48	M	LABR	PLZZZZ	USA
KIMK, MATIAS	28	M	LABR	PLZZZZ	USA
MARIA	30	F	W	PLZZZZ	USA
JOSEF	4	M	CHILD	PLZZZZ	USA
JOSEFA	1	F	CHILD	PLZZZZ	USA
BALLIN	1	M	CHILD	PLZZZZ	USA
KUCHTA, JAN	42	M	LABR	PLZZZZ	USA
SESKA, MICAL	35	M	LABR	PLZZZZ	USA
GLODZIAK, JOSEF	38	M	LABR	PLZZZZ	USA
SOPHIA	20	F	W	PLZZZZ	USA
SOWA, JOSEF	11	M	BY	PLZZZZ	USA
ZUBINSKI, FRANCIS	38	M	LABR	PLZZZZ	USA
JOSEFINE	29	F	W	PLZZZZ	USA
FRANCISKA	20	F	SP	PLZZZZ	USA
BERTISLAWA	4	F	CHILD	PLZZZZ	USA
JOHAN	.07	M	INFANT	PLZZZZ	USA
SIDORG, MICHAL	34	M	LABR	PLZZZZ	USA
DOROTHEA	30	F	W	PLZZZZ	USA
MARIA	5	F	CHILD	PLZZZZ	USA
BAWIAS, HENDRIK	25	M	FSHMN	PLZZZZ	***
HORNIK, SIMON	26	M	FSHMN	PLZZZZ	USA
MARTIN	20	M	FSHMN	PLZZZZ	USA
STOWA, RATHARIN	21	M	FSHMN	PLZZZZ	USA

PASSENGER	AGE	SEX	OCCUPATION	PRIV VIL DES
WALIK	14	M	FSHMN	PLZZZZUSA
KAWA, JAS.	28	M	FSHMN	PLZZZZUSA
ZOLONDEK, WOJTCH	28	M	FSHMN	PLZZZZUSA
SCHAURZ, JOSEF	14	M	FSHMN	PLZZZZUSA
MAJEWCYK, MICHAL	00	M	LABR	PLZZZZUSA
SOLTIS, JANOS	30	M	LABR	PLZZZZUSA
MACYAK, THOMAS	40	M	LABR	PLZZZZUSA
MAJERCZAK, JANOS	35	M	LABR	PLZZZZUSA
BIGERS, WOJTCH	11	M	BY	PLZZZZUSA
GUTLIEB, MATIAS	22	M	LABR	PLZZZZUSA
BEIZETZKE, STANISLAUS	20	M	LABR	PLZZZZUSA
LUDOVSKY, VINCENZ	29	M	LABR	PLZZZZUSA
SZYPAWSKY, WOJTCH	11	M	BY	PLZZZZUSA
KRAWCIK, PAL	36	M	LABR	PLZZZZUSA
BERES, PETER	27	M	LABR	PLZZZZUSA
ROMAN, JURA	29	M	LABR	PLZZZZUSA
DANO, JANOS	11	M	BY	PLZZZZUSA
MICHELCZAK, MICHEL	33	M	LABR	PLZZZZUSA
MAJEWSKY, FREDI	34	M	LABR	PLZZZZUSA
MARINCZAK, STEFAN	36	M	LABR	PLZZZZUSA
KONNAR, JANOS	11	M	BY	PLZZZZUSA
LINKOLOWSKY, JACOB	19	M	LABR	PLZZZZUSA
SZERZINSKY, JOSEF	30	M	LABR	PLZZZZUSA
SAWOZEVSKY, MARTIN	37	M	LABR	PLZZZZUSA
LAPINSKY, ADAM	36	M	LABR	PLZZZZUSA
SKOWSKY, WLADISL.	22	M	LABR	PLZZZZUSA
KONOSE, TEOFIL	11	M	LABR	PLZZZZUSA
JURPAK, JOHAN	28	M	LABR	PLZZZZUSA
FERKI, JANOS	37	M	LABR	PLZZZZUSA
KOSTUCHI, ANDREAS	38	M	LABR	PLZZZZUSA
ECKERT, FRANZ	22	M	LABR	PLZZZZUSA
NALEZCZINSKY, FRANZ	25	M	LABR	PLZZZZUSA
POBCTAC, JANOS	11	M	BY	PLZZZZUSA
WURAWSKY, WOJTCH	40	M	LABR	PLZZZZUSA
STEFANTI, JANOS	26	M	LABR	PLZZZZUSA
SCZERBO, JANOS	34	M	LABR	PLZZZZUSA
HALAS, GEORGI	40	M	LABR	PLZZZZUSA
PASTERNAK, GEORGI	11	M	BY	PLZZZZUSA
RUTLONSKY, FRANZ	38	M	LABR	PLZZZZUSA
MARIA	37	F	W	PLZZZZUSA
KARIE, WASIL	36	M	LABR	PLZZZZUSA
KUPREC, WOJTCH	48	M	LABR	PLZZZZUSA
BJEJ, THOMAS	53	M	LABR	PLZZZZUSA
MARIA	11	F	CH	PLZZZZUSA

SHIP: RUGIA

FROM: HAMBURG
TO: NEW YORK
ARRIVED: 15 MAY 1884

PASSENGER	AGE	SEX	OCCUPATION	PRIV VIL DES
SEGAL, WOLF	49	M	DLR	RRZZZZUSA
MARY---LSKI, CHEIM	38	M	DLR	RRZZZZUSA
U, TEWIE	18	M	UNKNOWN	RRZZZZUSA
--SEN--, ----STE	31	F	UNKNOWN	RRZZZZUSA
CHAIE	.11	M	INFANT	RRZZZZUSA
MONKA, ISAAC	8	M	CHILD	RRZZZZUSA
ORLTSCHUL, SCHIE	27	M	FARMER	RRZZZZUSA
SALOMOWITZ, LEOP.	58	M	LABR	RRZZZZUSA
SOPHIE	21	F	UNKNOWN	RRZZZZUSA
ROMALDO	19	M	CH	RRZZZZUSA
AGATHE	8	F	CHILD	RRZZZZUSA
PEUMANN, LEOP.	29	M	MLR	RRZZZZUSA
SOLINSKI, JOSEF	46	M	UNKNOWN	RRZZZZUSA
MARIANE	45	F	W	RRZZZZUSA
MARIANE	8	F	CHILD	RRZZZZUSA
IGNATZ	6	M	CHILD	RRZZZZUSA
U, SALI	37	F	W	RRZZZZUSA
RIWKE	7	F	CHILD	RRZZZZUSA
ESTHER	.11	F	INFANT	RRZZZZUSA
CHAIM	.01	M	INFANT	RRZZZZUSA
ABOLSOER, ELIAS	20	M	DLR	RRZZZZUSA
JACOBSOHN, JACOB	17	M	UNKNOWN	RRZZZZUSA
ZADICK, HANNI	24	F	UNKNOWN	RRZZZZUSA
ARANSKI, ISRAEL	24	M	DLR	RRZZZZUSA
LEIB	19	M	UNKNOWN	RRZZZZUSA
METISU, CHANE	27	F	UNKNOWN	RRZZZZUSA
ILIECKER, ABRAH.	18	M	TLR	RRZZZZUSA
MARCUS, ABR.	25	M	DLR	RRZZZZUSA
ECKERT, PETER	19	M	JNR	RRZZZZUSA
VOT, HARIER	21	M	FARMER	RRZZZZUSA
MAROSCHA, JONAS	40	M	LABR	RRZZZZUSA
JOSES	6	M	CHILD	RRZZZZUSA
ANELI	8	F	CHILD	RRZZZZUSA
DUDONIS, VINCENT	20	M	LABR	RRZZZZUSA
RASALSKA, ANNA	20	F	W	RRZZZZUSA
ANNA	.11	F	INFANT	RRZZZZUSA
KUSCHNISKA, APOLL.	18	F	SGL	RRZZZZUSA
ROMANOWSKY, VINCENT	26	M	LABR	RRZZZZUSA
WAGNER, MARG.	41	F	W	RRZZZZUSA
FRIEDR.	9	M	CHILD	RRZZZZUSA
ZIELIMSKA, JOH.	24	F	SGL	RRZZZZUSA
WISIELUOWSKI, NICOLEI	37	M	LABR	RRZZZZUSA
FRAWHKOWSKI, WILH.	42	M	UNKNOWN	RRZZZZUSA
MROCZINSKI, MICH.	30	M	LABR	RRZZZZUSA
LUBELSKY, BARUCH	39	M	PNR	RRZZZZUSA
JUDA	19	M	UNKNOWN	RRZZZZUSA
JASZGANITZ, SARA	15	F	SGL	RRZZZZUSA
ROGOW, MALKE	35	F	W	RRZZZZUSA
MOSES	8	M	CHILD	RRZZZZUSA
TAUBE	7	F	CHILD	RRZZZZUSA
MORDCHE	8	M	CHILD	RRZZZZUSA
SARA	6	F	CHILD	RRZZZZUSA
HENE	.11	F	INFANT	RRZZZZUSA
RUTKOWSKI, KASIM.	19	M	LABR	RRZZZZUSA
FRANZ	37	M	UNKNOWN	RRZZZZUSA
FROCZYKOWSKI, JAN	31	M	UNKNOWN	RRZZZZUSA
REICH, CARL	25	M	LABR	RRZZZZUSA
SICHENMAN, JAN	20	M	UNKNOWN	RRZZZZUSA
BUHEL, JOFN.	26	M	UNKNOWN	RRZZZZUSA
JENSEN, HEINR.	15	M	FARMER	RRZZZZUSA
GORDAN, LEA	15	F	SGL	RRZZZZUSA
GEID, KARL	22	M	CPTR	RRZZZZUSA
THENDA, SIMON	20	M	TLR	RRZZZZUSA
MROZINSKA, MARIANE	18	F	SGL	RRZZZZUSA
HELPEMD, ISRAEL	20	M	LABR	RRZZZZUSA
HORWITZ, SALOM.	22	M	LABR	RRZZZZUSA
FRAAS, CHIL.	68	M	MCHT	RRZZZZUSA
JOH.	45	F	W	RRZZZZUSA
GOLDRING, NATH.	17	M	MCHT	RRZZZZUSA

SHIP: FRISIA

FROM: HAMBURG AND HAVRE
TO: NEW YORK
ARRIVED: 16 MAY 1884

PASSENGER	AGE	SEX	OCCUPATION	PRIV VIL DES
BERMER, BARBARA	22	F	W	RRZZZZUSA
STANISLA.	2	F	CHILD	RRZZZZUSA
VALENTINE	.11	F	INFANT	RRZZZZUSA
FRIEDMANN, SALOMON	20	F	SGL	RRZZZZUSA
ZULIS, BALTRENIE	40	M	LABR	RRZZZZUSA
ANTON	37	M	LABR	RRZZZZUSA
MIKULSKY, CARL	48	M	LABR	RRZZZZUSA
STANISL.	19	M	LABR	RRZZZZUSA
JOSEF	19	M	LABR	RRZZZZUSA
RUJEWSKY, JAN'	29	M	LABR	RRZZZZUSA
ALLENA	22	F	W	RRZZZZUSA
KOTKY, IVAN	22	M	LABR	RRZZZZUSA
BUCKOVSKY, KASIMIR	43	M	LABR	RRZZZZUSA

PASSENGER	AGE	SEX	OCCUPATION	PRV	VIL	DES
LIMEISKI, ANTON	19	M	LABR	RR	ZZZZ	USA
DOMSKI, CASIMIR	36	M	LABR	RR	ZZZZ	USA
MADCIEFSKI, CASIMIR	36	M	LABR	RR	ZZZZ	USA
KOLENDERSKI, STANISLAV	20	M	LABR	RR	ZZZZ	USA
MUKOVSKY, VINCENT	30	M	LABR	RR	ZZZZ	USA
DETOD, JOSEF	24	M	LABR	RR	ZZZZ	USA
VALENITZ, JAN	30	M	LABR	RR	ZZZZ	USA
KUENZLI, ISAAC	40	M	DLR	PL	ZZZZ	USA
ROSALIE	38	F	W	PL	ZZZZ	USA
MOSES	22	M	S	PL	ZZZZ	USA
HIRSCH, CHEIM	35	M	MCHT	PL	ZZZZ	USA
JACOBSON, HERRM.	34	M	MCHT	RR	ZZZZ	USA

SHIP: KATIE

FROM: STETTIN
TO: NEW YORK
ARRIVED: 16 MAY 1884

PASSENGER	AGE	SEX	OCCUPATION	PRV	VIL	DES
SZAFRAN, MARIE	49	F	WO	PL	ZZZZ	USA
ANNSTARZA	22	F	UNKNOWN	PL	ZZZZ	USA
JOSEPHA	19	F	UNKNOWN	PL	ZZZZ	USA
STANISLAUS	17	M	UNKNOWN	PL	ZZZZ	USA
ANTON	11	M	UNKNOWN	PL	ZZZZ	USA
VALENTIN	10	M	UNKNOWN	PL	ZZZZ	USA
MARTHA	8	F	CHILD	PL	ZZZZ	USA
KOPACKA, JOSEPHA	19	F	UNKNOWN	PL	ZZZZ	USA
WISCHNIEWSKY, LEON	24	M	LABR	PL	ZZZZ	USA
GODNIARECK, JOSEPH	27	M	BLKSMH	PL	ZZZZ	USA
HEDWIG	27	F	W	PL	ZZZZ	USA
GODNIAREK, PELAGIA	2	F	CHILD	PL	ZZZZ	USA
CHELEWINSKY, MARIEANNA	23	F	UNKNOWN	PL	ZZZZ	USA
SLASINSKI, MICHEL	49	M	LABR	PL	ZZZZ	USA
KATHARINA	44	F	W	PL	ZZZZ	USA
FRANCISKA	16	F	D	PL	ZZZZ	USA
MARIANNA	15	F	UNKNOWN	PL	ZZZZ	USA
STANISLAWA	10	F	UNKNOWN	PL	ZZZZ	USA
WLADISLAW	4	M	CHILD	PL	ZZZZ	USA
BALZER, MARTIN	40	M	LABR	PL	ZZZZ	USA
CONSTANTIA	32	F	W	PL	ZZZZ	USA
JOSEPH	15	M	S	PL	ZZZZ	USA
MAGDALENA	9	F	CHILD	PL	ZZZZ	USA
VICTORIA	7	F	CHILD	PL	ZZZZ	USA
LUDWIG	1	M	CHILD	PL	ZZZZ	USA
LISSEWSKY, ALBERT	26	M	LABR	PL	ZZZZ	USA
GRODZICKI, WOJCIECH	42	M	UNKNOWN	PL	ZZZZ	USA
KATHARINA	40	F	W	PL	ZZZZ	USA
FRANZ	9	M	CHILD	PL	ZZZZ	USA
ELISABETH	6	F	CHILD	PL	ZZZZ	USA
JOHANN	4	M	CHILD	PL	ZZZZ	USA
FRANCISKA	2	F	CHILD	PL	ZZZZ	USA
MICHALINA	.04	F	INFANT	PL	ZZZZ	USA
ZIELINSKI, STANISLAW	16	M	LABR	PL	ZZZZ	USA
CONSTANTIA	20	F	UNKNOWN	PL	ZZZZ	USA
PRZESTWOR, JOSEPH	24	M	LABR	PL	ZZZZ	USA
SKROBANEK, SARCANDER	24	M	GDNR	PL	ZZZZ	USA
RICHWALSKI, LEOPOLD	48	M	LABR	PL	ZZZZ	USA
MARIANNE	49	F	W	PL	ZZZZ	USA
JEAN	16	M	S	PL	ZZZZ	USA
MARIANNE	4	F	CHILD	PL	ZZZZ	USA
REREK, MARTHA	17	F	UNKNOWN	PL	ZZZZ	USA
FADISCH, AMELIA	20	F	UNKNOWN	PL	ZZZZ	USA
PHILIPP	59	M	LABR	PL	ZZZZ	USA
RATAJCZAK, MARTIN	46	M	UNKNOWN	PL	ZZZZ	USA
STRZEMBKOWSKI, ANDRZY	33	M	UNKNOWN	PL	ZZZZ	USA
PACZYLK, JOSEPH	23	M	UNKNOWN	PL	ZZZZ	USA
PASTERNAK, PAUL	31	M	UNKNOWN	PL	ZZZZ	USA
EVA	42	F	W	PL	ZZZZ	USA
JOHANN	15	M	S	PL	ZZZZ	USA
KATHARINA	10	F	D	PL	ZZZZ	USA

PASSENGER	AGE	SEX	OCCUPATION	PRV	VIL	DES
ALBERT	5	M	CHILD	PL	ZZZZ	USA
SCZODARSKI, NICODEMUS	18	M	LABR	PL	ZZZZ	USA
DUETKIWICZ, FELIX	11	M	CH	PL	ZZZZ	USA
HADRISCH, FRANZ	23	M	LABR	PL	ZZZZ	USA
YZGDROCZ, IADWIGA	25	F	WO	PL	ZZZZ	USA
MARIEANNA	2	F	CHILD	PL	ZZZZ	USA
AGNES	.04	F	INFANT	PL	ZZZZ	USA
BOSIKOWSKI, PIETZ.	28	M	SHMK	PL	ZZZZ	USA
JABLOWSKY, FRANZISZECK	24	M	LABR	PL	ZZZZ	USA
HANKIEWICZ, JOSEPH	25	M	SMH	PL	ZZZZ	USA
CZESCHAK, PETER	27	M	LABR	PL	ZZZZ	USA
KUWIAK, JOSEPH	40	M	UNKNOWN	PL	ZZZZ	USA
MROZINSKI, ROSALIE	21	F	W	PL	ZZZZ	USA
FRANZ	1	M	CHILD	PL	ZZZZ	USA
PRZESTRO, BALZER	32	M	LABR	PL	ZZZZ	USA
RYMAKIEWICZ, WOYCIEK	32	M	SHMK	PL	ZZZZ	USA
MICHALINA	49	F	W	PL	ZZZZ	USA
MACHINSKA, MAGDALENA	30	F	W	PL	ZZZZ	USA
MARIE	1	F	CHILD	PL	ZZZZ	USA
PELAGIA	2	F	CHILD	PL	ZZZZ	USA
KAHN, JUDEL	31	M	UNKNOWN	RR	ZZZZ	USA

SHIP: MAIN

FROM: BREMEN
TO: NEW YORK
ARRIVED: 16 MAY 1884

PASSENGER	AGE	SEX	OCCUPATION	PRV	VIL	DES
KTONIECKA, KATARZYNA	24	F	W	RR	ZZZZ	USA
ZARZINSKA, THEOPHILIA	15	F	SVNT	RR	ZZZZ	USA
CZEPELSKI, JAN	26	M	LABR	RR	ZZZZ	USA
RABASZYNSKI, JAN	18	M	LABR	RR	ZZZZ	USA
LEWANDOWSKY, JOSEF	25	M	UNKNOWN	RR	ZZZZ	USA
OLSZTA, ANNA	40	F	W	RR	ZZZZ	USA
HELENE	9	F	CHILD	RR	ZZZZ	USA
WANDA	7	F	CHILD	RR	ZZZZ	USA

SHIP: ST. OF PENNSYLVANIA

FROM: GLASGOW AND LARNE
TO: NEW YORK
ARRIVED: 16 MAY 1884

PASSENGER	AGE	SEX	OCCUPATION	PRV	VIL	DES
KILIKOWSKI, NORDCHE	19	M	LABR	RR	ZZZZ	USA
SCHMUEL, ABRAHAM	27	M	UNKNOWN	RR	ZZZZ	USA
RYBSTEM, BERGEL	32	M	UNKNOWN	RR	ZZZZ	USA
TRAMBITZKY, JOSEPH	16	M	UNKNOWN	RR	ZZZZ	USA
WINER, JUDEL	23	M	UNKNOWN	RR	ZZZZ	USA
FRIEDMANN, JACOB	22	M	UNKNOWN	RR	ZZZZ	USA
HOHIANSK, IOSEL	29	M	PDLR	RR	ZZZZ	USA
SPANUR, MEUS	46	M	TLR	RR	ZZZZ	USA
GELT, MORITZ	11	M	UNKNOWN	RR	ZZZZ	USA
GRUZINSCHE, ISAAC	16	M	UNKNOWN	RR	ZZZZ	USA
SCHUSTER, MEIR	18	M	LABR	RR	ZZZZ	USA
SUSSAR, NETLE	35	M	UNKNOWN	RR	ZZZZ	USA
SCHWARG, ABRAHAM	28	M	UNKNOWN	RR	ZZZZ	USA
LEITY, LEISER	18	M	UNKNOWN	RR	ZZZZ	USA
LIHSMANN, ABRAHAM	28	M	UNKNOWN	RR	ZZZZ	USA
LAX, JANKEL	18	M	TLR	RR	ZZZZ	USA
HRAMER, DARG.	23	M	TDR	RR	ZZZZ	USA
WOLFER, MORISECH	45	M	UNKNOWN	RR	ZZZZ	USA
GIMOWITZ, D.	18	M	LABR	RR	ZZZZ	USA
FURMANSKI, MOSES	21	M	UNKNOWN	RR	ZZZZ	USA
LICHWITZ, SCHAGE	21	M	UNKNOWN	RR	ZZZZ	USA
ABRAHAMOWSCH, NOAH	37	M	UNKNOWN	RR	ZZZZ	USA

PASSENGER	AGE	SEX	OCCUPATION	PRV VIL DES
MOSES	10	M	UNKNOWN	RRZZZZUSA
SCHIMSCHEITZ, ISAAC	20	M	UNKNOWN	RRZZZZUSA
ROTH, SAMUEL	19	M	UNKNOWN	RRZZZZUSA
MANSCHER, MOSES	24	M	UNKNOWN	RRZZZZUSA
SUFFE, SCHFTER	23	M	UNKNOWN	RRZZZZUSA
ANDRICH, BENJAMIN	31	M	UNKNOWN	RRZZZZUSA
GRANAT, ISAAC	33	M	UNKNOWN	RRZZZZUSA
ABRAHAM	11	M	UNKNOWN	RRZZZZUSA
LIMIESKI, ABRAHAM	26	M	UNKNOWN	RRZZZZUSA
HOLEAB, LEIB	20	M	UNKNOWN	RRZZZZUSA
SACKS, H---	17	M	UNKNOWN	RRZZZZUSA
LAIBOWITZ, MARCUS	22	M	UNKNOWN	RRZZZZUSA
BALKIN, JACOB	44	M	UNKNOWN	RRZZZZUSA
BLAN, RESI	24	F	DMS	RRZZZZUSA
ABRAHAM	.04	M	INFANT	RRZZZZUSA
GLATT, RILCKE	21	M	LABR	RRZZZZUSA
MARITZKI, ODE	25	M	UNKNOWN	RRZZZZUSA
MITEB	1	M	CHILD	RRZZZZUSA
HISSEL, FRUME	18	M	LABR	RRZZZZUSA
HILLACK, SAMUEL	21	M	TLR	RRZZZZUSA
BLOCH, MOCHEL	23	M	LABR	RRZZZZUSA
JANKELEWSKY, HIRSCH	35	M	UNKNOWN	RRZZZZUSA
ROLLERY, ARON	35	M	UNKNOWN	RRZZZZUSA
SCHOR, CHAIM	44	M	UNKNOWN	RRZZZZUSA
ROSENFELD, ELRAM	32	M	UNKNOWN	RRZZZZUSA
HAHAN, JACOB	18	M	UNKNOWN	RRZZZZUSA
GITY, ABE	26	M	UNKNOWN	RRZZZZUSA
BLUM, GITTEL	24	M	UNKNOWN	RRZZZZUSA
SEILE	14	M	UNKNOWN	RRZZZZUSA
ROCHE	11	M	UNKNOWN	RRZZZZUSA
CHAIT, CHONON	41	M	LABR	RRZZZZUSA
HAPTAN, GISTAL	11	M	UNKNOWN	RRZZZZUSA
MALFSEN, OSCHY	18	M	UNKNOWN	RRZZZZUSA
ABRAHAM	18	M	UNKNOWN	RRZZZZUSA
HERING, CHAIM	41	M	UNKNOWN	RRZZZZUSA
BEHR	11	M	UNKNOWN	RRZZZZUSA
WOLF, ELIAS	35	M	UNKNOWN	RRZZZZUSA
SEID, EBIK	28	M	UNKNOWN	RRZZZZUSA
FRANKEL, SCHAIN	11	M	UNKNOWN	RRZZZZUSA
HRISMANSKI, ABRAHAM	16	M	LABR	RRZZZZUSA
FLEISCHMAN, ELISIK	19	M	UNKNOWN	RRZZZZUSA
LUBEIS, TOWEL	70	M	LABR	RRZZZZUSA
STALONSKI, LEISER	31	M	UNKNOWN	RRZZZZUSA
MINKUS, JACOB	20	M	UNKNOWN	RRZZZZUSA
MILYER, CHATZKEL	44	M	UNKNOWN	RRZZZZUSA
SCHABOSCWITZ, LEIB	34	M	UNKNOWN	RRZZZZUSA
HAILANBZK, NATHAN	30	M	UNKNOWN	RRZZZZUSA
LANGER, HINKLE	21	M	UNKNOWN	RRZZZZUSA
MECHEL	1	M	CHILD	RRZZZZUSA
HIRSCH, ABRAHAM	39	M	UNKNOWN	RRZZZZUSA
LEID, DAVID	39	M	UNKNOWN	RRZZZZUSA
MISCHE	17	M	UNKNOWN	RRZZZZUSA
HIRSCH	9	M	CHILD	RRZZZZUSA
BECKER, CHAIM	22	M	LABR	RRZZZZUSA
FRIEDMANN, JAN	20	M	TLR	RRZZZZUSA
JOIYAL	24	M	UNKNOWN	RRZZZZUSA
LYHMAN, ISER	17	M	UNKNOWN	RRZZZZUSA
ROSCHER, RAFAEL	25	M	UNKNOWN	RRZZZZUSA
ABRAMOWITZ, JACOB	36	M	UNKNOWN	RRZZZZUSA
SCHWARZ, MOSES	28	M	UNKNOWN	RRZZZZUSA
ELINKEWITZ, MEYER	26	M	PDLR	RRZZZZUSA
BUCHFIELD, J.	40	M	UNKNOWN	RRZZZZUSA
HOLZ, JACOB	39	M	UNKNOWN	RRZZZZUSA
CAROLINE	22	F	W	RRZZZZUSA
LANQIER, S.	21	M	LABR	RRZZZZUSA
C.	16	F	W	RRZZZZUSA
STOLAN, THE.	24	M	TLR	RRZZZZUSA
CHR.	21	F	W	RRZZZZUSA
DODIKOW, JANKEL	21	M	LABR	RRZZZZUSA
OSCHER, BEHR	11	M	UNKNOWN	RRZZZZUSA
BEST, CHAYKEL	26	M	UNKNOWN	RRZZZZUSA
HORESCHTER, HANICH	30	M	LABR	RRZZZZUSA
BERGER, LEIB	24	M	UNKNOWN	RRZZZZUSA
JULSMANSKI, ABRAM	19	M	LABR	RRZZZZUSA
GOLDFAIB, LEIB	24	M	TLR	RRZZZZUSA

PASSENGER	AGE	SEX	OCCUPATION	PRV VIL DES
SCHWARZ, ABRAHAM	28	M	UNKNOWN	PLZZZZUSA

SHIP: FULDA

FROM: BREMEN
TO: NEW YORK
ARRIVED: 17 MAY 1884

PASSENGER	AGE	SEX	OCCUPATION	PRV VIL DES
BERG, CHRISTIAN	43	M	FARMER	RRZZZZUSA
MARGARETTE	38	F	UNKNOWN	RRZZZZUSA
CATHARINE	17	F	UNKNOWN	RRZZZZUSA
CAROLINE	16	F	UNKNOWN	RRZZZZUSA
MARIE	7	F	CHILD	RRZZZZUSA
CHRISTIAN	6	M	CHILD	RRZZZZUSA
JOHANNES	4	M	CHILD	RRZZZZUSA
FRIEDRICH	3	M	CHILD	RRZZZZUSA
HEINRICH	2	M	CHILD	RRZZZZUSA
ALBERT	.01	M	INFANT	RRZZZZUSA
FICHTNER, JACOB	37	M	FARMER	RRZZZZUSA
DOROTHEA	38	F	UNKNOWN	RRZZZZUSA
JACOB	7	M	CHILD	RRZZZZUSA
WILHELM	4	M	CHILD	RRZZZZUSA
AUGUST	3	M	CHILD	RRZZZZUSA
ZIEGENHAGEL, FRIEDRICH	18	M	WVR	RRZZZZUSA
BRESSBER, JOHANN	20	M	FARMER	RRZZZZUSA
NATHAN, SATTLIEB	38	M	FARMER	RRZZZZUSA
U, CATHARINA	37	F	UNKNOWN	RRZZZZUSA
WATHGEMUTH, GOTTFRIED	20	M	FARMER	RRZZZZUSA
NATHAN, ELISABETH	15	F	UNKNOWN	RRZZZZUSA
JOHANN	13	M	FARMER	RRZZZZUSA
GOTTLIEB	7	M	CHILD	RRZZZZUSA
BARBARA	6	F	CHILD	RRZZZZUSA
CAROLINE	5	F	CHILD	RRZZZZUSA
RICHARD	3	M	CHILD	RRZZZZUSA
JULIUS	2	M	CHILD	RRZZZZUSA
DANIEL	.06	M	INFANT	RRZZZZUSA
THENVER, CAROLINE	68	F	UNKNOWN	RRZZZZUSA
CAROLINE	16	F	UNKNOWN	RRZZZZUSA
SCHLEICHT, JACOB	24	M	FARMER	RRZZZZUSA
MATHILDE	22	F	UNKNOWN	RRZZZZUSA
JACOB	00	M	UNKNOWN	RRZZZZUSA
CAROLINE	00	F	UNKNOWN	RRZZZZUSA
GEORG, HEINRICH	44	M	FARMER	RRZZZZUSA
CATHARINA	44	F	UNKNOWN	RRZZZZUSA
MARY	19	F	UNKNOWN	RRZZZZUSA
JOHANNE	7	M	CHILD	RRZZZZUSA
ROSINA	5	F	CHILD	RRZZZZUSA
JACOB	4	M	CHILD	RRZZZZUSA
U, CHRISTINE	2	F	CHILD	RRZZZZUSA
WILHELM	.08	M	INFANT	RRZZZZUSA
LANG, MARTIN	33	M	FARMER	RRZZZZUSA
ELISABETH	30	F	UNKNOWN	RRZZZZUSA
ELISABETH	7	F	CHILD	RRZZZZUSA
CAROLINE	4	F	CHILD	RRZZZZUSA
CARL	.08	M	INFANT	RRZZZZUSA

SHIP: RHYNLAND

FROM: ANTWERP
TO: NEW YORK
ARRIVED: 17 MAY 1884

PASSENGER	AGE	SEX	OCCUPATION	PRV VIL DES
KAREMORE, MASE	24	M	UNKNOWN	RRZZZZCH
MICH	3	M	CHILD	RRZZZZCH

SHIP: CITY OF MONTREAL

FROM: LIVERPOOL
TO: NEW YORK
ARRIVED: 19 MAY 1884

PASSENGER	AGE	SEX	OCCUPATION	PRV VIL DES
LESKI, ANDSEN	21	M	UNKNOWN	PLZZZZMN
SCHILLER, HERM.	26	M	UNKNOWN	PLZZZZNY
HAVANNIE, MARIA	26	F	W	PLZZZZNY
PETER	1	M	CHILD	PLZZZZNY
HANNAH	1	F	CHILD	PLZZZZNY
SKUPEN, JOSEF	38	M	LABR	PLZZZZNY
NORIK, ISTNA	10	M	CH	PLZZZZNY
KLAT, MAX	27	M	LABR	PLZZZZNY
PLOFFE, HEHHCH	35	M	UNKNOWN	PLZZZZNY
AUGUST	30	F	W	PLZZZZNY
BICK, ALBERT	32	M	LABR	PLZZZZBO
BRYTH, CARL	10	M	CH	PLZZZZBO
PECHTA, IGNATZ	27	M	LABR	PLZZZZNY
WIGROSTIK, FRANZ	47	M	UNKNOWN	PLZZZZNY
BRYMICIA, FRANKA	30	F	W	PLZZZZSFC
JOHANNA	1	F	CHILD	PLZZZZSFC
WICZORCK, ANTON	25	M	LABR	PLZZZZSFC
TECHNER, FRANZ	28	M	UNKNOWN	PLZZZZSFC
CHICON, THOS.	37	M	FARMER	PLZZZZNY
AGATHE	30	F	W	PLZZZZNY
KASSIMER	3	F	CHILD	PLZZZZNY
LUDIVIE	1	M	CHILD	PLZZZZNY
INVICH	5	M	CHILD	PLZZZZNY
KONICKNY, JACOB	35	M	LABR	PLZZZZNY
JANOWITZ, JOSEF	00	M	CH	PLZZZZNY
CZAYCHY, ANDREAS	24	M	LABR	PLZZZZNY
MARIANNE	20	F	W	PLZZZZNY
IGNATZ	1	M	CHILD	PLZZZZNY
LEFELDT, HEP.	00	M	LABR	PLZZZZMN
FRANKOWITZ, ALEX	11	M	CH	PLZZZZMN
POLAMO, FELIX	10	M	UNKNOWN	PLZZZZMN
FELITZ, GUGA	32	M	LABR	PLZZZZMN
KOROW, JAN	11	M	CH	PLZZZZMN
JUBCK, BOSCHAL	42	M	LABR	PLZZZZMN
MARKOWSKY, JOS	31	M	UNKNOWN	PLZZZZMN
PODLAZCK, PAUL	10	M	CH	PLZZZZMN
JOZOCK, CARL	46	M	LABR	PLZZZZCAL
STAVAS, JUDRY	11	M	CH	PLZZZZCAL
WILOSKOA, PAUIN	36	F	W	PLZZZZNY
VICTORIE	.11	F	INFANT	PLZZZZNY
ALEX	10	M	CH	PLZZZZNY
JAN	9	M	CHILD	PLZZZZNY
FABLONKA, MARIE	37	F	W	PLZZZZNY
BUMS	10	M	CH	PLZZZZNY
ISABELLA	2	F	CHILD	PLZZZZNY
WLADISLAW	1	M	CHILD	PLZZZZNY
SZECCA, IGNATZ	42	M	LABR	PLZZZZNO
FABLONKA, ALFANIA	1	F	CHILD	PLZZZZNY
KOBA, JOHAN	35	M	LABR	PLZZZZNY
KENIACH, JANS	9	M	CHILD	PLZZZZNY
SZECH, BATHAR	46	M	LABR	PLZZZZMN
GEORG, MOCH.	10	M	CH	PLZZZZMN
KAENT, ERNEST	24	M	LABR	PLZZZZNY
BOWIAH, JOHAN	11	M	CH	PLZZZZNY
KOLSOK, JOSEF	10	M	UNKNOWN	PLZZZZNY
KOSCHYH, JOB.	28	M	LABR	PLZZZZNY
THOMAS, ANTON	50	M	FARMER	RRZZZZNY
IGNODY, ALBERT	50	M	UNKNOWN	RRZZZZNY
MICHAEL, PAYSE	11	M	CH	RRZZZZNY
TOPEAH, JOSEF	45	M	FARMER	RRZZZZNY
MARIE	45	F	W	RRZZZZNY
ANNA	10	F	CH	RRZZZZNY
JAN	7	M	CHILD	RRZZZZNY
KORNAK, MICH.	11	M	UNKNOWN	RRZZZZNY
WANREAK, GURA	33	M	LABR	RRZZZZNY
PELTI, GICHO	3	M	CHILD	RRZZZZNY
FRANCISCA	30	F	W	RRZZZZNY
JAN	10	M	CH	RRZZZZNY
INATHEY	1	M	CHILD	RRZZZZNY
WINOWSKY, JAN	34	M	MNR	RRZZZZNY
MARIA	28	F	W	RRZZZZNY
CATH.	3	F	CHILD	RRZZZZNY
LUDOVIKA	1	F	CHILD	RRZZZZNY
AOOLONIA	1	F	CHILD	RRZZZZNY
BORDA, ADAM	45	M	LABR	RRZZZZTX
VICTORIA	39	F	W	RRZZZZTX
MICHL	00	M	CH	RRZZZZTX
JAN	2	M	CHILD	RRZZZZTX
EVA	1	F	CHILD	RRZZZZTX

SHIP: HAMMONIA

FROM: HAMBURG AND HAVRE
TO: NEW YORK
ARRIVED: 19 MAY 1884

PASSENGER	AGE	SEX	OCCUPATION	PRV VIL DES
LEWIT, CHANNE	40	F	W	RRZZZZUSA
REBECCA	8	F	CHILD	RRZZZZUSA
LINE	7	F	CHILD	RRZZZZUSA
DAVID	6	M	CHILD	RRZZZZUSA
LEISER	4	M	CHILD	RRZZZZUSA
JEGLICKY, CHINE	28	F	W	RRZZZZUSA
BENY	5	M	CHILD	RRZZZZUSA
PAUL	.11	M	INFANT	RRZZZZUSA
RUVKIND, CHAIM	15	M	BY	RRZZZZUSA
HARSIEL	8	M	CHILD	RRZZZZUSA
LEFS, MOSES	25	M	LABR	RRZZZZUSA
BOEGEN, LEISER	18	M	LABR	RRZZZZUSA
KLEIN, HARRIS	20	M	LABR	RRZZZZUSA
MORITZ	8	M	CHILD	RRZZZZUSA
FELLER, CHANNE	30	F	SGL	RRZZZZUSA
SCHURMANN, PESZA	26	F	W	RRZZZZUSA
CHEIM	.11	M	INFANT	RRZZZZUSA
CZOKAILA, ANTON	42	M	LABR	RRZZZZUSA
STANISL.	18	M	CH	RRZZZZUSA
JOSEF	8	M	CHILD	RRZZZZUSA
NECHOMOWICH, HILLEL	52	M	LABR	RRZZZZUSA
KEINDSO, JOSEF	26	F	W	RRZZZZUSA
HANNE	.11	F	INFANT	RRZZZZUSA
RUBSTEIN, WOLF	20	M	LABR	RRZZZZUSA
KLENOWITZ, KALMAN	42	M	LABR	RRZZZZUSA
MELTZER, HIRSCH	28	M	TLR	RRZZZZUSA
KREIMER, REIZEL	18	F	SGL	RRZZZZUSA
GRAJEWSKY, HIRSCH	19	M	LABR	RRZZZZUSA
EPSTEIN, DEBORA	40	F	W	RRZZZZUSA
REBECCA	19	F	CH	RRZZZZUSA
ISAAK	17	M	CH	RRZZZZUSA
SARA	8	F	CHILD	RRZZZZUSA
OSCAR	7	M	CHILD	RRZZZZUSA
MAX	6	M	CHILD	RRZZZZUSA
ROSA	4	F	CHILD	RRZZZZUSA
ARENBERG, JACOB	18	M	BRM	RRZZZZUSA
EPSTEIN, MAX	17	M	BRM	RRZZZZUSA
BERNSTEIN, LEISER	8	M	CHILD	RRZZZZUSA
SCHLOMANN, DAVID	8	M	CHILD	RRZZZZUSA
WITER, MOSES	40	M	TLR	RRZZZZUSA
KOPLANSKI, RUWER	38	M	DLR	RRZZZZUSA
KOHNOWITZ, ISAAK	14	M	DLR	RRZZZZUSA
ONI, MOSES	27	M	FELMO	RRZZZZUSA
KUALOWITZ, ANTON	20	M	LABR	RRZZZZUSA
BUJAWITZ, ANTON	20	M	LABR	RRZZZZUSA
WISCHNEVSKI, JOHANN	31	M	LABR	RRZZZZUSA
BRAUER, CHRIST.	35	M	LABR	RRZZZZUSA
DEJESKA, JOH.	24	M	LABR	RRZZZZUSA
DUSCHINSKI, MARZELLI	25	M	LABR	RRZZZZUSA
LEWIT, NOAH	.11	M	INFANT	RRZZZZUSA
EPSTEIN, REISE	5	F	CHILD	RRZZZZUSA
ZOLNOWSKI, WANDA	36	F	W	RRZZZZUSA

SHIP: FRISIA

FROM: HAMBURG
TO: NEW YORK
ARRIVED: 20 MAY 1884

PASSENGER	AGE	SEX	OCCUPATION	PRV VIL DES
ROSENBLUM, ARON	17	M	LABR	RRZZZZUSA
LINCUTHAL, DORA	20	F	UNKNOWN	RRZZZZUSA
MELSNER, SCHIER	16	M	CL	RRZZZZUSA
BLUM, LOEB.	23	M	TLR	RRZZZZUSA
JOSZINSKI, SAMUEL	31	M	LABR	RRZZZZUSA
KAPLAN, CHASKEL	21	M	LABR	RRZZZZUSA
KLAWONSKY, LEIB	21	M	MSN	RRZZZZUSA
REHDER, JOHN	21	M	SGL	RRZZZZUSA
ZEBROWSKI, FRANZ	41	M	UNKNOWN	RRZZZZUSA
BACHLIER, SAMUEL	21	M	TLR	RRZZZZUSA
PAIROSKOWSKI, KASIMIR	28	M	LABR	RRZZZZUSA
BUNTMANN, SAMUEL	15	M	UNKNOWN	RRZZZZUSA
BONNER, BASCHE	30	F	W	RRZZZZUSA
ALTER	8	M	CHILD	RRZZZZUSA
PIEWORSKI, CHAIE	45	F	W	RRZZZZUSA
KNAPP, WOLFF	40	M	LABR	RRZZZZUSA
LEISER	20	M	UNKNOWN	RRZZZZUSA
ZOKASER, SARA	16	F	SGL	RRZZZZUSA
GORDON, MALKE	32	F	UNKNOWN	RRZZZZUSA
RANSAK, HIRSCH	50	M	DLR	RRZZZZUSA
PESCHE	8	F	CHILD	RRZZZZUSA
BERMANN, SAMUEL	41	M	MCHT	RRZZZZUSA
BARDIN, JACOB	40	M	DLR	RRZZZZUSA
ROSENFELD, NATE.	19	M	UNKNOWN	RRZZZZUSA
CEKINSKAJA, ELENA	22	F	SGL	RRZZZZUSA
FUCHS, SALOMON	42	M	TLR	RRZZZZUSA
FLASCHKE, ASCHER	20	M	TLR	RRZZZZUSA
GRANER, LEWIN	17	M	MCHT	RRZZZZUSA
JANKEL, MOSES	32	M	DLR	RRZZZZUSA
MOCHOLOK, HERSCH	25	M	MCHT	RRZZZZUSA
MILLER, KARIEL	20	M	UNKNOWN	RRZZZZUSA
AXEBRED, CHAIM	35	M	UNKNOWN	RRZZZZUSA
ZLOKIEWITZ, NOCHEM	20	M	UNKNOWN	RRZZZZUSA
MOSKO	21	M	UNKNOWN	RRZZZZUSA
MILLER, JEKO	29	M	UNKNOWN	RRZZZZUSA
BLUM, LEA	20	F	SGL	RRZZZZUSA
LIPKE, ARON	33	M	LABR	RRZZZZUSA
BRACH, ISRAEL	20	M	TLR	RRZZZZUSA
CACILIE	20	F	W	RRZZZZUSA
SCHEINBERTH, ISRAEL	20	M	TLR	RRZZZZUSA
CHEIE	21	F	W	RRZZZZUSA
GOSZIGER, SALOMON	21	M	LABR	RRZZZZUSA
ZUCHOFA, JOSEPH	19	M	UNKNOWN	RRZZZZUSA
HORN, NATHAN	25	M	TLR	RRZZZZUSA
BEREMANN, GUSTE	22	F	SGL	RRZZZZUSA
HOFFMANN, CASPER	22	M	MCHT	RRZZZZUSA
KARR, FEIGE	30	F	W	RRZZZZUSA
JOSEPH	4	M	CHILD	RRZZZZUSA
DORA	3	F	CHILD	RRZZZZUSA
DYLOW, MARENS	25	M	LABR	RRZZZZUSA
GUMKOWSKI, LEO	46	M	UNKNOWN	RRZZZZUSA
SCHWEITZER, BARNEG	17	M	LABR	RRZZZZUSA
KROLL, MARENS	30	M	MUSN	RRZZZZUSA
ROSA	26	F	W	RRZZZZUSA
FRIDA	6	F	CHILD	RRZZZZUSA
BERTHA	4	F	CHILD	RRZZZZUSA
SARA	2	F	CHILD	RRZZZZUSA
FELIX	.11	M	INFANT	RRZZZZUSA
BREY, FRISIA	.01	F	INFANT	RR****USA

SHIP: GALLIA

FROM: LIVERPOOL AND QUEENSTOWN
TO: NEW YORK
ARRIVED: 21 MAY 1884

PASSENGER	AGE	SEX	OCCUPATION	PRV VIL DES
PACHULKA, MICHALINA	20	F	SP	RRZZZZUSA
TRASKO, FRANZ	24	M	LABR	RRZZZZUSA
MENSTEN, JACOB	30	M	UNKNOWN	RRZZZZUSA
PAULINA	21	F	W	RRZZZZUSA
ANDRE	.10	M	INFANT	RRZZZZUSA
PELECKY, ADAM	28	M	LABR	RRZZZZUSA
FRANZISKA	22	F	W	RRZZZZUSA
JOSEF	11	M	CH	RRZZZZUSA
JURETCK, ZERA	29	F	W	RRZZZZUSA
JOSEF	.11	M	INFANT	RRZZZZUSA
NATYCAK, ALKEM	32	M	LABR	RRZZZZUSA
CENDRICH, GUADORI	36	M	UNKNOWN	RRZZZZUSA
RACOWSKY, WOJTECK	28	M	UNKNOWN	RRZZZZUSA
CATHARINA	45	F	MA	RRZZZZUSA
ZEMMERMAN, JOHN	28	M	LABR	RRZZZZUSA
CASERSKY, VINCENT	28	M	LABR	RRZZZZUSA
MARIANNA	18	F	W	RRZZZZUSA
ZIMMERMANN, FRED	24	M	LABR	RRZZZZUSA
HANICH, JOSEF	21	M	UNKNOWN	RRZZZZUSA
MESEKAVITZ, MARAN	22	M	UNKNOWN	RRZZZZUSA
NAPOLUS, WARDUS	23	M	UNKNOWN	RRZZZZUSA
KERPOWITZ, ANDRES	34	M	UNKNOWN	RRZZZZUSA
ANTON	44	M	UNKNOWN	RRZZZZUSA
MATUREWITZ, JAN	23	M	UNKNOWN	RRZZZZUSA

SHIP: HELVETIA

FROM: LIVERPOOL
TO: NEW YORK
ARRIVED: 21 MAY 1884

PASSENGER	AGE	SEX	OCCUPATION	PRV VIL DES
ABRAHAM, ISIDOR	18	M	LABR	PLZZZZUSA
ASBRINK, P.W.	21	M	TLR	PLZZZZUSA
RASMUSSON, RASMUS	17	M	TLR	PLZZZZUSA
CHRISTINA	19	F	W	PLZZZZUSA
TERFALK, MARTIN	25	M	LABR	PLZZZZUSA
RYBERG, J.A.	24	M	LABR	PLZZZZUSA
BLOMSTEI, LIANDER	19	M	LABR	PLZZZZUSA
MASNI, J.	33	M	LABR	PLZZZZUSA
HANSON, AUGUST	20	M	LABR	PLZZZZUSA
KELEMOLN, MIKEL	34	M	BKR	PLZZZZUSA
HUGGBLIM, MIKKEL	26	M	SLR	PLZZZZUSA
WENTSHAN, GUSTAF	33	M	TLR	PLZZZZUSA
WITTI, ISAK	30	M	LABR	PLZZZZUSA
ANDERSON, AUG.	35	M	LABR	PLZZZZUSA
HANSEN, THOS.	36	M	TLR	PLZZZZUSA
RACHE, JOB.FERD.	23	M	MLR	PLZZZZUSA
GALWIN, HERMAN	17	M	BLKSMH	PLZZZZUSA
WAPP, AUGUST	25	M	UNKNOWN	PLZZZZUSA
MARIE	25	F	W	PLZZZZUSA
MINNA	3	F	CHILD	PLZZZZUSA
MARTIN	00	M	INF	PLZZZZUSA
SIMMILK, GUSTAF	18	M	MLDR	PLZZZZUSA
PLUSH, FRANS	33	M	LABR	PLZZZZUSA
LENCHTENBERGER, EMIL	31	M	BBR	PLZZZZUSA
KUSEMANN, FREDRICK	17	M	LABR	PLZZZZUSA
AUGUSTE	20	F	SP	PLZZZZUSA
WAGELFREI, MOSES	46	M	LABR	PLZZZZUSA
GOLDE	41	F	W	PLZZZZUSA
JACOB	21	M	LABR	PLZZZZUSA
R.	00	M	INF	PLZZZZUSA
GILBERT, JOSEPH	22	M	BCHR	PLZZZZUSA
ZENCOWICZ, JEN.	36	M	LABR	PLZZZZUSA

PASSENGER	AGE	SEX	OCCUPATION	PRVL	IVL	DES
GRISS, GISER	25	M	CPMKR	PL	ZZZZ	USA
WACUSKI, FRANCISK	37	M	LABR	PL	ZZZZ	USA
FRANCISKA	35	F	W	PL	ZZZZ	USA
JOSEFA	16	M	LABR	PL	ZZZZ	USA
JAN	11	M	CH	PL	ZZZZ	USA
FRANCISK	11	M	CH	PL	ZZZZ	USA
MARIE	8	F	CHILD	PL	ZZZZ	USA
ROSENBLUM, ISRAEL	17	M	LABR	PL	ZZZZ	USA
BRUNNER, LEOPOLD	28	M	LABR	PL	ZZZZ	USA
FRANZIISKA	26	F	W	PL	ZZZZ	USA
JOSEF	5	M	CHILD	PL	ZZZZ	USA
ANNA	3	F	CHILD	PL	ZZZZ	USA
FRANZISKA	00	F	INF	PL	ZZZZ	USA
ZASKONA, PETER	40	M	LABR	PL	ZZZZ	USA
ANNA	39	F	W	PL	ZZZZ	USA
FRANK	9	M	CHILD	PL	ZZZZ	USA
FRANZISKA	6	F	CHILD	PL	ZZZZ	USA
BART	3	M	CHILD	PL	ZZZZ	USA
ANTON	00	M	INF	PL	ZZZZ	USA
LORI	69	F	W	PL	ZZZZ	USA
KASERINE	24	F	W	PL	ZZZZ	USA
JAN	00	M	INF	PL	ZZZZ	USA
SANN, MARIE	14	F	SP	PL	ZZZZ	USA
KOLTER, DANIEL	28	M	TNSTH	PL	ZZZZ	USA
KUNINSKI, BARTS	40	M	CTL	PL	ZZZZ	USA
RUBIN, LAB.	20	M	BKR	PL	ZZZZ	USA
NEUMANN, MEYER	40	M	SHMK	PL	ZZZZ	USA
FRIEDMAN, JONATZ	30	M	LABR	PL	ZZZZ	USA
GRIM, JOSEF	30	M	LABR	PL	ZZZZ	USA
STALIVIKI, SOLOMON	27	M	FUR	PL	ZZZZ	USA
EPIBERG, ABRAHAM	41	M	LABR	PL	ZZZZ	USA
BOGES, SCHAIE	19	M	LABR	PL	ZZZZ	USA
SIZELMSKI, JOSEF	50	M	LABR	PL	ZZZZ	USA
MATULUNSKI, LAB.	39	M	LABR	PL	ZZZZ	USA
LEWIN, ERIK	19	M	BCHR	PL	ZZZZ	USA
GLUCK, ABRAHAM	30	M	MLDR	PL	ZZZZ	USA
DINABRWISKI, GRAEL	50	M	LABR	PL	ZZZZ	USA
FROK, BER.	16	M	LABR	PL	ZZZZ	USA
WERKSMANN, ELIE	33	M	FUR	PL	ZZZZ	USA
GUDEN, WYDER	30	M	FUR	PL	ZZZZ	USA
FRIEMAN, HERTZ	17	M	RPR	PL	ZZZZ	USA
MESLA, SIMON	31	M	LABR	PL	ZZZZ	USA
CHIROSKY, MARIANNA	28	F	W	PL	ZZZZ	USA
MICHAEL	28	M	LABR	PL	ZZZZ	USA
ALEX	00	M	INF	PL	ZZZZ	USA
COHEN, JACOB	30	M	LABR	PL	ZZZZ	USA
HIRSCH, JOSEF	30	M	TLR	PL	ZZZZ	USA
TARSLUNKO, BOSCHE	11	M	CH	PL	ZZZZ	USA
MOSCHE	10	M	CH	PL	ZZZZ	USA
WEISSLRUM, MOSCHE	20	M	PLH	PL	ZZZZ	USA
TAPKEWITZ, CHIWE	20	M	SHMK	PL	ZZZZ	USA
GROSMAN, PHILIP	20	M	LABR	PL	ZZZZ	USA
REBECCA	20	F	W	PL	ZZZZ	USA
FLEMRON, LERE	20	F	SP	PL	ZZZZ	USA
LAN, MEYER	20	M	BCHR	PL	ZZZZ	USA
MOSES	11	M	CH	PL	ZZZZ	USA
BALSAN, SOLOMON	18	M	TLR	PL	ZZZZ	USA
TEFLOR, ANNA	18	F	SP	PL	ZZZZ	USA
KARSKLER, JANOS	25	M	LABR	PL	ZZZZ	USA
PINEUS, JACOB	20	M	BKR	PL	ZZZZ	USA
ANGER	19	M	TLR	PL	ZZZZ	USA
HOCIZ, ABRAM	20	M	LABR	PL	ZZZZ	USA
RIBU, NOSSEN	45	M	TLR	PL	ZZZZ	USA
MULLER, RASMEL	17	M	SLR	PL	ZZZZ	USA
KRAJCIVSKY, HERS	19	M	LABR	PL	ZZZZ	USA
SIGUL, NOCHMAN	22	M	LABR	PL	ZZZZ	USA
LAISCKOWITZ, ABRAM	18	M	LABR	PL	ZZZZ	USA
FREYEL	20	F	W	PL	ZZZZ	USA
MICHALOWITZ, S.	21	M	SHMK	PL	ZZZZ	USA
KAPLAN, JOSSEL	20	M	LABR	PL	ZZZZ	USA
RASENZARCT, MAX	18	M	HRSMN	PL	ZZZZ	USA
RADENBAUM, RACHEL	22	F	W	PL	ZZZZ	USA
S.	00	F	INF	PL	ZZZZ	USA
KUNDSON, PEBRINE	27	F	W	PL	ZZZZ	USA
BERG, SWEN-J.	19	M	LABR	PL	ZZZZ	USA
SCHOOMLURTZ, MARCUS	30	M	TLR	PL	ZZZZ	USA
KWART, LEIB	30	M	TLR	PL	ZZZZ	USA
CHANE	20	M	TLR	PL	ZZZZ	USA
KLEIN, HERE	20	M	TLR	PL	ZZZZ	USA
LICHT, EGRIK	16	M	LABR	PL	ZZZZ	USA
BLASCHKO, MICHL.	30	M	LABR	PL	ZZZZ	USA
FRIEDMAN, ROSIE	17	F	SP	PL	ZZZZ	USA
ENZEL, BERNARD	10	M	CH	PL	ZZZZ	USA
SCHOWARZ, PHILIP	19	M	SHMK	PL	ZZZZ	USA
ELIAS	21	M	LABR	PL	ZZZZ	USA
GEISLER, TOBIAS	10	M	CH	PL	ZZZZ	USA
AXELBROD, CHAIN	20	M	TLR	PL	ZZZZ	USA

SHIP: CIRCASSIA

FROM: GLASGOW AND MOVILLE
TO: NEW YORK
ARRIVED: 22 MAY 1884

PASSENGER	AGE	SEX	OCCUPATION	PRVL	IVL	DES
HEILPESA, LEIB	20	M	CGRMKR	RR	ZZZZ	USA
HIRSCH	19	M	CGRMKR	RR	ZZZZ	USA
ZULOW, MENDEL	32	M	FLSH	RR	ZZZZ	USA
CHASINOWITZ, JOSEF	17	M	CGRMKR	RR	ZZZZ	USA
SCHICKOMSKY, SOLOMON	32	M	GZR	RR	ZZZZ	USA
SCHUSTER, PER	29	M	ART	RR	ZZZZ	USA
SCHUESKI, HIRSCH	28	M	DLR	RR	ZZZZ	USA
BERMAN, ISAAK	22	M	CGRMKR	RR	ZZZZ	USA
CHASANOWITZ, H.	19	M	TNSTH	RR	ZZZZ	USA
STOMA, MEYER	38	M	TLR	RR	ZZZZ	USA
START, JACOB	22	M	TLR	RR	ZZZZ	USA
MATYKOWSKY, H.	34	M	LABR	RR	ZZZZ	USA
KASKONITZ, MICHAEL	19	M	TLR	RR	ZZZZ	USA
FRIED, JOSEF	20	M	LABR	RR	ZZZZ	USA
JASSER, SOLOMON	18	M	GDSM	RR	ZZZZ	USA
DRABE, CHONE	30	M	TLR	RR	ZZZZ	USA
KAROIFSE, JANS	22	M	LABR	RR	ZZZZ	USA
RUIGER, SCH.	23	M	JNR	RR	ZZZZ	USA
SARA	22	F	W	RR	ZZZZ	USA
HULPERA, FREIDE	30	F	W	RR	ZZZZ	USA
NISCHE	9	F	CHILD	RR	ZZZZ	USA

SHIP: ERIN

FROM: LONDON
TO: NEW YORK
ARRIVED: 22 MAY 1884

PASSENGER	AGE	SEX	OCCUPATION	PRVL	IVL	DES
LIM, ANDRAS	40	M	UNKNOWN	PL	ZZZZ	USA
SHAPANSKY, SAMUEL	34	M	CPMKR	PL	ZZZZ	USA
STERM, ABRAM	10	M	CH	PL	ZZZZ	USA
PULSER, SOLOMON	20	M	LABR	PL	ZZZZ	USA
SCHAMES, MENDEL	40	M	CPMKR	PL	ZZZZ	USA
MASEK	11	M	CH	PL	ZZZZ	USA

SHIP: THOS. J. MAY

FROM: MEXICO
TO: NEW YORK
ARRIVED: 22 MAY 1884

PASSENGER	AGE	SEX	OCCUPATION	PRV VIL DES
JOHNSON, OTTO	35	M	SEMN	FNZZZZUNK
WISTERLAND, PETER	32	M	CPTR	FNZZZZUNK

SHIP: NOORDLAND

FROM: ANTWERP
TO: NEW YORK
ARRIVED: 23 MAY 1884

PASSENGER	AGE	SEX	OCCUPATION	PRV VIL DES
SPICZEL, FRZ.	20	M	UNKNOWN	PLZZZZNY
PRAIS, EVA	18	F	UNKNOWN	PLZZZZNY
LYZAG, CARL	21	M	UNKNOWN	PLZZZZNY
OSSOWSKI, ANT.	26	M	FARMER	PLZZZZNY
CAZARUCHZKA, TH.	30	M	UNKNOWN	PLZZZZNY
GILARSKI, MATH.	27	F	UNKNOWN	PLZZZZNY
MEAS	23	F	UNKNOWN	PLZZZZNY
URBUNK, JOS.	33	M	UNKNOWN	PLZZZZNY
SCHILINSKI, LEAS	25	M	UNKNOWN	PLZZZZNY
U, U	50	M	UNKNOWN	PLZZZZNY
U	40	F	UNKNOWN	PLZZZZNY
GRETZ, HIRSH	35	M	UNKNOWN	PLZZZZNY
KLOCHOWIAK, M.	18	M	UNKNOWN	PLZZZZNY
JWINSKI, JOH.	33	M	UNKNOWN	PLZZZZNY
MER.	22	F	UNKNOWN	PLZZZZNY
-----N	4	M	CHILD	PLZZZZNY
PET.	2	M	CHILD	PLZZZZNY
MARTHA	00	F	INF	PLZZZZNY

SHIP: STATE OF GEORGIA

FROM: GLASGOW AND LARNE
TO: NEW YORK
ARRIVED: 23 MAY 1884

PASSENGER	AGE	SEX	OCCUPATION	PRV VIL DES
BAAS, ISRAEL	20	M	LABR	PLZZZZUSA
SCHNEIDER, BENZEL	10	M	BY	RRZZZZUSA
BREMER, ABEL	24	M	PDLR	RRZZZZUSA
BLUM, GRITTMANN	11	M	BY	RRZZZZUSA
ANSCHEL, KIVA	18	M	LABR	RRZZZZUSA
HIRSCHOWITZ, SANDEL	18	M	LABR	RRZZZZUSA
SANDLER, JANKEL	18	M	LABR	RRZZZZUSA
BRANDE, CHAZKEL	18	M	LABR	RRZZZZUSA
FRUMENTOWITZ, JANKEL	21	M	PDLR	RRZZZZUSA
GITTELSOHN, JACOB	24	M	MLR	PLZZZZUSA
MASCHOWITZ, ITZIG	18	M	LABR	RRZZZZUSA
KAROLINSKY, INDEL	21	M	WCHMKR	PLZZZZUSA
KRUSSINSKY, LEA	26	F	W	PLZZZZUSA
RIWE	2	F	CHILD	PLZZZZUSA
KAHAN, WOLF	21	M	LABR	PLZZZZUSA
NAPASNICK, JANKEL	22	M	LABR	RRZZZZUSA
WOHLMANN, ELIAS	18	M	LABR	RRZZZZUSA
PLECKSYVA, JOSEPH	30	M	LABR	PLZZZZUSA
KATARINE	26	F	W	PLZZZZUSA
JOHANNE	16	F	SP	PLZZZZUSA
SENNISLOW	12	M	CH	PLZZZZUSA
WOITA	2	F	CHILD	PLZZZZUSA
VERONICA	.06	F	INFANT	PLZZZZUSA
LOMGENSKI, SCHEPSEL	33	M	LABR	PLZZZZUSA
JEANETTE	26	F	W	PLZZZZUSA
CHAIE	4	F	CHILD	PLZZZZUSA
JACOB	3	M	CHILD	PLZZZZUSA
GRABOWSKY, MICHAL	27	M	LABR	PLZZZZUSA
ZIRKELBACH, JORITZ	24	M	MLR	PLZZZZUSA
RADONSKI, ABRAHAM	16	M	LABR	PLZZZZUSA
RABINOWITZ, MANUEL	19	M	LABR	RRZZZZUSA
SKANTZIS, ADAM	20	M	LABR	RRZZZZUSA
BRIKSTANTIS, KLEMA	23	M	LABR	PLZZZZUSA
KRIGSCHIMS, RAUWA	19	M	LABR	PLZZZZUSA
SCHAKELOWITZ, JOSEPH	28	M	LABR	PLZZZZUSA
POPIRK, JANKEL	40	M	LABR	RRZZZZUSA
REICHMANN, WOLFF	40	M	PDLR	RRZZZZUSA
SCHMIETER, MOSES	19	M	PDLR	PLZZZZUSA
BAHRMANN, ABEL	20	M	PDLR	PLZZZZUSA
SCHMELESS, ISAC	30	M	PDLR	PLZZZZUSA
SERMANN, SALMON	36	M	PDLR	PLZZZZUSA
KRUGER, LEISER	33	M	TLR	PLZZZZUSA
GUTMANN, SCHMUEL	28	M	PDLR	PLZZZZUSA
KRISCHOWITZ, BERTHA	28	F	W	RRZZZZUSA
SOPHIE	3	F	CHILD	RRZZZZUSA
LESERSOHN, RISCHE	16	F	SP	RRZZZZUSA
HERSCHOWITZ, SUSSMAN	20	M	LABR	RRZZZZUSA
BLUM, FANI	18	F	SP	RRZZZZUSA
MULLER, MICHAEL	20	M	PDLR	RRZZZZUSA
PERLSTEIN, ROSE	40	F	W	RRZZZZUSA
ITZIK	3	M	CHILD	RRZZZZUSA
LIBOWITZ, JOSCHEL	34	M	PDLR	PLZZZZUSA
SILBERSTEIN, MEYER	22	M	LABR	RRZZZZUSA
LEWIN, SAMUEL	46	M	LABR	RRZZZZUSA
BERGER, ISAAC	27	M	TLR	PLZZZZUSA
ALTMANN, MORE	11	F	CH	PLZZZZUSA
LIBE	10	F	CH	PLZZZZUSA
BERNSTEIN, SCHONE	26	F	W	PLZZZZUSA
CHAJE	5	F	CHILD	PLZZZZUSA
FEIGE	3	F	CHILD	PLZZZZUSA
PRISCHMANN, HERSCHEL	20	M	LABR	RRZZZZUSA
SCHMITZATZKY, DAVID	20	M	LABR	RRZZZZUSA
SACHS, SCHMAJE	20	M	FARMER	RRZZZZUSA
SAJAWITZ, SCHMAJE	20	M	PDLR	RRZZZZUSA
JOSSELOWSKY, WOLF	30	M	LABR	RRZZZZUSA
JOREACH, LEISER	20	M	LABR	RRZZZZUSA
FEITCHMAN, ABRAHAM	24	M	LABR	RRZZZZUSA
MISCHELSOHN, HERZ	20	M	LABR	RRZZZZUSA
DAMSKY, MORITZ	18	M	PDLR	RRZZZZUSA
NOWAK, THOMAS	27	M	LABR	PLZZZZUSA
JUKOWSKY, CASIMIR	19	M	LABR	PLZZZZUSA
GOPINAS, PETTER	40	M	LABR	PLZZZZUSA
ROSENBERG, JOSEPH	46	M	LABR	PLZZZZUSA
BURACH, JACOB	26	M	LABR	RRZZZZUSA
SCHLOMRANKE, JOSEPH	34	M	LABR	RRZZZZUSA
SIMERNIS, JOHAN	33	M	LABR	PLZZZZUSA
RUTKOWSKY, FELIX	24	M	PDLR	PLZZZZUSA
CASIMIRA	21	F	W	PLZZZZUSA
THEKLA	.06	F	INFANT	PLZZZZUSA
SABOSCHITZKA, MARIE	43	F	W	PLZZZZUSA
VALERIA	17	F	SP	PLZZZZUSA
JOSEPH	9	M	CHILD	PLZZZZUSA
VERONICA	7	F	CHILD	PLZZZZUSA
AUCA	2	F	CHILD	PLZZZZUSA
LEOCADIA	1	F	CHILD	PLZZZZUSA
SPYCHALSKY, WANZ	26	M	LABR	PLZZZZUSA
APOLONIA	18	F	W	PLZZZZUSA
RANNA, BERTHA	13	F	CH	PLZZZZUSA
JACOBOWITZ, MARIE	18	F	SP	PLZZZZUSA
SAKERWISCH, VINCENZ	23	M	LABR	PLZZZZUSA
AMMALA, PRITA-M.	25	F	W	PLZZZZUSA
SULZKY, HERSCHEL	29	M	LABR	PLZZZZUSA
GLASER, OSCHE	26	M	LABR	PLZZZZUSA
MUROK, MOWSCHE	20	M	LABR	PLZZZZUSA
HOFMANN, HIRSCH	24	M	LABR	PLZZZZUSA
CHMILEWSKY, ABRAHAM	25	M	PDLR	PLZZZZUSA
PELZMANN, OSCHY	23	M	LABR	PLZZZZUSA
MOLAMED, KOPPEL	18	M	LABR	RRZZZZUSA
LIPSCHITZ, DAVID	16	M	LABR	RRZZZZUSA

PASSENGER	AGE	SEX	OCCUPATION	PRV	VIL	DES
ZODEK	30	M	LABR	RR	ZZZZ	USA
KIBOWITZ, ABRAHAM	32	M	LABR	RR	ZZZZ	USA
REISS, INDEL	20	M	LABR	RR	ZZZZ	USA
ELLA	22	F	W	RR	ZZZZ	USA
FLEISCHMANN, MOWSCHE	46	M	PDLR	RR	ZZZZ	USA
PATZ, ABRAHAM	19	M	PDLR	RR	ZZZZ	USA
MARGOLIS, SAM	16	M	LABR	RR	ZZZZ	USA
FUHRMANN, LEISER	19	M	LABR	RR	ZZZZ	USA
SOTNIK, ELJY	54	M	LABR	RR	ZZZZ	USA
SCHUSTER, MEYER	38	M	PDLR	RR	ZZZZ	USA
BREMER, MOWSCHE	18	M	PDLR	RR	ZZZZ	USA
SOLL, MOSES	18	M	LABR	RR	ZZZZ	USA
KLIVANSKY, BEHR	20	M	PDLR	PL	ZZZZ	USA
EISENMAN, MOWSCHE	50	M	PDLR	RR	ZZZZ	USA
GESELOWITZ, NOTEL	32	M	PDLR	PL	ZZZZ	USA
RATKIN, RAPHAEL	24	M	PDLR	RR	ZZZZ	USA
SEGAL, SIMON	18	M	PDLR	RR	ZZZZ	USA
ABRAMOWITZ, BARUCH	20	M	PDLR	PL	ZZZZ	USA
BLUMP, HERSCH	44	M	LABR	RR	ZZZZ	USA
STUZKER, MOTTEL	00	M	LABR	PL	ZZZZ	USA
HONIG, SPRINZE	18	F	SP	RR	ZZZZ	USA
BECHLER, SARAH	24	F	W	PL	ZZZZ	USA
DAMASK, SAMUEL	20	M	PDLR	RR	ZZZZ	USA
SILBER, JACOB	20	M	PDLR	RR	ZZZZ	USA
WOLKAFSKY, JOSEF	25	M	PDLR	RR	ZZZZ	USA
SKURVMANN, LEIB	18	M	PDLR	RR	ZZZZ	USA
SCHITZ, BANYEL	32	M	PDLR	RR	ZZZZ	USA
CITREN, HERSCHEL	21	M	PDLR	PL	ZZZZ	USA
ABRAHAMSEN, HERMAN	50	M	PDLR	PL	ZZZZ	USA
JOHANNA	50	F	W	PL	ZZZZ	USA
KANZEL, FRIEDRICH	22	M	SHMK	PL	ZZZZ	USA

SHIP: EIDER

FROM: BREMEN AND SOUTHAMPTON
TO: NEW YORK
ARRIVED: 24 MAY 1884

PASSENGER	AGE	SEX	OCCUPATION	PRV	VIL	DES
GABRIEL, FRIEDR.	42	M	LLD	RR	ZZZZ	USA
WILH.	43	F	W	RR	ZZZZ	USA
FRIEDR.	16	M	LABR	RR	ZZZZ	USA
CAROL.	19	F	UNKNOWN	RR	ZZZZ	USA
HEINR	10	M	CH	RR	ZZZZ	USA
---EDR.	9	M	CHILD	RR	ZZZZ	USA
---M.	8	M	CHILD	RR	ZZZZ	USA
AUG.	5	M	CHILD	RR	ZZZZ	USA
ANNA	.11	F	INFANT	RR	ZZZZ	USA
JULIUS	.11	M	INFANT	RR	ZZZZ	USA
RONKOWSKI, CAROL.	30	M	FARMER	RR	ZZZZ	USA
MATHILDE	29	F	W	RR	ZZZZ	USA
TOMASZYK, EDWARD	34	M	UNKNOWN	PL	ZZZZ	USA
ZAGACKI, JAN	32	M	FARMER	RR	ZZZZ	USA
MICHALY	28	M	UNKNOWN	RR	ZZZZ	USA
DEMBSKI, JOSEF	43	M	UNKNOWN	RR	ZZZZ	USA
DERLYGA, JOSEFA	00	F	W	RR	ZZZZ	USA
JANIELZA	.08	F	INFANT	RR	ZZZZ	USA
REDMANN, JULIUS	39	M	FARMER	RR	ZZZZ	USA
FLORENTINE	39	F	W	RR	ZZZZ	USA
WILHELM	16	M	UNKNOWN	RR	ZZZZ	USA
HEINRICH	8	M	CHILD	RR	ZZZZ	USA
PAULINE	2	F	CHILD	RR	ZZZZ	USA
ADOLF	.09	M	INFANT	RR	ZZZZ	USA
SCHROEDER, DAVID	37	M	FARMER	RR	ZZZZ	USA
HENRIETTE	19	F	UNKNOWN	RR	ZZZZ	USA
DAVID	15	M	UNKNOWN	RR	ZZZZ	USA
WILH.	9	F	CHILD	RR	ZZZZ	USA
MALWINE	7	F	CHILD	RR	ZZZZ	USA
GUSTAV	.03	M	INFANT	RR	ZZZZ	USA
NICKEL, ANDREAS	51	M	LABR	RR	ZZZZ	USA
ELISABETH	18	F	UNKNOWN	RR	ZZZZ	USA
ANNA	47	F	W	RR	ZZZZ	USA
HEINR.	16	M	UNKNOWN	RR	ZZZZ	USA
BERTHA	9	F	CHILD	RR	ZZZZ	USA
DOBASTEIN, MICHAEL	20	M	LABR	RR	ZZZZ	USA
SCHROEDER, MARIA	18	F	UNKNOWN	RR	ZZZZ	USA

SHIP: POLARIA

FROM: HAMBURG
TO: NEW YORK
ARRIVED: 25 MAY 1884

PASSENGER	AGE	SEX	OCCUPATION	PRV	VIL	DES
HARKIAVICZ, JUSTINA	25	F	WO	RR	ZZZZ	IA
JUSTINA	.07	F	INFANT	RR	ZZZZ	IA
ZAGURSKI, ALEXANDER	18	M	LABR	RR	ZZZZ	CH
BOWASSET, JURIS	25	M	LABR	PL	ZZZZ	NY
HORN, ABR.	41	M	TRDSMN	PL	ZZZZ	NY
REBECCA	41	F	W	PL	ZZZZ	NY
REGINA	7	F	CHILD	PL	ZZZZ	NY
CHAKEL	6	F	CHILD	PL	ZZZZ	NY
ABRAHAM	5	M	CHILD	PL	ZZZZ	NY
PINKUS	2	M	CHILD	PL	ZZZZ	NY
JOLLY	.06	F	INFANT	PL	ZZZZ	NY
ADAMOVIC, S.	45	M	LABR	PL	ZZZZ	NY
REICH, DAVID	23	M	UNKNOWN	PL	ZZZZ	NY
BERGER, AB.	29	M	UNKNOWN	PL	ZZZZ	NY
NOVOTNA, CATH.	22	F	UNKNOWN	PL	ZZZZ	NY
SEYNIENSKY, D.	15	M	TRDSMN	PL	ZZZZ	NY
GEADSAH, VALENT.	31	M	LABR	PL	ZZZZ	CH
SCHOPICCE, CATH.	24	F	UNKNOWN	PL	ZZZZ	CH
MESORICZ, JOSEF	20	M	TRDSMN	PL	ZZZZ	NY
MEYER, FISCHEL	38	M	UNKNOWN	PL	ZZZZ	NY
MAFFEROWICZ, BENNY	20	M	UNKNOWN	PL	ZZZZ	NY
RUBINSKI, CHAIM	28	M	UNKNOWN	PL	ZZZZ	NY
SCHOPIA, AD.	20	M	TRDSMN	PL	ZZZZ	NY
FRIDMANN, LEIB	25	M	TRDSMN	PL	ZZZZ	NY
ERIETZ, JACOB	24	M	UNKNOWN	PL	ZZZZ	NY
KASTAN, CHAIM	20	M	UNKNOWN	PL	ZZZZ	NY
MOSES	27	M	UNKNOWN	PL	ZZZZ	NY
DREESEN, ELSE	17	M	UNKNOWN	PL	ZZZZ	NY
ISAACKSON, ABR.	32	M	UNKNOWN	PL	ZZZZ	NY
WISCHNEFSKI, H.	35	M	UNKNOWN	PL	ZZZZ	NY
ELISABETH	35	F	W	PL	ZZZZ	NY
KANTAR, DAVID	20	M	TRDSMN	PL	ZZZZ	NY
KRUBSKY, JACOB	18	M	UNKNOWN	PL	ZZZZ	NY
SCHMILENSKY, JACOB	36	M	UNKNOWN	PL	ZZZZ	NY
DOBE	7	F	CHILD	PL	ZZZZ	NY
LEWIET, FEIGEL	32	M	TRDSMN	PL	ZZZZ	NY
LANSKI, HIRSCH	26	M	UNKNOWN	PL	ZZZZ	NY
FINKELSTEIN, LEIB	41	M	UNKNOWN	PL	ZZZZ	NY
ISAAC	7	M	CHILD	PL	ZZZZ	NY
RUBIN, MENDEL	22	M	TRDSMN	PL	ZZZZ	NY
FRAENKEL, CHAIM	32	M	TLR	PL	ZZZZ	NY
MATALSKI, SALAMON	19	M	UNKNOWN	PL	ZZZZ	NY
LEIB	7	M	CHILD	PL	ZZZZ	NY
ROSENTHAL, SALAMON	17	M	SHMK	PL	ZZZZ	NY
EPSTEIN, ABRAHAM	19	M	TLR	PL	ZZZZ	NY
HENRY	22	M	UNKNOWN	PL	ZZZZ	NY
FISCHEL, HENRIETTE	.05	F	INFANT	PL	ZZZZ	NY
RIWE	20	F	WO	PL	ZZZZ	NY
SEIBER, HIRSCH	23	M	TRDSMN	PL	ZZZZ	NY
RASCHE	21	F	W	PL	ZZZZ	NY
SCHLOME	.06	M	INFANT	PL	ZZZZ	NY
DAVID	.04	M	INFANT	PL	ZZZZ	NY
JASCH, JANKEL	20	M	LABR	PL	ZZZZ	NY
ERITZ, ISAH	7	M	CHILD	PL	ZZZZ	NY
RAPPAPOT, MOS.	18	M	TRDSMN	PL	ZZZZ	NY
RATBUS, WOLF	44	M	UNKNOWN	PL	ZZZZ	NY
SCHMAHL, BERNH	17	M	SMH	PL	ZZZZ	NY
JOENS, THOMA	18	F	SGL	PL	ZZZZ	NY

PASSENGER	AGE	SEX	OCCUPATION	PRV VIL DES
KOZUB, JAN	49	M	LABR	PLZZZZNY
AGNES	46	F	W	PLZZZZNY
THADDEUS	25	M	S	PLZZZZNY
JUSTINE	20	F	D	PLZZZZNY
SAWITSKI, SAMUEL	30	F	UNKNOWN	PLZZZZNY
PONTMINSKI, AN	30	M	UNKNOWN	PLZZZZNY
PODIONSKA, JACOB	30	M	UNKNOWN	PLZZZZNY
SOBIESCHENSKI, MICHEL	25	M	TRDSMN	PLZZZZNY
RICHTER, ARTHUR	24	M	LABR	PLZZZZUNK
KAES, JOSEF	26	M	LABR	PLZZZZUNK
VRYNDA, AND.	24	M	UNKNOWN	PLZZZZUNK
HARWATZ, SOFIE	31	F	WO	PLZZZZUNK
JAN	40	M	LABR	PLZZZZUNK
HILTWANN, BENJ.	25	M	UNKNOWN	PLZZZZUNK
SCHACHT, DAVID	21	M	UNKNOWN	PLZZZZUNK
MINNA	21	F	W	PLZZZZUNK
WINKOWSKI, JAN	40	M	LABR	PLZZZZUNK
POCHATZKA, SIMON	20	M	TRDSMN	PLZZZZUNK
KLONICK, FRANZ	22	M	BKR	PLZZZZUNK

SHIP: ASSYRIAN MONARCH

FROM: LONDON
TO: NEW YORK
ARRIVED: 26 MAY 1884

PASSENGER	AGE	SEX	OCCUPATION	PRV VIL DES
JACOBS, KATE	22	F	UNKNOWN	PLZZZZNY
JANE	2	F	CHILD	PLZZZZNY
BENJAMIN	1	M	CHILD	PLZZZZNY
STEPEN, MORRIS	18	M	LABR	PLZZZZNY
DEMTEAK, H.	34	M	LABR	PLZZZZNY
MELINKOFF, REBECCA	30	F	UNKNOWN	PLZZZZNY
HENRY	5	F	CHILD	PLZZZZNY
CACILIA	2	F	CHILD	PLZZZZNY
LEAH	00	F	INF	PLZZZZNY
MICHELSOHN, W.	22	M	LABR	PLZZZZNY
BERMAN, ISAAC	21	M	LABR	PLZZZZNY
SIMONS, JACOB	28	M	LABR	RRZZZZNY
MILLY	26	F	W	RRZZZZNY
MARKS	2	M	CHILD	RRZZZZNY
SAMUEL	00	M	INF	RRZZZZNY
SWISKARSKY, JACOB	37	M	LABR	PLZZZZNY
RACHAEL	35	F	W	PLZZZZNY
GOTTHETE	11	F	CH	PLZZZZNY
MARK	7	M	CHILD	PLZZZZNY
MARY	4	F	CHILD	PLZZZZNY
FRANKEL, ABR.	24	M	LABR	PLZZZZNY
KITHY	26	F	W	PLZZZZNY
SARAH	1	F	CHILD	PLZZZZNY
COHEN, HYNIAN	00	M	LABR	RRZZZZNY
GARRET, GEORGE	47	M	LABR	PLZZZZNY
CLARA	53	F	W	PLZZZZNY
ISAAC	18	M	LABR	PLZZZZNY
BENJAMIN	15	M	LABR	PLZZZZNY
HENRY	12	M	LABR	PLZZZZNY
HANNAH	10	F	CH	PLZZZZNY
PACHTER, DINAH	35	F	UNKNOWN	PLZZZZNY
MOSES	10	M	CH	PLZZZZNY
SAMUEL	7	M	CHILD	PLZZZZNY
WOLF	5	M	CHILD	PLZZZZNY
SOLOMON	3	M	CHILD	PLZZZZNY
JACOBS	2	M	CHILD	PLZZZZNY
HIRSCH, ABRAHAM	19	M	LABR	PLZZZZNY
NEBERLE, G.	28	M	LABR	PLZZZZNY
ANNA	24	F	W	PLZZZZNY
DORIS	18	F	UNKNOWN	PLZZZZNY
MARIE	16	F	UNKNOWN	PLZZZZNY
GOSINE	11	F	CH	PLZZZZNY
U	00	F	INF	PLZZZZNY
WILENIK, A.	18	M	LABR	RRZZZZNY

PASSENGER	AGE	SEX	OCCUPATION	PRV VIL DES
INAKER, B.	33	M	LABR	RRZZZZNY
VEGOF, ISRAEL	28	M	LABR	RRZZZZNY
KAPPELUSCH, W.	29	M	LABR	RRZZZZNY
KADLIBONSKY, ISRAEL	14	M	LABR	RRZZZZNY
BAROMOCH, D.	20	M	LABR	RRZZZZNY
LENOKON, J.	19	M	LABR	RRZZZZNY
SCHWARZ, SELIG	19	M	LABR	RRZZZZNY
UGBISKA, A.	18	M	LABR	PLZZZZNY
BIALOSUKY, ISAK	19	M	LABR	PLZZZZNY
CHIEPEZ, C.	32	M	LABR	PLZZZZNY
SAPOSEHEURIE, V.	18	M	LABR	PLZZZZNY
LEBENDIG, MOSES	22	M	LABR	PLZZZZNY
EPSRIEG, MOSES	19	M	LABR	PLZZZZNY
JOSEL	11	M	CH	PLZZZZNY
KAHA, SCHEMEL	24	M	LABR	PLZZZZNY
ALKES, S.	23	M	LABR	PLZZZZNY
GROJEWSKI, HERSEN	12	M	CH	PLZZZZNY
NERAT, JACOB	24	M	LABR	PLZZZZNY
WEINBURN, H.	19	M	LABR	PLZZZZNY
GAJEWSKY, M.	18	M	LABR	PLZZZZNY
JOSLACK, M.	19	M	LABR	PLZZZZNY
LIBERMANN, H.	24	M	LABR	PLZZZZNY
BAZAR, SARAH	12	F	CH	PLZZZZNY
VELANDA, S.	25	M	LABR	PLZZZZNY
SLABACKY, JOSEL	19	M	LABR	PLZZZZNY
SCHOSE, ISRAEL	30	M	LABR	PLZZZZNY
FISCHER, B.	12	M	CH	PLZZZZNY
LEVITE, L.	18	M	LABR	PLZZZZNY
CHIPPELLE, C.	00	M	LABR	PLZZZZNY
KESCHROOD, L.V.	30	M	LABR	PLZZZZNY
SCWALEWISTY, S.	32	M	LABR	RRZZZZNY
RUSSMANN, ISAK	52	M	LABR	PLZZZZNY
WOLF	11	M	CH	PLZZZZNY
VARWELL, V.W.	50	M	LABR	PLZZZZNY
KEITZ, ITZIK	22	M	LABR	PLZZZZNY
WALSSER, DAVID	28	M	LABR	RRZZZZNY
GROSSMAN, SALOMON	22	M	LABR	PLZZZZNY
ROSENBERG, GITKE	22	M	LABR	PLZZZZNY
RUCZKOWITZ, NAWIZINEC	21	M	LABR	PLZZZZNY
KASPAROWITZ, A.	12	M	CH	PLZZZZNY
BUDROWITZ, PETER	23	M	LABR	RRZZZZNY
ZUKOWSKI, P.	22	M	LABR	RRZZZZNY
FENSCHEWZKY, ALEX.	35	M	LABR	RRZZZZNY
ALBANSKY, V.W.	25	M	LABR	PLZZZZNY
PUTLITS, GUST.	21	M	LABR	PLZZZZNY
NIELSEN, N.H.	27	M	LABR	PLZZZZNY
JACOBSEN, J.	32	M	LABR	PLZZZZNY
PAULSON, H.	26	M	LABR	PLZZZZNY
DENNEKE, V.W.	26	M	LABR	PLZZZZNY
KASLOWSKY, M.	45	M	LABR	RRZZZZNY
M.	45	F	W	RRZZZZNY
P.	45	M	UNKNOWN	RRZZZZNY
E.	12	F	CH	RRZZZZNY
WINZKUNE, SIMON	20	M	LABR	PLZZZZNY
MIKEWITZ, W.	20	M	LABR	PLZZZZNY
SADOWSKY, C.	26	M	LABR	PLZZZZNY
STASKIWITZ, V.	23	M	LABR	RRZZZZNY
DAMALEWSKY, V.	22	M	LABR	RRZZZZNY
KARNILOWSKY, V.	27	M	LABR	RRZZZZNY
BALLUS, V.	30	M	LABR	PLZZZZNY
LEON, A.	23	M	LABR	PLZZZZNY
BALLUM, A.	38	M	LABR	RRZZZZNY
BRELIS, W.	23	M	LABR	RRZZZZNY
WOYTOLEMIS, A.	17	M	LABR	RRZZZZNY
BALKUS, J.	18	M	LABR	RRZZZZNY
JASKEWITZ, IGNAS	24	M	LABR	RRZZZZNY
STERNBERGER, V.	34	M	LABR	PLZZZZNY
HEFKE, ISAK-M.	18	M	LABR	PLZZZZNY
FRIEDMANN, CHANE	18	M	LABR	PLZZZZNY
WANGEROWITZ, ISAK	20	M	LABR	PLZZZZNY
GOLDBERG, E.	44	M	LABR	PLZZZZNY
VANIBACHER, SIMON	44	M	LABR	PLZZZZNY
TINKELSTEIN, H.	20	M	LABR	PLZZZZNY
NOWAKALSKY, S.	20	M	LABR	PLZZZZNY
SASLYNSKY, JANKEL	20	M	LABR	RRZZZZNY

PASSENGER	AGE	SEX	OCCUPATION	PRV VIL DES
KOCHANETZ, B.	25	M	LABR	RRZZZZNY
BROKIEWICKEY, J.	30	M	LABR	RRZZZZNY
WITTERSTEIN, W.	30	M	LABR	PLZZZZNY
S.	10	M	CH	PLZZZZNY
HERSCH	9	M	CHILD	PLZZZZNY
KELIE	00	M	INF	PLZZZZNY
LOMENTHAL, C.L.	20	M	LABR	PLZZZZNY
DREXLER, A.	18	M	LABR	RRZZZZNY
FRANKEL, MOSES	12	M	CH	RRZZZZNY
MORDOCHELOWITZ, M.	35	M	LABR	PLZZZZNY
SIEDENBERG, MARKUS	25	M	LABR	PLZZZZNY
BREINE	20	M	LABR	PLZZZZNY
BALYSTOKER, S.	20	M	LABR	PLZZZZNY
DOWITZ, L.	25	M	LABR	PLZZZZNY
BALYSTOKES, B.	00	M	INF	PLZZZZNY
MEYER, V.	25	M	LABR	PLZZZZNY
ZINCHOWIC, M.	20	M	LABR	PLZZZZNY
ROWSLAWSKI, I.	23	M	LABR	PLZZZZNY
RUDEZEWSKY, I.	20	M	LABR	RRZZZZNY
REARSKOWCHY, J.	30	M	LABR	RRZZZZNY
BOZYWSKY, F.	30	M	LABR	RRZZZZNY
BERNSTEIN, V.	20	M	LABR	RRZZZZNY
KARMA, R.	30	M	LABR	RRZZZZNY
WASFERSTEIN, M.	20	M	LABR	RRZZZZNY
LIENKELSTER, MOSKE	30	M	LABR	RRZZZZNY
GUITMANN, D.	8	M	CHILD	RRZZZZNY
KAVEWISK, ABRAHAM	20	M	LABR	PLZZZZNY
SOKALSKI, NOCHIM	20	M	LABR	PLZZZZNY
HORTIVITZ, J.	30	M	LABR	RRZZZZNY
ROSEN, ELIAS	20	M	LABR	RRZZZZNY
CONEWITZ, L.	20	M	LABR	RRZZZZNY
KAISER, LIEB	20	M	LABR	RRZZZZNY
GULMANN, W.	30	M	LABR	RRZZZZNY
BOUNSTEIN, S.	30	M	LABR	RRZZZZNY
SOLKAWITZ, H.	20	M	LABR	RRZZZZNY
C.	20	M	LABR	RRZZZZNY
SCHERENDSTEIN, C.	12	M	CH	RRZZZZNY
GUSTEIN, M.	25	M	CH	RRZZZZNY
ROTHERCHILD, C.	45	M	CH	PLZZZZNY
S.	30	M	CH	PLZZZZNY
N.	11	M	CH	PLZZZZNY
C.	10	M	CH	PLZZZZNY
V.	9	M	CHILD	PLZZZZNY
K.	00	M	INF	PLZZZZNY
JAWORSKA, J.	35	M	LABR	PLZZZZNY
MARGOSA	00	F	INF	PLZZZZNY
SPITZER, LIEBE	30	M	LABR	PLZZZZNY
CHANE	00	M	INF	PLZZZZNY
VIET, G.	16	M	LABR	PLZZZZNY
LEWIN, V.	30	M	LABR	PLZZZZNY
LEWISOHN, W.	30	M	LABR	PLZZZZNY
SCHONKARTZ, ITZAK	20	M	LABR	PLZZZZNY
ROSENBERG, R.	25	M	LABR	PLZZZZNY
BERNSTEIN, J.	29	M	LABR	PLZZZZNY
DUBOWSKY, VICTOR	35	M	LABR	PLZZZZNY
MAISOWITZ, M.	18	M	LABR	PLZZZZNY
MARSCHOWSKY, A.	20	M	LABR	PLZZZZNY

SHIP: AURANIA

FROM: LIVERPOOL AND QUEENSTOWN
TO: NEW YORK
ARRIVED: 26 MAY 1884

PASSENGER	AGE	SEX	OCCUPATION	PRV VIL DES
ARKOGUNGAS, ABRAM	21	M	LABR	FNZZZZUSA
MARTINS, MICHAEL	23	M	LABR	FNZZZZUSA

SHIP: EGYPT

FROM: LIVERPOOL
TO: NEW YORK
ARRIVED: 26 MAY 1884

PASSENGER	AGE	SEX	OCCUPATION	PRV VIL DES
LIPKIS, MOSES	17	M	LABR	RRZZZZUSA
SCHINER, LEIB	48	M	LABR	RRZZZZUSA
EDEL	17	F	SP	RRZZZZUSA
DORNSTEIN, MICHEL	18	F	SP	RRZZZZUSA
BAW, BERKO	17	F	SP	RRZZZZUSA
LINSCPLEVSKY, LEIB	33	M	LABR	RRZZZZUSA
BUCHLOLY, GEORGE	26	M	LABR	RRZZZZUSA
WESDMANN, JOE	34	M	LABR	RRZZZZUSA
KAYONSKY, MARTIN	56	M	LABR	RRZZZZUSA
LICHLENSTEIN, J.	18	M	LABR	RRZZZZUSA
BERLSOHN, SUS.	38	F	SP	RRZZZZUSA
FRENZOL, JOEL	20	M	LABR	RRZZZZUSA
LEVIN, JACOB	32	M	LABR	RRZZZZUSA
RIDISHKI, S.	20	M	LABR	RRZZZZUSA
PYGALL, HIRSEL	19	M	LABR	RRZZZZUSA
CHAMSVEL, ABRAHAM	31	M	LABR	RRZZZZUSA
SEPHANATON, MA.	20	M	LABR	RRZZZZUSA
FRUKT, G.	59	M	LABR	RRZZZZUSA
JOHNSON, JOHAN	33	M	LABR	RRZZZZUSA
TYPEWITZ, MENDEL	31	M	LABR	RRZZZZUSA
MORSHOM, HUGO	20	M	LABR	RRZZZZUSA
MECYNWSKI, KOSEL	20	M	LABR	RRZZZZUSA
SKIAHONSKI, JOSEF	24	M	LABR	RRZZZZUSA
DEKAS, FELIX	27	M	LABR	RRZZZZUSA
SCHISLAMAN, J.	18	M	LABR	RRZZZZUSA
ZUKERMANN, WOLF	24	M	LABR	RRZZZZUSA
GRASCHKEWSKI, S.	20	M	LABR	RRZZZZUSA
PRANKE, SELIG	29	M	LABR	RRZZZZUSA
FISCHKIN, MOSES	30	M	LABR	RRZZZZUSA
MERSOHN, MOSES	22	M	LABR	RRZZZZUSA
LUCKSON, L.	16	M	LABR	RRZZZZUSA
CRIETXHIN, JUDEL	35	M	LABR	RRZZZZUSA
SKLINDER, LEWIS	49	M	LABR	RRZZZZUSA
KONIG, LOUIS	22	M	LABR	RRZZZZUSA
KURZIN, JACOB	35	M	LABR	RRZZZZUSA
KOSINSKY, JACOB	21	M	LABR	RRZZZZUSA
WEISCHURLOWITZ, CH.	16	M	LABR	RRZZZZUSA
KLINGER, GODER	20	M	LABR	RRZZZZUSA
SCHAFRIN, PAUL	24	M	LABR	RRZZZZUSA
LIPWISKY, JOSEF	24	M	LABR	RRZZZZUSA
GOLDEN, LEIB	24	M	LABR	RRZZZZUSA
BABER, L.	20	M	LABR	RRZZZZUSA
LIPSCHITZ, KELMER	25	M	LABR	RRZZZZUSA
ROBINSOHN, CH.	35	M	LABR	RRZZZZUSA
LUSSANAUSWITZ, BERTHA	20	F	SP	RRZZZZUSA
ROGOLSKY, JOSEL	50	M	LABR	RRZZZZUSA
KLEIN, MOSES	31	M	LABR	RRZZZZUSA
LOSDEYSKY, L.	23	M	LABR	RRZZZZUSA
FRANKES, P.	34	M	LABR	RRZZZZUSA
T.	32	F	W	RRZZZZUSA
JOSEF	00	M	INF	RRZZZZUSA
WALEGAL, JOSEPH	40	M	LABR	RRZZZZUSA
SOFIA	40	F	W	RRZZZZUSA
JOSE	10	M	CH	RRZZZZUSA
MOSES	8	M	CHILD	RRZZZZUSA
WAIZEIK	00	M	INF	RRZZZZUSA
JEWANINSKI, CARL	23	M	LABR	RRZZZZUSA
POLAWONSKI, JOS.	30	M	LABR	RRZZZZUSA
SCHNEIDER, MOSES	22	M	LABR	RRZZZZUSA
KANOLSKI, HIRSCH	23	M	LABR	RRZZZZUSA
WOLF	11	M	CH	RRZZZZUSA
BEER, M.	20	M	LABR	RRZZZZUSA
JERE	17	F	W	RRZZZZUSA
SHIKER, DAVID	24	M	LABR	RRZZZZUSA
CHAIM	18	M	LABR	RRZZZZUSA
JODOLSKY, E.	26	M	LABR	RRZZZZUSA
LEWIN, JOSEPH	33	M	LABR	RRZZZZUSA
MICHAL	32	M	LABR	RRZZZZUSA

PASSENGER	AGE	SEX	OCCUPATION	PRIVIL	DES
TRETSCHMANN, C.	33	M	LABR	RRZZZZ	USA
JUAMSKY, ABR.	40	M	LABR	RRZZZZ	USA
BOLMONSKY, B.	45	M	LABR	RRZZZZ	USA
BORUSKY, LEIB	18	M	LABR	RRZZZZ	USA
PINKOWSKY, HIRSCH	44	M	LABR	RRZZZZ	USA
COCLEROWSKY, ISAAC	20	M	LABR	RRZZZZ	USA
TERDRE, T.	21	M	LABR	RRZZZZ	USA
SEGALL, SAMUEL	27	M	LABR	RRZZZZ	USA
GLUCKANAH, MOIDDE	28	M	LABR	RRZZZZ	USA
KRENOWITZ, A.	24	M	LABR	RRZZZZ	USA
HYECLES, H.	33	M	LABR	RRZZZZ	USA
GOLDHER, A.	27	M	LABR	RRZZZZ	USA
LEPODIS, SOPHIA	30	F	W	RRZZZZ	USA
F.	29	M	LABR	RRZZZZ	USA
LOUIS	27	M	LABR	RRZZZZ	USA
MEIKER, ISREL	27	M	LABR	RRZZZZ	USA
MASKOVIES, A.	24	M	LABR	RRZZZZ	USA
LEIGKANSKY, M.	25	M	LABR	RRZZZZ	USA
VILLIK, P.	29	M	LABR	RRZZZZ	USA
KUHEN, H.	18	M	LABR	RRZZZZ	USA
WERZEL, B.	12	M	CH	RRZZZZ	USA
WASCHKEWITZ, A.	24	M	LABR	RRZZZZ	USA
WILKAIDIS, J.	21	M	LABR	RRZZZZ	USA
CEDANAITIZ, JOSEF	24	M	LABR	RRZZZZ	USA
MALEDWITZ, MIKUS	28	M	LABR	RRZZZZ	USA
MORES, C.	20	M	LABR	RRZZZZ	USA
JOSES	21	M	LABR	RRZZZZ	USA
CHERITZ, JOSEF	19	M	LABR	RRZZZZ	USA
KELEIN, W.	27	M	LABR	RRZZZZ	USA
A.	29	M	LABR	RRZZZZ	USA
CICHAWSKY, MATHEW	31	M	LABR	RRZZZZ	USA
EVA	30	F	W	RRZZZZ	USA
BALH, R.	40	M	LABR	RRZZZZ	USA
FANNY	36	F	W	RRZZZZ	USA
H.	10	F	CH	RRZZZZ	USA
H.	11	F	CH	RRZZZZ	USA
SANDAK, MOSES	27	M	LABR	RRZZZZ	USA
HAINES, B.	31	M	LABR	RRZZZZ	USA
MASHAWITZ, MATHEW	36	M	LABR	RRZZZZ	USA
ROVSECTES, MATHEW	21	M	LABR	RRZZZZ	USA
BLACK, JOSE	31	M	LABR	RRZZZZ	USA
SEDI	30	F	W	RRZZZZ	USA
H.	27	F	SP	RRZZZZ	USA
BERTHA	11	F	CH	RRZZZZ	USA
PQUERO, MALY	24	M	LABR	RRZZZZ	USA
GOLDBERGER, WILLIAM	40	M	LABR	RRZZZZ	USA
BELLIE	36	F	W	RRZZZZ	USA
BELLIE	00	F	INF	RRZZZZ	USA
MIKOV, WEISS	32	M	LABR	RRZZZZ	USA
JACOBSON, SM.	21	M	LABR	RRZZZZ	USA
ANTRAGE, M.	30	M	LABR	RRZZZZ	USA
A.	25	F	W	RRZZZZ	USA
ANTON	10	M	CH	RRZZZZ	USA
L.	7	M	CHILD	RRZZZZ	USA
PIETER	6	M	CHILD	RRZZZZ	USA
BABTONE	3	M	CHILD	RRZZZZ	USA
PANKES, F.	26	M	LABR	RRZZZZ	USA
M.	21	F	W	RRZZZZ	USA
MASCHE, A.	21	M	LABR	RRZZZZ	USA
P.	20	F	W	RRZZZZ	USA
MOSES	2	M	CHILD	RRZZZZ	USA
LAUTMANN, L.	29	M	LABR	RRZZZZ	USA
VASILOWSKY, JOSEF	19	M	LABR	RRZZZZ	USA
JACOB, C.	29	M	LABR	RRZZZZ	USA
SARAH	23	F	W	RRZZZZ	USA
HELENA	2	F	CHILD	RRZZZZ	USA
BRAEMER, C.	26	M	LABR	RRZZZZ	USA
FISCHIANE, ROSI	29	M	LABR	RRZZZZ	USA
ALICE	27	F	W	RRZZZZ	USA
LAHY	24	F	SP	RRZZZZ	USA
JUSKIN, GOLDE	20	M	LABR	RRZZZZ	USA
KERSCHDERPER, R.	24	M	LABR	RRZZZZ	USA
BEKANAS, MATHEW	29	M	LABR	RRZZZZ	USA
BALLUBLOLT, B.	30	M	LABR	RRZZZZ	USA
MOSES, H.	27	M	LABR	RRZZZZ	USA

PASSENGER	AGE	SEX	OCCUPATION	PRIVIL	DES
W.	27	M	LABR	RRZZZZ	USA
HALLEMANN, I.	29	M	LABR	RRZZZZ	USA
BELI	25	F	W	RRZZZZ	USA
I.	21	F	SP	RRZZZZ	USA
GELIE	20	M	LABR	RRZZZZ	USA
MOSES	11	M	CH	RRZZZZ	USA
SEGALOWITZ, B.	40	M	LABR	RRZZZZ	USA
EVA	38	F	W	RRZZZZ	USA
CBERSTEIN, A.	20	M	LABR	RRZZZZ	USA
KALONSKY, JOSEF	21	M	LABR	RRZZZZ	USA
PAULOWSKY, JOE	19	M	LABR	RRZZZZ	USA
BEECHAN, MOSES	28	M	LABR	RRZZZZ	USA
LUCY	25	F	W	RRZZZZ	USA
SLADOWSKY, C.	21	M	LABR	RRZZZZ	USA
MAGNI, JABEL	21	M	LABR	RRZZZZ	USA
C.	19	F	W	RRZZZZ	USA
SPOTT, A.	40	M	LABR	RRZZZZ	USA
MARIA	38	F	W	RRZZZZ	USA
AULLAN	10	F	CH	RRZZZZ	USA
CA.	8	F	CHILD	RRZZZZ	USA
CATHERINA	00	F	INF	RRZZZZ	USA
KENFER, A.	20	M	LABR	RRZZZZ	USA
F.	21	M	LABR	RRZZZZ	USA
HORASKY, P.	20	M	LABR	RRZZZZ	USA
MASKAWITZ, R.	21	M	LABR	RRZZZZ	USA
LOBENSTEIN, I.	40	M	LABR	RRZZZZ	USA
LEBAGWITZ, M.	26	M	LABR	RRZZZZ	USA
PIEDLEK, MOSES	29	M	LABR	RRZZZZ	USA
MOSES	00	M	INF	RRZZZZ	USA
JACOB	00	M	INF	RRZZZZ	USA
MEYER, ASCHLOW	31	M	LABR	RRZZZZ	USA
CHAIS, IOKA	27	M	LABR	RRZZZZ	USA
BEEGER, J.B.	26	M	LABR	RRZZZZ	USA
HOWORSKY, BERNARD	29	M	LABR	RRZZZZ	USA
LEVIN, C.	19	M	LABR	RRZZZZ	USA
JEDIETZ, WOLF	29	M	LABR	RRZZZZ	USA
MOSES	18	M	LABR	RRZZZZ	USA
WELLIERAN, WOLF.	17	M	LABR	RRZZZZ	USA
SCHWAN, CARL	27	M	LABR	RRZZZZ	USA
KLAMBE, P.	29	M	LABR	RRZZZZ	USA
NOWAK, V.	31	M	LABR	RRZZZZ	USA
JACOB, S.	29	M	LABR	RRZZZZ	USA
WALONSKY, S.	37	M	LABR	RRZZZZ	USA
C.	31	F	W	RRZZZZ	USA
MOSES	00	M	INF	RRZZZZ	USA
RUPOWITZ, MAYER	26	M	LABR	RRZZZZ	USA
BERTHA	24	F	W	RRZZZZ	USA
EPSTEIN, MOSES	24	M	LABR	RRZZZZ	USA
SCHLOWITZ, S.	27	M	LABR	RRZZZZ	USA
AOOCHAKK, L.	24	M	LABR	RRZZZZ	USA
MINA	10	F	CH	RRZZZZ	USA
HOFERMANN, B.	25	M	LABR	RRZZZZ	USA
PAD, MOSES	28	M	LABR	RRZZZZ	USA
HELCHES, SCH.	27	M	LABR	RRZZZZ	USA
SUSAN	10	F	CH	RRZZZZ	USA
DAVIS, C.	21	M	LABR	RRZZZZ	USA
PRAGLER, L.	19	M	LABR	RRZZZZ	USA
CLEFLER, L.	16	M	LABR	RRZZZZ	USA
PREGAL, SCHELONU	23	M	LABR	RRZZZZ	USA
SCHOUBERGER, ARON	27	M	LABR	RRZZZZ	USA
SLASEFER, JACOB	26	M	LABR	RRZZZZ	USA
PAPU, W.	24	M	LABR	RRZZZZ	USA
MELABK, A.	21	M	LABR	RRZZZZ	USA
SCHAYWIA, JOSEF	19	M	LABR	RRZZZZ	USA
FEDER, M.	42	M	LABR	RRZZZZ	USA
BRUNDLER, S.	21	M	LABR	RRZZZZ	USA
MAKLSTEIN, C.	27	M	LABR	RRZZZZ	USA
RSCHEZANSKY, MOSES	24	M	LABR	RRZZZZ	USA
FRAEEH, MOSES	21	M	LABR	RRZZZZ	USA
SAMUELSEN, MOSES	31	M	LABR	RRZZZZ	USA
GEROVSKY, WAIEL	27	M	LABR	RRZZZZ	USA
BERNER, MYLER	24	M	LABR	RRZZZZ	USA
JAUDK, J.	21	M	LABR	RRZZZZ	USA
DWGILSCHIES, MOSES	21	M	LABR	RRZZZZ	USA
APYELSHIE, BEN	21	M	LABR	RRZZZZ	USA

PASSENGER	AGE	SEX	OCCUPATION	PRV VIL DES
GOLDNIG, A.	19	M	LABR	RRZZZZUSA
AOFSCHORT, ABRAHAM	23	M	LABR	RRZZZZUSA
RATHMAN, F.	27	M	LABR	RRZZZZUSA
SOBOH, LEIB	27	M	LABR	RRZZZZUSA
FERGENAM, G.	30	M	LABR	RRZZZZUSA
SCHENZUG, WOLF	29	M	LABR	RRZZZZUSA
SIDSIES, AUG.	25	M	LABR	RRZZZZUSA
FELIES, SELIG	26	M	LABR	RRZZZZUSA
RUBER, SAMUEL	34	M	LABR	RRZZZZUSA
A----, MOSES	18	M	LABR	RRZZZZUSA
JACOBSON, JOS.	30	M	LABR	RRZZZZUSA
WIENBURGER, P.	12	M	CH	RRZZZZUSA
BOYER, MOSES	28	M	LABR	RRZZZZUSA
ROSENGAT, MOSES	28	M	LABR	RRZZZZUSA
SCHAPREER, WOLF	34	M	LABR	RRZZZZUSA
GODLEWSKI, JACOB	21	M	LABR	RRZZZZUSA
RAZEICOWITZ, W.	19	M	LABR	RRZZZZUSA
ARANOWITZ, MOSES	17	M	LABR	RRZZZZUSA
KILANSKY, ABEL	17	M	LABR	RRZZZZUSA
FRANKPURT, AMANUEL	30	M	LABR	RRZZZZUSA
MODEL, WOLF	31	M	LABR	RRZZZZUSA
VEKA	11	F	CH	RRZZZZUSA
WASSERMAN, C.	20	M	LABR	RRZZZZUSA
SEUBER, H.	40	M	LABR	RRZZZZUSA
RABUCE---, P.	25	M	LABR	RRZZZZUSA
DUCK, NORMAN	30	M	LABR	RRZZZZUSA
HOLDTHER, J.	19	M	LABR	RRZZZZUSA
REZUCK, C.	18	M	LABR	RRZZZZUSA
SLEWENECK, MARTIN	35	M	LABR	RRZZZZUSA
R.	33	F	W	RRZZZZUSA
BRANER, REBUTA	18	M	LABR	RRZZZZUSA
KSAZANSKY, L.	29	M	LABR	RRZZZZUSA
KATZ, K.	21	M	LABR	RRZZZZUSA
SALK, MOSES	23	M	LABR	RRZZZZUSA
JANOWSKY, MICHAEL	19	M	LABR	RRZZZZUSA
MENATHA, C.	20	M	LABR	RRZZZZUSA
SKATERAN, MOSES	27	M	LABR	RRZZZZUSA
SCHATERAWITZ, N.	30	M	LABR	RRZZZZUSA
DENEYER, F.	24	M	LABR	RRZZZZUSA
JEEPEATER, C.	26	M	LABR	RRZZZZUSA

SHIP: SCHIEDAM

FROM: AMSTERDAM
TO: NEW YORK
ARRIVED: 26 MAY 1884

PASSENGER	AGE	SEX	OCCUPATION	PRV VIL DES
STOLOMEZ, CHASHE	32	F	NN	PLZZZZUSA
BELE	3	F	CHILD	PLZZZZUSA
SACHAROWITZ, BARUCH	29	M	SHMK	PLZZZZUSA
ZABLONOWITZ, GERSON	31	M	TNMK	PLZZZZUSA
RUCHBINDER, HENACH	21	M	LABR	PLZZZZUSA
KAPUTSCHWENTZ, M.	23	M	LABR	PLZZZZUSA
PERLMANN, BARUCH	22	M	LABR	PLZZZZUSA
SARAH	22	F	UNKNOWN	PLZZZZUSA
KRUSCHEWIKI, JANKEL	32	M	MACH	PLZZZZUSA
PERL	20	M	UNKNOWN	PLZZZZUSA
CHANE	.06	M	INFANT	PLZZZZUSA
HASE	.06	M	INFANT	PLZZZZUSA
TEIPER, MARCUS	21	M	TLR	PLZZZZUSA
RUCKIN, JOSSEL	39	M	BKR	PLZZZZUSA
CHODOUCH, REBECCA	20	F	UNKNOWN	PLZZZZUSA
KARDIN, SCHLOME	20	F	CGRMKR	PLZZZZUSA
TINZEWITZ, FRANZ	19	M	LABR	PLZZZZUSA
KUGEL, LEISER	20	M	TLR	PLZZZZUSA
KRESNEKOWITZ, SCHEI	30	M	TLR	PLZZZZUSA
GOLDBERG, JOSPEL	45	M	LABR	PLZZZZUSA
GESC, STANISLAW	20	M	LABR	PLZZZZUSA
ANDRUCHS, WINCENTY	27	M	LABR	PLZZZZUSA
ANNA	27	F	UNKNOWN	PLZZZZUSA

PASSENGER	AGE	SEX	OCCUPATION	PRV VIL DES
AGNES	.06	F	INFANT	PLZZZZUSA
KATRONA	1	F	CHILD	PLZZZZUSA
MACYENSKI, JAHANN	26	M	LABR	PLZZZZUSA
WITTEG, ANDREAS	40	M	LABR	PLZZZZUSA
KOMOSCHEWSKY, JAN	31	M	LABR	PLZZZZUSA
NOWATSKI, MATHIAS	24	M	LABR	PLZZZZUSA
POTHEYSKI, W.	34	M	LABR	PLZZZZUSA
KAPERSKY, HELENE	30	F	UNKNOWN	PLZZZZUSA
TOMACZ	10	M	CH	PLZZZZUSA
NOWATZKY, ALEX	21	M	LABR	PLZZZZUSA
SCHIFER, IGNATZ	14	M	LABR	PLZZZZUSA
BOTZEN, IGNATZ	11	M	CH	PLZZZZUSA
JINSEWITZ, JOHANN	37	M	LABR	PLZZZZUSA
CERWATZKI, JOHANN	26	M	LABR	PLZZZZUSA
MINSCHINSKY, STANISLAW	33	M	LABR	PLZZZZUSA
STEIN, MOSES	22	M	LABR	PLZZZZUSA
SCHULBERG, MOSES	19	M	CGRMKR	PLZZZZUSA
SCHEMIL	19	M	CGRMKR	PLZZZZUSA
KLEIMAN, MOSES	27	M	LABR	PLZZZZUSA
BARSCHANOWITZ, MOSES	22	M	LABR	PLZZZZUSA
LUKENBURG, ABRAHAM	35	M	LABR	PLZZZZUSA
KLEMPNER, RASER	36	M	LABR	PLZZZZUSA
KATEROWSKY, PERSCHE	18	M	LABR	PLZZZZUSA
PLITT, HERSCH	19	M	LABR	PLZZZZUSA
GUTMANN, CHAIM	18	M	LABR	PLZZZZUSA
BILIER, HERS	50	M	LABR	PLZZZZUSA
MIZL	9	M	CHILD	PLZZZZUSA
PINKUS, JENSE	25	M	LABR	PLZZZZUSA
WEBER, ADOLF	.06	M	INFANT	PLZZZZUSA
RYCHOK, ANTONIA	20	F	UNKNOWN	PLZZZZUSA
JOSEFA	1	F	CHILD	PLZZZZUSA
JOHANN	.03	M	INFANT	PLZZZZUSA
FUCHS, RASCHE	12	M	CH	PLZZZZUSA
JAWLEWITZ, CHOLE	20	M	UNKNOWN	PLZZZZUSA
ASHER, ATZCHOK	18	M	NN	PLZZZZUSA
LEIB	16	M	NN	PLZZZZUSA
FENZLER, FOREFITTEL	16	M	NN	PLZZZZUSA
KLEIN, SAMUEL	10	M	CH	PLZZZZUSA
EPSTEIN, MOSES	17	M	TLR	RRZZZZUSA
JAKULOWITZ, NOCHEM	40	M	NN	PLZZZZUSA
SHIA	20	F	NN	PLZZZZUSA
SCHWENGER, HERSCH	20	M	TLR	PLZZZZUSA
PETLUS, WOLF	41	M	TLR	PLZZZZUSA
GUTMAN, ZERLNU	20	F	NN	PLZZZZUSA
RAPAPORT, MOSES	18	M	TLR	PLZZZZUSA
SADECKA, CAROLINA	29	F	UNKNOWN	PLZZZZUSA
TAP, JANOS	37	M	LABR	PLZZZZUSA
WANSELAN, M.	22	M	FARMER	PLZZZZUSA
CEGLERSKI, W.	36	M	LABR	PLZZZZUSA
PETROSKI, MICH.	38	M	LABR	PLZZZZUSA
ANNA	27	F	UNKNOWN	PLZZZZUSA
WLADISLAW	8	M	CHILD	PLZZZZUSA
WANDA	6	F	CHILD	PLZZZZUSA
SIGMUND	.06	M	INFANT	PLZZZZUSA
SLUMINSKI, JAN	55	M	LABR	PLZZZZUSA
NADROSKI, W.	33	M	LABR	PLZZZZUSA
TISSLER, HIRSCH	24	M	LABR	PLZZZZUSA
SILBERMANN, U	59	M	LABR	PLZZZZUSA
ROSA	40	F	UNKNOWN	PLZZZZUSA
LINA	17	F	UNKNOWN	PLZZZZUSA
MEMM	17	F	UNKNOWN	PLZZZZUSA
HARUM	16	M	UNKNOWN	PLZZZZUSA
KATHE	12	F	UNKNOWN	PLZZZZUSA
NAZI	11	F	CH	PLZZZZUSA
HENDEL	.09	M	INFANT	PLZZZZUSA
GLUCK, PHILIPP	55	M	LABR	PLZZZZUSA
PEPI	55	F	UNKNOWN	PLZZZZUSA
LINA	15	F	UNKNOWN	PLZZZZUSA
KATE	17	F	UNKNOWN	PLZZZZUSA
KESSLER, MARCI	25	F	UNKNOWN	PLZZZZUSA
ARON	.06	M	INFANT	PLZZZZUSA
MANE	20	F	UNKNOWN	PLZZZZUSA
ATHELSOHN, SARA	20	F	UNKNOWN	PLZZZZUSA
MORSCHE	11	M	CH	PLZZZZUSA
CHANE	9	M	CHILD	PLZZZZUSA

PASSENGER	AGE	SEX	OCCUPATION	PRV VIL DES
KALMAN	1	M	CHILD	PLZZZZUSA
CHAIL	.03	M	INFANT	PLZZZZUSA
GRENZER, SARA	20	F	UNKNOWN	PLZZZZUSA
U, U	00	M	SHMK	PLZZZZUSA
SCHEWE	20	M	SHMK	PLZZZZUSA
FEIGE	1	F	CHILD	PLZZZZUSA
DAWSKY, PERE	44	F	NN	PLZZZZUSA
CHAIL	10	F	CH	PLZZZZUSA
CZULIK, MARIA	20	F	UNKNOWN	PLZZZZUSA
BRECZ, ANNA	20	F	UNKNOWN	PLZZZZUSA
LEVIN, SCHLOME	26	M	UNKNOWN	PLZZZZUSA
FENNE	27	F	UNKNOWN	PLZZZZUSA
JUCHINWETSKI, H.	18	M	UNKNOWN	PLZZZZUSA
CHANE	18	F	UNKNOWN	PLZZZZUSA
RUTENBERG, CHASKEL	26	M	LABR	PLZZZZUSA
DAWILOW, ISAK	16	M	LABR	PLZZZZUSA
LEVITIN, MICH.	29	M	LABR	RRZZZZUSA
PASILEMBRON, ABR.	25	M	LABR	RRZZZZUSA
KAPLAN, SOLOMON	23	M	LABR	RRZZZZUSA
BECHARSKY, CHAIM	30	M	LABR	RRZZZZUSA
TINKOWITZ, FLINE	23	F	UNKNOWN	RRZZZZUSA
ARON	20	M	LABR	RRZZZZUSA
TROSCH, DAVID	20	M	LABR	RRZZZZUSA
ROSEWSKY, JUDE	25	M	LABR	RRZZZZUSA
KABACZNIK, LABL.	20	M	LABR	RRZZZZUSA
SCHMIDWITZ, JOSEL	20	M	LABR	RRZZZZUSA
DJURA, IVAN	27	M	LABR	RRZZZZUSA
BRODER, SALOMON	24	M	LABR	RRZZZZUSA
CHOMCKY, JANKE	30	M	LABR	RRZZZZUSA
SCHAPIRO, NOCHEM	20	M	LABR	RRZZZZUSA
SCHIRBAK, ABRAHAM	25	M	PPMKR	RRZZZZUSA
RECHLIWITZ, CHANE	25	F	UNKNOWN	RRZZZZUSA
MARANDE, LEVDEGAR	23	M	LABR	RRZZZZUSA
ELLBOGEN, DWORE	40	M	LABR	RRZZZZUSA
RUSEL	10	M	CH	RRZZZZUSA
FISCHEL	12	M	CH	RRZZZZUSA
GEB	1	M	CHILD	RRZZZZUSA

SHIP: AUSTRAL

FROM: LIVERPOOL AND QUEENSTOWN
TO: NEW YORK
ARRIVED: 27 MAY 1884

PASSENGER	AGE	SEX	OCCUPATION	PRV VIL DES
SJOGREN, CARL-H.	38	M	LABR	FNZZZZNY
HAYER, HERMAN	25	M	LABR	FNZZZZNY
JACOBSEN, J.	21	M	LABR	FNZZZZNY
SJOGREEN, MATTS	27	M	LABR	FNZZZZNY
JOHUNESSON, J.	27	M	FARMER	FNZZZZUNK
JELINSKY, J.	20	M	FARMER	PLZZZZNY
NADOLSKY, JOSEF	33	M	LABR	PLZZZZNY
LORENZ, ANTON	36	M	LABR	PLZZZZNY
SAMOWSKY, JOS.	23	M	JNR	PLZZZZNY
SCHOLTOSKA, M.	20	F	SVNT	PLZZZZNY
MALOWSKY, LUDIVCIUS	20	F	SVNT	PLZZZZNY
SAMBROWSKY, L.	24	F	SVNT	PLZZZZNY
GLOWA, STEFAN	44	M	LABR	PLZZZZNY
JACOB	26	M	LABR	PLZZZZNY
AGECKOWSKY, MICHAEL	40	M	LABR	PLZZZZNY
GLOWA, JOHN	47	M	LABR	PLZZZZNY
LICHTINAN, B.	28	F	SVNT	PLZZZZNY
FREDIE	6	F	CHILD	PLZZZZNY
BIFKE	1	F	CHILD	PLZZZZNY
NORDKAWITZ, FEIGE	15	F	SVNT	PLZZZZNY
MILOSCHTAK, PETER	30	M	LABR	PLZZZZNY
SLANKILWICY, GEORG	30	M	LABR	PLZZZZNY
AGNES	30	F	UNKNOWN	PLZZZZNY
DOSEF	1	F	CHILD	PLZZZZNY
HANS	.06	M	INFANT	PLZZZZNY
HEIDCKA, HENDRICH	40	M	LABR	PLZZZZNY
HABAI, MOJCICH	45	F	SVNT	PLZZZZNY
CONSTANTINE	10	F	CH	PLZZZZNY
PAMKOLA, HANNA	30	F	SVNT	PLZZZZNY
SOPHIE	11	F	CH	PLZZZZNY
PETRUS	1	M	CHILD	PLZZZZNY
BICAKOWSKY, JOSEF	42	M	LABR	PLZZZZNY
HARMATOS, JACOB	30	M	LABR	PLZZZZNY
SOPHIE	30	F	UNKNOWN	PLZZZZNY
MARIE	11	F	CH	PLZZZZNY
JAN	3	M	CHILD	PLZZZZNY
MARIANA	1	F	CHILD	PLZZZZNY
PERDA, JOSEF	50	M	LABR	PLZZZZNY
AGATHA	40	F	UNKNOWN	PLZZZZNY
JOHN	11	M	CH	PLZZZZNY
B.	8	M	CHILD	PLZZZZNY
SIKORA, MOJCICK	34	M	LABR	PLZZZZNY
KIMGINDE	30	F	UNKNOWN	PLZZZZNY
JOSEF	5	M	CHILD	PLZZZZNY
MARIANNA	3	F	CHILD	PLZZZZNY
FRANZ	1	M	CHILD	PLZZZZNY
GERSCHE, ANTON	27	M	LABR	PLZZZZNY

SHIP: LESSING

FROM: HAMBURG
TO: NEW YORK
ARRIVED: 27 MAY 1884

PASSENGER	AGE	SEX	OCCUPATION	PRV VIL DES
WERDRAGER, MORDCHE	19	M	LABR	RRZZZZUSA
KARKLINSKI, RACHEL	20	F	SGL	RRZZZZUSA
JOSSEL	8	M	CHILD	RRZZZZUSA
SORKANSKI, BENJAMIN	20	M	LABR	RRZZZZUSA
KAHN, SAMUEL	40	M	UNKNOWN	RRZZZZUSA
U, U	18	M	UNKNOWN	RRZZZZUSA
BRIKER, MEMICHE	8	M	CHILD	RRZZZZUSA
RATH, MENDEL	54	M	DLR	RRZZZZUSA
JOSSEL	26	M	DLR	RRZZZZUSA
MINDEL	28	F	W	RRZZZZUSA
KOZA, JOSEPH	25	M	LABR	RRZZZZUSA
JOH.	23	M	LABR	RRZZZZUSA
GOZELNIK, FRANZ	24	M	LABR	RRZZZZUSA
FINKELSFEIN, FEIGE	18	F	SGL	RRZZZZUSA
KALWARISKI, BASCHE	20	F	SGL	RRZZZZUSA
GRINZBERG, MOSES	24	M	FARMER	RRZZZZUSA
PIAVNIK, ARON	30	M	DLR	RRZZZZUSA
GRANEWITZ, MENDEL	21	M	TLR	RRZZZZUSA
CHODOSIH, GERSON	24	M	TLR	RRZZZZUSA
RUTSTEIN, CZESNE	40	F	W	RRZZZZUSA
MOSES	.11	M	INFANT	RRZZZZUSA
HURWITZ, ISRAEL	23	M	DLR	RRZZZZUSA
---M----, U	20	M	LABR	RRZZZZUSA
AUGUST.	17	M	LABR	RRZZZZUSA
LINE	16	F	SGL	RRZZZZUSA
STEFANOWIEZ, FRANZISKA	22	F	SGL	RRZZZZUSA
VICTORIA	21	F	SGL	RRZZZZUSA
FARKESCH, JOSEPH	20	M	MCHT	RRZZZZUSA
CZARKOWSKI, PIOTR.	20	M	LABR	RRZZZZUSA
KOCHINSKAT, VINCENT	22	M	LABR	RRZZZZUSA
MOFULEWICZ, VINCENT	21	M	LABR	RRZZZZUSA
RAFALOWITZ, CHAIM	20	M	TLR	RRZZZZUSA
MESCHARES, DAVID	28	M	DLR	RRZZZZUSA
KARPELOW, ISRAEL	30	M	DLR	RRZZZZUSA
BILES, SARA	20	F	SGL	RRZZZZUSA
CHASCHE	20	F	SGL	RRZZZZUSA
RIBA, NOSSEN	20	M	LABR	RRZZZZUSA
ROTHSTEIN, FREIDE	40	F	W	RRZZZZUSA
CHAINE	8	M	CHILD	RRZZZZUSA
SELDE	6	F	CHILD	RRZZZZUSA
KERSCHT, JEZKO	15	M	LABR	RRZZZZUSA
GILLIS, SCHONE	18	F	SGL	RRZZZZUSA

PASSENGER	AGE	SEX	OCCUPATION	PRV VIL DES
KUGEL, LEISER	20	M	LABR	RRZZZZUSA
WENZIAL, ABRAM	44	M	LABR	RRZZZZUSA
JOZICKY, LINE	30	F	SGL	RRZZZZUSA
LOGOWSKY, SCHAJE	18	F	SGL	RRZZZZUSA
BLECKARSKY, CHAIM	35	M	LABR	RRZZZZUSA
SCHATTI, ABRAH.	43	M	LABR	RRZZZZUSA
PERLMANN, SELDE	18	F	SGL	RRZZZZUSA
SCHIFER	8	F	CHILD	RRZZZZUSA
WEGNER, ABRAHAM	18	M	SHMK	RRZZZZUSA
WIESGEDISKE, MARIE	18	F	SGL	RRZZZZUSA
ROSENGARD, JECHIEL	15	M	TNMK	RRZZZZUSA
RAHT, REBECCA	15	F	SGL	RRZZZZUSA
STONYA, REBECCA	18	F	SGL	RRZZZZUSA
FRANK, A-IFF---	34	F	W	RRZZZZUSA
RIWKE	.11	F	INFANT	RRZZZZUSA
PINCRIS, BER.	25	M	LABR	RRZZZZUSA
BONNER, SARA	18	F	SGL	RRZZZZUSA
STERLING, SUSE	28	F	W	RRZZZZUSA
SAMUEL	6	M	CHILD	RRZZZZUSA
LEILE	4	M	CHILD	RRZZZZUSA
OSCHER	.11	F	INFANT	RRZZZZUSA
WALLERSTEIN, CHAIM	16	M	LABR	RRZZZZUSA
VOLKMANN, MEYER	19	M	LABR	RRZZZZUSA
KRAP, CHANNE	18	F	SGL	RRZZZZUSA
MISCHNEVSKY, RACHEL	21	F	SGL	RRZZZZUSA
COHN, MORRIS	49	M	TLR	RRZZZZUSA
KOZEN, RASCHE	20	F	SGL	RRZZZZUSA
MARIASCHE	8	F	CHILD	RRZZZZUSA
DOMSKY, SZERNE	50	F	W	RRZZZZUSA
SCHEINE	24	F	W	RRZZZZUSA
MARIE	.11	F	INFANT	RRZZZZUSA
LEWINSOHN, SARA	8	F	CHILD	RRZZZZUSA
APFELBAUM, BULAN	17	M	LABR	RRZZZZUSA
FRIEDMANN, BEHR.	33	M	LABR	RRZZZZUSA
STERNBERG, MINNA	24	F	W	RRZZZZUSA
MEYER	.11	M	INFANT	RRZZZZUSA
KAPLAN, DWORE	20	F	SGL	RRZZZZUSA
WENGEROWITZ, ITZKO	20	M	LABR	RRZZZZUSA
FENSTER, JOSEPH	20	M	LABR	RRZZZZUSA
STILLER, ABRAHAM	20	M	LABR	RRZZZZUSA
POLIZINER, MEIER	17	M	MCHT	RRZZZZUSA
ITZKWITZ, DAVID	20	M	LABR	RRZZZZUSA
DODEL, JACOB	17	M	TLR	RRZZZZUSA
HOSKEL, ARON	16	M	LABR	RRZZZZUSA
RANSUK, SAMUEL	19	M	LABR	RRZZZZUSA
AISIK	18	M	LABR	RRZZZZUSA
LIEDER, PEREZ	16	M	DLR	RRZZZZUSA
LANDAN, REISIG	51	M	DLR	RRZZZZUSA
CHASEN, ARON	22	M	DLR	RRZZZZUSA
PILOWSKI, LASER	25	M	DLR	RRZZZZUSA
KASCHLESSKI, JOH.	25	M	LABR	RRZZZZUSA
KREINICH, JOSEF	18	M	LABR	RRZZZZUSA
WIENS, HEINR.	40	M	LABR	RRZZZZUSA
ELISABETH	38	F	W	RRZZZZUSA
PETER	9	M	CHILD	RRZZZZUSA
MARIE	4	F	CHILD	RRZZZZUSA
JACOB	.02	M	INFANT	RRZZZZUSA
GOERTZEN, HEINR.	40	M	LABR	RRZZZZUSA
MARIE	36	F	W	RRZZZZUSA
ANNE	8	F	CHILD	RRZZZZUSA
AUGUSTE	7	F	CHILD	RRZZZZUSA
KLAUS	8	M	CHILD	RRZZZZUSA
HEINR.	4	M	CHILD	RRZZZZUSA
JACOB	2	M	CHILD	RRZZZZUSA
JOH.	.03	M	INFANT	RRZZZZUSA
SKOWRCUSKI, JOSEF	32	M	LABR	RRZZZZUSA
RATOWSKI, HIRSCH	25	M	LABR	RRZZZZUSA
SCHONE	25	F	W	RRZZZZUSA
ABRAH.	3	M	CHILD	RRZZZZUSA
CHEIM	.11	M	INFANT	RRZZZZUSA
JERCHED	.01	F	INFANT	RRZZZZUSA
AHRENDT, JUGER	39	F	W	RRZZZZUSA
JENS	8	M	CHILD	RRZZZZUSA
MARIE	6	F	CHILD	RRZZZZUSA
NIELS	.11	M	INFANT	RRZZZZUSA

PASSENGER	AGE	SEX	OCCUPATION	PRV VIL DES
RUDDE, MAGDE.	20	F	SGL	RRZZZZUSA
ASMUSSEN, JOH.	16	M	LABR	RRZZZZUSA
SCHWEITZER, JOH.	26	M	FARMER	RRZZZZUSA
PETERS, JOH.	16	M	FARMER	RRZZZZUSA
JENSEN, SOREN	28	M	FARMER	RRZZZZUSA
NISSEN, JORGEN	17	M	FARMER	RRZZZZUSA
GOLDBERG, MARIANNE	26	F	W	RRZZZZUSA
ABRAM	.11	M	INFANT	RRZZZZUSA
LIPPMANN, DAVID	17	M	LABR	RRZZZZUSA
SEGAL, NATHAN	21	M	LABR	RRZZZZUSA
ZSCHIELACK, FRANZ	26	M	LABR	RRZZZZUSA
JOSEF	22	M	LABR	RRZZZZUSA
KYSOCKI, VINCENT	34	M	LABR	RRZZZZUSA
WERNER, AUGUST	30	M	LABR	RRZZZZUSA
MARIANNE	50	F	W	RRZZZZUSA
BEHRENDT, MARIANNE	56	F	W	RRZZZZUSA
FINKELSTEIN, MEYER	20	M	DLR	RRZZZZUSA
HOLLAND, ADOLPH	29	M	LABR	RRZZZZUSA
JULIUS	20	M	LABR	RRZZZZUSA
LEVIN, HIRSCH	22	M	LABR	RRZZZZUSA
FRIEDLANDER, DWINE	30	F	W	RRZZZZUSA
JOSEPH	7	M	CHILD	RRZZZZUSA
JACOB	5	M	CHILD	RRZZZZUSA
PINCUS	.11	M	INFANT	RRZZZZUSA
KACZEROWSKI, FELIX	36	M	LABR	RRZZZZUSA
HESCHELSON, GELLE	30	F	W	RRZZZZUSA
LEISER	.11	M	INFANT	RRZZZZUSA
MARIE, ESTHER	18	F	SGL	RRZZZZUSA
JANKELSON, CHAIN	25	M	TDR	RRZZZZUSA
BLUMBERG, ABRAHAM	22	M	LABR	RRZZZZUSA

SHIP: LAURENT

FROM: HAVRE
TO: NEW YORK
ARRIVED: 28 MAY 1884

PASSENGER	AGE	SEX	OCCUPATION	PRV VIL DES
CIESZKOWSKI, L.	13	M	MECH	PLZZZZCAL
HAHN, S.	22	M	CRR	RRZZZZNY

SHIP: BELGENLAND

FROM: ANTWERP
TO: NEW YORK
ARRIVED: 29 MAY 1884

PASSENGER	AGE	SEX	OCCUPATION	PRV VIL DES
PITJHYSUSKI, J.	27	M	CGRMKR	PLZZZZNY
ZOMSZAK, W.	18	M	LABR	PLZZZZNY
LINZOK, JOS.	22	M	LABR	PLZZZZNY
CIBETZKI, JUL.	19	M	UNKNOWN	PLZZZZPHI
LERBERG, GG.	36	M	PNTR	RRZZZZUNK
AUG.	36	F	UNKNOWN	RRZZZZUNK
PAUL	5	M	CHILD	RRZZZZUNK
EMMA	1	F	CHILD	RRZZZZUNK
MACKICWICZ, MARNE.	60	F	SVNT	PLZZZZNY
FRIEDGUT, BERN.	19	M	CGRMKR	RRZZZZNY
JANKE, HERM.	24	M	FARMER	RRZZZZNY
LASASKI, ABEL	30	M	UNKNOWN	RRZZZZNY
BASSIN, JOSEF	45	M	MCHT	RRZZZZNY
ANTON, RUMIE	45	F	SVNT	RRZZZZNY
LAREIGE	35	F	SVNT	RRZZZZNY
LIPPITZ, SARAH	18	F	SVNT	RRZZZZPA
AMOCHOWSKI, P.	31	M	HTR	RRZZZZUNK
BLOCK, FANNI	31	F	W	RRZZZZPA
S.	8	M	CHILD	RRZZZZPA

PASSENGER	AGE	SEX	OCCUPATION	PRV VIL DES
CHIL	6	M	CHILD	RRZZZZPA
KONRAD, GG.	50	M	LABR	PLZZZZNY
HARTING, MAR.	25	F	SVNT	RRZZZZNY
GLASZICK, AUG.	23	M	LABR	PLZZZZCH
FRANCIS	19	M	LABR	PLZZZZCH
NADEMORE	3	F	CHILD	PLZZZZCH
BUCKE, MICH.	30	M	LABR	PLZZZZPHI
KARCHER, J.	60	M	PVTR	PLZZZZPHI
MASH	50	F	UNKNOWN	PLZZZZPHI

SHIP: BOHEMIA

FROM: HAMBURG
TO: NEW YORK
ARRIVED: 29 MAY 1884

PASSENGER	AGE	SEX	OCCUPATION	PRV VIL DES
BIALISTOCKER, SALOMON	32	M	TLR	RRZZZZUSA
LINDENTHAL, CHAJE	35	F	W	RRZZZZUSA
LEWIN, FEIWEL	31	M	TLR	RRZZZZUSA
DEWITZ, LINE	20	F	SGL	RRZZZZUSA
EISENBERG, FREIDA	20	F	SGL	RRZZZZUSA
BOHLKE, FRIED.	40	M	LABR	RRZZZZUSA
KAMINSKY, CARL	48	M	LABR	RRZZZZUSA
ERNSTE.	36	F	W	RRZZZZUSA
LUDWIKA	.11	F	INFANT	RRZZZZUSA
NUCH, JOSEF	19	M	LABR	RRZZZZUSA
DAVID	18	M	LABR	RRZZZZUSA
DOBERSTEIN, ABRAH.	23	M	LABR	RRZZZZUSA
BUFMAN, FEWIE	23	M	LABR	RRZZZZUSA
GRUNHAUX, MICHEL	26	M	LABR	RRZZZZUSA
HALPERN, LEIB	16	M	LABR	RRZZZZUSA
HOLER, BARUH	25	M	LABR	RRZZZZUSA
LONIN, JUDA	36	M	LABR	RRZZZZUSA
GITTIN, RAPHEAL	32	M	LABR	RRZZZZUSA
ABRAH.	19	M	LABR	RRZZZZUSA
MANA, JOSEF	24	M	LABR	RRZZZZUSA
ISAACSON, LEIB	18	M	LABR	RRZZZZUSA
SISMER, JOHANN	18	M	LABR	RRZZZZUSA
SCHNEIDER, NOCHIM	17	M	TLR	RRZZZZUSA
BIALISTOCKI, SAMUEL	17	M	LABR	RRZZZZUSA
STURM, JULS.	40	M	CPTR	RRZZZZUSA
GEORG	9	M	CHILD	RRZZZZUSA
GRISSAS, ISRAEL	34	M	DLR	RRZZZZUSA
HRUTZKOM, CHATZKEL	15	M	SHPR	RRZZZZUSA
HIRSCHKOWITZ, BEHR.	40	M	LABR	RRZZZZUSA
WICHTOWSKI, FRANZ	26	M	LABR	RRZZZZUSA
TEOFILE	20	F	W	RRZZZZUSA
JAN	.09	M	INFANT	RRZZZZUSA
MIRZBILKI, ADAM	43	M	LABR	RRZZZZUSA
MACKINVICZ, JOSEF	40	M	LABR	RRZZZZUSA
G-----, ----ON	18	M	LABR	RRZZZZUSA
PESSEL	17	F	SGL	RRZZZZUSA
WEINBERG, FEIWUSCH	18	M	TLR	RRZZZZUSA
LEWINSOHN, JANKEL	57	M	BKR	RRZZZZUSA
CYRULNIKOUS, MICHEL	18	M	LABR	RRZZZZUSA
LEWITSCH, BERL.	46	M	TLR	RRZZZZUSA
RAPHAEL	18	M	CH	RRZZZZUSA
RACHEL	8	F	CHILD	RRZZZZUSA
BRANDEL	7	M	CHILD	RRZZZZUSA
DEJSEN, JENTE	16	F	SGL	RRZZZZUSA
ITTERS, LEA	46	F	W	RRZZZZUSA
ESTHER	16	F	CH	RRZZZZUSA
SCHONE	15	F	CH	RRZZZZUSA
BLURNE	8	F	CHILD	RRZZZZUSA
MEYER	7	M	CHILD	RRZZZZUSA
RASCHE	6	F	CHILD	RRZZZZUSA
SCHONE	5	F	CHILD	RRZZZZUSA
SPENDER, JULS.	28	M	LABR	RRZZZZUSA
MACZKELNAS, ANTON	25	M	LABR	RRZZZZUSA
BARUSZEWICZ, JOSEF	35	M	LABR	RRZZZZUSA

PASSENGER	AGE	SEX	OCCUPATION	PRV VIL DES
ARON	25	M	LABR	RRZZZZUSA
DUBASKE, PETERS	18	M	LABR	RRZZZZUSA
KUSNEROWSKI, FERD.	17	M	LABR	RRZZZZUSA
LICHTENBERG, AISIK	18	M	LABR	RRZZZZUSA
SIMON, JACOB	11	M	CH	RRZZZZUSA
SCHNIPA, MICHAEL	40	M	LABR	RRZZZZUSA
GWOSDINSHI, ROSALIE	25	F	SGL	RRZZZZUSA
KOLOSOWSKY, CASIMIR	27	M	LABR	RRZZZZUSA
ELISABETH	27	F	W	RRZZZZUSA
SUWALSKY, MOSES	19	M	LABR	RRZZZZUSA
WOLF, JACOB	20	M	DLR	RRZZZZUSA
CHACKEL, EISIK	21	M	TLR	RRZZZZUSA
ROGOWIN, MOSES	15	M	DLR	RRZZZZUSA
RODENSKY, SALOMEN	26	M	DLR	RRZZZZUSA
CHEIKLIN, LEIB	40	M	DLR	RRZZZZUSA
BININOWITZ, SCHONE	20	F	SGL	RRZZZZUSA
CZOLNO, BENTZE	34	M	DLR	RRZZZZUSA
REINHOLZ, JOHANN	24	M	BKR	RRZZZZUSA
MARIE	30	F	W	RRZZZZUSA
COHN, MEITE	26	F	W	RRZZZZUSA
ZITTE	.11	F	INFANT	RRZZZZUSA
ISAACSOHN, WOLF	23	M	MLR	RRZZZZUSA
KRINSKY, LURE	22	M	TLR	RRZZZZUSA
ARONSOHN, ABRAH.	29	M	LABR	RRZZZZUSA
GUTSTADT, MOSES	21	M	DLR	RRZZZZUSA
SCHAPIRO, LEIB	19	M	PNTR	RRZZZZUSA
BUSSTEIN, HILLEL	38	M	CGRMKR	RRZZZZUSA
LAZAR, CHANNE	40	F	W	RRZZZZUSA
U, MORRIS	40	M	TLR	RRZZZZUSA
AMALSKY, LEIB	19	M	LABR	RRZZZZUSA
SOSTOSKY, JUDEL	33	M	LABR	RRZZZZUSA
PASTOR, MINNA	17	F	SGL	RRZZZZUSA
KOLEF, JOSSEL	34	M	LABR	RRZZZZUSA
POSNICK, ABRAHAM	32	M	LABR	RRZZZZUSA
JEZSURAK, SARA	22	F	W	RRZZZZUSA
SAMUEL	.11	M	INFANT	RRZZZZUSA
GOLDENBERG, SCHONE	18	M	LABR	RRZZZZUSA
SCHAFFER, NATHAN	9	M	CHILD	RRZZZZUSA
FRIEDMANN, ISAAC	46	M	LABR	RRZZZZUSA
FISCHER, ABRAH.	14	M	LABR	RRZZZZUSA
LASAR, LIEBE	17	F	SGL	RRZZZZUSA
SCHAPIRA, BARUCH	17	M	LABR	RRZZZZUSA
POSGINCEWSKY, ABRAH.	18	M	DLR	RRZZZZUSA
M--------, CHAIN	17	M	LABR	RRZZZZUSA
LAWDOVSI-Z, JOSSEL	20	M	LABR	RRZZZZUSA
JANKELSON, ZOLMEN	19	M	DLR	RRZZZZUSA
WALLERSTEIN, LEA	25	F	W	RRZZZZUSA
BEHR.	.11	M	INFANT	RRZZZZUSA
GUTMANN, RACHEL	26	F	W	RRZZZZUSA
JOSSEL	.11	M	INFANT	RRZZZZUSA
TASCHMANN, ARON	23	M	LABR	RRZZZZUSA
SIEGEL, ESTHER	25	F	W	RRZZZZUSA
RAHEL	.11	F	INFANT	RRZZZZUSA
ABRAHAM	.01	M	INFANT	RRZZZZUSA
KOLENDA, ANNA	28	F	W	RRZZZZUSA
DAVID	8	M	CHILD	RRZZZZUSA
SALOMON	5	M	CHILD	RRZZZZUSA
FRIDA	.11	F	INFANT	RRZZZZUSA
MARWIANSKEI, PESCHE	8	F	CHILD	RRZZZZUSA
ABRAHAMSKY, SARA	50	F	W	RRZZZZUSA
MATHILDE	17	F	CH	RRZZZZUSA
HUGO	15	M	CH	RRZZZZUSA
GOLDBECK, META	70	F	W	RRZZZZUSA
RISCH, DORETHEA	28	F	W	RRZZZZUSA
EMIL	5	M	CHILD	RRZZZZUSA
LINCHER	4	M	CHILD	RRZZZZUSA
HERZBERG, FRIEDR.	27	M	APTC	RRZZZZUSA
GEORGE, HERRMANN	34	M	MECH	RRZZZZUSA
BOHLING, JOH.	26	M	WCHMKR	RRZZZZUSA
PICK, EMIL	25	M	MCHT	RRZZZZUSA
ZIMMERMANN, AUG.	30	M	MCHT	RRZZZZUSA
CARLSON, NIALS	38	M	LABR	RRZZZZUSA
GUSTAVA	33	F	W	RRZZZZUSA
ROBERT	.11	M	INFANT	RRZZZZUSA
SVENSON, JOHANNA	21	F	SGL	RRZZZZUSA

PASSENGER	AGE	SEX	OCCUPATION	PRIV	VIL	DES
BOSSGER, SELMA	18	F	SGL	RR	ZZZZ	USA
RISSLAND, RUD.	22	M	JNR	RR	ZZZZ	USA
HOFFMANN, OTTO	16	M	MUSN	RR	ZZZZ	USA
BRAUKMANN, GUSTAV	25	M	SHMK	RR	ZZZZ	USA
STAPL, HERRMANN	16	M	LABR	RR	ZZZZ	USA
KOEHLER, DOROTHEA	18	F	SGL	RR	ZZZZ	USA
SCHMIDZ, PETER	40	M	JNR	RR	ZZZZ	USA
ANNA	32	F	W	RR	ZZZZ	USA
CARL	5	M	CHILD	RR	ZZZZ	USA
MARY	.11	F	INFANT	RR	ZZZZ	USA
KRUSE, WILH.	25	M	LABR	RR	ZZZZ	USA
SENKEIS, ELISE	20	F	SGL	RR	ZZZZ	USA
ANNA	23	F	SGL	RR	ZZZZ	USA
KURZTISCH, HERRMANN	26	M	LABR	RR	ZZZZ	USA
PISCHKE, FRIEDR.	27	M	LABR	RR	ZZZZ	USA
THORSBERG, MARTIN	34	M	SEMN	RR	ZZZZ	USA
GLISBRADY, SCHERAN	38	M	SEMN	RR	ZZZZ	USA
BRAACH, ISAAK	33	M	SEMN	RR	ZZZZ	USA
TOMMER, HEINRICH	21	M	LABR	RR	ZZZZ	USA
NEIMARK, MOWSZA	18	F	SGL	RR	ZZZZ	USA
POEFFEL, EMIL	29	M	LABR	RR	ZZZZ	USA
GLADST-I-, EIDE	23	F	W	RR	ZZZZ	USA
FREIDA	8	F	CHILD	RR	ZZZZ	USA
BEILE	.11	F	INFANT	RR	ZZZZ	USA
WEINSTEIN, ISAAK	25	M	LABR	RR	ZZZZ	USA
SPEDER, DORA	24	F	W	RR	ZZZZ	USA
GUSTAV	3	M	CHILD	RR	ZZZZ	USA
SCHUETZ, JOSEF	19	M	LABR	RR	ZZZZ	USA
FRIEDR.	17	M	LABR	RR	ZZZZ	USA
SPEDER, JOH.	52	M	LABR	RR	ZZZZ	USA
JOH.	18	M	S	RR	ZZZZ	USA
NEIRMANN, MARIE	22	F	SGL	RR	ZZZZ	USA
ARENDZ, WILH.	37	M	SMH	RR	ZZZZ	USA
LOUISE	34	F	W	RR	ZZZZ	USA
MARTHA	5	F	CHILD	RR	ZZZZ	USA
PAUL	.11	M	INFANT	RR	ZZZZ	USA
CAROLINE	37	F	W	RR	ZZZZ	USA
KURZECHI, MARTIN	21	M	LABR	RR	ZZZZ	USA
DANTER, JOSEF	25	M	TNMK	RR	ZZZZ	USA
BOLEWSKY, JOSEF	24	M	DLR	RR	ZZZZ	USA
GUTMANN, JACOB	27	M	TLR	RR	ZZZZ	USA
FEIGE	28	F	W	RR	ZZZZ	USA
CHAIKLIN, SALOMON	23	M	DLR	RR	ZZZZ	USA
SALOMON	17	M	SMH	RR	ZZZZ	USA
TOMIAN, FOLK	17	M	LABR	RR	ZZZZ	USA
DARGESCHANSKY, CHAIN	36	M	MCHT	RR	ZZZZ	USA
JUTHEL, ARON	25	M	LABR	RR	ZZZZ	USA
IGOMATCH, DEBORA	40	F	W	RR	ZZZZ	USA
RISCHE	8	F	CHILD	RR	ZZZZ	USA
JOGMANN, SARAH	20	F	SGL	RR	ZZZZ	USA
LEIB	19	M	LABR	RR	ZZZZ	USA
HEYSE, AUGUST	35	M	SHMK	RR	ZZZZ	USA
GRUENBERG, LEISER	23	M	TLR	RR	ZZZZ	USA
ISAAK	10	M	S	RR	ZZZZ	USA
BUSBAUM, ABR.	23	M	BKR	RR	ZZZZ	USA
MARGRAF, MENDEL	22	M	DLR	RR	ZZZZ	USA
SCHAPIRO, CHEIM	24	M	DLR	RR	ZZZZ	USA
FENNE	22	F	W	RR	ZZZZ	USA
RABEWINSKY, MOSER	38	M	LABR	RR	ZZZZ	USA
FILKENSTEIN, STORNER	18	M	LABR	RR	ZZZZ	USA
KARKOWSKY, NACHMANN	19	M	LABR	RR	ZZZZ	USA
PERLOWITSCH, HIRSCH	25	M	LABR	RR	ZZZZ	USA
LOPVINSKY, TAUCHMANN	40	M	LABR	RR	ZZZZ	USA
MIZINSKY, JOSEPH	17	M	LABR	RR	ZZZZ	USA
PINKOWSKY, HIRSCH	20	M	LABR	RR	ZZZZ	USA
SKOFRUNISH, ISRAEL	20	M	LABR	RR	ZZZZ	USA
ROSENBERG, SARA	20	F	SGL	RR	ZZZZ	USA
GOLD, MENNEHE	25	F	W	RR	ZZZZ	USA
CHAIM	.11	M	INFANT	RR	ZZZZ	USA
GARFINKEL, BEILS.	26	F	W	RR	ZZZZ	USA
LEISER	4	M	CHILD	RR	ZZZZ	USA
SALOMON	.11	M	INFANT	RR	ZZZZ	USA
ECKERT, EDUARD	22	M	SDLR	RR	ZZZZ	USA
MIZKIEWCIZ, ANDREJ	60	M	LABR	RR	ZZZZ	USA
FRIEDMANN, LEIB	34	M	LABR	RR	ZZZZ	USA

PASSENGER	AGE	SEX	OCCUPATION	PRIV	VIL	DES
LANDSBERG, BLUME	50	F	W	RR	ZZZZ	USA
EIDEL	21	F	CH	RR	ZZZZ	USA
MARIANNE	8	F	CHILD	RR	ZZZZ	USA
LIEBE	7	F	CHILD	RR	ZZZZ	USA
DIGLETZ, SARA	18	F	SGL	RR	ZZZZ	USA
JOSNE, NISSEN	8	F	CHILD	RR	ZZZZ	USA
SACHS, JAHNKE	26	M	STMSN	RR	ZZZZ	USA

SHIP: RHEIN

FROM: BREMEN
TO: NEW YORK
ARRIVED: 29 MAY 1884

PASSENGER	AGE	SEX	OCCUPATION	PRIV	VIL	DES
KLEIN, SARA	20	F	NN	RR	ZZZZ	USA
PAULE	19	F	NN	RR	ZZZZ	USA

SHIP: STATE OF NEVADA

FROM: GLASGOW AND LARNE
TO: NEW YORK
ARRIVED: 30 MAY 1884

PASSENGER	AGE	SEX	OCCUPATION	PRIV	VIL	DES
BUDURG, WENZEL	29	M	LABR	PL	ZZZZ	USA
CHMORA, JOHANN	34	M	LABR	PL	ZZZZ	USA
GIBAS, JONAS	28	M	LABR	PL	ZZZZ	USA
ANNA	22	F	W	PL	ZZZZ	USA
JAN	.02	M	INFANT	PL	ZZZZ	USA
GOLUMBOVSKY, GEORG	22	M	LABR	PL	ZZZZ	USA
MALINOVSKY, SCHIDOR	27	M	LABR	PL	ZZZZ	USA
SCHUMLOM, CITT	27	F	W	PL	ZZZZ	USA
GUNKOZ, WALENTI	45	M	LABR	PL	ZZZZ	USA
LANKAN, JACOB	36	M	LABR	PL	ZZZZ	USA
PRECHORRAK, VINCENT	31	M	LABR	PL	ZZZZ	USA
MACZIS, JOSES	22	M	LABR	PL	ZZZZ	USA
WEISZNWAS, JOSES-M.	23	M	LABR	PL	ZZZZ	USA
MUTZKUS, JAN	28	M	LABR	PL	ZZZZ	USA
NIEMOZCNKA, CHRISTINE	26	F	W	PL	ZZZZ	USA
NEWIADOWSKY, BARLOL	40	M	LABR	PL	ZZZZ	USA
VICTORIA	16	F	W	PL	ZZZZ	USA
STANCHINSKY, PETER	42	M	LABR	PL	ZZZZ	USA
SCHIDLOWSKI, NISCHOW	23	M	LABR	PL	ZZZZ	USA
NISCHEN	20	F	W	PL	ZZZZ	USA
SCHOBOLSKI, ISRAEL	20	M	LABR	PL	ZZZZ	USA
STANKOWSKI, AUGUST	20	M	LABR	PL	ZZZZ	USA
WALMSKY, JONAS	30	M	LABR	PL	ZZZZ	USA
KOWASZ, WASIL	18	M	LABR	PL	ZZZZ	USA
EHRENREICH, JACOB	10	M	LABR	PL	ZZZZ	USA

SHIP: ELBE

FROM: BREMEN
TO: NEW YORK
ARRIVED: 31 MAY 1884

PASSENGER	AGE	SEX	OCCUPATION	PRIV	VIL	DES
SZUCH, L.	32	M	RTR	RR	ZZZZ	USA

PASSENGER	AGE	SEX	OCCUPATION	PRIV	DES
SHIP: ELYSIA					
FROM: UNKNOWN					
TO: NEW YORK					
ARRIVED: 31 MAY 1884					
JENDUSCHEK, JES.	45	M	LABR	RRZZZZ	USA
WASSERMAN, SALAMON	18	M	LABR	RRZZZZ	USA
SIDBOROSKI, NOCHAM	34	M	LABR	RRZZZZ	USA
MELGER, ZEIWEL	24	M	LABR	RRZZZZ	USA
TOSENDON, CHAIM-L.	25	M	LABR	RRZZZZ	USA
LEIB	12	M	CH	RRZZZZ	USA
GAWEL, MAESEY	35	M	LABR	RRZZZZ	USA
ALTMANIC, ABRAHAM-M.	22	M	LABR	RRZZZZ	USA
MUDNITZKI, ARON	18	M	LABR	RRZZZZ	USA
SARAH	17	F	SVNT	RRZZZZ	USA
ZICNICLOW, MOSES	18	F	SVNT	RRZZZZ	USA
DANER, CHAIM	20	M	LABR	RRZZZZ	USA
ITE	21	M	LABR	RRZZZZ	USA
WARSEHAWZIK, ISAAK	18	M	LABR	RRZZZZ	USA
LIEBSCHENTZ, ARON	30	M	LABR	RRZZZZ	USA
ELIAS	45	F	SVNT	RRZZZZ	USA
GIOSEH, PAUL	19	M	LABR	RRZZZZ	USA
STEPANSKY, VEIL	34	M	LABR	RRZZZZ	USA
MILLER, ABRAHAM	15	M	LABR	RRZZZZ	USA
DWORSKI, ISAAK	48	M	LABR	RRZZZZ	USA
PERETZ	10	M	CH	RRZZZZ	USA
LEWINSKI, WOLFE	43	M	LABR	RRZZZZ	USA
DWORSKIE, ANTON	28	M	LABR	RRZZZZ	USA
LASAR, NOACH	19	M	LABR	RRZZZZ	USA
KESPEZIK, HIRSCH	23	M	LABR	RRZZZZ	USA
FRIEDMANN, DAVID	25	M	LABR	RRZZZZ	USA
SHIP: CITY OF CHESTER					
FROM: LIVERPOOL AND QUEENSTOWN					
TO: NEW YORK					
ARRIVED: 02 JUNE 1884					
LOEFANICK, JACOB	52	M	LABR	RRZZZZ	NY
VERONICA	11	F	CH	RRZZZZ	NY
GOLASKY, JOSEPH	11	M	CH	RRZZZZ	NY
SCHLUWITZ, NUSSEN	34	M	LABR	RRZZZZ	NY
GOLDSTEIN, ABRAHAM	18	M	LABR	RRZZZZ	NY
CHAIE	20	F	W	RRZZZZ	NY
KUSRLEA, JACOB	35	M	FARMER	RRZZZZ	NY
LEDOKA	30	F	W	RRZZZZ	NY
HAMEN	1	F	CHILD	RRZZZZ	NY
HELENA	1	F	CHILD	RRZZZZ	NY
MYSLEVIE, ANTONIE	30	M	LABR	RRZZZZ	NY
ANDREY	27	F	W	RRZZZZ	NY
MODETZKY, ZINDRICH	11	F	CH	RRZZZZ	NY
FARRY, PAUL	37	M	FARMER	PLZZZZ	NY
LEVEC, FANOS	32	M	FARMER	PLZZZZ	NY
KOSECKY, ML.	11	M	CH	PLZZZZ	NY
FERRY, JAN	11	M	CH	PLZZZZ	NY
JANNLESVITZ, CASIMIR	32	M	LABR	PLZZZZ	NY
MATRICHEWITZ, ANTON	11	M	CH	PLZZZZ	NY
ERZA, NEMICK	20	M	LABR	PLZZZZ	NY
GEORG, MIKULA	11	M	CH	PLZZZZ	NY
KOZAH, WAVRIL	44	M	LABR	PLZZZZ	NY
ZAVISTACK, ADALBERT	11	M	CH	PLZZZZ	NY
KACINSKY, BONIFAC	38	M	FARMER	PLZZZZ	NY
MAGDALENA	34	F	W	PLZZZZ	NY
JOSEF	1	M	CHILD	PLZZZZ	NY
JANCEK	1	M	CHILD	PLZZZZ	NY
KRAPAITES, JAN	38	M	LABR	RRZZZZ	NY
VICTORIA	30	F	W	RRZZZZ	NY
SENZIK	10	M	CH	RRZZZZ	NY
VINCETS	1	M	CHILD	RRZZZZ	NY
RACWEK, JOSEF	25	M	LABR	PLZZZZ	NY
PIKULL, PHILLIPS	42	M	LABR	PLZZZZ	NY
JOSEF	11	M	CH	PLZZZZ	NY
JACOBSBY, JACOB	40	M	LABR	RRZZZZ	NY
MIHAL, STASSIK	42	M	LABR	RRZZZZ	NY
MATHIAS, MATEY	11	M	CH	RRZZZZ	NY
BASANY, CUBA	10	F	CH	RRZZZZ	NY
KAMINSKY, ADAM	26	M	LABR	RRZZZZ	NY
PENISKI, DOMK.	26	M	LABR	RRZZZZ	NY
RETEREZ, VINCENT	24	M	LABR	RRZZZZ	NY
REKEVEZ, JOS.	27	M	LABR	RRZZZZ	NY
WOZSEKONSKY, VINCENT	11	M	CH	RRZZZZ	NY
NEVANLIS, DOMK.	23	M	LABR	RRZZZZ	NY
BOHNISKY, DOMK.	11	M	CH	RRZZZZ	NY
WELENSKY, LEVER.	11	M	CH	RRZZZZ	NY
KEMPEL, EISIG	10	M	CH	RRZZZZ	NY
PERLMALTER, MINKE	56	F	W	PLZZZZ	NY
KMASKY, ELIAS-KUSCH.	29	M	LABR	RRZZZZ	NY
SWENTHAL, WOLF	25	M	LABR	RRZZZZ	NY
GLASER, WOLF	11	M	CH	RRZZZZ	NY
MILTKIN, MICHAEL	25	M	LABR	RRZZZZ	NY
LIEBE	20	F	W	RRZZZZ	NY
BLECK, ELIAS	30	M	LABR	RRZZZZ	NY
MEHR, ARON	24	M	LABR	RRZZZZ	NY
URGE, JACOB	50	M	LABR	RRZZZZ	NY
LEVISTON, LERBE	10	M	CH	RRZZZZ	NY
KAPPAPORT, HIRSCH	50	M	LABR	RRZZZZ	NY
MUSK, TOBIAS	11	M	CH	RRZZZZ	NY
BERNSTEIN, BENZEL	11	M	CH	RRZZZZ	NY
ORELSTEIN, HENE	19	M	LABR	RRZZZZ	NY
ZESANKE, RUBIN	11	M	CH	RRZZZZ	NY
LIPXHUTZ, SCHAUL.	64	M	LABR	RRZZZZ	MIL
MALKE	55	F	W	RRZZZZ	MIL
CHAIE	25	F	W	RRZZZZ	MIL
BRANE	22	F	UNKNOWN	RRZZZZ	MIL
MINDEL	11	F	CH	RRZZZZ	MIL
JACOB	1	M	CHILD	RRZZZZ	MIL
KRAWITZ, CHAIN	33	M	LABR	RRZZZZ	NY
SZOIWJE	33	F	W	RRZZZZ	NY
CHAIE	10	M	CH	RRZZZZ	NY
LEISER	8	F	CHILD	RRZZZZ	NY
JUDEL	6	F	CHILD	RRZZZZ	NY
SCHEPSEL	1	M	CHILD	RRZZZZ	NY
ISAAC	1	F	CHILD	RRZZZZ	NY
MINDES, ABR.	45	M	LABR	RRZZZZ	NY
CHAIE	40	F	W	RRZZZZ	NY
SCHEINE	1	F	CHILD	RRZZZZ	NY
FELDMANN, SCHWOTER	45	M	FARMER	RRZZZZ	NY
MALKE	40	F	W	RRZZZZ	NY
GEZI	11	F	CH	RRZZZZ	NY
RHEINE	9	F	CHILD	RRZZZZ	NY
TAUBER	5	F	CHILD	RRZZZZ	NY
JOSEF	1	F	CHILD	RRZZZZ	NY
RIFKE	1	F	CHILD	RRZZZZ	NY
ISAAC	11	M	CH	RRZZZZ	NY
VALENTIS, JONAS	11	M	CH	RRZZZZ	NY
ZROGANIS, JONAS	30	M	LABR	RRZZZZ	NY
KLOPMITH, JANOS	11	M	CH	PLZZZZ	NY
MATGIL, THOM.	25	M	LABR	PLZZZZ	NY
SCHIVEI, ANDRE	27	M	LABR	PLZZZZ	NY
LYTOPS, WILHELM	26	M	LABR	PLZZZZ	NY
BARENSKI, ANDI	21	M	LABR	PLZZZZ	NY
FRANCISCA	1	F	CHILD	PLZZZZ	NY
MARIA	1	F	CHILD	PLZZZZ	NY
STANISLAUS	11	M	CH	PLZZZZ	NY
ESEHNISKY, JOSEF	1	M	CHILD	PLZZZZ	NY
STARK, WALDMAR	37	M	LABR	PLZZZZ	NY

SHIP: INDIA

FROM: HAMBURG
TO: NEW YORK
ARRIVED: 02 JUNE 1884

PASSENGER	AGE	SEX	OCCUPATION	PRI	VIL	DES
TALISCH, MOS.	19	M	LABR	PL	ZZZZ	NY
BISKUP, WOJCECH	30	M	LABR	PL	ZZZZ	NY
SKINDZER, DOMINIK	22	M	LABR	RR	ZZZZ	NY
JAN	50	M	LABR	RR	ZZZZ	NY
WOJCIECHOWSKI, NIESDEM	33	M	LABR	RR	ZZZZ	NY
KUSEHNIERNFES, FRANZ	42	M	LABR	RR	ZZZZ	NY
DANIELOWITZ, NICODEM	42	M	LABR	RR	ZZZZ	NY
WILKANSKAS, ANDREAS	25	M	LABR	RR	ZZZZ	NY
RUBINSTEIN, WOLFF	34	M	TRDSMN	RR	ZZZZ	NY
BREKSTEIN, ELKE	7	M	CHILD	RR	ZZZZ	NY
RADZIEWCSKA, ROSALIE	21	F	WO	RR	ZZZZ	NY
LANIN, JACOBINE	22	F	SGL	RR	ZZZZ	NY
SLECHER, LEIB	33	M	TRDSMN	RR	ZZZZ	NY
LANGERT, SCHMUEL	7	M	CHILD	RR	ZZZZ	NY
SCHUMANN, SARA	33	F	WO	RR	ZZZZ	NY
ISRAEL	5	M	CHILD	RR	ZZZZ	NY
DAVID	6	M	CHILD	RR	ZZZZ	NY
WLODIJSTEWO, WLADISLAW	22	M	TRDSMN	RR	ZZZZ	NY

SHIP: WESTPHALIA

FROM: HAMBURG
TO: NEW YORK
ARRIVED: 02 JUNE 1884

PASSENGER	AGE	SEX	OCCUPATION	PRI	VIL	DES
FELDMANN, CHAIM	18	M	LABR	RR	ZZZZ	NY
KLEINER, CYRICL-A.	30	M	TLR	RR	ZZZZ	NY
ALPERN, JACOB	25	M	LABR	RR	ZZZZ	NY
RACHEL	23	F	WO	RR	ZZZZ	NY
PESCHEL	.11	F	INFANT	RR	ZZZZ	NY
GOLDENBERG, SALOMON	26	M	LABR	RR	ZZZZ	NY
BASCHE	20	F	WO	RR	ZZZZ	NY
STANKIEWICZ, EVA	20	F	WO	RR	ZZZZ	NY
ALZBETA	.03	F	INFANT	RR	ZZZZ	NY
BOTJRJINGE, MAGDALA.	20	F	SGL	RR	ZZZZ	NY
BARTESZKA, JOHN	18	M	LABR	RR	ZZZZ	NY
KERCHER, PETER	22	M	LABR	RR	ZZZZ	NY
STRECKER, ASMUS	31	M	BKBNDR	RR	ZZZZ	NY
FRANZ, GUSTAV	32	M	JNR	RR	ZZZZ	NY
FRIEDRICH, WILH.	27	M	SMH	RR	ZZZZ	NY
WALLERT, EDUARD	23	M	SMH	RR	ZZZZ	NY
DEGLAN, LEOPOLD	18	M	JNR	RR	ZZZZ	NY
FRANK, ISAAC	21	M	DLR	RR	ZZZZ	NY
BARDIN, JACOB	18	M	DLR	RR	ZZZZ	NY
CAPLAN, MEIER	18	M	DLR	RR	ZZZZ	NY
FINK, ISSER	50	M	LABR	RR	ZZZZ	NY
MIRCWISCHTAS, JOSAS	33	M	LABR	RR	ZZZZ	NY
KLAMOS, JURAS	18	M	WCHMKR	RR	ZZZZ	NY
KORTIM, MORDSCHE	31	F	DLR	RR	ZZZZ	NY
LIEBKIND, MOSER	15	M	DLR	RR	ZZZZ	NY
RUBIN, INDEL	23	M	DLR	RR	ZZZZ	NY
MICHE	19	M	DLR	RR	ZZZZ	NY
LIPMANN, SARA	40	F	W	RR	ZZZZ	NY
JACOB	18	M	CH	RR	ZZZZ	NY
GABRIEL	17	M	CH	RR	ZZZZ	NY
SKYNKUTE, MARIE	22	F	SGL	RR	ZZZZ	NY
STEPHANSEN, STEPHAN	21	M	FARMER	RR	ZZZZ	NY
BLOCH, DWARRE	46	F	W	RR	ZZZZ	NY
SARA	19	F	CH	RR	ZZZZ	NY
MEYER	17	M	CH	RR	ZZZZ	NY
BROZSCHOK	8	M	CHILD	RR	ZZZZ	NY
ISRAEL	7	M	CHILD	RR	ZZZZ	NY
ICLINLREN	5	F	CHILD	RR	ZZZZ	NY
K----B--G, MOSSES	25	M	DLR	RR	ZZZZ	NY
TANNEBAUM, TELKA	22	F	SGL	RR	ZZZZ	NY
BRODSKY, RACHEL	18	F	SGL	RR	ZZZZ	NY
MIDAKOMOWICH, MICH.	28	M	SMH	RR	ZZZZ	NY
BRODSKY, HENRY	25	M	LABR	RR	ZZZZ	NY
VALLY	25	F	W	RR	ZZZZ	NY
BRISCKMANN, LASKI	18	F	SGL	RR	ZZZZ	NY
RAGUCKA, ELSBETHA	22	F	SGL	RR	ZZZZ	NY
BRYINEWSKY, MAGDALENA	28	F	W	RR	ZZZZ	NY
ANTONAS	6	M	CHILD	RR	ZZZZ	NY
NAVICZKY, JEWA	20	F	SGL	RR	ZZZZ	NY
BIJAWOYTYS, JOSEF	30	M	LABR	RR	ZZZZ	NY
FRANCISCA	3	F	CHILD	RR	ZZZZ	NY
U, VICTORIA	.06	F	INFANT	RR	ZZZZ	NY
ANNA	28	F	W	RR	ZZZZ	NY
KASZEWITZ, MICHAEL	21	M	LABR	RR	ZZZZ	NY
DIAMANT, MAS.	20	M	LABR	RR	ZZZZ	NY
RIBINOWITZ, CHAIM	25	F	W	RR	ZZZZ	NY
MENNCHE	9	F	CHILD	RR	ZZZZ	NY
ISRAEL	.11	M	INFANT	RR	ZZZZ	NY
TANBE	.01	F	INFANT	RR	ZZZZ	NY
OLIENPOLSKY, DAVID	45	M	LABR	RR	ZZZZ	NY
ABRAH.	9	M	CHILD	RR	ZZZZ	NY
SILBERMANN, BEILE	24	F	W	RR	ZZZZ	NY
RUBEN	.01	M	INFANT	RR	ZZZZ	NY
SCHWEDE, BEILE	20	F	SGL	RR	ZZZZ	NY
FEINBERG, LIEBE	25	F	W	RR	ZZZZ	NY
CHAIM	5	F	CHILD	RR	ZZZZ	NY
MINE	7	F	CHILD	RR	ZZZZ	NY
SARA	8	F	CHILD	RR	ZZZZ	NY
PLINSA-K, MEYES	20	M	FARMER	RR	ZZZZ	NY
SCHOEMNANN, JANKEL	20	M	DLR	RR	ZZZZ	NY
SCHILMANN, CHASZE	17	F	SGL	RR	ZZZZ	NY
LUDWINOWSKY, SIMON	27	M	LABR	RR	ZZZZ	NY
WANSNANN, ROSA	28	F	W	RR	ZZZZ	NY
FRANZ	6	M	CHILD	RR	ZZZZ	NY
ANNA	5	F	CHILD	RR	ZZZZ	NY
JECMY	.11	F	INFANT	RR	ZZZZ	NY
LINE	.01	F	INFANT	RR	ZZZZ	NY
FAZENCBICK, PHILIPP	26	M	LABR	RR	ZZZZ	NY
KERCHER, ANTON	74	M	FARMER	RR	ZZZZ	NY
BARBARA	70	F	W	RR	ZZZZ	NY
ELISABETH	20	F	D	RR	ZZZZ	NY
JACOB	35	M	FARMER	RR	ZZZZ	NY
CATHR.	35	F	W	RR	ZZZZ	NY
HEINRICH	.11	M	INFANT	RR	ZZZZ	NY
ZOLLER, LUDWIG	36	M	FARMER	RR	ZZZZ	NY
CHRISTINE	28	F	W	RR	ZZZZ	NY
CHRISTINE	6	F	CHILD	RR	ZZZZ	NY
CATHRINA	3	F	CHILD	RR	ZZZZ	NY
MAGDAL	.11	F	INFANT	RR	ZZZZ	NY
RAEDLER, PAUL	43	M	LABR	RR	ZZZZ	NY
GERTRUD	36	F	W	RR	ZZZZ	NY
BENEDICT	22	M	CH	RR	ZZZZ	NY
ANTON	18	M	CH	RR	ZZZZ	NY
DOROTHEA	9	F	CHILD	RR	ZZZZ	NY
JOHANN	8	M	CHILD	RR	ZZZZ	NY
JOSEF	4	M	CHILD	RR	ZZZZ	NY
NICOLAUS	.11	M	INFANT	RR	ZZZZ	NY
HOST, JOH.	20	M	LABR	RR	ZZZZ	NY
POSCHNANN, LISBETH	29	F	SGL	RR	ZZZZ	NY
REDSIBONOWITSCH, PETER	20	M	LABR	RR	ZZZZ	NY
RUPRECHT, AUG.	35	M	LABR	RR	ZZZZ	NY
KIRSCHHORN, JACOB	22	M	LABR	RR	ZZZZ	NY
KASEGANSKY, PESCHE	18	F	SGL	RR	ZZZZ	NY
SAMUEL	8	M	CHILD	RR	ZZZZ	NY
SARA	5	F	CHILD	RR	ZZZZ	NY
MORDSCHE	3	F	CHILD	RR	ZZZZ	NY
FINKELSTEIN, ISAAC	19	M	LABR	RR	ZZZZ	NY
DWORRE	18	F	SGL	RR	ZZZZ	NY
BOSSINOW, MOSES	53	M	LABR	RR	ZZZZ	NY
LEON	50	F	W	RR	ZZZZ	NY
CHEIE	25	F	CH	RR	ZZZZ	NY
LEISER	6	M	CHILD	RR	ZZZZ	NY
ROSENGART, HIRSCH	30	M	LABR	RR	ZZZZ	NY

PASSENGER	AGE	SEX	OCCUPATION	PRV	VIL	DES
KRUPPE, WOLF	26	M	LABR	RR	ZZZZ	NY
RIWKE	20	F	W	RR	ZZZZ	NY
SIMCKE	4	F	CHILD	RR	ZZZZ	NY
SOLDE, CHANNE	40	F	W	RR	ZZZZ	NY
MUETZENMACHER, CHANZE	25	M	LABR	RR	ZZZZ	NY
PANOWSKY, SAMUEL	18	M	LABR	RR	ZZZZ	NY
NOCHUMOWITZ, SARA	18	F	SGL	RR	ZZZZ	NY
SLUTZKY, SALOMON	50	M	LABR	RR	ZZZZ	NY
BEHR.	8	M	CHILD	RR	ZZZZ	NY
MOSES	7	M	CHILD	RR	ZZZZ	NY
DAVID	5	M	CHILD	RR	ZZZZ	NY
FREYD, BAR.	40	M	LABR	RR	ZZZZ	NY
PESCHE	17	F	D	RR	ZZZZ	NY
SCHATZ, LEILE	47	M	LABR	RR	ZZZZ	NY
SHAPIRO, SALOMON	18	M	LABR	RR	ZZZZ	NY
ISAAC	17	M	LABR	RR	ZZZZ	NY
WARSCHAWSKY, SALOMON	19	M	LABR	RR	ZZZZ	NY
DANGELE, MATTHIAS	57	M	LABR	RR	ZZZZ	NY
LISCHZINSKY, ABRAH.	37	M	LABR	RR	ZZZZ	NY
DRATSCH, ISAAC	39	M	LABR	RR	ZZZZ	NY
ZARUBA, KASIMIR	55	M	LABR	RR	ZZZZ	NY
KAZUZONE, EVA	25	F	SGL	RR	ZZZZ	NY
GEDOMANSKI, ROSA	21	F	SGL	RR	ZZZZ	NY
FLEDERMANN, BEILE	20	F	SGL	RR	ZZZZ	NY
KASZUSANE, ANNA	21	F	SGL	RR	ZZZZ	NY
WEISSBROD, NOCHUM	18	M	LABR	RR	ZZZZ	NY
LEWINSKY, RACHEL	18	F	SGL	RR	ZZZZ	NY
FRIKIANSKY, JACOB	20	M	LABR	RR	ZZZZ	NY
WALKOWITZ, BENDIX	29	M	LABR	RR	ZZZZ	NY
IGLUN, SIDORES	25	M	LABR	RR	ZZZZ	NY
WENZELWAS, JONAS	34	M	LABR	RR	ZZZZ	NY
ANNA	27	F	W	RR	ZZZZ	NY
ALEX	20	M	LABR	RR	ZZZZ	NY
MARIA	18	F	SGL	RR	ZZZZ	NY
PETER	6	M	CHILD	RR	ZZZZ	NY
JAN	5	M	CHILD	RR	ZZZZ	NY
URSULA	3	F	CHILD	RR	ZZZZ	NY
AMBROS	.11	M	INFANT	RR	ZZZZ	NY
SCHERR, JOSEF	18	M	LABR	RR	ZZZZ	NY
ECKERT, LEONHARD	19	M	LABR	RR	ZZZZ	NY
SCKONKER, ISAAC	23	M	LABR	RR	ZZZZ	NY
PREZISWE, ABR.	18	M	LABR	RR	ZZZZ	NY
THYGESEN, LANST	59	M	LABR	RR	ZZZZ	NY
MARIA	50	F	W	RR	ZZZZ	NY
MIKKEL	9	F	CHILD	RR	ZZZZ	NY
ANNA	8	F	CHILD	RR	ZZZZ	NY
JOHANNSEN, ELENE	22	F	SGL	RR	ZZZZ	NY
GLUECK, IGNATZ	18	M	LABR	RR	ZZZZ	NY
RIWKE, SARA	9	F	CHILD	RR	ZZZZ	NY
LEWANDOWSKI, NATHAN	38	M	LABR	RR	ZZZZ	NY
SANDSTEIN, MORDSCHE	19	F	LABR	RR	ZZZZ	NY
REBECCA	20	F	W	RR	ZZZZ	NY
RUBINSTEIN, CHANNE	40	F	BKR	RR	ZZZZ	NY
AGINSKY, JOSEF	54	M	LABR	RR	ZZZZ	NY
KADISCHOWITZ, JACOB	32	M	LABR	RR	ZZZZ	NY
WIENANER, JOH.M.	25	M	LABR	RR	ZZZZ	NY
MOLENSKY, ROSA	44	F	W	RR	ZZZZ	NY
JACOB	20	M	S	RR	ZZZZ	NY
DAVIDA	16	F	D	RR	ZZZZ	NY
MIGAN-Z, ISRAEL	8	M	CHILD	RR	ZZZZ	NY
MITLENSTEIN, DANIEL	44	M	LABR	RR	ZZZZ	NY
CHAJE	44	F	W	RR	ZZZZ	NY
ISRAEL	9	M	CHILD	RR	ZZZZ	NY
CHANNE	8	M	CHILD	RR	ZZZZ	NY
GITTEL	7	F	CHILD	RR	ZZZZ	NY
RIWKE	3	F	CHILD	RR	ZZZZ	NY
SALOMON	.11	M	INFANT	RR	ZZZZ	NY
LEWIN, SCHEWA	38	F	W	RR	ZZZZ	NY
JACOB	9	M	CHILD	RR	ZZZZ	NY
STEINBERG, MOSES	23	M	CL	RR	ZZZZ	NY
ROSENTHAL, RACHEL	28	F	SGL	RR	ZZZZ	NY
ANDURSKI, ISAAC	32	M	LABR	RR	ZZZZ	NY
KASUZAWE, EVA	.11	F	INFANT	RR	ZZZZ	NY
SCHOLEMSKY, ROSA	.03	F	INFANT	RR	ZZZZ	NY

SHIP: BOTHNIA

FROM: LIVERPOOL AND QUEENSTOWN
TO: NEW YORK
ARRIVED: 03 JUNE 1884

PASSENGER	AGE	SEX	OCCUPATION	PRV	VIL	DES
SEMIDSKOWSKI, CASPAR	39	M	LABR	PL	ZZZZ	USA
SOLIKOVSKY, MICHAEL	21	M	LABR	PL	ZZZZ	USA
OLSEVSKY, JAN	40	M	LABR	PL	ZZZZ	USA
RACOVSKY, JULIUS	25	M	LABR	PL	ZZZZ	USA
SILAN, MICHAL	40	M	LABR	PL	ZZZZ	USA
ANDRAS	11	M	LABR	PL	ZZZZ	USA
TROFANOW, VASIL	25	M	LABR	PL	ZZZZ	USA
WOJTECH, MAI	45	M	LABR	PL	ZZZZ	USA
KATHERINA	38	F	W	PL	ZZZZ	USA
HEDWIKA	11	F	CH	PL	ZZZZ	USA
JOHN	10	M	CH	PL	ZZZZ	USA
MARIE	4	F	CHILD	PL	ZZZZ	USA
STANISLAW	.09	M	INFANT	PL	ZZZZ	USA
WIRBITZKY, HAVERIN	28	M	LABR	PL	ZZZZ	USA
WOLINSKY, BENJAMIN	32	M	PDLR	RR	ZZZZ	USA
ORLOW, ARON	35	M	SMH	RR	ZZZZ	USA
GALIN, SAM	42	M	PDLR	PL	ZZZZ	USA

SHIP: CANADA

FROM: HAVRE
TO: NEW YORK
ARRIVED: 03 JUNE 1884

PASSENGER	AGE	SEX	OCCUPATION	PRV	VIL	DES
CANDELIN, G.	23	M	ENGR	RR	ZZZZ	NY
SCHIFFMANN, SAMUEL	24	M	TLR	RR	ZZZZ	NY
STEIN, NOITE	21	M	HTR	RR	ZZZZ	NY
ADELE	24	F	UNKNOWN	RR	ZZZZ	NY
MUNDT, HERMANN	31	M	UNKNOWN	RR	ZZZZ	NY
BENTHIAN, EUGENE	23	M	CL	RR	ZZZZ	NY
MORITZ, CARL	21	M	CL	RR	ZZZZ	MIL
SEISTEMANN, JULES	38	M	LABR	RR	ZZZZ	NY

SHIP: GELLERT

FROM: HAMBURG AND HAVRE
TO: NEW YORK
ARRIVED: 03 JUNE 1884

PASSENGER	AGE	SEX	OCCUPATION	PRV	VIL	DES
IESCHONSKY, CHAIE	35	F	WO	RR	ZZZZ	USA
CHAIE	8	F	CHILD	RR	ZZZZ	USA
SCHIFF, MOSES-M.	34	M	LABR	RR	ZZZZ	USA
GERITZKI, MENDEL	17	M	LABR	RR	ZZZZ	USA
RAHU, RAUFMAN	36	M	LABR	RR	ZZZZ	USA
MINES, ARON	16	M	TLR	RR	ZZZZ	USA
DREUND, IGNATZ	25	M	MCHT	RR	ZZZZ	USA
WITA, MOSES	26	M	TLR	RR	ZZZZ	USA
BERKOWITZ, JACOB	36	M	DLR	RR	ZZZZ	USA
RAB, CHAIMS	35	M	DLR	RR	ZZZZ	USA
ELLERSTEIN, SCHIE	7	M	CHILD	RR	ZZZZ	USA
ARON, FANNY	38	F	W	RR	ZZZZ	USA
FRIED, BRONE	30	F	W	RR	ZZZZ	USA
RIWKE	8	F	CHILD	RR	ZZZZ	USA
ALTER	.11	M	INFANT	RR	ZZZZ	USA
BERG, LEHA	7	F	CHILD	RR	ZZZZ	USA
GOLDSTEIN, MOSES	20	M	TLR	RR	ZZZZ	USA
ROSENBERG, NACHE	27	F	W	RR	ZZZZ	USA
RUBEN	.11	M	INFANT	RR	ZZZZ	USA

PASSENGER	AGE	SEX	OCCUPATION	PRV VIL DES
MANU, JACOB	19	M	DLR	RRZZZZUSA
EMBON---, DUNE	19	F	SGL	RRZZZZUSA
BERMANN, ISRAEL	22	M	BCHR	RRZZZZUSA
SCHWARZ, SALY	14	F	SGL	RRZZZZUSA
LOSBERG, SARA	28	F	W	RRZZZZUSA
CHASCHE	8	F	CHILD	RRZZZZUSA
DAVID	.11	M	INFANT	RRZZZZUSA
RISCHE	.01	F	INFANT	RRZZZZUSA
COHN, RACHEL	22	F	W	RRZZZZUSA
JACHE	.06	F	INFANT	RRZZZZUSA
RUPPRECHT, MARIA	32	F	W	RRZZZZUSA
BARGE, ANNA	8	F	CHILD	RRZZZZUSA
RUPPRECHT, MARIA	7	F	CHILD	RRZZZZUSA
RUDERMAN, CHANE	10	F	CH	RRZZZZUSA
RUNENS, MARIC	39	M	LABR	RRZZZZUSA
UROWIK, SARA	18	F	W	RRZZZZUSA
ITZEHALK, ABRAM	15	M	LABR	RRZZZZUSA
JUNGMAN, HANY	18	F	SGL	RRZZZZUSA
MONERHAHN, ABRAHAM	20	M	LABR	RRZZZZUSA
LEIBMAN, CHAIM	22	M	DLR	RRZZZZUSA
RUMIN, JACOB	32	M	DLR	RRZZZZUSA
ALFONS	22	M	LABR	RRZZZZUSA
GRUNBERG, SCHOLEM	17	M	DLR	RRZZZZUSA
HOWENSKI, RONALD	22	M	LABR	RRZZZZUSA
LIEWEROWITZ, GOCHEL	18	M	DLR	RRZZZZUSA
GINSBURG, LEISER	38	M	DLR	RRZZZZUSA
BRIT, ABRAHAM	21	M	LABR	RRZZZZUSA
SCHTUB, SOLOMON	25	M	BCHR	RRZZZZUSA
WIESING, JOSEF	25	M	LABR	RRZZZZUSA
PAJESKE, JOSEF	18	M	LABR	RRZZZZUSA
ROSENBERG, ABRAM	20	M	LABR	RRZZZZUSA
RICHTER, CASSEL	14	M	LABR	RRZZZZUSA
STANOWIK, ELIAS	36	M	LABR	RRZZZZUSA
AESCHOWSKY, FALK	28	M	TLR	RRZZZZUSA
GORDAN, LEISER	22	M	DLR	RRZZZZUSA
FISCHELOWITZ, JACOB	22	M	JNR	RRZZZZUSA
GLEMBATZKY, BERNARD	19	M	DLR	RRZZZZUSA
BERKMAN, GEDALIE	19	M	DLR	RRZZZZUSA
ALISKEWITZ, ABRAHAM	36	M	TLR	RRZZZZUSA
BELLIN, HELLENE	25	F	SGL	RRZZZZUSA
SEMA--FER, ADOLF	46	M	DLR	RRZZZZUSA
ULRIKE	43	F	W	RRZZZZUSA
ELSE	8	F	CHILD	RRZZZZUSA
IDA	7	F	CHILD	RRZZZZUSA
ORES	6	M	CHILD	RRZZZZUSA
CURT	5	M	CHILD	RRZZZZUSA
LOCHMANN, S.	22	M	WCHMKR	RRZZZZUSA
FANNY	22	F	W	RRZZZZUSA
GRUNBAUM, DANIEL	27	M	PRNTR	RRZZZZUSA
ASCH, SALOMON	21	M	DLR	RRZZZZUSA
FOLTMAN, MARCUS	24	M	DLR	RRZZZZUSA
WERNER, MORDSCHEL	15	M	DLR	RRZZZZUSA
FISCHER, ABRAHAM	14	M	DLR	RRZZZZUSA
LEUKMAN, SCHMEREL	43	M	TLR	RRZZZZUSA
FARBER, JACOB	31	M	MCHT	PLZZZZUSA
HOFFMAN, GUSTAV	24	M	LABR	RRZZZZUSA
FREIDES, SCHEPSEL	31	M	DLR	RRZZZZUSA
AEPPEL, JACOB	30	M	DLR	RRZZZZUSA
WEINIK, SIMON	26	M	DLR	RRZZZZUSA
ROSTER, SALOMON	38	M	DLR	RRZZZZUSA
WISINSKI, ANTON	31	M	DLR	RRZZZZUSA
DIZINSKY, CHAMAULINE	25	F	W	RRZZZZUSA
MARAKIEWICZ, GOS.	40	M	LABR	RRZZZZUSA
DAMENIKE	25	F	W	RRZZZZUSA
VINCENT	.09	M	INFANT	RRZZZZUSA
GUTKIARIS, JACOB	25	M	LABR	RRZZZZUSA
ANTONIE	25	F	W	RRZZZZUSA
ZULRANSKI, ANDR.	24	M	LABR	RRZZZZUSA
REICHMANN, HANNE	54	F	W	RRZZZZUSA
FANNY	20	F	D	RRZZZZUSA
LUDWIG	.11	M	INFANT	RRZZZZUSA
JANOWSKY, LIBE	15	F	SGL	RRZZZZUSA
ILECHT, SCHILLIAN	18	M	LABR	RRZZZZUSA
HELPER, MEYER	16	M	LABR	RRZZZZUSA
MIERA, HESSE	40	F	W	RRZZZZUSA

PASSENGER	AGE	SEX	OCCUPATION	PRV VIL DES
SAMUEL	6	M	CHILD	RRZZZZUSA
GOLDE	4	F	CHILD	RRZZZZUSA
ESTHER	3	F	CHILD	RRZZZZUSA
JOSEF	.11	M	INFANT	RRZZZZUSA
SIMON	.01	M	INFANT	RRZZZZUSA
KANTOROWITZ, FEIGE	30	F	W	RRZZZZUSA
LEA	.02	F	INFANT	RRZZZZUSA
SALOMON, CHAI	18	F	SGL	RRZZZZUSA
GELLER, FEIGE	18	F	SGL	RRZZZZUSA
RUSSINSKY, ISRAEL	60	M	LABR	RRZZZZUSA
LIEBE	50	F	W	RRZZZZUSA
RIEREL	21	F	D	RRZZZZUSA
ABRAH.	.11	M	INFANT	RRZZZZUSA
KANTOROWITZ, FANI	29	F	LABR	RRZZZZUSA
BRAINE	.11	F	INFANT	RRZZZZUSA
RNOBLAUCH, LEIB	18	M	LABR	RRZZZZUSA
ROSTOWSKY, JACOB	40	M	LABR	RRZZZZUSA
MORRIS	10	M	S	RRZZZZUSA
LEVIN, ROSE	16	F	SGL	RRZZZZUSA
BONNER, CHAIM	20	M	LABR	RRZZZZUSA
ROM, ARRIEL	34	M	LABR	RRZZZZUSA
RAMINOWITZ, ROSE	27	F	W	RRZZZZUSA
BEHR	8	M	CHILD	RRZZZZUSA
GETTE	4	F	CHILD	RRZZZZUSA
JUDAS	.11	M	INFANT	RRZZZZUSA
KOWALEWS--IAN, ANT.	31	M	FARMER	RRZZZZUSA
GINSBERG, MOSES	25	M	DLR	RRZZZZUSA
NEUF----, SAMUEL	23	M	DLR	RRZZZZUSA
STALZOWE, ADELE	23	F	SGL	PLZZZZUSA
RAREMA, JOSEF	9	M	CHILD	PLZZZZUSA
SKALSKU, WAWZYNICE	35	M	LABR	PLZZZZUSA
RACHOWITZ, JOH.	26	M	LABR	PLZZZZUSA
MIEMIC, JACOB	25	M	LABR	PLZZZZUSA
EVA	38	F	W	PLZZZZUSA
AGATHE	5	F	CHILD	PLZZZZUSA
THEKLA	.06	F	INFANT	PLZZZZUSA
JATUCBA, JOH.	42	M	LABR	PLZZZZUSA
CATH.	40	F	W	PLZZZZUSA
STANISL.	8	M	CHILD	PLZZZZUSA
THOM	7	M	CHILD	PLZZZZUSA
JOH.	5	M	CHILD	PLZZZZUSA
JOSEF	.06	M	INFANT	PLZZZZUSA
CEASTE, SOFIA	27	F	SGL	PLZZZZUSA
MOTSISKI, JAN	29	M	LABR	PLZZZZUSA
RIEDLAND, SARA	38	F	W	RRZZZZUSA
GETTE	8	F	CHILD	RRZZZZUSA
LEIB	.11	M	INFANT	RRZZZZUSA
U, U	47	M	LABR	RRZZZZUSA
WILSKOWSKY, BETTE	25	F	W	RRZZZZUSA
MALKE	6	F	CHILD	RRZZZZUSA
LIEBEL	5	M	CHILD	RRZZZZUSA
ARON	.11	M	INFANT	RRZZZZUSA
MITTKOWSKY, BETTY	2	F	CHILD	RRZZZZUSA
MEYER, ITZE	17	M	TLR	RRZZZZUSA

SHIP: AMERICA

FROM: LIVERPOOL AND QUEENSTOWN
TO: NEW YORK
ARRIVED: 05 JUNE 1884

PASSENGER	AGE	SEX	OCCUPATION	PRV VIL DES
POLAZECKI, MORDECAI	36	M	LABR	RRZZZZUSA
ROSENWEIG, BEER	45	M	LABR	RRZZZZUSA
MALKE	35	F	W	RRZZZZUSA
MARIE	15	F	SVNT	RRZZZZUSA
DIANA	11	F	CH	RRZZZZUSA
EMIL	9	M	CHILD	RRZZZZUSA
STRACH, LEINER	25	F	SVNT	RRZZZZUSA
KLIM, ARMUN	10	M	CH	RRZZZZUSA
GROSS, MEYER	42	M	LABR	RRZZZZUSA

PASSENGER	AGE	SEX	OCCUPATION	PV RIL DES
TAUBE	38	F	W	RRZZZZUSA
HENE	19	M	LABR	RRZZZZUSA
ISAAC	17	M	LABR	RRZZZZUSA
MINA	11	F	CH	RRZZZZUSA
AARON	10	M	CH	RRZZZZUSA
IRAEL	9	M	CHILD	RRZZZZUSA
ABRAM	8	M	CHILD	RRZZZZUSA
BARA	3	F	CHILD	RRZZZZUSA
REBECCA	00	F	INF	RRZZZZUSA

SHIP: FURNESSIA

FROM: UNKNOWN
TO: NEW YORK
ARRIVED: 05 JUNE 1884

PASSENGER	AGE	SEX	OCCUPATION	PV RIL DES
PAPETZKIS, JURAS	28	M	LABR	PLZZZZUSA
PATRONE	28	F	W	PLZZZZUSA
HASIS	1	M	CHILD	PLZZZZUSA
ELSA	1	F	CHILD	PLZZZZUSA
BARNETT, SALOMON	40	M	LABR	PLZZZZUSA
SARAH	27	F	W	PLZZZZUSA
ARNASTOWSKI, MATHEAS	28	M	LABR	PLZZZZUSA
EVA	27	F	W	PLZZZZUSA
ZURKA, MACKE	32	M	LABR	PLZZZZUSA
LOHBERG, A.	25	M	LABR	PLZZZZUSA
MASEIKA, MATHEAS	29	M	LABR	PLZZZZUSA
DABKEWITZ, BALTRIS	26	M	LABR	PLZZZZUSA
RUBISIAK, IGNATZ	24	M	LABR	PLZZZZUSA
WENWSSES, JACUBES	23	M	LABR	PLZZZZUSA

SHIP: NURNBERG

FROM: BREMEN
TO: NEW YORK
ARRIVED: 05 JUNE 1884

PASSENGER	AGE	SEX	OCCUPATION	PV RIL DES
KOCHNICKI, ANTONIO	24	F	NN	RRZZZZUSA
MIULARSKI, FRANZISEK	22	M	LLD	RRZZZZUSA
KLEMOUSKI, JOSEF	25	M	LLD	RRZZZZUSA
RAPPAPORT, BRENDEL	40	M	LLD	RRZZZZUSA
BOESE, HEINR.	32	M	LABR	RRZZZZUSA
HELENE	32	F	W	RRZZZZUSA
AGANITA	4	F	CHILD	RRZZZZUSA
HELENE	2	F	CHILD	RRZZZZUSA
HEINR.	.06	M	INFANT	RRZZZZUSA
SOMMERFELD, LEONARD	27	M	FARMER	RRZZZZUSA
CATH.	30	F	W	RRZZZZUSA
ANNA	.11	F	INFANT	RRZZZZUSA
LEHRMANN, ANNA	23	F	NN	RRZZZZUSA
MARIE	19	F	NN	RRZZZZUSA
CASPAR, DAVID	24	M	LABR	RRZZZZUSA
EMILIE	28	F	W	RRZZZZUSA
ROBERT	00	M	CH	RRZZZZUSA
BAYER, JACOB	26	M	LABR	RRZZZZUSA
HELENE	23	F	W	RRZZZZUSA
GROW, PETER	36	M	FARMER	RRZZZZUSA
SUSANNE	26	F	W	RRZZZZUSA
KATH.	6	F	CHILD	RRZZZZUSA
PETER	4	M	CHILD	RRZZZZUSA
SUSANNA	.09	F	INFANT	RRZZZZUSA
KANNA, PETER	33	M	LABR	RRZZZZUSA
HELENE	30	F	W	RRZZZZUSA
HELENE	3	F	CHILD	RRZZZZUSA
PETER	2	M	CHILD	RRZZZZUSA
WILHELM	.09	M	INFANT	RRZZZZUSA
JUSTINE	.09	F	INFANT	RRZZZZUSA
EPP, JACOB	34	M	LABR	RRZZZZUSA
GERTRUD	30	F	W	RRZZZZUSA
JOHANN	7	M	CHILD	RRZZZZUSA
GERTRUDE	4	F	CHILD	RRZZZZUSA
AGATHE	2	F	CHILD	RRZZZZUSA
LEWEN, HEINR.	32	M	LLD	RRZZZZUSA
ELISABETH	32	F	W	RRZZZZUSA
KATH.	7	F	CHILD	RRZZZZUSA
HEINR.	4	M	CHILD	RRZZZZUSA
ELISABETH	2	F	CHILD	RRZZZZUSA
ZWIERTIENREZIN, VINCENT	25	M	LABR	RRZZZZUSA
KROKER, DAVID	35	M	PNTR	RRZZZZUSA
JACOB	8	M	CHILD	RRZZZZUSA
KATHARINA	35	F	W	RRZZZZUSA
DAVID	7	M	CHILD	RRZZZZUSA
HEINRICH	5	M	CHILD	RRZZZZUSA
KATHARINA	4	F	CHILD	RRZZZZUSA
MARIA	.09	F	INFANT	RRZZZZUSA
KRUSCZNA, SIMON	30	M	LABR	RRZZZZUSA

SHIP: WESTER

FROM: BREMEN
TO: NEW YORK
ARRIVED: 05 JUNE 1884

PASSENGER	AGE	SEX	OCCUPATION	PV RIL DES
MANTEC, GERTRUD	47	F	UNKNOWN	RRZZZZUSA
GORSKI, BONISLAW	28	M	LABR	PLZZZZUSA
PIESEH, JOH.	24	M	LABR	PLZZZZUSA
GOWKLAUZ, JACOB	22	M	MCHT	PLZZZZUSA
GEWURTZ, SCHMUEL	25	M	LABR	RRZZZZUSA
BEREND	10	M	CH	RRZZZZUSA
BLURUH, BENJ.	29	M	LABR	RRZZZZUSA
ANNA	24	F	W	RRZZZZUSA

SHIP: CITY OF RICHMOND

FROM: LIVERPOOL AND QUEENSTOWN
TO: NEW YORK
ARRIVED: 06 JUNE 1884

PASSENGER	AGE	SEX	OCCUPATION	PV RIL DES
AUGUSTIA, JOSEF	32	M	LABR	PLZZZZUSA
MARIE	30	F	W	PLZZZZUSA
FRANCISCA	9	F	CHILD	PLZZZZUSA
ANDRES	00	M	INF	PLZZZZUSA
HELMA	00	F	INF	PLZZZZUSA
SCHIELINSKY, EVA	22	F	SP	PLZZZZUSA
FRIEDMAN, NATHAN	39	M	LABR	PLZZZZUSA
BLAKOWSKY, LEONARD	11	M	LABR	PLZZZZUSA
WINLINZKI, ANTONI	29	M	LABR	PLZZZZUSA
NEWMAN, FANNY	20	F	SP	PLZZZZUSA
HERM.	00	F	INF	PLZZZZUSA
GUSTE	11	M	CH	PLZZZZUSA
RASSMAN, KALMAN	22	M	LABR	PLZZZZUSA
SARA	20	F	W	PLZZZZUSA
KAROL, FABIAN	40	M	LABR	PLZZZZUSA
LAGOS, FERENSTEIN	10	M	CH	PLZZZZUSA
DESBERGER, AUDEL	11	M	CH	PLZZZZUSA
WITZLIE, AUTAL	10	M	CH	PLZZZZUSA
JANOS, IURICHA	35	F	W	PLZZZZUSA
KULIS	11	M	CH	PLZZZZUSA
WALKO, ARON	37	M	LABR	PLZZZZUSA
M.	10	M	CH	PLZZZZUSA

PASSENGER	AGE	SEX	OCCUPATION	PRIVL	DES
BERKO, MICH.	31	F	W	PLZZZZ	USA
KUSSKO, JOS.	11	M	CH	PLZZZZ	USA
ODSEN, PETER	34	M	LABR	PLZZZZ	USA
MUSCHALEK, VOZE	44	M	LABR	PLZZZZ	USA
JOSWIEZAK, VAL.	43	M	LABR	PLZZZZ	USA
KUTUSKU, JOH.	35	M	LABR	PLZZZZ	USA
CATH.M.	25	F	W	PLZZZZ	USA
MICHELINE	11	F	CH	PLZZZZ	USA
FRANZESKA	00	F	INF	PLZZZZ	USA
JOSEPH	00	M	INF	PLZZZZ	USA
STROMER, MORITZ	17	M	LABR	PLZZZZ	USA
SZYBITZ, FRANZ	44	M	LABR	PLZZZZ	USA
KUTUSCHIK, M.	46	M	LABR	PLZZZZ	USA
MAGDALIE	60	F	W	PLZZZZ	USA
H.	6	M	CHILD	PLZZZZ	USA
GOLWONS, ANTONI	49	M	LABR	PLZZZZ	USA
PIKARSKA, MICHALINA	29	F	W	PLZZZZ	USA
JOSEFA	00	F	INF	PLZZZZ	USA
ANTONI	00	F	INF	PLZZZZ	USA
GWICKLENSKI, M.	23	F	LABR	PLZZZZ	USA
AMESCHKA	23	F	W	PLZZZZ	USA
SULKOVI, JACOB	36	M	LABR	PLZZZZ	USA
SUSANNE	36	F	W	PLZZZZ	USA
SUSANNE	00	F	INF	PLZZZZ	USA
ZIMMERMAN, MARIE	27	F	W	PLZZZZ	USA
SAM.	17	M	LABR	PLZZZZ	USA
AMALIE	00	F	INF	PLZZZZ	USA
ADELE	00	F	INF	PLZZZZ	USA
SAWALSTEIN, HIRSCH	11	M	CH	PLZZZZ	USA
PRESTEL, ANDRECUS	38	M	LABR	PLZZZZ	USA
URDOWSKA, LUDWIKA	38	M	LABR	PLZZZZ	USA
MARI	27	F	W	PLZZZZ	USA
SOFIA	3	F	CHILD	PLZZZZ	USA
JOHANNA	00	F	INF	PLZZZZ	USA
IV.	00	M	INF	PLZZZZ	USA
HARMANN, FRIED	34	M	LABR	PLZZZZ	USA
U, FRIED	43	F	W	PLZZZZ	USA
ORLOW, FRANZ	30	M	LABR	PLZZZZ	USA
CATH.	12	F	CH	PLZZZZ	USA
THEKLA	11	F	CH	PLZZZZ	USA
ADAM	10	M	CH	PLZZZZ	USA
MAISIL	9	M	CHILD	PLZZZZ	USA
LENORA	7	F	CHILD	PLZZZZ	USA
JAN	6	M	CHILD	PLZZZZ	USA
XAVER	2	M	CHILD	PLZZZZ	USA
LEVY	00	M	INF	PLZZZZ	USA
BIBA, MARIA	12	F	CH	PLZZZZ	USA
ZRIELNISKI, MICHAEL	22	M	LABR	PLZZZZ	USA
KALAMASCHINSKY, PETRONE	20	F	W	PLZZZZ	USA
HAGETTA, HED.	11	M	CH	PLZZZZ	USA
FEIZENBAUM, OSIAS	11	M	CH	PLZZZZ	USA
LECKLER, JOHN	38	M	LABR	PLZZZZ	USA
JANOS, JONES	29	M	LABR	PLZZZZ	USA
MATSON, ANDREW	29	M	LABR	PLZZZZ	USA
FRENK, JOHAN	28	M	LABR	PLZZZZ	USA
PEDUCK, ANDREAS	35	M	LABR	PLZZZZ	USA
KALISCH, WOYCICH	48	M	LABR	PLZZZZ	USA
JANOS, BRIM	23	F	W	PLZZZZ	USA
LANDAU, LUDWIG	27	M	LABR	PLZZZZ	USA
KOIZKOWSKY, JOH.	26	M	LABR	PLZZZZ	USA
BRENK, LAURENZ	44	M	LABR	PLZZZZ	USA
MARZEK, JAN	26	M	LABR	PLZZZZ	USA
KOLOWSKY, CARL	20	M	LABR	PLZZZZ	USA
BERGALSKA, CAROLINE	37	F	W	PLZZZZ	USA
MARIA	9	F	CHILD	PLZZZZ	USA
MAGNIRAN, L.	25	M	LABR	PLZZZZ	USA

PASSENGER	AGE	SEX	OCCUPATION	PRIVL	DES
SHIP: P CALAND					
FROM: ROTTERDAM					
TO: NEW YORK					
ARRIVED: 06 JUNE 1884					
ANDRUSKEVIC, WLADISLAW	27	M	LABR	PLZZZZ	USA
PARULA, MIKULA	33	M	SMH	PLZZZZ	USA
KASKOWSKI, FRANCISZ	20	M	FARMER	PLZZZZ	USA
KASKOWISKY, MARI	26	M	FARMER	PLZZZZ	USA
SHIP: WAESLAND					
FROM: ANTWERP					
TO: NEW YORK					
ARRIVED: 06 JUNE 1884					
SAULEC, HCH.	23	M	FARMER	RRZZZZ	MO
GRUNBERG, BERNE.	28	M	PRNTR	RRZZZZ	NY
PALOUS, FR.	15	M	FARMER	RRZZZZ	CIN
SHIP: WERRA					
FROM: BREMEN					
TO: NEW YORK					
ARRIVED: 07 JUNE 1884					
SPEYER, U-MR	24	M	TT	RRZZZZ	USA
U-MRS	19	F	TT	RRZZZZ	USA
SUNDERMANN, EDUARD	50	M	LABR	RRZZZZ	USA
MARIE	50	F	UNKNOWN	RRZZZZ	USA
MARIE	19	F	UNKNOWN	RRZZZZ	USA
EDUARD	17	M	LABR	RRZZZZ	USA
CORNELIUS	13	M	CH	RRZZZZ	USA
MARIE	7	F	CHILD	RRZZZZ	USA
GUENTHER, PETER	36	M	LLD	RRZZZZ	USA
MARGTH.	33	F	UNKNOWN	RRZZZZ	USA
ANNA	13	F	CH	RRZZZZ	USA
CARNELIUS	7	M	CHILD	RRZZZZ	USA
MARGTH.	7	F	CHILD	RRZZZZ	USA
PETER	6	M	CHILD	RRZZZZ	USA
AGVINSO	4	F	CHILD	RRZZZZ	USA
DANIEL	3	M	CHILD	RRZZZZ	USA
JOHANN	.11	M	INFANT	RRZZZZ	USA
ANNA	.11	F	INFANT	RRZZZZ	USA
EPP, CLAUS	52	M	LABR	RRZZZZ	USA
U, U	00	F	UNKNOWN	RRZZZZ	USA
FUNK, JOHANN	33	M	LABR	RRZZZZ	USA
MARIA	33	F	UNKNOWN	RRZZZZ	USA
MARIA	7	F	CHILD	RRZZZZ	USA
HELENE	6	F	CHILD	RRZZZZ	USA
-OHNE	00	F	CH	RRZZZZ	USA
ANNA	.03	F	INFANT	RRZZZZ	USA
EGER, SALOMON	67	M	LABR	RRZZZZ	USA
AUGUSTE	63	F	UNKNOWN	RRZZZZ	USA
JOHANN	35	M	LABR	RRZZZZ	USA
HEINR.	32	M	LABR	RRZZZZ	USA
CORNELIS	30	M	LABR	RRZZZZ	USA
JULIUS	25	M	LABR	RRZZZZ	USA
CATHARI.	41	F	UNKNOWN	RRZZZZ	USA
ELISABTH.	28	F	UNKNOWN	RRZZZZ	USA
ANNA	22	F	UNKNOWN	RRZZZZ	USA
PETERS, JOHANN	38	M	LABR	RRZZZZ	USA
KATHNA.	37	F	UNKNOWN	RRZZZZ	USA

PASSENGER	A G E	S E X	OCCUPATION	P R V	V I L	D E S
JOHANN	5	M	CHILD	RR	ZZZZ	USA
KATHNA.	7	F	CHILD	RR	ZZZZ	USA
ANNA	6	F	CHILD	RR	ZZZZ	USA
HELENE	.09	F	INFANT	RR	ZZZZ	USA
EICHENDORF, PETER	43	M	LABR	RR	ZZZZ	USA
JUSTINE	33	F	UNKNOWN	RR	ZZZZ	USA
JOHANN	7	M	CHILD	RR	ZZZZ	USA
JACOB	4	M	CHILD	RR	ZZZZ	USA
JUSTINE	.09	F	INFANT	RR	ZZZZ	USA
SCHMOR, JOHANN	43	M	LABR	RR	ZZZZ	USA
REGINE	42	F	UNKNOWN	RR	ZZZZ	USA
JOHANN	19	M	LABR	RR	ZZZZ	USA
JACOB	15	M	CH	RR	ZZZZ	USA
PETER	7	M	CHILD	RR	ZZZZ	USA
HEINR.	6	M	CHILD	RR	ZZZZ	USA
DAVID	2	M	CHILD	RR	ZZZZ	USA
ANNA	17	F	CH	RR	ZZZZ	USA
MARIA	6	F	CHILD	RR	ZZZZ	USA
KLEPP, LUDWIG	20	M	LABR	RR	ZZZZ	USA
KONOPATZKI, JUL.	5	M	CHILD	RR	ZZZZ	USA
BISLACK, MICHAEL	47	M	LLD	RR	ZZZZ	USA
KLEPP, AUG.	20	M	PNTR	RR	ZZZZ	USA
FELTENSTEIN, ROCHOLL	17	F	UNKNOWN	RR	ZZZZ	USA
LEWENSOHN, NATHAL	36	M	DLR	RR	ZZZZ	USA
LEWIN, DWER	18	M	DLR	RR	ZZZZ	USA
ISEKEIL, FRANZ	20	M	LABR	RR	ZZZZ	USA
FEINBERG, SALOMON	22	M	LABR	RR	ZZZZ	USA
----F, U	00	M	MCHT	RR	ZZZZ	USA
SONSTUVTIN, JACOB	35	M	MCHT	RR	ZZZZ	USA

SHIP: STATE OF NEBRASKA

FROM: GLASGOW AND LARNE
TO: NEW YORK
ARRIVED: 09 JUNE 1884

PASSENGER	A G E	S E X	OCCUPATION	P R V	V I L	D E S
BRANTHALH, IRAEL	17	M	LABR	RR	ZZZZ	USA
LITOWITZ, ISAAC	19	M	LABR	RR	ZZZZ	USA
MOSES	17	M	LABR	RR	ZZZZ	USA
CAUSCH, JOSSEL	54	M	LABR	RR	ZZZZ	USA
ROSA	50	F	W	RR	ZZZZ	USA
ERTIG, ABRAHAM	20	M	LABR	RR	ZZZZ	USA
RACHEL	20	F	W	RR	ZZZZ	USA
RESCHWIEDOWITZ, MOSES	28	M	LABR	RR	ZZZZ	USA
BERLIMER, ESTER	20	F	DMS	RR	ZZZZ	USA
NERLMANN, ISAAK	24	M	LABR	RR	ZZZZ	USA
GOLDBERG, DAVID	42	M	LABR	RR	ZZZZ	USA
LIPSCHITZ, ABRAHAM	22	M	LABR	RR	ZZZZ	USA
CHASAWITZ, JACOB	18	M	LABR	RR	ZZZZ	USA
ADINE, LEISER	17	M	LABR	RR	ZZZZ	USA
NAGUR, DAVID	18	M	LABR	RR	ZZZZ	USA
STUBSKO, LEIL	23	M	LABR	RR	ZZZZ	USA
SIMJENSKY, SCHLOME	23	M	LABR	RR	ZZZZ	USA
CHAIE	25	F	W	RR	ZZZZ	USA
SARAH	.05	F	INFANT	RR	ZZZZ	USA
NOWELOTZKY, CHAIM	16	M	LABR	RR	ZZZZ	USA
KLEIN, REGI	16	F	DMS	RR	ZZZZ	USA
HERSCHKOWITZ, BETTY	17	F	DMS	RR	ZZZZ	USA
JONKIN, ROBERT-K.	22	M	CL	RR	ZZZZ	USA
MARCZOWSKY, JACOB	33	M	LABR	RR	ZZZZ	USA
URBAS, MIKODEN	48	M	LABR	RR	ZZZZ	USA
JUKS, HIRSCH	18	M	LABR	RR	ZZZZ	USA
JEMMER, ABEL	19	M	LABR	RR	ZZZZ	USA
LEWIN, BENISH	23	M	LABR	RR	ZZZZ	USA
KAPLAN, SEMEL	19	M	LABR	RR	ZZZZ	USA
DAWIDOWITZ, JACOB	29	M	LABR	RR	ZZZZ	USA
EHRSOHN, SAMUEL	23	M	LABR	RR	ZZZZ	USA
LEWINSOHN, JOSEPH	17	M	LABR	RR	ZZZZ	USA
ARENSOHN, SCHOL	18	M	LABR	RR	ZZZZ	USA
ROSENGARD, HITTEL	21	M	LABR	RR	ZZZZ	USA
GALLUM, HIRSCH	39	M	LABR	RR	ZZZZ	USA
JIFFEL	22	M	LABR	RR	ZZZZ	USA
MINDER, NAPHTALI	55	M	LABR	RR	ZZZZ	USA
MASUR, MORDCHEL	50	M	LABR	RR	ZZZZ	USA
KLOSCHANDER, D.	26	M	LABR	RR	ZZZZ	USA
EVA	22	F	W	RR	ZZZZ	USA
FRIEDMAN, BENZEL	19	M	LABR	RR	ZZZZ	USA
MARGENSTEIN, GICALIA	32	M	LABR	RR	ZZZZ	USA
PINTUS	5	M	CHILD	RR	ZZZZ	USA
LIEBE	.07	M	INFANT	RR	ZZZZ	USA
BANICH	.07	M	INFANT	RR	ZZZZ	USA
MORGENSTEIN, ROSA	28	F	W	RR	ZZZZ	USA
SARAH	.11	F	INFANT	RR	ZZZZ	USA
HORDENSKY, HERSCHEL	37	M	LABR	RR	ZZZZ	USA
KAMIGUSSER, ISRAEL	40	M	LABR	RR	ZZZZ	USA
SCHMACH, CHAWE	24	F	W	RR	ZZZZ	USA
CHAIM	.03	M	INFANT	RR	ZZZZ	USA
KAPNER, LEISNER	28	M	LABR	RR	ZZZZ	USA
BACHNER, SALIMON	31	M	LABR	RR	ZZZZ	USA
KRAMER, DAVID	32	M	LABR	RR	ZZZZ	USA
JETTE	26	F	W	RR	ZZZZ	USA
GITTEL	5	F	CHILD	RR	ZZZZ	USA
DEBORAH	.09	F	INFANT	RR	ZZZZ	USA
HANNA	.09	F	INFANT	RR	ZZZZ	USA
ROSA	.09	F	INFANT	RR	ZZZZ	USA
BUDER, MORDCHE	35	M	LABR	RR	ZZZZ	USA
GOLD, FRIG	30	M	LABR	RR	ZZZZ	USA
SARAH	28	F	W	RR	ZZZZ	USA
KAPLAN, NOCHIM	18	M	LABR	RR	ZZZZ	USA
BEROWITSCH, MOSES	17	M	LABR	RR	ZZZZ	USA
GAHOVEK, WENZEL	21	M	LABR	RR	ZZZZ	USA
KABELKOWSKY, MORDCHE	36	M	LABR	RR	ZZZZ	USA
TAUBE	32	F	W	RR	ZZZZ	USA
CHANE	.05	F	INFANT	RR	ZZZZ	USA
GIBBART, HERMANN	25	M	LABR	RR	ZZZZ	USA
GRINSBERG, BEHR	30	M	LABR	RR	ZZZZ	USA
KATZ, ARON	36	M	LABR	RR	ZZZZ	USA
HIRSCH	11	M	CH	RR	ZZZZ	USA
WEINBERG, JENNY	18	F	DMS	RR	ZZZZ	USA
BERNSTEIN, MEYER	44	M	LABR	RR	ZZZZ	USA
CHAIE	17	F	DMS	RR	ZZZZ	USA
CHAIM	16	M	LABR	RR	ZZZZ	USA
BARANSKY, JANKEL	28	M	LABR	RR	ZZZZ	USA
NAVINSKY, JANKEL	11	M	CH	RR	ZZZZ	USA
BERCOWITZ, LEVI	25	M	LABR	RR	ZZZZ	USA
BETTY	18	F	W	RR	ZZZZ	USA
MOSCHKOWITZ, MARCUS	19	M	LABR	RR	ZZZZ	USA
BRICK, SAMUEL	30	M	LABR	RR	ZZZZ	USA
SIEGMUNDT	25	M	LABR	RR	ZZZZ	USA
NUNINSKY, ABRAHAM	20	M	LABR	RR	ZZZZ	USA
SANTAGKY, BEILE	22	F	DMS	RR	ZZZZ	USA
RASCHEL	18	F	DMS	RR	ZZZZ	USA
ROTH, YERGE	20	F	DMS	RR	ZZZZ	USA
NEUBERDT, RIWKE	18	F	DMS	RR	ZZZZ	USA
WELZ, SINNA	24	F	DMS	RR	ZZZZ	USA
MAZKOWSKY, MEYER	50	M	LABR	RR	ZZZZ	USA
ROSCHEL	48	F	W	RR	ZZZZ	USA
CHAME	10	F	CH	RR	ZZZZ	USA
SAMUEL	8	M	CHILD	RR	ZZZZ	USA
MARGULIES, HERSCH	36	M	LABR	RR	ZZZZ	USA
SOHUMANN, MICHAEL	23	M	LABR	RR	ZZZZ	USA
KRASSNER, LEIB	36	M	LABR	RR	ZZZZ	USA
SULOWITZ, RACHIMEL	19	F	DMS	RR	ZZZZ	USA
SEID, HENE	22	F	DMS	RR	ZZZZ	USA
LEWIN, MERE	19	F	DMS	RR	ZZZZ	USA
JOSSEL	10	M	CH	RR	ZZZZ	USA
RATINSKY, ADAM	30	M	LABR	RR	ZZZZ	USA
REKASOZIK, ADA	30	M	LABR	RR	ZZZZ	USA
MARUSCHA, MARTIN	26	M	LABR	RR	ZZZZ	USA
BENZIS, BENEDICT	25	M	LABR	RR	ZZZZ	USA
MARKUS, CHATZKEL	32	M	LABR	RR	ZZZZ	USA
FISCHLER, JOHANN	27	M	LABR	RR	ZZZZ	USA
WILENSKY, CHANNE	38	F	W	RR	ZZZZ	USA
KURLANZICK, JACOB	9	F	CHILD	RR	ZZZZ	USA
RIWKE	7	F	CHILD	RR	ZZZZ	USA

PASSENGER	AGE	SEX	OCCUPATION	PV RIVL	DES
SCHONE	5	F	CHILD	RRZZZZ	USA
MENDELSON, KEIL	19	F	DMS	RRZZZZ	USA
KOTTLER, ABRAHAM	25	M	LABR	RRZZZZ	USA
HELLMANN, ISAAK	25	M	LABR	RRZZZZ	USA
KARATOWSKY, J.	23	M	LABR	RRZZZZ	USA
CHAIE	20	F	W	RRZZZZ	USA
HURWITZ, MOSES	18	M	LABR	RRZZZZ	USA
GOLD, SAML.	42	M	LABR	RRZZZZ	USA
MENDELSOHN, C.	21	M	LABR	RRZZZZ	USA
KAHANY, ABEL	28	M	LABR	RRZZZZ	USA
JESEWITZ, JOSEPH	29	M	LABR	RRZZZZ	USA
FRANZELIS, JOSEPH	25	M	LABR	RRZZZZ	USA
HOCHRON, JACOB	40	M	LABR	RRZZZZ	USA
ARON	18	M	LABR	RRZZZZ	USA
SCHMULOWITZ, MENDEL	18	M	LABR	RRZZZZ	USA
ISAAK	16	M	LABR	RRZZZZ	USA
SOKOLOWSKI, MISCH	21	M	LABR	RRZZZZ	USA
GADRALOWSKY, PHILIPP	24	M	LABR	RRZZZZ	USA
ALBOWITZ, MORDCHE	36	M	LABR	RRZZZZ	USA
HOLOP, RABIN	18	M	LABR	RRZZZZ	USA
MISCHKUTZ, A.	22	M	LABR	RRZZZZ	USA
ABSCHUL, SALOMON	21	M	LABR	RRZZZZ	USA
BRASCH, ABRAHAM	29	M	LABR	RRZZZZ	USA
SCHMILANSKY, JETTE	23	F	DMS	RRZZZZ	USA
SCHUMANN, EIDE	35	F	W	RRZZZZ	USA
DIVIE	11	F	CH	RRZZZZ	USA
MOSES	9	M	CHILD	RRZZZZ	USA
SARAH	.07	F	INFANT	RRZZZZ	USA
GLASSMANN, JACOB	34	M	LABR	RRZZZZ	USA
KAMINSKY, CHAIM	42	M	LABR	RRZZZZ	USA
GOLDSTEIN, D.	50	M	LABR	RRZZZZ	USA
DAMDOWITZ, CHAIM	18	M	LABR	RRZZZZ	USA
BLOCK, JACOB	24	M	LABR	RRZZZZ	USA
MARCUS, LEIB	45	M	LABR	RRZZZZ	USA
MOSES	19	M	LABR	RRZZZZ	USA
HERSCHE, MOSES	18	M	LABR	RRZZZZ	USA
KAPLAN, SELIG	16	M	LABR	RRZZZZ	USA
MACHITOWITZ, MACHEM	18	M	LABR	RRZZZZ	USA
LEIBWITZ, CHAIM	19	M	LABR	RRZZZZ	USA
BAKOVSH, ABRAHAM	14	M	LABR	RRZZZZ	USA
KONGAD, LEIB	16	M	LABR	RRZZZZ	USA
POVELANSKI, JACOB	27	M	LABR	RRZZZZ	USA
MICHAEL, LISKA	27	M	LABR	RRZZZZ	USA
KUNSKEWOLSKY, JANE	00	M	LABR	RRZZZZ	USA
KRISSKI, ABRAHAM	20	M	LABR	RRZZZZ	USA
BEHRMANN, SAML.	43	M	LABR	RRZZZZ	USA
OPPENHEIM, CATZKEL	18	M	LABR	RRZZZZ	USA
JOSCHEL	25	M	LABR	RRZZZZ	USA
LEWINTHAL, ASCKNE	20	F	DMS	RRZZZZ	USA
POSTERNAK, JOSEF	11	M	CH	RRZZZZ	USA
RACHEL	9	F	CHILD	RRZZZZ	USA
SILBERMANN, MARITZ	25	M	LABR	RRZZZZ	USA
JEWITZEL, JAN	45	M	LABR	RRZZZZ	USA
CATHARINE	43	F	W	RRZZZZ	USA
VICTORIA	12	F	CH	RRZZZZ	USA
JOHANN	7	M	CHILD	RRZZZZ	USA
FRANZISCA	.06	F	INFANT	RRZZZZ	USA
JIWITZEL, JOSEPHA	.06	F	INFANT	RRZZZZ	USA
WICHTEROWITZ, ANTON	55	M	LABR	RRZZZZ	USA
ANNA	53	F	W	RRZZZZ	USA
JOSEPHA	20	F	DMS	RRZZZZ	USA
VICTORIA	16	F	DMS	RRZZZZ	USA
WEISS, PHILIPPE	20	M	LABR	RRZZZZ	USA
TENDRICH, KLARA	18	F	DMS	RRZZZZ	USA
DISCHKEWITZ, MICHAEL	52	M	LABR	RRZZZZ	USA
ROSALIE	42	F	W	RRZZZZ	USA
ADAM	13	M	CH	RRZZZZ	USA
MICHALIE	6	F	CHILD	RRZZZZ	USA
THOMAS	3	M	CHILD	RRZZZZ	USA
VINCENTI	.06	M	INFANT	RRZZZZ	USA
NEUMANN, CHAIM	24	M	LABR	RRZZZZ	USA
CHANE	30	F	W	RRZZZZ	USA
LIVINTON, SARAH	18	F	DMS	RRZZZZ	USA

SHIP: AMERIQUE

FROM: HAVRE
TO: NEW YORK
ARRIVED: 11 JUNE 1884

PASSENGER	AGE	SEX	OCCUPATION	PV RIVL	DES
GENIS, RACHEL	27	F	SMSTS	RRZZZZ	USA
MAX	3	M	CHILD	RRZZZZ	USA
FANNY	00	F	INF	RRZZZZ	USA
PAULINE	00	F	INF	RRZZZZ	USA
BRUSTEN, FANNY	32	F	FARMER	RRZZZZ	USA
ROSALIE	6	F	CHILD	RRZZZZ	USA

SHIP: BOLIVIA

FROM: GLASGOW AND MOVILLE
TO: NEW YORK
ARRIVED: 11 JUNE 1884

PASSENGER	AGE	SEX	OCCUPATION	PV RIVL	DES
SCHLEWSKY, LUD.	33	M	CL	PLZZZZ	USA
MARIA	21	F	UNKNOWN	PLZZZZ	USA

SHIP: GRECIAN MONARCH

FROM: LONDON
TO: NEW YORK
ARRIVED: 11 JUNE 1884

PASSENGER	AGE	SEX	OCCUPATION	PV RIVL	DES
LEWSKY, KOPPEL	20	M	BAT	RRZZZZ	USA
BERIL	40	M	BAT	RRZZZZ	USA
WACHS, MOSES	60	M	TLR	RRZZZZ	USA
ANNA	17	F	CH	RRZZZZ	USA
LEVI	11	M	CH	RRZZZZ	USA
KLEIN, JACOB	22	M	FUR	PLZZZZ	USA
GUTMAN, VICTOR	22	M	FUR	PLZZZZ	USA
BERGEN, ADOLPH	22	M	BKR	PLZZZZ	USA
ANNA	19	F	W	PLZZZZ	USA
CZERNAWSKY, MICH.	24	M	LABR	PLZZZZ	USA
MICHALINA	24	F	W	PLZZZZ	USA
PRETR.	.06	F	INFANT	PLZZZZ	USA
PROSCHUNSKA, KATE	24	F	NN	PLZZZZ	USA
BENLINSKI, WOLF	57	M	LABR	PLZZZZ	USA
KATE	53	F	W	PLZZZZ	USA
SARAH	20	F	CH	PLZZZZ	USA
ANNIE	18	F	CH	PLZZZZ	USA
SOFIA	16	F	CH	PLZZZZ	USA
MARY	11	F	CH	PLZZZZ	USA
MARKS	9	M	CHILD	PLZZZZ	USA
ROSENBERG, NATHAN	34	M	TLR	PLZZZZ	USA
BETSY	25	F	W	PLZZZZ	USA
PHILIP	8	M	CHILD	PLZZZZ	USA
KATE	2	F	CHILD	PLZZZZ	USA
WALDSTEIN, BETSY	30	F	W	PLZZZZ	USA
PHILIP	11	M	CH	PLZZZZ	USA
SARAH	10	F	CH	PLZZZZ	USA
ISRAEL	8	M	CHILD	PLZZZZ	USA
REBECCA	5	F	CHILD	PLZZZZ	USA
MARK	.09	M	INFANT	PLZZZZ	USA
LEVY, MOSES	00	M	LABR	PLZZZZ	USA
ANNIE	32	F	W	PLZZZZ	USA
REBECCA	15	F	CH	PLZZZZ	USA
RACHEL	11	F	CH	PLZZZZ	USA
SAMUEL	9	M	CHILD	PLZZZZ	USA
LILLY	6	F	CHILD	PLZZZZ	USA

PASSENGER	AGE	SEX	OCCUPATION	PRV VIL DES
ASHER	3	M	CHILD	PLZZZZUSA
BLUMAL	.11	M	INFANT	PLZZZZUSA
LEVINSOHN, REBECCA	28	F	W	PLZZZZUSA
JOS.	2	M	CHILD	PLZZZZUSA
ANNIE	.06	F	INFANT	PLZZZZUSA
WILK, REBECCA	59	F	NN	PLZZZZUSA
SOFIA	21	F	NN	PLZZZZUSA
MEIKEL, PHILIP	20	M	TLR	PLZZZZUSA
KRAMMAN, JOSEF	36	M	TLR	PLZZZZUSA
ZENZOWSKI, J.	53	M	LABR	PLZZZZUSA
LEVY, DAVID	35	M	LABR	PLZZZZUSA
STIFF, JUDAH	31	M	LABR	PLZZZZUSA
LINA	22	F	W	PLZZZZUSA
ROSA	.06	F	INFANT	PLZZZZUSA
ZCINSANG, MORRIS	18	M	BTMKR	PLZZZZUSA
COHEN, MARKS	24	M	LABR	PLZZZZUSA
BENIS, LEAH	22	M	LABR	PLZZZZUSA
BLUMENFIELD, SIMON	50	M	LABR	PLZZZZUSA
SALOMON	9	M	CHILD	PLZZZZUSA
COHEN, KATE	22	F	W	PLZZZZUSA
BETSY	.11	F	INFANT	PLZZZZUSA
DOLLASHINSKY, RACHEL	35	F	W	PLZZZZUSA
SARAH	10	F	CH	PLZZZZUSA
HENRY	8	M	CHILD	PLZZZZUSA
REBECCA	6	F	CHILD	PLZZZZUSA
GOLDA	4	F	CHILD	PLZZZZUSA
ABRAHAM	.11	M	INFANT	PLZZZZUSA
LERE, HANNAH	24	F	W	PLZZZZUSA
SARAH	4	F	CHILD	PLZZZZUSA
REBECCA	2	F	CHILD	PLZZZZUSA

SHIP: RHAETIA

FROM: HAMBURG
TO: NEW YORK
ARRIVED: 11 JUNE 1884

PASSENGER	AGE	SEX	OCCUPATION	PRV VIL DES
NOVYNSKI, WOLF.	40	M	LABR	RRZZZZUSA
DILZINJA, ANNA	18	F	SGL	RRZZZZUSA
WENDEL, CHATZKEL	50	M	TLR	RRZZZZUSA
CHABOTZKI, MEIER	44	M	TLR	RRZZZZUSA
CHODSOSH, GERSON	40	M	TLR	RRZZZZUSA
ROSENFELD, AUGUSTE	16	F	SGL	RRZZZZUSA
JESCHINOWSKI, SALOMON	45	M	TLR	RRZZZZUSA
SCHNEIDEROWITZ, ZALLEL	15	M	TLR	RRZZZZUSA
SPITALINK, JOSEF	25	M	TLR	RRZZZZUSA
KATZ, SARA	16	F	SGL	RRZZZZUSA
KERCHER, PETER	50	M	LABR	RRZZZZUSA
JOHANNE	57	F	W	RRZZZZUSA
JOH.	15	F	D	RRZZZZUSA
LOUISE	29	F	FARMER	RRZZZZUSA
JOH.	22	F	W	RRZZZZUSA
JOH.	.11	F	INFANT	RRZZZZUSA
DULKOWA, ANTONIE	53	F	W	RRZZZZUSA
JABLONSKA, GEORG.	21	M	LABR	RRZZZZUSA
ZINS, KOP.	15	M	LABR	RRZZZZUSA
SAMUELSON, SALOMON	25	M	TLR	RRZZZZUSA
ROIN, JACOB	23	M	SHMK	RRZZZZUSA
MARGOLIN, MOSES	25	M	DLR	RRZZZZUSA
RIWKEV, INDA	17	M	LABR	RRZZZZUSA
FORDONSKI, BERNK.	40	M	MCHT	RRZZZZUSA
POPPER, ANTON	19	M	MCHT	RRZZZZUSA
RADOMSKI, ANTON	20	M	LABR	RRZZZZUSA
ANDREJEWSKI, VALENTIN	45	M	LABR	RRZZZZUSA
PFENING, HANS	31	M	LABR	RRZZZZUSA
MARTIN	19	M	LABR	RRZZZZUSA
IDA	20	F	SGL	RRZZZZUSA
SIBERSKI, SAMUEL	21	M	DLR	RRZZZZUSA
SCHERBIN, JACOB	19	M	LABR	RRZZZZUSA
KAZLOWSKI, HANISL.	26	M	LABR	RRZZZZUSA
U, U	.11	M	INFANT	RRZZZZUSA
SCHTELBAUM, SARAH	26	F	W	RRZZZZUSA
MOSES	8	M	CHILD	RRZZZZUSA
MORDCHE	6	M	CHILD	RRZZZZUSA
JOSEPH	.11	M	INFANT	RRZZZZUSA
JACOBSOHN, SARAH	20	F	SGL	RRZZZZUSA
GROSSMANN, FREIDE	23	F	W	RRZZZZUSA
CHAINE	6	F	CHILD	RRZZZZUSA
LICBE	.11	M	INFANT	RRZZZZUSA
PALUESCH, SCHIC	54	M	DLR	RRZZZZUSA
GOLDBERGER, HERM.	35	M	LABR	RRZZZZUSA
FANNY	33	F	W	RRZZZZUSA
DORA	7	F	CHILD	RRZZZZUSA
SUSSMANN, SALWEN	45	M	LABR	RRZZZZUSA
WITTENSTEIN, MATHE	34	F	W	RRZZZZUSA
MASCHE	8	F	CHILD	RRZZZZUSA
ELKE	7	M	CHILD	RRZZZZUSA
JOSSEL	6	F	CHILD	RRZZZZUSA
HIRSCH	.11	M	INFANT	RRZZZZUSA
LENHOWITZ, MORITZ	30	M	LABR	RRZZZZUSA
STVAN, JAN	32	M	SHPR	RRZZZZUSA
MENYARS, ENGL.	22	M	STDNT	RRZZZZUSA
KREINAK, ANDR.	18	M	LABR	RRZZZZUSA
JAWORCZIK, ANDR.	20	M	LABR	RRZZZZUSA
PFLUGINSKI, VALENTIN	40	M	LABR	RRZZZZUSA
ALBERTINE	40	F	W	RRZZZZUSA
MARIE	8	F	CHILD	RRZZZZUSA
JULIE	7	F	CHILD	RRZZZZUSA
DWOLDISLAV	6	M	CHILD	RRZZZZUSA
EMILIE	5	F	CHILD	RRZZZZUSA
CLARA	3	F	CHILD	RRZZZZUSA
THEODOR	.09	M	INFANT	RRZZZZUSA
BERNAWICZ, STANISLAW	20	M	LABR	RRZZZZUSA
GLASSER, MANDEL	44	M	LABR	RRZZZZUSA
MALKOWSKI, MOSES	30	M	LABR	RRZZZZUSA
GUTMANN, MINNA	35	F	SGL	RRZZZZUSA
HELKER, ISRAEL	18	M	LABR	RRZZZZUSA
KUPER, CHASCHE	25	F	W	RRZZZZUSA
LEIZER	.11	F	INFANT	RRZZZZUSA
JALER, CHAIE	35	F	W	RRZZZZUSA
LICBE	8	F	CHILD	RRZZZZUSA
SARAH	.11	F	INFANT	RRZZZZUSA
JACOB	.01	M	INFANT	RRZZZZUSA
HASS, JOHANN	31	M	LABR	RRZZZZUSA
KAKOWSKA, KATH.	21	F	SGL	RRZZZZUSA
BEHLEJEWSKA, JULIANE	25	F	W	RRZZZZUSA
JOSEPHA	.11	F	INFANT	RRZZZZUSA
PILINOWSKY, RECHAME	40	F	W	RRZZZZUSA
LINE	8	F	CHILD	RRZZZZUSA
MINE	4	F	CHILD	RRZZZZUSA
RUBIN	6	M	CHILD	RRZZZZUSA
PESSE	.11	M	INFANT	RRZZZZUSA
ESTHER	.01	M	INFANT	RRZZZZUSA
GULEK, BEILE	40	F	W	RRZZZZUSA
RENDEL	18	F	CH	RRZZZZUSA
SCHIFRE	16	F	CH	RRZZZZUSA
JACOB	8	M	CHILD	RRZZZZUSA
REICHEL	7	F	CHILD	RRZZZZUSA
LIMAN	.11	M	INFANT	RRZZZZUSA
JARBURSKY, JOSEF	9	M	CHILD	RRZZZZUSA
HELIMARKA, JACOB	36	M	LABR	RRZZZZUSA
AGIIST, ITTA	20	F	W	RRZZZZUSA
JOSEF	.11	F	INFANT	RRZZZZUSA
LANKAJTIS, ADAM	35	M	LABR	RRZZZZUSA
MASENS	17	M	LABR	RRZZZZUSA
JOSEF	8	M	CHILD	RRZZZZUSA
SCHOILOWITZ, BENJAMIN	23	M	LABR	RRZZZZUSA
BERESIN, CLARA	28	F	W	RRZZZZUSA
MARIE	8	F	CHILD	RRZZZZUSA
TEPLITZ, ABRAHAM	20	M	WCHMKR	RRZZZZUSA
STENSILEWSKI, FRANZ	20	M	LABR	RRZZZZUSA
COHEN, ROSA	21	F	W	RRZZZZUSA
SARA	.11	F	INFANT	RRZZZZUSA
-ASCHE, SARA	.11	F	INFANT	RRZZZZUSA
STAMM, ARON	41	M	MCHT	RRZZZZUSA

PASSENGER	AGE	SEX	OCCUPATION	PRV	VIL	DES
SELAS, CARL	50	M	LABR	RR	ZZZZ	USA
BERNSSEIN, ISRAEL	36	M	LABR	RR	ZZZZ	USA
SCHIC	9	M	CHILD	RR	ZZZZ	USA
FINKELSTEIN, EBER	20	M	LABR	RR	ZZZZ	USA
KASDOR, DAVID	24	M	LABR	RR	ZZZZ	USA
ROSENHRANZ, BARUCH	46	M	TLR	RR	ZZZZ	USA
DAVID	18	M	CH	RR	ZZZZ	USA
HERM.	8	M	CHILD	RR	ZZZZ	USA
ABRAH.	7	M	CHILD	RR	ZZZZ	USA
FEIGE	6	M	CHILD	RR	ZZZZ	USA
JACUBOWITZ, BINE	29	F	W	RR	ZZZZ	USA
GISSEL	6	F	CHILD	RR	ZZZZ	USA
MORDCHE	.11	F	INFANT	RR	ZZZZ	USA
JUDA	49	M	LABR	RR	ZZZZ	USA
ESTHER	16	F	SGL	RR	ZZZZ	USA
KATZ, GITTEL	20	F	SGL	RR	ZZZZ	USA
ASCHLACK, DWORE	25	F	SGL	RR	ZZZZ	USA
BURNEIKA, OSIFS	23	M	LABR	RR	ZZZZ	USA
PLYSYNSKI, ANTON	20	M	LABR	RR	ZZZZ	USA
DONGINICK, STANISL.	18	M	LABR	RR	ZZZZ	USA
WINGITZKI, STORIAN	21	M	LABR	RR	ZZZZ	USA
MIGLIN, SEMAN	40	M	LABR	RR	ZZZZ	USA
PETER	19	M	LABR	RR	ZZZZ	USA
SODKE, HEINR.	33	M	LABR	RR	ZZZZ	USA
THIEL, JOACHIM	68	M	LABR	RR	ZZZZ	USA
FENSKI, CHR.	46	M	LABR	RR	ZZZZ	USA
LOUISE	44	F	W	RR	ZZZZ	USA
DANIEL	8	M	CHILD	RR	ZZZZ	USA
FRIEDR.	7	M	CHILD	RR	ZZZZ	USA
AMANDA	6	F	CHILD	RR	ZZZZ	USA
EMIL	5	M	CHILD	RR	ZZZZ	USA
JULIUS	4	M	CHILD	RR	ZZZZ	USA
MATHILDE	3	F	CHILD	RR	ZZZZ	USA
LUDWIG	2	M	CHILD	RR	ZZZZ	USA
LOUISE	1	F	CHILD	RR	ZZZZ	USA
EDUARD	20	M	LABR	RR	ZZZZ	USA
PAULINE	16	F	SGL	RR	ZZZZ	USA
FRIEDR.	30	M	LABR	RR	ZZZZ	USA
MALWINE	23	F	W	RR	ZZZZ	USA
RUDOLPH	3	M	CHILD	RR	ZZZZ	USA
ADOLPH	1	M	CHILD	RR	ZZZZ	USA
HULDA	.03	F	INFANT	RR	ZZZZ	USA
WENDS, CHR.	22	M	LABR	RR	ZZZZ	USA
LOUISE	23	F	W	RR	ZZZZ	USA
LADISCH, HEINR.	30	M	LABR	RR	ZZZZ	USA
WOLLENBERG, MOSES	23	M	TLR	RR	ZZZZ	USA
ZIELA	21	F	W	RR	ZZZZ	USA
LAKOLOWSKY, ANTON	31	M	LABR	RR	ZZZZ	USA
SYLDEROWICZ, ANASTASIA	26	F	SGL	RR	ZZZZ	USA
ZAMUSCHEWITZ, SCHEPSE	28	M	DLR	RR	ZZZZ	USA
KAMBERG, GUST.	25	M	SHMK	RR	ZZZZ	USA
SCHEINKER, CIPPE	30	F	WO	RR	ZZZZ	USA
ABRAH.	7	M	CHILD	RR	ZZZZ	USA
SARAH	5	F	CHILD	RR	ZZZZ	USA
HINDE	.11	F	INFANT	RR	ZZZZ	USA
UFFNER, RACHEL	28	F	WO	RR	ZZZZ	USA
SARA	.11	F	INFANT	RR	ZZZZ	USA
GLUCKLICH, BEILE	8	F	CHILD	RR	ZZZZ	USA
GORDON, SARAH	35	F	W	RR	ZZZZ	USA
ISAAC	8	M	CHILD	RR	ZZZZ	USA
CHEIE	5	M	CHILD	RR	ZZZZ	USA
JACOB	.11	M	INFANT	RR	ZZZZ	USA
BEILE	.01	M	INFANT	RR	ZZZZ	USA
LAPIDER, MOSES	21	M	LABR	RR	ZZZZ	USA
TOCKS, ETTE	25	F	W	RR	ZZZZ	USA
MEYER	4	M	CHILD	RR	ZZZZ	USA
LEIB	.11	M	INFANT	RR	ZZZZ	USA
BOBIER, LEO	50	M	W	RR	ZZZZ	USA
SAHOL, CHANNE	21	F	SGL	RR	ZZZZ	USA
HASHEL	8	M	CHILD	RR	ZZZZ	USA
BODE--W-T-, JOHANNE	26	F	W	RR	ZZZZ	USA
VICTORIA	4	F	CHILD	RR	ZZZZ	USA
STANISLAW	.11	M	INFANT	RR	ZZZZ	USA
BLUMBERG, JEANETTE	60	F	WO	RR	ZZZZ	USA
KOHN, CHAIE	26	F	SGL	RR	ZZZZ	USA
ZINN, SAMUEL	20	M	LABR	RR	ZZZZ	USA
REBECCA	20	F	W	RR	ZZZZ	USA

SHIP: WISCONSIN

FROM: LIVERPOOL AND QUEENSTOWN
TO: NEW YORK
ARRIVED: 11 JUNE 1884

PASSENGER	AGE	SEX	OCCUPATION	PRV	VIL	DES
KABAN, MOSES	47	M	LABR	PL	ZZZZ	USA
CHASLER, JAMHEN	18	M	LABR	PL	ZZZZ	USA
BROTSIEURTZ, AVAN	38	M	LABR	PL	ZZZZ	USA
MARIANNA	38	F	W	PL	ZZZZ	USA
JOSEPH	9	M	CHILD	PL	ZZZZ	USA
APOLINE	7	M	CHILD	PL	ZZZZ	USA
FRANZ	3	M	CHILD	PL	ZZZZ	USA
ANTONI	1	M	CHILD	PL	ZZZZ	USA
NOLANOWITZ, JOHAN	36	M	LABR	PL	ZZZZ	USA
MINES, BERL	36	M	LABR	PL	ZZZZ	USA
SCLIMK, JOHAN	43	M	LABR	PL	ZZZZ	USA
MARIA	34	F	W	PL	ZZZZ	USA
KLINTZE, PAUL	23	M	LABR	PL	ZZZZ	USA
BRAUN, AUG.	21	M	LABR	PL	ZZZZ	USA
HERMET, OTTO	22	M	LABR	PL	ZZZZ	USA
FRUDMAN, HIRSCH	39	M	LABR	PL	ZZZZ	USA
MANN, ISRAL	20	M	LABR	PL	ZZZZ	USA
LINBEH, WOLF	26	M	LABR	PL	ZZZZ	USA
CRERMAH, JOHAN	25	M	LABR	PL	ZZZZ	USA
PIORSNORSKI, MORRIS	17	M	LABR	PL	ZZZZ	USA
MEDOWSKY, ISRAL	32	M	LABR	PL	ZZZZ	USA
IOTTAD	24	F	W	PL	ZZZZ	USA
DEBORAH	9	F	CHILD	PL	ZZZZ	USA
JANE	8	F	CHILD	PL	ZZZZ	USA
JIRL	1	M	CHILD	PL	ZZZZ	USA
BAILI	1	M	CHILD	PL	ZZZZ	USA
COOKLEROW, CHANE	36	M	LABR	PL	ZZZZ	USA
CHASIE	30	F	W	PL	ZZZZ	USA
YUOSELL	7	M	CHILD	PL	ZZZZ	USA
ABRAHAM	3	M	CHILD	PL	ZZZZ	USA
BIRL	1	M	CHILD	PL	ZZZZ	USA
MOSES	1	M	CHILD	PL	ZZZZ	USA
SATULOWSKY, PINKA	60	M	LABR	PL	ZZZZ	USA
RAFLE	50	F	W	PL	ZZZZ	USA
MARIA	11	F	CH	PL	ZZZZ	USA
BELE	.06	M	INFANT	PL	ZZZZ	USA
MAUSTE	17	M	LABR	PL	ZZZZ	USA
SARAH	20	F	SP	PL	ZZZZ	USA
MARDELA	.07	F	INFANT	PL	ZZZZ	USA
ETHEL	17	F	SP	PL	ZZZZ	USA
SKELOWER, MAYER	30	M	LABR	PL	ZZZZ	USA
BOLER, CARL	27	M	LABR	PL	ZZZZ	USA
MAIDROWIZ, SCHMUEL	28	M	LABR	PL	ZZZZ	USA
KAPLOWITSCH, KARON	30	M	LABR	PL	ZZZZ	USA
HMEKE, GUSTAV	43	M	LABR	PL	ZZZZ	USA
KRAJENSKY, MATHIA	60	M	LABR	PL	ZZZZ	USA
PETER	43	M	LABR	PL	ZZZZ	USA
LUDIAN	31	M	LABR	PL	ZZZZ	USA
STAINS	11	M	CH	PL	ZZZZ	USA
WLADISLAW	4	M	CHILD	PL	ZZZZ	USA
SATALOWSKY, BENEUDT	27	M	LABR	PL	ZZZZ	USA
MERY	25	F	W	PL	ZZZZ	USA
SELDE	.07	M	INFANT	PL	ZZZZ	USA
WROBLEWIEG, ARON	24	M	LABR	PL	ZZZZ	USA
NISSEA	20	M	LABR	PL	ZZZZ	USA
GELLBLUM, MANI	24	M	LABR	PL	ZZZZ	USA
ROZASKA, SCHMUEL	38	M	LABR	PL	ZZZZ	USA
BEVCH, OSER	48	M	LABR	PL	ZZZZ	USA
HASMAN, WOLF	31	M	LABR	PL	ZZZZ	USA
ABBT, SLIRAB	50	M	LABR	PL	ZZZZ	USA
SHIRAH, CHATH.	50	F	W	PL	ZZZZ	USA

PASSENGER	AGE	SEX	OCCUPATION	PRV VIL DES
AGNES	18	F	SP	PLZZZZUSA
JOHANNA	16	F	SP	PLZZZZUSA
CATHA	11	F	CH	PLZZZZUSA
BRASCH, N.	57	M	LABR	PLZZZZUSA

SHIP: GENERAL WERDER

FROM: BREMEN
TO: NEW YORK
ARRIVED: 13 JUNE 1884

PASSENGER	AGE	SEX	OCCUPATION	PRV VIL DES
KUSTEL, RICHARD	31	M	FARMER	RRZZZZUSA
COHEN, JOCHIM	28	M	MUSN	RRZZZZUSA
THERESE	25	F	UNKNOWN	RRZZZZUSA
ROCHEL	6	M	CHILD	RRZZZZUSA
GITEL	3	M	CHILD	RRZZZZUSA
JACOB	.10	M	INFANT	RRZZZZUSA
LANT, GOTTLIEB	25	M	LABR	RRZZZZUSA
ELISABETH	25	F	W	RRZZZZUSA
BARBARA	3	F	CHILD	RRZZZZUSA
ELISABETH	.11	F	INFANT	RRZZZZUSA
STEIN, JOHANN	28	M	FARMER	RRZZZZUSA
CATHARINA	9	F	CHILD	RRZZZZUSA
F.	21	F	NN	RRZZZZUSA
MAGDALENA	19	F	NN	RRZZZZUSA
JOHANNES	16	M	LLD	RRZZZZUSA
EVA	13	F	CH	RRZZZZUSA
CHRISTINE	4	F	CHILD	RRZZZZUSA
ROSINE	2	F	CHILD	RRZZZZUSA
KEUFSCH, ABRAHAM	31	M	JNR	RRZZZZUSA
KATHARINA	30	F	W	RRZZZZUSA
ABRAHAM	6	M	CHILD	RRZZZZUSA
JACOB	.09	M	INFANT	RRZZZZUSA
PETER	.01	M	INFANT	RRZZZZUSA
PAUL	.01	M	INFANT	RRZZZZUSA

SHIP: WIELAND

FROM: HAMBURG
TO: NEW YORK
ARRIVED: 13 JUNE 1884

PASSENGER	AGE	SEX	OCCUPATION	PRV VIL DES
BACKSTROM, PAULINE	28	F	W	FNZZZZUSA
GEIVOWSKI, NICOLAI	32	M	DLR	RRZZZZUSA
HANDWERGER, ZIPPERLE	45	F	W	RRZZZZUSA
CHAIM	17	M	CH	RRZZZZUSA
ESTHER	15	F	CH	RRZZZZUSA
VORSTRAS, LEA	18	F	SGL	RRZZZZUSA
GOLDMANN, FEIGE	23	F	W	RRZZZZUSA
JACOB	.11	M	INFANT	RRZZZZUSA
UNBARSKY, MENDEL	18	M	SGL	RRZZZZUSA
SARNE, PAULINE	18	F	SGL	RRZZZZUSA
KAPLAN, HERM.	30	M	LABR	RRZZZZUSA
PAULINE	22	F	W	RRZZZZUSA
GOLDSTEIN, KOLLMANN	20	M	LABR	RRZZZZUSA
FLICKER, JACOB	20	M	LABR	RRZZZZUSA
KINRESCHKY, MOSES	20	M	LABR	RRZZZZUSA
RAHEL	20	F	W	RRZZZZUSA
SKLAROWSKY, SCHONE	18	F	SGL	RRZZZZUSA
SALK, SAMUEL	18	M	LABR	RRZZZZUSA
DAGMANN, FREIDE	27	F	W	RRZZZZUSA
PESCHE	.11	M	INFANT	RRZZZZUSA
MARIUS, CHAIE	20	F	SGL	RRZZZZUSA
ALEXANDER, CHAIE	9	F	CHILD	RRZZZZUSA
GOLDMANN, JOCHL	20	M	LABR	RRZZZZUSA

PASSENGER	AGE	SEX	OCCUPATION	PRV VIL DES
ALTMAN, CHANNE	15	F	SGL	RRZZZZUSA
ZUIKERMANN, ABRAH.	28	M	HTR	RRZZZZUSA
STEINBERG, JACOB	24	M	HTR	RRZZZZUSA
SEGAL, SCHLOME	17	F	LABR	RRZZZZUSA
WOLFINGER, MOSES	18	M	LABR	RRZZZZUSA
ANTON	15	M	LABR	RRZZZZUSA
AUKOWSKY, CATH.	38	F	SGL	RRZZZZUSA
JONAS, CAIEHE	34	F	W	RRZZZZUSA
DENNENBERG, MICHAEL	25	M	HTR	RRZZZZUSA
SCHEIME	20	F	W	RRZZZZUSA
MACKOWSKI, ROSA	40	F	W	RRZZZZUSA
LEISER	9	M	CHILD	RRZZZZUSA
BOBKI	4	M	CHILD	RRZZZZUSA
JACOB	.11	M	INFANT	RRZZZZUSA
PESCHE	17	F	SGL	RRZZZZUSA
KASCH, SCHEPSEL	42	M	CGRMKR	RRZZZZUSA
BENWITZ, LOUIS	22	M	LABR	RRZZZZUSA
LIEBE	21	F	W	RRZZZZUSA
MOSES	.11	M	INFANT	RRZZZZUSA
BERBENSKY, HANNE	50	F	W	RRZZZZUSA
FRANK, RAFAEL	18	M	MCHT	RRZZZZUSA
BRODER, USCHER	38	M	TLR	RRZZZZUSA
ISRAEL	18	M	LABR	RRZZZZUSA
BOLIUK, GERSON	20	M	BKBNDR	RRZZZZUSA
KONSER, HIRSCH	9	M	CHILD	RRZZZZUSA
WOYCINKI, ALB.	55	M	LABR	RRZZZZUSA
AGATHE	46	F	W	RRZZZZUSA
APPOLONIA	14	F	CH	RRZZZZUSA
PAUL	9	M	CHILD	RRZZZZUSA
HIRSCHDORFER, MOSES	32	M	LABR	RRZZZZUSA
BENDSTORF, HIRSCH	20	M	LABR	RRZZZZUSA
SPAT, BEILE	18	F	SGL	RRZZZZUSA
ORTH, JOH.	22	M	SMH	RRZZZZUSA
KOLSCHINSKI, CHATZKEL	21	M	LABR	RRZZZZUSA
PLOTKY, PESCHE	30	F	W	RRZZZZUSA
NOCHE	4	F	CHILD	RRZZZZUSA
BASCHE	.11	F	INFANT	RRZZZZUSA
SARA	.01	F	INFANT	RRZZZZUSA
GERSUOS, MICHAL	33	M	LABR	RRZZZZUSA
BODOWITZ, JUSTANZ	30	M	LABR	RRZZZZUSA
OSTROVSKY, PETER	19	M	LABR	RRZZZZUSA
MARTIN	27	M	LABR	RRZZZZUSA
ZLIVIE, JAN	28	M	LABR	RRZZZZUSA
MIKALAPMAS, KASIMIR	27	M	LABR	RRZZZZUSA
LONKEWITZ, MATEJ	45	M	LABR	RRZZZZUSA
HENZ, AUGUST	31	M	LABR	RRZZZZUSA
WILH.	27	F	W	RRZZZZUSA
REGINE	4	F	CHILD	RRZZZZUSA
HELENE	.11	F	INFANT	RRZZZZUSA
NORD, JOH.	25	M	LABR	RRZZZZUSA
ROSALIE	20	F	W	RRZZZZUSA
JOH.	.11	M	INFANT	RRZZZZUSA
ANNA	.01	F	INFANT	RRZZZZUSA
FRIEDR.	22	M	LABR	RRZZZZUSA
WILLEMS, JOHANN	25	M	LABR	RRZZZZUSA
KLIEWER, ABRAH.	35	M	LABR	RRZZZZUSA
WILH.	38	F	W	RRZZZZUSA
SUSANNE	9	F	CHILD	RRZZZZUSA
JACOB	8	M	CHILD	RRZZZZUSA
PETER	7	M	CHILD	RRZZZZUSA
ABRAHAM	6	M	CHILD	RRZZZZUSA
HEINR.	4	M	CHILD	RRZZZZUSA
GERHARD	2	M	CHILD	RRZZZZUSA
ANNA	.06	F	INFANT	RRZZZZUSA
BEGINSKI, MICHAEL	29	M	LABR	RRZZZZUSA
JUSTINE	21	F	W	RRZZZZUSA
ZIGELSKA, MARIANNE	27	F	W	RRZZZZUSA

PASSENGER	AGE	SEX	OCCUPATION	PRIV DES
SHIP: EMS				
FROM: UNKNOWN				
TO: NEW YORK				
ARRIVED: 14 JUNE 1884				
REIMER, ABRAHAM	37	M	FARMER	RRZZZZUSA
ANNA	37	F	NN	RRZZZZUSA
HELENE	16	F	NN	RRZZZZUSA
ANNA	14	F	NN	RRZZZZUSA
ABRAHAM	13	M	NN	RRZZZZUSA
AGNECA	8	F	CHILD	RRZZZZUSA
AGATHA	5	F	CHILD	RRZZZZUSA
CATHARINE	3	F	CHILD	RRZZZZUSA
MARIA	.11	F	INFANT	RRZZZZUSA
GOTTSCHALK, NATHAN	35	M	LABR	RRZZZZUSA
DISK, HEINR.	45	M	LABR	RRZZZZUSA
HELENE	45	F	NN	RRZZZZUSA
PETER	23	M	LLD	RRZZZZUSA
SUSANNE	22	F	NN	RRZZZZUSA
HELENE	21	F	NN	RRZZZZUSA
UNGER, DANIEL	31	M	LLD	RRZZZZUSA
ADELGUNDE	24	F	NN	RRZZZZUSA
JACOB-H.	2	M	CHILD	RRZZZZUSA
HELENE	3	F	CHILD	RRZZZZUSA
ROGINA, MATHIAS	37	M	LABR	RRZZZZUSA
DIRKS, WILHELM	36	M	FARMER	RRZZZZUSA
HELENE	37	F	NN	RRZZZZUSA
MARIE	10	F	NN	RRZZZZUSA
ANNA	2	F	CHILD	RRZZZZUSA
FADENRECHT, EDUARD	33	M	FARMER	RRZZZZUSA
CHARLOTTE	31	F	NN	RRZZZZUSA
RUDOLF	7	M	CHILD	RRZZZZUSA
MARIA	.03	F	INFANT	RRZZZZUSA
FERDINAND	68	M	FARMER	RRZZZZUSA
ADAMS, ABRAHAM	33	M	FARMER	RRZZZZUSA
JOHANN	5	M	CHILD	RRZZZZUSA
HEINRICH	4	M	CHILD	RRZZZZUSA
ANNA	6	F	CHILD	RRZZZZUSA
ABRAHAM	.09	M	INFANT	RRZZZZUSA
STEINGARD, JACOB	30	M	FARMER	RRZZZZUSA
CATHARINE	29	F	NN	RRZZZZUSA
ANNA	3	F	CHILD	RRZZZZUSA
CATHARINE	2	F	CHILD	RRZZZZUSA
JACOB	.01	M	INFANT	RRZZZZUSA
PETERS, ISAAC	31	M	FARMER	RRZZZZUSA
HELENE	33	F	NN	RRZZZZUSA
JACOB	7	M	CHILD	RRZZZZUSA
HEINR.	6	M	CHILD	RRZZZZUSA
ISAAC	5	M	CHILD	RRZZZZUSA
HELENE	1	F	CHILD	RRZZZZUSA
REMPEL, HEINR.	36	M	FARMER	RRZZZZUSA
MARGARETHA	31	F	NN	RRZZZZUSA
HEINRICH	3	M	CHILD	RRZZZZUSA
MARIA	4	F	CHILD	RRZZZZUSA
SAWATSKI, JACOB	35	M	FARMER	RRZZZZUSA
KATHERINA	33	F	NN	RRZZZZUSA
CONRADINE	4	F	CHILD	RRZZZZUSA
SUSANNE	2	F	CHILD	RRZZZZUSA
KATHARINE	1	F	CHILD	RRZZZZUSA
BREITENBADR, FRIEDR.	35	M	GZR	RRZZZZUSA
DAHLKE, HEINR.	30	M	FARMER	RRZZZZUSA
MARIE	38	F	NN	RRZZZZUSA
MARIE	6	F	CHILD	RRZZZZUSA
HERM.	2	M	CHILD	RRZZZZUSA
JACOB	.03	M	INFANT	RRZZZZUSA
SIEMENS, HELEN	27	F	NN	RRZZZZUSA
HELENE	2	F	CHILD	RRZZZZUSA
CORNELIE	.11	M	INFANT	RRZZZZUSA
JANZEN, JACOB	56	M	LABR	RRZZZZUSA
CATHARINE	53	F	NN	RRZZZZUSA
HEINRICH	22	M	LABR	RRZZZZUSA
JACOB	10	M	LABR	RRZZZZUSA
CATHARINE	15	F	NN	RRZZZZUSA
UNRAUTZ, ALBERT	25	M	LABR	RRZZZZUSA
HELENE	69	F	NN	RRZZZZUSA
WIENS, ARON	38	M	LABR	RRZZZZUSA
AGATHE	35	F	NN	RRZZZZUSA
ARON	9	M	CHILD	RRZZZZUSA
PETER	7	M	CHILD	RRZZZZUSA
DAVID	3	M	CHILD	RRZZZZUSA
ELISABETH	13	F	NN	RRZZZZUSA
HELENE	10	F	NN	RRZZZZUSA
BERNHARD	.02	M	INFANT	RRZZZZUSA
FAST, ABRAHAM	27	M	LABR	RRZZZZUSA
MARIA	23	F	NN	RRZZZZUSA
PETER	3	M	CHILD	RRZZZZUSA
ANNA	31	F	NN	RRZZZZUSA
WELENE	17	F	NN	RRZZZZUSA
SHIP: ISLAND				
FROM: COPENHAGEN				
TO: NEW YORK				
ARRIVED: 14 JUNE 1884				
PENSEN, HANS-P.	30	M	MSN	RRZZZZUSA
SHIP: POLYNESIA				
FROM: HAMBURG				
TO: NEW YORK				
ARRIVED: 14 JUNE 1884				
MENDEL, GESCH.	60	M	TRDSMN	RRZZZZNY
SUCKIS, SCH.	19	M	TRDSMN	RRZZZZNY
RUDERMANN, NATH.	43	M	LABR	RRZZZZNY
CHASCHKE	26	F	W	RRZZZZNY
ROSCHE	4	F	CHILD	RRZZZZNY
SCHIRFINSKY, M.	21	F	SGL	RRZZZZNY
RUSCHEL, R.	19	F	SGL	RRZZZZNY
KUPL--, ROSCH.	18	F	SGL	RRZZZZNY
ASGETT, LEISE	38	F	WO	RRZZZZNY
LIEBE	7	F	CHILD	RRZZZZNY
FEIGE	6	F	CHILD	RRZZZZNY
SCHOLEIN	5	F	CHILD	RRZZZZNY
HOCNIG, ROSE	7	F	CHILD	RRZZZZNY
MILDER, LINE	7	F	CHILD	RRZZZZNY
LEWITANSKY, BENJ.	17	M	TRDSMN	RRZZZZNY
PHILIPIS, PETRIS	24	M	TRDSMN	RRZZZZNY
LUBOWSKI, JOS.	36	M	TRDSMN	RRZZZZNY
ROSENBERG, SUN	28	M	LABR	RRZZZZMN
MOCKOVSKI, HIRSCH	20	M	SMH	RRZZZZNY
GRODBERG, BEILE	20	F	SGL	RRZZZZNY
STARGARD, ADOLF	24	M	JNR	RRZZZZNY
KLUMMEL, MARIE	19	F	SGL	RRZZZZNY
ZEBANSKY, MARIE	40	F	WO	RRZZZZNY
LEA	17	F	D	RRZZZZNY
PAULINE	13	F	D	RRZZZZNY
JOSEF	7	M	CHILD	RRZZZZNY
LEVINSON, ELIE	24	M	MCHT	RRZZZZNY
CZABAY, CATHA.	35	F	WO	PLZZZZNY
MICHAEL	4	M	CHILD	PLZZZZNY
COHN, JOEL	17	M	TRDSMN	RRZZZZNY
BERNHARDT, ALBERT	28	M	LABR	RRZZZZNY
VALIGEWSKI, LUDWIG	18	M	TRDSMN	RRZZZZNY
WEBER, RICHARD	40	M	TRDSMN	RRZZZZNY
KALWARINSKI, RIWEA	28	M	TRDSMN	RRZZZZNY
GENOVSKY, ANTONES	35	M	TRDSMN	RRZZZZNY

PASSENGER	AGE	SEX	OCCUPATION	PRIVL	DES
JOSEF	45	M	TRDSMN	RRZZZZ	NY
ROSE	35	F	W	RRZZZZ	NY
ANTON	7	M	CHILD	RRZZZZ	NY
WINCEZ	6	M	CHILD	RRZZZZ	NY
CASIMIR	3	M	CHILD	RRZZZZ	NY
JONAS	.05	M	INFANT	RRZZZZ	NY
HURWITZ, LEISER	35	M	TRDSMN	RRZZZZ	NY
ZERICE	30	F	W	RRZZZZ	NY
RUBEN	5	M	CHILD	RRZZZZ	NY
NATHAN	.08	M	INFANT	RRZZZZ	NY
BAKSCHANSKY, ISAAC	28	M	TRDSMN	RRZZZZ	NY
MINA	42	F	W	RRZZZZ	NY
ANNA	.05	F	INFANT	RRZZZZ	NY
JAKSEN, MOSES	25	M	TRDSMN	RRZZZZ	NY
REGINA	24	F	W	RRZZZZ	NY
ANNA	3	F	CHILD	RRZZZZ	NY
ABRAHAM	.07	M	INFANT	RRZZZZ	NY
JA----, JOSSEF	00	M	TRDSMN	RRZZZZ	NY
JEG-----, ISAAC	00	M	TRDSMN	RRZZZZ	NY
FER----, ABRAHAM	30	M	TRDSMN	RRZZZZ	NY
FEIN, SALOMON	7	M	CHILD	RRZZZZ	NY
SINGE----, MARCUS	00	M	TRDSMN	RRZZZZ	NY
SWIFETZKY, DAVID	21	M	TRDSMN	RRZZZZ	NY
COHN, ELIAS	20	M	TRDSMN	RRZZZZ	NY
GOLDE, ISAAC	23	M	TRDSMN	RRZZZZ	NY
KRUTZKOW, GABRIEL	50	M	TRDSMN	RRZZZZ	NY
BARUCH, JOSSEL	19	M	TRDSMN	RRZZZZ	NY
ESTHER	19	F	W	RRZZZZ	NY
VACHAMOWITZ, DAVID	18	M	TRDSMN	RRZZZZ	NY
ROMOWSKI, MEIER	26	M	TRDSMN	RRZZZZ	NY
WOLFF, VICTOR	22	M	TRDSMN	RRZZZZ	NY
KRUSINOWSKI, JOHANN	30	M	TRDSMN	RRZZZZ	NY
BARTKEWICZ, ANTON	35	M	TRDSMN	RRZZZZ	NY
BLAUSTEIN, SELIGM	26	M	TRDSMN	RRZZZZ	NY
SARA	24	F	W	RRZZZZ	NY
ZIEGE	.03	F	INFANT	RRZZZZ	NY
SCHELMSKI, MATHILDE	21	F	SGL	RRZZZZ	NY
MAGDALENE	18	F	SGL	RRZZZZ	NY
JUERGELITES, IWAN	20	M	LABR	RRZZZZ	NY
MARIANNE	22	F	W	RRZZZZ	NY
ABBAN, JOSEF	24	M	TRDSMN	RRZZZZ	NY
VOJCEC--, WLADUSCH	24	M	LABR	PLZZZZ	NY
SUTAWSKI, MICHEL	18	M	LABR	PLZZZZ	NY
BURGMANN, ESTI	17	F	SGL	PLZZZZ	NY
EHRENFELD, BERTHA	17	F	SGL	PLZZZZ	NY
PAULA	19	F	SGL	PLZZZZ	NY
UHR, ESTI	17	F	SGL	PLZZZZ	NY
EHRENFELD, MARIE	7	F	CHILD	PLZZZZ	NY
KORZEN, MARIE	18	F	SGL	PLZZZZ	NY
KHOSS, MARJANS	22	F	SGL	RRZZZZ	NY
HOLLANDER, JOS.	20	M	TRDSMN	RRZZZZ	NY
GOLDBERG, FEIGE	22	F	WO	RRZZZZ	NY
CJENE	.07	F	INFANT	RRZZZZ	NY
WOJTECHOVSKY, JOH	31	M	LABR	PLZZZZ	NY
WOGROVSKY, JOS.	25	M	LABR	PLZZZZ	NY
U, U	00	M	LABR	PLZZZZ	NY
KIVELSKY, JAN	45	M	LABR	RRZZZZ	NY
SLUMOS, JOHANN	24	M	LABR	RRZZZZ	NY
LEBSEC, ITZIG	19	M	LABR	RRZZZZ	NY
KORT, MEJA	19	M	LABR	RRZZZZ	NY
KRISBURG, LIPE	33	M	TRDSMN	RRZZZZ	NY
KANTEROWITZC, DAVID	34	M	TRDSMN	RRZZZZ	NY
ZIVEK, VICENTY	30	M	LABR	PLZZZZ	NY
JOSEFA	24	F	W	PLZZZZ	NY
WOLFF, HIRSCH	19	M	LABR	PLZZZZ	NY
LEHR, MOSES	23	M	TRDSMN	PLZZZZ	NY
ABRAHAM, EBNER	23	M	TRDSMN	PLZZZZ	NY
GRIMMAN, PACSEH	18	F	SGL	RRZZZZ	NY
PERMENBERG, JOCHIEL	28	M	JNR	PLZZZZ	NY

SHIP: ENGLAND

FROM: LIVERPOOL AND QUEENSTOWN
TO: NEW YORK
ARRIVED: 16 JUNE 1884

PASSENGER	AGE	SEX	OCCUPATION	PRIVL	DES
LAITMAN, H.	21	M	LABR	RRZZZZ	NY
LISA	22	F	W	RRZZZZ	NY
MARIA	4	F	CHILD	RRZZZZ	NY
SARVELA, JAHOB	32	M	LABR	RRZZZZ	NY
HARTBOY, MATZ	34	M	LABR	RRZZZZ	NY
JOHANSEN, GABR.	25	M	LABR	RRZZZZ	NY
LION, HIETI	31	M	LABR	RRZZZZ	NY
HASTBOY, JOH.	33	M	LABR	RRZZZZ	NY
KOSKI, JAHOB	20	M	LABR	RRZZZZ	NY
KARRE, JOHN	37	M	LABR	RRZZZZ	NY
PEKHI, JOHN	31	M	LABR	RRZZZZ	NY
WATAHA, W.	30	M	LABR	RRZZZZ	NY
LASSILA, M.	19	M	LABR	RRZZZZ	NY
PALLARE, I.	27	M	LABR	RRZZZZ	NY
HANKIMAKI, G.	28	M	LABR	RRZZZZ	NY
LOURI, MIKKI	29	M	LABR	RRZZZZ	NY
HYPPETI, JAKOB	21	M	LABR	RRZZZZ	NY
LIPPOLAT, MIKKI	40	M	LABR	RRZZZZ	NY
FALISO, JAHOB	40	M	LABR	RRZZZZ	NY
SARI, SOM	23	M	LABR	RRZZZZ	NY
KILO, ANTI	20	M	LABR	RRZZZZ	NY
GEMILA, M.	24	M	LABR	RRZZZZ	NY
IRAAS, JAHOB	21	M	LABR	RRZZZZ	NY
OSMANSKI, SOLOMON	22	M	LABR	RRZZZZ	NY
DONIGAN, MOSES-D.	11	M	CH	RRZZZZ	NY
JALVENSAN, AUGUST	23	M	LABR	RRZZZZ	NY
IWUKOWSKI, NILS	33	M	LABR	RRZZZZ	NY
KULPACA, MATHIAS	21	M	LABR	RRZZZZ	NY
KETZ, ELIAS	32	M	LABR	RRZZZZ	NY
KUJALA, MATHIAS	22	M	LABR	RRZZZZ	NY
LUUHANSEN, NILS	20	M	LABR	RRZZZZ	NY
LAULUGA, MICHAEL	22	M	LABR	RRZZZZ	NY
WHITTY, ASKED-Y.	23	M	LABR	RRZZZZ	NY
KANATI, KARL	28	M	LABR	RRZZZZ	NY
KEIGHTA, MARTIN	21	M	LABR	RRZZZZ	NY

SHIP: NORMANDIE

FROM: HAVRE
TO: NEW YORK
ARRIVED: 16 JUNE 1884

PASSENGER	AGE	SEX	OCCUPATION	PRIVL	DES
LEVY, SALOMON	33	M	MCHT	RRZZZZ	NY
SALANT, DAVID	25	M	SMH	RRZZZZ	NY
CHAIN, ELIE	20	M	SHMK	RRZZZZ	NY

SHIP: SUEVIA

FROM: HAMBURG
TO: NEW YORK
ARRIVED: 18 JUNE 1884

PASSENGER	AGE	SEX	OCCUPATION	PRIVL	DES
ERDMANN, MARTIN	64	M	LABR	RRZZZZ	USA
ELISABETH	53	F	W	RRZZZZ	USA
MARTIN	24	M	S	RRZZZZ	USA
JUSTINE	24	F	D	RRZZZZ	USA
ANDR.	23	M	S	RRZZZZ	USA
MARIE	19	F	D	RRZZZZ	USA

PASSENGER	AGE	SEX	OCCUPATION	PRV VIL DES
HEINR.	16	M	S	RRZZZZUSA
ELISABETH	15	F	D	RRZZZZUSA
MARIE	9	F	CHILD	RRZZZZUSA
MARIE	1	F	CHILD	RRZZZZUSA
ELISABETH	.03	F	INFANT	RRZZZZUSA
SCHULTZ, MICHEL	46	M	LABR	RRZZZZUSA
ELISABETH	43	F	W	RRZZZZUSA
HEINR.	22	M	CH	RRZZZZUSA
MARIE	17	F	CH	RRZZZZUSA
ELISABETH	9	F	CHILD	RRZZZZUSA
FLORENTINE	8	F	CHILD	RRZZZZUSA
MICHEL	7	M	CHILD	RRZZZZUSA
EDUARD	6	M	CHILD	RRZZZZUSA
MARTIN	5	M	CHILD	RRZZZZUSA
SAMUEL	1	M	CHILD	RRZZZZUSA
SCHWARZ, JACOB	26	M	LABR	RRZZZZUSA
KUHN, FRANZ	42	M	LABR	RRZZZZUSA
THERESE	40	F	W	RRZZZZUSA
THERESE	17	F	CH	RRZZZZUSA
DAVID	15	M	CH	RRZZZZUSA
JACOB	3	M	CHILD	RRZZZZUSA
HELENE	1	F	CHILD	RRZZZZUSA
EIBEL, EDUARD	36	M	LABR	RRZZZZUSA
ANNA	29	F	W	RRZZZZUSA
BARTH.	1	F	CHILD	RRZZZZUSA
RICHD.	17	M	LABR	RRZZZZUSA
CHARLOTTE	60	F	W	RRZZZZUSA
KOSCH, SAMUEL	33	M	LABR	RRZZZZUSA
WILHE.	32	F	W	RRZZZZUSA
HEINR.	9	M	CHILD	RRZZZZUSA
SAMUEL	8	M	CHILD	RRZZZZUSA
WILHE.	5	F	CHILD	RRZZZZUSA
MARIE	3	F	CHILD	RRZZZZUSA
CARL	1	M	CHILD	RRZZZZUSA
KOPACZEWSKI, JOHANN	46	M	LABR	RRZZZZUSA
MARIANNE	51	F	W	RRZZZZUSA
MICHAEL	58	M	LABR	RRZZZZUSA
ROGOW, HUNDI	25	F	W	RRZZZZUSA
MOSES	7	M	CHILD	RRZZZZUSA
BELA	4	F	CHILD	RRZZZZUSA
KOZLOWSKI, MICHAEL	22	M	LABR	RRZZZZUSA
FEINBERG, ARON	18	M	TLR	RRZZZZUSA
ROGOW, CAECILIC	1	F	CHILD	RRZZZZUSA
BLUMBERG, SCHEINE	17	F	SGL	RRZZZZUSA
KADLOWITZ, CHAJE	30	F	W	RRZZZZUSA
SCHOENE	1	F	CHILD	RRZZZZUSA
PESCHE	.03	F	INFANT	RRZZZZUSA
BONOF, BREINE	22	F	SGL	RRZZZZUSA
TUREK, ROSA	46	F	W	RRZZZZUSA
PAULINE	9	F	CHILD	RRZZZZUSA
GOLDBERG, ANSCHEL	43	M	LABR	RRZZZZUSA
BEILE	40	F	W	RRZZZZUSA
CHAIE	9	F	CHILD	RRZZZZUSA
MATEL	8	F	CHILD	RRZZZZUSA
JURGENSEN, BRUNU	26	M	STDNT	RRZZZZUSA
GIGUZINSKI, CHAIM	18	M	LKSH	RRZZZZUSA
FEINSTEIN, MAX	50	M	LABR	RRZZZZUSA
JONAS	9	M	CHILD	RRZZZZUSA
JASKOLSKI, ARON	23	M	LKSH	RRZZZZUSA
RAHEL	20	F	W	RRZZZZUSA
RAGOW, FEIWEL	20	M	WCHMKR	RRZZZZUSA
ISERSKY, LEIB	31	M	LABR	RRZZZZUSA
KOSSLER, CHAIM	22	M	LABR	RRZZZZUSA
KODOLOWITZ, RIWKE	6	M	CHILD	RRZZZZUSA
KOMINER, LEIB	37	M	LABR	RRZZZZUSA
MERE	35	F	W	RRZZZZUSA
RAHEL	9	F	CHILD	RRZZZZUSA
EPHRAIM	8	M	CHILD	RRZZZZUSA
BASCHE	7	M	CHILD	RRZZZZUSA
SAMUEL	4	M	CHILD	RRZZZZUSA
JACOB	3	M	CHILD	RRZZZZUSA
KAHN, HENNY	50	F	W	RRZZZZUSA
GOLDE	13	F	CH	RRZZZZUSA
SCHULMANN, ARON	51	M	GZR	RRZZZZUSA
KNEBEL, MOSES	21	M	UNKNOWN	RRZZZZUSA

PASSENGER	AGE	SEX	OCCUPATION	PRV VIL DES
ZIPPE	24	F	W	RRZZZZUSA
KAROLL, CHANE	61	F	W	RRZZZZUSA
SEGALL, ABRAM	19	M	DLR	RRZZZZUSA
SCHEINE	23	F	W	RRZZZZUSA
ROGOLSKY, MORDCHE	18	M	DLR	RRZZZZUSA
KABUCHER, ARON	45	M	DLR	RRZZZZUSA
KAUFFMANN, CHAIE	26	F	W	RRZZZZUSA
CHAIM	4	M	CHILD	RRZZZZUSA
HANNE	5	F	CHILD	RRZZZZUSA
RINGEL, JOCHEL	42	M	LABR	RRZZZZUSA
GRUENBAUM, RIFKE	50	M	TLR	RRZZZZUSA
FEIWEL	21	M	TLR	RRZZZZUSA
SCHAIE	19	M	TLR	RRZZZZUSA
SCHULGASSER, ELIAS	25	M	LABR	RRZZZZUSA
APPELBAUM, HIRSCH	37	M	LABR	RRZZZZUSA
STRUSSENBERG, ARON	27	M	LABR	RRZZZZUSA
STENKOWSKY, BERNHD.	19	M	LABR	RRZZZZUSA
STEINWITZ, ABRAH.	20	M	LABR	RRZZZZUSA
BASCHE	19	F	W	RRZZZZUSA
EICHENBERG, ISAAC	40	M	LABR	RRZZZZUSA
SWORSCHIN, MOSES	26	M	LABR	RRZZZZUSA
PARTSCHAK, ISRAEL	30	M	LABR	RRZZZZUSA
WOLF, SARAH	40	F	W	RRZZZZUSA
BEILE	10	F	CH	RRZZZZUSA
ISRAEL	7	M	CHILD	RRZZZZUSA
BEHR.	5	M	CHILD	RRZZZZUSA
WOLFF	1	M	CHILD	RRZZZZUSA
PENCIK, GITEL	31	F	W	RRZZZZUSA
ZANWEL	8	F	CHILD	RRZZZZUSA
HUNDE	4	F	CHILD	RRZZZZUSA
SARA	1	F	CHILD	RRZZZZUSA
SPORER, MUNKE	8	F	CHILD	RRZZZZUSA
SCHEINBART, PEISSACH	37	M	MSN	RRZZZZUSA
WARSCHOWITZ, RASCHE	34	F	W	RRZZZZUSA
ISAAC	12	M	CH	RRZZZZUSA
CHAIE	9	F	CHILD	RRZZZZUSA
BERL.	7	F	CHILD	RRZZZZUSA
MENASCHE	5	F	CHILD	RRZZZZUSA
JOSEF	1	M	CHILD	RRZZZZUSA
MARCUS	34	M	LABR	RRZZZZUSA
GOLDSCHMIDT, ISAAC	38	M	LABR	RRZZZZUSA
WSOLEK, ANTONI	30	M	LABR	RRZZZZUSA
KUCHEN, ICTEL	24	M	LABR	RRZZZZUSA
BIRN, ABE	25	M	LABR	RRZZZZUSA
ZANWEL, HENACH	12	M	LABR	RRZZZZUSA
HINDICK, FEIWEL	14	M	LABR	RRZZZZUSA
PENCIK, HENE	19	M	LABR	RRZZZZUSA

SHIP: CALIFORNIA

FROM: HAMBURG
TO: NEW YORK
ARRIVED: 19 JUNE 1884

PASSENGER	AGE	SEX	OCCUPATION	PRV VIL DES
WERLACHOWSKI, SEVERIN	45	M	LABR	PLZZZZNY
THERESE	35	F	W	PLZZZZNY
MARIE	11	F	D	PLZZZZNY
STANISLAUS	7	M	CHILD	PLZZZZNY
WOLFF, H.S.	14	M	S	PLZZZZNY
MORTENSEN, PETER	35	M	S	PLZZZZNY
CYPOWIERSKY, JACOB-H.	33	M	TRDSMN	RRZZZZNY
BROSILEWSKY, L.CH.	26	M	TRDSMN	RRZZZZNY
WINETZKI, JACOB	52	M	TRDSMN	RRZZZZNY
U, MINNA	19	F	W	RRZZZZNY
KLEIN, SAMUEL	37	M	SMH	RRZZZZNY
PINSA, KRASS	30	M	TRDSMN	RRZZZZNY
U, KRETE	28	F	W	RRZZZZNY
ADAMI	20	M	TRDSMN	RRZZZZNY
STRAWITZKI, PAULINE	25	F	SGL	RRZZZZNY
JALOWSKY, MOSES	17	M	TRDSMN	RRZZZZNY

PASSENGER	AGE	SEX	OCCUPATION	PRV	VIL	DES
SELPITZER, TODES	40	M	TRDSMN	RR	ZZZZ	NY
UNGARN, LEIB	20	M	TRDSMN	RR	ZZZZ	NY
ZUCKERMANN, SALOMON	31	M	TRDSMN	PL	ZZZZ	NY
KATZNIOWSKI, HERTZ	30	M	TRDSMN	RR	ZZZZ	NY
FRIEDEMANN, CHANE	37	M	TRDSMN	RR	ZZZZ	NY
GARFINKEL, SCHMUL	18	M	TRDSMN	RR	ZZZZ	NY
SCHULER, JANKEL	18	M	TRDSMN	RR	ZZZZ	NY
CHITIN, ABRAM	19	M	SHMK	RR	ZZZZ	NY
WEICHOWSKI, JOHANN	23	M	JNR	RR	ZZZZ	NY
ANNA	20	F	W	RR	ZZZZ	NY
SCHANDINSKI, MOSES	19	M	TRDSMN	RR	ZZZZ	NY
SALAMON	18	M	TRDSMN	RR	ZZZZ	NY
STEINBERG, GETTEL	22	F	WO	RR	ZZZZ	NY
GRUEMFELD, MENDEL	26	M	TRDSMN	RR	ZZZZ	NY
KLAUS, GEORG	.04	M	INFANT	RR	ZZZZ	NY
CHAIMORITZ, MOSES	18	M	TLR	RR	ZZZZ	NY
GOLDNIG, ISIDOR	17	M	TLR	RR	ZZZZ	NY
ISACSON, HIRSCH	27	M	PNTR	RR	ZZZZ	NY
LISECKA, AGNES	17	F	SGL	RR	ZZZZ	UNK
ROSENBERG, ITZIG	35	M	MCHT	RR	ZZZZ	UNK
REGANTOWISCH, MARIE	55	F	WO	RR	ZZZZ	WI
SOPHIE	21	F	D	RR	ZZZZ	WI
STRAUS, PAULINE	26	F	WO	RR	ZZZZ	WI
SCHULKE	3	M	CHILD	RR	ZZZZ	WI
SCHAIE	.07	M	INFANT	RR	ZZZZ	WI
MICHELSON, REBECKA	19	F	SGL	RR	ZZZZ	NY
ROSINE	21	F	W	RR	ZZZZ	NY
JOHANN	2	M	CHILD	RR	ZZZZ	NY
LUDWIG	.09	M	INFANT	RR	ZZZZ	NY
BREINAHY, MOSES	19	M	TRDSMN	RR	ZZZZ	NY
HIMMELHOCH, S.W.	66	M	TRDSMN	RR	ZZZZ	NY
HANNO	60	F	W	RR	ZZZZ	NY
REBECKA	22	F	D	RR	ZZZZ	NY
ROSCHEFSKA, MOSES	16	M	TRDSMN	RR	ZZZZ	NY
SILBERSOHN, ALTER	19	M	TRDSMN	RR	ZZZZ	NY
GROVZANSKI, MOSES	17	M	TRDSMN	RR	ZZZZ	NY
DISKMA, JUDEL	19	F	TRDSMN	RR	ZZZZ	NY
LIEBMANN, LEISER	20	M	TRDSMN	RR	ZZZZ	NY
ALPERO, CHAIN	33	M	TRDSMN	RR	ZZZZ	NY
BAS, ISRAEL	35	M	TRDSMN	RR	ZZZZ	NY
JUDEL	7	F	CHILD	RR	ZZZZ	NY
KOSINSKI, WOLF	6	M	CHILD	RR	ZZZZ	NY
PEHTOWSKI, SELIG	00	M	TRDSMN	RR	ZZZZ	NY
HEDELOWITZ, H.	48	M	TRDSMN	RR	ZZZZ	NY
FREDENBURG, SHONE	17	M	TRDSMN	RR	ZZZZ	NY
NEUFELD, NACHEVE	7	F	CHILD	RR	ZZZZ	NY
ROSENFELD, MALKE	24	F	WO	RR	ZZZZ	NY
RACHEL	4	F	CHILD	RR	ZZZZ	NY
LIENSKI, CHAIN	20	M	LABR	RR	ZZZZ	NY
DENUETER, AB.	42	M	LABR	RR	ZZZZ	NY
U, BERKOWIC	7	M	CHILD	RR	ZZZZ	NY
HANDELSMANN, LEA	50	F	WO	RR	ZZZZ	NY
GITEL	6	F	CHILD	RR	ZZZZ	NY
TEPLITZKI, MOSES	24	M	TRDSMN	RR	ZZZZ	NY
GEPNER, HIRSCH	19	M	TRDSMN	RR	ZZZZ	NY
BRENDSKI, MORDAHE	19	M	TRDSMN	RR	ZZZZ	NY
POLANSKI, LEISER	16	M	TRDSMN	RR	ZZZZ	NY
BIAGLINOWSKI, NOTE	25	M	TRDSMN	RR	ZZZZ	NY
DIEMONT, ARON	16	M	TRDSMN	RR	ZZZZ	NY
EPNER, CHAIE	25	M	TRDSMN	RR	ZZZZ	NY
MARKOWSKI, JANKEL	25	M	TRDSMN	RR	ZZZZ	NY
GERSCHOWITZ, DROVE	18	M	TRDSMN	RR	ZZZZ	NY
SCHERASCHEWSKI, EISIK	33	M	TRDSMN	RR	ZZZZ	NY
SCHEINE	35	F	W	RR	ZZZZ	NY
MEIER	7	M	CHILD	RR	ZZZZ	NY
GIETE	5	F	CHILD	RR	ZZZZ	NY
ARONSON, PESCHE-LEA	22	F	WO	RR	ZZZZ	NY
CHAIM	4	M	CHILD	RR	ZZZZ	NY
BRECHER, BARUCH	28	F	SGL	RR	ZZZZ	NY
MERRIS, ISAAC	28	M	LABR	RR	ZZZZ	NY
VIERTEL, FRAINS	25	F	WO	RR	ZZZZ	NY
HELENE	17	F	SGL	RR	ZZZZ	NY
KWELLER, GITEL	38	F	WO	RR	ZZZZ	NY
SCHLOWE	7	M	CHILD	RR	ZZZZ	NY
HUDES	6	M	CHILD	RR	ZZZZ	NY
DROWE	5	F	CHILD	RR	ZZZZ	NY
KLEINFUSS, MAX	28	M	LABR	RR	ZZZZ	NY
U, -----L	00	M	LABR	RR	ZZZZ	NY
HIRSCH, ISIDOR	00	M	CH	RR	ZZZZ	NY

SHIP: ODER

FROM: BREMEN
TO: NEW YORK
ARRIVED: 19 JUNE 1884

PASSENGER	AGE	SEX	OCCUPATION	PRV	VIL	DES
RYECHLICKYE, ANTON	40	M	LABR	RR	ZZZZ	USA
FRIES, ZERAFIA	29	F	NN	RR	ZZZZ	USA
GUSTAV	3	M	CHILD	RR	ZZZZ	USA

SHIP: EIDER

FROM: BREMEN AND SOUTHAMPTON
TO: NEW YORK
ARRIVED: 20 JUNE 1884

PASSENGER	AGE	SEX	OCCUPATION	PRV	VIL	DES
VONROSEN, N.	43	M	BRN	RR	ZZZZ	RSS
N.MRS	26	F	W	RR	ZZZZ	RSS
N.MRS	26	F	W	RR	ZZZZ	RSS
JANUSKIEWICZ, JUSTIN	29	M	MCHT	RR	ZZZZ	RSS
SAKOWSKI, AGATHE	22	F	NN	RR	ZZZZ	USA
NEUFELD, PETER	36	M	LABR	RR	ZZZZ	USA
AGATHE	29	F	W	RR	ZZZZ	USA
AGATHE	.10	F	INFANT	RR	ZZZZ	USA
SCHULZ, DAVID	35	M	LABR	RR	ZZZZ	USA
SARAH	35	F	W	RR	ZZZZ	USA
DAVID	4	M	CHILD	RR	ZZZZ	USA
ELISABETH	2	F	CHILD	RR	ZZZZ	USA
ABRAHAM	.06	M	INFANT	RR	ZZZZ	USA
SCHMIDT, CATHARINA	13	F	CH	RR	ZZZZ	USA
HOLZRICHTER, JOHANN	31	M	FARMER	RR	ZZZZ	USA
ANNA	26	F	W	RR	ZZZZ	USA
JOHANNA	4	F	CHILD	RR	ZZZZ	USA
MARIA	3	F	CHILD	RR	ZZZZ	USA
AGATHA	.11	F	INFANT	RR	ZZZZ	USA

SHIP: CITY OF MONTREAL

FROM: LIVERPOOL AND QUEENSTOWN
TO: NEW YORK
ARRIVED: 21 JUNE 1884

PASSENGER	AGE	SEX	OCCUPATION	PRV	VIL	DES
LAWRI, MATH	28	M	LABR	FN	ZZZZ	MI
LEPPANER, MANA	28	F	W	RR	ZZZZ	MI
DAVIDSON, VERRA-C.	4	F	CHILD	RR	ZZZZ	MI
KASKI, LOUIS	25	F	SVNT	RR	ZZZZ	MI
SIERMALA, H.	25	F	SVNT	RR	ZZZZ	MI
GURSEMN, MARIA	20	F	SVNT	RR	ZZZZ	MI
SIERMALA, MARIA	24	F	W	RR	ZZZZ	MI
VALMANSKY, MIKO	32	M	LABR	RR	ZZZZ	NY
STERNA, IGNATZ	49	M	LABR	RR	ZZZZ	NY
WOLFUL, HARHMAN	11	M	CH	RR	ZZZZ	NY
PROKOLSKY, LEIB	14	M	CH	RR	ZZZZ	NY
NORDEAS, EMIL	25	M	LABR	RR	ZZZZ	NY
SCHWARTENBUSH, JOHAN	11	M	CH	RR	ZZZZ	NY

PASSENGER	AGE	SEX	OCCUPATION	PV RIV IL DES
STANBUS, IVAN	23	M	LABR	RRZZZZNY
MODLEWOSKY, WOLF	34	M	LABR	RRZZZZNY
SHIELPA, WILHELM	23	M	LABR	RRZZZZNY
GERTZKI, RUD.	30	M	LABR	RRZZZZNY
KOHLMAN, EMIL	19	M	LABR	RRZZZZNY
JUNK, BEREL	28	M	JWLR	PLZZZZNY
SCHAPIRA, MUCHIN	48	M	LABR	PLZZZZNY
RUBOWITZ, ESTER	17	F	SVNT	PLZZZZNY
PELERSCHINSK, CHAREL	20	M	LABR	PLZZZZNY
SCHAMDE, RENKA	42	F	W	RRZZZZNY
ISITA	11	F	CH	RRZZZZNY
LEIB	10	F	CH	RRZZZZNY
ROSENBERG, SARA	38	F	W	RRZZZZNY
RESSEL	18	F	SVNT	RRZZZZNY
GITEL	11	M	CH	RRZZZZNY
ISAAK	10	M	CH	RRZZZZNY
MOSES	8	M	CHILD	RRZZZZNY
IDA	6	F	CHILD	RRZZZZNY
RAISA	6	F	CHILD	RRZZZZNY
ARGONISKY, JETTE	16	M	LABR	RRZZZZMA
JOHANN	19	M	LABR	RRZZZZMA
MAX	18	M	LABR	RRZZZZMA

SHIP: SPAIN

FROM: LIVERPOOL AND QUEENSTOWN
TO: NEW YORK
ARRIVED: 23 JUNE 1884

PASSENGER	AGE	SEX	OCCUPATION	PV RIV IL DES
MARYAKI, JACOB-P.	30	M	LABR	PLZZZZUSA
MARGUNKA, SUSANAH	29	F	SP	PLZZZZUSA
KATOZ, MOSES	32	M	LABR	PLZZZZUSA
MITTLESBACH, LEWIN	18	M	LABR	PLZZZZUSA
MELZER, ISAK	16	M	LABR	PLZZZZUSA
KALM, JOSEF	23	M	LABR	PLZZZZUSA
WEINIZEINER, F.	34	M	LABR	PLZZZZUSA
SIMON, A.	30	M	LABR	PLZZZZUSA
KENSORICK, N.	19	M	LABR	PLZZZZUSA
KANOWSKY, LEIB	20	M	LABR	PLZZZZUSA
MALKE	19	M	LABR	PLZZZZUSA
PANSON, K.	22	M	LABR	PLZZZZUSA
KATRE	20	F	W	PLZZZZUSA
KLEMFANS, J.	13	M	LABR	PLZZZZUSA
BUDROWSKY, ANIA	20	M	LABR	PLZZZZUSA
SCHERKAVSKY, MAX	16	M	LABR	PLZZZZUSA
ROWSKY, ISRAEL-ITEY	20	M	LABR	PLZZZZUSA
NACTIVBERG, KALEN	45	M	LABR	PLZZZZUSA
SEREISKI, MOSES	20	M	LABR	PLZZZZUSA
RITAWSKY, ARON	17	M	LABR	PLZZZZUSA
GUTHMAN, M.	32	M	LABR	PLZZZZUSA
JELOWITZ, J.	18	M	LABR	PLZZZZUSA
FERISHA, DAVID	18	M	LABR	PLZZZZUSA
GRAMMITZKI, J.	19	M	LABR	PLZZZZUSA
PORVAITZKA, SIMON	20	M	LABR	PLZZZZUSA
GORAN, R.	25	M	LABR	PLZZZZUSA

SHIP: MORAVIA

FROM: HAMBURG
TO: NEW YORK
ARRIVED: 24 JUNE 1884

PASSENGER	AGE	SEX	OCCUPATION	PV RIV IL DES
LUMBIANSKY, MOSES	45	M	DLR	RRZZZZUSA
FRAHIMOWIEZ, ANTONIA	30	F	W	RRZZZZUSA
ANTONIE	3	F	CHILD	RRZZZZUSA
ROSALIE	.11	F	INFANT	RRZZZZUSA
SZARAGOWSKY, LEIB	20	M	LABR	RRZZZZUSA
KOTLER, KARNEL	19	M	DLR	RRZZZZUSA
ESTHER	19	F	W	RRZZZZUSA
RIWKINDT, LEISER	18	M	DLR	RRZZZZUSA
LUTWINEN, ROSA	32	F	W	RRZZZZUSA
ANTON	4	M	CHILD	RRZZZZUSA
KWIETKANTKAS, WINZAS	22	M	LABR	RRZZZZUSA
WISKANTZKAS, JONAS	19	M	LABR	RRZZZZUSA
JONAS	28	M	LABR	RRZZZZUSA
SCHUKWITZ, ADAM	18	M	LABR	RRZZZZUSA
NORUSCHEWITZ, LUDWIG	25	M	LABR	RRZZZZUSA
FRANZISKA	22	F	W	RRZZZZUSA
ANTONINA	.06	F	INFANT	RRZZZZUSA
SOHRAMM, CARL	19	M	LABR	RRZZZZUSA
JABLONSKY, PAUL	39	M	LABR	RRZZZZUSA
GRANEWITZ, MENDEL	27	M	DLR	RRZZZZUSA
HEYMANN, SARA	45	F	W	RRZZZZUSA
HIRSCH	.11	M	INFANT	RRZZZZUSA
KAHN, CHAIE	9	F	CHILD	RRZZZZUSA
FEIGE	8	F	CHILD	RRZZZZUSA
KAPELOWITZ, RACHEL	25	F	W	RRZZZZUSA
BASCHE	.11	F	INFANT	RRZZZZUSA
KOLANTZIK, CASCHE	38	F	SGL	RRZZZZUSA
LEBANOWSKY, SEINE	20	F	SGL	RRZZZZUSA
SMOLINSKY, JOSEPH	24	M	LABR	RRZZZZUSA
KASPEROWITZ, ANNA	22	F	SGL	RRZZZZUSA
DANZIG, BEHR	29	M	LABR	RRZZZZUSA
BERENSTEIN, RACHEL	26	F	W	RRZZZZUSA
LEIB	7	M	CHILD	RRZZZZUSA
NACHMAN	5	M	CHILD	RRZZZZUSA
ARJE	.11	M	INFANT	RRZZZZUSA
ORLOFSKI, ARJE	16	M	LABR	RRZZZZUSA
ANTSCHELOWSKY, MEIER	50	M	LKSH	RRZZZZUSA
GOLDE	48	F	W	RRZZZZUSA
FRUME	16	F	CH	RRZZZZUSA
ZIWIE	8	F	CHILD	RRZZZZUSA
ARONSOHN, ESTHER	24	F	W	RRZZZZUSA
HINDE	3	F	CHILD	RRZZZZUSA
SCHEINE	.11	F	INFANT	RRZZZZUSA
BEILE	.01	F	INFANT	RRZZZZUSA
BARDOWSKI, ISAAC	22	M	LABR	RRZZZZUSA
ANNE	20	F	W	RRZZZZUSA
GENSBERG, SAMUEL	19	M	LABR	RRZZZZUSA
BONOF, ANNA	48	F	W	RRZZZZUSA
MINNA	50	F	W	RRZZZZUSA
SAMUEL	9	M	CHILD	RRZZZZUSA
ZAINEZKOWSKY, CHANNE	35	F	W	RRZZZZUSA
ETTEL	9	F	CHILD	RRZZZZUSA
RACHEL	7	F	CHILD	RRZZZZUSA
JOSCHE	4	F	CHILD	RRZZZZUSA
ISRAEL	9	M	CHILD	RRZZZZUSA
CIRLSTEIN, SAMUEL	46	M	LABR	RRZZZZUSA
RIEMER, MICHEL	15	M	LABR	RRZZZZUSA
GALIN, GOLDE	30	F	W	RRZZZZUSA
KOLINSKY, CHANNE	30	F	W	RRZZZZUSA
CHAJE	9	F	CHILD	RRZZZZUSA
DWORE	8	F	CHILD	RRZZZZUSA
KRECZMER, HEIN.	22	M	LABR	RRZZZZUSA
NOSSINOFF, JOSEF	31	M	MCHT	RRZZZZUSA
SLANDER, ISAAC	40	M	LABR	RRZZZZUSA
RIWKIN, LEIB	8	M	CHILD	RRZZZZUSA
BREINE	7	F	CHILD	RRZZZZUSA
JOCHEL	5	M	CHILD	RRZZZZUSA
CHANNE	.11	F	INFANT	RRZZZZUSA
JUDEL	.01	F	INFANT	RRZZZZUSA
ZWIRN, SOHMUEL	22	M	LABR	RRZZZZUSA
OLIKA, MENASCHE	25	F	SGL	RRZZZZUSA
SCHEINE	20	F	SGL	RRZZZZUSA
RATHAUS, JACOB	21	M	LABR	RRZZZZUSA
BRODE, JOSEF	20	M	LABR	RRZZZZUSA
MEINDEL, ABRAM	18	M	LABR	RRZZZZUSA
SKOWRONSKY, MOSES	60	M	LABR	RRZZZZUSA
NANES, CHAIE	50	M	DLR	RRZZZZUSA
KLOWANSKI, ISAAC	19	M	DLR	RRZZZZUSA

PASSENGER	AGE	SEX	OCCUPATION	PRIVL	DES
PERLAMNN, DAVID	20	M	DLR	RRZZZZ	USA
JUDILOWITZ, SELIG	24	M	DLR	RRZZZZ	USA
SALANT, WOLF	19	M	DLR	RRZZZZ	USA
SCHLUBINSKI, RUWEN	50	M	DLR	RRZZZZ	USA
CHAWE	50	F	W	RRZZZZ	USA
GITL	17	F	CH	RRZZZZ	USA
SLAWE	8	F	CHILD	RRZZZZ	USA
LEA	5	F	CHILD	RRZZZZ	USA
ISAAC	22	M	DLR	RRZZZZ	USA
REISEL	22	F	W	RRZZZZ	USA
CHAIM	.11	F	INFANT	RRZZZZ	USA
MONDSCHEIN, ABRAH.	21	M	LABR	RRZZZZ	USA
KOLETZKY, SARA	18	F	SGL	RRZZZZ	USA
ROSENFELD, JANKEL	21	M	LABR	RRZZZZ	USA
SRIEDENBERG, RACHEL	38	F	W	RRZZZZ	USA
GISCHE	9	F	CHILD	RRZZZZ	USA
JUDES	8	F	CHILD	RRZZZZ	USA
HIRSCH	4	M	CHILD	RRZZZZ	USA
GEISTEROWSKY, BEILE	40	F	W	RRZZZZ	USA
FREIDE	15	F	CH	RRZZZZ	USA
ISAAC	9	M	CHILD	RRZZZZ	USA
JACOB	8	M	CHILD	RRZZZZ	USA
JOHAN	5	M	CHILD	RRZZZZ	USA
GORDON, ETTEL	45	F	W	RRZZZZ	USA
SOMMER, HANNE	17	F	SGL	RRZZZZ	USA
MENDEL	14	F	SGL	RRZZZZ	USA
SCHIMANOWITZ, JOSEPH	19	M	CGRMKR	RRZZZZ	USA
SZIMONITZKY, ZYPE	18	F	SGL	RRZZZZ	USA
KONTZER, HERSCH	17	M	LABR	RRZZZZ	USA
RIWKE	9	F	CHILD	RRZZZZ	USA
DYLGILEWIE, CATH.	37	F	W	RRZZZZ	USA
MARIANE	9	F	CHILD	RRZZZZ	USA
ANNE	7	F	CHILD	RRZZZZ	USA
FRANK	.11	M	INFANT	RRZZZZ	USA
WOLENZUSNA, MARIANE	18	F	SGL	RRZZZZ	USA
PECZOWSKY, RACHEL	21	F	W	RRZZZZ	USA
ZIPE	.11	F	INFANT	RRZZZZ	USA
LASJER, BARUCH	30	M	LABR	RRZZZZ	USA
MEMTROITZ, JOHN	16	M	LABR	RRZZZZ	USA
KAPLAN, GUESCHE	25	F	W	RRZZZZ	USA
RACHEL	3	F	CHILD	RRZZZZ	USA
MOSES	.11	M	INFANT	RRZZZZ	USA
RUBINSTEIN, MERE	46	F	W	RRZZZZ	USA
MEYER	9	M	CHILD	RRZZZZ	USA
ESTHER	8	F	CHILD	RRZZZZ	USA
RUSCHE	4	F	CHILD	RRZZZZ	USA
SALOMON	.11	M	INFANT	RRZZZZ	USA
KLOPSKA, GOLDE	20	F	SGL	RRZZZZ	USA
SLEISCHER, SLATE	30	F	W	RRZZZZ	USA
HINDE	9	F	CHILD	RRZZZZ	USA
SUSEL	8	F	CHILD	RRZZZZ	USA
MANNE	5	F	CHILD	RRZZZZ	USA
SCHLOME	4	M	CHILD	RRZZZZ	USA
SEIDEMANN, WOLF	25	M	TLR	RRZZZZ	USA
HOCHDEINER, DAVID	18	M	LABR	RRZZZZ	USA
HURWITZ, MOSES	19	M	BRM	RRZZZZ	USA
RESNICK, SARA	18	F	SGL	RRZZZZ	USA
MATESUND, JONAS	26	M	LABR	RRZZZZ	USA
ANTONIE	21	F	W	RRZZZZ	USA
MATH.	7	M	CHILD	RRZZZZ	USA
SKOLNICK, MEYER	25	M	TLR	RRZZZZ	USA
PRASINSKI, ABRAH.	27	M	DLR	RRZZZZ	USA
SCHNEIDT, MOSES	32	M	DLR	RRZZZZ	USA
MAKOWSKI, SAM.	19	M	DLR	RRZZZZ	USA
ALSMANN, MOSCHE	15	M	LABR	RRZZZZ	USA
SUHRMANSKI, SORACH	30	M	DLR	RRZZZZ	USA
GELERT, BORECH	19	M	DLR	RRZZZZ	USA
GIEL, BEILA	28	F	W	RRZZZZ	USA
MOSCHONICK, MARCUS	50	M	TLR	RRZZZZ	USA
PAULINE	50	F	W	RRZZZZ	USA
ROBERT	7	M	CHILD	RRZZZZ	USA
KAMINOWSKI, HIRSCH	22	M	LABR	RRZZZZ	USA
GRUNBERG, NOCHUM	20	M	LABR	RRZZZZ	USA
LAPIDES, LUDWIG	17	M	LABR	RRZZZZ	USA
BEREK	16	M	LABR	RRZZZZ	USA
JOFFE, MERE	30	F	W	RRZZZZ	USA
ELKE	6	F	CHILD	RRZZZZ	USA
FEIGE	.11	F	INFANT	RRZZZZ	USA
SOSLAWSKI, MOSES	30	F	W	RRZZZZ	USA
MARIASCHE	.11	F	INFANT	RRZZZZ	USA
PALEG, SARA	20	F	SGL	RRZZZZ	USA
RACHEL	18	F	W	RRZZZZ	USA
REISEL	.11	F	INFANT	RRZZZZ	USA
FEINBERG, ISRAEL	20	M	LABR	RRZZZZ	USA
RISCHE	17	F	SGL	RRZZZZ	USA
ZLOTOJALECKI, SALOMON	20	M	LABR	RRZZZZ	USA
POTLEY, ISAAC	35	M	LABR	RRZZZZ	USA
GESCHE	25	F	W	RRZZZZ	USA
RIWKIN, MICHEL	60	M	LABR	RRZZZZ	USA
ETHE	45	F	W	RRZZZZ	USA
SCHEINE	18	F	CH	RRZZZZ	USA
RACHEL	9	F	CHILD	RRZZZZ	USA
CHERUETZKY, FRANK	13	M	LABR	RRZZZZ	USA
PAULINE	30	F	W	RRZZZZ	USA
JOSEPH	.11	M	INFANT	RRZZZZ	USA
SIMONOVICZ, ANOFRI	18	M	LABR	RRZZZZ	USA
WAITUKAITIS, JOHANN	18	M	LABR	RRZZZZ	USA
MATERIONLAITIS, JOSEF	29	M	LABR	RRZZZZ	USA
CATH.	29	F	W	RRZZZZ	USA
JOSEF	.02	M	INFANT	RRZZZZ	USA
SONKAYTYS, ALEXANDER	18	M	LABR	RRZZZZ	USA
STACHOWSKA, VERONIKA	17	F	SGL	RRZZZZ	USA
HELLSIN, CHONE	55	M	LABR	RRZZZZ	USA
HIRSCH	27	M	LABR	RRZZZZ	USA
KAPPEL, RIWE	19	M	LABR	RRZZZZ	USA
JOHANOWSKI, NESONEL	47	M	DLR	RRZZZZ	USA
PIWOWARSKI, ZIREL	9	M	CHILD	RRZZZZ	USA
CHASKEL	8	M	CHILD	RRZZZZ	USA
ISAAC	6	M	CHILD	RRZZZZ	USA
GRUN, SIMON	19	M	DLR	RRZZZZ	USA
REGINA	20	F	W	RRZZZZ	USA
STRAUSS, FELIX	18	M	BKBNDR	RRZZZZ	USA
BALDINGER, HERRM.	26	M	BKR	RRZZZZ	USA
KLEINFUSS, MAX	28	M	TLR	RRZZZZ	USA
ULFSKY, MOSES	32	M	TLR	RRZZZZ	USA
ARONOWITZ, ZALKE	19	F	UNKNOWN	RRZZZZ	USA
VISTEL, EFRAIM	25	M	LABR	RRZZZZ	USA
HELENE	17	F	W	RRZZZZ	USA
KWELLER, GITTEL	38	F	W	RRZZZZ	USA
HUDES	9	F	CHILD	RRZZZZ	USA
SCHLOME	8	F	CHILD	RRZZZZ	USA
DWORE	7	F	CHILD	RRZZZZ	USA
KIRSCH, ISIDOR	9	M	CHILD	RRZZZZ	USA
ESTERSOHN, EFRAIM	18	M	LABR	RRZZZZ	USA
KAPLANSKI, RUWEN	50	M	DLR	RRZZZZ	USA
LASCHER, SEMEL	20	M	DLR	RRZZZZ	USA
DOLGONOWSKY, GOLDE	20	F	SGL	RRZZZZ	USA
BEHR	.11	M	INFANT	RRZZZZ	USA
STERKOWSKI, SCHEWACH	25	M	LABR	RRZZZZ	USA
SARA	23	F	W	RRZZZZ	USA
LEA	.11	F	INFANT	RRZZZZ	USA
LEWTON, WOLF	35	M	LABR	RRZZZZ	USA
STAKEITIS, JOSEF	27	M	LABR	RRZZZZ	USA
CATH.	28	F	W	RRZZZZ	USA
MIKOS	.11	M	INFANT	RRZZZZ	USA
CONSTANTIN	.01	M	INFANT	RRZZZZ	USA
PASNOKITZ, MICHAL	35	M	LABR	RRZZZZ	USA
PIENTKOWSKY, JANKEL	35	M	LABR	RRZZZZ	USA
ZAREMBOWITZ, LIEBE	24	F	W	RRZZZZ	USA
SIWI	.11	F	INFANT	RRZZZZ	USA
HERSKOWITZ, JACOB	17	M	LABR	RRZZZZ	USA
SLEINDORF, MENDEL	18	M	LABR	RRZZZZ	USA
PODLASKY, MOSES	18	M	DLR	RRZZZZ	USA
WACHHOLDER, MOSES	17	M	DLR	RRZZZZ	USA
BLEICHMAN, ABRAH.	25	M	LABR	RRZZZZ	USA
BINE	30	F	W	RRZZZZ	USA
REICH, FRIED	45	M	FARMER	RRZZZZ	USA
HENRIETTE	45	F	W	RRZZZZ	USA
SELMA	14	F	D	RRZZZZ	USA
GLIFF, JOHANN	22	M	LABR	RRZZZZ	USA

PASSENGER	AGE	SEX	OCCUPATION	PRV VIL DES
HERSTEIN, LEIB	30	M	DLR	RRZZZZUSA
SIKOWSKI, SUSSEL	18	M	DLR	RRZZZZUSA
BRAWMANN, ISAAC	17	M	TLR	RRZZZZUSA
SCHEER, RUBIN	35	M	LABR	RRZZZZUSA
HOLSTEIN, MOSES	20	M	LABR	RRZZZZUSA
BELFER, CHAIM	54	M	LABR	RRZZZZUSA
RAHEL	54	F	W	RRZZZZUSA
CHAIE	25	F	CH	RRZZZZUSA
SCHOLEM	20	M	CH	RRZZZZUSA
MOSES	9	M	CHILD	RRZZZZUSA
SCHOLEM	.11	M	INFANT	RRZZZZUSA
BLAUSTEIN, ARON	20	M	LABR	RRZZZZUSA
GRAPENGETER, LUDWIG	46	M	LABR	RRZZZZUSA
GUTOWSKI, ANTON	30	M	LABR	RRZZZZUSA
MURSTEIN, ARON	18	M	LABR	RRZZZZUSA
KABAKER, HIRSCH	15	M	LABR	RRZZZZUSA
DANZIG, HINDE	24	F	SGL	RRZZZZUSA
SIEGEL, JACOB	48	M	LABR	RRZZZZUSA
MALTZ, JOSEPH	28	M	LABR	RRZZZZUSA
HERSTEIN, JANKEL	46	M	LABR	RRZZZZUSA
PINKELSTEIN, CHAIM	28	M	LABR	RRZZZZUSA
BRUDER, SALOMON	20	M	LABR	RRZZZZUSA
NIEDERMANN, MEYER	43	M	LABR	RRZZZZUSA
FRIED, MENDEL	27	M	LABR	RRZZZZUSA
ISAKOWITZ, ISAAC	19	M	LABR	RRZZZZUSA
KOLINSKY, MOSES	8	M	CHILD	RRZZZZUSA
PASSMANN, RIEWE	20	F	W	RRZZZZUSA
JUDEL	.11	F	INFANT	RRZZZZUSA
GORDON, SARA	27	F	W	RRZZZZUSA
AMALIE	13	F	CH	RRZZZZUSA
ROSA	5	F	CHILD	RRZZZZUSA
SALOMON	.11	M	INFANT	RRZZZZUSA
IDA	.01	F	INFANT	RRZZZZUSA
ANDERSON, JOH.W.	18	M	LABR	FNZZZZUSA
CARLSON, MAX	17	M	LABR	FNZZZZUSA
ED.	16	M	LABR	FNZZZZUSA
DANELOWITSCH, HINDA	18	F	SGL	RRZZZZUSA
LEBOCHKE, MORDCHE	34	M	TLR	RRZZZZUSA
WEISS, HUDES	18	F	SGL	RRZZZZUSA
KOMINOROSTEI, CHINE	23	F	SGL	RRZZZZUSA
AXELROD, CHEINE	17	M	LABR	RRZZZZUSA
LINDENTHAL, MARCUS	29	M	LABR	RRZZZZUSA
SLEISCHMANN, ISAAC	24	M	LABR	RRZZZZUSA
SINK, MOSES	32	M	LABR	RRZZZZUSA
ISAACSOHN, JACOB	19	M	LABR	RRZZZZUSA
PRACHERKRUG, JOH.	27	M	LABR	RRZZZZUSA
ROSENSOHN, CHAIM	29	M	LABR	RRZZZZUSA
KABATSCHNIK, JUDEL	21	M	LABR	RRZZZZUSA
SCHEINE	20	F	W	RRZZZZUSA
KRINTZMANN, JECHSEL	35	M	LABR	RRZZZZUSA
NOFOR, SCHEINE	19	F	SGL	RRZZZZUSA
ZIDRANSKI, ALB.	21	M	LABR	RRZZZZUSA
SCHMIT, ISRAEL	16	M	LABR	RRZZZZUSA
SELDMANN, CHASKEL	40	M	LABR	RRZZZZUSA
BLEICHMAN, HIRSCH	.03	M	INFANT	RRZZZZUSA
LEIB	21	M	LABR	RRZZZZUSA
DREI, SUSSMAN	33	M	LABR	RRZZZZUSA
FOW, SCHEIME	18	F	SGL	RRZZZZUSA
BER	17	M	LABR	RRZZZZUSA
SATENSTEIN, ISRAEL	15	M	LABR	RRZZZZUSA
KOHN, MOSES	17	M	LABR	RRZZZZUSA
RACHEL	17	F	SGL	RRZZZZUSA
ROSENZWEIG, JACOB	24	M	LABR	RRZZZZUSA
SCHUR, CHEIME	40	M	LABR	RRZZZZUSA
BLOCH, RAPHSEL	19	M	LABR	RRZZZZUSA
SEINSEUG, MENDEL	40	M	LABR	RRZZZZUSA
REICH, BARUCH	19	M	LABR	RRZZZZUSA
LEMPINCKI, ABRAH.	46	M	LABR	RRZZZZUSA
CHAIM	25	F	W	RRZZZZUSA
JACOB	9	M	CHILD	RRZZZZUSA
BEER, ISRAEL	33	M	LABR	RRZZZZUSA
WEINDOW, ROSA	16	F	W	RRZZZZUSA
RACHEL	.11	F	INFANT	RRZZZZUSA
LENE	4	F	CHILD	RRZZZZUSA
BRICH, DOBRE	17	M	LABR	RRZZZZUSA
LEINBIK, HIRSCH	16	M	LABR	RRZZZZUSA
HAUSMAN, EMANUEL	17	M	LABR	RRZZZZUSA
LORSCHINSKY, ROSA	50	F	W	RRZZZZUSA
KOPINSKY, SALOMON	40	M	LABR	RRZZZZUSA
ABRAM	8	M	CHILD	RRZZZZUSA
SARA	.11	F	INFANT	RRZZZZUSA
REIZE	9	F	CHILD	RRZZZZUSA
MOSES	5	M	CHILD	RRZZZZUSA
AWIDAM, SALMAN	19	M	LABR	RRZZZZUSA
ROSENBAUM, CHEIE	17	M	LABR	RRZZZZUSA
NAWENITZKI, REIWEL	21	M	LABR	RRZZZZUSA
SCHALMANN, JOSEL	20	M	LABR	RRZZZZUSA
GUSTMAN, EFRAIM	50	M	LABR	RRZZZZUSA
SCLIGMANN, ABRAH.	20	M	LABR	RRZZZZUSA

SHIP: LABRADOR

FROM: HAVRE
TO: NEW YORK
ARRIVED: 25 JUNE 1884

PASSENGER	AGE	SEX	OCCUPATION	PRV VIL DES
SPEKTER, JOSEPH	24	M	LKSH	RRZZZZNY
MURTZ, MOISE	27	M	SMH	RRZZZZNY
BABIETKY, LUDOMIR	27	M	SDLR	RRZZZZNY
HURWITZ, NATHAN	22	M	WCHMKR	RRZZZZNY
EISEMBERG, JONNAS	22	M	ATSN	RRZZZZNY

SHIP: HOLLAND

FROM: LONDON
TO: NEW YORK
ARRIVED: 26 JUNE 1884

PASSENGER	AGE	SEX	OCCUPATION	PRV VIL DES
FILEYSIGE, JHN.	20	M	MUSN	PLZZZZNY
EPTLIEY, JOS.	20	M	MUSN	PLZZZZNY
STAMLARDS, JAC.	20	M	MUSN	PLZZZZNY
LERRANTADING, FRANK	22	M	MUSN	PLZZZZNY

SHIP: HAMMONIA

FROM: HAMBURG AND HAVRE
TO: NEW YORK
ARRIVED: 27 JUNE 1884

PASSENGER	AGE	SEX	OCCUPATION	PRV VIL DES
ALLAND, FELIX	20	M	BBR	RRZZZZUSA
SIMON	18	M	TLR	RRZZZZUSA
RINALDO, MOSES	20	M	UNKNOWN	RRZZZZUSA
SAFIER, ZALLEL	40	M	LABR	RRZZZZUSA
CHAIE	8	M	CHILD	RRZZZZUSA
TONKONOGY, RACHEL	17	F	SGL	RRZZZZUSA
BEILE	14	F	SGL	RRZZZZUSA
ABRAHAM	9	M	CHILD	RRZZZZUSA
SCHIDOWSKY, CHAIE	22	F	W	RRZZZZUSA
ELIAS	.11	M	INFANT	RRZZZZUSA
POWIATOWSKY, LEIB	27	M	DLR	RRZZZZUSA
LEWIN, SCHLOME	33	M	DLR	RRZZZZUSA
FIUSCHNITZKI, MORDCHE	35	M	DLR	RRZZZZUSA
HOCHMANN, MOSES	9	M	CHILD	RRZZZZUSA
RAHEL	7	F	CHILD	RRZZZZUSA
FISCHEL, SCH---	40	M	LABR	RRZZZZUSA

PASSENGER	AGE	SEX	OCCUPATION	PRIVL	DES
KEGEL, JOSEPH	28	M	LABR	RRZZZZ	USA
RUBINOWITZ, MENDEL	19	M	LABR	RRZZZZ	USA
KRIKLANSKY, LIEBE	9	M	CHILD	RRZZZZ	USA
KWECZZINSKI, MORDCHE	28	M	DLR	RRZZZZ	USA
KIMSAL, MARIE	21	F	SGL	RRZZZZ	USA
AMBROSAVICH, ALZBETA	23	F	SGL	RRZZZZ	USA
STABIANSKI, ANNA	23	F	SGL	RRZZZZ	USA
KOWALEWSKI, STEFAN	22	M	LABR	RRZZZZ	USA
KETSCHEFSKI, SCHMUL	28	M	LABR	RRZZZZ	USA
JUDWERSKI, ZALLEL	18	M	CL	RRZZZZ	USA
KOHN, SCHEPSEL	25	M	HAMF	RRZZZZ	USA
DANSKE, MOSES	18	M	LABR	RRZZZZ	USA
UDWIN, MORDCHE	33	M	LABR	RRZZZZ	USA
LIEBE	9	M	CHILD	RRZZZZ	USA
NOWICK, BEHR.	23	M	LABR	RRZZZZ	USA
ELIAS	9	M	CHILD	RRZZZZ	USA
PALSER, ETTEL	27	F	W	RRZZZZ	USA
TAUBE	6	F	CHILD	RRZZZZ	USA
MICHALITZKY, BENJAMIN	25	M	TLR	RRZZZZ	USA
SCHIDORSKY, CHASKEL	47	M	LABR	RRZZZZ	USA
FUHRMANN, MEZER	20	M	CL	RRZZZZ	USA
JORSANSKY, MEZER	16	M	DLR	RRZZZZ	USA
SUBERSKI, HILLEL	15	M	CL	RRZZZZ	USA
ROSENGARTEN, NATHAN	51	M	WDMCHT	RRZZZZ	USA
BENJ.	18	M	S	RRZZZZ	USA
SCHALMANN, FREIDEL	25	F	W	RRZZZZ	USA
SORGE	4	F	CHILD	RRZZZZ	USA
JELIN, JERENZE	21	M	LABR	RRZZZZ	USA
HAIKOWSKY, MOSES	38	M	LABR	RRZZZZ	USA
MORETZKY, MARIUS	40	M	LABR	RRZZZZ	USA
SAZILLER, SALOMON	18	M	DLR	RRZZZZ	USA
KOSAKEWITZ, ETTEL	18	F	SGL	RRZZZZ	USA
CHANOWITZ, FISCHEL	48	M	TLR	RRZZZZ	USA
JELLIN, NOTE	18	M	TLR	RRZZZZ	USA
JANUSCHEWITZ, SOPHIE	20	F	SGL	RRZZZZ	USA
NAIDA, KASIMIR	27	M	LABR	RRZZZZ	USA
MARIE	30	F	W	RRZZZZ	USA
HELENE	.11	F	INFANT	RRZZZZ	USA
RZEPA, SALOMON	22	M	LABR	RRZZZZ	USA
KUCZINSKI, ABRAHAM	22	M	TLR	RRZZZZ	USA
SCHIFF, ISRAEL	18	M	TLR	RRZZZZ	USA
ARKIN, SIGMEMD	33	M	TLR	RRZZZZ	USA
FRIEDBERG, NATHAN	20	M	SHMK	RRZZZZ	USA
NAEVEN, BERTHA	30	F	W	RRZZZZ	USA
BERNSTEIN, ISRAEL	21	M	TLR	RRZZZZ	USA
JELOZAWSKY, ABRAHAM	19	M	TLR	RRZZZZ	USA
KATZ, FEIGE	17	F	SGL	RRZZZZ	USA
HOCHMANN, ISAAC	40	M	LABR	RRZZZZ	USA
RAHEL	35	F	W	RRZZZZ	USA
LEIB	.11	M	INFANT	RRZZZZ	USA
BERNSTEIN, ISRAEL	20	M	BKR	RRZZZZ	USA
PIETROWSKI, JOSEPH	18	M	LABR	RRZZZZ	USA
ROSENBERG, SCHEINE	25	F	SGL	RRZZZZ	USA
KUTTNER, MORDCHE	65	M	LABR	RRZZZZ	USA
KOSBORSKY, ELLE	25	F	W	RRZZZZ	USA
JACOB	.11	M	INFANT	RRZZZZ	USA
EISICK	.01	M	INFANT	RRZZZZ	USA
KAPILOW, CHAIE	25	F	W	RRZZZZ	USA
IDA	.11	F	INFANT	RRZZZZ	USA
ROPAIKA, ROSA	40	F	W	RRZZZZ	USA
EVA	8	F	CHILD	RRZZZZ	USA
VINCENZ	.11	M	INFANT	RRZZZZ	USA
FABELMANN, SELDE	18	F	SGL	RRZZZZ	USA
LUXENBURG, LEA	20	F	SGL	RRZZZZ	USA
SIREITZKY, ITTE	20	F	SGL	RRZZZZ	USA
GOLDBERG, TAUBE	38	F	W	RRZZZZ	USA
MALKE	18	F	CH	RRZZZZ	USA
ROSA	14	F	CH	RRZZZZ	USA
GERTRUDE	9	F	CHILD	RRZZZZ	USA
JOACHIM	8	M	CHILD	RRZZZZ	USA
SOPHIE	7	F	CHILD	RRZZZZ	USA
BEILE	6	F	CHILD	RRZZZZ	USA
FREIDE	5	F	CHILD	RRZZZZ	USA
CHARLOTTE	4	F	CHILD	RRZZZZ	USA
JULIE	.06	F	INFANT	RRZZZZ	USA

PASSENGER	AGE	SEX	OCCUPATION	PRIVL	DES
MARIE	.06	F	INFANT	RRZZZZ	USA
REINHERZ, HIRSCH	17	M	LABR	RRZZZZ	USA
SISKIND, JOACHIM	20	M	LABR	RRZZZZ	USA
ARINSTANN, CHANNE	17	F	SGL	RRZZZZ	USA
WASJERDAN, DORA	19	F	SGL	RRZZZZ	USA
KAILE, CHAIM	34	M	BCHR	RRZZZZ	USA
DLUGI, MOSES	36	M	LABR	RRZZZZ	USA
JUESOWSKY, WOLF	26	M	DLR	RRZZZZ	USA
PREUSF, HEINR.	30	M	DLR	RRZZZZ	USA
CHEI	25	F	SGL	RRZZZZ	USA
EPSTEIN, JACOB	40	M	LABR	RRZZZZ	USA
MARCUS	9	M	CHILD	RRZZZZ	USA
HODES, SCHOLEM	22	M	LABR	RRZZZZ	USA
BLOCH, NACHUM	20	M	CL	RRZZZZ	USA
KABACKER, CHATZKEL	19	M	LABR	RRZZZZ	USA
HRINSKY, ISRAEL	19	M	LABR	RRZZZZ	USA
SIDER, ABRAM	20	M	LABR	RRZZZZ	USA
CHASENOVITZ, LEIBEL	29	M	LABR	RRZZZZ	USA
LIFSCHITZ, DAVID	19	M	LABR	RRZZZZ	USA
AUDENITZKI, MOSES	20	M	LABR	RRZZZZ	USA
MAUED, SALOMON	19	M	LABR	RRZZZZ	USA
KARAFIOL, SCHOLEM	19	M	LABR	RRZZZZ	USA
SIEBART, JOSSEL	19	M	LABR	RRZZZZ	USA
SITVIN, JACOB	33	M	LABR	RRZZZZ	USA
ROSENBLUM, CHAIE	18	F	SGL	RRZZZZ	USA
FRANK, SOPHIE	20	F	SGL	RRZZZZ	USA
ROSEN, SAMUEL	9	M	CHILD	RRZZZZ	USA
ZITLANCK, BEER	60	M	LABR	RRZZZZ	USA
STEVE	55	F	W	RRZZZZ	USA
ESTHER	19	F	D	RRZZZZ	USA
WEINSTEIN, ISAAC	18	M	LABR	RRZZZZ	USA
ARMBON, TAUBE	23	F	W	RRZZZZ	USA
CHAIM	.09	F	INFANT	RRZZZZ	USA
HUTSCHINSKY, CHANNE	20	F	SGL	RRZZZZ	USA
PLOSKY, PINCUS	20	M	TLR	RRZZZZ	USA
PERLMANN, BEILE	21	F	SGL	RRZZZZ	USA
LINEWITZ, SCHLAME	42	M	LABR	RRZZZZ	USA
HELLMANN, FREIDE	15	F	SGL	RRZZZZ	USA
JOSSEL	9	M	CHILD	RRZZZZ	USA
ALBRECHT, AUGE.	20	F	SGL	RRZZZZ	USA
HABERMAS, EMILIE	18	F	SGL	RRZZZZ	USA
HEINRICH, EMILIE	19	F	SGL	RRZZZZ	USA
SCHOEPSEL, FRANK	20	M	LABR	RRZZZZ	USA
KRZZMICKI, STANISLAUS	48	M	LABR	RRZZZZ	USA
OLSZEWSKI, STANISLAUS	25	M	LABR	RRZZZZ	USA
RUBAT, MARTIN	22	M	LABR	RRZZZZ	USA
BEUERT, AUGUST	23	M	LABR	RRZZZZ	USA
GARFUNKEL, HEINR.	33	M	LABR	RRZZZZ	USA
WACHS, MEZER	31	M	LABR	RRZZZZ	USA
GEGLINISCHWESKI, FEIWEL	26	M	LABR	RRZZZZ	USA
LAKOJTS, JAN	37	M	LABR	RRZZZZ	USA
JESEITES, JOSEPH	21	M	LABR	RRZZZZ	USA
KITKUNAS, MATHS.	24	M	LABR	RRZZZZ	USA
GRYNIEWICZ, JOSEPH	21	M	LABR	RRZZZZ	USA
SKOP, MORDCHE	33	M	LABR	RRZZZZ	USA
NEUMANN, MARIE	30	F	W	RRZZZZ	USA
STEPHAN	9	M	CHILD	RRZZZZ	USA
JURKA	8	M	CHILD	RRZZZZ	USA
WLADIMIR	.11	M	INFANT	RRZZZZ	USA
LUDWIG	.01	M	INFANT	RRZZZZ	USA
ZSANI	15	F	SGL	RRZZZZ	USA
MARIE	9	F	CHILD	RRZZZZ	USA
STABIANSKA, ALEXDR.	19	M	LABR	RRZZZZ	USA
WOLPE, SARA	19	F	W	RRZZZZ	USA
DANIEN, ISAAC	26	M	LABR	RRZZZZ	USA
SCHWANDTNER, AUGST.	22	M	LABR	RRZZZZ	USA
ZUNK, CARL	18	M	LABR	RRZZZZ	USA
KAPLAN, ITZIG	31	M	LABR	RRZZZZ	USA
JAFFNER, DAVID	22	M	LABR	RRZZZZ	USA
BLOCHSTEIN, SUESSKIND	22	M	TLR	RRZZZZ	USA
HEKER, SCHMUL	19	M	LABR	RRZZZZ	USA
SCHOEVER, SALMEN	20	M	LABR	RRZZZZ	USA
ALTMANN, DAVID	21	M	LABR	RRZZZZ	USA
CHANNE	19	F	SGL	RRZZZZ	USA
MEKLER, GOLDE	26	F	W	RRZZZZ	USA

PASSENGER	AGE	SEX	OCCUPATION	PRIV	VIL	DES
CHAIE	.11	M	INFANT	RR	ZZZZ	USA
SABLODONSKI, CHAIM	25	M	DLR	RR	ZZZZ	USA
PREUSS, CHAIM	.09	M	INFANT	RR	ZZZZ	USA
TEFFER, SCHMUEL	28	M	LABR	RR	ZZZZ	USA
RACHEL	8	F	CHILD	RR	ZZZZ	USA
KLOTZ, MIRIAM	19	F	W	RR	ZZZZ	USA
SCHIDOWSKY, TERESA	.01	F	INFANT	RR	ZZZZ	USA
WALPE, ANNA	.09	F	INFANT	RR	ZZZZ	USA
CZEREN, ISRAEL	33	M	TLR	RR	ZZZZ	USA
FABERNECK, MORRIS	30	M	SHMK	RR	ZZZZ	USA
DORA	27	F	W	RR	ZZZZ	USA
RAHEL	4	F	CHILD	RR	ZZZZ	USA
SARAH	3	F	CHILD	RR	ZZZZ	USA
HANNAH	.11	F	INFANT	RR	ZZZZ	USA
SERERZ, ISAAC	20	M	TLR	RR	ZZZZ	USA
REBECCA	20	F	W	RR	ZZZZ	USA
COHN, FRIDA	20	F	SGL	RR	ZZZZ	USA
LOUISE	19	F	SGL	RR	ZZZZ	USA
FORNINA, OLGA	20	F	SGL	RR	ZZZZ	USA
HORNBORG, NADESCHDA	40	F	W	FN	ZZZZ	USA
HANNE	17	F	CH	FN	ZZZZ	USA
ANNA	15	F	CH	FN	ZZZZ	USA
JARELT	14	M	CH	FN	ZZZZ	USA
ELSA	9	F	CHILD	FN	ZZZZ	USA
IWANOW, NICOLAI	19	M	OFF	RR	ZZZZ	USA

SHIP: STATE OF INDIANA

FROM: GLASGOW AND LARNE
TO: NEW YORK
ARRIVED: 27 JUNE 1884

PASSENGER	AGE	SEX	OCCUPATION	PRIV	VIL	DES
LEWINGER, IGNAT	25	M	PDLR	PL	ZZZZ	USA
AMALIE	18	F	W	PL	ZZZZ	USA
FRIED, PINCUS	34	M	PDLR	PL	ZZZZ	USA
SAMUEL	10	M	CH	PL	ZZZZ	USA
KOLB, ONAS	19	M	PDLR	PL	ZZZZ	USA
HEFLER, ADOLF	20	M	PDLR	PL	ZZZZ	USA
KATZ, ITZIG	55	M	PDLR	PL	ZZZZ	USA
LEWIN, MENDEL	32	M	PDLR	PL	ZZZZ	USA
BAUM, JOHANN	27	M	PDLR	PL	ZZZZ	USA
LINER, SAMUEL	24	M	PDLR	PL	ZZZZ	USA
BARSCHATZKY, MOSON	18	M	PDLR	PL	ZZZZ	USA
SILBERMANN, ADOLPH	30	M	PDLR	PL	ZZZZ	USA
BERTHA	24	F	W	PL	ZZZZ	USA
MAX	5	M	CHILD	PL	ZZZZ	USA
ATTMANN, ISIDOR	20	M	PDLR	PL	ZZZZ	USA
BLOCK, MANDEL	39	M	PDLR	PL	ZZZZ	USA
OSIAS	17	M	PDLR	PL	ZZZZ	USA
KAZEW, SCHLOME	18	M	PDLR	PL	ZZZZ	USA
KABAN, ISRAEL	29	M	PDLR	PL	ZZZZ	USA
FINGERHUT, ISRAEL	24	M	PDLR	PL	ZZZZ	USA
BERTHA	20	F	W	PL	ZZZZ	USA
BLISNAK, MARIA	48	F	W	PL	ZZZZ	USA
SARAH	18	F	SP	PL	ZZZZ	USA
ELTE	00	F	INF	PL	ZZZZ	USA
WIENER, CAZILIE	21	F	SP	PL	ZZZZ	USA

SHIP: ANCHORIA

FROM: GLASGOW
TO: NEW YORK
ARRIVED: 28 JUNE 1884

PASSENGER	AGE	SEX	OCCUPATION	PRIV	VIL	DES
BENDELOWITZ, ARON	32	M	TLR	RR	ZZZZ	USA
GRUNBERG, WOLFF	21	M	LABR	RR	ZZZZ	USA
MATLIN, SOLOMON	54	M	CGRMKR	RR	ZZZZ	USA
SCHUJEWEITZ, ARON	26	M	LABR	RR	ZZZZ	USA
SCHUFSENSKA, ABRAHAM	19	M	LABR	RR	ZZZZ	USA
SYDRANSKI, HIRSCH	20	M	LABR	RR	ZZZZ	USA

SHIP: EGYPT

FROM: LIVERPOOL
TO: NEW YORK
ARRIVED: 28 JUNE 1884

PASSENGER	AGE	SEX	OCCUPATION	PRIV	VIL	DES
PERIS, ROBERT	50	M	LABR	PL	ZZZZ	USA
KELLWIAN, BARDZ	18	M	LABR	PL	ZZZZ	USA
JUNSOLA, JOHAN	26	M	LABR	FN	ZZZZ	USA
AJAIN, JOHAN	44	M	LABR	FN	ZZZZ	USA
GREVER, ALEX	20	M	LABR	FN	ZZZZ	USA
KANGAS, AN.	30	M	LABR	FN	ZZZZ	USA
HANONEN, EMILIA	33	F	W	FN	ZZZZ	USA
IDA	4	F	CHILD	FN	ZZZZ	USA
ISAK	2	M	CHILD	FN	ZZZZ	USA
HILDA	.07	F	INFANT	FN	ZZZZ	USA
ANNA	23	F	SP	FN	ZZZZ	USA
CLANSEN, ANDREAS	34	M	LABR	FN	ZZZZ	USA
FERNSTINA, MARY	6	F	CHILD	FN	ZZZZ	USA
SCHULZ, LOUIS	42	M	LABR	FN	ZZZZ	USA
OTTO	00	M	INF	FN	ZZZZ	USA
OLSON, HALVOR	27	M	LABR	FN	ZZZZ	USA
HAAKENSON, SIERIA	27	M	LABR	FN	ZZZZ	USA
JOHANN	4	M	CHILD	FN	ZZZZ	USA
ANNE	3	F	CHILD	FN	ZZZZ	USA
CHAIE	00	F	INF	FN	ZZZZ	USA
HALSH, ERIK	32	M	LABR	PL	ZZZZ	USA
MARIA	32	F	W	PL	ZZZZ	USA
JENNY	4	F	CHILD	PL	ZZZZ	USA
JOHAN	3	M	CHILD	PL	ZZZZ	USA
LINA	00	F	INF	PL	ZZZZ	USA
PERATOLNA, MARIA	22	F	SP	PL	ZZZZ	USA
OSTERBERG, HERMAN	19	M	LABR	PL	ZZZZ	USA
THORS, AUGUST	21	M	LABR	PL	ZZZZ	USA
FAETI, AJUKA	19	M	LABR	PL	ZZZZ	USA
NYHOLN, HENRIK	27	M	LABR	PL	ZZZZ	USA
KWIKANJAS, JOHAN	25	M	LABR	PL	ZZZZ	USA
ALLAGENAS, H.	35	M	LABR	PL	ZZZZ	USA
CHINSLINTIZKY, MOSES	19	M	LABR	PL	ZZZZ	USA
BALSEHER, JAUBE	23	M	LABR	PL	ZZZZ	USA
ISAKOWITZ, HIRSCH	30	M	LABR	PL	ZZZZ	USA
ABRAHAM	11	M	CH	PL	ZZZZ	USA
JANKEL, MARCUS	18	M	LABR	PL	ZZZZ	USA
SCHEER, WOLF	43	M	LABR	PL	ZZZZ	USA
PILL, HILLEL	17	M	LABR	PL	ZZZZ	USA
REUTENSKIN, JAKOB	25	M	LABR	PL	ZZZZ	USA
REISNER, BERL	11	M	CH	PL	ZZZZ	USA
KAJULINK, JOSEL	23	M	LABR	PL	ZZZZ	USA
WALNUATITZKI, JOSES	21	M	LABR	PL	ZZZZ	USA
KAZINSKI, MICHEL	19	M	LABR	PL	ZZZZ	USA
SALOWSKI, ELIAS	19	M	LABR	PL	ZZZZ	USA
CHAIE	20	M	LABR	PL	ZZZZ	USA
ELIASSOHN, CHANE	32	M	LABR	PL	ZZZZ	USA
FEDOREWSKY, JOHAN	30	M	LABR	PL	ZZZZ	USA
KLEWINSKY, HANNE	20	F	SP	PL	ZZZZ	USA
RUDOWSKY, MOSES	42	M	LABR	PL	ZZZZ	USA

PASSENGER	AGE	SEX	OCCUPATION	PRIVL	DES
RIFKE	36	F	W	PLZZZZ	USA
BOSCHE	8	M	CHILD	PLZZZZ	USA
SCHULEWITZ, CHAIM	45	M	LABR	PLZZZZ	USA
GOLDE	43	F	W	PLZZZZ	USA
MIBREL	16	F	SP	PLZZZZ	USA
ISRAEL	9	M	CHILD	PLZZZZ	USA
SARAH	6	F	CHILD	PLZZZZ	USA
JOSEF	5	M	CHILD	PLZZZZ	USA
ELKANA	00	M	INF	PLZZZZ	USA
STIEGLITZ, NAHTHAN	20	M	LABR	PLZZZZ	USA
MARGULIS, WOLF	37	M	LABR	PLZZZZ	USA
MARMANT, SIMON	24	M	LABR	PLZZZZ	USA
FEFERBLUM, S.	27	M	LABR	PLZZZZ	USA
SCHEGEL	26	M	LABR	PLZZZZ	USA
MORASKO, JAN	33	M	LABR	PLZZZZ	USA
LAURENATAS, JOSES	22	M	LABR	PLZZZZ	USA
UZERNETIZKY, ANTONES	27	M	LABR	PLZZZZ	USA
ANNA	25	F	W	PLZZZZ	USA
JAN	00	M	INF	PLZZZZ	USA
WEISSLULEWITZ, JOHAN	28	M	LABR	PLZZZZ	USA
BALLINSCHEILS, JOSES	20	M	LABR	PLZZZZ	USA
MARICKS, PATRONI	32	F	W	PLZZZZ	USA
N.	5	F	CHILD	PLZZZZ	USA
LUBERMANN, HERMAN	20	M	LABR	PLZZZZ	USA
KRAGERS, H.B.	53	M	LABR	PLZZZZ	USA
KIRSTEN	56	M	LABR	PLZZZZ	USA
JACOBINE	72	F	W	PLZZZZ	USA
BENDIX	20	F	SP	PLZZZZ	USA
SOLOFERT, RASMUS	22	M	LABR	PLZZZZ	USA
SORVIA, CARL-O.	22	M	LABR	PLZZZZ	USA
PUPINS, N.	40	M	LABR	PLZZZZ	USA
HOLKVAIN, HADLE	30	M	LABR	PLZZZZ	USA
MATHILDA	25	F	W	PLZZZZ	USA
MARTHA	24	F	SP	PLZZZZ	USA
SORVIG, JACOB-H.	25	M	LABR	PLZZZZ	USA
BASILAUTZ, GEORGE	59	M	LABR	PLZZZZ	USA
SACHO, MOSES	32	M	LABR	PLZZZZ	USA
BARON, JANKEL	40	M	LABR	PLZZZZ	USA
FRACHTENBERG, JOHN	30	M	LABR	PLZZZZ	USA
SERVIN, ALEX	49	M	LABR	PLZZZZ	USA
OBERMANN, ABRAHAM	45	M	LABR	PLZZZZ	USA
KARTUSKI, MANZE	26	M	LABR	PLZZZZ	USA
WOLF, PAUL	28	M	LABR	PLZZZZ	USA
PERSCH, HENRICH	22	M	LABR	PLZZZZ	USA
JAHN, ALBIN	35	M	LABR	PLZZZZ	USA
STEINTIZ, ANDREUS	29	M	LABR	PLZZZZ	USA
SCARETZKY, J.	36	M	LABR	PLZZZZ	USA
YURAWNER, JANKEL	24	M	LABR	PLZZZZ	USA
BLUCH, J.	35	M	LABR	PLZZZZ	USA
AURET, JANKEL	32	M	LABR	PLZZZZ	USA
SCIFFRIED, EDWARD	32	M	LABR	PLZZZZ	USA
LEMEL, MOSES	45	M	LABR	PLZZZZ	USA
DREMEL, K.	19	M	LABR	PLZZZZ	USA
FRADMANN, JACOB	47	M	LABR	PLZZZZ	USA
ROSA	46	F	W	PLZZZZ	USA
ADOLF	18	M	LABR	PLZZZZ	USA
METTA	19	F	SP	PLZZZZ	USA
ROSA	11	F	CH	PLZZZZ	USA
FANNY	9	F	CHILD	PLZZZZ	USA
FRIESTADER, FRANZ	26	M	LABR	PLZZZZ	USA
LABATVUZ, HIRSCH	26	M	LABR	PLZZZZ	USA
SUSKER, MATTES	20	M	LABR	PLZZZZ	USA
ZORAF, LEISER	42	M	LABR	PLZZZZ	USA
GERSTEIN, JOSSEL	22	M	LABR	PLZZZZ	USA
BLUMBERG, KALMAN	18	M	LABR	PLZZZZ	USA
ZODEK	19	M	LABR	PLZZZZ	USA
ISCHENOWITZKY, SCHLOME	40	M	LABR	PLZZZZ	USA
ABRAM	11	M	CH	PLZZZZ	USA
SCHER, JOSSEL	40	M	LABR	PLZZZZ	USA
SCHLUSKY, FREIAS	16	M	LABR	PLZZZZ	USA
JASBRUM, SCHLEIN	44	M	LABR	PLZZZZ	USA
MOSES	11	M	CH	PLZZZZ	USA
OTI, CHANS	20	M	LABR	PLZZZZ	USA
LOESCH, EMIL	38	M	LABR	PLZZZZ	USA
GOTTLIEF, MERVER	36	M	LABR	PLZZZZ	USA
SUDKASE, BERTHA	24	F	W	PLZZZZ	USA
HEDWIG	00	M	INF	PLZZZZ	USA
FRANKE, ALBERT	39	M	LABR	PLZZZZ	USA
EMMA	27	F	W	PLZZZZ	USA
HERZAY, GUSTAF	26	M	LABR	PLZZZZ	USA
DITTMANN, GUST.	28	M	LABR	PLZZZZ	USA
BEMIER, NATHAN	23	M	LABR	PLZZZZ	USA
MADER, CHRISTIAN	18	M	LABR	PLZZZZ	USA
BENZEL, HERZ	23	M	LABR	PLZZZZ	USA
ADLER, CAROLINE	6	F	CHILD	PLZZZZ	USA

SHIP: ELBE

FROM: BREMEN
TO: NEW YORK
ARRIVED: 28 JUNE 1884

PASSENGER	AGE	SEX	OCCUPATION	PRIVL	DES
WEGNER, JOH.	26	M	LABR	RRZZZZ	USA
CHARLOTTE	38	F	W	RRZZZZ	USA
ADOLFINE	15	F	NN	RRZZZZ	USA
TAMOCZ, ERWIN	52	M	LABR	RRZZZZ	USA
GRASULOWA, ANNA	29	F	NN	RRZZZZ	USA
JOSEF	.11	M	INFANT	RRZZZZ	USA
MERKIN, MOSES	32	M	FARMER	RRZZZZ	USA

SHIP: LYDIAN MONARCH

FROM: LONDON
TO: NEW YORK
ARRIVED: 28 JUNE 1884

PASSENGER	AGE	SEX	OCCUPATION	PRIVL	DES
ISAACS, LEWIS	18	M	TLR	RRZZZZ	NY
SIMONS, M.	18	M	TLR	RRZZZZ	NY
ARTER, SAM	20	M	GZR	PLZZZZ	NY
BEN	21	M	GZR	PLZZZZ	NY
ROBYITSKY, G.	25	M	BTMKR	PLZZZZ	BO
KORT, JOS.	29	M	BCHR	RRZZZZ	NY
LIPPMAN, M.	30	M	SHMK	RRZZZZ	NY
LIPCHICH, A.	63	M	NN	RRZZZZ	SP
HANSEN, M.	63	M	NN	RRZZZZ	UNK
INAKOWITCH, H.	26	M	TLR	PLZZZZ	NY
KROTZMAN, L.	24	M	TLR	PLZZZZ	NY
GOODMAN, B.	40	M	LABR	RRZZZZ	NY
H.	11	F	DMS	RRZZZZ	NY

SHIP: CITY OF CHICAGO

FROM: LIVERPOOL AND QUEENSTOWN
TO: NEW YORK
ARRIVED: 30 JUNE 1884

PASSENGER	AGE	SEX	OCCUPATION	PRIVL	DES
SILOKKA, KALLE	36	M	LABR	FNZZZZ	MI
ABRAMSON, MATTS	20	M	LABR	FNZZZZ	MI
ERIKSON, ELIAS	27	M	LABR	FNZZZZ	MI
DOBBER, MICHEL	24	F	SP	RRZZZZ	NY
MARIA, VALGA	20	F	SP	PLZZZZ	MN

PASSENGER	AGE	SEX	OCCUPATION	PRV	VIL	DES

SHIP: ST. OF PENNSYLVANIA

FROM: GLASGOW AND LARNE
TO: NEW YORK
ARRIVED: 30 JUNE 1884

PASSENGER	AGE	SEX	OCCUPATION	PRV	VIL	DES
MANDRIKS, WILLIAM	20	M	MCHT	RR	ZZZZ	USA
COLLIANDER, S.	19	M	MCHT	RR	ZZZZ	USA
MIGANOWSKI, LUDWIG	26	M	TLR	RR	ZZZZ	USA
BETHNIEWI, ABRAM	20	M	LABR	PL	ZZZZ	USA
BUSANSKY, UREL	20	M	PDLR	PL	ZZZZ	USA
GRABINSKY, OSIAS	24	M	SMH	PL	ZZZZ	USA
HURWITZ, SCHLOME	12	F	CH	PL	ZZZZ	USA
JOSEF, MORITZ	19	M	PDLR	PL	ZZZZ	USA
KAPBAN, NISSON	23	M	PDLR	PL	ZZZZ	USA
MARCUS, BAER	11	M	PDLR	PL	ZZZZ	USA
MULWITZKY, WULF	17	M	WVR	PL	ZZZZ	USA
NAVALL, CASSIMIR	35	M	PDLR	PL	ZZZZ	USA
SCHEIN, SUNDIL	38	M	PDLR	PL	ZZZZ	USA
SCHUSTER, SALOMON	23	M	PDLR	PL	ZZZZ	USA
CHAIE	24	F	W	PL	ZZZZ	USA
SARAH	.02	F	INFANT	PL	ZZZZ	USA
SEGALL, MOSES	26	M	PDLR	PL	ZZZZ	USA

SHIP: ZAANDAM

FROM: AMSTERDAM
TO: NEW YORK
ARRIVED: 30 JUNE 1884

PASSENGER	AGE	SEX	OCCUPATION	PRV	VIL	DES
NETERMAN, SAMUEL	31	M	BCHR	RR	ZZZZ	USA

SHIP: CIRCASSIA

FROM: GLASGOW AND MOVILLE
TO: NEW YORK
ARRIVED: 02 JULY 1884

PASSENGER	AGE	SEX	OCCUPATION	PRV	VIL	DES
GOLDBERG, PHILIP	26	M	TLR	RR	ZZZZ	USA
M.MRS	23	F	W	RR	ZZZZ	USA
GOLDA	.04	F	INFANT	RR	ZZZZ	USA
SACHS, RIVCKE	21	F	DMS	RR	ZZZZ	USA
ERSCHLER, SELIG	31	M	LABR	RR	ZZZZ	USA
AKERMANN, SAMUEL	22	M	DLR	RR	ZZZZ	USA
HANSON, AND.	23	M	LABR	RR	ZZZZ	USA
HIRSCH, CHAIM	33	M	LABR	RR	ZZZZ	USA
BOCHELSOHN, SCHLOSM	43	M	TLR	RR	ZZZZ	USA
SCHOPIRE, CHACKE	30	M	BKBNDR	RR	ZZZZ	USA

SHIP: GERMAIN

FROM: HAVRE
TO: NEW YORK
ARRIVED: 02 JULY 1884

PASSENGER	AGE	SEX	OCCUPATION	PRV	VIL	DES
KATZ, MARCUS	44	M	FARMER	RR	ZZZZ	NY
SARHA	35	F	UNKNOWN	RR	ZZZZ	NY
RUDOLPHE	12	M	UNKNOWN	RR	ZZZZ	NY
BERNARD	11	M	UNKNOWN	RR	ZZZZ	NY
FANCHEN	9	F	CHILD	RR	ZZZZ	NY
MARIE	10	F	UNKNOWN	RR	ZZZZ	NY
ANNA	3	F	CHILD	RR	ZZZZ	NY
ISRAEL	00	M	INF	RR	ZZZZ	NY
SCHALONITCH, SALOMON	21	M	WCHMKR	RR	ZZZZ	NY
SCOUROS, CHARLES	38	M	WCHMKR	RR	ZZZZ	NY

SHIP: CATALONIA

FROM: LIVERPOOL AND QUEENSTOWN
TO: NEW YORK
ARRIVED: 03 JULY 1884

PASSENGER	AGE	SEX	OCCUPATION	PRV	VIL	DES
WOLFF, SAML.	11	M	CH	RR	ZZZZ	NY
JOFF, SAML.	25	M	LABR	RR	ZZZZ	NY
MINSK, ELIAS	34	M	BCHR	RR	ZZZZ	NY
HANDELMANN, ANREL	38	M	LABR	RR	ZZZZ	NY
LPERLING, FEIBEL	17	M	LABR	RR	ZZZZ	NY

SHIP: DONAU

FROM: BREMEN
TO: NEW YORK
ARRIVED: 03 JULY 1884

PASSENGER	AGE	SEX	OCCUPATION	PRV	VIL	DES
MANSKY, CARL	19	M	FARMER	RR	ZZZZ	USA
SYLVESTER, CASIMIR	38	M	FARMER	RR	ZZZZ	USA
GIZEWSKA, EVA	25	F	NN	RR	ZZZZ	USA
MEROWITZ, CLARA	16	F	NN	RR	ZZZZ	USA

SHIP: RUGIA

FROM: HAMBURG
TO: NEW YORK
ARRIVED: 03 JULY 1884

PASSENGER	AGE	SEX	OCCUPATION	PRV	VIL	DES
RACHMIL, ABRAHAM	43	M	MUSN	RR	ZZZZ	USA
KRUPP, MOSES	37	M	LABR	RR	ZZZZ	USA
KANTOROWICZ, HERRM.	19	M	LABR	RR	ZZZZ	USA
RACHMIL, JACOB	40	M	MUSN	RR	ZZZZ	USA
CHAIM	9	M	CHILD	RR	ZZZZ	USA
KAPLAN, OFNER	38	M	MUSN	RR	ZZZZ	USA
LEIPZIGER, ABR.	43	M	MUSN	RR	ZZZZ	USA
ROCHMIL, JOSEF.	16	M	MUSN	RR	ZZZZ	USA
KAPLAN, MARCUS	16	M	MUSN	RR	ZZZZ	USA
KAPLOWITZ, CHAIM	37	M	SHMK	RR	ZZZZ	USA
JONAS	17	M	SHMK	RR	ZZZZ	USA
KOOPMANN, NICOLAUS	35	M	LABR	RR	ZZZZ	USA
KOPELOW, JACOB	17	M	LABR	RR	ZZZZ	USA
BLASBERG, HENDEL	18	M	SGL	RR	ZZZZ	USA
GOLDREICH, DAVID	40	M	LABR	RR	ZZZZ	USA
HANNE	18	F	CH	RR	ZZZZ	USA
MOSES	9	M	CHILD	RR	ZZZZ	USA
JEWEROWITZ, JACOB	26	M	LABR	RR	ZZZZ	USA
MANKE, CHEIC	24	F	SGL	RR	ZZZZ	USA
BOCK, LEA	19	M	SGL	RR	ZZZZ	USA
GITTEL, LEA	50	F	W	RR	ZZZZ	USA
CHANE	6	F	CHILD	RR	ZZZZ	USA
ZDROJEWSKY, RASCHE	36	F	W	RR	ZZZZ	USA
BEITE	9	F	CHILD	RR	ZZZZ	USA

PASSENGER	AGE	SEX	OCCUPATION	PRV VIL DES
ALTES	6	F	CHILD	RRZZZZUSA
CIREL	3	M	CHILD	RRZZZZUSA
GUTMANN, SALOMON	15	M	LABR	RRZZZZUSA
SALOMON, LEIB	9	M	CHILD	RRZZZZUSA
KOVVELA, J.HEINR.	21	M	SGL	RRZZZZUSA
SCHEIES, RABEL	19	M	SGL	RRZZZZUSA
NEUFELA, MARCUS	19	M	TLR	RRZZZZUSA
MESSER, JULS.	33	M	TLR	RRZZZZUSA
GARNOF--, HIRSCH	40	M	GLMK	RRZZZZUSA
SCHIMELOWITZ, BARUCH	19	M	LABR	RRZZZZUSA
ELPERN, LEWIN	19	M	LABR	RRZZZZUSA
WALLMANN, SIMON	21	M	LABR	RRZZZZUSA
GROSS, BEHR.	19	M	LABR	RRZZZZUSA
STARK, DAVID	28	M	LABR	RRZZZZUSA
WARSCHAWZIK, CHEIE	52	F	W	RRZZZZUSA
ELI	9	F	CHILD	RRZZZZUSA
SARA	8	F	CHILD	RRZZZZUSA
SCHMIED, MOSES	17	M	LABR	RRZZZZUSA
SCHIMANSKY, SCHOMSEL	20	M	LABR	RRZZZZUSA
SALEWSKY, MARIANE	27	F	SGL	RRZZZZUSA
BALTRUSCHAK, HEINR.	31	M	LABR	RRZZZZUSA
SCHILLER, CHRIST.	32	M	LABR	RRZZZZUSA
SINNOK-T, HEINR.	26	M	LABR	RRZZZZUSA
SIMON	21	M	LABR	RRZZZZUSA
MEYEROWITZ, BEHR.	8	M	CHILD	RRZZZZUSA
RAPLANSKY, BEHR.	55	M	SHMK	RRZZZZUSA
KAPLANSKY, SCHEINE	18	F	SGL	RRZZZZUSA
DAMSKY, JACOB	26	M	LABR	RRZZZZUSA
JUDELOWSKY, GERSON	22	M	LABR	RRZZZZUSA
KAROWSKY, HOFSCHI	22	M	LABR	RRZZZZUSA
HURWITZ, MEIER	25	M	JNR	RRZZZZUSA
SCHULMAN, BASCHE	37	F	SGL	RRZZZZUSA
BECKER, RIWE	33	F	SGL	RRZZZZUSA
HASINEIT, LEOPOLD	21	M	LABR	RRZZZZUSA
SCHUSDA, MICHEL	21	M	LABR	RRZZZZUSA
RWITZINSKY, ELISE	50	M	LABR	RRZZZZUSA
HIMELBAUM, MOSES	19	M	LABR	RRZZZZUSA
GROSSMANN, SUSSMANN	22	M	LABR	RRZZZZUSA
CAESILIE	20	F	W	RRZZZZUSA
GLIKSMANN, JACOB	20	M	LABR	RRZZZZUSA
SCHAMSCHENOWITZ, JOSSEL	50	M	LABR	RRZZZZUSA
GROBINER, SCHMUEL	30	M	LABR	RRZZZZUSA
STALL, REBECCA	30	F	W	RRZZZZUSA
BERTHA	8	F	CHILD	RRZZZZUSA
MEYEROWI--, LEIB	50	M	LABR	RRZZZZUSA
REBECCA	45	F	W	RRZZZZUSA
FREIDE	9	F	CHILD	RRZZZZUSA
FINKELSTEIN, ETTE	16	F	SGL	RRZZZZUSA
ELKE	9	F	CHILD	RRZZZZUSA
KNECHT, MELEZE	13	F	SGL	RRZZZZUSA
RESSLER, MARY	58	F	W	RRZZZZUSA
MESCHE	16	F	CH	RRZZZZUSA
MOSES	9	M	CHILD	RRZZZZUSA
STUPEL, EFRAIM	18	F	SGL	RRZZZZUSA
SAMUEL	8	M	CHILD	RRZZZZUSA
SIMONON, MEYER	19	M	TNMK	RRZZZZUSA
ITZIGSOHN, PINCUS	30	M	DLR	RRZZZZUSA
JORG, FREIDE	22	F	SGL	RRZZZZUSA
BARABAN, ISAAC	48	M	DLR	RRZZZZUSA
GOLDSTEIN, CHAIM	21	M	TLR	RRZZZZUSA
RUBIN, ROSA	17	F	SGL	RRZZZZUSA
DELLOWA, MARIANE	20	F	SGL	RRZZZZUSA
FRIEDBERG, JOSEPH	16	M	LABR	RRZZZZUSA
SCHIRADKOWSKY, LEIB	45	M	LABR	RRZZZZUSA
RUDA, ITTE	18	F	SGL	RRZZZZUSA
FINGERHUT, MOSES	36	M	LABR	RRZZZZUSA
ROSENBLATT, ROSA	25	F	W	RRZZZZUSA
RIWKE	3	F	CHILD	RRZZZZUSA
PINKUS	.11	M	INFANT	RRZZZZUSA
RATZKOWSKY, MALKE	16	F	SGL	RRZZZZUSA
DALABOWITZ, DAVID	39	M	SHMK	RRZZZZUSA
BRESUM, WINISKI	38	M	LABR	RRZZZZUSA
SCHWARZ, ALEXANDER	25	M	LABR	RRZZZZUSA
LIPSKY, DAVID	16	M	BRM	RRZZZZUSA
FRIEDMANN, SALOMON	65	M	LABR	RRZZZZUSA

PASSENGER	AGE	SEX	OCCUPATION	PRV VIL DES
GOLDE	48	F	W	RRZZZZUSA
LEISER	9	M	CHILD	RRZZZZUSA
SCHIFRE	6	F	CHILD	RRZZZZUSA
LESEROWITZ, SARA	70	F	W	RRZZZZUSA
REINOWITZ, FRUME	28	F	W	RRZZZZUSA
WILINSKI, MORITZ	22	M	TLR	RRZZZZUSA
SCHROTKOWSKY, ABRAM	20	M	LABR	RRZZZZUSA
TAUBE	20	F	W	RRZZZZUSA
JOG, BASCHE	34	F	W	RRZZZZUSA
SCHEINE	9	M	CHILD	RRZZZZUSA
MOSES	8	M	CHILD	RRZZZZUSA
CHAIC	7	M	CHILD	RRZZZZUSA
ELKE	5	F	CHILD	RRZZZZUSA
FREIDE	3	F	CHILD	RRZZZZUSA
LEA	.11	F	INFANT	RRZZZZUSA
CHAIC	.01	M	INFANT	RRZZZZUSA
ROMANOSKI, LEON	35	M	MCHT	RRZZZZUSA

SHIP: STATE OF GEORGIA

FROM: GLASGOW AND LARNE
TO: NEW YORK
ARRIVED: 03 JULY 1884

PASSENGER	AGE	SEX	OCCUPATION	PRV VIL DES
LEFROWITCH, EPHRAIM	26	M	PDLR	RRZZZZUSA
STEMBERG, MEYERS	22	M	PDLR	RRZZZZUSA
RUDALFSKI, MARKS	30	M	PDLR	RRZZZZUSA
ROCHSTEIN, BARNET	28	M	PDLR	RRZZZZUSA
LEIBE, RICHARD	31	M	WVR	RRZZZZUSA
MORSKES, ISRAEL	40	M	PDLR	RRZZZZUSA
BURUS, ROSE	18	F	SP	RRZZZZUSA
HORNSTEIN, ABRAHAM	18	M	LABR	RRZZZZUSA
WACHTEL, MORDCHE	21	M	LABR	RRZZZZUSA
KONSERSKY, MOSES	39	M	PDLR	RRZZZZUSA
BENITZKY, JACOB	64	M	WCHMKR	RRZZZZUSA
BERLOWITZ, NATHAN	33	M	LABR	RRZZZZUSA
JACOB	17	M	LABR	RRZZZZUSA
BARAN, MOSES	19	M	LABR	RRZZZZUSA
SAMBROWITZ, EPHRAIM	33	M	PDLR	RRZZZZUSA
BELFER, KILMAN	26	M	PDLR	RRZZZZUSA
SCHMIEGER, FEWEL	18	M	LABR	RRZZZZUSA
MULLER, WIGDOR	28	M	LABR	RRZZZZUSA
BOGION, SAMUEL	20	M	LABR	RRZZZZUSA
WAROTSCHNICK, BARUCH	18	M	LABR	RRZZZZUSA
SEGAL, HIRSCH	51	M	LABR	RRZZZZUSA
WEMEROWITZ, JACOB	33	M	LABR	RRZZZZUSA
SANDLER, LOSER	18	M	LABR	RRZZZZUSA
KRAMER, MENDEL	32	M	LABR	RRZZZZUSA
LOBOKUS, WINCENZ	24	M	LABR	RRZZZZUSA
STUHRMAN, ISAC	18	M	LABR	RRZZZZUSA
SKROTZKY, ANTON	42	M	LABR	RRZZZZUSA
JAN	11	M	LABR	RRZZZZUSA
KATZEK, JOEL	24	M	LABR	RRZZZZUSA
CHAIE	18	F	SP	RRZZZZUSA
GOLDBERG, BARUCH	12	M	BY	RRZZZZUSA
BERKOWITZ, GITEL	00	F	W	RRZZZZUSA
SAGER, CHAIE	00	M	LABR	RRZZZZUSA
LIEBE	41	F	W	RRZZZZUSA
LOEB	18	M	CH	RRZZZZUSA
MINDEL	7	F	CHILD	RRZZZZUSA
ROCHEL	5	F	CHILD	RRZZZZUSA
WEINBERG, LAZARUS	60	M	LABR	RRZZZZUSA
ITTE	44	F	W	RRZZZZUSA
JENTE	15	F	CH	RRZZZZUSA
LEAH	2	F	CHILD	RRZZZZUSA
SCHACHME	18	F	CH	RRZZZZUSA
NOZEN	26	M	LABR	RRZZZZUSA
BIALISTOTZKY, ABR.	19	M	PDLR	RRZZZZUSA
MARESTWO, ABR.	22	M	PDLR	RRZZZZUSA
EISTEN, NACHUM	30	M	PDLR	RRZZZZUSA

PASSENGER	AGE	SEX	OCCUPATION	PRIV	DES
BRAGOWSKY, MOSES	26	M	CMST	RRZZZZ	USA
FISCHER, DAVID	25	M	LABR	RRZZZZ	USA

SHIP: ASSYRIAN MONARCH

FROM: LONDON
TO: NEW YORK
ARRIVED: 05 JULY 1884

PASSENGER	AGE	SEX	OCCUPATION	PRIV	DES
SPIELMAN, REBECCA	48	F	W	PLZZZZ	NY
SAMUEL	16	M	LABR	PLZZZZ	NY
JOSEPH	11	M	CH	PLZZZZ	NY
SARAH	10	F	CH	PLZZZZ	NY
DORA	9	F	CHILD	PLZZZZ	NY
U, ISRAEL	8	M	CHILD	PLZZZZ	NY
GALONBECK, SHAPSEL	21	M	LABR	PLZZZZ	NY
RILL, FANNY	23	F	UNKNOWN	PLZZZZ	NY
STRAUSS, DINAH	23	F	UNKNOWN	PLZZZZ	NY
ABRAHAM	5	M	CHILD	PLZZZZ	NY
JACOBS, HANNAH	28	F	UNKNOWN	PLZZZZ	NY
ISAACS, A.	18	M	LABR	PLZZZZ	NY
NATHAN, REBECCA	24	F	W	PLZZZZ	NY
MAREUS	5	F	CHILD	PLZZZZ	NY
SARAH	2	F	CHILD	PLZZZZ	NY
MORRIS	00	U	INF	PLZZZZ	NY
HANDLER, JOSEPH	25	M	LABR	PLZZZZ	NY
GOLDBERG, JACOB	29	M	LABR	PLZZZZ	NY
HINDE	32	F	W	PLZZZZ	NY
JOSEPH	7	M	CHILD	PLZZZZ	NY
JAMES	5	M	CHILD	PLZZZZ	NY
ISAAC	3	M	CHILD	PLZZZZ	NY
SOLOMON	00	M	CH	PLZZZZ	NY
JACOBS, RACHAEL	56	F	UNKNOWN	PLZZZZ	NY
WACHYMSKI, W.	24	M	LABR	PLZZZZ	NY
ARONSBERG, A.	23	F	UNKNOWN	PLZZZZ	NY
KATE	00	F	INF	PLZZZZ	NY
BLUMENTHAL, P.	28	F	UNKNOWN	PLZZZZ	NY
SAMSON	6	M	CHILD	PLZZZZ	NY
SOLOMON	5	M	CHILD	PLZZZZ	NY
ESTHER	00	F	INF	PLZZZZ	NY
BRODSKY, M.	43	M	LABR	PLZZZZ	NY
HANNAH	40	F	W	PLZZZZ	NY
MOSES	16	M	LABR	PLZZZZ	NY
NESHAME	11	M	CH	PLZZZZ	NY
ISAAC	9	M	CHILD	PLZZZZ	NY
GENENDAL	5	F	CHILD	PLZZZZ	NY
EMANUEL	3	M	CHILD	PLZZZZ	NY
MORDECAI	2	M	CHILD	PLZZZZ	NY
JACOB	00	M	INF	PLZZZZ	NY
PRICE, L.S.	29	M	LABR	PLZZZZ	NY
HARRIS, JACOB	22	M	LABR	PLZZZZ	NY
SCHINER, H.	30	F	LABR	PLZZZZ	NY
SHERIS, HERJMAN	18	M	LABR	PLZZZZ	NY
LIMBERKOMP, RACHAEL	20	F	UNKNOWN	PLZZZZ	NY
HINDE	20	M	LABR	PLZZZZ	NY
MENDOZA, HENRY	00	M	LABR	PLZZZZ	NY
SLAPUK, H.	00	F	LABR	PLZZZZ	NY
WENTWORTH, REBECCA	40	F	W	PLZZZZ	NY
RACHAEL	13	F	W	PLZZZZ	NY
JOSEPH	11	M	CH	PLZZZZ	NY
JACOB	8	M	CHILD	PLZZZZ	NY
LEWIS	6	M	CHILD	PLZZZZ	NY
CLARA	4	F	CHILD	PLZZZZ	NY
COHEN, BLUMA	37	F	W	PLZZZZ	NY
LEWIS	14	M	LABR	PLZZZZ	NY
SARAH	12	F	CH	PLZZZZ	NY
JANE	12	F	CH	PLZZZZ	NY
KITTY	11	F	CH	PLZZZZ	NY
JESSIE	9	F	CHILD	PLZZZZ	NY
KATE	8	F	CHILD	PLZZZZ	NY

PASSENGER	AGE	SEX	OCCUPATION	PRIV	DES
RACHAEL	6	F	CHILD	PLZZZZ	NY
HYMAN	4	M	CHILD	PLZZZZ	NY
PHILLIPS, SAMUEL	51	M	LABR	PLZZZZ	NY
HANNAH	51	F	W	PLZZZZ	NY
JOHN	17	M	LABR	PLZZZZ	NY
MICHAEL	12	M	LABR	PLZZZZ	NY
SARAH	11	F	CH	PLZZZZ	NY
MARTHA	8	F	CHILD	PLZZZZ	NY
JOSEPH	7	M	CHILD	PLZZZZ	NY
LEWIS, ISAAC	26	M	LABR	PLZZZZ	NY
RACHAEL	25	F	W	PLZZZZ	NY
DAVID	4	M	CHILD	PLZZZZ	NY
FANNY	00	F	INF	PLZZZZ	NY
VANDERBERG, ANSELL	48	M	LABR	PLZZZZ	NY
JANE	48	F	W	PLZZZZ	NY
SOLOMON	25	M	LABR	PLZZZZ	NY
ABRAHAM	19	M	LABR	PLZZZZ	NY
MARY	12	F	UNKNOWN	PLZZZZ	NY
EMANUEL	11	M	CH	PLZZZZ	NY
JANE	10	F	CH	PLZZZZ	NY
SARAH	7	F	CHILD	PLZZZZ	NY
BUDKAUT, DINAH	24	F	W	PLZZZZ	NY
ABRAHAM	2	M	CHILD	PLZZZZ	NY
U, MICHAEL	00	M	INF	PLZZZZ	NY
MAGNUS, JULIA	25	F	W	PLZZZZ	NY
ROSE	6	F	CHILD	PLZZZZ	NY
RAPHAEL	4	M	CHILD	PLZZZZ	NY
HYAMS, HANNAH	34	F	W	PLZZZZ	NY
DEBORAH	11	F	CH	PLZZZZ	NY
LEAH	10	F	CH	PLZZZZ	NY
LEWIS	7	M	CHILD	PLZZZZ	NY
HYAM	5	F	CHILD	PLZZZZ	NY
U, SARAH	00	F	INF	PLZZZZ	NY
BLOCK, JACOB	43	M	LABR	PLZZZZ	NY
JULIA	42	F	W	PLZZZZ	NY
COHEN, REBECCA	38	F	W	PLZZZZ	NY
SARAH	20	F	W	PLZZZZ	NY
BOWMAN, MARY-A.	37	F	W	PLZZZZ	NY
ISRAEL	4	M	CHILD	PLZZZZ	NY
ELISABETH	9	F	CHILD	PLZZZZ	NY
RAPHAEL	8	M	CHILD	PLZZZZ	NY
ABRAHAM	5	M	CHILD	PLZZZZ	NY
JOSEPH	2	M	CHILD	PLZZZZ	NY
SYMONS, SARAH	24	F	W	PLZZZZ	NY
DEBORAH	5	F	CHILD	PLZZZZ	NY
NANCY	4	F	CHILD	PLZZZZ	NY
JANE	3	F	CHILD	PLZZZZ	NY
BETSY	00	F	INF	PLZZZZ	NY
LEONSEN, FANNY	35	F	W	PLZZZZ	NY
SOLOMON	11	M	CH	PLZZZZ	NY
JOSEPH	7	M	CHILD	PLZZZZ	NY
ISRAEL	5	M	CHILD	PLZZZZ	NY
ABRAHAM	3	M	CHILD	PLZZZZ	NY
SWANSKI, S.	00	F	UNKNOWN	PLZZZZ	NY
MAT.	3	M	CHILD	PLZZZZ	NY
VERA	00	F	INF	PLZZZZ	NY
JAFFE, ISAAC	25	M	LABR	PLZZZZ	NY
DAVIS, P.	00	M	LABR	PLZZZZ	NY
MYER, C.	00	M	LABR	PLZZZZ	NY
ALACK, W.	00	M	LABR	PLZZZZ	NY
POPLIS, LUD.W.	25	M	LABR	PLZZZZ	NY
BLUMER, KITTY	23	F	LABR	PLZZZZ	NY
U, K.	00	F	INF	PLZZZZ	NY
BETTS, ISAAC	00	M	LABR	PLZZZZ	NY
EMMA	26	F	W	PLZZZZ	NY
MARKS	7	M	CHILD	PLZZZZ	NY
REBECCA	4	F	CHILD	PLZZZZ	NY
SOLOMON	2	M	CHILD	PLZZZZ	NY
SARAH	00	F	INF	PLZZZZ	NY
VERLINCIA, J.	21	M	LABR	PLZZZZ	NY
ISAAC, WOOLF	00	M	LABR	PLZZZZ	NY
HEINEMAN, LOUIS	23	M	LABR	PLZZZZ	NY
EDELSTEIN, L.	21	M	LABR	PLZZZZ	NY
COHEN, LOUIS	30	M	LABR	PLZZZZ	NY
ZEFFER, M.	17	M	LABR	PLZZZZ	NY

PASSENGER	AGE	SEX	OCCUPATION	PRV	VIL	DES
KUAS, ANNA-K.	40	F	UNKNOWN	PL	ZZZZ	NY
KENDICH	8	F	CHILD	PL	ZZZZ	NY
MARIE	4	F	CHILD	PL	ZZZZ	NY
ALVINA	00	F	INF	PL	ZZZZ	NY

SHIP: CITY OF CHESTER

FROM: LIVERPOOL AND QUEENSTOWN
TO: NEW YORK
ARRIVED: 05 JULY 1884

PASSENGER	AGE	SEX	OCCUPATION	PRV	VIL	DES
LIKSON, LISA	18	F	SVNT	RR	ZZZZ	NY
NOWACKY, PAULINE	36	F	W	PL	ZZZZ	NY
BASCHEN, MOSES	45	F	FARMER	RR	ZZZZ	NY
MARIE	20	F	SVNT	RR	ZZZZ	NY
SARA	18	F	SVNT	RR	ZZZZ	NY
ISAAC	11	M	CH	RR	ZZZZ	NY
LENKULVER, JACOB	19	M	LABR	PL	ZZZZ	NY
SCHWARZ, FRANKEL	20	M	LABR	RR	ZZZZ	NY

SHIP: WERRA

FROM: BREMEN
TO: NEW YORK
ARRIVED: 05 JULY 1884

PASSENGER	AGE	SEX	OCCUPATION	PRV	VIL	DES
WOHLGEMUTH, CHAN.	27	M	FARMER	RR	ZZZZ	USA
ROSINE	26	F	UNKNOWN	RR	ZZZZ	USA
ROSINE	4	F	CHILD	RR	ZZZZ	USA
MATHILDE	3	F	CHILD	RR	ZZZZ	USA
JOHANN	2	M	CHILD	RR	ZZZZ	USA
CHRISTIAN	.02	M	INFANT	RR	ZZZZ	USA
BENTERS, JACOB	43	M	FARMER	RR	ZZZZ	USA
DOROTHEA	38	F	UNKNOWN	RR	ZZZZ	USA
ROSSIN, JOHANN	28	M	FARMER	RR	ZZZZ	USA
CHRISTINE	26	F	UNKNOWN	RR	ZZZZ	USA
CATHNA.	3	F	CHILD	RR	ZZZZ	USA
JOHANN	.11	M	INFANT	RR	ZZZZ	USA
HEISER, CHRISTNE.	22	F	UNKNOWN	RR	ZZZZ	USA
HOLZWOCEK, HCH.	34	M	FARMER	RR	ZZZZ	USA
FRIEDKE.	32	F	UNKNOWN	RR	ZZZZ	USA
JACOB	5	M	CHILD	RR	ZZZZ	USA
HEINR.	3	M	CHILD	RR	ZZZZ	USA
GOTTLIEB	.11	M	INFANT	RR	ZZZZ	USA
TIEGEL, FRIEDR.	25	M	LABR	RR	ZZZZ	USA
ANNA	23	F	UNKNOWN	RR	ZZZZ	USA
FRIEDR.	3	M	CHILD	RR	ZZZZ	USA
JOHANNES	.11	M	INFANT	RR	ZZZZ	USA
HEISER, LEONHARD	59	M	FARMER	RR	ZZZZ	USA
ROSINE	53	F	UNKNOWN	RR	ZZZZ	USA
ROSINE	18	F	UNKNOWN	RR	ZZZZ	USA
BARBARA	16	F	UNKNOWN	RR	ZZZZ	USA
JOHANNE	7	F	CHILD	RR	ZZZZ	USA
MICHAEL	6	M	CHILD	RR	ZZZZ	USA
CHRISTIAN	5	M	CHILD	RR	ZZZZ	USA
LACHMANN, LOT	21	M	FARMER	RR	ZZZZ	USA
HOLLWEGE, HCH.	21	M	FARMER	RR	ZZZZ	USA
HAMANN, HCH.	20	M	TNM	RR	ZZZZ	USA
RANCH, JACOB	20	M	LABR	RR	ZZZZ	USA
STEINBACH, CHRIST.	16	M	LABR	RR	ZZZZ	USA
BROSE, GOTTFR.	16	M	FARMER	RR	ZZZZ	USA
HEISER, JOHANNES	24	M	FARMER	RR	ZZZZ	USA
WOLPERT, HOSENS.	19	M	FARMER	RR	ZZZZ	USA

SHIP: AUSTRALIA

FROM: HAMBURG
TO: NEW YORK
ARRIVED: 07 JULY 1884

PASSENGER	AGE	SEX	OCCUPATION	PRV	VIL	DES
SALOMONS, MATILDE	19	F	SGL	RR	ZZZZ	NY
NEUMANN, ESTY	17	F	SGL	RR	ZZZZ	NY
DAVID	7	M	CHILD	RR	ZZZZ	NY
ARONSON, ARON	19	M	LABR	RR	ZZZZ	NY
GRIMBLATT, SANNE	50	F	W	RR	ZZZZ	NY
CHAWE	7	F	CHILD	RR	ZZZZ	NY
SARA	5	F	CHILD	RR	ZZZZ	NY
KAPLAN, HERZ	30	M	TDR	RR	ZZZZ	NY
HASSEWITZ, JONAS	25	M	LABR	RR	ZZZZ	NY
MARIE	25	F	W	RR	ZZZZ	NY
MARIE	.06	F	INFANT	RR	ZZZZ	NY
SCHMILEWSKI, RACHEL	30	F	WO	RR	ZZZZ	NY
HINDE	5	M	CHILD	RR	ZZZZ	NY
LEIB	2	M	CHILD	RR	ZZZZ	NY
ZIXINSKI, SALOMON	30	M	TDR	RR	ZZZZ	NY
WAWITZKI, GEORG	19	M	LABR	RR	ZZZZ	NY
OHRAFTOWITZ, MAGD.	20	F	W	RR	ZZZZ	NY
TEUBUER, CHRISTIAN	37	M	SMH	RR	ZZZZ	NY
KELLER, WOLF	32	M	TDR	PL	ZZZZ	NY
BERGMANN, NAPHT.	28	M	TDR	PL	ZZZZ	NY
KALMANOWITZ, ANNA	28	F	WO	RR	ZZZZ	NY
IRSCHFELD, MICHEL	19	M	TDR	RR	ZZZZ	NY
KAHN, HANNA	21	F	WO	RR	ZZZZ	NY
JACOB	.03	M	INFANT	RR	ZZZZ	NY
HILBERMANN, CHAIE	22	M	TDR	RR	ZZZZ	NY
WEISS, SALI	16	F	SGL	RR	ZZZZ	NY
NEUMANN, MARIE	20	F	SGL	RR	ZZZZ	NY
MEYERSON, ROSA	32	F	WO	RR	ZZZZ	NY
BLUME	11	M	S	RR	ZZZZ	NY
ETTE	6	M	CHILD	RR	ZZZZ	NY
MANDEL	5	M	CHILD	RR	ZZZZ	NY
ZIPE	3	F	CHILD	RR	ZZZZ	NY
SCHMIDT, MARIE	27	F	WO	RR	ZZZZ	NY
DAVID	6	M	CHILD	RR	ZZZZ	NY
EICHUER, HANS	18	M	LABR	RR	ZZZZ	NY
RAYMANOVSKY, VINCENT	20	M	LABR	RR	ZZZZ	NY
MEYER, ERNESTINE	33	M	LABR	RR	ZZZZ	NY
HEDWIG	5	F	CHILD	RR	ZZZZ	NY
SCHMIDT, HERM.	16	M	FARMER	RR	ZZZZ	CH
KASCHE, GUSTAV	29	M	SHMK	RR	ZZZZ	CH
AUGUSTE	29	F	W	RR	ZZZZ	CH
MARIE	4	F	CHILD	RR	ZZZZ	CH
WILLY	.07	M	INFANT	RR	ZZZZ	CH
GILL, WOYCECH	14	M	LABR	PL	ZZZZ	NY
NICOLAUS	7	M	CHILD	PL	ZZZZ	NY
BARADOWSKY, ISAC	26	M	TDR	RR	ZZZZ	NY
SALOMONOW, TAUBE	19	F	SGL	RR	ZZZZ	NY
FISCHER, ISRAEL	21	M	TDR	RR	ZZZZ	NY
CHANA	21	F	W	RR	ZZZZ	NY
WALOWSKY, MEYER	34	M	TDR	RR	ZZZZ	NY
DWORE	30	F	W	RR	ZZZZ	NY
CHAIKEL	7	F	CHILD	RR	ZZZZ	NY
JOEL	6	M	CHILD	RR	ZZZZ	NY
JACOB	.02	M	INFANT	RR	ZZZZ	NY
CHAINE	.11	M	INFANT	RR	ZZZZ	NY
GRODZKY, BAILE	40	F	WO	RR	ZZZZ	NY
BENZIEN	15	M	S	RR	ZZZZ	NY
SARA	.02	F	INFANT	RR	ZZZZ	NY
LUSTIG, FERD.	23	M	TDR	RR	ZZZZ	NY
LEIB, KAHAN	50	M	MNR	RR	ZZZZ	NY
LICHTMANN, LEIB	18	M	LABR	RR	ZZZZ	NY
SAROWITZ, BEITEL	53	M	TDR	RR	ZZZZ	NY
JOTE	53	F	W	RR	ZZZZ	NY
MALKOWITZ, ESTER	45	F	WO	RR	ZZZZ	NY
KOLVE	7	M	CHILD	RR	ZZZZ	NY
DOMINIC, ISAC	28	M	TLR	PL	ZZZZ	NY
LEIFERT, JULIUS	40	M	LABR	RR	ZZZZ	NY
MANDEINSK, MORITZ	22	M	LABR	RR	ZZZZ	NY

PASSENGER	AGE	SEX	OCCUPATION	PRIV	VIL	DES
ROSENWEIG, ASCHER	22	M	LABR	RR	ZZZZ	NY
BRODY, OREAS	22	M	PNTR	RR	ZZZZ	NY
FRIEDMANN, S.	35	M	LABR	RR	ZZZZ	NY
IDLER, LEIB	45	M	TLR	RR	ZZZZ	NY
FANNY	7	F	CHILD	RR	ZZZZ	NY
FRIEDE	6	F	CHILD	RR	ZZZZ	NY
JOACHIM	5	M	CHILD	RR	ZZZZ	NY
WERSTEIN, ABRAH.	20	M	TDR	RR	ZZZZ	NY
NESINSKE, BESAS	19	M	TDR	RR	ZZZZ	NY
SOUK--, ANNA	20	F	SGL	RR	ZZZZ	NY
VOGEL, SARAH	22	F	WO	RR	ZZZZ	NY
BEILE	7	F	CHILD	RR	ZZZZ	NY
PESCHE	6	F	CHILD	RR	ZZZZ	NY
NACHE	5	F	CHILD	RR	ZZZZ	NY
ISAAC	3	M	CHILD	RR	ZZZZ	NY
DWERCKE	.07	M	INFANT	RR	ZZZZ	NY
CHAIM	.07	M	INFANT	RR	ZZZZ	NY
STARK, LEIB	36	M	TDR	RR	ZZZZ	NY
KURE	7	F	CHILD	RR	ZZZZ	NY
JACH, SCHOL	18	M	TDR	RR	ZZZZ	NY
LANDAN, M.	7	M	CHILD	RR	ZZZZ	NY
ADAMUS, JOS.	21	M	TDR	RR	ZZZZ	NY
SAWICKY, PIOTR	16	M	TDR	RR	ZZZZ	NY
MEIROWITH, BEILE	19	F	SGL	RR	ZZZZ	NY
SEGALL, MALKE	36	F	WO	RR	ZZZZ	NY
ROSA	13	F	WO	RR	ZZZZ	NY
RACHEL	7	F	CHILD	RR	ZZZZ	NY
TAUBE	5	F	CHILD	RR	ZZZZ	NY
ZIPPE	3	F	CHILD	RR	ZZZZ	NY
SCHEINE	.07	F	INFANT	RR	ZZZZ	NY
LIBERMAN, MOSCHE	17	M	TDR	RR	ZZZZ	NY

SHIP: GELLERT

FROM: HAMBURG
TO: NEW YORK
ARRIVED: 07 JULY 1884

PASSENGER	AGE	SEX	OCCUPATION	PRIV	VIL	DES
EPSTEIN, ELJE	19	F	SGL	RR	ZZZZ	USA
RADZIEJEWSKA, GOLDE	28	F	W	RR	ZZZZ	USA
JENTE	9	M	CHILD	RR	ZZZZ	USA
LEISER	7	M	CHILD	RR	ZZZZ	USA
ISAAC	.11	M	INFANT	RR	ZZZZ	USA
KISCH, STEFAN	50	M	LABR	RR	ZZZZ	USA
WALDMANN, ROSA	13	F	SGL	RR	ZZZZ	USA
GORDON, LOUIS	38	M	TLR	RR	ZZZZ	USA
SEGELMANN, RAFAEL	19	M	WCHMKR	RR	ZZZZ	USA
SZEWTZKI, JOH.	19	M	LABR	RR	ZZZZ	USA
RZEMANISK, JOH.	28	M	LABR	RR	ZZZZ	USA
LANTERSTEIN, GESCHE	40	F	W	RR	ZZZZ	USA
CZERNE	18	F	CH	RR	ZZZZ	USA
MORDCHE	14	M	CH	RR	ZZZZ	USA
TROIZKE, MESCHULEM	24	M	DLR	RR	ZZZZ	USA
BRAD, LIEBE	18	F	SGL	RR	ZZZZ	USA
BILSKY, SAMUEL	17	M	TLR	RR	ZZZZ	USA
COHN, SARA	25	F	W	RR	ZZZZ	USA
TANLEK	.11	F	INFANT	RR	ZZZZ	USA
SADOSKI, IGNATZ	32	M	LABR	RR	ZZZZ	USA
SCHAPIRA, RACHEL	35	F	W	RR	ZZZZ	USA
ADOLF	9	M	CHILD	RR	ZZZZ	USA
SIMON	5	M	CHILD	RR	ZZZZ	USA
DINA	3	F	CHILD	RR	ZZZZ	USA
HANNE	6	F	CHILD	RR	ZZZZ	USA
KORINZKI, EVA	30	F	SGL	RR	ZZZZ	USA
HOVICZKAS, JURGIS	62	M	LABR	RR	ZZZZ	USA
GOTOWITZ, MORITZ	20	M	WCHMKR	RR	ZZZZ	USA
PETERSEN, CHARLES	24	M	FARMER	RR	ZZZZ	USA
RACZUM, JEZE	40	M	TLR	RR	ZZZZ	USA
PLAGER, BASCHE	36	F	W	RR	ZZZZ	USA
ITE	16	F	D	RR	ZZZZ	USA
LURIE, CHAIM	15	M	LABR	RR	ZZZZ	USA
BLUMBERG, ISAAC	18	M	LABR	RR	ZZZZ	USA
KLOT, MOSES	20	M	TLR	RR	ZZZZ	USA
SCHEINE	20	F	W	RR	ZZZZ	USA
PALMBAUN, PEISACH	50	M	BCHR	RR	ZZZZ	USA
JUDEL	18	M	S	RR	ZZZZ	USA
LUBIN, KUSSIEL	18	M	LABR	RR	ZZZZ	USA
HILFMAN, ABEL	9	M	CHILD	RR	ZZZZ	USA
LEBINSCH, MEIER	17	M	DLR	RR	ZZZZ	USA
FRIEDMAN, JANKEL	25	M	DLR	RR	ZZZZ	USA
BROCKMAN, SALOM.	16	M	LABR	RR	ZZZZ	USA
SHOWELSKY, MOSES-J.	19	M	DLR	RR	ZZZZ	USA
JUPOWITZ, ABR.B.	25	M	DLR	RR	ZZZZ	USA
ZIMANN, MEIER	24	M	LABR	RR	ZZZZ	USA
MATUWENITZ, MARIUS	25	M	LABR	RR	ZZZZ	USA
JUDELSOHN, MARKS	18	M	LABR	RR	ZZZZ	USA
PERCILSOWITZ, SCHEINE	18	F	SGL	RR	ZZZZ	USA
LEILE	57	M	LABR	RR	ZZZZ	USA
HOPPENHEIM, FEIGEL	18	F	SGL	RR	ZZZZ	USA
ROSENBERG, JENTE	36	F	W	RR	ZZZZ	USA
ANNA	9	F	CHILD	RR	ZZZZ	USA
BASCHE	8	F	CHILD	RR	ZZZZ	USA
SAMUEL	4	M	CHILD	RR	ZZZZ	USA
CHANNE	.11	F	INFANT	RR	ZZZZ	USA
MARGOLIES, SISEL	23	F	W	RR	ZZZZ	USA
SALOMON	.11	M	INFANT	RR	ZZZZ	USA
SKUROWSKY, GOLDE	30	F	W	RR	ZZZZ	USA
LEA	19	F	CH	RR	ZZZZ	USA
PEREL	7	M	CHILD	RR	ZZZZ	USA
ABRAHAM	4	M	CHILD	RR	ZZZZ	USA
HIRSCH	.11	M	INFANT	RR	ZZZZ	USA
MILSLESCHANSKY, IVAN	18	M	LABR	RR	ZZZZ	USA
DOBROWSKY, WLADISL.	26	M	LABR	RR	ZZZZ	USA
JOSEFA	22	F	W	RR	ZZZZ	USA
SCHAWELSKY, SARA	19	F	SGL	RR	ZZZZ	USA
JEFSEK, ANTONIA	50	F	W	RR	ZZZZ	USA
BRESLANER, HEIMAN	16	M	TLR	RR	ZZZZ	USA
GORDON, ISSER	23	M	LABR	RR	ZZZZ	USA
PERZIKOWIECZ, JACOB	9	M	CHILD	RR	ZZZZ	USA
ZESCHLANSKY, SAMUEL	23	M	TLR	RR	ZZZZ	USA
BASCHE	20	F	W	RR	ZZZZ	USA
PJEKER, JANKEL	21	M	SHMK	RR	ZZZZ	USA
RATZEN, LEISER	19	M	SHMK	RR	ZZZZ	USA
IZIKOWITZ, ABRAH.	21	M	SHMK	RR	ZZZZ	USA
EISIKOWITZ, ABRAH.	18	M	TNMK	RR	ZZZZ	USA
TKATZ, ISAAC	21	M	LABR	RR	ZZZZ	USA
DRASNY, PESACH	24	M	LABR	RR	ZZZZ	USA
DOBRZYNSKI, LESSER	18	M	MCHT	RR	ZZZZ	USA
ZLUMSKY, LEON	20	M	LABR	RR	ZZZZ	USA
PETZOLD, ERNZT	28	M	LABR	RR	ZZZZ	USA
MARTIN, ADOLF	16	M	SHMK	RR	ZZZZ	USA
WOLKOWISK, MOSES	18	M	LABR	RR	ZZZZ	USA
HOLGAITIS, JANOS	34	M	LABR	RR	ZZZZ	USA
GRUENBERG, HENOSH	9	M	CHILD	RR	ZZZZ	USA
ESTHER	8	F	CHILD	RR	ZZZZ	USA
WOLINSKY, SANDER	22	M	DLR	RR	ZZZZ	USA
PETTERSEN, KARL	17	M	LABR	RR	ZZZZ	USA
PER.	15	M	LABR	RR	ZZZZ	USA
UMANSKY, JOSEF	58	M	LABR	RR	ZZZZ	USA
GITTEL	55	F	W	RR	ZZZZ	USA
HENRIETTE	25	F	CH	RR	ZZZZ	USA
ESTHER	22	F	CH	RR	ZZZZ	USA
LEA	19	F	CH	RR	ZZZZ	USA
MARIE	16	F	CH	RR	ZZZZ	USA
UYZEICST, E.	55	M	LABR	RR	ZZZZ	USA
KRIMUNT, LEA	47	F	W	RR	ZZZZ	USA
ANETTA	16	F	CH	RR	ZZZZ	USA
ROSA	15	F	CH	RR	ZZZZ	USA
KLARA	9	F	CHILD	RR	ZZZZ	USA
MARIE	8	F	CHILD	RR	ZZZZ	USA
LOLA	7	F	CHILD	RR	ZZZZ	USA
VICTORIA	5	F	CHILD	RR	ZZZZ	USA
ARNOLD	2	M	CHILD	RR	ZZZZ	USA
BOSCHNIER, ALBERT	31	M	MCHT	RR	ZZZZ	USA
SILBERSTEIN, FISCHEL	30	M	LABR	RR	ZZZZ	USA

PASSENGER	AGE	SEX	OCCUPATION	PRV VIL DES
SLOTERENSKY, SARAH	16	F	SGL	RRZZZZUSA
KAPLAN, JACOB	24	M	SHMK	RRZZZZUSA
SARAH	20	F	W	RRZZZZUSA
PERLBERG, ISRAEL	21	M	JWLR	RRZZZZUSA
TANKEL, MENDEL	30	M	LABR	RRZZZZUSA
OSER, HIRSCH	10	M	CH	RRZZZZUSA
ABRAHAM	8	M	CHILD	RRZZZZUSA
KLEINSS, BASCHE	20	F	SGL	RRZZZZUSA
TER, DAVID	24	M	LABR	RRZZZZUSA
SCHERASCHEWSKY, CHAIM	16	M	LABR	RRZZZZUSA
WIESNA, JACOB	19	M	LABR	RRZZZZUSA
SEGAL, JACOB	28	M	LABR	RRZZZZUSA
MERENLANDER, JUDEL	20	M	LABR	RRZZZZUSA
EPHRAIM	19	M	LABR	RRZZZZUSA
KRIMKA, JOSSEL	18	M	TLR	RRZZZZUSA
DONOWITZ, MATEL	35	M	LABR	RRZZZZUSA
ABRAMOWITZ, MENDEL	19	M	LABR	RRZZZZUSA
SCHAPIRO, MOSES	42	M	LABR	RRZZZZUSA
RABINOWITZ, CHISSEL	30	M	LABR	RRZZZZUSA
MIEDLANSKY, SCHMERIEL	22	M	LABR	RRZZZZUSA
BUCH, DAVID	18	M	LABR	RRZZZZUSA
JAPKO, JOSSEL	37	M	LABR	RRZZZZUSA
TRANB, ESSOCH	30	M	LABR	RRZZZZUSA
SCHRAGI, GIETEL	20	F	SGL	RRZZZZUSA
GOLDSTEIN, SARAH	19	F	SGL	RRZZZZUSA
BRAUN, ROSA	17	F	SGL	RRZZZZUSA
AUSTERN, RIWKE	20	F	SGL	RRZZZZUSA
PETELOVSKY, HANNE	20	F	SGL	RRZZZZUSA
POTTS, TAUBE	18	F	SGL	RRZZZZUSA
BERNSTEIN, SCHEINE	30	F	W	RRZZZZUSA
LEA	.11	F	INFANT	RRZZZZUSA
ROSENTHAL, FEIWEL	45	M	LABR	RRZZZZUSA
BENZEL	9	M	CHILD	RRZZZZUSA
RUBENSTEIN, CHANNE	40	F	W	RRZZZZUSA
JACHWED	18	M	CH	RRZZZZUSA
LEA	16	F	CH	RRZZZZUSA
SARA	3	F	CHILD	RRZZZZUSA
CHAIE	.11	F	INFANT	RRZZZZUSA
ENDELMAN, LEA	36	F	W	RRZZZZUSA
MOSES	6	M	CHILD	RRZZZZUSA
OREL	.11	M	INFANT	RRZZZZUSA
BARANOWITZ, ESTHER	18	F	SGL	RRZZZZUSA
ABELSOHN, JUDEL	30	M	LABR	RRZZZZUSA
VAGT, WILH.	32	M	LABR	RRZZZZUSA
DECKSCHORT, AUGUST.	35	M	LABR	RRZZZZUSA
EPSTEIN, CHAIE	20	M	LABR	RRZZZZUSA
FRIEDMANSKY, JACOB	20	M	LABR	RRZZZZUSA
CHAIE	22	F	W	RRZZZZUSA
RUNDNUD, BEER	21	M	LABR	RRZZZZUSA
JABLONOWSKY, BERIL	20	M	LABR	RRZZZZUSA
GUROWSKY, BERL	25	M	LABR	RRZZZZUSA
BORUCKS, JETTE	23	F	W	RRZZZZUSA
JOSEF	.06	M	INFANT	RRZZZZUSA
HESCHENOWITZ, EIGE	18	F	SGL	RRZZZZUSA
HIRSCH	15	M	LABR	RRZZZZUSA
HEXHELSOHN, EPHRAIM	30	M	LABR	RRZZZZUSA
SIMANN, USIAS	36	M	LABR	RRZZZZUSA
FRIEDMANN, JACOB	18	M	LABR	RRZZZZUSA
DOBROWSKY, WLADISL.	.03	M	INFANT	RRZZZZUSA

SHIP: LESSING

FROM: HAMBURG AND HAVRE
TO: NEW YORK
ARRIVED: 07 JULY 1884

PASSENGER	AGE	SEX	OCCUPATION	PRV VIL DES
HERSCHMANN, ALTE	16	F	SGL	RRZZZZUSA
MARGOLINS, FISCHEL	18	M	FARMER	RRZZZZUSA
GERSON	9	M	CHILD	RRZZZZUSA
LEWIN, ABR.	19	M	MCHT	RRZZZZUSA
RAIGROTZKI, RIWKE	23	F	W	RRZZZZUSA
ISAAC	3	M	CHILD	RRZZZZUSA
ABR.	.11	M	INFANT	RRZZZZUSA
WOLFSOHN, CHAJE	15	F	SGL	RRZZZZUSA
LEWIN, ESTHER	26	F	W	RRZZZZUSA
SARA	.11	F	INFANT	RRZZZZUSA
BIRGER, BEILE	18	F	SGL	RRZZZZUSA
ZIMMERSSITZ, LIEBE	18	F	SGL	RRZZZZUSA
LEWIN, MOSES	18	M	LABR	RRZZZZUSA
SARA	9	F	CHILD	RRZZZZUSA
KORN, WOLF	14	M	LABR	RRZZZZUSA
U, U	18	M	LABR	RRZZZZUSA
FEINKOWITZ, FEIWEL	22	M	LABR	RRZZZZUSA
GLUECK, ISRAEL	31	M	LABR	RRZZZZUSA
SCHARGAWSKY, LORCH	31	M	LABR	RRZZZZUSA
BRENNER, MARKS	41	M	LABR	RRZZZZUSA
KLEINOWITZ, MOSES	17	M	LABR	RRZZZZUSA
KADNEZEWITZ, RUBEN	33	M	LABR	RRZZZZUSA
SCHAJE	40	F	W	RRZZZZUSA
LEA	7	F	CHILD	RRZZZZUSA
HILLEL	5	M	CHILD	RRZZZZUSA
WALANSKY, JANKEL	17	M	LABR	RRZZZZUSA
MARKS, ABRAM	25	M	LABR	RRZZZZUSA
TICOTSKI, JOSEPH	15	M	LABR	RRZZZZUSA
SLONINSKY, SELDE	21	F	W	RRZZZZUSA
DAVID	.06	M	INFANT	RRZZZZUSA
FEINBERG, ROSA	17	F	SGL	RRZZZZUSA
KOBUCKOW, SIMON	21	M	PNTR	RRZZZZUSA
NEBEL, JACOB	30	M	TLR	RRZZZZUSA
ROSENBERG, LOUISE	28	F	W	RRZZZZUSA
ITE	9	F	CHILD	RRZZZZUSA
WILOWISKI, FEIWEL	19	M	DLR	RRZZZZUSA
ROBINSKY, FEIGE	18	F	SGL	RRZZZZUSA
SKOP, BARUCH	16	M	JNR	RRZZZZUSA
BOLKIN, JULS.	19	M	LABR	RRZZZZUSA
DINWISKI, CHAJE	18	F	SGL	RRZZZZUSA
NEUMANN, HATTIE	17	F	SGL	RRZZZZUSA
DONEIF, SCHOLE	20	M	LABR	RRZZZZUSA
ABRAMOWITZ, ZALLEL	22	F	W	RRZZZZUSA
BASCHE	.11	F	INFANT	RRZZZZUSA
NENHOFF, JUDEL	53	M	LABR	RRZZZZUSA
COHN, SARA	30	F	W	RRZZZZUSA
CHEINE	7	F	CHILD	RRZZZZUSA
ABR.	.11	M	INFANT	RRZZZZUSA
FRUMSOHN, RACHEL	25	F	W	RRZZZZUSA
GOLDE	5	F	CHILD	RRZZZZUSA
SARA	.11	F	INFANT	RRZZZZUSA
BENJAMIN, BARUCH	20	M	LABR	RRZZZZUSA
BECKENSTAL, MOSES	20	M	DLR	RRZZZZUSA
MALISCHEWSKY, FEIWEL	18	M	TLR	RRZZZZUSA
FEINEMANN, LEIB	29	M	DLR	RRZZZZUSA
SCHREINER, JOEL	20	M	LABR	RRZZZZUSA
THAL, JOSEPH	23	F	DLR	RRZZZZUSA
KAHN, BENZEL	23	M	DLR	RRZZZZUSA
MEYER, TOBIAS	16	M	TLR	RRZZZZUSA
GERSCHOWITZ, MOSES	30	M	LABR	RRZZZZUSA
NEBEL, CHANNE	20	F	SGL	RRZZZZUSA
AKTARYNCH, ABRAH.	30	M	LABR	RRZZZZUSA
KOHN, MOSES	32	M	LABR	RRZZZZUSA
MENDEL	17	M	LABR	RRZZZZUSA
WILLER, HEINRICH	30	M	LABR	RRZZZZUSA
LIPSCHITZ, LEIB	18	M	LABR	RRZZZZUSA
LEWIN, BEINES	26	M	LABR	RRZZZZUSA
TSCHANOSILSKY, JOSEPH	24	M	LABR	RRZZZZUSA
NEUMANN, LEISER	19	M	LABR	RRZZZZUSA
ZWIETOWITZ, ABRAH.	23	M	TLR	RRZZZZUSA
SLAPAK, ARON	24	M	HAMF	RRZZZZUSA
KODUCZEWITZ, ABRAM	3	M	CHILD	RRZZZZUSA
SCHLUNHANTZKI, FRANZ	23	M	LABR	RRZZZZUSA
NEUMARK, HANNE	30	F	SGL	RRZZZZUSA
MANNFOLK, KARL	18	M	LABR	FNZZZZUSA
GUTMANN, SARA	22	F	SGL	RRZZZZUSA
WEINSTEIN, ABRAH.	17	M	TLR	RRZZZZUSA
GITTEL	15	F	SGL	RRZZZZUSA
BLOCH, BERTHA	47	M	TLR	RRZZZZUSA

PASSENGER	AGE	SEX	OCCUPATION	PRIVL	VIL	DES
NATHAN, CHARLES	45	M	DLR	RR	ZZZZ	USA
HIRSCH	15	M	S	RR	ZZZZ	USA
TANNSCHEIN, FREIDE	25	F	SGL	RR	ZZZZ	USA
GRUENFELS, CHANNE	18	F	SGL	RR	ZZZZ	USA
KOLIKOVSKY, JAN	20	M	LABR	RR	ZZZZ	USA
MATOLA, GEORG	23	M	LABR	RR	ZZZZ	USA
JURSKY, WLADISL.	22	M	LABR	RR	ZZZZ	USA
MARCHEWIC, JAN	22	M	LABR	RR	ZZZZ	USA
PRENGEL, GUST.	18	M	LABR	RR	ZZZZ	USA
STAWAJTYS, JAN	39	M	LABR	RR	ZZZZ	USA
MASIHEWITZ, JAN	18	M	LABR	RR	ZZZZ	USA
SCHAPIRA, BENZI	27	M	LABR	RR	ZZZZ	USA
MERBACH, BEILE	22	M	LABR	RR	ZZZZ	USA
FEINSTEIN, JOSSEL	25	M	LABR	RR	ZZZZ	USA
BLOCH, SIMCHE	34	M	LABR	RR	ZZZZ	USA
JEZKOWITZ, HIRSCH	19	M	LABR	RR	ZZZZ	USA
MILLER, LEIB	32	M	LABR	RR	ZZZZ	USA
ZINMANN, SELIG	26	M	LABR	RR	ZZZZ	USA
FARBER, GERSON	24	M	SHMK	RR	ZZZZ	USA
KLUSSKIN, ELIAS	24	M	TLR	RR	ZZZZ	USA
WALLEITEN, ELISABETH	35	F	SGL	RR	ZZZZ	USA
DRANGELIUS, VINCENTE	47	F	W	RR	ZZZZ	USA
SIMON	9	M	CHILD	RR	ZZZZ	USA
ANNA	3	F	CHILD	RR	ZZZZ	USA
ARENOWITZ, BEHR.	34	M	DLR	RR	ZZZZ	USA
BOMSZIG, HILLEL	22	M	DLR	RR	ZZZZ	USA
SOSNUTZKY, SCHINE	18	F	SGL	RR	ZZZZ	USA
RAGOLSKY, MARCUS	20	M	LABR	RR	ZZZZ	USA
SCHEINE	20	F	W	RR	ZZZZ	USA
SLOWINSKI, LEA	23	M	LABR	RR	ZZZZ	USA
VOGT, FRIEDR.	53	M	LABR	RR	ZZZZ	USA
JEWALENKO, CHANON	25	M	FARMER	RR	ZZZZ	USA
ROSA	19	F	W	RR	ZZZZ	USA
MILLER, MAURICE	22	M	LABR	RR	ZZZZ	USA
SURASKI, HODES	24	F	SGL	RR	ZZZZ	USA
LICHTENBERG, MARIE	55	F	WO	RR	ZZZZ	USA
HANNE	18	F	D	RR	ZZZZ	USA
WINIK, SCHIE	32	M	SHMK	RR	ZZZZ	USA
KRAWITZ, JOSEPH	34	M	DLR	RR	ZZZZ	USA
HANNA	32	F	W	RR	ZZZZ	USA
HERMANN	7	M	CHILD	RR	ZZZZ	USA
SAMUEL	5	M	CHILD	RR	ZZZZ	USA
TAUBE	2	F	CHILD	RR	ZZZZ	USA
HARRIS	.11	M	INFANT	RR	ZZZZ	USA
MILLER, HISS	23	M	ENGR	RR	ZZZZ	USA
ZAGALOWITZ, ISAAC	21	M	TNMK	RR	ZZZZ	USA
KOBYLAN-KY, ROMAIN	24	M	MECH	RR	ZZZZ	USA

SHIP: CANADA

FROM: HAVRE
TO: NEW YORK
ARRIVED: 09 JULY 1884

PASSENGER	AGE	SEX	OCCUPATION	PRIVL	VIL	DES
DE-ROTCHKOFF, U-MRS.	26	F	NN	RR	ZZZZ	NY
STEINDORFF, ISAAC	18	M	MECH	RR	ZZZZ	NY

SHIP: ETHIOPIA

FROM: GLASGOW AND MOVILLE
TO: NEW YORK
ARRIVED: 09 JULY 1884

PASSENGER	AGE	SEX	OCCUPATION	PRIVL	VIL	DES
DUBMEKY, ISRAEL	56	M	LABR	PL	ZZZZ	USA
NACL.	50	F	UNKNOWN	PL	ZZZZ	USA
BREMO	10	F	UNKNOWN	PL	ZZZZ	USA
BURGER, S.S.	34	F	UNKNOWN	RR	ZZZZ	USA
ISRAEL	15	M	UNKNOWN	RR	ZZZZ	USA
BENAZAWILSEH, NACHUM	75	M	LABR	RR	ZZZZ	USA
NORMON, ISRAEL	23	M	LABR	RR	ZZZZ	USA
MURSCHOWITCH, M.	30	M	LABR	RR	ZZZZ	USA
WASSON, JOSEF	23	M	LABR	RR	ZZZZ	USA
LENA	23	F	UNKNOWN	RR	ZZZZ	USA

SHIP: BELGENLAND

FROM: ANTWERP
TO: NEW YORK
ARRIVED: 11 JULY 1884

PASSENGER	AGE	SEX	OCCUPATION	PRIVL	VIL	DES
CAMITENK, ANNA	24	F	SVNT	PL	ZZZZ	MN

SHIP: CHATEAU YQUEN

FROM: BORDEAUX
TO: NEW YORK
ARRIVED: 11 JULY 1884

PASSENGER	AGE	SEX	OCCUPATION	PRIVL	VIL	DES
STOZLOISSKI, JEAN	28	M	TRDSMN	PL	ZZZZ	USA

SHIP: CITY OF RICHMOND

FROM: LIVERPOOL AND QUEENSTOWN
TO: NEW YORK
ARRIVED: 12 JULY 1884

PASSENGER	AGE	SEX	OCCUPATION	PRIVL	VIL	DES
REISCHIN, IFNE	29	M	LABR	PL	ZZZZ	USA
KRAUSHAAI, MOSES	33	M	LABR	PL	ZZZZ	USA
JETTE	10	M	CH	PL	ZZZZ	USA
DRILLING, BEZCK	53	M	LABR	PL	ZZZZ	USA
HANNA	19	F	SP	PL	ZZZZ	USA
DEWORA	10	F	CH	PL	ZZZZ	USA
DOBER	8	M	CHILD	PL	ZZZZ	USA

SHIP: INDIA

FROM: HAMBURG
TO: NEW YORK
ARRIVED: 13 JULY 1884

PASSENGER	AGE	SEX	OCCUPATION	PRIVL	VIL	DES
MOTLIN, HINDE	64	F	WO	RR	ZZZZ	NY
ABRAHAMSOHN, CHAIN	19	M	TDR	RR	ZZZZ	NY
LODZEISTEIN, CHR.	7	M	CHILD	RR	ZZZZ	NY
SLOTSKAMEN, RIWKE	56	F	WO	RR	ZZZZ	NY
SUSKIDOWITZ, ABELE	7	M	CHILD	RR	ZZZZ	NY
MANKE, AUGUSTE	22	F	SGL	RR	ZZZZ	IL
ZENDEL, FELIX	35	M	MCHT	RR	ZZZZ	NY
KI---ST, -ILM	00	M	TDR	RR	ZZZZ	NY
ABRAMOWITZ, ITE	00	F	SGL	RR	ZZZZ	NY
ORMLAND, NACH.	00	M	CGRMKR	RR	ZZZZ	NY

PASSENGER	AGE	SEX	OCCUPATION	PRV VIL DES
FEINBERG, RASCHE	24	F	WO	RRZZZZNY
MAIDELBERG, S.	35	M	WCHMKR	RRZZZZNY
WILENEZIK, ELIAS	46	M	TDR	RRZZZZNY
TAUBE	3	F	CHILD	RRZZZZNY
STRIWSS, CHARL.	53	F	WO	RRZZZZBAL
WILH.	23	F	D	RRZZZZBAL
CLARSSEN, WILHELM	24	M	CGRMKR	RRZZZZBAL
PETERSEN, P.	21	M	CGRMKR	RRZZZZBAL
GRUNBLATT, ESTER	24	F	SGL	PLZZZZNY
WALLACH, LEISE	18	F	SGL	PLZZZZNY
LITOWITZ, ELIAS	32	M	TDR	PLZZZZNY
ZEARNEWSKY, CHR.	16	F	SGL	PLZZZZNY
LEWENSTEIN, M.	19	M	TDR	PLZZZZNY
MAGID, ESTE	17	F	SGL	PLZZZZNY
CHJENC	20	F	SGL	PLZZZZNY
BERKSOHN, SIM.	17	M	LABR	PLZZZZNY
FELLMAN, LEWIN	23	M	TDR	PLZZZZNY
PERNIKOW, SAM.	17	M	TDR	PLZZZZNY
SCHEKIN, WENZEL	25	M	TDR	PLZZZZNY
ZUCKER, MOSES	45	M	TDR	PLZZZZNY
EMMER, SAMUEL	42	M	LABR	PLZZZZNY
KIRSMER, MOS.	20	M	TDR	RRZZZZNY
MER, DAVID	20	M	TDR	RRZZZZNY
FRIEDLAND, SCH.	20	M	TDR	RRZZZZNY
BRANDWEIN, JACOB	27	M	TDR	RRZZZZNY
PEPI	24	F	W	RRZZZZNY
SCHAPERON, BENJAMIN	32	M	TDR	RRZZZZNY
KULIKOWSKY, FRANZ	23	M	TDR	RRZZZZNY
KOZEK, BASCHKE	36	M	TDR	RRZZZZNY
MARKIR, LEISER	38	M	TDR	RRZZZZNY
RACHEL	17	F	W	RRZZZZNY
NACHMANN	7	M	CHILD	RRZZZZNY
ODE, MALKE	30	M	LABR	RRZZZZNY
JANKEL	7	M	CHILD	RRZZZZNY
CHATTEL	5	F	CHILD	RRZZZZNY
FEIGE	.11	F	INFANT	RRZZZZNY
BEESCHE	.02	F	INFANT	RRZZZZNY
TABOLOWSKY, ESTER	56	F	WO	RRZZZZNY
SMOLINK, LEIB	20	M	TDR	RRZZZZNY
JABLONOWSKI, JENTE	25	F	WO	RRZZZZNY
BENJAMIN	6	M	CHILD	RRZZZZNY
RIWKE	3	F	CHILD	RRZZZZNY
OSCAR	.07	M	INFANT	RRZZZZNY
BAYER, FRIEDEL	20	M	TDR	RRZZZZNY
ELBAUM, ISRAEL	19	M	TDR	RRZZZZNY
POMERANZ, JANKEL	18	M	TDR	RRZZZZNY
LIPSCHITZ, SALOMON	38	M	TDR	RRZZZZNY
TUGLAR, ABRAHAM	17	M	TDR	RRZZZZNY
MINARSCH, ZADEL	7	M	CHILD	RRZZZZNY
GRABMANN, MOSES	25	M	TDR	RRZZZZNY
SOMILSKI, ZOSSO	25	M	TDR	RRZZZZNY
WALK, ARON	29	M	TDR	RRZZZZNY
COHEN, JOSSEL	22	M	TDR	RRZZZZNY
CHAIM	23	M	TDR	RRZZZZNY
FUHRMANN, ARON	33	M	LABR	RRZZZZNY
BRAND, SARA	15	F	SGL	PLZZZZNY
UNGER, S.	20	F	WO	PLZZZZNY
JETTE	.09	F	INFANT	PLZZZZNY
TAPPER, RASCHE	29	F	WO	PLZZZZNY
MARCUS	7	M	CHILD	PLZZZZNY
CACILIE	6	F	CHILD	PLZZZZNY
LEON	4	M	CHILD	PLZZZZNY
SIGMUND	3	M	CHILD	PLZZZZNY
BLOHM, JOH.C.C.	26	M	LABR	RRZZZZNY
FESCHMANN, BASCHE	10	F	CH	RRZZZZNY
REIMSER, JOHANN	15	M	LABR	RRZZZZNY
TOMERSOND, AGATHE	22	F	UNKNOWN	RRZZZZNY
JAKUBOWSKY, VINC.	21	M	LABR	RRZZZZNY

SHIP: CARACAS

FROM: LA GUAIRA AND PUERTO CABELLO
TO: NEW YORK
ARRIVED: 14 JULY 1884

PASSENGER	AGE	SEX	OCCUPATION	PRV VIL DES
POPERT, PHILIPP	57	M	MCHT	RRZZZZUNK

SHIP: FURNESSIA

FROM: GLASGOW AND MOVILLE
TO: NEW YORK
ARRIVED: 15 JULY 1884

PASSENGER	AGE	SEX	OCCUPATION	PRV VIL DES
BRIETERMANN, HIRSCH	28	M	LABR	RRZZZZUSA
RACHEL	25	F	W	RRZZZZUSA
SARA	4	M	CHILD	RRZZZZUSA
ABR.	1	F	CHILD	RRZZZZUSA
REB.	.06	F	INFANT	RRZZZZUSA
GALZAR, JOHN	28	M	LABR	RRZZZZUSA
LEONORA	18	F	W	RRZZZZUSA
BERGMANN, ISAC	24	M	LABR	RRZZZZUSA
JENSOVA, WAK.	20	F	SVNT	RRZZZZUSA
HOIM, ABR.	20	M	LABR	RRZZZZUSA
CHAIE	23	F	W	RRZZZZUSA
SORE	.06	F	INFANT	RRZZZZUSA
LEINTH, CASKEL	26	F	SVNT	RRZZZZUSA
ROSS, DAVID	18	M	LABR	RRZZZZUSA
BUDWICK, ADOLF	11	M	CH	RRZZZZUSA
LEIKIHONER, ADOLF	18	M	LABR	RRZZZZUSA
WARSOISEKA, LEB	51	F	SVNT	RRZZZZUSA
SILLETRED, INGO	25	F	SVNT	RRZZZZUSA
SCHERNSKI, VICTOR	22	M	LABR	RRZZZZUSA
REGDA, FRANZ	49	M	LABR	RRZZZZUSA
FRAN.	47	F	W	RRZZZZUSA
JOHANN	3	F	CHILD	RRZZZZUSA
KATH.	5	F	CHILD	RRZZZZUSA
FRAN.	4	F	CHILD	RRZZZZUSA
THERESIA	20	F	SVNT	RRZZZZUSA
RUDOLF	11	M	CH	RRZZZZUSA
FRANZ	16	M	LABR	RRZZZZUSA
MARIE	22	F	SVNT	RRZZZZUSA
FARNBER, JOSEF	30	M	LABR	RRZZZZUSA

SHIP: AMERIQUE

FROM: HAVRE
TO: NEW YORK
ARRIVED: 16 JULY 1884

PASSENGER	AGE	SEX	OCCUPATION	PRV VIL DES
BORONSTEIN, SALOMON	24	M	TLR	RRZZZZUSA
GOLDREICH, MOISE	33	M	TLR	RRZZZZUSA

PASSENGER	AGE	SEX	OCCUPATION	PRIV	VIL	DES
SHIP: BOHEMIA						
FROM: HAMBURG						
TO: NEW YORK						
ARRIVED: 17 JULY 1884						
LIEBSCHUTZ, ESTHER	30	F	W	RR	ZZZZ	USA
TAUBE	7	F	CHILD	RR	ZZZZ	USA
FEIZEL	.11	F	INFANT	RR	ZZZZ	USA
FUDIRCH, FEGIER	27	M	JNR	RR	ZZZZ	USA
LAURA	23	F	W	RR	ZZZZ	USA
LOEWENSTEIN, SARA	19	F	SGL	RR	ZZZZ	USA
KASSEL, SARA	30	F	SGL	RR	ZZZZ	USA
VOLKWISCH, HERSCHEL	16	M	TLR	RR	ZZZZ	USA
LAMBERT, BERL	24	M	LABR	RR	ZZZZ	USA
KASCH, MOSES	19	M	TLR	RR	ZZZZ	USA
HIRSCH, ABR.	20	M	TLR	RR	ZZZZ	USA
SOMNACH, ABRAM	24	M	LABR	RR	ZZZZ	USA
BLUMBERG, MICHEL	9	M	CHILD	RR	ZZZZ	USA
LIPMANN, CHAJE	22	F	SGL	RR	ZZZZ	USA
PETIKOWSKI, JANKEL	17	M	LABR	RR	ZZZZ	USA
RUBIN, RIWE	19	F	SGL	RR	ZZZZ	USA
FAGORSKO, SARA	64	F	W	RR	ZZZZ	USA
MANNHEIMER, ELISE	24	F	SGL	RR	ZZZZ	USA
GOLDSTEIN, RACHEL	24	F	SGL	RR	ZZZZ	USA
SELAMITZKY, JANKEL	21	M	TLR	RR	ZZZZ	USA
RAPPOPORT, HANNE	26	F	SGL	RR	ZZZZ	USA
PODZAMKY, SEIBIEL	22	M	SHMK	RR	ZZZZ	USA
ENNR, DIEDRICH	36	M	LABR	RR	ZZZZ	USA
MARG.	36	F	W	RR	ZZZZ	USA
ELISAB.	13	F	CH	RR	ZZZZ	USA
JOH.	9	F	CHILD	RR	ZZZZ	USA
DIEDRICH	8	M	CHILD	RR	ZZZZ	USA
JACOB	7	M	CHILD	RR	ZZZZ	USA
PETER	5	M	CHILD	RR	ZZZZ	USA
MARG.	2	F	CHILD	RR	ZZZZ	USA
HEINR.	.01	M	INFANT	RR	ZZZZ	USA
FANKELOWITZ, TEWJE	21	M	LABR	RR	ZZZZ	USA
TROGAHN, AUGUSTE	23	F	SGL	RR	ZZZZ	USA
TRIRINSKI, MOSES	22	M	BCHR	RR	ZZZZ	USA
FRUME	23	F	W	RR	ZZZZ	USA
LIER, GEDALIE	17	M	TLR	RR	ZZZZ	USA
HUDERMANN, BERTHA	18	F	SGL	RR	ZZZZ	USA
FUARR, MATH.	43	M	LABR	RR	ZZZZ	USA
HAMUR, KARL	38	M	LABR	RR	ZZZZ	USA
BERNAR, ERIK	49	M	LABR	RR	ZZZZ	USA
KARL	31	M	LABR	RR	ZZZZ	USA
SZAMUTAT, FURGER	26	M	LABR	RR	ZZZZ	USA
PRIGOWSKY, FOREL	24	M	LABR	RR	ZZZZ	USA
AUZURTOWSKI, MAUSCHL	38	M	LABR	RR	ZZZZ	USA
LOEPP, PETER	37	M	LABR	RR	ZZZZ	USA
MARIE	32	F	W	RR	ZZZZ	USA
PETER	9	M	CHILD	RR	ZZZZ	USA
JACOB	7	M	CHILD	RR	ZZZZ	USA
JOH.	5	M	CHILD	RR	ZZZZ	USA
MARIE	3	F	CHILD	RR	ZZZZ	USA
SUSANNA	.09	F	INFANT	RR	ZZZZ	USA
SCHMELZINZER, ESTHER	18	F	SGL	RR	ZZZZ	USA
AUGUST, JUDITH	20	F	SGL	RR	ZZZZ	USA
SCHEWEL, PAUL	24	M	DLR	RR	ZZZZ	USA
SCHNEIDER, JOSSEL	25	M	DLR	RR	ZZZZ	USA
BEYERFELD, HENRIETTE	28	F	W	RR	ZZZZ	USA
JENNY	3	F	CHILD	RR	ZZZZ	USA
JOH.	30	F	SGL	RR	ZZZZ	USA
FAHRENBUCH, HEINR.	29	M	MCHT	RR	ZZZZ	USA
FRENDBERG, BENNEL	22	M	LABR	RR	ZZZZ	USA
WOLPERT, MEYER	32	M	LABR	RR	ZZZZ	USA
RABINOWITZ, DAVID	30	M	LABR	RR	ZZZZ	USA
SOM, HIRSCH	18	M	LABR	RR	ZZZZ	USA
SOHICK, MOSES	23	M	WCHMKR	RR	ZZZZ	USA
KREJNER, ESTHER	17	F	SGL	RR	ZZZZ	USA
SCHLUFREL, KUVA	42	F	W	RR	ZZZZ	USA
LEIBER, SCHEINDEL	16	F	SGL	RR	ZZZZ	USA
BRANER, HEINR.	24	M	LABR	RR	ZZZZ	USA
BERKOWITZ, LEOPOLD	16	M	LABR	RR	ZZZZ	USA
MICHAELSON, HANNE	35	F	W	RR	ZZZZ	USA
HEINE	22	F	SGL	RR	ZZZZ	USA
MARIE	9	F	CHILD	RR	ZZZZ	USA
SARA	8	F	CHILD	RR	ZZZZ	USA
ARON	3	M	CHILD	RR	ZZZZ	USA
DONS	.11	M	INFANT	RR	ZZZZ	USA
BAKANPIMONA, ROSALIE	18	F	SGL	RR	ZZZZ	USA
CHMIALEWSKI, JOHN	20	M	LABR	RR	ZZZZ	USA
JOSEF	19	M	LABR	RR	ZZZZ	USA
GRATS, ILIA	32	M	LABR	RR	ZZZZ	USA
MEJERSKA, ALEXANDRA	16	F	SGL	RR	ZZZZ	USA
LEYFER, GITTEL	15	F	SGL	RR	ZZZZ	USA
GOLD, NACHUM	17	M	JNR	RR	ZZZZ	USA
BUDZEWITZ, HANNE	26	F	W	RR	ZZZZ	USA
SARA	14	F	SI	RR	ZZZZ	USA
LEISER	7	M	CHILD	RR	ZZZZ	USA
ABRAHAM	4	M	CHILD	RR	ZZZZ	USA
ISAAC	2	M	CHILD	RR	ZZZZ	USA
LEA	.06	F	INFANT	RR	ZZZZ	USA
GINZBURG, HEINE	38	F	W	RR	ZZZZ	USA
FRENE	15	F	CH	RR	ZZZZ	USA
JANKEL	9	F	CHILD	RR	ZZZZ	USA
LECHOK	8	F	CHILD	RR	ZZZZ	USA
MARIE	7	F	CHILD	RR	ZZZZ	USA
MULLER, MORITZ	23	M	DLR	RR	ZZZZ	USA
SCHAEHOW, HIRSCH	16	M	DLR	RR	ZZZZ	USA
KARLON, HANNE	23	F	W	RR	ZZZZ	USA
ROSA	.01	F	INFANT	RR	ZZZZ	USA
RACHEL	15	F	SGL	RR	ZZZZ	USA
MARRUS, SARA	21	F	SGL	RR	ZZZZ	USA
HAMSA, AMRICH	28	F	W	RR	ZZZZ	USA
HANNE	6	F	CHILD	RR	ZZZZ	USA
MARIE	.06	F	INFANT	RR	ZZZZ	USA
SCHMARGEN, LEISER	20	M	LABR	RR	ZZZZ	USA
SCHEIT, SAMUEL	19	M	LABR	RR	ZZZZ	USA
KRANITZKI, MOSES	40	M	LABR	RR	ZZZZ	USA
KAHN, MENDEL	28	M	LABR	RR	ZZZZ	USA
CERVENKA, MARIE	21	F	SGL	RR	ZZZZ	USA
ELLENSTEIN, MAX	26	M	LABR	RR	ZZZZ	USA
ZUTEL, MATH	30	M	LABR	RR	ZZZZ	USA
ANNA	32	F	W	RR	ZZZZ	USA
STRASCHONER, DAVID	18	M	TLR	RR	ZZZZ	USA
ROSENBERG, MEIER	33	M	DLR	RR	ZZZZ	USA
NECHAME	28	F	W	RR	ZZZZ	USA
RACHEL	.06	F	INFANT	RR	ZZZZ	USA
JAFFE, CHIKEL	23	M	LABR	RR	ZZZZ	USA
PAU.	23	F	W	RR	ZZZZ	USA
SCHEINE	.06	F	INFANT	RR	ZZZZ	USA
FREILICH, MOSES	40	M	DLR	RR	ZZZZ	USA
MITTENTHAL, SARA	25	F	W	RR	ZZZZ	USA
JACOB	.11	M	INFANT	RR	ZZZZ	USA
ERSON, ISRAEL	20	M	LABR	RR	ZZZZ	USA
LEIE, SCHEINE	18	F	W	RR	ZZZZ	USA
MARCUS, LEIB	21	M	LABR	RR	ZZZZ	USA
GRUNA, JACOB	45	M	LABR	PL	ZZZZ	USA
PRIZOWSKI, JOSEF	.02	M	INFANT	RR	ZZZZ	USA
SCHELICHOWA, ANNA	20	F	SGL	RR	ZZZZ	USA
FEINBERG, HIRSCH	16	M	CL	RR	ZZZZ	USA
KLEIN, PHILIPP	26	M	SHMK	RR	ZZZZ	USA
SCHEZERBACK, HINDE	18	F	SGL	RR	ZZZZ	USA
KATZANCK, DAUBE	52	F	W	RR	ZZZZ	USA
ZIPE	17	F	D	RR	ZZZZ	USA
ISAAC	9	M	CHILD	RR	ZZZZ	USA
DAVIDSOHN, JETTE	22	F	SGL	RR	ZZZZ	USA
HOLMIKER, RACHEL	15	F	SGL	RR	ZZZZ	USA
GOLDOEDT, ITE	48	F	W	RR	ZZZZ	USA
SARA	17	F	CH	RR	ZZZZ	USA
BENRION	9	F	CHILD	RR	ZZZZ	USA
RACHMIEL	8	F	CHILD	RR	ZZZZ	USA
KREINER, SCHLAJE	60	M	DLR	RR	ZZZZ	USA
WITRIOL, NATHAN	19	M	PNTR	RR	ZZZZ	USA
LAGEWITZ, SARA	20	F	SGL	RR	ZZZZ	USA
ZIEGOLNICK, JULIUS	31	M	LABR	RR	ZZZZ	USA
BOLTANSKY, JOSEPH	40	M	DLR	RR	ZZZZ	USA

PASSENGER	AGE	SEX	OCCUPATION	PRV	VIL	DES
SCHLUSSEL, MOSES	18	M	DLR	RR	ZZZ	ZUSA
ROSENTHAL, AD.	33	M	DLR	RR	ZZZ	ZUSA
STAHLBERGER, KALMAN	24	M	DLR	RR	ZZZ	ZUSA
ZEISLER, AD.	24	M	DLR	RR	ZZZ	ZUSA
LEZIK, FRANZ	18	M	DLR	RR	ZZZ	ZUSA
ROSENTHAL, ROSA	42	F	W	RR	ZZZ	ZUSA
JETTE	18	F	CH	RR	ZZZ	ZUSA
BENJA	14	F	CH	RR	ZZZ	ZUSA
BERTHA	9	F	CHILD	RR	ZZZ	ZUSA
MORITZ	8	M	CHILD	RR	ZZZ	ZUSA
HERRM.	7	M	CHILD	RR	ZZZ	ZUSA
BETTI	5	F	CHILD	RR	ZZZ	ZUSA
MARIE	.11	F	INFANT	RR	ZZZ	ZUSA
MOSES	.11	M	INFANT	RR	ZZZ	ZUSA
FRIEDLAND, PESACH	24	M	LABR	RR	ZZZ	ZUSA
MOSES	13	M	LABR	RR	ZZZ	ZUSA
KOBILINE, MARIE	24	F	W	RR	ZZZ	ZUSA
MARIE	9	F	CHILD	RR	ZZZ	ZUSA
SALKOWITSCH, MEIER	20	M	TLR	RR	ZZZ	ZUSA
SCHILOSARSKY, JOSSEL	9	M	CHILD	RR	ZZZ	ZUSA
FAROB, PERL	18	F	SGL	RR	ZZZ	ZUSA
KOLENDERSKI, JAN	48	M	LABR	RR	ZZZ	ZUSA
KNOPINZ, ISAAC	19	M	LABR	RR	ZZZ	ZUSA
MISCHKINSKI, REISEL	19	F	SGL	RR	ZZZ	ZUSA
ANHAR, JONAR	43	M	LABR	RR	ZZZ	ZUSA
ANNE	33	F	W	RR	ZZZ	ZUSA
JAN	5	M	CHILD	RR	ZZZ	ZUSA
ANNA	3	F	CHILD	RR	ZZZ	ZUSA
MARIE	.11	F	INFANT	RR	ZZZ	ZUSA
JOHAR	17	M	LABR	RR	ZZZ	ZUSA
ANNE	40	F	W	RR	ZZZ	ZUSA
AUGUST	13	M	CH	RR	ZZZ	ZUSA
JOSEF	9	M	CHILD	RR	ZZZ	ZUSA
EVA	8	F	CHILD	RR	ZZZ	ZUSA
MARIE	6	F	CHILD	RR	ZZZ	ZUSA
BARBARA	.11	F	INFANT	RR	ZZZ	ZUSA
PRUSS, GOLDE	17	F	SGL	RR	ZZZ	ZUSA
WITTKIN, ETTE	18	F	SGL	RR	ZZZ	ZUSA
FINBERG, TAUBE	19	F	SGL	RR	ZZZ	ZUSA
SCHLIMAKOWSKY, ESTHER	24	F	W	RR	ZZZ	ZUSA
HRICZA, GEORG	34	F	W	RR	ZZZ	ZUSA
GOLOMBECK, ISAAC	25	F	WCHMKR	RR	ZZZ	ZUSA
GLUCKS, ABRAHAM	45	F	TLR	RR	ZZZ	ZUSA
LEWIN, JUDA	38	F	DLR	RR	ZZZ	ZUSA
KRIEGER, HIRSCHEL	40	F	LKSH	RR	ZZZ	ZUSA
BRAM, ISRAEL	24	F	TLR	RR	ZZZ	ZUSA
BERINSTEIN, BER	24	F	LABR	RR	ZZZ	ZUSA
SARA	23	F	W	RR	ZZZ	ZUSA
CHANNE	.09	F	INFANT	RR	ZZZ	ZUSA
FINKELSTEIN, WOLF	39	M	LABR	RR	ZZZ	ZUSA
PRZESINSKI, PESCHE	40	F	W	RR	ZZZ	ZUSA
HENNE	3	F	CHILD	RR	ZZZ	ZUSA
JOSEL	.11	M	INFANT	RR	ZZZ	***
GLASER, IDA	28	F	W	RR	ZZZ	ZUSA
PESCHE	8	F	CHILD	RR	ZZZ	ZUSA
LIEBE	7	F	CHILD	RR	ZZZ	ZUSA
ANNA	.11	F	INFANT	RR	ZZZ	ZUSA
SARA	.01	F	INFANT	RR	ZZZ	ZUSA
FANKOWITSCH, ANNE	23	F	SGL	RR	ZZZ	ZUSA
LIEBMANN, ISRAEL	15	M	LABR	RR	ZZZ	ZUSA
WOLF	9	M	CHILD	RR	ZZZ	ZUSA
WYTOWSKY, CHOSCHEL	18	F	SGL	RR	ZZZ	ZUSA
LYK, AUG.	26	F	SGL	RR	ZZZ	ZUSA
SCHAPIRO, ABRAM	35	M	LABR	RR	ZZZ	ZUSA
SKALAR, ISRAEL	26	M	SHMK	RR	ZZZ	ZUSA
FEINSEN, WOLF	18	M	DLR	RR	ZZZ	ZUSA
SUSSERWEIN, LEIB	43	M	DLR	RR	ZZZ	ZUSA
PORLUKAMS, VERONIKA	25	F	SGL	RR	ZZZ	ZUSA
LEWITE, SLATE	18	F	SGL	RR	ZZZ	ZUSA
STROKODAITIR, IGNATZ	23	M	LABR	RR	ZZZ	ZUSA
SACKS, MORDCHE	17	M	LABR	RR	ZZZ	ZUSA
SCHARATSCHEK, CHAIM	50	M	LABR	RR	ZZZ	ZUSA
JOBLONSKY, SALOMON	40	M	LABR	RR	ZZZ	ZUSA
TOKAR, SALOMON	22	M	MCHT	RR	ZZZ	ZUSA
RANSUK, ISRAEL	38	M	LABR	RR	ZZZ	ZUSA
ABEL	16	M	LABR	RR	ZZZ	ZUSA
ZADEKOWITZ, MOSES	18	M	LABR	RR	ZZZ	ZUSA
MARRUSNAUS, MATAWUSCH	23	M	LABR	RR	ZZZ	ZUSA
RACHELOWITZ, JOSEPH	23	M	LABR	RR	ZZZ	ZUSA
LEWITT, PERACH	17	M	LABR	RR	ZZZ	ZUSA
KOHN, SALOMON	43	M	LKSH	RR	ZZZ	ZUSA
GOLDSTEIN, ABRAHAM	20	M	DLR	RR	ZZZ	ZUSA

SHIP: SALIER

FROM: BREMEN
TO: NEW YORK
ARRIVED: 18 JULY 1884

PASSENGER	AGE	SEX	OCCUPATION	PRV	VIL	DES
SCHIEFELHEIN, HEINR.	26	M	FARMER	RR	ZZZ	ZUSA
BARBARA	26	F	W	RR	ZZZ	ZUSA
JOSEF	.06	M	INFANT	RR	ZZZ	ZUSA
ETZEL, JOSEF	31	M	JNR	RR	ZZZ	ZUSA
KATHR.	31	F	W	RR	ZZZ	ZUSA
GEORG	8	M	CHILD	RR	ZZZ	ZUSA
JOHANNES	5	M	CHILD	RR	ZZZ	ZUSA
JACOB	3	M	CHILD	RR	ZZZ	ZUSA
JOSEF	.11	M	INFANT	RR	ZZZ	ZUSA
SADLOSKA, ANTONIA	24	F	NN	RR	ZZZ	ZUSA
KASIMIR	.11	M	INFANT	RR	ZZZ	ZUSA
MILLER, ISAAC	26	M	JNR	RR	ZZZ	ZUSA
ANNA	19	F	W	RR	ZZZ	ZUSA
POKSEWSKZ, PAULINE	19	F	NN	RR	ZZZ	ZUSA
SCHMERL	11	M	CH	RR	ZZZ	ZUSA

SHIP: EIDER

FROM: BREMEN AND SOUTHAMPTON
TO: NEW YORK
ARRIVED: 19 JULY 1884

PASSENGER	AGE	SEX	OCCUPATION	PRV	VIL	DES
SEJPANSKY, FRANZISKA	19	F	W	RR	ZZZ	ZUSA
HELENE	.05	F	INFANT	RR	ZZZ	ZUSA
BLUM, RUDOLPH	25	M	MCHT	RR	ZZZ	ZUSA
WILHELMINE	21	F	NN	RR	ZZZ	ZUSA
HIRSCH, DAVID	50	M	LABR	RR	ZZZ	ZUSA
MEYER, ISAAK	16	M	NN	RR	ZZZ	ZUSA
WORONICHI, PIOTER	20	M	LABR	RR	ZZZ	ZUSA
URBANOWIC, ANTL.	27	F	NN	RR	ZZZ	ZUSA
GOZDZAWSKA, ANTL.	35	F	NN	RR	ZZZ	ZUSA
KRZESINSKA, JOSEFA	14	F	NN	RR	ZZZ	ZUSA

SHIP: STATE OF ALABAMA

FROM: GLASGOW AND LARNE
TO: NEW YORK
ARRIVED: 19 JULY 1884

PASSENGER	AGE	SEX	OCCUPATION	PRV	VIL	DES
LIPSCHITZ, BENZEL	45	M	PDLR	RR	ZZZ	ZNY
MORTEL	11	M	CH	RR	ZZZ	ZNY
JONE	9	M	CHILD	RR	ZZZ	ZNY
SCHUSTER, ETTEL	24	F	W	RR	ZZZ	ZNY
ESTHER	.07	F	INFANT	RR	ZZZ	ZNY
RAUCH, SPRINGE	38	F	W	RR	ZZZ	ZNY
HINDE	.09	F	INFANT	RR	ZZZ	ZNY

PASSENGER	AGE	SEX	OCCUPATION	PRV VIL DES
DEBORA	.09	F	INFANT	RRZZZZNY
BRAUDE, ARON	18	M	CGRMKR	RRZZZZNY
MARKER, ABE	18	M	TNSTH	RRZZZZNY
KAHN, DAVID	19	M	PDLR	RRZZZZPHI
WARAKUNSKY, ANTON	30	M	LABR	RRZZZZNY
MASOTIS, KASIMIR	22	M	LABR	RRZZZZOH
KRUM, SCHAIE	60	M	TLR	RRZZZZNY
ROCHE	00	F	W	RRZZZZNY
JAIVESOHN, SCHLOME	00	M	FARMER	RRZZZZNY
POTSCHINGE, MOSES	19	M	SHMK	RRZZZZNY
BARCKOWITZ, FRANZISKA	00	F	SVNT	RRZZZZNY
CHERARD, JUKIE	23	F	SVNT	RRZZZZNY
BARCHAN, SIMON	17	M	WVR	RRZZZZBO
KOWPKI, BERL	18	M	CGRMKR	RRZZZZNY
LETWIN, JACOB	25	M	TLR	RRZZZZNY
BALBROWSES, PETROS	19	M	LABR	RRZZZZNY
SOSNAWSKI, JUDE	00	M	BCHR	RRZZZZNY
EILSTEIN, KUSSIEL	33	M	PDLR	RRZZZZNY
ITTE	30	F	W	RRZZZZNY
KARL	.03	M	INFANT	RRZZZZNY
EPSTEIN, HERZ	20	M	PDLR	RRZZZZNY
GODAN, JAULE	34	F	W	RRZZZZNY
LEAH	6	F	CHILD	RRZZZZNY
KREINER, CHAIE	16	F	SVNT	RRZZZZNY
GRIENSBERG, KALMANN	19	M	CPMKR	RRZZZZNY
SCHLOM, SAML.	00	M	GZR	RRZZZZNY
BRAUN, BEHR.	00	M	PDLR	RRZZZZNY

SHIP: WIELAND

FROM: HAMBURG
TO: NEW YORK
ARRIVED: 21 JULY 1884

PASSENGER	AGE	SEX	OCCUPATION	PRV VIL DES
JOSSEL, ISIDOR	32	M	DLR	RRZZZZUSA
KRAWULSKI, WAWZENCE	28	M	LABR	RRZZZZUSA
MARCUSE, MINNA	25	F	SGL	RRZZZZUSA
ROSENBERG, MICHAEL	22	M	CGRMKR	RRZZZZUSA
KUPPE, SCHMER	28	M	MCHT	RRZZZZUSA
WIWATOWSKY, JOSEF	25	M	LABR	RRZZZZUSA
RUBENSOHN, HIRSCH	62	M	LABR	RRZZZZUSA
FEIGE	55	F	W	RRZZZZUSA
PESSE	25	F	CH	RRZZZZUSA
SCHEMA	20	F	CH	RRZZZZUSA
CHASSE	15	F	CH	RRZZZZUSA
HILLER, LEIB	48	M	LABR	RRZZZZUSA
SCHEINE	48	F	W	RRZZZZUSA
SARA	16	F	CH	RRZZZZUSA
MANES	9	M	CHILD	RRZZZZUSA
SCHNIDOWSKY, FEIGE	23	F	W	RRZZZZUSA
ABRAM	.03	M	INFANT	RRZZZZUSA
BRENNER, MOSES	31	M	LABR	RRZZZZUSA
BERGER, SCHLOME	20	M	LABR	RRZZZZUSA
KRULIK, WOLF	20	M	LABR	RRZZZZUSA
SOGALOWSKY, RACHEL	19	F	SGL	RRZZZZUSA
LECK, ISRAEL	35	M	JNR	RRZZZZUSA
LONDON, LEA	30	F	W	RRZZZZUSA
BENJ.	.11	M	INFANT	RRZZZZUSA
KASAGNE, CARL	17	M	LABR	RRZZZZUSA
GERBER, BENJAMIN	20	M	TLR	RRZZZZUSA
BERSCHE	20	F	W	RRZZZZUSA
PUPKA, MEIER	37	M	LABR	RRZZZZUSA
CHAIM	35	M	LABR	RRZZZZUSA
RIWE	33	F	W	RRZZZZUSA
CHLAST, SAMUEL	26	M	LABR	RRZZZZUSA
LONDON, LEWIN	30	M	LABR	RRZZZZUSA
ISAAC	4	M	CHILD	RRZZZZUSA
SCHECHTEL, BEREL	20	M	LABR	RRZZZZUSA
RAMBAR, MOSES	16	M	LABR	RRZZZZUSA
BLUMSTEIN, LEA	25	F	W	RRZZZZUSA
LEIB	4	M	CHILD	RRZZZZUSA
MOSES	.11	M	INFANT	RRZZZZUSA
WOLPE, MEIER	32	M	LABR	RRZZZZUSA
SCHIMBERG, ABRAH.	26	M	LABR	RRZZZZUSA
SILBERMANN, REISEL	20	M	SGL	RRZZZZUSA
RIKE	50	F	W	RRZZZZUSA
SAMUEL	14	M	LABR	RRZZZZUSA
SEGAL, SLOME	32	F	W	RRZZZZUSA
RIWKE	8	F	CHILD	RRZZZZUSA
SISCHLE	5	F	CHILD	RRZZZZUSA
ABR.	.11	M	INFANT	RRZZZZUSA
SCHIMEN	15	M	LABR	RRZZZZUSA
JANKEL	14	M	LABR	RRZZZZUSA
OPPENHEIM, FREIDE	42	F	SGL	RRZZZZUSA
BUSCHNEFSKY, HIRSCH	16	M	LABR	RRZZZZUSA
SILBERMANN, PHILIPP	20	M	LABR	RRZZZZUSA
FASSLER, DAVID	27	M	MCHT	RRZZZZUSA
MARKUSE, MAX	18	M	LABR	RRZZZZUSA
SKOP, ELIAS	43	M	LABR	RRZZZZUSA
ROSALIE	9	F	CHILD	RRZZZZUSA
GURSKI, THOMAS	40	M	LABR	RRZZZZUSA
GLUWATZKI, PAUL	50	M	LABR	RRZZZZUSA
SALOMEA	50	F	W	RRZZZZUSA
LOUISE	18	F	CH	RRZZZZUSA
JOH.	16	M	CH	RRZZZZUSA
BOLESLAV	9	M	CHILD	RRZZZZUSA
STEFAN	8	M	CHILD	RRZZZZUSA
ANNA	3	F	CHILD	RRZZZZUSA
BLUM, FANNI	28	F	SGL	RRZZZZUSA
LITPAK, SARA	15	F	SGL	RRZZZZUSA
EVA	3	F	CHILD	RRZZZZUSA
KURZMANN, HIRSCH	14	M	LABR	RRZZZZUSA
DOMBROWSKI, JULIANE	21	F	W	RRZZZZUSA
FRANZ	.03	M	INFANT	RRZZZZUSA
BLOTE, SARA	30	F	W	RRZZZZUSA
MEIER	9	M	CHILD	RRZZZZUSA
ETTE	5	F	CHILD	RRZZZZUSA
WASSERMANN, ROSA	25	F	W	RRZZZZUSA
DWORE	4	F	CHILD	RRZZZZUSA
AUERHORN, FEIGE	21	F	W	RRZZZZUSA
ABRAH.	.11	M	INFANT	RRZZZZUSA
LEISER	.01	M	INFANT	RRZZZZUSA
LASEROWITZ, LEA	40	F	W	RRZZZZUSA
NACHUM	6	M	CHILD	RRZZZZUSA
LEWIN, ROSA	33	F	W	RRZZZZUSA
HINDE	50	F	W	RRZZZZUSA
RACHEL	9	F	CHILD	RRZZZZUSA
REBECCA	3	F	CHILD	RRZZZZUSA
MINNA	9	F	CHILD	RRZZZZUSA
CHAIM	.11	M	INFANT	RRZZZZUSA
ROSENBERG, CHANNE	24	F	SGL	RRZZZZUSA
STOCKEL, FREIDE	16	F	SGL	RRZZZZUSA
ZEPPA, DINA	35	F	W	RRZZZZUSA
FREIDE	16	F	CH	RRZZZZUSA
SCHENDEL	6	M	CHILD	RRZZZZUSA
LEIB	4	M	CHILD	RRZZZZUSA
JANKEL	.11	M	INFANT	RRZZZZUSA
BLUME	.01	F	INFANT	RRZZZZUSA
RIMAN, CHAIM	26	M	LABR	RRZZZZUSA
FUCHS, SARA	9	F	CHILD	RRZZZZUSA
BRAUNE, FEIGE	26	F	W	RRZZZZUSA
MATEL	8	M	CHILD	RRZZZZUSA
JANKEL	6	M	CHILD	RRZZZZUSA
LOSZE	4	M	CHILD	RRZZZZUSA
WELTEL	.11	M	INFANT	RRZZZZUSA
SALANEZ, SIMON	21	M	LABR	RRZZZZUSA
SCHECHTMANN, ABR.	22	M	LABR	RRZZZZUSA
MARGULSKY, CHEIKEL	22	M	LABR	RRZZZZUSA
GUTKOWSKI, ISAAC	28	M	DLR	RRZZZZUSA
KOHN, ABRAH.	18	M	DLR	RRZZZZUSA
GLICKMANN, JANKEL	20	M	LKSH	RRZZZZUSA
SCHONE	20	F	W	RRZZZZUSA
GOLDSTEIN, SAMUEL	46	M	JNR	RRZZZZUSA
GINOWZKI, JOSEPH	17	M	CGRMKR	RRZZZZUSA
LEWINSOHN, CHANNE	9	F	CHILD	RRZZZZUSA

PASSENGER	AGE	SEX	OCCUPATION	PRV VIL DES
ETTEL	8	F	CHILD	RRZZZZUSA
CHAIM	7	M	CHILD	RRZZZZUSA
STEIER, OSIAS	26	M	LABR	RRZZZZUSA
BETTI	25	F	W	RRZZZZUSA
ESTHER	.11	F	INFANT	RRZZZZUSA
DWORE	.01	F	INFANT	RRZZZZUSA
WEINSTEIN, LIESE	20	F	SGL	RRZZZZUSA
KRITZER, MOSES	19	M	LABR	RRZZZZUSA
SCHAPLER, BEREK	23	M	LABR	RRZZZZUSA
BRENNERT, ISAAC	46	M	LABR	RRZZZZUSA
RUSZINSKI, ABRAM	20	M	LABR	RRZZZZUSA
GOTTHOLT, GERSON	60	M	LABR	RRZZZZUSA
OKUN, ARON	21	M	LABR	RRZZZZUSA
BEDNARSKI, MARIE	17	F	SGL	RRZZZZUSA
BISCHOFSWERDER, ABRAM	20	M	LABR	RRZZZZUSA
ETTENSOHN, RUWEN	50	M	LABR	RRZZZZUSA
MINDEL	48	F	W	RRZZZZUSA
ISAAC	8	M	CHILD	RRZZZZUSA
KAHN, OSCHER	9	M	CHILD	RRZZZZUSA
KOWAN, JACOB	22	M	LABR	RRZZZZUSA
KATZ, MOSES	32	M	LABR	RRZZZZUSA

SHIP: BOLIVIA

FROM: GLASGOW AND MOVILLE
TO: NEW YORK
ARRIVED: 22 JULY 1884

PASSENGER	AGE	SEX	OCCUPATION	PRV VIL DES
KOPPEL, JOSE	38	M	FARMER	RRZZZZUSA
MEGALAWSKY, S.	30	M	LABR	RRZZZZUSA
ANDRE, ANDRE	23	M	LABR	RRZZZZUSA
KISCH, H.	56	M	LABR	RRZZZZUSA
RUFFKIN, JOS.	23	M	TNSTH	RRZZZZUSA
SEGAL, SAM.	23	M	TNSTH	RRZZZZUSA
KOLTER, CHAIM	24	M	LABR	RRZZZZUSA
LEIPMANN, CHAINN	29	M	LABR	RRZZZZUSA
RAPPAPORT, MAN	15	M	LABR	RRZZZZUSA
RUBENSTEIN, JOSEF	17	M	CPR	RRZZZZUSA
ROSMUS, JOHAN	40	M	LABR	RRZZZZUSA

SHIP: WESTPHALIA

FROM: HAMBURG AND HAVRE
TO: NEW YORK
ARRIVED: 22 JULY 1884

PASSENGER	AGE	SEX	OCCUPATION	PRV VIL DES
SAGEL, JETTE	22	F	SGL	RRZZZZNY
SCHIMOKWITZ, SCHMUEL	18	M	LABR	RRZZZZNY
BUSCHINSKY, KASZMIRS	50	M	LABR	RRZZZZNY
BIALOWSKI, MORDSCHE	24	M	UNKNOWN	RRZZZZNY
EINFRANK, ISAAC	19	M	UNKNOWN	RRZZZZNY
SEGAL, BERKO	50	M	LABR	RRZZZZNY
MEER	9	M	CHILD	RRZZZZNY
DAVID	8	M	CHILD	RRZZZZNY
LEP, ISAAC	19	M	LABR	RRZZZZNY
TABESKEWITZ, KELMANN	44	M	LABR	RRZZZZNY
MEER, SLAVATYS	34	M	LABR	RRZZZZNY
GABOWITZ, KOPEL	50	M	LABR	RRZZZZNY
DROWITZ, OSSO	31	M	LABR	RRZZZZNY
KATZ, DINA	35	F	W	RRZZZZNY
TAUBE	9	F	CHILD	RRZZZZNY
SARA	8	F	CHILD	RRZZZZNY
RIWKE	6	F	CHILD	RRZZZZNY
ITTE	5	F	CHILD	RRZZZZNY
OSCHA	3	F	CHILD	RRZZZZNY

PASSENGER	AGE	SEX	OCCUPATION	PRV VIL DES
LEWINSKY, LEIB	19	M	LABR	RRZZZZNY
SCHIROCHINSKY, ROSA	18	F	SGL	RRZZZZNY
HANEBERG, SCHMUEL	16	M	LABR	RRZZZZNY
SILBERGLEID, CHEIE	30	F	SGL	RRZZZZNY
FRANK, SALOMON	17	M	LABR	RRZZZZNY
FRIEDMANN, MALKE	20	F	SGL	RRZZZZNY
CANAL, FREIDE	25	F	W	RRZZZZNY
ETTEL	.11	F	INFANT	RRZZZZNY
SOLVTAREFFSKAJA, SOFIE	22	F	W	RRZZZZNY
ISAAC	4	M	CHILD	RRZZZZNY
JOSEF	.11	M	INFANT	RRZZZZNY
GUREWITSCH, ISAAC	23	M	LABR	RRZZZZNY
ZISSEN, JUDKA	70	M	LABR	RRZZZZNY
FREDE	68	F	W	RRZZZZNY
HILEROWITZ, MOSES	25	M	BBR	RRZZZZNY
SCHERENKOWSKY, M.	50	M	LABR	RRZZZZNY
GUTMANN, RACHEL	28	F	W	RRZZZZNY
JACOB	6	M	CHILD	RRZZZZNY
ANNA	.11	F	INFANT	RRZZZZNY
ISETTE	.01	F	INFANT	RRZZZZNY
KAHN, HILLEL	50	F	LABR	RRZZZZNY
ISRAEL	9	M	CHILD	RRZZZZNY
TULERANSKY, SLOME	44	M	DLR	RRZZZZNY
RESI	40	F	W	RRZZZZNY
ROSA	23	F	CH	RRZZZZNY
MALKE	8	M	CHILD	RRZZZZNY
CHAIE	.11	M	INFANT	RRZZZZNY
SCHEINE	.01	F	INFANT	RRZZZZNY
SALINGER, MAX	18	M	LABR	RRZZZZNY
WALFOVITZ, MINNA	9	F	CHILD	RRZZZZNY
BEILES, MORDSCHE	19	F	LABR	RRZZZZNY
WALDMANN, MARIE	53	F	W	RRZZZZNY
EPSTEIN, SCHMUEL	22	M	LABR	RRZZZZNY
LEWITOW, REBECCA	32	F	W	RRZZZZNY
DAVID	7	M	CHILD	RRZZZZNY
SALMEN	6	M	CHILD	RRZZZZNY
LEISER	5	M	CHILD	RRZZZZNY
RASCHE	3	F	CHILD	RRZZZZNY
MICHAEL	.11	M	INFANT	RRZZZZNY
SIED, PESCHE	40	F	W	RRZZZZNY
LEIB	9	M	CHILD	RRZZZZNY
BREINE	8	F	CHILD	RRZZZZNY
HIRSCH	7	M	CHILD	RRZZZZNY
JENTE	5	F	CHILD	RRZZZZNY
HERTZBERG, HERM.	24	M	LABR	RRZZZZNY
LINE	20	F	W	RRZZZZNY
KROLL, LEIB	28	M	LABR	RRZZZZNY
MEMLOWSKY, GALE	50	F	W	RRZZZZNY
NEUMANN, REBECCA	9	F	CHILD	RRZZZZNY
ALTER	5	M	CHILD	RRZZZZNY
GREIGER, SAMUEL	19	M	LABR	RRZZZZNY
KORNFELD, HIRSCH	33	M	LABR	RRZZZZNY
SCHUTZ, FISCHEL	30	M	LABR	RRZZZZNY
FEIERMANN, ISAAC	22	M	LABR	RRZZZZNY
JERSE, STENIS	26	F	W	RRZZZZNY
AGETE	.11	F	INFANT	RRZZZZNY
MAGDA.	26	F	W	RRZZZZNY
ANNA	.11	F	INFANT	RRZZZZNY
SOBOLESKY, JAN	30	M	LABR	RRZZZZNY
EMMA	20	F	W	RRZZZZNY
JOSEF	.11	M	INFANT	RRZZZZNY
WILHELM	.01	M	INFANT	RRZZZZNY
LEWY, SCHIE	17	M	LABR	RRZZZZNY
GREYER, GEDALIA	20	F	SGL	RRZZZZNY
GUTMANN, MOSCHE	18	M	LABR	RRZZZZNY
SIEW, LIEBER	19	M	LABR	RRZZZZNY
WEIFS, PESCHE	26	F	W	RRZZZZNY
ABE	.11	M	INFANT	RRZZZZNY
NIFSELKOWSKY, JUDEL	24	M	LABR	RRZZZZNY
CHASCHE	20	F	W	RRZZZZNY
FRANK, JACOB	15	M	LABR	RRZZZZNY
GROBGELD, RISCHE	55	F	W	RRZZZZNY
NAUMANN, SARA	30	F	W	RRZZZZNY
ROSA	.11	F	INFANT	RRZZZZNY
BRAUN, SAMUEL	18	M	TLR	RRZZZZNY

PASSENGER	AGE	SEX	OCCUPATION	PRV VIL DES
SCHULMANN, CHAIE	18	F	SGL	RRZZZZNY
BELSOHN, NESCHE	20	F	SGL	RRZZZZNY
GERBER, PINCHOS	20	M	LABR	RRZZZZNY
CHANNE	20	F	W	RRZZZZNY
SUROWSKY, FRUME	23	F	SGL	RRZZZZNY
RICHMOND, SCHIFRE	19	F	SGL	RRZZZZNY
NIFSEN	9	F	CHILD	RRZZZZNY
MOSES	9	M	CHILD	RRZZZZNY
ARNKKER, BERL	44	M	DLR	RRZZZZNY
ETKE	16	F	D	RRZZZZNY
LUBIESKI, BASHE	17	F	SGL	RRZZZZNY
LEWIEN, ASHER	21	M	LABR	RRZZZZNY
LERGALOROWITZ, ABRAH.	21	M	LABR	RRZZZZNY
WALDMANN, FISHEL	44	M	HAMF	RRZZZZNY
POTRIGAL, HENOCH	17	M	TLR	RRZZZZNY
GOLDBERG, SCHEWA	30	F	W	RRZZZZNY
DEBORA	9	F	CHILD	RRZZZZNY
ZUCKER, GITTEL	25	F	W	RRZZZZNY
BEER	9	M	CHILD	RRZZZZNY
BECKER, JOH.	33	M	LABR	RRZZZZNY
CATHRA.	34	F	W	RRZZZZNY
CATHRA.	9	F	CHILD	RRZZZZNY
ABRAH.	8	M	CHILD	RRZZZZNY
JOHANN	5	M	CHILD	RRZZZZNY
CATHR.	69	F	W	RRZZZZNY
FLEMMING, HEINRICH	21	M	LABR	RRZZZZNY
BAUMANN, CORNELIUS	19	M	LABR	RRZZZZNY
BERG, HELENE	20	F	SGL	RRZZZZNY
PESNER, SCHLOME	36	M	LABR	RRZZZZNY
SCHEINBERG, CHAIE	60	F	W	RRZZZZNY
CHANNE	24	F	W	RRZZZZNY
U, RIWKE	.11	F	INFANT	RRZZZZNY
MISCHKINSKY, REISEL	35	F	W	RRZZZZNY
MOSES	.11	M	INFANT	RRZZZZNY
NISSELKOWSKY, LEAH	28	F	W	RRZZZZNY
MINNA	8	F	CHILD	RRZZZZNY
MASCHE	7	F	CHILD	RRZZZZNY
SELDE	6	F	CHILD	RRZZZZNY
CHAIE	.11	F	INFANT	RRZZZZNY
MEHL, MOSES	17	M	LABR	RRZZZZNY
BORKAN, SALOMON	20	M	LABR	RRZZZZNY
SARA	20	F	W	RRZZZZNY
KERBER, MOSES	20	M	SHMK	RRZZZZNY
PELKIEWICZ, TOMAS	19	M	LABR	RRZZZZNY
NACIS	28	M	LABR	RRZZZZNY
ARKIN, ALTE	29	F	W	RRZZZZNY
KOTTON, MOSES	24	M	LABR	RRZZZZNY
PENES, FRUME	27	F	W	RRZZZZNY
NISSELKOWSKI, CHANNE	28	F	W	RRZZZZNY
SARA	.11	F	INFANT	RRZZZZNY
ELKE	.01	F	INFANT	RRZZZZNY
BOLETZKI, MICHAEL	28	M	LABR	RRZZZZNY
MORENES, ISAAC	19	M	JWLR	RRZZZZNY
ZIMBERG, FEIGE	27	F	W	RRZZZZNY
MARIAMPOLSKY, ABRAH.	19	M	LABR	RRZZZZNY
ROSA, OSCAR	22	M	LABR	RRZZZZNY
JDIDIE, ABRAH.SLOMA	16	M	LABR	RRZZZZNY
PINEAS	10	M	S	RRZZZZNY
LINDE, SARAH	13	F	SGL	RRZZZZNY
TSCHASNY, RIWKE	26	F	W	RRZZZZNY
LEWI---, MEYER	40	M	TLR	RRZZZZNY
JACOBSEN, FANNY	18	F	SGL	RRZZZZNY
HETTY	11	F	SGL	RRZZZZNY
ROSENKRANZ, NESCHE	16	F	SGL	RRZZZZNY
NISSELKOWSKY, MOSES	.09	M	INFANT	RRZZZZNY
LEWIN, SARAMINKA	17	F	SGL	RRZZZZNY

SHIP: STATE OF NEBRASKA

FROM: GLASGOW AND LARNE
TO: NEW YORK
ARRIVED: 23 JULY 1884

PASSENGER	AGE	SEX	OCCUPATION	PRV VIL DES
WIVATENY, FRANZISKA	20	F	DMS	RRZZZZNY
ROGUTZKUS, JOSES	21	M	LABR	RRZZZZNY
MELDOSIS, MATIS	23	M	LABR	RRZZZZNY
JANKOWSKY, JORGE	25	M	LABR	RRZZZZNY
LEWY, ANNA	22	F	DMS	RRZZZZNY
GOLDMANN, LEW	19	M	LABR	RRZZZZNY
MARKOWITZ, CHANNE	17	M	LABR	RRZZZZNY
KAPLAN, JOSEF	33	M	LABR	RRZZZZNY
STEIN, JERSON	25	M	LABR	RRZZZZNY
GRABOWSKY, MEILACH	21	M	LABR	RRZZZZNY
KEIS, MICHAEL	30	M	LABR	RRZZZZNY
MOSSER, KAMMEIL	4	M	CHILD	RRZZZZNY
OREL	.10	M	INFANT	RRZZZZNY
RUSNAK, LOUISE	28	F	W	RRZZZZNY
LIZANSKY, ARON	19	M	LABR	RRZZZZNY
RISCH, PETER	32	M	LABR	RRZZZZNY
TANZIGER, LEIB	25	M	LABR	RRZZZZNY
LEWIT, ABRAHAM	27	M	LABR	RRZZZZNY
SARA	21	F	W	RRZZZZNY
CLARA	.11	F	INFANT	RRZZZZNY
SILBERMANN, M.	28	M	LABR	RRZZZZNY
GLATTSTEIN, ZALEL	28	M	LABR	RRZZZZNY
BALZWINIK, GEDALIE	16	M	LABR	RRZZZZNY
SCHUD, MOSES	45	M	LABR	RRZZZZNY
DAWIDOWITSCH, DAVID	23	M	LABR	RRZZZZNY
DRAKNER, SCHEFSEL	21	M	LABR	RRZZZZNY
JACOBSOHN, HERMANN	19	M	LABR	RRZZZZNY
ROSENTHAL, ISAAC	17	M	LABR	RRZZZZNY
BENUSCH, KASIMIR	25	M	LABR	RRZZZZNY
CHANIN, MOSES	19	M	LABR	RRZZZZNY
FEIGE	18	F	W	RRZZZZNY
MENDKOWITZ, ISAAK	23	M	LABR	RRZZZZNY
KAUFMANN, JECHIEL	26	M	LABR	RRZZZZNY
KLEWANSKY, HANNA	18	F	DMS	RRZZZZNY
GURSKY, OSCHER	35	M	LABR	RRZZZZNY
KAUFMANN, CHAIE	12	M	CH	RRZZZZNY
HIRSCH	8	M	CHILD	RRZZZZNY
MEYER	6	M	CHILD	RRZZZZNY
HOCHBERGER, REISE	33	F	W	RRZZZZNY
MENDEL	8	M	CHILD	RRZZZZNY
BREINDEL	.08	M	INFANT	RRZZZZNY
CHANNE	.08	M	INFANT	RRZZZZNY
MYTNIK, ISRAEL	22	M	LABR	RRZZZZNY
ELIASSOHN, BARUCH-A.	37	M	LABR	RRZZZZNY
KAPLAN, ABRAHAM	20	M	LABR	RRZZZZNY
KYHMANEN, ANTTI	23	M	FARMER	RRZZZZNY
LUKKABIBA, ISAAK	20	M	LABR	RRZZZZNY
MINZ, MOSES	38	M	LABR	RRZZZZNY
RUBINSTEIN, ABRAHAM	26	M	LABR	RRZZZZNY
KLIMPKE, GOTTLIEB	48	M	LABR	RRZZZZNY
BARCHAN, BERNHARD	26	M	LABR	RRZZZZNY
GARLICH, HEINRICH	28	M	LABR	RRZZZZNY

SHIP: ST LAURENT

FROM: HAVRE
TO: NEW YORK
ARRIVED: 24 JULY 1884

PASSENGER	AGE	SEX	OCCUPATION	PRV VIL DES
WITOWSKI, H.	40	M	MCHT	RRZZZZLOU
D.	9	M	CHILD	RRZZZZLOU
L.	6	M	CHILD	RRZZZZLOU
B.	4	M	CHILD	RRZZZZLOU

SHIP: ELBE

FROM: BREMEN
TO: NEW YORK
ARRIVED: 26 JULY 1884

PASSENGER	AGE	SEX	OCCUPATION	PRV VIL DES
ABRAHAMOWICZ, SORESTA	21	F	NN	RRZZZZUSA
DAVID	.11	M	INFANT	RRZZZZUSA
MOSES	.06	M	INFANT	RRZZZZUSA
ABRAHAMSON, SAL.	25	M	LABR	RRZZZZUSA
STEINBERG, SIEGM	27	M	LABR	RRZZZZUSA

SHIP: GRECIAN MONARCH

FROM: LONDON
TO: NEW YORK
ARRIVED: 26 JULY 1884

PASSENGER	AGE	SEX	OCCUPATION	PRV VIL DES
VALINSKY, JACOB	29	M	TLR	PLZZZZUSA
REBECCA	29	F	W	PLZZZZUSA
JUDAH	7	M	CHILD	PLZZZZUSA
BARUCH	5	M	CHILD	PLZZZZUSA
HZ.	3	M	CHILD	PLZZZZUSA
BELLA	1	F	CHILD	PLZZZZUSA
SIMPSON, MORRIS	32	M	TLR	PLZZZZUSA
RENBERG, ISRAEL	25	M	CGRMKR	RRZZZZUSA
M.	24	F	W	RRZZZZUSA
C.	1	F	CHILD	RRZZZZUSA
BARNETT, M.	19	M	TLR	PLZZZZUSA
CARLSTEIN, J.	22	M	TRVLR	RRZZZZUSA
MAGHATCH, L.	22	M	MCHT	PLZZZZUSA
LEVENE, N.	19	M	TLR	RRZZZZUSA
SILVERMAN, J.	24	M	TLR	PLZZZZUSA
SARAH	24	F	W	PLZZZZUSA
RACHAEL	1	F	CHILD	PLZZZZUSA
GOLDBERG, P.	20	M	TLR	RRZZZZUSA
J.	21	F	W	RRZZZZUSA
S.	1	F	CHILD	RRZZZZUSA
MENDELSON, A.	23	M	TLR	RRZZZZUSA
KATE	23	F	W	RRZZZZUSA
ISRAEL	1	F	CHILD	RRZZZZUSA
GRAYTSCHINSKY, H.	24	M	TLR	RRZZZZUSA
ESTHER	24	F	W	RRZZZZUSA
SARAH	11	F	CH	RRZZZZUSA
E.	2	F	CHILD	RRZZZZUSA
LOUIS	1	M	CHILD	RRZZZZUSA
PRANOWSKI, S.	28	M	LABR	PLZZZZUSA
AMBROSIER, MIAS	27	M	LABR	PLZZZZUSA
MATHEW, A.	24	M	PDLR	PLZZZZUSA
LANSMANN, M.	33	M	BKR	RRZZZZUSA
OKSYA, MORRIS	21	M	BKR	RRZZZZUSA

SHIP: NORMANDIE

FROM: HAVRE
TO: NEW YORK
ARRIVED: 28 JULY 1884

PASSENGER	AGE	SEX	OCCUPATION	PRV VIL DES
BLAUNSTEIN, RUSE	54	F	UNKNOWN	RRZZZZUNK
SAMUEL	20	M	UNKNOWN	RRZZZZUNK
JURESKY, HERMANN	25	M	PREST	PLZZZZNY
GLUCKMANN, MOISE	62	M	FUL	PLZZZZNY
SOPHIE	60	F	UNKNOWN	PLZZZZNY
ISIDORE	7	M	CHILD	PLZZZZNY
SAVIETZKI, LEONTINE	37	F	CK	PLZZZZNY
MILLON	16	M	UNKNOWN	PLZZZZNY
JACOB	12	M	UNKNOWN	PLZZZZNY
MOISE	9	M	CHILD	PLZZZZNY
SARAH	7	F	CHILD	PLZZZZNY
SILBERSTEIN, SALOMON	30	M	FARMER	PLZZZZNY
HERSCHMANN, NAEHOUM	20	M	POST	RRZZZZCT

SHIP: POLARIA

FROM: HAMBURG
TO: NEW YORK
ARRIVED: 28 JULY 1884

PASSENGER	AGE	SEX	OCCUPATION	PRV VIL DES
FERFELFAN, ABRAM	25	M	TLR	RRZZZZNY
PURJEZ, NETTE	25	F	SGL	PLZZZZNY
PRESENT, DAVID	17	M	TDR	RRZZZZUNK
NEPBACH, JOCHEL	26	M	JWLR	RRZZZZNY
GIRCH	22	M	WCHMKR	RRZZZZNY
ISCHES, BASCHE	17	F	SGL	RRZZZZOH
BARTNIK, ISRAEL	18	M	PTR	RRZZZZNY
RACHEL, FEIGE	19	M	PTR	RRZZZZNY
BIELE, RIFKE	20	F	SGL	RRZZZZNY
QUINT, SAMUEL	26	M	PNTR	RRZZZZNY
BERLINSKI, SUSKIND	19	M	BTH	RRZZZZNY
GROSS, MICHAEL	20	F	SGL	PLZZZZNY
PREROS, SALLY	21	F	SGL	PLZZZZNY
FINKEL, JONAS	19	M	TLR	RRZZZZNY
INSEL, RACHEL	40	F	SGL	RRZZZZNY
PORGES, JOHANNA	28	F	WO	PLZZZZNY
WOLPERT, HEINRICH	18	M	MCHT	RRZZZZNY
WITEMEANER, JOSEF	22	M	TDR	RRZZZZNY
GOLGUT, MAX.	22	M	TDR	RRZZZZNY
RITZPER, SCHAIL	32	M	TDR	RRZZZZNY
GROLL, ARON	23	M	TDR	RRZZZZNY
HERZBERG, ISIDOR	20	M	TDR	RRZZZZNY
MARLARSKI, HIRSCH	18	M	TDR	RRZZZZNY
RUBNINSKY, MOSES	23	M	TDR	RRZZZZNY
BOJARSKI, JOSEF	30	M	TDR	RRZZZZNY
RING, HERM.	28	M	TLR	PLZZZZNY
SIMBERG, SLAWA	26	F	WO	RRZZZZUNK
JOSEF	00	M	S	RRZZZZUNK
DAVID	.07	F	INFANT	RRZZZZUNK
GULBAS, CHAIE-ESTHER	20	F	SGL	RRZZZZNY
BARNET, NELE	19	F	WO	RRZZZZNY
MOSES	.03	M	INFANT	RRZZZZNY
WELLINGSTEIN, MARCUS	24	M	LABR	RRZZZZNY
SCHERR, ITZIG	20	M	TDR	RRZZZZNY
GOTTSTEIN, LAZAR	17	M	TDR	RRZZZZUNK
ROJSIR, TAMOR	26	M	LABR	RRZZZZNY
HENRY	6	M	CHILD	RRZZZZNY
MOSES	.08	M	INFANT	RRZZZZNY
U, MICHAEL	22	M	UNKNOWN	RRZZZZNY
LEWIN, MARCUS	21	M	TDR	RRZZZZNY
ZIPPER, SCHEINDEL	50	F	WO	PLZZZZNY
ARON	7	M	CHILD	PLZZZZNY
SAMUEL	00	M	S	PLZZZZNY
KLODAWSKY, CHEIN	21	M	TRDSMN	RRZZZZNY
FREID, BERL	42	M	TRDSMN	RRZZZZNY
GRIENWALD, CHEIN	21	M	TRDSMN	RRZZZZNY
GOLDBERG, A.	7	M	CHILD	RRZZZZNY
SEZAWINSKY, STANISLAUS	27	M	LABR	RRZZZZNY
IDOWITZ, DAVID	21	M	TRDSMN	RRZZZZNY
ANNA	20	F	W	RRZZZZNY
SEZAWINSKY, GUSTINA	22	F	SGL	RRZZZZNY
MILGRAM, FANNI	27	F	WO	PLZZZZNY
LINGER, CARL	34	M	MCHT	RRZZZZNY

PASSENGER	AGE	SEX	OCCUPATION	PRIVL	DES
SHIP: RHEATIA					
FROM: HAMBURG AND HAVRE					
TO: NEW YORK					
ARRIVED: 28 JULY 1884					
ROSENBERG, HILLEL	20	F	W	RRZZZZ	USA
BERNSTEIN, JOEL	20	M	SLR	RRZZZZ	USA
GOLDBERG, RACHEL	34	F	W	RRZZZZ	USA
ROSA	9	F	CHILD	RRZZZZ	USA
ISAAC	8	M	CHILD	RRZZZZ	USA
ARON	5	M	CHILD	RRZZZZ	USA
ABRAHAM	.05	M	INFANT	RRZZZZ	USA
THIEM, HENRIETTE	32	F	W	RRZZZZ	USA
HERTHA	7	F	CHILD	RRZZZZ	USA
CARL	6	M	CHILD	RRZZZZ	USA
ERNST	5	M	CHILD	RRZZZZ	USA
TEITELBAUM, PINCUS	18	M	LABR	RRZZZZ	USA
PERLMANN, CHAIM	17	M	LABR	RRZZZZ	USA
MELINOWICZ, JUDEL	43	M	LABR	RRZZZZ	USA
GOLDBERG, HENOCH	18	M	LABR	RRZZZZ	USA
BACZKOWSKI, BENCEL	20	M	LABR	RRZZZZ	USA
JROSCLINSKY, CHAWE	36	M	LABR	RRZZZZ	USA
SARASKY, CHANE	36	M	LABR	RRZZZZ	USA
EHRENBERG, FRANCET	33	F	W	RRZZZZ	USA
WOLF	11	M	INFANT	RRZZZZ	USA
GOLDSTEIN, LIEBE	34	F	W	RRZZZZ	USA
SARA	9	F	CHILD	RRZZZZ	USA
ETTEL	8	F	CHILD	RRZZZZ	USA
TAUBE	6	F	CHILD	RRZZZZ	USA
GRUNE	4	F	CHILD	RRZZZZ	USA
SIMON, MALKE	26	F	SGL	RRZZZZ	USA
SULKER, JACOB	14	M	DLR	RRZZZZ	USA
SCHLOBEDMANN, JOSSEL	18	M	DLR	RRZZZZ	USA
ROSENFELD, MAX.	22	M	DLR	RRZZZZ	USA
PODWERSKY, MOSES	45	M	DLR	RRZZZZ	USA
SAMUEL	17	M	CH	RRZZZZ	USA
PESACH	15	M	CH	RRZZZZ	USA
CHANE	9	F	CHILD	RRZZZZ	USA
RIWKE	8	F	CHILD	RRZZZZ	USA
TOBIASCHOW, DAVID	34	M	DLR	RRZZZZ	USA
NITSORG, MOSES	25	M	DLR	RRZZZZ	USA
SCHON, ARON	15	M	CGRMKR	RRZZZZ	USA
LICH, JOH.	39	M	TCHR	RRZZZZ	USA
ELIS.	37	F	W	RRZZZZ	USA
ROB.	3	M	CHILD	RRZZZZ	USA
HEINZ, JOH.	50	M	FARMER	RRZZZZ	USA
JAC.	30	M	FARMER	RRZZZZ	USA
PAULINE	30	F	W	RRZZZZ	USA
AMALIA	18	F	SGL	RRZZZZ	USA
JOH.	7	F	CHILD	RRZZZZ	USA
CATH.	15	F	CH	RRZZZZ	USA
HEINR.	28	M	FARMER	RRZZZZ	USA
SOPHIE	28	F	W	RRZZZZ	USA
JOH.	4	U	CHILD	RRZZZZ	USA
HEINR.	2	U	CHILD	RRZZZZ	USA
CHR.	20	F	FARMER	RRZZZZ	USA
JRUMSOH, JETTE	14	F	SGL	RRZZZZ	USA
RUWCNOWITZ, SARA	16	F	SGL	RRZZZZ	USA
LIPMANN, MORDCHE	30	M	LABR	RRZZZZ	USA
KALWARISKY, HIRSCH	16	M	LABR	RRZZZZ	USA
KLAWANSKY, FEIGE	18	F	SGL	RRZZZZ	USA
PARCZANSKY, LEA	60	F	W	RRZZZZ	USA
ABR.	22	M	LABR	RRZZZZ	USA
MOSES	18	M	LABR	RRZZZZ	USA
MEIER	15	M	LABR	RRZZZZ	USA
KOPSL	43	M	LABR	RRZZZZ	USA
MARWER, SARA	37	F	W	RRZZZZ	USA
SCHEWALH	9	F	CHILD	RRZZZZ	USA
CHAMM	8	F	CHILD	RRZZZZ	USA
JACOB	7	F	CHILD	RRZZZZ	USA
LEA	3	F	CHILD	RRZZZZ	USA
GORINSKY, R.	30	F	W	RRZZZZ	USA
CHAIM	5	F	CHILD	RRZZZZ	USA
GOTTL	.11	M	INFANT	RRZZZZ	USA
LEWINSKI, ITTE	32	F	W	RRZZZZ	USA
JOSEF	.11	M	INFANT	RRZZZZ	USA
SCHEDEWITZ, JETTE	18	F	SGL	RRZZZZ	USA
MENDEL, MOSES	18	M	LABR	RRZZZZ	USA
LEWITZ, JACOB	23	M	LABR	RRZZZZ	USA
RESNIK, J.	28	M	LABR	RRZZZZ	USA
MEYERSOHN, NECH.	14	M	LABR	RRZZZZ	USA
BRAWERMANN, HERM.	44	M	LABR	RRZZZZ	USA
ISAAC	9	M	CHILD	RRZZZZ	USA
MARCUS	8	M	CHILD	RRZZZZ	USA
WALDMANN, MENDEL	36	M	LABR	RRZZZZ	USA
BARCKAN, ABR.S.	27	M	LABR	RRZZZZ	USA
GRUNDFEST, MICHAL	30	M	LABR	RRZZZZ	USA
SONE	20	F	W	RRZZZZ	USA
PEOTNIC, MOSES	20	M	LABR	RRZZZZ	USA
GOLDMANN, LINE	17	F	SGL	RRZZZZ	USA
ROSENBERG, JANKELL	37	M	LABR	RRZZZZ	USA
WEIN, SARAH	17	F	SGL	RRZZZZ	USA
SCHONE	15	F	SGL	RRZZZZ	USA
MECHANICH, BERL	18	M	DLR	RRZZZZ	USA
WEIN, SAMUEL	46	M	LABR	RRZZZZ	USA
MAISLIN, MERE	18	F	SGL	RRZZZZ	USA
JACOB	8	M	CHILD	RRZZZZ	USA
RUBINSTEIN, MAYER	20	M	LABR	RRZZZZ	USA
KORABELNIK, ARON	20	M	LABR	RRZZZZ	USA
SCHEINBLUM, LEISER	19	M	LABR	RRZZZZ	USA
ROSENMANN, ITZEK	20	M	LABR	RRZZZZ	USA
GORITZKY, SALMEN	28	M	LABR	RRZZZZ	USA
SCHNAILOWITZ, ABR.	24	M	LABR	RRZZZZ	USA
HENNY	26	F	W	RRZZZZ	USA
GRABOWSKY, MORITZ	56	M	LABR	RRZZZZ	USA
WILENSKY, RUBIN	50	M	LABR	RRZZZZ	USA
GERSOHEN, JESSEL	27	M	LABR	RRZZZZ	USA
KRUK, HANNE	20	F	SGL	RRZZZZ	USA
WEIN, DAVID	47	M	LABR	RRZZZZ	USA
ROSA	9	F	CHILD	RRZZZZ	USA
BREN, ABRAM	37	M	LABR	RRZZZZ	USA
ROSA	.11	F	INFANT	RRZZZZ	USA
ROTH, MINNE	30	F	W	RRZZZZ	USA
SARAH	6	F	CHILD	RRZZZZ	USA
BARUCH	.11	F	INFANT	RRZZZZ	USA
SPITZ, MOSES	19	M	LABR	RRZZZZ	USA
KUENZEL, WENZEL	25	M	LABR	RRZZZZ	USA
WERNER, ESTHER	32	F	WO	RRZZZZ	USA
MALKE	7	F	CHILD	RRZZZZ	USA
LEOPOLD	5	M	CHILD	RRZZZZ	USA
FEIGE	.11	M	INFANT	RRZZZZ	USA
MENDELOWITZ, CHEIE	17	M	LABR	RRZZZZ	USA
HINSCH, GEORG	32	M	LABR	RRZZZZ	USA
MECHANIK, SPR.	60	M	LABR	RRZZZZ	USA
BLOTE, REISCHE	50	F	SGL	RRZZZZ	USA
WILANSKY, ABE	50	M	LABR	RRZZZZ	USA
FEIGE	50	F	W	RRZZZZ	USA
PESCHE	17	F	D	RRZZZZ	USA
BRASNICH, HERSCH	18	M	LABR	RRZZZZ	USA
WIKARY, JUSTINE	60	F	W	RRZZZZ	USA
MARIE	16	F	D	RRZZZZ	USA
JUDZENSKI, LUDWIG	45	M	LABR	RRZZZZ	USA
STAROZYJMSSKI, WIODZIMI	19	M	LABR	RRZZZZ	USA
KOWALSKI, STANISLAW	23	M	SLR	RRZZZZ	USA
WRONA, LEIB	19	M	SLR	RRZZZZ	USA
FELTENSTEIN, WOLF	51	M	LABR	RRZZZZ	USA
RASCHE	50	F	W	RRZZZZ	USA
CHANNE	19	F	CH	RRZZZZ	USA
CHAIME	16	F	CH	RRZZZZ	USA
DEBORA	9	F	CHILD	RRZZZZ	USA
MOSES	8	M	CHILD	RRZZZZ	USA
ALTER	.11	M	INFANT	RRZZZZ	USA
RANSUK, RUBEN	20	M	UNKNOWN	RRZZZZ	USA
SCHAPIRO, PERL	16	F	SGL	RRZZZZ	USA
GALINSHE, SARA	36	F	W	RRZZZZ	USA
ABR.	9	M	CHILD	RRZZZZ	USA
CHONE	8	M	CHILD	RRZZZZ	USA
HANNE	6	F	CHILD	RRZZZZ	USA

PASSENGER	AGE	SEX	OCCUPATION	PRV VIL DES
DINA	4	F	CHILD	RRZZZZUSA
SCHEINE	1	F	CHILD	RRZZZZUSA
GATTLIEBOWSKY, RACHEL	24	F	W	RRZZZZUSA
BERLE	.11	F	INFANT	RRZZZZUSA
BERWALD, LEISER	20	M	LABR	RRZZZZUSA
KOLTERS, CHAINE	30	M	LABR	RRZZZZUSA
WEINBERG, SAMUEL	18	M	LABR	RRZZZZUSA
RABITZKI, NAFTAL	20	M	LABR	RRZZZZUSA
JANKOLOWE, SCHAJE	20	M	SLR	RRZZZZUSA
NAMIRO, BOLESWA	20	M	LABR	RRZZZZUSA
GARDER, MICHEL	29	M	LABR	RRZZZZUSA
LUBOWITZ, BENZEL	24	M	LABR	RRZZZZUSA
FLARMANN, MASCHA	18	M	LABR	RRZZZZUSA
SPRINGER, HERM.	26	M	LABR	RRZZZZUSA
MEISTER, JUDEL	50	M	LABR	RRZZZZUSA
JEGLICKY, CHEIM	45	M	LABR	RRZZZZUSA
FRIEDR.	45	F	W	RRZZZZUSA
LEO	20	M	CH	RRZZZZUSA
GOLDE	18	M	CH	RRZZZZUSA
ADOLF	16	M	CH	RRZZZZUSA
RASCHKE	9	M	CHILD	RRZZZZUSA
LEO	8	M	CHILD	RRZZZZUSA
MENDEL	7	M	CHILD	RRZZZZUSA
ROTH, ABRAHAM	30	M	LABR	RRZZZZUSA
LEWITZKI, PESCHEL	24	M	LABR	RRZZZZUSA
HERZ, RAPHAEL	29	M	LABR	RRZZZZUSA
SCHUWLENSKY, GERSON	40	M	LABR	RRZZZZUSA
RASCHE	14	F	W	RRZZZZUSA
SCHMUEL	9	M	CHILD	RRZZZZUSA
RAEDEL, WILH.	29	M	MCHT	RRZZZZUSA
BERTHA	35	F	W	RRZZZZUSA
MONTEVE, JACOB	34	M	LABR	RRZZZZUSA
CHEIE	25	F	W	RRZZZZUSA
CHERMANN	4	F	CHILD	RRZZZZUSA
SARA	2	F	CHILD	RRZZZZUSA
LEIB	.11	U	INFANT	RRZZZZUSA
HALPERN, MOSES	18	M	MCHT	RRZZZZUSA
STRAUSF, ANNA	17	F	SGL	RRZZZZUSA
ZABLOCKA, PAULINE	24	F	SGL	RRZZZZUSA
KANTOR, CHAIM	31	M	LABR	RRZZZZUSA
KALWARISKY, HATE	20	F	SGL	RRZZZZUSA
COHN, ESTER	24	F	W	RRZZZZUSA
ARON	.11	M	INFANT	RRZZZZUSA
CHANNE	.01	F	INFANT	RRZZZZUSA
MEYERSOHN, BASCHE	33	F	W	RRZZZZUSA
MEINE	9	F	CHILD	RRZZZZUSA
MOSES	8	M	CHILD	RRZZZZUSA
CHAIM	.11	M	INFANT	RRZZZZUSA
GRENOWSKI, CHAJLEY	18	M	LABR	RRZZZZUSA
KROSZCJNSKI, LEIB	36	M	LABR	RRZZZZUSA
WALDMANN, HAME	46	F	W	RRZZZZUSA
SALI	9	F	CHILD	RRZZZZUSA
KORWIN, THEODOR	30	M	FARMER	RRZZZZUSA

SHIP: ST. OF PENNSYLVANIA

FROM: GLASGOW AND LARNE
TO: NEW YORK
ARRIVED: 31 JULY 1884

PASSENGER	AGE	SEX	OCCUPATION	PRV VIL DES
BRAFMANN, WOUCK	30	M	JNR	PLZZZZUSA
EISENSCHEER, MICHAL	25	M	JNR	PLZZZZUSA
SCHOMNEYER	23	M	SHMK	PLZZZZUSA
GOLDE	00	F	W	PLZZZZUSA
ERRMAN, SALOMON	23	M	TLR	PLZZZZUSA
KEILE	18	F	W	PLZZZZUSA
GELBLUM, ELVAIE	40	F	W	PLZZZZUSA
METTE	5	F	CHILD	PLZZZZUSA
PETTE	1	F	CHILD	PLZZZZUSA
GOLDBERG, ISRAEL	29	M	MUSN	PLZZZZUSA
JACOB	18	M	MUSN	PLZZZZUSA
GOLLECK, ABRAHAM	23	M	TLR	PLZZZZUSA
RASCH, FEIWEL	25	M	TLR	PLZZZZUSA
SCHNEIDER, ABRAHAM	23	M	TLR	PLZZZZUSA
LEIE	21	F	W	PLZZZZUSA
JOSSEL	.09	F	INFANT	PLZZZZUSA
WOTTKOWSKY, SCHMUEL	00	M	LABR	PLZZZZUSA
BLOCH, BENZEL	00	M	UNKNOWN	RRZZZZUSA
HIRSCHSOHN, LAVIN	25	M	GDSM	RRZZZZUSA
HOPP, LEIB	30	M	CPTR	RRZZZZUSA
KAPBAN, ITZIG	23	M	LABR	RRZZZZUSA
KLEIN, JACOB	22	M	HRDRS	RRZZZZUSA
POSCHWIZENSKY, JANKEL	30	M	SHMK	RRZZZZUSA
ZEASSA, JOSSEL	30	M	SHMK	RRZZZZUSA
SACHS, JOSEL	34	M	TLR	RRZZZZUSA

SHIP: SUEVIA

FROM: HAMBURG
TO: NEW YORK
ARRIVED: 01 AUGUST 1884

PASSENGER	AGE	SEX	OCCUPATION	PRV VIL DES
RABBINOWITZ, BERTHA	25	F	SGL	RRZZZZUSA
RICHMOND, FRUMES	20	F	SGL	RRZZZZUSA
PUNANSKY, LEA	17	F	SGL	RRZZZZUSA
KANOSSINSKI, PESCHE	40	F	SGL	RRZZZZUSA
LIEBERMANN, JOSSEL	50	M	LABR	RRZZZZUSA
GOLDIN, REISEL	40	F	W	RRZZZZUSA
MARCUS	18	M	CH	RRZZZZUSA
MOSES	16	M	CH	RRZZZZUSA
BREINE	9	F	CHILD	RRZZZZUSA
JOSEF	8	M	CHILD	RRZZZZUSA
ROCHE	7	M	CHILD	RRZZZZUSA
GOLDINGER, ODEL	42	F	W	RRZZZZUSA
LEA	9	F	CHILD	RRZZZZUSA
SCHLOME	8	F	CHILD	RRZZZZUSA
CHAWE	5	F	CHILD	RRZZZZUSA
RIEWKE	4	F	CHILD	RRZZZZUSA
ELI	.11	M	INFANT	RRZZZZUSA
LEWINSKY, LEIB	54	M	LABR	RRZZZZUSA
SCHAFIRO, CIREL	19	F	SGL	RRZZZZUSA
KOLMAN	15	M	LABR	RRZZZZUSA
GOTTLIEB, MANUEL	29	M	LABR	RRZZZZUSA
SKOP, MICHEL	14	M	LABR	RRZZZZUSA
BERGMANN, MENUCHE	15	F	SGL	RRZZZZUSA
GOLDENSOHN, DOBRE	19	F	SGL	RRZZZZUSA
MULLER, BENZEL	9	M	CHILD	RRZZZZUSA
STRASCH, MERE	17	F	SGL	RRZZZZUSA
NATHANSOHN, SIMON	14	M	LABR	RRZZZZUSA
BARZAINSKY, SARA	40	F	W	RRZZZZUSA
LEA	15	F	CH	RRZZZZUSA
KADICH	9	M	CHILD	RRZZZZUSA
BEHR	8	M	CHILD	RRZZZZUSA
CHANNE	6	F	CHILD	RRZZZZUSA
LEIB	4	M	CHILD	RRZZZZUSA
KOPPOLOWSKY, FEIBEL	24	M	LABR	RRZZZZUSA
PIELESCH, LEA	22	F	SGL	RRZZZZUSA
WIERUSCHOWSKI, ROSALIE	40	F	W	RRZZZZUSA
LIPKE	9	M	CHILD	RRZZZZUSA
FANNY	6	F	CHILD	RRZZZZUSA
MINNA	5	F	CHILD	RRZZZZUSA
VICTOR	4	M	CHILD	RRZZZZUSA
KORMANN, SELIG	19	M	LABR	RRZZZZUSA
WEISMANN, ROSA	27	F	W	RRZZZZUSA
REBECCA	6	F	CHILD	RRZZZZUSA
ABR.	3	M	CHILD	RRZZZZUSA
SALOMON	.09	M	INFANT	RRZZZZUSA
DOMISCHEWSKY, CHAIE	30	F	W	RRZZZZUSA
BASI	6	F	CHILD	RRZZZZUSA
FRUME	4	F	CHILD	RRZZZZUSA

PASSENGER	AGE	SEX	OCCUPATION	PRV VIL DES
SAMSON	.11	M	INFANT	RRZZZZUSA
OSCH, NACHMUND	17	M	MCHT	RRZZZZUSA
PENZACK, HANCHEN	17	F	SGL	PLZZZZUSA
HIRSCH	11	M	B	PLZZZZUSA
PESSEL	12	F	SI	PLZZZZUSA
MITTELMAN, ISRAEL	18	M	CL	RRZZZZUSA
BRESKER, CHANNE	30	F	W	RRZZZZUSA
BERKOWSKY, GITTEL	25	F	W	RRZZZZUSA
CHAIM	.11	M	INFANT	RRZZZZUSA
NEUMARK, MOSES	50	M	DLR	RRZZZZUSA
HINDE	50	F	W	RRZZZZUSA
RIEFKEL	9	F	CHILD	RRZZZZUSA
MALKE	7	F	CHILD	RRZZZZUSA
RACHEL	6	F	CHILD	RRZZZZUSA
OLAFF, JACOB	20	M	LABR	RRZZZZUSA
GRUNBERG, MEYER	19	M	LABR	RRZZZZUSA
LEWIN, DAVID	37	M	TLR	RRZZZZUSA
CHAIM	18	M	TLR	RRZZZZUSA
ORKO, ILKO	22	M	TLR	RRZZZZUSA
LEWIN, MICHEL	48	M	TLR	RRZZZZUSA
SCHAEFEL, HIRSCH	43	M	TLR	RRZZZZUSA
SCHWARZ, JANKEL	20	M	TLR	RRZZZZUSA
GLUCKSMAN, HENOCH	18	M	DLR	RRZZZZUSA
RATSCHIN, SIMON	17	M	LABR	RRZZZZUSA
DANGELEWITZ, CHONE	45	F	W	RRZZZZUSA
LIEBE	20	F	W	RRZZZZUSA
FEIGE	.11	F	INFANT	RRZZZZUSA
DOSCHEWSKY, LEWIN	18	M	LABR	RRZZZZUSA
BERNSTEIN, LEIB	17	M	LABR	RRZZZZUSA
BERGMAN, PINCHOS	55	M	LABR	RRZZZZUSA
BEILE	50	F	W	RRZZZZUSA
SARA	18	F	CH	RRZZZZUSA
ENOCH	9	M	CHILD	RRZZZZUSA
SCHLOME	8	F	CHILD	RRZZZZUSA
HINDE	7	F	CHILD	RRZZZZUSA
SCHIDLOWSKI, PINCHOS	52	M	LABR	RRZZZZUSA
GOLDE	9	F	CHILD	RRZZZZUSA
ROGALEN, CHAIM	32	M	LABR	RRZZZZUSA
GITTEL	28	F	W	RRZZZZUSA
ESTHER	9	F	CHILD	RRZZZZUSA
ABR.	7	M	CHILD	RRZZZZUSA
CHANNE	.11	F	INFANT	RRZZZZUSA
SINEITTO, GREGOR	41	M	LABR	RRZZZZUSA
SURGET, VINNACH	40	M	LABR	RRZZZZUSA
JAFFE, LINA	27	F	W	RRZZZZUSA
MARY	3	F	CHILD	RRZZZZUSA
ADOLPH	.11	M	INFANT	RRZZZZUSA
LEWITH, LEO	16	M	LABR	RRZZZZUSA
URWITZ, SEGEL	17	M	DLR	RRZZZZUSA
STUEZINTE, URSULA	20	F	SGL	RRZZZZUSA
MACZY, HANNE	24	F	W	RRZZZZUSA
SARA	.11	F	INFANT	RRZZZZUSA
JOSEF	.01	M	INFANT	RRZZZZUSA
SWIRSKY, PESACH	20	M	LABR	RRZZZZUSA
SEMULOWITZ, ABRAHAM	22	M	DLR	RRZZZZUSA
FEIGE	24	F	W	RRZZZZUSA
KINSBERG, ISRAEL	44	M	DLR	RRZZZZUSA
GOTTELWEIL, JERUCHIM	26	M	SHMK	RRZZZZUSA
SACHS, BARUCH	18	M	DLR	RRZZZZUSA
PROROKOW, WOLF	35	M	LABR	RRZZZZUSA
CHINE	22	F	W	RRZZZZUSA
HIRSCH	.11	M	INFANT	RRZZZZUSA
MINKOWSKI, ARON	54	M	LABR	RRZZZZUSA
BEILE	52	F	W	RRZZZZUSA
SCHEINE	23	F	D	RRZZZZUSA
SOBOLOW, BERL	34	M	LABR	RRZZZZUSA
BACHMANN, ISRAEL	33	M	LABR	RRZZZZUSA
LEWIN, SCHMUEL	32	M	LABR	RRZZZZUSA
SCHONBERG, JACOB	19	M	LABR	RRZZZZUSA
TURBERG, JACOB	20	M	LABR	RRZZZZUSA
BERMANN, RACHMIEL	22	M	LABR	RRZZZZUSA
HACK, SAMUEL	22	M	LABR	RRZZZZUSA
LURIE, SARA	17	F	SGL	RRZZZZUSA
ANGINITZKE, LINE	50	F	W	RRZZZZUSA
BRESKY, FREIDE	9	F	CHILD	RRZZZZUSA
LEA	7	F	CHILD	RRZZZZUSA
SARA	6	F	CHILD	RRZZZZUSA
SAMUEL	.06	M	INFANT	RRZZZZUSA
TIGER, ARON	20	M	CGRMKR	RRZZZZUSA
SPIRO, PHILIPP	48	M	LABR	RRZZZZUSA
GITTEL	16	F	D	RRZZZZUSA

SHIP: FULDA

FROM: BREMEN
TO: NEW YORK
ARRIVED: 02 AUGUST 1884

PASSENGER	AGE	SEX	OCCUPATION	PRV VIL DES
FREMEL, FRANZ	25	M	LABR	RRZZZZUSA
KASFEL, GITEL	33	M	LABR	RRZZZZUSA
RODE	7	M	CHILD	RRZZZZUSA
JULIUS	7	M	CHILD	RRZZZZUSA
SELINA	5	F	CHILD	RRZZZZUSA
JOSEF	3	M	CHILD	RRZZZZUSA
SELMA	.11	F	INFANT	RRZZZZUSA

SHIP: RUGIA

FROM: HAMBURG
TO: NEW YORK
ARRIVED: 05 AUGUST 1884

PASSENGER	AGE	SEX	OCCUPATION	PRV VIL DES
MOSKEWITZ, ST.	26	M	LABR	RRZZZZUSA
REPFELD, E.	20	M	MCHT	RRZZZZUSA
ROSENBEROF, G.	16	M	DLR	RRZZZZUSA
KIWI, F.	18	M	TLR	RRZZZZUSA
MARKEL, CH.	14	M	SGL	RRZZZZUSA
BLUSTEIN, CH.	16	M	SGL	RRZZZZUSA
BERGE, H.	27	M	TLR	RRZZZZUSA
DOBERSTEIN, F.	23	M	TLR	RRZZZZUSA
SIEBZICYER, D.	24	M	TLR	RRZZZZUSA
BABINSKY, K.	17	M	TLR	RRZZZZUSA
SLOWICKA, A.	43	F	W	RRZZZZUSA
EVA	23	F	CH	RRZZZZUSA
GEOWEY	7	M	CHILD	RRZZZZUSA
GUST, CARL	21	M	LABR	RRZZZZUSA
KREMER, P.	35	F	W	RRZZZZUSA
FACHE	13	F	CH	RRZZZZUSA
DOBRE	9	F	CHILD	RRZZZZUSA
FUERMANSKY, L.	20	F	SGL	RRZZZZUSA
SELICY	28	M	SHMK	RRZZZZUSA
KONESEHEWSKY, R.	45	F	W	RRZZZZUSA
FRIEDMANN, S.	25	F	W	RRZZZZUSA
SAMUEL	9	M	CHILD	RRZZZZUSA
BRODY, L.	30	M	DLR	RRZZZZUSA
MISCHKOWSKY, M.	40	F	W	RRZZZZUSA
SELDE	9	F	CHILD	RRZZZZUSA
ISRAEL	.11	M	INFANT	RRZZZZUSA
BOTWINKAN, LERN	22	M	LABR	RRZZZZUSA
HUGI, JETTE	24	F	W	RRZZZZUSA
CHEIE	3	F	CHILD	RRZZZZUSA
ESTHER	.11	F	INFANT	RRZZZZUSA
LEA	.01	F	INFANT	RRZZZZUSA
VESNIVSKI, G.	38	M	LABR	RRZZZZUSA
SAJEWICZ, SCH.	24	F	SGL	RRZZZZUSA
VONSEWITZ, F.	25	F	SGL	RRZZZZUSA
RUBIN, ELIAS	25	M	DLR	RRZZZZUSA
BLUSTEIN, W.	28	F	SGL	RRZZZZUSA
SARA	16	F	SGL	RRZZZZUSA
SCHAPIRA, JACOB	19	M	LABR	RRZZZZUSA

PASSENGER	AGE	SEX	OCCUPATION	PRIV	VIL	DES
BLUSTEIN, J.	16	M	LABR	RR	ZZZZ	USA
CZAWKOW, ABR.	19	M	LABR	RR	ZZZZ	USA
PIANKO, HERZ	20	M	LABR	RR	ZZZZ	USA
MANDEL, MOS.	28	M	LABR	RR	ZZZZ	USA
DINA	20	F	W	RR	ZZZZ	USA
GOLDBERG, S.	34	M	LABR	RR	ZZZZ	USA
DAVID	8	M	CHILD	RR	ZZZZ	USA
HILLMANN, FREIVE	65	F	SGL	RR	ZZZZ	USA
BIERMANN, MICHL.	36	M	LABR	RR	ZZZZ	USA
LOEWENSTEIN, ELIONE	20	F	SGL	RR	ZZZZ	USA
NOWARCZYK, JOS.	29	M	LABR	RR	ZZZZ	USA
KAHN, DAVID	20	M	TLR	RR	ZZZZ	USA
HOFFMANN, LEON	17	M	LABR	RR	ZZZZ	USA
URBAN, MARIE	18	F	SGL	RR	ZZZZ	USA
BACHICK, SCH.	20	F	SGL	RR	ZZZZ	USA
BEILE	19	F	SGL	RR	ZZZZ	USA
HOFFMANN, SCH.	17	F	SGL	RR	ZZZZ	USA
CHASCHER, HINDE	19	F	SGL	RR	ZZZZ	USA
KONZER, ISAAC	45	M	DLR	RR	ZZZZ	USA
RIWKE	50	F	W	RR	ZZZZ	USA
RASCHE	9	F	CHILD	RR	ZZZZ	USA
RACHEL	8	F	CHILD	RR	ZZZZ	USA
MUSEHER, MOSES	18	M	LABR	RR	ZZZZ	USA
PUTTER, M.	19	F	SGL	RR	ZZZZ	USA
SILBERMANN, CH.	20	F	W	RR	ZZZZ	USA
JOSSEL	.11	M	INFANT	RR	ZZZZ	USA
NEITZER, HIRSCH	50	M	DLR	RR	ZZZZ	USA
HENSEHE	18	F	D	RR	ZZZZ	USA
FARZOMBECK, F.	39	M	RAB	RR	ZZZZ	USA
MARTIN, JOSEF	35	M	CHMKR	RR	ZZZZ	USA
SCHACHTEL, MEYER	20	M	DLR	RR	ZZZZ	USA
BORRMANN, CH.	20	M	MCHT	RR	ZZZZ	USA
WACHSMANN, LEW.	52	M	MCHT	RR	ZZZZ	USA
SEREZOW, PESACH	40	M	LABR	RR	ZZZZ	USA
SCHECHTER, PERLE	41	F	W	RR	ZZZZ	USA
JOSEF	20	M	CH	RR	ZZZZ	USA
SAMUEL	18	M	CH	RR	ZZZZ	USA
GOLDE	15	F	CH	RR	ZZZZ	USA
SCHUSTER, ISAAC	19	M	SHMK	RR	ZZZZ	USA
SEGAL, ABR.	21	M	LABR	RR	ZZZZ	USA
GITTEL	22	F	W	RR	ZZZZ	USA
CHASHER, RIWE	16	F	SGL	RR	ZZZZ	USA
RASCHE	14	F	SGL	RR	ZZZZ	USA
BURSTEIN, MARC	32	M	DLR	RR	ZZZZ	USA
ITZKOWITZ, OSEH	17	M	DLR	RR	ZZZZ	USA
FRIEDMANN, SCHOL.	17	M	DLR	RR	ZZZZ	USA
KLINOWSKY, SARA	24	F	W	RR	ZZZZ	USA
TOBIAS	.11	M	INFANT	RR	ZZZZ	USA
BLOCH, HENE	25	F	W	RR	ZZZZ	USA
MOSES	.11	M	INFANT	RR	ZZZZ	USA
LUBUEKOW, JUDA	50	M	TLR	RR	ZZZZ	USA
BAMASCH, ROSA	19	F	SGL	RR	ZZZZ	USA
SCHEINACK, ISAAC	35	M	FARMER	RR	ZZZZ	USA
RUBINSOHN, WLF.	28	M	LABR	RR	ZZZZ	USA
MERKIN, JEB.	28	M	DLR	RR	ZZZZ	USA
FAZKA	24	F	W	RR	ZZZZ	USA
KRAUR, HEINR.	20	M	DLR	RR	ZZZZ	USA
WOCHUMOWITZ, LOBL.	62	M	TLR	RR	ZZZZ	USA
SARA	60	F	W	RR	ZZZZ	USA
ABELOWER, ISAAC	9	M	CHILD	RR	ZZZZ	USA
SCHLOMOWITZ, CH.	19	F	SGL	RR	ZZZZ	USA
JUDENKIRCH, BERNH.	30	M	CGRMKR	RR	ZZZZ	USA
MALZER, JUDA	20	F	FARMER	RR	ZZZZ	USA
URWITZ, HSCH.	35	M	LABR	RR	ZZZZ	USA
ARKIN, MOS.	20	M	LABR	RR	ZZZZ	USA
OLEWKEWITZ, FEIWE	18	M	LABR	RR	ZZZZ	USA
BERGMANN, ABR.	20	M	LABR	RR	ZZZZ	USA
KATORWOLOWSKY, B.	45	F	W	RR	ZZZZ	USA
SARA	9	F	CHILD	RR	ZZZZ	USA
MARIASCHE	8	F	CHILD	RR	ZZZZ	USA
MALKE	5	F	CHILD	RR	ZZZZ	USA
DWORE	4	F	CHILD	RR	ZZZZ	USA
COHN, MEYER	25	M	LABR	RR	ZZZZ	USA
RACHEL	23	F	W	RR	ZZZZ	USA
SAMUEL	.11	M	INFANT	RR	ZZZZ	USA
KALINSKY, JUDA	45	M	LABR	RR	ZZZZ	USA
XREIM, HENOCH	36	M	CGRMKR	RR	ZZZZ	USA
REICHENBACH, SAM.	30	M	DLR	RR	ZZZZ	USA
SESENENZKY, JOH.	26	M	LABR	RR	ZZZZ	USA
GRUNOWITZ, CLEM.	25	M	LABR	RR	ZZZZ	USA
GINKEWITZ, ANT.	21	F	W	RR	ZZZZ	USA
ALEX.	.11	M	INFANT	RR	ZZZZ	USA
SKIRTIMANSKY, M.	20	M	TLR	RR	ZZZZ	USA
JACOB	20	M	TLR	RR	ZZZZ	USA
LEA	20	F	W	RR	ZZZZ	USA
SOHLEIERMANN, M.	21	M	CPR	RR	ZZZZ	USA
JEGLITZ, C.	34	M	BKBNDR	RR	ZZZZ	USA
GOWDON, ISAAC	35	M	DLR	RR	ZZZZ	USA
CHAIM	9	M	CHILD	RR	ZZZZ	USA
BEILE	8	F	CHILD	RR	ZZZZ	USA
KLEIN, DWORE	14	F	SGL	RR	ZZZZ	USA
SARA	5	F	CHILD	RR	ZZZZ	USA
LICHTER, PRUME	42	F	W	RR	ZZZZ	USA
DEBORA	18	F	CH	RR	ZZZZ	USA
BARUCH	13	M	CH	RR	ZZZZ	USA
MOSES	8	M	CHILD	RR	ZZZZ	USA
LIPE	7	M	CHILD	RR	ZZZZ	USA
CHANNE	.11	M	INFANT	RR	ZZZZ	USA
PROLL, BENJAMIN	36	M	LABR	RR	ZZZZ	USA
NODELMANN, CH.	38	M	LABR	RR	ZZZZ	USA
SAFIR, BARUCH	30	M	LABR	RR	ZZZZ	USA
ISAAC	40	M	LABR	RR	ZZZZ	USA
SLOWEITZKY, SLOWE	18	M	LABR	RR	ZZZZ	USA
CHAIE	9	F	CHILD	RR	ZZZZ	USA
SMOLENSKI, BEILE	16	F	SGL	RR	ZZZZ	USA
RACHEL	38	F	W	RR	ZZZZ	USA
CHANNE	9	F	CHILD	RR	ZZZZ	USA
RIWKE	8	F	CHILD	RR	ZZZZ	USA
FREIDEL	6	F	CHILD	RR	ZZZZ	USA
MICHEL	3	M	CHILD	RR	ZZZZ	USA
WOLINSKI, FREUDE	28	F	W	RR	ZZZZ	USA
MASEHE	8	F	CHILD	RR	ZZZZ	USA
BEHR	4	M	CHILD	RR	ZZZZ	USA
REBECCA	.11	F	INFANT	RR	ZZZZ	USA
ELIAS	.01	M	INFANT	RR	ZZZZ	USA
NEUMEYER, FRANZ	33	M	JNR	RR	ZZZZ	USA
PETZILKA, FRANZ	29	M	LKSH	RR	ZZZZ	USA
MARIE	27	F	W	RR	ZZZZ	USA
FRANZ	4	M	CHILD	RR	ZZZZ	USA
AUGUST	2	M	CHILD	RR	ZZZZ	USA
BASS, BECHANE	36	F	W	RR	ZZZZ	USA
JR.	9	F	CHILD	RR	ZZZZ	USA
CH.	7	F	CHILD	RR	ZZZZ	USA
ITZ.	5	M	CHILD	RR	ZZZZ	USA
REB.	.11	F	INFANT	RR	ZZZZ	USA
DENTSEHMANN, BARUCH	40	M	LABR	RR	ZZZZ	USA

SHIP: LABRADOR

FROM: HAVRE
TO: NEW YORK
ARRIVED: 06 AUGUST 1884

PASSENGER	AGE	SEX	OCCUPATION	PRIV	VIL	DES
FREITENBERG, CALMANN	38	M	LKSH	PL	ZZZZ	NY
PARAH	37	F	UNKNOWN	PL	ZZZZ	NY
ANNA	4	F	CHILD	PL	ZZZZ	NY
JACOB	1	M	CHILD	PL	ZZZZ	NY

PASSENGER	AGE	SEX	OCCUPATION	PRIV	VIL	DES

SHIP: POLYNESIA

FROM: HAMBURG
TO: NEW YORK
ARRIVED: 06 AUGUST 1884

PASSENGER	AGE	SEX	OCCUPATION	PRIV	VIL	DES
REPOYNAKA, ANTONI	27	F	WO	PL	ZZZZ	IN
THEODOR	4	M	CHILD	PL	ZZZZ	IN
JADWIGA	2	M	CHILD	PL	ZZZZ	IN
LEAHADEA	.07	M	INFANT	PL	ZZZZ	IN
GAMDE, JOHANUS	25	M	LABR	RR	ZZZZ	NY
KAUTOROWITZ, SCHAUME	35	M	TRDSMN	RR	ZZZZ	NY
SCHUMACHER, HIRSCH	25	M	TRDSMN	RR	ZZZZ	NY
TRUMHIN, BEIR	34	M	TRDSMN	RR	ZZZZ	NY
TASMANN, ABR.	26	M	TRDSMN	RR	ZZZZ	NY
KRESEHCZ, BARUCH	21	M	SMH	RR	ZZZZ	NY
PUSCHNER, HERZ	20	M	JNR	RR	ZZZZ	NY
LEISEROWITZ, LEIZER	24	M	TRDSMN	RR	ZZZZ	NY
KLEISENGER, SCHULEM	24	M	LABR	RR	ZZZZ	NY
JOSEWITZ, CHRISTOPF	26	M	LABR	RR	ZZZZ	NY
LAPARINZKI, MOSES	19	M	LABR	RR	ZZZZ	NY
KAPAZINSKI, CHAIE	20	M	LABR	RR	ZZZZ	NY
KOPP, ITZIG	20	M	LABR	RR	ZZZZ	NY
HENE	20	M	LABR	RR	ZZZZ	NY
KOPPMANN, ISRAEL	20	M	LABR	RR	ZZZZ	NY
HEILPERA, LEISER	19	M	LABR	RR	ZZZZ	NY
MOLSCHAR, JOSEF	29	M	LABR	RR	ZZZZ	NY
ABRAMOWITZ, CHAIE	20	F	SGL	RR	ZZZZ	NY
FEIN, REITZEL	24	F	SGL	RR	ZZZZ	NY
SCHUBERT, LUDWIG	23	M	MCHT	RR	ZZZZ	NY
RAKIER, SAMUEL	30	M	LABR	RR	ZZZZ	NY
BOTWINIK, ISAK	56	M	TRDSMN	RR	ZZZZ	NY
KASCHE	56	F	W	RR	ZZZZ	NY
ELIAS	22	M	S	RR	ZZZZ	NY
REBECCA	17	F	D	RR	ZZZZ	NY
HAUSMANN, MOSES	25	M	TRDSMN	RR	ZZZZ	NY
ESTER	25	F	W	RR	ZZZZ	NY
CHAIE	18	F	SI	RR	ZZZZ	NY
BINDEL, SALOMON	20	M	LABR	RR	ZZZZ	NY
LESNER, PINCUS	39	M	TRDSMN	RR	ZZZZ	NY
NASEN	15	M	S	RR	ZZZZ	NY
COLM, HENRIETTE	35	M	WO	RR	ZZZZ	NY
CONRAD	7	M	CHILD	RR	ZZZZ	NY
JACOB	5	M	CHILD	RR	ZZZZ	NY
NATALIS	.04	F	INFANT	RR	ZZZZ	NY
SKOBATZSCH, ISIDOR	23	M	TRDSMN	RR	ZZZZ	NY
LAMPERT, NAFTALY	25	M	TRDSMN	RR	ZZZZ	NY
CAMER, MEYER	18	M	TLR	RR	ZZZZ	NY
MALKE	21	F	W	RR	ZZZZ	NY
NADELMANN, SIMON	23	M	MCHT	RR	ZZZZ	NY
FRAMBERG, ISRAEL	42	M	MCHT	RR	ZZZZ	NY
DUBOVSKI, ABRAM	43	M	MCHT	RR	ZZZZ	NY
HITZKI, ARON	22	M	LABR	RR	ZZZZ	NY
AUGUSTIN, JAN	22	M	LABR	RR	ZZZZ	NY
BANDMANN, ADOLF	30	M	LABR	PL	ZZZZ	NY
SCHAR, REIZEL	24	F	WO	PL	ZZZZ	NY
FEIGE	3	F	CHILD	PL	ZZZZ	NY
HANIK, HIRSCH	7	M	CHILD	PL	ZZZZ	NY
HOLLAINDER, SORE	50	F	WO	PL	ZZZZ	NY
BEILE	6	F	CHILD	PL	ZZZZ	NY
SARAS	5	M	CHILD	PL	ZZZZ	NY
ESTER	25	F	WO	PL	ZZZZ	NY
GOLDRINGER, FANNI	26	F	WO	PL	ZZZZ	NY
SOFIE	.08	F	INFANT	PL	ZZZZ	NY
FASKI, JACOB	44	M	LABR	PL	ZZZZ	NY
MELECH	7	M	CHILD	PL	ZZZZ	NY
HERZKI	6	M	CHILD	PL	ZZZZ	NY
GUSCHER	4	M	CHILD	PL	ZZZZ	NY
SIMON, MINNA	20	F	SGL	PL	ZZZZ	NY
GOLDBERG, PERIL	38	F	WO	PL	ZZZZ	NY
ISAK	14	M	S	PL	ZZZZ	NY
NATHAN	7	M	CHILD	PL	ZZZZ	NY
LEAH	6	F	CHILD	PL	ZZZZ	NY
CHINKA	4	F	CHILD	PL	ZZZZ	NY
MACHE	.08	F	INFANT	PL	ZZZZ	NY
CZYSEWSKI, ANTONIUS	22	M	LABR	PL	ZZZZ	NY
ORNER, OTTO	20	M	LABR	PL	ZZZZ	NY
SCHOR, HIRSCH	17	M	LABR	PL	ZZZZ	IL
LISLER, JONKEL	19	M	TRDSMN	RR	ZZZZ	NY
KREMINIZER, JOSEF	26	M	MCHT	RR	ZZZZ	NY
ELISE	2	F	CHILD	RR	ZZZZ	NY
ARNES, CHAIM	38	M	LABR	RR	ZZZZ	NY
GOLD, SAM.	20	M	LABR	RR	ZZZZ	NY
BELCZAN, HERSCHEL	55	M	LABR	RR	ZZZZ	NY
ABRAM	7	M	CHILD	RR	ZZZZ	NY
CEGAL, BENJAMIN	32	M	LABR	RR	ZZZZ	IL
ROSNAUSKI, JACOB	38	M	JNR	RR	ZZZZ	NY
JACOBSEN, LEA	22	F	SGL	RR	ZZZZ	NY
DAVIDOWSKI, EIDLE	16	F	SGL	RR	ZZZZ	NY
GRASNABYNSKE, LEIB	38	M	LABR	RR	ZZZZ	NY
SCHALA, MARCUS	31	M	BCHR	RR	ZZZZ	NY
PERLMUTTER, MARCUS	21	M	LABR	RR	ZZZZ	NY
BITMORSKY, MOSES	22	M	LABR	RR	ZZZZ	NY
ELIANSKY, ZODIK	21	M	HTR	RR	ZZZZ	NY
MOSKOWITZ, MAX	21	M	MCHT	RR	ZZZZ	NY
FELDMANN, JOSEF	34	M	MCHT	RR	ZZZZ	NY

SHIP: STATE OF INDIANA

FROM: GLASGOW AND LARNE
TO: NEW YORK
ARRIVED: 07 AUGUST 1884

PASSENGER	AGE	SEX	OCCUPATION	PRIV	VIL	DES
ELIASSOHN, JOSHUA	35	M	PDLR	RR	ZZZZ	USA
GLUECKSMAN, KALMAN	34	M	PDLR	RR	ZZZZ	USA
VIERTEL, PINKUS	20	M	PDLR	RR	ZZZZ	USA
WIRSBOWITZ, MOSES	25	M	PDLR	RR	ZZZZ	USA
LEWIN, ABRAHAM	18	M	PDLR	RR	ZZZZ	USA
ESTOROWITZ, LEIB	30	M	PDLR	RR	ZZZZ	USA
ZUCKOWITZ, SIEGMUND	20	M	FARMER	RR	ZZZZ	USA
INSZKON, STANISLAW	29	M	LABR	RR	ZZZZ	USA
SEGALL, MOSES	30	M	PDLR	RR	ZZZZ	USA
BERNSTEIN, ARM	42	M	PDLR	RR	ZZZZ	USA
POLIZINER, LONIS	23	M	PDLR	RR	ZZZZ	USA
BAGILZIK, DAVID	44	M	PDLR	RR	ZZZZ	USA
REBECCA	43	F	W	RR	ZZZZ	USA
BERTHA	10	F	CH	RR	ZZZZ	USA
MARKUS, REBEKKA	00	F	SP	RR	ZZZZ	USA
DONOWITZ, PESSEL	00	F	W	RR	ZZZZ	USA
FEIVEL	00	M	CH	RR	ZZZZ	USA
TEGNEDORF, TSCHERNITE	24	F	W	RR	ZZZZ	USA
FRIEDEL	3	M	CHILD	RR	ZZZZ	USA
NEUMANN, MEYER	26	M	PDLR	RR	ZZZZ	USA
CHAIE	24	F	W	RR	ZZZZ	USA
REBEKKA	1	F	CHILD	RR	ZZZZ	USA
WOLF	.04	M	INFANT	RR	ZZZZ	USA
GOLDBERG, CHANNE	29	F	W	RR	ZZZZ	USA
GOLDE	11	F	CH	RR	ZZZZ	USA
CHAIE	6	F	CHILD	RR	ZZZZ	USA
ABRAHAM	4	M	CHILD	RR	ZZZZ	USA
KRASNEGLOWE, ISRAEL	20	M	PDLR	RR	ZZZZ	USA
CHAIE	20	F	W	RR	ZZZZ	USA

PASSENGER	AGE	SEX	OCCUPATION	PRV VIL DES

SHIP: RHYNLAND

FROM: ANTWERP
TO: NEW YORK
ARRIVED: 08 AUGUST 1884

PASSENGER	AGE	SEX	OCCUPATION	PRV VIL DES
TIKS, CATH.	28	F	LABR	PLZZZZCH
VERA.	2	F	CHILD	PLZZZZCH
TRZ.	00	M	INF	PLZZZZCH
CHRISTOPH, A.	16	M	UNKNOWN	PLZZZZCH
WASCHEK, TH.	24	M	LABR	PLZZZZUNK
KUCKLL, JOH.	55	M	UNKNOWN	PLZZZZIL
MASSCILWO, PR.	31	M	UNKNOWN	RRZZZZUNK
H.	22	M	UNKNOWN	RRZZZZUNK
W.	1	M	CHILD	RRZZZZUNK
KOLLER, ROSA.	16	F	UNKNOWN	RRZZZZUNK
ETEL, GEO	20	M	UNKNOWN	RRZZZZNY

SHIP: HAMMONIA

FROM: HAMBURG AND HAVRE
TO: NEW YORK
ARRIVED: 11 AUGUST 1884

PASSENGER	AGE	SEX	OCCUPATION	PRV VIL DES
PHILLIPOWSKY SARA	38	F	W	RRZZZZUSA
BASCHE	.11	F	INFANT	RRZZZZUSA
LANGE, MEYER	18	M	MCHT	RRZZZZUSA
MEROWITSCH, BETTI	28	F	SGL	RRZZZZUSA
FLATOW, CHAIE	14	F	SGL	RRZZZZUSA
TAUBE	5	F	CHILD	RRZZZZUSA
LEIB	3	M	CHILD	RRZZZZUSA
BARON, TEWJE	18	M	CGRMKR	RRZZZZUSA
MOLOCH, RACHEL	21	F	SGL	RRZZZZUSA
STANISLOWSKI, ESTHER	23	F	W	RRZZZZUSA
ASCHER	3	M	CHILD	RRZZZZUSA
LIEFSCHITZ, MOSES	22	M	MCHT	RRZZZZUSA
MARIE	21	F	W	RRZZZZUSA
HOROWITZ, GIESE	40	F	W	RRZZZZUSA
HINDE	9	F	CHILD	RRZZZZUSA
ISAAC	8	M	CHILD	RRZZZZUSA
SARA	6	F	CHILD	RRZZZZUSA
CHEIM	5	M	CHILD	RRZZZZUSA
MICHEL	2	M	CHILD	RRZZZZUSA
TANNENBAUM, JACOB	23	M	TLR	RRZZZZUSA
FRANZISCA	24	F	W	RRZZZZUSA
ISAAC	9	M	CHILD	RRZZZZUSA
KARNOWSKY, CHALE	18	F	SGL	RRZZZZUSA
LEHMANN, ABR.	26	M	LABR	RRZZZZUSA
GLASER, MEYER	30	M	LABR	RRZZZZUSA
SARA	26	F	W	RRZZZZUSA
GITTEL	.11	F	INFANT	RRZZZZUSA
LIPNEWITZ, LEIB	18	M	LABR	RRZZZZUSA
TROZINSKI, EDM.	33	M	LABR	RRZZZZUSA
FRIEDOWSKI, TAUBE	25	F	W	RRZZZZUSA
HIRSCH	3	M	CHILD	RRZZZZUSA
LEIB	.06	M	INFANT	RRZZZZUSA
DIGROWSKI, ZIESLE	22	F	W	RRZZZZUSA
ITZKE	.11	M	INFANT	RRZZZZUSA
GORDON, GOLDE	23	F	W	RRZZZZUSA
ELKE	4	F	CHILD	RRZZZZUSA
RUCKE	.11	F	INFANT	RRZZZZUSA
WISCHIGRODSKY, MICHEL	17	M	LABR	RRZZZZUSA
JEKOWITZ, CHANNE	15	F	W	RRZZZZUSA
RACHEL	.11	F	INFANT	RRZZZZUSA
WOLF, FEIGE	23	F	W	RRZZZZUSA
CHEIE	4	F	CHILD	RRZZZZUSA
SAVORNE	.11	F	INFANT	RRZZZZUSA
DYANSKY, ILLER	18	M	LABR	RRZZZZUSA
ROSENTHAL, ITZKO	16	M	LABR	RRZZZZUSA
KAPLAN, NOCHIM	40	M	LABR	RRZZZZUSA
RUTKEWITZ, JOSEF	16	M	LABR	RRZZZZUSA
SCHWARZ, DAVID	50	M	LABR	RRZZZZUSA
GOLDE	40	F	W	RRZZZZUSA
SACK, JANKEL	40	M	LABR	RRZZZZUSA
JANNE	20	F	CH	RRZZZZUSA
ISRAEL	15	M	CH	RRZZZZUSA
REISEL	9	F	CHILD	RRZZZZUSA
GURIAN, JINNES	30	M	LABR	RRZZZZUSA
GDOLEWITZ, JANKEL	20	M	LABR	RRZZZZUSA
SCHENKER, EMILIE	37	F	W	RRZZZZUSA
REGINE	9	F	CHILD	RRZZZZUSA
HEINR.	8	M	CHILD	RRZZZZUSA
ROSA	7	F	CHILD	RRZZZZUSA
JOSEF	6	M	CHILD	RRZZZZUSA
ARNOLD	3	M	CHILD	RRZZZZUSA
FREIMANN, SCHAEHNE	20	M	LABR	RRZZZZUSA
DANTOWITZ, DAUBE	18	F	SGL	RRZZZZUSA
ZIPKIN, CHAIE	9	F	CHILD	RRZZZZUSA
BEREK, CHAIN	28	M	TLR	RRZZZZUSA
TOBACZNIKOW, J.	22	M	LABR	RRZZZZUSA
TIKOCINSKY, TAUBE	28	F	W	RRZZZZUSA
JOSEF	8	M	CHILD	RRZZZZUSA
SARA	6	F	CHILD	RRZZZZUSA
CHAJE	.11	F	INFANT	RRZZZZUSA
BORZION, GUTMANN	18	M	LABR	RRZZZZUSA
BEZUN, MORRIS	23	M	LABR	RRZZZZUSA
SARA	22	F	W	RRZZZZUSA
CHAIE	17	F	SGL	RRZZZZUSA
ADELSOHN, MEYER	6	M	CHILD	RRZZZZUSA
SEBANDOWSKI, CHAIE	28	F	W	RRZZZZUSA
TRUME	6	F	CHILD	RRZZZZUSA
DWOSCHE	.11	F	INFANT	RRZZZZUSA
FEINBERG, ARON	17	M	LABR	RRZZZZUSA
SOHN, AESCHE	18	F	SGL	RRZZZZUSA
GITTEL, NECHOME	9	F	CHILD	RRZZZZUSA
AT, ESTHER	18	F	SGL	RRZZZZUSA
NATELSOHN, ELKE	14	F	SGL	RRZZZZUSA
ADELSOHN, MOSES	27	M	LABR	RRZZZZUSA
MARIE	25	F	W	RRZZZZUSA
BERCH	.11	M	INFANT	RRZZZZUSA
GOLDSTEIN, ROSA	24	F	W	RRZZZZUSA
SENOEL	.11	M	INFANT	RRZZZZUSA
JACOB	.01	M	INFANT	RRZZZZUSA
WEINER, SARA	25	F	W	RRZZZZUSA
LESSER	6	M	CHILD	RRZZZZUSA
RADINSTEIN, EDUARD	20	M	LABR	RRZZZZUSA
SMILZ, ASRIEL	48	M	LABR	RRZZZZUSA
MOSES	28	M	LABR	RRZZZZUSA
ABE	10	M	S	RRZZZZUSA
LISMON, HIRSCH	30	M	LABR	RRZZZZUSA
CARLSON, CARL	25	M	LABR	RRZZZZUSA

SHIP: CALIFORNIA

FROM: HAMBURG
TO: NEW YORK
ARRIVED: 13 AUGUST 1884

PASSENGER	AGE	SEX	OCCUPATION	PRV VIL DES
WIMALHE, ABRAHAM	15	M	S	RRZZZZNY
LISCHNEWSKY, MARCZY	32	M	LABR	RRZZZZNY
GREBYNSKI, CHAIN	20	M	LABR	RRZZZZNY
GIMPELSON, JANKEL	43	M	TLR	RRZZZZNY
GOLDSCHMIDT, SALOMON	32	M	TRDSMN	RRZZZZNY
U, MAIER	17	M	TRDSMN	RRZZZZNY
DAVIDOWITZ, NATHAN	19	M	TRDSMN	RRZZZZNY
BLAN, SUMNE	23	F	WO	RRZZZZNY
WUNKOFSKY, DOMINIK	48	M	LABR	RRZZZZNY
DISNER, ANISDIL	21	M	LABR	RRZZZZNY
GERBER, RUDKE	18	F	SGL	RRZZZZNY

PASSENGER	AGE	SEX	OCCUPATION	PRV VIL DES
GUTSTEIN, HANNE	17	F	SGL	RRZZZZNY
KSOHNSON, MASCHE	30	M	LABR	RRZZZZNY
MEISTROWSKY, CHAWE	48	F	WO	RRZZZZNY
MUSZE	15	F	D	RRZZZZNY
DORETZIN, MENDEL	26	M	LABR	RRZZZZNY
MAYECK, BASCHE	17	F	SGL	RRZZZZNY
WEINGROTZ, SASSI	18	F	SGL	RRZZZZNY
SCHERSTER, SARA	19	F	SGL	RRZZZZNY
OSMIANCA, JOSEFINE	24	F	WO	RRZZZZNY
MARYANNE	5	F	CHILD	RRZZZZNY
JOSEFA	3	F	CHILD	RRZZZZNY
WOJTIKUNAS, KANMIR	24	M	LABR	RRZZZZUNK
CAHEN, SARA	14	F	WO	RRZZZZNY
SMOSCH, KREINE	22	F	WO	RRZZZZNY
JANTE	.04	M	INFANT	RRZZZZNY
BOEGIN, CHAIE	18	F	WO	RRZZZZNY
HIRSCH	.07	M	INFANT	RRZZZZNY
GRUENWALD, MOSES	19	M	TRDSMN	RRZZZZNY
ROSENWEIG, FRANZISKA	26	F	WO	RRZZZZNY
IDA	7	F	CHILD	RRZZZZNY
UBRICA	6	F	CHILD	RRZZZZNY
RUEDKE	4	F	CHILD	RRZZZZNY
MISTROSKI, BER.	50	M	TRDSMN	RRZZZZNY
KABATZNICK, TRUMME	45	F	WO	RRZZZZNY
CHAVE	18	F	D	RRZZZZNY
LEIB	15	M	S	RRZZZZNY
MASCHE	7	M	CHILD	RRZZZZNY
CHAIE	6	F	CHILD	RRZZZZNY
HANE	4	F	CHILD	RRZZZZNY
CHAIM	3	M	CHILD	RRZZZZNY
MISTROVSKI, MINE	18	F	SGL	RRZZZZNY
BALDEWSKI, JOHANNE	35	F	WO	RRZZZZNY
MANIZEWSKI, MAX	7	M	CHILD	RRZZZZNY
TARNOW, LADISLAUS	26	M	LABR	PLZZZZNY
BLASINSKY, KASIMIR	24	M	LABR	PLZZZZNY
GUTMANN, OTTO	18	M	SMH	RRZZZZNY
GOLDMANN, SCHMUL	19	M	SMH	RRZZZZNY
GORDON, OSCAR	22	M	WCHMKR	RRZZZZNY
PIANTKOWSKY, ABRAH.	42	M	TLR	RRZZZZNY
ZIELKE	42	F	W	RRZZZZNY
SUSMANN	25	M	S	RRZZZZNY
CHANE	18	F	D	RRZZZZNY
HIRSCH	.07	M	INFANT	RRZZZZNY
ROSCHKOWSKY, OSCAR	30	M	TRDSMN	RRZZZZNY

SHIP: CANADA

FROM: HAVRE
TO: NEW YORK
ARRIVED: 13 AUGUST 1884

PASSENGER	AGE	SEX	OCCUPATION	PRV VIL DES
PEINBERG, MARIA	20	F	NN	RRZZZZNY

SHIP: STATE OF GEORGIA

FROM: GLASGOW
TO: NEW YORK
ARRIVED: 13 AUGUST 1884

PASSENGER	AGE	SEX	OCCUPATION	PRV VIL DES
BAUM, BERTHA	15	F	SVNT	PLZZZZUSA
BANK, JONE	32	M	PDLR	PLZZZZUSA
CZECHANOWSKY, ABRAHAM	47	M	TLR	PLZZZZUSA
SCHEINE	16	M	TLR	PLZZZZUSA
JOSEF	11	M	CH	PLZZZZUSA
BARSCHOWITZ, JOSEF	18	M	PDLR	PLZZZZUSA
PECZINSKY, SCHLOME	18	M	TLR	PLZZZZUSA
EPNER, NITEN	19	M	TLR	PLZZZZUSA
TIEGEL	18	F	SVNT	PLZZZZUSA
TROELICH, WATZLAW	26	M	LABR	PLZZZZUSA
GESCHEDER, SAMUEL	31	M	PDLR	PLZZZZUSA
GOLDSTEIN, ARON	27	M	SMH	PLZZZZUSA
FELIN, ABRAHAM	00	M	PDLR	PLZZZZUSA
KUZINSKY, JOHANNE	00	F	SVNT	PLZZZZUSA
KUBINIS, EVA	20	F	SVNT	PLZZZZUSA
MATZKEBUAIR, MIRL	20	F	SVNT	PLZZZZUSA
MUNK, HIRSCH	45	F	LKSH	PLZZZZUSA
CHRENBACH, ROSALIE	40	F	W	PLZZZZUSA
ERNESTINE	11	F	CH	PLZZZZUSA
LENE	6	F	CHILD	PLZZZZUSA
SAMUEL	5	M	CHILD	PLZZZZUSA
APRENBACH, WALCHE	3	F	CHILD	PLZZZZUSA
PAULA	1	F	CHILD	PLZZZZUSA
WABODSKY, FRIEDE	30	F	W	PLZZZZUSA
BOSCHE	8	F	CHILD	PLZZZZUSA
FEIWEL	2	F	CHILD	PLZZZZUSA
SEMIKAS, ANARE	35	M	LABR	PLZZZZUSA
WEISKOLL, CINE	26	M	PDLR	PLZZZZUSA

SHIP: CITY OF RICHMOND

FROM: LIVERPOOL AND QUEENSTOWN
TO: NEW YORK
ARRIVED: 15 AUGUST 1884

PASSENGER	AGE	SEX	OCCUPATION	PRV VIL DES
PUHAKKA, LIESA	20	F	SP	FNZZZZUSA
RABINOWITZ, HEINRICH	34	M	LABR	FNADYNUSA

SHIP: EIDER

FROM: BREMEN AND SOUTHAMPTON
TO: NEW YORK
ARRIVED: 16 AUGUST 1884

PASSENGER	AGE	SEX	OCCUPATION	PRV VIL DES
HUPPMANN, JOSEPH	22	M	MCHT	RRZZZZUSA
TSCHEREMISSINOFF, STAAT	52	M	TT	RRZZZZUSA
TSCHEREMISSINOFF, DOROT	49	F	W	RRZZZZUSA
KIRASCHKEN, SOPHIE	35	F	W	RRZZZZUSA
LEON	14	M	CH	RRZZZZUSA
MICHAEL	11	M	CH	RRZZZZUSA
JOHANN	10	M	CH	RRZZZZUSA
SENIA	9	F	CHILD	RRZZZZUSA
ELISE	7	F	CHILD	RRZZZZUSA
NAUM	4	M	CHILD	RRZZZZUSA
SIMON	.09	M	INFANT	RRZZZZUSA
BACHAMAN, ISAAC	60	M	MCHT	RRZZZZUSA
ELISABETHA	65	F	W	RRZZZZUSA

SHIP: LESSING

FROM: HAMBURG AND HAVRE
TO: NEW YORK
ARRIVED: 16 AUGUST 1884

PASSENGER	AGE	SEX	OCCUPATION	PRV VIL DES
SALZSTEIN, ABRAM	19	M	WCHMKR	RRAHUIUSA
AMLISKA, MARIANNA	21	F	W	RRAHYCUSA

PASSENGER	AGE	SEX	OCCUPATION	PRV VIL DES
JOSEPH	.04	M	INFANT	RRAHYCUSA
RUDKEWITZ, JOSSEL	28	M	LABR	RRAHTOUSA
KANZELLAUM, SARA	18	F	SGL	RRAFWJUSA
SILLEZINGER, BETTI	16	F	SGL	RRAHSMUSA
ADOLF	9	M	CHILD	RRAHSMUSA
BRICKER, MINE	19	F	SGL	RRAHTFUSA
LEIB	9	M	CHILD	RRAHTFUSA
GELLURG, MOSES	17	M	LABR	RRAFWJUSA
CZIAPPENTE, K.	23	F	W	RRAHSWUSA
EMMA	2	F	CHILD	RRAHSWUSA
SCHLESINGER, REGI	14	F	SGL	RRAHRYUSA
HERM.	9	M	CHILD	RRAHRYUSA
GELLBERT, MINNA	23	F	W	RRZZZZUSA
FEIGE	.11	F	INFANT	RRZZZZUSA
HENOCHOWITZ, SOLOMON	21	M	TNR	RRAGRTUSA
GITTEL	20	F	W	RRAGRTUSA
WORSOWSKI, DOBNE	19	F	SGL	RRAHTFUSA
GORDON, JACOB	20	M	TLR	RRAHTFUSA
GOLDSCHMIDT, BENJAMIN	19	M	LABR	RRAFVGUSA
MAI, WOLF	23	M	LABR	RRAHTWUSA
BASCHER, MARIE	60	F	W	RRAHTWUSA
ROSENWALD, MOSES	19	M	LABR	RRAHTHUSA
SCHIFRIN, MIRIAM	23	F	W	RRZZZZUSA
CHASCHE	14	F	SGL	RRZZZZUSA
HANNE	8	F	CHILD	RRZZZZUSA
MARIE	.11	F	INFANT	RRZZZZUSA
BERTHA	.01	F	INFANT	RRZZZZUSA
NECHATOWITZ, MORCHE	18	F	SGL	RRZZZZUSA
LASDAN, SIMON	33	M	TLR	RRAGRTUSA
BLUMSTEIN, JOSSEL	64	M	WCHMKR	RRAHTCUSA
ADLER, MARIE	36	F	W	RRZZZZUSA
ETTEL	.11	F	INFANT	RRZZZZUSA
MARKOWITZ, KASRIEL	21	M	LABR	RRZZZZUSA
JIVAN, ESTHER	28	F	W	RRAHVVUSA
SCHAJE	.11	F	INFANT	RRAHVVUSA
ADLER, MOSES	8	M	CHILD	RRZZZZUSA
GOLDMANN, BASCHE	27	F	W	RRAHTOUSA
HEINR.	.11	M	INFANT	RRAHTOUSA
MAE	.01	F	INFANT	RRAHTOUSA
LEA	20	F	SGL	RRAHTOUSA
DOROTHEA	17	F	SGL	RRAHTOUSA
IDA	9	F	CHILD	RRAHTOUSA
JACOB	8	M	CHILD	RRAHTOUSA
HALLANGUIST, C.	24	M	CPRSMH	RRAHQHUSA
MATHE	23	F	W	RRAHQHUSA

SHIP: ASSYRIAN MONARCH

FROM: LONDON
TO: NEW YORK
ARRIVED: 18 AUGUST 1884

PASSENGER	AGE	SEX	OCCUPATION	PRV VIL DES
KRUSKANSKY, MORRIS	29	M	LABR	RRAHOONY
JUCIMANN, JACOB	24	M	LABR	RRZZZZNY

SHIP: AUSTRAL

FROM: LIVERPOOL AND QUEENSTOWN
TO: NEW YORK
ARRIVED: 18 AUGUST 1884

PASSENGER	AGE	SEX	OCCUPATION	PRV VIL DES
KOPPEL, DAVID	19	M	CGRMKR	RRZZZZCH
SOGELLOWICH, HUNRICH	31	M	LABR	RRZZZZNY
RUBENOWIC, JONN	18	M	BLKSMH	RRZZZZNY
SARKUSEAN, J.	18	M	BLKSMH	RRZZZZNY
JORDANSKY, HIRSCH	23	M	CPTR	RRZZZZNY
FISCHNER, ITZE	18	M	LABR	RRZZZZNY
CZYMECZUK, PELE	21	M	LABR	PLZZZZNY
BOGUS, VINCENT	24	M	LABR	PLZZZZNY
BAK, FRANZ	31	M	LABR	PLZZZZNY
ANNA	25	F	UNKNOWN	PLZZZZNY
S.	1	F	CHILD	PLZZZZNY
BOGUS, ANDREW	22	M	LABR	PLZZZZNY
MISTUR, VICTORIA	22	F	SVNT	PLZZZZNY
BUGAI, AGATHE	22	F	SVNT	PLZZZZNY
JACOB	48	M	LABR	PLZZZZNY
SOPHIE	34	F	UNKNOWN	PLZZZZNY
MARIE	9	F	CHILD	PLZZZZNY
FRANZ	1	M	CHILD	PLZZZZNY
ADBIERZCIHTEH, JOHAN	11	M	UNKNOWN	PLZZZZNY

SHIP: MORAVIA

FROM: HAMBURG
TO: NEW YORK
ARRIVED: 19 AUGUST 1884

PASSENGER	AGE	SEX	OCCUPATION	PRV VIL DES
PARNASS, LEA	55	F	W	PLAFWJUSA
TAUBE	18	F	D	PLAFWJUSA
VADEL, DAVID	40	F	PNTR	PLAHZPUSA
BANK, HANNA	40	F	W	PLAHZPUSA
BERK, JONN	54	M	LABR	PLAHSBUSA
ANNA	9	F	CHILD	PLAHSBUSA
HERRMAN, ADAM	21	M	LABR	PLAHSBUSA
ANNA	22	F	W	PLAHSBUSA
MASUTZKY, MOSES	18	M	LABR	PLAHYLUSA
ARONSTOM, DORIS	20	F	SGL	PLAHXHUSA
KOZMINSKI, LOUIS	21	M	LABR	PLAHWRUSA
LEWIN, HIRSCH	16	M	LABR	PLAHQUUSA
KOZMINSKI, MARIANNE	15	F	SGL	PLAHWRUSA
CZARNY, ISRAEL	34	M	LABR	PLAFWJUSA
KRESLOWSKI, SARA	18	F	SGL	PLAHZSUSA
ABRAHAM	9	M	CHILD	PLAHZSUSA
MARIE	8	F	CHILD	PLAHZSUSA
ITZKOWSKY, HEYMANN	21	M	LABR	PLAHVHUSA
BORTZIAN, GIOTEL	15	F	SGL	PLAHZSUSA
LATIN, CHAIM	19	M	LABR	PLAHZSUSA
FILOZOF, SAMUEL	19	M	MCHT	PLAFWJUSA
MELLA, CAECILIE	23	F	SGL	PLAHUNUSA
WEINSTEIN, SAMUEL	23	M	WCHMKR	RRZZZZUSA
ABEL	19	M	WCHMKR	RRZZZZUSA
WOLFSKY, GEORG	36	M	DLR	RRAHYNUSA
KURLANSKY, FUDEL	43	M	DLR	RRAHTNUSA
REBECA	40	F	W	RRAHTNUSA
LOUISE	19	F	CH	RRAHTNUSA
ROSALIE	9	F	CHILD	RRAHTNUSA
LUDWIG	8	M	CHILD	RRAHTNUSA
JACOB	6	M	CHILD	RRAHTNUSA
ELVAS	5	M	CHILD	RRAHTNUSA
BERTHA	.11	F	INFANT	RRAHTNUSA
REISMANN, SAMUEL	21	M	LABR	RRAHZSUSA
SUMELISHKY, DAVID	43	M	DLR	RRZZZZUSA
BEILE	40	F	W	RRZZZZUSA
JULK.	9	M	CHILD	RRZZZZUSA
JACOB	8	M	CHILD	RRZZZZUSA
SALOMON	4	M	CHILD	RRZZZZUSA
MALKE	.11	M	INFANT	RRZZZZUSA
KOPUELSKY, ISRAEL	18	M	LABR	RRAHZFUSA
BROD, RUBIN	26	M	MCHT	RRAHUSUSA
BIALISTOEZKY, SCHOLEM	35	M	PNTR	RRZZZZUSA
BERNSTEIN, DAVID	26	M	LABR	RRADOIUSA
FRANK, LEIB	19	M	LABR	RRAHWZUSA
SCHNEIMANN, FEIWEL	20	M	LABR	RRAHWZUSA
JACOB, SCHLOME	27	M	LABR	RRAHWZUSA
SCHAFRAN, ZALLEL	20	M	LABR	RRAHWZUSA

PASSENGER	AGE	SEX	OCCUPATION	PRV	VIL	DES
KLEINER, SUNDEL	20	M	LABR	RR	AHZI	USA
RUBENSTEIN, LEA	19	F	SGL	RR	AHTU	USA
JACOB	14	M	LABR	RR	AHTU	USA
KEMINSKY, MOSES	42	M	LABR	RR	AHWF	USA
BLUMKEN, ELIAS	18	M	LABR	RR	AHWF	USA
PRUSZLOVSKY, ABRAHAM	19	M	LABR	RR	AHSF	USA
SEIFER, MEILATH	28	M	LABR	RR	ZZZZ	USA
FRANK, SCHMUEL	26	M	LABR	RR	AHWZ	USA
WOLFROHN, HIRSCH	33	M	MCHT	RR	AHVA	USA
HERSCH, NATHAN	10	M	BY	RR	AHVA	USA
SEGALL, ISAAC	22	M	TLR	RR	AHVA	USA
GERDNIE, HIRSCH	16	M	TLR	RR	AHVA	USA
FEIWELOWITZ, ISAAC	20	M	CL	RR	AHVA	USA
MELZNER, ISRAEL	20	M	CL	RR	AHVA	USA
DRANER, BENJAMIN	32	M	DLR	RR	AHVA	USA
CHAIE	26	F	W	RR	AHVA	USA
DINE	8	F	CHILD	RR	AHVA	USA
KALMAN	2	M	CHILD	RR	AHVA	USA
POLLACK, MEYER	22	M	DLR	RR	AHVA	USA
GOLDBERG, CHAIKEL	36	M	LABR	RR	AHZP	USA
SCHAPIRO, JUDES	18	F	SGL	RR	AHVK	USA
NIESLOWA, PESA	22	F	SGL	RR	AHTW	USA
ZLOTNITZKA, GOLDE	55	F	W	RR	AHTW	USA
STADTMANN, JACOB	20	M	LABR	RR	AHZS	USA
LEA	19	F	W	RR	AHZS	USA
PAKOLSKY, LEIZER	65	M	LABR	RR	ZZZZ	USA
SIWE	45	F	W	RR	ZZZZ	USA
FEIGE	17	M	CH	RR	ZZZZ	USA
GERSON	23	M	CH	RR	ZZZZ	USA
BURGER, CHAIL	18	M	LABR	RR	AHZS	USA
LASNIETZKI, ISER	21	M	LABR	RR	AHZL	USA
FELLHAINDER, SAMUEL	32	M	LABR	RR	AHZS	USA
SZMULOWIS, LEON	20	M	LABR	RR	AFWJ	USA
STEPZENIS, MARIANNE	34	F	W	RR	AHZU	USA
U, U	.03	M	INFANT	RR	AHZU	USA
SBRASCHEEN, CHONON	20	M	SMH	RR	AHUZ	USA
MICHELSOHN, SCHEINE	14	F	SGL	RR	AHRZ	USA
KLEMPNER, PESCHE	45	F	W	RR	AHTM	USA
LEA	13	F	CH	RR	AHTM	USA
MEIER	9	M	CHILD	RR	AHTM	USA
SINEONE	17	F	SGL	RR	AHTM	USA
BERGRON, DEBORA	9	F	CHILD	RR	AHTQ	USA
LEWY, SARA	9	F	CHILD	RR	AHTQ	USA
SCHMOLL, UDEL	19	M	LABR	RR	ZZZZ	USA
WISCHNOWSKY, LEA	28	F	SGL	RR	AHTW	USA
LAZDZEISKY, BARUCH	25	M	WCHMKR	RR	AHRZ	USA
LEWIN, MEIER	44	M	LABR	RR	AEFL	USA
LURIE, LEISER	32	M	LABR	RR	ZZZZ	USA
KLEIN, BENNO	19	M	TNMK	RR	ZZZZ	USA
BECKER, ZIWIE	18	F	SGL	RR	AHRZ	USA
DWORSKI, RINEE	9	F	CHILD	RR	AHZL	USA
STEPSONNER, MARIAM	27	M	LABR	RR	AHZS	USA
MARIANNE	25	F	W	RR	AHZS	USA
BIEBER, MATHILDE	33	M	SGL	RR	AHZS	USA
BERESDA, DEMIAN	25	M	LABR	RR	AHZS	USA

SHIP: AMERIQUE

FROM: HAVRE
TO: NEW YORK
ARRIVED: 20 AUGUST 1884

PASSENGER	AGE	SEX	OCCUPATION	PRV	VIL	DES
DE-BESS, U-MRS.	25	F	NN	RR	ZZZZ	USA
GERF, SAMUEL	32	M	MCHT	RR	ZZZZ	USA
SWEDMANN, ISAAC	22	M	TNSTH	RR	ZZZZ	USA
KENTER, RUDOLPH	22	M	TNSTH	RR	ZZZZ	USA
SOLOVITZ, SIMON	26	M	GZR	RR	ZZZZ	USA
RABRUSCHI, SAMUEL	26	M	MCHT	RR	ZZZZ	USA

SHIP: DONAU

FROM: BREMEN
TO: NEW YORK
ARRIVED: 21 AUGUST 1884

PASSENGER	AGE	SEX	OCCUPATION	PRV	VIL	DES
SEGAL, FEIGE	16	F	NN	RR	ZZZZ	USA
ROSE	18	F	NN	RR	ZZZZ	USA
SCHUFRONE, MEYER	19	M	LABR	RR	ZZZZ	USA
KOHRAD, CAREL	42	F	NN	RR	ZZZZ	USA
PAULINE	16	F	NN	RR	ZZZZ	USA
HEINR.	8	M	CHILD	RR	ZZZZ	USA
ADELE	.09	F	INFANT	RR	ZZZZ	USA
LEWY, BERNH.	23	M	LABR	RR	ZZZZ	USA
KAHN, MOSES	41	M	CPTR	RR	ZZZZ	USA
SCHATIEL, LAZAR	41	M	JNR	RR	ZZZZ	USA
SCHALURO, HANNA	24	F	NN	RR	ZZZZ	USA

SHIP: WAESLAND

FROM: ANTWERP
TO: NEW YORK
ARRIVED: 22 AUGUST 1884

PASSENGER	AGE	SEX	OCCUPATION	PRV	VIL	DES
FIGNER, ANNA-MISS	26	F	UNKNOWN	RR	AEFL	RSS
PIERRE-MR	12	M	UNKNOWN	RR	AEFL	RSS
VERRA-ENGEL-MRS	42	F	UNKNOWN	RR	AEFL	RSS
HELLEN-MS	36	F	UNKNOWN	RR	AEFL	RSS
GUZOWSKY, BER.	27	M	UNKNOWN	PL	ZZZZ	USA
HEISER, ALEXIS	21	M	LABR	PL	AEFL	USA
W.	14	M	UNKNOWN	RR	ZZZZ	USA
MUCH, MAGOL.	41	F	UNKNOWN	RR	ZZZZ	USA
MAGD.	23	F	UNKNOWN	RR	ZZZZ	USA
MENDELSHONN, M.	50	M	FARMER	RR	ZZZZ	USA
U-MISS	16	F	UNKNOWN	RR	ZZZZ	USA
MILKONKA, FREZA	31	M	LABR	RR	ZZZZ	USA
CAROL	50	F	UNKNOWN	RR	ZZZZ	USA
VINE	7	F	CHILD	RR	ZZZZ	USA
AUT.	4	F	CHILD	RR	ZZZZ	USA
AND.	.11	M	INFANT	RR	ZZZZ	USA
MARIA	.05	F	INFANT	RR	ZZZZ	USA

SHIP: WERRA

FROM: BREMEN
TO: NEW YORK
ARRIVED: 23 AUGUST 1884

PASSENGER	AGE	SEX	OCCUPATION	PRV	VIL	DES
KASS, LEON	18	M	MUSN	RR	ZZZZ	USA
GUTMANN, TANTJE	19	F	UNKNOWN	RR	ZZZZ	USA
LAKOWSKY, ESTER	40	F	UNKNOWN	RR	ZZZZ	USA
FICHEN	7	F	CHILD	RR	ZZZZ	USA
ROBERT	6	M	CHILD	RR	ZZZZ	USA
MASHEL	3	M	CHILD	RR	ZZZZ	USA

PASSENGER	AGE	SEX	OCCUPATION	PRIVL	DES
SHIP: CITY OF BERLIN					
FROM: LIVERPOOL AND QUEENSTOWN					
TO: NEW YORK					
ARRIVED: 25 AUGUST 1884					
HERSCH, SEL	46	M	LABR	PLZZZ	ZUSA
OLEKSWER, JOSE	35	M	LABR	PLZZZ	ZUSA
JESSEY	14	F	SVNT	PLZZZ	ZUSA
YURSEL	9	M	CHILD	PLZZZ	ZUSA
UNTE	8	F	CHILD	PLZZZ	ZUSA
JACOB	5	M	CHILD	PLZZZ	ZUSA
JOH	00	M	INF	PLZZZ	ZUSA
NOVASAK, IAN	30	M	LABR	PLZZZ	ZUSA
SAWITZKI, JOSEF	20	M	LABR	PLZZZ	ZUSA
RUBENSTEIN, ISAAC	33	M	LABR	PLAHS	JUSA
BEILE	21	F	W	PLAHS	JUSA
ETTEL	8	F	CHILD	PLAHS	JUSA
ABRAHAM	1	M	CHILD	PLAHS	JUSA
HERSCHEL	1	M	CHILD	PLAHS	JUSA
NEAFIELD, ADOLPH	22	M	LABR	PLAHS	JUSA
FINKEL, ISEN	25	M	LABR	PLAHZ	SUSA
WEXANNURIS, IANKEL	28	M	LABR	PLZZZ	ZUSA
LEWIZ, ALBERT	27	M	LABR	PLAHX	MUSA
KOLBINN, WILHELM	29	M	LABR	PLAHY	XUSA
SHIP: GELLERT					
FROM: HAMBURG AND HAVRE					
TO: NEW YORK					
ARRIVED: 25 AUGUST 1884					
TSCHEROSKY, HIRSCH	22	M	LABR	PLAHT	FUSA
CHASIS, BENZIAN	22	M	RROFF	PLAFV	GUSA
FANNY	19	F	W	PLAFV	GUSA
HEDOWSKY, SAMUEL	18	M	LABR	PLAHR	ZUSA
ROSENTHAL, SAMUEL	17	M	LABR	PLAHZ	SUSA
STURM, SELIG	17	M	LABR	PLAHW	CUSA
ABRAMOWITZ, S.	15	F	SGL	RRZZZ	ZUSA
KORNITZ, KUSIEL	33	M	CGRMKR	RRAHS	HUSA
SIMON, FREIDE	50	F	W	RRZZZ	ZUSA
ROFALOWITZ, F.	44	M	TLR	RRZZZ	ZUSA
KADUCZOWITZ, HENN.	23	F	W	RRZZZ	ZUSA
GOLDBERG, HERM.	21	M	UNKNOWN	RRAHQ	UUSA
SELIG	40	M	UNKNOWN	RRAHQ	UUSA
SLATE	39	F	W	RRAHQ	UUSA
BERTHA	20	F	W	RRAHQ	UUSA
LINE	18	F	CH	RRAHQ	UUSA
PESACK	15	M	CH	RRAHQ	UUSA
SARA	9	F	CHILD	RRAHQ	UUSA
LEON	4	M	CHILD	RRAHQ	UUSA
DEBORA	.11	F	INFANT	RRAHQ	UUSA
SCHWARZMANN, HERSCH	19	M	CL	RRAHU	DUSA
POSTAWELSKY, MOSES	22	M	DLR	RRAHZ	SUSA
HENE	21	F	W	RRAHZ	SUSA
RAFALOWITZ, SCHEINE	.06	F	INFANT	RRZZZ	ZUSA
RAGOLSKY, H.	18	M	DLR	RRAHX	EUSA
BRAND, ABRAH.	31	M	DLR	RRAHX	EUSA
SILVERMANN, SOLOMON	41	M	DLR	RRAHX	EUSA
JACKUMOWITZ, VINCENT	21	M	SMH	RRAHS	PUSA
DOROWSKY, G.	20	F	W	RRAHT	FUSA
ISAAC	.06	M	INFANT	RRAHT	FUSA
RUDE, T.	56	F	W	RRAHT	FUSA
CHEIE	40	F	D	RRAHT	FUSA
ALSTER, DOBRE	36	F	W	RRAHT	FUSA
GITTE	16	F	CH	RRAHT	FUSA
G.	8	M	CHILD	RRAHT	FUSA
DEBORA	7	F	CHILD	RRAHT	FUSA
ELI	.11	M	INFANT	RRAHT	FUSA
GODLOWITZ, RACHEL	20	F	SGL	RRAHY	FUSA
HAROUR, LEIB	9	M	CHILD	RRAFW	JUSA
SILBARSTEIN, HASCHE	18	M	LABR	RRAFW	JUSA
GUTMANN, ARON	17	M	TLR	RRAHT	FUSA
KLEINOWITZ, REBECCA	35	F	W	RRAHZ	PUSA
ROSA	9	F	CHILD	RRAHZ	PUSA
ESTI	.11	F	INFANT	RRAHZ	PUSA
TALNISKY, JUDEL	20	M	LABR	RRAHW	WUSA
BLOCH, HERRYL	35	M	LABR	RRAHT	FUSA
FABER, MAX	19	M	PNTR	RRAHS	ZUSA
SOLOMONSKY, CHANNE	20	F	SGL	RRAHT	FUSA
SLABOTZKY, JOSSEL	19	M	DLR	RRAHV	UUSA
JANDURA, ANNA	30	F	W	RRAHV	UUSA
DUBOWSKY, ANTON	19	M	LABR	RRAHZ	PUSA
JANDURA, JENZE	.11	M	INFANT	RRAHZ	PUSA
ADELSKY, DANIEL	34	M	LABR	RRAHV	UUSA
HIRSCH, HARCUS	21	M	TLR	RRAHU	AUSA
ZEW, JOSEF	25	M	DLR	RRAHT	PUSA
KOPEZINSKY, CHAIM	33	M	DLR	RRAHT	PUSA
LEWIN, SOMON	38	M	DLR	RRAHT	PUSA
APERINSKY, ARON	19	M	LABR	RRAHY	YUSA
SCHAPIRO, PINKUS	19	M	LABR	RRAHX	LUSA
SARAH	19	F	W	RRAHX	LUSA
DANOWSKY, ABRAHAM	21	M	LABR	RRAHX	LUSA
BLOCH, HIRSCH	15	M	LABR	RRAHY	FUSA
SANDLER, LENDER	42	M	LABR	RRAHV	UUSA
RADISKANSKY, LEIB	20	M	BKBNDR	RRAHZ	SUSA
FRIEDMANN, LOUISE	7	F	CHILD	RRAFW	JUSA
SZANI	6	M	CHILD	RRAFW	JUSA
BERKOWITZ, NATHAN	9	M	CHILD	RRAFW	JUSA
LURIC, ISRAEL	20	M	SHMK	RRAHS	ZUSA
SARA	20	F	W	RRAHS	ZUSA
BERGER, RIWE	23	F	SGL	RRAHZ	SUSA
JAFFER, MOSES	25	M	LABR	RRAHY	RUSA
HURWITZ, RACHEL	50	F	SGL	RRAHZ	QUSA
WIGOTZKY, JACOB	30	M	DLR	RRAHV	UUSA
PIENERK, B.	19	M	MCHT	RRAHZ	DUSA
SCHARKOWITZ, HIRSCH	49	M	LABR	RRZZZ	ZUSA
KAMINSKY, PAUL	32	M	BCHR	RRAHZ	SUSA
LEVY, DAVID	42	M	LABR	RRZZZ	ZUSA
STUBER, CHRISTIAN	29	M	FARMER	RRAHV	BUSA
SAPPERSTEIN, EMMA	17	F	SGL	RRAHT	FUSA
GUTE	9	F	CHILD	RRAHT	FUSA
ROSENTAL, HERM.	17	M	MCHT	RRZZZ	ZUSA
LIEBERTHAL, HERM.	24	M	MCHT	RRZZZ	ZUSA
STRAUFS, ABRAHAM	19	M	GZR	RRAHY	MUSA
GOLDMANN, RACHEL	54	F	W	RRAHT	OUSA
GARBOLSKI, K.	18	M	LABR	RRAHQ	UUSA
LEO	17	M	SGL	RRAHQ	UUSA
KONIK, HERMAN	21	M	LABR	RRAHT	DUSA
MARIE	21	F	W	RRAHT	DUSA
BETTEN, MARCUS	20	M	SHMK	RRAHY	IUSA
TORLEK, WOLF	20	M	DLR	RRAHS	RUSA
SCHAPIRO, MOSES	21	M	LABR	RRAHT	FUSA
KURANTEI, ABL.	14	M	LABR	RRAHT	FUSA
GOFLA, OLGA	17	F	SGL	RRAHT	FUSA
ZMELBOW, BERTHA	16	F	SGL	RRAHT	FUSA
ALLECOFSKY, ANNA	18	F	SGL	RRAHT	FUSA
TATEREK, VALENTIN	30	M	LABR	RRAHZ	SUSA
JULIE	30	F	W	RRAHZ	SUSA
MARIE	8	F	CHILD	RRAHZ	SUSA
JOH.	4	M	CHILD	RRAHZ	SUSA
PAULINE	.06	F	INFANT	RRAHZ	SUSA
PREISS, HERM.	20	M	SHMK	RRAHZ	SUSA
EISIKOWITZ, PAULINE	19	F	SGL	RRZZZ	ZUSA
ZADORF, HIRSCH	20	M	CGRMKR	RRAHT	XUSA
ETTI	21	F	W	RRAHT	XUSA
FREIDMANN, MOSES	19	F	LABR	RRAHT	FUSA
KALWINSKY, REBECCA	40	F	W	RRAHT	FUSA
ROSALIE	16	F	CH	RRAHT	FUSA
FEIGE	9	M	CHILD	RRAHT	FUSA
ROSA	7	F	CHILD	RRAHT	FUSA
MOSES	4	M	CHILD	RRAHT	FUSA
SCHONE	3	F	CHILD	RRAHT	FUSA
FASTZIK, ISRAEL	19	M	LABR	RRZZZ	ZUSA

PASSENGER	AGE	SEX	OCCUPATION	PRV VIL DES
GOLDBERG, MEYER	20	M	JNR	RRAHTFUSA
SINGER, MOTEAS	19	M	SHMK	RRZZZZUSA
HANSAN, MEYER	21	M	LABR	RRZZZZUSA
FEITSCH, BARHUCH	22	M	LABR	RRAHVLUSA
BURH, WOLF	21	M	LABR	RRAHUVUSA
BOBLAWSKY, GEORG	17	M	DLR	RRAHWPUSA
LUBERZ, ISAAC	20	M	JNR	RRAHQUUSA
LUKOWSKY, MICHALINA	24	F	SGL	RRAHTNUSA
ROSENBAUM, KALMAN	46	M	GLMK	RRAFWJUSA
ISAAC	38	M	GLMK	RRAFWJUSA
JUDORSKI, Z.	18	M	CL	RRAHTFUSA
SEIDENBERG, IRMI	22	M	MCHT	RRAHOKUSA

SHIP: FURNESSIA

FROM: GLASGOW AND MOVILLE
TO: NEW YORK
ARRIVED: 26 AUGUST 1884

PASSENGER	AGE	SEX	OCCUPATION	PRV VIL DES
BEDUARKE, SELY	34	M	LABR	PLZZZZUSA
COCHANSKY, HENRY	34	M	LABR	PLZZZZUSA
FRECHEN, JACOB	55	M	LABR	PLZZZZUSA
HAFTREN, ISRAEL	30	M	LABR	PLZZZZUSA
LICHBENSTEIN, NACHEN	23	M	LABR	PLZZZZUSA
MEDAREWITZ, SILVESTA	26	M	LABR	PLZZZZUSA
MINNA	26	F	W	PLZZZZUSA
KISSBARIM, KISSEN	39	M	LABR	PLZZZZUSA
ORENLACH, ADAM	39	M	LABR	PLZZZZUSA
ROSESKANSKY, SAM	32	M	LABR	PLZZZZUSA
NAPEL, JACOB	54	M	LABR	PLZZZZUSA
NANNE	56	F	W	PLZZZZUSA
SUBERT, JAUH.	26	M	LABR	PLZZZZUSA
LAUD, BERIL	34	M	LABR	PLZZZZUSA
PERSON, JUGRID	23	F	W	PLZZZZUSA
SEGIN	.11	F	INFANT	PLZZZZUSA
MORWICH, MICH.	33	M	LABR	RRZZZZUSA
OLKEMTZKY, LEVA	18	M	LABR	RRZZZZUSA
PERLO, MARCUS	85	M	LABR	RRZZZZUSA
RYBAK, LEIBE	26	F	W	RRZZZZUSA
ABRAHAM	1	M	CHILD	RRZZZZUSA
DAVID	.03	M	INFANT	RRZZZZUSA
SCHUMIDOWSKY, LAZAR	22	M	LABR	RRZZZZUSA
SILBER, SAM	20	M	LABR	RRZZZZUSA
STURMAN, SALOMON	30	M	LABR	RRZZZZUSA
SOKOLSKY, DAVID	30	M	LABR	RRZZZZUSA
SHAS, ARON	19	M	LABR	RRZZZZUSA
LUPNER, JUDE	11	M	LABR	RRZZZZUSA
SCHLEN, MOSES	22	M	LABR	RRZZZZUSA
WEHMANN, SARAH	19	F	LABR	RRZZZZUSA
LEVERSI, SAM	22	M	LABR	RRZZZZUSA

SHIP: BOHEMIA

FROM: HAMBURG
TO: NEW YORK
ARRIVED: 27 AUGUST 1884

PASSENGER	AGE	SEX	OCCUPATION	PRV VIL DES
PORBOHUE, JACOB	16	M	PNTR	RRAHXHUSA
IDA	18	F	SGL	RRAHXHUSA
YCHUMANN, HELENE	46	F	W	RRAHXHUSA
ANNA	4	F	CHILD	RRAHXHUSA
SIEGFRIED	3	M	CHILD	RRAHXHUSA
KASCHATZKY, CHANC	28	M	LABR	RRAHZNUSA
LOBSENS, ISON	17	M	LABR	RRAHTKUSA
REDLER, DAVID	22	M	CL	RRAFWJUSA

PASSENGER	AGE	SEX	OCCUPATION	PRV VIL DES
MARKIER, SONDREL	25	M	SCP	RRAHTFUSA
BELYER, LEIBISCH	40	M	TLR	RRAHTJUSA
RUDERMANN, ARON	17	M	LABR	RRAHUKUSA
YBIRSCH, LIPKA	9	M	CHILD	RRAHYCUSA
ZIMMERMANN, NOAH	30	M	LABR	RRAHUKUSA
KOSIK, CHAIM	19	M	SCHM	RRAHZDUSA
COHN, BEILE	25	F	SGL	RRAHZMUSA
NEUMANN, BEILE	25	F	W	RRZZZZUSA
SOPRA, ANNA	28	F	W	RRZZZZUSA
SARAH	5	F	CHILD	RRZZZZUSA
WESTPHALEN, MAGDA	26	F	W	RRZZZZUSA
ANNA	9	F	CHILD	RRZZZZUSA
MAX	7	F	CHILD	RRZZZZUSA
ANNA	5	F	CHILD	RRZZZZUSA
JOHS	2	F	CHILD	RRZZZZUSA
SEELIE	1	F	CHILD	RRZZZZUSA
HUGO	.11	F	INFANT	RRZZZZUSA
SOHVER, EMIL	26	M	LABR	RRZZZZUSA
SORENSEN, MARIE	16	F	SGL	RRZZZZUSA
FLEIMOWSKI, GESEPH	26	M	TLR	RRZZZZUSA
KWUCZINSEWSKI, GOH	51	M	LABR	RRAHZFUSA
PAULINE	48	F	W	RRAHZFUSA
LODER, AUGUSTE	35	F	W	RRAHTIUSA
GEORTLER, AUGUSTE	43	F	W	RRAAKHUSA
HELENE	15	F	D	RRAAKHUSA
KEORNER, ANNA	20	F	SGL	RRAAKHUSA
EUDE, HUGO	23	M	LABR	RRAAKHUSA
GLEOOKSMANN, SAMUEL	28	M	LABR	RRAHTNUSA
NATALIE	28	F	W	RRAHTNUSA
SCHAPEIRO, DAVID	60	M	TCHR	RRAHZPUSA
LEA	55	F	W	RRAHZPUSA
HERRM	14	M	S	RRAHZPUSA
YANSZAK, VICTORIA	22	F	SGL	RRAHYUUSA
LEIB	.11	U	INFANT	RRAHYUUSA
UNTERBERGER, SAMUEL	56	M	LABR	RRZZZZUSA
SARA	18	F	D	RRZZZZUSA
RABINOWITZ, KIEWE	35	F	W	RRZZZZUSA
SOHACHTMANN, DAVID	17	M	LABR	RRAHTKUSA
SUFSMANN, MORDOHE	39	M	LABR	RRAHQDUSA
SCHMOLENSKY, LEA	36	F	W	RRZZZZUSA
LIEBE	18	F	CH	RRZZZZUSA
DEIL	21	F	CH	RRZZZZUSA
SLATA	8	F	CHILD	RRZZZZUSA
BASCHE	6	F	CHILD	RRZZZZUSA
CHAIM	.11	F	INFANT	RRZZZZUSA
SUSSHOLZ, CHAIM	32	M	TLR	RRAFWJUSA
GUTENTAG, SALOMON	24	M	DLR	RRAFWJUSA
ESTEROF, GERSON	22	M	TLR	RRAHTUUSA
SKLOWSKY, ISRAEL	42	M	CHMKR	RRZZZZUSA
HITLIN, NOCHEN	50	M	TLR	RRAHZOUSA
LEIZES	9	M	CHILD	RRAHZOUSA
COHN, ABRAM	6	M	CHILD	RRAHYCUSA
KROM, SEWOLON	34	M	LABR	RRAHWOUSA
BLUMENBERG, JOSEF	22	M	LABR	RRAHZJUSA
PALS, HERSOH	30	M	LABR	RRAFWJUSA
SUSCHKOWITZ, SALOMON	55	M	TLR	RRZZZZUSA
KAHNOWITZ, ABRAH	20	M	MLR	RRAHUKUSA
RAD, MORITZ	20	M	LABR	RRAHZPUSA
FALLADER, MICHLE	47	F	W	RRAHZMUSA
DAVID	18	U	UNKNOWN	RRAHZMUSA
FENER, ADOLF	24	M	LABR	RRAHXNUSA
KUSZNER, ABRAM	40	M	LABR	RRAHZPUSA
GUTE	40	F	W	RRAHZPUSA
RIWE	60	F	M	RRAHZPUSA
HERZ	9	F	CHILD	RRAHZPUSA
MOSES	4	U	CHILD	RRAHZPUSA
MENASSE	5	U	CHILD	RRAHZPUSA
WILKOWISCHKI, BAR	64	M	LABR	RRAHVJUSA
YOSEF	28	M	LABR	RRAHVJUSA
SCHEINE	26	F	W	RRAHVJUSA
BEINISCH	4	F	CHILD	RRAHVJUSA
ROSCHE	2	F	CHILD	RRAHVJUSA
ROSES	.06	F	INFANT	RRAHVJUSA
GOLDMANN, REFKA	19	F	SGL	RRAHZSUSA
HOLDINSKA, MARIANNE	32	F	SGL	RRAHZSUSA

PASSENGER	AGE	SEX	OCCUPATION	PRV	VIL	DES
COHEN, HANNA	21	F	SGL	RR	AHWY	USA
CHAJE	18	M	LABR	RR	AHWY	USA
SAJE	9	M	CHILD	RR	AHWY	USA
GLUSKIN, BASCHE	20	F	SGL	RR	AHVO	USA
DON, DVORA	19	F	SGL	RR	AHVO	USA
KAUFMANN, SCHOLEM	35	M	LABR	RR	AHZS	USA
PERILSTEIN, SCHMUL	38	M	TLR	RR	AHZS	USA
ROBISOHN, NOCHIM	35	F	W	RR	AHZS	USA
BRAUN, SCHEIMEN	21	M	DLR	RR	ZZZZ	USA
STUTZKY, LUDIO	19	M	TLR	RR	AHVP	USA
LONDON, LOSER	40	M	LABR	RR	AHWG	USA
STOLOWSKY, IAS	20	M	LABR	RR	AHWG	USA
CLAFF, MINNA	18	M	SGL	RR	AHZP	USA
FISCHEL, NACHUM	17	M	LABR	RR	AHZS	USA
GOLDSTEIN, MALI	43	F	W	RR	AHSP	USA
FESCHEL	9	F	CHILD	RR	AHSP	USA
LEIB	8	F	CHILD	RR	AHSP	USA
JOSEF	4	F	CHILD	RR	AHSP	USA
ROSA	.11	F	INFANT	RR	AHSP	USA
WOLF	.01	F	INFANT	RR	AHSP	USA
ISAACS, ELI	9	M	CHILD	RR	AHSP	USA
WELRO, SALOMON	46	M	LABR	RR	AHWS	USA
ISRAEL	.11	M	INFANT	RR	AHWS	USA
SARASON, GOLDE	19	F	SGL	RR	AHSY	USA
LEWIN, HIRSCH	42	M	SHMK	RR	AHXI	USA
PRUSKI, MOSES	24	M	SHMK	RR	AHXI	USA
GABRILOWITZ, SALOMON	33	M	LABR	RR	AHZN	USA
MARGOLIS, CHAIM	20	M	LABR	RR	AHZS	USA
SCHIMELES, BEHR	19	M	LABR	RR	AHUV	USA
KATSCHESCHINSKY, ZIPPI	19	F	SGL	RR	AHVT	USA
LIDWINOWSKI, SIMCHE	21	M	LABR	RR	AHYZ	USA
NOCHOOSKY, SAMUEL	21	M	LABR	RR	AHYZ	USA
MICHOLOWSKY, ESTHER	22	F	SGL	RR	AHYZ	USA
GLOBE, FREIBUSCH	21	M	TLR	RR	AHWL	USA
RECHMANN, ABRAHAM	21	M	TLR	RR	AHWL	USA
IACOBSOHN, LEISER	21	M	LABR	RR	AHSQ	USA
SACHS, LIEBE	28	F	W	RR	AHSQ	USA
CHANNE	9	F	CHILD	RR	AHSQ	USA
ZIPPE	6	F	CHILD	RR	AHSQ	USA
CHAJE	3	F	CHILD	RR	AHSQ	USA

SHIP: ST LAURENT

FROM: HAVRE
TO: NEW YORK
ARRIVED: 27 AUGUST 1884

PASSENGER	AGE	SEX	OCCUPATION	PRV	VIL	DES
SANDEWSKI, GITOS	22	M	SP	RR	ADXW	NY
JOSEPH	1	M	CHILD	RR	ADXW	NY
SCHWARLOWSKI, ELIE	20	M	CLGYMN	RR	ADXW	NY
KAHN, LEON	20	M	CLGYMN	RR	ADXW	NY
LEVY, ABRAHAM	20	M	CLGYMN	RR	ADXW	NY
GEDANSKI, WOLFF	24	M	UNKNOWN	PL	ZZZZ	NY
DORA	23	F	UNKNOWN	PL	ZZZZ	NY
MANRICE	1	M	CHILD	PL	ZZZZ	NY
JOKOLOWSKI, MICHEL	25	M	CPRSMH	PL	ADXW	OH
BELLA	30	F	CPRSMH	PL	ADXW	NY

SHIP: CITY OF MONTREAL

FROM: LIVERPOOL AND QUEENSTOWN
TO: NEW YORK
ARRIVED: 30 AUGUST 1884

PASSENGER	AGE	SEX	OCCUPATION	PRV	VIL	DES
KEMNEL, D.	45	M	TLR	PL	ZZZZ	NY
ESTREL	40	M	TLR	PL	ZZZZ	NY
OSIAS	17	M	LABR	PL	ZZZZ	NY
GROELS	16	F	SVNT	PL	ZZZZ	NY
MARIA	11	F	CH	PL	ZZZZ	NY
PAUL	7	M	CHILD	PL	ZZZZ	NY
RACHEL	5	F	CHILD	PL	ZZZZ	NY
MAYER	1	F	CHILD	PL	ZZZZ	NY
GOLDSTEIN, MOSES	23	F	LABR	PL	AHQC	NY
DESBOR, LEIB	23	F	LABR	PL	ZZZZ	NY
BLUFFSTEIN, ISAAC	18	F	LABR	PL	AHQD	NY

SHIP: ELBE

FROM: BREMEN
TO: NEW YORK
ARRIVED: 30 AUGUST 1884

PASSENGER	AGE	SEX	OCCUPATION	PRV	VIL	DES
KRUKOW, NICOLAUS	23	M	MCHT	PL	AHOO	USA
TARUTINOW, NICOLAUS	27	M	MCHT	PL	AHOO	USA
HEIDEBRECHT, ANNA	21	F	NN	PL	AHTF	USA
SCHRODER, HEINR.	21	M	LABR	RR	ZZZZ	USA
ANNA	29	F	NN	RR	ZZZZ	USA
ANDREAS	69	M	LABR	RR	ZZZZ	USA
CATH.	5	F	CHILD	RR	ZZZZ	USA
HEINRICH	3	M	CHILD	RR	ZZZZ	USA
ANDREAS	.06	M	INFANT	RR	ZZZZ	USA
HILDEBRANDT, JOHANN	45	M	LABR	RR	ZZZZ	USA
ANNA	44	F	NN	RR	ZZZZ	USA
MARIA	18	F	NN	RR	ZZZZ	USA
PETER	10	M	NN	RR	ZZZZ	USA
LEWIN, LIEBE	18	F	NN	RR	AAKH	USA
HALPEIN, ABRAHAM	10	M	LABR	RR	ZZZZ	USA

SHIP: STATE OF ALABAMA

FROM: GLASGOW AND LARNE
TO: NEW YORK
ARRIVED: 30 AUGUST 1884

PASSENGER	AGE	SEX	OCCUPATION	PRV	VIL	DES
FEINBERG, JOEL	40	M	LABR	RR	ZZZZ	NY
SUNDEL	17	M	LABR	RR	ZZZZ	NY
MELBR, SCHLOME	19	M	JNR	RR	ZZZZ	NY
GARFINKEL, LEIB	25	M	LABR	RR	ZZZZ	NY
SANDLER, TADERS	18	M	LABR	RR	ZZZZ	NY
ULINSKY, BEHR	19	M	LABR	RR	ZZZZ	NY
PROP, MOSES	45	M	LABR	RR	ZZZZ	NY
HURWITZ, SAMUEL	18	M	JNR	RR	ZZZZ	BO
AKINEWSKY, CHAJE	19	F	SVNT	RR	ZZZZ	CH
BAMSLAK, CHAJE	00	F	W	RR	ZZZZ	NY
SCHLOME	.03	F	INFANT	RR	ZZZZ	NY
SCHIMANZIG, SCHIMON	00	M	LABR	RR	ZZZZ	NY
BERL	00	M	BY	RR	ZZZZ	NY
SKYSH, GRETA-A.	00	F	SVNT	RR	ZZZZ	UNK
RATSCHISKY, F.	30	M	CGRMKR	RR	ZZZZ	NY
GZESCHLAK, THEOPHIL	40	M	LABR	RR	ZZZZ	NY
FELDHERD, HELEN	20	F	SVNT	RR	ZZZZ	NY
WERNGARNSKY, MEYER	32	M	LABR	RR	ZZZZ	NY

PASSENGER	AGE	SEX	OCCUPATION	PRV VIL DES
ZUCKERMANN, SEGELINE	24	F	W	RRZZZZNY
BESSE	9	F	CHILD	RRZZZZNY
TECHAROWITZ, BLUME	24	F	W	RRZZZZNY
RIFKE	3	F	CHILD	RRZZZZNY

SHIP: WESTPHALIA

FROM: HAMBURG AND HAVRE
TO: NEW YORK
ARRIVED: 30 AUGUST 1884

PASSENGER	AGE	SEX	OCCUPATION	PRV VIL DES
ROSENTHAL, JACOB	28	M	LABR	RRAFWJNY
HERWITZ, FRENDE	40	F	W	RRZZZZNY
JACOB	9	M	CHILD	RRZZZZNY
REISKE	8	F	CHILD	RRZZZZNY
MAX	4	M	CHILD	RRZZZZNY
MICHEL	.11	M	INFANT	RRZZZZNY
FLEISCHER, CHANNE	18	F	SGL	RRZZZZNY
SOGILOWITZ, CHAIE	20	F	SGL	RRZZZZNY
BLUMBERG, MOSES	20	M	LABR	RRZZZZNY
BERLUNSKE, KADESCH	18	M	CL	RRAHUSNY
CYRELSON, CHAIM	48	M	LABR	RRZZZZNY
FEINBERG, CHAJE	27	F	W	RRADIMNY
PEISACH	9	M	CHILD	RRADIMNY
SILPE	5	F	CHILD	RRADIMNY
FEIGE	.11	F	INFANT	RRADIMNY
JABLONSKY, ABRAHAM	27	M	TLR	RRAHTUNY
LEA	19	F	W	RRAHTUNY
GORDON, FEIGE	25	F	SGL	RRZZZZNY
CZICHIES, ABRAM	27	M	TLR	RRZZZZNY
BERBMANN, CHEIE	19	F	SGL	RRZZZZNY
KUNE	18	F	SGL	RRZZZZNY
REZI	9	F	CHILD	RRZZZZNY
REISKISS, OSCHER	24	F	W	RRZZZZNY
JACOB	.11	M	INFANT	RRZZZZNY
LEA	.01	F	INFANT	RRZZZZNY
KRANKOWSKY, EBELL	18	M	TLR	RRZZZZNY
COHEN, HANNE	24	F	W	RRZZZZNY
RACHEL	.11	F	INFANT	RRZZZZNY
SINGER, DWORE	26	F	W	RRZZZZNY
MOSES	.11	M	INFANT	RRZZZZNY
SILBERGLEIT, FEITEL	39	M	SHMK	RRAHTONY
JESCHE	24	F	W	RRAHTONY
MAUSCHE	7	F	CHILD	RRAHTONY
GERSON	4	M	CHILD	RRAHTONY
MINNI	.03	F	INFANT	RRAHTONY
SLODAWNIK, ISAAC	17	M	DLR	RRADIMNY
GOLDSTEIN, MAX	20	M	TLR	RRZZZZNY
BAFF, EISIK	32	M	UNKNOWN	RRAHVUNY
MANNPOVSKY, ISRAEL	19	M	LABR	RRZZZZNY
FEINBERG, TAUBE	26	F	W	RRZZZZNY
URIE	9	F	CHILD	RRZZZZNY
MOSES	7	M	CHILD	RRZZZZNY
SARA	.11	F	INFANT	RRZZZZNY
SUSSKIND, CHAIE	20	F	SGL	RRAHVANY
REICHER, SALOMON	42	M	LABR	RRZZZZNY
KIWE	8	F	CHILD	RRZZZZNY
MADER, BREINE	9	F	CHILD	RRZZZZNY
BUNSELMANN, ELISAS	20	M	LABR	RRZZZZNY
OLKENISKY, ARON	20	M	LABR	RRZZZZNY
ZACK, BENESCH	53	M	DLR	RRZZZZNY
SLATCKE	46	F	W	RRZZZZNY
MORDSCHE	13	F	CH	RRZZZZNY
JACOB	9	M	CHILD	RRZZZZNY
ELISE	8	F	CHILD	RRZZZZNY
SINE	5	F	CHILD	RRZZZZNY
ZIPRE	.11	F	INFANT	RRZZZZNY
JOEL	.01	M	INFANT	RRZZZZNY
KOLMA, CHEIE	21	F	SGL	RRAHTFNY
LWIE, LENA	29	F	W	RRAHTFNY
TAUBE	4	F	CHILD	RRAHTFNY
MENDEL	.09	M	INFANT	RRAHTFNY
WEINSTEIN, REBECCA	19	F	SGL	RRAHTFNY
SCHNAPER, MOSES	17	M	DLR	RRAHTFNY
WOLOWITZ, CHAIE	22	F	SGL	RRAHTONY
SCHENKMANN, SARA	42	F	W	RRZZZZNY
CHAIE	17	F	CH	RRZZZZNY
SALOMON	7	M	CHILD	RRZZZZNY
ED	5	M	CHILD	RRZZZZNY
GOSCHANSKY, ITZIG	23	M	LABR	RRZZZZNY
CHAIM	14	M	LABR	RRZZZZNY
KARNEWSKY, SIMON	14	M	LABR	RRZZZZNY
WILKOWSLY, SARA	20	F	SGL	RRZZZZNY
FEIGE	9	F	CHILD	RRZZZZNY
GOLDE	7	F	CHILD	RRZZZZNY
RUMSKY, CHAIE	20	F	SGL	RRZZZZNY
COHN, HARRIS	20	M	LABR	RRZZZZNY
BRANDSTEIN, CHAIE	23	F	SGL	RRAHOKNY
ENDELMANN, ELIAS	9	M	CHILD	RRAHOKNY
STANDWARSKY, ISRAEL	20	M	LABR	RRZZZZNY
BLUMBERG, FRIDA	19	F	SGL	RRZZZZNY
WEINSTEIN, ISRAEL	9	M	CHILD	RRZZZZNY
ZESARSKY, JOCHEL	17	M	LABR	RRZZZZNY
KOTKIN, SALOMON	23	M	LABR	RRZZZZNY
SACH, CHAIM	24	M	LABR	RRZZZZNY
ROSENBLUM, MARIA	18	F	SGL	RRZZZZNY
KAHN, PESCHE	30	F	W	RRZZZZNY
BROSCHE	7	F	CHILD	RRZZZZNY
BEILE	6	F	CHILD	RRZZZZNY
SCHALEMOWITZ, GOLDE	19	F	SGL	RRZZZZNY
FLEISCHER, CHAIE	16	F	SGL	RRZZZZNY
PERLSTEN, SALOMON	24	M	SHMK	RRZZZZNY
LEWY, SAMUEL	19	M	MSN	RRAHTFNY
DINE	19	F	W	RRAHTFNY
WILDAWER, LEIBE	9	M	CHILD	RRAHTFNY
DANIELIS, JAN	30	M	LABR	RRZZZZNY
LAZAROWITZ, SCHMEINDEL	8	M	CHILD	RRZZZZNY
KAMZEN, MAREUS	16	M	WCHMKR	RRZZZZNY
RUDOMINSKY, SAMUEL	20	M	TLR	RRZZZZNY
CHANE	20	F	W	RRZZZZNY
HOPENSTEIN, ISAAC	17	M	DLR	RRZZZZNY
ROSENBERG, BERUCH	19	M	WCHMKR	RRZZZZNY
RUDOMINSKY, SIM.	.03	M	INFANT	RRZZZZNY

SHIP: AUSTRALIA

FROM: HAMBURG
TO: NEW YORK
ARRIVED: 01 SEPTEMBER 1884

PASSENGER	AGE	SEX	OCCUPATION	PRV VIL DES
DOGALLIS, VINCENT	19	M	LABR	RRZZZZNY
HUTTNER, JOS.	18	M	SMH	PLZZZZNY
SCHLECHTER, JANKEL	33	M	TLR	RRZZZZNY
GOLDE	20	F	W	RRZZZZNY
HERSTEIN, SALOMON	19	M	TRDSMN	RRZZZZNY
ABRAMAN, ABRAHAM	45	M	MCHT	RRZZZZNY
FEIGE	27	F	W	RRZZZZNY
PIMSKI, MEYER	18	M	PTR	RRZZZZNY
ESTER	23	F	W	RRZZZZNY
CHAIKIM, MOSES	21	M	SMH	RRZZZZNY
CHAIKE	18	F	W	RRZZZZNY
DORF, CHANE	25	F	WO	RRZZZZNY
ZIERL	.07	F	INFANT	RRZZZZNY
BERGMANN, ELIAS	27	M	TRDSMN	PLZZZZOH
SCHLUSINGER, CHIEL	30	M	TRDSMN	PLZZZZNY
KUPER, PETER	17	M	TRDSMN	RRZZZZNY
BLUMFELD, HIRSCH	24	M	TLR	RRZZZZNY
DAUMANN, HERM.	20	M	TRDSMN	RRZZZZNY
PATACHINSKY, ABRAHAM	20	M	TRDSMN	RRZZZZNY
ARONSWITZ, CHANE	20	F	WO	RRZZZZNY

PASSENGER	AGE	SEX	OCCUPATION	PRV	VIL	DES
MOSES	.04	M	INFANT	RR	ZZZZ	NY
KUERTZER, NETTE	35	F	WO	RR	ZZZZ	NY
KOHATZKY, MENDEL	17	M	TRDSMN	RR	ZZZZ	NY
FRIEDMANN, LEIBKA	18	M	TRDSMN	RR	ZZZZ	NY
SCHOENHAUS, FIGA	23	F	SGL	RR	ZZZZ	NY
FALKE, GUSTAV	32	M	LABR	RR	ZZZZ	NE
SCHILDAY, ABRAM	29	M	MCHT	PL	ZZZZ	NY
PUSCTSFEDSKI, SCHOLEM	17	M	LABR	RR	ZZZZ	NY
ULANPERT, ELIAS	16	M	LABR	RR	ZZZZ	NY
FEINSTEIN, SAM.	16	M	LABR	RR	ZZZZ	NY
KRANZOWKI, CHASCHE	7	M	CHILD	RR	ZZZZ	NY
KROM, LIEBE	18	F	SGL	RR	ZZZZ	NY
BERELEWITZ, GOLDE	53	F	WO	RR	ZZZZ	NY
FRIES, SCHOLEM	24	M	TRDSMN	RR	ZZZZ	NY
ISRAEL, BERNHD.	27	M	SHMK	RR	ZZZZ	NY
DUBORSKY, CHAMI	26	M	TLR	RR	ZZZZ	NY
LIPSCHITZ, JOSEF	18	M	MCHT	RR	ZZZZ	NY
KAPLAN, LEN	18	F	SGL	RR	ZZZZ	NY
SCHIER, ARTHUR	24	M	TRDSMN	RR	ZZZZ	NY
CHAWIN, JOSEF	39	M	LABR	RR	ZZZZ	NY
CHAIE	36	F	W	RR	ZZZZ	NY
ABRAHAM	19	M	S	RR	ZZZZ	NY
HELLEL	18	M	S	RR	ZZZZ	NY
MENDEL	13	M	S	RR	ZZZZ	NY
CHAIM	00	M	S	RR	ZZZZ	NY
JANKEL	00	M	S	RR	ZZZZ	NY
ESTER	4	F	CHILD	RR	ZZZZ	NY
RAHEL	3	F	CHILD	RR	ZZZZ	NY
ZWIKOVSKI, DORA	16	F	SGL	RR	ZZZZ	NY
LEWIN, RAHEL	17	F	SGL	RR	ZZZZ	NY
APPELBAUM, CHAI	55	F	WO	RR	ZZZZ	UNK
KALBER, SIMON	24	M	TRDSMN	RR	ZZZZ	IL
OPPENHEIN, TAUBE	21	F	WO	RR	ZZZZ	NY
NANNY	.03	F	INFANT	RR	ZZZZ	NY
MUSSLER, BRAME	40	F	WO	RR	ZZZZ	NY
GOLDE	15	F	D	RR	ZZZZ	NY
MOSES	7	M	CHILD	RR	ZZZZ	NY
PESSEL	6	M	CHILD	RR	ZZZZ	NY
LAIZER	4	M	CHILD	RR	ZZZZ	NY
BRATSPIES, CHANE	21	F	SGL	RR	ZZZZ	NY
PAUDSEHEIN, SAM.	22	M	LABR	RR	ZZZZ	NY
SOFIE	17	F	SI	RR	ZZZZ	NY
LAUDE, MORSCHEL	21	M	MCHT	PL	ZZZZ	NY
REIBER, MARCUS	18	M	LABR	RR	ZZZZ	NY
HERRMANN, INDEL	34	M	LABR	RR	ZZZZ	NY
SCHAPIRO, HIRSCH	16	M	LABR	RR	ZZZZ	NY
SASNOWSKY, JANKEL	20	M	TNR	RR	ZZZZ	NY
ZUCKERBAUM, JUDKE	38	M	JNR	RR	ZZZZ	NY
NIKNISS, BENJAMIN	44	M	CGRMKR	RR	ZZZZ	NY
SCHAROW, SALAM.	19	M	MCHT	RR	ZZZZ	NY
PUNZICK, CHAIM	20	M	MCHT	RR	ZZZZ	NY
KOTTGES, JOSEF	48	M	TCHR	RR	ZZZZ	NY
WILSCHEN, JACOB	20	M	TRDSMN	RR	ZZZZ	NY
ASSA, MARRIS	18	M	TRDSMN	RR	ZZZZ	NY

SHIP: NORMANDIE

FROM: HAVRE
TO: NEW YORK
ARRIVED: 01 SEPTEMBER 1884

PASSENGER	AGE	SEX	OCCUPATION	PRV	VIL	DES
KOLOGRIVOFF, JEAN	40	M	DIP	RR	ZZZZ	UNK
ABDANK-ABAKANOWICZ, BRU	31	M	UNKNOWN	RR	ZZZZ	PA
SIEDMANN, FLORENTINE	28	F	DRSMKR	RR	ZZZZ	NY
HENRIETTE	7	F	CHILD	RR	ZZZZ	NY
MORITZ	00	M	INF	RR	ZZZZ	NY
LEON	00	M	INF	RR	ZZZZ	NY
GOLDENBERG, WOLF	21	M	BLDR	RR	ZZZZ	NY

SHIP: GALLIA

FROM: LIVERPOOL AND QUEENSTOWN
TO: NEW YORK
ARRIVED: 02 SEPTEMBER 1884

PASSENGER	AGE	SEX	OCCUPATION	PRV	VIL	DES
SMDYK, CSCOW	25	M	GENT	PL	ZZZZ	USA

SHIP: BOLIVIA

FROM: GLASGOW AND MOVILLE
TO: NEW YORK
ARRIVED: 03 SEPTEMBER 1884

PASSENGER	AGE	SEX	OCCUPATION	PRV	VIL	DES
GUTMAN, CHAIN	26	M	LABR	PL	AFWJ	USA
KLANE	26	F	W	PL	AFWJ	USA
LEON	.06	M	INFANT	PL	AFWJ	USA
WERSLOWSKY, SELY	26	M	LABR	RR	ZZZZ	USA
ROSENTHAL, MARCUS	52	M	LABR	RR	ZZZZ	USA

SHIP: VALENCIA

FROM: UNKNOWN
TO: NEW YORK
ARRIVED: 03 SEPTEMBER 1884

PASSENGER	AGE	SEX	OCCUPATION	PRV	VIL	DES
ASKELIN, CONRAD	56	M	CPTR	FN	ZZZZ	UNK

SHIP: WESTERNLAND

FROM: ANTWERP
TO: NEW YORK
ARRIVED: 03 SEPTEMBER 1884

PASSENGER	AGE	SEX	OCCUPATION	PRV	VIL	DES
NEYT, CLAS	24	M	LABR	PL	ZZZZ	DYT
BADER, JOS.	28	M	TLR	PL	ZZZZ	NY
HENBLEIN, C.	24	M	FARMER	PL	ZZZZ	UNK
M.	23	F	UNKNOWN	PL	ZZZZ	UNK
M.	1	M	CHILD	PL	ZZZZ	UNK
M.	1	F	CHILD	PL	ZZZZ	UNK
STOLOWSKA, M.	25	F	UNKNOWN	PL	ZZZZ	PHI
MCH.	00	M	INF	PL	ZZZZ	PHI
ROTKOWSKI, INAS	19	M	LABR	PL	ZZZZ	CH
JOS.	17	F	UNKNOWN	PL	ZZZZ	CH
PRUB, INUR	23	F	UNKNOWN	PL	ZZZZ	PHI
NETZNER, AM	44	F	UNKNOWN	PL	ZZZZ	PHI
ROSA	15	F	UNKNOWN	PL	ZZZZ	PHI
REBA	12	F	UNKNOWN	PL	ZZZZ	PHI
SAC	7	M	CHILD	PL	ZZZZ	PHI
MAKA	10	F	UNKNOWN	PL	ZZZZ	PHI
JASTON, JOS.	40	M	LABR	PL	ZZZZ	NY
PET.	39	F	UNKNOWN	PL	ZZZZ	NY
MAGD.	9	F	CHILD	PL	ZZZZ	NY
WEH.	7	M	CHILD	PL	ZZZZ	NY
MAR.	5	F	CHILD	PL	ZZZZ	NY
ANNA	00	F	INF	PL	ZZZZ	NY
LARNUTZKA, M.	33	F	UNKNOWN	PL	ZZZZ	NY

PASSENGER	AGE	SEX	OCCUPATION	PV RIV	D E S
SHIP: WISCONSIN					
FROM: LIVERPOOL AND QUEENSTOWN					
TO: NEW YORK					
ARRIVED: 03 SEPTEMBER 1884					
SEGAR, SAMUEL	18	M	LABR	PLZZZ	ZUSA
SHIP: HUNGARIA					
FROM: HAMBURG					
TO: NEW YORK					
ARRIVED: 04 SEPTEMBER 1884					
ROSITZKY, SALOMON	36	M	LABR	RRZZZ	ZUSA
DURKSEN, JACOB	44	M	FARMER	RRZZZ	ZUSA
CATH.	40	F	W	RRZZZ	ZUSA
PETER	16	M	S	RRZZZ	ZUSA
CATHARINE	14	F	CH	RRZZZ	ZUSA
ANNA	9	F	CHILD	RRZZZ	ZUSA
JACOB	8	M	CHILD	RRZZZ	ZUSA
HELENE	5	F	CHILD	RRZZZ	ZUSA
MARIE	3	F	CHILD	RRZZZ	ZUSA
ROSENSTEIN, CHASKEL	18	M	TLR	RRZZZ	ZUSA
RESNILOW, BAR	38	M	TLR	RRZZZ	ZUSA
CHEIE	22	F	W	RRZZZ	ZUSA
TEPLITZKY, MEYER	23	M	TLR	RRZZZ	ZUSA
SMELANSKY, SAL.	16	M	TLR	RRZZZ	ZUSA
ETZMANN, MARIE	20	F	SGL	RRZZZ	ZUSA
SALOMONSKY, SAM.	23	M	BCHR	RRAHW	EUSA
ZIPPI	22	F	W	RRAHW	EUSA
LEWIN, ISRAEL	22	M	CGRMKR	RRAHT	FUSA
CHAJE	22	F	W	RRAHT	FUSA
RIWE	.11	F	INFANT	RRAHT	FUSA
SAJES, ABRAHAM	20	M	CL	RRAHT	FUSA
CHASSILOW, HIRSCH	26	M	DLR	RRZZZ	ZUSA
MANNHEIM, CHAIM	27	M	DLR	RRADO	IUSA
BURSTEIN, FALK	16	M	TLR	RRADO	IUSA
RAWITZ, ITZIK	36	M	TLR	RRZZZ	ZUSA
WOLPERT, LEISER	20	M	CL	RRADO	IUSA
KOHANE, SARAH	19	F	SGL	RRZZZ	ZUSA
LAU, WILHELM	36	M	LABR	RRZZZ	ZUSA
ROSMANN, BEHR	18	M	TLR	RRZZZ	ZUSA
KOPFZUCKER, SCHACHUE	26	M	LABR	RRAFW	JUSA
SARA	23	F	W	RRAFW	JUSA
MOSES	.11	M	INFANT	RRAFW	JUSA
ROSENFELD, ABRAHAM	35	M	LABR	RRAFW	JUSA
TAUNENBAUM, LEISER	26	M	LABR	RRZZZ	ZUSA
MALKE	27	F	W	RRZZZ	ZUSA
SIMON	.11	M	INFANT	RRZZZ	ZUSA
ASCHENFARB, SAMUEL	26	M	BKBNDR	RRAFW	JUSA
KELLERMANN, KISSEL	37	M	LABR	RRAFW	JUSA
MILEWSKI, JOHS.	31	M	LABR	RRZZZ	ZUSA
MARIE	24	F	W	RRZZZ	ZUSA
JOHN	23	M	LABR	RRZZZ	ZUSA
HOROWITZ, JETTE	20	F	SGL	RRAHU	FUSA
PALUKAJTIS, JAN	19	M	LABR	RRAHV	JUSA
GERTZ, MEYER	38	M	MCHT	RRZZZ	ZUSA
BEITLER, BASCHE	26	F	W	RRAHZ	SUSA
CHANNE	.11	F	INFANT	RRAHZ	SUSA
TIMM, AMALIE	25	F	W	RRZZZ	ZUSA
RATINITZ, FREIDE	27	F	W	RRAHT	UUSA
ITE	8	F	CHILD	RRAHT	UUSA
FEIGE	8	M	CHILD	RRAHT	UUSA
GRUNSTEIN, RACHEL	19	F	SGL	RRAHT	UUSA
MEDLOWITZ, FRAME	50	F	W	RRAHT	UUSA
ARONSOHN, WOLF	38	M	LABR	RRAHT	UUSA
MINNIE	8	F	CHILD	RRAHT	UUSA
MATEKOWSKY, ETTE	26	F	W	RRAHZ	SUSA
SCHLOME	.11	M	INFANT	RRAHZ	SUSA
NISSELKOWSKY, SARA	24	F	W	RRAHZ	SUSA
MOSES	.11	M	INFANT	RRAHZ	SUSA
BEILER, MINE	9	F	CHILD	RRAHZ	SUSA
BELA	6	F	CHILD	RRAHZ	SUSA
KRONITZKI, DAVID	22	M	SHMK	RRZZZ	ZUSA
REBECCA	21	F	W	RRZZZ	ZUSA
SELIG	.11	M	INFANT	RRZZZ	ZUSA
JACOB	.01	M	INFANT	RRZZZ	ZUSA
KAPLAN, TAUBE	35	F	W	RRAHT	UUSA
SARA	6	F	CHILD	RRAHT	UUSA
LEINE	4	F	CHILD	RRAHT	UUSA
METZNIK, JANKEL	9	M	CHILD	RRAHT	UUSA
ROSEN, HIRSCH	9	M	CHILD	RRAHT	SUSA
BERGKOWICZ, AISIK	35	M	MSN	RRAHT	FUSA
KAPLAN, HANNE	56	F	W	RRAHT	FUSA
ESTHER	18	F	D	RRAHT	FUSA
KOLEF, SIMON	9	M	CHILD	RRZZZ	ZUSA
LURIA, FEIGE	19	F	SGL	RRZZZ	ZUSA
FALCK, BREINDEL	39	F	W	RRADO	IUSA
BEILE	9	F	CHILD	RRADO	IUSA
CHANNE	8	F	CHILD	RRADO	IUSA
FARBER, ROSA	17	F	SGL	RRADO	IUSA
ETTEL	6	F	CHILD	RRADO	IUSA
KATZSCHOWSKI, MIRIAM	28	F	W	RRAHT	SUSA
ISAAK	9	M	CHILD	RRAHT	SUSA
SIMON	7	M	CHILD	RRAHT	SUSA
MOTEL	5	M	CHILD	RRAHT	SUSA
DRESCHE	3	F	CHILD	RRAHT	SUSA
WIERNIK, DINA	30	F	W	RRAHT	SUSA
SCHEPSEL	9	F	CHILD	RRAHT	SUSA
CHANNE	8	F	CHILD	RRAHT	SUSA
ROSENTHAL, ORKE	20	M	LABR	RRADO	IUSA
CHEIE	18	F	W	RRADO	IUSA
URANSKI, SISCHLE	18	F	SGL	RRAHT	SUSA
KOLEF, ESTER	14	F	SGL	RRAHZ	NUSA
AKSEBROD, SCHIFRE	15	F	SGL	RRAHT	UUSA
FUCHS, OZER	30	M	TLR	RRZZZ	ZUSA
BATNER, LEIB	28	M	BCHR	RRZZZ	ZUSA
GOLDSTEIN, ITZIG	30	M	DLR	RRZZZ	ZUSA
VEHOU, CHARLES	35	M	LABR	RRAHV	OUSA
SALAWEICIK, HIRSCH	20	M	LABR	RRZZZ	ZUSA
LOHWAK, LEIB	34	M	LABR	RRAHZ	PUSA
MIRIAM	30	F	W	RRAHZ	PUSA
WOLF	.11	M	INFANT	RRAHZ	PUSA
LUXENBERG, THERESE	18	F	SGL	RRAHT	FUSA
GRODZINSKY, CIREL	40	F	W	RRAHT	OUSA
PUTTERMANN, LEIBUSCH	30	M	LABR	RRAHT	OUSA
BROCHE	24	F	W	RRAHT	OUSA
CHEINE	.11	F	INFANT	RRAHT	OUSA
IDSAL, HERMANN	19	M	WCHMKR	RRZZZ	ZUSA
REIBSTEIN, RACHEL	19	F	SGL	RRAHT	FUSA
SCHNEIDER, SCHONE	23	F	SGL	RRAHT	FUSA
ZIPEIS, MENDEL	19	M	LABR	RRAHU	TUSA
BEDNERKOWITZ, ISAAC	20	M	LABR	RRAHU	TUSA
NECHE	20	F	W	RRAHU	TUSA
REICH, SUSANNE	50	F	W	RRAHU	TUSA
JASKOWITZ, JOSEF	5	M	CHILD	RRAHU	TUSA
TOMELIN-, MARIE	24	F	SGL	RRZZZ	ZUSA
KADISOHN, JOSEPH	59	M	DLR	RRZZZ	ZUSA
JENTE	58	F	W	RRZZZ	ZUSA
GRADZIENSKI, SALOMON	9	M	CHILD	RRAHT	OUSA
BAUM, SCHAJE	30	M	LABR	RRAFW	JUSA
CHEIE	21	F	W	RRAFW	JUSA
JOSSEL	8	M	CHILD	RRAFW	JUSA
BLUM, CHEIE	21	F	SGL	RRZZZ	ZUSA
KROWITZKY, RUBEN	24	M	LABR	RRZZZ	ZUSA
SLOTNITZKY, LEISER	34	M	LABR	RRAHZ	SUSA
SCH--B--, HERM.	17	M	LABR	RRZZZ	ZUSA
LEA	19	F	SGL	RRZZZ	ZUSA
BLUM, WILHELM	26	M	LABR	RRZZZ	ZUSA
RACHELSOHN, MEYER	17	M	LABR	RRZZZ	ZUSA
PASCHEMINSKI, ESCHIS	17	M	LABR	RRZZZ	ZUSA
ALEXANDROWITZ, ANNA	19	F	SGL	RRAHW	HUSA
KATZLOWSKY, ANTONIE	37	M	LABR	RRZZZ	ZUSA

PASSENGER	AGE	SEX	OCCUPATION	PRV	VIL	DES
SHIP: ODER						
FROM: BREMEN						
TO: NEW YORK						
ARRIVED: 04 SEPTEMBER 1884						
LEWANDOWSKA, ANTONIA	19	F	NN	RR	ZZZZ	USA
WARNZEWSKA, ANTONI	23	M	FARMER	RR	ZZZZ	USA
CHELMICKA, FRANZISKA	20	F	NN	RR	ZZZZ	USA
FRIEDMANN, ROCHE	26	F	NN	RR	ZZZZ	USA
GANERIF	10	F	CH	RR	ZZZZ	USA
SCHMINKE	8	F	CHILD	RR	ZZZZ	USA
GOLKA	4	F	CHILD	RR	ZZZZ	USA
LASKI	.11	F	INFANT	RR	ZZZZ	USA
SEIDMANN, ELSE	40	F	NN	RR	ZZZZ	USA
GERSKI, DAVID	22	M	LABR	RR	ZZZZ	USA
PENA	19	F	NN	RR	ZZZZ	USA
SEIDMANN, ETTKE	17	F	NN	RR	ZZZZ	USA
SCHEJE	10	F	CH	RR	ZZZZ	USA
JACOB	8	M	CHILD	RR	ZZZZ	USA
SHIP: STATE OF NEBRASKA						
FROM: GLASGOW AND LARNE						
TO: NEW YORK						
ARRIVED: 04 SEPTEMBER 1884						
FELDMANN, S.	19	M	LABR	RR	ZZZZ	NY
ARKEN, MENDEL	22	M	LABR	RR	ZZZZ	NY
BRENYVOGEL, ANSHEL	24	M	LABR	RR	ZZZZ	NY
REICHMANN, HIRSCH	50	M	LABR	RR	ZZZZ	NY
WEISGOLD, ABRAHAM	25	M	LABR	RR	ZZZZ	NY
BLEIN, MICHEL	19	M	LABR	RR	ZZZZ	NY
BARAWITZ, SCHEPSEL	24	M	LABR	RR	ZZZZ	NY
FRIEDMANN, DAVID	36	M	LABR	RR	ZZZZ	NY
RUBENSTEIN, MINNA	24	F	DMS	RR	ZZZZ	NY
LITRON, NOTE	40	M	LABR	RR	ZZZZ	NY
JOSSEL	12	M	CH	RR	ZZZZ	NY
SEGALAWITZ, RACHMIEL	26	M	LABR	RR	ZZZZ	NY
SWENZISKY, ADAM	23	M	LABR	RR	ZZZZ	NY
MELAMED, SUNDE	32	M	LABR	RR	ZZZZ	NY
C.S.	20	F	W	RR	ZZZZ	NY
TAUBE	2	F	CHILD	RR	ZZZZ	NY
NATHAN	.03	F	INFANT	RR	ZZZZ	NY
GESLER, SCHEINE	20	F	DMS	RR	ZZZZ	NY
BERNSTEIN, SCHMIDT	39	M	LABR	RR	ZZZZ	NY
SHIP: FULDA						
FROM: BREMEN						
TO: NEW YORK						
ARRIVED: 06 SEPTEMBER 1884						
KRAUSE, CONSTANTIN	46	M	LABR	RR	ZZZZ	USA
SOCHOSELSKY, ISAAC	19	M	MCHT	RR	ZZZZ	USA
SHIP: GRECIAN MONARCH						
FROM: LONDON						
TO: NEW YORK						
ARRIVED: 06 SEPTEMBER 1884						
MICHELSON, J.	24	M	NN	RR	ADAX	NY
BORDSKY, ADOLPH	17	M	UNKNOWN	RR	AHQH	PA
ARTISKY, LEAH	31	F	NN	RR	AHQH	CH
GETTA	1	F	CHILD	RR	AHQH	CH
MOSES, BERTHA	29	F	NN	PL	ZZZZ	NY
SELINA	15	F	CH	PL	ZZZZ	NY
ABR.	11	M	CH	PL	ZZZZ	NY
SARAH	00	F	UNKNOWN	PL	ZZZZ	NY
REBECCA	3	F	CHILD	PL	ZZZZ	NY
ROSE	1	F	CHILD	PL	ZZZZ	NY
HOLANDER, ESIHN	34	F	NN	PL	AEFL	NY
ROSENBERG, FANNY	24	F	UNKNOWN	PL	AHOO	BAL
BERNHARD	4	M	CHILD	PL	AHOO	BAL
HANY	3	M	CHILD	PL	AHOO	BAL
HOFMAN	1	M	CHILD	PL	AHOO	BAL
CAPLAN, ISAAC	19	M	TLR	PL	AEFL	NY
LEITZ, ROSA	19	F	NN	PL	AEFL	NY
SCHEFER, B.	18	M	TLR	RR	ZZZZ	NY
WARGA, WOLF	36	M	NN	RR	ZZZZ	TX
HERZMARK, N.	35	M	NN	RR	ZZZZ	TX
SILBERFELDT, J.	18	M	NN	RR	ZZZZ	TX
MILHANSKY, N.	22	M	LABR	RR	ZZZZ	TX
COHEN, E.	22	M	LABR	RR	ZZZZ	TX
VILANDER, E.	35	M	TLR	RR	ZZZZ	NY
BERG, LONIS	45	M	TLR	RR	ZZZZ	NY
FENERSTOCK, JACOB	25	M	TLR	RR	ZZZZ	NY
C.	23	F	TLR	RR	ZZZZ	NY
A.	1	M	CHILD	RR	ZZZZ	NY
SHIP: SCHIEDAM						
FROM: AMSTERDAM						
TO: NEW YORK						
ARRIVED: 06 SEPTEMBER 1884						
LIEBERMAN, JUDEL	17	M	CGRMKR	RR	ZZZZ	USA
SHIP: CITY OF CHICAGO						
FROM: LIVERPOOL AND QUEENSTOWN						
TO: NEW YORK						
ARRIVED: 08 SEPTEMBER 1884						
ROSENBERG, ISRAEL	32	M	CPTR	RR	ACBF	NY
KREISSMANN, JOZE	52	F	W	RR	ACBF	NY
STOZELITZ, AND.	40	M	LABR	RR	ACBF	NY
AGNES	41	F	W	RR	ACBF	NY
JOHANA	11	M	CH	RR	ACBF	NY
MARIA	8	F	CHILD	RR	ACBF	NY
ANDREAS	4	M	CHILD	RR	ACBF	NY
ANTON	2	M	CHILD	RR	ACBF	NY
LUDWIG	00	M	INF	RR	ACBF	NY
SACHANAS, JOHAN	45	M	LABR	RR	ACBF	NY
ADIZO	16	F	SP	RR	ACBF	NY
AGNES	3	F	CHILD	RR	ACBF	NY
GOTTFRIED, ANCHEL	31	M	LABR	RR	ACBF	NY
LOEVICK, SAML.	30	M	LABR	RR	ACBF	NY
CLANI	26	F	W	RR	ACBF	NY

PASSENGER	AGE	SEX	OCCUPATION	PRV VIL DES
SOLOMON	3	M	CHILD	RRACBFNY
FRIEDE	00	F	INF	RRACBFNY
SCHWARTZE, MINNA	30	F	W	RRACBFNY
CECELLI	8	F	CHILD	RRACBFNY
SOFIA	6	F	CHILD	RRACBFNY
ANNA	5	F	CHILD	RRACBFNY
MARIA	00	F	INF	RRACBFNY
ROTERSTEIN, JORG	18	F	SP	RRACBFNY
ROSENWERG, ANNA	18	F	W	RRACBFNY
VICTOR	21	M	LABR	RRACBFNY
MAGEELKA, FRANZ	27	M	LABR	RRACBFNY
ELI	21	F	W	RRACBFNY
HEITMANN	00	F	INF	RRACBFNY
KLEPPER, ARN	28	M	LABR	RRACBFNY
ROSENBAUM, LIA	36	F	W	RRACBFNY
HIRCH	18	M	SP	RRACBFNY
ARN	6	M	CHILD	RRACBFNY
FARCIL	4	M	CHILD	RRACBFNY
RIFKA	00	F	INF	RRACBFNY
FRANKEL, BLOOMES	40	F	W	RRACBFNY
ISRAEL	9	M	CHILD	RRACBFNY
REBECCA	6	F	CHILD	RRACBFNY
WOLF	2	M	CHILD	RRACBFNY
ABRAM	7	M	CHILD	RRACBFNY

SHIP: KAETIE

FROM: UNKNOWN
TO: NEW YORK
ARRIVED: 08 SEPTEMBER 1884

PASSENGER	AGE	SEX	OCCUPATION	PRV VIL DES
PRYGODSINSKI, MICHAEL	15	M	LABR	PLZZZZNY
WESCHOLOWSKA, JULIE	47	F	WO	PLZZZZNY
MARIE	17	F	D	PLZZZZNY
FRANZISKA	71	F	D	PLZZZZNY
ANICZAK, WOICIECH	22	M	LABR	PLZZZZNY
KALASCH, JADRIDA	19	F	UNKNOWN	PLZZZZNY
SWORSKI, VALERIAN	32	M	MSN	PLZZZZNY
DOROTHEA	40	F	W	PLZZZZNY
COHN, ELIAS	15	M	LABR	PLZZZZNY

SHIP: WIELAND

FROM: HAMBURG
TO: NEW YORK
ARRIVED: 08 SEPTEMBER 1884

PASSENGER	AGE	SEX	OCCUPATION	PRV VIL DES
KAPILOWSKY, ABRAM	21	M	DLR	RRZZZZUSA
KESTEL, DOBRE	30	F	W	RRZZZZUSA
DEVORE	7	F	CHILD	RRZZZZUSA
JANKEL	.11	F	INFANT	RRZZZZUSA
GOTTLIEB, HANNE	35	F	W	RRZZZZUSA
HERMANN	8	M	CHILD	RRZZZZUSA
ISRAEL	7	M	CHILD	RRZZZZUSA
RESI	8	F	CHILD	RRZZZZUSA
BARUSH	6	F	CHILD	RRZZZZUSA
FANNY	.11	F	INFANT	RRZZZZUSA
MARIA, PETRA	9	M	CHILD	RRZZZZUSA
KRAMA, JONAS	16	M	LABR	RRZZZZUSA
ZWERN, CHAIE	24	F	W	RRZZZZUSA
ESTHER	.11	F	INFANT	RRZZZZUSA
JOSPANN, FEIWE	21	F	SGL	RRZZZZUSA
GOLDBERGER, ESTIE	48	F	W	RRZZZZUSA
HANNE	20	F	SGL	RRZZZZUSA
LENE	17	F	SGL	RRZZZZUSA
DOBREWDISKY, SALOMON	50	M	TLR	RRZZZZUSA
GRUENSTEIN, DAVID	40	M	DLR	RRZZZZUSA
DEVORE	40	F	W	RRZZZZUSA
CHAIE	17	F	D	RRZZZZUSA
CHRAST, JOSEFA	36	F	W	RRZZZZUSA
MARIE	9	F	CHILD	RRZZZZUSA
BLOCK, EMILIE	19	F	SGL	RRZZZZUSA
LUDWIG	15	M	FARMER	RRZZZZUSA
POWLAWSKA, ANTONIE	30	F	W	RRZZZZUSA
JAN	.11	M	INFANT	RRZZZZUSA
COHN, SELIG	33	M	LABR	RRZZZZUSA
FEIN, CHAIE	48	F	W	RRZZZZUSA
PERLE	9	F	CHILD	RRZZZZUSA
ETTEL	8	F	CHILD	RRZZZZUSA
DAVID	5	M	CHILD	RRZZZZUSA
HIRSCH	3	M	CHILD	RRZZZZUSA
ALTERMANN, LEA	14	F	SGL	RRZZZZUSA
BEILE	9	F	CHILD	RRZZZZUSA
LUVIC, FEIGEL	18	F	SGL	RRZZZZUSA
BREIBATZ, SAMUEL	9	M	CHILD	RRZZZZUSA
FRIEDLAND, SARA	23	F	W	RRZZZZUSA
LEIB	4	M	CHILD	RRZZZZUSA
SALOMON	.11	M	INFANT	RRZZZZUSA
LUDMANN, JANNE	19	F	SGL	RRZZZZUSA
BEINES	9	M	CHILD	RRZZZZUSA
MEYEROWITZ, HIRSCH	34	M	HAMF	RRZZZZUSA
ARONSOHN, ARON	48	M	MCHT	RRZZZZUSA
SCHEINE	48	F	W	RRZZZZUSA
PRUN, ABRAHAM	23	M	MCHT	RRZZZZUSA
ROSA	22	F	W	RRZZZZUSA
ARONSOHN, RUBEN	9	M	CHILD	RRZZZZUSA
LEISER	8	M	CHILD	RRZZZZUSA
ZIBULSKY, LEISER	43	M	MCHT	RRZZZZUSA
EDELMAN, JOSEF	32	M	MCHT	RRZZZZUSA
KAPLAN, LEISER	41	M	MCHT	RRZZZZUSA
WEISS, NACHUM	24	M	MCHT	RRZZZZUSA
SCHEIGILOWITZ, ISAAC	39	M	MCHT	RRZZZZUSA
LIPMANOW, ISAAC	21	M	CPTR	RRZZZZUSA
MICHALOW, RACHEL	22	F	SGL	RRZZZZUSA
ABRAMOWITZ, JACOB	19	M	DLR	RRZZZZUSA
TERPUTZKY, RACHEL	21	F	SGL	RRZZZZUSA
RADYN, ADOLF	35	M	RE	RRZZZZUSA
JOHE.	32	F	W	RRZZZZUSA
HERM.	5	M	CHILD	RRZZZZUSA
MAX	4	M	CHILD	RRZZZZUSA
PAUL	.11	M	INFANT	RRZZZZUSA
HELENE	.01	F	INFANT	RRZZZZUSA
HERSTEIN, ISIDOR	22	M	CGRMKR	RRZZZZUSA
GOTTLIEB, MOSES	9	M	CHILD	RRZZZZUSA
RUBENSTEIN, MENDEL	26	M	DLR	RRZZZZUSA
ARONSOHN, BER.	20	M	LABR	RRZZZZUSA
LIPMANN, CHAIN	19	M	LABR	RRZZZZUSA
LASER, LEONH.	24	M	LABR	RRZZZZUSA
LINE	24	M	MCHT	RRZZZZUSA
DONINGER, OTTO	16	M	BKR	RRZZZZUSA
SCHELOWITZ, AARON	22	M	CL	RRZZZZUSA
FEIN, LINA	18	F	SGL	RRZZZZUSA
SILBERSOHN, CHAIE	45	F	W	RRZZZZUSA
MOSES	18	M	S	RRZZZZUSA
TRUPIANSKY, ESTHER	18	F	SGL	RRZZZZUSA
SUSMANOWITZ, SISEL	19	F	W	RRZZZZUSA
HASFELD, KICHAEL	32	M	SLR	RRZZZZUSA
RIDEL, ISRAEL	29	M	TLR	RRZZZZUSA
MARGOSEHINSKY, SAMUEL	28	M	DLR	RRZZZZUSA
MARGASCHINSKY, REBECCA	26	F	W	RRZZZZUSA
WIERKOWSKY, HIRSCH	31	M	DLR	RRZZZZUSA
FREIDE	28	F	W	RRZZZZUSA
RICOKIND, ARON	22	M	CL	RRZZZZUSA
MANSKY, SARA	21	F	SGL	RRZZZZUSA
KAHLER, BENJAMIN	36	M	DLR	RRZZZZUSA
LEWINSKY, RAHLE	32	F	W	RRZZZZUSA
BELA	9	F	CHILD	RRZZZZUSA
GOLDMANN, FEIGE	65	F	W	RRZZZZUSA
MERANE	5	F	CHILD	RRZZZZUSA
SHAPIRO, MOSES	20	M	TLR	RRZZZZUSA

PASSENGER	AGE	SEX	OCCUPATION	PRV VIL DES
ESTER	21	F	W	RRZZZZUSA
WITTENSTEIN, LEIB	19	M	MCHT	RRZZZZUSA
HOFFMAN, ERNST	30	M	LABR	RRZZZZUSA
WARREN, SALIE	20	F	SGL	RRZZZZUSA
HIFERD, VICHE	18	F	SGL	RRZZZZUSA
KULICK, CHANNE	20	F	SGL	RRZZZZUSA
LAN, KALLMAN	20	M	DLR	RRZZZZUSA
CHANNE	20	F	W	RRZZZZUSA
FEINBERG, LEIB	17	M	BRM	RRZZZZUSA
WALATZKI, JERAN	23	M	LABR	RRZZZZUSA
WOIDZKI, BENEDICT	26	M	LABR	RRZZZZUSA
ZOSSEK, ELIAS	17	M	LABR	RRZZZZUSA
NOVASILTSOW, BARBA.	50	F	SGL	RRZZZZUSA

SHIP: EMS

FROM: BREMEN
TO: NEW YORK
ARRIVED: 09 SEPTEMBER 1884

PASSENGER	AGE	SEX	OCCUPATION	PRV VIL DES
KOMAREZ, JACOB	30	M	LABR	RRZZZZUSA
KOMACZ, ABRAHAM	50	M	LABR	RRZZZZUSA
VEGE	46	F	NN	RRZZZZUSA
BERTRAM	15	M	CL	RRZZZZUSA
GORIO	10	M	CH	RRZZZZUSA
ESTER	23	F	NN	RRZZZZUSA
MESTIM	2	M	CHILD	RRZZZZUSA
ROTHSTEIN, ABEL	27	M	BRR	RRZZZZUSA
DERACZYNSKI, LEIB	23	M	LLD	RRZZZZUSA
SCHLUOHTUS, JENNY	40	F	NN	RRZZZZUSA
RODBECK, SARAH	38	F	NN	RRZZZZUSA
HERSK	10	M	CH	RRZZZZUSA
ABRAHAM	5	M	CHILD	RRZZZZUSA
LIEBE	.11	F	INFANT	RRZZZZUSA
CHAIE	18	F	NN	RRZZZZUSA
HANNA	.01	F	INFANT	RRZZZZUSA
SILBERSTEIN, REBECCA	24	F	NN	RRZZZZUSA
JACOB	4	M	CHILD	RRZZZZUSA
SCHEIDL	.11	M	INFANT	RRZZZZUSA
STROHBACH, JOSEF	18	M	FARMER	RRZZZZUSA
DOGART, ROSE	60	F	NN	RRZZZZUSA
ZLATE	18	F	NN	RRZZZZUSA
POLOSKY, MATKE	10	F	CH	RRZZZZUSA
NICHE	45	F	NN	RRZZZZUSA
HUDES	17	M	FARMER	RRZZZZUSA
BIALOPLOCKI, MARIA	38	F	NN	RRZZZZUSA
ANTONIE	6	F	CHILD	RRZZZZUSA
VICTORIA	3	F	CHILD	RRZZZZUSA
PIETRE	.09	M	INFANT	RRZZZZUSA
KEWISCH, SALUTA-MAEZ	27	F	NN	RRZZZZUSA
ALEXANDER	6	M	CHILD	RRZZZZUSA
JANTZEN, HEINR.	54	M	FARMER	RRZZZZUSA
BARBARA	52	F	NN	RRZZZZUSA
JOHANN	22	M	FARMER	RRZZZZUSA
JACOB	20	M	FARMER	RRZZZZUSA
CORNELIUS	18	M	FARMER	RRZZZZUSA
MARIE	14	F	CH	RRZZZZUSA
BARBARA	12	F	CH	RRZZZZUSA
DAVID	8	M	CHILD	RRZZZZUSA
PENNER, JOHANNES	33	M	FARMER	RRZZZZUSA
HELENE	28	F	NN	RRZZZZUSA
CATHARINA	9	F	CHILD	RRZZZZUSA
HEINRICH	7	M	CHILD	RRZZZZUSA
HELENE	5	F	CHILD	RRZZZZUSA
MARIA	.11	F	INFANT	RRZZZZUSA
JANTZEN, JOHANN	60	M	FARMER	RRZZZZUSA
CATHARINE	58	F	NN	RRZZZZUSA
HEINRICH	22	M	FARMER	RRZZZZUSA
JOHANN	20	M	FARMER	RRZZZZUSA
HERMANN	17	M	FARMER	RRZZZZUSA
ALEXANDER	14	M	FARMER	RRZZZZUSA
UNRAH, PETER	41	M	FARMER	RRZZZZUSA
HELENE	28	F	NN	RRZZZZUSA
PETER	5	M	CHILD	RRZZZZUSA
ANNA	69	F	NN	RRZZZZUSA
JOHANN	.03	M	INFANT	RRZZZZUSA
CORNELIUS	43	M	FARMER	RRZZZZUSA
HELENE	37	F	NN	RRZZZZUSA
ELISABETH	17	F	CH	RRZZZZUSA
ANNA	15	F	CH	RRZZZZUSA
AGNETA	13	F	CH	RRZZZZUSA
JOHANN	10	M	CH	RRZZZZUSA
PETER	7	M	CHILD	RRZZZZUSA
CORNELIUS	.11	M	INFANT	RRZZZZUSA
DIRKS, TOBIAS	25	M	LABR	RRZZZZUSA
EVA	26	F	NN	RRZZZZUSA
JOHANNES	4	M	CHILD	RRZZZZUSA
ABRAHAM	2	M	CHILD	RRZZZZUSA
ABRAHAM	23	M	FARMER	RRZZZZUSA
MARIA	20	F	NN	RRZZZZUSA
ABRAHAM	.06	M	INFANT	RRZZZZUSA
WIEBE, BERNHARD	24	M	FARMER	RRZZZZUSA
CATHARINE	23	F	NN	RRZZZZUSA
HEINRICH	.01	M	INFANT	RRZZZZUSA
CORNELIUS	22	M	NN	RRZZZZUSA
ANNA	18	F	NN	RRZZZZUSA
KLAAFSEN, MAXIC	54	F	NN	RRZZZZUSA
JACOB	17	M	FARMER	RRZZZZUSA
HELENE	8	F	CHILD	RRZZZZUSA
GRENEC, HEINRICH	48	M	FARMER	RRZZZZUSA
HELENE	19	F	NN	RRZZZZUSA
JACOB	15	M	FARMER	RRZZZZUSA
ISAAK	10	M	CH	RRZZZZUSA
PETER	6	M	CHILD	RRZZZZUSA
FAST, GERHARD	30	M	FARMER	RRZZZZUSA
CATHARINA	33	F	NN	RRZZZZUSA
GERHARD	10	M	CH	RRZZZZUSA
JOHANNES	7	M	CHILD	RRZZZZUSA
JACOB	1	M	CHILD	RRZZZZUSA
WILHELM	.06	M	INFANT	RRZZZZUSA
ALBRECHT, HEINR.	38	M	FARMER	RRZZZZUSA
HELINE	37	F	NN	RRZZZZUSA
HEINRICH	10	M	CH	RRZZZZUSA
FRANZ	8	M	CHILD	RRZZZZUSA
HELENE	5	F	CHILD	RRZZZZUSA
ABRAHAM	3	M	CHILD	RRZZZZUSA
MARTENS, JOHANN	34	M	FARMER	RRZZZZUSA
MARIA	34	F	NN	RRZZZZUSA
CORNELIA	9	F	CHILD	RRZZZZUSA
MARIA	7	F	CHILD	RRZZZZUSA
ANNA	4	F	CHILD	RRZZZZUSA
WEGELI, HEINRICH	45	M	FARMER	RRZZZZUSA
CATHARINE	45	F	NN	RRZZZZUSA
MARGARETHE	18	F	NN	RRZZZZUSA
ANNA	8	F	CHILD	RRZZZZUSA
ANNA	4	F	CHILD	RRZZZZUSA
PETER	10	M	CH	RRZZZZUSA
JOHANNES	.09	M	INFANT	RRZZZZUSA
PENNER, ANNA	38	F	NN	RRZZZZUSA

SHIP: RHAETIA

FROM: HAMBURG
TO: NEW YORK
ARRIVED: 09 SEPTEMBER 1884

PASSENGER	AGE	SEX	OCCUPATION	PRV VIL DES
OBRONEZKA, BER.	27	M	LABR	RRZZZZUSA
LEWISHAU, LEO	20	M	LABR	RRZZZZUSA
EPSTEIN, CHANNE	42	F	SGL	RRZZZZUSA
PUNKOWSKY, SARA	55	F	W	RRZZZZUSA

PASSENGER	AGE	SEX	OCCUPATION	PV VIL DES
MITTEL	9	F	CHILD	RRZZZZUSA
HERSCH	8	M	CHILD	RRZZZZUSA
BLIZNAK, SCHIE	55	M	LABR	RRZZZZUSA
SAMBITOL, NECHE	20	F	SGL	RRZZZZUSA
GARSANY, LEVIN	27	M	LABR	RRZZZZUSA
JACOBY, CATHRN.	54	M	LABR	RRZZZZUSA
BESNIHOW, MOSES	31	M	LABR	RRZZZZUSA
MICHEL	18	M	LABR	RRZZZZUSA
EPSTEIN, LEWIN	40	M	TCHR	RRZZZZUSA
AUGUSTE	17	F	CH	RRZZZZUSA
JACOB	9	M	CHILD	RRZZZZUSA
TAUBE	8	F	CHILD	RRZZZZUSA
SELDE	7	F	CHILD	RRZZZZUSA
FRADEL	6	F	CHILD	RRZZZZUSA
FEIVEL	5	M	CHILD	RRZZZZUSA
MIRIAM	4	F	CHILD	RRZZZZUSA
LIPMANN, MERE	9	F	CHILD	RRZZZZUSA
GARTEN, SARA	22	F	SGL	RRZZZZUSA
PUNKOWSKY, MORDCHE	46	M	LABR	RRZZZZUSA
HADES	46	F	W	RRZZZZUSA
RACHEL	17	F	CH	RRZZZZUSA
RIWE	3	F	CHILD	RRZZZZUSA
SARA	.11	F	INFANT	RRZZZZUSA
SCHAIERMANN, SALOMON	15	M	LABR	RRZZZZUSA
BABINTZKA, BEILE	20	F	SGL	RRZZZZUSA
SELITZ	20	M	LABR	RRZZZZUSA
PODWOZINSKA, PESCHE	18	F	SGL	RRZZZZUSA
TRIZINSKA, SCHIFRA	20	F	SGL	RRZZZZUSA
SHIEGELSKI, RUBEN	20	M	LABR	RRZZZZUSA
TRAKT, GERSON	26	M	LKSH	RRZZZZUSA
GUTMANN, ABEL	15	M	CL	RRZZZZUSA
ROTTENBERG, SHEINIKE	20	M	LABR	RRZZZZUSA
MENKUPSKI, ABR.	19	M	LABR	RRZZZZUSA
SIMANSKY, CHAIM	22	F	SGL	RRZZZZUSA
MARGULES, JENNY	24	F	W	RRZZZZUSA
KAPLAN, SALOMON	17	M	MSN	RRZZZZUSA
SLOWOTIZKI, JOSEF	19	M	SHMK	RRZZZZUSA
SUWALSKI, WOLF	9	M	CHILD	RRZZZZUSA
LIECHTZICHER, CHAIM	17	M	CL	RRZZZZUSA
POSTANITZ, ISRAEL	18	M	CL	RRZZZZUSA
ROTHSTEIN, SALOMON	18	M	CCHMN	RRZZZZUSA
KLEIN, DAVID	15	M	LABR	RRZZZZUSA
SCHWARZ, MINNA	24	F	SGL	RRZZZZUSA
ISAAC	29	M	LABR	RRZZZZUSA
ABRAMOWITZ, ABRAM	9	M	CHILD	RRZZZZUSA
LOSES, BENJ.	18	M	LABR	RRZZZZUSA
JAFFE, ABEL	18	M	CL	RRZZZZUSA
CHANNE	19	F	W	RRZZZZUSA
OGNIS, MIREL	19	F	W	RRZZZZUSA
MINNA	19	F	SGL	RRZZZZUSA
KOWIR, RACHEL	52	F	W	RRZZZZUSA
FAERBER, BENJ.	35	M	DYR	RRZZZZUSA
BLUM, NISSEN	47	M	DLR	RRZZZZUSA
REBECCA	46	F	W	RRZZZZUSA
THERESE	19	F	CH	RRZZZZUSA
DORA	15	F	CH	RRZZZZUSA
MARIE	9	F	CHILD	RRZZZZUSA
ISIDOR	8	M	CHILD	RRZZZZUSA
MAN	8	M	CHILD	RRZZZZUSA
JUL.	6	M	CHILD	RRZZZZUSA
SALOMON	.11	M	INFANT	RRZZZZUSA
SACHS, ZALLEL	25	M	CGRMKR	RRZZZZUSA
DERWINSKY, OSIAS	32	M	LABR	RRZZZZUSA
MARGULES, JENNY	.07	F	INFANT	RRZZZZUSA
MICHAEL, GOLDE	33	F	W	RRZZZZUSA
MOSES	9	M	CHILD	RRZZZZUSA
CHEIE	8	F	CHILD	RRZZZZUSA
RACHEL	4	F	CHILD	RRZZZZUSA
FANNY	3	F	CHILD	RRZZZZUSA
BRODSKI, ISRAEL	52	M	CGRMKR	RRZZZZUSA

SHIP: DEVONIA

FROM: GLASGOW AND MOVILLE
TO: NEW YORK
ARRIVED: 10 SEPTEMBER 1884

PASSENGER	AGE	SEX	OCCUPATION	PV VIL DES
BLUMENFELD, LEHAM	40	M	LABR	RRACBFUSA
DAVID	21	M	LABR	RRACBFUSA
CHEIM	19	M	LABR	RRACBFUSA
SEWICHE	16	F	LABR	RRACBFUSA
ARADIL	14	M	NN	RRACBFUSA
RACHEL	11	F	CH	RRACBFUSA
MAUP.	5	F	CHILD	RRACBFUSA
SUBSCHILTZ, FENGER	45	F	NN	RRADBQUSA
UDA	11	F	CH	RRADBQUSA
VENEZIA	3	F	CHILD	RRADBQUSA
JULIUS	20	M	SMH	RRADBQUSA
BORTMAN, NECHA	14	F	CH	RRADBQUSA
GROSO, MORRIS	35	M	JWLR	RRADBQUSA
JOHNSLER, MERE	26	F	NN	RRZZZZUSA
KARRHE	1	F	CHILD	RRZZZZUSA
FLARENGAGER, FRIEDRICH	27	M	LABR	RRACBFUSA
FRIMRENNAV, MORITZ	43	M	MCHT	RRACBFUSA

SHIP: LABRADOR

FROM: HAVRE
TO: NEW YORK
ARRIVED: 11 SEPTEMBER 1884

PASSENGER	AGE	SEX	OCCUPATION	PV VIL DES
ACHIKE, GUBINSKI	30	M	UNKNOWN	RRZZZZNY
SARAH	26	F	UNKNOWN	RRZZZZNY
LINA	5	F	CHILD	RRZZZZNY
LOUIS	3	M	CHILD	RRZZZZNY
JOSEPH	00	M	INF	RRZZZZNY
SOGERMANN, MICHEL	15	M	NN	RRZZZZNY
TLANKCHTEIN, ANGEL	16	M	NN	RRZZZZNY
VACTCHTER, AMIENS	68	M	NN	RRZZZZNY
SCTRIKONSKY, AARON	28	M	NN	RRZZZZNY

SHIP: ST. OF PENNSYLVANIA

FROM: GLASGOW AND LARNE
TO: NEW YORK
ARRIVED: 11 SEPTEMBER 1884

PASSENGER	AGE	SEX	OCCUPATION	PV VIL DES
BARENFUSS, RUBIN	27	M	CPMKR	RRZZZZUSA
PERLE	25	F	W	RRZZZZUSA
MALKE	.06	F	INFANT	RRZZZZUSA
FISCHER, LOB.	19	M	CPMKR	RRZZZZUSA
GARLE, ELIAS	53	M	MCHT	RRZZZZUSA
MARIE	10	F	CH	RRZZZZUSA
MARCUS, BARSCHE	28	F	W	RRZZZZUSA
RAKEL	1	F	CHILD	RRZZZZUSA
MARGOLIN, MEYER	22	M	MCHT	RRZZZZUSA
GROSS, HIRSCH	12	M	CH	RRZZZZUSA
MICH, BERL	18	M	MCHT	RRZZZZUSA
MARSAN, SAWEL	46	M	LABR	RRZZZZUSA
RESSITIS, ANTON	36	M	LABR	RRZZZZUSA
STINANIS, MARTIN	50	M	LABR	RRZZZZUSA
JULIE	40	F	W	RRZZZZUSA
ELWIRA	16	F	SP	RRZZZZUSA
ZODEKOW, MINNA	22	F	W	RRZZZZUSA
ZABEL	.03	F	INFANT	RRZZZZUSA

PASSENGER	AGE	SEX	OCCUPATION	PRV	VIL	DES
LIFFONEN, CARL	25	M	LABR	RR	ZZZ	ZUSA
SOEDERBERG, HILDA	25	F	SP	RR	ZZZ	ZUSA

SHIP: CITY OF CHESTER

FROM: LIVERPOOL AND QUEENSTOWN
TO: NEW YORK
ARRIVED: 12 SEPTEMBER 1884

PASSENGER	AGE	SEX	OCCUPATION	PRV	VIL	DES
KROOPMANN, BARUCH	44	M	FARMER	RR	ACB	DNY
RIVE	36	F	W	RR	ACB	DNY
ALTE	6	F	CHILD	RR	ACB	DNY
CHAIE	5	F	CHILD	RR	ACB	DNY
LEIB	1	F	CHILD	RR	ACB	DNY
AMOLSKY, PEREL	21	M	LABR	RR	ACB	DNY
EHR, BERMAN	19	M	LABR	RR	AEF	LNY
RABINOWITZ, JACOB	20	M	LABR	RR	AFW	JNY

SHIP: PENNLAND

FROM: ANTWERP
TO: NEW YORK
ARRIVED: 12 SEPTEMBER 1884

PASSENGER	AGE	SEX	OCCUPATION	PRV	VIL	DES
GOLOMBOESKA, AL.	30	F	LABR	RR	ZZZ	ZUNK
FR.	9	M	CHILD	RR	ZZZ	ZUNK
AN.	7	F	CHILD	RR	ZZZ	ZUNK
TH.	5	M	CHILD	RR	ZZZ	ZUNK
JOS.	3	F	CHILD	RR	ZZZ	ZUNK
ROS.	.06	F	INFANT	RR	ZZZ	ZUNK
ALBETER, J.	33	M	CPR	RR	AEF	LUNK
SCHLEIMACHER, Q.	21	F	CPTR	RR	AEF	LNY
KLEINE, TEH.	22	M	CPTR	RR	ZZZ	ZSTL
FZ.	25	M	FARMER	RR	ZZZ	ZSTL
ORT, MATH.	43	M	SHMK	RR	ZZZ	ZUNK
NEICHER, JOH.	31	M	SHMK	RR	ZZZ	ZUNK
SEHNITGER, MAH.	21	M	SHR	RR	ZZZ	ZBUF

SHIP: EIDER

FROM: BREMEN AND SOUTHAMPTON
TO: NEW YORK
ARRIVED: 13 SEPTEMBER 1884

PASSENGER	AGE	SEX	OCCUPATION	PRV	VIL	DES
WERBELOWSKY, MARY	34	F	W	RR	ZZZ	ZRSS
BENJAMIN	.06	M	INFANT	RR	ZZZ	ZRSS
HERSTEIN, CHANE	20	F	NN	RR	ZZZ	ZUSA
WEBELOWSKI, NEIB	31	F	W	RR	ZZZ	ZUSA
HANNI	18	F	NN	RR	ZZZ	ZUSA
MOSES	.06	M	INFANT	RR	ZZZ	ZUSA
CZIRLE	11	F	CH	RR	ZZZ	ZUSA
LINA	7	F	CHILD	RR	ZZZ	ZUSA
SCHULTZ, HELENE	19	F	NN	RR	ZZZ	ZUSA
MORKOWITZ, SALLI	16	F	NN	RR	ZZZ	ZUSA
ZUCKMANSKY, FLORA	19	F	NN	RR	ZZZ	ZUSA

SHIP: AUSTRAL

FROM: LIVERPOOL AND QUEENSTOWN
TO: NEW YORK
ARRIVED: 15 SEPTEMBER 1884

PASSENGER	AGE	SEX	OCCUPATION	PRV	VIL	DES
MICHALSKI, L.	20	M	UNKNOWN	RR	ZZZ	ZNY
EBEINEKE, ISRAEL	18	M	LABR	RR	ZZZ	ZNY
SEGALL, REINE	20	M	SVNT	RR	ZZZ	ZNY

SHIP: INDIA

FROM: HAMBURG
TO: NEW YORK
ARRIVED: 15 SEPTEMBER 1884

PASSENGER	AGE	SEX	OCCUPATION	PRV	VIL	DES
FISCHER, JOHANN	25	M	LABR	RR	ZZZ	ZNY
SIVOLKIN, KALMANN	23	M	MCHT	RR	ZZZ	ZMRL
LINA	19	F	W	RR	ZZZ	ZMRL
SIEF, E.F.	32	M	TCHR	RR	ZZZ	ZMRL
DEMBROWSKA, MARIA	36	F	WO	RR	ZZZ	ZNY
JULIA	12	F	D	RR	ZZZ	ZNY
HEINRICH	5	M	CHILD	RR	ZZZ	ZNY
ROSENZWEIG, SIMON	30	M	WCHMKR	RR	ZZZ	ZNY
SAMUEL, ALTER	23	M	SMH	RR	ZZZ	ZNY
GOLDBLAD, HENDSCHE	21	F	WO	PL	ZZZ	ZNY
ESTHER	7	F	CHILD	PL	ZZZ	ZNY
EISIK	4	M	CHILD	PL	ZZZ	ZNY
KAPLAN, HIRSCH	29	M	MCHT	RR	ZZZ	ZNY
DWORE	26	F	W	RR	ZZZ	ZNY
KABATZNIK, LEISER	58	M	UNKNOWN	RR	ZZZ	ZNY
KURTZELINK, ARON	52	M	UNKNOWN	RR	ZZZ	ZNY
KIREL	47	F	W	RR	ZZZ	ZNY
ABRAHAM	19	M	S	RR	ZZZ	ZNY
FRIEMANN, CHARLOTTE	25	F	WO	PL	ZZZ	ZNY
LOUISE	.03	F	INFANT	PL	ZZZ	ZNY
JACOB	.11	M	INFANT	PL	ZZZ	ZNY
NEN, LINA	25	F	SGL	RR	ZZZ	ZNY
MILOVSKY, HIRSCH	56	M	LABR	RR	ZZZ	ZNY
DINE	51	F	W	RR	ZZZ	ZNY
KAPUZNICH, BINE	19	M	JNR	RR	ZZZ	ZNY
GITTEL	20	F	W	RR	ZZZ	ZNY
FISCHMANN, R.	23	F	WO	PL	ZZZ	ZNY
SARAH	.04	F	INFANT	PL	ZZZ	ZNY
BIENENSTOK, MALKE	18	F	SGL	PL	ZZZ	ZNY
SAMELA, DAVID	42	M	JNR	RR	ZZZ	ZNY
LEIB	7	F	CHILD	RR	ZZZ	ZNY
ANERBACH, MEYER	23	M	SDLR	RR	ZZZ	ZNY
ALTSCHUL, ISAAC	20	M	JNR	RR	ZZZ	ZNY
BASE	20	F	W	RR	ZZZ	ZNY
STORN, R.	26	M	LABR	RR	ZZZ	ZNY
PICARSKY, EIS.	33	F	WO	RR	ZZZ	ZNY
JACOB	7	M	CHILD	RR	ZZZ	ZNY
SAWSKY, FRIDR.	28	F	WO	RR	ZZZ	ZNY
ABRAHAM	6	M	CHILD	RR	ZZZ	ZNY
CALMANN	.04	M	INFANT	RR	ZZZ	ZNY
MATTENSON, ISAAK	20	M	LABR	RR	ZZZ	ZNY
GRAUTZ, CHAIE	28	F	WO	RR	ZZZ	ZNY
SALI	6	M	CHILD	RR	ZZZ	ZNY
ZIPPKE	3	M	CHILD	RR	ZZZ	ZNY
JACOB	.07	M	INFANT	RR	ZZZ	ZNY
PODOSCHOWO, SCHOLEM	18	M	LABR	RR	ZZZ	ZNY
PISSICCHOWNA, MARIA	30	F	SGL	RR	ZZZ	ZNY
KARPEMTER, FANNY	20	F	SGL	RR	ZZZ	ZNY
RUTSTEIN, ARON	50	M	LABR	RR	ZZZ	ZNY
PURWIN, FEIGE	29	F	WO	RR	ZZZ	ZNY
JUDEL	6	M	CHILD	RR	ZZZ	ZNY
DAVID	5	M	CHILD	RR	ZZZ	ZNY
SALOMON	.09	M	INFANT	RR	ZZZ	ZNY

PASSENGER	AGE	SEX	OCCUPATION	PRV VIL DES
ARENGERD, ISAAC	19	M	LABR	RRZZZZNY
BASTLIST, S.	32	F	WO	RRZZZZNY
SARAH	8	F	CHILD	RRZZZZNY
ROCHEL	4	F	CHILD	RRZZZZNY
MARIA	.07	F	INFANT	RRZZZZNY
FEISTEL, BASCHE-M.	15	F	SGL	RRZZZZNY
OZAROFF, LIEBE	26	F	WO	RRZZZZNY
DIRSAKHE	3	F	CHILD	RRZZZZNY
PERL	.06	M	INFANT	RRZZZZNY
BRODERSEN, CHAJE	21	F	WO	RRZZZZNY
SORE	7	F	CHILD	RRZZZZNY
KAHN, MALKE	29	F	WO	RRZZZZNY
HINDE	7	F	CHILD	RRZZZZNY
TENN	6	F	CHILD	RRZZZZNY
BINKE	4	F	CHILD	RRZZZZNY
SOKOLOWA, JENTE-L.	24	F	SGL	RRZZZZNY

SHIP: SUEVIA

FROM: HAMBURG AND HAVRE
TO: NEW YORK
ARRIVED: 15 SEPTEMBER 1884

PASSENGER	AGE	SEX	OCCUPATION	PRV VIL DES
KAPLAN, SCHMUEL	20	M	LABR	RRAHTRUSA
LIEBE	20	F	W	RRAHTRUSA
ETTE	15	F	SGL	RRAHTRUSA
IDOWITZ, MOSES	17	M	LABR	RRAHTRUSA
KIDAUSKY, SIMON	15	M	LABR	RRAHTRUSA
BREITMAN, NEHEMIE	18	F	SGL	RRAHTUUSA
KAPPERISCH, SCHMUEL	21	M	LABR	RRAHTFUSA
GRUNBERG, LINA	20	F	SGL	RRZZZZUSA
ANTONETTE	18	F	SGL	RRZZZZUSA
ILWOLOWITZ, JULIUS	27	M	TLR	RRAGRTUSA
JOH.	29	F	W	RRAGRTUSA
MARTIN	5	M	CHILD	RRAGRTUSA
EMMA	.11	F	INFANT	RRAGRTUSA
SACKS, BLUME	15	F	SGL	RRAHSWUSA
GRINBERG, ARON-L.	27	M	DLR	RRZZZZUSA
CLARA	25	F	W	RRZZZZUSA
HIRSCHKOWITZ, JACOB	23	M	LABR	RRZZZZUSA
ZIRILA	21	F	W	RRZZZZUSA
FANNY	9	F	CHILD	RRZZZZUSA
BABAUSKI, SCHONE	18	F	SGL	RRZZZZUSA
CHAIE	16	F	SGL	RRZZZZUSA
SPITZ, MEYER	21	M	TNR	RRZZZZUSA
NEISNER, SCHER	19	M	TLR	RRZZZZUSA
RUBENSTEIN, CHAIM	41	M	LABR	RRZZZZUSA
YESINA, RACHEL	32	F	W	RRZZZZUSA
SALLY	7	F	CHILD	RRZZZZUSA
LEVI	5	M	CHILD	RRZZZZUSA
SCHINBERG, ABRAH.	9	M	CHILD	RRZZZZUSA
TROCZKI, WLADISL.	22	F	SGL	RRZZZZUSA
PARNESS, MORDSCHE	24	M	MCHT	RRAHUIUSA
FEIGE	21	F	W	RRAHUIUSA
ABR.	.11	M	INFANT	RRAHUIUSA
HELENE	.01	F	INFANT	RRAHUIUSA
KURLANCZIK, WOLF	44	M	LABR	RRAHTFUSA
RIWE	9	F	CHILD	RRAHTFUSA
MEITE	8	F	CHILD	RRAHTFUSA
RUBEN	7	M	CHILD	RRAHTFUSA
JENTE	6	M	CHILD	RRAHTFUSA
MOSES	4	M	CHILD	RRAHTFUSA
EIGE	14	M	CH	RRAHTFUSA
RUPIN, BERMAN	20	M	TLR	RRAHTFUSA
BARDIN, JUDEL	18	M	LABR	RRZZZZUSA
WISANSKY, CHIENNE	35	F	W	RRZZZZUSA
MINNA	13	F	CH	RRZZZZUSA
MEIER	8	M	CHILD	RRZZZZUSA
GROSS, HANNE	9	F	CHILD	RRZZZZUSA
SUCHOWSKY, MINNA	18	F	SGL	RRZZZZUSA
PUN, ITTE	22	F	SGL	RRZZZZUSA
LEWINSTEIN, BENZEL	18	M	LABR	RRZZZZUSA
BAJARSKI, GITTEL	28	F	W	RRAHVUUSA
LEIB	.11	M	INFANT	RRAHVUUSA
SACKS, SLATE	45	F	W	RRAHSWUSA
SCHONE	9	F	CHILD	RRAHSWUSA
MILNIK, SAMUEL	9	F	CHILD	RRAHSWUSA
NICHELOWSKI, ROSA	70	F	W	RRZZZZUSA
LEA	28	F	W	RRZZZZUSA
MINNA	9	F	CHILD	RRZZZZUSA
MOSES	7	M	CHILD	RRZZZZUSA
SELDE	5	M	CHILD	RRZZZZUSA
MOSES	3	M	CHILD	RRZZZZUSA
SCHONE	.11	F	INFANT	RRZZZZUSA
ROGALSKI, ABRAH.	19	M	LABR	RRZZZZUSA
SMALOWICZ, WOLF	22	M	LABR	RRZZZZUSA
CIRLSTEIN, LAJE	18	F	SGL	RRAHTSUSA
SCHAPIRO, LEIB	33	F	SGL	RRZZZZUSA
DUSKIN, RACHEL	24	F	W	RRZZZZUSA
CHAIM	4	M	CHILD	RRZZZZUSA
SEGER, NEUME	15	F	SGL	RRAHZSUSA
DELUS, MATH.	22	M	LABR	RRAHZSUSA
STOPEK, FREIDE	42	F	W	RRZZZZUSA
CHAIM	15	F	CH	RRZZZZUSA
MALI	9	F	CHILD	RRZZZZUSA
ABRAH.	7	M	CHILD	RRZZZZUSA
ABDOCH	3	M	CHILD	RRZZZZUSA
HILLELSEN, HILLE	18	M	TLR	RRZZZZUSA
LICHTENSTEIN, ISAAC	18	M	LABR	RRZZZZUSA
MARCUS, JOSEPH	28	M	JNR	RRZZZZUSA
SINKELSTEIN, DAVID	23	M	LABR	RRZZZZUSA
GUTMANN, LEISER	18	M	LABR	RRZZZZUSA
BARANOWSKY, SIMON	19	M	TLR	RRZZZZUSA
URKOWITZ, MOSES	34	M	LABR	RRZZZZUSA
LAO, SALOMON	23	M	LABR	RRZZZZUSA
LEWINSTEIN, CHIENNE	50	F	W	RRZZZZUSA
LESROWITZ, MENDEL	19	M	LABR	RRAHTSUSA
EPSTEIN, GERSON	19	M	LABR	RRZZZZUSA
SELSCHER, ITZKE	18	M	LABR	RRAEFLUSA
ROSEDE	19	F	SGL	RRAEFLUSA
SILBERSTEIN, LOUIS	28	M	SMH	RRZZZZUSA
SELMANOWITZ, JACOB	25	M	DLR	RRZZZZUSA
ZENSOR, ADAM	16	M	UMKR	RRAFWJUSA
SCHMIDT, BERL	35	M	SMH	RRZZZZUSA
FROMMER, ABRAH.	15	M	MLR	RRZZZZUSA
SABASEWITZ, ISAAC	29	M	DLR	RRZZZZUSA
LEWINSOHN, SALOMON	33	M	DLR	RRZZZZUSA
ESTHER	25	F	W	RRZZZZUSA
KURLAREZIK, CHASCHE	20	F	SGL	RRAHTFUSA
MATSCHIS, BALTREMEI	23	M	LABR	RRZZZZUSA
KRUMSOHN, ASRIEL	17	M	LABR	RRADOIUSA
SOKOLOFF, DAVID	24	M	SMH	RRAHQUUSA
REISS, HERRM.	26	M	TCHR	RRAHQUUSA
BRAUM, SAMUEL	28	M	SDLR	RRZZZZUSA
JACHE	28	F	W	RRZZZZUSA
ABRAH.	3	M	CHILD	RRZZZZUSA
JIH.	.11	M	INFANT	RRZZZZUSA
ARIE	21	M	BKBNDR	RRZZZZUSA
ABR.	26	M	MCHT	RRZZZZUSA
LATSCHICK, MICHAEL	24	M	JNR	RRAHUIUSA
ITTELSOHN, SALOMON	28	M	CGRMKR	RRAHTFUSA
EPSTEIN, CHAIE	26	F	W	RRAFWJUSA
DAVID	6	M	CHILD	RRAFWJUSA
SCHAIE	4	F	CHILD	RRAFWJUSA
CZERNE	3	F	CHILD	RRAFWJUSA
MARIANNE	.01	F	INFANT	RRAFWJUSA
JOSEPH	.11	M	INFANT	RRAFWJUSA
RABIUS, ARON	25	M	WVR	RRZZZZUSA
STEIN, SARA	28	F	W	RRZZZZUSA
MICHEL	9	M	CHILD	RRZZZZUSA
DAVID	4	M	CHILD	RRZZZZUSA
LEWITSCH, CIPE	42	F	W	RRAHOKUSA
BEILE	19	F	CH	RRAHOKUSA
SALOMON	6	M	CHILD	RRAHOKUSA
RACHEL	.11	F	INFANT	RRAHOKUSA

PASSENGER	AGE	SEX	OCCUPATION	PRV VIL DES
KEMPINSKY, ABRAH.	65	M	TLR	RRZZZZUSA
EIDELSOHN, MICHEL	18	F	SGL	RRAHSWUSA
POSNANSKY, REGINE	17	F	SGL	RRZZZZUSA
BEHRMANN, LEIB	59	M	LABR	RRAHTFUSA
CHAIE	57	F	W	RRAHTFUSA
ZUDIKOF, CHINE	20	F	SGL	RRAHTFUSA
DOBRE	22	F	SGL	RRAHTFUSA
SEYSKIND, DAVID	18	M	LABR	RRAGRTUSA
LINE	14	F	SGL	RRAGRTUSA
SIRAPSKE, JUDEL	20	M	LABR	RRZZZZUSA
OFFENBERG, LASER	20	M	LABR	RRZZZZUSA
SESBROT, JONAS	36	M	LABR	RRZZZZUSA
REBECCA	16	F	D	RRAHUFUSA
ASCHER	14	F	D	RRAHUFUSA
KOZLOWSKY, MICHAEL	33	M	MSN	RRZZZZUSA
STOPEK, TAUBE	.11	M	INFANT	RRZZZZUSA
HERING, DAVID	16	M	CGRMKR	RRZZZZUSA
SAGOLSKY, SCHEFFEL	30	M	LABR	RRZZZZUSA
HACK, DAVID	20	M	LABR	RRZZZZUSA

SHIP: ANCHORIA

FROM: GLASGOW
TO: NEW YORK
ARRIVED: 17 SEPTEMBER 1884

PASSENGER	AGE	SEX	OCCUPATION	PRV VIL DES
BLUM, JOSEF	17	M	TLR	RRZZZZUSA
DANANKIRSCH, EDW.	19	M	LITGR	RRZZZZUSA
ADOLPH	20	M	BKPR	RRZZZZUSA
GOLDSTEIN, JACOB-S.	31	M	LABR	RRZZZZUSA
KIRS, STEF.	25	M	LABR	RRZZZZUSA
STEINBERG, ISRAEL	14	M	UNKNOWN	RRZZZZUSA

SHIP: BREMEN

FROM: BREMEN
TO: NEW YORK
ARRIVED: 18 SEPTEMBER 1884

PASSENGER	AGE	SEX	OCCUPATION	PRV VIL DES
BECKER, ISAAK	59	M	LABR	RRZZZZUSA
JULIUS	8	M	CHILD	RRZZZZUSA
SIMON	7	M	CHILD	RRZZZZUSA
HECKER, ABRAHAM	55	M	LABR	RRZZZZUSA
KASSEL, FRIDRICH	25	M	LABR	RRZZZZUSA
SLANT, TANT	30	F	NN	RRZZZZUSA
DUWIT	8	M	CHILD	RRZZZZUSA
HIRSAT	6	M	CHILD	RRZZZZUSA
AREND	4	M	CHILD	RRZZZZUSA
LEIB	1	M	CHILD	RRZZZZUSA
SAGIRIN, SAPSETA	20	F	NN	RRZZZZUSA
KRASNE, LECH.	20	F	NN	RRZZZZUSA
SOWOKINS, MARCELLA	34	F	NN	RRZZZZUSA
JOSEF	8	M	CHILD	RRZZZZUSA
ANNA	6	F	CHILD	RRZZZZUSA
MARIANNE	5	F	CHILD	RRZZZZUSA
CASIMIR	3	M	CHILD	RRZZZZUSA
JOSEF	.10	M	INFANT	RRZZZZUSA
STUCZKOWNA, JOSEFA	20	F	NN	RRZZZZUSA
KIESEN, MAX	20	M	LABR	RRZZZZUSA
ANNA	16	F	NN	RRZZZZUSA

SHIP: CANADA

FROM: HAVRE
TO: NEW YORK
ARRIVED: 18 SEPTEMBER 1884

PASSENGER	AGE	SEX	OCCUPATION	PRV VIL DES
DE-KORSAK, U-MRS	24	F	NN	RRZZZZCIN

SHIP: FRISIA

FROM: HAMBURG
TO: NEW YORK
ARRIVED: 18 SEPTEMBER 1884

PASSENGER	AGE	SEX	OCCUPATION	PRV VIL DES
ZABARSKI, THEODORE	41	F	W	RRZZZZUSA
MARTHA	18	F	D	RRZZZZUSA
KLAIVENSKY, HILLEL	15	M	MSN	RRZZZZUSA
DRAN, MOSES-A.	18	M	SHMK	RRZZZZUSA
BAWILSKI, JOSEF	18	M	CGRMKR	RRAHTFUSA
CHAIE	49	F	W	RRAHTFUSA
SHALANSKY, RIWKE	17	F	SGL	RRZZZZUSA
BAERMANN, CHAIE	25	F	W	RRZZZZUSA
FEIN	.06	M	INFANT	RRZZZZUSA
SCHPRINSKY, HENE	20	F	SGL	RRAHTSUSA
KABELSKY, ABRAHAM	20	M	LABR	RRZZZZUSA
LOPEROWITZ, ZIPE	21	F	W	RRZZZZUSA
HIRSCH	22	M	LABR	RRZZZZUSA
FRIEDMANN, LIEB	20	M	LABR	RRAHTFUSA
CHACKELOWITZ, NOCHEM	51	M	LABR	RRZZZZUSA
KOKOCZKY, SCHEIME	23	F	W	RRAHTOUSA
WAVZE	5	M	CHILD	RRAHTOUSA
BARUCH	.11	M	INFANT	RRAHTOUSA
STOLOWITZ, MORDCHE	9	M	CHILD	RRAHTOUSA
LEIB	8	M	CHILD	RRAHTOUSA
TRELING, LEA	20	F	SGL	RRADOIUSA
LAPIR, JETTE	29	F	W	RRZZZZUSA
PESCHE	8	F	CHILD	RRZZZZUSA
JACOB	.11	M	INFANT	RRZZZZUSA
LEIBOWITZ, RACHLE	19	F	SGL	RRZZZZUSA
JACUBOWSKY, ROSA	30	F	W	RRZZZZUSA
HEYMANN	4	M	CHILD	RRZZZZUSA
COHN, HULDA	21	F	SGL	RRZZZZUSA
STRALEVSKY, ETTEL	41	F	W	RRADOIUSA
SARA	9	F	CHILD	RRADOIUSA
SCHOBEDMANN, WOLF	38	M	LABR	RRZZZZUSA
MEISCHOWITZ, DAVID	18	M	LABR	RRZZZZUSA
LEWIN, MOSES	17	M	LABR	RRZZZZUSA
FRIEDMANN, PESSE	20	F	SGL	RRAHTFUSA
CHAIKLOWITZ, MENUCH	8	F	CHILD	RRZZZZUSA
CHACZINSKY, JOSEL	24	M	TLR	RRZZZZUSA
MALZ, RUWEN	15	M	TLR	RRZZZZUSA
MIRWISCH, SCHEIE	33	M	TLR	RRZZZZUSA
ACHRAP, MOSES	20	M	CGRMKR	RRZZZZUSA
LOEWEN, JOSSEL	41	M	LABR	RRZZZZUSA
KAJCHUTZ, EVA	22	F	W	RRZZZZUSA
ANTONIE	.11	F	INFANT	RRZZZZUSA
TACZYDOWSKI, VINCENTI	24	M	LABR	RRAHZSUSA
ORLUCK, JOSSEL	30	M	LABR	RRZZZZUSA
MICHELSOHN, FRIEDE	25	F	W	RRAHSPUSA
SAMUEL	3	M	CHILD	RRAHSPUSA
DINA	.11	F	INFANT	RRAHSPUSA
BIALISTOK, SCHIRE	18	F	SGL	RRAHZRUSA
TOBIAS, NOCHIMN	27	M	TLR	RRACONUSA
JACOBSTEIN, ALTE	9	F	CHILD	RRZZZZUSA
LELONKA, CIREL	38	F	W	RRZZZZUSA
MARIANNE	.11	F	INFANT	RRZZZZUSA
SCHIMANOWITZ, NESCHE	50	F	W	RRAHSPUSA
SCHWARZ, CHAIE	27	F	W	RRAHSPUSA
FEDALIA	4	F	CHILD	RRAHSPUSA

PASSENGER	AGE	SEX	OCCUPATION	PRVL	VIL	DES
FREIDE	.11	F	INFANT	RR	AHSP	USA
SILBERMANN, MOSS	30	M	LABR	RR	AFVG	USA
ALISE	22	F	W	RR	AFVG	USA
MOSES	.11	M	INFANT	RR	AFVG	USA
ZUCKERMANN, CHANNE	20	F	W	RR	ZZZZ	USA
SARA	.11	F	INFANT	RR	ZZZZ	USA
SPINCHE	.11	F	INFANT	RR	ZZZZ	USA
RIWKIN, LEIB	16	F	SGL	RR	ZZZZ	USA
BEGUN, HENE	16	F	SGL	RR	AHOK	USA
SEGAL, CHANNE	42	F	W	RR	ZZZZ	USA
CHAIE	22	F	CH	RR	ZZZZ	USA
ALTER	9	M	CHILD	RR	ZZZZ	USA
DAVID	8	M	CHILD	RR	ZZZZ	USA
BASCHE	6	M	CHILD	RR	ZZZZ	USA
BREINDEL	4	M	CHILD	RR	ZZZZ	USA
BEILE	.06	F	INFANT	RR	ZZZZ	USA
BERL	.06	M	INFANT	RR	ZZZZ	USA
LICHTENSTEIN, CHAIM	18	M	LABR	RR	AFWJ	USA
BRANDE, HILLEL	30	M	HRSDLR	RR	ZZZZ	USA
FLATAN, ISRAEL	40	M	LABR	RR	ADOI	USA
BEILE	17	F	CH	RR	ADOI	USA
LESSER	9	M	CHILD	RR	ADOI	USA
BOROWSKY, ISAAK	22	M	JNR	RR	AHXH	USA
FREITELSOHN, ABRAH.	25	M	TLR	RR	AHTF	USA
SALOMON	16	M	TLR	RR	AHTF	USA
SEGALL, ARON	22	M	JNR	RR	ZZZZ	USA
LANDARSKY, SIMON	29	M	LABR	RR	ZZZZ	USA
SAMUEL	9	M	CHILD	RR	ZZZZ	USA
KAMINACZ, SCHONE	30	F	W	RR	AHTR	USA
GITTE	5	F	CHILD	RR	AHTR	USA
JUDA	.11	F	INFANT	RR	AHTR	USA
BLOCK, LIPMAN	23	M	TLR	RR	AHVA	USA
FINHELSTEIN, SELMA	22	F	SGL	RR	AHVA	USA
WECKER, RACHEL	22	F	SGL	RR	ZZZZ	USA
SKAPLAN, SOCHER	20	M	MCHT	RR	ACON	USA
BRAUN, CHAIM	29	M	MCHT	RR	ZZZZ	USA
KOHLER, JUL.	44	M	SHMK	RR	ADOI	USA
GUSTINE	38	F	W	RR	ADOI	USA
GRODE, RUDOLF	41	M	SHMK	RR	ADOI	USA
SCHNEIDERREITH, GEORG	30	M	LABR	RR	ADOI	USA
BAKOWITZ, SIMON	20	M	LABR	RR	AHTF	USA
PISCHMER, DWORE	20	F	SGL	RR	AHTF	USA
SIBALSKY, SIMON	18	M	CGRMKR	RR	AHTF	USA
ABRAHAM	20	M	CGRMKR	RR	AHTF	USA
SONN, ISRAL	20	M	LABR	RR	AHTF	USA
FEIGE	20	F	W	RR	AHTF	USA
PISCHUNER, LEISER	20	M	LABR	RR	AHTF	USA
BERNSTEIN, BER.	16	M	LABR	RR	AHTF	USA
PINKOWSKY, RACHEL	47	F	W	RR	AHTF	USA
EIGE	15	F	CH	RR	AHTF	USA
CHASKEL	9	M	CHILD	RR	AHTF	USA
ESTHER	6	F	CHILD	RR	AHTF	USA
MOSES	.11	M	INFANT	RR	AHTF	USA
FINKEL, ELIAS	22	M	TLR	RR	ZZZZ	USA
ROSENBERG, HINDE	42	F	W	RR	ZZZZ	USA
CHASCHE	18	F	CH	RR	ZZZZ	USA
LIEBE	15	F	CH	RR	ZZZZ	USA
RACHEL	8	F	CHILD	RR	ZZZZ	USA
HILLEL	9	M	CHILD	RR	ZZZZ	USA
MENDEL	6	M	CHILD	RR	ZZZZ	USA
ELIE	.11	M	INFANT	RR	ZZZZ	USA
FINKELSTEIN, MENUCHE	42	F	W	RR	ZZZZ	USA
SCHMUEL	9	M	CHILD	RR	ZZZZ	USA
SOIKE, LEIB	21	M	SHMK	RR	ZZZZ	USA
KRIWITZKI, CIEWIE	20	F	SGL	RR	AGRT	USA
NIMEROWSKY, DAVID	45	M	LABR	RR	ZZZZ	USA
ROSA	17	F	CH	RR	ZZZZ	USA
W.	14	M	BY	RR	ZZZZ	USA
FINKEL, EIDEL	20	F	SGL	RR	ZZZZ	USA
JEZYN, SAMUEL	17	M	CHMKR	RR	ZZZZ	USA
BERNSTEIN, RACHEL	40	F	W	RR	AHSW	USA
JENTE	9	F	CHILD	RR	AHSW	USA
SCHOLOM	7	M	CHILD	RR	AHSW	USA
HOSCHE	5	F	CHILD	RR	AHSW	USA
NOCHMANN	.11	M	INFANT	RR	AHSW	USA
ROMEK, BASCHE	40	F	W	RR	ZZZZ	USA
JECHID	16	M	CH	RR	ZZZZ	USA
ARON	9	M	CHILD	RR	ZZZZ	USA
SCHWARZ, ROSA	16	F	SGL	RR	ZZZZ	USA

SHIP: RHYNLAND

FROM: ANTWERP
TO: NEW YORK
ARRIVED: 19 SEPTEMBER 1884

PASSENGER	AGE	SEX	OCCUPATION	PRVL	VIL	DES
KASHELECK, A.	50	F	UNKNOWN	PL	ZZZZ	WI
STANISLAWSKI, A.	44	F	UNKNOWN	PL	ZZZZ	UNK
FRZ.	18	M	UNKNOWN	PL	ZZZZ	UNK
M.	15	F	UNKNOWN	PL	ZZZZ	UNK
LOR	7	F	CHILD	PL	ZZZZ	UNK
PAL	5	F	CHILD	PL	ZZZZ	UNK
RODUNSEL, E.	21	M	UNKNOWN	PL	ZZZZ	UNK
GEZESKOWICH, ST.	20	M	UNKNOWN	PL	ZZZZ	UNK
ANTA.	8	F	CHILD	PL	ZZZZ	UNK

SHIP: STATE OF INDIANA

FROM: GLASGOW AND LARNE
TO: NEW YORK
ARRIVED: 19 SEPTEMBER 1884

PASSENGER	AGE	SEX	OCCUPATION	PRVL	VIL	DES
OLTARSH, GUTE	00	F	W	RR	ZZZZ	USA
MOSES	2	M	CHILD	RR	ZZZZ	USA
NEWLER, PEREZ	26	M	CGRMKR	RR	ZZZZ	USA
BASCHE	23	F	W	RR	ZZZZ	USA
BEHRINGSOHN, SEINE	56	F	W	RR	ZZZZ	USA
LEITES, EPHRAIM	18	M	DYR	RR	ZZZZ	USA
STOCK, ABRAHAM	21	M	SMH	RR	ZZZZ	USA
JAROWSKY, ANTON	24	M	LABR	RR	ZZZZ	USA
KRANS, ISAAC	45	M	TLR	RR	ZZZZ	USA
SILBERSTEIN, JOSEPH	19	M	CL	RR	ZZZZ	USA
GRUENGOLD, MORDCHE	18	M	PDLR	RR	ZZZZ	USA
MICHALOWSKY, MICHAIL	28	M	PDLR	RR	ZZZZ	USA

SHIP: CITY OF RICHMOND

FROM: LIVERPOOL AND QUEENSTOWN
TO: NEW YORK
ARRIVED: 20 SEPTEMBER 1884

PASSENGER	AGE	SEX	OCCUPATION	PRVL	VIL	DES
KATZ, SACKUE	28	M	LABR	RR	ZZZZ	USA
KOTVITZ, SAM.	38	M	UNKNOWN	RR	ZZZZ	USA
KOVITZ, HARY	10	M	CH	RR	ZZZZ	USA
GERBEROWITZ, IOSSELL	23	M	LABR	RR	ZZZZ	UNK
EIJEL, SIMON	19	M	UNKNOWN	RR	ZZZZ	UNK
JOSEFSON, CARL	31	M	UNKNOWN	RR	ZZZZ	UNK
MUKER	38	M	UNKNOWN	RR	ZZZZ	UNK
MITCHELL, CHAS.B.	25	M	LABR	RR	ZZZZ	LON

SHIP: EGYPTIAN MONARCH

FROM: LONDON
TO: NEW YORK
ARRIVED: 20 SEPTEMBER 1884

PASSENGER	AGE	SEX	OCCUPATION	PRV VIL DES
FRILYHE, ANDR.	34	M	LABR	PLZZZZNY
CHEPHER, SCHNERE	21	M	LABR	PLZZZZNY
CROUHOLMO, ALEX	29	M	CPTR	FNZZZZTX

SHIP: HAMMONIA

FROM: HAMBURG AND HAVRE
TO: NEW YORK
ARRIVED: 20 SEPTEMBER 1884

PASSENGER	AGE	SEX	OCCUPATION	PRV VIL DES
ISAAK, ISRAEL	19	M	LABR	RRZZZZUSA
CHRAPOF, FUDEL	18	M	LABR	RRZZZZUSA
BENTZIG, ANDR.	16	M	BKR	RRZZZZUSA
EINSOHN, ITTE	24	F	SGL	RRZZZZUSA
ZWOBAT, MARIE	55	F	W	RRZZZZUSA
ROGASCH, ELIZABETH	32	F	W	RRZZZZUSA
ANNA	9	F	CHILD	RRZZZZUSA
WILEH.	8	M	CHILD	RRZZZZUSA
EMILIE	7	F	CHILD	RRZZZZUSA
GOTTL.	5	M	CHILD	RRZZZZUSA
JULIANNA	3	F	CHILD	RRZZZZUSA
JULS.	.11	M	INFANT	RRZZZZUSA
RAABNER, KATI	18	F	SGL	RRZZZZUSA
SKLARSKYE, SARA	19	F	SGL	RRZZZZUSA
FEIN, BEILE	18	F	SGL	RRZZZZUSA
EFRAIM	9	M	CHILD	RRZZZZUSA
SKICHIDLOWE, GITTEL	25	F	W	RRZZZZUSA
SAMUEL	3	M	CHILD	RRZZZZUSA
JOSSEL	.09	M	INFANT	RRZZZZUSA
LUBIEC, ANNA	36	F	W	RRZZZZUSA
STEFANIE	9	F	CHILD	RRZZZZUSA
MARIE	8	F	CHILD	RRZZZZUSA
JOSEPHA	6	F	CHILD	RRZZZZUSA
WLADISLAW	.11	M	INFANT	RRZZZZUSA
BRANYL, JETTE	32	F	W	RRZZZZUSA
ALTER	4	M	CHILD	RRZZZZUSA
MOTES	.11	M	INFANT	RRZZZZUSA
WENKER, DOBRE	38	F	W	RRZZZZUSA
CHAJE	.11	F	INFANT	RRZZZZUSA
ROSENBERG, ELIAS	30	M	LABR	RRZZZZUSA
LINE	27	F	W	RRZZZZUSA
LINE	3	F	CHILD	RRZZZZUSA
ISACK	.11	M	INFANT	RRZZZZUSA
JUNE	26	F	W	RRZZZZUSA
MARTHA	4	F	CHILD	RRZZZZUSA
ADOLF	.11	M	INFANT	RRZZZZUSA
SAMKOWIE, JOB.	18	F	SGL	RRZZZZUSA
SKLARSKY, ABRAM	15	M	LABR	RRZZZZUSA
BAPKA, BREINE	16	F	SGL	RRZZZZUSA
SCHAPIRO, TOBIAS	20	M	TLR	RRZZZZUSA
GRUENHOLZ, LEIB	20	M	TLR	RRZZZZUSA
MUELLER, ALBERT	43	M	MCHT	RRZZZZUSA
BERNSTEIN, PERETZ	17	M	DLR	RRZZZZUSA
LEWIN, SALOMON	20	M	DLR	RRZZZZUSA
ZAHN, CHARLOTTE	27	F	W	RRZZZZUSA
REGINA	.11	F	INFANT	RRZZZZUSA
SEHAT, CHAJIM	24	M	LABR	RRZZZZUSA
MOSES	26	M	LABR	RRZZZZUSA
LIEHTENSTEIN, ESTHER	17	F	SGL	RRZZZZUSA
ROLETSKY, SAMUEL	22	M	MCHT	RRZZZZUSA
SULEZKA, CATHA.	21	F	W	RRZZZZUSA
JOSEFA	.11	F	INFANT	RRZZZZUSA
KARTUN, LEA	25	F	W	RRZZZZUSA
ABRAH.	9	M	CHILD	RRZZZZUSA
DOBRE	.11	F	INFANT	RRZZZZUSA
JACOB	.01	M	INFANT	RRZZZZUSA
ALBANOWICZ, SIOTR.	18	M	LABR	RRZZZZUSA
HIRSCHOSITZ, EIDE	18	F	SGL	RRZZZZUSA
ROSENBAUM, PESCHE	21	F	W	RRZZZZUSA
MICHELEM	.11	M	INFANT	RRZZZZUSA
REBECCA	.11	F	INFANT	RRZZZZUSA
GITOWSKYE, ALBT.	17	F	SGL	RRZZZZUSA
GARBE, KALMAN	24	M	BKR	RRZZZZUSA
LEVY, JOSEF	21	M	MLR	RRZZZZUSA
GIRSCHOWITZ, ROSE	20	F	SGL	RRZZZZUSA
ALPERN, ARON	45	M	CGRMKR	RRZZZZUSA
HANDELSMANN, HANNE	29	F	W	RRZZZZUSA
ALTE	.08	F	INFANT	RRZZZZUSA
ZUBROWITZ, CHEINE	28	F	W	RRZZZZUSA
JETE	9	F	CHILD	RRZZZZUSA
ROSENKRANZ, ZIPE	23	F	W	RRZZZZUSA
JACOB	.11	M	INFANT	RRZZZZUSA
FRIEDMANN, CHANNE	23	F	W	RRZZZZUSA
JOSSEL	.11	M	INFANT	RRZZZZUSA
LEWIN, ISRAEL	43	M	DLR	RRZZZZUSA
CHANNE	40	F	W	RRZZZZUSA
SARA	16	F	CH	RRZZZZUSA
FANNY	15	F	CH	RRZZZZUSA
SCHEINE	6	F	CHILD	RRZZZZUSA
RACHEL	5	F	CHILD	RRZZZZUSA
BORIS	22	M	LABR	RRZZZZUSA
GOLDSTEIN, CHAIM	25	M	DLR	RRZZZZUSA
KRUKOWSKY, LEO	18	M	ENGR	RRZZZZUSA
DOBROCZYENA, MEYER	40	M	LABR	RRZZZZUSA

SHIP: QUEEN

FROM: LONDON
TO: NEW YORK
ARRIVED: 20 SEPTEMBER 1884

PASSENGER	AGE	SEX	OCCUPATION	PRV VIL DES
GOODSTONE, MORRIS	30	M	PNTR	PLZZZZUNK
WOYLAND, BERTHA	24	M	SVNT	PLZZZZNY
GOLD, WOLF	30	M	LABR	PLZZZZPHI
INESSER, RACH.	33	F	W	PLZZZZNY
LOUISE	11	F	CH	PLZZZZNY
BETSY	9	F	CHILD	PLZZZZNY
HARRY	7	M	CHILD	PLZZZZNY
SOPHIA	1	F	CHILD	PLZZZZNY
HARRIS, JANE	15	F	SVNT	PLZZZZNY
BONDER, JOSEPH	30	M	TLR	PLZZZZCH
SILVERMANN, JULIUS	27	M	CGRMKR	PLZZZZNY
LENYRITSKY, J.C.	23	M	LABR	PLZZZZNY
JILES, PAULINE	17	F	SVNT	PLZZZZNY
MINDELOWITZ, SIMON	21	M	TLR	RRZZZZNY
MENCH, EMANUEL	30	M	TLR	RRZZZZNY

SHIP: WERRA

FROM: BREMEN
TO: NEW YORK
ARRIVED: 20 SEPTEMBER 1884

PASSENGER	AGE	SEX	OCCUPATION	PRV VIL DES
STEBACTZKY, U	54	M	GEN	RRZZZZUSA
SACHO, REBECCA	19	F	UNKNOWN	RRZZZZUSA
EMMA	.10	F	INFANT	RRZZZZUSA
DOROTHEA	.10	F	INFANT	RRZZZZUSA
LEVIN, ESTER	22	F	UNKNOWN	RRZZZZUSA

PASSENGER	AGE	SEX	OCCUPATION	PV RIVL	DES
HOLLAND, AD.	23	M	LABR	RRZZZZ	USA
LEA	7	F	CHILD	RRZZZZ	USA
ZISEL	18	M	LABR	RRZZZZ	USA
KUSZEWSKA, NATHALIA	27	F	UNKNOWN	RRZZZZ	USA
MARIANNA	00	F	UNKNOWN	RRZZZZ	USA

SHIP: ALASKA

FROM: LIVERPOOL AND QUEENSTOWN
TO: NEW YORK
ARRIVED: 22 SEPTEMBER 1884

PASSENGER	AGE	SEX	OCCUPATION	PV RIVL	DES
JOSEPHTHAL, HEWCICH	17	M	LABR	PLZZZZ	USA

SHIP: RUGIA

FROM: HAMBURG
TO: NEW YORK
ARRIVED: 22 SEPTEMBER 1884

PASSENGER	AGE	SEX	OCCUPATION	PV RIVL	DES
GOLDBAUM, HERRSCH	50	M	DLR	RRZZZZ	USA
FEIGE	42	F	W	RRZZZZ	USA
SCHUKSMITH, JOSNA	32	M	SHMK	RRZZZZ	USA
GRESINGER, FRIEDE	48	M	SHMK	RRZZZZ	USA
EMANUEL	9	M	CHILD	RRZZZZ	USA
JOSNOWITZ, BERTHA	21	F	SGL	RRZZZZ	USA
MALKES, TONI	46	F	W	RRZZZZ	USA
JUDES	18	F	CH	RRZZZZ	USA
MEYER	9	M	CHILD	RRZZZZ	USA
BASCHE	8	F	CHILD	RRZZZZ	USA
SOMMER, ESTHER	49	F	W	RRZZZZ	USA
BAUMGART, SAMUEL	46	M	LABR	RRZZZZ	USA
JEANNET	29	M	LABR	RRZZZZ	USA
SOMMER, MORITZ	17	M	LABR	RRZZZZ	USA
BAUMGARTEN, JOSEPH	21	M	LABR	RRZZZZ	USA
KEMPNER, LEON	14	M	SCH	RRZZZZ	USA
EICHSTADT, WILH.	27	M	TNR	RRZZZZ	USA
BILAWOSKY, ABRAHAM	17	M	LABR	RRZZZZ	USA
KREISSMANN, CIPE	33	F	W	RRZZZZ	USA
REBECCA	8	F	CHILD	RRZZZZ	USA
RACHEL	6	F	CHILD	RRZZZZ	USA
BERTHA	4	F	CHILD	RRZZZZ	USA
JECHUL	3	M	CHILD	RRZZZZ	USA
LOWENSTEIN, HERRM.	47	M	LABR	RRZZZZ	USA
THERESE	35	F	W	RRZZZZ	USA
NETTI	9	F	CHILD	RRZZZZ	USA
JOSEPPINE	6	F	CHILD	RRZZZZ	USA
KARTUN, REBECCA	32	F	W	RRZZZZ	USA
MORDCHE	7	M	CHILD	RRZZZZ	USA
BUFF, LEIB	26	M	S	RRZZZZ	USA
BOES, HERM.	22	M	S	RRZZZZ	USA
FRIDA	21	F	W	RRZZZZ	USA
JOB.	4	M	CHILD	RRZZZZ	USA
LEWINSKY, NOCHEM	8	M	CHILD	RRZZZZ	USA
WINNER, DAUBE	23	M	SGL	RRZZZZ	USA
NAIGOFF, EVA	22	F	W	RRZZZZ	USA
DINA	.09	F	INFANT	RRZZZZ	USA
HEIMANN, SIMON	19	M	LABR	RRZZZZ	USA
BERKOWITZ, DAVID	20	M	LABR	RRZZZZ	USA
GUDINSKY, MACZE	36	F	W	RRZZZZ	USA
JOSSEL	9	M	CHILD	RRZZZZ	USA
CHAJE	4	F	CHILD	RRZZZZ	USA
SEGAL, KEITE	26	F	W	RRZZZZ	USA
SARA	5	F	CHILD	RRZZZZ	USA
ESTHER	.11	F	INFANT	RRZZZZ	USA
FEIGE	.01	F	INFANT	RRZZZZ	USA
SEGALOWITZ, LEA	45	F	W	RRZZZZ	USA
SARA	8	F	CHILD	RRZZZZ	USA
BUKEWITZ, MINNA	15	F	SGL	RRZZZZ	USA
BUSCHKES, FEIWEL	9	M	CHILD	RRZZZZ	USA
CHAIE	8	M	CHILD	RRZZZZ	USA
SCHUSTER, ISSER	40	M	LABR	RRZZZZ	USA
RAPHAEL	9	M	CHILD	RRZZZZ	USA
POTATNIK, SARA	28	F	SGL	RRZZZZ	USA
BRANDY, MOSES	53	M	LABR	RRZZZZ	USA
SELDE	41	F	W	RRZZZZ	USA
RIWE	18	F	CH	RRZZZZ	USA
SARA	8	F	CHILD	RRZZZZ	USA
MOSES	6	M	CHILD	RRZZZZ	USA
SCHONMANN, ALTE	9	F	CHILD	RRZZZZ	USA
BLOCK, LEA	50	F	W	RRZZZZ	USA
CHAIE	13	F	CH	RRZZZZ	USA
HODES	8	F	CHILD	RRZZZZ	USA
WEINBERG, FEIWEL	20	M	LABR	RRZZZZ	USA
ROSENBLUM, BERTHA	25	F	SGL	RRZZZZ	USA
SCHAPIRA, SCHEINE	23	F	W	RRZZZZ	USA
SCHEINE	4	F	CHILD	RRZZZZ	USA

SHIP: SERVIA

FROM: LIVERPOOL
TO: NEW YORK
ARRIVED: 22 SEPTEMBER 1884

PASSENGER	AGE	SEX	OCCUPATION	PV RIVL	DES
NEFTEL, U-MR	53	M	SGN	RRZZZZ	USA
U-MRS	50	F	W	RRZZZZ	USA
COOK, E.MISS	20	F	SVNT	RRZZZZ	USA
GULCKE, IT.MR	58	M	MD	RRZZZZ	USA
DMAMOW, H.MR	27	M	MCHT	RRZZZZ	USA
KAWSKY, DE-PAUL-MR	31	M	GENT	RRZZZZ	USA

SHIP: STATE OF GEORGIA

FROM: GLASGOW AND LARNE
TO: NEW YORK
ARRIVED: 23 SEPTEMBER 1884

PASSENGER	AGE	SEX	OCCUPATION	PV RIVL	DES
SEMANDOCHISK, ANNA	40	F	W	PLZZZZ	NY
ANNA	8	F	CHILD	PLZZZZ	NY
ROSA	5	F	CHILD	PLZZZZ	NY
CRIADA, JANKO	23	M	LABR	PLZZZZ	NY
RIVCBAK, ACTOM	20	M	LABR	PLZZZZ	NY
JANCA	19	M	LABR	PLZZZZ	NY
POSEWANSKY, CHANNE	52	F	W	PLZZZZ	NY
ESTHER	17	F	SVNT	PLZZZZ	NY

SHIP: CIRCASSIA

FROM: GLASGOW AND MOVILLE
TO: NEW YORK
ARRIVED: 24 SEPTEMBER 1884

PASSENGER	AGE	SEX	OCCUPATION	PV RIVL	DES
SOCHOR, GABRIEL	32	M	LABR	RRZZZZ	USA
JOSEPH	8	M	CHILD	RRZZZZ	USA
JACHUA	6	F	CHILD	RRZZZZ	USA

PASSENGER	AGE	SEX	OCCUPATION	PRIVL	DES
ETHEL	00	F	INF	RRZZZZ	USA
NORRGARG, ERICK	24	M	LABR	RRZZZZ	UNK
BLUSE, JOHANN	21	M	LABR	RRZZZZ	UNK
MAMCLUND, ISRAEL	24	M	LABR	RRZZZZ	UNK
MATTERS, MATTS	21	M	LABR	RRZZZZ	UNK
NYBACK, CHRISHAN	29	M	LABR	RRZZZZ	UNK
OLSSON, JOHAN	20	M	LABR	RRZZZZ	USA
SILBERFIELD, ISRAEL	18	M	DLR	RRZZZZ	USA
KROHMANN, JOSEF	23	M	TLR	RRZZZZ	USA
SOHALL, MOSES	18	M	SHMK	RRZZZZ	USA
BLUMBIN, BERKER	20	M	PRNTR	RRZZZZ	USA
BARODARKIN, JACOB	24	M	MACH	RRZZZZ	USA
HANNA	27	F	W	RRZZZZ	USA
KLAPST, ARON	26	M	GLVR	RRZZZZ	USA
ABRAHAM	14	M	GLVR	RRZZZZ	USA
HEINR.	4	M	CHILD	RRZZZZ	USA
SARA	1	F	CHILD	RRZZZZ	USA
WNRUH, AUG.	16	M	JNR	RRZZZZ	USA
BOSE, ANDREAS	33	M	LLD	RRZZZZ	USA
HELENE	34	F	W	RRZZZZ	USA
HEINR	5	M	CHILD	RRZZZZ	USA
PETER	4	M	CHILD	RRZZZZ	USA
HELENE	2	F	CHILD	RRZZZZ	USA
GOLDBATH, BIERKA	30	F	NN	RRZZZZ	USA
JETTE	7	F	CHILD	RRZZZZ	USA
LENE	8	F	CHILD	RRZZZZ	USA
MARIA	2	F	CHILD	RRZZZZ	USA
LENA	.03	F	INFANT	RRZZZZ	USA
MARKMEIER, BASCHE	18	F	NN	RRZZZZ	USA
BORANSKY, LINA	28	F	NN	RRZZZZ	USA

SHIP: SAINT GERMAIN

FROM: HAVRE
TO: NEW YORK
ARRIVED: 24 SEPTEMBER 1884

PASSENGER	AGE	SEX	OCCUPATION	PRIVL	DES
MARKA, SPITZ	21	M	TLR	RRZZZZ	UNK

SHIP: CALAND

FROM: ROTTERDAM
TO: NEW YORK
ARRIVED: 25 SEPTEMBER 1884

PASSENGER	AGE	SEX	OCCUPATION	PRIVL	DES
REHHER, CARL	20	M	TLR	RRZZZZ	USA
NILSCH, AUGUST	42	M	STCTR	RRAEFL	USA
PAUL	17	M	STCTR	RRAEFL	USA

SHIP: DONAU

FROM: BREMEN
TO: NEW YORK
ARRIVED: 25 SEPTEMBER 1884

PASSENGER	AGE	SEX	OCCUPATION	PRIVL	DES
UNRUH, BENJ.	58	M	FARMER	RRZZZZ	USA
LENE	44	F	W	RRZZZZ	USA
ELISAB.	18	F	CH	RRZZZZ	USA
SUSANNE	00	F	CH	RRZZZZ	USA
MARIA	10	F	CH	RRZZZZ	USA
JUSTINE	8	F	CHILD	RRZZZZ	USA
CORNELIUS	6	M	CHILD	RRZZZZ	USA
CATH.	2	F	CHILD	RRZZZZ	USA
BENJAMIN	.09	M	INFANT	RRZZZZ	USA
NEUMANN, PETER	53	M	FARMER	RRZZZZ	USA
MARG.	50	F	W	RRZZZZ	USA
GERHARD	16	M	CH	RRZZZZ	USA
MARG.	10	F	CH	RRZZZZ	USA
PETER	4	M	CHILD	RRZZZZ	USA
BULLER, DAVID	44	M	LABR	RRZZZZ	USA
SARA	39	F	W	RRZZZZ	USA
VOGT, CATH.	74	F	NN	RRZZZZ	USA
BULLER, CATH.	16	F	CH	RRZZZZ	USA
DAVID	11	M	CH	RRZZZZ	USA
PETER	6	M	CHILD	RRZZZZ	USA

SHIP: POLARIA

FROM: HAMBURG
TO: NEW YORK
ARRIVED: 25 SEPTEMBER 1884

PASSENGER	AGE	SEX	OCCUPATION	PRIVL	DES
VONBRENNER, A.BRAND	20	M	CGRMKR	RRZZZZ	NY
IDA	24	F	W	RRZZZZ	NY
SAMUEL	.07	M	INFANT	RRZZZZ	NY
PASCHILSKY, BELE	24	F	WO	RRZZZZ	NY
ARONOWITZ, CHAIE-R.	28	F	WO	RRZZZZ	NY
FREIDE	7	F	CHILD	RRZZZZ	NY
CHASKEL, HERZMANN	15	M	LABR	RRZZZZ	NY
ISRALEIK, JUD.	28	M	TLR	RRZZZZ	NY
GELART, PEASCH	42	M	TLR	RRZZZZ	NY
MUELLER, HELENE	18	F	SGL	PLZZZZ	NY
DAVIDSOHN, MARIA	19	F	SGL	RRZZZZ	NY
BARTELS, SAMUEL	32	M	LABR	RRZZZZ	NY
SCHNEIDER, ADOLF	24	M	JNR	RRZZZZ	NY
CWIEFACH, ALTER	30	M	LABR	PLZZZZ	NY
ABRAHAM	28	M	LABR	PLZZZZ	NY
LASSER, SALOMON	31	M	LABR	RRZZZZ	NY
HANNA	23	F	W	RRZZZZ	NY
LINA	.05	F	INFANT	RRZZZZ	NY
KAPLAN, CHANE	3	F	CHILD	RRZZZZ	NY
MAX	.04	M	INFANT	RRZZZZ	NY
BOSE, GOSSEL	20	M	LABR	RRZZZZ	NY
TELESCHA, PINS.	26	M	TLR	RRZZZZ	NY
KAEMLER, MICHEL	22	M	TRDSMN	RRZZZZ	NY
LEWIN, NASSEN	25	M	TRDSMN	RRZZZZ	NY
BAGATYTYS, MACI	30	M	LABR	RRZZZZ	PA
EMILIE	28	F	W	RRZZZZ	PA
MICHAEL	5	M	CHILD	RRZZZZ	PA
MEYERWITZ, MAGKEL	18	M	LABR	RRZZZZ	IL
SCHNEIDEROWITZ, BEREL	21	M	LABR	RRZZZZ	NY
BASKIN, JANKEL	19	M	LABR	RRZZZZ	OH
MENDEL	17	M	LABR	RRZZZZ	OH
STARKENTHIN, BAREL	32	M	TLR	RRZZZZ	NY
RIEBCUS, ABRAH.	16	M	MCHT	RRZZZZ	NY
MELJER, BEILE	32	F	WO	RRZZZZ	UNK
VILEIMANN, ABR.	25	M	TDR	RRZZZZ	UNK
MARIANE	20	F	W	RRZZZZ	UNK
BAKAL, SCHLOME	33	M	JNR	RRZZZZ	NY
SCHWARZBERG, MEYER	22	M	TRDSMN	RRZZZZ	NY
GEDALJE	19	M	TRDSMN	RRZZZZ	NY
GINSBERG, FEIGE	22	F	WO	RRZZZZ	NY
ZIREL	.11	F	INFANT	RRZZZZ	NY
TAUBE	.02	F	INFANT	RRZZZZ	NY
SCHRINKE, MART.	33	M	LABR	RRZZZZ	NY
LOUISE	29	F	W	RRZZZZ	UNK
JOHANN	4	M	CHILD	RRZZZZ	UNK
MARIA	.04	F	INFANT	RRZZZZ	UNK
LIPSCHEITZ, CHAIM	22	M	SMH	RRZZZZ	NY
HELENE	32	F	W	RRZZZZ	NY

PASSENGER	AGE	SEX	OCCUPATION	PRV VIL	DES
WIFSCH, DAVID	19	M	LKSH	RRZZZZ	NY
SARAH	22	F	W	RRZZZZ	NY
JUDEL--, F-------	00	F	SGL	RRZZZZ	NY
CHAIM	17	F	SGL	RRZZZZ	NY

SHIP: ELBE

FROM: BREMEN
TO: NEW YORK
ARRIVED: 27 SEPTEMBER 1884

PASSENGER	AGE	SEX	OCCUPATION	PRV VIL	DES
HOFFRICHTER, AUGUSTE	39	F	NN	RRZZZZ	USA
MARIE	36	F	NN	RRZZZZ	USA
PAULINE	6	F	CHILD	RRZZZZ	USA
HAAS, GEORG	22	M	FARMER	RRZZZZ	USA
MASSHALTER, DAVID	21	M	FARMER	RRZZZZ	USA
HEIBEL, PHILIPP	21	M	LABR	RRZZZZ	USA
FUST, GEORG	21	M	LABR	RRZZZZ	USA
DORLINGER, GOTTL.	21	M	LABR	RRZZZZ	USA
PENZ, CHRIST.	21	M	LABR	RRZZZZ	USA
MARTEL, GEORG	21	M	LABR	RRZZZZ	USA
HIEB, WILH.	21	M	LABR	RRZZZZ	USA
HAAS, JOHANN	21	M	LABR	RRZZZZ	USA
GROSZ, JACOB	30	M	FARMER	RRZZZZ	USA
CAROLINE	30	F	NN	RRZZZZ	USA
CAROLINE	25	F	NN	RRZZZZ	USA
JACOB	4	M	CHILD	RRZZZZ	USA
CATHAR.	3	F	CHILD	RRZZZZ	USA
CHRISTIAN	.11	M	INFANT	RRZZZZ	USA
LATNER, JACOB	20	M	FARMER	RRZZZZ	USA
ROSINA	28	F	NN	RRZZZZ	USA
CATHARINE	2	F	CHILD	RRZZZZ	USA
ROSINA	.04	F	INFANT	RRZZZZ	USA
KESSLER, CHRISTIAN	28	M	FARMER	RRZZZZ	USA
CHRISTINE	24	F	NN	RRZZZZ	USA
OP, DAWID	43	M	FARMER	RRZZZZ	USA
CATH.	37	F	NN	RRZZZZ	USA
JACOB	11	M	CH	RRZZZZ	USA
DANIEL	10	M	CH	RRZZZZ	USA
JOHANN	8	M	CHILD	RRZZZZ	USA
CATHARINE	6	F	CHILD	RRZZZZ	USA
CHRISTIAN	2	M	CHILD	RRZZZZ	USA
ROSINA	.06	F	INFANT	RRZZZZ	USA
NIES, JOHANN	40	M	FARMER	RRZZZZ	USA
BARB.	38	F	NN	RRZZZZ	USA
JACOB	16	M	FARMER	RRZZZZ	USA
ROSINA	11	F	CH	RRZZZZ	USA
BARBARA	9	F	CHILD	RRZZZZ	USA
CAROLINA	5	F	CHILD	RRZZZZ	USA
EVA	3	F	CHILD	RRZZZZ	USA
CHRISTIANE	1	F	CHILD	RRZZZZ	USA
-I--DER, JOHANN	00	M	FARMER	RRZZZZ	USA
FRIEDERIKE	22	F	NN	RRZZZZ	USA
JOHANN	1	M	CHILD	RRZZZZ	USA
FUCHS, JACOB	25	M	FARMER	RRZZZZ	USA
MAGDALENE	23	F	NN	RRZZZZ	USA
JACOB	3	M	CHILD	RRZZZZ	USA
CHRISTINE	1	F	CHILD	RRZZZZ	USA
SCHUMACHER, FRIEDRICH	26	M	LABR	RRZZZZ	USA
BARBARA	23	F	NN	RRZZZZ	USA
REGINA	.02	F	INFANT	RRZZZZ	USA
BENDER, MICHAEL	34	M	FARMER	RRZZZZ	USA
MAGDALENE	32	F	NN	RRZZZZ	USA
FRIEDRICH	6	M	CHILD	RRZZZZ	USA
MICHAEL	4	M	CHILD	RRZZZZ	USA
JACOB	3	M	CHILD	RRZZZZ	USA
JOHANN	1	M	CHILD	RRZZZZ	USA
VOEGELE, JOHANN	35	M	FARMER	RRZZZZ	USA
FRIEDERIKE	23	F	NN	RRZZZZ	USA
FRIEDERIKE	4	F	CHILD	RRZZZZ	USA
JOHANN	8	M	CHILD	RRZZZZ	USA
ROSINE	6	F	CHILD	RRZZZZ	USA
FRIEDRICH	2	M	CHILD	RRZZZZ	USA
CHRISTIAN	.06	M	INFANT	RRZZZZ	USA
SCHAFER, JOHANNES	24	M	FARMER	RRZZZZ	USA
ROSINE	20	F	NN	RRZZZZ	USA
CHRIST.	.10	M	INFANT	RRZZZZ	USA
KEIM, MARGARETHE	40	F	NN	RRZZZZ	USA
CHRISTIAN	18	M	LABR	RRZZZZ	USA
JACOB	11	M	CH	RRZZZZ	USA
JOHANN	8	M	CHILD	RRZZZZ	USA
WILLY	5	M	CHILD	RRZZZZ	USA
FRIEDERIKE	7	F	CHILD	RRZZZZ	USA
CHRISTOF	2	M	CHILD	RRZZZZ	USA
WEISFER, GOTTLIEB	45	M	FARMER	RRZZZZ	USA
CATHARINE	39	F	NN	RRZZZZ	USA
GOTTLIEB	19	M	FARMER	RRZZZZ	USA
JACOB	17	M	FARMER	RRZZZZ	USA
JOHANN	14	M	CH	RRZZZZ	USA
CHRISTOF	11	M	CH	RRZZZZ	USA
CATHARINA	10	F	CH	RRZZZZ	USA
CHRISTIAN	8	M	CHILD	RRZZZZ	USA
WEISFNER, FRIEDRICH	5	M	CHILD	RRZZZZ	USA
ROSINA	2	F	CHILD	RRZZZZ	USA
WILHELM	.08	M	INFANT	RRZZZZ	USA
LOB, DANIEL	43	M	FARMER	RRZZZZ	USA
MAGDALENE	41	F	NN	RRZZZZ	USA
DANIEL	15	M	LABR	RRZZZZ	USA
MAGDALENE	13	F	CH	RRZZZZ	USA
JOHANN	8	M	CHILD	RRZZZZ	USA
ROSINA	4	F	CHILD	RRZZZZ	USA
CHRISTIAN	2	M	CHILD	RRZZZZ	USA
HOP, REGINE	65	F	FARMER	RRZZZZ	USA
MORIZ, JACOB	36	M	NN	RRZZZZ	USA
CATH.	34	F	NN	RRZZZZ	USA
CATH.	13	F	CH	RRZZZZ	USA
JACOB	11	M	CH	RRZZZZ	USA
FRIEDRICH	10	M	CH	RRZZZZ	USA
JOHANN	5	M	CHILD	RRZZZZ	USA
PHILIPP	3	M	CHILD	RRZZZZ	USA
CARL	.11	M	INFANT	RRZZZZ	USA
KAREL, CHRIST.	34	M	FARMER	RRZZZZ	USA
ELISABETH	00	F	NN	RRZZZZ	USA
CHRISTIAN	10	M	CH	RRZZZZ	USA
JACOB	9	M	CHILD	RRZZZZ	USA
JOHANN	7	M	CHILD	RRZZZZ	USA
MAGDALENE	3	F	CHILD	RRZZZZ	USA
CHRISTIAN	1	M	CHILD	RRZZZZ	USA
LISABETH	.06	F	INFANT	RRZZZZ	USA
MEYER, CHRISTIAN	24	M	FARMER	RRZZZZ	USA
CATHARINE	24	F	NN	RRZZZZ	USA
BLOMHART, CHRISTIAN	00	M	FARMER	RRZZZZ	USA
MAGDALENE	38	F	NN	RRZZZZ	USA
CATHARINE	22	F	NN	RRZZZZ	USA
JACOB	18	M	FARMER	RRZZZZ	USA
FRIEDRICH	15	M	CH	RRZZZZ	USA
JACOB	5	M	CHILD	RRZZZZ	USA
MARIA	2	F	CHILD	RRZZZZ	USA
BIEBER, JACOB	48	M	LABR	RRZZZZ	USA
CHRISTIANE	42	F	NN	RRZZZZ	USA
JACOB	00	M	FARMER	RRZZZZ	USA
JOHANN	15	M	NN	RRZZZZ	USA
HEINRICH	6	M	CHILD	RRZZZZ	USA
FRIEDRICH	4	M	CHILD	RRZZZZ	USA
CHRISTIAN	2	M	CHILD	RRZZZZ	USA
MAGDALENE	19	F	CH	RRZZZZ	USA
ROSINE	12	F	CH	RRZZZZ	USA
BARBARA	10	F	CH	RRZZZZ	USA
CAROLINE	8	F	CHILD	RRZZZZ	USA
JACOBER, FRIEDRICH	32	M	FARMER	RRZZZZ	USA
CHRISTIANE	31	F	NN	RRZZZZ	USA
FRIEDRICH	8	M	CHILD	RRZZZZ	USA
JACOB	6	M	CHILD	RRZZZZ	USA
MAGDALENE	4	F	CHILD	RRZZZZ	USA
CHRISTIAN	2	M	CHILD	RRZZZZ	USA

PASSENGER	AGE	SEX	OCCUPATION	PV RIVL	DES
LISABETTA	.09	F	INFANT	RRZZZZ	USA
SCHRITZ, JOHANN	34	M	FARMER	RRZZZZ	USA
CHRISTINE	26	F	NN	RRZZZZ	USA
JOHANN	8	M	CHILD	RRZZZZ	USA
ROSINE	6	F	CHILD	RRZZZZ	USA
CARL	4	M	CHILD	RRZZZZ	USA
GEIGLE, JACOB	35	M	FARMER	RRZZZZ	USA
CATHAR.	33	F	NN	RRZZZZ	USA
ADAM	5	M	CHILD	RRZZZZ	USA
CATHARINE	3	F	CHILD	RRZZZZ	USA
JOHANNE	.11	F	INFANT	RRZZZZ	USA
SIELER, MAGDALENE	65	F	NN	RRZZZZ	USA
LENNO, ADAM	23	M	FARMER	RRZZZZ	USA
CHRISTINE	23	F	NN	RRZZZZ	USA
KLEIM, JACOB	23	M	FARMER	RRZZZZ	USA
CHRISTINE	24	F	NN	RRZZZZ	USA
CATHARINE	4	F	CHILD	RRZZZZ	USA
JACOB	2	M	CHILD	RRZZZZ	USA
WITTMEIER, SIMON	27	M	FARMER	RRZZZZ	USA
CHRISTINE	26	F	NN	RRZZZZ	USA
SIMON	4	M	CHILD	RRZZZZ	USA
FRIEDRICH	.06	M	INFANT	RRZZZZ	USA
DUDACEH, KATHARINE	00	F	INF	RR****	USA
MAIER, CHRISTIAN	00	M	INF	RR****	USA

SHIP: CITY OF BERLIN

FROM: LIVERPOOL AND QUEENSTOWN
TO: NEW YORK
ARRIVED: 29 SEPTEMBER 1884

PASSENGER	AGE	SEX	OCCUPATION	PV RIVL	DES
BLOCHALF, BERNH	23	M	LABR	RRADAX	NY
KOZEMNSKI, U-MR	21	M	LABR	PLZZZZ	NY
ESTHEN	18	F	W	PLZZZZ	NY
MAZIAS, S.S.	26	M	LABR	RRZZZZ	NY

SHIP: CITY OF ROME

FROM: LIVERPOOL AND QUEENSTOWN
TO: NEW YORK
ARRIVED: 29 SEPTEMBER 1884

PASSENGER	AGE	SEX	OCCUPATION	PV RIVL	DES
SWALA, J.	22	M	LABR	PLZZZZ	NY
HARRIS, LAZARUS	44	M	GENT	PLZZZZ	NY
SCHAFFAN, JOHANN	31	M	PREST	PLZZZZ	NY

SHIP: OREGON

FROM: LIVERPOOL AND QUEENSTOWN
TO: NEW YORK
ARRIVED: 29 SEPTEMBER 1884

PASSENGER	AGE	SEX	OCCUPATION	PV RIVL	DES
YAARA, JOHN	38	M	LABR	FNZZZZ	USA
AHOLA, EMANUEL	27	M	LABR	FNZZZZ	USA
LYNDOYS, JOHN	28	M	SEMN	FNZZZZ	USA
MAUKINAN, YISIK	43	M	SEMN	FNZZZZ	USA
YAKKILA, YAAKOF	29	M	SEMN	FNZZZZ	USA
MISILA, JABOT	40	M	SEMN	FNZZZZ	USA
KIOVIAHO, KARL	25	M	LABR	FNZZZZ	USA
KALLINKI, JOHAN	42	M	LABR	FNZZZZ	USA
VISAGA, KARL	35	M	LABR	FNZZZZ	USA
OJOLA, JACOB	29	M	LABR	FNZZZZ	USA
FILFPOLA, MATTS	24	M	LABR	FNZZZZ	USA
OJALA, JOHAN	18	M	LABR	FNZZZZ	USA
JOHAN-G.	20	M	LABR	FNZZZZ	USA
LATHI, JOHAN	22	M	LABR	FNZZZZ	USA
LETHMAKI, JOHN-F.	20	M	LABR	FNZZZZ	USA
KALLIKOSKI, JOHN-J.	40	M	LABR	FNZZZZ	USA
KIVIALIC, MATHI	21	M	LABR	FNZZZZ	USA
WINANS, D.KAF.	24	M	GENT	RRZZZZ	USA

SHIP: MORAVIA

FROM: HAMBURG
TO: NEW YORK
ARRIVED: 30 SEPTEMBER 1884

PASSENGER	AGE	SEX	OCCUPATION	PV RIVL	DES
STRUMBIGLOWSKY, EGGE	20	F	W	RRAHUV	USA
EBEL, PHILIPP	31	M	FARMER	RRZZZZ	USA
ELISABETH	22	F	W	RRZZZZ	USA
ELISABETH	2	F	CHILD	RRZZZZ	USA
SOPHIE	.06	F	INFANT	RRZZZZ	USA
KOENIG, FRANZ	36	M	FARMER	RRZZZZ	USA
ROSINE	31	F	W	RRZZZZ	USA
JOHE.	8	M	CHILD	RRZZZZ	USA
JACOB	6	M	CHILD	RRZZZZ	USA
ROSINE	2	F	CHILD	RRZZZZ	USA
EMILIE	.03	F	INFANT	RRZZZZ	USA
SCHERER, LUDWIG	32	M	FARMER	RRZZZZ	USA
ELISABETH	27	F	W	RRZZZZ	USA
CATHA.	3	F	CHILD	RRZZZZ	USA
CHRIST.	2	F	CHILD	RRZZZZ	USA
MARKOFSKI, JACOBUS	33	M	LABR	RRAHZS	USA
BONKOWSKY, JOSEPH	20	M	MLR	RRACON	USA
WEIMANN, LEIB	20	M	LABR	RRZZZZ	USA
WOLF, ISAAC	29	M	TCHR	RRZZZZ	USA
JETTE	27	F	W	RRZZZZ	USA
MINNA	.11	F	INFANT	RRZZZZ	USA
ABRAHAM	.01	M	INFANT	RRZZZZ	USA
LUKAT, BERTHA	18	F	SGL	RRZZZZ	USA
JOHE.	15	F	SGL	RRZZZZ	USA
MILLMANN, BETTI	24	F	SGL	RRAFVG	USA
WODORISKA, ELIAS	9	F	CHILD	RRAFVG	USA
HURWITZ, LINE	20	F	SGL	RRAHSW	USA
ALMAN, LEVIN	17	M	LABR	RRZZZZ	USA
GETZ, SARA	29	F	W	RRZZZZ	USA
FREIDE	7	F	CHILD	RRZZZZ	USA
ISAAC	.09	F	INFANT	RRZZZZ	USA
REIF, MENDEL	31	M	MSN	RRAHTA	USA
GETZ, MANNE	5	F	CHILD	RRAHTA	USA
KOTWICKI, MICHAL	57	M	FARMER	RRZZZZ	USA
MACHLIN, MORCHY	53	M	LABR	RRZZZZ	USA
MATZNER, ALVIS	29	M	JNR	RRZZZZ	USA

SHIP: ETHIOPIA

FROM: GLASGOW AND MOVILLE
TO: NEW YORK
ARRIVED: 02 OCTOBER 1884

PASSENGER	AGE	SEX	OCCUPATION	PV RIVL	DES
STERN, GEO	19	M	PRNTR	RRAEFL	USA
JOHNKE, HARSINS	35	M	PDLR	RRAEFL	USA
SCHNEIDER, GEORG	30	M	JNR	RRZZZZ	USA
MOSEHOWETZ, CLARK	24	M	UNKNOWN	PLZZZZ	USA
SCAOWSKY, SALAMON	35	M	TLR	PLAEFL	USA

PASSENGER	AGE	SEX	OCCUPATION	PRV	VIL	DES

SHIP: LESSING

FROM: HAMBURG
TO: NEW YORK
ARRIVED: 02 OCTOBER 1884

PASSENGER	AGE	SEX	OCCUPATION	PRVVILDES
BAUER, DAVID	25	M	TLR	RRZZZZUSA
ALEXANDER, MARY	15	F	SGL	RRAHTFUSA
GUTFREUND, GUSTAV	17	M	MCHT	RRACONUSA
BIKAWITZKI, RISCHE	35	F	W	RRZZZZUSA
MORITZ	9	M	CHILD	RRZZZZUSA
SARA	9	F	CHILD	RRZZZZUSA
WISCHLATSCHI, JOH.	38	M	LABR	RRAHZSUSA
MARGA.	31	F	W	RRAHZSUSA
ANTKOWIAK, MARIE	24	F	W	RRAHZSUSA
ROSALIE	.11	F	INFANT	RRAHZSUSA
FISCHMANN, LEOPOLD	20	M	APTC	RRAHWQUSA
FINKELPORT, JOSEF	20	M	FARMER	RRAHWQUSA
KANTOR, CHAIN	24	M	DLR	RRAHTFUSA
CHAJE	22	F	W	RRAHTFUSA
SINGERMANN, MOSES	41	M	UNKNOWN	RRZZZZUSA
ELKE	34	F	W	RRZZZZUSA
EPHRAIM	18	M	S	RRZZZZUSA
ALBERT	9	M	CHILD	RRZZZZUSA
ISAAC	7	M	CHILD	RRZZZZUSA
SIMON	3	M	CHILD	RRZZZZUSA
WULF	.11	M	INFANT	RRZZZZUSA
ABRAHAM	35	M	DLR	RRZZZZUSA
ABRAMS, SCHOLEM	21	M	DLR	RRZZZZUSA
BITSCHER, JACOB	20	M	TNMK	RRAHQUUSA
JAFEC, ELIAS	26	M	BCHR	RRZZZZUSA
RAFFELOWITZ, MARY	21	F	SGL	RRAHQUUSA
LADER, ELIAS	57	M	DLR	RRZZZZUSA
CHANE	8	F	CHILD	RRZZZZUSA
ROTELIENUS, JONAS	48	M	LABR	RRAHSWUSA
BLUMENTHAL, ISRAEL	14	M	LABR	RRAHTFUSA
PANKOWSKA, JOSEFA	30	F	SGL	RRZZZZUSA
TUZIKESWIES, THEOPHILE	24	M	LABR	RRZZZZUSA
MANSCHAGEN, GREGOR	25	M	LABR	RRAFZDUSA
DASCHKOWSKI, WLADISL.	42	M	LABR	RRAFZDUSA
HELENE	18	F	D	RRAFZDUSA
SWERLICHOWSKY, CARL	21	M	LABR	RRAFZDUSA
ARKIN, ABRAM	18	M	LABR	RRZZZZUSA
GERSON, CHAIM	20	M	LABR	RRZZZZUSA
LIPSCHITZ, NACHMANN	18	M	LABR	RRAFVGUSA
BARKE, ALEXANDER	32	M	LABR	RRAHQUUSA
NONTROWITZ, PIOTER	21	M	LABR	RRAHQUUSA
WIETKEWITZ, ADOLF	21	M	LABR	RRAHQUUSA
BERKOWSKY, SALOMON	20	M	LABR	RRAHZSUSA

SHIP: BELGENLAND

FROM: ANTWERP
TO: NEW YORK
ARRIVED: 04 OCTOBER 1884

PASSENGER	AGE	SEX	OCCUPATION	PRVVILDES
BARB, VICT.	25	M	LABR	PLZZZZUNK
WYTATERISH, JOH.	30	M	LABR	PLZZZZUNK
M.	2	M	CHILD	PLZZZZUNK
FR.	7	F	CHILD	PLZZZZUNK
ROMA	7	F	CHILD	PLZZZZUNK
KLOSOWSKI, MICH.	23	M	LABR	RRZZZZUNK
AN.	24	F	LABR	RRZZZZUNK
FITZLOWSKA, ED.	00	F	HSWF	RRZZZZPHI
JUCHOVOSKI, EM.	8	F	CHILD	RRZZZZPHI
BERGMANN, DAN	22	M	GLSMKR	RRZZZZCOU
FRONCIG, H.	20	M	SMH	RRZZZZMIL

SHIP: FULDA

FROM: BREMEN
TO: NEW YORK
ARRIVED: 04 OCTOBER 1884

PASSENGER	AGE	SEX	OCCUPATION	PRVVILDES
BIER, PHILIPP	38	M	LABR	RRZZZZUSA
ANNA	35	F	UNKNOWN	RRZZZZUSA
LOUISE	14	F	CH	RRZZZZUSA
HEINRICH	11	M	LABR	RRZZZZUSA
FRIEDRICH	9	M	CHILD	RRZZZZUSA
ALEXANDER	5	M	CHILD	RRZZZZUSA
JOHANNES	2	M	CHILD	RRZZZZUSA
DAVID	.06	M	INFANT	RRZZZZUSA
ABRAHAMS, ELISABETH	20	F	UNKNOWN	RRZZZZUSA
HEINRICH	.03	M	INFANT	RRZZZZUSA
SEILER, CATHA.	24	F	UNKNOWN	RRZZZZUSA
MARIA	14	F	CH	RRZZZZUSA
PAULS, PETER	20	M	FARMER	RRZZZZUSA
ALBRECHT, HEINR.	40	M	LLD	RRZZZZUSA
HELENE	39	F	UNKNOWN	RRZZZZUSA
HEINRICH	8	M	CHILD	RRZZZZUSA
ANNA	6	F	CHILD	RRZZZZUSA
JACOB	4	M	CHILD	RRZZZZUSA
JANTZEN, ABRAHAM	32	M	LABR	RRZZZZUSA
CATHA.	33	F	UNKNOWN	RRZZZZUSA
JOHANNES	9	M	CHILD	RRZZZZUSA
CATHA.	7	F	CHILD	RRZZZZUSA
HEINRICH	5	M	CHILD	RRZZZZUSA
CLAAFSEN, ARON	35	M	LABR	RRZZZZUSA
HELENE	42	F	UNKNOWN	RRZZZZUSA
JOHANNES	10	M	CH	RRZZZZUSA
JUSTINE	9	F	CHILD	RRZZZZUSA
DIRKS, BENJAMIN	50	M	FARMER	RRZZZZUSA
AGNESA	48	F	UNKNOWN	RRZZZZUSA
JACOB	22	M	LABR	RRZZZZUSA
FRIEDRICH	22	M	LABR	RRZZZZUSA
HEINRICH	18	M	FARMER	RRZZZZUSA
PETER	15	M	FARMER	RRZZZZUSA
ISAAC	13	M	FARMER	RRZZZZUSA
GERHARD	11	M	FARMER	RRZZZZUSA
DAVID	9	M	CHILD	RRZZZZUSA
HELENE	6	F	CHILD	RRZZZZUSA
TOEWS, JACOB	46	M	FARMER	RRZZZZUSA
MARIE	46	F	UNKNOWN	RRZZZZUSA
JOHANNES	18	M	FARMER	RRZZZZUSA
CORNELIUS	15	M	FARMER	RRZZZZUSA
DAVID	14	M	FARMER	RRZZZZUSA
CATHARINA	12	F	CH	RRZZZZUSA
LOUISE	00	F	CH	RRZZZZUSA
ANNA	7	F	CHILD	RRZZZZUSA
HEINRICH	22	M	LABR	RRZZZZUSA
ANNA	20	F	UNKNOWN	RRZZZZUSA
MARIE	.09	F	INFANT	RRZZZZUSA
ENZ, MARIA	56	F	UNKNOWN	RRZZZZUSA
HLAGGBLOM, AUG.	28	M	PNTR	RRZZZZUSA
EDLA	25	F	UNKNOWN	RRZZZZUSA
LANDENBERGER, JOH.	30	M	FARMER	RRZZZZUSA
EVA	28	F	UNKNOWN	RRZZZZUSA
WILL, JACOB	20	M	MCHT	RRZZZZUSA
KRAIN, CHRISTINE	22	F	UNKNOWN	RRZZZZUSA

PASSENGER	AGE	SEX	OCCUPATION	PRV	VIL	DES

SHIP: STATE OF NEVADA

FROM: GLASGOW
TO: NEW YORK
ARRIVED: 04 OCTOBER 1884

PASSENGER	AGE	SEX	OCCUPATION	PRV VIL DES
JOSELOWITZ, J.	30	M	PDLR	RRZZZZUSA
KANICHOWSKY, S.	22	M	PDLR	RRZZZZUSA
J.	20	F	W	RRZZZZUSA
MULLER, H.	41	M	PDLR	RRZZZZUSA
SUTKER, U-MR	19	M	TLR	RRZZZZUSA
SUCHART, F.	19	M	TLR	RRZZZZUSA
G.	20	F	W	RRZZZZUSA
DYNRA, M.	55	M	LABR	PLZZZZUSA
KERSCH, J.	18	M	LABR	PLZZZZUSA
OHARMIK, B.	18	F	W	PLZZZZUSA
SOLONOWITZ, A.	24	M	LABR	PLZZZZUSA
L.	22	M	LABR	PLZZZZUSA
WIKOWSKY, N.	40	M	LABR	PLZZZZUSA
J.	42	F	W	PLZZZZUSA
M.	10	M	CH	PLZZZZUSA
J.	5	M	CHILD	PLZZZZUSA
HAAG, A.	15	M	CH	FNZZZZUSA
D.	11	F	CH	FNZZZZUSA

SHIP: CITY OF MONTREAL

FROM: LIVERPOOL AND QUEENSTOWN
TO: NEW YORK
ARRIVED: 06 OCTOBER 1884

PASSENGER	AGE	SEX	OCCUPATION	PRV VIL DES
NASMAN, HERMAN	17	M	LABR	FNZZZZPA
ROCHEMAKI, PAULINE	22	F	W	FNZZZZNY
WEATTAR	1	F	CHILD	FNZZZZNY
SIEIN, JUST.	18	M	UNKNOWN	FNZZZZWI
MASSALOFF, I.	34	M	MECH	FNADXWNY

SHIP: GELLERT

FROM: HAMBURG AND HAVRE
TO: NEW YORK
ARRIVED: 06 OCTOBER 1884

PASSENGER	AGE	SEX	OCCUPATION	PRV VIL DES
LAPIN, LINA	18	F	SGL	FNAHZSUSA
GEORG	17	M	LABR	FNAHZSUSA
BLASKE, CARL	30	M	LABR	RRZZZZUSA
HEUTWIG, FRANZ	30	M	LABR	RRZZZZUSA
SCHKLAR, ISAAC	19	M	LABR	RRAHZSUSA
ISCHWED	15	M	LABR	RRAHZSUSA
ALBERT, CATH.	26	F	W	RRZZZZUSA
ALFRED	1	M	CHILD	RRZZZZUSA
ERNA	.05	F	INFANT	RRZZZZUSA
PAUSTIAN, MINNA	18	F	SGL	RRZZZZUSA
BAUER, ALMA	40	F	W	RRAHQDUSA
VALENTINE	.11	F	INFANT	RRAHQDUSA
KOEHNBERG, MELANIE	30	F	SGL	RRAHQDUSA

SHIP: GENERAL WERDER

FROM: BREMEN
TO: NEW YORK
ARRIVED: 06 OCTOBER 1884

PASSENGER	AGE	SEX	OCCUPATION	PRV VIL DES
GARDORSKY, EDUARD	49	M	FARMER	RRZZZZRSS
JOHANN	12	M	CH	RRZZZZRSS
WAGNER, ANDR.	36	M	FARMER	RRZZZZRSS
BAUERT, FRIEDR.	26	M	LABR	RRZZZZRSS
CAROL	23	F	W	RRZZZZRSS
CAROL	3	F	CHILD	RRZZZZRSS
MAGDLA.	.09	F	INFANT	RRZZZZRSS
LIETZ, HEINR.	52	M	FARMER	RRZZZZRSS
CHRISTINE	40	F	W	RRZZZZRSS
FRIEDR.	17	M	FARMER	RRZZZZRSS
JOHANN	6	M	CHILD	RRZZZZRSS
ANDREAS	5	M	CHILD	RRZZZZRSS
HEINR.	1	M	CHILD	RRZZZZRSS
CAROLINE	4	F	CHILD	RRZZZZRSS
ELISABETH	.11	F	INFANT	RRZZZZRSS
KRAFT, DANIEL	46	M	LABR	RRZZZZRSS
CATHA.	46	F	W	RRZZZZRSS
CATHA.	20	F	CH	RRZZZZRSS
CATHA.	6	F	CHILD	RRZZZZRSS
ROSINE	5	F	CHILD	RRZZZZRSS
GEORG	7	M	CHILD	RRZZZZRSS
CHRISTINE	.11	F	INFANT	RRZZZZRSS
LEFFLER, PHILIPP	20	M	FARMER	RRZZZZRSS
LOWER, EDUARD	20	M	FARMER	RRZZZZRSS
HESCHELE, JOSEF	19	M	FARMER	RRZZZZRSS
KRAMER, GOTTL.	22	M	FARMER	RRZZZZRSS
OLTKE, DOROTHEA	22	F	NN	RRZZZZRSS
HEBERLE, GEORG	15	M	LABR	RRZZZZRSS
WAGNER, CATH.	21	F	NN	RRZZZZRSS
TAROLOWSKA, KATZMIRA	36	F	W	RRZZZZRSS
BAUSCH, FRANZ	19	M	FARMER	RRZZZZRSS
GRUEN, LEOPOLD	22	M	FARMER	RRZZZZRSS

SHIP: MARTHA

FROM: UNKNOWN
TO: NEW YORK
ARRIVED: 06 OCTOBER 1884

PASSENGER	AGE	SEX	OCCUPATION	PRV VIL DES
HAINEMAN, BRISTE	40	F	WO	FNZZZZNY
JOHANN	11	M	CH	FNZZZZNY
GUSTAV	1	M	CHILD	FNZZZZNY
ADOLPH	2	M	CHILD	FNZZZZNY
ANNI	27	F	SGL	FNZZZZNY

SHIP: FURNESSIA

FROM: GLASGOW
TO: NEW YORK
ARRIVED: 08 OCTOBER 1884

PASSENGER	AGE	SEX	OCCUPATION	PRV VIL DES
MARTIN, U-MRS	24	F	SVNT	PLZZZZUSA
BROMAN, J.J.E.	26	M	LABR	RRZZZZUSA
CUCLAND, G.G.E.	36	M	LABR	RRZZZZUSA
ISRAELSAM, M.G.	30	M	LABR	RRZZZZUSA
SGOGREM, C.	47	F	NN	RRZZZZUSA
SACK, J.	22	M	LABR	PLZZZZUSA

PASSENGER	AGE	SEX	OCCUPATION	PRV	VIL	DES

SHIP: GALLIA

FROM: LIVERPOOL AND QUEENSTOWN
TO: NEW YORK
ARRIVED: 08 OCTOBER 1884

PASSENGER	AGE	SEX	OCCUPATION	PRV	VIL	DES
MARTENSEN, RUDOLPH-V.	33	M	BNKR	RR	ZZZZ	USA

SHIP: LEERDAM

FROM: ROTTERDAM
TO: NEW YORK
ARRIVED: 08 OCTOBER 1884

PASSENGER	AGE	SEX	OCCUPATION	PRV	VIL	DES
LAMPINSUM, JOHAN-ELIAS	41	M	TLR	FN	ZZZZ	USA

SHIP: POLYNESIA

FROM: HAMBURG
TO: NEW YORK
ARRIVED: 09 OCTOBER 1884

PASSENGER	AGE	SEX	OCCUPATION	PRV	VIL	DES
BRIDOWSKY, JANKEL	50	M	PNTR	RR	ZZZZ	NY
MARTISDRACK, JOH.	44	M	LABR	PL	ZZZZ	UNK
JOHANNA	35	F	W	PL	ZZZZ	UNK
DONOTEK, ROSINE	18	F	SI	PL	ZZZZ	UNK
MATSCHAK, GEORG	15	F	D	PL	ZZZZ	UNK
FRANZ	7	M	CHILD	PL	ZZZZ	UNK
ROSALIE	.04	F	INFANT	PL	ZZZZ	UNK
KUBAN, JOSEF	36	M	LABR	PL	ZZZZ	UNK
ANNA	36	F	W	PL	ZZZZ	UNK
ROSINE	7	F	CHILD	PL	ZZZZ	UNK
ANNA	6	F	CHILD	PL	ZZZZ	UNK
JOSEF	5	M	CHILD	PL	ZZZZ	UNK
PAUL	3	M	CHILD	PL	ZZZZ	UNK
CELESTINA	2	F	CHILD	PL	ZZZZ	UNK
FRANZ	.07	M	INFANT	PL	ZZZZ	UNK
WOLLEK, FRANZ	36	M	LABR	PL	ZZZZ	UNK
JOHANNE	36	F	W	PL	ZZZZ	UNK
FRANZ	00	M	S	PL	ZZZZ	UNK
MARIA	6	F	CHILD	PL	ZZZZ	UNK
ANNA	3	F	CHILD	PL	ZZZZ	UNK
FISCH, PINKUS	16	M	LABR	PL	ZZZZ	NY
CHASCHES, JOSEPH	17	M	LABR	RR	ZZZZ	NY

SHIP: ODER

FROM: BREMEN
TO: NEW YORK
ARRIVED: 10 OCTOBER 1884

PASSENGER	AGE	SEX	OCCUPATION	PRV	VIL	DES
HANKE, REINHARD	28	M	MLR	RR	ZZZZ	USA

SHIP: WAESLAND

FROM: ANTWERP
TO: NEW YORK
ARRIVED: 10 OCTOBER 1884

PASSENGER	AGE	SEX	OCCUPATION	PRV	VIL	DES
HUCZMANN, HEH.	19	M	STDNT	RR	ZZZZ	RSS
HELLWIG, J.	35	M	FRMN	PL	ZZZZ	UNK

SHIP: EMS

FROM: BREMEN
TO: NEW YORK
ARRIVED: 11 OCTOBER 1884

PASSENGER	AGE	SEX	OCCUPATION	PRV	VIL	DES
HOFER, MICHAEL	43	M	SMH	RR	ZZZZ	USA
LOUISE	20	F	NN	RR	ZZZZ	USA
MARGARETHE	17	F	NN	RR	ZZZZ	USA
CHARLOTTE	16	F	NN	RR	ZZZZ	USA
EVA	17	F	NN	RR	ZZZZ	USA
AMALIE	7	F	CHILD	RR	ZZZZ	USA
ALBERT	6	M	CHILD	RR	ZZZZ	USA
ROSENBERG, ISAAK	33	M	MCHT	RR	ZZZZ	USA
REBECCA	24	F	NN	RR	ZZZZ	USA
MARIE	.06	F	INFANT	RR	ZZZZ	USA
MAUCH, PETER	31	M	FARMER	RR	ZZZZ	USA
CATHARINE	30	F	NN	RR	ZZZZ	USA
CATHARINE	9	F	CHILD	RR	ZZZZ	USA
ELISABETH	4	F	CHILD	RR	ZZZZ	USA
PETER	1	M	CHILD	RR	ZZZZ	USA
REMBALD, ADAM	37	M	FARMER	RR	ZZZZ	USA
MAGDALENE	36	F	NN	RR	ZZZZ	USA
ADAM	10	M	NN	RR	ZZZZ	USA
CATHARINE	9	F	CHILD	RR	ZZZZ	USA
CARL	7	M	CHILD	RR	ZZZZ	USA
GOTTLIEB	5	M	CHILD	RR	ZZZZ	USA
HEINRICH	4	M	CHILD	RR	ZZZZ	USA
PFUFF, MICHAEL	22	M	FARMER	RR	ZZZZ	USA
RETMANN, GEORG	32	M	FARMER	RR	ZZZZ	USA
EVA	30	F	NN	RR	ZZZZ	USA
GEORG	2	M	CHILD	RR	ZZZZ	USA
PETER	00	M	NN	RR	ZZZZ	USA
SALTONES, WINCAS	28	M	LABR	RR	ZZZZ	USA
MARIA	27	F	NN	RR	ZZZZ	USA
ANTONIA	.11	F	INFANT	RR	ZZZZ	USA
WEHL, FRIEDRICH	37	M	FARMER	RR	ZZZZ	USA
MARGARETHE	35	F	NN	RR	ZZZZ	USA
MARGARETHE	4	F	CHILD	RR	ZZZZ	USA
CATHARINE	2	F	CHILD	RR	ZZZZ	USA
GEISLER, CHRISTIAN	25	M	FARMER	RR	ZZZZ	USA
CHRISTINA	25	F	NN	RR	ZZZZ	USA
PETER	1	M	CHILD	RR	ZZZZ	USA

SHIP: LYDIAN MONARCH

FROM: LONDON
TO: NEW YORK
ARRIVED: 11 OCTOBER 1884

PASSENGER	AGE	SEX	OCCUPATION	PRV	VIL	DES
PRISE, REBECCA	28	F	UNKNOWN	PL	ZZZZ	NY
SARAH	10	F	UNKNOWN	PL	ZZZZ	NY
FANNY	6	F	CHILD	PL	ZZZZ	NY
HART, B.	30	M	CGRMKR	PL	ZZZZ	NY
ESTHER	32	F	UNKNOWN	PL	ZZZZ	NY

PASSENGER	AGE	SEX	OCCUPATION	PRIVL	DES
DANIEL	.06	M	INFANT	PLZZZZ	NY
ASHER	2	M	CHILD	PLZZZZ	NY
PHILIPP	26	M	CGRMKR	PLZZZZ	NY
HARWACK	24	F	UNKNOWN	PLZZZZ	NY
DANIEL	2	M	CHILD	PLZZZZ	NY

SHIP: SILESIA

FROM: HAMBURG
TO: NEW YORK
ARRIVED: 11 OCTOBER 1884

PASSENGER	AGE	SEX	OCCUPATION	PRIVL	DES
LASEROFF, PAULIE	22	F	SGL	PLAHTF	USA
BULEWITZ, MATZEI	21	M	LABR	PLAHSW	USA
MACZEIBUTI, MAGDALENE	17	F	SGL	PLAHZS	USA
KORSCHASKI, KAITE	15	F	SGL	PLAFVG	USA
ANEKIS, JOSEF	21	M	LABR	PLAHSW	USA
BERGEL, JOSEF	21	M	LABR	PLAHSW	USA
BUKIWITZ, MAGDALENE	21	F	SGL	PLAHSW	USA
NIEMEYK, MARIANNE	22	F	W	PLAHUI	USA
CASIMIR	.09	M	INFANT	PLAHUI	USA
OSTROWSKA, ANTONIA	30	F	W	PLAHUI	USA
CONSTANZE	4	F	CHILD	PLAHUI	USA
WLADISLAW	3	M	CHILD	PLAHUI	USA
STANISLAWA	.09	F	INFANT	PLAHUI	USA
BENZION, JOSEF	17	M	CGRMKR	RRZZZZ	USA
FESCHINSKA, JOSEFA	26	F	SGL	RRZZZZ	USA
SOILINSKI, JOSEF	40	M	LABR	RRAHUI	USA
KOLIZINSKY, CHIENE	20	F	W	RRZZZZ	USA
SAHILEGOWSKI, MICHEL	27	M	SHMK	RRAHUI	USA
FRITZ, JOHANN	42	M	LABR	RRZZZZ	USA
SCHONE	18	F	D	RRZZZZ	USA
RAAN, HEINRICH	24	M	LABR	RRAHUI	USA
JASTER, AUGUST	21	M	LABR	RRAHUI	USA
WIESE, HERMAN	23	M	LABR	RRAHUI	USA
AMSTERDAM, BEILE	34	F	W	PLZZZZ	USA
FEIGE	11	F	CH	PLZZZZ	USA
BRANE	9	M	CHILD	PLZZZZ	USA
FRADE	8	F	CHILD	PLZZZZ	USA
JACOB	5	M	CHILD	PLZZZZ	USA
RIUWKE	2	F	CHILD	PLZZZZ	USA
BODENDORF, AUGUST	24	M	JNR	RRZZZZ	USA

SHIP: WESTPHALIA

FROM: HAMBURG AND HAVRE
TO: NEW YORK
ARRIVED: 11 OCTOBER 1884

PASSENGER	AGE	SEX	OCCUPATION	PRIVL	DES
SMOLIANSKY, JOSSEL	20	M	CGRMKR	RRAHOK	NY
JABLOWITZ, RIWE	50	F	W	RRADOI	NY
CHEIE	19	F	D	RRADOI	NY
PERLSTEIN, SARAH	40	F	W	RRZZZZ	NY
ROSA	13	F	CH	RRZZZZ	NY
TAUBE	9	F	CHILD	RRZZZZ	NY
KIWE	8	F	CHILD	RRZZZZ	NY
FETZI	5	F	CHILD	RRZZZZ	NY
LIEBE	3	F	CHILD	RRZZZZ	NY
ABRAH.	.11	M	INFANT	RRZZZZ	NY
AMBROSIOWICZ, MICHALINE	18	F	SGL	RRAHZS	NY
SCHIMAMOINZOWA, VICTORI	40	F	W	RRAHZS	NY
SCHIMAMOINZOWA, STANISL	8	M	CHILD	RRAHZS	NY
LAPIDUS, MAWICE	19	M	MCHT	RRAFWJ	NY
NATALIE	18	F	SGL	RRAFWJ	NY
FISCHER, GEORG	30	M	LABR	RRAHZS	NY

SHIP: ARIZONA

FROM: LIVERPOOL AND QUEENSTOWN
TO: NEW YORK
ARRIVED: 13 OCTOBER 1884

PASSENGER	AGE	SEX	OCCUPATION	PRIVL	DES
PLOWINSKI, BARBARA	35	F	W	PLZZZZ	USA
ELIANA	60	F	W	PLZZZZ	USA
MARIANNA	10	F	CH	PLZZZZ	USA
JOSEPHA	8	F	CHILD	PLZZZZ	USA
BROTSEDA	6	F	CHILD	PLZZZZ	USA
WLADISLAW	3	M	CHILD	PLZZZZ	USA
ANTONIN	.10	M	INFANT	PLZZZZ	USA

SHIP: AURANIA

FROM: LIVERPOOL
TO: NEW YORK
ARRIVED: 13 OCTOBER 1884

PASSENGER	AGE	SEX	OCCUPATION	PRIVL	DES
GUDEBZER, MARTIN	35	M	LABR	PLAFWJ	USA
ONDIZ, ANDREAS	26	M	LABR	PLAFWJ	USA

SHIP: AUSTRAL

FROM: LIVERPOOL AND QUEENSTOWN
TO: NEW YORK
ARRIVED: 13 OCTOBER 1884

PASSENGER	AGE	SEX	OCCUPATION	PRIVL	DES
AUGUSTENOWITZ, FRANZ	44	M	LABR	PLZZZZ	NY
PONDO, JAN	39	M	LABR	PLZZZZ	NY
PETRONELLA	35	F	W	PLZZZZ	NY
FRANCISCH	8	M	CHILD	PLZZZZ	NY
ADAM	6	M	CHILD	PLZZZZ	NY
ELEONORA	1	F	CHILD	PLZZZZ	NY
SLOVZAK, LEONA	43	F	SVNT	PLZZZZ	NY
PACZKO, JAN	40	M	LABR	PLZZZZ	NY
CATHARINA	26	F	W	PLZZZZ	NY
JUDRZE	3	M	CHILD	PLZZZZ	NY
JASONITE	.06	F	INFANT	PLZZZZ	NY
GRODZINSLI, SLOVENTA	50	F	SVNT	PLZZZZ	NY
VICTORIA	27	F	UNKNOWN	PLZZZZ	NY
JOSEF	3	M	CHILD	PLZZZZ	NY
WANDA	1	F	CHILD	PLZZZZ	NY
JUREK, JAN	45	M	LABR	PLZZZZ	NY
CHAPLEN, MOSES	17	M	TRVLR	PLZZZZ	NY
SCHAPIRA, BER	47	M	TRVLR	PLZZZZ	NY

SHIP: CITY OF CHICAGO

FROM: LIVERPOOL AND QUEENSTOWN
TO: NEW YORK
ARRIVED: 13 OCTOBER 1884

PASSENGER	AGE	SEX	OCCUPATION	PRIVL	DES
ROSENBAUM, PAULINA	27	F	W	PLADBQ	NY
FUSTER, U-MRS	32	F	LDY	PLADAX	NY
U-MR	26	M	GENT	PLADAX	NY
ISAAK	12	M	BY	PLADAX	NY

PASSENGER	AGE	SEX	OCCUPATION	PV RI VL	DES

SHIP: EIDER

FROM: BREMEN AND SOUTHAMPTON
TO: NEW YORK
ARRIVED: 13 OCTOBER 1884

PASSENGER	AGE	SEX	OCCUPATION	PV RI VL	DES
HERMANN, H.H.	17	M	LABR	RRZZZZ	USA
MOTTENSTADT, H.H.	17	M	LABR	RRZZZZ	USA
BIEKE, J.H.	18	F	W	RRZZZZ	USA
SCHEURMANN, F.W.	67	M	JNR	RRZZZZ	USA
LUTTERKORT, C.H.	17	M	JNR	RRZZZZ	USA
RIEKE, A.M.	20	M	JNR	RRZZZZ	USA
GRUNDMANN, H.H.	29	M	LABR	RRZZZZ	USA
FREROK, AUG.FRDR.	14	M	NN	RRZZZZ	USA
NIEMANN, FRITZ	17	M	FARMER	RRZZZZ	USA
PEPERKORN, FRIEDR.	17	M	FARMER	RRZZZZ	USA
WITTSTHIESEN, CLANS.	35	M	TLR	RRZZZZ	USA

SHIP: STATE OF ALABAMA

FROM: GLASGOW AND LARNE
TO: NEW YORK
ARRIVED: 13 OCTOBER 1884

PASSENGER	AGE	SEX	OCCUPATION	PV RI VL	DES
HOBZMANN, ABRAHAM	22	M	LABR	RRZZZZ	NY
KLEMHEY, DAVID	26	M	JNR	RRZZZZ	NY
HESCHE	22	F	W	RRZZZZ	NY
DELNI	.02	F	INFANT	RRZZZZ	NY
KRANZUWUS, JO.	22	M	FARMER	RRZZZZ	NY

SHIP: BOHEMIA

FROM: HAMBURG
TO: NEW YORK
ARRIVED: 15 OCTOBER 1884

PASSENGER	AGE	SEX	OCCUPATION	PV RI VL	DES
REIKES, ASCHOR	24	M	LABR	RRZZZZ	USA
JACOB, HIRSCH	28	M	LABR	RRZZZZ	USA
SOPHIE	24	F	W	RRZZZZ	USA
GNIP, TAUBE	50	F	W	RRABBX	USA
DAVID	18	M	CH	RRABBX	USA
PESCHE	16	F	CH	RRABBX	USA
G.	9	M	CHILD	RRABBX	USA
MALKOWITZ, MARIA	26	F	W	RRAHZS	USA
ELISABETA	.09	F	INFANT	RRAHZS	USA
ZICH, MORITZ	22	M	LABR	RRZZZZ	USA
SURAWY, SOPHIE	22	F	SGL	RRAEFL	USA
SENDAROWITZ, HERRSCH	18	M	LABR	RRAHTU	USA
FELDMANN, LASER	28	M	MCHT	RRAEFL	USA
SCHWARZ, WILH.	32	F	W	RRAHTF	USA
OTTO	9	M	CHILD	RRAHTF	USA
HUGO	8	M	CHILD	RRAHTF	USA
LEVI	4	M	CHILD	RRAHTF	USA
PARLOW, DORETTE	26	F	W	RRAHZS	USA
ANNA	5	F	CHILD	RRAHZS	USA
KAHN, KALMAN	15	M	LABR	RRAHTF	USA
SACK, MEIER	19	M	LABR	RRZZZZ	USA
LORENZ, WILHELM	44	M	LABR	RRZZZZ	USA
COHN, ESTHER	45	F	W	RRAHTF	USA
BELLE	18	F	D	RRAHTF	USA
MEIER	9	M	CHILD	RRAHTF	USA
BOSLIN, MARCUS	22	M	LABR	RRZZZZ	USA
SCHEIKUN, LEWI	19	F	SGL	RRZZZZ	USA
STABUNOW, GEORG	32	M	LABR	RRAHZS	USA
ANG.	29	F	W	RRAHZS	USA
FINKELBERG, GOSEPP	25	M	DLR	RRZZZZ	USA

SHIP: BOLIVIA

FROM: GLASGOW AND MOVILLE
TO: NEW YORK
ARRIVED: 15 OCTOBER 1884

PASSENGER	AGE	SEX	OCCUPATION	PV RI VL	DES
PABOFORI, ICARE	32	M	TNSTH	RRZZZZ	USA
REISMANN, JANKEL	17	M	LABR	RRZZZZ	USA
BARCKI, SIMON	17	M	LKSH	RRZZZZ	USA
THOMASEN, TEODOR	20	M	PNTR	RRZZZZ	USA
DINGIAN, G.K.	23	M	SHMK	RRZZZZ	USA
HARORHINE	18	M	SHMK	RRZZZZ	USA
PASHGIAN, HORRAN	24	M	SHMK	RRZZZZ	USA

SHIP: STATE OF NEBRASKA

FROM: GLASGOW AND LARNE
TO: NEW YORK
ARRIVED: 15 OCTOBER 1884

PASSENGER	AGE	SEX	OCCUPATION	PV RI VL	DES
KOWOLCZIK, MACZEI	32	M	LABR	RRZZZZ	PA
HUBRIAK, DEWOS	26	M	LABR	RRZZZZ	PA
MELMANN, ISAAC	23	M	LABR	RRZZZZ	PA
CHOROSZCZAK, SANDER	12	M	CH	RRZZZZ	PA
RODZANIC, PEDRO	19	M	LABR	RRZZZZ	NY
ADAMIAC, MICHAEL	21	M	LABR	RRZZZZ	NY
HUNCZA, AFTEN	26	M	LABR	RRZZZZ	PA
HUBRIAK, TOMKO	25	M	LABR	RRZZZZ	PA
PERKOWSKY, STANISLAW	19	M	LABR	RRZZZZ	NY
MOCHOWSKY, JAN	22	M	LABR	RRZZZZ	PA
FINKELSTEIN, MENDEL	22	M	JNR	RRZZZZ	NY
SCHAW, CHAIM	40	M	DLR	RRZZZZ	NY
MARIE	20	F	W	RRZZZZ	NY
EPHRAIM	00	M	CH	RRZZZZ	NY
BEILE	8	F	CHILD	RRZZZZ	NY
FEIGE	.11	F	INFANT	RRZZZZ	NY
ROHEL	.02	M	INFANT	RRZZZZ	NY
ROSENFELD, CHAWE	31	F	W	RRZZZZ	NY
SAMUEL	9	M	CHILD	RRZZZZ	NY
WITTE	8	F	CHILD	RRZZZZ	NY
GITTEL	6	F	CHILD	RRZZZZ	NY
GEDALIE	1	M	CHILD	RRZZZZ	NY
SARAH	.02	F	INFANT	RRZZZZ	NY
HASOWSKY, HIRSCH	17	M	LABR	RRZZZZ	NY
MAZHSMACZ, STANISLAW	20	M	LABR	RRZZZZ	UNK
BAZHINSKY, JOSEPH	23	M	LABR	RRZZZZ	NY
ROSENBERG, ESTHER	20	F	SVNT	RRZZZZ	NY
HURWITZ, MERE	22	F	W	RRZZZZ	NY
ISRAEL	2	M	CHILD	RRZZZZ	NY
ITTE	1	F	CHILD	RRZZZZ	NY
BANDURA, JOHAN	40	M	LABR	RRZZZZ	NY
FRIEDMANN, NISAN	24	M	MLR	RRZZZZ	NY

SHIP: EGYPT

FROM: LIVERPOOL
TO: NEW YORK
ARRIVED: 18 OCTOBER 1884

PASSENGER	AGE	SEX	OCCUPATION	PRV VIL DES
JOWICK, ALOF-P.	72	M	LABR	RRAGUZUSA
JOHANSON, IDA	24	F	SP	RRAGUZUSA
WILSON, EMMA	21	F	SP	RRAGUZUSA
JOSEFSON, CHRISTINA	19	F	SP	RRAGUZUSA
LARSEN, GUSTOF	59	M	LABR	RRAGUZUSA
NILSON, ANDERS	59	M	LABR	RRAGUZUSA
GUSTOFA	45	F	W	RRAGUZUSA
CARL	14	M	LABR	RRAGUZUSA
AMANDA	10	F	CH	RRAGUZUSA
GELINA	4	F	CHILD	RRAGUZUSA
MACTHILDA	5	F	CHILD	RRAGUZUSA
SVENSON, ANDERS	51	M	LABR	RRAGUZUSA
CARL	16	M	LABR	RRAGUZUSA
JOHANSON, AMANDA	17	F	SP	RRAGUZUSA
BORJINSON, BUJIR	19	M	LABR	RRAGUZUSA
AGNER, JOHANNA	24	F	SP	RRAGUZUSA
JANSEN, A.A.	22	M	LABR	RRAGUZUSA
BORG, ANNA-C.	22	F	SP	RRAGUZUSA
LORISA	18	F	SP	RRAGUZUSA
MANNERBERG, AUGUSTA	25	F	SP	RRAGUZUSA
JOHANSEN, CARL	21	M	LABR	RRAGUZUSA
BENGSTROM, CARL	27	M	LABR	RRAGUZUSA
PETTERSON, JOHAN	20	M	LABR	RRAGUZUSA
ESKOLA, GAISA	24	M	LABR	RRAGUZUSA
SULAMPSA, MIKKI	22	M	LABR	FNZZZZUSA
SMITH, SOLOMON	40	M	LABR	FNZZZZUSA
BALDER, PETER	14	M	LABR	FNZZZZUSA
EKLEMD, AUGUSTA	36	F	W	FNZZZZUSA
MAGNAS	11	M	CH	FNZZZZUSA
EROLD	7	M	CHILD	FNZZZZUSA
JOHANNA	9	F	CHILD	FNZZZZUSA
BERTA	00	F	INF	FNZZZZUSA
ANDERSON, CAROLINA	24	F	SP	FNAGUZUSA
ANGERSCHETER, AUGUSTA	20	F	SP	FNAGUZUSA
ANDERSON, ANNA-E.	32	F	W	FNAGUZUSA
OLIVIA	10	F	CH	FNAGUZUSA
BROSTROEM, KURT-A.	22	M	LABR	FNAGUZUSA
DAHLMAN, JOHAN	40	M	LABR	FNAGUZUSA
JOHANSON, AUGUST	34	M	LABR	FNAGUZUSA
ELIASON, ELIAS	53	M	LABR	FNAGUZUSA
KALLISKOSKA, ELIAS	25	M	LABR	FNAGUZUSA
THOREIN, ALFRED	24	M	LABR	FNZZZZUSA
CHRISTIANSEN, AUGUSTA	21	F	SP	FNZZZZUSA
DOLGVIST, THELKA	18	F	SP	FNZZZZUSA
CARLSEN, MATHILDA	23	F	SP	FNAGUZUSA
JOHANSON, HANNAH	25	F	SP	FNAGUZUSA
STEN, EMIL	20	M	LABR	FNAGUZUSA
LJNUG, CLAUS	50	M	LABR	FNAGUZUSA
MACTHEA, ANTON	30	M	LABR	FNAGUZUSA
LUNDLEZ, ANDERS	22	M	LABR	FNAGUZUSA
ANNA	26	F	SP	FNAGUZUSA
MARTENSEN, MARTHA	19	F	SP	FNAGUZUSA
HACKSELD, AXEL	30	M	MACH	FNAGUZUSA
FIGER, ANNA-J.	43	F	W	FNAGUZUSA
MATHILDA	41	F	W	FNAGUZUSA
OLGA	8	F	CHILD	FNAGUZUSA
ELFRID	4	M	CHILD	FNAGUZUSA
ANNA	00	F	INF	FNAGUZUSA

SHIP: ITALY

FROM: LONDON
TO: NEW YORK
ARRIVED: 18 OCTOBER 1884

PASSENGER	AGE	SEX	OCCUPATION	PRV VIL DES
LINDENELIT, DUBOIS	22	M	LABR	RRZZZZPHI
FANNY	20	F	W	RRZZZZPHI
STRASHIMSKI, H.	25	M	LABR	RRZZZZNY
LEHIMANN, JOS.	32	M	LABR	RRZZZZNY
STONKES, JOHN	22	M	LABR	RRZZZZNY
LICOVMOVITCH, HAYAM	26	M	LABR	PLZZZZNY
RABONSKI, DAVID	12	M	LABR	PLZZZZNY
STOIN, FRED	26	M	LABR	PLZZZZNY
URLAINES, JULIA	21	F	UNKNOWN	RRZZZZNY
GOSHOWITZ, HARRIS	18	M	LABR	RRZZZZNY
LAMBITOC, WM.	19	M	LABR	RRZZZZNY
ROFFMSON, HARRIS	20	M	LABR	RRZZZZNY
LISINSKI, MYER	20	M	LABR	PLZZZZNY

SHIP: NEDERLAND

FROM: ANTWERP
TO: NEW YORK
ARRIVED: 18 OCTOBER 1884

PASSENGER	AGE	SEX	OCCUPATION	PRV VIL DES
REINKE, W.	19	M	LABR	PLZZZZUNK
WAEBEL, CHR.	20	F	NN	PLZZZZNY

SHIP: WERRA

FROM: BREMEN AND SOUTHAMPTON
TO: NEW YORK
ARRIVED: 18 OCTOBER 1884

PASSENGER	AGE	SEX	OCCUPATION	PRV VIL DES
SCHANER, PHILIPP	34	M	FARMER	RRZZZZUSA
BARBARA	33	F	UNKNOWN	RRZZZZUSA
BARBARA	6	F	CHILD	RRZZZZUSA
PHILIPP	3	M	CHILD	RRZZZZUSA
CATHARINA	2	F	CHILD	RRZZZZUSA
JACOB	.04	M	INFANT	RRZZZZUSA
KAPPEL, FR.	21	M	FARMER	RRZZZZUSA
HOLLWEGER, FRIEDR.	56	M	FARMER	RRZZZZUSA
CATHARINA	54	F	UNKNOWN	RRZZZZUSA
CHRISTINE	7	F	CHILD	RRZZZZUSA
CHRISTIAN	19	M	FARMER	RRZZZZUSA
GOTTLIEB	16	M	FARMER	RRZZZZUSA
LIPPERT, JOHANN	27	M	FARMER	RRZZZZUSA
CATH.	24	F	UNKNOWN	RRZZZZUSA
CHRISTINE	20	F	UNKNOWN	RRZZZZUSA
AUGUST	2	M	CHILD	RRZZZZUSA
EPHRAIM	.09	M	INFANT	RRZZZZUSA
DESKE, JOHANN	26	M	FARMER	RRZZZZUSA
CAROLINE	23	F	UNKNOWN	RRZZZZUSA
CAROLINE	.04	F	INFANT	RRZZZZUSA
KLOOZ, FRIEDR.	38	M	FARMER	RRZZZZUSA
CHRISTINE	34	F	UNKNOWN	RRZZZZUSA
CHRISTINE	6	F	CHILD	RRZZZZUSA
MARG.	4	F	CHILD	RRZZZZUSA
CATHARINA	3	F	CHILD	RRZZZZUSA
MAGDALENA	.09	F	INFANT	RRZZZZUSA
MUTSCHLER, KAJOB	33	M	FARMER	RRZZZZUSA
CATHARINA	34	F	UNKNOWN	RRZZZZUSA
ELISABETH	7	F	CHILD	RRZZZZUSA

PASSENGER	AGE	SEX	OCCUPATION	PRI VIL DES
MARGARETHE	.10	F	INFANT	RRZZZZUSA
REICH, ANDR.	20	M	FARMER	RRZZZZUSA
MAGIN, EMIL	16	M	FARMER	RRZZZZUSA
RUDOLF, LUDW.	44	M	FARMER	RRZZZZUSA
CATHRINA	39	F	UNKNOWN	RRZZZZUSA
LUDWIG	19	M	FARMER	RRZZZZUSA
CHRISTINA	15	F	UNKNOWN	RRZZZZUSA
LOUISE	13	F	UNKNOWN	RRZZZZUSA
CATHARINA	7	F	CHILD	RRZZZZUSA
JOHANN	6	M	CHILD	RRZZZZUSA
GEORG	5	M	CHILD	RRZZZZUSA
MAGDALENA	4	F	CHILD	RRZZZZUSA
PAULINE	3	F	CHILD	RRZZZZUSA
AUGUST	.11	M	INFANT	RRZZZZUSA
WEISS, PHILIPP	44	M	FARMER	RRZZZZUSA
ANNA	42	F	UNKNOWN	RRZZZZUSA
ELISAB.	21	F	UNKNOWN	RRZZZZUSA
FRIDERIKE	12	F	UNKNOWN	RRZZZZUSA
CHRISTINE	7	F	CHILD	RRZZZZUSA
JOHANN	6	M	CHILD	RRZZZZUSA
PHILIPP	3	M	CHILD	RRZZZZUSA
FREDERICH	4	M	CHILD	RRZZZZUSA
JACOB	2	M	CHILD	RRZZZZUSA
REIMER, HEINR.	41	M	FARMER	RRZZZZUSA
ELISAB.	39	F	UNKNOWN	RRZZZZUSA
CHRISTINE	15	F	UNKNOWN	RRZZZZUSA
FREIDR.	7	M	CHILD	RRZZZZUSA
MARG.	6	F	CHILD	RRZZZZUSA
JOHANN	5	M	CHILD	RRZZZZUSA
CAROLINE	3	F	CHILD	RRZZZZUSA
ELISABETH	.11	F	INFANT	RRZZZZUSA
THURN, FRIEDR.	24	M	FARMER	RRZZZZUSA
CHRISTINE	22	F	UNKNOWN	RRZZZZUSA
JOHANN	19	M	FARMER	RRZZZZUSA
CHRISTINE	.11	F	INFANT	RRZZZZUSA
SCHMIDT, CATHARINA	17	F	UNKNOWN	RRZZZZUSA
LEICHT, JOHANN	26	M	FARMER	RRZZZZUSA
CATHARINA	28	F	UNKNOWN	RRZZZZUSA
JACOB	7	M	CHILD	RRZZZZUSA
JOHANN	70	M	FARMER	RRZZZZUSA
MAGD.	35	F	UNKNOWN	RRZZZZUSA
FREDERIKE	18	F	UNKNOWN	RRZZZZUSA
AMAN, HEINR.	45	M	FARMER	RRZZZZUSA
ROSINA	40	F	UNKNOWN	RRZZZZUSA
JOHANN	18	M	FARMER	RRZZZZUSA
FRITZ	14	M	FARMER	RRZZZZUSA
JACOB	7	M	CHILD	RRZZZZUSA
ROSINA	6	F	CHILD	RRZZZZUSA
CHRISTIAN	4	M	CHILD	RRZZZZUSA
LOUISE	3	F	CHILD	RRZZZZUSA
MAGD.	.09	F	INFANT	RRZZZZUSA
FREDERIKE	72	F	UNKNOWN	RRZZZZUSA
WOLF, CHRIST.	26	M	FARMER	RRZZZZUSA
MARG.	27	F	UNKNOWN	RRZZZZUSA
MARG.	5	F	CHILD	RRZZZZUSA
CHRISTIAN	2	M	CHILD	RRZZZZUSA
CHRISTIANA	.05	F	INFANT	RRZZZZUSA
LICHT, FRIEDR.	27	M	LLD	RRZZZZUSA
FREDERIKE	25	F	UNKNOWN	RRZZZZUSA
WENZ, FRIEDR.	21	M	FARMER	RRZZZZUSA
KUIPPEL, JOHANN	20	M	FARMER	RRZZZZUSA
ALDINGER, JOH.	17	M	FARMER	RRZZZZUSA
HAFNER, EMANUEL	18	M	FARMER	RRZZZZUSA
LAMMEL, JOH.	19	M	FARMER	RRZZZZUSA
SCHUMACHER, JOH.	20	M	FARMER	RRZZZZUSA
MULLER, ALBERT	48	M	FARMER	RRZZZZUSA
WITHMAIER, JOH.	23	M	FARMER	RRZZZZUSA
CATH.	20	F	UNKNOWN	RRZZZZUSA
CATH.	.04	F	INFANT	RRZZZZUSA
WALTER, JOHANN	29	M	FARMER	RRZZZZUSA
LEOPOLDINE	29	F	UNKNOWN	RRZZZZUSA
ROSINE	4	F	CHILD	RRZZZZUSA
JOHANN	3	M	CHILD	RRZZZZUSA
RETTEL, JOHANN	23	M	FARMER	RRZZZZUSA
LUDW.	15	M	FARMER	RRZZZZUSA

PASSENGER	AGE	SEX	OCCUPATION	PRI VIL DES
MARTIN	17	M	FARMER	RRZZZZUSA
WANNER, PHILIPP	26	M	FARMER	RRZZZZUSA
CATH.	23	F	UNKNOWN	RRZZZZUSA
FRIEDR.	.09	M	INFANT	RRZZZZUSA
HOFFMANN, JACOB	32	M	FARMER	RRZZZZUSA
CATH.	24	F	UNKNOWN	RRZZZZUSA
MAGD.	6	F	CHILD	RRZZZZUSA
JOHANN	5	M	CHILD	RRZZZZUSA
CATH.	3	F	CHILD	RRZZZZUSA
CHRESTINE	.09	F	INFANT	RRZZZZUSA
BOSCHE, JACOB	22	M	FARMER	RRZZZZUSA
MAIDINGER, FRIEDR.	00	M	FARMER	RRZZZZUSA
CATH.	00	F	UNKNOWN	RRZZZZUSA
ANDREAS	00	M	UNKNOWN	RRZZZZUSA
KUPMANN, JACOB	24	M	FARMER	RRZZZZUSA
JUST, CHRIST.	24	M	FARMER	RRZZZZUSA
ELISABETH	22	F	UNKNOWN	RRZZZZUSA
CARL	.11	M	INFANT	RRZZZZUSA
BETZLER, JOH.	19	M	UNKNOWN	RRZZZZUSA
FMR, JOH.	19	M	UNKNOWN	RRZZZZUSA
BECKER, DAVID	29	M	UNKNOWN	RRZZZZUSA
PHILIPPE	24	F	UNKNOWN	RRZZZZUSA
JACOB	2	M	CHILD	RRZZZZUSA
AUGUST	.11	M	INFANT	RRZZZZUSA
BEINDER, JACOB	25	M	FARMER	RRZZZZUSA
CHRESTINA	23	F	UNKNOWN	RRZZZZUSA
JOHANN	2	M	CHILD	RRZZZZUSA
CHRESTINE	.03	F	INFANT	RRZZZZUSA
MARTEL, PHILIPP	19	M	FARMER	RRZZZZUSA
BECKER, PHILIPP	19	M	FARMER	RRZZZZUSA
MAIER, ADAM	18	M	FARMER	RRZZZZUSA
PETZ, MICHAEL	22	M	FARMER	RRZZZZUSA
MAGDALENE	22	F	UNKNOWN	RRZZZZUSA
ELISABETH	20	F	UNKNOWN	RRZZZZUSA
ELISABETH	19	F	UNKNOWN	RRZZZZUSA
RALL, JACOB	26	M	FARMER	RRZZZZUSA
MAGD.	23	F	UNKNOWN	RRZZZZUSA
JOHANN	20	M	FARMER	RRZZZZUSA
DOROTHEA	21	F	UNKNOWN	RRZZZZUSA
SCHMIDT, JOHANN	26	M	FARMER	RRZZZZUSA
ELISAB.	20	F	UNKNOWN	RRZZZZUSA
FRIEDERIKE	.09	F	INFANT	RRZZZZUSA
WEIDINGER, ADAM	31	M	FARMER	RRZZZZUSA
MAGD.	28	F	UNKNOWN	RRZZZZUSA
MAGD.	7	F	CHILD	RRZZZZUSA
CHRISTINE	4	F	CHILD	RRZZZZUSA
ADAM	.03	M	INFANT	RRZZZZUSA
FREY, MARTIN	40	M	FARMER	RRZZZZUSA
ELISAB.	30	F	UNKNOWN	RRZZZZUSA
HEINR.	17	M	FARMER	RRZZZZUSA
JOHANN	15	M	FARMER	RRZZZZUSA
CATHARINE	6	F	CHILD	RRZZZZUSA
JACOB	4	M	CHILD	RRZZZZUSA
EVA	.09	F	INFANT	RRZZZZUSA
ELISABETH	00	F	UNKNOWN	RRZZZZUSA
PFEIPPER, GOTTL.	00	M	FARMER	RRZZZZUSA
CHREITINE	43	F	UNKNOWN	RRZZZZUSA
CATH.	21	F	UNKNOWN	RRZZZZUSA
MAGDALENE	17	F	UNKNOWN	RRZZZZUSA
GOTTL.	12	M	UNKNOWN	RRZZZZUSA
GRETEL	7	F	CHILD	RRZZZZUSA
ELISABETH.	6	F	CHILD	RRZZZZUSA
JOHANN	4	M	CHILD	RRZZZZUSA
ROSINE	2	F	CHILD	RRZZZZUSA
BECKER, FRIEDR.	56	M	FARMER	RRZZZZUSA
FRIEDERIKE	53	F	UNKNOWN	RRZZZZUSA
ADOLF	7	M	CHILD	RRZZZZUSA
ANDRAS	17	M	FARMER	RRZZZZUSA
FRIEKE	70	F	UNKNOWN	RRZZZZUSA
HUFF, GR.	40	M	FARMER	RRZZZZUSA
BARBARA	00	F	UNKNOWN	RRZZZZUSA
ELISABETH	25	F	UNKNOWN	RRZZZZUSA
CHRISTIAN	4	M	CHILD	RRZZZZUSA
MAGD.	.03	F	INFANT	RRZZZZUSA
RIEP, G.	31	M	FARMER	RRZZZZUSA

PASSENGER	AGE	SEX	OCCUPATION	PRV VIL DES
CHRISTINE	27	F	UNKNOWN	RRZZZZUSA
JACOB	7	M	CHILD	RRZZZZUSA
PHILIPPINE	4	F	CHILD	RRZZZZUSA
AUGUST	3	M	CHILD	RRZZZZUSA
FESCHER, CHRISTIAN	28	M	FARMER	RRZZZZUSA
CAROLINE	26	F	UNKNOWN	RRZZZZUSA
CHRISTINE	4	F	CHILD	RRZZZZUSA
CHRISTIAN	.09	M	INFANT	RRZZZZUSA
GIMPEL, SIMON	45	M	FARMER	RRZZZZUSA
BARBARA	41	F	UNKNOWN	RRZZZZUSA
BARBARA	20	F	UNKNOWN	RRZZZZUSA
CATH.	18	F	UNKNOWN	RRZZZZUSA
CAROLINE	15	F	UNKNOWN	RRZZZZUSA
SIMON	13	M	UNKNOWN	RRZZZZUSA
JOHANN	7	M	CHILD	RRZZZZUSA
ELISABETH	6	F	CHILD	RRZZZZUSA
WILH.	3	F	CHILD	RRZZZZUSA
HEINR.	2	M	CHILD	RRZZZZUSA
SCHLACHTERLE, ELISABETH	18	F	UNKNOWN	RRZZZZUSA
RADEN, CHRIST	20	M	FARMER	RRZZZZUSA
PITZ, PHILIPP	20	M	FARMER	RRZZZZUSA
RIEP, HEINR.	18	M	FARMER	RRZZZZUSA
WACKER, PHIL.	52	M	FARMER	RRZZZZUSA
CATH.	51	F	UNKNOWN	RRZZZZUSA
CAROLINE	7	F	CHILD	RRZZZZUSA
JOHANN	15	M	FARMER	RRZZZZUSA
JOHANN	19	M	FARMER	RRZZZZUSA
MAISCH, CHRIST.	00	M	FARMER	RRZZZZUSA
CATH.	00	F	UNKNOWN	RRZZZZUSA
CATH.	00	F	UNKNOWN	RRZZZZUSA
JACOB	18	M	FARMER	RRZZZZUSA
LUDW.	7	M	CHILD	RRZZZZUSA
ROSINE	4	F	CHILD	RRZZZZUSA
LISBETH	2	F	CHILD	RRZZZZUSA
JOHANN	.09	M	INFANT	RRZZZZUSA
OBERLANDER, JACOB	28	M	FARMER	RRZZZZUSA
BARBARA	26	F	UNKNOWN	RRZZZZUSA
JACOB	4	M	CHILD	RRZZZZUSA
FRIEDR.	3	M	CHILD	RRZZZZUSA
ADAM	.03	M	INFANT	RRZZZZUSA
TUPPER, JACOB	26	M	FARMER	RRZZZZUSA
FRIEDKE	32	F	UNKNOWN	RRZZZZUSA
ROSINE	.09	F	INFANT	RRZZZZUSA
SCHMIDT, HEINR.	20	M	FARMER	RRZZZZUSA
KRAUS, WILH.	28	M	FARMER	RRZZZZUSA
CATH.	25	F	UNKNOWN	RRZZZZUSA
EMILIE	4	F	CHILD	RRZZZZUSA
CATHARINA	2	F	CHILD	RRZZZZUSA
BARBARA	.06	F	INFANT	RRZZZZUSA
FRICH, ADAM	26	M	FARMER	RRZZZZUSA
ROSINE	23	F	UNKNOWN	RRZZZZUSA
EUTZE, CHRISTOF	49	M	FARMER	RRZZZZUSA
ELISAB.	51	F	UNKNOWN	RRZZZZUSA
CHRISTINA	23	F	UNKNOWN	RRZZZZUSA
LORENZ	24	M	FARMER	RRZZZZUSA
ELISAB.	20	F	UNKNOWN	RRZZZZUSA
JOHANNE	19	F	UNKNOWN	RRZZZZUSA
WILH.	13	M	FARMER	RRZZZZUSA
SCHECK, CHRISTIANNE	18	F	UNKNOWN	RRZZZZUSA
KLEMMER, FRIEDR.	22	M	FARMER	RRZZZZUSA
WENZLAPF, JAKOB	23	M	FARMER	RRZZZZUSA
CHRISTINE	23	F	UNKNOWN	RRZZZZUSA
HIEB, FRIEDR.	25	M	FARMER	RRZZZZUSA
MAGD.	21	F	UNKNOWN	RRZZZZUSA
GOTTL.	2	M	CHILD	RRZZZZUSA
CAROLINE	.11	F	INFANT	RRZZZZUSA
BALTHASAR	18	M	FARMER	RRZZZZUSA
WILH.	20	M	FARMER	RRZZZZUSA
SCHAUER, JACOB	19	M	FARMER	RRZZZZUSA
ARTHEL, DOROTHEA	56	F	UNKNOWN	RRZZZZUSA
BECKER, JACOB	40	M	FARMER	RRZZZZUSA
CHRISTINE	36	F	UNKNOWN	RRZZZZUSA
CARL	7	M	CHILD	RRZZZZUSA
JACOB	5	M	CHILD	RRZZZZUSA
PAULINE	2	F	CHILD	RRZZZZUSA

PASSENGER	AGE	SEX	OCCUPATION	PRV VIL DES
MAGD.	.02	F	INFANT	RRZZZZUSA
ROTH, G.	53	M	BRR	RRZZZZUSA
MARG.	34	F	UNKNOWN	RRZZZZUSA
GEORG	15	M	UNKNOWN	RRZZZZUSA
GRETCHEN	7	F	CHILD	RRZZZZUSA
FAUTH, CHRISTOF	35	M	FARMER	RRZZZZUSA
ROSINE	30	F	UNKNOWN	RRZZZZUSA
ROSINE	5	F	CHILD	RRZZZZUSA
CATHARINA	3	F	CHILD	RRZZZZUSA
CHRISTINE	2	F	CHILD	RRZZZZUSA
MAGD.	.08	F	INFANT	RRZZZZUSA
FRICHY, JONAS	30	M	FARMER	RRZZZZUSA
SUSANNE	25	F	UNKNOWN	RRZZZZUSA
JOSEF	.11	M	INFANT	RRZZZZUSA
ALBRECHT, ROSINE	58	F	UNKNOWN	RRZZZZUSA
WILH.	21	M	FARMER	RRZZZZUSA
JOHANN	17	M	FARMER	RRZZZZUSA
ROSINE	15	M	FARMER	RRZZZZUSA
BOLLINGER, CARL	22	M	FARMER	RRZZZZUSA
GURSZA, JOSEF	40	M	FARMER	RRZZZZUSA
SUP, G.	25	M	FARMER	RRZZZZUSA
GROCHOL, WASIL	24	M	FARMER	RRZZZZUSA
TENIMK, JANOS	35	M	FARMER	RRZZZZUSA
BATZAR, ANDRAS	31	M	FARMER	RRZZZZUSA
ANTONIK, G.	35	M	FARMER	RRZZZZUSA
KARFENSTEIN, JAC.	22	M	FARMER	RRZZZZUSA

SHIP: CITY OF CHESTER

FROM: LIVERPOOL AND QUEENSTOWN
TO: NEW YORK
ARRIVED: 20 OCTOBER 1884

PASSENGER	AGE	SEX	OCCUPATION	PRV VIL DES
WACHA, FRANZ	27	M	LABR	RRACBFCLE
GUDOLOWITZ, ARON	40	M	LABR	RRACBFNY
MAUKSWITZ, SCHMUEL	19	M	LABR	RRACBFNY
DISTOLATOV, MISCHE	25	M	LABR	RRACBFNY
PUDLEWITZ, MARIAME	35	F	SVNT	RRACBFNE
HARRIES, ALEX	28	M	CL	RRADBQNY

SHIP: WIELAND

FROM: HAMBURG
TO: NEW YORK
ARRIVED: 20 OCTOBER 1884

PASSENGER	AGE	SEX	OCCUPATION	PRV VIL DES
BERMANN, HARRIET	20	F	SGL	RRZZZZUSA
WIGUSIN, ISAAC	56	M	TLR	RRZZZZUSA
LEWITZKI, CHAIM	57	M	DLR	RRZZZZUSA
LABAN	14	M	CH	RRZZZZUSA
FAGA	17	F	CH	RRZZZZUSA
ALT, SARA	18	F	SGL	RRZZZZUSA
SARA	18	F	SGL	RRZZZZUSA
ZAMIZEWSKA, JOSEFA	24	F	W	RRZZZZUSA
JON	.11	M	INFANT	RRZZZZUSA
SCHWARZ, ANNA	22	F	SGL	RRZZZZUSA
BERNSTEIN, LINE	19	F	SGL	RRZZZZUSA
MOSES	17	M	LABR	RRZZZZUSA
ROTH, JACOB	40	M	LABR	RRZZZZUSA
EVA	38	F	W	RRZZZZUSA
EVA	17	F	CH	RRZZZZUSA
SUSANNE	16	F	CH	RRZZZZUSA
JACOB	14	M	CH	RRZZZZUSA
PETER	9	M	CHILD	RRZZZZUSA
CHRISTINE	2	F	CHILD	RRZZZZUSA

PASSENGER	AGE	SEX	OCCUPATION	PRIV	VIL	DES
ANDR.	.11	M	INFANT	RR	ZZZZ	USA
KLUNDT, WILH.	23	M	LABR	RR	ZZZZ	USA
SCHLUMPERT, LEIB	34	M	LABR	RR	ZZZZ	USA
WISNEWSKI, FRANZ	48	M	LABR	RR	ZZZZ	USA
LASS, CARL	20	M	FARMER	RR	ZZZZ	USA
PERLHEIM, CATHA.	25	F	SGL	RR	ZZZZ	USA
MACZINSKI, ADAM	22	M	LABR	RR	ZZZZ	USA
BUCHSBAUM, SIGMD.	27	M	LABR	RR	ZZZZ	USA

SHIP: CALIFORNIA

FROM: HAMBURG
TO: NEW YORK
ARRIVED: 21 OCTOBER 1884

PASSENGER	AGE	SEX	OCCUPATION	PRIV	VIL	DES
BOMINSKY, B.	24	M	LABR	RR	ZZZZ	NY
WEINBAUM, MA.	18	F	SGL	RR	ZZZZ	NY
TEMA	16	F	SGL	RR	ZZZZ	NY
UNKNOWN, GUSTAV	21	M	S	RR	ZZZZ	NY
BOTGINSKY, JOSEF	24	F	SGL	RR	ZZZZ	NY
HODAK, MARIA	19	F	W	RR	ZZZZ	NY
MOJARY, ADAM	38	M	LABR	RR	ZZZZ	NY
BRENBAUM, SIG.	42	M	TCHR	RR	ZZZZ	NY
EMILIE	38	F	W	RR	ZZZZ	NY
JACOB	7	M	CHILD	RR	ZZZZ	NY
MORITZ	6	M	CHILD	RR	ZZZZ	NY
GISELLA	5	M	CHILD	RR	ZZZZ	NY
SAMUEL	3	M	CHILD	RR	ZZZZ	NY
WOTENSKY, GEORG	22	M	LABR	RR	ZZZZ	PA
HELENE	21	F	W	RR	ZZZZ	PA
RIMSCHA, CA.	26	F	W	RR	ZZZZ	PA
VICTORIA	5	F	CHILD	RR	ZZZZ	PA
STANISLAUS	00	M	INF	RR	ZZZZ	PA
HOLTGOTT, S.J.	35	M	TCHR	RR	ZZZZ	PA
REGINA	30	F	W	RR	ZZZZ	PA
ANNA	7	F	CHILD	RR	ZZZZ	PA
PAULINE	6	F	CHILD	RR	ZZZZ	PA
KORNER, CLARA	28	F	WO	RR	ZZZZ	PA
CLARA	7	F	CHILD	RR	ZZZZ	PA
THEODOR	5	M	CHILD	RR	ZZZZ	PA
LEWIN, CATH.	20	F	TCHR	RR	ZZZZ	NY
CHASKE	19	F	SI	RR	ZZZZ	NY
MISKOWSKY, PAULI.	38	F	WO	RR	ZZZZ	NY
PESCHY	14	F	CH	RR	ZZZZ	NY
SOFIE	10	F	CH	RR	ZZZZ	NY
CLAI	7	M	CHILD	RR	ZZZZ	NY
ICZAAK	5	M	CHILD	RR	ZZZZ	NY
MISHE	3	M	CHILD	RR	ZZZZ	NY
MINKOWSKY, SAMUEL	6	M	CHILD	RR	ZZZZ	NY
WOSS, FRID	56	M	LABR	RR	ZZZZ	NY

SHIP: BOTHNIA

FROM: LIVERPOOL AND QUEENSTOWN
TO: NEW YORK
ARRIVED: 22 OCTOBER 1884

PASSENGER	AGE	SEX	OCCUPATION	PRIV	VIL	DES
ASHEROWSKY, MARY	36	F	W	PL	ZZZZ	USA
ISRAEL	34	M	DLR	PL	ZZZZ	USA
ISRAEL	11	M	CH	PL	ZZZZ	USA
HERMAN	10	M	CH	PL	ZZZZ	USA
LEAH	9	F	CHILD	PL	ZZZZ	USA
DAVID	8	M	CHILD	PL	ZZZZ	USA
HERMAN, MAURIA	26	M	TLR	PL	ZZZZ	USA

SHIP: DEVONIA

FROM: GLASGOW AND MOVILLE
TO: NEW YORK
ARRIVED: 22 OCTOBER 1884

PASSENGER	AGE	SEX	OCCUPATION	PRIV	VIL	DES
HAMBEY, MOSES	18	M	LABR	RR	ZZZZ	USA

SHIP: RHAETIA

FROM: HAMBURG
TO: NEW YORK
ARRIVED: 22 OCTOBER 1884

PASSENGER	AGE	SEX	OCCUPATION	PRIV	VIL	DES
KOCZOROWSKY, ANDREAS	25	M	LABR	RR	ZZZZ	USA
BAHREN, MOSES	23	M	PH	RR	ZZZZ	USA
ZARIZANSKY, SAMUEL	29	M	BBR	RR	ZZZZ	USA
LINK, CHR.	40	M	FARMER	RR	ZZZZ	USA
ANNA	36	F	W	RR	ZZZZ	USA
ELISABETH	14	F	CH	RR	ZZZZ	USA
GRD.	13	M	CH	RR	ZZZZ	USA
CATHRINA	7	F	CHILD	RR	ZZZZ	USA
CHR.	4	M	CHILD	RR	ZZZZ	USA
CAROLINE	.11	F	INFANT	RR	ZZZZ	USA
WERNER, CHRIST.	50	F	W	RR	ZZZZ	USA
PETER	23	M	CH	RR	ZZZZ	USA
DAVID	21	M	CH	RR	ZZZZ	USA
SALOMON	9	M	CHILD	RR	ZZZZ	USA
GOTTLIEB	7	M	CHILD	RR	ZZZZ	USA
ADAM	6	M	CHILD	RR	ZZZZ	USA
JULIE	4	F	CHILD	RR	ZZZZ	USA
RICCHE	20	F	CH	RR	ZZZZ	USA
HEGEL, DAVID	20	M	FARMER	RR	ZZZZ	USA
ELISABETH	20	F	SGL	RR	ZZZZ	USA
CATH.	16	F	SGL	RR	ZZZZ	USA
KNISSEL, GEORG	21	M	FARMER	RR	ZZZZ	USA
ZARICZANSKI, MEYER	32	M	MCHT	RR	ZZZZ	USA

SHIP: CANADA

FROM: HAVRE
TO: NEW YORK
ARRIVED: 23 OCTOBER 1884

PASSENGER	AGE	SEX	OCCUPATION	PRIV	VIL	DES
KOBATRKY, U-MR	29	M	PUB	RR	ZZZZ	NY

SHIP: ARCHIMEDE

FROM: UNKNOWN
TO: NEW YORK
ARRIVED: 24 OCTOBER 1884

PASSENGER	AGE	SEX	OCCUPATION	PRIV	VIL	DES
FRANCESCA, GOTTFRID	30	M	UNKNOWN	RR	ZZZZ	NY

PASSENGER	AGE	SEX	OCCUPATION	PRIVL	DES
SHIP: CITY OF RICHMOND					
FROM: LIVERPOOL AND QUEENSTOWN					
TO: NEW YORK					
ARRIVED: 25 OCTOBER 1884					
WARBERG, HENRY	20	M	LABR	RRACBF	USA
BERGHOTZ, MICHAEL	11	M	CH	PLZZZZ	USA
KACZBERG, MOSES	19	M	LABR	PLZZZZ	USA
SHIP: ELBE					
FROM: BREMEN					
TO: NEW YORK					
ARRIVED: 25 OCTOBER 1884					
MICHELSON, BRONISLA.	30	F	NN	RRZZZZ	USA
EDMEMD	8	M	CHILD	RRZZZZ	USA
REGINA	5	F	CHILD	RRZZZZ	USA
HEISS, JOH.	45	M	FARMER	RRZZZZ	USA
MAGDALENE	42	F	W	RRZZZZ	USA
MARGARETHE	18	F	CH	RRZZZZ	USA
JOHANN	16	M	CH	RRZZZZ	USA
JACOB	11	M	CH	RRZZZZ	USA
MATHILDE	6	F	CHILD	RRZZZZ	USA
MAGDALENE	2	F	CHILD	RRZZZZ	USA
FISCHER, CHRIST.	40	M	FARMER	RRZZZZ	USA
DOROTHEA	37	F	W	RRZZZZ	USA
CHRISTIAN	13	M	CH	RRZZZZ	USA
MAGDALENE	11	F	CH	RRZZZZ	USA
KATHARINA	5	F	CHILD	RRZZZZ	USA
CHRISTINE	3	F	CHILD	RRZZZZ	USA
ROSINE	2	F	CHILD	RRZZZZ	USA
JOHANNE	.11	F	INFANT	RRZZZZ	USA
FEIKERT, GOTTL.	24	M	LABR	RRZZZZ	USA
CATHARINA	21	F	W	RRZZZZ	USA
BOSCHER, JOH.	57	M	FARMER	RRZZZZ	USA
CATHARINA	54	F	W	RRZZZZ	USA
JOHANN	22	M	FARMER	RRZZZZ	USA
AUGUST	18	M	FARMER	RRZZZZ	USA
JACOB	15	M	FARMER	RRZZZZ	USA
CAROLINA	11	F	CH	RRZZZZ	USA
CHRISTINE	.11	F	INFANT	RRZZZZ	USA
HERR, CATHARINA	18	F	NN	RRZZZZ	USA
GEORG	1	M	CHILD	RRZZZZ	USA
CHRISTIAN	4	M	CHILD	RRZZZZ	USA
NEUFERT, GEORG	20	M	FARMER	RRZZZZ	USA
KETTERLING, JAC.	28	M	FARMER	RRZZZZ	USA
CATHARINA	19	F	W	RRZZZZ	USA
MEHLHAFF, FRZ.	20	M	FARMER	RRZZZZ	USA
STEBNER, HEINR.	30	M	LABR	RRZZZZ	USA
CHRISTINE	28	F	W	RRZZZZ	USA
MAGDALENA	5	F	CHILD	RRZZZZ	USA
CHRISTINE	3	F	CHILD	RRZZZZ	USA
ALBINE	.04	F	INFANT	RRZZZZ	USA
MEHLHAFF, FR.	18	M	FARMER	RRZZZZ	USA
HAAS, GG.	25	M	LABR	RRZZZZ	USA
CATHARINA	21	F	W	RRZZZZ	USA
JACOB	14	M	LABR	RRZZZZ	USA
CATHARINA	.11	F	INFANT	RRZZZZ	USA
HAGEL, JOH.	24	M	FARMER	RRZZZZ	USA
LISABETH	25	F	W	RRZZZZ	USA
ADAM	20	M	FARMER	RRZZZZ	USA
CHARLOTTE	75	F	NN	RRZZZZ	USA
HAAS, JAC.	31	M	FARMER	RRZZZZ	USA
BARBETTE	29	F	W	RRZZZZ	USA
JACOB	6	M	CHILD	RRZZZZ	USA
CATHARINA	2	F	CHILD	RRZZZZ	USA
CHRISTINE	.01	F	INFANT	RRZZZZ	USA
SPENGER, JOH.	36	M	FARMER	RRZZZZ	USA
CATHARINA	25	F	W	RRZZZZ	USA
JOHANN	3	M	CHILD	RRZZZZ	USA
CATHARINA	.11	F	INFANT	RRZZZZ	USA
MELHOF, ROSINE	18	F	NN	RRZZZZ	USA
DRESSLER, ADAM	56	M	FARMER	RRZZZZ	USA
MARGARETHA	56	F	W	RRZZZZ	USA
MICHEL	40	M	FARMER	RRZZZZ	USA
IDA	17	F	NN	RRZZZZ	USA
ELISABETH	15	F	NN	RRZZZZ	USA
DANIEL	10	M	CH	RRZZZZ	USA
RIEB, FRIEDA	29	M	FARMER	RRZZZZ	USA
BARBA.	25	F	W	RRZZZZ	USA
JACOB	1	M	CHILD	RRZZZZ	USA
FRIEDA	.06	F	INFANT	RRZZZZ	USA
JUNKER, GG.	30	M	FARMER	RRZZZZ	USA
MARGARETHA	25	F	W	RRZZZZ	USA
JOHANN	2	M	CHILD	RRZZZZ	USA
CHRISTINE	.05	F	INFANT	RRZZZZ	USA
RIEGER, JOHANN	25	M	FARMER	RRZZZZ	USA
BARBARA	26	F	W	RRZZZZ	USA
BARBA.	.11	F	INFANT	RRZZZZ	USA
ALBRECHT, U	18	M	FARMER	RRZZZZ	USA
MORTEL, JHIL.	20	M	FARMER	RRZZZZ	USA
FRIEDKE	22	F	NN	RRZZZZ	USA
AUGUST	17	M	W	RRZZZZ	USA
SCHNEIDER, JOHS.	39	M	FARMER	RRZZZZ	USA
CATHARINA	30	F	W	RRZZZZ	USA
MATTHIAS	14	M	FARMER	RRZZZZ	USA
MICHAEL	8	M	CHILD	RRZZZZ	USA
MARIANNE	5	F	CHILD	RRZZZZ	USA
AGNES	3	F	CHILD	RRZZZZ	USA
ANTON	2	M	CHILD	RRZZZZ	USA
FRANZISKA	.06	F	INFANT	RRZZZZ	USA
MUELLER, FR.	31	M	FARMER	RRZZZZ	USA
BARBARA	23	F	W	RRZZZZ	USA
MAGDALENA	2	F	CHILD	RRZZZZ	USA
FRIEDRIEL	1	M	CHILD	RRZZZZ	USA
JOHANN	.10	M	INFANT	RRZZZZ	USA
HOCHHALTER, FR.	35	M	FARMER	RRZZZZ	USA
MAGDALENA	36	F	W	RRZZZZ	USA
CATHARINA	11	F	CH	RRZZZZ	USA
JACOB	10	M	CH	RRZZZZ	USA
CHRISTINE	8	F	CHILD	RRZZZZ	USA
BARBARA	6	F	CHILD	RRZZZZ	USA
MAGDALENA	3	F	CHILD	RRZZZZ	USA
FRIEDRICH	.11	M	INFANT	RRZZZZ	USA
KRAINER, CHRISTOPH	24	M	FARMER	RRZZZZ	USA
MAGDALENA	22	F	W	RRZZZZ	USA
FRIEDRICH	.03	M	INFANT	RRZZZZ	USA
CHRISTINE	.01	F	INFANT	RRZZZZ	USA
MEIER, JOH.	25	M	FARMER	RRZZZZ	USA
LISABETHA	25	F	W	RRZZZZ	USA
PHILIPP	1	M	CHILD	RRZZZZ	USA
ADAM	.02	M	INFANT	RRZZZZ	USA
MUNCH, CONR.	27	M	FARMER	RRZZZZ	USA
HOF, SIMON	26	M	FARMER	RRZZZZ	USA
MATHILDA	26	F	W	RRZZZZ	USA
JOHANN	1	M	CHILD	RRZZZZ	USA
MATHILDE	.01	F	INFANT	RRZZZZ	USA
CARL	29	M	FARMER	RRZZZZ	USA
BARBETHA	24	F	W	RRZZZZ	USA
ADAM	2	M	CHILD	RRZZZZ	USA
CATHARINA	.05	F	INFANT	RRZZZZ	USA
FEIST, JOS.	22	M	FARMER	RRZZZZ	USA
SIMON	20	M	W	RRZZZZ	USA
MEIDINGER, AD.	26	M	FARMER	RRZZZZ	USA
BARBARA	22	F	W	RRZZZZ	USA
CATHARINA	2	F	CHILD	RRZZZZ	USA
ADOLF	.06	M	INFANT	RRZZZZ	USA
BOZE, VAL.	37	M	FARMER	RRZZZZ	USA
WILHELMINE	27	F	W	RRZZZZ	USA
CAROLINE	15	F	FARMER	RRZZZZ	USA
DOROTHEA	11	F	CH	RRZZZZ	USA
CHRISTINE	10	F	CH	RRZZZZ	USA

PASSENGER	AGE	SEX	OCCUPATION	PRV	VIL	DES
CATHARINA	8	F	CHILD	RR	ZZZZ	USA
ADOLF	6	M	CHILD	RR	ZZZZ	USA
MAGDALENA	5	F	CHILD	RR	ZZZZ	USA
AUGUSTE	3	F	CHILD	RR	ZZZZ	USA
ADAM	2	M	CHILD	RR	ZZZZ	USA
JOHANN	.10	M	INFANT	RR	ZZZZ	USA
SPITZER, GG.	26	M	FARMER	RR	ZZZZ	USA
ELISABTH.	23	F	W	RR	ZZZZ	USA
CHRISTOPH	.06	M	INFANT	RR	ZZZZ	USA
BRESSLER, ADAM	23	M	FARMER	RR	ZZZZ	USA
MAGDALENA	21	F	W	RR	ZZZZ	USA
MAGDALENA	.06	F	INFANT	RR	ZZZZ	USA
STREIFEL, JOH.	35	M	FARMER	RR	ZZZZ	USA
LISABETHA	28	F	W	RR	ZZZZ	USA
MATTHIAS	7	M	CHILD	RR	ZZZZ	USA
CATHARINA	3	F	CHILD	RR	ZZZZ	USA
BARBARA	1	F	CHILD	RR	ZZZZ	USA
FEIST, NIC.	24	M	FARMER	RR	ZZZZ	USA
RICHARD	25	M	FARMER	RR	ZZZZ	USA
MOSES	.05	M	INFANT	RR	ZZZZ	USA
MICHAEL	26	M	FARMER	RR	ZZZZ	USA
LOUISE	25	F	W	RR	ZZZZ	USA
LISABETHA	2	F	CHILD	RR	ZZZZ	USA
JOHANNE	.03	F	INFANT	RR	ZZZZ	USA
HOF, ADAM	32	M	FARMER	RR	ZZZZ	USA
MAGDALENA	33	F	W	RR	ZZZZ	USA
CORNELIA	1	F	CHILD	RR	ZZZZ	USA
MARGARETHA	.01	F	INFANT	RR	ZZZZ	USA
BECKER, HERM.	38	M	FARMER	RR	ZZZZ	USA
MARGARETHA	32	F	W	RR	ZZZZ	USA
HEINRICH	3	M	CHILD	RR	ZZZZ	USA
CARL	.11	M	INFANT	RR	ZZZZ	USA
WEBER, MARIA	10	F	CH	RR	ZZZZ	USA
BRAUN, WENDELIN	28	M	FARMER	RR	ZZZZ	USA
EVA	25	F	W	RR	ZZZZ	USA
FRANZ	7	M	CHILD	RR	ZZZZ	USA
WENDELIN	5	M	CHILD	RR	ZZZZ	USA
BARBARA	.02	F	INFANT	RR	ZZZZ	USA
FEIST, MICH.	43	M	FARMER	RR	ZZZZ	USA
LISABETTA	40	F	W	RR	ZZZZ	USA
JOSEF	14	M	FARMER	RR	ZZZZ	USA
EVA	11	F	CH	RR	ZZZZ	USA
BARBARA	9	F	CHILD	RR	ZZZZ	USA
JOHANNE	7	F	CHILD	RR	ZZZZ	USA
ANTON	2	F	CHILD	RR	ZZZZ	USA
HOLZER, JOHS.	24	M	FARMER	RR	ZZZZ	USA
LISABETH	20	F	W	RR	ZZZZ	USA
LISABETH	.05	F	INFANT	RR	ZZZZ	USA
SCHAPIRA, M.	38	M	LABR	RR	ZZZZ	USA
DESSAN, PINKUS	19	M	LABR	RR	ZZZZ	USA
KOHN, NOCHMATJE	45	M	LABR	RR	ZZZZ	USA
MANSCHEL	18	M	LABR	RR	ZZZZ	USA
BEHLA	16	F	NN	RR	ZZZZ	USA

SHIP: ST. OF PENNSYLVANIA

FROM: GLASGOW AND LARNE
TO: NEW YORK
ARRIVED: 25 OCTOBER 1884

PASSENGER	AGE	SEX	OCCUPATION	PRV	VIL	DES
AMISCHINSKI, CHAIE	55	M	BCKM	PL	ZZZZ	USA
TEWKY	55	F	W	PL	ZZZZ	USA
KATZ, LEIB	16	M	LABR	PL	ZZZZ	USA
GWOZDZ, JOSEF	36	M	MCHT	PL	ZZZZ	USA
LUCIE	28	F	W	PL	ZZZZ	USA
MARGA	7	F	CHILD	PL	ZZZZ	USA
WLADISLAUS	5	M	CHILD	PL	ZZZZ	USA
KASIMIR	.07	M	INFANT	PL	ZZZZ	USA
BOGONISHOW, PETER	18	M	LABR	RR	ZZZZ	USA
JACOBLEW, ANDREI	23	M	LABR	RR	ZZZZ	USA
WASILI	18	M	LABR	RR	ZZZZ	USA
LUCKMANN, JEKEL	20	M	CGRMKR	RR	ZZZZ	USA
SEID, BESSEL	19	M	PPHGR	RR	ZZZZ	USA

SHIP: HABSBURG

FROM: BREMEN
TO: NEW YORK
ARRIVED: 27 OCTOBER 1884

PASSENGER	AGE	SEX	OCCUPATION	PRV	VIL	DES
LIPJETZ, RAPHAEL	19	M	FARMER	RR	ZZZZ	USA
STERN, CAECILIE	25	F	W	RR	ZZZZ	NY
LINA	2	F	CHILD	RR	ZZZZ	NY
SCHMERTLOWITZ, SALOMON	24	M	FARMER	RR	ZZZZ	NY
EVA	19	F	W	RR	ZZZZ	NY
SHAKOTIM, VINCENT	18	M	LABR	RR	ZZZZ	NY

SHIP: SUEVIA

FROM: HAMBURG AND HAVRE
TO: NEW YORK
ARRIVED: 27 OCTOBER 1884

PASSENGER	AGE	SEX	OCCUPATION	PRV	VIL	DES
SPISAK, FRIDA	42	F	W	RR	ZZZZ	USA
WAITUKAITIS, JAN	20	M	LABR	RR	ZZZZ	USA
GRIGALUS, SIMON	20	M	LABR	RR	AHZS	USA
KLINKENSTEIN, HYMAN	21	M	UNKNOWN	RR	AFWJ	USA
WOLF, CARL	22	M	CCHMN	RR	AFWJ	USA
ZWIGHAFT, MOSES	24	M	MCHT	RR	ZZZZ	USA
BOCK, FRIEDR.	26	M	LABR	RR	ZZZZ	USA
WERNER, JOHANN	56	M	LABR	RR	ZZZZ	USA
WILH.	18	M	LABR	RR	ZZZZ	USA
STERN, MICH.	31	M	LABR	RR	ZZZZ	USA
CAROLINE	18	F	SGL	RR	ZZZZ	USA
WALTER, MATTIS	36	M	LABR	RR	ZZZZ	USA
HENRIETTE	33	F	W	RR	ZZZZ	USA
EDUARD	9	M	CHILD	RR	ZZZZ	USA
ANNA	8	F	CHILD	RR	ZZZZ	USA
BERTHA	.11	F	INFANT	RR	ZZZZ	USA
LEEVEN, ABR.	30	M	FARMER	RR	ZZZZ	USA
HELENE	29	F	W	RR	ZZZZ	USA
JACOB	5	M	CHILD	RR	ZZZZ	USA
PETER	3	M	CHILD	RR	ZZZZ	USA
ABRAH.	2	M	CHILD	RR	ZZZZ	USA
HEINR.	.11	M	INFANT	RR	ZZZZ	USA
UNRUH, HEINR.	51	M	FARMER	RR	ZZZZ	USA
HEINR.	24	M	CH	RR	ZZZZ	USA
ELISE	20	F	CH	RR	ZZZZ	USA
JOH.	18	M	CH	RR	ZZZZ	USA
MARIE	16	F	CH	RR	ZZZZ	USA
ANNA	14	F	CH	RR	ZZZZ	USA
CORNELIUS	9	M	CHILD	RR	ZZZZ	USA
MARTENS, ISAAC	20	M	FARMER	RR	ZZZZ	USA
KOPP, PETER	18	M	FARMER	RR	ZZZZ	USA
BUCHMUELLER, WILH.	48	M	LABR	RR	ZZZZ	USA
MARGA.	46	F	W	RR	ZZZZ	USA
ELISE	18	F	CH	RR	ZZZZ	USA
HEINR.	20	M	CH	RR	ZZZZ	USA
CHARLOTTE	18	F	CH	RR	ZZZZ	USA
KAFTAN, LUDWIG	18	M	LABR	RR	ZZZZ	USA
SCHWARZ, MICHAEL	68	M	FARMER	RR	ZZZZ	USA
JUSTINE	34	F	W	RR	ZZZZ	USA
JOH.	7	M	CHILD	RR	ZZZZ	USA
ABR.	2	M	CHILD	RR	ZZZZ	USA
REISSWIG, GEORG	29	M	FARMER	RR	ZZZZ	USA

PASSENGER	AGE	SEX	OCCUPATION	PRVL	VILE	DES
MARGA.	24	F	W	RR	ZZZZ	USA
HEINR.	6	M	CHILD	RR	ZZZZ	USA
WERNER, ANTON	47	M	FARMER	RR	ZZZZ	USA
REGINE	47	F	W	RR	ZZZZ	USA
CHRISTINE	20	F	CH	RR	ZZZZ	USA
ROSINE	18	F	CH	RR	ZZZZ	USA
GOTTLIEB	14	F	CH	RR	ZZZZ	USA
CHR.	25	M	CH	RR	ZZZZ	USA
DAVID	7	M	CHILD	RR	ZZZZ	USA
JOHANN	23	M	FARMER	RR	ZZZZ	USA
ROSINE	23	F	W	RR	ZZZZ	USA
CAROLINE	4	F	CHILD	RR	ZZZZ	USA
AMALIE	.06	F	INFANT	RR	ZZZZ	USA
HOST, MICHAEL	54	M	JNR	RR	ZZZZ	USA
MARGARETH	48	F	W	RR	ZZZZ	USA
HEINRICH	18	M	CH	RR	ZZZZ	USA
PETRA, ELISABETH	19	F	SGL	RR	ZZZZ	USA
MAGDALENA	17	F	SGL	RR	ZZZZ	USA
HOST, MICHAEL	29	M	LABR	RR	ZZZZ	USA
MARIE	27	F	W	RR	ZZZZ	USA
LISABET	6	F	CHILD	RR	ZZZZ	USA
CATHA.	5	F	CHILD	RR	ZZZZ	USA
JACOB	4	M	CHILD	RR	ZZZZ	USA
JOHANN	2	M	CHILD	RR	ZZZZ	USA
MARGA.	.03	F	INFANT	RR	ZZZZ	USA
JACOB	30	M	LABR	RR	ZZZZ	USA
BARBA.	27	F	W	RR	ZZZZ	USA
ELISAB.	5	F	CHILD	RR	ZZZZ	USA
ULMER, JOHANNES	35	M	LABR	RR	ZZZZ	USA
MARGA.	28	F	W	RR	ZZZZ	USA
MARGE.	4	F	CHILD	RR	ZZZZ	USA
JOHANNES	3	M	CHILD	RR	ZZZZ	USA
JACOB	2	M	CHILD	RR	ZZZZ	USA
GOTTLIEB	.03	M	INFANT	RR	ZZZZ	USA

SHIP: CITY OF ROME

FROM: LIVERPOOL
TO: NEW YORK
ARRIVED: 28 OCTOBER 1884

PASSENGER	AGE	SEX	OCCUPATION	PRVL	VILE	DES
COHEN, LOUIS	27	M	LABR	PL	ZZZZ	NY
ABIA	31	M	UNKNOWN	PL	ZZZZ	NY
KATE	25	F	W	PL	ZZZZ	NY
REBECCA	4	F	CHILD	PL	ZZZZ	NY
ESTHER	1	F	CHILD	PL	ZZZZ	NY

SHIP: FRISIA

FROM: HAMBURG
TO: NEW YORK
ARRIVED: 28 OCTOBER 1884

PASSENGER	AGE	SEX	OCCUPATION	PRVL	VILE	DES
MACOLAZ, JACOB	18	M	LABR	PL	AFVG	USA
GOLDFARB, JANKEL	24	M	FARMER	RR	ZZZZ	USA
ROSENFELD, MOSES	19	M	LABR	RR	ZZZZ	USA
ZWIC, GEORG	21	M	LABR	RR	AEGT	USA
TRAUTMANN, CONSTANTIN	21	M	LABR	RR	AEGT	USA
PICHLER, ANTON	33	M	STWD	RR	AHTN	USA
BAER, MARIE	32	F	W	RR	AHQH	USA

SHIP: GERMAIN

FROM: HAVRE
TO: NEW YORK
ARRIVED: 30 OCTOBER 1884

PASSENGER	AGE	SEX	OCCUPATION	PRVL	VILE	DES
GONZALES, MM.	23	F	UNKNOWN	PL	ZZZZ	NY
BRAMTLEFTKEY, FRANCOIS	22	M	PNR	RR	ZZZZ	NY

SHIP: GRECIAN MONARCH

FROM: LONDON
TO: NEW YORK
ARRIVED: 30 OCTOBER 1884

PASSENGER	AGE	SEX	OCCUPATION	PRVL	VILE	DES
WEINTRAUB, D.	27	F	LABR	PL	ZZZZ	NY
S.	5	M	CHILD	PL	ZZZZ	NY
J.	00	M	INF	PL	ZZZZ	NY
GROFINSKY, N.	58	F	W	RR	ZZZZ	NY

SHIP: PENNLAND

FROM: ANTWERP
TO: NEW YORK
ARRIVED: 31 OCTOBER 1884

PASSENGER	AGE	SEX	OCCUPATION	PRVL	VILE	DES
CZARNETZKI, FRANZ	20	M	LABR	PL	ZZZZ	NY
OLINSKA, MAR.	21	F	SVNT	PL	ZZZZ	UNK
HONIZKE, B.	20	F	SVNT	PL	ZZZZ	MIL
RUEZINSKI, N.	16	M	FARMER	PL	ZZZZ	CH
A.	11	M	FARMER	PL	ZZZZ	CH
EVANS, S.	30	M	LABR	PL	ZZZZ	UNK
MOTTES, S.	35	F	UNKNOWN	PL	ZZZZ	UNK
EVANS, N.	00	M	INF	PL	ZZZZ	UNK
S.	00	M	INF	PL	ZZZZ	UNK
A.	5	M	CHILD	PL	ZZZZ	UNK
BENTZIG, O.	22	M	LABR	PL	ZZZZ	NY
JARZENKEWITZ, M.	28	F	UNKNOWN	RR	ZZZZ	NY
JOS.	00	F	INF	RR	ZZZZ	NY
KENUKOWSKI, M.	20	F	SVNT	PL	ZZZZ	UNK
RUZINSKI, A.	15	M	LABR	PL	ZZZZ	PA
KARNOWSKI, M.	18	M	SHMK	PL	ZZZZ	PA

SHIP: RHEIN

FROM: BREMEN
TO: NEW YORK
ARRIVED: 31 OCTOBER 1884

PASSENGER	AGE	SEX	OCCUPATION	PRVL	VILE	DES
GIETROWSKA, MARIANNE	20	F	NN	RR	ZZZZ	USA
ARCICZEWSKY, STANISL.	24	M	LABR	RR	ZZZZ	USA
WEISS, PHILIPP	21	M	LABR	RR	ZZZZ	USA
BECKER, LEISER	24	M	GDSM	RR	ZZZZ	USA
KIRSCHMANN, CHRISTIAN	48	M	FARMER	RR	ZZZZ	USA
CHRISTINA	48	F	W	RR	ZZZZ	USA
SOPHIE	18	F	NN	RR	ZZZZ	USA
CAROL.	11	F	CH	RR	ZZZZ	USA
JOHANN	9	M	CHILD	RR	ZZZZ	USA
HILKONICH, JOSSEL	26	M	LABR	RR	ZZZZ	USA

SHIP: STATE OF INDIANA

FROM: GLASGOW AND LARNE
TO: NEW YORK
ARRIVED: 31 OCTOBER 1884

PASSENGER	AGE	SEX	OCCUPATION	PRV VIL DES
FRIEDWALD, SELMANN	35	M	PDLR	RRZZZZUSA
SURAWIN, MOSES	21	M	WCHMKR	RRZZZZUSA
FEIN, SCHMUEL	17	M	PDLR	RRZZZZUSA
DINE, JOSEPH	27	M	PDLR	RRZZZZUSA
PESCHKIN, DAVID	40	M	PNTR	RRZZZZUSA
CHAIM	18	M	TNSTH	RRZZZZUSA
GODOWSKY, LIPKA	15	M	MUSN	RRZZZZUSA
PASSMAK, CHAIM	48	M	MUSN	RRZZZZUSA
GRATSCHOFF, NICOLAI	26	M	ENGR	RRZZZZUSA
STEFANOWITZ, STANISLAW	23	M	LABR	PLZZZZUSA
MIZINSKY, FELIX	26	M	LABR	PLZZZZUSA
WARNER, GEORG	21	M	LABR	PLZZZZUSA
CHIRUPECK, MARIE	21	F	W	PLZZZZUSA
JOSEPH	2	M	CHILD	PLZZZZUSA

SHIP: FULDA

FROM: UNKNOWN
TO: NEW YORK
ARRIVED: 01 NOVEMBER 1884

PASSENGER	AGE	SEX	OCCUPATION	PRV VIL DES
VANROSO, U	41	M	TT	RRZZZZUSA
U	36	F	TT	RRZZZZUSA
MOTSCHER, CHRISTIAN	34	M	LABR	RRZZZZUSA
MARTHA	24	F	UNKNOWN	RRZZZZUSA
CATHARINA	8	F	CHILD	RRZZZZUSA
MARIA	7	F	CHILD	RRZZZZUSA
CHRISTIAN	6	M	CHILD	RRZZZZUSA
GOTTLIEB	21	M	FARMER	RRZZZZUSA
KIRSCHEMANN, JACOB	26	M	FARMER	RRZZZZUSA
ELISABETH	23	F	UNKNOWN	RRZZZZUSA
EMILIE	.11	F	INFANT	RRZZZZUSA
MALKIEWICZ, FRANZ	27	F	LABR	RRZZZZUSA
VILANOWSKI, FRANZ	29	F	FARMER	RRZZZZUSA
KRENZER, ANTON	40	F	FARMER	RRZZZZUSA
HANNES, ANTON	27	F	FARMER	RRZZZZUSA
KNOPP, EDWARD	22	F	FARMER	RRZZZZUSA
WOLFF, CHRISTIAN	29	F	LABR	RRZZZZUSA
EVA	26	F	UNKNOWN	RRZZZZUSA
FRIEDRICH	.11	M	INFANT	RRZZZZUSA
BRESSLER, LORENZ	44	M	FARMER	RRZZZZUSA
ADAM	17	M	FARMER	RRZZZZUSA
JOHANN	4	M	CHILD	RRZZZZUSA
REINSCHMIDT, JACOB	18	M	FARMER	RRZZZZUSA
HEINRICH	28	M	FARMER	RRZZZZUSA
FRIEDERIKE	20	F	UNKNOWN	RRZZZZUSA
WILHELM	.11	M	INFANT	RRZZZZUSA
NUSS, LUDWIG	54	M	FARMER	RRZZZZUSA
MARGA	54	F	UNKNOWN	RRZZZZUSA
SCHMEDENSKY, RASCHKE	18	M	LABR	RRZZZZUSA
TESCHE	15	M	LABR	RRZZZZUSA
LEIBRANDT, ISAAC	79	M	FARMER	RRZZZZUSA
AGATHA	69	F	UNKNOWN	RRZZZZUSA
ELISE	26	F	UNKNOWN	RRZZZZUSA
JACOB	.09	M	INFANT	RRZZZZUSA
JOHANN	23	M	FARMER	RRZZZZUSA
ELISE	20	F	UNKNOWN	RRZZZZUSA
GOTTLIEB	2	M	CHILD	RRZZZZUSA
UNGER, FRIEDA	48	F	UNKNOWN	RRZZZZUSA
GOTTLIEB	7	M	CHILD	RRZZZZUSA
CONRAD, JACOB	7	F	CHILD	RRZZZZUSA
ROSINE	48	F	UNKNOWN	RRZZZZUSA
MATHILDE	18	F	UNKNOWN	RRZZZZUSA
HEINRICH	16	M	FARMER	RRZZZZUSA
ROSINE	8	F	CHILD	RRZZZZUSA
JOHANN	7	M	CHILD	RRZZZZUSA
WILHELM	6	M	CHILD	RRZZZZUSA
GUSTAV	4	M	CHILD	RRZZZZUSA
JOHANNES	2	M	CHILD	RRZZZZUSA
FRITZ, FRIEDRICH	34	M	FARMER	RRZZZZUSA
ELISE	30	F	UNKNOWN	RRZZZZUSA
JOHANN	8	M	CHILD	RRZZZZUSA
CHRISTINE	6	F	CHILD	RRZZZZUSA
JACOB	3	M	CHILD	RRZZZZUSA
ELISABETH	.06	F	INFANT	RRZZZZUSA
UNGER, WILHELM	18	M	FARMER	RRZZZZUSA
GALL, CARL	22	M	TCHR	RRZZZZUSA
BARBARA	24	F	UNKNOWN	RRZZZZUSA
CATHARINA	4	F	CHILD	RRZZZZUSA
FISCHER, JOHANN	25	M	FARMER	RRZZZZUSA
CAROLINE	23	F	UNKNOWN	RRZZZZUSA
AGNES	3	F	CHILD	RRZZZZUSA
ROSINE	.09	F	INFANT	RRZZZZUSA
JOHANN	14	M	FARMER	RRZZZZUSA
SCHICK, LUDWIG	61	M	FARMER	RRZZZZUSA
MAGDA	56	F	UNKNOWN	RRZZZZUSA
CARL	36	M	FARMER	RRZZZZUSA
ROSINE	36	F	UNKNOWN	RRZZZZUSA
ROSINE	8	F	CHILD	RRZZZZUSA
JOHANNES	6	M	CHILD	RRZZZZUSA
WILHELM	4	M	CHILD	RRZZZZUSA
JACOB	.11	M	INFANT	RRZZZZUSA
BAUER, LUDWIG	52	M	FARMER	RRZZZZUSA
JOHANNA	48	F	UNKNOWN	RRZZZZUSA
FRIEDRICH	26	M	FARMER	RRZZZZUSA
ELISE	26	F	UNKNOWN	RRZZZZUSA
MAGDA	.04	F	INFANT	RRZZZZUSA
FRITZ, ADAM	29	M	FARMER	RRZZZZUSA
CHRISTINE	25	F	UNKNOWN	RRZZZZUSA
JOHANN	.07	M	INFANT	RRZZZZUSA
PILTZ, HEINRICH	32	M	FARMER	RRZZZZUSA
ROSINE	26	F	UNKNOWN	RRZZZZUSA
HEINRICH	4	M	CHILD	RRZZZZUSA
ANDRAS	3	M	CHILD	RRZZZZUSA
NIETZ, FRIEDRICH	25	M	LABR	RRZZZZUSA
ELISABETH	23	F	UNKNOWN	RRZZZZUSA
FRIEDRICH	2	M	CHILD	RRZZZZUSA
ROSINE	.03	F	INFANT	RRZZZZUSA
BARBARA	64	F	UNKNOWN	RRZZZZUSA
BARBARA	20	F	UNKNOWN	RRZZZZUSA
SAENGER, JOHANN	27	M	LLD	RRZZZZUSA
MARGA	25	F	UNKNOWN	RRZZZZUSA
FISCHER, CARL	53	M	LABR	RRZZZZUSA
MARGA	50	F	UNKNOWN	RRZZZZUSA
BARBARA	21	F	UNKNOWN	RRZZZZUSA
ANTON	18	M	TNM	RRZZZZUSA
JOSEF	16	M	BRR	RRZZZZUSA
STELAN	14	M	JNR	RRZZZZUSA
ADELHEN	8	F	CHILD	RRZZZZUSA
ADAM	6	M	CHILD	RRZZZZUSA
CATHARINA	4	F	CHILD	RRZZZZUSA
MARTIN	30	M	FARMER	RRZZZZUSA
ELISE	28	F	UNKNOWN	RRZZZZUSA
JOSEF	5	M	CHILD	RRZZZZUSA
GRETE	2	F	CHILD	RRZZZZUSA
FERDINAND	25	M	FARMER	RRZZZZUSA
LUDWIKA	27	F	UNKNOWN	RRZZZZUSA
JOHANN	2	M	CHILD	RRZZZZUSA
CARL	.09	M	INFANT	RRZZZZUSA
JACOB	32	M	FARMER	RRZZZZUSA
HELENE	30	F	UNKNOWN	RRZZZZUSA
MATHIAS	8	M	CHILD	RRZZZZUSA
CATHARINA	6	F	CHILD	RRZZZZUSA
GRETIHEN	.03	F	INFANT	RRZZZZUSA
FICHTNER, GOTTLIEB	24	M	FARMER	RRZZZZUSA
JOHANNES	18	M	FARMER	RRZZZZUSA
GEORG, CHRIST	24	M	FARMER	RRZZZZUSA
HARSCH, LEONARD	32	M	FARMER	RRZZZZUSA

PASSENGER	AGE	SEX	OCCUPATION	PRV VIL DES
CHARLOTTE	25	F	UNKNOWN	RRZZZZUSA
CATHARINA	6	F	CHILD	RRZZZZUSA
JACOB	4	M	CHILD	RRZZZZUSA
HEINRICH	3	M	CHILD	RRZZZZUSA
MARIE	2	F	CHILD	RRZZZZUSA
METZGER, MAGDA	50	F	UNKNOWN	RRZZZZUSA
FRIEDR.	22	M	FARMER	RRZZZZUSA
JOHANN	19	M	FARMER	RRZZZZUSA
ROSINE	17	F	UNKNOWN	RRZZZZUSA
CHRISTINE	14	F	UNKNOWN	RRZZZZUSA
JACOB	13	M	FARMER	RRZZZZUSA
CHRISTIAN	27	M	FARMER	RRZZZZUSA
CATHARINA	25	F	UNKNOWN	RRZZZZUSA
CHRISTIAN	2	M	CHILD	RRZZZZUSA
SCHUHMACHER, CHRISTIAN	43	M	FARMER	RRZZZZUSA
CATHARINA	32	F	UNKNOWN	RRZZZZUSA
FRIEDRICH	16	M	FARMER	RRZZZZUSA
ELISE	8	F	CHILD	RRZZZZUSA
FRIEDERIKE	7	F	CHILD	RRZZZZUSA
CHRISTOF	4	M	CHILD	RRZZZZUSA
CATHARINA	2	F	CHILD	RRZZZZUSA
ROSINE	.09	F	INFANT	RRZZZZUSA
BECK, JOHANN	26	M	LLD	RRZZZZUSA
ELISE	23	F	UNKNOWN	RRZZZZUSA
KUBLE, JOHANN	19	M	FARMER	RRZZZZUSA
BAUERSBERGER, JOHANN	20	M	FARMER	RRZZZZUSA
RATH, CHRISTIAN	22	M	FARMER	RRZZZZUSA
PISCHKE, ANDRAS	30	M	LABR	RRZZZZUSA

SHIP: HAMMONIA

FROM: HAMBURG AND HAVRE
TO: NEW YORK
ARRIVED: 01 NOVEMBER 1884

PASSENGER	AGE	SEX	OCCUPATION	PRV VIL DES
DUNSKYE, TAUBE	24	F	W	RRZZZZUSA
ABRAM	4	M	CHILD	RRZZZZUSA
CHAIM	3	M	CHILD	RRZZZZUSA
STERNBERG, SIEGFRIED	18	M	SCH	RRZZZZUSA
U, U	29	M	SMH	RRZZZZUSA
EDELMANN, ABEL	54	M	TLR	RRZZZZUSA
WEINSTEIN, ISAAC	39	M	SMH	RRZZZZUSA
PREUTKI, SALOMON	21	M	LABR	RRZZZZUSA
ROGOZINSKI, PINKUS	23	M	TLR	RRZZZZUSA
GORDON, OLGA	25	F	W	RRZZZZUSA
SAMUEL	7	M	CHILD	RRZZZZUSA
GITTEL	5	F	CHILD	RRZZZZUSA
MOSES	.11	M	INFANT	RRZZZZUSA
AUSTROWA, MAGAL.	30	F	W	RRZZZZUSA
AUGUSTIN	.11	M	INFANT	RRZZZZUSA
CHISHOREWICZ, JOH.	23	M	LABR	RRZZZZUSA
EFFROTH, KASRIEL	36	M	LABR	RRZZZZUSA
LEBER, EFRAIM	23	M	LABR	RRZZZZUSA
FEIN, FEIWEL	18	M	TLR	RRZZZZUSA
SCHIMELIS, PINCHOS	55	M	DLR	RRZZZZUSA
SARA	50	F	W	RRZZZZUSA
KARLOWETSCH, JOSEF	35	M	LABR	RRZZZZUSA
MAKAREWITSCH, JOSEF	36	M	LABR	RRZZZZUSA
NOWETZKI, STANISLAUS	20	M	LABR	RRZZZZUSA
JERUSALEMSKYE, CHAIM	33	M	LABR	RRZZZZUSA
SAVRINO, ISRAEL	22	M	LABR	RRZZZZUSA
BAUDELEVSKYE, JOHANN	40	M	LABR	RRZZZZUSA
CHASANOVSKYE, ALTER	18	M	LABR	RRZZZZUSA
WLADISLAWSKYE, JACOB	20	M	DLR	RRZZZZUSA
FAJOK, JOH.	23	M	FARMER	RRZZZZUSA
SCHNEIDER, JACOB	24	M	FARMER	RRZZZZUSA
KUTLER, TEWIE	18	F	SGL	RRZZZZUSA
ORANSKY, CHAIE	50	F	W	RRZZZZUSA
ZIPPE	25	F	W	RRZZZZUSA
MOSES	.11	M	INFANT	RRZZZZUSA

PASSENGER	AGE	SEX	OCCUPATION	PRV VIL DES
FREIDE	9	F	CHILD	RRZZZZUSA
HENOCH	8	M	CHILD	RRZZZZUSA
REBECCA	3	F	CHILD	RRZZZZUSA
WIEHNE	.11	F	INFANT	RRZZZZUSA

SHIP: OREGON

FROM: LIVERPOOL AND QUEENSTOWN
TO: NEW YORK
ARRIVED: 03 NOVEMBER 1884

PASSENGER	AGE	SEX	OCCUPATION	PRV VIL DES
JACOBSON, OSCAR	20	M	LABR	FNZZZZUSA
HEIR, MARIE	50	F	MA	FNZZZZUSA
LANDAN, ELLA	22	F	SP	FNZZZZUSA
FELDSTEIN, SOLOMON	26	M	LABR	FNZZZZUSA
KEISARI, JHS.	16	M	LABR	FNZZZZUSA
KAHRO, MATTS	35	M	LABR	FNZZZZUSA
JUSA, ERIK	20	M	LABR	FNZZZZUSA
JOKILA, VALENTINE	20	M	LABR	FNZZZZUSA
IKKOLA, JOHAN	19	M	LABR	FNZZZZUSA
KETTULA, MATTS	35	M	LABR	FNZZZZUSA
LINDHOLM, KARL	30	M	LABR	FNZZZZUSA
MAKI, ERIK	40	M	LABR	FNZZZZUSA
AHLBACK, MATHILDA	21	F	SVNT	FNZZZZUSA
LUTHASAARI, ELIAS	20	M	LABR	FNZZZZUSA
SERKILE, ISAK	20	M	LABR	FNZZZZUSA
ISOAHO, GUSTAF	39	M	LABR	FNZZZZUSA
KAHRO, ELIAS	45	M	LABR	FNZZZZUSA
AUSSONIEMI, SOLOMON	35	M	LABR	FNZZZZUSA
ISAKSON, OSCAR	23	M	LABR	FNZZZZUSA
MANNINEN, EMANUEL	23	M	LABR	FNZZZZUSA
HOGPOLA, HENRIK	35	M	LABR	FNZZZZUSA
JURIN, JOHAN	34	M	LABR	FNZZZZUSA
ISOAHO, JOHAN	18	M	LABR	FNZZZZUSA
PYYLAMPI, SOLOMON	37	M	LABR	FNZZZZUSA
JACOB	19	M	LABR	FNZZZZUSA
IKKOLA, JHS.	22	M	LABR	FNZZZZUSA
PYYLAMPI, ERIK	37	M	LABR	FNZZZZUSA
IKKOLA, GUSTAF	22	M	LABR	FNZZZZUSA
KEMETSO, WENDLA	23	F	SP	FNZZZZUSA
GOLDBERG, E.W.	50	M	JNLST	PLZZZZUSA
WHISTLER, ROLAND-W.	26	M	LWYR	RRZZZZUSA

SHIP: RUGIA

FROM: HAMBURG
TO: NEW YORK
ARRIVED: 05 NOVEMBER 1884

PASSENGER	AGE	SEX	OCCUPATION	PRV VIL DES
AKSTIMULE, PETRONELLO	18	M	SGL	RRZZZZUSA
OKTNOVICH, VICENTE	45	M	LABR	RRZZZZUSA
NIEDERMANN, ABRAH.	19	M	TLR	RRZZZZUSA
KROTSCHINSKY, JACOB	15	M	LABR	RRZZZZUSA
ROSENSOHN, RIWKE	40	F	W	RRZZZZUSA
HINDE	19	F	CH	RRZZZZUSA
CHANNE	17	F	CH	RRZZZZUSA
SCHONE	15	F	CH	RRZZZZUSA
CHAIM	9	F	CHILD	RRZZZZUSA
RAHEL	8	F	CHILD	RRZZZZUSA
WILH.	6	M	CHILD	RRZZZZUSA
SIMON	4	M	CHILD	RRZZZZUSA
SAMUEL	.11	M	INFANT	RRZZZZUSA
MISCHKOWITZ, CHAIM	18	M	LABR	RRZZZZUSA
MORCUSE, TAUCHEN	23	M	LABR	RRZZZZUSA
RUBEN, MOSES	17	M	LABR	RRZZZZUSA

PASSENGER	AGE	SEX	OCCUPATION	PRIVIL	DES
KRATZOW, JACOB	21	M	LABR	RRZZZZ	USA
JOFFE, PESCHE	24	F	W	RRZZZZ	USA
BENJUMIN	.11	M	INFANT	RRZZZZ	USA
POLINER, LEISER	17	M	DLR	RRZZZZ	USA
SCHERMANN, JOSEPH	20	M	TLR	RRZZZZ	USA
LEA	18	F	SGL	RRZZZZ	USA
LIZEROWSKY, MOSES	19	M	CGRMKR	RRZZZZ	USA
HEYMANN, JACOB	15	M	LABR	RRZZZZ	USA
LIPSKY, MOSES	50	M	LABR	RRZZZZ	USA
LIPSCHITZ, ABRAH.	19	M	TLR	RRZZZZ	USA
RIBAK, JOSEPH	30	M	LABR	RRZZZZ	USA
SCHLASE, NICOLAY	25	M	MCHT	RRZZZZ	USA
GOLDE, RIWKE	64	F	W	RRZZZZ	USA
MARIANNE	40	F	W	RRZZZZ	USA
MOSES	9	M	CHILD	RRZZZZ	USA
LEIB	8	M	CHILD	RRZZZZ	USA
WITT, JOHANNE	30	F	SGL	RRZZZZ	USA
BOSCH, GITTEL	26	F	W	RRZZZZ	USA
ISRAEL	6	M	CHILD	RRZZZZ	USA
SARA	3	F	CHILD	RRZZZZ	USA
LOSCHOWSKY, ISAAC	17	M	LABR	RRZZZZ	USA
LEVINSTEIN, CHAIE	22	F	W	RRZZZZ	USA
SARA	.06	F	INFANT	RRZZZZ	USA
SCHILLING, PAULINE	20	F	SGL	RRZZZZ	USA
ANDR.	22	M	LABR	RRZZZZ	USA
MATZKEWITZ, ANNIE	22	F	SGL	RRZZZZ	USA
BERNSTEIN, LEWIN	18	M	MSN	RRZZZZ	USA
KLEINFUSS, ARON	30	M	TLR	RRZZZZ	USA
PONSIOKI, JOSEF	18	M	LABR	RRZZZZ	USA
SCHALESCHOTZKI, TAUBE	20	F	SGL	RRZZZZ	USA
ABRAMOWITZ, JONAS	20	M	LABR	RRZZZZ	USA
LIPSCHITZ, JOEL	00	M	TLR	RRZZZZ	USA
BROUDY, ISAAC	21	M	DLR	RRZZZZ	USA
GOLDBERG, HIRSCH	22	M	JNR	RRZZZZ	USA
KLEINSCHMIDT, FRIEDE	22	F	SGL	RRZZZZ	USA
GOTZ, PHILIPP	27	M	FARMER	RRZZZZ	USA
CAROLINE	25	F	W	RRZZZZ	USA
ROSINE	3	F	CHILD	RRZZZZ	USA
FRIEDR.	.11	F	INFANT	RRZZZZ	USA
GIESE, JOH.	33	M	FARMER	RRZZZZ	USA
ELISAB.	29	F	W	RRZZZZ	USA
FRIEDR.	6	F	CHILD	RRZZZZ	USA
JOH.	2	M	CHILD	RRZZZZ	USA
PHIL.	.09	M	INFANT	RRZZZZ	USA
BALENSKY, ELISAB.	20	F	SGL	RRZZZZ	USA
KOMFOLD, FANNY	23	F	SGL	RRZZZZ	USA

SHIP: LABRADOR

FROM: HAVRE
TO: NEW YORK
ARRIVED: 07 NOVEMBER 1884

PASSENGER	AGE	SEX	OCCUPATION	PRIVIL	DES
PETRAKOWSKY, JACOB	15	M	NN	RRZZZZ	NY
MULHSTEIN, HENRI	14	M	NN	RRZZZZ	NY

SHIP: AUSTRALIA

FROM: HAMBURG
TO: NEW YORK
ARRIVED: 08 NOVEMBER 1884

PASSENGER	AGE	SEX	OCCUPATION	PRIVIL	DES
KOZTOWSKI, ED.	24	M	MCHT	PLZZZZ	IL
WOLTANOWSKA, ANNA	25	F	WO	PLZZZZ	IL
OSOGOWISCH, VALERI	27	F	WO	PLZZZZ	IL
LADISLAUS	7	M	CHILD	PLZZZZ	IL
LUBLINSKI, RAPHAEL	46	M	LABR	RRZZZZ	NY
SARAH	44	F	WO	RRZZZZ	NY
IDA	20	F	D	RRZZZZ	NY
FAUCH	12	M	S	RRZZZZ	NY
TAUBE	7	F	CHILD	RRZZZZ	NY
RACHEL	6	F	CHILD	RRZZZZ	NY
ARTENSTEIN, CHAIM	26	M	LABR	RRZZZZ	NY
KETTLERVON, SCHITRE	14	F	SGL	RRZZZZ	NY
MASLINKOW, CHAJE	59	F	WO	RRZZZZ	NY
ISAAC	7	M	CHILD	RRZZZZ	NY
ALIK	5	M	CHILD	RRZZZZ	NY
GRUFT, BERL	26	M	TRDSMN	PLZZZZ	NY
FENER, JUDA	21	M	TRDSMN	PLZZZZ	NY
SILBERMANN, DAVID	19	M	LABR	PLZZZZ	NY
WALKOWSKY, SAM	28	M	MCHT	RRZZZZ	NY
FEIER, LEOP.	27	M	TU	RRZZZZ	NY
PIECZANSKY, CH.	21	M	LABR	RRZZZZ	NY
SILBERSTEIN, D.	26	M	BRR	RRZZZZ	NY
HARRIES	20	M	MLR	RRZZZZ	NY

SHIP: CIRCASSIA

FROM: GLASGOW AND MOVILLE
TO: NEW YORK
ARRIVED: 08 NOVEMBER 1884

PASSENGER	AGE	SEX	OCCUPATION	PRIVIL	DES
FLASCHAL, EMANUEL	30	M	CL	PLZZZZ	USA

SHIP: RHYNLAND

FROM: ANTWERP
TO: NEW YORK
ARRIVED: 08 NOVEMBER 1884

PASSENGER	AGE	SEX	OCCUPATION	PRIVIL	DES
HUBERT, PETER	19	M	CPTR	RRZZZZ	NY
MERGEN, WM.	22	M	CPTR	RRZZZZ	NY
FULBRECK, C.	22	M	UNKNOWN	PLZZZZ	PHI
GOTZ, J.	18	M	UNKNOWN	PLZZZZ	UNK
JANCZESKI, M.	40	M	UNKNOWN	PLZZZZ	USA
NAGEN, P.	19	F	UNKNOWN	PLZZZZ	IL
HNILMANN, K.	26	F	UNKNOWN	PLZZZZ	PHI
TOMSAK, J.	19	M	UNKNOWN	PLZZZZ	NY
CLZEWSKI, ANT.	21	M	UNKNOWN	RRZZZZ	UNK

SHIP: DONAU

FROM: BREMEN
TO: NEW YORK
ARRIVED: 10 NOVEMBER 1884

PASSENGER	AGE	SEX	OCCUPATION	PRIVIL	DES
SALZMANN, JEKE	28	M	FARMER	RRZZZZ	USA
RICH.	20	M	FARMER	RRZZZZ	USA
KOPPLER, GOTTL.	19	M	LABR	RRZZZZ	USA
STEINBACH, CHRIST.	21	M	LABR	RRZZZZ	USA
SEWGER, FRIEDR.	21	M	LABR	RRZZZZ	USA
SCHERPINSKY, GOTTLIEB	20	M	LABR	RRZZZZ	USA
BROZINSKI, LEAN	21	M	LABR	RRZZZZ	USA
THIESSEN, JACOB	54	M	FARMER	RRZZZZ	USA
CATH.	44	F	W	RRZZZZ	USA

PASSENGER	AGE	SEX	OCCUPATION	PRV VIL DES
FRANZ	19	M	CH	RRZZZZUSA
MARIE	16	F	CH	RRZZZZUSA
JACOB	14	M	CH	RRZZZZUSA
HEINR.	11	M	CH	RRZZZZUSA
JUSTINE	9	F	CHILD	RRZZZZUSA
JOHANN	7	M	CHILD	RRZZZZUSA
GERHARD	4	M	CHILD	RRZZZZUSA
TRAHTENBERG, FEIGE	19	F	NN	RRZZZZUSA
ZICL	18	F	NN	RRZZZZUSA

SHIP: EMS

FROM: BREMEN
TO: NEW YORK
ARRIVED: 10 NOVEMBER 1884

PASSENGER	AGE	SEX	OCCUPATION	PRV VIL DES
NIKOLSKY, LUGASV.	47	M	TT	RRZZZZUSA
ROSA	20	F	NN	RRZZZZUSA
LUGAS	5	M	CHILD	RRZZZZUSA
WILHELM	4	M	CHILD	RRZZZZUSA
MARIA	1	F	CHILD	RRZZZZUSA
SCHOEBERG, WILHELMINE	19	F	NN	RRZZZZUSA
AMANN, JOHANN	33	M	FARMER	RRZZZZUSA
CHRISTINE	24	F	NN	RRZZZZUSA
JOHANN	8	M	CHILD	RRZZZZUSA
JACOB	6	M	CHILD	RRZZZZUSA
CHRISTINE	4	F	CHILD	RRZZZZUSA
FRIEDRIKE	.02	F	INFANT	RRZZZZUSA
RAN, FRIEDRIKE	21	F	NN	RRZZZZUSA
ROSLER, WILHELM	27	M	FARMER	RRZZZZUSA
FRIEDRIKE	26	F	NN	RRZZZZUSA
WILHELM	.09	M	INFANT	RRZZZZUSA
GIENGER, JOHANN	45	M	FARMER	RRZZZZUSA
CHRISTINE	45	F	NN	RRZZZZUSA
CATHARINE	17	F	NN	RRZZZZUSA
PETER	15	M	NN	RRZZZZUSA
ADAM	13	M	CH	RRZZZZUSA
MARGARETHE	10	F	CH	RRZZZZUSA
ELISABETH	3	F	CHILD	RRZZZZUSA
DOROTHEA	.09	F	INFANT	RRZZZZUSA
MEYER, RUDOLF	64	M	FARMER	RRZZZZUSA
RAIDE, GOTTLIEB	30	M	FARMER	RRZZZZUSA
CHRISTINE	24	F	NN	RRZZZZUSA
CHRISTINE	4	F	CHILD	RRZZZZUSA
MAGDALENE	2	F	CHILD	RRZZZZUSA
GOTTLIEB	.11	M	INFANT	RRZZZZUSA
ROBMANN, BLILE	55	M	LABR	RRZZZZUSA
GOLDE	18	F	NN	RRZZZZUSA
WACKER, JACOB	53	M	FARMER	RRZZZZUSA
BARBARA	52	F	NN	RRZZZZUSA
CHRISTIAN	19	M	FARMER	RRZZZZUSA
CARL	15	M	NN	RRZZZZUSA
PHILIPP	10	M	CH	RRZZZZUSA
LUDWIG	9	M	CHILD	RRZZZZUSA
SATTLER, KATHARINE	50	F	NN	RRZZZZUSA
CARL	20	M	FARMER	RRZZZZUSA
CHRISTIAN	15	M	NN	RRZZZZUSA
CONSTANTIN	10	M	CH	RRZZZZUSA
FERDINAND	9	M	CHILD	RRZZZZUSA
EDUARD	4	M	CHILD	RRZZZZUSA
MARIA	2	F	CHILD	RRZZZZUSA
STUECKLER, LUDWIG	28	M	FARMER	RRZZZZUSA
CATHARINE	23	F	NN	RRZZZZUSA
ZIEGLER, WILH.	34	M	FARMER	RRZZZZUSA
CATHARINE	27	F	NN	RRZZZZUSA
JACOB	2	M	CHILD	RRZZZZUSA
BECK, JACOB	28	M	FARMER	RRZZZZUSA
CATHARINE	29	F	NN	RRZZZZUSA
HOLLGEISER, FRIEDR.	29	M	FARMER	RRZZZZUSA
MARIA	24	F	NN	RRZZZZUSA
GOTTLOB	2	M	CHILD	RRZZZZUSA
FRIEDRICH	.10	M	INFANT	RRZZZZUSA
SCHELL, GOTTLOB	9	M	CHILD	RRZZZZUSA
HOLLGEISER, JACOB	16	M	FARMER	RRZZZZUSA
FORST, JACOB	33	M	FARMER	RRZZZZUSA
CAROLINE	27	F	NN	RRZZZZUSA
CAROLINE	6	F	CHILD	RRZZZZUSA
LISABETH	4	F	CHILD	RRZZZZUSA
RIEKE	3	F	CHILD	RRZZZZUSA
CATHARINE	1	F	CHILD	RRZZZZUSA
WUEST, PETER	32	M	FARMER	RRZZZZUSA
ELISABETH	29	F	NN	RRZZZZUSA
PETER	5	M	CHILD	RRZZZZUSA
CATHARINE	4	F	CHILD	RRZZZZUSA
PAULINE	.05	F	INFANT	RRZZZZUSA
FRANZ, ANDREAS	32	M	LABR	RRZZZZUSA
CHARLOTTE	26	F	NN	RRZZZZUSA
HARTMANN, LISETTE	56	F	NN	RRZZZZUSA

SHIP: LESSING

FROM: HAMBURG AND HAVRE
TO: NEW YORK
ARRIVED: 10 NOVEMBER 1884

PASSENGER	AGE	SEX	OCCUPATION	PRV VIL DES
U, LOUISE	25	F	W	RRZZZZUSA
ROBINSON, JOEL	18	M	LABR	RRZZZZUSA
PODEWSKI, ELKE	32	F	W	RRAFWJUSA
SIMISCHE	8	F	CHILD	RRAFWJUSA
DAVID	6	M	CHILD	RRAFWJUSA
HINDE	5	F	CHILD	RRAFWJUSA
PHILIPOWSKY, BARUCH	18	M	LABR	RRAHZSUSA
ZUCKERMANN, ZIWIE	20	F	SGL	RRAGRTUSA
GINETZISCHKY, WOLF	14	M	LABR	RRAGRTUSA
VKEMIANSKY, ISIDOR	19	M	LABR	RRZZZZUSA
MARKUS, ADLPH.	25	M	LABR	RRZZZZUSA
HECHT, MATHILDE	24	F	SGL	RRAHZSUSA
ROSCHINSKY, ISAAC	33	M	TNR	RRZZZZUSA
FILACSCHI, JOSEF	9	M	CHILD	RRZZZZUSA
U, FRANZ	8	M	CHILD	RRZZZZUSA
ISACOWITZ, JACOB	40	M	LABR	RRAHTFUSA
ETTE	15	F	D	RRAHTFUSA
SCHMUL	14	M	S	RRAHTFUSA
ZALLEL	9	M	CHILD	RRAHTFUSA
KAN, ISAAC	16	M	LABR	RRAHRZUSA
SARA	20	F	W	RRAHRZUSA
SZIMEC	.05	M	INFANT	RRAHRZUSA
KREMER, NACHEM	20	M	TLR	RRAHTFUSA
FELDMANN, ELIAS	48	M	DLR	RRAHOKUSA
BEHR.	21	M	DLR	RRAHOKUSA
SCHOCHAT, JOZE	31	M	DLR	RRAHOKUSA
LEWITAN, LEA	23	F	SGL	RRAHTUUSA
SINISCHI, CASPAR.	24	M	LABR	RRZZZZUSA
GOWA, JOH.	22	M	LABR	RRZZZZUSA
SMETANA, FRANZ	27	M	LABR	RRZZZZUSA
CHAINN, BARUCH	19	M	LABR	RRAHUVUSA
MARIANNE	22	F	W	RRAHUVUSA
TIGER, NESCHE	42	F	W	RRZZZZUSA
RACHEL	9	F	CHILD	RRZZZZUSA
DRESSER, CHAIM	24	M	LABR	RRAHTUUSA
JUDELWITZ, ELY	19	M	LABR	RRZZZZUSA
HECHT, WILH.	17	M	LABR	RRZZZZUSA
DANOWSKI, CZIHY	20	F	LABR	RRAHZSUSA
LEIKE	.08	F	INFANT	RRAHZSUSA
BERNSTEIN, HIRSCH	19	M	LABR	RRAGRTUSA
LEICHENHAUS, SARA	20	F	SGL	RRAHTUUSA
SCHLAMINKAT, BARBA.	20	F	SGL	RRZZZZUSA
SCHWINGELI, SYLVESTER	24	M	LABR	RRZZZZUSA
LITTWEITES, ANTONAS	22	M	LABR	RRZZZZUSA
CAPLAN, TAUBE	22	F	SGL	RRAHVLUSA

PASSENGER	A G E	S E X	OCCUPATION	P R V / V I L / D E S
WILENZIG, JOSEF	21	M	LABR	RRAHTFUSA
LEIBSON, JUDEL	28	F	W	RRAHZSUSA
CHAIM	00	M	S	RRAHZSUSA
SCHUBERT, ANNA	27	F	W	RRAHQDUSA
WILLI	5	F	CHILD	RRAHQDUSA
ELSE	2	F	CHILD	RRAHQDUSA
ALFRED	.11	M	INFANT	RRAHQDUSA
GABRIELSOHN, BATHSEBA	19	F	SGL	RRAHVLUSA
CHESINS, JERSI	24	M	LABR	RRZZZZUSA
MILGRAMM, NOCHIM	25	M	LABR	RRZZZZUSA
BANK, WOLF	21	M	LABR	RRZZZZUSA
SARAH	22	F	W	RRZZZZUSA

SHIP: STATE OF GEORGIA

FROM: GLASGOW AND LARNE
TO: NEW YORK
ARRIVED: 10 NOVEMBER 1884

PASSENGER	A G E	S E X	OCCUPATION	P R V / V I L / D E S
SANDSTEIN, RASES	24	M	PDLR	PLZZZZNY
SIMON, MOSES	21	M	PDLR	PLZZZZNY
BEDER, HEINRICH	40	M	LABR	PLZZZZNY
WEISFMANN, REGINE	22	F	W	PLZZZZNY
MALI	.02	F	INFANT	PLZZZZNY
GOLDSCHMIED, FRIDA	23	F	WI	PLZZZZNY
SALLY	00	F	CH	PLZZZZNY
SELINSKA, PAULINE	22	F	SVNT	PLZZZZNY
STALMAKOWSKY, FRANZ	36	M	LABR	PLZZZZNY
FARDERISKY, FEIWEL	22	M	PDLR	PLZZZZNY
SCHULDIENER, JOSEF	22	M	PDLR	PLZZZZNY
FEIN, HIRCH	23	M	PDLR	PLZZZZNY
OSKOWITZ, HILLET	33	M	PDLR	PLZZZZNY
KINSCHI, MEYER	22	M	PDLR	PLZZZZNY
LIPMANN, ISRAEL	27	M	PDLR	PLZZZZNY
ESTHER	23	F	W	PLZZZZNY
JANOS, HRABACK	38	M	LABR	PLZZZZNY

SHIP: ETHIOPIA

FROM: GLASGOW AND MOVILLE
TO: NEW YORK
ARRIVED: 13 NOVEMBER 1884

PASSENGER	A G E	S E X	OCCUPATION	P R V / V I L / D E S
LUDAFSOHKIN, JEWELL	24	M	PRNTR	RRZZZZUSA
ZEMANSKA, MAX	18	M	LABR	RRZZZZUSA
CZAWAMATOF, SALOMON	25	M	PDLR	RRZZZZUSA
PICK, JOHANNA	25	F	UNKNOWN	RRZZZZUSA
IDA	5	F	CHILD	RRZZZZUSA
OLGA	3	F	CHILD	RRZZZZUSA
ALICE	.02	F	INFANT	RRZZZZUSA

SHIP: THE QUEEN

FROM: LONDON
TO: NEW YORK
ARRIVED: 13 NOVEMBER 1884

PASSENGER	A G E	S E X	OCCUPATION	P R V / V I L / D E S
LAKINSKY, H.	48	F	W	PLZZZZNY
F.	15	F	CH	PLZZZZNY
M.	11	M	CH	PLZZZZNY
L.	9	F	CHILD	PLZZZZNY
A.	8	F	CHILD	PLZZZZNY
KOHANOFF, R.	48	F	W	PLZZZZNY
M.	17	M	S	PLZZZZNY
G.	2	M	CHILD	PLZZZZNY
JABLONSKY, G.	35	F	W	PLZZZZNY
J.	11	F	CH	PLZZZZNY
HERSCHERSZ, J.	30	M	TLR	PLZZZZNY
M.	28	F	W	PLZZZZNY
J.	5	F	CHILD	PLZZZZNY
G.	.10	F	INFANT	PLZZZZNY
REMENOVITZ, A.	28	M	MECH	RRZZZZNY
CHORKIN, A.H.	21	M	TLR	RRZZZZNY
JACOBS, S.	23	M	TLR	RRZZZZNY

SHIP: MORAVIA

FROM: HAMBURG
TO: NEW YORK
ARRIVED: 14 NOVEMBER 1884

PASSENGER	A G E	S E X	OCCUPATION	P R V / V I L / D E S
ZERNEMANN, CHAIM	23	M	LABR	RRZZZZUSA
HLAMETH, RIWKE	21	F	W	RRZZZZUSA
JACOB	.11	M	INFANT	RRZZZZUSA
MOSES	.01	M	INFANT	RRZZZZUSA
WEIMANN, LEA	19	F	SGL	RRAHTFUSA
WISATZKY, JOSEF	23	M	LABR	RRZZZZUSA
RABINOWITZ, SCHEPSEL	23	M	LABR	RRZZZZUSA
KRIEGEL, JACOB	17	M	LABR	RRAHTUUSA
DUSCHKY, KNISSIEL	21	M	LABR	RRAHTFUSA
BEECHERMANN, MORITZ	21	M	LABR	RRZZZZUSA
MATHILDE	19	F	W	RRZZZZUSA
WIEDZETZKI, ISAAK	21	M	LABR	RRZZZZUSA
SCHMIDT, JACOB	25	M	LABR	RRZZZZUSA
CHRISTINE	26	F	W	RRZZZZUSA
ROSINE	4	F	CHILD	RRZZZZUSA
PHILIPP	18	M	LABR	RRZZZZUSA
BACKER, AUGUST	29	M	LABR	RRZZZZUSA
ELISABETH	25	F	W	RRZZZZUSA
JULIANE	73	F	W	RRZZZZUSA
FUEHRER, JACOB	26	M	LABR	RRAFQVUSA
ELISABETH	25	F	W	RRAFQVUSA
JACOB	5	M	CHILD	RRAFQVUSA
ALEXANDER	.03	M	INFANT	RRAFQVUSA
FALT, JACOB	41	M	LABR	RRAEGTUSA
ANNA	31	F	W	RRAEGTUSA
JOHANN	9	M	CHILD	RRAEGTUSA
ANNA	.03	F	INFANT	RRAEGTUSA
IHRKE, LUDWIG	46	M	FARMER	RRZZZZUSA
ERNESTINE	49	F	W	RRZZZZUSA
WILH.	13	M	CH	RRZZZZUSA
KOCK, CARL	23	M	FARMER	RRZZZZUSA
BRONNEMEIER, PHILIPP	21	M	LABR	RRAFQVUSA
DORA	21	F	W	RRAFQVUSA
KRANS, JOHANN	33	M	LABR	RRZZZZUSA
BARBA.	31	F	W	RRZZZZUSA
LIDA	.11	F	INFANT	RRZZZZUSA
LUTZ, ANTONIN	28	M	FARMER	RRZZZZUSA
ELIZA	25	F	W	RRZZZZUSA
GOTTLIEB	2	M	CHILD	RRZZZZUSA
JACOB	.11	M	INFANT	RRZZZZUSA
KRIEG, JOH.	27	M	FARMER	RRZZZZUSA
MARGE.	27	F	W	RRZZZZUSA
CATHE.	20	F	SGL	RRZZZZUSA
CATHE.	2	F	CHILD	RRZZZZUSA
--ARGE.	.11	F	INFANT	RRZZZZUSA
ULMER, CHRISTIAN	32	M	FARMER	RRZZZZUSA
CATHA.	30	F	W	RRZZZZUSA
CARL	9	M	CHILD	RRZZZZUSA
CATH.	7	F	CHILD	RRZZZZUSA

PASSENGER	AGE	SEX	OCCUPATION	PRIV	VIL	DES
ELISE	5	F	CHILD	RR	ZZZZ	USA
CHRISTINE	2	F	CHILD	RR	ZZZZ	USA
CHRISTIAN	.11	M	INFANT	RR	ZZZZ	USA
HRITSCHELKRAUS, KOWL	51	M	FARMER	RR	ZZZZ	USA
LOUISA	50	F	W	RR	ZZZZ	USA
CATHA.	21	F	CH	RR	ZZZZ	USA
JACOB	19	M	CH	RR	ZZZZ	USA
CARL	17	M	CH	RR	ZZZZ	USA
CHRISTINA	15	F	CH	RR	ZZZZ	USA
CHRISTIAN	9	M	CHILD	RR	ZZZZ	USA
GOTTLIEB	7	M	CHILD	RR	ZZZZ	USA
HUBER, JACOB	40	M	FARMER	RR	ZZZZ	USA
JOHE.	42	F	W	RR	ZZZZ	USA
CHRISTINE	14	F	CH	RR	ZZZZ	USA
GEORG	5	M	CHILD	RR	ZZZZ	USA
MARGA.	3	F	CHILD	RR	ZZZZ	USA
ELISE	.11	F	INFANT	RR	ZZZZ	USA
FISCHER, PHILIPP	24	M	FARMER	RR	ZZZZ	USA
BARBA.	25	F	W	RR	ZZZZ	USA
BARBA.	2	F	CHILD	RR	ZZZZ	USA
ROZINE	2	F	CHILD	RR	ZZZZ	USA
PHILIPP	.03	M	INFANT	RR	ZZZZ	USA
RENZ, JACOB	34	M	FARMER	RR	ZZZZ	USA
BARBA.	32	F	W	RR	ZZZZ	USA
CONRAD	9	M	CHILD	RR	ZZZZ	USA
MARGA.	8	F	CHILD	RR	ZZZZ	USA
DAVID	19	M	LABR	RR	ZZZZ	USA
CARL	22	M	LABR	RR	ZZZZ	USA
ELISE	19	F	SGL	RR	ZZZZ	USA
HEINE, PHILIPP	39	M	FARMER	RR	ZZZZ	USA
JULIANE	39	F	W	RR	ZZZZ	USA
JACOB	20	M	CH	RR	ZZZZ	USA
PHILIPP	18	M	CH	RR	ZZZZ	USA
JULIANE	18	F	CH	RR	ZZZZ	USA
EVA	17	F	CH	RR	ZZZZ	USA
DAVID	13	M	CH	RR	ZZZZ	USA
CHRISTIAN	7	M	CHILD	RR	ZZZZ	USA
HEINRICH	5	M	CHILD	RR	ZZZZ	USA
SOPHIA	2	F	CHILD	RR	ZZZZ	USA
JACOB	.11	M	INFANT	RR	ZZZZ	USA
STARIKOW, MICHAEL	17	M	MCHT	RR	AFVG	USA
SCHULZ, FOJOMNA	36	F	W	RR	ZZZZ	USA
REINHOLV	.11	M	INFANT	RR	ZZZZ	USA
KRADER, SARA	20	F	SGL	RR	ZZZZ	USA
COHN, LEWINS	15	M	LABR	RR	ZZZZ	USA
BENJAMIN	19	M	LABR	RR	ZZZZ	USA
PRYSYKAT, ANNA	50	F	W	RR	ZZZZ	USA
AMANDA	14	F	CH	RR	ZZZZ	USA
FRANKFURTER, RIWKE	18	F	SGL	RR	ZZZZ	USA
FINKELBERG, CHASCHE	50	F	W	RR	ZZZZ	USA
RACHEL	20	F	CH	RR	ZZZZ	USA
MINNIE	14	F	CH	RR	ZZZZ	USA
BEHR	8	M	CHILD	RR	ZZZZ	USA
ARONSOHN, MARCUS	51	M	LABR	RR	AHTS	USA
SARA	32	F	W	RR	AHTS	USA
PESACH	9	F	CHILD	RR	AHTS	USA
DWORE	7	F	CHILD	RR	AHTS	USA
MALKE	.11	F	INFANT	RR	AHTS	USA
SALNIK, LEIB	16	M	LABR	RR	ZZZZ	USA
SCHMUGLER, SIMON	48	M	LABR	RR	ZZZZ	USA
DREYER, MEYER	39	M	LABR	RR	ZZZZ	USA
FRIEDMANN, FREIDE	42	F	W	RR	ZZZZ	USA
RACHEL	16	F	CH	RR	ZZZZ	USA
ISRAEL	9	M	CHILD	RR	ZZZZ	USA
BASCHE	4	F	CHILD	RR	ZZZZ	USA
MENDEL	.11	M	INFANT	RR	ZZZZ	USA
KOFMANN, MOSES	40	M	HRCTR	RR	ZZZZ	USA
MERE	30	F	W	RR	ZZZZ	USA
JOACHIM	7	M	CHILD	RR	ZZZZ	USA
BERL	.06	M	INFANT	RR	ZZZZ	USA
HELZIN, JOSSEL	40	M	LKSH	RR	ZZZZ	USA
GOLDBERG, WOLF	24	M	LABR	RR	ZZZZ	USA
GRODNIK, DAVID	36	M	LABR	RR	ZZZZ	USA
EIDES, SCHMUL	16	M	LABR	RR	ZZZZ	USA
KARTUM, LUSCHE	27	F	SGL	RR	ZZZZ	USA
ABELOWITZ, JOSSEL	24	M	LABR	RR	ZZZZ	USA
ROMEKAT, IWAN	22	M	LABR	RR	AHTF	USA
RUSSIANOW, ELIE	25	M	TLR	RR	AHTU	USA
RUSSOW, MOSES	24	M	TLR	RR	AHTU	USA
RIWKIN, MIREL	30	F	W	RR	AHSL	USA
CHAINE	7	F	CHILD	RR	AHSL	USA
DOBRE	4	F	CHILD	RR	AHSL	USA
ITZIG	.11	M	INFANT	RR	AHSL	USA
KATZ, FRADEL	18	F	SGL	RR	ZZZZ	USA
KAMINSKY, SYLVESTER	20	M	LABR	RR	ZZZZ	USA
GOLD, CHANNE	20	F	W	RR	AHYC	USA
WOLF	9	M	CHILD	RR	AHYC	USA
BERL	.11	M	INFANT	RR	AHYC	USA
GREENBERG, LOEB	19	M	LABR	RR	AHSW	USA
BUCHMANN, RACHEL	14	F	SGL	RR	ZZZZ	USA
SEGAL, RACHEL	18	F	SGL	RR	AHTF	USA
BEILE	20	F	SGL	RR	AHTF	USA
BIALESTOTSKY, SCHMUL	17	M	LABR	RR	AHQU	USA
SAWATZKI, LIEBE	23	F	W	RR	ZZZZ	USA
ROSA	.11	F	INFANT	RR	ZZZZ	USA
DAVID	.01	M	INFANT	RR	ZZZZ	USA
ABRAMOWITZ, JACOB	22	M	DLR	RR	ZZZZ	USA
TIGER, SELIG	35	M	DLR	RR	ZZZZ	USA
FEINBERG, ISSER	42	M	LABR	RR	AHZS	USA
SAWATZKI, SIESSEL	19	F	SGL	RR	ZZZZ	USA
DOLINSKY, CHAIE	19	F	SGL	RR	AHZS	USA
FERTZIG, BREINE	19	F	SGL	RR	AHZS	USA
RIPINSKY, JOSEF	21	M	FARMER	RR	ZZZZ	USA
HUTMACHER, DAVID	19	M	LABR	RR	ZZZZ	USA
BRONISLOWSKY, SAMUEL	21	M	LABR	RR	ZZZZ	USA
LUXEMBURG, MOSES	23	M	LABR	RR	ZZZZ	USA
GELBART, SARA	36	F	SGL	RR	ZZZZ	USA
ABRAMS, FEIBUSCH	18	M	TLR	RR	AHTD	USA
GOLDENSOHN, MOSES	38	M	LABR	RR	AHSW	USA
GRUENSTEIN, CHAIE	18	F	SGL	RR	AHSW	USA
ARON	17	M	LABR	RR	AHSW	USA
KAUFMANN, CHANNE	35	F	W	RR	AHQU	USA
ESTHER	15	F	CH	RR	AHQU	USA
DINA	9	F	CHILD	RR	AHQU	USA
AMBROSEWITZ, PETER	26	M	LABR	RR	ZZZZ	USA
JEDWAP, FEIGE	16	F	SGL	RR	ZZZZ	USA
HERUSCHSOHN, DAVID	18	M	LABR	RR	AHSW	USA
BOROWSKY, BARUCH	20	M	LABR	RR	ZZZZ	USA
ISAAC	20	M	LABR	RR	ZZZZ	USA
SCHAPEL	20	M	LABR	RR	ZZZZ	USA
STANKOWITZ, MARTIN	30	M	LABR	RR	AHTR	USA
ROSA	25	F	W	RR	AHTR	USA
LUCASEWITZ, JOSEF	20	M	LABR	RR	AHTR	USA
KASPEROWITZ, JOSEF	23	M	LABR	RR	AHTR	USA
KRAKOWSKY, MARIE	20	F	SGL	RR	AHTR	USA
PONIBASA, MARIA	18	F	SGL	RR	AHTR	USA
AVISENIS, STASIS	48	M	LABR	RR	AHTR	USA
ANTON	36	M	LABR	RR	AHTR	USA
MAGDAL	26	F	W	RR	AHTR	USA
MARIE	5	F	CHILD	RR	AHTR	USA
ANNA	.11	F	INFANT	RR	AHTR	USA
JOSEF	.01	M	INFANT	RR	AHTR	USA
EDELMANN, JOH.	15	M	LABR	RR	ZZZZ	USA

SHIP: NOORDLAND

FROM: ANTWERP
TO: NEW YORK
ARRIVED: 14 NOVEMBER 1884

PASSENGER	AGE	SEX	OCCUPATION	PRIV	VIL	DES
SALOWOWICZ, F.	40	F	W	PL	ZZZZ	UNK
WAD	00	M	UNKNOWN	PL	ZZZZ	UNK
L.	9	M	CHILD	PL	ZZZZ	UNK
H.	7	M	CHILD	PL	ZZZZ	UNK
F.	3	M	CHILD	PL	ZZZZ	UNK

PASSENGER	AGE	SEX	OCCUPATION	PRV VIL DES
C.	00	F	INF	PLZZZZUNK
SLOTHY, J.	24	F	W	PLZZZZUNK
S.	4	F	CHILD	PLZZZZUNK
M.	2	F	CHILD	PLZZZZUNK
NAWOVTZIS, M.	32	F	W	PLZZZZUNK
JOH.	7	M	CHILD	PLZZZZUNK
ANT.	5	M	CHILD	PLZZZZUNK
MAR.	00	M	INF	PLZZZZUNK
KUBERA, MAR.	38	F	W	PLZZZZUNK
A.	10	M	CH	PLZZZZUNK
ER.	8	F	CHILD	PLZZZZUNK
L.	5	F	CHILD	PLZZZZUNK
L.	3	F	CHILD	PLZZZZUNK
KAS.	00	M	INF	PLZZZZUNK
LUCZAICIONA, FR.	40	F	W	PLZZZZUNK
BACHIWIAN, C.	25	F	W	PLZZZZUNK
ZAP, FR.	32	M	LABR	PLZZZZPHI
EM.	27	F	LABR	PLZZZZPHI
H.	3	M	CHILD	PLZZZZPHI
BUFSKI, A.	22	M	LABR	PLZZZZUNK
NOWISCITES, M.	26	M	LABR	RRZZZZNY
FISCHERE, H.	43	M	LABR	PLZZZZNY
CA.	38	F	UNKNOWN	PLZZZZNY
PETER	17	M	UNKNOWN	PLZZZZNY
EM.	11	M	CH	PLZZZZNY
CH.	5	M	CHILD	PLZZZZNY
AUG.	00	M	INF	PLZZZZNY
GRUNNIG, W.	43	M	SMH	PLZZZZNY
EVA	38	F	UNKNOWN	PLZZZZNY
ROB.	17	M	CH	PLZZZZNY
GIWIE	3	M	CHILD	PLZZZZNY
DEMFNICK, A.	11	M	CH	PLZZZZUNK
POLARKE, JOH.	22	M	LABR	PLZZZZPHI
GRUNINGER, A.	27	F	SVNT	PLZZZZPHI

SHIP: STATE OF NEVADA

FROM: GLASGOW
TO: NEW YORK
ARRIVED: 14 NOVEMBER 1884

PASSENGER	AGE	SEX	OCCUPATION	PRV VIL DES
ANKISKY, L.	22	M	PPHGR	RRZZZZUSA
BLOSH, A.	18	M	LABR	RRZZZZUSA
BEHRMANN, J.	24	M	PDLR	RRZZZZUSA
HRZ.	22	F	W	RRZZZZUSA
DENTSCH, A.	20	M	PDLR	RRZZZZUSA
GOLDSTEIN, J.	22	M	PDLR	RRZZZZUSA
FEDIDJE, S.	22	M	PDLR	RRZZZZUSA
SOMMES, W.	21	M	PDLR	RRZZZZUSA
SCHABES, R.	20	M	LABR	RRZZZZUSA
SILBERSTEIN, J.	00	M	PDLR	RRZZZZUSA
SCHACHNOWSKY, H.	25	M	LABR	RRZZZZUSA
SCHWARZ, J.	17	M	PDLR	RRZZZZUSA
WEINSTEIN, C.	19	M	PDLR	RRZZZZUSA
JASKOWITZ, J.	23	M	PDLR	RRZZZZUSA
ISRAEL, W.	29	M	PDLR	RRZZZZUSA
JAGEDNITZKY, H.	40	M	PDLR	RRZZZZUSA
JAKON, M.	25	M	PDLR	RRZZZZUSA
S.	20	M	PDLR	RRZZZZUSA
JAFFE, FELIX	19	M	PDLR	RRZZZZUSA
WEINBERG, RESI	11	F	CH	RRZZZZUSA
KONOR, MOSES	00	M	SHMK	RRZZZZUSA

SHIP: EIDER

FROM: BREMEN AND SOUTHAMPTON
TO: NEW YORK
ARRIVED: 15 NOVEMBER 1884

PASSENGER	AGE	SEX	OCCUPATION	PRV VIL DES
SCHROB, JOH.PET.	33	M	LABR	RRZZZZUSA
KATHA.	28	F	W	RRZZZZUSA
SLOMINSKY, HIRSCH	27	M	FARMER	RRZZZZUSA
MINNA	30	F	W	RRZZZZUSA
DORA	7	F	CHILD	RRZZZZUSA
RACHEL	4	F	CHILD	RRZZZZUSA
BUCH, ABEL	32	M	FARMER	RRZZZZUSA
RAFAEL	10	M	CH	RRZZZZUSA
WEICHL, MARA	30	M	FARMER	RRZZZZUSA
REGINE	21	F	W	RRZZZZUSA
REGINE	.11	F	INFANT	RRZZZZUSA
WEICHEL, PETER	.01	M	INFANT	RRZZZZUSA
MITZEL, PETER	29	M	FARMER	RRZZZZUSA
BARBA.	21	F	W	RRZZZZUSA
JACOB	.06	M	INFANT	RRZZZZUSA
WALLINGER, JOHS.	28	M	FARMER	RRZZZZUSA
BARBA.	22	F	W	RRZZZZUSA
BASTIAN, PHILIPP	26	M	LABR	RRZZZZUSA
DOROTHEA	26	F	W	RRZZZZUSA
ELISABETH	.01	F	INFANT	RRZZZZUSA
GUTMUELLER, MICHAEL	35	M	FARMER	RRZZZZUSA
KATHA.	34	F	W	RRZZZZUSA
JOH.	9	M	CHILD	RRZZZZUSA
FRIEDR.	00	M	CH	RRZZZZUSA
CAROLE.	4	F	CHILD	RRZZZZUSA
CHRISTE.	3	F	CHILD	RRZZZZUSA
CHRISTN.	.11	M	INFANT	RRZZZZUSA
BAUER, JOHANN	29	M	FARMER	RRZZZZUSA
CHRISTE.	26	F	W	RRZZZZUSA
MARGE.	.11	F	INFANT	RRZZZZUSA
CATHA.	.01	F	INFANT	RRZZZZUSA
MUELLER, ANDREAS	25	M	FARMER	RRZZZZUSA
ELISABETH	23	F	W	RRZZZZUSA
BENZ, CHRIST.	27	M	FARMER	RRZZZZUSA
JULIANE	26	F	W	RRZZZZUSA
CHRIST.	.11	M	INFANT	RRZZZZUSA
PUCKELBERGER, DOROTHEA	22	F	NN	RRZZZZUSA
GRAF, ELIAB	19	F	W	RRZZZZUSA
SCHNEIDER, MARTHA	.01	F	INFANT	RRZZZZUSA
KLUND, MICHAEL	40	M	FARMER	RRZZZZUSA
BARBA.	35	F	W	RRZZZZUSA
CATHA.	9	F	CHILD	RRZZZZUSA
BARBA.	7	F	CHILD	RRZZZZUSA
JOHANN	4	M	CHILD	RRZZZZUSA
EDUARD	1	M	CHILD	RRZZZZUSA
MARGA	.03	F	INFANT	RRZZZZUSA
JOHANN	27	M	FARMER	RRZZZZUSA
NADEL, MATHIAS	22	M	FARMER	RRZZZZUSA
DOROTHEA	21	F	W	RRZZZZUSA
GEISLER, JOHANNES	22	M	LABR	RRZZZZUSA
WILHE.	19	F	NN	RRZZZZUSA
CHRISTOF	16	M	CH	RRZZZZUSA
ANDREAS	18	F	CH	RRZZZZUSA
NODEL, GOTTLIEB	57	M	FARMER	RRZZZZUSA
CHRISTE.	55	F	W	RRZZZZUSA
GOTTLIEB	20	M	FARMER	RRZZZZUSA
CHRISTE.	18	F	NN	RRZZZZUSA
ANNA-MA.	17	F	NN	RRZZZZUSA
ANTON	16	M	LABR	RRZZZZUSA
JUSTE.	7	F	CHILD	RRZZZZUSA
JULIANE	27	F	NN	RRZZZZUSA
GRAMLICH, ANDRAS	39	M	FARMER	RRZZZZUSA
SALOMEA	39	F	W	RRZZZZUSA
ANDRAS	14	M	NN	RRZZZZUSA
BARBA.	11	F	CH	RRZZZZUSA
LOUISE	6	F	CHILD	RRZZZZUSA
CATHA.	.11	F	INFANT	RRZZZZUSA
HIRSCH, SIMON	28	M	FARMER	RRZZZZUSA

PASSENGER	AGE	SEX	OCCUPATION	PRV VIL DES
ELISABETH	25	F	W	RRZZZZUSA
SIMON	2	M	CHILD	RRZZZZUSA
FRIEDA	.06	F	INFANT	RRZZZZUSA
FELICK, GOTTLIEB	18	M	LABR	RRZZZZUSA
MARGE.	21	F	NN	RRZZZZUSA
BASTIAN, JACOB	30	M	FARMER	RRZZZZUSA
CHRISTA	24	F	W	RRZZZZUSA
GOTTLIEB	.09	M	INFANT	RRZZZZUSA
ROHLHEISER, JOHS.	34	M	TLR	RRZZZZUSA
KATHA.	28	F	W	RRZZZZUSA
KATHA.	6	F	CHILD	RRZZZZUSA
LISBETH	2	F	CHILD	RRZZZZUSA
ANNA	.03	F	INFANT	RRZZZZUSA
GLUND, JACOB	29	M	FARMER	RRZZZZUSA
MARIA	31	F	W	RRZZZZUSA
CARL	5	M	CHILD	RRZZZZUSA
JACOB	4	M	CHILD	RRZZZZUSA
AUGUST	3	M	CHILD	RRZZZZUSA
ELISABETH	.11	F	INFANT	RRZZZZUSA
HOFER, HEINR.	45	M	FARMER	RRZZZZUSA
KATHA.	40	F	W	RRZZZZUSA
ELISAB.	16	F	NN	RRZZZZUSA
FRIEDR.	5	M	CHILD	RRZZZZUSA
KATHA.	4	F	CHILD	RRZZZZUSA
CHRIST.	3	M	CHILD	RRZZZZUSA
EVA	1	F	CHILD	RRZZZZUSA
LUTZ, MICHAEL	27	M	FARMER	RRZZZZUSA
KATHA.	25	F	W	RRZZZZUSA
EMILIE	1	F	CHILD	RRZZZZUSA
RUDWICE, ERDMANN	35	M	FARMER	RRZZZZUSA
ELISABETHA	26	F	W	RRZZZZUSA
REMBALD, ERNST	41	M	FARMER	RRZZZZUSA
FRIEDKE.	38	F	W	RRZZZZUSA
CHRISTE.	13	F	NN	RRZZZZUSA
JACOB	9	M	CHILD	RRZZZZUSA
MICHAEL	8	M	CHILD	RRZZZZUSA
PETER	7	M	CHILD	RRZZZZUSA
LOUISE	5	F	CHILD	RRZZZZUSA
CHRIST.	2	M	CHILD	RRZZZZUSA
CATHA.	1	F	CHILD	RRZZZZUSA
ROTH, ADAM	29	M	FARMER	RRZZZZUSA
CAROLE.	24	F	W	RRZZZZUSA
CATHA.	3	F	CHILD	RRZZZZUSA
ADAM	2	M	CHILD	RRZZZZUSA
CAROLE.	.08	F	INFANT	RRZZZZUSA
IDER, HEINR.	29	M	FARMER	RRZZZZUSA
CHRISTE.	29	F	W	RRZZZZUSA
HEINR.	4	M	CHILD	RRZZZZUSA
BARBA.	3	F	CHILD	RRZZZZUSA
SIMON	2	M	CHILD	RRZZZZUSA
FRIEDRICH	.05	M	INFANT	RRZZZZUSA
SALAMON, ESTER	18	F	NN	RRZZZZUSA

SHIP: CITY OF CHICAGO

FROM: LIVERPOOL AND QUEENSTOWN
TO: NEW YORK
ARRIVED: 17 NOVEMBER 1884

PASSENGER	AGE	SEX	OCCUPATION	PRV VIL DES
KOBBAS, ELIZA	12	F	CH	RRACBFNY

SHIP: GENERAL WERDER

FROM: BREMEN
TO: NEW YORK
ARRIVED: 17 NOVEMBER 1884

PASSENGER	AGE	SEX	OCCUPATION	PRV VIL DES
KOOP, THOMAS	39	M	LABR	RRZZZZUSA
SARA	35	F	W	RRZZZZUSA
SARA	6	F	CHILD	RRZZZZUSA
MARIE	7	F	CHILD	RRZZZZUSA
CATHA.	.09	F	INFANT	RRZZZZUSA
PANKRATZ, ABRAM	30	M	LABR	RRZZZZUSA
EVA	24	F	W	RRZZZZUSA
AGNES	5	F	CHILD	RRZZZZUSA
ABRAM	4	M	CHILD	RRZZZZUSA
KLONIWSKI, STANISLOW	13	M	CH	RRZZZZUSA
BRAUN, JACOB	33	M	LABR	RRZZZZUSA
HELENE	23	F	W	RRZZZZUSA
JACOB	4	M	CHILD	RRZZZZUSA
HELENE	4	F	CHILD	RRZZZZUSA
AGATHE	4	F	CHILD	RRZZZZUSA
ELISABETH	.06	F	INFANT	RRZZZZUSA
KLAWANSKY, -ATSEN	14	M	FARMER	RRZZZZUSA
PERNER, WILHELM	40	M	LABR	RRZZZZUSA
UNRUH, DAVID	21	M	LABR	RRZZZZUSA
HELENE	21	F	W	RRZZZZUSA
LENZ, EMILIE	21	F	NN	RRZZZZUSA
CAPLAN, SALOMON	20	M	LABR	RRZZZZUSA

SHIP: P CALAND

FROM: ROTTERDAM
TO: NEW YORK
ARRIVED: 17 NOVEMBER 1884

PASSENGER	AGE	SEX	OCCUPATION	PRV VIL DES
ELIASTEN, MOSES	20	M	MCHT	RRZZZZUSA

SHIP: FURNESSIA

FROM: GLASGOW
TO: NEW YORK
ARRIVED: 20 NOVEMBER 1884

PASSENGER	AGE	SEX	OCCUPATION	PRV VIL DES
KAHN, WOLFF	58	M	LABR	RRZZZZUSA
CHAWE	55	F	NN	RRZZZZUSA

SHIP: BELGENLAND

FROM: ANTWERP
TO: NEW YORK
ARRIVED: 21 NOVEMBER 1884

PASSENGER	AGE	SEX	OCCUPATION	PRV VIL DES
ZAREMBA, A.	30	M	LABR	PLZZZZUNK
HOFT, ANN	32	F	HSWF	PLZZZZUNK
OTT.	9	F	CHILD	PLZZZZUNK
AUG.	7	F	CHILD	PLZZZZUNK
H.	5	F	CHILD	PLZZZZUNK
R.	3	F	CHILD	PLZZZZUNK
O.	00	F	INF	PLZZZZUNK

PASSENGER	AGE	SEX	OCCUPATION	PRV	VIL	DES
JURISCH, L.	50	F	HSWF	PL	ZZZZ	WI
ELE.	18	F	UNKNOWN	PL	ZZZZ	WI
M.	14	M	CH	PL	ZZZZ	WI
V.	11	M	CH	PL	ZZZZ	WI
DRZEWIUKE, VIC.	28	M	SMH	PL	ZZZZ	PHI
VIC.	30	F	UNKNOWN	PL	ZZZZ	PHI
P.	5	M	CHILD	PL	ZZZZ	PHI
BOB	2	M	CHILD	PL	ZZZZ	PHI
KANIECKA, K.	20	F	HSWF	PL	ZZZZ	UNK
A.	00	F	INF	PL	ZZZZ	UNK
MARTSCHENH, JOHN	00	M	LABR	PL	ZZZZ	WI
U	00	M	LABR	PL	ZZZZ	WI
U	00	M	LABR	PL	ZZZZ	WI
U	00	F	CH	PL	ZZZZ	WI
TECH, JOH	23	M	BTMKR	PL	AHCJ	NY
CONRAD, FERD.	24	M	CPR	RR	ZZZZ	NY
SWAZDINBA, L.	27	F	HSWF	PL	ZZZZ	UNK
J.	3	F	CHILD	PL	ZZZZ	UNK
M.	00	M	INF	PL	ZZZZ	UNK
SCEMUN, CL.	29	M	FARMER	PL	AAQH	NY

SHIP: POLARIA

FROM: HAMBURG
TO: NEW YORK
ARRIVED: 21 NOVEMBER 1884

PASSENGER	AGE	SEX	OCCUPATION	PRV	VIL	DES
POBLOZECK, ANDR.	21	M	LABR	RR	ZZZZ	NY
FOTH, AUG.	30	M	FARMER	RR	ZZZZ	UNK
ELISABETH	25	F	W	RR	ZZZZ	UNK
MARIA	2	F	CHILD	RR	ZZZZ	UNK
ERNESTINE	.08	F	INFANT	RR	ZZZZ	UNK
ROLNICK, HIRSCH	28	M	TRDSMN	RR	ZZZZ	NY
FRIEDMAN, H.	28	M	TRDSMN	RR	ZZZZ	NY
ETTEL	21	F	W	RR	ZZZZ	NY
CZICHOWITZ, JAN	40	M	LABR	RR	ZZZZ	NY
EVA	30	F	W	RR	ZZZZ	NY
JULIE	7	F	CHILD	RR	ZZZZ	NY
KOWALTZY, ALEAND.	19	M	LABR	RR	ZZZZ	NY
WIETRA, SIGMUND	21	M	LABR	RR	ZZZZ	NY
PELKA, JOHANNES	29	M	JNR	RR	ZZZZ	OH
ECKERT, ELISE	47	F	WO	RR	ZZZZ	OH
HEINR.	19	M	S	RR	ZZZZ	OH
MINNA	17	F	D	RR	ZZZZ	OH
BARTEL, ELISE	81	F	WO	RR	ZZZZ	NY
ELISE	41	F	WO	RR	ZZZZ	NY
CHAR, JACOB	31	M	LABR	RR	ZZZZ	KS
EVA	26	F	W	RR	ZZZZ	KS
ELVIRA	.06	F	INFANT	RR	ZZZZ	KS
GEROLD	50	M	LABR	RR	ZZZZ	UNK
EVA	52	F	W	RR	ZZZZ	UNK
HEINR.	16	M	S	RR	ZZZZ	UNK
ALBERTINE	7	F	CHILD	RR	ZZZZ	UNK
DOMSKY, MEYER	18	M	TRDSMN	RR	ZZZZ	NY
WOLF, BENZEL	28	M	TRDSMN	RR	ZZZZ	NY
ABEL, ABRAHAM	22	M	TRDSMN	RR	ZZZZ	NY
SCHWARZ, FREINDL	22	F	WO	PL	ZZZZ	NY
ISRAEL	.04	M	INFANT	PL	ZZZZ	NY
BISGEIER, LEA	17	F	SGL	PL	ZZZZ	NY
ASCHER, ABRAHAM	40	M	TRDSMN	PL	ZZZZ	NY
FRIEMENT	35	F	W	PL	ZZZZ	NY
FEIGE	.07	F	INFANT	PL	ZZZZ	NY
SCHRANK, CHANE	18	F	SGL	PL	ZZZZ	NY
SCHWARTZ, JACOB	18	M	LABR	PL	ZZZZ	NY
MONTAZ, MARCUS	40	M	LABR	PL	ZZZZ	NY
MINDEL	40	F	W	PL	ZZZZ	NY
MOSES	4	M	CHILD	PL	ZZZZ	NY
RIEWKE	.08	F	INFANT	PL	ZZZZ	NY
LANDE, MASE	20	M	LITGR	RR	ZZZZ	NY
BOBLEWSKY, MEYER	21	M	TRDSMN	RR	ZZZZ	NY
WARSCHEFSKY, JOSEF	18	M	TRDSMN	RR	ZZZZ	NY
WISCHZIKINSKY, JANKEL	18	M	MCHT	RR	ZZZZ	NY
CHAID, SCHLOME	46	M	TLR	RR	ZZZZ	NY
NOCHANE	20	F	D	RR	ZZZZ	NY
CASSEL, JANKEL	22	M	TLR	RR	ZZZZ	NY
DITZNERSTEIN, CHATZKEL	11	M	TRDSMN	RR	ZZZZ	NY
TEILE, HERM.	37	M	TRDSMN	RR	ZZZZ	NY
ROSENBLUM, MORITZ	20	M	WVR	RR	ZZZZ	NY
FEMMER, RACHEL	48	F	WO	RR	ZZZZ	OH
SCHMALHENSER, SARAH	26	F	SGL	PL	ZZZZ	OH
FEILER, BLUME	7	F	CHILD	PL	ZZZZ	OH
COHN, ARON	00	M	TRDSMN	RR	ZZZZ	NY
LEIHMANN, REISL	18	F	SGL	PL	ZZZZ	NY
FINKELSTEIN, HIRSCH	19	M	LABR	RR	ZZZZ	NY
ARONSOHN, RUB.	24	M	MCHT	RR	ZZZZ	NY
RADINSKY, JOS.	40	M	LABR	RR	ZZZZ	NY
SIEDER, JACOB	30	M	LABR	RR	ZZZZ	NY
APELBAUM, MARCUS	40	M	LABR	RR	ZZZZ	NY
KLEIN, ESTER	40	F	WO	RR	ZZZZ	NY
PERL.	12	M	CH	RR	ZZZZ	NY
TAUBE	7	F	CHILD	RR	ZZZZ	NY
MOSES	6	M	CHILD	RR	ZZZZ	NY
LEISER	5	M	CHILD	RR	ZZZZ	NY
RIWKE	.09	F	INFANT	RR	ZZZZ	NY
SACHAROWITZ, TAUBE	24	F	WO	RR	ZZZZ	NY
HINDE	3	F	CHILD	RR	ZZZZ	NY
RETRICH, JOHAN	27	M	LABR	RR	ZZZZ	NY
KOSMAR, VINAK	40	M	LABR	RR	ZZZZ	NY
HENOSCH, ASCH.	21	M	FARMER	RR	ZZZZ	NY
KANTZKOWALZTI, CH.	22	M	MCHT	RR	ZZZZ	NY
MOKEL, PINKUS	22	M	MCHT	RR	ZZZZ	NY
KOWALSCHICK, LEON	40	M	LABR	PL	ZZZZ	NY
RFEFFERKORN, SAMUEL	19	M	CL	RR	ZZZZ	NY
BROKMANN, M.	19	M	CL	RR	ZZZZ	NY
M.	19	M	CL	RR	ZZZZ	NY
OKONKY, JOHANN	28	M	LABR	RR	ZZZZ	NY
JOSEFA	.06	F	INFANT	RR	ZZZZ	NY
LEWERENTZ, AUGUST	23	M	LABR	RR	ZZZZ	NY
LIPSCHITZ, CARL	21	M	LABR	RR	ZZZZ	NY
GRINSPA, RAPHAEL	16	M	LABR	RR	ZZZZ	PHI
KAPLAN, MAX.	17	M	LABR	RR	ZZZZ	NY
GOFER, JACOB	16	M	LABR	RR	ZZZZ	NY
BESKIR, ESSIG	22	M	WCHMKR	RR	ZZZZ	UNK
GLUECKSTEIN, JACOB	21	M	SHMK	RR	ZZZZ	NY
TOMMEL, ABRAH.	22	M	LABR	RR	ZZZZ	NY
GROSSMAN, BARUCH	21	M	LABR	RR	ZZZZ	NY
GIWOWSKA, SCHMUL	21	M	LABR	RR	ZZZZ	NY
ENDELMAN, CHATZ.	21	M	LABR	RR	ZZZZ	NY
SATASTJONI, LUDOWIKA	22	F	WO	RR	ZZZZ	NY
SARA	.04	F	INFANT	RR	ZZZZ	NY

SHIP: SILESIA

FROM: HAMBURG
TO: NEW YORK
ARRIVED: 21 NOVEMBER 1884

PASSENGER	AGE	SEX	OCCUPATION	PRV	VIL	DES
SONOLENSKY, REBECCA	20	F	SGL	RR	AHSW	USA
AROTZKIN, BAMET	38	M	LABR	RR	ZZZZ	USA
CHAIM	18	M	LABR	RR	ZZZZ	USA
TRAUM, RACHEL	40	F	W	RR	ZZZZ	USA
RIWKE, GITTEL	7	F	CHILD	RR	ZZZZ	USA
JANKEL	.11	M	INFANT	RR	ZZZZ	USA
RIWKE	9	F	CHILD	RR	ZZZZ	USA
MARKOWSKI, HIRSCH	20	M	DLR	RR	ZZZZ	USA
IWJANSKI, HIRSCH	24	M	DLR	RR	AHTF	USA
LEIB	18	M	DLR	RR	AHTF	USA
FILD, NATAN	35	M	DLR	RR	ZZZZ	USA
PAULINE	35	F	W	RR	ZZZZ	USA
META	24	F	SI	RR	ZZZZ	USA

PASSENGER	AGE	SEX	OCCUPATION	PRV VIL DES
ERIK	3	M	CHILD	RRZZZZUSA
RABINOWITZ, HIRSCH	43	M	WCHMKR	RRZZZZUSA
ANTSCHELOWITZ, PEREZ	9	M	CHILD	RRAHQUUSA
RABINOWITZ, CHAIM	23	M	DYR	RRAHQUUSA
LEWIN, NOTE	19	M	TLR	RRZZZZUSA
KOPPEL	19	M	DYR	RRZZZZUSA
SCHMADSACK, ESTHER	22	F	W	RRZZZZUSA
PSADJE	6	M	CHILD	RRZZZZUSA
LEIDEN, MEYER	19	M	LABR	RRAHTFUSA
WABNIK, RASCHE	22	F	SGL	RRAHTFUSA
POSKO, MOSES	18	M	LABR	RRAGRTUSA
ANNA	9	F	CHILD	RRAGRTUSA
ROSENBERG, RIWKE	18	F	SGL	RRZZZZUSA
GOLDANSKY, GISCHE	32	F	W	RRZZZZUSA
CHAIM	8	M	CHILD	RRZZZZUSA
MOSES	7	M	CHILD	RRZZZZUSA
MARIASCHE	5	F	CHILD	RRZZZZUSA
MOTEL	.11	M	INFANT	RRZZZZUSA
ELKE	.01	F	INFANT	RRZZZZUSA
KOSAK, SARAH	30	F	W	RRZZZZUSA
JENTE	9	F	CHILD	RRZZZZUSA
ESTHE	8	F	CHILD	RRZZZZUSA
PIECHOCZKA, EMILIE	19	F	SGL	RRZZZZUSA
HARN, RICKEL	21	F	SGL	RRZZZZUSA
RACHEL	18	F	SGL	RRZZZZUSA
SEGALOWSKY, BEILE	18	F	SGL	RRAHTQUSA
SEITZ, SALOMON	28	M	FARMER	RRAHTUUSA
JOSEF	16	M	FARMER	RRAHTUUSA
LEWNI, ZADEL	45	M	LABR	RRAHTOUSA
IVAN, RUBEN	19	M	LABR	RRZZZZUSA
WYST, HEINRICH	52	M	LABR	RRAEGTUSA
ANNA	49	F	W	RRAEGTUSA
HEINACH	22	M	CH	RRAEGTUSA
JOHANNE	20	F	CH	RRAEGTUSA
JOH.	19	M	CH	RRAEGTUSA
PETER	18	M	CH	RRAEGTUSA
CHRISTINE	16	F	CH	RRAEGTUSA
MARIE	9	F	CHILD	RRAEGTUSA
CATHARINA	8	F	CHILD	RRAEGTUSA
CARE	3	M	CHILD	RRAEGTUSA
KAPELE, CARL	25	M	LABR	RRAEGTUSA
MARG.	24	F	W	RRAEGTUSA
LOUISE	2	F	CHILD	RRAEGTUSA
SCHOLDLING, GITTEL	29	M	FARMER	RRZZZZUSA
CATH.	29	F	W	RRZZZZUSA
HEINRICH	5	M	CHILD	RRZZZZUSA
CATH.	2	F	CHILD	RRZZZZUSA
MARG.	.03	F	INFANT	RRZZZZUSA
DELL, LUDWIG	39	M	FARMER	RRZZZZUSA
CH.	39	F	W	RRZZZZUSA
JOHANN	14	M	CH	RRZZZZUSA
LUDWIG	6	M	CHILD	RRZZZZUSA
CHRISTIAN	2	M	CHILD	RRZZZZUSA
HEINRICH	.03	M	INFANT	RRZZZZUSA
HURWITZ, ROSA	24	F	W	RRAHTFUSA
PAULINE	3	F	CHILD	RRAHTFUSA
REGINA	.11	F	INFANT	RRAHTFUSA
BUCHMULLER, JOHANN	42	M	FARMER	RRZZZZUSA
ANNA	42	F	W	RRZZZZUSA
CHARLOTTE	7	F	CHILD	RRZZZZUSA
CATH.	5	F	CHILD	RRZZZZUSA
JOHANES	2	M	CHILD	RRZZZZUSA
ELISABETH	.02	F	INFANT	RRZZZZUSA
WEINSTEIN, JACOB	22	M	JNR	RRAHTFUSA
KOWALUTI, VINCENT	25	M	LABR	RRAHZSUSA
KOTHINKA	22	F	W	RRAHZSUSA
SCHULTZ, ISRAEL	21	M	TLR	RRAHTKUSA
JENNER, CHAUS	23	M	PNTR	RRZZZZUSA
TRIEDE, IGNATZ	18	M	MCHT	RRZZZZUSA
GRANSWITZ, FISCHEL	20	M	DLR	RRZZZZUSA
PUPKIN, ISAAC	19	M	CL	RRAHTFUSA
BACHRACH, JOSEF	18	M	CL	RRAHTFUSA
KORNBLUTH, CHAIM	18	M	LABR	RRZZZZUSA
GOLDMANN, JACOB	15	M	LABR	RRZZZZUSA
ASCHER, TEME	21	M	LABR	RRZZZZUSA

PASSENGER	AGE	SEX	OCCUPATION	PRV VIL DES
MARTIN	24	M	LABR	RRZZZZUSA
TRUSKY, TAIWES	19	M	DLR	RRZZZZUSA
LAPIN, WOLF	18	M	DLR	RRAHVOUSA
JORDAN, MINE	25	F	W	RRZZZZUSA
SAMUEL	.03	M	INFANT	RRZZZZUSA
SIEGER, LEISER	21	M	FARMER	RRAHTFUSA
SARA	20	F	W	RRAHTFUSA
LEA	17	F	SGL	RRAHTFUSA
GOLDSTEIN, CHANNE	5	F	CHILD	RRZZZZUSA
SKLIANSKY, NOCHEM	28	M	LABR	RRAHTSUSA
KATZ, LUNCHE	27	M	DLR	RRAHVAUSA
CHANNE	23	F	W	RRAHVAUSA
GESCHE	24	F	SGL	RRAHVAUSA
EIDECHER, MARIE	24	F	W	RRZZZZUSA
GUSTAV	4	M	CHILD	RRZZZZUSA
OTTO	2	M	CHILD	RRZZZZUSA
JULIUS	.11	M	INFANT	RRZZZZUSA
TREGLAR, BERTHA	24	F	SGL	RRAHVAUSA
PILSER, CIREL	20	F	W	RRAHTKUSA
JACOB	.11	M	INFANT	RRAHTKUSA
PODLIPSKY, WOLF	18	M	LABR	RRAHZSUSA
LEWIN, PESCHE	16	F	SGL	RRZZZZUSA
CAPLAN, SMERL	17	M	LABR	RRAHZPUSA
NUPBAUM, GEILE	9	F	CHILD	RRZZZZUSA
GOLDIN, HANNE	20	F	SGL	RRZZZZUSA
MOROSZIWITZ, FEIGE	9	F	CHILD	RRAHTFUSA
MIRAN, JULIUS	24	M	LABR	RRAHZSUSA
KASLER, LUDWIG	29	M	LABR	RRAHZSUSA
KASIR, WOBEL	18	M	LABR	RRAHZSUSA
SCHWARTZ, ADOLF	17	M	LABR	RRAHZSUSA
BRANDY, PESCHE	45	F	W	RRAHSWUSA
SAMUEL	9	M	CHILD	RRAHSWUSA
ABRAHAM	8	M	CHILD	RRAHSWUSA
MEYER	6	M	CHILD	RRAHSWUSA
ISRAEL	3	M	CHILD	RRAHSWUSA
KARAMOWSKY, JACOB	9	M	CHILD	RRZZZZUSA
JANDELSKY, JANKEL	21	M	LABR	RRZZZZUSA
RUBENSTEIN, BEHR	22	M	LABR	RRZZZZUSA
BORNSTEIN, RACHEL	9	F	CHILD	RRZZZZUSA
LEA	8	F	CHILD	RRZZZZUSA
BOTHSCHILDT, MORITZ	18	M	LABR	RRAHSPUSA
LAUPER, BEILE	19	F	SGL	RRZZZZUSA
MAGARINER, BERNHARD	22	M	LABR	RRZZZZUSA
TREGLER, AMANDO	.11	F	INFANT	RRAHVAUSA
PARCZENSKA, ANASTASIE	.10	F	INFANT	RRZZZZUSA

SHIP: CITY OF CHESTER

FROM: LIVERPOOL AND QUEENSTOWN
TO: NEW YORK
ARRIVED: 22 NOVEMBER 1884

PASSENGER	AGE	SEX	OCCUPATION	PRV VIL DES
SATZBERG, MEYER	32	M	LABR	RRACBFNY
WALSMAN, JACOB	24	M	LABR	RRAGUZNY

SHIP: ODER

FROM: BREMEN AND SOUTHAMPTON
TO: NEW YORK
ARRIVED: 22 NOVEMBER 1884

PASSENGER	AGE	SEX	OCCUPATION	PRV VIL DES
GETMANN, YECHIEL	19	M	MCHT	RRZZZZUSA
PLOSKYE, NOCHMANN	18	M	MCHT	RRZZZZUSA
GLUCKMANN, CHEIM-LEIB	30	M	LABR	RRZZZZUSA
HANZ, FAINL	30	M	FARMER	RRZZZZUSA

PASSENGER	AGE	SEX	OCCUPATION	PRIV	VIL	DES
ELISABETH	27	F	NN	RR	ZZZZ	USA
ROSALIA	3	F	CHILD	RR	ZZZZ	USA
FISCHER, GOTTLIEB	34	M	FARMER	RR	ZZZZ	USA
KATHARINA	30	F	NN	RR	ZZZZ	USA
MARIA	10	F	CH	RR	ZZZZ	USA
CAROLINE	8	F	CHILD	RR	ZZZZ	USA
ROSINE	5	F	CHILD	RR	ZZZZ	USA
CHRISTINE	3	F	CHILD	RR	ZZZZ	USA
HAAS, FRIEDRICH	65	M	FARMER	RR	ZZZZ	USA
MUELLER, JOHAN	38	M	FARMER	RR	ZZZZ	USA
SABINE	25	F	NN	RR	ZZZZ	USA
CATHARINA	9	F	CHILD	RR	ZZZZ	USA
GRETE	5	F	CHILD	RR	ZZZZ	USA
CAROLINE	3	F	CHILD	RR	ZZZZ	USA
JOHAN	.06	M	INFANT	RR	ZZZZ	USA
ADAM	29	M	FARMER	RR	ZZZZ	USA
CAROLINE	22	F	NN	RR	ZZZZ	USA
CHRISTINE	4	F	CHILD	RR	ZZZZ	USA
FRIEDRICH	2	M	CHILD	RR	ZZZZ	USA
JOHANN	.06	M	INFANT	RR	ZZZZ	USA
SCHWEIGERT, GOTTLIEB	28	M	FARMER	RR	ZZZZ	USA
MARIA	29	F	NN	RR	ZZZZ	USA
FRIEDRICH	4	M	CHILD	RR	ZZZZ	USA
MARIA	3	F	CHILD	RR	ZZZZ	USA
CONRAD	.06	M	INFANT	RR	ZZZZ	USA
DANIEL	19	M	UNKNOWN	RR	ZZZZ	USA
STASSEL, CHRISTIAN	72	M	FARMER	RR	ZZZZ	USA
STADEL, DOROTHEA	32	F	NN	RR	ZZZZ	USA
CHRISTIAN	5	M	CHILD	RR	ZZZZ	USA
CHRISTIANE	3	F	CHILD	RR	ZZZZ	USA
CHRISTINE	24	F	UNKNOWN	RR	ZZZZ	USA
WEIFS, FRIEDRICH	84	M	FARMER	RR	ZZZZ	USA
JOHANNA	68	F	NN	RR	ZZZZ	USA
SAENSLER, ROSINE	24	F	NN	RR	ZZZZ	USA
ZELLER, JOHANNES	47	M	LLD	RR	ZZZZ	USA
ELISABETH	47	F	NN	RR	ZZZZ	USA
JACOB	22	M	FARMER	RR	ZZZZ	USA
GEORG	17	M	FARMER	RR	ZZZZ	USA
GOTTLIEB	10	M	CH	RR	ZZZZ	USA
JOHAN	8	M	CHILD	RR	ZZZZ	USA
ADOLF	6	M	CHILD	RR	ZZZZ	USA
JULIUS	4	M	CHILD	RR	ZZZZ	USA
ELISABETH	20	F	UNKNOWN	RR	ZZZZ	USA
HEIM, ANDREAS	22	M	LABR	RR	ZZZZ	USA
STUEBER, AMALIA	20	F	NN	RR	ZZZZ	USA
WOLFERT, ANDREAS	19	M	FARMER	RR	ZZZZ	USA
JULIANE	17	F	NN	RR	ZZZZ	USA
PFEIFFER, ANDREAS	50	M	FARMER	RR	ZZZZ	USA
ROSINE	50	F	NN	RR	ZZZZ	USA
MICHAL	19	M	FARMER	RR	ZZZZ	USA
ANDREAS	17	M	FARMER	RR	ZZZZ	USA
GOTTLIEB	15	M	NN	RR	ZZZZ	USA
JOHANN	11	M	CH	RR	ZZZZ	USA
CONRAD	9	M	CHILD	RR	ZZZZ	USA
CHRISTIAN	6	M	CHILD	RR	ZZZZ	USA
SCHAEDLER, ADAM	24	M	FARMER	RR	ZZZZ	USA
CATHARINA	32	F	NN	RR	ZZZZ	USA
CATHARINA	6	F	CHILD	RR	ZZZZ	USA
ANDREAS	1	M	CHILD	RR	ZZZZ	USA
HAAR, LENA	18	F	NN	PL	ZZZZ	USA
WOLSKE, ERNST	23	M	TLR	PL	ZZZZ	USA
KRAFT, JOHAN	32	M	FARMER	RR	ZZZZ	USA
MARTHA	30	F	NN	RR	ZZZZ	USA
MARIANNE	6	F	CHILD	RR	ZZZZ	USA
STEPHAN	4	M	CHILD	RR	ZZZZ	USA
JOHANNE	00	F	INF	RR	ZZZZ	USA
MARGARET	00	F	INF	RR	ZZZZ	USA
MASTEL, PETER	28	M	FARMER	RR	ZZZZ	USA
CATHARINA	28	F	NN	RR	ZZZZ	USA
KASIMIR	7	M	CHILD	RR	ZZZZ	USA
BENDIK	2	M	CHILD	RR	ZZZZ	USA
FRANZISKA	.09	F	INFANT	RR	ZZZZ	USA
JOACHIM, JACOB	00	M	FARMER	RR	ZZZZ	USA
WILHELMINE	00	F	NN	RR	ZZZZ	USA
MARIA	10	F	CH	RR	ZZZZ	USA

PASSENGER	AGE	SEX	OCCUPATION	PRIV	VIL	DES
JACOB	8	M	CHILD	RR	ZZZZ	USA
DOROTHEA	2	F	CHILD	RR	ZZZZ	USA
SCHEINDEL, SALOMON	00	M	MCHT	RR	ZZZZ	USA
MARKUS	00	M	NN	RR	ZZZZ	USA
ESLA	7	F	CHILD	RR	ZZZZ	USA
SEINLER	17	M	UNKNOWN	RR	ZZZZ	USA
SORKEL, CHONE	33	M	LABR	RR	ZZZZ	USA
RUMS, JOHANNES	39	M	FARMER	RR	ZZZZ	USA
BARBARA	00	F	NN	RR	ZZZZ	USA
LUCADA	14	F	CH	RR	ZZZZ	USA
CAROLINE	5	F	CHILD	RR	ZZZZ	USA
NICOLAUS	4	M	CHILD	RR	ZZZZ	USA
ELISABETH	.09	F	INFANT	RR	ZZZZ	USA
STALER, ISRAEL	47	M	MCHT	RR	ZZZZ	USA
BEILE, ROCHE	40	M	MCHT	RR	ZZZZ	USA
LEILE	.11	F	INFANT	RR	ZZZZ	USA

SHIP: STATE OF NEBRASKA

FROM: GLASGOW AND LARNE
TO: NEW YORK
ARRIVED: 22 NOVEMBER 1884

PASSENGER	AGE	SEX	OCCUPATION	PRIV	VIL	DES
BABIESKI, ABRAHAM	21	M	TLR	RR	ZZZZ	NY
PAULINA	20	F	W	RR	ZZZZ	NY
KARUZANSKI, ISAK	20	M	CGRMKR	RR	ZZZZ	NY
HORWITZ, LEIB	19	M	CGRMKR	RR	ZZZZ	NY
EDELMANN, NATHAN	18	M	BKPR	RR	ZZZZ	NY
JOHANN	10	M	CH	RR	ZZZZ	NY
MASS, RUBIN	21	M	SMH	RR	ZZZZ	NY
RABINOWITZ, BOHER	18	M	CGRMKR	RR	ZZZZ	BAL
WINCENTE, ANDREAS	00	M	FARMER	RR	ZZZZ	NY
KALMANN, MEYER	58	M	TLR	RR	ZZZZ	NY
JETTE	58	F	W	RR	ZZZZ	NY
MULLER, CHAIE	26	F	W	RR	ZZZZ	NY
ESTHER	6	F	CHILD	RR	ZZZZ	NY
MOSES	.10	M	INFANT	RR	ZZZZ	NY
WESCH, MOSES	21	M	BRR	RR	ZZZZ	NY
KORNUSKY, MICHL.	26	M	LKSH	RR	ZZZZ	NY

SHIP: WERRA

FROM: BREMEN AND SOUTHAMPTON
TO: NEW YORK
ARRIVED: 22 NOVEMBER 1884

PASSENGER	AGE	SEX	OCCUPATION	PRIV	VIL	DES
LUBSCHITZ, LAB.	20	M	MLR	RR	ZZZZ	USA
FRIEDMANN, BRINDEL	27	F	UNKNOWN	RR	ZZZZ	USA
CHANNE	.10	F	INFANT	RR	ZZZZ	USA
SCHIMINSKY, ROZIALYA	20	F	UNKNOWN	RR	ZZZZ	USA
BLITZBLUM, MEYER	22	M	LABR	RR	ZZZZ	USA
MARTHA	21	F	UNKNOWN	RR	ZZZZ	USA
ROTT, JOHANN	34	M	LABR	RR	ZZZZ	USA
FRIEDERIKE	32	F	UNKNOWN	RR	ZZZZ	USA
JOHANN	15	M	LABR	RR	ZZZZ	USA
FRIEDRICH	7	M	CHILD	RR	ZZZZ	USA
MAGDALENA	6	F	CHILD	RR	ZZZZ	USA
CHRISTIAN	5	M	CHILD	RR	ZZZZ	USA
AUGUST	5	M	CHILD	RR	ZZZZ	USA
JACOB	4	M	CHILD	RR	ZZZZ	USA
ADAM	.11	M	INFANT	RR	ZZZZ	USA
MALLOCK, PETER	40	M	FARMER	RR	ZZZZ	USA
DOROTHEA	35	F	UNKNOWN	RR	ZZZZ	USA
CATHARINA	15	F	UNKNOWN	RR	ZZZZ	USA
DOROTHEA	7	F	CHILD	RR	ZZZZ	USA

PASSENGER	AGE	SEX	OCCUPATION	PRIV	VIL	DES
PETER	7	M	CHILD	RR	ZZZZ	USA
CHRISTINE	6	F	CHILD	RR	ZZZZ	USA
ELISE	4	F	CHILD	RR	ZZZZ	USA
JOHANN	2	M	CHILD	RR	ZZZZ	USA
GEORG	.11	M	INFANT	RR	ZZZZ	USA

SHIP: WESTPHALIA

FROM: HAMBURG AND HAVRE
TO: NEW YORK
ARRIVED: 22 NOVEMBER 1884

PASSENGER	AGE	SEX	OCCUPATION	PRIV	VIL	DES
LUBICZ, MORDSCHE	35	M	DLR	RR	ZZZZ	NY
FRANKEL, F.	17	M	DLR	RR	ZZZZ	NY
ADLER, ETTA	50	F	W	RR	ZZZZ	NY
MARY	18	F	D	RR	ZZZZ	NY
PANTOWSKA, SARA	50	F	W	RR	ZZZZ	NY
SCHNIPISCKY, RASCHAMIE	36	F	W	RR	AHSW	NY
ABRAM	8	M	CHILD	RR	AHSW	NY
SIME	9	F	CHILD	RR	AHSW	NY
VICTOR	.11	F	INFANT	RR	AHSW	NY
FEINBERG, HITZLE	20	M	LABR	RR	AHTF	NY
WEISSMANN, JUDE	22	M	LABR	RR	ZZZZ	NY
TARTULSKY, HIRSCH	20	M	TLR	RR	AHZS	NY
KOHN, IDA	40	F	W	RR	ZZZZ	NY
CHANNE	9	F	CHILD	RR	ZZZZ	NY
MICHEL	5	M	CHILD	RR	ZZZZ	NY
HILLEL	.11	F	INFANT	RR	ZZZZ	NY
SMOLARZ, JOEL	40	M	DLR	RR	ZZZZ	NY
GEVOSSKY, DAB.	22	M	LABR	RR	ZZZZ	NY
COHN, MERC.	30	F	W	RR	ZZZZ	NY
SCHEPSEL	.11	F	INFANT	RR	ZZZZ	NY
GOLLER, SARA	20	F	W	RR	AFWJ	NY
LEA	.11	F	INFANT	RR	AFWJ	NY
FUHRMANN, MERE	20	F	SGL	RR	ZZZZ	NY
ANNA	18	F	SGL	RR	ZZZZ	NY
EMISOHN, FEITEL	40	M	LABR	RR	AHTF	NY
SCHEINE	35	F	W	RR	AHTF	NY
FEIGE	9	F	CHILD	RR	AHTF	NY
CHEIE	7	F	CHILD	RR	AHTF	NY
ODES	3	M	CHILD	RR	AHTF	NY
JACOB	.11	M	INFANT	RR	AHTF	NY
LIPSCHITZ, JOSEF	21	M	DLR	RR	AHTF	NY
ETTE	20	F	W	RR	AHTF	NY
HIRSCHOWITZ, SCHEWACH	43	M	LABR	RR	ZZZZ	NY
RUBRECHT, FEIGE	26	F	W	RR	AFWJ	NY
ISAAC	7	M	CHILD	RR	AFWJ	NY
KLUFT, ISAAC	32	M	MCHT	RR	AHWE	NY
SOPHIE	30	F	W	RR	AHWE	NY
ABRAH.	4	M	CHILD	RR	AHWE	NY
GRADOSKY, JUNDEL	21	M	LABR	RR	ZZZZ	NY
ITE	19	F	W	RR	ZZZZ	NY
KUJENKOWSKY, ANDR.	40	M	LABR	RR	ZZZZ	NY
WEINTRAUB, SCHRACHNE	20	M	LABR	RR	AHTF	NY
SCHANKSTAEDT, MARCUS	58	M	MCHT	RR	AGRT	NY
HANDEL	54	F	W	RR	AGRT	NY
FRANKEL, SALOMON	18	M	LABR	RR	AHWP	NY
MARCUS	19	M	LABR	RR	AHWP	NY
SALEWITZIG, MENDEL	18	M	LABR	RR	ZZZZ	NY
CHATENOWSKY, ABRAH.	32	M	LABR	RR	AHQU	NY
ZADEKOW, EPHRAIM	21	M	LABR	RR	ZZZZ	NY
WACHS, ISAAC	42	M	LABR	RR	AFVG	NY
WAISS, ISAAC	37	M	LABR	RR	AFVG	NY
ANKUDEWITZ, ANNA	30	F	W	RR	ZZZZ	NY
PETER	4	M	CHILD	RR	ZZZZ	NY
ANTON	.11	M	INFANT	RR	ZZZZ	NY
DEOEDZINSKY, IGNATZ	21	M	LABR	RR	ZZZZ	NY
ROTSCHKULIS, MIKOLAI	26	M	LABR	RR	ZZZZ	NY
BENEDICT	20	M	LABR	RR	ZZZZ	NY
BATHEIDIS, FRANZ	24	M	LABR	RR	ZZZZ	NY
TURMANN, ARON	50	M	LABR	RR	ZZZZ	NY
PERLE	45	F	W	RR	ZZZZ	NY
REBECCA	9	F	CHILD	RR	ZZZZ	NY
HINDE	8	F	CHILD	RR	ZZZZ	NY
MARKER, JUDEL	19	M	LABR	RR	AFWJ	NY
LEA	19	F	W	RR	AFWJ	NY
KRINGEL, ABRAHAM	30	M	LABR	RR	AHSW	NY
DIMANT, SAMUEL	20	M	LABR	RR	AHZS	NY
GRASNOPOLSKY, OFSCHI	20	M	LABR	RR	AHZS	NY
FRIEDMANN, HIRSCH	40	M	LABR	RR	AHZS	NY
MIZUNSKY, RISCHE	40	F	W	RR	AHZS	NY
CHAIE	18	F	CH	RR	AHZS	NY
ENNE	9	F	CHILD	RR	AHZS	NY
BASCHE	8	F	CHILD	RR	AHZS	NY
ABRAHAM	6	M	CHILD	RR	AHZS	NY
RAHEL	.11	F	INFANT	RR	AHZS	NY
SPECTOR, ROSA	18	F	SGL	RR	ZZZZ	NY
PETER, SCHEINE	25	F	W	RR	AHTK	NY
ABRAM	5	M	CHILD	RR	AHTK	NY
ESTHER	.11	F	INFANT	RR	AHTK	NY
BREITMANN, SLATE	13	F	SGL	RR	AHZS	NY
KAPERSOHN, ABRAHAM	18	M	LABR	RR	ZZZZ	NY
HEIMANN, TAUBE	29	F	SGL	RR	ZZZZ	NY
GUTKOWSKY, LEIB	30	M	TLR	RR	AHTF	NY
HAYMANN, ELIAS	48	M	LABR	RR	ZZZZ	NY
DOBKIN, RIWKE	24	F	SGL	RR	ZZZZ	NY
ABRAMOWITZ, NACHEM	19	M	MSN	RR	AHTF	NY
KURLANCZIK, CHAIE	17	M	MSN	RR	AHTF	NY
SCHEINFELD, MOSES	6	M	CHILD	RR	AHTF	NY
LIPARECK, MICHAEL	21	M	BKR	RR	AHTF	NY
LOWECUSKY, PIOTER	35	M	BKR	RR	AHTF	NY
SILBERMANN, DAVID	34	M	LABR	RR	ZZZZ	NY
SCHEINFELDT, FREIDA	28	F	W	RR	AHTF	NY
MARCUS	8	M	CHILD	RR	AHTF	NY
HINDE	1	F	CHILD	RR	AHTF	NY
LEIBOWITZ, WOLF	22	M	TLR	RR	ZZZZ	NY
ETTEL	20	F	W	RR	ZZZZ	NY
FINKELSTEIN, MARCUS	20	M	LABR	RR	ZZZZ	NY
TITZKOWSK-, PIOTER	20	M	LABR	RR	ZZZZ	NY
BERUH	20	M	LABR	RR	ZZZZ	NY
GLAZMANN, ISAAC	20	M	LABR	RR	ZZZZ	NY
SCHECHTMANN, DOBE	20	F	SGL	RR	ZZZZ	NY
WEINSTEIN, MOSES	27	M	LABR	RR	ZZZZ	NY
DONIAN, SARA	18	F	SGL	RR	ZZZZ	NY
MEYER, JOHANN	24	M	FARMER	RR	ZZZZ	NY

SHIP: INDIA

FROM: HAMBURG
TO: NEW YORK
ARRIVED: 28 NOVEMBER 1884

PASSENGER	AGE	SEX	OCCUPATION	PRIV	VIL	DES
TAUBER, PANKEL	20	M	LKSH	RR	ZZZZ	NY
JETTE	25	F	W	RR	ZZZZ	NY
FREUDT, CHANE	24	F	WO	RR	ZZZZ	NY
ABRAHAM	.06	M	INFANT	RR	ZZZZ	NY
CZYMOITIS, MORDCSHE	16	M	TRDSMN	RR	ZZZZ	NY
BERINSTEIN, MEYER	19	M	TRDSMN	RR	ZZZZ	NY
LAWTOCHUN, FRANZ	26	M	LABR	RR	ZZZZ	NY
HIRSCH, HUDE	20	M	LABR	RR	ZZZZ	NY
ROSALIE	20	F	W	RR	ZZZZ	NY
RADIK, CHANE	39	F	WO	RR	ZZZZ	NY
SURO	7	F	CHILD	RR	ZZZZ	NY
JETTE	6	F	CHILD	RR	ZZZZ	NY
JOSEF	5	M	CHILD	RR	ZZZZ	NY
ABRAHAM	3	M	CHILD	RR	ZZZZ	NY
BERSCH	.04	M	INFANT	RR	ZZZZ	NY
SCHAUER, MORSCHE	20	M	LABR	RR	ZZZZ	NY
GOLDBERG, SOLME	20	F	SGL	RR	ZZZZ	NY
GROSSMANN, CHATZKE	37	M	LABR	RR	ZZZZ	NY

PASSENGER	AGE	SEX	OCCUPATION	PV RI VL	D E S
WOLFF	35	M	LABR	RRZZZZ	NY
STEINBERG, ERTEL	7	M	CHILD	RRZZZZ	NY
LISCHAZINSKY, ERNST	21	F	SGL	RRZZZZ	NY
SLOMNISKY, MOSES	20	M	MCHT	RRZZZZ	NY
ISAAC	23	M	MCHT	RRZZZZ	NY
LIPSCHITZ, ABRAHAM	23	M	FARMER	RRZZZZ	NY
CHAIM	23	M	FARMER	RRZZZZ	NY
DEMBRONSKY, JUDE	22	M	SMH	RRZZZZ	NY
JOS, LEISER	20	M	JNR	RRZZZZ	NY
KLEIN, DAVID	26	M	SHMK	RRZZZZ	NY
LIPPKES, MOSES	21	M	CL	RRZZZZ	NY
FRIEDA	20	F	W	RRZZZZ	NY
ELIMELECH, LEIB	18	M	MSN	RRZZZZ	NY
RADIN, ABRAH.	35	M	LABR	RRZZZZ	NY
FASCHINOWSKY, SCHARGE	43	M	LABR	RRZZZZ	NY
SKARSKY, POSACH	23	M	LABR	RRZZZZ	NY
LEAH	23	F	W	RRZZZZ	NY
BLAUSKIN, MORDCHE	7	M	CHILD	RRZZZZ	NY
SPATM, NICOL	47	M	LABR	RRZZZZ	NY
JOHANN	15	M	LABR	RRZZZZ	NY
GELLER, KALKI	40	F	WO	PLZZZZ	NY
HELENE	16	F	D	PLZZZZ	NY
LUDWILLE	7	F	CHILD	PLZZZZ	NY
DAVID	12	M	S	PLZZZZ	NY
EDMUND	6	M	CHILD	PLZZZZ	NY
ADOLF	5	M	CHILD	PLZZZZ	NY
ARON	4	M	CHILD	PLZZZZ	NY
HUGO	2	M	CHILD	PLZZZZ	NY
BREFAN, WACIL	24	M	LABR	PLZZZZ	NY
MOSKO, PETRO	25	M	LABR	PLZZZZ	NY
BLAGKO, MEKOLACK	25	M	LABR	PLZZZZ	NY
HOROWITZ, ISAK	42	M	TRDSMN	RRZZZZ	NY
GESCHER	42	F	W	RRZZZZ	NY
BERTHA	10	F	D	RRZZZZ	NY
OSCAR	7	M	CHILD	RRZZZZ	NY
LEIB	5	M	CHILD	RRZZZZ	NY
EMMA	3	F	CHILD	RRZZZZ	NY
MARIA	.07	F	INFANT	RRZZZZ	NY
BELLMANN, LUBE	36	F	WO	RRZZZZ	NY
EMMA	13	F	D	RRZZZZ	NY
ABRAHAM	7	M	CHILD	RRZZZZ	NY
MAX	5	M	CHILD	RRZZZZ	NY
OSCAR	4	M	CHILD	RRZZZZ	NY
HERMANN	3	M	CHILD	RRZZZZ	NY
JEMDSCHER, H.	.07	M	INFANT	RRZZZZ	NY
LEWIN, MOSES	22	M	TR	RRZZZZ	NY
USCH, TOBIAS	17	M	TR	RRZZZZ	NY
SILBERMANN, MOSES	22	M	TRDSMN	RRZZZZ	NY
ZIMMERMANN, ESTE	29	F	WO	RRZZZZ	NY
LEON	15	M	S	RRZZZZ	NY
TAUBE	12	F	D	RRZZZZ	NY
JOSEF	7	M	CHILD	RRZZZZ	NY
ABRAHAM	6	M	CHILD	RRZZZZ	NY
RACHEL	5	F	CHILD	RRZZZZ	NY
JOHANN	4	M	CHILD	RRZZZZ	NY
NUKIN, LEISER	32	M	TRDSMN	RRZZZZ	NY
WEISS, GEBR.	30	M	LABR	RRZZZZ	NY
SAMUEL, BENJ.	18	M	CL	RRZZZZ	NY
EISENBERG, JANCO	20	M	LABR	RRZZZZ	NY
FEINSTEIN, LEIB	50	M	TRDSMN	RRZZZZ	PHI
MAYERS, IDEL	35	F	WO	RRZZZZ	PHI
WENIG, BERTHA	25	F	SGL	RRZZZZ	NY
HOLLAND, ANTONIE	32	F	SGL	RRZZZZ	NY
LASCHANSKI, D.	16	M	LABR	RRZZZZ	NY
BRANDO, BRANNO	20	F	SGL	RRZZZZ	NY
HORWITZ, REBECKA	48	F	W	RRZZZZ	NY
ESTER	12	F	D	RRZZZZ	NY
HANA	17	F	D	RRZZZZ	NY
JANKEL	55	M	LABR	RRZZZZ	NY
BACHARACH, CHANE-J.	35	M	TRDSMN	RRZZZZ	NY
PRINOWITZ, LOBE-M.	40	F	WO	RRZZZZ	NY
XHAIE	10	F	D	RRZZZZ	NY
SCHOLEIN	7	M	CHILD	RRZZZZ	NY
RUBEN	6	M	CHILD	RRZZZZ	NY
MAGALIS, CHANE	26	F	WO	RRZZZZ	NY
HIRSCH	.11	M	INFANT	RRZZZZ	NY
HANNA	.01	F	INFANT	RRZZZZ	NY
COHN, ABRAHAM	29	M	TLR	RRZZZZ	NY
BRODSKY, E.D.	54	M	TLR	RRZZZZ	NY
GENESE	42	F	W	RRZZZZ	NY
MEYER	17	M	S	RRZZZZ	NY
MAM	12	F	D	RRZZZZ	NY
SDWORE	10	F	D	RRZZZZ	NY
ISRAEL	6	M	CHILD	RRZZZZ	NY
JESSER	3	M	CHILD	RRZZZZ	NY
JACOB	.04	M	INFANT	RRZZZZ	NY
DUMBER, MORITZ	29	M	TRDSMN	RRZZZZ	NY
ROSE	29	F	W	RRZZZZ	NY
ISAAC	3	M	CHILD	RRZZZZ	NY
RADLE	.05	F	INFANT	RRZZZZ	NY
BARON, HEINRICH	21	M	LABR	RRZZZZ	NY
HANNE	21	M	LABR	RRZZZZ	NY
SCREISKO, ELIAS	50	M	TRDSMN	RRZZZZ	NY
FEIVE	49	F	W	RRZZZZ	NY
CHONE	00	M	LABR	RRZZZZ	NY
MARCUS, CHASER	00	M	LABR	RRZZZZ	NY
FERN, NACHUM	00	M	LABR	RRZZZZ	NY
GOLDSTEIN, ABRAHAM	18	M	LABR	RRZZZZ	NY
FENCK, DWORE	30	F	WO	RRZZZZ	NY
SORE	3	F	CHILD	RRZZZZ	NY
ABRAHAM	.08	M	INFANT	RRZZZZ	NY

SHIP: WAESLAND

FROM: ANTWERP
TO: NEW YORK
ARRIVED: 28 NOVEMBER 1884

PASSENGER	AGE	SEX	OCCUPATION	PV RI VL	D E S
KNAUER, FRANZ-MR	33	M	ENGR	PLZZZZ	USA
BRAND, AUG.	22	M	BCHR	RRZZZZ	USA
PETERSHON, AUG.	45	M	LABR	RRZZZZ	USA
M.	42	M	LABR	RRZZZZ	USA
C.	10	M	UNKNOWN	RRZZZZ	USA
ROSTCK, H.	37	M	UNKNOWN	RRZZZZ	USA
J.	40	F	UNKNOWN	RRZZZZ	USA
REDL, BACTZENS	21	M	UNKNOWN	RRZZZZ	USA
FEICHEST, M.	26	M	TLR	RRZZZZ	USA
BECKER, LEOP.	26	M	SMH	RRZZZZ	USA
NAPOKOI, J.	24	M	LABR	RRZZZZ	USA
L.	00	M	INF	RRZZZZ	USA
K.	00	M	INF	RRZZZZ	USA
MOYAK, M.	21	M	LABR	PLZZZZ	USA
MAR.	8	F	CHILD	PLZZZZ	USA
AG.	6	F	CHILD	PLZZZZ	USA
V.	.09	M	INFANT	PLZZZZ	USA

SHIP: WIELAND

FROM: HAMBURG
TO: NEW YORK
ARRIVED: 28 NOVEMBER 1884

PASSENGER	AGE	SEX	OCCUPATION	PV RI VL	D E S
KELLERMANN, GITTEL	32	F	SGL	RRZZZZ	USA
FREIDE	16	F	SGL	RRZZZZ	USA
JELLA, MIRKA	20	F	W	RRZZZZ	USA
CHAIE	.03	F	INFANT	RRZZZZ	USA
GLAS, JANKEL	22	M	TLR	RRZZZZ	USA
WIELANS, JOHANN	53	M	LABR	RRZZZZ	USA
JUSTINE	40	F	W	RRZZZZ	USA
ANNA	17	F	CH	RRZZZZ	USA

PASSENGER	AGE	SEX	OCCUPATION	PRV VIL DES
JACOB	16	M	CH	RRZZZZUSA
HEINRICH	13	M	CH	RRZZZZUSA
FRIEDR.	9	M	CHILD	RRZZZZUSA
WIEB, ISAAC	34	M	LABR	RRZZZZUSA
MARIA	30	F	W	RRZZZZUSA
SUSANNE	8	F	CHILD	RRZZZZUSA
ISAAC	6	M	CHILD	RRZZZZUSA
CATHA.	4	F	CHILD	RRZZZZUSA
MARIE	3	F	CHILD	RRZZZZUSA
JACOB	.11	M	INFANT	RRZZZZUSA
NORD, MARTIN	18	M	LABR	RRZZZZUSA
CHORONZYTSKI, JUDEL	43	M	DLR	RRZZZZUSA
WOLBERG, GITTEL	20	F	SGL	RRZZZZUSA
LICHTBLAN, TAUBE	20	F	SGL	RRZZZZUSA
COHN, PHILIPP	37	M	LABR	RRZZZZUSA
SALOMEA	22	F	W	RRZZZZUSA
KANTLER, CARL	19	M	LABR	RRZZZZUSA
CHORENZITZKY, JACHOLD	24	M	LABR	RRZZZZUSA
SARA	23	F	W	RRZZZZUSA
GLODMANN, MOSES	20	M	DLR	RRZZZZUSA
WARSCHOWSKY, JUDA	20	M	LABR	RRZZZZUSA
RAWSK, DAVID	20	M	LABR	RRZZZZUSA
RINBERG, LEIB	20	M	FARMER	RRZZZZUSA
TORKLER, HENRIETTE	26	F	W	RRZZZZUSA
EDMUND	4	M	CHILD	RRZZZZUSA
HERM.	.11	M	INFANT	RRZZZZUSA
KOSAK, SALOMON	23	M	JNR	RRZZZZUSA
ABRAHAM, LEIB	29	M	TLR	RRZZZZUSA
SCHUELKE, CARL	48	M	LABR	RRZZZZUSA
ANNA	49	F	W	RRZZZZUSA
EDUARD	9	M	CHILD	RRZZZZUSA
RUDOLPH	8	M	CHILD	RRZZZZUSA
HERRM.	7	M	CHILD	RRZZZZUSA
ERNST	4	M	CHILD	RRZZZZUSA
GROSS, ELGER	18	M	MCHT	RRZZZZUSA
MODEZULSKA, ANNA	18	F	SGL	RRZZZZUSA
TASCHMOWSKY, CHANNE	20	F	SGL	RRZZZZUSA
SARA	18	F	SGL	RRZZZZUSA
ROSENBERG, SCHEINE	48	F	SGL	RRZZZZUSA
FRANKEL, JUDEL	21	M	LABR	RRZZZZUSA
CHAIE	20	F	W	RRZZZZUSA
GRUENGARD, ISAAC	33	M	LABR	RRZZZZUSA
POPKEWITZ, HIRSCH	25	M	LABR	RRZZZZUSA
PASCHILINSKI, MEYER	21	M	LABR	RRZZZZUSA
SCHEINE	19	F	W	RRZZZZUSA
STEINBERG, AVESER	21	M	LABR	RRZZZZUSA
EPSTEIN, OSIAS	26	M	LABR	RRZZZZUSA
GRODZINSKY, ABRAHAM	21	M	LABR	RRZZZZUSA
DIMANT, JUDA	21	M	SHMK	RRZZZZUSA
LEA	20	F	W	RRZZZZUSA
RATZKOWSKY, JACOB	21	M	LABR	RRZZZZUSA
ROSBAD, CHANNE	19	F	TNMK	RRZZZZUSA
ABRAHAMSON, ISAAC	20	M	TLR	RRZZZZUSA
MASCINSKI, RACHEL	28	F	W	RRZZZZUSA
PESCHE	3	F	CHILD	RRZZZZUSA
MINNIE	.11	F	INFANT	RRZZZZUSA
GUMBINSKI, MORDCHE	20	M	LABR	RRZZZZUSA
FRIEDMANN, FREIDE	22	F	W	RRZZZZUSA
ABRAHAM	.11	M	INFANT	RRZZZZUSA
PODHAISKA, CARL	31	M	WTR	RRZZZZUSA

SHIP: ALSATIA

FROM: GLASGOW AND MOVILLE
TO: NEW YORK
ARRIVED: 29 NOVEMBER 1884

PASSENGER	AGE	SEX	OCCUPATION	PRV VIL DES
HYEYINSKI, FRANCOIS-H.	32	M	GENT	RRACBFUSA
EMILIE	28	F	LDY	RRACBFUSA
NAVIGOKY, ELIAS	49	M	TLR	RRAHQUUSA
KALMEN	11	M	NN	RRAHQUUSA
ARONSELM, JACOB	16	M	CL	RRZZZZUSA
SHIEKY, PHILOPH	18	M	MCHT	RRZZZZUSA
SALNITSKI, SALOMON	40	M	MCHT	RRZZZZUSA

SHIP: EGYPT

FROM: LIVERPOOL
TO: NEW YORK
ARRIVED: 29 NOVEMBER 1884

PASSENGER	AGE	SEX	OCCUPATION	PRV VIL DES
SCHWARTZ, JACOB	24	M	LABR	PLZZZZUSA
RUBENGIT, ISAAC	19	M	LABR	PLZZZZUSA
KUKURUK, MORITZ	21	M	LABR	PLZZZZUSA
PHILIP, LOUIS	20	M	LABR	PLZZZZUSA
AWRENS, M.	21	M	LABR	RRZZZZUSA
FACTTOACKE, J.	23	M	LABR	RRZZZZUSA
BLORM, HARRIS	21	M	LABR	RRZZZZUSA

SHIP: MAIN

FROM: BREMEN
TO: NEW YORK
ARRIVED: 29 NOVEMBER 1884

PASSENGER	AGE	SEX	OCCUPATION	PRV VIL DES
KLEG, SIMON	20	M	LABR	RRZZZZUSA

SHIP: PENNSYLVANIA

FROM: GLASGOW AND LARNE
TO: NEW YORK
ARRIVED: 29 NOVEMBER 1884

PASSENGER	AGE	SEX	OCCUPATION	PRV VIL DES
ALEXANDER, ANNA	35	F	W	PLZZZZUSA
STROGOWSKY, LEIB	21	M	TLR	PLZZZZUSA
ODES, RASCHE	00	M	LABR	RRZZZZUSA
SUWOWLES, FEIGE	00	F	W	RRZZZZUSA
TEITELBAUM, MEYER	00	M	BKR	RRZZZZUSA
JUDES	38	F	W	RRZZZZUSA
RASCHE	16	M	LABR	RRZZZZUSA
PUN, MANCE	11	M	CH	RRZZZZUSA
FEIM, LEA	46	F	W	RRZZZZUSA
JOSEPH	11	M	CH	RRZZZZUSA
SUTE	1	F	CHILD	RRZZZZUSA

SHIP: GERMANIC

FROM: LIVERPOOL
TO: NEW YORK
ARRIVED: 01 DECEMBER 1884

PASSENGER	AGE	SEX	OCCUPATION	PRV VIL DES
LUBIC, GOM.	32	M	LABR	RRZZZZUSA
WOERFFEL, C.J.	38	M	UNKNOWN	RRADBQRSS

SHIP: SERVIA

FROM: LIVERPOOL
TO: NEW YORK
ARRIVED: 01 DECEMBER 1884

PASSENGER	AGE	SEX	OCCUPATION	PRV VIL DES
ABERG, NILS-J.	24	M	UNKNOWN	FNZZZZUSA
NSMEN, JACOB	22	M	UNKNOWN	FNZZZZUSA
FAHL, ANTON	22	M	UNKNOWN	FNZZZZUSA
SUNDSTREM, ADRIEN	22	M	UNKNOWN	FNZZZZUSA
EKMERTENCK, G.	28	M	UNKNOWN	FNZZZZUSA

SHIP: BOHEMIA

FROM: HAMBURG
TO: NEW YORK
ARRIVED: 03 DECEMBER 1884

PASSENGER	AGE	SEX	OCCUPATION	PRV VIL DES
GAMBROOK, MEYER	19	M	DLR	RRZZZZUSA
SCHAVLINSKI, JUDES	42	F	W	RRZZZZUSA
JANKEL	18	M	CH	RRZZZZUSA
MEYER	14	M	CH	RRZZZZUSA
ARON	9	M	CHILD	RRZZZZUSA
ARON	8	M	CHILD	RRZZZZUSA
RUWEN	7	M	CHILD	RRZZZZUSA
TAUBE	6	M	CHILD	RRZZZZUSA
ISAAK	.11	M	INFANT	RRZZZZUSA
KANIGORSKI, ROSALIE	25	F	W	RRAGDUUSA
MARTHA	6	F	CHILD	RRAGDUUSA
ANTON	5	M	CHILD	RRAGDUUSA
AGNES	3	M	CHILD	RRAGDUUSA
MAX	.09	M	INFANT	RRAGDUUSA
MARKOS, SOLOMON	22	M	TLR	RRZZZZUSA
LIPSCHUTZ, REBECCA	36	F	W	RRZZZZUSA
LEA	19	F	CH	RRZZZZUSA
GITTEL	17	F	CH	RRZZZZUSA
PESIE	9	M	CHILD	RRZZZZUSA
LISKIND	5	M	CHILD	RRZZZZUSA
TROTZKI, SCHEINE	25	F	W	RRAHTFUSA
SALOMON	.11	M	INFANT	RRAHTFUSA
HAUSMANN, HEINRID	27	M	BCHR	RRACBFUSA
SCHAPIRO, ARON	9	M	CHILD	RRAHSZUSA
JACOB	8	M	CHILD	RRAHSZUSA
KRUMIK, ABR.	19	M	LABR	RRZZZZUSA
NEMES, ADOLF	31	M	LABR	RRAHSZUSA
SCHAPIRO, MERE	38	F	SGL	RRAHSZUSA
RUFF, OSCHER	19	M	LABR	RRAHTFUSA
POLIWODA, MORITZ	22	M	BCHR	RRAFZDUSA
GOULD, CHAIM	34	M	LABR	RRAHTFUSA
JESCHOWSKY, LEISER	9	M	CHILD	RRAHTFUSA
SCHLOME	8	M	CHILD	RRAHTFUSA
LEWIN, MINNIE	48	F	W	RRAGRTUSA
WOJNOWSKY, FRANZISKA	24	F	SGL	RRAGRTUSA
NEUMILLER, PHILIPP	30	M	LABR	RRABPNUSA
MARIE	33	F	W	RRABPNUSA
JOH	9	M	CHILD	RRABPNUSA
CHRISTINE	2	F	CHILD	RRABPNUSA
LOUISE	.06	F	INFANT	RRABPNUSA
JMBIG, JOSEF	23	M	LABR	RRZZZZUSA
OSCAR	27	F	W	RRZZZZUSA
BERTHA	2	F	CHILD	RRZZZZUSA
OLGA	.11	F	INFANT	RRZZZZUSA
WIENER, FRIEDR.	28	M	LABR	RRZZZZUSA
JOHANNA	31	F	W	RRZZZZUSA
WENISKI, ALEX	24	M	LABR	RRAHZSUSA
MIENLIS, JOSEF	24	M	LABR	RRAHZSUSA
BOGATZ, EMMA	18	F	SGL	RRZZZZUSA
LISSOWITZKY, LEISER	18	F	BCHR	RRZZZZUSA
KESSLER, THEODOR	26	M	DLR	RRAFWJUSA
GRUNSPAN, HIRSA	21	M	CL	RRAHVAUSA
MASIS, KASIMIR	24	M	LABR	RRZZZZUSA
MAGDA	22	F	W	RRZZZZUSA
WISGELNA, JURGIS	21	M	LABR	RRAHZSUSA
MARKUS, CHAIE	20	M	TLR	RRZZZZUSA
GEVIEKOS, G.	40	M	LABR	RRAHZSUSA

SHIP: DEVONIA

FROM: GLASGOW AND MOVILLE
TO: NEW YORK
ARRIVED: 03 DECEMBER 1884

PASSENGER	AGE	SEX	OCCUPATION	PRV VIL DES
BARNETT, B.	27	M	TLR	RRZZZZUSA
U-MRS	30	F	NN	RRZZZZUSA
SANDOWKY, LISSER	21	M	SHMK	PLZZZZUSA
MALKI	23	F	NN	PLZZZZUSA
KEVIATKAWSKY, S.	24	F	NN	PLZZZZUSA
WASSERMAN, B.	10	M	CH	PLZZZZUSA
CHARCS, JUDOR	10	M	CH	RRZZZZUSA
FANNY	19	F	NN	RRZZZZUSA
LEDERHAUDLER, J.	23	M	MCHT	RRZZZZUSA
GUSKIND, NACHEM	23	M	LABR	RRZZZZUSA
LISERAKY, CHAIM	19	M	TLR	RRZZZZUSA
FELDMAAN, M.	32	M	SHMK	RRZZZZUSA
SCHLACHHAUS, E.	28	M	LABR	PLZZZZUSA
GRASSFELD, ELIAS	23	M	UNKNOWN	PLZZZZUSA
WEINBERGER, A.	28	M	LABR	PLZZZZUSA
KARNGOLD, F.	18	M	CGRMKR	RRZZZZUSA

SHIP: WESTERNLAND

FROM: ANTWERP
TO: NEW YORK
ARRIVED: 03 DECEMBER 1884

PASSENGER	AGE	SEX	OCCUPATION	PRV VIL DES
MEYER, CZ.	43	F	UNKNOWN	PLZZZZNY
OLWSKI, J.	28	M	FARMER	PLZZZZNY
KOLOWSKA, M.	20	F	UNKNOWN	PLZZZZUNK
MA.	10	F	CH	PLZZZZUNK
OSHKINSKA, HR.	18	F	UNKNOWN	PLZZZZPLY
PLAWATZKI, C.	25	F	SDLR	PLAEABNY
GOETZ, W.	19	F	UNKNOWN	PLZZZZUNK
JEHGURSKI, U	20	M	LABR	PLAEABUNK
EHLERT, P.	25	M	TLR	PLZZZZCH
WISNIEWSKI, L.	22	M	LABR	PLZZZZUNK
MEYER, OTTO	9	M	CHILD	PLZZZZMIL
F.	6	M	CHILD	PLZZZZMIL
AD.	3	F	CHILD	PLZZZZMIL
OLGA	00	F	INF	PLZZZZMIL
MERGER, JOS.	29	F	UNKNOWN	PLZZZZNY
FISCHMIKEL, A.	20	M	SMH	PLZZZZNY
RABUSCS, MAR.	30	F	UNKNOWN	PLZZZZNY
DVORIEH, J.	23	M	SHMK	RRZZZZNY

PASSENGER	AGE	SEX	OCCUPATION	PRVIL	DES
SHIP: STATE OF ALABAMA					
FROM: GLASGOW AND LARNE					
TO: NEW YORK					
ARRIVED: 05 DECEMBER 1884					
BERNSTEIN, HIRSCH	22	M	FARMER	RRZZZZ	NY
BERNOWICZ, JACOB	22	M	BKBNDR	RRZZZZ	NY
CHINCZEWITZ, JAN	00	M	FARMER	RRZZZZ	CH
CHESZEITES, OSSIF	30	M	LABR	RRZZZZ	MI
DAVIDSOHN, PASSEL	42	M	MCHT	RRZZZZ	OH
DAVID, MEYER	25	M	MCHT	RRZZZZ	NY
ESTHER	00	F	NN	RRZZZZ	NY
FAUST, WLADISHAW	00	M	LABR	RRZZZZ	UNK
FRIEDMANN, ELIAS	22	M	MCHT	RRZZZZ	NY
GALITZKI, JACOB	00	M	TLR	RRZZZZ	NY
HIRSCHAWICZ, CHAIM	30	M	LABR	RRZZZZ	NY
KAHNUS, BARUCH	00	M	CBLR	RRZZZZ	NY
LIEHT, DAVID	00	M	LABR	RRZZZZ	PHI
LEONI, EYSECK	00	M	LABR	RRZZZZ	MO
LUKOCZITZ, BERNT	00	M	LABR	RRZZZZ	CH
MERKEL, NOCHERN	00	M	MCHT	RRZZZZ	BAL
OSSILOWSKI, FELIX	00	M	LABR	RRZZZZ	UNK
PAUKMANN, MEYER	50	M	TLR	RRZZZZ	NY
PAJE	44	F	W	RRZZZZ	NY
HING	00	M	NN	RRZZZZ	NY
PERIL	00	M	NN	RRZZZZ	NY
PREGGER, MOSES	00	M	CBLR	RRZZZZ	NY
DINOWSKY, DOBE	00	F	DRSMKR	RRZZZZ	NY
RASANSKI, -APHILIA	00	F	MDW	RRZZZZ	NY
SALZMANN, MEYER	24	M	TLR	RRZZZZ	NY
JURGOSTEIN, DEBORAH	11	F	CH	RRZZZZ	NY
SENATOR, ABRAHAM	55	M	CBLR	RRZZZZ	PHI
SESITZKY, BENZEL	35	M	CK	RRZZZZ	NY
LINA	33	F	W	RRZZZZ	NY
SEMIN, OLGA	19	F	NN	RRZZZZ	NY
OLGA	18	F	NN	RRZZZZ	NY
REBEKKA	17	F	NN	RRZZZZ	NY
WILEZEWSKI, STANISL.	20	M	LABR	RRZZZZ	MI
ZUCHOHWSKI, HODES	60	F	W	RRZZZZ	NY
ELIAS	10	M	CH	RRZZZZ	NY
GOLDE	8	F	CHILD	RRZZZZ	NY
ZARVEL, HIRSCH	21	M	CBLR	RRZZZZ	NY
SHIP: FULDA					
FROM: BREMEN					
TO: NEW YORK					
ARRIVED: 06 DECEMBER 1884					
BOLLMANN, OSCAR	24	M	TT	RRAHQD	USA
SHULZ, JACOB	45	M	FARMER	RRZZZZ	USA
CATHARINA	42	F	UNKNOWN	RRZZZZ	USA
JACOB	19	M	FARMER	RRZZZZ	USA
CHRISTINE	20	F	UNKNOWN	RRZZZZ	USA
JOSEF	17	M	FARMER	RRZZZZ	USA
BARBARA	14	F	CH	RRZZZZ	USA
DANIEL	8	M	CHILD	RRZZZZ	USA
CATHARINA	7	F	CHILD	RRZZZZ	USA
CHRISTIAN	6	M	CHILD	RRZZZZ	USA
ROSINE	.11	F	INFANT	RRZZZZ	USA
HERMANN, JACOB	24	M	FARMER	RRZZZZ	USA
MARGA	24	F	UNKNOWN	RRZZZZ	USA
WALDEMAR	.11	M	INFANT	RRZZZZ	USA
NAGEL, FRIEDR.	44	M	LABR	RRAFQV	USA
JACOB	20	M	LABR	RRAFQV	USA
GEORG	17	M	LABR	RRAFQV	USA
OLDENBACH, HEINRICH	35	M	LABR	RRAEGT	USA
CHRISTINE	34	F	UNKNOWN	RRAEGT	USA
RENZLER, JOHANN	50	M	LABR	RRZZZZ	USA
CHRISTINE	44	F	UNKNOWN	RRZZZZ	USA
GEORG	25	M	LABR	RRZZZZ	USA
HULDA	24	F	UNKNOWN	RRZZZZ	USA
ELISE	.05	F	INFANT	RRZZZZ	USA
ANDREAS	16	M	LABR	RRZZZZ	USA
ELISABETH	20	F	UNKNOWN	RRZZZZ	USA
HURWITZ, MAX	18	M	LABR	RRZZZZ	USA
SHIP: POLYNESIA					
FROM: HAMBURG					
TO: NEW YORK					
ARRIVED: 06 DECEMBER 1884					
FINN, AD.	33	M	MCHT	RRZZZZ	NY
LOWENTHAL, MORDSCHE	20	M	LABR	RRZZZZ	NY
MORDEL, WOLF	20	M	LABR	RRZZZZ	NY
REGKO, DAVID	18	M	LRCTR	RRZZZZ	NY
ITE	18	F	W	RRZZZZ	NY
GOLDBERG, HENOCH	33	M	JNR	RRZZZZ	NY
DWORE	26	F	W	RRZZZZ	NY
WILASKIS, CHAIN	24	M	TRDSMN	RRZZZZ	NY
GELBAITIS, JOS.	40	M	LABR	RRZZZZ	NY
ANNA	31	F	W	RRZZZZ	NY
MATHEUS	7	M	CHILD	RRZZZZ	NY
MAGA	5	F	CHILD	RRZZZZ	NY
ANNA	3	F	CHILD	RRZZZZ	NY
BLOCH, JOSEF	18	M	TRDSMN	RRZZZZ	NY
HONIGFELD, ABRAH.	38	M	TRDSMN	PLZZZZ	UNK
CHANE	7	F	CHILD	PLZZZZ	UNK
LIBSCHUETZ, BOREL	40	M	MCHT	RRZZZZ	NY
WEINBERG, SAUL	42	M	TRDSMN	PLZZZZ	NY
NEUSTADT, LEIB	33	M	TRDSMN	RRZZZZ	PA
HANSEN, PETER-P.	21	M	FARMER	RRZZZZ	UNK
MARLITZKI, WOLF.	21	M	LABR	RRZZZZ	NY
MOSKE, GAMELES	17	M	LABR	RRZZZZ	NY
SOMMER, LEISER	20	M	LABR	RRZZZZ	NY
ZEBULSKY, PAUL	33	M	LABR	RRZZZZ	NY
KLIMUT, LEIE	18	F	SGL	PLZZZZ	NY
ISRAELSKY, ARON	18	M	TRDSMN	RRZZZZ	NY
ABRAMOWITZ, WOLF	35	M	TRDSMN	RRZZZZ	NY
URDOMMSKY, ELKE	20	F	WO	RRZZZZ	NY
MALTE	.07	F	INFANT	RRZZZZ	NY
KADISCHES, HIRSCH	21	M	TRDSMN	RRZZZZ	NY
ZNOFE	18	F	W	RRZZZZ	NY
SHIP: HABSBURG					
FROM: BREMEN					
TO: NEW YORK					
ARRIVED: 08 DECEMBER 1884					
LEVIN, JENTE	22	M	LABR	RRZZZZ	NY
ISRAEL, SIMON	20	M	CL	RRZZZZ	NY
BROTMANN, ARON	32	M	PDLR	RRZZZZ	NY
LEHOPP, JOHANN	45	M	JNR	RRZZZZ	UNK
CATHARINA	43	F	W	RRZZZZ	UNK
JOHANNA	15	F	CH	RRZZZZ	UNK
JACOB	10	M	CH	RRZZZZ	UNK
CATHARINA	2	F	CHILD	RRZZZZ	UNK
CARL	.09	M	INFANT	RRZZZZ	UNK
NIKANT, FERDINAND	54	M	FARMER	RRZZZZ	NY
CONSTANZIA	53	F	W	RRZZZZ	NY
FERDINAND	27	M	FARMER	RRZZZZ	NY

PASSENGER	AGE	SEX	OCCUPATION	PRV VIL DES
OTTILIE	28	F	SVNT	RRZZZZNY
EDUARD	21	M	LABR	RRZZZZNY
JOHANN	18	M	LABR	RRZZZZNY
HELENE	17	F	SVNT	RRZZZZNY
ATALIA	17	F	SVNT	RRZZZZNY
ADOLF	11	M	CH	RRZZZZNY
GAEDE, JOHANN	45	M	LABR	RRZZZZNY
SARAH	46	F	W	RRZZZZNY
HEINRICH	17	M	CH	RRZZZZNY
JOHANN	15	M	CH	RRZZZZNY
JACOB	14	M	CH	RRZZZZNY
EVA	7	F	CHILD	RRZZZZNY
ELISABETH	2	F	CHILD	RRZZZZNY
COHN, CHAIN	30	F	W	RRZZZZNY
BIRKI	10	F	CH	RRZZZZNY
DAVID	3	M	CHILD	RRZZZZNY
CHEIM	.09	F	INFANT	RRZZZZNY
LADICSEWITZ, SELDE	18	F	SVNT	RRZZZZNY
DAWIDOWITZ, ANNA	18	F	SVNT	RRZZZZPA
SARAZECK, SARAH	16	F	SVNT	RRZZZZNY
SCHOPP, ELISABETH	4	F	CHILD	RRZZZZUNK

SHIP: OREGON

FROM: LIVERPOOL AND QUEENSTOWN
TO: NEW YORK
ARRIVED: 08 DECEMBER 1884

PASSENGER	AGE	SEX	OCCUPATION	PRV VIL DES
LUBANSKY, PAUL	40	M	LABR	PLZZZZUSA
SZEPULN, JANOS	24	M	LABR	PLZZZZUSA
LISKA, GEORGE	11	M	CH	PLZZZZUSA
MUZALA, PETER	20	M	LABR	PLZZZZUSA
SUVATSA, MICHL.	11	M	CH	PLZZZZUSA
PUCHALA, JANOS	11	M	CH	PLZZZZUSA
RAGA, MARIE	17	F	SP	PLZZZZUSA
POLATSEK, ELISE	11	F	CH	PLZZZZUSA
WLADIMIR, W.	32	M	MSNY	RRZZZZUSA
GEDEON	40	M	MSNY	RRZZZZUSA
MITWZAD	22	M	MSNY	RRZZZZUSA
BLUMENTHAL, M.	28	M	FRR	RRZZZZUSA

SHIP: SUEVIA

FROM: HAMBURG
TO: NEW YORK
ARRIVED: 09 DECEMBER 1884

PASSENGER	AGE	SEX	OCCUPATION	PRV VIL DES
ALTSCHULER, LEON	30	M	WVR	RRZZZZUSA
LISESKI, JAN	45	M	LABR	RRZZZZUSA
EVA	45	F	W	RRZZZZUSA
RADTKE, AUGUST	28	M	LKSH	RRZZZZUSA
EMILIE	22	F	W	RRZZZZUSA
AUGUST	3	M	CHILD	RRZZZZUSA
GUSTAV	.11	M	INFANT	RRZZZZUSA
ROSENTHAL, RUBIN	55	M	LABR	RRZZZZUSA
TAUBE	18	F	SGL	RRAHSEUSA
CHAZEROWSKY, ANNA	38	F	W	RRZZZZUSA
JUDEL	.11	F	INFANT	RRZZZZUSA
SCHILINITZKI, JETTE	20	F	SGL	RRZZZZUSA
WOLFSOHN, MALKE	19	F	SGL	RRZZZZUSA
CHANITE, JOSUA	20	M	LABR	RRZZZZUSA
GRUENBLATT, BREINE	30	F	W	RRZZZZUSA
JELITZKY	.11	F	INFANT	RRZZZZUSA
KALITZKY	.11	F	INFANT	RRZZZZUSA
SLAKKE	9	F	CHILD	RRZZZZUSA
POKOCZEWSKY, JOSSEL	22	M	LABR	RRZZZZUSA
JOSSEL	9	M	CHILD	RRZZZZUSA
FRIEDMANN, SARA	18	F	SGL	RRAHUTUSA
WACHSMANN, SZINA	24	F	SGL	RRAFVGUSA
SCHAJEWITZ, LEIB	22	M	DLR	RRZZZZUSA
FINKELGOR, ALTER	9	M	CHILD	RRZZZZUSA
GOLDBERG, CHAIM	67	M	TLR	RRAFWJUSA
FRIEDLAENDER, CHAIM	21	M	DLR	RRZZZZUSA
GOLDMANN, BERL	16	M	LABR	RRZZZZUSA
RIWKE	9	F	CHILD	RRZZZZUSA
CHAIE	8	F	CHILD	RRZZZZUSA
JACOB	7	M	CHILD	RRZZZZUSA
SCHIENAN	6	M	CHILD	RRZZZZUSA
SCHWARTZ, SELIG	18	M	TNMK	RRZZZZUSA
NOCHINSKY, SAMUEL	20	M	LABR	RRAHVOUSA
BERNSTEIN, CHASKEL	52	M	LABR	RRZZZZUSA
MINNA	50	F	W	RRZZZZUSA
TAUBE	17	F	CH	RRZZZZUSA
MOSES	9	M	CHILD	RRZZZZUSA
RUBINOWITZ, ABEL	17	M	LABR	RRZZZZUSA
CHANITE, SARA	19	F	SGL	RRZZZZUSA
WILENZIK, ISAAC	19	M	LABR	RRZZZZUSA
SIMIAWITZ, LIPMAN	24	M	LABR	RRZZZZUSA
KATZEWITZ, SCHAJE	9	M	CHILD	RRZZZZUSA
ISRAEL	8	M	CHILD	RRZZZZUSA
MELER, BEHR	37	M	LABR	RRAHTFUSA
ROSENTHAL, JOSSEL	43	M	LABR	RRZZZZUSA
DOMBROWSKI, CAROLE.	45	F	W	RRZZZZUSA
LEWAR, MOSES	23	M	LABR	RRAHVUUSA
ROSER	22	F	W	RRAHVUUSA
BIRNBAUM, LEON	25	M	LABR	RRAHVUUSA
WOLFFORF, CHAIM	21	M	ENGR	RRAFWJUSA
SCHACH, RACHEL	17	F	SGL	RRAGRTUSA
DOBBERSTEIN, CHAJE	22	F	SGL	RRAHTUUSA
GINSBERG, ISRAEL	16	M	LKSH	RRZZZZUSA
ZIWIE	22	F	SGL	RRZZZZUSA
SORESOHN, ISAAC	19	M	UPHST	RRAHTFUSA
BURSTEIN, LEIB	36	M	LABR	RRAHTFUSA

SHIP: CANADA

FROM: HAVRE
TO: NEW YORK
ARRIVED: 13 DECEMBER 1884

PASSENGER	AGE	SEX	OCCUPATION	PRV VIL DES
FOEL, ROME	26	M	TLR	RRZZZZNY

SHIP: RHAETIA

FROM: HAMBURG
TO: NEW YORK
ARRIVED: 13 DECEMBER 1884

PASSENGER	AGE	SEX	OCCUPATION	PRV VIL DES
GOLDBERG, LIEBE	22	F	W	RRZZZZUSA
LEIB	17	M	LABR	RRZZZZUSA
LINE	.11	F	INFANT	RRZZZZUSA
FEINBLUM, SALOMON	9	M	CHILD	RRZZZZUSA
LEWIN, JACOB	18	M	LABR	RRZZZZUSA
JASHAU, BERL	18	M	DLR	RRZZZZUSA
NATRA, MARCUS	22	M	TLR	RRZZZZUSA
FRIEDMANN, MOSES	50	M	LABR	RRZZZZUSA
REBECCA	17	F	CH	RRZZZZUSA
SHLOME	9	M	CHILD	RRZZZZUSA
CHAIM	8	M	CHILD	RRZZZZUSA
SCHUCK, FEIGE	27	F	W	RRZZZZUSA

PASSENGER	AGE	SEX	OCCUPATION	PRV VIL DES
DEBORA	8	F	CHILD	RRZZZZUSA
LERA	6	M	CHILD	RRZZZZUSA
RESNIJKOW, LIEBE	21	F	SGL	RRZZZZUSA
ROSENFELD, J.	20	F	SGL	RRZZZZUSA
LEVISOHN, SCHEINE	15	F	SGL	RRZZZZUSA
JAMSKI, JONE	17	M	DLR	RRZZZZUSA
HONVITZ, HILLEL	25	M	DLR	RRZZZZUSA
LEWISOHN, LEIB	21	M	DLR	RRZZZZUSA
LEBEWOHL, LEISER	17	M	DLR	RRZZZZUSA
SELMANN, SALOMON	21	M	DLR	RRZZZZUSA
CHAIE	18	M	DLR	RRZZZZUSA
KAMINSKY, ELY	21	M	DLR	RRZZZZUSA
KUNTZKOWITZ, DAVID	21	M	DLR	RRZZZZUSA
OSSELSON, GERSON	50	M	DLR	RRZZZZUSA
HATZ, ABR.	20	M	DLR	RRZZZZUSA
KASZYNSKA, FRANZKA.	19	F	SGL	RRZZZZUSA
KUCERITZ, ANDR.	27	M	LABR	RRZZZZUSA
GRINGART, GERSON	18	M	BCHR	RRZZZZUSA
REDER, CHAIL	36	F	W	RRZZZZUSA
ALTER	2	M	CHILD	RRZZZZUSA
RICKEL	1	M	CHILD	RRZZZZUSA
KAMPOS, MICHAEL	20	M	LABR	RRZZZZUSA
FINKELMANN, ABRAH.	18	M	LABR	RRZZZZUSA
LUBLINER, SCHMUL	19	M	LABR	RRZZZZUSA

SHIP: ANCHORIA

FROM: GLASGOW
TO: NEW YORK
ARRIVED: 15 DECEMBER 1884

PASSENGER	AGE	SEX	OCCUPATION	PRV VIL DES
ANTONAS, ALEX	21	M	UNKNOWN	RRZZZZUSA
COHEN, ELIAS	19	M	PDLR	RRZZZZUSA
KISCH, BERKA	50	M	DPR	RRZZZZUSA
KAUKANTZKOS, IOSEL	21	M	LABR	RRZZZZUSA
SEGALOWICZ, MICHAEL	22	M	UNKNOWN	RRZZZZUSA
UKAS, ADOMAS	21	M	UNKNOWN	RRZZZZUSA

SHIP: EMS

FROM: BREMEN
TO: NEW YORK
ARRIVED: 15 DECEMBER 1884

PASSENGER	AGE	SEX	OCCUPATION	PRV VIL DES
FISCHER, PHILIPP	27	M	FARMER	RRZZZZUSA
FRIEDRIKE	28	F	NN	RRZZZZUSA
ELISABETH	2	F	CHILD	RRZZZZUSA
CAHTARINE	1	F	CHILD	RRZZZZUSA
JOHANN	.06	M	INFANT	RRZZZZUSA
BERLINSKY, DAV.	14	M	FARMER	RRZZZZUSA
GUTMANN, MOSES	64	M	MCHT	RRZZZZUSA
SUSAR	62	F	NN	RRZZZZUSA
LIEBE	20	M	FARMER	RRZZZZUSA
ISRELSKY, ETTY	18	M	FARMER	RRZZZZUSA
MOLDENHAUER, JOH.	31	M	FARMER	RRZZZZUSA
LOUISE	32	F	NN	RRZZZZUSA
CHRISTINA	18	F	NN	RRZZZZUSA
ANDREAS	17	M	LABR	RRZZZZUSA
GOTTFRIED	13	M	CH	RRZZZZUSA
EVALINA	10	F	CH	RRZZZZUSA
FERDINAND	8	M	CHILD	RRZZZZUSA
MATHILDE	.09	F	INFANT	RRZZZZUSA
CATHARINE	.09	F	INFANT	RRZZZZUSA
CHRISTIAN	.06	M	INFANT	RRZZZZUSA
ROSTOWSKY, EVA	18	F	NN	RRZZZZUSA

SHIP: PENNLAND

FROM: ANTWERP
TO: NEW YORK
ARRIVED: 15 DECEMBER 1884

PASSENGER	AGE	SEX	OCCUPATION	PRV VIL DES
WITTKOWSKA, MARZ.	60	M	FARMER	RRAHTRUNK
JABUKE, WILH.	23	M	LABR	PLZZZZMIL
SCHALINSKA, FELCE.	20	F	SVNT	PLZZZZPHI
SPILSKY, J.	15	F	SVNT	PLAEABUNK
JABUKE, AUG.	21	M	LABR	PLZZZZMIL
RENKAWITCZ, ANNA	24	M	FARMER	PLZZZZIL
FISCHMANN, M.	50	M	TLR	PLZZZZNY
WALANSKA, SABA.	40	F	SVNT	PLACXZUNK
BORNSTEIN, SAM.	25	M	CGRMKR	RRZZZZUNK
SYSMANSKY, K.	60	F	W	RRZZZZUNK
HEALICKE, V.	27	M	STCL	RRZZZZNY
KEON, AUG.	00	M	LABR	RRZZZZNY
REIXECK, FZ.	00	M	LABR	RRZZZZNY

SHIP: STATE OF INDIANA

FROM: GLASGOW AND LARNE
TO: NEW YORK
ARRIVED: 15 DECEMBER 1884

PASSENGER	AGE	SEX	OCCUPATION	PRV VIL DES
HELFENBEIN, ARON	27	M	CPTR	RRZZZZUSA
ALEXANDROWITZ, GERSON	35	M	PDLR	RRZZZZUSA
MILES, ISRAEL	16	M	PDLR	RRZZZZUSA
SANDLER, FEIWEL	37	M	PDLR	RRZZZZUSA
RUTENBERG, MARCUS	19	M	PDLR	RRZZZZUSA
WILLENZIG, RUBEN	24	M	PDLR	RRZZZZUSA
KLEINE, FEIGE	26	F	W	RRZZZZUSA
RIWKE	.06	F	INFANT	RRZZZZUSA
ZUCKER, SARAH	35	F	W	RRZZZZUSA
FISCHEL	1	M	CHILD	RRZZZZUSA
MUEHLSTEIN, BARUCH	45	M	PDLR	RRZZZZUSA
MUSKE.	45	F	W	RRZZZZUSA
MOSES	11	M	CH	RRZZZZUSA
MATHIS	8	M	CHILD	RRZZZZUSA
CHAIM	6	M	CHILD	RRZZZZUSA
RACHEL	5	F	CHILD	RRZZZZUSA
MENACHE	2	M	CHILD	RRZZZZUSA
ETTEL	.09	F	INFANT	RRZZZZUSA
BEHRMAN, SAMUEL	25	M	PDLR	RRZZZZUSA
KATZ, ITZIK	22	M	WCHMKR	RRZZZZUSA
PERSON, MOSES-L.	22	M	PDLR	RRZZZZUSA
FREIDE	19	F	W	RRZZZZUSA
KERSTEIN, AUGUST	19	M	LABR	RRZZZZUSA
LIPNIK, MEYER	19	M	PDLR	RRZZZZUSA
FINKELSTEIN, SOLOMON	40	M	PDLR	RRZZZZUSA
EDELSTEIN, BENJAMIN	23	M	PDLR	RRZZZZUSA
CHARITON, MOSES	44	M	LABR	RRZZZZUSA
LEWITH, BARUCH	22	M	PDLR	RRZZZZUSA
RABINOWITZ, JOSEPH	24	M	PDLR	RRZZZZUSA
BRANNSTEIN, CHIEL	22	M	BRR	RRZZZZUSA
BAENDELMANN, LEIB	28	M	LKSH	RR7ZZZUSA
ALEXOWITZ, MARIA	27	F	W	PLZZZZUSA
MARIA	6	F	CHILD	PLZZZZUSA
HELENA	1	F	CHILD	PLZZZZUSA
MEIRICH, LIPMANN	29	M	PDLR	PLZZZZUSA
FLATOW, ABRAHAM	22	M	PDLR	PLZZZZUSA

PASSENGER	AGE	SEX	OCCUPATION	PRV VIL DES

SHIP: RUGIA

FROM: HAMBURG
TO: NEW YORK
ARRIVED: 18 DECEMBER 1884

PASSENGER	AGE	SEX	OCCUPATION	PRV VIL DES
KOLIKANT, ABRAH.	39	M	DLR	RRZZZZUSA
LIMONOWITZ, MOSES	35	M	DLR	RRZZZZUSA
WOLFSOHN, LEWIN	38	M	DLR	RRZZZZUSA
GOLDBERG, BERL	21	M	UNKNOWN	RRZZZZUSA
ALTMANN, SALI	16	F	CH	RRZZZZUSA
ADOLF	9	M	CHILD	RRZZZZUSA
SUESSKIND, BENJAMIN	32	M	LABR	RRZZZZUSA
RESI	27	F	W	RRZZZZUSA
LEISER	4	M	CHILD	RRZZZZUSA
OSVSIKY, JACOB	31	M	LABR	RRZZZZUSA
WEISSBERG, SCHEVE	26	F	W	RRZZZZUSA
LEIB	6	M	CHILD	RRZZZZUSA
ETTEL	4	F	CHILD	RRZZZZUSA
WITOSTHKER, MAX	25	M	LABR	RRZZZZUSA
SANDILON, ISAAC	18	M	DLR	RRZZZZUSA
ASSWARITZ, JEZOK	18	M	UNKNOWN	RRZZZZUSA
FEIN, FENONSEL	18	M	DLR	RRZZZZUSA
JAFFE, CHONE	27	M	MSN	RRZZZZUSA
GARFINKEL, RACHEL	31	F	W	RRZZZZUSA
PAULINE	9	F	CHILD	RRZZZZUSA
MARIE	5	F	CHILD	RRZZZZUSA
SCHMUEL	9	M	CHILD	RRZZZZUSA
CHASKEL	7	M	CHILD	RRZZZZUSA
LIBOFSKY, MOSCHE	8	F	CHILD	RRZZZZUSA
BUTAITIS, DOMINIK	23	M	FARMER	RRZZZZUSA
KRAM, MENDEL	32	M	DLR	RRZZZZUSA
TAUBE	18	F	SGL	RRZZZZUSA
BRAWNIANA, MARCUS	20	M	LABR	RRZZZZUSA
COHEN, BASCHE	20	F	SGL	RRZZZZUSA
MELLER, PESACH	18	M	LABR	RRZZZZUSA
SCHAPIRO, MARIANE	29	F	W	RRZZZZUSA
BLAN, DEBORA	24	F	W	RRZZZZUSA
REBECCA	8	F	CHILD	RRZZZZUSA
LEBERWURST, HERMAN	30	M	MSN	RRZZZZUSA

SHIP: CIRCASSIA

FROM: GLASGOW AND MOVILLE
TO: NEW YORK
ARRIVED: 19 DECEMBER 1884

PASSENGER	AGE	SEX	OCCUPATION	PRV VIL DES
EDELMAN, KERVE	19	M	LABR	RRZZZZUSA
ROMANOWSKY, JUDEL	24	M	TLR	RRZZZZUSA
ALEXANDEWITZ, WOLF	8	M	CHILD	RRZZZZUSA
LOUIS	.06	M	INFANT	RRZZZZUSA
RUBELSKI, ZEMACH	40	M	TLR	RRZZZZUSA
NOHA, IGNATZ	23	M	LABR	RRZZZZUSA
KAROLINE	11	F	CH	RRZZZZUSA
BAUM, MITKE	26	F	W	RRZZZZUSA
BECKY	6	F	CHILD	RRZZZZUSA
AARON	3	M	CHILD	RRZZZZUSA
ANNIE	2	F	CHILD	RRZZZZUSA
HARRY	.05	M	INFANT	RRZZZZUSA
ETTINGER, TAUBE	40	F	W	RRZZZZUSA
MOSES	20	M	CGRMKR	RRZZZZUSA
MENDEL	16	M	CGRMKR	RRZZZZUSA
JUDEL	11	M	CH	RRZZZZUSA
LENA	4	F	CHILD	RRZZZZUSA
ISRAEL	2	M	CHILD	RRZZZZUSA
BECKSYANSKI, JAN.	25	M	LABR	RRZZZZUSA
KULAK, PAUL	25	M	LABR	RRZZZZUSA
GOLDSTEIN, BEN.	21	M	DLR	RRZZZZUSA
KLOPOT, SCHAIE	20	M	GLVR	RRZZZZUSA
RAIHINITSH, MORDCHE	22	M	DLR	RRZZZZUSA

SHIP: CALIFORNIA

FROM: HAMBURG
TO: NEW YORK
ARRIVED: 22 DECEMBER 1884

PASSENGER	AGE	SEX	OCCUPATION	PRV VIL DES
MEYER, HEINR.	19	M	FARMER	RRZZZZNY
STEINWARZER, BEHR	22	M	TLR	RRZZZZNY
FEILER, GEORG	26	M	FARMER	RRZZZZNY
KUMIN, NOCHEM	35	M	TRDSMN	RRZZZZNY
DEIBE, MOS.	26	M	TRDSMN	RRZZZZNY
GDIMAN, HIRSCH	24	M	CGRMKR	RRZZZZNY
HAPTIC, LIEBE	50	F	WO	RRZZZZNY
KUSINEWITZ, LIEBE	19	F	SGL	RRZZZZNY
SCHARLOT, FANI	20	F	SGL	RRZZZZNY
GOLDMANN, ABR.	19	M	TRDSMN	RRZZZZNY
BARCKSTEIN, LOCHER-B.	22	M	TRDSMN	RRZZZZNY
RUVE	21	F	W	RRZZZZNY
BOBSOWSKY, PESCHE	18	F	SGL	RRZZZZNY
GROSBORG, HERSCH	18	M	TRDSMN	RRZZZZNY
POSESIORSKY, ROCHANE	17	F	SGL	RRZZZZNY
SOROWSKY, M.L.	22	F	WO	RRZZZZNY
KABAZNIK, PACHE	22	F	SGL	RRZZZZNY
GLUCKMANN, SIM.	17	M	CL	RRZZZZNY
MATEL	18	M	SGL	RRZZZZNY
BRAUN, MENDEL	22	M	CPTR	RRZZZZNY
BORN, ROSA	19	F	SGL	RRZZZZNY
KUSTIN, ABRAH.	23	M	MCHT	RRZZZZNY
SYNGA, JOSES	21	M	LABR	RRZZZZNY
GOTTHOFER, IDEL	23	M	TLR	PLZZZZNY
KIERACZ, MICH.	24	M	LABR	PLZZZZUNK
KIERZIENSKY, ARNOLD	19	M	LABR	RRZZZZNY
ADELMANN, JESCHE	21	M	TRDSMN	RRZZZZNY
KATZ, JOSEPH	32	M	TRDSMN	RRZZZZNY
ETTA	24	F	W	RRZZZZNY
LIEBE	.07	F	INFANT	RRZZZZNY
SCHMERZ, ROSA	22	F	W	PLZZZZNY
COHN, PAPY	7	M	CHILD	PLZZZZNY
SEINDEL	6	F	CHILD	PLZZZZNY
HERMANN	5	M	CHILD	PLZZZZNY
ABRAHAM	3	M	CHILD	PLZZZZNY
SCHMERZ, FEIGE	.04	F	INFANT	PLZZZZNY
ZEMPLINER, SCHOL.	20	M	TRDSMN	RRZZZZNY
SEINDEL	20	F	W	RRZZZZNY
NOWINITZKY, LEIB	21	M	TLR	RRZZZZNY
ZADIK, JOSEPH	23	M	TRDSMN	RRZZZZNY
LEVIN, JOHANNA	21	F	SGL	RRZZZZNY
FRANK, ALEXANDER	19	M	TRDSMN	RRZZZZNY
LEVIN, NATALIE	18	F	SGL	RRZZZZNY
WILNISKY, PINS	21	F	LABR	RRZZZZNY
ELISABETH	26	F	W	RRZZZZNY

SHIP: EIDER

FROM: BREMEN AND SOUTHAMPTON
TO: NEW YORK
ARRIVED: 22 DECEMBER 1884

PASSENGER	AGE	SEX	OCCUPATION	PRV VIL DES
SCHUELER, JOHANN	20	M	FARMER	RRZZZZUSA
NOVICKI, VINCENTY	14	M	CH	RRZZZZUSA
MARIANNA	17	F	CH	RRZZZZUSA
BREITLING, JACOB	22	M	LABR	RRZZZZUSA
GOTTLIEB	20	M	LABR	RRZZZZUSA

PASSENGER	AGE	SEX	OCCUPATION	PRV	VIL	DES
STUEKLER, LUDWIG	58	M	FARMER	RR	ZZZZ	USA
CHRISTE.	58	F	W	RR	ZZZZ	USA
BRENNEISEN, DOROTHEA	21	F	NN	RR	ZZZZ	USA
RAILE, ANDREAS	28	M	FARMER	RR	ZZZZ	USA
ROSINA	28	F	W	RR	ZZZZ	USA
BARBA.	2	F	CHILD	RR	ZZZZ	USA
FRIEDRICH	.06	M	INFANT	RR	ZZZZ	USA
MICHAEL	33	M	FARMER	RR	ZZZZ	USA
KATHA.	30	F	W	RR	ZZZZ	USA
KATHA.	9	F	CHILD	RR	ZZZZ	USA
MICHAEL	7	M	CHILD	RR	ZZZZ	USA
JACOB	6	M	CHILD	RR	ZZZZ	USA
MAGDARINA	4	F	CHILD	RR	ZZZZ	USA
JOHANN	3	M	CHILD	RR	ZZZZ	USA
DAVID	2	M	CHILD	RR	ZZZZ	USA
ELISAB.	.06	F	INFANT	RR	ZZZZ	USA
MEYER, EMILIE	28	F	W	RR	ZZZZ	USA
WANDA	7	F	CHILD	RR	ZZZZ	USA
PABEL	2	M	CHILD	RR	ZZZZ	USA
GISCHNITZKA, REBECCA	30	F	W	RR	ZZZZ	USA
DAVID	7	M	CHILD	RR	ZZZZ	USA
ISAAC	4	M	CHILD	RR	ZZZZ	USA
IDA	5	F	CHILD	RR	ZZZZ	USA
BORUCH	2	M	CHILD	RR	ZZZZ	USA

SHIP: STATE OF GEORGIA

FROM: GLASGOW AND LARNE
TO: NEW YORK
ARRIVED: 22 DECEMBER 1884

PASSENGER	AGE	SEX	OCCUPATION	PRV	VIL	DES
GURIN, LEISER	00	M	LABR	PL	ZZZZ	NY
ZIRINSKY, MINE	00	F	W	PL	ZZZZ	NY
MOSES	00	M	CH	PL	ZZZZ	NY
PRASOWSKY, JUDEL	22	M	LABR	PL	ZZZZ	NY
BARKEN, SAMUEL	21	M	LABR	PL	ZZZZ	NY
GRIN, JETE	00	F	CH	PL	ZZZZ	NY
KOHLBALT, ABRAHAM	30	M	LABR	PL	ZZZZ	NY
JETTE	25	F	W	PL	ZZZZ	NY
LEZAGERSKA, PAUL	43	M	LABR	PL	ZZZZ	NY
KUPER, SIMON	28	M	LABR	PL	ZZZZ	NY
LEWINSON, JOSEF	19	M	LABR	PL	ZZZZ	NY
KUBANICK, ELIAS	21	M	LABR	PL	ZZZZ	NY
ROSS, BERL	20	M	LABR	PL	ZZZZ	NY
LIMANSKY, ISAAK	21	M	LABR	PL	ZZZZ	NY
ARONOWITZ, FEIGE	50	F	W	PL	ZZZZ	NY
BASSE	00	F	NN	PL	ZZZZ	NY
BERALOWITZ, JESSIE	46	M	LABR	PL	ZZZZ	NY
SCHOLSFMANN, BASKE	21	M	LABR	PL	ZZZZ	NY
BERNSTEIN, ISAAK	24	M	LABR	PL	ZZZZ	NY
GOLDE	22	F	W	PL	ZZZZ	NY
LEVINBERG, ELIAS	00	M	LABR	PL	ZZZZ	NY
RAKONSKY, DAVID	20	M	LABR	PL	ZZZZ	NY
IWAKOWSKY, JOSEF	22	M	LABR	PL	ZZZZ	NY
LAPIDOWSKY, MORDCHE	21	M	LABR	PL	ZZZZ	NY
GLUECK, BENUS	23	M	LABR	PL	ZZZZ	NY
BLECKON, JOSEF	21	M	TNSTH	PL	ZZZZ	NY
KANTOR, CHANE	00	F	W	PL	ZZZZ	NY
ABRAHAM	.11	M	INFANT	PL	ZZZZ	NY

SHIP: GELLERT

FROM: HAMBURG AND HAVRE
TO: NEW YORK
ARRIVED: 23 DECEMBER 1884

PASSENGER	AGE	SEX	OCCUPATION	PRV	VIL	DES
LACHOWSKY, LOUIS	28	M	MUSN	PL	ACBF	USA
STOFFER, ADAM	29	M	FARMER	PL	ACBF	USA
EVA	22	F	W	PL	ACBF	USA
MAGDAL.	.02	F	INFANT	PL	ACBF	USA
FRIEDR.	17	M	FARMER	PL	ACBF	USA
PFEIFFER, JOHS.	44	M	FARMER	PL	ACBF	USA
BARBA.	42	F	W	PL	ACBF	USA
CHRISTE.	18	F	CH	PL	ACBF	USA
CATHA.	16	F	CH	PL	ACBF	USA
CAROLINE	12	F	CH	PL	ACBF	USA
LISE	9	F	CHILD	PL	ACBF	USA
JOHS.	8	M	CHILD	PL	ACBF	USA
BARBA.	2	F	CHILD	PL	ACBF	USA
FILIP	.03	M	INFANT	PL	ACBF	USA
MUNTSCH, MARGA.	18	F	SGL	PL	ACBF	USA
LISE	13	F	CH	PL	ACBF	USA
CATHA.	5	F	CHILD	PL	ACBF	USA
WEBER, JOH.	29	M	LABR	PL	ACBF	USA
CATHA.	27	F	W	PL	ACBF	USA
GOTTL.	4	M	CHILD	PL	ACBF	USA
FOWA	1	M	CHILD	PL	ACBF	USA
CHR.	.09	M	INFANT	PL	ACBF	USA
FRIEDR.	17	M	FARMER	PL	ACBF	USA
HOFFMANN, PETER	42	M	LABR	PL	ACBF	USA
ELISABETH	40	F	W	PL	ACBF	USA
MARGA	22	F	D	PL	ACBF	USA
SCHRADER, CARL	18	M	FARMER	PL	ACBF	USA
ULMER, FRIEDR.	33	M	FARMER	PL	ACBF	USA
CATHA.	26	F	W	PL	ACBF	USA
CATHA.	6	F	CHILD	PL	ACBF	USA
JACOB	4	M	CHILD	PL	ACBF	USA
CHRISTE.	2	F	CHILD	PL	ACBF	USA
FRIEDR.	.02	M	INFANT	PL	ACBF	USA
ANNA	17	F	SGL	PL	ACBF	USA
GOTTLOB	27	M	FARMER	PL	ACBF	USA
SOFIE	27	F	W	PL	ACBF	USA
CHRISTE.	5	F	CHILD	PL	ACBF	USA
JACOB	3	M	CHILD	PL	ACBF	USA
GOTTL.	2	M	CHILD	PL	ACBF	USA
SOFIE	1	F	CHILD	PL	ACBF	USA
FRIEDR.	.02	M	INFANT	PL	ACBF	USA
BARBA.	66	F	W	PL	ACBF	USA
BLOCKKOLB, SALOMON	41	M	FARMER	PL	ACBF	USA
BARBA.	38	F	W	PL	ACBF	USA
MARIE	15	F	CH	PL	ACBF	USA
SUSANNE	13	F	CH	PL	ACBF	USA
BARBA.	9	F	CHILD	PL	ACBF	USA
JOHS.	8	M	CHILD	PL	ACBF	USA
JACOB	7	M	CHILD	PL	ACBF	USA
SALOMON	2	M	CHILD	PL	ACBF	USA
GOTTL.	.09	M	INFANT	PL	ACBF	USA
ZWEIGHOFF, JACOB	18	M	LABR	PL	ACBF	USA
WARTOWSKY, LIPE	35	M	DLR	PL	ACBF	USA
MATUKAJENTA, JEVA	22	F	W	PL	ACBF	USA
GOLDFAGEN, ABRAM	24	M	JNR	PL	ACBF	USA
MEYEROWITZ, CHAIM	30	M	LABR	PL	ACBF	USA
ELFOND, BENDER	19	M	SMH	PL	ACBF	USA
ZIMMER, RUWEN	36	M	LABR	PL	ACBF	USA
GITTELMANN, SCHLOME	22	F	LABR	PL	ACBF	USA
BACKSCHT, SAMUEL	39	M	DLR	PL	ACBF	USA
SCHLIEWE, JOH.	38	M	LABR	PL	ACBF	USA
SCHOECK, JOH.	55	M	LABR	PL	ACBF	USA
CATHA.	42	F	LABR	PL	ACBF	USA
GOTTFR.	9	F	CHILD	PL	ACBF	USA
WILH.	8	M	CHILD	PL	ACBF	USA
HANNE	5	F	CHILD	PL	ACBF	USA
PHEIL, ROBERT	24	M	FARMER	PL	ACBF	USA
HAMMERMEISTER, AUG.	21	M	LABR	PL	ACBF	USA

PASSENGER	AGE	SEX	OCCUPATION	PRIV	DES
LOUISE	22	F	W	PLACBF	USA
RICHTER, EMMA	24	F	SGL	PLACBF	USA
HUMMEL, STEFAN	21	M	LABR	PLACBF	USA
BUCKING, LOUIS	00	M	UNKNOWN	PLACBF	USA
MUNSCH, ANDR.	42	M	LABR	PLACBF	USA
LOUISE	39	F	W	PLACBF	USA
ANDR.	16	M	CH	PLACBF	USA
ELISABETH	4	F	CHILD	PLACBF	USA
CHRIST.	2	M	CHILD	PLACBF	USA
CHRISTE.	.08	F	INFANT	PLACBF	USA
HEIDE, JOCHIM	00	U	UNKNOWN	PLACBF	USA
ZIEBAR, RUD.	21	M	LABR	PLACBF	USA
SCHIMANSKY, JOSEF	18	M	LABR	PLACBF	USA
GRAJUDA, MARIANE	18	F	W	PLACBF	USA
USWALLS, MICHEL	21	M	LABR	PLACBF	USA
CHABAS, HERRM.	31	M	LABR	PLACBF	USA
HELENE	24	F	W	PLACBF	USA
ROSENBLATT, SALOMON	25	M	APTC	PLACDS	USA

SHIP: LAKE NEPIGON

FROM: LIVERPOOL
TO: NEW YORK
ARRIVED: 23 DECEMBER 1884

PASSENGER	AGE	SEX	OCCUPATION	PRIV	DES
COHEN, NATHAN	21	M	JNR	RRZZZZ	NY
BETESA	22	F	W	RRZZZZ	NY
HERENA	2	F	CHILD	RRZZZZ	NY
GOLDSTEIN, SARAH	18	F	SVNT	PLZZZZ	MRL
SIMON, OLE	24	M	MECH	RRZZZZ	NY
FALKEN, BENJ.	36	M	MECH	RRZZZZ	NY
FARBER, HANS	21	M	MECH	RRZZZZ	NY

SHIP: ST SIMON

FROM: HAVRE
TO: NEW YORK
ARRIVED: 23 DECEMBER 1884

PASSENGER	AGE	SEX	OCCUPATION	PRIV	DES
BROUNDER, G.	29	M	MECH	RRZZZZ	NY

SHIP: NOORDLAND

FROM: ANTWERP
TO: NEW YORK
ARRIVED: 27 DECEMBER 1884

PASSENGER	AGE	SEX	OCCUPATION	PRIV	DES
BERTSCH, JAC.	24	M	FARMER	RRZZZZ	UNK
MARG.	24	F	UNKNOWN	RRZZZZ	UNK
KETTLING, FR.	20	M	FARMER	RRZZZZ	UNK
GOTTL.	18	M	UNKNOWN	RRZZZZ	UNK
LEICHT, CH.	30	F	FARMER	RRZZZZ	UNK
CARL	23	M	UNKNOWN	RRZZZZ	UNK
DAVID	26	M	FARMER	RRZZZZ	UNK
ELIS	28	F	UNKNOWN	RRZZZZ	UNK
LOUISE	3	F	CHILD	RRZZZZ	UNK
ELIS	2	F	CHILD	RRZZZZ	UNK
CHRIST.	00	F	INF	RRZZZZ	UNK
EHERT, JACOB	27	M	FARMER	RRZZZZ	UNK
MAGD.	24	F	UNKNOWN	RRZZZZ	UNK
MAGD.	3	F	CHILD	RRZZZZ	UNK
JOH.	2	M	CHILD	RRZZZZ	UNK
CHRIST.	00	F	INF	RRZZZZ	UNK
NIETZKE, GOTL.	27	M	FARMER	RRZZZZ	UNK
ROS.	23	F	UNKNOWN	RRZZZZ	UNK
GOTL.	00	M	INF	RRZZZZ	UNK
DEG, CHR.	19	M	UNKNOWN	RRZZZZ	UNK
GOHRIG, JOH.	33	M	FARMER	RRZZZZ	UNK
ELIS.	24	F	UNKNOWN	RRZZZZ	UNK
JOH.	00	M	INF	RRZZZZ	UNK
MUELLER, MART.	39	M	FARMER	RRZZZZ	UNK
FR.	35	F	UNKNOWN	RRZZZZ	UNK
CATH.	11	F	CH	RRZZZZ	UNK
MARIE	9	F	CHILD	RRZZZZ	UNK
JOHN	8	M	CHILD	RRZZZZ	UNK
PHIL	4	M	CHILD	RRZZZZ	UNK
CHR.	00	M	INF	RRZZZZ	UNK
SINGER, ANDR.	20	M	FARMER	RRZZZZ	UNK
SCHAIDT, MART.	22	M	FARMER	RRZZZZ	UNK
DAEG, CONRAD	23	M	FARMER	RRZZZZ	UNK
MARIE	27	F	UNKNOWN	RRZZZZ	UNK
JOHN	10	M	CH	RRZZZZ	UNK
GOTTL.	9	M	CHILD	RRZZZZ	UNK
WILDEMUTH, P.	22	M	FARMER	RRZZZZ	UNK
MAGD.	19	F	UNKNOWN	RRZZZZ	UNK
TRAUTMANN, GUST.	25	M	FARMER	RRZZZZ	UNK
ELIS	20	F	UNKNOWN	RRZZZZ	UNK
DEWALT, JAC.	30	M	FARMER	RRZZZZ	UNK
MARG.	25	F	UNKNOWN	RRZZZZ	UNK
BENS, GG.	37	M	FARMER	RRZZZZ	UNK
M.	40	F	UNKNOWN	RRZZZZ	UNK
G.	18	M	UNKNOWN	RRZZZZ	UNK
A.	10	M	CH	RRZZZZ	UNK
MARG.	8	F	CHILD	RRZZZZ	UNK
CATH.	6	F	CHILD	RRZZZZ	UNK
FISH	4	M	CHILD	RRZZZZ	UNK
JAC.	00	M	INF	RRZZZZ	UNK
KUCHLA, M.	28	F	W	PLZZZZ	PHI
ROS.	00	F	INF	PLZZZZ	PHI
SCHMIDT, PETER	26	M	FARMER	RRZZZZ	UNK
MAGD.	24	F	UNKNOWN	RRZZZZ	UNK
CHR.	3	F	CHILD	RRZZZZ	UNK
JOHN	39	M	FARMER	RRZZZZ	UNK
WILHE.	37	F	UNKNOWN	RRZZZZ	UNK
WILHE.	17	F	UNKNOWN	RRZZZZ	UNK
JACOB	13	M	CH	RRZZZZ	UNK
MAGD.	3	F	CHILD	RRZZZZ	UNK
PAUL	00	M	INF	RRZZZZ	UNK
SPERLE, CHRIST.	22	M	FARMER	RRZZZZ	UNK
MANTHEC, F.	20	M	FARMER	RRZZZZ	UNK
BAUERT, CH.	19	M	FARMER	RRZZZZ	UNK
SZIERBACHER, CATH.	17	F	SVNT	RRZZZZ	UNK
MUELLER, MART.	8	M	CHILD	RRZZZZ	UNK
PHILIPINE	00	F	INF	RR****	UNK

SHIP: ETHIOPIA

FROM: GLASGOW AND MOVILLE
TO: NEW YORK
ARRIVED: 29 DECEMBER 1884

PASSENGER	AGE	SEX	OCCUPATION	PRIV	DES
REHAK, MARIA	18	F	HP	PLZZZZ	USA
ARONOWITZ, HERRM.	19	M	LABR	PLZZZZ	USA
HOFMANN, KAUFMANN	33	M	LABR	RRZZZZ	USA
KREMVAT, MOSES	26	M	LABR	RRZZZZ	USA
KAUH, KARL	20	M	LABR	RRZZZZ	USA
MANASCHEWITZ, WOLF	21	M	LABR	RRZZZZ	USA

PASSENGER	AGE	SEX	OCCUPATION	PRV	VIL	DES
SHIP: MORAVIA						
FROM: HAMBURG						
TO: NEW YORK						
ARRIVED: 29 DECEMBER 1884						
MORRIS, DAVID	19	M	WCHMKR	RR	AHTF	USA
SIEFS, HEINR.	30	M	LABR	RR	AHZS	USA
FRIEDR.	23	M	LABR	RR	AHZS	USA
USCHEKOWSKY, ROSA	40	F	W	RR	AHWE	USA
JOSEF	15	M	CH	RR	AHWE	USA
WOLF	12	M	CH	RR	AHWE	USA
LASKOSKA, MARIANNE	22	F	SGL	RR	ZZZZ	USA
BOROWIAK, ANTONIA	23	F	SGL	RR	ZZZZ	USA
LEWINSBERG, BASCHE	23	F	W	RR	ZZZZ	USA
SAMUEL	.11	M	INFANT	RR	ZZZZ	USA
NOWICK, ISAAC	32	M	DLR	RR	ZZZZ	USA
FEINSOD, CHAIM	36	M	DLR	RR	ZZZZ	USA
WARSCHAWSKI, SCHOLEM	38	M	DLR	RR	ZZZZ	USA
ROSENBERG, SAMUEL	29	M	DLR	RR	AHZS	USA
BERTHA	19	F	W	RR	AHZS	USA
LEIBSOHN, NOCHUM	17	M	DLR	RR	AHZS	USA
IGELSKI, ROSA	19	F	SGL	RR	AHZS	USA
ROSENBLUM, ABRAM	18	M	FARMER	RR	ZZZZ	USA
KRIGER, CHAIM	19	M	TLR	RR	AFWJ	USA
PALUBINSKY, JONAS	22	M	LABR	RR	AHZS	USA
MATIZACTIS, JAN	23	M	LABR	RR	AHZS	USA
KOSTOSKI, MIKOLEI	20	M	LABR	RR	AHZS	USA
BORNSTEIN, MEYER	20	M	LABR	RR	ZZZZ	USA
KESTENBAUM, JACOB	21	M	LABR	RR	ZZZZ	USA
SOKOLEWSKY, JOSEF	21	M	LABR	RR	ZZZZ	USA
MATISIEWIEG, ANTON	21	M	LABR	RR	ZZZZ	USA
RAMENOWSKY, CATHE.	20	F	SGL	RR	ZZZZ	USA
GOLDBERG, TAUBE	49	F	W	RR	AHSW	USA
SCHIMEN	8	M	CHILD	RR	AHSW	USA
SHIP: NEVADA						
FROM: GLASGOW AND LARNE						
TO: NEW YORK						
ARRIVED: 29 DECEMBER 1884						
BECKER, TOBIAS	24	M	TLR	RR	ZZZZ	USA
BALUTA, J.	22	M	LABR	RR	ACBF	USA
DAVIDSOHN, JOS.	40	M	UPHST	RR	AHUU	USA
L.	38	F	W	RR	AHUU	USA
M.	10	F	CH	RR	AHUU	USA
J.	9	F	CHILD	RR	AHUU	USA
H.	.08	M	INFANT	RR	AHUU	USA
SCHLAMA, M.	20	M	TLR	PL	ZZZZ	USA
HEINSCHINKER, J.	20	M	LABR	PL	ZZZZ	USA
SCHASERS, J.	00	M	PDLR	PL	ZZZZ	USA
R.	00	F	CH	PL	ZZZZ	USA
RIES, O.	00	M	LABR	PL	ZZZZ	USA
SHIP: ODER						
FROM: BREMEN AND SOUTHAMPTON						
TO: NEW YORK						
ARRIVED: 30 DECEMBER 1884						
KURTZ, MOSES	21	M	MCHT	PL	ZZZZ	USA
AARON	19	M	UNKNOWN	PL	ZZZZ	USA
LEVY	24	M	UNKNOWN	PL	ZZZZ	USA
SHIP: RHEIN						
FROM: BREMEN AND SOUTHAMPTON						
TO: NEW YORK						
ARRIVED: 30 DECEMBER 1884						
LICHTENSTEIN, JOSEF	21	M	LABR	RR	ZZZZ	USA
ALEXANDER, ERNESTINE	19	F	NN	RR	AEUW	USA
RATZLAFF, JACOB	54	M	LABR	RR	ZZZZ	USA
HELENA	50	F	W	RR	ZZZZ	USA
JACOB	28	M	LABR	RR	ZZZZ	USA
SUSANNE	21	F	NN	RR	ZZZZ	USA
BENJAMIN	19	M	LABR	RR	ZZZZ	USA
ANNA	16	F	NN	RR	ZZZZ	USA
HELENE	14	F	CH	RR	ZZZZ	USA
FRANZ	8	M	CHILD	RR	ZZZZ	USA
SHIP: RICHMOND						
FROM: LIVERPOOL AND QUEENSTOWN						
TO: NEW YORK						
ARRIVED: 30 DECEMBER 1884						
BORONSKY, J.	32	M	LABR	RR	ZZZZ	USA
LEWITHON, LEIB	59	M	LABR	RR	ZZZZ	USA
LEMER, A.	22	M	LABR	RR	ZZZZ	USA
SELIG, JAC.	20	M	LABR	RR	ZZZZ	USA
LEWITON, L.	21	M	LABR	RR	ZZZZ	USA
GROHSCHICH, CHR.	24	M	LABR	RR	ZZZZ	USA
MICZKIWSKI, DANIEL	26	M	LABR	PL	ZZZZ	USA
LSGELINA, PETRO	28	M	LABR	PL	ZZZZ	USA
SHIP: WESTPHALIA						
FROM: HAMBURG						
TO: NEW YORK						
ARRIVED: 30 DECEMBER 1884						
SHAR, HERRM.	19	M	LABR	RR	ZZZZ	USA
ZLOTOWSKY, MOSES	25	M	LABR	RR	AHZS	USA
SCHEINE	22	F	W	RR	AHZS	USA
SPITZ, BARUCH	21	M	LABR	RR	ZZZZ	USA
KATZ, ARON	22	M	LABR	RR	ZZZZ	USA
STIEM, FRITZ	22	M	LABR	RR	AHUI	USA
PINIAK, ALIAS	17	M	LABR	RR	AHZD	USA
ALMAN, ELIAS	24	M	LABR	RR	ZZZZ	USA
MARGOLIS, ZAMEL	25	M	LABR	RR	AFZD	USA
SKALNIK, MORITZ	23	M	LABR	RR	AFZD	USA
SUVISLOWO, MISKE	25	M	LABR	RR	AFZD	USA
APENSTEN, ABRAHAM	59	M	LABR	RR	AHSW	USA
MOSES	26	M	LABR	RR	AHSW	USA
CHASES, HELENE	20	F	SGL	RR	AHWP	USA
AUGUSTE	18	F	SGL	RR	AHWP	USA
ANNA	17	F	SGL	RR	AHWP	USA
GLAGOWSKY, SARA	30	F	W	RR	ZZZZ	USA
RACHEL	4	F	CHILD	RR	ZZZZ	USA
CHARLOTTE	.11	F	INFANT	RR	ZZZZ	USA
TOMASCHEWSKY, ANDR.	29	M	LABR	RR	AFZD	USA
LECHMANN, LAZAR	22	M	LABR	RR	AHVA	USA
HOFFMANN, ISER	18	M	LABR	RR	AHZS	USA
PRODER, MILK	22	F	SGL	RR	ZZZZ	USA
ANINTO, BAER	17	M	LABR	RR	ZZZZ	USA
JACOB	13	M	B	RR	ZZZZ	USA
NEUMANN, MARIE	22	F	SGL	RR	ZZZZ	USA

PASSENGER	AGE	SEX	OCCUPATION	PRIVIL	DES
WEIZENBLUT, STANISL.	65	M	MCHT	RRAFWJ	USA
GOLDSTEIN, MOSES	24	M	LABR	RRZZZZ	USA
SPALT, SIMON	30	M	TLR	RRZZZZ	USA
JUNGERMANN, MORRIS	32	M	DLR	RRZZZZ	USA
MUEHLSTEIN, HERRM.	31	M	LABR	RRZZZZ	USA

SHIP: BOTHNIA

FROM: LIVERPOOL AND QUEENSTOWN
TO: NEW YORK
ARRIVED: 31 DECEMBER 1884

PASSENGER	AGE	SEX	OCCUPATION	PRIVIL	DES
WOLFE, MORRIS	20	M	TLR	RRZZZZ	USA
HAKKILA, JACOB	33	M	LABR	FNZZZZ	USA
LAOMA, JEREMIAS	25	M	LABR	PLZZZZ	USA
TULIKKA, JOHANNES	20	M	LABR	PLZZZZ	USA
NEKUNEN, MICHAEL	27	M	LABR	RRZZZZ	USA
NIKKUNEN, JOHAN	19	M	LABR	RRZZZZ	USA
KAATAN, JACOB	20	M	LABR	PLZZZZ	USA
KUHLBERG, MATTS.J.	27	M	LABR	PLZZZZ	USA

SHIP: FURNESSIA

FROM: GLASGOW
TO: NEW YORK
ARRIVED: 31 DECEMBER 1884

PASSENGER	AGE	SEX	OCCUPATION	PRIVIL	DES
GARFANKEL, SAMUEL	22	M	SHMK	PLACBF	USA
ELIZE	20	F	W	PLACBF	USA
SELZMACHER, SELDE	22	F	W	PLACBF	USA
LEIEC	3	F	CHILD	PLACBF	USA
ISRAEL	2	F	CHILD	PLACBF	USA
CHUNELEWSKY, MOSES	18	M	SHMK	PLACBF	USA
FRANK, JANKEL	22	M	TLR	PLACBF	USA

SHIP: CITY OF CHESTER

FROM: LIVERPOOL AND QUEENSTOWN
TO: NEW YORK
ARRIVED: 02 JANUARY 1885

PASSENGER	AGE	SEX	OCCUPATION	PRIVIL	DES
BARNITZKA, LUDWIGA	22	F	SVNT	PLACBF	USA
KEILER, HELENE	25	F	SVNT	PLACBF	NY

SHIP: ST OF PENNSYLVANIA

FROM: GLASGOW
TO: NEW YORK
ARRIVED: 02 JANUARY 1885

PASSENGER	AGE	SEX	OCCUPATION	PRIVIL	DES
HOCHENBERGER, MOSES	30	M	MCHT	PLAHWX	USA
PAGOIMONSKY, ELIAS	17	M	MCHT	PLAHVA	USA
ROSENBEND, LUDWIG	21	M	CL	PLAHWV	USA
ROSOF, SISCHE	21	F	TLR	PLAHXY	USA
WEINSCHENKER, NACHUM	49	M	LABR	RRZZZZ	USA

PASSENGER	AGE	SEX	OCCUPATION	PRIVIL	DES
FREIDA	37	F	W	RRZZZZ	USA
SARAH	17	F	SVNT	RRZZZZ	USA
RASH	11	F	CH	RRZZZZ	USA
MOCHEL	7	M	CHILD	RRZZZZ	USA

SHIP: SALIER

FROM: BREMEN
TO: NEW YORK
ARRIVED: 05 JANUARY 1885

PASSENGER	AGE	SEX	OCCUPATION	PRIVIL	DES
VONTURISE, ROBERT	17	M	TT	RRAHOO	USA
SLUZYNSKA, CAROLINE	24	F	NN	RRZZZZ	USA
STANISLAUS	2	M	CHILD	RRZZZZ	USA

SHIP: WIELAND

FROM: HAMBURG
TO: NEW YORK
ARRIVED: 05 JANUARY 1885

PASSENGER	AGE	SEX	OCCUPATION	PRIVIL	DES
ROSENTHAL, CHAIE	50	F	W	RRZZZZ	USA
WOLF	9	M	CHILD	RRZZZZ	USA
KLECZEWSKI, LEIB	18	M	BKR	RRZZZZ	USA
HINDE	21	F	W	RRZZZZ	USA
GARNER, SCHIE	21	M	LABR	RRZZZZ	USA
ROSENKRANZ, DAVID	20	M	DLR	RRZZZZ	USA
MEYERSOHN, ELIAS	20	M	LABR	RRZZZZ	USA
WITEPSKI, ABRAHAM	18	M	LABR	RRZZZZ	USA
EISENBERG, MAX	20	M	LABR	RRZZZZ	USA
NIEDBOLSKI, SALOMON	24	M	TLR	RRZZZZ	USA
STOKOWSKI, KASIMIR	20	M	LABR	RRZZZZ	USA
BROMBERG, KAPEL	18	M	LABR	RRZZZZ	USA
BAHR, OTTILIE	19	F	SGL	RRZZZZ	USA
ROSENTHAL, ABRAHAM	24	M	DLR	RRZZZZ	USA
FELDMANN, ZIPE	19	F	SGL	RRZZZZ	USA
FRIEDLAENDER, SCHEINE	45	F	W	RRZZZZ	USA
POLISOF, SAMUEL	22	M	LABR	RRZZZZ	USA
ISRAEL, SCHEINE	24	F	W	RRZZZZ	USA
SCHOLEM	5	M	CHILD	RRZZZZ	USA
MALMIK, ABR.H.	22	M	PTR	RRZZZZ	USA
SCHWAND, SCHLAR	32	M	LABR	RRZZZZ	USA
ROSENBLUM, BASCHE	19	F	SGL	RRZZZZ	USA

SHIP: ALSATIA

FROM: GLASGOW
TO: NEW YORK
ARRIVED: 09 JANUARY 1885

PASSENGER	AGE	SEX	OCCUPATION	PRIVIL	DES
PETZULIS, M.	20	M	LABR	RRACBF	USA
WOLENTZES, A.	21	M	LABR	RRACBF	USA
LEZO, B.	40	M	SHMK	RRACBF	USA
KATALINSKY, A.	24	M	TLR	RRACBF	USA
BUCEK, K.	22	M	PMBR	RRACBF	USA
DUBKIS, MENDEL	18	M	PMBR	RRACBF	USA

PASSENGER	AGE	SEX	OCCUPATION	PV RI VL	DES

SHIP: MINHO

FROM: RIO DE JANEIRO
TO: NEW YORK
ARRIVED: 09 JANUARY 1885

PASSENGER	AGE	SEX	OCCUPATION	PRV VIL	DES
JOPATTI, ENGENE	24	M	AGNTTH	PLZZZZ	NY

SHIP: AUSTRALIA

FROM: HAMBURG
TO: NEW YORK
ARRIVED: 10 JANUARY 1885

PASSENGER	AGE	SEX	OCCUPATION	PRV VIL	DES
DREYER, BENJ.	22	M	LABR	RRZZZZ	NY
SIBIOWSKY, KOPPEL	22	M	MCHT	RRZZZZ	NY
HEYMANNSOHN, JAC.	33	M	MCHT	RRZZZZ	NY
ROSENBERG, KREMDE	18	F	SGL	RRZZZZ	NY
HILLER, MAIER	48	F	WO	PLZZZZ	NY
PERL	7	M	CHILD	PLZZZZ	NY
PIAWNIK, CHAIE	27	F	WO	RRZZZZ	NY
SLAWE	.04	F	INFANT	RRZZZZ	NY
WEINSTOCK, JETTE	16	F	SGL	RRZZZZ	NY
GERSCHONSKY, JOSEL	50	M	TLR	RRZZZZ	NY
SCHMULNIK, MICH.L.	19	M	TLR	RRZZZZ	NY
LEON, MONTVILA	37	M	JNR	RRZZZZ	NY
DREY, FEIWISH	20	M	TRDSMN	RRZZZZ	NY
HARIG, BEREL	20	M	TRDSMN	RRZZZZ	NY
NIEMKIEWICZ, JOSEF	40	M	LABR	RRZZZZ	PA
MAKARCWICZ, JOSEF	40	M	LABR	RRZZZZ	PA
SALZ, NOSEN	17	M	MCHT	PLZZZZ	NY
BARTEL, NICODEMUS	33	M	LABR	RRZZZZ	NY

SHIP: STATE OF NEBRASKA

FROM: GLASGOW
TO: NEW YORK
ARRIVED: 13 JANUARY 1885

PASSENGER	AGE	SEX	OCCUPATION	PRV VIL	DES
FERBER, SAMUEL	35	M	DYR	RRZZZZ	NY
WASCHILIES, ANTON	23	M	FARMER	RRZZZZ	NY
JAKOHOFSKY, CONSTANTIN	45	M	NOTPUB	RRZZZZ	NY
SCHONINSKY, ANTON	33	M	LABR	RRZZZZ	NY
SKOPOWSKY, RUBEN	22	M	TLR	RRZZZZ	NY
DORF, MORITZ	17	M	SHMK	RRZZZZ	NY
BAUMANN, MORITZ	24	M	CNF	RRZZZZ	TN
ROSALIE	21	F	W	RRZZZZ	TN
HAUPTMANN, JACOB	39	M	TLR	RRZZZZ	NY
JOSEPH	9	M	CHILD	RRZZZZ	NY
ADOLPH	42	M	TLR	RRZZZZ	NY
SALZARIN	18	F	CH	RRZZZZ	NY
HELENA	15	F	CH	RRZZZZ	NY
JOSEF	8	M	CHILD	RRZZZZ	NY
BALSAM, F.	23	M	TLR	RRZZZZ	NY
SCHIPPA, CHAJE	37	F	W	RRZZZZ	NY
RITKE	.11	F	INFANT	RRZZZZ	NY
DORTCHE	1	F	CHILD	RRZZZZ	NY

SHIP: WYOMING

FROM: LIVERPOOL
TO: NEW YORK
ARRIVED: 15 JANUARY 1885

PASSENGER	AGE	SEX	OCCUPATION	PRV VIL	DES
SAWALZKI, SEELIG	22	M	GZR	PLZZZZ	USA

SHIP: MAIN

FROM: BREMEN
TO: NEW YORK
ARRIVED: 12 JANUARY 1885

PASSENGER	AGE	SEX	OCCUPATION	PRV VIL	DES
KIRSCHMANN, LUDWIG	23	M	FARMER	RRZZZZ	USA
CAROLINE	22	F	W	RRZZZZ	USA
ELISABETH	.03	F	INFANT	RRZZZZ	USA
KLEIN, JOHANN	12	M	FARMER	RRZZZZ	USA
ROSENSTEIN, ABRAHAM	30	M	FARMER	RRZZZZ	USA
RAHAN, LOEB	14	M	FARMER	RRAHVA	USA
GRUENSPAN, CLAUS	36	M	MCHT	RRAHVA	USA
HUCK, HEINR.	35	M	MCHT	RRZZZZ	USA
TREYMANN, SCHAGE	54	F	W	RRZZZZ	USA
WITSCHE	46	F	W	RRZZZZ	USA
WILHELM	25	M	MCHT	RRZZZZ	USA
ABRAHAM	23	M	MCHT	RRZZZZ	USA
MOSES	15	M	MCHT	RRZZZZ	USA
LEON	.11	M	INFANT	RRZZZZ	USA
SKEERKE, SAMUEL	54	M	LABR	RRZZZZ	USA
ABRAHAM	9	M	CHILD	RRZZZZ	USA
LEVENSOHN, DAVID	35	M	LABR	RRZZZZ	USA

SHIP: BOHEMIA

FROM: HAMBURG
TO: NEW YORK
ARRIVED: 16 JANUARY 1885

PASSENGER	AGE	SEX	OCCUPATION	PRV VIL	DES
TURZIN, MEYER	20	M	CGRMKR	RRZZZZ	USA
TRAUBE, SELIG	22	M	DLR	RRZZZZ	USA
ROTHSTEIN, JOSSEL	30	M	LABR	RRZZZZ	USA
BABANEKI, ESTER	20	F	SGL	RRZZZZ	USA
CHARSEH, OSCHER-L.	19	M	MCHT	RRZZZZ	USA
ROSETTE	22	F	W	RRZZZZ	USA
KNOP, CHAZKEL	29	M	DLR	RRAHTA	USA
BRIDAWSKY, MOSES	19	M	DLR	RRAHTA	USA
OPPENHEIM, ARON	21	M	LABR	RRZZZZ	USA
KANSKY, ISSER	22	M	SMH	RRZZZZ	USA
TACHNA, ELIAS	22	M	DLR	RRZZZZ	USA
ROCHIK, CZEZNE	52	F	W	RRAHVA	USA
ZIONLUM	19	M	S	RRAHVA	USA
DAVID	14	M	S	RRAHVA	USA
MARKOWITZ, DEBORA	20	F	SGL	RRZZZZ	USA
WILKOMIRSKY, JOSSEL	40	M	LABR	RRAHTF	USA
GUSZKA, HODIES	18	F	SGL	RRAHTW	USA
SCHINIKOWITZ, ISRAEL	43	M	LABR	RRZZZZ	USA
PROLHER, MOSES	20	M	LABR	RRZZZZ	USA
FIKELSTEIN, JENTE	58	F	W	RRZZZZ	USA
LEISER	17	M	LABR	RRZZZZ	USA
BERG, CARL	23	M	BKBNDR	RRZZZZ	USA
MALERSKI, SCHMUEL	28	M	DLR	RRZZZZ	USA
HONIGSBAUM, MALKE	15	F	SGL	RRAHZL	USA
LIPSCHITZ, MEYER	24	M	DLR	RRAHZL	USA

PASSENGER	AGE	SEX	OCCUPATION	PRIVIL	DES
LEWIN, JACOB	15	M	DLR	RRAHZL	USA
WLOSOWITCH, MENDEL	23	M	TLR	RRZZZZ	USA
RANDIS, GEORG	35	M	LABR	RRZZZZ	USA
SALMAS, MARIANNE	22	F	W	RRZZZZ	USA
ALBERTINE	.11	F	INFANT	RRZZZZ	USA
ROGINETZKY, JEIK	46	M	DLR	RRZZZZ	USA
KRELETZ, BEINUSZ	26	M	TLR	RRZZZZ	USA
STANKEWICZ, JACOB	34	M	LABR	RRZZZZ	USA
MILEUC, JAN	31	M	LABR	RRZZZZ	USA
JANCZIK, MATHEUS	30	M	LABR	RRZZZZ	USA

SHIP: DEVONIA

FROM: GLASGOW AND LONDONDERRY
TO: NEW YORK
ARRIVED: 16 JANUARY 1885

PASSENGER	AGE	SEX	OCCUPATION	PRIVIL	DES
STRECSKZ, DAVID	30	M	LABR	RRZZZZ	USA
KWIALKANSKY, CHAION	23	M	SHMK	RRZZZZ	USA
BRODDER, JOSEF	28	M	TLR	RRZZZZ	USA
KWIATKAARKY, MOSES	18	M	LABR	RRZZZZ	USA
MESSASSNIK, SIMON	28	M	CGRMKR	RRZZZZ	USA
JAODSER, BEILE	18	F	UNKNOWN	RRZZZZ	USA
ZLATOWSKI, ANNA	22	F	UNKNOWN	RRZZZZ	USA
SAROMBAWITSD, S.	19	M	LABR	RRZZZZ	USA

SHIP: ST GERMAIN

FROM: HAVRE
TO: NEW YORK
ARRIVED: 16 JANUARY 1885

PASSENGER	AGE	SEX	OCCUPATION	PRIVIL	DES
JAWOSKI, LE-COMTE-MR.	29	M	UNKNOWN	PLZZZZ	HLU

SHIP: WESTERNLAND

FROM: ANTWERP
TO: NEW YORK
ARRIVED: 16 JANUARY 1885

PASSENGER	AGE	SEX	OCCUPATION	PRIVIL	DES
GOTZ, HZ.	50	M	JNR	PLZZZZ	USA
ARTZYNSKA, ROSALIE	25	F	UNKNOWN	PLZZZZ	NY
ANNA	00	F	INF	PLZZZZ	NY

SHIP: NECKAR

FROM: BREMEN
TO: NEW YORK
ARRIVED: 19 JANUARY 1885

PASSENGER	AGE	SEX	OCCUPATION	PRIVIL	DES
ZUCKERMANN, BARUCH	36	M	LABR	RRZZZZ	USA
JOBE	28	F	W	RRZZZZ	USA
BEREND	7	M	CHILD	RRZZZZ	USA
WOLF	3	M	CHILD	RRZZZZ	USA
ISRAEL	.11	M	INFANT	RRZZZZ	USA

PASSENGER	AGE	SEX	OCCUPATION	PRIVIL	DES
LEWE, DAVID	20	M	FARMER	RRZZZZ	USA
NEUMANN, CARL	34	M	FARMER	RRZZZZ	USA
SAMELSOHN, FREIDE	32	F	NN	RRZZZZ	USA
SALOMON	10	M	CH	RRZZZZ	USA
HEN.	5	M	CHILD	RRZZZZ	USA
JOSEPH	1	M	CHILD	RRZZZZ	USA
CHANE	11	F	CH	RRZZZZ	USA
SILBERMANN, CHAJE	21	F	NN	RRZZZZ	USA
HEEDER, SIMON	28	M	SHMK	RRZZZZ	USA
FRIEDERIKE	24	F	W	RRZZZZ	USA
ELISABETH	.09	F	INFANT	RRZZZZ	USA
ERDMANN, CHRIST.	18	M	LABR	RRZZZZ	USA
KAHAN, LASAR	20	M	LABR	RRZZZZ	USA
PATZ, HELENA	20	F	NN	RRZZZZ	USA
SAPIRA, JUNDL.	11	M	CH	RRZZZZ	USA

SHIP: ARIZONA

FROM: LIVERPOOL AND QUEENSTOWN
TO: NEW YORK
ARRIVED: 20 JANUARY 1885

PASSENGER	AGE	SEX	OCCUPATION	PRIVIL	DES
CHEPP, N.MR	30	M	GENT	RRAAKH	RSS
FRENDENBERG, U-MR	27	M	GENT	RRADBQ	RSS

SHIP: PAVONIA

FROM: LIVERPOOL AND QUEENSTOWN
TO: NEW YORK
ARRIVED: 22 JANUARY 1885

PASSENGER	AGE	SEX	OCCUPATION	PRIVIL	DES
PERKART, AUGUST	35	M	TLR	RRZZZZ	UNK

SHIP: STATE OF ALABAMA

FROM: GLASGOW AND LARNE
TO: NEW YORK
ARRIVED: 22 JANUARY 1885

PASSENGER	AGE	SEX	OCCUPATION	PRIVIL	DES
BEBATZKY, NOCHERN	30	M	MSN	RRZZZZ	NY
KATZ, ARIYDER	40	M	LABR	RRZZZZ	NY
JANKELOWITZ, SAMUEL	20	M	JNR	RRZZZZ	PHI
MENDELSOHN, BENGEL	26	M	TLR	RRZZZZ	CH
SURTILA, JOSEPH	38	M	LABR	RRZZZZ	NY
PAPPURPORT, EISECK	33	M	LABR	RRZZZZ	NY
SCHAPIRO, SCHMUEL	20	M	LABR	RRZZZZ	NY
ZUNELOWITZ, MICHEL	20	M	BLKSMH	RRZZZZ	PHI

SHIP: CANADA

FROM: HAVRE
TO: NEW YORK
ARRIVED: 23 JANUARY 1885

PASSENGER	AGE	SEX	OCCUPATION	PRV VIL	DES
BOBRINSKY, U-MRS	26	F	NN	RRZZZZ	NY
SCHITSLING, MICHEL	27	M	CBTMKR	RRZZZZ	NY
BEZZENKOWSKI, SCHAL	22	M	CBTMKR	RRZZZZ	NY

SHIP: GENERAL WERDER

FROM: BREMEN AND SOUTHAMPTON
TO: NEW YORK
ARRIVED: 23 JANUARY 1885

PASSENGER	AGE	SEX	OCCUPATION	PRV VIL	DES
SCHMIDT, CHRISTIAN	22	M	FARMER	RRZZZZ	USA
EVA	34	F	W	RRZZZZ	USA
JULA	6	F	CHILD	RRZZZZ	USA
CHRISTIAN	4	M	CHILD	RRZZZZ	USA
HEINRICH	.06	M	INFANT	RRZZZZ	USA
ZIMMERMANN, CHRISTIAN	24	M	LLD	RRZZZZ	USA

SHIP: LESSING

FROM: HAMBURG
TO: NEW YORK
ARRIVED: 23 JANUARY 1885

PASSENGER	AGE	SEX	OCCUPATION	PRV VIL	DES
WOD, SAMUEL	40	M	MCHT	RRAHTF	USA
ZERWITZ, MATHEUS	42	M	LABR	RRAFWJ	USA
GRINSPAN, CHAIE	19	F	SGL	RRAHTR	USA
GARKE, BER.	19	M	LABR	RRAHWU	USA
MLINASCH, BEILE	20	F	SGL	RRAHVU	USA
GERSON	9	M	CHILD	RRAHVU	USA
SILBERMANN, SOLOMON	31	M	LABR	RRAHTP	USA
KLEINBODT, NOACH.	65	M	LABR	RRAHYQ	USA

SHIP: SUEVIA

FROM: HAMBURG
TO: NEW YORK
ARRIVED: 23 JANUARY 1885

PASSENGER	AGE	SEX	OCCUPATION	PRV VIL	DES
HERING, ANNA	35	F	W	RRAFVG	USA
BARANOW, ABRAHAM	20	M	LABR	RRAGRT	USA
FINKELSTEIN, TAUBE	22	F	SGL	RRAHTL	USA
BATEIR, PIOTR	21	M	LABR	RRZZZZ	USA
JOCHONOW, HIRSCH	45	M	TLR	RRAHTF	USA
AMBROSE, PETER	36	M	LABR	RRZZZZ	USA
LEUFELD, FENNY	45	F	W	RRZZZZ	USA
STAVSKY, SCHIMSCHON	30	M	LABR	RRAHVX	USA
FREY, ALBERT	29	M	LABR	RRAHVX	USA
ABELSOHN, SAM.	40	M	DLR	RRAHSL	USA
REUBEN	9	M	CHILD	RRAHSL	USA
LUTH, CLAUS	58	M	LABR	RRAHSL	USA
PISTEL, JOH.	28	M	LABR	RRZZZZ	USA
LEWKOWIETZ, ESTHER	35	F	W	RRAHTF	USA
CHAIE	9	F	CHILD	RRAHTF	USA
CHAZKEL	8	F	CHILD	RRAHTF	USA
ABRAHAM	5	M	CHILD	RRAHTF	USA
HIRSZENFELD, JOSEPH	33	M	MECH	RRAFWJ	USA
GOLDFARB, ISAAC	21	M	LABR	RRAHZS	USA
FELTENSTEIN, ABRAM	19	M	LABR	RRAHZS	USA
JEDWABNIK, BERKO	23	M	LABR	RRAHZS	USA
KOPELOWITZ, MAIER	31	M	LABR	RRAHZS	USA
MIRAK, RIWKE	70	M	LABR	RRAHZS	USA
AUSCHLAWSKI, OSCHER	53	M	LABR	RRZZZZ	USA
CHAIE	14	F	D	RRZZZZ	USA
ZARESZAWSKI, JOSSEL	26	M	LABR	RRAHSP	USA

SHIP: STATE OF INDIANA

FROM: GLASGOW AND LARNE
TO: NEW YORK
ARRIVED: 24 JANUARY 1885

PASSENGER	AGE	SEX	OCCUPATION	PRV VIL	DES
SCHATZ, SCHINAJE	58	M	PDLR	RRZZZZ	USA
GOLDMANN, CHAWNE	21	M	LABR	RRZZZZ	USA
SKLASKE, JOSSEL	27	M	LABR	RRZZZZ	USA
ZIEGELSTREICH, JOSEPH	22	M	LABR	RRAFWJ	USA
TISCHLER, DAVID	19	M	PDLR	RRAFWJ	USA
JITOWSKY, CHAIM	20	M	PDLR	RRZZZZ	USA
WINKELMANN, FEIWEL	20	M	PDLR	RRZZZZ	USA
WERNARRA, JOSEPH	42	M	LABR	RRAEAB	USA
WOLPERT, JACOB	19	M	PDLR	RRZZZZ	USA
FEINSTEIN, GITTEL	19	F	SP	RRZZZZ	USA
FILLIPATIS, SIMON	21	M	LABR	RRZZZZ	USA
HARMINTZ, JUERGENS	22	M	CPTR	RRZZZZ	USA
RUBEN, SORECH	22	M	PDLR	RRZZZZ	USA
KOZAK, MICHAEL	25	M	LABR	RRAEAB	USA
JOHAN	22	M	LABR	RRAEAB	USA
ANTON	27	M	LABR	RRAEAB	USA

SHIP: PENNLAND

FROM: ANTWERP
TO: NEW YORK
ARRIVED: 26 JANUARY 1885

PASSENGER	AGE	SEX	OCCUPATION	PRV VIL	DES
ZOLLENTKEWITZ, E.	22	F	FARMER	RRZZZZ	PHI
BRUCHMANN, C.D.	22	M	TLR	RRZZZZ	PHI
JUSALOWSKI, N.	00	M	FARMER	RRZZZZ	PHI
U	00	F	FARMER	RRZZZZ	PHI
U	00	F	CH	RRZZZZ	PHI
SCHWEL, M.	64	M	LABR	RRZZZZ	PHI
B.	57	F	LABR	RRZZZZ	PHI
JOSE	26	F	LABR	RRZZZZ	PHI
FRZ.	18	M	LABR	RRZZZZ	PHI
AMELIA	16	F	LABR	RRZZZZ	PHI

SHIP: SPAIN

FROM: LIVERPOOL
TO: NEW YORK
ARRIVED: 26 JANUARY 1885

PASSENGER	AGE	SEX	OCCUPATION	PRV VIL	DES
KALTON, ISRAEL	11	M	CH	PLZZZZ	USA
EMMA	9	F	CHILD	PLZZZZ	USA

PASSENGER	AGE	SEX	OCCUPATION	PRV VIL DES
PAUL	8	M	CHILD	PLZZZZUSA
JACOB	5	M	CHILD	PLZZZZUSA
KNOLTON, NATH.	30	M	LABR	PLZZZZUSA
ROSENBLOOM, JANE	36	F	W	RRZZZZUSA
ROSA	10	F	CH	RRZZZZUSA
ESTHER	8	F	CHILD	RRZZZZUSA
JULIUS	4	M	CHILD	RRZZZZUSA
REBECCA	1	F	CHILD	RRZZZZUSA
GOLD, LEWIS	34	M	LABR	RRZZZZUSA
MONA	28	F	W	RRZZZZUSA
JOSEPH	2	M	CHILD	RRZZZZUSA
DENLACH, ELIAS	28	M	LABR	RRZZZZUSA
REBECCA	26	F	W	RRZZZZUSA
DOLERA	1	F	CHILD	RRZZZZUSA
KOLTON, CHEZYA	2	F	CHILD	RRZZZZUSA

SHIP: WERRA

FROM: BREMEN
TO: NEW YORK
ARRIVED: 26 JANUARY 1885

PASSENGER	AGE	SEX	OCCUPATION	PRV VIL DES
RODLER, PETER	45	M	FARMER	RRZZZZNY
MARIA	46	F	UNKNOWN	RRZZZZNY
AGNESA	18	F	UNKNOWN	RRZZZZNY
BARBARA	16	F	UNKNOWN	RRZZZZNY
EVA	7	F	CHILD	RRZZZZNY
ESTACH	5	F	CHILD	RRZZZZNY
MAGDALENA	2	F	CHILD	RRZZZZNY
KROGER, FRIEDKE	19	F	UNKNOWN	RRZZZZNY
ELISE	17	F	UNKNOWN	RRZZZZNY
BODLER, JAKOB	23	M	FARMER	RRZZZZNY
AGATHE	18	F	UNKNOWN	RRZZZZNY
MEIDINGER, ADAM	38	M	FARMER	RRZZZZNY
FRIEDERIKE	37	F	UNKNOWN	RRZZZZNY
EVA	14	F	UNKNOWN	RRZZZZNY
CATHARINA	7	F	CHILD	RRZZZZNY
ADAM	6	M	CHILD	RRZZZZNY
JACOB	2	M	CHILD	RRZZZZNY
CHRISTINE	.02	F	INFANT	RRZZZZNY
JAC.	33	M	FARMER	RRZZZZNY
ROSINE	33	F	UNKNOWN	RRZZZZNY
CATH.	7	F	CHILD	RRZZZZNY
EVA	6	F	CHILD	RRZZZZNY
ADAM	4	M	CHILD	RRZZZZNY
JACOB	3	M	CHILD	RRZZZZNY
GOTTL.	.11	M	INFANT	RRZZZZNY
CHRISTINE	.01	F	INFANT	RRZZZZNY
DOPP, JOHANN	35	M	FARMER	RRZZZZNY
CATH.	26	F	UNKNOWN	RRZZZZNY
CATH.	5	F	CHILD	RRZZZZNY
LISA	4	F	CHILD	RRZZZZNY
BEATA	.11	F	INFANT	RRZZZZNY
GEHRING, ADAM	42	M	FARMER	RRZZZZNY
MAGD.	39	F	UNKNOWN	RRZZZZNY
CATH.	16	F	UNKNOWN	RRZZZZNY
JACOB	7	M	CHILD	RRZZZZNY
MARGAR.	2	F	CHILD	RRZZZZNY
CATH.	.04	F	INFANT	RRZZZZNY
MULLER, VALENTIN	22	M	FARMER	RRZZZZNY
CHRISTINE	18	F	UNKNOWN	RRZZZZNY
HEINR.	.01	M	INFANT	RRZZZZNY
LAUB, GOTTL.	42	M	FARMER	RRZZZZNY
CATHARINA	44	F	UNKNOWN	RRZZZZNY
MARG.	17	F	UNKNOWN	RRZZZZNY
HEINR.	1	M	CHILD	RRZZZZNY
CATH.	3	F	CHILD	RRZZZZNY
FRIEDR.	2	M	CHILD	RRZZZZNY
JUREISAN, JANOS	25	M	LABR	RRZZZZNY

SHIP: POLARIA

FROM: HAMBURG
TO: NEW YORK
ARRIVED: 27 JANUARY 1885

PASSENGER	AGE	SEX	OCCUPATION	PRV VIL DES
CHARAIS, SCHIB-S.	23	M	MCHT	RRZZZZNY
SANDLER, SAMUEL	30	M	JNR	RRZZZZNY
SARAH	30	F	W	RRZZZZNY
CHAYE	6	F	CHILD	RRZZZZNY
TUROMUS	2	M	CHILD	RRZZZZNY
LEIBE	.06	F	INFANT	RRZZZZNY
CHAST, LOLLET	23	M	TLR	RRZZZZNY
BERKOWITZ, DAV.	21	M	JNR	RRZZZZNY
MELZER, CHACHEL	22	M	JNR	RRZZZZNY
SIEGEL, RIFLE	7	F	CHILD	RRZZZZNY
ABRUTIN, SALOMON	27	M	TLR	RRZZZZNY
MOOR, CHRIST.	23	M	LABR	RRZZZZNY
CAROLINE	22	F	W	RRZZZZNY
WILHELM	20	M	B	RRZZZZNY
GOTTFRIED	17	M	B	RRZZZZNY
JOHANN	7	M	CHILD	RRZZZZNY
BARBARA	4	F	CHILD	RRZZZZNY
AUGUST	.09	M	INFANT	RRZZZZNY
WILKUMSKY, SELIG	21	M	TRDSMN	RRZZZZNY
HERR, ROB.	18	M	MCHT	RRZZZZNY
FLICKER, LEISER	17	M	LABR	PLZZZZNY
SITZBERG, BENETH	41	M	MCHT	RRZZZZNY
BROMER, FERD.	28	M	SMH	RRZZZZNY
FUHRMA, BEHR.	36	M	LABR	RRZZZZNY
SZALLIMANN, BEND.	20	M	LABR	RRZZZZNY
NOVAK, LEIB	21	M	LABR	RRZZZZNY
SLAWA, JOH.	50	M	LABR	RRZZZZNY

SHIP: CIRCASSIA

FROM: GLASGOW AND MOVILLE
TO: NEW YORK
ARRIVED: 29 JANUARY 1885

PASSENGER	AGE	SEX	OCCUPATION	PRV VIL DES
KLANANSKY, JACOB	28	M	LABR	RRZZZZUSA
LEVY, ISAC	24	M	CGRMKR	RRZZZZUSA
BIBROWSKY, SIGINUND	18	M	CL	RRZZZZUSA
GOLDSTEIN, HARRIS	33	M	SHMK	RRZZZZUSA
KUSHIN, SOLOMON	21	M	DLR	RRZZZZUSA
MASSONOIZ, AUGUSTINE	20	M	DLR	RRZZZZUSA
SCHUPIRA, GITEL	38	M	DLR	RRZZZZUSA
SARA	11	F	CH	RRZZZZUSA
DAVID	10	M	CH	RRZZZZUSA

SHIP: HABSBURG

FROM: BREMEN
TO: NEW YORK
ARRIVED: 29 JANUARY 1885

PASSENGER	AGE	SEX	OCCUPATION	PRV VIL DES
LAPIDOS, ISAAC	24	M	LABR	RRZZZZNY
LEWY, HIRSCH	16	M	LABR	RRZZZZNY
NOWIDROWSKY, SCHOPSE	30	M	BKR	RRZZZZNY
SALZMANN, ABRAHAM	20	M	LABR	RRZZZZNY
PBASSKE, HEINRICH	20	M	LABR	RRZZZZNY
SCHLEIHS, CHRISTIAN	23	M	FARMER	RRZZZZNY
MEYER, CARL	19	M	TCHR	RRZZZZNY
GARNESCHIL, MICHAEL	21	M	FARMER	RRZZZZNY

PASSENGER	AGE	SEX	OCCUPATION	PRV VIL DES
DASSKO, JOHANN	30	M	LABR	RRZZZZNY
STOFFKO, PAUL	20	M	LABR	RRZZZZNY
TURIK, MICHAEL	34	M	LABR	RRZZZZNY
KALEKOWSKI, JOHANN	25	M	LABR	RRZZZZNY
SASCHER, POTACZECK	26	M	LABR	RRZZZZNY
LUTZ, JOHANN	33	M	FARMER	RRZZZZNY
CATHARINA	28	F	W	RRZZZZNY
MARGARETTA	4	F	CHILD	RRZZZZNY
CATHARINA	2	F	CHILD	RRZZZZNY
ROSINA	.09	F	INFANT	RRZZZZNY
OHRMANN, GOTTLIEB	25	M	FARMER	RRZZZZNY
BARBARA	25	F	W	RRZZZZNY
WILHELMINE	.06	F	INFANT	RRZZZZNY
BANMESBERGER, HEINRICH	35	M	FARMER	RRZZZZNY
MARIE	38	F	W	RRZZZZNY
CHRISTINE	18	F	CH	RRZZZZNY
LONISA	11	F	CH	RRZZZZNY
CHRISTIAN	7	M	CHILD	RRZZZZNY
MARIE	6	F	CHILD	RRZZZZNY
MARGARETHA	4	F	CHILD	RRZZZZNY
CHRISTINA	2	F	CHILD	RRZZZZNY
JACOB	.10	M	INFANT	RRZZZZNY
PUSKAR, MARIE	24	F	SVNT	RRZZZZNY
WARYA, BOJKA	22	F	SVNT	RRZZZZNY

SHIP: SCYTHIA

FROM: LIVERPOOL AND QUEENSTOWN
TO: NEW YORK
ARRIVED: 30 JANUARY 1885

PASSENGER	AGE	SEX	OCCUPATION	PRV VIL DES
JOHANSON, EDWARD	25	M	ENGR	RRZZZZUNK

SHIP: RHEIN

FROM: BREMEN
TO: NEW YORK
ARRIVED: 02 FEBRUARY 1885

PASSENGER	AGE	SEX	OCCUPATION	PRV VIL DES
SCHNIDER, MARIANNE	21	F	NN	RRZZZZUSA
EMILIE	.09	F	INFANT	RRZZZZUSA

SHIP: STATE OF GEORGIA

FROM: GLASGOW
TO: NEW YORK
ARRIVED: 02 FEBRUARY 1885

PASSENGER	AGE	SEX	OCCUPATION	PRV VIL DES
RAVALYIK, PESACH	20	M	DLR	PLZZZZNY
STIMBOCK, MOSES	00	M	DLR	PLZZZZNY
U	00	M	DLR	PLZZZZNY
BENJAMIN	00	M	CH	PLZZZZNY
OLSEN, STRUTON	20	M	SHMK	PLZZZZNY
JANKEL	45	M	SHMK	PLZZZZNY
GRUNDWARK, FISCHEL	35	M	DLR	PLZZZZNY
BLECHER, JUAEL	44	M	DLR	PLZZZZNY
CZERWANKA, JAN	27	M	LABR	PLZZZZNY
ZOK, SEBASTIAN	25	M	LABR	PLZZZZNY
KELLAR, WADIE	45	M	LABR	PLZZZZNY
ARON	12	M	CH	PLZZZZNY

PASSENGER	AGE	SEX	OCCUPATION	PRV VIL DES
LUBINEZYCK, SCHOLEM	32	M	GDSM	RRZZZZNY
CHANE	30	F	W	RRZZZZNY
ABRAHAM	5	M	CHILD	RRZZZZNY
MOSES	2	M	CHILD	RRZZZZNY
DURILATIES, JOSSEL	40	M	DLR	RRZZZZNY
ROSENBERG, NACHMAN	34	M	JNR	RRZZZZNY
SECHEL, NAFTALY	19	M	LABR	RRZZZZNY
SLATZEN, HERMANN	26	M	CL	RRZZZZNY
MOSES	19	M	CL	RRZZZZNY
GRUNBERG, JACOB	13	M	LABR	RRZZZZNY
SERSCHKEY, LEISER	40	M	LABR	RRZZZZNY
OMCHKA, MIKAEL	29	M	LABR	RRZZZZNY

SHIP: CITY OF RICHMOND

FROM: LIVERPOOL AND QUEENSTOWN
TO: NEW YORK
ARRIVED: 03 FEBRUARY 1885

PASSENGER	AGE	SEX	OCCUPATION	PRV VIL DES
NAUERTERSKY, SIMON	32	M	LABR	RRAFWJUSA
LARENZ, MICH.	25	M	LABR	RRAFWJUSA
SCHONONG, MAUSCHELL	19	M	LABR	RRAFWJUSA
MISLEY, ANNA	32	F	W	RRAFWJUSA
LAMMAUSTER, WERDELL	17	M	LABR	RRZZZZUSA

SHIP: ELBE

FROM: BREMEN
TO: NEW YORK
ARRIVED: 03 FEBRUARY 1885

PASSENGER	AGE	SEX	OCCUPATION	PRV VIL DES
HARDLE, JOH.	44	M	FARMER	RRZZZZUSA
BARBARA	40	F	W	RRZZZZUSA
LOUISE	16	F	CH	RRZZZZUSA
CHRISTINE	6	F	CHILD	RRZZZZUSA
JULIANE	3	F	CHILD	RRZZZZUSA
JACOB	.06	M	INFANT	RRZZZZUSA
HAUSANER, KARL	39	M	FARMER	RRZZZZUSA
JOHANNE	27	F	W	RRZZZZUSA
KARL	14	M	CH	RRZZZZUSA
JOHANNE	9	F	CHILD	RRZZZZUSA
KATHARINE	5	F	CHILD	RRZZZZUSA
ROSINE	2	F	CHILD	RRZZZZUSA
DAJNEV, WASIL	18	M	LABR	RRZZZZUSA
JANNI, MICHAL	29	M	LABR	RRZZZZUSA
MIKOLAI, JONAS	29	M	LABR	RRZZZZUSA
MARCUNKO, JONAS	30	M	LABR	RRZZZZUSA
RIBAR, JURA	31	M	LABR	RRZZZZUSA
PALURIK, ANDR.	26	M	LABR	RRZZZZUSA
LITAWEE, JANOS	22	M	LABR	RRZZZZUSA
GIRALSKI, JOS.	34	M	LABR	RRZZZZUSA
HRITZ, JURKO	21	M	LABR	RRZZZZUSA
GABRIEL, SUS.	20	F	NN	RRZZZZUSA
PECKAR, RAWL	27	M	LABR	RRZZZZUSA
GOEBEL, JACOB	29	M	FARMER	RRZZZZUSA
CATHARINE	26	F	W	RRZZZZUSA
JACOB	.11	M	INFANT	RRZZZZUSA
TUFFLER, FRIEDR.	43	M	FARMER	RRZZZZUSA
BARBARA	42	F	W	RRZZZZUSA
CATHARINE	18	F	NN	RRZZZZUSA
FRIEDRICH	11	M	CH	RRZZZZUSA
DAVID	9	M	CHILD	RRZZZZUSA
JOHANN	7	M	CHILD	RRZZZZUSA
CHRISTINE	5	F	CHILD	RRZZZZUSA
MAGDALENE	.11	F	INFANT	RRZZZZUSA

PASSENGER	AGE	SEX	OCCUPATION	PRVIL	DES
ZULTY, FEIGE	42	M	LABR	RRZZZZ	USA

SHIP: SERVIA

FROM: LIVERPOOL
TO: NEW YORK
ARRIVED: 05 FEBRUARY 1885

PASSENGER	AGE	SEX	OCCUPATION	PRVIL	DES
EPSTEIN, RENNIE	38	F	MCHT	RRZZZZ	USA
CHEANE	17	F	SVNT	RRZZZZ	USA
BASCHKE	10	F	CH	RRZZZZ	USA
LEAH	6	F	CHILD	RRZZZZ	USA
MENASCHE	4	F	CHILD	RRZZZZ	USA

SHIP: CITY OF CHESTER

FROM: LIVERPOOL AND QUEENSTOWN
TO: NEW YORK
ARRIVED: 07 FEBRUARY 1885

PASSENGER	AGE	SEX	OCCUPATION	PRVIL	DES
DAVIES, SOLOMON	17	M	LABR	RRACBF	NY
COZTLONSKI, JOSEPH	25	M	CL	RRADBQ	NY
RAPIEFF, JOHN.J.MR	32	M	GENT	RRADBQ	NY

SHIP: ETHIOPIA

FROM: GLASGOW
TO: NEW YORK
ARRIVED: 07 FEBRUARY 1885

PASSENGER	AGE	SEX	OCCUPATION	PRVIL	DES
JOSEPH, CHAIM	28	M	LABR	PLZZZZ	USA
SYMERSKA, JADWEGA	50	F	UNKNOWN	PLZZZZ	USA
GOMBETA, J.	31	M	LABR	PLZZZZ	USA

SHIP: INDIA

FROM: HAMBURG
TO: NEW YORK
ARRIVED: 07 FEBRUARY 1885

PASSENGER	AGE	SEX	OCCUPATION	PRVIL	DES
WACHMANN, ARON	19	M	BKBNDR	RRZZZZ	NY
OLKONITZKYE, B.	19	M	TRDSMN	RRZZZZ	NY
REYNECK, SCH.BAR.	18	M	LABR	RRZZZZ	IL
KAHAN, JACOB	22	M	TRDSMN	RRZZZZ	IL
KOPNICKI, EISECK	50	M	TRDSMN	RRZZZZ	IL
JUDEL	24	M	TRDSMN	RRZZZZ	IL
KOLNICKE, ANTON	22	M	SHMK	RRZZZZ	IL
TIALEK, MICHAL	26	M	LABR	RRZZZZ	IL
WICHDOWITZ, SELG.	18	M	CL	RRZZZZ	NY
MILLNER, JOS.	22	M	CL	RRZZZZ	NY
ITZ.	20	M	SHMK	RRZZZZ	NY
MENDELMAN, MOSES	38	M	LABR	RRZZZZ	NY
JARETZKI, JAKOB	50	M	LABR	RRZZZZ	NY
AGNES	50	F	W	RRZZZZ	NY
JAN	2	M	CHILD	RRZZZZ	NY

PASSENGER	AGE	SEX	OCCUPATION	PRVIL	DES
DULKOWICZ, MARIANN	00	M	LABR	RRZZZZ	NY
TEMMER, DAVD.	18	M	LABR	RRZZZZ	NY

SHIP: STATE OF NEVADA

FROM: GLASGOW AND LARNE
TO: NEW YORK
ARRIVED: 07 FEBRUARY 1885

PASSENGER	AGE	SEX	OCCUPATION	PRVIL	DES
ARNOSKY, L.	00	M	CGRMKR	RRZZZZ	USA
FRICOLMAN, L.	00	M	PDLR	RRZZZZ	USA
HALLERMAN, L.	00	M	PDLR	RRZZZZ	USA
KRYSUZYNSKY, J.	00	M	PDLR	RRZZZZ	USA
KAHN, J.	00	M	CL	RRZZZZ	USA
KAPLAN, E.	00	M	SHMK	RRZZZZ	USA
MARKOWSKY, S.	00	M	LABR	RRZZZZ	USA
C.	00	F	W	RRZZZZ	USA
S.	00	M	CH	RRZZZZ	USA
A.	00	F	CH	RRZZZZ	USA
L.	00	F	CH	RRZZZZ	USA
MARGOLIS, U	00	M	LABR	RRZZZZ	USA
NEUMAN, A.	28	M	SHMK	RRZZZZ	USA
NATHANSON, B.	00	M	PDLR	RRZZZZ	USA
SCHAPIRO, M.	49	M	PDLR	RRZZZZ	USA
SCHIVISKY, J.	00	M	BKR	RRZZZZ	USA
SCHIRAKANER, M.	26	M	LABR	RRZZZZ	USA
WOTTKOW, W.	36	M	LABR	RRZZZZ	USA

SHIP: ALASKA

FROM: LIVERPOOL AND QUEENSTOWN
TO: NEW YORK
ARRIVED: 09 FEBRUARY 1885

PASSENGER	AGE	SEX	OCCUPATION	PRVIL	DES
BERGMAN, SAMUEL	52	M	TLR	PLZZZZ	USA
ANNAH	45	F	W	PLZZZZ	USA
LOUIS	19	F	SP	PLZZZZ	USA
DORA	17	F	SP	PLZZZZ	USA
SARAH	15	F	SP	PLZZZZ	USA
HARRY	14	M	CH	PLZZZZ	USA
MARY	11	F	CH	PLZZZZ	USA
ISAAC	10	M	CH	PLZZZZ	USA
ESTHER	8	F	CHILD	PLZZZZ	USA
BERTHA	5	F	CHILD	PLZZZZ	USA
ROSE	2	F	CHILD	PLZZZZ	USA

SHIP: FULDA

FROM: BREMEN
TO: NEW YORK
ARRIVED: 09 FEBRUARY 1885

PASSENGER	AGE	SEX	OCCUPATION	PRVIL	DES
AMBRULEWITZ, STANISLAUS	19	M	LABR	RRZZZZ	USA
PERMANN, JACOB	31	M	FARMER	RRZZZZ	USA
CATHARINA	29	F	UNKNOWN	RRZZZZ	USA
FRIEDRICH	8	M	CHILD	RRZZZZ	USA
CATHARINA	7	F	CHILD	RRZZZZ	USA
CAROLINE	5	F	CHILD	RRZZZZ	USA
MARGA	2	F	CHILD	RRZZZZ	USA
JACOB	.05	M	INFANT	RRZZZZ	USA

PASSENGER	AGE	SEX	OCCUPATION	PRV	VIL	DES

SHIP: NOORDLAND

FROM: ANTWERP
TO: NEW YORK
ARRIVED: 09 FEBRUARY 1885

PASSENGER	AGE	SEX	OCCUPATION	PRVVILDES
BREMER, G.	25	M	FARMER	RRZZZZUNK

SHIP: ODER

FROM: BREMEN AND SOUTHAMPTON
TO: NEW YORK
ARRIVED: 09 FEBRUARY 1885

PASSENGER	AGE	SEX	OCCUPATION	PRVVILDES
ELERMANN, JACOB	44	M	FARMER	RRZZZZUSA
JOHANNE	42	F	NN	RRZZZZUSA
ROSINE	21	F	NN	RRZZZZUSA
JACOB	20	M	FARMER	RRZZZZUSA
DAVID	18	M	FARMER	RRZZZZUSA
JOHANNE	10	F	NN	RRZZZZUSA
MARGARETHE	8	F	CHILD	RRZZZZUSA
FRIEDRICH	7	M	CHILD	RRZZZZUSA
AUGUST	3	M	CHILD	RRZZZZUSA
CHRISTIAN	.06	M	INFANT	RRZZZZUSA
GALINAITIS, ANTON	36	M	LABR	RRZZZZUSA

SHIP: CARACAS

FROM: UNKNOWN
TO: NEW YORK
ARRIVED: 11 FEBRUARY 1885

PASSENGER	AGE	SEX	OCCUPATION	PRVVILDES
ABRAMOFF, ABRAMO	35	M	UNKNOWN	RRZZZZUNK

SHIP: GALLIA

FROM: LIVERPOOL AND QUEENSTOWN
TO: NEW YORK
ARRIVED: 12 FEBRUARY 1885

PASSENGER	AGE	SEX	OCCUPATION	PRVVILDES
FINK, LOUIS	35	M	PDLR	PLZZZZUSA
ZEIDMANN, NILS	43	M	PDLR	PLZZZZUSA
STERIN, JACOB	19	M	TRVLR	RRZZZZUSA
COHEN, MARKS	30	M	TLR	RRZZZZUSA
GOLDBERG, ELLIS	36	M	MCHT	RRZZZZUSA

SHIP: LAKE HURON

FROM: LIVERPOOL
TO: NEW YORK
ARRIVED: 12 FEBRUARY 1885

PASSENGER	AGE	SEX	OCCUPATION	PRVVILDES
SCHMER, SOLOMON	35	M	LABR	PLZZZZNY
SOLOMON, EISON	18	M	LABR	RRZZZZBO

PASSENGER	AGE	SEX	OCCUPATION	PRV	VIL	DES

SHIP: FURNESSIA

FROM: GLASGOW
TO: NEW YORK
ARRIVED: 13 FEBRUARY 1885

PASSENGER	AGE	SEX	OCCUPATION	PRVVILDES
PASTUROWSKY, BERGEMMANN	23	M	LABR	RRZZZZUSA
WITZ-CITZKS, KASIMIR	24	M	LABR	RRZZZZUSA

SHIP: BELGENLAND

FROM: ANTWERP
TO: NEW YORK
ARRIVED: 14 FEBRUARY 1885

PASSENGER	AGE	SEX	OCCUPATION	PRVVILDES
KICZINA, ELISAB.	23	F	UNKNOWN	PLZZZZNY
JOSEPH	.10	M	INFANT	PLZZZZNY

SHIP: CITY OF BERLIN

FROM: LIVERPOOL AND QUEENSTOWN
TO: NEW YORK
ARRIVED: 14 FEBRUARY 1885

PASSENGER	AGE	SEX	OCCUPATION	PRVVILDES
BARKIN, SCHOLEM	36	M	LABR	RRZZZZNY

SHIP: EMS

FROM: BREMEN
TO: NEW YORK
ARRIVED: 14 FEBRUARY 1885

PASSENGER	AGE	SEX	OCCUPATION	PRVVILDES
VIATRE, GITKE	24	F	NN	RRZZZZUSA
ABRAHAM	.11	M	INFANT	RRZZZZUSA
FINKELSTEIN, HEINR.	4	M	CHILD	RRZZZZUSA
GITTELSOHN, SAM.	19	M	LABR	RRZZZZUSA

SHIP: RHAETIA

FROM: HAMBURG
TO: NEW YORK
ARRIVED: 14 FEBRUARY 1885

PASSENGER	AGE	SEX	OCCUPATION	PRVVILDES
LASSOWSHA, MARIANNE	25	F	SGL	RRZZZZUSA
WISNEFSKY, FRANZ	40	M	LABR	RRZZZZUSA
MAY, HIRSCH	59	M	MCHT	RRZZZZUSA
GIDALIN, GITE	36	F	W	RRZZZZUSA
ABL.	9	M	CHILD	RRZZZZUSA
SIEMHE	9	F	CHILD	RRZZZZUSA
MUSCHA	8	F	CHILD	RRZZZZUSA
DOLZA	5	M	CHILD	RRZZZZUSA
RACHEL	.11	F	INFANT	RRZZZZUSA
MENOWITZ, FREIDE	22	F	W	RRZZZZUSA
CHEIE	.06	F	INFANT	RRZZZZUSA

PASSENGER	AGE	SEX	OCCUPATION	PRVL	VILE	DES
HELPER, SARAH	30	F	W	RR	ZZZZ	USA
MOSES	9	M	CHILD	RR	ZZZZ	USA
SEINCHE	6	M	CHILD	RR	ZZZZ	USA
ESTER	.11	F	INFANT	RR	ZZZZ	USA
TACHNOWSKY, BENJAMIN	18	M	TLR	RR	ZZZZ	USA
NASANSIN, DAVID	26	M	LABR	RR	ZZZZ	USA
FISCHER, EDWARD	18	M	LABR	RR	ZZZZ	USA
GRUNBLATT, NOCHEM	35	M	DLR	RR	ZZZZ	USA
SCHMARKOWITZ, MOSES	50	M	DLR	RR	ZZZZ	USA
ABRAHAM	9	M	CHILD	RR	ZZZZ	USA
ENOWITZ, CHAIM	33	M	DLR	RR	ZZZZ	USA
ANDRONIK, J.	40	M	PSTR	RR	ZZZZ	USA
BENON, JOSEF	50	M	LABR	RR	ZZZZ	USA
MOSSERZOWITZ, SARUCH	22	M	LABR	RR	ZZZZ	USA
WILANSKY, ABRAHAM	15	M	LABR	RR	ZZZZ	USA
ROSENBERG, HINAE	20	F	SGL	RR	ZZZZ	USA

SHIP: ST. OF PENNSYLVANIA

FROM: GLASGOW AND LARNE
TO: NEW YORK
ARRIVED: 14 FEBRUARY 1885

PASSENGER	AGE	SEX	OCCUPATION	PRVL	VILE	DES
BRENDOW, SIMON	00	M	TLR	RR	ZZZZ	USA
BERNSTEIN, FRIDEL	40	M	UNKNOWN	RR	AHTF	USA
SCHEINE	26	F	W	RR	AHTF	USA
CHATZKEL	9	M	CHILD	RR	AHTF	USA
NACHMEN	2	M	CHILD	RR	AHTF	USA
BASCHKE	1	F	CHILD	RR	AHTF	USA
MOSES	42	M	MCHT	RR	ZZZZ	USA
EFRAIMSON, ADAM	30	M	MCHT	RR	AFWJ	USA
HOLLAENDER, WOLF	28	M	FARMER	RR	ZZZZ	USA
HOFMAN, SCHLOME	37	M	MCHT	RR	ZZZZ	USA
KAHAN, REBECCA	20	F	SVNT	RR	ZZZZ	USA
LASREROW, CHAJE	20	F	SVNT	RR	ZZZZ	USA
LEWINSKY, JEIWUSCH	18	M	TLR	RR	ZZZZ	USA
SARAH	11	F	CH	RR	ZZZZ	USA
MACIEJEWSKA, VICTORIA	26	F	W	RR	ZZZZ	USA
PERLOWITZ, ABRAHAM	25	M	TLR	RR	ZZZZ	USA
RICKELSON, J.	18	M	TLR	RR	ZZZZ	USA
SABIN, LEIB	60	M	MCHT	RR	ZZZZ	USA
HESSL.	26	M	MCHT	RR	ZZZZ	USA
SAML.	10	M	CH	RR	ZZZZ	USA
BEIMOWSKI, WICENTI	32	M	LABR	PL	ZZZZ	USA
PAULME	22	F	W	PL	ZZZZ	USA
KAHOLEWSKA, STANISLAUS	00	M	LABR	PL	ZZZZ	USA
JONAS, ISAAC	46	M	CGRMKR	PL	AFWJ	USA
MASELEITIS, PESSE	45	M	LABR	PL	ZZZZ	USA
MOZKEWITZ, NIKADIM	30	M	LABR	PL	ZZZZ	USA

SHIP: CITY OF CHICAGO

FROM: LIVERPOOL AND QUEENSTOWN
TO: NEW YORK
ARRIVED: 15 FEBRUARY 1885

PASSENGER	AGE	SEX	OCCUPATION	PRVL	VILE	DES
GALTZ, WENNUN	23	M	LABR	PL	ACBF	CH
WERDKA, STEFAN	29	M	LABR	PL	ACBF	CH
CAMBILASK, THOMAS	27	M	LABR	PL	ACBF	CH
LISAH, PETRO	23	M	LABR	PL	ACBF	CH
PERON, AND.	25	M	LABR	PL	ACBF	CH

SHIP: SALIER

FROM: BREMEN
TO: NEW YORK
ARRIVED: 16 FEBRUARY 1885

PASSENGER	AGE	SEX	OCCUPATION	PRVL	VILE	DES
SCHNEIDER, SARAH	16	F	UNKNOWN	RR	ZZZZ	USA
SZECINSKA, EMILIE	22	F	NN	RR	ZZZZ	USA
MUELLER, CARL	22	M	FARMER	RR	AHTF	USA
PAULUS	16	M	FARMER	RR	AHTF	USA

SHIP: POLYNESIA

FROM: HAMBURG
TO: NEW YORK
ARRIVED: 17 FEBRUARY 1885

PASSENGER	AGE	SEX	OCCUPATION	PRVL	VILE	DES
GULUS, M.	24	F	WO	PL	ZZZZ	NY
JOHANN	.09	M	INFANT	PL	ZZZZ	NY
BANDEL, MEIND.E.	48	F	WO	RR	ZZZZ	NY
ESTER	7	F	CHILD	RR	ZZZZ	NY
JUDES	6	M	CHILD	RR	ZZZZ	NY
SALOMON	5	M	CHILD	RR	ZZZZ	NY
MOCZIZOK, PIOTER	24	M	LABR	PL	ZZZZ	NY
BOROWSKY, ABR.M.	21	M	SHMK	RR	ZZZZ	NY
HOLZBERG, SCHOCHMA	30	M	TRDSMN	RR	ZZZZ	NY
NOSCHE	25	F	WO	RR	ZZZZ	NY
ROPPORT, JOH	49	M	TRDSMN	RR	ZZZZ	NY
SIND, HERM.	23	M	BRR	RR	ZZZZ	NY
GOLDSTEIN, ABR.	27	M	LABR	RR	ZZZZ	NY
KUSCHELUH, KOPEL	44	M	TRDSMN	RR	ZZZZ	NY
PODRAJA, ANDR.	27	M	LABR	PL	ZZZZ	NY
KOGLOWA, PAULA	40	F	WO	PL	ZZZZ	NY
WALEH	7	M	CHILD	PL	ZZZZ	NY
BARTUCH	6	M	CHILD	PL	ZZZZ	NY
ROSENHRAM, JACOB	22	M	MCHT	PL	ZZZZ	NY
MARCUS, BEMNI	18	F	SGL	PL	ZZZZ	NY
FRISCH, DAVID	31	F	BCHR	RR	ZZZZ	NY
KARNOWSKY, H.	30	F	WO	RR	ZZZZ	NY
LORE	7	F	CHILD	RR	ZZZZ	NY
JENTE	4	F	CHILD	RR	ZZZZ	NY
BIALAS, VALENTIN	24	M	LABR	PL	ZZZZ	NY
PAWET, W.	22	M	LABR	PL	ZZZZ	NY
REYE, KOPI	23	M	LABR	PL	ZZZZ	NY
CHREBACK, SANCHO	20	M	LABR	PL	ZZZZ	NY
BOGUSLAWSKY, MARIA	40	F	TRDSMN	RR	ZZZZ	NY
LASSINECZ, MATT.	55	F	TRDSMN	PL	ZZZZ	NY
MORZAH, ANN.	20	F	WO	PL	ZZZZ	NY
MARIANNE	.08	F	INFANT	PL	ZZZZ	NY
TOHARIZCH, JOH.	36	M	LABR	PL	ZZZZ	NY
SIEPAURTZ, KASI	28	M	LABR	RR	ZZZZ	NY
WELLENCHUTE, DOMES	21	M	LABR	RR	ZZZZ	NY
PINCUS, Y.	38	M	TRDSMN	RR	ZZZZ	NY
BRUCHE	28	F	W	RR	ZZZZ	NY
LEAH	.11	F	INFANT	RR	ZZZZ	NY
ABRAHAM	.01	M	INFANT	RR	ZZZZ	NY

PASSENGER	AGE	SEX	OCCUPATION	PRIV	VIL	DES

SHIP: WYOMING

FROM: LIVERPOOL
TO: NEW YORK
ARRIVED: 18 FEBRUARY 1885

PASSENGER	AGE	SEX	OCCUPATION	PV	VIL	DES
SUITZKI, CHAIM	39	M	LABR	RR	ZZZZ	USA

SHIP: MORAVIA

FROM: HAMBURG
TO: NEW YORK
ARRIVED: 19 FEBRUARY 1885

PASSENGER	AGE	SEX	OCCUPATION	PV	VIL	DES
GEDSARSKY, MORDSCHE	15	F	SGL	RR	AHSW	USA
SPURO, BERNH.	30	M	DLR	RR	AFWJ	USA
GETTE	30	F	W	RR	AFWJ	USA
WESCHER, CHAJE	19	F	SGL	RR	AHTF	USA
CAP, SCHONE	28	F	W	RR	ZZZZ	USA
WESCHER, MOSES	18	M	TLR	RR	AHTF	USA
BERKOWITZ, BARUCH	22	M	LABR	RR	AHYT	USA
BLOCK, SCHLOME	15	M	LABR	RR	AHTF	USA
RADSTEIN, JOSEF	19	M	LABR	RR	AHYH	USA
REBECCA	20	F	W	RR	AHYH	USA
COHN, MENUCHE	16	F	W	RR	ZZZZ	USA
SARA	.11	F	INFANT	RR	ZZZZ	USA
RIWKE	.01	F	INFANT	RR	ZZZZ	USA
LEWINTHAL, ITE	23	F	W	RR	AHSP	USA
ELIAS	.11	M	INFANT	RR	AHSP	USA
CHANNE	.01	F	INFANT	RR	AHSP	USA
LEWINSOHN, ISAAC	19	M	DLR	RR	AHTS	USA
PREISE, SCHEMEN	21	M	DLR	RR	AHXL	USA
SCHWARZ, MORITZ	18	M	PNTR	RR	AHVG	USA

SHIP: STATE OF NEBRASKA

FROM: GLASGOW AND LARNE
TO: NEW YORK
ARRIVED: 19 FEBRUARY 1885

PASSENGER	AGE	SEX	OCCUPATION	PV	VIL	DES
KLOPOT, SURICK	28	M	GLVR	RR	ZZZZ	NY
HOCHLEHNER, MOSES	20	M	FARMER	RR	ZZZZ	NY
KEMLER, MALKE	40	F	W	RR	ZZZZ	NY
LEAH	15	F	D	RR	ZZZZ	NY
LALEL	2	F	CHILD	RR	ZZZZ	NY
FREITKE	1	F	CHILD	RR	ZZZZ	NY
BORKOW, LEO	25	M	SHMK	RR	ZZZZ	NY
BINJAS, CHAIM	30	M	PDLR	RR	ZZZZ	BO
NECHANE	22	F	W	RR	ZZZZ	BO
LENSUSKY, MENOST	35	M	WCHMKR	RR	ZZZZ	NY
KAPLAN, LEISER	30	M	PDLR	RR	ZZZZ	NY

SHIP: ALSATIA

FROM: GLASGOW
TO: NEW YORK
ARRIVED: 20 FEBRUARY 1885

PASSENGER	AGE	SEX	OCCUPATION	PV	VIL	DES
MCLANICD, NACHINNI	17	M	PDLR	RR	AFVG	USA
ENTERICK, S.	18	M	TNR	RR	ACBF	USA

SHIP: WAESLAND

FROM: ANTWERP
TO: NEW YORK
ARRIVED: 20 FEBRUARY 1885

PASSENGER	AGE	SEX	OCCUPATION	PV	VIL	DES
BARANSKI, JOS.	24	M	FARMER	PL	ZZZZ	NY
MALONOWSKI, H.	66	M	MSN	PL	ZZZZ	NY
MARIA	40	F	MSN	PL	ZZZZ	NY
ODANSKI, MICHEL	26	M	TLR	PL	ZZZZ	PHI

SHIP: CALIFORNIA

FROM: HAMBURG
TO: NEW YORK
ARRIVED: 21 FEBRUARY 1885

PASSENGER	AGE	SEX	OCCUPATION	PV	VIL	DES
RUBINSTEIN, SCH.	25	M	TRDSMN	RR	ZZZZ	NY
KOPAL, ROHEL	30	F	WO	RR	ZZZZ	NY
ABRAHAM	3	M	CHILD	RR	ZZZZ	NY
CHAW	.05	M	INFANT	RR	ZZZZ	NY
NOTH	18	M	B	RR	ZZZZ	NY
KOSELWITZ, ABRAHAM	23	M	TRDSMN	RR	ZZZZ	NY
HIGER, HYPOLT	21	M	CL	RR	ZZZZ	NY
LOSSAU, FRIEDRICH	22	M	LABR	RR	ZZZZ	NY
BUCHAWATZKI, JOSEF	22	M	TRDSMN	RR	ZZZZ	NY
KANAPKY, ABRAHAM	34	M	LABR	RR	ZZZZ	NY
LUCHOWITZ, JACOB	18	M	LABR	RR	ZZZZ	NY
LIBOWIN, LIEBE	55	F	WO	RR	ZZZZ	NY
MALKE	20	F	WO	RR	ZZZZ	NY
LEWINSOHN, LOUIS	30	M	TRDSMN	RR	ZZZZ	NY
SOMMER, BEER	38	M	TRDSMN	RR	ZZZZ	NY
MARIWJANSKY, M.	19	M	LABR	RR	ZZZZ	NY
BERLINER, HIRSCH-E.	26	M	BCHR	RR	ZZZZ	NY

SHIP: MAIN

FROM: BREMEN
TO: NEW YORK
ARRIVED: 21 FEBRUARY 1885

PASSENGER	AGE	SEX	OCCUPATION	PV	VIL	DES
ITZKOWITZ, BERNAN	31	M	LABR	RR	ZZZZ	USA
ABRAHAMOWITZ, FEIWEL	18	M	LABR	RR	ZZZZ	USA
SCHMIEGA, CARL	24	M	FARMER	RR	ZZZZ	USA
WINGER, HERM.	23	M	FARMER	RR	ZZZZ	USA
SCHLESINGER, SALOMON	30	M	LABR	RR	ZZZZ	USA

PASSENGER	AGE	SEX	OCCUPATION	PRIV	VILE	DES

SHIP: GELLERT

FROM: HAMBURG AND HAVRE
TO: NEW YORK
ARRIVED: 23 FEBRUARY 1885

PASSENGER	AGE	SEX	OCCUPATION	PRIV	VILE	DES
LEWIN, SCHAIE	20	M	LABR	RR	ZZZZ	USA
BAUM, MICHAEL	13	M	CH	RR	ZZZZ	USA
SCHAFER, ITZEHOK	38	M	LABR	RR	ZZZZ	USA
HIRSKOWITZ, TAUBE	25	F	SGL	RR	ZZZZ	USA
ZODIKOW, LEA	45	F	W	RR	ZZZZ	USA
SORACH	9	M	CHILD	RR	ZZZZ	USA
ROSA	8	F	CHILD	RR	ZZZZ	USA
SEGERMANN, HIRSCH	37	M	LABR	RR	ZZZZ	USA
PUNENSKY, FEIWE	40	M	LABR	RR	ZZZZ	USA
POJARER, LEIB	31	M	LABR	RR	ZZZZ	USA
BERNSTEIN, JETTE	18	F	SGL	RR	ZZZZ	USA
JAVERKOWSKY, BENDET	19	M	PNTR	RR	ZZZZ	USA
ZLOTNITZKY, PERL	9	F	CHILD	RR	ZZZZ	USA

SHIP: AURANIA

FROM: LIVERPOOL
TO: NEW YORK
ARRIVED: 24 FEBRUARY 1885

PASSENGER	AGE	SEX	OCCUPATION	PRIV	VILE	DES
BRAMSTEIN, RACHAEL	16	F	SP	PL	ZZZZ	USA
WEINBERG, D.	42	M	TLR	PL	ZZZZ	USA
ZUCHOVSKI, MOSES	26	M	LABR	PL	ZZZZ	USA
HANDMACHER, MARDOCHE	32	M	LABR	PL	ZZZZ	USA
CITRISSTAUM, MORITZ	25	M	LABR	PL	ZZZZ	USA
ZALI	23	M	LABR	PL	ZZZZ	USA
JUHOBOWITCH, ZADIK	18	M	LABR	PL	ZZZZ	USA
BRAMSTEIN, EWADIL	38	M	LABR	PL	ZZZZ	USA

SHIP: EDAM

FROM: AMSTERDAM
TO: NEW YORK
ARRIVED: 24 FEBRUARY 1885

PASSENGER	AGE	SEX	OCCUPATION	PRIV	VILE	DES
WURIAN, WASIL	11	M	LABR	RR	ZZZZ	USA
FEDOR	17	M	LABR	RR	ZZZZ	USA

SHIP: VALENCIA

FROM: CURACAO
TO: NEW YORK
ARRIVED: 24 FEBRUARY 1885

PASSENGER	AGE	SEX	OCCUPATION	PRIV	VILE	DES
MULNER, R.	36	M	MCHT	PL	ZZZZ	CAN

SHIP: WESTPHALIA

FROM: HAMBURG
TO: NEW YORK
ARRIVED: 25 FEBRUARY 1885

PASSENGER	AGE	SEX	OCCUPATION	PRIV	VILE	DES
PIETKIEWIECZ, FRANZA.	43	F	W	RR	ZZZZ	USA
JEAN	40	M	LABR	RR	ZZZZ	USA
WRONISLAW	18	M	CH	RR	ZZZZ	USA
ANTON	9	M	CHILD	RR	ZZZZ	USA
LOCHNER, JETTE	20	F	SGL	RR	ZZZZ	USA
TESCHLENSKY, ALEXANDER	21	M	LABR	RR	ZZZZ	USA
MANC, ROBERT	21	M	LABR	RR	ZZZZ	USA
LEWIN, JUNA	23	M	LABR	RR	ZZZZ	USA
BROETMANN, BAUSCH	21	M	LABR	RR	ZZZZ	USA
SADOWITZ, RIWKE	47	F	W	RR	ZZZZ	USA
ZUCKERMANN, DAVID	32	M	DLR	RR	ZZZZ	USA
WOLFF	29	M	DLR	RR	ZZZZ	USA
STEINKE, CAROLINE	23	F	SGL	RR	ZZZZ	USA
ALBERTINE	24	F	SGL	RR	ZZZZ	USA
LEINSINGER, ITSCHKO	30	M	LABR	RR	ZZZZ	USA
CYNAMON, ISRAEL	18	M	LABR	RR	ZZZZ	USA
BARSTEIN, HERSCH	42	M	LABR	RR	ZZZZ	USA
JAEDE, HEINR.	33	M	LABR	RR	ZZZZ	USA
BERGSTEIN, CHAIE	20	F	SGL	RR	ZZZZ	USA
BESSER, CHIEL	9	M	CHILD	RR	ZZZZ	USA
WILCZINSKI, HEINR.	19	M	LABR	RR	ZZZZ	USA
HENACH	9	M	CHILD	RR	ZZZZ	USA
DIAMANT, GERSON	25	M	TLR	RR	ZZZZ	USA
SCHILLIK, MORITZ	19	M	LABR	RR	ZZZZ	USA
RIKMANN, CHAIM	40	M	LABR	RR	ZZZZ	USA
HERSLIKOWITZ, MORITZ	20	M	TLR	RR	ZZZZ	USA
FEIWEL	27	M	TLR	RR	ZZZZ	USA
ICEK	26	M	TLR	RR	ZZZZ	USA
HEIMANN, WOLF	42	M	LABR	RR	ZZZZ	USA
FEIZELOWITZ, HERRM.	40	M	LABR	RR	ZZZZ	USA
HEIMANN, JASKA	9	M	CHILD	RR	ZZZZ	USA
BABREVYE, CHANNE	12	F	SGL	RR	ZZZZ	USA
ROSENSTEIN, BENJAMIN	21	M	SHMK	RR	ZZZZ	USA

SHIP: DEVONIA

FROM: GLASGOW AND MOVILLE
TO: NEW YORK
ARRIVED: 26 FEBRUARY 1885

PASSENGER	AGE	SEX	OCCUPATION	PRIV	VILE	DES
ZANERRA, F.	34	M	MCHT	RR	ZZZZ	USA
IRANOFF, C.U.	36	M	MCHT	RR	ZZZZ	USA
W.	20	F	NN	RR	ZZZZ	USA

SHIP: ST GERMAIN

FROM: HAVRE
TO: NEW YORK
ARRIVED: 26 FEBRUARY 1885

PASSENGER	AGE	SEX	OCCUPATION	PRIV	VILE	DES
LEON, FRANCK	20	M	HTR	RR	ZZZZ	NY

SHIP: CITY OF CHICAGO

FROM: LIVERPOOL AND QUEENSTOWN
TO: NEW YORK
ARRIVED: 02 MARCH 1885

PASSENGER	AGE	SEX	OCCUPATION	PRV VIL DES
DREXELL, HY.	33	M	GENT	RRADXWNY
U-MRS	28	F	W	RRADXWNY

SHIP: NECKAR

FROM: UNKNOWN
TO: NEW YORK
ARRIVED: 02 MARCH 1885

PASSENGER	AGE	SEX	OCCUPATION	PRV VIL DES
ZINICWICZ, EVA	28	F	UNKNOWN	RRZZZZNY
KOLSKY, DAVID	28	M	DLR	RRZZZZNY
LINIEWITZ, WOICHIN	8	M	CHILD	RRZZZZNY
WLATI	5	M	CHILD	RRZZZZNY
MICHEL	2	M	CHILD	RRZZZZNY
JOH.	.03	M	INFANT	RRZZZZNY
WALMKEWITZ, JAN	30	M	LABR	RRZZZZNY
KARRICKY, ANTON	40	M	LABR	RRZZZZNY
KUBOWSKY, ANTON	23	M	LABR	RRZZZZNY
WALMKEWITZ, AMALIA	11	F	CH	RRZZZZUNK

SHIP: WERRA

FROM: BREMEN AND SOUTHAMPTON
TO: NEW YORK
ARRIVED: 02 MARCH 1885

PASSENGER	AGE	SEX	OCCUPATION	PRV VIL DES
GOEBEL, FRIEDR.	37	M	FARMER	RRZZZZNY
MARGARETHE	32	F	UNKNOWN	RRZZZZNY
JACOB	7	M	CHILD	RRZZZZNY
ROSINA	6	F	CHILD	RRZZZZNY
CHRISTINE	4	F	CHILD	RRZZZZNY
FRIEDR.	2	M	CHILD	RRZZZZNY
KRAIN, MICHAEL	65	M	FARMER	RRZZZZNY
RUBARA	65	F	UNKNOWN	RRZZZZNY
KIRCHHOFF, JOHANN	24	F	FARMER	RRZZZZNY
GOLSCHE, NICOLAUS	27	M	FARMER	RRZZZZNY
SALOMOE	23	F	UNKNOWN	RRZZZZNY

SHIP: LEERDAM

FROM: ROTTERDAM
TO: NEW YORK
ARRIVED: 03 MARCH 1885

PASSENGER	AGE	SEX	OCCUPATION	PRV VIL DES
JACOBSON, JAC.	25	M	LABR	RRAFVGUSA

SHIP: SCYTHIA

FROM: LIVERPOOL AND QUEENSTOWN
TO: NEW YORK
ARRIVED: 05 MARCH 1885

PASSENGER	AGE	SEX	OCCUPATION	PRV VIL DES
KROPTOWSKI, HIRSCH	52	M	OPTC	RRADBQUNK

SHIP: NUERNBERG

FROM: BREMEN
TO: NEW YORK
ARRIVED: 06 MARCH 1885

PASSENGER	AGE	SEX	OCCUPATION	PRV VIL DES
LICHTENSTEIN, LEISER	32	M	LABR	RRZZZZUSA
SALOMOVITZ-SCHONBAUMARR	17	M	LABR	RRZZZZUSA
ROSENKOWITZ, ISRAEL	11	M	CH	RRZZZZUSA
HILLE, ADOLF	30	M	LABR	RRZZZZUSA
JULIANE	21	F	W	RRZZZZUSA
REINHOLD	.11	M	INFANT	RRZZZZUSA
MULLER, CAROL.	29	F	NN	RRZZZZUSA
MERGNER, HERM.	25	M	WVR	RRZZZZUSA
ANARITZKI, BERTHA	44	F	NN	RRZZZZUSA
HELLMER, WILH.	32	M	LABR	RRZZZZUSA
IDA	21	F	W	RRZZZZUSA
ALMA	.03	F	INFANT	RRZZZZUSA
KOMASA, JOHANN	23	M	FARMER	RRZZZZUSA
ZELAZNY, FRANZ	64	M	FARMER	RRZZZZUSA
AUGUSTE	54	F	W	RRZZZZUSA
MARKIEWITZ, AGATHA	40	F	W	RRZZZZUSA
JAVA	11	F	CH	RRZZZZUSA
DONEWA	8	F	CHILD	RRZZZZUSA
LAWAN	6	M	CHILD	RRZZZZUSA
AGATHA	3	F	CHILD	RRZZZZUSA
ZODES, MEYER	42	M	SMH	RRZZZZUSA
ORSE	17	F	NN	RRZZZZUSA

SHIP: BOHEMIA

FROM: HAMBURG
TO: NEW YORK
ARRIVED: 07 MARCH 1885

PASSENGER	AGE	SEX	OCCUPATION	PRV VIL DES
ZIANOWCIZ, DOMINIK	25	M	LABR	RRZZZZUSA
FELTENSTEIN, MARIE	16	F	SGL	RRAHTFUSA
CHAIKILOWITZ, PINDIOS	20	M	DLR	RRZZZZUSA
BROVERMANN, MOSES	19	M	JNR	RRZZZZUSA
HEIZIKOWITZ, SCHLOME	19	M	LABR	RRAHVUUSA
ANDERS, MARIE	20	F	SGL	RRZZZZUSA
SELIZER, CARL	20	M	MCHT	RRAHQHUSA
HINZE, EMIL	38	F	W	RRAHQHUSA
DRACHLE, CHAJKEL	28	M	LABR	RRAHSXUSA
MALZ, DAVID	23	M	LABR	RRZZZZUSA
GEDE, ROBERT	28	M	TNR	RRAHZSUSA
LEWIN, SUSSMANN	23	M	DLR	RRZZZZUSA
KANTOROWIECZ, FALK	42	M	DLR	RRAHTFUSA
JABLONOWSKI, HENE	20	F	SGL	RRAHZSUSA
HENE	.11	F	INFANT	RRAHZSUSA
GUTKOWSKY, MAX	22	M	DLR	RRAHZSUSA
LEWITAR, HIRSCH	59	M	DLR	RRAHZSUSA
MARKINSKY, SALOMON	22	M	DLR	RRAHZSUSA
ADELMAN, GITTEL	17	F	SGL	RRAGRTUSA
DOBROWSKY, SARAH	18	F	SGL	RRZZZZUSA
SEGAL, MINNA	36	F	SGL	RRZZZZUSA

PASSENGER	AGE	SEX	OCCUPATION	PRV	VIL	DES
SEIMANN, HINDE	18	F	SGL	RR	ZZZZ	USA
TAWROGER, CHAIE	18	F	SGL	RR	ZZZZ	USA
SELIGAMNN, SALOMON	34	M	LABR	RR	ZZZZ	USA
WISCHEN, SCHLOME	20	M	LABR	RR	ZZZZ	USA
NESZIK, CHAIM	23	M	LABR	RR	ZZZZ	USA
GROSS, ISRAEL	39	M	LABR	RR	ZZZZ	USA
KLEIN, JACOB	19	M	LABR	RR	AHVU	USA
EISENBERG, HIRSCH	22	M	LABR	RR	AHVU	USA
ZEDEKOW, MALKE	9	F	CHILD	RR	ZZZZ	USA
SCHLOME	8	F	CHILD	RR	ZZZZ	USA
KOPELOWITZ, HESCHEL	25	M	DLR	RR	AGRT	USA
STEINSCHNEIDER, BERTHA	22	F	SGL	RR	ZZZZ	USA
ATLAS, TINE	21	F	SGL	RR	ZZZZ	USA
WOITSCHACH, JANOS	35	M	LABR	RR	AHSW	USA
ROSZKEWITZ, FRANZ	38	M	LABR	RR	AHSW	USA
SOBOLEWSKY, JAN	27	M	LABR	RR	AHSW	USA
WILENSKY, KASEMIER	24	M	LABR	RR	AHSW	USA
BLAGAWITZ, ANDRZI	27	M	LABR	RR	AHSW	USA
GORINSKY, KAROL	20	M	LABR	RR	AHSW	USA
GREISZKONIS, VIENCENTY	21	M	LABR	RR	ZZZZ	USA
KANINSKY, SCHOLEM	36	M	LABR	RR	ZZZZ	USA
KIRSTEIN, MOSES	24	M	DLR	RR	AHZS	USA
ZEGELSKI, JULIAN	23	M	JNR	RR	ZZZZ	USA
WALDER, WIEBKE	29	F	SGL	RR	ZZZZ	USA
BERNSTEIN, NATHAN	19	M	LABR	RR	ZZZZ	USA

SHIP: DONAU

FROM: BREMEN
TO: NEW YORK
ARRIVED: 07 MARCH 1885

PASSENGER	AGE	SEX	OCCUPATION	PRV	VIL	DES
KAPLAN, LEA	40	F	UNKNOWN	RR	ZZZZ	USA
SCHIKEN	11	M	CH	RR	ZZZZ	USA
DOBIR	7	M	CHILD	RR	ZZZZ	USA
HAWER	5	M	CHILD	RR	ZZZZ	USA
ELKA	4	F	CHILD	RR	ZZZZ	USA
LEIB	.09	M	INFANT	RR	ZZZZ	USA
LIPKOWITZ, HATZKE	18	F	INF	RR	ZZZZ	USA
PRESCHBERG, JITESEK	44	M	LABR	RR	ZZZZ	USA
LEIJZEROWICK, ESTHER	7	F	CHILD	RR	ZZZZ	USA

SHIP: PENNLAND

FROM: ANTWERP
TO: NEW YORK
ARRIVED: 07 MARCH 1885

PASSENGER	AGE	SEX	OCCUPATION	PRV	VIL	DES
LIGNANT, J.	25	M	LABR	RR	ZZZZ	NY
M.	24	F	LABR	RR	ZZZZ	NY

SHIP: SPAIN

FROM: LIVERPOOL
TO: NEW YORK
ARRIVED: 07 MARCH 1885

PASSENGER	AGE	SEX	OCCUPATION	PRV	VIL	DES
PISTER, LEISER	18	M	LABR	PL	ZZZZ	USA
GEIGER, CHAIM	30	M	LABR	PL	ZZZZ	USA
GOLDSMITH, REBECCA	22	F	SP	PL	ZZZZ	USA
LEILE	36	F	W	PL	ZZZZ	USA
BASTE	4	F	CHILD	PL	ZZZZ	USA

SHIP: CITY OF RICHMOND

FROM: LIVERPOOL AND QUEENSTOWN
TO: NEW YORK
ARRIVED: 09 MARCH 1885

PASSENGER	AGE	SEX	OCCUPATION	PRV	VIL	DES
LEVY, SCHONE-M.	18	M	LABR	PL	AFWJ	USA
ANDSIAK, ANDREAS	41	M	LABR	PL	AFWJ	USA

SHIP: ELBE

FROM: BREMEN
TO: NEW YORK
ARRIVED: 09 MARCH 1885

PASSENGER	AGE	SEX	OCCUPATION	PRV	VIL	DES
RATOWSKI, JESEK	19	M	LABR	RR	ZZZZ	USA
ROSENSTEIN, A.	16	M	LABR	RR	ZZZZ	USA

SHIP: OREGON

FROM: LIVERPOOL AND QUEENSTOWN
TO: NEW YORK
ARRIVED: 09 MARCH 1885

PASSENGER	AGE	SEX	OCCUPATION	PRV	VIL	DES
STACH, JOHN	23	M	LABR	PL	ZZZZ	USA
MILLER, JOE	25	M	LABR	PL	ZZZZ	USA

SHIP: STATE OF INDIANA

FROM: GLASGOW AND LARNE
TO: NEW YORK
ARRIVED: 09 MARCH 1885

PASSENGER	AGE	SEX	OCCUPATION	PRV	VIL	DES
MIHALY, LUZA	25	M	LABR	RR	ZZZZ	USA
JANOTZKI, PETER	28	M	LABR	RR	ZZZZ	USA
GULYAS, GYORGY	25	M	LABR	RR	ZZZZ	USA
HOSTMAR, ANDRAS	25	M	LABR	RR	ZZZZ	USA
KAVINSKY, JOSEF	22	M	LABR	RR	ZZZZ	USA
VOTOLACI, JAN	28	M	LABR	RR	ZZZZ	USA
TABICIS, STEFAN	22	M	LABR	RR	ZZZZ	USA
KUCHTA, ANDRE	33	M	LABR	RR	ZZZZ	USA
MICKOLE, SEREPITA	16	M	LABR	RR	ZZZZ	USA
FECN, FENJI	24	M	LABR	RR	ZZZZ	USA
KUCHTE, TEKU	22	M	LABR	RR	ZZZZ	USA
FOJISK, VLANE	21	M	LABR	RR	ZZZZ	USA
FRIEDMANN, HIRSCH	21	M	LABR	RR	ZZZZ	USA
MICHUK, FEIBEL	18	M	LABR	RR	ZZZZ	USA
W---D, MENDEL	00	M	LABR	RR	ZZZZ	USA
GASTMANN, DAVID	31	M	PDLR	RR	ZZZZ	USA
WASSERTRAUM, MARCUS	26	M	PDLR	RR	ZZZZ	USA
ROTH, DAVID	27	M	PDLR	RR	ZZZZ	USA
OPPENHEIM, ISAAC	25	M	PDLR	RR	ZZZZ	USA

PASSENGER	AGE	SEX	OCCUPATION	PRV VIL DES
GRUNBERG, NATHAN	30	M	PDLR	RRZZZZUSA
RAPEDENSKY, MORDCHE	44	M	PDLR	RRZZZZUSA
GAURIEL	21	M	PDLR	RRZZZZUSA
ROSEN, MARCUS	45	M	PDLR	RRZZZZUSA
SALZBERG, BENJAMIN	23	M	PDLR	RRZZZZUSA
WAD, BENZEL	26	M	PDLR	RRZZZZUSA
FISCHKES, JOSSEL	22	M	PDLR	RRZZZZUSA
EILENTUCH, ABRAHAM	22	M	PDLR	RRZZZZUSA
USSER, SAMUEL	34	M	PDLR	RRZZZZUSA
MICHELSOHN, ABRAHAM	26	M	PDLR	RRZZZZUSA
DANOWSKY, KUSID	26	M	PDLR	RRZZZZUSA
KAHAN, LEISER	33	M	PDLR	RRZZZZUSA
BURCHOWITZ, MEYER	26	M	PDLR	RRZZZZUSA
ROSEN, DAVID	17	M	PDLR	RRZZZZUSA
SAITZ, KOPPEL	25	M	PDLR	RRZZZZUSA
WEISENHOLZ, MOSES	30	M	PDLR	RRZZZZUSA
KLAMICK, JUDEL	32	M	PDLR	RRZZZZUSA
RUBENOWITZ, ISAAC	22	M	PDLR	RRZZZZUSA
SCHWARZMANN, NATHAN	43	M	PDLR	RRZZZZUSA
LEISERWITZ, LEISER	18	M	PDLR	RRZZZZUSA
JERESELAMSKY, RUCHEL	11	F	CH	RRZZZZUSA
FRIEDMANN, DAVID	49	M	PDLR	RRZZZZUSA
KUTCHEWITZKY, JANCKEL	26	M	PDLR	RRZZZZUSA
LOB, ABRAHAM	22	M	PDLR	RRZZZZUSA
MAGYNAS, ABRAHAM	00	M	PDLR	RRZZZZUSA
SPITERS, ABRAHAM	27	M	CGRMKR	RRZZZZUSA
LEVI, MARCUS	34	M	SHMK	RRZZZZUSA
RACZKOWSKI, LOUIS	30	M	PDLR	RRZZZZUSA
ROTHSCHILD, CHAIM	42	M	TLR	RRZZZZUSA
RIBOLOWSKY, MORITZ	33	M	TLR	RRZZZZUSA
ZACHARIAS, DAVID	38	M	TLR	RRZZZZUSA
KARTES, MINDE	10	F	CH	RRZZZZUSA
PEHRMANN, MORITZ	48	M	PDLR	RRZZZZUSA
RIFKE	39	F	W	RRZZZZUSA
ARON	11	M	CH	RRZZZZUSA
JAKOB	10	M	CH	RRZZZZUSA
SCHWAGE	9	M	CHILD	RRZZZZUSA
SIMON	2	M	CHILD	RRZZZZUSA
FANNY	9	F	CHILD	RRZZZZUSA
SCHESKKS	8	F	CHILD	RRZZZZUSA
WALKOWSKY, MEYER	50	M	PDLR	RRZZZZUSA
MERE	32	F	W	RRZZZZUSA
LEIB	10	M	CH	RRZZZZUSA
ZUKUSCHINSKY, CHAJE	00	F	W	RRZZZZUSA
KACZWINSKI, DORKA	00	F	W	RRZZZZUSA
ZA---RIA, CHANNE	00	F	W	RRZZZZUSA
FUTER, MARIA	00	F	SP	RRZZZZUSA
OLSENOVIC, MARIANNE	00	F	SP	RRZZZZUSA
HOLSTEIN, MALKE	00	F	W	RRZZZZUSA
SCHAPSE	00	M	CH	RRZZZZUSA

SHIP: WIELAND

FROM: HAMBURG
TO: NEW YORK
ARRIVED: 09 MARCH 1885

PASSENGER	AGE	SEX	OCCUPATION	PRV VIL DES
KOLISCHISKOWO, RUBEN	17	M	DLR	RRZZZZUSA
TAPPELBERG, RACHMIL	23	M	DLR	RRZZZZUSA
RUBINOWITZ, ANNA	28	F	W	RRZZZZUSA
ISAAC	9	M	CHILD	RRZZZZUSA
HINDE	7	F	CHILD	RRZZZZUSA
DAVID	4	M	CHILD	RRZZZZUSA
RUDOLPH, ARON	25	M	BKR	RRZZZZUSA
FRINK, ESCHE	24	M	LABR	RRZZZZUSA
MENDEL, SARAH	15	F	SGL	RRZZZZUSA
TROCKOZIMER, FALK	14	M	LABR	RRZZZZUSA
BALTREMOWITZ, LEIB	38	M	LABR	RRZZZZUSA
ARONSKY, LEISER	9	M	CHILD	RRZZZZUSA
RUBENSTEIN, BENJAMIN	25	M	LABR	RRZZZZUSA
BLUMBERG, JUDEL	48	M	LABR	RRZZZZUSA
JOSSEL	14	M	CH	RRZZZZUSA
ETTEL	9	M	CHILD	RRZZZZUSA
KRIWERUTZKY, SARA	22	F	W	RRZZZZUSA
JEKE	.11	F	INFANT	RRZZZZUSA
SABEWITZ, OSCHIKY	17	M	LABR	RRZZZZUSA
KNOLL, NOCHEM-D.	9	M	CHILD	RRZZZZUSA
SCHLEIMOWITZ, HIRSCH	30	M	LABR	RRZZZZUSA
ASRALOWITZ, SANDER	55	M	LABR	RRZZZZUSA
EITNER, FRIEDR.	35	M	DLR	RRZZZZUSA

SHIP: SUEVIA

FROM: HAMBURG AND HAVRE
TO: NEW YORK
ARRIVED: 10 MARCH 1885

PASSENGER	AGE	SEX	OCCUPATION	PRV VIL DES
MILLING, BEN	16	M	LABR	RRAFWJUSA
SARA	18	F	SGL	RRAFWJUSA
SEGALOWITZ, ELI	35	M	LABR	RRAHTUUSA
KATZELENBOGEN, ABRAHAM	25	M	LABR	RRAHTUUSA
PORTUVI, LEIB	27	M	LABR	RRAHTUUSA
AXELBRAD, BER	40	M	LABR	RRAHTUUSA
SERZOWSKY, MORDCHE	27	M	LABR	RRAHTUUSA
SELDMANN, OWSIE	25	M	LABR	RRAHTUUSA
HELDTKE, FRIED	32	M	LABR	RRAHTFUSA
ERNEST.	24	F	W	RRAHTFUSA
MATH.	.11	M	INFANT	RRAHTFUNK
IDA	.01	F	INFANT	RRAHTFUSA
OTTO	26	M	LABR	RRAHTFUSA
AUG.	21	F	SGL	RRAHTFUSA
EDWARD	9	M	CHILD	RRAHTFUSA
LEWIN, DINE	38	F	W	RRAHTFUSA
PESCHE	15	F	CH	RRAHTFUSA
CHATZKEL	9	F	CHILD	RRAHTFUSA
JACOB	8	M	CHILD	RRAHTFUSA
CHASCHE	6	M	CHILD	RRAHTFUSA
JUDEL	.11	F	INFANT	RRAHTFUSA
WULFBERG, ISAAC	42	M	LABR	RRZZZZUSA
SCHAJEWITZ, OSCHER	38	M	LABR	RRZZZZUSA
GORDON, LOEB	15	M	LABR	RRZZZZUSA
ASIKOWITZ, GOLDE	35	F	W	RRAHTFUSA
ZERNE	9	F	CHILD	RRAHTFUSA
PESE	7	F	CHILD	RRAHTFUSA
SCHEINE	5	F	CHILD	RRAHTFUSA
SAMUEL	4	M	CHILD	RRAHTFUSA
DINA	.11	F	INFANT	RRAHTFUSA
BOGDENSKI, KACOB	40	M	TLR	RRAHTNUSA
JUDEL	22	M	TLR	RRAHTNUSA
TRACK, MINNA	22	F	SGL	RRAHTNUSA
MACKOWITZ, MOSES	19	M	LABR	RRZZZZUSA
KORNOWSKY, ARON	50	M	LABR	RRAHTFUSA
GARBARSKI, ABRAHAM	16	M	LABR	RRAHTRUSA
CHAIMSOHN, EISIK	18	M	SMH	RRZZZZUSA
LEFKOWITZ, DWORE	28	F	W	RRAHTNUSA
HINDE	4	F	CHILD	RRAHTNUSA
GELBTRUNK, LEVY	26	M	LABR	RRAFWJUSA
GUTMANN, MEYER	19	M	MSN	RRZZZZUSA
FEIGE	24	F	SGL	RRZZZZUSA
SILBERMANN, DAVID	27	M	LABR	RRAFVGUSA
SAFER, MOSES	19	M	LABR	RRZZZZUSA
JECHAS, PALKO	36	M	LABR	RRZZZZUSA
KELWATER, LUDW.	17	M	LABR	RRAHZSUSA
KARLOWITZ, PETER	20	M	LABR	RRAHZSUSA
SCHMIDTKE, MATHIAS	20	M	LABR	RRAHZSUSA
PROWITZKY, PESSE	34	F	W	RRZZZZUSA
RIWKE	9	F	CHILD	RRZZZZUSA
ALTER	4	M	CHILD	RRZZZZUSA
MOSES	.11	M	INFANT	RRZZZZUSA
JOSSE	.01	M	INFANT	RRZZZZUSA

PASSENGER	AGE	SEX	OCCUPATION	PRIVL	DES
TOPIEL, DRESEL	20	F	W	RRAFWJ	USA
PINKUS	.11	M	INFANT	RRAFWJ	USA
JAINBOWITZ, MEGER	17	M	LABR	RRZZZZ	USA
NIZEZELSKI, JIKO	25	M	LABR	RRAGRT	USA
PELSER, LENE	40	F	W	RRAHVA	USA
RAHEL	9	F	CHILD	RRAHVA	USA
ISRAEL	8	M	CHILD	RRAHVA	USA
TAUBE	7	F	CHILD	RRAHVA	USA
GOLDE	5	F	CHILD	RRAHVA	USA
BEHR	.11	M	INFANT	RRAHVA	USA

SHIP: AUSTRALIA

FROM: HAMBURG
TO: NEW YORK
ARRIVED: 12 MARCH 1885

PASSENGER	AGE	SEX	OCCUPATION	PRIVL	DES
GERSCHEWITZ, LEISER	34	M	JNR	RRZZZZ	NY
OLINKER, MOSES	33	M	JNR	RRZZZZ	NY
SCHLEPOCK, GEDALIE	33	M	BCHR	RRZZZZ	NY
LEWITOWITZ, BERL	38	M	TRDSMN	RRZZZZ	NY
ROCHEL	16	F	SGL	RRZZZZ	NY
SCHLOWITZKI, SELIG	50	M	TRDSMN	RRZZZZ	NY
WALWANUIS, SIGM.	24	M	LABR	RRZZZZ	NY
ORANOWITZ, ANTON	34	M	LABR	RRZZZZ	NY
WALWAUIS, CHRIST	41	M	LABR	RRZZZZ	NY
KOSTAWSKY, PETER	33	M	LABR	RRZZZZ	NY
WEINTROP, LEIB	24	M	TRDSMN	PLZZZZ	NY
HOROWITZ, L.	24	M	TNM	PLZZZZ	NY
SAFFIER, SAL.	25	M	TRDSMN	PLZZZZ	NY
MAURER, SISEL	20	F	SGL	PLZZZZ	NY
CHALAP, JACOB	18	M	TLR	RRZZZZ	NY
BEER, PEHLOMA	30	M	TRDSMN	RRZZZZ	NY
MAKEL, JULIUS	42	M	LABR	RRZZZZ	NY
CHRISTIAN	7	M	CHILD	RRZZZZ	NY
PEHAWTRINIKY, JAN	14	M	G	RRZZZZ	NY
RUBINSTEIN, JACOB	22	M	TRDSMN	RRZZZZ	NY
ZEN, BENJAMIN	24	M	TLR	RRZZZZ	NY
ISAAK, ABRAHAM	28	M	TLR	RRZZZZ	NY
WEEZER, CHAIM	24	M	TLR	RRZZZZ	NY
CHAWE	18	F	W	RRZZZZ	NY
GOLDSTEIN, MARCUS	27	M	BBR	RRZZZZ	NY
FREIDE	22	F	W	RRZZZZ	NY
KORPER, MOSES	25	M	TLR	RRZZZZ	NY
SPIRO, MICHE	24	M	TRDSMN	RRZZZZ	NY
FREINOWITZ, MOSES	39	M	TRDSMN	RRZZZZ	NY
BRUTO, BERN.	22	M	MCHT	RRZZZZ	NY
OBELINSKI, FEIGE	20	M	LABR	RRZZZZ	NY
ZUCKERMAN, PASCHKI	35	F	WO	RRZZZZ	NY
GOLDE	7	F	CHILD	RRZZZZ	NY
FREDERIK	6	M	CHILD	RRZZZZ	NY
ETTEN	4	M	CHILD	RRZZZZ	NY
LEBBEN	.11	F	INFANT	RRZZZZ	NY
ADDA	.02	F	INFANT	RRZZZZ	NY
OBLINSKY, ISRAEL	18	M	LABR	RRZZZZ	NY
KATTMANN, MOS.L.	20	M	TRDSMN	RRZZZZ	NY
JOSDOWITZ, HINSCH-L.	17	M	JNR	RRZZZZ	NY
CHANE	19	F	W	RRZZZZ	NY
MULLER, NATHAN	25	M	SMH	PLZZZZ	NY
MARKIBUTZKI, SELIG	27	M	TRDSMN	RRZZZZ	NY
KRAWITZKI, JOSEL	39	M	TRDSMN	RRZZZZ	NY
WEISKY, JOHEM	33	M	LABR	RRZZZZ	NY
GRUMINSKY, SCHMUL	19	M	TRDSMN	RRZZZZ	NY

SHIP: STATE OF GEORGIA

FROM: GLASGOW
TO: NEW YORK
ARRIVED: 12 MARCH 1885

PASSENGER	AGE	SEX	OCCUPATION	PRIVL	DES
ELISKEWITZ, LEIBE	46	M	DLR	RRZZZZ	NY
ABRAHAM	11	M	CH	RRZZZZ	NY
NICOLAWSKY, ATZIG	25	M	LABR	RRZZZZ	NY
RITTER, JACOB	38	M	LABR	RRZZZZ	NY
BERGMANN, ISSER	54	M	PDLR	RRZZZZ	NY
KRARKOWITZ, LASCHE	28	F	W	RRZZZZ	NY
ITTE	.11	F	INFANT	RRZZZZ	NY

SHIP: CITY OF BERLIN

FROM: LIVERPOOL AND QUEENSTOWN
TO: NEW YORK
ARRIVED: 14 MARCH 1885

PASSENGER	AGE	SEX	OCCUPATION	PRIVL	DES
JAROSKY, IGNATZ	30	M	LABR	PLZZZZ	NY
HIRSCHOWSKY, KERSCH	39	M	LABR	PLZZZZ	PHI
WILPAWSKY, MARKUS	39	M	LABR	PLZZZZ	NY
KLEWANSKY, ICKEL	16	M	LABR	PLZZZZ	NY
NORRIS, JESIS	25	M	LABR	PLZZZZ	NY
OFRONOK, JOSEICK	24	M	LABR	PLZZZZ	NY
BEDINA, JOSEF	44	M	LABR	PLZZZZ	NY
STINCEK, KASIMIR	27	M	LABR	PLZZZZ	NY
VADA, JAN	44	M	LABR	PLZZZZ	NY

SHIP: FULDA

FROM: BREMEN
TO: NEW YORK
ARRIVED: 14 MARCH 1885

PASSENGER	AGE	SEX	OCCUPATION	PRIVL	DES
DUBKOWSKI, BASCHE	27	F	UNKNOWN	RRZZZZ	USA
SCHEMANN, DAVID	20	M	TLR	RRZZZZ	USA
CHANE	22	F	UNKNOWN	RRZZZZ	USA
BAWLAWSKY, FEIGA	60	F	UNKNOWN	RRZZZZ	USA
GENENEILBS, JETA	22	F	UNKNOWN	RRZZZZ	USA
CAECILIA	.11	F	INFANT	RRZZZZ	USA
GRUCSTANSKY, MEYER	34	M	LABR	RRZZZZ	USA

SHIP: RHEIN

FROM: BREMEN AND SOUTHAMPTON
TO: NEW YORK
ARRIVED: 14 MARCH 1885

PASSENGER	AGE	SEX	OCCUPATION	PRIVL	DES
SPIEGEL, ICZAK	24	M	LABR	RRZZZZ	USA
GOLDSCHNEIDER, ZENTE	36	F	NN	RRZZZZ	USA
LENE	8	F	CHILD	RRZZZZ	USA
GITMAN	6	M	CHILD	RRZZZZ	USA
SAZA	1	F	CHILD	RRZZZZ	USA
GLICKMANN, MARTHA	60	F	NN	RRZZZZ	USA
NELKEN, ADOLF	18	M	LABR	RRAHOK	USA
LOMBARSKI, ISRAEL	18	M	TRVLR	RRADGO	USA
BALTIONSKY, BRANE	43	F	NN	RRAEFL	USA

PASSENGER	AGE	SEX	OCCUPATION	PRIVIL	DES
DORA	18	F	NN	RRAEFL	USA
JACOB	8	M	CHILD	RRAEFL	USA
MOSES	6	M	CHILD	RRAEFL	USA
BRODER, ABRAHAM	32	M	MCHT	RRADGO	USA
SIGAS, GUSCHAN	44	M	LABR	RRADGO	USA
BERENSTEIN, LOUIS	30	M	DLR	RRZZZZ	USA
ROSENBLUM, SIMON	45	M	DLR	RRZZZZ	USA
RICKE	43	F	W	RRZZZZ	USA
GEORG	8	M	CHILD	RRZZZZ	USA
LEVIN, ABRAHAM	14	M	NN	RRADGO	USA
MASCHEWITZ, ESTER	36	F	NN	RRADGO	USA
SIMON	10	M	CH	RRADGO	USA
SAMUEL	7	M	CHILD	RRADGO	USA
ISIDOR	4	M	CHILD	RRADGO	USA
ROSALIE	.09	F	INFANT	RRADGO	USA
ROSENZWEIG, ESTER	22	F	NN	RRAHOK	USA
SALOMON	.11	M	INFANT	RRAHOK	USA
GLUECKMANN, VEIGL.	24	M	BCHR	RRAEFL	USA

SHIP: NORMANDIE

FROM: HAVRE
TO: NEW YORK
ARRIVED: 16 MARCH 1885

PASSENGER	AGE	SEX	OCCUPATION	PRIVIL	DES
VILEMBERG, JACOB	30	M	HAMF	RRZZZZ	CAN
MAYER	31	M	HAMF	RRZZZZ	CAN

SHIP: RUGIA

FROM: HAMBURG
TO: NEW YORK
ARRIVED: 17 MARCH 1885

PASSENGER	AGE	SEX	OCCUPATION	PRIVIL	DES
MOLLINA, ITZIG	35	M	DLR	RRZZZZ	USA
MOSES, VALENTIN	40	M	LABR	RRZZZZ	USA
CERNINSKY, FRANZ.	41	M	LABR	RRZZZZ	USA
WOHASEWSKY, JOSEPH	44	M	LABR	RRZZZZ	USA
SERANKOWSKY, ANTON	22	M	LABR	RRZZZZ	USA
MUSCHIKOWSKI, WOLF.	58	M	LABR	RRZZZZ	USA
METNIK, SCHIFRE	35	F	W	RRZZZZ	USA
BEILE	16	F	CH	RRZZZZ	USA
SARA	9	F	CHILD	RRZZZZ	USA
ETTE	6	F	CHILD	RRZZZZ	USA
TOKARSKY, SCHOLEM.	19	M	BKBNDR	RRZZZZ	USA
ALEXANDER, BORNACH	35	M	DLR	RRZZZZ	USA
KLEIN, ARON	26	M	LABR	RRZZZZ	USA
SCHARNITZKY, ELKE	22	F	W	RRZZZZ	USA
KEILE	4	F	CHILD	RRZZZZ	USA
FRUME	.11	F	INFANT	RRZZZZ	USA
SOTARSKY, MARIANNE	18	F	SGL	RRZZZZ	USA
COHN, DEBORA	26	F	W	RRZZZZ	USA
SARA	3	F	CHILD	RRZZZZ	USA
ISAAC	.11	M	INFANT	RRZZZZ	USA
RASELOWITSCH, ALSIL.	20	F	SGL	RRZZZZ	USA
GLASSER, PHILIPP	28	M	DLR	RRZZZZ	USA
LEBEDON, SCHLOME	36	M	LABR	RRZZZZ	USA
EHRLICH, ABRAM.	45	M	LABR	RRZZZZ	USA
MORRIS, LIEBE	34	F	W	RRZZZZ	USA
HENKE	5	F	CHILD	RRZZZZ	USA
LAZAR	.11	M	INFANT	RRZZZZ	USA
SPIWAK, NECHAME	18	F	SGL	RRZZZZ	USA
CHAIC	16	F	SGL	RRZZZZ	USA
JANKOWSKY, REBECCA	20	F	SGL	RRZZZZ	USA
DEUTSCH, CHAIC	50	F	W	RRZZZZ	USA

PASSENGER	AGE	SEX	OCCUPATION	PRIVIL	DES
MERRVOITZ, HARRY.	26	M	LABR	RRZZZZ	USA
SONBERG, VICTOR	21	M	LABR	RRZZZZ	USA
GLASSER, SUENDEL	45	M	MCHT	RRZZZZ	USA
LURZALL, HERRMANN	22	M	LABR	RRZZZZ	USA
RIFFER, JOSEF	23	M	LABR	RRZZZZ	USA
IWASCHEFSKI, KOSIS	24	M	LABR	RRZZZZ	USA
BUSCHEWITZ, JACOB	24	M	LABR	RRZZZZ	USA
KOHLOWSKY, IGNATZ	21	M	SHMK	RRZZZZ	USA
BITTERN, JOSEF	20	M	FARMER	RRZZZZ	USA
BONATH, CHRISTINE	42	F	W	RRZZZZ	USA
FRITZ	9	M	CHILD	RRZZZZ	USA
GUSTAV	5	M	CHILD	RRZZZZ	USA
JOSEPH	.11	M	INFANT	RRZZZZ	USA
KIRSEN, CZERNE	30	F	W	RRZZZZ	USA
SARA	20	F	SGL	RRZZZZ	USA
LEISER	8	M	CHILD	RRZZZZ	USA
GUTE	5	M	CHILD	RRZZZZ	USA
DUKTOR, ITZIG	30	M	LABR	RRZZZZ	USA
HEDEMAN, MARIE	25	F	SGL	RRZZZZ	USA
HILKOWITZ, REBECCA	45	F	W	RRZZZZ	USA
ROSALIE	18	F	CH	RRZZZZ	USA
ELKE	16	F	CH	RRZZZZ	USA
SAMPEL	13	M	CH	RRZZZZ	USA
SCHLEMSE	12	M	CH	RRZZZZ	USA
HILLER	9	M	CHILD	RRZZZZ	USA
CHANNE	6	M	CHILD	RRZZZZ	USA
LEVI, RACHEL	36	F	W	RRZZZZ	USA
MARIE	35	F	W	RRZZZZ	USA
DEGER	16	M	CH	RRZZZZ	USA
SARA	9	F	CHILD	RRZZZZ	USA
MERIKE	7	F	CHILD	RRZZZZ	USA
HIRSCHEL	5	M	CHILD	RRZZZZ	USA
U, JETTE	3	F	CHILD	RRZZZZ	USA
DRESMI, SARA	20	F	SGL	RRZZZZ	USA
PERLSTEIN, MEILACH	9	M	CHILD	RRZZZZ	USA
KUPOWICZ, MINNA	18	F	SGL	RRZZZZ	USA
RABINOWIZ, SIMON	52	M	DLR	RRZZZZ	USA
FINKELSTEIN, HEIGE	19	F	SGL	RRZZZZ	USA
KIRCHNER, NOCHCUS	26	M	LABR	RRZZZZ	USA
BEILE	25	F	W	RRZZZZ	USA
WEINSTEIN, ABRAM.	52	M	LABR	RRZZZZ	USA
JOSEPF, REBECCA	35	F	W	RRZZZZ	USA
FEIGE	9	F	CHILD	RRZZZZ	USA
RACHEL	8	F	CHILD	RRZZZZ	USA
MOSES	7	M	CHILD	RRZZZZ	USA
ITZIG	7	M	CHILD	RRZZZZ	USA
DRON.	5	M	CHILD	RRZZZZ	USA
SCHLOME	4	M	CHILD	RRZZZZ	USA

SHIP: NOORDLAND

FROM: ANTWERP
TO: NEW YORK
ARRIVED: 19 MARCH 1885

PASSENGER	AGE	SEX	OCCUPATION	PRIVIL	DES
FIAMKOWIAK, A.	24	M	FARMER	PLZZZZ	MIL
BONJSKI, J.	24	M	FARMER	PLZZZZ	PHI
PH.	17	M	FARMER	PLZZZZ	PHI
JAC.	15	M	UNKNOWN	PLZZZZ	PHI
FRANKONSKI, F.	15	M	LABR	PLZZZZ	NY
ZARONSKI, J.	19	M	FARMER	PLZZZZ	DET
POLACHOWSKI, S.	21	M	FARMER	PLZZZZ	PHI
MACHINS, AN.	22	M	FARMER	PLZZZZ	UNK
CHEREPONOW, SPIRO	33	M	UNKNOWN	RRZZZZ	NY
FRANKOWICEK, JOSA.	00	F	INF	PLZZZZ	MIL

SHIP: STATE OF NEVADA

FROM: GLASGOW AND LARNE
TO: NEW YORK
ARRIVED: 19 MARCH 1885

PASSENGER	AGE	SEX	OCCUPATION	PV VIL DES
BURSTEIN, S.	18	M	LABR	RRZZZZUSA
DIMINTI, J.	25	M	LABR	RRAHZSUSA
DLUZNICWICZ, C.	55	F	W	RRZZZZUSA
GZUJEWICZ, J.	22	M	LABR	RRAHTFUSA
GRODZINSKY, M.	20	M	SHMK	RRZZZZUSA
HONBLUTH, M.	20	M	CL	RRZZZZUSA
HESSENREICH, P.	33	M	PDLR	RRZZZZUSA
MALKE	30	F	W	RRZZZZUSA
SCHONE	48	F	W	RRZZZZUSA
GOLDBERG, MOSES	16	M	PDLR	RRZZZZUSA
C.	2	F	CHILD	RRZZZZUSA
HIRSCH	.09	M	INFANT	RRZZZZUSA
KANIMOTZKY, J.	20	M	LABR	RRZZZZUSA
CHAIE	20	F	W	RRZZZZUSA
BERKE	2	F	CHILD	RRZZZZUSA
LEISEROWITZ, C.	00	M	PDLR	RRZZZZUSA
LEWNISKEY, L.	40	M	LABR	RRAHZSUSA
OSNITZKY, M.	22	M	UNKNOWN	RRAHTOUSA
PRINZESZNIK, J.	22	M	TLR	RRZZZZUSA
REUNAS, M.	22	M	CL	RRAFVGUSA
ROSENBLATT, J.	30	M	LABR	RRZZZZUSA
RIER, GERSON	34	M	BCHR	RRZZZZUSA
STEPHAN, A.	26	M	LABR	RRAHTFUSA
SCHAPIRA, S.	31	M	CL	RRAEFLUSA
SALKANOWITZ, L.	40	M	LABR	RRACBFUSA
SIGISMUND, C.	50	M	PDLR	RRZZZZUSA
J.	19	F	SVNT	RRZZZZUSA
STEIN, J.	29	M	SHMK	RRZZZZUSA
C.	26	F	W	RRZZZZUSA
ITZIG	1	M	CHILD	RRZZZZUSA
WANGA, J.	23	M	LABR	RRZZZZUSA
WORTSCH, S.	23	M	LABR	RRZZZZUSA
CHARLIK, A.	20	M	TLR	PLZZZZUSA
GAZIENDZNISKY, A.	00	M	LABR	PLZZZZUSA
ITZIGSOHN, J.	22	M	CL	PLZZZZUSA
JOSELOWITZ, E.	00	F	W	PLZZZZUSA
CHAJE	00	F	CH	PLZZZZUSA
ISRAEL	00	M	CH	PLZZZZUSA
MAIN	00	M	CH	PLZZZZUSA
HIRSCHEL	.03	F	INFANT	PLZZZZUSA
OKOMESKY, C.	22	M	SHMK	PLAHQUUSA
SERESCHEWSKY, F.	17	F	SVNT	PLAHQUUSA
SCHNEIES, RIFKE	27	F	W	PLZZZZUSA
PESSA	1	F	CHILD	PLZZZZUSA
ZIMNOWITZ, J.	18	M	TLR	PLZZZZUSA
SCHACTA, L.	35	M	GDSM	PLZZZZUSA

SHIP: EMS

FROM: BREMEN
TO: NEW YORK
ARRIVED: 21 MARCH 1885

PASSENGER	AGE	SEX	OCCUPATION	PV VIL DES
GAIKOROSKI, VALENTIN	27	M	LABR	RRZZZZUSA
MALECKI, MATHIAS	31	M	LABR	RRZZZZUSA
KACZMARSKI, ALEX	27	M	JNR	RRZZZZUSA
SZALWINSKI, WOJCIECK	42	M	LABR	RRZZZZUSA
DULRUSKI, WOJCECH	21	M	LABR	RRZZZZUSA
DYLINSKI, WLADISLAW	25	M	SHMK	RRZZZZUSA
DOERR, GOTTLIEB	38	M	FARMER	RRADGOUSA
CHRISTINE	34	F	NN	RRADGOUSA
CHRISTINE	10	F	CH	RRADGOUSA
JACOB	8	M	CHILD	RRADGOUSA
AUGUST	6	M	CHILD	RRADGOUSA
EVA	3	F	CHILD	RRADGOUSA
JUNKER, HEYMANN	48	M	LABR	RRAFWJUSA
NATALIE	18	F	NN	RRAFWJUSA
LEVISOHN, MAX	28	M	FARMER	RRADGOUSA

SHIP: LESSING

FROM: HAMBURG AND HAVRE
TO: NEW YORK
ARRIVED: 21 MARCH 1885

PASSENGER	AGE	SEX	OCCUPATION	PV VIL DES
MOSCHOWITZ, MOSES	14	M	LABR	RRAHTFUSA
BRODICK, YENATZ	21	M	LABR	RRZZZZUSA
JOMALEK, JOSEF	24	M	LABR	RRZZZZUSA
HANKE, AUGUST	32	M	MCHT	RRAAXLUSA
MUELLER, FRANK-E.	43	M	BCHR	RRAAXLUSA
KLEINMAN, HASER	18	M	TLR	RRZZZZUSA
ROCHELSCHA, TODORIS	35	M	LABR	RRAHTQUSA
ZIMMERMAN, CHR.	56	M	FARMER	RRZZZZUSA
WILHE.	60	F	W	RRZZZZUSA
GROCHOWSKI, ANNA	24	F	SGL	RRAGRTUSA
BALUTA, MARRIN	25	M	LABR	RRAHZSUSA
ODER, SAMUEL	18	M	LABR	RRAHTRUSA
FARECTSTEIN, ISRAEL	18	M	LABR	RRAHTRUSA
SCHLACHTER, CHASKEL	45	M	LABR	RRAHVUUSA
SCHAUZ, CHRISTIAN	47	M	FARMER	RRAETSUSA
JOHE.	46	F	W	RRAETSUSA
BARBARA	20	F	CH	RRAETSUSA
MATHS	18	M	CH	RRAETSUSA
GEORG	16	M	CH	RRAETSUSA
CAECILIE	14	F	CH	RRAETSUSA
ELISABETH	9	F	CHILD	RRAETSUSA
JOACHIM	8	M	CHILD	RRAETSUSA
CHRISTIAN	7	M	CHILD	RRAETSUSA
MARIANNE	5	F	CHILD	RRAETSUSA
BERGER, FRANZ	25	M	FARMER	RRAETSUSA
MUELLER, JACOB	35	M	LABR	RRACNZUSA
ISABELLA	32	F	W	RRACNZUSA
ELISABETH	8	F	CHILD	RRACNZUSA
GOTTL.	6	M	CHILD	RRACNZUSA
EMILIE	4	F	CHILD	RRACNZUSA
STEIGER, JACOB	31	M	FARMER	RRACNZUSA
CAROLINE	27	F	W	RRACNZUSA
CATHA.	7	F	CHILD	RRACNZUSA
GOTTL.	5	M	CHILD	RRACNZUSA
ELISABETH	3	F	CHILD	RRACNZUSA
MAEHRER, JACOB	27	M	FARMER	RRACNZUSA
MARIE	26	F	W	RRACNZUSA
CAROLINE	4	F	CHILD	RRACNZUSA
CATHA.	2	F	CHILD	RRACNZUSA
PHILIPP	.09	M	INFANT	RRACNZUSA
ZIMMERMANN, PHILIPP	16	M	FARMER	RRACNZUSA
SCHAEFER, MATHS.	36	M	FARMER	RRAETSUSA
MARGO	35	F	W	RRAETSUSA
CASPAR	13	M	CH	RRAETSUSA
PETER	7	M	CHILD	RRAETSUSA
FRANZISCA	9	F	CHILD	RRAETSUSA
ANNA	4	F	CHILD	RRAETSUSA
PHILIPP	2	M	CHILD	RRAETSUSA
ZIMMERMANN, EVA	19	F	SGL	RRAFQVUSA
LOUISE	22	F	SGL	RRAFQVUSA
STAN, TEOFIL	32	M	MCHT	RRAFWJUSA
GEWONOWITZ, GOTTL.	27	M	LABR	RRAHZSUSA
KUSCHINSKY, CARL	27	M	LABR	RRAHZSUSA
BORIS, IWAN	26	M	LABR	RRAHZSUSA
ZABULSKI, ADAM	24	M	LABR	RRAHZSUSA
JURCIKANOSH, MATHS.	28	M	LABR	RRAHZSUSA
ABCINNIS, ANTON	23	M	LABR	RRAHZSUSA
SCHEGELSKI, MATHS.	26	M	LABR	RRAHZSUSA

PASSENGER	AGE	SEX	OCCUPATION	PRV VIL DES
WOWONISS, VINCENT	28	M	LABR	RRAFZDUSA
ROMANOWSKI, FRANZ	25	M	LABR	RRAHZSUSA
ANNA	22	F	W	RRAHZSUSA
LUDWIKA	.09	F	INFANT	RRAHZSUSA
STUCK, ANTON	30	M	LABR	RRAHZSUSA
KELLER, MARTIN	27	M	LABR	RRAHZSUSA
ANTONINA	30	F	W	RRAHZSUSA
VITEL	.11	M	INFANT	RRAHZSUSA
EVA	.11	F	INFANT	RRAHZSUSA
WOROTKI, WOITECH	33	M	LABR	RRAHZSUSA
WATJELSKI, STANISLAUS	20	M	LABR	RRAHZSUSA
JACUBOWSKI, JACOB	26	M	LABR	RRAHZSUSA
MICHALINE	24	F	W	RRAHZSUSA
CASIMIR	.09	M	INFANT	RRAHZSUSA
RUKOWSKI, VINCENT	21	M	LABR	RRAHZSUSA
FEINBERG, ROSA	26	F	W	RRAHTFUSA
HANNE	.11	F	INFANT	RRAHTFUSA
ITTE	.11	F	INFANT	RRAHTFUSA
RITKOWITZ, SCHLOME	35	M	SHMK	RRAHZNUSA
SCHIDELSKY, BARUCH	21	M	TLR	RRAHTFUSA
ABERSTEIN, ISAAC	34	M	TLR	RRZZZZUSA
LISZINSKI, LEA	45	F	W	RRZZZZUSA
KEMELGOR, LEIB	42	M	LABR	RRAHTFUSA
WICHNE	42	F	W	RRAHTFUSA
ABRAHAM	9	M	CHILD	RRAHTFUSA
RUBEN	4	M	CHILD	RRAHTFUSA
MUSCHE	.11	M	INFANT	RRAHTFUSA
LISZINSKI, PERLE	18	F	SGL	RRZZZZUSA
MOSES	6	M	CHILD	RRZZZZUSA
GITTEL	5	F	CHILD	RRZZZZUSA
SCHKOLNIK, SALMEN	20	M	JNR	RRAHTFUSA
TONI	20	F	W	RRAHTFUSA
GOLDFISCH, JANTOW	36	M	DLR	RRZZZZUSA
KITKIN, NOFTEL	25	M	STWD	RRAHUVUSA
JALOWSKI, CHASKEL	43	M	JNR	RRAHVUUSA
GLUECKFELD, WOLF	40	M	JNR	RRAHVUUSA
BERNSTEIN, BEILE	18	F	SGL	PLZZZZUSA
WILDSTEIN, SIMON	23	M	LABR	PLZZZZUSA
MILLER, LEWI	34	M	TLR	RRZZZZUSA
KAPLAN, HIRSCH	34	M	MCHT	RRAHTRUSA
SCHAPIRA, CHEIM	40	M	MCHT	RRZZZZUSA
PODCAR, BASCHE	20	F	SGL	RRAHVLUSA
CIMBALISCH, MARCUS	22	M	MCHT	RRAFWJUSA
CZIKOWSKI, FRANZ	23	M	LABR	RRAHZSUSA
UWANOWICZ, ANTON	23	M	LABR	RRAHZSUSA
BUSA, FRANZ	33	M	LABR	RRAHZSUSA
LISCENSKA, ANTON	22	M	LABR	RRAHZSUSA
CZIREWSKI, JACOB	22	M	LABR	RRAHZSUSA
JOFFE, SALOMON	19	M	WCHMKR	RRAGRTUSA
PODGAR, SASCHE	16	F	SGL	RRAHVLUSA

SHIP: ODER

FROM: BREMEN
TO: NEW YORK
ARRIVED: 23 MARCH 1885

PASSENGER	AGE	SEX	OCCUPATION	PRV VIL DES
SEGADOWITZ, FAMIZ	25	F	NN	RRZZZZUSA
MOSES	2	M	CHILD	RRZZZZUSA
CHAJE	.09	F	INFANT	RRZZZZUSA
MEYERSOHN, SZEINE-LEA	50	F	NN	RRZZZZUSA
ANNA	20	F	NN	RRZZZZUSA
MISCHKOWSKYE, STEFAN	28	M	LABR	RRZZZZUSA
SCHUKOWSKYE, JOH.	27	M	LABR	RRZZZZUSA
WEINK, JACOB	24	M	LABR	RRZZZZUSA
FONKEWITZ, FRANZ	25	M	LABR	RRZZZZUSA
GESCHINSKYE, PAUL	24	M	LABR	RRZZZZUSA
SZEMETZKYE, MICH.	17	M	LABR	RRZZZZUSA
NEULART, FRIED	34	M	LABR	RRZZZZUSA
BARDEWICK, B.M.	30	M	LABR	RRZZZZUSA

PASSENGER	AGE	SEX	OCCUPATION	PRV VIL DES
CIESLACK, PETER	7	M	CHILD	RRZZZZUSA
FRANK	9	M	CHILD	RRZZZZUSA
JOHANN	16	M	CH	RRZZZZUSA
ANTON	18	M	FARMER	RRZZZZUSA
BRANGOLZ, BAER	23	M	LABR	RRZZZZUSA
RICKOWSKYE, JOHANN	50	M	LABR	RRZZZZUSA
ANETTE	23	F	NN	RRZZZZUSA
KAUFMANN, BARBARA	33	F	NN	RRZZZZUSA
MARCUS	10	M	CH	RRZZZZUSA
LEHA, ETTA	22	F	NN	RRZZZZUSA
ETTE	.09	F	INFANT	RRZZZZUSA
BRAUN, B.M.	28	M	LABR	RRZZZZUSA
KRANZ, JOHANN	34	M	FARMER	RRZZZZUSA
MARGARETHA	31	F	NN	RRZZZZUSA
JOHANN	8	M	CHILD	RRZZZZUSA
MARGARETHA	2	F	CHILD	RRZZZZUSA
CATHARINA	.04	F	INFANT	RRZZZZUSA
POST, CHRISTINE	20	F	NN	RRZZZZUSA
COCHLER, CONRAD	30	M	LABR	RRZZZZUSA
CATHARINA	22	F	NN	RRZZZZUSA
CATHARINA	2	F	CHILD	RRZZZZUSA
JOHANN	.02	M	INFANT	RRZZZZUSA
CHRISTOFFERS, CARL	16	M	CH	RRZZZZUSA
HOFFMAN, RIWKE	20	F	NN	RRZZZZUSA
LEISER	8	M	CHILD	RRZZZZUSA
CAPSCHE	3	M	CHILD	RRZZZZUSA

SHIP: FRISIA

FROM: HAMBURG
TO: NEW YORK
ARRIVED: 25 MARCH 1885

PASSENGER	AGE	SEX	OCCUPATION	PRV VIL DES
DLUGAR, ABRAH.	38	M	LABR	RRZZZZUSA
ANILOWSKY, ANTONIE	21	F	SGL	RRZZZZUSA
MARIE	18	F	CH	RRZZZZUSA
GRUENBERG, MARKUS	18	M	LABR	RRZZZZUSA
HIRSCHBERG, ITZIG	28	M	DLR	RRZZZZUSA
BERTMANN, ABEL	20	M	DLR	RRZZZZUSA
FRANKEL, JANKEL	36	M	DLR	RRZZZZUSA
SIMON, JONE	52	M	DLR	RRZZZZUSA
BRANDIS, NOACH	20	M	DLR	RRZZZZUSA
JOSINSKY, WLADISL.	29	M	LABR	RRZZZZUSA
KOLISKY, JOSEPH	22	M	LABR	RRZZZZUSA
WANDEL, LEOPOLD	25	M	LABR	RRZZZZUSA

SHIP: POLARIA

FROM: HAMBURG
TO: NEW YORK
ARRIVED: 25 MARCH 1885

PASSENGER	AGE	SEX	OCCUPATION	PRV VIL DES
SUBRAS, STANISL.	24	M	LABR	RRZZZZNY
ZELINSKI, KARL	22	M	LABR	RRZZZZNY
GRAJEWSKI, STEFAN	43	M	LABR	RRZZZZBAL
BALUSCHEWITZ, MART.	21	M	LABR	RRZZZZNY
TWAROWSKA, ADELE	22	F	WO	RRZZZZNY
SPEBECK, V.	42	M	LABR	PLZZZZNY
WOREK, TH.	35	M	LABR	PLZZZZNY
WAGNER, JOS.	25	M	LABR	PLZZZZNY
BUBAZKI, JOS.	18	M	LABR	PLZZZZNY
FISCH, ROSA	32	F	WO	PLZZZZNY
ROSA	7	F	CHILD	PLZZZZNY
ISAAK	5	M	CHILD	PLZZZZNY
PERITZ	00	M	CH	PLZZZZNY

PASSENGER	AGE	SEX	OCCUPATION	PRV	VIL	DES
POSIWANSKY, J.H.	19	M	EGR	RR	ZZZZ	NY
POSIEWANSKY, SARAH	7	F	CHILD	RR	ZZZZ	NY
KONJETZIN, MICHAL	28	M	LABR	PL	ZZZZ	NY
SOFIE	23	F	W	PL	ZZZZ	NY
BARTOLICH, JAN	30	M	LABR	PL	ZZZZ	NY
RENDA, PAVEL	26	M	LABR	PL	ZZZZ	NY
KUSCHER, ANDR.	40	M	LABR	PL	ZZZZ	NY
GOTTLIEB, CHANE	21	M	MCHT	RR	ZZZZ	NY
MELACH, MEHR.	23	M	TLR	RR	ZZZZ	NY
NEWAWITZKY, CHAIM	30	M	TLR	RR	ZZZZ	NY
NACHOWITZ, BEREK	37	M	TLR	RR	ZZZZ	NY
BRUSCHUK, WOLF	30	M	TLR	RR	ZZZZ	NY
LUTKUS, STANISLAUS	20	M	LABR	RR	ZZZZ	NY
STANISLAW, MAKELN	20	M	LABR	RR	ZZZZ	NY
ENGELHARDT, ESTER	34	F	WO	RR	ZZZZ	IL
FANNY	7	F	CHILD	RR	ZZZZ	IL
ROZEL	5	F	CHILD	RR	ZZZZ	IL
REBECKA	2	F	CHILD	RR	ZZZZ	IL
NIEDEL, LEIBACH	21	M	TRDSMN	PL	ZZZZ	NY
GRABINOW, ABRAH.	20	M	TRDSMN	RR	ZZZZ	NY
GOTTLIEB, MICHEL	34	M	LABR	PL	ZZZZ	NY
HAWYLACK, PETER	20	M	FARMER	PL	ZZZZ	IL
MACZECRC, SIMON	46	M	LABR	PL	ZZZZ	NY
SOLEK, JANOS	31	M	LABR	PL	ZZZZ	NY
STEFAN, JOHANN	38	M	LABR	PL	ZZZZ	NY
KOPACZ, STEFAN	27	M	LABR	PL	ZZZZ	NY
OSSIP, JANCIPE	18	M	LABR	PL	ZZZZ	NY
ROZBOLLUS, ISCHACK	36	M	LABR	PL	ZZZZ	NY
PEDRAGA, JAN	30	M	LABR	PL	ZZZZ	NY
KAPURKA, STASCH	30	M	LABR	PL	ZZZZ	NY
MARIA	25	F	W	PL	ZZZZ	NY
SCHWRAWETZ, THEKLA	24	F	SGL	PL	ZZZZ	NY
REMITZKO, PANKO	24	M	LABR	PL	ZZZZ	NY
TWORECK, CATHA.	22	F	WO	PL	ZZZZ	NY
HEINRICH	.06	F	INFANT	PL	ZZZZ	NY
ROSINDE, HANNAH	28	F	WO	RR	ZZZZ	NY
ABRAHAM	6	M	CHILD	RR	ZZZZ	NY
MATHILDE	4	F	CHILD	RR	ZZZZ	NY
STEPNER, FEIGE	21	F	SGL	RR	ZZZZ	NY
HIRSCH	19	M	TRDSMN	RR	ZZZZ	NY
RABINOWITZ, ESTER	18	F	SGL	RR	ZZZZ	NY
DOLINSKI, ASCHE	26	F	WO	RR	ZZZZ	NY
ESTER	4	F	CHILD	RR	ZZZZ	NY
MESCHE	.07	F	INFANT	RR	ZZZZ	NY
SEINER, BENJAMIN	21	M	LABR	RR	ZZZZ	NY
SOBOLOWSKI, JAC.	23	M	LABR	RR	ZZZZ	NY
SCHNEIDERMANN, CHR.	17	M	LABR	RR	ZZZZ	NY
MALZ, MEYER	26	M	BKR	RR	ZZZZ	NY
KAPLAN, MOS.	36	M	MCHT	RR	ZZZZ	NY
GUTMANN, RURI	53	F	WO	RR	ZZZZ	NY
KOPPEL, GORD.	22	M	CGRMKR	RR	ZZZZ	NY

SHIP: BOTHNIA

FROM: LIVERPOOL AND QUEENSTOWN
TO: NEW YORK
ARRIVED: 26 MARCH 1885

PASSENGER	AGE	SEX	OCCUPATION	PRV	VIL	DES
SIMONS, SAMUEL	26	M	LABR	PL	ZZZZ	USA

SHIP: BELGENLAND

FROM: ANTWERP
TO: NEW YORK
ARRIVED: 27 MARCH 1885

PASSENGER	AGE	SEX	OCCUPATION	PRV	VIL	DES
ESSEZYNENAY, P.	21	M	JNR	RR	ZZZZ	USA

SHIP: ETHIOPIA

FROM: UNKNOWN
TO: NEW YORK
ARRIVED: 27 MARCH 1885

PASSENGER	AGE	SEX	OCCUPATION	PRV	VIL	DES
ORTNEA, MORITZ	19	M	MCHT	RR	ZZZZ	USA
PANEMIMSKY, MOSES	50	M	CPTR	RR	ZZZZ	USA
HIRSCH	24	M	UNKNOWN	RR	ZZZZ	USA
GERSCH, MENDEL	18	M	UNKNOWN	RR	ZZZZ	USA
WADZINSKY, ARON	23	M	TLR	RR	ZZZZ	USA
LEWIN, HILLEL	24	M	TLR	RR	ZZZZ	USA
SCHINDELMAN, LEOPOLD	40	M	MACH	RR	ZZZZ	USA
U, MARIA	21	F	UNKNOWN	RR	ZZZZ	USA
MLENASSKY, PEISSACH	19	M	LABR	RR	ZZZZ	USA
MANSCHEWITZ, MANDEL	32	M	PDLR	RR	ZZZZ	USA
CHALOV, DAVID	20	M	CPTR	RR	ZZZZ	USA
KAZCENNER, JACOB	20	M	LABR	RR	ZZZZ	USA
OLETZKY, LAIE	20	F	LABR	RR	ZZZZ	USA
LIS, JOHAN	23	M	LABR	PL	ZZZZ	USA
NOWCEKI, HYPOLD	57	M	UNKNOWN	PL	ZZZZ	USA
JACOB, JOHAN	26	M	UNKNOWN	PL	ZZZZ	USA
LEVIN, HANE	30	M	UNKNOWN	PL	ZZZZ	USA
LEPIL, JAKOB	45	M	UNKNOWN	PL	ZZZZ	USA
U, MARIE	30	F	LABR	PL	ZZZZ	USA
DIMONT, MOSES	27	M	TRVLR	PL	ZZZZ	USA
PETER, JANOS	33	M	UNKNOWN	PL	ZZZZ	USA

SHIP: EIDER

FROM: BREMEN AND SOUTHAMPTON
TO: NEW YORK
ARRIVED: 28 MARCH 1885

PASSENGER	AGE	SEX	OCCUPATION	PRV	VIL	DES
BUDZINSKI, PETER	23	M	LABR	RR	ZZZZ	USA
GURSKI, ANTON	22	M	LABR	RR	ZZZZ	USA
BINEWITZ, CONSTN.	25	M	LABR	RR	ZZZZ	USA
INDELOWITZ, SAMUEL	30	M	LABR	RR	ZZZZ	USA
LIWAK, SIME	22	F	NN	RR	ZZZZ	USA
SCHULZ, JOHANN	23	M	LABR	RR	ZZZZ	USA
CHRISTE.	22	F	W	RR	ZZZZ	USA
JOHANN	.05	M	INFANT	RR	ZZZZ	USA
REMPFER, GEORG	63	M	LABR	RR	ZZZZ	USA
CATHA.	16	F	CH	RR	ZZZZ	USA
GEORG	28	M	LABR	RR	ZZZZ	USA
FRIEDKE.	24	F	W	RR	ZZZZ	USA
CHRISTN.	4	M	CHILD	RR	ZZZZ	USA
PAULINE	.03	F	INFANT	RR	ZZZZ	USA
BREITLING, DOROTHEA	18	F	NN	RR	ZZZZ	USA
SCHULZ, JACOB	24	M	FARMER	RR	ZZZZ	USA
WILHE.	26	F	W	RR	ZZZZ	USA
FRIEDKE.	2	F	CHILD	RR	ZZZZ	USA
ELISAB.	.06	F	INFANT	RR	ZZZZ	USA
KORUBOWSKY, FRANZ	21	M	LABR	RR	ZZZZ	USA
ANTON	25	M	LABR	RR	ZZZZ	USA
BERGOWITZ, MARIAN	21	M	LABR	RR	ZZZZ	USA

PASSENGER	AGE	SEX	OCCUPATION	PRIVL	DES
GRYMIEWICZ, ANNA	27	F	W	RRZZZZ	USA
JOSEF	3	M	CHILD	RRZZZZ	USA
KASIMIR	.11	M	INFANT	RRZZZZ	USA
SCOTOITZKY, WOJCIECH	23	M	LABR	RRZZZZ	USA
PRETOZYK, JULIAN	21	M	LABR	RRZZZZ	USA
ROW, MATHIAS	25	M	LABR	RRZZZZ	USA
KOLAKOWSKI, JAN	33	M	LABR	RRZZZZ	USA
WISCHNEWSKY, VALENTIN	27	M	LABR	RRZZZZ	USA
GROCHOWALSKY, ANTON	40	M	LABR	RRZZZZ	USA
BEULLEJEWSKI, FRANZICEK	34	M	LABR	RRZZZZ	USA
SLAWICKI, CONSTN.	24	M	LABR	RRZZZZ	USA
GEHRINGER, GEORG	48	M	FARMER	RRZZZZ	USA
LISABETHA	44	F	W	RRZZZZ	USA
JACOB	17	M	FARMER	RRZZZZ	USA
MAGDA.	16	F	NN	RRZZZZ	USA
CARL	9	M	CHILD	RRZZZZ	USA
ELISE	5	F	CHILD	RRZZZZ	USA
EDUARD	3	M	CHILD	RRZZZZ	USA
JOHANN	.06	M	INFANT	RRZZZZ	USA
HOEPFER, JACOB	27	M	FARMER	RRZZZZ	USA
CATHA.	22	F	W	RRZZZZ	USA
AUG.	3	M	CHILD	RRZZZZ	USA
JACOB	1	M	CHILD	RRZZZZ	USA
BARBA.	.01	F	INFANT	RRZZZZ	USA
BECKER, CHRISTA.	47	M	FARMER	RRZZZZ	USA
CATHA.	36	F	W	RRZZZZ	USA
HEINR.	4	M	CHILD	RRZZZZ	USA
CARL	1	M	CHILD	RRZZZZ	USA
DROEGE, WILHE.	37	F	W	RRZZZZ	USA
RICHD.	7	M	CHILD	RRZZZZ	USA
LUTZ, MICHAEL	63	M	FARMER	RRZZZZ	USA
FRIEDKE.	63	F	W	RRZZZZ	USA
CHRISTN.	11	M	CH	RRZZZZ	USA
SANTER, CAROLE.	22	F	NN	RRZZZZ	USA
LUTZ, ADAM	32	M	FARMER	RRZZZZ	USA
ROSINE	32	F	W	RRZZZZ	USA
ADAM	8	M	CHILD	RRZZZZ	USA
WILHE.	7	F	CHILD	RRZZZZ	USA
JOHANN	4	M	CHILD	RRZZZZ	USA
ROSINE	.03	F	INFANT	RRZZZZ	USA
JACOB	21	M	FARMER	RRZZZZ	USA
LEHNOR, ADAM	31	M	LABR	RRZZZZ	USA
PHILIPPINE	27	F	W	RRZZZZ	USA
CATHA.	10	F	CH	RRZZZZ	USA
RUDOLF	9	M	CHILD	RRZZZZ	USA
ADAM	5	M	CHILD	RRZZZZ	USA
EMILIE	1	F	CHILD	RRZZZZ	USA
MICHAEL	.01	M	INFANT	RRZZZZ	USA
SEILER, DAVID	24	M	LABR	RRZZZZ	USA
ULMER, LUDWIG	18	M	LABR	RRZZZZ	USA
CHRISTN.	16	M	LABR	RRZZZZ	USA
SOBOLEWSKI, JOSEF	18	M	FARMER	RRZZZZ	USA
ANISCHEWSKI, JACOB	37	M	FARMER	RRZZZZ	USA
KATHA.	34	F	W	RRZZZZ	USA
MARIA	4	F	CHILD	RRZZZZ	USA
MARTIN	33	M	FARMER	RRZZZZ	USA
KATHA.	37	F	W	RRZZZZ	USA
KATHA.	3	F	CHILD	RRZZZZ	USA
LUCAS, JACOB	27	M	FARMER	RRZZZZ	USA
KATHA.	24	F	W	RRZZZZ	USA
JACOB	.11	M	INFANT	RRZZZZ	USA
FRIEDR.	57	M	FARMER	RRZZZZ	USA
CHRISTE.	50	F	W	RRZZZZ	USA
ISRAEL	18	M	FARMER	RRZZZZ	USA
PHILIPP	15	M	CH	RRZZZZ	USA
SALOME	11	M	CH	RRZZZZ	USA
MAGDA.	10	F	CH	RRZZZZ	USA
CATHA.	4	F	CHILD	RRZZZZ	USA
JOHANNES	23	M	FARMER	RRZZZZ	USA
GOTTLIEBE	18	F	W	RRZZZZ	USA
ADAM	.03	M	INFANT	RRZZZZ	USA
STROBEL, GOTTLIEB	33	M	FARMER	RRZZZZ	USA
FRIEDKE.	28	F	W	RRZZZZ	USA
SALOME	10	M	CH	RRZZZZ	USA
FRIEDR.	8	M	CHILD	RRZZZZ	USA
JACOB	4	M	CHILD	RRZZZZ	USA
JOHANN	2	M	CHILD	RRZZZZ	USA
GOTTLIEB	.03	M	INFANT	RRZZZZ	USA
DENOSKI, ANTON	31	M	LABR	RRZZZZ	USA
MIHALSKI, FRANZ	30	M	LABR	RRZZZZ	USA

SHIP: MAIN

FROM: BREMEN
TO: NEW YORK
ARRIVED: 28 MARCH 1885

PASSENGER	AGE	SEX	OCCUPATION	PRIVL	DES
CIBILIWITSCH, BEILE	18	F	DRSMKR	RRZZZZ	USA
CELANIC	3	F	CHILD	RRZZZZ	USA
SMATELNIK, LEIE	23	F	W	RRZZZZ	USA
NOTES, BEILE-CHAJE	24	F	W	RRZZZZ	USA
VEIGE	2	F	CHILD	RRZZZZ	USA
CZIKANOWICZ, MAGDL.	40	F	W	RRZZZZ	USA
MARIA	19	F	D	RRZZZZ	USA
ANTON	8	M	CHILD	RRZZZZ	USA
JOSEF	6	M	CHILD	RRZZZZ	USA
KAZANIK, BARUCH-MENDEL	34	M	LABR	RRZZZZ	USA
TAUBE	10	F	CH	RRZZZZ	USA
HERMANN	11	M	CH	RRZZZZ	USA
WIEICHOSKI, JOSEF	18	M	LABR	RRZZZZ	USA
MASULEWITZ, HERSCH-MEYE	17	M	CL	RRZZZZ	USA
LEWIN, MOSES	36	M	MCHT	RRZZZZ	USA
MEYER, BLASSBERG	46	M	MCHT	RRZZZZ	USA
ROGAS, FRANZ	23	M	MCHT	RRZZZZ	USA
FRANZISKA	19	F	W	RRZZZZ	USA
MUSZUKEWCIZ, JAN	32	M	FARMER	RRZZZZ	USA
WENGEZENOWITZ, WLADISLA	25	M	LABR	RRZZZZ	USA
DANIELOWITZ, BOSELOW	24	M	LABR	RRZZZZ	USA
JASZINSKI, JAN	22	M	LABR	RRZZZZ	USA
SZIMSIRSKI, MICHAL	24	M	LABR	RRZZZZ	USA
MILEWSKI, FRANZ	22	M	LABR	RRZZZZ	USA
TAROWITSCH, R.	40	M	LABR	RRZZZZ	USA

SHIP: ST. OF PENNSYLVANIA

FROM: GLASGOW AND LARNE
TO: NEW YORK
ARRIVED: 28 MARCH 1885

PASSENGER	AGE	SEX	OCCUPATION	PRIVL	DES
FISCHMANN, TRUEL	38	M	MCHT	RRACBF	USA
HENE	32	F	W	RRACBF	USA
CHAIE	12	F	CH	RRACBF	USA
EILVA	7	F	CHILD	RRACBF	USA
BENZEL	3	M	CHILD	RRACBF	USA
GITTELMANN, SAML.	37	M	MCHT	RRACBF	USA
SARA	38	F	W	RRACBF	USA
BENZEL	10	M	CH	RRACBF	USA
ELIAS	8	M	CHILD	RRACBF	USA
ABRAHAM	5	M	CHILD	RRACBF	USA
FISCHEL	.09	M	INFANT	RRACBF	USA
GRODETZKY, MICHEL	38	M	SMH	RRACBF	USA
JANOS, TIRPAK	40	M	LABR	RRAARR	USA
ROBINSON, MERVYN	35	M	FARMER	RRAFTP	USA

PASSENGER	AGE	SEX	OCCUPATION	PRV	IVL	DES

SHIP: AURANIA

FROM: LIVERPOOL
TO: NEW YORK
ARRIVED: 30 MARCH 1885

PASSENGER	AGE	SEX	OCCUPATION	PRV	IVL	DES
FRIEDLICH, ARON	30	M	LABR	RR	AHOO	USA
LOCBEH	7	M	CHILD	RR	AHOO	USA
SARAH	6	F	CHILD	RR	AHOO	USA
KAUFMANN	4	M	CHILD	RR	AHOO	USA
ADA	2	F	CHILD	RR	AHOO	USA
KAZLONE, MICHOLOC	54	M	NN	RR	AHQH	USA
SOPHIE	40	F	W	RR	AHQH	USA
VICTOR	14	M	CH	RR	AHQH	USA
LIVEZ, PHILIP	32	M	MCHT	RR	ZZZZ	USA

SHIP: HAMMONIA

FROM: HAMBURG AND HAVRE
TO: NEW YORK
ARRIVED: 30 MARCH 1885

PASSENGER	AGE	SEX	OCCUPATION	PRV	IVL	DES
OSCMANN, SALOMON	19	M	BBR	RR	ZZZZ	USA
GROFSBELD, MORITZ	24	M	DLR	RR	ZZZZ	USA
SCHOENFELD, JACOB	33	M	DLR	RR	ZZZZ	USA
WARSCHOFSKY, JACOB	20	M	DLR	RR	ZZZZ	USA
ORCHINSKY, FISCHEL	33	M	DLR	RR	ZZZZ	USA
NYMANN, MOSSEL	18	M	W	RR	ZZZZ	USA
SCHWARZ, ELLI	35	F	TLR	RR	ZZZZ	USA
CHANNE	26	F	W	RR	ZZZZ	USA
RIWKE	10	F	CH	RR	ZZZZ	USA
FREIDE	.04	F	INFANT	RR	ZZZZ	USA
RIWKE	50	F	W	RR	ZZZZ	USA
MIKOLAJSAS, JECSY	23	M	LABR	RR	ZZZZ	USA
LEVIN, ROFLE	19	F	SGL	RR	ZZZZ	USA
LIBBE	6	F	CHILD	RR	ZZZZ	USA
MEHLICHEINCKER, MOSES	26	M	LABR	RR	ZZZZ	USA
EDLER, JOHANNA	41	F	W	RR	ZZZZ	USA
KODISZKY, SARA	24	F	SGL	RR	ZZZZ	USA
MISHINSKY, ROSA	62	F	SGL	RR	ZZZZ	USA
MEYERS, SARA	34	F	W	RR	ZZZZ	USA
RIGELHOP, RIWKE	18	F	SGL	RR	ZZZZ	USA
BORNSTEIN, JADLEK	19	M	WCHMKR	RR	ZZZZ	USA
FRIEDMANN, SCHASCHE	30	M	W	RR	ZZZZ	USA
RACHEL	8	F	CHILD	RR	ZZZZ	USA
CHANNE	6	F	CHILD	RR	ZZZZ	USA
CHAIM	.11	M	INFANT	RR	ZZZZ	USA
LEIB	.01	M	INFANT	RR	ZZZZ	USA
KANCER, RECHAME	48	F	W	RR	ZZZZ	USA
SEIKE	9	M	CHILD	RR	ZZZZ	USA
KALKE	7	M	CHILD	RR	ZZZZ	USA
NOTTE	4	M	CHILD	RR	ZZZZ	USA
KRAUSE, MICHAEL	31	M	LABR	RR	ZZZZ	USA
KUBE, ROL.	41	M	LABR	RR	ZZZZ	USA
PODGAR, SAMUEL	42	M	LABR	RR	ZZZZ	USA
SEIKE	36	F	W	RR	ZZZZ	USA
MALKE	9	F	CHILD	RR	ZZZZ	USA
REBECCA	7	F	CHILD	RR	ZZZZ	USA
REIFKE	4	F	CHILD	RR	ZZZZ	USA

SHIP: ARIZONA

FROM: LIVERPOOL AND QUEENSTOWN
TO: NEW YORK
ARRIVED: 31 MARCH 1885

PASSENGER	AGE	SEX	OCCUPATION	PRV	IVL	DES
PRIESCHOFF, JOSEF	23	M	LABR	RR	ZZZZ	USA
DOLZCLECKI, ANTON	20	M	LABR	PL	ZZZZ	USA

SHIP: INDIA

FROM: HAMBURG
TO: NEW YORK
ARRIVED: 01 APRIL 1885

PASSENGER	AGE	SEX	OCCUPATION	PRV	IVL	DES
GRABOWSKY, MICHAEL	33	M	LABR	RR	ZZZZ	NY
MACHATZKY, STANISLAUS	35	M	LABR	RR	ZZZZ	NY
DUBROWITZ, MARIE	18	F	SGL	RR	ZZZZ	OH
LEWIN	12	M	CH	RR	ZZZZ	OH
SCHABEL, BAER	16	M	LABR	RR	ZZZZ	OH
KAPLAN, MOSES	30	M	TRDSMN	RR	ZZZZ	IL
WITZ, SALOMON	25	M	BKR	RR	ZZZZ	NY
HANSEN, HEINRICH	16	M	FARMER	RR	ZZZZ	NY
SALOMON, KALMAN	33	M	LABR	PL	ZZZZ	NY
ROSSNER, HERM.	18	M	LABR	PL	ZZZZ	NY
BODNOS, FRANZ	50	M	LABR	PL	ZZZZ	NY
BODNAR, MOSES	15	M	LABR	PL	ZZZZ	NY
KEMPLER, JOHANN	24	M	TRDSMN	PL	ZZZZ	NY
JETTI	23	F	W	PL	ZZZZ	NY
MARIA	20	F	SI	PL	ZZZZ	NY
FICHTENBAUM, SIMON	25	F	WO	PL	ZZZZ	NY
ISRAEL	3	M	CHILD	PL	ZZZZ	NY
GNIADEK, JOSEPH	20	M	LABR	PL	ZZZZ	NY
PROPF, LION	17	M	LABR	RR	ZZZZ	IL
LIPPKE, FISCHEL	30	M	LABR	RR	ZZZZ	NY
LEISER, SCHLOME	28	M	LABR	RR	ZZZZ	BAL
LEISERSOHN, RIFEL	16	M	LABR	RR	ZZZZ	UNK
BERNSTEIN, OSCHIES	20	M	LABR	RR	ZZZZ	NY
FRANZ, BROENIC	30	M	LABR	PL	ZZZZ	NY
BAZONDEK, WLADISLAW	30	M	LABR	PL	ZZZZ	NY
IWANEC, KASIMIR	36	M	LABR	PL	ZZZZ	NY
JULIANE	25	F	W	PL	ZZZZ	NY
JOSEF	5	M	CHILD	PL	ZZZZ	NY
MARIA	2	F	CHILD	PL	ZZZZ	NY
VICTORIA	6	F	CHILD	PL	ZZZZ	NY
MAROZANTE	68	F	UNKNOWN	PL	ZZZZ	NY
ODANIK, JACOB	19	M	LABR	PL	ZZZZ	NY
WOJTAR, JAN	27	M	LABR	PL	ZZZZ	NY
GOCAK, WOJTEK	34	M	LABR	PL	ZZZZ	NY
POTEMPA, JAN	40	M	LABR	PL	ZZZZ	NY
ROGUS, JACOB	19	M	LABR	PL	ZZZZ	NY
WEGOS, JOSEF	24	M	LABR	PL	ZZZZ	NY
POSTEL, FREMA	16	M	LABR	PL	ZZZZ	NY
LEWIN, CHARLES	40	M	LABR	RR	ZZZZ	NY
REDONSKI, FERD.	54	M	LABR	PL	ZZZZ	NY
ROSBRAND, JOHANN	52	M	LABR	PL	ZZZZ	NY
ROMDIMSKY, JOS.	24	M	LABR	PL	ZZZZ	NY
SCHUMDS, WOYTISCH	21	M	LABR	PL	ZZZZ	NY
DREYER, JOSSEL	26	M	FARMER	RR	ZZZZ	NY
GLAESER, JON	00	M	TRDSMN	RR	ZZZZ	NY
SEIDEMANN, WOLF	7	M	CHILD	RR	ZZZZ	NY
ZULLIN, ANDREAS	36	F	WO	PL	ZZZZ	NY
MARIANNE	7	F	CHILD	PL	ZZZZ	NY
MICHAEL	.06	M	INFANT	PL	ZZZZ	NY
KARPOWITZ, JOHANN	31	M	FARMER	PL	ZZZZ	NY

SHIP: WERRA

FROM: BREMEN
TO: NEW YORK
ARRIVED: 01 APRIL 1885

PASSENGER	AGE	SEX	OCCUPATION	PRV VIL DES
STIRCITZKY, WOPCIECH	20	M	LABR	RRZZZZNY
GEORGI, MARIE	21	F	UNKNOWN	RRZZZZNY
ACKERMANN, CATHA.	40	F	UNKNOWN	RRZZZZNY
JACOB	19	M	FARMER	RRZZZZNY
ANDREAS	17	M	FARMER	RRZZZZNY
PETER	7	M	CHILD	RRZZZZNY
GEORG	5	M	CHILD	RRZZZZNY
JOHANN	3	M	CHILD	RRZZZZNY
SOPHIE	2	F	CHILD	RRZZZZNY
FISCHER, MICHAEL	42	M	FARMER	RRZZZZNY
CATHA.	40	F	UNKNOWN	RRZZZZNY
ROSINA	19	F	UNKNOWN	RRZZZZNY
FRIEDR.	17	M	FARMER	RRZZZZNY
CATHA.	7	F	CHILD	RRZZZZNY
LISABETH	6	F	CHILD	RRZZZZNY
JACOB	5	M	CHILD	RRZZZZNY
CAROLINA	4	F	CHILD	RRZZZZNY
MAGDALENE	2	F	CHILD	RRZZZZNY
JOHANN	00	M	INF	RRZZZZNY
KANZ, MICHAEL	36	M	FARMER	RRZZZZNY
CATHA.	30	F	UNKNOWN	RRZZZZNY
JACOB	4	M	CHILD	RRZZZZNY
CHRIST.	3	M	CHILD	RRZZZZNY
CATHA.	.03	F	INFANT	RRZZZZNY
ZIMMERMANN, JACOB	30	M	FARMER	RRZZZZNY
ELISABETH	24	F	UNKNOWN	RRZZZZNY
JACOB	3	M	CHILD	RRZZZZNY
JOHANN	2	M	CHILD	RRZZZZNY
ELISABETH	.06	F	INFANT	RRZZZZNY
BERNSTEIN, JANOS	42	M	LABR	RRZZZZNY

SHIP: AMERIQUE

FROM: HAVRE
TO: NEW YORK
ARRIVED: 02 APRIL 1885

PASSENGER	AGE	SEX	OCCUPATION	PRV VIL DES
KOKOTKIEWICZ, ANTONIE	34	M	MSN	RRZZZZUSA
LOUISE	40	F	NN	RRZZZZUSA
ANDIE	28	M	NN	RRZZZZUSA
HEDWIGE	15	F	CH	RRZZZZUSA
JOSEPHINE	10	F	CH	RRZZZZUSA
ELISABETH	8	F	CHILD	RRZZZZUSA
CASIMIR	5	M	CHILD	RRZZZZUSA
LOUIS	00	M	INF	RRZZZZUSA
JEAN	00	M	INF	RRZZZZUSA

SHIP: MORAVIA

FROM: HAMBURG
TO: NEW YORK
ARRIVED: 02 APRIL 1885

PASSENGER	AGE	SEX	OCCUPATION	PRV VIL DES
PUCHALSKI, JAN	37	M	LABR	RRAHYCUSA
WLADISL.	27	M	LABR	RRAHYCUSA
PELNIKOWSKYE, APPOLLONA	40	M	LABR	RRZZZZUSA
JANISCHEWSKY, FRANZ	25	M	LABR	RRZZZZUSA
FALSYN, MONIKA	27	F	W	RRZZZZUSA
ANTON	4	M	CHILD	RRZZZZUSA
GICSEWSKA, EVA	22	F	SGL	RRZZZZUSA
UCZENSKI, FRANZ	23	M	LABR	RRZZZZUSA
KWIATKOWSKA, JOSEFA	25	F	W	RRAHYCUSA
SOFIE	.08	F	INFANT	RRAHYCUSA
LEKIECKI, JAN	22	F	LABR	RRAHSWUSA
ALEXANDROWITZ, SARA	42	F	W	RRZZZZUSA
LEISER	9	M	CHILD	RRZZZZUSA
MORDSCHE	6	F	CHILD	RRZZZZUSA
BOJANOWSKY, MICHAEL	24	M	LABR	RRAHUFUSA
URZDOWSKY, FRANZ	25	M	LABR	RRAHUFUSA
KAKOTZKA, FRANZA.	20	F	SGL	RRAHUFUSA
ENDELMANN, LEA	22	F	SGL	RRZZZZUSA
ESTER	20	F	SGL	RRZZZZUSA
BLUME	9	M	CHILD	RRZZZZUSA
CHELSCHACK, FRANZ	21	M	LABR	RRAHZSUSA
WESTLAND, JULIAN	28	M	LABR	RRAHZSUSA
DOBJERG, JAN	36	M	LABR	RRAHZSUSA
SCHOSTAC, DWASSI	50	F	W	RRZZZZUSA
RIEFKE	20	F	CH	RRZZZZUSA
SARA	17	F	CH	RRZZZZUSA
CHANE	9	M	CHILD	RRZZZZUSA
OSIAS	5	M	CHILD	RRZZZZUSA
ESTER	.11	F	INFANT	RRZZZZUSA
HORN, STANISLAWA	19	F	SGL	RRZZZZUSA
GLAESER, AUGUSTE	29	F	SGL	RRZZZZUSA
WERTHER, JOSEPH	35	M	LABR	RRZZZZUSA
CATHA.	35	F	W	RRZZZZUSA
JOH.	.03	M	INFANT	RRZZZZUSA
SCHILLKALIS, STANISL.	21	M	LABR	RRAHTFUSA
SCHAMNAITIA, FRANZ	25	M	LABR	RRAHTFUSA
SIGMANLOWICZ, VINCENT	15	M	LABR	RRAHTFUSA
WIRSCHIKALSKI, JOH.	22	M	LABR	RRAHTFUSA
SKINKIS, VINCENT	28	M	LABR	RRAHTFUSA
MOSSAITIR, ANTON	20	M	LABR	RRAHZSUSA
ANTON	24	M	LABR	RRAHZSUSA
JARONIN	27	M	LABR	RRAHZSUSA
AGNISKA	20	F	W	RRAHZSUSA
KROLL, AUGUST	20	M	LABR	RRZZZZUSA
MISCHKOWSKYE, ZLATE	16	F	SGL	RRZZZZUSA
MARZINKO, SOPHIE	18	F	SGL	RRZZZZUSA
VERONA	16	F	SGL	RRZZZZUSA
SLOMATINSKY, FRAIN	21	M	LABR	RRZZZZUSA
WOLKOWITZ, SENDER	24	M	LABR	RRZZZZUSA
BRUDNER, LOUIS	26	M	LABR	RRAGRTUSA
STACHEL	22	F	SGL	RRAGRTUSA
BASCHE	15	F	SGL	RRAGRTUSA
DOBBERSTEIN, DAVID	55	M	LABR	RRAHOKUSA
JULS.	26	M	DLR	RRAHOKUSA
RADZIEWICZ, JANISL.	20	M	LABR	RRZZZZUSA
GROSSKOWKA, JOSEFA	42	F	W	RRAHYCUSA
FRANZ	15	M	CH	RRAHYCUSA
JAN	9	M	CHILD	RRAHYCUSA
HENDRIK	8	M	CHILD	RRAHYCUSA
HELENE	7	F	CHILD	RRAHYCUSA
IGNATZ	2	M	CHILD	RRAHYCUSA
DZIERZENKO, HIPOLIT	45	M	LABR	RRAHUFUSA

SHIP: STATE OF NEBRASKA

FROM: GLASGOW AND LARNE
TO: NEW YORK
ARRIVED: 02 APRIL 1885

PASSENGER	AGE	SEX	OCCUPATION	PRV VIL DES
HELLMANN,, HIPOLIT	28	M	PDLR	RRZZZZNY
BIROCZAK, MICHAEL	46	M	PDLR	RRZZZZNY
KOMERA, ANNA	18	F	SVNT	RRZZZZNY
GAJCER, GEORG	22	M	GZR	RRZZZZNY
KASCELAK, JOSEF	27	M	PDLR	RRZZZZNY
WASKO, JANKA	29	F	SVNT	RRZZZZNY

PASSENGER	AGE	SEX	OCCUPATION	PRIV	VIL	DES
KIZKO, ANDREAS	29	M	LABR	RR	ZZZZ	NY
DUMOSCA, JOSEF	23	M	DLR	RR	ZZZZ	NY
LAZAROWITZ, JOSEF	30	M	DLR	RR	ZZZZ	NY
ELLENA	9	F	CHILD	RR	ZZZZ	NY
ANNA	6	F	CHILD	RR	ZZZZ	NY
SIMKO, ANADKO	34	M	PDLR	RR	ZZZZ	NY
MIKOLAJ, MEUSICEK	34	M	LABR	RR	ZZZZ	NY
STEFAN, KOLENZE	49	M	LABR	PL	ZZZZ	NY
SABANSKY, JOSEF	27	M	LABR	PL	ZZZZ	NY
FEDOR, LEGAN	34	M	LABR	PL	ZZZZ	NY
JOSEF, GOVEC	37	M	LABR	PL	ZZZZ	NY
SNELOFF, SPERIDON	23	M	LABR	RR	ZZZZ	NY
IFISCHOFF, ISAAC	22	M	LABR	RR	ZZZZ	NY
GUSCHOROWSKY, JAN	37	M	LABR	RR	ZZZZ	NY
KANOPKA, JAN	23	M	LABR	RR	ZZZZ	NY
SACKCZEWSKI, TEOPHIL	18	M	LABR	RR	ZZZZ	NY
MELINAWSKY, JOSEF	24	M	LABR	RR	ZZZZ	NY
BARTEL, MICHAL	00	M	LABR	RR	ZZZZ	NY
LISCHEWSKY, JAN	24	M	LABR	RR	ZZZZ	NY
ALEXER, JAN	00	M	LABR	RR	ZZZZ	NY
WAWCZIN, JACOB	22	M	LABR	RR	ZZZZ	NY
LINKOWITZ, KASIMIR	24	M	LABR	RR	ZZZZ	NY
JUCHS, PEISACH	30	M	CCHMN	RR	ZZZZ	NY
KRASOWITZ, ANTON	28	M	LABR	RR	ZZZZ	NY
SABULEWITZ, ENDRES	36	M	LABR	RR	ZZZZ	NY
KARBSTEIN, AUGUST	27	M	LABR	RR	ZZZZ	NY
JANKOWSKY, MICHAL	25	M	LABR	RR	ZZZZ	NY
BASCHKEWITZ, MISLAR	30	M	LABR	RR	ZZZZ	NY
KOVAKOSKY, WALDRISLAUS	26	M	LABR	RR	ZZZZ	NY
LISSITCA, JAN	26	M	LABR	RR	ZZZZ	NY
FRANZISKA	23	F	W	RR	ZZZZ	NY
BORIA.	.09	F	INFANT	RR	ZZZZ	NY
LARSINSKY, THEOPHIL	20	M	LABR	RR	ZZZZ	NY
SALESCHKINSKY, FRANZ	25	M	LABR	RR	ZZZZ	NY
PIKROWSKY, JAN	27	M	LABR	RR	ZZZZ	NY
CAZCEFASKY, VALENTINE	19	M	LABR	RR	ZZZZ	NY
SCHWARTZ, FRANZ	20	M	LABR	RR	ZZZZ	NY
MILANSKY, MICHAEL	19	M	LABR	RR	ZZZZ	NY
PINTOWSKY, ABR.	00	M	LABR	RR	ZZZZ	NY
ROCHANSKY, IGNATZ	00	M	LABR	RR	ZZZZ	NY

SHIP: WAESLAND

FROM: ANTWERP
TO: NEW YORK
ARRIVED: 02 APRIL 1885

PASSENGER	AGE	SEX	OCCUPATION	PRIV	VIL	DES
SCHMITZ, P.	29	M	UNKNOWN	RR	ZZZZ	NY
JACOBS, L.	22	F	UNKNOWN	RR	ZZZZ	NY
LEIMET, M.	46	M	LABR	RR	ZZZZ	NY
HURK, MS.	36	M	LABR	RR	ZZZZ	NY
LEIMET, M.	17	M	LABR	RR	ZZZZ	NY
KOWALSKI, ANT.	27	M	MSN	RR	ZZZZ	NY
LINDEN, G.	25	M	LABR	RR	ZZZZ	NY
HASSELBACK, S.	18	M	UNKNOWN	RR	ZZZZ	NY
LONGE, C.E.	21	M	LABR	RR	ZZZZ	STL
GUNTHAS, C.	20	F	LABR	RR	ZZZZ	NY
KIESER, J.	26	M	LABR	RR	ZZZZ	NY
MARENS, J.	32	M	LABR	RR	ZZZZ	NY
MILLER, J.	26	M	SHMK	RR	ZZZZ	NY
SCHERER, P.	56	M	LABR	RR	ZZZZ	CH
MULLER, J.	21	M	LABR	RR	ZZZZ	NY
MEYERS, G.	25	M	LABR	RR	ZZZZ	NY
GTOFFEL, J.	31	M	LABR	RR	ZZZZ	BUF
SEHRAMM, G.	27	M	LABR	RR	ZZZZ	CH
KOLAZENSKI, J.	30	M	LABR	RR	ZZZZ	NY
SKAZENSKA, R.	19	M	LABR	RR	ZZZZ	CH
WISNIEWNOSKI, A.	36	M	LABR	RR	ZZZZ	NY
RUPCZEMCSKI, W.	17	M	LABR	RR	ZZZZ	CH
RONZE, E.	26	F	LABR	RR	ZZZZ	UNK
WOLSKI, M.	26	M	UNKNOWN	RR	ZZZZ	NY
J.	16	M	LABR	RR	ZZZZ	NY
POPROSKI, S.	36	M	TLR	RR	ZZZZ	MIL
PATZKOWSKI, S.	57	M	LABR	RR	ZZZZ	UNK
A.	47	F	UNKNOWN	RR	ZZZZ	UNK
M.	10	F	LABR	RR	ZZZZ	UNK
J.	5	F	CHILD	RR	ZZZZ	UNK
POLENSKI, L.	27	M	UNKNOWN	RR	ZZZZ	PHI
ROHLKA, J.	21	F	LABR	RR	ZZZZ	NY
W.	17	F	LABR	RR	ZZZZ	MIL
HUMERSKA, W.	27	F	LABR	RR	ZZZZ	MIL
JESKE, R.	21	M	LABR	RR	ZZZZ	UNK
ONDREZCOWSKI, O.F.	18	M	LABR	RR	ZZZZ	BUF
GODONSKI, G.	46	M	LABR	RR	ZZZZ	NY
PARONS, J.G.	19	M	TLR	RR	ZZZZ	CH
STAZSAK, J.	33	M	UNKNOWN	RR	ZZZZ	NY
SZEZYKA, B.	24	F	LABR	RR	ZZZZ	NY
POBLOMSKI, S.	16	M	LABR	RR	ZZZZ	NY

SHIP: CITY OF RICHMOND

FROM: LIVERPOOL AND QUEENSTOWN
TO: NEW YORK
ARRIVED: 03 APRIL 1885

PASSENGER	AGE	SEX	OCCUPATION	PRIV	VIL	DES
WIKOWSKY, ANTON	37	M	LABR	PL	ZZZZ	USA

SHIP: CITY OF ROME

FROM: LIVERPOOL AND QUEENSTOWN
TO: NEW YORK
ARRIVED: 03 APRIL 1885

PASSENGER	AGE	SEX	OCCUPATION	PRIV	VIL	DES
BUDAK, ANDREY	40	M	LABR	RR	ZZZZ	USA
BROWSKY, MATHEI	19	M	LABR	RR	ZZZZ	USA
BUZAK, LEON	44	M	LABR	RR	ZZZZ	USA
BUBERICK, WOITICH	45	M	LABR	RR	ZZZZ	USA
GEDAK, HEDOR	21	M	LABR	RR	ZZZZ	USA
KACAR, VINCENTY	40	M	LABR	RR	ZZZZ	USA
STOZELCIK, PAWEL	40	M	LABR	RR	ZZZZ	USA
SELASKA, MICHAL	29	M	LABR	RR	ZZZZ	USA

SHIP: ENGLAND

FROM: LIVERPOOL AND QUEENSTOWN
TO: NEW YORK
ARRIVED: 04 APRIL 1885

PASSENGER	AGE	SEX	OCCUPATION	PRIV	VIL	DES
RSACHOWITZ, MOSES	33	M	LABR	RR	ZZZZ	NY

PASSENGER	AGE	SEX	OCCUPATION	PRV VIL DES

SHIP: CITY OF CHICAGO

FROM: LIVERPOOL AND QUEENSTOWN
TO: NEW YORK
ARRIVED: 06 APRIL 1885

PASSENGER	AGE	SEX	OCCUPATION	PRV VIL DES
JAKOLOWSKI, FRANZ	25	M	SHMK	RRAFZDNY
STALL, MORRIS	23	M	CPMKR	RRADBQNY
COLEMAN, J.	40	M	CPMKR	RRADBQNY
SAM.	11	M	CH	RRADBQNY

SHIP: ELBE

FROM: BREMEN
TO: NEW YORK
ARRIVED: 06 APRIL 1885

PASSENGER	AGE	SEX	OCCUPATION	PRV VIL DES
SCHELZE, G.	40	M	LABR	RRZZZZUSA
FRIEDR.	8	M	CHILD	RRZZZZUSA
FEISTER, C.	28	M	LABR	RRZZZZUSA
EMILIE	25	F	W	RRZZZZUSA
AMALIE	.11	F	INFANT	RRZZZZUSA
SANDER, PAULINS	20	F	NN	RRZZZZUSA
SCHATSCHNEIDER, EVA	50	F	LABR	RRZZZZUSA
HEINRICH, ANNA	23	F	NN	RRZZZZUSA
EMMA	24	F	NN	RRZZZZUSA
SCHMIDT, HENRIETTE	24	F	NN	RRZZZZUSA
LAEMMLE, D.	54	M	FARMER	RRZZZZUSA
KLIPPE, JOHANN	.11	M	INFANT	RRZZZZUSA
LAEMMLE, CHRISTIANE	50	F	W	RRZZZZUSA
JACOB	8	M	CHILD	RRZZZZUSA
DAVID	5	M	CHILD	RRZZZZUSA
WOLF, G.	25	M	FARMER	RRZZZZUSA
LOUISE	25	F	W	RRZZZZUSA
LOUISE	.11	F	INFANT	RRZZZZUSA
SCHAEFFER, PHIL.	19	M	LABR	RRZZZZUSA
HINGER, A.	58	M	LABR	RRZZZZUSA
CAROLINE	52	F	W	RRZZZZUSA
CAROLINE	23	F	CH	RRZZZZUSA
FRIEDRICH	17	M	LABR	RRZZZZUSA
MARGARETHE	16	F	CH	RRZZZZUSA
ROSINE	9	F	CHILD	RRZZZZUSA
FRIEDERIKE	2	F	CHILD	RRZZZZUSA
KLEIN, F.	41	M	FARMER	RRZZZZUSA
CHRISTINE	36	F	W	RRZZZZUSA
FRIEDRICH	6	M	CHILD	RRZZZZUSA
MAGDALENE	4	F	CHILD	RRZZZZUSA
JACOB	.11	M	INFANT	RRZZZZUSA
WEIN, JOHANN	25	M	FARMER	RRZZZZUSA
LISABETH	21	F	W	RRZZZZUSA
JOHANN	.05	M	INFANT	RRZZZZUSA
KLIPPE, G.	25	M	FARMER	RRZZZZUSA
MAGDAL.	25	F	W	RRZZZZUSA
GEORG	3	M	CHILD	RRZZZZUSA
WOLF, JOHANN	40	M	FARMER	RRZZZZUSA
FRIEDERIKE	33	F	W	RRZZZZUSA
JOHANNE	16	F	CH	RRZZZZUSA
GEORG	11	M	CH	RRZZZZUSA
ELISABETH	4	F	CHILD	RRZZZZUSA
FRIEDRICH	.11	M	INFANT	RRZZZZUSA
FISCHER, KARL	49	M	FARMER	RRZZZZUSA
KATHARINA	32	F	W	RRZZZZUSA
ELISABETH	17	F	CH	RRZZZZUSA
JACOB	22	M	LABR	RRZZZZUSA
FRIEDERIKE	9	F	CHILD	RRZZZZUSA
KARL	16	M	LABR	RRZZZZUSA
MAGDALENE	5	F	CHILD	RRZZZZUSA
CHRISTINE	.06	F	INFANT	RRZZZZUSA
AMANN, FRIEDRICH	40	M	FARMER	RRZZZZUSA
BETCA	36	F	W	RRZZZZUSA
FRIEDRICH	16	M	LABR	RRZZZZUSA
CHRISTINE	9	F	CHILD	RRZZZZUSA
JOHANN	5	M	CHILD	RRZZZZUSA
HEINRICH	3	M	CHILD	RRZZZZUSA
EVA	1	F	CHILD	RRZZZZUSA
JACOB	.03	M	INFANT	RRZZZZUSA
LAMMLE, JOHANN	33	M	FARMER	RRZZZZUSA
MAGDALENE	28	F	W	RRZZZZUSA
LUDWIG	11	M	CH	RRZZZZUSA
ELISABETH	7	F	CHILD	RRZZZZUSA
MAGDALENE	5	F	CHILD	RRZZZZUSA
KIERLE, CHRISTIAN	42	M	FARMER	RRZZZZUSA
CHRISTINE	41	F	W	RRZZZZUSA
CHRISTIAN	19	M	LABR	RRZZZZUSA
KARL	18	M	LABR	RRZZZZUSA
DAVID	16	M	LABR	RRZZZZUSA
JOHANN	10	M	CH	RRZZZZUSA
FRIEDERIKE	7	F	CHILD	RRZZZZUSA
HEINRICH	4	M	CHILD	RRZZZZUSA
BUCSING, WILHELM	20	M	LABR	RRZZZZUSA
MALESZKA, FRANZ	24	M	LABR	RRZZZZUSA
BUEHMANN, MINNA	19	F	NN	RRZZZZUSA
LINA	17	F	NN	RRZZZZUSA
STEGMANN, FRIEDRICH	35	M	LABR	RRZZZZUSA
KAMINSKA, ANNA	22	F	NN	RRZZZZUSA
KATRUSKI, JAN	40	M	LABR	RRZZZZUSA
GRABOWSKI, ANDREAS	38	M	LABR	RRZZZZUSA
MURAWSKA, KATHARINA	20	F	NN	RRZZZZUSA
SIKARSKA, EMILIE	27	F	NN	RRZZZZUSA
JOSEFA	.11	F	INFANT	RRZZZZUSA
LINERSKI, IGNAZ	25	M	LABR	RRZZZZUSA
HEIT, ADAM	26	M	FARMER	RRZZZZUSA
MAGDAL.	21	F	W	RRZZZZUSA
HERSE, FRIEDRICH	30	M	FARMER	RRZZZZUSA
ANNA	30	F	W	RRZZZZUSA
ANNA	3	F	CHILD	RRZZZZUSA
FRIEDRICH	2	M	CHILD	RRZZZZUSA
WILHELM	.11	M	INFANT	RRZZZZUSA
MEYER, FAEVL	32	M	FARMER	RRZZZZUSA
CHRISTINE	23	F	W	RRZZZZUSA
FRIEDERIKE	1	F	CHILD	RRZZZZUSA
CHRISTINE	.05	F	INFANT	RRZZZZUSA
SCHOIPLE, FRIEDRICH	36	M	FARMER	RRZZZZUSA
EVA	30	F	W	RRZZZZUSA
FRIEDRICH	9	M	CHILD	RRZZZZUSA
JOHANN	5	M	CHILD	RRZZZZUSA
CHRISTIAN	00	M	CH	RRZZZZUSA
JOHANNA	19	M	CH	RRZZZZUSA
WILDERMUTH, ADAM	58	M	FARMER	RRZZZZUSA
WOLF, MARITN	22	M	FARMER	RRZZZZUSA
MARIE	24	F	W	RRZZZZUSA
FRIEDRICH	1	M	CHILD	RRZZZZUSA
AMANN, PHILIPP	47	M	FARMER	RRZZZZUSA
CHRISTINE	41	F	W	RRZZZZUSA
CHRISTINE	21	F	CH	RRZZZZUSA
HEINRICH	10	M	CH	RRZZZZUSA
JOHANN	10	M	CH	RRZZZZUSA
JACOB	8	M	CHILD	RRZZZZUSA
RICKE	4	F	CHILD	RRZZZZUSA
CHRISTIAN	3	M	CHILD	RRZZZZUSA
MEYER, CARL	34	M	FARMER	RRZZZZUSA
BARBARA	32	F	W	RRZZZZUSA
KARL	6	M	CHILD	RRZZZZUSA
BARBARA	4	F	CHILD	RRZZZZUSA
JOHANN	1	M	CHILD	RRZZZZUSA
MAGDALENA	.02	F	INFANT	RRZZZZUSA
HEINS, DANIEL	60	M	FARMER	RRZZZZUSA
KATHARINA	59	F	W	RRZZZZUSA
CHRISTINE	24	F	CH	RRZZZZUSA
DOROTHEA	20	F	CH	RRZZZZUSA
SCHIMLE, MARTIN	39	M	FARMER	RRZZZZUSA
ROSINA	37	F	W	RRZZZZUSA
HEINRICH	5	M	CHILD	RRZZZZUSA
JOHANN	3	M	CHILD	RRZZZZUSA

PASSENGER	AGE	SEX	OCCUPATION	PRV VIL DES
FRIEDERIKA	.02	F	INFANT	RRZZZZUSA
PAWLAK, A.	34	M	LABR	RRZZZZUSA
KURLE, CHRISTINE	1	F	CHILD	RRZZZZUSA
RITTEL, GEORG	27	M	FARMER	RRZZZZUSA
CHRISTINE	23	F	W	RRZZZZUSA
GEORG	.11	M	INFANT	RRZZZZUSA
WOLF, JOHANN	42	M	FARMER	RRZZZZUSA
FRIEDERIKE	35	F	W	RRZZZZUSA
JOHANNES	17	M	LABR	RRZZZZUSA
JACOB	8	M	CHILD	RRZZZZUSA
CHRISTIAN	6	M	CHILD	RRZZZZUSA
GEORG	3	M	CHILD	RRZZZZUSA
GOTTLIEB	.03	M	INFANT	RRZZZZUSA
MERKEL, FRIEDRICH	35	M	LABR	RRZZZZUSA
MARGARETTIE	33	F	W	RRZZZZUSA
ELISABETH	7	F	CHILD	RRZZZZUSA
CHRISTINE	5	F	CHILD	RRZZZZUSA
JOHANNES	4	M	CHILD	RRZZZZUSA
WOLF, FRIEDRICH	40	M	FARMER	RRZZZZUSA
MARGARETHE	39	F	W	RRZZZZUSA
FRIEDRICH	17	M	LABR	RRZZZZUSA
JOHANNES	15	M	CH	RRZZZZUSA
KAROLINE	11	F	CH	RRZZZZUSA
MARGARETTE	9	F	CHILD	RRZZZZUSA
JACOB	7	M	CHILD	RRZZZZUSA
CHRISTINE	4	F	CHILD	RRZZZZUSA
CHRISTIAN	2	M	CHILD	RRZZZZUSA
SCHPIERE, PHIL.	20	M	FARMER	RRZZZZUSA
FRIEDRICH	18	M	FARMER	RRZZZZUSA
PISCHKE, MARGARETTA	27	F	NN	RRZZZZUSA
JOHANN	5	M	CHILD	RRZZZZUSA
FRIEDRICH	3	M	CHILD	RRZZZZUSA
KATHARINA	2	F	CHILD	RRZZZZUSA
CHRISTINE	1	F	CHILD	RRZZZZUSA
MAGDALENA	.06	F	INFANT	RRZZZZUSA
SCHACK, JOHANN	28	M	FARMER	RRZZZZUSA
KATHARINA	24	F	W	RRZZZZUSA
KONRAD	.03	M	INFANT	RRZZZZUSA
SCHOCK, CHRISTIAN	26	M	LABR	RRZZZZUSA
CHRISTINE	25	F	W	RRZZZZUSA
CHRISTIAN	2	M	CHILD	RRZZZZUSA
JOHANN	.11	M	INFANT	RRZZZZUSA
GRAF, EWALD	21	M	FARMER	RRZZZZUSA
JOHANN	39	M	FARMER	RRZZZZUSA
CHRISTNE	39	F	W	RRZZZZUSA
JACOB	18	M	LABR	RRZZZZUSA
KATHARINA	16	F	CH	RRZZZZUSA
JOHANN	13	M	CH	RRZZZZUSA
ADOLPH	11	M	CH	RRZZZZUSA
DEWALD	7	M	CHILD	RRZZZZUSA
CHRISTINE	4	F	CHILD	RRZZZZUSA
AUGUST	1	M	CHILD	RRZZZZUSA
LAMARIC, HEINRICH	44	M	FARMER	RRZZZZUSA
SCHMELE, GOTTFRIED	47	M	LABR	RRZZZZUSA
WILHELMINE	41	F	W	RRZZZZUSA
WILHELM	11	M	CH	RRZZZZUSA
PAUL	6	M	CHILD	RRZZZZUSA
RICHARD	2	M	CHILD	RRZZZZUSA
MARTHA	.02	F	INFANT	RRZZZZUSA
PAULINE	20	F	UNKNOWN	RRZZZZUSA
U	00	M	LABR	RRZZZZUSA
WILHELMINE	15	F	CH	RRZZZZUSA
HERMANN	11	M	CH	RRZZZZUSA
HEINRICH	9	M	CHILD	RRZZZZUSA
WALTER, GRITZ	23	M	LABR	RRZZZZUSA
EBEL, WILHELM	71	M	LABR	RRZZZZUSA
KATHARINA	64	F	W	RRZZZZUSA

SHIP: UMBRIA

FROM: LIVERPOOL AND QUEENSTOWN
TO: NEW YORK
ARRIVED: 07 APRIL 1885

PASSENGER	AGE	SEX	OCCUPATION	PRV VIL DES
SAANILA, HISKIA	35	M	LABR	FNZZZZUSA
ANTINLUOMA, AND.	25	M	LABR	FNZZZZUSA
LUOMA, GUSTAF	25	M	LABR	FNZZZZUSA
JUIFALE, FHD.A.	25	M	LABR	FNZZZZUSA
LADRALA, NILLS-A.	25	M	LABR	FNZZZZUSA
KALAVNARI, JACOB	19	M	LABR	FNZZZZUSA
JOHN	24	M	LABR	FNZZZZUSA

SHIP: WESTERNLAND

FROM: ANTWERP
TO: NEW YORK
ARRIVED: 09 APRIL 1885

PASSENGER	AGE	SEX	OCCUPATION	PRV VIL DES
HARTAL, N.MR	56	M	GENT	FNAHQHNY

SHIP: NECKAR

FROM: BREMEN
TO: NEW YORK
ARRIVED: 11 APRIL 1885

PASSENGER	AGE	SEX	OCCUPATION	PRV VIL DES
TSZELOMSKI, FRANCA.	20	F	SVNT	RRZZZZNY
REAJEWSKA, ANNA	26	F	SVNT	RRZZZZNY
SCHEIFELE, CHRISTOF	59	M	LABR	RRZZZZNY
CATHA.	17	F	UNKNOWN	RRZZZZNY
ELISAB.	15	F	UNKNOWN	RRZZZZNY
LAMMLE, FRIEDR.	30	M	FARMER	RRZZZZNY
CATHA.	25	F	UNKNOWN	RRZZZZNY
DAVID	2	M	CHILD	RRZZZZNY
ELISABETH	.05	F	INFANT	RRZZZZNY
FISCHER, ELISAB.	18	F	SVNT	RRZZZZNY
KAUL, JACOB	63	M	FARMER	RRZZZZNY
ELISAB.	60	F	UNKNOWN	RRZZZZNY
JACOB	36	M	FARMER	RRZZZZNY
CATHA.	33	F	UNKNOWN	RRZZZZNY
CATHARINA	8	F	CHILD	RRZZZZNY
MARGA.	6	F	CHILD	RRZZZZNY
ROSINA	5	F	CHILD	RRZZZZNY
JACOB	4	M	CHILD	RRZZZZNY
MAGDA.	2	F	CHILD	RRZZZZNY
ELISAB.	.03	F	INFANT	RRZZZZNY
CHRIST.	24	M	LABR	RRZZZZNY
REGINA	22	F	UNKNOWN	RRZZZZNY
CATHA.	2	F	CHILD	RRZZZZNY
MAGDA.	.02	F	INFANT	RRZZZZNY
STEINWALD, WILHM.	30	M	FARMER	RRZZZZNY
MARGA.	20	F	UNKNOWN	RRZZZZNY
MARGA.	4	F	CHILD	RRZZZZNY
JOHANN	2	M	CHILD	RRZZZZNY
ELISABETH	.01	F	INFANT	RRZZZZNY

SHIP: FULDA

FROM: BREMEN
TO: NEW YORK
ARRIVED: 13 APRIL 1885

PASSENGER	AGE	SEX	OCCUPATION	PV RI VL DES
HELLEDAG, S.	60	M	TT	RRAEFLUSA
ULMER, LUDWIG	00	M	FARMER	RRZZZZUSA
DOROTHEA	42	F	UNKNOWN	RRZZZZUSA
CHRISTINE	18	F	UNKNOWN	RRZZZZUSA
LISBETH	8	F	CHILD	RRZZZZUSA
CAHTARINA	7	F	CHILD	RRZZZZUSA
LOUISE	5	F	CHILD	RRZZZZUSA
CAROLINE	3	F	CHILD	RRZZZZUSA
RICKE	2	F	CHILD	RRZZZZUSA
DIETE, HEINRICH	50	M	FARMER	RRZZZZUSA
CATHARINA	49	F	UNKNOWN	RRZZZZUSA
CHRISTINE	25	F	UNKNOWN	RRZZZZUSA
PHILIPPINE	15	F	CH	RRZZZZUSA
CHRISTIAN	8	M	CHILD	RRACDUUSA
ELISABETH	7	F	CHILD	RRACDUUSA
EVA	4	F	CHILD	RRACDUUSA
JOHANN	2	M	CHILD	RRACWPUSA
BARBARA	.06	F	INFANT	RRZZZZUSA
JACOB	24	M	FARMER	RRZZZZUSA
CAROLINE	24	F	UNKNOWN	RRZZZZUSA
CAHTARINA	.03	F	INFANT	RRZZZZUSA
ULLMER, JACOB	24	M	FARMER	RRZZZZUSA
CAROLINE	25	F	UNKNOWN	RRZZZZUSA
CATHARINE	2	F	CHILD	RRZZZZUSA
GOTTLIEB	.09	M	INFANT	RRZZZZUSA
SEILER, JACOB	56	M	FARMER	RRZZZZUSA
EVA	48	F	UNKNOWN	RRZZZZUSA
JACOB	28	M	FARMER	RRZZZZUSA
CATHERINA	20	F	UNKNOWN	RRZZZZUSA
LISABETH	18	F	CH	RRZZZZUSA
LINA	16	F	CH	RRZZZZUSA
GRETHE	8	F	CHILD	RRACBRUSA
GOTTLIEB	7	M	CHILD	RRZZZZUSA
LISE	6	F	CHILD	RRZZZZUSA
HIRSCH, JOSEF	37	M	FARMER	RRZZZZUSA
CATHARINA	36	F	UNKNOWN	RRZZZZUSA
LISBETH	15	F	CH	RRZZZZUSA
JOHANN	8	M	CHILD	RRZZZZUSA
JACOB	7	M	CHILD	RRZZZZUSA
LUDWIG	6	M	CHILD	RRAAKHUSA
CHRISTINE	4	F	CHILD	RRAAKHUSA
WAGNER, JOHANN	32	M	FARMER	RRAAKHUSA
MARIA	27	F	UNKNOWN	RRAAKHUSA
HEINRICH	4	M	CHILD	RRAAKHUSA
PAUL	.04	M	INFANT	RRAAKHUSA
ODENBACH, JOHANN	36	M	FARMER	RRZZZZUSA
ROSINA	34	F	UNKNOWN	RRZZZZUSA
JOHANN	8	M	CHILD	RRZZZZUSA
ELISABETH	7	F	CHILD	RRZZZZUSA
HEINRICH	4	M	CHILD	RRZZZZUSA
FRIEDRICH	2	M	CHILD	RRZZZZUSA
SCHMIDT, JACOB	43	M	FARMER	RRZZZZUSA
WILHELMINE	40	F	UNKNOWN	RRZZZZUSA
CAROLINE	15	F	UNKNOWN	RRZZZZUSA
JACOB	13	M	FARMER	RRZZZZUSA
CARL	8	M	CHILD	RRZZZZUSA
CHRISTIAN	7	M	CHILD	RRZZZZUSA
MICHAEL	4	M	CHILD	RRAAKHUSA
PETER	.09	M	INFANT	RRAAKHUSA
HEINRICHSON, HEINRICH	45	M	FARMER	RRAAKHUSA
CHRISTINE	43	F	UNKNOWN	RRAAKHUSA
ELEONORE	22	F	UNKNOWN	RRZZZZUSA
PAULINE	21	F	UNKNOWN	RRZZZZUSA
CHRISTINE	17	F	UNKNOWN	RRZZZZUSA
WILHELM	8	M	CHILD	RRZZZZUSA
MARIE	5	F	CHILD	RRZZZZUSA
ROSINE	2	F	CHILD	RRZZZZUSA
SEILER, FRIEDRICH	43	M	FARMER	RRZZZZUSA
MARGA.	41	F	UNKNOWN	RRZZZZUSA
MAGA.	16	F	CH	RRZZZZUSA
GOTTLIEB	14	M	FARMER	RRZZZZUSA
LISABETH	8	F	CHILD	RRZZZZUSA
JACOB	7	M	CHILD	RRZZZZUSA
CATHARINA	6	F	CHILD	RRZZZZUSA
JOHANNES	3	M	CHILD	RRZZZZUSA
HEINRICHSON, PETER	74	M	LABR	RRZZZZUSA

SHIP: WESTPHALIA

FROM: HAMBURG AND HAVRE
TO: NEW YORK
ARRIVED: 13 APRIL 1885

PASSENGER	AGE	SEX	OCCUPATION	PV RI VL DES
GLICK, ISAAC	47	M	DLR	RRAHTFUSA
GOLE, FRANZ	39	M	LABR	RRAHZSUSA
WILHELMINE	32	F	W	RRAHZSUSA
GUSTAV	5	M	CHILD	RRAHZSUSA
ANNA	.11	F	INFANT	RRAHZSUSA
KRZYKWA, MARAY	28	F	W	RRAHZSUSA
STANISLAUS	24	M	LABR	RRAHZSUSA
KOWALEWSKI, FELIX	.09	M	INFANT	RRAHZSUSA

SHIP: POLYNESIA

FROM: HAMBURG
TO: NEW YORK
ARRIVED: 14 APRIL 1885

PASSENGER	AGE	SEX	OCCUPATION	PV RI VL DES
MEWAZOWSKI, AND.	19	M	LABR	RRZZZZNY
MORKOZATIN, J.	23	M	LABR	RRZZZZNY
ZOLOWNA, VICTORIA	30	F	SGL	RRZZZZNY
PAULICH, PIETRO	25	M	LABR	PLZZZZCH
ROSA	25	F	W	PLZZZZCH
ROLLUCH, JESSE	25	M	LABR	PLZZZZCH
NOWACK, SAMUEL	25	M	W	PLZZZZCH
PLAVKOW, STANISL.	26	M	W	PLZZZZCH
JALIA	24	F	W	PLZZZZCH
LEGAN, CONRAD	24	M	LABR	PLZZZZCH
PAJAK, JAN	43	M	LABR	PLZZZZCH
ZING, WAZIG	50	M	LABR	PLZZZZCH
BORZIJEWSKI, JAN	52	M	LABR	PLZZZZCH
RONITZKI, PETER	37	M	LABR	PLZZZZNY
OZEIZOCK, FR.	38	M	LABR	PLZZZZNY
PITROWSKI, JOS.	48	M	LABR	PLZZZZNY
ROTKOWITZ, THS.	28	M	LABR	PLZZZZNY
ROVSDOWA, VICTA.	20	F	SGL	PLZZZZNY
BIRGAH, JOAN	33	M	LABR	PLZZZZNY
HELENE	28	F	W	PLZZZZNY
MOSES	7	F	CHILD	PLZZZZNY
LUTEN	6	M	CHILD	PLZZZZNY
JOSEPH	.07	M	INFANT	PLZZZZNY
BOCHADLER, JOSEPH	26	M	LABR	PLZZZZNY
GRADZIN, MILANE	35	F	W	PLZZZZNY
JEAN	4	M	CHILD	PLZZZZNY
REISKI, STANISL.	29	M	LABR	PLZZZZNY
LEKLA	24	F	W	PLZZZZNY
WAWZIN, REBRA	36	M	LABR	PLZZZZNY
MADUZA, JEAN	24	M	LABR	PLZZZZNY
DZIZA, ST.	23	M	LABR	PLZZZZNY
VINZENTE, BOWAR	40	M	LABR	PLZZZZNY
KODZAVA, PIETRO	18	M	LABR	PLZZZZNY
POWOJEK, JOREH	55	M	LABR	PLZZZZNY
TEDERKA, AND.	24	M	LABR	PLZZZZNY

PASSENGER	AGE	SEX	OCCUPATION	PRV	VIL	DES
KURZAWA, JOSEPH	38	M	FARMER	PL	ZZZZ	CH
BORONAWSKA, A.	19	M	FARMER	PL	ZZZZ	CH
JEDWICK, MARIA	28	F	WO	PL	ZZZZ	NY
JULIA	7	F	CHILD	PL	ZZZZ	NY
LUDWIG	4	M	CHILD	PL	ZZZZ	NY
OLESCHANSKI, W.	29	M	UNKNOWN	PL	ZZZZ	CH
POZDOL, MARIA	22	M	UNKNOWN	PL	ZZZZ	CH
DOMSKA, MARIA	22	F	WO	PL	ZZZZ	CH
BOCHNIA, CAROL.	7	F	CHILD	PL	ZZZZ	STL
BORCHARDH, HEINR.	30	M	LABR	PL	ZZZZ	STL
ULRIKE	28	F	W	PL	ZZZZ	STL
FRANZ	7	M	CHILD	PL	ZZZZ	STL
LAGE, ADOLPH	23	M	LABR	RR	ZZZZ	NY
GUTER, JOHANA	28	M	LABR	RR	ZZZZ	NY
SCHOENBROD, MARIA	27	F	W	RR	ZZZZ	NY
LEA	7	F	CHILD	RR	ZZZZ	NY
SOPHIE	6	F	CHILD	RR	ZZZZ	NY
DORA	3	F	CHILD	RR	ZZZZ	NY
NAUM	.06	M	INFANT	RR	ZZZZ	NY
MORDARSCH	30	M	UNKNOWN	RR	ZZZZ	CH
BORCHARDH, W.	2	M	CHILD	RR	ZZZZ	CH
KOSLA, RUNIGUND	11	F	CH	PL	ZZZZ	CH
JADVICE, AM.	7	M	CHILD	PL	ZZZZ	CH
KARZIAK, JADWIG	19	M	SGL	PL	ZZZZ	CH
LUDOMILLA	17	F	SGL	PL	ZZZZ	CH
BARAN, ANDREZ	20	M	LABR	PL	ZZZZ	CH
WANTUCH, WAZSIA	59	M	LABR	PL	ZZZZ	CH
STEINETZKIWICZ, JOS.	35	M	LABR	PL	ZZZZ	MIL
PETERS, AD.	33	M	LABR	PL	ZZZZ	MIL
MARIA	26	F	W	PL	ZZZZ	MIL
RUV.	6	M	CHILD	PL	ZZZZ	MIL
ADOLF	.08	M	INFANT	PL	ZZZZ	MIL
TALMITZ, ANTERSIC	20	F	TLR	RR	ZZZZ	CH
ROSANOWSKY, FR.	34	M	LABR	RR	ZZZZ	NY
MATALOWIS, FRANZ	35	M	LABR	RR	ZZZZ	NY
ROHIFHA, JOS.	25	M	LABR	RR	ZZZZ	NY
MARZIKOWITCH, JEAN	26	M	LABR	RR	ZZZZ	NY
MAZIGO, JOS.	22	M	LABR	RR	ZZZZ	NY
KRIZINSKI, ANT.	26	M	LABR	RR	ZZZZ	NY
DEDEWITSCH, G.	24	M	LABR	RR	ZZZZ	NY
JANKOFSKY, SL.	26	M	LABR	RR	ZZZZ	NY
BIREL, JOAN	24	M	LABR	RR	ZZZZ	NY

SHIP: SERVIA

FROM: LIVERPOOL AND QUEENSTOWN
TO: NEW YORK
ARRIVED: 14 APRIL 1885

PASSENGER	AGE	SEX	OCCUPATION	PRV	VIL	DES
MARTYN, MARTRIS	23	F	SVNT	RR	ZZZZ	USA
JOHNSON, MARTIN	40	M	TLR	FN	ZZZZ	USA
STAMBERGER, FRANK	45	M	TLR	FN	ZZZZ	USA
KAUTOLA, JOH.J.	49	M	UNKNOWN	FN	ZZZZ	USA
IKALA, JACOB-J.	31	M	LABR	FN	ZZZZ	USA
KAUGAS, JOH.E.	33	M	TNR	FN	ZZZZ	USA
KASKI, JOHAN	42	M	TNR	FN	ZZZZ	USA
SYKORA, WENZEL	42	M	LABR	PL	ZZZZ	USA
LEBZ, GOTHARD	61	M	GENT	RR	ZZZZ	USA

SHIP: GELLERT

FROM: HAMBURG
TO: NEW YORK
ARRIVED: 15 APRIL 1885

PASSENGER	AGE	SEX	OCCUPATION	PRV	VIL	DES
CYTROWSKI, ADAM	25	M	LABR	RR	ZZZZ	USA
BUDANOWICZ, ADAM	26	M	LABR	RR	ZZZZ	USA
GLADKOWSKI, ANTON	42	M	LABR	RR	ZZZZ	USA
JASINSKY, LUDWIG	21	M	STDNT	RR	ZZZZ	USA
DONKSCHA, PAUL	20	M	STDNT	RR	ZZZZ	USA
BRZSKIEWICZ, MICHAEL	19	M	LABR	RR	ZZZZ	USA
KARPOWICZ, EVA	24	F	W	RR	ZZZZ	USA
MARIE	.11	F	INFANT	RR	ZZZZ	USA
EISENBAUM, SAMUEL	26	M	LABR	RR	ZZZZ	USA
WACZKOWSKY, ANTON	27	M	LABR	RR	ZZZZ	USA
PROTROWSKY, VALENTIN	20	M	LABR	RR	ZZZZ	USA
MALLINOWSKI, JOSEF	25	M	LABR	RR	ZZZZ	USA
JAN	30	M	LABR	RR	ZZZZ	USA
LISESCKI, FRANZ	21	M	LABR	RR	ZZZZ	USA
ALEX, JOH.	30	M	LABR	RR	ZZZZ	USA
CEPJEJUS, MICH.	40	M	LABR	RR	ZZZZ	USA
SMOLINSKY, ANTON	18	M	LABR	RR	ZZZZ	USA
GISEFSKY, VALENTIN	20	M	LABR	RR	ZZZZ	USA
SCHIZERSFSKY, MARIANNA	18	F	SGL	RR	ZZZZ	USA
WA--O, JINDRO	52	M	LABR	RR	ZZZZ	USA
ZILINSKY, MICH.	13	M	LABR	RR	ZZZZ	USA
KRALA, ANNA	20	F	SGL	RR	ZZZZ	USA
DIRKS, FRIEDR.	50	M	LABR	RR	ZZZZ	USA
GUSTAV	22	M	LABR	RR	ZZZZ	USA
REINHOLD	18	M	LABR	RR	ZZZZ	USA
KRAL, JOSEF	22	M	LABR	RR	ZZZZ	USA
MORASAS, CARL	25	M	LABR	RR	ZZZZ	USA
HOCHA, JOH.	28	M	LABR	RR	ZZZZ	USA
SCHAFFER, ADAM	24	M	LABR	RR	ZZZZ	USA
ADAMEI--, ED.	24	M	LABR	RR	ZZZZ	USA
ROSENTHAL, MAX	19	M	STDNT	RR	ZZZZ	USA

SHIP: PENNLAND

FROM: ANTWERP
TO: NEW YORK
ARRIVED: 17 APRIL 1885

PASSENGER	AGE	SEX	OCCUPATION	PRV	VIL	DES
NEMITZ, AUG.	13	M	LABR	PL	ZZZZ	UNK
JUKALI, FES.	20	M	LABR	PL	ZZZZ	NY
ROSA	2	F	CHILD	PL	ZZZZ	NY
NIC, HUCKSCHER	45	M	UNKNOWN	RR	ZZZZ	NY
PODYMSKI, HERM.	29	M	CPTR	RR	ZZZZ	CH
MARIE	27	F	CPTR	RR	ZZZZ	CH
REINHOLD	.11	F	INFANT	RR	ZZZZ	CH
ZUTKOWSKI, WILH.	35	M	CPTR	RR	ZZZZ	CH

SHIP: BOHEMIA

FROM: HAMBURG
TO: NEW YORK
ARRIVED: 18 APRIL 1885

PASSENGER	AGE	SEX	OCCUPATION	PRV	VIL	DES
LEWANDOWSKY, FRANZ	21	M	LABR	RR	ZZZZ	USA
WEIHER, GUSTAV	26	M	FARMER	RR	AHTF	USA
SCHNEIDER, LUDWIG	50	M	LABR	RR	AHZS	USA
THEODOR	24	M	LABR	RR	AHZS	USA
AUGUST	18	M	LABR	RR	AHZS	USA

PASSENGER	AGE	SEX	OCCUPATION	PRV	VIL	DES
SHIP: CALIFORNIA						
FROM: HAMBURG						
TO: NEW YORK						
ARRIVED: 18 APRIL 1885						
SKURA, STANISLAUS	24	M	LABR	PL	ZZZZ	CH
MUNDROCK, MARIE	20	F	SGL	PL	ZZZZ	CH
CHRIENZECK, VOJCEH	28	M	LABR	PL	ZZZZ	CH
CATHARINA	46	F	W	PL	ZZZZ	CH
BRZACK, JOS.	25	M	LABR	PL	ZZZZ	CH
KRAWJEZT, SIMON	52	M	LABR	PL	ZZZZ	CH
CAHTARINA	45	F	W	PL	ZZZZ	CH
JOHEMNA	7	F	CHILD	PL	ZZZZ	CH
SIMON	.07	M	INFANT	PL	ZZZZ	CH
CHANICLEWITZ, FRANZ	40	M	LABR	PL	ZZZZ	CH
KOSSIACK, JAN	16	M	LABR	PL	ZZZZ	NY
BOBITZ, PETRESELLA	22	F	SGL	PL	ZZZZ	NY
CAROL, MICTOS	26	M	LABR	PL	ZZZZ	NY
SHIP: EMS						
FROM: BREMEN						
TO: NEW YORK						
ARRIVED: 18 APRIL 1885						
HEER, DANIEL	30	M	LABR	PL	AFWJ	USA
DUFFERT, DANIEL	23	M	LABR	PL	AFWJ	USA
KOWALSKI, PETER	36	M	LABR	RR	ZZZZ	USA
GENTSCH, IDA	37	F	NN	RR	ZZZZ	USA
ELISE	9	F	CHILD	RR	ZZZZ	USA
HEDWIG	8	F	CHILD	RR	ZZZZ	USA
ARTHUR	5	M	CHILD	RR	ZZZZ	USA
MULZOF, MICHAL	18	M	LABR	RR	ZZZZ	USA
TREFTS, JOHANN	26	M	FARMER	RR	ZZZZ	USA
FRIEDERICKE	24	F	NN	RR	ZZZZ	USA
SHIP: STATE OF INDIANA						
FROM: GLASGOW AND LARNE						
TO: NEW YORK						
ARRIVED: 18 APRIL 1885						
GUTFARB, MARCUS	20	M	PDLR	RR	ZZZZ	USA
BAD, HIRSCH	20	M	PDLR	RR	ZZZZ	USA
SELIGSOHN, WOLF	29	M	PDLR	RR	AHTF	USA
MARINOWSKY, KASIMIR	22	M	LABR	RR	ACBF	USA
STELLMANDA, KASIMIR	31	M	LABR	RR	ACBF	USA
SANDOLE, KASIMIR	33	M	LABR	RR	ZZZZ	USA
SHIP: CELTIC						
FROM: LIVERPOOL AND QUEENSTOWN						
TO: NEW YORK						
ARRIVED: 20 APRIL 1885						
JACOBSWITZ, JACOB	25	M	TLR	RR	ADAX	USA
EMMA	30	F	W	RR	ADAX	USA
HYAM	11	M	CH	RR	ADAX	USA
JOSEPH	10	M	CH	RR	ADAX	USA
JULIE	9	F	CHILD	RR	ADAX	USA
RACHAEL	8	F	CHILD	RR	ADAX	USA
ANNETE	6	F	CHILD	RR	ADAX	USA
SARAH	4	F	CHILD	RR	ADAX	USA
ROSA	1	F	CHILD	RR	ADAX	USA
DAVY	.01	M	INFANT	RR	ADAX	USA
SHIP: HOHENZOLLEN						
FROM: BREMEN						
TO: NEW YORK						
ARRIVED: 20 APRIL 1885						
RIEG, AUGUST	31	M	LABR	RR	ZZZZ	USA
AUGUSTA	28	F	W	RR	ZZZZ	USA
AUGUSTA	8	F	CHILD	RR	ZZZZ	USA
EMILIE	17	F	NN	RR	ZZZZ	USA
WERZBINSKA, EMILIE	35	F	W	RR	AHVU	USA
JOSEF	8	M	CHILD	RR	AHVU	USA
LADISL.	5	M	CHILD	RR	AHVU	USA
STANISL.	4	M	CHILD	RR	AHVU	USA
STASCHA	.10	M	INFANT	RR	AHVU	USA
BEDNARSKI, JACOB	20	M	MCHT	RR	ZZZZ	USA
MARIANNE	23	F	NN	RR	ZZZZ	USA
MARZIPEWSKY, MARGOTT	55	M	LABR	RR	AHWD	USA
STACTOWIAK, JOSEF	28	M	LABR	RR	AHWD	USA
STANISLAWA	19	F	W	RR	AHWD	USA
SHIP: MARTHA						
FROM: UNKNOWN						
TO: NEW YORK						
ARRIVED: 20 APRIL 1885						
KENDROW, JOSEPH	28	M	LABR	RR	AHWD	CH
SOPHIA	24	F	SGL	RR	AHWD	CH
CYLKOWSKI, JOHN	57	M	LABR	RR	AHWD	CH
IGNACY	21	M	LABR	RR	AHWD	CH
VOJTIN, GUSTAV	26	M	LABR	RR	AHWD	IA
ANDERSON, ERICK	25	M	LABR	RR	AHWD	MI
SHIP: PARENTI						
FROM: CAPE TOWN						
TO: NEW YORK						
ARRIVED: 22 APRIL 1885						
FRIELMS, JOHAN-CARL	68	M	FARMER	RR	ZZZZ	USA
MARIA-CATHARINA	56	F	WO	RR	ZZZZ	USA
SOPHIA	31	F	WO	RR	ZZZZ	USA
MARIA-CATHARINA	32	F	WO	RR	ZZZZ	USA
ANA-LISABETH	20	F	WO	RR	ZZZZ	USA
CATARINA-ELISABETH	18	F	CH	RR	ZZZZ	USA
MARIA-ELISABETH	50	F	WO	RR	ZZZZ	USA
JOHAN-FREDERICH	35	M	FARMER	RR	ZZZZ	USA
CHRISTIAN	10	M	CH	RR	ZZZZ	USA
ANA-CATHARINA	8	F	CHILD	RR	ZZZZ	USA
FREDERICK	6	M	CHILD	RR	ZZZZ	USA
MARIA-CATHARINA	4	F	CHILD	RR	ZZZZ	USA

PASSENGER	AGE	SEX	OCCUPATION	PRIV	VIL	DES
CARL-FREDERICK	2	M	CHILD	RR	ZZZZ	USA
CATHARINA-ELISABETH	32	F	WO	RR	ZZZZ	USA
HENNING, MARIA	24	F	WO	RR	ZZZZ	UNK
HEINNING, BERTHA	2	F	CHILD	RR	ZZZZ	UNK

SHIP: SUEVIA

FROM: HAMBURG
TO: NEW YORK
ARRIVED: 22 APRIL 1885

PASSENGER	AGE	SEX	OCCUPATION	PRIV	VIL	DES
PUCH, ISAAC	24	M	DLR	RRAH	VU	USA
RACZKOWSKY, VALENTIN	20	M	LABR	RRAH	UI	USA
PLITTA, IGNATZ	29	M	LABR	RRAH	SU	USA
KOPKA, WLADISL.	26	M	LABR	RRAH	SU	USA
MARIANNE	24	F	W	RRAH	SU	USA
KWIATKOWSKI, JOH.	25	M	LABR	RRAH	ZS	USA
ANNA	17	F	SGL	RRAH	ZS	USA
WYDRACHOWSKI, JOSEF	18	M	LABR	RRAH	SV	USA

SHIP: ALSATIA

FROM: GLASGOW AND MOVILLE
TO: NEW YORK
ARRIVED: 23 APRIL 1885

PASSENGER	AGE	SEX	OCCUPATION	PRIV	VIL	DES
SILVERMAN, ISAAC	23	M	LABR	RR	ZZZZ	USA
J.MS	20	F	W	RR	ZZZZ	USA
BENJ.	.08	M	INFANT	RR	ZZZZ	USA
HARRIS, LEVI	18	M	LABR	RR	ZZZZ	USA

SHIP: BALTIC

FROM: LIVERPOOL AND QUEENSTOWN
TO: NEW YORK
ARRIVED: 24 APRIL 1885

PASSENGER	AGE	SEX	OCCUPATION	PRIV	VIL	DES
WOENSOFSKY, MOSES	30	M	GENT	RR	ZZZZ	USA
U-MRS	24	F	W	RR	ZZZZ	USA
M.	23	F	SP	RR	ZZZZ	USA
MST	4	M	CHILD	RR	ZZZZ	USA

SHIP: RHYNLAND

FROM: ANTWERP
TO: NEW YORK
ARRIVED: 24 APRIL 1885

PASSENGER	AGE	SEX	OCCUPATION	PRIV	VIL	DES
KIBRICK, A.	37	M	DT	RR	ZZZZ	USA
KNICMINSKI, ANT.	22	M	FARMER	RR	ZZZZ	UNK
GERT.	20	F	UNKNOWN	RR	ZZZZ	UNK
STANISL.	.06	M	INFANT	RR	ZZZZ	UNK
LAZNECZAK, AND.	18	M	FARMER	RR	ZZZZ	UNK
PAWLOWSKA, CATH.	38	F	FARMER	RRAF	WJ	CH
RUD.	16	M	CH	RRAF	WJ	CH
ANNA	9	F	CHILD	RRAF	WJ	CH
PAUL	8	M	CHILD	RRAF	WJ	CH
WILL, FRIED	32	M	FARMER	RR	ZZZZ	MIL
BERTHA	35	F	UNKNOWN	RR	ZZZZ	MIL
GUST.	9	M	CHILD	RR	ZZZZ	MIL
OTTO	7	M	CHILD	RR	ZZZZ	MIL
EMIL	4	M	CHILD	RR	ZZZZ	MIL
REBOWSKI, MATS	44	M	LABR	RR	ZZZZ	MIL
TRASZEWSKI, JAS.	47	M	FARMER	RRAF	WJ	NY
ANNA	45	F	UNKNOWN	RRAF	WJ	NY
ANT.	14	M	CH	RRAF	WJ	NY
ALOIZAK	3	M	CHILD	RRAF	WJ	NY
CONST.	4	M	CHILD	RRAF	WJ	NY
DOMBLOWSKI, W.	55	M	CPTR	RR	ZZZZ	PHI
M.	54	F	UNKNOWN	RR	ZZZZ	PHI
PRZOZOWSKI, J.	31	M	LABR	RR	ZZZZ	NY
BRZONA, N.	25	M	LABR	RR	ZZZZ	NY
PLOTZINSKI, J.	40	M	LABR	RR	ZZZZ	NY
KA.	50	F	UNKNOWN	RR	ZZZZ	NY
JULA.	18	F	CH	RR	ZZZZ	NY
FLASZINSKA, JOS.	23	M	LABR	RRAH	OO	NY
JUL.	2	F	CHILD	RRAH	OO	NY
STAW	00	M	LABR	RRAH	OO	NY
SULINCKA, MA.	1	F	CHILD	RRAH	OO	NY
MEHECWZEWSKA, MA.	22	F	UNKNOWN	RRAF	WJ	NY
--K.	00	M	INF	RRAF	WJ	NY
LOEMAN, M.	27	F	UNKNOWN	RR	ZZZZ	NY
MA.	22	F	UNKNOWN	RR	ZZZZ	NY
KUROWSKI, E.	25	M	LABR	RR	ZZZZ	NY
JANCZAC, MINE	25	M	LABR	RR	ZZZZ	NY
MA.	20	F	UNKNOWN	RR	ZZZZ	NY
BAKOWSKA, J.J	15	M	LABR	RRAG	RT	USA
FIBIKOSKA, M.	25	F	SVNT	RRAG	RT	UNK
NIEWOLOK, J.	21	F	SVNT	RR	ZZZZ	MIL
M.	20	F	SVNT	RR	ZZZZ	MIL
WINDOZSKI, J.	40	M	SMH	RR	ZZZZ	MIL
M.	40	F	UNKNOWN	RR	ZZZZ	MIL
A.	7	M	CHILD	RR	ZZZZ	MIL
A.	3	F	CHILD	RR	ZZZZ	MIL
M.	2	F	CHILD	RR	ZZZZ	MIL
A.	00	M	INF	RR	ZZZZ	MIL
KWARZINSKI, A.	21	M	LABR	RR	ZZZZ	CH
GALZ, J.	21	M	LABR	RR	ZZZZ	MIL
KURECKI, FR.	28	M	LABR	RR	ZZZZ	NY
THEES, M.	42	F	CH	RR	ZZZZ	NY
HADINACK, JOH.	28	M	FARMER	RR	ZZZZ	PRI
CATH.	20	F	FARMER	RR	ZZZZ	PRI
CATH.	3	F	CHILD	RR	ZZZZ	PRI
LUDW.	.06	M	INFANT	RR	ZZZZ	PRI
JANKOWSKA, MA.	22	F	UNKNOWN	RR	ZZZZ	NY

SHIP: DONAU

FROM: BREMEN
TO: NEW YORK
ARRIVED: 25 APRIL 1885

PASSENGER	AGE	SEX	OCCUPATION	PRIV	VIL	DES
MALOBPSCHE, MART.	30	M	LABR	RR	ZZZZ	USA
PAULINE	26	F	W	RR	ZZZZ	USA
MARIANNE	.11	F	INFANT	RR	ZZZZ	USA
SAWITZKA, JADWIGA	16	F	NN	RR	ZZZZ	USA
FEIST, FRANZ	53	M	FARMER	RR	ZZZZ	USA
BARB.	53	F	W	RR	ZZZZ	USA
FRANCISCA	16	F	CH	RR	ZZZZ	USA
JOSEPH	10	M	CH	RR	ZZZZ	USA
PETER	9	M	CHILD	RR	ZZZZ	USA
GUTMULLER, LUDW.	50	M	FARMER	RR	ZZZZ	USA
CATH.	49	F	W	RR	ZZZZ	USA
MARG.	14	F	CH	RR	ZZZZ	USA
MAGD.	9	F	CHILD	RR	ZZZZ	USA

PASSENGER	AGE	SEX	OCCUPATION	PRV VIL DES
ICH.	23	M	FARMER	RRZZZZUSA
CATH.	23	F	W	RRZZZZUSA
WALL, JACOB	28	M	FARMER	RRZZZZUSA
ANNA	30	F	W	RRZZZZUSA
FRIEDERIKE	1	F	CHILD	RRZZZZUSA
KRAIN, FRIEDR.	28	M	FARMER	RRZZZZUSA
MARG.	21	F	W	RRZZZZUSA
MARIA	3	F	CHILD	RRZZZZUSA
CHRISTINA	1	F	CHILD	RRZZZZUSA
DAROTHEA	19	F	NN	RRZZZZUSA
POLLINGER, JACOB	27	M	FARMER	RRZZZZUSA
CATH.	24	F	W	RRZZZZUSA
MERGELL, JACOB	26	M	FARMER	RRZZZZUSA
BARB.	24	F	W	RRZZZZUSA
ELISAB.	1	F	CHILD	RRZZZZUSA
CATH.	.09	F	INFANT	RRZZZZUSA
KRAIN, JACOB	26	M	FARMER	RRZZZZUSA
GRETE	25	F	W	RRZZZZUSA
CAROL.	2	F	CHILD	RRZZZZUSA
CATH.	.10	F	INFANT	RRZZZZUSA
REICH, EVA	20	F	NN	RRZZZZUSA
MEIER, JAC.	26	M	FARMER	RRZZZZUSA
CATH.	24	F	W	RRZZZZUSA
EVA	1	F	CHILD	RRZZZZUSA
CATH.	.02	F	INFANT	RRZZZZUSA
BENG, JACOB	26	M	BCHR	RRZZZZUSA
CHRISTINE	26	F	W	RRZZZZUSA
MAGD.	3	F	CHILD	RRZZZZUSA
CHRISTINA	.11	F	INFANT	RRZZZZUSA
STRACH, FEIBAH	11	F	NN	RRZZZZUSA
WAGEMANN, CHRIST.	29	M	LABR	RRZZZZUSA
MARG.	25	F	W	RRZZZZUSA
ADOLPH	1	M	CHILD	RRZZZZUSA
EHRENMANN, JAC.	28	M	LABR	RRZZZZUSA
THERESE	26	F	W	RRZZZZUSA
CHRIST.	2	M	CHILD	RRZZZZUSA
CATH.	.04	F	INFANT	RRZZZZUSA
MAGD.	22	F	NN	RRZZZZUSA
CHRISTIAN	9	M	CHILD	RRZZZZUSA
KLEIN, PETER	45	M	FARMER	RRZZZZUSA
CATH.	40	F	W	RRZZZZUSA
JOH.	19	M	FARMER	RRZZZZUSA
CATH.	14	F	CH	RRZZZZUSA
MARG.	14	F	CH	RRZZZZUSA
MAGD.	9	F	CHILD	RRZZZZUSA
ROLINA	7	F	CHILD	RRZZZZUSA
JACOB	4	M	CHILD	RRZZZZUSA
BARB.	2	F	CHILD	RRZZZZUSA
MARIA	.06	F	INFANT	RRZZZZUSA
JOB, ICH.	23	M	FARMER	RRZZZZUSA
CAROL.	23	F	W	RRZZZZUSA
CATH.	2	F	CHILD	RRZZZZUSA
JACOB	.06	M	INFANT	RRZZZZUSA
MELAF, ICH.	22	M	FARMER	RRZZZZUSA
CHRISTINE	23	F	W	RRZZZZUSA
BENZ, FRIEDR.	52	M	FARMER	RRZZZZUSA
ELISAB.	40	F	W	RRZZZZUSA
FRIEDR.	19	M	FARMER	RRZZZZUSA
BARB.	22	F	W	RRZZZZUSA
ELISAB.	9	F	CHILD	RRZZZZUSA
CHRISTINA	7	F	CHILD	RRZZZZUSA
GEORG	4	M	CHILD	RRZZZZUSA
JOHANN	1	M	CHILD	RRZZZZUSA
THUM, FRIEDR.	28	M	CPTR	RRZZZZUSA
CATH.	21	F	W	RRZZZZUSA
FRIEDR.	.11	M	INFANT	RRZZZZUSA
EBERHANDT, GEORG	32	M	LABR	RRZZZZUSA
MARG.	27	F	W	RRZZZZUSA
CATH.	.11	F	INFANT	RRZZZZUSA
CATH.	79	F	NN	RRZZZZUSA

SHIP: EIDER

FROM: BREMEN AND SOUTHAMPTON
TO: NEW YORK
ARRIVED: 25 APRIL 1885

PASSENGER	AGE	SEX	OCCUPATION	PRV VIL DES
WERBITZKY, MARTIN	28	M	LABR	RRZZZZUSA
KUNDERT, ANDREAS	40	M	LABR	RRZZZZUSA
CATH.	36	F	W	RRZZZZUSA
CATH.	14	F	NN	RRZZZZUSA
SCHLAT, MICHAEL	45	M	FARMER	RRZZZZUSA
MAGD.	41	F	W	RRZZZZUSA
FRIEDR.	17	M	FARMER	RRZZZZUSA
JACOB	10	M	CH	RRZZZZUSA
GEORG.	7	M	CHILD	RRZZZZUSA
JOHANN	6	M	CHILD	RRZZZZUSA
CATH.	16	F	NN	RRZZZZUSA
MAGD.	4	F	CHILD	RRZZZZUSA
SCHMIDT, CONRAD	23	M	LABR	RRZZZZUSA
CATH.	23	F	W	RRZZZZUSA
LUDWIG	.11	M	INFANT	RRZZZZUSA
ADAM, JACOB	39	M	LABR	RRZZZZUSA
CHRIST.	38	F	W	RRZZZZUSA
JACOB	11	M	CH	RRZZZZUSA
CATH.	7	F	CHILD	RRZZZZUSA
GEORG	6	M	CHILD	RRZZZZUSA
JOHANN	4	M	CHILD	RRZZZZUSA
FRIEDR.	.10	M	INFANT	RRZZZZUSA
HERTEL, JACOB	45	M	LABR	RRZZZZUSA
ROSINA	41	F	W	RRZZZZUSA
JACOB	19	M	LABR	RRZZZZUSA
FRIEDR.	17	M	LABR	RRZZZZUSA
JOHANN	13	M	NN	RRZZZZUSA
CHRIST.	6	M	CHILD	RRZZZZUSA
CARL	.06	M	INFANT	RRZZZZUSA
CATH.	16	F	NN	RRZZZZUSA
FRIEDR.	7	F	CHILD	RRZZZZUSA
ROSINA	4	F	CHILD	RRZZZZUSA
CHRISTINA	.11	F	INFANT	RRZZZZUSA
KIEBLER, ADAM	32	M	LABR	RRZZZZUSA
CHRIST.	30	F	W	RRZZZZUSA
CHRIST.	7	F	CHILD	RRZZZZUSA
CATHARINA	6	F	CHILD	RRZZZZUSA
DAVID	2	M	CHILD	RRZZZZUSA
JOHANNES	.11	M	INFANT	RRZZZZUSA
ERLENBAUSCH, MAGD.	32	F	W	RRZZZZUSA
CHRIST.	7	F	CHILD	RRZZZZUSA
FRIEDR.	6	M	CHILD	RRZZZZUSA
MAGD.	4	F	CHILD	RRZZZZUSA
FRIEDK.	.11	F	INFANT	RRZZZZUSA
BECHTOLDT, FRIEDR.	26	M	FARMER	RRZZZZUSA
CATH.	23	F	W	RRZZZZUSA
CATH.	.11	F	INFANT	RRZZZZUSA
CHRIST.	.01	F	INFANT	RRZZZZUSA
SANTER, BERNH.	40	M	FARMER	RRZZZZUSA
CHRIST.	36	F	W	RRZZZZUSA
CHRIST.	16	F	NN	RRZZZZUSA
CATH.	13	F	NN	RRZZZZUSA
GRETE	10	F	CH	RRZZZZUSA
MAGD.	7	F	CHILD	RRZZZZUSA
JOHANN	6	M	CHILD	RRZZZZUSA
BARB.	5	F	CHILD	RRZZZZUSA
LOUISE	3	F	CHILD	RRZZZZUSA
EBERHARD	.11	M	INFANT	RRZZZZUSA
KUNDERT, JACOB	7	M	CHILD	RRZZZZUSA
KLEIN, FRIEDR.	51	M	FARMER	RRZZZZUSA
BARB.	43	F	W	RRZZZZUSA
JOHANN	20	M	FARMER	RRZZZZUSA
EDWARD	18	M	FARMER	RRZZZZUSA
FRIEDR.	.11	M	INFANT	RRZZZZUSA
ROSINE	4	F	CHILD	RRZZZZUSA

PASSENGER	AGE	SEX	OCCUPATION	PRIV	VIL	DES

SHIP: LESSING

FROM: HAMBURG AND HAVRE
TO: NEW YORK
ARRIVED: 25 APRIL 1885

PASSENGER	AGE	SEX	OCCUPATION	PV		DES
STIPPELMANN, ISAAC	50	M	UNKNOWN	RR	AHSX	USA
HENE	35	F	W	RR	AHSX	USA
HECHT, JOSEPH	30	M	LABR	RR	AFVG	USA
SABIEZYNSKA, MARIANNE	30	F	W	RR	AHZT	USA
ANNA	9	F	CHILD	RR	AHZT	USA
MARIANNE	8	F	CHILD	RR	AHZT	USA
LICHTMANN, G.	29	M	LABR	RR	AHTF	USA
KOSZERKIEWICZ, ABRAM	43	M	LABR	RR	AHUF	USA
HEINIG, FRANZ	31	M	MSN	RR	ZZZZ	USA
EMMA	4	F	CHILD	RR	ZZZZ	USA
CLARA	3	F	CHILD	RR	ZZZZ	USA
CHAUS, ANTON	16	M	LABR	RR	ZZZZ	USA
SOKOLOWSKY, FRANZ	24	M	LABR	RR	AHYC	USA
HANNKO, AUGUST	40	M	LABR	RR	AHYC	USA
SLAJINSKI, JOSEF	25	M	LABR	RR	AHYC	USA
ARONWITZ, JANKEL	45	M	FARMER	RR	AHSA	USA
ADAMSKI, WLADISL.	23	M	LABR	RR	AHWB	USA
RESKOWSKI, CONSTANTIN	26	M	LABR	RR	ZZZZ	USA
STOLZ, ANTON	25	M	LABR	RR	ZZZZ	USA
JANKOWSKI, JAN	42	M	LABR	RR	AHZT	USA
DOBLANSKI, ANDRZY	20	M	LABR	RR	ZZZZ	USA
JABLONSKY, JAN	26	M	LABR	RR	ZZZZ	USA
BYCZINSKI, ADOLPH	40	M	LABR	RR	AHUF	USA
CHORUSCH, JOSEPH	19	M	LABR	RR	AHUF	USA
JANKOWSKA, HELENE	25	F	SGL	RR	AFWJ	USA
SLAWICKA, EVA	21	F	SGL	RR	AHVE	USA
MARIE	54	F	W	RR	AHVE	USA
JANKOWSKI, ANTON	17	M	MCHT	RR	AFWJ	USA
CHSAN, ABRAHAM	30	M	MCHT	RR	ZZZZ	USA
KLEINER, ESTHER	30	F	W	RR	AHXQ	USA
SARA	9	F	CHILD	RR	AHXQ	USA
GETTE	7	F	CHILD	RR	AHXQ	USA
GOLDE	1	F	CHILD	RR	AHXQ	USA
JACOB	.05	M	INFANT	RR	AHXQ	USA
MATECKA, VERINIKA	26	F	W	RR	AHYC	USA
FRANZISKA	20	F	SGL	RR	AHYC	USA
MARIANNE	17	F	SGL	RR	AHYC	USA
FELIX	.11	M	INFANT	RR	AHYC	USA
BRUMMER, JANKEL	35	M	LABR	RR	AHWQ	USA
GOLDFARB, ARON	18	M	DLR	RR	AHQU	USA

SHIP: STATE OF ALABAMA

FROM: GLASGOW AND LARNE
TO: NEW YORK
ARRIVED: 25 APRIL 1885

PASSENGER	AGE	SEX	OCCUPATION	PV		DES
AUGUSTIN, C.	55	M	INKP	RR	ZZZZ	NY
FYZMADO, U	26	M	LABR	RR	ZZZZ	NY
HANSEL, JOH.	35	M	INKP	RR	ZZZZ	NY
HORN, ARTHUR	25	M	SHPKR	RR	ZZZZ	NY
JANKOWITZ, M.	20	M	CL	RR	ZZZZ	NY
NITKIN, L.	17	M	CL	RR	ZZZZ	NY
RADRUMIES, M.	45	M	LABR	RR	ZZZZ	NY
WOGEL, DAVID	20	M	TLR	RR	ZZZZ	NY
WITKALRAK, JAN	35	M	LABR	RR	ZZZZ	PHI
ESBILLA	34	F	W	RR	ZZZZ	PHI
ANTONIE	8	F	CHILD	RR	ZZZZ	PHI
LUDWIG	5	M	CHILD	RR	ZZZZ	PHI
THOMAS	00	M	NN	RR	ZZZZ	PHI
FRANZISKA	.03	F	INFANT	RR	ZZZZ	PHI

SHIP: RUGIA

FROM: HAMBURG
TO: NEW YORK
ARRIVED: 28 APRIL 1885

PASSENGER	AGE	SEX	OCCUPATION	PV		DES
CHOMICOVO, MICHALINE	26	F	SGL	RR	ZZZZ	USA
SAKOVICOCH, JOSEFA	26	F	W	RR	ZZZZ	USA
EMILIE	3	F	CHILD	RR	ZZZZ	USA
DRILONG, STANISL.	19	M	LABR	RR	ZZZZ	USA
SAVINSKY, ANTON	22	M	LABR	RR	ZZZZ	USA
KRIVECKY, VINCENTE	20	M	LABR	RR	ZZZZ	USA
CZEZAITIS, MARIANNE	18	F	SGL	RR	ZZZZ	USA
JANKOWSKI, BERNARD	23	M	LABR	RR	ZZZZ	USA
SCHUSTA, VERONICA	26	F	W	RR	ZZZZ	USA
FRANZ	.11	M	INFANT	RR	ZZZZ	USA
SIERACZKA, ANTONIA	20	F	SGL	RR	ZZZZ	USA
MEYER, JAN	36	M	LABR	RR	ZZZZ	USA
JOSEFA	27	F	W	RR	ZZZZ	USA
CONSTANTIN	7	M	CHILD	RR	ZZZZ	USA
EVA	1	F	CHILD	RR	ZZZZ	USA
WACHS, MORITZ	21	M	LABR	RR	ZZZZ	USA
KAROSCH, EVYRA	23	M	LABR	RR	ZZZZ	USA
REIN, MAX	21	M	DLR	RR	ZZZZ	USA
PAULINE	20	F	W	RR	ZZZZ	USA
DOMBROWSKY, FRANZ	19	M	LABR	RR	ZZZZ	USA
LEVITAN, CHAIM	24	M	DLR	RR	ZZZZ	USA
KATZ, ALTER	26	M	MUSN	RR	ZZZZ	USA
KETHA, WALCK	22	M	LABR	RR	ZZZZ	USA
DRZONKIEWSKI, ANTON	26	M	LABR	RR	ZZZZ	USA
KURILOWSKI, MARIANNE	8	F	CHILD	RR	ZZZZ	USA
DEMBROWSKI, ROSA	23	F	W	RR	ZZZZ	USA
MARY	2	F	CHILD	RR	ZZZZ	USA
ROSENBAUM, HERSCH	14	M	LABR	RR	ZZZZ	USA
LEPNIZKI, DAVID	30	M	LABR	RR	ZZZZ	USA
MELTZER, ISAAC	19	M	DLR	RR	ZZZZ	USA
ZUCKERMANN, ABRAH.	24	M	LABR	RR	ZZZZ	USA
PVEKARSCH, JOSEF	23	M	LABR	RR	ZZZZ	USA
ROMANOWSKI, JOSEF	18	M	LABR	RR	ZZZZ	USA
WOLTOLEWITZ, ANTON	50	M	LABR	RR	ZZZZ	USA
SEWOK, ANTON	20	M	LABR	RR	ZZZZ	USA
HEFZEL, JURE	33	M	LABR	RR	ZZZZ	USA
DOLEOS, ANNA	20	F	SGL	RR	ZZZZ	USA
IVAN, JURE	16	M	LABR	RR	ZZZZ	USA
SZVINZEWSKI, STANISL.	21	M	LABR	RR	ZZZZ	USA
MOSCHLEWSKI, MOSES	15	M	TLR	RR	ZZZZ	USA
GOLDSTEIN, HANCHEN	9	F	CHILD	RR	ZZZZ	USA
TWINE	6	F	CHILD	RR	ZZZZ	USA
LEWITH, MARIE	30	F	W	RR	ZZZZ	USA
SARA	9	F	CHILD	RR	ZZZZ	USA
MOSES	8	M	CHILD	RR	ZZZZ	USA
ISAAC	6	M	CHILD	RR	ZZZZ	USA
ANNA	4	F	CHILD	RR	ZZZZ	USA
REISEL	.03	M	INFANT	RR	ZZZZ	USA
FISCHBEIN, JONAS	27	M	LABR	RR	ZZZZ	USA
RIWKE	27	F	W	RR	ZZZZ	USA
SPRINZE	.11	F	INFANT	RR	ZZZZ	USA
WIERZBICKI, CHAIM	20	M	LABR	RR	ZZZZ	USA
LAZRES, MAYER	19	M	TLR	RR	ZZZZ	USA
SEFEN, SALOMON	36	M	LABR	RR	ZZZZ	USA
FRIEDMANN, NAFTALI	35	M	LABR	RR	ZZZZ	USA
LADOWSKY, JOSEPH	27	M	LABR	RR	ZZZZ	USA
SUPKEWICH, PESACH	35	M	LABR	RR	ZZZZ	USA
ISKOWSKU, ISAAC	18	M	LABR	RR	ZZZZ	USA
BARRAN, ARON	18	M	LABR	RR	ZZZZ	USA
OKIM, PAUL	18	M	LABR	RR	ZZZZ	USA
CHALETZKY, JOSEF	36	M	LABR	RR	ZZZZ	USA
HERMANN, ISAAC	23	M	LABR	RR	ZZZZ	USA
GOTTDIENER, RAZAR	25	M	LABR	RR	ZZZZ	USA
FEIMANN, ELIAS	16	M	LABR	RR	ZZZZ	USA
RUDZINSKI, PIOTR	32	M	LABR	RR	ZZZZ	USA
SLOMANSKI, ICHON	26	M	LABR	RR	ZZZZ	USA
SREDNITZKY, MORDCHE	18	M	LABR	RR	ZZZZ	USA
RINKOWSKY, ICKO	23	M	LABR	RR	ZZZZ	USA

PASSENGER	AGE	SEX	OCCUPATION	PRV	VIL	DES
FRIEDMANN, BENJAMIN	23	M	LABR	RR	ZZZZ	USA
GOTTLIEB, CHAIM	27	M	LABR	RR	ZZZZ	USA
RINKOWSKY, GEDALIA	27	F	SGL	RR	ZZZZ	USA
JACZUNSKI, VICTOR	27	M	LABR	RR	ZZZZ	USA
GAJEWSKI, STANISLAW	28	M	LABR	RR	ZZZZ	USA
MIROWNA, MARIANNE	18	F	SGL	RR	ZZZZ	USA
ICKOWSKY, ABR.	18	M	LABR	RR	ZZZZ	USA
LUZINER, ABR.	43	M	LABR	RR	ZZZZ	USA
BENDER, PHILIPP	26	M	FARMER	RR	ZZZZ	USA
ELISAB.	24	F	W	RR	ZZZZ	USA
JACOB	3	M	CHILD	RR	ZZZZ	USA
CATH.	.11	F	INFANT	RR	ZZZZ	USA
CAROL.	.01	F	INFANT	RR	ZZZZ	USA
FRIEDR.	47	M	LABR	RR	ZZZZ	USA
CATH.	47	F	W	RR	ZZZZ	USA
MARTIN	24	M	CH	RR	ZZZZ	USA
CATH.	23	F	CH	RR	ZZZZ	USA
JOH.	22	M	CH	RR	ZZZZ	USA
CAROL.	20	F	CH	RR	ZZZZ	USA
CATH.	11	F	CH	RR	ZZZZ	USA
PHILIPP	10	M	CH	RR	ZZZZ	USA
HENBEL, JOHANN	27	M	LABR	RR	ZZZZ	USA
CATH.	24	F	W	RR	ZZZZ	USA
FRIEDR.	3	F	CHILD	RR	ZZZZ	USA
KETTLING, GEORG	48	M	LABR	RR	ZZZZ	USA
MARIE	45	F	W	RR	ZZZZ	USA
MARG.	19	F	CH	RR	ZZZZ	USA
ELISAB.	17	F	CH	RR	ZZZZ	USA
GEORG	4	M	CHILD	RR	ZZZZ	USA
MAGD.	2	F	CHILD	RR	ZZZZ	USA
CHRISTIAN	.11	M	INFANT	RR	ZZZZ	USA
VALENTIN	40	M	LABR	RR	ZZZZ	USA
ELISAB.	35	F	W	RR	ZZZZ	USA
JOHANNES	12	M	CH	RR	ZZZZ	USA
CATH.	10	F	CH	RR	ZZZZ	USA
MARIE	8	F	CHILD	RR	ZZZZ	USA
CHRISTINE	7	F	CHILD	RR	ZZZZ	USA
ELISE	4	F	CHILD	RR	ZZZZ	USA
ROSINE	.11	F	INFANT	RR	ZZZZ	USA

SHIP: CIRCASSIA

FROM: GLASGOW AND MOVILLE
TO: NEW YORK
ARRIVED: 29 APRIL 1885

PASSENGER	AGE	SEX	OCCUPATION	PRV	VIL	DES
ZACZKEWICZ, LUD.	24	M	LABR	RR	ZZZZ	USA
GADOWSKY, ART.	23	M	LABR	RR	ZZZZ	USA
ECHERT, FRANZ	24	M	LABR	RR	ZZZZ	USA
ZELINSKY, JOSEF	34	M	LABR	RR	ZZZZ	USA
OLREWSKY, ANT.	24	M	LABR	RR	ZZZZ	USA
DOMBOWSKY, DOM.	19	M	LABR	RR	ZZZZ	USA
BECHER, JOSEF	25	M	LABR	RR	ZZZZ	USA
BOJOWSKY, GEORG.	24	M	LABR	RR	ZZZZ	USA
HOWSEY, CHARLOTTE	24	F	W	RR	ZZZZ	USA
DAVID	4	M	CHILD	RR	ZZZZ	USA
AMELIA	4	F	CHILD	RR	ZZZZ	USA
SAMUEL	3	M	CHILD	RR	ZZZZ	USA
ROSA	1	F	CHILD	RR	ZZZZ	USA
GABRESTIC, JULIAN	32	M	LABR	RR	ZZZZ	USA

SHIP: WERRA

FROM: BREMEN AND SOUTHAMPTON
TO: NEW YORK
ARRIVED: 30 APRIL 1885

PASSENGER	AGE	SEX	OCCUPATION	PRV	VIL	DES
BURSTEIN, MOSES	26	M	LABR	RR	ZZZZ	NY
FUHRMANN, SCHLIEMEN	24	M	LABR	RR	ZZZZ	NY
LEWKOW, SIMON	18	M	MCHT	RR	ZZZZ	NY
SARGALOWITSCH, ELIAS	24	M	MCHT	RR	ZZZZ	NY
WISKOWSKI, JOH.	21	M	LABR	RR	ZZZZ	NY
CHEINKES, RACHEL	24	M	LABR	RR	ZZZZ	NY
ITZIG	2	M	CHILD	RR	ZZZZ	NY
LUKASZEWJE, LUDW.	26	M	LABR	RR	ZZZZ	UNK
WITINEWSKI, MARYANNE	40	F	UNKNOWN	RR	ZZZZ	UNK
ANTON	22	M	LABR	RR	ZZZZ	UNK
STANISLAW	17	M	LABR	RR	ZZZZ	UNK
DWORE	6	F	CHILD	RR	ZZZZ	UNK
JOHANN	4	M	CHILD	RR	ZZZZ	UNK
KLEIN, ADOLF	17	M	LABR	RR	ZZZZ	UNK
PRIEBE, WILHELM	34	M	LABR	RR	ZZZZ	UNK
WITHN.	31	F	UNKNOWN	RR	ZZZZ	UNK
MARTIN	7	M	CHILD	RR	ZZZZ	UNK
MATHILDE	4	F	CHILD	RR	ZZZZ	UNK
EMILIE	.06	F	INFANT	RR	ZZZZ	UNK
TEFER, MOSZEK	33	M	LABR	RR	ZZZZ	NY
GABRYS, VICTOR	16	M	LABR	RR	ZZZZ	NY
ZOZYCKI, STANISL.	18	M	LABR	RR	ZZZZ	NY
GRABOWSKY, FRZ.	24	M	LABR	RR	ZZZZ	NY
SKOTOWSKY, ANT.	26	M	LABR	RR	ZZZZ	NY
DIPA, STANISLAW	16	M	LABR	RR	ZZZZ	NY
BIRRUS, HANE	30	F	UNKNOWN	RR	ZZZZ	NY
KRENSCHEWSKY, G.	27	F	UNKNOWN	RR	ZZZZ	NY
LABR, G.	27	F	UNKNOWN	RR	ZZZZ	NY
BURKOWSKI, PETER	27	F	UNKNOWN	RR	ZZZZ	NY
ESTEN, FR.	26	F	UNKNOWN	RR	ZZZZ	NY
ROWNE, SAMUEL	37	F	UNKNOWN	RR	ZZZZ	NY

SHIP: WYOMING

FROM: LIVERPOOL AND QUEENSTOWN
TO: NEW YORK
ARRIVED: 30 APRIL 1885

PASSENGER	AGE	SEX	OCCUPATION	PRV	VIL	DES
RACHAN, JANOS	45	F	MA	PL	ZZZZ	USA
ASTAZLIVCEZ, KAJ.	36	M	LABR	PL	ZZZZ	USA

SHIP: NOORDLAND

FROM: ANTWERP
TO: NEW YORK
ARRIVED: 01 MAY 1885

PASSENGER	AGE	SEX	OCCUPATION	PRV	VIL	DES
SMITH, J.	25	M	LABR	PL	ADBQ	USA
ANT.	20	M	LABR	PL	ADBQ	USA
M.	00	M	INF	PL	ADBQ	USA
JOS.	22	M	LABR	PL	ADBQ	USA
JOH.	22	M	LABR	PL	ADBQ	USA
BARBIGE, B.	23	M	STDNT	RR	ZZZZ	USA
GORSKI, V.	60	M	FARMER	PL	ZZZZ	USA
CONSTANT.	50	M	FARMER	PL	ZZZZ	USA
ROSALIA	32	F	UNKNOWN	PL	ZZZZ	USA

PASSENGER	AGE	SEX	OCCUPATION	PRV VIL DES

SHIP: WESTER

FROM: BREMEN
TO: NEW YORK
ARRIVED: 01 MAY 1885

PASSENGER	AGE	SEX	OCCUPATION	PRV VIL DES
SCHIDLER, AUG.	16	M	LABR	RRZZZZUSA
ZAMMOTH, ADOLF	21	M	LABR	RRZZZZUSA
SCHICHINOWITZ, LEIBE	24	M	LABR	RRZZZZUSA
FENTIK, JULIANNA	22	F	NN	RRZZZZUSA
SCHICKOWSKY, ROMAN	35	M	LABR	RRZZZZUSA
SLOVINSKY, JOSEF	21	M	LABR	RRZZZZUSA

SHIP: CITY OF CHESTER

FROM: LIVERPOOL AND QUEENSTOWN
TO: NEW YORK
ARRIVED: 02 MAY 1885

PASSENGER	AGE	SEX	OCCUPATION	PRV VIL DES
HALFENBERG, LEON	24	M	CL	RRADAXNY
JEANETTE	19	F	W	RRADAXNY
SCHARJON, VINCENT	24	M	LABR	RRACBFNY
WABICZIUS, MENKA	22	F	SVNT	RRACBFNY

SHIP: ELBE

FROM: BREMEN
TO: NEW YORK
ARRIVED: 04 MAY 1885

PASSENGER	AGE	SEX	OCCUPATION	PRV VIL DES
SUFFER, CHAIM	36	M	LABR	RRZZZZUSA
JOSEPH	7	M	CHILD	RRZZZZUSA
WRUBEL, JANKEL	18	M	LABR	RRZZZZUSA
FASANBACH, MEYER	20	M	LABR	RRZZZZUSA
PATARKA, ABRAHAM	18	M	LABR	RRZZZZUSA
GATSKE, ANDREAS	28	M	BLKSMH	RRZZZZUSA
CZENINSKY, STANISL.	35	M	LABR	RRZZZZUSA
HEFTKE, ANDREAS	26	M	LABR	RRZZZZUSA
DUDE, GUSTAV	30	M	LABR	RRZZZZUSA
WILHELMINE	26	F	W	RRZZZZUSA
ERNST	.11	M	INFANT	RRZZZZUSA
KISLMANN, AUG.	20	M	LABR	RRZZZZUSA
HATZ, AUGUST	26	M	FARMER	RRZZZZUSA
DOMBROWSKY, JOSEPH	36	M	LABR	RRZZZZUSA
PODSCHOLOPSKI, IGNATZ	32	M	LABR	RRZZZZUSA
BEZOSA, JANKEL	20	M	LABR	RRZZZZUSA
STERN, DAVID	33	M	MCHT	RRZZZZUSA
JANKELOWITZ, POSSEL	23	M	LABR	RRZZZZUSA
MALA, MEYER	26	M	LABR	RRZZZZUSA
FAVORSKYY, ALEX.	31	M	LABR	RRZZZZUSA
BOMBERSKY, JOSEF	19	M	LABR	RRZZZZUSA
BRANDT, CHRISTOPH	51	M	CPTR	RRZZZZUSA
WILH.	48	F	W	RRZZZZUSA
HERMANN	15	M	CH	RRZZZZUSA
WILH.	13	F	CH	RRZZZZUSA
WILH.	10	M	CH	RRZZZZUSA
MARIE	9	F	CHILD	RRZZZZUSA
JOHANN	6	M	CHILD	RRZZZZUSA
WAZATER, AL.	14	F	NN	RRZZZZUSA
SLAWSKA, MARIANNA	40	F	NN	RRZZZZUSA
BABONAWICZ, ABRAM	30	M	LABR	RRZZZZUSA
FREID, BORTZIG	40	M	LABR	RRZZZZUSA
LEIB	25	M	LABR	RRZZZZUSA
WOJTKE, CARL	25	M	FARMER	RRZZZZUSA
SCHULZ, FR.	35	M	LABR	RRZZZZUSA
BRETZKE, GUST.	24	M	LABR	RRZZZZUSA
EWALD, U	33	M	DYR	RRZZZZUSA
BANETZKY, SIMON	30	M	LABR	RRZZZZUSA
RINDFLEISCH, JOS.	20	M	TCHR	RRZZZZUSA
FRANK, JOHANNES	54	M	WVR	RRZZZZUSA
PHILIPPINE	53	F	W	RRZZZZUSA
CATHARINE	15	F	CH	RRZZZZUSA
KESSLER, JUSTINE	22	F	NN	RRZZZZUSA
HOOCK, H.	26	M	TLR	RRZZZZUSA
NEUBAUER, LUISE	20	F	NN	RRZZZZUSA
NEUMANN, GUSTAV	36	M	BKPR	RRZZZZUSA
RISTOCK, MARIANNA	35	F	NN	RRZZZZUSA
JOHANN	7	M	CHILD	RRZZZZUSA
FERDINAND	6	M	CHILD	RRZZZZUSA
G-AN, FERDINAND	20	M	FARMER	RRZZZZUSA
PLOTNICK, MICHAEL	40	M	LABR	RRZZZZUSA

SHIP: ETRURIA

FROM: LIVERPOOL AND QUEENSTOWN
TO: NEW YORK
ARRIVED: 04 MAY 1885

PASSENGER	AGE	SEX	OCCUPATION	PRV VIL DES
OLLUS, MAT.	41	M	LABR	FNZZZZUSA
JASTULA, HECKKI	27	M	CPTR	FNZZZZUSA
RAF, JACOB	24	M	LABR	FNZZZZUSA
LEPPUS, MATS	26	M	LABR	FNZZZZUSA

SHIP: AUSTRALIA

FROM: HAMBURG
TO: NEW YORK
ARRIVED: 05 MAY 1885

PASSENGER	AGE	SEX	OCCUPATION	PRV VIL DES
SCHUCKOPSKI, JAC.	23	M	LABR	RRZZZZNE
PAKUTA, THEKLA	26	F	WO	PLZZZZIL
KARDOCK, SOS.	21	M	LABR	RRZZZZNY
MATTOK, MEUH.	32	M	LABR	PLZZZZIL
SIRCE, WOIZEK	47	M	LABR	PLZZZZIL
MEUHALEWICZ, SORAEL	18	M	TLR	RRZZZZNY
PELAWICZ, RAF.	50	M	TLR	RRZZZZNY
SENDATZ, BERG.	38	M	TLR	RRZZZZNY
MARKERT, SOH.	26	M	JNR	RRZZZZNY
SOHANNISSOHN, C.	31	M	LABR	RRZZZZNY
WINKEL, WILH.	23	M	MSN	RRZZZZIL
MAYER, M.	17	M	MCHT	RRZZZZNY
ZIELEWICZ, PETER	24	M	LABR	RRZZZZNY
CATHARINE	24	F	W	RRZZZZNY
MARIANNE	.10	F	INFANT	RRZZZZNY
DAVID, AUGUST	25	M	LABR	RRZZZZIL
MATUGOWSKI, JOH.	48	M	LABR	RRZZZZNY
SARAMINSKY, M.	46	M	LABR	RRZZZZNY
BELAIK, STANISLAUS	17	M	LABR	PLZZZZPA
SCHAFFLER, SAFFET.	25	F	WO	PLZZZZPA
RET.MISS	.06	F	INFANT	PLZZZZPA
KLAPPER, JACOB	30	M	LABR	PLZZZZIL
BERKOWITZ, SCHEINDEL	17	F	WO	PLZZZZNY
LIBITZKI, ABRAHAM	42	M	FARMER	RRZZZZIL
NECHANE	35	F	W	RRZZZZIL
BENYIAL	7	F	CHILD	RRZZZZIL
SASEFI	6	M	CHILD	RRZZZZIL
CHAIM	4	M	CHILD	RRZZZZIL
PILTROVICH, LIBY	17	F	SGL	RRZZZZUNK
STOLCZ, ANTON	15	M	LABR	RRZZZZUNK

PASSENGER	AGE	SEX	OCCUPATION	PRIVL	DES
SCHER, RAICHEL	19	F	SGL	PLZZZZ	NY
BIEDRON, PETER	40	M	LABR	PLZZZZ	NY
VICTORIA	27	F	W	PLZZZZ	NY
HANNCHEN	.07	F	INFANT	PLZZZZ	NY
HIRSCH, WOLF	15	M	SHMK	PLZZZZ	NY
MEYER	22	M	LABR	PLZZZZ	NY
SEYE	16	M	LABR	PLZZZZ	NY
SCHOTTLAND, DWORE	40	F	WO	PLZZZZ	NY
CHAME	6	F	CHILD	PLZZZZ	NY
NEIZUR, FEIGE	18	F	SGL	PLZZZZ	NY
GOSKA, HELENE	19	F	SGL	PLZZZZ	NY
KUSCH, MARYA	20	F	SGL	PLZZZZ	NY
CYWIK, HEDWIGA	22	F	SGL	PLZZZZ	NY
SABYKA, CAROLINE	7	F	CHILD	PLZZZZ	NY
WICHERT, WLADISL.	15	M	FARMER	RRZZZZ	NY
PASLAWSKI, CH.	49	F	WO	RRZZZZ	NY
PESCHE	20	F	WO	RRZZZZ	NY
UNGARN, BREZEL	7	F	CHILD	PLZZZZ	NY
TAZBERECK, MARYA	20	F	SGL	PLZZZZ	IL
GADACZ, WEW.	40	F	WO	PLZZZZ	IL
MARIA	2	F	CHILD	PLZZZZ	IL
GARITZKA, FRANZISCA	20	F	WO	PLZZZZ	IL
MARY	4	F	CHILD	PLZZZZ	IL
JOLER, ABRAH.	20	M	LABR	PLZZZZ	NY
OCHSMANN, JENTE	7	M	CHILD	RRZZZZ	NY
BELGRADT, S.	19	M	TRDSMN	RRZZZZ	NY
KOPPER, LEISER	18	M	TRDSMN	RRZZZZ	NY
FREGE, ALB.J.	45	M	TLR	RRZZZZ	NY
SCHANBORN, JAN.	41	M	TLR	RRZZZZ	NY
BLICHSCHLIS, JANKEL	21	M	SHMK	RRZZZZ	NY
ARONOWITZ, HIRSCH	22	M	TRDSMN	RRZZZZ	NY
ABROVOMITZ, LEISER	22	M	TRDSMN	RRZZZZ	NY
LISLIPER, M.	26	M	TRDSMN	RRZZZZ	NY
KREBS, ANNA	23	F	WO	RRZZZZ	NY
FRIEDMAN, JAC.	54	M	TRDSMN	RRZZZZ	NY
SALI	56	F	W	RRZZZZ	NY
SPIELMANN, H.	37	M	MCHT	PLZZZZ	NY
KLEIN, LAZ.	32	M	TRDSMN	RRZZZZ	NY
ROSA	26	F	W	RRZZZZ	NY
MORITZ	7	M	CHILD	RRZZZZ	NY
PAULA	4	F	CHILD	RRZZZZ	NY
JACOB	6	M	CHILD	RRZZZZ	NY
BELA	.10	F	INFANT	RRZZZZ	NY
ABRAHAM	16	M	B	RRZZZZ	NY
U	.01	F	INFANT	RRZZZZ	NY
HAMBERG, SAM.	33	M	TRDSMN	RRZZZZ	NY
LEWY, SAM.	38	M	TRDSMN	RRZZZZ	NY
GRAZYMOKA, JOSEFA	33	F	WO	RRZZZZ	NY
RABINOWITZ, LAZAR	26	M	LABR	RRZZZZ	NY
FELENIEWSKY, FELIX	24	M	LABR	RRZZZZ	NY
OMILANOWITZ, JOHN	20	M	LABR	RRZZZZ	NY
MATSCHILEWITZ, PIOTR	23	M	LABR	RRZZZZ	NY
STRACHI, JOS.	31	M	LABR	RRZZZZ	NY
MICHAEL	27	M	LABR	RRZZZZ	NY
CASPEROWITZ, VINCENT	19	M	LABR	RRZZZZ	UNK
GRUSEWITZ, JURIS	35	M	LABR	RRZZZZ	NY
WIESLAWSKY, JOSES	24	M	LABR	RRZZZZ	NY
GRABLEWSKY, SIMON	25	M	LABR	RRZZZZ	UNK
SCHINKOWITZ, JOSES	30	M	LABR	RRZZZZ	NY
KOWALEWSKY, JAN	24	M	LABR	RRZZZZ	NY
CZESNY, ANTONIE	22	M	LABR	RRZZZZ	NY
KALINSKY, JOS.	20	F	SGL	RRZZZZ	NY
RACHEL	18	M	LABR	RRZZZZ	NY
ZADIDAW, CHAIM	22	M	LABR	RRZZZZ	NY
MAN, JUDA	18	M	LABR	RRZZZZ	NY
PLACH, JOS.	22	M	LABR	RRZZZZ	NY
SCHULZ, HENRIETTE	38	F	W	RRZZZZ	IL
ZISSAN, FRANZ	24	M	LABR	PLZZZZ	NY
RACHMANN, JAN	22	M	LABR	PLZZZZ	NY
BARAN, MICH.	24	M	LABR	PLZZZZ	NY
NEWA, JAS.	24	M	LABR	PLZZZZ	NY
SPORA, MICH.	27	M	LABR	PLZZZZ	NY
JOS.	28	M	LABR	PLZZZZ	NY
MARIANNE	20	F	SGL	PLZZZZ	NY
PRZYWORN, ANTONIA	47	M	LABR	PLZZZZ	NY
GRABOWS, MARC	42	M	LABR	PLZZZZ	NY
JOCHARSROWITZ, MOS.	40	M	LABR	PLZZZZ	NY
BRZINSKY, ANNA	34	F	WO	PLZZZZ	NY
MART.	43	M	LABR	PLZZZZ	NY
SILBER, ABR.M.	21	M	LABR	RRZZZZ	NY
BROZOWSKY, T.	41	M	LABR	RRZZZZ	NY
GRUDOWSKY, JOS.	47	M	LABR	RRZZZZ	NY
LEWIN, SCHMUEL	20	M	LABR	RRZZZZ	NY
EPSTEIN, LEISER	25	M	TRDSMN	RRZZZZ	NY
LIPITZ, ISAAK	24	M	TRDSMN	RRZZZZ	NY
RANUS, ERIK	33	M	SHMK	RRZZZZ	NY
SCHMUSS, NATHAN	18	M	SHMK	RRZZZZ	NY
BENCHIS, FISCHEL	16	M	SHMK	RRZZZZ	NY
SCHMALTOWSKY, H.	26	M	SHMK	RRZZZZ	NY
DEBORA	27	M	SHMK	RRZZZZ	NY
STABINSKY, MOSES	24	M	SLR	RRZZZZ	NY
FREID, SALOM.	16	M	TRDSMN	RRZZZZ	NY
BATZKOWSKA, ABR.	43	M	TRDSMN	RRZZZZ	NY
KAHAN, BERE	7	M	CHILD	RRZZZZ	NY
SAWOLSKY, M.	17	M	LABR	RRZZZZ	NY
SILBERSTEIN, W.	29	M	LABR	RRZZZZ	NY

SHIP: WIELAND

FROM: HAMBURG
TO: NEW YORK
ARRIVED: 05 MAY 1885

PASSENGER	AGE	SEX	OCCUPATION	PRIVL	DES
ZINDA, JOSEPH	17	M	LABR	RRZZZZ	USA
ZIMMERMANN, BERL	26	M	TLR	RRZZZZ	USA
STEIN, CHAJE	35	F	W	RRZZZZ	USA
JANKEL	3	M	CHILD	RRZZZZ	USA
PERE	.11	F	INFANT	RRZZZZ	USA
MERMANN, RACHEL	9	F	CHILD	RRZZZZ	USA
KOHN, MOSES	29	M	DLR	RRZZZZ	USA
SABLOTZKI, ANDR.	31	M	LABR	RRZZZZ	USA
BALTRODOWSKY, MOSES	18	M	LABR	RRZZZZ	USA
KOHEN, CHAIM	21	M	DLR	RRZZZZ	USA
WOLF, HENRIETTE	31	F	W	RRZZZZ	USA
BOKALSKA, FRANCISKA	60	F	W	RRZZZZ	USA
MARTHA	7	F	CHILD	RRZZZZ	USA
FRANZ	5	M	CHILD	RRZZZZ	USA
SCHILOSORSKY, CHANNE	18	F	SGL	RRZZZZ	USA
LAPIDUS, SALOMON	25	M	DLR	RRZZZZ	USA
CZIMCISKI, ANTON	26	M	LABR	RRZZZZ	USA
GELER, SARAH	22	F	SGL	RRZZZZ	USA
FLEISCHMANN, CHANNE	24	F	W	RRZZZZ	USA
GITTKA	.11	F	INFANT	RRZZZZ	USA
LEIZER	36	M	DLR	RRZZZZ	USA
LAPIDUS, JANKEL	35	M	DLR	RRZZZZ	USA
HOLPEROWITZ, LEIB	23	M	DLR	RRZZZZ	USA
POSNAK, NOCHEM	23	M	DLR	RRZZZZ	USA
KAHN, LEIB	20	M	LABR	RRZZZZ	USA
LIPSCHITZ, ELIAS	18	M	LABR	RRZZZZ	USA
MILLER, ITE	28	F	W	RRZZZZ	USA
ISRAEL	8	M	CHILD	RRZZZZ	USA
BASCHE	4	F	CHILD	RRZZZZ	USA
STALLER, ISAAC	26	M	LABR	RRZZZZ	USA
KOSIOLKOWSKI, ZELEG	19	M	DLR	RRZZZZ	USA
CHAIKELOWITZ, JOSSEL	18	M	LABR	RRZZZZ	USA
ISRAELOWITZ, ISRAEL	46	M	LABR	RRZZZZ	USA
SCHNEIDER, HIRSCH	19	M	LABR	RRZZZZ	USA
BABIS, DWORE	55	F	W	RRZZZZ	USA
GITTELMANN, SARA	20	F	SGL	RRZZZZ	USA
REICH, HANNE	16	F	SGL	RRZZZZ	USA
MORITZ	9	M	CHILD	RRZZZZ	USA
STRASSBERG, ABRAHAM	35	M	LABR	RRZZZZ	USA
MOSKOWITZ, SALOMON	20	M	LABR	RRZZZZ	USA
JACOBSOHN, BEILE	40	F	W	RRZZZZ	USA
OEHRTZKI, IGNATZ	28	M	LABR	RRZZZZ	USA

PASSENGER	AGE	SEX	OCCUPATION	PRIVL	VIL	DES
NUTZ, JACOB	18	M	CTW	RR	ZZZZ	USA
ELISABETH	15	F	SGL	RR	ZZZZ	USA
FALKENBERG, CARL	45	M	MLR	RR	ZZZZ	USA
HENRIETTE	48	F	W	RR	ZZZZ	USA
WILH.	14	F	CH	RR	ZZZZ	USA
FRANZ	9	M	CHILD	RR	ZZZZ	USA
DOROTHEA	7	F	CHILD	RR	ZZZZ	USA
DEEFSKI, JOH.	32	M	LABR	RR	ZZZZ	USA
JURECIK, JANOS	35	M	LABR	RR	ZZZZ	USA
SKONT, JOSEF	38	M	LABR	RR	ZZZZ	USA
KURONSKI, JANOS	41	M	LABR	RR	ZZZZ	USA
LOFFELHOLZ, JETTE	22	F	SGL	RR	ZZZZ	USA
GRUNFELD, MOSES	56	M	LABR	RR	ZZZZ	USA
ZYCINSKI, FRANZ	26	M	MLR	RR	ZZZZ	USA
KADZUISKA, ANNA	38	F	W	RR	ZZZZ	USA
GOLDSCHMIDT, ARON	9	M	CHILD	RR	ZZZZ	USA
SCHREIBER, DAVID	20	M	TLR	RR	ZZZZ	USA
TILNICK, GOLDE	17	F	SGL	RR	ZZZZ	USA
RYDZINSKI, LADISL.	40	M	LABR	RR	ZZZZ	USA
BLAZIEWSKY, JAN	22	M	LABR	RR	ZZZZ	USA
BLACHIEWITZ, JOSEPH	24	M	LABR	RR	ZZZZ	USA
SADOWSKY, FRANZ	21	M	LABR	RR	ZZZZ	USA
SIMONSKY, JOSEF	28	M	LABR	RR	ZZZZ	USA
SABLONY, JOS.	28	M	LABR	RR	ZZZZ	USA
MULLER, W.	20	M	LABR	RR	ZZZZ	USA
ELIZAR, RUBEN	20	M	LABR	RR	ZZZZ	USA
KURKEWITZ, SAMUEL	9	M	CHILD	RR	ZZZZ	USA
SCHRAGE, PESYCH	17	M	MSN	RR	ZZZZ	USA
DOMBROWSKY, JAN	32	M	LABR	RR	ZZZZ	USA
EISNER, SOPHIE	17	F	SGL	RR	ZZZZ	USA
ISRAESKY, NOCH.	18	M	LABR	RR	ZZZZ	USA
SKOLSKY, MOSES	19	M	LABR	RR	ZZZZ	USA
REINBLINKER, MENDEL	20	M	LABR	RR	ZZZZ	USA
RUBENSTEIN, JANKEL	23	M	LABR	RR	ZZZZ	USA
MICHELSON, ABRAH.	23	M	SHMK	RR	ZZZZ	USA
GOLDENSTEIN, ARON	27	M	LABR	RR	ZZZZ	USA
ZINSERENKA, PENCUS	22	M	LABR	RR	ZZZZ	USA
STEFANIK, TEKLA	18	F	SGL	RR	ZZZZ	USA
FRIEDMANN, LIEBE	25	F	W	RR	ZZZZ	USA
GITTEL	5	M	CHILD	RR	ZZZZ	USA
SAMUEL	2	M	CHILD	RR	ZZZZ	USA
ROSMIERSKA, CONSTANTIA	20	M	SGL	RR	ZZZZ	USA
ANNA	22	M	SGL	RR	ZZZZ	USA
WIEZBIEZKI, VINCENT	18	M	LABR	RR	ZZZZ	USA
ZABROWSKY, CHAJE	18	M	LABR	RR	ZZZZ	USA
GRUSKA, FEIWEL	26	M	LABR	RR	ZZZZ	USA
GOLDENSOHN, JANKEL	13	M	LABR	RR	ZZZZ	USA
ARONSOHN, OSCHER	25	M	LABR	RR	ZZZZ	USA
EHRENSTEIN, SCHANE	16	M	LABR	RR	ZZZZ	USA
RIZEWSKA, ANNA	30	F	W	RR	ZZZZ	USA
VICTOR	.11	M	INFANT	RR	ZZZZ	USA
LEFKOWITZ, MOSES	52	M	LABR	RR	ZZZZ	USA
HANNE	48	F	W	RR	ZZZZ	USA
ARON, MARIS	27	M	LABR	RR	ZZZZ	USA
DINE, SORE	18	F	SGL	RR	ZZZZ	USA
ROSENDORF, JUDE	20	F	SGL	RR	ZZZZ	USA
SCHEIGER, MOSES	30	M	MCHT	RR	ZZZZ	USA
FLASCHMANN, MINE	27	F	SGL	RR	ZZZZ	USA
CZESLIK, WOLF	30	M	LABR	RR	ZZZZ	USA
MUNZ, ESTHER	31	F	W	RR	ZZZZ	USA
LEO	4	M	CHILD	RR	ZZZZ	USA
SORE	.11	F	INFANT	RR	ZZZZ	USA
GEHART, SAL.	18	M	LABR	RR	ZZZZ	USA
BERKER, MINNA	28	F	W	RR	ZZZZ	USA
WILLY	6	M	CHILD	RR	ZZZZ	USA
RECHTMANN, LEISER	22	M	LABR	RR	ZZZZ	USA
KOKOWSKY, SORE	25	F	SGL	RR	ZZZZ	USA
REMANOWSKY, SALOMON	28	M	MCHT	RR	ZZZZ	USA
USCHERWITZ, MORDCHE	20	M	MCHT	RR	ZZZZ	USA
LEWINSOHN, JOSEL	21	M	MCHT	RR	ZZZZ	USA
SORE	18	F	W	RR	ZZZZ	USA
LEIBSOHN, ABE	26	M	LABR	RR	ZZZZ	USA

SHIP: ETHIOPIA

FROM: GLASGOW AND MOVILLE
TO: NEW YORK
ARRIVED: 06 MAY 1885

PASSENGER	AGE	SEX	OCCUPATION	PRIVL	VIL	DES
LACHN, JAN	24	M	LABR	RR	ZZZZ	USA
DANCEWICZ, FRANCISZEK	22	M	LABR	RR	ZZZZ	USA
ANDROLEWICZ, JOSEF	26	M	LABR	RR	ZZZZ	USA
PRENF, JOHUS	31	M	MSN	RR	ZZZZ	USA
RAMENSKY, RASMER	21	M	SMH	RR	ZZZZ	USA
FOLP, JACOB	27	M	LABR	RR	ZZZZ	USA
SLOVIEMS, JOSEF	23	M	LABR	RR	ZZZZ	USA
MIKOLAMETSCH, MALEZ	30	M	LABR	RR	ZZZZ	USA
SABALEWSKI, GABRIEL	20	M	LABR	RR	ZZZZ	USA
RIES, LUDWIG	22	M	CPTR	RR	ZZZZ	USA
RYDZEWSKI, HAWER	20	M	LABR	RR	ZZZZ	USA
SKROTZKO, FRANCISZEK	20	M	LABR	RR	ZZZZ	USA
WAKS, ELIAS	43	M	MCHT	RR	ZZZZ	USA
BLONDKANN, JOSEF	30	M	LABR	RR	ZZZZ	USA

SHIP: GREECE

FROM: UNKNOWN
TO: NEW YORK
ARRIVED: 06 MAY 1885

PASSENGER	AGE	SEX	OCCUPATION	PRIVL	VIL	DES
WOLINSKY, FRANK	25	M	LABR	RR	ZZZZ	NY
LESINSKY, STANISLAUS	22	M	LABR	RR	ZZZZ	NY
KANUNSKI, JACOB	23	M	LABR	RR	ZZZZ	NY
LENN, LONO	22	M	LABR	RR	ZZZZ	NY
SCHULTZ, NATHAN	40	M	LABR	RR	ZZZZ	NY

SHIP: AMERIQUE

FROM: HAVRE
TO: NEW YORK
ARRIVED: 08 MAY 1885

PASSENGER	AGE	SEX	OCCUPATION	PRIVL	VIL	DES
KOENIG, M.	24	M	FARMER	FN	ZZZZ	USA

SHIP: BELGENLAND

FROM: ANTWERP
TO: NEW YORK
ARRIVED: 09 MAY 1885

PASSENGER	AGE	SEX	OCCUPATION	PRIVL	VIL	DES
WARGI, MARY	29	F	FARMER	PL	ZZZZ	MIL
ISER	6	F	CHILD	PL	ZZZZ	MIL
MARY	4	F	CHILD	PL	ZZZZ	MIL
ANTON	00	M	INF	PL	ZZZZ	MIL
VANGOLA, GEORG.	27	M	BKR	PL	ADBQ	NY
RINAY, SAL.	23	M	JWLR	RR	ZZZZ	NY
MISTISZINSKA, JOS.	23	M	LABR	PL	ZZZZ	UNK
PYMEROWSKI, JOHN	19	M	LABR	PL	ZZZZ	NY
FRANZ	17	M	LABR	PL	ZZZZ	NY
SCOTT, MORDCHE	27	F	SVNT	PL	ZZZZ	NY
AUGUST	9	M	CHILD	PL	ZZZZ	NY
ROSEK, JOHN	35	M	LABR	PL	ZZZZ	PRI

PASSENGER	AGE	SEX	OCCUPATION	PRV IVL	DES
MARY	30	F	UNKNOWN	PLZZZZ	PRI
CATH.	8	F	CHILD	PLZZZZ	PRI
JOSEPH	6	M	CHILD	PLZZZZ	PRI
FRANZ	4	M	CHILD	PLZZZZ	PRI
PAJEWSKI, JOHN	19	M	LABR	PLZZZZ	CH
ITZEWSKI, MARIE	10	F	CH	PLZZZZ	UNK
BJOSKA, WAG.	25	F	SVNT	PLZZZZ	NY
ANNA	17	F	CH	PLZZZZ	NY
ANNA	5	F	CHILD	PLZZZZ	NY
HANISLAS	4	M	CHILD	PLZZZZ	NY
ANDREAS	2	M	CHILD	PLZZZZ	NY
JOHANN	.06	M	INFANT	PLZZZZ	NY
LIMOWE, ALEX	22	M	LABR	PLAFVG	NY
JAMASUNS, JEAN	21	M	BKR	PLZZZZ	UNK
SCHNEIBLER, CARL.	28	M	FARMER	RRZZZZ	NY
ELIS	28	F	UNKNOWN	RRZZZZ	NY
OSTER, JOS.	21	M	LABR	RRZZZZ	NY
SCHNEIBLER, CHRIST.	4	F	CHILD	RRZZZZ	NY
PAULINE	3	F	CHILD	RRZZZZ	NY
ROSINE	.06	F	INFANT	RRZZZZ	NY
ENGELHARDT, HCH.	28	M	LABR	RRZZZZ	NY
MARG.	25	F	UNKNOWN	RRZZZZ	NY
GRENTZLER, JOS.	18	M	LABR	RRZZZZ	NY
ENGELHARDT, HCH.	4	M	CHILD	RRZZZZ	NY
ALEX	3	M	CHILD	RRZZZZ	NY
ROSINE	00	F	INF	RRZZZZ	NY

SHIP: CITY OF CHICAGO

FROM: LIVERPOOL AND QUEENSTOWN
TO: NEW YORK
ARRIVED: 09 MAY 1885

PASSENGER	AGE	SEX	OCCUPATION	PRV IVL	DES
CZEZWSKA, FRANK	21	M	LABR	RRACBF	USA
JOHN	18	M	LABR	RRACBF	USA

SHIP: FULDA

FROM: BREMEN AND SOUTHAMPTON
TO: NEW YORK
ARRIVED: 09 MAY 1885

PASSENGER	AGE	SEX	OCCUPATION	PRV IVL	DES
KELLER, AD.	51	M	LABR	RRZZZZ	USA
HOLLENDA, FR.	30	M	LABR	RRZZZZ	USA
SCHRANK, ETTEL	17	M	WTR	RRZZZZ	USA
HONIG, MINDEL	19	M	LABR	RRZZZZ	USA
MUELLER, JOS.	26	M	LABR	RRADIJ	USA
KUCHARSKI, MICH.	22	M	LABR	RRADIJ	USA
PALISCHAWSKI, BRUNISLAW	26	M	ENGR	RRZZZZ	USA
BERENS, STANISL.	23	M	ENGR	RRZZZZ	USA
U, U	00	M	FARMER	RRZZZZ	USA
VIRGINIA	42	F	UNKNOWN	RRZZZZ	USA
NATALIA	16	F	CH	RRZZZZ	USA
ALFRED	17	M	FARMER	RRZZZZ	USA
FRIED	13	M	FARMER	RRZZZZ	USA
ARNOLD	8	M	CHILD	RRZZZZ	USA
ARTHUR	6	M	CHILD	RRZZZZ	USA
LUDWIG	4	M	CHILD	RRZZZZ	USA
PHILIPPE	2	M	CHILD	RRZZZZ	USA
MARGOT, LOUISE	54	F	UNKNOWN	RRZZZZ	USA
ALWEN, PHILIPP	47	M	FARMER	RRZZZZ	USA
ANNE	38	M	UNKNOWN	RRZZZZ	USA
FRIEDR.	17	M	FARMER	RRZZZZ	USA
DAVID	15	M	FARMER	RRZZZZ	USA
CATHA.	14	F	CH	RRZZZZ	USA
EDUARD	8	M	CHILD	RRZZZZ	USA
ROSALIA	4	F	CHILD	RRZZZZ	USA
RUDOLF	3	M	CHILD	RRZZZZ	USA
EUGEN	2	M	CHILD	RRZZZZ	USA
U, U	.02	F	INFANT	RRZZZZ	USA

SHIP: ODER

FROM: BREMEN AND SOUTHAMPTON
TO: NEW YORK
ARRIVED: 09 MAY 1885

PASSENGER	AGE	SEX	OCCUPATION	PRV IVL	DES
ROM, DAVID	20	M	LABR	RRZZZZ	USA
NATHASON, MAN	24	M	LABR	RRZZZZ	USA
MESCHER, MEYER	30	M	LABR	RRZZZZ	USA
ROCKIS, NATHAN	32	M	LABR	RRZZZZ	USA
FRIDKIND, MEYER	18	M	LABR	RRZZZZ	USA
JEMA, MEITA	18	M	LABR	RRZZZZ	USA
LEPARD, ISR.SALMEN	18	M	LABR	RRZZZZ	USA
THON, JOHAN	38	M	LABR	RRZZZZ	USA
KOLINSKI, DWORE	47	F	NN	RRAHSP	USA
CHAMIN	18	M	MCHT	RRAHSP	USA
ANNA	8	F	CHILD	RRAHSP	USA
SALOMON	10	M	CH	RRAHSP	USA
BAUSKE, FRIEDR.	45	M	FARMER	RRZZZZ	USA
ADELINE	38	F	NN	RRZZZZ	USA
FRANZ	10	M	CH	RRZZZZ	USA
HERMANN	8	M	CHILD	RRZZZZ	USA
OTTO	4	M	CHILD	RRZZZZ	USA
ANNA	.01	F	INFANT	RRZZZZ	USA
LUDWIG	70	M	FARMER	RRZZZZ	USA
MOLL, BERTHA	17	F	CH	RRAAKH	USA
WESOLOWSKA, KATARZINA	29	F	NN	RRZZZZ	USA
WALLERSTEIN, JADE	20	M	LABR	RRAHZS	USA
ABRAHAMS, JOSEPH	17	M	LABR	RRZZZZ	USA
HIRSCHFELD, ISAAC	34	M	LABR	RRZZZZ	USA
STANKIEWITZ, VERONIKA	31	F	NN	RRZZZZ	USA
VERONIKA	2	F	CHILD	RRZZZZ	USA
MANKOWICZ	.09	M	INFANT	RRZZZZ	USA
KOHN, JACOB	17	M	LABR	RRAHRZ	USA
RUTKOWSI, ROSALIA	18	F	NN	RRZZZZ	USA
SAZILLER, MOLDEKA	36	M	LABR	RRZZZZ	USA
SALINGER, MOSES	12	M	CH	RRZZZZ	USA
GARTIN, SCHAJE	18	M	LABR	RRZZZZ	USA
KOLBER, SCHAHSE	25	F	NN	RRZZZZ	USA
LISSOWSKI, CASIMIR	23	M	LABR	RRZZZZ	USA
BACHULSKI, MARCUS	64	M	LABR	RRZZZZ	USA
SCHLACHTER, MEYER	15	M	LABR	RRZZZZ	USA
LEFF, ITZEHOK	32	M	LABR	RRZZZZ	USA
ISAAC	18	M	LABR	RRZZZZ	USA
RABINOWITZ, ROCHE	18	M	NN	RRZZZZ	USA
SMOLEWSKI, VINCENZ	30	M	LABR	RRZZZZ	USA
FEINBERG, JOSEPH	4	M	CHILD	RRZZZZ	USA
MEYER	10	M	CH	RRZZZZ	USA
SEIDENBERG, BARUCH	65	M	LABR	RRZZZZ	USA
CHANNE	18	M	LABR	RRZZZZ	USA
MOTTIE	11	F	CH	RRZZZZ	USA
SILBERMANN, CLARA	18	F	NN	RRZZZZ	USA
DAVIDSON, MILAS	24	M	LABR	RRZZZZ	USA
KLINOWSKA, ULLIANE	45	F	NN	RRZZZZ	USA
SOGACKA, MICHALINE	17	F	NN	RRZZZZ	USA
SUSA	2	F	CHILD	RRZZZZ	USA
HELENKA	.03	F	INFANT	RRZZZZ	USA
MARIANNE	31	F	NN	RRZZZZ	USA
MAAS, MOSES	19	M	LABR	RRZZZZ	USA
RATHNER, ROFEL	18	M	LABR	RRZZZZ	USA
PRESSMAN, ISRAEL	20	M	LABR	RRZZZZ	USA
LEWITE, SEIC	19	M	LABR	RRZZZZ	USA
COHN, REBECKA	17	F	NN	RRZZZZ	USA
EDELBERG, ROCHE	24	M	LABR	RRZZZZ	USA

PASSENGER	AGE	SEX	OCCUPATION	PRV	VIL	DES
KOBELOWITZ, MOSES	17	M	LABR	RR	ZZZZ	USA

SHIP: ST. OF PENNSYLVANIA

FROM: GLASGOW AND LARNE
TO: NEW YORK
ARRIVED: 09 MAY 1885

PASSENGER	AGE	SEX	OCCUPATION	PRV	VIL	DES
BIER, I.	18	M	LABR	PL	ZZZZ	USA
ROZINTKO, S.	24	M	LABR	PL	ZZZZ	USA
BRZINSKY, A.	36	M	LABR	PL	ZZZZ	USA
DAPKIS, I.	22	M	LABR	PL	ZZZZ	USA
DZURA, I.	25	M	LABR	PL	ZZZZ	USA
LEIER, I.	30	M	LABR	PL	ZZZZ	USA
FISCHBEIN, N.	23	M	SHMK	PL	ZZZZ	USA
Z.	22	F	W	PL	ZZZZ	USA
CZELWOKIACH, J.	37	M	LABR	PL	ZZZZ	USA
FORTENTZER, J.	19	M	LABR	PL	ZZZZ	USA
GLADER, F.	23	M	LABR	PL	ZZZZ	USA
GRABOWSKY, I.	24	M	LABR	PL	ZZZZ	USA
J.	22	M	LABR	PL	ZZZZ	USA
GRIBOWITZ, G.	33	M	LABR	PL	ZZZZ	USA
GUTERMANN, K.	16	M	LABR	PL	ZZZZ	USA
HELLER, K.	17	M	LABR	PL	ZZZZ	USA
JANISCHER, I.	27	M	LABR	PL	ZZZZ	USA
JAMISLAW, K.	25	M	LABR	PL	ZZZZ	USA
JANILEWITZ, J.	30	M	LABR	PL	ZZZZ	USA
ISTEN, S.	18	M	LABR	PL	ZZZZ	USA
D.	16	M	LABR	PL	ZZZZ	USA
KARUCHOWSKI, S.	26	M	LABR	PL	ZZZZ	USA
KANECHOWSKI, E.	9	F	CHILD	PL	ZZZZ	USA
G.	1	M	CHILD	PL	ZZZZ	USA
KARP, S.	28	M	LABR	PL	ZZZZ	USA
KASLOWSKY, M.	25	M	LABR	PL	ZZZZ	USA
KERKELS, M.	30	M	LABR	PL	ZZZZ	USA
KOBERSKY, I.	25	M	LABR	PL	ZZZZ	USA
KOPSCHINSKY, F.	28	M	LABR	PL	ZZZZ	USA
KROWUT, V.	28	M	LABR	PL	ZZZZ	USA
LOTOJA, I.	26	M	LABR	PL	ZZZZ	USA
SACKS, S.	48	M	LABR	PL	ZZZZ	USA
LEBERAN, L.	17	M	LABR	PL	ZZZZ	USA
LICEMSKY, A.	28	M	LABR	PL	ZZZZ	USA
LISOTTE, W.	24	M	LABR	PL	ZZZZ	USA
A.	25	F	W	PL	ZZZZ	USA
R.	7	M	CHILD	PL	ZZZZ	USA
LUCKOWITZ, J.	27	M	LABR	PL	ZZZZ	USA
MARSALES, J.	25	M	LABR	PL	ZZZZ	USA
MASKETAWIS, I.	32	M	LABR	PL	ZZZZ	USA
MATISCHKA, F.	40	M	LABR	PL	ZZZZ	USA
MIKOBOLSKI, L.	30	M	LABR	PL	ZZZZ	USA
WETEZROVE, H.	11	M	LABR	PL	ZZZZ	USA
MOSIO, A.	19	M	LABR	PL	ZZZZ	USA
OLESOWSKY, I.	21	M	LABR	PL	ZZZZ	USA
PASVO, D.	36	M	LABR	PL	ZZZZ	USA
A.	25	F	W	PL	ZZZZ	USA
PAWLOWSKY, I.	21	M	LABR	PL	ZZZZ	USA
REINSCHAK, V.	35	M	LABR	PL	ZZZZ	USA
L.	27	F	W	PL	ZZZZ	USA
ROSCHOW, H.	19	M	LABR	PL	ZZZZ	USA
ROSENBLUTH, B.	27	M	LABR	PL	ZZZZ	USA
SAPISCHKA, K.	25	F	W	PL	ZZZZ	USA
SCHNOR, B.	19	F	SP	PL	ZZZZ	USA
SEITZ, M.	22	M	LABR	PL	ZZZZ	USA
SIMON, A.	18	M	CL	PL	ZZZZ	USA
I.	15	M	LABR	PL	ZZZZ	USA
SINEWSKY, I.	26	M	WCHMKR	PL	ZZZZ	USA
SIMONKA, P.	25	M	LABR	PL	ZZZZ	USA
STANBOWSKY, A.	26	M	LABR	PL	ZZZZ	USA
P.	28	M	LABR	PL	ZZZZ	USA
STANISLAUS, S.	29	M	LABR	PL	ZZZZ	USA
STEPANOWICZ, A.	16	M	LABR	PL	ZZZZ	USA
UNGIRACZY, P.	20	M	LABR	PL	ZZZZ	USA
URBANOISY, U.	20	M	LABR	PL	ZZZZ	USA
VITETZKY, M.	26	M	LABR	PL	ZZZZ	USA
WAZENJOCK, G.	35	M	LABR	PL	ZZZZ	USA
WALACK, I.	30	M	LABR	PL	ZZZZ	USA
WASCHIPSKY, S.	39	M	LABR	PL	ZZZZ	USA
WIENIEWSKI, I.	44	M	LABR	PL	ZZZZ	USA
F.	35	F	W	PL	ZZZZ	USA
O.	2	M	CHILD	PL	ZZZZ	USA
WITETZKI, I.	40	M	LABR	PL	ZZZZ	USA
WAHISCHKA, I.	27	M	LABR	PL	ZZZZ	USA
ZAWATSCHKY, R.	20	M	LABR	PL	ZZZZ	USA
V.	24	M	LABR	PL	ZZZZ	USA
POSCHATZEWSKI, L.	25	M	TLR	PL	ZZZZ	USA
S.	18	F	W	PL	ZZZZ	USA
HIRSCHITZKI, M.	25	F	MCHT	RR	ZZZZ	USA
BARATIS, A.	22	F	LABR	RR	ZZZZ	USA
REGEL, M.	25	F	MCHT	RR	ZZZZ	USA
F.	17	F	W	RR	ZZZZ	USA
BLUMENTHAL, S.	20	M	MCHT	RR	ZZZZ	USA
CHACHAM, C.	23	M	MCHT	RR	ZZZZ	USA
E.	20	F	W	RR	ZZZZ	USA
DEMMAN, I.	25	M	LABR	RR	ZZZZ	USA
DIBOWSKY, A.	00	M	LABR	RR	ZZZZ	USA
ELTENBEY, S.	40	M	LABR	RR	ZZZZ	USA
GALWER, I.	17	M	MCHT	RR	ZZZZ	USA
GARRASCH, F.	29	M	LABR	RR	ZZZZ	USA
GOLDBERG, N.	32	M	LABR	RR	ZZZZ	USA
GRABOWSKI, M.	29	M	LABR	RR	ZZZZ	USA
GRINBERG, S.	27	M	LABR	RR	ZZZZ	USA
JABLOWSKY, B.	31	M	LABR	RR	ZZZZ	USA
KAPLAN, C.	25	M	LABR	RR	ZZZZ	USA
KROLEWYETSKY, I.	17	M	LABR	RR	ZZZZ	USA
LEVITHAN, I.	25	M	LABR	RR	ZZZZ	USA
MATULEWICZK, H.	35	M	LABR	RR	ZZZZ	USA
H.	18	F	W	RR	ZZZZ	USA
MOGOSKI, S.	20	M	LABR	RR	ZZZZ	USA
MOTHEL, S.	32	M	HRDRS	RR	ZZZZ	USA
M.	20	F	W	RR	ZZZZ	USA
POSNAK, M.	25	M	MCHT	RR	ZZZZ	USA
PERM, H.	22	M	MCHT	RR	ZZZZ	USA
PLATZ, I.	19	M	MCHT	RR	ZZZZ	USA
RIWELSKY, G.	20	M	MCHT	RR	ZZZZ	USA
SAVILOWITZ, C.	24	M	MCHT	RR	ZZZZ	USA
SCHAPIRO, I.	27	M	MCHT	RR	ZZZZ	USA
SLOTNILOW, I.	25	M	MCHT	RR	ZZZZ	USA
SOLINSKY, O.	48	M	MCHT	RR	ZZZZ	USA
SOTZKY, I.	20	M	MCHT	RR	ZZZZ	USA
SAROKA, C.	22	M	MCHT	RR	ZZZZ	USA
STELLER, M.	29	M	MCHT	RR	ZZZZ	USA
STARSASIS, H.	23	M	MCHT	RR	ZZZZ	USA
I.	23	M	MCHT	RR	ZZZZ	USA
STICH, S.	28	M	MCHT	RR	ZZZZ	USA
WAITAKU, S.	24	M	MCHT	RR	ZZZZ	USA
ZOTNIK, R.	32	M	MCHT	RR	ZZZZ	USA
HEIMAN, A.	27	M	MCHT	RR	ZZZZ	USA
SCHMULZON, I.	30	M	MCHT	RR	ZZZZ	USA
WARDER, I.	35	M	MCHT	RR	ZZZZ	USA

SHIP: FURNESSIA

FROM: GLASGOW
TO: NEW YORK
ARRIVED: 11 MAY 1885

PASSENGER	AGE	SEX	OCCUPATION	PRV	VIL	DES
LISCIAK, ANNA	29	F	NN	RR	ZZZZ	USA
KRISSO, MORDEL	27	M	NN	RR	ZZZZ	USA
SOHNABEL, S.	27	M	LABR	RR	ZZZZ	USA
SHERMAN, J.	27	M	LABR	RR	ZZZZ	USA

PASSENGER	AGE	SEX	OCCUPATION	PRIVL	DES
ROFFES, CHU	37	M	LABR	RRZZZZ	USA
PLEMACK, MUACHEM	35	M	LABR	RRZZZZ	USA
LUFKOW, BERL	18	M	LABR	RRZZZZ	USA
KARP, NILSEN	17	M	LABR	RRZZZZ	USA
ABRAHAM	37	M	LABR	RRZZZZ	USA
KUSCHNER, S.	19	M	LABR	RRZZZZ	USA
KISSEL, DAVID	30	M	LABR	RRZZZZ	USA
CHUSES, MAY	32	M	LABR	RRZZZZ	USA
SCHUNLANS, WOLF	18	M	LABR	RRZZZZ	USA
SELIG	16	M	LABR	RRZZZZ	USA
KATHARIHA, LIBA	18	F	NN	PLZZZZ	USA
FENNOSKY, GEORG	18	M	LABR	PLZZZZ	USA
LABLONSKY, F.	31	M	LABR	PLZZZZ	USA
SUARSKY, LUDWIG	34	M	LABR	PLZZZZ	USA
SKALSKI, JAN.	22	M	LABR	PLZZZZ	USA
SZURFAL, JOSEF	36	M	LABR	PLZZZZ	USA
SZORYS, PIOTR	45	M	LABR	PLZZZZ	USA
RUTZIK, ANTON	40	M	LABR	PLZZZZ	USA
PTARZYASKI, JAN	45	M	LABR	PLZZZZ	USA
BOKOWSKI, J.	50	M	LABR	PLZZZZ	USA
MICHALEK, JOHAN	25	M	LABR	PLZZZZ	USA
MACHOWITZ, B.	25	M	LABR	PLZZZZ	USA
LIEFER, B.	20	M	LABR	PLZZZZ	USA
LITKI, AND	23	M	LABR	PLZZZZ	USA
KEVKEWITZ, ISAK	17	M	LABR	PLZZZZ	USA
KNUSELKI, LUKASS	30	M	LABR	PLZZZZ	USA
JADERSELKI, S.	28	M	LABR	PLZZZZ	USA
HURSOITZ, M.	19	M	LABR	PLZZZZ	USA
HUSCHKOWITZ, B.	30	M	LABR	PLZZZZ	USA
GOLDGLUECK, MOSES	20	M	LABR	PLZZZZ	USA
GENSOWITCH, URESSIN	20	M	LABR	PLZZZZ	USA
GJERT, F.	28	M	LABR	PLZZZZ	USA
JERAKSCHAK, GEORG	21	M	LABR	PLZZZZ	USA
GPANG, HANS	35	M	LABR	PLZZZZ	USA
FEDORSKI, JAN	23	M	LABR	PLZZZZ	USA
ERCKS, GARN	38	M	LABR	PLZZZZ	USA
DENARSKY, MICHAEL	28	M	LABR	PLZZZZ	USA
DRAZBA, F.	34	M	LABR	PLZZZZ	USA
BARONOWSKY, K.	42	M	LABR	PLZZZZ	USA
BOYANOWSKY, JHI.	28	M	LABR	PLZZZZ	USA
BAZKO, ANNA	17	F	NN	PLZZZZ	USA
BARBUSZ, S.	36	M	LABR	PLZZZZ	USA
ANDROSZ, FETIZKO	30	M	LABR	PLZZZZ	USA
SORI, ANDREAS	45	M	LABR	PLZZZZ	USA
SOHANNA	46	F	W	PLZZZZ	USA
GOTH, ANTON	26	M	UNKNOWN	PLZZZZ	USA
CARL	10	M	LABR	PLZZZZ	USA
DEINBOZAK, ANNA	30	F	NN	PLZZZZ	USA
SOFIA	9	F	CHILD	PLZZZZ	USA
JUNA	4	F	CHILD	PLZZZZ	USA
MARIA	00	F	INF	PLZZZZ	USA
BODIN, FEREMLI	35	M	LABR	PLZZZZ	USA
JOHANNA	24	F	W	PLZZZZ	USA

SHIP: HELVETIA

FROM: LIVERPOOL
TO: NEW YORK
ARRIVED: 11 MAY 1885

PASSENGER	AGE	SEX	OCCUPATION	PRIVL	DES
BUDZROSCK, JOS.	24	M	LABR	PLAADQ	USA
PULKOWSKI, IGEN	36	M	LABR	PLAADQ	USA
KALPISKY, JACOB	31	M	LABR	RRZZZZ	USA
SORDECK, JOSEF	35	M	LABR	RRZZZZ	USA
KARIABUK, PARTI	32	M	LABR	RRAHQH	USA
KETCHSHAK, JOSEF	30	M	LABR	RRZZZZ	USA
KARONWITCH, STH.	21	M	CTHR	PLZZZZ	USA
HAREWITH, KLAUDER	20	M	TLR	PLZZZZ	USA
HENRICKSON, HENRY	30	M	LABR	FNZZZZ	USA

SHIP: SERVIA

FROM: LIVERPOOL AND QUEENSTOWN
TO: NEW YORK
ARRIVED: 11 MAY 1885

PASSENGER	AGE	SEX	OCCUPATION	PRIVL	DES
NUSITOLA, MATO	19	M	LABR	RRZZZZ	USA
GABRIEL, SALOMON	30	M	LABR	RRZZZZ	USA
FARMIAS, JOHAN	30	M	LABR	FNZZZZ	USA
ESASS, MICHEL	20	M	LABR	FNZZZZ	USA
DUKTVIG, LEANDER	29	M	LABR	FNZZZZ	USA
YRYAS, MICHEL	27	M	LABR	FNZZZZ	USA
YLLIHANLACA, AND.	22	M	LABR	FNZZZZ	USA
SANTA, JON	38	M	LABR	FNZZZZ	USA
HENRY	30	M	LABR	FNZZZZ	USA
MARIA	18	F	SP	FNZZZZ	USA
PYSTO, ANDREAS	28	M	LABR	FNZZZZ	USA
ABRAM	25	M	LABR	FNZZZZ	USA
NYLAND, THES.	34	M	LABR	FNZZZZ	USA
ERIK	24	M	LABR	FNZZZZ	USA
KULLMAN, WILHELM	35	M	LABR	FNZZZZ	USA
KASKOLA, ERIK	21	M	LABR	FNZZZZ	USA
JATH, CARL	32	M	LABR	FNZZZZ	USA

SHIP: MORAVIA

FROM: HAMBURG
TO: NEW YORK
ARRIVED: 12 MAY 1885

PASSENGER	AGE	SEX	OCCUPATION	PRIVL	DES
NIEDERMANN, CHAIN-S.	14	M	LABR	RRZZZZ	USA
WAJSERSTEIN, MENDEL	30	M	TLR	RRAHTO	USA
MACHOWITZ, CHOE	50	F	W	RRADOI	USA
ABR.	9	M	CHILD	RRADOI	USA
ROSENFELD, MOSES	15	M	LABR	RRZZZZ	USA
SCHEIMANN, EISER	26	M	DLR	RRAHTF	USA
WEINER, ISAAC	33	M	LABR	RRZZZZ	USA
EINNEHMER, SCHAI	22	M	UNKNOWN	RRZZZZ	USA
GOLDBERG, HIRSCHEL	16	M	DLR	RRZZZZ	USA
NARAGELSKI, ABRAHAM	17	M	DLR	RRAHZS	USA
OSCHICHO, JANKEL	14	M	DLR	RRZZZZ	USA
STEIN, JANKEL-M.	28	M	LABR	RRZZZZ	USA
SAMSEBER, FREUDE	38	F	W	RRAHSP	USA
SCHEPSEL	9	M	CHILD	RRAHSP	USA
SALMEN	8	M	CHILD	RRAHSP	USA
BLUME	5	F	CHILD	RRAHSP	USA
RIWKE	3	F	CHILD	RRAHSP	USA
PETTERSON, CAROLINE	61	F	W	FNZZZZ	USA
MARIE	35	F	D	FNZZZZ	USA
DANEYGER, SALOMON	17	M	LABR	RRZZZZ	USA
DAVIDSOHN, SAMUEL	16	M	LABR	RRAHZS	USA
KRAWTSCHUG, MARIAN	20	F	SGL	RRZZZZ	USA
ROLNICKI, CH.	19	M	FARMER	RRZZZZ	USA
TRILETZKI, GENIS	20	M	LABR	RRZZZZ	USA
LEIPHAHN, ABRAHAM	18	M	LABR	RRAHTF	USA
PAMNUNSKY, MALKE	44	F	W	RRAHTR	USA
KORDULANZINSKYE, JOSEFA	20	F	SGL	RRZZZZ	USA
PITZEKNE, DAVID	9	M	CHILD	RRZZZZ	USA
JOFFE, TAUBE	19	F	SGL	RRZZZZ	USA
LEWIN, LOUIS	20	M	LABR	RRAHTF	USA
LEWINSKYE, SARAH	26	F	W	RRZZZZ	USA
CHANNE	3	F	CHILD	RRZZZZ	USA
DAVID	.11	M	INFANT	RRZZZZ	USA
ROGOWSKI, CHANNE	54	F	UNKNOWN	RRAHTF	USA
RAHEL	30	F	F	RRAHTF	USA
ITTE	18	F	F	RRAHTF	USA
SALEWEIZIG, TRUNE	24	F	SGL	RRZZZZ	USA
LEVENSKY, REBECCA	22	F	SGL	RRZZZZ	USA
RABITZKYE, MICHLE	20	F	W	RRZZZZ	USA

PASSENGER	AGE	SEX	OCCUPATION	PRV VIL DES
PAVA, BANE.	9	F	CHILD	RRZZZZUSA
IWANSKY, WOLF.	21	M	LABR	RRAHTFUSA
SCHOSTACK, BASCHE	23	F	W	RRZZZZUSA
BENJAMIN	.11	M	INFANT	RRZZZZUSA
HOFFMAN, MARIE	41	F	W	RRAHVAUSA
LOUIS	9	M	CHILD	RRAHVAUSA
PERSY	8	M	CHILD	RRAHVAUSA
SANDER, MORDCHE	23	M	DLR	RRAHTFUSA
LINTGE, HIRSCH	25	M	TLR	RRZZZZUSA
GILLE	18	F	W	RRZZZZUSA
KAHN, LAZAR	18	M	LABR	RRAHTFUSA
KOHN, FACL	22	M	LABR	RRZZZZUSA
SCHERESEWSKI, MALKE	28	F	W	RRZZZZUSA
SLOM	9	M	CHILD	RRZZZZUSA
CHEIE	6	F	CHILD	RRZZZZUSA
LEA	5	F	CHILD	RRZZZZUSA
PAWARSKY, RUBEN	20	M	LABR	RRAHTFUSA
SORESEN, JAMES	31	M	FARMER	FNZZZZUSA
WARSCHOFSKI, CHANNE	45	F	W	FNAHTRUSA
SARAH	20	F	CH	FNAHTRUSA
FREIDE	16	F	CH	FNAHTRUSA
SCHULKE	9	F	CHILD	FNAHTRUSA
CHAIM	8	M	CHILD	FNAHTRUSA
DOLE	6	F	CHILD	FNAHTRUSA
CHAIKE	3	F	CHILD	FNAHTRUSA
GUTMANN, LEIB	18	M	DLR	RRZZZZUSA
LEVIN, WOLF.	18	M	DLR	RRZZZZUSA
OLINSKYE, ESCHKIEL	54	M	DLR	RRAHZSUSA
RAFELOWITSCH, CHAIM	21	M	TLR	RRZZZZUSA
LEWIN, LIPPE	50	F	W	RRAHUKUSA
BRODNOWSKYE, NOAH.	8	M	CHILD	RRAHZSUSA
KAPLAN, SALOMON	23	M	LABR	RRAHUKUSA
SUNKOWSKYE, WLADISL.	30	M	LABR	RRZZZZUSA
PAULINE	37	F	W	RRZZZZUSA
BRONISLAW	9	M	CHILD	RRZZZZUSA
WANDA	7	F	CHILD	RRZZZZUSA
SOFIE	5	F	CHILD	RRZZZZUSA
MARIANNE	3	F	CHILD	RRZZZZUSA
WITTLIEB, HERMANN	30	M	LABR	RRZZZZUSA
LIVKE, MARIE	18	F	SGL	RRZZZZUSA
BOBTER, MEYER	19	M	LABR	RRZZZZUSA
HELLMANN, JOSEF	16	M	LABR	RRZZZZUSA
ANGERS, BENDET	42	M	LABR	RRZZZZUSA
WISNOFSKYE, SELDE	36	F	W	RRZZZZUSA
PELSER	9	M	CHILD	RRZZZZUSA
LEISER	5	M	CHILD	RRZZZZUSA
JOSEF	3	M	CHILD	RRZZZZUSA
WILLIE	.11	M	INFANT	RRZZZZUSA
LIBAN, JOSSEL	25	M	LABR	RRZZZZUSA
SKOSS, ISAAC	9	M	CHILD	RRZZZZUSA
SELTZER, ABR.	32	M	LABR	RRAHUKUSA
KANTROWITZ, MASCHI	19	M	LABR	RRAHUKUSA
ROSSENBISS, SAMUEL	50	M	DLR	RRAFWJUSA
LEA	50	F	W	RRAFWJUSA
SIMSCHE	18	F	CH	RRAFWJUSA
CHAJE	16	F	CH	RRAFWJUSA
BEILIS, BEILE	16	F	SGL	RRAFWJUSA
LIPSCHITZ, CHANNE	40	F	W	RRAFWJUSA
SCHAPIRO, SCHLOME	20	M	LABR	RRAHTUUSA
AKELRATH, CHAIE	18	F	D	RRAHUKUSA
JOSSEL	50	M	LABR	RRAHUKUSA
RODE	45	F	W	RRAHUKUSA
BLANSTEIN, ISAAC	23	M	LABR	RRAHTUUSA
SZAFFER, SZLANA	16	F	SGL	RRZZZZUSA
MISZKINSKY, LEIZER	20	M	LABR	RRZZZZUSA
SAVLANSKYE, DORA	30	F	W	RRZZZZUSA
LEA	9	F	CHILD	RRZZZZUSA
ISAAC	8	M	CHILD	RRZZZZUSA
MARCUS	3	M	CHILD	RRZZZZUSA
SALOMON	6	M	CHILD	RRZZZZUSA
CHANNE	4	F	CHILD	RRZZZZUSA
RAW, SAMUEL	45	M	TLR	RRAHVAUSA
RZATKOWSKI, SIMON	24	M	LABR	RRAHZSUSA
MEIEROWITZ, ABRAHAM	22	M	LABR	RRZZZZUSA
SWERDLOFF, GINESE	18	F	SGL	RRZZZZUSA
STRICWEN, HELENE	17	F	SGL	RRZZZZUSA
MARKOWITZ, TRUME	18	F	SGL	RRZZZZUSA
SCHAFORNIK, CHAIE	30	F	SGL	RRZZZZUSA
FEIGE	65	F	W	RRZZZZUSA
MOLASCH, WILLIAM	21	M	LABR	RRZZZZUSA
PAWLASKI, ANTON	22	M	LABR	RRZZZZUSA
JOSEPHA	28	F	W	RRZZZZUSA
RINGEL, OSCHER	9	M	CHILD	RRZZZZUSA
SARLANSKI, ANNA	30	F	W	RRZZZZUSA
LIPPMANN, ABRAHAM	28	M	SHMK	RRAHUKUSA
GELLER, SCHLOME	20	M	LABR	RRZZZZUSA
TOPERANSKI, FRAJEN	28	M	TLR	RRZZZZUSA
MARIANNE	28	F	W	RRZZZZUSA
SEGAL, BENJAMIN	19	M	CL	RRZZZZUSA
LOWINGER, ADOLF	34	M	LABR	RRZZZZUSA
BETTI	24	F	W	RRZZZZUSA
FRANZ	5	M	CHILD	RRZZZZUSA
BERTALOM.	3	M	CHILD	RRZZZZUSA
SANDER	.06	M	INFANT	RRZZZZUSA
GONDULA, JANOS	36	M	LABR	RRZZZZUSA
ANNA	32	F	W	RRZZZZUSA
PODLESNYE, JUSTA	15	F	SGL	RRZZZZUSA
KLAWANSKY, BENJAMIN	23	M	DLR	RRZZZZUSA
LEWIN, ALBRECHE	18	M	LABR	RRAHTFUSA
MOSES	9	M	CHILD	RRAHTFUSA
MARCUS	8	M	CHILD	RRAHTFUSA
RUDOMIEC, GERSON	30	M	TLR	RRZZZZUSA
RUDENER, ARON	23	M	DLR	RRZZZZUSA
BERGER, BERNHD.	25	M	SHMK	RRZZZZUSA
KLEIN, ETTEL	18	F	SGL	RRZZZZUSA
FRIEDLAND, SAMUEL	22	M	TLR	RRAHSZUSA
FLAKS, MOSES	22	M	TLR	RRAHTUUSA
ZEMANSKI, JONAS	30	M	LABR	RRZZZZUSA
ZYWOKA, JONAS	24	M	LABR	RRZZZZUSA
PAJAWJAS, SIMON	34	M	LABR	RRZZZZUSA
ZUCKERMANN, SALI	18	F	SGL	RRZZZZUSA
ROTTENBERG, HANNE	13	F	SGL	RRAHTFUSA
PINCUS, ABRAHAM	40	M	MLR	RRZZZZUSA
BREWIG, DAVID	20	M	LABR	RRZZZZUSA
FINKELMANN, HINDE	19	F	SGL	RRAHVUUSA
GROSSMANN, CHAIM	35	M	TLR	RRZZZZUSA
KORNAINSKI, OSCHER	18	M	SHMK	RRAHVUUSA
SZYMANOWICZ, ANTON	37	M	LABR	RRAHZSUSA
ANTONINA	44	F	W	RRAHZSUSA
BENEWSKI, ANTON	21	M	LABR	RRAHZSUSA
KREIBJACH, SYELVESTER	18	M	LABR	RRAHVUUSA
SOLEWSKYE, WLADISLAW	25	M	LABR	RRAHVUUSA
MIGLAZEWSKI, IGNATZ	25	M	LABR	RRAHVUUSA
PAULINE	26	F	W	RRAHVUUSA
MICHAEL	.11	M	INFANT	RRAHVUUSA
JOSEPH	.01	M	INFANT	RRAHVUUSA
TILETZKI, JOSEPH	26	M	LABR	RRAHZSUSA
STIBATOW, VINCENTI	26	M	LABR	RRAHZSUSA
ANNA	25	F	W	RRAHZSUSA
MACZKIEWICZ, PETER	29	M	LABR	RRAHZSUSA
CATHA.	29	F	W	RRAHZSUSA
DANIEL, MARCUS	38	M	LABR	RRAFVGUSA
LEISER	15	M	LABR	RRAFVGUSA
KORITZKI, ABRAHAM	18	M	LABR	RRAHZSUSA
TOPARANSKY, GORDON	.02	M	INFANT	RRZZZZUSA
ROTH, ABRAHAM	32	M	CPR	RRAHTFUSA
RES, LAZARUS	49	M	MUSN	RRZZZZUSA
FRIEDLANDER, ESTER	18	F	SGL	RRZZZZUSA
GOLDSTEIN, GENTE	18	F	SGL	RRZZZZUSA
ARONSOHN, ABRAHAM	23	M	LABR	RRZZZZUSA
MOSES	17	M	LABR	RRZZZZUSA
JENTE	20	F	SGL	RRZZZZUSA
ALTE	29	F	W	RRZZZZUSA
LEA	6	F	CHILD	RRZZZZUSA
BRANE	.11	F	INFANT	RRZZZZUSA
BAUMGARTEN, MARA	32	F	W	RRAAKHUSA
HULDA	8	F	CHILD	RRAAKHUSA
MOSES, ARON	38	M	LABR	RRAHTFUSA
KALITZKY, CHAIM	16	M	LABR	RRZZZZUSA
LINGER, SIMON	31	M	SHMK	RRZZZZUSA

PASSENGER	AGE	SEX	OCCUPATION	PRVVIL	DES
LEA	18	F	W	RRZZZZ	USA
LAPNITZKY, SCHOLEM	19	M	LABR	RRAHTF	USA
LANWICA, MOSES	35	F	W	RRAFVG	USA
GITTEL	6	F	CHILD	RRAFVG	USA
SAMUEL	3	M	CHILD	RRAFVG	USA
GOLDE	.11	F	INFANT	RRAFVG	USA
ORANSKI, BEILE	18	F	SGL	RRAHTF	USA
CHAJE	17	F	SGL	RRAHTF	USA
MICKLACZEMIS, PIOTR	16	M	LABR	RRAHRZ	USA
WROBLEWSKA, TEOFILA	20	F	W	RRAHRZ	USA
JOH.	.11	F	INFANT	RRAHRZ	USA
KAHN, TAUBE	18	F	SGL	RRAHVU	USA
RUEZINSKI, JAN	28	M	LABR	RRZZZZ	USA
BENCKOSKI, WOJCEH	65	M	LABR	RRAHLP	USA
ZUEGE, WILH.	16	M	LABR	RRAAKH	USA
KOHN, DORA	55	F	W	RRZZZZ	USA
ESTER	16	F	CH	RRZZZZ	USA
HERM.	9	M	CHILD	RRZZZZ	USA
BERGER, IDA	16	F	SGL	RRZZZZ	USA
RUBEN, BERL.	15	M	LABR	RRAHVV	USA
JACOB	8	M	CHILD	RRAHVV	USA
OSMANSCHI, MOSES	20	M	DLR	RRZZZZ	USA
BECWRINOWICZ, LEISER	30	M	LABR	RRZZZZ	USA
RUBIN, SARA	42	F	W	RRAHVU	USA
SIMON	9	M	CHILD	RRAHVU	USA
TEPERMANN, ROBERT	18	M	LKSH	RRZZZZ	USA
RABINOWITZ, BARUCH	34	M	LABR	RRZZZZ	USA
MALCHE	32	F	W	RRZZZZ	USA
BARUCH	5	M	CHILD	RRZZZZ	USA
FEIGE	4	F	CHILD	RRZZZZ	USA
JANKE	.11	M	INFANT	RRZZZZ	USA
PFEFFERSNUNOF, CHAIM	20	M	LABR	RRZZZZ	USA
BLANK, SCHWAIGE	21	F	SGL	RRZZZZ	USA
KAUFMANN, FEIGE	40	F	W	RRZZZZ	USA
ALTER	4	M	CHILD	RRZZZZ	USA
HENOG	3	M	CHILD	RRZZZZ	USA
MALE	.09	F	INFANT	RRZZZZ	USA
SCHARNOZOF, SIMON	20	M	SHMK	RRACON	USA
OWALSKY, IGNATZ	50	M	LABR	RRZZZZ	USA
BERG, PHILIPP	15	M	LABR	RRZZZZ	USA
CHASROMACK, A.S.	24	M	LABR	RRZZZZ	USA
RADETZKI, MICHAEL	29	M	LABR	RRAHUI	USA
AMALIE	30	F	W	RRAHUI	USA
WILHE.	3	M	CHILD	RRAHUI	USA
OTTILIE	.11	F	INFANT	RRAHUI	USA
WISNEWSKYE, JOH.	28	M	LABR	RRAHUI	USA
BILITZKI, JOSEF	24	M	MLR	RRAHUI	USA
RANZUK, LEA	40	F	W	RRZZZZ	USA
BEILE	7	F	CHILD	RRZZZZ	USA
ABE	5	M	CHILD	RRZZZZ	USA
RUVE	.06	F	INFANT	RRZZZZ	USA
BARBAR, MOSES	25	M	CL	RRZZZZ	USA
SCHLONEOWITZ, HERSCH.	22	M	BCHR	RRAHTF	USA
KALWA, LOUISE	39	F	W	RRAHTF	USA
KAUFMANN, ABR.	37	M	MCHT	RRZZZZ	USA
SIEGEL, MEIER	52	M	DLR	RRAEFL	USA
FEIGE	49	F	W	RRAEFL	USA
INDE	15	F	CH	RRAEFL	USA
ISAAC	8	M	CHILD	RRAEFL	USA
ESTER	6	F	CHILD	RRAEFL	USA
TEINER, ISAAC	20	M	LABR	RRZZZZ	USA
KUEHNEL, JOSEPH	48	M	FARMER	RRZZZZ	USA
FERST, MENDEL	38	M	DLR	RRAHWR	USA
LIEBE	36	F	W	RRAHWR	USA
ALIE	9	F	CHILD	RRAHWR	USA
CHANNE	4	F	CHILD	RRAHWR	USA
ABR.	.06	M	INFANT	RRAHWR	USA
BRENNER, LEIB	20	M	DLR	RRAGRT	USA
SZORSKA, LOSER	17	M	SHMK	RRZZZZ	USA
OJOROLZINKY, ISRAEL	27	M	LABR	RRAHTO	USA
LURINSKY, FRELENS	25	M	LABR	RRZZZZ	USA
BASKATAS, MOSES	50	M	TCHR	RRAHZS	USA
MENDILOWIZ, DWORE	50	F	W	RRAHTF	USA
BLOSKI, ITCKO	18	M	LABR	RRAGRT	USA
STREICHMANN, OSINA	24	M	LABR	RRZZZZ	USA
HASENPOD, SELIG	18	M	LABR	RRAGRT	USA
ROSAISKY, SIMON	33	M	LABR	RRZZZZ	USA
RACHEL	32	F	W	RRZZZZ	USA
MOSES	8	M	CHILD	RRZZZZ	USA
PEISACH	6	M	CHILD	RRZZZZ	USA
HARRIS	4	M	CHILD	RRZZZZ	USA
JACOB	.11	M	INFANT	RRZZZZ	USA
ROWELSKY, LEAK	40	F	W	RRZZZZ	USA
ISIDOR	9	M	CHILD	RRZZZZ	USA
NATHAN	8	M	CHILD	RRZZZZ	USA
REBECCA	7	F	CHILD	RRZZZZ	USA
BENJAMIN	6	M	CHILD	RRZZZZ	USA
ADOLF	5	M	CHILD	RRZZZZ	USA
ANNA	3	F	CHILD	RRZZZZ	USA
ROSALIE	.11	F	INFANT	RRZZZZ	USA
HIRSCHBEIN, HENDEL	26	M	FELMO	RRZZZZ	USA
FELIX	17	M	GZR	RRZZZZ	USA
PERIL, SARA	25	F	SGL	RRZZZZ	USA
BRUSOWSKI, LEIB	14	M	LABR	RRZZZZ	USA
MAUSOWITZ, ANNA	23	F	W	RRZZZZ	USA
MELA	2	F	CHILD	RRZZZZ	USA
POJAST, ITZIG	25	M	MCHT	RRZZZZ	USA
BEILE	21	F	W	RRZZZZ	USA
DWORE	3	F	CHILD	RRZZZZ	USA
PINKUS	.11	M	INFANT	RRZZZZ	USA
POPPER, ISRAEL	19	M	LABR	RRZZZZ	USA
ZFAS, MARIANE	20	F	SGL	RRAHVU	USA
PENMUNSKY, RACHEL	23	F	SGL	RRAHTF	USA
RABINOWITZ, SAMUEL	12	M	CH	RRAHVA	USA
RUBENSTEIN, HENOCH	21	M	DLR	RRAHTR	USA
REIZEL, CHAINE	20	F	SGL	RRAHTR	USA
RABINSKY, JANKEL	9	M	CHILD	RRAHTR	USA
WALDMANN, ABR.	27	M	MUSN	RRZZZZ	USA
MARIAN	22	M	TLR	RRZZZZ	USA
DANGELAJCKI, CHAIE	26	F	SGL	RRZZZZ	USA
ACROWITZ, GEO	45	M	DLR	RRAHUF	USA
JACOBOWITZ, ISIDOR	40	M	TLR	RRAHUF	USA
RABOTKI, SALOMON	20	M	GZR	RRAHUF	USA
GRIMGART, CHAIE	18	F	SGL	RRZZZZ	USA
ROSENBLUM, HENRY	20	M	DLR	RRAHTR	USA
GOLDSTEIN, HESSAK	20	M	DLR	RRAHTR	USA
MOSCHEFSKI, SARAH	25	F	W	RRZZZZ	USA
CHAINE	4	F	CHILD	RRZZZZ	USA
ZUVIE	2	M	CHILD	RRZZZZ	USA
BERLOWITZ, GABRIEL	50	M	DLR	RRAHVA	USA
BREILE	45	F	W	RRAHVA	USA
JOSEPH	9	M	CHILD	RRAHVA	USA
MERLOWITZ, CHASKER	8	M	CHILD	RRAHVA	USA
NIZEJEWSKA, CATHA.	20	F	SGL	RRZZZZ	USA
LEMDOCIMTE, MARIE	28	F	SGL	RRAHZS	USA
GOLDSTEIN, RACHEL	24	F	W	RRZZZZ	USA
ISRAEL	3	M	CHILD	RRZZZZ	USA
LEVI	.11	F	INFANT	RRZZZZ	USA
ETKOFSKI, MENASSE	53	M	LABR	RRAHZS	USA
FESCHEL	53	F	W	RRAHZS	USA
BEILE	9	F	CHILD	RRAHZS	USA
CEPLA, ROSALIE	33	F	W	RRAHZS	USA
JOSEF	9	M	CHILD	RRAHZS	USA
FRANZ	8	M	CHILD	RRAHZS	USA
BEINESCHOWITZ, RUBEN	18	M	DLR	RRZZZZ	USA
STONER, HERSCHEL	37	M	WVR	RRZZZZ	USA
SZISZKAIS, STEINE	38	M	DLR	RRZZZZ	USA
SAKOLOFSKI, MARIANE	24	F	W	RRAHTR	USA
MAGDA.	6	F	CHILD	RRAHTR	USA
KOBAKKER, LIZZIE	16	F	SGL	RRAHTR	USA
BADULES, MARIE	19	F	SGL	RRAHZS	USA
LEWINSTEIN, SCHER.	25	M	MCHT	RRAHTR	USA
JANOWSKY, CHAJE	28	F	W	RRAHSW	USA
GABRIEL	.11	M	INFANT	RRAHSW	USA
TIESER, CHAJE	21	F	W	RRZZZZ	USA
GABRIEL	.11	M	INFANT	RRZZZZ	USA
ANSCHELOWITZ, CHAJE	23	F	W	RRZZZZ	USA
KUSIL	.11	M	INFANT	RRZZZZ	USA
JANKOWSKY, JACHMAN	20	M	LABR	RRAHVO	USA
ROSENFELDT, SCHIFE	16	M	LABR	RRZZZZ	USA

PASSENGER	AGE	SEX	OCCUPATION	PRIV	VIL	DES
JANKEL	20	M	LABR	RR	ZZZZ	USA
ROSENSOHN, MICHLE	30	F	W	RR	AHSW	USA
PESCHE	9	F	CHILD	RR	AHSW	USA
SARAH	6	F	CHILD	RR	AHSW	USA
RICOKE	5	F	CHILD	RR	AHSW	USA
FINKELSTEIN, BEILE	18	F	SGL	RR	ZZZZ	USA
FEILE	9	M	CHILD	RR	ZZZZ	USA
KURNICK, MARCUS	40	M	DLR	RR	AFWJ	USA
BLUME	30	F	W	RR	AFWJ	USA
BODHIAIKOWICZ, MORDCHE	18	M	LABR	RR	AHVU	USA
PERL, SARAH	25	F	W	RR	ZZZZ	USA
JETTE	.11	F	INFANT	RR	ZZZZ	USA
FINKELMANN, MENDEL	40	M	DLR	RR	AHVU	USA
CHALK	18	F	SGL	RR	AHVU	USA
GOLDBERG, SARA	28	F	SGL	RR	ZZZZ	USA
KWIJAD, ISRAEL	16	M	TLR	RR	ZZZZ	USA
DAVIDSOHN, JOSEPH	13	M	CH	RR	ZZZZ	USA
SCHIMPKLOWITZ, ABEL	15	M	MCHT	RR	ZZZZ	USA
GOLDSTEIN, MEYER	20	M	MCHT	RR	AHTF	USA
ROBLENSKY, LEISER	22	M	MCHT	RR	AHZS	USA
FRIEDA	22	F	W	RR	AHZS	USA
KALAMAN, JACOB	23	M	LABR	RR	AHTW	USA
WINSCHINSKY, ABR.	34	M	LABR	RR	AHTW	USA
BRANOWITZ, NOCHIM	17	M	LABR	RR	ZZZZ	USA
GOLDCHER, MISCHKE	20	M	LABR	RR	ZZZZ	USA
KATSOVLOTZKI, ABR.	18	M	LABR	RR	AHTQ	USA
FOLLEDER, BENJAMIN	20	M	LABR	RR	AHTQ	USA
LENZNER, MEIER	19	M	LABR	RR	ZZZZ	USA
KRUTZKOW, SIMCHE	40	F	W	RR	AHVA	USA
ISRAEL	9	M	CHILD	RR	AHVA	USA
SARAH	5	F	CHILD	RR	AHVA	USA
ABR.	.11	M	INFANT	RR	AHVA	USA
LUBRINSKI, ABR.J.	33	M	LABR	RR	AHZS	USA
GOLDSCHER, LEA	16	F	SGL	RR	ZZZZ	USA
LADOWITZ, ISRAEL	26	M	LABR	RR	ZZZZ	USA
CHANNE	17	F	SGL	RR	ZZZZ	USA
BRODUWITZ, ABR.	65	M	LABR	RR	AHWP	USA
MAZUTZKYE, SCHONE	21	F	SGL	RR	ZZZZ	USA
SCHMUEL	19	M	LABR	RR	ZZZZ	USA
SCHMERZ, ASCHER	18	M	LABR	RR	ZZZZ	USA
WEISS, GOLDE	18	F	SGL	RR	ZZZZ	USA
KRATSDKOF, BASCHE	23	F	SGL	RR	AHVA	USA
MEDHIRSKY, LIEBE	20	F	W	RR	ZZZZ	USA
SETKE	.11	F	INFANT	RR	ZZZZ	USA
KRUGER, RUDOLF	36	M	CPTR	RR	ZZZZ	USA
SCHLEKISS, SIMON	18	M	DLR	RR	ZZZZ	USA
KATTILUS, MATHIES	46	M	DLR	RR	ZZZZ	USA
MARIE	18	F	W	RR	ZZZZ	USA
PABOLINSKI, ANSER.	40	M	DLR	RR	AHTR	USA
MACZKIEWICZ, ANTONIA	4	F	CHILD	RR	AHTF	USA
PAUL	3	M	CHILD	RR	AHTF	USA
FRIEDMANN, GOTTEL	19	M	LABR	RR	AHTF	USA
PAWALEWSKI, ANTON	.11	M	INFANT	RR	ZZZZ	USA

SHIP: RHAETIA

FROM: HAMBURG AND HAVRE
TO: NEW YORK
ARRIVED: 12 MAY 1885

PASSENGER	AGE	SEX	OCCUPATION	PRIV	VIL	DES
MARCKS, CHEIM	18	M	SHMK	RR	ZZZZ	USA
EPSTEIN, BARNET	24	M	DLR	RR	ZZZZ	USA
MORITZ	20	M	CGRMKR	RR	ZZZZ	USA
CSINSKI-, STANISL.	40	M	LABR	RR	ZZZZ	USA
WISNEWSKI, PAUL	40	M	LABR	RR	ZZZZ	USA
WARZYNSKI, IGNATZ	30	M	LABR	RR	ZZZZ	USA
KALISCHEWSKI, JAN	38	M	LABR	RR	ZZZZ	USA
LISTEWSKY, FRANZ	20	M	LABR	RR	ZZZZ	USA
SCHNEIDER, JOSEPH	21	M	SMH	RR	ZZZZ	USA
BITSCHIK, HERZ	30	M	DLR	RR	ZZZZ	USA
KARPASS, GEORG	17	M	LABR	RR	ZZZZ	USA
BAILKIS, MATHIAS	27	M	LABR	RR	ZZZZ	USA
FRIEDMANN, SCHOLEM	18	M	LABR	RR	ZZZZ	USA
ABRAHAM	9	M	CHILD	RR	ZZZZ	USA
MOSES	8	M	CHILD	RR	ZZZZ	USA
BASCH, DAVID	27	M	HAMF	RR	ZZZZ	USA
TAKTOR, ABRAHAM	18	M	GZR	RR	ZZZZ	USA
SCHWARTZMANN, ISRAEL	16	M	DLR	RR	ZZZZ	USA
RUBINOWITZ, ELIAS	52	M	TLR	RR	ZZZZ	USA
STANKE, ERNST	51	M	FARMER	RR	ZZZZ	USA
JOHANNE	54	F	W	RR	ZZZZ	USA
ERNESTINE	19	F	CH	RR	ZZZZ	USA
LOUISE	9	F	CHILD	RR	ZZZZ	USA
JAKUBOWSKY, VINCENT	18	M	LABR	RR	ZZZZ	USA
FELDMANN, MARTIN	26	M	LABR	RR	ZZZZ	USA
GODACKOWITZ, PIOTR	30	M	LABR	RR	ZZZZ	USA
PALEWITZ, VINCENT	18	M	LABR	RR	ZZZZ	USA
DRENGOWSKI, STANISLAUS	24	M	LABR	RR	ZZZZ	USA
LADISLAWA	24	F	W	RR	ZZZZ	USA
WITTENBERG, ISIDOR	25	F	W	RR	ZZZZ	USA
ROBINOWITZ, MARCUS	9	M	CHILD	RR	ZZZZ	USA
NORODWORSKI, NAFTALIE	17	F	SGL	RR	ZZZZ	USA
CHIDCKE, MEYER	35	M	LABR	RR	ZZZZ	USA
JERSCHOW, ISRAEL	25	M	LABR	RR	ZZZZ	USA
BOLITZ, CARL	29	M	FARMER	RR	ZZZZ	USA
WALL, CHRISTIAN	44	M	FARMER	RR	ZZZZ	USA
LOUISE	43	F	W	RR	ZZZZ	USA
MATHILDE	14	F	CH	RR	ZZZZ	USA
JACOB	9	M	CHILD	RR	ZZZZ	USA
ELISABETH	8	F	CHILD	RR	ZZZZ	USA
DOROTHEA	7	F	CHILD	RR	ZZZZ	USA
WILHELM	1	M	CHILD	RR	ZZZZ	USA
HORSCH, HEINRICH	27	M	FARMER	RR	ZZZZ	USA
CATHARINE	24	F	W	RR	ZZZZ	USA
JACOB	1	M	CHILD	RR	ZZZZ	USA
BECK, CONRAD	28	M	FARMER	RR	ZZZZ	USA
SOPHIE	28	F	W	RR	ZZZZ	USA
WAGNER, FRIEDR.	60	M	FARMER	RR	ZZZZ	USA
MARGA.	60	F	W	RR	ZZZZ	USA
MATHE.	19	F	D	RR	ZZZZ	USA
UNGER, FRIEDR.	14	M	FARMER	RR	ZZZZ	USA
WAGNER, FRIEDR.	28	M	FARMER	RR	ZZZZ	USA
DOROTHEA	24	F	W	RR	ZZZZ	USA
FRIEDR.	5	M	CHILD	RR	ZZZZ	USA
OTTILIE	4	F	CHILD	RR	ZZZZ	USA
WILHELM	.06	M	INFANT	RR	ZZZZ	USA
SCHAEFFERT, JOHANN	34	M	LABR	RR	ZZZZ	USA
TROESER, FRIEDR.	24	M	LABR	RR	ZZZZ	USA
ROSINE	20	F	W	RR	ZZZZ	USA
MATHE.	21	F	SGL	RR	ZZZZ	USA
CAHTA.	13	F	SGL	RR	ZZZZ	USA
JOHS.	16	M	FARMER	RR	ZZZZ	USA
WILH.	9	M	CHILD	RR	ZZZZ	USA
MARIE	7	F	CHILD	RR	ZZZZ	USA
FISCHES, JOHS.	57	M	FARMER	RR	ZZZZ	USA
DOROTHEA	57	F	W	RR	ZZZZ	USA
KYMANN, CATHA.	28	F	W	RR	ZZZZ	USA
MARIE	3	F	CHILD	RR	ZZZZ	USA
ROBINOWITZ, BASCHE	22	F	SGL	RR	ZZZZ	USA
WERSCHNOWSKI, LEIB	22	M	FARMER	RR	ZZZZ	USA
MAX	16	M	FARMER	RR	ZZZZ	USA
FOSEN, DAVID	34	M	LABR	RR	ZZZZ	USA
FISCHKIER, MOSES	19	M	LABR	RR	ZZZZ	USA
MATTSON, MATTHS.	23	M	FARMER	FN	ZZZZ	USA
ECKLUND, FRED.	27	M	FARMER	FN	ZZZZ	USA
KARLSON, KARL	30	M	FARMER	FN	ZZZZ	USA
K.JOHN	21	M	FARMER	FN	ZZZZ	USA
SMICZKOWSKI, JOH.	24	M	LABR	RR	ZZZZ	USA
ROSINSKY, FRANZ	23	M	LABR	RR	ZZZZ	USA
ZYMANN, JOSEF	.06	M	INFANT	RR	ZZZZ	USA
ATLAS, MEYER	40	M	DLR	RR	ZZZZ	USA
JUNGKUNZ, CARL	23	M	LABR	RR	ZZZZ	USA
GABERT, GUSTAV	27	M	LABR	RR	ZZZZ	USA
SCHIKOWSKI, JOSEF	30	M	LABR	RR	ZZZZ	USA
CHAZAN, LEA	25	F	W	RR	ZZZZ	USA

PASSENGER	AGE	SEX	OCCUPATION	PRIVL	DES
LEISER	.11	M	INFANT	RRZZZZ	USA
ROGOW, SALOMON	20	M	DLR	RRZZZZ	USA
JAWORSKI, JOSEF	16	M	LABR	RRZZZZ	USA
HONY, HERSCHEL	18	M	LABR	RRZZZZ	USA
HALPERN, CHAIM	25	M	TNR	RRZZZZ	USA
SCHMUEL	28	M	TNR	RRZZZZ	USA
CHAIMSOHN, MARCUS	30	M	SMH	RRZZZZ	USA
LIWSCHUETZ, LEIB	20	M	CGRMKR	RRZZZZ	USA
PRZESLAWSKI, VICTORIA	32	F	W	PLZZZZ	USA
ANNA	6	F	CHILD	PLZZZZ	USA
JOSEF	4	M	CHILD	PLZZZZ	USA
FAKLIESZ	1	M	CHILD	PLZZZZ	USA
WELF, SARA	24	F	MD	PLZZZZ	USA

SHIP: SALIER

FROM: BREMEN
TO: NEW YORK
ARRIVED: 12 MAY 1885

PASSENGER	AGE	SEX	OCCUPATION	PRIVL	DES
SLER, GOLDE	20	F	NN	RRZZZZ	USA
WOLDMANN, JOS.	21	M	LABR	RRZZZZ	USA
RABINOWITZ, SCHIME	22	F	NN	RRZZZZ	USA
SARAH	20	F	NN	RRZZZZ	USA
WEBER, ROCHEL-ETTEL	24	M	NN	RRZZZZ	USA
SEIX, CAL.	25	M	NN	RRZZZZ	USA
WERNER, RIEWE	20	F	NN	RRZZZZ	USA
GLUECKEICH, SAM.	17	M	DLR	RRZZZZ	USA
STIEBEL, BERL.	18	M	DLR	RRZZZZ	USA
PINDRAK, WOLF	25	M	DLR	RRZZZZ	USA
WELTMANN, TRIESCHE	25	M	DLR	RRZZZZ	USA
SCHERMANN, ABRAHAM	20	M	DLR	RRZZZZ	USA
HUTMAUHER, HIRSCH	22	M	DLR	RRZZZZ	USA
WASCHNESK, LIEBER	22	M	DLR	RRZZZZ	USA
DANELEKAD, ANNA	36	F	NN	RRZZZZ	USA
ANNA	11	F	CH	RRZZZZ	USA
MARIE	8	F	CHILD	RRZZZZ	USA
LOTTE	6	F	CHILD	RRZZZZ	USA
JOHANNA	4	F	CHILD	RRZZZZ	USA
JOSEF	.02	M	INFANT	RRZZZZ	USA
AUGUSTE	.02	F	INFANT	RRZZZZ	USA
URBAN, HELEN	18	F	NN	RRZZZZ	USA
FRIEDMANN, FRED.	28	M	LABR	RRZZZZ	USA
RACHEL	24	F	W	RRZZZZ	USA
FRIEDBERG, SAM.	24	M	LABR	RRZZZZ	USA
IROTZKY, HARRIS	26	M	NN	RRZZZZ	USA
LEWITH, MORITZ	40	M	NN	RRZZZZ	USA
LEFF, ZORACH	15	M	NN	RRZZZZ	USA
BESNIEWSKY, MOTRI-O.	26	F	NN	RRZZZZ	USA
EISE, MIRE	9	F	CHILD	RRZZZZ	USA
MIRJE, SEIFERT	.09	F	INFANT	RRZZZZ	USA
BLUMENTHAL, IDA	17	F	NN	RRZZZZ	USA
ROHAN, SEPEL	19	M	NN	RRZZZZ	USA
LIPSCHITZ, MOSES	28	M	DLR	RRZZZZ	USA
GELBBLUM, ABRAHAM	26	M	DLR	RRZZZZ	USA
LOWENBERG, BABETTE	22	F	NN	RRZZZZ	USA
RIED, SAREN	21	M	DLR	RRZZZZ	USA
HERMANN	19	M	DLR	RRZZZZ	USA
BALSER, LEIB	24	M	DLR	RRZZZZ	USA
HERR, LIPMANN	23	M	DLR	RRZZZZ	USA
SADEWSKY, ANTONIUS	42	M	DLR	RRZZZZ	USA
HANNAH	27	F	W	RRZZZZ	USA
VINCENTZ	5	M	CHILD	RRZZZZ	USA
ADELA	4	F	CHILD	RRZZZZ	USA
ALEXANDER	1	M	CHILD	RRZZZZ	USA
RUNDA, F.	48	M	DLR	RRZZZZ	USA
RACHEL	47	F	W	RRZZZZ	USA
LEISER	23	M	NN	RRZZZZ	USA
CHEJE	20	M	NN	RRZZZZ	USA
CHANE	17	F	NN	RRZZZZ	USA
GITTEL	25	F	NN	RRZZZZ	USA
EISIG	21	M	NN	RRZZZZ	USA
PORT, ELENE	25	F	NN	RRZZZZ	USA
MARIE	11	F	NN	RRZZZZ	USA
FANNY	6	F	CHILD	RRZZZZ	USA
LINA	4	F	CHILD	RRZZZZ	USA
GERBER, ELIAS	25	M	DLR	RRZZZZ	USA
HISKOWITZ, CONSTANT.	45	M	DLR	RRZZZZ	USA
ROSALIE	40	F	W	RRZZZZ	USA
VLADEK	11	M	CH	RRZZZZ	USA
JAN	5	M	CHILD	RRZZZZ	USA
SIZMUND	4	M	CHILD	RRZZZZ	USA
WANDA	3	F	CHILD	RRZZZZ	USA
VIETA	.06	F	INFANT	RRZZZZ	USA
ZELINSKI, JACOB	35	M	DLR	RRZZZZ	USA
FRANZISKA	30	F	W	RRZZZZ	USA
MAGDELOWSKY, ABTAH.	29	M	DLR	RRZZZZ	USA
HIRSCHFELD, TOHAS	17	M	DLR	RRZZZZ	USA
SCHAJEWITZ, ABE	20	M	DLR	RRZZZZ	USA
KERNA, STEFAN	25	M	DLR	RRZZZZ	USA
BROMNSTEIN, JANKEL	26	M	DLR	RRZZZZ	USA
RUBINSTEIN, MEYER	34	M	DLR	RRZZZZ	USA
KASKE	28	F	W	RRZZZZ	USA
SARAH	4	F	CHILD	RRZZZZ	USA
GETEL	.11	F	INFANT	RRZZZZ	USA
BORN, DANIEL	20	M	CL	RRZZZZ	USA
LEWIN, CHAWE	40	M	DLR	RRZZZZ	USA
WOLPERT, LEA	24	F	NN	RRZZZZ	USA
BLUME	25	F	NN	RRZZZZ	USA
ARON	30	M	NN	RRZZZZ	USA
MUSER, JOHANUS	30	M	NN	RRZZZZ	USA
PRANEITIS, FRANE	20	M	NN	RRZZZZ	USA
NADRIZIME, EPHR.	38	M	NN	RRZZZZ	USA
GOLSTEIN, B.	25	M	NN	RRZZZZ	USA

SHIP: ENGLAND

FROM: LIVERPOOL AND QUEENSTOWN
TO: NEW YORK
ARRIVED: 13 MAY 1885

PASSENGER	AGE	SEX	OCCUPATION	PRIVL	DES
KLEIN, ABRAHAM	46	M	DRS	RRZZZZ	USA
WEKLU, ZELDA	26	F	SP	FNZZZZ	USA
WARILU, MARY	21	F	SP	FNZZZZ	USA
ANDERDOTTER, GRETTE	24	F	SP	FNZZZZ	USA
PENTILA, MATHEU	26	M	LABR	FNZZZZ	USA
WEIKALA, MATHEU	27	M	LABR	FNZZZZ	USA
PELANDER, MATHIAS	20	M	LABR	FNZZZZ	USA
WITALA, MATHIAS	27	M	LABR	FNZZZZ	USA
GEDDALA, JOH.	20	M	LABR	FNZZZZ	USA
KRIMTALA, MATHIAS	20	M	LABR	FNZZZZ	USA
LANTA, ANNA	29	F	SP	FNZZZZ	USA
PUMALA, MATHIAS	23	M	LABR	FNZZZZ	USA
UREFE	35	F	W	FNZZZZ	USA
SOFIE	.06	F	INFANT	FNZZZZ	USA
HAKALA, ESAIUS	23	M	LABR	FNZZZZ	USA
SAPPARE, JOH	39	M	LABR	FNZZZZ	USA
MAHOSHI, JACOB	28	M	LABR	FNZZZZ	USA
WILBONSEN, JACOB	30	M	LABR	FNZZZZ	USA
KOZALH, JOHANNA	23	F	SP	FNZZZZ	USA
SKARBECK, H.	26	M	LABR	FNZZZZ	USA
BALKEWY, JOH	25	M	LABR	FNZZZZ	USA
SEOMOT, CONST.	20	M	LABR	FNZZZZ	USA
POLANES, LUD.	27	M	LABR	FNZZZZ	USA
ABOWSKI, ARON	21	M	LABR	FNZZZZ	USA
KHTONERANSKA, JUTBY	34	M	LABR	FNZZZZ	USA
POVICK, BERKE	30	M	LABR	FNZZZZ	USA
SOME, LOCKET	11	M	CH	FNZZZZ	USA
PADOVSKY, JACOB	20	M	LABR	FNZZZZ	USA
LAMHENRAD, BORUCH	11	M	CH	FNZZZZ	USA

PASSENGER	AGE	SEX	OCCUPATION	PRV VIL DES
LIFCHIT, PESCHE	22	M	LABR	FNZZZZUSA
RAHN, WOLF	20	M	LABR	FNZZZZUSA
KASPAR, JOSEFE	24	M	LABR	FNZZZZUSA
HENHEL, ESEL	24	M	LABR	FNZZZZUSA
MASKINUZ, LUSIN	26	M	LABR	FNZZZZUSA
SMUMHE, MHLOME	11	M	CH	FNZZZZUSA
HICHETOVSHE, JOSEF	27	M	LABR	FNZZZZUSA
OKRENTONE, SIMON	28	M	LABR	FNZZZZUSA
GOSCHANSKY, HILLET	27	M	LABR	FNZZZZUSA
RUTSHOBY, MOSES	11	M	CH	FNZZZZUSA
CHURGIN, ALB.	25	M	LABR	FNZZZZUSA
KAPLAN, H.	25	M	LABR	FNZZZZUSA
WEINSTEIN, CH.	24	M	LABR	FNZZZZUSA
FISCHEL, JACOB	25	M	LABR	FNZZZZUSA
WOLFSEHN, WLH.	18	F	SP	FNZZZZUSA
HINDA	20	F	SP	FNZZZZUSA
REBECKA	.06	F	INFANT	FNZZZZUSA
WARCHAFSKY, J.	24	M	LABR	FNZZZZUSA
GIBSMAN, MOSES	22	M	LABR	FNZZZZUSA
ROWIN, JENNIF.	18	F	SP	FNZZZZUSA
FISCHER, JOSEF	11	M	CH	FNZZZZUSA
ROBIN, K.	17	M	LABR	FNZZZZUSA
KARSCH, WOLF	27	M	LABR	FNZZZZUSA
WIDIS, FOBIUS	21	M	LABR	FNZZZZUSA
WILLIS, ISACK	11	M	CH	FNZZZZUSA
RABMSOVIT, ABR.	22	M	LABR	FNZZZZUSA
KAPLIN, HENDEL	27	M	LABR	FNZZZZUSA

PASSENGER	AGE	SEX	OCCUPATION	PRV VIL DES
DOBRSINEWSKI, CHAGE	36	M	LABR	RRZZZZNY
SCHEPEL	11	M	UNKNOWN	RRZZZZNY
BROCHE	10	F	UNKNOWN	RRZZZZNY
ERSCHEL	7	F	CHILD	RRZZZZNY
RITKA	5	F	CHILD	RRZZZZNY
ITKE	5	F	CHILD	RRZZZZNY
RASCHKE	4	F	CHILD	RRZZZZNY
SCHOLENKE	2	F	CHILD	RRZZZZNY
WIJOST, JANKO	10	M	UNKNOWN	RRZZZZNY
DECHICHOWITZ, MADYSLAW	32	M	LABR	RRZZZZUNK
WOJEKOWSKA, STANISLAWA	18	F	UNKNOWN	RRZZZZUNK
GRODZEWSKY, RIVE	36	M	UNKNOWN	RRZZZZNY
BEREL	15	F	UNKNOWN	RRZZZZNY
HASCHE	11	F	UNKNOWN	RRZZZZNY
PERSCHE	8	F	CHILD	RRZZZZNY
LEISCHE	7	F	CHILD	RRZZZZNY
ERDLE	5	F	CHILD	RRZZZZNY
GITLE	.01	F	INFANT	RRZZZZNY
JATSCHKA, JANKOW	26	M	UNKNOWN	RRZZZZNY
LENE	25	F	UNKNOWN	RRZZZZNY
ITZKOWITZ, SCHANNE	19	F	UNKNOWN	RRZZZZNY
SEIDER, NUCHEN	20	F	UNKNOWN	RRZZZZNY
GLADSTEIN, ROSALIE	28	F	UNKNOWN	RRZZZZNY
RIFKE, SARAH	36	F	UNKNOWN	RRZZZZUNK
MONIS	10	F	UNKNOWN	RRZZZZUNK
ANNA	8	F	CHILD	RRZZZZUNK

SHIP: HOHENSTAUFEN

FROM: BREMEN
TO: NEW YORK
ARRIVED: 13 MAY 1885

PASSENGER	AGE	SEX	OCCUPATION	PRV VIL DES
LASNITZKA, MIREL	23	M	LABR	RRZZZZNY
SCHWELGIN, AUG.	23	M	LABR	RRZZZZNY
SCHNITTKOWSKA, JADWIGA	17	F	LABR	RRZZZZNY
CERECZKIEWICZ, JULIANNA	28	F	UNKNOWN	RRZZZZNY
WISNIEWSK, VICTORIA	28	F	UNKNOWN	RRZZZZNY
VICTORIA	4	F	CHILD	RRZZZZNY
LEISER, ABRAHAM	27	M	FARMER	RRZZZZNY
JELLIN, DOBE	17	F	UNKNOWN	RRZZZZNY
DOBE	16	F	UNKNOWN	RRZZZZNY
LYDMANN, JAN	29	M	LABR	RRZZZZNY
SCHKOLNICK, BEILE	12	M	UNKNOWN	RRZZZZNY
JANKE	8	M	CHILD	RRZZZZNY
LISETTE	7	F	CHILD	RRZZZZNY
MESCHLE	3	M	CHILD	RRZZZZNY
COHN, MOSCH-WOLF	31	M	LABR	RRZZZZNY
JETTE	31	F	UNKNOWN	RRZZZZNY
SCOLNIK, NECHAME	58	F	UNKNOWN	RRZZZZNY
RIKE	18	F	UNKNOWN	RRZZZZNY
GURZYNSKY, JOSEF	24	M	LABR	RRZZZZIL
NADROSKI, JADINGER	39	M	FARMER	RRZZZZNY
JOHN	8	M	CHILD	RRZZZZNY
JOSEF	.06	M	INFANT	RRZZZZNY
MUHLEWITSCH, IGNAZ	30	M	FARMER	RRZZZZUNK
STOLZKE, FRANZISKA	21	F	UNKNOWN	RRZZZZNY
MATIAKOWSKA, FRANZISKA	21	F	UNKNOWN	RRZZZZNY
VOYDA, JAN	22	M	LABR	RRZZZZNY
BLOCK, HENE	34	F	UNKNOWN	RRZZZZUNK
SCHMIDT, BEILE	16	M	LABR	RRZZZZNY
SCHULZ, JOH.	23	F	LABR	RRZZZZNY
KAMENTZ, U	25	M	LABR	RRZZZZNY
ROHEL, JENNY	24	F	UNKNOWN	RRZZZZNY
MARSCHE	3	F	CHILD	RRZZZZNY
CRONMANN, JERMA	26	M	UNKNOWN	RRZZZZNY
JANKEL	3	F	CHILD	RRZZZZNY
MESCHE	.09	F	INFANT	RRZZZZNY
KINSKI, LENA	25	F	UNKNOWN	RRZZZZNY

SHIP: NEVADA

FROM: LIVERPOOL AND QUEENSTOWN
TO: NEW YORK
ARRIVED: 13 MAY 1885

PASSENGER	AGE	SEX	OCCUPATION	PRV VIL DES
KULIKOWSKI, I.	22	M	LABR	PLZZZZUSA
POTROSEHEITSY, I.	21	M	LABR	PLZZZZUSA
JAKUBOWSKY, I.	27	M	LABR	PLZZZZUSA
POTESCHINSKY, H.	33	M	LABR	PLZZZZUSA
BUKOWSKY, S.	23	M	LABR	PLZZZZUSA
CRESLIESKI, JAN	33	M	LABR	PLZZZZUSA
LESIROWITZ, SAM	40	M	LABR	PLZZZZUSA
HUSCHESSKY, O.	20	M	LABR	PLZZZZUSA
LMIGEWICY, JAN	35	M	LABR	PLZZZZUSA
SCHTERETITZKY, I.	26	M	LABR	PLZZZZUSA
KLAWANSKY, I.	23	M	LABR	PLZZZZUSA
INSEHOTZKI, I.	27	M	LABR	PLZZZZUSA
HRUDMANN, I.	29	M	LABR	PLZZZZUSA
MUSCHIRARSKY, SAM	40	M	LABR	PLZZZZUSA
RICHIKOWSKY, M.	40	M	LABR	PLZZZZUSA
DOBKICAREY, ANTON	24	M	LABR	PLZZZZUSA
GRODSINSKY, M.	24	M	LABR	PLZZZZUSA
SADOWSKY, I.	26	M	LABR	PLZZZZUSA
KAFIGINSKY, A.	27	M	LABR	PLZZZZUSA
BICHTMAN, I.	11	M	LABR	PLZZZZUSA
LUKWITZ, M.	37	M	LABR	PLZZZZUSA
WOTRASHERITZ, M.	35	M	LABR	PLZZZZUSA
BARBINSKI, B.	25	M	LABR	PLZZZZUSA
MARANSKY, A.	40	M	LABR	PLZZZZUSA
STANKEWITZ, I.	28	M	LABR	PLZZZZUSA
GBUBOKYKY, CHARM	23	M	LABR	PLZZZZUSA
BROSKY, H.	23	M	LABR	PLZZZZUSA
KUPOWSKY, B.	17	M	LABR	PLZZZZUSA
SCHLOMAWITZ, ITZIG	30	M	LABR	PLZZZZUSA
SOHEROWINSKY, I.	30	M	LABR	PLZZZZUSA
LERNISKI, A.	20	M	LABR	PLZZZZUSA
SNARSKY, L.	21	M	LABR	PLZZZZUSA
HITROWITZ, M.	24	M	LABR	PLZZZZUSA
MOLLASCHIWITZ, G.	17	M	LABR	PLZZZZUSA
SPRENSKY, H.	27	F	W	PLZZZZUSA
JOSEPHA	24	M	LABR	PLZZZZUSA
KLEMONT, A.	28	M	LABR	PLZZZZUSA

PASSENGER	AGE	SEX	OCCUPATION	PV RI VL	DES
PIKARSKI, A.	11	M	LABR	PLZZZZ	USA
CHIMLOWSKY, I.	27	M	LABR	PLZZZZ	USA
HEILELEWITZ, L.	18	M	LABR	PLZZZZ	USA
JACHINOWITZ, M.	30	M	LABR	PLZZZZ	USA
BROSUNSKY, I.	32	M	LABR	PLZZZZ	USA
MISKY, S.	19	M	LABR	PLZZZZ	USA
CHANOWITZ, I.	55	M	LABR	PLZZZZ	USA
DWORE	50	F	W	PLZZZZ	USA
ESTHER	15	F	CH	PLZZZZ	USA
CHANE	8	M	CHILD	PLZZZZ	USA

SHIP: WAESLAND

FROM: ANTWERP
TO: NEW YORK
ARRIVED: 14 MAY 1885

PASSENGER	AGE	SEX	OCCUPATION	PV RI VL	DES
HARTMANN, J.	23	M	LABR	RRZZZZ	NY
HAAS, J.	44	M	LABR	RRZZZZ	PHI
J.	24	M	LABR	RRZZZZ	PHI
OSINKI, JH.	21	M	LABR	PLZZZZ	NY
ZEBRONSKI, JOS.	15	M	LABR	PLZZZZ	UNK
FAMMNEZ, ANT.	70	M	LABR	PLZZZZ	UNK
FRANZ	55	M	LABR	PLZZZZ	UNK
CZENETSKI, FR.	26	M	LABR	PLZZZZ	NY
ROSA	22	F	SVNT	PLZZZZ	NY
MAR.	2	F	CHILD	PLZZZZ	NY
JOH.	00	M	INF	PLZZZZ	NY
GANSTER, AUG.	36	M	LABR	RRZZZZ	NY
AUG.	7	M	CHILD	RRZZZZ	NY
LUD.	4	M	CHILD	RRZZZZ	NY
PETER	3	M	CHILD	RRZZZZ	NY
STEYMANN, C.	19	M	BCHR	PLZZZZ	NY
LIPSKY, J.	15	M	LABR	PLZZZZ	MIL
LITNTRESKA, MARIE	30	F	LABR	PLZZZZ	UNK
NOE	6	M	CHILD	PLZZZZ	UNK
ANNA	4	F	CHILD	PLZZZZ	UNK
FUNK, CH.	30	M	LABR	RRZZZZ	UNK
ROS.	28	F	UNKNOWN	RRZZZZ	UNK
JOH.	5	M	CHILD	RRZZZZ	UNK
WIL.	3	M	CHILD	RRZZZZ	UNK
SOLOMON	00	M	INF	RRZZZZ	UNK
JAMSREMEZ, AD.	25	M	CPTR	RRZZZZ	UNK
JOS.	25	F	UNKNOWN	RRZZZZ	UNK
LINKA, JAC.	30	M	LABR	PLZZZZ	PIT
M.	28	F	UNKNOWN	PLZZZZ	PIT
W.	4	M	CHILD	PLZZZZ	PIT
M.	2	F	CHILD	PLZZZZ	PIT
EM.	00	M	INF	PLZZZZ	PIT
RISTONE, C.	22	F	LABR	PLZZZZ	NY
TRUCHAUSS, J.	49	M	LABR	PLAGAL	NY
KAUF, SOPH.	28	F	TLR	PLZZZZ	NY
ROB.	11	M	UNKNOWN	PLZZZZ	NY
J.	9	M	CHILD	PLZZZZ	NY
FISCHER, ANNA	15	F	SVNT	PLZZZZ	NY
ROTZ, S.	17	M	MSN	PLZZZZ	PHI

SHIP: HAMMONIA

FROM: HAMBURG AND HAVRE
TO: NEW YORK
ARRIVED: 15 MAY 1885

PASSENGER	AGE	SEX	OCCUPATION	PV RI VL	DES
TIKOTZKI, BREINE	18	M	SGL	RRZZZZ	USA
LEVIT, JUDE	42	M	DLR	RRZZZZ	USA
NOWODWORSKY, JANKEL	35	M	LABR	RRZZZZ	USA
LOEB, HENA	7	M	CHILD	RRZZZZ	USA
SIMON	6	M	CHILD	RRZZZZ	USA
JACOB	.06	M	INFANT	RRZZZZ	USA
KAMBER, SCHEINE	38	F	W	RRZZZZ	USA
SARA	16	F	CH	RRZZZZ	USA
MALKE	9	M	CHILD	RRZZZZ	USA
REICHEL	8	M	CHILD	RRZZZZ	USA
MINNA	6	F	CHILD	RRZZZZ	USA
LUWELSKY, MARY	15	F	SGL	RRZZZZ	USA
JASKOWIAK, VALENTIN	43	M	LABR	RRZZZZ	USA
MARIANNE	40	F	W	RRZZZZ	USA
JOSEF	8	M	CHILD	RRZZZZ	USA
CASIMIR	.11	M	INFANT	RRZZZZ	USA
HALPERU, GUDIC	40	F	W	RRZZZZ	USA
RIWKE	5	F	CHILD	RRZZZZ	USA
JOSSEL	.11	M	INFANT	RRZZZZ	USA
LEISEROWITZ, SARA	19	F	SGL	RRZZZZ	USA
MALKE	9	F	CHILD	RRZZZZ	USA
ROGOWCE, MINZE	50	F	W	RRZZZZ	USA
CHLIBOWSKY, ISRAEL	27	M	LABR	RRZZZZ	USA
ABRAHAM	9	M	CHILD	RRZZZZ	USA
BLUM, WOLF	26	M	LABR	RRZZZZ	USA
PIALKOWITZ, FEIGE	23	F	W	RRZZZZ	USA
TAUBE	.11	F	INFANT	RRZZZZ	USA
LEZAL, LIEBE	30	F	W	RRZZZZ	USA
FEIGE	7	F	CHILD	RRZZZZ	USA
BERKSON, DAVID	50	M	LABR	RRZZZZ	USA
WIGRANSKY, CH.	20	F	W	RRZZZZ	USA
ROSEL	4	F	CHILD	RRZZZZ	USA
GESULLA	5	F	CHILD	RRZZZZ	USA
HAGENBERG, MEYER	18	M	LABR	RRZZZZ	USA
OLIENPOLSKY, KEILE	.11	F	INFANT	RRZZZZ	USA
KEILE	.11	F	INFANT	RRZZZZ	USA
SIMPSON, JERUCHIM	40	M	LABR	RRZZZZ	USA
SAMUEL	25	M	LABR	RRZZZZ	USA
SIEW, JOSEF	17	M	LABR	RRZZZZ	USA
BLASCHKE, MICHAEL	40	M	LABR	RRZZZZ	USA
REMPINSKY, WLADISLAW	20	M	LABR	RRZZZZ	USA
SOBOLEWSKA, TUCOPHILA	38	F	W	RRZZZZ	USA
JAN	9	M	CHILD	RRZZZZ	USA
JULIA	8	F	CHILD	RRZZZZ	USA
STANISLAW	.11	M	INFANT	RRZZZZ	USA
BOCHMANN, BERULE	21	M	LABR	RRZZZZ	USA
TAMENHAMN, CHATZKEL	21	M	SGL	RRZZZZ	USA
SEGAL, MINA	20	F	SGL	RRZZZZ	USA
LITWIN, ISAAC	19	M	TLR	RRZZZZ	USA
RIBOWSKY, BER	26	M	BCHR	RRZZZZ	USA
SIDER, PESCHE	20	M	SGL	RRZZZZ	USA
HUBERMANN, MANES	19	M	DLR	RRZZZZ	USA
LITWIN, ABRAHAM	37	M	TLR	RRZZZZ	USA
MARGOWSKI, CHANNE	23	M	DLR	RRZZZZ	USA
MEYSLING, JOH.	23	M	LABR	RRZZZZ	USA
HULDA	25	F	W	RRZZZZ	USA
WILLI	.11	M	INFANT	RRZZZZ	USA
LEWITZKY, MARTIN	19	M	MCHT	RRZZZZ	USA
SCHUCIDER, SCHAJE	26	M	LABR	RRZZZZ	USA
SIDER, JANKEL	19	M	LABR	RRZZZZ	USA
JOSEF	9	M	CHILD	RRZZZZ	USA
OLIENPOLSKY, DWORA	32	F	W	RRZZZZ	USA
CHANNE	9	M	CHILD	RRZZZZ	USA
LIEBE	7	M	CHILD	RRZZZZ	USA
CHAIN	4	M	CHILD	RRZZZZ	USA
KRUCK, JAEF	24	M	LABR	RRZZZZ	USA
RASUCHOWITZ, TAUBE	18	F	SGL	RRZZZZ	USA
RUDERMANN, UECHAME	14	M	SGL	RRZZZZ	USA
FEICKTOROWSKY, MEYER	24	M	LABR	RRZZZZ	USA
ISRAEL	9	M	CHILD	RRZZZZ	USA
SMOLENSKI, CHASCHE	40	F	W	RRZZZZ	USA
MEIER	9	M	CHILD	RRZZZZ	USA
HODES	8	M	CHILD	RRZZZZ	USA
DOBRE	7	M	CHILD	RRZZZZ	USA
JACOB	3	M	CHILD	RRZZZZ	USA
JOSEPH	.11	M	INFANT	RRZZZZ	USA
JATKOWSKI, GITTEL	50	F	W	RRZZZZ	USA

PASSENGER	AGE	SEX	OCCUPATION	PRV VIL DES
KOHEN, HIRSCH	17	M	DLR	RRZZZZUSA
SANDLER, CHAN.	17	M	SGL	RRZZZZUSA
BERKSON, JANKEL	18	M	LABR	RRZZZZUSA
ITE	30	F	W	RRZZZZUSA
CHRISTENSEN, CHRISTINE	53	F	W	RRZZZZUSA
ANNA	15	F	CH	RRZZZZUSA
MOTTE	20	F	CH	RRZZZZUSA
CHRISTIANNE	.11	F	INFANT	RRZZZZUSA
PETERS, JACOB	18	M	FARMER	RRZZZZUSA
SCHUEDEN, THEODOR	17	M	FARMER	RRZZZZUSA
AHRENSDORF, PETER	27	M	FARMER	RRZZZZUSA
SOPHIE	62	F	W	RRZZZZUSA
JACOB, MARG.	27	F	SGL	RRZZZZUSA
MAUSSEN, SOPHIE	14	F	SGL	RRZZZZUSA
MARIE	9	F	CHILD	RRZZZZUSA
SCHULZ, PETER	51	M	FARMER	RRZZZZUSA
WIEBKE	50	F	W	RRZZZZUSA
ANNA	16	F	CH	RRZZZZUSA
EMMA	9	F	CHILD	RRZZZZUSA
CHRISTIAN	8	M	CHILD	RRZZZZUSA
GRAM, CATHARINA	42	F	FARMER	RRZZZZUSA
BERTEL	16	M	CH	RRZZZZUSA
KAREN	14	M	CH	RRZZZZUSA
ANNA	9	F	CHILD	RRZZZZUSA
NISS	7	M	CHILD	RRZZZZUSA
KRISTINA	.11	F	INFANT	RRZZZZUSA
HANSEN, ELISABETH	53	F	W	RRZZZZUSA
MARIE	21	F	D	RRZZZZUSA
BERTRAMSEN, CHRISTIANE	38	F	W	RRZZZZUSA
ANNE	17	F	CH	RRZZZZUSA
MARIE	9	F	CHILD	RRZZZZUSA
BERTHA	8	F	CHILD	RRZZZZUSA
PAULA	6	F	CHILD	RRZZZZUSA

SHIP: HERMANN

FROM: BREMEN
TO: NEW YORK
ARRIVED: 15 MAY 1885

PASSENGER	AGE	SEX	OCCUPATION	PRV VIL DES
POTZVERSKI, MINDEL	30	M	LABR	RRZZZZUSA
CACILIE	2	F	CHILD	RRZZZZUSA
FROMME	.01	F	INFANT	RRZZZZUSA
LEMPISKY, RICKE	19	M	LABR	RRZZZZUSA
GROSTEL, ROSALIE	31	F	NN	RRZZZZUSA
PERNSTEIN, BASCHE	32	M	LABR	RRZZZZUSA
JUDKE	7	M	CHILD	RRZZZZUSA
NAFAEH	6	M	CHILD	RRZZZZUSA
JANKO	3	M	CHILD	RRZZZZUSA
ABRAM	2	M	CHILD	RRZZZZUSA
RIFKE	.01	F	INFANT	RRZZZZUSA
PLONTKE, GOTTLIEB	60	M	LABR	RRZZZZUSA
EMILIE	35	F	NN	RRZZZZUSA
DUKSIEL, JACOB	36	M	NN	RRZZZZUSA
ROSINE	31	F	NN	RRZZZZUSA
THEODOR	7	M	CHILD	RRZZZZUSA
CAROLINE	3	F	CHILD	RRZZZZUSA
GATON, ALEXANDER	49	M	FARMER	RRZZZZUSA
ERNST	19	M	FARMER	RRZZZZUSA
LYDIA	18	F	NN	RRZZZZUSA
MAUS, CATHERINA	20	F	NN	RRZZZZUSA
FRIEDRICH	20	M	FARMER	RRZZZZUSA
SCHELL, LUDWIG	30	M	FARMER	RRZZZZUSA
SINGEIS, EDNARD	19	M	FARMER	RRZZZZUSA
PREISS, MIKE	20	F	NN	RRZZZZUSA
EMILIE	14	F	NN	RRZZZZUSA
SKINSKY, JACOB	40	M	LABR	RRZZZZUSA
DOFYRR, JACOB	30	M	LABR	RRZZZZUSA
KLOSS, JOH.	26	M	LABR	RRZZZZUSA
LINKIWICZ, NICOL	17	M	LABR	RRZZZZUSA
PARTNOI, FELIG	38	M	LABR	RRZZZZUSA
GAITEL	16	M	LABR	RRZZZZUSA
ROSEWITZ, PETER	36	M	LABR	RRZZZZUSA
ASCHUKUMES, AMROS	20	M	LABR	RRZZZZUSA
LICHTHEIN, SCHLEIME	49	M	LABR	RRZZZZUSA
PATURA, LAZAR	17	M	LABR	RRZZZZUSA
BODSTEIN, JUDAS	24	M	LABR	RRZZZZUSA
KRONITZ, LAZER	17	M	LABR	RRZZZZUSA
KREMITZ, SCHOLEM	20	M	LABR	RRZZZZUSA
BUDERMANN, NEIKE	18	M	LABR	RRZZZZUSA
SCHULTZ, JOH.	23	M	LABR	RRZZZZUSA
WIEZERKIEWICZ, FRANK	18	M	LABR	RRZZZZUSA
GRUNHAUS, SCHMUEL	18	M	LABR	RRZZZZUSA
SANDLER, SORE	18	M	LABR	RRZZZZUSA
NEPPNER, SASSKIND	21	M	LABR	RRZZZZUSA
LIFSCHITZ, SORE	20	M	LABR	RRZZZZUSA
LEWIN, MOSES	22	M	LABR	RRZZZZUSA
PRANSKY, HIRSCH	22	M	LABR	RRZZZZUSA

SHIP: KAETIE

FROM: STETTIN
TO: NEW YORK
ARRIVED: 15 MAY 1885

PASSENGER	AGE	SEX	OCCUPATION	PRV VIL DES
RATTLEN, SARA	50	F	WO	RRZZZZUSA
GESCHKE, AUGUST	34	M	LABR	RRZZZZUSA
EMILIE	38	F	W	RRZZZZUSA
PAUL	3	M	CHILD	RRZZZZUSA
EMILIE	6	F	CHILD	RRZZZZUSA
JOHANNES	1	M	CHILD	RRZZZZUSA
WELT, MARTIN	40	M	LABR	RRZZZZUSA
AUGUSTE	37	F	W	RRZZZZUSA
BERTHA	10	F	D	RRZZZZUSA
AUGUSTE	8	F	CHILD	RRZZZZUSA
MARIA	6	F	CHILD	RRZZZZUSA
JOHANNA	5	F	CHILD	RRZZZZUSA
OTTO	.06	M	INFANT	RRZZZZUSA
DEMBINSKI, MARIA	30	F	SP	RRZZZZUSA
ANNA	30	F	SP	RRZZZZUSA
MARARWSKI, WALENTIN	28	M	LABR	RRZZZZUSA
JOSEPHA	28	F	W	RRZZZZUSA
PAPOMOTA	50	F	WO	RRZZZZUSA
GRAVARACK, JOSEF	35	M	LABR	RRZZZZUSA
KRIMM	27	M	LABR	RRZZZZUSA
FABER, FEIBEL	20	M	LABR	RRZZZZUSA
DORA	16	F	SI	RRZZZZUSA
EVA	15	F	SI	RRZZZZUSA
SCHURMAN, ABRAHAM	32	M	LABR	RRZZZZUSA
BERNSTEIN, HIRSCH	34	M	LABR	RRZZZZUSA
REBECCA	28	F	W	RRZZZZUSA
FANNI	4	F	CHILD	RRZZZZUSA
JACOB	1	M	CHILD	RRZZZZUSA
JANKOVS, ESRAEL	19	M	LABR	RRZZZZUSA
JABOULSKY, SIMON	19	M	LABR	RRZZZZUSA
DREES, AUGUST	26	M	SHMK	RRZZZZUSA
ZAGORSKI, MICHAEL	39	M	SHMK	RRZZZZUSA
MAGDALENE	28	F	W	RRZZZZUSA
MARIA	2	F	CHILD	RRZZZZUSA
PIROCH, ALBRECHT	42	M	LABR	RRZZZZUSA
APPOLINA	29	F	W	RRZZZZUSA
JOHANN	25	M	FARMER	RRZZZZUSA
LENACH, DAVID	15	M	LABR	RRZZZZUSA
ITREY	58	M	LABR	RRZZZZUSA
KASPRAWITZ, JOHAN	24	M	LABR	RRZZZZUSA

PASSENGER	AGE	SEX	OCCUPATION	PRIVL	DES
SHIP: RHEIN					
FROM: BREMEN AND SOUTHAMPTON					
TO: NEW YORK					
ARRIVED: 15 MAY 1885					
LEVINSOHN, HIRSCH	22	M	LABR	RRZZZZ	USA
GROSSNIAUM, MAX	35	M	LABR	RRZZZZ	USA
GOLDMANN, ESTHER	42	F	NN	RRZZZZ	USA
REISEL	19	F	NN	RRZZZZ	USA
MARCUS	18	M	NN	RRZZZZ	USA
HENOCH	10	M	CH	RRZZZZ	USA
MALI	20	F	NN	RRZZZZ	USA
ISAAC	19	M	LABR	RRZZZZ	USA
SCHWARZMANN, HERMANN	19	M	TRVLR	RRZZZZ	USA
SHIP: CITY OF RICHMOND					
FROM: LIVERPOOL AND QUEENSTOWN					
TO: NEW YORK					
ARRIVED: 16 MAY 1885					
LOWENOHN, C.	18	M	LABR	RRAFWJ	NY
BERLOWITZ, W.	19	M	LABR	RRAFWJ	NY
SHIP: EMS					
FROM: BREMEN					
TO: NEW YORK					
ARRIVED: 16 MAY 1885					
VANBACKMETEFF, U-MRS	27	F	NN	RRZZZZ	USA
SCHINKOMENKOFF, ANNA	19	F	SVNT	RRZZZZ	USA
FISCHER, CARL	70	M	LLD	RRAFVG	USA
CAROLINA	60	F	NN	RRAFVG	USA
RIEB, PHILIPP	32	M	LABR	RRAFWJ	USA
CAROLINE	20	F	NN	RRAFWJ	USA
FRIEDRICH	8	M	CHILD	RRAFWJ	USA
PHILIPP	7	M	CHILD	RRAFWJ	USA
CATHALINE	4	F	CHILD	RRAFWJ	USA
U	00	F	NN	RRAFWJ	USA
U	.03	M	INFANT	RRAFWJ	USA
DOCTIR, GOTTLIEB	52	M	LABR	RRAFWJ	USA
MAGDALINE	46	F	NN	RRAFWJ	USA
JOHANN	20	M	LABR	RRAFWJ	USA
GOTTLIEB	18	M	LABR	RRAFWJ	USA
FRIEDRICH	14	M	CL	RRAFWJ	USA
PHILIPP	8	M	CHILD	RRAFWJ	USA
CHRISTIAN	6	M	CHILD	RRAFWJ	USA
AUGUST	2	M	CHILD	RRAFWJ	USA
EVA	10	F	NN	RRAFWJ	USA
REICH, CHRISTIANE	26	F	NN	RRAFWJ	USA
WITTMAYER, CHRIST.	49	M	LABR	RRAFWJ	USA
ROSINE	21	F	NN	RRAFWJ	USA
ELISE	19	F	NN	RRAFWJ	USA
BARBARA	17	F	NN	RRAFWJ	USA
GOTTLIEB	10	M	NN	RRAFWJ	USA
CHRISTIAN	7	M	CHILD	RRAFWJ	USA
HANK, PETER	33	M	LABR	RRZZZZ	USA
MARGARETHA	34	F	NN	RRZZZZ	USA
PETER	9	M	CHILD	RRZZZZ	USA
GEORG	8	M	CHILD	RRZZZZ	USA
EVA	7	F	CHILD	RRZZZZ	USA
CAROLINE	6	F	CHILD	RRZZZZ	USA
FRIEDRICH	1	M	CHILD	RRZZZZ	USA
JACOB	.05	M	INFANT	RRZZZZ	USA
LEHMABEL, JOHANN	27	M	LABR	RRZZZZ	USA
CATHARINE	27	F	NN	RRZZZZ	USA
JACOB	3	M	CHILD	RRZZZZ	USA
ADAM	2	M	CHILD	RRZZZZ	USA
CATHARINE	.01	F	INFANT	RRZZZZ	USA
LINK, CHRISTIAN	33	M	LABR	RRZZZZ	USA
CHRISTINE	30	F	NN	RRZZZZ	USA
GOTTLIEB	3	M	CHILD	RRZZZZ	USA
SOPHIE	3	F	CHILD	RRZZZZ	USA
EMILIE	1	F	CHILD	RRZZZZ	USA
CAROLINE	.03	F	INFANT	RRZZZZ	USA
LATNER, HEIMICH	27	M	LABR	RRZZZZ	USA
ROSINE	26	F	NN	RRZZZZ	USA
DANIEL	3	M	CHILD	RRZZZZ	USA
HEINRICH	.06	M	INFANT	RRZZZZ	USA
UNGER, JACOB	27	M	LABR	RRZZZZ	USA
CATHARINE	26	F	NN	RRZZZZ	USA
FRIDRICKE	.02	F	INFANT	RRZZZZ	USA
BRO---ER, JOH.	27	M	LABR	RRZZZZ	USA
U	26	F	NN	RRZZZZ	USA
JOHANN	.11	M	INFANT	RRZZZZ	USA
TROSTER, CHRISTOF	55	M	LABR	RRZZZZ	USA
CHRISTINE	54	F	NN	RRZZZZ	USA
SCHAFFER, CHRISTOFF	62	M	LABR	RRZZZZ	USA
CHRISTINE	60	F	NN	RRZZZZ	USA
ROSINE	14	F	NN	RRZZZZ	USA
SPRINGER, FRIEDRICH	29	M	LABR	RRZZZZ	USA
MAGDALENE	27	F	NN	RRZZZZ	USA
FRIEDRICH	7	M	CHILD	RRZZZZ	USA
CAROLINE	4	F	CHILD	RRZZZZ	USA
JOHANN	.11	M	INFANT	RRZZZZ	USA
MAYTONSKY, WIC.	20	M	LABR	RRAFWJ	USA
MOSS, MICHAEL	48	M	LABR	RRAFWJ	USA
MARGARETHE	32	F	NN	RRAFWJ	USA
PETER	18	M	LABR	RRAFWJ	USA
HEINRICH	17	M	LABR	RRAFWJ	USA
ROSINE	7	F	CHILD	RRAFWJ	USA
JOHANN	4	M	CHILD	RRAFWJ	USA
MAGDALENE	2	F	CHILD	RRAFWJ	USA
BRANDNER, JOH.	55	M	LABR	RRAFWJ	USA
ROSINE	50	F	NN	RRAFWJ	USA
CHRISTINE	14	M	NN	RRAFWJ	USA
FRIEDRICH	10	M	NN	RRAFWJ	USA
ELISABETH	23	F	NN	RRAFWJ	USA
BARBARA	22	F	NN	RRAFWJ	USA
CHRISTINE	17	F	NN	RRAFWJ	USA
ROSINE	7	F	CHILD	RRAFWJ	USA
BUGLER, GEORG	36	M	LABR	RRAFWJ	USA
CHRISTINE	34	F	NN	RRAFWJ	USA
MARGARETHE	57	F	NN	RRAFWJ	USA
GOTTLIEB	4	M	CHILD	RRAFWJ	USA
HEINRICH	3	M	CHILD	RRAFWJ	USA
GEORG	1	M	CHILD	RRAFWJ	USA
WITTMEYER, SIMON	55	M	LABR	RRAFWJ	USA
CATHARINE	.01	F	INFANT	RRAFWJ	USA
MOSS, JOHANN	27	M	LABR	RRAFWJ	USA
MARGARETHE	25	F	NN	RRAFWJ	USA
ELISABETH	4	F	CHILD	RRAFWJ	USA
JOHANN	2	M	CHILD	RRAFWJ	USA
HEINRICH	.02	M	INFANT	RRAFWJ	USA
FRIEDRICH	21	M	LABR	RRAFWJ	USA
SMOLINSKI, NICOLAUS	39	M	LABR	RRAFWJ	USA
CHRISTINE	22	F	NN	RRAFWJ	USA
ELISABETH	4	F	CHILD	RRAFWJ	USA
JOHANN	2	M	CHILD	RRAFWJ	USA
WILHELM	.02	M	INFANT	RRAFWJ	USA
KIRSCHMANN, CHRIST.	33	M	LABR	RRAFWJ	USA
PHILIPPINE	12	F	NN	RRAFWJ	USA
JACOB	10	M	NN	RRAFWJ	USA
CATHARINE	9	F	CHILD	RRAFWJ	USA
CHRISTIAN	7	M	CHILD	RRAFWJ	USA
JOHANN	4	M	CHILD	RRAFWJ	USA
FRIEDRICH	2	M	CHILD	RRAFWJ	USA

PASSENGER	AGE	SEX	OCCUPATION	PRV VIL DES
CATHARINE	54	F	NN	RRAFWJUSA
MAGDALENE	19	F	NN	RRAFWJUSA
MAGDALENE	.09	F	INFANT	RRAFWJUSA
ZIMPEL, MICHEL	32	M	LABR	RRAFWJUSA
CATHARINE	20	F	NN	RRAFWJUSA
JOHANN	2	M	CHILD	RRAFWJUSA
HUBER, PETER	25	M	LABR	RRAFWJUSA
MARGARETHE	23	F	NN	RRAFWJUSA
PETER	3	M	CHILD	RRAFWJUSA
CATHARINE	20	F	NN	RRAFWJUSA
SCHAFFER, JACOB	39	M	LABR	RRZZZZUSA
CATHARINE	35	F	NN	RRZZZZUSA
JOHANN	16	M	LABR	RRZZZZUSA
CATHARINE	2	F	CHILD	RRZZZZUSA
JACOB	4	M	CHILD	RRZZZZUSA
STROBEL, JOHANNES	46	M	LABR	RRZZZZUSA
DOROTHEA	45	F	NN	RRZZZZUSA
JOHANN	16	M	LABR	RRZZZZUSA
JACOB	14	M	NN	RRZZZZUSA
FRIEDRICH	7	M	CHILD	RRZZZZUSA
FLEMMER, PETER	46	M	LABR	RRZZZZUSA
PAULINE	32	F	NN	RRZZZZUSA
CAROLINE	18	F	NN	RRZZZZUSA
PETER	12	M	NN	RRZZZZUSA
GUSTAV	10	M	NN	RRZZZZUSA
CAROLINE	10	F	NN	RRZZZZUSA
HUMMER, HEINR.	19	M	FARMER	RRZZZZUSA
ULRICH, JOHANN	24	M	FARMER	RRZZZZUSA
WOLFER, JOHANNES	64	M	FARMER	RRZZZZUSA
RENTSCHLER, JOH.	35	M	FARMER	RRZZZZUSA
JULIANE	30	F	NN	RRZZZZUSA
FRIERIKE	3	F	CHILD	RRZZZZUSA
LISABETHA	6	F	CHILD	RRZZZZUSA
JACOB	5	M	CHILD	RRZZZZUSA
JOHANN	.11	M	INFANT	RRZZZZUSA
JOHANN	48	M	FARMER	RRZZZZUSA
CATHARINE	57	F	NN	RRZZZZUSA
ENTZMINGER, JACOB	32	M	LABR	RRZZZZUSA
CATHARINE	24	F	NN	RRZZZZUSA
CATHARINE	7	F	CHILD	RRZZZZUSA
EVA	3	F	CHILD	RRZZZZUSA
JACOB	.04	M	INFANT	RRZZZZ***
ANNE-MARIA	19	F	NN	RRZZZZUSA
WALKER, JACOB	43	M	FARMER	RRAEIYUSA
MAGDALENE	39	F	NN	RRAEIYUSA
FRIEDRICH	17	M	FARMER	RRAEIYUSA
MAGDALENE	15	F	NN	RRAEIYUSA
JACOB	10	M	NN	RRAEIYUSA
JOHANN	9	M	CHILD	RRAEIYUSA
CHRISTIAN	8	M	CHILD	RRAEIYUSA
JULIANE	6	F	CHILD	RRAEIYUSA
LUDWIG	4	M	CHILD	RRAEIYUSA
ROSINA	2	F	CHILD	RRAEIYUSA
SIEBER, PHILIPP	46	M	FARMER	RRZZZZUSA
MAGDALENE	40	F	NN	RRZZZZUSA
EVA	17	F	NN	RRZZZZUSA
CATHARINA	17	F	NN	RRZZZZUSA
MARIA	10	F	NN	RRZZZZUSA
HEIRICH	4	M	CHILD	RRZZZZUSA
ELISABETH	15	F	NN	RRZZZZUSA
ADAM	7	M	CHILD	RRZZZZUSA
PETER	4	M	CHILD	RRZZZZUSA
GOTTLIEB	.01	M	INFANT	RRZZZZUSA
PUMMERENKE, GOTTL.	21	M	FARMER	RRZZZZUSA
ANDREAS	18	M	FARMER	RRZZZZUSA
BECKER, CHRISTIAN	25	M	FARMER	RRZZZZUSA
CAROLINE	23	F	NN	RRZZZZUSA
OTTILIA	.11	F	INFANT	RRZZZZUSA
BARBARA	21	F	NN	RRZZZZUSA
NILL, JACOB	19	M	FARMER	RRZZZZUSA
STERK, JOHANNES	25	M	FARMER	RRZZZZUSA
ROSINA	22	F	NN	RRZZZZUSA
JOHANNES	2	M	CHILD	RRZZZZUSA
LOUISE	.03	F	INFANT	RRZZZZUSA
LOUISE	18	F	NN	RRZZZZUSA
TITUS, JOHANN	51	M	FARMER	RRZZZZUSA
CATHARINE	49	F	NN	RRZZZZUSA
JOHANNUS	23	M	FARMER	RRZZZZUSA
JACOB	17	M	FARMER	RRZZZZUSA
GEORG	9	M	CHILD	RRZZZZUSA
EMANUEL	5	M	CHILD	RRZZZZUSA
ADOLF	2	M	CHILD	RRZZZZUSA
REGINA	10	F	NN	RRZZZZUSA
KAMPF, JACOB	28	M	FARMER	RRZZZZUSA
CAROLINE	27	F	NN	RRZZZZUSA
JACOB	7	M	CHILD	RRZZZZUSA
MICHAEL	4	M	CHILD	RRZZZZUSA
MATHEUS	.03	M	INFANT	RRZZZZUSA
KASH, PETER	31	M	FARMER	RRZZZZUSA
EVA	26	F	NN	RRZZZZUSA
JULIUS	4	M	CHILD	RRZZZZUSA
SIELER, PETER	27	M	FARMER	RRZZZZUSA
ELISABETH	22	F	NN	RRZZZZUSA
BAUER, JACOB	25	M	FARMER	RRZZZZUSA
CATHRINE	19	F	NN	RRZZZZUSA
STEPPER, GOTTLIEB	19	M	FARMER	RRZZZZUSA
NITZKE, CHRISTOPH	40	M	FARMER	RRZZZZUSA
ROSINA	35	F	NN	RRZZZZUSA
CATHARINE	17	F	NN	RRZZZZUSA
JACOB	16	M	FARMER	RRZZZZUSA
MATHIUS	15	M	FARMER	RRZZZZUSA
CHRISTOPH	11	M	NN	RRZZZZUSA
ROSINA	10	F	NN	RRZZZZUSA
JOHANN	8	M	CHILD	RRZZZZUSA
CAROLINE	6	F	CHILD	RRZZZZUSA
CHRISTIAN	4	M	CHILD	RRZZZZUSA
CHRISTIAN	4	M	CHILD	RRZZZZUSA
WAHL, FRIEDRICH	23	M	FARMER	RRZZZZUSA
MARGARETHE	21	F	NN	RRZZZZUSA
JOHANN	.01	M	INFANT	RRZZZZUSA
WILHELM	26	M	FARMER	RRZZZZUSA
CHRISTINE	22	F	NN	RRZZZZUSA
BOSERT, FRIEDRICH	24	M	FARMER	RRZZZZUSA
CHRISTINE	21	F	NN	RRZZZZUSA
SKALEY, FRIEDR.	38	M	FARMER	RRZZZZUSA
CAROLINE	32	F	NN	RRZZZZUSA
FRIEDR.	13	M	NN	RRZZZZUSA
GOTTLIEB	10	M	NN	RRZZZZUSA
JACOB	7	M	CHILD	RRZZZZUSA
MATHIUS	4	M	CHILD	RRZZZZUSA
SUSANNE	2	F	CHILD	RRZZZZUSA
MAXIA	.11	F	INFANT	RRZZZZUSA
SAMUEL	18	M	FARMER	RRZZZZUSA
GOTTFRIED	16	M	FARMER	RRZZZZUSA
DOBLER, MATHIUS	26	M	FARMER	RRZZZZUSA
CAROLINE	26	F	NN	RRZZZZUSA
JACOB	3	M	CHILD	RRZZZZUSA
GOTTLIEB	.08	M	INFANT	RRZZZZUSA
HAMMEL, JOHANNUS	24	M	FARMER	RRZZZZUSA
MEYER, MICHAEL	18	M	FARMER	RRZZZZUSA
REISER, GOTTFRIED	30	M	FARMER	RRZZZZUSA
SUSANNE	26	F	NN	RRZZZZUSA
ELISABETH	2	F	CHILD	RRZZZZUSA
JOHANN	.06	M	INFANT	RRZZZZUSA

SHIP: GALLIA

FROM: LIVERPOOL AND QUEENSTOWN
TO: NEW YORK
ARRIVED: 18 MAY 1885

PASSENGER	AGE	SEX	OCCUPATION	PRV VIL DES
HOZACKA, MDEA	31	M	LABR	PLZZZZUSA
BADNAVANSKA, MARIE	26	F	UNKNOWN	PLZZZZUSA
BODAK, ONDIA	46	M	LABR	PLZZZZUSA
KROK, JACOR	40	M	LABR	PLZZZZUSA

PASSENGER	AGE	SEX	OCCUPATION	PRV VIL DES
GORENDSTEIN, SCHAMAY	18	M	LABR	PLZZZZUSA
DAVID	10	M	LABR	PLZZZZUSA
SVERSKY, WACK.	59	M	LABR	PLZZZZUSA
SOFIA	56	F	W	PLZZZZUSA
RUMOLA	10	F	CH	PLZZZZUSA
BART, ISRAEL	29	M	PDLR	PLZZZZUSA
NASKA	30	F	W	PLZZZZUSA
KALOLE, IEFSKA	24	F	SP	PLZZZZUSA
ANNA	11	F	CH	PLZZZZUSA
NOSELSKY, ITKA	10	F	CH	PLZZZZUSA
LECHSEK, BAELOLN	29	M	LABR	PLZZZZUSA
ROCHAUK, JANOS	24	M	LABR	PLZZZZUSA
ZUBOWSKY, AUG.	23	M	LABR	PLZZZZUSA
DARENSKY, FRANZ	42	M	LABR	PLZZZZUSA
JENKORSKY, JAN	23	M	LABR	PLZZZZUSA
HEDNEFSKY, ALEX	30	M	LABR	PLZZZZUSA
KOEMAK, FRENKS	33	M	LABR	PLZZZZUSA
STRUMISCKY, ADOLF	50	M	LABR	PLZZZZUSA
ZULKOVSKY, MICHAL	47	M	LABR	PLZZZZUSA
ZAW, PALE	35	M	LABR	PLZZZZUSA
MISKO, JUNCA	26	M	LABR	PLZZZZUSA
MARIE	18	F	SP	PLZZZZUSA
PETRO	16	M	LABR	PLZZZZUSA

SHIP: HABSBURG

FROM: BREMEN
TO: NEW YORK
ARRIVED: 18 MAY 1885

PASSENGER	AGE	SEX	OCCUPATION	PRV VIL DES
MULLER, FIDEL	16	M	LABR	RRZZZZNY
CAPTAN, CHARLES	32	M	LABR	RRZZZZNY
MAREUS, ISRAEL-ARON	18	M	LABR	RRZZZZNY
TUBIRE, JANKEL	18	M	LABR	RRZZZZNY
LUBERINSKI, BARTOLOMI	45	M	LABR	RRZZZZNY
WINITZKI, ISAAC-WOLF	23	M	LABR	RRZZZZNY
SCHMOLLER, JOEL	18	M	LABR	RRAGRTNY
TRYMANN, ALBERT-BIRON	20	M	LABR	RRAHUFNY
ANNENBERG, MIREL	19	M	LABR	RRAHUFNY
BATTJER, AUGUST	19	M	LABR	RRZZZZNY
KESSEL, WOLF	15	M	LABR	RRZZZZNY
ROMANOWSKY, FRANZ	20	M	LABR	RRZZZZNY
KNEG, RUBEN	15	M	LABR	RRAHUFNY
NIEBDOLSKI, FRANZ	26	M	LABR	RRAHTFNY
SCHMIDT, JACOB	25	M	LABR	RRAHTFNY
KANTROWITZ, KIMRIS	29	M	LABR	RRAHTFNY
LIHWANKORAKI, HEINRICH	18	M	LABR	RRZZZZNY
WASENFUSS, CARL	21	M	FARMER	RRZZZZNY
GUROSKI, JOSEF	38	M	LABR	RRAGRTNY
GOUSWROWSKI, JOSEFARE	20	M	LABR	RRAHTFNY
NEVACZELSKI, JOSEF	20	M	LABR	RRAHTFNY
SACHARSKI, STANISLAW	34	M	LABR	RRAHTFNY
JIMBELMANN, PETER	23	M	LABR	RRZZZZNY
AXSEL, CARL	17	M	LABR	RRAAZFNY
WACHSCHICZ, CHRISTOPF	30	M	LABR	RRAHTFNY
ANNA	28	F	W	RRAHTFNY
PAUL	5	M	CHILD	RRAHTFNY
WIDEWSKI, BEILE-GOLDE	30	M	LABR	RRZZZZNY
NACHERN	17	M	LABR	RRZZZZNY
ZEITAC	14	M	LABR	RRZZZZNY
ESTHER	7	F	CHILD	RRZZZZNY
SCH.	2	F	CHILD	RRZZZZNY
NISCHE	.09	F	INFANT	RRZZZZNY
FELDMANN, MOJE-HEIDE	18	M	LABR	RRZZZZNY
MAUSCHE	14	M	LABR	RRZZZZNY
ENHEN, SCHMEIDER	7	M	CHILD	RRZZZZNY
SEGAL, GRETE	30	F	W	RRZZZZNY
FEGE	4	F	CHILD	RRZZZZNY
SEL.	2	M	CHILD	RRZZZZNY
SCHIK	3	F	CHILD	RRZZZZNY

PASSENGER	AGE	SEX	OCCUPATION	PRV VIL DES
SELDA	.04	F	INFANT	RRZZZZNY
LAROJENSKA, JULIANNE	30	F	W	RRZZZZNY
ANNA	10	F	CH	RRZZZZNY
ANTONIA	7	F	CHILD	RRZZZZNY
STANISLAWA	6	F	CHILD	RRZZZZNY
BRUNISLAW	5	M	CHILD	RRZZZZNY
MATZ, MENDEL	45	M	LABR	RRZZZZNY
MARIE	50	F	W	RRZZZZNY
KRUWANT, RIFKE-LEA	40	F	W	RRZZZZNY
SUNACHE	12	F	CH	RRAHTFNY
SALEMO	7	M	CHILD	RRAHTFNY
FEIGEL	4	M	CHILD	RRAHTFNY
BYANAN	18	M	CH	RRAHTFNY
RAPPAPORT, HERSCH	44	M	LABR	RRAHTFNY
SENIE	38	F	W	RRAHTFNY
MARETTA	11	F	CH	RRAHTFNY
AHTE	7	F	CHILD	RRAHTFNY
GLASER, DORA-LIEBE	30	F	W	RRZZZZIL
ANTON	7	M	CHILD	RRZZZZIL
TIBEL	5	M	CHILD	RRZZZZIL
ABEL	3	M	CHILD	RRZZZZIL
GRINHALL, SARAH	22	F	W	RRAHZHNY
DAVID	3	M	CHILD	RRAHZHNY
BRENI	1	M	CHILD	RRAHZHNY
PENNAR, EMILIA	48	F	W	RRAHZHNY
HANNA	7	F	CHILD	RRAHZHNY
EMILIE	5	F	CHILD	RRAHZHNY
GOKOWSKA, EMILIA	36	F	W	RRZZZZMI
FRANZ	7	M	CHILD	RRZZZZMI
JULIAN	5	M	CHILD	RRZZZZMI
DZURALINA	4	F	CHILD	RRZZZZMI
DALKE, MARGARETHE	31	F	W	RRZZZZNY
MARGARETHE	10	F	CH	RRZZZZNY
FRIEDA	7	F	CHILD	RRZZZZNY
GOTTLIEB	2	M	CHILD	RRZZZZNY
EHRLICH, ESTER-BROCHE	22	F	CH	RRAHOKNY
ABRAHAM	4	M	CHILD	RRAHOKNY
ABENER	.09	M	INFANT	RRAHOKNY
GRUNICH, GOTTFRIED	73	M	FARMER	RRZZZZNY
MARIE	66	F	W	RRZZZZNY
PACKENBERGER, LORENZ	26	M	LABR	RRZZZZNY
JULIANE	22	F	W	RRZZZZNY
FRIEDRICH	1	M	CHILD	RRZZZZNY
ELISABETH	.05	F	INFANT	RRZZZZNY
LORENZ	60	M	FARMER	RRZZZZNY
DOROTHEA	55	F	W	RRZZZZNY
MARIA	23	F	D	RRZZZZNY
KATHARINA	20	F	D	RRZZZZNY
ELISABETH	17	F	D	RRZZZZNY
HOMEIER, FRIEDRICH	34	M	FARMER	RRZZZZNY
CATHARINA	29	F	W	RRZZZZNY
CATHARINA	7	F	CHILD	RRZZZZNY
CHRISTIAN	4	M	CHILD	RRZZZZNY
LOUISE	2	F	CHILD	RRZZZZNY
WEICHS, JOHANN	26	M	FARMER	RRZZZZNY
CHRISTINE	28	F	W	RRZZZZNY
JOHANN	4	M	CHILD	RRZZZZNY
CHRISTINE	1	F	CHILD	RRZZZZNY
SIHOCK, HEINRICH	55	M	FARMER	RRZZZZNY
LOUISE	24	M	CH	RRZZZZNY
KATHARINE	20	M	CH	RRZZZZNY
HANNA	5	M	CHILD	RRZZZZNY
ROTHLINGER, CHRISTIAN	32	M	FARMER	RRZZZZNY
REGINA	31	F	W	RRZZZZNY
CHRISTIAN	7	M	CHILD	RRZZZZNY
PHILIPP	4	M	CHILD	RRZZZZNY
CAROLINE	4	F	CHILD	RRZZZZNY
ROSINA	.11	F	INFANT	RRZZZZNY
GRUNEICH, GOTTLIEB	26	M	FARMER	RRZZZZNY
CATHARINA	23	F	W	RRZZZZNY
JACOB	2	M	CHILD	RRZZZZNY
JOHANN	.04	M	INFANT	RRZZZZNY
MARTIN, WILHELM	26	M	FARMER	RRAAJXUNK
ELISABETH	23	F	W	RRAAJXUNK
CATHARINA	.10	F	INFANT	RRAAJXUNK

PASSENGER	AGE	SEX	OCCUPATION	PRV VIL DES
SIEBERG, LUDWIG	23	M	FARMER	RRAAJXUNK
MARIE	24	F	W	RRAAJXUNK
FUHRER, PHILIPP	57	M	FARMER	RRAAJXUNK
CHARLOTTE	45	F	W	RRAAJXUNK
ADAM	21	M	FARMER	RRAAJXUNK
HEINRICH	21	M	CH	RRAAJXUNK
PETER	14	M	CH	RRAAJXUNK
FRIEDRICH	9	M	CHILD	RRAAJXUNK
DAVID	3	M	CHILD	RRAAJXUNK
CHRISTINE	17	F	CH	RRAAJXUNK
JOHANNE	9	F	CHILD	RRAAJXUNK
CATHARINA	7	F	CHILD	RRAAJXUNK
BARBARA	4	F	CHILD	RRAAJXUNK
SOPHIE	.11	F	INFANT	RRAAJXUNK
WEISS, KARL	39	M	FARMER	RRZZZZUNK
LOUISE	36	F	W	RRZZZZUNK
GEORG	16	M	CH	RRZZZZUNK
JOHANNES	13	M	CH	RRZZZZUNK
WILLIAM	7	M	CHILD	RRZZZZUNK
JACOB	4	M	CHILD	RRZZZZUNK
MARTHA	1	F	CHILD	RRZZZZUNK
KNECHT, FERDINAND	37	M	FARMER	RRAEFLUNK
CATHARINA	33	F	W	RRAEFLUNK
THERESA	11	F	CH	RRAEFLUNK
IMMANUEL	9	M	CHILD	RRAEFLUNK
JOHANNES	.07	M	INFANT	RRAEFLUNK
LIDIA	6	F	CHILD	RRAEFLUNK
AMALIA	3	F	CHILD	RRAEFLUNK
SUKOS, WILHELM	34	M	LABR	RRAEFLUNK
CAROLINE	33	F	W	RRAEFLUNK
ELISABETH	19	F	CH	RRAEFLUNK
EDUARD	7	M	CHILD	RRAEFLUNK
MARIE	6	F	CHILD	RRAEFLUNK
JOHANNE	4	F	CHILD	RRAEFLUNK
LIDIA	.11	F	INFANT	RRAEFLUNK
SCHOCK, PETER	51	M	FARMER	RRAEFLUNK
MARIA	41	F	W	RRAEFLUNK
CHRISTIAN	17	M	CH	RRAEFLUNK
PHILIPP	13	M	CH	RRAEFLUNK
PETER	7	M	CHILD	RRAEFLUNK
DOROTHEA	5	F	CHILD	RRAEFLUNK
JACOB	2	M	CHILD	RRAEFLUNK
ROSINE	.11	M	INFANT	RRAEFLUNK
LITZ, WILHELMINE	22	M	W	RRAEFLUNK
ELISABETH	1	M	CHILD	RRAEFLUNK
BANIK, KARL	35	M	FARMER	RRZZZZUNK
KAROLINE	34	F	W	RRZZZZUNK
JOHANNES	6	M	CHILD	RRZZZZUNK
LIDIA	5	F	CHILD	RRZZZZUNK
EDUARD	3	M	CHILD	RRZZZZUNK
MATHILDE	3	F	CHILD	RRZZZZUNK
PAULINE	1	F	CHILD	RRZZZZUNK
BERTHA	.03	F	INFANT	RRZZZZUNK
BOBINSKI, THOMAS	31	M	FARMER	RRZZZZNY
L.	26	F	W	RRZZZZNY
PATROSKI, MACHI	73	M	FARMER	RRZZZZNY
PODALOK, ANDREA	30	M	FARMER	RRZZZZNY
STANISLAVA	22	F	W	RRZZZZNY
ANTON	.11	M	INFANT	RRZZZZNY
TABESKA, FRANCISKA	60	F	UNKNOWN	RRZZZZNY
HEINE, HELENE	32	M	LABR	RRZZZZNY
CHRISTIAN	30	F	W	RRZZZZNY
CATHARINA	5	F	CHILD	RRZZZZNY
AMALIE	.04	F	INFANT	RRZZZZNY
KRINGER, WELHELMINE	24	F	SVNT	RRZZZZNY
BINGER, JULIE	30	F	SVNT	RRZZZZNY
KLEIN, GESHA	16	F	SVNT	RRAGRTNY
GOTTLIEB, SAM-GITTEL	21	F	W	RRAHOKNY
LIEBE-GRETE	.10	F	INFANT	RRAHOKNY
BATZLAFF, MARIA	19	F	SVNT	RRZZZZNY
KRUZESKA, EMILIA	20	F	SVNT	RRZZZZNY
KRAZESKI, WLADISLAWA	18	F	SVNT	RRZZZZNY
SGURZEWSKA, THEOPHILA	25	F	SVNT	RRZZZZNY
ZAREMBA, ANNA	20	F	SVNT	RRZZZZNY

SHIP: POLARIA

FROM: HAMBURG
TO: NEW YORK
ARRIVED: 18 MAY 1885

PASSENGER	AGE	SEX	OCCUPATION	PRV VIL DES
POJUS, JERUCHEM	26	M	TRDSMN	RRZZZZIL
FRANNE	24	F	W	RRZZZZIL
HERSCH	.11	F	INFANT	RRZZZZIL
FEIGE	.01	M	INFANT	RRZZZZIL
HERSCHKOWITZ, LEIB	42	F	UNKNOWN	RRZZZZIL
SAX, ARON	27	M	TRDSMN	RRZZZZCIN
KOENIGSBERG, ISRAEL	22	M	TRDSMN	RRZZZZCIN
SCHMULJAN, JAKOB	15	M	TRDSMN	RRZZZZCIN
DEKAZ, LUDWIKA	20	F	TRDSMN	RRZZZZCH
WALZOK, CATHARINA	25	F	SGL	RRZZZZCH
POJUS, JAN	23	M	LABR	PLZZZZCH
JOSEFA	30	F	W	PLZZZZCH
GERBER, MAX	21	M	UPHST	RRZZZZCH
GOLDSTEIN, JANKEL	20	M	TRDSMN	RRZZZZCH
OREK, MOSCHE-A.	30	M	LABR	RRZZZZCH
LECHLE	27	F	W	RRZZZZCH
CHAIE	3	F	CHILD	RRZZZZCH
CHANNE	.06	F	INFANT	RRZZZZCH
MOSES, MENDEL	18	M	LABR	RRZZZZNY
LIEB, ABRAH.	25	M	LABR	RRZZZZSP
PERL	25	F	W	RRZZZZSP
STIEMER	.06	M	INFANT	RRZZZZUNK
SENDAROWSKY, GERSCH	26	M	CGRMKR	RRZZZZNY
CHAIE	25	F	W	RRZZZZNY
SCHMUEL	.08	M	INFANT	RRZZZZNY
MEISNER, ISRAEL	45	M	TRDSMN	RRZZZZNY
LEWIN, PESACH-J.	18	M	TLR	RRZZZZCH
MEISLIN, SORE-K.	41	F	WO	RRZZZZCH
MAYER	7	M	CHILD	RRZZZZCH
BETTY	6	F	CHILD	RRZZZZCH
SCHNEIT, YSHIA-VELRIN	25	M	TCHR	RRZZZZCH
PESA	24	F	W	RRZZZZCH
BURSZTYN, CHAINE	40	F	WO	RRZZZZNY
RACHEL	7	F	CHILD	RRZZZZNY
GLADSTEIN, CHAJE	45	F	WO	RRZZZZNY
LIEBE	19	M	CH	RRZZZZNY
LEIX	17	F	CH	RRZZZZNY
GISANY, HIRSCH	25	M	BBR	RRZZZZNY
DOMIN, ANNE	36	F	WO	PLZZZZNY
JAN	7	M	CHILD	PLZZZZNY
MARGARETHE	6	F	CHILD	PLZZZZNY
ROSALIE	5	F	CHILD	PLZZZZNY
JULIUS	3	M	CHILD	PLZZZZNY
CAROLINE	.07	F	INFANT	PLZZZZNY
ZABA, ANNA	48	F	WO	PLZZZZCH
JAN	15	M	CH	PLZZZZCH
WOICZIK	7	M	CHILD	PLZZZZCH
MARIANNE	5	F	CHILD	PLZZZZCH
KREMER, ABRAH.	37	M	LABR	PLZZZZNY
BUTZEK, HIRSCH	17	M	TRDSMN	PLZZZZNY
DOBBERMANN, LAIB	26	M	TRDSMN	PLZZZZIL
GREINBERG, LEA	30	F	WO	PLZZZZIL
RACHEL	7	F	CHILD	PLZZZZNY
JANKEL	6	F	CHILD	PLZZZZNY
BERAK	5	F	CHILD	PLZZZZNY
GRENBERG, MEYER	2	M	CHILD	PLZZZZNY
ELKE	.06	F	INFANT	PLZZZZNY
POJUS, ROSA	40	F	WO	PLZZZZNY
LEA	20	F	D	PLZZZZNY
DINA	11	F	D	PLZZZZNY
CHASCHA	7	F	CHILD	PLZZZZNY
CHEJA	6	F	CHILD	PLZZZZNY
SZENY, ANT.	17	M	LABR	PLZZZZNY
KOWALEWSKY, MICH.	27	M	LABR	PLZZZZNY
SZIPONSKY, ALEX.	34	M	LABR	PLZZZZWI
MURAWSKA, AL.	21	M	LABR	PLZZZZWI
GONKA, THS.	18	M	LABR	PLZZZZNY
SOUCHA, MARIANNE	21	F	SGL	PLZZZZNY

PASSENGER	AGE	SEX	OCCUPATION	PRV VIL DES
BORITZA, JOS.	35	M	LABR	PLZZZZNY
STANNOCH, ALB.	28	M	LABR	PLZZZZNY
MORTE, FRANZ	25	M	LABR	PLZZZZNY
ZENSCHAN, JAN	24	M	LABR	PLZZZZIL
WIELEK, JENDR.	24	M	LABR	PLZZZZIL
STARCZIK, JAN	20	M	LABR	PLZZZZIL
KUTTA, JAN	20	M	LABR	PLZZZZIL
KELIAN, PIETRO	24	M	LABR	PLZZZZNY
KWITTEC, WOISZIK	28	M	LABR	PLZZZZCH
ADAM, STARZ	22	M	LABR	PLZZZZCH
STEMPEK, STANISL.	45	M	LABR	PLZZZZUNK
ANNA	40	F	W	PLZZZZUNK
JOSEF	13	M	CH	PLZZZZUNK
JACOB	7	M	CHILD	PLZZZZUNK
JAN	5	M	CHILD	PLZZZZUNK
STANISLAUS	3	M	CHILD	PLZZZZUNK
ANNA	2	F	CHILD	PLZZZZUNK
WODASCH, JAN	24	M	LABR	PLZZZZUNK
SCHREDE, MICH.	24	M	LABR	PLZZZZUNK
WEBSCHETZ, SIMON	36	M	LABR	PLZZZZNY
OSENS, MATH.	25	M	LABR	PLZZZZNY
OSTROWSK, STAN.	23	M	LABR	PLZZZZNY
KARNOWSKY, RAFFAEL	31	M	LABR	PLZZZZNY
KORNTWIETZ, DAWID	20	M	LABR	PLZZZZNY
PARADOWSKY, ADAM	38	M	LABR	RRZZZZNY
HAMEL, H.	31	M	SMH	RRZZZZNY
NOMACK, SAM.ANT.	27	M	LABR	PLZZZZNY
HOLLANDER, RICKE	7	F	CHILD	PLZZZZNY
BERNHANT, SAMUEL	39	M	LABR	PLZZZZNY
DEBORAH	25	F	W	PLZZZZNY
MORITZ	6	M	CHILD	PLZZZZNY
ENGEL, ALOIS	24	M	LKSH	RRZZZZNY
GRELL, JACOB	21	M	MCHT	PLZZZZNY
SABODKIN, MOSES	26	M	TRDSMN	RRZZZZNY
PAUL	25	F	W	RRZZZZNY
CHANNE	10	F	CH	RRZZZZNY
MAIER	.01	F	INFANT	RRZZZZNY
PLUM, JACOB	32	M	BKR	RRZZZZCH
BEISOWSKY, JOSEF	22	M	LABR	RRZZZZCH
KISCHEWITZKI, W.	34	M	LABR	RRZZZZCH
BERNAL, MARIANE	24	F	WO	PLZZZZCH
LUDOWIGA	3	F	CHILD	PLZZZZCH
ANTONINA	.06	F	INFANT	PLZZZZCH
CHODEROWSKI, CASIMIR	43	M	BRDKP	RRZZZZCH
MARIANE	40	F	W	RRZZZZCH
IGNATZ	7	M	CHILD	RRZZZZCH
JAN	6	M	CHILD	RRZZZZCH
JOHANN	.04	M	INFANT	RRZZZZCH
WOBLEWSKY, WLADISLAV	25	M	SMH	RRZZZZCH
FANIK, BOLESLAW	21	M	LABR	RRZZZZCH
NARDOWSKY, CLEMENS	19	M	BRDKP	RRZZZZCH
GUDDEL, VINCENTY	28	M	BRDKP	RRZZZZCH
SCHIMON, ADAM	19	M	BRDKP	RRZZZZCH
MISCHEWITZ, JAN	26	M	LABR	RRZZZZCH
WIENKIEWSKY, VICTOR	20	M	LABR	RRZZZZCH
VOTTE, FELIX	21	M	SGL	RRZZZZCH
MISCHNIEWITZ, FRANCISCA	26	F	SGL	RRZZZZMI
SUSASNISKY, ANT.	26	F	SGL	RRZZZZNY
KONBA, BARTOL	47	M	LABR	RRZZZZIL
ANNA	50	F	W	RRZZZZIL
KATHARINA	25	F	D	RRZZZZIL
MARIE	17	F	D	RRZZZZIL
BETTI	12	F	D	RRZZZZIL
MARTONS	28	M	LABR	RRZZZZIL
KATHARINA	25	F	W	RRZZZZIL
JOSEF	1	M	CHILD	RRZZZZIL
SCHIMCHOWITZ, THEBUS	21	M	TRDSMN	RRZZZZIL
ABRAHAM	25	M	W	RRZZZZIL
HOCHMAN, PINKUS	27	M	TRDSMN	RRZZZZIL
SCHAJE	23	F	W	RRZZZZIL
KOMFROST, FRANZ	26	M	LABR	PLZZZZIL
VZTBECKI, JOSEF	23	M	LABR	PLZZZZIL
DITTERMAN, NACFM.	39	M	TLR	RRZZZZNY
KREINE	35	F	W	RRZZZZNY
BANK, SANDEL	16	M	LABR	PLZZZZIL

PASSENGER	AGE	SEX	OCCUPATION	PRV VIL DES
FLADE, EMIL	15	M	LABR	PLZZZZIL
JESOWSKY, SCHANIE	22	F	SGL	RRZZZZNY
BARANOWSKY, JULIA	23	F	LABR	RRZZZZNY
BALTRICHEITES, JAN	25	M	LABR	RRZZZZNY
LANSCHEITIS, JAN	27	M	LABR	RRZZZZNY
NATHANSON, BROCHE	34	F	TRDSMN	RRZZZZIL
BLOCH, ITZIG	28	M	TRDSMN	RRZZZZIL
PRINZ, ROSA	24	F	WO	RRZZZZIL
WILHELM	.09	M	INFANT	RRZZZZIL
SCHWANOWITZ, BETTY	18	F	SGL	RRZZZZIL
CARLOVECK, JOSEF	25	M	TLR	RRZZZZIL
WANEZAK, CATHERINA	37	F	SGL	RRZZZZIL
LIPSCHUETZ, SCHLOME	14	M	SGL	RRZZZZIL
CHERKOWITSCH, LUCIA	18	F	SGL	RRZZZZCH
MACHERCBERG, LEISER	17	M	TDR	RRZZZZCH
KOBAKER, JOSEF	15	M	TDR	RRZZZZNY
MENDELSTAM, ABRAH.	36	M	PNTR	RRZZZZIL
SIMROCK, SCHMUL	7	M	CHILD	RRZZZZIL
MATROWSKY, SORE	22	F	WO	RRZZZZNY
BENJAMIN	.06	M	INFANT	RRZZZZNY
EDEL, SARA	45	F	WO	RRZZZZNY
MICHEL	7	M	CHILD	RRZZZZNY
JOSEF	4	M	CHILD	RRZZZZNY
JACOB	3	M	CHILD	RRZZZZNY
SCHLEIM	2	F	CHILD	RRZZZZNY
DORRENSTEIN, RACHEL	18	F	SGL	PLZZZZIL
GREINBERG, J.H.	50	M	TRDSMN	PLZZZZNY
MONHEIT, CHANNE	19	F	SGL	PLZZZZIL
MUENZ, PAULINA	28	F	SGL	RRZZZZIL
GREEN, DUBEY	48	F	WO	PLZZZZNY
LEIBIS	18	F	D	PLZZZZNY
SARAH	20	F	D	PLZZZZNY
KOHN, GITAL	25	F	WO	RRZZZZNY
CHAIN	.07	F	INFANT	RRZZZZNY
ROSENBERG, JOHAM	32	M	FARMER	RRZZZZIL
PIONMETZKI, ISRAEL	26	M	TRDSMN	RRZZZZNY
GOLDE	25	F	W	RRZZZZNY
BASING, HERMANN	16	M	TDR	RRZZZZNY
TISCHLER, EVA	40	F	WO	RRZZZZBO
ROSA	17	F	D	RRZZZZBO
CLARY	6	F	CHILD	RRZZZZBO
MARIANA	5	F	CHILD	RRZZZZBO
ARON	4	M	CHILD	RRZZZZBO
FELD, FRITZ	50	M	TRDSMN	RRZZZZIL
CHAIM	46	F	W	RRZZZZIL
HANNA	9	F	CHILD	RRZZZZIL
LEWY	6	M	CHILD	RRZZZZIL
ROSALIN	4	F	CHILD	RRZZZZIL
BALAIA	11	F	CH	RRZZZZIL
POLONCZER, GITEL	14	F	SGL	PLZZZZIL
ZELLER, RAFAEL	14	M	CH	PLZZZZNY
BAUM----, OLGA	65	F	SGL	RRZZZZIL
ARTHUR	11	M	CH	RRZZZZIL
PATZKOWSKY, ANTON	58	M	LABR	PLZZZZOH
CATHERINA	55	F	W	PLZZZZOH
TEOFILA	19	F	CH	PLZZZZOH
CATHERINA	16	F	CH	PLZZZZOH
HECHT, ROCHE	50	F	WO	RRZZZZNY
REBECA	30	F	D	RRZZZZNY
LEIB	11	M	CH	RRZZZZNY
SCHLEINN	7	M	CHILD	RRZZZZNY
BARUCH	6	M	CHILD	RRZZZZNY
BEER	4	M	CHILD	RRZZZZNY
SCHINE	2	F	CHILD	RRZZZZNY
LEWY, CHAWA	62	F	WO	RRZZZZNY
KAUFMAN, MEYER	20	M	SHMK	RRZZZZMN
RICHARD	24	M	MCHT	RRZZZZNY
BIELSKI, MOSES	23	M	TRDSMN	RRZZZZNY
BIALE, ARON	16	M	TLR	RRZZZZNY
KAHN, ITZIG	22	M	MLR	RRZZZZNY
DAN, ITZIG	29	M	TRDSMN	RRZZZZIL
CHAIE	30	F	W	RRZZZZIL
CHANKE	7	F	CHILD	RRZZZZIL
LIEBKE	3	F	CHILD	RRZZZZIL
CHANNE	.08	F	INFANT	RRZZZZIL

PASSENGER	AGE	SEX	OCCUPATION	PRIV	VIL	DES
GOLDSTEIN, BRANZE	25	F	WO	RR	ZZZZ	NY
BERTHA	3	F	CHILD	RR	ZZZZ	NY
BERNSTEIN, ESTER	50	F	WO	RR	ZZZZ	NY
BLOCH, NOAH	30	M	SMH	RR	ZZZZ	NY
KURZOW, BENJAM.	35	M	PRTR	RR	ZZZZ	NY
SMIGELSKI, CARL	18	M	WO	RR	ZZZZ	NY
SCHMUR, ROCHE	17	F	SGL	PL	ZZZZ	NY
KIVE	6	M	CHILD	PL	ZZZZ	NY
MEYER	5	M	CHILD	PL	ZZZZ	NY
HOLLAENDER, IGNATZ	7	M	CHILD	PL	ZZZZ	NY
POMPA, ANDREY	30	M	LABR	PL	ZZZZ	NY
JANOWSKY, MENDEL	20	M	TRDSMN	RR	ZZZZ	NY
GOLDBERG, CHANNE	22	F	WO	RR	ZZZZ	NY
MAGID, NISSEN	45	M	TDR	RR	ZZZZ	NY
GITEL	40	F	W	RR	ZZZZ	NY
RASMEL	7	M	CHILD	RR	ZZZZ	NY
MENDEL	6	M	CHILD	RR	ZZZZ	NY
THERESE	5	F	CHILD	RR	ZZZZ	NY
EINBERG, ARON	17	M	TDR	RR	ZZZZ	NY
GARKOWSKY, STANISLAUS	28	M	TDR	RR	ZZZZ	NY
MARY	25	F	W	RR	ZZZZ	NY
MEYER, AUGUSTE	25	F	WO	RR	ZZZZ	NY
MAGMUSSEN, GUSTAV	39	M	TDR	RR	ZZZZ	NY
CHRISTINE	50	F	W	RR	ZZZZ	NY
KUKEL, CHANE	23	F	SGL	RR	ZZZZ	NY
U, U	00	M	LABR	RR	ZZZZ	NY
MUSCATENBRUT, LOSER	20	M	TLR	RR	ZZZZ	NY
TINCENSKY, JACOB	30	M	MCHT	RR	ZZZZ	NY
APTER, WILHELM	23	M	MCHT	PL	ZZZZ	NY
SECHZACH, VALENT.	30	M	LABR	PL	ZZZZ	NY
PANHEWITZ, VICTOR	25	M	TRDSMN	RR	ZZZZ	NY
BUSLAVSKY, ANT.	30	M	TRDSMN	RR	ZZZZ	NY
FINGERBAUM, JOSEL	39	M	TRDSMN	RR	ZZZZ	NY
MERETZKO, SELIG	33	M	TRDSMN	RR	ZZZZ	NY
SEGALL, MOSES	20	M	TRDSMN	RR	ZZZZ	NY
RUBENOWITZ, JUDEL	35	M	TRDSMN	RR	ZZZZ	NY
FREIMANN, ITZIG	21	M	SHMK	RR	ZZZZ	NY
SARA	18	F	W	RR	ZZZZ	NY
SCHAPERA, EFRAIM	45	M	SMH	RR	ZZZZ	NY
NEUMAN, MARCUS	22	M	TLR	RR	ZZZZ	NY
BEILE	19	F	W	RR	ZZZZ	NY
BERG, ABRAH.	20	M	TRDSMN	RR	ZZZZ	NY
AXELRAD, ISAC	36	M	TRDSMN	RR	ZZZZ	NY
FEITELSOHN, MATHS.	20	M	TRDSMN	RR	ZZZZ	NY
KOSLAWSKY, MATHS.	26	M	LABR	RR	ZZZZ	NY
SAWITZKI, MATHS.	33	M	LABR	RR	ZZZZ	NY
AEROLSKY, MORDSCHE	19	M	LABR	RR	ZZZZ	NY
HEITIGMAN, KADISCH	43	M	TRDSMN	RR	ZZZZ	NY
RABINOWICZ, LEIB	39	M	TRDSMN	RR	ZZZZ	NY
KOT, SCHULEM	18	M	TRDSMN	RR	ZZZZ	NY
WEINSTEIN, ISRAEL	19	M	LABR	RR	ZZZZ	NY
KAHN, HIRSCH	37	M	LABR	RR	ZZZZ	NY
MOSES	7	M	CHILD	RR	ZZZZ	NY
BURMAN, SCHMUL	18	M	LABR	RR	ZZZZ	NY
DEGIELA, VICTORIA	20	F	SGL	RR	ZZZZ	NY
MAIREM, BERNHD.	18	M	LABR	RR	ZZZZ	NY
TRON, BARUCH	18	M	LABR	RR	ZZZZ	NY
JANKEL, ANNA	16	F	LABR	RR	ZZZZ	NY
OSCHMAN, CHAIE	25	M	LABR	RR	ZZZZ	NY
BIALYSTOZKY, ISRAEL	35	M	TDR	RR	ZZZZ	NY
MENACH	27	F	W	RR	ZZZZ	NY
SAMUEL	5	M	CHILD	RR	ZZZZ	NY
ISACK	.06	M	INFANT	RR	ZZZZ	NY
LOESCHER, ADOLF	35	M	BKR	RR	ZZZZ	NY
DEHUTEZ, ANNARI	18	F	FARMER	RR	ZZZZ	NY
KASIMES, JAN	22	M	FARMER	RR	ZZZZ	NY
BUNGE, GUSTAV	29	M	FARMER	RR	ZZZZ	NY

SHIP: FRISIA

FROM: HAMBURG
TO: NEW YORK
ARRIVED: 19 MAY 1885

PASSENGER	AGE	SEX	OCCUPATION	PRIV	VIL	DES
PRAHST, CAROL.	23	F	SGL	RR	ZZZZ	USA
BLAUSTEIN, CHANNE	30	F	W	RR	ZZZZ	USA
WOLF	9	M	CHILD	RR	ZZZZ	USA
ISAAC	00	M	CH	RR	ZZZZ	USA
JUDA	5	M	CHILD	RR	ZZZZ	USA
CHEIE	9	F	CHILD	RR	ZZZZ	USA
LEA	5	F	CHILD	RR	ZZZZ	USA
ANNE	3	F	CHILD	RR	ZZZZ	USA
FINKELSTEIN, CHANNE	27	F	W	RR	ZZZZ	USA
CHANNE	.11	F	INFANT	RR	ZZZZ	USA
PEPLITZ, RIWKE	25	F	W	RR	ZZZZ	USA
CERIL	.11	F	INFANT	RR	ZZZZ	USA
LENE	.01	F	INFANT	RR	ZZZZ	USA
CHMILEWSKY, SCHEINE	30	F	W	RR	ZZZZ	USA
RIWKE	6	F	CHILD	RR	ZZZZ	USA
MIRKE	.11	M	INFANT	RR	ZZZZ	USA
JACOBSEN, JACOB	9	M	CHILD	RR	ZZZZ	USA
JOSEF	7	M	CHILD	RR	ZZZZ	USA
ALTUCH, ZERUCHINS	16	M	LABR	RR	ZZZZ	USA
KAZIOL, EPHRAIM	33	M	LABR	RR	ZZZZ	USA
KONDRIETEIS, SIMON	26	M	LABR	RR	ZZZZ	USA
AREXINA, MARIANNE	17	F	SGL	RR	ZZZZ	USA
WEIN, LEIZER	44	M	DLR	RR	ZZZZ	USA
HERSCH, ABR.	30	M	LABR	RR	ZZZZ	USA
WEMZLOW, THOMAS	25	M	LABR	RR	ZZZZ	USA
BENDEICSKY, MARTIN	24	M	LABR	RR	ZZZZ	USA
BROCHMANN, ABR.	24	M	WCHMKR	RR	ZZZZ	USA
BERTHA	22	F	W	RR	ZZZZ	USA
EISNER, WOLFF	23	M	DLR	RR	ZZZZ	USA
AWRED, SCHACHNE	19	F	SGL	RR	ZZZZ	USA
GRANAT, HIRSCH	44	M	TLR	RR	ZZZZ	USA
KANTOROWITZ, ESCHE	20	F	SGL	RR	ZZZZ	USA
PREDRETKOWSKA, MARIANNE	26	F	SGL	RR	ZZZZ	USA
KAMINSKY, ANTON	19	M	LABR	RR	ZZZZ	USA
ROSENSTRAM, ERIK	39	M	SEMN	FN	ZZZZ	USA
BOGNI, CHAIM	14	M	LABR	FN	ZZZZ	USA
MARINKOWITZ, TOMAS	21	M	LABR	FN	ZZZZ	USA
KOWALEWSKA, INZA	16	F	SGL	FN	ZZZZ	USA
ALESKOWITZ, LIPPMAN	35	M	LABR	FN	ACBF	USA
SEGALOWITZ, SCHELHM	21	F	W	FN	ACBF	USA
MARIANE	3	F	CHILD	FN	ACBF	USA
GOLOWJENITZ, LOSZE	23	F	SGL	FN	ACBF	USA
ALESKOWITZ, LIPPMAN	23	M	LABR	FN	ACBF	USA
GRUENSTEIN, SIMON	17	M	MCHT	FN	ACBF	USA
KALMANOWITZ, BENJAMIN	20	M	LABR	FN	ACBF	USA
GRODNICH, CHS.	35	M	LABR	FN	ACBF	USA
MIKULSCHAMSKY, MEYER	20	M	LABR	FN	ACBF	USA
BACHERACH, BASCHE	20	F	SGL	FN	ACBF	USA
GROSSMANN, JOSEF	15	M	LABR	FN	ACBF	USA
ABRAHAM	9	M	CHILD	FN	ACBF	USA
HEIMAN	8	F	CHILD	FN	ACBF	USA
ZUCKERMANN, GERSON	20	M	LABR	FN	ACBF	USA
LEWIN, FEIBEL	30	F	W	FN	ACBF	USA
RACHEL	9	F	CHILD	FN	ACBF	USA
PERETZ	8	M	CHILD	FN	ACBF	USA
JUDEL	6	F	CHILD	FN	ACBF	USA
LEILE	4	M	CHILD	FN	ACBF	USA
LIBNOWSKY, SAMUEL	34	M	DLR	FN	ACBF	USA
WITTO, BEIB	19	F	SGL	FN	ACBF	USA
CHOROTZKI, SALOMON	18	M	LABR	FN	ACBF	USA
HIRSCH	16	M	LABR	FN	ACBF	USA
MEIER	15	M	LABR	FN	ACBF	USA
BOGIN, MUCHE	14	F	SGL	FN	ACBF	USA
BIRSOHN, KEILE	27	F	W	FN	ACBF	USA
DAVID	4	M	CHILD	FN	ACBF	USA
MOSES	.11	M	INFANT	FN	ACBF	USA
GITTEL	.01	F	INFANT	FN	ACBF	USA
RABINOWITZ, RUWEN	60	M	TCHR	FN	ACBF	USA

PASSENGER	AGE	SEX	OCCUPATION	PRVL	VIL	DES
MOSTOWNITZKY, CHAIM	20	M	DLR	FN	ACBF	USA
SCHACH, SELIG	20	M	LABR	FN	ACBF	USA
PIASECKI, ADAM	23	M	LABR	FN	ACBF	USA
GOLDMANN, JUDA	28	M	SGL	FN	ACBF	USA
SACK, NATHAN	17	M	LABR	FN	ACBF	USA
DEBORA	19	F	SGL	FN	ACBF	USA
HERRM.	18	M	LABR	FN	ACBF	USA
DOBRE	45	F	W	FN	ACBF	USA
LIEBERSTEIN, LEIB	37	M	SMH	FN	ACBF	USA
LIEHT, OSCHER	19	M	DLR	FN	ACBF	USA
BERLINSKY, RIWKE	40	F	W	FN	ACBF	USA
BEISEL	9	M	CHILD	FN	ACBF	USA
JACOB	8	M	CHILD	FN	ACBF	USA
KAPLAN, MOSES	26	M	LABR	FN	ACBF	USA
PILOISKY, TAUBE	45	F	W	FN	ACBF	USA
BEILE	17	F	CH	FN	ACBF	USA
ISAAC	14	M	CH	FN	ACBF	USA
CHEMIN	9	M	CHILD	FN	ACBF	USA
WOLFF	8	M	CHILD	FN	ACBF	USA
SCHER, JACOB	53	M	TLR	FN	ACBF	USA
BRZOZN, SPRINGE	40	F	W	FN	ACBF	USA
ISAAC	8	M	CHILD	FN	ACBF	USA
FEIGE	4	M	CHILD	FN	ACBF	USA
JACOB	.11	M	INFANT	FN	ACBF	USA
MENASE	.01	M	INFANT	FN	ACBF	USA
BERLINSKI, MOSES	40	M	LABR	FN	ACBF	USA
CHASCHE	18	F	SGL	FN	ACBF	USA
BRAUN, MEIER	19	M	TLR	FN	ACBF	USA
WIBUSKI, BEILE	17	F	SGL	FN	ACBF	USA
CHIEDE, SCHEINE	56	F	W	FN	ACBF	USA
CHAJE	25	F	W	FN	ACBF	USA
JUDES	.10	M	INFANT	FN	ACBF	USA
LINKNISKY, ABRAHAM	14	M	LABR	FN	ACBF	USA
IPP, MEYER	50	M	LABR	FN	ACBF	USA
ROTH, NOEHR	9	M	CHILD	FN	ACBF	USA
BALTROWITZ, NOSSEN	18	M	LABR	FN	ACBF	USA
KABOZNICK, SAMUEL	16	M	LABR	FN	ACBF	USA
GOLDSCHMIDT, PESACH	26	M	DLR	FN	ACBF	USA
ROSENBERG, RUBEN	33	M	DLR	FN	ACBF	USA
GORDON, ELIAS	15	M	DLR	FN	ACBF	USA
ISRAELSKY, JUDEL	13	F	CH	FN	ACBF	USA
BARANOWITZ, LEISER	40	M	DLR	FN	ACBF	USA
ABR.	9	M	CHILD	FN	ACBF	USA
STEIN, CLARA	20	F	W	FN	ACBF	USA
SOFIE	.11	F	INFANT	FN	ACBF	USA
SPUDIA, MATHS.	46	M	LABR	FN	ACBF	USA
ROSENBLUM, FRUME	38	F	W	FN	ACBF	USA
MEYER	17	M	CH	FN	ACBF	USA
MOSES	9	M	CHILD	FN	ACBF	USA
MORDSCHE	8	M	CHILD	FN	ACBF	USA
FREUDE	6	F	CHILD	FN	ACBF	USA
ETTIE	4	F	CHILD	FN	ACBF	USA
STEINBERG, SCHOLEM	17	M	DLR	FN	ACBF	USA
SCHEFFELOWIZ, SALOMON	19	M	LABR	FN	ACBF	USA
HOLLBERG, ISRAEL	16	M	LABR	FN	ACBF	USA
PASWENZINSKI, SARA	26	F	W	FN	ACBF	USA
RIWE	.11	F	INFANT	FN	ACBF	USA
WEISSBERG, ESTHER	19	F	SGL	FN	ACBF	USA
ULNIK, ESTHER	15	F	SGL	FN	ACBF	USA
KLABANSKY, RACHEL	50	F	W	FN	ACBF	USA
MAX	23	M	LABR	FN	ACBF	USA
HIRSCH, JOSEF	18	M	LABR	FN	ACBF	USA
BARAN, LEIB	15	M	LABR	FN	ACBF	USA
KASCDOI, BEREL	17	M	LABR	FN	ACBF	USA
FRIEDMANN, SCHMUEL	18	M	LABR	FN	ACBF	USA
ROTMEIER, LEWIN	48	M	CPTR	FN	ACBF	USA
MOLDOWSKY, SCHLOME	25	M	TLR	FN	ACBF	USA
KASPEROWICZ, JOSEFA	22	F	SGL	FN	ACBF	USA
CZECINSKI, ELKE	60	F	W	FN	ACBF	USA
RUMELZIK, ANTON	24	M	LABR	FN	ACBF	USA
POTOCKI, JOSEF	22	M	LABR	FN	ACBF	USA
KASPEROWICZ, ALEXANDER	29	M	LABR	FN	ACBF	USA
UZDESKA, HINDE	22	F	SGL	FN	ACBF	USA
BRODOWSKY, ISAAC	17	M	LABR	FN	ACBF	USA
FLECKER, JULIE	40	F	W	FN	ACBF	USA
MORITZ	14	M	CH	FN	ACBF	USA
HEIMANN	9	M	CHILD	FN	ACBF	USA

SHIP: STATE OF INDIANA

FROM: GLASGOW AND LARNE
TO: NEW YORK
ARRIVED: 21 MAY 1885

PASSENGER	AGE	SEX	OCCUPATION	PRV	VIL	DES
HALLMANN, CHIEL	30	M	CGRMKR	FN	AFVG	USA
FANI	26	F	W	FN	AFVG	USA
SZWERBIN, ALEXANDER	25	M	LABR	PL	ZZZZ	USA
ANTONIE	30	F	W	PL	ZZZZ	USA
POLUSK, LAURIN	26	M	LABR	PL	ZZZZ	USA
JUZE	27	F	W	PL	ZZZZ	USA
KRESCHEFSKY, FELIX	27	M	LABR	PL	ZZZZ	USA
HANNA	26	F	W	PL	ZZZZ	USA
ANNA	1	F	CHILD	PL	ZZZZ	USA
STAJ, MICHAEL	26	M	LABR	PL	ZZZZ	USA
MARIANNE	20	F	W	PL	ZZZZ	USA
KATARZYNE	18	F	SP	PL	ZZZZ	USA
JAN	.09	M	INFANT	PL	ZZZZ	USA
BORZAK, WOIZ	33	M	LABR	PL	ZZZZ	USA
PETRONELA	28	F	W	PL	ZZZZ	USA
JAN	3	M	CHILD	PL	ZZZZ	USA
FRANZISCHEK	1	M	CHILD	PL	ZZZZ	USA
ALLINA	.01	F	INFANT	PL	ZZZZ	USA
ROSEL, JAN	40	M	LABR	PL	ZZZZ	USA
KATAZINA	33	F	W	PL	ZZZZ	USA
JOSEF	8	M	CHILD	PL	ZZZZ	USA
WAJICIH	7	M	CHILD	PL	ZZZZ	USA
LUDWICK	4	M	CHILD	PL	ZZZZ	USA
JENDRESSY	2	M	CHILD	PL	ZZZZ	USA
ZOBAWA, FELIX	36	M	LABR	PL	ZZZZ	USA
AGATHE	24	F	W	PL	ZZZZ	USA
JOSEPHA	3	F	CHILD	PL	ZZZZ	USA
PAULUS	1	M	CHILD	PL	ZZZZ	USA
DARGEWITZ, CONSTANTIN	28	M	LABR	PL	ZZZZ	USA
APPOLINA	26	F	W	PL	ZZZZ	USA
LEON	5	M	CHILD	PL	ZZZZ	USA
FEIWEROWITZ, KIWE	10	F	CH	PL	AGRT	USA
POLACK, LIEBE	20	F	SP	RR	ZZZZ	USA
KAPLAN, ELIAS	36	M	LABR	RR	ZZZZ	USA
LUBACZ, MARCUS	16	M	LABR	RR	ZZZZ	USA
TWAWG, JOSEF	36	M	LABR	RR	ZZZZ	USA
KRYSOFSKI, JOSEF	43	M	LABR	RR	ZZZZ	USA
MIESERITZ, ELIAS	37	M	PDLR	RR	ADAT	USA
KAPLAN, SALOMON	26	M	TLR	RR	ZZZZ	USA
ZENZUR, HIRSCH	19	M	PDLR	RR	ZZZZ	USA
LUKASEWICH, MARCUS	21	M	LABR	RR	ZZZZ	USA
SKABEIJI, JURGES	55	M	LABR	RR	ACBF	USA
KESSMIS, ANTONIO	26	M	LABR	RR	ACBF	USA
WARNICSKI, JONA	30	M	LABR	RR	ACBF	USA
GOLAMBECK, HIRSCH	48	M	LABR	RR	ACBF	USA
JANKOWITZ, MARKUS	19	M	PDLR	RR	ACBF	USA
INOTZIG, PIOHE	40	M	LABR	RR	ZZZZ	USA
KOWALEWSKY, JANKO	37	M	LABR	RR	ZZZZ	USA
PAVELACK, MARTIN	34	M	LABR	RR	ZZZZ	USA
WOIZNEK, JAKOB	35	M	LABR	RR	ZZZZ	USA
SCHIMKOWITZ, JOSEF	20	M	LABR	RR	ZZZZ	USA
MICHAEL	22	M	LABR	RR	ZZZZ	USA
RASKEWITZ, CONSTANTIN	25	M	LABR	RR	ZZZZ	USA
BOGDEN, ANTONIO	20	M	LABR	RR	ZZZZ	USA
GABINKEWITZ, JOSEF	21	M	LABR	RR	ZZZZ	USA
KRAPNISKI, LEON	31	M	LABR	RR	ZZZZ	USA
SENK, THOMAS	30	M	LABR	RR	ZZZZ	USA
HOFFMAN, KONSTANTIN	30	M	LABR	RR	ZZZZ	USA
ANDREWITZ, FRANZ	42	M	LABR	RR	ZZZZ	USA
BORSCHEWITZ, STANISLAW	27	M	LABR	RR	ZZZZ	USA
MAKULSKI, TEOPHIL	25	M	LABR	RR	ZZZZ	USA

PASSENGER	AGE	SEX	OCCUPATION	PRV VIL DES
ABRAMOWITZ, ANTON	52	M	LABR	RRZZZZUSA
KONTAROWITZ, ANTON	27	M	LABR	RRZZZZUSA
BALINSK, VINCENTI	24	M	LABR	RRZZZZUSA
SPARA, JAN	50	M	LABR	RRZZZZUSA
OSCHKIMUS, JAN	30	M	LABR	RRZZZZUSA
ZEGNIS, VINCENTZ	26	M	LABR	RRZZZZUSA
ANDKOWSKY, PAUL	26	M	LABR	RRZZZZUSA
DOMELINSKY, FELIX	55	M	LABR	RRZZZZUSA
ADREWITZ, FRANTZ	24	M	LABR	RRZZZZUSA
KOZLOWSKY, JAN	32	M	LABR	RRZZZZUSA
CZESCHLIK, JOHAN	30	M	LABR	RRZZZZUSA
MINHIRSKY, FRANZ	22	M	LABR	RRZZZZUSA
KLINOWITZ, IGNATZ	36	M	LABR	RRZZZZUSA
BARULA, VINCENTI	25	M	LABR	RRZZZZUSA
CCKAUSKI, WOJICICH	33	M	LABR	RRZZZZUSA
ZAPOLOWSKY, THOMAS	30	M	LABR	RRZZZZUSA
WOGLULKAWICZ, LAURIS	45	M	LABR	RRACBFUSA
RUBSEWITZ, CONSTANTIN	23	M	LABR	RRZZZZUSA
WENCKEWITCH, MATEUS	38	M	LABR	RRZZZZUSA
KAZIMIR	10	M	CH	RRZZZZUSA
COHEN, ABRAHAM	28	M	PDLR	RRZZZZUSA
SHRINZ, DAVID	19	M	LABR	RRAHVUUSA
FERNBACK, MOSES	30	M	SHMK	RRAHTFUSA
WULFF, BEHR.	15	M	SHMK	RRACBFUSA
RABINOWITZ, ABRAHAM	26	M	LABR	RRACBFUSA
KLAWANSKI, JANKEL	25	M	CPTR	RRZZZZUSA
LEWIN, SAMUEL	49	M	CPTR	RRZZZZUSA
BRANDSOHN, HOSEL	15	M	TLR	RRZZZZUSA
FISCH, MOSES	17	M	TLR	RRACBFUSA
FLEISCHER, ISRAEL	26	M	PDLR	RRACBFUSA
EPSTEIN, MEYER	19	M	PDLR	RRAHQUUSA
LOSLAHN, DAVID	30	M	PDLR	RRZZZZUSA
KRAISIN, LEON	23	M	PDLR	RRACBFUSA
SCHINIEBOWITZ, ISRAEL	11	M	CH	RRAGRTUSA
JOSEL, ABRAHAM	35	M	PDLR	RRAGRTUSA
MORDECHOWITZ, SELMAN	26	M	PDLR	RRAGRTUSA
FEINBERG, HANSER	11	M	CH	RRAGRTUSA
INDELSOHN, ISRAEL	20	M	PDLR	RRAGRTUSA
CARABELLICK, NAPOLI	24	M	PDLR	RRAGRTUSA
JUDKOFFSKY, BEER	20	M	PDLR	RRZZZZUSA
GANONSKY, ABRAHAM	15	M	PDLR	RRAHVUUSA
GLAGOWSKY, LEZER	20	M	PDLR	RRAHVUUSA
WITEBSKY, ISSER	18	M	PDLR	RRZZZZUSA
KUSCH, SIMON	21	M	PDLR	RRAHOKUSA
KALKUT, ISRAEL	32	M	PDLR	RRZZZZUSA
SILBERMANN, MOSES	17	M	PDLR	RRZZZZUSA
FEIWEROWITZ, DAVID	17	M	PDLR	RRAGRTUSA
ANDREWITZ, JACOB	42	M	PDLR	RRZZZZUSA
BALTINSKI, JOSEF	35	M	PDLR	RRZZZZUSA

SHIP: BRITISH KING

FROM: LIVERPOOL AND QUEENSTOWN
TO: NEW YORK
ARRIVED: 22 MAY 1885

PASSENGER	AGE	SEX	OCCUPATION	PRV VIL DES
FACHUR, MORDCHE	21	M	LABR	PLZZZZUSA
RUDELIZ, PITRO	23	M	LABR	PLZZZZUSA
KATKUSKY, JANKEL	20	M	LABR	PLZZZZUSA
KRAMARSKY, SCHRUNEL	40	M	LABR	PLZZZZUSA
CHALUPOWITZ, JACOB	45	M	LABR	PLZZZZUSA
STIPIKOW, SCHEBSEL	25	M	LABR	PLZZZZUSA
DWORE	25	F	W	PLZZZZUSA
KOHN, JACOB	25	M	LABR	PLZZZZUSA
SCHAWELSKY, SCHLOME	53	M	LABR	PLZZZZUSA
CHACKO, SCHMULKA	16	M	LABR	PLZZZZUSA
FARGOWSKY, BERL	25	M	LABR	PLZZZZUSA
MARGENSOWITZ, MARIANNE	24	M	LABR	PLZZZZUSA
SCHIERMANN, SARIE	17	F	SP	PLZZZZUSA
RADOFSKY, MENDEL	18	M	LABR	PLZZZZUSA
KUHR, SUXEL	29	F	SP	PLZZZZUSA
DANKO, JANOS	29	M	LABR	PLZZZZUSA
BERMANN, OSCHER	28	M	LABR	PLZZZZUSA
OWSCHA	11	M	CH	PLZZZZUSA
STAURI, VINCENT	30	M	LABR	PLZZZZUSA
MARIANA	27	F	W	PLZZZZUSA
ANNA	.02	F	INFANT	PLZZZZUSA
GRODUNSKY, MICHAEL	37	M	LABR	PLZZZZUSA
MACKTIGALE, SARA	24	F	SP	PLZZZZUSA
MALDOWSKY, SCHIC	15	M	LABR	PLZZZZUSA
REN	19	M	LABR	PLZZZZUSA
FUNK, SOLOMON	29	M	LABR	PLZZZZUSA
SENNA	23	F	W	PLZZZZUSA
HADES, MICHAEL	23	M	LABR	PLZZZZUSA
EISIK, BEER	25	M	LABR	PLZZZZUSA
FRIEDMANN, PESCHE	10	F	CH	PLZZZZUSA
GRABOWSKI, LIPMANN	33	M	LABR	PLZZZZUSA
PANTOFFEL, MERDCHE	28	M	LABR	PLZZZZUSA
SENKUOONA, FRANZ	25	M	LABR	PLZZZZUSA
ALZ	16	M	LABR	PLZZZZUSA
STRONEVSKI, FELIX	16	M	LABR	PLZZZZUSA
ASCH, ABR.	26	M	LABR	PLZZZZUSA
MLAVER, SAM	49	M	LABR	PLZZZZUSA
SCHWARTZMANN, ABR.	51	M	LABR	PLZZZZUSA
FLEISCHER, DAVID	30	M	LABR	PLZZZZUSA
KORECHY, ANTON	20	M	LABR	PLZZZZUSA
DABROVSKI, JOS.	25	M	LABR	PLZZZZUSA
FRANKREICH, SAM	23	M	LABR	PLZZZZUSA
SELTER	20	F	SP	PLZZZZUSA
ESSER, JOSEF	50	M	LABR	PLZZZZUSA
KUBALA, ADAM	25	M	LABR	PLZZZZUSA
MAZIK	11	M	CH	PLZZZZUSA
MAINALD, SAM	26	M	CH	PLZZZZUSA
MANTAVSKI, PIETRO	23	M	CH	PLZZZZUSA
JUTELMANN, NATHAN	18	M	CH	PLZZZZUSA
KRAUINK, BENJIMAN	23	M	CH	PLZZZZUSA
SAICHOWSKY, JOSEPH	50	M	CH	PLZZZZUSA
ZACHUMBA, VOJTIECH	27	M	CH	PLZZZZUSA
MIK, MARTIN	23	M	CH	PLZZZZUSA
JUSMANN, ISAAC	45	M	CH	PLZZZZUSA
SCHIMANSKY, JUDEL	16	M	CH	PLZZZZUSA
SEGAL, CHAIM	50	M	CH	PLZZZZUSA
PEREL	48	F	W	PLZZZZUSA
SCHEWE	17	F	SP	PLZZZZUSA
ZIPPE	15	F	SP	PLZZZZUSA
JOSSEL	9	M	CHILD	PLZZZZUSA
SARRAH	5	F	CHILD	PLZZZZUSA
SCHADEK, ADAM	23	M	LABR	PLZZZZUSA
VICTORIA	40	F	W	PLZZZZUSA
ROSALIA	19	F	SP	PLZZZZUSA
CASPER	18	M	LABR	PLZZZZUSA
MICH.	16	M	LABR	PLZZZZUSA
ANNA	11	F	CH	PLZZZZUSA
JACOB	4	M	CHILD	PLZZZZUSA
ANNA	2	F	CHILD	PLZZZZUSA
PTASEHEK, ANNA	11	F	CH	PLZZZZUSA
FISCHGOLD, ABRAH.	25	M	LABR	RRZZZZUSA
KASEMIA, MUDIA	25	M	LABR	RRZZZZUSA
FRACHLENBERG, SCHAJE	22	M	LABR	RRZZZZUSA
ZIRELSTEIN, MOSES	18	M	LABR	RRZZZZUSA
GOLDFARD, BEN	28	M	LABR	RRZZZZUSA
JAHR, MOSES	25	M	LABR	RRZZZZUSA
JAFFER, SCHMUEL	11	M	CH	RRZZZZUSA
RUG, MICHAEL	40	M	LABR	RRZZZZUSA
ELISABETH	36	F	W	RRZZZZUSA
MARIANNA	9	F	CHILD	RRZZZZUSA
ANTONIN	7	M	CHILD	RRZZZZUSA
JULIANNA	6	F	CHILD	RRZZZZUSA
ANDELA	4	F	CHILD	RRZZZZUSA
CAROLINA	.08	F	INFANT	RRZZZZUSA
CZUKOWSKY, ADAM	26	M	LABR	RRZZZZUSA
JEDEWIN, DOMENIK	18	M	LABR	RRZZZZUSA
MALGLON	36	M	LABR	RRZZZZUSA
SUDUGZKI, JAN	33	M	LABR	RRZZZZUSA
ANNA	34	F	W	RRZZZZUSA

PASSENGER	AGE	SEX	OCCUPATION	PRV VIL DES
JAN	3	M	CHILD	RRZZZZUSA
CATH.	.09	F	INFANT	RRZZZZUSA
WENICKY, SAM.	23	M	LABR	RRZZZZUSA
FLYSGSON, LEIB	19	M	LABR	RRZZZZUSA
HANSON, KON.	40	M	LABR	RRZZZZUSA

SHIP: CALAND

FROM: ROTTERDAM
TO: NEW YORK
ARRIVED: 22 MAY 1885

PASSENGER	AGE	SEX	OCCUPATION	PRV VIL DES
MEDZUKEWITZ, SIMON	35	M	LABR	RRZZZZUSA
TEIL, MARCUS	18	M	LABR	RRACTCUSA
LAPKIN, REINA	15	F	NN	PLZZZZUSA
GUT, BLAZE	29	M	LABR	PLZZZZUSA
SCHWANNERFER, NOACHIM	19	M	LABR	PLZZZZUSA
LEGEN, SANDEL	42	M	LABR	PLZZZZUSA
SCHOPIRA, OSKAR	18	M	MCHT	PLZZZZUSA
SANUM, RUBIN	23	M	MCHT	PLZZZZUSA
LAVIN, ABEL	25	M	MCHT	PLZZZZUSA
MANSOLF, JOHANN	41	M	MCHT	PLZZZZUSA
STOCKZINSKY, LEVI	19	M	MCHT	PLAHVUUSA
CHEWIN, IZAK	20	M	MCHT	PLZZZZUSA
HIRSCHLUKAN, SCHMUEL	33	M	MCHT	PLZZZZUSA
TRUNNEN, ELIAS	30	M	MCHT	PLZZZZUSA
TAITSCH, LEIB	25	M	MCHT	PLZZZZUSA
SOHNEK, BEEN	20	M	MCHT	PLZZZZUSA
KOZIK, IGNATZ	26	M	LABR	PLZZZZUSA
HERMANN, FEIGE	22	M	LABR	PLZZZZUSA
CARMEN, DEUTSCH	16	F	NN	PLZZZZUSA
LAPKIN, SAMUEL	20	M	LABR	PLZZZZUSA
STAUL, CHUNNE	30	M	LABR	PLZZZZUSA
LAPKIN, ITZKO	25	M	TLR	PLZZZZUSA
SOSSMAN, ABRAHAM	47	M	TLR	PLZZZZUSA
LIDKIN, LEIB	52	M	TLR	PLZZZZUSA
MASCHUK, ESTHER	20	F	NN	PLZZZZUSA
WASSERSBROM, LOUIS	18	M	LABR	PLZZZZUSA
TOUBELOWSKI, BERKO	16	M	LABR	PLZZZZUSA
MIKOBITES, JONAS	24	M	LABR	PLZZZZUSA
MIKNEWITZ, CARL	30	M	LABR	PLZZZZUSA
BRUDEWITZ, JONAS	22	M	LABR	PLZZZZUSA
SCHILUNKES, MIKAS	20	M	LABR	PLZZZZUSA
VICTORIA	24	F	NN	PLZZZZUSA

SHIP: INDIA

FROM: HAMBURG
TO: NEW YORK
ARRIVED: 22 MAY 1885

PASSENGER	AGE	SEX	OCCUPATION	PRV VIL DES
KOSSAKOWSKY, IGN.	26	M	LABR	RRZZZZIL
BARONOWSKY, V.	25	M	LABR	RRZZZZNY
BRUSAKUS, A.	19	M	LABR	RRZZZZNY
KIRSCHNALSKY, M.	14	M	TDR	RRZZZZNY
PERLMANN, JOSS.	24	M	TDR	RRZZZZNY
KROZINSKE, L.	50	M	TRDSMN	RRZZZZNY
SCHANE	40	F	W	RRZZZZNY
DAVID	12	M	S	RRZZZZNY
FEREL	4	F	CHILD	RRZZZZNY
CHAIE	.11	F	INFANT	RRZZZZNY
LEISER	.02	M	INFANT	RRZZZZNY
KIRSCHMANSKY, MOS.	18	M	TDR	RRZZZZNY
GOLDBERG, ETTEL	65	F	WI	RRZZZZIL
LICE	25	F	WO	RRZZZZIL
BRANITZKI	7	F	CHILD	RRZZZZIL
REFKI	6	F	CHILD	RRZZZZIL
BEILKE	5	F	CHILD	RRZZZZIL
SAMKE	2	F	CHILD	RRZZZZIL
MUCKE	.08	F	INFANT	RRZZZZIL
KAMINSKA, DOWE	28	F	WO	RRZZZZNY
ROSA	.06	F	INFANT	RRZZZZNY
KUSCHNER, SAL.	17	M	TDR	RRZZZZNY
CHANE	16	F	SI	RRZZZZNY
KAIKOFSKY, JOS.	35	M	LABR	RRZZZZUNK
MAICZE, SAM.	19	M	TDR	RRZZZZPA
NIERMANN, HIRSCH	20	M	TDR	RRZZZZNY
FLAMM, ROSA	32	F	SGL	RRZZZZNY
WIZBUDZKI, ZAB.	16	F	SGL	RRZZZZNY
WALTER, JULIANE	16	F	SGL	RRZZZZUNK
CAROLINE	23	F	SGL	RRZZZZUNK
OPATZKI, ANDREAS	25	M	TDR	RRZZZZNY
GOLDMANN, ISIDOR	19	M	TDR	RRZZZZNY
MEDNICK, LEISER	42	M	TDR	RRZZZZNY
ORWITT, KASIMIR	38	M	TDR	RRZZZZNY
BEHRMANN, BL.	46	M	TDR	RRZZZZNY
ITZKOWITZ, CHAZKEL	25	M	TDR	RRZZZZNY
KLATZKI, H.	45	M	TDR	RRZZZZNY
SLATE	45	F	W	RRZZZZNY
CHANE	13	F	D	RRZZZZNY
NECHE	7	M	CHILD	RRZZZZNY
HERSCHMAN, MARC.	30	M	TDR	RRZZZZNY
PICHOFA, SUSANNE	17	F	SGL	PLZZZZNY
BIRMANN, MEYER	18	M	TDR	RRZZZZNY
RUBENS, B.	22	F	WO	RRZZZZNY
MINNA	.06	F	INFANT	RRZZZZNY
JAFFE, CHANE	16	M	MCHT	RRZZZZNY
WRONSKA, MARYANA	30	F	SGL	PLZZZZIL
DZIKOWSKA, JOSEFA	43	F	WO	RRZZZZNY
ALEXANDER	7	M	CHILD	RRZZZZNY
STANISLAUS	6	M	CHILD	RRZZZZNY
LUDWIKA	5	F	CHILD	RRZZZZNY
JULIAN	4	M	CHILD	RRZZZZNY
FRUDE	00	F	D	RRZZZZNY
WASILOWSKI, JULIAN	40	M	FARMER	RRZZZZNY
KANZIS, KANZINI	36	M	LABR	RRZZZZNY
GOTTLIEB, MARK	36	M	TDR	RRZZZZNY
FELSENFELD, CHACO	17	F	SGL	RRZZZZNY
FRIEDMANN, JACOB	18	M	TDR	RRZZZZNY
WASSERSTRAUTH, ISRAEL	19	M	TDR	RRZZZZNY
CHACE	18	F	W	RRZZZZNY
SURDEN, JUREK	28	M	LABR	PLZZZZNY
SCHRAGE, NOAH	35	M	MCHT	PLZZZZNY
BRANDTEVSEIN, SAM.	21	M	TDR	RRZZZZNY
REISENFELD, RIWKE	18	F	SGL	RRZZZZNY
ABLEC, MARIE	21	F	SGL	RRZZZZNY
WONIEZ, JOHANN	55	M	LABR	RRZZZZIL
GROFSMANN, MARIE	16	F	SGL	RRZZZZCLE
GROSS, SALIG	21	M	LABR	PLZZZZNY
KRESLA	20	F	W	PLZZZZNY
KORN, LIPMANN	49	M	LABR	PLZZZZNY
SILBERG, JACOB	16	M	TRDSMN	RRZZZZNY
FUDICK, LEIB	35	M	TRDSMN	RRZZZZNY
SCHIRKNES, ANDR.	34	M	TRDSMN	RRZZZZNY
PERLMANN, DWOSCHE	15	M	TRDSMN	RRZZZZNY
BRAUN, ABEL	22	M	TRDSMN	RRZZZZNY
MIRUS, JOSSEL	32	M	TRDSMN	RRZZZZNY
ROSKIS, NOAH	42	M	TRDSMN	RRZZZZNY
KRAWICZ, HERSCH	34	M	TRDSMN	RRZZZZNY
FUCHS, CHANE	28	M	TRDSMN	RRZZZZNY
OMERTUS, JAN	30	M	LABR	RRZZZZNY
KURLANDER, JEN.	42	M	LABR	RRZZZZNY
SCHNEIDERSTEIN, NOTE	45	M	LABR	RRZZZZCAN
FREIDE	43	F	W	RRZZZZCAN
ALFER	.06	M	INFANT	RRZZZZCAN
CHANE	13	F	D	RRZZZZCAN
MEIER	65	M	S	RRZZZZCAN
EITEL	64	M	S	RRZZZZCAN
P----SKY, PESUCH	00	M	UNKNOWN	RRZZZZNY
ITTE	30	F	W	RRZZZZNY

PASSENGER	AGE	SEX	OCCUPATION	PRVL	VIL	DES
KUNE	6	M	CHILD	RR	ZZZZ	NY
REISEL	3	F	CHILD	RR	ZZZZ	NY
ELKE	.07	M	INFANT	RR	ZZZZ	NY
TRINKELSTEIN, WOLF	27	M	FARMER	RR	ZZZZ	NY
SCHIKIEREWITZ, WOLF	32	M	TDR	RR	ZZZZ	NY
FINKELSTEIN, KATHI	26	F	WO	RR	ZZZZ	NY
THERESE	.11	F	INFANT	RR	ZZZZ	NY
SARA	.02	F	INFANT	RR	ZZZZ	NY
STEINBOLZ, DAVID	26	M	TRDSMN	RR	ZZZZ	NY
SEGELEWITZ, FREIDE	25	F	SGL	RR	ZZZZ	NY
SACHS, ITZIG	44	M	TDR	RR	ZZZZ	IL
ESTER	40	F	W	RR	ZZZZ	IL
ANNA	18	F	D	RR	ZZZZ	IL
SIMCHE	18	M	S	RR	ZZZZ	IL
MARCUS	7	M	CHILD	RR	ZZZZ	IL
SCHOKEN	6	M	CHILD	RR	ZZZZ	IL
LEIB	5	F	CHILD	RR	ZZZZ	IL
LOWENTHAL, DINA	45	F	WO	RR	ZZZZ	IL
NALLIE	6	F	CHILD	RR	ZZZZ	IL
MIRWIS, CROME	18	M	TDR	RR	ZZZZ	BO
MANESEWIC, SARAH	20	F	SGL	RR	ZZZZ	BO
LUNIC, RUBEN	18	M	TRDSMN	RR	ZZZZ	NY
JACOBSOHN, SCHOL	20	M	TRDSMN	RR	ZZZZ	BAL
THURSCHWELL, NATHAN	41	M	TRDSMN	PL	ZZZZ	NY
BEILE	21	F	W	PL	ZZZZ	NY
GITTEL	.06	F	INFANT	PL	ZZZZ	NY

SHIP: NECKAR

FROM: BREMEN
TO: NEW YORK
ARRIVED: 22 MAY 1885

PASSENGER	AGE	SEX	OCCUPATION	PRVL	VIL	DES
ASMUS, ARTHUR	19	M	CL	RR	ZZZZ	NY
SIMULOWITZ, LEHAIM	23	M	LABR	RR	ZZZZ	NY
CAPLAN, CHAIM	25	M	LABR	RR	ZZZZ	NY
STULZ, STANISLAV	19	M	LABR	RR	ZZZZ	NY
LEWIN, SELIG	21	M	LABR	RR	ZZZZ	NY
IDA	8	F	CHILD	RR	ZZZZ	NY
MOKOILIS, ANTONY	18	F	SVNT	RR	ZZZZ	PA
AGATHA	12	F	CH	RR	ZZZZ	PA
ELENDE	13	F	CH	RR	ZZZZ	PA
STRYKAJLYV, MAGDA.	30	F	SVNT	RR	ZZZZ	PA
MAGDA.	3	F	CHILD	RR	ZZZZ	PA
SAL.	.09	M	INFANT	RR	ZZZZ	PA
TISCH, CHAJE	18	M	LABR	RR	ZZZZ	PA
BLOCK, FR.	30	M	LABR	RR	ZZZZ	IL
HEITE	26	F	UNKNOWN	RR	ZZZZ	IL
SCHAPSE	2	M	CHILD	RR	ZZZZ	IL
SARA	.06	F	INFANT	RR	ZZZZ	IL
KRAIN, MICHAEL	25	M	FARMER	RR	ADNB	NY
LISBETH	23	F	UNKNOWN	RR	ADNB	NY
JACOB	.02	M	INFANT	RR	ADNB	NY
PISCHKE, WILH.	34	M	FARMER	RR	ADNB	NY
MAGDAL.	30	F	UNKNOWN	RR	ADNB	NY
MARGAR.	8	F	CHILD	RR	ADNB	NY
LUDWIG	6	M	CHILD	RR	ADNB	NY
JOHANN	4	M	CHILD	RR	ADNB	NY
CATHARINE	2	F	CHILD	RR	ADNB	NY
MAGDALINA	.08	F	INFANT	RR	ADNB	NY
WILD, JOHANN	35	M	LABR	RR	ADNB	NY
CAHTARINE	32	F	UNKNOWN	RR	ADNB	NY
CATHERINE	8	F	CHILD	RR	ADNB	NY
CAROLINE	7	F	CHILD	RR	ADNB	NY
JACOB	5	M	CHILD	RR	ADNB	NY
CHRISTINE	2	F	CHILD	RR	ADNB	NY
MAGDAL.	.04	F	INFANT	RR	ADNB	NY

SHIP: CITY OF BERLIN

FROM: LIVERPOOL AND QUEENSTOWN
TO: NEW YORK
ARRIVED: 23 MAY 1885

PASSENGER	AGE	SEX	OCCUPATION	PRVL	VIL	DES
MAUO, ED.F.	24	M	LABR	RR	ACBF	UNK
JOHANNA	23	F	W	RR	ACBF	UNK
MARIA	4	F	CHILD	RR	ACBF	UNK
DOBROWOLSKY, KARL	50	M	FARMER	RR	ACBF	NY
JOHANNA	18	M	FARMER	RR	ACBF	NY
BRASAUTZKY, JOSEF	24	M	LABR	RR	ACBF	NY
HALELUIS, VINCENT	35	M	LABR	RR	ACBF	NY
RUBINSKI, ISAK	18	M	LABR	RR	ACBF	NY
PRUSS, MARIUS	20	M	LABR	RR	ACBF	NY
SCHILOWILDS, LEIB	18	M	LABR	RR	ACBF	NY
FNIKEL, MANDEL	19	M	LABR	RR	ACBF	NY
KALMAUSK, RUBEUS	25	M	LABR	RR	ACBF	NY
ROCHMANN, JUDI	18	M	LABR	RR	ACBF	NY
WOLPHU, ISIDOR	22	M	LABR	RR	ACBF	NY
KAPLAN, LIEB	25	M	FARMER	RR	ACBF	NY
RAPAPORT, OWEZU	20	M	LABR	RR	ACBF	NY
HILKILA, SUSAN	20	M	LABR	FN	ZZZZ	CH
JORTONILLE, JUS.	21	M	LABR	PL	ZZZZ	CH
ALENAUCITIS, JOHANN	22	M	LABR	PL	ZZZZ	CH
STILLMARK, AUT.	17	M	LABR	PL	ZZZZ	CH

SHIP: EIDER

FROM: BREMEN AND SOUTHAMPTON
TO: NEW YORK
ARRIVED: 23 MAY 1885

PASSENGER	AGE	SEX	OCCUPATION	PRVL	VIL	DES
BADER, CHRIST.	48	M	LABR	RR	ZZZZ	USA
JOHANNE	48	F	W	RR	ZZZZ	USA
ANTON	18	M	LABR	RR	ZZZZ	USA
KATHARINE	16	F	NN	RR	ZZZZ	USA
WILHELM	10	M	CH	RR	ZZZZ	USA
HEINRICH	7	M	CHILD	RR	ZZZZ	USA
LEHR, JOHANN	49	M	LABR	RR	ZZZZ	USA
CHRISTE	45	F	W	RR	ZZZZ	USA
BARBARA	22	F	NN	RR	ZZZZ	USA
ANDREAS	24	M	LABR	RR	ZZZZ	USA
EMMA	18	F	NN	RR	ZZZZ	USA
CHRIST.	16	F	NN	RR	ZZZZ	USA
JOHANN	14	M	NN	RR	ZZZZ	USA
MAGD.	4	F	CHILD	RR	ZZZZ	USA
VALENTIN	2	M	CHILD	RR	ZZZZ	USA
HELENA	.11	F	INFANT	RR	ZZZZ	USA
BRUNNEMEYER, GEORG	33	M	LABR	RR	ZZZZ	USA
MARG.	31	F	W	RR	ZZZZ	USA
GEORG	8	M	CHILD	RR	ZZZZ	USA
CATH.	5	F	CHILD	RR	ZZZZ	USA
SOFIA	4	F	CHILD	RR	ZZZZ	USA
JACOB	2	M	CHILD	RR	ZZZZ	USA
LIESBETH	.11	F	INFANT	RR	ZZZZ	USA
CONRAD	.11	M	INFANT	RR	ZZZZ	USA
GOLDBLUM, ERTEL	23	M	FARMER	RR	ZZZZ	USA
LIPPE	.06	M	INFANT	RR	ZZZZ	USA
TRILLING, MARIE	19	F	NN	RR	ZZZZ	USA
HOCHSTATTER, JACOB	60	M	LABR	RR	ZZZZ	USA
LOUISE	48	F	W	RR	ZZZZ	USA
KATHARINE	22	F	NN	RR	ZZZZ	USA
JACOB	13	M	NN	RR	ZZZZ	USA
LOUISE	13	F	NN	RR	ZZZZ	USA
BARBARA	13	F	NN	RR	ZZZZ	USA
JOHANNES	7	M	CHILD	RR	ZZZZ	USA
MAGD.	4	F	CHILD	RR	ZZZZ	USA
FAUL, CARL	32	M	LABR	RR	ZZZZ	USA

PASSENGER	AGE	SEX	OCCUPATION	PRV VIL DES
KATH.	28	F	W	RRZZZZUSA
KATH.	7	F	CHILD	RRZZZZUSA
ROSINE	4	F	CHILD	RRZZZZUSA
BARBARA	3	F	CHILD	RRZZZZUSA
HEINBUCH, JOHANNES	23	M	LABR	RRZZZZUSA
CHRIST.	20	F	NN	RRZZZZUSA
CHRIST.	17	F	NN	RRZZZZUSA
ZACKER, DAVID	19	M	LABR	RRZZZZUSA
POSONSKY, JACOB	52	M	LABR	RRZZZZUSA
FURGENSON, REINHOLD	19	M	LABR	RRZZZZUSA
PASOPSKY, SAMUEL	20	M	LABR	RRZZZZUSA
MEIDINGER, JOHANN	40	M	FARMER	RRAAXFUSA
MAGD.	40	F	W	RRAAXFUSA
CHRIST.	18	M	FARMER	RRAAXFUSA
FRIEDR.	15	M	NN	RRAAXFUSA
CHRIST.	7	F	CHILD	RRAAXFUSA
CATH.	6	F	CHILD	RRAAXFUSA
JACOB	5	M	CHILD	RRAAXFUSA
ADOLF	3	M	CHILD	RRAAXFUSA
JOHANN	.11	M	INFANT	RRAAXFUSA
SKOMETZKI, JOHANNES	20	M	LABR	RRZZZZUSA
RIEGER, FREDR.	24	M	FARMER	RRAAXFUSA
CATH.	22	F	W	RRAAXFUSA
MATHEUS	.06	M	INFANT	RRAAXFUSA
ROSIN, GEORG	26	M	FARMER	RRAAXFUSA
CATH.	27	F	W	RRAAXFUSA
CHRIST.	2	F	CHILD	RRAAXFUSA
CATH.	.09	F	INFANT	RRAAXFUSA
SCHAMBER, ANNA	47	F	W	RRZZZZUSA
BAR, JOH.	23	M	FARMER	RRZZZZUSA
SUSANNE	14	F	NN	RRZZZZUSA
ANNA	11	F	CH	RRZZZZUSA
CHRIST.	7	M	CHILD	RRZZZZUSA
REINHOLD	5	M	CHILD	RRZZZZUSA

SHIP: GELLERT

FROM: HAMBURG AND HAVRE
TO: NEW YORK
ARRIVED: 23 MAY 1885

PASSENGER	AGE	SEX	OCCUPATION	PRV VIL DES
SZPURADOWSKI, IGNATZ	20	M	BBR	RRZZZZUSA
LEVINSOHN, HINDE	15	M	SGL	RRAHTFUSA
MIDRED, SCHIMCHE	35	M	TLR	RRAHVUUSA
RHEINWASSER, SARA	50	F	W	RRZZZZUSA
BENENSOHN, SARA	19	F	SGL	RRAHTFUSA
KULVINSKY, SCHOLEM	19	M	LABR	RRAHTUUSA
LEORNAEWSKI, KADISCH	50	M	TLR	RRAHVUUSA
LEWINSOHN, HASCHE	40	F	W	RRAHVUUSA
MALE	17	F	CH	RRAHVUUSA
HIRSCH	9	M	CHILD	RRAHVUUSA
ETTEL	7	M	CHILD	RRAHVUUSA
NESKE	5	M	CHILD	RRAHVUUSA
PESACH, RIWKE	18	F	SGL	RRZZZZUSA
SAUDELSKY, MINNA	22	F	SGL	RRZZZZUSA
BECKER, MAIE	25	F	W	RRZZZZUSA
BIRL	3	M	CHILD	RRZZZZUSA
BREINE	.11	F	INFANT	RRZZZZUSA
JOFFE, FISCHMANN	13	M	LABR	RRZZZZUSA
SCHEWIHSKY, ABRAH.	16	M	LABR	RRZZZZUSA
ISMUSCH, PAULINE	18	F	SGL	RRAHTFUSA
MUSE	17	F	SGL	RRAHTFUSA
ARANSOHN, ESTA	24	F	SGL	RRZZZZUSA
REST, SALOMON	22	M	BRM	RRZZZZUSA
SCHNEIDEROWITZ, MOSES	30	M	LABR	RRAGRTUSA
PINAUSKY, JACOB	45	M	LABR	RRZZZZUSA
DINA	40	F	W	RRZZZZUSA
WEINBERG, JEUTE	25	F	SGL	RRADOIUSA
BEILIS, HANNE	27	F	W	RRZZZZUSA
MENUCHE	9	F	CHILD	RRZZZZUSA
JOSEF	8	M	CHILD	RRZZZZUSA
BENLAMIN	.11	M	INFANT	RRZZZZUSA
FRIEDMANN, BETTI	17	F	SGL	RRAHTFUSA
KARPOWITZ, LEA	18	F	SGL	RRAHZSUSA
SCHAPIRO, ZISSEL	18	F	SGL	RRZZZZUSA
BER, GEDALIE	13	F	SGL	RRZZZZUSA
FRENKEL, M.	27	M	LABR	RRZZZZUSA
SAJE	40	M	LABR	RRZZZZUSA
BECKER, LEIBUSCH	15	M	LABR	RRZZZZUSA
SAPIRSTEIN, FEIGE	40	F	W	RRAHTFUSA
EISIG	8	M	CHILD	RRAHTFUSA
ZINE	6	F	CHILD	RRAHTFUSA
SCHIE	2	F	CHILD	RRAHTFUSA
FRENKEL, CHANNE	18	F	SGL	RRAHTSUSA
HERSCH	9	M	CHILD	RRAHTSUSA
WASSERSTROM, SCHEIDEL	35	F	W	RRZZZZUSA
ISAAC	4	M	CHILD	RRZZZZUSA
WOLF	5	M	CHILD	RRZZZZUSA
ZIREL	.11	M	INFANT	RRZZZZUSA
VOWINSKA, MARIASCHE	18	F	SGL	RRAHVUUSA
EHRLICH, FRINNET	42	F	W	RRZZZZUSA
BORDO, JOSEPH	44	M	LABR	RRABQBUSA
POLIMER, MENASSE	34	M	LABR	RRZZZZUSA
RINDEL, PERL	16	M	SGL	RRZZZZUSA
SONNENFELD, MENDEL	32	M	LABR	RRZZZZUSA
LOUISE	21	F	W	RRZZZZUSA
FRINA	14	F	SGL	RRZZZZUSA
CHEIE	.11	F	INFANT	RRZZZZUSA
LEWIN, MOSES	49	M	DLR	RRAHTUUSA
MICHELSOHN, ANDR.	58	M	LABR	RRZZZZUSA
MARIE	56	F	W	RRZZZZUSA
EMANUEL	16	M	CH	RRZZZZUSA
PAULINE	15	F	CH	RRZZZZUSA
SCHUB, JACOB	22	M	DLR	RRZZZZUSA
GITTEL	20	F	W	RRZZZZUSA
HARTWIG, JOHANN	32	M	LABR	RRAHZSUSA
REHTMANN, MASCHE	45	F	W	RRAHTFUSA
SCHLOME	7	F	CHILD	RRAHTFUSA
ABR.	6	M	CHILD	RRAHTFUSA
BROCHE	4	F	CHILD	RRAHTFUSA
MOSES	3	M	CHILD	RRAHTFUSA
CHAVE	2	F	CHILD	RRAHTFUSA
MARKSON, BARUCH	19	F	MCHT	RRAHZSUSA
DOMBRAWSKA, MARIANNE	30	F	W	RRZZZZUSA
FRANZISKA	3	F	CHILD	RRZZZZUSA
ANNA	19	F	SGL	RRZZZZUSA
KLODOWSKY, ESTHER	24	F	SGL	RRZZZZUSA
BERDER, LEIMANN	18	F	W	RRZZZZUSA
JACOB	.11	M	INFANT	RRZZZZUSA
KELLMANN, MAYER	18	M	LABR	RRZZZZUSA
RACHWIL, SAMUEL	14	M	BKBNDR	RRZZZZUSA
LUKIS, DOBRA	16	F	SGL	RRAHUFUSA
RUBELSKI, GERSON	22	M	LABR	RRAHTFUSA
SCHEINFELD, ISAAK	20	M	DLR	RRZZZZUSA
SLOZNIK, RUBEN	30	M	DLR	RRZZZZUSA
WERBLUNSKI, HIRSCH	16	M	LABR	RRZZZZUSA
STEINGER, FEIGE	23	F	W	RRAHTOUSA
NOSSEN	4	M	CHILD	RRAHTOUSA
WIZOZKY, CHOJE	17	M	LABR	RRAHVUUSA
GORDT, HILLEL	23	M	LABR	RRAHVUUSA
SUSSMANOWITZ, HUIDE	24	F	W	RRZZZZUSA
RIWE	.06	F	INFANT	RRZZZZUSA
WITKOWSKA, CONSTANCIA	26	F	W	RRAHSWUSA
LEOCADIA	4	M	CHILD	RRAHSWUSA
SCHEF, BEILE	67	F	W	RRZZZZUSA
FEIGE	18	F	D	RRZZZZUSA
SCHOLDT, PETER	35	M	LABR	RRAHZSUSA
GINSBURG, SAMUEL	17	M	LABR	RRAHVUUSA
KUPPERMANN, MOSES	45	M	LABR	RRZZZZUSA
BRODSKY, JACOB	22	M	DLR	RRAHTFUSA
GLUCK, MOSES	22	M	DLR	RRZZZZUSA
KAPLAN, CHAIE	23	M	SHMK	RRZZZZUSA
FIGA, ULRICH	16	M	TLR	RRAHUIUSA
OPENHEIM, BEN	42	M	PRNTR	RRAHTFUSA
LICHTENSTEIN, KEILE	22	F	SGL	RRZZZZUSA

PASSENGER	AGE	SEX	OCCUPATION	PRV VIL DES
FISCHEL	64	M	TU	RRZZZZUSA
SCHMULOWITZ, ESTHER	35	F	W	RRZZZZUSA
ISRAEL	9	M	CHILD	RRZZZZUSA
TAUBE	8	M	CHILD	RRZZZZUSA
MALE	6	M	CHILD	RRZZZZUSA
ISAAC	5	M	CHILD	RRZZZZUSA
CZERNE	45	F	CH	RRZZZZUSA
SARA	2	F	CHILD	RRZZZZUSA
SPUDER, AUGUSTE	16	F	SGL	RRAHZSUSA
AMALIE	20	F	SGL	RRAHZSUSA
TRULING, CHASKEL	17	M	DLR	RRZZZZUSA
RUBINOWITZ, LIEBE	29	F	W	RRZZZZUSA
DAVID	8	M	CHILD	RRZZZZUSA
ROSA	.11	F	INFANT	RRZZZZUSA
KLOTZ, MERE	19	F	SGL	RRZZZZUSA
MARKOWSKY, GITTEL	30	F	W	RRZZZZUSA
MOSES	4	M	CHILD	RRZZZZUSA
SEGELOWITZ, LIEBE	23	F	W	RRZZZZUSA
LEIZAL	8	F	CHILD	RRZZZZUSA
MASCHE	.11	F	INFANT	RRZZZZ***
SCHOJE, DOHE	18	F	SGL	RRZZZZUSA
STOZNIK, LIEBE	27	F	SGL	RRZZZZUSA
KIRZNAUSKY, SCHEINE	43	F	SGL	RRAHZSUSA
GRUNFELDER, TIELE	18	F	SGL	RRZZZZUSA
LEWITTE, FEIWEL	34	M	TLR	RRZZZZUSA
NEMZINSKY, ISRAEL	29	M	DLR	RRZZZZUSA
LEWIN, SARA	28	F	W	RRAGRTUSA
RAPHAEL	4	M	CHILD	RRAGRTUSA
SCH.	.02	M	INFANT	RRAGRTUSA

SHIP: AURANIA

FROM: LIVERPOOL AND QUEENSTOWN
TO: NEW YORK
ARRIVED: 25 MAY 1885

PASSENGER	AGE	SEX	OCCUPATION	PRV VIL DES
SUSKO, MICHAEL	30	M	LABR	RRAHOOUSA
TYMCIK, PAUL	27	M	LABR	RRAHOOUSA
HOSCHFALD, CUS.	30	M	FARMER	RRAHOOUSA
DORETHA	27	F	W	RRAHOOUSA
LOFA	7	F	CHILD	RRAHOOUSA
BALZI	.08	M	INFANT	RRAHOOUSA
ZANTORSKY, FRANZ	18	M	LABR	RRAHOOUSA
TILKO, ANTON	34	M	LABR	RRAHOOUSA
MALEGKI, IRAN	28	M	LABR	RRAHOOUSA
DUDINSKY, IGNATZ	28	M	LABR	RRAHOOUSA
ISKOVSKY, TOMAS	23	M	LABR	RRAHOOUSA
ROBEK, FUDEL	23	M	LABR	RRAHOOUSA
SCTULDER, SAMUEL	19	M	LABR	RRAHOOUSA
BANUVITZ, TIZI	30	M	LABR	RRAHOOUSA

SHIP: WESTPHALIA

FROM: HAMBURG
TO: NEW YORK
ARRIVED: 25 MAY 1885

PASSENGER	AGE	SEX	OCCUPATION	PRV VIL DES
NIESZEWSKI, M.	30	M	MCHT	RRZZZZUSA
ABBE, BER.	12	M	CH	RRZZZZUSA
STOLOW, MOSCHE	35	M	LABR	RRAHQHUSA
LEWKOWITZ, LEWIN	46	M	LABR	RRZZZZUSA
COHN, SCHMUEL	19	M	LABR	RRZZZZUSA
GOLDSTEIN, SELDE	26	F	W	RRZZZZUSA
DAVID	2	M	CHILD	RRZZZZUSA
BASCHE	.11	M	INFANT	RRZZZZUSA
FINKELBRAND, BEREIK	34	M	DLR	RRAHZNUSA
MERE	25	F	W	RRAHZNUSA
MOSES	4	M	CHILD	RRAHZNUSA
BROCHE	9	F	CHILD	RRAHZNUSA
BARANOWSKY, ESSEL	45	M	TLR	RRZZZZUSA
BERMAN, BERKE	16	M	TLR	RRZZZZUSA
BINSKY, KALMAN	18	M	SHMK	RRZZZZUSA
TATARSKY, ABRAM	28	M	TNMK	RRZZZZUSA
CHANNE	26	F	W	RRZZZZUSA
BREINLE	.11	F	INFANT	RRZZZZUSA
SARA	.11	F	INFANT	RRZZZZUSA
COHN, BARUCH	50	M	DLR	RRAHVOUSA
FRENSEL, SCHACHNE	14	F	SGL	RRZZZZUSA
KASCH, MEYER	22	M	CGRMKR	RRAHVUUSA
PRESSEISEN, BARUCH	54	M	TLR	RRZZZZUSA
JOSEPH	18	M	BKR	RRZZZZUSA
MARISE	15	F	SGL	RRZZZZUSA
HAMDURSKY, MERE	19	F	SGL	RRZZZZUSA
WALCK, SARA	35	F	W	RRAHSZUSA
JECHIEL	9	F	CHILD	RRAHSZUSA
HANNE	5	F	CHILD	RRAHSZUSA
ABE	3	M	CHILD	RRAHSZUSA
CHAWE	.11	F	INFANT	RRAHSZUSA
BERKANG, LEA	18	F	W	RRAHSZUSA
ESTHER	.06	F	INFANT	RRAHSZUSA
SCHEONES, LEIB	43	M	LABR	RRZZZZUSA
JOSSEL	9	M	CHILD	RRZZZZUSA
CZIEZELSKY, LEIB	20	M	TLR	RRAHTSUSA
MICHEL, CHANNE	19	F	SGL	RRAHWZUSA
RACHEL	9	F	CHILD	RRAHWZUSA
PREGLER, LEOPOLD	18	M	SMH	RRZZZZUSA
TERSKA, LOUISE	17	F	SGL	RRZZZZUSA
GURNA, FRANZA.	30	F	W	RRZZZZUSA
VACLAV	10	M	CH	RRZZZZUSA
SIEGMUND	7	M	CHILD	RRZZZZUSA
SOPHIE	4	F	CHILD	RRZZZZUSA
STEFAN	.11	F	INFANT	RRZZZZUSA
ROSENBLUM, SCHOLEM	19	M	DLR	RRAHTFUSA
KLEIN, TORKASZ	14	M	LABR	RRZZZZUSA
LEIFER, JOSEPH	23	M	LABR	RRZZZZUSA
KUSEL, CHEIE	20	F	SGL	RRAHTFUSA
BARUCH	9	M	CHILD	RRAHTFUSA
GITTEL	8	M	CHILD	RRAHTFUSA
GOLDBERG, JACOB	23	M	LABR	RRZZZZUSA
DINA	21	F	SGL	RRZZZZUSA
KALWARSKY, REIZE	22	F	SGL	RRZZZZUSA
MORDSCHE	16	M	LABR	RRZZZZUSA
KALWARISKY, GIMPEL	22	M	LABR	RRZZZZUSA
IPP, ISAAC	25	M	DLR	RRAHTFUSA
PRAEGER, HERSCHEL	50	M	LABR	RRZZZZUSA
LEWKOWITZ, KOPPEL	30	M	LABR	RRZZZZUSA
MUELLER, ISRAEL	50	M	DLR	RRZZZZUSA
ROCKMANOWSKY, FRIDEY	35	F	W	RRZZZZUSA
REBECCA	9	F	CHILD	RRZZZZUSA
LOUIS	8	M	CHILD	RRZZZZUSA
KONTORSKI, M.	46	M	LABR	RRZZZZUSA
ROCKMANOWSKY, SARA	.11	F	INFANT	RRZZZZUSA
SUSANNE	.01	F	INFANT	RRZZZZUSA
MARK, SARA	40	F	W	RRAHZSUSA
GELLO, ICHNO	36	M	LABR	RRZZZZUSA
MARCELLO	9	M	CHILD	RRZZZZUSA
JURGEN	8	M	CHILD	RRZZZZUSA
JOSEF	16	M	CH	RRZZZZUSA
JAN	14	M	CH	RRZZZZUSA
ELISAB.	40	F	W	RRZZZZUSA
PRIVALSKY, WOLF	35	M	TCHR	RRAHVUUSA
GERSON	9	M	CHILD	RRAHVUUSA
MASCHE	6	M	CHILD	RRAHVUUSA
MELLNER, CHAIM	22	M	DLR	RRAHUIUSA
CHIEWAK, NOCHIM	24	M	LABR	RRAHVUUSA
KUPLINSKY, CHEIM	30	M	CGRMKR	RRAHVUUSA
WISCHINSKI, ABRAHAM	24	M	DLR	RRZZZZUSA
ROJEWSKI, WAURZEWICZ	30	M	LABR	RRZZZZUSA
BERGER, JOSEL-M.	30	M	TLR	RRAHTOUSA
BALSAM, ELIAKIN	30	M	SHMK	RRZZZZUSA

PASSENGER	AGE	SEX	OCCUPATION	PRIVL	DES
ROSENFELD, JACUS	17	M	LABR	RRZZZZ	USA
ARSTEIN, NECHE	55	F	W	RRAHSL	USA
DOBOSZYNSKA, THEOPHILA	50	F	W	RRAHSW	USA
MARIE	20	F	CH	RRAHSW	USA
CAROLINE	16	F	CH	RRAHSW	USA
JULIE	9	F	CHILD	RRAHSW	USA
MISCHKUEZ, CHEIM	17	M	LABR	RRZZZZ	USA
URKINTE, ANNA	23	F	SGL	RRAHZS	USA
SCHIFROWITSCH, WOLF	20	M	KNSMH	RRZZZZ	USA
ROSENTHAL, DAVE	18	M	CGRMKR	RRAHZS	USA
COHN, YANKEL	16	M	LABR	RRZZZZ	USA
ADELSOHN, MOSES	19	M	TLR	RRZZZZ	USA
BAJUCZ, ISTVAN	17	M	LABR	RRZZZZ	USA
SMENASTIS, PETER	18	M	LABR	RRAHZS	USA
PERLBERG, ISAAC	20	M	LABR	RRZZZZ	USA
WIEBENZICH, MINNA	16	F	SGL	RRZZZZ	USA
GORDON, CHAJE	20	F	SGL	RRAHSZ	USA
JASDEBSKI, ANTON	31	M	LABR	RRAHZS	USA
RATSTEIN, CHANNE	19	F	SGL	RRZZZZ	USA
SALOMYR, CHAIM	30	M	LABR	RRAHTF	USA
SCHAPIRO, RASCHE	28	F	W	RRZZZZ	USA
ARON	9	M	CHILD	RRZZZZ	USA
ISRAEL	5	M	CHILD	RRZZZZ	USA
SARA	3	F	CHILD	RRZZZZ	USA
SCHLAPOVSBERSKY, ABRAH.	8	M	CHILD	RRZZZZ	USA
PEISACH	9	M	CHILD	RRZZZZ	USA
SCHAPIRO, KREIWE	60	F	W	RRZZZZ	USA

SHIP: HOHENZOLLEN

FROM: BREMEN
TO: NEW YORK
ARRIVED: 26 MAY 1885

PASSENGER	AGE	SEX	OCCUPATION	PRIVL	DES
STUTA, WACZ.	23	M	LABR	RRZZZZ	USA
RATZACKI, ANNA	27	F	W	RRAHTO	USA
JAN	5	M	CHILD	RRAHTO	USA
MICHALINA	4	F	CHILD	RRAHTO	USA
WLADISLAUS	.01	M	INFANT	RRAHTO	USA
PALKE, JACOB	28	M	LABR	RRAHTO	USA
NIEMOWITZKI, JACOB	24	M	LABR	RRAHUC	USA
JARMAWICZ, MICHAEL	30	M	LABR	RRAHXR	USA
CLYFTA, CARL	22	M	LABR	RRZZZZ	USA
BALTIMORE, JANKEL	17	M	LABR	RRAHZC	USA
LATTAWITZ, GITTE	18	F	NN	RRAHZC	USA
BANK, FRICH	46	F	W	RRAHZC	USA
SELIG	17	M	LABR	RRAHZC	USA
BLUME	7	M	CHILD	RRAHZC	USA
RATCHKOWITZ, M.	19	M	LABR	RRAHZC	USA
WANOSKY, SELIG	18	M	LABR	RRAHZC	USA
CHAPUMOWITZ, HIRSCH	20	M	LABR	RRAHZC	USA
VALENTA, PAULINE	20	F	NN	RRAHZC	USA
ANTONIA	7	F	CHILD	RRAHZC	USA
NOWAK, JOSEF	25	M	LABR	RRAHZC	USA
BARZENKA, ROSALIA	22	F	NN	RRAHZC	USA
WIEDOCZIK, F.	34	M	LABR	RRAHZC	USA
WENJEZKAWSKI, JULIANA	40	F	NN	RRAHZC	USA
MARTHA	9	F	CHILD	RRAHZC	USA
SINGER, MASER	40	M	LABR	RRZZZZ	USA
RASACKI, EMIL	20	M	LABR	RRZZZZ	USA
WENTHAL, ISRAEL	33	M	LABR	RRZZZZ	USA
KAZNECKI, LUDWIG	50	M	LABR	RRAHTE	USA
HALPERD, SELIG	16	M	LABR	RRAHTE	USA
NASECAWICZ, FRANZ	50	M	LABR	RRAHTE	USA
LIFSCHITZ, LEISER	25	M	LABR	RRAHXO	USA
MINDEL, LEIB	30	M	LABR	RRAHTF	USA
LEIBGOLD, ROSA	2	F	CHILD	RRAHTF	USA
TUCHTEN, DAVID	50	M	LABR	RRAHTF	USA
LUSTIG, B.	15	M	LABR	RRAHTF	USA
CASIMIR, MARY	30	F	W	RRAHTF	USA

PASSENGER	AGE	SEX	OCCUPATION	PRIVL	DES
ERNST	3	M	CHILD	RRAHTF	USA
VICTORIA	.05	F	INFANT	RRAHTF	USA
BERKAM, WILHELM	24	M	LABR	RRAHTT	USA
JAHNKE, AUGUST	30	M	LABR	RRAHTT	USA
ERNESTINE	40	F	W	RRAHTT	USA
HERMANN	3	M	CHILD	RRAHTT	USA
MATHILDE	.01	F	INFANT	RRAHTT	USA
SCHULTZE, ADOLF	18	M	LABR	RRAHTT	USA
KLUTIS, FRANZ	14	M	NN	RRAHTT	USA
GUBSTEIN, CLASCHE	46	M	LABR	RRAHTT	USA
MARIANNE	7	F	CHILD	RRAHTT	USA
DAVID	5	M	CHILD	RRAHTT	USA
MEHLMAN, LEISER	22	M	LABR	RRAHTT	USA
RUBIN, R.	25	F	W	RRAFVG	USA
BL.	7	M	CHILD	RRAFVG	USA
CHAVE	6	F	CHILD	RRAFVG	USA
BRUDA	5	M	CHILD	RRAFVG	USA
GERALHAWSKY, FRANZ	26	M	LABR	RRAFVG	USA
KOBILUS, ANTON	21	M	LABR	RRAFVG	USA
BEERMANN, HERSCH	43	M	LABR	RRAFVG	USA
MATTLE	40	F	W	RRAFVG	USA
LEIE	19	M	LABR	RRAFVG	USA
ESTER	16	F	NN	RRAFVG	USA
ISAAC	7	M	CHILD	RRAFVG	USA

SHIP: NUERNBERG

FROM: BREMEN
TO: NEW YORK
ARRIVED: 26 MAY 1885

PASSENGER	AGE	SEX	OCCUPATION	PRIVL	DES
CHIBOLOWSKI, MATHIAS	21	M	LABR	RRZZZZ	USA
SCHWEWLING, FEIWEL	29	M	LABR	RRZZZZ	USA
ZIWE	29	F	W	RRZZZZ	USA
HIRSCH	8	M	CHILD	RRZZZZ	USA
LESER	5	M	CHILD	RRZZZZ	USA
MOSCHER	1	M	CHILD	RRZZZZ	USA
HANNA	.02	F	INFANT	RRZZZZ	USA
SUNDERMANN, ABRAHAM	22	M	LABR	RRZZZZ	USA
AUGUST	59	M	LABR	RRZZZZ	USA
ELISABETH	48	F	W	RRZZZZ	USA
MARIA	17	F	NN	RRZZZZ	USA
ANNA	15	F	NN	RRZZZZ	USA
SAHRA	13	F	CH	RRZZZZ	USA
HERMANN	11	M	CH	RRZZZZ	USA
SALOMON	5	M	CHILD	RRZZZZ	USA
DUBROWSKI, MOSES-ARON	27	M	LABR	RRZZZZ	USA
RATAJIZCZAK, MARCIAN	57	M	LABR	RRZZZZ	USA
WIESE, CHRISTOF	56	M	LABR	RRZZZZ	USA
STZACKIEWICZ, VICTOW	26	M	LABR	RRZZZZ	USA
HAPPKE, CHRISTIAN	27	M	LABR	RRZZZZ	USA
SILBERSTEIN, SOHARNE	45	F	W	RRZZZZ	USA
PERL	2	F	CHILD	RRZZZZ	USA
ESTER	.03	F	INFANT	RRZZZZ	USA
RAFALOWITZ, HERTZ	17	M	LABR	RRZZZZ	USA
RESOHMANN, LACI	18	F	NN	RRZZZZ	USA
BLAT, ABRAHAM	17	M	LABR	RRZZZZ	USA
MAIKEWITZ, MROHAEL	40	M	LABR	RRZZZZ	USA
MAGDLA.	40	F	W	RRZZZZ	USA
MARIA	10	F	CH	RRZZZZ	USA
JONES	5	M	CHILD	RRZZZZ	USA
FITZENT	3	M	CHILD	RRZZZZ	USA
MAGDA.	.06	F	INFANT	RRZZZZ	USA
WOLF, ARON	24	M	LABR	RRZZZZ	USA
HEIHE	22	M	LABR	RRZZZZ	USA
FANNA, LIEBE	20	M	LABR	RRZZZZ	USA
GUETHE, LEINE	20	M	LABR	RRZZZZ	USA
NARUMSKY, DAVID	30	M	LABR	RRZZZZ	USA
BYEN, HENDEL	18	M	LABR	RRZZZZ	USA
GRASS, ELIAS	26	M	LABR	RRZZZZ	USA

PASSENGER	AGE	SEX	OCCUPATION	PRIV	VIL	DES
KWUK, RUBEN	38	M	LABR	RRZZ	ZZ	USA
KEIMER, ABRAHAM	18	M	LABR	RRZZ	ZZ	USA
MANASEWITSCH, BEIMESD	18	F	NN	RRZZ	ZZ	USA
RABINOWITZ, ITZIG	22	M	LABR	RRZZ	ZZ	USA
KATZ, LEOPOLD	18	M	LABR	RRZZ	ZZ	USA
SOKMULSOHN, ABEL	10	M	CH	RRZZ	ZZ	USA
SKOLL, SARAH	18	F	NN	RRZZ	ZZ	USA
MUELLER, SIMON	16	M	LABR	RRZZ	ZZ	USA
OSER, CHANE	38	M	LABR	RRZZ	ZZ	USA
LEWIN	17	M	LABR	RRZZ	ZZ	USA
BEREHOWITZ, FEIGE	32	M	LABR	RRZZ	ZZ	USA
BERE	18	M	LABR	RRZZ	ZZ	USA
BERELOWITZ, JACOBA	10	M	CH	RRZZ	ZZ	USA
SOHWIKE	7	M	CHILD	RRZZ	ZZ	USA
DORA	5	F	CHILD	RRZZ	ZZ	USA
HIRSCH	3	M	CHILD	RRZZ	ZZ	USA
FRIEDMANN, BERIL	16	M	FARMER	RRZZ	ZZ	USA
BERKER, ZABEL	18	M	FARMER	RRZZ	ZZ	USA
LANDE, DAVID	19	M	FARMER	RRZZ	ZZ	USA
GITTE, CHAJE	17	M	FARMER	RRZZ	ZZ	USA
HUWSCHAWITZ, FEIGE	20	M	LABR	RRZZ	ZZ	USA
MARKEL, CLARA	30	F	W	RRZZ	ZZ	USA
SOHUME	1	M	CHILD	RRZZ	ZZ	USA
LEISEWITZ, JANKEL	24	M	LABR	RRZZ	ZZ	USA
FRIDA	.06	F	INFANT	RRZZ	ZZ	USA

SHIP: ANCHORIA

FROM: GLASGOW
TO: NEW YORK
ARRIVED: 27 MAY 1885

PASSENGER	AGE	SEX	OCCUPATION	PRIV	VIL	DES
BLUMENTHAL, J.	21	M	LABR	RRAC	BF	USA
ABRAHAMSON, E.	40	M	PDLR	RRAC	BF	USA
BONCK, ISIDOR	32	M	PDLR	RRAC	BF	USA
COCONEWITZ, D.	36	M	LABR	RRAC	BF	USA
DOSTVR, JACOB	20	M	CGRMKR	RRAC	BF	USA
DRAUGIALAS, P.	20	M	LABR	RRAC	BF	USA
EIDLER, J.	24	M	LABR	RRAC	BF	USA
FRANK, ANTON	40	M	LABR	RRAC	BF	USA
GRAKOWITZ, F.	30	M	LABR	RRAC	BF	USA
GOLDBERGER, ABEL	41	M	PDLR	RRAC	BF	USA
GOLDBERG, BORUCH	17	M	PDLR	RRAC	BF	USA
HANS, JANRAS	40	M	LABR	RRAC	BF	USA
JANETZKY, F.	25	M	LABR	RRAC	BF	USA
JOSTAITIS, VINCENTY	48	M	LABR	RRAC	BF	USA
MATHEWS	20	M	LABR	RRAC	BF	USA
JOSEF	24	M	LABR	RRAC	BF	USA
KELMINSKY, M.	23	M	LABR	RRAC	BF	USA
KOHONT, M.	23	M	LABR	RRAC	BF	USA
KIWSCHNER, JACOB	34	M	TLR	RRZZ	ZZ	USA
RACHEL	30	F	NN	RRZZ	ZZ	USA
GITEL	45	F	NN	RRZZ	ZZ	USA
ISAC	8	M	CHILD	RRZZ	ZZ	USA
KROHNERT, O.	34	M	LABR	RRZZ	ZZ	USA
ANELA	30	F	NN	RRZZ	ZZ	USA
LEWIN, INDEL	34	M	LABR	RRAF	VG	USA
LANBOVSKY, SCHAINE	27	M	PDLR	RRAH	TU	USA
MARRSOW, SCH.	24	M	LABR	RRZZ	ZZ	USA
MILNER, ISAAC	44	M	LABR	RRZZ	ZZ	USA
MATZNER, LEIRE	19	M	SHMK	RRZZ	ZZ	USA
MICHELEWITZ, ZINDEL	18	M	PDLR	RRAC	BF	USA
PICKUS, ARON	17	M	TLR	RRAH	TU	USA
ROZE, ST.	28	M	LABR	RRAC	BF	USA
ROTHBART, JOEL	20	M	LABR	RRAC	BF	USA
ROMKEWITZ, CARL	00	M	LABR	RRAC	BF	USA
ROSENTHAL, S.	18	M	LABR	RRAC	BF	USA
RIEHMANN, ISRAEL	35	M	LABR	RRAC	BF	USA
STIRSCH	18	M	LABR	RRAC	BF	USA
ROSNEKOWITSCH, MOSES	23	M	LABR	RRAC	BF	USA

PASSENGER	AGE	SEX	OCCUPATION	PRIV	VIL	DES
RINE	22	F	NN	RRAC	BF	USA
RADOSKI, SCTLOMA	19	M	BLKSMH	RRAC	BF	USA
ROSENS, LEON	3	M	CHILD	RRAC	BF	USA
MARIE	2	F	CHILD	RRAC	BF	USA
SALOMON	1	M	CHILD	RRAC	BF	USA
FISCHEL	1	M	CHILD	RRAC	BF	USA
SOPHIA	00	F	UNKNOWN	RRAC	BF	USA
RISOWTKY, MICHL.	38	M	LABR	RRAC	BF	USA
SCHUSTER, LIEBE	20	F	SVNT	RRAC	BF	USA
ZETASGEWSKI, JAN	22	M	LABR	RRAC	BF	USA
STAHBAUM, H.	32	M	BKR	RRAC	BF	USA
SEIDEMANN, S.	20	M	GDSM	RRAC	BF	USA
SOLOK, SCHMUL	30	M	TLR	RRAC	BF	USA
SALISTINSKI, SANE	16	M	PDLR	RRAC	BF	USA
SCHCOR, J.	18	M	PDLR	RRAC	BF	USA
SCHESTKA, MORDCKE	17	M	PDLR	RRAC	BF	USA
JASCHMANN, A.	25	M	TLR	RRAC	BF	USA
JAW, STIRSCH	18	M	PDLR	RRAC	BF	USA
ULANOWSKY, JACOB	30	M	MD	RRAC	BF	USA
WEIN, J.	18	M	PDLR	RRAC	BF	USA
WIRZBIME, M.	36	M	LABR	RRAC	BF	USA
JOHANNA	19	F	NN	RRAC	BF	USA

SHIP: WERRA

FROM: BREMEN
TO: NEW YORK
ARRIVED: 27 MAY 1885

PASSENGER	AGE	SEX	OCCUPATION	PRIV	VIL	DES
CZERWCZKI, ROB.	39	M	LABR	RRZZ	ZZ	NY
ZACHARSKY, STEFAN	27	M	LABR	RRZZ	ZZ	NY
GRABOWSKY, UNPELT	21	M	LABR	RRZZ	ZZ	NY
GRUENWALD, DANIEL	31	M	LABR	RRZZ	ZZ	NY
BANDER, ALEXANDER	48	M	FARMER	RRZZ	ZZ	IL
JUSTINE	48	F	UNKNOWN	RRZZ	ZZ	IL
JULIUS	19	M	FARMER	RRZZ	ZZ	NY
AUGUSTE	14	F	CH	RRZZ	ZZ	NY
PAULINE	7	F	CHILD	RRZZ	ZZ	NY
ALESIE	5	F	CHILD	RRZZ	ZZ	NY
VEIT, LUDW.	52	M	FARMER	RRZZ	ZZ	NY
HELENE	34	F	UNKNOWN	RRZZ	ZZ	NY
MATHILDE	16	F	CH	RRZZ	ZZ	NY
WILHELM	7	M	CHILD	RRZZ	ZZ	NY
WILHELMINE	4	F	CHILD	RRZZ	ZZ	NY
SCHULZ, ERDMANN	45	M	TLR	RRZZ	ZZ	NY
KATHNA.	46	F	UNKNOWN	RRZZ	ZZ	NY
JOHANN	15	M	CH	RRZZ	ZZ	NY
LEWY, CUNZ	32	M	LABR	RRZZ	ZZ	NY
SCHIMAUNSKY, JOSEF	29	M	LABR	RRZZ	ZZ	NY
HOMANN, GG.	28	M	FARMER	RRZZ	ZZ	NY
MARIE	25	F	UNKNOWN	RRZZ	ZZ	NY
GEORG	4	M	CHILD	RRZZ	ZZ	NY
ROSINI	3	F	CHILD	RRZZ	ZZ	NY
JACOB	.06	M	INFANT	RRZZ	ZZ	NY
BETTERMANN, PETER	25	M	FARMER	RRZZ	ZZ	NY
CAROLINE	21	F	UNKNOWN	RRZZ	ZZ	NY
LISBETH	00	F	UNKNOWN	RRZZ	ZZ	NY

PASSENGER	AGE	SEX	OCCUPATION	PV RI VL	DES

SHIP: WISCONSIN

FROM: LIVERPOOL AND QUEENSTOWN
TO: NEW YORK
ARRIVED: 27 MAY 1885

PASSENGER	AGE	SEX	OCCUPATION	PV RI VL	DES
PRABUTTER, ERES	43	M	LABR	PLZZZZ	USA
KESTEL, SALOMON	24	M	LABR	PLZZZZ	USA
NWEHINSKY, ANTON	50	M	LABR	PLZZZZ	USA
GERSTENFIELD, DOBE	20	F	SP	PLZZZZ	USA
STOLASKY, JOS.	28	M	LABR	PLZZZZ	USA
CHRISTENSEN, AOGE	22	F	SP	PLZZZZ	USA
SAREWICZ, ANTON	27	M	LABR	PLZZZZ	USA
CHAPAWICZKI, AUGUSTIN	19	F	SP	PLZZZZ	USA
HOROWICZ, HILBL	19	F	SP	PLZZZZ	USA
BORKA, THEODOR	27	M	LABR	PLZZZZ	USA
CHRONSTY, ISRAEL-M.	22	M	LABR	PLZZZZ	USA
LEWINSKY, ABR.	19	M	LABR	PLZZZZ	USA
SOLA, ANDREAS	41	M	LABR	PLZZZZ	USA
ILONA	44	F	W	PLZZZZ	USA
FREIDALES, JOSEF	29	M	LABR	PLZZZZ	USA
KEWICZ, ONOFRA	26	F	SP	PLZZZZ	USA
KRAPOWICZ, IRWIN	24	M	LABR	PLZZZZ	USA
NADOA, ABR.	28	M	LABR	PLZZZZ	USA
FRANKEL, MENDEL	22	M	LABR	PLZZZZ	USA
MUSCAT, ALBERT	23	M	LABR	PLZZZZ	USA
HESBERG, GUSTAV	28	M	LABR	PLZZZZ	USA
MEYER, SACHAM	35	M	LABR	PLZZZZ	USA
KAHN, ABR.	20	M	LABR	PLZZZZ	USA
LAUGSAU, MENDEL	35	M	LABR	PLZZZZ	USA
SARAH	21	F	SP	PLZZZZ	USA
ROSA	.08	F	INFANT	PLZZZZ	USA
MARCUS	19	F	SP	PLZZZZ	USA
MED, BARRUCH	22	M	LABR	PLZZZZ	USA
FHIRKENHOFF, CHAIM	25	M	LABR	PLZZZZ	USA
MIRL	22	M	LABR	PLZZZZ	USA
BANK, OMDA	22	M	LABR	PLZZZZ	USA

SHIP: CITY OF ROME

FROM: LIVERPOOL AND QUEENSTOWN
TO: NEW YORK
ARRIVED: 28 MAY 1885

PASSENGER	AGE	SEX	OCCUPATION	PV RI VL	DES
RODYKA, ABRAHAM	21	M	LABR	PLAEFL	USA

SHIP: BALTIC

FROM: LIVERPOOL AND QUEENSTOWN
TO: NEW YORK
ARRIVED: 29 MAY 1885

PASSENGER	AGE	SEX	OCCUPATION	PV RI VL	DES
BRADREN, CHINST	18	M	FARMER	RRZZZZ	USA
CHOSOWSKY, TOBIAS	40	M	SLSMN	RRZZZZ	USA
SARAH	40	F	W	RRZZZZ	USA
LEIL, JACOB	19	M	TU	RRZZZZ	USA
SAMUEL	11	M	SCH	RRZZZZ	USA
JACOB	10	M	SCH	RRZZZZ	USA
ZONIACH	8	M	CHILD	RRZZZZ	USA
EHAS	4	M	CHILD	RRZZZZ	USA
REUBEN	.10	M	INFANT	RRZZZZ	USA
CHESOWSKY, TIEGEN	21	M	TU	RRZZZZ	USA
RACHEL	19	F	W	RRZZZZ	USA
CHAYE	18	F	SVNT	RRZZZZ	USA

PASSENGER	AGE	SEX	OCCUPATION	PV RI VL	DES
PASQUALL, CARRIA	29	M	FARMER	RRZZZZ	USA
FRANCOSES, RUSSE	37	M	FARMER	RRZZZZ	USA
COSTO, PECTRO	49	M	FARMER	RRZZZZ	USA
MARIE	43	F	W	RRZZZZ	USA
GUSMAN, MOSES	23	M	SHMK	RRZZZZ	USA
SOFIE	22	F	W	RRZZZZ	USA
ALEXANDER	19	M	SHMK	RRZZZZ	USA
ABRAHAM	.10	M	INFANT	RRZZZZ	USA
SEIDNE, SOLOMON	27	M	MSN	RRZZZZ	USA
BESSY	22	F	W	RRZZZZ	USA
MAX	.08	M	INFANT	RRZZZZ	USA
BERGES, SOLOMON	20	M	MNR	RRZZZZ	USA
KATIZ, JASSEL	27	M	MNR	RRZZZZ	USA
SLONMUSKI, SIMON	24	M	REF	RRZZZZ	USA
SUNSKOWKE, IGUATUZ	41	M	FARMER	RRZZZZ	USA
BORCEWSKY, ANTON	44	M	GZR	RRZZZZ	USA
ZORSKEY, MICH	26	M	GZR	RRZZZZ	USA
VYCTOR, SYLVERST	40	M	FARMER	RRZZZZ	USA
JADECKY, JOH.	28	M	FARMER	RRZZZZ	USA
MORASKY, PETRO	15	M	FARMER	RRZZZZ	USA
ADAMZEK, JAN	29	F	SP	RRZZZZ	USA
PEMSTINGAS, ARON	25	M	MACH	RRZZZZ	USA
KAPIS, HARZUNA	34	M	MACH	RRZZZZ	USA
SCHALANKE, MARIE	16	F	SVNT	RRZZZZ	USA
PELZER, MARIAN	27	F	SVNT	RRAFWJ	USA
KASEZYNSKU, FRANZ	28	M	MUSN	RRAFWJ	USA
FRACZKOWSKY, MENDEL	29	M	FARMER	RRAFWJ	USA
KOSLOWSKY, MARIE	26	F	SVNT	RRAFWJ	USA
KERICK, WOLF	22	M	IMKR	RRAFWJ	USA
RAFALIN, MARY-E.	17	F	SP	RRAFWJ	USA
SILBER, FRANKEL-W.	25	M	MECH	RRAFWJ	USA
GRUZ, CH.	23	M	UNKNOWN	RRAEAB	USA
FISKE, REINK	25	M	UNKNOWN	RRAEAB	USA
FINKELSTEIN, MOSES	25	M	BTMKR	RRAEAB	USA
HAMUEL	36	M	BTMKR	RRAEAB	USA
ROCHOVSKY, ALEX	35	M	CL	RRAFWJ	USA

SHIP: PENNLAND

FROM: ANTWERP
TO: NEW YORK
ARRIVED: 29 MAY 1885

PASSENGER	AGE	SEX	OCCUPATION	PV RI VL	DES
KAJAWSKA, A.	50	M	FNR	PLZZZZ	NY
JARMUECZ, ELIST	22	F	SVNT	RRZZZZ	CH
URBANOWSKI, FRIZ	30	F	UNKNOWN	RRZZZZ	DET
MINE	28	F	UNKNOWN	RRZZZZ	DET
ANTON	5	M	CHILD	RRZZZZ	DET
CRADE, SAHIA	18	F	SVNT	RRAHSL	UNK
BISKUP, AGNES	31	F	W	RRZZZZ	NY
FR.	10	F	CH	RRZZZZ	NY
MAR.	4	F	CHILD	RRZZZZ	NY
ANNA	2	F	CHILD	RRZZZZ	NY
KLEINBERG, E.	36	M	TLR	RRAEFL	NY
RUDINSKI, D.	27	M	LABR	PLZZZZ	UNK
JAUMKO, D.	25	M	LABR	PLAHOO	UNK
KOSOWSKI, A.	24	M	LABR	PLAHOO	UNK
ISKOWITZ, A.	20	M	LABR	PLAHOO	PA
SOKA, I.	19	M	LABR	RRZZZZ	CH
FORMANSKI, S.	17	M	LABR	RRAFZD	UNK
JACCOLA, URESTE	38	M	LABR	RRZZZZ	NY
GABRIEL, THOMAS	50	M	UNKNOWN	RRZZZZ	WI
AGNES, THOMAS	50	M	UNKNOWN	RRZZZZ	WI
DESKE, MICH.	60	M	UNKNOWN	PLZZZZ	UNK
ANNA	58	F	UNKNOWN	PLZZZZ	UNK
ELL	10	F	UNKNOWN	PLZZZZ	UNK
OTTO	8	F	CHILD	PLZZZZ	UNK
ROCKERT, JUL.	15	M	UNKNOWN	RRZZZZ	NY
JUL.	9	M	CHILD	RRZZZZ	NY
LUDMELLA, J.	22	F	SVNT	RRZZZZ	UNK

PASSENGER	AGE	SEX	OCCUPATION	PRIV	VIL	DES
SHAPERO, B.	15	M	LABR	RRZZZZ		UNK
DORABIALA, AUT.	20	M	LABR	PLZZZZ		CH
MEYRAH	16	M	LABR	PLZZZZ		CH
MAIZICK, HERM.	18	M	LABR	PLZZZZ		CH
MATHILD	15	F	LABR	PLZZZZ		CH
BURROWSKI, F.	20	M	UNKNOWN	RRZZZZ		NY
BOBLE, EVA	24	F	SVNT	RRZZZZ		NY
ANNA	.09	F	INFANT	RRZZZZ		NY
LINDERBAUM, S.	20	M	MLR	RRAFVG		MI
STARRES	22	M	MLR	RRAFVG		MI

SHIP: ZAANDAM

FROM: AMSTERDAM
TO: NEW YORK
ARRIVED: 30 MAY 1885

PASSENGER	AGE	SEX	OCCUPATION	PRIV	VIL	DES
SHERMAN, LUBISH	20	M	MCHT	PLZZZZ		USA
NACHAURE	24	F	UNKNOWN	PLZZZZ		USA
MARKOWSKY, FRANZ	26	M	UNKNOWN	PLZZZZ		USA
HERMAN, NACHUM	25	M	UNKNOWN	PLZZZZ		USA
STABINSKY, JAW.	23	M	UNKNOWN	PLZZZZ		USA
KRAEZEK, ANDREAS	34	M	UNKNOWN	PLZZZZ		USA
MANDELER, NORSCHE	16	M	UNKNOWN	PLZZZZ		USA
LERNER, BERB.	33	M	UNKNOWN	PLZZZZ		USA
CHAIA	11	F	UNKNOWN	PLZZZZ		USA
SCHADOWSKY, JUDE	19	M	NN	PLZZZZ		USA
SINDENBAUM, SALOMON	50	M	MCHT	PLZZZZ		USA
KUGELENSKY, JAN	52	M	NN	PLZZZZ		USA
ANTON	25	M	NN	PLZZZZ		USA
JOSEPH	23	M	NN	PLZZZZ		USA
VAVORINE	37	F	NN	PLZZZZ		USA
VERONIKA	44	F	NN	PLZZZZ		USA
ADAM	1	M	CHILD	PLZZZZ		USA
CATHARINA	23	F	NN	PLZZZZ		USA
EVA	3	F	CHILD	PLZZZZ		USA
ALEXANDER	20	M	NN	PLZZZZ		USA
NADEL, U	25	F	NN	PLZZZZ		USA
DORA	1	F	CHILD	PLZZZZ		USA
PILTER, MOSES	25	M	NN	PLZZZZ		USA
OSTROW, ISRAEL	34	M	NN	PLZZZZ		USA
URNOKOR, MEYER	43	M	NN	PLZZZZ		USA
BERISCH, EISIG	32	M	NN	PLZZZZ		USA
CURCKUKER, CHASKEL	16	M	NN	PLZZZZ		USA
SULWELD, LIEBISCH	26	M	NN	PLZZZZ		USA
BLIER, LIECHE	32	M	MCHT	PLZZZZ		USA
MESCHEZUWSKY, SENDER	45	M	MCHT	PLZZZZ		USA
CHEIE	19	M	NN	PLZZZZ		USA
MINDE	11	F	NN	PLZZZZ		USA
LIEB, SELIG	22	M	MCHT	PLZZZZ		USA
PENZAH, ADOLF	24	M	MCHT	PLZZZZ		USA
BILLET, SAMREL	30	M	MCHT	PLZZZZ		USA
BRUMAN, JOHEL	53	M	MCHT	PLZZZZ		USA
BRODOWIL, BENJAMIN	20	M	MCHT	PLZZZZ		USA
NACHUM	20	F	MCHT	PLZZZZ		USA
KATOWSKY, HINDE	23	F	MCHT	PLZZZZ		USA
LEIB	4	M	CHILD	PLZZZZ		USA
BRONSKY, JOSEPH	41	M	NN	PLZZZZ		USA
PALUH, JAN	45	M	NN	PLZZZZ		USA
GALOCZ, JANOS	23	M	NN	PLZZZZ		USA
LORENZ, JOSEPH	42	M	NN	PLZZZZ		USA
PALUH, JAN	35	M	NN	PLZZZZ		USA
SELIGA, VALENTIN	45	M	NN	PLZZZZ		USA
GALOCZ, VALENTIN	23	M	NN	PLZZZZ		USA
SCHWEITZIG, JANHEL	16	M	NN	PLZZZZ		USA
TSCHESCHAREH, MICHEL	44	M	NN	PLZZZZ		USA
GUBELZ, CARL	27	M	MCHT	PLZZZZ		USA
BANECH, KARZINA	16	F	NN	PLZZZZ		USA
PODBORESH, ENAEL	33	M	NN	PLZZZZ		USA
STORTZ, HERMAN	17	M	NN	PLZZZZ		USA
SEMEITER, VINCENTZ	20	M	NN	PLZZZZ		USA
JAKUBOWITZ, OSCHER	50	M	NN	PLZZZZ		USA
ODELS, ABRAHAM	21	M	NN	PLZZZZ		USA
KULIKOWSKY, MICHEL	40	M	NN	PLZZZZ		USA
WITNOWSKY, JULIUS	31	M	NN	PLZZZZ		USA
CUSEL, BENZEL	19	M	NN	PLZZZZ		USA
CLAFTER, SAM	10	M	NN	PLZZZZ		USA
JACOBSON, ISAAK	27	M	NN	PLZZZZ		USA
POPILSKY, LEIER	19	M	NN	PLZZZZ		USA
BOBKERS, HIRSCH	40	M	NN	PLZZZZ		USA
SEW, LEIB	29	M	NN	PLZZZZ		USA
TEIGES	25	M	NN	PLZZZZ		USA
SAMSON	1	M	CHILD	PLZZZZ		USA
BRAM, BE---	16	F	NN	PLZZZZ		USA
SCHERMAN, LUBISH	20	M	MCHT	PLZZZZ		USA
NACHAURE	24	F	MCHT	PLZZZZ		USA
MARKOWSKY, FRANZ	26	M	MCHT	PLZZZZ		USA
HERMAN, NACHAM	25	M	MCHT	PLZZZZ		USA
STABINSKY, JAN	23	M	MCHT	PLZZZZ		USA
KRAEZEH, ANDREAS	34	M	MCHT	PLZZZZ		USA
MANDELER, NORSCHE	16	M	MCHT	PLZZZZ		USA
LERNER, BERB.	33	M	MCHT	PLZZZZ		USA
CHAIA	11	F	MCHT	PLZZZZ		USA
SCHADOWSKY, JUDE	19	M	NN	PLZZZZ		USA
SINDENBAUM, SALOMON	50	M	MCHT	PLZZZZ		USA
KUDELEWSKY, JAN	52	M	NN	PLZZZZ		USA
ANTON	25	M	NN	PLZZZZ		USA
JOSEPH	23	M	NN	PLZZZZ		USA
VAVORINE	37	F	NN	PLZZZZ		USA
VERONIKA	44	F	NN	PLZZZZ		USA
ADAM	1	M	CHILD	PLZZZZ		USA
CATHARINA	23	F	NN	PLZZZZ		USA
EVA	3	F	CHILD	PLZZZZ		USA
ALEXANDER	20	M	NN	PLZZZZ		USA
VADEL, U	00	F	NN	PLZZZZ		USA
JANOTSCHEF, ELISABETH	17	F	NN	PLZZZZ		USA
HORHAUS, AMALIE	52	F	NN	PLZZZZ		USA
FRANKE, LOUISE	21	F	NN	PLZZZZ		USA
GREIMER, WMIL	26	M	NN	PLZZZZ		USA
SCHULEM, FREIDE	22	F	NN	PLZZZZ		USA
ISRAEL	1	M	CHILD	PLZZZZ		USA
COHN, JACOB	30	M	MCHT	PLZZZZ		USA
SCHEIER, JACOB	40	M	MCHT	PLZZZZ		USA
STAVITKE, WINE	20	F	MCHT	PLZZZZ		USA
LEBBA, MASHES	20	M	NN	PLZZZZ		USA
BRODER, SIMON	41	M	NN	PLZZZZ		USA
LUCKERM, MAX	20	M	NN	PLZZZZ		USA
KRAMER, ALEX	21	M	MCHT	PLZZZZ		USA
KLEINKOPF, SALOMON	10	M	MCHT	PLZZZZ		USA
BRAUN, ROSA	29	F	NN	PLZZZZ		USA
HELENA	1	F	CHILD	PLZZZZ		USA
LARNORD, HIRSCH	35	M	NN	PLZZZZ		USA
GRAFLIN, HERSCH	23	M	BCK	PLZZZZ		USA
SENANTPE, MOVIE	20	M	CPTR	PLZZZZ		USA
SENATZKES, PEPSCHE	19	M	LABR	PLZZZZ		USA
BUSHIRES, JANOSH	20	M	NN	PLZZZZ		USA
SILBERMAN, SENDER	15	M	LABR	PLZZZZ		USA
BEZEICKAS, JORASH	25	M	LABR	PLZZZZ		USA
GROSS, HANR	20	M	LABR	PLZZZZ		USA
FRANZ	20	M	LABR	PLZZZZ		USA

SHIP: CELTIC

FROM: LIVERPOOL AND QUEENSTOWN
TO: NEW YORK
ARRIVED: 01 JUNE 1885

PASSENGER	AGE	SEX	OCCUPATION	PRIV	VIL	DES
LUCTZER, DEL.	20	M	LABR	PLACBF		USA
SALTZ, HUE	18	F	SP	PLACBF		USA
LUBIANKER, SIEGINA	27	M	LABR	PLACBF		USA

PASSENGER	AGE	SEX	OCCUPATION	PRV VIL DES
SCHUN, SIMON	24	M	LABR	PLACBFUSA
JENTERBLEAN, ARSCHER	32	M	LABR	PLACBFUSA
MEHR, BAR.	29	M	LABR	PLACBFUSA
ALODACK, JOSEPH	33	M	LABR	PLACBFUSA
ASSILOWICZ, MANN	34	M	LABR	PLACBFUSA
LOTRACK, JOSEF	26	M	LABR	PLACBFUSA
KAPLAN, SELIG	32	M	LABR	PLACBFUSA
AFSCHER, ABRAH.	29	M	LABR	PLACBFUSA
AFSEHER, FREIDE	27	F	W	PLACBFUSA
ROSENER, LEVY	40	M	LABR	PLACBFUSA
JUGE, SALOMON	34	M	LABR	PLACBFUSA
MUSHE, RUD.	26	M	LABR	PLACBFUSA
BODANOWITZ, ALEXANDER	29	M	LABR	PLACBFUSA

SHIP: CIRCASSIA

FROM: GLASGOW AND MOVILLE
TO: NEW YORK
ARRIVED: 01 JUNE 1885

PASSENGER	AGE	SEX	OCCUPATION	PRV VIL DES
RAUCECK, RACHAEL	23	M	DLR	RRZZZZUSA
SCLUWEL	2	F	CHILD	RRZZZZUSA
MARIANN	1	F	CHILD	RRZZZZUSA
HOSEL, FRANTSZEK	24	M	LABR	RRZZZZUSA
SCHEIR, WORMS	24	M	TLR	RRZZZZUSA
DANEL, JOSEPH	21	M	DLR	RRZZZZUSA
SOSMOWSKI, SCHLAUM	20	M	TLR	RRZZZZUSA
RASIHTZ, JERWHERE	22	M	DLR	RRZZZZUSA
KIMIMAWSKI, MOSES	21	M	DLR	RRZZZZUSA
SIEMBERG, NOTE	22	M	DLR	RRZZZZUSA
CHAIN	22	M	DLR	RRZZZZUSA
MARGOLIS, MOTEL	17	M	DLR	RRZZZZUSA
HOLANDER, SCHLOME	19	M	DLR	RRZZZZUSA
ABERSOHN, SAYA	18	M	DLR	RRZZZZUSA
SURETZ, CHAIN	45	M	DLR	RRZZZZUSA
ABRAMSHON, HANNAH	31	M	MCHT	RRZZZZUSA
BRIEMER, SHOEL.	28	M	FARMER	RRZZZZUSA
HANNA	25	F	UNKNOWN	RRZZZZUSA
ELICHO	1	M	CHILD	RRZZZZUSA
JUSKOWITZ, CHANI	19	M	DLR	RRZZZZUSA
DANYOLA, ANDRIE	31	M	DLR	RRZZZZUSA
DZIEZIETA, VINCENTZ	59	M	DLR	RRZZZZUSA
MAGDALENN	55	F	W	RRZZZZUSA
KEURTZ, CARL.STAN.	31	M	DLR	RRZZZZUSA
SABAL, JANOS	26	M	LABR	RRZZZZUSA
DZAENTA, ANTONIS	33	M	DLR	RRZZZZUSA
MARIANN	23	F	W	RRZZZZUSA
NEMCKI, MAEZES	30	M	DLR	RRZZZZUSA
SCHYERBACK, ALORDE	24	M	DLR	RRZZZZUSA
GITE	24	F	W	RRZZZZUSA
GERSON	14	M	CH	RRZZZZUSA
DARENZ, CASIS	20	M	LABR	RRZZZZUSA
STANKOWITZ, JAN.	19	M	DLR	RRZZZZUSA
BATINSKI, JOSEPH	31	M	DLR	RRZZZZUSA
KOHANA, CHAIN	19	M	DLR	RRZZZZUSA
ESTER	18	F	SP	RRZZZZUSA
JARLESKI, DAVID	23	M	DLR	RRZZZZUSA
GRAMMAN, MORDCHE	25	M	DLR	RRZZZZUSA
DOBE	19	F	W	RRZZZZUSA
SEARCHI, SAMUEL	16	M	CH	RRZZZZUSA
MOSES	11	M	CH	RRZZZZUSA
MENDEL, HALPERN	17	F	LKSH	RRZZZZUSA
MIKOLSKI, LIEBEL	44	M	DLR	RRZZZZUSA
ULBRECH, FERDINAND	20	M	DLR	RRZZZZUSA
WANKOFFI, NEDIKE	28	M	UNKNOWN	RRZZZZUSA
SAHMELSON, LESSER	21	M	DLR	RRZZZZUSA
FANNY	20	F	W	RRZZZZUSA
KOSEHO, ABRAHAM	20	M	TLR	RRZZZZUSA
MANN, MENDEL	29	M	DLR	RRZZZZUSA
SCHALERWITZ, ITZIG	18	M	DLR	RRZZZZUSA

PASSENGER	AGE	SEX	OCCUPATION	PRV VIL DES
ABELSOHN, NIEBEL	10	F	CH	RRZZZZUSA
FRIEDLAND, BARUCH	20	M	DLR	RRZZZZUSA
FAUSTE, PAUL	23	M	UNKNOWN	RRZZZZUSA
SCHIE	2	F	CHILD	RRZZZZUSA
BILEISKOI, GITEL	24	M	DLR	RRZZZZUSA
BILEISKI, LITTEL	1	F	CHILD	RRZZZZUSA
GERST, CHAYE	17	M	LABR	RRZZZZUSA
ROSA	14	F	SP	RRZZZZUSA
GEIST, JITO	28	M	SP	RRZZZZUSA
HERSCH	1	F	CHILD	RRZZZZUSA
SIMONS, ISAAC	22	M	DLR	RRZZZZUSA
WOLFF, FRASKER	34	M	DLR	RRZZZZUSA
VEIBEL, HAIN	25	M	TLR	RRZZZZUSA
KATZ, JACOFINCO	21	F	SVNT	RRZZZZUSA
FALBE, ELIAS	26	M	DLR	RRZZZZUSA
CHEINE	20	F	W	RRZZZZUSA
MOSFEWICK, SAMUEL	24	M	DLR	RRZZZZUSA
ASPERIN, CAIN	40	M	DLR	RRZZZZUSA
HURNICH	11	M	CH	RRZZZZUSA
BISKI, NACHMAN	20	M	UNKNOWN	RRZZZZUSA
JACKOWSKI, MOSES	23	M	JNR	RRZZZZUSA
BERSHON, DZORZE	18	M	DLR	RRZZZZUSA
MARCUS, WOLF	45	M	DLR	RRZZZZUSA
ABRAHAM	10	M	CH	RRZZZZUSA
BALEISKI, JANTHEL	2	F	CHILD	RRZZZZUSA

SHIP: ELBE

FROM: BREMEN
TO: NEW YORK
ARRIVED: 01 JUNE 1885

PASSENGER	AGE	SEX	OCCUPATION	PRV VIL DES
KRAWITZ, BENZEL	36	M	LABR	RRZZZZUSA
SELIERMANN, CHAJE	20	M	NN	RRZZZZUSA
LEWIST, HANNELL	11	M	CH	RRZZZZUSA
RADEWICH, ANNA	27	F	NN	RRZZZZUSA
PERNSELICTSEH, MARG.	16	F	CH	RRZZZZUSA
OSTROWSKY, RALLY	22	M	NN	RRZZZZUSA
LESMIEWSKI, JULIA	33	M	NN	RRZZZZUSA
JACOB	8	M	CHILD	RRZZZZUSA
FANNI	7	F	CHILD	RRZZZZUSA
OSTROWSKI, LEA	21	F	NN	RRZZZZUSA
OSTER, WILHELM	22	M	LABR	RRZZZZUSA
PFAFF, PHILIPP	24	M	LABR	RRZZZZUSA
ELISABETH	22	F	W	RRZZZZUSA
PHILIPP	1	M	CHILD	RRZZZZUSA
WERRE, CHRISTIAN	32	M	FARMER	RRZZZZUSA
MARIA	26	F	W	RRZZZZUSA
CHRISTIAN	6	M	CHILD	RRZZZZUSA
FRIEDRICH	5	M	CHILD	RRZZZZUSA
HEINRICH	3	M	CHILD	RRZZZZUSA
BERTHA	.11	F	INFANT	RRZZZZUSA
MACIEJEWSKI, PAUL	33	M	NN	RRZZZZUSA
PEIT, MOSCHE	25	M	LABR	RRZZZZUSA
LIEBE	.02	F	INFANT	RRZZZZUSA
SCHERMANN, CHARA-SORE	20	F	NN	RRZZZZUSA
KONSTANTZWOWSKI, FEIGE	16	F	CH	RRZZZZUSA
RIWKA	50	F	NN	RRZZZZUSA
SELMME	12	M	CH	RRZZZZUSA
DONI	10	F	CH	RRZZZZUSA
SAGE	8	F	CHILD	RRZZZZUSA
SEHOENWALD, ILKE	18	F	CH	RRZZZZUSA
ELSKE	16	F	CH	RRZZZZUSA
MEYER, GOTTLIEB	12	M	CH	RRZZZZUSA
REIZIG, ROCHEL	8	M	CHILD	RRZZZZUSA
SANTS, SEIN	24	M	LABR	RRZZZZUSA
SOLIDASKI, MOSES	40	M	LABR	RRZZZZUSA
SEHWARZ, ROSE	26	F	NN	RRZZZZUSA
EDDY	.03	F	INFANT	RRZZZZUSA
LECWEN, JACOB	26	M	LABR	RRZZZZUSA

PASSENGER	AGE	SEX	OCCUPATION	PRV	VIL	DES

SHIP: ETRURIA

FROM: LIVERPOOL AND QUEENSTOWN
TO: NEW YORK
ARRIVED: 01 JUNE 1885

PASSENGER	AGE	SEX	OCCUPATION	PRV	VIL	DES
HOFFERING, ABRAHAM	57	M	MCHT	RR	ZZZZ	EN

SHIP: STATE OF ALABAMA

FROM: GLASGOW AND LARNE
TO: NEW YORK
ARRIVED: 01 JUNE 1885

PASSENGER	AGE	SEX	OCCUPATION	PRV	VIL	DES
BASOPSKY, ABRAHAM	25	M	LABR	RR	ZZZZ	NY
BUCZKOWSKY, JOSEPH	25	M	SDLR	RR	ZZZZ	CH
BRAUDE, MOSES	18	M	LABR	RR	ZZZZ	NY
BOROV, SCHEBSEL	25	M	SMH	RR	ZZZZ	NY
CHAIKA, SOLEM	28	M	CBLR	RR	ZZZZ	NY
CHONIAK, S.	36	M	LABR	RR	ZZZZ	PIT
FRESHMANN, O.	19	M	NN	RR	ZZZZ	NY
FREINSTEIN, MOSES	38	M	TLR	RR	ZZZZ	NY
FLINSAN, LEVI	20	M	CBLR	RR	ZZZZ	NY
GRUNBERG, R.	25	M	LABR	RR	ZZZZ	NY
GLUCK, MOSES	30	M	LABR	RR	ZZZZ	NY
GASUKA, FRANZ	35	M	LABR	RR	ZZZZ	NY
JELINSKI, L.	40	M	LABR	RR	ZZZZ	NY
JAKSCH, JAN	40	M	LABR	RR	ZZZZ	NY
JAKUBOWSKY, JULIAN	28	M	LABR	RR	ZZZZ	NY
KATCHAR, LEOB	22	M	LABR	RR	ZZZZ	NY
KALY, JARGEL	24	M	CBLR	RR	ZZZZ	NY
KAHN, JOSSEL	44	M	CBLR	RR	ZZZZ	NY
TURETZKES, JONNAS	20	M	LABR	RR	ZZZZ	NY
RAMEN, MARCUS	19	M	LABR	RR	ZZZZ	NY
KIRSCHSOHN, EPHRAIM	12	M	NN	RR	ZZZZ	NY
KASTOWSKY, FRANZ	26	M	LABR	RR	ZZZZ	NY
SUNDENSKY, A.	19	M	CBLR	RR	ZZZZ	NY
LEVIN, ISAAC	32	M	CBLR	RR	ZZZZ	NY
LEVETA, BIER	25	M	LABR	RR	ZZZZ	NY
LIPSCHITZ, BARUCH	59	M	GZR	RR	ZZZZ	NY
LEVIN, MARCUS	30	M	CBLR	RR	ZZZZ	NY
SARA	21	F	W	RR	ZZZZ	NY
LIEBERMANN, H.	24	M	SMH	RR	ZZZZ	NY
M---, PEREZ	28	M	CBLR	RR	ZZZZ	NY
U	22	M	CBLR	RR	ZZZZ	NY
MUHLMANN, ISRAEL	29	M	BKBNDR	RR	ZZZZ	NY
KATHI	28	F	W	RR	ZZZZ	NY
ABRAHAM	8	M	CHILD	RR	ZZZZ	NY
ZERLE	5	M	CHILD	RR	ZZZZ	NY
DAVID	1	M	CHILD	RR	ZZZZ	NY
MANTZENBAUM, ALEX.	22	M	LABR	RR	ZZZZ	NY
MEYER, JOSEPH	00	M	CBLR	RR	ZZZZ	NY
NIJEKO, MICHAEL	26	M	LABR	RR	ZZZZ	NY
FRANZISCA	26	F	W	RR	ZZZZ	NY
RUBEL, SIMON	28	M	LABR	RR	ZZZZ	NY
RUDIKLEY, S.	19	M	CBLR	RR	ZZZZ	NY
RUBISCHOWITZ, ANTONIO	40	M	LABR	RR	ZZZZ	NY
LURANDERSTEIN, ABRAHAM	20	M	CBLR	RR	ZZZZ	NY
SCHENE	19	F	W	RR	ZZZZ	NY
SEMANN, J.	35	M	LABR	RR	ZZZZ	NY
SMOLLER, JITTKE	28	F	W	RR	ZZZZ	NY
RACHEL	7	F	CHILD	RR	ZZZZ	NY
SATINSKI, STANISLAU	35	M	CBLR	RR	ZZZZ	NY
MAXIMILIAN	30	M	JNR	RR	ZZZZ	NY
KONSTANTIN	24	M	SMH	RR	ZZZZ	NY
SCHUGAMANN, ETKE	22	F	NN	RR	ZZZZ	NY
SCHMILETZKY, NOTE	26	M	LABR	RR	ZZZZ	NY
SACHS, BEILE	52	F	NN	RR	ZZZZ	NY
JETTE	29	F	W	RR	ZZZZ	NY
MAX	11	M	NN	RR	ZZZZ	NY
SOPHIE	10	F	NN	RR	ZZZZ	NY
MARIE	4	F	CHILD	RR	ZZZZ	NY
HERMANN	1	M	CHILD	RR	ZZZZ	NY
ISRAEL	.03	M	INFANT	RR	ZZZZ	NY
SIGMUND, VINCENT	27	M	LABR	RR	ZZZZ	NY
THEDAK, ERZRBEK	00	F	NN	RR	ZZZZ	NY
WAKS, EBRAIM	37	M	CBLR	RR	ZZZZ	NY
WISMEWSKY, PAUL	24	M	LABR	RR	ZZZZ	NY
LEVINSKY, ISAAC	19	M	LABR	RR	ZZZZ	NY

SHIP: WYOMING

FROM: LIVERPOOL AND QUEENSTOWN
TO: NEW YORK
ARRIVED: 03 JUNE 1885

PASSENGER	AGE	SEX	OCCUPATION	PRV	VIL	DES
DROBINSKY, PRINCUS	32	F	MA	RR	ZZZZ	USA
WOLPE, RUCKIN	26	F	SP	RR	ZZZZ	USA
JOSENOWITZ, MOSCHE	48	M	FARMER	RR	ZZZZ	USA
LIRCH	48	F	W	RR	ZZZZ	USA
SIKENE	19	F	SP	RR	ZZZZ	USA
HINDE	9	F	CHILD	RR	ZZZZ	USA
ELIAS	8	M	CHILD	RR	ZZZZ	USA
ESTER	7	F	CHILD	RR	ZZZZ	USA
MAKOWSKY, OWSCHE	18	M	LABR	RR	AAJX	USA
GOLDSTEIN, SACO	20	M	FARMER	RR	ZZZZ	USA
RIWKE	20	F	W	RR	ZZZZ	USA
MAKOWSKY, BEER	21	M	CL	RR	ZZZZ	USA
BREMIS, SCHMIRL	25	M	FARMER	PL	ZZZZ	USA
RIFKE	20	F	W	PL	ZZZZ	USA
BURSTEIN, PESACH	26	M	GZR	RR	ZZZZ	USA
PINKEL, WOLF	2	M	CHILD	RR	ZZZZ	USA
SCHONFELD, BERL	19	M	SDLR	RR	ZZZZ	USA
FRITZKE, MOJSE	19	F	SP	RR	ZZZZ	USA
SISSMORSKY, ABR.	27	M	MNR	RR	ZZZZ	USA
SIMON, ISAAC	19	M	PMBR	RR	ACBF	USA
DARZKIN, MARITZ	19	F	SP	RR	ACBF	USA

SHIP: POLYNESIA

FROM: HAMBURG
TO: NEW YORK
ARRIVED: 04 JUNE 1885

PASSENGER	AGE	SEX	OCCUPATION	PRV	VIL	DES
TUMPOWITZ, ALB.	50	M	TRDSMN	RR	ZZZZ	NY
ARONSON, RUBEN	36	M	TRDSMN	RR	ZZZZ	NY
HIRSCHSON, LEIB	26	M	TRDSMN	RR	ZZZZ	NY
MELANCK, MOSES	48	M	TRDSMN	RR	ZZZZ	NY
WARKOL, ISRAEL	26	M	TRDSMN	RR	ZZZZ	NY
HABER, BRIL.	21	M	CL	RR	ZZZZ	NY
LUBIN, RUBEL	50	F	WO	RR	ZZZZ	NY
MISCHNITZKY, SALOM.	18	M	TRDSMN	RR	ZZZZ	NY
KOLETZKI, JAKOB	38	M	TRDSMN	RR	ZZZZ	NY
KALETZKI, JUDEL	30	M	TRDSMN	RR	ZZZZ	NY
BLUM, WOLF	40	M	TRDSMN	RR	ZZZZ	NY
JACOBSTEIN, JACOB	43	M	TRDSMN	RR	ZZZZ	NY
RUBINSTEIN, CHAIM	37	M	TRDSMN	RR	ZZZZ	NY
SIMON	34	M	TRDSMN	RR	ZZZZ	NY
KAEHN, MOSES	45	M	TRDSMN	RR	ZZZZ	NY
LANDAN, MOSES	20	M	LABR	PL	ZZZZ	NY
NOL, ESIG	42	M	TRDSMN	RR	ZZZZ	NY
SARETZKY, JUDEL	38	M	TLR	RR	ZZZZ	NY
EIDELMANN, SCHAIE	33	M	TLR	RR	ZZZZ	NY
KEUMINSKY, JUDEL	27	M	TRDSMN	RR	ZZZZ	NY

PASSENGER	AGE	SEX	OCCUPATION	PRIVIL	DES
KAACHMALNICK, JS.	43	M	TRDSMN	RRZZZZ	NY
HAENDLER, MARCUS	18	M	LABR	PLZZZZ	IL
SPIRA, BENSION	20	M	FARMER	PLZZZZ	IL
BUBELSKY, EPHRAIM	28	M	SHMK	RRZZZZ	NY
ZUPOWITZ, MICH.	27	M	TRDSMN	RRZZZZ	NY
WILDE, THADAEUS	35	M	MCHT	RRZZZZ	NY
ROMANOWSKA, LEON	7	M	CHILD	RRZZZZ	NY
SZWEIJKART, BRUNISL.	11	F	F	RRZZZZ	NY
SACK, LISI	20	M	TRDSMN	RRZZZZ	NY
ALTMANN, CUNE	00	F	WO	RRZZZZ	NY
SCHLUNKE	7	M	CHILD	RRZZZZ	NY
LEWY, WOLF	30	M	TRDSMN	RRZZZZ	NY
FLEISCHER, ISRAEL	20	M	BCHR	RRZZZZ	NY
IDDE	20	F	WO	RRZZZZ	NY
FRUME	6	F	CHILD	RRZZZZ	NY
LISANSKI, B.	42	M	TRDSMN	RRZZZZ	NY
KOEHL	43	F	W	RRZZZZ	NY
SAMUEL	15	M	CH	RRZZZZ	NY
LEIB	6	M	CHILD	RRZZZZ	NY
GOLDE	7	F	CHILD	RRZZZZ	NY
MARSCHAK, ISRAEL	16	M	TRDSMN	RRZZZZ	NY
DEMBROWSKY, SAL.	23	M	TRDSMN	RRZZZZ	NY
RITZMANN, FUDISCH	36	F	WO	RRZZZZ	NY
ROSCHLE	7	F	CHILD	RRZZZZ	NY
DAVID	6	M	CHILD	RRZZZZ	NY
KUBALSKY, MAYER	20	M	LABR	RRZZZZ	NY
REFKE	6	F	CHILD	RRZZZZ	NY
SCHEINKER, ROCHEL	40	F	WO	RRZZZZ	NY
EMMA	15	F	CH	RRZZZZ	NY
KARAGINSKI, FITZOCH	7	M	CHILD	RRZZZZ	NY
SCHITZ, HELMANN	22	M	TRDSMN	RRZZZZ	NY
SCHUSTER, ISRAEL	20	M	TRDSMN	RRZZZZ	NY
KATZ, ABR.	30	M	TRDSMN	RRZZZZ	NY
LACHS, TONI	18	F	BRM	RRZZZZ	NY
MOSESSOHN, ZEM.	59	M	LABR	RRZZZZ	NY
FEIGE	58	F	W	RRZZZZ	NY
KRENSTEIN, ELKES	24	F	WO	RRZZZZ	NY
MIELKE	4	M	CHILD	RRZZZZ	NY
MOSES	.07	M	INFANT	RRZZZZ	NY
PLAWSKA, ROSALIE	40	F	WO	RRZZZZ	NY
STEFANIE	7	M	CHILD	RRZZZZ	NY
STANISLAUS	6	M	CHILD	RRZZZZ	NY
EDUARD	5	M	CHILD	RRZZZZ	NY
ALEXANDER	4	M	CHILD	RRZZZZ	NY
FURMANSKI, WOYE	17	M	LABR	PLZZZZ	NY
GRETTMANN, CHR.R.	34	F	WO	RRZZZZ	NY
GIDEL	6	F	CHILD	RRZZZZ	NY
ISRAEL	5	M	CHILD	RRZZZZ	NY
RUCHAREL	3	M	CHILD	RRZZZZ	NY
LEHE	.08	F	INFANT	RRZZZZ	NY
SCHMIDT, KOPPEL	15	M	TDR	RRZZZZ	NY
ZULONIS, EV.M.	17	F	SGL	RRZZZZ	NY
ELISABETH	15	F	SGL	RRZZZZ	NY
DAVITSCH, F.	28	F	WO	RRZZZZ	NY
MOISCHE	.08	F	INFANT	RRZZZZ	NY
DOMBROWSKY, PETER	26	M	LABR	RRZZZZ	NY
BURKATSCH, JOSEPH	16	M	LABR	RRZZZZ	NY
MAKSCHUR, ANTON	48	M	LABR	RRZZZZ	NY
MAGOT, ITZIG	25	M	LABR	RRZZZZ	NY
KOLETSKY, HIRSCH	33	M	LABR	RRZZZZ	NY
FRANKOWSKY, ITZIG	18	M	LABR	RRZZZZ	NY
KULIK, CHAZKO	18	F	SGL	RRZZZZ	NY
KALEWSKY, SCHMUEHL	35	M	TDR	RRZZZZ	NY
JELITZKY, BERTHA	18	F	SGL	RRZZZZ	NY
COHN, SCHIMCHE	38	M	TDR	RRZZZZ	NY
SLOTOFATECKO, PETEZ	16	M	TDR	RRZZZZ	NY
STEINBERG, CHAJE	18	F	SGL	RRZZZZ	IL
LASS, HEYMANN	7	M	CHILD	RRZZZZ	NY
HERMANN	6	M	CHILD	RRZZZZ	NY
RATOVSKY, HIRSCH	54	M	LABR	RRZZZZ	NY
MECHLER, SOFIE	42	F	WO	PLZZZZ	NY
ALPERIN, JERRIE	18	F	SGL	PLZZZZ	NY
SILBERMANN, MINNA	28	F	SGL	RRZZZZ	NY
GRINSPAN, LEA	36	F	WO	RRZZZZ	NY
FAKEL	17	M	CH	RRZZZZ	NY
MIREL	11	F	CH	RRZZZZ	NY
RIFKE	7	F	CHILD	RRZZZZ	NY
MENCHE	4	M	CHILD	RRZZZZ	NY
MORDSCHE	.06	M	INFANT	RRZZZZ	NY
FROST, HERZ	20	M	LABR	PLZZZZ	IL
RUSNACK, JOHN	23	M	LABR	PLZZZZ	IL
KWEZYNSKI, REISEL	33	F	WO	RRZZZZ	MA
TAUBE	4	F	CHILD	RRZZZZ	MA
ROMAN	2	M	CHILD	RRZZZZ	MA
KWITSCHINSKY, MARY	19	F	SGL	RRZZZZ	MA
CHANE	17	F	SGL	RRZZZZ	MA
ZILLI	7	F	CHILD	RRZZZZ	MA
SALOMON	6	M	CHILD	RRZZZZ	MA
MOBZA	30	M	TRDSMN	RRZZZZ	MA
LEBOWITZ, MICHAEL	19	M	TRDSMN	RRZZZZ	NY
HEBBELN, MARGARETHE	48	F	W	RRZZZZ	NY
CLAUS	7	M	CHILD	RRZZZZ	NY
HANS	6	M	CHILD	RRZZZZ	NY
RUDOLF	4	M	CHILD	RRZZZZ	NY
KRIEGER, MAX	25	M	LABR	RRZZZZ	PA
FINKELSTEIN, SARA	35	F	WO	RRZZZZ	NY
MOSCHE	6	M	CHILD	RRZZZZ	NY
GITEL	.06	F	INFANT	RRZZZZ	NY
FETTBROD, SZENGE	40	F	WO	RRZZZZ	NY
RACHEL	20	F	D	RRZZZZ	NY
JOSEF	4	M	CHILD	RRZZZZ	NY
ELKE	7	M	CHILD	RRZZZZ	NY
FANNY	.03	F	INFANT	RRZZZZ	NY
KURSCHON, BERNHARD	18	M	LABR	RRZZZZ	NY
ROESTER, FEIGE	17	F	SGL	PLZZZZ	NY
SCHMIGELSKY, ABEL	18	M	TDR	RRZZZZ	NY
BERNSTEIN, CHASLER	23	M	TDR	RRZZZZ	NY
FREIDMANN, MOSES	28	M	TDR	RRZZZZ	NY
KALMANN, KALMAN	50	M	FARMER	RRZZZZ	IL
HVOL	50	F	W	RRZZZZ	IL
ANNA	6	F	CHILD	RRZZZZ	IL
SILBERSTEIN, JENTE	00	F	SGL	RRZZZZ	IL
REINFELDT, SARA	18	F	SGL	PLZZZZ	NY
WESTREICH, HERMANN	19	F	SGL	PLZZZZ	NY
GOLDNER, NOCHE	19	F	SGL	PLZZZZ	NY
ROSENTHAL, ISRAEL	30	M	MCHT	RRZZZZ	NY
KLEIN, MATHILDE	19	F	SGL	RRZZZZ	NY
GOLDBERG, NATHAN	22	M	TDR	RRZZZZ	NY
TAUB, SAMUEL	17	M	TDR	RRZZZZ	NY
KATZ, LEIB	7	M	CHILD	RRZZZZ	NY
ANNA	6	F	CHILD	RRZZZZ	NY
KELLO	7	M	CHILD	RRZZZZ	NY
ROSENFELD, DAVID	21	M	PRTR	PLZZZZ	NY
ROSA	21	F	W	PLZZZZ	NY
GELB, ZIPORA	15	F	SGL	PLZZZZ	NY
KANWIESER, ELIAS	25	M	TDR	PLZZZZ	NY
CHAIE	22	F	W	PLZZZZ	NY
FRZYNAGEL, HIRSCH	38	M	TDR	PLZZZZ	NY
JOSSI, CHAIM	21	M	TNMK	RRZZZZ	NY
EMMA	27	F	W	RRZZZZ	NY
PERLMANN, M.	00	M	TDR	RRZZZZ	IL
EVA	20	F	W	RRZZZZ	IL
PRUSZINSKY, CATHARIN.	20	F	SGL	RRZZZZ	IL
RCESCHKE, FRANZ	22	M	LABR	RRZZZZ	IL
KUSOVIA, ANTON	20	M	TDR	RRZZZZ	IL
LASIC, THS.	36	M	TLR	RRZZZZ	IL
SALUL, FAUHEL	26	M	TDR	RRZZZZ	IL
KAPPE, ERNST	34	M	LABR	RRZZZZ	IL
RUTKOVSKY, ANDREJ	35	M	LABR	RRZZZZ	IL
GOLDSCHI, CHANE	17	F	SGL	RRZZZZ	IL
MECHANIK, LUCIE	19	F	SGL	RRZZZZ	IL
BOJNUCHI, BRUNO	11	M	CH	RRZZZZ	IL
BERNSTEIN, ISRAEL	28	M	TDR	RRZZZZ	IL
WALLACH, JOS.	35	M	LABR	PLZZZZ	IL
SZYMASZCK, TOMASI	24	M	LABR	PLZZZZ	IL
FRANKOWA, LUDW.	27	M	LABR	PLZZZZ	IL
CARYLA, JAN	25	M	LABR	PLZZZZ	IL
WILOCKA, JANISKA	57	M	LABR	PLZZZZ	IL
SCHAPIRA, CHAJE	18	M	LABR	PLZZZZ	IL
TECKER, MOSES	49	M	JNR	RRZZZZ	IL

PASSENGER	AGE	SEX	OCCUPATION	PRV VIL DES
BECKER, SCHOLEM	24	M	TDR	RRZZZZIL
LUDSJEWITZ, ANTONIE	28	F	WO	RRZZZZIL
WASSER, ABRAHAM	28	M	TDR	PLZZZZNY
COHAN, ELISAS	25	M	JNR	RRZZZZNY
NEBESKY, ANTON	32	M	FARMER	RRZZZZNY
NEMEC, FRANZ	17	M	FARMER	RRZZZZNY
MOWITZ, JAKOB	34	M	TDR	RRZZZZNY
WERTHHEIM, IDA	19	F	SGL	RRZZZZNY
ROSI	15	F	CH	RRZZZZNY
FALCK, CHANE	21	M	SGL	RRZZZZNY
LOEWENTHAL, ISAAC	22	M	SHMK	RRZZZZNY
KWITSCHINSKY, DAV.	7	M	CHILD	RRZZZZNY
LURIN, NACH.	25	M	TRDSMN	RRZZZZNY
CHAIA	22	F	W	RRZZZZNY
SKLOVSKY, SCHMUHL	20	M	TRDSMN	RRZZZZIL
ISAAC	18	M	TRDSMN	RRZZZZIL
SCHLOMER	17	M	TRDSMN	RRZZZZNY
DWORE	13	F	SGL	RRZZZZNY
SARAZINSKY, WACLAR	23	M	TRDSMN	RRZZZZNY
PERL	22	M	TRDSMN	RRZZZZNY
GARFINKEL, MOSES	18	M	TDR	PLZZZZNY
ZEMBA, JOSEF	34	M	FARMER	PLZZZZNY
GABRIELE	28	F	W	PLZZZZNY
JOSEF	4	M	CHILD	PLZZZZNY
MARIE	.09	F	INFANT	PLZZZZNY
LOEWENTHAL, RIWKE	32	F	WO	RRZZZZNY
ETTEL	.06	M	INFANT	RRZZZZNY
STEPANEK, MACI	40	M	LABR	PLZZZZNY

SHIP: STATE OF NEVADA

FROM: GLASGOW AND LARNE
TO: NEW YORK
ARRIVED: 04 JUNE 1885

PASSENGER	AGE	SEX	OCCUPATION	PRV VIL DES
JUSCHKIA, G.	40	M	PDLR	RRZZZZUSA
ITNINITZ, J.	18	M	LABR	RRZZZZUSA
TERRTELBAUM, S.	18	M	LABR	RRZZZZUSA
JAFFE, A.	23	M	PDLR	RRZZZZUSA
KATZ, J.	34	M	SHMK	RRZZZZUSA
KUTINOW, A.	48	M	LABR	RRZZZZUSA
NEWITZKY, P.	27	M	LABR	RRZZZZUSA
J.	16	F	SVNT	RRZZZZUSA
THOS.	11	M	CH	RRZZZZUSA
NEUMAN, F.	48	M	TLR	RRZZZZUSA
SCHLACTER, E.	41	M	PDLR	RRZZZZUSA
ZAMEN, A.	16	M	LABR	RRZZZZUSA
ZANWURTZ, M.	49	M	TLR	RRZZZZUSA
WARNOSKY, J.	28	M	PDLR	RRZZZZUSA
JARMINEITES, V.	21	M	LABR	PLZZZZUSA
DARKINA, O.	21	M	LABR	PLZZZZUSA
EISENMANN, T.	28	M	PDLR	PLZZZZUSA
FINK, S.	25	M	PDLR	PLZZZZUSA
DD.	23	M	PDLR	PLZZZZUSA
FASINECCKE, J.	31	M	LABR	PLZZZZUSA
KLINTZKY, J.	30	M	LABR	PLZZZZUSA
KOLICZEK, K.	00	F	W	PLZZZZUSA
MOROWSKI, F.	23	M	LABR	PLZZZZUSA
MOSES, H.	24	M	WTR	PLZZZZUSA
OCKOCKI, M.	22	M	LABR	PLZZZZUSA
PRONDINCKI, J.	33	M	LABR	PLZZZZUSA
CATH.	39	F	W	PLZZZZUSA
JAN	9	M	CHILD	PLZZZZUSA
SECMAN, M.	26	M	PDLR	PLZZZZUSA
SCHWARZBERG, J.	26	M	PDLR	PLZZZZUSA

SHIP: BOHEMIA

FROM: HAMBURG
TO: NEW YORK
ARRIVED: 05 JUNE 1885

PASSENGER	AGE	SEX	OCCUPATION	PRV VIL DES
ORTMANN, FEIBUCH	48	M	LABR	RRZZZZUSA
SARA	18	F	SGL	RRZZZZUSA
HKATTON, SAM.	34	M	LABR	RRZZZZUSA
DROGEL	33	F	W	RRZZZZUSA
LEIB	4	M	CHILD	RRZZZZUSA
HINDE	3	F	CHILD	RRZZZZUSA
MORGMSTEIN, GOSAN	34	M	LABR	RRAHTLUSA
CORALSKA, FRIDA	22	F	SGL	RRZZZZUSA
BERCSLAFSKI, SCHMUEL	20	M	LABR	RRAHZSUSA
FRIEDMANN, CHAJE	16	F	SGL	RRZZZZUSA
SCHAFFER, ESTHER	40	F	W	RRAHZSUSA
MORDSCHE	9	F	CHILD	RRAHZSUSA
SCHAIE	8	F	CHILD	RRAHZSUSA
CHAJE	5	F	CHILD	RRAHZSUSA
GERSON	.11	M	INFANT	RRAHZSUSA
SCHREIBER, MOTEL	20	M	DLR	RRAHXXUSA
REINIS, SELMAN	28	M	MCHT	RRAFVGUSA
SAFIR, BARUCH	38	M	TLR	RRZZZZUSA
SECKZICS, MOSES-K.	20	M	DLR	RRAHXXUSA
KANTROWITZ, ISRAEL	18	M	TLR	RRZZZZUSA
KAPLAN, FREIDE	21	F	SGL	RRZZZZUSA
KABATZNIK, SCHEINE	36	F	W	RRZZZZUSA
SALMEN	9	M	CHILD	RRZZZZUSA
BEILE	6	M	CHILD	RRZZZZUSA
WOWISCHICK, NACHANKE	18	M	LABR	RRZZZZUSA
TIKOTZKE, CHAIE	16	F	SGL	RRAHVUUSA
ARONOWITZ, CHANNE	18	F	SGL	RRZZZZUSA
BERLINSKY, ELIAS	20	M	LABR	RRZZZZUSA
TOKER, MATUS.	29	M	LABR	RRAHTUUSA
STARESTER, KIEWE	24	F	W	RRAHTFUSA
ROSI	.11	M	INFANT	RRAHTFUSA
POLANSKY, RIEWKE	30	F	W	RRZZZZUSA
GITTEL	50	F	W	RRZZZZUSA
SARA	9	F	CHILD	RRZZZZUSA
DAVID	8	M	CHILD	RRZZZZUSA
ELI	6	M	CHILD	RRZZZZUSA
MOSES	4	M	CHILD	RRZZZZUSA
CKODASCH, CHONE	15	M	LABR	RRZZZZUSA
KOLAHOWSKY, YAN	38	M	TLR	RRZZZZUSA
KAPLAN, CHEIM	21	M	LABR	RRAHTRUSA
GOLDSMITH, CHANNE	20	F	SGL	RRAHTRUSA
ABRAMS, RASCHE	20	F	SGL	RRAHUVUSA
LIEBKE	8	F	CHILD	RRAHUVUSA
STORSINSKY, MIRIAM	17	M	LABR	RRZZZZUSA
KLON, LEA	56	F	W	RRAHTFUSA
LASKY, ESKIEL	16	M	LABR	RRZZZZUSA
PAWA, BOTSCHER	9	M	CHILD	RRAHSWUSA
ROSENGARD, FEIGE	25	F	W	RRZZZZUSA
ESTHER	6	F	CHILD	RRZZZZUSA
JOCHEM	3	M	CHILD	RRZZZZUSA
BERG, ABRAH.	58	M	DLR	RRAGRTUSA
HASKEL, SCHLOMA	17	M	DLR	RRZZZZUSA
LINDER, CHAIM	33	M	SHMK	RRAHZSUSA
SARA	3	F	CHILD	RRAHZSUSA
ROSA	.09	F	INFANT	RRAHZSUSA
JOCHWED	30	F	W	RRAHZSUSA
MARLAM, ELKE	36	F	W	RRZZZZUSA
PASCHEL	9	F	CHILD	RRZZZZUSA
ESTHER	8	F	CHILD	RRZZZZUSA
ERTEK	5	M	CHILD	RRZZZZUSA
CHAJE	4	F	CHILD	RRZZZZUSA
ROSA	2	F	CHILD	RRZZZZUSA
ALOFZIN, FREIDE	38	F	W	RRZZZZUSA
BACHE	9	F	CHILD	RRZZZZUSA
SCHOLEM	6	M	CHILD	RRZZZZUSA
HIRSCH	4	M	CHILD	RRZZZZUSA
GENISKA, JOSEFA	20	F	W	RRZZZZUSA
MARIANNE	.11	F	INFANT	RRZZZZUSA

PASSENGER	AGE	SEX	OCCUPATION	PRV	VIL	DES
KONZENSKI, ISIDOR	16	M	LABR	RRZZ	ZZ	USA
STEIN, MENDEL	31	M	SHMK	RRAH	VA	USA
SLAVE	17	F	SGL	RRAH	VA	USA
ROTOWSKI, CHAIM-J.	18	M	LABR	RRAH	TW	USA
MEHLTRAEGER, MORITZ	38	M	MD	RRAH	QH	USA
MORETZKI, MORITZ	34	M	DLR	RRZZ	ZZ	USA
CHAIM	13	F	CH	RRZZ	ZZ	USA
KOHN, EMMA	22	F	W	RRAF	VG	USA
JACOB	5	M	CHILD	RRAF	VG	USA
PAUL	6	M	CHILD	RRAF	VG	USA
FREUDE	9	M	CHILD	RRAF	VG	USA
META	15	F	SGL	RRAF	VG	USA
LILLY	.11	F	INFANT	RRAF	VG	USA
HANNE	.11	F	INFANT	RRAF	VG	USA
WEINSTEIN, JOEL	9	M	CHILD	RRAF	VG	USA
GEIRARIZA, SARA	25	F	W	RRZZ	ZZ	USA
MEIER	7	M	CHILD	RRZZ	ZZ	USA
JUDA	3	F	CHILD	RRZZ	ZZ	USA
WEINER, ELIAS	25	M	TNMK	RRZZ	ZZ	USA
RACHEL	7	F	CHILD	RRZZ	ZZ	USA
SKLAR, TAUBE	35	F	W	RRZZ	ZZ	USA
SARA	18	F	CH	RRZZ	ZZ	USA
SCHULER, SCHOLEM	23	M	JWLR	RRZZ	ZZ	USA
WALDSTEIN, RUWEN	15	M	LABR	RRZZ	ZZ	USA
LOKATIS, NATHAN	22	M	LABR	RRZZ	ZZ	USA
LURES, STANISLAUS	20	M	LABR	RRZZ	ZZ	USA
SCHEICHER, ABRAM.	20	M	LABR	RRZZ	ZZ	USA
MARKOW, LESER	32	M	LABR	RRZZ	ZZ	USA
HANNA	8	F	CHILD	RRZZ	ZZ	USA
PERSCHEL	4	F	CHILD	RRZZ	ZZ	USA
KAPLAN, ISAAC	34	M	CTW	RRAF	VG	USA
ROSA	34	F	W	RRAF	VG	USA
WACH, FRIEDR.H.	52	M	LABR	RRZZ	ZZ	USA
MARGA.	32	F	W	RRZZ	ZZ	USA
HERM.	25	M	CH	RRZZ	ZZ	USA
BERTHA	23	F	CH	RRZZ	ZZ	USA
EMMA	21	F	CH	RRZZ	ZZ	USA
MINNA	9	F	CHILD	RRZZ	ZZ	USA
PHILIPPINE	8	F	CHILD	RRZZ	ZZ	USA
EDUARD	7	M	CHILD	RRZZ	ZZ	USA
JULS.	5	M	CHILD	RRZZ	ZZ	USA
EMIL	3	M	CHILD	RRZZ	ZZ	USA
WILH.	.06	M	INFANT	RRZZ	ZZ	USA
SCHUMANN, CARL	40	M	FARMER	RRZZ	ZZ	USA
CAROLINE	22	F	W	RRZZ	ZZ	USA
ROSA	.11	F	INFANT	RRZZ	ZZ	USA
STUECKLE, WILH.	27	M	LABR	RRZZ	ZZ	USA
ROSINE	22	F	W	RRZZ	ZZ	USA
WILH.	.09	M	INFANT	RRZZ	ZZ	USA
ELLWANGER, MICHAEL	16	M	FARMER	RRZZ	ZZ	USA
DORA	28	F	W	RRZZ	ZZ	USA
FRIEDR.	29	M	FARMER	RRZZ	ZZ	USA
AMALIE	21	F	W	RRZZ	ZZ	USA
WILH.	3	M	CHILD	RRZZ	ZZ	USA
HEINR.	.09	M	INFANT	RRZZ	ZZ	USA
ELISABETH	68	F	W	RRZZ	ZZ	USA
ROSINE	17	F	SGL	RRZZ	ZZ	USA
GEORG	37	M	FARMER	RRZZ	ZZ	USA
CATHA.	31	F	W	RRZZ	ZZ	USA
CARL	9	M	CHILD	RRZZ	ZZ	USA
JACOB	8	M	CHILD	RRZZ	ZZ	USA
CATHA	7	F	CHILD	RRZZ	ZZ	USA
CHRISTINE	4	F	CHILD	RRZZ	ZZ	USA
WILHE.	3	F	CHILD	RRZZ	ZZ	USA
WILH	.09	M	INFANT	RRZZ	ZZ	USA
JACOB	19	M	FARMER	RRZZ	ZZ	USA
PHILIPP	46	M	LABR	RRZZ	ZZ	USA
ANNA	35	F	W	RRZZ	ZZ	USA
PHILIPP	9	M	CHILD	RRZZ	ZZ	USA
CATHA.	8	F	CHILD	RRZZ	ZZ	USA
MINNA	4	F	CHILD	RRZZ	ZZ	USA
AUGUSTI	2	F	CHILD	RRZZ	ZZ	USA
JACOB	48	M	FARMER	RRZZ	ZZ	USA
ANNA	45	F	W	RRZZ	ZZ	USA
FRDKE.	9	F	CHILD	RRZZ	ZZ	USA
CARL	8	M	CHILD	RRZZ	ZZ	USA
AUGUST	7	M	CHILD	RRZZ	ZZ	USA
ELISE	6	F	CHILD	RRZZ	ZZ	USA
FRIEDR.	4	M	CHILD	RRZZ	ZZ	USA
WILH.	.11	M	INFANT	RRZZ	ZZ	USA
MARSZABKIEWICZ, ANDR.	23	M	LABR	RRAH	ZS	USA
KOWALSKI, JOH.	29	M	LABR	RRAH	ZS	USA
ANNA	22	F	W	RRAH	ZS	USA
WROBESKI, ANNA	50	F	W	RRAH	SW	USA
KOP, JETTE	18	F	SGL	RRZZ	ZZ	USA
MARKS, MICHAEL	38	M	DLR	RRZZ	ZZ	USA
REICHER, GULD.	30	F	W	RRZZ	ZZ	USA
CHANNE	9	F	CHILD	RRZZ	ZZ	USA
MOSES	7	M	CHILD	RRZZ	ZZ	USA
EFRAIM	4	M	CHILD	RRZZ	ZZ	USA
RACHEL	3	F	CHILD	RRZZ	ZZ	USA
SCHNIFFMANN, CHANNE	18	F	SGL	RRAH	TU	USA
BLOOM, LIEBE	33	F	W	RRZZ	ZZ	USA
CHATZKEL	5	M	CHILD	RRZZ	ZZ	USA
SARA	2	F	CHILD	RRZZ	ZZ	USA
DOBE	8	F	CHILD	RRZZ	ZZ	USA
STRAIKE, JANOS	37	M	LABR	RRZZ	ZZ	USA
WINKLER, BARUCH	24	M	LABR	RRZZ	ZZ	USA
BINGER, SARA	19	F	SGL	RRAG	RT	USA
KOPELEWITZ, SIMON	14	M	LABR	RRAG	RT	USA
MENDELSTEIN, CHANNE	13	F	SGL	RRZZ	ZZ	USA
GITTEL	9	F	CHILD	RRZZ	ZZ	USA
CAPLAN, JACOB	26	M	DLR	RRZZ	ZZ	USA
DELTNES, JOSEPH	20	M	LABR	RRAE	AB	USA
MARIE	20	F	W	RRAE	AB	USA
STAROSZESKI, JOSEF	32	M	LABR	RRAH	UF	USA
MARIE	30	F	W	RRAH	UF	USA
ANTON	6	M	CHILD	RRAH	UF	USA
JAN	4	M	CHILD	RRAH	UF	USA
ABRAHANSON, GESCHE	21	F	SGL	RRAE	FL	USA
KARNOW, ANNA	35	F	W	RRZZ	ZZ	USA
RUBEN	9	M	CHILD	RRZZ	ZZ	USA
NOCHEM	5	M	CHILD	RRZZ	ZZ	USA
JOSEPH	4	M	CHILD	RRZZ	ZZ	USA
ISAAC	.09	M	INFANT	RRZZ	ZZ	USA
SIEGEL, BAER	13	M	CH	RRZZ	ZZ	USA
ISOFSKY, ANTON	22	M	LABR	RRAH	ZS	USA
BRZOZOWAK, ANTONINA	18	F	SGL	RRAH	ZS	USA
KELLNER, SUSANNE	28	F	W	RRAH	ZS	USA
MARZEL	2	M	CHILD	RRAH	ZS	USA
OLGA	.04	F	INFANT	RRAH	ZS	USA
KAHN, CIREL	29	F	W	RRAH	TF	USA
SCHMUEL	7	M	CHILD	RRAH	TF	USA
BENJAMIN	5	M	CHILD	RRAH	TF	USA
BEILE	3	M	CHILD	RRAH	TF	USA
WEINBERG, HIRSCH	19	M	TLR	RRAE	FL	USA
GAZEWER, CHAINE	58	M	TLR	RRAF	VG	USA
ROSENSTEIN, BARUCH	23	M	EGR	RRZZ	ZZ	USA
SINGER, KREIM	30	F	W	RRAH	TF	USA
CHAIM	8	M	CHILD	RRAH	TF	USA
ABRAH.	7	M	CHILD	RRAH	TF	USA
FEIGE	6	F	CHILD	RRAH	TF	USA
MOSES	5	M	CHILD	RRAH	TF	USA
JOSEF	4	M	CHILD	RRAH	TF	USA
MINNA	.11	F	INFANT	RRAH	TF	USA
LOEWENSTEIN, ISAAC	16	M	DLR	RRZZ	ZZ	USA
LINDE, SELDE	19	F	SGL	RRAB	QB	USA
MICHELSOHN, NOCHEM	43	M	DLR	RRAB	QB	USA
BEREL	9	M	CHILD	RRAB	QB	USA
HELLMANN, NOCHUME	30	F	W	RRAB	QB	USA
ISAAC	7	M	CHILD	RRAB	QB	USA
ANNE	6	F	CHILD	RRAB	QB	USA
MERE	.11	F	INFANT	RRAB	QB	USA
GUTTMANN, JESSEL	42	M	DLR	RRAB	QB	USA
GEBHART, TAUBE	17	F	SGL	RRAB	QB	USA
MICHELSOHN, SARA	29	F	W	RRAB	QB	USA
CHAJE	14	F	CH	RRAB	QB	USA
MINNA	9	F	CHILD	RRAB	QB	USA
BECKY	.11	M	INFANT	RRAB	QB	USA
REISEL	.01	M	INFANT	RRAB	QB	USA

PASSENGER	AGE	SEX	OCCUPATION	PRV VIL DES
BRAUNSTEIN, ISAAC	53	M	TLR	RRAFVGUSA
MIRLE	49	F	W	RRAFVGUSA
HIRSCHFELD, M.	33	M	TCHR	RRZZZZUSA
ALTE	26	F	W	RRZZZZUSA
SAMUEL	9	M	CHILD	RRZZZZUSA
ALEXANDRA	4	M	CHILD	RRZZZZUSA
ROSA	.11	F	INFANT	RRZZZZUSA
LEDER, JETTE	19	F	SGL	RRZZZZUSA
RIEKE	17	F	SGL	RRZZZZUSA
KARASAK, JACOB	58	M	TLR	RRAHOKUSA
CHERKASKY, MARCUS	17	M	TLR	RRZZZZUSA
SLOMIANSKY, JOCHEL	19	M	LABR	RRAHQUUSA
MISCINKIEWICZ, ANTON	18	M	LABR	RRAHZSUSA
JAMBOWSKY, JEZEKIEL	29	M	TCHR	RRAHTFUSA
JABLONSKY, JACOB	19	M	TLR	RRAHTUUSA
LEWIN, JOCHEN	36	M	HAMF	RRZZZZUSA
KOSTASCHINSKY, ISRAEL	25	M	TLR	RRZZZZUSA
GRUNSTEIN, MARCUS	20	M	TNMK	RRAHVUUSA
SARA	19	F	SGL	RRAHVUUSA
ESTHER	9	F	CHILD	RRAHVUUSA
WISCHNEWSKY, JOSEPH	25	M	LABR	RRZZZZUSA
ANNA	.11	F	INFANT	RRZZZZUSA
ANTONIE	.11	F	INFANT	RRZZZZUSA
KONOWNO, ANNA	16	F	SGL	RRZZZZUSA
SAGARZELSKI, KATHA.	18	F	SGL	RRZZZZUSA
BARTNICKI, MOSES	45	M	LABR	RRZZZZUSA
KILLIKEWITSCH, JULS.	17	M	LABR	RRZZZZUSA
RABINOWITZ, ARON	26	M	FELMO	RRAHRKUSA
SCHULMANN, DAVID	35	M	TLR	RRAHRKUSA
SLAVE	33	F	W	RRAHRKUSA
SCHEIM	9	M	CHILD	RRAHRKUSA
SALOMON	7	M	CHILD	RRAHRKUSA
BLUME	3	M	CHILD	RRAHRKUSA
SUSCHE	2	F	CHILD	RRAHRKUSA
MOSES	1	M	CHILD	RRAHRKUSA
LEDWINOWISKY, BEILE	19	F	SGL	RRADOIUSA
DIMENT, ISRAEL	44	M	BKR	RRADOIUSA
LIDMANN, MEIER	60	M	DLR	RRAHTFUSA
COHEN, ABRAH.	20	M	DLR	RRZZZZUSA
PESCHE	20	F	W	RRZZZZUSA
ABR.	6	M	CHILD	RRZZZZUSA
BLOTNIZKI, JAC.	20	M	LABR	RRAHTRUSA
JOSEM, JUEDEL	17	M	LABR	RRZZZZUSA
PERLEMANN, ISAAC	19	M	LABR	RRAHUVUSA
REDER, BLUME	14	F	SGL	RRZZZZUSA
RACHEL	7	F	CHILD	RRZZZZUSA
KATZ, JACOB	50	M	LABR	RRZZZZUSA
BEILE	18	F	SGL	RRZZZZUSA
SACHERMANN, ELI	21	M	LABR	RRZZZZUSA
TARKUS, DANIEL	19	M	LABR	RRZZZZUSA
DOMBROWSKY, RASCHE	16	F	SGL	RRAHUVUSA
CHANNE	12	F	CH	RRAHUVUSA
KANTAN, JANKEL	19	M	LABR	RRZZZZUSA
SILANSKY, ICKO	23	M	DLR	RRAGRTUSA
ABRAHAM	9	M	CHILD	RRAGRTUSA
PREISMANN, JETTE	16	F	SGL	RRZZZZUSA
ADLER, MEYER	33	M	DLR	RRZZZZUSA
GINZBERG, PASSE	19	F	SGL	RRZZZZUSA
CHAIN	5	M	CHILD	RRZZZZUSA
ARINOWITZ, LACHARIAS	22	M	LABR	RRAGRTUSA
PARCANIK, SPRINGE	16	F	SGL	RRZZZZUSA
SCHACHNOWSKY, BEILE	20	F	SGL	RRZZZZUSA
BALSAM, MOSES	24	M	LABR	RRZZZZUSA
FELDSTEIN, HARRIS	25	M	LABR	RRZZZZUSA
SCHANE	19	F	W	RRZZZZUSA
KALTBLUT, NOCHIM	35	M	LABR	RRZZZZUSA
DAVID	8	M	CHILD	RRZZZZUSA
BERLOWITZ, ANNA	26	F	SGL	RRAHZSUSA
KOSALIEWICH, JERSY	25	M	JNR	RRAHSWUSA
KARABAWITZ, FRANZ	29	M	JNR	RRAHSWUSA
MARKIEWITZ, ANUF	19	M	JNR	RRAHSWUSA
DANNSCHAWITZ, JOSEF	18	M	JNR	RRAHSWUSA
SPITZER, GEDALIE	20	M	JNR	RRZZZZUSA
MAJEWSKI, LORENZ	30	M	JNR	RRAFWJUSA
SCHUKEWITZ, JERSY	25	M	JNR	RRAHSWUSA
BERSKIS, JACOB	30	M	JNR	RRAHZSUSA
KOHN, WILH.	25	M	LABR	RRAHOKUSA
LEDER, GITTEL	13	F	SGL	RRZZZZUSA
ORTMANN, SCHEWE	8	F	CHILD	RRZZZZUSA
STARKEWITZ, ANTON	18	M	LABR	RRAHSWUSA
LINDNER, KARL	00	M	INF	RR****USA
TYNAK, JANOS	00	M	INF	RR****USA

SHIP: WESER

FROM: BREMEN
TO: NEW YORK
ARRIVED: 05 JUNE 1885

PASSENGER	AGE	SEX	OCCUPATION	PRV VIL DES
GRUNHAUS, F.N.	18	M	LABR	RRZZZZUSA
ROSCIERSKY, JAN	35	M	LABR	RRZZZZUSA
MENTIGEL, EMMA	28	F	NN	RRZZZZUSA
DUSCHECK, CLAM	37	F	NN	RRZZZZUSA
MARIANNA	19	F	NN	RRZZZZUSA
CAROLINA	14	F	NN	RRZZZZUSA
MATHILDE	6	F	CHILD	RRZZZZUSA
EIDER, CILAWE	33	F	NN	RRZZZZUSA
ANNA	.11	F	INFANT	RRZZZZUSA
ABELOW, HARRIS	27	M	LABR	RRZZZZUSA
OWYER	5	M	CHILD	RRZZZZUSA
WEINSTEIN, NATHAN	17	M	LABR	RRZZZZUSA
LUXENBERG, ROSE	22	F	NN	RRZZZZUSA
KABACZNIK, RISZE	50	M	LABR	RRZZZZUSA
FROHN, KALIGMANN	20	M	DLR	RRZZZZUSA
ESTER	17	F	NN	RRZZZZUSA
DUDKIN, MAYER	36	M	LABR	RRZZZZUSA
ADELINA	32	F	NN	RRZZZZUSA
PETER	15	M	NN	RRZZZZUSA
SCHAVE	10	F	NN	RRZZZZUSA
NACHTORE	8	F	CHILD	RRZZZZUSA
RUCHEL	2	F	CHILD	RRZZZZUSA
HUDI	.04	F	INFANT	RRZZZZUSA
KROYAK, MICHAEL	35	M	LABR	RRZZZZUSA
SOPLOCK, JOSEPH	20	M	LABR	RRZZZZUSA
KULACZEWSKY, JANOS	25	M	LABR	RRZZZZUSA
SACKS, MOSES	19	M	DLR	RRZZZZUSA
HIRSCH	13	M	DLR	RRZZZZUSA
FLAMME, CLAIM	19	M	DLR	RRZZZZUSA
BEILE, CH.	19	M	DLR	RRZZZZUSA
SILBERMANN, RIWE	18	M	DLR	RRZZZZUSA
BLOME, ISRAEL	16	M	DLR	RRZZZZUSA
GLUCK, SARAH	18	F	NN	RRZZZZUSA
BREBER, WOLF	57	M	DLR	RRZZZZUSA
SAWER, FANNY	20	F	NN	RRZZZZUSA
CHAJE	29	M	DLR	RRZZZZUSA
SUSMANN, B.	30	M	DLR	RRZZZZUSA
SUSKE	18	M	DLR	RRZZZZUSA
FESCHBEIN, RASSIE	27	F	NN	RRZZZZUSA
HANNA	7	F	CHILD	RRZZZZUSA
HODES	4	M	CHILD	RRZZZZUSA
ESTER	.11	F	INFANT	RRZZZZUSA

SHIP: CITY OF CHESTER

FROM: LIVERPOOL AND QUEENSTOWN
TO: NEW YORK
ARRIVED: 06 JUNE 1885

PASSENGER	AGE	SEX	OCCUPATION	PRV VIL DES
STROM, HENNRICH	32	M	FARMER	RRAGUZCT
KUCK, ANDERS	22	M	FARMER	RRAGUZNY

PASSENGER	AGE	SEX	OCCUPATION	PRV VIL DES
STRUVESS, HEINRICH	25	M	GM	RRAGUZNY
BACKS, PETER	19	M	CRT	RRAGUZNY
MARTENS, MARIA	55	F	SVNT	RRAGUZUNK
GOLDSTEIN, WM.	32	M	WVR	RRADAXPHI

SHIP: FULDA

FROM: BREMEN
TO: NEW YORK
ARRIVED: 06 JUNE 1885

PASSENGER	AGE	SEX	OCCUPATION	PRV VIL DES
REANERT, ADOLF	19	M	LABR	RRZZZZUSA
HABERMAS, EMILIE	20	F	UNKNOWN	RRZZZZUSA
FRDINAND	16	M	LABR	RRZZZZUSA
HOFFNER, MATHAUS	17	M	FARMER	RRZZZZUSA
MAIS, CHRIST	23	M	FARMER	RRZZZZUSA
KATHARINA	24	F	UNKNOWN	RRZZZZUSA
HETZEL, CHRISTOF	40	M	FARMER	RRZZZZUSA
CHASER, LIPPE	36	M	FARMER	RRZZZZUSA
EISINGER, HCH.	28	M	LABR	RRZZZZUSA
MARG.	28	F	UNKNOWN	RRZZZZUSA
GUSTAV	6	M	CHILD	RRZZZZUSA
MAGDALENA	3	F	CHILD	RRZZZZUSA
ANDREAS	.11	M	INFANT	RRZZZZUSA
RUDOLF	.11	M	INFANT	RRZZZZUSA
WEIST, JOHANN	25	M	FARMER	RRZZZZUSA
BARBARA	26	F	UNKNOWN	RRZZZZUSA
BARBARA	2	F	CHILD	RRZZZZUSA
CAROLINA	.11	F	INFANT	RRZZZZUSA
JOHANNES	.01	M	INFANT	RRZZZZUSA
LEVY, JACOB	32	M	FARMER	RRZZZZUSA
CAROLINE	29	F	UNKNOWN	RRZZZZUSA
CAROLINE	8	F	CHILD	RRZZZZUSA
DOROTHEA	4	F	CHILD	RRZZZZUSA
SOPHIA	2	F	CHILD	RRZZZZUSA
JACOB	.09	M	INFANT	RRZZZZUSA
LUTZ, GOTTLIEB	35	M	FARMER	RRZZZZUSA
MAGD.	31	F	UNKNOWN	RRZZZZUSA
GUSTAV	8	M	CHILD	RRZZZZUSA
MAGD.	6	F	CHILD	RRZZZZUSA
ADOLF	.10	M	INFANT	RRZZZZUSA

SHIP: MAIN

FROM: BREMEN
TO: NEW YORK
ARRIVED: 06 JUNE 1885

PASSENGER	AGE	SEX	OCCUPATION	PRV VIL DES
WARLIKAWSKY, MICHAEL	34	M	MCHT	RRZZZZUSA
ZANGWIL, ABRAHAM	16	M	MCHT	RRZZZZUSA
SACHAROFF, ALEXANDER	35	M	FARMER	RRZZZZUSA
HELENE	4	F	CHILD	RRZZZZUSA
WILHELM	37	M	FARMER	RRZZZZUSA
WASZELEWSKI, ADAM	40	M	FARMER	RRZZZZUSA
KOTSCHERONSKY, ROSALIE	24	F	W	RRZZZZUSA
STANISLAW	1	M	CHILD	RRZZZZUSA
SCHADLER, JOHANN	14	M	FARMER	RRZZZZUSA
ROHRS, MATHILDE	38	F	W	RRZZZZUSA
EMMA	9	F	CHILD	RRZZZZUSA
GEORG	8	M	CHILD	RRZZZZUSA
FRITZ	6	M	CHILD	RRZZZZUSA
BRUNO	3	M	CHILD	RRZZZZUSA
KITSCHA, JULIANNA	67	F	W	RRZZZZUSA
WISCHNENSKY, JOHANN	31	M	FARMER	RRZZZZUSA
BRAJEWSKI, WAWORZYN	19	M	LABR	RRZZZZUSA

PASSENGER	AGE	SEX	OCCUPATION	PRV VIL DES
CHALAD, FRANZ	25	M	LABR	RRZZZZUSA
KOZANSKI, JOSEF	21	M	LABR	RRZZZZUSA
SEHSCH, MICHAEL	43	M	FARMER	RRZZZZUSA
ROSINE	33	F	W	RRZZZZUSA
HEINRICH	18	M	FARMER	RRZZZZUSA
EVA	15	F	D	RRZZZZUSA
ROSINE	9	F	CHILD	RRZZZZUSA
DOROTHEA	8	F	CHILD	RRZZZZUSA
JACOB	6	M	CHILD	RRZZZZUSA
ELISABETH	5	F	CHILD	RRZZZZUSA
KATHARINE	2	F	CHILD	RRZZZZUSA
MICHAEL	.01	M	INFANT	RRZZZZUSA
SCHMIDT, ROSINE	17	F	SVNT	RRZZZZUSA

SHIP: RHYNLAND

FROM: ANTWERP
TO: NEW YORK
ARRIVED: 06 JUNE 1885

PASSENGER	AGE	SEX	OCCUPATION	PRV VIL DES
BLUHM, W.	19	M	SHMK	RRAEFLNY
GORNY, JOH.	22	M	CPTR	RRZZZZUNK
PRIKYL, F.	25	F	UNKNOWN	RRZZZZNY
M.	3	F	CHILD	RRZZZZNY
ANT.	1	F	CHILD	RRZZZZNY
JUL.	.06	F	INFANT	RRZZZZNY

SHIP: WIELAND

FROM: HAMBURG
TO: NEW YORK
ARRIVED: 06 JUNE 1885

PASSENGER	AGE	SEX	OCCUPATION	PRV VIL DES
GROSS, AUGUST	26	M	LABR	RRZZZZUSA
DAVIDOWSKY, SARA	27	F	W	RRZZZZUSA
CHONE	5	M	CHILD	RRZZZZUSA
CHAJE	.09	F	INFANT	RRZZZZUSA
SCHEINHAUS, ALTER	20	M	LABR	RRZZZZUSA
JANKOWIAK, FRANZ	33	M	LABR	RRZZZZUSA
JEFKA	33	F	W	RRZZZZUSA
SYMEAK, ROMAN	44	M	LABR	RRZZZZUSA
HODKOVSKY, STEFAN	27	M	LABR	RRZZZZUSA
SANIN, NICOLAUS	35	M	LABR	RRZZZZUSA
LINITZKY, ARJE	17	M	MCHT	RRZZZZUSA
COHEN, SALOMON	20	M	DLR	RRZZZZUSA
TAUBE	22	F	W	RRZZZZUSA
DWORE	3	F	CHILD	RRZZZZUSA
ASRIEL	.11	M	INFANT	RRZZZZUSA
LIPSCHITZ, NECHANIE	35	F	W	RRZZZZUSA
MEYER	9	M	CHILD	RRZZZZUSA
ABRAH.	8	M	CHILD	RRZZZZUSA
PAVEL	6	M	CHILD	RRZZZZUSA
DERFELD, HERSCH	38	M	LABR	RRZZZZUSA
FEIGE	40	F	W	RRZZZZUSA
ABRAH.	18	F	CH	RRZZZZ***
BOBI	6	F	CHILD	RRZZZZUSA
OCHSMANN, ISAAC	28	F	LABR	RRZZZZUSA
GOLDSTEIN, LEIB	27	F	LABR	RRZZZZUSA
HALPERN, ARIE	20	F	TLR	RRZZZZUSA
KOTON, JENTE	44	F	W	RRZZZZUSA
MATES	15	M	CH	RRZZZZUSA
JUDEL	9	M	CHILD	RRZZZZUSA
JACOB	8	M	CHILD	RRZZZZUSA
ANIBROSAITIS, AUGUST	50	M	LABR	RRZZZZUSA
MISCHKIND, JULIE	30	F	W	RRZZZZUSA

PASSENGER	AGE	SEX	OCCUPATION	PRV VIL DES
JOSEPHA	20	F	SI	RRZZZZUSA
ANNA	17	F	SI	RRZZZZUSA
JACOB	8	M	CHILD	RRZZZZUSA
ROSA	4	F	CHILD	RRZZZZUSA
HIRSCH	.06	M	INFANT	RRZZZZUSA
SIMON, ABRAM	18	M	LABR	RRZZZZUSA
GOLDMANN, WOLF	23	M	LABR	RRZZZZUSA
GITTEL	17	F	SGL	RRZZZZUSA
STANKEWITZ, JOSEF	30	M	LABR	RRZZZZUSA
AMBROSEWICK, BOLTEN	32	M	LABR	RRZZZZUSA
ZIELENIAK, JOSEF	28	M	LABR	RRZZZZUSA
ELISABETH	20	F	W	RRZZZZUSA
ELISABETH	.11	F	INFANT	RRZZZZUSA
ZANGWILL, SARA	14	F	W	RRZZZZUSA
SCHENI	5	M	CHILD	RRZZZZUSA
GURSKY, MOSES	16	M	LABR	RRZZZZUSA
WESOTZKI, SCHEINE	30	M	WVR	RRZZZZUSA
LEIB	31	M	WVR	RRZZZZUSA
BAS, ABRAHAM	16	M	LABR	RRZZZZUSA
ELLWANGER, WILH.	36	M	FARMER	RRZZZZUSA
WILH.	36	M	FARMER	RRZZZZUSA
MINE	4	F	CHILD	RRZZZZUSA
MATTES, MICHAEL	30	M	FARMER	RRZZZZUSA
MARIE	28	F	W	RRZZZZUSA
MARIE	8	F	CHILD	RRZZZZUSA
JOH.	1	M	CHILD	RRZZZZUSA
WILHELM	.01	M	INFANT	RRZZZZUSA
BREZINA, JULS	24	M	LABR	RRZZZZUSA
BLANK, EUGENIE	18	F	SGL	RRZZZZUSA
MASENIE, FRANZ	23	M	LABR	RRZZZZUSA
GROSCHOVSKY, ANTON	18	M	LABR	RRZZZZUSA
KOVALEVSKY, JOSEF	25	M	LABR	RRZZZZUSA
DUBOWSKY, JEG.	22	M	LABR	RRZZZZUSA
WOLTE, MORRIS	16	M	LABR	RRZZZZUSA

SHIP: LEERDAM

FROM: ROTTERDAM
TO: NEW YORK
ARRIVED: 08 JUNE 1885

PASSENGER	AGE	SEX	OCCUPATION	PRV VIL DES
LEIBNITZ, JOSEPH	29	M	LABR	PLZZZZUSA
LESCHEZEMSKY, M.	24	M	LABR	PLZZZZUSA
CSCHERENSKA, FREIDE	20	F	UNKNOWN	PLZZZZUSA
JOSEL	.06	M	INFANT	PLZZZZUSA
WEINSTEIN, SCHOLEM	20	M	LABR	PLZZZZUSA
ROCHEL	25	F	UNKNOWN	PLZZZZUSA
MASCHE	.06	F	INFANT	PLZZZZUSA
TERESE	.06	F	INFANT	PLZZZZUSA
STUBEK, ARIE	18	M	FARMER	PLZZZZUSA
PERAUTZLER, ROCHEL	40	M	FARMER	PLZZZZUSA
SKAZINSKY, MOSES	19	M	FARMER	PLZZZZUSA
POMERANZ, LIEWE	20	M	LABR	PLZZZZUSA
BRANSTEIN, MARE	41	M	LABR	PLZZZZUSA
CHACE	45	F	UNKNOWN	PLZZZZUSA
ELIAS	18	M	LABR	PLZZZZUSA
MOSES	16	M	LABR	PLZZZZUSA
SARAH	8	F	CHILD	PLZZZZUSA
BENJAMIN	5	M	CHILD	PLZZZZUSA
SCHENKER, JOSEPH	24	M	TLR	PLZZZZUSA
LINGER, SIEGFRIED	18	M	FARMER	PLZZZZUSA
GUTMAN, BERL	24	M	FARMER	PLZZZZUSA
HOCHWELD, GODEL	28	M	MCHT	PLAHOKUSA
MEISLER, LEIB	25	M	MCHT	PLAHOKUSA
PIZAREANSKY, NACH.	18	M	MCHT	PLZZZZUSA
ABRAHAM	18	M	MCHT	PLZZZZUSA
BURSTEIN, BARUCH	18	M	MCHT	PLZZZZUSA
SCHMIDTISH, SALOMON	20	M	MCHT	PLZZZZUSA
KATZMELLEN, JACOB	40	M	MCHT	PLZZZZUSA
SORE	18	F	UNKNOWN	PLZZZZUSA

PASSENGER	AGE	SEX	OCCUPATION	PRV VIL DES
ISAAC	21	M	MCHT	PLZZZZUSA
CAUSAN, ANNA	19	F	UNKNOWN	PLZZZZUSA
CHINKIS, DAVID	30	F	UNKNOWN	PLZZZZUSA
AZRIEL	5	F	CHILD	PLZZZZUSA
CHURK, CHASKEL	45	M	MCHT	PLZZZZUSA
TEWIE	23	F	UNKNOWN	PLZZZZUSA
SCHMUEL	28	M	MCHT	PLZZZZUSA
JASOLOWITZ, ELIAS	27	M	MCHT	PLZZZZUSA
PUCH, JACOB	39	M	MCHT	PLZZZZUSA
DONAITIS, JOSES	28	M	MCHT	PLZZZZUSA
ARMENSKIED, MATIS	35	M	MCHT	PLZZZZUSA
PAGER, JOSEF	22	M	MCHT	PLZZZZUSA

SHIP: ETHIOPIA

FROM: GLASGOW AND MOVILLE
TO: NEW YORK
ARRIVED: 09 JUNE 1885

PASSENGER	AGE	SEX	OCCUPATION	PRV VIL DES
KOOP, JULIUS	24	M	SHMK	RRZZZZUSA
BARSTENHAVEN, EDWARD	25	M	LABR	RRZZZZUSA

SHIP: ERGO

FROM: TRINIDAD
TO: NEW YORK
ARRIVED: 11 JUNE 1885

PASSENGER	AGE	SEX	OCCUPATION	PRV VIL DES
HAMILTON, LEO	35	M	FSHMN	RRZZZZNY

SHIP: RUGIA

FROM: HAMBURG
TO: NEW YORK
ARRIVED: 11 JUNE 1885

PASSENGER	AGE	SEX	OCCUPATION	PRV VIL DES
SCHRANGK, PETER	27	M	LABR	RRZZZZUSA
GUTTMANN, MOSES	40	M	MUSN	RRZZZZUSA
CHELNIER, HEINR.	19	M	CGRMKR	RRZZZZUSA
HERMANN, CHRIST.	35	M	LABR	RRZZZZUSA
DOROTHEA	22	F	W	RRZZZZUSA
FRIED.	17	M	CH	RRZZZZUSA
MARIE	9	F	CHILD	RRZZZZUSA
CAROL.	7	F	CHILD	RRZZZZUSA
ZANDER, MARIE	20	F	SGL	RRZZZZUSA
OMANSKI, MAMUS	18	M	LABR	RRZZZZUSA
SCHINDEL, RACHEL	28	F	W	RRZZZZUSA
JOS.	7	M	CHILD	RRZZZZUSA
TAUBE	.11	F	INFANT	RRZZZZUSA
OLINSKY, RIWKE	20	F	SGL	RRZZZZUSA
ROSENSOHN, ITTE	20	F	SGL	RRZZZZUSA
TERKIANSKY, RACHEL	23	F	W	RRZZZZUSA
DAVID	.11	M	INFANT	RRZZZZUSA
BOGUS, FRANZ	18	M	LABR	RRZZZZUSA
ORLOWSKY, KAZIMIR	27	M	LABR	RRZZZZUSA
STERNSTEIN, MASCHE	23	F	W	RRZZZZUSA
ELI	.11	M	INFANT	RRZZZZUSA
NEUMANN, DWORE	15	F	SGL	RRZZZZUSA
GOLDSTEIN, ITTE	31	F	W	RRZZZZUSA
JACOB	4	M	CHILD	RRZZZZUSA

PASSENGER	AGE	SEX	OCCUPATION	PRV VIL DES
CHEIE	2	F	CHILD	RRZZZZUSA
CHAWE	.11	F	INFANT	RRZZZZUSA
LIBOWITZ, CHAJE	17	F	SGL	RRZZZZUSA
ALIBUDA, ANDR.	24	M	LABR	RRZZZZUSA
NATHAN, CHAJE	18	F	SGL	RRZZZZUSA
MARKS, HIRSCH	9	M	CHILD	RRZZZZUSA
BENNE	8	M	CHILD	RRZZZZUSA
SCHAEFFER, BLUNN	14	M	LABR	RRZZZZUSA
KAUFMANN, RASCHE	20	F	SGL	RRZZZZUSA
HALSBAND, MASE	18	M	FARMER	RRZZZZUSA
SCHWARTZ, LEOPOLD	30	M	FARMER	RRZZZZUSA
ROSA	24	F	W	RRZZZZUSA
ROSA	.11	F	INFANT	RRZZZZUSA
EMANUEL	.01	M	INFANT	RRZZZZUSA
CHASZNISKY, CHAIM	40	M	TLR	RRZZZZUSA
MARIE	33	F	W	RRZZZZUSA
SAPERSTEIN, AISIK	30	M	SHMK	RRZZZZUSA
ROTHMANN, BEREL	28	M	DLR	RRZZZZUSA
SILBERMANN, JOSEL	40	M	TLR	RRZZZZUSA
SPITZ, NATHAN	28	M	SHMK	RRZZZZUSA
DOMBLEWSKA, MICHALINE	33	F	W	RRZZZZUSA
ANDR.	7	M	CHILD	RRZZZZUSA
AGNESKA	3	F	CHILD	RRZZZZ***
ROSALIE	.06	F	INFANT	RRZZZZUSA
TREY, SARA	30	F	SGL	RRZZZZUSA
ZANDER, DERGI	25	M	LABR	RRZZZZUSA
SKLAMBERG, RUWEN	15	M	LABR	RRZZZZUSA
TANNENBAUM, WILH.	30	M	LABR	RRZZZZUSA
MESTER, SIGM.	9	M	CHILD	RRZZZZUSA
LANGERT, ENE	20	F	SGL	RRZZZZUSA
DEWORA	18	F	SGL	RRZZZZUSA
NAGEL, JACOB	36	M	FARMER	RRZZZZUSA
JACOB	9	M	CHILD	RRZZZZUSA
MARG.	8	F	CHILD	RRZZZZUSA
ELISE	4	F	CHILD	RRZZZZUSA
HEINR.	.11	M	INFANT	RRZZZZUSA
SCHAPIRA, MOSES	16	M	DLR	RRZZZZUSA
ENGELMANN, HIRSCH	67	M	DLR	RRZZZZUSA
GRODZINSKI, ISAAC	27	M	DLR	RRZZZZUSA
BIRGER, FENTE	28	F	W	RRZZZZUSA
SARA	.11	F	INFANT	RRZZZZUSA
MOSES	.01	M	INFANT	RRZZZZUSA
DUNSKY, ISAAC	20	M	LABR	RRZZZZUSA
LEIPNER, MORDEHE	19	M	LABR	RRZZZZUSA
ZAWOTZKY, J---L	15	M	LABR	RRZZZZUSA
RUBINSKY, MINNA	21	F	SGL	RRZZZZUSA
LIEBERMANN, SARA	50	F	W	RRZZZZUSA
ISAAC	9	M	CHILD	RRZZZZUSA
DWORE	7	F	CHILD	RRZZZZUSA
BILINSKY, SIMON	20	M	LABR	RRZZZZUSA
SLOTOWSKY, ABRAHAM	15	M	LABR	RRZZZZUSA
SIFSCHUTZ, ITTE	40	F	W	RRZZZZUSA
MPORDCHE	9	M	CHILD	RRZZZZUSA
ABRAM	8	M	CHILD	RRZZZZUSA
NACHMAN	4	M	CHILD	RRZZZZUSA
RIFKE	.11	F	INFANT	RRZZZZUSA
SOLINSKY, LEA	35	F	SGL	RRZZZZUSA
ESTHER	20	F	SGL	RRZZZZUSA
LICHTENSTEIN, LEISER	18	M	LABR	RRZZZZUSA
ANKESTIS, ISAAC	18	M	LABR	RRZZZZUSA
HELMLING, ALFRED	28	M	MCHT	RRZZZZUSA
GOLDBERG, L.	60	M	LABR	RRZZZZUSA
ROTH, FANNY	14	F	SGL	RRZZZZUSA
SOKOL, HERSCH	17	M	LABR	RRZZZZUSA
WELSCH, GUENDEL	45	F	W	RRZZZZUSA
WILENSKY, SCHEIN	17	F	SGL	RRZZZZUSA
SALMONOWITZ, GERSON	35	M	LABR	RRZZZZUSA
GUSTEL	30	F	W	RRZZZZUSA
ESTHER	8	F	CHILD	RRZZZZUSA
SALOMON	6	M	CHILD	RRZZZZUSA
FANNY	.11	F	INFANT	RRZZZZUSA
KOBSA, SIGMUND	39	M	MCHT	RRZZZZUSA
KUBIS, JULIE	20	F	SGL	RRZZZZUSA
ANTONIE	9	F	CHILD	RRZZZZUSA
STEINBERG, GIESSE	32	F	W	RRZZZZUSA
ZIEREL	9	M	CHILD	RRZZZZUSA
LEIL	8	M	CHILD	RRZZZZUSA
ELKE	5	F	CHILD	RRZZZZUSA
BASCHE	3	F	CHILD	RRZZZZUSA
MORDCHE	.11	M	INFANT	RRZZZZUSA
NEUMANN, SALOM.	20	M	LABR	RRZZZZUSA
MARIANNE	20	F	W	RRZZZZUSA
TORONCZYK, CHAIM	19	M	LABR	RRZZZZUSA
GINSBERG, MORDCHE	20	M	LABR	RRZZZZUSA
ELKE	18	F	W	RRZZZZUSA
SIMON, CHAIM	35	M	LABR	RRZZZZUSA
STEINBERG, PICEK	40	M	LABR	RRZZZZUSA
LOWITZ, FEITEL	34	M	JNR	RRZZZZUSA
ZELINSKY, INSEN	19	M	LABR	RRZZZZUSA
EDELSOHN, MARK	23	M	TLR	RRZZZZUSA
GOLDBERG, LEISER	19	M	LABR	RRZZZZUSA
RUBEL, JANKEL	18	M	LABR	RRZZZZUSA
BEDUARICKA, JOH.	32	F	W	RRZZZZUSA
HIRSCH	9	M	CHILD	RRZZZZUSA
A.	7	M	CHILD	RRZZZZUSA
D.	4	F	CHILD	RRZZZZUSA
RUWEN, HIRSCH	20	M	LABR	RRZZZZUSA
BARKOWITZ, NOCHEM	20	M	LABR	RRZZZZUSA
MAMPEL, LEISER	19	M	LABR	RRZZZZUSA
STEIN, CHONE	20	M	LABR	RRZZZZUSA
FRANKEL, ROSA	18	F	SGL	RRZZZZUSA
ARKIN, SARA	24	F	SGL	RRZZZZUSA
MEIER	24	M	LABR	RRZZZZUSA
MOSENTZNITZ, MORRIS	22	M	JWLR	RRZZZZUSA
MILLER, ROSA	19	F	SGL	RRZZZZUSA
CHEILEWSKI, BERL	18	M	LABR	RRZZZZUSA
CHAIE	9	F	CHILD	RRZZZZUSA
ONIKELSKI, ITTE	20	F	SGL	RRZZZZUSA
ISRAEL	19	M	LABR	RRZZZZUSA
MILLERMANN, JACOB	34	M	TLR	RRZZZZUSA
ZELIKOWITZ, ETTE	15	F	SGL	RRZZZZUSA
BIRGER, SELIG	31	M	LABR	RRZZZZUSA
DUBICKI, ANTON	25	M	LABR	RRZZZZUSA
DOBRZANSKY, MARC	18	M	LABR	RRZZZZUSA
BRICKMANN, JAC.	33	M	LABR	RRZZZZUSA
LIWSTEIN, SANIE	35	F	SGL	RRZZZZUSA
HORBARG, BEREL	9	F	CHILD	RRZZZZUSA
GARBER, JORDAN	28	F	DLR	RRZZZZUSA
FREI, LEO	19	M	FARMER	RRZZZZUSA
OLSTEIN, ELKE	20	F	SGL	RRZZZZUSA
RUBINSIHN, TEWIE	19	M	DLR	RRZZZZUSA
ORELOWITZ, ISAAC	22	M	DLR	RRZZZZUSA
FRIEDMANN, ITE	20	F	SGL	RRZZZZUSA
GOLDMANN, SLADI	9	M	CHILD	RRZZZZUSA
SCHULBERG, DAVID	18	M	LABR	RRZZZZUSA
BORNSTEIN, RIWE	13	F	SGL	RRZZZZUSA

SHIP: BRITISH EMPIRE

FROM: LIVERPOOL
TO: NEW YORK
ARRIVED: 13 JUNE 1885

PASSENGER	AGE	SEX	OCCUPATION	PRV VIL DES
KEZINITZKI, JANKEL	24	M	LABR	RRZZZZUSA
LITTLI, FRIEDRICH	20	M	LABR	RRZZZZUSA

PASSENGER	AGE	SEX	OCCUPATION	PRV VIL DES

SHIP: CITY OF CHICAGO

FROM: LIVERPOOL AND QUEENSTOWN
TO: NEW YORK
ARRIVED: 13 JUNE 1885

PASSENGER	AGE	SEX	OCCUPATION	PRV VIL DES
GROSS, SALMON	23	M	LABR	RRACBFIL
HACEWROWITZ, ITZIG	22	M	LABR	RRACBFNY
LASCHER, ISAAC	37	M	LABR	RRACBFNY
FOCKER, DANL.	26	M	LABR	RRACBFNY
SCHALL, FEIVEL	32	M	LABR	RRACBFNY
HILLNE, JOHAN	30	M	LABR	RRAGUZNY
LANGER, ELIAS	16	M	LABR	RRAGUZNY
FASS, NAIHUM	53	M	LABR	RRAGUZNY
NORSCH.	25	M	LABR	RRAGUZNY
SCHIMANOHY, HYPOLITE	49	M	LABR	RRAGUZNY
WEINER, SALAMON	18	M	LABR	RRACBFNY
SOPITZESKY, ABRAHAM	21	M	LABR	RRACBFNY
BENDER, JULIUS	19	M	LABR	RRACBFNY
GOLDGRAD, ELIAS	24	M	LABR	RRACBFNY
ERSLI, MAX	17	M	LABR	RRACBFNY
MENDEHEWITZ, MENDEL	25	M	LABR	RRACBFNY
RUBENSTEIN, MORITZ	17	M	CL	RRACBFNY
JANNER, BENDICT	22	M	LABR	RRACBFNY
LUNER, ISAK	19	M	LABR	PLZZZZNY
GROSSMAN, CATH.	32	F	W	PLACBFCH
FANNY	9	F	CHILD	PLACBFCH
AMUTH	00	F	INF	PLACBFCH

SHIP: NORDLAND

FROM: ANTWERP
TO: NEW YORK
ARRIVED: 13 JUNE 1885

PASSENGER	AGE	SEX	OCCUPATION	PRV VIL DES
TRUNCK, JOSEPH	22	M	MCHT	RRZZZZATR

SHIP: CALIFORNIA

FROM: HAMBURG
TO: NEW YORK
ARRIVED: 15 JUNE 1885

PASSENGER	AGE	SEX	OCCUPATION	PRV VIL DES
ROPPENWIL, SALE	58	F	WO	RRZZZZIL
MOGELER, SEBBA	15	F	SGL	RRZZZZMA
RADEHOWSKY, RAUHALL	29	F	WO	RRZZZZNY
MISCHEWSKY, CHAIM	19	M	LABR	RRZZZZNY
TRUCHATCKUT, MAGDA	34	F	SGL	RRZZZZNY
LABOWITZ, HENRI	20	M	LABR	PLZZZZNY
HANNE	19	F	W	PLZZZZNY
FRANKEL, ABRAHAM	23	M	TDR	PLZZZZCH
HOCHOW, FALERSEN	27	M	TDR	RRZZZZNY
SCHAPIRA, SALOMON	23	M	TDR	RRZZZZNY
KALBERG, ITZIG	18	M	TDR	RRZZZZNY
GETZ, AWE	21	M	TDR	RRZZZZUNK
MALMEWSKI, H.	26	M	TDR	RRZZZZNY
GUELEWITZ, MENDEL	19	M	LABR	RRZZZZNY
HOMIACK, THOMAS	28	M	LABR	PLZZZZNY
UBIACK, TH.	28	M	LABR	PLZZZZNY
RODUAR, JANOS	28	M	LABR	PLZZZZNY
ULBRUH, DAVID	28	M	LABR	PLZZZZNY
GRIESBACH, JANOS	20	M	LABR	PLZZZZNY
KLINGER, MEYER	50	M	TDR	PLZZZZNY
FIEDLER, BRE.	25	M	MCHT	RRZZZZNY
LUTKIES, JOSEF	23	M	TDR	RRZZZZNY
MERLIS, OSWAS	30	M	TDR	RRZZZZNY
BEREWSKY, BERNER	38	M	BCHR	RRZZZZCH
SARA	38	F	W	RRZZZZCH
JOSEF	17	M	S	RRZZZZCH
ERNESTINE	7	F	CHILD	RRZZZZCH
ALEXANDER	4	M	CHILD	RRZZZZCH
AMALIE	.06	F	INFANT	RRZZZZCH
LEBOWITZ, MAX	30	M	TDR	RRZZZZCH
HIRSCH	54	M	TDR	RRZZZZCH
GETS, FEIWEL	18	F	SGL	RRZZZZNY
MOSCHI	16	F	SGL	RRZZZZNY
KATZENELBAGEN, MENDEL	7	M	CHILD	RRZZZZNY
SUSFMANN, ESTER	24	F	WO	RRZZZZNY
CHAIE	.06	M	INFANT	RRZZZZNY
BRESLER, MATEL	35	F	WO	RRZZZZPA
FEIGE	7	F	CHILD	RRZZZZPA
BEREL	6	F	CHILD	RRZZZZPA
PESCHE	4	M	CHILD	RRZZZZPA
STONDT, JOSEF	40	M	LABR	PLZZZZIL
MARIANNE	29	F	W	PLZZZZIL
CATHARINA	7	F	CHILD	PLZZZZIL
JOHANN	5	M	CHILD	PLZZZZIL
FRIEDERIKE	2	F	CHILD	PLZZZZIL
FOLGEMANN, ANNA	36	F	WO	PLZZZZIL
NATHAN	.06	M	INFANT	PLZZZZIL
SCHETZER, ARON	15	M	LABR	RRZZZZUNK
MENDORF, MALINA	25	F	SGL	RRZZZZPA
FORREL, LEIB	30	M	FARMER	RRZZZZIL
CHAIM	7	M	CHILD	RRZZZZIL
BOBKE	5	M	CHILD	RRZZZZIL
SOLM, PAULINE	19	F	SGL	RRZZZZMA
POLINSKY, FEIGE	18	F	SGL	RRZZZZIL
NIELSEN, CHRISTEN	34	M	FARMER	RRZZZZNY
CAROLINE	30	F	W	RRZZZZNY
ANNE	7	F	CHILD	RRZZZZNY
JACOB	5	M	CHILD	RRZZZZNY
HAASE, AUGUSTE	16	M	FARMER	RRZZZZDAV
HABRZLEWITZ, LUDWIG	30	M	MSN	PLZZZZIL
THEKLA	34	F	W	PLZZZZIL
MARIANSKI, BERL	18	F	SGL	RRZZZZNY
LIEBE	7	F	CHILD	RRZZZZNY
MOSES	6	M	CHILD	RRZZZZNY
KANEMALSKY, ABRAM	18	M	TDR	RRZZZZNY
SCHNAPESKY, LEISER	24	M	TDR	RRZZZZIL
FAJANK, MARIANNE	18	F	SGL	PLZZZZPIT
MARKS, SARA	30	F	WO	RRZZZZNY
BASCHE	7	F	CHILD	RRZZZZNY
ISRAEL	6	M	CHILD	RRZZZZNY
NACHUM	3	M	CHILD	RRZZZZNY
MALESZEG, ANDREZEY	33	M	LABR	PLZZZZNY
ROTMANN, ANNA	30	F	WO	RRZZZZNY
DUDEZATIS, MAGDA	21	F	SGL	RRZZZZNY
KOBACKER, CHATZEL	15	F	SGL	RRZZZZNY
KANTROWITZ, ROW.	33	F	TDR	RRZZZZNY
RIFKE	30	F	W	RRZZZZNY
TAUBE	.11	F	INFANT	RRZZZZNY
KEILE	.02	M	INFANT	RRZZZZNY
KUTZINSKI, CHAIM	19	M	TDR	RRZZZZNY
FASHULSKI, FRANZ	25	M	LABR	RRZZZZNY
FORREL, LOISE	32	F	WO	RRZZZZNY
SPERGER, DAVID	36	M	TDR	RRZZZZNY
HUBSCHMANN, LEOP.	26	M	TDR	RRZZZZNY
PIERKOWSKI, ANTON	28	M	LABR	RRZZZZNY
FUDELSKI, ITZIG	7	M	CHILD	RRZZZZNY
LIEBMANN, MOSSEL	20	M	LABR	RRZZZZNY
FEGNIST, JOSEL	27	M	LABR	RRZZZZNY
TRLIS, ANTON	00	M	LABR	RRZZZZNY
TRACTHUY, IWAN	19	M	LABR	RRZZZZNY
RUGALSKY, MEND.	48	M	TDR	RRZZZZNY
CHIEWE	45	F	W	RRZZZZNY
BASSE	16	F	D	RRZZZZNY
FEIGE	7	F	CHILD	RRZZZZNY
REISFEL	6	F	CHILD	RRZZZZNY
SELIG	5	M	CHILD	RRZZZZNY

PASSENGER	AGE	SEX	OCCUPATION	PRV VIL DES
MOSES	3	M	CHILD	RRZZZZNY
BERKMANN, ROCHAME	19	F	SGL	RRZZZZNY
PLATZKI, SELIG	24	M	TDR	RRZZZZNY
FRIEDMANN, JACOB	20	M	TDR	RRZZZZNY
GINSBERG, MEYER	30	M	TDR	RRZZZZNY
SALMONOWITZ, SALM.	26	M	TDR	RRZZZZNY
GRUNSPAN, ISRAEL	27	M	TDR	RRZZZZNY
IPEISKY, FAI.	38	M	TDR	RRZZZZNY
STRITZEL, MARCUS	27	M	LABR	PLZZZZNY
MULLER, ESTER	22	F	WO	RRZZZZNY
ZADUK	5	M	CHILD	RRZZZZNY
GRUNSKI, CHANE	23	F	WO	RRZZZZNY
LEISER	2	M	CHILD	RRZZZZNY
ASCHER	.06	M	INFANT	RRZZZZNY
LEIBGOTT, LEIB	25	M	TDR	RRZZZZNY
GEISCHOWITZ, ESTER	40	F	WO	RRZZZZNY
JABEL	7	F	CHILD	RRZZZZNY
SUSMANN	6	M	CHILD	RRZZZZNY
MASCHE	5	F	CHILD	RRZZZZNY
MASTE	5	F	CHILD	RRZZZZNY
MARIE	4	F	CHILD	RRZZZZNY
CHATZEL	18	M	LABR	RRZZZZNY
KALMANN, LOUIS	17	M	LABR	RRZZZZNY
ITZIKOWITZ, CHEINE	19	F	SGL	RRZZZZNY
LANDE, ISAAC-M.	16	M	TDR	RRZZZZNY
MUDELSKY, F.	38	M	LABR	RRZZZZNY
ZURECHT	38	F	W	RRZZZZNY
KATZ, LISSY	19	F	SGL	RRZZZZNY
LEWIS, IDA	20	F	SGL	RRZZZZNY
GOLDFARB, MOSES	20	M	TDR	RRZZZZNY
FRIEDMANN, MOSES	30	M	LABR	PLZZZZNY
THAN, MENDE	26	M	LABR	PLZZZZNY
SANERBRUNN, LEIB	30	M	LABR	PLZZZZNY
NEUMARK, EPP.	32	M	CGRMKR	PLZZZZNY

SHIP: DONAU

FROM: BREMEN
TO: NEW YORK
ARRIVED: 15 JUNE 1885

PASSENGER	AGE	SEX	OCCUPATION	PRV VIL DES
CLEBANSKI, FANNY	22	F	NN	RRZZZZUSA
GARFEROWITZ, ETTEL	15	F	CH	RRZZZZUSA
LEWAK, SORE	20	F	NN	RRZZZZUSA
LEWI, MORDER	22	M	LABR	RRZZZZUSA
GUMBINER, AROW	19	M	LABR	RRZZZZUSA
LEKOWSKY, HYMANN	20	M	LABR	RRZZZZUSA
FINKOWSKA, JOSEPHA	30	F	NN	RRZZZZUSA
WADYSLAW	9	M	CHILD	RRZZZZUSA
GROS, FANNY	32	F	NN	RRZZZZUSA
HERMANN	7	M	CHILD	RRZZZZUSA
JACOB	6	M	CHILD	RRZZZZUSA
THEFALA	4	F	CHILD	RRZZZZUSA
SCHAFER, CARL	38	M	LABR	RRZZZZUSA
MARIE	38	F	W	RRZZZZUSA
KRENITZKY, NOCHEN	7	M	CHILD	RRZZZZUSA
KIRS, JUDA	38	F	NN	RRZZZZUSA
BRANNSOHN, ITZKA	55	M	MCHT	RRZZZZUSA
PZORSKY, MINNA	18	F	NN	RRZZZZUSA
DIMAN, WACAK	55	M	FARMER	RRZZZZUSA
SIEWITZ, WOLL	21	M	LABR	RRZZZZUSA
LEWIEN, LEVIN	26	M	LABR	RRZZZZUSA
LIBSKER, MOSES	18	M	LABR	RRZZZZUSA
GLOCKFELD, RACHEL	22	F	NN	RRZZZZUSA
MERELE	.11	F	INFANT	RRZZZZUSA
SCHAINO, SCHARNEL	35	M	FARMER	RRZZZZUSA
BLEM, JACOB	34	M	FARMER	RRZZZZUSA
CATH.	36	F	W	RRZZZZUSA
CATH.	16	F	CH	RRZZZZUSA
AMALIE	13	F	CH	RRZZZZUSA
MARG.	10	F	CH	RRZZZZUSA
ELISAB.	10	F	CH	RRZZZZUSA
AMALIE	7	F	CHILD	RRZZZZUSA
EMILIE	6	F	CHILD	RRZZZZUSA
HEINR.	3	M	CHILD	RRZZZZUSA
ALIS, ARNOLD	14	M	CH	RRZZZZUSA
PALINTZKI, DAVID	16	M	CL	RRZZZZUSA
NEUERMANN, MICH.	17	M	SMH	RRZZZZUSA
LASOWSKY, MOSES	26	M	SMH	RRZZZZUSA
TOBIAS, HAMIR	24	M	SMH	RRZZZZUSA
HANNA	3	F	CHILD	RRZZZZUSA
SELME	3	F	CHILD	RRZZZZUSA
JACOB	.08	M	INFANT	RRZZZZUSA
PASS, CHAIM	50	M	FARMER	RRZZZZUSA
MEISTER, MORDCHE	17	M	FARMER	RRZZZZUSA
CHAJE, SANDEL	18	F	NN	RRZZZZUSA
FELDENHEIM, ESTHER	19	F	NN	RRZZZZUSA
DECZEWSKO, MARIA	24	F	NN	RRZZZZUSA
FRANZ	.06	M	INFANT	RRZZZZUSA
WEHL, MICHEL	32	M	FARMER	RRZZZZUSA
CHRISTINA	29	F	W	RRZZZZUSA
CHRISTINA	4	F	CHILD	RRZZZZUSA
BARBARA	2	F	CHILD	RRZZZZUSA
JACOB	.07	M	INFANT	RRZZZZUSA
DOROGHCHTER, SALOMON	20	M	CL	RRZZZZUSA

SHIP: EDAM

FROM: AMSTERDAM
TO: NEW YORK
ARRIVED: 15 JUNE 1885

PASSENGER	AGE	SEX	OCCUPATION	PRV VIL DES
SCHENKIS, ANTON	00	M	UNKNOWN	PLZZZZUSA
JUDKIEWIETZ, HIRSCH	35	M	MCHT	PLAFVGUSA
HECDEL	26	F	UNKNOWN	PLAFVGUSA
SANDHAUS, ISAAK	28	M	UNKNOWN	PLZZZZUSA
BRAND, GRETEL	17	F	UNKNOWN	PLZZZZUSA
BEREK, BOCHEL	30	F	UNKNOWN	PLZZZZUSA
ZIFI	1	F	CHILD	PLZZZZUSA

SHIP: ST. OF PENNSYLVANIA

FROM: GLASGOW AND LARNE
TO: NEW YORK
ARRIVED: 15 JUNE 1885

PASSENGER	AGE	SEX	OCCUPATION	PRV VIL DES
BARZKI, NACHMIR	41	M	MCHT	RRZZZZUSA
ABRAHAM	19	M	MCHT	RRZZZZUSA
BLAN, MOSES	25	M	PNTR	RRZZZZUSA
BREST, ABRAHAM	24	M	PNTR	RRZZZZUSA
FEITELMANN, ISAAC	26	M	MCHT	RRZZZZUSA
MOSES	23	M	MCHT	RRZZZZUSA
FIBAK, RUDOLF	28	M	LABR	RRZZZZUSA
GARB, NIDEL	30	M	MCHT	RRZZZZUSA
GERSTEIN, TAUBE	20	F	SP	RRZZZZUSA
GOLDE	18	F	SP	RRZZZZUSA
GRIMBAUM, DAVID	49	M	TLR	RRZZZZUSA
HIRSCHKOWITZ, MENDEL	24	M	MCHT	RRZZZZUSA
HIMMELHOCH, WOLF	19	M	MCHT	RRZZZZUSA
KALMICK, SCHLOM	33	M	MCHT	RRZZZZUSA
SCHAIE	27	F	W	RRZZZZUSA
GRI----	4	F	CHILD	RRZZZZUSA
KAPLAN, HERRMAN	18	M	TLR	RRZZZZUSA
KUVINSK, GERONIME	38	M	LABR	RRAHTFUSA
KINNSO, FRANZISK	22	M	LABR	RRAHTFUSA

PASSENGER	AGE	SEX	OCCUPATION	PRV VIL DES
LITTMAN, ROSA	43	F	W	RRZZZZUSA
MOTTEK, MICHAL	30	M	LABR	RRZZZZUSA
PERL, JACOB-J.	20	M	MCHT	RRZZZZUSA
PROST, ALBERT	26	M	SMH	RRAHTFUSA
SCHRER, SALMEN	23	M	MCHT	RRZZZZUSA
SCHELOKOWSKY, THS.	20	M	LABR	RRZZZZUSA
STENDER, MENDEL	24	M	MCHT	RRZZZZUSA

SHIP: FURNESSIA

FROM: GLASGOW AND MOVILLE
TO: NEW YORK
ARRIVED: 16 JUNE 1885

PASSENGER	AGE	SEX	OCCUPATION	PRV VIL DES
ANDRAS, CANDA	21	M	LABR	RRZZZZUSA
BARKA, MAYER	22	M	DLR	RRZZZZUSA
BIRMANN, THOSCH	26	M	JNR	RRZZZZUSA
PINARSKY, LEISER	24	M	TLR	RRZZZZUSA
CZAJEWSKI, TH.	23	M	FARMER	RRZZZZUSA
GABRELOWITZ, FEIBISCH	20	M	TNSTH	RRZZZZUSA
GOOBMANN, SEIDE	18	M	TLR	RRZZZZUSA
GEDALJE	18	M	TLR	RRZZZZUSA
SANDEL	18	M	TLR	RRZZZZUSA
HOSS, LEISER	14	M	CL	RRZZZZUSA
HAINTSCH, STAN	23	M	FARMER	RRZZZZUSA
KURNITZ, KALMANN	30	M	DLR	RRZZZZUSA
KIVLASCH, STEFAN	21	M	FARMER	RRZZZZUSA
KATZ, SELIG	35	M	DLR	RRZZZZUSA
KOSDAN, CHAIN	41	M	TLR	RRZZZZUSA
KWINOZUCKI, CHANE	20	M	MCHT	RRZZZZUSA
KRIPLANSKI, SALOMON	36	M	SHMK	RRZZZZUSA
NICINEN, MOSES	48	M	DLR	RRZZZZUSA
RUBIN, EISIK	18	M	LABR	RRZZZZUSA
SCHWAT, SAMUEL	22	M	LABR	RRZZZZUSA
HOFFMANN, HUGO	15	M	DLR	RRZZZZUSA
SAFRANCK, FRANZ	24	M	LABR	RRZZZZUSA
DLUGATS, CHAIN	17	M	LABR	RRZZZZUSA
SEGALSON, ABRAHAM	20	M	HTR	RRZZZZUSA
SOBRAWSKY, SELIG	22	M	DLR	RRZZZZUSA
HVAL, JACOB	20	M	DLR	RRZZZZUSA
STEINBERG, SCHIE	20	M	DLR	RRZZZZUSA
WOLLF, IZTIG	52	M	TU	RRZZZZUSA
CZACHMANETZSK, ADAM	20	M	TLR	RRZZZZUSA
GRIMBLALL, BASCHE	45	F	NN	RRZZZZUSA
POLLACK, BASCHE	28	F	NN	RRZZZZUSA
WEINSTEIN, MARCUS	28	M	DLR	RRZZZZUSA
BASCHE	20	F	W	RRZZZZUSA
GARBOG, MICHAL-LIP.	20	M	DLR	RRZZZZUSA
HEINE	21	F	W	RRZZZZUSA
KAIKIN, SELMINE	27	F	NN	RRZZZZUSA
HERSCH	10	M	CH	RRZZZZUSA
MOSES	8	M	CHILD	RRZZZZUSA
WOLF	5	M	CHILD	RRZZZZUSA
MEYER	1	F	CHILD	RRZZZZUSA
KISCHOLEFSKY, THOM.	44	M	FARMER	RRZZZZUSA
JUSTINE	37	F	W	RRZZZZUSA
ANNA	19	F	CH	RRZZZZUSA
JOSEFA	8	F	CHILD	RRZZZZUSA
WLADISLAW	6	M	CHILD	RRZZZZUSA
JOSEFA	1	F	CHILD	RRZZZZUSA
KALNEZEWITSCH, PERRY	36	M	FARMER	RRZZZZUSA
ANNA	26	F	W	RRZZZZUSA
JAN	20	M	FARMER	RRZZZZUSA
URSULA	1	F	CHILD	RRZZZZUSA
KROST, WOLF	26	M	DLR	RRZZZZUSA
RACHEL	26	F	W	RRZZZZUSA
U, LIEBE	1	F	CHILD	RRZZZZUSA
ROSAITZKI, HIRSCH	44	M	DLR	RRZZZZUSA
JOSSEL	11	M	CH	RRZZZZUSA
ROSENTHAL, WOLFF	20	M	DLR	RRZZZZUSA
LIPPEL	18	F	W	RRZZZZUSA

SHIP: GALLIA

FROM: LIVERPOOL AND QUEENSTOWN
TO: NEW YORK
ARRIVED: 16 JUNE 1885

PASSENGER	AGE	SEX	OCCUPATION	PRV VIL DES
PONTTA, JOHAN	17	M	LABR	FNZZZZUSA
MACUPAA, ISACK	26	M	LABR	FNZZZZUSA
LAURILA, TOMAS	43	M	LABR	FNZZZZUSA
SLEGG, OTTO	36	M	LABR	FNZZZZUSA
MAFELA, MATT	27	M	LABR	FNZZZZUSA
OHKLA, JAKOB	17	M	LABR	FNZZZZUSA
MULLO, JAKOB	37	M	LABR	FNZZZZUSA
KULELBERG, MAT	48	M	LABR	FNZZZZUSA
TENPA, ISACK	16	M	LABR	FNZZZZUSA
KUHLBERG, MATTS.F.	26	M	LABR	FNZZZZUSA
KALLIAUFRAD, ESIAS	30	M	LABR	FNZZZZUSA
PRUNGO, JOHAN	37	M	LABR	FNZZZZUSA
PITTANSKI, JOHN	33	M	LABR	FNZZZZUSA
TONOGRARI, MATTS	17	M	LABR	FNZZZZUSA
PARK, MATTS	23	M	LABR	FNZZZZUSA
TURRA, JOHAN	23	M	LABR	FNZZZZUSA
KORSSI, SOFIA	28	F	SP	FNZZZZUSA
WAREWMAA, SARNIA	24	F	SP	FNZZZZUSA
SALMON, ANNA-L.	29	F	UNKNOWN	FNZZZZUSA
ADA.	4	F	CHILD	FNZZZZUSA
MATTI	3	F	CHILD	FNZZZZUSA
WEKOLONSKY, WARDJLA	27	M	LABR	PLZZZZUSA
COMMEUB, EDWARD	29	M	DYR	PLZZZZUSA
OLSON, ANDERS	50	M	LABR	RRZZZZUSA
SIGRI	40	F	W	RRZZZZUSA
CHRISTEN	10	F	CH	RRZZZZUSA
OLAF	6	M	CHILD	RRZZZZUSA
MARIE	3	F	CHILD	RRZZZZUSA
ANDERS	4	M	CHILD	RRZZZZUSA
PULINTER, GRAIL	36	M	LABR	RRZZZZUSA
PERLINSTEE, BUE.	17	M	LABR	RRZZZZUSA
LANZ, SISIL	34	F	UNKNOWN	RRZZZZUSA
COLMAN	9	M	CHILD	RRZZZZUSA
HARM.	8	M	CHILD	RRZZZZUSA
MICHEL	7	M	CHILD	RRZZZZUSA

SHIP: CANADA

FROM: UNKNOWN
TO: NEW YORK
ARRIVED: 17 JUNE 1885

PASSENGER	AGE	SEX	OCCUPATION	PRV VIL DES
BROZENSKY, FRANZITHES	25	M	LABR	PLZZZZUSA
ELISABETH	17	F	W	PLZZZZUSA
SCHAPERA, SAMUEL	22	M	UNKNOWN	RRZZZZUSA
MYERKAT, ISAK	18	M	LABR	RRZZZZUSA
SCHONFELD, ABRAHAM	17	M	LABR	RRZZZZUSA
OSHER, KESSER	36	M	LABR	RRZZZZUSA
FINKELMAN, BENIESI	33	M	LABR	RRZZZZUSA
FREIDEL, JACOB	23	M	LABR	RRZZZZUSA
BERNSTEIN, MEYER	21	M	NN	RRZZZZUSA
MORGULIES, JANKEL	31	M	LABR	RRZZZZUSA
EDELMAN, ABRAHAM	30	M	BTMKR	RRZZZZUSA
OFREWSKY, DONESES	35	M	LABR	PLZZZZUSA
KITKENRE, KARL	42	M	LABR	PLZZZZUSA
WILBANEN, JAKOB	23	M	SLD	PLZZZZUSA
RAGAMAKI, JAKOB	30	M	SLD	PLZZZZUSA

PASSENGER	AGE	SEX	OCCUPATION	PRIVL	DES
HANCE, JOSEF	34	M	SLD	PLZZZZ	USA
KALLIONKA, ISAK	32	M	SLD	PLZZZZ	USA
SCHWARTZ, GITEL	20	M	JWLR	PLZZZZ	USA
TRILLING, BULE	22	M	NN	PLZZZZ	USA
DAVIS, REBECCA	59	F	UNKNOWN	PLZZZZ	USA
ABRAMOWITZ, HUMICE	29	F	NN	RRZZZZ	USA
JACOB	2	F	CHILD	RRZZZZ	USA
JENNY	.07	M	INFANT	RRZZZZ	USA
STEINER, SAMUEL	21	M	TLR	RRZZZZ	USA
SINBERG, MOSES	27	M	LABR	PLZZZZ	USA
FOKS, MARKS	23	M	LABR	RRZZZZ	USA
SANDELMAN, ISAAC	22	M	FARMER	RRZZZZ	USA
MANNA, SALOMON	18	M	FARMER	PLZZZZ	USA
SEGAL, SALOMON	19	M	CPMKR	RRZZZZ	USA
RATBONSE, SIMON	21	M	UNKNOWN	RRZZZZ	USA
BERUSTEIN, HOFMAN	21	M	LABR	RRZZZZ	USA
GERTZINAN, MIDIAM	39	M	LABR	RRZZZZ	USA
MALKE	19	M	UNKNOWN	RRZZZZ	USA
CHAWE-TOBE	17	M	UNKNOWN	RRZZZZ	USA
NECHAMIE	15	M	CH	RRZZZZ	USA
DEBORAH	11	M	CH	RRZZZZ	USA
ISOCOB	10	M	CH	RRZZZZ	USA
COHEN, FEIGE	24	M	LABR	RRZZZZ	USA
ABRAMI	19	M	UNKNOWN	RRZZZZ	USA
JOSEPH	17	M	CH	RRZZZZ	USA
AARON	11	M	CH	RRZZZZ	USA
JONAS	10	M	CH	RRZZZZ	USA
REDE	8	M	CHILD	RRZZZZ	USA
MOTTEL	6	M	CHILD	RRZZZZ	USA
KAUFMAN, LEON	21	M	UNKNOWN	RRZZZZ	USA
MUNLEVSKY, LOTZTONS	20	M	TLR	RRZZZZ	USA

SHIP: RHAETIA

FROM: HAMBURG
TO: NEW YORK
ARRIVED: 17 JUNE 1885

PASSENGER	AGE	SEX	OCCUPATION	PRIVL	DES
FINK, KOPPEL	14	M	DLR	RRZZZZ	USA
HURWITZ, MENDEL	24	M	LABR	RRZZZZ	USA
SITEOFSKY, MARCUS	15	M	LABR	RRZZZZ	USA
JANKEL	18	M	LABR	RRZZZZ	USA
GRZIBALSKI, CAROLINE	39	F	W	RRZZZZ	USA
FRANZ	8	M	CHILD	RRZZZZ	USA
JOSEF	5	M	CHILD	RRZZZZ	USA
STEFANI	4	F	CHILD	RRZZZZ	USA
DAVIDOW, MALKE	54	F	W	RRZZZZ	USA
EPSTEIN, REBECCA	31	F	W	RRZZZZ	USA
SAUL	6	M	CHILD	RRZZZZ	USA
ENOCH	4	M	CHILD	RRZZZZ	USA
HARLIEB, LEIB	32	M	HAMF	RRZZZZ	USA
STRZELESKI, MARIANNE	28	F	SGL	RRZZZZ	USA
CHASEN, CHIM	49	F	W	RRZZZZ	USA
ISOMAKI, GUSTAV	24	M	FARMER	RRZZZZ	USA
GUSTAFSON, GUSTAF	26	M	FARMER	RRZZZZ	USA
COHN, MARIASSE	13	F	SGL	RRZZZZ	USA
WASSERMANN, MENDEL	33	M	DLR	RRZZZZ	USA
FREID, LEIB	30	M	LABR	RRZZZZ	USA
HARFELD, MATEL	25	F	W	RRZZZZ	USA
MORDSCHE	4	M	CHILD	RRZZZZ	USA
LONDON, JACOB	20	M	SMH	RRZZZZ	USA
BRESLANER, LEIBEL	38	M	TLR	RRZZZZ	USA
FRANK, MEYER	42	M	LABR	RRZZZZ	USA
SINGER, SCHOLEM	35	M	BKBNDR	RRZZZZ	USA
ANNSKIEWICSZ, LUDWIKA	35	F	SGL	RRZZZZ	USA
LOUKTA, PAUL	24	M	LABR	RRZZZZ	USA
ZOSTKOW, SARA	23	F	W	RRZZZZ	USA
CHEIM	4	M	CHILD	RRZZZZ	USA
HENOCH	.11	M	INFANT	RRZZZZ	USA
GUTMANN, CHAIM	21	M	DLR	RRZZZZ	USA

PASSENGER	AGE	SEX	OCCUPATION	PRIVL	DES
STEIN, ABR.ISAAC	29	M	TNSTH	RRZZZZ	USA
BDIL, LIEBE	26	F	W	RRZZZZ	USA
ABRAHAM	.11	M	INFANT	RRZZZZ	USA
LOSDEN, JACOB	15	M	DLR	RRZZZZ	USA
SIEGEL, FEIWEL	17	M	DLR	RRZZZZ	USA
LEWITAN, CASHE	20	F	SGL	RRZZZZ	USA
SCHMILOWSKY, HERM.	18	M	LABR	RRZZZZ	USA
LEVINSOHN, NECHE	44	F	W	RRZZZZ	USA
REINE	9	F	CHILD	RRZZZZ	USA
MARIASCHE	8	F	CHILD	RRZZZZ	USA
BOROWSKIJ, ROSA	18	F	SGL	RRZZZZ	USA
WIURKOSKA, MARIANNE	22	F	SGL	RRZZZZ	USA
ANTENSSVIKA, ERKKI	51	M	FARMER	RRZZZZ	USA
HANTALA, HERM.	28	M	FARMER	RRZZZZ	USA
MAFINSSVIKA, NICOLAI	23	M	FARMER	RRZZZZ	USA
LEWIN, JACOB	25	M	DLR	RRZZZZ	USA
WEINBERG, LEISER	25	M	LABR	RRZZZZ	USA
BLASKA, ANNA	27	F	W	RRZZZZ	USA
JUSTINE	19	F	SGL	RRZZZZ	USA
CAROLINE	3	F	CHILD	RRZZZZ	USA
MICHAEL	.11	M	INFANT	RRZZZZ	USA
AITIS, ABRAHAM	14	M	TLR	RRZZZZ	USA
WULF, PESCHE	19	F	SGL	RRZZZZ	USA
NEUERMANN, SARA	20	F	SGL	RRZZZZ	USA
GOLDBERG, ARON	39	M	LABR	RRZZZZ	USA
GRUENSPAHN, SCHMUEL	29	M	LABR	RRZZZZ	USA
FURMANSKY, LOEB	47	M	LABR	RRZZZZ	USA
PESCHE	50	F	W	RRZZZZ	USA
LEA	16	F	CH	RRZZZZ	USA
GOLDFARB, JUDA	28	F	LABR	RRZZZZ	USA
LIPSCHUETZ, ISRAEL	18	M	LABR	RRZZZZ	USA
KRIKSTANSKY, CHAIE	40	F	W	RRZZZZ	USA
SOBEL, LIEBE	8	F	CHILD	RRZZZZ	USA
SEHERBACK, MEYER	26	M	LABR	RRZZZZ	USA
SANDLER, JUDES	39	M	W	RRZZZZ	USA
CHAIM	18	M	CH	RRZZZZ	USA
PESCHE	16	M	CH	RRZZZZ	USA
SCHMUEL	7	M	CHILD	RRZZZZ	USA
ABRAM	5	M	CHILD	RRZZZZ	USA
SELDE	.11	M	INFANT	RRZZZZ	USA
GOLANSKY, MOSES	18	M	LABR	RRZZZZ	USA
GOLDE	20	F	LABR	RRZZZZ	USA
RAKOWITZ, SCHEINE	18	M	SGL	RRZZZZ	USA
GUDOWSKY, CHAIM	18	M	LABR	RRZZZZ	USA
ARONOWSKY, KADISCH	43	M	LABR	RRZZZZ	USA
ROCHE	40	F	W	RRZZZZ	USA
AMOLSKY, ITTE	17	F	SGL	RRZZZZ	USA
CHOLDNEWITZ, CHAIE	24	F	W	RRZZZZ	USA
FRUME	.10	F	INFANT	RRZZZZ	USA
LIPOLTZ, LIEBE	20	F	W	RRZZZZ	USA
CHONE	.10	F	INFANT	RRZZZZ	USA
KROM, ITTE	55	F	W	RRZZZZ	USA
JENTE	30	F	D	RRZZZZ	USA
ELMICHMICHSKY, SALOMON	31	M	LABR	RRZZZZ	USA
SCHEWE	29	F	W	RRZZZZ	USA
LUBA	9	M	CHILD	RRZZZZ	USA
TAUBE	7	F	CHILD	RRZZZZ	USA
SCHOENE	5	F	CHILD	RRZZZZ	USA
DAVID	.03	M	INFANT	RRZZZZ	USA
MATLIN, HIRSCH	20	M	LABR	RRZZZZ	USA
DAVIDSOHN, MENDEL-H.	17	M	LABR	RRZZZZ	USA
EPSTEIN, NAFTOLI	26	M	DLR	RRZZZZ	USA
LEW, MOSES	50	M	LABR	RRZZZZ	USA
HIRSCH	9	M	CHILD	RRZZZZ	USA
JENTE	8	F	CHILD	RRZZZZ	USA
GOLEB	7	M	CHILD	RRZZZZ	USA
SCEZENA, JOSEPHOTA	30	F	W	RRZZZZ	USA
MARIE	1	F	CHILD	RRZZZZ	USA
BRENSILBER, M.	27	M	JNR	RRZZZZ	USA
FANNY	18	F	W	RRZZZZ	USA
ANNA	18	F	SI	RRZZZZ	USA
ABRAM	00	M	INF	RRZZZZ	USA
WECHSLER, MOSES	25	M	JNR	RRZZZZ	USA
ROSA	20	F	W	RRZZZZ	USA
ROSA	46	F	M	RRZZZZ	USA

PASSENGER	AGE	SEX	OCCUPATION	PRV VIL DES
ITZIG	9	M	CHILD	RRZZZZUSA
ELISABETH	7	F	CHILD	RRZZZZUSA
ANNA	1	F	CHILD	RRZZZZUSA
HOFFMANN, CUBER	35	M	BKR	RRZZZZUSA
SCHIRER, JACOB	18	M	LABR	RRZZZZUSA
HURWITZ, JACOB	21	M	LABR	RRZZZZUSA
SCHUMACHER, PETER	35	M	LABR	RRZZZZUSA
MICHEL, CATHA.	23	F	SGL	RRZZZZUSA
FAIN, RISCHE	20	F	SGL	RRZZZZUSA
POMASKI, VALERIAN	27	M	SMH	RRZZZZUSA
KLINOWSKY, JOH.	26	M	LABR	RRZZZZUSA
STEINERT, MAX	53	M	LABR	RRZZZZUSA
HELENE	50	F	W	RRZZZZUSA
ANNA	2	F	CHILD	RRZZZZUSA
SCHUHMACHER, SAMUEL	16	M	CL	RRZZZZUSA
LIEB, FEIGE	17	F	SGL	RRZZZZUSA
ELBERT, CHAIM	25	M	MCHT	RRZZZZUSA
CHRISTEL	27	F	W	RRZZZZUSA
JOCHIM	2	M	CHILD	RRZZZZUSA
ROSA	.06	F	INFANT	RRZZZZUSA
ARKIN, JOSEPH	26	M	LABR	RRZZZZUSA
FAIN, DAVID	30	M	LABR	RRZZZZUSA
BECKER, SALOMON	46	M	LABR	RRZZZZUSA
SARA	46	F	W	RRZZZZUSA
EFRAIM	16	M	CH	RRZZZZUSA
BIOLISTOCKY, ESTHER	24	F	SGL	RRZZZZUSA
ZEMACH, MEYER	22	F	SGL	RRZZZZUSA
SALOMON	9	M	CHILD	RRZZZZUSA
RIWOLDE, HIRSCH	60	M	DLR	RRZZZZUSA
BLEIER, LEA	25	F	W	RRZZZZUSA
TELA	3	F	CHILD	RRZZZZUSA
JAGELSKI, JAN	23	M	LABR	RRZZZZUSA
MEYER, EMILIE	26	F	SGL	RRZZZZUSA
DWORETZKY, MORITZ	26	M	LABR	RRZZZZUSA
MARKNICSKI, OREN	28	M	SMH	RRZZZZUSA
BIOBLOLOTSKY, BARUCH	60	M	DLR	RRZZZZUSA

SHIP: BELGENLAND

FROM: ANTWERP
TO: NEW YORK
ARRIVED: 18 JUNE 1885

PASSENGER	AGE	SEX	OCCUPATION	PRV VIL DES
ROEBER, FRIEDA-MRS	25	F	SLR	RRAAKHNY
CROPIK, SUSNE.	40	F	SVNT	PLZZZZNY
MARIANNE	10	F	CH	PLZZZZNY
ANNA	8	F	CHILD	PLZZZZNY
JOH.	2	F	CHILD	PLZZZZNY
RACZKIS, A.	20	M	UNKNOWN	PLAFTMUNK
NOWASZYCK, MICH.	30	M	LABR	PLZZZZNY
ANT.	17	M	LABR	PLZZZZNY
MICH.	10	M	CH	PLZZZZNY
MARA.	8	F	CHILD	PLZZZZNY
CATH.	6	F	CHILD	PLZZZZNY
AGNES	3	F	CHILD	PLZZZZNY
JOS.	00	M	INF	PLZZZZNY
PETTER, RUD.	17	M	LABR	PLZZZZUNK
SPIES, JR.	28	M	JWLR	PLAEGCNY
FISCHER, A.	24	M	LABR	PLAEGCNY
SPIES, JAC.	00	M	INF	RRZZZZNY
SIEBEL, FCH.	64	M	GDNR	RRAESMCIN
NOWASEWSKI, VAL.	25	M	LABR	RRZZZZNY
KALINA, ADA.	18	M	MCHT	PLZZZZCH
SELBERSTEIN, CAR.	20	M	MCHT	PLZZZZCH
JOMZAK, JOH.	31	M	LABR	PLZZZZNY
ELIS	30	F	UNKNOWN	PLZZZZNY
JOH.	15	M	CH	PLZZZZNY
JON	12	M	CH	PLZZZZNY
FRZ.	10	M	CH	PLZZZZNY
MAR.	8	F	CHILD	PLZZZZNY

PASSENGER	AGE	SEX	OCCUPATION	PRV VIL DES
VAL.	2	M	CHILD	PLZZZZNY
JOS.	00	M	INF	PLZZZZNY
SELBERSTEIN, DAVID	9	M	CHILD	PLAFTMSTL

SHIP: NEVADA

FROM: LIVERPOOL AND QUEENSTOWN
TO: NEW YORK
ARRIVED: 18 JUNE 1885

PASSENGER	AGE	SEX	OCCUPATION	PRV VIL DES
GOLDBERG, ISRAEL	40	M	LABR	RRZZZZUSA
HERSCHSOHN, RACHEL	19	F	SP	RRZZZZUSA
FRENK, USGA	33	M	LABR	RRZZZZUSA
SCHNAPE, ABR.	41	M	LABR	RRZZZZUSA
ZICOWICZ, OH.	23	M	LABR	RRZZZZUSA
WOLK, Z.	28	M	LABR	RRZZZZUSA
BLAZAR, NOCHMAN	32	M	LABR	RRZZZZUSA
GOFFORT, MARTIN	47	M	LABR	RRZZZZUSA
ANNA	28	F	W	RRZZZZUSA
STANISLAUS	11	F	CH	RRZZZZUSA
VINCENTE	3	M	CHILD	RRZZZZUSA
LEVY, MORCHE	20	F	W	RRZZZZUSA
CHAIM	20	F	W	RRZZZZUSA
SOLOMON	00	M	INF	RRZZZZUSA
FREIMAN, JOSEF	00	M	LABR	RRZZZZUSA
ROSALIE	29	F	W	RRZZZZUSA
SIMON	9	M	CHILD	RRZZZZUSA
FANNY	6	F	CHILD	RRZZZZUSA
WILLY	7	M	CHILD	RRZZZZUSA
BELLA	3	F	CHILD	RRZZZZUSA
VUGMAUN, SIMON	21	M	LABR	RRZZZZUSA

SHIP: SIMON

FROM: HAVRE
TO: NEW YORK
ARRIVED: 18 JUNE 1885

PASSENGER	AGE	SEX	OCCUPATION	PRV VIL DES
BORAK, MATHAN	28	M	CPMKR	PLZZZZNY
NINA	29	F	W	PLZZZZNY

SHIP: MARTHA

FROM: UNKNOWN
TO: NEW YORK
ARRIVED: 19 JUNE 1885

PASSENGER	AGE	SEX	OCCUPATION	PRV VIL DES
BONNER, PAULINE	23	F	SVNT	RRZZZZNY
IFNALD, CATHARINE	38	F	WO	RRZZZZMI
EMMA	11	F	CH	RRZZZZMI
MARIE	10	F	CH	RRZZZZMI
JACOB	8	M	CHILD	RRZZZZMI
BERNHARD	7	M	CHILD	RRZZZZMI
FANNY	6	F	CHILD	RRZZZZMI
ANNA	5	F	CHILD	RRZZZZMI
FRED	3	M	CHILD	RRZZZZMI
SALOMON	.10	M	INFANT	RRZZZZMI
MERA	1	F	CHILD	RRZZZZMI
SANDAN, FERDINAND	29	M	LABR	PLZZZZWI
LOUISE	29	F	W	PLZZZZWI

PASSENGER	AGE	SEX	OCCUPATION	PRV VIL DES
GLEMRICH	10	M	CH	PLZZZZWI
EDWARD	3	M	CHILD	PLZZZZWI
EMILIE	.06	F	INFANT	PLZZZZWI
IDELLMANCZEWSKI, FRANZ	16	M	LABR	PLZZZZMI
IUMMIENNY, IGNATZ	42	M	LABR	PLZZZZMN
SCHAFFMAN, ESTER	18	F	WVR	PLZZZZIL
I.F.	19	M	WVR	PLZZZZIL
M.F.	29	M	WVR	PLZZZZIL
KOSS, BERUHARD	16	M	TRDSMN	RRZZZZUNK
KAPSLAN, HANNACH	20	F	SVNT	RRZZZZIL
FRIEDMANN, JOSEPH	30	M	LABR	RRZZZZIL
GELINKI, VALENTINE	27	M	LABR	RRZZZZDET
JESKE, MICHAEL	45	M	FARMER	RRZZZZUNK
CHRISTINE	10	F	D	RRZZZZUNK
PLAGENTER, MARTIN	25	M	LABR	PLZZZZUNK
SUBITY, SARAH	20	F	NN	RRZZZZUNK
YATOK, ESTER	18	F	NN	RRZZZZUNK
STAGIBLOM, ADRIAN	23	M	INWKR	FNZZZZMN

SHIP: RHEIN

FROM: BREMEN AND SOUTHAMPTON
TO: NEW YORK
ARRIVED: 19 JUNE 1885

PASSENGER	AGE	SEX	OCCUPATION	PRV VIL DES
BOSENGWITZ, DAVID	36	M	LABR	RRZZZZUSA
BLOSTEIN, PENSACH	19	M	LABR	RRZZZZUSA
LANDMAN, HINDE	30	F	NN	RRZZZZUSA
LEIB	5	M	CHILD	RRZZZZUSA
HINDE	.09	F	INFANT	RRZZZZUSA
SPETGANG, MARIANNE	35	F	NN	RRZZZZUSA
ESTER	.04	F	INFANT	RRZZZZUSA
BANTE, NESSEL	.11	M	INFANT	RRZZZZUSA
NESSEL	52	F	NN	RRZZZZUSA
CZYZEWSKA, MARIANNA	26	F	NN	RRZZZZUSA
FUNKELSTEIN, CLAIR	35	M	LABR	RRZZZZUSA
TABERT, JACOB	31	M	LABR	RRZZZZUSA
SCHMIDT, CORNELIUS	32	M	LABR	RRZZZZUSA
HELENE	30	F	W	RRZZZZUSA
PETER	3	M	CHILD	RRZZZZUSA
MARIE	.03	F	INFANT	RRZZZZUSA
WIENS, JOHANN	46	M	FARMER	RRZZZZUSA
AGATHE	39	F	W	RRZZZZUSA
ELISE	16	F	NN	RRZZZZUSA
JOHANN	18	M	FARMER	RRZZZZUSA
DAVID	14	M	CH	RRZZZZUSA
AUGUSTE	6	F	CHILD	RRZZZZUSA
ANNA	4	F	CHILD	RRZZZZUSA
WEIN, SALOMON	19	M	TRVLR	RRZZZZUSA
MIERAN, HEINRICH	44	M	LABR	RRZZZZUSA
HELENA	36	F	W	RRZZZZUSA
DIETRICH	16	M	LABR	RRZZZZUSA
HELENA	4	F	CHILD	RRZZZZUSA
JOHANN	.11	M	INFANT	RRZZZZUSA
HOLZRICHTER, HEINRICH	36	M	LABR	RRZZZZUSA
BARBARA	39	F	W	RRZZZZUSA
MARIE	11	F	CH	RRZZZZUSA
HEINRICH	10	M	CH	RRZZZZUSA
PETER	8	M	CHILD	RRZZZZUSA
CATHARINE	7	F	CHILD	RRZZZZUSA
ANNA	4	F	CHILD	RRZZZZUSA
JACOB	3	M	CHILD	RRZZZZUSA
BARBARA	.02	F	INFANT	RRZZZZUSA
RULEIN, CHAJE	33	F	NN	RRZZZZUSA
CHAINE	8	F	CHILD	RRZZZZUSA
GERSON	6	M	CHILD	RRZZZZUSA
ROSCHKE	4	F	CHILD	RRZZZZUSA
IDELSOHN, ISRAEL	20	M	TRVLR	RRZZZZUSA
KLUFT, SALOMON	23	M	LABR	RRZZZZUSA
POWNITZKY, PIETR	22	M	LABR	RRZZZZUSA

PASSENGER	AGE	SEX	OCCUPATION	PRV VIL DES
WERNER, ANDR.	46	M	SDLR	RRZZZZUSA
KATRINA	47	F	W	RRZZZZUSA
JOHANN	14	M	CH	RRZZZZUSA
PAUL	8	M	CHILD	RRZZZZUSA
JACOB	5	M	CHILD	RRZZZZUSA
ELISE	4	F	CHILD	RRZZZZUSA
LEFKOWITZ, MARCUS	17	M	LABR	RRZZZZUSA
SOMNER, MOSES	15	M	NN	RRZZZZUSA
WOICICOWSKI, F.	18	M	LABR	RRZZZZUSA
SCHALASCHAWICZ, VINCENT	33	M	LABR	RRZZZZUSA
FRANZISCA	26	F	W	RRZZZZUSA
ANNA	7	F	CHILD	RRZZZZUSA
VERONICA	5	F	CHILD	RRZZZZUSA
PETRONELLI	.09	F	INFANT	RRZZZZUSA
MATHIAS	18	M	LABR	RRZZZZUSA
KWETINSKY, KATHRINE	22	F	NN	RRZZZZUSA
TEITELMANN, RELE	19	M	LABR	RRZZZZUSA
BARACH, SCHIFRA	37	F	NN	RRZZZZUSA
SLATE	6	M	CHILD	RRZZZZUSA
PERRE	5	M	CHILD	RRZZZZUSA
HIRSCH	3	M	CHILD	RRZZZZUSA
JANKE	.06	M	INFANT	RRZZZZUSA
GAST, MATHILDE	21	F	NN	RRZZZZUSA
SCHULZ, AUGUSTA	20	F	NN	RRZZZZUSA
STRACHUNSKY, JOHN	18	M	MCHT	RRZZZZUSA
WASILEWSKI, MARIANNE	30	F	NN	RRZZZZUSA
ANNA	18	F	NN	RRZZZZUSA

SHIP: W A SCHOLTEN

FROM: ROTTERDAM
TO: NEW YORK
ARRIVED: 19 JUNE 1885

PASSENGER	AGE	SEX	OCCUPATION	PRV VIL DES
ROTSCHILD, JOSEF	20	M	TLR	PLZZZZUSA
SPIEGEL, JOSEF	19	M	TLR	PLZZZZUSA
ROSENBLEN, MOSES	32	M	TLR	PLZZZZUSA
BRAUN, NECHE	19	M	SLSMN	PLZZZZUSA
PEKA, IZAK	34	M	SLSMN	PLZZZZUSA
SCHEERE, BASSE	10	F	UNKNOWN	PLZZZZUSA
KAPLAN, SIMSOM	45	M	LABR	PLZZZZUSA
BARON, CHANE	53	M	SHMK	PLZZZZUSA
GONDELWITZ, HERSCH	22	M	SHMK	PLZZZZUSA
BACKNER, ROBERT	33	M	SMH	PLZZZZUSA
BEIS, JOHAN	20	M	SHMK	PLZZZZUSA
NEUBAUER, ROBERT	20	M	SMH	PLZZZZUSA
LAVEL, SCHMUL	40	M	TLR	PLZZZZUSA
LEIBWITZ, HIRSCH	40	M	TLR	PLZZZZUSA
GODJE, PESACH	23	M	SLSMN	PLZZZZUSA
FRIEDMANN, SCHEIL	12	M	SLSMN	PLZZZZUSA
KORBE, OCHER	22	M	TLR	PLZZZZUSA
ETEL	20	M	BDMKR	PLZZZZUSA
LUBERSKI, PESACH	24	M	CPTR	PLZZZZUSA
GONRANSKI, SAMUEL	20	M	SLSMN	PLZZZZUSA
FICHEL	22	M	SLSMN	PLZZZZUSA
ROSENBERG, SAMUEL	20	M	SLSMN	PLZZZZUSA
GONIANSKI, FRANE	20	F	JNR	PLZZZZUSA
MIOCH, BARUSCH	30	M	CPMKR	PLZZZZUSA
DRISMAN, CHANNE	30	F	UNKNOWN	PLZZZZUSA
KORN, SOLOMON	16	M	UNKNOWN	PLZZZZUSA
SMOLSKI, ABRAH.	20	M	SLSMN	PLZZZZUSA
FRIEDMAN, I.J.	30	M	SHMK	PLZZZZUSA
HERCZOWITZ, ADOLF	24	M	PIMK	PLZZZZUSA
HAUSKI, MOSES	21	M	UNKNOWN	PLZZZZUSA
GUTELWEIN, BEHR	24	M	SMH	PLZZZZUSA
SCHMITTMANN, FEIWEL	20	M	SLSMN	PLZZZZUSA
GLOSMANN, MOSCH.	19	M	CGRMKR	PLZZZZUSA
STEINMAN, ABRAHAM	19	M	LKSH	PLZZZZUSA
BRADEN, SAMUEL	20	M	TLR	PLZZZZUSA
STANBERG, ABRAHAM	30	M	TLR	PLZZZZUSA

PASSENGER	AGE	SEX	OCCUPATION	PRV VIL DES
KLAWBUS, DOMENK	43	M	SLSMN	PLZZZZUSA
SAMONUSKI, SAUL	19	M	MLR	PLZZZZUSA
PUNSKI, H.	20	M	SLSMN	PLZZZZUSA
RADIETZKI, NOACHUM	35	M	SLSMN	PLZZZZUSA
KERNICK, RENI	27	M	SLSMN	PLZZZZUSA
BUCHLES, NOACH	21	M	SLSMN	PLZZZZUSA
GARNOWSKI, RUBEN	19	M	STNER	PLZZZZUSA
KRIM, JACHANE	41	M	TIR	PLZZZZUSA
DIRSCHENFELD, ZIPE	19	F	UNKNOWN	PLZZZZUSA
LABOWSKI, WOLF	50	M	SLSMN	PLZZZZUSA
LEIB	19	M	SLSMN	PLZZZZUSA
MEDENITZ, ABRAHAM	33	M	SLSMN	PLZZZZUSA
ROMEINZKUS, ANTAMAS	22	M	MLR	PLZZZZUSA
KATZ, MOISCHE	23	F	UNKNOWN	PLZZZZUSA
WIPLIG, PINCUS	40	M	UNKNOWN	PLZZZZUSA
LES, CHANE	22	M	TLR	PLZZZZUSA
JADSMINSKI, JOSAS	24	M	UNKNOWN	PLZZZZUSA
STRUMPE, SELIG	46	M	LABR	PLZZZZUSA
GRISALUS, TAMASES	25	M	LABR	PLZZZZUSA
MATUSEWSKI, W.	21	M	TLR	PLZZZZUSA
SPIELVOGEL, PINKUS	30	M	TLR	PLZZZZUSA
MARCUS, NOSE	46	M	SLSMN	PLZZZZUSA
SOVICHOI, ANTON	44	M	SLSMN	PLZZZZUSA
NASS, JACOB	24	M	UMKR	PLZZZZUSA
GOLD, DAVID	00	M	SLSMN	PLZZZZUSA
WINTERGRUN, MALKE	17	F	UNKNOWN	PLZZZZUSA
BERMANN, LEA	35	F	UNKNOWN	PLZZZZUSA
LEISER	5	M	CHILD	PLZZZZUSA
RACHEL	9	F	CHILD	PLZZZZUSA
SORK, BASCHE	27	F	UNKNOWN	PLZZZZUSA
MEIER	4	M	CHILD	PLZZZZUSA
MATEL	.06	M	INFANT	PLZZZZUSA
JOUNKEL	.06	M	INFANT	PLZZZZUSA
AROWITZ, OSCAR	46	M	UNKNOWN	PLZZZZUSA
TOUCHEL	40	M	UNKNOWN	PLZZZZUSA
BRODT, JONAS	30	M	SLSMN	PLZZZZUSA
SARA	30	F	UNKNOWN	PLZZZZUSA
FANNY	7	F	CHILD	PLZZZZUSA
BETTI	6	F	CHILD	PLZZZZUSA
DAVID	4	M	CHILD	PLZZZZUSA
MAX	.06	M	INFANT	PLZZZZUSA
OTTILIE	.06	F	INFANT	PLZZZZUSA
PULER, CHANE	40	F	UNKNOWN	PLZZZZUSA
JETTE	10	M	UNKNOWN	PLZZZZUSA
SCHAPIRO, TUNTJE	30	F	UNKNOWN	PLZZZZUSA
SAMUEL	11	M	UNKNOWN	PLZZZZUSA
HIRWITZ, SARA	24	F	UNKNOWN	PLZZZZUSA
ABRAHAM	2	M	CHILD	PLZZZZUSA
HOCHMAN, ISRAEL	34	M	CPMKR	PLZZZZUSA
RACHEL	30	F	CPMKR	PLZZZZUSA
MALKE	.06	F	INFANT	PLZZZZUSA
SAMUEL	.06	M	INFANT	PLZZZZUSA
BLATH, MOSES	24	M	BKR	PLZZZZUSA
ESTHER	20	F	UNKNOWN	PLZZZZUSA
MOTSCHE	24	F	UNKNOWN	PLZZZZUSA
SCHEWE	.06	F	INFANT	PLZZZZUSA
CARL, MARIA	20	F	UNKNOWN	PLZZZZUSA
HAVIR	5	F	CHILD	PLZZZZUSA

SHIP: CITY OF RICHMOND

FROM: LIVERPOOL
TO: NEW YORK
ARRIVED: 20 JUNE 1885

PASSENGER	AGE	SEX	OCCUPATION	PRV VIL DES
PANTREFFA, B.	36	M	LABR	PLZZZZUSA
LINSKY, M.	18	M	LABR	PLZZZZUSA
LYKS, MATHIAS	33	M	LABR	PLACBFUSA
JOHANN, K.	40	M	LABR	PLACBFUSA
EBERHARD, FRED	36	M	LABR	PLACBFUSA
W.	30	F	W	PLACBFUSA
G.	9	M	CHILD	PLACBFUSA
A.	7	M	CHILD	PLACBFUSA
W.	4	M	CHILD	PLACBFUSA
R.	3	F	CHILD	PLACBFUSA
C.	00	F	INF	PLACBFUSA
SALKARD, WOLF	35	M	LABR	RRZZZZUSA
GOLDE	36	F	W	RRZZZZUSA
MARK	11	M	CH	RRZZZZUSA
SARAH	8	F	CHILD	RRZZZZUSA
B.	5	F	CHILD	RRZZZZUSA
RACHEL	00	F	INF	RRZZZZUSA
GODSTENI, J.	24	M	LABR	RRZZZZUSA
SARAH	23	F	W	RRZZZZUSA
SARAH	00	F	INF	RRZZZZUSA
RUBERT, JAC.	23	M	LABR	RRZZZZUSA
EBASCHOFF, J.	22	M	LABR	RRZZZZUSA
MAYER, DAVID	30	M	LABR	RRZZZZUSA
KONIGSDORF, B.	18	M	LABR	RRZZZZUSA

SHIP: EIDER

FROM: BREMEN AND SOUTHAMPTON
TO: NEW YORK
ARRIVED: 20 JUNE 1885

PASSENGER	AGE	SEX	OCCUPATION	PRV VIL DES
THIEL, EDUARD	18	M	LABR	RRZZZZUSA
KOWITZKI, STANISLAUS	24	M	LKSH	RRZZZZUSA
WARGENTIN, JOHANN	43	M	LABR	RRZZZZUSA
SARAH	19	F	NN	RRZZZZUSA
ANNA	16	F	CH	RRZZZZUSA
AUGA.	13	F	CH	RRZZZZUSA
MARGA.	9	F	CHILD	RRZZZZUSA
JOHANN	7	M	CHILD	RRZZZZUSA
KATHA.	2	F	CHILD	RRZZZZUSA
GOTTLIEB, MORITZ	33	M	LABR	RRZZZZUSA
SKATKIEWICZ, STANISL.	17	M	LABR	RRZZZZUSA
SYPROWICZ, ANTON	16	M	LABR	RRZZZZUSA
KLEEMAN, ABRAHAM	40	M	BKR	RRZZZZUSA
FRUMOWSKY, SALMON	33	M	TLR	RRZZZZUSA
RITTENBERG, EFRAIM	33	M	LABR	RRZZZZUSA
LEGEN, IHLA	20	F	NN	RRZZZZUSA
LERNER, SURKE	15	M	CH	RRZZZZUSA
HIMMELSTERN, RACHEL	20	F	NN	RRZZZZUSA
ITZIG	12	M	CH	RRZZZZUSA
MACHMANN, SEUL-ISRAEL	24	M	TNSTH	RRZZZZUSA
DOBRE	21	F	W	RRZZZZUSA
BASELER, AUGUSTE	25	F	NN	RRZZZZUSA
LINDE, JECHIEL-SCH.	18	M	LABR	RRZZZZUSA
GARBOWSKY, ISRAEL	17	M	LABR	RRZZZZUSA
FISCHMANN, ISRAEL	9	M	CHILD	RRZZZZUSA
JATKOWSKY, JANKEL	18	M	SHMK	RRZZZZUSA
RACHEL	20	F	W	RRZZZZUSA
KAMINSKY, JOSEPH	26	M	LABR	RRZZZZUSA
NEUMANN, RACHEL	50	F	WI	RRZZZZUSA
MINNA	28	F	WI	RRZZZZUSA
ARON	9	M	CHILD	RRZZZZUSA
ZEIL, LEIE	16	F	CH	RRZZZZUSA
SAMA, JACOB-LEIB	17	M	SHMK	RRZZZZUSA

PASSENGER	AGE	SEX	OCCUPATION	PRIVIL	DES
SHIP: MORAVIA					
FROM: HAMBURG					
TO: NEW YORK					
ARRIVED: 23 JUNE 1885					
GOLDBERG, MINNA	25	F	W	RRAHUV	USA
EISIK	.06	M	INFANT	RRAHUV	USA
WOGA, SOPHIE	40	M	UNKNOWN	RRZZZZ	USA
JACOB	15	M	CH	RRZZZZ	USA
LIEBE	9	F	CHILD	RRZZZZ	USA
JULIUS	8	M	CHILD	RRZZZZ	USA
SCHUHLER, ABRAHAM	16	M	BRM	RRZZZZ	USA
BERZINSKY, ISAAC	20	M	TLR	RRZZZZ	USA
KYONSKOSKOWNA, ANNA	20	F	SGL	RRAHWP	USA
BOMBE, ALTER	27	M	TLR	RRZZZZ	USA
SALOZIZZE, HIRSCH	18	M	LKSH	RRAHOK	USA
KOPPLER, LEA	28	F	W	RRZZZZ	USA
SCHIA	5	F	CHILD	RRZZZZ	USA
NEUWIRTH, SARA	19	F	SGL	RRZZZZ	USA
SOPACZINSKY, PESCHE	44	F	W	RRAHZS	USA
MOSES	9	M	CHILD	RRAHZS	USA
ABR.	8	M	CHILD	RRAHZS	USA
BLUME	6	F	CHILD	RRAHZS	USA
GITTEL	3	F	CHILD	RRAHZS	USA
HORN, LINE	23	F	SGL	RRADOI	USA
SBEZNICK, FANE	20	F	SGL	RRAHTS	USA
HERZKOWITZ, SALI	19	F	SGL	RRZZZZ	USA
SARA	21	F	SGL	RRZZZZ	USA
BRIK, MALKE	16	F	SGL	RRZZZZ	USA
LEWINSOHN, NISKA	19	F	SGL	RRZZZZ	USA
KOHN, ABRAHAM	18	M	LABR	RRZZZZ	USA
EDELSTEIN, ABR.	19	M	LABR	RRZZZZ	USA
WALKOWSKI, VINCENT	35	M	LABR	RRAHSW	USA
CZWIKOWSKI, JAN.	20	M	LABR	RRAHZS	USA
ZYLINSKA, JOSEPH	18	F	SGL	RRAHZS	USA
LEWANOWICZ, TEOFILA	27	F	W	RRAHZS	USA
MARIE	.03	F	INFANT	RRAHZS	USA
GOLDBERG, CHANNE	18	F	SGL	RRZZZZ	USA
WEINGUT, MEYER	20	M	TLR	RRZZZZ	USA
BUCCWIG, FELIX	15	M	LABR	RRZZZZ	USA
JULIAN	9	M	CHILD	RRZZZZ	USA
LUP, WILH.	19	F	SGL	RRZZZZ	USA
TIMM, HENRY	48	M	SHMK	RRZZZZ	USA
NEJEREZIK, SESHIES	17	M	LABR	RRZZZZ	USA
GRUNFELD, SARA	16	F	SGL	RRZZZZ	USA
REVKIN, RACHEL	17	F	SGL	RRAHOK	USA
ISRAELEWITZ, SARA	18	F	SGL	RRAHTF	USA
TIGUR, ISAAC	20	M	LABR	RRAGRT	USA
RACHMANN, HIRSCH	14	M	LABR	RRZZZZ	USA
LINE	18	F	SGL	RRZZZZ	USA
MICHALOWSKY, CHAWE	18	F	CH	RRZZZZ	USA
LEIB	13	F	CH	RRZZZZ	USA
MOSES	9	F	CHILD	RRZZZZ	USA
STAWEANSKY, MENDEL	18	F	LABR	RRAHTS	USA
SALZMANN, MOSES	18	F	LABR	RRAHTS	USA
KOLBER, NIC.	22	F	CPTR	RRAHTS	USA
WEISS, BENNO	67	F	STCTR	RRAHTS	USA
HIRSCHFELD, ISAAC	18	F	SHMK	RRZZZZ	USA
KRULEWIETZKI, CHAZKEL	19	F	LABR	RRZZZZ	USA
BRODKE, ARON	19	F	HRCTR	RRAHTU	USA
KODESCH, HARRIS	29	F	LABR	RRZZZZ	USA
ROTHSCHILDT, MARKS	19	F	DLR	RRZZZZ	USA
SOSNARSKI, SAMUEL	30	F	DLR	RRZZZZ	USA
HURWITZ, DWORA	16	F	SGL	RRAHTO	USA
MUHELSOHN, CHINE	19	F	SGL	RRAHRZ	USA
BERANK, JOHN	40	M	BCHR	RRAHRZ	USA
JOHN	23	M	STDNT	RRAHRZ	USA
SEGAL, LEISER	20	M	SHMK	RRZZZZ	USA
ALIPOWITZ, SUSSKIND	35	M	GZR	RRZZZZ	USA
BERNSTEIN, FEIGE	14	F	SGL	RRZZZZ	USA
WOZTKIWIC, ADAM	20	M	LABR	RRAHZS	USA
GIESBRECHT, FRANZ	30	M	LABR	RRZZZZ	USA
MARIE	27	F	W	RRZZZZ	USA
MARIE	.11	F	INFANT	RRZZZZ	USA
MALINOWSKA, ROSALIE	35	F	W	RRZZZZ	USA
BABRINK	9	F	CHILD	RRZZZZ	USA
MATHEUS	7	M	CHILD	RRZZZZ	USA
BERGMANN, WILH.	54	F	W	RRZZZZ	USA
FISCHMANN, LEISER	32	M	LABR	RRZZZZ	USA
BRUME	32	F	W	RRZZZZ	USA
PINKUS	9	M	CHILD	RRZZZZ	USA
SCHIFRE	4	F	CHILD	RRZZZZ	USA
NACHUM	.11	M	INFANT	RRZZZZ	USA
ARON	36	M	LABR	RRZZZZ	USA
KEILE	36	F	W	RRZZZZ	USA
SCHIFRE	9	F	CHILD	RRZZZZ	USA
ABR.	7	M	CHILD	RRZZZZ	USA
RACHEL	.11	F	INFANT	RRZZZZ	USA
ZUKOWSKY, BALTROM	45	M	LABR	RRAHTF	USA
ROMANOWSKY, JOH.	25	M	LABR	RRAHZS	USA
BROJAT, GEORG	21	M	LABR	RRAHZS	USA
PAULIKAT, JURGES	25	M	LABR	RRAHZS	USA
LADEN, MORDEHE	30	M	CPTR	RRZZZZ	USA
JENTE	28	F	W	RRZZZZ	USA
SCHLOME	.11	M	INFANT	RRZZZZ	USA
GLASS, SCHAJE	20	F	SGL	RRAFWJ	USA
SCHMULEWICZ, JACOB	21	M	LABR	RRAHTN	USA
KOHEN, ABEL	22	M	LABR	RRZZZZ	USA
SAUL	17	M	LABR	RRZZZZ	USA
UBOWIEZA, RACHEL	46	F	W	RRZZZZ	USA
ABRAHAM	9	M	CHILD	RRZZZZ	USA
ELIAS	6	M	CHILD	RRZZZZ	USA
IGELSKI, MOSES	19	M	LABR	RRZZZZ	USA
BRODOWSKY, WOLF	19	M	LABR	RRZZZZ	USA
ELDSTEIN, LIEBE	20	F	SGL	RRZZZZ	USA
WIENITZKI, HENOCH	42	M	LABR	RRZZZZ	USA
SAKOL, FRUME	22	F	W	RRAHZS	USA
STERA	.11	F	INFANT	RRAHZS	USA
BOROWITZ, ZIREL	22	F	W	RRAHZS	USA
FEIGEL	4	M	CHILD	RRAHZS	USA
NUCHEM	.11	M	INFANT	RRAHZS	USA
SCHUHMANN, JANKEL	34	M	LABR	RRZZZZ	USA
ABELMANN, RACHEL	19	F	SGL	RRAHVA	USA
TEINSTEIN, MOSES	15	M	LABR	RRZZZZ	USA
SCHULUM, BERTHA	20	F	SGL	RRZZZZ	USA
LASIHER, SCHEINE	26	F	W	RRZZZZ	USA
LIEBE	18	F	SGL	RRZZZZ	USA
MARIANNE	6	F	CHILD	RRZZZZ	USA
LEISER	4	M	CHILD	RRZZZZ	USA
SCHULMANN, FEIGE	38	F	W	RRZZZZ	USA
GENESCHE	8	F	CHILD	RRZZZZ	USA
NACHAME	6	F	CHILD	RRZZZZ	USA
ALTER	4	M	CHILD	RRZZZZ	USA
SAKS, SCHOLEM	18	M	LABR	RRZZZZ	USA
WILPON, RACHEL	20	F	SGL	RRAHTU	USA
KUBILIUS, ANTON	42	M	LABR	RRAHSW	USA
BADUNSKY, CHAIM	19	M	BRR	RRAGRT	USA
WEINBERG, ITZIG	35	M	LABR	RRAHTN	USA
LEA	20	F	W	RRAHTN	USA
LEWIN, GITTEL	19	F	SGL	RRAHOK	USA
MINDEL	17	F	SGL	RRAHOK	USA
KODALOWSKY, IVAN	23	M	LABR	RRAHZS	USA
SIMKIWITZ, CONSTANTIN	24	M	LABR	RRAHZS	USA
PAWLOWITZ, ANTON	25	M	LABR	RRAHZS	USA
LANG, MEYER	33	M	MCHT	RRZZZZ	USA
LAUPHEAR, S.E.	27	M	DLR	RRZZZZ	USA
KAZIN, USCHER	27	M	BRM	RRZZZZ	USA
ALLSCHWANG, MARCUS	18	M	LABR	RRZZZZ	USA
FEITZ, ISAAC	27	M	DLR	RRZZZZ	USA
JACOB, FEIG.	21	M	LABR	RRZZZZ	USA
SCHELLER, AUGUST	35	M	LABR	RRZZZZ	USA
NAGEL, CAROLINA	31	F	W	RRABPN	USA
EMILIE	.06	F	INFANT	RRABPN	USA
PRUSKY, ABRAHAM	18	M	LABR	RRZZZZ	USA
RUDNITZKI, WOLF	35	M	LABR	RRAHTN	USA
SKRIPZE, SAMUEL	25	M	LABR	RRZZZZ	USA
SEWERKOWSKI, SARA	18	F	W	RRZZZZ	USA
LEIB	.06	M	INFANT	RRZZZZ	USA

PASSENGER	AGE	SEX	OCCUPATION	PRV	VIL	DES
RIEB, FEIGE	20	F	W	RR	ZZZZ	USA
SCHAIE	.11	F	INFANT	RR	ZZZZ	USA
CIREL	.01	F	INFANT	RR	ZZZZ	USA
MEYEROWIECZ, BENJ.SEVEZ	17	M	LABR	RR	ZZZZ	USA
WEINBERG, SIMON	21	M	LABR	RR	ZZZZ	USA
MIEL, MENDE	30	M	LABR	RR	ZZZZ	USA
ULOGALKE, GERSON	40	M	FELMO	RR	ZZZZ	USA
OPPENHEIM, JOH.	30	M	DLR	RR	AHTF	USA
BLOCK, LEOPOLD	49	M	LABR	RR	AHZS	USA
SUSANNE	13	F	CH	RR	AHZS	USA
JOH.	9	M	CHILD	RR	AHZS	USA
KAPLAN, JOSEF	34	M	LABR	RR	AHTF	USA
KARTUM, JOSEF	28	M	BRR	RR	AHTF	USA
RUBENSTEIN, JANKEL	22	M	TLR	RR	AHTF	USA
RATH, DANIEL	43	M	FARMER	RR	ZZZZ	USA
MARG.	40	F	W	RR	ZZZZ	USA
CATH.	19	F	CH	RR	ZZZZ	USA
JACOB	14	M	CH	RR	ZZZZ	USA
CAROLINE	9	F	CHILD	RR	ZZZZ	USA
ELISABETH	8	F	CHILD	RR	ZZZZ	USA
GOTTLIEB	3	M	CHILD	RR	ZZZZ	USA
DANIEL	7	M	CHILD	RR	ZZZZ	USA
SCHENK, HEINR.	60	M	FARMER	RR	ZZZZ	USA
GLUCK, MARY	40	F	W	RR	ZZZZ	USA
JANKEL	9	M	CHILD	RR	ZZZZ	USA
FEIGE	8	F	CHILD	RR	ZZZZ	USA
MEIER	4	M	CHILD	RR	ZZZZ	USA
FRIGINSKY, SCHMUEL	19	M	MLR	RR	ZZZZ	USA
GARBER, JANKEL	30	M	LABR	RR	ZZZZ	USA
WEINTRAUB, JACOB	17	M	LABR	RR	AFWJ	USA
BRIARSKY, SCHEINE	50	F	W	RR	ZZZZ	USA
GOLDMANN, ESTER	22	F	SGL	RR	ZZZZ	USA
SKRIPZE, PESSE	40	F	W	RR	ZZZZ	USA
JACOB	9	M	CHILD	RR	ZZZZ	USA
SCHLOMOWITZ, JUDEL	26	M	BCHR	RR	ZZZZ	USA
KAPLAN, JANKEL	18	M	PNTR	RR	ZZZZ	USA
ROSENBERG, JACOB	32	M	TNM	RR	ZZZZ	USA
RIEB, NACHUM	26	M	DLR	RR	ZZZZ	USA
RUBINSTEIN, JACOB	16	M	DLR	RR	ZZZZ	USA
GLASS, DAVID	20	M	SHMK	RR	ZZZZ	USA
SCHUMSKI, GEDALIE	32	M	CGRMKR	RR	ZZZZ	USA
WEINSCHELBAUM, MICHEL	31	M	TNM	RR	ZZZZ	USA
SCHERMANN, ISAAC	27	M	DLR	RR	ZZZZ	USA
BURBAN, MEIER	26	M	BCHR	RR	AHUS	USA
MAZOR, JOSEPH	40	M	DLR	RR	ZZZZ	USA
PAPKSIN, MORDCHE	9	F	CHILD	RR	ZZZZ	USA
KUNE	8	F	CHILD	RR	ZZZZ	USA
LUKOWELSKY, FISCHEL-SEN	12	M	BY	RR	ZZZZ	USA
WEISLOWITZ, JOSEPH	22	M	LABR	RR	ZZZZ	USA
LACZENSKY, SCHLOME	28	M	LABR	RR	AFWJ	USA
LUPMANN, SCHAPSE	47	M	LABR	RR	ZZZZ	USA
ALTEMANN, ABR.L.	34	M	MCHT	RR	AHTF	USA
WOHLMANN, MARIANNA	19	F	SGL	RR	ZZZZ	USA
KRZYKWA, FRANZ	27	M	LABR	RR	AHZS	USA
SELWER, ARON	16	M	LABR	RR	ZZZZ	USA
FINKELBURG, RIWKE	23	F	W	RR	ZZZZ	USA
MORDCHE	.11	F	INFANT	RR	ZZZZ	USA
NESCHE, CHAIE	24	F	W	RR	AGRT	USA
ESTER	.11	F	INFANT	RR	AGRT	USA
RATOSKY, CHASE	22	F	SGL	RR	ZZZZ	USA
SCHEINE	19	F	SGL	RR	ZZZZ	USA
HACK, BEREL	40	M	JNR	RR	ZZZZ	USA
EX, FRUMET	48	M	LABR	RR	ZZZZ	USA
RAIGROTZKI, GOLDE	16	F	SGL	RR	AHRZ	USA
NATELSOHN, ISAAC	16	M	TLR	RR	ZZZZ	USA
GETZMANN, MARIE	21	F	SGL	RR	ZZZZ	USA
LEISER, RIWKE	24	F	W	RR	AHTW	USA
GERSON	5	M	CHILD	RR	AHTW	USA
HINDE	4	F	CHILD	RR	AHTW	USA
FRUMET	.11	M	INFANT	RR	AHTW	USA
ARONOWITZ, LEA	20	F	SGL	RR	AHTF	USA
GOTTSTEIN, ISAAC	16	M	LABR	RR	ZZZZ	USA
BOSICKI, PINKUS	25	M	LABR	RR	ZZZZ	USA
GERSON, CHANNE	24	F	SGL	RR	ZZZZ	USA
HARSON, BESSIE	9	F	CHILD	RR	ZZZZ	USA
SCHMIDT, MARG.	51	F	W	RR	ZZZZ	USA
NICOLAUS	8	M	CHILD	RR	ZZZZ	USA
BEJFOWITZ, CHAJE	56	F	W	RR	ZZZZ	USA
GOLDSCHMIDT, CHAIE	20	F	SGL	RR	AHTF	USA
OLITZKI, RAHEL	48	F	W	RR	ZZZZ	USA
ROSENBERG, DAVID	34	M	LABR	RR	ZZZZ	USA
LIEBE	34	F	W	RR	ZZZZ	USA
TAUBE	6	F	CHILD	RR	ZZZZ	USA
JOSEPH	5	M	CHILD	RR	ZZZZ	USA
LEPPERL	.11	M	INFANT	RR	ZZZZ	USA
BENECKE, JOHANN	26	M	PNTR	RR	ZZZZ	USA
OPPENHEIM, BERUCH	55	M	LABR	RR	ZZZZ	USA
HOFFMANN, HUBERT	16	M	LABR	RR	ZZZZ	USA
BARSCH, AUGUST	28	M	BRR	RR	ZZZZ	USA
ANTONIN	24	F	W	RR	ZZZZ	USA
MAX	2	M	CHILD	RR	ZZZZ	USA
WALTER, GUSTAV	21	M	LABR	RR	ZZZZ	USA
EMILIE	27	F	W	RR	ZZZZ	USA
MATZEL, FRIEDR.	29	M	LABR	RR	ZZZZ	USA
OTTILIE	22	F	W	RR	ZZZZ	USA
ERNST	.03	M	INFANT	RR	ZZZZ	USA
CRASMUS, GUSTAV	31	M	LABR	RR	ACTC	USA
ROSINA	23	F	W	RR	ACTC	USA
ADOLPH	4	M	CHILD	RR	ACTC	USA
WILH.	3	M	CHILD	RR	ACTC	USA
MARIE	.11	F	INFANT	RR	ACTC	USA
PRONOWSKI, FRANZ	20	M	LABR	RR	ZZZZ	USA
OPPENHEIM, BARUCH	55	M	LABR	RR	ZZZZ	USA
HOFFMANN, HUBERT	16	M	LABR	RR	ZZZZ	USA
BARSCH, AUGUST	28	M	BRR	RR	ZZZZ	USA
ANTONIN	24	F	W	RR	ZZZZ	USA
MAX	2	M	CHILD	RR	ZZZZ	USA
WALTER, GUSTAV	21	M	LABR	RR	ZZZZ	USA
EMILIE	27	F	W	RR	ZZZZ	USA
MATZEL, FRIEDR.	29	M	LABR	RR	ZZZZ	USA
OTTILIE	22	F	W	RR	ZZZZ	USA
ERNST	.03	M	INFANT	RR	ZZZZ	USA
CRASMUS, GUSTAV	31	M	LABR	RR	ACTC	USA
ROSINA	28	F	W	RR	ACTC	USA
ADOLPH	4	M	CHILD	RR	ACTC	USA
WILH.	3	M	CHILD	RR	ACTC	USA
MARIE	.11	F	INFANT	RR	ACTC	USA
PRONOWSKI, FRANZ	20	M	LABR	RR	ZZZZ	USA
RADOLA, STEFAN	25	M	CTW	RR	ACTQ	USA
BLAGEJEZIK, JOH.	26	M	DLR	RR	ZZZZ	USA
FURGENSEN, MAGD.	18	F	SGL	RR	AHZS	USA
FRITZ	48	M	LABR	RR	AHZS	USA
MARIE	44	F	W	RR	AHZS	USA
JOH.	9	M	CHILD	RR	AHZS	USA
PEILLY, JACOB	55	M	LABR	RR	AHZS	USA
ANNA	58	F	W	RR	AHZS	USA
PORPEL, EISIG	20	F	TLR	RR	AHTF	USA
GLASMANN, SAM.	17	F	WCHMKR	RR	AHOK	USA
ROBINSKY, SCHIE	22	F	LABR	RR	ZZZZ	USA
PELONOW, ESTER	18	F	SGL	RR	AGRT	USA
RICKEL, RESSIE	26	F	W	RR	AHTF	USA
SCHEEL	2	M	CHILD	RR	AHTF	USA
HIRSCH	.06	M	INFANT	RR	AHTF	USA
WERBOLOWSKY, CHAIE	30	F	W	RR	AHSW	USA
HANNE	8	F	CHILD	RR	AHSW	USA
RIWKE	6	F	CHILD	RR	AHSW	USA
MINE	3	F	CHILD	RR	AHSW	USA
SAWERKORWSKI, KOPPEL	40	M	LABR	RR	AHZS	USA
SCHEINE	17	F	CH	RR	AHZS	USA
S.	9	F	CHILD	RR	AHZS	USA
NASCHANOWITZ, GERSCHEL	9	M	CHILD	RR	AHZS	USA
GARBOWSKY, RACHEL	23	F	SGL	RR	AHZS	USA
GITTEL, TAUBE	30	F	W	RR	AHTF	USA
ABRAHAM	.11	M	INFANT	RR	AHTF	USA
BERETZ, MAROJE	22	M	LABR	RR	ZZZZ	USA
ENGELSKY, ANNA	25	F	W	RR	ZZZZ	USA
ANNA	5	F	CHILD	RR	ZZZZ	USA
KASCHE	2	F	CHILD	RR	ZZZZ	USA
CHAINOWSKY, FREIDE	15	F	SGL	RR	AHZS	USA
SILVERMANN, SARA	19	F	SGL	RR	ZZZZ	USA

PASSENGER	AGE	SEX	OCCUPATION	PRIV	DES
KOHEN, SALOMON	30	M	LABR	RRAHZS	USA
BLAUSTEIN, MEYER	14	M	LABR	RRZZZZ	USA
HEYMANN, DAVID	20	M	DLR	RRZZZZ	USA
ZLOSOW, LEIB	35	M	LABR	RRAHTO	USA
MENDEL	25	M	CH	RRAHTO	USA
HIRSCH	12	M	CH	RRAHTO	USA
BARGETEIN, NESCHE	40	M	W	RRAHZS	USA
MICHEL	9	M	CHILD	RRAHZS	USA
JONAS	8	M	CHILD	RRAHZS	USA
ISAAC	7	M	CHILD	RRAHZS	USA
GOLDSTEIN, ESTER	45	F	W	RRZZZZ	USA
ROSA	15	F	D	RRZZZZ	USA
ROSENSTEIN, JACOB	40	M	LABR	RRZZZZ	USA
OSCHINSKY, SAUNY	18	F	SGL	RRAHZS	USA
SCHMIDT, CHAIE	25	F	W	RRAHZS	USA
MOSES	.11	M	INFANT	RRAHZS	USA
BIRGER, CHAIE	16	F	SGL	RRAHZS	USA
PESKALISKY, ROSA	18	F	SGL	RRAHOK	USA
SALOMON, MORITZ	45	M	LABR	RRAHUI	USA
ISAACSOHN, LEWIN	45	M	DLR	RRZZZZ	USA
NANKIN, HIRSCH	20	M	BCHR	RRZZZZ	USA
RADITZKY, ISRAEL	23	M	LABR	RRAFVG	USA
MARG.	20	F	SGL	RRAFVG	USA
JOSEF	21	M	LABR	RRAFVG	USA
REISEL	21	F	SGL	RRAFVG	USA
PREIS, LEISER	16	M	LABR	RRZZZZ	USA
RUSCHE	17	F	SGL	RRZZZZ	USA
ENIGSOHN, SCHERMER	17	M	LABR	RRZZZZ	USA
KRAWANSKY, ABR.	22	M	LABR	RRZZZZ	USA
MUHELOWSKY, LEISER	18	M	LABR	RRZZZZ	USA
SPERLING, PERETZ	20	M	LABR	RRZZZZ	USA
LEWINSKY, SIMON	20	M	LABR	RRAHZS	USA
ASCHINSKY, JOSEF	24	M	LABR	RRAHZS	USA
SARA	24	F	W	RRAHZS	USA
LEWIE	.11	F	INFANT	RRAHZS	USA
ALEXANDER, HANNE	17	F	SGL	RRAHSW	USA
BAROWSKY, MOSES	35	M	LABR	RRAHSW	USA
KRAMEL, SCHOLEM	35	M	LABR	RRAHSW	USA
JUDE	35	F	W	RRAHSW	USA
SAMUEL	17	M	CH	RRAHSW	USA
CHANNE	14	F	CH	RRAHSW	USA
ITZIG	8	M	CHILD	RRAHSW	USA
SCHIFFRE	7	F	CHILD	RRAHSW	USA
GERSOHN, CH.	.06	M	INFANT	RRZZZZ	USA

SHIP: ENGLAND

FROM: LIVERPOOL
TO: NEW YORK
ARRIVED: 24 JUNE 1885

PASSENGER	AGE	SEX	OCCUPATION	PRIV	DES
LEVISON, D.	20	M	UNKNOWN	RRADBQ	NY
ASBERG, AUG.	29	M	LABR	RRAHQH	CAL
KELKONAFSA, ISAK	35	M	LABR	RRAHQH	NY
DALBERG, W.	22	M	LABR	RRAHQH	CAL
BASSOJA, MATTE	21	M	LABR	RRAHQH	NY
WESTERLING, ANDERS	23	M	LABR	RRAHQH	NY
GUTMAN, H.	19	F	SP	PLZZZZ	NY
BLOSTEIN, MOSES	22	M	TNSTH	PLADAX	NY

SHIP: WERRA

FROM: BREMEN
TO: NEW YORK
ARRIVED: 24 JUNE 1885

PASSENGER	AGE	SEX	OCCUPATION	PRIV	DES
KOHN, RODEL	38	M	LABR	RRZZZZ	NY
LOUIS, MARTIL	25	M	LABR	RRZZZZ	NY
KAUFMANN, MARIE	20	F	UNKNOWN	RRZZZZ	NY
CHAJETINSKY, MOSES	17	M	LABR	RRZZZZ	NY
TUCHMACHER, LIEBE	23	F	UNKNOWN	RRZZZZ	NY
BEILE	3	F	CHILD	RRZZZZ	NY
HEIMANN, ABE	23	M	LABR	RRZZZZ	NY
BEILE	22	F	UNKNOWN	RRZZZZ	NY
SELDE	.03	F	INFANT	RRZZZZ	NY
RODOWITZ, HELENE	36	F	UNKNOWN	RRZZZZ	NY
HANNE	7	F	CHILD	RRZZZZ	NY
RIFKA	6	F	CHILD	RRZZZZ	NY
ALTE	5	F	CHILD	RRZZZZ	NY
ESTER	2	F	CHILD	RRZZZZ	NY
KLUG, THERESE	40	F	UNKNOWN	RRZZZZ	NY
FREIBERGER, NECHE	26	M	LABR	RRZZZZ	PHI
ISAAC	6	M	CHILD	RRZZZZ	PHI
SURECH	20	F	UNKNOWN	RRZZZZ	PHI
DEIBE	.11	F	INFANT	RRZZZZ	PHI
TARULONIS, ANTONIE	20	F	UNKNOWN	RRZZZZ	NY
SCHULKIN, SCHEINE	18	F	UNKNOWN	RRZZZZ	NY
STECHER, RICKE	18	F	UNKNOWN	RRZZZZ	NY
KARPILOW, LEISER	16	M	LABR	RRZZZZ	NY
ROTHMANN, DIETHMANN	40	M	LABR	RRZZZZ	NY
ENGEL, BARBARA	56	F	UNKNOWN	RRZZZZ	NY
JOSEF	27	M	FARMER	RRZZZZ	NY
THEODOR	14	M	LABR	RRZZZZ	NY
GALUMBICK, FRADE	33	F	UNKNOWN	RRZZZZ	NY
HEIKE	7	F	CHILD	RRZZZZ	NY
BURG	6	M	CHILD	RRZZZZ	NY
RAHE	3	F	CHILD	RRZZZZ	NY
FLACKS, MENNCHA	18	F	CH	RRZZZZ	NY
WOHLE, WITTE	16	F	CH	RRZZZZ	NY
KURAN, ITTE	7	F	CHILD	RRZZZZ	NY
GALUMBICK, BAER	26	M	LABR	RRZZZZ	NY
FUENFER, LEYER	35	M	LABR	RRZZZZ	NY

SHIP: STATE OF GEORGIA

FROM: GLASGOW AND LARNE
TO: NEW YORK
ARRIVED: 25 JUNE 1885

PASSENGER	AGE	SEX	OCCUPATION	PRIV	DES
GOLDBLATT, SHEINE	39	F	W	RRZZZZ	USA
RACHE	9	F	CHILD	RRZZZZ	USA
LEWINE	1	M	CHILD	RRZZZZ	USA
LICKER, BRACK	30	M	SHMK	RRZZZZ	USA
SHEINE	24	F	W	RRZZZZ	USA
SARAH	1	F	CHILD	RRZZZZ	USA
NOCHUN, LEISER	49	M	LABR	RRZZZZ	USA
RACHIE	28	F	W	RRZZZZ	USA
BERTHA	6	F	CHILD	RRZZZZ	USA
LINA	1	F	CHILD	RRZZZZ	USA
SINGER, CHENNE	33	F	W	RRZZZZ	USA
BEILE	6	F	CHILD	RRZZZZ	USA
CHANNE	3	F	CHILD	RRZZZZ	USA
JANKEL	2	M	CHILD	RRZZZZ	USA
LEISER	.10	M	INFANT	RRZZZZ	USA
KHAN, CHATZKEL	37	M	MCHT	RRZZZZ	USA
BRANDE, MEYER	7	M	CHILD	RRZZZZ	USA
HIRCHFILD, DAVID	58	M	DR	RRZZZZ	USA
EMMA	52	F	W	RRZZZZ	USA
HENRY	23	F	W	RRZZZZ	USA

PASSENGER	AGE	SEX	OCCUPATION	PRV VIL DES
HINDE	16	F	SVNT	RRZZZZUSA
ROCHEC	00	F	CH	RRZZZZUSA
BLANSTEIN, CHAEVS	28	F	W	RRZZZZUSA
MALK	7	F	CHILD	RRZZZZUSA
CHANNE	2	F	CHILD	RRZZZZUSA
EGOLNIZER, SAMUEL	23	M	JNR	RRZZZZUSA
CHAEVE	20	F	W	RRZZZZUSA
HORONETZKY, JOSEPH	49	M	LABR	PLZZZZUSA
CHRISTINA	35	F	W	PLZZZZUSA
ROMAL	2	M	CHILD	PLZZZZUSA
MATINESCH	.04	F	INFANT	PLZZZZUSA
SCHEFFLER, NILINS	50	M	LABR	PLZZZZUSA
CAROLINE	41	F	W	PLZZZZUSA
SKINKATIS, MARAINE	20	F	SVNT	PLZZZZUSA
GRAUSTIN, GENESCHO	26	F	W	PLZZZZUSA
REBECCA	17	F	SVNT	PLZZZZUSA
ROCHEL, HELINA	17	F	SVNT	RRZZZZUSA
MANSKI, SARAH	44	F	SVNT	RRZZZZUSA
JACHMER, RACHEL	20	F	SVNT	RRZZZZUSA
CHIE, DAVID	25	M	MLR	RRZZZZUSA
BEER, MARCUS	18	M	LABR	RRZZZZUSA
AEPPELMAN, LEIB	31	M	LABR	RRZZZZUSA
NACHUMSON, EISI	40	M	LABR	RRZZZZUSA
PINKUS	10	M	CH	RRZZZZUSA
PEPORT, MEYER	34	M	LABR	RRZZZZUSA
LICKER, RAPHAEL	28	M	PDLR	RRZZZZUSA
WASSERMANN, ARON	29	M	LABR	RRZZZZUSA
SOSCHUHMACHER, ISAAK	29	M	LABR	RRZZZZUSA
PODOSCH, SCHOLEM	26	M	TLR	RRZZZZUSA
SOBOROWSKY, MOSES	21	M	LABR	RRZZZZUSA
SELKOWIZ, HIRSCH	27	M	LABR	RRZZZZUSA
KOHE, BERSCH	18	M	LABR	RRZZZZUSA
KLAS, MOSES	19	M	LABR	RRZZZZUSA
BRANDT, TOBIAS	21	M	LABR	RRZZZZUSA
ZIMMENT, CHATZKEL	17	M	CL	RRZZZZUSA
ANNENBERG, MEYER	18	M	LABR	RRZZZZUSA
MALCHE	20	F	W	RRZZZZUSA
OSKOWSKY, ARON	29	M	LABR	RRZZZZUSA
SCHKALMIK, HIRSCH	37	M	LABR	RRZZZZUSA
LEWIN, PHILIP	19	M	JNR	RRZZZZUSA
TABERGANSKY, WILH	22	M	TCHR	RRZZZZUSA
GRANSTEIN, MOSES	50	M	JNR	RRZZZZUSA
RADVID, JOSEF	26	M	LABR	PLZZZZUSA
MISCBIE, STANISLAUS	28	M	LABR	PLZZZZUSA
ZICK, VICTOR	25	M	LABR	PLZZZZUSA
MARSCHANY, JAHON	45	M	DSTLR	PLZZZZUSA
WIMMET, CARL	45	M	LABR	PLZZZZUSA
WYSOTSKY, SEGMUND	20	M	LABR	PLZZZZUSA
SKOWKATIS, MARTIN	30	M	LABR	PLZZZZUSA
DAVCETIS, JOSEF	32	M	LABR	PLZZZZUSA
ISOLATIS, JURGIS	23	M	LABR	PLZZZZUSA
VOGT, JULIUS	28	M	LABR	PLZZZZUSA
SAHI, MICHAELL	32	M	LABR	PLZZZZUSA
SLUJIK, JOHANN	00	M	LABR	PLZZZZUSA
HADSCHWRECK, JOH.	25	M	LABR	PLZZZZUSA
MELIKAN, JOH.	30	M	LABR	PLZZZZUSA
DAKUT, MAZE	37	M	LABR	PLZZZZUSA
KARALNING, ZISHI	22	M	LABR	PLZZZZUSA
ZEMAVZUCK, JACOB	25	M	LABR	PLZZZZUSA
JERKA, GURA	25	M	LABR	PLZZZZUSA
GRESZKI, ANDREAS	50	M	LABR	PLZZZZUSA
MARKAMA, JAKENS	22	M	LABR	PLZZZZUSA
SCHUDI, JOSEF	32	M	LABR	PLZZZZUSA
JOSEF	20	M	LABR	PLZZZZUSA
PAUL	18	M	LABR	PLZZZZUSA
KUKLIS, OSIJ	25	M	LABR	PLZZZZUSA
LAPATA, ANTON	27	M	LABR	PLZZZZUSA
JANSOWSKY, ABR.	60	M	LABR	PLZZZZUSA
KARMOLNIECKY, LEONH	31	M	BCHR	PLZZZZUSA

SHIP: WAESLAND

FROM: ANTWERP
TO: NEW YORK
ARRIVED: 25 JUNE 1885

PASSENGER	AGE	SEX	OCCUPATION	PRV VIL DES
WITKOWSKI, EMLE.	28	F	SVNT	PLZZZZCH
THEO	3	M	CHILD	PLZZZZCH
IDA	2	F	CHILD	PLZZZZCH
EMIL	00	M	INF	PLZZZZCH
CHRISTOPH, WILHME.	52	M	LABR	PLZZZZCH
EMMA	9	F	CHILD	PLZZZZCH
FOLESKI, PEL.	26	M	LABR	PLZZZZNY
LORENZI, C.	43	F	SVNT	PLZZZZUNK
C.	43	F	SVNT	PLZZZZUNK
FOLLOWSKY, C.	25	M	SDLR	PLZZZZSFC

SHIP: CITY OF ROME

FROM: LIVERPOOL
TO: NEW YORK
ARRIVED: 26 JUNE 1885

PASSENGER	AGE	SEX	OCCUPATION	PRV VIL DES
FREEMAN, SIMON	26	M	LABR	RRZZZZUSA
LIST, ITZAG	50	M	LABR	RRZZZZUSA
SICHER, SCHOLEM	28	M	LABR	RRZZZZUSA
GOLDSTEIN, MEYER-LEIB	14	M	LABR	RRZZZZUSA
EDER, LUD.	37	M	LABR	RRZZZZUSA
PACJE	20	M	LABR	RRZZZZUSA
CHAGE	17	M	LABR	RRZZZZUSA
LEVY, BARNETT	37	M	LABR	RRZZZZUSA
PARTUSE, LIESER	18	M	LABR	RRZZZZUSA
PERCHNAM, LK.	34	M	LABR	RRZZZZUSA
JUCKER, SIMON	44	M	LABR	RRZZZZUSA
ROCHEL	43	F	W	RRZZZZUSA
SCHEINE	11	M	CH	RRZZZZUSA
SCHOLEM	10	M	CH	RRZZZZUSA
JOSSEL	9	M	CHILD	RRZZZZUSA
BARUCH	7	M	CHILD	RRZZZZUSA
SANDAMUNSKY, PERTCHES	20	M	LABR	RRZZZZUSA
HEWGBERG, JULIUS	28	M	LABR	RRZZZZUSA
WOLFSOHEN, U.B.W.	35	M	LABR	RRZZZZUSA
LOUIS	9	M	CHILD	RRZZZZUSA
ROSENBERG, ABRAM	50	M	LABR	RRZZZZUSA
MOSES	11	M	CH	RRZZZZUSA
KAWITZ, EMANUEL	18	M	LABR	RRAGRTUSA
KUGUVIC, NORDCHE	19	M	LABR	RRAGRTUSA

SHIP: HAMMONIA

FROM: HAMBURG AND HAVRE
TO: NEW YORK
ARRIVED: 27 JUNE 1885

PASSENGER	AGE	SEX	OCCUPATION	PRV VIL DES
TARNOPOLSKY, SCHMESEL	29	M	DYR	RRZZZZUSA
MARCUS	20	M	LABR	RRZZZZUSA
ULLBERT, SCHEBSAY	27	M	TLR	RRZZZZUSA
STRAUSS, ANNA	78	F	W	RRZZZZUSA
NITSCH, AUGE.	42	F	W	RRZZZZUSA
WILH.	8	F	CHILD	RRZZZZUSA
ELISE	4	F	CHILD	RRZZZZUSA
GRUENFELD, DWORE	19	F	SGL	RRZZZZUSA
SCHAPIRO, WULL	24	M	LABR	RRZZZZUSA
SARA	30	F	W	RRZZZZUSA

PASSENGER	AGE	SEX	OCCUPATION	PRV VIL DES
MINE	4	F	CHILD	RRZZZZUSA
SELMANNS, CHAJE	19	F	SGL	RRZZZZUSA
KATZ, CHAJE	56	F	W	RRZZZZUSA
MOSES	23	M	SHMK	RRZZZZUSA
RIWKE	21	F	W	RRZZZZUSA
CHASKEL	.09	F	INFANT	RRZZZZUSA
KWIASKOWKY, TEOFILA	25	M	LABR	RRZZZZUSA
GORDON, SCHIMER	17	M	BKBNDR	RRZZZZUSA
ROMANFISKY, RUBEN	15	M	LABR	RRZZZZUSA
HENSCHEL, CHASZE	18	F	SGL	RRZZZZUSA
FINGERZWEIZ, MOSES	9	M	CHILD	RRZZZZUSA
BARTNOY, MENIZC	20	M	TLR	RRZZZZUSA
DELLER, ELISE	25	M	JNR	RRZZZZUSA
ACHERMANN, CHAIM	18	M	TLR	RRZZZZUSA
KOCHSUCH, JACOB	19	M	JWLR	RRZZZZUSA
POTTENBRINIK, LEA	36	F	W	RRZZZZUSA
POTTABRINIK, DAVID	6	M	CHILD	RRZZZZUSA
BRUK, JOSEFA	20	F	SGL	RRZZZZUSA
KRAHINNICH, JOH.	20	M	LABR	RRZZZZUSA
KUNCITS, MARIE	19	F	SGL	RRZZZZUSA
PERLMANN, HASON	17	M	TLR	RRZZZZUSA
MARKOWITZ, JENNY	19	F	SGL	RRZZZZUSA
KASCHMEREWITZ, LEIB	18	M	FELMO	RRZZZZUSA
WALDSTEIN, MARCUS	34	M	DLR	RRZZZZUSA
SLOTHIN, SARA	22	F	W	RRZZZZUSA
ILOTE	.11	M	INFANT	RRZZZZUSA
KATZ, ISAAC	57	M	TLR	RRZZZZUSA
CHEIE	51	F	W	RRZZZZUSA
COHEN, ABRAHAM	21	M	PRNTR	RRZZZZUSA
LINKIEWICZ, HELENE	25	F	W	RRZZZZUSA
ANTONIE	.11	F	INFANT	RRZZZZUSA
MALINA, LOUIS	28	M	FARMER	RRZZZZUSA
GORDON, BUNE	30	F	W	RRZZZZUSA
MALKE	8	F	CHILD	RRZZZZUSA
SCHONEMANN, ISRAEL	22	M	LABR	RRZZZZUSA
SCHEINKER, MAL.	18	F	SGL	RRZZZZUSA
HOEHCHE, WILH.	27	M	LABR	RRZZZZUSA
AUGUSTE	22	F	W	RRZZZZUSA
MALLINA, MARI	22	F	W	RRZZZZUSA
GOLOZEWSKI, STANISL.	23	M	LABR	RRZZZZUSA
WARTELSKY, MARCUS	22	M	LABR	RRZZZZUSA
RESNIHOWITZ, HIRSCH	23	M	DLR	RRZZZZUSA
FREIDE	20	F	W	RRZZZZUSA
ABRAHAMS, M.	17	M	LABR	RRZZZZUSA
GRANET, SILHE	40	F	W	RRZZZZUSA
GITTA	18	F	CH	RRZZZZUSA
FEIN, ICHE	20	M	LABR	RRZZZZUSA
WARSCHAWSKY, MANNEL	19	M	LABR	RRZZZZUSA
CUTIN, MINDEL	20	F	W	RRZZZZUSA
CHATZKEL	6	M	CHILD	RRZZZZUSA
ZECHMANN, ESTER	21	F	SGL	RRZZZZUSA
GIDNISKY, HIRSCH	20	M	FARMER	RRZZZZUSA
BERNSTEIN, CHAIE	18	F	SGL	RRZZZZUSA
GRANET, SARAH	5	F	CHILD	RRZZZZUSA
JOSEFEITIS, AMALIE	24	F	SGL	RRZZZZUSA
EPHSTEIN, ALBRT.	32	M	LABR	RRZZZZUSA
KONITZ, ANDR.	24	M	LABR	RRZZZZUSA
MIROSLAWSKI, SCHOLEM	9	M	CHILD	RRZZZZUSA
HERZMANN, MARTIN	45	M	LABR	RRZZZZUSA
CAROLINE	36	F	W	RRZZZZUSA
MARIE	9	F	CHILD	RRZZZZUSA
ELISABETH	8	F	CHILD	RRZZZZUSA
CARL	4	M	CHILD	RRZZZZUSA
JOHN	2	M	CHILD	RRZZZZUSA
KWATIR, LORENZ	70	M	LABR	RRZZZZUSA
ELISABETH	68	F	W	RRZZZZUSA
HEINR.	24	M	UNKNOWN	RRZZZZUSA
FRIEDSICHS, MICHAEL	42	M	FARMER	RRZZZZUSA
BARBR.	48	F	W	RRZZZZUSA
MARIE	18	F	CH	RRZZZZUSA
HUEBNER, ANDR.	66	M	FARMER	RRZZZZUSA
EMILIE	18	F	W	RRZZZZUSA
JOH.	.06	M	INFANT	RRZZZZUSA
GOTTLIEBER, MARTA	21	F	SGL	RRZZZZUSA
BUCHHOLZ, EPHRAIM	42	M	FARMER	RRZZZZUSA
MARGTHA.	36	F	W	RRZZZZUSA
CATHR.	13	F	CH	RRZZZZUSA
DOROTHEA	9	F	CHILD	RRZZZZUSA
EMANUEL	2	M	CHILD	RRZZZZUSA
CARL	.09	M	INFANT	RRZZZZUSA
MATHIES, JOH.	23	M	FARMER	RRZZZZUSA
CATHR.	22	F	W	RRZZZZUSA
GRUEN, PETER	36	M	FARMER	RRZZZZUSA
DOROTHEA	32	F	W	RRZZZZUSA
JOH.	9	M	CHILD	RRZZZZUSA
DOROTHEA	8	F	CHILD	RRZZZZUSA
EMILIE	.11	F	INFANT	RRZZZZUSA
BERNSTEIN, MENDEL	20	M	LABR	RRZZZZUSA
ABRAHAM	16	M	CH	RRZZZZUSA
FISCHE	9	M	CHILD	RRZZZZUSA
ADAMAJTIS, JOSEF	24	M	LABR	RRZZZZUSA
PUKALKO, FRANZ	21	M	LABR	RRZZZZUSA
COHN, ALTER	19	M	LABR	RRZZZZUSA
JANHLEWITZ, FISCHEL	34	M	LABR	RRZZZZUSA
SCHLEMOWITZ, BER.	20	M	LABR	RRZZZZUSA
BIRNAM, CHAIM	31	M	LABR	RRZZZZUSA
GLOZMANN, SCHOLEM	34	M	LABR	RRZZZZUSA
KRISTAL, ABRAHAM	20	M	LABR	RRZZZZUSA
LAPIDUS, ABE.	20	M	LABR	RRZZZZUSA
FEINSINGER, DAVID	20	M	LABR	RRZZZZUSA

SHIP: CITY OF BERLIN

FROM: LIVERPOOL AND QUEENSTOWN
TO: NEW YORK
ARRIVED: 29 JUNE 1885

PASSENGER	AGE	SEX	OCCUPATION	PRV VIL DES
HINDERSON, HANA-A.	21	F	W	RRAEWSMI
ANNA	00	F	INF	RRAEWSMI
WALLSDOTTER, LISA	23	F	SP	RRAEWSNY
ABRAMSON, ELZA	18	M	LABR	RRAEWSNE
KERSTULA, JOHAN-F.	12	M	CH	RRAEWSNY
TIEKER, ERICK	50	M	LABR	RRAEWSNY
ETSTRAND, FRANS-W.	20	M	LABR	RRAEWSNY
RATRAND, RICHARD	16	M	LABR	RRAEWSNY
NECAIAJOWSKI, LUDWIG	23	M	LABR	RRACBFNO
RAMTHAL, SOLOMON	22	M	LABR	RRACBFOH
FREIDKIN, ISAK	18	M	LABR	RRACBFIN
SCHAFE, LEIB	11	M	CH	RRACBFIN
TABAS, NEV---L--	20	M	CH	RRACBFIN
RALLYNMIDIS, AUBAI	20	M	CH	RRACBFIN
JUTESWO----, AUSTIN	58	M	CH	RRACBFIN
ITZIG	27	M	CH	RRACBFIN
MERFLEREZKY, JACOB	23	M	CH	RRACBFIN
ZOMALA, JACOB	34	M	LABR	FNZZZZNE
MARIA	34	F	W	FNZZZZNE
TUKULA, ANDRES	20	M	LABR	FNZZZZNY
IRA, HORNA	26	M	LABR	FNZZZZNY
KOLFRAM----, ANNA	17	F	SP	FNZZZZNY
LIPERUCKTA, JOSEF	19	M	LABR	FNZZZZNY
JATTENSSA, KAJSA	30	M	LABR	FNZZZZNY
KERTUSA, JANS-F.	18	M	LABR	FNZZZZNY
JOSIERNITZKI, JESCHES	20	M	LABR	FNACBFNY
SEGABROSKI, CHONE	26	M	LABR	FNACBFNY
SZYDKODSKI, JAN	20	M	LABR	FNACBFNY
RADENSKY, SAUL	38	M	LABR	FNACBFNY
JASCHRISCH, SCHMUL	18	M	LABR	FNACBFNY
SCHMULORITZ, JOSEL	29	M	LABR	FNACBFNY

PASSENGER	AGE	SEX	OCCUPATION	PRI V	VIL	DES
SHIP: ELBE						
FROM: BREMEN						
TO: NEW YORK						
ARRIVED: 29 JUNE 1885						
GOLDENBERG, SARAH	11	F	CH	RR	ZZZZ	USA
RIFKE	14	F	CH	RR	ZZZZ	USA
JACOB	9	M	CHILD	RR	ZZZZ	USA
KUPCINSKY, JOSEF	23	M	LABR	RR	ZZZZ	USA
VISCHENSOHN, BERTHA	22	M	NN	RR	ZZZZ	USA
STUETZKI, HIRSCH	21	M	LABR	RR	ZZZZ	USA
GILES, INDA	70	F	NN	RR	ZZZZ	USA
LEO	30	M	LABR	RR	ZZZZ	USA
ETTE	10	F	CH	RR	ZZZZ	USA
LERCHE	8	F	CHILD	RR	ZZZZ	USA
CHAJE	6	F	CHILD	RR	ZZZZ	USA
ROCHE	2	F	CHILD	RR	ZZZZ	USA
ROSE	.09	F	INFANT	RR	ZZZZ	USA
TUCHMANN, LIEBE	23	F	NN	RR	ZZZZ	USA
BEILE	3	F	CHILD	RR	ZZZZ	USA
GEBRENBLATT, SCHIMMEL	18	M	MCHT	RR	ZZZZ	USA
SOHA, ALBERT	30	M	LABR	RR	ZZZZ	USA
BARMANOWITZ, SAL.	18	M	LABR	RR	ZZZZ	USA
ZALLEL	19	M	LABR	RR	ZZZZ	USA
WARKENTIN, HEINR.	38	M	FARMER	RR	ZZZZ	USA
MARGA.	37	F	W	RR	ZZZZ	USA
HEINR.	11	M	CH	RR	ZZZZ	USA
JACOB	9	M	CHILD	RR	ZZZZ	USA
ANNA	6	M	CHILD	RR	ZZZZ	USA
HELENE	4	M	CHILD	RR	ZZZZ	USA
WIRKSEN, JOHANN	47	M	FARMER	RR	ZZZZ	USA
AGATHE	49	F	W	RR	ZZZZ	USA
HEINR.	26	M	FARMER	RR	ZZZZ	USA
JOHANN	15	M	FARMER	RR	ZZZZ	USA
AGATHE	25	F	NN	RR	ZZZZ	USA
KATHERINE	21	F	NN	RR	ZZZZ	USA
JUSTINE	18	F	NN	RR	ZZZZ	USA
EVA	11	F	CH	RR	ZZZZ	USA
PREPOZ, LEIB	18	M	MCHT	RR	ZZZZ	USA
GRATZ, WILHELM	11	M	CH	RR	ZZZZ	USA
ROSE	29	F	CH	RR	ZZZZ	USA
LEIFER, LAZAR	45	M	LABR	RR	ZZZZ	USA
SAKOL, SARA	45	F	NN	RR	ZZZZ	USA
MOSES	11	M	CH	RR	ZZZZ	USA
THIESEN, ARON	44	M	LABR	RR	ZZZZ	USA
ANNA	34	F	W	RR	ZZZZ	USA
ANNA	12	F	CH	RR	ZZZZ	USA
MARIE	11	F	CH	RR	ZZZZ	USA
CATHARINA	7	F	CHILD	RR	ZZZZ	USA
HEINRICH	5	M	CHILD	RR	ZZZZ	USA
ARON	2	M	CHILD	RR	ZZZZ	USA
SUSANE	.04	F	INFANT	RR	ZZZZ	USA
AGNETHA	.04	F	INFANT	RR	ZZZZ	USA
SHIP: ETRURIA						
FROM: LIVERPOOL AND QUEENSTOWN						
TO: NEW YORK						
ARRIVED: 29 JUNE 1885						
ALLILOMUNA, JOHAN	30	M	LABR	RR	AEWS	USA
NICMOLOLA, A.K.	40	M	LABR	RR	AEWS	USA
PUMICOLA, JOHAN	21	M	LABR	RR	AEWS	USA
LAMELA, F.J	22	M	LABR	RR	AEWS	USA
SEWANIER, MATTS	00	M	LABR	RR	AEWS	USA
KASMICZ, ANDERS	20	M	LABR	RR	AEWS	USA
SIOLA, ABRAM	24	M	LABR	RR	AEWS	USA
HENDENS, MARIA-S.	58	F	LABR	RR	AEWS	USA
ELLEN	17	F	SP	RR	AEWS	USA
JUFOLA, GRETA	20	F	SP	RR	AEWS	USA
LINBUL, MATT	60	M	CPTR	RR	AEWS	USA
LISA	57	F	W	RR	AEWS	USA
RALLI	11	M	CH	RR	AEWS	USA
FORSTER, MARIE	32	F	MSN	RR	AEWS	USA
HILDA	11	F	CH	RR	AEWS	USA
SACARIAS	10	M	CH	RR	AEWS	USA
HILDA	5	F	CHILD	RR	AEWS	USA
JENNY	4	F	CHILD	RR	AEWS	USA
HELMA	2	F	CHILD	RR	AEWS	USA
SILANSSVA, JOHAN	28	M	FARMER	RR	AEWS	USA
MARIE	26	F	W	RR	AEWS	USA
JOHAN	8	M	CHILD	RR	AEWS	USA
ALBERT	4	M	CHILD	RR	AEWS	USA
AUG.	.08	M	INFANT	RR	AEWS	USA
SIKKILA, JOSHUA	37	M	FARMER	RR	AEWS	USA
HANNA	30	F	W	RR	AEWS	USA
MARIA	4	F	CHILD	RR	AEWS	USA
ELI	3	M	CHILD	RR	AEWS	USA
MCKIRSHEIM, AUG.	38	M	LABR	RR	AEWS	USA
POMNALA, JACOB	30	M	LABR	RR	AEWS	USA
ANNA-L.	30	F	W	RR	AEWS	USA
NIEMER, JOSHUA	36	M	FARMER	RR	AEWS	USA
ANNA-L.	33	F	W	RR	AEWS	USA
JULIUS	11	M	CH	RR	AEWS	USA
MARGA	10	F	CH	RR	AEWS	USA
OSCAR	8	M	CHILD	RR	AEWS	USA
JOSHUA	4	M	CHILD	RR	AEWS	USA
SELMA	.06	F	INFANT	RR	AEWS	USA
JOHANSEN, ISACK	30	M	SEMN	RR	AEWS	USA
SHIP: FRISIA						
FROM: HAMBURG						
TO: NEW YORK						
ARRIVED: 30 JUNE 1885						
SCHAPIRP, ABRAHAM	60	M	DLR	RR	ZZZZ	USA
BEILE	20	F	SGL	RR	ZZZZ	USA
KOSSOWITZKY, JUDITH	17	F	SGL	RR	ZZZZ	USA
GISS, MOSES	30	M	DLR	RR	ZZZZ	USA
LEWIN, JACOB	5	M	CHILD	RR	ZZZZ	USA
ROSENBERG, SALOMON	25	M	DLR	RR	ZZZZ	USA
KUTZEWITZKY, WOLF	55	M	LABR	RR	ZZZZ	USA
REISE	20	F	SGL	RR	ZZZZ	USA
EPSTEIN, CHAIM	24	M	DLR	RR	ZZZZ	USA
KOHANOWSKI, LEIB	30	M	DLR	RR	ZZZZ	USA
LEWIN, CHAWE	23	F	W	RR	ZZZZ	USA
SALOMON	.11	M	INFANT	RR	ZZZZ	USA
MAINET, LESSER	19	M	DLR	RR	ZZZZ	USA
SPARK, PESSE	40	F	W	RR	ZZZZ	USA
GASSKOWSKI, MOSES	20	M	LABR	RR	ZZZZ	USA
RODNAR, CLARA	60	F	W	RR	ZZZZ	USA
SANDOR, LAJOS	9	M	CHILD	RR	ZZZZ	USA
EIDELMANN, TOBIAS	28	M	LABR	RR	ZZZZ	USA
GABORKIND, OSIAS	30	M	LABR	RR	ZZZZ	USA
SCHUESKIN, LEIB	32	M	LABR	RR	ZZZZ	USA
SALK, CHASKEL	35	M	LABR	RR	ZZZZ	USA
GRUNSPAHN, MARCUS	53	M	LABR	RR	ZZZZ	USA
SARA	48	F	W	RR	ZZZZ	USA
JOSEF	23	M	CH	RR	ZZZZ	USA
ROSA	17	F	CH	RR	ZZZZ	USA
MALKE	9	F	CHILD	RR	ZZZZ	USA
BEILE	7	F	CHILD	RR	ZZZZ	USA
GOWBOLTZ, BER.	18	M	LABR	RR	ZZZZ	USA
DOHN, DWORE	30	F	W	RR	ZZZZ	USA
RAHEL	.06	F	INFANT	RR	ZZZZ	USA
KOWENSKY, MOSES	36	M	LABR	RR	ZZZZ	USA
FREIDE	14	F	CH	RR	ZZZZ	USA

PASSENGER	AGE	SEX	OCCUPATION	PRV	VIL	DES
KOCHENBERG, MERE	35	F	SGL	RR	ZZZZ	USA
STARK, LEIB	35	M	DLR	RR	ZZZZ	USA
SOMMERFELDT, ISAAC	15	M	LABR	RR	ZZZZ	USA
GERHARD, JACOB	12	M	CH	RR	ZZZZ	USA
KORNTEIER, FEIGE	35	F	W	RR	ZZZZ	USA
RIWKE	15	F	CH	RR	ZZZZ	USA
HINDE	7	F	CHILD	RR	ZZZZ	USA
ABRAH.	4	M	CHILD	RR	ZZZZ	USA
NOCHEM	8	M	CHILD	RR	ZZZZ	USA
LEFTZOWITZ, NATHAN	14	M	LABR	RR	ZZZZ	USA
SAMUEL	14	M	LABR	RR	ZZZZ	USA
FRANKENSTEIN, RACHEL	28	F	W	RR	ZZZZ	USA
JOSEF	5	M	CHILD	RR	ZZZZ	USA
FEITEL	.11	M	INFANT	RR	ZZZZ	USA
COHEN, SCHEINE	25	F	SGL	RR	ZZZZ	USA
SEGAL, LEJA	30	F	W	RR	ZZZZ	USA
NESCHE	8	F	CHILD	RR	ZZZZ	USA
FRENKEL, ARON	36	M	DLR	RR	ZZZZ	USA
LEWENBERG, MENDEL	16	M	LABR	RR	ZZZZ	USA
DEGOTZKY, CHASKEL	35	M	GZR	RR	ZZZZ	USA
HENE	35	F	W	RR	ZZZZ	USA
LEIB	9	M	CHILD	RR	ZZZZ	USA
HENOCH	.11	M	INFANT	RR	ZZZZ	USA
PATELOWITZ, SAMUEL	16	M	LABR	RR	ZZZZ	USA
ADLER, CHASCHE	16	F	LABR	RR	ZZZZ	USA
LOEW, MAX	17	M	MCHT	RR	ZZZZ	USA
PITROWSKA, PITRO	27	M	LABR	RR	ZZZZ	USA
LEWIN, RIWKE	25	F	SGL	RR	ZZZZ	USA
SCHWABSKY, ABRAH.	19	M	LABR	RR	ZZZZ	USA
BARGMANN, ISAAC	53	M	SEMN	RR	ZZZZ	USA
JABLONSKY, ESTHER	17	F	SGL	RR	ZZZZ	USA
ROTH, FRIEDR.	21	M	FARMER	RR	ZZZZ	USA
CATH.	15	F	SGL	RR	ZZZZ	USA
GOTTFRIED	9	M	CHILD	RR	ZZZZ	USA
GENSBERG, MOSES	17	M	DLR	RR	ZZZZ	USA
DEMBOWITZ, SIMON	21	M	LABR	RR	ZZZZ	USA
STEINERT, SCHIE	20	F	LABR	RR	ZZZZ	USA
ROSA	21	F	W	RR	ZZZZ	USA
ZION, JOSEF	18	M	LABR	RR	ZZZZ	USA
DINER, BARSCHI	50	M	SGL	RR	ZZZZ	USA
WIDNOWSKY, ISAAC	16	M	LABR	RR	ZZZZ	USA
BLOCH, PAULINE	16	F	SGL	RR	ZZZZ	USA
SEGAL, GITTEL	45	F	W	RR	ZZZZ	USA
LEA	18	F	CH	RR	ZZZZ	USA
TAUBE	8	F	CHILD	RR	ZZZZ	USA
SCHMUL	6	M	CHILD	RR	ZZZZ	USA
TIKORSKY, JOSSEL	46	M	LABR	RR	ZZZZ	USA
BOWER, MEYER	20	M	LABR	RR	ZZZZ	USA
CZANOWITZ, SUSSEL	18	F	SGL	RR	ZZZZ	USA
MATSON, KAISER	33	M	W	RR	ZZZZ	USA
HULDA	9	F	CHILD	RR	ZZZZ	USA
EINAR	7	M	CHILD	RR	ZZZZ	USA
WAZNISKI, MASCHKE	19	M	SGL	RR	ZZZZ	USA
SIMON, LEIB	25	M	LABR	RR	ZZZZ	USA
PESCHE	18	F	SGL	RR	ZZZZ	USA
SCHILMAN, MARIASCHE	9	F	CHILD	RR	ZZZZ	USA
CZERNOWSKY, SOFIE	16	F	SGL	RR	ZZZZ	USA
PEN, GERSON	25	M	LABR	RR	ZZZZ	USA
BLACK, SARA	20	F	SGL	RR	ZZZZ	USA
DREGLITZI, JENNI	18	F	SGL	RR	ZZZZ	USA
BLUMARSOHN, CHAIM	14	M	LABR	RR	ZZZZ	USA
RACZKOWSKY, MAX	21	M	TLR	RR	ZZZZ	USA
JANGERMANN, CHAJE	19	F	SGL	RR	ZZZZ	USA
JANKELOWITZ, ZERINE	17	F	SGL	RR	ZZZZ	USA
SIMON, LEIB	33	M	LABR	RR	ZZZZ	USA
MARGOL, SARA	17	F	SGL	RR	ZZZZ	USA
CHIRALSKY, SARA	21	F	SGL	RR	ZZZZ	USA
CHASKELOWITZ, BRANE	18	F	SGL	RR	ZZZZ	USA
LAN, ISAAC	17	M	LABR	RR	ZZZZ	USA
LEWIN, BORKO	20	M	LABR	RR	ZZZZ	USA
JANKEL	19	M	LABR	RR	ZZZZ	USA
MOSESSOHN, JANKEL	14	M	LABR	RR	ZZZZ	USA
GOTTLIEB, SCHLOME	12	M	CH	RR	ZZZZ	USA
TECK, BENJAMIN	35	M	LABR	RR	ZZZZ	USA
WIERZBELOWSKY, MARCIN	22	M	LABR	RR	ZZZZ	USA
GOLDE	23	F	W	RR	ZZZZ	USA
HERSCH	.11	M	INFANT	RR	ZZZZ	USA
FALK	.11	M	INFANT	RR	ZZZZ	USA
RACHMANN, JOSSEL	20	M	LABR	RR	ZZZZ	USA
NUDELMANN, ESTHER	25	F	W	RR	ZZZZ	USA
ISRAEL	9	M	CHILD	RR	ZZZZ	USA
CHANNE	7	F	CHILD	RR	ZZZZ	USA
HIRSCH	3	M	CHILD	RR	ZZZZ	USA
PESSE	.11	F	INFANT	RR	ZZZZ	USA
BACHERACH, ISAAC	28	M	DLR	RR	ZZZZ	USA
LEWIN, FISCHEL	20	M	DLR	RR	ZZZZ	USA
GIWORSKY, OREL	20	M	LABR	RR	ZZZZ	USA
DANIEL, SANY	18	M	DLR	RR	ZZZZ	USA
BRUCHIS, ISAAC	26	M	LABR	RR	ZZZZ	USA
MARIANNE	20	F	W	RR	ZZZZ	USA
SALOMON	23	M	LABR	RR	ZZZZ	USA
MARAWSKY, LEIB	23	M	LABR	RR	ZZZZ	USA
SOFIE	19	F	W	RR	ZZZZ	USA
GEISSAN, ISRAEL	20	M	LABR	RR	ZZZZ	USA
SPOLSKY, ABRAH.	28	M	LABR	RR	ZZZZ	USA
FINKENSTEIN, ARON	50	M	LABR	RR	ZZZZ	USA
EDELMANN, ARON	32	M	LABR	RR	ZZZZ	USA
ISCHLANDSKY, WOLF	20	M	LABR	RR	ZZZZ	USA
RASCHMANN, FEIGE	19	M	LABR	RR	ZZZZ	USA
BUZOWA, KATTE	27	F	W	RR	ZZZZ	USA
JOHA.	.11	F	INFANT	RR	ZZZZ	USA

SHIP: ANCHORIA

FROM: GLASGOW
TO: NEW YORK
ARRIVED: 01 JULY 1885

PASSENGER	AGE	SEX	OCCUPATION	PRV	VIL	DES
GRINAITZI, CECIMIR	32	M	LABR	RR	ZZZZ	USA
LERI, REUBEN	30	M	TLR	RR	ZZZZ	USA
LIBOSCHOWSKY, ISAK	37	M	DLR	RR	ZZZZ	USA
LUSTGARTEN, SIMON	38	M	CPTR	RR	ZZZZ	USA
LIPSCHUTZ, LIPMAN	43	M	PDLR	RR	ZZZZ	USA
MAHLER, JANKEL	20	M	PDLR	RR	ZZZZ	USA
RUDASZEWSKY, ISAK	22	M	PDLR	RR	ZZZZ	USA
LUSTAVSEN, SIMON	32	M	PDLR	RR	ZZZZ	USA
SABOLOWSKY, SAUL	19	M	PDLR	RR	ZZZZ	USA
SLEIKAS, JOHN.	40	M	LABR	RR	ZZZZ	USA
SCHWARZ, SCHMUEL	22	M	LABR	RR	ZZZZ	USA

SHIP: WESTERNLAND

FROM: ANTWERP
TO: NEW YORK
ARRIVED: 01 JULY 1885

PASSENGER	AGE	SEX	OCCUPATION	PRV	VIL	DES
CLOWETZEK, OTTO	00	U	INF	PL	ZZZZ	NY
LEVANDOWSKI, S.	18	M	LABR	PL	ZZZZ	NY

PASSENGER	AGE	SEX	OCCUPATION	PRV	VIL	DES

SHIP: WISCONSIN

FROM: LIVERPOOL AND QUEENSTOWN
TO: NEW YORK
ARRIVED: 01 JULY 1885

PASSENGER	AGE	SEX	OCCUPATION	PRV	VIL	DES
CHARMIOWICZ, ISRAEL	20	M	CL	PL	AFVG	USA
KROOKS, SIMON-E.	39	M	ATSN	PL	AFWJ	UNK
MARIA	35	F	W	PL	AFWJ	UNK
MAJA-G.	8	F	CHILD	PL	AFWJ	USA
EMANUEL	4	F	CHILD	PL	AFWJ	USA
KRONSTEDT, MARTIN	44	M	CPTR	PL	ZZZZ	USA
KAYSA	38	F	W	PL	ZZZZ	USA
EMANUEL	4	M	CHILD	PL	ZZZZ	USA
HELLMAN, LARS-G.	30	M	FARMER	PL	ZZZZ	UNK
STORGARD, GUSTAV	26	M	FARMER	PL	ZZZZ	USA
JANSON, MATTS-J.	28	M	MLR	PL	ZZZZ	UNK
SKARA, EDLA-J.	22	F	SP	PL	AFWJ	USA
JAFS, ANNA-M.	26	F	SP	PL	AFWJ	USA
ABRAMOWITZ, MINSCH	20	F	LABR	PL	ACBF	USA
MAILACH, FEIWEL	36	F	LABR	PL	ZZZZ	USA
BREIT, NAPHTAL	34	F	PNTR	RR	ZZZZ	USA
KOTT, HERSCH	20	F	CL	RR	AFVG	USA
BIRNKRART, MORITZ	35	F	FARMER	PL	ZZZZ	USA
ITE	32	F	W	PL	ZZZZ	USA
ARON	9	M	CHILD	PL	ZZZZ	USA
SAMUEL	6	M	CHILD	PL	ZZZZ	USA
SARAH	.08	F	INFANT	PL	ZZZZ	USA
MARCUS	.08	M	INFANT	PL	ZZZZ	USA
FELSENFELD, JACOB	40	M	BKPR	PL	ZZZZ	USA
JOSEF	30	M	BKPR	PL	ZZZZ	USA
BERGER, PINCUS	28	M	UNKNOWN	PL	ZZZZ	USA
SCHECHMANN, CHAIE	20	M	LABR	PL	ACBF	USA

SHIP: STATE OF INDIA

FROM: LIVERPOOL AND QUEENSTOWN
TO: NEW YORK
ARRIVED: 02 JULY 1885

PASSENGER	AGE	SEX	OCCUPATION	PRV	VIL	DES
BROWN, WILLIAM	46	M	SLR	FN	ZZZZ	USA
KOPELANSKY, CHATZKEL	18	M	PDLR	FN	AHTF	USA
RAIWID, MOSES	20	M	PDLR	RR	ZZZZ	USA
LEWITHAN, MENASCHE	17	M	PDLR	RR	ZZZZ	USA
PALOWIN, LEIB	19	M	PDLR	RR	AHWE	USA
KRAUS, MOWSHA	41	M	PDLR	RR	ZZZZ	USA
MITTELMAN, MORDCHE	20	M	PDLR	RR	AHSX	USA
KANTER, HIRSCH	18	M	PDLR	RR	AHTF	USA
SHEIN, HIRSCH	32	M	PDLR	RR	ZZZZ	USA
FRIEDMANN, LEOPOLD	21	M	PDLR	RR	AEFL	USA
HIRSCHOWITZ, HILLEL	22	M	PDLR	RR	ZZZZ	USA
FREIMANN, SLEIM	36	M	PDLR	RR	ZZZZ	USA
SACHS, CHAIM	21	M	PDLR	RR	ACBF	USA
STERN, MEYER	55	M	PDLR	RR	ACBF	USA
GRUNBERG, LAASER	33	M	PDLR	RR	ZZZZ	USA
GAUNER, GELMAAN	19	M	PDLR	RR	AHTF	USA
KAHL, SAMUEL	45	M	BCHR	RR	AHTF	USA
SCHAPIRO, ZECHIEL	21	M	LABR	RR	ZZZZ	USA
KORWAARSHIK, NOSSAN	17	M	PDLR	RR	AHTF	USA
FRIEDLAUDER, BEHR	18	M	LABR	RR	AEFL	USA
KREMER, SOLOMON	11	M	BY	RR	ZZZZ	USA
TRIEBER, MENDEL	28	M	PDLR	RR	ZZZZ	USA
HIRSCH	18	M	PDLR	RR	ZZZZ	USA
GROTKE, LOUIS	32	M	PDLR	PL	ZZZZ	USA
ZORN, NATHAN	26	M	LABR	PL	ZZZZ	USA
BAKEWICZ, JOHAN	28	M	LABR	PL	ZZZZ	USA
SAMBAKORA, FRANZ	22	M	LABR	PL	ZZZZ	USA
SALZULSKE, MATHER	23	M	LABR	PL	ZZZZ	USA
FOROWSKY, VINCAL	26	M	LABR	PL	ZZZZ	USA
CHEOLOWSKY, ZIZEL	26	F	SP	RR	ZZZZ	USA
SUSSE	20	F	SP	RR	ZZZZ	USA
MALKE	15	F	SP	RR	ZZZZ	USA
SAMPOWSKY, VERONIKA	21	F	SP	PL	ZZZZ	USA
CHEOLOWSKY, JOSEPH	50	M	PDLR	PL	ACBF	USA
CHAJE	46	F	W	PL	ACBF	USA
MICHAEL	9	M	CHILD	PL	ACBF	USA
JAKOB	8	M	CHILD	PL	ACBF	USA
JETTE	1	F	CHILD	PL	ACBF	USA
FRIEDMANN, MEYER	39	M	PDLR	PL	AEFL	USA
GRETAL	29	F	W	PL	AEFL	USA
JOHAN	5	M	CHILD	PL	AEFL	USA
DWORA	1	F	CHILD	PL	AEFL	USA
SALKOW, PESSE	30	F	W	RR	ZZZZ	USA
CHAIM	2	M	CHILD	RR	ZZZZ	USA
BACZATZKI, MARCUS	39	M	PDLR	RR	ACBF	USA
REBECCA	39	F	W	RR	ACBF	USA
BEER	11	M	CH	RR	ACBF	USA
ISAAC	9	M	CHILD	RR	ACBF	USA
WOLF	7	M	CHILD	RR	ACBF	USA
ROSA	5	F	CHILD	RR	ACBF	USA

SHIP: BALTIC

FROM: LIVERPOOL AND QUEENSTOWN
TO: NEW YORK
ARRIVED: 03 JULY 1885

PASSENGER	AGE	SEX	OCCUPATION	PRV	VIL	DES
TESKA, SCOFIL	31	M	LABR	RR	AGRT	USA
HAGGENMILLER, FRIZ	27	M	LABR	RR	AGRT	USA
BASCHKASKI, JOH	37	F	W	RR	AGRT	USA
JOSEFA	6	F	CHILD	RR	AGRT	USA
DAWINOWITSCH, M.	36	F	W	RR	AGRT	USA
BEN	4	M	CHILD	RR	AGRT	USA
EIMHORN, JOSEF	40	M	LABR	RR	AGRT	USA
KOLWEITAS, PETER	30	M	LABR	RR	AGRT	USA
MAWIKAS, VICENTE	27	M	LABR	RR	AGRT	USA
ALEXINAS, CASE	32	M	LABR	RR	AGRT	USA
CATH.	25	F	W	RR	AGRT	USA
FRANZISCA	3	M	CHILD	RR	AGRT	USA
ELISABETH	.09	F	INFANT	RR	AGRT	USA
PELESCH, JOSEPH	31	M	LABR	RR	AGRT	USA
MARIE	28	F	W	RR	AGRT	USA
BRITASCHKEN, BERN.	29	M	LABR	RR	AGRT	USA
FRIEDERIKA	28	F	W	RR	AGRT	USA
GOROAN, BARRICK	27	M	LABR	RR	AGRT	USA
DAMECKI, IGNATZ	36	M	LABR	RR	AGRT	USA
ANTONINA	35	F	W	RR	AGRT	USA
HAAK, ISAAC	29	M	LABR	RR	AGRT	USA
LIW, WOLF	30	M	LABR	RR	AGRT	USA
WEHLER, ISRAEL	29	M	LABR	RR	AGRT	USA
CHISTAK, TANKEL	6	M	CHILD	RR	AGRT	USA
STIPLEMAN, CHA.	38	M	LABR	RR	AGRT	USA
PIKOWSKY, ABTAH.	36	M	LABR	RR	AGRT	USA
JORGENSEN, GEORG	27	M	LABR	RR	AGRT	USA
KATZ, SCHMERL	30	M	LABR	RR	AGRT	USA
SARAH	21	F	SVNT	RR	AGRT	USA
HENNOCK	22	M	LABR	RR	AGRT	USA
BRANDE, SCHIEMEN	26	M	LABR	RR	AGRT	USA
SCHASVENSTEIN, ARON	21	M	LABR	RR	AGRT	USA

PASSENGER	AGE	SEX	OCCUPATION	PRV	VIL	DES
SHIP: CIRCASSIA						
FROM: GLASGOW AND MOVILLE						
TO: NEW YORK						
ARRIVED: 06 JULY 1885						
SEGAL, KAFMAN	57	M	DLR	RR	ZZZZ	USA
LEOPOLD	16	M	DLR	RR	ZZZZ	USA
ZARNOWSKI, LEWY	28	M	LABR	RR	ZZZZ	USA
SEGALOF, SOLOMON	20	M	MSN	RR	ZZZZ	USA
NEUBERG, CHAIM	34	M	CGRMKR	RR	ZZZZ	USA
KULLMAN, D.	28	M	CL	RR	ZZZZ	USA
BENGIANOWSKI, H.	21	M	CGRMKR	RR	ZZZZ	USA
CHOCHUM, LIBE	22	F	UNKNOWN	RR	ZZZZ	USA
SAGOR, JOSEF	25	M	DLR	RR	ZZZZ	USA
GIWOSKI, MECH.	26	M	SMH	RR	ZZZZ	USA
ROSALIA	18	F	W	RR	ZZZZ	USA
SHIP: FULDA						
FROM: BREMEN						
TO: NEW YORK						
ARRIVED: 06 JULY 1885						
MARK, LEONARD	17	M	LABR	RR	ZZZZ	USA
KEISER, RIVE	33	F	UNKNOWN	RR	AEFL	USA
BASCH, RACHEL	50	F	UNKNOWN	RR	ZZZZ	USA
LORA	24	F	UNKNOWN	RR	ZZZZ	USA
MASCHKE	10	F	UNKNOWN	RR	ZZZZ	USA
STETTIN, FERDINAND	18	M	LABR	RR	ZZZZ	USA
HAMING, SARAH	36	F	UNKNOWN	RR	ZZZZ	USA
REBECCA	7	F	CHILD	RR	ZZZZ	USA
BROWN, HASKEL	34	M	LABR	RR	ZZZZ	USA
SCHNEIDEROWSKY, ALTER	20	M	LABR	RR	ZZZZ	USA
SENIE	8	F	CHILD	RR	ZZZZ	USA
HARSCHLAWSKY, ROSA	28	F	UNKNOWN	RR	ZZZZ	USA
DORA	5	F	CHILD	RR	ZZZZ	USA
SIMON	3	M	CHILD	RR	ZZZZ	USA
KALAFUT, AGNES	24	F	UNKNOWN	RR	ZZZZ	USA
AGNES	.10	F	INFANT	RR	ZZZZ	USA
WODOTEPKI, FREIDE	50	F	UNKNOWN	RR	ZZZZ	USA
SCHNEIDEROWSKY, ALTE	23	M	FARMER	RR	ZZZZ	USA
REWNO, RESSI	22	F	UNKNOWN	RR	ZZZZ	USA
SARA	.11	F	INFANT	RR	ZZZZ	USA
SHIP: GOTTARDO						
FROM: PALERMO						
TO: NEW YORK						
ARRIVED: 06 JULY 1885						
SDRIKOWSKI, FERDINAND	30	M	RE	PL	ZZZZ	USA
SIEDLISKA, MARIA-FRANCI	42	F	RE-MERCY	PL	ZZZZ	USA
LUBWIDEKA, MARIA-RAFFAE	26	F	RE-MERCY	PL	ZZZZ	USA
LUBWIDEKA, LAURETA-TECL	22	F	RE-MERCY	PL	ZZZZ	USA
CZAMOWSKA, MARIA-PAOLA	28	F	RE-MERCY	PL	ZZZZ	USA
SZREMINSKA, TEOFILA-TAR	26	F	RE-MERCY	PL	ZZZZ	USA
SADWSHA, ELISABETTA-CEC	29	F	RE-MERCY	PL	ZZZZ	USA
KIJENSKA, ANNA-EVANGELI	27	F	RE-MERCY	PL	ZZZZ	USA
CRAPPI, GIOVANNA-ANGELA	23	F	RE-MERCY	PL	ZZZZ	USA
SIERPINICA, GIMEPPINA-S	25	F	RE-MERCY	PL	ZZZZ	USA
PAREIK, ANNA-FILOMENA	24	F	RE-MERCY	PL	ZZZZ	USA
LUKASZEWIS, CAROLINA-AG	21	F	RE-MERCY	PL	ZZZZ	USA
LECHERT, TEOFILA	7	F	CHILD	PL	ZZZZ	USA
MIECINAO	4	M	CHILD	PL	ZZZZ	USA
SHIP: NECKAR						
FROM: BREMEN						
TO: NEW YORK						
ARRIVED: 06 JULY 1885						
CORDES, JOH.HEINR.	72	M	UNKNOWN	RR	ZZZZ	NY
STERN, JEANT	26	M	MCHT	RR	AEFL	NY
DALUGE, RUDOLF	16	M	LABR	RR	ADNI	NY
GUSTMANN, TAB.	16	M	LABR	RR	ZZZZ	NY
LEICHES, AARON	24	M	DLR	RR	ZZZZ	NY
BERNSTEIN, JACOB	18	M	DLR	RR	ZZZZ	NY
ZUDEK, CHAIM-JOSSEL	18	M	CL	RR	ZZZZ	NY
TAUBE	11	F	UNKNOWN	RR	ZZZZ	NY
ZLATNITZKI, TAUBE	33	F	UNKNOWN	RR	ZZZZ	NY
LEDI	8	F	CHILD	RR	ZZZZ	NY
LIEBE	7	F	CHILD	RR	ZZZZ	NY
SELDE	3	F	CHILD	RR	ZZZZ	NY
MIER	.11	M	INFANT	RR	ZZZZ	NY
STURN, FREDRICH	87	M	UNKNOWN	RR	ZZZZ	NY
MARIE	32	F	SVNT	RR	ZZZZ	NY
JULIUS	14	M	UNKNOWN	RR	ZZZZ	NY
LEONORE	10	F	UNKNOWN	RR	ZZZZ	NY
FRIEDERIKE	9	F	CHILD	RR	ZZZZ	NY
COHN, ISIDOR	23	M	DLR	RR	AHVA	NY
CHAGE	25	F	UNKNOWN	RR	AHVA	NY
P.	.10	F	INFANT	RR	AHVA	NY
TEWE	.01	F	INFANT	RR	AHVA	NY
BUCZA, JOCHEN	42	M	LABR	RR	AGRT	NY
SEHAPIRO, RUBEN	50	M	DLR	RR	ZZZZ	NY
M.	11	M	UNKNOWN	RR	ZZZZ	NY
JOHNI	8	M	CHILD	RR	ZZZZ	NY
KEIZER, RACHEL	18	F	SVNT	RR	ZZZZ	NY
SZARKOWSKY, LEA	44	F	UNKNOWN	RR	ZZZZ	UNK
ISRAEL	11	M	UNKNOWN	RR	ZZZZ	UNK
ESTER	10	F	UNKNOWN	RR	ZZZZ	UNK
WOTH, CORNELIUS	35	M	FARMER	RR	ZZZZ	UNK
EVA	25	F	UNKNOWN	RR	ZZZZ	UNK
AGNES	6	F	CHILD	RR	ZZZZ	UNK
WILHELMINE	3	F	CHILD	RR	ZZZZ	UNK
WILHELM	.09	M	INFANT	RR	ZZZZ	UNK
BOGDAN, JOSEG	25	M	SMH	RR	ZZZZ	UNK
LATZMITZKY, SARA	16	F	SVNT	RR	ZZZZ	NY
LIMLE, CHERIM	41	M	DLR	RR	ZZZZ	NY
MISCHKE	41	F	UNKNOWN	RR	ZZZZ	NY
GABRIEL	17	M	DLR	RR	ABHT	NY
JUDIT	17	F	SVNT	RR	ABHT	NY
ABRAHAM	7	M	CHILD	RR	ABHT	NY
CHASIN, LEISER	28	M	LABR	RR	ZZZZ	NY
MASKEWICZ, ANNA	20	F	SVNT	RR	AAER	NY
SILBERMANN, MARCUS	28	M	UNKNOWN	RR	AAER	NY
ESTHER	19	F	SVNT	RR	AAER	NY
SCHAFEROWITZ, ESTER	17	F	SVNT	RR	ZZZZ	NY
KASE, SARAH	20	F	SVNT	RR	ZZZZ	NY
RIVE	20	F	SVNT	RR	ZZZZ	NY
CHAPIEL, TAUBE	18	F	SVNT	RR	ZZZZ	NY
GURNER, FREIDE	18	F	SVNT	RR	ZZZZ	NY
ZUCKERBAUM, LEIBE	28	F	SVNT	RR	ZZZZ	NY
WIENKE, STANISLAWA	19	F	SVNT	RR	ZZZZ	NY

PASSENGER	AGE	SEX	OCCUPATION	PV RI VL	DES
SHIP: P CALAND					
FROM: ROTTERDAM					
TO: NEW YORK					
ARRIVED: 06 JULY 1885					
KUTZNER, ANTON	00	M	MCHT	PLZZZ	ZUSA
LUZIKA	00	F	NN	PLZZZ	ZUSA
JACOBSON, GOLDE	35	F	NN	PLZZZ	ZUSA
ROSENBERG, WILH.	16	M	LABR	PLZZZ	ZUSA
GABERLAY, GABRIEL	11	M	NN	PLZZZ	ZUSA
BAURAS, ADAMAS	34	M	LABR	PLZZZ	ZUSA
BINDEN, SELIG	20	M	MCHT	PLZZZ	ZUSA
KORULN, GUSTAV	26	M	LABR	PLABV	EUSA
MARIA	20	F	NN	PLABV	EUSA
ELISABETH	.06	F	INFANT	PLABV	EUSA
FRANKEL, SALOMON	42	M	LABR	RRZZZ	ZUSA
ISAK	9	M	CHILD	RRZZZ	ZUSA
ROSIN	10	F	NN	RRZZZ	ZUSA
SHIP: SERVIA					
FROM: LIVERPOOL AND QUEENSTOWN					
TO: NEW YORK					
ARRIVED: 06 JULY 1885					
SANAALAINEU, PELTER	31	M	LABR	RRZZZ	ZUNK
MILLER, AUD.	41	M	LABR	RRZZZ	ZNY
FELIN, JOHANN	20	M	LABR	RRZZZ	ZNY
SROISKA, ABRAM	25	M	LABR	RRZZZ	ZNY
SHIP: SUEVIA					
FROM: HAMBURG					
TO: NEW YORK					
ARRIVED: 06 JULY 1885					
WESTERMINKER, GITTEL	50	F	W	RRAHX	FUSA
GRUENBERG, LCHIFRE	18	F	SGL	RRAHS	WUSA
HEURWITZ, MOSES	21	M	LABR	RRAHS	WUSA
KRASULES, JOSEF	21	M	LABR	RRZZZ	ZUSA
OKOLAWSKY, OSIP	33	M	LABR	RRZZZ	ZUSA
ZAROZAN, FENTI	20	F	SGL	RRAHU	OUSA
MALKE	9	F	CHILD	RRAHU	OUSA
KRAMER, IDA	16	F	SGL	RRZZZ	ZUSA
ROCHE-SPRINGL	18	F	SGL	RRZZZ	ZUSA
RABINOWITZ, ESTHER	30	F	W	RRAHU	OUSA
NOCHIM	6	M	CHILD	RRAHU	OUSA
SARA	4	F	CHILD	RRAHU	OUSA
WOLF, LEISER	17	M	FELMO	RRAHU	OUSA
FRANK, ESTHER	50	F	W	RRAHS	WUSA
ZEREWITZ, NECHAME	13	F	SGL	RRAHS	WUSA
LASER, LENE	20	F	SGL	RRAHU	OUSA
LAKEN--KY, JOSEF	16	M	LABR	RRAGR	TUSA
OPP--NN, BASCHE	42	F	W	RRAHS	WUSA
DWORE	19	F	D	RRAHS	WUSA
SAM	9	M	CHILD	RRAHS	WUSA
PREBRODSKY, TANCHUNN	38	M	LABR	RRAHZ	SUSA
SOROSON, MAUSCHE	9	M	CHILD	RRAHZ	SUSA
SOHIDORSKY, MALKE	16	F	SGL	RRAHZ	SUSA
SOHAITZKI, SEINE	26	F	W	RRAHZ	HUSA
RUSIEL	7	M	CHILD	RRAHZ	HUSA
ISRAEL	4	M	CHILD	RRAHZ	HUSA
ISAAC	.11	M	INFANT	RRAHZ	HUSA
MATZKOWSKY, MOSES	15	M	LABR	RRAHZ	SUSA
GOLDENSCHLAG, VICTOR	20	M	LABR	RRAHO	KUSA
TURIEN, RACHEL	17	F	SGL	RRZZZ	ZUSA
SAUMELSOHN, CHAINE	43	F	SGL	RRZZZ	ZUSA
WABEZKY, FRANZ	21	M	LABR	RRZZZ	ZUSA
LIPPMANN, JOSEF	53	M	LABR	RRAHX	XUSA
HANNE	18	F	SGL	RRAHX	XUSA
BRUNSTEIN, ISAAC	21	M	LABR	RRAHW	NUSA
NATHAN, PAULINE	14	F	SGL	RRAHU	OUSA
CASSA	58	F	W	RRAHU	OUSA
BERLINSKY, MOSES	19	M	LABR	RRAHU	UUSA
PER, SARA	40	F	W	RRAHU	OUSA
MOSES	9	M	CHILD	RRAHU	OUSA
REBECCA	8	F	CHILD	RRAHU	OUSA
JETTE	7	F	CHILD	RRAHU	OUSA
ANNA	4	F	CHILD	RRAHU	OUSA
SEIDENBERG, GOLDE	18	F	SGL	RRAHU	UUSA
ESTHER	16	F	SGL	RRAHU	UUSA
BERLINSKY, SARA	19	F	SGL	RRAHU	UUSA
GALITZKY, JUDE	9	M	CHILD	RRAFV	GUSA
ARON	6	M	CHILD	RRAFV	GUSA
REBECCA	5	F	CHILD	RRAFV	GUSA
ABRAM	4	M	CHILD	RRAFV	GUSA
HERNN	3	M	CHILD	RRAFV	GUSA
LEISER	.11	M	INFANT	RRAFV	GUSA
ISCHER, FISCHI	35	F	W	RRAHZ	IUSA
IANKEL	9	M	CHILD	RRAHZ	IUSA
IENTI	6	F	CHILD	RRAHZ	IUSA
LEIB	8	M	CHILD	RRAHZ	IUSA
HOELES	5	M	CHILD	RRAHZ	IUSA
MIRI	.11	F	INFANT	RRAHZ	IUSA
KABATZINK, GOLDE	37	M	LABR	RRAHW	KUSA
HEINDE	20	F	W	RRAHW	KUSA
ARON	.11	M	INFANT	RRAHW	KUSA
KOHN, LEIB	9	M	CHILD	RRAHU	XUSA
FRIEDERIKE	8	F	CHILD	RRAHU	XUSA
CHAINN	7	F	CHILD	RRAHU	XUSA
SIMON	5	M	CHILD	RRAHU	XUSA
WAGMANN, RACHEL	63	F	W	RRAHT	ZUSA
SCHAPIRO, FEIGE	18	F	W	RRAHO	KUSA
SOBELA--, JOSEF	27	M	BKSL	RRAHO	KUSA
GOLDBLATT, LOUIS	20	M	DLR	RRAHX	PUSA
KAPLAN, MEDLOCH	16	M	PRNTR	RRAHZ	SUSA
GERSCHNNECK, LASAR	18	M	DLR	RRAHQ	UUSA
BUTSCHIER, IAN	35	M	LABR	RRZZZ	ZUSA
BALNATZ, SIMON	38	M	LABR	RRZZZ	ZUSA
ANDEKER, FERD	49	M	LABR	RRZZZ	ZUSA
JANTOWSKY, CARL	47	M	LABR	RRZZZ	ZUSA
STRASEMOGEL, MORITZ	17	M	DLR	RRAFW	JUSA
DENGATSCH, MINNA	45	F	W	RRAHQ	UUSA
SIMON	17	M	CH	RRAHQ	UUSA
LAZARUS	18	M	CH	RRAHQ	UUSA
FEFLENSTEIN, SCHEINE	52	F	SGL	RRAHU	OUSA
GRAJOWSKA, ELISABETH	24	F	SGL	RRAHU	OUSA
KARLOWSKI, PIOTRO	40	M	LABR	RRAHZ	SUSA
CZAWLOWSKI, STANISLAV	21	M	LABR	RRZZZ	ZUSA
BARANOWSKI, FRANZ	29	M	LABR	RRAHZ	SUSA
ZEICHODOLSKI, STANISLAV	28	M	LABR	RRAHZ	SUSA
SAK, SARA	35	F	SGL	RRAHZ	EUSA
RANISCHEFSKY, GOLDE	26	F	W	RRAHV	FUSA
SALOMON	.11	M	INFANT	RRAHV	FUSA
ROSENTHAL, ELERINE	20	F	SGL	RRAHV	RUSA
SIMCHUL, SOHEFFEL	27	M	LABR	RRAHU	JUSA
RUSZINSKI, PAUL	38	M	LABR	RRAHU	JUSA
LUTA, IAGNATZ	18	M	LABR	RRAHZ	SUSA
ZDANCEWITZ, MONICA	19	F	SGL	RRAHT	GUSA
MILEWSKI, FRANZ	33	M	LABR	RRAHT	GUSA
JOSEFA	33	F	W	RRAHT	GUSA
ANTON	9	M	CHILD	RRAHT	GUSA
OSCHA	.11	M	INFANT	RRAHT	GUSA
STANISLAV	.01	M	INFANT	RRAHT	GUSA
LEBER, LARIA	21	F	SGL	RRZZZ	ZUSA
FICHAL, EISIK	20	M	LABR	RRAHU	OUSA
MILLNER, BLUME	30	F	SGL	RRAHZ	JUSA
PROPP, RESSE	30	F	W	RRAHZ	QUSA

PASSENGER	AGE	SEX	OCCUPATION	PRI VIL DES
ELIAS	7	M	CHILD	RRAHZQUSA
BERICK, LEA	60	F	W	RRAHUMUSA
BEREL	18	F	CH	RRAHUMUSA
PESSE	9	F	CHILD	RRAHUMUSA
PEGALL, SARA	20	F	SGL	RRAHUOUSA
JACOB	20	M	LABR	RRAHUOUSA
JELLE	19	F	SGL	RRAHUOUSA
PLOCKER, CHAINNE	25	F	W	RRAHTKUSA
SALLEB	.11	F	INFANT	RRAHTKUSA
RES, CHAJE	20	F	SGL	RRAHUOUSA
ROTHSCHILD, ROCHEL	28	F	SGL	RRZZZZUSA
DERONKE, JOSEF	22	M	DLR	RRAHSOUSA
FREID, LEIB	22	M	DLR	RRAHXDUSA
LIPIANSKI, BENZEL	18	M	BCHR	RRAHVRUSA
RACHEL	20	F	SGL	RRAHVRUSA
MARIANOW, PINC	21	M	DLR	RRAHOOUSA
GUTKOWSKI, ABRAHAM	9	M	CHILD	RRAHUUUSA
UEHENNAS	8	M	CHILD	RRAHUUUSA
KLIBANSKI, ISAAC	15	M	LABR	RRAHUVUSA
SLOMOWA, ESTHER	22	F	W	RRAHUOUSA
RACHNIB	9	F	CHILD	RRAHUOUSA
LISKY	7	F	CHILD	RRAHUOUSA
DAVID	5	M	CHILD	RRAHUOUSA
SUNLH, FEIVEL	20	M	TLR	RRAHUOUSA
BENKENDOFF, SAUL	20	M	TLR	RRAHUTUSA
WARSCHAFSKY, ABRAHAM	17	M	JNR	RRAHVCUSA
DAVID	50	M	TLR	RRAHVCUSA
SLATE	48	F	W	RRAHVCUSA
ROSA	18	F	D	RRAHVCUSA
SEHMEREL	9	M	CHILD	RRAHVCUSA
SAPIRO, SIMNE	30	F	W	RRAHTOUSA
HERM	9	M	CHILD	RRAHTOUSA
CHAWE	6	F	CHILD	RRAHTOUSA
DINA	.11	F	INFANT	RRAHTOUSA
WITTENBERG, LEA	40	F	W	RRAHUOUSA
RUBINOWITZ, CHAIE	40	F	W	RRAHWAUSA
SARA	9	F	CHILD	RRAHWAUSA
ISAAC	7	M	CHILD	RRAHWAUSA
MALKE	4	F	CHILD	RRAHWAUSA
BREINE	.11	F	INFANT	RRAHWAUSA
WILENSKY, MARIE	40	F	W	RRZZZZUSA
HELTMANN, ARON	46	M	JWLR	RRAHVYUSA
MENDEL	16	M	JWLR	RRAHVYUSA
RACHELSOHN, ESTHER	16	F	SGL	RRAHSWUSA
ABRAM	9	M	CHILD	RRAHSWUSA
GORR, ROCHE	20	F	SGL	RRAHUOUSA
RAEZKOWSKY, JUDE	17	M	LABR	RRAHSWUSA
ARAT, SINCHE	16	M	LABR	RRAHUTUSA
LEWIN, HIELEL	19	M	LABR	RRAHQUUSA
JAKOWITZ, DAVID	17	M	LABR	RRAHUTUSA
JACOBOWITZ, CHANE	50	F	W	RRZZZZUSA
LEWY, SALOMON	25	M	MSN	RRAHVAUSA
ROSA	39	F	CH	RRAHVAUSA
RIWKE	9	M	CHILD	RRAHVAUSA
CHAIE	8	F	CHILD	RRAHVAUSA
LEA	.11	F	INFANT	RRAHVAUSA
SCHMECKCARSKY, BASCHE	20	F	SGL	RRAHTRUSA
CHLEBOWSKY, JOSEF	46	M	CPR	RRAHYCUSA
FEINSTEINER, BENZEL	25	M	JNR	RRAHUVUSA
SACKWEINER, ISAAC	35	M	MCHT	RRAHSGUSA
RUORR, HERM	34	M	LABR	RRAEFLUSA
MEIROWITZ, ABE	23	M	LABR	RRAHTRUSA
BEKKER, NATHAN	18	M	LABR	RRAHSWUSA
WEIFS, MOSES	19	M	HTR	RRAHUTUSA
RANFMANN, MARIASCHE	21	F	W	RRZZZZUSA
MOSCHE	25	M	LABR	RRZZZZUSA
GILSTEIN, CHAIM	25	M	LABR	RRZZZZUSA
MICHALOWITZ, MENDEL	41	M	LABR	RRAHWEUSA
ESTHER	20	F	W	RRAHWEUSA
ZRAEL	.06	M	INFANT	RRAHWEUSA
KALINER, MEYER	20	M	LABR	RRAHUOUSA
BEILE	19	F	W	RRAHUOUSA
MATZ, SIMON	20	M	DLR	RRAHZIUSA
CHAICHE	21	F	W	RRAHZIUSA
FREIFMANN, NACHMEN	26	M	LABR	RRAHZIUSA

PASSENGER	AGE	SEX	OCCUPATION	PRI VIL DES
SCHELEWITZ, JOHANN	50	M	LABR	RRAHZIUSA
RATOWSKY, CHAIM	21	M	LABR	RRAHTWUSA
GLANZ, HERM	20	M	LABR	RRAHUOUSA
STARAND, NOTE	26	M	LABR	RRAHZBUSA
LIEBE	25	F	W	RRAHZBUSA
PALAIBIS, PANLIS	20	M	UNKNOWN	RRAHYEUSA
FELDMANN, ABE	20	M	SHMK	RRAHUOUSA
ROSENSAN, LEISER	52	M	DLR	RRZZZZUSA
CHEIC	50	F	W	RRZZZZUSA
ROSA	18	F	CH	RRZZZZUSA
BEHR	9	M	CHILD	RRZZZZUSA
HIRSCH	7	M	CHILD	RRZZZZUSA
ABRAM	5	M	CHILD	RRZZZZUSA
RARLINSKY, LEA	18	F	SGL	RRAHUOUSA
BECKER, ABRAHAM	20	M	LABR	RRAHUOUSA
KAPPEL	21	M	LABR	RRAHUOUSA
RASINSKY, MARCUS	17	M	LABR	RRAHTBUSA
GOLDBLATT, MIRIAM	30	F	W	RRAHTAUSA
MOSES	8	M	CHILD	RRAHTAUSA
FEIWEL	4	M	CHILD	RRAHTAUSA
JACOB	.11	M	INFANT	RRAHTAUSA
WEINSTEIN, HIRSCH	37	M	LABR	RRAHTBUSA
BERUSTOCH, MORITZ	26	M	LABR	RRAFWJUSA
TIKOZINSKI, ISIDOR	21	M	LABR	RRAHSPUSA
GLUECH, SALOMON	21	M	LABR	RRAHUPUSA
CHAIE	22	F	W	RRAHUPUSA
GERBER, MORDSCHE	20	M	LABR	RRAHTRUSA
PESCHE	22	F	W	RRAHTRUSA
ROSENBLATT, JANKEL	21	M	LABR	RRZZZZUSA
GRAJEWSKY, SARA	30	F	W	RRAHVUUSA
SCHUMEL	9	M	CHILD	RRAHVUUSA
TANBE	8	F	CHILD	RRAHVUUSA
CHAIM	7	M	CHILD	RRAHVUUSA
SALKA	5	F	CHILD	RRAHVUUSA
LEISER	3	M	CHILD	RRAHVUUSA
ZIPPE	.11	F	INFANT	RRAHVUUSA
ROMINSKI, ISRAEL	18	M	LABR	RRAHVDUSA
SCHNISZOWSKY, CHAINE	35	F	W	RRAHZSUSA
SCHMUEL	9	M	CHILD	RRAHZSUSA
WOLF	7	M	CHILD	RRAHZSUSA
BEILE	.11	F	INFANT	RRAHZSUSA
FRIEDMANN, DWORE	29	F	W	RRAHXWUSA
EPRHRAIM	7	M	CHILD	RRAHXWUSA
SALLEL	6	F	CHILD	RRAHXWUSA
PANBE	.11	F	INFANT	RRAHXWUSA
FINKELSTEIN, HANNE	19	F	UNKNOWN	RRAHXWUSA
SCHWARZ, JOSEF	15	M	LABR	RRAHXWUSA
SCHLOMA, CHAIM	15	M	LABR	RRAHXUUSA
STAM, JACOB	43	M	LABR	RRAHZSUSA
BARANSKY, ANDRAS	24	M	LABR	RRAHUOUSA

SHIP: HELVETIA

FROM: LIVERPOOL
TO: NEW YORK
ARRIVED: 07 JULY 1885

PASSENGER	AGE	SEX	OCCUPATION	PRI VIL DES
HAATMAKI, JOHAN	25	M	LABR	RRAFWJUSA
SEPPELA, HILMA	23	M	LABR	RRAFWJUSA
KALIKA, CRUTZ	59	F	SP	RRAFWJUSA
CARLSON, HELENA	18	F	SP	RRAFWJUSA
KNUTILA, ISAKO	27	M	LABR	RRAFWJUSA
HANILO, M.L.	20	M	LABR	RRAFWJUSA
JACOBSEN, MARTIN	19	M	LABR	RRAFWJUSA
HETURI, HERMAN	31	M	LABR	RRAFWJUSA
MALUNG, JOH.	27	M	LABR	RRAFWJUSA
EILOS, ELIAS	30	M	LABR	RRAFWJUSA
SUSANNA	31	F	W	RRAFWJUSA
SUSANNA	11	F	CH	RRAFWJUSA
HYBLA, SOPHIA	26	F	LABR	RRAFWJUSA

PASSENGER	AGE	SEX	OCCUPATION	PRV VIL DES
KEITTI, JOH.	28	F	LABR	RRAFWJUSA
HYVA, JACOB	26	F	LABR	RRAFWJUSA

SHIP: POLARIA

FROM: HAMBURG
TO: NEW YORK
ARRIVED: 08 JULY 1885

PASSENGER	AGE	SEX	OCCUPATION	PRV VIL DES
MISKEWICZ, SILVESTER	27	M	TRDSMN	RRZZZZNY
SAMUELS, PUSCH	21	M	WCHMKR	RRZZZZNY
STEIN, MORITZ	25	M	TRDSMN	RRZZZZNY
DEITSCH, JOS.	39	M	LABR	RRZZZZNY
LEVY, ARON	18	M	TRDSMN	RRZZZZNY
FEDERMANN, HANUAH	22	F	WO	RRZZZZUNK
JULIA	3	F	CHILD	RRZZZZUNK
SCHAPIRA, LIEBE	18	F	SGL	RRZZZZNY
SAFIER, JACOB	19	M	TRDSMN	RRZZZZWI
SAPIRO, JUDEL	25	M	TNM	RRZZZZPA
REICHEL, EST.I.	38	F	WO	RRZZZZNY
ABRAHAM	7	M	CHILD	RRZZZZNY
CHANE	6	F	CHILD	RRZZZZNY
MELKE	5	F	CHILD	RRZZZZNY
SALOMON	3	M	CHILD	RRZZZZNY
JASCHE	.06	F	INFANT	RRZZZZNY
SAMUEL	39	M	TRDSMN	RRZZZZNY
CZILESOHN, RICH.	17	F	SGL	RRZZZZNY
REMSCHREIBERT, HIRSCH	18	M	TLR	RRZZZZNY
MASCHICK, ISRAEL	17	M	TLR	RRZZZZNY
TEMMEA	18	F	SI	RRZZZZNY
KAPLAN, JACOB	20	M	TRDSMN	RRZZZZNY
KLEINMANN, SAMUEL	18	M	SHMK	RRZZZZPA
ROTMANN, ABRAHAM	20	M	TRDSMN	RRZZZZNY
SCHORF, SORE	29	F	WO	RRZZZZNY
COHN, ABRAH.	18	M	LABR	RRZZZZNY
ENGELBERG, CHAINE	25	F	LABR	PLZZZZNY
DAVID	3	M	CHILD	PLZZZZNY
JOSEF	.07	M	INFANT	PLZZZZNY
KOSCHES, ELIAS	20	M	CGRMKR	PLZZZZNY
WITTKOWSKY, FISCHEL	20	M	TRDSMN	PLZZZZNY
LEWIN, JOSEPH	22	M	TRDSMN	PLZZZZNY
BUTINSKY, CESAR	20	M	TRDSMN	PLZZZZNY
KAPPENMACHER, BERB.	28	M	BBR	PLZZZZNY
ALTER	7	M	CHILD	PLZZZZNY
WEINTRAUB, UNKNOWN	44	M	LABR	RRZZZZNY
MINNE	41	F	W	RRZZZZNY
TAUBE	17	F	D	RRZZZZNY
SUSSE	11	F	D	RRZZZZNY
ALTER	6	M	CHILD	RRZZZZNY
BLUMEFELD, P.	30	M	TLR	RRZZZZNY
PAULINE	26	F	W	RRZZZZNY
JUD.	6	M	CHILD	RRZZZZNY
AXENFELD, ABRAH.	26	M	LABR	RRZZZZNY
BIEL, ANDREAS	37	M	LABR	PLZZZZNY
GORDON, FEIGE	16	F	SGL	PLZZZZNY
WEGMEISTER, SIMON	18	M	MCHT	PLZZZZNY
ARBNER, LEISER	20	M	TRDSMN	PLZZZZNY
GABUTZKY, CHR.	20	M	TRDSMN	PLZZZZNY
LUWINSKI, JOSSEL	00	M	TRDSMN	PLZZZZNY
FUNK, LEIB	00	M	LABR	PLZZZZNY
JACOBSON, RUB.	19	M	LKSH	PLZZZZNY
CHASEN, L.	18	F	WO	PLZZZZNY
SCHUL	.05	F	INFANT	PLZZZZNY
HARLIP, ELIAS	46	M	LABR	PLZZZZNY
HANNE	40	F	W	PLZZZZNY
LEA	20	F	D	PLZZZZNY
ARON	15	M	S	PLZZZZNY
MOSES	12	M	S	PLZZZZNY
HEISCHI	7	F	CHILD	PLZZZZNY
ISRAEL	6	M	CHILD	PLZZZZNY
----TE	5	F	CHILD	PLZZZZNY
FORENSKI, CHAS.	22	M	TRDSMN	PLZZZZUNK
SELKEN, SUSKIND	18	M	CL	PLZZZZNY
AGATHE	19	F	SI	PLZZZZNY
CHASEN, JACOB	20	M	TRDSMN	PLZZZZUNK
GROSS, RACHEL	18	F	W	PLZZZZNY
STEINBERG, FRIDA	30	F	WO	PLZZZZUNK
SCHEINE	5	F	CHILD	PLZZZZUNK
NACHUM	4	M	CHILD	PLZZZZUNK
ODER, SCH.J.	17	M	TRDSMN	PLZZZZUNK
LEWINSOHN, FEIGE	16	F	SGL	PLZZZZNY
KREISER, HIRSCH	20	M	MCHT	PLZZZZNY
SOBEL, CHAJE	26	F	WO	PLZZZZNY
LIOS	7	F	CHILD	PLZZZZNY
SALOMON	5	M	CHILD	PLZZZZNY
SCHABAD, BELLA-R.	45	F	WO	PLZZZZCH
TOKARSKY, FEIGE	20	F	WO	PLZZZZCH
DAVIDSON, LEIB	20	M	TRDSMN	PLZZZZCH
GORDON, LEIB	35	M	FARMER	PLZZZZCH
HAKOVSKA, SARA	13	F	SGL	PLZZZZCH
BEIK, MARIA	21	F	SGL	PLZZZZUNK
CIESLISKOSKA, CAROLINE	27	F	WO	RRZZZZNY
KOLATER	.06	F	INFANT	RRZZZZNY
GROSSMANN, PEPI	17	F	SGL	RRZZZZNY
LEICHTER, IDA	28	F	W	PLZZZZNY
CHAIM	26	M	LABR	PLZZZZNY
SLAWECK, LEIB	20	M	FARMER	RRZZZZNY
GERKOW, LEIB	17	M	TRDSMN	RRZZZZNY
UNKNOWN, HENRY	21	M	LABR	RRZZZZCH
-USSACH, PINCUS	00	M	LABR	RRZZZZCH
BLOM, SOPHIE	19	F	SGL	RRZZZZMA
LEIB	55	M	LABR	RRZZZZMA
BELA	50	F	W	RRZZZZMA
JACOB, SARA	15	F	SGL	RRZZZZNY
GIETEL	40	F	WO	RRZZZZNY
NICHAN	7	M	CHILD	RRZZZZNY
LEIB	6	M	CHILD	RRZZZZNY
MEIBRUCH, HIRSCH	38	M	TDR	PLZZZZNY
GELESMAN, HIRSCH	39	M	TDR	PLZZZZNY
MOSKOWITZ, SIMON	35	M	LABR	PLZZZZNY
GEFFKEN, ISAAC	20	M	TDR	RRZZZZIA
ADELMAN, RACHEL	17	F	SGL	RRZZZZIA
EPSTEIN, SELIG	19	M	LABR	RRZZZZNY
SEHEWACH, ABRAHAM	40	M	LABR	RRZZZZNY
LICHTENSTEIN, CZERNE	28	F	WO	RRZZZZNY
FEDOR	6	M	CHILD	RRZZZZNY
PAULINE	4	F	CHILD	RRZZZZNY
REBECHA	.09	F	INFANT	RRZZZZNY
WERSCHANRSKY, REISEL	19	F	SGL	RRZZZZNY
PRASS, JACOB	36	M	TRDSMN	RRZZZZNY
MARKORD, ITTE	17	F	SGL	RRZZZZNY
BLUM, CHAIE	20	F	SGL	RRZZZZNY
SCHNEIDER, JUDEL	28	M	TRDSMN	RRZZZZNY
BERK, BEHR	18	M	TRDSMN	RRZZZZNY
FRIEDLANDER, ITTE	23	F	SGL	RRZZZZNY
VOLKOW, RIWE	28	F	WO	RRZZZZNY
LEAH	.10	F	INFANT	RRZZZZNY
KATZ, PINCUS	00	M	LABR	RRZZZZNY
BLUME	19	F	W	RRZZZZNY
COLEL	.07	F	INFANT	RRZZZZNY
REITZ, ABRAH.	16	M	LABR	RRZZZZNY
PALANDT, M.	19	M	LABR	RRZZZZNY
TRECCSTEDT, B.	38	M	TRDSMN	RRZZZZNY
COHN, JACOB	19	M	BRM	RRZZZZNY

PASSENGER	AGE	SEX	OCCUPATION	PRV	VIL	DES

SHIP: ST LAURENT

FROM: HAVRE
TO: NEW YORK
ARRIVED: 08 JULY 1885

RASZEK, ANDRE	26	M	SHMK	PL	ZZZZ	NY

SHIP: WYOMING

FROM: LIVERPOOL AND QUEENSTOWN
TO: NEW YORK
ARRIVED: 08 JULY 1885

KOIG, JOSEF	15	M	PMBR	RR	ZZZZ	USA
LINKEH, MOSES	26	M	GZR	RR	ZZZZ	USA
GOLGSHAUB, SEIDE	19	M	LABR	RR	ZZZZ	USA
KAHN, SRADIG	27	M	BLKSMH	RR	ZZZZ	USA
SCRAPRO, SAM.	18	M	SDLR	RR	ZZZZ	USA
CLAINK, MINNIE	11	F	CH	RR	ZZZZ	USA

SHIP: PENNLAND

FROM: ANTWERP
TO: NEW YORK
ARRIVED: 09 JULY 1885

JAHUKE, MEIKE-MRS	56	F	SLSMN	RR	ZZZZ	USA
PIOCHOWIAK, WOJ.	45	M	LABR	RR	ZZZZ	NY
MALUSIAK, FRZ.	19	M	LABR	RR	ZZZZ	NY
SAMSON, JUL.	30	M	MNR	PL	ZZZZ	NY
CATH.	36	F	MNR	PL	ZZZZ	NY
PET.	8	M	CHILD	PL	ZZZZ	NY
MARIE	6	F	CHILD	PL	ZZZZ	NY
JOHN	3	M	CHILD	PL	ZZZZ	NY
MATHA.	00	F	INF	PL	ZZZZ	NY

SHIP: CITY OF CHESTER

FROM: LIVERPOOL AND QUEENSTOWN
TO: NEW YORK
ARRIVED: 10 JULY 1885

MAKIBALO, AUGUSTA	23	F	SVNT	PL	AGUZ	MN
HILDA-S.	25	F	SVNT	PL	AGUZ	MN
LEION, TELA-A.	18	F	SVNT	PL	AGUZ	CH
TILON, MARIA-J.	25	F	SVNT	PL	AGUZ	CH
PAUKALA, SELINA	25	F	SVNT	PL	AGUZ	MN
GRENMBYR, RICH.	21	M	TNMK	PL	ADED	NY
KARKAITER, JONAS	25	M	LABR	PL	ACBF	NY
ANNA	23	F	W	PL	ACBF	NY
ANNA	1	F	CHILD	PL	ACBF	NY
DELIGNER, JOS.	20	M	LABR	PL	ACBF	NY
LEMDER, KAZIS	22	M	LABR	PL	ADBQ	NY
KANMAN, ELGIN	19	M	TLR	PL	ADED	NY
ELINA	21	F	W	PL	ADED	NY
FRANK, ABRAHAM	25	M	TLR	PL	ADED	NY
ELINA	25	F	W	PL	ADED	NY
GLUCKUMANN, J.	29	M	MSN	PL	ADBQ	NY
FANNY	24	F	W	PL	ADBQ	NY
TUCK	3	M	CHILD	PL	ADBQ	NY
U	00	M	INF	PL	ADBQ	NY
COHEN, JACOB	30	M	LABR	PL	ADBQ	NY
JANE	19	F	SVNT	PL	ADBQ	NY

SHIP: STATE OF ALABAMA

FROM: GLASGOW AND LARNE
TO: NEW YORK
ARRIVED: 10 JULY 1885

MISLUTERZ, SALOMON	00	M	UNKNOWN	RR	ZZZZ	NY
PRING, PEPI	00	F	NN	RR	ZZZZ	NY
ELLICHOWITZ, EFRAIM	00	M	LABR	RR	ZZZZ	NY
FAMELSOHN, L.	00	M	UNKNOWN	RR	ZZZZ	OH
FAST, JACOB	00	M	LABR	RR	ZZZZ	NY
FINKELMANN, MARCUS	00	M	UNKNOWN	RR	ZZZZ	BO
FISCHBEIN, S.	00	M	UNKNOWN	RR	ZZZZ	NY
FRUNTSEH, J.	00	M	LABR	RR	ZZZZ	NY
GRIKETIS, JOHANN	00	M	LABR	RR	ZZZZ	NY
GORDON, MENDEL	00	M	UNKNOWN	RR	ZZZZ	OH
M.	00	M	LABR	RR	ZZZZ	NY
GALANZIK, E.	00	M	LABR	RR	ZZZZ	NY
GINSBERG, CHANE	00	M	UNKNOWN	RR	ZZZZ	NY
SARAH	00	F	W	RR	ZZZZ	NY
PAULINE	00	F	NN	RR	ZZZZ	NY
ROSE	00	F	NN	RR	ZZZZ	NY
BERNAND	00	M	NN	RR	ZZZZ	NY
GENDLER, MOSES	00	M	SMH	RR	ZZZZ	NY
GORKOWSKI, JAN	00	M	BBR	RR	ZZZZ	MO
JARLINSKY, HERSCH	28	M	LABR	RR	ZZZZ	NY
JOSEFOWICZ, STEFAN	44	M	SMH	RR	ZZZZ	PHI
WARZILLA	23	F	SVNT	RR	ZZZZ	PHI
KRASSA, EMANUEL	43	M	LABR	RR	ZZZZ	NY
EMIL	11	M	CH	RR	ZZZZ	NY
HKOVICTZ, ARON	37	M	UNKNOWN	RR	ZZZZ	NY
LUEFFER, A.	26	M	LABR	RR	ZZZZ	NY
NAITES, STEPHAN	23	M	LABR	RR	ZZZZ	NY
DAFSCHES, KASJMIR	30	M	LABR	RR	ZZZZ	NY
SCHWESTES, A.	23	M	LABR	RR	ZZZZ	NY
PENHOF, MEYER	28	M	HTR	RR	ZZZZ	NY
CHASCHE	20	F	W	RR	ZZZZ	NY
GDALJE	.01	F	INFANT	RR	ZZZZ	NY
SUCHAJ, P.	22	M	LABR	RR	ZZZZ	MO
SCHWARTZ----, P.	00	U	UNKNOWN	RR	ZZZZ	NY
SEMIN, LINA	20	F	NN	RR	ZZZZ	NY
SCHNEIDERMANN, ELIAS	24	M	UNKNOWN	RR	ZZZZ	MO
SPRINGE	22	F	W	RR	ZZZZ	MO
WEINBERG, L.	40	M	UNKNOWN	RR	ZZZZ	NY
ZACHILOW, JULIAN	22	M	LABR	RR	ZZZZ	MO
ZIEGLER, HIRSCH	16	M	CBLR	RR	ZZZZ	NY

SHIP: EMS

FROM: BREMEN
TO: NEW YORK
ARRIVED: 11 JULY 1885

MICKADISCH, MARTHA	20	F	NN	RR	AHOO	USA
OLSCHEWSKY, JOSEF	40	M	LABR	RR	AFWJ	USA
GRUENBERG, MAX	20	M	LABR	RR	ZZZZ	USA
WRONA, REGINA	18	F	NN	RR	ZZZZ	USA
HIRSCH	19	M	LABR	RR	ZZZZ	USA
MAROS, WINCENTY	25	M	LABR	RR	AFWJ	USA

PASSENGER	AGE	SEX	OCCUPATION	PRVL	VIL	DES
WOLLMANN, CARL	32	M	LABR	RR	ZZZZ	USA
ANNA	24	F	NN	RR	ZZZZ	USA
MARIA	5	F	CHILD	RR	ZZZZ	USA
BERTHA	2	F	CHILD	RR	ZZZZ	USA
LOUISE	.02	F	INFANT	RR	ZZZZ	USA
BUKEWICZ, VINCENTY	31	M	LABR	RR	ZZZZ	USA
WIRSBOLOWSKY, JOSEF	32	M	LABR	RR	ZZZZ	USA
BUZANSKY, BARILE	18	F	NN	RR	ZZZZ	USA
MEHR, SCHEWA	30	F	NN	RR	ZZZZ	USA
ELLI	10	F	CH	RR	ZZZZ	USA
HEINRICH	8	M	CHILD	RR	ZZZZ	USA
DAVIDOWITZ, MARIANNE	30	F	NN	RR	ZZZZ	USA
BENJAMIN	10	M	CH	RR	ZZZZ	USA
KASRIL	8	M	CHILD	RR	ZZZZ	USA
ISAAC	7	M	CHILD	RR	ZZZZ	USA
MEYER	5	M	CHILD	RR	ZZZZ	USA
ESCHER	3	M	CHILD	RR	ZZZZ	USA
BLOUSTEIN, ARSIK	19	M	LABR	RR	AFWJ	USA
SLOTINSKY, RUCHE	28	F	NN	RR	AFWJ	USA
SCHMUL	8	M	CHILD	RR	AFWJ	USA
BASSE	.11	F	INFANT	RR	AFWJ	USA

SHIP: GENERAL WERDER

FROM: BREMEN AND SOUTHAMPTON
TO: NEW YORK
ARRIVED: 11 JULY 1885

PASSENGER	AGE	SEX	OCCUPATION	PRVL	VIL	DES
DEMBYE, MORITZ	35	M	LABR	RR	ZZZZ	USA
WAGNER, SORE	22	F	NN	RR	ZZZZ	USA
MUELLER, CIWZE	44	F	NN	RR	ZZZZ	USA
BEILE	11	F	CH	RR	ZZZZ	USA
ABREMKE	10	M	CH	RR	ZZZZ	USA
SCHMULKE	8	M	CHILD	RR	ZZZZ	USA
PENTAR, SCHL.	35	M	LABR	RR	ZZZZ	USA
CONTS, SORI	35	F	NN	RR	ZZZZ	USA
DAVIDSON, ABRAHAM	16	M	LABR	RR	ZZZZ	USA
ISAAC	31	M	LABR	RR	ZZZZ	USA
SLOTINSKYE, RACHE	28	F	NN	RR	ZZZZ	USA
BASSE	8	F	CHILD	RR	ZZZZ	USA
SETEMBAS	.11	M	INFANT	RR	ZZZZ	USA
PISKORSKI, ADAM	30	M	LABR	RR	ZZZZ	USA
SKULNIK, MORITZ	36	M	LABR	RR	ZZZZ	USA
PANIMS, PEISACH	15	M	LABR	RR	ZZZZ	USA
GENDEL, MENDEL	31	M	LABR	RR	ZZZZ	USA
BRZOZONSKI, CHANE	40	F	NN	RR	ZZZZ	USA
JOCHIM	17	M	CH	RR	ZZZZ	USA
JANKEL	17	M	CH	RR	ZZZZ	USA
MASCH	11	F	CH	RR	ZZZZ	USA
MANSCHEL	6	M	CHILD	RR	ZZZZ	USA
WURUBLEWSKI, CHANE	40	F	NN	RR	ZZZZ	USA
LEIB	16	M	CH	RR	ZZZZ	USA
BADASCH, CHAJE	20	F	NN	RR	ZZZZ	USA
RANTNER, CHAIS	20	F	NN	RR	ZZZZ	USA
ROCHANGER, ANTON	33	M	LABR	RR	ZZZZ	USA
BLUM, KALMAN	25	M	LABR	RR	ZZZZ	USA
WYESZYNSKI, JOSEPH	20	M	LABR	RR	ZZZZ	USA
WOLSKI, JOSEPH	35	M	LABR	RR	ZZZZ	USA
SMOLEWSKI, FEIGE	18	M	FARMER	RR	ZZZZ	USA
WOLFF, BAROF	15	M	FARMER	RR	ZZZZ	USA
LEWKOWICZ, MICH.	22	M	LABR	RR	ZZZZ	USA
WEINER, HIRSCH	18	M	LABR	RR	ZZZZ	USA
MARYOWSKYE, ABRAHAM	20	M	DLR	RR	ZZZZ	USA
ZAKRZEWSKI, ALEXANDER	29	M	FARMER	RR	ZZZZ	USA
HELENA	28	F	NN	RR	ZZZZ	USA
ALEXANDER	4	M	CHILD	RR	ZZZZ	USA
JOHAN	2	M	CHILD	RR	ZZZZ	USA
JOSEPH	1	M	CHILD	RR	ZZZZ	USA
BLAUSS, JOHAN	51	M	FARMER	RR	ZZZZ	USA
RATZLAFF, BENJAMIN	19	M	TLR	RR	ZZZZ	USA
HERMANN, FERDINAND	27	M	LABR	RR	ZZZZ	USA
GRASOFSKY, PAULA	26	F	NN	RR	ZZZZ	USA
SIMON	4	M	CHILD	RR	ZZZZ	USA
ANNA	2	F	CHILD	RR	ZZZZ	USA
EMMA	.08	F	INFANT	RR	ZZZZ	USA
KUEZEWITZ, JULIA	37	F	NN	RR	ZZZZ	USA

SHIP: WESTPHALIA

FROM: HAMBURG AND HAVRE
TO: NEW YORK
ARRIVED: 11 JULY 1885

PASSENGER	AGE	SEX	OCCUPATION	PRVL	VIL	DES
JARGOSTEIN, CHASZE	44	F	W	RR	AHTR	USA
LIEBE	20	F	CH	RR	AHTR	USA
LEA	9	F	CHILD	RR	AHTR	USA
CHAIM	8	F	CHILD	RR	AHTR	USA
GITTEL	7	F	CHILD	RR	AHTR	USA
JANKUNER, NOCHIM	42	M	LABR	RR	AHZS	USA
ZIWIE	34	F	W	RR	AHZS	USA
ISAAC	9	M	CHILD	RR	AHZS	USA
BENJAMIN	8	M	CHILD	RR	AHZS	USA
ABRAH.	7	M	CHILD	RR	AHZS	USA
MOSES	6	M	CHILD	RR	AHZS	USA
FEIGE	.11	F	INFANT	RR	AHZS	USA
JALOWITZ, JACOB	19	M	LABR	RR	AHTF	USA
LAPIDUSOHN, ETTEL	40	F	W	RR	AHTF	USA
JENNY	18	F	CH	RR	AHTF	USA
CHAIE	9	F	CHILD	RR	AHTF	USA
REBECCA	5	F	CHILD	RR	AHTF	USA
MORDSCHE	4	F	CHILD	RR	AHTF	USA
RUSSE	3	F	CHILD	RR	AHTF	USA
ROSA	.06	F	INFANT	RR	AHTF	USA
WILCZEK, ASCHER	20	M	LABR	RR	AHTW	USA
RUBINSKY, NOSEM	44	M	CL	RR	ZZZZ	USA
WINETZKY, BASSE	18	F	SGL	RR	ZZZZ	USA
SCHANBROWSKY, JESKA	16	F	SGL	RR	AGRT	USA
ENGEL, GOLDE	17	F	SGL	RR	AHTU	USA
GWILDIES, HEINR.	33	M	LABR	RR	AHZS	USA
LUDWIG, AUGUST	32	M	LABR	RR	AHZS	USA
K-I--T, MARIE	16	F	SGL	RR	AHZS	USA
STANAT, SIGMUND	29	M	LABR	RR	AHZS	USA
BROSTOWSKY, SCHLOMA	32	M	DLR	RR	AHZS	USA
CASPERSKY, KALMAN	15	M	DLR	RR	AHZS	USA
KANTER, HARRIS	28	M	DLR	RR	AHZS	USA
DWORELISKY, CHARLES	30	M	DLR	RR	ZZZZ	USA
KAUFMANN, BEILE	16	F	SGL	RR	ZZZZ	USA
KUSNEB, HODE	17	F	SGL	RR	AHTF	USA
CARABELNIK, RACHEL	45	F	W	RR	ZZZZ	USA
PAULINE	18	F	CH	RR	ZZZZ	USA
SAMUEL	15	M	CH	RR	ZZZZ	USA
MOSES	9	M	CHILD	RR	ZZZZ	USA
KASCHINSKY, MOSES	21	M	TLR	RR	AHZS	USA
RAPPEPORT, MOJES	23	M	TNR	RR	ZZZZ	USA
NICOLAI, FERD.	23	M	SMH	RR	ZZZZ	USA
DOERR, JULS.	21	M	CTW	RR	ZZZZ	USA
SROGOWITZ, CHANNE	20	M	CGRMKR	RR	AHWP	USA
GITTEL	20	F	W	RR	AHWP	USA
BRAUN, JACOB	20	M	LABR	RR	AHZS	USA
ELKE	18	F	W	RR	AHZS	USA
ROSEN, RUBEN	18	M	TLR	RR	ZZZZ	USA
ULMER, JACOB	46	M	FARMER	RR	AFQV	USA
ELISABETH	35	F	W	RR	AFQV	USA
SOPHIE	8	F	CHILD	RR	AFQV	USA
CARL	4	M	CHILD	RR	AFQV	USA
WILH	3	M	CHILD	RR	AFQV	USA
CARL	.06	M	INFANT	RR	AFQV	USA
PILHJANOKI, GUSTAVA	18	F	SGL	FN	ZZZZ	USA
SCHACOKISCH, HANNA	26	F	SGL	RR	ZZZZ	USA
BARANOWITSCH, CHAIE	45	F	W	RR	ZZZZ	USA

PASSENGER	AGE	SEX	OCCUPATION	PRV VIL DES
BEHR	9	M	CHILD	RRZZZZUSA
JOSSEL	8	M	CHILD	RRZZZZUSA
ELIAS	6	M	CHILD	RRZZZZUSA
ETTEL	4	F	CHILD	RRZZZZUSA
EDELMANN, CHASZE	40	F	W	RRZZZZUSA
JANKEL	18	M	CH	RRZZZZUSA
LEIB	9	M	CHILD	RRZZZZUSA
ISAAC	8	M	CHILD	RRZZZZUSA
WODNYCK, SARA	28	F	W	RRZZZZUSA
JOSEF	5	M	CHILD	RRZZZZUSA
ABRAH.	.11	M	INFANT	RRZZZZUSA
LANB, ISAAC	50	M	LABR	RRZZZZUSA
ESTHER	48	F	W	RRZZZZUSA
FRUMET	21	F	CH	RRZZZZUSA
MALKE	8	F	CHILD	RRZZZZUSA
FEINSTEIN, SAMUEL	40	M	LABR	RRZZZZUSA
SARA	37	F	W	RRZZZZUSA
MOSES	.11	M	INFANT	RRZZZZUSA
MINNA	68	F	W	RRZZZZUSA
KUTTNER, BELLA	18	F	SGL	RRZZZZUSA
KAPLAN, ESRA	9	F	CHILD	RRAHTRUSA
WERNER, DAVID	25	M	LABR	RRAHUFUSA
SHERMANN, LOUIS	39	M	LABR	RRAHTUUSA
PERLENFEIND, GOTTL.	25	M	LABR	RRAFQVUSA
EVA	24	F	W	RRAFQVUSA
GOTTLOB	.09	M	INFANT	RRAFQVUSA
LEWINSOHN, DAVID	25	M	BCHR	RRAHSLUSA
MINE	20	F	W	RRAHSLUSA
LANDAU, JEFIN	58	M	LABR	RRAEFLUSA
SCHNEIDER, LEISER	17	M	LABR	RRAHTFUSA
AMBROSEWITZ, ADAM	30	M	LABR	RRAHZSUSA
SYLVESTER	25	M	LABR	RRAHZSUSA
SCHUSSEL, SIMON	37	M	DLR	RRZZZZUSA
LILIE	40	F	W	RRZZZZUSA
JACOB	10	M	CH	RRZZZZUSA
ESTHER	11	F	CH	RRZZZZUSA
LAUB, ISAAC	.06	M	INFANT	RRZZZZUSA
SCHAMARIN, NICOLAI	38	M	ENGR	RRAHQHUSA
SOPHIE	26	F	W	RRAHQHUSA
GOLDSTEIN, MAYER	40	M	DLR	RRZZZZUSA
ESTHER	35	F	W	RRZZZZUSA
BERLA	9	F	CHILD	RRZZZZUSA
HOGA	8	F	CHILD	RRZZZZUSA
ISAAC	7	M	CHILD	RRZZZZUSA
JACOB	4	M	CHILD	RRZZZZUSA

SHIP: ZAANDAM

FROM: AMSTERDAM
TO: NEW YORK
ARRIVED: 11 JULY 1885

PASSENGER	AGE	SEX	OCCUPATION	PRV VIL DES
CLAUSEN, ABEL	19	M	LABR	PLZZZZUSA
SCHMIRAWSKI, KASIS	40	M	MCHT	PLZZZZUSA
KATRE	45	F	UNKNOWN	PLZZZZUSA
ANDREAS	17	M	CH	PLZZZZUSA
ZANAS	7	M	CHILD	PLZZZZUSA
ELARIANA	1	F	CHILD	PLZZZZUSA
KAGLS	.06	M	INFANT	PLZZZZUSA
SCHUPENES, KASIS	26	M	UNKNOWN	PLZZZZUSA
ELISE	00	F	UNKNOWN	PLZZZZUSA
BAKEN, CHAIE	00	M	UNKNOWN	PLZZZZUSA
FRAISE, CHARIE	00	M	UNKNOWN	PLZZZZUSA
DLOVITZ, OSFCHER	00	M	UNKNOWN	PLZZZZUSA
CURAN, HILLEL	27	M	UNKNOWN	PLZZZZUSA
FELDMAN, HERMANA	27	F	UNKNOWN	PLZZZZUSA
ZIRMSCHI, SORE	30	M	MCHT	PLZZZZUSA
ROSA	7	F	CHILD	PLZZZZUSA
ALTER	3	M	CHILD	PLZZZZUSA
DWORA	.06	F	INFANT	PLZZZZUSA
SLACEWER, SALOMON	35	M	MCHT	PLZZZZUSA
PEKARSKEY, CARL	22	M	MCHT	PLZZZZUSA
SLATOWSKIJ, HIRSCH	32	M	MCHT	PLZZZZUSA
PEKARSKEY, JACOB	32	M	MCHT	PLZZZZUSA
REICHWEIN, ANNA	49	F	UNKNOWN	PLZZZZUSA

SHIP: LESSING

FROM: HAMBURG
TO: NEW YORK
ARRIVED: 13 JULY 1885

PASSENGER	AGE	SEX	OCCUPATION	PRV VIL DES
ROSTOWSKY, SARA	35	F	W	PLAHVAUSA
WOLF	9	M	CHILD	PLAHVAUSA
LEA	6	F	CHILD	PLAHVAUSA
EHREN, DOBRE	18	F	SGL	RRZZZZUSA
BARZOWSKY, BASCHE	18	F	SGL	RRAHTFUSA
BAROW, ISSER	17	M	LABR	RRZZZZUSA
MIRIAM	16	F	SGL	RRZZZZUSA
MADSEN, GEORGINE	54	F	W	FNZZZZUSA
KOWALSKA, SCHOLASTIKA	48	F	W	RRZZZZUSA
BRONISLAV	9	M	CHILD	RRZZZZUSA
WLADISLAWA	7	F	CHILD	RRZZZZUSA
COHEN, HANNE	22	F	SGL	RRZZZZUSA
KRUPIENSKA, CATHA.	29	F	W	RRAHTGUSA
ANTONINA	.11	F	INFANT	RRAHTGUSA
GOLDOFT, NOCHEN	16	M	UPHST	RRZZZZUSA
SAUL	9	M	CHILD	RRZZZZUSA
APPELSOHN, LIEBE	34	F	W	RRZZZZUSA
MOTEL	7	M	CHILD	RRZZZZUSA
SAMUEL	4	M	CHILD	RRZZZZUSA
DAVID	.11	M	INFANT	RRZZZZUSA
KATRORCK, MIRIAM	26	F	W	RRZZZZUSA
JOCHE.	.11	F	INFANT	RRZZZZUSA
MIKLISCHANSKY, SAMUEL	46	M	LABR	RRZZZZUSA
SARA	44	F	W	RRZZZZUSA
SARA	9	F	CHILD	RRZZZZUSA
RACHEL	6	F	CHILD	RRZZZZUSA
LIBOWITZ, RACHEL	46	F	W	RRZZZZUSA
ANNA	14	F	CH	RRZZZZUSA
ISAAC	7	M	CHILD	RRZZZZUSA
SCHEINE	5	F	CHILD	RRZZZZUSA
JANOWSKY, LEIB	33	M	LABR	RRAHVUUSA
LIKUTZKY, MEYER	18	M	LABR	RRAHSWUSA
SCHEINKER, EMILIE	37	F	W	RRAFWJUSA
MORRIS	9	M	CHILD	RRAFWJUSA
ROSALIE	8	F	CHILD	RRAFWJUSA
JOSEPH	7	M	CHILD	RRAFWJUSA
ARON	5	M	CHILD	RRAFWJUSA
PASTERNACK, CHAIE	35	F	W	RRAFVGUSA
DWORE	15	F	CH	RRAFVGUSA
SWED, VICTOR	19	M	FARMER	FNZZZZUSA
GOLDBERG, ABRAH.	20	M	MCHT	FNZZZZUSA
ZIEVERS, CHAIM	34	M	LABR	FNZZZZUSA
STERNBERG, BERNHD.	27	M	LABR	FNZZZZUSA
ROSA	21	F	W	FNZZZZUSA
SOLTOK, SCHIJE	18	M	LABR	FNZZZZUSA
ZOGELOWITZ, ABRAM	9	M	CHILD	FNZZZZUSA
TOBIAS, BERISCH	20	M	LABR	FNZZZZUSA
GUT, MARCUS	19	M	LABR	FNZZZZUSA
SOLL, LASER	19	M	LABR	FNZZZZUSA
ABRAMOWITZ, NATHAN	19	M	LABR	FNZZZZUSA
FRIEDACH, SIMON	22	M	LABR	FNZZZZUSA
ASEH, ROSA	19	F	SGL	FNAGRTUSA
BERTHA	15	F	SGL	FNAGRTUSA
KUSCHNER, CHAIM	21	M	JNR	FNZZZZUSA
POLIPP, JOHANN	19	M	JNR	FNZZZZUSA
ACHILOWITZ, NOCHEM	18	M	JNR	FNZZZZUSA
DELANSKY, BEILE	18	F	SGL	FNZZZZUSA
RACHEL	9	F	CHILD	FNZZZZUSA

PASSENGER	AGE	SEX	OCCUPATION	PRV	VIL	DES
KABATSCHNICK, ISAAC	9	M	CHILD	FN	ZZZZ	USA
HARWITZ, CHAIC	42	F	W	FN	ZZZZ	USA
JETTE	19	F	CH	FN	ZZZZ	USA
FANNY	13	F	CH	FN	ZZZZ	USA
JENNY	12	F	CH	FN	ZZZZ	USA
BERTHA	5	F	CHILD	FN	ZZZZ	USA
SARA	7	F	CHILD	FN	ZZZZ	USA
GLUECKMANN, ABRAHAM	40	M	LABR	FN	AFWJ	USA
SUSSMANN, ISIDOR	47	M	LABR	FN	ACON	USA
AUGUSTE	45	F	W	FN	ACON	USA
IDA	18	F	CH	FN	ACON	USA
BERTHA	9	F	CHILD	FN	ACON	USA
ULRIKE	8	F	CHILD	FN	ACON	USA
WILLY	5	M	CHILD	FN	ACON	USA
TOMKEWITZ, DOMINICK	22	M	LABR	FN	AHZS	USA
KATYRSKY, JAN	19	M	LABR	FN	AHZS	USA
BILOZOR, PIOTR	25	M	LABR	FN	AHZS	USA
LEYMEL, FRANZ	21	M	LABR	FN	AHZS	USA
RETTER, CARL	38	M	FARMER	FN	AFQV	USA
BAECKER, RIWE	18	F	SGL	FN	AHTF	USA
KUPPEMANN, SIMON	18	M	LABR	FN	ZZZZ	USA
BASZ, MIRL.	25	F	W	FN	ZZZZ	USA
HENACH	.11	M	INFANT	FN	ZZZZ	USA
CHAWES, MOSZES	25	F	W	FN	ZZZZ	USA
LEBSE	.06	M	INFANT	FN	ZZZZ	USA
FRUME	4	M	CHILD	FN	ZZZZ	USA
USIAK, FRANK	21	M	LABR	FN	ZZZZ	USA
ANTONINA	20	F	W	FN	ZZZZ	USA
SILBERSCHN, NOCHUM	19	M	LABR	FN	AHWE	USA
EISENBERG, SAMUEL	18	M	LABR	FN	AHZS	USA
LIPINSKY, SORACH	18	F	LABR	FN	AHZS	USA
NECHAMKES, MISKO	21	M	SMH	FN	AFVG	USA
PINCUS	19	M	SMH	FN	AFVG	USA
MARKS, SARAH	35	F	W	FN	AHTO	USA
TAUBE	7	F	CHILD	FN	AHTO	USA
SALOMON	4	M	CHILD	FN	AHTO	USA
ROSENFELD, MEYER	19	M	CPMKR	FN	AHZS	USA
KOTLER, ISAAC	26	M	LABR	FN	ZZZZ	USA
STOLOWSKY, LIPPE	20	F	SGL	FN	ZZZZ	USA
SMOLENSKI, SCHEINE	50	F	W	FN	ZZZZ	USA
ETTEL	21	F	W	FN	ZZZZ	USA
GNESCHE	12	F	CH	FN	ZZZZ	USA
LEIB	9	M	CHILD	FN	ZZZZ	USA
HIRSCH	7	M	CHILD	FN	ZZZZ	USA
KOWALSKI, ISRAEL	43	M	LABR	FN	ZZZZ	USA
FRIEDMANN, CHAIE-RUSKI	28	F	W	FN	ZZZZ	USA
ESTHER	.11	F	INFANT	FN	ZZZZ	USA
KAPLANSKI, FEIGE	47	F	W	FN	ZZZZ	USA
KREIM	19	M	CH	FN	ZZZZ	USA
SARA	11	F	CH	FN	ZZZZ	USA
JOSEPH	5	M	CHILD	FN	ZZZZ	USA
LEWINSKI, MOSES	42	M	SHMK	FN	ZZZZ	USA
NOCHIMSON, ABEL	25	M	DLR	FN	ZZZZ	USA
CHRISTAL, ISAAC	18	M	LABR	FN	ZZZZ	USA
FELLHAENDLER, JACOB	30	M	UNKNOWN	FN	AHZS	USA

SHIP: ETHIOPIA

FROM: GLASGOW AND MOVILLE
TO: NEW YORK
ARRIVED: 14 JULY 1885

PASSENGER	AGE	SEX	OCCUPATION	PRV	VIL	DES
PREGER, THERESA	27	F	HP	RR	ZZZZ	USA
FUCHS, HIRSET	20	M	WVR	RR	ZZZZ	USA
SCHNAPERA, MOSES	27	M	BXMR	RR	ZZZZ	USA
KRASCHANSKI, MORDCHE	32	M	LABR	RR	ZZZZ	USA
KOPASING, MARIA	38	F	HP	PL	ZZZZ	USA
FRENDEL, SENDER	16	M	LABR	PL	ZZZZ	USA
KOMENDA, KARL	28	M	SMH	PL	ZZZZ	USA
U, BARBARA	27	F	UNKNOWN	PL	ZZZZ	USA

SHIP: INDIA

FROM: HAMBURG
TO: NEW YORK
ARRIVED: 14 JULY 1885

PASSENGER	AGE	SEX	OCCUPATION	PRV	VIL	DES
TERENZEK, SMUEL	17	M	LABR	RR	ZZZZ	NY
DOBROWITZ, ABR.E.	20	M	TU	RR	ZZZZ	NY
SEIDEL, ABR.H.	20	M	LABR	RR	ZZZZ	NY
GUSTAJTESS, JOS.	20	M	LABR	RR	ZZZZ	NY
PCEK, ISRAEL-H.	20	M	TRDSMN	RR	ZZZZ	NY
TENDLER, LEIB	32	M	CNF	RR	ZZZZ	NY
OKANEWITZ, SCH.	55	M	TRDSMN	RR	ZZZZ	NY
MOSER	7	M	CHILD	RR	ZZZZ	NY
HARRIES, SAM.	17	M	TRDSMN	RR	ZZZZ	NY
OKERN, FEIGEL	19	F	SGL	RR	ZZZZ	NY
WEISSMANN, CHAIM	25	M	TRDSMN	RR	ZZZZ	STL
HEMSMAN, JETTE	20	F	SGL	RR	ZZZZ	NY
CZAZKA, BERG.	59	M	TLR	RR	ZZZZ	NY
SLATI	43	F	W	RR	ZZZZ	NY
RINKEWITZ, WLADISLAUS	27	M	LABR	RR	ZZZZ	NY
MEHRSTEIN, JANKEL	34	M	JNR	RR	ZZZZ	NY
LEWINSKY, SARA	50	F	WO	RR	ZZZZ	NY
CHAIE	7	M	CHILD	RR	ZZZZ	NY
FEIGE	6	M	CHILD	RR	ZZZZ	NY
JENTE	60	F	UNKNOWN	RR	ZZZZ	NY
TEITELBAUM, NACHM.	26	M	TDR	PL	ZZZZ	NY
HINDE	18	F	WO	PL	ZZZZ	NY
MORENSKOWA, ARNOLD	19	M	LABR	RR	ZZZZ	NY
SCHAPIRA, MARCUS	40	M	LABR	RR	ZZZZ	NY
KATZ, ITZIG	31	M	LABR	RR	ZZZZ	NY
BERGMAN, ELIAS	30	M	LABR	RR	ZZZZ	NY
GRABSEZERI, B.	27	M	LABR	RR	ZZZZ	NY
BERNTH, KARL	24	M	LABR	RR	ZZZZ	NY

SHIP: BOTHNIA

FROM: LIVERPOOL AND QUEENSTOWN
TO: NEW YORK
ARRIVED: 15 JULY 1885

PASSENGER	AGE	SEX	OCCUPATION	PRV	VIL	DES
KOHN, NATHAN	30	M	SHMK	PL	ZZZZ	NY

SHIP: CITY OF CHICAGO

FROM: LIVERPOOL AND QUEENSTOWN
TO: NEW YORK
ARRIVED: 17 JULY 1885

PASSENGER	AGE	SEX	OCCUPATION	PRV	VIL	DES
BAWELT, MAT.	35	M	CPMKR	PL	AARR	NY
PINCKANKUS, PEUBB	32	F	W	PL	AEWS	NY
RODD, NILL	19	M	LABR	PL	AEWS	NY

PASSENGER	AGE	SEX	OCCUPATION	PRV	VIL	DES

SHIP: MAIN

FROM: BREMEN
TO: NEW YORK
ARRIVED: 17 JULY 1885

PASSENGER	AGE	SEX	OCCUPATION	PRV VIL DES
PETESCHINSKI, JANKEL	14	M	LABR	RRZZZZUSA
SIRVANSKI, FREIDE	20	M	LABR	RRZZZZUSA
RUSKYE, BENJAMIN	35	M	LABR	RRZZZZUSA
HARRIS	15	M	LABR	RRZZZZUSA
NAUJOHAS, JOHANN	30	M	LABR	RRZZZZUSA
BOEHNIC, MARIA	17	F	SVNT	RRZZZZUSA
CZIZELSKI, DWORE	50	F	W	RRZZZZUSA
HENE	15	F	D	RRZZZZUSA
MEYERS, PERCHE	18	F	SVNT	RRZZZZUSA
HINZ, CHRISTINE	39	F	SVNT	RRZZZZUSA
LORGE, FERIE	27	F	SVNT	RRZZZZUSA
RZESZEWSKY, ESTER	18	F	SVNT	RRZZZZUSA
PUSCHNER, SARA	22	F	W	RRZZZZUSA
LENZE	.06	F	INFANT	RRZZZZUSA
CHERJCIKAS, MICHAEL	30	M	LABR	RRZZZZUSA
ANNA	32	F	W	RRZZZZUSA
TRASJESKI, IGNATZ	40	M	LABR	RRZZZZUSA
MARIANNE	30	F	W	RRZZZZUSA
STANISLAUS	10	M	CH	RRZZZZUSA
ANTONIE	6	F	CHILD	RRZZZZUSA
AMALIE	1	F	CHILD	RRZZZZUSA
JOSEF	.03	M	INFANT	RRZZZZUSA

SHIP: STATE OF NEVADA

FROM: GLASGOW AND LARNE
TO: NEW YORK
ARRIVED: 17 JULY 1885

PASSENGER	AGE	SEX	OCCUPATION	PRV VIL DES
BADDASCH, W.	11	M	CH	RRZZZZUSA
BLANSTEIN, C.	33	M	LAD	RRZZZZUSA
REB.	2	F	CHILD	RRZZZZUSA
CLARA	1	F	CHILD	RRZZZZUSA
BOCKANTZ, N.	24	M	BTDR	RRZZZZUSA
H.	22	F	W	RRZZZZUSA
BENJAMINOWITZ, B.	20	M	PDLR	RRZZZZUSA
CHATZ, J.	26	M	SHMK	RRZZZZUSA
EHRLICH, J.	33	M	PDLR	RRZZZZUSA
EDELMANN, L.	49	M	PDLR	RRZZZZUSA
M.	42	F	W	RRZZZZUSA
R.	00	F	CH	RRZZZZUSA
S.	4	F	CHILD	RRZZZZUSA
EMMA	1	F	CHILD	RRZZZZUSA
GRINKER, J.	18	M	PDLR	RRZZZZUSA
JENNY	12	F	CH	RRZZZZUSA
FYGNA, J.	36	M	TNSTH	RRZZZZUSA
GRUSCHKOWITZ, A.	18	M	SHMK	RRZZZZUSA
GRAJAR, S.	52	M	TLR	RRZZZZUSA
P.	45	F	W	RRZZZZUSA
C.	11	F	CH	RRZZZZUSA
E.	10	M	CH	RRZZZZUSA
S.	1	F	CHILD	RRZZZZUSA
GRUNER, A.	39	M	TLR	RRZZZZUSA
GRONBERG, L.	19	M	LABR	RRZZZZUSA
GLASS, J.	46	M	PDLR	RRZZZZUSA
HUTT, S.	19	M	TLR	RRZZZZUSA
JOSSELOWITZ, L.	23	M	JNR	RRZZZZUSA
KAUFMAN, A.	27	M	SHMK	RRZZZZUSA
KEISER, B.	42	M	PDLR	RRZZZZUSA
GOLDENBERG, A.	18	M	PDLR	RRZZZZUSA
KASKA, J.	25	M	LABR	RRZZZZUSA
KELEREJKA, H.	20	M	SHMK	RRZZZZUSA
KAHN, J.	21	M	PDLR	RRZZZZUSA
KADAN, P.	23	F	SVNT	RRZZZZUSA
MEHIEK, C.	24	M	MLR	RRZZZZUSA
MOTSCHELENIC, A.	21	M	CL	RRZZZZUSA
NOCHIM, C.	32	M	SHMK	RRZZZZUSA
R.	26	F	W	RRZZZZUSA
A.	00	M	CH	RRZZZZUSA
U, U	.03	F	INFANT	RRZZZZUSA
PAJELOWITZ, A.	25	M	LABR	RRZZZZUSA
PORT, M.	21	M	SHMK	RRZZZZUSA
RIBA, J.	20	M	LABR	RRZZZZUSA
RULONITZ, S.	20	M	LABR	RRZZZZUSA
E.	36	F	W	RRZZZZUSA
STUCK, JD.	31	M	CL	RRZZZZUSA
SEELMAN, J.	18	M	PDLR	RRZZZZUSA
SARAMACK, P.	12	M	CH	RRZZZZUSA
SCHOHAN, W.	19	M	LABR	RRZZZZUSA
SALMEROWITZ, M.	26	M	DSTLR	RRZZZZUSA
SEGALL, S.	18	M	PDLR	RRZZZZUSA
STROHM, C.	39	M	PDLR	RRZZZZUSA
STRANICKIS, A.	24	M	LABR	RRZZZZUSA
WOLK, R.	19	F	SVNT	RRZZZZUSA

SHIP: EIDER

FROM: BREMEN AND SOUTHAMPTON
TO: NEW YORK
ARRIVED: 18 JULY 1885

PASSENGER	AGE	SEX	OCCUPATION	PRV VIL DES
MAZKEWITZ, MARTIN	28	M	LABR	RRZZZZUSA

SHIP: LEERDAM

FROM: ROTTERDAM
TO: NEW YORK
ARRIVED: 18 JULY 1885

PASSENGER	AGE	SEX	OCCUPATION	PRV VIL DES
KWITSCHAN, KARL	00	M	SMH	PLZZZZUSA
AMALIA	28	F	UNKNOWN	PLZZZZUSA
NATHALIA	10	F	CH	PLZZZZUSA
GADULSKI, PAUL	33	M	LABR	PLZZZZUSA
DROSZESKY, FELIX	00	M	LABR	PLZZZZUSA
ILONKE, C-ERE	00	F	UNKNOWN	RRZZZZUSA
STORCH, BARBA.	17	F	UNKNOWN	RRZZZZUSA
SLOWOWIZKI, ABRAH.	25	M	MCHT	RRZZZZUSA
MASE, MOSE	00	M	MCHT	RRZZZZUSA
GRESCHEWIECH, MARTIN	28	F	UNKNOWN	RRZZZZUSA
GEREDCKY, PERL	00	F	UNKNOWN	RRZZZZUSA
SCHMUL	14	M	UNKNOWN	RRZZZZUSA
HIRSCHKOWITZ, U	00	F	UNKNOWN	RRZZZZUSA
GOREDECKY, EINIZ	00	M	UNKNOWN	RRZZZZUSA
KANN, U	00	M	LABR	RRZZZZUSA
MICHALSKY, MARTHA	25	F	UNKNOWN	RRZZZZUSA

SHIP: AURANIA

FROM: LIVERPOOL AND QUEENSTOWN
TO: NEW YORK
ARRIVED: 20 JULY 1885

PASSENGER	AGE	SEX	OCCUPATION	PRV	VIL	DES
WIEMAN, NILS	43	M	LABR	RR	ZZZZ	USA
ENGLUND, ERICK	22	M	LABR	RR	ZZZZ	USA
PAKKALA, S.M.	22	M	LABR	RR	ZZZZ	USA
RUHIJOWI, MARIE	22	F	SP	RR	ZZZZ	USA
LATTER, JULIUS	21	M	LABR	RR	ZZZZ	USA
HAPAGANGES, ALT.	18	M	LABR	RR	ZZZZ	USA
MATILA, JACOB	35	M	LABR	RR	ZZZZ	USA
BROSATZ, SALMAN	50	M	LABR	RR	AFZD	USA
LAPIN, RACHAEL	28	F	MA	RR	AFZD	USA
REBECCA	4	F	CHILD	RR	AFZD	USA
ROSA	2	F	CHILD	RR	AFZD	USA
MORGEMART, VICTOR	45	M	CL	RR	AFZD	USA
SCHEY, A.C.	50	M	LABR	RR	AFZD	USA
PWATSCH, FANNY	31	F	MA	RR	AFZD	USA
HAWEY	7	M	CHILD	RR	AFZD	USA
DAVIES, REIS	19	M	TLR	RR	AFZD	USA
WESTMAN, GUST.E.	23	M	LABR	RR	ZZZZ	USA
AUG.	20	M	LABR	RR	ZZZZ	USA
SUSSMAN, PAUL	22	M	LABR	RR	ZZZZ	USA
RAYMOND, CHAS.	20	F	SP	RR	ZZZZ	USA
MARK, HERM.	28	M	LABR	RR	ZZZZ	USA
H-----, JUD.	32	M	LABR	RR	ZZZZ	USA
GIBBINS, RICHD.	22	M	LABR	RR	ZZZZ	USA
MACLAZ, ED.J.	22	M	LABR	RR	ZZZZ	USA
PHILLIPS, GUFFITH	52	M	FARMER	RR	ZZZZ	USA
ROBINSON, JOSEPH	40	M	FARMER	RR	ZZZZ	USA
BICK, IWANCES	32	M	FARMER	RR	ZZZZ	USA
FICK----, WILH	47	M	TRVLR	RR	ZZZZ	USA
MARG-LI, OTTO	40	M	FARMER	RR	ZZZZ	USA

SHIP: FURNESSIA

FROM: UNKNOWN
TO: NEW YORK
ARRIVED: 20 JULY 1885

PASSENGER	AGE	SEX	OCCUPATION	PRV	VIL	DES
GRUND, SCHULEN	20	M	LABR	RR	ZZZZ	USA
KAUFMANN, HIRSCH	25	M	LABR	RR	ZZZZ	USA
LEWI, MENDEL	28	M	LABR	RR	ZZZZ	USA
ROSITZKI, GEMMANN	23	M	LABR	RR	ZZZZ	USA
BRAUN, SOPHIE	23	F	NN	RR	ZZZZ	USA
BARBAK, CHAJE	22	F	NN	RR	ZZZZ	USA
ABRAMOWICZ, JOSEPH	30	M	LABR	PL	ZZZZ	USA
KOPCZAK, J.	39	M	LABR	PL	ZZZZ	USA
MARIA	35	F	W	PL	ZZZZ	USA
JULIANA	10	F	CH	PL	ZZZZ	USA
ANGELIA	6	F	CHILD	PL	ZZZZ	USA
MARIA	2	F	CHILD	PL	ZZZZ	USA
JOSEF	29	M	LABR	PL	ZZZZ	USA
CHRISTIENSEN, NICLO-J.	26	M	FARMER	PL	ZZZZ	USA

SHIP: SPAIN

FROM: LIVERPOOL
TO: NEW YORK
ARRIVED: 20 JULY 1885

PASSENGER	AGE	SEX	OCCUPATION	PRV	VIL	DES
HINKA, JOH.E.	18	M	LABR	FN	ZZZZ	USA
AMANTA	21	F	SP	FN	ZZZZ	USA
MAHELA, MAT.	18	M	LABR	FN	ZZZZ	USA
JAWRELA, A.L.	25	M	LABR	FN	ZZZZ	USA
DAVIS, ANNA	18	F	SP	FN	ZZZZ	USA
SEIKA, GUSTAF	56	M	LABR	FN	ZZZZ	USA
LOUISA	56	F	W	FN	ZZZZ	USA
KALJANTEN, ANNA	40	F	SP	FN	ZZZZ	USA
AUGUST	4	F	CHILD	FN	ZZZZ	USA
CHAPIMKY, ABRAM	60	M	LABR	PL	ZZZZ	USA
SARA	58	F	W	PL	ZZZZ	USA
NUCHE	18	M	LABR	PL	ZZZZ	USA
NUMITALO, SIMON	40	M	LABR	FN	ZZZZ	USA
SANMILA, JAKOB	59	M	LABR	FN	ZZZZ	USA
ESAIASON, JOH.	39	M	LABR	FN	ZZZZ	USA
SOISKA, JOHAN	49	M	LABR	FN	ZZZZ	USA
BLEKI, JAKOB	36	M	LABR	FN	ZZZZ	USA
SILJANBAVA, JOH.	20	M	LABR	FN	ZZZZ	USA
KOSKI, JACOB	19	M	LABR	FN	ZZZZ	USA
EVA	33	F	W	FN	ZZZZ	USA
PORENEN, EMIL	18	M	LABR	FN	ZZZZ	USA
LAKARI, JOHN	35	M	LABR	FN	ZZZZ	USA
JEMTILA, JACOB	23	M	LABR	FN	ZZZZ	USA
KANGAS, MARIA	39	F	SP	FN	ZZZZ	USA
HELINA	6	F	CHILD	FN	ZZZZ	USA
SALAPAKKA, JOH.	19	M	LABR	FN	ZZZZ	USA
HOK, JOSEPHINA	24	F	SP	FN	ZZZZ	USA
BARKINEN, KAISA	25	F	SP	FN	ZZZZ	USA
HINKA, ERIK	56	M	LABR	FN	ZZZZ	USA
EFROSINE	54	F	W	FN	ZZZZ	USA
HENRIK	11	M	CH	FN	ZZZZ	USA
PETTER	10	M	CH	FN	ZZZZ	USA
MANSIKKA, JOH.	42	M	LABR	FN	ZZZZ	USA
SELLER, ABRAHAM	36	M	LABR	RR	ZZZZ	USA
BASE	26	F	W	RR	ZZZZ	USA
GSEL	7	M	CHILD	RR	ZZZZ	USA
PESSE	3	M	CHILD	RR	ZZZZ	USA
MOSES	1	M	CHILD	RR	ZZZZ	USA
KELIALKOV, ANELA	45	F	SP	FN	ZZZZ	USA
LUBELCALL, JAN	15	M	LABR	FN	ZZZZ	USA

SHIP: NEVADA

FROM: LIVERPOOL AND QUEENSTOWN
TO: NEW YORK
ARRIVED: 22 JULY 1885

PASSENGER	AGE	SEX	OCCUPATION	PRV	VIL	DES
FLINK, MATTS-K.	23	M	LABR	FN	ZZZZ	USA
BRANDBOCHER, ANDERS	31	M	LABR	FN	ZZZZ	USA

SHIP: ST. OF PENNSYLVANIA

FROM: GLASGOW AND LARNE
TO: NEW YORK
ARRIVED: 22 JULY 1885

PASSENGER	AGE	SEX	OCCUPATION	PRV	VIL	DES
BRAND, JACOB	45	M	MCHT	PL	ZZZZ	USA
JOSCHWED	35	F	W	PL	ZZZZ	USA

PASSENGER	AGE	SEX	OCCUPATION	PRV VIL DES
RUBIN	4	M	CHILD	PLZZZZUSA
OSCHER	3	M	CHILD	PLZZZZUSA
FEST, JACOB	22	M	MCHT	PLZZZZUSA
LANGENANER, JOSEF	18	M	MCHT	PLZZZZUSA
MANN, JOSSEL	22	M	MCHT	PLZZZZUSA
MOHUR, LEIB	32	M	LABR	PLZZZZUSA
NEZER, HERM.	26	M	MCHT	PLZZZZUSA
VEBERALL, CHAIM	35	M	MCHT	PLZZZZUSA
WLINSTEIN, MOSES	28	M	MCHT	PLACTCUSA
RINGER, LEAH	20	F	W	PLAHTFUSA
--AR--E, JACHKE	38	M	MCHT	RRZZZZUSA
DREICZE, SCHIC	16	M	MCHT	RRZZZZUSA
WIGOTZKI, CHAIM	19	M	MCHT	RRZZZZUSA
EICKELBERG, CHAIM	46	M	MCHT	RRZZZZUSA
SIMON	19	M	MCHT	RRZZZZUSA
ENDELMAN, JULIUS	19	M	MCHT	RRZZZZUSA
FANNY	20	F	W	RRZZZZUSA
FRIEDMAN, SALOMON	45	M	MCHT	RRZZZZUSA
FREIWUSCH, DAVID	25	M	HTR	RRAAKHUSA
JOHANNA	21	F	W	RRAAKHUSA
GERSON, MOSES	33	M	MCHT	RRAGRTUSA
HAMSCHLAG, LEIB	23	M	MCHT	RRZZZZUSA
HERSOHN, HERZ	43	M	MCHT	RRZZZZUSA
ITZIKOW, BEER	30	M	MCHT	RRAHTFUSA
JAKNOWITZ, ARON	25	M	MCHT	RRAHTFUSA
KAHAN, SALOMON	20	M	CGRMKR	RRZZZZUSA
KARCTZKI, FREIDE	18	F	SP	RRAHTFUSA
KACMIZOWICZ, NACHUME	00	M	MCHT	RRZZZZUSA
KOLTAN, LEIB	00	M	MCHT	RRAHVUUSA
KOLVERINSKY, ABRAHAM	26	M	MCHT	RRAFVGUSA
SZENDLA	23	F	W	RRAFVGUSA
ARON	1	M	CHILD	RRAFVGUSA
KRUGER, JANKEL	18	M	MCHT	RRAHTFUSA
LIPTZIK, BEHR.	33	M	MCHT	RRZZZZUSA
MEROWITZ, SALOMON	00	M	MCHT	RRZZZZUSA
ITZIG	00	M	MCHT	RRZZZZUSA
MOWSCHEWITZ, RACHEL	30	F	W	RRAHTFUSA
MOSES	2	M	CHILD	RRAHTFUSA
SARAH	.04	F	INFANT	RRAHTFUSA
RECHNIKOWSKI, CHAIME	36	F	W	RRZZZZUSA
DEBORAH	8	F	CHILD	RRZZZZUSA
ZIRLE	9	F	CHILD	RRZZZZUSA
GITKE	5	F	CHILD	RRZZZZUSA
RIETZ, ARIE	42	M	MCHT	RRAHTFUSA
ROSENTZKI, AWRAN	00	M	MCHT	RRZZZZUSA
RUSSKIN, PESASCH	26	M	MCHT	RRAHQUUSA
SOFIE	24	F	W	RRAHQUUSA
SCHAFER, SAML.	17	M	MCHT	RRZZZZUSA
SCHIER, ABRAHAM	30	M	TLR	RRZZZZUSA
BABE	19	F	W	RRZZZZUSA
SCHIMICKLER, ABRAHAM	20	M	MCHT	RRAGRTUSA
SEGAL, MICHEL	22	M	MCHT	RRAHVAUSA
CECILIE	19	F	W	RRAHVAUSA
SISKINDOWITZ, HANSEL	50	M	MCHT	RRAHSLUSA
CHASCHE	00	F	CH	RRAHSLUSA
U, U	00	M	BKBNDR	RRAGRTUSA
U	19	M	FARMER	RRZZZZUSA
U	00	M	FARMER	RRZZZZUSA
U	00	F	W	RRZZZZUSA
ZWICK, SCHLOME	8	F	CHILD	RRZZZZUSA
RUBEN	3	M	CHILD	RRZZZZUSA

SHIP: BOHEMIA

FROM: HAMBURG
TO: NEW YORK
ARRIVED: 23 JULY 1885

PASSENGER	AGE	SEX	OCCUPATION	PRV VIL DES
JAFFE, HIRSCH	14	M	LABR	RRZZZZUSA
STARK, ISAAC	18	M	LABR	RRAHTFUSA
ROSENTHAL, MALKE	17	F	SGL	RRAHZSUSA
RACHEL	15	F	SGL	RRAHZSUSA
LUBELSKI, LEIBUS	15	M	CH	RRZZZZUSA
SEGEL, UDEL	18	M	LABR	RRAHTFUSA
GOLDBERG, BEER	34	M	DLR	RRAHTFUSA
FEIERSTEIN, ABRAH.	17	M	JNR	RRZZZZUSA
GARMSCHICK, MOSES	15	M	LABR	RRZZZZUSA
ZEEW, SELDY	19	F	W	RRZZZZUSA
CHMILEWSKY, JOCHWED	20	M	DLR	RRZZZZUSA
ALBT.	18	M	DLR	RRZZZZUSA
ISAKOWITZ, GOLDE	18	F	SGL	RRAHOOUSA
GORDON, ROSA	38	F	W	RRZZZZUSA
ELLIA	9	F	CHILD	RRZZZZUSA
DAVID	8	M	CHILD	RRZZZZUSA
LEIB	6	M	CHILD	RRZZZZUSA
SALOMON	4	M	CHILD	RRZZZZUSA
LESER	.11	M	INFANT	RRZZZZUSA
MAKLER, MUCHEM	48	M	LABR	RRZZZZUSA
LEA	48	F	W	RRZZZZUSA
ROSA	28	F	W	RRZZZZUSA
GEDULJI	3	F	CHILD	RRZZZZUSA
BRENNER, FANNY	30	F	W	RRAHTFUSA
LEIZER	8	M	CHILD	RRAHTFUSA
LIPE	7	F	CHILD	RRAHTFUSA
CHAIE	5	F	CHILD	RRAHTFUSA
JANKEL, SAUL	24	M	DLR	RRZZZZUSA
RIWKE	18	F	W	RRZZZZUSA
JANKOWSKY, LIEBE	46	F	W	RRZZZZUSA
FREUND, FANNY	26	F	W	RRZZZZUSA
ROSA	.02	F	INFANT	RRZZZZUSA
MICHELSON, RISZE	40	F	W	RRAGRTUSA
SCHMUEL	9	M	CHILD	RRAGRTUSA
TAUBE	8	F	CHILD	RRAGRTUSA
CHAIE	7	F	CHILD	RRAGRTUSA
CHATZKEL	2	M	CHILD	RRAGRTUSA
KRAWITZ, LIEBE	8	F	CHILD	RRAGRTUSA
FINKELSTEIN, DAVID	45	M	LABR	RRAHYFUSA
SARA	4	F	CHILD	RRAHYFUSA
JITTE	.10	F	INFANT	RRAHYFUSA
URIN, MERE	20	F	W	RRAHYFUSA
BRENNER, SARA	30	F	W	RRAHTFUSA
ISRAEL	8	M	CHILD	RRAHTFUSA
JETTE	21	F	W	RRAHTFUSA
SHREMSKY, CHONE	31	M	DLR	RRZZZZUSA
URIN, JENTE-GILH.	16	F	SGL	RRAHYFUSA
HEYMANN, LOUIS	19	M	MCHT	RRAHZSUSA
HIRSCHFELD, ROSE	16	F	SGL	RRAHVAUSA
ALESCHNOWITZ, OSIAS	20	M	DLR	RRZZZZUSA
KAMINSKY, VICTORIA	45	F	W	PLZZZZUSA
LEBLANG, ZIWIE	42	M	DLR	PLZZZZUSA
MIRL	18	F	CH	PLZZZZUSA
SERLAN, ANNA	25	F	W	RRZZZZUSA
WELWEL	.11	M	INFANT	RRZZZZUSA
CHASINOWITZ, ESTHER	22	F	W	RRZZZZUSA
DAVID	10	M	CH	RRZZZZUSA
TAUBE	45	F	W	RRZZZZUSA
RASCHE	6	F	CHILD	RRZZZZUSA
CHENYE	6	M	CHILD	RRZZZZUSA
SCHIMMEL, EMILIE	20	F	SGL	RRZZZZUSA
PAULINE	15	F	SGL	RRZZZZUSA
BODERSKY, MARTIN	27	M	LABR	RRZZZZUSA
PUGULIS, PAULINE	26	F	SGL	RRAHTFUSA
SAK, LIEB	20	M	LABR	RRZZZZUSA
SKOLL, HANNA	20	F	SGL	RRZZZZUSA
SARETZKY, CISECK	19	M	DLR	RRAHVAUSA
GORDON, RIWKE	40	F	W	RRZZZZUSA
ARKE	8	M	CHILD	RRZZZZUSA
PADZIWILIS, ANTON	22	M	LABR	RRAHTFUSA
LANGE, ERNST	32	M	LABR	RRAFQVUSA
ALMGANSOWE, AGNES	49	F	SGL	RRAHZSUSA
PALASKY, LEIB	30	M	LABR	RRZZZZUSA
KALETZKY, ISRAEL	19	M	LABR	RRZZZZUSA
RIMIL, ABRAHAM	38	M	DLR	RRZZZZUSA
KAHN, JECHIEL	37	M	DLR	RRZZZZUSA
BLUMBERG, TEWIE	16	M	DLR	RRZZZZUSA

PASSENGER	AGE	SEX	OCCUPATION	PRV VIL DES
CHRISTAL, ISAAK	18	M	LABR	RRZZZZUSA
ASCH, ABRAHAM	16	M	DLR	RRZZZZUSA
GORDON, JOSEPH	4	M	CHILD	RRZZZZUSA
BEHR, MOSES	16	M	TLR	RRZZZZUSA
KOHN, MEYER	21	M	DLR	RRZZZZUSA
LEFKOWICZ, CHARLOTTE	22	F	SGL	RRZZZZUSA
SCHRANK, SCHMIL	24	M	LABR	PLZZZZUSA
APPELBAUM, JANKEL	35	M	CGRMKR	RRZZZZUSA
FRIEDMANN, ZEMACH	18	M	LABR	RRAHTFUSA
NODEK, JAN	40	M	LABR	PLZZZZUSA
WIERCZBIDKE, VALENTY	29	M	LABR	PLZZZZUSA
DANKOWSKA, SCLOKIJA	20	F	SGL	PLZZZZUSA
UZUPS, PAVEL	52	M	LABR	RRZZZZUSA
ANNA	55	F	W	RRZZZZUSA
MAGDL.	20	F	CH	RRZZZZUSA
ELIASOWITZ, NECHEMIA	26	M	MLR	RRZZZZUSA
STAMINSKY, SALOMON	35	M	LABR	RRAEFLUSA
DANSON, ISAAC	15	M	LABR	RRAGRTUSA
AUGUSCHEWISCH, FOGEL	27	F	W	RRZZZZUSA
SAMUEL	6	M	CHILD	RRZZZZUSA
SALOMON	4	M	CHILD	RRZZZZUSA
HURWITZ, SCHEIN	22	F	W	RRZZZZUSA
NACHAME	.11	F	INFANT	RRZZZZUSA
KROWN, MARIE	28	F	W	RRZZZZUSA
DOBE	6	F	CHILD	RRZZZZUSA
SCHIFRE	4	F	CHILD	RRZZZZUSA
CHRISTOF, CHAJE	17	F	SGL	RRZZZZUSA
ZISKYN, ANNA	18	F	SGL	PLZZZZUSA
KOHONTZ, MARIA	14	F	SGL	PLZZZZUSA
CZACKA, JOHANN	35	M	LABR	RRZZZZUSA
CATHA.	27	F	W	RRZZZZUSA
SCHITAS, JOHANN	25	M	FARMER	RRZZZZUSA
DIETTENER, MAGDA.	24	F	SGL	RRZZZZUSA
HODISCH, MAGDA.	22	F	SGL	RRZZZZUSA
SUMMERGRAD, BARUCH	22	M	LABR	RRAHTUUSA
OKNER, SALOMON	20	M	LABR	RRAHTUUSA
STRUMP, JETTE	17	F	SGL	PLZZZZUSA
SINDEL, TILLE	9	F	CHILD	PLZZZZUSA
SCHRECK, CHAIE	22	F	W	PLZZZZUSA
LEUCHTER, CHAJI	12	F	SGL	PLZZZZUSA
SCHOTTLAND, BLUME	41	F	W	PLZZZZUSA
SARA	6	F	CHILD	PLZZZZUSA
CHICE	5	F	CHILD	PLZZZZUSA
ELIAS	9	M	CHILD	PLZZZZUSA
KUPFERMANN, ANNA	20	F	SGL	PLZZZZUSA
FRAKIN, ISAAC	18	M	LABR	PLAHTUUSA
SINGER, SARAH	23	F	W	PLAHTUUSA
ABRAHAM	.11	M	INFANT	PLAHTUUSA
SCHWADIS, EUGENIE	22	F	SGL	PLAGRTUSA
TRAUTMANN, ADAM	33	M	LABR	PLAFQVUSA
BARBARA	28	F	W	PLAFQVUSA
ADAM	7	M	CHILD	PLAFQVUSA
CAROLINE	5	F	CHILD	PLAFQVUSA
ENDELMANN, CHANNE	50	F	W	RRZZZZUSA
SCHEINE	21	F	CH	RRZZZZUSA
CHIENE	19	F	CH	RRZZZZUSA
SCHMIDT, CHRISTOF.	47	M	FARMER	RRZZZZUSA
MARIA	47	F	W	RRZZZZUSA
PHILIPP	16	M	CH	RRZZZZUSA
ADAM	12	M	CH	RRZZZZUSA
CATHA.	22	F	CH	RRZZZZUSA
CHRISTOF	8	M	CHILD	RRZZZZUSA
FLATOW, ANNA	27	F	SGL	RRZZZZUSA
REBECCA	19	F	SGL	RRZZZZUSA
MORAWITZ, CHAIM	35	M	DLR	RRZZZZUSA
STROKA, JANE	44	M	DLR	PLZZZZUSA
ROSENNAUM, SCHEINE	19	F	SGL	RRZZZZUSA
MERE	17	F	SGL	RRZZZZUSA
GOLDBERG, RIWKE	37	F	W	RRAHZSUSA
CHAIE	.11	F	INFANT	RRAHZSUSA
ROSENKRANZ, SLAM.D.	22	F	SGL	RRAHVJUSA
SCHERESCHEWSKY, BERMAN	30	M	LABR	RRAHVAUSA
SIMON	9	M	CHILD	RRAHVAUSA
ROSS, CZERNE	28	F	W	RRAHVAUSA
REBECCA	5	F	CHILD	RRAHVAUSA
FRATJE	.11	M	INFANT	RRAHVAUSA
JUDELSKY, SAMUEL	9	M	CHILD	RRAHVJUSA
FINGERHUT, ARON	20	M	DLR	RRACXZUSA
TOLTZE	.11	F	INFANT	RRACXZUSA
OBZENIK, SCHEINE	18	F	SGL	RRZZZZUSA
KIMMEL, RACHEL	28	F	W	PLZZZZUSA
CHESKEL	6	F	CHILD	PLZZZZUSA
MARIANE	4	F	CHILD	PLZZZZUSA
BENJAMIN	.11	M	INFANT	PLZZZZUSA
BENJAMIN, SAMUEL	45	M	LABR	PLAEHVUSA
KAPLAN, NOCHEM	15	M	LABR	PLAHTRUSA
JUDEL	24	M	LABR	PLAHTRUSA
MELTZER, SCHMUL	18	M	GDSM	PLAHTFUSA
PROPP, R.PESCHE	30	F	W	PLAHTFUSA
CHAIE	9	F	CHILD	PLAHTFUSA
ISAREL	4	M	CHILD	PLAHTFUSA
CHAJE	.11	M	INFANT	PLAHTFUSA
BAERMANN, BERTHA	20	F	SGL	PLAHVAUSA
ZAWACKA, ANTONIA	25	F	W	RRZZZZUSA
AGATHE	4	F	CHILD	RRZZZZUSA
AUSTERM, JOSEPH-S.	17	M	DLR	RRAHZSUSA
PAZERSKI, HIRSCH	21	M	DLR	RRZZZZUSA
AURON, MOSES	38	M	DLR	RRAHRZUSA
WILNER, HENOCH	44	M	DLR	RRAHSWUSA
ISABLINSKY, HYMANN	40	M	LABR	RRAHQUUSA
MILLER, CHAIE	18	F	SGL	RRAHSWUSA
NEUFELD, BEALE	9	F	CHILD	RRZZZZUSA
STORCH, JOSEF	24	M	LABR	RRACTCUSA
LEON	19	M	LABR	RRACTCUSA
LEIE	24	F	W	RRACTCUSA
JOSEF	9	M	CHILD	RRACTCUSA
DRILACH, JOCHEN	45	M	DLR	PLZZZZUSA
DIENSTAG, JACOB	25	M	DLR	PLZZZZUSA
FINGERHUT, ARON-S.	20	M	DLR	PLZZZZUSA
HERRMANN, PERETZ	24	M	DLR	PLZZZZUSA
SCHNEIDER, DANIEL	28	M	LABR	RRZZZZUSA
KAPLAN, SCHMUL	9	M	CHILD	RRAHTRUSA
CHATZKE	5	F	CHILD	RRAHTRUSA
ZEREL	3	F	CHILD	RRAHTRUSA
SCHNEIDER, CAROLINE	28	F	W	RRZZZZUSA
DANIEL	5	M	CHILD	RRZZZZUSA
LOUISE	3	F	CHILD	RRZZZZUSA
PAULINE	2	F	CHILD	RRZZZZUSA
REINHOLD	.06	M	INFANT	RRZZZZUSA
BUSCH, NATHAN	44	M	DLR	RRAGVPUSA
LUBSOHN, MORDCHE	17	M	LABR	RRAHTRUSA
LINE	7	F	CHILD	RRAHTRUSA
KAPLAN, MOSES	19	M	BCHR	RRAHZSUSA
SORESMANN, ZADEK	19	M	DLR	RRAEFLUSA
MENDEL	16	M	DLR	RRAEFLUSA
PATZERSKI, CHAINE	21	F	SGL	RRZZZZUSA
RABINOWITZ, MARCUS	22	M	LABR	RRAFVGUSA
LOUIS	16	M	DLR	RRAFVGUSA
CICZKOWSKA, ABRAHAM	23	M	BCHR	RRZZZZUSA
SARAH	23	F	W	RRZZZZUSA
FURMANOWITZ, RACHEL	18	F	SGL	RRZZZZUSA
BARAITZKY, ISRAEL	9	M	CHILD	RRZZZZUSA
LEBEN, LEIB	30	M	LABR	RRAHWHUSA

SHIP: NOORDLAND

FROM: ANTWERP
TO: NEW YORK
ARRIVED: 23 JULY 1885

PASSENGER	AGE	SEX	OCCUPATION	PRV VIL DES
RINTKIEWICZ, U	22	F	UNKNOWN	RRZZZZNY
MILKE	22	F	UNKNOWN	RRZZZZNY
KRULIKMOVA, U	19	F	UNKNOWN	RRZZZZUNK
REX, SARIS	17	M	UNKNOWN	RRZZZZNY

PASSENGER	AGE	SEX	OCCUPATION	PRV VIL DES

SHIP: BRITISH QUEEN

FROM: LONDON
TO: NEW YORK
ARRIVED: 24 JULY 1885

PASSENGER	AGE	SEX	OCCUPATION	PRV VIL DES
KAISER, PAULINE	35	F	W	PLZZZZUSA
FANNY	18	F	W	PLZZZZUSA

SHIP: CITY OF ROME

FROM: LIVERPOOL
TO: NEW YORK
ARRIVED: 24 JULY 1885

PASSENGER	AGE	SEX	OCCUPATION	PRV VIL DES
BACKAR, SALMAN	20	M	LABR	RRZZZZUSA
HANZASCHI	23	M	LABR	RRZZZZUSA
EPSTEIN, PHIL.	24	M	LABR	RRZZZZUSA

SHIP: CITY OF RICHMOND

FROM: LIVERPOOL AND QUEENSTOWN
TO: NEW YORK
ARRIVED: 25 JULY 1885

PASSENGER	AGE	SEX	OCCUPATION	PRV VIL DES
KADUMSKY, ARON	20	M	LABR	PLZZZZUSA

SHIP: EDAM

FROM: AMSTERDAM
TO: NEW YORK
ARRIVED: 25 JULY 1885

PASSENGER	AGE	SEX	OCCUPATION	PRV VIL DES
STUNBERG, CHAYO	22	F	SVNT	RRZZZZUSA
HROMOWITCH, JOS.	28	M	FARMER	RRZZZZUSA
FRIEDMAN, SALOMON	33	M	FARMER	RRZZZZUSA
STANKOWITCH, JOSEF	23	M	UNKNOWN	RRAHTFUSA
ANNA	29	F	UNKNOWN	RRAHTFUSA
VACLAW	10	M	UNKNOWN	RRAHTFUSA
RADETZKY, SIMON	26	M	UNKNOWN	RRAHOKUSA
ESTHER	20	F	UNKNOWN	RRAHOKUSA
MASHE	10	M	UNKNOWN	RRAHOKUSA
SCHEI	10	M	UNKNOWN	RRAHOKUSA
LEISE	.11	M	INFANT	RRAHOKUSA
RADIKOW, ITZIG	20	M	UNKNOWN	RRAHTFUSA
ELYHOL, BACHEL	16	M	UNKNOWN	RRZZZZUSA
DORNSTREICH, TEIWEB	28	M	UNKNOWN	RRZZZZUSA
JAWITZ, WOLF	26	M	UNKNOWN	RRZZZZUSA
HENNI	20	F	UNKNOWN	RRZZZZUSA
BASSI	.09	F	INFANT	RRZZZZUSA
BERGER, MOSES	25	M	UNKNOWN	RRZZZZUSA
SERNER, ELKE	19	F	UNKNOWN	RRZZZZUSA
SCHETZBERG, JACOB	30	M	UNKNOWN	RRZZZZUSA
STARMOSKY, ABRAHAM	18	M	UNKNOWN	RRZZZZUSA
ROSENFELD, MICHEL	21	M	UNKNOWN	RRAHTFUSA
BRANDY, JUDEL	20	M	UNKNOWN	RRAHTFUSA
REINES, ABRAHAM	58	M	UNKNOWN	RRZZZZUSA
CHAJO	50	F	UNKNOWN	RRZZZZUSA
BONI	18	M	UNKNOWN	RRZZZZUSA
SALOMON	7	M	CHILD	RRZZZZUSA
FANNY	18	F	UNKNOWN	RRZZZZUSA
MENDEL	14	M	UNKNOWN	RRZZZZUSA
RUBEN	9	M	CHILD	RRZZZZUSA
MOSES	12	M	UNKNOWN	RRZZZZUSA
WEINSTROCK, BORIS	22	M	UNKNOWN	RRAFVGUSA
BRANSTEIN, NANNA	24	M	UNKNOWN	RRAFVGUSA
GRUNBERG, ROSA	17	F	UNKNOWN	RRAFVGUSA
WEINSTEIN, SCHLOME	20	M	UNKNOWN	RRZZZZUSA
MULLER, ABE	17	M	UNKNOWN	RRAHTFUSA
RACHEL	20	F	UNKNOWN	RRAHTFUSA
KONIG, CHAIN	18	M	UNKNOWN	RRAGRTUSA
RACHEL	21	F	UNKNOWN	RRAGRTUSA

SHIP: KAETIE

FROM: UNKNOWN
TO: NEW YORK
ARRIVED: 25 JULY 1885

PASSENGER	AGE	SEX	OCCUPATION	PRV VIL DES
SCHWARTZ, ROBERT	22	M	LABR	RRZZZZUSA
HAMENTZKI, ROCHE	33	F	W	RRZZZZUSA
LIEBESCHEINE	9	F	CHILD	RRZZZZUSA
RIWEESTER	7	F	CHILD	RRZZZZUSA
LOTE	5	F	CHILD	RRZZZZUSA
TIBEFEIGE	3	F	CHILD	RRZZZZUSA
DYNIL	1	M	CHILD	RRZZZZUSA
GABOWITZ, EICHEL	45	M	LABR	PLZZZZUSA
DEBORAH	20	F	D	PLZZZZUSA
SARAH	17	F	D	PLZZZZUSA
LEA	15	F	D	PLZZZZUSA
WOLFLEIB	13	M	S	PLZZZZUSA
TATAKOWSKY, HEIMAN	21	M	LABR	RRZZZZUSA
SCHWARTZ, MARCUS	21	M	LABR	RRZZZZUSA
MARIL, MOSES	21	M	LABR	RRZZZZUSA
GINSBERG, FISCHEL	48	M	FA	RRZZZZUSA
ROSIA	22	F	D	RRZZZZUSA
FEIWUSCH, CHONE	32	F	W	RRZZZZUSA
TOBA	26	F	UNKNOWN	RRZZZZUSA
ROCHEL	4	M	CHILD	RRZZZZUSA
ITZIG	1	M	CHILD	RRZZZZUSA
KANTROWITZ, BERNARD	45	M	MCHT	RRZZZZUSA
R.	18	F	D	RRZZZZUSA
DHAPROK, ROCHEL	20	F	UNKNOWN	RRZZZZUSA
CYNAMEN, H.	20	M	LABR	RRZZZZUSA
KARMZEN, D.	18	M	LABR	RRZZZZUSA
CHOVER, MOTEL	20	M	LABR	RRZZZZUSA
OCIDILSKI, SLOMAN	35	M	LABR	RRZZZZUSA
FEINSTEIN, ISAAC	35	M	LABR	RRZZZZUSA
ISAAC	36	M	LABR	RRZZZZUSA
BIEBERSTEIN, ISR.ISAAC	43	M	PNTR	RRZZZZUSA
STURMAK, ANNE	19	F	W	RRZZZZUSA
BECKMANN, SAMUEL	33	M	LABR	RRZZZZUSA
SWIDERSKOW, MARIANNA	23	F	W	RRZZZZUSA
ACKSNER, MICHAEL	48	M	FARMER	RRZZZZUSA
KATHARINA	45	F	W	RRZZZZUSA
KATHARINA	17	F	D	RRZZZZUSA
JACOB	14	M	S	RRZZZZUSA
GEORG	9	M	CHILD	RRZZZZUSA
ELISABETH	2	F	CHILD	RRZZZZUSA
MINA	1	F	CHILD	RRZZZZUSA
BRANSTEIN, SALEM	16	M	MCHT	RRZZZZUSA
TESKE, KAROLINE	46	F	WO	RRZZZZUSA
ELISABETH	56	F	M	RRZZZZUSA
ELISABETH	7	F	CHILD	RRZZZZUSA
FRIEDERIKE	5	F	CHILD	RRZZZZUSA
JACOB	2	M	CHILD	RRZZZZUSA
CARL	27	M	CH	RRZZZZUSA
FLACKS, FEIG.	24	F	W	RRZZZZUSA
JANKEL	1	M	CHILD	RRZZZZUSA

PASSENGER	AGE	SEX	OCCUPATION	PRV VIL DES
JACOBOWE, CHAIBE	51	F	W	RRZZZZUSA
LEA	10	F	D	RRZZZZUSA
FEIGE	20	F	D	RRZZZZUSA
CHAINE	25	F	D	RRZZZZUSA
CHAIBE	25	F	D	RRZZZZUSA
FRIEDE	5	F	CHILD	RRZZZZUSA
LAPIN, FANNY	26	F	D	RRZZZZUSA
TUHRMANN, FEIGE	1	F	CHILD	RRZZZZUSA
LAOIN, FEIWER	50	M	LABR	RRZZZZUSA
HANTUSKY, ISRAEL	32	M	LABR	RRZZZZUSA
ESTHER	27	F	W	RRZZZZUSA
SALOMON	6	M	CHILD	RRZZZZUSA
ARON	1	M	CHILD	RRZZZZUSA
BERGMANN, MINDEL	40	F	W	RRZZZZUSA
LAUBE	2	F	CHILD	RRZZZZUSA
SYLBERSTEIN, ABRAHAM	44	M	LABR	RRZZZZUSA
EINHORN, MAX	23	M	LABR	RRZZZZUSA
HENRIKSSON, HEINRIK	25	M	CPTR	FNZZZZUSA
RAPPONN, LIZA	28	F	SVNT	FNZZZZUSA
KAEJELNOHO, ANNA	18	F	SVNT	FNZZZZUSA
EDLUND, CARL-J.	15	M	BY	FNZZZZUSA
AUGUSTE	16	F	UNKNOWN	FNZZZZUSA
CAROLINE	48	F	SVNT	FNZZZZUSA
EUGENIE	11	F	CH	FNZZZZUSA
GUNNERI, JUSTINE	32	F	SVNT	FNZZZZUSA
JOHN	9	M	CHILD	FNZZZZUSA
MARY	6	F	CHILD	FNZZZZUSA
KERSTI, KARL-W.	18	M	LABR	FNZZZZUSA
MORTO, LISE	28	F	SVNT	FNZZZZUSA
MARIA	25	F	SVNT	FNZZZZUSA
HOGEMASKI, GUSTAV	25	M	LABR	FNZZZZUSA
WOROME, KACOB	26	M	LABR	FNZZZZUSA
EKORANTO, LENA	27	F	SVNT	FNZZZZUSA
RENTE, LISA	34	F	SVNT	FNZZZZUSA
WAMLIN, JOHAN	35	M	LABR	FNZZZZUSA

SHIP: SALIER

FROM: BREMEN
TO: NEW YORK
ARRIVED: 25 JULY 1885

PASSENGER	AGE	SEX	OCCUPATION	PRV VIL DES
OTTER, ELISE	40	F	NN	FNAHQHUSA
SCHELMINSKI, JOSEF	24	M	LABR	FNAGRTUSA
STACHEWITZ, PIOTR	23	M	LABR	FNAGRTUSA
WILK, CASE	20	M	B	FNAGRTUSA
STEINBACH, CHAJE	13	M	NN	FNAGRTUSA
ZATHIN, LAZARUS	50	M	NN	RRZZZZUSA
SOFIA	16	F	NN	RRZZZZUSA
HANNE	14	F	NN	RRZZZZUSA
SLEINE	10	F	CH	RRZZZZUSA
LEISER	7	M	CHILD	RRZZZZUSA
BEIZINAK, DARVE	25	F	NN	RRAFWJUSA
HERSCH	.09	M	INFANT	RRAFWJUSA
MOLOWSKY, MOSES	31	M	NN	RRAFWJUSA
GOLDSTEIN, HIRSCH	12	M	CH	RRAHQDUSA
KAPILANSKY, LEIB	20	M	NN	RRAHQDUSA
OKUMINSKY, FRODEL	20	F	NN	RRAHQDUSA
MOSCHEL	21	M	NN	RRAHQDUSA
TROTZKY, HIRSCH	20	M	NN	RRAHQDUSA
RUDELPH, ZELIG	18	M	LABR	RRAHQDUSA
GARBER, RUBEN	25	M	NN	RRAHTFUSA
IGILITZKY, ANNA	20	F	NN	RRAHTFUSA

SHIP: WIELAND

FROM: HAMBURG
TO: NEW YORK
ARRIVED: 25 JULY 1885

PASSENGER	AGE	SEX	OCCUPATION	PRV VIL DES
MALTOVSKY, KAZIMIR	20	M	LABR	RRZZZZUSA
WILK, LOUIS	17	M	LABR	RRZZZZUSA
WORTMANN, CHAIM	22	M	CGRMKR	RRZZZZUSA
SALOMON, TAUBE	18	F	SGL	RRZZZZUSA
ZAROCH	52	M	DLR	RRZZZZUSA
KURSOWE, CHANNE	43	F	W	RRZZZZUSA
RACHEL	13	F	CH	RRZZZZUSA
ROSA	5	F	CHILD	RRZZZZUSA
WOLF	9	M	CHILD	RRZZZZUSA
SIGEL, FEIGE	20	F	SGL	RRZZZZUSA
KLEINMANN, LEIB	19	M	DLR	RRZZZZUSA
RABINOWITZ, LEIZER	19	M	DLR	RRZZZZUSA
WITTMANN, SARAH	9	F	CHILD	RRZZZZUSA
SCHRAMEK, MOIS	23	M	LABR	PLZZZZUSA
ANNA	19	F	W	PLZZZZUSA
MOUSKI, ESTHER	24	F	W	RRZZZZUSA
LEISER	4	M	CHILD	RRZZZZUSA
SARA	.11	F	INFANT	RRZZZZUSA
CITRINBLATT, MEIER	40	M	DLR	RRZZZZUSA
WOLFSOHN, BENJAMIN	19	M	DLR	RRZZZZUSA
SCHEFFER, ROSA	34	F	W	RRZZZZUSA
ALFRED	11	M	CH	RRZZZZUSA
BENJAMIN	5	M	CHILD	RRZZZZUSA
JOSEF	4	M	CHILD	RRZZZZUSA
ISRAEL	3	M	CHILD	RRZZZZUSA
HARRICH	.06	M	INFANT	RRZZZZUSA
KERCHERR, SAMUEL	30	M	TLR	RRZZZZUSA
KRAMER, JACOB	18	M	LABR	RRZZZZUSA
STEIN, HITTEL	40	M	TLR	RRZZZZUSA
AUERBACH, ABRAH.	31	M	MCHT	RRZZZZUSA
BRECKSTEIN, GALIA	25	F	W	RRZZZZUSA
TAUBE	6	F	CHILD	RRZZZZUSA
MACZKIEWICZ, SARAH	20	F	SGL	RRZZZZUSA
COHN, MAYER	20	M	DLR	RRZZZZUSA
HELFGOTT, THEODOR	45	M	BCHR	PLZZZZUSA
SARA	43	F	W	PLZZZZUSA
SIEGMUNDT	16	M	S	PLZZZZUSA
ISRAEL	8	M	CHILD	PLZZZZUSA
GUTTMANN, SERNA	38	F	W	RRZZZZUSA
LIEBE	5	F	CHILD	RRZZZZUSA
MERE	3	F	CHILD	RRZZZZUSA
BRAZNE, LITMANN	34	M	DLR	RRZZZZUSA
SUSNITZKI, ABRAH.	32	M	BCHR	RRZZZZUSA
KRUGER, MOSES	36	M	DLR	RRZZZZUSA
SAMUEL, LUDWIG	43	M	LABR	RRZZZZUSA
OTTO	9	F	CHILD	RRZZZZUSA
OTHILIE	9	F	CHILD	RRZZZZUSA
LEO	.09	M	INFANT	RRZZZZUSA
SCHENK, DOROTHEA	17	F	SGL	RRZZZZUSA
LOSSBERG, TAUBE	18	F	SGL	RRZZZZUSA
WILEMSKY, JENKEL	43	M	LABR	RRZZZZUSA
HASER, SCHMUEL	46	M	LABR	RRZZZZUSA
FUCHS, CHANE	20	F	W	PLZZZZUSA
BERNHARD	37	M	DLR	PLZZZZUSA
GRINBERG, MORDECHE	20	M	LABR	RRZZZZUSA
LEWIN, ARON	18	M	DLR	RRZZZZUSA
PASUR, LEIB	18	M	TNM	RRZZZZUSA
WASILAWSKA, ANNA	25	F	W	RRZZZZUSA
JURAS	8	M	CHILD	RRZZZZUSA
ANNA	2	F	CHILD	RRZZZZUSA
JACUBOWITZ, FRANZ	22	F	W	RRZZZZUSA
JOZAS	.09	M	INFANT	RRZZZZUSA
FELDMANN, JOSEF	32	M	LABR	RRZZZZUSA
RUBINSKY, DAVID	20	M	DLR	RRZZZZUSA
HERBST, TEIL	25	M	DLR	RRZZZZUSA
MECHUME, ABRAH.	36	M	LABR	RRZZZZUSA
ZIMEHRE	6	F	CHILD	RRZZZZUSA
WOLTMANN, DAVID	30	M	DLR	RRZZZZUSA

PASSENGER	AGE	SEX	OCCUPATION	PRV VIL DES
PASUR, LENA	18	F	SGL	RRZZZZUSA
GOLDFLAUM, RACHEL	34	F	SGL	RRZZZZUSA
GRODZIENSKI, MARCUS	21	M	BKLYR	RRZZZZUSA
RENNENBAUM, LEWIS	49	M	INMKR	RRZZZZUSA
MAYER	46	M	DLR	RRZZZZUSA
KOSZEWSKY, JOHANN	32	M	CK	RRZZZZUSA

SHIP: DONAU

FROM: BREMEN
TO: NEW YORK
ARRIVED: 27 JULY 1885

PASSENGER	AGE	SEX	OCCUPATION	PRV VIL DES
FERZMANOFSKY, CONSTANTY	36	M	TT	RRAFWJNY
WOSKEWICZ, ANTON	32	M	LABR	RRZZZZNY
BARBARA	24	F	W	RRZZZZNY
MAGDA	3	F	CHILD	RRZZZZNY
JAN	.08	M	INFANT	RRZZZZNY
PAUSA, MATEJ	40	F	W	RRZZZZNY

SHIP: ETRURIA

FROM: LIVERPOOL AND QUEENSTOWN
TO: NEW YORK
ARRIVED: 27 JULY 1885

PASSENGER	AGE	SEX	OCCUPATION	PRV VIL DES
MALKANAKI, HERN.	34	M	LABR	FNZZZZUSA
SALOWAKI, JOH.E.	29	M	LABR	FNZZZZUSA
NYLAND, GUSTAF	29	M	LABR	FNZZZZUSA
WARB, JOHAN	26	M	LABR	FNZZZZUSA
ILKA, ERIK-M.	37	M	LABR	FNZZZZUSA
KOYNINEMA, A.	18	M	LABR	FNZZZZUSA
KORPI, HELMA	11	F	CH	FNZZZZUSA
MARENSON, M.	27	F	CL	RRZZZZCAN

SHIP: RUGIA

FROM: HAMBURG
TO: NEW YORK
ARRIVED: 28 JULY 1885

PASSENGER	AGE	SEX	OCCUPATION	PRV VIL DES
DANEIS, DAVID	42	M	DLR	RRZZZZUSA
LOUISE	18	F	D	RRZZZZUSA
TILLES, SALOMON	38	M	LABR	PLZZZZUSA
LEA	31	F	W	PLZZZZUSA
GUSTAV	7	M	CHILD	PLZZZZUSA
EHRUN	2	M	CHILD	PLZZZZUSA
SAWICKER, ELISABETH	28	F	W	PLZZZZUSA
JOSEF	14	M	UNKNOWN	PLZZZZUSA
GOLDSTEIN, PESSE	64	F	W	PLZZZZUSA
PETRAT, GEORGE	24	M	LABR	RRZZZZUSA
BIRNBAUM, SCHEPSEL	18	F	LABR	RRZZZZUSA
SUDLOWITZ, MALKE	28	F	W	RRZZZZUSA
IDA	.11	F	INFANT	RRZZZZUSA
MEYEROWITZ, ELKONS	18	M	TLR	RRZZZZUSA
ESPORUD, ZALLEL	53	F	DLR	RRZZZZUSA
MECHANIK, GEDALIE	40	F	CPTR	RRZZZZUSA
ROSENFELD, SALY	40	F	LABR	RRZZZZUSA
BAROWSKY, ISIDOR	20	F	TBCMNFTR	RRZZZZUSA
HERSCHKOWITZ, ABRAM	35	M	DLR	PLZZZZUSA
DUSTMANN, FEIDEL	20	M	DLR	RRZZZZUSA
HERRMANN, SIMON	47	M	MCHT	PLZZZZUSA
RUDZIEWITZ, JOSEF	18	M	DLR	RRZZZZUSA
TOZORSKY, FRUME	56	F	SGL	RRZZZZUSA
SCHECHMEISTER, MENDEL	22	M	SHMK	RRZZZZUSA
APPELBAUM, RACHEL	55	F	W	RRZZZZUSA
HELBER, GRETE	18	F	SGL	RRZZZZUSA
FACHMANN, FANNY	16	F	SGL	PLZZZZUSA
BIMBERG, SHANE	20	F	SGL	PLZZZZUSA
BIDZINSKY, FRANZ	47	M	LABR	PLZZZZUSA
STANISLAUS	9	M	CHILD	PLZZZZUSA
ANNA	45	F	W	PLZZZZUSA
FRANZ	6	M	CHILD	PLZZZZUSA
ANNA	4	F	CHILD	PLZZZZUSA
BEDNAR, THERESE	21	F	SGL	PLZZZZUSA
CERNA, FRANZISKA	32	F	SGL	PLZZZZUSA
KIRSTBEIN, REBECCA	26	F	W	RRZZZZUSA
WALTER	4	M	CHILD	RRZZZZUSA
IDA	.11	F	INFANT	RRZZZZUSA
MELTZER, JACOB-L.	45	M	DLR	RRZZZZUSA
PRIWA	20	F	D	RRZZZZUSA
JOHANN	16	M	S	RRZZZZUSA
KIRSTEIN, SLATE	45	F	W	RRZZZZUSA
BARUCH	9	M	CHILD	RRZZZZUSA
GOLDSCHMIDT, MOSES	17	M	DLR	RRZZZZUSA
BER	8	M	CHILD	RRZZZZUSA
KIRSTEIN, CHAYME-W.	18	M	DLR	RRZZZZUSA
SARA	9	F	CHILD	RRZZZZUSA
SUMERACKI, JAN	50	M	LABR	PLZZZZUSA
BUDA, BREINE	30	F	W	PLZZZZUSA
GERSON	6	M	CHILD	PLZZZZUSA
CHAIM	4	M	CHILD	PLZZZZUSA
RACHEL	.11	F	INFANT	PLZZZZUSA
BLUMENFELD, ABRAHAM	39	M	SHMK	PLZZZZUSA
SCHLESINGER, CHAIM	60	F	W	PLZZZZUSA
GALL, JOHANN	47	M	FARMER	PLZZZZUSA
KOTCZINERA, VINCENT	44	M	FARMER	PLZZZZUSA
NOWAK, LEIE	23	F	SGL	RRZZZZUSA
TILLES, R.	00	F	INF	RR****USA

SHIP: ABYSSINIA

FROM: LIVERPOOL AND QUEENSTOWN
TO: NEW YORK
ARRIVED: 29 JULY 1885

PASSENGER	AGE	SEX	OCCUPATION	PRV VIL DES
ISACKSON, ISAACK	20	M	FARMER	FNZZZZUSA
LUDISCHINSKI, SAMUEL	27	M	SHMK	FNZZZZUSA
STENMAN, JACOB-A.	21	M	BKR	RRZZZZUSA
VENDEL, SAMUEL	16	M	TDR	RRZZZZUSA
JASINSKY, ADAM	32	M	BLKSMH	RRZZZZUSA
KOPERKIDWITZ, FRANZ	30	M	BBR	RRZZZZUSA
BRAWIEZ, CHAIM	23	M	TLR	RRZZZZUSA
GLOSONSKI, DAVID	21	M	TLR	RRZZZZUSA
LEITLIN, SIMON	40	M	PDLR	RRZZZZUSA
EPSTEIN, ISAAC	17	M	BKPR	RRZZZZUSA

SHIP: STATE OF GEORGIA

FROM: GLASGOW AND LARNE
TO: NEW YORK
ARRIVED: 29 JULY 1885

PASSENGER	AGE	SEX	OCCUPATION	PRV VIL DES
LESSERN, CHAWE	22	F	SVNT	RRZZZZUSA
ABELSOHN, KALE	18	F	SVNT	RRZZZZUSA

PASSENGER	AGE	SEX	OCCUPATION	PRV VIL DES
KALIN, MOSES	22	M	LABR	RRZZZZUSA
ROSEN	23	F	W	RRZZZZUSA
MORUSWEITE, HINRITTE	35	F	W	PLZZZZUSA
EMILIE	10	F	CH	PLZZZZUSA
ANNA	7	F	CHILD	PLZZZZUSA
H.	2	F	CHILD	PLZZZZUSA
HELENE	1	F	CHILD	PLZZZZUSA
FRIEDMANN, MISSLE	21	F	W	PLZZZZUSA
F.	.06	F	INFANT	PLZZZZUSA
JADLOWITZ, ABEL	32	M	LABR	PLZZZZUSA
L.	32	F	W	PLZZZZUSA
MARIA	10	F	CH	PLZZZZUSA
CHANA	7	F	CHILD	PLZZZZUSA
ANNA	5	F	CHILD	PLZZZZUSA
GUDLOWITZ, ROSALIE	1	F	CHILD	PLZZZZUSA
FORCH.	.02	F	INFANT	PLZZZZUSA
FLANELL, ISAAK	30	M	FARMER	PLZZZZUSA
LEA	29	F	W	PLZZZZUSA
ZACK, JOSEPH	18	M	BCHR	RRZZZZUSA
ROCKOWITZKY, WENDE	45	M	PDLR	RRZZZZUSA
ECKEL, HURWITZ	32	M	PDLR	RRZZZZUSA
KAPLIN, BENGEL	00	M	PDLR	RRZZZZUSA
LURGIE, ELIE	00	M	PDLR	RRZZZZUSA
FELDMANN, ISAAC	00	M	CL	RRZZZZUSA
PLOTEL, ITZIG	00	M	PDLR	RRZZZZUSA
IM----AN, PINCUS	00	M	LABR	RRZZZZUSA
MELANIF, ITZIG	00	M	PDLR	RRZZZZUSA
ZADIKON, CHAIE	00	M	PDLR	RRZZZZUSA
JOEL	00	M	PDLR	RRZZZZUSA
KLONFUSS, HIRCH	00	M	PDLR	RRZZZZUSA
SILBERT, MECH.	00	M	LABR	RRZZZZUSA
JOSEPH	00	M	PDLR	RRZZZZUSA
KAPLIN, HIRCH	00	M	PDLR	RRZZZZUSA
RITTERD, BEN.	00	M	CL	RRZZZZUSA
WALDMANN, OSIAS	00	M	PDLR	RRZZZZUSA
REIS, ISRAEL	00	M	PH	RRZZZZUSA
CHARONSKY, MINDEL	00	M	TLR	PLZZZZUSA
WEISSBACHT, JACOB	00	M	BCHR	PLZZZZUSA
BERKOWITZ, BEER	00	M	TLR	PLZZZZUSA
AVTERKIETZ, AUGUST	00	M	LABR	PLZZZZUSA
HOLM, CARL	00	M	LABR	PLZZZZUSA
PAULUS, LUTZKUS	00	M	LABR	PLZZZZUSA
LICH---, JACOB	00	M	LABR	PLZZZZUSA
FRIEDMANN, U	00	M	LABR	PLZZZZUSA
BORON, JAN	00	M	LABR	PLZZZZUSA
SIGALL, MOZAL	00	M	LABR	PLZZZZUSA
PJEUCCA, ABEL	00	M	LABR	PLZZZZUSA
WEPZINSKY, CARL	40	M	LABR	PLZZZZUSA
WORLBUG, EPHRAIM	11	M	CH	PLZZZZUSA

SHIP: BELGENLAND

FROM: ANTWERP
TO: NEW YORK
ARRIVED: 30 JULY 1885

PASSENGER	AGE	SEX	OCCUPATION	PRV VIL DES
GROSS, B.	21	M	LRDRS	RRZZZZIL
KALINOWSKI, A.	22	M	LABR	PLZZZZUNK
MALOWKOWSKI, J.	36	M	LABR	PLZZZZNY
CEGAL, M.	19	M	MCHT	RRZZZZIL
M.	10	M	UNKNOWN	RRZZZZIL
BETTY	11	F	UNKNOWN	RRZZZZIL
HARRIS, SAL.	35	M	TRDSMN	RRAHVUNY
BLACHSTEIN, J.	20	M	BBR	RRADBQNY
BLASKO, JULIANE	32	F	W	PLZZZZUNK
ANNA	10	F	UNKNOWN	PLZZZZUNK

SHIP: CALIFORNIA

FROM: HAMBURG
TO: NEW YORK
ARRIVED: 31 JULY 1885

PASSENGER	AGE	SEX	OCCUPATION	PRV VIL DES
WEINSTEIN, SCH.	19	M	CL	RRZZZZNY
KOSTRINSKY, MOS.	19	M	TLR	RRZZZZNY
KAPLAN, CHAIM	45	M	TLR	RRZZZZNY
KROHN, LEISER	20	M	SGL	RRZZZZIL
SCHIRWINSKI, MORSCHE	28	M	LABR	RRZZZZNY
FEIGEL	25	F	W	RRZZZZNY
JACOB	.11	M	INFANT	RRZZZZNY
SLATE	.02	F	INFANT	RRZZZZNY
PESTENAK, ABR.	25	M	LABR	RRZZZZNY
CHANE	20	F	W	RRZZZZNY
SARAH	.06	F	INFANT	RRZZZZNY
SALOMON, TH.	15	M	LABR	RRZZZZNY
STIRNSREIN, JANKEL	17	M	LKSH	RRZZZZNY
RAWEKOWITZ, JELLIE	24	F	WO	RRZZZZIL
GROSSMANN, ABR.	47	M	TRDSMN	RRZZZZIL
BERTHA	43	F	W	RRZZZZIL
MEYER	21	M	S	RRZZZZIL
PINCUS	12	M	S	RRZZZZIL
DAVID	7	M	CHILD	RRZZZZIL
BERTHA	7	F	CHILD	RRZZZZIL
ROSE	.06	F	INFANT	RRZZZZIL
BESPALITZ, CHANE	17	F	SGL	RRZZZZIL
SALOM.	25	M	BLKSMH	RRZZZZIL
M.	22	F	W	RRZZZZIL
ALTER	7	M	CHILD	RRZZZZIL
SABELOWITZ, LOUISE	14	M	BY	RRZZZZIL
FRIEDMANN, FANNY	33	F	WO	RRZZZZIL
CHARLES	6	M	CHILD	RRZZZZIL
KRON, JANKEL	18	M	TRDSMN	RRZZZZIL
BERTIN, AYS	15	F	SGL	RRZZZZUNK
ENTE	16	F	SGL	RRZZZZUNK
WANG, CHANE	23	F	WO	PLZZZZNY
S.	.05	F	INFANT	PLZZZZNY
SCHUHAM, SIMCHE	20	M	BKMR	PLZZZZIL
PICHLOWSUKA, KAZIMIR	36	M	LABR	PLZZZZNY
KEFFNER, SAMUEL	23	M	LABR	PLZZZZNY
GOLDBERG, DAVID	28	M	BKR	PLZZZZNY
KAPLAN, CHASSEL	20	M	LABR	RRZZZZNY
FEILANDER, SALI	19	F	SGL	RRZZZZNY
FRIEDZAHN, SARA	17	F	SGL	RRZZZZNY
ISRAELSON, ABRAM	18	M	LABR	RRZZZZIL
FURST, FLORA	34	F	WO	RRZZZZNY
SOFIA	7	F	CHILD	RRZZZZNY
HENRIETTE	6	F	CHILD	RRZZZZNY
BELLA	.05	F	INFANT	RRZZZZNY
LICHTMANN, ZALLOB	26	M	LABR	RRZZZZNY
FEINERSON, ROSALIE	31	F	WO	RRZZZZNY
NATALKE	7	F	CHILD	RRZZZZNY
DRURIK, THEKLA	60	F	WO	PLZZZZNY
ANNA	16	F	D	PLZZZZNY
I.	18	F	D	PLZZZZNY
MEINEIKE, W.	39	M	FARMER	PLZZZZUNK
BOSHE	37	F	W	PLZZZZUNK
MARIA	7	F	CHILD	PLZZZZUNK
FREDZAPA, ELIAS	26	M	TDR	RRZZZZIL
ROSA	23	F	W	RRZZZZIL
ZUCKER, MORDCHE	30	F	WO	PLZZZZNY
ROSING, L.	40	M	JNR	RRZZZZNY
KOPORCZYNSKI, RUD.	25	M	LABR	RRZZZZNY
BUSZAN, BERNHARD	32	M	FARMER	PLZZZZWI
HAUPT, ISENG	16	F	SGL	RRZZZZNY
SEMMI.	.10	F	INFANT	RRZZZZNY
CERN, LOUIS	20	M	MCHT	RRZZZZUNK
GILLIS, BERIL	25	F	WO	RRZZZZIL
LEWIN, SCHEINE	17	F	SGL	RRZZZZNY
GETEL	16	F	SGL	RRZZZZNY
TABIA	7	F	CHILD	RRZZZZNY
ABRAHAM	6	M	CHILD	RRZZZZNY

PASSENGER	AGE	SEX	OCCUPATION	PRIV	VIL	DES
MEYER	5	M	CHILD	RR	ZZZZ	NY
BELLA	5	F	CHILD	RR	ZZZZ	NY
KAPLAN, RACHEL	51	F	SGL	RR	ZZZZ	PA
WALKAWITSCH, BASCHE	35	F	WO	RR	ZZZZ	NY
KRISSIEL	7	M	CHILD	RR	ZZZZ	NY
GITEL	5	F	CHILD	RR	ZZZZ	NY
LATT, JOSEF	26	M	SMH	RR	ZZZZ	IL
WANDLER, MOSES	24	M	LABR	PL	ZZZZ	NY
TAOHNE, BRAINE	23	F	WO	RR	ZZZZ	NY
HERMANN	.07	M	INFANT	RR	ZZZZ	NY
SALOMON, LILLE	16	F	SGL	RR	ZZZZ	NY
KATZ, MARIA	16	F	SGL	RR	ZZZZ	NY
GOLDSMITH, SARA	7	F	CHILD	PL	ZZZZ	NY
ESTER	5	F	CHILD	PL	ZZZZ	NY
SROSTAK, W.	29	M	LABR	PL	ZZZZ	NY
BESCHOWITZ, ITZIG	46	M	TDR	RR	ZZZZ	NY

SHIP: CITY OF BERLIN

FROM: LIVERPOOL
TO: NEW YORK
ARRIVED: 31 JULY 1885

PASSENGER	AGE	SEX	OCCUPATION	PRIV	VIL	DES
ANDERSON, FRILA-L.	30	F	W	RR	AEWS	KS
PORISIE, ERRICKA	4	F	CHILD	RR	AEWS	KS
PORISSE, HERMAN	2	M	CHILD	RR	AEWS	KS
HENDERSON, AMANDA-S.	36	F	W	RR	AEWS	BO
BERTHA	4	F	CHILD	RR	AEWS	BO
HILDA	2	F	CHILD	RR	AEWS	BO
ZACHIESON, LOUISA	17	F	SP	RR	AEWS	KS
CHUMPLAN, MICH.	19	M	FARMER	RR	ACBF	WI

SHIP: WERRA

FROM: BREMEN
TO: NEW YORK
ARRIVED: 31 JULY 1885

PASSENGER	AGE	SEX	OCCUPATION	PRIV	VIL	DES
BAKHMEKFT, G.	38	M	TT	RR	ZZZZ	NY
BURGER, HENNY	35	F	UNKNOWN	RR	ZZZZ	NY
CHAIN	7	F	CHILD	RR	ZZZZ	NY
HIRKE	6	F	CHILD	RR	ZZZZ	NY
ALTE	.10	F	INFANT	RR	ZZZZ	NY
SALOMON	3	M	CHILD	RR	ZZZZ	NY
PARZKOWICZ, PORIGIN	40	F	UNKNOWN	RR	ZZZZ	NY
APOLONA	30	F	UNKNOWN	RR	ZZZZ	NY
STANISLAUS	5	M	CHILD	RR	ZZZZ	NY
JOSEFA	6	F	CHILD	RR	ZZZZ	NY
ROSA	.06	F	INFANT	RR	ZZZZ	NY
LUDWIKA	3	F	CHILD	RR	ZZZZ	NY
DOSCHKOWITZ, CHARLOTTE	36	F	UNKNOWN	RR	ZZZZ	NY
MARIE	3	F	CHILD	RR	ZZZZ	NY
REINHOLD	.11	M	INFANT	RR	ZZZZ	NY
WENDER, SARAH	33	F	UNKNOWN	RR	ZZZZ	NY
PERSE	7	F	CHILD	RR	ZZZZ	NY
JOWEL	6	F	CHILD	RR	ZZZZ	NY
LEIBE	5	F	CHILD	RR	ZZZZ	NY
SIMON	4	M	CHILD	RR	ZZZZ	NY
MICHEL	4	M	CHILD	RR	ZZZZ	NY
ZIPPE	3	F	CHILD	RR	ZZZZ	NY
NAWICKA, ELEONORE	25	F	UNKNOWN	RR	ZZZZ	NY
DELLITZKI, WICENTY	30	F	UNKNOWN	RR	ZZZZ	NY
NORRGARD, JOHANSON	21	M	LABR	RR	ZZZZ	NY
AUCEWIZ, TERFIL	30	M	LABR	RR	ZZZZ	NY
LEPZOW, WLADISLAW	20	M	LABR	RR	ZZZZ	NY

PASSENGER	AGE	SEX	OCCUPATION	PRIV	VIL	DES
LUKASEWICZ, VICTORIA	25	F	UNKNOWN	RR	ZZZZ	NY
JACOBSOHN, DORA	22	F	UNKNOWN	RR	ZZZZ	NY
JACOB	.05	M	INFANT	RR	ZZZZ	NY
WECHSLER, CHAIM	4	M	CHILD	RR	ZZZZ	NY
RADZIEWICZ, JULIUS	25	M	LABR	RR	ZZZZ	NY
DAUCKCZA, LUDW.	27	M	LABR	RR	ZZZZ	NY
GYRZEWICZ, AUGUSTIN	23	M	LABR	RR	ZZZZ	NY
SYTKEWICZ, STEFAN	21	M	LABR	RR	ZZZZ	NY
GUDAITIS, ANTONY	25	M	LABR	RR	ZZZZ	NY
ABRAHAM, BLUME	18	M	FARMER	RR	ZZZZ	NY

SHIP: W A SCHOLTEN

FROM: ROTTERDAM
TO: NEW YORK
ARRIVED: 01 AUGUST 1885

PASSENGER	AGE	SEX	OCCUPATION	PRIV	VIL	DES
KUZINSKI, SIEGFRIED	18	M	SLSMN	RR	ZZZZ	USA
FEINSTEIN, K.	17	M	SLSMN	RR	ZZZZ	USA
COHN, FRIEDE	30	F	UNKNOWN	RR	ZZZZ	USA
MOSES	5	F	CHILD	RR	ZZZZ	USA
ISRAEL	6	F	CHILD	RR	ZZZZ	USA
SABLUDOWSKA, ESTHER	26	F	UNKNOWN	RR	ZZZZ	USA
INDA, MICHAEL	00	M	UNKNOWN	RR	ZZZZ	USA
LINKA, VINCENTE	6	M	CHILD	RR	ZZZZ	USA
LITVAK, BARUCH	33	M	GUL	RR	ZZZZ	USA
SABLUDOWSK-, MOSES	12	M	CH	RR	ZZZZ	USA
WOLF	.06	M	INFANT	RR	ZZZZ	USA
AVIDAN, JANKEL	20	M	SLSMN	RR	ZZZZ	USA
GERSINSKI, DAVID	18	M	UNKNOWN	RR	ZZZZ	USA
GRUNBLADZ, MAX	26	M	MCHT	RR	ZZZZ	USA
AUGUSTE	26	F	UNKNOWN	RR	ZZZZ	USA
IDA	7	F	CHILD	RR	ZZZZ	USA
JACOB	5	M	CHILD	RR	ZZZZ	USA
MAX	3	M	CHILD	RR	ZZZZ	USA
FREIDE	.06	F	INFANT	RR	ZZZZ	USA
ARTHUR	.06	M	INFANT	RR	ZZZZ	USA
ROTHBLUM, IDA	17	F	CH	RR	ZZZZ	USA
SPIELBERG, ISRAEL	22	M	SLSMN	RR	ZZZZ	USA
AVIDAN, BERL	23	M	SLSMN	RR	ZZZZ	USA
RACHEL	30	F	UNKNOWN	RR	ZZZZ	USA
BERKOWITZ, ELIAS	22	M	SHMK	RR	ZZZZ	USA
RUBENSTEIN, OCHER	37	M	BRR	RR	ZZZZ	USA
IZAK	12	M	CH	RR	ZZZZ	USA
ABRAM	11	M	CH	RR	ZZZZ	USA
LEWIN, MEJER	20	M	JNR	RR	ZZZZ	USA
GORDAN, JOSEL	33	M	SLSMN	RR	ZZZZ	USA
LEA	24	F	UNKNOWN	RR	ZZZZ	USA
MOSES	4	M	CHILD	RR	ZZZZ	USA
STANIN, JOSEPH	20	M	LABR	RR	ZZZZ	USA
MILKOWSKI, MEYER	36	M	TLR	RR	ZZZZ	USA
RAWITOKIS, JOSEPH	22	M	LABR	RR	ZZZZ	USA
GRUNDWAK, BEER	33	M	TNM	RR	ZZZZ	USA
DAVIE, SCHLOME	19	M	LABR	RR	ZZZZ	USA
FRIEDMAN, MOSES	20	M	GUL	RR	ZZZZ	USA
WIEL, BENJAMIN	20	M	SMH	RR	ZZZZ	USA
CREIS, CHEIM	20	M	JNR	RR	ZZZZ	USA
STOLNIK, JOSEF	23	M	SLSMN	RR	ZZZZ	USA
RIESFEN, JOHANNES	24	M	LABR	RR	ZZZZ	USA

SHIP: SERVIA

FROM: LIVERPOOL.AND QUEENSTOWN
TO: NEW YORK
ARRIVED: 03 AUGUST 1885

PASSENGER	AGE	SEX	OCCUPATION	PRI VIL DES
SOKOLOWSKY, FRANZ	50	M	LABR	PLZZZZNY
BOSTA, VOYTEG	18	M	LABR	PLZZZZNY
ECLENBERG, HANS	33	M	LABR	RRZZZZMA
KUPMAN, LASSI	22	M	LABR	FNZZZZIL
MARGA	21	F	W	FNZZZZIL
ALAMA	3	F	CHILD	FNZZZZIL
ERIKA	19	F	SP	FNZZZZIL
MARJA	2	F	CHILD	FNZZZZIL
ANNA	.09	F	INFANT	FNZZZZIL

SHIP: ANCHORIA

FROM: GLASGOW
TO: NEW YORK
ARRIVED: 05 AUGUST 1885

PASSENGER	AGE	SEX	OCCUPATION	PRI VIL DES
GOLDBERG, ABRAHAM	21	M	DLR	FNACBFUSA
KASSEL, MOSES	38	M	DLR	FNACBFUSA
ROSE	56	F	NN	FNACBFUSA
KLIWANSKY, MOSES	54	M	GDSM	FNACBFUSA
LEPLEWSKI, SOL.	33	M	DLR	FNACBFUSA
BELA	28	F	NN	FNACBFUSA
ESTER	2	F	CHILD	FNACBFUSA
MESMER, JACOB	30	M	MUSN	FNACBFUSA
NUSSBAUM, JACOB	21	M	DSTLR	FNACBFUSA
MOSES	20	M	DSTLR	FNACBFUSA
OLANDER, SOL.	20	M	LABR	FNACBFUSA
STRAUPINSKY, MARCUS	46	M	BBR	FNACBFUSA
SPIRER, HERMAN	28	M	TLR	FNACBFUSA
MAIER	11	M	CH	FNACBFUSA
WEISBRAUT, ITZIG	19	M	PH	FNACBFUSA

SHIP: ENGLAND

FROM: LIVERPOOL AND QUEENSTOWN
TO: NEW YORK
ARRIVED: 05 AUGUST 1885

PASSENGER	AGE	SEX	OCCUPATION	PRI VIL DES
LIMDBUG, SIMON	20	M	BRKR	FNADBQNY
SHELKY, HENRY	26	M	TLR	FNADBQNY
SILBERMANN, HYMAN	22	M	CBTMKR	FNADBQNY
SMITHMAN, ARON	27	M	CBTMKR	FNADBQNY
DAVIS, MORRIS	21	M	CBTMKR	FNADBQNY
EDELSTEIN, MILLRAE	28	M	CPMKR	FNADBQNY
ISAKERMAN, MORRIS	43	M	LABR	FNADBQNY
ROSENBERG, ROSA	35	F	W	FNADAXCH
JOHN	10	M	CH	FNADAXCH
ABRAHAM	8	M	CHILD	FNADAXCH
HYMAN	4	M	CHILD	FNADAXCH
ISAREL	1	M	CHILD	FNADAXCH
COHIN, AMELIA	8	F	CHILD	FNADAXNY
HANNAH	6	F	CHILD	FNADAXNY
RACHEL	4	F	CHILD	FNADAXNY
LEWIS	2	M	CHILD	FNADAXNY
SILOERMANN, ABRAHAM	19	M	CBTMKR	FNADBQNY
LAHON, BENJ.	19	M	BCHR	FNADBQNY
CHIMETOWSKY, MYER	21	M	FUR	FNADBQPHI
BISKHOP, ABRAHAM	20	M	CPMKR	FNADBQNY
FREEDMAN, MARKS	25	M	TLR	FNADBQNY
BROMBERG, ZELLA	55	F	W	FNAFVHNY
SCHULTZ, MORRIS	22	M	TLR	FNADAXCH
REBECCA	19	F	W	FNADAXCH
MASHORES, WOLF	37	M	CPMKR	FNADBQNY
SARAH	36	F	W	FNADBQNY
RENLIN	17	M	CPMKR	FNADBQNY
CHASKEL	15	M	CH	FNADBQNY
DAVISE	11	M	CH	FNADBQNY
NATHAN, ISAAC	2	M	CHILD	FNADBQNY
RACHEL	.06	F	INFANT	FNADBQNY
ABRAHAM, HARRIS	31	M	TLR	FNADBQNY
BELTOTERES, BREL.	22	F	SP	FNAHQHUNK
MARIA	19	F	SP	FNAHQHUNK
WAULEN, MARIA	21	F	SP	RRZZZZNY
LUEKKI, ANNA	40	F	W	RRZZZZNY
JOHAN	10	M	CH	RRZZZZNY
MATTIUS	8	M	CHILD	RRZZZZNY
ERSON, JOHN-E.	60	M	LABR	FNZZZZNY
MARIA	50	F	W	FNZZZZIA
MAYHANNSON, IDA	19	F	SP	FNZZZZNY
EDWARD	10	M	CH	FNZZZZNY
MATILA, HEINRICK	35	M	LABR	FNZZZZCAL
LUNKE, KRILU	30	F	W	FNZZZZNY
JOHAN	4	M	CHILD	FNZZZZNY
SEREFINA	1	F	CHILD	FNZZZZNY
HALPEN, M.	19	M	BLKSMH	FNADBQUNK
COHN, LEDALJE	30	M	SHMK	FNADBQNY
SARA	11	F	CH	FNADBQNY
LAZAR	10	M	CH	FNADBQNY
LUGERMAN, JACOB	35	M	CGRMKR	FNADBQNY
ROSSKOVSKY, C.	23	M	TLR	FNADBQNY
LAZAM, WOLF	19	M	WCHMKR	FNADBQNY
WASHAN, ZIPPE	32	M	LABR	FNADBQNY
HAGU, GUSTAFIN	42	F	W	FNADBQNY
CATTE	8	F	CHILD	FNADBQNY
JOHAN	14	M	LABR	FNADBQNY
E.	3	M	CHILD	FNADBQNY
KILLINCEN, JACOB	44	M	LABR	FNAHQHNY
BOLIKKA, MATHIAS	25	M	LABR	FNZZZZNY
JOKKOLU, MARIN	23	M	LABR	FNZZZZNY
MIELKY, MATHEUS	31	M	TLR	RRZZZZNY
EPSTEIN, MOSES	19	M	TLR	RRZZZZNY
LERASJUMSKY, OSHAR	30	M	JNR	RRAHQUNY
BERLY	22	M	JNR	RRAHQUNY
CHARLES	3	M	CHILD	RRAHQUNY
LONUS	1	M	CHILD	RRAHQUNY
MOSEP, FANNIE	22	F	SP	RRADBQNY

SHIP: RHAETIA

FROM: HAMBURG
TO: NEW YORK
ARRIVED: 05 AUGUST 1885

PASSENGER	AGE	SEX	OCCUPATION	PRI VIL DES
MELTZER, SARA-OLGA	31	F	W	RRZZZZUSA
JONARICHA	9	M	CHILD	RRZZZZUSA
CLARA	9	F	CHILD	RRZZZZUSA
AUATINISCH, WOLF	19	M	LKSH	RRZZZZUSA
DAMSKY, HIRSCH	18	M	LABR	RRAHTFUSA
TEIBEL, ILKE	22	F	SGL	RRAHTFUSA
WOLKOW, ICHINE-B.	23	F	W	RRZZZZUSA
SALOMON	.11	M	INFANT	RRZZZZUSA
BUKANSKI, RUWEN	33	M	TNMK	RRAHTFUSA
POLAY, FRUME	54	F	W	RRZZZZUSA
ROCHEL	17	F	CH	RRZZZZUSA
LEWSCHE	15	F	CH	RRZZZZUSA
GUDELMANN, BERTHA	20	F	SGL	RRZZZZUSA
LIP, SOPHIE	20	F	SGL	RRZZZZUSA
DWORA, ANNA	24	F	W	RRAHZSUSA

PASSENGER	AGE	SEX	OCCUPATION	PRV VIL DES
RUBIN	5	M	CHILD	RRAHZSUSA
MEYER	3	M	CHILD	RRAHZSUSA
DAVID	.09	M	INFANT	RRAHZSUSA
MEYER, HEINRICH	48	M	DLR	RRAHZSUSA
BIELEMANN, FRED	53	M	MCHT	RRAHZSUSA
FISKEL, ABRAHAM-H.	30	M	TNMK	RRAHVUUSA
DWAROLISKY, JUDEL	50	M	FARMER	RRAHTFUSA
MALCHEN	45	F	W	RRAHTFUSA
EINTRACHT, BLINNE	27	F	W	RRACTCUSA
ROMAN	7	M	CHILD	RRACTCUSA
ALFRED	5	M	CHILD	RRACTCUSA
SALI	3	F	CHILD	RRACTCUSA
KOSSAN, ANNA	22	F	SGL	RRZZZZUSA
MELTZER, MARK	18	M	MCHT	RRZZZZUSA
ZAJIN, JOSEFA	25	F	W	RRZZZZUSA
STANISLAWA	2	F	CHILD	RRZZZZUSA
CATHARINA	.09	F	INFANT	RRZZZZUSA
PISTOL, ANNA	40	F	W	PLZZZZUSA
SOPHIE	.09	F	INFANT	PLZZZZUSA
SEMIL, SALMON	16	F	SGL	PLZZZZUSA
SEMMEL, BETTY	20	F	SGL	PLZZZZUSA
OBINSKI, SCHMUEL	42	M	TLR	PLAHTFUSA
HANNA	35	F	W	PLAHTFUSA
ALTER	.11	M	INFANT	PLAHTFUSA
KAMLARY, ABRAHAM	18	M	TLR	PLAHUFUSA
MARIE	23	F	W	PLAHUFUSA
DWORE	20	F	SGL	PLAHUFUSA
GINOWSKY, FREIDE	38	F	W	PLAHXHUSA
FANNI	9	M	CHILD	PLAHXHUSA
IDA	9	F	CHILD	PLAHXHUSA
CHARLOTTE	7	F	CHILD	PLAHXHUSA
HANNCHEN	4	F	CHILD	PLAHXHUSA
ARON	.11	M	INFANT	PLAHXHUSA
RUDOLF, SELMA	19	F	SGL	PLAHXHUSA
LIBOMIERSKY, PEISECH	50	M	SMH	RRZZZZUSA
TURKUS, WILH.	22	M	CGRMKR	RRZZZZUSA
FISCHMANN, JUDA	20	M	TLR	RRZZZZUSA
SEGAL, LEIB	20	M	DLR	RRZZZZUSA
WOLOZINSKI, JOSEF	21	M	LABR	RRZZZZUSA
MILLITAL, JUL.	30	M	LABR	RRZZZZUSA
HUBECK, JOSEPH	50	M	LABR	RRZZZZUSA
KIMEL, JOHANN	39	M	JNR	PLZZZZUSA
THERESE	26	F	W	PLZZZZUSA
JOHANN	9	M	CHILD	PLZZZZUSA
FERDINAND	4	M	CHILD	PLZZZZUSA
ANNA	4	F	CHILD	PLZZZZUSA
WALIAH, GEORG	25	M	JNR	PLZZZZUSA
GELNER, FRANZ	42	M	JNR	PLZZZZUSA
MELTZER, SELIG	23	M	LABR	PLZZZZUSA
MAKAREWICZEN, AGATHE	25	F	W	RRZZZZUSA
AGATHE	4	F	CHILD	RRZZZZUSA
MARIE	.06	F	INFANT	RRZZZZUSA
SCHOENEWICZ, HERM.	19	M	LABR	RRAHUFUSA
GODAT, ANNA	19	F	SGL	RRZZZZUSA
RISNISS, ANTON	20	M	LABR	RRAFZDUSA

SHIP: STATE OF INDIANA

FROM: GLASGOW AND LARNE
TO: NEW YORK
ARRIVED: 05 AUGUST 1885

PASSENGER	AGE	SEX	OCCUPATION	PRV VIL DES
COHEN, NISCHUM	16	M	BCHR	RRZZZZUSA
LEIB	14	M	BCHR	RRZZZZUSA
KAUFMANN, GOTTLIEB	17	M	CL	RRAHTFUSA
MEER, DAVID	20	M	JWLR	RRZZZZUSA
CHOSER, OSSIAS	20	M	UNKNOWN	RRACBFUSA
LEW, MOSES	22	M	SHMK	RRZZZZUSA
BARUCH, ABRAHAM	22	M	SHMK	RRZZZZUSA
LISCHINSKY, ABRAHAM	39	M	LABR	RRZZZZUSA

PASSENGER	AGE	SEX	OCCUPATION	PRV VIL DES
REDMANN, BEER	19	M	LABR	RRACBFUSA
MILLNER, MOSES	20	M	TLR	RRZZZZUSA
SUDALKIS, JAKOB	20	M	PDLR	RRZZZZUSA
LIPSCHITZ, BERNHARD	20	M	PDLR	RRZZZZUSA
FEIL, JACOB	21	M	PDLR	RRAFVGUSA
JERSCHEWSKY, KOPPEL	37	M	PDLR	RRZZZZUSA
KISMAR, ITZIG	19	M	PDLR	RRACBFUSA
JAFFE, GERSON	30	M	PDLR	RRZZZZUSA
SALZMANN, MOSES	38	M	PDLR	RRACBFUSA
PAWROWSKY, FRANZ	00	M	LABR	RRAHUIUSA
LAPIDUS, WOLFF	49	M	PDLR	RRAFWJUSA
SCHMUCK, LEIB	24	M	PDLR	PLZZZZUSA
GRESCHAR, FRANZ	38	M	LABR	PLZZZZUSA
DUDES, FANNI	22	F	SP	PLAFVGUSA
LENARS, ZINE	17	F	SP	RRZZZZUSA
FEINSTEIN, JOSEF	24	M	PDLR	RRAHTFUSA
CHAIE	23	F	W	RRAHTFUSA
JACOB	11	M	CH	RRAHTFUSA
MOSES	2	M	CHILD	RRAHTFUSA
RACHEL	1	F	CHILD	RRAHTFUSA
BIEBER, MENDEL	33	M	PDLR	RRZZZZUSA
FEIGE	29	F	W	RRZZZZUSA
JACOB	11	M	CH	RRZZZZUSA
CHAIM	9	M	CHILD	RRZZZZUSA
ZIMCHE	8	M	CHILD	RRZZZZUSA
LEIB	5	M	CHILD	RRZZZZUSA
SCHONE	2	F	CHILD	RRZZZZUSA
FALK	.03	M	INFANT	RRZZZZUSA
ECKHOFF, ISRAEL	39	M	PDLR	RRZZZZUSA
SCHEINDEL	30	F	W	RRZZZZUSA
BERTHA	12	F	CH	RRZZZZUSA
ABRAHAM	3	M	CHILD	RRZZZZUSA
COHN, ARJE	32	M	TCHR	RRZZZZUSA
ROCHEL	30	F	W	RRZZZZUSA
SLOME	11	M	CH	RRZZZZUSA
SCHEINDE	7	F	CHILD	RRZZZZUSA
DAVID	3	M	CHILD	RRZZZZUSA
BASCHE	.03	F	INFANT	RRZZZZUSA
LEWARS, BEER	7	M	CHILD	RRZZZZUSA
DEBORA	3	F	CHILD	RRZZZZUSA
SALZMANN, GITEL	9	F	CHILD	RRACBFUSA

SHIP: WISCONSIN

FROM: LIVERPOOL AND QUEENSTOWN
TO: NEW YORK
ARRIVED: 05 AUGUST 1885

PASSENGER	AGE	SEX	OCCUPATION	PRV VIL DES
BENJAKOWSKY, BENJAMIN	34	M	LABR	RRZZZZUSA
K-ZNIER, MORDEKE	31	M	LABR	RRZZZZUSA
KULIN, HERON.	44	M	LABR	RRZZZZUSA
NIKAISKI, GERG.	33	M	LABR	RRZZZZUSA
WINKOSST, WILHELM	56	M	LABR	RRZZZZUSA

SHIP: WAESLAND

FROM: ANTWERP
TO: NEW YORK
ARRIVED: 06 AUGUST 1885

PASSENGER	AGE	SEX	OCCUPATION	PRV VIL DES
GROBLEWSKY, I.	33	M	TLR	PLZZZZNY
ALSTROM, H.	20	M	TLR	FNZZZZNY
GASZEZYNSKI, A.	23	M	CPTR	RRZZZZUNK
WOCHOWSKI, I.	21	M	MSN	PLZZZZNY
CICHANSKI, A.	17	M	LABR	PLZZZZCH

PASSENGER	AGE	SEX	OCCUPATION	PRV VIL DES
KATARZYNA, PAUL	24	M	SMH	PLZZZZMIL
JASN.	00	F	INF	PLZZZZMIL
MICH.	00	M	INF	PLZZZZMIL

SHIP: BALTIC

FROM: LIVERPOOL AND QUEENSTOWN
TO: NEW YORK
ARRIVED: 07 AUGUST 1885

PASSENGER	AGE	SEX	OCCUPATION	PRV VIL DES
BARENSBLUD, ISAC	16	M	FARMER	PLAGRTUSA
BUNDOKER, PEJUNCHER	20	M	FARMER	PLAGRTUSA
KATRE	21	F	SVNT	PLAGRTUSA
NEIGER, ARON	31	M	CK	PLAGRTUSA
RAPAPORT, AB.	29	M	LABR	PLAGRTUSA
BERTE	23	F	W	PLAGRTUSA
BORIS	.10	F	INFANT	PLAGRTUSA
GOLDENBURG, EPHRAIM	18	M	LABR	PLAFWJUSA
KAPERUS, JANKEL	26	M	LABR	PLAFWJUSA
GOTHERSTROM, KARL-W.	21	M	LABR	PLAFWJUSA
HENITS, THEODOR	25	M	LABR	PLAFWJUSA
IWEN	22	M	LABR	PLAFWJUSA

SHIP: FULDA

FROM: BREMEN
TO: NEW YORK
ARRIVED: 07 AUGUST 1885

PASSENGER	AGE	SEX	OCCUPATION	PRV VIL DES
MANSFELD, RACHAL	46	M	LABR	PLAEFLUSA
LEITZE	8	F	CHILD	PLAEFLUSA
SOKOLOWSKI, FRIEDRICH	40	M	LABR	PLAEXKUSA
JULIANE	36	F	UNKNOWN	PLAEXKUSA
JULIANE	14	F	UNKNOWN	PLAEXKUSA
AMALIE	8	F	CHILD	PLAEXKUSA
DAVID	.11	M	INFANT	PLAEXKUSA
EHRHARDT, JOSEPH	47	M	LABR	PLAEXKUSA
ELISE	29	F	UNKNOWN	PLAEXKUSA

SHIP: GRECIAN MONARCH

FROM: LONDON
TO: NEW YORK
ARRIVED: 07 AUGUST 1885

PASSENGER	AGE	SEX	OCCUPATION	PRV VIL DES
DELANS, J.H.MR	39	F	NN	RRZZZZBO
A.J.MR	17	M	CH	RRZZZZBO

SHIP: HAMMONIA

FROM: HAMBURG AND HAVRE
TO: NEW YORK
ARRIVED: 07 AUGUST 1885

PASSENGER	AGE	SEX	OCCUPATION	PRV VIL DES
BAHOWSKY, MORACHE	19	M	TLR	RRZZZZUSA
HENCHEW, SALOMON	20	M	LABR	RRZZZZUSA
SCHAFMEN, JANKEL	19	M	SMH	RRZZZZUSA
DANOWIZ, SCHAI	22	M	LABR	RRZZZZUSA
ESSEL	22	F	W	RRZZZZUSA
KIZALEWSKI, MARIANNE	30	F	W	RRZZZZUSA
MARG.	.11	F	INFANT	RRZZZZUSA
ZUHOWSHOWA, CATHARINA	24	F	SGL	RRZZZZUSA
ABRAMOWICZ, FEINWISCH	25	M	LABR	RRZZZZUSA
WOLF, FRANK	26	M	WRT	RRZZZZUSA
LUBLINSKI, JACOB	27	M	LABR	RRZZZZUSA
OKUN, CHEIM	19	M	LABR	RRZZZZUSA
FISCHER, EMILIE	29	F	SGL	RRZZZZUSA
GOLDBERG, BERTA	18	F	SGL	RRZZZZUSA
ELIAS	16	M	LABR	RRZZZZUSA
KAHN, LEIB	16	M	LABR	RRZZZZUSA
BOSENGART, SARA	48	F	W	RRZZZZUSA
LEIB	9	M	CHILD	RRZZZZUSA
MORDCHE	8	M	CHILD	RRZZZZUSA

SHIP: RHEIN

FROM: BREMEN AND SOUTHAMPTON
TO: NEW YORK
ARRIVED: 07 AUGUST 1885

PASSENGER	AGE	SEX	OCCUPATION	PRV VIL DES
BRAUMSTEIN, DINA	27	F	NN	RRZZZZUSA
LEWKE	6	F	CHILD	RRZZZZUSA
LEIB	5	M	CHILD	RRZZZZUSA
SCHENIDEL	3	M	CHILD	RRZZZZUSA
LEWITT, ABRAHAM	24	M	TT	RRZZZZUSA
GITTEL	23	F	W	RRZZZZUSA
SAMUEL	.05	M	INFANT	RRZZZZUSA
ACKERMANN, ELKE	27	F	NN	RRZZZZUSA
SAMUEL	6	M	CHILD	RRZZZZUSA
FEGE	4	F	CHILD	RRZZZZUSA
CHAINE	2	F	CHILD	RRZZZZUSA
AARON	.09	M	INFANT	RRZZZZUSA
ELFBE, ROCHEL	23	F	NN	RRZZZZUSA
UDEL	2	F	CHILD	RRZZZZUSA
ITZIG	.04	M	INFANT	RRZZZZUSA
LEWITH, PINKA	15	F	NN	RRZZZZUSA
DUBCZANSKY, SORE	34	F	NN	RRZZZZUSA
RIFKE	7	F	CHILD	RRZZZZUSA
REBECCA	6	F	CHILD	RRZZZZUSA
ELISAR	5	M	CHILD	RRZZZZUSA
CHAIDE	3	F	CHILD	RRZZZZUSA
AARON	.11	M	INFANT	RRZZZZUSA
IUROWITZ, SARA	20	F	NN	RRZZZZUSA
BRUCK, DAVID	24	M	LABR	RRZZZZUSA
BOGOSER, STEFANOS	27	M	LABR	RRZZZZUSA
ACHENBACH, JACOB	27	M	LABR	RRZZZZUSA
METZLER, PETER	22	M	LABR	RRZZZZUSA
PETRUCZEWICZ, ADAM	30	M	LABR	RRZZZZUSA
NEUBLATT, REBECCA	20	F	NN	RRZZZZUSA
SCHOEMER, NUTE	28	F	NN	PLZZZZUSA
WARDOWSKY, ROCHAN	17	F	NN	RRZZZZUSA
ALBERT	19	M	LABR	RRZZZZUSA
ETKINS, JACOB	35	M	TT	RRZZZZUSA
HARRIS, DAVID	28	M	LABR	RRZZZZUSA
ARIS, MARIE	20	F	NN	RRZZZZUSA
RUCHWALSKY, MARE	18	M	LABR	RRZZZZUSA
PREISMANN, WOLF	16	M	NN	RRZZZZUSA

PASSENGER	AGE	SEX	OCCUPATION	PRV VIL DES
LOBKACZ, ANTONIE	23	M	LABR	RRZZZZUSA
BUCZEWICZ, AUGUST	30	M	LABR	RRZZZZUSA
AGATHE	10	F	CH	RRZZZZUSA
AUGUSTIN	7	M	CHILD	RRZZZZUSA
MARIA	6	F	CHILD	RRZZZZUSA
SZIMANSKI, JAN	28	M	LABR	RRZZZZUSA
LEVIN, ISAAC	24	M	LABR	RRZZZZUSA

SHIP: CIRCASSIA

FROM: GLASGOW AND MOVILLE
TO: NEW YORK
ARRIVED: 10 AUGUST 1885

PASSENGER	AGE	SEX	OCCUPATION	PRV VIL DES
SALZBERG, LEON	19	M	DLR	RRZZZZUSA
GOLDBERG, ABRAHAM	26	M	TLR	RRZZZZUSA
HAIDIN, SAM.	20	M	DRG	RRZZZZUSA
SCHEFZ, KOPEL	18	M	DLR	RRZZZZUSA
BRUIN, MATHAN	22	M	DLR	RRZZZZUSA
WOSLEMSKI, WILHELM	22	M	LKSH	RRZZZZUSA

SHIP: GALLIA

FROM: LIVERPOOL AND QUEENSTOWN
TO: NEW YORK
ARRIVED: 10 AUGUST 1885

PASSENGER	AGE	SEX	OCCUPATION	PRV VIL DES
HAANELA, KAISA	18	F	SP	RRZZZZUSA
RUFMENIN, NICHOLAS	26	M	SEMN	RRZZZZUSA
KARSSIKA, H.M.	18	M	SEMN	RRZZZZUSA
RONKANEN, ANNA	35	F	MA	RRZZZZUSA
JOH.	11	F	CH	RRZZZZUSA
CARL	10	M	CH	RRZZZZUSA
ANNA	8	F	CHILD	RRZZZZUSA
AB.	4	M	CHILD	RRZZZZUSA
MORBAMMEN, ANNA	30	F	MA	RRZZZZUSA
WOLBORG	8	M	CHILD	RRZZZZUSA
STENA	4	M	CHILD	RRZZZZUSA
JACOB	2	M	CHILD	RRZZZZUSA
ANNA	.06	F	INFANT	RRZZZZUSA
EISEWKOW, RISSIL	33	F	SVNT	PLZZZZUSA

SHIP: SCHIEDAM

FROM: AMSTERDAM
TO: NEW YORK
ARRIVED: 10 AUGUST 1885

PASSENGER	AGE	SEX	OCCUPATION	PRV VIL DES
DIADAK, JOSEF	26	M	LABR	RRZZZZUSA
TUSKA, PAUL	25	M	LABR	RRZZZZUSA
SCHANKIN, ABRAH.	40	M	LABR	RRZZZZUSA

SHIP: SUEVIA

FROM: HAMBURG
TO: NEW YORK
ARRIVED: 10 AUGUST 1885

PASSENGER	AGE	SEX	OCCUPATION	PRV VIL DES
LUNGLEBER, SLAH	46	F	W	RRZZZZUSA
LEWANDOWSKA, SOFIA	16	F	SGL	RRZZZZUSA
DOMROWSKA, MARIANNA	23	F	SGL	RRAHUFUSA
GERSCHENOWITZ, CHAIN	38	F	W	RRZZZZUSA
CHANNE	9	F	CHILD	RRZZZZUSA
ABRAHAM	8	M	CHILD	RRZZZZUSA
REISEL	7	M	CHILD	RRZZZZUSA
LAZARUS	6	M	CHILD	RRZZZZUSA
DAVID	3	M	CHILD	RRZZZZUSA
PERL, JAS-L.	27	M	TLR	RRAHTOUSA
MENSEL, SAMUEL	16	M	TLR	RRAHUFUSA
SPIRO, JACOB	15	M	LABR	RRZZZZUSA
IGLIG, PESCHE	22	F	W	RRAHTFUSA
ISAAC	4	M	CHILD	RRAHTFUSA
SEREISKY, SARA	18	F	SGL	RRAHTFUSA
SMARKOWITZ, PESCHE	45	F	W	RRAHTFUSA
ANNA	.09	F	INFANT	RRAHTFUSA
SPARBERG, DAVID	50	M	DLR	RRAHTFUSA
DWORSKY, ISRAEL	32	M	LABR	RRAHZSUSA
COHN, REISEL	27	F	W	RRADOIUSA
GOTTLIEB	9	M	CHILD	RRADOIUSA
JOEHE	00	F	CH	RRADOIUSA
GOLDBERG, ISAAC	26	M	TNMK	RRAFVGUSA
RANHUT, CARL	17	M	BBR	RRZZZZUSA
ACALAJENK, MAGDAL.	22	F	SGL	RRAHTRUSA
MINZER, ROSA	30	F	W	RRZZZZUSA
SARA	8	F	CHILD	RRZZZZUSA
JOSSEL	7	F	CHILD	RRZZZZUSA
MOSES	6	M	CHILD	RRZZZZUSA
ISAAC	.11	M	INFANT	RRZZZZUSA
NEUFELD, OLGA	38	F	SGL	RRZZZZUSA
SONIE	15	F	SGL	RRZZZZUSA
LIPNIAK, ABRAHAM	50	M	DLR	RRAHTOUSA
BERKER, LEA	50	F	W	RRAHZIUSA
SCHWEIDZER, LEIZER	25	M	DLR	RRAFWJUSA
GRUNBLATT, ABRAHAM	9	M	CHILD	RRAHTFUSA
PFUND, CARL-W.	28	M	UNKNOWN	RRZZZZUSA
EISENBERG, JACOB	23	M	LABR	RRAHOKUSA
MINZER, ISAAC	18	M	LABR	RRAHOKUSA
BARUCH	32	M	LABR	RRAHOKUSA
PERBOHNER, MARIE	17	F	SGL	RRAHXHUSA
KERSUR, ISAAC	26	M	TCHR	RRZZZZUSA
GESANSKA, JACHNE	33	F	W	RRZZZZUSA
SELIG	9	M	CHILD	RRZZZZUSA
SIMON	8	M	CHILD	RRZZZZUSA
PILIKANSKY, PAUL	6	M	CHILD	RRZZZZUSA
GELBERD, HERSCH	29	M	LABR	RRZZZZUSA
GOLDE	25	F	W	RRZZZZUSA
JACOB	.11	M	INFANT	RRZZZZUSA
OSTRY, ROSA	40	F	W	RRAHZSUSA
ELISE	3	F	CHILD	RRAHZSUSA
FEIT, SCHENU	23	F	W	RRADOIUSA
BEILE	48	F	W	RRADOIUSA
ROSA	18	F	SGL	RRADOIUSA
LEWITHAN, CHUER	48	F	W	RRAHTFUSA
RODE	18	F	CH	RRAHTFUSA
MOSES	9	M	CHILD	RRAHTFUSA
EFARIN	5	M	CHILD	RRAHTFUSA
GERSON	6	M	CHILD	RRAHTFUSA
TASTEL	8	M	CHILD	RRAHTFUSA
ARNOWSKY, ABRAHAM	56	M	LABR	RRAHTFUSA
FRIEDLIH, CHAS	25	F	W	RRZZZZUSA
BASI	9	F	CHILD	RRZZZZUSA
ITZIG	8	M	CHILD	RRZZZZUSA
JACOB	.11	M	INFANT	RRZZZZUSA
HARMEL, JACOB	20	M	PNTR	RRZZZZUSA
GINSBERG, FISCHEL	20	F	SGL	RRZZZZUSA

PASSENGER	AGE	SEX	OCCUPATION	PRIV	VIL	DES
SHIP: WYOMING						
FROM: LIVERPOOL AND QUEENSTOWN						
TO: NEW YORK						
ARRIVED: 11 AUGUST 1885						
FELDMANN, LIEB	35	F	SP	RR	ZZZZ	USA
PRACZINCHY, ABR.	41	F	FARMER	RR	ZZZZ	USA
FEIGE	21	F	SP	RR	ZZZZ	USA
RUZ, ISAACH	32	M	LABR	RR	ZZZZ	USA
SILBER, JACOB	46	M	MNR	PL	ZZZZ	USA
HANNA	44	F	W	PL	ZZZZ	USA
BERTHA	17	F	SP	PL	ZZZZ	USA
DANIEL	11	M	CH	PL	ZZZZ	USA
ESTER	9	F	CHILD	PL	ZZZZ	USA
FAUBE	.09	M	INFANT	PL	ZZZZ	USA
LEVIORCH, MICH.	25	M	FARMER	PL	ZZZZ	USA
FERGE	23	F	W	PL	ZZZZ	USA
SALOMON	.11	M	INFANT	PL	ZZZZ	USA
STANITZKI, SALOMON	21	M	GZR	PL	ZZZZ	USA
MISCHEVISKI, JACOB	19	M	GZR	RR	ZZZZ	USA
KRONSTADT, AMSCHEL	47	M	FARMER	RR	ZZZZ	USA
MARIESCO	25	F	SP	RR	ZZZZ	USA
MALKE	11	F	CH	RR	ZZZZ	USA
ODER	.10	M	INFANT	RR	ZZZZ	USA
PARAH	.10	M	INFANT	RR	ZZZZ	USA
SILBERSTEIN, JANKE	27	M	LABR	RR	ZZZZ	USA
ROSENTHAL, GESEL	15	F	SP	RR	ZZZZ	USA
HURWITZ, ISRAEL	19	M	CL	RR	ZZZZ	USA
ROSENZWERG, ABEL	18	M	LABR	RR	ZZZZ	USA
SHIP: STATE OF ALABAMA						
FROM: GLASGOW AND LARNE						
TO: NEW YORK						
ARRIVED: 13 AUGUST 1885						
AWGENBLUCK, MEIER	20	M	CMMSR	RR	ZZZZ	NY
BAWN, LIEB	28	M	CMMSR	RR	ZZZZ	NY
GUSTE	20	M	CMMSR	RR	ZZZZ	NY
FANNY	1	F	CHILD	RR	ZZZZ	NY
COHAN, MORRIS	28	M	TLR	RR	ZZZZ	PVD
FREIBUG, WOLF	45	M	CMMSR	RR	ZZZZ	NY
GLUR, JACOB	17	M	CMMSR	RR	ZZZZ	NY
FRANKEL, ABRAM	31	M	CMMSR	RR	ZZZZ	NY
GRUNSSON, ISAAC	24	M	CMMSR	RR	ZZZZ	STL
GRUNBERG, HIRSCH	20	M	SMH	RR	ZZZZ	NY
SCHEME	25	F	NN	RR	ZZZZ	PHI
ABRAHAM	1	M	CHILD	RR	ZZZZ	PHI
SCHEINE	1	F	CHILD	RR	ZZZZ	PHI
HIRSCH	25	M	CMMSR	RR	ZZZZ	NY
KLISOWZITZKY, NECHAME	40	F	W	RR	ZZZZ	NY
SELDE	19	F	NN	RR	ZZZZ	NY
SAMUEL	11	M	NN	RR	ZZZZ	NY
ISAAK	6	M	CHILD	RR	ZZZZ	NY
HENER, ISAAK	37	M	CMMSR	RR	ZZZZ	NY
KUVILN, JEREMIAZ	57	M	CMMSR	RR	ZZZZ	NY
SOPHIE	52	F	UNKNOWN	RR	ZZZZ	NY
KREMETZUK, ABRAH.	28	M	CMMSR	RR	ZZZZ	NY
LESER, ISIA	21	M	CMMSR	RR	ZZZZ	NY
RACHEL	20	F	NN	RR	ZZZZ	NY
LUBSCHIK, BISI	21	M	PH	RR	ZZZZ	NY
MELLER, FRANK	24	M	LABR	RR	ZZZZ	NY
ROSENTHAL, UNKNOWN	43	M	CMMSR	RR	ZZZZ	NY
DAVID	19	M	STDNT	RR	ZZZZ	CH
STEMBUG, CHAMRE	26	F	W	RR	ZZZZ	NY
JACOB	7	M	CHILD	RR	ZZZZ	NY
SARA	3	F	CHILD	RR	ZZZZ	NY
SANE	3	F	CHILD	RR	ZZZZ	NY

PASSENGER	AGE	SEX	OCCUPATION	PRIV	VIL	DES
SIWKIN, JULIE	21	M	NN	RR	ZZZZ	CH
VZUMZE, AGNES	19	F	LABR	RR	ZZZZ	CH
TISPACH, SEBASTIAN	25	M	CMMSR	RR	ZZZZ	CH
GRENZER, SALOMON	27	M	TLR	RR	ZZZZ	CH
GOLDFLASS, ARON	42	M	TLR	RR	ZZZZ	CH
SCHIL.	23	F	NN	RR	ZZZZ	CH
KATTIE	8	F	CHILD	RR	ZZZZ	CH
ROSA	6	F	CHILD	RR	ZZZZ	CH
ANNA	5	F	CHILD	RR	ZZZZ	CH
REBECCA	2	F	CHILD	RR	ZZZZ	CH
IDA	4	F	CHILD	RR	ZZZZ	CH
JUDA	20	F	NN	RR	ZZZZ	CH
MARIA	14	F	NN	RR	ZZZZ	CH
HADES, HERRMANN	46	M	TCHR	RR	ZZZZ	BO
HOSSICK, VALENTIN	22	M	LABR	RR	ZZZZ	NY
VOZARA, GYULA	18	M	LABR	RR	ZZZZ	NY
WARSCHAFSKI, ISAAC	30	M	LABR	RR	ZZZZ	CH
SHIP: CITY OF CHESTER						
FROM: LIVERPOOL AND QUEENSTOWN						
TO: NEW YORK						
ARRIVED: 14 AUGUST 1885						
WILKO, KAYSA	26	F	W	FN	ZZZZ	MI
EDLA-K.	1	F	CHILD	FN	ZZZZ	MI
JACOBS, ISAC	32	M	PNTR	FN	ADAX	NY
KATIE	20	F	W	FN	ADAX	NY
U	1	F	CHILD	FN	ADAX	NY
TILSEY, JOS.H.	34	M	BRR	RR	ZZZZ	PTT
GUMMERAS, H.E.	23	M	GENT	RR	ADBQ	NY
BRANDER, K.W.	49	M	GENT	RR	ADBQ	NY
WINSTEN, C.W.	56	M	GENT	RR	ADBQ	NY
SHIP: NECKAR						
FROM: BREMEN						
TO: NEW YORK						
ARRIVED: 14 AUGUST 1885						
BALLINOWER, FANNY	20	F	SVNT	RR	ZZZZ	NY
SCHICK, HIZZI	18	F	SVNT	RR	ZZZZ	NY
RUBINOWITZ, ITTE	44	F	UNKNOWN	RR	ZZZZ	NY
SAL.	16	M	DLR	RR	ZZZZ	NY
BERNH.	15	M	UNKNOWN	RR	ZZZZ	NY
KALINOWER, LEIB	41	M	LABR	RR	ZZZZ	NY
RACHAL	39	F	UNKNOWN	RR	ZZZZ	NY
NECTE	14	F	UNKNOWN	RR	ZZZZ	NY
ERDEL	12	F	UNKNOWN	RR	ZZZZ	NY
KOSLOWSKA, JOSEFA	30	F	UNKNOWN	RR	ZZZZ	OH
FRAMZ.	58	F	UNKNOWN	RR	ZZZZ	OH
MICHAEL	4	M	CHILD	RR	ZZZZ	OH
STANISL.	2	M	CHILD	RR	ZZZZ	OH
HORWITZ, FRANZ	40	M	LABR	RR	ZZZZ	MO
HEICHE	11	F	UNKNOWN	RR	ZZZZ	MO
ESTER	9	F	CHILD	RR	ZZZZ	MO
UHR.	7	F	CHILD	RR	ZZZZ	MO
NURE	5	F	CHILD	RR	ZZZZ	MO
RUBIN, RUCHIN	45	F	UNKNOWN	RR	ZZZZ	OH
BESE	12	F	UNKNOWN	RR	ZZZZ	OH
WIEN, CHARIA	22	F	UNKNOWN	RR	ZZZZ	NY
MENDEL	.11	M	INFANT	RR	ZZZZ	NY
FAST, TOBA	30	F	UNKNOWN	RR	ZZZZ	NY
BASSI	5	F	CHILD	RR	ZZZZ	NY
SCHEGE	2	F	CHILD	RR	ZZZZ	NY

PASSENGER	AGE	SEX	OCCUPATION	PRV VIL DES
KATZ, JOSEPH	40	M	LABR	RRZZZZNY
FISCHLER	8	F	CHILD	RRZZZZNY
SCHI	7	F	CHILD	RRZZZZNY
PINES	2	F	CHILD	RRZZZZNY
STELNACH, ANGELA	27	F	UNKNOWN	RRZZZZNY
SIGMIND	4	M	CHILD	RRZZZZNY
THEODOR	.04	M	INFANT	RRZZZZNY
LOMZINSKI, T.	28	M	LABR	RRZZZZNY
MORE	17	F	UNKNOWN	RRZZZZNY
TROME	3	F	CHILD	RRZZZZNY
DENENBRUSKY, ESTER	30	F	UNKNOWN	RRZZZZNY
JENCHEL	10	F	UNKNOWN	RRZZZZNY
FROME	4	F	CHILD	RRZZZZNY
SCHLEIME	3	F	CHILD	RRZZZZNY
MENDEL	.09	M	INFANT	RRZZZZNY
LEWINSKY, MICH.	40	M	LABR	RRZZZZNY
DWERKE	12	M	UNKNOWN	RRZZZZNY
SORKE	8	M	CHILD	RRZZZZNY
MIRKE	7	M	CHILD	RRZZZZNY
TEFKE	5	M	CHILD	RRZZZZNY
GOSKE	3	M	CHILD	RRZZZZNY
ALTER, ALKE	10	M	UNKNOWN	RRZZZZNY
COHEN, JACOB	17	M	LABR	RRZZZZNY
LEVINSOHN, MOSES	58	M	DLR	RRZZZZNY
BERLOWITZ, ELLA	19	F	SVNT	RRZZZZNY
GRUNSTEIN, ERNST	32	M	LABR	RRZZZZNY
GLUCK, SCHAPSEL	20	M	LABR	RRZZZZNY
BALLINOM, GER.	17	M	LABR	RRZZZZNY
SKULINK, DAVID	18	M	LABR	RRZZZZOH

SHIP: EMS

FROM: BREMEN
TO: NEW YORK
ARRIVED: 15 AUGUST 1885

PASSENGER	AGE	SEX	OCCUPATION	PRV VIL DES
SAWADSKY, JOH.	26	M	JNR	RRAHOOUSA
ENNS, JOHANNES	23	M	LABR	RRAHOOUSA
TEICHREW, KATHAR.	23	F	NN	RRAHOOUSA
REIMER, HEINRICH	24	M	LABR	RRAHOOUSA
COHEN, JANKI	42	M	LABR	RRAFWJUSA
ZALEWSKA, CATHAR.	25	F	NN	RRAHOOUSA
BLUME, JACOB	52	M	LABR	RRAGRTUSA
MALKA	19	F	NN	RRAGRTUSA
BENZEL	18	M	LABR	RRAGRTUSA
ROSAVA	10	F	NN	RRAGRTUSA
BENDER	9	M	CHILD	RRAGRTUSA
DIECKSTEIN, DRESI	38	F	NN	RRZZZZUSA
BEILE	3	F	CHILD	RRZZZZUSA
STRAUSSBERG, MALKE	40	F	NN	RRAHOOUSA
HANNA	16	F	NN	RRAHOOUSA
JOSEPH	13	M	NN	RRAHOOUSA
MAUSOHE	10	F	NN	RRAHOOUSA
SCHIFER	9	F	CHILD	RRAHOOUSA
RACHEL	8	F	CHILD	RRAHOOUSA
JANKEL	7	M	CHILD	RRAHOOUSA
LEIBEL	6	F	CHILD	RRAHOOUSA
ELKE	3	F	CHILD	RRAHOOUSA
CLAUSOH, ABRAHAM	20	M	LABR	RRAGRTUSA
KUNZE, MARTHA	6	F	CHILD	RRAGRTUSA
BENZSKOWA, ANNA	25	F	NN	RRAGRTUSA
MAGDALENE	.02	F	INFANT	RRAGRTUSA
KEBEISKY, MASE	30	M	LABR	RRAFWJUSA
DOBBE, CHAJE	26	F	NN	RRAFWJUSA
WOLFF	.11	M	INFANT	RRAFWJUSA
ABRAHAM, ISAAC	30	M	FARMER	RRAFWJUSA
SCHOENE, RACHEL	20	F	NN	RRAFWJUSA
SILBERMANN, JOSEF	21	M	LABR	RRAFWJUSA

SHIP: POLYNESIA

FROM: HAMBURG
TO: NEW YORK
ARRIVED: 15 AUGUST 1885

PASSENGER	AGE	SEX	OCCUPATION	PRV VIL DES
KOSIBA, THERESE	24	F	WO	PLZZZZNY
THERESE	.07	F	INFANT	PLZZZZNY
BUECHNER, ANNA	25	F	WO	RRZZZZNY
AUGUST	.07	M	INFANT	RRZZZZNY
MALWITE, OTTILIE	24	F	WO	RRZZZZNY
EDUARD	.06	M	INFANT	RRZZZZNY
HURT, FRANK	16	M	LABR	PLZZZZNY
LASDOWSKY, PINE	20	M	LABR	RRZZZZNY
ARON, JOSEF	63	M	LABR	RRZZZZNY
SLUMBA, JOSEF	36	M	LABR	RRZZZZNY
MURAKOVA, MAGD.	40	F	WO	RRZZZZNY
AGNES	3	F	CHILD	RRZZZZNY
FRAWSISKA	.07	F	INFANT	RRZZZZNY
STAWITZKI, MENDEL	25	M	LABR	PLZZZZNY
GROSSMAN, ZACHOR	25	M	LABR	PLZZZZNY
FRIEDMANN, H.	39	M	LABR	PLZZZZNY
BOCKY	15	F	CH	PLZZZZNY
SCHARF, GERSON	22	M	LABR	PLZZZZNY
LAPIDIS, TOBI.ROSZA	15	M	LABR	RRZZZZNY
SCHLOMOWITZ, C.	35	F	WO	RRZZZZIL
GITTEL	7	F	CHILD	RRZZZZIL
MIREL	5	F	CHILD	RRZZZZIL
SCHOLOM	3	M	CHILD	RRZZZZIL
RAMENOCKI, CHANE	16	M	LABR	RRZZZZIL
JOHANNSKY, CHANE	25	F	WO	RRZZZZNY
LEWOFSKY, BARUCH	28	M	SDLR	RRZZZZNY
BERNSTEIN, SCHMUHL	53	M	TDR	RRZZZZNY
FEIGE	50	F	W	RRZZZZNY
JOSEF	7	M	CHILD	RRZZZZNY
DYLINSKA, VERONIKA	27	F	WO	RRZZZZNY
LUBELSKI, PECHI	30	F	SGL	RRZZZZNY
GRINBERG, ABRAHAM	18	M	LABR	RRZZZZNY
BASCHE	19	F	W	RRZZZZNY
SEMECOSKY, LEA	50	F	WO	RRZZZZNY
HENDELOWITZ, SARAH	35	F	WO	RRZZZZNY
SARAH	7	F	CHILD	RRZZZZNY
NACHUM	6	M	CHILD	RRZZZZNY
DAVID	5	M	CHILD	RRZZZZNY
MOSES	3	M	CHILD	RRZZZZNY
CHAIM	.05	M	INFANT	RRZZZZNY
ZEHCHOWSKA, ROSZA	35	F	WO	RRZZZZIL
ESTER	6	F	CHILD	RRZZZZIL
ELKE	.06	F	INFANT	RRZZZZIL
BRILL, ABRAH.	35	M	TRDSMN	RRZZZZIL
BERGER, SAMUEL	19	M	UNKNOWN	RRZZZZNY
JACHERMANSKY, WOLF	18	M	TRDSMN	RRZZZZNY
RAGOLSKY, JUDEL	30	M	BKR	RRZZZZNY
GOLDMANN, CHAIM	36	M	TRDSMN	RRZZZZNY
LEWIN, ISAAC	50	M	TRDSMN	RRZZZZNY

SHIP: AURANIA

FROM: LIVERPOOL AND QUEENSTOWN
TO: NEW YORK
ARRIVED: 17 AUGUST 1885

PASSENGER	AGE	SEX	OCCUPATION	PRV VIL DES
GUNSTIEN, MANDE	33	M	LABR	RRZZZZUSA
HANNE	23	F	W	RRZZZZUSA
NOTIE	9	F	CHILD	RRZZZZUSA
NECKLIN	3	F	CHILD	RRZZZZUSA
GENSTEIN, HUNDA	.08	M	INFANT	RRZZZZUSA
POKOLULWSKY, JACOB	25	M	LABR	RRZZZZUSA
SARAH	19	F	W	RRZZZZUSA

PASSENGER	AGE	SEX	OCCUPATION	PRVL	VIL	DES
WOLF	.06	F	INFANT	RR	ZZZZ	USA
CZEWZYNSKI, HAMIOL	28	M	LABR	PL	ZZZZ	USA

SHIP: ETHIOPIA

FROM: GLASGOW AND MOVILLE
TO: NEW YORK
ARRIVED: 17 AUGUST 1885

PASSENGER	AGE	SEX	OCCUPATION	PRVL	VIL	DES
SANGSTER, ANDREAS	35	M	SEMN	RR	ZZZZ	USA
JAFFE, CHAWE	37	M	DLR	RR	ZZZZ	USA
MECHANIK, BERNHARD	19	M	DLR	RR	ZZZZ	USA
BASCHENKOWITZ, GEDALJE	19	M	DLR	RR	ZZZZ	USA
KORSNESKI, JOSEF	23	M	FDRS	RR	ZZZZ	USA

SHIP: MORAVIA

FROM: HAMBURG
TO: NEW YORK
ARRIVED: 18 AUGUST 1885

PASSENGER	AGE	SEX	OCCUPATION	PRVL	VIL	DES
MILLNER, SARA	45	F	W	RR	ZZZZ	USA
CHAJE	20	F	D	RR	ZZZZ	USA
DAMLOWIG, ROSALIE	20	F	SGL	RR	ZZZZ	USA
SILBERHERR, SALOMON	25	M	JWLR	RR	ZZZZ	USA
GOLDBERG, SARAH	35	M	TLR	RR	ZZZZ	USA
SILBERMANN, LISE	21	F	W	RR	ZZZZ	USA
PESACH	.11	F	INFANT	RR	ZZZZ	USA
BASCHE	.01	F	INFANT	RR	ZZZZ	USA
DUBOWSKY, MOSES	19	M	MCHT	RR	ZZZZ	USA
FREID, BEILE	50	F	W	RR	ZZZZ	USA
LEA	18	F	D	RR	ZZZZ	USA
WANDA, BLIMA	49	F	W	RR	ZZZZ	USA
GOLDSTEIN, MERE	29	F	W	RR	ZZZZ	USA
MINNA	9	F	CHILD	RR	ZZZZ	USA
BEHSE	8	F	CHILD	RR	ZZZZ	USA
MOSES	4	M	CHILD	RR	ZZZZ	USA
HEYMANN	.11	M	INFANT	RR	ZZZZ	USA
HOLSMANN, BRAINE	13	F	SGL	RR	ZZZZ	USA
WOLF, DORA	18	F	SGL	RR	ZZZZ	USA
KOPELMANN, JACOB	18	M	LABR	RR	ZZZZ	USA
BUERGER, HENRY	30	M	LABR	RR	ZZZZ	USA
ORTSCHIK	.11	M	INFANT	RR	ZZZZ	USA
MARGULOFF, DORA	21	F	SGL	RR	ZZZZ	USA
MAGOLINSKY, RACHEL	21	F	SGL	RR	ZZZZ	USA
ROTHSTEIN, RUBEN	19	M	DLR	RR	ZZZZ	USA
SINGER, CHACZA	23	F	SGL	RR	ZZZZ	USA
MANNA, MOLLI	19	F	SGL	RR	ZZZZ	USA
EPSTEIN, HEIMANN	28	M	DLR	RR	ZZZZ	USA
LAPIDUS, BASCHE	25	F	W	RR	ZZZZ	USA
JACOB	6	M	CHILD	RR	ZZZZ	USA
RUBINSTEIN, DWORE	17	F	SGL	RR	ZZZZ	USA
LEWIN, LIEBE	30	F	W	RR	ZZZZ	USA
BEILE	14	F	CH	RR	ZZZZ	USA
GABRIEL	9	M	CHILD	RR	ZZZZ	USA
MARCUS	5	M	CHILD	RR	ZZZZ	USA
LEISER	3	M	CHILD	RR	ZZZZ	USA
WOLF	.11	M	INFANT	RR	ZZZZ	USA
LAPIDUS, LIEBMANN	25	M	DLR	RR	ZZZZ	USA
NAGORNOSKI, BRUNON	28	M	SMH	RR	ZZZZ	USA
SCHIDLOWER, MARKUS	17	M	CL	RR	ZZZZ	USA
CZEINBEKER, BEILE	35	F	W	RR	ZZZZ	USA
CHEIE	9	F	CHILD	RR	ZZZZ	USA
CHAIN	8	M	CHILD	RR	ZZZZ	USA
JUDEL	7	F	CHILD	RR	ZZZZ	USA
BERL	5	M	CHILD	RR	ZZZZ	USA
SILBERSTEIN, SARAH	32	F	W	RR	ZZZZ	USA
HENE	9	F	CHILD	RR	ZZZZ	USA
LEIB	8	M	CHILD	RR	ZZZZ	USA
HIRSCH	6	M	CHILD	RR	ZZZZ	USA
ITZIG	5	M	CHILD	RR	ZZZZ	USA
SCHWARZBERG, MPSES	42	M	LABR	RR	ZZZZ	USA
EFFENDI, MEINES	46	M	FARMER	RR	ZZZZ	USA
FRUME	50	F	W	RR	ZZZZ	USA
LONDON, JETI	16	F	SGL	RR	ZZZZ	USA
ETIL	60	F	W	RR	ZZZZ	USA
PIETROWSKI, ANTON	21	M	LABR	RR	ZZZZ	USA
BERMANN, ITZIG	20	M	DLR	RR	ZZZZ	USA
LEWINSOHN, JOHLA	40	F	W	RR	ZZZZ	USA
RACHEL	20	F	CH	RR	ZZZZ	USA
ESTHER	9	F	CHILD	RR	ZZZZ	USA
LEA	8	F	CHILD	RR	ZZZZ	USA
RUBEN	7	M	CHILD	RR	ZZZZ	USA
SAMUEL	5	M	CHILD	RR	ZZZZ	USA
RONNA	4	F	CHILD	RR	ZZZZ	USA
DWORSKI, PESCHE	24	F	W	RR	ZZZZ	USA
MOSES	.11	M	INFANT	RR	ZZZZ	USA
BOGACKI, JANKEL	20	M	LABR	RR	ZZZZ	USA
WILKOF, ISAAC	18	M	CCHMKR	RR	ZZZZ	USA
ROSENCRANZ, CHANNE	40	F	W	RR	ZZZZ	USA
CHORA	18	F	CH	RR	ZZZZ	USA
CHAJE	7	F	CHILD	RR	ZZZZ	USA
FRIEDR.	6	M	CHILD	RR	ZZZZ	USA
LEGHE	5	M	CHILD	RR	ZZZZ	USA
JEWEROWITZ, BEIL	18	F	SGL	RR	ZZZZ	USA
BLUMENTHAL, MORITZ	23	M	DLR	RR	ZZZZ	USA
MICZYNSKI, RIWKE	30	F	W	RR	ZZZZ	USA
LEISER	9	M	CHILD	RR	ZZZZ	USA
NACHMEN	8	M	CHILD	RR	ZZZZ	USA
ITE	4	F	CHILD	RR	ZZZZ	USA
ANSCHER, RACHEL	17	F	SGL	RR	ZZZZ	USA
MAGILEWSKI, BASI	20	M	LABR	RR	ZZZZ	USA
OPPELMANN, SELIG	39	M	SGL	RR	ZZZZ	USA
SLOMOWITZ, SARA	19	F	SGL	RR	ZZZZ	USA
SMITH, REBECCA	20	F	SGL	RR	ZZZZ	USA
OPPENHEIM, RIWKE	36	F	W	RR	ZZZZ	USA
ROZENKRANZ, SASSEL	8	M	CHILD	RR	ZZZZ	USA
SARA	5	F	CHILD	RR	ZZZZ	USA
MARKOWITZ, DAVID	19	M	LABR	RR	ZZZZ	USA
DIEMANSCHEIN, P.H.	29	M	TCHR	RR	ZZZZ	USA
JOHANNE	26	F	W	RR	ZZZZ	USA
JULIUS	3	M	CHILD	RR	ZZZZ	USA
SARA	.09	F	INFANT	RR	ZZZZ	USA
KRAFT, HERMANN	17	M	LABR	RR	ZZZZ	USA
BLUM, REBECCA	30	F	W	RR	ZZZZ	USA
SARA	9	F	CHILD	RR	ZZZZ	USA
GERSON	6	M	CHILD	RR	ZZZZ	USA
LEIB	3	M	CHILD	RR	ZZZZ	USA
CHATZKO	.06	M	INFANT	RR	ZZZZ	USA
SCHESTUKOWSKY, SAM.	31	M	BCHR	RR	ZZZZ	USA
BIALISTOCKY, ANNIE	32	F	W	RR	ZZZZ	USA
JACOB	2	M	CHILD	RR	ZZZZ	USA
RUBEN	8	M	CHILD	RR	ZZZZ	USA
DOBRE	3	M	CHILD	RR	ZZZZ	USA
BERUSCH	.11	M	INFANT	RR	ZZZZ	USA
RIWKE	.11	F	INFANT	RR	ZZZZ	USA
BERNSTEIN, ISRAEL	19	M	LABR	RR	ZZZZ	USA
TSCHORIK, MENDEL	36	M	SHMK	RR	ZZZZ	USA
ROSENWALD, SARAH	56	F	W	RR	ZZZZ	USA
PRZYBITOWSKI, FRANZ	42	M	LABR	RR	ZZZZ	USA
ROSEMANN, LEIB	19	M	LABR	RR	ZZZZ	USA
ANNA	20	F	W	RR	ZZZZ	USA
WEINACH, SARA	31	F	W	RR	ZZZZ	USA
LEISER	3	M	CHILD	RR	ZZZZ	USA
JACOB	9	M	CHILD	RR	ZZZZ	USA
SCHEINE	6	F	CHILD	RR	ZZZZ	USA
JANKOWSKY, KEIB	30	F	W	RR	ZZZZ	USA
JACOB	9	M	CHILD	RR	ZZZZ	USA
ABRAHAM	8	M	CHILD	RR	ZZZZ	USA
SCHEINE	3	F	CHILD	RR	ZZZZ	USA

PASSENGER	AGE	SEX	OCCUPATION	PRV VIL DES
PLODKE, SALOMON	19	M	DLR	RRZZZZUSA
LIEBOWITZ, RULKIN	18	M	LABR	RRZZZZUSA
UNGAR, JOSEF	16	M	LABR	RRZZZZUSA
JUNGERMANN, ROSA	31	F	W	RRZZZZUSA
HULDA	4	F	CHILD	RRZZZZUSA
HENRY	.11	M	INFANT	RRZZZZUSA
JACOB	.01	M	INFANT	RRZZZZUSA
MITLARSCH, SELIG	17	M	TLR	RRZZZZUSA
ROLINECK, SELIG	8	M	CHILD	RRZZZZUSA
SELIGMANN, MARGOLA	32	F	W	RRZZZZUSA
SALTZE	4	M	CHILD	RRZZZZUSA
MICHAEL	.11	M	INFANT	RRZZZZUSA
KAPLAN, SAMUEL	22	M	LABR	RRZZZZUSA
DESSAUER, ABRAHAM	41	M	LABR	RRZZZZUSA
PLUNTOWSKY, JOSEPHINE	21	F	W	RRZZZZUSA
JOSEPHINE	.09	F	INFANT	RRZZZZUSA
ROSENWALD, EMIL	21	M	LABR	RRZZZZUSA
GALINSKY, HANNE	18	F	SGL	RRZZZZUSA
RUBEN, LEA	15	F	SGL	RRZZZZUSA
LEWIN, FEIGE	53	F	W	RRZZZZUSA
HIRSCHFELD, REISEL	30	F	W	RRZZZZUSA
SCHEINDEL	9	F	CHILD	RRZZZZUSA
ETTEL	7	F	CHILD	RRZZZZUSA
JETTE	4	F	CHILD	RRZZZZUSA
AWRUM	.11	M	INFANT	RRZZZZUSA
MEYER	.01	M	INFANT	RRZZZZUSA
POLLENBAUM, KILWE	65	M	LABR	RRZZZZUSA
HURWITZ, OSCHER	53	F	W	RRZZZZUSA
MULLER, MORITZ	30	M	LABR	RRZZZZUSA
RIWKE	28	F	W	RRZZZZUSA
SAMUEL	24	M	LABR	RRZZZZUSA
POLSKY, SCHACHNE	20	M	LABR	RRZZZZUSA
SARA	18	F	W	RRZZZZUSA
LEWIN, EIGE	18	F	SGL	RRZZZZUSA
GUTMANN, LEA	50	F	W	RRZZZZUSA
FEIGE	9	F	CHILD	RRZZZZUSA
KAPLAN, GITTEL	34	F	W	RRZZZZUSA
JENTE	17	F	SGL	RRZZZZUSA
BLUMBERG, MALKE	22	F	SGL	RRZZZZUSA
LENHOFF, MEYER	20	M	LABR	RRZZZZUSA
ROTHSTEIN, CHANNE	16	F	SGL	RRZZZZUSA
RASCHE	9	F	CHILD	RRZZZZUSA
GLUCKSTEIN, CHANNE	24	F	W	RRZZZZUSA
MORDCHE	9	M	CHILD	RRZZZZUSA
GOLDE	.11	F	INFANT	RRZZZZUSA
MENDELSOHN, PESCHE	26	F	W	RRZZZZUSA
ROSA	.11	F	INFANT	RRZZZZUSA
KOROWITZ, RACHEL	18	F	SGL	RRZZZZUSA
MANDEL, PINCUS	23	M	LABR	RRZZZZUSA
LEWIN, RISCHE	17	F	SGL	RRZZZZUSA
LEWINBERG, KURIEL	20	M	TLR	RRZZZZUSA
KAPLAN, DAVID	21	M	DLR	RRZZZZUSA
COHEN, DWORE	26	F	W	RRZZZZUSA
SCHEINE	.03	F	INFANT	RRZZZZUSA
TURJANSKI, CHAJE	25	F	W	RRZZZZUSA
FANNY	.11	F	INFANT	RRZZZZUSA
SCHNEEMANN, SALMEN	24	M	LABR	RRZZZZUSA
SMOSKOWITZ, CHAJE	53	F	W	RRZZZZUSA
SCHMUEL	9	M	CHILD	RRZZZZUSA
LIKUWETZKI, LIEBE	30	F	W	RRZZZZUSA
ROSENWEIG, CHAIN	5	M	CHILD	RRZZZZUSA
PALHIEL	4	M	CHILD	RRZZZZUSA
LEIB	.11	M	INFANT	RRZZZZUSA
LEHMANN, HENNY	18	F	SGL	RRZZZZUSA
TRAUB, JUDEL	22	M	LABR	RRZZZZUSA
LEWIN, JACOB	44	M	LABR	RRZZZZUSA
CHAIE	17	F	D	RRZZZZUSA
MEDANSKY, MORDCHE	15	M	LABR	RRZZZZUSA
KRAM, CHAIE	40	F	W	RRZZZZUSA
BEIB	20	F	W	RRZZZZUSA
FEIGE	18	F	CH	RRZZZZUSA
MOTHEL	9	M	CHILD	RRZZZZUSA
SALOMON	8	M	CHILD	RRZZZZUSA
KAHN, SARA	28	F	W	RRZZZZUSA
REITZE	8	F	CHILD	RRZZZZUSA
RACHEL	6	F	CHILD	RRZZZZUSA
LEIB	.11	M	INFANT	RRZZZZUSA
SCHEINE	.11	F	INFANT	RRZZZZUSA
ENGELSTEIN, ISAAC	30	M	DLR	RRZZZZUSA
MARKS, RUBIN	25	M	DLR	RRZZZZUSA
WARSCHAESKI, ARON	20	M	DLR	RRZZZZUSA
WOLF	20	M	DLR	RRZZZZUSA
FRIEDMANN, CHANNE	38	F	W	RRZZZZUSA
MENUCHE	15	M	S	RRZZZZUSA
JURSCHKOWSKY, CHAZEL	25	M	DLR	RRZZZZUSA
MULLER, ETEL	.09	F	INFANT	RRZZZZUSA
ASSONSKY, MEYER	20	M	LABR	RRZZZZUSA
SELIGMANN, RACHEL	00	F	INF	RR****USA

SHIP: HELVETIA

FROM: LIVERPOOL
TO: NEW YORK
ARRIVED: 19 AUGUST 1885

PASSENGER	AGE	SEX	OCCUPATION	PRV VIL DES
GRAMMER, WOLF	24	M	LABR	RRAFVGUSA
LIPSCHITZ, MORRIS	21	M	LABR	RRZZZZUSA
DUBROF, DAVID	22	M	LABR	RRZZZZUSA
SWARTZBERG, BENJAMIN	20	M	LABR	RRAFWJUSA
MAGGNY, GUST.	30	M	LABR	RRZZZZUSA
ANITJEWI, KASJA	23	M	LABR	RRZZZZUSA
SVEN, VAILO	27	F	SP	RRAHQHUSA
DRABEK, TEREZA	24	F	SP	RRAHQHUSA
KADLEC, JAN	25	M	LABR	RRAFWJUSA
WALTE, OSCAR	19	M	LABR	RRAFWJUSA
RUBINSTEIN, ISRAEL	45	M	LABR	RRZZZZUSA

SHIP: CITY OF ROME

FROM: LIVERPOOL
TO: NEW YORK
ARRIVED: 20 AUGUST 1885

PASSENGER	AGE	SEX	OCCUPATION	PRV VIL DES
WOLFF, ABRAH.	35	M	LABR	RRZZZZUSA
LEWITAU, N--J	33	M	LABR	RRZZZZUSA
LENA	26	F	W	RRZZZZUSA
SELAVJE	2	F	CHILD	RRZZZZUSA
MELNIK, HZZ.	20	M	LABR	RRZZZZUSA
HERGETOWITZ, E.	42	M	LABR	RRZZZZUSA
ROLEGROWSKY, S.	30	M	LABR	RRZZZZUSA
FISAK, ANDRES	40	M	LABR	RRZZZZUSA
HARRIS, W.	45	F	MA	RRZZZZUSA
ABM.	11	M	CH	RRZZZZUSA
ROSIE	10	F	CH	RRZZZZUSA
MARION	9	F	CHILD	RRZZZZUSA
ARON	8	M	CHILD	RRZZZZUSA
EVA	6	F	CHILD	RRZZZZUSA
KOWELWKI, A.	27	M	LABR	RRZZZZUSA
ISRABOVIEC, N.	22	M	LABR	RRZZZZUSA
ROSENGART, ELI	19	M	LABR	RRZZZZUSA
CHAJEN, J.DEN.C.	22	M	LABR	RRZZZZUSA
MEYER, KARL	30	M	LABR	RRACBFUSA
SABLATZKI, J.	30	F	SVNT	RRZZZZUSA

SHIP: STATE OF NEVADA

FROM: GLASGOW AND LARNE
TO: NEW YORK
ARRIVED: 20 AUGUST 1885

PASSENGER	AGE	SEX	OCCUPATION	PRV VIL DES
ARONSTEIN, S.	35	M	WCHMKR	RRZZZZUSA
M.	28	F	W	RRZZZZUSA
N.	7	F	CHILD	RRZZZZUSA
L.	5	F	CHILD	RRZZZZUSA
L.	2	M	CHILD	RRZZZZUSA
S.	.09	F	INFANT	RRZZZZUSA
BARDIN, J.	50	M	LABR	RRZZZZUSA
KRESCHOZKY, J.	10	M	PDLR	RRZZZZUSA
BRANDE, P.	43	M	BY	RRZZZZUSA
BERG, W.	31	M	PDLR	RRZZZZUSA
SCHLESNITZKI, E.	23	M	PDLR	RRZZZZUSA
KOBELINSKI, J.	26	M	PDLR	RRZZZZUSA
LANSKI, S.	10	M	CH	RRZZZZUSA
BLIDER, H.	20	M	LABR	RRZZZZUSA
CZONTKOW, L.	48	M	PDLR	RRZZZZUSA
CHLADEK, J.	68	M	LABR	RRZZZZUSA
CZORKOW, B.	30	M	LABR	RRZZZZUSA
L.	30	F	W	RRZZZZUSA
D.	1	M	CHILD	RRZZZZUSA
L.	.03	F	INFANT	RRZZZZUSA
M.	42	M	LABR	RRZZZZUSA
G.	20	F	W	RRZZZZUSA
N.	.06	F	INFANT	RRZZZZUSA
E.	26	M	LABR	RRZZZZUSA
DAMSKY, C.	30	F	W	RRZZZZUSA
D.	11	M	CH	RRZZZZUSA
S.	8	M	CHILD	RRZZZZUSA
M.	6	M	CHILD	RRZZZZUSA
M.	1	M	CHILD	RRZZZZUSA
DUBZANSKY, C.	31	M	PDLR	RRZZZZUSA
EDELSTEIN, A.	34	M	PDLR	RRZZZZUSA
FELMAN, M.	31	M	PDLR	RRZZZZUSA
FEINSINGER, D.	38	M	LABR	RRZZZZUSA
FAUN, H.	10	M	PDLR	RRZZZZUSA
GERSCHUM, H.	2	M	CHILD	RRZZZZUSA
GOLDFARB, M.	60	M	PDLR	RRZZZZUSA
B.	25	M	PDLR	RRZZZZUSA
R.	23	M	PDLR	RRZZZZUSA
GRUNWALD, S.	39	M	PDLR	RRZZZZUSA
GLAND, A.	35	M	LABR	RRZZZZUSA
C.	11	M	CH	RRZZZZUSA
HEYMANN, M.	40	M	PDLR	RRZZZZUSA
JAFFE, A.	28	M	PDLR	RRZZZZUSA
KAUFMANN, R.	21	F	SVNT	RRZZZZUSA
KIRSTEIN, J.	23	M	BCHR	RRZZZZUSA
LILOWSKY, D.	31	F	SVNT	RRZZZZUSA
LEHR, L.	21	M	GDSM	RRZZZZUSA
MANDELBAUM, J.	30	M	BCHR	RRZZZZUSA
NALITZKY, S.	21	M	TLR	RRZZZZUSA
L.	18	M	TLR	RRZZZZUSA
NACHUMSOHN, S.	23	F	W	RRZZZZUSA
S.	3	M	CHILD	RRZZZZUSA
F.	1	F	CHILD	RRZZZZUSA
PRIVALSKY, S.	20	M	SHMK	RRZZZZUSA
R.	18	F	W	RRZZZZUSA
RUBENSTEIN, C.	24	F	SVNT	RRZZZZUSA
RUTTENBERG, B.	45	M	PDLR	RRZZZZUSA
WIRKOWSKY, S.	11	M	CH	RRZZZZUSA
ROBINSON, J.	20	M	PDLR	RRZZZZUSA
RACZKOWSKI, A.	12	M	CH	RRZZZZUSA
ROSENFELD, A.	25	M	UNKNOWN	RRZZZZUSA
JUSSWEIN, M.	18	M	SHMK	RRZZZZUSA
C.	18	F	W	RRZZZZUSA
SCHIFRES, H.	22	M	CL	RRZZZZUSA
JIN, F.	19	M	CL	RRZZZZUSA
SORG, J.	32	M	PDLR	RRZZZZUSA
SCHENFEIN, A.	26	M	LABR	RRZZZZUSA
E.	24	F	W	RRZZZZUSA
WARRIN, S.	19	F	SVNT	RRZZZZUSA
WIGDIRSOHN, J.	21	M	PDLR	RRZZZZUSA
BRALOBROTZKY, K.	23	M	SHMK	PLZZZZUSA
S.	21	M	PDLR	PLZZZZUSA
ELI	10	F	CH	PLZZZZUSA
CHSOWITZ, J.	21	M	LABR	PLZZZZUSA
KAMMINSKY, S.	34	M	BKR	PLZZZZUSA
PREGSELSKY, M.	23	M	LABR	PLZZZZUSA
ROSENBLATT, M.	26	M	CL	PLZZZZUSA
SCHUMSKY, J.	18	M	TLR	PLZZZZUSA
SCHWARTZBARD, A.	20	M	PDLR	PLZZZZUSA
M.	30	F	W	PLZZZZUSA
MAKOVER, H.	40	M	TLR	PLZZZZUSA

SHIP: CITY OF CHICAGO

FROM: LIVERPOOL AND QUEENSTOWN
TO: NEW YORK
ARRIVED: 21 AUGUST 1885

PASSENGER	AGE	SEX	OCCUPATION	PRV VIL DES
BLOCK, JOHAN	22	M	TCHR	PLACBFNY
MAGALENDE, ADAM	27	M	PDLR	PLACBFNY
SCHENZNAS, GEORG	24	M	PDLR	PLACBFNY
LEITRUM, ARON	19	M	JNR	PLACBFNY
RAGSOWSKY, ISAK	22	M	TNSTH	PLACBFNY
SCHLOGAN, SCHLOME	00	M	JNR	PLACBFIL
SILBERTSEN, JUL.	18	M	CL	PLACBFPHI
JEPLISH, ZAL.	26	M	BKR	PLACBFNY
HOKALA, GRETA	21	F	SP	PLAEWSNY
HETNILLA, JOHANA	25	F	SP	PLAEWSNY
KROBEL, THS.L.	28	M	LABR	PLACBFNY
AGNES	28	F	W	PLACBFNY
MARIE	8	F	CHILD	PLACBFNY
CMOLEN	2	F	CHILD	PLACBFNY
JOHAN	00	F	INF	PLACBFNY
PETER	00	M	INF	PLACBFNY

SHIP: EIDER

FROM: BREMEN AND SOUTHAMPTON
TO: NEW YORK
ARRIVED: 22 AUGUST 1885

PASSENGER	AGE	SEX	OCCUPATION	PRV VIL DES
FILIPOWSKA, THAKLA	32	F	W	RRZZZZUSA
MARIE	13	F	NN	RRZZZZUSA
GULKOWSKA, MARIE	53	F	W	RRZZZZUSA
ENNOCH, FISCKEL	20	M	MCHT	RRZZZZUSA
CLAWANSKY, CHANE	18	F	NN	RRZZZZUSA
BERMANN, JOSSEL	22	F	NN	RRZZZZUSA
CLAWANSKY, JOSEF	12	M	CH	RRZZZZUSA
FEIGE	36	F	NN	RRZZZZUSA
KROKIN, HARRIS	29	M	LABR	RRZZZZUSA
BROKOFSKY, JOHANN	47	M	FARMER	RRAETZUSA
MARIA	43	F	W	RRAETZUSA
JACOB	20	M	FARMER	RRAETZUSA
ELISAB.	18	F	NN	RRAETZUSA
HEINR.	14	M	NN	RRAETZUSA
MARIA	10	F	CH	RRAETZUSA
CHRISTA	8	F	CHILD	RRAETZUSA
WILHELM	4	M	CHILD	RRAETZUSA
PAULINE	.07	F	INFANT	RRAETZUSA
BERMANN, CHANE	18	F	NN	RRAARRUSA

PASSENGER	AGE	SEX	OCCUPATION	PRV	VIL	DES

SHIP: GENERAL WERDER

FROM: BREMEN AND SOUTHAMPTON
TO: NEW YORK
ARRIVED: 22 AUGUST 1885

PASSENGER	AGE	SEX	OCCUPATION	PV	VL	DES
NOBLE, LYDIA	28	F	NN	RR	AHQD	RSS
MARIA	.05	F	INFANT	RR	AHQD	RSS
MAGRYKE, CAROLINE	50	F	NN	RR	AFDK	USA
LANDE, MOSES	25	M	LABR	RR	ZZZZ	USA
GUNTZER, LAZERUS	20	M	LABR	RR	ZZZZ	USA
DAMBROWSKY, CHAIA	30	F	NN	RR	ZZZZ	USA
JENKEL	4	M	CHILD	RR	ZZZZ	USA
HEDEZ	.03	F	INFANT	RR	ZZZZ	USA
SKARSKY, ABRAHAM	40	M	LABR	RR	AFTS	USA
ALPERN, MATLE	20	F	NN	RR	ZZZZ	USA
MATJINETZKY, CHANINA	61	F	NN	RR	ZZZZ	USA
BOSIA	28	F	NN	RR	ZZZZ	USA
SACKS, SARA	3	F	CHILD	RR	ZZZZ	USA
HIRSCH	4	M	CHILD	RR	ZZZZ	USA
RABNER, FANNI	18	F	NN	RR	ZZZZ	USA
DWIN, HULDA	19	F	NN	RR	ZZZZ	USA
HOINACKA, MARIANNA	27	F	NN	RR	ZZZZ	USA
WADALOF	6	F	CHILD	RR	ZZZZ	USA
STANISLAUS	4	M	CHILD	RR	ZZZZ	USA
DORA	.09	F	INFANT	RR	ZZZZ	USA
KLIBANSKY, MARIANNE	30	F	NN	RR	ZZZZ	USA
SCHEL	24	M	LABR	RR	ZZZZ	USA
ITZIG	8	M	CHILD	RR	ZZZZ	USA
LIBAH	7	F	CHILD	RR	ZZZZ	USA
BLOCK, BAZZEWA	48	F	NN	RR	ZZZZ	USA
PARAR	17	F	NN	RR	ZZZZ	USA
BEREK	8	F	CHILD	RR	ZZZZ	USA
MARSCHEA	5	F	CHILD	RR	ZZZZ	USA
SOWA	9	F	CHILD	RR	ZZZZ	USA
GEHMANN, LENE	30	F	NN	RR	ZZZZ	USA
RADANIS, BORIS	19	M	LABR	RR	ZZZZ	USA
WIEMEINITZ, ISAAC	20	M	TLR	RR	ZZZZ	USA
LACH, CHROIM	19	M	LABR	RR	ZZZZ	USA
GOLDSTEIN, JETTE	18	F	NN	RR	ZZZZ	USA

SHIP: MARTHA

FROM: STETTIN
TO: NEW YORK
ARRIVED: 22 AUGUST 1885

PASSENGER	AGE	SEX	OCCUPATION	PV	VL	DES
TRAWINSKY, FRANZISKA	26	F	W	PL	ZZZZ	CH
JOSEPH	7	M	CHILD	PL	ZZZZ	CH
HARIE	.09	F	INFANT	PL	ZZZZ	CH
SPERBER, O.	26	M	FARMER	PL	ZZZZ	STL
STAMMEISER, L.	21	M	TLR	PL	ZZZZ	***
BERMANN, ITTE	30	F	W	RR	ZZZZ	CIN
MARRIS	11	M	CH	RR	ZZZZ	CIN
SARAHFIREDE	10	F	CH	RR	ZZZZ	CIN
RALA	6	F	CHILD	RR	ZZZZ	CIN
SALOMON	4	M	CHILD	RR	ZZZZ	CIN
STEINBERG, HANNA	55	F	WO	RR	ZZZZ	DET
SPOING, LIBBY	22	F	SVNT	RR	ZZZZ	OH
MINOLLA	18	F	SVNT	RR	ZZZZ	OH
GOLDBERG, RAFAEL	35	M	TRDSMN	RR	ZZZZ	CH
BURKENFELD, FANNY	17	F	SVNT	PL	ZZZZ	ALB
EYMAN, SARAH	22	F	WO	RR	ZZZZ	CH
SANDAU, PAULINE	25	F	WO	RR	ZZZZ	IL
AUGUSTE	4	F	CHILD	RR	ZZZZ	IL
RABENOWITZ, LEAB	20	M	TRDSMN	RR	ZZZZ	IL
PLUNGE, JOSEPH	31	M	LABR	RR	ZZZZ	CH
RUBEN, RUTH	23	F	WO	RR	ZZZZ	CAN
HASE	17	M	LABR	RR	ZZZZ	CAN
CHAIN	7	M	CHILD	RR	ZZZZ	CAN
VEWACH	00	M	CH	RR	ZZZZ	CAN
KREMER, LEISER	17	M	TRDSMN	RR	ZZZZ	LAN
JENKOWSKI, MENDEL	49	M	MLR	RR	ZZZZ	NY
FANNY	31	F	W	RR	ZZZZ	NY
AMALIE	17	F	CH	RR	ZZZZ	NY
LEWIN	11	M	CH	RR	ZZZZ	NY
ELIAS	10	M	CH	RR	ZZZZ	NY
BLUME	8	F	CHILD	RR	ZZZZ	NY
JUDE	3	F	CHILD	RR	ZZZZ	NY
HINDE	7	F	CHILD	RR	ZZZZ	NY
SMEIL	6	M	CHILD	RR	ZZZZ	NY
NAPHTALIN, MENDEL	47	M	TRDSMN	RR	ZZZZ	NY
EYMAN, DAVID	19	M	SHGLR	RR	ZZZZ	NY
ENGERMANN, LINE	30	F	WO	RR	ZZZZ	CH
MARIE	10	F	CH	RR	ZZZZ	CH
JOHANNE	5	F	CHILD	RR	ZZZZ	CH
DAVID	1	M	CHILD	RR	ZZZZ	CH
ENGARMANN, HERRMANN	.02	M	INFANT	RR	ZZZZ	CH
SANDAU, MARIA	.11	F	INFANT	RR	ZZZZ	IL
PESKE, FREDRICH	56	M	LABR	RR	ZZZZ	UNK
BARBARA	27	F	SI	RR	ZZZZ	UNK
BARBARA	22	F	W	RR	ZZZZ	UNK
LYOLIA	.03	F	INFANT	RR	ZZZZ	UNK
GANGAS, MATTS.	19	M	LABR	FN	ZZZZ	NE
VESTLAND, JOSEPHINE	34	F	SVNT	FN	ZZZZ	MI
HULDA	6	F	CHILD	FN	ZZZZ	MI
STINA	4	F	CHILD	FN	ZZZZ	MI
OLZA, IDA-P.	20	F	SVNT	FN	ZZZZ	MI

SHIP: FURNESSIA

FROM: UNKNOWN
TO: NEW YORK
ARRIVED: 24 AUGUST 1885

PASSENGER	AGE	SEX	OCCUPATION	PV	VL	DES
MOYLAKI, MINIE	25	M	LABR	PL	ZZZZ	USA
ROSALIA	25	F	NN	PL	ZZZZ	USA
ABRAMOZ, WOCHEN	14	M	LABR	RR	ZZZZ	USA
BUSGAN, LEWY	30	M	LABR	RR	ZZZZ	USA
BROIDI, MORDCHE	50	M	LABR	RR	ZZZZ	USA
COMBERG, J.	21	M	LABR	RR	ZZZZ	USA
GRONBERG, JUDEL	24	M	LABR	RR	ZZZZ	USA
HOLDUBER, JANKEL	21	M	LABR	RR	ZZZZ	USA
KATZ, JAKEL	25	M	LABR	RR	ZZZZ	USA
BRAINI	22	F	NN	RR	ZZZZ	USA

SHIP: ZAANDAM

FROM: AMSTERDAM
TO: NEW YORK
ARRIVED: 24 AUGUST 1885

PASSENGER	AGE	SEX	OCCUPATION	PV	VL	DES
FROIJ, ABRAHAM	20	M	MCHT	RR	ZZZZ	USA
RHACHEL	20	F	NN	RR	ZZZZ	USA
SCHULZ, CHASKEL	24	M	MCHT	RR	ZZZZ	USA
PERLBERGER, ISAK	20	M	MCHT	RR	ZZZZ	USA
MIGAWA, WERONICA	30	F	UNKNOWN	PL	ZZZZ	USA
SIEBERMAN, LOUIS	29	M	MCHT	PL	ZZZZ	USA
KROMBERG, SCHLONIE	37	F	UNKNOWN	PL	ZZZZ	USA
BEIDE, SEIB	19	M	UNKNOWN	PL	ZZZZ	USA
SCHMULEWSCHEWKY, BEILE	24	M	UNKNOWN	PL	ZZZZ	USA
BREUWE	1	F	CHILD	PL	ZZZZ	USA
HIRSCH, ELIAS	26	M	MCHT	PL	ZZZZ	USA
SALOMON	22	M	MCHT	PL	ZZZZ	USA

PASSENGER	AGE	SEX	OCCUPATION	PRV VIL DES
JUSTIG, RACHEL	25	F	UNKNOWN	PLZZZZUSA
GERBER, ABRAHAM	34	M	UNKNOWN	PLZZZZUSA
BARNEH	5	F	CHILD	PLZZZZUSA
DORATHA, OLEV	24	F	UNKNOWN	PLZZZZUSA
JOSEPH	1	F	CHILD	PLZZZZUSA
REIBSTEIN, WOLF	20	M	MCHT	PLZZZZUSA
MARKSEN, CHASKEL	20	M	UNKNOWN	PLZZZZUSA
SIEM, HIERSCH	26	M	MCHT	PLZZZZUSA
GOLDFINGER, MORITZ	30	M	UNKNOWN	PLZZZZUSA
SCHIEBOWSKI, ANGELA	33	F	UNKNOWN	PLZZZZUSA
ZIEKERMAN, CHEMJE	17	M	UNKNOWN	PLZZZZUSA
KOHN, CHEINE	26	M	UNKNOWN	PLZZZZUSA

SHIP: GERMAIN

FROM: HAVRE
TO: NEW YORK
ARRIVED: 25 AUGUST 1885

PASSENGER	AGE	SEX	OCCUPATION	PRV VIL DES
DESMIRNOFF, NELLIE-MRS	29	F	NN	RRZZZZNY
NELLIE-MRS	7	F	CHILD	RRZZZZNY

SHIP: AUSTRALIA

FROM: HAMBURG
TO: NEW YORK
ARRIVED: 26 AUGUST 1885

PASSENGER	AGE	SEX	OCCUPATION	PRV VIL DES
GOLDSTEIN, ED.	30	F	WO	RRZZZZIL
JUDEL	7	M	CHILD	RRZZZZIL
TABA	5	F	CHILD	RRZZZZIL
JUDES	.10	M	INFANT	RRZZZZIL
NOERENT, NIELS	45	F	WO	RRZZZZNY
BRONISLAW	23	M	S	RRZZZZNY
CANILLA	7	F	CHILD	RRZZZZNY
STANISLAUS	6	M	CHILD	RRZZZZNY
JOSEPHTA	5	F	CHILD	RRZZZZNY
LADISLAUS	4	M	CHILD	RRZZZZNY
MARIYA	3	F	CHILD	RRZZZZNY
BERNHARD	2	M	CHILD	RRZZZZNY
KASIMER	.07	F	INFANT	RRZZZZNY
WEINBERG, ROSINE	7	F	CHILD	PLZZZZNY
CZIRLSTEIN, JANKEL	43	M	TRDSMN	RRZZZZUNK
LIEBERS, ROSA	24	F	WO	RRZZZZUNK
SARAH	.09	F	INFANT	RRZZZZUNK
STANBER, GABRIEL	38	M	TLR	PLZZZZUNK
ACHTABOWSKA, FRANCIS	17	M	SGL	RRZZZZUNK
HIRSCH, PINKUS	7	M	CHILD	PLZZZZUNK
BARDIN, HELENE	17	F	SGL	RRZZZZIL
MASCHKEWITZ, MUND	51	F	WO	RRZZZZIL
TAUBE	16	F	D	RRZZZZIL
MAKOWSKA, CATHARINA	30	F	SGL	PLZZZZWI
KOWALEWSKY, ANTON	27	M	LABR	PLZZZZPA
KOSENSTEIN, NACHUM	20	M	BRR	RRZZZZNY
PRIBBENOW, TAUL	26	M	LABR	RRZZZZNY
AMEN, EDWARD	44	M	TRDSMN	RRZZZZNY
KAUFMANN, SAMUEL	19	M	TRDSMN	RRZZZZUNK
FEINBERG, HIRSCH	15	M	TRDSMN	RRZZZZUNK
DIKLER, NIC.	25	M	LABR	RRZZZZUNK
NEWASCHEWSKY, P.	25	M	LABR	RRZZZZUNK
WEDSINSKY, BRONISL.	17	M	SHMK	PLZZZZNY
DEUTSCH, CHAN-M.	50	F	WO	RRZZZZNY
DEMITZ, MINNA	23	F	SGL	RRZZZZNY
FEMBERG, LENA	20	F	WO	RRZZZZUNK
HIRSCH	.07	M	INFANT	RRZZZZUNK

PASSENGER	AGE	SEX	OCCUPATION	PRV VIL DES
GRUNSTEIN, SORE	20	F	WO	RRZZZZIL
STEPONECK, ANNA	53	F	WO	RRZZZZIL
ANTONIE	29	F	D	RRZZZZIL
WOICECB	.11	M	INFANT	RRZZZZIL
SLEYS	.01	M	INFANT	RRZZZZIL
GRABOWSKA, ROSA	17	F	SGL	PLZZZZNY
WALINOWSKI, JOSEF	27	M	MCHT	RRZZZZUNK
ZEGULSKI, JOSEF	23	M	MCHT	RRZZZZUNK
BRUIZI, ANTON	23	M	MCHT	RRZZZZUNK
HEROWSOHN, MARCUS	30	M	MCHT	RRZZZZUNK
CHOWAINER, DIMKE	18	M	LABR	PLZZZZNY
KROLIKOWSKI, WILH.	17	M	LABR	PLZZZZNY

SHIP: FRISIA

FROM: HAMBURG
TO: NEW YORK
ARRIVED: 27 AUGUST 1885

PASSENGER	AGE	SEX	OCCUPATION	PRV VIL DES
ROSENBAUM, ELY	15	M	TU	RRZZZZUSA
HARRIS, JOSEF	33	M	BKBNDR	RRZZZZUSA
SCHMITAJUNSKY, BERL-L.	16	M	LABR	RRZZZZUSA
GORDON, ISAAC	18	M	WCHMKR	RRZZZZUSA
SCHLAMOWSKY, ABRAH.	15	M	TLR	RRZZZZUSA
FRIDMANN, CILA	33	F	W	RRZZZZUSA
MAX	6	M	CHILD	RRZZZZUSA
SELIG	5	M	CHILD	RRZZZZUSA
BERNHD.	4	M	CHILD	RRZZZZUSA
KANTER, FANNY	20	F	SGL	RRZZZZUSA
LIPSCHUTZ, BREIN	31	F	W	RRZZZZUSA
WOLFF	9	M	CHILD	RRZZZZUSA
JOSEF	8	M	CHILD	RRZZZZUSA
LEA	6	F	CHILD	RRZZZZUSA
RUSKOWSKY, JAC.	19	M	LABR	RRZZZZUSA
KETORACKI, JOS.	25	M	LABR	RRZZZZUSA
PEHOLSKY, PAUL	28	M	LABR	RRZZZZUSA
FRANZA.	18	F	W	RRZZZZUSA
IGNATZ	21	M	LABR	RRZZZZUSA
GOLDFINGER, RACHEL	16	F	SGL	RRZZZZUSA
BARON, MOSES	33	M	LABR	RRZZZZUSA
SCHEINE	9	F	CHILD	RRZZZZUSA
BIRGER, RACHEL	35	F	W	RRZZZZUSA
LEIB	8	M	CHILD	RRZZZZUSA
JOCHEL	6	M	CHILD	RRZZZZUSA
CHENE	4	M	CHILD	RRZZZZUSA
SISSEL	3	M	CHILD	RRZZZZUSA
MARIE	.11	M	INFANT	RRZZZZUSA
ALEXANDER, ESTHER	45	F	W	RRZZZZUSA
CHAIM	14	M	CH	RRZZZZUSA
ELK, REBECCA	19	F	SGL	RRZZZZUSA
LIBOWITZ, MORDCHE	19	M	LABR	RRZZZZUSA
BECKER, CHAIE	18	F	SGL	RRZZZZUSA
MENDELSOHN, SCHLOME	12	M	LABR	RRZZZZUSA
KOBATZNIK, EIDEL	32	F	W	RRZZZZUSA
MENDEL	9	M	CHILD	RRZZZZUSA
LEIB	4	M	CHILD	RRZZZZUSA
RIWKE	.11	F	INFANT	RRZZZZUSA
KOPINOS, H.BERK.	42	M	TLR	RRZZZZUSA
ROSA	38	F	W	RRZZZZUSA
SCHIFFRE	18	F	CH	RRZZZZUSA
JACOB	16	F	CH	RRZZZZUSA
MAGDA.	9	F	CHILD	RRZZZZUSA
HENDE	8	F	CHILD	RRZZZZUSA
LEIB	7	M	CHILD	RRZZZZUSA
HOSSEM	6	M	CHILD	RRZZZZUSA
SCHREIBER, AMALIE	23	F	W	RRZZZZUSA
WILH.	3	M	CHILD	RRZZZZUSA
WEINSTEIN, ISRAEL	18	M	CL	RRZZZZUSA
SINGER, RACHEL	26	F	W	RRZZZZUSA
ABRAMOWITZ, GLEIKE	43	F	W	RRZZZZUSA

PASSENGER	AGE	SEX	OCCUPATION	PRV VIL DES
ABRAH.	9	M	CHILD	RRZZZZUSA
SCHOLEM	7	M	CHILD	RRZZZZUSA
ROTHENBERG, RACHEL	13	F	SGL	RRZZZZUSA
BERISCH	9	M	CHILD	RRZZZZUSA
LEWINSOHN, HANNE	20	F	SGL	RRZZZZUSA
EHRLICH, MARCUS	20	M	LABR	RRZZZZUSA
RADOWSKY, CHASCHE	32	F	W	RRZZZZUSA
SAMUEL	8	M	CHILD	RRZZZZUSA
JOSEPH	6	M	CHILD	RRZZZZUSA
RUBEN	.11	M	INFANT	RRZZZZUSA
SCHULZ, SCHOLEM	32	M	LABR	RRZZZZUSA
KANTOR, CHASZE	18	F	SGL	RRZZZZUSA
MANUS, MAYER	25	M	LABR	RRZZZZUSA
ROTENBERG, GITTEL	37	F	W	RRZZZZUSA
MARY	8	F	CHILD	RRZZZZUSA
BERNSTEIN, LAZAR	5	M	CHILD	RRZZZZUSA
SCHOEN, BENNA	21	F	MCHT	RRZZZZUSA
ZIMERMANN, SARA	24	F	W	RRZZZZUSA
ELIAS	.11	M	INFANT	RRZZZZUSA
JETZALL, LASAR	18	M	CL	RRZZZZUSA
GINSBERG, NECHANE	17	F	SGL	RRZZZZUSA
MORELL, JOSEF	19	M	LABR	RRZZZZUSA
STEIN, AMALIE	52	F	W	RRZZZZUSA
CLARA	30	F	W	RRZZZZUSA
CARL	9	M	CHILD	RRZZZZUSA
CART.	4	M	CHILD	RRZZZZUSA
HEINRICH, LEON	18	M	CL	RRZZZZUSA
TYLIKA, FRANZA.	23	F	SGL	RRZZZZUSA
GRUENWALD, LEIB	42	M	LABR	RRZZZZUSA
SPAHN, JULIANE	48	F	W	RRZZZZUSA
MARIE	18	F	CH	RRZZZZUSA
JACOB	9	F	CHILD	RRZZZZUSA
HANS	8	F	CHILD	RRZZZZUSA
CATHA.	7	F	CHILD	RRZZZZUSA
PETER	4	M	CHILD	RRZZZZUSA
BALSKY, RACHEL	22	M	SGL	RRZZZZUSA
GOLDSTEIN, P.	36	M	LABR	RRZZZZUSA
MILLER, L.	19	M	LABR	RRZZZZUSA
BLUM, SCHEINE	30	F	SGL	RRZZZZUSA
GOLDBERG, BECKI	28	F	W	RRZZZZUSA
BENDICT	.11	M	INFANT	RRZZZZUSA
SMILY, RACHEL	24	F	W	RRZZZZUSA
REBECCA	4	F	CHILD	RRZZZZUSA
BERTHA	.11	F	INFANT	RRZZZZUSA
ISAAC, ABRAHAM	9	M	CHILD	RRZZZZUSA
BERNE, SARA	34	F	W	RRZZZZUSA
REBECCA	9	F	CHILD	RRZZZZUSA
MOSES	8	M	CHILD	RRZZZZUSA
ISAAC	7	M	CHILD	RRZZZZUSA
OSCHER	6	M	CHILD	RRZZZZUSA
JACOBSEN, SARAH	16	F	SGL	RRZZZZUSA
SAX, RACHEL	20	F	SGL	RRZZZZUSA
GRAJNOWSKY, JACOB	20	M	LABR	RRZZZZUSA
LEJTERMANN, ABRAH.	25	M	DLR	RRZZZZUSA
JENNY	25	F	W	RRZZZZUSA
MAY, ARON	20	M	SMH	RRZZZZUSA
ROSENBERG, J.	32	F	TNMK	RRZZZZUSA
COHEN, ELI	18	M	CPMKR	RRZZZZUSA
SELIGMANN, KEILE	28	F	W	RRZZZZUSA
ABRAH.	8	M	CHILD	RRZZZZUSA
DAVID	6	M	CHILD	RRZZZZUSA
MINNA	.11	F	INFANT	RRZZZZUSA
RADZIEWITZ, VINCENT	50	M	LABR	RRZZZZUSA
GRABOWSKY, JOH.	42	M	CPTR	RRZZZZUSA
GALEWITZ, SIGMD.	22	M	LABR	RRZZZZUSA
SILINSKY, IGNATZ	20	M	LABR	RRZZZZUSA
EISENBERG, ARON	17	M	LABR	RRZZZZUSA
JETTE	14	F	SGL	RRZZZZUSA
GLUECKMANN, JOSEF	32	M	LABR	RRZZZZUSA
MASKOWITZ, DAVID	33	M	JWLR	RRZZZZUSA
MISTURSKY, ESTHER	31	F	W	RRZZZZUSA
MENDEL	9	M	CHILD	RRZZZZUSA
MIUCHEN	8	F	CHILD	RRZZZZUSA
JOSSEL	.11	M	INFANT	RRZZZZUSA
SCHIRMANN, MICHEL	36	M	LABR	RRZZZZUSA

PASSENGER	AGE	SEX	OCCUPATION	PRV VIL DES
PINCUS, BEILE	30	F	W	RRZZZZUSA
SARA	5	F	CHILD	RRZZZZUSA
IDA	4	F	CHILD	RRZZZZUSA
PREISS, BREINE	18	F	SGL	RRZZZZUSA
SLOLOWSKY, SCHEINE	18	F	SGL	RRZZZZUSA
KASPEN, ESTHER	30	F	W	RRZZZZUSA
MORITZ	3	M	CHILD	RRZZZZUSA
RUBINSKY, DWORE	19	F	SGL	RRZZZZUSA
FRIEDMANN, SLATI	40	F	W	RRZZZZUSA
SAMUEL	9	M	CHILD	RRZZZZUSA
CHEINE	7	F	CHILD	RRZZZZUSA
LIE, RACHEL	19	F	SGL	RRZZZZUSA
KARLINSKY, LEIB	55	M	W	RRZZZZUSA
RACHEL	21	F	W	RRZZZZUSA
FREIDE	.11	F	INFANT	RRZZZZUSA
KLISCHINSKY, TAUBE	20	F	SGL	RRZZZZUSA
STEFANOWSKA, NECHA	16	F	SGL	RRZZZZUSA
SEYENSKY, MARCUS	43	M	DLR	RRZZZZUSA
LEA	40	F	W	RRZZZZUSA
KLEINSCHMIDT, WOLFF	35	M	LABR	RRZZZZUSA
ELIAS	9	M	CHILD	RRZZZZUSA
MINA	8	F	CHILD	RRZZZZUSA
LEA	6	M	CHILD	RRZZZZUSA
CHANNE	5	F	CHILD	RRZZZZUSA
ABRAH.	.11	M	INFANT	RRZZZZUSA
CARABELNIK, RACHEL	30	F	W	RRZZZZUSA
TEWIE	4	M	CHILD	RRZZZZUSA
ARON	3	M	CHILD	RRZZZZUSA
LIPPMANN, MOSES	17	M	LABR	RRZZZZUSA
ISRAELSKY, LEIB	25	M	LABR	RRZZZZUSA
SCHWISKY, ISIDOR	35	M	LABR	RRZZZZUSA
ROSA	24	F	W	RRZZZZUSA
FLORA	5	F	CHILD	RRZZZZUSA
JACOB	2	M	CHILD	RRZZZZUSA
LEWINSKY, SALOMON	21	M	SHMK	RRZZZZUSA
WIGANSKY, CHAIE	19	F	SGL	RRZZZZUSA
LITOWJETZKI, MINNA	18	F	SGL	RRZZZZUSA

SHIP: RHYNLAND

FROM: ANTWERP
TO: NEW YORK
ARRIVED: 27 AUGUST 1885

PASSENGER	AGE	SEX	OCCUPATION	PRV VIL DES
SUNDER, JACOB	39	M	UNKNOWN	RRAGRTNY

SHIP: ST. OF PENNSYLVANIA

FROM: GLASGOW
TO: NEW YORK
ARRIVED: 27 AUGUST 1885

PASSENGER	AGE	SEX	OCCUPATION	PRV VIL DES
ABENSOHN, ASUEL	00	M	CGRMKR	RRAFWJUSA
ESTHER	00	F	W	RRAFWJUSA
RACHEL	00	F	CH	RRAFWJUSA
ABRAHAM	9	M	CHILD	RRAFWJUSA
JUDEL	5	F	CHILD	RRAFWJUSA
FREICH	1	F	CHILD	RRAFWJUSA
LEWIN, HOSCHEL	1	M	CHILD	RRAFWJUSA
ARMSTEIN, ABRAHAM	2	M	CHILD	RRAHTUUSA
BAGISCHER, LADA	00	M	SHMK	RRZZZZUSA
BALSU, LEA	00	F	W	RRZZZZUSA
JUDEL	00	F	CH	RRZZZZUSA
BENJAS, SAMUEL	35	M	FARMER	RRZZZZUSA
CHAGES, LARB.	00	M	MCHT	RRZZZZUSA

PASSENGER	AGE	SEX	OCCUPATION	PRV VIL DES
CHWATZKY, CHAIM	00	M	TLR	RRZZZZUSA
PIAMANT, SCHMUL	21	M	SHMK	RRZZZZUSA
EDELSOHN, JACOB	19	M	MCHT	RRAHTUUSA
ELK, SCHMUEL	16	M	MCHT	RRZZZZUSA
FLEISCHER, SARAH	36	F	W	RRZZZZUSA
FURST, RUBIN	39	M	DYR	RRZZZZUSA
GRABOWSKI, ISRAEL	30	M	LABR	RRZZZZUSA
GRADOWITZ, HIRSCH	23	M	MCHT	RRZZZZUSA
GRODZINSKA, ELKE	23	F	W	RRAHQUUSA
SEIDI	1	F	CHILD	RRAHQUUSA
GROSSMAN, NACHAME	18	F	W	RRZZZZUSA
HARDSTEIN, FREIDE	17	F	SVNT	RRZZZZUSA
HJANSKY, EISA	20	M	SMH	RRZZZZUSA
HANNA	14	F	SVNT	RRZZZZUSA
JAKABOWSKY, JOSEF	23	M	SMH	RRZZZZUSA
ELKE	22	F	W	RRZZZZUSA
KRABOWSKY, JOSEF	27	M	SHMK	RRZZZZUSA
KRINDELKEMP, U	60	F	W	RRZZZZUSA
KOBEFLER, BENJAMIN	19	M	LABR	RRAHTFUSA
KINSKOWOLSK, SALOMON	19	M	MCHT	RRZZZZUSA
KOPMAN, SCHOLEM	22	M	TLR	RRZZZZUSA
LACHMANOWITZ, ARON	24	M	BCHR	RRZZZZUSA
MILHANIK, SALOMON	17	M	JNR	RRZZZZUSA
MILNER, NAWTOLI	60	M	LABR	RRZZZZUSA
MIRWISCH, SAMUEL	18	M	MCHT	RRZZZZUSA
ESTHER	19	F	W	RRZZZZUSA
MOSKOWIYZ, BEILE	22	F	W	RRZZZZUSA
SUSSE	2	F	CHILD	RRZZZZUSA
OLENSTEIN, MEITE	42	F	W	RRZZZZUSA
SARAH	10	F	CH	RRZZZZUSA
RACHEL	7	F	CHILD	RRZZZZUSA
ISAREL	00	M	CH	RRZZZZUSA
TERLMAN, M.	00	M	UNKNOWN	RRZZZZUSA
MEIER	18	M	UNKNOWN	RRZZZZUSA
PFFER, JUDEL	14	M	TLR	RRZZZZUSA
RAPPEPORT, HERMANN	21	M	TLR	RRZZZZUSA
RESCH, ISACH	39	M	LABR	RRZZZZUSA
RUBIN, JOSSEL	21	M	SMH	RRZZZZUSA
SCHUNDT, HIREL	55	M	UNKNOWN	RRZZZZUSA
SILBA, RAFAEL	20	M	SMH	RRAHTFUSA
STEIN, MARCUS	21	M	SMH	RRAHTFUSA
TROMP, ESTHER	42	F	SVNT	RRZZZZUSA
TRUBA, MOSEL	41	M	MCHT	RRZZZZUSA
WOLKOFF, ANNA	27	F	W	RRZZZZUSA
ELSA	18	F	SVNT	RRZZZZUSA
EDMUNDT	17	M	LABR	RRZZZZUSA
JOHANN	13	M	LABR	RRZZZZUSA
ZAYKINOWSKI, MENDEL	30	M	MCHT	RRZZZZUSA
ZESTATSKY, LOBEL	21	M	TLR	RRZZZZUSA
BERKOWITZ, ROSA	35	F	W	RRZZZZUSA
HERMANN	6	M	CHILD	RRZZZZUSA
BELY	3	F	CHILD	RRZZZZUSA
SCHARMIL	1	M	CHILD	RRZZZZUSA

SHIP: ABYSSINIA

FROM: LIVERPOOL AND QUEENSTOWN
TO: NEW YORK
ARRIVED: 28 AUGUST 1885

PASSENGER	AGE	SEX	OCCUPATION	PRV VIL DES
SILBERMAN, LEIB	45	M	UNKNOWN	PLZZZZUSA
BERNSHEM, LEIB	57	M	TLR	PLZZZZUSA
SCHUCHER, LEIB	31	F	SP	RRZZZZUSA
HEINSHEIN, ADELE	57	F	MA	RRZZZZUSA
WENMAUN, PETER	23	M	PNTR	PLZZZZUSA
REIMANN, BEREL	27	M	LABR	PLZZZZUSA
GLEICK, HIRSCH	27	M	BLKSMH	PLZZZZUSA
SALOMON	20	M	BLKSMH	PLZZZZUSA
SAMNEL, EMMA	16	F	SVNT	PLZZZZUSA
HATOWSKI, ISRAEL	43	M	PDLR	PLZZZZUSA
BENJAMIN	18	M	WCHMKR	PLZZZZUSA
LEVITAK, MOSES	26	M	SHMK	PLZZZZUSA
KEAN, WOLF	25	M	TLR	PLZZZZUSA
SCHMEID, SCHLOME	22	M	TLR	PLZZZZUSA
LIPSCHUTZ, LEVY	20	M	BKPR	PLZZZZUSA
DUBINN, SALOMON	16	M	PDLR	PLZZZZUSA
BOEJDANOW, ANTONIA	20	F	SVNT	PLZZZZUSA
ERSON, INGRID-C.	60	M	MNR	FNZZZZUSA
SIGG, GUSTYVA	55	F	MA	FNZZZZUSA
CAROLINE	11	F	CH	FNZZZZUSA
CHLAWOWITZ, BARNEH	31	M	FLABR	FNZZZZUSA

SHIP: CITY OF RICHMOND

FROM: LIVERPOOL
TO: NEW YORK
ARRIVED: 28 AUGUST 1885

PASSENGER	AGE	SEX	OCCUPATION	PRV VIL DES
SPIELER, P.	30	F	W	RRZZZZUSA
HERM.	4	F	CHILD	RRZZZZUSA
CHREUSTINE, A.	35	M	LABR	RRZZZZUSA
M.	35	F	W	RRZZZZUSA
G.	17	M	LABR	RRZZZZUSA
BUCK, H.	35	M	LABR	RRZZZZUSA
MENDEL, JACOB	23	M	LABR	RRZZZZUSA
RACHMANN, DAVID	22	M	LABR	PLZZZZUSA
LEVY, R.	30	M	LABR	PLZZZZUSA
M.	27	F	W	PLZZZZUSA
H.	00	M	INF	PLZZZZUSA
S.	30	F	W	PLZZZZUSA
S.	9	F	CHILD	PLZZZZUSA
K.	6	F	CHILD	PLZZZZUSA
H.	00	M	INF	PLZZZZUSA
REHUALSKA, P.	30	M	LABR	PLZZZZUSA
FREYMANN, MATILDA	40	F	W	PLZZZZUSA
F.	9	F	CHILD	PLZZZZUSA
S.	6	F	CHILD	PLZZZZUSA

SHIP: SALIER

FROM: BREMEN
TO: NEW YORK
ARRIVED: 28 AUGUST 1885

PASSENGER	AGE	SEX	OCCUPATION	PRV VIL DES
PASCHINSAWA, BELIROYA	11	F	CH	PLAGRTUSA
KIV, DAVID	20	M	NN	PLAHOKUSA
MINDEL, LOUIS	20	M	NN	PLAHOKUSA
ABRAMOWITZ, RIWE	22	F	NN	PLAHOKUSA
EPSTEIN, MERE	28	F	NN	PLAHOKUSA
SALOMON	6	M	CHILD	PLAHOKUSA
VEITEL	5	F	CHILD	PLAHOKUSA
EIDER	.09	F	INFANT	PLAHOKUSA
GERSTENOWITZ, JUDA	30	M	NN	RRZZZZUSA
EPSTEIN, ESTER	20	F	NN	RRZZZZUSA
KATZ, ROCHEL	36	M	NN	RRZZZZUSA
JACOB	9	M	CHILD	RRZZZZUSA
WIRDE	8	F	CHILD	RRZZZZUSA
CHEINE	.09	F	INFANT	RRZZZZUSA
LIPOWITZKY, SAM.	15	M	CH	RRZZZZUSA
PODLEPSKIZ, LOEB	15	M	CH	RRZZZZUSA
DUNECZISCHAK, ANNA	22	F	CH	RRZZZZUSA
ANNA	1	F	CHILD	RRZZZZUSA
PESELLAR, VINBA	25	M	NN	RRZZZZUSA
GOLDSTEIN, JAC.	30	M	NN	RRZZZZUSA
LEWISOHN, REBECCA	33	F	NN	RRZZZZUSA

PASSENGER	AGE	SEX	OCCUPATION	PV RIV	VIL	DES
SCHAWEL	33	F	NN	RR	ZZZZ	USA
LINA	11	F	CH	RR	ZZZZ	USA
PAULINE	8	F	CHILD	RR	ZZZZ	USA
MOSES	9	M	CHILD	RR	ZZZZ	USA
WILCZINSKI, HERM.	16	M	LABR	RR	ZZZZ	USA
REGINA	22	F	NN	RR	ZZZZ	USA
ITZIG, OSCAR	00	M	NN	RR	ZZZZ	USA
KER, MINNA	20	F	NN	RR	ZZZZ	USA

SHIP: WESTPHALIA

FROM: HAMBURG AND HAVRE
TO: NEW YORK
ARRIVED: 28 AUGUST 1885

PASSENGER	AGE	SEX	OCCUPATION	PV RIV	VIL	DES
HAUPTMANN, SAMUEL	26	M	BRR	RR	ZZZZ	USA
GLUECKSMANN, EVA	19	F	SGL	RR	ZZZZ	USA
LOEWENSOHN, MOSES	56	M	DLR	RR	ZZZZ	USA
MINNA	55	F	W	RR	ZZZZ	USA
BRAUN, SEFTEL	26	M	TNMK	RR	ZZZZ	USA
SARA	23	F	W	RR	ZZZZ	USA
ISRAEL	.02	M	INFANT	RR	ZZZZ	USA
KRAMER, IDA	40	F	W	RR	ZZZZ	USA
CHANNE	16	F	CH	RR	ZZZZ	USA
HIRSCH	9	M	CHILD	RR	ZZZZ	USA
SCHIFFRE	8	F	CHILD	RR	ZZZZ	USA
DAVID	5	M	CHILD	RR	ZZZZ	USA
JUDEL	3	F	CHILD	RR	ZZZZ	USA
BENJ.	.11	M	INFANT	RR	ZZZZ	USA
SPIGLE, RACHEL	.11	F	INFANT	RR	ZZZZ	USA
MAKOWER, ESTHER	33	F	W	RR	ZZZZ	USA
SARA	6	F	CHILD	RR	ZZZZ	USA
POCI	5	F	CHILD	RR	ZZZZ	USA
CHASKEL	.11	F	INFANT	RR	ZZZZ	USA
KINZAR, LEIZER	25	M	LABR	RR	ZZZZ	USA
CHARZANSKY, LIEBE	16	F	SGL	RR	ZZZZ	USA
MASUR, BER.	25	M	LABR	RR	ZZZZ	USA
NOWODWORSKY, REISEL	25	F	W	RR	AHRZ	USA
SCHOLEM	8	M	CHILD	RR	AHRZ	USA
ELIAS	7	M	CHILD	RR	AHRZ	USA
SARA	3	F	CHILD	RR	AHRZ	USA
JENNY	.11	F	INFANT	RR	AHRZ	USA
ROSENBLUM, JANKEL	22	M	LABR	RR	ADOI	USA
BLUME	21	F	W	RR	ADOI	USA
RUF, JUDEL	22	F	SGL	RR	ADOI	USA
BERMANN, CHASKEL	44	M	DLR	RR	ZZZZ	USA
KAUFMANN, DAVID	20	M	LABR	RR	ZZZZ	USA
GRUNSTEIN, KOLEF	55	M	LABR	RR	ZZZZ	USA
PIZURKY, JANKEL	21	M	LABR	RR	ZZZZ	USA
BUELEWICZ, KASIMIR	24	M	LABR	RR	AHZS	USA
LERBOWITZ, SCHOVE	19	F	SGL	RR	ZZZZ	USA
PLOTSCHINSKA, RIVKE	40	F	W	RR	ZZZZ	USA
RACHEL	19	F	CH	RR	ZZZZ	USA
SCHMAKA	9	F	CHILD	RR	ZZZZ	USA
BENJ.	8	M	CHILD	RR	ZZZZ	USA
SELIG	7	M	CHILD	RR	ZZZZ	USA
CHANNE	5	F	CHILD	RR	ZZZZ	USA
LEWINTHAL, JUDEL	60	F	W	RR	ZZZZ	USA
KOEN, MOSES	19	M	MCHT	RR	AGRT	USA
KOWALSKI, GEORG	16	M	FARMER	RR	ZZZZ	USA
MAGGEL, JEREMIAS	19	M	LABR	RR	ZZZZ	USA
SCHAPIRO, MARIANNE	18	F	SGL	RR	ZZZZ	USA
STEINARD, LEA	58	F	W	RR	ADOI	USA
ARKIN, REBECCA	45	F	W	RR	ZZZZ	USA
PESCHE	8	F	CHILD	RR	ZZZZ	USA
HURWITZ, CHANNE	25	F	W	RR	ZZZZ	USA
ABRAH.	.11	M	INFANT	RR	ZZZZ	USA
MELTZER, ROSALIE	30	F	W	RR	ZZZZ	USA
ALTE	9	F	CHILD	RR	ZZZZ	USA
JOSSEL	6	M	CHILD	RR	ZZZZ	USA
ARKIN, MARCUS	26	M	LABR	RR	ZZZZ	USA
KATZ, ITZIG	40	M	TLR	RR	AHTF	USA
RAMBACH, RUBEN	55	M	LABR	RR	AHTF	USA
RODBORD, JUDAS	26	F	W	RR	ZZZZ	USA
MERE	.11	F	INFANT	RR	ZZZZ	USA
ABRAMOWITZ, NATHAN	21	M	SDLR	RR	ZZZZ	USA
SPIGLE, NANCY	28	F	W	RR	ZZZZ	USA
MORITZ, AUG.	22	M	LABR	RR	ZZZZ	USA
SAAK, ISAAC	38	M	DLR	RR	ZZZZ	USA
GRUNSTEIN, ETTE	35	F	W	RR	ZZZZ	USA
JACOB	9	M	CHILD	RR	ZZZZ	USA
RACHEL	8	F	CHILD	RR	ZZZZ	USA
FARBMANN, HIRSCH	22	M	MCHT	RR	ZZZZ	USA
LEWIN, SCHLOME	18	M	LABR	RR	AGRT	USA
CHASEKOW, LEIB	55	M	DLR	RR	AHZS	USA
TAUCHUM	2	M	CHILD	RR	AHZS	USA
GINSBURG, SAMUEL	7	M	CHILD	RR	AHZS	USA
SCHUMACHER, ISTEL	14	M	LABR	RR	ZZZZ	USA
SCHARKIN, BEILE	24	F	W	RR	ZZZZ	USA
ABRAH.	.11	M	INFANT	RR	ZZZZ	USA
ROSENGARTEN, RACHEL	23	F	SGL	RR	AHZJ	USA
LANGLEBEN, HERRM.	37	M	DLR	RR	ZZZZ	USA
GRANJEWITZ, BEILE	40	F	W	RR	ADOI	USA
KABEL, HENRY	25	M	FARMER	RR	AHZS	USA
JOSEF	23	F	W	RR	AHZS	USA
HENRICH, BOLESLAV	21	M	CL	RR	AHZS	USA
MALINOWITZ, REBECCA	21	F	W	RR	ACDS	USA
ANNA	.09	F	INFANT	RR	ACDS	USA

SHIP: EGYPT

FROM: LIVERPOOL
TO: NEW YORK
ARRIVED: 29 AUGUST 1885

PASSENGER	AGE	SEX	OCCUPATION	PV RIV	VIL	DES
PICAROVICZ, ABRAHAM	37	M	LABR	RR	AFVG	USA
AMALIE	39	F	W	RR	AFVG	USA
V.	8	M	CHILD	RR	AFVG	USA
LINE	4	M	CHILD	RR	AFVG	USA
SARAH	1	F	CHILD	RR	AFVG	USA
BLEMSHIN, B.	21	M	LABR	RR	ADBQ	USA
ESCONER, MENDEL-F.	19	M	LABR	RR	ADBQ	USA
SHORNESS, LEIB	26	M	LABR	RR	ADBQ	USA
BAGNEL, ISAAC	20	M	LABR	RR	ADBQ	USA
HOLTZMAN, MEYER	21	M	LABR	RR	ADBQ	USA
BARNETT, JACOB	21	M	LABR	RR	ADBQ	USA
ESENBERG, HERMAN	46	M	LABR	RR	ADBQ	USA
ROSSMAN, SOLOMAN	19	M	LABR	RR	ADBQ	USA
CHERSLEN, MOSES	16	M	LABR	RR	ADBQ	USA
ROSENBLAN, MECH.	18	M	LABR	RR	ADBQ	USA
GERBER, HERMAN	25	M	LABR	RR	ADBQ	USA
JACOBSON, CATH.	47	F	W	RR	ZZZZ	USA
PETER	17	M	LABR	RR	ZZZZ	USA
ZLLIONSKY, JANKEL	20	M	LABR	RR	ZZZZ	USA
HILLELSOHN, LEIB	18	M	LABR	RR	ZZZZ	USA
POCRIVOLSKI, MOSES	20	M	LABR	RR	ZZZZ	USA
AMSHEWITH, JOSUS	20	M	LABR	RR	AFVG	USA
LIPSCIL, MOSES	16	M	LABR	RR	AFVG	USA
LANDEN, NILS	33	M	LABR	RR	AFVG	USA
HALL, ENOCK	21	M	LABR	RR	AFVG	USA
IRASTENCKZ, SUSE	18	M	LABR	RR	AFVG	USA
GOLDENBERG, JACOB	22	M	LABR	RR	AFVG	USA
BROCK, ABRAHAM	24	M	LABR	RR	ADBQ	USA
LORSSE, K.	20	M	LABR	RR	ADBQ	USA
LEVI, JOHN	41	M	LABR	RR	AFVG	USA
BERNSLAIN, SOLOMAN	24	M	LABR	RR	AFVG	USA
MARS, L.	27	M	LABR	RR	AFVG	USA
SCHABES, MOSES	18	M	LABR	RR	AFVG	USA
BALKSADSKY, SAMUEL	20	M	LABR	RR	AFVG	USA
MASCKANSKY, R.	30	M	LABR	RR	AFVG	USA

PASSENGER	AGE	SEX	OCCUPATION	PRIV	VIL	DES
SCHEINE	9	M	CHILD	RR	AFVG	USA
GASCHEN	7	M	CHILD	RR	AFVG	USA
HINDE	3	M	CHILD	RR	AFVG	USA
SALEWAIZEK, C.	25	M	LABR	RR	AFVG	USA
HISLE, GOLDE	52	M	LABR	RR	AFVG	USA
WALKEWOCTZKY, MARIA	30	F	W	RR	AFVG	USA
MARIA	8	F	CHILD	RR	AFVG	USA
CARL	00	M	INF	RR	AFVG	USA
E.	00	M	INF	RR	AFVG	USA
SHAYONIS, JACOB	34	M	LABR	RR	AFVG	USA
M.	22	M	LABR	RR	AFVG	USA
HARRIS	6	M	CHILD	RR	AFVG	USA
BENONI, H.	28	M	LABR	RR	AFVG	USA
JOHANNA	32	F	W	RR	AFVG	USA
METZKEWITZ, JONAS	25	M	LABR	RR	AFVG	USA
WISCHEWSKY, EVA	24	F	W	RR	ADBQ	USA
VALPEN, SOLOMAN	26	M	LABR	RR	ADBQ	USA
LEIB	20	M	LABR	RR	ADBQ	USA
BOLOCSKY, LEAH	30	F	W	RR	AFVG	USA
BENJAMIN	10	M	CH	RR	AFVG	USA
MOSES	6	M	CHILD	RR	AFVG	USA
HEYANE	00	M	INF	RR	AFVG	USA
LEVIN, ANNA	35	F	W	RR	AFVG	USA
PENETAS	10	F	CH	RR	AFVG	USA
B.	3	M	CHILD	RR	AFVG	USA
BOAS, DORA	26	F	W	RR	AFVG	USA
LEAH	8	F	CHILD	RR	AFVG	USA
SARAH	7	F	CHILD	RR	AFVG	USA
BETSY	3	F	CHILD	RR	ZZZZ	USA
OSCAR	2	M	CHILD	RR	ZZZZ	USA
JOHANSTON, MARIA	18	F	SP	RR	ZZZZ	USA

SHIP: LEERDAM

FROM: ROTTERDAM
TO: NEW YORK
ARRIVED: 29 AUGUST 1885

PASSENGER	AGE	SEX	OCCUPATION	PRIV	VIL	DES
MARKOW, MOSES	43	M	MCHT	RR	ZZZZ	USA
APPENHEIM, BEHR	46	M	MCHT	RR	ZZZZ	USA
BASCHE	23	M	MCHT	RR	ZZZZ	USA
GRUNBERGER, RON	20	F	UNKNOWN	RR	ZZZZ	USA
TOBIAS, TILNER	26	M	LABR	RR	ZZZZ	USA
FRIDRICH	19	M	LABR	RR	ZZZZ	USA
LEVINSOHN, SCHEINE	40	M	MCHT	RR	ZZZZ	USA
JONATHAN	10	M	CH	RR	ZZZZ	USA
SAMUEL	11	M	CH	RR	ZZZZ	USA

SHIP: WERRA

FROM: BREMEN
TO: NEW YORK
ARRIVED: 29 AUGUST 1885

PASSENGER	AGE	SEX	OCCUPATION	PRIV	VIL	DES
SEHR, GG.	65	M	TT	RR	ZZZZ	NY
MRS.G.	64	F	UNKNOWN	RR	ZZZZ	NY
GRISS, WILHM.	32	M	TT	RR	ZZZZ	NY
CATHA.	29	F	UNKNOWN	RR	ZZZZ	NY
WILHM.	7	M	CHILD	RR	ZZZZ	NY
LILIA	6	F	CHILD	RR	ZZZZ	NY
MARGTHE.	5	F	CHILD	RR	ZZZZ	NY
AMALIA	4	F	CHILD	RR	ZZZZ	NY
LEONA	.11	F	INFANT	RR	ZZZZ	NY
POSOPSKY, PAULINE	41	F	UNKNOWN	RR	ZZZZ	NY
MARIE	18	F	CH	RR	ZZZZ	NY
ANETTE	16	F	CH	RR	ZZZZ	NY
ELISE	7	F	CHILD	RR	ZZZZ	NY
ROSALIE	6	F	CHILD	RR	ZZZZ	NY
MICHAEL	5	M	CHILD	RR	ZZZZ	NY
HANS	3	M	CHILD	RR	ZZZZ	NY
RIEDINGER, JACOB	30	M	FARMER	RR	ZZZZ	NY
SUSANNA	30	F	UNKNOWN	RR	ZZZZ	NY
JACOB	7	M	CHILD	RR	ZZZZ	NY
CHRISTINE	5	F	CHILD	RR	ZZZZ	NY
HEYMANN, DAV.	20	M	LABR	RR	ZZZZ	NY
TICHLER, CARL	22	M	FARMER	RR	ZZZZ	NY
SOPHIE	19	F	UNKNOWN	RR	ZZZZ	NY
WETTENBERG, ESTER	29	F	UNKNOWN	RR	ZZZZ	NY
DAVID	7	M	CHILD	RR	ZZZZ	NY
BEILE	6	F	CHILD	RR	ZZZZ	NY
JOSSEL	3	M	CHILD	RR	ZZZZ	NY
ROBENVIVET, CHAIN	32	M	LABR	RR	ZZZZ	NY
MUELLER, ROB.	22	M	JNR	PL	ZZZZ	NY

SHIP: LESSING

FROM: HAMBURG
TO: NEW YORK
ARRIVED: 31 AUGUST 1885

PASSENGER	AGE	SEX	OCCUPATION	PRIV	VIL	DES
KASANOWICZ, SCHMUEL	20	M	TLR	RR	ZZZZ	USA
FEIN, TAUBE	23	F	W	RR	ZZZZ	USA
ISAAC	.11	M	INFANT	RR	ZZZZ	USA
FINKELSTEIN, LEA	52	F	W	RR	AFWJ	USA
TWARDOWSKI, HEYMANN	21	M	LABR	RR	ZZZZ	USA
LINE	20	F	W	RR	ZZZZ	USA
PERLSOHN, ABR.	20	M	DLR	RR	AHSW	USA
FUCHS, ANNA	18	F	SGL	RR	AHUF	USA
MUELLER, FISCHEL	23	M	LABR	RR	ZZZZ	USA
SCHROCTLIN, MICHAEL	32	M	LABR	RR	AEGT	USA
CATHE.	29	F	W	RR	AEGT	USA
ANNA	7	F	CHILD	RR	AEGT	USA
JACOB	5	M	CHILD	RR	AEGT	USA
HEINRICH	3	M	CHILD	RR	AEGT	USA
SCHMIDT, HENRY	28	M	LABR	RR	AEGT	USA
ELISABETH	27	F	W	RR	AEGT	USA
CATHA.	6	F	CHILD	RR	AEGT	USA
ELISABETH	4	F	CHILD	RR	AEGT	USA
MARES	2	F	CHILD	RR	AEGT	USA
HEINR.	.09	M	INFANT	RR	AEGT	USA
NUSS, PETER	15	M	LABR	RR	AEGT	USA
SCHMIDT, ELISABETH	18	F	SGL	RR	AEGT	USA
APPELBAUM, ROSA	23	F	SGL	RR	ZZZZ	USA
FELDBERG, SARAH	18	F	SGL	RR	ZZZZ	USA
WEINBERG, MINNA	19	F	SGL	RR	AHTR	USA
MEIERSOHN, LEIZER	16	M	LABR	RR	ZZZZ	USA
FRIEDMANN, JACOB	9	M	CHILD	RR	ZZZZ	USA
SUROWSKY, SCHLOME	17	M	LABR	RR	ZZZZ	USA
BERCZIM, LEIB	33	M	LABR	RR	ZZZZ	USA
SILBERMANN, ARON-T.	22	M	LABR	RR	AHTF	USA
HOCHMANN, FEIGE	58	F	W	RR	ZZZZ	USA
ZIGLINOWSKY, YSAAC	20	M	DLR	RR	ZZZZ	USA
JANKELSOHN, DAVID	45	M	DLR	RR	AHTR	USA
LIEBE	45	F	W	RR	AHTR	USA
PERLE	17	F	CH	RR	AHTR	USA
ESTHER	9	F	CHILD	RR	AHTR	USA
BENJ.	8	M	CHILD	RR	AHTR	USA
JAC.	7	M	CHILD	RR	AHTR	USA
MERE	6	M	CHILD	RR	AHTR	USA
HERSCH	5	M	CHILD	RR	AHTR	USA
JAFE, ANNA	16	F	SGL	RR	AHTF	USA
KOWALSKI, LEON	21	M	LABR	RR	AHUI	USA
TURCZAN, ITTE	39	F	W	RR	ZZZZ	USA
SARA	17	F	CH	RR	ZZZZ	USA
BEINE	9	M	CHILD	RR	ZZZZ	USA

PASSENGER	AGE	SEX	OCCUPATION	PRV	VIL	DES
BRAUNSTEIN, BERNHARD	30	M	DLR	RR	ZZZZ	USA
SALOMONOW, SALOMON	19	M	LABR	RR	AHTU	USA
MORDCHELES, NEH.	50	M	DLR	RR	ZZZZ	USA
FREIDE	50	F	W	RR	ZZZZ	USA
HONSKY, SARA	28	F	W	RR	ZZZZ	USA
CHANNE	4	F	CHILD	RR	ZZZZ	USA
GOLDFARB, JHE.	22	F	SGL	RR	ZZZZ	USA
LEVITA, ABRAH.	25	M	DLR	RR	ZZZZ	USA
SCHAPIRA, CLARA	26	F	W	RR	ZZZZ	USA
RASCHE	7	F	CHILD	RR	ZZZZ	USA
RACHEL	6	F	CHILD	RR	ZZZZ	USA
JOSSEL	5	M	CHILD	RR	ZZZZ	USA
HIRSCH	.11	M	INFANT	RR	ZZZZ	USA
SABLODOWSKY, SARA	16	F	SGL	RR	ZZZZ	USA
SUROWITZ, TAUBE	27	F	W	RR	ZZZZ	USA
ELIAS	13	M	CH	RR	ZZZZ	USA
MICHEL	6	M	CHILD	RR	ZZZZ	USA
JENNY	4	F	CHILD	RR	ZZZZ	USA
LEISER	.06	M	INFANT	RR	ZZZZ	USA
SILBERMANN, ABR.	18	M	LABR	RR	ZZZZ	USA
EMSZINSKI, RACHEL	18	F	SGL	RR	AHSW	USA
NOTTEL, SCHEVE	25	F	W	RR	AHTF	USA
DWORE	.11	F	INFANT	RR	AHTF	USA
ABRAHAMOWITZ, MARIE	44	F	W	RR	AFVG	USA
DAVID	9	M	CHILD	RR	AFVG	USA
ISAAC	8	M	CHILD	RR	AFVG	USA
KRAETZNER, HARRIS	20	M	DLR	RR	ZZZZ	USA
ZWISON, ISAAC	9	M	CHILD	RR	AHTR	USA
SIDELSKI, ETTEL	28	F	W	RR	AHTF	USA
DWORE	.11	F	INFANT	RR	AHTF	USA
REBECCA	20	F	SGL	RR	AHTF	USA
PORT, NECHAME	24	F	SGL	RR	AHTF	USA
GOSPODAR, LINA	19	F	SGL	RR	AHTF	USA
LAPIDES, ANNA	20	F	SGL	RR	ZZZZ	USA
BROMBERG, JOSEPH	35	M	LABR	RR	ZZZZ	USA
CHANNE	22	F	W	RR	ZZZZ	USA
NOCHIM	.11	M	INFANT	RR	ZZZZ	USA
NADELMANN, JACOB	16	M	LABR	RR	ZZZZ	USA
GINTZBERG, ESTHER	32	F	W	RR	ZZZZ	USA
HIRSCH	4	M	CHILD	RR	ZZZZ	USA
MENNCHE	.11	M	INFANT	RR	ZZZZ	USA
SUMBERG, RISCHE	24	F	SGL	RR	AHTU	USA
ROMANOW, ABR.	24	M	LABR	RR	AHTU	USA
JUDAC, DAVID	32	M	LABR	RR	AHTU	USA
KRETUNTKO, MOSES	18	M	LABR	RR	ZZZZ	USA
WILANSKY, HENE	26	F	W	RR	ZZZZ	USA
SALOMON	.11	M	INFANT	RR	ZZZZ	USA
SALOMON	.11	M	INFANT	RR	ZZZZ	USA
APOTHEKER, JUDE	20	M	LABR	RR	AHTU	USA
OLKENITZKI, ALTE	20	F	W	RR	ZZZZ	USA
PESCHE	.11	F	INFANT	RR	ZZZZ	USA
MISCHNITZKI, EFRAIM	14	M	LABR	RR	ZZZZ	USA
FINKELSTEIN, JACOB	53	M	LABR	RR	ZZZZ	USA
HENE	20	F	SGL	RR	ZZZZ	USA
WOLFF, MALKE	44	F	W	RR	AHTR	USA
RACHEL	9	F	CHILD	RR	AHTR	USA
SARA	5	F	CHILD	RR	AHTR	USA
SAMUEL	8	M	CHILD	RR	AHTR	USA
ARON	.11	M	INFANT	RR	AHTR	USA
METER, ITZKO	27	M	CL	RR	AHTR	USA
LEKUTZKIJ, SCHLUM	20	M	LABR	RR	ADOI	USA
RUBINOWITZ, KOPPEL	20	M	LABR	RR	ZZZZ	USA
ITZKOWITZ, ISAAC	20	M	LABR	RR	ZZZZ	USA
DINA	10	F	W	RR	ZZZZ	USA
PRES, BEREL	20	M	LABR	RR	ZZZZ	USA
SUROWITZ, GITTEL	3	F	CHILD	RR	ZZZZ	USA
POLIWODA, ESTHER	50	F	W	RR	ZZZZ	USA
REITZE	24	F	W	RR	ZZZZ	USA
ELISE	2	F	CHILD	RR	ZZZZ	USA
FELSMANN, ANDR.	21	M	LABR	RR	ZZZZ	USA
KELLNER, PAUL	26	M	TCHR	RR	ZZZZ	USA
FLORA	28	F	W	RR	ZZZZ	USA
ALEXANDER	1	M	CHILD	RR	ZZZZ	USA
RUDOLPH	.06	M	INFANT	RR	ZZZZ	USA

SHIP: POLARIA

FROM: HAMBURG
TO: NEW YORK
ARRIVED: 31 AUGUST 1885

PASSENGER	AGE	SEX	OCCUPATION	PRV	VIL	DES
SCHNEIDER, S.D.	36	M	LABR	RR	ZZZZ	NY
SOHAMSE	28	F	W	RR	ZZZZ	NY
GRIESE	7	F	CHILD	RR	ZZZZ	NY
ALEXANDER	4	M	CHILD	RR	ZZZZ	NY
HERRMANN	5	M	CHILD	RR	ZZZZ	NY
SUMHUBER, EMMA	20	F	SGL	RR	ZZZZ	UNK
MEISEL, MERRI	30	F	SGL	RR	ZZZZ	CH
HIRSCH	15	M	CH	RR	ZZZZ	CH
ISAAK	7	M	CHILD	RR	ZZZZ	CH
CHAWE	6	M	CHILD	RR	ZZZZ	CH
MILLER, SEBKA	27	F	WO	RR	ZZZZ	NY
MARIA	.07	F	INFANT	RR	ZZZZ	NY
RABINOWITZ, CHR.	32	F	WO	RR	ZZZZ	CH
LEIBEL	7	F	CHILD	RR	ZZZZ	CH
HEINSCHEL	6	F	CHILD	RR	ZZZZ	CH
FEIGEL	3	F	CHILD	RR	ZZZZ	CH
KOHAN, FEIGE	25	F	WO	RR	ZZZZ	CH
BLOOM, JOSEF	17	M	LABR	RR	ZZZZ	CH
JACOB	7	M	CHILD	RR	ZZZZ	CH
SOCSKIN, MORDEL	20	M	SVNT	RR	ZZZZ	STL
LEWY, ESTER	40	F	WO	RR	ZZZZ	NY
WILSCHINSKY, MINNA	28	F	WO	RR	ZZZZ	NY
LEWIN, RACHEL	7	F	CHILD	RR	ZZZZ	NY
STIRBNER	5	M	CHILD	RR	ZZZZ	NY
MECHANITZKI, AYRIEL	35	M	LABR	RR	ZZZZ	CH
BOICESKY, R.L.	26	F	WO	RR	ZZZZ	NY
WOLFF	4	M	CHILD	RR	ZZZZ	NY
JANKEL	3	M	CHILD	RR	ZZZZ	NY
FRENKEL, ESTER	35	F	WO	RR	ZZZZ	NY
CHAIM	7	M	CHILD	RR	ZZZZ	NY
JANKEL	3	F	CHILD	RR	ZZZZ	NY
RIWKE	.10	F	INFANT	RR	ZZZZ	NY
SCHLOM, ELIAS	22	M	TRDSMN	RR	ZZZZ	NY
SCHULHOFF, REBECKA	28	F	WO	RR	ZZZZ	EMA
MOSES	7	M	CHILD	RR	ZZZZ	EMA
JEIHEDA	5	F	CHILD	RR	ZZZZ	EMA
CHITSEHCK, RIFKE	38	F	WO	RR	ZZZZ	NY
RACHEL	6	F	CHILD	RR	ZZZZ	NY
ESTHER	.09	F	INFANT	RR	ZZZZ	NY

SHIP: STATE OF GEORGIA

FROM: GLASGOW AND LARNE
TO: NEW YORK
ARRIVED: 01 SEPTEMBER 1885

PASSENGER	AGE	SEX	OCCUPATION	PRV	VIL	DES
BRYOZA, BELA	14	F	CH	PL	ZZZZ	USA
SCHMALANG, SCHIRO	22	M	LABR	PL	ZZZZ	USA
LARRE	22	F	W	PL	ZZZZ	USA
ERRE	11	M	CH	PL	ZZZZ	USA
SILBERSTEIN, LEA	25	F	W	PL	ZZZZ	USA
ITE	.08	F	INFANT	PL	ZZZZ	USA
BARSCHAN, RIEFKE	41	F	W	PL	ZZZZ	USA
STEFANIE	15	F	CH	PL	ZZZZ	USA
ADOLF	10	M	CH	PL	ZZZZ	USA
DEBOWSKY, RACHEL	24	F	W	RR	ZZZZ	USA
MEYER	.03	M	INFANT	RR	ZZZZ	USA
HELMANN, GERSON	20	M	PDLR	RR	ZZZZ	USA
RAHE	22	F	W	RR	ZZZZ	USA
SEGAL, SARA	30	F	W	RR	ZZZZ	USA
URIE	10	F	CH	RR	ZZZZ	USA
JECHIEL	8	M	CHILD	RR	ZZZZ	USA
DAVID	6	M	CHILD	RR	ZZZZ	USA

PASSENGER	AGE	SEX	OCCUPATION	PRIVL	DES
MALKE	2	F	CHILD	RRZZZZ	USA
SCHIKMANN, WOLFE	35	M	LABR	RRZZZZ	USA
SUSSEL	34	F	W	RRZZZZ	USA
CHAJE	2	F	CHILD	RRZZZZ	USA
MALKE	1	F	CHILD	RRZZZZ	USA
LEWITA, SARAH	31	F	W	RRZZZZ	USA
REIZEL	1	F	CHILD	RRZZZZ	USA
CHAMINKES, CHAZKE	30	F	W	RRZZZZ	USA
BEILE	8	M	CHILD	RRZZZZ	USA
ETHEL	6	F	CHILD	RRZZZZ	USA
EIDEL	3	M	CHILD	RRZZZZ	USA
RACHEL	1	M	CHILD	RRZZZZ	USA
PREISS, SUSSMAN	35	F	W	RRZZZZ	USA
JANKELL	10	M	CH	RRZZZZ	USA
ARONWITZ, WOLFF	00	M	PDLR	RRZZZZ	USA
CZENE	20	F	W	RRZZZZ	USA
WEINSTEIN, LEIB	29	M	PDLR	RRZZZZ	USA
FEIGE	27	F	W	RRZZZZ	USA
HANI	3	F	CHILD	RRZZZZ	USA
ABRAHAM	.06	M	INFANT	RRZZZZ	USA
WILENZIECK, JUDEL	45	M	PDLR	PLZZZZ	USA
FRIEDMANN, NACHIM	22	M	PDLR	PLZZZZ	USA
FILET, GUSTAV	45	M	PDLR	PLZZZZ	USA
NEUMANN, LOUIS	32	M	PDLR	PLZZZZ	USA
GOLEZYNSKI, ANTON	22	M	PDLR	PLZZZZ	USA
GOLDHANDLER, CHAIN	23	M	PDLR	PLZZZZ	USA
LIPPERT, MAX	23	M	PDLR	PLZZZZ	USA
LEWIN, RUBERT	30	M	LABR	RRZZZZ	USA
STARSS, SAMUEL	22	M	LABR	RRZZZZ	USA
KARFENTRAEGLER, ABEBAIL	37	M	LABR	RRZZZZ	USA
LEWIN, MOSES	35	M	LABR	RRZZZZ	USA
RASCH, EISIG	38	M	LABR	RRZZZZ	USA
RAZINCKY, JAKOB	26	M	LABR	RRZZZZ	USA
MICHACHKY, STANISLAUS	30	M	LABR	RRZZZZ	USA
GARBARSKY, ABRAHAM	20	M	LABR	RRZZZZ	USA
GROSS, BARUCH	21	M	LABR	RRZZZZ	USA
BASSKIND, DAVID	18	M	LABR	RRZZZZ	USA
SCHIMKOWITZ, MARCUS	19	M	PDLR	RRZZZZ	USA
MICHELSKY, MARCUS	18	M	PDLR	RRZZZZ	USA
MOSES, ISRAEL	19	M	PDLR	RRZZZZ	USA
MOWSCHAUS, ISAAK	26	M	PDLR	RRZZZZ	USA
GRUNFELD, A.	18	M	PDLR	RRZZZZ	USA
EFRON, MOSES	22	M	PDLR	RRZZZZ	USA
OLONA, SAKOUR	23	M	LABR	RRZZZZ	USA
CHAWALITZ, GEO	20	M	LABR	RRZZZZ	USA
BUNAK, JAN	18	M	LABR	RRZZZZ	USA
ONTACHER, CHAIM	25	M	LABR	RRZZZZ	USA
JECIM, JACOB	18	M	LABR	RRZZZZ	USA
LEWIN, GERSON	22	M	PDLR	RRZZZZ	USA
FEINAZ, JACHEL	45	M	LABR	RRZZZZ	USA
KAUFFMAN, MORDCHE	44	M	LABR	RRZZZZ	USA
WEISBROD, SELMAN	24	M	LABR	RRZZZZ	USA
SACHE, LEIB	11	M	CH	RRZZZZ	USA
HUTTELMANN, SCHWEIBEL	19	M	LABR	RRZZZZ	USA
BECKER, BENI	20	M	LABR	RRZZZZ	USA
MALKOWSKY, FISCHEL	45	M	LABR	RRZZZZ	USA
KATZ, NAFTALI	18	M	LABR	RRZZZZ	USA

SHIP: LABRADOR

FROM: HAVRE
TO: NEW YORK
ARRIVED: 02 SEPTEMBER 1885

PASSENGER	AGE	SEX	OCCUPATION	PRIVL	DES
ARNOLD, JACOB	28	F	DRSMKR	RRZZZZ	NY
PATRIS, JACOB	00	F	DRSMKR	RRZZZZ	NY

SHIP: NOORDLAND

FROM: ANTWERP
TO: NEW YORK
ARRIVED: 02 SEPTEMBER 1885

PASSENGER	AGE	SEX	OCCUPATION	PRIVL	DES
FZOFANOUSKI, FR.	38	M	UNKNOWN	RRZZZZ	NY
KASKOWSKA, W.	25	M	UNKNOWN	RRZZZZ	NY
STAPIRA, EST.	21	M	UNKNOWN	RRACBF	NY

SHIP: CITY OF WASHINGTON

FROM: UNKNOWN
TO: NEW YORK
ARRIVED: 03 SEPTEMBER 1885

PASSENGER	AGE	SEX	OCCUPATION	PRIVL	DES
GOFITITS, VICHI	20	M	STDNT	RRZZZZ	NY

SHIP: CITY OF BERLIN

FROM: LIVERPOOL AND QUEENSTOWN
TO: NEW YORK
ARRIVED: 04 SEPTEMBER 1885

PASSENGER	AGE	SEX	OCCUPATION	PRIVL	DES
WROBELOWITZ, MO.	00	F	INF	RRACBF	WI
JAILETOWITZ, JANKEL	35	M	LABR	RRACBF	NY
CHANNE	30	F	W	RRACBF	NY
GOLD	2	M	CHILD	RRACBF	NY
ITZIG	00	M	INF	RRACBF	NY
NERBELOWITZ, FREIDE	28	F	W	RRACBF	NY
CHANE	4	F	CHILD	RRACBF	NY
BARRSCHE	2	M	CHILD	RRACBF	NY
ZICHERMANN, NESCHMANN	30	M	LABR	RRACBF	NY
CZEMERCOWSKI, MARCEI	23	M	LABR	RRACBF	NY
FREEDSTEIN, RUEN	22	M	LABR	RRADBQ	NY

SHIP: DONAU

FROM: BREMEN
TO: NEW YORK
ARRIVED: 04 SEPTEMBER 1885

PASSENGER	AGE	SEX	OCCUPATION	PRIVL	DES
LEWIT, MERET	24	F	NN	RRZZZZ	USA
SEGAL, TAUBE	30	F	NN	RRZZZZ	USA
LYNKOWSKI, CHRIST	18	M	LABR	RRZZZZ	USA
RISLEWITZ, MART.	18	M	LABR	RRZZZZ	USA
BERMANN, JANKEL	20	M	FARMER	RRZZZZ	USA
SCHAPIRO, BACHEL	38	F	NN	RRZZZZ	USA
ISAAK	7	M	CHILD	RRZZZZ	USA
DAVID	5	M	CHILD	RRZZZZ	USA
PAIE	.08	F	INFANT	RRZZZZ	USA
EIHELDINGER, JOS.	23	M	FARMER	RRZZZZ	USA
WEBER, JOS.	45	M	FARMER	RRZZZZ	USA
SCHAPIRO, ARNCH.	20	M	LABR	RRZZZZ	USA
GORDON, ABRAH.	16	M	FARMER	RRZZZZ	USA
SCHAPIRO, TILLE	16	F	NN	RRZZZZ	USA
BANNER, JOHANNA	35	F	NN	RRZZZZ	USA
LESE	7	F	CHILD	RRZZZZ	USA
ABEL	6	F	CHILD	RRZZZZ	USA

PASSENGER	AGE	SEX	OCCUPATION	PRV VIL DES
BASKE	3	F	CHILD	RRZZZZUSA
JUNSZACZKA, ANNA	18	F	NN	RRZZZZUSA
SCHAPIRO, RACHEL	30	F	NN	RRZZZZUSA
LIEBKE	7	F	CHILD	RRZZZZUSA
HENE	4	F	CHILD	RRZZZZUSA
CHASTELKEWITZ, ESTHER	35	F	NN	RRZZZZUSA
GITTEL	4	F	CHILD	RRZZZZUSA
FREUD	7	F	CHILD	RRZZZZUSA
ROSKE	6	F	CHILD	RRZZZZUSA
RUSCHINSKI, FRUMA	50	M	FARMER	RRZZZZUSA
HIE	17	M	CH	RRZZZZUSA
TRICH	7	M	CHILD	RRZZZZUSA
BESCHE	6	F	CHILD	RRZZZZUSA
DAVID	6	M	CHILD	RRZZZZUSA
SARAH	30	F	NN	RRZZZZUSA
TACHA	7	F	CHILD	RRZZZZUSA
BEIE	5	F	CHILD	RRZZZZUSA
SALOMO	4	M	CHILD	RRZZZZUSA
BEILE	2	F	CHILD	RRZZZZUSA
BRASCHE	.03	F	INFANT	RRZZZZUSA
STOHN, ERI	30	F	NN	RRZZZZUSA
HENNY	7	F	CHILD	RRZZZZUSA
ABRAHAM	4	M	CHILD	RRZZZZUSA
SZAJA	.02	F	INFANT	RRZZZZUSA
DEWARSKY, CHANNA	40	F	NN	RRZZZZUSA
BESCHE	7	F	CHILD	RRZZZZUSA
BESCHE	6	F	CHILD	RRZZZZUSA
JOSEL	4	M	CHILD	RRZZZZUSA
PELKIN, SARAH	30	F	NN	RRZZZZUSA
RAVE	4	F	CHILD	RRZZZZUSA
BEREL	.04	M	INFANT	RRZZZZUSA
GARSON, BERUH	28	M	FARMER	RRZZZZUSA
MATTI, STEPHAN	30	M	FARMER	RRZZZZUSA
KLIWANOWSKY, MOSES	21	M	CL	RRZZZZUSA
SLOWINSKY, MARGOLES	29	F	NN	RRZZZZUSA
ABRAHAM	.10	M	INFANT	RRZZZZUSA
LEWNSOHN, MARCUS	35	M	FARMER	RRZZZZUSA
REBECCA	33	F	W	RRZZZZUSA
ANNA	11	F	CH	RRZZZZUSA
SARAH	7	F	CHILD	RRZZZZUSA
JACOB	7	M	CHILD	RRZZZZUSA
REIL	5	M	CHILD	RRZZZZUSA
MARCUS	.10	M	INFANT	RRZZZZUSA
WEIDENBACH, HEINR.	22	M	FARMER	RRZZZZUSA
TRAUTNER, LUDW.	21	M	FARMER	RRZZZZUSA
BATASCHINKA, TRINA	18	F	NN	RRZZZZUSA
BLOCK, SARAH	40	F	NN	RRZZZZUSA
FREIDE	.07	F	INFANT	RRZZZZUSA
BROSOWSKY, CHAIN	30	F	NN	RRZZZZUSA
RISCHINSKY, JOS.	23	M	LABR	RRZZZZUSA
MONICA	4	F	CHILD	RRZZZZUSA
AHER	.10	F	INFANT	RRZZZZUSA
BLOCK, ROCHEL	11	F	CH	RRZZZZUSA
ALEXANDROWITZ, PESCHE	23	F	W	RRZZZZUSA
FRUNZ, ISRAEL	59	M	CPTR	RRZZZZUSA
KAHLMANN, ALB.	20	M	CPTR	RRZZZZUSA
TUHRMANN, FEIDEL	7	F	CHILD	RRZZZZUSA
TOPILSKY, SORE	30	F	NN	RRZZZZUSA
CHAWE	7	F	CHILD	RRZZZZUSA
HIRSCH	6	M	CHILD	RRZZZZUSA

SHIP: ELBE

FROM: BREMEN
TO: NEW YORK
ARRIVED: 05 SEPTEMBER 1885

PASSENGER	AGE	SEX	OCCUPATION	PRV VIL DES
FUNK, CORNELIUS	48	M	LABR	RRZZZZUSA
ELISAB.	44	F	W	RRZZZZUSA
ELISAB.	20	F	NN	RRZZZZUSA
ANNA	17	F	NN	RRZZZZUSA
HELENE	15	F	CH	RRZZZZUSA
MARIE	12	F	CH	RRZZZZUSA
AGATHA	4	F	CHILD	RRZZZZUSA
MARY	.06	F	INFANT	RRZZZZUSA
CATH.	.03	F	INFANT	RRZZZZUSA
SCHULZ, DAVID	43	M	LABR	RRZZZZUSA
ELISAB.	38	F	W	RRZZZZUSA
HELENE	6	F	CHILD	RRZZZZUSA
BENJAMIN	4	M	CHILD	RRZZZZUSA
ELISAB.	2	F	CHILD	RRZZZZUSA
RIFFEL, GEORG	34	M	LABR	RRZZZZUSA
MARG.	20	F	W	RRZZZZUSA
JOHANN	8	M	CHILD	RRZZZZUSA
DAVID	4	M	CHILD	RRZZZZUSA
GEORG	.06	M	INFANT	RRZZZZUSA
WEDEL, B.	29	M	CPTR	RRZZZZUSA
CATH.	30	F	W	RRZZZZUSA
MARIA	7	F	CHILD	RRZZZZUSA
CAMELIUS	5	M	CHILD	RRZZZZUSA
FUNK, HEINR.	46	M	FARMER	RRZZZZUSA
ANNA	43	F	W	RRZZZZUSA
MARIA	17	F	CH	RRZZZZUSA
ANNA	15	F	CH	RRZZZZUSA
SUSANNA	13	F	CH	RRZZZZUSA
HEINRICH	10	M	CH	RRZZZZUSA
MARY	2	F	CHILD	RRZZZZUSA
ESAN, CORNELIUS	48	M	LABR	RRZZZZUSA
HELENE	45	F	W	RRZZZZUSA
HEINRICH	20	M	LABR	RRZZZZUSA
CORNELIUS	18	M	LABR	RRZZZZUSA
HELENE	11	F	CH	RRZZZZUSA
MARY	7	F	CHILD	RRZZZZUSA
REINER, CORNELIUS	23	M	LABR	RRZZZZUSA
ECK, PETER	46	M	FARMER	RRZZZZUSA
AGNES	47	F	W	RRZZZZUSA
JACOB	20	M	FARMER	RRZZZZUSA
JOHANN	16	M	FARMER	RRZZZZUSA
TOBIAS	14	M	CH	RRZZZZUSA
BENJAMIN	12	M	CH	RRZZZZUSA
PETER	9	M	CHILD	RRZZZZUSA
HELENE	2	F	CHILD	RRZZZZUSA
KOPP, ISAAC	52	M	MCHT	RRZZZZUSA
CATH.	28	F	NN	RRZZZZUSA
CATH.	3	F	CHILD	RRZZZZUSA
ISAAC	.09	M	INFANT	RRZZZZUSA
KROEKER, FRANZ	23	M	LABR	RRZZZZUSA
ELISAB.	22	F	W	RRZZZZUSA
SCHMIDT, DAVID	50	M	FARMER	RRZZZZUSA
EVA	48	F	W	RRZZZZUSA
PETER	17	M	FARMER	RRZZZZUSA
AGNES	15	F	CH	RRZZZZUSA
JACOB	14	M	CH	RRZZZZUSA
ANNA	12	F	CH	RRZZZZUSA
HEINZ	8	M	CHILD	RRZZZZUSA
DANIEL	6	M	CHILD	RRZZZZUSA
DAVID	1	M	CHILD	RRZZZZUSA
TUNK, JACOB	33	M	FARMER	RRZZZZUSA
MARIE	20	F	W	RRZZZZUSA
JACOB	1	M	CHILD	RRZZZZUSA
MARIE	.01	F	INFANT	RRZZZZUSA
JANZEN, HEINE	49	M	FARMER	RRZZZZUSA
ANNA	50	F	W	RRZZZZUSA
JACOB	17	M	FARMER	RRZZZZUSA
MARIE	14	F	CH	RRZZZZUSA
FRANZ	10	M	CH	RRZZZZUSA
KOOP, GERHARD	23	M	FARMER	RRZZZZUSA
CATH.	21	F	W	RRZZZZUSA
ANNA	2	F	CHILD	RRZZZZUSA
MARIE	.01	F	INFANT	RRZZZZUSA
WIENZ, DIETRICH	50	M	FARMER	RRZZZZUSA
LOUISE	26	F	NN	RRZZZZUSA
AGATA	18	F	NN	RRZZZZUSA
MARIA	16	F	NN	RRZZZZUSA
ANNA	12	F	NN	RRZZZZUSA

PASSENGER	AGE	SEX	OCCUPATION	PRV VIL DES
DAVID	10	M	NN	RRZZZZUSA
SCHAPIRO, SLOTE	66	M	LABR	RRZZZZUSA
HARTIG, CLARA	21	F	NN	RRZZZZUSA
BECK, HANS	32	M	LABR	RRZZZZUSA
TIGER, CARL	40	M	FARMER	RRZZZZUSA
LINA	20	F	W	RRZZZZUSA
BERTHA	18	F	CH	RRZZZZUSA
SZACHNOWSKY, RIVA	23	F	NN	RRZZZZUSA
MEISCHE	.09	M	INFANT	RRZZZZUSA
FRIEDMANN, BEILE	19	F	NN	RRZZZZUSA
SCHICK, PHILIPP	25	M	LABR	RRZZZZUSA
LITISEWSKY, FRANK	36	M	FARMER	RRZZZZUSA
HINDIN, LEIL	50	M	FARMER	RRZZZZUSA
JUL.	45	F	W	RRZZZZUSA
FRIED.	17	M	FARMER	RRZZZZUSA
HIRSCH	8	M	CHILD	RRZZZZUSA
SIMON	5	M	CHILD	RRZZZZUSA
LUDGIN, BOCHE-SEIL	20	F	NN	RRZZZZUSA
MEYER	7	M	CHILD	RRZZZZUSA
MARIA	4	F	CHILD	RRZZZZUSA

SHIP: INDIA

FROM: HAMBURG
TO: NEW YORK
ARRIVED: 07 SEPTEMBER 1885

PASSENGER	AGE	SEX	OCCUPATION	PRV VIL DES
FRIEDMANN, HIRSCHE	24	F	WO	RRZZZZNY
LEIBE	.06	M	INFANT	RRZZZZNY
KOZEL, BERKA	27	M	LABR	RRZZZZNY
SKAP, SALOM.	20	M	LABR	RRZZZZNY
ROGALSKI, MINSCHER	46	F	WO	RRZZZZIL
HERTZ	12	M	S	RRZZZZIL
FEIGEL	20	F	D	RRZZZZIL
BRAUNSTEIN, JOSEF	40	M	MCHT	RRZZZZUNK
PESCHE	22	F	D	RRZZZZUNK
BALKOSADSKY, LOUIS	19	M	LABR	RRZZZZNY
TAPALOWSKY, SARA	50	F	WO	RRZZZZNY
ANNA	7	F	CHILD	RRZZZZNY
ELKA	6	F	CHILD	RRZZZZNY
LORBET, BELA	37	F	WO	RRZZZZNY
CHANE	12	F	D	RRZZZZNY
MOSES	7	M	CHILD	RRZZZZNY
LEZZIE	.06	F	INFANT	RRZZZZNY
JANKEL	5	M	CHILD	RRZZZZNY
BUNTMANN, HANNA	20	F	SGL	RRZZZZNY
KIRSTEIN, SIEGM.	19	M	MCHT	RRZZZZIL
ZELMA, JOSEFA	60	F	SGL	RRZZZZIL
SUESMANN, RABE	46	F	WO	RRZZZZIL
BERTHA	7	F	CHILD	RRZZZZIL
DETTELBAUM, B.	24	F	SGL	RRZZZZIL
WALCROKY, FRANZ	28	M	LABR	RRZZZZNY
MENDELSOHN, LEOPOLD	34	M	SHMK	RRZZZZIL
SALOMONSOHN, SCHLOM	22	M	JNR	RRZZZZIL
BUBEN, MARCUS	21	M	TRDSMN	RRZZZZNY
FETUKER, SORE	23	F	WO	RRZZZZNY
SASHE	.07	M	INFANT	RRZZZZNY
KRAWICZ, LEIB	23	M	TRDSMN	RRZZZZNY
SCHLOME	26	M	TRDSMN	RRZZZZNY
COHN, CHAJE	20	F	SGL	RRZZZZNY
SCHWEIDSTEIN, JOEL	18	M	TRDSMN	RRZZZZNY
KATZ, TODEL	7	M	CHILD	RRZZZZNY
LUKZAJTES, JACOB	17	M	LABR	RRZZZZNY
ADAM	20	M	LABR	RRZZZZNY
BERNSTEIN, CHR.B.	20	F	WO	RRZZZZNY
MALKE, BASSIE	13	F	CH	RRZZZZNY
EDEL, SALOM	7	M	CHILD	RRZZZZNY
FELDMANN, HIRSCH	16	M	LABR	RRZZZZNY
BRADSTEIN, HIRSCH	21	M	LABR	RRZZZZNY
CHANS	20	F	W	RRZZZZNY

PASSENGER	AGE	SEX	OCCUPATION	PRV VIL DES
HELPERT, M.	39	M	LABR	RRZZZZNY
KATSCHKE, CHAIM	45	M	LABR	RRZZZZIL
WULF, BENZIL	35	M	LABR	RRZZZZNY
TEMPKA, MAX	35	M	LABR	RRZZZZPA

SHIP: LA NORMANDIE

FROM: HAVRE
TO: NEW YORK
ARRIVED: 07 SEPTEMBER 1885

PASSENGER	AGE	SEX	OCCUPATION	PRV VIL DES
CHASCHEWSKY, NICOLAI-MR	35	M	UNKNOWN	RRZZZZNY
ROTTARY, U-MR	28	M	UNKNOWN	RRZZZZMX
SIGESMOND, S.B.MR	51	M	UNKNOWN	RRZZZZBAL
ARECINAKI, KAZNNIAR	24	M	UNKNOWN	PLZZZZCAN
SOSNOWSKY, BERNAW	20	M	SDLR	PLZZZZNY
RUDZKI, EADENSY	20	M	SDLR	PLZZZZNY

SHIP: RUGIA

FROM: HAMBURG
TO: NEW YORK
ARRIVED: 07 SEPTEMBER 1885

PASSENGER	AGE	SEX	OCCUPATION	PRV VIL DES
ARONOWSKI, ABR.	17	M	CGRMKR	RRZZZZUSA
KAPLAN, JOS.	19	M	BCHR	RRZZZZUSA
ARONOWSKI, LIESEL	39	M	CL	RRZZZZUSA
PICARIKI, RACHEL	27	F	W	RRZZZZUSA
JULS	6	M	CHILD	RRZZZZUSA
LINI	4	F	CHILD	RRZZZZUSA
MAX	.09	M	INFANT	RRZZZZUSA
GOLTER, SCHRIM	26	F	W	RRZZZZUSA
ARON	.11	M	INFANT	RRZZZZUSA
LUCINDE	4	F	CHILD	RRZZZZUSA
REIHOLD	.11	M	INFANT	RRZZZZUSA
FREDERIKSEN, CHRISTINE	36	F	W	RRZZZZUSA
ANNA	3	F	CHILD	RRZZZZUSA
HOPPE, CHS.H.	37	M	LABR	RRZZZZUSA
BENDER, JOHANNE	64	F	W	RRZZZZUSA
STUKEROWITZ, TH.	21	M	CL	RRZZZZUSA
PILONSKY, MOSES	20	M	MUSN	RRZZZZUSA
FOBLONSKY, MOSES	24	M	BKMR	RRZZZZUSA
BEERFELD, FRIEDEL	27	M	TLR	RRZZZZUSA
TAUBE	20	F	W	RRZZZZUSA
HOTENBERG, MEYER	18	M	TLR	RRZZZZUSA
ROSENBLUM, NOTTE	18	M	TLR	RRZZZZUSA
KRUL, DWORE	9	F	CHILD	RRZZZZUSA
LAU, RACHEL	30	F	W	RRZZZZUSA
SALMEN	9	M	CHILD	RRZZZZUSA
ROSENBLUM, FRUME	9	F	CHILD	RRZZZZUSA
WOLFF, FRIDR.	20	M	LABR	RRZZZZUSA
LEVY, PEREL	50	F	W	RRZZZZUSA
MADREL	9	F	CHILD	RRZZZZUSA
P--N, RACHEL	28	F	W	RRZZZZUSA
FRIEDR.	.04	M	INFANT	RRZZZZUSA
POKROWSKY, ASCHER	20	M	TLR	RRZZZZUSA
SCHON, SIMON	20	M	TLR	RRZZZZUSA
NORDMAN, NATHALIE	21	F	SGL	RRZZZZUSA
BERKOWITZ, RIVKE	17	F	SGL	RRZZZZUSA
GITTEL	60	F	W	RRZZZZUSA
BERNSTEIN, MOSES	22	M	LABR	RRZZZZUSA
ROSA	18	F	W	RRZZZZUSA
NIMEROWSKI, FEIGE	18	F	SGL	RRZZZZUSA
JANKEL	12	F	SI	RRZZZZUSA
REBECCA	9	F	CHILD	RRZZZZUSA

PASSENGER	A G E	S E X	OCCUPATION	P R V	V I L	D E S
SAHRA	8	F	CHILD	RR	ZZZZ	USA
MOTTE	4	F	CHILD	RR	ZZZZ	USA
GITTEL	2	F	CHILD	RR	ZZZZ	USA
MLAMETH, CIPPE	24	F	W	RR	ZZZZ	USA
JUDEL	.04	F	INFANT	RR	ZZZZ	USA
BRAUN, ABRECH	54	M	LABR	RR	ZZZZ	USA
BERNHARD	19	M	CH	RR	ZZZZ	USA
JULIE	15	F	CH	RR	ZZZZ	USA
FANNY	12	F	CH	RR	ZZZZ	USA
WOLF, ELKA	18	F	SGL	RR	ZZZZ	USA
NUEMAN, SCHMUEL	28	M	DLR	RR	ZZZZ	USA
ROSENBERG, RACHEL	32	F	W	RR	ZZZZ	USA
VICTOR	9	M	CHILD	RR	ZZZZ	USA
GITTE	7	F	CHILD	RR	ZZZZ	USA
GISCHE	6	F	CHILD	RR	ZZZZ	USA
EGE	3	F	CHILD	RR	ZZZZ	USA
IDA	.11	F	INFANT	RR	ZZZZ	USA
SILBERSTEIN, MOSES	21	M	MCHT	RR	ZZZZ	USA
SOPHIE	18	F	W	RR	ZZZZ	USA
KANTOR, MORITZ	24	M	JWLR	RR	ZZZZ	USA
MASCHE	20	F	W	RR	ZZZZ	USA
WESTEN, REBECCA	20	F	SGL	RR	ZZZZ	USA
KORN, PAIE	30	F	W	RR	ZZZZ	USA
RIVE	9	F	CHILD	RR	ZZZZ	USA
JASEL	.11	F	INFANT	RR	ZZZZ	USA
SCHNEE, LINE	20	F	SGL	RR	ZZZZ	USA
WITSCHKI, FLIA	17	M	MCHT	RR	ZZZZ	USA
ANNETHE	20	F	SGL	RR	ZZZZ	USA
JAKOBOWITZ, RACHEL	20	F	SGL	RR	ZZZZ	USA
ROCK, FEIGE	23	F	SGL	RR	ZZZZ	USA
KATZ, ALTER	6	M	CHILD	RR	ZZZZ	USA
MOSCHKOWITZ, MARIE	39	F	W	RR	ZZZZ	USA
ZURANSKY, MARTIN	26	M	LABR	RR	ZZZZ	USA
ROSALIE	19	F	W	RR	ZZZZ	USA
WOLLMANN, RUD.	24	M	LABR	RR	ZZZZ	USA
KON, VANIEL	23	M	LABR	RR	ZZZZ	USA
JOSEFA	18	F	W	RR	ZZZZ	USA
WICKSTEIN, SARA	18	F	SGL	RR	ZZZZ	USA
REIMAN, DORA	21	F	W	RR	ZZZZ	USA
LEISER	.11	M	INFANT	RR	ZZZZ	USA
GUDDEWICZEWA, URSULA	19	F	SGL	RR	ZZZZ	USA
ACKERMANN, KONSTANTIN	25	M	LABR	RR	ZZZZ	USA
LUDOWIKA	20	F	W	RR	ZZZZ	USA
STANISLAUS	9	M	CHILD	RR	ZZZZ	USA
ADAMOWITZ, PROKIEDA	27	F	W	RR	ZZZZ	USA
APPELSTEIN, GETTO	22	F	SGL	RR	ZZZZ	USA
STRAGONSKI, DAVID	14	M	TLR	RR	ZZZZ	USA
RYBACH, ARON	20	M	MCHT	RR	ZZZZ	USA
MORIMOND, JOSEPH	20	M	LABR	RR	ZZZZ	USA
MARGOWITZ, RIWKE	16	F	SGL	RR	ZZZZ	USA
BURSTEIN, CHLAWNE	40	M	PRWKR	RR	ZZZZ	USA
JESNER, SARA	20	F	SGL	RR	ZZZZ	USA
LEWKOWITZ, ISAAC	20	M	TLR	RR	ZZZZ	USA
CHAIT, JACOB	32	M	LABR	RR	ZZZZ	USA
SARA	9	F	CHILD	RR	ZZZZ	USA
GRADENSKI, FEIGE	16	F	SGL	RR	ZZZZ	USA
LINDENBAITH, ANNA	17	F	SGL	RR	ZZZZ	USA
BENZIG, ANDR.	21	M	JNR	RR	ZZZZ	USA
HERSCHBERG, SCHEINE	20	F	SGL	RR	ZZZZ	USA
GOLDSTEIN, RACHEL	17	F	SGL	RR	ZZZZ	USA
RACHAME	50	F	W	RR	ZZZZ	USA
GOSCHER, LOUIS	23	M	LABR	RR	ZZZZ	USA
RACHEL	22	F	W	RR	ZZZZ	USA
COHN, SAMUEL	22	M	LABR	RR	ZZZZ	USA
POLLACK, HANNE	36	F	W	RR	ZZZZ	USA
DAVID	.11	M	INFANT	RR	ZZZZ	USA
CHARNASS, RACHEL	17	F	SGL	RR	ZZZZ	USA
PETERS, HEIN	28	M	FARMER	RR	ZZZZ	USA
SARA	25	F	W	RR	ZZZZ	USA
HELENE	2	F	CHILD	RR	ZZZZ	USA
PETER	.11	M	INFANT	RR	ZZZZ	USA
ELISABETH	.01	F	INFANT	RR	ZZZZ	USA
REWS, PETER	60	M	FARMER	RR	ZZZZ	USA
SARA	45	F	W	RR	ZZZZ	USA
ELISABETH	22	F	CH	RR	ZZZZ	USA

PASSENGER	A G E	S E X	OCCUPATION	P R V	V I L	D E S
MARIE	16	F	CH	RR	ZZZZ	USA
PETER	14	M	CH	RR	ZZZZ	USA
GUSTAV	12	M	CH	RR	ZZZZ	USA
ABR.	9	M	CHILD	RR	ZZZZ	USA
JOHANN	8	M	CHILD	RR	ZZZZ	USA
NEUFELD, JOHN	42	M	FARMER	RR	ZZZZ	USA
JOHN	30	F	W	RR	ZZZZ	USA
EVA	16	F	CH	RR	ZZZZ	USA
JOHN	15	M	CH	RR	ZZZZ	USA
HEIN	12	M	CH	RR	ZZZZ	USA
PETER	9	M	CHILD	RR	ZZZZ	USA
MARIE	2	F	CHILD	RR	ZZZZ	USA
HERRMANN, JOHN	21	M	MCHT	RR	ZZZZ	USA
LINDROSS, HERRMANN	20	M	SEMN	FN	ZZZZ	USA
SCHWARZBERG, ABRAHAM	21	M	UNKNOWN	RR	ZZZZ	USA
OESTERLING, AUG.	42	M	FARMER	RR	ZZZZ	USA
ELISABETH	34	F	W	RR	ZZZZ	USA
PETER	7	M	CHILD	RR	ZZZZ	USA
WILH.	4	M	CHILD	RR	ZZZZ	USA
ELISABETH	.06	F	INFANT	RR	ZZZZ	USA
WILH.	20	M	CH	RR	ZZZZ	USA
TAUBE, ARINA	47	F	W	RR	ZZZZ	USA
MARIE	19	F	CH	RR	ZZZZ	USA
HELENE	15	F	CH	RR	ZZZZ	USA
SOPHIE	9	F	CHILD	RR	ZZZZ	USA
NICOLAI	9	M	CHILD	RR	ZZZZ	USA
PUCZKANER, SIMON	36	M	LABR	RR	ZZZZ	USA
SMARGON, CHAIE	35	F	W	RR	ZZZZ	USA
PERETZ	9	M	CHILD	RR	ZZZZ	USA
JANKEL	8	M	CHILD	RR	ZZZZ	USA
LEIB	7	M	CHILD	RR	ZZZZ	USA
CHASKE	5	M	CHILD	RR	ZZZZ	USA
LUOKERMANN, JASSEL	9	M	CHILD	RR	ZZZZ	USA

SHIP: ANCHORIA

FROM: GLASGOW
TO: NEW YORK
ARRIVED: 08 SEPTEMBER 1885

PASSENGER	A G E	S E X	OCCUPATION	P R V	V I L	D E S
AJAHRING, SOOL.	21	F	SVNT	RR	ACBF	USA
BERUSHOWITZ, BILLED	29	M	PDLR	RR	ACBF	USA
BIRALYSTAKA, RACHEL	21	F	NN	RR	ACBF	USA
GUTTEL	22	F	NN	RR	ACBF	USA
WATALSKI, REISEL	14	M	CH	RR	ACBF	USA
DEMANT, CHAJE	20	F	SVNT	RR	ACBF	USA
FEINBERG, SARA	17	F	DRSMKR	RR	ACBF	USA
UZIL	12	F	CH	RR	ACBF	USA
CHAJE	10	F	CH	RR	ACBF	USA
JEKEL, JUDEL	19	M	PDLR	RR	ACBF	USA
MULLER, ROSHE	18	F	SVNT	RR	ACBF	USA
REICHEL, MAX	17	M	LKSH	RR	ACBF	USA
ROSENKOWITZ, LEA	22	F	NN	RR	ACBF	USA
MOSES	1	M	CHILD	RR	ACBF	USA
SCHAPIRA, ABRAHAM	45	M	DLR	RR	AFVG	USA
CHANE	43	M	NN	RR	AFVG	USA
CHAJEM	15	M	CH	RR	AFVG	USA
DAVID	11	M	CH	RR	AFVG	USA
BEILE	10	M	CH	RR	AFVG	USA
RACHEL	7	F	CHILD	RR	AFVG	USA
ISAAC	5	M	CHILD	RR	AFVG	USA
LEKAR	2	M	CHILD	RR	AFVG	USA

SHIP: FULDA

FROM: BREMEN
TO: NEW YORK
ARRIVED: 09 SEPTEMBER 1885

PASSENGER	AGE	SEX	OCCUPATION	PV RI VL DES
KOSZOREK, ALEXANDER	26	M	FARMER	RRAEFLUSA
BINDER, MARY	30	F	UNKNOWN	RRAEFLUSA
HELKE	8	F	CHILD	RRAEFLUSA
NACHANKA	7	F	CHILD	RRAEFLUSA
BENJAMIN	4	M	CHILD	RRAEFLUSA
LOUIS	3	M	CHILD	RRAEFLUSA
SELMA	.11	F	INFANT	RRAEFLUSA
FRANK, NECHANE	30	M	FARMER	RRAEFLUSA
CAPITI	8	F	CHILD	RRAEFLUSA
NASINSKA	4	F	CHILD	RRAEFLUSA
ICHNA	.11	F	INFANT	RRAEFLUSA
ROSENBLUM, SAMUEL	26	M	CGRMKR	RRAHOKUSA
ELIAS, JUDOZA	17	F	CH	RRAHOKUSA
ROSENBLUM, DEVORA	18	F	CH	RRAHOKUSA
BECK, CHAIE	3	F	CHILD	RRAHOKUSA

SHIP: WISCONSIN

FROM: LIVERPOOL AND QUEENSTOWN
TO: NEW YORK
ARRIVED: 09 SEPTEMBER 1885

PASSENGER	AGE	SEX	OCCUPATION	PV RI VL DES
MEYEROWICZ, MORDSHE	27	M	LABR	RRAGRTUSA
KAPLAN, LEISER-ISAAC	19	M	LABR	RRAGRTUSA
MOSSESOHN, MOSES	28	M	LABR	RRZZZZUSA
SERGINSKY, SCHMUBL	19	M	LABR	RRAFWJUSA
FERG.	18	M	LABR	RRAFWJUSA

SHIP: STATE OF INDIANA

FROM: GLASGOW AND LARNE
TO: NEW YORK
ARRIVED: 10 SEPTEMBER 1885

PASSENGER	AGE	SEX	OCCUPATION	PV RI VL DES
KELNI, HIRSCH	26	M	LABR	RRAHOKUSA
BEREL	26	M	PDLR	RRAHOKUSA
GILLESCH, BEREL	16	M	PDLR	RRZZZZUSA
KELNI, NATHAN	20	M	PDLR	RRAHOKUSA
SCHANHAM, ABRAHAM	20	M	PDLR	RRZZZZUSA
LOEWENTHAL, ABRAHAM	24	M	PDLR	RRAHOKUSA
KIZNIK, MOSES	18	M	PDLR	RRZZZZUSA
STATKEWITZ, HERSCH	28	M	PDLR	RRZZZZUSA
KELNI, FEIGE	43	M	PDLR	RRAHOKUSA
NEUMANN, THEODOR	25	M	LABR	RRACBFUSA
MARKUS, JOSEPH	19	M	SHMK	RRZZZZUSA
SCHOCHET, LEISER	19	M	TLR	RRZZZZUSA
EFRACKEN, MARCUS	20	M	CL	RRZZZZUSA
SIW, NATHAN	19	M	WCHMKR	RRZZZZUSA
SCHONBRECHT, JOSSEL	24	M	PDLR	RRAHOKUSA
HIRSCH	22	M	PDLR	RRAHOKUSA
EISENBERG, NOAH	22	M	PDLR	RRAHOKUSA
GEWALKOWSKY, ISAAK	18	M	BKR	RRACBFUSA
NOAK, JOSEPH	28	M	LABR	RRABUTUSA
MANDEL, JOSEPH	31	M	CGRMKR	PLZZZZUSA
MONATE, ALTER	34	M	PDLR	PLZZZZUSA
BERGTHAL, LEIZER	24	M	TLR	PLZZZZUSA
OLLENSFUNNER, ISRAEL-BA	46	M	PDLR	PLZZZZUSA
OLLENSFUNNER, RAPHAEL	12	M	CH	PLZZZZUSA
BADER, ELIAS	60	M	PDLR	PLZZZZUSA
WOLFENSOHN, FEIGE	17	F	SP	PLZZZZUSA
KELNI, PEREL	20	F	SP	PLAHOKUSA
DRUCK, JETTE	21	F	SP	RRZZZZUSA
TAUBER, REBEKKA	20	F	SP	RRZZZZUSA
GORFUSS, HELENA	43	F	SP	RRACSDUSA
SCHOENBRETT, KATARINE	20	F	SP	RRAHOKUSA
DEBORAH	16	F	SP	RRAHOKUSA
SAKOVIC, JOSEPH	27	M	LABR	PLZZZZUSA
MAGDA	20	F	W	PLZZZZUSA
SCHAD, EIDEL	20	F	W	RRZZZZUSA
DAVID	2	M	CHILD	RRZZZZUSA
MOLKE	.03	F	INFANT	RRZZZZUSA
SCHINEBECKER, SARAH	30	F	W	RRZZZZUSA
ESTHER	2	F	CHILD	RRZZZZUSA
SCHINBRETT, SCHLOME	45	M	DLR	RRAHOKUSA
CHANE	45	F	W	RRAHOKUSA
ITZIG	14	M	CH	RRAHOKUSA
SHIFRE	12	F	CH	RRAHOKUSA
FEIGE	9	F	CHILD	RRAHOKUSA
GITEL	5	F	CHILD	RRAHOKUSA
MOSES	7	M	CHILD	RRAHOKUSA
RUNIE	4	F	CHILD	RRAHOKUSA
RIFKE	1	F	CHILD	RRAHOKUSA
NOAH	.03	M	INFANT	RRAHOKUSA
KELNI, BARUCH	43	F	PDLR	RRAHOKUSA
CHANE	43	F	W	RRAHOKUSA
RIFKE	12	F	CH	RRAHOKUSA
ESTHER	9	F	CHILD	RRAHOKUSA
LEA	5	F	CHILD	RRAHOKUSA
HINDE	4	F	CHILD	RRAHOKUSA
CHAJE	.03	F	INFANT	RRAHOKUSA
CHASEN, LEIB	24	M	PDLR	RRAHTFUSA
ZIPE	20	F	W	RRAHTFUSA
MULLER, ITZIG	23	M	PDLR	RRAHOKUSA
BASIL	20	F	W	RRAHOKUSA
RUME	.09	F	INFANT	RRAHOKUSA
KRULL, EISIK	40	M	TCHR	RRZZZZUSA
MALKE	36	F	W	RRZZZZUSA
JOSSEL	8	M	CHILD	RRZZZZUSA
CHANNE	5	F	CHILD	RRZZZZUSA
ISRAEL	2	M	CHILD	RRZZZZUSA
ESTHER	2	F	CHILD	RRZZZZUSA
SIMON	.06	M	INFANT	RRZZZZUSA
AMSCHINSKY, NISEN	38	M	PDLR	PLZZZZUSA
NESCHE	28	F	W	PLZZZZUSA
CHANNE	2	F	CHILD	PLZZZZUSA
MARIE	.06	F	INFANT	PLZZZZUSA
ROSENFELD, ABRAHAM	60	M	PDLR	PLZZZZUSA
HINDE	45	F	W	PLZZZZUSA
JOSEPH	13	M	CH	PLZZZZUSA
CHAJE	11	F	CH	PLZZZZUSA
REBEKKA	9	F	CHILD	PLZZZZUSA
CHANE	7	F	CHILD	PLZZZZUSA
HENY	5	F	CHILD	PLZZZZUSA
FEIGE	1	F	CHILD	PLZZZZUSA
WOLFENSOHN, ISAAC	34	M	GZR	PLZZZZUSA
DWORA	33	F	W	PLZZZZUSA
CHAZKEL	12	M	CH	PLZZZZUSA
NISSEN	9	M	CHILD	PLZZZZUSA
BARUCH	5	M	CHILD	PLZZZZUSA
WOLFENSON, BERUSCH	.10	M	INFANT	PLZZZZUSA
RAPPAPORT, GEDALJE	35	M	PDLR	PLZZZZUSA
MATHIE	26	F	W	PLZZZZUSA
ITE	1	F	CHILD	PLZZZZUSA
SCHLOME	.09	M	INFANT	PLZZZZUSA

SHIP: BELGENLAND

FROM: ANTWERP
TO: NEW YORK
ARRIVED: 11 SEPTEMBER 1885

PASSENGER	AGE	SEX	OCCUPATION	PRIV	VIL	DES
SEGAL, C.	25	F	UNKNOWN	RR	ZZZZ	STL
LEIE	7	F	CHILD	RR	ZZZZ	NY
KARL	45	M	UNKNOWN	RR	ZZZZ	NY
ZUCKERMANN, S.	40	M	MCHT	RR	AHZS	NY
LUBELESKI, B.	19	M	MACH	RR	ADBQ	NY
POGWATCHIK, P.	27	M	UNKNOWN	RR	ZZZZ	IL
SCHMITT, BERHE.	45	F	W	RR	ZZZZ	USA
M.	17	F	CH	RR	ZZZZ	USA
C.	4	M	CHILD	RR	ZZZZ	USA
FELINSKI, A.	31	M	BKR	PL	ZZZZ	NY

SHIP: EMS

FROM: BREMEN
TO: NEW YORK
ARRIVED: 12 SEPTEMBER 1885

PASSENGER	AGE	SEX	OCCUPATION	PRIV	VIL	DES
ORINTOWITZ, ANTONIA	24	F	NN	PL	AFWJ	USA
PAUL	4	M	CHILD	PL	AFWJ	USA
KAHN, ABRAHAM	17	M	MCHT	PL	AGRT	USA
PODSELWER, DAVID	16	M	MCHT	PL	AGRT	USA
BRUNN, LOUISE	24	F	NN	RR	ZZZZ	USA
DICK, ISAAK	50	M	LABR	RR	AFWJ	USA
BATSCHKA, JOSEFA	28	F	NN	RR	AFWJ	USA
MARI	9	F	CHILD	RR	AFWJ	USA
RUDOLF	7	M	CHILD	RR	AFWJ	USA
HEDWIG	4	F	CHILD	RR	AFWJ	USA

SHIP: WIELAND

FROM: HAMBURG
TO: NEW YORK
ARRIVED: 12 SEPTEMBER 1885

PASSENGER	AGE	SEX	OCCUPATION	PRIV	VIL	DES
BALTER, ARON	30	M	DLR	RR	ZZZZ	USA
CORDTS, BERUH.	14	M	LABR	RR	ZZZZ	USA
ABRAMOWITZ, J.	30	M	LABR	RR	ZZZZ	USA
ESTER	28	F	W	RR	ZZZZ	USA
BREINE	.09	F	INFANT	RR	ZZZZ	USA
SCHTALOWITZ, BENJAMIN	18	M	CBTMKR	RR	ZZZZ	USA
CHAINE	24	M	CBTMKR	RR	ZZZZ	USA
LESCHE	22	F	SGL	RR	ZZZZ	USA
KOMITZ, CHAIM	44	M	MCHT	RR	ZZZZ	USA
FEIWE	9	F	CHILD	RR	ZZZZ	USA
PACZEWICZ, STANISL.	28	M	JNR	RR	ZZZZ	USA
LUDW.	26	M	JNR	RR	ZZZZ	USA
ANTON	24	M	LABR	RR	ZZZZ	USA
ALMA	21	F	SGL	RR	ZZZZ	USA
SCHEBERS, BASCHE	45	F	SGL	RR	ZZZZ	USA
KOPERSKY, ULIANE	40	F	W	RR	ZZZZ	USA
SUSSEL	9	F	CHILD	RR	ZZZZ	USA
MULHNER, CARL	26	M	JNR	RR	ZZZZ	USA
EMILIE	23	F	W	RR	ZZZZ	USA
EMILIE	5	F	CHILD	RR	ZZZZ	USA
CARL	4	M	CHILD	RR	ZZZZ	USA
SWARTZ, RIWE	20	M	SGL	RR	ZZZZ	USA
RACHEL	18	M	SGL	RR	ZZZZ	USA
CHAWE	16	M	SGL	RR	ZZZZ	USA
GRUNBERG, ABRAM	23	M	DLR	RR	ZZZZ	USA
BERCHOWITZ, ABRAHAM	20	M	DLR	RR	ZZZZ	USA
COHN, SARAH	25	F	W	RR	ZZZZ	USA
JANKEL	.11	M	INFANT	RR	ZZZZ	***
WETENSTEIN, KIWE	50	M	DLR	RR	ZZZZ	USA
CHAWE	50	F	W	RR	ZZZZ	USA
RACHEL	17	F	CH	RR	ZZZZ	USA
DAVID	13	M	CH	RR	ZZZZ	USA
ISRAEL	9	M	CHILD	RR	ZZZZ	USA
HOFFMANN, JETTE	15	F	SGL	RR	ZZZZ	USA
DOWIDOWITZ, CHINE	19	F	SGL	RR	ZZZZ	USA
PRESSMANN, MOSES-J.	27	M	LABR	RR	ZZZZ	USA
BRESSLER, MICHAEL	36	M	LABR	RR	ZZZZ	USA
FAKTOR, MOSES	25	M	LABR	RR	ZZZZ	USA
OPPENHEIM, BREINE	27	F	W	RR	ZZZZ	USA
ELIAS	33	M	LABR	RR	ZZZZ	USA
RAHEL	4	F	CHILD	RR	ZZZZ	USA
SUSEL	.11	F	INFANT	RR	ZZZZ	USA
DOBRY, SUSSKIND	19	M	BBR	RR	ZZZZ	USA
KRUPINSKI, FRANZ	27	M	LABR	RR	ZZZZ	USA
BALICKI, ANDR.	27	M	LABR	RR	ZZZZ	USA
SZENTACZKA, VALERIA	19	F	SGL	RR	ZZZZ	USA
BERNHARD, ABRAM	45	M	LABR	RR	ZZZZ	USA
RUMBERG, DINE	25	F	W	RR	ZZZZ	USA
ABRAM	15	M	B	RR	ZZZZ	USA
KOHN, LENA	16	F	SGL	RR	ZZZZ	USA
RAFSKI, ASRIEL	34	M	LABR	RR	ZZZZ	USA
GUTTMANN, HEINR.	36	M	LABR	RR	ZZZZ	USA

SHIP: W A SCHOLTEN

FROM: ROTTERDAM
TO: NEW YORK
ARRIVED: 14 SEPTEMBER 1885

PASSENGER	AGE	SEX	OCCUPATION	PRIV	VIL	DES
TOEMAN, MICHAEL	20	M	LABR	RR	ZZZZ	USA
DOLITOWSKI, H.	22	M	LABR	RR	ZZZZ	USA
MIGOLOWSKY, MISCHEL	18	M	LABR	RR	ZZZZ	USA
PLOMNEUFELS, SALMEN	19	M	CGRMKR	RR	ZZZZ	USA
SLOMNIK, ABRAHAM	26	M	LABR	RR	ZZZZ	USA
MILINATZKISCH, ISSAS	00	M	LABR	RR	ZZZZ	USA
ANELKE	20	F	UNKNOWN	RR	ZZZZ	USA
MICHALOWSKY, SCHMAL	32	M	TLR	RR	ZZZZ	USA
DAVID	19	M	TLR	RR	ZZZZ	USA
GITTEL	7	F	CHILD	RR	ZZZZ	USA

SHIP: CIRCASSIA

FROM: GLASGOW AND MOVILLE
TO: NEW YORK
ARRIVED: 15 SEPTEMBER 1885

PASSENGER	AGE	SEX	OCCUPATION	PRIV	VIL	DES
BENZLER, SALMON	43	M	SHMK	RR	ZZZZ	USA
MOSES	11	M	NN	RR	ZZZZ	USA
LEURIN, NISSAN	16	M	LABR	RR	ZZZZ	USA
LAURIE, FRAN	25	M	LABR	RR	ZZZZ	USA
INMER	20	M	LABR	RR	ZZZZ	USA
SCHILAWSKY, BENGEL	35	M	MCHT	RR	ZZZZ	USA
LERSOWITZ, JANKEL	35	M	DLR	RR	ZZZZ	USA
THORKELSEN, INGEBERG	48	F	W	RR	ZZZZ	USA
BAIL	11	M	NN	RR	ZZZZ	USA
JON	10	M	NN	RR	ZZZZ	USA
JANKELOWITZ, JONE	23	M	DLR	RR	ZZZZ	USA
SORE	22	F	W	RR	ZZZZ	USA
BOOME	2	F	CHILD	RR	ZZZZ	USA

PASSENGER	AGE	SEX	OCCUPATION	PRV VIL DES
MORCH	1	F	CHILD	RRZZZZUSA
INEGEROWITZ, ABRAHAM	18	M	DLR	RRZZZZUSA

SHIP: RHAETIA

FROM: HAMBURG
TO: NEW YORK
ARRIVED: 15 SEPTEMBER 1885

PASSENGER	AGE	SEX	OCCUPATION	PRV VIL DES
GLASSMANN, ESTER	23	F	SGL	RRAHOKUSA
NOCHEM	25	M	LABR	RRAHOKUSA
MAYRICH, ROSALIE	35	F	W	RRZZZZUSA
CAROLINE	15	F	CH	RRZZZZUSA
SCHLOME	9	M	CHILD	RRZZZZUSA
MARCUS	7	M	CHILD	RRZZZZUSA
FEIGE	5	F	CHILD	RRZZZZUSA
SCHUMKLER, CHAIM	18	M	LABR	RRAHOKUSA
LEWIN, JETTE	36	F	W	RRZZZZUSA
LOTH	.11	F	INFANT	RRZZZZUSA
SALOMON	.01	M	INFANT	RRZZZZUSA
KLANIECKA, ROSALIE	65	F	W	RRAHTWUSA
KANKEL, JENTE	17	F	SGL	RRAFWJUSA
CAPLAN, BINE	25	F	SGL	RRZZZZUSA
MANDEL, REITSCHEL	18	F	SGL	RRZZZZUSA
SILBERSTEIN, SARA	21	F	SGL	RRZZZZUSA
STEINSCHMATZ, ISAAC	28	M	DLR	RRAFVGUSA
SURANSKYE, JACOB	28	M	LABR	RRAHZSUSA
JOHE.	27	F	W	RRAHZSUSA
SEDONIE	.11	F	INFANT	RRAHZSUSA
GUSTAVE	.01	F	INFANT	RRAHZSUSA
WEINSTOCK, ISRAEL	43	M	LABR	RRAFVGUSA
MILLER, ISSER	17	M	LABR	RRZZZZUSA
FURMER, BALIJ	9	M	CHILD	RRAHZSUSA
JACOB	8	M	CHILD	RRAHZSUSA
KAPLAN, ARON	18	M	LABR	RRAFWJUSA
RAPPEPORT, MAX	17	M	LABR	RRAFWJUSA
REICH, MORDCH.	36	F	W	RRAFWJUSA
BERTHA	.11	F	INFANT	RRAFWJUSA
STEINSCHMALZ, LEA	25	F	W	RRAFVGUSA
SCHLIEMAN	5	M	CHILD	RRAFVGUSA
DEMBROWSKI, JACOB	27	M	LABR	RRACONUSA
GEMBROWITZ, FRANZ	29	M	LABR	RRZZZZUSA
OLEZYSKYE, DAVID	22	M	LABR	RRZZZZUSA
WASYLOWSKYE, MOSES	17	M	LABR	RRZZZZUSA
FEIGERISCH, BENZIN	22	M	LABR	RRZZZZUSA
WASYLOWSKYE, JANKEL	19	M	MCHT	RRZZZZUSA
BERNCKMANN, JANKEL	26	M	MCHT	RRZZZZUSA
HECHT, CARL	60	M	LABR	RRZZZZUSA
MARIE	56	F	W	RRZZZZUSA
TALEINDER, APPOLINA	22	F	SGL	RRZZZZUSA
JANUSZEC, JOH.	18	M	LABR	RRAHZSUSA
SLOWITZKYE, JOH.	21	M	LABR	RRAHZSUSA
LAPOTE, PAULINE	24	F	SGL	RRAEFLUSA
GERSTENKVEN, NORME	20	F	SGL	RRAHTOUSA
SZILL, MICHAEL	28	M	LABR	RRAHYCUSA
KRANICKI, JOSEF	24	M	LABR	RRAHYCUSA

SHIP: SPAIN

FROM: LIVERPOOL
TO: NEW YORK
ARRIVED: 15 SEPTEMBER 1885

PASSENGER	AGE	SEX	OCCUPATION	PRV VIL DES
JUCHANSKY, CACITRE	32	F	SP	RRAHUENY
BLUMA	1	M	CHILD	RRAHUENY
YANKIN	.06	F	INFANT	RRAHUENY
SADKIN, HARRIS	20	M	LABR	RRZZZZNY
BRENNER, ABRAHAM	22	M	LABR	RRZZZZNY
GREENSPAN, RENBIN	33	M	LABR	RRZZZZNY
JETTA	29	F	W	RRZZZZNY
TERESE, KAISA	35	F	SP	RRZZZZNY
KAISA	11	F	CH	RRZZZZNY
JACOB	4	M	CHILD	RRZZZZNY
CARL	3	M	CHILD	RRZZZZNY
LASANEN, HY.	30	M	LABR	FNZZZZNY
KOPAKKOLA, NINA	22	F	SP	RRZZZZNY
ISAKSON, JOSEPHINE	25	F	SP	RRZZZZNY
MITTAL, MARID	40	F	SP	PLZZZZNY
ISAK	15	M	LABR	PLZZZZNY
JOHAN	11	M	CH	PLZZZZNY
JAKOB	9	M	CHILD	PLZZZZNY
SAMUEL	5	M	CHILD	PLZZZZNY
GERBROVA, HOLGO	17	F	SP	PLAHUENY
JUCKARSKY, CACITRE	23	F	SP	PLAHUENY
FRIDMANSKI, WOLF	20	M	LABR	RRZZZZNY
KLEMOLA, MATHIAS	28	M	LABR	FNZZZZNY
KETOMAKI, JOHN	38	M	LABR	FNZZZZNY
KARIKKA, JOHANNA	21	F	SP	FNZZZZNY
KAHA, JOSEF	25	M	BKR	RRZZZZNY
SKOLVIK, SACHER	21	M	LABR	RRZZZZNY
GOLDSTEIN, GOTZE	19	M	LABR	RRZZZZNY
ROCHEL	19	F	W	RRZZZZNY
EPSTEIN, ROCHTEL	32	F	SP	RRAHUENY
MERE	1	F	CHILD	RRAHUENY
MEDVINIK, ABRAHAM	38	M	LABR	RRZZZZNY
GRINSBERG, JOSEL	43	M	SHMK	RRAHTUNY
WOLF	3	M	CHILD	RRAHTUNY
CHAJE	4	M	CHILD	RRAHTUNY
BARNSTEIN, ROCHTEL	26	F	SP	RRZZZZNY
SARAH	1	F	CHILD	RRZZZZNY
KOLB, LAZAR	22	M	LABR	RRZZZZNY
SCHAPIRA, LEIB	18	M	LABR	RRZZZZNY
SHEYER	22	M	LABR	RRZZZZNY
PREISKEL, GERSEL	18	M	LABR	RRZZZZNY
LESSEN, MOSES	21	M	GDSM	RRZZZZNY
SILBERSKY, CHAIM	20	M	LABR	RRZZZZNY
MEYEROWITZ, MEYER	20	M	LABR	RRZZZZNY
CHAIE	20	F	W	RRZZZZNY
BREMSTEIN, JOSEL	33	M	LABR	RRZZZZNY
ROCHEL	25	F	W	RRZZZZNY
BERL	7	M	CHILD	RRZZZZNY
SORE	5	M	CHILD	RRZZZZNY
GOLDE	4	F	CHILD	RRZZZZNY
RINKE	1	M	CHILD	RRZZZZNY
GETEL	1	F	CHILD	RRZZZZNY
SPECTOR, SELIG	24	M	LABR	RRZZZZNY
LONZET, FERNKEL	26	M	GDSM	RRZZZZNY
KEJSLER, CHAIM	30	M	LABR	RRZZZZNY
LEWSCHE	30	F	W	RRZZZZNY
JENTE	9	M	CHILD	RRZZZZNY
NOAH	7	M	CHILD	RRZZZZNY
FENKEL	1	M	CHILD	RRZZZZNY
BLUMA	1	F	CHILD	RRZZZZNY
HOPPENFELD, DAVID	20	M	TLR	RRAFWJNY
LUSKERMAN, JANKEL	25	M	MCHT	RRZZZZNY
JANKULE, CHAIM	22	M	LABR	PLZZZZNY
CHANE	18	F	W	PLZZZZNY
CHAIE	1	M	CHILD	PLZZZZNY
CHAWE	50	F	SP	PLZZZZNY
ABRAHAM	67	M	LABR	PLZZZZNY
LEIBE	46	F	W	PLZZZZNY
LEIKE	16	F	SP	PLZZZZNY
GOLDE	11	F	CH	PLZZZZNY
REIBERG, CHAWE	50	F	SP	RRZZZZNY
CHAIE	17	F	SP	RRZZZZNY
FRIEDMAN, JOCHE	36	F	SP	RRAGDDNY
CHAIM	9	M	CHILD	RRAGDDNY
BEILE	8	M	CHILD	RRAGDDNY
SPRIMA	1	M	CHILD	RRAGDDNY
KRUGER, WILH.	29	M	LABR	RRAGDDNY

PASSENGER	AGE	SEX	OCCUPATION	PRV	VIL	DES
RAJKOWSKY, REBECKA	46	F	SP	RR	ZZZZ	NY
LISE	15	F	SP	RR	ZZZZ	NY
SORE	11	F	CH	RR	ZZZZ	NY

SHIP: WAESLAND

FROM: ANTWERP
TO: NEW YORK
ARRIVED: 18 SEPTEMBER 1885

PASSENGER	AGE	SEX	OCCUPATION	PRV	VIL	DES
CHRUSTSCHOW, PETER	18	M	FARMER	RR	AHQH	NY

SHIP: CITY OF CHESTER

FROM: LIVERPOOL AND QUEENSTOWN
TO: NEW YORK
ARRIVED: 19 SEPTEMBER 1885

PASSENGER	AGE	SEX	OCCUPATION	PRV	VIL	DES
STODD, AUGUST	23	M	LABR	RR	ZZZZ	UNK
BERGGRIST, ARON	19	M	LABR	FN	ZZZZ	WI
WAZERDOWSKY, SWEZ	25	M	GZR	RR	ZZZZ	NY

SHIP: EIDER

FROM: BREMEN AND SOUTHAMPTON
TO: NEW YORK
ARRIVED: 19 SEPTEMBER 1885

PASSENGER	AGE	SEX	OCCUPATION	PRV	VIL	DES
HERTER, ROSINA	29	F	NN	RR	ZZZZ	USA
CLARBLATT, AREL	12	M	CH	RR	ZZZZ	USA
CHONE	10	F	CH	RR	ZZZZ	USA
CIZANKE	7	F	CHILD	RR	ZZZZ	USA
MINA	4	F	CHILD	RR	ZZZZ	USA
MANOFZEWITSCH, JOS.	42	M	BCHR	RR	ZZZZ	USA
JANTZEN, LEANDER	41	M	MCHT	RR	AEMA	USA
MARIE	15	F	CH	RR	AEMA	USA
EMILIE	11	F	CH	RR	AEMA	USA
MARGA.	8	F	CHILD	RR	AEMA	USA
GAIER, JOHANN	46	M	FARMER	RR	ZZZZ	USA
BARBA.	46	F	W	RR	ZZZZ	USA
CHRISTN.	21	M	FARMER	RR	ZZZZ	USA
MAGDA.	19	F	NN	RR	ZZZZ	USA
ROSINA	17	F	NN	RR	ZZZZ	USA
CHARLE.	16	F	CH	RR	ZZZZ	USA
EMIL	7	M	CHILD	RR	ZZZZ	USA
LIDIA	.01	F	INFANT	RR	ZZZZ	USA
HITRO, MICH.	26	M	LABR	RR	ZZZZ	USA
BARGEN, JOHANN	36	M	LABR	RR	ZZZZ	USA
MARIA	26	F	W	RR	ZZZZ	USA
SUSANNA	11	F	CH	RR	ZZZZ	USA
JOHANN	10	M	CH	RR	ZZZZ	USA
MARIE	3	F	CHILD	RR	ZZZZ	USA
ELISABETH	1	F	CHILD	RR	ZZZZ	USA
ABRAHAM	.03	M	INFANT	RR	ZZZZ	USA
JANZEN, CORNINS	24	M	LABR	RR	ZZZZ	USA

SHIP: HAMMONIA

FROM: HAMBURG AND HAVRE
TO: NEW YORK
ARRIVED: 19 SEPTEMBER 1885

PASSENGER	AGE	SEX	OCCUPATION	PRV	VIL	DES
BANONEWSKI, ANNA	40	F	W	RR	ZZZZ	USA
EMMA	7	F	CHILD	RR	ZZZZ	USA
MARIANNE	5	F	CHILD	RR	ZZZZ	USA
CZIN, AREI	21	M	TLR	RR	AFWJ	USA
PAJAST, CHAJ.J.	18	F	SGL	RR	AFWJ	USA
GROSSAH, LUDW.	23	M	LABR	RR	AFWJ	USA
FRIEDMANN, HELENE	28	F	W	RR	AFWJ	USA
NASCHEL	9	M	CHILD	RR	AFWJ	USA
JOSEL	4	M	CHILD	RR	AFWJ	USA
SPRINZE	8	M	CHILD	RR	AFWJ	USA
BENTE	6	M	CHILD	RR	AFWJ	USA
KONINSKY, PIET.	23	M	LABR	RR	AHTR	USA
FEINBERG, ANNA	25	F	W	RR	ZZZZ	USA
WLALINOWSKA, LUDOVIKA	24	F	SGL	RR	ZZZZ	USA
KAPLAN, JACOB	15	M	LABR	RR	AHSL	USA
FEIWEL, LEISER	23	M	LABR	RR	AHZP	USA
SCHASKUNSKY, ELKE	18	F	SGL	RR	AHZP	USA
ROSENTHAL, NOCHEM	18	M	LABR	RR	AHQU	USA
RABINOWITZ, META	30	M	MCHT	RR	ZZZZ	USA
FEINBERG, ANNA	5	F	CHILD	RR	ZZZZ	USA
POSAZANIS, ANTONINA	23	F	W	RR	ZZZZ	USA
JANEH	.11	M	INFANT	RR	ZZZZ	USA
KRAINIAK, JOSEFA	28	F	W	RR	ZZZZ	USA
ANNA	9	F	CHILD	RR	ZZZZ	USA

SHIP: RHEIN

FROM: BREMEN AND SOUTHAMPTON
TO: NEW YORK
ARRIVED: 19 SEPTEMBER 1885

PASSENGER	AGE	SEX	OCCUPATION	PRV	VIL	DES
DUMBOWSKY, FRIDERIKE	19	F	NN	RR	ZZZZ	USA
JANKEL	.09	F	INFANT	RR	ZZZZ	USA
MELTZER, ESTER	19	F	NN	RR	ZZZZ	USA
EPHRAIM	.01	M	INFANT	RR	ZZZZ	USA
SANDOWSKY, NOCHEM	37	M	LABR	RR	ZZZZ	USA
PITONOK, CHAIL	21	F	NN	RR	ZZZZ	USA
PESSE	.09	F	INFANT	RR	ZZZZ	USA
SCHLACHTER, ALEXANDER	11	M	NN	RR	ZZZZ	USA
DELINSKY, NESCHE	28	F	NN	RR	ZZZZ	USA
ROSA	2	F	CHILD	RR	ZZZZ	USA
BASCHE	.11	F	INFANT	RR	ZZZZ	USA
HERZIG, JETTE	19	F	NN	RR	ZZZZ	USA
ALBERSTA, PAUL	20	M	LABR	RR	ZZZZ	USA
LADSCHICK, AUGUSTE	29	F	NN	RR	ZZZZ	USA
EMIL	6	M	CHILD	RR	ZZZZ	USA
KURJANSKE, RIWE	27	F	NN	RR	ZZZZ	USA
SLABOTKA, SARA	20	F	NN	RR	ZZZZ	USA
LEF, SCHMUEL	20	M	TRVLR	RR	ZZZZ	USA
KIRMOWSKY, LEIB	19	M	TRVLR	RR	ZZZZ	USA

PASSENGER	AGE	SEX	OCCUPATION	PRV	VIL	DES

SHIP: CALIFORNIA

FROM: HAMBURG
TO: NEW YORK
ARRIVED: 21 SEPTEMBER 1885

PASSENGER	AGE	SEX	OCCUPATION	PRV VIL DES
LUBELSKY, HANE	22	F	SGL	RRZZZZNY
SILBERMANN, LEIE	18	F	SGL	RRZZZZNY
GREINER, LIBE	20	M	SHMK	RRZZZZNY
LEVY, BENZ	26	F	SGL	RRZZZZNY
HAIMANICH, B.D.	33	M	CGRMKR	RRZZZZNY
LEIPONER, NACH.	45	M	TRDSMN	RRZZZZNY
FREIDMANN, J.	7	M	CHILD	RRZZZZNY
POLAK, JUDEL	7	M	CHILD	RRZZZZNY
HOSSMANN, MARIA	32	F	WO	RRZZZZNY
CHANE	7	F	CHILD	RRZZZZNY
LEIB	3	M	CHILD	RRZZZZNY
ABRAHAM	.10	M	INFANT	RRZZZZNY
HAUPT, FERD.	23	M	LABR	RRZZZZUNK
ERNESTINE	24	F	W	RRZZZZUNK
EMIL	2	M	CHILD	RRZZZZUNK
ALFRED	.06	M	INFANT	RRZZZZUNK
SCHUMACHER, AUGUSTE	17	F	SGL	RRZZZZNY
PONTI, WILH.	72	F	L	RRZZZZNY
KUZCZA, MARIA	65	F	WO	RRZZZZIL
ALEYANDROWISCH, SARAH	30	F	WO	RRZZZZNY
ETTEL	7	F	CHILD	RRZZZZNY
ELIAS	6	M	CHILD	RRZZZZNY
PEFHE	4	F	CHILD	RRZZZZNY
CHESE	.10	F	INFANT	RRZZZZNY
WEISS, CHAIN-L.	25	F	WO	RRZZZZNY
HIRSCH	.10	M	INFANT	RRZZZZNY
ROSA	.02	F	INFANT	RRZZZZNY
LIKONISKA, MAGD.	19	F	SGL	RRZZZZNY
SCHAD, MENDEL	20	M	LABR	RRZZZZNY
PETRIUS, CHAIM	23	M	TNSTH	RRZZZZNY
HINKE	18	F	W	RRZZZZNY
MILOWSKI, JOHN	35	M	LABR	RRZZZZNY
SEGOWSKI, M.	7	M	CHILD	RRZZZZNY
KPETZ, H.JOHANN	37	M	JNR	RRZZZZNY
LEUHAITES, TH.	27	M	LABR	RRZZZZPIT
COHN, PLEVE	22	F	SGL	RRZZZZNY
HERMANN, SORE	40	F	WO	RRZZZZNY
LEWIN, FEIA	36	F	WO	RRZZZZNY
ESTER	16	F	D	RRZZZZNY
CHAIM	7	M	CHILD	RRZZZZNY
FEIDEL	5	M	CHILD	RRZZZZNY
MOSES	4	M	CHILD	RRZZZZNY
REBECCA	.10	F	INFANT	RRZZZZNY
FEIGE	.02	F	INFANT	RRZZZZNY
OHSMARM, CHAIN	42	F	WO	RRZZZZNY
SOLNICK, FRONE	50	M	UNKNOWN	RRZZZZNY
JETTE	23	F	D	RRZZZZNY
MOSES	6	M	CHILD	RRZZZZNY
PETRINSKI, SCHLOME	.03	M	INFANT	RRZZZZNY

SHIP: ETRURIA

FROM: LIVERPOOL AND QUEENSTOWN
TO: NEW YORK
ARRIVED: 21 SEPTEMBER 1885

PASSENGER	AGE	SEX	OCCUPATION	PRV VIL DES
DE-RENTHAL, U-BARONESS	40	F	MA	RRADBQUSA
CASTIA	9	M	CHILD	RRADBQUSA

SHIP: STATE OF ALABAMA

FROM: GLASGOW AND LARNE
TO: NEW YORK
ARRIVED: 21 SEPTEMBER 1885

PASSENGER	AGE	SEX	OCCUPATION	PRV VIL DES
BERNSTEIN, LEISER	20	M	UNKNOWN	RRZZZZNY
BERMANN, ABRAHAM	19	M	UNKNOWN	RRZZZZNY
BLANSTEIN, CHAIE	39	F	W	RRZZZZNY
SCHEINE	16	F	NN	RRZZZZNY
LIEBE	9	F	CHILD	RRZZZZNY
MICH.	8	M	CHILD	RRZZZZNY
DUEL	3	F	CHILD	RRZZZZNY
DAVIDOWITZ, CHANE	20	M	LABR	RRZZZZNY
DOBRES, MENDEL	28	M	GZR	RRZZZZNY
FLORA	26	F	W	RRZZZZNY
MAX	5	M	CHILD	RRZZZZNY
GRETE	1	F	CHILD	RRZZZZNY
HIRSCH, HERMANN	17	M	UNKNOWN	RRZZZZNY
KAHN, ITZIG	29	M	TLR	RRZZZZNY
LEWIN, JENKEL	41	F	W	RRZZZZNY
SCHEINE	4	F	CHILD	RRZZZZNY
MEYERSON, HINDE	40	F	W	RRZZZZNY
SARAH	18	F	NN	RRZZZZNY
MIKUZINSKY, GEDALIE	24	M	LABR	RRZZZZCH
WOLFF	37	M	UNKNOWN	RRZZZZCH
SARAH	31	F	W	RRZZZZCH
JEROCHIM	8	M	CHILD	RRZZZZCH
ELISCHEN	6	F	CHILD	RRZZZZCH
REZNICK, JACOB	38	M	BCHR	RRZZZZNY
ROSENTHAL, WIEHNE	45	F	W	RRZZZZNY
RUBIN	11	M	NN	RRZZZZNY
JUDEL	9	F	CHILD	RRZZZZNY
SCHIMONOWITZ, LEIB-H.	33	M	UNKNOWN	RRZZZZNY
SINGEREWITZ, BERTIE	51	M	UNKNOWN	RRZZZZNY
LEIE	50	F	W	RRZZZZNY
JETTE	17	F	NN	RRZZZZNY
FRUME	30	F	SVNT	RRZZZZNY
SCH---OWIK, JACOB	00	M	UNKNOWN	RRZZZZNY
WILSENFELD, ARON	25	M	LABR	RRZZZZNY
SAMUEL	00	M	LABR	RRZZZZNY
ZUCKER, REWI	00	F	W	RRZZZZNY
SAMUEL	4	M	CHILD	RRZZZZNY
JURA	1	F	CHILD	RRZZZZNY

SHIP: ETHIOPIA

FROM: GLASGOW AND MOVILLE
TO: NEW YORK
ARRIVED: 22 SEPTEMBER 1885

PASSENGER	AGE	SEX	OCCUPATION	PRV VIL DES
SACHS, LERI	32	F	UNKNOWN	RRZZZZUSA
BENJAMIN	11	M	UNKNOWN	RRZZZZUSA
RIEZE	8	F	CHILD	RRZZZZUSA
BEROCH	4	M	CHILD	RRZZZZUSA
INTI	5	F	CHILD	RRZZZZUSA
MENDELSIHN, P.	18	M	BCHR	RRZZZZUSA
FILMAN, L.	33	M	BKR	RRZZZZUSA

PASSENGER	AGE	SEX	OCCUPATION	PRV VIL DES

SHIP: WESTERNLAND

FROM: ANTWERP
TO: NEW YORK
ARRIVED: 23 SEPTEMBER 1885

PASSENGER	AGE	SEX	OCCUPATION	PRV VIL DES
SESOROWITZ, SARAH	18	F	UNKNOWN	RRZZZZUNK
SORBODA, FRANTZ	23	M	FARMER	PLZZZZSTL
KANEFSKY, JOHN	56	M	FARMER	PLZZZZNY
GRANSWOKA, R.	18	F	UNKNOWN	PLZZZZUSA
WANAGUSKA, MATHA.	21	F	UNKNOWN	PLZZZZCH
W.	00	F	INF	PLZZZZCH
MALYSIAK, MARIE	37	F	UNKNOWN	PLZZZZUNK
MICH.	00	M	INF	PLZZZZUNK
SABATI, P.	42	M	BKR	RRZZZZNY
JANKOWSKI, K.	17	F	UNKNOWN	RRZZZZUNK
KNISCHE, RICHAL	17	F	UNKNOWN	RRZZZZUNK
SARAH	11	F	CH	RRZZZZUNK
POMOWSKMAT, FR.	26	F	UNKNOWN	PLZZZZUNK
FUSKO	12	F	CH	PLZZZZUNK
OLSCHOWSKI, AD.	23	M	FARMER	PLZZZZSTL

SHIP: SCHIEDAM

FROM: AMSTERDAM
TO: NEW YORK
ARRIVED: 24 SEPTEMBER 1885

PASSENGER	AGE	SEX	OCCUPATION	PRV VIL DES
MASSUR, BETTY	40	F	NN	RRZZZZUSA
ORELIA	16	F	NN	RRZZZZUSA
U	00	F	NN	RRZZZZUSA
DAVID	10	M	NN	RRZZZZUSA
JANOS	10	M	NN	RRZZZZUSA
ELLA	9	F	CHILD	RRZZZZUSA
BENNO	7	M	CHILD	RRZZZZUSA
PFEFFER, WOLF	32	M	LABR	RRZZZZUSA
GUTEL	24	F	UNKNOWN	RRZZZZUSA
CHAINE	1	F	CHILD	RRZZZZUSA
MALKE	.04	F	INFANT	RRZZZZUSA
CAHN, SCHOLEM	20	F	TLR	RRZZZZUSA
LOORE	20	F	UNKNOWN	RRZZZZUSA
SCHWARZBERG, LEWOSCH	22	F	UNKNOWN	RRZZZZUSA
JACOB	3	M	CHILD	RRZZZZUSA
LEVORE	1	F	CHILD	RRZZZZUSA
KASSEMIROVO, SIMON	40	M	LABR	RRAHTFUSA
RAWOTZKIS, JURGES	20	M	LABR	RRZZZZUSA
ROSENBERG, JACOB	20	M	BKR	RRZZZZUSA
KAUFMANN, ISIDOR	22	M	MCHT	RRAEFLUSA
MILLUER, ABRAHAM	22	M	TLR	RRZZZZUSA
PARES, WOLF	42	M	TLR	RRAFVGUSA

SHIP: SUEVIA

FROM: HAMBURG AND HAVRE
TO: NEW YORK
ARRIVED: 24 SEPTEMBER 1885

PASSENGER	AGE	SEX	OCCUPATION	PRV VIL DES
DE-COCK, FANNY	36	F	W	RRAHQHUSA
TANTO, HERMINE	26	F	SGL	RRAEFLUSA
ELOISA	35	F	SGL	RRAEFLUSA
HALPERN, RIWE	33	F	W	RRAGRTUSA
CH.	9	F	CHILD	RRAGRTUSA
REBECCA	.11	F	INFANT	RRAGRTUSA
LIBOWITZ, LEIB	23	M	TLR	RRZZZZUSA
WEISS, CLARA	33	F	W	RRZZZZUSA
HANNA	6	F	CHILD	RRZZZZUSA
RABEL	.11	F	INFANT	RRZZZZUSA
DAMSKY, CHAJE	17	F	SGL	RRZZZZUSA
ZUCKERMANN, LEMACH	41	M	LABR	RRAGRTUSA
MARKSOHN, ABRAM	27	M	LABR	RRZZZZUSA
SCHAPIRO, MOSES	9	M	CHILD	RRZZZZUSA
ROSA	7	F	CHILD	RRZZZZUSA
CILINSKY, HELENE	50	F	W	RRZZZZUSA
GRABOWSKY, NICOL	27	M	LABR	RRZZZZUSA
CHMILEWSKA, KATH.	20	F	SGL	RRZZZZUSA
JOSEPHINE	23	F	W	RRZZZZUSA
ZLBE	3	M	CHILD	RRZZZZUSA
MARISCHNA	2	F	CHILD	RRZZZZUSA

SHIP: CITY OF CHICAGO

FROM: LIVERPOOL AND QUEENSTOWN
TO: NEW YORK
ARRIVED: 25 SEPTEMBER 1885

PASSENGER	AGE	SEX	OCCUPATION	PRV VIL DES
BRUGLANSKI, FR.	28	M	LABR	RRACBFNY
KUTULKA, ANTON-S.	20	M	LABR	RRACBFNY
BIGUGRUNSKI, BALLIUS	20	M	LABR	RRACBFNY

SHIP: KAETIE

FROM: UNKNOWN
TO: NEW YORK
ARRIVED: 25 SEPTEMBER 1885

PASSENGER	AGE	SEX	OCCUPATION	PRV VIL DES
RAWITSCH, SARA	18	F	GL	RRZZZZUSA
PLASCHANSKY, CHASA	20	F	W	RRZZZZUSA
GLUCKSOHN, ISAAC	31	M	LABR	RRZZZZUSA
MENSKRIN, REBECCA	40	F	W	RRZZZZUSA
KAYLA	20	F	CH	RRZZZZUSA
ELLA	17	F	CH	RRZZZZUSA
SCHNEIDER	11	M	CH	RRZZZZUSA
ABIE	10	M	CH	RRZZZZUSA
MARIE	7	F	CHILD	RRZZZZUSA
ABRAHAM	4	M	CHILD	RRZZZZUSA

SHIP: STATE OF NEVADA

FROM: GLASGOW AND LARNE
TO: NEW YORK
ARRIVED: 25 SEPTEMBER 1885

PASSENGER	AGE	SEX	OCCUPATION	PRV VIL DES
ZEERMANN, MOSES	18	M	LABR	RRZZZZUSA
RACHEL	20	F	W	RRZZZZUSA
FERNBERG, SELDA	50	F	W	RRZZZZUSA
ETEL	23	F	SVNT	RRZZZZUSA
MALKE	19	F	SVNT	RRZZZZUSA
MALKE	12	F	SVNT	RRZZZZUSA
GRATT, SALOMON	18	M	CGRMKR	RRZZZZUSA
GOLLERUP, C.	20	M	PDLR	RRZZZZUSA
SARAH	22	F	W	RRZZZZUSA
GREIDBERG, JACOB	22	M	PDLR	RRZZZZUSA
KATZ, JANKEL	26	M	PDLR	RRZZZZUSA
BIRMAN, W.	18	M	PDLR	RRZZZZUSA

PASSENGER	AGE	SEX	OCCUPATION	PRIV	VIL	DES
ISRAEL	11	M	PDLR	RR	ZZZZ	USA
LYDIA	23	F	W	RR	ZZZZ	USA
OSEMANN, C.	22	F	W	RR	ZZZZ	USA
ISRAEL	1	M	CHILD	RR	ZZZZ	USA
ROSLOWSKY, O.	20	M	LABR	RR	ZZZZ	USA
SPARKOWSKY, U.	25	M	LABR	RR	ZZZZ	USA
SCHLOMONITZ, B.	25	F	W	RR	ZZZZ	USA
JEMACH	3	F	CHILD	RR	ZZZZ	USA
SATZOSKI, MEIER	17	M	PDLR	RR	ZZZZ	USA
MISEL	18	M	PDLR	RR	ZZZZ	USA
SCHLOMONITZ, J.	18	M	PDLR	RR	ZZZZ	USA
WEISSMAN, A.	42	M	PDLR	RR	ZZZZ	USA
WRESCHINSKY, J.	60	M	PDLR	RR	ZZZZ	USA
EVA	54	F	W	RR	ZZZZ	USA
ERNESTINE	22	F	SVNT	RR	ZZZZ	USA
GOLSKOWSKY, MARIANE	23	F	W	PL	ZZZZ	USA
WANDA	.06	F	INFANT	PL	ZZZZ	USA
GRADISK, PAULINA	26	F	W	PL	ZZZZ	USA
STANISLAW	1	M	CHILD	PL	ZZZZ	USA
PEDSKENITZ, JOSEPHA	21	F	W	PL	ZZZZ	USA
BARBARA	1	F	CHILD	PL	ZZZZ	USA

SHIP: NECKAR

FROM: BREMEN
TO: NEW YORK
ARRIVED: 26 SEPTEMBER 1885

PASSENGER	AGE	SEX	OCCUPATION	PRIV	VIL	DES
BOLECHEWITZ, MARIE	33	F	SVNT	RR	ZZZZ	NY
SCHAPIRA, RUBEN	40	M	LABR	RR	ZZZZ	NY
SCHMETZ, WILH.	25	M	LABR	RR	ZZZZ	NY
ROSALIE	22	F	UNKNOWN	RR	ZZZZ	NY
ALBERT	23	M	LABR	RR	ZZZZ	NY
ADOLPH	.01	M	INFANT	RR	ZZZZ	NY
NIEDZINSKI, ADAM	20	M	LABR	RR	ZZZZ	PHI
RATHNER, MOSES	48	M	MCHT	RR	ZZZZ	NY
ESTER	42	F	UNKNOWN	RR	ZZZZ	NY
SAMUEL	23	M	MCHT	RR	ZZZZ	NY
GAITON	11	M	UNKNOWN	RR	ZZZZ	NY
ROSALIE	7	F	CHILD	RR	ZZZZ	NY
ELSE	3	F	CHILD	RR	ZZZZ	NY

SHIP: WERRA

FROM: BREMEN AND SOUTHAMPTON
TO: NEW YORK
ARRIVED: 26 SEPTEMBER 1885

PASSENGER	AGE	SEX	OCCUPATION	PRIV	VIL	DES
NICKEL, HEINR.	64	M	LABR	RR	ZZZZ	USA
HELENE	45	F	NN	RR	ZZZZ	USA
HEINR.	27	M	LABR	RR	ZZZZ	USA
PETER	16	M	LABR	RR	ZZZZ	USA
GERHARD	14	M	LABR	RR	ZZZZ	USA
MARIA	7	F	CHILD	RR	ZZZZ	USA
FRANZ	6	M	CHILD	RR	ZZZZ	USA
ELISABETH	5	F	CHILD	RR	ZZZZ	USA
JACOB	4	M	CHILD	RR	ZZZZ	USA
JOHANN	.11	M	INFANT	RR	ZZZZ	USA
CORNELIUS	.11	M	INFANT	RR	ZZZZ	USA
KNOPFLE, JACOB	43	M	LABR	RR	ZZZZ	USA
MAGDALENE	43	F	NN	RR	ZZZZ	USA
JACOB	19	M	LABR	RR	ZZZZ	USA
ELISABETH	14	F	NN	RR	ZZZZ	USA
JOHANNES	13	M	LABR	RR	ZZZZ	USA
DOROTHEA	7	F	CHILD	RR	ZZZZ	USA

PASSENGER	AGE	SEX	OCCUPATION	PRIV	VIL	DES
MAGD.	6	F	CHILD	RR	ZZZZ	USA
CHRISTINE	5	F	CHILD	RR	ZZZZ	USA
ADAM	3	M	CHILD	RR	ZZZZ	USA
CATH.	.11	F	INFANT	RR	ZZZZ	USA
MAIER, GOTTL.	24	M	NN	RR	ZZZZ	USA
REGINE	21	F	NN	RR	ZZZZ	USA
SAUTTER, ANDREAS	41	M	LABR	RR	ZZZZ	USA
KATH.	38	F	NN	RR	ZZZZ	USA
BARBARA	16	F	NN	RR	ZZZZ	USA
JOHANNES	13	M	NN	RR	ZZZZ	USA
ELISABETH	4	F	CHILD	RR	ZZZZ	USA
CHRISTINA	.09	F	INFANT	RR	ZZZZ	USA
ROHRL, MARIE	7	F	CHILD	RR	ZZZZ	USA
SURNAME, ELISABETH	30	F	NN	RR	ZZZZ	USA
LANGE, EMMA	16	F	NN	RR	ZZZZ	USA
MOLL, SOPHIE	25	F	NN	RR	ZZZZ	USA
ZWIANDOWSKI, EDMUND	37	M	LABR	RR	ZZZZ	USA
MICHALINE	39	F	NN	RR	ZZZZ	USA
LUCIA	15	F	NN	RR	ZZZZ	USA
BOLLISLAUS	7	M	CHILD	RR	ZZZZ	USA
STANISLAUS	5	M	CHILD	RR	ZZZZ	USA
MATHILDE	3	F	CHILD	RR	ZZZZ	USA
HELENE	.03	F	INFANT	RR	ZZZZ	USA

SHIP: FRISIA

FROM: HAMBURG AND HAVRE
TO: NEW YORK
ARRIVED: 28 SEPTEMBER 1885

PASSENGER	AGE	SEX	OCCUPATION	PRIV	VIL	DES
ZEMBUZER, BEILE	28	F	SGL	RR	ZZZZ	USA
SCHILDOWSKY, RACHEL	55	F	W	RR	ZZZZ	USA
BIFSCHIETZ, BENJAMIN	20	M	MCHT	RR	ZZZZ	USA
BLONSKI, PETER	25	M	LABR	RR	ZZZZ	USA
AGNISKA	22	F	W	RR	ZZZZ	USA
SCHNEIDER, PAULINE	32	F	W	RR	ZZZZ	USA
LEISER	.11	M	INFANT	RR	ZZZZ	USA
BEILE	.11	F	INFANT	RR	ZZZZ	USA

SHIP: FURNESSIA

FROM: UNKNOWN
TO: NEW YORK
ARRIVED: 28 SEPTEMBER 1885

PASSENGER	AGE	SEX	OCCUPATION	PRIV	VIL	DES
INSALMAN, PETER	41	M	LABR	PL	ZZZZ	USA
GRAJOWSKI, LEIB	35	F	NN	PL	ZZZZ	USA
NUMAN, REBECCA	18	F	NN	PL	ZZZZ	USA
LOSCHINAWSKI, JOSSEL	34	M	LABR	RR	ZZZZ	USA
ORINSKY, BEOR	23	M	DLR	RR	ZZZZ	USA

SHIP: P CALAND

FROM: ROTTERDAM
TO: NEW YORK
ARRIVED: 28 SEPTEMBER 1885

PASSENGER	AGE	SEX	OCCUPATION	PRIV	VIL	DES
WUGMAN, OSSEI	40	M	MCHT	RR	AFVG	USA
WORWICH, HIRSCH	28	M	MCHT	RR	AFVG	USA
DETMER, HENRY	26	M	MCHT	RR	AFVG	USA

PASSENGER	AGE	SEX	OCCUPATION	PRV	VIL	DES
LISS, JULIUS	21	M	FARMER	RR	ZZZZ	USA
ROTTENARI, CAROLINE	56	F	NN	RR	ZZZZ	USA
ALBERT	26	M	MCHT	RR	ZZZZ	USA

SHIP: ENGLAND

FROM: LIVERPOOL AND QUEENSTOWN
TO: NEW YORK
ARRIVED: 29 SEPTEMBER 1885

PASSENGER	AGE	SEX	OCCUPATION	PRV	VIL	DES
LINTULAHLU, MINNA	20	F	SP	FN	ZZZZ	NY
SAPPANIEMA, MATT.	25	F	SP	FN	AHQH	NY
HULLALU, ITAI	19	F	SP	FN	ZZZZ	NY
SOCDBURG, ANNA	29	F	SP	FN	ZZZZ	NY
E.	7	M	CHILD	FN	ZZZZ	NY
KOSKINUMU, PETER	15	M	LABR	FN	ZZZZ	NY
ALBERT	11	M	CH	FN	ZZZZ	NY
WOLLBERG, REINE	40	F	W	FN	ACBF	NY
ENOK	8	M	CHILD	FN	ACBF	NY
SCHAPE	4	M	CHILD	FN	ACBF	NY
HULULU, ABRAHAM	45	M	LABR	RR	ZZZZ	NY

SHIP: MORAVIA

FROM: HAMBURG
TO: NEW YORK
ARRIVED: 29 SEPTEMBER 1885

PASSENGER	AGE	SEX	OCCUPATION	PRV	VIL	DES
KRIZNIAK, MARG.	26	F	W	RR	ZZZZ	USA
BOLESLAVA	9	F	CHILD	RR	ZZZZ	USA
JOSEF	7	M	CHILD	RR	ZZZZ	USA
HELENE	2	F	CHILD	RR	ZZZZ	USA
GLASER, JENNY	18	F	SGL	RR	ZZZZ	USA
GLASSMANN, PESSE	20	F	SGL	RR	ZZZZ	USA
FREIMANN, JOSEF	18	M	LABR	RR	ZZZZ	USA
LINKE, PEREL	30	F	W	RR	ZZZZ	USA
FANNY	9	F	CHILD	RR	ZZZZ	USA
LEIB	5	M	CHILD	RR	ZZZZ	USA
FREIMANN, ELISABETH	16	F	SGL	RR	ZZZZ	USA

SHIP: NEVADA

FROM: LIVERPOOL AND QUEENSTOWN
TO: NEW YORK
ARRIVED: 29 SEPTEMBER 1885

PASSENGER	AGE	SEX	OCCUPATION	PRV	VIL	DES
WENTSKOWSKY, JOHAN	33	M	LABR	RR	ACBF	USA
HELEN	35	F	W	RR	ACBF	USA
PETER	10	M	CH	RR	ACBF	USA
ANNA	9	F	CHILD	RR	ACBF	USA
ELINE	6	F	CHILD	RR	ACBF	USA
HANS	4	M	CHILD	RR	ACBF	USA
MARIE	00	F	INF	RR	ACBF	USA
HELENE	11	F	CH	RR	ACBF	USA
LILZA, DINA	36	F	JWLR	RR	AEFL	USA
THYRA	9	F	CHILD	RR	AEFL	USA

SHIP: MAIN

FROM: BREMEN
TO: NEW YORK
ARRIVED: 01 OCTOBER 1885

PASSENGER	AGE	SEX	OCCUPATION	PRV	VIL	DES
DOBSLOV, HEINR.	44	M	FARMER	RR	ZZZZ	USA
ANNA	42	F	W	RR	ZZZZ	USA
MATHILDE	15	F	D	RR	ZZZZ	USA
PAULINE	11	F	CH	RR	ZZZZ	USA
AUGUSTINE	9	F	CHILD	RR	ZZZZ	USA
ANNA	7	F	CHILD	RR	ZZZZ	USA
MARTHA	4	F	CHILD	RR	ZZZZ	USA
EMILIE	2	F	CHILD	RR	ZZZZ	USA
BERTHA	.10	F	INFANT	RR	ZZZZ	USA

SHIP: ELBE

FROM: BREMEN
TO: NEW YORK
ARRIVED: 03 OCTOBER 1885

PASSENGER	AGE	SEX	OCCUPATION	PRV	VIL	DES
WIZBILKA, ULIANNA	18	F	NN	RR	ZZZZ	USA
LUPKA, CARL.	58	F	NN	RR	ZZZZ	USA
INSZKANSKI, ANTANIE	42	F	NN	RR	ZZZZ	USA
LZENKAWSKA, ANNA	19	F	NN	RR	ZZZZ	USA
RYMMAR, JULIANNA	20	F	NN	RR	ZZZZ	USA
ELKIND, ARON	20	M	LABR	RR	ZZZZ	USA
GOLDENBERG, SCHMUEL	29	M	SDLR	RR	ZZZZ	USA
DAVID	9	M	CHILD	RR	ZZZZ	USA
TOSZKAWSKA, ANNA	28	M	NN	RR	ZZZZ	USA
VINCENT	5	M	CHILD	RR	ZZZZ	USA
JOHANN	3	M	CHILD	RR	ZZZZ	USA
ANNA	.03	F	INFANT	RR	ZZZZ	USA

SHIP: GEISER

FROM: COPENHAGEN AND STETTIN
TO: NEW YORK
ARRIVED: 03 OCTOBER 1885

PASSENGER	AGE	SEX	OCCUPATION	PRV	VIL	DES
KAUTLO, ABRAHAM-JOH.	31	M	LABR	FN	ZZZZ	USA
REPLIN, AMANDA-MS	22	F	NN	FN	ZZZZ	USA

SHIP: ZAANDAM

FROM: AMSTERDAM
TO: NEW YORK
ARRIVED: 03 OCTOBER 1885

PASSENGER	AGE	SEX	OCCUPATION	PRV	VIL	DES
SCHLONOWITZ, DAVID	19	M	LABR	PL	ZZZZ	USA
BARMINSKO, WASILI	27	M	MCHT	RR	ZZZZ	USA
ALEXANDER	35	M	MCHT	RR	ZZZZ	USA

PASSENGER	AGE	SEX	OCCUPATION	PRV	VIL	DES

SHIP: POLYNESIA

FROM: HAMBURG
TO: NEW YORK
ARRIVED: 05 OCTOBER 1885

PASSENGER	AGE	SEX	OCCUPATION	PRV VIL DES
BANESKAUTZKES, ANT.	25	M	LABR	RRZZZZUNK
STRAWINSKY, TH.	26	M	LABR	RRZZZZUNK
AGATHE	27	F	W	RRZZZZUNK
FALK, STABON	50	M	LABR	RRZZZZNY
GILLIG, MAX	00	M	BCHR	RRZZZZIA
DUBITZKI, RASEL	20	F	SGL	RRZZZZWI
JURGENS, HERM.	34	M	LABR	RRZZZZNY
CAROLINE	30	F	W	RRZZZZNY
CARL	3	M	CHILD	RRZZZZNY
MARTHA	.07	F	INFANT	RRZZZZNY
KRISTALL, REBECCA	22	F	WO	RRZZZZNY
JENNIE	.11	F	INFANT	RRZZZZNY
FRIEDERIKE	.01	F	INFANT	RRZZZZNY
WILSCHINSKY, BERTHOLD	18	M	TDR	RRZZZZPA
COHN, RACHEL	31	F	WO	RRZZZZNY
BIRMANN	4	M	CHILD	RRZZZZNY
SABOLKA, FRANZ	25	M	MLR	RRZZZZNY
TINK, DEBORA	22	F	WO	RRZZZZNY

SHIP: WESTPHALIA

FROM: HAMBURG
TO: NEW YORK
ARRIVED: 05 OCTOBER 1885

PASSENGER	AGE	SEX	OCCUPATION	PRV VIL DES
MOSYKEWITZ, ROSALIE	22	F	SGL	RRZZZZUSA
LODZEWISZA, FR.MILKE	38	M	LABR	RRAHZSUSA
SIMONSKY, B.	19	M	DLR	RRZZZZUSA
SIKORSKI, JOSEF	40	M	GDNR	RRZZZZUSA
SCHMIDT, MAX	22	M	MCHT	RRAAZQUSA
FROMM, CARL	74	M	MCHT	RRZZZZUSA
ERNESTINE	64	F	W	RRZZZZUSA
RUCZENIECS, JOH.	25	M	LABR	RRZZZZUSA
JANOS	24	M	LABR	RRZZZZUSA
AMBROZEMIEZEZ, VINCENT	22	M	LABR	RRZZZZUSA
BERGMANN, HYMANN	17	M	LABR	RRZZZZUSA
APPELBAUM, ITTEL	19	F	SGL	RRAHTFUSA
MOIN, ARON	23	M	LABR	RRAHTFUSA
TEIFER, BERNHARD	27	M	CGRMKR	RRACONUSA
KOPPELMANN, JULIAN	31	M	PH	RRAFWJUSA
LUDORF, VINCENT	22	M	LABR	RRAHZSUSA
GLOWATSKI, STANISLAUS	23	M	LABR	RRAHZSUSA
DAMILOWITZ, ANTON	38	M	LABR	RRAHZSUSA
WISZGINDE, ANTON	22	M	LABR	RRAHZSUSA
MAGDALENE	19	F	W	RRAHZSUSA
PASNESZ, MALKE	22	F	SGL	RRAFVGUSA
CARLSON, AMANDA	22	F	SGL	FNZZZZUSA
DAMSKY, TAUBE	35	F	W	FNAHTFUSA
JANKEL	.11	F	INFANT	FNAHTFUSA
BUKEWIZOWA, JADWIGA	40	F	W	FNAHTFUSA
ALBINE	9	F	CHILD	FNAHTFUSA
ANTON	3	M	CHILD	FNAHTFUSA
LANGLEBEN, CHINE	17	F	SGL	RRZZZZUSA
ROSENTHAL, KATI	25	F	W	RRZZZZUSA
ETTEL	5	F	CHILD	RRZZZZUSA
LASOS	3	M	CHILD	RRZZZZUSA
BERTA	.11	F	INFANT	RRZZZZUSA
MATALEWICOWA, MARG.	24	F	W	RRAHZSUSA
JOS.	.06	M	INFANT	RRAHZSUSA
LEWANOWITZ, VINCENT	19	M	LABR	RRAHZSUSA
MICULA, VINCENT	20	M	LABR	RRAHZSUSA
REGUNAS, JANOS	26	M	LABR	RRAHZSUSA
GRADILIS, VINCENT	22	M	LABR	RRAHZSUSA

PASSENGER	AGE	SEX	OCCUPATION	PRV VIL DES
URBANOW, ANNA	18	F	SGL	RRAHZSUSA
FREIMANN, BENJAMIN	20	M	LABR	RRAHTFUSA
GLESER, GITTEL	29	F	W	RRAHTFUSA
RACHEL	6	F	CHILD	RRAHTFUSA
ABRAHAM	5	M	CHILD	RRAHTFUSA
SAMUEL	.11	M	INFANT	RRAHTFUSA
SARA	.11	M	INFANT	RRAHTFUSA
RUKOWIZKI, ROMAN	35	M	FARMER	RRZZZZUSA
LEMUS, LUDWIKA	25	F	W	RRAHZSUSA
OTTO	9	M	CHILD	RRAHZSUSA
EMMA	7	F	CHILD	RRAHZSUSA
BUTTEL, W.	16	M	LABR	RRAHZSUSA

SHIP: FULDA

FROM: BREMEN
TO: NEW YORK
ARRIVED: 07 OCTOBER 1885

PASSENGER	AGE	SEX	OCCUPATION	PRV VIL DES
BERSER, ISAAC	8	M	CHILD	RRAEFLUSA
MOSES	7	M	CHILD	RRAEFLUSA
MARKWART, DAVID	20	M	FARMER	RRAEFLUSA
MARTHA	18	F	UNKNOWN	RRAEFLUSA
JURKO, MIHALY	30	M	LABR	RRAEFLUSA
KRAVETZ, JAKOB	30	M	LABR	RRAEFLUSA

SHIP: ST LAURENT

FROM: HAVRE
TO: NEW YORK
ARRIVED: 08 OCTOBER 1885

PASSENGER	AGE	SEX	OCCUPATION	PRV VIL DES
EARNEST, W.	40	M	MCHT	RRZZZZCH
AUG.	17	F	NN	RRZZZZNY
W.	1	M	CHILD	RRZZZZNY

SHIP: STATE OF GEORGIA

FROM: GLASGOW AND LARNE
TO: NEW YORK
ARRIVED: 08 OCTOBER 1885

PASSENGER	AGE	SEX	OCCUPATION	PRV VIL DES
ROSSITZKY, JUDA	25	F	W	RRZZZZUSA
MEYER	2	M	CHILD	RRZZZZUSA
ARPUTSCHUWNA, ANNA	20	F	NN	RRZZZZUSA
MICHAJOW, ANTONINA	38	F	W	RRZZZZUSA
IWAN	10	M	CH	RRZZZZUSA
ANNA	7	F	CHILD	RRZZZZUSA
KONCTANTA	3	F	CHILD	RRZZZZUSA
ANTONIA	2	F	CHILD	RRZZZZUSA
CALTA	1	F	CHILD	RRZZZZUSA
GRUENBERG, SIMON	18	M	PDLR	RRZZZZUSA
BREIKYSKO, ANTON	19	M	LABR	RRZZZZUSA
STALANIS, VINCENT	45	M	LABR	RRZZZZUSA

PASSENGER	AGE	SEX	OCCUPATION	PRIV	VIL	DES

SHIP: EMS

FROM: BREMEN
TO: NEW YORK
ARRIVED: 10 OCTOBER 1885

PASSENGER	AGE	SEX	OCCUPATION	PV	VIL	DES
HUPE, FRITZ	27	M	FARMER	RR	AFWJ	USA
SABOL, MIKE	16	F	CH	RR	ZZZZ	USA
SADOWSKY, WENZEL	28	M	LABR	RR	ZZZZ	USA
ANNA	28	F	NN	RR	ZZZZ	USA
ANTON	4	M	CHILD	RR	ZZZZ	USA
MARIANNE	3	F	CHILD	RR	ZZZZ	USA
ANNA	.11	F	INFANT	RR	ZZZZ	USA
CAASSEN, PETRO	25	M	LABR	RR	AFWJ	USA
MARGARETHE	20	F	NN	RR	AFWJ	USA

SHIP: LESSING

FROM: HAMBURG AND HAVRE
TO: NEW YORK
ARRIVED: 10 OCTOBER 1885

PASSENGER	AGE	SEX	OCCUPATION	PV	VIL	DES
LEBOWITZ, SALMEN	21	M	TNMK	RR	AHTF	USA
LUKASZEWSKA, KATHE.	40	F	W	RR	ZZZZ	USA
FELIX	16	M	CH	RR	ZZZZ	USA
VERONIKA	9	F	CHILD	RR	ZZZZ	USA
ANGELA	7	F	CHILD	RR	ZZZZ	USA
KRZESLAWSKA, CHANNE	18	F	SGL	RR	AHZS	USA
JOZE	9	M	CHILD	RR	AHZS	USA
RACHEL	8	F	CHILD	RR	AHZS	USA
MOSES	6	M	CHILD	RR	AHZS	USA
RUBINSTEIN, SALOMEN	18	M	LABR	RR	AHZS	USA
GARFUNKEL, ISAAC	33	M	DLR	RR	ZZZZ	USA
KLARA	25	F	W	RR	ZZZZ	USA
ASSIEL	9	M	CHILD	RR	ZZZZ	USA
MALKE	9	M	CHILD	RR	ZZZZ	USA
PEREL	50	F	W	RR	ZZZZ	USA
LEWIN, PHILIPP	24	M	LABR	RR	ZZZZ	USA
FRIEDMANN, RECHAME	33	F	W	RR	AHSW	USA
MANASSE	9	M	CHILD	RR	AHSW	USA
CHAIE	6	F	CHILD	RR	AHSW	USA
NECHE	5	F	CHILD	RR	AHSW	USA
HINDE	3	F	CHILD	RR	AHSW	USA
JACOB	.11	M	INFANT	RR	AHSW	USA
SALZSTEIN, IDA	24	F	SGL	RR	AFWJ	USA
LENBUSCHEL, MAX	46	M	MCHT	RR	AFWJ	USA
ROSA	40	F	W	RR	AFWJ	USA
STANISLAUS	17	M	CH	RR	AFWJ	USA
ERNESTINE	15	F	CH	RR	AFWJ	USA
DOROTHEA	9	F	CHILD	RR	AFWJ	USA
BERTHOLD	8	M	CHILD	RR	AFWJ	USA
THEODOR	4	M	CHILD	RR	AFWJ	USA
WISO, ANNA	20	F	SGL	RR	ZZZZ	USA
ROGNO, JOSEFA	18	F	SGL	RR	ZZZZ	USA
STRIGOWSKA, MARIANNE	18	F	SGL	RR	AHZS	USA

SHIP: LA NORMANDIE

FROM: HAVRE
TO: NEW YORK
ARRIVED: 12 OCTOBER 1885

PASSENGER	AGE	SEX	OCCUPATION	PV	VIL	DES
BELLENGER, MARIE-MRS	28	F	NN	PL	ZZZZ	NY
ABRAHAM, SALOMON	32	M	MCHT	RR	ZZZZ	NY

SHIP: LEERDAM

FROM: ROTTERDAM
TO: NEW YORK
ARRIVED: 12 OCTOBER 1885

PASSENGER	AGE	SEX	OCCUPATION	PV	VIL	DES
MEJERSOHN, JANKEL	38	M	LABR	RR	ZZZZ	USA
MEYER	9	M	CHILD	RR	ZZZZ	USA
OTTENSE, ZALLER	54	M	LABR	RR	ZZZZ	USA
GOTZHAN, JANKEL	30	M	LABR	RR	ZZZZ	USA
ELESTERBERG, KRIST	18	M	LABR	RR	ZZZZ	USA
LINGRAN, HELENE	25	M	LABR	RR	ZZZZ	USA
SARECZOMSKY, MEYER	25	M	LABR	RR	ZZZZ	USA
BRAUN, ADOLF	42	M	LABR	RR	ZZZZ	USA
BALENSEUS, SIMON	25	M	LABR	RR	ZZZZ	USA
BALTROME	42	M	LABR	RR	ZZZZ	USA
WALICH, MARIS	24	F	NN	RR	ZZZZ	USA
KERN, ALIVIA	26	M	MCHT	RR	ZZZZ	USA
NIATHA, HEIDY	26	F	NN	RR	ZZZZ	USA
ESSIG	55	F	NN	RR	ZZZZ	USA
HOEKS, FRANZ	24	M	LABR	RR	ZZZZ	USA
HERUTOFER, MADSCHE	18	M	LABR	RR	ZZZZ	USA

SHIP: ANCHORIA

FROM: GLASGOW
TO: NEW YORK
ARRIVED: 14 OCTOBER 1885

PASSENGER	AGE	SEX	OCCUPATION	PV	VIL	DES
BRANDSTEIN, JANKEL-L.	35	M	PDLR	RR	ZZZZ	USA
BAYOLAGTIS, BALTRAS	30	M	LABR	RR	ZZZZ	USA
CSURY, KARA	35	F	NN	RR	ZZZZ	USA
JOHANN	.11	M	INFANT	RR	ZZZZ	USA
KRORTKOWSKI, JOS.	26	M	LABR	RR	ZZZZ	USA
MAJTKOWITZ, V.	23	M	LABR	RR	ZZZZ	USA
MULLER, FRED.	45	M	STCTR	RR	ZZZZ	USA
RATUSCHMUSKI, BALTRAS	30	M	LABR	RR	ZZZZ	USA
WURSCHUPSKI, SAML.	36	M	MUSN	RR	ZZZZ	USA
ZALLER, MENDEL	23	M	DYR	RR	ZZZZ	USA

SHIP: BOHEMIA

FROM: HAMBURG
TO: NEW YORK
ARRIVED: 15 OCTOBER 1885

PASSENGER	AGE	SEX	OCCUPATION	PV	VIL	DES
SCHULTZ, MARIE	29	F	SGL	RR	AHTF	USA
PAULUKANIS, BERNARDIN	20	F	LABR	RR	ZZZZ	USA
WALLINICZ, VINCENTI	30	F	LABR	RR	ZZZZ	USA
ANNA	18	F	SGL	RR	ZZZZ	USA
TEZERNIKOWSKY, JOKER	33	M	LABR	RR	ZZZZ	USA
CHEI	28	F	W	RR	ZZZZ	USA
LOB.	7	M	CHILD	RR	ZZZZ	USA
JOEL	5	M	CHILD	RR	ZZZZ	USA
LIESE	3	F	CHILD	RR	ZZZZ	USA
GOLDMANN, LEIB	18	M	SMH	RR	ZZZZ	USA
KONAPKA, AGISKA	40	F	W	RR	ZZZZ	USA
JOSEF	5	M	CHILD	RR	ZZZZ	USA
VINCENS	3	M	CHILD	RR	ZZZZ	USA
PETRUS	.06	M	INFANT	RR	ZZZZ	USA
KUCZYNSKI, MICHAEL	26	M	LABR	RR	AHTF	USA
WEISSMANN, CHAJE	44	F	W	RR	ZZZZ	USA
GERSTON	22	M	WVR	RR	ZZZZ	USA
SARA	9	F	CHILD	RR	ZZZZ	USA

PASSENGER	AGE	SEX	OCCUPATION	PRV VIL DES
MARIUS	8	M	CHILD	RRZZZZUSA
GIEHOWICZ, CASIMIR	18	M	LABR	RRAHTFUSA
EPSTEIN, LEIB	42	M	DLR	RRZZZZUSA
RICKLE	33	F	W	RRZZZZUSA
ANNA	8	F	CHILD	RRZZZZUSA
JOSEPH	6	M	CHILD	RRZZZZUSA
CHATZKEL	4	F	CHILD	RRZZZZUSA
MALKE	.11	F	INFANT	RRZZZZUSA
SCHECHANOWITZ, MARIUS	28	M	SHMK	RRZZZZUSA
BERTHA	27	F	W	RRZZZZUSA
DOROTHEA	5	F	CHILD	RRZZZZUSA
SAMUEL	.11	M	INFANT	RRZZZZUSA

SHIP: CITY OF ROME

FROM: LIVERPOOL
TO: NEW YORK
ARRIVED: 16 OCTOBER 1885

PASSENGER	AGE	SEX	OCCUPATION	PRV VIL DES
KAMENSKY, MOSES	41	M	MCHT	RRAHQHUSA
HANNA	36	F	W	RRAHQHUSA
GREJ.	12	F	CH	RRAHQHUSA
M.	10	F	CH	RRAHQHUSA
LEVIS	9	F	CHILD	RRAHQHUSA
BERTHA	7	F	CHILD	RRAHQHUSA
NORDWELL, FRK.	31	M	LABR	RRZZZZUSA
MACULAT, J.	35	M	LABR	RRZZZZUSA
NAEL, K.	25	M	LABR	RRZZZZUSA
SCHINK, J.	18	F	SVNT	RRZZZZUSA
ABDI	17	F	SVNT	RRZZZZUSA
MARTINSON, HY.	5	M	CHILD	RRZZZZUSA

SHIP: STATE OF INDIANA

FROM: GLASGOW AND LARNE
TO: NEW YORK
ARRIVED: 16 OCTOBER 1885

PASSENGER	AGE	SEX	OCCUPATION	PRV VIL DES
RISKIND, ABRAHAM	24	M	BKR	RRAHQUUSA
BEER, BACK	31	M	CL	RRAHTFUSA
DOBROWSKY, JOSEPH	18	M	CGRMKR	RRZZZZUSA
SEIDMAN, MARCUS	35	M	CGRMKR	RRAHVUUSA
ARONSTEIN, JUDEL	33	M	PDLR	RRZZZZUSA
UNISKAWITZ, PAUL	25	M	LABR	RRZZZZUSA
DIAMAND, ROSA	36	F	W	RRAHOKUSA
LINA	10	F	CH	RRAHOKUSA
SOPHIA	7	F	CHILD	RRAHOKUSA
NELLY	4	F	CHILD	RRAHOKUSA
GRODZINSKY, DOBE	19	F	SP	RRAHQUUSA
WOROBIEFF, DIMITRE	18	F	CL	RRACBFUSA

SHIP: DONAU

FROM: BREMEN
TO: NEW YORK
ARRIVED: 17 OCTOBER 1885

PASSENGER	AGE	SEX	OCCUPATION	PRV VIL DES
GOLDSTEIN, LEISER	24	M	LABR	RRZZZZUSA
WIENOZ, GERHARD	48	M	LABR	RRZZZZUSA
ELISAB.	44	F	W	RRZZZZUSA
MARG.	19	F	CH	RRZZZZUSA
ELISAB.	17	F	CH	RRZZZZUSA
ANDREAS	12	M	CH	RRZZZZUSA
HEINRICH	9	M	CHILD	RRZZZZUSA
JOHANN	7	M	CHILD	RRZZZZUSA
MARIE	3	F	CHILD	RRZZZZUSA
STARKEL, JACOB	39	M	TLR	RRZZZZUSA
CATH.	38	F	W	RRZZZZUSA
JACOB	18	M	TLR	RRZZZZUSA
EMILIE	13	F	CH	RRZZZZUSA
FRIEDR.	10	M	CH	RRZZZZUSA
EMMANUEL	9	M	CHILD	RRZZZZUSA
LIDIA	6	F	CHILD	RRZZZZUSA
JOH.	5	M	CHILD	RRZZZZUSA
NATHANACH	2	F	CHILD	RRZZZZUSA
KUCULAWA, MAG.N.	25	F	NN	RRZZZZUSA
SUSS, JOH.	55	M	FARMER	RRZZZZUSA
MARG.	50	F	W	RRZZZZUSA
BERTHA	18	F	CH	RRZZZZUSA
MAGD.	77	F	NN	RRZZZZUSA
LAUF, ROBERT	23	M	LABR	RRZZZZUSA
MATHILDE	23	F	W	RRZZZZUSA
SUSS, JOH.	30	M	LABR	RRZZZZUSA
CATH.	31	F	W	RRZZZZUSA
CHRISTOPH	9	M	CHILD	RRZZZZUSA
JOHANN	6	M	CHILD	RRZZZZUSA
MEIDINGER, ADAM	64	M	BCHR	RRZZZZUSA
CATH.	64	F	W	RRZZZZUSA
JOH.	27	M	BCHR	RRZZZZUSA
MAGD.	27	F	W	RRZZZZUSA
JACOB	5	M	CHILD	RRZZZZUSA
CHRIST.	3	F	CHILD	RRZZZZUSA
EVA	.03	F	INFANT	RRZZZZUSA
KLARBLATT, TAUBE	28	F	NN	RRZZZZUSA
JOSEL	3	M	CHILD	RRZZZZUSA
RIFE	.01	F	INFANT	RRZZZZUSA
BRUMMEIER, PHIL.	40	M	LABR	RRZZZZUSA
ELISAB.	36	F	W	RRZZZZUSA
MARG.	14	F	CH	RRZZZZUSA
HEINRICH	7	M	CHILD	RRZZZZUSA
FRIEDR.	5	M	CHILD	RRZZZZUSA
LOUISE	3	F	CHILD	RRZZZZUSA

SHIP: WIELAND

FROM: HAMBURG
TO: NEW YORK
ARRIVED: 17 OCTOBER 1885

PASSENGER	AGE	SEX	OCCUPATION	PRV VIL DES
MIELNIKOW, SARA	25	F	W	RRZZZZUSA
BREME	3	F	CHILD	RRZZZZUSA
CHAJE	.09	M	INFANT	RRZZZZUSA
DOBRSINEWSKY, CHAIE	25	F	W	RRZZZZUSA
EPHRAIM	.11	M	INFANT	RRZZZZUSA
JACOB	.01	M	INFANT	RRZZZZUSA
MAYROWITZ, MENDEL	46	M	LABR	RRZZZZUSA
FRUMSOHN, BEILE	25	F	W	RRZZZZUSA
JOSEF	.10	M	INFANT	RRZZZZUSA
KRESPOWITZ, SIMON	20	M	LABR	RRZZZZUSA
KRUGER, FERD.	25	M	FARMER	RRZZZZUSA
BOBROWSKI, JOSEPH	21	M	LABR	RRZZZZUSA
CZYDLOWSKI, GEORG	21	M	LABR	RRZZZZUSA
EPSTEIN, BREME	42	F	W	RRZZZZUSA
RAPPEPORT, ROSA	20	F	SGL	RRZZZZUSA

SHIP: CITY OF MONTREAL

FROM: LIVERPOOL AND QUEENSTOWN
TO: NEW YORK
ARRIVED: 19 OCTOBER 1885

PASSENGER	AGE	SEX	OCCUPATION	PRV	VIL	DES
AGATHE, MOS.SCHAYE	33	M	TCHR	RR	AEF	LNY

SHIP: EDAM

FROM: AMSTERDAM
TO: NEW YORK
ARRIVED: 19 OCTOBER 1885

PASSENGER	AGE	SEX	OCCUPATION	PRV	VIL	DES
KARZASICROWSKY, KATHARI	17	F	SVNT	PL	ZZZ	ZUSA

SHIP: EIDER

FROM: BREMEN AND SOUTHAMPTON
TO: NEW YORK
ARRIVED: 19 OCTOBER 1885

PASSENGER	AGE	SEX	OCCUPATION	PRV	VIL	DES
WYSOCKI, FRANZISEK	46	M	LABR	PL	AHT	FUSA
FRANZISKA	36	F	W	PL	AHT	FUSA
APOLONIA	9	F	CHILD	PL	AHT	FUSA
ANTON	3	F	CHILD	PL	AHT	FUSA
FELLER, JOSEF	65	M	LABR	RR	ZZZ	ZUSA
MAGDA.	60	F	W	RR	ZZZ	ZUSA
ROGUS	22	M	LABR	RR	ZZZ	ZUSA
ELISAB.	21	F	NN	RR	ZZZ	ZUSA
KAUK, JOH.	34	M	FARMER	RR	ZZZ	ZUSA
MARGE.	34	F	W	RR	ZZZ	ZUSA
CHRISTN.	9	M	CHILD	RR	ZZZ	ZUSA
JOHANN	2	M	CHILD	RR	ZZZ	ZUSA
ROSALIE	.08	F	INFANT	RR	ZZZ	ZUSA
EVA	19	F	NN	RR	ZZZ	ZUSA
BARBARA	11	F	CH	RR	ZZZ	ZUSA
ROSINE	9	F	CHILD	RR	ZZZ	ZUSA
CHRIST.	25	M	FARMER	RR	ZZZ	ZUSA
CATHA.	23	F	W	RR	ZZZ	ZUSA
FUEHRER, CHRIST.	23	M	LABR	RR	ZZZ	ZUSA
LISABETH	23	F	W	RR	ZZZ	ZUSA
KAUK, DAVID	22	M	LABR	RR	ZZZ	ZUSA
WOELLER, ROCHUS	16	M	LABR	RR	AHY	KUSA
THOMAS	20	M	LABR	RR	AHY	KUSA
KALMBERGER, ANDREAS	20	M	FARMER	RR	ZZZ	ZUSA
SCHAECHFERLE, GOTTFRIED	37	M	FARMER	RR	ZZZ	ZUSA
ELISAB.	38	F	W	RR	ZZZ	ZUSA
GOTTFR.	13	M	CH	RR	ZZZ	ZUSA
KATHA.	11	F	CH	RR	ZZZ	ZUSA
HEINR.	10	M	CH	RR	ZZZ	ZUSA
JACOB	8	M	CHILD	RR	ZZZ	ZUSA
JOHANN	6	M	CHILD	RR	ZZZ	ZUSA
WILHELM	4	M	CHILD	RR	ZZZ	ZUSA
ANDREAS	2	M	CHILD	RR	ZZZ	ZUSA
EDUARD	.01	M	INFANT	RR	ZZZ	ZUSA
ENGEL, JOHANN	18	M	LABR	RR	ZZZ	ZUSA
FRIEDR.	16	M	LABR	RR	ZZZ	ZUSA
HUTNAN, LUKACZ	17	M	LABR	RR	ZZZ	ZUSA
CZERVENAK, JANOS	18	M	LABR	RR	ZZZ	ZUSA
SCHOTT, MIHAL	17	M	LABR	RR	ZZZ	ZUSA

SHIP: ETRURIA

FROM: LIVERPOOL AND QUEENSTOWN
TO: NEW YORK
ARRIVED: 19 OCTOBER 1885

PASSENGER	AGE	SEX	OCCUPATION	PRV	VIL	DES
ANDECK, LOB.	32	M	FARMER	RR	ZZZ	ZUSA
ROSE	30	F	W	RR	ZZZ	ZUSA
SAMUEL	5	M	CHILD	RR	ZZZ	ZUSA
MALKE	3	M	CHILD	RR	ZZZ	ZUSA
MEYER	.08	M	INFANT	RR	ZZZ	ZUSA

SHIP: AUSTRALIA

FROM: HAMBURG
TO: NEW YORK
ARRIVED: 20 OCTOBER 1885

PASSENGER	AGE	SEX	OCCUPATION	PRV	VIL	DES
BRICK, ABRAH.	20	M	CGRMKR	RR	ZZZ	ZNY
SCHITTMANN, CHR.	30	M	TRDSMN	RR	ZZZ	ZUNK
HOWBINSKI, MOSES	18	M	TDR	RR	ZZZ	ZIL
NATANSON, BERNH.	13	M	TRDSMN	RR	ZZZ	ZNY
WEINSCHENKER, SCHMUL	65	M	TLR	RR	ZZZ	ZIL
GOLDSTEIN, SARAH	24	F	W	RR	ZZZ	ZIL
ABRAHAM	21	M	LABR	RR	ZZZ	ZIL
ZCLEZZCZI, HIRSCH	10	M	CH	RR	ZZZ	ZNY
NOWICKI, JOS.	24	M	PRNTR	RR	ZZZ	ZNY
STREICH, ANT.	24	M	CL	RR	ZZZ	ZNY
KURIATKOWSKI, MAR.	30	M	LABR	RR	ZZZ	ZNY

SHIP: RUGIA

FROM: HAMBURG
TO: NEW YORK
ARRIVED: 20 OCTOBER 1885

PASSENGER	AGE	SEX	OCCUPATION	PRV	VIL	DES
PERLSTEIN, GNESCHE	20	F	W	RR	ZZZ	ZUSA
SARA	.11	F	INFANT	RR	ZZZ	ZUSA
SOEPFER, GEDALIE	17	F	SGL	RR	ZZZ	ZUSA
SZECZEPANSKI, JOHANNE	41	F	W	RR	ZZZ	ZUSA
FLATAR, JACOB	27	M	LABR	RR	ZZZ	ZUSA
DOROTHEA	31	F	W	RR	ZZZ	ZUSA
LEWIN	9	M	CHILD	RR	ZZZ	ZUSA
SOLHY, DAVID	29	M	DLR	RR	ZZZ	ZUSA
AUGUSTE	25	F	W	RR	ZZZ	ZUSA
SALOMON	6	M	CHILD	RR	ZZZ	ZUSA
RIECKE	3	F	CHILD	RR	ZZZ	ZUSA
FANNY	.02	F	INFANT	RR	ZZZ	ZUSA
BAUMANN, HEYMANN	23	M	MCHT	RR	ZZZ	ZUSA
BILEWITZ, BENJAMIN	26	M	LABR	RR	ZZZ	ZUSA
DORA	25	F	W	RR	ZZZ	ZUSA
LAZAR	7	M	CHILD	RR	ZZZ	ZUSA
HERM.	.11	M	INFANT	RR	ZZZ	ZUSA
SMOLENSKI, SAMUEL	19	M	LABR	RR	ZZZ	ZUSA
SEHETZKI, MAX	23	M	MCHT	RR	ZZZ	ZUSA
SKOP, LEOPOLD	15	M	LABR	RR	ZZZ	ZUSA
MEIL, ERNST	21	M	LABR	RR	ZZZ	ZUSA
SALATKO, ALEX	19	M	LABR	RR	ZZZ	ZUSA

SHIP: CANADA

FROM: HAVRE
TO: NEW YORK
ARRIVED: 21 OCTOBER 1885

PASSENGER	AGE	SEX	OCCUPATION	PRV VIL	DES
LEWITA, P.	32	M	ART	PLZZZZ	NY

SHIP: RHEIN

FROM: BREMEN AND SOUTHAMPTON
TO: NEW YORK
ARRIVED: 22 OCTOBER 1885

PASSENGER	AGE	SEX	OCCUPATION	PRV VIL	DES
MALAKOWA, ANTONIA	50	F	NN	RRZZZZ	USA
SCHAETSCHURSKI, VICTOR	21	M	LABR	RRZZZZ	USA
WATKOWSKI, MICHAEL	30	M	LABR	RRZZZZ	USA
VALENTA	22	F	W	RRZZZZ	USA
GRAJSZEWSKA, ISRAEL.	18	M	TRVLR	RRZZZZ	USA
MENDELOWITZ, CHAIE	41	F	NN	RRZZZZ	USA
SARAH	11	F	CH	RRZZZZ	USA
ISAAC	9	M	CHILD	RRZZZZ	USA
AARON	7	M	CHILD	RRZZZZ	USA
LINA	6	F	CHILD	RRZZZZ	USA
JETTE	5	F	CHILD	RRZZZZ	USA
LEIB	3	F	CHILD	RRZZZZ	USA
MERKEL, ADAM	30	M	LABR	RRZZZZ	USA
CHRISTINE	30	F	W	RRZZZZ	USA
EVA	7	F	CHILD	RRZZZZ	USA
PHILIPP	4	M	CHILD	RRZZZZ	USA
CHRISTINE	3	F	CHILD	RRZZZZ	USA
JACOB	.09	M	INFANT	RRZZZZ	USA
ELISABETH	60	F	NN	RRZZZZ	USA
CAROLINE	16	F	CH	RRZZZZ	USA
GIDT, ALEXANDER	19	M	LABR	RRAAZQ	USA
WOLF, HEINRICH	27	M	LABR	RRZZZZ	USA
ROSINE	26	F	W	RRZZZZ	USA
HEINRICH	3	M	CHILD	RRZZZZ	USA
HEINRICH	53	M	LABR	RRZZZZ	USA
CATHARINE	50	F	W	RRZZZZ	USA
CATHARINE	20	F	NN	RRZZZZ	USA
CHRISTIAN	15	M	CH	RRZZZZ	USA
FRIEDERIKE	7	F	CHILD	RRZZZZ	USA
LIPPERT, JOHANN	20	M	LABR	RRZZZZ	USA
HORNING, JOHANN	29	M	TLR	RRZZZZ	USA
CHRISTINE	22	F	W	RRZZZZ	USA
JOHANN	.01	M	INFANT	RRZZZZ	USA
STREICH, LUDWIG	39	M	LABR	RRZZZZ	USA
ERNESTINE	38	F	W	RRZZZZ	USA
WILHELMINE	13	F	CH	RRZZZZ	USA
CARL	7	M	CHILD	RRZZZZ	USA
FERDINAND	5	M	CHILD	RRZZZZ	USA
MARIA	2	F	CHILD	RRZZZZ	USA
ADOLF	.11	M	INFANT	RRZZZZ	USA
ZDROGERZKOWNA, GOSEPPA	35	F	NN	RRZZZZ	USA
MALL	7	F	CHILD	RRZZZZ	USA
ABRAHAM	3	M	CHILD	RRZZZZ	USA
CHAIE	.02	M	INFANT	RRZZZZ	USA
KRAUSE, FRIEDRICH	40	M	LABR	RRZZZZ	USA
LEUFORST, LUDWIG	20	M	LABR	RRZZZZ	USA
ADOLF	18	M	LABR	RRZZZZ	USA

SHIP: CITY OF CHESTER

FROM: LIVERPOOL AND QUEENSTOWN
TO: NEW YORK
ARRIVED: 23 OCTOBER 1885

PASSENGER	AGE	SEX	OCCUPATION	PRV VIL	DES
FREDSON, MARY	33	F	SVNT	RRAGUZ	KS
HENTE, ALBERTINA	30	F	SVNT	FNZZZZ	KS
BUDKEWITZKY, ANTON	41	M	LABR	FNACBF	PIT
HALLONER, FRANZ	22	M	LABR	FNAGUZ	MI
MARTEN, J.	30	M	FARMER	FNADAX	NY
KLEMENTILDA, KAYSA	24	F	SVNT	RRZZZZ	KS
SYMON, JACOB	23	M	CL	RRZZZZ	CH
FANNIE	23	F	W	RRZZZZ	CH
SARAH	1	F	CHILD	RRZZZZ	CH
CAZELET, U-MR	24	M	GENT	RRADBQ	FL
SIBRANOF, MANE.	57	F	LDY	RRADBQ	NY
MADLA.	32	F	LDY	RRADBQ	NY

SHIP: MARTHA

FROM: UNKNOWN
TO: NEW YORK
ARRIVED: 23 OCTOBER 1885

PASSENGER	AGE	SEX	OCCUPATION	PRV VIL	DES
KLEIER, HEINRICH	23	M	MCHT	RRZZZZ	NY
MINDT, JACOB	37	M	LABR	RRZZZZ	UNK
CHRISTINA	34	F	W	RRZZZZ	UNK
ELISABETHA	11	F	CH	RRZZZZ	UNK
JACOB	9	M	CHILD	RRZZZZ	UNK
HEINRICH	6	M	CHILD	RRZZZZ	UNK
PETER	3	M	CHILD	RRZZZZ	UNK
EMILIE	2	F	CHILD	RRZZZZ	UNK
CARL.	.06	M	INFANT	RRZZZZ	UNK
SCHINDLER, ANDREAS	75	M	FARMER	RRZZZZ	UNK
JACOBINE	68	F	W	RRZZZZ	UNK
JOHANNES	40	M	CH	RRZZZZ	UNK
JULIANNE	40	F	CH	RRZZZZ	UNK
MICHAEL	20	M	CH	RRZZZZ	UNK
JACOB	13	M	CH	RRZZZZ	UNK
ELISABETH	15	F	CH	RRZZZZ	UNK
ROSINE	7	F	CHILD	RRZZZZ	UNK
CHRISTINE	4	F	CHILD	RRZZZZ	UNK
DOROTHEA	.11	F	INFANT	RRZZZZ	UNK
WEISS, ADAM	25	M	FARMER	RRZZZZ	UNK
ROSINE	20	F	W	RRZZZZ	UNK
CHRISTINE	.02	F	INFANT	RRZZZZ	UNK
JASPRITZ, KATHARINA	14	F	SVNT	RRZZZZ	UNK
SEILA, KATHARINA	13	F	SVNT	RRZZZZ	UNK
STERN, PHILIPP	52	M	FARMER	RRZZZZ	UNK
LOUISE	37	F	W	RRZZZZ	UNK
DANIEL	20	M	CH	RRZZZZ	UNK
ADAM	18	M	CH	RRZZZZ	UNK
JOHANNES	9	M	CHILD	RRZZZZ	UNK
BERTULA, MATHILDE	19	F	SVNT	FNZZZZ	NE
OJE, JOHANN-H.	28	M	LABR	FNZZZZ	NE

PASSENGER	AGE	SEX	OCCUPATION	PRIV	VIL	DES

SHIP: STATE OF ALABAMA

FROM: GLASGOW AND LARNE
TO: NEW YORK
ARRIVED: 23 OCTOBER 1885

PASSENGER	AGE	SEX	OCCUPATION	PV	D
BLAUSTEIN, UDEL	32	F	W	RRZZZZ	NY
CHAIE	1	F	CHILD	RRZZZZ	NY
BUNYACRUSKY, MARIE	19	F	NN	RRZZZZ	NY
FRIEDMAN, BEER	24	M	TLR	RRZZZZ	NY
GESCHPERT, JAS.	27	M	LABR	RRZZZZ	NY
GRANCWITACH, WILH.	32	M	TLR	RRZZZZ	NY
HAENDEL, MARIE	17	F	SVNT	RRZZZZ	NY
JABLOKOWITZ, ADOLPH	16	M	JNR	RRZZZZ	NY
KATAR, MAX	16	M	LABR	RRZZZZ	NY
NUSSENSOHN, HERMANN	16	M	LABR	RRZZZZ	NY
KURINSKY, JOSEPH	18	M	LABR	RRZZZZ	NY
NOTKIN, BERTHA	30	F	NN	RRZZZZ	NY
PIOTZ, ZIMOTEUS	24	M	FARMER	RRZZZZ	NY
SCHIMANOWITZ, JONAS	22	M	LABR	RRZZZZ	NY
MARIANNE	15	F	CH	RRZZZZ	NY
SAVILE, MENDEL	30	F	UNKNOWN	RRZZZZ	NY
BOLINE	23	F	W	RRZZZZ	NY
LIBEL	.01	F	INFANT	RRZZZZ	NY
SAROSY, JULIA	20	F	INF	RRZZZZ	NY
TRAUB, JACOB	18	M	CMST	RRZZZZ	NY
WOLFBERG, MOSES	31	M	UNKNOWN	RRZZZZ	NY

SHIP: WERRA

FROM: BREMEN AND SOUTHAMPTON
TO: NEW YORK
ARRIVED: 23 OCTOBER 1885

PASSENGER	AGE	SEX	OCCUPATION	PV	D
SCHUMACHER, FRANZ	36	M	LABR	RRZZZZ	USA
MAGDALA.	33	F	UNKNOWN	RRZZZZ	USA
JOHANNA	16	F	CH	RRZZZZ	USA
ANNA	14	F	CH	RRZZZZ	USA
CATHA	9	F	CHILD	RRZZZZ	USA
JOHANNES	4	M	CHILD	RRZZZZ	USA
JOSEF	2	M	CHILD	RRZZZZ	USA
MAGDA.	.11	F	INFANT	RRZZZZ	USA
KELLER, JOHANNA	37	M	FARMER	RRZZZZ	USA
CATHA.	32	F	UNKNOWN	RRZZZZ	USA
WILHELM	9	M	CHILD	RRZZZZ	USA
CASPAR	7	M	CHILD	RRZZZZ	USA
MARIA	4	F	CHILD	RRZZZZ	USA
JOHANNES	3	M	CHILD	RRZZZZ	USA
ANTON	.11	M	INFANT	RRZZZZ	USA
WERISBICK, JOSEF	27	M	FARMER	RRZZZZ	USA
SCHUMACHER, JOSEF	27	M	FARMER	RRZZZZ	USA
BARBARA	22	F	UNKNOWN	RRZZZZ	USA
JOSEF	2	M	CHILD	RRZZZZ	USA
CATHA.	.11	F	INFANT	RRZZZZ	USA
DYLENSKA, VERONICA	24	F	UNKNOWN	RRZZZZ	USA
MIEHL, HCH.	22	M	LABR	RRZZZZ	USA
JANS, CARL	17	M	UNKNOWN	RRZZZZ	USA
HOFFART, LUDWIG	30	M	FARMER	RRAHYK	USA
MARGARETHE	30	F	UNKNOWN	RRAHYK	USA
MARIANNE	7	F	CHILD	RRAHYK	USA
SCHATA	4	F	CHILD	RRAHYK	USA
BARBARA	2	F	CHILD	RRAHYK	USA
JOHANNES	.06	M	INFANT	RRAHYK	USA
CARL	14	M	CH	RRAHYK	USA
JOSEF	30	M	LABR	RRAHYK	USA
MARIANNE	28	F	UNKNOWN	RRAHYK	USA
MAGDALENE	2	F	CHILD	RRAHYK	USA
JOSEF	.06	M	INFANT	RRAHYK	USA
BAUMDTARK, ANTON	32	M	FARMER	RRAHYK	USA
CHRISTINE	28	F	UNKNOWN	RRAHYK	USA
PETER	2	M	CHILD	RRAHYK	USA
FRANZ	.09	M	INFANT	RRAHYK	USA
HOFFARTH, JOSEF	23	M	FARMER	RRAHYK	USA
CAROLINE	19	F	UNKNOWN	RRAHYK	USA
BERTSCH, JOHANNES	31	M	FARMER	RRAHYK	USA
MAGDALENE	30	F	UNKNOWN	RRAHYK	USA
ANTON	11	M	CH	RRAHYK	USA
ROSINE	5	F	CHILD	RRAHYK	USA
VALENTIN	2	M	CHILD	RRAHYK	USA
ANDRES	.06	M	INFANT	RRAHYK	USA
WEICHEL, BALTHASAR	27	M	FARMER	RRAHYK	USA
MICHEL, BARBARA	25	F	UNKNOWN	RRAHYK	USA
BERNHARD	4	M	CHILD	RRAHYK	USA
LIZABETH	2	F	CHILD	RRAHYK	USA
MARGARETHE	.06	F	INFANT	RRAHYK	USA
KELLER, ANTON	26	M	FARMER	RRAHYK	USA
ANNA	23	F	UNKNOWN	RRAHYK	USA
WARLINGER, SEBASTIAN	24	M	FARMER	RRAHYK	USA
EVA	21	F	UNKNOWN	RRAHYK	USA
SEBASTIAN	.06	M	INFANT	RRAHYK	USA
CACILIA	58	F	UNKNOWN	RRAHYK	USA
TATES	31	M	FARMER	RRAHYK	USA
MARGARETHE	30	F	UNKNOWN	RRAHYK	USA
SYLVESTER	5	M	CHILD	RRAHYK	USA
ANTON	.06	M	INFANT	RRAHYK	USA
ROST, PHIL.	38	M	FARMER	RRAFQV	USA
EVA	39	F	UNKNOWN	RRAFQV	USA
JACOB	9	M	CHILD	RRAFQV	USA
HCH.	7	M	CHILD	RRAFQV	USA
FILIP	5	M	CHILD	RRAFQV	USA
EVA	2	F	CHILD	RRAFQV	USA
CHRISTOF	.06	M	INFANT	RRAFQV	USA
FUEHRER, FILIP	24	M	FARMER	RRAFQV	USA
SOPHIE	18	F	UNKNOWN	RRAFQV	USA
CARL	.06	M	INFANT	RRAFQV	USA
THOMAS, BALTH.	23	M	FARMER	RRAHYK	USA
VOELLER, JOS.	22	M	FARMER	RRAHYK	USA
LEON	17	M	FARMER	RRAHYK	USA
GIESI, JOSEF	29	M	FARMER	RRZZZZ	USA
CLARA	23	F	UNKNOWN	RRZZZZ	USA
MARIA	1	F	CHILD	RRZZZZ	USA
CATHA.	.03	F	INFANT	RRZZZZ	USA
HARTMANN, JOHAN	26	M	FARMER	RRZZZZ	USA
CHRISTINE	26	F	UNKNOWN	RRZZZZ	USA
WILHELMNE.	2	F	CHILD	RRZZZZ	USA
ADAM	.06	M	INFANT	RRZZZZ	USA
WLM.	18	M	FARMER	RRZZZZ	USA
ATTELMANN, CHRISTF.	20	M	FARMER	RRZZZZ	USA
BITTERMANN, AUG.	31	M	FARMER	RRZZZZ	USA
TRIWKE	28	F	UNKNOWN	RRZZZZ	USA
MARGA.	5	F	CHILD	RRZZZZ	USA
AUGUST	1	M	CHILD	RRZZZZ	USA
JACOB	.01	M	INFANT	RRZZZZ	USA
FISCHER, CATHA.	32	F	UNKNOWN	RRZZZZ	USA
BECHTOLD, FRIED.	25	M	FARMER	RRZZZZ	USA
LISABETH	19	F	UNKNOWN	RRZZZZ	USA
RENZ, FRIED.	28	M	FARMER	RRZZZZ	USA
ROSINA	30	F	UNKNOWN	RRZZZZ	USA
ROSINA	5	F	CHILD	RRZZZZ	USA
BARBARA	3	F	CHILD	RRZZZZ	USA
CHRISTINA	1	F	CHILD	RRZZZZ	USA
WAGNER, GEORG	27	M	FARMER	RRZZZZ	USA
MARIE	23	F	UNKNOWN	RRZZZZ	USA
MAGDA.	2	F	CHILD	RRZZZZ	USA
JACOB	.09	M	INFANT	RRZZZZ	USA
SEGAL, SAL.	21	M	LABR	RRZZZZ	USA
GRANOT, HARRIS	33	M	LABR	RRZZZZ	USA
JALVALINSKY, M.	20	M	LABR	RRZZZZ	USA

PASSENGER	AGE	SEX	OCCUPATION	PRIV	DES
SHIP: W A SCHOLTEN					
FROM: ROTTERDAM					
TO: NEW YORK					
ARRIVED: 24 OCTOBER 1885					
JONSON, ERIKE	20	F	UNKNOWN	FNZZZZ	USA
SWENSON, EMILIE	31	F	UNKNOWN	FNZZZZ	USA
ERIKSON, VICTOR	40	M	CL	FNZZZZ	USA
JOHNSON, SERENA	20	F	UNKNOWN	FNZZZZ	USA
BEERMAN, M.	20	M	SLSMN	RRZZZZ	USA
BERNECHER, MOSES	30	M	SLSMN	RRZZZZ	USA
SHIP: ASSYRIAN MONARCH					
FROM: LONDON					
TO: NEW YORK					
ARRIVED: 26 OCTOBER 1885					
GOLAM, MOSES	19	M	LABR	PLZZZZ	NY
HERMAN	24	M	LABR	PLZZZZ	NY
SCHMUGLARSKY, ISAAC	19	M	TLR	RRZZZZ	NY
GRANUK, EHREN	36	M	CPMKR	PLZZZZ	NY
SHIP: ETHIOPIA					
FROM: GLASGOW AND MOVILLE					
TO: NEW YORK					
ARRIVED: 26 OCTOBER 1885					
BLOCH, CHANE	34	M	BKR	RRZZZZ	USA
ELKE	4	F	CHILD	RRZZZZ	USA
JUDETH	3	M	CHILD	RRZZZZ	USA
JOPPER, JOACHIM	19	M	TLR	RRZZZZ	USA
GRILLMAN, MOSES	17	M	LABR	RRZZZZ	USA
WEINBERG, MOSCHE	19	M	PDLR	RRZZZZ	USA
LURCOWSKY, JOSEPH	27	M	FARMER	RRZZZZ	USA
WERMUNSKY, ABRAHAM	12	M	CH	RRZZZZ	USA
KLEIN, WOLF	21	M	LABR	RRZZZZ	USA
GRAMMANN, JACOB	23	M	LABR	RRZZZZ	USA
BASHE	20	M	LABR	RRZZZZ	USA
GRUNBERG, JOSSEL	11	M	CH	RRZZZZ	USA
MICHAEL	9	M	CHILD	RRZZZZ	USA
SHIP: POLARIA					
FROM: HAMBURG					
TO: NEW YORK					
ARRIVED: 26 OCTOBER 1885					
SCHWEGAT, H.	54	M	SEMN	RRZZZZ	NY
MINNA	50	F	W	RRZZZZ	NY
EUGEN	24	M	S	RRZZZZ	NY
HULDA	22	F	D	RRZZZZ	NY
OLGA	15	F	CH	RRZZZZ	NY
ANNA	10	F	CH	RRZZZZ	NY
MINNA	7	F	CHILD	RRZZZZ	NY
BREST, ALBERT	20	M	TRDSMN	RRZZZZ	NY
HENTSCHEL, JOS.	23	M	SHMK	RRZZZZ	IL
SCHEIMANN, ZIPKI	30	F	WO	RRZZZZ	NY
MUNCKE	7	M	CHILD	RRZZZZ	NY
BRUCHE	5	F	CHILD	RRZZZZ	NY
SCHEINE	.11	F	INFANT	RRZZZZ	NY
SARAH	.02	F	INFANT	RRZZZZ	NY
KOPPEL, MARCUS	00	M	WCHMKR	RRZZZZ	NY
AKROLINSKY, ABR.	32	M	WCHMKR	RRZZZZ	NY
ANNA	27	F	W	RRZZZZ	NY
MAX.	7	M	CHILD	RRZZZZ	NY
WALTER	.10	M	INFANT	RRZZZZ	NY
SAMUEL	.02	M	INFANT	RRZZZZ	NY
BERKOWITZ, NISSER	30	M	MCHT	RRZZZZ	NY
ROSENBLUM, DINE	29	F	WO	RRZZZZ	NY
EIDEL	4	M	CHILD	RRZZZZ	NY
CHAINE	.06	F	INFANT	RRZZZZ	NY
KUNDZICZ, LUDWIG	19	M	LABR	RRZZZZ	NY
LIDERSKY, ABEL	19	M	MCHT	RRZZZZ	NY
LEWISOHN, ISAC	18	M	MCHT	RRZZZZ	NY
BRAUN, NIECHE	50	M	MCHT	RRZZZZ	NY
RELMKY, MOSES	17	M	MCHT	RRZZZZ	NY
FRIED, FRUNE	27	F	SGL	RRZZZZ	NY
ELIAS	6	M	CHILD	RRZZZZ	NY
MARCUS	4	M	CHILD	RRZZZZ	NY
LEWITANSKY, DAVID	19	M	MSNY	RRZZZZ	IL
PAWATARYS, MAGD.	18	F	SGL	RRZZZZ	UNK
RUDOLPF, ANNA	25	F	WO	RRZZZZ	NY
ANNA	.08	F	INFANT	RRZZZZ	NY
BIERBAUM, MEYER	30	M	TRDSMN	RRZZZZ	NY
LIPNITZKI, JOS.	36	M	LABR	RRZZZZ	NY
RAICHE	36	F	W	RRZZZZ	NY
ZUDECK	7	M	CHILD	RRZZZZ	NY
ABRAHAM	6	M	CHILD	RRZZZZ	NY
SONI	5	M	CHILD	RRZZZZ	NY
ROSA	3	F	CHILD	RRZZZZ	NY
NISSEN	.10	F	INFANT	RRZZZZ	NY
LEIE	.10	F	INFANT	RRZZZZ	NY
ROSENSTEIN, ROSA	20	F	SGL	RRZZZZ	NY
GUTSCHE, LOUISE	39	F	MLR	RRZZZZ	NY
HUDACZIK, MICH.	20	M	LABR	RRZZZZ	NY
COHN, KOPEL	25	M	TRDSMN	RRZZZZ	NY
SIGOL, SAMUEL	35	M	TRDSMN	RRZZZZ	NY
RABENWITZ, PERL.	18	M	TRDSMN	RRZZZZ	NY
LIPSCHUTZ, SUSMANN	21	M	TRDSMN	RRZZZZ	NY
BRENNER, BER.	45	M	TRDSMN	RRZZZZ	NY
SILBERMANN, EICH.	25	M	PDLR	RRZZZZ	NY
SUWAL, MOSCHE	20	M	PDLR	RRZZZZ	NY
WOLGIN, MARIE	16	F	SGL	RRZZZZ	NY
SCHAR, VICTOR	18	M	TRDSMN	RRZZZZ	NY
HORSCH, MARIE	24	F	SGL	RRZZZZ	NY
ROSENBLUM, MORITZ	23	M	TRDSMN	RRZZZZ	NY
SHIP: SERVIA					
FROM: LIVERPOOL AND QUEENSTOWN					
TO: NEW YORK					
ARRIVED: 26 OCTOBER 1885					
SCHUCHAI, CHAIM	52	M	LABR	RRZZZZ	NY
ARON	21	M	LABR	RRZZZZ	NY
LESS, ITZIG	33	M	LABR	RRZZZZ	NY
HORBAL, PAUL	25	M	LABR	RRZZZZ	NY
HONITSCHAK, PETER	26	M	LABR	RRZZZZ	NY

PASSENGER	AGE	SEX	OCCUPATION	PRV	VIL	DES
SHIP: SPAIN						
FROM: LIVERPOOL						
TO: NEW YORK						
ARRIVED: 26 OCTOBER 1885						
ALTHNER, AARON	40	M	TLR	PL	ZZZZ	NY
JANGA, KAJA-L.	20	F	SP	FN	ZZZZ	NY
HUSHMAN, ASHER	27	M	TLR	FN	AFVG	NY
TORVANIEME, JOHAN	23	M	LABR	FN	ZZZZ	NY
KINNONON, CALL	25	M	LABR	FN	ZZZZ	NY
ERIKSON, OTTO	25	M	LABR	FN	ZZZZ	NY
KAIVAS, AMANDA	29	F	SP	FN	ZZZZ	NY
PAWLOH, MACKALINS	45	M	LABR	PL	ZZZZ	NY
MARIANE	19	F	SP	PL	ZZZZ	NY
MIETOJ	17	F	SP	PL	ZZZZ	NY
FRANCISCA	15	F	CH	PL	ZZZZ	NY
VERONEHA	6	F	CHILD	PL	ZZZZ	NY
SIMON	4	M	CHILD	PL	ZZZZ	NY
SEODOVOWIG, MAX.	19	M	LABR	RR	ZZZZ	NY
FEIN, CHAIN	19	M	LABR	RR	ZZZZ	NY
FRIEDLAND, JANKEL	18	M	LABR	RR	ZZZZ	NY
JAKOWSKY, AND.	40	M	LABR	RR	ZZZZ	NY
SHIP: RHAETIA						
FROM: HAMBURG						
TO: NEW YORK						
ARRIVED: 27 OCTOBER 1885						
KRYNSKA, JOSEFINE	32	F	W	RR	ZZZZ	USA
ANNA	3	F	CHILD	RR	ZZZZ	USA
KANBELNIK, SAMUEL	46	M	DLR	RR	ZZZZ	USA
KRAMER, GERSON	30	M	DLR	RR	ABQB	USA
ZOSTKOPF, SARA	30	F	W	RR	ZZZZ	USA
RIWKE	7	F	CHILD	RR	ZZZZ	USA
CHAIM	.11	M	INFANT	RR	ZZZZ	USA
ISAAC, SIMON	21	F	SGL	RR	AHTN	USA
KARNOWSKY, SARA	17	F	SGL	RR	ZZZZ	USA
FUGLER, MICHEL	15	M	LABR	RR	AHTF	USA
WALLERSTEIN, HIRSCH	38	M	TLR	RR	ZZZZ	USA
KAHAN, FREIDE	26	F	W	RR	ZZZZ	USA
ABRAHAM	4	M	CHILD	RR	ZZZZ	USA
HINDE	.11	F	INFANT	RR	ZZZZ	USA
MAUSACK, ITZACK	16	M	LABR	RR	ZZZZ	USA
ROSENBERG, RUSKA	29	F	SGL	RR	AEFL	USA
SASLANSKY, ALEXANDER	18	M	LABR	RR	ZZZZ	USA
ROSENBERG, STERINA	23	F	W	RR	AHQU	USA
THEKLA	.11	F	INFANT	RR	AHQU	USA
DAVID, AEFRED	30	M	MCHT	RR	ZZZZ	USA
ZEGLINSKY, ADAM	30	M	LABR	RR	AFWJ	USA
JOSEFA	28	F	W	RR	AFWJ	USA
JOSEFA	9	F	CHILD	RR	AFWJ	USA
WEINSTEIN, BORRIS	33	M	LABR	RR	ZZZZ	USA
RACKMANN, LEIB	34	M	LABR	RR	ZZZZ	USA
GRUENBER, ISAAC	31	M	DLR	RR	ZZZZ	USA
MESE, DAVID	17	M	DLR	RR	ZZZZ	USA
DEMBROWSKY, JACOB	15	M	TLR	RR	AHTF	USA
STEIN, WULF	17	M	TLR	RR	ZZZZ	USA
SCHAPIRO, SCHENE	8	F	CHILD	RR	ZZZZ	USA
MARKER, JANKEL	9	M	CHILD	RR	ZZZZ	USA
MICHEWITZ, MALE	19	F	SGL	RR	AHZS	USA
GRIVES, MORDSCHEL	40	M	DLR	RR	AHTF	USA
SCHEINE	33	F	W	RR	AHTF	USA
WOLF	8	M	CHILD	RR	AHTF	USA
SAMUEL	7	M	CHILD	RR	AHTF	USA
FREIDE	5	F	CHILD	RR	AHTF	USA
MICHEL	4	M	CHILD	RR	AHTF	USA
CHAIE	.11	M	INFANT	RR	AHTF	USA
MOSES	.01	M	INFANT	RR	AHTF	USA
DUPINSCHKY, JOSEPH	33	M	LABR	RR	AHTF	USA
BRAUN, HERMANN	16	M	CGRMKR	RR	ZZZZ	USA
GOLNUT, FREIDE	22	F	SGL	RR	ZZZZ	USA
KATZ, SAMUEL	26	M	DLR	RR	AHVA	USA
MARKOWSKY, NESCHE	20	F	W	RR	ZZZZ	USA
ZIPE	.11	F	INFANT	RR	ZZZZ	USA
WALDMANN, MORITZ	18	M	CL	RR	AHVU	USA
AWNER, SCHAGE	35	M	TCHR	RR	ZZZZ	USA
ROGASINSKY, SCHAPSA	27	M	TLR	RR	ZZZZ	USA
MANKOWITZ, BERTHA	18	F	SGL	RR	AEFL	USA
PISKIN, SIMON	19	M	LABR	RR	ZZZZ	USA
RADIN, CHAWE	34	F	W	RR	ZZZZ	USA
KRESTANSKY, GERSON	9	M	CHILD	RR	ZZZZ	USA
KREMPANSKY, SCHAP.	8	M	CHILD	RR	ZZZZ	USA
FUEZI, MARIE	19	F	SGL	RR	ZZZZ	USA
BER, CHATZKEL	20	M	DLR	RR	ZZZZ	USA
SILBERBLATT, MEYER	27	M	DLR	RR	AADE	USA
SAKOWSKA, ELKA	33	F	W	RR	ZZZZ	USA
SAMUNOWSKY, ARON	26	M	LABR	RR	ZZZZ	USA
GOLDBERG, KOPPEL	27	M	LABR	RR	ZZZZ	USA
KAMINSKY, ROBERT	15	M	LABR	RR	ZZZZ	USA
LEERMANN, ARON	19	M	LABR	RR	ZZZZ	USA
SILDWETZKI, LEIB	22	M	LABR	RR	ZZZZ	USA
KOHN, WOLF	20	M	LABR	RR	ZZZZ	USA
SCHIMANSKY, JOH.	29	M	LABR	RR	ZZZZ	USA
ANGELIKA	20	F	W	RR	ZZZZ	USA
ANNA	14	F	SGL	RR	ZZZZ	USA
LUDOWIKA	.11	F	INFANT	RR	ZZZZ	USA
GINSBERG, JECHID	26	F	W	RR	ZZZZ	USA
ARON	4	M	CHILD	RR	ZZZZ	USA
ROSA	.11	F	INFANT	RR	ZZZZ	USA
ISRAEL, ABRAM	15	M	LABR	RR	AHTD	USA
FREID, IDA	40	F	W	RR	ZZZZ	USA
HERSCH	9	M	CHILD	RR	ZZZZ	USA
CHANE	8	F	CHILD	RR	ZZZZ	USA
MARGT.	18	F	SGL	RR	ZZZZ	USA
LEA	15	F	CH	RR	ZZZZ	USA
KASOD, ABE	21	M	LABR	RR	ZZZZ	USA
BRAUN, JETTE	16	F	SGL	RR	AHZS	USA
LIWINSKY, NICHE	27	F	W	RR	AHSW	USA
LEIB	7	M	CHILD	RR	AHSW	USA
SARA	4	F	CHILD	RR	AHSW	USA
CHANNE	.11	F	INFANT	RR	AHSW	USA
SIMON, CHANNE	45	F	W	RR	ZZZZ	USA
CHAIE	8	F	CHILD	RR	ZZZZ	USA
SIEMON	6	M	CHILD	RR	ZZZZ	USA
SANOTZKI, SCHOLEM	40	M	LABR	RR	AHSW	USA
REBECCA	38	F	W	RR	AHSW	USA
MEDOWNIK, ESTER	28	F	W	RR	ZZZZ	USA
CHASKEL	.11	F	INFANT	RR	ZZZZ	USA
GROSCH, ESTER	20	F	W	RR	ZZZZ	USA
SAMUEL	20	M	LABR	RR	ZZZZ	USA
SEREISKI, SESTNA	23	M	DLR	RR	AHZS	USA
LEWINSON, SCHEPSE	17	F	SGL	RR	AHZS	USA
GUDELSKI, SCHABSAI	45	M	TCHR	RR	AHZS	USA
DOCKTORSKI, RACHEL	40	F	W	RR	ZZZZ	USA
ESTER	9	F	CHILD	RR	ZZZZ	USA
HIRSCH	8	M	CHILD	RR	ZZZZ	USA
PESSE	7	F	CHILD	RR	ZZZZ	USA
HANNE	4	F	CHILD	RR	ZZZZ	USA
LAPIDOWSKI, SAMUEL	21	M	DLR	RR	ZZZZ	USA
FREUD, ISRAEL	6	M	CHILD	RR	ZZZZ	USA
LONDON, BERNHD.	28	M	DLR	RR	ZZZZ	USA
DWORE	26	F	W	RR	ZZZZ	USA
ADELE	2	F	CHILD	RR	ZZZZ	USA
DAVID	.06	M	INFANT	RR	ZZZZ	USA
SILBERMANN, ABR.	19	M	DLR	RR	ZZZZ	USA
SANOTZKI, CHAIM	9	M	CHILD	RR	AHSW	USA
JACOB	8	M	CHILD	RR	AHSW	USA
PERES, LEIB	13	M	CH	RR	AHTF	USA
NOVINBOSKY, LEIB	24	M	LABR	RR	AHSW	USA
RAPHALSON, MOSES	9	M	CHILD	RR	ZZZZ	USA
BARK, ABRAH.	20	M	TLR	RR	AHYC	USA
RAUSUK, BERE	19	M	LABR	RR	ZZZZ	USA

PASSENGER	AGE	SEX	OCCUPATION	PRIV	VIL	DES
ROSENTHAL, LEIB	19	M	LABR	RR	ZZZZ	USA
SCHAUTER, PETER	.01	M	INFANT	RR	ZZZZ	USA
KINTTEL, JASNIS	29	M	FARMER	RR	ZZZZ	USA
MARIE	24	F	W	RR	ZZZZ	USA
JACOB	35	M	FARMER	RR	ZZZZ	USA
FREDERIKE	33	F	W	RR	ZZZZ	USA
KUSTINE	11	F	CH	RR	ZZZZ	USA
FREDERIKE	10	F	CH	RR	ZZZZ	USA
MARIE	6	F	CHILD	RR	ZZZZ	USA
ZARATIC	4	M	CHILD	RR	ZZZZ	USA
JACOB	3	M	CHILD	RR	ZZZZ	USA
ELISATH.	.11	F	INFANT	RR	ZZZZ	USA
GOETZ, PAUL	35	M	FARMER	RR	ZZZZ	USA
MARIE	30	F	W	RR	ZZZZ	USA
PAUL	6	M	CHILD	RR	ZZZZ	USA
FRIEDR.	4	M	CHILD	RR	ZZZZ	USA
JOH.	2	M	CHILD	RR	ZZZZ	USA
MARGA.	.06	F	INFANT	RR	ZZZZ	USA
BAUER, RUDOLPH	21	M	LABR	RR	ZZZZ	USA
ABRAHAM, MORITZ	22	M	DLR	RR	AHSW	USA
FYNDALA, ANNA	17	F	SGL	RR	ZZZZ	USA
NOVEMBER, GITTEL	15	F	SGL	RR	ZZZZ	USA

SHIP: STATE OF NEVADA

FROM: GLASGOW AND LARNE
TO: NEW YORK
ARRIVED: 29 OCTOBER 1885

PASSENGER	AGE	SEX	OCCUPATION	PRIV	VIL	DES
BENINSOHN, MERE	30	F	W	RR	ZZZZ	USA
ROSA	.10	F	INFANT	RR	AHTU	USA
BRESCHEL, M.	18	M	PDLR	RR	AHTU	USA
BARSKI, SALOMON	35	M	PDLR	RR	AFVG	USA
BOMANN, ITY	22	M	WCHMKR	RR	ZZZZ	USA
DENELEWSKY, ISRAEL	20	M	PDLR	RR	AHVA	USA
GLASSMAN, M.	34	M	ENGR	RR	ZZZZ	USA
HERSCHBERG, J.	17	M	CL	RR	AHTN	USA
LICHT, F.	22	M	LABR	RR	AHVA	USA
MEDWEDOWSKI, B.	32	M	LABR	RR	AFVG	USA
SACK, M.	17	M	TLR	RR	AHUI	USA
STEZSAK, L.	24	M	CGRMKR	RR	AHUI	USA
LICHTENSTEIN, S.	24	F	W	RR	AFVG	USA
F.	1	F	CHILD	RR	AFVG	USA
LEWIN, DD.	15	M	TLR	RR	AHTD	USA
MICAS, W.	23	M	LABR	PL	ZZZZ	USA
SALUZKA, A.	24	F	W	PL	ZZZZ	USA
F.	1	M	CHILD	PL	ZZZZ	USA
ZUREWITZ, J.	50	M	LABR	PL	ZZZZ	USA

SHIP: CITY OF CHICAGO

FROM: LIVERPOOL AND QUEENSTOWN
TO: NEW YORK
ARRIVED: 30 OCTOBER 1885

PASSENGER	AGE	SEX	OCCUPATION	PRIV	VIL	DES
DONAWITCZ, JAKOB	20	M	LABR	PL	ACBF	NY
BRADS, M.	18	M	LABR	PL	ACBF	NY
BENJAMENOWICZ, WLH.	55	M	TLR	PL	ACBF	NY
MORITZ	22	M	TLR	PL	ACBF	NY
MANUEL, HARRIS	24	M	TLR	RR	ZZZZ	NY
SANDOWITZ, SALMON	30	M	CGRMKR	RR	ACBF	NY
PONEMANSKI, ABRAHAM	18	M	LABR	RR	ACBF	NY
SEGALL, MENDAL	20	M	WVR	RR	ACBF	NY
HALPERN, JOSEL	20	M	LABR	RR	ACBF	NY
ABRAMOWITZ, RACHEL	20	F	W	RR	ACBF	NY
KAPOL, MOSES	19	M	SHMK	RR	ACBF	NY
ESTHER	19	F	SP	RR	ACBF	NY

SHIP: HAMMONIA

FROM: HAMBURG AND HAVRE
TO: NEW YORK
ARRIVED: 30 OCTOBER 1885

PASSENGER	AGE	SEX	OCCUPATION	PRIV	VIL	DES
TOMASAJLIS, STANISLAUS	36	M	LABR	RR	ZZZZ	USA
MARIANNE	36	F	W	RR	ZZZZ	USA
MAGDALENE	.09	F	INFANT	RR	ZZZZ	USA
LESZINSKY, ROSA	22	F	SGL	RR	ZZZZ	USA
MINE	23	F	W	RR	ZZZZ	USA
GOLDE	.11	F	INFANT	RR	ZZZZ	USA
RODNEWSKY, GESENDEL	18	F	SGL	RR	ZZZZ	USA
SCHIMKOWSKY, ESTER	30	F	W	RR	ZZZZ	USA
SCHMUEL	.11	M	INFANT	RR	ZZZZ	USA
LITTMAN, ANNA	21	F	SGL	RR	AHTF	USA
DOROWCKY, SIMON	17	M	LABR	RR	AHTF	USA
VINIK, SARA	25	F	SGL	RR	AHTF	USA
SODORE, HIRSCH	42	M	DLR	RR	AHTF	USA
PREKORSKY, HIRSCH	9	M	CHILD	RR	AHTF	USA
MOSKOWCKY, RIWKE	24	M	W	RR	AHTF	USA
JOSEF	.11	M	INFANT	RR	AHTF	USA
SCHAMILSKY, PESACH	30	M	LABR	RR	AHTF	USA
BRAVEMANN, ADA	28	F	W	RR	ZZZZ	USA
CHAIM	9	M	CHILD	RR	ZZZZ	USA
PINE	8	M	CHILD	RR	ZZZZ	USA
MOSES	4	M	CHILD	RR	ZZZZ	USA
LAPUCK, ITTE	48	F	W	RR	ZZZZ	USA
DOBE	23	F	CH	RR	ZZZZ	USA
MOSES	9	M	CHILD	RR	ZZZZ	USA
BEILE	6	M	CHILD	RR	ZZZZ	USA
FEIGE	.11	M	INFANT	RR	ZZZZ	USA
BARHER, CERNE	30	F	SGL	RR	ZZZZ	USA
BILTZENES, JURGEN	23	M	LABR	RR	ZZZZ	USA
MATHILDE	27	F	W	RR	ZZZZ	USA
VERONIKA	4	F	CHILD	RR	ZZZZ	USA
JOSEF	.11	M	INFANT	RR	ZZZZ	USA
WICZNONIKAS, SIMON	29	M	LABR	RR	ZZZZ	USA
BADONAS, CASIS	33	M	LABR	RR	ZZZZ	USA
WEIJSFELDT, ABRAHAM	25	M	LABR	RR	ZZZZ	USA
BAMNEH, JACOB	30	M	LABR	RR	ZZZZ	USA
LEPINSKI, SCHEBSEL	17	M	LABR	RR	ZZZZ	USA
ASCHEROWITZ, ASCHER	41	M	MCHT	RR	ZZZZ	USA
BINGER, BEREIH	20	M	DLR	RR	ZZZZ	USA
AMSINSKY, MARCUS	25	M	DLR	RR	ZZZZ	USA
BRAUN, HIRSCH	31	M	LABR	RR	ZZZZ	USA
AMALIE	32	F	W	RR	ZZZZ	USA
JACOB	16	M	CH	RR	ZZZZ	USA
KIEWE	6	F	CHILD	RR	ZZZZ	USA
FREIDE	4	F	CHILD	RR	ZZZZ	USA
BERNH.	3	F	CHILD	RR	ZZZZ	USA
MARIE	.11	F	INFANT	RR	ZZZZ	USA
FEDKE	.01	F	INFANT	RR	ZZZZ	USA
GRABOWSKI, MOSES	18	M	DLR	RR	ZZZZ	USA
MOSHOWITZ, ISRAEL	23	M	LABR	RR	ZZZZ	USA
BERMAN, LEISER	22	M	LABR	RR	ZZZZ	USA
LEWIN, LEIB	45	M	LABR	RR	ZZZZ	USA
PHILIPOWSKI, ABRAHAM	25	M	LABR	RR	ZZZZ	USA
KRONIWITZKY, HERRMANN	25	M	LABR	RR	ZZZZ	USA
DUBERSTEIN, MAX.	28	M	LABR	RR	ADOI	USA
AUGUSTE	24	F	W	RR	ADOI	USA
DAVID	4	M	CHILD	RR	ADOI	USA
LEOPOLD	.11	M	INFANT	RR	ADOI	USA
LAKOME, CHAIE	17	F	SGL	RR	ZZZZ	USA
BROZD, LEIME	28	F	W	RR	AHTU	USA
ITTE	4	F	CHILD	RR	ZZZZ	USA
BURESTEIN, SARAH	22	F	W	RR	ZZZZ	USA

PASSENGER	AGE	SEX	OCCUPATION	PRV VIL DES
CHEWJE	.11	F	INFANT	RRZZZZUSA
TAUBE	.01	F	INFANT	RRZZZZUSA
PATZ, CHAIM	18	F	SGL	RRZZZZUSA
GOLDSTEIN, MOSES	30	M	LABR	RRAHSLUSA
BAUMANN, HIRSCH	20	M	LABR	RRZZZZUSA
MURNITZ, ABRAHAM	21	M	TLR	RRZZZZUSA
MICHELSOHN, FEIWEL	15	M	SHMK	RRAHRZUSA
ZALACHINSKY, MARG.	18	F	SGL	RRAHZSUSA
KIEDAISCH, ERNST	24	M	LABR	RRAHZSUSA
MARIANNE	19	F	W	RRAHZSUSA
MAX.	2	M	CHILD	RRAFAJUSA
JOHNE.	.02	F	INFANT	RRAFAJUSA
GABRIEL, BERTA	27	F	SGL	RRAFAJUSA
STREUBEL, ANNA	21	F	W	RRAFAJUSA
HEDWIG	4	F	CHILD	RRAFAJUSA
MARIE	.11	F	INFANT	RRAFAJUSA
SLOSONESKY, CHEIM	22	M	CNF	RRZZZZUSA
BUKATMANN, AARON	18	M	CL	RRAGRTUSA
KNITTEL, JACOB	58	M	FARMER	RRZZZZUSA
MARGA.	54	F	W	RRZZZZUSA
WILH.	14	M	CH	RRZZZZUSA
PETERSEN, KATARINA	61	F	SGL	RRAHTUUSA
SENESY, NACHMEN	40	M	DLR	RRAHTUUSA
WOLPOW, LOUISE	22	M	DLR	RRAHTUUSA
SPITZ, ARON	34	M	DLR	RRZZZZUSA
KRAJCWICH, JOH.	39	M	LABR	RRZZZZUSA
PETSITZA, ANNA	20	F	SGL	RRZZZZUSA
SOBOLSKI, JANKEL	20	M	DLR	RRZZZZUSA
FRANKEL, ABRAH.	15	M	LABR	RRZZZZUSA
NOAH	40	M	LABR	RRZZZZUSA
SARA	40	F	W	RRZZZZUSA
FRAENHEL, FREUDE	20	F	CH	RRZZZZUSA
MINNA	9	F	CHILD	RRZZZZUSA
KIWI	7	F	CHILD	RRZZZZUSA
ISRAEL	5	M	CHILD	RRZZZZUSA
FELSCHITZ, FEIGE	20	F	W	RRZZZZUSA
TUMPOWSKY, BEREL	25	M	LABR	RRZZZZUSA
PERLEISKI, MENDEL	20	M	LABR	RRZZZZUSA
BENDISSA, ELI	20	M	LABR	RRZZZZUSA
LESKIN, MORITZ	25	M	SDLR	RRZZZZUSA
FRANK, MEYER	43	M	DLR	RRZZZZUSA
SCHIEW, MEYER	24	M	DLR	RRZZZZUSA
LEVINOWSKY, LEISER	21	M	BCHR	RRAHZSUSA
WALENSKY, JACOB	21	M	BRR	RRAHZSUSA
BERMAN, APL.	19	M	LABR	RRAHZSUSA
ENGLE, MOSES	17	M	BBR	RRZZZZUSA
LOPATIN, HELENE	24	F	SGL	RRAHQHUSA
BORLETZKI, SAVELLI	38	M	SHMK	RRZZZZUSA
KILIEW, MARTIN	35	M	SHMK	RRZZZZUSA
SZIMOWCIZ, MOWSZA	60	M	LABR	RRAHTRUSA
RIEKE	60	F	W	RRAHTRUSA
CAPLAN, BENJAMIN	8	M	CHILD	RRAHTRUSA

SHIP: WAESLAND

FROM: ANTWERP
TO: NEW YORK
ARRIVED: 30 OCTOBER 1885

PASSENGER	AGE	SEX	OCCUPATION	PRV VIL DES
DREWS, ACH.	24	M	LABR	RRZZZZNY
BERTHA	24	F	UNKNOWN	RRZZZZNY
WILH.	50	F	UNKNOWN	RRZZZZNY
LOUISE	50	F	UNKNOWN	RRZZZZNY
U, MINNA	.02	F	INFANT	RRZZZZNY

SHIP: ELBE

FROM: BREMEN
TO: NEW YORK
ARRIVED: 31 OCTOBER 1885

PASSENGER	AGE	SEX	OCCUPATION	PRV VIL DES
BRANDT, SCHMUL	32	M	FARMER	RRZZZZUSA
BROW, DANIEL	19	M	LABR	RRZZZZUSA
REICHEL, PHILIPP	34	M	FARMER	RRZZZZUSA
APERTE, MICHEL	32	M	FARMER	RRZZZZUSA
REGINA	21	F	W	RRZZZZUSA
NICOLAUS	4	M	CHILD	RRZZZZUSA
U, GEORG	.09	M	INFANT	RRZZZZUSA
NEIS, JACOB	28	M	FARMER	RRZZZZUSA
MAGARETHE	25	F	NN	RRZZZZUSA
ANTON	.10	M	INFANT	RRZZZZUSA
GLATT, ANTON	23	M	FARMER	RRZZZZUSA
CATHARINE	20	F	W	RRZZZZUSA
ROSALIE	8	F	CHILD	RRZZZZUSA
ZAHN, ANTON	30	M	FARMER	RRZZZZUSA
MAGDALENE	23	F	W	RRZZZZUSA
MARTIN	2	M	CHILD	RRZZZZUSA
TI--, JOS.	35	M	FARMER	RRZZZZUSA
AGNES	33	F	W	RRZZZZUSA
CAROLINE	10	F	CH	RRZZZZUSA
FRANZ	6	M	CHILD	RRZZZZUSA
ANTON	4	M	CHILD	RRZZZZUSA
JACOB	2	M	CHILD	RRZZZZUSA
JOSEPH	.03	M	INFANT	RRZZZZUSA
HELD, JACOB	32	M	FARMER	RRZZZZUSA
BARBARA	25	F	W	RRZZZZUSA
MAGDALENE	5	F	CHILD	RRZZZZUSA
MATHIAS	2	M	CHILD	RRZZZZUSA
ZAHN, CONST.	25	M	FARMER	RRZZZZUSA
MARIE	24	F	W	RRZZZZUSA
ELISE	18	F	CH	RRZZZZUSA
ANTON	3	M	CHILD	RRZZZZUSA
JOSEF	2	M	CHILD	RRZZZZUSA
ADAM	.07	M	INFANT	RRZZZZUSA
VOELLER, JOHANNES	28	M	FARMER	RRZZZZUSA
KATHARINE	26	F	W	RRZZZZUSA
DUERMS	2	M	CHILD	RRZZZZUSA
GRETHE	.09	F	INFANT	RRZZZZUSA
SCHAEFER, PAUL	40	M	FARMER	RRZZZZUSA
CATHARINE	44	F	W	RRZZZZUSA
JACOB	16	M	CH	RRZZZZUSA
BERNH.	9	M	CHILD	RRZZZZUSA
FRANZ	7	M	CHILD	RRZZZZUSA
LISABETH	5	F	CHILD	RRZZZZUSA
FIND, ANTON	34	M	FARMER	RRZZZZUSA
THERSENA	30	F	W	RRZZZZUSA
JOHANNES	6	M	CHILD	RRZZZZUSA
ROCHNUS	3	M	CHILD	RRZZZZUSA
BERNHARD	.06	M	INFANT	RRZZZZUSA
NEIS, GEORG	54	M	FARMER	RRZZZZUSA
FRANCISCA	52	F	NN	RRZZZZUSA
MARGARETHE	18	F	CH	RRZZZZUSA
CATHARINE	16	F	CH	RRZZZZUSA
JOSEF	14	M	CH	RRZZZZUSA
HELENA	6	F	CHILD	RRZZZZUSA
GRANBINSKY, SAUMN.	23	M	LABR	RRZZZZUSA
BENJAMIN	30	M	LABR	RRZZZZUSA

SHIP: NECKAR

FROM: BREMEN
TO: NEW YORK
ARRIVED: 31 OCTOBER 1885

PASSENGER	AGE	SEX	OCCUPATION	PRV VIL DES
FEIN, ARJE	26	F	WO	RRZZZZNY
KAPLAN, JUDEL	17	F	WO	RRZZZZNY
HER, HEIDMER	31	F	SVNT	RRZZZZNY
FRUMER	18	F	SVNT	RRZZZZNY
CHIMEN	11	F	SVNT	RRZZZZNY
PLUTZKE, MEISSE	17	F	SVNT	RRZZZZNY
ROSENFELD, FRINE	32	F	SVNT	RRZZZZNY
PLUTZKE, PESSY	17	F	SVNT	RRZZZZNY
WEINDORF, GERSON	20	M	LABR	RRZZZZNY
KLAASSEN, HEINR.	27	M	LABR	RRZZZZNY
ANNA	27	F	UNKNOWN	RRZZZZNY
HEINR.	1	M	CHILD	RRZZZZNY
JOHANN	.01	M	INFANT	RRZZZZNY
SUCKAN, ABRAHAM	42	M	FARMER	RRZZZZNY
CATHARINA	39	F	UNKNOWN	RRZZZZNY
ABRAHAM	16	M	UNKNOWN	RRZZZZNY
SUSANNE	14	F	UNKNOWN	RRZZZZNY
PETER	11	M	UNKNOWN	RRZZZZNY
CATH.	8	F	CHILD	RRZZZZNY
MARG.	6	F	CHILD	RRZZZZNY
HELENE	3	F	CHILD	RRZZZZNY
PINIEWITSCH, JAN.	25	M	FARMER	RRZZZZNY
FRANSKEH, JOSEPH	28	M	FARMER	RRZZZZNY
GEGETZK, JOSEPH	25	M	FARMER	RRZZZZNY
PLAKSI, ISAAC	17	M	UNKNOWN	RRZZZZCH
JONKE, PETER	44	M	FARMER	RRZZZZNY
MARIE	44	F	UNKNOWN	RRZZZZNY
PETER	16	M	FARMER	RRZZZZNY
JOHANN	14	M	UNKNOWN	RRZZZZNY
MARIE	9	F	CHILD	RRZZZZNY
EPHRAIM	9	M	CHILD	RRZZZZNY
ELISABETH	5	F	CHILD	RRZZZZNY
FLORENTINE	4	F	CHILD	RRZZZZNY
FRANZ	2	M	CHILD	RRZZZZNY
JACOB	11	M	UNKNOWN	RRZZZZNY
LIEBERMANN, BELIE	25	F	UNKNOWN	RRZZZZNY
HEIBUSCH	13	M	UNKNOWN	RRZZZZNY
FRANK, MERE	35	F	UNKNOWN	RRZZZZNY
LOEB	11	M	UNKNOWN	RRZZZZNY
LEMAKE	10	F	UNKNOWN	RRZZZZNY
NISSE	7	F	CHILD	RRZZZZNY
RIFKE	3	F	CHILD	RRZZZZNY
ROSMANN, LEIB	37	M	LABR	RRZZZZNY
SCHIEMANN, JAC.	19	M	LABR	RRZZZZPA
PAUL	22	M	LABR	RRZZZZPA
SIMON, PINKE	20	F	SVNT	RRZZZZNY
LAPPE, CHANE	28	F	SVNT	RRZZZZNY
NONNMANN, CHANE	2	F	CHILD	RRZZZZNY
ALWINE	.02	F	INFANT	RRZZZZNY
DITTMANN, FRIEDR.	34	M	LABR	RRZZZZNY
AUGUST	.09	M	INFANT	RRZZZZNY
TEMPLIN, PAULINE	23	F	UNKNOWN	RRZZZZNY
FERDINAND	.09	M	INFANT	RRZZZZNY
BUDKEWICZ, MARY	22	F	UNKNOWN	RRZZZZNY
CASIMIR	2	M	CHILD	RRZZZZNY
PIKOWSKA, CAROL.	20	F	SVNT	RRZZZZNY
SCHMIDT, FRIEDR.	32	M	FARMER	RRZZZZNY
MARG.	31	F	UNKNOWN	RRZZZZNY
FRIEDR.	7	M	CHILD	RRZZZZNY
MARG.	5	F	CHILD	RRZZZZNY
BARB.	.06	F	INFANT	RRZZZZNY
FISCHER, ADAM	32	M	FARMER	RRZZZZNY
ELISABETH	28	F	UNKNOWN	RRZZZZNY
MARIE	2	F	CHILD	RRZZZZNY
JACOB	4	M	CHILD	RRZZZZNY
SUSANNE	.09	F	INFANT	RRZZZZNY
GRIESSI, HEINR.	26	M	FARMER	RRZZZZNY
CATH.	25	F	UNKNOWN	RRZZZZNY
JOHANNES	3	M	CHILD	RRZZZZNY
WILHELN	.06	M	INFANT	RRZZZZNY
LEWIN, NOSSEM	15	M	LABR	RRZZZZNY
MARKOWITZ, MORZE	18	F	SVNT	RRZZZZNY
SOFELA, WAZINECZANA	31	F	UNKNOWN	RRZZZZNY
ZAPEJEWSKA	24	F	UNKNOWN	RRZZZZNY
KAMINSKA, ALEX	21	M	LABR	RRZZZZNY
FRANZISCA	21	F	UNKNOWN	RRZZZZNY
BENSO, ANNA	26	F	UNKNOWN	RRZZZZNY
ANNA	.11	F	INFANT	RRZZZZNY
KRAEMAR, LEISER	15	M	LABR	RRZZZZNY
JANCOWICZ, S.	52	M	LABR	RRZZZZNY
SZERNO, M.	22	M	LABR	RRZZZZNY
PALRUTZKY, JACOB	32	M	LABR	RRZZZZNY
FLATON, ARON	37	M	LABR	RRZZZZNY
DRESMER, ISIDOR	25	M	LABR	RRZZZZNY
JOSEFOWITZ, CARL	22	M	LABR	RRZZZZNY
VALENESICK, F.	19	M	FARMER	RRZZZZNY
STEIN, MORITZ	22	M	LABR	RRZZZZNY

SHIP: FURNESSIA

FROM: GLASGOW
TO: NEW YORK
ARRIVED: 03 NOVEMBER 1885

PASSENGER	AGE	SEX	OCCUPATION	PRV VIL DES
DWORKIND, ISAC	24	M	LABR	RRZZZZUSA
ISAC	24	M	LABR	RRZZZZUSA
KOLM, ISAC	26	M	PRNTR	RRZZZZUSA
GRUN, LEIB	35	M	DLR	RRZZZZUSA
KORLUNKI, MORDSCHE	23	M	DLR	RRZZZZUSA
BERLINERBLAN, JOSEPH	11	M	NN	RRZZZZUSA
KOZAK, JANKEL	42	M	SHMK	RRZZZZUSA
LASOR	20	M	SHMK	RRZZZZUSA
ROMSCH, JACOB	22	M	DLR	RRZZZZUSA
SCHAPIRA, JOSEPH	23	M	DLR	RRZZZZUSA
SCHMINGLER, LEISER	32	M	DLR	RRZZZZUSA
SCHWARZMANN, BEER	30	M	DLR	RRZZZZUSA
SEGALL, ITZIG	21	M	LABR	RRZZZZUSA
LANKISCHKI, MENDEL	20	M	DLR	RRZZZZUSA
SARDINA	19	F	W	RRZZZZUSA
ROTTER, ITZIG	54	M	OPTC	RRZZZZUSA
MALKE	45	F	W	RRZZZZUSA
BERLA	18	F	W	RRZZZZUSA
RALE	16	F	W	RRZZZZUSA
SAMUEL	11	M	NN	RRZZZZUSA
SADOW, FEIWEL	23	M	TLR	RRZZZZUSA
JETTE	22	F	W	RRZZZZUSA
LORE	2	F	CHILD	RRZZZZUSA
MORDSCHE	.06	M	INFANT	RRZZZZUSA
LECHMANN, ABRAHAM	22	M	TNSTH	RRZZZZUSA
SOSSI	20	F	W	RRZZZZUSA
ROSSMANN, BRAINE	17	F	SVNT	RRZZZZUSA

SHIP: GALLIA

FROM: LIVERPOOL AND QUEENSTOWN
TO: NEW YORK
ARRIVED: 03 NOVEMBER 1885

PASSENGER	AGE	SEX	OCCUPATION	PRV VIL DES
RUBIN, SOLOMON	22	M	LABR	RRZZZZUSA
FREDRICKSON, ANDERS	54	M	LABR	FNZZZZUSA
HIRSCH, JOSEPH	21	M	LABR	FNZZZZUSA
PITTERSON, PITTER-W.	27	M	LABR	FNAEWSUSA
WALLI, JACOB	32	M	LABR	FNZZZZUSA

SHIP: FULDA

FROM: BREMEN
TO: NEW YORK
ARRIVED: 04 NOVEMBER 1885

PASSENGER	AGE	SEX	OCCUPATION	PRV VIL DES
SCHINEN, SUSSMAN	20	M	MCHT	RRZZZZUSA
PLITMANN, SLINE	23	M	NN	RRZZZZUSA
PEREL	4	M	CHILD	RRZZZZUSA
HAHNKE, JOHANN	42	M	FARMER	RRZZZZUSA
CAROLINE	24	F	NN	RRZZZZUSA
LYDIA	18	F	NN	RRZZZZUSA
SALOMINE	8	F	CHILD	RRZZZZUSA
JUSTINE	6	F	CHILD	RRZZZZUSA
MATHILDE	5	F	CHILD	RRZZZZUSA
SOPHIE	2	F	CHILD	RRZZZZUSA
MUND, CHRIST.	43	M	FARMER	RRZZZZUSA
CAROLINE	42	F	NN	RRZZZZUSA
ROSINE	17	F	NN	RRZZZZUSA
JOHANNES	14	M	FARMER	RRZZZZUSA
JOHANNA	8	F	CHILD	RRZZZZUSA
FERDINAND	6	M	CHILD	RRZZZZUSA
JACOB	5	M	CHILD	RRZZZZUSA
GOTTLIEF	.09	M	INFANT	RRZZZZUSA
GOTTLIEF	20	M	FARMER	RRZZZZUSA
BOLAFF, DANIEL	25	M	FARMER	RRZZZZUSA
LOUISE	23	F	NN	RRZZZZUSA
ABELITA	.07	F	INFANT	RRZZZZUSA
HENKE, DAVID	23	M	FARMER	RRZZZZUSA
SCHMIRER, JACOB	39	M	FARMER	RRZZZZUSA
CHRISTINE	38	F	NN	RRZZZZUSA
MARIA	13	F	NN	RRZZZZUSA
MAGDA	8	F	CHILD	RRZZZZUSA
CAROLINE	6	F	CHILD	RRZZZZUSA
SALOMINE	2	F	CHILD	RRZZZZUSA
SCHLATCZ, ANDREAS	29	M	FARMER	RRZZZZUSA
FRIEDRIKE	20	F	NN	RRZZZZUSA
JOHANN	.10	M	INFANT	RRZZZZUSA
SCHULZ, JUSTINE	42	F	NN	RRZZZZUSA
SCHUH, JOHANN	29	M	FARMER	RRZZZZUSA
EVA	29	F	NN	RRZZZZUSA
CATHARINE	8	F	CHILD	RRZZZZUSA
MAGDA	6	F	CHILD	RRZZZZUSA
MARIE	3	F	CHILD	RRZZZZUSA
JOSEF	.03	M	INFANT	RRZZZZUSA
LIEBHAHN, WANDELIN	31	M	FARMER	RRAHYKUSA
MARIANNE	24	F	NN	RRAHYKUSA
SYLVESTER	.03	F	INFANT	RRAHYKUSA
SCHUH, BERNHARD	32	M	FARMER	RRAHYKUSA
ROSALIA	26	F	NN	RRAHYKUSA
FRAMZ	.10	M	INFANT	RRAHYKUSA
WELTER, BERNHARD	38	M	FARMER	RRZZZZUSA
BARBARA	37	F	NN	RRZZZZUSA
PAUL	7	M	CHILD	RRZZZZUSA
LISABETH	6	F	CHILD	RRZZZZUSA
CATHARINA	2	F	CHILD	RRZZZZUSA
GRAUMANN, CARL	33	M	FARMER	RRZZZZUSA
CAROLINE	32	F	NN	RRZZZZUSA
LYDIA	8	F	CHILD	RRZZZZUSA
JOHANN	7	M	CHILD	RRZZZZUSA
EMIL	6	M	CHILD	RRZZZZUSA
GUSTAV	5	M	CHILD	RRZZZZUSA
MARIE	2	F	CHILD	RRZZZZUSA
MUND, CAROLINE	7	F	CHILD	RRZZZZUSA
SCHMIERER, JOHANN	43	M	FARMER	RRAAYZUSA
CATHRINA	43	F	NN	RRAAYZUSA
JOHANN	17	M	NN	RRAAYZUSA
CHRISTINA	14	F	NN	RRAAYZUSA
MARGA	8	F	CHILD	RRAAYZUSA
JACOB	7	M	CHILD	RRAAYZUSA
MAGDA	5	F	CHILD	RRAAYZUSA
SALAMINA	2	F	CHILD	RRAAYZUSA
FRANZ	23	M	FARMER	RRZZZZUSA
FRIEDERIKE	22	F	NN	RRZZZZUSA
CAROLINE	.08	F	INFANT	RRZZZZUSA
FRAUTMANN, FRIEDRICH	22	M	FARMER	RRZZZZUSA
OCHSNER, NICOLAUS	21	M	FARMER	RRZZZZUSA
KARPITOW, LEIZI	22	F	NN	RRAAYZUSA
FEINE	19	F	NN	RRAAYZUSA

SHIP: INDIA

FROM: HAMBURG
TO: NEW YORK
ARRIVED: 04 NOVEMBER 1885

PASSENGER	AGE	SEX	OCCUPATION	PRV VIL DES
FRACHTMANN, ROSALIE	40	F	WO	PLZZZZNY
HEINRICH	7	M	CHILD	PLZZZZNY
ADOLF	5	M	CHILD	PLZZZZNY
SARAH	.06	F	INFANT	PLZZZZNY
SAPIRA, HARRIS	20	M	TRDSMN	RRZZZZNY
HORSTNOWITZ, IGNATZIA	28	F	WO	RRZZZZNY
TUROWSKY, JAN	25	M	LABR	RRZZZZNY
ROSE, JOHANN	24	M	MCHT	RRZZZZUNK
WEINSTEIN, MOSES	27	M	TLR	RRZZZZNY
HEIDEN, SAMUEL	40	M	JWLR	RRZZZZNY
JETZER, EPHRAIM	20	M	TLR	RRZZZZNY
KOPELWITZ, MORDSCHEL	16	M	SHMK	RRZZZZNY
FINGERHUT, RIWE	40	F	WO	RRZZZZNY
PINCUS	8	M	CHILD	RRZZZZNY
HIRSCH	5	M	CHILD	RRZZZZNY
BRAINE	.05	F	INFANT	RRZZZZNY
BLANKITZKI, ABRAHAM	19	M	LABR	RRZZZZNY
LYSKOWSKI, JOSEF	21	M	TDR	RRZZZZIL
LESCHITZKI, MOAH	20	M	TDR	RRZZZZNY
SCHERESCHEWSKA, PESSE-L	21	F	WO	RRZZZZUNK
WEITZMANN, BEILE	20	F	SGL	RRZZZZNY
COHN, HIRSCH	39	M	TRDSMN	PLZZZZNY
MARCUS, LINA	40	F	WO	RRZZZZNY
HORTSCHE	6	F	CHILD	RRZZZZNY
DAKOVKA, ABRAHAM	28	M	TRDSMN	RRZZZZNY
OSWITSCHINSKA, MARIA	22	F	WO	PLZZZZNY
GOLBERG, JANKEL	26	M	TRDSMN	RRZZZZPHI
CHANE	20	F	W	RRZZZZPHI
GORKE, EMIL	23	M	LABR	RRZZZZPHI
NATALIE	.10	M	INFANT	RRZZZZPHI
MAGETTMANN, MOSES	30	M	TRDSMN	RRZZZZIL
CHANE	14	F	D	RRZZZZIL
KUBOLSKI, LEIB	13	F	BY	RRZZZZNY
KANICK, ROSALIE	70	F	WO	RRZZZZNY

SHIP: SCHIEDAM

FROM: AMSTERDAM
TO: NEW YORK
ARRIVED: 04 NOVEMBER 1885

PASSENGER	AGE	SEX	OCCUPATION	PRV VIL DES
KACKUR, JOHANNES	20	M	FARMER	RRZZZZUSA
SAMSKAR, JOHANNES	24	M	FARMER	RRZZZZUSA
WESTMAN, JONAS	30	M	FARMER	RRZZZZUSA
OLSTEIN, JACOB	20	M	MCHT	RRAHTFUSA
FRIEDMANN, SAMUEL	21	M	LABR	RRZZZZUSA
SENATOR, SALOMON	21	M	MCHT	RRAHTFUSA
MENDELSOHN, ISRAEL	19	M	CGRMKR	RRZZZZUSA
PATREIKA, LEIB	10	M	MCHT	RRZZZZUSA
SCHLESSINGER, HESSE	32	M	LABR	RRZZZZUSA
JANOWITZ, SCHMUL	26	M	LABR	RRZZZZUSA
KUSCHNER, MAY	29	M	SHMK	RRZZZZUSA
SCHAPIRA, MOSES	32	M	BKR	RRZZZZUSA

PASSENGER	AGE	SEX	OCCUPATION	PRV VIL DES
WALSTEIN, MOSES	20	M	CGRMKR	RRZZZZUSA
WINIK, ALTER	20	M	SDLR	RRZZZZUSA
MULSTEIN, MOSES	52	M	TLR	RRZZZZUSA
KRAWZ, ABR.	45	M	LABR	RRZZZZUSA
KARASCHNITZ, ITSCHIG	26	M	TLR	RRZZZZUSA
WASFERZENG, ELIAS	43	M	MCHT	RRAHUGUSA
NEUDORF, SALOMON	22	M	BKR	RRZZZZUSA
NISCHUNIS, IWIGES	22	M	LABR	RRZZZZUSA
MATUSEWITZ, VINCENT	24	M	LABR	RRZZZZUSA
SARMSKARS, MATS	20	M	FARMER	RRZZZZUSA
KINSERIS, ANDREAS	30	M	LABR	RRZZZZUSA
JAFFE, JANKEL	49	M	LABR	RRZZZZUSA
WEBER, CHAINE	20	M	TLR	RRZZZZUSA
JOHANOWSKY, PESCHE	24	F	UNKNOWN	RRZZZZUSA
CHAINE	.06	F	INFANT	RRZZZZUSA
PACZENKA, LEIB	20	M	LABR	RRZZZZUSA
MOSES	.06	M	INFANT	RRZZZZUSA
FUCHS, RACHEL	26	F	UNKNOWN	RRAHUGUSA
SARAH	1	F	CHILD	RRAHUGUSA
MARKURIZ, JURGI	20	M	LABR	RRZZZZUSA
STANKIWITZ, JOSEPH	20	M	LABR	RRZZZZUSA
LITKAR, JOSEPH	25	M	LABR	RRZZZZUSA
ANNA	20	F	UNKNOWN	RRZZZZUSA

SHIP: SUEVIA

FROM: HAMBURG
TO: NEW YORK
ARRIVED: 04 NOVEMBER 1885

PASSENGER	AGE	SEX	OCCUPATION	PRV VIL DES
KAFTAL, JOSEF	36	M	TCHR	RRAFWJNY
SARA	25	F	W	RRAFWJNY
MORUSON, STANISLAUS	51	M	LABR	RRAHZSNY
JAKUBOWSKY, BERUH	30	M	LABR	RRAHZSNY
TARGEWITZ, IGNATZ	23	M	LABR	RRAHZSNY
SCHULZ, ALEX	28	M	LABR	RRAHZSNY
KALEWITZKI, CHINE	18	F	SGL	RRAHUUNY
DAHRMANN, WILH.	27	M	LABR	RRAHUUNY
MANKOWSKA, AGNES	28	F	W	RRZZZZNY
WOLKOWITZ, DWORE	32	F	W	RRAHSWNY
FEIGE	9	F	CHILD	RRAHSWNY
LEIB	7	M	CHILD	RRAHSWNY
SMALINSKA, ANNA	30	F	W	RRZZZZNY
CHAJE	3	M	CHILD	RRZZZZNY
LINA	3	F	CHILD	RRZZZZNY
MICHEL	.11	M	INFANT	RRZZZZNY
GUZMANN, JACOB	24	M	LABR	RRZZZZNY
COHN, DAVID	40	M	LABR	RRZZZZNY
RACHEL	40	F	W	RRZZZZNY
MARIE	9	F	CHILD	RRZZZZNY
MARK, ROSA	9	F	CHILD	RRZZZZNY
FINKELHORN, CHEI	16	F	SGL	RRZZZZNY
BREGOWSKI, ZERNE	25	F	SGL	RRAHTFNY
JANSOHN, LOUISE	28	F	SGL	RRAEFLNY
MARGEEST, JOSEF	28	M	LABR	RRZZZZNY
COHEN, DAVID	22	M	LABR	RRZZZZNY
BECKERMANN, THERESE	28	F	W	RRZZZZNY
NATHAN	8	M	CHILD	RRZZZZNY
ELKAN	4	M	CHILD	RRZZZZNY
BERTHA	3	F	CHILD	RRZZZZNY
JULS	2	M	CHILD	RRZZZZNY
MARTHA	.09	F	INFANT	RRZZZZNY
DOBRIMANN, ELISAR	38	M	LABR	RRZZZZNY
KERESZTURI, JOSEF	25	M	LABR	RRZZZZNY
WODOSFOLWI, KARL	25	M	LABR	RRZZZZNY
MEINS, WOLF	27	M	LABR	RRZZZZNY
FINKELHAAR, BENJAMIN	15	M	LABR	RRZZZZNY
ROM, MOSES	16	M	LABR	RRZZZZNY
HILESAN, HILLUL	38	M	LABR	RRZZZZIL
MINNA	30	F	W	RRZZZZIL
EMMA	9	F	CHILD	RRZZZZIL
ADOLPH	8	M	CHILD	RRZZZZIL
ROSA	6	F	CHILD	RRZZZZIL
BERTHA	4	F	CHILD	RRZZZZIL
SOHEFTELIWITZ, SARA	19	F	SGL	RRZZZZIL
BLUMENTHAL, HANNE	22	F	SGL	RRZZZZIL
FRANK, BEHR	50	M	LABR	RRZZZZIL
GEZELOWITZ, HERM.	22	M	LABR	RRZZZZPA
BERMANN, LEA	19	F	SGL	RRAHTFPA
SOHOIKI, PEISSAAK	9	M	CHILD	RRAHTFPA
SOHAVI	8	F	CHILD	RRAHTFPA
SARA	7	F	CHILD	RRAHTFPA
CHANNE	6	F	CHILD	RRAHTFPA
BLEIWESS, JOEL	34	M	LABR	RRZZZZUSA
JULKA	25	F	W	RRZZZZUSA
HANNA	6	F	CHILD	RRZZZZUSA
GUSTAV	3	M	CHILD	RRZZZZUSA
JEANELLA	.11	F	INFANT	RRZZZZUSA
HAMOLSKY, MENASCHE	20	F	SGL	RRZZZZUNK
SEGLARSKY, ESTHER	34	F	W	RRAHZSIL
MAX	9	M	CHILD	RRAHZSIL
CHAIME	6	F	CHILD	RRAHZSIL
NATHAN	7	M	CHILD	RRAHZSIL
ERNA	.11	F	INFANT	RRAHZSIL
LITONNIZ, JOSE	20	M	DLR	RRZZZZUSA
ADAMUS, FRANZ	17	M	LABR	RRZZZZUSA
GELBART, ROSALIE	30	F	W	RRZZZZUSA
RACHEL	9	F	CHILD	RRZZZZUSA
PESSEL	4	M	CHILD	RRZZZZUSA
HOPTMANN, WOLF	5	M	CHILD	RRZZZZUSA
PINCUS	3	M	CHILD	RRZZZZUSA
LEIB	.11	M	INFANT	RRZZZZUSA
SENDACK, ANNA	19	F	SGL	RRAHTOUSA
MAGID, CHINA	20	F	SGL	RRZZZZUSA
USOHER, SOHINDEL	9	F	CHILD	RRZZZZUSA
PERL	5	F	CHILD	RRZZZZUSA
KAHAN, HADASZEL	22	F	SGL	RRAHTRUSA
ZALMEN, ABRAHAM	18	M	DLR	RRAHVUUSA
PESCHWEDSKI, CHAIN	19	M	TLR	RRZZZZUSA
MORRIS, SARA	21	F	W	RRZZZZNY
ABRAHAM	.11	M	INFANT	RRZZZZNY
ABRAHAMS, HIRSCH	20	M	DLR	RRZZZZNY
PESCHE	20	F	SGL	RRZZZZNY
FRANKEL, SARA	18	F	SGL	RRZZZZNY
BONITZKI, MOSES	19	M	MCHT	RRZZZZNY
SANDELOWSKY, LEIB	21	M	LABR	RRZZZZNY
CHASIE	18	F	W	RRZZZZNY
BIRNBACH, SELIG	25	M	DLR	RRAHUYNY
SENDER, SOHOLEM	19	M	TLR	RRAHTONY
STRAUBING, RACHEL	28	F	W	RRZZZZNY
CHAWE	9	F	CHILD	RRZZZZNY
EFRAIM	.11	M	INFANT	RRZZZZNY
FRUME	.01	F	INFANT	RRZZZZNY
KAUFMANN, NAFTALI	32	M	DLR	RRZZZZNY
STANISKER, SALAREN	20	M	DLR	RRZZZZNY
PINKOWSKI, ARON	47	M	DLR	RRZZZZNY
DINENSOHN, WOLF	15	M	DLR	RRAHZSNY
LITOWITZ, CHINE	42	F	W	RRZZZZNY
BASCHE	9	F	CHILD	RRZZZZNY
SOHEIN	.11	F	INFANT	RRZZZZNY
LESOHINSKY, CHAIM	19	M	DLR	RRZZZZNY
MIRWIS, ISAAC	32	M	DLR	RRZZZZNY
HEROHANOWITZ, EIDEL	26	F	SGL	RRZZZZNY
KOHN, RUDOLPH	18	M	DT	RRAHQHNY

PASSENGER	AGE	SEX	OCCUPATION	PRV VIL DES

SHIP: NEVADA

FROM: LIVERPOOL AND QUEENSTOWN
TO: NEW YORK
ARRIVED: 05 NOVEMBER 1885

PASSENGER	AGE	SEX	OCCUPATION	PRV VIL DES
MICHA, AND.	41	M	LABR	RRZZZZUSA
DOLKOWITZ, RAE	19	F	SP	RRZZZZUSA
SALZWERSZ, MAR.	38	M	LABR	RRZZZZUSA
JERGENBAUM, BER.	17	M	LABR	RRZZZZUSA
SILBERMANN, LIT.	26	M	LABR	RRZZZZUSA
KLIVANSKY, JAC.	42	M	LABR	RRZZZZUSA
KLATSCHEUTZ, LEIR	34	M	LABR	RRZZZZUSA
SANERNITZ, SAM.	25	M	LABR	RRZZZZUSA
KANEL, KAN	48	M	LABR	RRZZZZUSA

SHIP: WESTERNLAND

FROM: ANTWERP
TO: NEW YORK
ARRIVED: 05 NOVEMBER 1885

PASSENGER	AGE	SEX	OCCUPATION	PRV VIL DES
KALINA, FR.	22	M	LABR	RRZZZZSTL

SHIP: ST. OF PENNSYLVANIA

FROM: GLASGOW AND LARNE
TO: NEW YORK
ARRIVED: 06 NOVEMBER 1885

PASSENGER	AGE	SEX	OCCUPATION	PRV VIL DES
MACHNIS, SIEGFR.	22	M	STDNT	RRAAKHUSA
KATSON, EMIL	21	M	SLR	FNZZZZUSA
CHMELNITZKY, MOSES	55	M	TLR	FNAFVGUSA
PESCHE	50	F	W	FNAFVGUSA
LIEBE	20	F	W	FNAFVGUSA
CHANNE	.03	F	INFANT	FNAFVGUSA
CZELES, SCHIWACH	19	M	MCHT	RRZZZZUSA
FEINSTEN, SCHMUL	19	M	MCHT	RRZZZZUSA
GLASER, SIMON	31	M	MCHT	RRZZZZUSA
SIM.	26	F	W	RRZZZZUSA
MOSES	12	M	CH	RRZZZZUSA
JAKOB	00	M	CH	RRZZZZUSA
HEIN.	8	M	CHILD	RRZZZZUSA
SENI	6	F	CHILD	RRZZZZUSA
SARAH	1	F	CHILD	RRZZZZUSA
GOLDBERG, WOLF	27	M	CPMKR	RRZZZZUSA
GRUENBAUM, SCHIME	35	F	W	RRZZZZUSA
BEILE	17	F	SP	RRZZZZUSA
ABRAHAM	12	M	CH	RRZZZZUSA
GOHMBERG, MOSES	20	M	TLR	RRZZZZUSA
HIRSCHOWITZ, BEER	30	M	TLR	RRZZZZUSA
HENRIETTA	30	F	W	RRZZZZUSA
BERNHARD	11	M	CH	RRZZZZUSA
ISIDOR	8	M	CHILD	RRZZZZUSA
SIMON	4	M	CHILD	RRZZZZUSA
PAUL	3	M	CHILD	RRZZZZUSA
BARUCH	2	M	CHILD	RRZZZZUSA
GERMAN	.03	M	INFANT	RRZZZZUSA
JASLOWSKI, MEYER	50	M	TLR	RRAHZSUSA
MARANZ, SCHMUL	24	M	UNKNOWN	RRZZZZUSA
MINES, CHANNE	17	F	SP	RRZZZZUSA
SAKOZINSKY, HIRSCH	21	M	MCHT	RRZZZZUSA
MARIANE	21	F	SP	RRZZZZUSA
SCHMOKOVSKY, BENJAMIN	23	M	MCHT	RRZZZZUSA
SCHWALNITZKY, CHAIM	16	M	PPHGR	RRAFVGUSA
SKIVAK, CHASKEL	19	M	MCHT	RRAHXXUSA
TAGER, MEIER	20	M	MCHT	RRZZZZUSA

SHIP: CITY OF RICHMOND

FROM: LIVERPOOL
TO: NEW YORK
ARRIVED: 07 NOVEMBER 1885

PASSENGER	AGE	SEX	OCCUPATION	PRV VIL DES
BONESKY, SCHMUL	17	M	LABR	PLZZZZUSA
SCHNEIDER, SCHMUL	22	M	LABR	PLZZZZUSA
CHAMOWSKY, JOSEPH	27	M	LABR	PLZZZZUSA
GIBJENSKY, J.	21	M	LABR	PLZZZZUSA
MARJULSKY, HIRSCH	20	M	LABR	PLZZZZUSA
SEHMANN, ISAC	21	M	LABR	PLZZZZUSA
SALLYSOHN, B.	28	M	LABR	PLZZZZUSA
KRONEWBERG, ARON	20	M	LABR	PLZZZZUSA
GRAMEWITZ, M.	46	M	LABR	PLZZZZUSA
GREEMANN, K.	20	M	LABR	PLZZZZUSA
NIPODWIT, M.	38	M	LABR	PLZZZZUSA
DUMBELSKY, ABRAM	17	M	LABR	PLZZZZUSA
FREDOWSKY, JANKEL	20	M	LABR	PLZZZZUSA
KATTERINE, ABRAM	26	M	LABR	PLZZZZUSA
SLADONSKY, ABRAM	20	M	LABR	PLZZZZUSA
WEISSMAN, C.	18	M	LABR	PLZZZZUSA
SEHWARTZ, JACOB	32	M	LABR	PLZZZZUSA
BERLOWITZ, MOSES	28	M	LABR	PLZZZZUSA
DEMBROWSKY, LEISER	24	M	LABR	PLZZZZUSA
STOLMTZ, J.	20	M	LABR	PLZZZZUSA
WEDERTZKI, JOSEPH	25	M	LABR	PLZZZZUSA
EPSTIN, JOSEF	19	M	LABR	PLZZZZUSA
KASCHKIS, JOSEF	24	M	LABR	PLZZZZUSA
KOSCHNISKY, K.	26	M	LABR	PLZZZZUSA
KOHANY, FINNA	16	F	SVNT	PLZZZZUSA
GOLDBERG, ISRAEL	19	M	LABR	PLZZZZUSA
JOSEF	19	M	LABR	PLZZZZUSA
MARGOMSKY, LEIB	19	M	LABR	PLZZZZUSA
HARRIS, B.	11	M	CH	PLZZZZUSA
M.	9	M	CHILD	PLZZZZUSA
MOSES	7	M	CHILD	PLZZZZUSA
DEMANT, M.	30	M	LABR	PLZZZZUSA
EWA	21	F	W	PLZZZZUSA
BERMANN, ZETTA	3	F	CHILD	PLZZZZUSA
SILBERMANN, BERKISS	20	M	LABR	PLZZZZUSA
GRANEWITZ, DAVID	11	M	CH	PLZZZZUSA
ISTWAN, HEDGEN	34	M	LABR	PLZZZZUSA
E.E.	20	F	W	PLZZZZUSA
W.A.	11	M	CH	PLZZZZUSA
FRIEDMANN, JACOB	30	M	LABR	PLZZZZUSA
ISAAC	11	M	CH	PLZZZZUSA
L.	10	M	CH	PLZZZZUSA
JANOWSKE, P.	38	M	LABR	PLZZZZUSA
AXELROD, ABM.	59	M	LABR	PLACBFUSA
LENA	55	F	W	PLACBFUSA
DEBERAH	18	F	SVNT	PLACBFUSA
CELIA	16	F	SVNT	PLACBFUSA
FINKELSTEIN, LEA	50	F	W	PLZZZZUSA
ISKOWITZ, ELLY	55	F	W	PLZZZZUSA
ODESS, Z.	22	F	W	PLZZZZUSA
MINNA	00	F	INF	PLZZZZUSA
GRODSZIMSKY, LEON	19	M	LABR	PLAHOOUSA

PASSENGER	AGE	SEX	OCCUPATION	PRV	VIL	DES
SHIP: EMS						
FROM: BREMEN						
TO: NEW YORK						
ARRIVED: 07 NOVEMBER 1885						
KLINOWSKI, ANTON	18	M	FARMER	PL	AHOO	USA
KUCH, GEORG	25	M	FARMER	PL	AFWJ	USA
LOUISE	25	F	NN	PL	AFWJ	USA
ANTONINA	.11	M	INFANT	PL	AFWJ	USA
REINKE, ANDREAS	45	M	FARMER	PL	AFWJ	USA
LOUISE	40	F	NN	PL	AFWJ	USA
DANIEL	21	M	FARMER	PL	AFWJ	USA
CHRISTINE	18	F	NN	PL	AFWJ	USA
JULIANE	21	F	NN	PL	AFWJ	USA
SOPHIE	4	F	CHILD	PL	AFWJ	USA
JOHANN	3	M	CHILD	PL	AFWJ	USA
EMILIE	.03	F	INFANT	PL	AFWJ	USA
ANDREAS	.01	M	INFANT	PL	AFWJ	USA
KROLL, JOHANN	47	M	FARMER	RR	ZZZZ	USA
CATHARINE	40	F	NN	RR	ZZZZ	USA
CHRISTIAN	17	M	FARMER	RR	ZZZZ	USA
SOPHIE	14	F	CH	RR	ZZZZ	USA
GOTTFRIED	10	F	CH	RR	ZZZZ	USA
DANIEL	8	F	CHILD	RR	ZZZZ	USA
MATHILDE	3	F	CHILD	RR	ZZZZ	USA
JOHANN	.09	M	INFANT	RR	ZZZZ	USA
WEISS, SAMUEL	17	M	FARMER	RR	AHOO	USA
GROSS, CAROLINE	21	F	NN	RR	AHOO	USA
SCHNEIDER, GOTTLIEB	41	M	FARMER	RR	AHOO	USA
ROSINE	35	F	NN	RR	AHOO	USA
JOHANNES	16	M	CH	RR	AHOO	USA
CHRISTIAN	13	M	CH	RR	AHOO	USA
EMANUEL	10	M	CH	RR	AHOO	USA
SPOHIE	2	F	CHILD	RR	AHOO	USA
BIETZ, GOTTLIEB	36	M	FARMER	RR	AHOO	USA
CHRISTINA	36	F	NN	RR	AHOO	USA
JOHANN	10	M	CH	RR	AHOO	USA
GOTTLIEB	10	M	CH	RR	AHOO	USA
GOTTFRIED	8	M	CHILD	RR	AHOO	USA
JACOB	.05	M	INFANT	RR	AHOO	USA
MARIA	6	F	CHILD	RR	AHOO	USA
LIDIA	2	F	CHILD	RR	AHOO	USA
ANNA-MARIA	69	F	NN	RR	AHOO	USA
PATZER, EMANUEL	17	M	FARMER	RR	AHOO	USA
WEISS, JACOB	22	M	LABR	RR	AHOO	USA
HAWENSCHILD, JOSEF	24	M	FARMER	RR	AHOO	USA
PELZEL, JOHANN	32	M	FARMER	RR	ZZZZ	USA
AMALIE	30	F	NN	RR	ZZZZ	USA
JOHANN	10	M	CH	RR	ZZZZ	USA
FRANZ	7	M	CHILD	RR	ZZZZ	USA
BERNHARD	1	M	CHILD	RR	ZZZZ	USA
CONRAD	.09	M	INFANT	RR	ZZZZ	USA
JAROSCH, JOHANN	25	M	LABR	RR	ZZZZ	USA
BARBARA	14	F	CH	RR	ZZZZ	USA
MARIA	1	F	CHILD	RR	ZZZZ	USA
HAWENSCHILD, JOH.	28	M	FARMER	RR	ZZZZ	USA
FRANZISKA	28	F	NN	RR	ZZZZ	USA
JOSEF	8	M	CHILD	RR	ZZZZ	USA
THERESE	7	F	CHILD	RR	ZZZZ	USA
CAROLINE	4	F	CHILD	RR	ZZZZ	USA
JOH.	2	M	CHILD	RR	ZZZZ	USA
MARIA	.09	F	INFANT	RR	ZZZZ	USA
GRUENEICH, CARL	37	M	FARMER	RR	AFWJ	USA
JUSTINE	36	F	NN	RR	AFWJ	USA
CHRISTIAN	6	M	CHILD	RR	AFWJ	USA
MATHILDE	4	F	CHILD	RR	AFWJ	USA
MAGDALENE	2	F	CHILD	RR	AFWJ	USA
FRIEDERICKE	.10	F	INFANT	RR	AFWJ	USA
LEMKE, CHRISTIAN	31	M	FARMER	RR	AFWJ	USA
CAROLINE	29	F	NN	RR	AFWJ	USA
DANIEL	5	M	CHILD	RR	AFWJ	USA
CHRISTINE	3	F	CHILD	RR	AFWJ	USA
CHRISTIAN	1	M	CHILD	RR	AFWJ	USA

PASSENGER	AGE	SEX	OCCUPATION	PRV	VIL	DES
FRIES, JOHANN	34	M	FARMER	RR	AFWJ	USA
JULIANE	26	F	NN	RR	AFWJ	USA
ADAM	8	M	CHILD	RR	AFWJ	USA
JOHANN	6	M	CHILD	RR	AFWJ	USA
MICHAEL	3	M	CHILD	RR	AFWJ	USA
CHRISTIAN	1	M	CHILD	RR	AFWJ	USA
LANGE, JOHANN	27	M	FARMER	RR	AFWJ	USA
LOUISE	25	F	NN	RR	AFWJ	USA
MICHAEL	2	M	CHILD	RR	AFWJ	USA
JOHANN	.06	M	INFANT	RR	AFWJ	USA
RIEHL, DANIEL	30	M	FARMER	RR	AFWJ	USA
SOPHIE	22	F	NN	RR	AFWJ	USA
MARIA	2	F	CHILD	RR	AFWJ	USA
AUGUST	.02	M	INFANT	RR	AFWJ	USA
HINZ, CHRISTOPH	26	M	FARMER	RR	AESF	USA
SOPHIE	24	F	NN	RR	AESF	USA
SAMUEL	3	M	CHILD	RR	AESF	USA
LOUISE	61	F	NN	RR	AESF	USA
SUSANNA	21	F	NN	RR	AESF	USA
MARTIN	13	M	CH	RR	AESF	USA
BELZ, CHRISTIAN	25	M	FARMER	RR	AESF	USA
ANNA	22	F	NN	RR	AESF	USA
JULIANE	.05	F	INFANT	RR	AESF	USA
WIEGE, MICHAEL	27	M	FARMER	RR	AESF	USA
SUSANNE	26	F	NN	RR	AESF	USA
CHRISTINE	2	F	CHILD	RR	AESF	***
SOPHIE	.06	F	INFANT	RR	AESF	USA
BILLIGMEIER, LUDWIG	26	M	FARMER	RR	AESF	USA
JULIANE	22	F	NN	RR	AESF	USA
JULIANE	3	F	CHILD	RR	AESF	USA
JOHANN	.09	M	INFANT	RR	AESF	USA
JUSTINA	18	F	CH	RR	AESF	USA
BELZ, DANIEL	58	M	FARMER	RR	ZZZZ	USA
CAROLINE	37	F	NN	RR	ZZZZ	USA
JACOB	15	M	CH	RR	ZZZZ	USA
ELISABETH	13	F	CH	RR	ZZZZ	USA
CAROLINE	5	F	CHILD	RR	ZZZZ	USA
MATHILDE	3	F	CHILD	RR	ZZZZ	USA
SPRECHER, MICHAEL	45	M	FARMER	RR	ZZZZ	USA
CAROLINE	43	F	NN	RR	ZZZZ	USA
ALFRED	18	M	CH	RR	ZZZZ	USA
DAVID	15	M	CH	RR	ZZZZ	USA
JOHANNES	10	M	CH	RR	ZZZZ	USA
MAGDALENE	8	F	CHILD	RR	ZZZZ	USA
MICHAEL	4	M	CHILD	RR	ZZZZ	USA
RIEHL, CHRISTIAN	27	M	FARMER	RR	ZZZZ	USA
REGINA	22	F	NN	RR	ZZZZ	USA
LOUISE	2	F	CHILD	RR	ZZZZ	USA
SONNERFELD, FRIEDR.	18	M	FARMER	RR	ZZZZ	USA
PETER, KARL	19	M	FARMER	RR	ZZZZ	USA
KIFIUS, ALEXANDER	30	M	FARMER	RR	AAMJ	USA
KLAUCK, CHRIST.	46	M	LABR	RR	AFWJ	USA
JULIE	45	F	NN	RR	AFWJ	USA
WILHELM	20	M	FARMER	RR	AFWJ	USA
JOHANN	18	M	FARMER	RR	AFWJ	USA
JACOB	15	M	CH	RR	AFWJ	USA
SAMUEL	9	M	CHILD	RR	AFWJ	USA
WILHELMINE	7	F	CHILD	RR	AFWJ	USA
GOTTLIEB	15	M	CH	RR	AFWJ	USA
JOHANNES	14	M	CH	RR	AFWJ	USA
LOUISE	10	F	CH	RR	AFWJ	USA
WALL, PHILIPP	28	M	FARMER	RR	AFWJ	USA
CATHARINE	28	F	NN	RR	AFWJ	USA
CHRISTINE	4	F	CHILD	RR	AFWJ	USA
PHILIPP	2	M	CHILD	RR	AFWJ	USA
CATHARINE	.05	F	INFANT	RR	AFWJ	USA
GEORG, HEINRICH	38	M	FARMER	RR	AFWJ	USA
MARIA	37	F	NN	RR	AFWJ	USA
MARGARETHE	10	F	CH	RR	AFWJ	USA
MARIA	9	F	CHILD	RR	AFWJ	USA
HEINRICH	6	M	CHILD	RR	AFWJ	USA
JOHANN	3	M	CHILD	RR	AFWJ	USA
ROSE	1	F	CHILD	RR	AFWJ	USA
GATZKI, GOTTLIEB	53	M	FARMER	RR	ZZZZ	USA
JUSTINE	50	F	NN	RR	ZZZZ	USA

PASSENGER	AGE	SEX	OCCUPATION	PRV	VIL	DES
FERDINAND	23	M	FARMER	RR	ZZZZ	USA
SOPHIE	23	F	NN	RR	ZZZZ	USA
AUGUST	19	M	FARMER	RR	ZZZZ	USA
SCHEIFELE, CHRIST.	32	M	FARMER	RR	ZZZZ	USA
CHRISTINE	29	F	NN	RR	ZZZZ	USA
CHRISTIAN	5	M	CHILD	RR	ZZZZ	USA
HEINRICH	4	M	CHILD	RR	ZZZZ	USA
LISBETH	1	F	CHILD	RR	ZZZZ	USA
JOHANN	.05	M	INFANT	RR	ZZZZ	USA
VOSSLER, FRIEDRICH	44	M	FARMER	RR	AHOO	USA
FRIEDRICKE	31	F	NN	RR	AHOO	USA
JOHANNES	17	M	CL	RR	AHOO	USA
FRIEDRICH	14	M	CH	RR	AHOO	USA
CHRISTINE	21	F	NN	RR	AHOO	USA
DOROTHEA	19	F	NN	RR	AHOO	USA
MARIA	10	F	CH	RR	AHOO	USA
EDUARD	9	M	CHILD	RR	AHOO	USA
MATHILDE	5	F	CHILD	RR	AHOO	USA
CATHARINE	3	F	CHILD	RR	AHOO	USA
JACOB	1	M	CHILD	RR	AHOO	USA
MAASS, FRIEDERIKE	59	F	NN	RR	AHOO	USA
MAGDALENE	16	F	CH	RR	AHOO	USA
KRUEGER, JULIANE	21	F	NN	RR	AHOO	USA
BADER, SAMUEL	36	M	FARMER	RR	AFWJ	USA
LISBETH	33	F	NN	RR	AFWJ	USA
JOHANN	14	M	CH	RR	AFWJ	USA
EMANUEL	8	M	CHILD	RR	AFWJ	USA
DANIEL	6	M	CHILD	RR	AFWJ	USA
WILHELM	4	M	CHILD	RR	AFWJ	USA
GOTTLIEB	1	M	CHILD	RR	AFWJ	USA
LUCAS, GOTTLIEB	24	M	FARMER	RR	AFWJ	USA
LOUISE	22	F	NN	RR	AFWJ	USA
ADAM	.04	M	INFANT	RR	AFWJ	USA
CHRISTIAN	55	M	LABR	RR	AFWJ	USA
CAROLINE	41	F	NN	RR	AFWJ	USA
ROSINA	24	F	NN	RR	AFWJ	USA
CAROLINE	17	F	CH	RR	AFWJ	USA
STROBEL, CHRISTIAN	22	M	FARMER	RR	AFWJ	USA
JACOB	18	M	FARMER	RR	AFWJ	USA
JOHANN	16	M	FARMER	RR	AFWJ	USA
STOECKER, FRIEDRICH	59	M	FARMER	RR	AFWJ	USA
CATHARINE	50	F	NN	RR	AFWJ	USA
FRIEDERIKE	15	F	NN	RR	AFWJ	USA
GOTTFRIED	10	M	CH	RR	AFWJ	USA
JACOB	9	M	CHILD	RR	AFWJ	USA
GOTTLIEB	7	M	CHILD	RR	AFWJ	USA
JACOB	18	M	FARMER	RR	AFWJ	USA
PELZEL, FRANZ	22	M	FARMER	RR	AGRT	USA
MUELLER, JOHANN	28	M	FARMER	RR	AGRT	USA
WILHELMINE	29	F	NN	RR	AGRT	USA
GOTTFRIED	8	M	CHILD	RR	AGRT	USA
JOHANN	6	M	CHILD	RR	AGRT	USA
GUSTAV	4	M	CHILD	RR	AGRT	USA
MATHILDE	.11	F	INFANT	RR	AGRT	USA
GOTTLIEB	28	M	FARMER	RR	AGRT	USA
CHRISTINE	24	F	NN	RR	AGRT	USA
DANIEL	3	M	CHILD	RR	AGRT	USA
MATHILDE	.11	F	INFANT	RR	AGRT	USA
BLUM, ANDREAS	25	M	FARMER	RR	AGRT	USA
CATHARINA	19	F	NN	RR	AGRT	USA
LYDIA	11	F	CH	RR	AGRT	USA
HILLIGES, CARL	33	M	FARMER	RR	AFWJ	USA
CAROLINE	27	F	NN	RR	AFWJ	USA
EMANUEL	9	M	CHILD	RR	AFWJ	USA
EDUARD	7	M	CHILD	RR	AFWJ	USA
JOHANN	2	M	CHILD	RR	AFWJ	USA
CHRISTINE	4	F	CHILD	RR	AFWJ	USA
THEODOR	.03	M	INFANT	RR	AFWJ	USA
JANKELSOHN, CHAJEK	30	M	LABR	RR	AGRT	USA
ZARABA, MARTIN	21	M	LABR	RR	AGRT	USA

SHIP: PERSIAN MONARCH

FROM: LONDON
TO: NEW YORK
ARRIVED: 07 NOVEMBER 1885

PASSENGER	AGE	SEX	OCCUPATION	PRV	VIL	DES
JONNESTEIN, E.	26	F	NN	RR	ZZZZ	NY
ETTY	6	F	CHILD	RR	ZZZZ	NY
SARAH	.06	F	INFANT	RR	ZZZZ	NY
JOSENBERG, MOSES	25	M	TLR	RR	ZZZZ	NY
BREMER, B.	22	M	HTR	RR	ZZZZ	NY
SHEDDIN, REBECCA	21	F	NN	PL	ZZZZ	NY
JOHN, F.	25	M	WTR	PL	ZZZZ	NY

SHIP: ABYSSINIA

FROM: LIVERPOOL AND QUEENSTOWN
TO: NEW YORK
ARRIVED: 09 NOVEMBER 1885

PASSENGER	AGE	SEX	OCCUPATION	PRV	VIL	DES
CRINCESSON, ALEX	18	M	LABR	RR	ZZZZ	USA
ROSNER, ARON	28	M	LABR	RR	ZZZZ	USA
MORDHESY, LIEB	24	F	SP	RR	ZZZZ	USA
BICKRSTEIN, SIMON	18	M	LABR	RR	ZZZZ	USA
MICHELMANN, ELIAS	20	M	LABR	RR	ZZZZ	USA
SRIME	22	F	W	RR	ZZZZ	USA
KUPPERMANN, OFZIS	22	M	LABR	RR	ZZZZ	USA
CHASE	23	F	W	RR	ZZZZ	USA
MEONIH, MILECH	37	M	PNTR	RR	ZZZZ	USA
DINE, JERE	20	F	MA	RR	ZZZZ	USA
JACOB	1	M	CHILD	RR	ZZZZ	USA
FISCHER, JESCHEF	20	M	LABR	RR	ZZZZ	USA
SARA	20	F	W	RR	ZZZZ	USA
SINZEL, SARAH	28	F	MA	RR	ZZZZ	USA
MINNA	9	F	CHILD	RR	ZZZZ	USA
HARRY	7	M	CHILD	RR	ZZZZ	USA
ROSA	5	F	CHILD	RR	ZZZZ	USA
LINA	1	F	CHILD	RR	ZZZZ	USA
JEHNER, SAML.	28	M	LABR	RR	ZZZZ	USA
SIRTMANN, HERM.	26	M	LABR	RR	ZZZZ	USA
ERNESTINE	23	F	W	RR	ZZZZ	USA
CHAIE	58	F	MA	RR	ZZZZ	USA
ISAAC	6	M	CHILD	RR	ZZZZ	USA
ARON	3	M	CHILD	RR	ZZZZ	USA
WOLF, SALOMON	26	M	LABR	RR	ZZZZ	USA

SHIP: AURANIA

FROM: LIVERPOOL AND QUEENSTOWN
TO: NEW YORK
ARRIVED: 09 NOVEMBER 1885

PASSENGER	AGE	SEX	OCCUPATION	PRV	VIL	DES
FEGNER, JOHAN	25	M	LABR	RR	ZZZZ	OH
SERDKUS, JONAS	30	M	LABR	RR	ZZZZ	OH

PASSENGER	A G E	S E X	OCCUPATION	P V R I V L	D E S
SHIP: MORAVIA					
FROM: HAMBURG					
TO: NEW YORK					
ARRIVED: 12 NOVEMBER 1885					
LUBIN, JOE	21	M	TLR	RRZZZZ	USA
FRANKENHEIM, ARON-M.	21	M	DLR	RRAHTK	USA
PETRANDKOWA, MAGDALENA	19	F	SGL	RRZZZZ	USA
BATIER, PETRONELLA	65	M	LABR	RRAHSW	USA
CZISEWSKA, JOSPE	18	F	SGL	RRAHTO	USA
HOLLANDER, IWA	42	M	TLR	RRZZZZ	USA
LACKER, ABRAHAM	18	M	TLR	RRZZZZ	USA
ANDENITZKI, RUWEN	14	M	LABR	RRZZZZ	USA
RANDINATIS, MATHS.	23	M	TLR	RRAHZS	USA
PETRALSKA, PAULUS	18	M	LABR	RRAHZS	USA
JEGLIS, CASIS	23	M	LABR	RRAHZS	USA
KOSAKIEWICZ, JOH.	22	M	SMH	RRZZZZ	USA
SCHLUTZKIN, RINIE	60	F	W	RRZZZZ	USA
PINELIS, BEILE	45	F	W	RRZZZZ	USA
WOLF, SALOMON	50	M	LABR	RRAFVG	USA
WOLF	9	M	CHILD	RRAFVG	USA
GUCZKOWSKI, ANTON	22	M	LABR	RRAHZS	USA
KARNEZUCH, FRANZ	23	M	LABR	RRAHZS	USA
BUSCHKIEWICZ, JOSEF	22	M	LABR	RRAHZS	USA
SADLER, FEIGE	22	F	W	RRAFVG	USA
MARIUS	.11	F	INFANT	RRAFVG	USA
SANDLER, ALTER	20	F	W	RRAFVG	USA
MINNA	.06	F	INFANT	RRAFVG	USA
GRUENHEIN, PINDRES	24	M	LABR	RRZZZZ	USA
ISSEROH, ZIPORA	18	F	SGL	RRZZZZ	USA
WEISS, NAZI	18	F	SGL	RRZZZZ	USA
ZELMER, SAM.	20	M	LABR	RRZZZZ	USA
BRZEZINSKA, MARIANNA	23	F	W	RRZZZZ	USA
FRANZISKA	.11	F	INFANT	RRZZZZ	USA
GOCAZ, HAJE	23	F	SGL	RRZZZZ	USA
KOJMONA, ROSALIE-SZARA	22	M	LABR	RRAHZS	USA
FAGUS, ANTON	22	M	LABR	RRZZZZ	USA
MICKELMANN, JOSEPH	16	M	DLR	RRZZZZ	USA
RODANSKY, NOCHUM	19	M	LABR	RRZZZZ	USA
LIPOWSKY, FRANZ	29	M	MCHT	RRZZZZ	USA
KROSNEPOLSKY, JACOB	24	M	LABR	RRZZZZ	USA
SCHEIM	27	F	W	RRZZZZ	USA
ISAAC	3	M	CHILD	RRZZZZ	USA
CHAIN	.11	M	INFANT	RRZZZZ	USA
BAYER, MORDCHE	23	M	LABR	RRZZZZ	USA
BESMANN, BLUME	46	F	W	RRZZZZ	USA
MOSES	6	M	CHILD	RRZZZZ	USA
GEOFSKI, ABRAHAM	54	M	LABR	RRZZZZ	USA
FRIEDER.	22	F	SGL	RRZZZZ	USA
BLUME	16	F	SGL	RRZZZZ	USA
HEYMANN, KOPEL	30	M	DLR	RRZZZZ	USA
CHANOWIJ, CHAIN	16	M	DLR	RRAHSW	USA
KAPLAU, LEIB	65	M	DLR	RRAHSW	USA
KAHN, JANKEL	19	M	LABR	RRZZZZ	USA
LEWIN, ISSAC	23	M	APTC	RRZZZZ	USA
WILIMEILIS, AUGUST	38	M	LABR	RRAHTR	USA
TOMAITIS, AUGUST	22	M	LABR	RRAHTR	USA
SPOLINSKI, VINCENT	22	M	LABR	RRAHTR	USA
KASNOWSKA, WINTESCH	23	M	LABR	RRZZZZ	USA
KRAVETZKI, RUNEW	24	M	LABR	RRZZZZ	USA
KOPEL, SALOMON	21	M	LABR	RRAHVL	USA
PESCHE	20	F	W	RRAHVL	USA
CHYL, RIWKE	20	F	W	RRZZZZ	USA
CHEWKE	.11	F	INFANT	RRZZZZ	USA
GRUENSTEIN, HELENE	30	F	W	RRZZZZ	USA
GRUNSTEIN, CHAWE	5	F	CHILD	RRZZZZ	USA
RIWKE	3	F	CHILD	RRZZZZ	USA
BALTSCHE	.11	F	INFANT	RRZZZZ	USA
ROGACZINSKI, ANDR.	30	M	LABR	RRZZZZ	USA
CZENSKOWSKA, NATHAN	28	M	BCHR	RRZZZZ	USA
SIELICHA, ANNA	19	F	SGL	RRZZZZ	USA
WILENSKY, RIWKE	15	F	SGL	RRAHTR	USA
RAISCHOPSKI, JONE	18	M	TLR	RRAHTR	USA
LINICK, ROCHEN	17	M	LABR	RRZZZZ	USA
KRAMER, NECHAME	50	F	W	RRAHTF	USA
EIDEL	24	F	W	RRAHTF	USA
ISSAC	3	F	CHILD	RRAHTF	USA
CHAIN	2	F	CHILD	RRAHTF	USA
HIRSCH	.06	F	INFANT	RRAHTF	USA
GINGOLD, TADRES	16	M	LABR	RRZZZZ	USA
LEMPITTZ--, CHEIN	45	F	W	RRAHTO	USA
RACHEL	18	F	CH	RRAHTO	USA
JOSSEL	9	M	CHILD	RRAHTO	USA
SIMON	8	M	CHILD	RRAHTO	USA
GROSSMANN, SALOMON	24	M	LABR	RRZZZZ	USA
KANNER, BREINDIL	30	F	W	RRZZZZ	USA
ISAAC	9	M	CHILD	RRZZZZ	USA
MOSES	8	M	CHILD	RRZZZZ	USA
BERTUSCH	.11	M	INFANT	RRZZZZ	USA
KNOP, TAUBE	19	F	SGL	RRZZZZ	USA
MINDEL	15	F	SGL	RRZZZZ	USA
GINSBURG, ISAAC	9	M	CHILD	RRAHVL	USA
EMANUEL	8	M	CHILD	RRAHVL	USA
SHIP: ST GERMAIN					
FROM: HAVRE					
TO: NEW YORK					
ARRIVED: 12 NOVEMBER 1885					
BEWSCHEVSKY, SALMON	23	M	PHRS	RRZZZZ	NY
MENDEL, LEIB	33	M	UNKNOWN	RRZZZZ	CH
SHIP: STATE OF NEBRASKA					
FROM: GLASGOW AND LARNE					
TO: NEW YORK					
ARRIVED: 13 NOVEMBER 1885					
KROINICH, ERGA	26	F	SVNT	RRZZZZ	NY
SEGALL, CHENE	25	M	SMH	RRZZZZ	BUF
RACHEL	21	F	W	RRZZZZ	BUF
JOEL	.07	M	INFANT	RRZZZZ	BUF
GROSSER, NATHAN	36	M	PNTR	RRZZZZ	STL
FELDMAN, JACOB	38	M	CGRMKR	RRZZZZ	STL
MORD, MOSES	24	M	LABR	RRZZZZ	NY
WALSCHINSKY, WOLF	50	M	LABR	RRZZZZ	NY
JOHN	8	M	CHILD	RRZZZZ	NY
MARIANNA	2	F	CHILD	RRZZZZ	NY
GITTELMAN, FISHELL	60	M	TLR	RRZZZZ	CLE
RIWKE	54	F	W	RRZZZZ	CLE
JACOB	16	M	LABR	RRZZZZ	CLE
FRODEL	10	F	CH	RRZZZZ	CLE
POTASEH, JOSEPH	19	M	TLR	RRZZZZ	NY
RACHEL	19	F	SVNT	RRZZZZ	NY
ISSER	19	F	TLR	RRZZZZ	NY
HIRSCHOWITZ, DAVID	40	M	LABR	RRZZZZ	NY
SKOP, ISAAK	9	M	CHILD	RRZZZZ	NY
SCHEPSEL	4	F	CHILD	RRZZZZ	NY
ABRAHAM	.11	M	INFANT	RRZZZZ	NY
WANIE, EDJE	21	M	LABR	RRZZZZ	NY
CHANE	24	F	W	RRZZZZ	NY
GERDEN, MANES	27	M	CMST	RRZZZZ	NY
MARKEWITZ, MARIE	28	F	W	RRZZZZ	NY
AUBAN	.11	M	INFANT	RRZZZZ	NY
MANTSCHOWSKY, BARUCH	40	M	PDLR	RRZZZZ	CH
HILLEWITZ, CHASSE	22	F	SVNT	RRZZZZ	NY
ISSERMANN, HERMANN	20	M	PDLR	RRZZZZ	NY

PASSENGER	AGE	SEX	OCCUPATION	PRV VIL DES
ANTOLICK, JANUS	30	M	LABR	RRZZZZNY
GEDOWIN, JANUS	11	M	CH	RRZZZZNY
STERNBERG, MOSES	19	M	FARMER	RRZZZZPHI
LEWIT, JACOB	28	M	FARMER	RRZZZZPHI
SKERICZVAK, WASIL	23	M	LABR	RRZZZZNY
SLEPAK, WASIL	25	M	LABR	RRZZZZNY
MARCHOW, GREGOR	26	M	LABR	RRZZZZNY
WILSCHELSKY, RACHEL	18	F	SVNT	RRZZZZNY
KOWOLSKI, SMICHE	19	M	TLR	RRZZZZNY
FRIEDMANN, SIMON	35	M	PDLR	RRZZZZNY
LOB.	8	M	CHILD	RRZZZZNY
DULZKI, CHAJEM	34	M	PDLR	RRZZZZNY
KONSCHAL, FRIEDRICH	25	M	SHMK	RRZZZZNY
DIKSHAL, EMILIE	46	F	W	RRZZZZNY
AUGUST	8	M	CHILD	RRZZZZNY

SHIP: EIDER

FROM: BREMEN AND SOUTHAMPTON
TO: NEW YORK
ARRIVED: 14 NOVEMBER 1885

PASSENGER	AGE	SEX	OCCUPATION	PRV VIL DES
ROSENBLUM, ROSALIA	16	F	CH	RRZZZZUSA
SARAH	30	F	NN	RRZZZZUSA
MICHALIS	11	M	CH	RRZZZZUSA
BLOCH, JOSEF	21	M	FARMER	RRZZZZUSA
GRONEWALD, MARIE	22	F	NN	RRZZZZUSA
ALTMANN, MORITZ	21	M	MCHT	RRZZZZUSA
ELL, JOHANNES	43	M	FARMER	RRZZZZUSA
CATHA.	39	F	W	RRZZZZUSA
FRANZ	20	M	FARMER	RRZZZZUSA
ELISABETH	20	F	NN	RRZZZZUSA
JOHANNES	11	M	CH	RRZZZZUSA
ROCHUS	9	M	CHILD	RRZZZZUSA
JOSEF	4	M	CHILD	RRZZZZUSA
JULIANE	.09	F	INFANT	RRZZZZUSA
WEICHEL, JOSEF	28	M	FARMER	RRZZZZUSA
CHRISTINE	26	F	W	RRZZZZUSA
BARBARA	6	F	CHILD	RRZZZZUSA
FRANZ	3	M	CHILD	RRZZZZUSA
ANTON	.09	M	INFANT	RRZZZZUSA
REINBOLD, IGNATZ	30	M	FARMER	RRZZZZUSA
BARBARA	28	F	W	RRZZZZUSA
JOHANNE	7	F	CHILD	RRZZZZUSA
JOSEF	6	M	CHILD	RRZZZZUSA
ANNA	2	F	CHILD	RRZZZZUSA
ANTON	.09	M	INFANT	RRZZZZUSA
BRANNAGEL, CASIMIR	20	M	FARMER	RRZZZZUSA
PHILIPPINE	22	F	W	RRZZZZUSA
MARGARETHE	.07	F	INFANT	RRZZZZUSA
HOFFARTH, BALTHASAR	33	M	FARMER	RRZZZZUSA
CATHA.	32	F	W	RRZZZZUSA
MARGA.	4	F	CHILD	RRZZZZUSA
MARIE	3	F	CHILD	RRZZZZUSA
JOSEF	1	M	CHILD	RRZZZZUSA
MICHAEL	.06	M	INFANT	RRZZZZUSA
SCHNEIDER, FELIX	21	M	FARMER	RRZZZZUSA
SANDLER, ROCHUS	19	M	FARMER	RRZZZZUSA
EISENZIMMER, PETER	28	M	FARMER	RRZZZZUSA
MARIE	27	F	W	RRZZZZUSA
MARIE	9	F	CHILD	RRZZZZUSA
PETER	4	M	CHILD	RRZZZZUSA
ROCHUS	1	M	CHILD	RRZZZZUSA
JUNG, PHILIPPINE	19	F	NN	RRZZZZUSA
WEICHEL, ANTON	33	M	FARMER	RRZZZZUSA
CAROLINE	25	F	W	RRZZZZUSA
BARBARA	11	F	CH	RRZZZZUSA
MARGARETHE	9	F	CHILD	RRZZZZUSA
CATHARINE	6	F	CHILD	RRZZZZUSA
FRANZ	.06	M	INFANT	RRZZZZUSA

PASSENGER	AGE	SEX	OCCUPATION	PRV VIL DES
SCHOL, JACOB	19	M	FARMER	RRZZZZUSA
HARTMANN, ANTON	20	M	FARMER	RRZZZZUSA
VOELLER, ANTON	20	M	FARMER	RRZZZZUSA
MATERI, WENDELIN	28	M	FARMER	RRZZZZUSA
MAGDE.	25	F	W	RRZZZZUSA
MARTIN	.01	M	INFANT	RRZZZZUSA
RICHTER, WILHELM	32	M	FARMER	RRZZZZUSA
CHRISTE.	26	F	W	RRZZZZUSA
SOPHIE	4	F	CHILD	RRZZZZUSA
FRANZ, JOHANN	23	M	FARMER	RRZZZZUSA
ENSMINGER, JACOB	31	M	FARMER	RRZZZZUSA
SUSANNA	28	F	W	RRZZZZUSA
LOUISE	4	F	CHILD	RRZZZZUSA
GOETZ, SOPHIE	19	F	NN	RRZZZZUSA
VOLLER, ANTON	20	M	LABR	RRZZZZUSA
PFEIFFER, WILH.	25	M	LABR	RRZZZZUSA
MARIANNE	20	F	W	RRZZZZUSA
MARIANNE	1	F	CHILD	RRZZZZUSA
ROMALTUS	.06	M	INFANT	RRZZZZUSA
LITZINGER, TOMAS	20	M	LABR	RRZZZZUSA
SCHLACHTER, MAX	27	M	LABR	RRAAHUUSA

SHIP: MAIN

FROM: BREMEN
TO: NEW YORK
ARRIVED: 14 NOVEMBER 1885

PASSENGER	AGE	SEX	OCCUPATION	PRV VIL DES
OBERZAHN, JOHAN	33	M	LABR	RRZZZZUSA
GUTFREUND, JOSEF	50	M	LABR	RRZZZZUSA
KORYWECKY, JOSEF	20	M	LABR	RRZZZZUSA
MISCHKE, THEOFIE	26	M	LABR	RRZZZZUSA
HECTOR	22	M	LABR	RRZZZZUSA
SUPRONOWICZ, PETER	41	M	LABR	RRZZZZUSA
GRUCHOWSKI, IGNATZI	22	M	LABR	RRZZZZUSA
LEUMER, JAN	30	M	LABR	RRZZZZUSA
DUBOCZINSKI, BRONISLA	22	M	LABR	RRZZZZUSA
TREMOWSKI, FRANZ	20	M	LABR	RRZZZZUSA
AGNIST, LENA	18	F	SVNT	RRZZZZUSA
GINZBURG, ZELDA	18	F	SVNT	RRZZZZUSA
KUSZWIRSKY, ZODEK	21	F	SVNT	RRZZZZUSA
ZABORNE, MARIANNE	40	F	W	RRZZZZUSA
JAN	13	M	CH	RRZZZZUSA
ANNETTE	8	F	CHILD	RRZZZZUSA
EDWARD	4	M	CHILD	RRZZZZUSA
SIMON, LIEBE	33	F	W	RRZZZZUSA
RODE	11	F	CH	RRZZZZUSA
DWORE	9	F	CHILD	RRZZZZUSA
CHAJE	8	F	CHILD	RRZZZZUSA
MOSES	4	M	CHILD	RRZZZZUSA
JOSEF	2	M	CHILD	RRZZZZUSA
SYRUB, JOSEF	19	M	LABR	RRZZZZUSA
GESCHBACH, GABE	25	F	SVNT	RRZZZZUSA
JACOB, GABE	23	F	SVNT	RRZZZZUSA
RIED, BEILE	20	F	SVNT	RRZZZZUSA
WEISS, SALI	18	F	SVNT	RRZZZZUSA
GLUECK, BERTHA	18	F	SVNT	RRZZZZUSA
FELDMANN, DWORE	38	F	W	RRZZZZUSA
BEMION	10	M	CH	RRZZZZUSA
SALMEN	8	M	CHILD	RRZZZZUSA
FISCHEL	.01	M	INFANT	RRZZZZUSA
TIEDJE, HERM.	17	M	LABR	RRZZZZUSA
FRIEDMANN, DWORE	30	F	SVNT	RRZZZZUSA
MONTBARON, EDWARD	27	M	LABR	RRZZZZUSA
BUDMINSKI, KARL	30	M	LABR	RRZZZZUSA
ALMA	27	F	W	RRZZZZUSA
CARL	.03	M	INFANT	RRZZZZUSA
EDMUND	.03	M	INFANT	RRZZZZUSA

SHIP: PENNLAND

FROM: ANTWERP
TO: NEW YORK
ARRIVED: 15 NOVEMBER 1885

PASSENGER	AGE	SEX	OCCUPATION	PRV VIL DES
GOPZEVICH, MICH.	18	M	LABR	RRZZZZCH
PETER	15	M	LABR	RRZZZZCH
ACCONSOFF, ISC.	25	M	BTMKR	RRZZZZNY
KORDOS, MAR.	25	F	W	RRZZZZUNK
JOSEPH	00	M	INF	RRZZZZUNK
DERFERT, CONST.	24	F	W	RRZZZZUNK
JOS.	00	M	INF	RRZZZZUNK
BRENNER, H.	25	M	LABR	RRZZZZUNK
ELIS.	20	F	LABR	RRZZZZUNK
HEL.	00	M	INF	RRZZZZUNK

SHIP: ALASKA

FROM: LIVERPOOL AND QUEENSTOWN
TO: NEW YORK
ARRIVED: 16 NOVEMBER 1885

PASSENGER	AGE	SEX	OCCUPATION	PRV VIL DES
APPELTING, ISAAC	40	M	MRNR	RRZZZZUNK

SHIP: CALIFORNIA

FROM: HAMBURG
TO: NEW YORK
ARRIVED: 16 NOVEMBER 1885

PASSENGER	AGE	SEX	OCCUPATION	PRV VIL DES
NOMBERZIG, CHAIC	17	F	SGL	RRZZZZWI
ZIPPEL, ARON	33	M	LABR	RRZZZZNY
FARBSTEIN, F.	21	M	TRDSMN	RRZZZZNY
SMOLENSKY, REBECKA	18	F	SGL	RRZZZZIL
JOSEPH	17	M	B	RRZZZZIL
MEISLEWSKY, BREINE	16	F	SGL	RRZZZZIL
KAPLAN, REBECCA	18	F	SGL	RRZZZZIL
PRAISE, STAITE	19	F	SGL	RRZZZZNY
KORSZEK, RUBIN	45	M	TLR	RRZZZZNY
KAISER, KOSEL	28	M	TLR	RRZZZZNY
TUCHOSCHINSKO, CHANE	20	F	WO	RRZZZZMO
ABRAHAM	.06	M	INFANT	RRZZZZMO
GERTZ, SCHOLIM	7	M	CHILD	RRZZZZNY
ROSENSTEIN, ROSA	24	F	WO	RRZZZZNY
MIRELA	5	F	CHILD	RRZZZZNY
ANNY	.08	F	INFANT	RRZZZZNY
GOLDSTEIN, RACHEL	59	F	WO	RRZZZZIL
KERSCHENBAUM, MENASKE	30	F	WO	RRZZZZNY
TICHTERMANN, ABR.	36	M	FUR	RRZZZZNY
BESSE, JOSEF	20	M	TRDSMN	RRZZZZNY
GRUENWALD, GEORG	18	M	SMH	RRZZZZNY
TEITELBAUM, WOLF	24	M	SMH	RRZZZZNY
SAMUEL, VICTOR	55	M	TDR	RRZZZZNY
SANKEL	6	M	CHILD	RRZZZZNY
FEIN, LEA	27	F	W	RRZZZZNY
SCHANDER	3	M	CHILD	RRZZZZNY
FULA	.05	F	INFANT	RRZZZZNY
LEDERER, E.	13	M	LABR	RRZZZZNY
RUDEL, EFFE	28	F	WO	RRZZZZNY
DOROTHEA	4	F	CHILD	RRZZZZNY
HEIDTMANN, ANNA	27	F	W	RRZZZZNY
ZEIKOKEITISCH, JOS.	32	M	LABR	RRZZZZNY
WEISCHMIS, ANDR.	21	M	LABR	RRZZZZNY
TORAFF, SALOM.	24	M	TRDSMN	RRZZZZNY
BRANNSTEIN, JAC.	18	M	TRDSMN	RRZZZZNY
SCHUR, TOBIAS	39	M	TRDSMN	RRZZZZNY
SCHAFFIER, MOWSKE	45	M	WCHMKR	RRZZZZNY
RIWK	20	F	UNKNOWN	RRZZZZNY
CHELMER, ROSA	22	F	SGL	RRZZZZNY
ZERFANSKOWSKY, P.	25	M	LABR	RRZZZZNY
WEINSTEIN, ELKE	20	F	WO	RRZZZZNY
HIRSCH	7	M	CHILD	RRZZZZNY
CHANE	5	F	CHILD	RRZZZZNY
GOLDSTEIN, SAM.	20	M	LABR	RRZZZZNY
BLADKOWSKY, MOS.	24	M	LABR	RRZZZZNY
LEFKOWITZ, MOSES	30	M	TDR	RRZZZZNY

SHIP: ETRURIA

FROM: LIVERPOOL AND QUEENSTOWN
TO: NEW YORK
ARRIVED: 16 NOVEMBER 1885

PASSENGER	AGE	SEX	OCCUPATION	PRV VIL DES
KUTZ, MARCUS	36	M	LABR	RRZZZZUSA
NELSON, MARIE	52	F	MA	FNZZZZUSA
KEINDA, LINA-S.	30	F	MA	FNZZZZUSA
NILSON, WILHELA.	11	F	CH	FNZZZZUSA
ELIZ	7	F	CHILD	FNZZZZUSA
FULDA	4	F	CHILD	FNZZZZUSA

SHIP: GELLERT

FROM: HAMBURG AND HAVRE
TO: NEW YORK
ARRIVED: 16 NOVEMBER 1885

PASSENGER	AGE	SEX	OCCUPATION	PRV VIL DES
JOFFE, MOSES	57	M	LABR	RRZZZZUSA
SCHIMOWITZ, MOSES	19	M	TCHR	RRZZZZUSA
LOZAZYSKI, MORDCHE	40	M	DLR	RRZZZZUSA
BERNSTEIN, MEYER	20	M	DLR	RRZZZZUSA
BIERBISZKI, JUDEL	20	M	BCHR	RRZZZZUSA
FRAENKEL, FANNY	14	F	SGL	RRAHTRUSA
PUTTERMANN, HERSCH	45	M	LABR	RRZZZZUSA
HELLERSTEIN, SCHMUL	42	M	DLR	RRZZZZUSA
GOLDSTEIN, JACOB	28	M	LABR	RRZZZZUSA
KOHN, MOSES	18	M	LABR	RRAHZSUSA
NORKEWICH, AUGUST	20	M	LABR	RRAHSWUSA
LEMKCITIS, JOSEPH	21	M	LABR	RRZZZZUSA
SMULIJAN, HORACE	36	M	DLR	RRZZZZUSA
GERSCHUIN, JACOB	39	M	DLR	RRAHVLUSA
ROSEN, HIRSCH	25	M	DLR	RRZZZZUSA
CHRISTALL, RACHEL	30	F	W	RRZZZZUSA
LIEBE	5	M	CHILD	RRZZZZUSA
NAFTALI	3	M	CHILD	RRZZZZUSA
ROSENFELD, JACOB	19	M	DLR	RRZZZZUSA
MINA	19	F	W	RRZZZZUSA
FEHRMANN, LEA	27	F	W	RRZZZZUSA
ISRAEL	.11	M	INFANT	RRZZZZUSA
RUBEL, ABRAM	21	M	LABR	RRZZZZUSA
GRANITZER, CHAIM	36	F	WO	RRAHTUUSA
PRUSSAK, PHILIPP	31	M	CGRMKR	RRAHUIUSA
ISKA	31	F	W	RRAHUIUSA
ARTHUR	3	M	CHILD	RRAHUIUSA
ZUCKERMANN, LINA	54	F	W	RRZZZZUSA
MAX	11	M	CH	RRZZZZUSA
RACHEL	7	F	CHILD	RRZZZZUSA
ADEL	2	F	CHILD	RRZZZZUSA

PASSENGER	AGE	SEX	OCCUPATION	PRV	VIL	DES

SHIP: LESSING

FROM: HAMBURG
TO: NEW YORK
ARRIVED: 16 NOVEMBER 1885

PASSENGER	AGE	SEX	OCCUPATION	PRV VIL DES
PERELDICK, SCHMUEL	24	M	LABR	RRAFVGUSA
CHAJE	60	F	M	RRAFVGUSA
LEIDE, MIREL	20	F	SGL	RRAHTFUSA
BUMMOWITZ, ISAAC	23	M	LABR	RRZZZZUSA
KAMINSKY, PESCHE	17	F	SGL	RRZZZZUSA
JERMAJMAS, JERMOAL	17	M	LABR	RRZZZZUSA
BUNIMOWITZ, RACHE	23	F	SGL	RRZZZZUSA
WOLINSKY, SCHEINDEL	30	F	W	RRZZZZUSA
HEIGE	9	F	CHILD	RRZZZZUSA
LIEBE	9	F	CHILD	RRZZZZUSA
HINDE	7	F	CHILD	RRZZZZUSA
DWORE	5	F	CHILD	RRZZZZUSA
LEIB	3	M	CHILD	RRZZZZUSA
RUMBERG, ABR.	9	M	CHILD	RRZZZZUSA
MUNE, ACHEM	34	M	SHMK	RRZZZZUSA
GAJAZ, GETZEL	26	M	DLR	RRZZZZUSA
MOSES	18	M	DLR	RRZZZZUSA
GUTMANN, LEVECK	29	M	TLR	RRZZZZUSA
KORPIEL, HERTZ	18	M	TLR	RRZZZZUSA
BARETZKI, MOSES	39	M	JNR	RRZZZZUSA
CYTRON, SALOMON	50	M	DLR	RRZZZZUSA
ROSALIE	59	F	W	RRZZZZUSA
LEONORE	19	F	CH	RRZZZZUSA
BERNSTEIN, SCHIFRE	52	F	W	RRAFVGUSA
PAWA, CHAIE	18	F	SGL	RRAFVGUSA
GOLDSTEIN, TAUBE	17	F	SGL	RRAHSWUSA
CHMILEWSKI, SUSSEL	20	M	TLR	RRZZZZUSA
GITTEL	20	F	W	RRZZZZUSA
GOLDSTEIN, ISAAC	18	M	WCHMKR	RRAHSWUSA
CUTNOW, CHAIE	20	F	W	RRZZZZUSA
HENE	6	F	CHILD	RRZZZZUSA
JOSEPH	8	M	CHILD	RRZZZZUSA
NOCHAME	3	F	CHILD	RRZZZZUSA
HORN, MARIE	17	F	SGL	RRZZZZUSA
SEGAL, BANE	16	F	SGL	RRZZZZUSA
JUDES	9	F	CHILD	RRZZZZUSA
HAMER, REISEL	44	F	W	RRZZZZUSA
JACOB	14	M	CH	RRZZZZUSA
MORITZ	9	M	CHILD	RRZZZZUSA
SEGALL, LIEBE	55	F	W	RRZZZZUSA
KISSIN, JOSEF	20	M	LABR	RRZZZZUSA
WEITZ, MOSES	19	M	LABR	RRAHWEUSA

SHIP: NORMANDIE

FROM: HAVRE
TO: NEW YORK
ARRIVED: 16 NOVEMBER 1885

PASSENGER	AGE	SEX	OCCUPATION	PRV VIL DES
DESELENKOFF, EUGENE	36	M	OFF	RRZZZZNY

SHIP: DEVONIA

FROM: GLASGOW
TO: NEW YORK
ARRIVED: 18 NOVEMBER 1885

PASSENGER	AGE	SEX	OCCUPATION	PRV VIL DES
BARANOWITSCH, PEISACH	29	M	TLR	RRACBFUSA
BERELOWITZ, HIRSCH	19	M	PDLR	RRACBFUSA
CHOLINZKI, CHASKEL	31	M	JNR	RRACBFUSA
LEIB	21	M	NN	RRACBFUSA
CHAMELIS, ISAAC	19	M	PDLR	RRACBFUSA
FRIEDKIN, DAR.	30	M	SHMK	RRACBFUSA
GLACHENHUS, LIPE	20	M	JNR	RRACBFUSA
GORDON, LEISER	19	M	LABR	RRACBFUSA
GERBER, BENZEL	33	M	BCHR	RRACBFUSA
HOFMANN, LEIB	58	M	PNTR	RRACBFUSA
ESTER	40	F	NN	RRACBFUSA
CHAJEN	17	M	CH	RRACBFUSA
RIWKE	11	M	CH	RRACBFUSA
ABRAHAM	10	M	CH	RRACBFUSA
KOLMAN	5	M	CHILD	RRACBFUSA
PAULINE	2	F	CHILD	RRACBFUSA
SALOMON	.09	M	INFANT	RRACBFUSA
HALPERT, ISRAEL	40	M	LABR	RRACBFUSA
HILLEL, CYNAMON	34	M	LABR	RRACBFUSA
LEWIS, MOSES	20	M	LABR	RRACBFUSA
JANKEL	27	M	LABR	RRACBFUSA
LASER, MECHMIE	37	M	LABR	RRACBFUSA
RACHINSKI, MOSES	20	M	LABR	RRACBFUSA
RUBENSTEIN, DAV.J.	24	M	LABR	RRACBFUSA
ROSENFELD, MEYER	40	M	LABR	RRACBFUSA
SCHONFELD, BENZIN	21	M	LABR	RRACBFUSA
SCHLEME, ARON	35	M	LABR	RRACBFUSA
LEBE	10	M	CH	RRACBFUSA
FINKELSTEIN, SAML.	20	M	LABR	RRACBFUSA
WASLAWSKI, SCELIG	23	M	LABR	RRACBFUSA
SARA	20	F	NN	RRACBFUSA
JAFFE, SAML.	24	M	LABR	RRACBFUSA
LEWIN, MOSES	16	M	LABR	RRACBFUSA

SHIP: STATE OF GEORGIA

FROM: GLASGOW AND LARNE
TO: NEW YORK
ARRIVED: 19 NOVEMBER 1885

PASSENGER	AGE	SEX	OCCUPATION	PRV VIL DES
BERTIMER, JULIUS	27	M	TLR	PLZZZZUSA
FELLNER, LEIBISCH	31	M	PDLR	PLZZZZUSA
BRODITZKY, MOTTEL	25	M	PDLR	PLZZZZUSA
KLINKOWSTEIN, JAKOB	19	M	PDLR	PLZZZZUSA
POLOKOWSKY, TEOFIL	30	M	LABR	PLZZZZUSA
LEISEROWITCH, MARCUS	20	M	PDLR	RRZZZZUSA
WEISSMANN, CHAINE	43	M	PDLR	RRZZZZUSA
JOSEF	21	M	PDLR	RRZZZZUSA
ARONOWITZ, SCHOLEM	20	M	TLR	RRZZZZUSA
SCHEIDNER, SAMUEL	44	M	LABR	RRZZZZUSA
FINKELDEUTCH, ITZIG	20	M	PDLR	RRZZZZUSA
KITCHFELAN, JEGA	56	F	SP	PLZZZZUSA
FRIEDMAN, GITTEL	19	F	SP	PLZZZZUSA
NEUER, ROSA	22	F	SP	RRZZZZUSA
LEWINSON, BARUCH	30	M	LABR	PLZZZZUSA
DOROTHEA	30	F	W	PLZZZZUSA
FANNY	5	F	CHILD	PLZZZZUSA
JOSEF	3	M	CHILD	PLZZZZUSA
SALOMON	2	M	CHILD	PLZZZZUSA
PAULINE	1	F	CHILD	PLZZZZUSA
JEGENDORFF, JETE	34	F	W	PLZZZZUSA
FIEDEL	1	F	CHILD	PLZZZZUSA
BLAUMSTEIN, HIRSCH	30	M	PDLR	PLZZZZUSA

PASSENGER	AGE	SEX	OCCUPATION	PRVIL	DES
REFKE	25	F	W	PLZZZ	USA
DAVID	2	M	CHILD	PLZZZ	USA
MOSES	1	M	CHILD	PLZZZ	USA
MISCHELSKY, LEIE	38	F	W	PLZZZ	USA
ELKE	3	F	CHILD	PLZZZ	USA
SARAH	5	F	CHILD	PLZZZ	USA
KERKE	2	M	CHILD	PLZZZ	USA
MERKE	1	M	CHILD	PLZZZ	USA
METOR, CHALENA	28	F	W	PLZZZ	USA
SARAH	5	F	CHILD	PLZZZ	USA
MALER, DREZEL	38	F	W	RRZZZ	USA
ALTE	9	F	CHILD	RRZZZ	USA
NECHANNE	1	M	CHILD	RRZZZ	USA
ISRAEL, HIRSCH	28	M	LABR	RRZZZ	USA
ROSALIE	30	F	W	RRZZZ	USA
HERMANN	2	M	CHILD	RRZZZ	USA
MINICK, LEA	45	F	W	RRZZZ	USA
PEREL	11	F	CH	RRZZZ	USA
KALMAN	10	M	CH	RRZZZ	USA
JOSEL	5	M	CHILD	RRZZZ	USA
MAIA	18	F	W	RRZZZ	USA

SHIP: CITY OF BERLIN

FROM: LIVERPOOL AND QUEENSTOWN
TO: NEW YORK
ARRIVED: 20 NOVEMBER 1885

PASSENGER	AGE	SEX	OCCUPATION	PRVIL	DES
SPRENGEIN, ARON	40	M	LABR	RRACBF	NY
SZAPACKER, MARCUS	24	F	SVNT	RRACBF	NY
JOSEF	00	M	INF	RRACBF	NY
MARIA	00	F	INF	RRACBF	NY
KOSUNSKA, MARIA	30	F	W	RRAARR	WI
WILHELM	8	M	CHILD	RRAARR	WI
MADESTAI	6	M	CHILD	RRAARR	WI
MONICA	4	F	CHILD	RRAARR	WI
ALBERT	3	M	CHILD	RRAARR	WI
MODZERESKO, ANA	22	F	W	RRACBF	NY
KOSINSKA, ANNA	00	F	INF	RRACBF	NY
MOSES, MOSES	44	M	FARMER	RRACBF	NY
HRITZKO, ISIDOR	20	M	LABR	RRACBF	NY
SCHLENSKO, SAMUEL	18	M	LABR	RRACBF	NY
ESTER	19	F	SVNT	RRACBF	NY
KREMNER, LEIB	19	M	LABR	RRACBF	NY
ARELSAD, HERMAN	29	M	CL	RRACBF	NY
JOSEF	23	M	CL	RRACBF	NY
LAPIDUS, ISRAEL	29	M	CL	RRACBF	NY
SLEPIAN, BAER	24	M	MNR	RRACBF	NY
RUBIN, LEISER	35	M	MNR	RRACBF	NY
ABRAHAM, MANE	23	M	MNR	RRACBF	NY
SLANKO, EISIG	30	M	MECH	RRACBF	NY
SACHANORSKA, SACHER	46	F	W	RRACBF	NY
JANKO	17	F	SVNT	RRACBF	NY
RENSER	8	M	CHILD	RRACBF	NY
NEGEL, ABRAHAM	31	M	TLR	RRACBF	NY
JACKOB	23	M	TLR	RRACBF	NY
SHADLOWZIN, ABRAHAM	19	M	LABR	RRACBF	NY
NUFSBAUM, ABRAHAM	19	M	LABR	RRACBF	NY
KERSLA, MANZA	18	M	SVNT	RRACBF	NY
SHRENUSCH, LEIRE	43	F	W	RRACBF	NY
ARON	10	M	CH	RRACBF	NY
CZERNICK, MOSES	22	M	LABR	RRACBF	NY
ARONOWITSCH, LORE	21	M	LABR	RRACBF	NY
KRON, BERNHD.	23	M	LABR	RRACBF	NY
DE-GILLERT, MADL.THEODO	31	F	AR	RRACBF	NY

SHIP: DONAU

FROM: BREMEN
TO: NEW YORK
ARRIVED: 20 NOVEMBER 1885

PASSENGER	AGE	SEX	OCCUPATION	PRVIL	DES
SCHLARSKI, BORUCH	24	F	NN	RRZZZ	USA
DAVIS, BASCHE	24	F	NN	RRZZZ	USA
KOPCZOWSKY, CHAIE	19	F	NN	RRZZZ	USA
ABRAMSKY, JOSEL	18	F	NN	RRZZZ	USA
ANSENBERG, FRADEL	20	F	NN	RRZZZ	USA
FEDERMANN, DWOIRE	17	F	NN	RRZZZ	USA
WELSON, NACHMANN	54	M	FARMER	RRZZZ	USA
HINDE	48	F	W	RRZZZ	USA
CHAIN	10	M	CH	RRZZZ	USA
KALIK, WILH.	36	M	MCHT	RRZZZ	USA
SCHOLL, WENDELIN	23	M	FARMER	RRZZZ	USA
FETSCH, PETER	24	M	FARMER	RRZZZ	USA
KONOPATZKE, ADAM	34	M	FARMER	RRZZZ	USA
KONOPATZKI, THOTINE	28	F	NN	RRZZZ	USA
EMILIE	8	F	CHILD	RRZZZ	USA
CARL	5	M	CHILD	RRZZZ	USA
ANNA	.05	F	INFANT	RRZZZ	USA
MILDER, GISELA	18	F	NN	RRZZZ	USA
TSCHINKOWITZ, LEIBEL	18	F	NN	RRZZZ	USA
SELIKOWITZ, JENTE	35	F	NN	RRZZZ	USA
JANKEL	11	M	CH	RRZZZ	USA
NEACH	11	M	CH	RRZZZ	USA
BORACH	3	M	CHILD	RRZZZ	USA
OSCHOFSKI, MARCIN	22	M	LABR	RRZZZ	USA
ACKSTOROWITSCH, MARCIN	30	M	LABR	RRZZZ	USA
TOMASCHEWSKI, MARTIN	20	M	LABR	RRZZZ	USA
REINHOLD, BALTHASAR	38	M	LABR	RRZZZ	USA
LISBETH	34	F	W	RRZZZ	USA
JACOB	11	M	CH	RRZZZ	USA
ADAM	10	M	CH	RRZZZ	USA
MARTIN	7	M	CHILD	RRZZZ	USA
PHILIPPINE	4	F	CHILD	RRZZZ	USA
HELENE	2	F	CHILD	RRZZZ	USA
PUCHALSKI, WLADISLAW	21	M	LABR	RRZZZ	USA
VEDRA, FRANK	20	M	LABR	RRZZZ	USA
ROSENBERG, MARKS	34	M	BCHR	RRZZZ	USA
ROMMER, JEZKO	30	M	FARMER	RRZZZ	USA
RAKSZIOWNA, MICHALINE	19	F	NN	RRZZZ	USA
BIETZ, JOH.	34	M	NN	RRZZZ	USA
MAGD.	28	F	W	RRZZZ	USA
PAULINE	8	F	CHILD	RRZZZ	USA
JOHANN	7	M	CHILD	RRZZZ	USA
CHRISTIANE	4	F	CHILD	RRZZZ	USA
WILK, LOUISE	60	F	NN	RRZZZ	USA
ENOMINGER, WILH.	27	M	SMH	RRZZZ	USA
WILHE.	20	F	W	RRZZZ	USA
FREICHEL, MARIE	68	F	NN	RRZZZ	USA
MERGIKOWITZ, LEIB	20	M	SMH	RRZZZ	USA
BARTON, ANDR.	24	M	LABR	RRZZZ	USA
JOH.	32	M	LABR	RRZZZ	USA
KAWALERTSCHIK, HENNI	30	F	NN	RRZZZ	USA
UNATOWSKI, CAROL.	24	F	NN	RRZZZ	USA
BERTHA	11	F	CH	RRZZZ	USA
ANNA	6	F	CHILD	RRZZZ	USA
JULIE	5	F	CHILD	RRZZZ	USA

PASSENGER	AGE	SEX	OCCUPATION	PRIVL	DES

SHIP: WERRA

FROM: BREMEN AND SOUTHAMPTON
TO: NEW YORK
ARRIVED: 21 NOVEMBER 1885

PASSENGER	AGE	SEX	OCCUPATION	PRIVL	DES
CORDES, LINA	18	F	NN	RRAETV	USA
HEINSEL, HEINR.	16	M	FARMER	RRZZZZ	USA
SONIPNIRSKA, PAULINA	43	F	NN	RRZZZZ	USA
SIPNEWSKA, CARL	15	M	NN	RRZZZZ	USA
KARTOWICZ, JOHN	20	M	FARMER	RRZZZZ	USA
LAGODNY, MARIANNE	22	F	NN	RRZZZZ	USA
SEKOWSKY, MORTEL	30	M	LABR	RRZZZZ	USA
BESER	25	F	W	RRZZZZ	USA
STENZEL, JAN	29	M	LABR	RRZZZZ	USA
SCHAPIRO, HODE	18	F	NN	RRZZZZ	USA
GRONAN, BALTHASAR	22	M	LABR	RRZZZZ	USA
SKOPP, MATHILDE	11	F	NN	RRZZZZ	USA
ROSALIE	9	F	CHILD	RRZZZZ	USA
FANNY	8	F	CHILD	RRZZZZ	USA

SHIP: EGYPTIAN MONARCH

FROM: LONDON
TO: NEW YORK
ARRIVED: 23 NOVEMBER 1885

PASSENGER	AGE	SEX	OCCUPATION	PRIVL	DES
JACOBS, ABRAHAM	21	M	TLR	RRADBQ	NY
TIECO, LIEL	35	M	TLR	RRADBQ	NY
RIGA, S.	24	M	WCHMKR	RRADBQ	HAT
BROWN, MAX	27	M	TLR	RRADBQ	NY
RACHENE	27	F	W	RRADBQ	NY

SHIP: KATIE

FROM: UNKNOWN
TO: NEW YORK
ARRIVED: 23 NOVEMBER 1885

PASSENGER	AGE	SEX	OCCUPATION	PRIVL	DES
SENGERMAN, RUBIN	18	M	SHMK	RRZZZZ	USA
GRABOWSKY, PAUL	15	M	LABR	PLZZZZ	USA
EHRLICH, A.J.	17	M	TLR	RRZZZZ	USA
SINDJEWSKY, ABRAHAM	17	M	SHMK	RRZZZZ	USA
ZOMONTOWSKY, FEIGE	30	F	W	RRAHZS	USA
DAVID	1	M	CHILD	RRAHZS	USA
MOLLINSA, BRITE-L.	31	F	SVNT	FNZZZZ	OR
JOHAN-A.	6	M	CHILD	FNZZZZ	OR
HERWIK	3	M	CHILD	FNZZZZ	OR

SHIP: LEERDAM

FROM: ROTTERDAM
TO: NEW YORK
ARRIVED: 23 NOVEMBER 1885

PASSENGER	AGE	SEX	OCCUPATION	PRIVL	DES
KOSINER, MARKUS	28	F	LABR	RRZZZZ	USA
NASSELSKYE, ISIDOR	21	M	MCHT	RRZZZZ	USA
LANGER, JAKOB	25	M	MCHT	RRZZZZ	USA
WILK, ARON	22	M	LABR	RRZZZZ	USA
PLATOI, MOSES	22	M	MCHT	RRZZZZ	USA
STIRB, BENJAMIN	48	M	MCHT	RRZZZZ	USA
PASLOTKY, SARAH	25	F	NN	RRZZZZ	USA
WOLF	6	M	CHILD	RRZZZZ	USA
GIEBER	5	M	CHILD	RRZZZZ	USA
DODIS, JEOLDS	25	F	CH	RRZZZZ	USA
HIRSCH	.06	M	INFANT	RRZZZZ	USA
SEGALL, JOSEF	34	M	LABR	RRZZZZ	USA
SCHEIVACHS, CHOSCHE	40	M	LABR	RRZZZZ	USA
SARAH	7	F	CHILD	RRZZZZ	USA
ISAAC	5	M	CHILD	RRZZZZ	USA
HIRSCH	.03	M	INFANT	RRZZZZ	USA
SEGALL, JOSEFF	34	M	LABR	RRZZZZ	USA
SEHWOCH, CHASCHE	40	M	LABR	RRZZZZ	USA
SARAH	7	F	CHILD	RRZZZZ	USA
ISAAC	5	M	CHILD	RRZZZZ	USA
HIRSCH	.03	M	INFANT	RRZZZZ	USA

SHIP: OREGON

FROM: LIVERPOOL AND QUEENSTOWN
TO: NEW YORK
ARRIVED: 23 NOVEMBER 1885

PASSENGER	AGE	SEX	OCCUPATION	PRIVL	DES
WELDOOSKY, CHAGE	20	F	SP	RRZZZZ	NY
COHEN, ISAAC	23	M	MACH	RRZZZZ	NY
DERBYN, ANTON	30	M	LABR	RRZZZZ	DET
LATONEYKI, LEBRISCH	22	M	LABR	RRZZZZ	DET
JASELOVETZ, GERSON	18	M	LABR	RRZZZZ	NY
HERSCHOVETZ, HERSCH	20	M	LABR	RRZZZZ	NY
GULMANN, KYIG	19	M	LABR	RRZZZZ	NY
REDNEKOWITSCH, SCHOLENN	20	M	LABR	RRZZZZ	NY
KATZ, MOSES	22	M	LABR	RRZZZZ	NY
BURLOCK, ZUSKU	23	F	W	RRZZZZ	NY
JOHN	.10	M	INFANT	RRZZZZ	NY

SHIP: CIRCASSIA

FROM: UNKNOWN
TO: NEW YORK
ARRIVED: 24 NOVEMBER 1885

PASSENGER	AGE	SEX	OCCUPATION	PRIVL	DES
RUBEN, ABRAHAM	20	M	SHMK	RRZZZZ	USA
MICHEL	20	M	SHMK	RRZZZZ	USA
SAFFER, JACOB	34	M	DLR	RRZZZZ	USA
DORIS	32	F	W	RRZZZZ	USA
ADOLPH	6	M	CHILD	RRZZZZ	USA
AMALIA	1	F	CHILD	RRZZZZ	USA
COHN, ABRAHAM	33	M	UNKNOWN	RRZZZZ	USA
JOHANNA	33	F	W	RRZZZZ	USA
SOPHIA	7	F	CHILD	RRZZZZ	USA
LOUIS	5	M	CHILD	RRZZZZ	USA
HERMAN	2	M	CHILD	RRZZZZ	USA
RAHEL	1	F	CHILD	RRZZZZ	USA
ZELICHOWSO, ISRAEL	23	M	FARMER	RRZZZZ	USA
MARIE	23	F	W	RRZZZZ	USA
ZIMS, TAUBE	20	F	SVNT	RRZZZZ	USA
WALZ, PINKUSS	20	M	BBR	RRZZZZ	USA
PERI	19	F	W	RRZZZZ	USA
SANGIANSKY, HIRSCH	39	M	DLR	RRZZZZ	USA
SARAH	38	F	W	RRZZZZ	USA
LOUIS	12	M	CH	RRZZZZ	USA
CHAIN-J.	10	M	CH	RRZZZZ	USA
FREUDE	8	F	CHILD	RRZZZZ	USA
BENZEL	5	M	CHILD	RRZZZZ	USA

PASSENGER	AGE	SEX	OCCUPATION	PRV VIL DES
BEREL	3	F	CHILD	RRZZZZUSA
WEINSTEIN, VICTOR	22	M	CL	RRZZZZUSA
WAZNISKI, HENOCK	21	M	CPMKR	RRZZZZUSA
RAW, JANKEL	21	M	LABR	RRZZZZUSA
MALENNOSCH, IWAN	21	M	LABR	RRZZZZUSA
CHACHAUSKI, CHAIN-H.	22	M	DLR	RRZZZZUSA
KRAM, WOLFF	18	M	WCHMKR	RRZZZZUSA
LIPSCHUTZ, MARCUS	17	M	DLR	RRZZZZUSA
KUCPI, FEIWEL	18	M	DLR	RRZZZZUSA
SCHLOME, JASER	20	M	GDSM	RRZZZZUSA
SCHARF, DAVID	21	M	DLR	RRZZZZUSA
CALPER, ELIE	18	M	CL	RRZZZZUSA
NOWECHOWITZ, NOAH	23	M	DLR	RRZZZZUSA
BLUMSTEIN, NISSEN	31	M	DLR	RRZZZZUSA
BLUM, ABRAH.K.	44	M	DLR	RRZZZZUSA
ISRAEL	8	M	CHILD	RRZZZZUSA
DROP, MICHEL	51	M	MCHT	RRZZZZUSA
MAKITA, MARCIAH	25	M	LABR	RRZZZZUSA
MAKOWSKI, FRANZ	34	M	LABR	RRZZZZUSA
CHARNAS, SCHIMAN	21	M	DLR	RRZZZZUSA
POMAK, PROKOP	25	M	DLR	RRZZZZUSA
KIRWAT, JACOB	48	M	TLR	RRZZZZUSA
SEGOLL, JACOB	36	M	DLR	RRZZZZUSA
KOCHWISKY, CHAIM-J.	36	M	DLR	RRZZZZUSA

SHIP: BOHEMIA

FROM: HAMBURG
TO: NEW YORK
ARRIVED: 25 NOVEMBER 1885

PASSENGER	AGE	SEX	OCCUPATION	PRV VIL DES
FROMBERG, CHAIM	20	F	SGL	RRZZZZUSA
LEIB	9	F	CHILD	RRZZZZUSA
MACIEJEWSKA, THERESE	30	F	SGL	RRZZZZUSA
HERZBERG, BEHR	41	M	DLR	RRZZZZUSA
LAMBRECHT, MATHIAS	55	M	LABR	RRAGHKUSA
CHRISTINE	55	F	W	RRAGHKUSA
ELISABETH	12	F	CH	RRAGHKUSA
JACOB	9	M	CHILD	RRAGHKUSA
REICHERT, MICHAEL	24	M	FARMER	RRAGHKUSA
CAROLINE	25	F	W	RRAGHKUSA
WILHE.	2	F	CHILD	RRAGHKUSA
CATHE.	55	F	W	RRAGHKUSA
SYBILLA	27	F	SGL	RRAGHKUSA
GINGER, LUDWIG	38	M	FARMER	RRAGHKUSA
EVA	24	F	W	RRAGHKUSA
CAROLINE	4	F	CHILD	RRAGHKUSA
MAGDE.	3	F	CHILD	RRAGHKUSA
EVA	.11	F	INFANT	RRAGHKUSA
LUDWIG	14	M	FARMER	RRAGHKUSA
ERESMANN, CONRAD	35	M	FARMER	RRAGHKUSA
CAROLINE	35	F	W	RRAGHKUSA
MARG.	9	F	CHILD	RRAGHKUSA
NOWOTHNY, FERD.	49	M	FARMER	RRZZZZUSA
TRDKE.	49	F	W	RRZZZZUSA
FRANZ	20	M	CH	RRZZZZUSA
GEORG	15	M	CH	RRZZZZUSA
MARG.	13	F	CH	RRZZZZUSA
MINNA	8	F	CHILD	RRZZZZUSA
GOESTADT, WILHE.	29	F	W	RRZZZZUSA
EMIL	6	M	CHILD	RRZZZZUSA
GEDERITZ, WLADISLAV	23	M	LABR	RRZZZZUSA
TEKULSKY, ISRAEL	50	M	DLR	RRZZZZUSA
KOLESKI, ANTHONY	30	M	TU	RRAHZSUSA
SILBERBERG, RACHEL	21	F	SGL	RRZZZZUSA
RUSANSKI, MENDEL	30	M	DLR	RRZZZZUSA
CZERLOW, DWORE	18	F	SGL	RRZZZZUSA
ROCHIGALSKI, ABRAH.	50	M	DLR	RRAHSWUSA
BALINIAS, DOMINIK	22	M	LABR	RRZZZZUSA
ZELOWSKY, JUDEL	26	M	LABR	RRZZZZUSA

PASSENGER	AGE	SEX	OCCUPATION	PRV VIL DES
SEWKA	9	M	CHILD	RRZZZZUSA
GULOWSKI, ANTON	18	F	W	RRZZZZUSA
GRUSCHKE, SCHAPIRO	13	F	SGL	RRZZZZUSA
KAUFMANN, RACHEL	40	F	W	RRZZZZUSA
ELI	9	M	CHILD	RRZZZZUSA
LEIB	7	M	CHILD	RRZZZZUSA
LEISER	.11	M	INFANT	RRZZZZUSA
KLAPPER, CHAIE	40	F	W	RRAHTUUSA
RACHEL	9	F	CHILD	RRAHTUUSA
GREBMANN, ISAAC	43	M	LABR	RRZZZZUSA
KATZ, JANKEL	22	M	LABR	RRZZZZUSA
MEIKA, LEA	20	F	SGL	RRZZZZUSA
LEPINEITAS, JAN	27	M	LABR	RRZZZZUSA
WINICKIS, VALT.	29	M	LABR	RRAHTKUSA
JELIZUN, T.	28	M	LABR	RRZZZZUSA
MARIANN	36	F	W	RRZZZZUSA
JERR.	6	F	CHILD	RRZZZZUSA
ANNA	4	F	CHILD	RRZZZZUSA
WENZEL	.06	M	INFANT	RRZZZZUSA
OCIMTA, TOBIAS	42	M	LABR	RRZZZZUSA
RACHEL	43	F	W	RRZZZZUSA
ELKE	16	F	CH	RRZZZZUSA
LEA	14	F	CH	RRZZZZUSA
HIRSCH	9	M	CHILD	RRZZZZUSA
MARIE	8	F	CHILD	RRZZZZUSA
CHANNE	7	F	CHILD	RRZZZZUSA
TRUNE	15	F	SGL	RRZZZZUSA
RITZ, EDUARD	22	M	LABR	RRZZZZUSA
SABORSKY, THOMAS	17	M	LABR	RRAHZDUSA
SOHWINKOWSKY, PIETRO	18	M	LABR	RRAHZDUSA
BIND, ANNA	23	F	SGL	RRZZZZUSA
SCHLACHTER, ZADEK	55	M	LABR	RRAHYCUSA
SCHWARZ, MARCUS	20	M	LABR	RRAHYCUSA
JOHN, BEINISCH	9	M	CHILD	RRZZZZUSA
CHILLA, ANNE	21	F	SGL	RRZZZZUSA
MASCHOFSKY, NICOLAUS	26	M	LABR	RRZZZZUSA
JUSTINE	27	F	W	RRZZZZUSA
ROSALIE	3	F	CHILD	RRZZZZUSA
FRANZ	.02	M	INFANT	RRZZZZUSA
JAROSCHEFSKY, JOH.	52	M	LABR	RRZZZZUSA
JASZIMBOWITZ, MOSES	18	M	LABR	RRZZZZUSA
CHASKEL, JACOB	26	M	LABR	RRAHYCUSA
KLEIN, MEYER	35	M	LABR	RRZZZZUSA
MEHL, JACOB	19	M	LABR	RRZZZZUSA
SEIFFER, OSCAR	19	M	LABR	RRZZZZUSA
MEHL, CHEINE	16	M	LABR	RRZZZZUSA
NESSKE, JOHANN	23	M	FARMER	RRZZZZUSA
BELINSOHN, JACOB	21	M	DLR	RRAGRTUSA
TIKOTZKI, JUDES	16	M	LABR	RRZZZZUSA
MARGOLIS, WOLF	21	M	DLR	RRZZZZUSA
TASCHMONSKI, JENTE	44	F	W	RRAHZSUSA
ETTEL	9	F	CHILD	RRAHZSUSA
ZIPE	8	F	CHILD	RRAHZSUSA
FROMBERG, FEIGE	8	F	CHILD	RRZZZZUSA
DUBERSTEIN, ARON	20	M	DLR	RRZZZZUSA
CURANSKY, CHAJE	18	F	SGL	RRAHTRUSA
GOLDBERG, SALOMON	32	M	BCHR	RRZZZZUSA
CINAMON, LOUIS	20	M	TLR	RRAHVVUSA
REIF, CHANNE	30	F	W	RRAHWOUSA
SAMUEL	9	M	CHILD	RRAHWOUSA
MARGOLIS, ISAAC	48	M	DLR	RRAHTSUSA
HINDE	45	F	W	RRAHTSUSA
ANNA	20	F	CH	RRAHTSUSA
LEIRE	18	F	CH	RRAHTSUSA
IDA	9	F	CHILD	RRAHTSUSA
BERTHA	8	F	CHILD	RRAHTSUSA
ELIAS	.11	M	INFANT	RRAHTSUSA
KAPLAN, LEIB	24	M	DLR	RRAHTAUSA
LOEWENSTEIN, SIMCHA	29	M	DLR	RRZZZZUSA
PUSCHIN, ISSER	33	M	DLR	RRZZZZUSA
RIWICKI, ISRAEL	37	M	LABR	RRAHOKUSA
MANE	30	F	W	RRAHOKUSA
SARA	9	F	CHILD	RRAHOKUSA
MORDCHE	5	F	CHILD	RRAHOKUSA
MOSES	2	M	CHILD	RRAHOKUSA

PASSENGER	AGE	SEX	OCCUPATION	PRIV	VIL	DES
LIEBE	55	F	W	RR	AHOK	USA
BERLINSKI, CHAIM	19	M	DLR	RR	ZZZZ	USA
SZULI, THERESE	20	F	SGL	RR	ZZZZ	USA
GALUB, ISAAC	18	M	DLR	RR	AHTU	USA
GANS, ARON	22	M	DLR	RR	ZZZZ	USA
TABAZNIK, ALTER	21	M	MCHT	RR	ZZZZ	USA
BASCHE	20	F	W	RR	ZZZZ	USA
SAKON, PINKUS	30	M	MCHT	RR	ZZZZ	USA
KONITZKY, OSCHER	19	M	MCHT	RR	ZZZZ	USA
DANELSKY, ABRAHAM	37	M	LABR	RR	ZZZZ	USA
ESTHER	30	F	W	RR	ZZZZ	USA
MORDCHE	15	F	CH	RR	ZZZZ	USA
SARA	9	F	CHILD	RR	ZZZZ	USA
HINDE	8	F	CHILD	RR	ZZZZ	USA

SHIP: ENGLAND

FROM: LIVERPOOL AND QUEENSTOWN
TO: NEW YORK
ARRIVED: 25 NOVEMBER 1885

PASSENGER	AGE	SEX	OCCUPATION	PRIV	VIL	DES
LICHTENSTEIN, M.	33	M	BND	RR	ADAX	TX
MOSSES, BARET	38	M	BKR	RR	ADBQ	BAL
KARLUN, ANNA	18	F	SP	RR	AGUZ	NY
MARK, BETTY	15	F	SP	RR	ZZZZ	NY
PHILIPOSKI, TEOD.	50	M	LABR	PL	ZZZZ	OH
VOGEL, SIMA	18	M	TLR	PL	ZZZZ	OH
BICSATSCH, ANNA	18	F	SP	RR	ZZZZ	OH
WICATIDER, CRIKER	39	M	UNKNOWN	FN	ZZZZ	OH
SOFIER	29	F	W	FN	ZZZZ	OH
LIMDEN, JOEL	24	M	SEMN	FN	ZZZZ	OH
GUSTOF	20	M	LABR	FN	ZZZZ	OH
SETLESINGER, SCHIMON	25	M	LABR	FN	ACBF	OH
FRIL, ADAM	53	M	LABR	FN	AFVG	OH
LUDVIKA	48	F	W	FN	AFVG	OH
JACOB	22	M	LABR	FN	AFVG	OH
CARL	18	M	LABR	FN	AFVG	OH
WILHELMINA	20	F	SP	FN	AFVG	OH
PETER	10	M	CH	FN	AFVG	OH
CHRISTIAN	8	M	CHILD	FN	AFVG	OH
GOTTLEIB	4	M	CHILD	FN	AFVG	OH
ADAM	.01	M	INFANT	FN	AFVG	OH
GORONTSON, MOSES	20	M	BKLYR	FN	AGRT	OH
BROLOWSKY, MIORCTEN	22	M	LABR	RR	ZZZZ	OH
BACHER, BLEMIL	20	M	LABR	FN	ZZZZ	OH
MENDELSOHN, SAMUEL	25	M	MCHT	FN	AFWJ	OH
SIMON, GUSKA	11	M	CH	FN	ACBF	OH
U, SHAUSCHE	9	M	CHILD	FN	ACBF	OH

SHIP: WYOMING

FROM: LIVERPOOL
TO: NEW YORK
ARRIVED: 25 NOVEMBER 1885

PASSENGER	AGE	SEX	OCCUPATION	PRIV	VIL	DES
BRAMSTEIN, MOISCHE	21	F	SP	PL	ZZZZ	USA

SHIP: LYDIAN MONARCH

FROM: LONDON
TO: NEW YORK
ARRIVED: 27 NOVEMBER 1885

PASSENGER	AGE	SEX	OCCUPATION	PRIV	VIL	DES
RUBENSTEIN, H.	35	M	JNR	RR	ZZZZ	NY
R.	28	F	JNR	RR	ZZZZ	NY
A.	8	F	CHILD	RR	ZZZZ	NY
D.	5	F	CHILD	RR	ZZZZ	NY
S.	3	F	CHILD	RR	ZZZZ	NY
R.	.01	M	INFANT	RR	ZZZZ	NY
ZOLSOCK, A.	24	M	TLR	PL	ZZZZ	NY

SHIP: NOORDLAND

FROM: ANTWERP
TO: NEW YORK
ARRIVED: 27 NOVEMBER 1885

PASSENGER	AGE	SEX	OCCUPATION	PRIV	VIL	DES
DAWIDOWICZ, IG.	18	M	LABR	RR	ZZZZ	UNK
DANGERT, JAN	30	M	LABR	RR	ZZZZ	UNK
GORECKI, STANISL.	58	M	LABR	RR	ZZZZ	NY
VICTORIA	50	F	LABR	RR	ZZZZ	NY
ANNELLA	11	F	LABR	RR	ZZZZ	NY
STOKBISKY, M.	29	F	HTR	RR	ADBQ	NY

SHIP: RHEIN

FROM: BREMEN AND SOUTHAMPTON
TO: NEW YORK
ARRIVED: 27 NOVEMBER 1885

PASSENGER	AGE	SEX	OCCUPATION	PRIV	VIL	DES
KLEIN, LECO	23	F	NN	RR	ZZZZ	USA
HIRSCH	.11	M	INFANT	RR	ZZZZ	USA
AWNER, RABMOWITZ	32	M	LABR	RR	ZZZZ	USA
ZIGRACK, WOJCIECH	25	M	LABR	RR	ZZZZ	USA
KLUCZEWSKY, CHANE	20	F	NN	RR	ZZZZ	USA
PALKOWITZ, BOINSCH	29	M	PDLR	RR	ZZZZ	USA
PINEWSKI, FRANZISZ	31	M	LABR	RR	ZZZZ	USA
WAIKIKAUCKINSTE, ANTONI	18	F	NN	RR	ZZZZ	USA
JAFFE, DICHA	32	F	NN	RR	ZZZZ	USA
WOLF	9	M	CHILD	RR	ZZZZ	USA
ROCHEL	7	M	CHILD	RR	ZZZZ	USA
HERMS	6	M	CHILD	RR	ZZZZ	USA
ABEH	5	M	CHILD	RR	ZZZZ	USA
BREME	3	F	CHILD	RR	ZZZZ	USA
MOSEH	.11	M	INFANT	RR	ZZZZ	USA
BUTOWITZ, BARACH.	45	M	LABR	RR	ZZZZ	USA
LEDA	42	F	W	RR	ZZZZ	USA
JOSSEL	6	M	CHILD	RR	ZZZZ	USA
RACHEL	11	F	CH	RR	ZZZZ	USA
GERWANSKA, WILHELMINE	28	F	NN	RR	ZZZZ	USA
MOCOWICZ, CASIMIR	40	M	LABR	RR	ZZZZ	USA
REINSCHMIDT, MATHIAS	25	M	LABR	RR	ZZZZ	USA
CHRISTINE	22	F	W	RR	ZZZZ	USA
MARTIN	.11	M	INFANT	RR	ZZZZ	USA
RENTER, LOUISE	26	F	NN	RR	ZZZZ	USA
WAISZNIS, MATHIAS	23	M	LABR	RR	ZZZZ	USA
BUSCHANSKY, LEBEL.	19	M	SHMK	RR	ZZZZ	USA
KEVASCHNESCH, GERTRUDE	25	F	NN	RR	ZZZZ	USA
GRABOWSKI, JOHN.	24	M	LABR	RR	ZZZZ	USA
MARIE	24	F	W	RR	ZZZZ	USA
ANNA	.04	F	INFANT	RR	ZZZZ	USA

PASSENGER	AGE	SEX	OCCUPATION	PV RIVL	DES
ZIELINSKY, TOMASY	65	M	LABR	RRZZZZ	USA
SOGKOWSKA, LEVCADIA	21	F	NN	RRZZZZ	USA
HELENE	.09	F	INFANT	RRZZZZ	USA

SHIP: STATE OF INDIANA

FROM: GLASGOW AND LARNE
TO: NEW YORK
ARRIVED: 27 NOVEMBER 1885

PASSENGER	AGE	SEX	OCCUPATION	PV RIVL	DES
LEWETIN, JACOB	22	M	PDLR	RRZZZZ	USA
GELLERMAN, BENZIN	36	M	PDLR	RRZZZZ	USA
SCHMILK, BERTHZIA	24	M	PDLR	RRZZZZ	USA
REICH, CHATZKEL	20	M	PDLR	RRADOI	USA
KAPLAN, JANKEL	24	M	PDLR	RRAHZP	USA
LEON	16	M	PDLR	RRAHZP	USA
JOSEPHER, JOSEPH	35	M	PDLR	RRZZZZ	USA
BLOCH, MOSES	21	M	PDLR	RRZZZZ	USA
KIEWITZKY, LEIB	22	M	TLR	RRAHOK	USA
CHASSIN, LEIB	23	M	PDLR	RRZZZZ	USA
SCHWARZ, OREL	25	M	PDLR	RRZZZZ	USA
CHAROWSKY, JOHAN	60	M	LABR	RRAARR	USA
JOSEF	12	M	LABR	RRAARR	USA
WLADISLAUS	22	M	LABR	RRAARR	USA
BIESONER, HIRSCH	20	M	PDLR	PLZZZZ	USA
UKRAINZIK, BERNHARD	11	M	CH	PLAFWJ	USA
KINTOP, JAN	22	M	PDLR	PLAFWJ	USA
KLEMETISCH, ABRAM	26	M	PDLR	PLZZZZ	USA
ROSENTHAL, CHANE	50	M	PDLR	PLACBF	USA
SELIG	8	M	CHILD	PLACBF	USA
SLUTZINSKY, HERMAN	37	M	TNSTH	RRZZZZ	USA
RALE	30	F	W	RRZZZZ	USA
BENJAMIN	2	M	CHILD	RRZZZZ	USA
MALKE	.09	F	INFANT	RRZZZZ	USA
UNTERBERG, FEIGE	28	F	W	RRZZZZ	USA
SELDE	5	F	CHILD	RRZZZZ	USA
HELIK	4	M	CHILD	RRZZZZ	USA
PAZNANSKI, LAZAR	21	M	PDLR	RRAGRT	USA
JETTE	21	F	W	RRAGRT	USA
ZADIKOW, SALMON	21	M	BKBNDR	RRAHTF	USA
GOLDE	25	F	W	RRAHTF	USA
BUTENSKY, GERSON	26	M	PDLR	RRADGO	USA
SCHEITE	26	F	W	RRADGO	USA
HUHNERFELD, SELIG	38	M	TLR	PLZZZZ	USA
ROSA	28	F	W	PLZZZZ	USA
CZEWEK, CHAIM	20	M	TLR	PLAFWJ	USA
HELENE	19	F	W	PLAFWJ	USA
ZEDEWSKI, RACHEL	55	F	W	PLAFWJ	USA

SHIP: WIELAND

FROM: HAMBURG
TO: NEW YORK
ARRIVED: 27 NOVEMBER 1885

PASSENGER	AGE	SEX	OCCUPATION	PV RIVL	DES
BALL, ISAAC	32	M	CPTR	FNZZZZ	USA
WELZEWSKY, FEIBEL	36	M	PNTR	RRZZZZ	USA
PANZISKI, CHAJE-F.	20	F	SGL	RRZZZZ	USA
SAMUEL	.11	M	INFANT	RRZZZZ	USA
NEUMANN, SARA	26	F	W	RRZZZZ	USA
DWORE	18	F	SGL	RRZZZZ	USA
BROCHE	4	F	CHILD	RRZZZZ	USA
HERSCH	6	M	CHILD	RRZZZZ	USA
MANKEWITZ, SARA	34	F	W	RRZZZZ	USA
LEIB	9	M	CHILD	RRZZZZ	USA
WOLF	8	M	CHILD	RRZZZZ	USA
ELI	7	F	CHILD	RRZZZZ	USA
MOSES	4	M	CHILD	RRZZZZ	USA
SAVIC, IRAN	27	M	LABR	RRZZZZ	USA
KUBUKNITIS, ANTONIS	18	M	LABR	RRZZZZ	USA
BUKEVITZ, KAZIMIR	18	M	LABR	RRZZZZ	USA
BIMGARDA, AUGUST	27	M	LABR	RRZZZZ	USA
CONRADI, PETER	39	M	LABR	RRZZZZ	USA
SCHAJES, RIWE	23	F	SGL	RRZZZZ	USA
WASINSKY, JOSEF	26	M	LABR	RRZZZZ	USA
KRAINIK, JOSEF	22	M	LABR	RRZZZZ	USA
ROTKOWSKI, JOSEF	25	M	LABR	RRZZZZ	USA
MORDSKE, MARIANNE	18	F	SGL	RRZZZZ	USA
BERLOWITZ, MEYER	40	M	TLR	RRZZZZ	USA
ITZIG	20	M	TLR	RRZZZZ	USA
CHANIDE, JUDEL	20	M	LABR	RRZZZZ	USA
WERBELEWSKI, EI---SCH	20	M	DLR	RRZZZZ	USA
KLIBANSKY, LAZAR	26	M	DLR	RRZZZZ	USA
KALSTEIN, ABEL	20	M	TLR	RRZZZZ	USA
KOPCZANSKI, HIRSCH	20	M	TLR	RRZZZZ	USA
WENGLINSKI, LEON	18	M	WCHMKR	RRZZZZ	USA
SCHERKSNER, MOSES	15	M	DLR	RRZZZZ	USA
DOBROCZINSKI, LEIBUSCH	27	M	DLR	RRZZZZ	USA
HILEROWITZ, SAMUEL	9	M	CHILD	RRZZZZ	USA
GRUENBERG, JANKEL	26	M	DLR	RRZZZZ	USA
NOCHEME	17	M	DLR	RRZZZZ	USA
LINDE, SAMUEL	20	M	DLR	RRZZZZ	USA
TOTARSKI, SUSSMANN	19	M	LABR	RRZZZZ	USA
KALINOWSKY, ANTON	33	M	LABR	RRZZZZ	USA
DOBIDEITIS, MATHEUS	20	M	LABR	RRZZZZ	USA
RABANOWITSCH, JULS.	25	M	LABR	RRZZZZ	USA
LUTKEWITSCH, JOSEF	22	M	LABR	RRZZZZ	USA
GORBATZ, LEIB	19	M	LABR	RRZZZZ	USA
GRODENSKY, SCHOLEM	22	M	LABR	RRZZZZ	USA
KIEL, HERSCH	16	M	TLR	RRZZZZ	USA
GERSON	9	M	CHILD	RRZZZZ	USA
SKUTZKI, NOCHEM	40	M	LABR	RRZZZZ	USA
MALKE	37	F	W	RRZZZZ	USA
LEIB	.11	M	INFANT	RRZZZZ	USA
CHAIE	.01	F	INFANT	RRZZZZ	USA
EISENBERG, LEVY	21	M	SHMK	RRZZZZ	USA
PETRUS, KONSTANTINUS	24	M	LABR	RRZZZZ	USA
FRIEDMANN, HIRSCH	21	M	TLR	RRZZZZ	USA
OLZEWSKI, SZYMON	63	M	DLR	RRZZZZ	USA
TOMASCHEWSKI, ANTON	20	M	PNTR	RRZZZZ	USA
WASCHILEWSKI, BOGESLAW	24	M	LABR	RRZZZZ	USA
MANKEWICZ, SORE	.04	F	INFANT	RRZZZZ	USA

SHIP: CITY OF CHESTER

FROM: LIVERPOOL AND QUEENSTOWN
TO: NEW YORK
ARRIVED: 28 NOVEMBER 1885

PASSENGER	AGE	SEX	OCCUPATION	PV RIVL	DES
NORDLUNG, ALMA-L.	22	F	SVNT	FNZZZZ	NY
JOSEFINA	25	F	SVNT	FNZZZZ	NY
KAARIALA, KONSLOND	22	M	LABR	FNZZZZ	MI
BLOCK, I.	21	M	LABR	FNADAX	NY

PASSENGER	AGE	SEX	OCCUPATION	PRIV	VIL	DES

SHIP: ELBE

FROM: BREMEN
TO: NEW YORK
ARRIVED: 28 NOVEMBER 1885

PASSENGER	AGE	SEX	OCCUPATION	PV	VIL	DES
MROZENSKA, CATHARINA	40	F	NN	RR	ZZZZ	USA
FISCHER, JOHANN	62	M	FARMER	RR	ZZZZ	USA
CAROLINE	46	F	W	RR	ZZZZ	USA
LOUISE	19	F	CH	RR	ZZZZ	USA
AUGUST	18	F	LABR	RR	ZZZZ	USA
JUSTINA	14	F	CH	RR	ZZZZ	USA
SUSANNA	11	F	CH	RR	ZZZZ	USA
JOHANN	4	M	CHILD	RR	ZZZZ	***
KURZ, PETER	24	M	FARMER	RR	ZZZZ	USA
MARIE	24	F	W	RR	ZZZZ	USA
EDUARD	.01	M	INFANT	RR	ZZZZ	USA
RIETZ, MICHEL	27	M	FARMER	RR	ZZZZ	USA
CATHARINE	21	F	W	RR	ZZZZ	USA
EMILIE	2	F	CHILD	RR	ZZZZ	USA
KIEN, SAMUEL	.09	M	INFANT	RR	ZZZZ	***
SCHLEICHNER, DORETHEA	43	F	NN	RR	ZZZZ	USA
LOUISE	23	F	NN	RR	ZZZZ	USA
ROSINA	17	F	NN	RR	ZZZZ	USA
JOHANN	6	M	CHILD	RR	ZZZZ	USA
RIETZ, SAMUEL	.06	M	INFANT	RR	ZZZZ	USA
MARGUART, JOSEPH	29	M	FARMER	RR	ZZZZ	USA
BARBARA	24	F	W	RR	ZZZZ	USA
THERESE	4	F	CHILD	RR	ZZZZ	USA
MARIE	2	F	CHILD	RR	ZZZZ	USA
JOSEF	.06	M	INFANT	RR	ZZZZ	USA

SHIP: ETHIOPIA

FROM: GLASGOW AND MOVILLE
TO: NEW YORK
ARRIVED: 30 NOVEMBER 1885

PASSENGER	AGE	SEX	OCCUPATION	PV	VIL	DES
HIRSCH, ISAAC	20	M	TLR	RR	ZZZZ	USA
ASRIN, MENDEL-MARY	49	M	LABR	RR	ZZZZ	USA
DIMIN, BER.	42	M	UNKNOWN	RR	ZZZZ	USA
SILVERZ, JAN	23	M	LABR	RR	ZZZZ	USA
WANALANIS, ACHALVIS	24	M	LABR	RR	ZZZZ	USA
KASULITZ, KASNNER	22	M	LABR	RR	ZZZZ	USA
GURKMAN, JOSSEL	19	M	TNSTH	RR	ZZZZ	USA
SCHONOP, SCHLEME	50	F	UNKNOWN	RR	ZZZZ	USA
ISAK	19	M	LABR	RR	ZZZZ	USA
KUSNITZ, MOSES	24	M	LABR	RR	ZZZZ	USA
SCHMANSKI, BERNHARD	33	M	LABR	RR	ZZZZ	USA
MEYERSEN, SCHLOME	21	M	LABR	RR	ZZZZ	USA
BLUMENTHAL, ISAK	30	M	LABR	RR	ZZZZ	USA
LEMANGO, DAVID	20	M	PDLR	RR	ZZZZ	USA
FRECSIN, ISAAC	22	M	TLR	RR	ZZZZ	USA
ESTHER	20	F	UNKNOWN	RR	ZZZZ	USA
KAZMIR, ANNA	35	F	HP	PL	ZZZZ	USA
SLOWENSKY, MARIA	21	F	HSKPR	PL	ZZZZ	USA
STEFAN	2	M	CHILD	PL	ZZZZ	USA
KAMMOWSKY, SAMUEL	21	M	MCHT	PL	ZZZZ	USA
SEGMUNDSEN, JOEL	30	M	MCHT	PL	ZZZZ	USA

SHIP: GEISER

FROM: COPENHAGEN
TO: NEW YORK
ARRIVED: 30 NOVEMBER 1885

PASSENGER	AGE	SEX	OCCUPATION	PV	VIL	DES
KENGSHAUG, OLE-O.	30	M	SHMK	FN	ZZZZ	USA

SHIP: POLYNESIA

FROM: HAMBURG
TO: NEW YORK
ARRIVED: 30 NOVEMBER 1885

PASSENGER	AGE	SEX	OCCUPATION	PV	VIL	DES
JERELSKY, CHAIE	17	F	SGL	RR	ZZZZ	NY
JAMSSYO, ANDR.	23	M	LABR	PL	ZZZZ	NY
ROSNER, HIRSCH	39	M	TDR	PL	ZZZZ	NY
MECKEN, FRIMET	24	F	SGL	PL	ZZZZ	NY
JOCHEN, MOSES	26	M	TRDSMN	PL	ZZZZ	NY
BOTMANN, CHAIM	23	M	TRDSMN	PL	ZZZZ	NY
HIRSCH	21	M	TRDSMN	PL	ZZZZ	NY
PENOR, SIMON	29	M	TRDSMN	PL	ZZZZ	NY
KOTBE, MARCUS	27	M	TRDSMN	PL	ZZZZ	NY
WECHSEBAUM, HANNY	35	F	WO	PL	ZZZZ	NY
CITLY	7	E	CHILD	PL	ZZZZ	NY
MALEY	6	F	CHILD	PL	ZZZZ	NY
MARCUS	6	M	CHILD	PL	ZZZZ	NY
ABRAHAM	.08	M	INFANT	PL	ZZZZ	NY
BAND, JOS.	21	M	TLR	PL	ZZZZ	NY
BERNSTEIN, HIRSCH	28	M	MCHT	RR	ZZZZ	IL
SKLAWSKY, SORE	40	F	WO	RR	ZZZZ	NY
GITEL	7	F	CHILD	RR	ZZZZ	NY
CHAIM	6	M	CHILD	RR	ZZZZ	NY
ESTHER	4	F	CHILD	RR	ZZZZ	NY
DOBER	2	M	CHILD	RR	ZZZZ	NY
ABRAHAM	.05	M	INFANT	RR	ZZZZ	NY
SPITZ, ARON	25	M	LABR	RR	ZZZZ	OH
STOBAR, ABRAH.	20	M	LABR	RR	ZZZZ	PIT
GRUETZHAENDLER, S.L.	20	M	SHMK	RR	ZZZZ	NY
KAPPNER, CHANE	24	F	WO	PL	ZZZZ	NY
SCHEIA	6	F	CHILD	PL	ZZZZ	NY
LEIA	.07	F	INFANT	PL	ZZZZ	NY
WRONSKI, JEHUDA	21	M	BCHR	RR	ZZZZ	IL
LITTACKLER, MOSECHEL	20	M	TRDSMN	RR	ZZZZ	NY
PLOZARIUS, VICTOR	20	M	LABR	RR	ZZZZ	NY
ROSALIA	21	F	SI	RR	ZZZZ	NY
BERMANN, RIWKE	20	F	WO	RR	ZZZZ	NY
RICHEL	.06	F	INFANT	RR	ZZZZ	NY
WIGOTZKY, LAZAR	36	M	TDR	RR	ZZZZ	NY
JAPETHINSKI, CIWJE	26	F	WO	RR	ZZZZ	NY
JANKEL	.08	M	INFANT	RR	ZZZZ	NY
BESCHKIN, CHANE	18	F	SGL	RR	ZZZZ	CH
BUCKO, MARYANNE	24	F	WO	RR	ZZZZ	NY
STANISLAWE	.06	F	INFANT	RR	ZZZZ	NY
MARYELKA	3	F	CHILD	RR	ZZZZ	NY
MEYER, AUGUSTE	40	F	W	RR	ZZZZ	NY
WITTY	7	M	CHILD	RR	ZZZZ	NY
MARIA	6	F	CHILD	RR	ZZZZ	NY
CARL	5	M	CHILD	RR	ZZZZ	NY
GORNSKA, MARIANNE	44	F	WO	RR	ZZZZ	IL
WITSCHINSKA, ARON	24	M	TLR	PL	ZZZZ	NY
LESCHKOWITZ, LEISER	24	M	CL	PL	ZZZZ	NY
CHILL, ARON	21	M	TLR	PL	ZZZZ	NY
GARTNER, ESTER	22	F	SGL	PL	ZZZZ	NY
FRIED, SALOMON	19	M	TLR	RR	ZZZZ	NY
BLOCKMANN, JAC.F.	22	M	TRDSMN	RR	ZZZZ	NY
LITMANN, SUSE	19	F	SGL	PL	ZZZZ	NY
SCHEWA	17	F	SGL	PL	ZZZZ	NY
MANSKY, SARAH	19	F	WO	RR	ZZZZ	NY

PASSENGER	AGE	SEX	OCCUPATION	PRV VIL DES
ABRAH.	5	M	CHILD	RRZZZZNY
DAVID	7	M	CHILD	RRZZZZNY
GACTNER, SAMUEL	24	M	LABR	PLZZZZNY
KLEINSCHMIDT, OLYMPHIE	21	F	SGL	RRZZZZNY
LEONIDA	17	F	SGL	RRZZZZNY
KARFIELD, FRADEL	29	F	WO	PLZZZZNY
MARIA	6	F	CHILD	PLZZZZNY
RYCZKOWSKA, ANNE	24	F	WO	PLZZZZNY
JOSEPH	5	M	CHILD	PLZZZZNY
THILE	.06	F	INFANT	PLZZZZNY
TEDER, MORITZ	24	M	FARMER	PLZZZZNY

SHIP: RUGIA

FROM: HAMBURG
TO: NEW YORK
ARRIVED: 30 NOVEMBER 1885

PASSENGER	AGE	SEX	OCCUPATION	PRV VIL DES
ZURSKI, GEORGE	22	M	LABR	RRZZZZUSA
SWETICAS, ANDREAS	21	M	LABR	RRZZZZUSA
SCHEIMANN, HIRSCH	40	M	TNMK	RRZZZZUSA
FRIEDMANN, SCHMUEL	35	M	DLR	RRZZZZUSA
CHAWEZ, DWORE	18	F	SGL	RRZZZZUSA
BIMMERMANN, CAROLINE	69	F	W	RRZZZZUSA
JOSEF	13	M	S	RRZZZZUSA
ROTHKOWSKY, JOSEF	20	M	LABR	RRZZZZUSA
LIROTA, BERCK	20	M	LABR	RRZZZZUSA
DAMIAN, MARIAN	22	M	LABR	RRZZZZUSA
BETOWSKY, JOS.	20	M	LABR	RRZZZZUSA
SZNIPKUTIS, GEORGE	21	M	LABR	RRZZZZUSA
SINDEROJANSKI, MARIAN	25	M	LABR	RRZZZZUSA
MEYCROWITS, JASSE	19	M	LABR	RRZZZZUSA
KRALNIK, CHAIC	19	M	LABR	RRZZZZUSA
SILMANN, HINDE	30	F	W	RRZZZZUSA
CZERNE	9	F	CHILD	RRZZZZUSA
HIEBE	8	F	CHILD	RRZZZZUSA
NECHAME	5	F	CHILD	RRZZZZUSA
HERSCHEL	.11	M	INFANT	RRZZZZUSA
WEINSTEIN, SARA	40	F	W	RRZZZZUSA
BEILE	15	F	SGL	RRZZZZUSA
JOSEPH	9	M	CHILD	RRZZZZUSA
LEA	8	F	CHILD	RRZZZZUSA
MIKAS, ALITA	23	M	LABR	RRZZZZUSA
RUBINSTEIN, SAMUEL	21	M	LABR	RRZZZZUSA
GEWOELT, JOSSEL	23	M	LABR	RRZZZZUSA
PUKOWSKY, CARL	45	M	LABR	RRZZZZUSA
KATZEP, CHAIM	35	M	LABR	RRZZZZUSA
REINSTEIN, SAMUEL	21	M	LABR	RRZZZZUSA
KOPELOW, MARTIN	18	M	LABR	RRZZZZUSA
ZERWITZ, HECHE	26	F	W	RRZZZZUSA
SAMUEL	.11	M	INFANT	RRZZZZUSA
STEINMANN, JOSEPF	26	M	TLR	RRZZZZUSA
BERKMENN, JSRAEL	22	M	LABR	RRZZZZUSA
BRODOWITZ, SCHEIME	20	F	W	RRZZZZUSA
HERSCH	.11	M	INFANT	RRZZZZUSA
PODEWZE, CHAJE	9	M	CHILD	RRZZZZUSA

SHIP: UMBRIA

FROM: LIVERPOOL
TO: NEW YORK
ARRIVED: 30 NOVEMBER 1885

PASSENGER	AGE	SEX	OCCUPATION	PRV VIL DES
HAGGETIOM, JOHAN	39	M	LABR	RRZZZZNY
ROSENSHALL, WOLF	19	M	LABR	RRZZZZNY
SEGAL, RUDOLF	21	M	LABR	RRZZZZNY
NIKOLN, JOSEPH	27	M	LABR	RRZZZZNY
MARK	28	M	LABR	RRZZZZNY
RADOM, ANT	23	M	LABR	RRZZZZNY

SHIP: ARIZONA

FROM: LIVERPOOL AND QUEENSTOWN
TO: NEW YORK
ARRIVED: 01 DECEMBER 1885

PASSENGER	AGE	SEX	OCCUPATION	PRV VIL DES
MINTEL, RIVKE	17	F	SP	RRZZZZUSA
FINKELSTEIN, KAHMEN	23	F	SP	RRZZZZUSA
CHANE	20	F	SP	RRZZZZUSA
KALMAR	15	F	SP	RRZZZZUSA
SISKIN, WOLF	23	M	LABR	RRZZZZUSA

SHIP: STATE OF NEVADA

FROM: GLASGOW AND LARNE
TO: NEW YORK
ARRIVED: 03 DECEMBER 1885

PASSENGER	AGE	SEX	OCCUPATION	PRV VIL DES
PANNOW, C.	37	F	W	RRZZZZUSA
MOSES	.03	M	INFANT	RRZZZZUSA
GRIMSGAN, JOS.	34	M	CL	RRZZZZUSA
ST.	34	F	W	RRZZZZUSA
WAHNROSS, B.	63	F	SVNT	RRZZZZUSA
BOGATZKY, B.	00	M	PNTR	RRZZZZUSA
SISTEL, B.	19	M	PDLR	RRZZZZUSA
Z.	18	M	PDLR	RRZZZZUSA
KOSTLICKY, J.	24	M	LABR	RRZZZZUSA
SLISKA, C.	26	M	JNR	RRZZZZUSA
SCHASONAS, ALEX	22	M	LABR	RRZZZZUSA
SCHACKER, M.	34	M	CL	RRZZZZUSA
WITTFELD, LEON	27	M	LABR	RRZZZZUSA
K.	23	F	W	RRZZZZUSA
ZNKOWSKI, M.	30	M	LABR	PLZZZZUSA
LEWANDOWSKY, F.	26	M	LABR	PLZZZZUSA
MASLOWSKY, W.	23	M	LABR	PLZZZZUSA
MAKOWSKY, J.	41	M	LABR	PLZZZZUSA
TIEZESKI, J.	31	M	SHMK	PLZZZZUSA
ZELLEN, S.	48	M	TLR	PLZZZZUSA
WESELOWSKY, S.	37	M	LABR	PLZZZZUSA

SHIP: BELGENLAND

FROM: ANTWERP
TO: NEW YORK
ARRIVED: 04 DECEMBER 1885

PASSENGER	AGE	SEX	OCCUPATION	PRV VIL DES
GOLDBERG, N.	24	M	TLR	PLADBQPHI

SHIP: CITY OF CHICAGO

FROM: LIVERPOOL AND QUEENSTOWN
TO: NEW YORK
ARRIVED: 05 DECEMBER 1885

PASSENGER	AGE	SEX	OCCUPATION	PRIV	VIL	DES
PASCHKANSKI, JOSEF	40	M	BCHR	PL	ACBF	CAN
SLODOWNIKI, LAB.	23	M	LABR	PL	ACBF	NY
BITTERN, MODCHE	22	M	PDLR	PL	ACBF	NY
DUNDEROWIKZ, ANTON	26	M	LABR	PL	ACBF	NY
MAHSCHAWZKY, WHANN	35	M	LABR	PL	ACBF	NY
DEMISKY, LUMAR	30	M	LABR	PL	ACBF	NY
MAPALSKY, MICHEL	32	M	LABR	PL	ACBF	NY
SUKOWSKY, LADIREZ	20	M	LABR	PL	ACBF	NY
PUK, JONAS	40	M	PDLR	PL	ACBF	NY
SCHLUSHERS, BUL	29	M	PDLR	PL	ACBF	NY
PESASCHOWSKY, JOSEL	18	M	PDLR	PL	ACBF	NY
BRISKU, ISAK	17	M	PDLR	PL	ACBF	IL
KURAKEIT, AUG.	21	M	LABR	PL	ACBF	NY
WOLK, JANAS	23	M	LABR	PL	ACBF	NY
ABRAMSKY, JUDEL	24	M	PDLR	PL	ACBF	NY
CZARNE, SNIDIL	21	M	PDLR	PL	ACBF	NY
AFIRFLON, MARTSS	32	M	TLR	PL	ACBF	PHI
WEIP, MARKUM	26	M	LABR	PL	ACBF	NY
LEBOWITZ, LENA	18	F	SP	PL	ACBF	NY
JOSEF	19	M	LABR	PL	ACBF	NY
NENBERG, LENA	22	F	SP	PL	ACBF	NY
SURE	40	F	W	PL	ACBF	NY
ROTHSTEIN, ISSAC	35	M	MKR	PL	ACBF	NY
ETTEL	30	F	W	PL	ACBF	NY
LERSE	11	F	CH	PL	ACBF	NY
DREPEL	9	F	CHILD	PL	ACBF	NY
DAK-	7	M	CHILD	PL	ACBF	NY
ISEDEL	9	M	CHILD	PL	ACBF	NY
BONN	4	M	CHILD	PL	ACBF	NY
ABERSSON, GRITEL	16	F	SP	PL	ACBF	NY
RIVKE	7	F	CHILD	PL	ACBF	NY

SHIP: EMS

FROM: BREMEN
TO: NEW YORK
ARRIVED: 05 DECEMBER 1885

PASSENGER	AGE	SEX	OCCUPATION	PRIV	VIL	DES
SCHNEIDERONSKY, ALTR.	28	M	LABR	PL	AFWJ	USA
MUTZ, GEORG	34	M	FARMER	PL	AGRT	USA
FRIEDRICKE	33	F	NN	PL	AGRT	USA
CATHARINE	13	F	NN	PL	AGRT	USA
JOHANNES	10	M	NN	PL	AGRT	USA
FRIEDRICH	8	M	CHILD	PL	AGRT	USA
JACOB	6	M	CHILD	PL	AGRT	USA
MAGDALENE	4	F	CHILD	PL	AGRT	USA
CHRISTIAN	.05	M	INFANT	PL	AGRT	USA
MEIER, JACOB	35	M	FARMER	PL	AFWJ	USA
KAROLINE	33	F	NN	PL	AFWJ	USA
KATHARINE	14	F	NN	PL	AFWJ	USA
FRIEDRIKE	9	F	CHILD	PL	AFWJ	USA
JACOB	.11	M	INFANT	PL	AFWJ	USA
KABZAN, MARTIN	23	M	LABR	PL	AGRT	USA
SILBERSTEIN, RACHEL	14	F	NN	PL	AGRT	USA
GROSCHOWSKY, BERINE	30	F	NN	PL	AGRT	USA
ENNS, PETER	53	M	FARMER	PL	AGRT	USA
EVA	29	F	NN	PL	AGRT	USA
DAVID	22	M	LABR	PL	AGRT	USA
JOHANN	17	M	LABR	PL	AGRT	USA
GERHARD	14	M	NN	PL	AGRT	USA
ELIZABETH	16	F	NN	PL	AGRT	USA
ANNA	3	F	CHILD	PL	AGRT	USA
EVA	5	F	CHILD	PL	AGRT	USA
DIEDRICH	4	M	CHILD	PL	AGRT	USA
CATHARINE	.09	F	INFANT	PL	AGRT	USA
SARATA, JOSEL	22	M	FARMER	PL	AGRT	USA
JARDANSKY, MOSES	21	M	LABR	PL	AFWJ	USA
KORAPCZIK, DWORE	24	F	NN	PL	AGRT	USA
CHAJE	4	F	CHILD	PL	AGRT	USA
LEIE	.06	F	INFANT	PL	AGRT	USA
HINDE	.04	F	INFANT	PL	AGRT	USA
GORYEL, LUDWIKA	25	F	NN	PL	AGRT	USA
JOHANNA	3	F	CHILD	PL	AGRT	USA
BONISLAWA	.11	F	INFANT	PL	AGRT	USA
BERGMANN, EMANUEL	30	M	LABR	PL	AGRT	USA
PETSCH, CONRAD	31	M	FARMER	RR	ZZZZ	USA
ROSINE	31	F	NN	RR	ZZZZ	USA
CAROLINE	5	F	CHILD	RR	ZZZZ	USA
JACOB	2	M	CHILD	RR	ZZZZ	USA
CHRISTIANE	.06	F	INFANT	RR	ZZZZ	USA
MARCOWSKA, ZABELJA	30	F	NN	RR	AGRT	USA
GEFKA	5	F	CHILD	RR	AGRT	USA
KAPLAN, LEISER	34	M	MCHT	RR	AFWJ	USA
SINGER, LEISER	30	M	MCHT	RR	AFWJ	USA
ROSA	23	F	NN	RR	AFWJ	USA
ADLER, MICHLE	20	M	LABR	RR	AFWJ	USA

SHIP: W A SCHOLTEN

FROM: ROTTERDAM
TO: NEW YORK
ARRIVED: 07 DECEMBER 1885

PASSENGER	AGE	SEX	OCCUPATION	PRIV	VIL	DES
SCHAPIRO, LEIB	18	M	SLSMN	RR	ZZZZ	USA
LEWI, ADOLF	23	M	SLSMN	RR	ZZZZ	USA

SHIP: AURANIA

FROM: LIVERPOOL AND QUEENSTOWN
TO: NEW YORK
ARRIVED: 08 DECEMBER 1885

PASSENGER	AGE	SEX	OCCUPATION	PRIV	VIL	DES
LEWES, CHAS	32	M	LABR	RR	ZZZZ	NY
SARAH	25	F	W	RR	ZZZZ	NY
HOURVITZ, SIMON	21	M	LABR	RR	ZZZZ	NY
SCHWARTZOTIEW, JOSEF	18	M	LABR	PL	ZZZZ	NY
GERTER, JACOB	21	M	LABR	PL	ZZZZ	NY
HERVENG, PINKUS	24	M	LABR	PL	ZZZZ	CH
GRUNBERG, SAM.	19	M	LABR	PL	ZZZZ	NY

SHIP: FURNESSIA

FROM: GLASGOW
TO: NEW YORK
ARRIVED: 10 DECEMBER 1885

PASSENGER	AGE	SEX	OCCUPATION	PRIV	VIL	DES
KRONGELB, HIRSCH	18	M	BKLYR	RR	ZZZZ	USA
LACHS, ISAAC	27	M	DLR	RR	ZZZZ	USA
STORSKY, LEOPOLD	18	M	DLR	RR	ZZZZ	USA
ELIAS	10	M	UNKNOWN	RR	ZZZZ	USA
ROSENBERG, DANIEL	22	M	CL	FN	ZZZZ	USA
KRAWITZ, ROSA	19	F	HP	RR	ZZZZ	USA
LARNERRA, F.	26	M	CK	RR	ZZZZ	USA

PASSENGER	AGE	SEX	OCCUPATION	PRIVL	DES

SHIP: NEVADA

FROM: LIVERPOOL AND QUEENSTOWN
TO: NEW YORK
ARRIVED: 10 DECEMBER 1885

PASSENGER	AGE	SEX	OCCUPATION	PRIVL	DES
HANTZER, LEID	42	M	WCHMKR	PLZZZ	ZUSA
SLATE	42	F	W	PLZZZ	ZUSA
CHONE	9	M	CHILD	PLZZZ	ZUSA
RAHEL	7	F	CHILD	PLZZZ	ZUSA
ITZE	00	F	INF	PLZZZ	ZUSA
SCHENI	4	F	CHILD	PLZZZ	ZUSA
GILL, SARAH	35	F	W	PLZZZ	ZUSA
LAZARUS	10	M	CH	PLZZZ	ZUSA
SIMON	10	M	CH	PLZZZ	ZUSA
CALLMAN	8	M	CHILD	PLZZZ	ZUSA
PHILLIP	4	M	CHILD	PLZZZ	ZUSA
U	.06	F	INFANT	PLZZZ	ZUSA

SHIP: HELVETIA

FROM: LIVERPOOL
TO: NEW YORK
ARRIVED: 11 DECEMBER 1885

PASSENGER	AGE	SEX	OCCUPATION	PRIVL	DES
BERMAN, CHAWE	44	M	LABR	PLZZZ	ZUSA
CHAIE	18	M	LABR	PLZZZ	ZUSA
RACHE	10	M	CH	PLZZZ	ZUSA
BEILE	11	M	CH	PLZZZ	ZUSA
ABRAM	9	M	CHILD	PLZZZ	ZUSA
HERSCH	7	M	CHILD	PLZZZ	ZUSA
BEWON	.07	M	INFANT	PLZZZ	ZUSA
KAPECSTA, MAX	20	M	LABR	PLZZZ	ZUSA
MADLEWICH, JACOB	18	M	LABR	PLZZZ	ZUSA
SANOS, LUKA	17	M	LABR	PLZZZ	ZUSA
CYAKA	20	M	LABR	PLZZZ	ZUSA
BREIERSTEIN	24	M	LABR	PLZZZ	ZUSA

SHIP: LABRADOR

FROM: HAVRE
TO: NEW YORK
ARRIVED: 11 DECEMBER 1885

PASSENGER	AGE	SEX	OCCUPATION	PRIVL	DES
BACKRA, MOISE	35	M	UNKNOWN	RRZZZ	ZNY
BERR, SCHLEIN	13	M	CH	RRZZZ	ZNY

SHIP: EIDER

FROM: BREMEN AND SOUTHAMPTON
TO: NEW YORK
ARRIVED: 12 DECEMBER 1885

PASSENGER	AGE	SEX	OCCUPATION	PRIVL	DES
ROGALSKY, HERM.	25	M	LABR	RRZZZ	ZUSA
NEUMANN, ABRAH.	23	M	LABR	RRZZZ	ZUSA
HEINR.	21	M	FARMER	RRZZZ	ZUSA
URANSKY, CAROLL	32	F	NN	RRZZZ	ZUSA
JUDELOWITZ, PESCHE	24	F	W	RRZZZ	ZUSA

SHIP: ST. OF PENNSYLVANIA

FROM: GLASGOW AND LARNE
TO: NEW YORK
ARRIVED: 12 DECEMBER 1885

PASSENGER	AGE	SEX	OCCUPATION	PRIVL	DES
CAHN, HIRSCH	30	M	MCHT	RRADG	OUSA
FEIGE	28	F	NN	RRADG	OUSA
SARAH	2	F	CHILD	RRADG	OUSA
REBECCA	.06	F	INFANT	RRADG	OUSA
DOMBROWSKY, MATLUS	19	M	LABR	RRZZZ	ZUSA
ELTEMAN, GERSCHEN	26	M	SHMK	RRZZZ	ZUSA
SELIG	20	M	SHMK	RRZZZ	ZUSA
FELDHUHN, MICHEL	22	M	TLR	RRZZZ	ZUSA
FINKELSTEIN, SCHIMKEL	26	F	NN	RRZZZ	ZUSA
INNERFELD, JAEL	21	M	MCHT	RRZZZ	ZUSA
FEIGE	20	F	NN	RRZZZ	ZUSA
KAPLAN, SELIG	30	M	SHMK	RRADG	OUSA
DOBRE	26	F	NN	RRADG	OUSA
OLGA	2	F	CHILD	RRADG	OUSA
FEMOEL	1	M	CHILD	RRADG	OUSA
KAUFMAN, SCHNNIL	35	M	TLR	RRZZZ	ZUSA
KRUEGER, LESER	21	M	TLR	RRZZZ	ZUSA
KMISCHINSKY, JANCKEL	20	M	SHMK	RRZZZ	ZUSA
JETTE	18	F	NN	RRZZZ	ZUSA
LEWIN, ISRAEL	32	M	CPR	RRADG	OUSA
SARAH	27	F	NN	RRADG	OUSA
JETTE	2	F	CHILD	RRADG	OUSA
REILE	.09	F	INFANT	RRADG	OUSA
PANSMANSKY, CHAIM	21	M	MCHT	RRZZZ	ZUSA
PALAWER, HIRSCH	21	M	TLR	RRZZZ	ZUSA
POPOW, IWAN	25	M	MCHT	RRZZZ	ZUSA
RATINETZKY, ELIAS	17	M	TLR	RRZZZ	ZUSA
SALOMOWITZ, SCHNEIA	21	M	TKR	RRZZZ	ZUSA
SCHARFSTEIN, CHAIM	21	M	TLR	RRZZZ	ZUSA
SCHAPIRA, MOSES	22	M	BKR	RRZZZ	ZUSA
SILBERMAN, MORITZ	21	M	TLR	RRZZZ	ZUSA
BEILE	18	F	NN	RRZZZ	ZUSA
ZELONKA, CHAIE	17	F	NN	RRZZZ	ZUSA
SCHANE	00	F	NN	RRZZZ	ZUSA
CHAIM	8	M	CHILD	RRZZZ	ZUSA

SHIP: CITY OF RICHMOND

FROM: LIVERPOOL
TO: NEW YORK
ARRIVED: 14 DECEMBER 1885

PASSENGER	AGE	SEX	OCCUPATION	PRIVL	DES
OSSILUS, INO	19	M	LABR	PLZZZ	ZUSA
LIDSBNITZKE, JACOB	28	M	LABR	PLZZZ	ZUSA
UGO	20	M	LABR	PLZZZ	ZUSA
ROSENBERG, MELL	22	M	LABR	PLZZZ	ZUSA
MENCHLOWITZ, JOSEL	20	M	LABR	PLZZZ	ZUSA
WOLKENBERG, W.	19	M	LABR	PLZZZ	ZUSA
GONDOS, JOHN	22	M	LABR	PLZZZ	ZUSA
JEGBRA, W.	40	M	FARMER	PLZZZ	ZUSA
FRANK, ESEK	36	M	FARMER	PLZZZ	ZUSA
LIPLITZKE, ALTER	44	M	FARMER	PLZZZ	ZUSA
GOLDBERG, SIMON	20	M	LABR	PLZZZ	ZUSA
WEIN, G.	17	M	LABR	PLZZZ	ZUSA
BURGU, L.	21	M	LABR	PLZZZ	ZUSA
ALLASTE, ABRU	21	M	LABR	PLZZZ	ZUSA
KAPLUN, ISAC	11	M	CH	PLZZZ	ZUSA
GRINZMAN, V.	20	M	LABR	PLZZZ	ZUSA
BERMANN, A.	40	M	LABR	PLZZZ	ZUSA
KNESCHOWSKY, DAVICE	26	M	LABR	PLZZZ	ZUSA
BEER, M.	20	M	LABR	PLZZZ	ZUSA
SCHMDT, L.	21	M	LABR	PLZZZ	ZUSA
FINKELSTEIN, ABHN	29	M	LABR	PLZZZ	ZUSA

PASSENGER	AGE	SEX	OCCUPATION	PRIV	VIL	DES
ABEL, KAPHEL	19	F	SVNT	PL	ZZZZ	USA
BACSO, E.	25	F	SVNT	PL	ZZZZ	USA
KASIMER, MARIA	25	F	SVNT	PL	ZZZZ	USA
KISEL, IDA	18	F	SVNT	PL	ZZZZ	USA
KUBLOWSKY, JOHANNA	26	F	SVNT	PL	ZZZZ	USA
BEREUSTER, O.	26	M	LABR	PL	ZZZZ	USA
SOPHIA	28	F	W	PL	ZZZZ	USA
JASCHPAN, H.	36	F	W	PL	ZZZZ	USA
J.	18	F	NRS	PL	ZZZZ	USA
L.	11	M	CH	PL	ZZZZ	USA
KIRSTEN, C.	18	M	LABR	PL	ZZZZ	USA
ROSENBERG, C.	16	F	NRS	PL	ZZZZ	USA
LIPINSKY, L.	11	M	CH	PL	ZZZZ	USA
KRASCHEWSKI, J.	8	M	CHILD	PL	ZZZZ	USA
KUSCHINSKY, JAN	35	M	LABR	PL	AAYK	USA
STRASE, J.	20	M	LABR	PL	AAYK	USA
OSSILUS, A.	27	M	LABR	PL	AAYK	USA
DUBOSARSKY, S.	34	M	LABR	PL	AAYK	USA
GOZIKOWSKE, ALTER	44	M	LABR	PL	AAYK	USA

SHIP: ETRURIA

FROM: LIVERPOOL AND QUEENSTOWN
TO: NEW YORK
ARRIVED: 14 DECEMBER 1885

PASSENGER	AGE	SEX	OCCUPATION	PRIV	VIL	DES
LODER, MEIN	50	M	LABR	RR	ZZZZ	USA
LIELARGNY, ALBERT	27	M	LABR	RR	AFWJ	USA
ROSENTHAL, SOLOMON	50	M	LABR	RR	AFWJ	USA
STAHL, BUEL	26	F	SP	RR	AFWJ	USA
BIMIEG, JUDITH	18	F	SP	RR	AFWJ	USA

SHIP: NECKAR

FROM: BREMEN
TO: NEW YORK
ARRIVED: 14 DECEMBER 1885

PASSENGER	AGE	SEX	OCCUPATION	PRIV	VIL	DES
PISKORSKA, ELISABETH	25	F	UNKNOWN	RR	ZZZZ	PIT
MARINKA	.11	F	INFANT	RR	ZZZZ	PIT
FEINBERG, MORDCHE	23	F	UNKNOWN	RR	ZZZZ	BAL
MEYER	6	M	CHILD	RR	ZZZZ	BAL
LIEBE	1	F	CHILD	RR	ZZZZ	BAL
OUARD, REBECCA	20	F	SVNT	RR	ZZZZ	NY
HEGENER, ADOLF	23	M	ENGR	RR	AHXH	NY
TURAWICZ, ADAM	20	M	FARMER	RR	ZZZZ	UNK
NONNENMACHER, MARTIN	65	M	LABR	RR	ZZZZ	NY
ALZUL, RIWE	55	F	UNKNOWN	RR	ZZZZ	NY
FAEKBER, GITTEL	19	M	DLR	RR	ZZZZ	NY

SHIP: RHAETIA

FROM: HAMBURG
TO: NEW YORK
ARRIVED: 14 DECEMBER 1885

PASSENGER	AGE	SEX	OCCUPATION	PRIV	VIL	DES
STEIN, CIWJE	34	F	W	RR	ZZZZ	USA
HILLEL	9	M	CHILD	RR	ZZZZ	USA
JANKEL	8	M	CHILD	RR	ZZZZ	USA
RACHEL	7	F	CHILD	RR	ZZZZ	USA
HIRSCH	4	M	CHILD	RR	ZZZZ	USA
SOMASCHEFSKY, VINZENS	18	M	LABR	RR	ZZZZ	USA
STEIN, LEA	28	F	W	RR	ZZZZ	USA
SARA	5	F	CHILD	RR	ZZZZ	USA
JOSHE	4	M	CHILD	RR	ZZZZ	USA
ZEIDEL, ABRAM	26	M	LABR	RR	ZZZZ	USA
TAUBE	20	F	W	RR	ZZZZ	USA
WOWE	8	F	CHILD	RR	ZZZZ	USA
FREIDE	9	F	CHILD	RR	ZZZZ	USA
BOLA	.11	F	INFANT	RR	ZZZZ	USA
PRAUTMANN, GEORG	32	M	LABR	RR	ZZZZ	USA
CHRISTINE	29	F	W	RR	ZZZZ	USA
KATH.	7	F	CHILD	RR	ZZZZ	USA
LISABETH	4	F	CHILD	RR	ZZZZ	USA
CAROLINE	.11	F	INFANT	RR	ZZZZ	USA
JOHANN	.01	M	INFANT	RR	ZZZZ	USA
KOPLITZKI, MORDCHE	41	M	LABR	RR	ZZZZ	USA
LINKE, GOTTLIEB	37	M	LABR	RR	ZZZZ	USA
PHILIPPINE	35	F	W	RR	ZZZZ	USA
CHRISTIAN	8	M	CHILD	RR	ZZZZ	USA
JACOB	4	M	CHILD	RR	ZZZZ	USA
EVA	.11	F	INFANT	RR	ZZZZ	USA
MAGDALENE	.01	F	INFANT	RR	ZZZZ	USA
SURULINSKY, VICTOR	20	M	DLR	RR	ZZZZ	USA
NARKEWICZ, PAULINE	30	F	W	RR	ZZZZ	USA
JOSEFA	8	F	CHILD	RR	ZZZZ	USA
JACOB	6	M	CHILD	RR	ZZZZ	USA
JOSEF	4	M	CHILD	RR	ZZZZ	USA
BRAVERMANN, OSCHER	38	M	LABR	RR	ZZZZ	USA
ABRAH.	9	M	CHILD	RR	ZZZZ	USA
HAASE, FRIEDR.	22	M	LABR	RR	ZZZZ	USA
RUDKOWSKY, JAN	26	M	LABR	RR	ZZZZ	USA
DIETZ, HEINR.	40	M	FARMER	RR	ZZZZ	USA
MARIANE	30	F	W	RR	ZZZZ	USA
AMALIE	5	F	CHILD	RR	ZZZZ	USA
WILHELM	2	M	CHILD	RR	ZZZZ	USA
MARIE	.11	F	INFANT	RR	ZZZZ	USA
PALUCH, ISAAC	58	M	LABR	RR	ZZZZ	USA
PERLSTEIN, SIMON	40	M	LABR	RR	ZZZZ	USA
KOBATZNIK, ROSA	19	F	SGL	RR	ZZZZ	USA
MIKLISCHANSKY, BENJ.	45	M	LABR	RR	ZZZZ	USA
SATNICK, EVA	28	F	W	RR	ZZZZ	USA
MERIAM	6	F	CHILD	RR	ZZZZ	USA
BEILE	5	F	CHILD	RR	ZZZZ	USA
LICHTENFELD, LASSIEL	21	M	TLR	RR	ZZZZ	USA
UDZIWJAK, ELJE	22	M	DLR	RR	ZZZZ	USA
LIPSKY, BETTY	65	F	W	RR	ZZZZ	USA
EISENBERG, JENTE	9	M	CHILD	RR	ZZZZ	USA
KANTOR, ISRAEL	28	M	DLR	RR	ZZZZ	USA
MARIE	25	F	W	RR	ZZZZ	USA
HANCHEN	3	F	CHILD	RR	ZZZZ	USA
OSCHER	.11	M	INFANT	RR	ZZZZ	USA
SEGALLOWSKY, PESCHE	44	F	W	RR	ZZZZ	USA
LEISER	9	M	CHILD	RR	ZZZZ	USA
FRUME	8	F	CHILD	RR	ZZZZ	USA
RIWE	3	F	CHILD	RR	ZZZZ	USA
HIRSCH	6	M	CHILD	RR	ZZZZ	USA
NEICHUMCIL, DANIEL	22	M	LABR	RR	ZZZZ	USA
MANDEL, MARIE	32	F	W	RR	ZZZZ	USA
ALBERT	8	M	CHILD	RR	ZZZZ	USA
RICHARD	6	M	CHILD	RR	ZZZZ	USA
JURICK	5	M	CHILD	RR	ZZZZ	USA
MARTHA	.11	F	INFANT	RR	ZZZZ	USA
POLINSKI, GUSTAV	24	M	LABR	RR	ZZZZ	USA
PELROCE, JAN	60	M	LABR	RR	ZZZZ	USA
JUDASCHEWITZ, ISAAC	21	M	LABR	RR	ZZZZ	USA
SCHAFER, ABEL	54	M	DLR	RR	ZZZZ	USA
CHEIE	50	F	W	RR	ZZZZ	USA
SOPHIE	17	F	CH	RR	ZZZZ	USA
HINDE	9	F	CHILD	RR	ZZZZ	USA
KOZLOWSKI, JOSEF	38	M	LABR	RR	ZZZZ	USA
HORBATZEWSKO, JOSEF	40	M	LABR	RR	ZZZZ	USA
PITKIEWICZ, JOSEPH	33	M	CPTR	RR	ZZZZ	USA
SILBERLING, SHEIE	40	M	DLR	RR	ZZZZ	USA
SIFERT, SARA	40	F	W	RR	ZZZZ	USA

PASSENGER	AGE	SEX	OCCUPATION	PRIVL	DES
DWORA	15	F	CH	RRZZZZ	USA
ABRAM	9	M	CHILD	RRZZZZ	USA
HERZKI	6	F	CHILD	RRZZZZ	USA
LIEBE	4	F	CHILD	RRZZZZ	USA
PROSE, SIMON	38	M	DLR	RRZZZZ	USA
CHANNE	29	F	W	RRZZZZ	USA
BLEIWESS, ABRAH.	36	M	LABR	RRZZZZ	USA
SPIELER, CHAIM	35	M	LABR	RRZZZZ	USA
DEUF, FEISEL	22	F	SGL	RRZZZZ	USA
RIEDEL, ENGEL	26	F	SGL	RRZZZZ	USA
FINDLING, LEA	18	F	SGL	RRZZZZ	USA
REUH, SCHEIE	18	F	SGL	RRZZZZ	USA
SCHABORSCH, JITEL	58	F	W	RRZZZZ	USA
WOLZANSKI, JANKEL	40	M	LABR	RRZZZZ	USA
SCHOME	26	F	W	RRZZZZ	USA
MALKE	9	F	CHILD	RRZZZZ	USA
CHEIE	8	F	CHILD	RRZZZZ	USA
LIEBE	4	F	CHILD	RRZZZZ	USA
REBECCA	.11	F	INFANT	RRZZZZ	USA
CHAIME	.01	M	INFANT	RRZZZZ	USA
SCHEFFERT, MANE	16	M	LABR	RRZZZZ	USA
PELGUS, EMILIE	20	F	SGL	RRZZZZ	USA
SELIGMANN, CHAIM	24	M	DLR	RRZZZZ	USA
POTASCHINSKI, LIEPE	20	M	LABR	RRZZZZ	USA

SHIP: ZEELAND

FROM: ANTWERP
TO: NEW YORK
ARRIVED: 15 DECEMBER 1885

PASSENGER	AGE	SEX	OCCUPATION	PRIVL	DES
SCHWALZKA, WILHELMINA	21	F	W	PLZZZZ	USA
CHR.	18	F	SP	PLZZZZ	USA
SPINGER, EMELINE	21	F	SP	PLZZZZ	USA
BONNSKI, M.	18	M	FARMER	PLZZZZ	USA
POLOKA, AL.	22	M	LABR	PLZZZZ	USA
M.	11	F	UNKNOWN	PLZZZZ	USA
WISA, MAG.	48	F	W	PLZZZZ	USA

SHIP: SUEVIA

FROM: HAMBURG
TO: NEW YORK
ARRIVED: 16 DECEMBER 1885

PASSENGER	AGE	SEX	OCCUPATION	PRIVL	DES
BRETSCHNEIDER, CHRISTOP	19	M	LABR	RRZZZZ	NY
ULLRICH, JACOB	28	M	LABR	RRZZZZ	UNK
JOHANNA	28	F	W	RRZZZZ	UNK
CATHARINA	4	F	CHILD	RRZZZZ	UNK
JACOB	3	M	CHILD	RRZZZZ	UNK
HEINRICH	.09	M	INFANT	RRZZZZ	UNK
KNOLL, KATHARINA	51	F	W	RRZZZZ	UNK
ELISABETH	17	F	CH	RRZZZZ	UNK
CATHARINE	9	F	CHILD	RRZZZZ	UNK
HAGEL, PETER	28	M	LABR	RRZZZZ	UNK
ELISABETH	28	F	W	RRZZZZ	UNK
ELISABETH	4	F	CHILD	RRZZZZ	UNK
BENDER, MARTIN	25	M	LABR	RRZZZZ	UNK
CHRISTINE	24	F	W	RRZZZZ	UNK
CATHARINE	1	F	CHILD	RRZZZZ	UNK
MARTIN	.11	M	INFANT	RRZZZZ	UNK
HAASE, GEORG	59	M	LABR	RRZZZZ	UNK
CATHARINA	56	F	W	RRZZZZ	UNK
KLEIN, ELISABETH	40	F	W	RRZZZZ	UNK
HEINRICH	21	M	LABR	RRZZZZ	UNK

PASSENGER	AGE	SEX	OCCUPATION	PRIVL	DES
JOHANN	16	M	LABR	RRZZZZ	UNK
RIEB, CHRISTOPH	39	M	LABR	RRZZZZ	UNK
CAROLINA	37	F	W	RRZZZZ	UNK
KNOLL, PETER	22	M	LABR	RRZZZZ	UNK
CHRISTINE	20	F	W	RRZZZZ	UNK
BEHRENDT, JACOB	32	M	LABR	RRZZZZ	UNK
CHRISTINE	30	F	W	RRZZZZ	UNK
LUDWIG	7	M	CHILD	RRZZZZ	UNK
CHRISTINE	3	F	CHILD	RRZZZZ	UNK
ELISABETH	.09	F	INFANT	RRZZZZ	UNK
ENGEL, JOHANN	21	M	LABR	RRZZZZ	UNK
CHMILEWSKI, STANISL.	25	M	LABR	RRAHZS	UNK
MORROS, JAN	23	M	LABR	RRAHZS	OH
REINGOLD, RASHE	20	F	SGL	RRZZZZ	NY
RIS, ASCHER	18	M	LABR	RRZZZZ	NY
ROSENFELD, DAVID	18	M	LABR	RRAHTF	NY
LINA	9	F	CHILD	RRAHTF	NY
KLEIN, LEDY	36	F	W	RRZZZZ	IL
ILON	16	F	SGL	RRZZZZ	IL
KONAR	6	M	CHILD	RRZZZZ	IL
ROTH, SZANI	23	F	W	RRZZZZ	MN
KABAKER, MINDEL	45	F	W	RRZZZZ	MN
BEILE	20	F	CH	RRZZZZ	MN
ETHEL	18	F	CH	RRZZZZ	MN
JACOB	15	M	CH	RRZZZZ	MN
ISAAC	9	M	CHILD	RRZZZZ	MN
JOSEPH	9	M	CHILD	RRZZZZ	MN
MOSES	7	M	CHILD	RRZZZZ	MN
SCHLOME	4	M	CHILD	RRZZZZ	MN
GUDCZEWSKI, PETER	22	M	LABR	RRAHZS	NE
OLORWACZ, ANTON	27	M	LABR	RRAHZS	NE
MAKONEER, JULS.	20	M	TLR	RRZZZZ	NE
CHROSLOWSKI, JOSEPH	19	M	LABR	RRAHZS	NE
FEUER, FRANZ	18	M	SMH	RRZZZZ	NE
KANTROWITZ, HERSCH	55	M	DLR	RRAFWJ	NE
NOCHE	42	F	W	RRAFWJ	NE
GABRIEL	9	M	CHILD	RRAFWJ	NE
SARA	8	F	CHILD	RRAFWJ	NE
DRACHENFELD, LEIB	40	M	DLR	RRZZZZ	UNK
MALAMUDES, LEIB	49	M	LABR	RRZZZZ	UNK
BRUNN	30	F	W	RRZZZZ	UNK
BEKALEWICK, LEIB	22	M	LABR	RRZZZZ	UNK
SASCHE	18	F	W	RRZZZZ	UNK
TAUZEWSKI, SARA	20	F	SGL	RRZZZZ	MO
BRENNER, RACHEL	9	F	CHILD	RRAHVU	NY
SIERALSKI, EMANUEL	20	M	TNMK	RRZZZZ	NY
MEISEL, SCHAJE	20	F	W	RRAHVU	NY
EPSTEIN, ABR.	20	M	LABR	RRAHVU	NY
MELCH, BEILE-BASCHE	20	F	W	RRAHVU	NY
MENISKA	.09	F	INFANT	RRAHVU	NY
PUNATZKY, PESSACH	35	M	LABR	RRAGRT	CH
HALUB, HINDE	28	F	SGL	RRAHTU	CH
SUREK, JULIE	24	F	W	RRZZZZ	NY
JOSEPH	9	M	CHILD	RRZZZZ	NY
MARIA	8	F	CHILD	RRZZZZ	NY
JULIUS	5	M	CHILD	RRZZZZ	NY
JOHANN	3	M	CHILD	RRZZZZ	NY
ELISABETH	.11	F	INFANT	RRZZZZ	NY
WOGT, CLARA	26	F	W	RRZZZZ	PHI
PAULINE	15	F	SGL	RRZZZZ	PHI
AGNES	3	F	CHILD	RRZZZZ	PHI
JULIE	.09	F	INFANT	RRZZZZ	PHI
-UY, MICHAEL	30	M	LABR	RRZZZZ	NY
SOHEN, OTTO	19	M	LABR	RRZZZZ	IL
BRANDT, KARL	32	M	LABR	RRZZZZ	IL
HOLDSTEIN, DOROTHEA	24	F	SGL	RRAHZD	NY
SCHWARZ, CHAZKEL	30	M	LABR	RRAHTU	NY
HOLDSTEIN, BARNET	21	M	TLR	RRAHZD	NY
SIGELZKY, ABRAM	55	M	DLR	RRZZZZ	NY
CHAJE	54	F	W	RRZZZZ	NY
CHAWE	14	F	CH	RRZZZZ	NY
RACHEL	3	F	CHILD	RRZZZZ	NY
ROSTUD, RAFFEL	18	M	LABR	RRZZZZ	UNK
EPSTEIN, JOHEINE	18	F	W	RRZZZZ	NY
CHAJE	.11	F	INFANT	RRZZZZ	NY

PASSENGER	AGE	SEX	OCCUPATION	PRV IL	DES
SAMUELOWITZ, MARTIN	23	M	LABR	RRZZZZ	NY
AGNESKA	21	F	W	RRZZZZ	NY
AGNESKA	.03	F	INFANT	RRZZZZ	NY
SCHLIFKOWSKA, ALEXANDRA	50	F	W	RRAHZS	NY
SIGNITZKY, OSSER	40	M	DLR	RRZZZZ	OH
LEWITZKO, ARON	30	M	LABR	RRZZZZ	NY
LEWIT, SALOMON	21	M	MCHT	RRZZZZ	NY
STEINDORF, MOSES	21	M	LABR	RRZZZZ	NE
BELSIN, SAMUEL	21	M	LABR	RRZZZZ	NE
SEGALOWSKY, JOSEF	22	M	LABR	RRZZZZ	NE
SPANER, TAUBE	16	F	W	RRZZZZ	NE
SIMON	9	M	CHILD	RRZZZZ	NE
LEWISOHN, HELENE	19	F	SGL	RRAHVA	NY

SHIP: WISCONSIN

FROM: LIVERPOOL
TO: NEW YORK
ARRIVED: 17 DECEMBER 1885

PASSENGER	AGE	SEX	OCCUPATION	PRV IL	DES
ROSENBERG, MORITZ	26	M	GZR	RRZZZZ	USA
CHIOSTOWSKY, MIEZISLOW	21	M	SDLR	PLZZZZ	USA
SEIDENBERG, PREIDE	20	F	SP	PLZZZZ	USA
NISSEN	11	M	CH	PLZZZZ	USA
DEBORA	.09	F	INFANT	PLZZZZ	USA
SCHANCK, JOHANNES	28	M	LABR	RRZZZZ	USA
SAVITZKY, FELIX	30	M	FARMER	RRZZZZ	USA
GIBORAWSKY, SAM.	17	M	CPTR	RRZZZZ	USA
EPSUCH, SCHEBERN	23	M	CPTR	RRZZZZ	USA
GIBROWSKY, FRIEDE	19	F	SP	RRZZZZ	USA
MERKUSON, MEUREL	28	F	SP	RRZZZZ	USA
IMELOWITZ, SOLOMON	37	M	GZR	RRZZZZ	USA
MENDEL	40	F	W	RRZZZZ	USA

SHIP: AUSTRALIA

FROM: HAMBURG
TO: NEW YORK
ARRIVED: 18 DECEMBER 1885

PASSENGER	AGE	SEX	OCCUPATION	PRV IL	DES
BENDZUS, CASIMIR	20	M	FARMER	RRZZZZ	NY
BEHRMANN, ALB.	32	M	MCHT	RRZZZZ	NY
HENDSACHER, REISEL	24	F	SGL	RRZZZZ	NY
LEWIT, BEILE	16	F	SGL	RRZZZZ	NY
BENDZUS, THEOPHIL	23	M	LABR	RRZZZZ	NY
ROTHSTEIN, PESCHE	30	M	BKR	RRZZZZ	NY
LILE	30	F	W	RRZZZZ	NY
LEWITTA, HEIL.LEA	50	F	WO	RRZZZZ	UNK
PLAGING, FRIEDR.	32	M	LABR	RRZZZZ	UNK
RUBIN, DAVID	20	M	UNKNOWN	RRZZZZ	UNK
RADATZ, JOH.	50	M	LABR	RRZZZZ	UNK
WIESE, CAROLINE	48	F	WO	RRZZZZ	NY
EMMA	7	F	CHILD	RRZZZZ	NY
OTTILIE	6	F	CHILD	RRZZZZ	NY
HAPKE, PAULINE	22	F	WO	RRZZZZ	NY
BERTHA	2	F	CHILD	RRZZZZ	NY
LUDWIG	.11	M	INFANT	RRZZZZ	NY
DOGROWSKY, SLAWE	19	F	SGL	RRZZZZ	NY
TUBIANSKI, SZMERL	19	M	LABR	RRZZZZ	NY
KARANBAN, ELIAS	25	M	TRDSMN	RRZZZZ	NY
SCHLUBSKI, MARCUS	27	M	TRDSMN	RRZZZZ	NY
CZOSNOK, WOLFF	39	M	MCHT	PLZZZZ	NY
MASER, KLEMENZ	42	M	LABR	PLZZZZ	NY
REPAK, TIMKO	42	M	LABR	PLZZZZ	NY
AFTEN	31	M	LABR	PLZZZZ	NY

PASSENGER	AGE	SEX	OCCUPATION	PRV IL	DES
MARCHUT, JAN	40	M	LABR	PLZZZZ	NY
DENZ, VOSSIL	40	M	LABR	PLZZZZ	NY
RUSSIN, JAN	24	M	LABR	PLZZZZ	NY
PARTAK, JOH.	33	M	LABR	PLZZZZ	NY
MURVA, PAUL	41	M	LABR	PLZZZZ	NY
RELIGIN, MITRO	48	M	LABR	PLZZZZ	NY
MORZAN, ANTON	40	M	LABR	PLZZZZ	NY
KADYN, PIETRO	16	M	LABR	PLZZZZ	NY
SCHLEINZ, ANTON	20	M	LABR	PLZZZZ	NY
JARZAMBOWSKA, MARYANNE	38	F	WO	RRZZZZ	NY
AGNES	7	F	CHILD	RRZZZZ	NY
JOHANNA	6	F	CHILD	RRZZZZ	NY
STANISLAUS	4	M	CHILD	RRZZZZ	NY
PIOKOWSKI, JAN	16	M	LABR	RRZZZZ	NY

SHIP: STATE OF NEBRASKA

FROM: GLASGOW AND LARNE
TO: NEW YORK
ARRIVED: 18 DECEMBER 1885

PASSENGER	AGE	SEX	OCCUPATION	PRV IL	DES
KLICHOFSTEIN, MORITZ	16	M	SLSMN	RRZZZZ	NY
ARNOSTAWSKI, WINCENTY	19	M	LABR	RRZZZZ	NY
KUSCHANSKY, JOSEF	25	M	LABR	RRZZZZ	NY
OLSCHEWSKY, JOSEF	19	M	LABR	RRZZZZ	NY
BONER, JULIUS	21	M	CL	RRZZZZ	NY
KANTOR, MICHEL	44	M	TLR	RRZZZZ	NY
CHANNE	43	F	W	RRZZZZ	NY
MOSES	8	M	CHILD	RRZZZZ	NY
JOSEPH	8	M	CHILD	RRZZZZ	NY
ESTHER	6	F	CHILD	RRZZZZ	NY
LEA	4	F	CHILD	RRZZZZ	NY
CHANNE	2	F	CHILD	RRZZZZ	NY
MATTE	1	F	CHILD	RRZZZZ	NY
KUTZIRKA, PESTER	35	M	LABR	RRZZZZ	NY
BENEDEK, DUSZAR	30	M	LABR	RRZZZZ	NY
PACKATZKI, RIWE	38	F	W	RRZZZZ	BO
MENDEL	9	M	CHILD	RRZZZZ	BO
SALOMON	6	M	CHILD	RRZZZZ	BO
ZINKE	5	F	CHILD	RRZZZZ	BO
LAIB	4	F	CHILD	RRZZZZ	BO
JETTE	1	F	CHILD	RRZZZZ	BO
BOTEROSEN, ISRAEL	00	M	TCHR	RRZZZZ	NY
NIELUBER, RIFKE	23	M	PDLR	RRZZZZ	NY
JACOBSEN, MENDEL	23	M	LABR	RRZZZZ	UNK
CAPRIS, MEILOCH	27	M	CCHBLDR	RRZZZZ	NY
VAGEL, ESTHER	38	F	W	RRZZZZ	NY
LEPERT, SAM.	18	M	LABR	RRZZZZ	NY
EPPEL, MOSES	22	M	LABR	RRZZZZ	CIN
BLANKFELD, HIRSCH	19	M	FARMER	RRZZZZ	IL

SHIP: WERRA

FROM: BREMEN AND SOUTHAMPTON
TO: NEW YORK
ARRIVED: 19 DECEMBER 1885

PASSENGER	AGE	SEX	OCCUPATION	PRV IL	DES
POTMEIDER, FANNY	15	F	NN	RRZZZZ	USA
ZWET, ABR.ABBE	33	M	LABR	RRZZZZ	USA
ANNA	26	F	W	RRZZZZ	USA
MICHAL	.09	M	INFANT	RRZZZZ	USA
BACZELOWSKI, MAYANNA	32	F	W	RRZZZZ	USA
KLMEC.	4	F	CHILD	RRZZZZ	USA

PASSENGER	AGE	SEX	OCCUPATION	PRIV	VIL	DES

SHIP: ALASKA

FROM: LIVERPOOL AND QUEENSTOWN
TO: NEW YORK
ARRIVED: 21 DECEMBER 1885

PASSENGER	AGE	SEX	OCCUPATION	PRIV	VIL	DES
MELA, HERMANN	38	M	MCHT	RR	ZZZZ	USA
PIKUS, RUBEN	18	M	SLR	RR	ZZZZ	USA
KIRMANN, BENJAMIN	22	M	SLR	RR	ZZZZ	USA
COPLANEKY, I.	20	M	CGRMKR	RR	ZZZZ	USA

SHIP: NORMANDIE

FROM: HAVRE
TO: NEW YORK
ARRIVED: 21 DECEMBER 1885

PASSENGER	AGE	SEX	OCCUPATION	PRIV	VIL	DES
BONIS, CHARLES-MR.	23	M	NN	RR	ZZZZ	NY

SHIP: SCHIEDAM

FROM: AMSTERDAM
TO: NEW YORK
ARRIVED: 22 DECEMBER 1885

PASSENGER	AGE	SEX	OCCUPATION	PRIV	VIL	DES
BRITZK, JANKEL	35	M	LABR	RR	ZZZZ	USA
LIPSCHILZ, EPHRAIM	23	M	LABR	RR	ZZZZ	USA
SILBER, ABRAHAM	28	M	MCHT	RR	ZZZZ	USA
LATUSCHEWITZ, ITZIGS	20	M	MCHT	RR	ZZZZ	USA
RADSCHUNES, JURGES	30	M	MCHT	RR	ZZZZ	USA
LIPMAN, LEIB	18	M	LABR	RR	ZZZZ	USA
GLUCFELD, HIRSCH	24	M	LABR	RR	ZZZZ	USA
GELLBLADT, MOSES	35	M	LABR	RR	ZZZZ	USA

SHIP: DEVONIA

FROM: GLASGOW
TO: NEW YORK
ARRIVED: 23 DECEMBER 1885

PASSENGER	AGE	SEX	OCCUPATION	PRIV	VIL	DES
BUEZKIER, SALAMON	18	M	PDLR	RR	ACBF	USA
CONRAD, MATHIAS	32	M	LABR	RR	ACBF	USA
DEMPSKI, ADAM	21	M	LABR	RR	ACBF	USA
RUBEN, DAVID	37	M	LABR	RR	ACBF	USA
ROSENBERG, JOSEL	27	M	LABR	RR	ACBF	USA
SAFRAN, ANTON	23	M	LABR	RR	ACBF	USA
ZUPPER, JEAN	22	M	LABR	RR	ACBF	USA

SHIP: MORAVIA

FROM: HAMBURG
TO: NEW YORK
ARRIVED: 23 DECEMBER 1885

PASSENGER	AGE	SEX	OCCUPATION	PRIV	VIL	DES
MASER, MANDEL	19	M	LABR	RR	ZZZZ	USA
PREIGE, DINA	51	F	W	RR	AHTR	USA
CHANNIE	16	F	SGL	RR	AHTR	USA
GORDON, RACHEL	20	F	SGL	RR	ZZZZ	USA
KURIPSKY, FELIX	22	M	LABR	RR	AHZS	USA
FRIEDMANN, MORITZ	50	M	MCHT	RR	ZZZZ	USA
SILBER, JANKEL	38	M	DLR	RR	AHTF	USA
BURKOWSKA, JATH.	30	F	W	RR	ZZZZ	USA
JULIE	4	F	CHILD	RR	ZZZZ	USA
KAZIMIR	.11	M	INFANT	RR	ZZZZ	USA
KATH.	.11	F	INFANT	RR	ZZZZ	USA
SCHULMANN, ROSA	45	F	W	RR	AHTF	USA
GITTEL	9	F	CHILD	RR	AHTF	USA
MAYER, ADOLF	19	M	LABR	RR	AHZS	USA
SAHANEIGUTE, MARTHA	28	F	SGL	RR	AHZS	USA
MILONTZISTI, MAGDALENA	28	F	SGL	RR	AHZS	USA
FROMMENSOHN, ISRAEL	18	M	LABR	RR	ZZZZ	USA
GRANOWSKY, ITE	16	F	SGL	RR	ZZZZ	USA
SUCHOWSKI, MARIE	19	F	SGL	RR	AHTF	USA
NEUMARK, ELY	21	M	LABR	RR	ZZZZ	USA
ROSS, FEIGE	40	F	W	RR	AHZN	USA
MICHEL	9	M	CHILD	RR	AHZN	USA
JACOB	6	M	CHILD	RR	AHZN	USA
KRALNICK, CHANNE	35	F	W	RR	ZZZZ	USA
BABE	9	F	CHILD	RR	ZZZZ	USA
JANTE	7	F	CHILD	RR	ZZZZ	USA
MARIANNE	3	F	CHILD	RR	ZZZZ	USA
MAB.	.11	F	INFANT	RR	ZZZZ	USA
KOTADRINSKI, ADOLPH	40	M	DLR	RR	ZZZZ	USA
WRUBLEWSKI, ANTON	28	M	LABR	RR	AHOO	USA

SHIP: POLARIA

FROM: HAMBURG
TO: NEW YORK
ARRIVED: 24 DECEMBER 1885

PASSENGER	AGE	SEX	OCCUPATION	PRIV	VIL	DES
CZATKUS, ANT.	25	M	LABR	RR	ZZZZ	NY
LUBOWICZ, E.	35	M	LABR	RR	ZZZZ	NY
BUCHHOLZ, HEINRICH	18	M	LABR	RR	ZZZZ	IL
WILHELM	16	M	LABR	RR	ZZZZ	IL
KWOST, WM.	19	M	LABR	RR	ZZZZ	UNK
WYSOCKI, KASEMIR	25	M	LABR	RR	ZZZZ	UNK
CLEMENS	15	M	LABR	RR	ZZZZ	UNK
PREIZE, JOH.SOND.	25	M	CL	RR	ZZZZ	NY
BRONZA, MARIANNA	31	F	WO	RR	ZZZZ	UNK
MARIA	6	F	CHILD	RR	ZZZZ	UNK
ELISABETH	5	F	CHILD	RR	ZZZZ	UNK
CATHARINA	3	F	CHILD	RR	ZZZZ	UNK
DEMBINSKI, GERSCHE	22	M	BCHR	RR	ZZZZ	NY
MILINKI, MALKE	19	F	SGL	RR	ZZZZ	NY
ROSA	17	F	SGL	RR	ZZZZ	NY
MEYER	7	M	CHILD	RR	ZZZZ	NY
GIDZINSKY, LEON	19	M	TRDSMN	RR	ZZZZ	UNK
KLUGE, FRIEDR.	75	M	FARMER	RR	ZZZZ	NY
HULDA	56	F	W	RR	ZZZZ	NY
REICH, CHAIM	18	M	TRDSMN	RR	ZZZZ	NY
CLAFF, BENNY	19	M	TRDSMN	RR	ZZZZ	NY
PREIZE, HIRSCH	18	M	TRDSMN	RR	ZZZZ	NY
JONNGETOB, JACOB	23	M	TRDSMN	RR	ZZZZ	NY
FINK, MALKE	24	F	WO	RR	ZZZZ	NY
ELI	3	F	CHILD	RR	ZZZZ	NY
GOLDFARB, FELIG	22	M	TDR	RR	ZZZZ	NY

PASSENGER	AGE	SEX	OCCUPATION	PRV	VIL	DES
SROBECK, MORDSCHE	21	F	SGL	RR	ZZZZ	NY

SHIP: STATE OF GEORGIA

FROM: GLASGOW AND LARNE
TO: NEW YORK
ARRIVED: 24 DECEMBER 1885

PASSENGER	AGE	SEX	OCCUPATION	PRV	VIL	DES
COCHAN, SARAH	43	F	W	RR	ZZZZ	USA
MARIANE	19	F	NN	RR	ZZZZ	USA
HIRSCH	6	M	CHILD	RR	ZZZZ	USA
CHANNE	4	F	CHILD	RR	ZZZZ	USA
WOISZECK, ADOLF	35	M	LABR	RR	ZZZZ	USA
WEISSBAD, SIMON	22	M	TLR	RR	ZZZZ	USA
KOWALSKY, MOSES	22	M	LABR	RR	ZZZZ	USA
ESTHERMANN, SAMUEL	24	M	TLR	RR	ZZZZ	USA
SCHERZON, SCHIMON	27	M	TLR	RR	ZZZZ	USA
BAROWSKY, GEO	29	M	LABR	RR	ZZZZ	USA
BACK, HIRSCH	37	M	TLR	RR	ZZZZ	USA
BIRMSTEIN, HIRSCH	23	M	TLR	RR	ZZZZ	USA
SCHMITMANN, WOLF	35	M	TLR	RR	ZZZZ	USA
EISENTZICK, JECHIEL	23	M	TLR	RR	ZZZZ	USA
REICHELSOHN, MOSES	24	M	TLR	RR	ZZZZ	USA
MARGOLIS, CHATZKEL	32	M	SHMK	RR	ZZZZ	USA
ZIEGELNICKY, HIRSCH	20	M	LABR	RR	ZZZZ	USA
JEDASOWSKY, MARCUS	25	M	TLR	RR	ZZZZ	USA
BALTIANSKY, ABR.	18	M	CGRMKR	RR	ZZZZ	USA
GOLDBLATT, FEIWEL	23	M	PDLR	RR	ZZZZ	USA
SZEFFTEL, SCHMANN	22	M	WVR	RR	ZZZZ	USA
KUGEL, DAVID	20	M	WCHMKR	RR	ZZZZ	USA
HERZMANN, NAFTALI	21	M	WCHMKR	RR	ZZZZ	USA
WONKOW, ISAAK	39	M	MSN	RR	ZZZZ	USA
BJALL, ELIAS	19	M	JNR	RR	ZZZZ	USA
REIBSTEIN, M---S	00	M	PDLR	RR	ZZZZ	USA
NACHEM	20	M	PDLR	RR	ZZZZ	USA
SLASKIN, SAMUEL	27	M	PDLR	RR	ZZZZ	USA
FRANKIB, JUDOR	30	M	PDLR	RR	ZZZZ	USA
PAIKIS, ANTONI	36	M	LABR	RR	ZZZZ	USA
JANDYES, JANOS	29	M	LABR	RR	ZZZZ	USA
SCHMIETAS, ANTONI	29	M	LABR	RR	ZZZZ	USA
SCHMALANSKA, MICKA	28	M	LABR	RR	ZZZZ	USA

SHIP: CITY OF BERLIN

FROM: LIVERPOOL AND QUEENSTOWN
TO: NEW YORK
ARRIVED: 26 DECEMBER 1885

PASSENGER	AGE	SEX	OCCUPATION	PRV	VIL	DES
DOMBROWSKY, CARNICZ	31	M	LABR	RR	ACBF	PIT
RABINOWISZ, MARCUS	18	M	LABR	RR	ACBF	NY
SCHOLENSKY, HERMANN	21	M	LABR	RR	ACBF	NY
JUDELOWITZ, ISAK	24	M	LABR	RR	ACBF	NY

SHIP: MAIN

FROM: BREMEN
TO: NEW YORK
ARRIVED: 26 DECEMBER 1885

PASSENGER	AGE	SEX	OCCUPATION	PRV	VIL	DES
FISCHER, REICHEL	28	M	LABR	RR	ZZZZ	USA
GUSTAV	11	M	CH	RR	ZZZZ	USA
ISAAK	8	M	CHILD	RR	ZZZZ	USA
JORKEL	3	M	CHILD	RR	ZZZZ	USA
SEGAL, M----	24	M	LABR	RR	ZZZZ	USA
SIMON, JACOB	30	M	LABR	RR	ZZZZ	USA
GLIEDER, DAVID	28	M	LABR	RR	ZZZZ	USA
BOTSCHENIK, SCHENDEL	35	M	LABR	RR	ZZZZ	USA
ARON	18	M	LABR	RR	ZZZZ	USA
LOEB	.01	M	INFANT	RR	ZZZZ	USA
SCHMIDTKE, JOHANN	21	M	LABR	RR	ZZZZ	USA
GRISS, MARIE	19	F	SVNT	RR	ZZZZ	USA
AUGUSTE	16	F	CH	RR	ZZZZ	USA
HOJNECKA, VERONIKA	23	F	W	RR	ZZZZ	USA
LEON	.01	M	INFANT	RR	ZZZZ	USA
WAJEWSKI, ADAM	31	M	LABR	RR	ZZZZ	USA
SCHREIBMANN, MOSES	54	M	PDLR	RR	ZZZZ	USA

SHIP: P CALAND

FROM: ROTTERDAM
TO: NEW YORK
ARRIVED: 26 DECEMBER 1885

PASSENGER	AGE	SEX	OCCUPATION	PRV	VIL	DES
TRESZANSKY, ELIE	20	M	MCHT	RR	ZZZZ	USA
MENESEWITKY, MOSES	20	M	SHMK	RR	ZZZZ	USA
GELNSON, ABRAHM	21	M	PDLR	RR	ZZZZ	USA

SHIP: PERSIAN MONARCH

FROM: LONDON
TO: NEW YORK
ARRIVED: 26 DECEMBER 1885

PASSENGER	AGE	SEX	OCCUPATION	PRV	VIL	DES
STEINBERG, JULIUS	54	M	UNKNOWN	PL	ZZZZ	NY
ESTHER	32	F	W	PL	ZZZZ	NY
ISAAC	10	M	CH	PL	ZZZZ	NY
ALFRED	8	M	CHILD	PL	ZZZZ	NY
FINEAT	6	M	CHILD	PL	ZZZZ	NY
PAULINE	5	F	CHILD	PL	ZZZZ	NY
TERESA	3	F	CHILD	PL	ZZZZ	NY
KATE	3	F	CHILD	PL	ZZZZ	NY
GOLDSTEIN, DAVID	20	M	TLR	RR	ZZZZ	NY
GOLDMAN, LOUIS	21	M	TLR	RR	ZZZZ	NY
COHEN, LOUIS	24	M	TLR	PL	ZZZZ	NY

PASSENGER	AGE	SEX	OCCUPATION	PRV	VIL	DES

SHIP: ARIZONA

FROM: LIVERPOOL
TO: NEW YORK
ARRIVED: 28 DECEMBER 1885

PASSENGER	AGE	SEX	OCCUPATION	PRV VIL DES
LEIDNE, FRIEDNE	50	F	W	PLZZZZUSA
FALCKE, BEIDE	15	F	SP	PLZZZZUSA
KOMMITAL, MOSES	17	M	LABR	PLZZZZUSA
SCHEFFEL, ISAACK	52	M	UNKNOWN	PLZZZZUSA
FROSSER, ISAACK	28	M	UNKNOWN	PLZZZZUSA

SHIP: SERVIA

FROM: LIVERPOOL AND QUEENSTOWN
TO: NEW YORK
ARRIVED: 28 DECEMBER 1885

PASSENGER	AGE	SEX	OCCUPATION	PRV VIL DES
ZEDELKO, SIM.	21	M	LABR	RRZZZZBAL
VEBOS, MIK.	28	M	LABR	RRZZZZNY
JOOL, JANOS	38	M	LABR	RRZZZZNY
SUNDELL, YET	22	M	LABR	RRZZZZMI
SUMNISKY, JOHAN	24	M	LABR	RRZZZZNY
SIMESKY, DRAJ.	24	M	LABR	RRZZZZNY
RATNER, MICHAEL	18	M	LABR	RRZZZZNY
PUSCHUAK, ISRAEL	40	M	LABR	RRZZZZNY
NICO, JOSEF	40	M	LABR	RRZZZZNY
KALCOK, WASIL	20	M	LABR	RRZZZZNY
GUSTAFSON, LEAR	27	M	LABR	RRZZZZPIT
GULLBERG, VALENTINIE	25	M	LABR	RRZZZZPIT
MILLER, HENDRIK	40	M	MCHT	RRZZZZPIT

SHIP: CIRCASSIA

FROM: GLASGOW AND MOVILLE
TO: NEW YORK
ARRIVED: 29 DECEMBER 1885

PASSENGER	AGE	SEX	OCCUPATION	PRV VIL DES
SCHERESCHEWSKY, ISAK	21	M	JNR	RRZZZZUSA
IDA	21	F	W	RRZZZZUSA
BISCHOWSKI, F.	52	M	DLR	RRZZZZUSA
PASCHE	23	F	W	RRZZZZUSA
KOBEKOWSKY, RACHMEL	21	M	DLR	RRZZZZUSA
AROSSOHN, BEHR	44	M	DLR	RRZZZZUSA
SOREMSKI, ANTON	28	M	MLR	RRZZZZUSA
HIRMANN, Z.	25	M	LABR	RRZZZZUSA
GERTSCH, JUSIS	24	M	LABR	RRZZZZUSA
KUTZKI, JULIUS	22	M	MLR	RRZZZZUSA
WAGNER, EDWARD	22	M	BCHR	RRZZZZUSA
HIRSCH, LUD.	20	M	DLR	RRZZZZUSA
BEER, CHAIN	20	M	TLR	RRZZZZUSA
JOSEFER, LIPMANN	21	M	DLR	RRZZZZUSA
SCHAPIRA, MOSES	30	M	TLR	RRZZZZUSA
BLOCH, BERNES	23	M	DSTLR	RRZZZZUSA
POLLAK, JOSEF	21	M	UNKNOWN	RRZZZZUSA
MICHALOWSKY, IDA	20	F	TLR	RRZZZZUSA
JOSEL	42	M	DLR	RRZZZZUSA
SALOMON	11	M	NN	RRZZZZUSA

SHIP: GELLERT

FROM: HAMBURG
TO: NEW YORK
ARRIVED: 29 DECEMBER 1885

PASSENGER	AGE	SEX	OCCUPATION	PRV VIL DES
KRANITZKY, BRONISLAVA	27	F	W	RRZZZZUSA
ANNA	4	F	CHILD	RRZZZZUSA
ALEXANDER	2	M	CHILD	RRZZZZUSA
MARIE	.11	F	INFANT	RRZZZZUSA
PANTER, PAULINA	25	F	W	RRZZZZUSA
CARL	4	M	CHILD	RRZZZZUSA
JOHANN	35	M	LABR	RRZZZZUSA
GERNISEWSKI, CASIMIR	23	M	LABR	RRAHZSUSA
BAUNSZEWSKI, FRANCISZEK	22	M	LABR	RRAHZSUSA
KORBA, ISTVAN	26	M	LABR	RRAHZSUSA
KATEL, VACLAV	21	M	LABR	RRAHZSUSA
MARIE	20	F	W	RRAHZSUSA
KITAI, MOSES	20	M	TLR	RRZZZZUSA
FEIN, CHASCHE	22	F	W	RRAHTFUSA
SAMUEL	.11	M	INFANT	RRAHTFUSA
CHAIMSON, SARA	19	F	SI	RRAHTFUSA
BEN	9	F	CHILD	RRAHTFUSA
KIRSTEIN, MARIE	34	F	W	RRAEFLUSA
ANDREAS	25	M	MCHT	RRAEFLUSA
KIZIWREK, FRANZISKA	20	F	W	RRZZZZUSA
BRONISOWA	.11	M	INFANT	RRZZZZUSA
LOWOCHOWSKI, JACOB	42	M	LABR	RRAHZSUSA
RUBIN, MMIRIAM	16	F	SGL	RRAHSLUSA
RUBINSKI, GITTEL	19	F	SGL	RRAHTRUSA
SONNENSTRAHL, LEWIN	60	M	DLR	RRZZZZUSA
ORLOWSKI, JACOB	29	M	SHMK	RRZZZZUSA
WILNER, BENJAMIN	52	M	DLR	RRZZZZUSA
CITRINBAUM, BASCHE	20	F	W	RRZZZZUSA
CILLI	.11	F	INFANT	RRZZZZUSA
BINOWITZ, HELENE	24	F	SGL	RRAHQHUSA
EMMA	27	F	SGL	RRAHQHUSA
BULWA, SCHEIE	33	F	W	RRZZZZUSA
MEIER	8	M	CHILD	RRZZZZUSA
CZAPPER, ZALKE	24	M	LABR	RRZZZZUSA
GUTMANN, BARIS	40	M	CGRMKR	RRAHVUUSA
KAWABOWSKI, JULIUS	37	M	LABR	RRAHZSUSA
LAMPKE, JOHN	36	M	LABR	RRAHZSUSA
SNEGOTZKI, LUDW.	25	M	LABR	RRAHZSUSA
SZEGLINSKI, LEVY	17	M	LABR	RRAHZSUSA
OSMANSKI, WLADISLAUS	17	M	LABR	RRAHZSUSA
SAITZINSKI, JOSEF	24	M	SHMK	RRAHZSUSA
KOSCIEMBA, MICHAEL	29	M	LABR	RRAHZSUSA
GRZEBSKI, LORENZ	22	M	LABR	RRAHZSUSA
ZABOROWSKI, FRANZ	60	M	LABR	RRAHZSUSA
EVA	60	F	W	RRAHZSUSA
ROMAN	9	M	CHILD	RRAHZSUSA
KASMIRA	7	F	CHILD	RRAHZSUSA
THOMAS	25	M	LABR	RRAHZSUSA
ZUCKERMANN, SARA	21	F	SGL	RRZZZZUSA

SHIP: SPAIN

FROM: LIVERPOOL
TO: NEW YORK
ARRIVED: 30 DECEMBER 1885

PASSENGER	AGE	SEX	OCCUPATION	PRV VIL DES
FRISHBANE, SIMON	23	M	HTR	PLZZZZNY
BELENVUSS, SAM.	47	M	FARMER	RRZZZZNY
MEYER	11	M	CH	RRZZZZNY
LEIDENBERG, ABRAHAM	21	M	SHMK	PLZZZZNY
BUCK, BESSIE	25	F	SP	PLADBQNY
MACKS	1	M	CHILD	PLADBQNY
COHEN, REBECCA	20	F	SP	PLADBQNY

PASSENGER	AGE	SEX	OCCUPATION	PRIV	VIL	DES
KOLLAK, OF.	24	M	HTR	RR	ZZZZ	NY
LEBROVITZ, CH.	20	M	LABR	RR	ZZZZ	NY
BROVANER, BERL	19	M	LABR	PL	ZZZZ	NY
LIPMAN, JANKEL	22	M	SMH	PL	ZZZZ	NY
KAHN, LOUIS	24	M	SING	PL	ZZZZ	NY
SARA	20	F	W	PL	ZZZZ	NY
ALPERN, ARIE	52	M	SMH	RR	ZZZZ	NY
NURSHOBE, NESMON	20	M	WCHMKR	RR	ZZZZ	NY
LUBROMICHY, JOS.	20	M	LABR	PL	ZZZZ	NY
TEKLA	21	F	SP	PL	ZZZZ	NY
NAPTHAEL	18	M	LABR	PL	ZZZZ	NY
ANITOWSKY, JOS.	26	M	LABR	RR	ZZZZ	NY
URBAN, JAN	25	M	LABR	RR	ZZZZ	NY
YABLONSKY, JANKEL	25	M	LABR	RR	ZZZZ	NY

SHIP: INDIA

FROM: HAMBURG
TO: NEW YORK
ARRIVED: 31 DECEMBER 1885

PASSENGER	AGE	SEX	OCCUPATION	PRIV	VIL	DES
LACKOWSKI, BAS.	26	M	LABR	RR	ZZZZ	NY
NADOLNI, FRANZ	22	M	LABR	RR	ZZZZ	NY
FLOSSMANN, THERESE	20	F	SGL	RR	ZZZZ	IL
MOLOLETNIO, WOLF	18	M	LABR	RR	ZZZZ	NY
LEWANZYK, ANT.	20	M	LABR	RR	ZZZZ	NY
TYBURSKA, ELEONORE	30	F	WO	PL	ZZZZ	IL
JOSEPH	.10	M	INFANT	PL	ZZZZ	IL
GESCHWANDE, ANNA	36	F	WO	RR	ZZZZ	MO
COPOLD	8	M	CHILD	RR	ZZZZ	MO
HANCHEN	4	F	CHILD	RR	ZZZZ	MO
JEWEROWITZ, B.	22	M	MCHT	RR	ZZZZ	NY
KAISERKETISS, A.	27	M	LABR	RR	ZZZZ	NY
KNEIDLER, WILH.	21	M	BLKSMH	RR	ZZZZ	NY
TURMANNSKY, SCHL.	30	M	MLR	RR	ZZZZ	NY

SHIP: MARTHA

FROM: UNKNOWN
TO: NEW YORK
ARRIVED: 31 DECEMBER 1885

PASSENGER	AGE	SEX	OCCUPATION	PRIV	VIL	DES
LICHTENSTEIN, J.	35	M	TRDSMN	RR	ZZZZ	NY
SCHWARTZ, E.	18	M	TRDSMN	RR	ZZZZ	CH
GOLDSTEIN, MARCUS	35	M	JNR	RR	ZZZZ	NY
JOSEPH	6	M	CHILD	RR	ZZZZ	NY
BADOWSKI, JULIAN	18	M	SHMK	RR	ZZZZ	NY

SHIP: CITY OF CHESTER

FROM: LIVERPOOL AND QUEENSTOWN
TO: NEW YORK
ARRIVED: 02 JANUARY 1886

PASSENGER	AGE	SEX	OCCUPATION	PRIV	VIL	DES
LUSKAN, LEIB	18	M	LABR	RR	AHQH	BAL
JOSEFNATES, JOSEF	30	M	LABR	RR	AHQH	BAL
BARTKUS, JURGIS	26	M	LABR	RR	AHQH	NY
JEMS, PAUL	24	M	LABR	RR	AHQH	NY
RUBINOWITSCH, RUBIN	21	M	UNKNOWN	RR	AHQH	NY
RUBINSTEIN, RUBIN	41	M	UNKNOWN	RR	AHQH	NY
RUDELSKI, WOLF	24	M	LABR	RR	AHQH	NY
CERSKI, JANKEL	33	M	LABR	RR	AHQH	NY
SCHNEIDER, HERSCH	17	M	LABR	RR	AHQH	CH
HIRSCHOWITZ, DAVID	20	M	LABR	RR	AHQH	CH
ATLEFMANN, SAM.	17	M	LABR	RR	AHQH	CH
KOMTLUM, ITZIG	50	M	FARMER	PL	ZZZZ	CH
MILLER, M.	35	F	W	PL	ADBQ	PA

SHIP: RHEIN

FROM: HAVRE
TO: NEW YORK
ARRIVED: 02 JANUARY 1886

PASSENGER	AGE	SEX	OCCUPATION	PRIV	VIL	DES
ANTEU, CARL-JULIUS	30	M	MCHT	RR	ZZZZ	NY
PATENSON, LEON	17	M	LABR	RR	AHOK	NY
SCHMUL, SEBUL	32	M	PDLR	RR	ZZZZ	NY
BOBLOWSKI, SALOMON	28	M	PDLR	RR	ZZZZ	NY
SIEF, JOSSEL	20	M	PDLR	RR	ZZZZ	NY
FLEISIHMANN, FISCHL	42	M	LABR	RR	ZZZZ	NY
KAKTOCKSKY, WLADESKI	24	M	LABR	RR	ZZZZ	NY
POHUSKO, MAZE	20	M	LABR	RR	ZZZZ	NY
SENGERMANN, MOSES	30	M	LABR	RR	ZZZZ	NY
WOLFF, JOHANN	28	M	FARMER	RR	ACZG	NY
MARIA	27	F	W	RR	ACZG	NY
CHRISTINA	4	F	CHILD	RR	ACZG	NY
MARIA	3	F	CHILD	RR	ACZG	NY
WEPHART, JOHANN	22	M	FARMER	RR	ACZG	NY
CHRISTINE	20	F	W	RR	ACZG	NY
WAGNER, JOHANN	34	M	FARMER	RR	ACZG	NY
PAULINA	30	F	W	RR	ACZG	NY
MARIA	6	F	CHILD	RR	ACZG	NY
PAULINE	2	F	CHILD	RR	ACZG	NY
HALM, CATHARINE	65	F	M	RR	ACZG	NY
MULLER, PHILIPP	28	M	FARMER	RR	ZZZZ	NY
PAULINE	24	F	W	RR	ZZZZ	NY
SCHWAMM, ADAM	29	M	FARMER	RR	ZZZZ	NY
MAGDALENA	24	F	W	RR	ZZZZ	NY
ROSINA	18	F	SVNT	RR	ZZZZ	NY
GOTTFRIED	.09	M	INFANT	RR	ZZZZ	NY
BRAUN, MARCUS	9	M	CHILD	RR	ZZZZ	NY
MORITZ	5	M	CHILD	RR	ZZZZ	NY
ETEL	7	F	CHILD	RR	ZZZZ	NY
HERMANN	.11	M	INFANT	RR	ZZZZ	NY
SUHOSKI, FELIX	32	M	PDLR	RR	ZZZZ	UNK
ISEFATA	30	F	W	RR	ZZZZ	UNK
FRANZISKA	7	F	CHILD	RR	ZZZZ	UNK
MILIAN	5	M	CHILD	RR	ZZZZ	UNK
VERONIKA	2	F	CHILD	RR	ZZZZ	UNK
ANNA	.03	F	INFANT	RR	ZZZZ	UNK
MAUMIORT, JOSEF	40	M	LABR	RR	ZZZZ	NY
DAVID	7	M	CHILD	RR	ZZZZ	NY
LUBIK	6	M	CHILD	RR	ZZZZ	NY
PATENSON, MARIE	17	F	SVNT	RR	AHOK	NY
ETTENSON, LINA	20	F	SVNT	RR	AFWJ	NY
EHRLICH, CHAJE	52	F	W	RR	ZZZZ	NY

SHIP: STATE OF INDIANA

FROM: GLASGOW AND LARNE
TO: NEW YORK
ARRIVED: 02 JANUARY 1886

PASSENGER	AGE	SEX	OCCUPATION	PRIV	VIL	DES
HORELKOWITZ, NOHEM	60	F	PDLR	RR	ZZZZ	USA
CHANE	60	F	W	RR	ZZZZ	USA

PASSENGER	AGE	SEX	OCCUPATION	PRIV VIL DES
RAM, ISAAK	26	M	PDLR	RRAHTFUSA
KAMINCKI, SCHUMEN	34	M	PDLR	RRAHTUUSA
TOCHEN, CHONE	22	M	PDLR	RRZZZZUSA
AXELRAD, LEISER	23	M	PDLR	RRAHTUUSA
MARINICZ, RIGOWO	30	M	LABR	RRZZZZUSA
PITZULIS, JOSEF	20	M	LABR	RRZZZZUSA
JAKUBOWITZ, RIGOWO	40	M	LABR	RRZZZZUSA
SEGLIN, CHAIM	45	M	SPM	RRAHTFUSA
KIRSCHUER, CHATZKEL	37	M	LABR	RRACSDUSA
BORSUK, JOSEF	38	M	LABR	RRACBFUSA
STEINBERG, SOLOMON	27	M	PDLR	RRZZZZUSA
NEUMENJONSKY, BEREL	30	M	PDLR	RRAHTPUSA
GRAJWER, RIFKE	23	F	W	RRAHTUUSA
BEER	1	M	CHILD	RRAHTUUSA
JACHLES, CHANNE	50	F	W	RRAHTFUSA
CLARA	17	F	SP	RRAHTFUSA
MASCHE	10	F	CH	RRAHTFUSA
RAM, ROSA	18	F	SP	RRAHTFUSA
CHAJE	24	F	W	RRAHTFUSA
BENJAMIN	00	M	CH	RRAHTFUSA
SCHINWETTER, SCHENDEL	30	F	W	RRZZZZUSA
FEIGE	10	F	CH	RRZZZZUSA
BINE	2	F	CHILD	RRZZZZUSA
RIFKE	1	F	CHILD	RRZZZZUSA

SHIP: SWITZERLAND

FROM: ANTWERP
TO: NEW YORK
ARRIVED: 02 JANUARY 1886

PASSENGER	AGE	SEX	OCCUPATION	PRIV VIL DES
BELINSKY, C.	24	M	TRVLR	RRADBQNY
SMOLIK, MARIA	34	F	UNKNOWN	PLZZZZNY
WARIS, JAC.	41	M	CBTMKR	PLADBQNY

SHIP: BOHEMIA

FROM: HAMBURG
TO: NEW YORK
ARRIVED: 05 JANUARY 1886

PASSENGER	AGE	SEX	OCCUPATION	PRIV VIL DES
LIEM, MAX	36	M	MCHT	PLAHOOUSA
MARIE	36	F	W	PLAHOOUSA
VAN-DEN-DEHLE, ELISABET	24	F	SGL	PLAHOOUSA
VAN-DEN-DEHLE, CARL	13	M	BY	PLAHOOUSA
IANUTZKY, SALOMON	23	M	DLR	PLAHTFUSA
RIWKIN, CHAIE	20	F	SGL	PLAHVOUSA
RIWKE	15	F	SGL	PLAHVOUSA
BELNOSKY, SILVESTER	20	M	LABR	RRZZZZUSA
KELMANN, ARON	34	M	DLR	RRZZZZUSA
MAHARAM, HIRSCH	54	M	DLR	RRAHWEUSA
SZIZERBECH, CHAIM	17	M	LABR	RRZZZZUSA
KURLANCZIK, MEILACH	27	M	ENGR	RRAHTFUSA
BLOCH, SARAH	17	F	SGL	RRAHTFUSA
WEIMOVSKY, HIRSCH	55	M	TLR	RRAHRZUSA
SEGAL, ANNIE	20	F	SGL	RRAHTFUSA
NUSBAUM, JANKEL	25	M	DLR	RRAHZSUSA
MALINIAK, MISKO	24	M	LABR	RRAHZSUSA
JUSKO, ZIALA	9	M	CHILD	RRAHZSUSA
EISENBERG, CHIENNE	17	F	SGL	RRAHZSUSA
LINE	18	F	SGL	RRAHZSUSA

SHIP: CALIFORNIA

FROM: HAMBURG
TO: NEW YORK
ARRIVED: 05 JANUARY 1886

PASSENGER	AGE	SEX	OCCUPATION	PRIV VIL DES
SILBERSTEIN, SANDER	25	M	CL	PLZZZZNY
GAZOVER, FEIGE	48	F	WO	RRZZZZNY
HUDZE	21	F	WO	RRZZZZNY
SCHMUEL	7	M	CHILD	RRZZZZNY
DWOSKIN, SHEYE	17	M	TRDSMN	RRZZZZIL
JANKEL	49	M	TRDSMN	RRZZZZIL
FINKEL, DAVID	20	M	TLR	RRZZZZIA
BOWELSKA, EMMA	25	F	SGL	RRZZZZUNK
FINK, CHASKEL	26	M	TLR	RRZZZZNY
WEISMANN, MOSES	16	M	LABR	RRZZZZPA
GOLDBERG, ABRAHAM	20	M	TLR	RRZZZZPA
GOLDSTEIN, BERL	17	M	TLR	RRZZZZPA

SHIP: ENGLAND

FROM: LIVERPOOL
TO: NEW YORK
ARRIVED: 05 JANUARY 1886

PASSENGER	AGE	SEX	OCCUPATION	PRIV VIL DES
KASPER, NATHAN	25	M	GNMKR	RRADEDNY
KATILLOPER, ALEX	23	M	PDLR	PLZZZZNY
YONDEK, CHAN	35	F	W	PLZZZZNY
ABRAHAM	10	M	CH	PLZZZZNY
DWORE	4	F	CHILD	PLZZZZNY
FISCHEL	3	F	CHILD	PLZZZZNY
TISSE	2	F	CHILD	PLZZZZNY
POMERANIN, CHAGE	29	F	LABR	PLZZZZNY
LOVENSOHN, JANEY	50	F	W	PLADBQCH
JELIUS, ANNIE	40	F	W	PLADBQCH
FANY	17	F	SP	PLADBQCH
DEBORAH	11	F	CH	PLADBQCH
JACOB	7	M	CHILD	PLADBQCH
SARAH	4	F	CHILD	PLADBQCH
FLOREN	2	F	CHILD	PLADBQCH
ISAAC	00	M	INF	PLADBQCH
MAKOVE, MOSES	32	M	TLR	PLADBQNY
PRESDNER, PESAIT	48	M	TLR	RRZZZZNY
BERLOWIT, LE.	18	M	TLR	RRZZZZNY
GONSEN, ABRAHAM	50	M	PDLR	RRZZZZNY
HERSCHKOWIT, MOSES	40	M	TLR	RRZZZZNY
FRANK, JOSEL	15	M	PDLR	RRZZZZNY
HOCHSTERD, ABRAHAM	23	M	PDLR	RRADBQNY
JUTOWETZ, MOSES	20	M	PDLR	RRZZZZNY
GOLDBERG, CHAIM	36	M	LABR	RRZZZZNY
DAVISE, L.	21	F	W	RRADBQNY
CHARLES	2	M	CHILD	RRADBQNY
SALOMON, RACHEL	1	F	CHILD	RRADBQNY
REBECCA	28	F	W	RRADBQNY
LESSIE	11	M	CH	RRADBQNY
VAUL.	9	M	CHILD	RRADBQNY
DAVID	5	M	CHILD	RRADBQNY
SARAH	3	F	CHILD	RRADBQNY
FINKELSTEIN, SOLOMON	29	M	PDLR	RRZZZZBO

SHIP: GALLIA

FROM: LIVERPOOL AND QUEENSTOWN
TO: NEW YORK
ARRIVED: 05 JANUARY 1886

PASSENGER	AGE	SEX	OCCUPATION	PRIVILEGE	DES
SHURE, MAX	28	M	CL	RRADAX	USA
STANCOFF, FR.	27	M	LABR	RRZZZZ	USA
STOWOSKA, ANASTASIA	18	F	SP	PLZZZZ	USA
LANA, DINA	30	M	CPMKR	PLZZZZ	USA

SHIP: ABYSSINIA

FROM: LIVERPOOL
TO: NEW YORK
ARRIVED: 06 JANUARY 1886

PASSENGER	AGE	SEX	OCCUPATION	PRIVILEGE	DES
PESNAK, LEON	26	M	LABR	PLADAX	USA
BORGAILLA, JOHAN	35	M	LABR	PLADAX	USA
VAGLITA, MICHAEL	28	M	LABR	PLADAX	USA
BLATZKA, MICHAEL	28	M	LABR	PLADAX	USA

SHIP: AMERIQUE

FROM: HAVRE
TO: NEW YORK
ARRIVED: 06 JANUARY 1886

PASSENGER	AGE	SEX	OCCUPATION	PRIVILEGE	DES
NOVASSELSKI, U-MRS	19	F	UNKNOWN	RRZZZZ	USA

SHIP: EGYPTIAN MONARCH

FROM: GLASGOW
TO: NEW YORK
ARRIVED: 06 JANUARY 1886

PASSENGER	AGE	SEX	OCCUPATION	PRIVILEGE	DES
DAVIS, JACOB	22	M	SHMK	RRZZZZ	NY
WOLF, ARAK	29	M	BKR	RRZZZZ	NY
HYMAN, GODFREY	29	M	MACH	RRAAQH	NY
FRIEDMAN, JOSEPH	26	M	MACH	RRAAQH	NY
COHEN, DEBORAH	26	F	W	RRAAQH	NY
GUSTAV	23	M	TLR	RRAAQH	NY
ROSENDAL, M.	24	M	TLR	RRAAQH	PHI
MANDEL, PHILLIP	20	M	MACH	RRAAQH	NY
YOURMASH, ISAAC	21	M	TLR	RRAAQH	NY
GOLUSKIN, HENRY	20	M	TLR	RRAAQH	NY
MARKS, LASARUS	23	M	TLR	RRAAQH	NY

SHIP: PENNLAND

FROM: ANTWERP
TO: NEW YORK
ARRIVED: 06 JANUARY 1886

PASSENGER	AGE	SEX	OCCUPATION	PRIVILEGE	DES
DE-NAWAKOWSKI, H.	30	M	MCHT	RRAFWJ	NY

SHIP: WESER

FROM: HAVRE
TO: NEW YORK
ARRIVED: 06 JANUARY 1886

PASSENGER	AGE	SEX	OCCUPATION	PRIVILEGE	DES
ANZILEWITZ, DAVID	18	M	FARMER	RRZZZZ	USA
SZUSTAKONOSKA, MAGD.	33	F	NN	RRZZZZ	USA

SHIP: BRITANNIC

FROM: LIVERPOOL AND QUEENSTOWN
TO: NEW YORK
ARRIVED: 11 JANUARY 1886

PASSENGER	AGE	SEX	OCCUPATION	PRIVILEGE	DES
KEHRT, ARON	27	M	LABR	RRACBF	USA
BAHR.	25	M	LABR	RRACBF	USA
SCHELMETZSKY, MOSES	28	M	LABR	RRACBF	USA
BOCKERT, FRITZ	29	M	LABR	RRACBF	USA
EMILIE	27	F	W	RRACBF	USA
IRMA	.10	M	INFANT	RRACBF	USA
ANDREZEWSKY, ADAM	26	M	LABR	RRACBF	USA

SHIP: STATE OF NEVADA

FROM: GLASGOW AND LARNE
TO: NEW YORK
ARRIVED: 11 JANUARY 1886

PASSENGER	AGE	SEX	OCCUPATION	PRIVILEGE	DES
ELIASCHOWITZ, J.	53	M	LABR	RRZZZZ	USA
GORNOLESAK, M.	21	U	SVNT	RRZZZZ	USA
GIRDON, E.	33	U	PNTR	RRZZZZ	USA
MARZIN, KATH.	20	F	SVNT	RRZZZZ	USA
SUSMANN, S.	10	U	CH	RRZZZZ	USA
M.	8	U	CHILD	RRZZZZ	USA
ESHR.	5	U	CHILD	RRZZZZ	USA
G.	40	F	W	RRZZZZ	USA
SIMON, S.	23	U	SVNT	RRZZZZ	USA
SCHMUL, S.	22	M	PDLR	RRZZZZ	USA
JASTROW, ABR.	19	M	LABR	RRZZZZ	USA
---MERMAN, S.	22	U	UNKNOWN	RRZZZZ	USA
BURSTEIN, U	00	U	LABR	PLZZZZ	USA
BRYSINSKI, U	28	U	LABR	PLZZZZ	USA
FRIEMAN, M.	45	U	LABR	PLZZZZ	USA
GABELMAN, S.	46	M	PDLR	PLZZZZ	USA
SEIDEN, N.	32	U	LABR	PLZZZZ	USA

PASSENGER	AGE	SEX	OCCUPATION	PRIVL	DES

SHIP: AURANIA

FROM: LIVERPOOL AND QUEENSTOWN
TO: NEW YORK
ARRIVED: 12 JANUARY 1886

PASSENGER	AGE	SEX	OCCUPATION	PRIVL	DES
FINN, JUDAH	22	M	LABR	RRZZ	ZZUSA
SONDAY, MARK	27	M	LABR	RRZZ	ZZUSA
LEVY, ABRAHAM	22	M	LABR	RRZZ	ZZUSA
ZACHARIAS, ABRAHAM	24	M	LABR	RRZZ	ZZUSA
MATILONES, PARIN	21	M	LABR	RRZZ	ZZUSA
FALKOWITZ, SAML.	19	M	LABR	RRZZ	ZZUSA
BLOCH, ISRAEL	25	M	LABR	RRZZ	ZZUSA
MALAZMICY, KASMER	21	M	LABR	RRZZ	ZZUSA
CYASS, LAURENTI	26	M	LABR	RRZZ	ZZUSA
LASTOWSKI, ANTON	21	M	LABR	RRZZ	ZZUSA
KATILA, NILS	26	M	LABR	FNZZ	ZZUSA

SHIP: CANADA

FROM: HAVRE
TO: NEW YORK
ARRIVED: 14 JANUARY 1886

PASSENGER	AGE	SEX	OCCUPATION	PRIVL	DES
SOLINSKI, SALOMON	37	M	UNKNOWN	PLZZ	ZZNY

SHIP: ETHIOPIA

FROM: GLASGOW AND MOVILLE
TO: NEW YORK
ARRIVED: 14 JANUARY 1886

PASSENGER	AGE	SEX	OCCUPATION	PRIVL	DES
ENCHORN, MOSES	43	M	MCHT	RRZZ	ZZUSA
U, CHANE	70	M	MCHT	RRZZ	ZZUSA
GEDNANCKY, NOCHAN	23	M	PDLR	RRZZ	ZZUSA
SUSKISS, EBER	31	M	PDLR	RRZZ	ZZUSA
DORAWITZ, JANKEL	38	M	PDLR	RRZZ	ZZUSA
ALTMANN, BENJAMIN	27	M	PDLR	RRZZ	ZZUSA
RUDMAN, ISRAEL	35	M	PDLR	RRZZ	ZZUSA
GUDELSKY, ISRAEL	21	M	PDLR	RRZZ	ZZUSA
GITEL	20	M	PDLR	RRZZ	ZZUSA
SCHOCHET, LEIB	20	M	DLR	RRZZ	ZZUSA
GORDON, ITZIG	20	M	BKBNDR	RRZZ	ZZUSA
BUSCHEL, JUDA	23	M	TLR	RRZZ	ZZUSA
U, BUNE	18	M	TLR	RRZZ	ZZUSA
BUDWINCEZ, CHAMI	22	M	TLR	RRZZ	ZZUSA
BASHA, HEINRICH	20	M	SCP	RRZZ	ZZUSA
ALPERN, SCHOLEM	33	M	PDLR	RRZZ	ZZUSA
KATZ, ABRAHAM	43	M	DSTLR	RRZZ	ZZUSA
BERKOWITZ, CHANE	20	F	TLR	RRZZ	ZZUSA
MAZKUWICZ, ANTON	22	M	LABR	RRZZ	ZZUSA
ROHEF, ABRAHAM	30	M	MSN	RRZZ	ZZUSA
SELZER, BARACK	33	M	BRR	RRZZ	ZZUSA
FRIED, ISAAC	35	M	FARMER	RRZZ	ZZUSA
KURZHORN, SARAH-B.	21	F	UNKNOWN	RRZZ	ZZUSA
IROTZKI, SAMUEL	20	M	MCHT	RRZZ	ZZUSA

SHIP: LESSING

FROM: HAMBURG
TO: NEW YORK
ARRIVED: 14 JANUARY 1886

PASSENGER	AGE	SEX	OCCUPATION	PRIVL	DES
EKEHRIN, SARA	25	F	W	RRZZ	ZZUSA
WOLF	.11	M	INFANT	RRZZ	ZZUSA
QUINTY, JOSEPH	16	M	LABR	RRAG	RTUSA
FISCHKIN, SCHMUEL	38	M	LABR	RRZZ	ZZUSA
KAPLAN, RACHEL	18	F	SGL	RRZZ	ZZUSA
NATKIN, ARON	37	M	MCHT	RRAH	TRUSA
GRABER, ISAAC	18	M	LABR	RRAH	UYUSA
ADELSOHN, SCHAIE	70	M	DLR	RRAH	RZUSA
SILBERSOHN, RIWKE	18	F	SGL	RRAH	ZSUSA
DAVIDSOHN, ABEL	50	M	LABR	RRZZ	ZZUSA
FELMANN, MICHEL	19	M	LABR	RRZZ	ZZUSA
FLEISCHER, ELIAS	21	M	BCHR	RRZZ	ZZUSA
JAKUBOWSKI, ANIKI	20	M	LABR	RRAH	ZSUSA
OLSCHEWITZ, JACOB	19	M	JNR	RRZZ	ZZUSA
ROSENSTEIN, DAVID	28	M	TLR	RRZZ	ZZUSA
BANDELIN, MOSES	28	M	DLR	RRAH	TRUSA
SILBERMANN, SALOMON	66	M	DLR	RRAH	ZSUSA
MINNA	55	F	W	RRAH	ZSUSA
LINDENTHAL, ESTHER	36	F	W	RRZZ	ZZUSA
CHASCHE	9	F	CHILD	RRZZ	ZZUSA
CHASKEL	8	M	CHILD	RRZZ	ZZUSA
WOLF	7	M	CHILD	RRZZ	ZZUSA
SCHEINE	6	F	CHILD	RRZZ	ZZUSA
MALKE	4	F	CHILD	RRZZ	ZZUSA
CHANNE	.11	F	INFANT	RRZZ	ZZUSA
PATZ, MEIER	29	M	DLR	RRAH	TFUSA
POSTAWNIK, MERE	60	F	W	RRZZ	ZZUSA
PANOR, ARON	9	M	CHILD	RRZZ	ZZUSA
FREIDE	8	F	CHILD	RRZZ	ZZUSA
SEIDENBERG, CHAIM	9	M	CHILD	RRZZ	ZZUSA
RUDERMANN, ISRAEL	27	M	TLR	RRZZ	ZZUSA
ITZIG	34	M	TLR	RRZZ	ZZUSA
SEPOWICZ, JUDE	50	M	LABR	RRAG	RTUSA
CHAWKE	19	M	CH	RRAG	RTUSA
JACKE	8	M	CHILD	RRAG	RTUSA
ITE	6	F	CHILD	RRAG	RTUSA
FISCHBEIN, RACHEL	22	F	SGL	RRZZ	ZZUSA
ALESZKEWITZ, DAVID	31	M	DLR	RRZZ	ZZUSA
CHUDA, AGNES	28	F	SGL	RRZZ	ZZUSA
TOSMANN, SIMCHE	22	M	MCHT	RRAH	TUUSA

SHIP: RHYNLAND

FROM: ANTWERP
TO: NEW YORK
ARRIVED: 15 JANUARY 1886

PASSENGER	AGE	SEX	OCCUPATION	PRIVL	DES
ANDERS, CHRISTIAN	40	M	SHMK	RRAE	FLUNK
KATHA.	40	F	UNKNOWN	RRAE	FLUNK
PETER	21	M	SHMK	RRAE	FLUNK
ELISA	13	F	CH	RRAE	FLUNK
CAROLINA	5	F	CHILD	RRAE	FLUNK
LYDIA	3	F	CHILD	RRAE	FLUNK
SCHLEY, WLADISLAUS	21	M	SMH	RRZZ	ZZNY

PASSENGER	AGE	SEX	OCCUPATION	PRV	VIL	DES

SHIP: CITY OF RICHMOND

FROM: LIVERPOOL
TO: NEW YORK
ARRIVED: 16 JANUARY 1886

PASSENGER	AGE	SEX	OCCUPATION	PV RI VL	DES
MAJOV, J.	26	M	LABR	PLZZZZ	USA
WENTZORNEV, J.	22	M	LABR	PLZZZZ	USA
EDELMANN, DAVID	19	M	LABR	PLAHTU	USA
MANEKOWSKI, ISRAEL	22	M	LABR	PLAHTU	USA
NOEL, ABRAM	34	M	LABR	PLAHTU	USA
KRASAYNSKI, JAN	22	M	LABR	PLAHTU	USA
BREITMANN, LEVY	22	M	LABR	PLAHTU	USA
BRODEI, JACOB	22	M	LABR	PLAHTU	USA

SHIP: NECKAR

FROM: BREMEN
TO: NEW YORK
ARRIVED: 16 JANUARY 1886

PASSENGER	AGE	SEX	OCCUPATION	PV RI VL	DES
LONDON, SARAH	40	F	SVNT	RRZZZZ	NY
LASKOWETZ, ESTER	30	F	UNKNOWN	RRZZZZ	NY
ELIAS	7	M	CHILD	RRZZZZ	NY
ETTEL	5	M	CHILD	RRZZZZ	NY
WEINBERGER, LOUIS	18	M	LABR	RRZZZZ	NY
GARMEISE, HIRSCH	17	M	LABR	RRZZZZ	NY
SCHWIMMER, LEIB	22	M	FARMER	RRZZZZ	NY
STEIN, JAKOB	15	M	FARMER	RRZZZZ	NY
SCHNEIDER, JOSEF	30	M	FARMER	RRZZZZ	NY
DUCHMANN, FICHE	22	M	FARMER	RRZZZZ	NY
KETOWITZ, JOSEF	33	M	FARMER	RRZZZZ	NY
LENIATOWA, MEJER	29	M	SMH	RRZZZZ	NY

SHIP: OREGON

FROM: LIVERPOOL AND QUEENSTOWN
TO: NEW YORK
ARRIVED: 18 JANUARY 1886

PASSENGER	AGE	SEX	OCCUPATION	PV RI VL	DES
PERSKI, ISAK	35	M	FLABR	RRZZZZ	NY
WEINS, FRIDA	26	F	MA	RRZZZZ	NY
D.	2	M	CHILD	RRZZZZ	NY
PYE, SAUL-MOSES	23	M	INMNGR	RRZZZZ	NY
PINKUS, RICHARD	20	M	TRVLR	RRZZZZ	RSS
BLOCK, RAFAEL	24	M	LABR	RRZZZZ	NY
ASCHOZOWITZ, MOSES	27	M	LABR	RRZZZZ	NY
SCHRERMANN, MARDOKE	48	M	FLABR	RRZZZZ	NY
KOHM, JOSEF	45	M	LABR	RRZZZZ	BAL
SWEK, LIEB	42	M	FLABR	RRZZZZ	NY
HELLMANN, PETER	19	M	UNKNOWN	RRZZZZ	NY
SEICHES, SAMUEL	11	M	CH	RRZZZZ	NY
AOMIVITYKI, JULIUS	23	M	FLABR	RRZZZZ	NY
GLORIA, HOSEA	38	M	LABR	RRZZZZ	NY
LAPALATSKY, LESSER	20	M	LABR	RRZZZZ	BO
HARISKY, WOLF	19	M	LABR	RRZZZZ	NY
GARTINKER, BENJAMIN	16	M	LABR	RRZZZZ	NY
MULLER, CONSTANTIN	33	M	HTR	RRZZZZ	BO
KUSCHILEWSKY, LIEB	22	M	LABR	RRZZZZ	NY
HACHMANN	10	M	CH	RRZZZZ	NY
CHROST, BENJAMIN	28	M	LABR	RRZZZZ	NY
ABELSON, SAPIR	21	M	LABR	RRZZZZ	CH
JOSEY, ISRAEL	28	M	FLABR	RRZZZZ	CH
LAHAL, ISAK	22	M	LABR	RRZZZZ	CH
DORTMANN, ELIAS	36	M	LABR	RRZZZZ	NY
KALB, DAVID	29	M	LABR	PLZZZZ	NY
WEISER, GERMANN	24	M	LABR	PLZZZZ	NY
LIPSCHITZ, MENDEL	25	M	LABR	PLZZZZ	NY
FORDONSKI, BARUCH	40	M	TLR	PLZZZZ	NY
HENCKEL, MORRIS	20	M	MARWKR	PLZZZZ	CH
BROWN, ADELE	43	M	LABR	PLZZZZ	NY
IABER, JACOB	20	M	LABR	PLZZZZ	NY
SALTSMANN, SALMEN	24	M	FLABR	PLZZZZ	NY
KARPERTEG, ADALBERT	20	M	LABR	PLZZZZ	BO
GETGER, MOSES	24	M	LABR	PLZZZZ	NY
PELLER, LEON	23	M	LABR	PLZZZZ	NY
REBECCA	18	F	W	PLZZZZ	NY

SHIP: RUGIA

FROM: HAMBURG
TO: NEW YORK
ARRIVED: 19 JANUARY 1886

PASSENGER	AGE	SEX	OCCUPATION	PV RI VL	DES
SALWEITZIG, LEIB	25	M	LABR	RRZZZZ	USA
KOHN, ABRAH.	23	M	MCHT	RRZZZZ	USA
KASAWA, ADAM	33	M	LABR	RRZZZZ	USA
KAPUL, SCHMEREL	21	M	LABR	RRZZZZ	USA
LOKSCHEWITZ, B.	20	M	MCHT	RRZZZZ	USA
POLIVODY, LEIB	36	M	DLR	RRZZZZ	USA
SLOTE, ZIRE	23	F	SGL	RRZZZZ	USA
HERM.	35	M	TLR	RRZZZZ	USA
KRASKY, LEISER	26	M	DLR	RRZZZZ	USA
WEISSBART, BER.	65	M	DLR	RRZZZZ	USA
BUCHMANN, ISAAC	17	M	GLMK	RRZZZZ	USA
FREIMARK, TAUBE	25	F	W	RRZZZZ	USA
FREIDE	6	F	CHILD	RRZZZZ	USA
KEILE	.11	F	INFANT	RRZZZZ	USA
ITE	.11	F	INFANT	RRZZZZ	USA
BALTROSCHANK, JOSEF	26	M	DLR	RRZZZZ	USA

SHIP: LABRADOR

FROM: HAVRE
TO: NEW YORK
ARRIVED: 20 JANUARY 1886

PASSENGER	AGE	SEX	OCCUPATION	PV RI VL	DES
LUCKZICKI, LADISLAS-MR	30	M	UNKNOWN	RRZZZZ	USA
CARLONE, ANATOLIO	26	M	NN	RRZZZZ	USA

SHIP: BALTIC

FROM: LIVERPOOL AND QUEENSTOWN
TO: NEW YORK
ARRIVED: 23 JANUARY 1886

PASSENGER	AGE	SEX	OCCUPATION	PV RI VL	DES
FORSMAN, EDW.	20	M	LABR	RRZZZZ	USA
WIESNEUSKA, BARBARA	44	F	W	RRAGRT	USA
NARA-ANNA	9	F	CHILD	RRAGRT	USA
STANISLAUS	3	M	CHILD	RRAGRT	USA
ARANSKI, BESSIE	30	F	W	RRAGRT	USA
ANN	.08	F	INFANT	RRAGRT	USA

PASSENGER	AGE	SEX	OCCUPATION	PRIVL	DES

SHIP: EMS

FROM: BREMEN
TO: NEW YORK
ARRIVED: 23 JANUARY 1886

PASSENGER	AGE	SEX	OCCUPATION	PRIVL	DES
OSCHSNER, JOHANN	29	M	FARMER	RRAFQVUSA	
NISSEN, FRANZ	41	M	FARMER	RRABPSUSA	
MARIA	20	F	NN	RRABPSUSA	
FRANZ	17	M	FARMER	RRABPSUSA	
JOHANN	13	M	NN	RRABPSUSA	
JACOB	14	M	NN	RRABPSUSA	
HELENE	10	F	NN	RRABPSUSA	
PETER	8	M	CHILD	RRABPSUSA	
ELISABETH	10	F	NN	RRABPSUSA	
CATHARINA	6	F	CHILD	RRABPSUSA	
ANNA	4	F	CHILD	RRABPSUSA	
KINDSWATER, JOH.	33	M	TLR	RRAFWJUSA	
AYLIS	33	F	NN	RRAFWJUSA	
CONRAD	7	M	CHILD	RRAFWJUSA	
STOLOZINSKI, FRANZ	22	M	FARMER	RRAFWJUSA	
PODOLSKY, WOLF	34	M	LABR	RRAEFLUSA	
BURRUSS, HERRE	13	M	NN	RRAFWJUSA	
SAMUILL	8	M	CHILD	RRAFWJUSA	
WASSERKRUG, JAKEL	24	M	LABR	RRAFWJUSA	
ESTHER	21	F	NN	RRAFWJUSA	
HERSCH	.11	M	INFANT	RRAFWJUSA	
GUT, DAVID	30	M	LABR	RRZZZZUSA	
SCHREIBER, MICHAEL	31	M	LABR	RRZZZZUSA	
ROSA	26	F	NN	RRZZZZUSA	

SHIP: ST. OF PENNSYLVANIA

FROM: GLASGOW AND LARNE
TO: NEW YORK
ARRIVED: 23 JANUARY 1886

PASSENGER	AGE	SEX	OCCUPATION	PRIVL	DES
ABELSOHN, ITZIG	26	M	MCHT	RRZZZZUSA	
ABRAMOWITZ, JOSEEL	44	M	MCHT	RRZZZZUSA	
ALKEROWITZ, BARUCH	25	M	MCHT	RRZZZZUSA	
BERNSTEIN, CHAIE	30	F	W	RRZZZZUSA	
ABRAHAM	2	M	CHILD	RRZZZZUSA	
CHAIT, NOAH	56	M	MCHT	RRZZZZUSA	
CHAIFETZ, LEIB	23	M	MCHT	RRZZZZUSA	
DIMSKY, HIRSCH	50	M	MCHT	RRZZZZUSA	
MOSES	26	M	MCHT	RRZZZZUSA	
EYTIES, LEIB	52	M	LABR	RRACBFUSA	
FRIEDMANN, GOLDE	22	F	SVNT	RRZZZZUSA	
GELBERT, CHASKEL	35	M	MCHT	RRZZZZUSA	
LEJA	11	F	SVNT	RRZZZZUSA	
GESCHENSTEIN, JOEL	18	M	MCHT	RRZZZZUSA	
GRUSCHKE, LEIB	18	M	MCHT	RRACBFUSA	
HAAKE, SARAH	46	F	W	RRZZZZUSA	
LILLA	17	F	NN	RRZZZZUSA	
ANNE	10	F	NN	RRZZZZUSA	
JETTE	7	F	CHILD	RRZZZZUSA	
PICHS	.01	M	INFANT	RRZZZZUSA	
JUDKOWSKY, SIMON	00	M	MCHT	RRZZZZUSA	
KAHN, PEISACH	53	M	MCHT	RRZZZZUSA	
KAPLAN, JACOB	23	M	JNR	RRZZZZUSA	
LERNER, ELIAR	22	M	LABR	RRACBFUSA	
LYN, MALIE	47	F	NN	RRAHVUUSA	
MALZER, RACHMIEL	24	M	MCHT	RRZZZZUSA	
NAGUZ, MARCUS	22	M	MCHT	RRAHUFUSA	
ORZECH, ISRAEL	23	M	MCHT	RRZZZZUSA	
PETROWSKA, JOSEF	30	M	LABR	RRZZZZUSA	
PFLANMENBAUM, SCHMUEL	32	M	MCHT	RRACSDUSA	
BERTHA	23	F	W	RRACSDUSA	
MARTHA	3	F	CHILD	RRACSDUSA	
SALOMON	2	M	CHILD	RRACSDUSA	
ISIDOR	.07	M	INFANT	RRACSDUSA	
PIKUS, ABRAH.	28	M	MCHT	RRZZZZUSA	
RESOLOWSKY, JOSEF	58	M	SHMK	RRAHTOUSA	
ROSENBLATH, MEYER	43	M	SHMK	RRZZZZUSA	
SCHACHNOWITZ, CHAIM	26	M	MCHT	RRZZZZUSA	
SCHAPIRO, DOROTHEA	23	F	W	RRZZZZUSA	
JOSEF	3	M	CHILD	RRZZZZUSA	
MAX	.02	M	INFANT	RRZZZZUSA	
SCHNIDER, A.	22	M	JNR	RRACBFUSA	
ISIDOR	.06	M	INFANT	RRACBFUSA	
SCHUR, DAVID	35	M	SHMK	RRZZZZUSA	
BLUME	33	F	W	RRZZZZUSA	
SUCHER	8	M	CHILD	RRZZZZUSA	
SELDE	3	F	CHILD	RRZZZZUSA	
SELZER, BEER	30	M	MCHT	RRAGRTUSA	
TORBMAN, DAVID	24	M	MCHT	RRZZZZUSA	
ZILEWSKI, ABRAHAM	30	M	MCHT	RRZZZZUSA	
ZILEWITZ, GEISCHE	21	F	W	RRZZZZUSA	
SARAH	.03	F	INFANT	RRZZZZUSA	

SHIP: RHAETIA

FROM: HAMBURG
TO: NEW YORK
ARRIVED: 27 JANUARY 1886

PASSENGER	AGE	SEX	OCCUPATION	PRIVL	DES
LESCHEN, LOEB	13	M	BY	RRZZZZUSA	
RACHEL	19	F	SGL	RRZZZZUSA	
VOLGEN, LEA	18	F	SGL	RRZZZZUSA	
FISCHELOWITZ, ARON	19	M	DLR	RRZZZZUSA	
BULKEWITSCH, MARIANE	18	F	SGL	RRZZZZUSA	
STEINBERG, SARA	20	F	SGL	RRZZZZUSA	
KADESCHEWITZ, ISRAEL	20	M	DLR	RRZZZZUSA	
MIELLER, BEREL	23	M	DLR	RRZZZZUSA	
ALPER, SALOMON	34	M	MCHT	RRZZZZUSA	
BOGIN, CHASCHE	18	F	SGL	RRZZZZUSA	
ZYDKY, MODKY	29	M	DLR	RRZZZZUSA	
FISCHMANN, HIRSCH	18	M	DLR	RRZZZZUSA	
HILLEWITZ, JOSEF	60	M	LABR	RRZZZZUSA	
PALE, MOSES	19	M	SHMK	RRZZZZUSA	
KREMER, LEIB	28	M	DLR	RRZZZZUSA	
SCHAPIRO, ABRAHAM	23	M	DLR	RRZZZZUSA	
MENZINSKI, SELIG	19	M	DLR	RRZZZZUSA	
TAUB, ARON	45	M	DLR	RRZZZZUSA	
RAPPEPORT, LEA	20	F	SGL	RRZZZZUSA	
WOLPERT, URIAS	35	M	DLR	RRZZZZUSA	
KAPELOW, FEIGE	24	M	LABR	RRZZZZUSA	
STRAZUNSKI, JACOB	25	M	UNKNOWN	RRZZZZUSA	
MARIE	22	F	W	RRZZZZUSA	
HERZ	1	M	CHILD	RRZZZZUSA	
ERNESTINE	.06	F	INFANT	RRZZZZUSA	
BRECKSTEIN, SARA	25	F	SGL	RRZZZZUSA	
KUBITZKI, LEON	17	M	LABR	RRZZZZUSA	
TRAINOWSKY, JOSSEL	33	M	DLR	RRZZZZUSA	
MULLBERG, MOSES	19	M	TLR	RRZZZZUSA	
KANELL, MOSES	26	M	LABR	RRZZZZUSA	
OLENDERSKY, CHAZKEL	27	M	LABR	RRZZZZUSA	
DWARKOWSKY, RAPHAEL	30	M	LABR	RRZZZZUSA	
KUNTSCHIK, BENJAMIN	23	M	LABR	RRZZZZUSA	
SCHLOME	18	M	LABR	RRZZZZUSA	
ECKMANN, SAMUEL	17	M	MCHT	RRZZZZUSA	
WERSCHINOWSKI, JACOB	29	M	DLR	RRZZZZUSA	

PASSENGER	AGE	SEX	OCCUPATION	PRIV	VIL	DES

SHIP: POLYNESIA

FROM: HAMBURG
TO: NEW YORK
ARRIVED: 28 JANUARY 1886

PASSENGER	AGE	SEX	OCCUPATION	PRIV	VIL	DES
FRIEDMANN, SAMUEL	18	M	CL	RR	ZZZZ	NY
ROSENBERG, LINA	18	F	SGL	RR	ZZZZ	NY
MARIA	20	F	SGL	RR	ZZZZ	NY
SCHORR, JUDA	22	M	TDR	RR	ZZZZ	NY
MOGOWITZKI, MOPP	25	M	TDR	RR	ZZZZ	NY
SOLOWEJEZIK, BER.	20	M	TDR	RR	ZZZZ	NY
FRANKEL, MOPP.	24	M	TDR	RR	ZZZZ	NY
STEG, M.	22	F	SGL	RR	ZZZZ	NY
GITE	19	F	SGL	RR	ZZZZ	NY
KRAMM, LEA	36	F	LABR	RR	ZZZZ	NY
CHAIE	12	F	D	RR	ZZZZ	NY
MALKE	7	F	CHILD	RR	ZZZZ	NY
LEISER	6	M	CHILD	RR	ZZZZ	NY
URI	6	F	CHILD	RR	ZZZZ	NY
ISAK	3	M	CHILD	RR	ZZZZ	NY
MAR.	.10	M	INFANT	RR	ZZZZ	NY
KOHN, MARCUS	00	M	BBR	RR	ZZZZ	NY
REBECCA	23	F	SI	RR	ZZZZ	NY
FRIEDMANN, P.	22	F	WO	RR	ZZZZ	NY
I.	.06	M	INFANT	RR	ZZZZ	NY
MARKUS, JUDEL	16	M	LABR	RR	ZZZZ	UNK
DEU, CHAN	30	F	WO	RR	ZZZZ	CH
RIVKIN, BACHELA	37	F	WO	RR	ZZZZ	NY
REUSCHMANSKY, H.	37	F	WO	RR	ZZZZ	NY
SAMUEL	7	M	CHILD	RR	ZZZZ	NY
JOUSS.	6	F	CHILD	RR	ZZZZ	NY
DWORE	.05	F	INFANT	RR	ZZZZ	NY
HEVES, BARB.	19	F	SGL	RR	ZZZZ	NY
CZEMBALMOS, MARIA	20	F	SGL	RR	ZZZZ	NY
JAFFA, N.	21	M	MCHT	RR	ZZZZ	CH
PLUTACH, CATH.	22	F	SGL	RR	ZZZZ	UNK

SHIP: STATE OF NEBRASKA

FROM: GLASGOW AND LARNE
TO: NEW YORK
ARRIVED: 28 JANUARY 1886

PASSENGER	AGE	SEX	OCCUPATION	PRIV	VIL	DES
ROSENBERG, FAWEISCH	42	M	JWLR	RR	ZZZZ	NY
BERNSTEIN, SELIG	27	M	SHMK	RR	ZZZZ	NY
KADSCHOWITZ, WAR.	28	F	W	RR	ZZZZ	NY
FEIGE	.11	F	INFANT	RR	ZZZZ	NY
KUKISCH, MORDCHE	40	M	PDLR	RR	ZZZZ	NY
GLASER, SCHMUEL	20	M	TLR	RR	ZZZZ	NY
LEWIN, SCHINEN	16	M	LABR	RR	ZZZZ	NY
SCHOBALT, HERZ	25	M	LABR	RR	ZZZZ	NY
FISCHER, RUBIN	21	M	FARMER	RR	ZZZZ	NY
KOWALSKI, WLADISLAW	20	M	TLR	RR	ZZZZ	NY
MARIA	20	F	W	RR	ZZZZ	NY
HUDZE, FEIGE	21	F	SVNT	RR	ZZZZ	NY
LEMDIN, ANDR.	00	M	MCHT	RR	ZZZZ	NY
KORALLISCHAK, JACOB	48	M	MCHT	RR	ZZZZ	NY
CZARA---, U	00	F	UNKNOWN	RR	ZZZZ	NY

SHIP: BELGENLAND

FROM: ANTWERP
TO: NEW YORK
ARRIVED: 29 JANUARY 1886

PASSENGER	AGE	SEX	OCCUPATION	PRIV	VIL	DES
RABAGDEK, M.	60	F	SVNT	PL	ZZZZ	NY
WALLACHOWSKI, H.	24	F	CK	PL	ADBQ	NY
COHEN, JOS.	24	F	LABR	PL	ADBQ	NY
CROOK, PHIL.	22	F	TLR	PL	ADBQ	NY

SHIP: MAIN

FROM: BREMEN
TO: NEW YORK
ARRIVED: 29 JANUARY 1886

PASSENGER	AGE	SEX	OCCUPATION	PRIV	VIL	DES
ARANOWITZ, FEIGE	28	F	W	RR	ZZZZ	USA
HIRSCH	3	M	CHILD	RR	ZZZZ	USA
DWORE	.09	F	INFANT	RR	ZZZZ	USA
WODELEWSKI, MARIA	26	F	W	RR	ZZZZ	USA
JOSEF	3	M	CHILD	RR	ZZZZ	USA
MARIA	.09	F	INFANT	RR	ZZZZ	USA

SHIP: ASSYRIAN MONARCH

FROM: LONDON
TO: NEW YORK
ARRIVED: 30 JANUARY 1886

PASSENGER	AGE	SEX	OCCUPATION	PRIV	VIL	DES
GEINSTANSKY, REBECCA	22	F	W	RR	ZZZZ	NY
JOSEPH	.06	M	INFANT	RR	ZZZZ	NY
--HEN, RAPHAEL	21	M	PK	RR	ZZZZ	NY
JAFFE, JULIUS	29	M	CRR	RR	ZZZZ	NY
KRIENDEL	26	F	W	RR	ZZZZ	NY
FANNY	.06	F	INFANT	RR	ZZZZ	NY
LENDER, SHEINE	33	F	W	RR	ZZZZ	NY
LOUISA	9	F	CHILD	RR	ZZZZ	NY
JOSEPH	7	M	CHILD	RR	ZZZZ	NY
ANNETTA	5	F	CHILD	RR	ZZZZ	NY
AARON	2	M	CHILD	RR	ZZZZ	NY
ALEXANDER	.06	M	INFANT	RR	ZZZZ	NY
GLOYOWSKY, LEAH	30	F	W	RR	ZZZZ	NY
RACHAEL	9	F	CHILD	RR	ZZZZ	NY
JUDAH	7	F	CHILD	RR	ZZZZ	NY
BUNIA	2	F	CHILD	RR	ZZZZ	NY
SERECHOWSKY, ROSE	38	F	W	RR	ZZZZ	NY
SCHMAZA	7	F	CHILD	RR	ZZZZ	NY
BENJAMIN	2	M	CHILD	RR	ZZZZ	NY
HIRSCHOWITZ, SALOMON	26	M	TLR	RR	ZZZZ	NY
FANNY	25	F	W	RR	ZZZZ	NY
GOLDE	2	F	CHILD	RR	ZZZZ	NY
REBECCA	.06	F	INFANT	RR	ZZZZ	NY

SHIP: CITY OF BERLIN

FROM: LIVERPOOL AND QUEENSTOWN
TO: NEW YORK
ARRIVED: 30 JANUARY 1886

PASSENGER	AGE	SEX	OCCUPATION	PRIV	VIL	DES
PAPWISKA, MARY-IAUR	14	F	SVNT	RR	ADAX	NY
KOPAS, GEORGE	39	M	LABR	RR	ADAX	NY
KUZMITZ, PAUL	30	M	LABR	RR	ADAX	NY
LYZYNSKI, JAN	16	M	LABR	RR	ADAX	NY
ROGAS, CONSTANTIN	36	M	LABR	RR	ACBF	NY
KUZMITZ, MITRO	40	M	LABR	RR	ACBF	PA
NALENTY, MICOLAY	33	M	LABR	RR	ACBF	PA
MITRAH, AFTAN	11	M	CH	RR	ACBF	PA

SHIP: EIDER

FROM: BREMEN
TO: NEW YORK
ARRIVED: 30 JANUARY 1886

PASSENGER	AGE	SEX	OCCUPATION	PRIV	VIL	DES
IPP, ISAAC	18	M	BLKSMH	RR	ZZZZ	USA
BUCHHALTER, OSCAR	25	M	BKBNDR	RR	ZZZZ	USA
JULIUS	14	M	NN	RR	ZZZZ	USA
PISZKOWSKA, LUDWIGA	40	F	W	RR	ZZZZ	USA
STEFANI	17	F	NN	RR	ZZZZ	USA
KRAUSE, SAMUEL	46	M	FARMER	RR	ZZZZ	USA
BEATE	44	F	W	RR	ZZZZ	USA
BEATE	23	F	NN	RR	ZZZZ	USA
GOTTLIEB	21	M	FARMER	RR	ZZZZ	USA
MICHAEL	14	M	NN	RR	ZZZZ	USA
JULIANE	10	F	CH	RR	ZZZZ	USA
ROSINE	8	F	CHILD	RR	ZZZZ	USA
SAMUEL	6	M	CHILD	RR	ZZZZ	USA
MARTHA	.10	F	INFANT	RR	ZZZZ	USA

SHIP: CELTIC

FROM: LIVERPOOL AND QUEENSTOWN
TO: NEW YORK
ARRIVED: 01 FEBRUARY 1886

PASSENGER	AGE	SEX	OCCUPATION	PRIV	VIL	DES
KATZ, SAMUEL	20	M	LABR	RR	ACBF	USA
BEINER, SAUL	25	M	LABR	RR	ACBF	USA
LEHMANN, AUGUST	27	M	LABR	RR	ACBF	USA
MARIA	27	F	W	RR	ACBF	USA
BANETS, ANDIE	29	M	LABR	RR	ACBF	USA
ROOZOKO, MAKAL	28	M	LABR	RR	ACBF	USA
AISCHITZ, NIKOLAI	27	M	LABR	RR	ACBF	USA
KUCHTA, JITSHKO	29	M	LABR	RR	ACBF	USA
KEMARIZTZ, WASIL	31	M	LABR	RR	ACBF	USA
LEBREMSEHI, STEFAN	26	M	LABR	RR	ACBF	USA
WANAZSARE, FRANC	27	M	LABR	RR	ACBF	USA
KUSCHAISKIT, HJERONING	22	M	LABR	RR	ACBF	USA
RUTZKI, BERIL	24	M	LABR	RR	ACBF	USA
ROSKEVITZ, ANDREAS	23	M	LABR	RR	ACBF	USA
BLOHIM, FRIEDERICH	29	M	LABR	RR	ACBF	USA
MARPE, CARL	30	M	LABR	RR	ACBF	USA

SHIP: EGYPT

FROM: LIVERPOOL
TO: NEW YORK
ARRIVED: 01 FEBRUARY 1886

PASSENGER	AGE	SEX	OCCUPATION	PRIV	VIL	DES
GOLDIN, J.	20	M	LABR	RR	ZZZZ	USA
BERSKER, ARON	23	M	LABR	RR	ZZZZ	USA
HASER, S.	33	M	LABR	RR	ZZZZ	USA
KAKONSKY, ABR.	24	M	LABR	RR	ZZZZ	USA
PILEWSKY, CHON	21	M	LABR	RR	ZZZZ	USA
APPELBAUM, L.	16	M	LABR	RR	ZZZZ	USA
GUBITZKY, S.	42	M	LABR	RR	ZZZZ	USA
SERAYSKY, BRUNO	21	M	LABR	RR	ZZZZ	USA
RUKTER, H.	36	M	LABR	RR	ZZZZ	USA
MILLNER, M.	26	M	LABR	RR	ZZZZ	USA
GOLD, MEYER	25	M	LABR	RR	ZZZZ	USA
BARON, B.	45	M	LABR	RR	ZZZZ	USA
ARNDS, W.	31	M	LABR	RR	ZZZZ	USA
HARLEGRAF, ALBERT	32	M	LABR	RR	ZZZZ	USA
WILLNIK, C.	28	M	LABR	RR	ZZZZ	USA
RITKOWSKY, A.	31	M	LABR	RR	ZZZZ	USA
SURNAN, MOSES	48	M	LABR	RR	ZZZZ	USA
PATVINSEN, MOSES	37	M	LABR	RR	ZZZZ	USA
SCHIFF, HAIG	46	M	LABR	RR	ZZZZ	USA
POSTESSIK, J.	26	M	LABR	RR	ZZZZ	USA
MELLER, S.	29	M	LABR	RR	ZZZZ	USA
SAVOSKI, JOSEPH	44	M	LABR	RR	ZZZZ	USA
MULLER, S.	36	M	LABR	RR	ZZZZ	USA
KOERSKY, ELIAS	21	M	LABR	RR	ZZZZ	USA
MOSES, J.	31	M	LABR	RR	ZZZZ	USA
BERSIG, C.	16	M	LABR	RR	ZZZZ	USA
POLLINNY, S.	24	M	LABR	RR	ZZZZ	USA
ROENTTAL, ABRAHAM	30	M	LABR	RR	ZZZZ	USA
LEIBOWITZ, ANNI	18	M	LABR	RR	ZZZZ	USA
PETTERSEN, LILLIE	23	M	LABR	RR	ZZZZ	USA
LARSON, LAIS	39	M	LABR	RR	ZZZZ	USA
GELTLER, JOHAN	11	M	CH	RR	ZZZZ	USA
ANN	9	F	CHILD	RR	ZZZZ	USA
KRONNAN, C.	28	M	LABR	RR	ZZZZ	USA
C.	10	M	CH	RR	ZZZZ	USA
PAVEL	8	M	CHILD	RR	ZZZZ	USA
ZETTEL, RACHEL	30	F	SP	RR	ZZZZ	USA
KLUGE, MINA	32	F	SP	RR	ZZZZ	USA
LEWITZKY, PAWRUSHA	21	M	LABR	RR	ZZZZ	USA
LARSON, JACOB	40	M	LABR	RR	ZZZZ	USA
NILS	28	M	LABR	RR	ZZZZ	USA

SHIP: GALLIA

FROM: LIVERPOOL AND QUEENSTOWN
TO: NEW YORK
ARRIVED: 02 FEBRUARY 1886

PASSENGER	AGE	SEX	OCCUPATION	PRIV	VIL	DES
MALAMUD, ISAAC	21	M	LABR	RR	ZZZZ	USA
RIFKA	18	F	W	RR	ZZZZ	USA
KRIKAUT, ANNA	44	F	MA	PL	ZZZZ	USA
BUTHA	10	F	CH	PL	ZZZZ	USA
ROBINSON, SAN.	35	M	TLR	PL	ZZZZ	USA

SHIP: ST GERMAIN

FROM: HAVRE
TO: NEW YORK
ARRIVED: 02 FEBRUARY 1886

PASSENGER	AGE	SEX	OCCUPATION	PRV VIL DES
HARKRI, ALEXANDER	23	M	CMPR	RRZZZZNY

SHIP: SUEVIA

FROM: HAMBURG
TO: NEW YORK
ARRIVED: 02 FEBRUARY 1886

PASSENGER	AGE	SEX	OCCUPATION	PRV VIL DES
AUGSBURG, CARL	28	M	CL	RRAEFLNY
ROGINSKI, JULIAN	31	M	LABR	RRAHZSNY
WIZEWSKI, ANTON	20	M	LABR	RRAHZSNY
BUDZKOW, JACOB	20	M	LABR	RRZZZZNY
SINKIEWICZ, MARIE	18	F	SGL	RRAHZSNY
KRUPNIK, SALOMON	33	M	LABR	RRZZZZCIN
RACHEL	25	F	W	RRZZZZCIN
SARA	.06	F	INFANT	RRZZZZCIN
DAVID	.06	M	INFANT	RRZZZZCIN
ONIKELSKI, CHAIE	40	F	W	RRZZZZCIN
SAMUEL	9	M	CHILD	RRZZZZCIN
ARON	8	M	CHILD	RRZZZZCIN
BARUCH	5	M	CHILD	RRZZZZCIN
SILBERMANN, ANNA	20	F	SGL	RRZZZZNY
FISCHER, PETER	23	M	LABR	RRAHZSCH
SIMKEWITZ, JOSEF	20	M	LABR	RRAHTFCIN
JOSEFA	24	F	SGL	RRAHTFCIN
MARIE	14	F	SGL	RRAHTFCIN
RUBEL, STANISL.	25	M	LABR	RRAHTFNY
PROHARSKI, ANTON	18	M	LABR	RRAHZDNY
LIES, MOSES-L.	35	M	SHMK	RRZZZZNY
MAYID, JUDEL	20	M	LABR	RRAHZDNY
KRZEMINSKY, JOHN	16	M	LABR	RRAHZDNY
JOSEF	13	M	S	RRAHZDNY
WODEK	8	M	CHILD	RRAHZDNY
PIOTRE	5	F	CHILD	RRAHZDNY
MARIANNE	9	F	CHILD	RRAHZDNY
RUBINSTEIN, JACOB	26	M	DLR	RRZZZZNY
ROSENBLUTH, MAYER	40	M	DLR	RRZZZZNY
SACK, MARIUS	39	M	DLR	RRZZZZNY
MINNA	35	F	W	RRZZZZNY
ABEL	16	M	CH	RRZZZZNY
SOHIWE	14	F	CH	RRZZZZNY
ETTEL	9	F	CHILD	RRZZZZNY
CHENE	8	F	CHILD	RRZZZZNY
NOTE	7	F	CHILD	RRZZZZNY
CHENE	6	F	CHILD	RRZZZZNY
ASCHKENAZY, ISAAC	22	M	DLR	RRZZZZCH
NUSTER, ELIAS	16	M	DLR	RRZZZZCH
ROST, JOSEF	23	M	DLR	RRZZZZCH
PITZELE, SAUL	26	M	DLR	RRZZZZCH
WEISSEL, MARCUS	23	M	DLR	RRZZZZNY
VIERZIG, LEIB	35	M	DLR	RRZZZZNY
REDMANN, PETER	36	M	FELMO	RRZZZZNY
GIWOWSKY, ELIAS	18	M	LABR	RRZZZZNY
PODLISKY, LEISER	20	M	LABR	RRZZZZNY
ARENOWSKY, VICENT	31	M	LABR	RRAHUFNY
MALIMOWICZ, JOSEF	37	M	SHMK	RRAHUFNY
GABLOWSKI, FRANZ	25	M	LABR	RRAHZSNY
LIEZ, REISEL	13	F	SGL	RRZZZZCH
SANDETZKI, BEILE	16	F	SGL	RRZZZZCH
SIDELSKI, HIRSCH	16	M	LABR	RRAHSWCH
TUCHMANN, ABRAHAM	20	M	TLR	RRZZZZNY
FRIEDMANN, LEIB	46	M	TLR	RRAHSWNY
BARBANELSKY, CHAIN	29	M	LABR	RRZZZZNY
MASOHKOWITZ, JUDEL	23	M	LABR	RRZZZZNY
ADLER, JANKEL	26	M	LABR	RRZZZZNY
BERG, MOSES	32	M	LABR	RRZZZZNY
WEISS, DAVID	35	M	LABR	RRZZZZNY
ELPERN, JANKEL	31	M	LABR	RRZZZZNY
SOHIEF, SALOMON	37	M	LABR	RRAHTUNY
WIELENZIK, SLAH.	24	F	W	RRAHVJNY
FRUME	4	F	CHILD	RRAHVJNY
ESTHER	.11	F	INFANT	RRAHVJNY
NUEMANN, TOBIAS	26	M	LABR	RRZZZZCIN
ESTHER	21	F	W	RRZZZZCIN
GERSOHN, MEYER	27	M	LABR	RRZZZZNY
MASUR; SESSE	28	F	SGL	RRZZZZNY
BAUTENBERG, BAR.	22	M	LABR	RRZZZZNY
GURIAN, CHAIM	45	M	LABR	RRZZZZNY
KASPES, CHAIM	20	M	LABR	RRAGRTNY

SHIP: STATE OF GEORGIA

FROM: GLASGOW AND LARNE
TO: NEW YORK
ARRIVED: 05 FEBRUARY 1886

PASSENGER	AGE	SEX	OCCUPATION	PRV VIL DES
PERSKI, CHANE	17	F	SVNT	RRZZZZUSA
LACKAUVOURTSCH, JUDE	23	M	LABR	RRZZZZUSA
SULKANVOURTSCH, CHANE	18	F	W	RRZZZZUSA
KIETA, JACOB	38	M	LABR	PLZZZZUSA
STARZOVSKI, WJOCIEK	19	M	CPTR	PLZZZZUSA
PROWIDZKY, CHRAWZISCHEK	27	M	SHMK	PLZZZZUSA
SEITHEL, LESSER	23	M	LABR	RRZZZZUSA
BERENDSOHN, MARCUS	26	M	BBR	RRZZZZUSA
SEGALOWETZ, HIRSCH	00	M	UNKNOWN	RRZZZZUSA
GERSCHAU, BERKO	21	M	MACH	RRZZZZUSA
LEGALOWTZKY, BORUCH	25	M	LABR	RRZZZZUSA
MAZI, LEIB	23	M	SHMK	RRZZZZUSA
WEINSTEIN, KARSEIT	25	M	DLR	RRZZZZUSA
PERSKY, MEYER	42	M	PDLR	RRZZZZUSA
FAPMANN, ISAAC	42	M	PNTR	RRZZZZUSA
DREISS, NACHAN	24	M	PDLR	RRZZZZUSA
EPPELBAUM, SELIG	18	M	TNSTH	RRZZZZUSA
KOPPENHEIM, SCHLAMINE	28	M	PDLR	RRZZZZUSA
HARITZ, NECHOMIR	26	M	DLR	RRZZZZUSA
KISCHBEIN, SCHMIND	23	M	LABR	RRZZZZUSA
KROW, LIPPO	26	M	TLR	RRZZZZUSA
TREMBITZKI, ABRAHAM	44	M	TLR	RRZZZZUSA
FRAT, FARIFEL	45	M	SLMK	RRZZZZUSA
SPESZKTOTOW, FEOD.	30	M	LABR	RRZZZZUSA
ALPERA, ABRAHAM	23	M	GZR	RRZZZZUSA
FORT, GEROCHED	21	M	MACH	RRZZZZUSA
GLACHENHUS, LEISER	25	M	LABR	RRZZZZUSA
BERMANN, ISAAC	40	M	PDLR	RRZZZZUSA
PAKUTZKI, MOSS.	26	M	SLMK	RRZZZZUSA
RUBENSTEIN, ISRAEL	29	M	SHMK	RRZZZZUSA
LALDIN, ABRAHAM	40	M	SDLR	RRZZZZUSA
JALLOWSKY, AARON	50	M	SLR	RRZZZZUSA

SHIP: WAESLAND

FROM: ANTWERP
TO: NEW YORK
ARRIVED: 05 FEBRUARY 1886

PASSENGER	AGE	SEX	OCCUPATION	PRV VIL DES
KALINA, CHS.	42	M	LABR	RRZZZZIL

PASSENGER	AGE	SEX	OCCUPATION	PRV	VIL	DES
SHIP: CITY OF CHESTER						
FROM: LIVERPOOL AND QUEENSTOWN						
TO: NEW YORK						
ARRIVED: 06 FEBRUARY 1886						
SCHERATZKI, MENDEL	17	M	TLR	RR	ZZZZ	NY

PASSENGER	AGE	SEX	OCCUPATION	PRV	VIL	DES
SHIP: BRITANNIC						
FROM: LIVERPOOL AND QUEENSTOWN						
TO: NEW YORK						
ARRIVED: 08 FEBRUARY 1886						
MONTAGUE, HENRY	29	M	MLR	RR	ACBF	USA
ELIZA	27	F	W	RR	ACBF	USA
JOHN	4	M	CHILD	RR	ACBF	USA
HANSON, AUG.	31	M	LABR	RR	ACBF	USA
NICKOLSON, JOHN	29	M	LABR	RR	ACBF	USA
HILLJE, JOHANN	29	M	FARMER	RR	ACBF	USA
OLTMANNS, GERH.	31	M	FARMER	RR	ACBF	USA
MONTAGUE, ANNA	25	F	SP	RR	ACBF	USA
AIXEIC, HENRI	27	M	LABR	RR	ACBF	USA

PASSENGER	AGE	SEX	OCCUPATION	PRV	VIL	DES
SHIP: AURANIA						
FROM: LIVERPOOL AND QUEENSTOWN						
TO: NEW YORK						
ARRIVED: 09 FEBRUARY 1886						
SONNENTHAL, WILHELM	29	M	LABR	RR	ZZZZ	NY
ISAAC	11	M	CH	RR	ZZZZ	NY
EISLER, HIRSCH	25	M	LABR	RR	ZZZZ	NY
KAHN, MINDEL	20	M	LABR	RR	ZZZZ	NY
MATHILLA, IDA	20	F	SP	RR	ZZZZ	OH
MARIE	18	F	SP	RR	ZZZZ	OH
AMCHA	17	F	SP	RR	ZZZZ	OH
DAKOVSKY, MIKLOS	20	M	LABR	RR	ZZZZ	NY
SCHOSTAC, JOSEF	26	M	LABR	RR	ZZZZ	NY
GRIFFIN, JOSEF	52	M	LABR	RR	ZZZZ	NY
ALTMAN, MOSES	22	M	LABR	RR	ZZZZ	NY
GOLDSTEIN, ABRAM	25	M	LABR	RR	ZZZZ	NY
SODERHOLM, WILHM.	33	M	LABR	RR	ZZZZ	MA
MARKINZOLK, CARL-E.	29	M	LABR	RR	ZZZZ	MA
WESTERBACH, CARL	36	M	LABR	RR	ZZZZ	MA
SIMONS, JOHAN	38	M	LABR	RR	ZZZZ	MA
DEPPIN, EDWARD	30	M	MCHT	RR	ZZZZ	NY

PASSENGER	AGE	SEX	OCCUPATION	PRV	VIL	DES
SHIP: GENERAL WERDER						
FROM: BREMEN AND SOUTHAMPTON						
TO: NEW YORK						
ARRIVED: 11 FEBRUARY 1886						
FRIEDMANN, RUSCHE	17	F	NN	RR	ACBR	USA
ZDROJEWSKI, FRANS	24	M	LABR	RR	ZZZZ	USA
LEWENDOSKI, MICHAL	28	M	LABR	RR	ZZZZ	USA
LANG, KARL	22	M	LABR	RR	AFQV	USA

PASSENGER	AGE	SEX	OCCUPATION	PRV	VIL	DES
SHIP: MORAVIA						
FROM: HAMBURG						
TO: NEW YORK						
ARRIVED: 12 FEBRUARY 1886						
SCHUHR, BENJAMIN	26	M	PNTR	RR	AHXH	USA
BANKAT, GEORG	45	M	MCHT	RR	AEFL	USA
REIS, SCHIE	20	M	DLR	RR	AEFL	USA
KORN, LEIB	39	M	DLR	RR	ZZZZ	USA
ALPER, ABE	32	M	DLR	RR	ZZZZ	USA
SAMUEL	48	M	DLR	RR	ZZZZ	USA
KITZINSKI, JANKE	40	M	JNR	RR	AHZS	USA
ZODOWSKI, JOH.	19	M	TLR	RR	AHZS	USA
PETROWITZ, MICHAL	19	M	TLR	RR	AHZS	USA
DEMONTOWITZ, VINCENT	27	M	LABR	RR	AHZS	USA
SCHETELOW, GELDO	18	F	SGL	RR	AHXC	USA
WARCZAWER, MALKE	50	F	W	RR	AHZM	USA
GETTE	20	F	D	RR	AHZM	USA
GROLL, ARON	24	M	PNTR	RR	AHTF	USA
RINKOWSKY, LUDW.	27	M	LABR	RR	AHZS	USA
FEGE, EDEL	26	F	W	RR	AHZP	USA
MENDEL	.11	F	INFANT	RR	AHZP	USA
ESTERSOHN, LEA	50	F	W	RR	AHSW	USA
BERNSTEIN, CHAJE	30	F	SGL	RR	AFWJ	USA
PALTROWIK, JUL.	20	M	DLR	RR	AHTO	USA
MYLOCZNIK, ELIAS	19	M	LABR	RR	AHTF	USA
SASKE, JUDEL	22	M	LABR	RR	ZZZZ	USA
MISCHKINEL, MEILACH	9	M	CHILD	RR	ZZZZ	USA
KOMMEL, ANNA	20	F	SGL	RR	AHSL	USA
MALICKI, MATHEUS	33	M	LABR	RR	AHZS	USA
GELEM, DAVID	42	M	LABR	RR	AHSP	USA
MORITZ, GEDALI	21	M	LABR	RR	AHZR	USA
STEDR, MORRIS	20	M	LABR	RR	AHTF	USA
SZYMANOWSKI, AUGUSTIN	38	M	LABR	RR	AHZS	USA

PASSENGER	AGE	SEX	OCCUPATION	PRV	VIL	DES
SHIP: ST LAURENT						
FROM: HAVRE						
TO: NEW YORK						
ARRIVED: 12 FEBRUARY 1886						
KROWINSKI, ABRAHAM	30	M	TLR	RR	ZZZZ	NY
ADELE	20	F	TLR	RR	ZZZZ	NY

PASSENGER	AGE	SEX	OCCUPATION	PRV	VIL	DES
SHIP: ACAPULCO						
FROM: PANAMA						
TO: NEW YORK						
ARRIVED: 13 FEBRUARY 1886						
MANASSEVITZ, R.	40	M	MCHT	RR	ZZZZ	USA
MEYERS, P.	38	M	LABR	RR	ZZZZ	RSS

PASSENGER	AGE	SEX	OCCUPATION	PRV	VIL	DES

SHIP: PERSIAN MONARCH

FROM: LONDON
TO: NEW YORK
ARRIVED: 13 FEBRUARY 1886

PASSENGER	AGE	SEX	OCCUPATION	PRV	VIL	DES
SALLON, S.	19	M	BLKSMH	RR	ZZZZ	USA
GOLDING, J.	22	M	CPR	RR	ZZZZ	USA
RAPHAL, M.	21	M	WTRPR	PL	ZZZZ	USA
ROSENBERG, W.	18	M	BTMKR	PL	ZZZZ	USA
GLICKSMAN, S.	22	M	TLR	PL	ZZZZ	USA
SCHWESTER, M.	21	M	TLR	RR	ZZZZ	USA
SCHUWANIC, F.	21	M	BTMKR	RR	ZZZZ	USA
PORTER, J.	20	M	CPTR	RR	ZZZZ	USA
SCHOENERMANN, J.	27	M	MACH	RR	ZZZZ	USA
GORDON, D.	19	M	TRVLR	PL	ZZZZ	USA
SKOLINICK, J.	22	M	BTMKR	RR	ZZZZ	USA
LEWIKOFF, H.	19	M	UNKNOWN	RR	ZZZZ	USA
K---A--EC, M.	22	M	BTMKR	RR	ZZZZ	USA
POLACK, A.	20	M	TLR	RR	ZZZZ	USA
COHEN, A.	42	M	TLR	PL	ZZZZ	USA

SHIP: CIRCASSIA

FROM: GLASGOW AND MOVILLE
TO: NEW YORK
ARRIVED: 15 FEBRUARY 1886

PASSENGER	AGE	SEX	OCCUPATION	PRV	VIL	DES
AMBROSCH, STEFAN	19	M	LABR	RR	ZZZZ	USA
CACILIA	17	F	SVNT	RR	ZZZZ	USA
MOSKOWITZ, SUCHE	24	M	LABR	RR	ZZZZ	USA
ELIAN, ABRAHAM	40	M	TNSTH	RR	ZZZZ	USA
SILBERSTER, SALOMON	59	M	DLR	RR	ZZZZ	USA
BRISINSKY, ED.	29	M	JNR	RR	ZZZZ	USA
AMELIA	20	F	W	RR	ZZZZ	USA
MANDEL, MOSES	40	M	SHMK	RR	ZZZZ	USA
DINA	33	F	W	RR	ZZZZ	USA
SONIA	4	F	CHILD	RR	ZZZZ	USA
ELIANA	1	F	CHILD	RR	ZZZZ	USA
LASER	.03	M	INFANT	RR	ZZZZ	USA
JASSEROVSKY, BOLESLAW	24	M	FARMER	RR	ZZZZ	USA
SCHICHTER, MOSES	43	M	TLR	RR	ZZZZ	USA
NUCHOMOWSKY, LIPE	23	M	SMH	RR	ZZZZ	USA
SCHOLEN, SOLOMON	38	M	JNR	RR	ZZZZ	USA
LASER, ADOLF	26	M	LABR	RR	ZZZZ	USA
ROTHENSTEIN, ELIAS	25	M	LABR	RR	ZZZZ	USA
KATZ, LEISER	59	M	TLR	RR	ZZZZ	USA
EPPSTEIN, VASSEL	40	M	DLR	RR	ZZZZ	USA

SHIP: FULDA

FROM: BREMEN
TO: NEW YORK
ARRIVED: 15 FEBRUARY 1886

PASSENGER	AGE	SEX	OCCUPATION	PRV	VIL	DES
MOKAITES, JOSEF	56	M	LABR	RR	AEFL	USA
ANNA	64	F	UNKNOWN	RR	AEFL	USA
AGATHE	17	F	UNKNOWN	RR	AEFL	USA
MANA	6	F	CHILD	RR	AEFL	USA

SHIP: HERMANN

FROM: BREMEN
TO: NEW YORK
ARRIVED: 15 FEBRUARY 1886

PASSENGER	AGE	SEX	OCCUPATION	PRV	VIL	DES
SALKOWSKA, JULIANE	22	F	NN	RR	AFWJ	USA
DOMBROWSKY, ABRAH.	19	M	TLR	RR	ZZZZ	USA
SMOLINSKY, DAVID	19	M	SHMK	RR	ZZZZ	USA
BOTLINSKY, ITZIG	13	M	CH	RR	ZZZZ	USA
FRANK, BARUCH	14	M	CH	RR	ZZZZ	USA

SHIP: OREGON

FROM: LIVERPOOL AND QUEENSTOWN
TO: NEW YORK
ARRIVED: 15 FEBRUARY 1886

PASSENGER	AGE	SEX	OCCUPATION	PRV	VIL	DES
GUTMANN, ISRAEL	23	M	TLR	RR	ZZZZ	NY
GREENBERG, SCHEMOINER	35	M	MCHT	RR	ZZZZ	NY
HELLER, MOSES	11	M	CH	RR	ZZZZ	NY
HAMSTER, MARCUS	24	M	LABR	RR	ZZZZ	NY
LITZOWITZ, ABEL	11	M	CH	RR	ZZZZ	NY
UKSON, USHER	20	M	LABR	RR	ZZZZ	NY
ALBERT, NATHAN	27	M	LABR	RR	ZZZZ	NY
BEICOVITZ, HARRIS	21	M	TLR	RR	ZZZZ	NY
KISCHWORA, JULIAN	28	M	LABR	RR	ZZZZ	NY
GEBER, JOAN	17	M	LABR	RR	ZZZZ	NY
BECKER, MARY	11	F	SP	RR	ZZZZ	NY
ABRAMOWITZ, ZIPPI	25	F	MA	RR	ZZZZ	NY
ISAAK	20	M	MCHT	RR	ZZZZ	NY
SAFFER, ANNIE	36	F	W	RR	ZZZZ	NY
HARRY	11	M	CH	RR	ZZZZ	NY
FRIEDMANN, BERTHA	20	F	SP	RR	ZZZZ	NY
SARA	16	F	SP	RR	ZZZZ	NY

SHIP: SPAIN

FROM: LIVERPOOL
TO: NEW YORK
ARRIVED: 15 FEBRUARY 1886

PASSENGER	AGE	SEX	OCCUPATION	PRV	VIL	DES
ARONSKY, RACHEL	26	F	SP	PL	ZZZZ	NY
LEAH	6	F	CHILD	PL	ZZZZ	NY
BRENAN, HERR.	44	M	LABR	PL	AHQD	NY
HOFFMAN, S.	42	M	LABR	PL	AHQD	NY
FINKELSTEIN, F.	20	M	LABR	PL	ZZZZ	NY
BRAUN, JOSEPH	45	M	LABR	PL	ZZZZ	NY
ELIZA	40	F	W	PL	ZZZZ	NY
ONKEL, RACHEL	18	F	SP	PL	ZZZZ	NY
ABSWITZY, KANZY	35	F	SP	PL	ZZZZ	NY
HANS	9	M	CHILD	PL	ZZZZ	NY
MARIE	6	F	CHILD	PL	ZZZZ	NY
JOSEF	3	F	CHILD	PL	ZZZZ	NY
WILHELM	1	F	CHILD	PL	ZZZZ	NY
BRAUN, LISSA	8	F	CHILD	PL	ZZZZ	NY
ISIDOR	6	M	CHILD	PL	ZZZZ	NY
MARTHA	1	F	CHILD	PL	ZZZZ	NY
MORTON, HENRICH	40	M	LABR	RR	ZZZZ	NY
PAJALA, JACOB	30	M	LABR	RR	ZZZZ	NY
BERGSTROM, C.J.	20	M	LABR	RR	ZZZZ	NY
SEIR, W.	20	M	LABR	RR	ZZZZ	NY
HESSMANN, TRANCE	40	M	LABR	PL	ZZZZ	NY
GRUNBERG, ABRAHAM	39	M	LABR	RR	ZZZZ	NY

PASSENGER	AGE	SEX	OCCUPATION	PRV VIL DES
KRANETZIK, ARIE	25	M	LABR	PLZZZZNY
CHAWSKI, MODCHE	36	M	LABR	RRZZZZNY
BAKALOV, LEIB	50	M	LABR	PLZZZZNY
GRABOWSKY, SCHMUF	49	M	LABR	RRZZZZNY
MOSES, ISAAC	32	M	LABR	PLZZZZNY
STEIGBURGER, SOLOMON	26	M	LABR	PLZZZZNY
FINKE, MARIE	19	F	SP	PLZZZZNY
ROTZEN, ABRAHAM	24	M	LABR	PLZZZZNY

SHIP: STATE OF INDIANA

FROM: GLASGOW AND LARNE
TO: NEW YORK
ARRIVED: 15 FEBRUARY 1886

PASSENGER	AGE	SEX	OCCUPATION	PRV VIL DES
OPMAT, JOSEPH	26	M	LABR	RRZZZZUSA
KESLER, SANDER	00	M	PDLR	RRAHTAUSA
MELTZER, JACOB-M.	30	M	JNR	RRZZZZUSA
JACOB	36	M	PDLR	RRZZZZUSA
SCHMUL	30	M	GZR	RRAGRTUSA
BUMINOWITZ, FEIVE	30	M	PDLR	RRZZZZUSA
SCHELLMANN, MOSES	36	M	TLR	RRZZZZUSA
DUBINSKI, MOSES	22	M	PDLR	RRZZZZUSA
KATZ, MOSES	00	M	PDLR	RRZZZZUSA
RUDENSKI, JECHEM	00	M	TLR	RRZZZZUSA
U, U	00	M	SHMK	RRZZZZUSA
SCHONHANS, JACOB	00	M	PDLR	RRZZZZUSA
ELLMAN, MOSES	24	M	TLR	RRZZZZUSA
SKLUT, SCHMUEL	00	M	SHMK	RRZZZZUSA
CHATZKEL	35	M	GZR	RRAGRTUSA
ASF, GERSCHOW	31	M	TLR	RRZZZZUSA
GETLIN, BEHR.	15	M	PDLR	RRAGRTUSA
KASNYSOHN, LEIB	23	M	TLR	RRZZZZUSA
HALPERT, HIRSCH	22	M	SMH	RRZZZZUSA
ABE	00	M	BCHR	RRZZZZUSA
GOZEWER, SCHMUEL	40	M	PDLR	RRZZZZUSA
MAGED, WOLF	26	M	PDLR	RRAHTRUSA
PIASKOWSKY, BARUCH	45	M	PDLR	PLZZZZUSA
JALONSKI, SIMCHE	38	M	TLR	RRZZZZUSA
ROTHBART, ABRAHAM	20	M	JNR	RRAHTFUSA
CHANNE	20	F	W	RRAHTFUSA

SHIP: GELLERT

FROM: HAMBURG
TO: NEW YORK
ARRIVED: 16 FEBRUARY 1886

PASSENGER	AGE	SEX	OCCUPATION	PRV VIL DES
LAPISE, CHANNE	30	F	W	RRAHXGUSA
BARANOWSKY, URKE	4	F	CHILD	RRAHXGUSA
BEILE	.11	F	INFANT	RRAHXGUSA
WOJWODA, BERTHOL	21	M	FARMER	RRAHZSUSA
LEMANOWSKY, CHAIM	20	M	LABR	RRAHVUUSA
FRIEDSTEIN, CHAIM	23	M	MCHT	RRZZZZUSA
ALEER, RUWEN	20	M	TLR	RRAHXGUSA
SCHEINE	18	F	W	RRAHXGUSA
KOLISCHKO, KASIMIR	25	M	FARMER	RRAFVGUSA
BERGMAN, BERTHA	37	F	W	RRAGRTUSA
KLEIN, JOSEPH	19	M	TLR	RRAHZEUSA
WOLPE, ELIAS	16	M	LABR	RRAHZEUSA
BOGANTZ, JACOB	22	M	MCHT	RRAHTFUSA
KASSEL, DAVID	39	M	DLR	RRAHTFUSA
FANNY	35	F	W	RRAHTFUSA
LEWIN	9	M	CHILD	RRAHTFUSA
MOSES	6	M	CHILD	RRAHTFUSA
KALMAN	5	M	CHILD	RRAHTFUSA
ISRAEL	2	M	CHILD	RRAHTFUSA
LUBERSTEIN, LEISER	23	M	DLR	RRAHTUUSA
SOKOLSKI, TAMCHEN	32	M	TLR	RRAHUKUSA
LAPIDES, DAVID	18	M	SHMK	RRAHUKUSA
GALUB, N.	27	M	TLR	RRAHUKUSA
HEILPERN, LEIB	20	M	DLR	RRAHUKUSA
GAFFIN, CHAIM	19	M	DLR	RRAHUKUSA
PLOTKIN, JACOB	24	M	JNR	RRAHUKUSA
DULEWSKI, JAN	27	M	TLR	RRAHZSUSA
BAYARSKI, JOSSEL	21	M	PNTR	RRAHUQUSA
COHN, ESTHER	55	F	W	RRAHSWUSA
BANDERER, CHAJE	20	M	LABR	RRAHSWUSA
LEWINKIND, ISAAC	24	M	DLR	RRAHOOUSA
KAHN, MASCHE	27	F	W	RRAHSWUSA
ISRAEL	4	M	CHILD	RRAHSWUSA
ROSEL	2	F	CHILD	RRAHSWUSA
LEIKUTZKY, MOSES	30	M	LABR	RRAHZUUSA
MAINSON, SARE	20	F	SGL	RRAHTRUSA
AUGUS, JOHN	16	M	LABR	RRAHVUUSA

SHIP: NEVADA

FROM: LIVERPOOL
TO: NEW YORK
ARRIVED: 18 FEBRUARY 1886

PASSENGER	AGE	SEX	OCCUPATION	PRV VIL DES
BABUNSKY, D.	32	M	BBR	PLZZZZUSA

SHIP: GRECIAN MONARCH

FROM: LONDON
TO: NEW YORK
ARRIVED: 19 FEBRUARY 1886

PASSENGER	AGE	SEX	OCCUPATION	PRV VIL DES
KERSTER, JETTE-D.	35	F	NN	PLZZZZNY

SHIP: PENNLAND

FROM: ANTWERP
TO: NEW YORK
ARRIVED: 19 FEBRUARY 1886

PASSENGER	AGE	SEX	OCCUPATION	PRV VIL DES
LEVONE, F.	21	M	LABR	RRZZZZNY
LIBHOFSKI, B.	21	M	LABR	RRZZZZNY

SHIP: EMS

FROM: BREMEN
TO: NEW YORK
ARRIVED: 20 FEBRUARY 1886

PASSENGER	AGE	SEX	OCCUPATION	PRV VIL DES
ZADIK, GDAL	22	M	LABR	RRAFVGUSA
MARKUS, MOSES	30	M	MCHT	RRAFQVUSA
FRIEDMANN, JACOB	30	M	LABR	RRAFQVUSA

PASSENGER	AGE	SEX	OCCUPATION	PRV	VIL	DES
LEWY, ISAACK	25	M	MCHT	RR	AFQV	USA
JACOBSOHN, CHAJE	20	F	NN	RR	AFQV	USA

SHIP: KATIE

FROM: STETTIN
TO: NEW YORK
ARRIVED: 20 FEBRUARY 1886

PASSENGER	AGE	SEX	OCCUPATION	PRV	VIL	DES
KOHOKOLEWSKA, JULIA	36	F	W	RR	ZZZZ	USA
CONSTANTIA	7	F	CHILD	RR	ZZZZ	USA
CYNAMON, JACOB	18	M	LABR	RR	ZZZZ	USA
MANIKOWSKA, MARGAR.	28	F	W	PL	ZZZZ	USA
STANISLAUS	2	M	CHILD	PL	ZZZZ	USA
BTITZBLAN, JITTE	24	F	WI	RR	ZZZZ	USA
KASPROVICZ, ANNA	18	F	CH	PL	ZZZZ	USA

SHIP: AUSTRALIA

FROM: HAMBURG
TO: NEW YORK
ARRIVED: 22 FEBRUARY 1886

PASSENGER	AGE	SEX	OCCUPATION	PRV	VIL	DES
LISNEWSKI, JOS.	27	M	LABR	RR	ZZZZ	NY
STANKIEWITZ, JAN	30	M	LABR	RR	ZZZZ	NY
BARUSKOWSKY, ANT.	26	M	LABR	RR	ZZZZ	NY
TCHETSCHAKOWSKI, JOS.	38	M	MLR	RR	ZZZZ	NY
AGATHE	32	F	W	RR	ZZZZ	NY
WADEK	5	M	CHILD	RR	ZZZZ	NY
MATHILDE	4	F	CHILD	RR	ZZZZ	NY
ALEXANDER	2	M	CHILD	RR	ZZZZ	NY
MAX	.09	M	INFANT	RR	ZZZZ	NY
ZUHLMANN, ROB.	19	M	LABR	RR	ZZZZ	NY
MEROWITZ, LEISER	26	M	TRDSMN	RR	ZZZZ	NY
REISEL	20	F	W	RR	ZZZZ	NY
GARFINKEL, REISEL	20	F	SGL	RR	ZZZZ	NY
NOOISNECKI, SCHEYE	19	M	TDR	RR	ZZZZ	NY
FRIEDA	19	F	W	RR	ZZZZ	NY
HOROWITZ, P.	20	M	UNKNOWN	RR	ZZZZ	NY
GODELSKY, ABR.J.	55	M	TRDSMN	RR	ZZZZ	NY
LUCHT, CHAYE	23	F	WO	RR	ZZZZ	NY
LEIB	.08	M	INFANT	RR	ZZZZ	NY
RUNTMANN, JOS.	50	M	LABR	RR	ZZZZ	IL
FISCHER, DAVID	22	M	TLR	RR	ZZZZ	NY
JOCHELSEN, ITZIG	22	M	LABR	RR	ZZZZ	NY
GLOSSER, MOSES	33	M	LABR	RR	ZZZZ	NY
LEWIN, SALOM.	21	M	TDR	RR	ZZZZ	NY
BERTHA	19	F	W	RR	ZZZZ	NY
ROSENBLUTH, ISAAC	7	M	CHILD	RR	ZZZZ	NY
BEREL	5	M	CHILD	RR	ZZZZ	NY
FUNKELSTEIN, FEIWEL	20	M	TDR	RR	ZZZZ	NY
DOMBROWSKY, ANNA	30	F	WO	RR	ZZZZ	NY
ANNA	.09	F	INFANT	RR	ZZZZ	NY
KILL, HANNI	24	M	SGL	RR	ZZZZ	NY
ROSENBLUETH, ELIAS	25	M	JNR	RR	ZZZZ	NY
STALEZ, SCHMUL	26	M	JNR	RR	ZZZZ	NY
ISAAK	19	M	JNR	RR	ZZZZ	NY
BAZOFEL, ASCHER	24	M	TRDSMN	RR	ZZZZ	NY
GLASER, MOSES	38	M	GZR	RR	ZZZZ	NY
ISAAC	20	M	GZR	RR	ZZZZ	NY

SHIP: CITY OF RICHMOND

FROM: LIVERPOOL
TO: NEW YORK
ARRIVED: 22 FEBRUARY 1886

PASSENGER	AGE	SEX	OCCUPATION	PRV	VIL	DES
LUKES, L.	28	M	LABR	PL	ZZZZ	USA
WILEMSKY, HENDLE	23	M	LABR	PL	ZZZZ	USA
SOKOLOW, SIMON	24	M	LABR	PL	ZZZZ	USA
WERSHIL, H.	20	M	LABR	PL	ZZZZ	USA
WITOWSKA, SIMON	33	M	LABR	PL	ZZZZ	USA
CERRESPK, A.	30	F	W	PL	ZZZZ	USA
JOHAN	13	M	CH	PL	ZZZZ	USA
HORSTENKE, CHRIS	9	M	CHILD	PL	ZZZZ	USA
MITOWSKA, THOS.	34	M	LABR	PL	ZZZZ	USA
ZAWADYKZ, ANTON	22	M	LABR	PL	ZZZZ	USA
VADGALES, ANTON	26	M	LABR	PL	ZZZZ	USA
DAMAGALSKY, A.	21	F	W	PL	ZZZZ	USA
ANTON	21	M	LABR	PL	ZZZZ	USA
HUDAK, G.	31	M	LABR	PL	ZZZZ	USA
BODNAR, JANOS	25	M	LABR	PL	ZZZZ	USA
FINKEL, BERNARD	21	M	LABR	PL	ZZZZ	USA
GOLLOK, C.	18	M	LABR	PL	ZZZZ	USA
HIRETZ, A.	37	M	LABR	PL	ZZZZ	USA
PIPAS, JEHNA	29	F	W	PL	ZZZZ	USA
MICHALZ, F.	44	M	LABR	PL	ZZZZ	USA
GOLDBLATT, L.	30	M	LABR	PL	AHTU	USA
MAJOR, VAIL	25	M	LABR	PL	AHTU	USA
KOSKOWITZ, JASAK	45	M	LABR	PL	AHTU	USA
SPEIGLE, L.	25	M	LABR	PL	AHTU	USA
ROTH, JOSEF	20	M	LABR	PL	AHTU	USA
JURKS, PETER	35	M	LABR	PL	AHTU	USA
JENDRI, P.	30	M	LABR	PL	AHTU	USA
IVAN, DIMON	32	M	LABR	PL	AHTU	USA
PETER	11	M	CH	PL	AHTU	USA
P.	10	M	CH	PL	AHTU	USA
MATNAS, MICHL.	41	M	LABR	PL	AHTU	USA
N.	11	M	CH	PL	AHTU	USA
JEDOR, J.	26	M	LABR	PL	AHTU	USA
STOJACK, MICHL.	35	M	LABR	PL	AHTU	USA
KIRTZ, BERL	20	M	LABR	PL	AHTU	USA
FELDSCHER, ARON	23	M	LABR	PL	AHTU	USA
SCHOCHTER, B.	35	M	LABR	PL	AHTU	USA
SACLONDNI, JANOS	18	M	LABR	PL	AHTU	USA
ANDERAS, W.	10	M	CH	PL	AHTU	USA
FERIN, ROSEN	18	M	LABR	PL	AHTU	USA
KATZ, B.	32	M	LABR	PL	AHTU	USA
KAVLER, KISSIC	33	M	LABR	PL	AHTU	USA
FREIBERG, MOSES	32	M	LABR	PL	AHTU	USA
EMIL	11	F	CH	PL	AHTU	USA
SCHMERT, JOHANN	26	M	LABR	PL	AHTU	USA
MARIA	18	F	W	PL	AHTU	USA

SHIP: STATE OF NEVADA

FROM: GLASGOW AND LARNE
TO: NEW YORK
ARRIVED: 22 FEBRUARY 1886

PASSENGER	AGE	SEX	OCCUPATION	PRV	VIL	DES
BAIRISS, L.	55	M	JNR	RR	ZZZZ	USA
BASISTE, M.	25	F	W	RR	ZZZZ	USA
GOLDE	3	F	CHILD	RR	ZZZZ	USA
SARAH	1	F	CHILD	RR	ZZZZ	USA
COLEJORSKY, E.	26	M	PDLR	RR	AFVG	USA
ERSAND, M.	30	M	ENGR	RR	AHTB	USA
FELDMANN, M.	41	M	SHMK	RR	AHTB	USA
LOFONSSON, J.	22	M	FARMER	RR	AGUZ	USA
MIHAL, K.	21	M	LABR	RR	ZZZZ	USA
MALETZKIN, K.	42	M	CGRMKR	RR	ZZZZ	USA

PASSENGER	AGE	SEX	OCCUPATION	PRV	VIL	DES
MARKOWITZ, C.	22	F	W	RR	ZZZZ	USA
TILLE	.09	F	INFANT	RR	ZZZZ	USA
ROZMANSKY, A.	16	M	ENGR	RR	ZZZZ	USA
ROSSANDEL, A.	35	M	LABR	RR	ZZZZ	USA
RUDERMANN, S.	16	M	TLR	RR	ZZZZ	USA
RABINOW, C.	22	M	MLR	RR	ZZZZ	USA
SCHULMANN, L.	25	F	W	RR	ZZZZ	USA
BASCHE	.09	F	INFANT	RR	ZZZZ	USA
SCHAVELOWSKY, A.	35	M	TLR	RR	ZZZZ	USA
U, U	00	U	SHMK	RR	ZZZZ	USA

SHIP: KEHRWIEDER

FROM: HAMBURG
TO: NEW YORK
ARRIVED: 23 FEBRUARY 1886

PASSENGER	AGE	SEX	OCCUPATION	PRV	VIL	DES
BUSCHBAUM, MOTEL	20	M	TCHR	RR	ZZZZ	NY
ABRAHAM	20	M	TCHR	RR	ZZZZ	NY
KIRSCHBAUM, SAM.	23	M	BKR	RR	ZZZZ	NY
GALLON, MAUSCH	46	M	LABR	RR	ZZZZ	NY
PAISCHE	38	F	W	RR	ZZZZ	NY
IDA	7	F	CHILD	RR	ZZZZ	NY
SARAH	6	F	CHILD	RR	ZZZZ	NY
TOBIAS	.10	M	INFANT	RR	ZZZZ	NY
PALUSCH, ISAAC	37	M	SHMK	RR	ZZZZ	NY
MARGOLI, SCHONON	18	M	LABR	RR	ZZZZ	NY
MOSEL, SAMUEL	42	M	LABR	RR	ZZZZ	NY
SCHIFFENHAUS, ABR.	26	M	LABR	RR	ZZZZ	NY
SCHLIPEL, BEHR.JANK	32	M	LABR	RR	ZZZZ	NY
REITZ, ISRAEL	34	M	LABR	RR	ZZZZ	NY
PINCHOWITZ, SIM.	20	M	LABR	RR	ZZZZ	NY
DANISCHKOWITZ, SCH.	20	M	LABR	RR	ZZZZ	NY
KASDAN, PETR.	20	M	LABR	RR	ZZZZ	NY
LEWIN, ABR.E.	28	M	LABR	RR	ZZZZ	NY
RUBENSCHIK, JAENKEL	36	M	LABR	RR	ZZZZ	NY
MILINOWITZ, LEIB	27	M	LABR	RR	ZZZZ	NY
HAHN, MAYER	17	M	LABR	RR	ZZZZ	NY
FEITELOWICZ, LEISER	44	M	LABR	RR	ZZZZ	NY
BAMEN, ITZIG	40	M	SHMK	RR	ZZZZ	NY
ARSCHENOWSKY, FEIGE-R.	18	M	SGL	RR	ZZZZ	NY
FUSCZAK, QUILLE	20	F	SGL	PL	ZZZZ	NY
SELTZER, MEYER	16	M	LABR	PL	ZZZZ	NY
SCHNITTMANN, LANKOW	26	M	LABR	PL	ZZZZ	NY
LEWIN, MOSES	28	M	LABR	PL	ZZZZ	NY
LEDER, JAHEW	28	M	LABR	PL	ZZZZ	NY
LOUIS, EISSIG	23	M	LABR	PL	ZZZZ	NY
LAPIDUS, BENJ.	17	M	LABR	PL	ZZZZ	NY
SCHULMANN, FEIRA	27	M	LABR	PL	ZZZZ	NY
HURWITZ, FEINE	26	M	LABR	PL	ZZZZ	NY
GRINES, SCHAJE	26	M	LABR	PL	ZZZZ	NY
SEGALOWITZ, LEIB	22	M	LABR	PL	ZZZZ	NY
LIPJAN, HERTZ	21	M	LABR	PL	ZZZZ	NY
ISACKSOHN, NACH	48	M	LABR	PL	ZZZZ	NY
STANGE, ALEXANDER	21	M	MCHT	PL	ZZZZ	NY
BONIFACIUS, SAW.	27	M	MCHT	RR	ZZZZ	NY
RABENOWITZ, JAC.	28	M	TRDSMN	RR	ZZZZ	NY
GOLDSCHMIDT, NACHI	33	M	TLR	RR	ZZZZ	NY
JOSEPH, ZELIG	18	M	TRDSMN	RR	ZZZZ	NY
SIMSON, LINA	35	F	WO	RR	ZZZZ	NY
SOPHIE	6	F	CHILD	RR	ZZZZ	NY
JOHANNA	5	F	CHILD	RR	ZZZZ	NY
JULIA	.09	F	INFANT	RR	ZZZZ	NY
JANNO	3	F	CHILD	RR	ZZZZ	NY
GITTE, CONRT.	43	M	UNKNOWN	RR	ZZZZ	NY
FLATDEC, JACOB	20	M	LABR	RR	ZZZZ	NY

SHIP: CANADA

FROM: HAVRE
TO: NEW YORK
ARRIVED: 24 FEBRUARY 1886

PASSENGER	AGE	SEX	OCCUPATION	PRV	VIL	DES
REHFELD, ALEX.	18	M	TLR	PL	ZZZZ	NY

SHIP: INDIA

FROM: HAMBURG
TO: NEW YORK
ARRIVED: 25 FEBRUARY 1886

PASSENGER	AGE	SEX	OCCUPATION	PRV	VIL	DES
SCHERKO, STEPH.	23	M	LABR	RR	ZZZZ	NY
LUSEHKE, CARL	30	M	LABR	RR	ZZZZ	NY
CHANOWSKI, ALEXANDR	7	M	CHILD	RR	ZZZZ	NY
SEROCHA, EMILIAN	22	M	LABR	RR	ZZZZ	NY
WOSENKO, JAN	25	M	LABR	RR	ZZZZ	NY
LUSCHKA, MIKOLA	27	M	LABR	RR	ZZZZ	NY
GOLDSEHER, ABRAH.	60	M	TRDSMN	RR	ZZZZ	NY
FEINTUCH, LASER	24	M	TRDSMN	RR	ZZZZ	NY
EICHEL, MOSES	37	M	TRDSMN	RR	ZZZZ	NY
EIDMANN, SAM	38	M	TRDSMN	RR	ZZZZ	NY
GOLDSOHER, SORE	25	F	WO	RR	ZZZZ	NY
JANKEL	.06	M	INFANT	RR	ZZZZ	NY
GOLDSTEIN, MEIER	20	M	MCHT	PL	ZZZZ	NY
HIRSCH, JAC.	42	M	TRDSMN	RR	ZZZZ	NY
SABLODOWSKY, JOSSEL	37	M	TRDSMN	RR	ZZZZ	NY
SCHUCHMANN, MOSES	40	M	TRDSMN	RR	ZZZZ	NY
MEYER	37	M	TRDSMN	RR	ZZZZ	NY
KULISCA, ABRAH.	19	M	TRDSMN	RR	ZZZZ	NY
EDELMANN, LEIB	33	M	TRDSMN	RR	ZZZZ	NY
MARGOLIN, BER	35	M	TRDSMN	RR	ZZZZ	NY
ECHERMANN, ABR.	25	M	TRDSMN	RR	ZZZZ	NY
KOPELOWITZ, JACOB	27	M	TRDSMN	RR	ZZZZ	NY
AXELROD, SARAH	18	F	SGL	RR	ZZZZ	NY
KOHN, ISAAC	23	M	TRDSMN	RR	ZZZZ	NY
KEIFMANN	50	M	TRDSMN	RR	ZZZZ	NY
CHAIT, ARON	37	M	TRDSMN	RR	ZZZZ	NY
MARGOLIN, MEYER	33	M	TRDSMN	RR	ZZZZ	NY
BASCHOA, JOSCHESCHEL	23	M	TRDSMN	RR	ZZZZ	NY
MATZOLOWITZ, BERL	28	M	TRDSMN	RR	ZZZZ	NY
KREINER, CHANS	36	M	TRDSMN	RR	ZZZZ	NY
FEIN, JUDEL	37	M	TRDSMN	RR	ZZZZ	NY
KOHN, ABRAH.	26	M	TRDSMN	RR	ZZZZ	NY
ENGELSOHN, CH.	28	M	TRDSMN	RR	ZZZZ	NY
KIRSCHNER, SCHMUEL	35	M	TRDSMN	RR	ZZZZ	NY
LAUERSKI, IGNADAS	22	M	TRDSMN	RR	ZZZZ	NY
OKYNEWITZ, WLADISLAW	28	M	TRDSMN	RR	ZZZZ	NY
KETZOWITZ, SCHMUEL	18	M	TRDSMN	RR	ZZZZ	NY
GOLDSTEIN, SAMUEL	30	M	LABR	PL	ZZZZ	NY
HOTZ, DAUL.	22	M	LABR	PL	ZZZZ	NY
RITOW, SELM.	22	M	LABR	PL	ZZZZ	NY
RUDENSKI, LEISER	23	M	TRDSMN	RR	ZZZZ	NY
BERMANN, ISRAEL	27	M	TRDSMN	RR	ZZZZ	NY
ELIAS	18	M	TRDSMN	RR	ZZZZ	NY
KATZENOWITZ, SAL.	20	M	TRDSMN	RR	ZZZZ	NY
BERMANN, BERL	17	M	TRDSMN	RR	ZZZZ	NY
SCHMIDT, SIEG.	26	M	UNKNOWN	RR	ZZZZ	NY

PASSENGER	AGE	SEX	OCCUPATION	PRV	VIL	DES

SHIP: ENGLAND

FROM: LIVERPOOL
TO: NEW YORK
ARRIVED: 26 FEBRUARY 1886

PASSENGER	A	S	OCCUPATION	PV		D
GOLDSTEIN, ESTER	24	F	W	RR	ADBQ	NY
BIKEY	.11	F	INFANT	RR	ADBQ	NY
SCHUPITZEY, MARK	27	M	TLR	RR	ADBQ	NY
COHEN, ISAAC	21	M	TLR	RR	ADBQ	NY
MARAIS, ADOLPH	24	M	SHPKR	RR	ADBQ	NY
AGUS, ROSALIE	20	F	SP	RR	ADBQ	NY
COHEN, MAR.	33	M	TLR	RR	ADBQ	NY
BRAUER, L.	18	F	SP	RR	ADBQ	NY
MULF, MARK	27	M	TLR	RR	ADBQ	NY
GOLDSTEIN, LEO	30	M	LABR	RR	ADBQ	NY
ANNE	11	F	CH	RR	ADBQ	NY
DELBY	5	M	CHILD	RR	ADBQ	NY
PATLIKOR, M.	11	M	HTR	RR	ADBQ	LIP

SHIP: RYNLAND

FROM: ANTWERP
TO: NEW YORK
ARRIVED: 26 FEBRUARY 1886

PASSENGER	A	S	OCCUPATION	PV		D
HANAUER, ADAM	28	M	MCHT	RR	AFWJ	NY
RAFEL, MARK	21	M	SLR	RR	ADBQ	NY

SHIP: DONAU

FROM: BREMEN
TO: NEW YORK
ARRIVED: 01 MARCH 1886

PASSENGER	A	S	OCCUPATION	PV		D
SIMON, MENUCHE	48	F	NN	RR	ZZZZ	USA
CHAIE	11	F	NN	RR	ZZZZ	USA
MORDCHE	9	F	CHILD	RR	ZZZZ	USA
SCHMIDT, MARIE	59	F	NN	RR	ZZZZ	USA

SHIP: EIDER

FROM: BREMEN
TO: NEW YORK
ARRIVED: 01 MARCH 1886

PASSENGER	A	S	OCCUPATION	PV		D
LEMCHTER, SARAH	22	F	W	RR	AHYB	USA
ABRAH.	.01	M	INFANT	RR	AHYB	USA
FEIGE	19	F	NN	RR	AHYB	USA

SHIP: ALASKA

FROM: LIVERPOOL AND QUEENSTOWN
TO: NEW YORK
ARRIVED: 02 MARCH 1886

PASSENGER	A	S	OCCUPATION	PV		D
LAKOFSKY, EDWARD	27	M	CBTMKR	RR	ZZZZ	USA
MARY	25	F	W	RR	ZZZZ	USA
HURWITZ, DAVID	18	M	FLABR	RR	ZZZZ	USA
GORDOLON, JACOB	18	M	FLABR	RR	ZZZZ	USA
GERL, EMANUEL	13	M	FLABR	RR	ZZZZ	USA
GLAICH, WILCHELM	11	M	CH	RR	ZZZZ	USA
AGSERN, JUDA	30	M	TLR	RR	ZZZZ	USA
SPORINE, LADIK	44	M	TLR	RR	ZZZZ	USA
KURCINSKY, SIMCHE	28	M	FLABR	RR	ZZZZ	USA
SCHACHET, MEYER	48	M	CGRMKR	RR	ZZZZ	USA
GRUNHAUS, ABRAHAM	25	M	FLABR	RR	ZZZZ	USA
SCHAPIRA, SHEIRL	28	M	FLABR	RR	ZZZZ	USA
WISCHOWAB, GITEL	20	F	MA	RR	ZZZZ	USA
RACHEL	1	F	CHILD	RR	ZZZZ	USA

SHIP: BOHEMIA

FROM: HAMBURG
TO: NEW YORK
ARRIVED: 03 MARCH 1886

PASSENGER	A	S	OCCUPATION	PV		D
JUSHAL, RAHEL	32	F	W	RR	AHTF	USA
PESCHE	4	F	CHILD	RR	AHTF	USA
GESSY	.11	F	INFANT	RR	AHTF	USA
HEPKIN, HERMANN	10	M	DLR	RR	AHTF	USA
NEWZOWITZ, IGNATZ	36	M	LABR	RR	AHZS	USA
GERULAT, GETTE	25	F	W	RR	AHSW	USA
MARIANNE	.11	F	INFANT	RR	AHSW	USA
PICZNIK, EFIRA	40	F	W	RR	AFVG	USA
ROSA	20	F	D	RR	AFVG	USA
SUSSKIND, MARIUS	30	M	BKR	RR	AGRT	USA
FRASKOLASKY, KONSTANTIN	30	M	LABR	RR	AHVQ	USA
PAUL, MARIE	33	F	SGL	RR	AHYP	USA
MORITZ, MINNA	26	F	SGL	RR	AHYP	USA
GLINKA, MENDEL	16	M	LABR	RR	AHTO	USA
RUDNIK, MOSES	25	M	DLR	RR	AHYK	USA
PACKRASKY, JUDEL	35	M	BKBNDR	RR	AHSW	USA
PODBEREZKY, DAVID	34	M	DLR	RR	AHXS	USA
TODT, NOCHEM	37	M	DLR	RR	AHXS	USA
HONZA, JAN	29	M	LABR	RR	AHXS	USA
BESLAPSKY, MOSES	20	M	LABR	RR	ZZZZ	USA
FADLER, EVA	19	F	SGL	RR	ZZZZ	USA
POLIVODY, ISAAC	19	M	TNMK	RR	AHYD	USA
WILKOMIRSKY, CIRL	40	F	W	RR	AHYK	USA
HINDE	17	F	D	RR	AHYK	USA
MINNIK, MORDSCHE	34	M	DLR	RR	AHVU	USA
ZALKE, JOSSEL	44	M	TLR	RR	AHZH	USA
PAZNOKECZ, CHAIM	32	M	TLR	RR	AHZH	USA
LEWTON, BERL	31	M	TLR	RR	AHZH	USA
MARKEL, DAVID	18	M	TLR	RR	AHZH	USA
SCHLEPIAN, SARA	30	F	SGL	RR	AHQH	USA
KAIKOWSKY, JAN	28	M	LABR	RR	AHZS	USA
BETKE, FRIEDR.	25	M	LABR	RR	AHZS	USA
PANTER, MICH.	24	M	LABR	RR	AHZS	USA
JANFELD, FRANZ	25	M	LABR	RR	AHZS	USA

SHIP: GALLIA

FROM: LIVERPOOL AND QUEENSTOWN
TO: NEW YORK
ARRIVED: 03 MARCH 1886

PASSENGER	AGE	SEX	OCCUPATION	PRI	VIL	DES
RIBACK, ISAAC	25	M	LABR	RR	ACBF	USA
GEBEL, MAX	40	M	LABR	RR	ACBF	USA
GOL, JOSEF	35	M	LABR	RR	ACBF	USA
PAWLIKAWSKY, WAL.	24	M	LABR	RR	ACBF	USA
KALATA, JOSEF	26	M	LABR	RR	ACBF	USA
SCHLASER, LEIB	28	M	LABR	RR	ACBF	USA
GRUNBERG, KILTEN	28	M	LABR	RR	ACBF	USA
WISCHNOWITH, ANNA	27	F	MA	PL	ZZZZ	USA
MARY	3	F	CHILD	PL	ZZZZ	USA
AURY, ISAAC	5	M	CHILD	PL	ACBF	USA
ALBITU, ABRAHAM	20	M	LABR	PL	ACBF	USA
SROLUK, HER	23	M	LABR	PL	ACBF	USA
JACOBOWITCH, MEYER	48	M	LABR	PL	ACBF	USA
COHAN, SCH.	18	M	LABR	PL	ACBF	USA
KATZ, SCHOLEM	46	M	LABR	PL	ACBF	USA
MALOSCHEWITZ, ISAAC	27	M	LABR	PL	ACBF	USA
ROSUMNER, MARCUS	40	M	GDSM	PL	ACBF	USA
CHAIN	24	M	GDSM	PL	ACBF	USA
MARYELAN, JOHAN	46	M	LABR	RR	ZZZZ	USA
RONICKY, MIHAL	11	M	LABR	RR	ZZZZ	USA
TIMBALACK, JULIAN	20	M	LABR	RR	ZZZZ	USA
MESAR, MIHAL	40	M	LABR	RR	ZZZZ	USA
MIRDALE, MIHAL	36	M	LABR	RR	AHQD	USA
HUSE, MEIER	22	M	TLR	RR	ACBF	USA
GIEM, ISAAC	20	M	LABR	RR	ACBF	USA
JURKE, NILS	21	M	LABR	RR	ACBF	USA
CAHN, BENJ.	23	M	LABR	RR	ACBF	USA
KREUTZKY, ABRAHAM	20	M	LABR	RR	ACBF	USA
GLOTZER, BEN.	30	M	MNFTR	RR	ADBQ	USA
LEWIS, LOUIS	30	M	TLR	RR	ADBQ	USA
AUGRIG, FEIGE	.11	F	INFANT	RR	ACBF	USA
SCHAPUS, FREIDE	1	F	CHILD	RR	ACBF	USA
RIBELOWSKY, BLUME	31	F	MA	RR	ACBF	USA
GEDALIE	9	F	CHILD	RR	ACBF	USA
JUDEL	5	M	CHILD	RR	ACBF	USA
ROSEL	.04	F	INFANT	RR	ACBF	USA
JAFFE, EASTER	46	F	MA	RR	ACBF	USA
GITEL	23	F	SVNT	RR	ACBF	USA
MIREL	8	M	CHILD	RR	ACBF	USA
SCHAFUS, CHASSE	38	F	MA	RR	ACBF	USA
WOLF	7	M	CHILD	RR	ACBF	USA
NAWRASKE, SREN	15	M	LABR	RR	ACBF	USA
SARAH	11	F	CH	RR	ACBF	USA
BERKOWITZ, JER.	33	F	MA	RR	ACBF	USA
SARA	7	F	CHILD	RR	ACBF	USA
JACOB	3	M	CHILD	RR	ACBF	USA
WILLENBERG, DINE	20	F	SVNT	RR	ACBF	USA
LEA	18	F	SVNT	RR	ACBF	USA
RITZ, CH.	35	F	MA	RR	ACBF	USA
ISRAEL	4	M	CHILD	RR	ACBF	USA
CHURE	.05	F	INFANT	RR	ACBF	USA
AURIG, CAR.	30	F	MA	RR	ACBF	USA
JOS.	11	M	CH	RR	ACBF	USA
JETTE	9	F	CHILD	RR	ACBF	USA
JENTE	7	F	CHILD	RR	ACBF	USA

SHIP: EGYPTIAN MONARCH

FROM: LONDON
TO: NEW YORK
ARRIVED: 04 MARCH 1886

PASSENGER	AGE	SEX	OCCUPATION	PRI	VIL	DES
DUISMAN, JACOB	23	M	CBTMKR	RR	ZZZZ	NY
RESS, MARK	23	M	TLR	RR	ZZZZ	NY
LORAH	26	F	W	RR	ZZZZ	NY
LUDWIG	1	M	CHILD	RR	ZZZZ	NY
ARYA	00	F	INF	RR	ZZZZ	NY
LALTZ, MOZIS	18	M	B	RR	ZZZZ	NY
FEELIZ, OLGE	20	F	CPMKR	RR	ZZZZ	NY

SHIP: LABRADOR

FROM: HAVRE
TO: NEW YORK
ARRIVED: 04 MARCH 1886

PASSENGER	AGE	SEX	OCCUPATION	PRI	VIL	DES
DEGESSLER, NICOLAS	47	M	COL	RR	ZZZZ	USA

SHIP: RUGIA

FROM: HAMBURG
TO: NEW YORK
ARRIVED: 04 MARCH 1886

PASSENGER	AGE	SEX	OCCUPATION	PRI	VIL	DES
TEKOFSKY, SAL.	40	M	DLR	RR	ZZZZ	USA
ROSENBLUM, WOLF	19	M	BKR	RR	ZZZZ	USA
MILKEWITZ, LENENT	29	M	LABR	RR	ZZZZ	USA
CAROLINE	27	F	W	RR	ZZZZ	USA
ULEWITZ, JAN	25	M	LABR	RR	ZZZZ	USA
SLESKIN, PETER	23	M	FARMER	RR	ZZZZ	USA
PLECHARSKY, ANTON	36	M	LABR	RR	ZZZZ	USA
KOLASZYNSKY, JOSEPH	38	M	LABR	RR	ZZZZ	USA
SAVICKY, PETER	35	M	LABR	RR	ZZZZ	USA
HARTMANN, JUL.	34	M	LABR	RR	ZZZZ	USA
HERRMANN, MORITZ	18	M	MCHT	RR	ZZZZ	USA
HALPER, JANKEL	42	M	DLR	RR	ZZZZ	USA
HIRSCH	9	M	CHILD	RR	ZZZZ	USA
COHN, MASCHA	20	F	W	RR	ZZZZ	USA
RACHEL	.11	M	INFANT	RR	ZZZZ	USA
CASS, JACOB	26	M	DLR	RR	ZZZZ	USA
STEINBERG, LINE	16	F	SGL	RR	ZZZZ	USA
BROZONSKY, WILIE	40	F	W	RR	ZZZZ	USA
MERE	14	F	CH	RR	ZZZZ	USA
SUSSEL	9	F	CHILD	RR	ZZZZ	USA
RACHIMIEL	3	M	CHILD	RR	ZZZZ	USA
OHLSCHEWSKY, PAUL	21	M	LABR	RR	ZZZZ	USA
MARCHUND, VINCENT	45	M	LABR	RR	ZZZZ	USA
KING, ABRAH.	18	M	TLR	RR	ZZZZ	USA
KARNOWSKI, SCHOLEM	45	M	DLR	RR	ZZZZ	USA
SCHIFMANN, DAVID	28	M	TLR	RR	ZZZZ	USA
HURWITZ, ESTER	22	F	W	RR	ZZZZ	USA
EFRAIM	.11	M	INFANT	RR	ZZZZ	USA
WILK, SCHIMEN	15	M	TLR	RR	ZZZZ	USA
SINGER, JANKEL	38	M	TLR	RR	ZZZZ	USA
SKAWRONECK, ISRAEL	26	M	SHMK	RR	ZZZZ	USA
ERNST, JULS.	24	M	LABR	RR	ZZZZ	USA
HAF, AUG.	22	M	LABR	RR	ZZZZ	USA
PLICKOWSKY, JAC.	18	M	SHMK	RR	ZZZZ	USA
MAGID, BASCHE	16	F	SGL	RR	ZZZZ	USA
PLIKOWSKY, FREID.	20	F	W	RR	ZZZZ	USA

PASSENGER	AGE	SEX	OCCUPATION	PRV VIL DES
GITTEL	.11	F	INFANT	RRZZZZUSA
GOLDSTEIN, CHAIM	21	M	DLR	RRZZZZUSA
FRIEDMANN, NATHAN	17	M	DLR	RRZZZZUSA
WINKELMANN, LOUIS	19	M	DLR	RRZZZZUSA
MOSCHKOWITZ, EISSIK	36	M	LABR	RRZZZZUSA
FLATAN, CHAIE	19	F	SGL	RRZZZZUSA
ROSENBERG, SALMEN	17	M	LABR	RRZZZZUSA
STOFA, MIHAL	24	M	LABR	RRZZZZUSA
PASHIG, ANDR.	32	M	LABR	RRZZZZUSA
BERESH, JANOS	49	M	LABR	RRZZZZUSA
PALBERG, REINHOLD	25	M	MCHT	RRZZZZUSA

SHIP: CITY OF BERLIN

FROM: LIVERPOOL AND QUEENSTOWN
TO: NEW YORK
ARRIVED: 05 MARCH 1886

PASSENGER	AGE	SEX	OCCUPATION	PRV VIL DES
DANIELSON, JOHAN	49	M	LABR	RRAGUZNY

SHIP: LYDIAN MONARCH

FROM: LONDON
TO: NEW YORK
ARRIVED: 05 MARCH 1886

PASSENGER	AGE	SEX	OCCUPATION	PRV VIL DES
WAGNER, A.	20	M	TLR	RRZZZZNY
DANSIK, M.	28	M	BCHR	RRZZZZNY
KUDIRSKY, A.	21	M	TLR	RRZZZZNY
LEVY, M.	26	M	TLR	RRZZZZNY
SARAH	24	F	UNKNOWN	RRZZZZNY
IDA	.03	F	INFANT	RRZZZZNY
JESSIR, J.	19	M	TLR	RRZZZZNY
JASKOLSKY, B.	19	M	MECH	RRZZZZNY
KATSCHEROFF, J.	23	M	HTR	RRZZZZNY
LEVY, J.	20	M	FUR	RRZZZZNY
HEWIC, L.	39	M	MCHT	RRZZZZNY

SHIP: MARTHA

FROM: STETTIN
TO: NEW YORK
ARRIVED: 05 MARCH 1886

PASSENGER	AGE	SEX	OCCUPATION	PRV VIL DES
GOTTLIEB, HEYMANN	35	M	TRDSMN	RRZZZZCLE
SOHNABEL, RICHARD	24	M	LABR	PLZZZZWI
PRZGSIEK, IGNATZ	22	M	LABR	PLZZZZMI
FRANKOWIAK, MARIA	15	F	SVNT	PLZZZZMI
MUELLER, ESTER-RACHEL	45	F	WO	RRZZZZNY
MARISOHE	19	F	CH	RRZZZZNY
TAUBER	17	F	CH	RRZZZZNY
ZIRZEN, ABE.	17	M	CH	RRZZZZNY
FRONIE	9	M	CHILD	RRZZZZNY
JOSEF	7	M	CHILD	RRZZZZNY
SARASCHU, E.	26	M	UNKNOWN	PLZZZZNY

SHIP: STATE OF NEBRASKA

FROM: GLASGOW AND LARNE
TO: NEW YORK
ARRIVED: 05 MARCH 1886

PASSENGER	AGE	SEX	OCCUPATION	PRV VIL DES
MATGAN, MICH.	25	M	LABR	RRZZZZNY
WASYL	18	M	LABR	RRZZZZNY
GOJVOS, JANOS	42	M	LABR	RRZZZZNY
PROJTGO, GEORG	25	M	LABR	RRZZZZNY
PETROWITZKI, ABRAHAM	47	M	DLR	RRZZZZUNK
JOSEPH	27	M	DLR	RRZZZZUNK
SCHERMANN, JOSEF	27	M	DLR	RRZZZZNY
BIER, FEIWE	20	M	DLR	RRZZZZNY
BAJER, ABRAHAM	42	M	DLR	RRZZZZNY
SODOWSKY, BER	28	M	DLR	RRZZZZNY
ZERTES, CHAIM	30	M	DLR	RRZZZZNY
STEINMANN, MOSES-L.	28	M	DLR	RRZZZZNY
SORNOW, ISAAC	30	M	DLR	RRZZZZNY
ATOA, ZODECK	23	M	DLR	RRZZZZNY
LAPIDUS, BER	25	M	DLR	RRZZZZNY
NECHANNE	25	F	NN	RRZZZZNY
SARETZKI, SCHEPSEL	33	M	DLR	RRZZZZNY
GIRSON, SCHEPSEL	23	M	DLR	RRZZZZNY
RULSTEIN, ABRAHAM	33	M	DLR	RRZZZZNY
ZUCKERMANN, DEBORA	20	F	NN	RRZZZZNY
CHEIFEL, ROCHA	19	F	NN	RRZZZZNY
RUDNIK, MOSES	23	M	DLR	RRZZZZNY
KARBENEK, CHAIM	18	M	DLR	RRZZZZNY
NICOLAJEWSKY, ABRAHAM	31	M	DLR	RRZZZZNY
DOLGON, MEYER-A.	27	M	DLR	RRZZZZNY
LIBERMANN, SCHULEM	60	M	DLR	RRZZZZNY
BECKER, MOSES	33	M	DLR	RRZZZZNY
GORETZKY, JOSEF	30	M	MSN	RRZZZZNY
KAPLAN, ZEMACH	37	M	DLR	RRZZZZNY
WEINER, SCHLOME	22	M	MLR	RRZZZZNY
KARPEL, JANKEL-L.	34	M	DLR	RRZZZZNY
BATNISKY, MARY-ANN	42	F	W	RRZZZZNY
LETONSKY, JOS.	24	M	LABR	RRZZZZNY

SHIP: WESER

FROM: BREMEN
TO: NEW YORK
ARRIVED: 05 MARCH 1886

PASSENGER	AGE	SEX	OCCUPATION	PRV VIL DES
PODLYISKI, JOSEF	60	M	LABR	RRZZZZUSA
DUB, E.	30	M	LABR	RRZZZZUSA
SIMON	10	M	NN	RRZZZZUSA
SALEN	8	M	CHILD	RRZZZZUSA

SHIP: WERRA

FROM: BREMEN AND SOUTHAMPTON
TO: NEW YORK
ARRIVED: 06 MARCH 1886

PASSENGER	AGE	SEX	OCCUPATION	PRV VIL DES
MULLER, BERMANN	36	M	LABR	RRZZZZUSA
KAPLAN, HARRIS	38	M	LABR	RRZZZZUSA
SCHORK, AUGUST	40	M	FARMER	RRZZZZUSA
CHRISTIANE	36	F	W	RRZZZZUSA
MARIA	15	F	NN	RRZZZZUSA
CATH.	8	F	CHILD	RRZZZZUSA
CHRISTIANE	4	F	CHILD	RRZZZZUSA

PASSENGER	AGE	SEX	OCCUPATION	PRV VIL DES
LYDIA	3	F	CHILD	RRZZZZUSA
JACOB	.11	M	INFANT	RRZZZZUSA
EPHROSINE	22	F	NN	RRZZZZUSA
HORMANY, JACOB	24	M	FARMER	RRZZZZUSA
FRANZ, FRIEDR.	25	M	LABR	RRZZZZUSA
ROSINE	24	F	W	RRZZZZUSA
MARIE	.03	F	INFANT	RRZZZZUSA
NEUFELD, PETER	48	M	FARMER	RRZZZZUSA
CATH.	47	F	W	RRZZZZUSA
CATH.	20	F	NN	RRZZZZUSA
ANNA	16	F	NN	RRZZZZUSA
ANGANITA	14	F	NN	RRZZZZUSA
ELISABETH	12	F	CH	RRZZZZUSA
MARIA	11	F	CH	RRZZZZUSA
JACOB	7	M	CHILD	RRZZZZUSA
SUSANNE	1	F	CHILD	RRZZZZUSA
KERSEH, ABRAHAM	21	M	BCHR	RRZZZZUSA
ROSENBERG, MEYER	18	M	TLR	RRZZZZUSA
MINNA	19	F	NN	RRZZZZUSA
ALPERSTEIN, PERRE	24	F	NN	RRZZZZUSA
KOROPCZIK, HENNE	50	F	NN	RRZZZZUSA

SHIP: AURANIA

FROM: LIVERPOOL AND QUEENSTOWN
TO: NEW YORK
ARRIVED: 08 MARCH 1886

PASSENGER	AGE	SEX	OCCUPATION	PRV VIL DES
NILKUWITZ, ISRAEL	22	M	LABR	PLZZZZBO
STANDEL, JOSEF	24	M	LABR	PLZZZZNY
FUHRMANN, HIRSCH	20	M	LABR	PLZZZZNY
HINDEL, ISRAEL	30	M	LABR	PLZZZZNY
DAMN, HIRSCH	16	M	LABR	PLZZZZNY
BUNZELL, DAVID	46	M	LABR	PLZZZZNY
HASLOWSKY, ABR.	23	M	LABR	PLZZZZNY
SCHINWALS, FRANK	33	M	LABR	PLZZZZNY
KAPPAM, SAM	23	M	LABR	PLZZZZNY
OCKRA, SELIZ	18	M	LABR	PLZZZZNY
ZLATT	20	M	LABR	PLZZZZNY
AHLER, DAVID	22	M	LABR	PLZZZZNY
WIMTHOKY, ANTON	34	M	LABR	PLZZZZNY
WESSETRISKY, ANTON	23	M	FARMER	PLZZZZNY
WILM.	44	M	FARMER	PLZZZZNY
MS.	38	F	W	PLZZZZNY
FRED.	11	M	CH	PLZZZZNY
JOSEF	9	M	CHILD	PLZZZZNY
FELIX	4	M	CHILD	PLZZZZNY
MARIANE	3	F	CHILD	PLZZZZNY
FOATSTERIC, ADAM	26	M	LABR	PLZZZZNY
TOPSCHIWSKY, DAVID	42	M	LABR	PLZZZZNY
FROGSOTH, JACOB	30	M	LABR	PLZZZZNY
FRESESIN, MICHAEL	30	M	LABR	PLZZZZNY
RUSTAKOF, MOSES	36	M	LABR	PLZZZZNY

SHIP: DEVONIA

FROM: GLASGOW
TO: NEW YORK
ARRIVED: 08 MARCH 1886

PASSENGER	AGE	SEX	OCCUPATION	PRV VIL DES
YOUKEL, AX.	19	M	TLR	PLACBFUSA
ABRAMOWITZ, ADAM	45	M	LABR	PLACBFUSA
BOSHIN, HIRSCH	25	M	BLKSMH	PLACBFUSA
CHALOSEN, MARKUS	19	M	PDLR	PLACBFUSA
SCHOVE	22	M	PDLR	PLACBFUSA
GOLDBLATT, SALMON	24	M	PDLR	PLACBFUSA
GLASMAN, NAFTAL.	22	M	PDLR	PLACBFUSA
MIR.	23	M	PDLR	PLACBFUSA
GLEITER, MOSCHE	21	M	BLKSMH	PLACBFUSA
HIRSCHKOWITZ, NOCHEN	26	M	LABR	PLACBFUSA
KATZ, SCHLOME	50	M	MCHT	PLACBFUSA
KOGEL, LEISER	30	M	TLR	PLACBFUSA
KALEDER, MICHAL	28	M	LABR	PLACBFUSA
KOSGNEWSKI, JOSEFA	23	F	W	PLACBFUSA
ALEXANDRA	.09	F	INFANT	PLACBFUSA
KALIMOWITZ, ABRAHAM	23	M	PDLR	PLACBFUSA
LICHTERMANN, IZIG	26	M	SHMK	PLACBFUSA
LEVIN, B.	26	M	PDLR	PLACBFUSA
LECHOWITZ, ARON	31	M	PDLR	PLACBFUSA
MUCSHITZ, IVAN	24	M	LABR	PLACBFUSA
OLVER, ANTON	26	M	LABR	PLACBFUSA
PELKIEWITZ, JAN	34	M	SHMK	PLACBFUSA
PERKOWSKI, VINICK	24	M	LABR	PLACBFUSA
SALOMON	21	M	PDLR	PLACBFUSA
RUBINTZIK, MORDCHE	25	M	BLKSMH	PLACBFUSA
RITZKIN, ITZIG	21	M	MECH	PLACBFUSA
RUBENSTEIN, ELIE	28	M	PDLR	PLACBFUSA
SCHANMSCKI, DAV.	20	M	TLR	PLACBFUSA
SLONIKOWSKI, FRANZ	21	M	LABR	PLACBFUSA
SCHNEIDER, FRANZ	30	M	LABR	PLACBFUSA
ULOJURS, ABRAHAM	22	M	PDLR	PLACBFUSA

SHIP: EGYPT

FROM: LIVERPOOL
TO: NEW YORK
ARRIVED: 08 MARCH 1886

PASSENGER	AGE	SEX	OCCUPATION	PRV VIL DES
ZUMARD, JOSEPH	34	M	LABR	PLAEFLUSA
JOHONER, MOSES	29	M	LABR	PLAEFLUSA
E.	27	M	LABR	PLAEFLUSA
KONIG, E.	36	M	LABR	PLAEFLUSA
WASPONSKY, GABRIEL	27	M	LABR	PLAEFLUSA
LOENE, ABR.	30	M	LABR	PLAAECUSA
RYBACK, JACOB	25	M	LABR	PLAAECUSA
LECHEWITZ, LEIB	55	M	LABR	PLAAECUSA
LEGER	10	M	CH	PLAAECUSA
WASSIKOWSKY, MEYER	26	M	LABR	PLAAECUSA
KAMINSKY, K.	30	M	LABR	PLAAECUSA
APPLBAUM, H.	26	M	LABR	PLAAECUSA
KRAVIT, WOLF	26	M	LABR	PLAAECUSA
KOGEL, MAX	20	M	LABR	RRZZZZUSA
LEVI, I.	20	M	LABR	RRZZZZUSA
ARHWITZ, S.	28	M	LABR	RRZZZZUSA
GREENBERG, SOLOMON	33	M	LABR	RRZZZZUSA
SLARSEWETZ, E.	25	M	LABR	RRZZZZUSA
MOWDSA, JOSEPH	24	M	LABR	RRZZZZUSA
BERRINAS, I.	28	M	LABR	RRZZZZUSA
CERSOVSKY, M.	25	M	LABR	RRZZZZUSA
RUBIN, P.	26	M	LABR	RRZZZZUSA
SCHUNNER, JOS.	26	M	LABR	RRADBQUSA
MEDNICK, MOSES	19	M	LABR	RRADBQUSA
KOCH, BERL	20	M	LABR	RRADBQUSA
HERKOWSKY, M.	25	M	LABR	RRADBQUSA
LEVI, JACOB	19	M	LABR	RRADBQUSA
GASFMERT, ABRAHAM	25	M	LABR	RRADBQUSA
EDELSTEIN, B.	19	M	LABR	RRADBQUSA
ARONSKY, M.	47	M	LABR	RRADBQUSA
HASDEN, S.	24	M	LABR	RRADBQUSA
FELDSMANN, LEVI	22	M	LABR	RRADBQUSA
HYKOFSKY, M.	19	M	LABR	RRADBQUSA
RESNIK, JOSEF	25	M	LABR	RRADBQUSA
KOSTELSKY, BERHE	46	M	LABR	RRADBQUSA
WACHTER, FRED	39	M	LABR	RRADBQUSA
MATOWSKY, SIMON	40	M	LABR	RRADBQUSA

PASSENGER	AGE	SEX	OCCUPATION	PRV VIL DES
FERLER, S.	20	M	LABR	RRADBQUSA
BECKAURT, S.	19	M	LABR	RRADBQUSA
FETENHA, M.	27	M	LABR	RRADBQUSA
SARAH	20	F	W	RRACBFUSA

SHIP: HELVETIA

FROM: LIVERPOOL
TO: NEW YORK
ARRIVED: 08 MARCH 1886

PASSENGER	AGE	SEX	OCCUPATION	PRV VIL DES
PEDVISON, RUDOLF	39	M	LABR	RRZZZZUSA
COHEN, JACOB	28	M	LABR	RRZZZZUSA
LUGAR, LAUGH	29	M	LABR	RRZZZZUSA
CARLSON, JULIUS	22	M	LABR	RRZZZZUSA
GOLDFRED, LAUB	24	M	LABR	RRZZZZUSA

SHIP: LESSING

FROM: HAMBURG
TO: NEW YORK
ARRIVED: 08 MARCH 1886

PASSENGER	AGE	SEX	OCCUPATION	PRV VIL DES
FINKELSTEIN, LIEBE	30	F	W	RRAHTFUSA
FEIGE	.11	M	INFANT	RRAHTFUSA
SIESKIND, SOLOMON	18	M	LABR	RRAHTNUSA
HADINITZ, ISAAC	20	M	MCHT	RRAHYGUSA
T.	18	F	W	RRAHYGUSA
RABINOWITZ, BORIS	16	M	LABR	RRAHTUUSA
SEOLIN, JOSEPH	19	M	LABR	RRAHTUUSA
GORDITZ, ABRAHAM	28	M	LABR	RRAHTUUSA
KOPERMANN, MICHEL	31	M	LABR	RRAHTUUSA
STEMPELMANN, BENJAMIN	38	M	TLR	RRAGRTUSA
RUTOWITSCH, LOUIS	47	M	LABR	RRAHQHUSA
GRUNBERG, JUDES	27	F	W	RRAHQUUSA
LEAH	4	F	CHILD	RRAHQUUSA
DAVID	.11	M	INFANT	RRAHQUUSA
KROK, ISAAC	25	M	JNR	RRAHZAUSA
EISENSTEIN, RIVKA	50	F	W	RRAHSCUSA
ARUNISS, LEIB	40	M	LABR	RRAHZSUSA
ISAAC	43	M	LABR	RRAHZSUSA
DZIEWULSKI, LEONHARD	33	M	UNKNOWN	RRAHTYUSA
AMALIE	29	F	W	RRAHTYUSA
WANDA	.09	F	INFANT	RRAHTYUSA
GOLDIN, SCHEINE	17	F	SGL	RRAHTUUSA
SCHWARZBURG, JOSEF	23	M	DLR	RRAHTKUSA
BECKER, NOCHIM	23	M	DLR	RRAHYJUSA
OCHSENBURG, ARON	28	M	TLR	RRAHTUUSA
KORNBLUM, ANNA	26	F	SGL	RRAHQUUSA
MESCHEL, SCHAJ.	25	M	CGRMKR	RRAHUEUSA
MICHELSON, CHR.	38	M	MCHT	RRAHTFUSA
LEWIN, J.	38	M	DLR	RRAGRTUSA
KUNZEWEICZKY, ELIAS	19	M	DLR	RRZZZZUSA
SCHULTE, ANTON	23	M	LABR	RRAHZSUSA
WISCHNIEWSKY, LUDWIG	28	M	LABR	RRAHZSUSA
KRUPETZKI, J.	25	M	UNKNOWN	RRAHZSUSA
LIPNAZKY, TAMARE	40	F	W	RRAHZSUSA
FREIDE	6	F	CHILD	RRAHZSUSA
FRUME	18	F	W	RRAHZSUSA
ELIAS	6	M	CHILD	RRAHZSUSA
GOZORSKY, ABRAHAM	24	M	TLR	RRAHZSUSA
LEWITAN, ARJE	35	M	DLR	RRAHSPUSA
GURWITZ, LEISER	44	M	LABR	RRAHZKUSA
KOSLOWSKY, LEISER	49	M	LABR	RRAHZKUSA
KORZOWSKY, JOSEF	24	M	MCHT	RRAHWTUSA
KOLISCHEWSKY, ANTON	34	M	LABR	RRAHTFUSA
TUROWSKY, JOSEF	30	M	LABR	RRAHTFUSA
TYRINSKY, MARIA	28	M	LABR	RRAHTFUSA
KOWALSCHINSKY, JOS.	16	M	LABR	RRAHTFUSA
JAN	28	M	LABR	RRAHTFUSA
SOBISINSKA, PAULINE	20	M	LABR	RRAHTFUSA
BIRUBANN, MAX.	22	M	CRTMK	RRAHVUUSA
EIDELES, MOSES	50	M	CL	RRAHUVUSA
ZIMONIEWSKI, JULIAN	23	M	FARMER	RRAHVIUSA
GRUNSTEIN, ISRAEL	24	M	FARMER	RRAHSWUSA
MARGELIS, CHAIM	45	M	FARMER	RRAHSWUSA

SHIP: NEDERLAND

FROM: ANTWERP
TO: NEW YORK
ARRIVED: 08 MARCH 1886

PASSENGER	AGE	SEX	OCCUPATION	PRV VIL DES
KOWALOWSKI, H.	18	M	TLR	PLZZZZUNK
PREZINSKI, TH.	24	M	LABR	PLZZZZUNK
GABEL, HEB.	23	F	MUSN	PLZZZZNY
SAR.	19	F	MUSN	PLZZZZNY
EMEL	18	F	MUSN	PLZZZZNY

SHIP: POLARIA

FROM: HAMBURG
TO: NEW YORK
ARRIVED: 08 MARCH 1886

PASSENGER	AGE	SEX	OCCUPATION	PRV VIL DES
LACOMY, DAVID	38	M	TLR	RRZZZZNY
KORNBLUM, DAVD.	57	M	MCHT	RRZZZZNY
PACHIWISCJI, R.	21	M	LABR	RRZZZZNY
BELLONISKY, MALIAS	20	M	LABR	RRZZZZNY
DANKS, OSSIP	23	M	LABR	RRZZZZNY
JUWARZAWICZ, VINE	20	M	LABR	RRZZZZNY
LEBOLSKY, AUG.	26	M	BKR	RRZZZZNY

SHIP: GERMAIN

FROM: HAVRE
TO: NEW YORK
ARRIVED: 09 MARCH 1886

PASSENGER	AGE	SEX	OCCUPATION	PRV VIL DES
BAUNN, LIEB	22	M	CL	RRZZZZNY

SHIP: WYOMING

FROM: LIVERPOOL AND QUEENSTOWN
TO: NEW YORK
ARRIVED: 09 MARCH 1886

PASSENGER	AGE	SEX	OCCUPATION	PRV VIL DES
PAUL, JOHN	28	M	FARMER	PLZZZZUSA
MARY	50	F	W	PLZZZZUSA
FRANK	10	M	CH	PLZZZZUSA

PASSENGER	AGE	SEX	OCCUPATION	PRIV	VIL	DES
FRANCISEN	1	F	CHILD	PL	ZZZZ	USA
GRUN, ESJE	22	F	SP	PL	ZZZZ	USA
BEZMEREWICZ, ANTON	28	M	CPTR	PL	ZZZZ	USA
ANDRASEWSKY, PAULA	21	M	CPTR	PL	ZZZZ	USA
GRUMBERG, GOTZEL	24	M	FARMER	PL	ZZZZ	USA
FEIGE	20	F	W	PL	ZZZZ	USA

SHIP: BELGENLAND

FROM: ANTWERP
TO: NEW YORK
ARRIVED: 12 MARCH 1886

PASSENGER	AGE	SEX	OCCUPATION	PRIV	VIL	DES
SZMEITAROWITZ, M.	30	F	WO	PL	ZZZZ	NY
SZMYTEROWICZ, A.	50	M	LABR	PL	ZZZZ	NY

SHIP: MAIN

FROM: BREMEN
TO: NEW YORK
ARRIVED: 12 MARCH 1886

PASSENGER	AGE	SEX	OCCUPATION	PRIV	VIL	DES
NOCHAMKIN, MICKE	36	F	W	RR	ZZZZ	USA
ESTER	15	F	D	RR	ZZZZ	USA
SIMON	8	M	CHILD	RR	ZZZZ	USA
CHAJE	9	M	CHILD	RR	ZZZZ	USA
FREIDE	6	F	CHILD	RR	ZZZZ	USA

SHIP: ST. OF PENNSYLVANIA

FROM: GLASGOW AND LARNE
TO: NEW YORK
ARRIVED: 12 MARCH 1886

PASSENGER	AGE	SEX	OCCUPATION	PRIV	VIL	DES
ARBECK, A.	37	M	MCHT	RR	ZZZZ	USA
BERENSOHN, B.	24	M	MCHT	RR	ZZZZ	USA
BITZKOWSKY, L.	28	M	MCHT	RR	ZZZZ	USA
BLOCK, SCHANI	38	M	MCHT	RR	ZZZZ	USA
BODO, KATHARINA	22	F	NN	RR	ZZZZ	USA
CHADOWITZ, AISIK	25	M	JNR	RR	AHTU	USA
CHAIFETZ, JANSKEL	28	M	MCHT	RR	ZZZZ	USA
PAN, BENZION	42	M	MCHT	RR	ZZZZ	USA
FEINSTEIN, DAVID	25	M	TLR	RR	ZZZZ	USA
FREIMAN, ISAAC	43	M	MCHT	RR	ZZZZ	USA
PINIL, ABRAH.JUR.	28	M	PT	RR	ZZZZ	USA
GELBJOHN, MAR.	27	M	JNR	RR	ZZZZ	USA
GITTIN, MORDSCHE	40	M	MCHT	RR	ZZZZ	USA
GRIDZINSKY, ISAAC	55	M	MCHT	RR	AFVG	USA
HIRSCH	10	M	NN	RR	AFVG	USA
HERSCHMANN, HERZ	40	M	MCHT	RR	AHTO	USA
HOLLANDER, CHAIME	18	M	TLR	RR	ZZZZ	USA
ITLIAS, PETRO	40	M	LABR	RR	AHZS	USA
KAPUTIN, MICHAL	24	M	LABR	RR	ZZZZ	USA
KATZ, ASIAS	27	M	MCHT	RR	ZZZZ	USA
KUZEL, ISAAC-MOSES	22	M	BCHR	RR	AHTU	USA
LEVIN, LEISER	44	M	TLR	RR	ZZZZ	USA
LIACHOWSKI, ARON	25	M	TLR	RR	ZZZZ	USA
MANIZEWITZ, ABRAM	28	M	MCHT	RR	ZZZZ	USA
MINNA	20	F	NN	RR	ZZZZ	USA
PASCHE	18	F	NN	RR	ZZZZ	USA
MICHELOWITZKY, B.	22	M	LABR	RR	ZZZZ	USA
MUDRI, KONSTANTIN	27	M	LABR	RR	ZZZZ	USA
MIRSNISKY, DAVID	48	M	LABR	RR	ZZZZ	USA
JOSSEL	20	M	LABR	RR	ZZZZ	USA
NEFACH, SCHLOMAH	23	M	MCHT	RR	ZZZZ	USA
DEWOSCHE	20	F	NN	RR	ZZZZ	USA
ORSEWITZ, SCHLOME	38	M	CPTR	RR	ZZZZ	USA
PERSKY, CHAIM	24	M	MCHT	RR	ZZZZ	USA
PRESSMON, MICHEL	36	M	JNR	RR	AHTU	USA
RUBEMANN, ISAC	28	M	MCHT	RR	ZZZZ	USA
RUBINSTEIN, MOSES-C.	36	M	TLR	RR	ZZZZ	USA
RUITSTEIN, MORDSCHE	35	M	TLR	RR	ZZZZ	USA
MOSES	34	M	TLR	RR	ZZZZ	USA
SCHNEIDER, FEIWEL	23	M	JNR	RR	ZZZZ	USA
OZIAS	34	M	JNR	RR	ZZZZ	USA
SCHMIDT, JOSEF	19	M	JNR	RR	ZZZZ	USA
JACOB	16	M	JNR	RR	ZZZZ	USA
AISIC	20	M	JNR	RR	ZZZZ	USA
SECHOWITZ, PJATRO	24	M	LABR	RR	ZZZZ	USA
SANOLENSKY, STANISL.	20	M	LABR	RR	ZZZZ	USA
SKOWANSKY, MICHAEL	30	M	LABR	RR	ZZZZ	USA
STASCHINUS, JAN	00	M	LABR	RR	ZZZZ	USA
WIGOWITZ, MORDSCHE	40	M	MCHT	RR	ZZZZ	USA
RASCHE	40	F	NN	RR	ZZZZ	USA
ABRAHAM	00	M	NN	RR	ZZZZ	USA
CHAIM	11	M	NN	RR	ZZZZ	USA
MOSES	10	M	NN	RR	ZZZZ	USA
CHANNE	1	F	CHILD	RR	ZZZZ	USA
SARAH	7	F	CHILD	RR	ZZZZ	USA
WISCHNEWSKI, FRANZ	28	M	FARMER	RR	ZZZZ	USA
VERONIKA	25	F	NN	RR	ZZZZ	USA
LEWIN, SALOMON	21	M	TLR	RR	AHTU	USA

SHIP: CITY OF CHESTER

FROM: LIVERPOOL AND QUEENSTOWN
TO: NEW YORK
ARRIVED: 15 MARCH 1886

PASSENGER	AGE	SEX	OCCUPATION	PRIV	VIL	DES
GRUCHALD, THOM.	24	M	LABR	PL	ZZZZ	NY
PAULAK, FRANZ	24	M	LABR	PL	ADAX	PA

SHIP: OREGON

FROM: LIVERPOOL AND QUEENSTOWN
TO: NEW YORK
ARRIVED: 15 MARCH 1886

PASSENGER	AGE	SEX	OCCUPATION	PRIV	VIL	DES
BERMAN, ISRAEL	18	M	LABR	RR	ZZZZ	NY
FARBIRE, THEODORES	33	M	LABR	RR	ZZZZ	NY
BARNER, ANDERS	19	M	LABR	RR	ZZZZ	NY
BLATTMAN, ISAAC	33	M	LABR	RR	ZZZZ	NY
BLUMENSTEIN, JOSEPH	35	M	FARMER	RR	ZZZZ	NY
ERWENEZIK, MORDCKE	50	M	LABR	RR	ZZZZ	NY
BEERMANN, SELINA	50	M	LABR	RR	ZZZZ	NY
SCHEINE	20	M	LABR	RR	ZZZZ	NY
BAUMBLIT, SAMUEL	50	M	LABR	RR	ZZZZ	NY
SEIDE	20	M	LABR	RR	ZZZZ	NY
ZOREL	18	M	LABR	RR	ZZZZ	NY
EPHRAIM	17	M	LABR	RR	ZZZZ	NY
RIBAKOFF, VICTOR	24	M	FARMER	RR	ZZZZ	NY
KALNASY, THERESE	20	F	SP	RR	ZZZZ	NY
COHEN, ROSA	51	F	MA	PL	ZZZZ	MN
MAURICE	19	M	CL	PL	ZZZZ	MN
WILLIAM	16	M	CL	PL	ZZZZ	MN

PASSENGER	AGE	SEX	OCCUPATION	PRVL	VIL	DES
SAVENA, MICHAEL	30	M	LABR	PL	ZZZZ	NY
KOLODEY, IGNAZ	29	M	TLR	PL	ZZZZ	NY
POINANSKI, FRANZ	25	M	LABR	PL	ZZZZ	NY
BRAUSMANE, ROSA	35	F	MA	PL	ZZZZ	NY
SUSSE	16	F	SP	PL	ZZZZ	NY
MARIE	11	F	SP	PL	ZZZZ	NY
NATHAN	8	M	CHILD	PL	ZZZZ	NY
JACOB	6	M	CHILD	PL	ZZZZ	NY

SHIP: ARIZONA

FROM: LIVERPOOL AND QUEENSTOWN
TO: NEW YORK
ARRIVED: 16 MARCH 1886

PASSENGER	AGE	SEX	OCCUPATION	PRVL	VIL	DES
BECKER, SAML.	19	M	FARMER	PL	AHQH	USA

SHIP: BRITANNIC

FROM: LIVERPOOL AND QUEENSTOWN
TO: NEW YORK
ARRIVED: 16 MARCH 1886

PASSENGER	AGE	SEX	OCCUPATION	PRVL	VIL	DES
WASERITZ, ANNA	18	F	SVNT	PL	ACBF	USA
JORSEF, KURNA	22	F	SVNT	PL	ACBF	USA
ISTARANGUE, H.CUDAY	28	F	W	PL	ACBF	USA
BUDAY, ANDREAS	4	M	CHILD	PL	ACBF	USA
U	.10	F	INFANT	PL	ACBF	USA
RASMUSAN, BIRDINCUS	21	M	LABR	PL	ACBF	USA
STERMLANN, SET.	31	M	LABR	PL	ACBF	USA
HOLENBERG, FRANZ	29	M	LABR	PL	ACBF	USA
JANGAR, JOSEF	27	M	LABR	PL	ACBF	USA
BILINKIN, MOSES	31	M	LABR	PL	ACBF	USA
SCHEIKEL	28	M	LABR	PL	ACBF	USA
SZEZUPAK, BORIS	41	M	LABR	PL	ACBF	USA
ANNITA	39	F	W	PL	ACBF	USA
OFSE	8	F	CHILD	PL	ACBF	USA
LEON	15	M	LABR	PL	ACBF	USA
CAECILIAN	14	F	SP	PL	ACBF	USA
BEAHILENSKY, MANUEL	29	M	FARMER	PL	ACBF	USA
SILBERSTEIN, H.	27	M	FARMER	PL	ACBF	USA

SHIP: ST LAURENT

FROM: HAVRE
TO: NEW YORK
ARRIVED: 18 MARCH 1886

PASSENGER	AGE	SEX	OCCUPATION	PRVL	VIL	DES
SCHMOLL, ALFRED	23	M	CL	RR	ZZZZ	NY

SHIP: ASSYRIAN MONARCH

FROM: LONDON
TO: NEW YORK
ARRIVED: 19 MARCH 1886

PASSENGER	AGE	SEX	OCCUPATION	PRVL	VIL	DES
LEBOWITZ, SIMON	29	M	TRVLR	RR	ADBQ	NY
ROSENBERG, ISAAC	26	M	TLR	RR	ADBQ	NY
SOLFF, MORRIS	20	M	TLR	RR	ADBQ	NY
SOLOMONS, ISRAEL	20	M	TLR	RR	ADBQ	NY
WOLFF, AARON	24	M	TLR	RR	ADBQ	NY
FANNY	22	F	W	RR	ADBQ	NY
ROSENBRANTZ, AARON	46	M	TLR	RR	ADBQ	NY
CLARA	38	F	W	RR	ADBQ	NY
HERRMANN	17	M	LABR	RR	ADBQ	NY
LEVY	10	M	CH	RR	ADBQ	NY
GETHE	4	M	CHILD	RR	ADBQ	NY
ABRAHAM	2	M	CHILD	RR	ADBQ	NY
BONK, ---DEL	56	M	HMRMN	RR	ADBQ	NY
FRIDA	40	F	W	RR	ADBQ	NY
BERTHA	15	F	DMS	RR	ADBQ	NY
HANNAH	11	F	CH	RR	ADBQ	NY
ISAAC	10	M	CH	RR	ADBQ	NY
MOSES	8	M	CHILD	RR	ADBQ	NY
ROSE	7	F	CHILD	RR	ADBQ	NY
SIMON	6	M	CHILD	RR	ADBQ	NY
BERGER, SOLOMON	32	M	TLR	RR	ADBQ	NY
PUNKA, MARY-ANN	18	F	DMS	RR	ADBQ	NY
WOOLF, ISAAC	32	M	TLR	RR	ADBQ	NY
ZIPPLE, LEVY	25	M	TLR	RR	ADBQ	NY
BRUNK, NATHAN	22	M	BRM	RR	ADBQ	NY
KOLING, HIRSCH	27	M	TLR	RR	ADBQ	NY
GANK, BARUK	28	M	TLR	RR	ADBQ	NY
NADLAR, HIRSCH	24	M	TLR	RR	ADBQ	NY
NENBERGER, SAMUEL	18	M	TLR	RR	ADBQ	NY
ISAACSON, JACOB	22	M	TLR	RR	ADBQ	NY
LEVY, D.	25	M	SHMK	RR	ADBQ	NY
SOLOMONS, A.	36	M	MACH	RR	ADBQ	NY

SHIP: RHAETIA

FROM: HAMBURG
TO: NEW YORK
ARRIVED: 19 MARCH 1886

PASSENGER	AGE	SEX	OCCUPATION	PRVL	VIL	DES
HERZBERG, NICOLAI	16	M	LABR	RR	ZZZZ	USA
MAKOWEN, DWORE	26	F	W	RR	ZZZZ	USA
NISSEN	8	M	CHILD	RR	ZZZZ	USA
LEIBEL	7	M	CHILD	RR	ZZZZ	USA
KRUK, RIWKE	38	F	W	RR	ZZZZ	USA
DAVID	34	M	TRDSMN	RR	ZZZZ	USA
CHANE	16	M	CH	RR	ZZZZ	USA
SCHMEIC	9	M	CHILD	RR	ZZZZ	USA
PERE	9	F	CHILD	RR	ZZZZ	USA
ABRAHAM	.11	M	INFANT	RR	ZZZZ	USA
TURECK, ABRAHAM	44	M	TRDSMN	RR	ZZZZ	USA
BERNOWSKE, ITE	17	F	SGL	RR	ZZZZ	USA
DISMANOWITZ, ELIAS	44	M	TLR	RR	ZZZZ	USA
PICOSCH, ROSA	30	F	W	RR	ZZZZ	USA
ESTER	7	F	CHILD	RR	ZZZZ	USA
ANSCHEL	.11	M	INFANT	RR	ZZZZ	USA
MICHELSKY, WULF	40	M	LABR	RR	ZZZZ	USA
SCHUP, RUWIN	51	M	TLR	RR	ZZZZ	USA
ZARNOW, FEWEL	26	M	TLR	RR	ZZZZ	USA
MIENUCHES, MUSCHEL	35	M	TLR	RR	ZZZZ	USA
U, U	00	M	TLR	RR	ZZZZ	USA
LEIB, JOHN	9	M	CHILD	RR	ZZZZ	USA
SNITMANN, MENDEL	38	M	TLR	RR	ZZZZ	USA
MOBSCHIKOW, DAVID	25	M	TLR	RR	ZZZZ	USA

PASSENGER	AGE	SEX	OCCUPATION	PV RIVL DES
ZUKERBERG, ISRAEL	18	M	TLR	RRZZZZUSA
SCHMIDT, LEISER	25	M	TLR	RRZZZZUSA
BREINKEN, NOCHUM	15	M	FUR	RRZZZZUSA
CZERNEWITZ, SALOMON	20	M	SHMK	RRZZZZUSA
RUPPERWASSER, ABRAH.	22	M	LABR	RRZZZZUSA
BERKOWITZ, SARAH	23	F	SGL	RRZZZZUSA
DEMBOWSKA, MALGEZALA	18	F	SGL	RRZZZZUSA
FRANKFURT, SALOMON	18	F	LABR	RRZZZZUSA
PAUL, JOHN	37	F	LABR	RRZZZZUSA
BERSON, LEON	24	F	LABR	RRZZZZUSA
MISCHKIN, LEISER	16	F	MCHT	RRZZZZUSA
ALPEROWITZ, ISRAEL	32	F	LABR	RRZZZZUSA
KANOWITZ, SCHOUL	26	F	LABR	RRZZZZUSA
SIESKEWITZ, SALOMON	20	F	LABR	RRZZZZUSA
HURWITZ, MOSES	40	F	LABR	RRZZZZUSA
HERSCHBERG, JACOB	22	F	LABR	RRZZZZUSA
LIEBE	23	F	W	RRZZZZUSA
KEMMELHOR, FEIWE	18	F	SGL	RRZZZZUSA
CHANIE	19	F	SGL	RRZZZZUSA
JOFFE, ABRAHAM	40	M	LABR	RRZZZZUSA
DICKSTEIN, JOSCHE	45	M	LABR	RRZZZZUSA
ROSENBLATT, SAMUEL	42	M	SHMK	RRZZZZUSA
LINK, SARA	22	F	W	RRZZZZUSA
BERLINSKY, SARA	3	F	CHILD	RRZZZZUSA
WITKIN, CHAIM	32	M	TRDSMN	RRZZZZUSA
LEWIKOSKY, BEILE	26	F	W	RRZZZZUSA
SARA	14	F	SI	RRZZZZUSA
RONY	.11	M	INFANT	RRZZZZUSA
SCHAPIRO, MINNA	24	F	W	RRZZZZUSA
JOSEPH	9	M	CHILD	RRZZZZUSA
SARAH	1	F	CHILD	RRZZZZUSA
AHRENDT, BER	58	M	TRDSMN	RRZZZZUSA
HINDE	50	F	W	RRZZZZUSA
GITEL	19	F	CH	RRZZZZUSA
CHANE	16	F	CH	RRZZZZUSA
WOLLOTZKY, MOSES	28	M	JNR	RRZZZZUSA
BATTCHEN, RUBEN	19	M	TLR	RRZZZZUSA
SAMUEL	46	M	TLR	RRZZZZUSA
NAWISSELSKY, MICHAEL	27	M	TLR	RRZZZZUSA
JURGELL, JOSEF	28	M	TLR	RRZZZZUSA
LEWIN, JOSSEL	34	M	TRDSMN	RRZZZZUSA
CHODOSCH, MICHEL	48	M	TLR	RRZZZZUSA
KANOWALOWA, ESCHKE	40	F	W	RRZZZZUSA
GERSON	15	M	TLR	RRZZZZUSA
SCHWIRSKI, MALKE	24	F	SGL	RRZZZZUSA
LUKASZEWSKI, STANISLAV	22	M	LABR	RRZZZZUSA
LOMAS, LEIB	42	M	MCHT	RRZZZZUSA
FRANKOWSKI, CHAII	40	F	W	RRZZZZUSA
LASER	9	M	CHILD	RRZZZZUSA
ABRAHAM	5	M	CHILD	RRZZZZUSA
JAILE	9	F	CHILD	RRZZZZUSA
LEISER	7	M	CHILD	RRZZZZUSA
MIELINKER, DEBORA	25	F	W	RRZZZZUSA
CHAIM	25	M	LABR	RRZZZZUSA
SCHKOLNITZ, CHAIM	19	M	LABR	RRZZZZUSA
MOSENSOHN, SCHLOME	17	M	LABR	RRZZZZUSA
SZYMANOWSKI, ED.	43	M	LABR	RRZZZZUSA
ROSALIE	36	F	W	RRZZZZUSA
JOSEFA	9	F	CHILD	RRZZZZUSA
PAULNE	5	F	CHILD	RRZZZZUSA
JULIANA	3	F	CHILD	RRZZZZUSA
FRANZ	.03	M	INFANT	RRZZZZUSA
SZYMANSKI, MARTIN	37	M	LABR	RRZZZZUSA
GRABITZKI, BRUNISLAW	43	M	LABR	RRZZZZUSA
PIURKOWSKI, JOHANN	38	M	LABR	RRZZZZUSA
STRASANSKI, CHANIE	20	F	SGL	RRZZZZUSA
SCHNEIDMANN, MARCUS	19	M	JNR	RRZZZZUSA
WIDEMINSKY, JAN	25	M	LABR	RRZZZZUSA
GINSBERG, MONES	23	M	LABR	RRZZZZUSA
MINKOWSKY, POWEL	33	M	LABR	RRZZZZUSA
KRUPNITZKY, MOSES	30	M	JNR	RRZZZZUSA
REPEZINSKI, MINNA	20	F	SGL	RRZZZZUSA
BALBERITZKY, ISRAEL	17	M	BKBNDR	RRZZZZUSA
ARANOWIECZ, ISAAC	20	M	BKBNDR	RRZZZZUSA
GLASER, SCHMERL	19	M	LABR	RRZZZZUSA

SHIP: WAESLAND

FROM: ANTWERP
TO: NEW YORK
ARRIVED: 19 MARCH 1886

PASSENGER	AGE	SEX	OCCUPATION	PV RIVL DES
COHEN, MARX	26	M	LABR	RRAHQDCH

SHIP: ELBE

FROM: BREMEN
TO: NEW YORK
ARRIVED: 20 MARCH 1886

PASSENGER	AGE	SEX	OCCUPATION	PV RIVL DES
ULISKEY, REBECCA	19	F	SVNT	RRZZZZUSA

SHIP: STATE OF INDIANA

FROM: GLASGOW AND LARNE
TO: NEW YORK
ARRIVED: 20 MARCH 1886

PASSENGER	AGE	SEX	OCCUPATION	PV RIVL DES
ALPERON, ELIAS	51	M	TLR	RRZZZZUSA
SALOMON	28	M	TLR	RRZZZZUSA
FECHLNER, BERTHOLD	22	M	SPNR	RRZZZZUSA
KEMP, DAVID	38	M	PDLR	RRZZZZUSA
BASSE, SCHLOME	20	M	PDLR	RRZZZZUSA
SEGALL, SCHAJE	21	M	PDLR	RRZZZZUSA
GRUEND, LEIB	49	M	PDLR	RRAHTUUSA
BRAGADIR, JOSEPH	35	M	PDLR	RRAHTUUSA
LEISER	11	M	CH	RRAHTUUSA
KWIDTEK, MORDCHE	46	M	PDLR	RRAHTOUSA
ISRAEL	31	M	PDLR	RRAHTOUSA
WELT, MEILECH	29	M	PDLR	PLZZZZUSA
BRONOWSKI, NOCHIM	24	M	PDLR	PLZZZZUSA
MUCHAN, MOSES	25	M	TLR	PLZZZZUSA
BATZ, USIEL	25	M	PDLR	PLZZZZUSA
SCHIWEK, CHAIM	34	M	TLR	PLZZZZUSA
SCHIRKOWSKY, ABRAHAM	18	M	TLR	PLZZZZUSA
RITZ, JASCHZAK	36	M	LABR	PLZZZZUSA
LAGAN, FEIWEL	30	M	SHMK	PLZZZZUSA
FISCH, MOSES	44	M	JNR	PLZZZZUSA
SABRODSKY, JOSEF	32	M	LABR	PLACBFUSA
RATZKOWSKY, MICHAL	39	M	LABR	PLZZZZUSA
MICHAL	26	M	LABR	PLZZZZUSA
ZWISCHDOCK, JOSEPH	9	M	CHILD	PLZZZZUSA
JOSEPH	7	M	CHILD	PLZZZZUSA
SKALSKA, VIKTORIA	39	F	W	PLZZZZUSA
ANTONIE	4	F	CHILD	PLZZZZUSA
WILK, JOSEPH	33	M	LABR	PLZZZZUSA
GADWEGA	25	F	W	PLZZZZUSA
ANTONIA	4	F	CHILD	PLZZZZUSA
MARIANNA	.09	F	INFANT	PLZZZZUSA
WEISSGARBER, RIWKE	25	F	W	PLZZZZUSA
BASCHE	3	F	CHILD	PLZZZZUSA
LEIB	2	F	CHILD	PLZZZZUSA
SCHAPIRO, MINNA	36	F	W	PLAHSZUSA
ALTE	6	F	CHILD	PLAHSZUSA
PESCHE	2	F	CHILD	PLAHSZUSA
MEYER	2	M	CHILD	PLAHSZUSA
RARRIS, ANJA	44	F	W	RRZZZZUSA
SUNWEZKA, DOMINIKE	22	F	SP	PLZZZZUSA
PANIMUNSKY, SORE	27	F	W	PLACBFUSA
RAPHAEL, ZIWEL	23	F	W	PLAFWJUSA

PASSENGER	AGE	SEX	OCCUPATION	PRVL	DES
SHIP: CALIFORNIA					
FROM: HAMBURG					
TO: NEW YORK					
ARRIVED: 22 MARCH 1886					
BOGORSKY, WOLF	26	M	MCHT	RRZZZZ	IL
GRODZIS, LAMBUS	18	M	LABR	RRZZZZ	NY
MATOURS, PRAMHA	22	M	LABR	RRZZZZ	NY
MIKAS, VINCENT	22	M	LABR	RRZZZZ	NY
MINKILLIS, KASEMIR	39	M	LABR	RRZZZZ	IL
SCHURKMANN, HERM.MORDHE	27	M	TRDSMN	RRZZZZ	NY
KUNITZKI, SCHLOM	35	M	TRDSMN	RRZZZZ	NY
BERMANN, ABRAHAM	49	M	TRDSMN	RRZZZZ	NY
SELDIN, CHAIM	37	M	TLR	RRZZZZ	NY
TIHERINN, OSCAR	24	M	TLR	RRZZZZ	NY
GREBIN, ISAAC	36	M	TLR	RRZZZZ	NY
ZUKERMANN, KALM	30	M	TLR	RRZZZZ	NY
MILIKOWSKY, ABRAHAM	26	M	TLR	RRZZZZ	NY
WITSEMANN, JULIUS	27	M	SMH	RRZZZZ	NY
PASSMANN, NOCH	29	M	TLR	RRZZZZ	NY
SEGOLOWITZ, ABRAHAM	32	M	TLR	RRZZZZ	NY
SINGER, ELKE	40	F	WO	RRZZZZ	NY
MEREL	7	F	CHILD	RRZZZZ	NY
CHAIE	6	F	CHILD	RRZZZZ	NY
SKLUT, SAB.B.	34	M	TRDSMN	RRZZZZ	NY
BURIMOWITZ, SAL.	27	M	TRDSMN	RRZZZZ	NY
SEGALL, SCHLOME	32	M	TRDSMN	RRZZZZ	NY
CHAIKER, CH.SCH.	21	M	TRDSMN	RRZZZZ	NY
FELDMANN, DAVID	29	M	TRDSMN	RRZZZZ	NY
RONG.	21	F	W	RRZZZZ	NY
GOUSCHMANN, HERSCH	25	M	TRDSMN	RRZZZZ	NY
WOLPANSKY, MORDCHE	43	M	TRDSMN	RRZZZZ	NY
RUBENZICK, MOSES	43	M	TRDSMN	RRZZZZ	NY
BESEMER, JOSEF	40	M	TRDSMN	RRZZZZ	NY
KAMIN, JOSEF	31	M	TRDSMN	RRZZZZ	NY
OSCHEROWITZ, ISRAEL	51	M	TRDSMN	RRZZZZ	NY
ZERGES, SCH.CHATZ.	21	M	TRDSMN	RRZZZZ	NY
ZUIKERMANN, SALOMON	17	M	TRDSMN	RRZZZZ	NY
HINNENBERG, SCH.	27	M	TRDSMN	RRZZZZ	NY
MORSON, ABRAHAM	18	M	TRDSMN	RRZZZZ	NY
RESIL, ISRAEL-S.	22	M	TRDSMN	RRZZZZ	NY
GURPBURG, SALOMON	23	M	TRDSMN	RRZZZZ	NY
IGEL, SIEGMUND	24	M	TRDSMN	RRZZZZ	NY
KOWALEWSKY, STEFAN	26	M	JNR	RRZZZZ	NY
MOSUG, NICOLAI	24	M	LABR	RRZZZZ	NY
SEHMICK, IWAN	25	M	LABR	RRZZZZ	NY
LUMIKOWSKY, JOSEF	17	M	LABR	RRZZZZ	NY
TUSCHINSKY, ANTON	44	M	LABR	RRZZZZ	NY
ANETTA	28	F	W	RRZZZZ	NY
RUBIN, GITE	29	F	WO	RRZZZZ	NY
TAUBE	6	F	CHILD	RRZZZZ	NY
JOSEF	.07	M	INFANT	RRZZZZ	NY
HOROVITZ, ABRAHAM	19	M	LABR	RRZZZZ	NY
SCHNIDER, MOSCHE	32	M	MCHT	RRZZZZ	NY
DERFLER, SALMAN	42	M	MCHT	RRZZZZ	NY
BLUCHER, JOSEF	24	M	LABR	RRZZZZ	NY
SCHLUSSEL, MORDCHE	18	M	LABR	RRZZZZ	NY
GOLDMANN, JAC.	18	M	LABR	RRZZZZ	NY
SCHLUSSEL, ABRAHAM	47	M	MCHT	RRZZZZ	NY
GARFUNKEL, WOLF	17	M	MCHT	RRZZZZ	NY
BOTWINIK, HIRSCH	23	M	MCHT	RRZZZZ	NY
ITKIN, ISRAEL	26	M	MCHT	RRZZZZ	NY
LIPMANN, MEYER	18	M	MCHT	RRZZZZ	NY
LEVITOR, SALOMON	7	M	CHILD	RRZZZZ	NY
WOLSKY, WLADISLAW	30	M	FARMER	RRZZZZ	NY
AUGUSTE	38	F	W	RRZZZZ	NY
ADELE	7	F	CHILD	RRZZZZ	NY
BRUNISLAW	6	M	CHILD	RRZZZZ	NY
MUHLAN, HEINRICH	38	M	LABR	RRZZZZ	NY
MIDLAWSKI, LEISER	36	M	GDNR	RRZZZZ	NY
KUDNITZKY, FEIGE	20	F	WO	RRZZZZ	NY
RUBIN, SELIG	19	M	LABR	RRZZZZ	NY
DUKOR, ISAAC	32	M	LABR	RRZZZZ	NY
WEINER, HIRSCH	42	F	WO	RRZZZZ	NY
LABA	7	F	CHILD	RRZZZZ	NY
WOLF	6	M	CHILD	RRZZZZ	NY
KABAN, MOSES	26	M	LABR	RRZZZZ	NY
CHMELL, ABRAHAM	26	M	LABR	RRZZZZ	NY
KRASNER, JUDA	23	M	LABR	RRZZZZ	NY
SERSCHER, BENSIAN	25	M	LABR	RRZZZZ	NY
STEINBINK, ISRAEL	30	M	LABR	RRZZZZ	NY
FUCHS, RUBIN	22	M	GDSM	RRZZZZ	NY
MARIA	18	F	W	RRZZZZ	NY
SHIP: CITY OF CHICAGO					
FROM: LIVERPOOL AND QUEENSTOWN					
TO: NEW YORK					
ARRIVED: 22 MARCH 1886					
VETE, CAL.	39	M	PNTR	RRADAX	NY
GRUNBERG, M.	22	M	CPRSMH	RRACDS	NE
EISENSTEIN, CHAIM	45	M	LABR	RRACBF	NY
MITH, HULDE	28	F	W	RRACBF	CH
HANNA	2	F	CHILD	RRACBF	CH
JA-	00	F	INF	RRACBF	CH
NEUMANN, SCHEMDEL	50	F	W	RRACBF	NY
CHANNE	11	F	CH	RRACBF	NY
FUL.	10	M	CH	RRACBF	NY
SHIP: EMS					
FROM: BREMEN					
TO: NEW YORK					
ARRIVED: 22 MARCH 1886					
BENNER, KARL	45	M	MNR	RRZZZZ	USA
KUPFERMANN, JACOB	26	M	MNR	RRAHTU	USA
SHIP: P CALAND					
FROM: ROTTERDAM					
TO: NEW YORK					
ARRIVED: 22 MARCH 1886					
PORTNOWITZ, SHASKA	52	F	NN	PLZZZZ	USA
RIHEL	10	F	NN	PLZZZZ	USA
SHIP: WESTPHALIA					
FROM: HAMBURG					
TO: NEW YORK					
ARRIVED: 22 MARCH 1886					
MATISON, TERLE	19	F	SGL	RRZZZZ	USA
MENDELSOHN, LEISER	18	M	LABR	RRZZZZ	USA
ELI	21	M	LABR	RRZZZZ	USA
ANSCHELOWITZ, SALOMON	20	M	LKSH	RRZZZZ	USA

PASSENGER	AGE	SEX	OCCUPATION	PRIV	VIL	DES
BARKAN, SALOMON	24	M	TLR	RR	ZZZZ	USA
ESKIND, SELIG	19	M	LABR	RR	ZZZZ	USA
KANOWITZ, ISAAK	50	M	LABR	RR	ZZZZ	USA
MORDSCHE	4	M	CHILD	RR	ZZZZ	USA
LEWIN, LEISER	36	M	SMH	RR	ZZZZ	USA
ABRAMOWITZ, ISRAEL	42	M	CGRMKR	RR	ZZZZ	USA
LISCHE	40	F	W	RR	ZZZZ	USA
HUTTMANN, JANKEL	18	M	CL	RR	ZZZZ	USA
MORE	20	M	DLR	RR	ZZZZ	USA
ZEITMANN, SARAH	20	F	W	RR	ZZZZ	USA
KALINSKY, JACOB	20	M	LABR	RR	ZZZZ	USA
ESTHER	19	F	W	RR	ZZZZ	USA
SIMSCHELOWITZ, SALOMON	43	M	DLR	RR	ZZZZ	USA
NOSSEN	20	M	MCHT	RR	ZZZZ	USA
ROST, EISICK	20	M	MCHT	RR	ZZZZ	USA
BENDRELS, CHRISTOPH	42	M	LABR	RR	ZZZZ	USA
MARTIN	9	M	CHILD	RR	ZZZZ	USA
PLUTZIS, ANTON	26	M	LABR	RR	ZZZZ	USA
TUKER, TAUBE	22	F	SGL	RR	ZZZZ	USA
ARKIN, REBECA	17	F	SGL	RR	ZZZZ	USA
TUDRITZKI, ASRIEL	28	M	LABR	RR	ZZZZ	USA
NIEDZWETZKY, MEYER	43	M	LABR	RR	ZZZZ	USA
SCHEINDLINGER, ESTHER	23	F	SGL	RR	ZZZZ	USA
OSAWSKY, ITE	22	F	SGL	RR	ZZZZ	USA
SEWKOWICZ, BETSI	35	F	W	RR	ZZZZ	USA
LIEBE	9	F	CHILD	RR	ZZZZ	USA
ISRAEL	7	M	CHILD	RR	ZZZZ	USA
ELI	.11	M	INFANT	RR	ZZZZ	USA
KLEIN, SIMON	16	M	LABR	RR	ZZZZ	USA
LONDON, MORITZ	27	M	LABR	RR	ZZZZ	USA
JENNY	21	F	W	RR	ZZZZ	USA
KORN, ABRAM	24	M	LABR	RR	ZZZZ	USA
BLAUSTEIN, DAVID	25	M	TCHR	RR	ZZZZ	USA
ROSALIE	25	F	W	RR	ZZZZ	USA
TOROWITZ, PESCHE	21	F	SGL	RR	ZZZZ	USA
CZANETZKY, JOSEF	22	M	LABR	RR	ZZZZ	USA
OKUSCHEWSKY, CYPRIAND	28	M	LABR	RR	ZZZZ	USA
PUCHALSKY, ANTON	50	M	LABR	RR	ZZZZ	USA
JOSEFA	23	F	SGL	RR	ZZZZ	USA

SHIP: CIRCASSIA

FROM: GLASGOW AND MOVILLE
TO: NEW YORK
ARRIVED: 23 MARCH 1886

PASSENGER	AGE	SEX	OCCUPATION	PRIV	VIL	DES
ROSEK, JENKS.	36	M	LABR	RR	ZZZZ	USA
SUCHOW, CHAJIM	18	M	DLR	RR	ZZZZ	USA
CHOSEWONITZ, BENZI	36	M	DLR	RR	ZZZZ	USA
PALL, ABRAM	43	M	DLR	RR	ZZZZ	USA
ANCHELOWITZ, HIRSCH	16	M	DLR	RR	ZZZZ	USA
EPSTEIN, ABRAHAM	26	M	DLR	RR	ZZZZ	USA
BORCHOWITZ, ABRAM	17	M	LABR	RR	ZZZZ	USA
JASENOWSKY, KASIMIR	28	M	LABR	RR	ZZZZ	USA
DEVSKY, JASER	24	M	LABR	RR	ZZZZ	USA
KLATZKI, SCHACHNE	23	M	DLR	RR	ZZZZ	USA
KRAWITZ, NACHEM	26	M	DLR	RR	ZZZZ	USA
KATZ, ISRAEL	24	M	DLR	RR	ZZZZ	USA
GROSS, MARKUS	38	M	DLR	RR	ZZZZ	USA
BABLO, INDRI	38	M	LABR	RR	ZZZZ	USA
RIGL, PAUL	33	M	LABR	RR	ZZZZ	USA
WINANCKY, MICHAL	23	M	LABR	RR	ZZZZ	USA
JANOS, DEBRO	23	M	LABR	RR	ZZZZ	USA
SEJKO, JOSEPH	27	M	LABR	RR	ZZZZ	USA
BUJANOWSKI, ANTONI	27	M	LABR	RR	ZZZZ	USA
MASEL, SCHLOME	23	M	LABR	RR	ZZZZ	USA
WOSLOWSKY, OHIS	18	M	DLR	RR	ZZZZ	USA
EIDELMANN, MOSES	24	M	DLR	RR	ZZZZ	USA
GORDON, ELZE	26	M	DLR	RR	ZZZZ	USA
KUPPESOTCH, SCHLOME	19	M	LABR	RR	ZZZZ	USA
NOLL, JUDEL	26	M	LABR	RR	ZZZZ	USA
GALEMBE, JANKEL	35	M	LABR	RR	ZZZZ	USA
BLUMENTHAL, HYMAN	21	M	CL	RR	ZZZZ	USA
KOVALSKY, MIHAL	40	M	DLR	RR	ZZZZ	USA
CAZARYK, JANOS	21	M	DLR	RR	ZZZZ	USA
KOSCO, MIHAL	21	M	DLR	RR	ZZZZ	USA
SPIRKO, PETER	19	M	LABR	RR	ZZZZ	USA
LUSAY, JANOS	28	M	LABR	RR	ZZZZ	USA
KOVALSKY, ELIAS	44	M	LABR	RR	ZZZZ	USA
BERECKY, MIHAL	37	M	LABR	RR	ZZZZ	USA
SIDOR, JANOS	24	M	LABR	RR	ZZZZ	USA
KRAINE, MIHAL	18	M	LABR	RR	ZZZZ	USA
RINODACKO, WARDAS	30	M	LABR	RR	ZZZZ	USA
FRIEDLAND, ITZIG	27	M	LABR	RR	ZZZZ	USA
MAGIR, OWSCHECI	30	M	LABR	RR	ZZZZ	USA
DEVSKY, ALEXANDRINA	20	F	W	RR	ZZZZ	USA
MAJULSKY, MAGGIE	16	F	SVNT	RR	ZZZZ	USA
GEORG, MITRO	24	M	LABR	RR	ZZZZ	USA
LOJECK, MIHAL	20	M	LABR	RR	ZZZZ	USA
DZANBO, JOSEF	17	M	LABR	RR	ZZZZ	USA
JIZIOKA, MIHAL	28	M	LABR	RR	ZZZZ	USA
CABAK, PAUL	29	M	LABR	RR	ZZZZ	USA

SHIP: POLYNESIA

FROM: HAMBURG
TO: NEW YORK
ARRIVED: 24 MARCH 1886

PASSENGER	AGE	SEX	OCCUPATION	PRIV	VIL	DES
GURINSKA, STEPHAN	36	M	LABR	RR	ZZZZ	NY
TALER, AB.	27	M	LABR	RR	ZZZZ	NY
ADLER, LEIB	35	M	LABR	RR	ZZZZ	NY
MUHEBORN, MICH.	30	M	LABR	RR	ZZZZ	NY
BERLIN, ELIAS	37	M	LABR	RR	ZZZZ	NY
SCHMALL, HIRSCH	27	M	LABR	RR	ZZZZ	NY
JOCHENOWITZ, JOH.	37	M	LABR	RR	ZZZZ	NY
SCHUALL, LEO	18	M	LABR	RR	ZZZZ	NY
ROSENTHAL, HANS	00	M	LABR	RR	ZZZZ	NY
MARCUS, CHAIE	35	F	WO	RR	ZZZZ	NY
MOSCHE	11	F	D	RR	ZZZZ	NY
MALHE	7	M	CHILD	RR	ZZZZ	NY
ALTER	6	M	CHILD	RR	ZZZZ	NY
JONTEL	5	M	CHILD	RR	ZZZZ	NY
BRENNER, ZARA	25	F	SGL	RR	ZZZZ	NY

SHIP: SPAIN

FROM: LIVERPOOL
TO: NEW YORK
ARRIVED: 24 MARCH 1886

PASSENGER	AGE	SEX	OCCUPATION	PRIV	VIL	DES
LEPELSTREM, M.	26	M	LABR	RR	ZZZZ	NY
LOUIS, E.	34	M	LABR	RR	ADBQ	NY
WEINBERG, DAVID	26	M	LABR	RR	ADBQ	NY
SCHMITZ, JAGNES	22	M	LABR	RR	ADBQ	NY
RUDA, HARRIS	28	M	LABR	RR	ZZZZ	NY
KLENEY, EMANUEL	10	M	CH	RR	ADBQ	NY
HARRIS	9	M	CHILD	RR	ADBQ	NY
POLAK, MENDEL	22	M	LABR	RR	ZZZZ	NY
JACOB, MENDEL	20	M	LABR	RR	ZZZZ	NY
HIRSCH, S.	21	M	LABR	RR	ZZZZ	NY
LEWESGERM, HINDE	36	M	LABR	RR	ZZZZ	NY
REBECKE	11	F	CH	RR	ZZZZ	NY
LICHE	10	M	CH	RR	ZZZZ	NY
SCHUFFE	6	M	CHILD	RR	ZZZZ	NY

PASSENGER	AGE	SEX	OCCUPATION	PRIVL	DES
MOLKE	4	M	CHILD	RRZZ	ZZNY
BRENER, MENDEL	15	M	LABR	RRZZ	ZZNY
FURLONG, ABE	25	M	LABR	RRZZ	ZZNY
STEMFRER, MOSER	32	M	LABR	RRZZ	ZZNY
ISAK	28	M	LABR	RRZZ	ZZNY
LAN, MENACHE	34	M	LABR	RRZZ	ZZNY
LAHN, MENACHE	34	M	LABR	RRZZ	ZZNY
MICKALY, IGNATZ	29	M	LABR	RRZZ	ZZNY
GORDON, MICHEL	18	M	LABR	RRZZ	ZZNY
SCHIMINOWCELTZ, MICHEL	26	M	LABR	PLZZ	ZZNY
PLIANSKY, MOSES	19	M	LABR	RRZZ	ZZNY
LESSNELOVFITZ, FRANZ	22	M	LABR	RRZZ	ZZNY
HAPLAN, GERSON	25	M	LABR	RRZZ	ZZNY
KOTZKEWITZ, LEIZER	24	M	LABR	RRZZ	ZZNY
GRUNDE, LEIZER	26	M	LABR	RRZZ	ZZNY
FUBRECK, KARMUCKE	16	M	LABR	RRZZ	ZZNY
HAPSLAN, EPHR.	30	M	LABR	RRZZ	ZZNY
WARKAN, SCHUNE.	40	M	LABR	RRZZ	ZZNY
OKOV, FENKE	33	M	LABR	RRZZ	ZZNY
GRIMHAIS, JUDE	28	M	LABR	RRZZ	ZZNY
ETERMAN, LEIZER	18	M	LABR	RRZZ	ZZNY
ELPERN, NOTER	24	M	LABR	RRZZ	ZZNY
LIPPERSEN, GABRIEL	26	M	LABR	RRZZ	ZZNY
MELZER, LACHARNE	44	M	LABR	RRZZ	ZZNY
MENHALOCK, B.	21	M	LABR	RRZZ	ZZNY
SCWARTZ, FANNIE	19	F	SP	RRZZ	ZZNY
WALLACK, ABM.	33	M	LABR	RRZZ	ZZNY
PREIS, LEIZER	18	M	LABR	RRZZ	ZZNY
POLAKOF, CHAIM	19	M	LABR	RRZZ	ZZNY
MANHECH, S.	19	M	LABR	RRZZ	ZZNY
SCHUHAN, JANKE	38	M	LABR	RRZZ	ZZNY
KEWITZ, NICHOF	30	M	LABR	RRZZ	ZZNY
KENKUSKY, ALEX	23	M	LABR	RRZZ	ZZNY
ETERMAN, NOCHEIM	19	M	LABR	RRZZ	ZZNY
SCHAPER, JUDI	24	M	LABR	RRZZ	ZZNY
KSINTYKY, JAKE	21	M	LABR	RRZZ	ZZNY
CHAVIE	25	F	W	RRZZ	ZZNY
HARRIET	3	F	CHILD	RRZZ	ZZNY
BANK, JOSEL	22	F	SP	RRZZ	ZZNY
CHWELL, JAN.	50	M	LABR	RRZZ	ZZNY
MODCHE, AL.	50	M	LABR	RRZZ	ZZNY
MOLINSKY, HAN.	25	F	SP	RRZZ	ZZNY
JOSEF	4	M	CHILD	RRZZ	ZZNY
ABM.	3	M	CHILD	RRZZ	ZZNY
KOLTEZKY, ABM.	20	M	LABR	RRZZ	ZZNY
TISKKOFSH, ABM.	25	M	LABR	RRZZ	ZZNY
LEVEN, ANISHEL	23	M	LABR	RRZZ	ZZNY
LEEBERMAN, E.	34	M	LABR	RRZZ	ZZNY
KIRCHEL	18	M	LABR	RRZZ	ZZNY
LIPPSTEIN, M.	28	M	LABR	RRZZ	ZZNY
FELSEN, ARIE	26	M	LABR	RRZZ	ZZNY
WALKE, CHANE	18	M	LABR	RRZZ	ZZNY
SCHIMEL, ISAK	18	M	LABR	RRZZ	ZZNY
STAVNITZKY, S.	20	M	LABR	RRZZ	ZZNY
JANO	24	M	LABR	RRZZ	ZZNY
SCHOVBES, S.	32	M	LABR	RRZZ	ZZNY
WEIMBERG, S.	31	M	LABR	RRZZ	ZZNY
WEINER, S.	25	M	LABR	RRZZ	ZZNY
LEIBSKOVSKY, M.	18	M	LABR	RRZZ	ZZNY
PANTSCHER, MAX.	60	M	LABR	RRZZ	ZZNY
GOLDSTEIN, MAX.	24	M	LABR	RRZZ	ZZNY
CHAIE	21	M	LABR	RRZZ	ZZNY
JONKEL	5	M	CHILD	RRZZ	ZZNY
ACRIMIN, A.	22	M	LABR	RRZZ	ZZNY
RUSTHAL, BERL	43	M	LABR	RRZZ	ZZNY
RUBEN, LEIB	44	M	LABR	RRZZ	ZZNY
CEMBLENK, JUIDE	34	F	SP	RRZZ	ZZNY
ESTHER	11	F	CH	RRZZ	ZZNY
WASKEWITZ, F.	20	F	SP	RRZZ	ZZNY
WILLONAK, ABM.	45	M	LABR	RRZZ	ZZNY
SAFRIOVITZ, F.	19	M	LABR	RRZZ	ZZNY
RUBENSTEIN, M.	52	M	LABR	RRZZ	ZZNY
RINVERMANE, S.	45	M	LABR	RRZZ	ZZNY
HAREVITZ, T.	18	M	LABR	RRZZ	ZZNY
TELESCHOWITZ, A.	22	M	LABR	RRZZ	ZZNY
RONE	26	F	W	RRZZ	ZZNY
SCHEPXLEVITZ, H.	36	M	LABR	RRZZ	ZZNY
BORODVICK, M.	20	M	LABR	RRZZ	ZZNY
ABRAMSOHN, S.	22	M	LABR	RRZZ	ZZNY
TUCKER, JACOB	21	M	LABR	RRZZ	ZZNY
CHOSE	20	F	W	RRZZ	ZZNY
KRASNOPOLSKY, E.	44	M	LABR	RRZZ	ZZNY
TERVEL	11	M	CH	RRZZ	ZZNY
ZLASCHEL	9	M	CHILD	RRZZ	ZZNY
ISRAIL, K.	26	M	LABR	RRZZ	ZZNY
KRASNOPOLSKY, B.	35	M	LABR	RRZZ	ZZNY
TUNK, WOLF	23	M	LABR	RRZZ	ZZNY
DANTE, WOLF	30	M	LABR	RRZZ	ZZNY
PEWROVSKY, T.	35	M	LABR	RRZZ	ZZNY
SERGASKY, ABE.	18	M	LABR	RRZZ	ZZNY
TEIGEN, JACOB	25	M	LABR	RRZZ	ZZNY
HERBER, MODCH.	25	M	LABR	RRZZ	ZZNY
LEWSCHUD, S.	25	M	TLR	RRAD	BQNY
TENICHOWICZ, LEO	23	F	SP	RRZZ	ZZNY
SOLOMON	1	F	CHILD	RRZZ	ZZNY
LEIB	00	F	CH	RRZZ	ZZNY
REIBEN, S.	40	M	LABR	RRZZ	ZZNY
HANDLER, A.	18	M	LABR	RRZZ	ZZNY
MOWSOHN, L.	21	M	LABR	RRZZ	ZZNY
A.	22	F	SP	RRZZ	ZZNY
INKA, WEITZEN	42	M	LABR	RRZZ	ZZNY
CHIDACK, MARIE	26	F	SP	RRZZ	ZZNY
NISHLA, SUSANA	20	F	SP	RRZZ	ZZNY

SHIP: RHEIN

FROM: BREMEN
TO: NEW YORK
ARRIVED: 26 MARCH 1886

PASSENGER	AGE	SEX	OCCUPATION	PRIVL	DES
COMEZARSKA, ZIPE	17	M	LABR	RRZZ	ZZUSA
BABANSKI, FRIEDE	38	F	NN	RRZZ	ZZUSA
SARA	10	F	CH	RRZZ	ZZUSA
MARIE	7	F	CHILD	RRZZ	ZZUSA
BERTHA	6	F	CHILD	RRZZ	ZZUSA
REBECCA	4	F	CHILD	RRZZ	ZZUSA
T.	3	F	CHILD	RRZZ	ZZUSA
KOENIG, PETER	44	M	LABR	RRZZ	ZZUSA
CAROLINE	41	F	W	RRZZ	ZZUSA
MARIE	20	F	NN	RRZZ	ZZUSA
EMILIE	18	F	NN	RRZZ	ZZUSA
OTTO	15	M	NN	RRZZ	ZZUSA
WILHELM	7	M	CHILD	RRZZ	ZZUSA
RUDOLF	6	M	CHILD	RRZZ	ZZUSA
ALFRED	22	M	LABR	RRZZ	ZZUSA
ARTHUR	5	M	CHILD	RRZZ	ZZUSA
JOHANNES	4	M	CHILD	RRZZ	ZZUSA
ROBERT	.09	M	INFANT	RRZZ	ZZUSA
SCHMIDT, LUDWIG	33	M	LABR	RRZZ	ZZUSA
BARBARA	48	F	W	RRZZ	ZZUSA
LUDWIG	22	M	LABR	RRZZ	ZZUSA
WILHELMINE	20	F	NN	RRZZ	ZZUSA
JOHANN	17	M	LABR	RRZZ	ZZUSA
PETER	6	M	CHILD	RRZZ	ZZUSA
LUDWIG	.01	M	INFANT	RRZZ	ZZUSA
MULLER, AUGUST	50	M	CPTR	RRZZ	ZZUSA
HINZ, CARL	43	M	LABR	RRZZ	ZZUSA
ANNA	44	F	W	RRZZ	ZZUSA
GEORG	19	M	LABR	RRZZ	ZZUSA
LOUISE	18	F	SVNT	RRZZ	ZZUSA
CAROLINE	16	F	NN	RRZZ	ZZUSA
REGINE	10	F	CH	RRZZ	ZZUSA
CATHARINE	7	F	CHILD	RRZZ	ZZUSA
CHRISTIAN	6	M	CHILD	RRZZ	ZZUSA
MANNEH	1	M	CHILD	RRZZ	ZZUSA

PASSENGER	AGE	SEX	OCCUPATION	PRIV	DES
BOBNAJTES, JADWIGA	30	F	NN	RRZZZZ	USA
JERA	11	F	CH	RRZZZZ	USA
PETER	2	M	CHILD	RRZZZZ	USA
ANKODOWICZ, JURAN	28	M	LABR	RRZZZZ	USA

SHIP: CITY OF RICHMOND

FROM: LIVERPOOL
TO: NEW YORK
ARRIVED: 29 MARCH 1886

PASSENGER	AGE	SEX	OCCUPATION	PRIV	DES
OXVINSKY, LOUIS	26	M	LABR	RRAFWJ	USA
LEOWIN, JACOB	40	M	LABR	RRAFWJ	USA
ZUCKERMANN, JOSEF	35	M	LABR	RRAFWJ	USA
ZWISEN, J.	24	M	LABR	RRAFWJ	USA
L.	22	F	W	RRAFWJ	USA
SRAB, E.	18	M	LABR	RRAFWJ	USA
IUSCAK, MATHIAS	26	M	LABR	RRAFWJ	USA
GENDRA, PETER	21	M	LABR	RRAFWJ	USA
ADELSOHN, ABHM.	37	M	LABR	RRAFWJ	USA
MUE.	10	M	CH	RRAFWJ	USA
GINZBURG, M.	27	M	LABR	RRAHOO	USA
RUCK, BEHR.	47	M	LABR	RRAHOO	USA
SATZ, SOLOMON	36	M	LABR	RRAHQD	USA
HAYERFT, P.	56	M	LABR	RRAHOO	USA
R.	7	M	CHILD	RRAHOO	USA
PER.	5	M	CHILD	RRAHOO	USA
KERSAK, G.	18	M	LABR	RRAHOO	USA
IOGAR, B.	18	M	LABR	RRAHOO	USA

SHIP: STATE OF NEVADA

FROM: GLASGOW AND LARNE
TO: NEW YORK
ARRIVED: 29 MARCH 1886

PASSENGER	AGE	SEX	OCCUPATION	PRIV	DES
DURDA, F.	27	M	LABR	PLZZZZ	USA
FROLICH, C.	18	M	PDLR	PLAHSN	USA
HELLMANREICH, I.	22	M	PDLR	PLZZZZ	USA
KARMA, A.	26	M	LABR	PLZZZZ	USA
OSCHNITZ, A.	27	M	LABR	PLZZZZ	USA
RAWSKY, L.	28	M	SMH	PLZZZZ	USA
SZUNANSKY, J.	35	M	PDLR	PLZZZZ	USA
ELISE	27	F	W	PLZZZZ	USA
STYCLESKI, J.	27	M	LABR	PLZZZZ	USA
SHRINSKY, B.	27	M	LABR	PLZZZZ	USA
SAZULLA, N.	26	M	LABR	PLZZZZ	USA
U, U	25	F	W	RRZZZZ	USA
H.	.04	F	INFANT	RRZZZZ	USA
BERMANN, W.	17	M	PDLR	RRZZZZ	USA
BINDERMANN, C.	25	F	W	RRZZZZ	USA
BASCOLKO, M.	28	M	LABR	RRZZZZ	USA
CHONKLIN, L.	19	M	TLR	RRZZZZ	USA
DUBINSKY, A.	24	M	PDLR	RRZZZZ	USA
DAER, G.	48	M	PDLR	RRZZZZ	USA
FUNT, G.	24	M	TLR	RRAHTU	USA
HALPEN, E.	22	M	PDLR	RRAHTU	USA
JAFFE, E.	28	F	W	RRAHTU	USA
M.	.09	M	INFANT	RRAHTU	USA
JOKELEWITZ, S.	50	M	TLR	RRZZZZ	USA
KOSCHNOMITZ, L.	18	M	PDLR	RRZZZZ	USA
KURSCHNER, I.	25	M	PDLR	RRZZZZ	USA
KATZ, K.	24	M	PDLR	RRZZZZ	USA
KALY	31	M	TLR	RRZZZZ	USA
KOLISKA, M.	18	F	SVNT	RRAGRT	USA
KALMANN, G.	31	M	MCHT	RRZZZZ	USA
KAHN, W.	24	M	CL	RRZZZZ	USA
KESTIL, S.	54	M	PDLR	RRZZZZ	USA
KATZ, H.	20	M	PDLR	RRZZZZ	USA
LEVI	24	F	W	RRZZZZ	USA
A.	.04	F	INFANT	RRZZZZ	USA
GURWITCH, A.	18	F	W	RRZZZZ	USA
K.	.10	F	INFANT	RRZZZZ	USA
LAPIDUS, S.	24	M	BKR	RRZZZZ	USA
LIMIS, H.	45	F	W	RRZZZZ	USA
F.	1	F	CHILD	RRZZZZ	USA
B.	23	F	W	RRZZZZ	USA
S.	18	F	NN	RRZZZZ	USA
LEIHM, G.	37	M	BKR	RRAHTF	USA
LOWENSTEIN, A.	22	M	PDLR	RRAHTF	USA
MENDLOWITZ, M.	21	M	PDLR	RRZZZZ	USA
MADWEIZICK, M.	18	M	PDLR	RRZZZZ	USA
U, U	00	M	PDLR	RRZZZZ	USA
CZRAK, M.	21	M	PDLR	RRZZZZ	USA
PATCHUTZKY, C.	18	M	TLR	RRZZZZ	USA
PEHRMANN, A.	27	M	CGRMKR	RRZZZZ	USA
MEVIESNE, M.	12	M	CH	RRZZZZ	USA
RETZKI, M.	30	M	LABR	RRZZZZ	USA
ROLICK, J.	25	M	PDLR	RRZZZZ	USA
RUDMIKI, C.	21	M	PDLR	RRZZZZ	USA
RUDURK, A.	33	M	TLR	RRZZZZ	USA
RODKOWITZ, S.	24	M	GLMK	RRZZZZ	USA
SARETSKI, M.	26	M	PDLR	RRZZZZ	USA
E.	25	M	SMH	RRZZZZ	USA
SACKI, P.	27	M	PDLR	RRAHTU	USA
U-MRS	21	F	W	RRAHTU	USA
A.	1	M	CHILD	RRAHTU	USA
SAWN, D.	27	M	TNSTH	RRZZZZ	USA
SILBERMAN, R.	47	F	W	RRZZZZ	USA
A.	21	F	NN	RRZZZZ	USA
SIMON, RUB.	21	M	LABR	RRZZZZ	USA
SHAPIRO, E.	15	M	CGRMKR	RRZZZZ	USA
SEGAL, C.	18	F	W	RRZZZZ	USA
I.	00	F	CH	RRZZZZ	USA
WEISS, D.	31	M	PDLR	RRZZZZ	USA
WEINHAUS, C.	26	M	PDLR	RRZZZZ	USA
WASILEWSKY, M.	29	M	TLR	RRZZZZ	USA
WOLPERT, W.	19	M	BRR	RRZZZZ	USA
WATTENBERG, D.	50	M	BKR	RRZZZZ	USA
U, C.	40	M	TLR	RRZZZZ	USA
----NAN, S.	19	M	PDLR	RRZZZZ	USA
O.	23	M	CGRMKR	RRZZZZ	USA
ZINKIN, H.	33	M	PDLR	RRZZZZ	USA

SHIP: EIDER

FROM: BREMEN
TO: NEW YORK
ARRIVED: 30 MARCH 1886

PASSENGER	AGE	SEX	OCCUPATION	PRIV	DES
BOGDANOWITZ, VINCENT	27	M	LABR	RRZZZZ	USA
AGATHE	21	F	W	RRZZZZ	USA
MARCEL	3	M	CHILD	RRZZZZ	USA
KIANANSIS, JUSTIN	20	M	LABR	RRZZZZ	USA
ADOMAITIS, BATTROMER	30	M	LABR	RRZZZZ	USA
SZADOWSKY, JAN	30	M	LABR	RRZZZZ	USA
KALKSTEIN, JAS.	25	M	LABR	RRZZZZ	USA
BINKOWSKY, WLAD.	20	M	LABR	RRZZZZ	USA
MASCHKEWICZ, ANT.	24	M	LABR	RRZZZZ	USA
TOWADETZKY, STANISL.	20	M	LABR	RRZZZZ	USA
EISEDAWITSCH, ANT.	24	M	LABR	RRZZZZ	USA
SKRENANS, ANT.	25	M	LABR	RRZZZZ	USA
WOITAKUM, BART.	25	M	LABR	RRZZZZ	USA
CHRISTER, MOSES	19	M	LABR	RRZZZZ	USA
LUBISCH, LION	16	M	LABR	RRZZZZ	USA

PASSENGER	AGE	SEX	OCCUPATION	PRV	VIL	DES
ZEGELSKI, FRANZ	35	M	LABR	RR	ZZZZ	USA

SHIP: SUEVIA

FROM: HAMBURG
TO: NEW YORK
ARRIVED: 30 MARCH 1886

PASSENGER	AGE	SEX	OCCUPATION	PRV	VIL	DES
STEPANO, GEORG	23	M	ENGR	RR	AFVG	USA
SCHMILOWSKY, ISAAC	60	M	TLR	RR	AHWU	USA
ARON	16	M	S	RR	AHWU	USA
SCHAPIRO, ABRAM	18	M	DLR	RR	AHZO	USA
MURKEND, WOLF	23	M	TLR	RR	AHZO	USA
PALEVS, SIMON	46	M	DLR	RR	AHZO	USA
REICHELSOHN, MARIASCHE	17	F	SGL	RR	AHZO	USA
ARON	22	M	BCHR	RR	AHZO	USA
MODANSKY, PESCHE	40	F	W	RR	AHZL	USA
MOSES	9	M	CHILD	RR	AHZL	USA
ISRAEL	8	M	CHILD	RR	AHZL	USA
CHAIE	4	F	CHILD	RR	AHZL	USA
CHASCHE	.11	F	INFANT	RR	AHZL	USA
LANGLEBEN, CHANNE	25	F	SGL	RR	AHZL	USA
ZEGELITZKI, ABRAM	40	M	LABR	RR	AHZL	USA
GOTLIBOWSKI, ELIAS	37	M	DLR	RR	AHZL	USA
GOLDSTEIN, L.	9	M	CHILD	RR	AHVU	USA
SLONITZKY, BEREL	20	M	DLR	RR	AHZL	USA
BLECHER, MOSES	32	M	DLR	RR	AHTF	USA
MENKIS, SAMUEL	28	M	DLR	RR	AHVU	USA
LUBARTOW, CHANNE	30	F	W	RR	AHZG	USA
RACHMIL	.11	M	INFANT	RR	AHZG	USA
APEL, HIRSCH	45	M	DLR	RR	AHWI	USA
GITTEL	47	F	W	RR	AHWI	USA
LENE	9	F	CHILD	RR	AHWI	USA
RUJNOWITZ, CHAIM	40	M	DLR	RR	AHTF	USA
LUDWIN, FRUME	9	F	CHILD	RR	AHZL	USA
DONELCZYK, ANTONY	28	M	LABR	RR	AHYA	USA
DALENYA, FRANZ	28	M	LABR	RR	AHZS	USA
SAKS, BASCHE	20	F	SGL	RR	AHZS	USA
BENERT, LEIB	19	M	LABR	RR	ZZZZ	USA
GANS, GELLA	19	F	SGL	RR	AHYB	USA
ZULKIS, MARCUS	40	M	LABR	RR	AHYB	USA
FUCHS, HINDE	22	F	W	RR	AHSN	USA
HERSES	.11	M	INFANT	RR	AHSN	USA
GLAS, ANNA	17	F	SGL	RR	AHYS	USA
RIGELHOF, LOTTI	22	F	SGL	RR	AHUY	USA
ZEBRONETZKY, MEYER	22	M	LABR	RR	AHUY	USA
MENDELSOHN, SCHASCHE	25	F	W	RR	AHZR	USA
RIWKE	.11	F	INFANT	RR	AHZR	USA
SLABODSKY, SARA	24	F	W	RR	AHSK	USA
SALMEN	.03	M	INFANT	RR	AHSK	USA
KRIMKO, ESTHER	19	F	W	RR	AHXZ	USA
FISCHEL	50	F	W	RR	AHXZ	USA
ABRAHAM	.06	M	INFANT	RR	AHXZ	USA
LEWIT, DAVID	47	M	DLR	RR	AHRZ	USA
NISSEL	21	M	DLR	RR	AHRZ	USA
ALEXANDER, ABRAM	40	M	LABR	RR	AHTN	USA
KOPPELMANN, JACOB	23	M	LABR	RR	ZZZZ	USA
LEA	32	F	W	RR	ZZZZ	USA
EIDEL	20	M	LABR	RR	ZZZZ	USA
MINE	8	F	CHILD	RR	ZZZZ	USA
PESSE	5	F	CHILD	RR	ZZZZ	USA
EIYE	.11	F	INFANT	RR	ZZZZ	USA
DAVID	.01	M	INFANT	RR	ZZZZ	USA
WOLLMER, CHAIKEL	44	M	DLR	RR	ZZZZ	USA
LANDWEIL, LEIB	30	M	LABR	RR	AHZR	USA
LEF, HIRSCHEL	20	M	LABR	RR	AHZR	USA
LANGUNUS, ANTON	18	M	LABR	RR	AHZS	USA
KULAN, STANISL.	25	M	LABR	RR	AHZS	USA
SCHWENSKY, J.	21	M	LABR	RR	AHZS	USA
PROTASIEWICZ, FR.	20	M	LABR	RR	AHZS	USA
TOROSCHIEWICZ, FR.	18	M	LABR	RR	AHZS	USA
SARALO, LUDWIG	26	M	LABR	RR	AHZS	USA
TONALIS, VINCENT	22	M	LABR	RR	AHZS	USA
RANDT, FRANZ	27	M	LABR	RR	AHZS	USA
ZILINSKY, ANTON	29	M	LABR	RR	ZZZZ	USA
KOSOWA, PETER	24	M	LABR	RR	ZZZZ	USA
RUCINSKY, ANDREAS	24	M	LABR	RR	ZZZZ	USA
STEIN, FRANK	26	M	LABR	RR	AHWH	USA
BRIGOLIS, JURGIS	23	M	LABR	RR	ZZZZ	USA
KRAUTSCHEW, VICENTI	20	M	LABR	RR	AHUB	USA
LAWITZKI, JAN	18	M	LABR	RR	AHUB	USA
GRUSCHKIN, PEITR	20	M	LABR	RR	AHUB	USA
MALINOWSKY, FELIX	21	M	LABR	RR	AHZS	USA
PILARSKI, MARCIN	31	M	LABR	RR	AHZS	USA
FRANKOWSKI, PAWEL	26	M	LABR	RR	AHZS	USA
JIFSUBITIS, JOKIM	43	M	LABR	RR	AHZS	USA
ZIMONOWITZ, JOH.	39	M	LABR	RR	AHZS	USA
ANDRUSCHIEWICZ, ANTON	21	M	LABR	RR	AHZS	USA
WILLART, JOCHIM	50	M	LABR	RR	AHZS	USA
DANIELLE	15	F	D	RR	AHZS	USA
JOSEF	9	M	CHILD	RR	AHZS	USA
DENOWICZ, ANTON	48	M	LABR	RR	AHZS	USA
JANNSCH, JOSEPH	21	M	LABR	RR	AHZS	USA

SHIP: ETHIOPIA

FROM: GLASGOW AND MOVILLE
TO: NEW YORK
ARRIVED: 31 MARCH 1886

PASSENGER	AGE	SEX	OCCUPATION	PRV	VIL	DES
REIGER, SCHLEMON	30	M	BBR	RR	ZZZZ	USA
MENCOVORSAY, JACOB	21	M	TLR	RR	ZZZZ	USA
ESTHER	20	F	UNKNOWN	RR	ZZZZ	USA
WEINHAUS, ITZIG	30	M	TLR	RR	ZZZZ	USA
KUTSCHAITIS, JACOB	23	M	TLR	RR	ZZZZ	USA
ELPEROWITSCH, SELMAR	22	M	LABR	RR	ZZZZ	USA
ABRAHAM	11	M	UNKNOWN	RR	ZZZZ	USA
LAUDSMANN, JUDEL	38	M	PDLR	RR	ZZZZ	USA
JOPKOWITZ, SCHLOME	26	M	CPTR	RR	ZZZZ	USA
LASER	40	M	HTR	RR	ZZZZ	USA
SCHEFFHNANN, SELIG	30	M	PDLR	RR	ZZZZ	USA
WICKNOR, NATHAN	29	M	TLR	RR	ZZZZ	USA
JETTI	20	M	TLR	RR	ZZZZ	USA

SHIP: GALLIA

FROM: LIVERPOOL AND QUEENSTOWN
TO: NEW YORK
ARRIVED: 31 MARCH 1886

PASSENGER	AGE	SEX	OCCUPATION	PRV	VIL	DES
BANAS, JOSEF	43	M	LABR	PL	ZZZZ	USA
WONSIK, YAN	40	M	LABR	PL	ZZZZ	USA
BILEYCKI, PETER	30	M	LABR	PL	ZZZZ	USA
FEINMAN, ABEL	23	M	TLR	PL	ZZZZ	USA
WINEROWSKY, ISAAC	17	M	LABR	PL	ZZZZ	USA
ABRAMSON, ASRIEL	18	M	LABR	RR	ZZZZ	USA
KUMMEL, ELKE	17	F	SVNT	RR	ZZZZ	USA
SAML.	53	M	LABR	RR	ZZZZ	USA
BRENNER, LINA	17	F	MA	RR	ZZZZ	USA
DIRKORSKY, MICHAL	30	M	BLKSMH	RR	ZZZZ	USA
MAZARSKY, THEOPHIL	41	M	LABR	RR	ZZZZ	USA
CHOMITZ, VINCENTE	30	M	LABR	RR	ZZZZ	USA
SALMERADON, TIVAN	21	M	PNTR	RR	ADXW	USA
GOLDSTEIN, GALLIL	28	M	TLR	RR	ZZZZ	USA
SCHENAMIS, MENDEL	20	M	LABR	RR	ZZZZ	USA

PASSENGER	AGE	SEX	OCCUPATION	PV VIL DES
MARKOWITZ, ABRAHAM	25	M	LABR	RRZZZZUSA
GIACOMOZ, PASLO	40	M	LABR	RRZZZZUSA
WARSHASKY, JOHN	50	M	MCHT	RRADBQUSA

SHIP: GELLERT

FROM: HAMBURG AND HAVRE
TO: NEW YORK
ARRIVED: 02 APRIL 1886

PASSENGER	AGE	SEX	OCCUPATION	PV VIL DES
GINZBERG, IANKEL	23	M	LABR	RRAGRTUSA
KASDTON, SIMON	23	M	LABR	RRAGRTUSA
HEIHENBERG, HIRSCH	48	M	GLSMKR	RRAHTFUSA
LABORKRANZ, ISAAC	18	M	GLSMKR	RRAHTFUSA
RIGELHOP, CHAINE	19	F	SGL	RRZZZZUSA
BIRGER, RACHEL	28	F	W	RRZZZZUSA
JOFFE, JACOB	16	M	DLR	RRAEFLUSA
BLAUSTEIN, FAITEL	20	M	LABR	RRZZZZUSA
GASRINSKI, WLADISL.	36	M	LABR	RRZZZZUSA
PAULINE	27	F	W	RRZZZZUSA
ANASTASIA	4	F	CHILD	RRAFWJUSA
ERSIHELOWITZ, HESCHEL	48	M	TLR	RRAFWJUSA
DAVILOWITZ, ANADIE	31	M	TLR	RRAHSTUSA
ROSENBERG, ARON	25	M	TLR	RRAHSDUSA
ELPER, JUDIS	22	F	SGL	RRAHSEUSA
PARBER, LASER	20	M	MCHT	RRAHSEUSA
WIELIK, IGNATIV	24	M	LABR	RRAGRTUSA
ISKOWITZ, JACOB	35	M	LABR	RRAGRTUSA
MIELLER, ILEL	35	M	LABR	RRAGRTUSA
CHANNE	9	F	CHILD	RRAGRTUSA
ABRAMSKY, MOSES	27	M	DLR	RRZZZZUSA
RACHE	28	F	W	RRZZZZUSA
JUDE	9	M	CHILD	RRZZZZUSA
ABBE	.11	M	INFANT	RRZZZZUSA
SIHOSCHENSKY, BAER	26	M	LABR	RRAHWJUSA
ACHAPIRO, NATHAN	26	M	LABR	RRAHXBUSA
GILDENFEIN, MARCUS	22	M	LABR	RRAHTUUSA
SEGELOWITZ, ISAAC	20	M	LABR	RRAHTUUSA
FEIN, ISAAC	30	M	LABR	RRAHTUUSA
GRUENHAUS, JOSEF	34	M	LABR	RRAHTUUSA
LOWEN, ELIAS	23	M	LABR	RRAHWJUSA
GOLULE, ABRAHAM	26	M	LABR	RRAHWJUSA
IDISCHKEWITZ, ESTHER	24	F	W	RRAHVMUSA
SWIERSKY, ROSA	18	F	SGL	RRAHTFUSA
KURLANDZIK, MORRUS	16	M	MCHT	RRAHTFUSA
CHURGIN, BERL	23	M	TLR	RRAHTUUSA
GEPAT, LUDWIG	21	M	JNR	RRZZZZUSA
LIRULNIK, FEIVEL	20	F	SGL	RRAHZQUSA
TRUSFUSS, BENDET	21	M	DLR	RRAEFLUSA
AURICK, JULS	27	M	WVR	RRAHTNUSA
SALATZKI, MICHAEL	60	M	LABR	RRAGRTUSA
SARA	9	F	CHILD	RRAGRTUSA
GITTEL	8	F	CHILD	RRAGRTUSA
ARINOWITZ, ITE	22	F	W	RRAGRTUSA
MOSES	.11	M	INFANT	RRAGRTUSA
ROSLEWITZ, JOSEF	30	M	TLR	RRAHVWUSA
LEWIN, TANNCHEN	27	M	MCHT	RRZZZZUSA
PAKUTSKI, ISAAK	45	M	MCHT	RRZZZZUSA
RULTINAK, TANNSHE	27	M	MCHT	RRZZZZUSA
CHURGEL, ABRAHAM	17	M	MCHT	RRZZZZUSA
GARMAISE, ISRAEL	39	M	MCHT	RRZZZZUSA
AKLUTH, ABRAM	40	M	SMH	RRAHYWUSA
SALATZKY, GITTEL	20	F	SGL	RRAGRTUSA
SILBERMANN, IGNATZ	19	M	LABR	RRAHTKUSA
ARANOWSKY, SARA	30	F	W	RRAGRTUSA
CHAWE	9	F	CHILD	RRAGRTUSA

SHIP: PENNLAND

FROM: ANTWERP
TO: NEW YORK
ARRIVED: 03 APRIL 1886

PASSENGER	AGE	SEX	OCCUPATION	PV VIL DES
KOCHLER, H.MISS	29	F	BRR	RRZZZZPTL
NORDWIND, JUL.	18	M	SLSMN	PLZZZZNY
AGONSKI, L.	45	M	TLR	RRZZZZNY
POLLOCK, ABR.	26	M	TLR	RRZZZZNY

SHIP: PERSIAN MONARCH

FROM: LONDON
TO: NEW YORK
ARRIVED: 03 APRIL 1886

PASSENGER	AGE	SEX	OCCUPATION	PV VIL DES
SYLVESTON, J.	30	M	MACH	RRZZZZNY
ALICE	26	F	MACH	RRZZZZNY
MATILDA	2	F	CHILD	RRZZZZNY
LEVY, MAURICE	22	M	TLR	PLZZZZNY
HANNAH	20	F	TLR	PLZZZZNY
AARONS, LOUIS	27	M	TLR	PLZZZZUNK
ZAZARAZEH, ABRAHAM	21	M	TLR	PLZZZZNY
SYMON, BENJAMIN	21	M	TLR	RRZZZZBAL
LOWEN, MOS.	33	M	MCHT	RRZZZZNY
RICHTER, PHILIP	26	M	TLR	PLZZZZNY
WACHTER, ISRAEL	24	M	TLR	PLZZZZPHI
DORAH	21	F	TLR	PLZZZZPHI

SHIP: WERRA

FROM: BREMEN AND SOUTHAMPTON
TO: NEW YORK
ARRIVED: 05 APRIL 1886

PASSENGER	AGE	SEX	OCCUPATION	PV VIL DES
SCHIWALSKY, VINCENT	22	M	LABR	RRZZZZUSA
SULCOZKI, PETER	21	M	LABR	RRZZZZUSA
BROMINSKI, JAN	21	M	LABR	RRZZZZUSA
RACHILEWIS, WRATL.	25	M	LABR	RRZZZZUSA
BILDER, JOHS.	33	M	FARMER	RRZZZZUSA
KATHA.	28	F	W	RRZZZZUSA
MARIA	4	F	CHILD	RRZZZZUSA
MARTIN	3	M	CHILD	RRZZZZUSA
CHRISTIAN	.05	M	INFANT	RRZZZZUSA
BODEMER, GOTTL.	55	M	FARMER	RRZZZZUSA
JUSTINE	57	F	W	RRZZZZUSA
ELISABETH	19	F	NN	RRZZZZUSA
WALS, JACOB	31	M	FARMER	RRZZZZUSA
EVA	28	F	W	RRZZZZUSA
CAROLINE	6	F	CHILD	RRZZZZUSA
JOHANNES	2	M	CHILD	RRZZZZUSA
JACOB	.04	M	INFANT	RRZZZZUSA
MEYER, CHRISTIAN	23	M	FARMER	RRZZZZUSA
PENER	20	F	W	RRZZZZUSA
EMILIE	.06	F	INFANT	RRZZZZUSA
PERSCH, CHRIST.	23	M	FARMER	RRZZZZUSA
LAI, JOHANN	22	M	FARMER	RRZZZZUSA
WALZ, GOTTL.	18	M	FARMER	RRZZZZUSA
BINDERWALD, JOHANNES	28	M	FARMER	RRZZZZUSA
MARG.	25	F	W	RRZZZZUSA
KATHA.	4	F	CHILD	RRZZZZUSA
JOHANNES	3	M	CHILD	RRZZZZUSA
MICHAEL	.03	M	INFANT	RRZZZZUSA

PASSENGER	AGE	SEX	OCCUPATION	PRV VIL DES
PREIDLING, JOH.	16	M	CH	RRZZZZUSA
SWASINSKI, JOSEF	30	M	PDLR	RRZZZZUSA
ZAGAKI, JOSEF	24	M	LABR	RRZZZZUSA
GROSCHOWSKY, BERNHD.	19	M	LABR	RRZZZZUSA
OLSINA, WOLF	19	M	MCHT	RRAEFLUSA
SCHRAMM, DANIEL	39	M	FARMER	RRZZZZUSA
ELISAB.	39	F	W	RRZZZZUSA
KATHA.	3	F	CHILD	RRZZZZUSA
JACOB	.02	M	INFANT	RRZZZZUSA
SCHAEDLER, ANDREAS	33	M	FARMER	RRZZZZUSA
HELENE	32	F	W	RRZZZZUSA
LOUISE	3	F	CHILD	RRZZZZUSA
LOUISE	1	F	CHILD	RRZZZZUSA
ELISAB.	.08	F	INFANT	RRZZZZUSA
TAUBLER, GOTTLIEB	18	M	FARMER	RRZZZZUSA
ANDREAS	.10	M	INFANT	RRZZZZUSA
MEYER, CHRIST.	35	M	FARMER	RRZZZZUSA
CAROLE.	35	F	W	RRZZZZUSA
FRIEDR.	3	M	CHILD	RRZZZZUSA
CHRISTA.	.08	F	INFANT	RRZZZZUSA
BEGLER, FRIEDR.	35	M	FARMER	RRZZZZUSA
KATHA.	33	F	W	RRZZZZUSA
JOHANNES	7	M	CHILD	RRZZZZUSA
GOTTL.	5	M	CHILD	RRZZZZUSA
KATHA.	2	F	CHILD	RRZZZZUSA
FRIEDR.	.06	M	INFANT	RRZZZZUSA
UHLMANNSICK, HEINR.	18	M	LABR	PLZZZZUSA
SCHUCK, CHAIM	19	M	LABR	PLZZZZUSA
GOLDWACH, JOSEF	36	M	LABR	PLZZZZUSA
TIDRACH, ARON	21	M	LABR	PLZZZZUSA
DOCTOR, JACOB	26	M	LABR	RRZZZZUSA
MARGA.	24	F	W	RRZZZZUSA
JACOB	2	M	CHILD	RRZZZZUSA
GOTTL.	.11	M	INFANT	RRZZZZUSA
MANDJAK, HANJA	20	M	LABR	RRAHTFUSA
HOLWEGER, ROSINA	30	F	W	RRAHTFUSA
JOH.	4	M	CHILD	RRAHTFUSA
JACOB	3	M	CHILD	RRAHTFUSA
ROSINA	.06	F	INFANT	RRAHTFUSA
BERTSCH, STANISL.	28	M	LABR	RRZZZZUSA
ANNA	23	F	W	RRZZZZUSA
ANNA	.11	F	INFANT	RRZZZZUSA
MAGDA.	.01	F	INFANT	RRZZZZUSA
FETTICH, WENDELIN	37	M	LABR	RRZZZZUSA
CATHA.	27	F	W	RRZZZZUSA
LIPPOLD	.11	M	INFANT	RRZZZZUSA
HEGELL, EMANUEL	37	M	FARMER	RRZZZZUSA
MARGARITHA	36	F	W	RRZZZZUSA
IGNATZ	10	M	CH	RRZZZZUSA
JACOB	8	M	CHILD	RRZZZZUSA
EMIL	7	M	CHILD	RRZZZZUSA
THOMAS	5	M	CHILD	RRZZZZUSA
JOSEF, FRANZ	4	M	CHILD	RRZZZZUSA
FRANZ	2	M	CHILD	RRZZZZUSA
PETER	.03	M	INFANT	RRZZZZUSA
ANTON	1	M	CHILD	RRZZZZUSA

SHIP: ABYSSINIA

FROM: LIVERPOOL AND QUEENSTOWN
TO: NEW YORK
ARRIVED: 09 APRIL 1886

PASSENGER	AGE	SEX	OCCUPATION	PRV VIL DES
MADZIKOWSKY, BARTR.	24	M	FLABR	RRZZZZUSA
GRUNDKOWSKY, ANTONI	22	M	FLABR	RRZZZZUSA
DYENBOWA, JACOB	24	M	FLABR	RRZZZZUSA
TRILATI, FRANS	40	M	FLABR	RRZZZZUSA
GRALA, JOSEPH	42	M	CLR	RRZZZZUSA
MOSEHEKA, JOSEPH	19	M	FLABR	RRZZZZUSA
JACUBOWSKY, JAN	18	M	FLABR	RRZZZZUSA
JACOBROWSKY, AMBROSENA	34	M	MNR	RRZZZZUSA
NIEMCZINSKY, JEYKA	35	M	PDLR	RRZZZZUSA
HENDRIKSEN, NILS	37	M	MRNR	RRZZZZUSA

SHIP: AMERICA

FROM: LIVERPOOL
TO: NEW YORK
ARRIVED: 09 APRIL 1886

PASSENGER	AGE	SEX	OCCUPATION	PRV VIL DES
WESTERNINE, L.	28	F	W	RRZZZZUSA
MATHILDA	5	F	CHILD	RRZZZZUSA
J.	7	F	CHILD	RRZZZZUSA
M.	00	F	INF	RRZZZZUSA
ERLANSEN, PAUL	26	M	LABR	RRZZZZUSA
ERIKSON, PEDER	18	M	LABR	RRZZZZUSA
KLEINSWUTT, W.	50	M	LABR	RRZZZZUSA
M.	45	F	W	RRZZZZUSA
K.	25	M	LABR	RRZZZZUSA
M.	23	F	SP	RRZZZZUSA
H.	24	M	LABR	RRZZZZUSA
M.	3	M	CHILD	RRZZZZUSA
SEUSKY, J.	40	F	W	RRZZZZUSA
C.	10	F	CH	RRZZZZUSA
F.	9	F	CHILD	RRZZZZUSA
G.	6	F	CHILD	RRZZZZUSA
M.	00	F	INF	RRZZZZUSA
BRYELA, KASPER	32	M	LABR	RRZZZZUSA
FOLGEWGAK, JOSE	32	M	LABR	RRZZZZUSA
STANK, JAN	26	M	LABR	RRZZZZUSA
KIWLAK, A.	27	M	LABR	RRZZZZUSA
PERIER, S.	26	M	LABR	RRZZZZUSA
TONEGAK, F.	25	M	LABR	RRZZZZUSA
ROWNAN, MOSES	16	M	LABR	RRZZZZUSA
PILERENG--, V.	11	M	CH	RRZZZZUSA
PALUGIS, N.	23	M	LABR	RRZZZZUSA
SEMIN, A.	25	M	LABR	RRZZZZUSA
KALINOWSKI, JOSEF	26	M	LABR	RRZZZZUSA
GARCUSIZ, R.	26	M	LABR	RRZZZZUSA
BARCINTZ, JOSEF	29	M	LABR	RRZZZZUSA

SHIP: ANCHORIA

FROM: GLASGOW AND MOVILLE
TO: NEW YORK
ARRIVED: 09 APRIL 1886

PASSENGER	AGE	SEX	OCCUPATION	PRV VIL DES
WIDLANSKI, SORE-ROCHE	30	F	W	RRZZZZUSA
FRUME	9	F	CHILD	RRZZZZUSA
CHANE	7	F	CHILD	RRZZZZUSA
RIWE	1	F	CHILD	RRZZZZUSA
MOSES	21	M	LABR	RRZZZZUSA
GISCHE	17	M	LABR	RRAHZSUSA
ELFEMOWE, RASSE	40	F	W	RRAHZSUSA
MARECHE	11	F	CH	RRAHZSUSA
JOSEF	9	M	CHILD	RRAHZSUSA
MENDEL	5	M	CHILD	RRAHZSUSA
MUOCHE	1	F	CHILD	RRAHZSUSA
FAIN, ELKE	40	F	W	RRAHZSUSA
MOSCHE	10	F	CH	RRAHZSUSA
HANNE	6	F	CHILD	RRAHZSUSA
FEIGE	6	F	CHILD	RRAHZSUSA
MEIER	1	M	CHILD	RRAHTUUSA
KOMMEL, ABEL	20	M	PDLR	RRZZZZUSA
ETTEL	22	F	W	RRZZZZUSA

PASSENGER	AGE	SEX	OCCUPATION	PRV VIL DES
CHONDEKOWSKI, ABRAM	27	M	LABR	RRZZZZUSA
SCHANDEL	20	F	W	RRZZZZUSA
PUSA, NOJTECH	26	M	LABR	RRAHZSUSA
MARIAN	26	F	W	RRAHZSUSA
GALASCINSKY, VINCENT	27	M	W	RRAHZSUSA
KAPLAN, ADOLF	20	M	DLR	RRAHVUUSA
LEWIN, BEREL	28	M	LABR	RRAGRTUSA
TYKTYN, ABRAHAM	18	M	LABR	RRAHVUUSA
MERZALSKI, KASIMIR	36	M	LABR	RRAHTFUSA
FERNNES, JOSEPH	22	M	LABR	RRAHTFUSA
BALTEINE, SIGMUND	28	M	LABR	RRAHTFUSA
ZIANNES, JOSEPH	22	M	LABR	RRAHTFUSA
JOSEFEITIS, JOSEF	24	M	LABR	RRAHTFUSA
DUNOV, ALTER	19	M	LABR	RRAHTUUSA
WEINSTEIN, NATHAN	19	M	LABR	RRAHQUUSA
DUNOV, ITZIG	47	M	LABR	RRAHTUUSA
STOBETMANN, WOLF	40	M	LABR	RRAHTFUSA
HEBELMANN, RUBIN	27	M	LABR	RRAHTFUSA
IWINTZIG, ISRAEL	19	M	LABR	RRAHTUUSA
TURETZKY, ABRAHAM	27	M	LABR	RRAHTUUSA
DOGOWSKY, SCHAJE	44	M	LABR	RRAHTFUSA
PREK, E.JRAELOWITZ	36	M	LABR	RRAHTFUSA
BREITMANN, WOLF	26	M	LABR	RRAHTUUSA
SCHWALOWITZ, LEIB	19	M	LABR	RRAEFLUSA
EPHRAIM, SAMUEL	17	M	LABR	RRAHZSUSA
HURWITZ, SCHLOME	33	M	LABR	RRAGRTUSA
GABRIELSOHN, MOSES	21	M	MSN	RRZZZZUSA
GLUCKMANN, MOSECHEK	22	M	LABR	RRAHTFUSA
ABRAMOWITZ, RACHMIL	19	M	LABR	RRAGRTUSA
SURDUT, JANKEL	42	M	LABR	RRAHTFUSA
KURTZON, BERL	35	M	LABR	RRAHTUUSA
RODMAN, HODEL	19	M	LABR	RRAHTUUSA
ISAKOW, REBEKA	20	F	HP	RRAHTUUSA

SHIP: CANADA

FROM: HAVRE
TO: NEW YORK
ARRIVED: 09 APRIL 1886

PASSENGER	AGE	SEX	OCCUPATION	PRV VIL DES
STAMM, RACHEL	42	F	NN	RRZZZZNY
SARAH	12	F	NN	RRZZZZNY
ISAAC	10	M	NN	RRZZZZNY
REBECCA	7	F	CHILD	RRZZZZNY
SAMUEL	3	M	CHILD	RRZZZZNY
MARCUS, JOSEPH	25	M	HTR	RRZZZZNY
LEONTINE	22	F	NN	RRZZZZNY
BERNARD	1	M	CHILD	RRZZZZNY

SHIP: MORAVIA

FROM: HAMBURG
TO: NEW YORK
ARRIVED: 09 APRIL 1886

PASSENGER	AGE	SEX	OCCUPATION	PRV VIL DES
CHAEMOWICZ, SCHEIL	19	M	LABR	RRZZZZUSA
SBIEGOSKI, IGNATZ	32	M	LABR	RRZZZZUSA
CZASGOVSKI, STANISLAUS	25	M	LABR	RRAHZSUSA
BRZCZINSKI, JOSEPH	34	M	LABR	RRAHZSUSA
LENGER, JANOS	48	M	LABR	RRAHZSUSA
BONKALIK, FRANZ	18	M	LABR	RRAHZSUSA
ISGUR, SIMON	21	M	TNMK	RRAHTUUSA
SIMKA	18	F	W	RRAHTUUSA
KILIAN, WILH.	30	M	LABR	RRZZZZUSA
AREFFIOVNA, ANNE	27	F	SGL	RRZZZZUSA
SPIRIDON	32	M	LABR	RRZZZZUSA
WENDLOWSKY, FELIX	16	M	LABR	RRZZZZUSA
LAWITAN, SLATTE	40	F	W	RRZZZZUSA
ELIAS	9	M	CHILD	RRZZZZUSA
STEFFENSON, PETER	30	M	FARMER	RRZZZZUSA
EISENBERG, SAMUEL	18	M	CGRMKR	RRAHVUUSA
BERMANN, CHANNE	30	F	W	RRZZZZUSA
JOSEPH	5	M	CHILD	RRZZZZUSA
PACKHEIZER, MORITZ	26	M	SHMK	RRZZZZUSA
PAULINE	24	F	W	RRZZZZUSA
STRELZIN, CHAIM	31	M	DLR	RRZZZZUSA
MUELLER, NOACH	35	M	DLR	RRZZZZUSA
GOLDE	29	F	W	RRZZZZUSA
LEOPOLD	5	M	CHILD	RRZZZZUSA
BERTHA	4	F	CHILD	RRZZZZUSA
ROSA	.11	F	INFANT	RRZZZZUSA
PROPP, MEIER	28	M	CL	RRAHVAUSA
LACK, JOSSEL	18	M	SHMK	RRZZZZUSA
LIPSMANNOW, ROSA	18	F	SGL	RRZZZZUSA
SCHWARZ, FRIEDE	7	F	CHILD	RRAHTOUSA
GLADOWSKY, JAN	22	M	FARMER	RRAHUFUSA
LEISMEISTER, GEORG	40	M	FARMER	RRACOVUSA
KATHA	37	F	W	RRACOVUSA
SEBASTIAN	17	M	CH	RRACOVUSA
FERD.	9	M	CHILD	RRACOVUSA
ADAM	7	M	CHILD	RRACOVUSA
LUDWIG	5	M	CHILD	RRACOVUSA
MARGA	4	F	CHILD	RRACOVUSA
MARIE	2	F	CHILD	RRACOVUSA
JOHL	.06	F	INFANT	RRACOVUSA
SCHUMACHER, JOSEF	35	M	LABR	RRAHYKUSA
ANGONES	33	F	W	RRAHYKUSA
FRANZ	9	M	CHILD	RRAHYKUSA
EMANUEL	8	M	CHILD	RRAHYKUSA
PETER	.11	M	INFANT	RRAHYKUSA
MARIANE	5	F	CHILD	RRAHYKUSA
MAGDAL	3	F	CHILD	RRAHYKUSA
ADAM	27	M	FARMER	RRAHYKUSA
MARIE	22	F	W	RRAHYKUSA
JOHS.	.09	M	INFANT	RRAHYKUSA
ULEM, FRANZ	32	M	LABR	RRAHYKUSA
MAGD.	28	F	W	RRAHYKUSA
ANT.	7	M	CHILD	RRAHYKUSA
SEBASTIAN	3	M	CHILD	RRAHYKUSA
KRISTINE	15	F	SGL	RRAHYKUSA
FROTMANN, JOH.	29	M	FARMER	RRABIJUSA
MARGARETHA	23	F	W	RRABIJUSA
FISCHER, JOSEF	23	M	LABR	RRAHYKUSA
SCHANDER, KASAMIER	29	M	FARMER	RRAHYKUSA
BARBA.	26	F	W	RRAHYKUSA
JOH.	4	M	CHILD	RRAHYKUSA
MICH.	3	M	CHILD	RRAHYKUSA
WENDELBIN	2	M	CHILD	RRAHYKUSA
KASIMIR	.04	M	INFANT	RRAHYKUSA
MILLER, ENGELBART	44	M	FARMER	RRABIJUSA
ROSINE	42	F	W	RRABIJUSA
CATHE.	7	F	CHILD	RRABIJUSA
MARIE	5	F	CHILD	RRABIJUSA
BARBA.	2	F	CHILD	RRABIJUSA
SCHUMACHER, PAUL	29	M	W	RRAHYKUSA
MAGDALENA	25	F	CH	RRAHYKUSA
CATHA.	4	F	CHILD	RRAHYKUSA
JOHS.	2	M	CHILD	RRAHYKUSA
ZANN, ADAM	49	M	FARMER	RRABIJUSA
ELISABETH	50	F	W	RRABIJUSA
ADAM	9	M	CHILD	RRABIJUSA
URIEK, EGIDENS	49	M	FARMER	RRABIJUSA
ELISABETH	44	F	W	RRABIJUSA
CAECILLE	24	F	CH	RRABIJUSA
CLARA	26	F	CH	RRABIJUSA
MICH.	18	M	CH	RRABIJUSA
MAGDALENA	16	F	CH	RRABIJUSA
CATHA.	9	F	CHILD	RRABIJUSA
THEOD.	7	M	CHILD	RRABIJUSA
BRAUNAGEL, MARIANNE	48	F	W	RRAHYKUSA

PASSENGER	AGE	SEX	OCCUPATION	PRV VIL DES
MARIE	20	F	CH	RRAHYKUSA
ANTON	17	M	CH	RRAHYKUSA
MAGD.	9	F	CHILD	RRAHYKUSA
EVA	4	F	CHILD	RRAHYKUSA
SILL, SEBASTIAN	25	M	FARMER	RRABIJUSA
BARBA.	22	F	W	RRABIJUSA
WILH.	.06	M	INFANT	RRABIJUSA
SCHUMACHER, SEBASTIAN	31	M	FARMER	RRAHYKUSA
MARIANNE	26	F	W	RRAHYKUSA
JOSEF	9	M	CHILD	RRAHYKUSA
MARIANNE	8	F	CHILD	RRAHYKUSA
FRANZ	5	M	CHILD	RRAHYKUSA
BARBA.	2	F	CHILD	RRAHYKUSA
KELLER, FINJES	33	M	FARMER	RRABIJUSA
ANNA	00	F	W	RRABIJUSA
JOSEF	5	M	CHILD	RRABIJUSA
PETRONELLA	3	M	CHILD	RRABIJUSA
LUCAS	.11	M	INFANT	RRABIJUSA
MILLER, JOHS.	29	M	FARMER	RRABIJUSA
THERESE	20	F	W	RRABIJUSA
JOHS.	.11	M	INFANT	RRABIJUSA
LADRER, SEBASTIAN	57	M	FARMER	RRACOVUSA
ROSALIE	30	F	W	RRACOVUSA
JOHS.	24	M	CH	RRACOVUSA
SEBASTIAN	17	M	CH	RRACOVUSA
SEBASTIAN	9	M	CHILD	RRACOVUSA
GEORG	6	M	CHILD	RRACOVUSA
MARIANNE	4	F	CHILD	RRACOVUSA
PHILIPP	20	M	FARMER	RRACOVUSA
MARIE	22	F	W	RRACOVUSA
ANTON	3	M	CHILD	RRACOVUSA
ANNA	.09	F	INFANT	RRACOVUSA
ROSALIE	.09	F	INFANT	RRACOVUSA
BRAUN, ABRAHAM	24	M	LABR	RRZZZZUSA
LOUS	22	M	LABR	RRZZZZUSA
BERTHA	19	F	SGL	RRZZZZUSA
SMOLEWITZ, GIKEL	17	F	SGL	RRAHTOUSA
KALMA, MOSES	22	M	DLR	RRZZZZUSA
BENEDIKT, MIKOS	29	M	LABR	RRAHYCUSA
EWIGTER, RUBEN	42	M	LABR	RRZZZZUSA
PRENOKY, NADCINGI	36	M	LABR	RRAHTSUSA
BROKOWITZ, JENNY	25	F	W	RRAFVGUSA
SAMUEL	6	M	CHILD	RRAFVGUSA
PERLBERG, CHEINE	20	F	SGL	RRAHZRUSA
SISSLER, JOSEF	31	M	LABR	RRZZZZUSA
STOCKLITZKY, SCHOLEW	19	M	LABR	RRZZZZUSA
GITTEL	19	F	W	RRZZZZUSA
SCHASE	.11	F	INFANT	RRZZZZUSA
GUTTMANN, SARA	22	F	SGL	RRZZZZUSA
JUNDELSKY, LIERB	45	F	W	RRAHXWUSA
SCHWED	18	M	CH	RRAHXWUSA
TAUBE	7	M	CHILD	RRAHXWUSA
MOSES	5	M	CHILD	RRAHXWUSA
GROSSMANN, DAVID	17	M	LABR	RRZZZZUSA
SDANOWICZ, FRANZ	24	M	LABR	RRZZZZUSA
IGNATZ	23	M	LABR	RRZZZZUSA
SALACH, JAN	49	M	LABR	RRZZZZUSA
WEZOLAK, ALEXANDER	27	M	LABR	RRZZZZUSA
FEIGE	24	F	W	RRZZZZUSA
KLAPPER, JACOB	42	M	TLR	RRZZZZUSA
SCHELINSKI, ABRAM	46	M	TU	RRZZZZUSA
FEIGE	18	F	SGL	RRZZZZUSA
EISEN, DAVID	25	M	BCHR	RRZZZZUSA
FEIGE	19	F	SGL	RRZZZZUSA
STARK, HENOCH	42	M	JNR	RRZZZZUSA
WEINBERGER, ABRAM	20	M	CL	RRZZZZUSA
HANNER, ISRAEL	45	M	TLR	RRZZZZUSA
MALKE	9	F	CHILD	RRZZZZUSA
ALTWEIS, CHAINE	23	M	TLR	RRZZZZUSA
RZATHOWSKI, ANDRE	26	M	LABR	RRZZZZUSA
KOWALEWSKI, FRANZ	31	M	LABR	RRAHZSUSA
DONIGOWSKI, KASIMIR	24	M	LABR	RRAHZSUSA
CHALIELOWSKI, JOSEF	26	M	LABR	RRAHZSUSA
SEINOWS, LEA	43	F	W	RRAHZSUSA
ABRAH.	15	M	CH	RRAHZSUSA

PASSENGER	AGE	SEX	OCCUPATION	PRV VIL DES
HEIDE	9	M	CHILD	RRAHZSUSA
HIRSCH	8	M	CHILD	RRAHZSUSA
ETHL.	7	F	CHILD	RRAHZSUSA
GITTEL	.11	F	INFANT	RRAHZSUSA
SCHEBSEE	5	F	CHILD	RRAHZSUSA

SHIP: STATE OF GEORGIA

FROM: GLASGOW AND LARNE
TO: NEW YORK
ARRIVED: 09 APRIL 1886

PASSENGER	AGE	SEX	OCCUPATION	PRV VIL DES
TRUMPOSCHOWSKY, PERIE	22	F	SVNT	RRZZZZUSA
FAERBER, CHINKE	50	F	SVNT	RRZZZZUSA
GRODZINSKY, ZELIJA	50	F	W	RRZZZZUSA
DLUZELINSKY, JACOBINE	18	F	SVNT	RRZZZZUSA
KRONWALL, AUGUSTA	37	F	SVNT	RRZZZZUSA
SCHIMINZIZ, ISRAEL	40	M	LABR	RRZZZZUSA
FROMME	32	F	W	RRZZZZUSA
NOAH	3	M	CHILD	RRZZZZUSA
BRAINE	5	F	CHILD	RRZZZZUSA
THERESE	1	F	CHILD	RRZZZZUSA
JENTE	.04	F	INFANT	RRZZZZUSA
BANDELL, NATHAN	27	M	LABR	RRZZZZUSA
ETHEL	18	F	W	RRZZZZUSA
BLANSKY, GEO	28	M	LABR	RRZZZZUSA
PATRONIA	23	F	W	RRZZZZUSA
GROGER, PETER	27	M	LABR	RRZZZZUSA
FANNY	22	F	W	RRZZZZUSA
MAJEWSKY, LUDWIG	52	M	LABR	RRZZZZUSA
MARGAIN	37	F	W	RRZZZZUSA
LUDWIG	.06	M	INFANT	RRZZZZUSA
WEINSTEIN, MESCHE	29	F	W	RRZZZZUSA
REBECCA	4	F	CHILD	RRZZZZUSA
JACOB	2	M	CHILD	RRZZZZUSA
JUDA	.10	F	INFANT	RRZZZZUSA
DLUGELINSKY, FELIG	34	M	PDLR	RRZZZZUSA
JACOB	24	M	PDLR	RRZZZZUSA
SCHICHTOR, ANTON	20	M	LABR	RRZZZZUSA
MILLER, FRANZ	18	M	LABR	RRZZZZUSA
MASLOWSKY, WALTER	20	M	LABR	RRZZZZUSA
RODEWALT, PAUL	24	M	PDLR	RRZZZZUSA
FEGELMANN, KOPEL	29	M	BKR	RRZZZZUSA
SCHEMARKES, MATHIAS	25	M	LABR	RRZZZZUSA
HANS	28	M	LABR	RRZZZZUSA
KAZEW, SALOMON	21	M	LABR	RRZZZZUSA
LEIB, DAVID	22	M	LABR	RRZZZZUSA
BEHR	19	M	LABR	RRZZZZUSA
WASCHLEWSKY, ANTON	22	M	LABR	RRZZZZUSA
GERZOWSKY, ARON	22	M	LABR	RRZZZZUSA
STANKOWITZ, TADENZ	26	M	LABR	RRZZZZUSA
PRYSKEWITZ, JAKOB	36	M	LABR	RRZZZZUSA
REISK, JOSEPH	26	M	LABR	RRZZZZUSA
WOLSKY, PIETRO	22	M	LABR	RRZZZZUSA
JEKEWITZ, LEOPOLD	23	M	LABR	RRZZZZUSA
SACKOWITZ, ANTONIE	33	M	LABR	RRZZZZUSA
VISCJENSKY, PIETRO	36	M	LABR	RRZZZZUSA
KABAKOWSKY, ANTON	42	M	LABR	RRZZZZUSA
MICIROWITZ, ADAM	23	M	LABR	RRZZZZUSA
SIENKOWSKY, ANTON	26	M	LABR	RRZZZZUSA
KAPILOWITZ, LEIB	26	M	LABR	RRZZZZUSA
TROTZKI, JOSEPH	24	M	LABR	RRZZZZUSA
LESKO, KONSTANTIN	20	M	LABR	RRZZZZUSA
SACKEWSKY, PETER	37	M	LABR	RRZZZZUSA
RAMOMONSKY, ADAM	21	M	LABR	RRZZZZUSA
GERZUMSKY, BENDIX	33	M	LABR	RRZZZZUSA
TRATZKY, SIMON	36	M	LABR	RRZZZZUSA
BURSITSKY, FRANZISECK	25	M	LABR	RRZZZZUSA
ISIDOR, MICHALIE	00	M	LABR	RRZZZZUSA
MAJOCAC, JAN	43	M	LABR	RRZZZZUSA

PASSENGER	AGE	SEX	OCCUPATION	PV VIL DES
GRESLEWITZ, JACOB	28	M	LABR	RRZZZZUSA
BURSTEIN, RUBEN	32	M	TLR	RRZZZZUSA
JABLONSKY, JACOB	30	M	TLR	RRZZZZUSA
KAMMINSKY, VICTOR	45	M	LABR	RRZZZZUSA
BUERN, ISRAEL	33	M	LABR	RRZZZZUSA
DIEDOWSKY, JOSEF	22	M	LABR	RRZZZZUSA
SINKEWITZ, ANTON	27	M	LABR	RRZZZZUSA
FRANZ	11	M	LABR	RRZZZZUSA
PROSSER, JOSSEL	42	M	LABR	RRZZZZUSA
SYDREWSKA, JANOS	20	M	LABR	RRZZZZUSA
KLAWANSKY, BINNE	22	M	LABR	RRZZZZUSA
SOBOLEWSKY, OSIFS	28	M	LABR	RRZZZZUSA
MARDAS, MICHEL	36	M	LABR	RRZZZZUSA
ALEXANDER, PIETRO	30	M	LABR	RRZZZZUSA
DWORKIN, CHAIM	50	M	LABR	RRZZZZUSA
LASEWNICK, NACHEM	19	M	LABR	RRZZZZUSA
RUBIN, MENDEL	19	M	LABR	RRZZZZUSA
KASSELOWITZ, ISRAEL	21	M	LABR	RRZZZZUSA
AXELROD, ISAAC	24	M	LABR	RRZZZZUSA
KAREWITZ, AISIK	42	M	LABR	RRZZZZUSA
KARL, NACHEM	24	M	LABR	RRZZZZUSA
ALGIMOWITCH, SIMON	25	M	LABR	RRZZZZUSA
SILBERMANN, CATZKEL	24	M	LABR	RRZZZZUSA
JACOB	11	M	LABR	RRZZZZUSA
DINENINJ, FRANCIS	25	M	LABR	RRZZZZUSA

SHIP: ENGLAND

FROM: LIVERPOOL AND QUEENSTOWN
TO: NEW YORK
ARRIVED: 10 APRIL 1886

PASSENGER	AGE	SEX	OCCUPATION	PV VIL DES
RUVAN, M.	35	M	GLVR	RRADAXNY
SCHUSHER, ASRIEL	19	M	FARMER	RRZZZZNY
KATZ, JULIUS	26	M	LABR	RRAAKHNY
ROMAN, S.	26	M	LABR	RRADBQNY
ISAACS, S.	22	F	SP	RRADBQNY
E.	24	F	SP	RRADBQNY
LEWIN, J.	33	F	TLR	PLZZZZNY
LYOM, ABRAHAM	29	M	TLR	PLADBQCH
BREGOWSKY, SAM	26	M	TLR	RRZZZZNY
FREGIL, SCHLOME	27	M	TLR	RRADAXNY
BLUM	10	M	CH	RRADAXNY
MENDELSOHN, ROSA	30	F	W	RRZZZZCH
MALKE	4	F	CHILD	RRZZZZCH
R.	1	M	CHILD	RRZZZZCH
COHN, ISRAEL	20	M	LABR	RRADAXNY
NIEL, E.I.O.	28	M	TRVLR	RRADBQNY
FLETYKE, MAREUS	19	M	LABR	RRADAXNY
LALLINSKY, SALOMON	16	M	LABR	RRADAXNY
HEMBALIES, SUGER	25	M	LABR	RRADAXNY
COHN, ALEXANDER	28	M	TLR	PLZZZZNY
TRUDEL	30	M	TLR	PLZZZZNY
CHER, ABRAHAM	21	M	TLR	PLZZZZNY
HOLLMSKOWITZ, ABRAHAM	21	M	TLR	PLZZZZNY
KOSTRINSKY, SCHLOME	57	M	LABR	PLZZZZNY
REZNIK, ADOLPF	28	M	CPTR	RRZZZZNY
KRUSWITZ, EPHRAIM	26	M	LABR	RRACBFNY
KLOP, HIRSCH	26	M	LABR	RRACBFNY
VERALL, PAMEL	20	M	LABR	RRAHTUNY
GROWSKY, NILSEN	30	M	LABR	RRACBFNY
SHAZVAN, SHONE	22	M	LABR	RRACBFNY
NINKOW, DAVID	31	M	LABR	RRACBFNY
RUFKA	22	M	LABR	RRACBFNY
EPIRIE, SHLOME	24	M	LABR	RRACBFNY
HALPERIN, SHLOME	24	M	LABR	RRACBFNY
EPIRIE, HINDEL	26	M	LABR	RRACBFNY
EPEROWITZ, ISAK	24	M	LABR	RRACBFNY
EPRIN, RUBEN	18	M	LABR	RRACBFNY
SCHULMANN, SCHINA	44	F	W	RRZZZZNY
MARCUS	12	M	CH	RRZZZZNY
SIEL	10	M	CH	RRZZZZNY
MOSES	5	M	CHILD	RRZZZZNY
KILNIK, VICTOR	18	M	WVR	RRZZZZNY
BREWSKY, B.	26	M	GLSR	RRZZZZNY
KOPELOWIC, JOSEF	26	M	CGRMKR	RRZZZZNY
EPRIM, JACOB	11	M	CH	RRZZZZNY
GWIGNAMIER, MOSES	28	M	TBCL	RRZZZZNY
LIEPTENSTEIN, SALMON	35	M	WVR	RRZZZZNY
CHRINHAM, GOLDE	19	F	SP	PLZZZZNY
SCHIMON, WALKI	17	M	LABR	PLZZZZNY
HIRSCH, LAZER	20	M	LABR	PLZZZZNY
MEMEL	19	M	LABR	PLZZZZNY
BLANSKY, CHASKEL	19	M	LABR	PLZZZZNY
KAPLIN, LEIL	20	M	TLR	PLZZZZNY
LEWIN, SAMUEL	24	M	PNTR	RRZZZZNY
CECILLA	18	F	W	RRZZZZNY
KALSPAVIER, CHONE	36	F	TLR	RRZZZZNY
KOZEL, MOD.	36	F	TLR	RRAEWSNY
BRALASTEVSKY, SUGER	50	F	TLR	RRAEWSNY
BUKOWITZ, ABR.	28	F	SMH	RRAEWSNY
SCHNEIDER, MEYER	40	F	LABR	RRAEWSNY
KELINGOP, BOROR-OSCAR	22	F	LABR	RRAEWSNY
WAGNER, J.	22	F	LABR	RRAEWSNY
PAIOD, CHAIM	47	F	LABR	RRAEWSNY
PAPER, SALOMON	26	F	FARMER	RRZZZZNY
DEBORAH	24	F	W	RRZZZZNY
REBECCA	1	F	CHILD	RRZZZZNY
SCHUSON, G.	18	F	SP	RRZZZZNY
PEREL	11	M	CH	RRZZZZNY
MAHEL	22	M	LABR	RRZZZZNY
REBECCA	1	F	CHILD	RRZZZZNY
MALKE	11	M	CH	RRZZZZNY
SARAH	9	F	CHILD	RRZZZZNY
JACOB	7	M	CHILD	RRZZZZNY
FURE	1	M	CHILD	RRZZZZNY
MUSHMANN, MENDEL	23	M	LABR	RRAEWSNY
RUBIN, JOEL	24	M	LABR	RRACBFNY
BERGER, CHAIM	26	M	LABR	RRACBFNY
HOWSKY, MICHAEL	30	M	LABR	RRACBFNY
FIHTELLAY, HIRSCH	24	M	LABR	PLZZZZNY
ESTHER	18	F	SP	PLZZZZNY
ESTHER	16	F	SP	PLZZZZNY
MAYER	10	M	CH	PLZZZZNY
SCHAPIRA, BERL	25	M	LABR	PLZZZZNY
KALEY, SCHEINE	17	M	LABR	PLZZZZNY
MOSHENIN, LEIB	29	M	LABR	PLZZZZNY
SOSCHINSKY, F.	38	M	LABR	PLZZZZNY
SLOBATZKI, SAM.	22	M	TLR	PLAHTUNY
RUBIN, LEIB	17	M	LABR	PLAHTUNY
RUCHLSOHN, CERIK	24	M	TLR	PLAHTUNY
GOVEKOW, FISCHEL	25	M	LABR	PLAHTUNY
GORSKORE, L.	27	M	LABR	PLAHTUNY
KLONTERSKY, LOCKE	27	M	LABR	PLADBQNY
KONSECK, LEIB	52	M	TLR	PLADBQNY
RUCHELSON, HIRSCH	23	M	PRNTR	PLAHTUNY
ROSENTHAL, H.	20	F	SP	PLZZZZNY
LUDENBERG, LISKIN	19	M	SHMK	PLZZZZNY
KELE	20	F	W	PLZZZZNY
SCHAPIRA, PERETZ	37	M	LABR	RRZZZZNY
WOGKSCHANER, ALEXANDER	35	M	CPTR	RRZZZZNY
LOOBECK, SCHMUEL	25	M	LABR	PLZZZZNY
LEOM, HIRSCH	35	M	LABR	PLZZZZNY
LEVOTZKY, STANISLAV	29	M	LABR	PLACBFNY
JAKEWITZ, ANTON	23	M	LABR	PLACBFNY
SCRUBA, VER.	21	M	LABR	PLACBFNY
GREYERSKY, ST.	25	M	LABR	PLACBFNY
PRITREI, ANTON	22	M	LABR	PLACBFNY
RYBACK, ABRAHAM	20	M	LABR	PLACBFNY
WACHT, SAMUEL	20	M	LABR	PLACBFNY
LIPPMAN, WOLF	38	M	LABR	PLACBFNY
KUGAL, CHAIM	39	M	LABR	PLACBFNY

PASSENGER	AGE	SEX	OCCUPATION	PV RIV	D ES
SHIP: FULDA					
FROM: BREMEN					
TO: NEW YORK					
ARRIVED: 10 APRIL 1886					
KRANI, JACOB	23	M	FARMER	PLAHO	KUSA
LOUISE	21	F	UNKNOWN	PLAHO	KUSA
JACOB	.11	F	INFANT	PLAHO	KUSA
CHRISTIAN	35	M	FARMER	PLAHO	KUSA
MAGDALENA	30	F	UNKNOWN	PLAHO	KUSA
NATHAN	8	M	CHILD	PLAHO	KUSA
CHRISTIAN	4	M	CHILD	PLAHO	KUSA
CHRISTINE	3	F	CHILD	PLAHO	KUSA
JACOB	.11	M	INFANT	PLAHO	KUSA
SCHAUER, MARTIN	57	M	FARMER	PLAHO	KUSA
CAROLINE	55	F	UNKNOWN	PLAHO	KUSA
JACOB	20	M	FARMER	PLAHO	KUSA
FRISCHEISEN, FRIEDR.	21	M	FARMER	PLAHO	KUSA
DOBRZCINSKA, SARAH	23	F	UNKNOWN	PLAHO	KUSA
ISIDOR	6	M	CHILD	PLAHO	KUSA
ISAAC	3	M	CHILD	PLAHO	KUSA
EPSTEIN, HERM.	24	M	MCHT	PLAHO	KUSA
KOBAZINSKY, FRANZ	30	M	SMH	RRZZZ	ZUSA
JADWIGA	25	F	UNKNOWN	RRZZZ	ZUSA
JADWIGA	.11	F	INFANT	RRZZZ	ZUSA
MASAINSKY, MARSELLY	25	M	LABR	RRZZZ	ZUSA
KLIMASCHEWSKI, JOSEF	42	M	BCHR	RRZZZ	ZUSA
BEWSKI, PAUL	38	M	LABR	RRZZZ	ZUSA
STANIEWICZ, STANISLAUS	20	M	LABR	RRZZZ	ZUSA
RUTHIEWICZ, LEON	33	M	LABR	RRZZZ	ZUSA
SHIP: CITY OF BERLIN					
FROM: LIVERPOOL AND QUEENSTOWN					
TO: NEW YORK					
ARRIVED: 12 APRIL 1886					
RAGASCHNITZ, JOSEF	25	M	LABR	RRACB	FNY
AMMELEWSKI, SLAREDUS	18	M	LABR	RRACB	FNY
BREKOP, ANDREAS	37	M	LABR	RRACB	FNY
FRANCISCO	21	F	W	RRACB	FNY
FREGMUSKIC, HAURIE	30	F	W	RRACB	FNY
ELIAS	5	M	CHILD	RRACB	FNY
CHAE	4	M	CHILD	RRACB	FNY
MCAWK	00	F	INF	RRACB	FNY
TREUND, MOSES	36	M	LABR	RRACB	FNY
SOKOLOWSKI, SANCKO	40	M	FARMER	RRACB	FNY
LISSEL	36	F	W	RRACB	FNY
SAMUEL	35	M	LABR	RRACB	FNY
CHALIN	00	M	CH	RRACB	FNY
HERSCH	9	M	CHILD	RRACB	FNY
KALMAN	00	M	INF	RRACB	FNY
ROGINI	9	M	CHILD	RRACB	FNY
MAUMDERS, ISRAEL	39	M	LABR	RRACB	FNY
MATI	10	M	CH	RRACB	FNY
ETAZSTZ, MOSES	40	M	LABR	RRACB	FNY
IDA	36	F	SVNT	RRACB	FNY
STRUGATZ, FREIDE	18	F	SVNT	RRACB	FNY
MARIE	16	F	SVNT	RRACB	FNY
ESACK, JESENSKY	30	M	FARMER	RRACB	FNY
SARA	00	F	W	RRACB	FNY
JULS.	00	F	INF	RRACB	FNY
ISTVANY, BARTHO	29	M	LABR	RRACB	FNY
STAKOWIAK, JOSEPH	22	M	LABR	RRACB	FNY
JOS.	22	M	LABR	RRACB	FNY
RAMALL, SUSMAN	26	M	LABR	RRACB	FNY
SITTWITZ, WOLF	49	M	LABR	RRACB	FOH
JETTE	50	F	W	RRACB	FOH
NATHAN	15	M	LABR	RRACB	FOH
HANNA	10	M	CH	RRACB	FOH
SHIP: INDIA					
FROM: HAMBURG					
TO: NEW YORK					
ARRIVED: 12 APRIL 1886					
BRILL, LEIB	19	M	SMH	RRZZZ	ZNY
APEL, MENDEL	18	M	CL	RRZZZ	ZNY
SPOTTER, ZITTER	18	F	SGL	RRZZZ	ZNY
MALLER, JACOB	29	M	TLR	RRZZZ	ZNY
GOLDSCHMIDT, ESTER	20	M	SHMK	RRZZZ	ZNY
JANKOWSKY, MARCIN	28	M	LABR	RRZZZ	ZPA
KATHARINA	23	F	W	RRZZZ	ZPA
JOSEPH	7	M	CHILD	RRZZZ	ZPA
LEOWENTHAL, ZYPKA	42	M	LABR	RRZZZ	ZNY
CHAIE	17	F	CH	RRZZZ	ZNY
BASHHE.	10	F	CH	RRZZZ	ZNY
LEIB	7	M	CHILD	RRZZZ	ZNY
CHITKE	6	F	CHILD	RRZZZ	ZNY
JACOB	5	M	CHILD	RRZZZ	ZNY
BARNAH	4	M	CHILD	RRZZZ	ZNY
BASCHKE	.11	F	INFANT	RRZZZ	ZNY
PETSCHKE	.02	F	INFANT	RRZZZ	ZNY
LEWIN, ZONA	40	F	WO	RRZZZ	ZNY
RIFFLE	14	F	CH	RRZZZ	ZNY
KUSSIEL	11	F	CH	RRZZZ	ZNY
BERGSCH	7	M	CHILD	RRZZZ	ZNY
ZIPKE	6	F	CHILD	RRZZZ	ZNY
JACOB	5	M	CHILD	RRZZZ	ZNY
CRIVITZ, SALMON	36	M	TRDSMN	RRZZZ	ZNY
FEINBERG, STUSE-SLATE	34	F	WO	RRZZZ	ZNY
SARAH	15	F	CH	RRZZZ	ZNY
PAPE	7	M	CHILD	RRZZZ	ZNY
CHAIME	5	F	CHILD	RRZZZ	ZNY
BRANS	.06	M	INFANT	RRZZZ	ZNY
FRAENKEL, MOSES	24	M	LABR	RRZZZ	ZNY
MILUMES, JAN	18	M	LABR	RRZZZ	ZNY
ANICKER, SARA	38	F	WO	RRZZZ	ZNY
MOSES	18	M	CH	RRZZZ	ZNY
BEILE	19	F	CH	RRZZZ	ZNY
SCHIFRE	18	F	CH	RRZZZ	ZNY
TRENE	7	F	CHILD	RRZZZ	ZNY
WITKOWER, JULI	28	F	WO	RRZZZ	ZNY
ETTEL	7	F	CHILD	RRZZZ	ZNY
BERNSTEIN, ROSA	24	F	WO	RRZZZ	ZNY
MOSES	.09	M	INFANT	RRZZZ	ZNY
BLUMENTHAL, CHAN.L.	40	F	WO	RRZZZ	ZNY
JUDES	7	M	CHILD	RRZZZ	ZNY
SCHIFFRE	4	F	CHILD	RRZZZ	ZNY
PESACH	6	M	CHILD	RRZZZ	ZNY
SCHWEITZER, JOH.	32	M	FRR	PLZZZ	ZNY
GLESNER, PH.	38	M	CPTR	PLZZZ	ZNY
MICHA, WEGE	25	M	LABR	PLZZZ	ZNY
KAUFER, SALOM.	51	M	TRDSMN	PLZZZ	ZNY
BENGEL, MAX	26	M	LABR	PLZZZ	ZNY
SCHIKSNEL, LEOP.	21	M	LABR	PLZZZ	ZNY
JAN	26	M	LABR	PLZZZ	ZNY
JACUBOWITZ, VINC.	26	M	LABR	PLZZZ	ZNY
BARYCZ, MACY	20	M	LABR	PLZZZ	ZNY
JACUBOWITZ, MACY	18	M	LABR	PLZZZ	ZNY
IGLUNISCTZ, A.	22	M	LABR	PLZZZ	ZNY
STRONKIEWSKY, R.	26	M	LABR	PLZZZ	ZNY
POWTENIC, KASIMIR	21	M	LABR	RRZZZ	ZNY
ZUZUNGERIVITECH, F.	24	M	LABR	RRZZZ	ZNY
SOKOLOWSKI, CAS.	31	M	LABR	RRZZZ	ZNY
ABEGIAMARS, ANT.	23	M	LABR	RRZZZ	ZNY
SCHLECHTER, HERM.	24	M	TRDSMN	RRZZZ	ZNY

PASSENGER	A G E	S E X	OCCUPATION	P V D / R I E / V L S
LEFKOWITZ, ESTER	21	F	SGL	RRZZZZNY
ROSCHBAUM, LUBISCH	26	M	TRDSMN	RRZZZZNY
SIEGEL, ARI	34	M	TRDSMN	RRZZZZNY
ASCHENBERG, JUL.	36	M	TRDSMN	RRZZZZNY

SHIP: WIELAND

FROM: HAMBURG
TO: NEW YORK
ARRIVED: 12 APRIL 1886

PASSENGER	A G E	S E X	OCCUPATION	P V D / R I E / V L S
KATZ, CIPE	50	F	W	RRZZZZUSA
JANOS	17	M	CH	RRZZZZUSA
FEIGE	9	M	CHILD	RRZZZZUSA
SAMUEL	8	M	CHILD	RRZZZZUSA
CHAIE	7	F	CHILD	RRZZZZUSA
BETSCHLAND, GUSTAV	27	M	LABR	RRZZZZUSA
GARETZKY, FRANZ	25	M	LABR	RRZZZZUSA
MOTSCHKEWICZ, SCHMRED	26	M	LABR.	RRZZZZUSA
BARANOWSKY, JOSEF	24	M	LABR	RRZZZZUSA
ADAMOWITZ, WOJCECH	24	M	LABR	RRZZZZUSA
RADOWSKY, MARTIN	29	M	LABR	RRZZZZUSA
PIETROWSKY, ANTON	33	M	LABR	RRZZZZUSA
KUNSCHALSKY, WOJTECH	22	M	LABR	RRZZZZUSA
BUNETZKY, JOSEPH	22	M	LABR	RRZZZZUSA
REDMEWSKY, IGNATZ	24	M	LABR	RRZZZZUSA
KWIATKOWSKY, JOHANN	21	M	LABR	RRZZZZUSA
PRUSEN, SCHOLEM	16	M	LABR	RRZZZZUSA
WALLERSTEIN, CZENTE	50	F	W	RRZZZZUSA
LEWIN, LEISER-J.	30	M	LABR	RRZZZZUSA
DENOWSKI, JEROMIN	17	M	LABR	RRZZZZUSA
BETSCHLAND, MARIANNE	20	F	SGL	RRZZZZUSA
KOSCHNITZKI, MARTIN	27	M	LABR	RRZZZZUSA
MARIEMKEWICZ, FRANZ	25	M	LABR	RRZZZZUSA
MARIE	23	F	W	RRZZZZUSA
RITZKE, FRIEDR.	48	M	LABR	RRZZZZUSA
JAZLENSKY, IGNATZ	37	M	LABR	RRZZZZUSA
ABRAMOWITZ, JOCHE	40	F	W	RRZZZZUSA
ESTHER	17	F	CH	RRZZZZUSA
ISAAC	9	M	CHILD	RRZZZZUSA
MICHAEL	8	M	CHILD	RRZZZZUSA
JENNY	6	F	CHILD	RRZZZZUSA
SCHWARZ, HANNE	58	F	W	RRZZZZUSA
BIRNBAUM, LEA	54	F	W	RRZZZZUSA
ROSCHTE	3	F	CHILD	RRZZZZUSA
SARA	2	F	CHILD	RRZZZZUSA
JABLONSKY, MURKO	9	M	CHILD	RRZZZZUSA
WOLFF, WILHE.	21	F	SGL	RRZZZZUSA
GRUSKAS, J.	25	M	LABR	RRZZZZUSA
TRULIS, WLADISLAW	24	M	MCHT	RRZZZZUSA

SHIP: HABSBURG

FROM: BREMEN
TO: NEW YORK
ARRIVED: 13 APRIL 1886

PASSENGER	A G E	S E X	OCCUPATION	P V D / R I E / V L S
MICHERSKI, PAUL	25	M	LABR	RRAHUFNY
GRABOWSKY, STANISLAUS	32	M	LABR	RRAHUFNY
MARZKIEWITZ, FRANZ	25	M	LABR	RRAHUFNY
KUTINGA, JAN	23	M	LABR	RRAHUFNY
MASCHINSKI, KASIMIR	27	M	LABR	RRAHUFNY
SCHULZ, THEODOR	27	M	FARMER	RRZZZZNY
MALASEWSKY, PETER	22	M	LABR	RRAHOKNY
BABICKI, ANTON	34	M	LABR	RRZZZZIL
GELINSKI, ANTON	45	M	LABR	RRZZZZOH
BAROZKI, FRANZ	35	M	LABR	RRZZZZOH
ROSENSTEIN, SIMON	16	M	LABR	RRZZZZNY
TREICHER, STANISLAUS	21	M	LABR	RRZZZZNY
STANKOWSKY, LEON	24	M	LABR	RRZZZZNY
LICHTENFELS, EMIL	13	M	LABR	RRZZZZNY
SARCIVIC, STANISL.	26	M	LABR	RRAHOKNY
ANDRASKIEWITZ, SYLVESTE	28	M	LABR	RRAHOKNY
BUTKIEWITZ, ANTON	30	M	LABR	RRAHOKNY
SOBOLEWSKY, ANTON	25	M	LABR	RRAHOKNY
KUPINSKY, JAN	21	M	LABR	RRAHOKNY
PUTRAZEMSKY, ANT.	26	M	LABR	RRAHOKNY
GURADOWSKY, PETER	32	M	LABR	RRAHOKNY
KUPINSKY, ANTON	27	M	LABR	RRAHOKNY
SCHNEIDER, JOSEF	28	M	LABR	RRAHOKNY
RUTZKOWSKY, VINCENZ	35	M	LABR	RRAHOKNY
RUSTUKO, VIKTOR	27	M	LABR	RRAFVGNY
KASMULOWICZ, WOYCEK	26	M	LABR	RRZZZZNY
FANDREY, VINCENT	25	M	LABR	RRZZZZMA
KOBRENSKY, JOHANN	30	M	LABR	RRAHOONY
BODZKY, FRANZ	45	M	LABR	RRAHOONY
MARLESKY, IGNAZ	28	M	LABR	RRZZZZNY
LEBADOWSKY, PETER	37	M	LABR	RRZZZZNY
JOSEF	35	M	LABR	RRZZZZNY
BUGINSKY, ANTON	25	M	LABR	RRZZZZNY
OSOWSKY, CASIMIR	37	M	LABR	RRZZZZNY
GORSKY, THEODOR	20	M	LABR	RRZZZZNY
ZELESKY, ALBERT	17	M	LABR	RRZZZZNY
GORDOWSKY, MARCELL	22	M	LABR	RRZZZZNY
PEBOSCHEWSKY, FRANZ	22	M	LABR	RRZZZZNY
DETTMER, FRANZ	15	M	LABR	RRZZZZNY
WIESMIVSKY, JOSEF	29	M	LABR	RRZZZZNY
ZORSALSKI, STEFAN	30	M	LABR	RRZZZZNY
DETTMER, JAKOB	46	M	LABR	RRZZZZNY
HAMMERBACHER, HEINRICH	26	M	LABR	RRZZZZNY
KLUG, THEODOR	25	M	LABR	RRADDQNY
WITK, WILHELM	30	M	LABR	RRAHOONY
SATSKOW, ANTON	26	M	LABR	RRAHOONY
ALBRECHT, AUGUST	46	M	LABR	RRAHOONY
STUEWE, ALBERT	26	M	FARMER	RRZZZZNY
ALVINE	22	F	W	RRZZZZNY
CARL	.09	M	INFANT	RRZZZZNY
PUTZIGER, PAULINE	33	F	W	RRZZZZNY
SALIE	11	F	CH	RRZZZZNY
SARAH	10	F	CH	RRZZZZNY
LINA	10	F	CH	RRZZZZNY
MAX	6	M	CHILD	RRZZZZNY
MISKWEWIC, JAN	33	M	FARMER	RRZZZZNY
FRANZISKA	31	F	W	RRZZZZNY
CASIMIR	7	M	CHILD	RRZZZZNY
LEONARDI	5	M	CHILD	RRZZZZNY
COLLENDO, MARIANNE	23	F	W	RRZZZZNY
ROBERTO	2	M	CHILD	RRZZZZNY
ALEXANDER	.09	M	INFANT	RRZZZZNY
KOPZUECKER, MIRYAM	26	F	W	RRAEFLNY
MANES	4	M	CHILD	RRZZZZNY
LEWANDOWSKY, JOHANN	24	M	LABR	RRAGRTNY
AGNES	19	F	W	RRAGRTNY
MARIE	.09	F	INFANT	RRAGRTNY
ANNZKIEWICZ, VINCENTA	23	F	SVNT	RRZZZZNY
NARUSCEWICZ, URSULA	20	F	SVNT	RRZZZZNY
PETRUSKA, MARIA	15	F	SVNT	RRZZZZNY
WASILEWSKY, ANDREAS	22	M	LABR	RRZZZZNY
LUDWIGA	16	F	SVNT	RRZZZZNY
PAGOSKOI, FRANZISKA	9	F	CHILD	RRZZZZNY
BINDOWSKY, RACHEL	20	F	SVNT	RRZZZZNY
PANOWSKY, ROSALIA	24	F	SVNT	RRZZZZNY

PASSENGER	AGE	SEX	OCCUPATION	PRIV	VIL	DES
SHIP: BRITANNIC						
FROM: LIVERPOOL AND QUEENSTOWN						
TO: NEW YORK						
ARRIVED: 14 APRIL 1886						
SCHUDTIG, MICHAEL	22	M	LABR	RR	AC	BFUSA
RATH	20	M	LABR	RR	AC	BFUSA
SASEBASITZKI, AUG.	28	M	LABR	RR	AC	BFUSA
GRAFTMEYER, EMIL	27	M	LABR	RR	AC	BFUSA
GUMITE, ANTON	30	M	LABR	RR	AC	BFUSA
RYEPIEWSKY, JULIAN	32	M	LABR	RR	AC	BFUSA
ANAISHLOWITZ, IVAN	27	M	LABR	RR	AC	BFUSA
LICHBYEHLER, JACOB	26	M	LABR	RR	AC	BFUSA
KANARIK, ABRAHAM	28	M	LABR	RR	AC	BFUSA
SCHMIDT, ELISABETH	23	F	W	RR	AC	BFUSA
ANNA	10	F	CH	RR	AC	BFUSA
GORCAS, BERTHE	28	F	SVNT	RR	AC	BFUSA
ORZICK, CARL	23	M	LABR	RR	AC	BFUSA
BROSCH, JACOB	29	M	LABR	RR	AC	BFUSA
SHITZKI, BENJAMIN	27	M	LABR	RR	AC	BFUSA
CHUIN, JACOB	23	M	LABR	RR	AC	BFUSA
SHITZKI, BENJAMIN	24	M	LABR	RR	AC	BFUSA
LEURIE, ABRAHAM	24	M	LABR	RR	AC	BFUSA
HALFERN, BENJAMIN	21	M	LABR	RR	AC	BFUSA
SCHRENICK, DAVID	29	M	LABR	RR	AC	BFUSA
ARENOWSKY, LEIB	31	M	LABR	RR	AC	BFUSA
MULLER, EMMA	39	F	SVNT	RR	AC	BFUSA
SABME, CYMIA	34	F	W	RR	AC	BFUSA
MARIA	.11	F	INFANT	RR	AC	BFUSA
CATALNI, SWANKO	26	F	SVNT	RR	AC	BFUSA
SHIP: DEVONIA						
FROM: GLASGOW						
TO: NEW YORK						
ARRIVED: 16 APRIL 1886						
ANMOWITZKY, FEIGE	23	F	NN	RR	AC	BFUSA
ANDESKEN, CHRISTINE	31	F	SVNT	RR	AC	BFUSA
CHORON, MENNE	19	F	SVNT	RR	AC	BFUSA
HEINSKE, BERTHA	29	F	NN	RR	AC	BFUSA
LUDWIG	1	M	CHILD	RR	AC	BFUSA
PILETZKI, MARIEN	23	F	SVNT	RR	AC	BFUSA
TERESIA	19	F	SVNT	RR	AC	BFUSA
SKESKU, FILE	20	F	SVNT	RR	AC	BFUSA
DRESTINAMSKI, LEYE	26	F	NN	RR	AC	BFUSA
WOLF	2	M	CHILD	RR	AC	BFUSA
BELIE	1	F	CHILD	RR	AC	BFUSA
GOLMUBOWIEZ, BASCHE	40	F	NN	RR	AC	BFUSA
HANNA	12	F	NN	RR	AC	BFUSA
SARA	9	F	CHILD	RR	AC	BFUSA
MINKE	1	M	CHILD	RR	AC	BFUSA
FEIST, C.	30	M	LABR	RR	AC	BFUSA
MARIA	30	F	NN	RR	AC	BFUSA
LORENZ	4	M	CHILD	RR	AC	BFUSA
MAGDALENA	2	F	CHILD	RR	AC	BFUSA
DANIEL	.03	M	INFANT	RR	AC	BFUSA
FRANCISCA	.03	F	INFANT	RR	AC	BFUSA
JODEROWITZ, ELIAS	48	M	LABR	RR	AC	BFUSA
HERMANN	11	M	NN	RR	AC	BFUSA
ZULANUS, MATEI	38	M	LABR	RR	AC	BFUSA
FRANZISCA	34	F	NN	RR	AC	BFUSA
ANTONIUM	2	M	CHILD	RR	AC	BFUSA
MARIE	1	F	CHILD	RR	AC	BFUSA
BAKOWITZ, HIRSCH	36	M	TLR	RR	AC	BFUSA
BOKEJES, S.	27	M	LABR	RR	AC	BFUSA
BANIS, STAN.	35	M	LABR	RR	AC	BFUSA
BURAUS, KAZIMIR	30	M	LABR	RR	AC	BFUSA
BUREUS, IRAN	30	M	LABR	RR	AC	BFUSA
DUMS, ADAM	22	M	LABR	RR	AC	BFUSA
GSCHIMKOWSKI, JOSEF	24	M	LABR	RR	AC	BFUSA
GOLDBERG, A.	17	M	LABR	RR	AC	BFUSA
GRAIMERS, JAN	20	M	LABR	RR	AC	BFUSA
STEIN, LUDWIG	19	M	LABR	RR	AC	BFUSA
JOHANN	20	M	BLKSMH	RR	AC	BFUSA
HAUSTRAT, F.	20	M	LABR	RR	AC	BFUSA
KASDAN, W.	32	M	LABR	RR	AC	BFUSA
KASPARONIE, K.	25	M	LABR	RR	AC	BFUSA
KABNER, A.	19	M	LABR	RR	AC	BFUSA
MYHL	19	M	LABR	RR	AC	BFUSA
LEWIN, SCHMUEL	34	M	LABR	RR	AC	BFUSA
S.	35	M	LABR	RR	AC	BFUSA
PLISZOWIS, M.	25	M	LABR	RR	AC	BFUSA
KUDNIK, M.	34	M	LABR	RR	AC	BFUSA
SEITER, ITZIG	33	M	LABR	RR	AC	BFUSA
SOBRASS, SIMON	22	M	LABR	RR	AC	BFUSA
SLUZKI, PETER	30	M	LABR	RR	AC	BFUSA
SCHNEIDER, CHR.	40	M	LABR	RR	AC	BFUSA
SLEST, LEOPOLD	29	M	LABR	RR	AC	BFUSA
SOWASEWICZ, MICHAEL	25	M	LABR	RR	AC	BFUSA
URBANISS, FRANZ	30	M	LABR	RR	AC	BFUSA
WATCHULIS, S.	20	M	LABR	RR	AC	BFUSA
WISOCKY, SIMON	26	M	LABR	RR	AC	BFUSA
WARNA, MATHAI	23	M	LABR	RR	AC	BFUSA
ZIEDANIS, M.	35	M	LABR	RR	AC	BFUSA
SHIP: ELBE						
FROM: BREMEN						
TO: NEW YORK						
ARRIVED: 16 APRIL 1886						
HINZ, DANIEL	40	M	FARMER	RR	ZZ	ZZNY
WILH.	33	F	UNKNOWN	RR	ZZ	ZZNY
DANIEL	2	M	CHILD	RR	ZZ	ZZNY
JOHANN	.04	M	INFANT	RR	ZZ	ZZNY
REPP, LOUISE	19	F	UNKNOWN	RR	ZZ	ZZNY
GUNY, ALBERT	26	M	FARMER	RR	AE	QQNY
BOSSERT, JOH.	25	M	FARMER	RR	ZZ	ZZUNK
DOROTHEA	19	F	UNKNOWN	RR	ZZ	ZZUNK
FRIEDR.	50	M	FARMER	RR	ZZ	ZZUNK
ROSINA	50	F	UNKNOWN	RR	ZZ	ZZUNK
GOTTLIEB	14	M	UNKNOWN	RR	ZZ	ZZUNK
FRIED.	19	F	SVNT	RR	ZZ	ZZUNK
SELMA	17	F	SVNT	RR	ZZ	ZZUNK
MARIA	8	F	CHILD	RR	ZZ	ZZUNK
LYDIA	5	F	CHILD	RR	ZZ	ZZUNK
MULLER, HEINR.	31	M	FARMER	RR	ZZ	ZZUNK
ROSINA	29	F	UNKNOWN	RR	ZZ	ZZUNK
MATH.	3	M	CHILD	RR	ZZ	ZZUNK
JACOB	.09	M	INFANT	RR	ZZ	ZZUNK
BOLOSCHOWITZ, STANISL.	20	M	LABR	RR	ZZ	ZZNY
KOSMOSKY, PETER	22	M	LABR	RR	ZZ	ZZNY
WOLECHOWITZ, ANDREY	21	M	LABR	RR	ZZ	ZZNY
FRADRICH, SIMON	21	M	LABR	RR	ZZ	ZZNY
REISER, SIMON	22	M	FARMER	RR	ZZ	ZZUNK
JUSTINE	17	F	UNKNOWN	RR	ZZ	ZZUNK
GROTT, DANIEL	28	M	LABR	RR	ZZ	ZZUNK
CHRIST.	23	F	UNKNOWN	RR	ZZ	ZZUNK
MATHILDE	2	F	CHILD	RR	ZZ	ZZUNK
HILLER, SIMON	17	M	FARMER	RR	ZZ	ZZUNK
BRUDNER, LOUIS	23	M	MCHT	RR	ZZ	ZZNY

PASSENGER	AGE	SEX	OCCUPATION	PRV	VIL	DES

SHIP: STATE OF NEBRASKA

FROM: GLASGOW AND LARNE
TO: NEW YORK
ARRIVED: 16 APRIL 1886

PASSENGER	AGE	SEX	OCCUPATION	PRV	VIL	DES
ROMANOW, MOSES	30	M	DLR	RR	ZZZZ	NY
SUWITZSKI, JOSEPH	23	M	TLR	RR	ZZZZ	NY
REISNER, DAVID	36	M	DLR	RR	ZZZZ	NY
SUCHKO, MICHAEL	30	M	LABR	RR	ZZZZ	NY
GOSTINKEL, CHANE	35	F	SVNT	RR	ZZZZ	NY
KLEIN, LEISER	40	M	PDLR	RR	ZZZZ	NY
SUSCHKO, MICHAEL	30	M	LABR	RR	ZZZZ	NY
GOSTINKEL, CHANE	35	F	SVNT	RR	ZZZZ	NY
KLEIN, LEISER	40	M	PDLR	RR	ZZZZ	NY
SCHNEEMEISS, MICHAEL	20	M	PDLR	RR	ZZZZ	NY
OLSCHAF--, PAUL	26	M	TLR	RR	ZZZZ	NY
MARIA	27	F	W	RR	ZZZZ	NY
LEONA	.06	F	INFANT	RR	ZZZZ	NY
SANDIK, ANDRES	27	M	LABR	RR	ZZZZ	NY
LESCHKO, BAB.	27	M	LABR	RR	ZZZZ	NY
GOBEWITZ, WLADISLAW	23	M	SHMK	RR	ZZZZ	NY
SOBEWITZ, STANISLAW	11	M	CH	RR	ZZZZ	NY
KUSEREWITZ, FRANZ	30	M	LABR	RR	ZZZZ	NY
MROZEK, KARL	26	M	LABR	RR	ZZZZ	NY
JURGAS, LUSCHOS	38	M	LABR	RR	ZZZZ	NY
SCHLESINGER, SCHMUL	22	M	JNR	RR	ZZZZ	NY
KLEIN, SCH.	30	M	LABR	RR	ZZZZ	NY
NAUSOLOWITZ, JAN	24	M	LABR	RR	ZZZZ	NY
MIGELANSKI, JOSEF	23	M	LABR	RR	ZZZZ	NY
RABOCESTY, RAMEL	26	M	LABR	RR	ZZZZ	NY
WASCHELZSKI, JOSEF	18	M	PDLR	RR	ZZZZ	NY
MASALOWITZ, AUG.	31	M	LABR	RR	ZZZZ	NY
DEULSCH, MOSES	22	M	DLR	RR	ZZZZ	NY
RAKOWSKI, KONSTANTIN	26	M	LABR	RR	ZZZZ	NY
TELEWI, MORDCHE	35	M	LABR	RR	ZZZZ	NY
ROSTKE, ISTWAN	35	M	LABR	RR	ZZZZ	NY
BAROLKE, KARAL	25	M	LABR	RR	ZZZZ	NY
KOLWEK, JANOS	30	M	LABR	RR	ZZZZ	NY
NEWLAIAWSKI, H.	25	M	LABR	RR	ZZZZ	NY
DAUSKUS, FRANZ	23	M	TLR	RR	ZZZZ	NY
RINIWITZ, JACOB	25	M	FARMER	RR	ZZZZ	NY

SHIP: CITY OF CHESTER

FROM: LIVERPOOL
TO: NEW YORK
ARRIVED: 17 APRIL 1886

PASSENGER	AGE	SEX	OCCUPATION	PRV	VIL	DES
ARCHER, MARIAN	17	F	SVNT	RR	AFWJ	NY
HEGIEK, ANNA	20	F	SVNT	RR	AFWJ	NY
RVOTKA, ANNA	24	F	SVNT	RR	AFWJ	NY
FAIRANCE, MARIO	23	F	SVNT	RR	AFWJ	NY
GWORCK, WOJSICK	24	M	LABR	PL	ZZZZ	BUF
BERRA, FRANZ	16	M	LABR	PL	AFWJ	BUF
PENKALSKI, ANTON	40	M	LABR	PL	AFWJ	BUF
SOPLAWSKI, ANTON	24	M	MNR	PL	ACBF	BUF
ANNEGAL, TOMAS	25	M	LABR	PL	ACBF	MI
MARIANA	23	F	W	PL	ACBF	MI
U, U	00	F	INF	PL	ACBF	MI
SINISCHOK, PAVEL	38	M	LABR	PL	AFWJ	NY
WALCZEWSKI, FOINAZ	45	M	LABR	PL	AFWJ	NY
RAKONITZ, MICHAEL	57	M	LABR	PL	ACBF	NY
BIDUS, AGNITJA	17	F	SVNT	PL	AFWJ	NY
WISNEWSKY, MARIE	48	F	W	PL	ACBF	NY
JOSEFA	20	F	SVNT	PL	ACBF	NY
FRANCESCA	18	F	SVNT	PL	ACBF	NY
SYLOCSNIK, ISIDOR	21	M	LABR	PL	AFWJ	NY
REBENSKI, KURINKO	18	M	LABR	PL	AFWJ	NY
SZAROTZON, ANTON	34	M	LABR	PL	AFWJ	NY
CRUPECK, SIMON	26	M	LABR	PL	ACBF	NY
CILELLA, JAN	32	M	LABR	PL	ACBF	NY
GEMPEL, WASKO	32	M	LABR	PL	ACBF	NY
PLASKO, ANT.	51	M	LABR	PL	AFWJ	NY
WEINA, ANDRY	32	M	LABR	PL	AFWJ	NY
REWAK, OMEPRI	53	M	LABR	PL	AFWJ	NY
WACHWAN, THEODOR	11	M	CH	PL	ACBF	NY
STOSSACK, HANVILLE	30	M	LABR	PL	AFWJ	NY
LUPASCH, ANNA	20	F	SVNT	PL	AFWJ	NY
PISCH, ASSAFAT	11	M	CH	PL	AFWJ	NY
MATHJALEK, JAN	24	M	LABR	PL	AFWJ	NY
GRUMMER, DAVID	44	M	LABR	PL	ACBF	NY
GITERMAN, PERL	27	M	LABR	PL	AFWJ	NY
MUSKER, HILLARG	27	M	LABR	PL	ACBF	NY
GLUS, DORKA	18	M	LABR	PL	ACBF	NY
KOWALSZIK, ANDY	20	M	LABR	PL	AFWJ	NY
WOCHUFSKY, ADDASY	19	M	LABR	PL	ACBF	NY
MISLOCKY, OSEF	20	M	LABR	PL	AFWJ	NY
KOWABZIK, PHILIPP	34	M	LABR	PL	ACBF	NY
WYKOWSKY, WASIL	11	M	CH	PL	ACBF	NY
SCHUNAWSKY, FRANZ	24	M	LABR	PL	ACBF	NY
BRUSDA, STEPHEN	37	M	LABR	PL	AFWJ	NY
SASSKOWSKY, ANTON	25	M	LABR	PL	ACBF	NY
WASCHELEWSKY, JOSEF	38	M	LABR	PL	ACBF	NY
LESCHINSKY, JUKASCH	27	M	LABR	PL	ACBF	NY
BENARSKY, JAN	23	M	LABR	PL	ACBF	NY
BORESKY, PETER	40	M	LABR	PL	ACBF	NY
CATHARINE	40	F	W	PL	ACBF	NY
POPLAWSKI, JOSEFA	20	F	SVNT	PL	ACBF	BUF
KARBOWIAK, JAN	42	M	MNR	PL	ACBF	NY
KATZ, LEIB	35	M	LABR	PL	AAJV	HTD
ETEL	22	M	LABR	PL	AAJV	HTD
MALKE	10	M	CH	PL	AAJV	HTD
U, BEILE	9	M	CHILD	PL	AAJV	HTD
MEIER	6	M	CHILD	PL	AAJV	HTD
LEA	00	F	INF	PL	AAJV	HTD
NOTA	32	F	W	PL	AAJV	HTD
NORDCHE	11	F	CH	PL	AAJV	HTD
BACH, IDA	30	F	W	PL	AEFL	NY
ELIAS	3	F	CHILD	PL	AEFL	NY
JACOB	00	M	INF	PL	AEFL	NY
WOLFSKY, THOMAS	26	M	LABR	PL	AFWJ	NY
GAFFE, SIEGMUND	26	M	LABR	RR	ZZZZ	NY
KREMSKY, MORITZ	18	M	PH	RR	AFWJ	NY
SCHARF, SIMON	23	M	LABR	RR	ACBF	NY
DUNTKUSKY, MADISLOW	30	M	LABR	RR	ACBF	NY
HRIAT, MICHL.	32	M	LABR	RR	ACBF	NY
JANKO, PLAM	28	M	LABR	RR	AFWJ	NY
HABAS, MIKOS	20	M	LABR	RR	AFWJ	NY
BURGHARD, HANAS	20	M	LABR	RR	ZZZZ	NY
SCHULMESSLER, MICHL.	29	M	LABR	RR	ZZZZ	NY
HANNA	25	F	W	RR	ZZZZ	NY
SCHMIDT, ADAM	31	M	UNKNOWN	RR	ZZZZ	NY
KATARINA	28	F	W	RR	ZZZZ	NY
MARIUS	3	M	CHILD	RR	ZZZZ	NY
MEIER, MICHAEL	50	M	LABR	RR	ZZZZ	KS
MICHAEL	38	M	LABR	RR	ZZZZ	KS
U-MRS	37	F	W	RR	ZZZZ	KS
CATHARINE	16	F	SVNT	RR	ZZZZ	KS
ELIZABETH	15	F	SVNT	RR	ZZZZ	KS
JOSEPH	11	M	CH	RR	ZZZZ	KS
STOLIKA, JOHN-S.	29	M	LABR	RR	ACBF	NY
BURGHARDT, HASPAR	40	M	LABR	RR	ZZZZ	NY
U-MRS	39	F	W	RR	ZZZZ	NY
CATHARINE	18	F	SP	RR	ZZZZ	NY
U, U	10	M	CH	RR	ZZZZ	NY
U	7	F	CHILD	RR	ZZZZ	NY
STEHLYKE, MARIE	18	F	SVNT	RR	AFWJ	NY
GERTWITZ, MARIETTA	57	F	W	PL	ZZZZ	NY
PECOTZE, ANGELICA	18	F	SP	PL	ZZZZ	NY

SHIP: EGYPTIAN MONARCH

FROM: LONDON
TO: NEW YORK
ARRIVED: 17 APRIL 1886

PASSENGER	AGE	SEX	OCCUPATION	PRV VIL DES
COHEN, PHILLIP	36	M	TLR	PLZZZZNY
LEAH	35	F	W	PLZZZZNY
JULIA	11	F	CH	PLZZZZNY
SARAH	7	F	CHILD	PLZZZZNY
HARRIS	4	M	CHILD	PLZZZZNY
LESSIR	00	M	INF	PLZZZZNY
SCHNEIDER, BENJAMIN	22	M	TLR	PLZZZZNY
GOLDSTICK, SOLOMAN	42	M	BTMKR	PLZZZZPHI
LACHS, SIMON	34	M	MCHT	RRZZZZNY
KATI	34	F	W	RRZZZZNY
HERMAN	12	M	CH	RRZZZZNY
MERRIS	4	M	CHILD	RRZZZZNY

SHIP: EMS

FROM: BREMEN
TO: NEW YORK
ARRIVED: 17 APRIL 1886

PASSENGER	AGE	SEX	OCCUPATION	PRV VIL DES
NEUMANN, DAVID	19	M	CL	RRAHOOUSA
SCHLAT, JOHANN	28	M	FARMER	RRAFWJUSA
CATHARINE	20	F	NN	RRAFWJUSA
CHARLOTTE	4	F	CHILD	RRAFWJUSA
ANNA	.08	F	INFANT	RRAFWJUSA
SOHEIFELL, JOH.	24	M	FARMER	RRAFWJUSA
EMILIE	24	F	NN	RRAFWJUSA
ELISABETH	.04	F	INFANT	RRAFWJUSA
BALLINGER, JOH.	43	M	LABR	RRAFWJUSA
CATHARINE	38	F	NN	RRAFWJUSA
ROSINA	18	F	CH	RRAFWJUSA
CATHARINE	16	F	CH	RRAFWJUSA
DOROTHEA	10	F	CH	RRAFWJUSA
JOHANNE	10	F	CH	RRAFWJUSA
MARGARETHE	8	F	CHILD	RRAFWJUSA
MARIA	6	F	CHILD	RRAFWJUSA
ELISABETH	3	F	CHILD	RRAFWJUSA
MATHIAS	.11	M	INFANT	RRAFWJUSA

SHIP: NOORDLAND

FROM: ANTWERP
TO: NEW YORK
ARRIVED: 17 APRIL 1886

PASSENGER	AGE	SEX	OCCUPATION	PRV VIL DES
ITZRAKA, ANT.	20	F	UNKNOWN	PLZZZZUNK
STARKOWSKY, IVAN	35	M	UNKNOWN	PLZZZZNY
LECIGKOWSKY, CLARA	24	F	UNKNOWN	RRZZZZNY
STEPHAN	2	M	CHILD	RRZZZZNY
BRUN	00	M	INF	RRZZZZNY
MASLONICH, JOH.	25	M	LABR	RRZZZZIL
DEKEROFF, H.	33	M	LABR	RRZZZZNY

SHIP: EGYPT

FROM: LIVERPOOL
TO: NEW YORK
ARRIVED: 19 APRIL 1886

PASSENGER	AGE	SEX	OCCUPATION	PRV VIL DES
REFKEVSKY, CASSE	18	M	LABR	RRZZZZUSA
MORITZ	8	M	CHILD	RRZZZZUSA
RUPPE, JOHAN	48	M	LABR	RRZZZZUSA
KOSIG, JOHAN	31	M	LABR	RRZZZZUSA
ANTON	31	M	LABR	RRZZZZUSA
MICHE, GEORG	33	M	LABR	RRZZZZUSA
SCHANER, JOSEPH	44	M	LABR	RRZZZZUSA
KOSIG, MATHIAS	25	M	LABR	RRZZZZUSA
HAUSER, MARIE	35	F	SP	RRZZZZUSA
MORENS, JANKEL	22	M	LABR	RRZZZZUSA
HORKOWITZ, MICHAL	25	M	LABR	RRZZZZUSA
ORAHEROCTZ, SELIG	22	M	LABR	RRZZZZUSA
BELFIER, ITZIG	26	M	LABR	RRZZZZUSA
BREINE	24	F	W	RRZZZZUSA
ROSA	3	F	CHILD	RRZZZZUSA
BERGEN, CHANCE	18	M	LABR	PLZZZZUSA
GERZOT, PRUDENT	27	M	LABR	PLZZZZUSA
GELBERT, HIRSCH	26	M	LABR	PLZZZZUSA
PERLMAN, MOSES	26	M	LABR	PLZZZZUSA
CLAIRE	20	M	LABR	PLZZZZUSA
GRABOWSKY, PAVEL	45	M	LABR	PLZZZZUSA
KALM, ALE	46	M	LABR	PLZZZZUSA
PESEL	15	M	LABR	PLZZZZUSA
DAVID	11	M	CH	PLZZZZUSA
SILHA, VOYTECH	26	M	LABR	PLZZZZUSA
PRELOWITZ, SAREH	20	F	W	PLZZZZUSA
DOBE	10	F	INF	PLZZZZUSA
FEKEL, MIHAL	31	M	LABR	PLZZZZUSA
KETZ, LEIZER	24	M	LABR	PLZZZZUSA
WOLFSON, LEIB	19	M	LABR	PLZZZZUSA
LIBINSKY, MISL.	20	M	LABR	PLZZZZUSA
MICHALOWITZ, LEIB	33	M	LABR	PLZZZZUSA

SHIP: FURNESSIA

FROM: UNKNOWN
TO: NEW YORK
ARRIVED: 19 APRIL 1886

PASSENGER	AGE	SEX	OCCUPATION	PRV VIL DES
MODCHE, MLAMED	28	M	DLR	RRZZZZUSA
MUFFER, BETLEM	28	M	LABR	RRZZZZUSA
MINTA, JANATZA	33	M	NN	PLZZZZUSA
MARGARITHA	33	F	NN	PLZZZZUSA
FRANZ	3	M	CHILD	PLZZZZUSA
JOHANN	1	M	CHILD	PLZZZZUSA
AKREMOWITZ, ALEXANDER	20	M	LABR	PLZZZZUSA
BROSINSKY, GUSTAV	34	M	LABR	PLZZZZUSA
BUSCHA, LEON	33	M	LABR	PLZZZZUSA
THOMAS	25	M	LABR	PLZZZZUSA
DUCZMAH, JAN	25	M	LABR	PLZZZZUSA
FILARSKI, LEON	24	M	LABR	PLZZZZUSA
GUBAS, LUDWIG	18	M	LABR	PLZZZZUSA
JAPCZENSKI, JOHAN	43	M	LABR	PLZZZZUSA
JESOWIT, JAN	26	M	LABR	PLZZZZUSA
JODISS, AUGUST	35	M	LABR	PLZZZZUSA
KREGLOWSKY, STAN.	27	M	LABR	PLZZZZUSA
KROCZAK, JOSEF	37	M	LABR	PLZZZZUSA
KOSO, JEAN	33	M	LABR	PLZZZZUSA
LISEFSKY, MICHAEL	29	M	LABR	PLZZZZUSA
LICHOWITZ, ANTONI	40	M	LABR	PLZZZZUSA
LIBERSKI, MICHAEL	25	M	LABR	PLZZZZUSA
LUCZAK, JOSEF	26	M	LABR	PLZZZZUSA
MILCINKY, KAZIMIR	20	M	LABR	PLZZZZUSA

PASSENGER	AGE	SEX	OCCUPATION	PRVIL	DES
MITEK, JAN	47	M	LABR	PLZZZZ	USA
NOWICKA, ANNA	29	F	NN	PLZZZZ	USA
WENZIL	3	F	CHILD	PLZZZZ	USA
POLFANOWITCH, JOSEPH	22	M	LABR	PLZZZZ	USA
REMOWITZ, ADAM	26	M	LABR	PLZZZZ	USA
ROSWONKOWSKI, JULIUS	20	M	LABR	PLZZZZ	USA
SASCHER, BARTOL	23	M	LABR	PLZZZZ	USA
STANISCHEWSKI, PETER	31	M	LABR	PLZZZZ	USA
SKOWRANSKI, ANTON	21	M	LABR	PLZZZZ	USA
STACEVICZ, LUDWIG	23	M	LABR	PLZZZZ	USA
SWINKUNAS, JONAS	26	M	LABR	PLZZZZ	USA
JURAS	22	M	LABR	PLZZZZ	USA
SZIBARNA, PETER	33	M	LABR	PLZZZZ	USA
SELENISS, JOHANN	22	M	LABR	PLZZZZ	USA
STEGEVIST, K.	40	M	LABR	PLZZZZ	USA
STADUSCKI, WOJCIECK	24	M	LABR	PLZZZZ	USA
TAMAS, JOHAN	28	M	LABR	PLZZZZ	USA
VIGINTY	23	M	LABR	PLZZZZ	USA
URBAN, VIGENTY	20	M	LABR	PLZZZZ	USA
WOLUTZKI, JAN	22	M	LABR	PLZZZZ	USA
WUCK, JAN	24	M	LABR	PLZZZZ	USA
WEIZUNES, JOSEF	30	M	LABR	PLZZZZ	USA
WALINSKI, SALOMON	27	M	DLR	PLZZZZ	USA
ZAWGOWSKI, MICHAEL	27	M	LABR	PLZZZZ	USA
ZOLMEROWITZ, JAN	42	M	LABR	PLZZZZ	USA
JOSEFA	36	F	NN	PLZZZZ	USA
VERONICA	21	F	SVNT	PLZZZZ	USA
ZUG, JOSEF	30	M	LABR	PLZZZZ	USA

SHIP: LESSING

FROM: HAMBURG
TO: NEW YORK
ARRIVED: 19 APRIL 1886

PASSENGER	AGE	SEX	OCCUPATION	PRVIL	DES
KOSLOWSKY, JAN	25	M	LABR	RRZZZZ	USA
BARTOSCHEWITZSCH, JOHAN	17	F	SGL	RRZZZZ	USA
KAMINSKY, BUCHARD	47	M	LABR	RRAHTK	USA
ANTONIE	35	F	W	RRAHTK	USA
TRUCHAN, FRANZIZEK	42	M	LABR	RRAHZS	USA
PODRUGAL, ANTON	30	M	LABR	RRAHZS	USA
MATTIZEK, JOHANNA	16	F	SGL	RRAHVA	USA
ZAWICKI, FRANZ	20	M	LABR	RRZZZZ	USA
SCHARSCHEWSKY, JAN	23	M	LABR	RRZZZZ	USA
STANKIEWICZ, JOH.	38	M	LABR	RRAHZS	USA
URBANOWICZ, VINCENT	25	M	LABR	RRAHZS	USA
GABUNOWSKI, THEODOR	26	M	LABR	RRAHUH	USA
KOSSEK, ANTON	19	M	LABR	RRAHUH	USA
OLECKI, JAN	18	M	LABR	RRAHUH	USA
BREHMER, OTTILIE	19	F	SGL	RRAHUH	USA
ANNA	21	F	SGL	RRAHUH	USA
DOROPINSKI, CATHA.	28	F	SGL	RRAHUH	USA
WIENER, CHARLOTTE	18	F	SGL	RRAHVU	USA

SHIP: RUGIA

FROM: HAMBURG
TO: NEW YORK
ARRIVED: 19 APRIL 1886

PASSENGER	AGE	SEX	OCCUPATION	PRVIL	DES
BANK, LOEB	26	M	DLR	RRZZZZ	USA
ROSENGARD, JENTE	46	F	W	RRZZZZ	USA
RIWKE	8	F	CHILD	RRZZZZ	USA
SARA	4	F	CHILD	RRZZZZ	USA
LEVINSOHN, JS.	18	M	LABR	RRZZZZ	USA
LASKY, LIEBE	27	F	W	RRZZZZ	USA
ABRAM	6	M	CHILD	RRZZZZ	USA
LEA	4	F	CHILD	RRZZZZ	USA
ELI	3	F	CHILD	RRZZZZ	USA
RIEWKA	.11	F	INFANT	RRZZZZ	USA
ROSENGARG, SCHEINE	45	F	W	RRZZZZ	USA
MOTTEL	8	F	CHILD	RRZZZZ	USA
ROSA	4	F	CHILD	RRZZZZ	USA
UDZEWICH, ANNA	30	F	W	RRZZZZ	USA
MARIE	9	F	CHILD	RRZZZZ	USA
JOSEF	5	M	CHILD	RRZZZZ	USA
VORONIKA	.11	F	INFANT	RRZZZZ	USA
WALANCHA, FEIWEL	38	M	LABR	RRZZZZ	USA
LEVIN, GELE	18	F	SGL	RRZZZZ	USA
PERCIKOWITZ, BEILE	14	F	SGL	RRZZZZ	USA
GINSBERG, FEIGE	35	F	W	RRZZZZ	USA
NAFTALI	9	M	CHILD	RRZZZZ	USA
ABRAM	6	M	CHILD	RRZZZZ	USA
LIEBE	4	F	CHILD	RRZZZZ	USA
ZALINGER, SARA	23	F	W	RRZZZZ	USA
RIEWKE	18	F	SGL	RRZZZZ	USA
RACHEL	4	F	CHILD	RRZZZZ	USA
LEIB	.11	M	INFANT	RRZZZZ	USA
STRAUSS, JOHAN	30	M	LABR	RRZZZZ	USA
MARIAE.	24	F	W	RRZZZZ	USA
KARTUSKI, FEIGE	23	F	W	RRZZZZ	USA
SALOMON	.02	M	INFANT	RRZZZZ	USA
ROSENSTADT, ADOLF	20	M	MCHT	RRZZZZ	USA
ZYDOWSKY, JAC.	21	M	LABR	RRZZZZ	USA
SACHAROWITZ, ZILKE	25	F	W	RRZZZZ	USA
MOSES	.11	M	INFANT	RRZZZZ	USA
WIETRICZKA, JOSEPHA	36	F	W	RRZZZZ	USA
BARSCHKOWSKI, FRANZA.	55	F	W	RRZZZZ	USA
DOMINIK	28	M	LABR	RRZZZZ	USA
ANNA	23	F	SGL	RRZZZZ	USA
STEFAN	23	M	LABR	RRZZZZ	USA
ANNA	16	F	SGL	RRZZZZ	USA
KOWALSKY, NICOL.	35	M	LABR	RRZZZZ	USA
SCHELASCHEWITZ, AUG.	45	M	LABR	RRZZZZ	USA
KOWARSKY, RINE	17	F	SGL	RRZZZZ	USA
FINKELSTEIN, JOS.	32	M	DLR	RRZZZZ	USA
WASOWSKI, CARL	27	M	JNR	RRZZZZ	USA
AXEN, ANT.	28	M	JNR	RRZZZZ	USA
WINAKENGER, JOH.	40	M	JNR	RRZZZZ	USA
BIRDIS, JOH.	20	M	JNR	RRZZZZ	USA
KEDEAMER, JEAN	20	M	JNR	RRZZZZ	USA
BOSCH, ANT.	33	M	JNR	RRZZZZ	USA
JOSCHEWITZ, MATTH.	20	M	JNR	RRZZZZ	USA
GROSSER, THEOD.	24	M	JNR	RRZZZZ	USA
EISENKOPF, GOLDE	24	F	W	RRZZZZ	USA
CHANNE	.09	F	INFANT	RRZZZZ	USA
BERNSTEIN, AUGUSTE	22	F	W	RRZZZZ	USA
SALOMON	.09	M	INFANT	RRZZZZ	USA
RIEGER, LEIB	51	M	DLR	RRZZZZ	USA
STERANKA, ONUFRI	47	M	DLR	RRZZZZ	USA
SACHS, JOSEF	18	M	LABR	RRZZZZ	USA
GORECKA, HELENE	26	F	SGL	RRZZZZ	USA
LOPETOWSKY, THOS.	38	M	LABR	RRZZZZ	USA
POGORSELAK, ANDREY	26	M	LABR	RRZZZZ	USA
SZAKOCZUS, ADAM	19	M	LABR	RRZZZZ	USA
JUDELOWITZ, HANNA	28	F	W	RRZZZZ	USA
SARA	9	F	CHILD	RRZZZZ	USA
MORITZ	8	M	CHILD	RRZZZZ	USA
RAHEL	7	F	CHILD	RRZZZZ	USA
ESTHER	5	F	CHILD	RRZZZZ	USA
GERBER, RIECKE	35	F	W	RRZZZZ	USA
ABR.	4	M	CHILD	RRZZZZ	USA
JECKET	.09	M	INFANT	RRZZZZ	USA
WEISS, SANDOR	23	M	MCHT	RRZZZZ	USA
WLIEDERZINSKY, CHEIM	34	M	LABR	RRZZZZ	USA
KRISTOL, JOSEF	38	M	LABR	RRZZZZ	USA
SARA	16	F	W	RRZZZZ	USA
ROTHSCHILD, JUDEL	26	M	LABR	RRZZZZ	USA
OKEN, ZLATE	22	F	W	RRZZZZ	USA
SCHIFRE	.11	F	INFANT	RRZZZZ	USA

PASSENGER	AGE	SEX	OCCUPATION	PRIV	DES
NEUMAN, JOSSEL	19	M	DLR	RRZZZZ	USA
GUTCHEN, HIRSCH	36	M	FELMO	RRZZZZ	USA

SHIP: BELGENLAND

FROM: ANTWERP
TO: NEW YORK
ARRIVED: 22 APRIL 1886

PASSENGER	AGE	SEX	OCCUPATION	PRIV	DES
TERANKLE, A.	23	M	GENT	RRAHUF	USA

SHIP: ZAANDAM

FROM: AMSTERDAM
TO: NEW YORK
ARRIVED: 24 APRIL 1886

PASSENGER	AGE	SEX	OCCUPATION	PRIV	DES
KLEIN, KARL	22	M	BCHR	PLZZZZ	USA
ECKER, JOSEPH	45	M	LABR	PLZZZZ	USA
ELISABETH	47	F	UNKNOWN	PLZZZZ	USA
STEPHEN	6	M	CHILD	PLZZZZ	USA
JULIANA	9	F	CHILD	PLZZZZ	USA
SAURE, W.MARIA	37	F	NN	PLZZZZ	USA
ECHER, FRANZ	35	M	LABR	PLZZZZ	USA
MARIA	23	F	UNKNOWN	PLZZZZ	USA
URIOVIES, LORENZ	30	M	FARMER	PLZZZZ	USA
MARIA	27	F	UNKNOWN	PLZZZZ	USA
CATHARINA	9	F	CHILD	PLZZZZ	USA
PETER	8	M	CHILD	PLZZZZ	USA
LORENZ	7	M	CHILD	PLZZZZ	USA
ANNA	4	F	CHILD	PLZZZZ	USA
KAISER, MATHIAS	34	M	BKLYR	PLZZZZ	USA
EISINGER, MICHAEL	34	M	LABR	PLZZZZ	USA
HADL, JOHAN	30	M	LABR	PLZZZZ	USA
HELLER, ANTON	35	M	LABR	PLZZZZ	USA
MARIA	29	F	UNKNOWN	PLZZZZ	USA
CATH.	10	F	UNKNOWN	PLZZZZ	USA
JOSEF	8	M	CHILD	PLZZZZ	USA
MARIA	4	F	CHILD	PLZZZZ	USA
GANDL, THERESIA	24	F	NN	PLZZZZ	USA

SHIP: ST LAURENT

FROM: HAVRE
TO: NEW YORK
ARRIVED: 27 APRIL 1886

PASSENGER	AGE	SEX	OCCUPATION	PRIV	DES
BEINWASSER, HEINRICH	17	M	NN	RRZZZZ	NY
PIADA	12	F	NN	RRZZZZ	NY
GENNY	9	F	CHILD	RRZZZZ	NY
KUPFSTEIN, MAX	13	M	NN	RRZZZZ	NY

INDEX